UNIVERSITY CASEBOOK SERIES®

THE LAW OF BIODIVERSITY AND ECOSYSTEM MANAGEMENT

THIRD EDITION

by

JOHN COPELAND NAGLE
John N. Matthews Professor of Law
University of Notre Dame

J.B. RUHL
David Daniels Allen Distinguished Chair in Law
Vanderbilt University Law School

KALYANI ROBBINS
Associate Professor of Law
University of Akron

FOUNDATION PRESS
2013

THOMSON REUTERS™

© 2002, 2006 FOUNDATION PRESS
© 2013 by THOMSON REUTERS / FOUNDATION PRESS
    1 New York Plaza, 34th Floor
    New York, NY 10004
    Phone Toll Free (877) 888-1330
    Fax (646) 424-5201
    foundation-press.com

Printed in the United States of America

ISBN: 978-1-60930-032-6

Mat #41171622

In memory of Patricia Campbell Nagle

J.C.N.

To Lisa, Grant, and Grayson

J.B.R.

For Skyler and Maxfield

K.R.

PREFACE TO THE THIRD EDITION

The third edition of this book features one familiar theme and two new ones. The familiar theme is change. The law of biodiversity is like a pendulum that swings back-and-forth depending on broader political changes. The first edition of the book appeared during the Bush Administration, the second edition at the beginning of the Obama Administration, and we are completing this book one week before we learn whether the next four years will present a Romney Administration or the second term of the Obama Administration. The specific rules governing biodiversity have shifted with the wider political winds, but the underlying questions raised by endangered species, ecosystem management, and the legal protection of biodiversity persist regardless of who holds office at a particular moment.

One of the new features of this edition is the addition of three chapters addressing climate change. We are the beneficiary of a decade of thinking about how climate change will affect biodiversity that has developed since we first wrote this book. We expect that new scientific understandings – and perhaps new laws – will continue to shape the response in this area in particular. The materials that we include here provide the latest account of how the law is involved in the efforts to protect biodiversity from the effects of climate change.

The final new feature of this edition is the most exciting one. Kalyani Robbins has joined us for this edition of the book, and the book is already better for it. Kalyani has quickly developed into a leading scholar on a variety of issues related to the law of biodiversity. Her insight has helped us reshape old materials and develop new ones. We can only hope that the law is as successful at incorporating new ideas as this book has been thanks to Kalyani's work.

JOHN COPELAND NAGLE
J.B. RUHL
KALYANI ROBBINS

November 2012

PREFACE TO THE SECOND EDITION

In the Preface to the first edition of this book, we observed that the field of law captured by the topics of biodiversity and ecosystem management is changing rapidly and that the second edition of the book would contain many differences from the first. We were right in one respect, but wrong in another.

Structurally, this second edition is very much like the first. The only change we have made is to divide what was one chapter on "extreme ecosystems" into two separate chapters—one covering "fragile ecosystems" and the other covering "human-dominated ecosystems." We did this to reflect the increasing attention those two ecosystem types are receiving given the policy challenges they present. There were no sweeping changes I the law of biodiversity and ecosystem management that required any further tinkering with the basic skeleton of the book.

On the other hand, the law of biodiversity and ecosystem management has changed in details substantially since the first edition, owing primarily to the change of administrations in the White House. Federal policy under the Clinton Administration drove the initial phase of initiatives to recognize biodiversity conservation as an important goal and to integrate it into law and policy through the Endangered Species Act and the broader framework of ecosystem management. Many of those initiatives, particularly those having to do with the Endangered Species Act, were instituted during the mid-1990s, but just as many were put in place during the closing days of the Administration. The incoming Bush Administration put a screeching halt to the latter, and slowly began revisiting the former. By the time the first edition was published, however, the Bush Administration had made little headway toward defining its approach to biodiversity and ecosystem management. The first edition thus provided a snapshot of the law of biodiversity conservation and ecosystem management with full knowledge it was on the brink of change.

Indeed, the administrative reform effort picked up steam not long thereafter, and many changes to previous policies, albeit policies that had not been in place for very long, soon began to unfold. Not surprisingly, supporters of Clinton Administration policies challenged virtually all of these policy changes in the courts, with some success. The law of biodiversity and ecosystem management, in other words, remains in flux, and we have attempted in this second edition to capture not only where the law now stands, but how the process of change transpired in the agencies and the courts (Congress has remained essentially inert on the topic). There is no chapter in the first three parts of the book, covering biodiversity, the Endangered Species Act, and ecosystem management policy, that has not been touched by this process. We have no delusions, to say the least, that more change is not around the corner for all three of those topics. Nevertheless, the magnitude and direction of changes in the four years since the first edition suggested to use the need for a second edition pulling it all together in one volume rather than issuing what would have been a very long and intricate supplement.

Just as with the first edition, we have many people to thank for helping us with this important milestone. We had the help of many students in our respective classes who identified strengths and weaknesses in the first edition. We are also grateful to faculty adopters of the first edition who provided feedback. The deans and faculty of our law schools, Notre Dame and Florida State University, continued their unwavering support of our work, and we may have procrastinated in the necessary hard work involved had it not been for the support of John Bloomquist at Foundation Press. Last, but not least by a long shot, we thank our wives, Lisa Nagle and Lisa LeMaster, and families for patience and support.

We welcome comments on this second edition, on both its strengths and areas for improvement. Please direct any feedback to John Nagle (nagle.8@nd.edu) or J.B. Ruhl (jruhl@law.fsu.edu).

JOHN COPELAND NAGLE
J.B. RUHL

PREFACE TO THE FIRST EDITION

It is unlikely that this book would have been published ten years ago. Biodiversity and ecosystem management were far from household words in the early 1990s, and had only begun to emerge in the sciences as relevant ways of thinking about the environment and human impacts on it. Law, always a straggler, was far behind in this case. A law school text on biodiversity and ecosystem management written in 1990, even by the most inventive of authors, would have been quite thin. Its market would have been even more slim, as few law schools had strayed in their curriculum beyond the traditional offerings of a survey course on environmental law and, maybe, another on natural resources law.

Much has changed since then. In 1999, the National Geographic Society declared biodiversity one of six subjects shaping our destiny and devoted an issue of *National Geographic* to the topic. Despite that sea change in the sciences, the law of biodiversity and ecosystem management has only begun to coalesce. After passing the 1990 Clean Air Act amendments, Congress has been unable to reach a consensus in support of any new major environmental law initiatives. That has left biodiversity far off Congress' radar screen. Nevertheless, as recent years have shown, Congress is not the only potent force of change in environmental law. Federal courts and agencies have interpreted federal laws—in many cases laws that have remained virtually unchanged for decades—in ways that have opened to door to the formation of policy on questions central to biodiversity conservation and ecosystem management. Many states have also lived up to the ideal of states as the laboratory of innovation when it comes to biodiversity and ecosystem management. Suffice it to say that, as much as has happened in the sciences, law has finally discovered biodiversity and ecosystem management as core subjects of environmental regulation and begun the process of catching the law up with the science.

We have attempted in this book to capture where the law at present stands in that regard. To do so, we begin in Part I with an overview of the topic that shows how law and science gradually are fusing. The materials introduce the student to the important threshold issues that face the development of a law of biodiversity, including defining what biodiversity is, choosing among different policy approaches for its protection, and finding the appropriate levels of administration—federal, tribal, state, and local— for implementing those policies.

Part II then covers the law that has emerged as the centerpiece of federal biodiversity policy—the Endangered Species Act. Famous for its lofty aspiration of conserving imperiled species and their ecosystems, and infamous to many for how it goes about doing so, perhaps no federal environmental law wields such power and produces as much controversy as does the Endangered Species Act. Our coverage in Part II walks the student through the mechanics and policy of the framework provisions of the law, covering the identification of threatened and endangered species and their critical habitat, the duties that apply to federal agencies once a species is "listed," and the strong prohibitions that apply to all persons and governments against harming protected species. Over time the latter of these themes–the so-called "take"prohibition that applies to private and public landowners alike—has moved the center of gravity for the Endangered Species Act from primarily a federal agency concern to having substantial impact on local land use decisions around the nation, which has in turn led the law to become engulfed in property rights issues. Part II thus also covers the emerging innovations in endangered species policy that may prove in the long run to promote both biodiversity conservation and flexibility for landowners.

Notwithstanding its broad scope and potent authorities, the Endangered Species Act falls far short of providing a comprehensive biodiversity conservation law. Yet, along with endangered species protection, a patchwork of existing state and federal laws can go a long way toward broad coverage of biodiversity conservation values. The difficulty is in how to describe that amalgam of laws. We have chosen the approach in Part III that seems most consistent with the way in which biodiversity is discussed at policy levels—as a core objective of ecosystem management. As then Secretary of the Interior Bruce Babbitt once quipped, in congressional testimony no less, an ecosystem can be anything from a raindrop to the planet. The point is that ecosystems, and their biological diversity, can be defined at very small, reductionist scales, or very large, holistic scales, or somewhere in between. For the convenience of presentation, we have chosen the middle ground, dividing coverage of ecosystem management according to different types of ecosystems we felt would be familiar to any student, but without violating sound scientific treatment of the topic.

Indeed, the science of ecology—the study of ecosystems—has forged bold new paths in recent years in tandem with the increased understanding of the importance of biological diversity. An important overarching theme of much of this new work in ecology is the dynamic, open nature of ecosystems and the processes which are in constant flux. We are increasingly appreciating that ecosystems involve complex interrelations, adaptive strategies for dealing with disturbance, and a sustainability that depends on change. Boundaries and parts have little meaning in such open systems. Yet humans have a difficult time managing chaos. Administrative convenience necessitates some division and compartmentalization of complex management problems, even if at the expense of a perfect description of the subject matter. Indeed, this, so far, has been the case for the web of laws oriented—more accurately, being reoriented—toward ecosystem management. So, while we recognize that forests and wetlands may overlap, it is useful, particularly given the structure of the law, to give them separate coverage in this text.

Consistent with that approach, the chapters in Part III are organized based on types of ecosystems. The first series of chapters covers conventional divisions of ecosystem types into forests, grasslands, freshwater, and coastal and marine. The bundles of laws associated with managing these ecosystem regimes are covered in each corresponding chapter. The theme in these chapters is the conservation of biodiversity values in ecosystems that have not been significantly degraded by human intrusion, or at least which can be recovered to that state. Some ecosystems, however, such as coral reefs, islands, and deserts, present dire circumstances as a result of their critical dynamics. There are also ecosystems no longer capable of being defined without reference to human presence. These human-dominated ecosystems include lands in agricultural, recreational, and urban uses. Far from unimportant in terms of biodiversity conservation, scientists increasingly are finding that these two extreme ecosystem types play an important role in overall biodiversity conservation goals. Accordingly, we cover them in the final chapter of Part III.

Parts I through III provide an ample framework for understanding the law of biodiversity conservation and ecosystem management in the United States. But, as we have observed, at a more holistic level the entire planet must be managed as an ecosystem. Biodiversity knows no political boundaries. Thus, in Part IV we turn to issue of global biodiversity. The law of global biodiversity is forming on two levels. First, recognizing that local events can have profound impacts on global biodiversity, many nations have started to shape their domestic laws to take transboundary effects into account. Simultaneously, the international community has begun to develop conventions for managing the "big picture" of biodiversity through international law in its customary, bilateral, and multilateral forms.

As unlikely as it is that this text would have been published ten years ago, it is equally likely that it will not resemble its present form in ten years. This field of law is changing rapidly. That we can even call it a field of law today suggests we have moved far and fast in the past decade. There is no reason to believe that this momentum will be lost, or that the field will be considered to have "matured," any time in the near future. But the materials covered in this book will always be known as the beginning of the law of biodiversity and ecosystem management, and are likely always to be important in that respect even if they fade from day-to-day prominence as the field evolves. Law students who use this first edition of the text thus can say they got into the topic of biodiversity and ecosystem management law at the ground floor. Where the law of biodiversity and ecosystem management goes from here is anyone's call, but wherever that may be, we plan to be there every step of the way and, through subsequent editions of this book, to record the journey.

Our road traveled thus far would not have been possible without the assistance of many. Numerous student research assistants contributed countless hours finding source materials: Ryan Carson, Vinette Godelia, Sean Moloney, Kyle Payne, Susan Lyndrup, Wes Wheeler, and Kristina Zurcher. Many colleagues at other institutions offered invaluable insight on drafts and on the topic in general. Chief among them was Rob Fischman, who meticulously reviewed many of the chapters and provided comments well beyond the call of duty. Also thanks in this department go to Jim Salzman, Oliver Houck, Marc Miller, Jim Salzman, and Buzz Thompson. Students in our respective biodiversity law seminars also endured early drafts and helped us immensely in refining the materials to provide what we hope other instructors and students will find a teachable, probing, and informative text. Dean Patricia O'Hara of the Notre Dame Law School and Dean Don Weidner of the Florida State University College of Law provided generous support of our research. We also thank our publisher, Steve Errick, for having the vision to chart new ground in the field of environmental law texts.

Of course, like all those before us who conceived law school texts with starry-eyed vision, jumped for joy upon receiving a publication agreement, and then found out just how much work it would be after all, we owe or deepest thanks to our families, who patiently supported us every page of the way, particularly our wives: Lisa Nagle and Lisa LeMaster. We welcome comments on the text, on both its strengths and areas for improvement. They may be sent to John Nagle (nagle.8@nd.edu) or J. B. Ruhl (jruhl@law.fsu.edu).

JOHN COPELAND NAGLE

J.B. RUHL

ACKNOWLEDGMENTS

The authors gratefully acknowledge the permissions granted to reproduce the following materials.

Books and Articles

Adams, Jonathan S., Bruce A. Stein and Lynn S. Kutner, "Biodiversity: Our Precious Heritage," in "Precious Heritage: The Status of Biodiversity in the United States" (Bruce A. Stein, Lynn S. Kutner & Jonathan S. Adams eds., 2000). Reprinted with permission of Oxford University Press.

Barrera-Hernandez, Lila Katz de, and Alastair R. Lucas, "Environmental Law in Latin America and the Caribbean: Overview and Assessment," 12 Georgetown International Environmental Law Review 207 (1999). Reprinted with permission of the publisher, Georgetown International Environmental Law Journal © 1999, and the authors.

Babbitt, Bruce, "Between the Flood and the Rainbow: Our Covenant to Protect the Whole of Creation," 2 Animal Law 1 (1996). Reprinted with permission of Animal Law and the author.

Blair, John M., Scott L. Collins, and Alan K. Knapp, "Ecosystems As Functional Units In Nature," 14 Natural Resources & Env't 150 (2000). Reprinted by permission of the American Bar Association copyright © 2000.

Bowden, Matthew M., "An Overview of the National Estuary Program," 11 Natural Resouces & Env't 35 (Fall 1996). Reprinted by permission of the American Bar Association copyright © 1996.

Dickson, Barnabas, "CITES in Harare: A Review of the Tenth Conference of the Parties," Colorado Journal of International Environmental Law, 1997 Year Book 55. Reprinted by permission of the author and the Colorado Journal of International Environmental Law.

Green, Martha Hodgkins, "How Green Is My Valley?," 47 Nature Conservancy 18 (Sept. / Oct. 1997). Reprinted by permission of the Nature Conservancy.

Grumbine, R. Edward, "What Is Ecosystem Management?," 8 Conservation Biology 27 (1994). Reprinted with permission by Blackwell Science, Inc.

Hodas, David, NEPA, Ecosystem Management and Environmental Accounting, 14 Natural Resources & Env't 185 (2000). Reprinted by permission of the American Bar Association copyright © 2000.

Hsu, Shi-Ling and James E. Wilen, "Ecosystem Management and the 1996 Sustainable Fisheries Act," 24 Ecology L.Q. 799 (1997). Reprinted from Ecology Law Quarterly, vol. 24, no. 4, pp. 799–811, by permission of Ecology Law Quarterly and the authors. Copyright © 1997 by the Regents of the University of California.

Hughes, Harry R. and Thomas W. Burke, Jr., "The Cleanup of the Nation's Largest Estuary: A Test of Political Will," 11 Natural Resources & Env't 30 (Fall 1996). Reprinted by permission of the American Bar Association copyright © 1996.

"In re Fund for Animals Ltd.," Administrative Appeals Tribunal, 9 A.L.D. 622 (1986). Reprinted with permission of LexisNexis Butterworths.

Karkkainen, Bradley C., "Biodiversity and Land," 83 Cornell Law Review 1 (1997). Reprinted by permission of the author and the Cornell Law Review.

Kelly, Christopher R. and James A. Lodoen, "Federal Farm Program Conservation Initiatives: Past, Present, and Future," 9 Natural Resources & Env't 17 (Winter 1995). Reprinted by permission of the American Bar Association copyright © 1995.

Morell, Virginia, "New Mammals Discovered by Biology's New Explorers," 273 Science 1491 (1996). Reprinted with permission from Science, vol. 273, page 1491. Copyright © 1996 American Association for the Advancement of Science.

National Research Council, "The Bering Sea Ecocystem" (1996). Reprinted with permission of National Academy Press.

Postel, Sandra and Stephen Carpenter, "Freshwater Ecosystem Services," in "Nature's Services: Societal Dependence on Natural Ecosystems" (Gretchen Dailey ed. 1997). Reprinted with permission of Island Press copyright © 1997.

Ruhl, J.B. and Christopher Lant, Tim Loftus, Steven Kraft, Jane Adams, and Leslie Duram, "Proposal for a Model State Watershed Management Act," 33 Envtl. L. 929 (2003). Reprinted with permission of the authors.

Ruhl, J.B. and R. Juge Gregg, "Integrating Ecosystem Services Into Environmental Law: A Case Study of Wetlands Mitigation Banking," 20 Stan. Envtl. L.J. 365 (2001). Reprinted by permission of the authors and the Stanford Environmental Law Journal.

Ruhl, J.B., "Ecosystem Management, The Endangered Species Act, and the Seven Degrees of Relevance," 14 Natural Resources & Env't 156 (2000). Reprinted by permission of the American Bar Association copyright © 2000.

Ruhl, J.B., "The Disconnect Between Environmental Assessment and Adaptive Management," 36 Trends 1 (July-Aug. 2005). Reprinted by permission of the American Bar Association copyright © 2005.

Salzman, James, "Valuing Ecosystem Services," 24 Ecology L.Q. 887 (1997). Reprinted from Ecology Law Quarterly, vol. 4. no. 4, pp. 887-903, by permission of Ecology Law Quarterly and the author. Copyright © 1997 by Ecology Law Quarterly.

Taylor, William E. and Mark Gerath, "The Watershed Protection Approach: Is the Promise About to Be Realized?," 11 Natural Resources & Env't 16 (Fall 1996). Reprinted by permission of the American Bar Association copyright © 1996.

Thompson, Barton H., Jr., "Markets for Nature," 25 Wm. & Mary Envtl. Law & Pol'y Rev. 261 (2000). Reprinted with permission of the William and Mary Environmental Law and Policy Review.

Thompson, Rebecca, "'Ecosystem Management'– Great Idea, But What Is It, Will It Work, and Who Will Pay?," 9 Natural Resources & Env't 42 (Winter 1995). Reprinted by permission of the American Bar Association copyright © 1995.

United Nations Conference on Environment and Development: Convention on Biological Diversity, 31 International Legal Materials 818 (1992). Reprinted by permission of the Secretariat of the Convention on Biological Diversity.

United Nations Food and Agriculture Organization, Code of Conduct for Responsible Fisheries. Copyright (c) 2001 Food and Agriculture Organization of the United Nations. Reprinted with permission of the Food and Agriculture Organization of the United Nations.

Watermolen, D.J., C. Bleser, D. Zastrow, J. Christenson, D.R. Lentz and 20 co-authors. 2000. Executive Summary Pp. Iii-xviii in "Wisconsin Statewide Karner Blue Butterfly Habitat Conservation Plan and Environmental Impact Statement." 2 Vols. Madison: Wisconsin Department of Natural Resources. Reprinted by permission of the Wisconsin Department of Nature Resources.

World Trade Organization Appellate Body, "United States – Import Prohibition of Certain Shrimp and Shrimp Products," WT/DS58/AB/R; (98-3899); AB-1998-4, 1998 WTO DS LEXIS 13 (1998). Reprinted by permission of the World Trade Organization.

Illustrations

1990 Total Water Withdrawals illustration, United States Geological Survey.

Alabama red-bellied turtle, photograph by Robert H. Mount. Reproduced by permission of the Alabama Department of Archives and History.

Apalachicola-Chattahoochee-Flint River Basin map, United States Army Corps of Engineers.

Atlas of America's Polluted Waters, United States Environmental Protection Agency.

Blackburn's sphinx moth, photograph by W.P. Mull.

Caimen yacare, photograph by David S. Kirshner.

CALFED Problem and Solution Areas map, CALFED.

California condor, photograph, collection of the Arizona Ecological Field Services Office of the United States Fish and Wildlife Service.

California gnatcatcher, photograph by Arnold Small, United States Fish and Wildlife Service.

Chequamegon-Nicolet National Forest, photograph by United States Forest Service.

Chesapeake Bay Watershed map, Chesapeake Bay Program.

Coastal Zone Management Program map, National Ocean Service.

Dead crab, photograph by United States Environmental Protection Agency.

Delhi Sands Flower-Loving Fly, photograph by Guy Bruyea.

Devil's Hole photograph, National Park Service.

Ecoregions map, United States Bureau of Land Management.

Ecosystem Units map, United States Fish and Wildlife Service.

Entry to Cimarron National Grassland, photograph by United States Forest Service.

Glacier Bay photograph, National Park Service.

Illinois cave amphipod, photograph by Steve Taylor, Center for Biodiversity, Illinois Natural History Survey.

Karner blue butterfly, photograph by Ann B. Swengel.

Key deer, photograph by Gerald Ludwig, United States Fish and Wildlife Service.

Klamath River Basin map, National Research Council.

Loach minnow, photograph by Marty Jakle, United States Fish and Wildlife Service.

Lower Keys marsh rabbit, photograph by Beth Forys.

Marine Protected Areas map, National Ocean Service.

Mississippi River Basin with Gulf of Mexico Hypoxia map, United States Environmental Protection Agency.

National Forest Lands map, United States Forest Service.

New York City Water Supply map, New York City Department of Environmental Protection.

Overall National Coastal Condition chart, United States Environmental Protection Agency.

Percentage of wetland losses map, United States Geological Survey.

Phase I Inventory of Current EPA Efforts to Protect Ecosystems map, United States Environmental Protection Agency.

Piping plover, photograph by J.P. Mattson, United States Fish and Wildlife Service.

Principal Oxidized Nitrogen Airsheds map, United States Environmental Protection Agency and National Oceanic and Atmospheric Administration.

Proposed Darby Prairie National Wildlife Refuge map, United States Fish and Wildlife Service.

Public Lands Managed by the Bureau of Land Management map, Bureau of Land Management.

Shawnee National Forest map, United States Forest Service.

Shawnee National Forest, photograph by United States Forest Service.

Southeast Orlando land use map, Planning and Development Department, City of Orlando, Florida.

The White Marlin illustration, National Marine Fisheries Service.

Watershed Information Network Atlas map, United States Environmental Protection Agency.

Watersheds of National Estuaries map, United States Environmental Protection Agency.

White Marlin Open, photograph by Angel Bolinger, Maryland Department of Natural Resources.

SUMMARY OF CONTENTS

PART 1. BIODIVERSITY

PART 2. THE ENDANGERED SPECIES ACT

PART 3. MANAGING ECOSYSTEM DIVERSITY

PART 4. GLOBAL BIODIVERSITY

PART 5. MAJOR THREATS TO BIODIVERSITY AND ECOSYSTEMS

PART 2. THE ENDANGERED SPECIES ACT

TABLE OF CONTENTS

PART 1. BIODIVERSITY

PART 4. GLOBAL BIODIVERSITY

PART 5. MAJOR THREATS TO BIODIVERSITY AND ECOSYSTEMS

TABLE OF CASES

The principal cases are in bold type.

UNIVERSITY CASEBOOK SERIES ®

THE LAW OF BIODIVERSITY AND ECOSYSTEM MANAGEMENT

THIRD EDITION

PART 1

BIODIVERSITY

CHAPTER 1

THE PROBLEM OF THE DELHI SANDS FLOWER-LOVING FLY

Long ago, the Santa Ana winds picked up sand from several creeks and deposited it over about 35,000 acres of land located about sixty miles east of the Pacific Ocean in southern California. Thus were born the Delhi sand dunes (also known as the Colton Dunes), the only inland sand dune system in the Los Angeles basin. At first glance, the dunes are inhabited only by blowing sand and scattered shrubs. But contrary to the popular image of deserts as barren of wildlife, desert ecosystems are in fact teeming with birds, insects, reptiles, mammals and plants. The Delhi Sands are a good example of what one finds in a coastal sage scrub ecosystem. Birds such as Western meadowlarks and burrowing owls frequent the area. The San Diego horned lizard and the legless lizard live in the dunes, as do insects such as the Delhi sands metalmark butterfly and the Delhi sands Jerusalem cricket. The onset of night entices the Los Angeles pocket mouse, the San Bernardino kangaroo rat and other small mammals to survey the land. Primrose, goldfields and other wildflowers flourish after the winter rains, replaced later in the year by the wild buckwheat and the colorful butterflies that the plant attracts. The yellow flowers of telegraph weeds appear in the summer.

The Delhi sands

2

Increasingly, though, the Delhi Sands are home to many people, too. The area had long been inhabited by many different Native American peoples, including the Serrano, the Cahuilla, the Chemehuevi and the Mojave. Spanish and Mormon missionaries traveled across the land during the eighteenth and early nineteenth centuries, and the first European settlements in what is now western San Bernardino and Riverside Counties began after California became a state in 1850 and after the railroad reached the area in the early 1870's. The city of Colton, for example, was first settled in 1874 and named after a Civil War general who also served as the vice president of the Southern Pacific Railroad. The settlers immediately began planting citrus orchards despite concerns that the land was inadequate for farming. The citrus thrived in the warm climate once irrigated water was delivered from the nearby Santa Ana River, and much of the land was cultivated for grapes, oranges and other fruits by the late 1800's. Dairies, residential homes, and commercial and industrial development were the next to appear on the scene.

The results of the human settlements have not been especially attractive. The California Portland Cement Company mined Slover Mountain for over 100 years, leaving a pile of granite and no dunes in its wake. Similar enterprises have taken the sand for road fill and other purposes. Junk yards and petroleum tank farms abound. The Southern Pacific Railroad and Interstate 10 bisect the area. A landfill, a sewage treatment facility and many illegally dumped cars are also nearby. Off-road vehicle enthusiasts alter the terrain of the little bit of the dunes that remains.

Yet the land is in great demand. The population of Colton, in the heart of the dunes, grew from 45,000 in 1995 to 52,000 in 2005. San Bernardino and Riverside Counties were second to Las Vegas in population growth between 2000 and 2005, jumping 15.3% to a total of 3.75 million residents. The additional people bring additional demands for housing, shopping, offices, road, and other facilities to be built on the previously barren land. The attractiveness of the area has spiked land prices to as high as $160,000 per acre.

The human population of the dunes is as diverse as the wildlife population. Nearly sixty percent of the residents of Colton, for example, are of Hispanic origin. Another fifteen percent of Colton's residents are African-Americans, Asians, or Native Americans. The city's median family income is only slightly above $35,000, making it one of the poorest cities in California. The closure of many military bases and the loss of defense jobs in San Bernardino County caused the region to suffer a significant economic recession beginning in the 1980's. The economic plight of the area was illustrated by the creation of the Agua Mansa Enterprise Zone, which was established by San Bernardino and Riverside Counties and the cities of Colton, Rialto and Riverside in an effort to lure economic development to a 10,000 acre site in the region. The 1986 environmental study preceding the creation of the enterprise zone assured that there were no rare or endangered species living on the affected land.

The view of the dunes today, with I-10 in the foreground and the sand mining operation in the background.

The growth in the human population has produced a corresponding shrinkage of the original Delhi sands. Most of the original dunes were destroyed by the onset of agricultural uses at the end of the nineteenth century. Over the next one hundred years, commercial, industrial and residential development eliminated much of the remaining dunes. A shopping center replaced seventy acres of dunes in the early 1990s, and a county park split another segment of the dunes in 1998. Only about forty square miles of dunes—or about two percent of the original sands—exist in several patches stretching between the cities of Colton and Mira Loma.

As the Delhi sands have disappeared, so has the native wildlife. Pringle's monardella, a wildflower that once grew only in the Delhi sands, has already gone extinct. The number of meadowlarks and burrowing owls has diminished as their habitats have been converted into human uses, though both birds have displayed a surprising resiliency in the presence of bulldozers and landfills and the like. And the area is the still the only place on earth where the Delhi Sands Flower–Loving Fly clings to life.

The Fly—known to entomologists as *Rhaphiomidas terminatus abdominalis*—is colored orangish and brown, with dark brown oval spots on its abdomen and emerald green eyes. It is one-inch long, much larger than a common house fly. The Fly undergoes a metamorphosis from egg to larva to pupa to adult fly over a three-year period. Once it emerges from the sand at the end of the three years, an individual Fly lives for about a week in August and September. The Flies are active during the heat of the day, with females burrowing into the sand to deposit about forty eggs at one time. The Flies remain inactive during cloudy, rainy or windy conditions. The Fly is only found in the Delhi sands.

The Delhi-Sands Flower Loving Fly

photo by Guy Bruyea

The Fly is one of nearly 85,000 species of flies that scientists have identified around the world so far. It is one of a dozen species that comprise the *Rhaphiomidas* genus. The Fly is distinguished from the other species within the *Rhaphiomidas* genus—all of which live in arid and semi-arid parts of California, Arizona, New Mexico and northern Mexico—by its bi-colored abdomen and its widely separated eyes. The Fly is actually a sub-species of the *Rhaphiomidas terminatus* species. Its companion subspecies and closest relative—the El Segundo Flower–Loving Fly—lived in the sand dunes north of downtown Los Angeles until the dunes were replaced by runways upon the construction of Los Angeles International Airport in the 1960s. That fly was thought to be extinct until a tiny remnant population was recently discovered surviving in a fragment of dune habitat close to LAX.

As its name suggests, the Fly loves flowers. It hovers like a humming-bird as it removes nectar from the native buckwheat flowers with its long tubular proboscis. It flies low, preferring sparsely vegetated areas. The Fly is a pollinator. It is one of a small group of flies that are pollinators. Other flower-loving flies survive elsewhere. For example, the acton flower-loving fly pollinates an endangered Californian plant known as the Santa Ana wooly-star.

Entomologists do not know a whole lot about the Fly. The first Fly was collected in 1888, but it was not until a century later that the Fly was iden-tified as a separate subspecies. The Fly probably lived throughout the full historic extent of the Delhi Sands, though we will never be sure about that.

Entomologists do not know what the larval flies-in-waiting eat during their three years underground. Nor is there any indication that the Fly provides any nutritional, medicinal or other tangible benefit to people.

The Fly survives in just five locations within an eight mile radius along the border of San Bernardino and Riverside Counties. No one knows for sure how many Flies are alive today, though estimates run from a couple hundred to less than a thousand. What everyone agrees upon, though, is that the number of Flies is shrinking and that the species may soon become extinct.

The Fly faces a variety of threats to its survival. Birds, reptiles, dragonflies, and ants sometimes attack and kill a larval or adult Fly. Pesticides used for agricultural purposes eliminate the native vegetation upon which the Fly appears to rely for its survival. Native plants have been smothered by local dairies that have dumped tons of cow manure on sections of the dunes—often without the landowner's permission—thus providing nutrient-rich soil for exotic plants. Mustard, cheeseweed, the Russian thistle, and other plants that are new to the area affect the soil in a way that is harmful to the Fly. The native vegetation is trampled by offroad vehicle riders and removed for fire control efforts. The Fly lives best in those few areas that have yet to be disturbed by human activities. Also, the fact that so few populations of the Fly still exist makes the entire species vulnerable to catastrophic events such as fires and droughts. The small, scattered populations reduce the genetic variability of the Fly—and thus, its ability to respond to environmental stresses—as well.

Mostly, though, the Fly is on the brink of extinction because the Delhi sands are disappearing in the wake of human development. An estimated 98% of the Fly's original habitat has been destroyed. By 1993, the Delhi sands that remained were threatened by a host of residential, commercial and industrial development projects. The most notable development to threaten the Fly was a hospital. Plans to replace San Bernardino's aging County Medical Center began in the late 1970s. County officials designed a large regional medical center that could resist earthquakes and satisfy the demands of federal health officials. The site selected for the hospital was a vacant piece of land just north of I-10 in Colton. By September 1993, the county was finally ready to break ground for its new Arrowhead Regional Medical Center.

Meanwhile, the Fly had attracted the attention of Greg Ballmer, a staff researcher in entomology at the University of California at Riverside. Ballmer viewed the Fly as "spectacular," yet he quickly became concerned about its plight. The rapid residential, commercial and industrial development of the region posed a grave threat to the survival of the dunes ecosystem, and thus to the survival of the Fly. So Ballmer did what any smart entomologist would do: he filed a petition with the United States Fish & Wildlife Service (FWS) to list the Fly as "endangered" under the Endangered Species Act of 1973.

Congress had enacted the ESA in 1973 during the heyday of federal environmental legislation. The proponents of the law evoked images of bald eagles, grizzly bears, alligators and other national symbols that were on the brink of disappearing from this land. Almost immediately, though, the ESA was deployed to protect much less popular creatures. The listing of the snail darter as endangered just months after the ESA became law resulted in the Supreme Court's decision in Tennessee Valley Authority v. Hill, 437 U.S. 153 (1978), confirming that the multi-million dollar Tellico Dam project could not be completed because of the threat that the dam posed to the snail darter's survival. In more recent years, the law's application to the northern spotted owl became a focal point for broader debates between the timber industry and environmentalists in the Pacific Northwest.

Ballmer had asked the FWS to list the Fly because of the urgency of the development pressures on all of the Fly's remaining habitat. The agency did not act until September 1993, when it agreed to add the Fly to the list of endangered species on an emergency basis. That also happened to be the day before construction was to begin on San Bernardino County's new hospital project smack in the middle of some of the Fly's prime habitat. At the first meeting between local officials and the FWS, a FWS employee surveyed the scene and suggested that nearby I-10—the major east-west highway between the San Bernardino Valley and Los Angeles— would have to be closed two months each year when the Fly was above ground.

Local officials were stuck. They protested to Congress. And they tried to cut a deal with the FWS. At first, the parties agreed that the hospital could be built if it was moved three hundred feet to the north and if the county established a refuge for the Fly. The "refuge" was vacant land adjacent to the hospital that was bordered by orange plastic fencing. Happily, the Flies loved the fencing. Then the county realized that they would need to build a new electrical substation to power the hospital; that resulted in seven more acres for the refuge. But when the county sought permission to reconfigure the roads in the area surrounding the hospital, the FWS balked. The county sued, joined by local developers, claiming that the ESA could not be constitutionally applied to regulate construction projects involving a species like the Fly that lived in only one state and that it was not involved in interstate commerce itself. The district court held that such an application of the ESA was constitutional, as did a divided D.C. Circuit, and any hope for a constitutional exit disappeared in June 1998 when the Supreme Court denied certiorari. *See* National Ass'n of Home Builders v. Babbit, 949 F.Supp. 1 (D.D.C.1996), *aff'd*, 130 F.3d 1041 (D.C.Cir.1997), *cert. denied*, 524 U.S. 937 (1998).

The Fly, thanks to the ESA, now occupied a position of great strength in future discussions about the development of the region. A host of developments were challenged because of their possible impact on the Fly and its remaining habitat. The projects included:

- A 2.8 million square foot WalMart distribution facility to be built in the dunes near Colton.

- A 27 hole golf course and accompanying 202 home development slated for Fontana which a city official defended because the sighting of a couple of Flies there over a two-year period is "just not enough science to put people's land at risk."
- A truck stop and industrial center to be built by Kaiser Ventures, which estimates that the project could create 5,300 jobs and $75 million per year to the San Bernardino County economy.
- A cement plant and a facility that produces sidewalk pavers in Rialto that was blocked by a federal court when the FWS claimed that the plant would wipe out a major portion of the Fly's habitat, but which the FWS approved in 1999 when the company agreed to set aside 30.5 acres of land for Fly habitat.
- A large project that would include new homes, theaters and restaurants in Fontana.
- The proposal of Viny Industries, a paper products company, to create 400 jobs by building on sixty acres of land in Colton.
- A $110 million plant to make fiberboard from recycled waste wood which opened in the Agua Mansa Industrial Center in May 1999 only after the industrial center contributed $450,000 to purchase other habitat for the Fly.

In August 2002, a single Fly was discovered on a parcel of land where the city of Colton had hoped to build a small-scale replica of an historic majorleague sports complex. The project immediately stalled. The city finally abandoned it in 2006, complaining that the FWS "took a project and doubled it in price and shrunk it down over a fly." The hospital itself finally opened in March 1999 after the county set aside a total of twelve acres of land for a Fly refuge. The county estimated that moving the site of the hospital, establishing the Fly preserves, and otherwise accommodating the Fly cost the county nearly $3,000,000.

The Fly also interfered with environmental cleanup activities in the area. When petroleum leaking from a nearby tank farm contaminated the groundwater, the presence of the Fly underground so complicated any remediation work that the tank farm owner planned to wait for the plume of contamination to migrate past the Fly's habitat. Additionally, the vacant, sandy land favored by the Fly was an attractive spot for the illegal dumping of trash, including abandoned appliances, used diapers, and yard debris. Local officials wanted to remove that trash, but the FWS insisted that the trash must be picked up by hand instead of by the ordinary heavy machinery that could disturb the Fly larvae that are buried in the sand. To prevent additional trash from being dumped in the area, Riverside and Colton enacted ordinances authorizing the forfeiture of any vehicle used to transport trash that is dumped in the sands. Other local towns are considering similar ordinances, in part because of concerns that they will become havens from trash dumpers who fear the more stringent sanctions imposed in neighboring communities.

In early 1999, Fontana officials warned that the Fly could cause the city to default on $42 million in municipal bonds. The city had issued the bonds in 1991 to build streets, sewers, lighting, and other improvements on vacant land adjacent to a small shopping center. The possibility that the Fly lives on the land prevented the expected commercial development of the land, and when the landowner stopped paying taxes on the land, the city began to use its reserve funds to pay the bondholders. The Fly did facilitate one source of new employment: developers hired consultants to determine the extent of the presence of the Fly in the area. It was only when the landowner paid its taxes after one such survey failed to find any Flies on the property that Fontana barely avoided defaulting on the bonds in October 1999.

The Fly continued to block the proposed road construction projects that resulted in the commerce clause litigation. Colton officials and the FWS had not reached an agreement that would permit the realignment of roads near the new hospital despite meetings held throughout 1999. Similarly, when Riverside County asked the FWS for permission to build new ramps for I-15 in Mira Loma, the federal agency responded that the county would need to establish a 200 acre preserve for the Fly. The agency reasoned that although the ramps would only displace a little more than eight acres of Fly habitat, the effect on the Fly of the accompanying development and increased traffic justified a larger reserve. The purchase of that much land would cost the county as much as $32 million in an area where land sells for up to $160,000 an acre, which would make the Fly reserve more expensive than the highway ramps themselves. More generally, when officials representing Colton, Fontana, Rialto and other local cities met with the FWS in July 1999 to propose setting aside 850 acres of land for Fly habitat in exchange for permission to develop throughout the area, they were told that FWS biologists were seeking 2,100 acres that could cost $220 million to purchase. Much of that land—including a former dairy in Ontario—would have to be rehabilitated in order to serve as viable habitat for the Fly.

The Fly was vilified. Fontana Mayor David Eshleman complained that the Fly "is costing the Inland Empire thousands of jobs and millions of dollars. I think we should issue fly swatters to everyone." Colton's city manager estimated the stalled development, uncollected tax revenue, and lost jobs attributable to the Fly as totaling $661 million. Local residents were quick to offer their own reactions to the predicament: one man claimed that the Fly "larva is the same I've seen in tequila bottles being imported here from Mexico," and a woman worried that children and schools were "an endangered species that gets no help." Julie Biggs, the Colton city attorney, characterized the Fly's habitat as "a bunch of dirt and weeds." Jerry Eaves, the chairman of the San Bernardino County Board of Supervisors, stated that "the Endangered Species Act was intended to save eagles and bears. Personally, I don't think we should be spending this money to save cockroaches, snails and flies." Advocates for reform of the ESA seized on the controversy as an example of the kinds of problems that the law created, with the "people vs. flies" argument being voiced frequently.

The Fly has been featured on network television news shows, leading newspapers across the country, *National Geographic*, and other national media. CBS described it as "superfly, with the power to stop bulldozers." The *Los Angeles Times* reported that the Fly could become "the snail darter of the 1990s." Many portrayals of the Fly have been unsympathetic. The *Washington Post* described the Fly as "a creature that spends most of its life underground, living as a fat, clumsy, enigmatic maggot." The *Washington Times* editorialized that "one could build the flies their own mansion in Beverly Hills . . . fill it up from top to bottom with leftover potato salad and other fly delicacies, and it would still be cheaper than the royal estate Fish & Wildlife has in mind for them."

By contrast, UCLA professor Rudy Mattoni described the Fly as "a national treasure in the middle of junkyards. . . It's a fly you can love. It's beautiful." A FWS official told CNN that the Fly "isn't as charismatic as a panda bear or a sea otter, but that doesn't make it any less important." Another FWS official insisted that "the value of the fly to mankind is a very difficult thing to judge. It's much more of a moral issue. Do we have the right to destroy another creature when we, in our day-to-day activities, have the ability not to destroy a creature?" The statement of county supervisor Jerry Eaves that the ESA was not intended to save flies provoked a letter to the editor of the *Los Angeles Times* complaining that "developers and their minions in public office will go to any length to satisfy their corporate greed." Environmentalists also emphasized the importance of the dune ecosystem rather than the Fly. Greg Ballmer, the entomologist who proposed the Fly's listing under the ESA, explained that the Fly "is an umbrella species in that preserving its habitat preserves for posterity the entire community with which it lives." A FWS biologist reminded that "every ecosystem has its intrinsic value, and maybe we can't quite put a dollar value on it. But every time one disappears, it's an indication that something else is wrong." Dan Silver, the head of the Endangered Habitats League, asserted that the ESA "is saving Riverside County from itself, its own short-sightedness. It is forcing people to take a longer view."

Having lost in the courts, the local communities turned to Congress. They paid $48,000 for a Washington lobbyist to persuade Congress to remove the Fly from the list of protected species. Democratic state representative Joe Baca introduced a resolution in the California legislature calling for lifting of the ESA's protection of the Fly; the voters rewarded him by electing him to Congress in 1999. Republican Senate candidate Matt Fong was not so fortunate in 1998: he campaigned against the Fly's impact on development in the region, but he lost to incumbent Senator Barbara Boxer, a supporter of the ESA. The lobbying effort continued in 2002 when Colton Mayor Deirdre Bennett wielded a giant flyswatter while speaking at a press conference denouncing the Fly and its protectors. "To us and the majority of Americans with any common sense at all," protested Mayor Bennett, flies "are pests, nothing more, nothing less—pests we have historically grown up swatting." The protected status of the Fly survived all of these efforts.

Another strategy involved the crafting of a habitat conservation plan (HCP) that would set aside some land for habitat for the Fly and other wildlife while allowing other land—including wildlife habitat—to be developed. Eleven local cities joined San Bernardino County in planning a HCP that would encompass over 300,000 acres of land comprised of eight different kinds of ecosystems and containing the Fly and other rare species such as the San Bernardino kangaroo rat and the Santa Ana River woolystar. Several years of negotiations failed to produce an agreeable plan. Indeed, Colton and other nearby cities and counties temporarily withdrew from their negotiations with the FWS in the summer of 2002, claiming that the anticipated $3 million cost of setting aside 33 acres as habitat for the Fly amounted to "legalized extortion." A FWS spokesperson responded that the agency has worked with cities all across the country "in partnership to develop a plan that makes biological sense and balance the conservation needs of the species and opportunity for economic development." The federal Department of the Interior provided local communities with nearly three million dollars in grants in 2003 for the purchase of some of the Fly's habitat and for the continued preparation of the habitat conservation plan.

Meanwhile, both economic development and protection of the Fly proceeded on a piecemeal basis. The typical approach involved a landowner agreeing to set aside some of its property to serve as habitat for the Fly in exchange for FWS permission to build on another part of its property. In other instances a developer simply paid for the purchase of other land that could be used by the Fly. For example, in August 2000 the developer of a warehouse project agreed to pay $82,500 so that a community group could purchase habitat for the Fly. But neither side was really satisfied by such arrangements: environmentalists worried that the haphazard patches of protected land would not sustain a healthy population of the Fly, while developers watched as their proposed building sites remained vacant as the economic boom of the 1990s ended.

In June 2005, the FWS reached an agreement with Vulcan Materials Company, an Alabama rock and asphalt business that acquired land in Colton as a result of recent corporate mergers. According to the agreement, 150 acres of land owned by Vulcan will be permanently preserved as part of a new conservation bank containing habitat for the Fly. Greg Ballmer described the land as the largest undeveloped parcel remaining in the Colton Dunes ecosystem. The conservation bank will be expanded as other businesses donate land that can serve as habitat for the Fly in order to receive development credits from the FWS. The first sale from the conservation bank occurred in January 2006, when a commercial developer paid $300,000 for two credits, thus preserving two acres of habitat in order to obtain FWS approval to develop five acres of degraded habitat elsewhere in the area. Such conservation banks have become common throughout the nation, but this was the first such bank designed to protect a rare insect.

But even that device frustrated the city officials in Colton. In January 2006, the city council worried about the amount of lands set aside "by open space conservation agreements, easements, and other contractual mechanisms by their owners to insure that these properties will never be used for anything except open space conservation and Delhi Fly Habitat, despite the properties' current land use and zoning designations which may allow for some reasonable development." Accordingly, the city council passed an emergency ordinance requiring the rezoning of any protected land as "Open Space" and the receipt of a conditional use permit before any land within the city may be encumbered with an easement or other device to protect the Fly. At the same time, Mayor Bennett again asked the FWS to delist the Fly, claiming that (1) there is already sufficient habitat to protect the Fly; (2) the FWS had improperly acted as if critical habitat had been designated for the Fly without going through the formal designation process; (3) the recovery plan for the Fly is ambiguous and not achievable; and perhaps most strikingly, (4) the Fly is in fact an invasive species that is not native to the area, and actually threatens the native species there. The FWS rejected the city's claims.

So government officials, developers, environmentalists, and other interested parties are still debating the needs of the Fly, the dunes, and the people who live there. The FWS continues to meet with local county and city officials in an effort to resolve both specific proposed projects and the broader issues raised by the Fly. Scientists are trying to breed the Fly in captivity, though they have not succeeded yet. Private efforts to help the Fly have begun, such as the work of volunteers and local students to restore a four-acre right-of-way owned by Southern California Edison. Nonetheless, scientists and federal officials still fear that the Fly will go extinct early this century despite all of the efforts to save it.

NOTES & QUESTIONS

1. Assume that you are a billionaire who wants to protect the Delhi Sands and the Fly at all costs. What would you do?

Assume that you are an attorney for an environmental group that wants to protect the Delhi Sands and the Fly. What would you advise?

Assume that you are the land use attorney for the City of Colton, and that you have been asked to report on how to protect the Delhi Sands and the Fly while still accounting for human needs in the economically depressed city. What would you recommend?

2. The saga of the dunes and the Fly raises nearly every imaginable question about the relationship between biodiversity and the law. How would you answer the following questions:

- Why should we preserve the Delhi Sands? Why should we preserve the Fly?
- What cost should we be willing to pay to save the dunes or the Fly?
- Should we be more concerned about saving ecosystems like the dunes, or individuals species like the Fly?
- Are some species more worth saving than others? Who should make that decision?

- What role should private efforts play in preserving the dunes and the Fly? What role should the law play?
- Are the dunes and the Fly best protected by international law, federal law, state law, or some combination of such laws?
- Who should pay the costs of protecting the Fly and the Delhi Sands ecosystem?

3. September 23, 2003 marked the tenth anniversary of the listing of the Fly. The Riverside *Press Enterprise* noted the event by remarking "[m]illions spent, millions lost in 10 years to accommodate a rare fly that has bedeviled developers and government officials from Colton to Mira Loma." What report do you expect to read on the twentieth anniversary of the listing of the Fly in 2013?

4. We do not know how the story of the Delhi Sands and the Fly will end. In that respect, the saga is typical of most modern controversies involving biodiversity, as will become obvious as we consider the stories of other ecosystems and species throughout this book. Meanwhile, the best sources of updates on the Fly and the related controversy are the reports of the *Press–Entrorprise* (the Riverside newspaper available on LEXIS or Westlaw). For additional material on the Fly's happenings to date, *see, e.g.*, Determination of Endangered Status for the Delhi Sands Flower–Loving Fly, 58 Fed. Reg. 49881 (1993); U.S. FISH AND WILDLIFE SERVICE, PACIFIC REGION, FINAL RECOVERY PLAN FOR THE DELHI SANDS FLOWER–LOVING FLY (1997); National Ass'n of Home Builders v. Babbitt, 130 F.3d 1041 (D.C.Cir.1997), *cert. denied*, 524 U.S. 937 (1998); JOHN COPELAND NAGLE, LAW'S ENVIRONMENT: HOW THE LAW SHAPES THE PLACES WE LIVE 50-92 (2010) (chapter describing Colton's experience with the Fly and with a variety of other environmental challenges); Kenneth J. Kingsley, *Behavior of the Delhi Sands Flower-Loving Fly (Diptera: Mydidae), A Little–Known Endangered Species*, 89 ANNALS OF THE ENTOMOLOGICAL SOC'Y OF AMERICA 883 (1996).

CHAPTER 2

AN OVERVIEW OF BIODIVERSITY

Chapter Outline:
A. Types of Biodiversity
B. Why We Care About Biodiversity
C. Threats to Biodiversity

People have long pondered the biological wealth of this world with a mixture of wonder, fear, awe, and concern. The term "biodiversity" itself was not coined until the 1980s, when the eminent Harvard biologist Edward O. Wilson popularized it. *See* EDWARD O. WILSON, THE DIVERSITY OF LIFE 15 (1992) (referring to "[b]iological diversity—'biodiversity' in the new parlance"). By 1992, the Convention on Biological Diversity defined biological diversity as "the variability among living organisms from all sources, including, *inter alia*, terrestrial, marine and other aquatic ecosystems and the ecological complexes of which they are a part; this includes diversity within species, between species and of ecosystems." That statement only begins to hint at the vast range of plant, animal, and other life encompassed by the idea of biodiversity. Biodiversity means many things to many people, though the core understanding of the breadth of life on this planet pervades all of the multiple definitions.

This chapter seeks to provide an elementary guide to the nature of biodiversity. It explains what biodiversity means, why it is important, and what threatens its existence today. Each of these topics has elicited far more thoughtful scientific study than can be captured in this overview. The best sources to consult for a sense of the vast scientific and popular literature that has examined the nature of biodiversity just in the past few years include PRECIOUS HERITAGE: THE STATUS OF BIODIVERSITY IN THE UNITED STATES 7–10 (Bruce A. Stein, Lynn S. Kutner & Jonathan S. Adams eds., 2000), a joint product of the Nature Conservancy and the Association for Biodiversity Information, NATIONAL RESEARCH COUNCIL, PERSPECTIVES ON BIODIVERSITY: VALUING ITS ROLE IN AN EVERCHANGING WORLD (1999); REED F. NOSS & ALLEN Y. COOPERRIDER, SAVING NATURE'S LEGACY: PROTECTING AND RESTORING BIODIVERSITY (1994); and WORLD CONSERVATION MONITORING CENTRE, GLOBAL BIODIVERSITY: STATUS OF THE EARTH'S LIVING RESOURCES (Brian Groombridge ed. 1992). And for an excellent interactive tour of biodiversity, conservation biology, and environmental science, try the CD-ROM *Conserving Earth's Biodiversity with E.O. Wilson*, prepared by Edward O. Wilson and Dan L. Perlman.

A. TYPES OF BIODIVERSITY

Jonathan S. Adams, Bruce A. Stein & Lynn S. Kutner, *Biodiversity: Our Precious Heritage*

Precious Heritage: The Status of Biodiversity in the United States 7–10.
(Bruce A. Stein, Lynn S. Kutner & Jonathan S. Adams eds., 2000).

From the Devils Hole pupfish to the delicate spring ecosystems at Ash Meadows to the Mohave Desert, from genes to species to ecosystems to landscapes: Each is part of the fabric of life. Each is a component of biodiversity. But what is biodiversity? Although the term is now common, many people are bewildered by it. Still others use it in an all-encompassing way to refer to any and all nature.

Biodiversity is, in essence, the full array of life on Earth. The most tangible manifestations of this concept are the species of plants, animals, and microorganisms that surround us. Yet biodiversity is more than just the number and diversity of species, as immense as that might be. It also includes the genetic material that makes up those species. And at a higher level, it includes the natural communities, ecosystems, and landscapes of which species are a part. The concept of biodiversity includes both the variety of these things and the variability found within and among them. Biodiversity also encompasses the processes—both ecological and evolutionary—that allow life on Earth to continue adapting and evolving.

While the term *biodiversity* was coined and popularized only recently, the concept is as old as the human desire to know and name all the creatures of the earth. Nature's daunting complexity demands some method of differentiating among its various components. Four of the principal levels of biological organization are genes, species, ecosystems, and landscapes.

Genetic diversity refers to the unique combinations of genes found within and among organisms. Genes, composed of DNA sequences, are the fundamental building blocks of life. The complexes of genes found within individual organisms, and their frequencies of occurrence within a population, are the basic levels at which evolution occurs. Genetic variability is an important trait in assuring the long-term survival of most species, since it allows them to respond to unpredictable changes in their environment.

Species diversity encompasses the variety of living organisms inhabiting an area. This is most commonly gauged by the number of different of organisms—for instance, the number of different birds or plants in a state, country, or ecosystem. While species are the most widely understood aspect of biodiversity, it is actually the individual populations that together make up a species that are the focus of on-the-ground conservation efforts.

Ecological diversity refers to the higher-level organization of different species into natural communities, and the interplay between these communities and the physical environment that forms ecosystems. Interactions are key to ecological diversity. This includes interactions among different species—predators and prey, for instance, or pollinators and flowers—as well as interaction among these species and the physical processes, such as nutrient cycling or periodic fires, that are essential to maintain ecosystem functioning.

Landscape diversity refers to the geography of different ecosystems across a large area and the connection among them. Natural communities and ecosystems change across the landscape in response to environmental gradients such as climate, soils, or altitude and form characteristic mosaics. Understanding the patterns among these natural ecosystems and how they relate to other landscape features, such as farms, cities, and roads, is key to maintaining such regional diversity.

Conservation of biodiversity requires attention to each of these levels, because all contribute to the persistence of life on Earth. More than most people realize, humans rely on wild biological resources for food and shelter. Genes from wild plants, for instance, allow plant breeders to develop disease-resistant crops or increase crop yields, passing along the benefits of biodiversity to farmers and ultimately consumers. Similarly, medicines derived from plants, animals, and especially microbes are an established part of the Western pharmacy and include such widely used medications as aspirin, penicillin, and digitalis. The emerging biotechnology industry, perhaps more than any other, depends on such wild genetic resources. Indeed, a crucial piece of the technology that enables scientists and industry to easily multiply strands of DNA—and thereby create useful commercial products—derives from the bacterium *Thermus aquaticus*, first discovered in a hot spring in Yellowstone National Park.

The value of these biodiversity goods is enormous, but even so it is just a fraction of the value of the ecosystem services on which human life depends, such as waste assimilation, climate regulation, water supply and regulation, erosion control and sediment retention, soil formation, waste treatment, and pollination. Ecosystem services, however, are largely outside the financial markets and therefore are ignored or undervalued. By one rough estimate the value of ecosystem services for the entire biosphere is $33 trillion, nearly double the global gross national product.

When most people think about biodiversity, however, they think not about ecosystems and their services but rather about species. Yet scientists still don't know how many species share the planet with us. Estimates vary by an order of magnitude. A conservative guess is roughly 14 million species, only one-eighth supports far more species than previously believed, from tremendous numbers of beetles living in the canopy of tropical trees to bacteria inhabiting rocks more than a mile beneath the earth's surface.

Individual species, like the pupfishes of the desert Southwest, form threads in the lustrous ecological tapestry of the United States. Further examination reveals a dense weave of thousands of species, many found nowhere else. Together these threads spell out superlatives: tallest, largest, oldest. Topping out at more than 360 feet in height, northern California's redwoods (*Sequoia sempervivens*) are the tallest trees in the world. Their close relatives the giant sequoias (*Sequoiadendron giganteum*) rank among the most massive living things on Earth, and bristlecone pines (*Pinus longaeva*), overlooking the Owens Valley near the summit of eastern California's White Mountains, are the world's oldest living trees, some dating back nearly 5,000 years.

The difference between two species can be visually obvious, as with the Devils Hole and Owens pupfish, or so subtle that only sophisticated molecular techniques can reveal the distinctions. Nonetheless, scientists have documented more than 200,000 species from the United States, and the true number of species living here is probably at least double this figure. By any measure, the United States is home to an exceptionally diverse flora and fauna. On a global scale the nation is particularly noteworthy for certain groups of organisms, including salamanders, coniferous plants, and freshwater fishes, turtles, mussels, snails, and crayfishes. The United States harbors nearly 16,000 species of vascular plants, about 9% of the world's total mammal species, and about 10% of known freshwater fishes worldwide.

This wealth of life owes a great deal to the nation's size and location. While covering only about 6% of the earth's total land area, the United States spans nearly a third of the globe, extending more than 120 degrees of longitude from eastern Maine to the tip of the Aleutian chain, and 50 degrees in latitude from Point Barrow above the Arctic Circle to the southern tip of Hawaii below the tropic of Cancer. Together with this expanse of terrain comes a variety of topographic features and climates, from Death Valley to Mt. McKinley. This range of climates has given rise to a wide array of ecological types, from tundra and subarctic conifer forests called taiga, to deserts, prairie, boreal forest, deciduous forests, temperate rain forest, and even tropical rain forests.

While still far from complete, the process of documenting the nation's ecological diversity suggests that the United States is also extraordinary from an ecological perspective. For example, of the 14 biome types worldwide that represent major ecosystem groups, the United States contains 12, more than any other country. Three biomes—temperate broadleaf forests, temperate grasslands, and mixed mountain systems—are particularly well represented: At least 10% of their area occurs in the United States. Around the world and on a more detailed scale within the United States, ecologists have also identified relatively large areas, known as ecoregions, that in ecological terms function more or less as a unit. With 21 of 28 globally defined ecoregions, the United States is also the most diverse country in the world from an ecoregional perspective.

On a much finer ecological scale, natural heritage ecologists have identified more than 4,500 distinct vegetation communities in the United States. This figure is likely to grow as additional inventory and classification work proceeds, and we can project that on the order to 7,000 to 9,000 natural and seminatural vegetation associations ultimately will be documented from the United States.

NOTES & QUESTIONS

1. What does the term biodiversity mean? Is the term biodiversity really just a synonym for "life on earth?" For a chart listing several other similar, though not identical, definitions, and an analysis of the conceptual problems presented by the idea of biological diversity, see DAN L. PERLMAN & GLENN ADELSON, BIO-DIVERSITY: EXPLORING VALUES AND PRIORITIES IN CONSERVATION (1997).

2. The different types of biodiversity can be viewed along a continuum from the characteristics of individual organisms to the features of vast tracts of land. The same term "biodiversity" is used in each instance because the extent of the biological resources is important at the micro level, the macro level, and everywhere in-between.

Genetic diversity tends to be treated as an issue that is distinct from the other kinds of biodiversity. The value of such diversity is its avoidance of the negative adaptive and reproductive consequences of limiting a species to a population of genetically similar individuals. Much variation in genes requires biological and chemical analysis to detect. Genetic diversity may also be seen in variation among individuals in anatomy and behavior. The genetic differences in Douglas fir trees, for example, are evident in their response to cold and to moisture. Most discussions of genetic diversity occur in either of two contexts: the preservation of seeds for agricultural purposes, and the prevention of in-breeding among endangered animals. Contemporary farming practices often rely upon genetically uniform crops, which present a threat of widespread crop failure if those crops cannot combat a certain pest or disease. Consequently, many environmentalists and agricultural reformers promote seed banks, variation in crops, and other means of achieving greater genetic diversity in agriculture. The importance of genetic diversity in preventing extinction is revealed in the extent of the southern California habitat of the arroyo toad that needs to be protected for the species to survive. "Populations on the periphery of the species range or in atypical ecological environments are important for maintaining the genetic diversity of the species which could be essential to evolutionary adaptation to changing climatic and environmental conditions." The protection of the arroyo toad thus required 22 discrete habitat units totaling over 182,000 acres. *See* Final Designation of Critical Habitat for the Arroyo Toad, 66 Fed. Reg. 9414, 9419–26 (2001). A similar challenge is presented by the genetic similarity of all cheetahs: "The fastest animal on land, an apparent model of evolutionary fitness, is also as inbred as the average lab mouse." Richard Conniff, *Cheetahs: Ghosts of the Grasslands*, NAT'L GEO., Dec. 1999, at 20.

Species diversity is the most familiar form of biodiversity. It is the only kind of biodiversity protected by its own federal law—the Endangered Species Act (ESA)—and by international treaties such as the Convention on the International Trade in Endangered Species (CITES). Yet it is surprisingly difficult to identify what constitutes a "species." Why are there eight distinct species of bears: Asiatic black bears, American black bears, brown bears, the giant panda, polar bears, sloth bears, spectacled bears, and sun bears? Why are the Siberian tiger, the South China tiger, the Indo-Chinese tiger, and the Bengal tiger viewed as members of the same species (albeit different subspecies)? Why was it not until 2001 that scientists decided that African elephants actually constitute two distinct species, African forest elephants and African savannah elephants? *See* Alfred L. Roca et al., *Genetic Evidence for Two Species of Elephant*

in Africa, 293 SCIENCE 1473 (2001). Why not treat all tigers and leopards and jaguars as members of a single species of large, orange, carnivorous cats? Which characteristics should be relevant in determining the identity of a species? While there is no definitive answer to such questions, the most common understanding of what constitutes a species is attributed to Harvard evolutionary biologist Ernst Mayr: "A species is a reproductive community of populations, reproductively isolated from other populations, that occupies a specific niche in nature." ERNST MAYR, THE GROWTH OF BIOLOGICAL THOUGHT 273 (1982). Mayr's explanation does not solve the definitional problem, though, as evidenced by the struggle to decide what constitutes a "species" for purposes of the ESA, recounted below at pages 147–54.

Ecosystem diversity has gained increasing attention in recent years. That attention is reflected in the countless scientific conferences examining many kinds of ecosystems, the popular concern about specific types of ecosystems such as wetlands and rainforests, and the attention that ecosystems have received pursuant to the collection of state and federal laws considered in Part III. There are still few laws that are specifically designed to protect a wide collection of different kinds of ecosystems, though many environmentalists favor the enactment of something like an "Endangered Ecosystem Act" modeled on the existing ESA. *See, e.g.*, Julie B. Bloch, *Preserving Biological Diversity in the United States: The Case for Moving to an Ecosystems Approach to Protect the Nation's Biological Wealth*, 10 PACE ENVTL. L. REV. 175, 217–22 (1992) (advocating a federal "Ecosystems Protection Act").

Yet the idea of an "ecosystem" is even more difficult to define than a "species." The general idea is of a community of organisms found in a particular geographical area. That community is dynamic and its borders cannot always be ascertained. Nonetheless, a variety of types of ecosystems have been recognized. For example, "[a]n ecosystem can be a vegetation type, a plant association, a natural community, or a habitat defined by floristics, structure, age, geography, condition, or other ecologically relevant factors. Thus, virgin and old-growth forests, pitcher plant (*Sarracenia* spp.) bogs, ungrazed sagebrush steppe, wetlands, (general or specific types), Midwestern oak (*Quercus* spp.) savanna, vernal pools, free-flowing rivers, and seagrass meadows are ecosystem types." Reed F. Noss, Edward T. LaRoe III & J. Michael Scott, *Endangered Ecosystems of the United States: A Preliminary Assessment of Loss and Degradation*, 28 BIOLOGICAL REP. 1, 3 (1995), *available at* http://biology.usgs.gov/pubs/ecosys.htm.

Landscape diversity refers to the collection of different kinds of ecosystems. Many areas contain multiple ecosystems, such as grasslands, wetlands and forests. The diversity of ecosystems, and the resulting diverse landscapes becomes visible only from a regional perspective. The next category—ecoregions—describes "large landscapes that can be distinguished from other regions on the basis of climate, physiography, soils, species composition patterns (biogeography) and other variables." NOSS & COOPERRIDER, *supra*, at 11. Finally, a "biome" is a "major regional community of plants and animals with similar life forms and environmental conditions." M. Lynne Corn, *Ecosystems, Biomes, and Watersheds: Definitions and Use*, CRS Rep.No. 93–655 ENR, at 4 (1993). The fourteen biomes of the world are tropical humid forests, subtropical/temperate rain forests/woodlands, temperate needleleaf forests/woodlands, tropical dry forests/woodlands, temperate broadleaf forests, evergreen scle-

rophyllous forests, warm deserts/semideserts, tropical grasslands/savannas, temperate grasslands, mixed island systems, tundra communities, mixed mountain systems, cold-winter deserts, and lake systems. *See* Mark T. Bryer et al., *More Than the Sum of the Parts: Diversity and Status of Ecological Systems*, in PRECIOUS HERITAGE, *supra*, at 206 (providing a map of the world's biomes).

This previously undescribed honeyeater is the first new species of bird to be found in New Guinea in more than 60 years.

Wild Mekong: New Species In 2010 from the Forests, Wetlands and Waters of the Greater Mekong, Asia's Land of Rivers

World Wildlife Fund, 2011.
http://awsassets.panda.org/downloads/greater_mekong_species_report_web_ready_version_nov_14_2011_1.pdf.

A new monkey, a self-cloning skink, five carnivorous plants, and a unique leaf warbler are among the 208 species newly described by science in the Greater Mekong region during 2010. In total 145 plants, 28 reptiles, 25 fish, 7 amphibians, 2 mammals and 1 bird have been discovered in the last year.

This rate of discovery marks Asia's land of rivers as one of the last frontiers for new species discoveries on our planet.

The Greater Mekong region of Southeast Asia through which the Mekong river flows comprises the countries of Cambodia, Laos, Myanmar, Thailand, Vietnam and China (including Yunnan province). The region is home to some of the planet's most endangered and charismatic wild species including tiger, Asian elephant, Mekong dolphin and Mekong giant catfish,

in addition to hundreds of newly discovered species. Between 1997 and 2009 an incredible 1,376 species were discovered by science across this region alone. . .

PSYCHEDELIC GECKO (Cnemaspis psychedelica)

A new psychedelic gecko species was discovered this past year on Hon Khoai Island, Ca Mau Province, Ngoc Hien District, 18 km off the southern tip of the Ca Mu Peninsula in southern Vietnam.

The new species is unique in that it displays a remarkable psychedelic pattern of bright orange appendages; a dense, yellow neck overlying thick, black, lines; and a blue-gray body bearing yellow bars on its bright-orange sides. It also differs from all other species of Cnemaspis in size.

Psychedelic gecko

Cnemaspis psychedelica is the third endemic species of Cnemaspis from Vietnam and brings the total number of species in Vietnam to six. Its occurrence on one of 92 islands in Rach Gia Bay highlights the necessity for further surveys of these little known islands according to scientists, who are just beginning to reveal the surprising degree of endemism and diversity in the area. This further emphasises that the full extent of the Greater Mekong's biological diversity remains unknown to science.

Cnemaspis psychedelica is known only from the tiny (roughly 8 km2) Hon Khoai Island. The island reaches approximately 320m at its highest point, with thick forest cover sloping gently down to a mangrove-lined coast. Scattered across the lowlands of the island are small to massive boulders that provide the habitat for *Cnemaspis psychedelica*.

Some 75 species from the *Cnemaspis* are now found across Asia.

NOTES & QUESTIONS

1. We continue to discover new species at a rapid rate. Arizona State University's International Institute for Species Exploration reported that 19,232 species were discovered in 2009. *See* International Institute for Species Exploration: 2011 SOS State of Observed Species: A Report on Our Knowledge of Earth's Species (2012), http://timgostony.com/iisetemp/SOS2011_FINALr.pdf. Vietnam has hosted some of the most remarkable finds in recent years, including the Vu Quang ox—also known as the soala—that was known only to villagers living near the mountainous rainforests in northern Vietnam until a British biologist made the ox the largest mammal discovered in nearly a century. It and other species in the area had remained hidden in part because war and trade embargoes prevented scientists from exploring the area. *See* Eugene Linden, *Ancient Creatures in a Lost World: In An Isolated Region that Divides Vietnam and Laos, Scientists Find a Trove of New Species*, TIME, June 20, 1994, at 52.

Species belonging to other classes are discovered far more frequently than mammals and birds. Entomologists are always finding new insects, such as the hundreds of beetles that Smithsonian Institution scientist Terry Erwin found in a single tree in the Panamanian rain forest. Nearly 1,000 new species of mollusks have been identified in the Florida Keys since 1995. In 1994, biologists found a tree that had been thought to have been extinct for 60 million years in a canyon in Wollemi National Park north of Sydney. Nor are such discoveries limited to remote, uninhabited parts of the world. Three new species of spiders were found by collectors in a forest preserve outside of Chicago in 2000. A new species of ant was discovered in a potted plant in a Washington, D.C. office. Besides these individual species, entirely new ecosystems continue to be discovered, especially in the virgin forests of the Amazon.

2. The ongoing discovery of new species of wildlife and plants presents obvious challenges to any estimate of the total number of species in the world. Scientists believe that "[t]he majority of species on Earth have yet to be discovered," guessing that we have identified as few as ten percent of the species that live throughout the world. ANDREW BEATTIE & PAUL EHRLICH, WILD SOLUTIONS:

How Biodiversity is Money in the Bank 9 (2001). Perhaps it should be surprising, then, that estimates regarding the amount of biodiversity vary greatly. Medieval scientists assumed that the total number of species in the world was constrained by the capacity of Noah's ark. Today's scientists guess that the total number of species ranges anywhere from one million to 100 million. The proper methodology for calculating the number of species is often contested as scientists disagree about how to extrapolate from the relatively small number of known species to the admittedly unknown total number of species. The methodology and contours of that debate are well summarized in Nigel E. Stork, *The Magnitude of Global Biodiversity and Its Decline*, in THE LIVING PLANET IN CRISIS 10–21 (1999); WORLD CONSERVATION MONITORING CENTRE, *supra*, at 17–38; NORMAN MYERS, THE SINKING ARK (1979). It is important to remember, though, that "biodiversity is not just a numbers game," and that "[w]hen we consider species richness at any scale smaller than the biosphere, quality is more important than quantity." NOSS & COOPERRIDER, *supra*, at 4.

3. Whatever number is accurate, it is apparent that biodiversity is not distributed evenly throughout the world. On a local level, the number of species increases as the area of land increases. For example, if ten species live on one acre of land, then 20 species would be expected on 32 acres of land. But the amount of land is not the sole determiner of the extent of biodiversity. "Life does not lie evenly across the landscape. For a variety of reasons—evolution, geography, climate, or historical accident, to name a few—some places harbor more species than others." Stephen J. Chaplin, *The Geography of Imperilment: Targeting Conservation Toward Critical Biodiversity Areas*, in PRECIOUS HERITAGE, *supra*, at 187. Maps of the homes of endangered species in the United States display a concentration along the Pacific Coast, Florida, and the Appalachians, with relatively few rare species in the northeast or the central Great Plains. *See id.* at 162–83 (illustrating the distribution of biodiversity nationwide according to several different measures). The tendency of biodiversity to concentrate in certain areas has led conservationists to focus on so-called "hot spots" where the most biodiversity is found. One study identified six such hot spots in the United States:

- *Hawai'i*, whose isolation has resulted in a remarkable collection of plant and animal life, including many striking forest birds;
- *The southern Appalachians*, where rivers teem with unique fish and mussels;
- *The San Francisco Bay area*, which features many endemic plants and vernal pool invertebrates;
- *Coastal and interior southern California*, where an array of birds, fish, plants, and insects—including the Delhi Sands Flower-Loving Fly—live in coastal sage scrub and grassland ecosystems;
- *The Florida panhandle*, whose woodlands, bays and rivers host an exceptional array of reptiles and amphibians; and
- *The Death Valley region*, where unusual fish, snails, and plants survive amidst the harsh desert environment.

Id. at 188–99. These hotspots only begin to show how much biodiversity exists close to home. As one study concluded, "By any measure, the United States is home to an exceptionally diverse flora and fauna. On a global scale the nation is particularly noteworthy for certain groups of organisms, including salamanders, coniferous plants, and freshwater fishes, turtles, mussels, snails, and crayfishes." Jonathan S. Adams, Bruce A. Stein & Lynn S. Kutner, *Biodiversity: Our Precious Heritage 9*, in PRECIOUS HERITAGE, *supra*, at 9; *see also* Bruce A. Stein et al., *A Remarkable Array: Species Diversity in the United States*, in PRECIOUS HERITAGE, *supra*, at 55–92 (detailing the number and kinds of species that live in the United States).

Of course, the United States is only one of a number of places blessed with abundant biodiversity. Russell Miettermeier, whose work for Conservation International is discussed in the *Science* article, has coauthored two books documenting biological hotspots around the world. The first book describes 25 of those places, including the tropical Andes, the Caribbean, Madagascar and Indian Ocean islands, the Caucasus, the mountains of south-central China, and southwest Australia. *See* RUSSELL A. MITTERMEIER, NORMAN MYERS & CRISTINA GOETTSCH MITTERMEIER, HOTSPOTS: EARTH'S BIOLOGICALLY RICHEST AND MOST ENDANGERED TERRESTRIAL ECOREGIONS (1999). The importance of such hotspots is demonstrated by such statistics as the occurrence of 70% of all vascular plants within the 1.44% of the earth's surface occupied by the hotspots; and the presence of 35.5% of all bird, mammal, reptile and amphibian species only in those hotspots. *Id.* at 34, 37. The second book, published five years later, identified "six previously overlooked areas [that] qualify for hotspot status," including the Madrean Pine-Oak Woodlands of northern Mexico and the southwestern United States, the mountains of central Asia, and Japan. RUSSELL MITTERMEIER ET AL., HOTSPOTS REVISITED: EARTH'S BIOLOGICALLY RICHEST AND MOST ENDANGERED TERRESTRIAL ECOREGIONS 29 (2004). For another list of hotspots, and a proposed Vital Ecosystems Preservation Act to protect them, *see* JOHN CHARLES KUNICH, ARK OF THE BROKEN COVENANT: PROTECTING THE WORLD'S BIODIVERSITY HOTSPOTS (2003).

B. WHY WE CARE ABOUT BIODIVERSITY

Testimony of Dr. Michael Grever, *Medicinal Uses of Plants; Protection for Plants Under the Endangered Species Act: Hearing Before the Subcommittee on Environment and Natural Resources of the House Committee on Merchant Marine and Fisheries*

United States House of Representatives, 1993.
103d Cong., 1st Sess., pp. 20–32.

I am Dr. Michael Grever, Associate Director for the Developmental Therapeutics Program (DTP) of the National Cancer Institutes's (NCI) Division of Cancer Treatment, at the National Institutes of Health (NIH)... Thank you for the opportunity to appear before you today to discuss the NCI's efforts to locate and develop medicinal compounds from plants to combat cancer and HIV (human immunodeficiency virus) infection and its sequelae. NCI is exploring and supporting a broad spectrum of ways to combat these two diseases, from prevention and diagnosis through treatment to rehabilitation and psychosocial care of patients. Drug development from natural products is just one avenue of emphasis; but until we can completely prevent cancer or HIV infection from occurring, it is an extremely important part of our effort to develop and design more effective and less toxic treatments.

In 1993, over 1 million new cases of cancer will be diagnosed in the United States and about 526,000 people will die of the disease. Since cancer incidence increases with age, most cases occur in adults at mid-life or older. There has been a steady rise in the cancer mortality rate in the United States in the last 50 years, with the major causes of this increase being lung, prostate, and breast cancers. The impact of cancer in general on minority and underserved populations is disproportionately great.

AIDS (acquired immune deficiency syndrome) was recognized as a distinctive syndrome over ten years ago and since then NCI has been involved in multiple disciplines of AIDS research. AIDS is not the primary mission of NCI; however, NCI leads the NIH's efforts in pediatric AIDS clinical studies, making advances in the identification and evaluation of potential therapies for HIV-infected children. Similarly, NCI heads efforts to develop therapies for HIV-associated malignancies, and has developed an extensive and comprehensive program to design and develop anti-HIV drug therapies. Following the discovery of the antiviral action of AZT (azidothymidine), ddi (dideoxyinosine), and ddc (dideoxycytidine) in the intramural NCI in the mid-1980's, the cancer drug screen was adapted for anti-HIV drug screening.

For our natural products drug screening effort to be at all successful, we must have available to us a multitude of species to study, and preservation of the species is critical to this effort. Global consumption patterns, perverse policy incentives and population pressures threaten biodiversity worldwide. In the countryside, exploitative resource management practices deplete soil and contaminate water supplies; deforestation for farming, pasture and building material leads to erosion and heavy flooding. The resulting disappearance of natural habitats has profound economic, environmental and scientific consequences. Among the ultimate consequences will be a loss of raw materials from which medicinal products might be developed.

BACKGROUND

Throughout the ages humans have looked to nature as a source of medicines for the treatment of a wide variety of diseases. Plants have formed the basis for sophisticated systems of traditional medicine, which have been in existence for thousands of years throughout the globe. Microorganisms and marine organisms have, however, played lesser roles in such traditional systems.

Natural products also play an essential role in the health care systems of developed countries, in providing new types of biologically active substances that either cannot be made chemically or would not have been conceived by chemists. Well-known examples of plant-derived medicinal agents include the antimalarial drug quinine, the analgesics codeine and morphine, the tranquilizer reserpine, and the cardiac glycoside, digitalis. The role of microbial fermentations has been predominant in the development of antibiotics, with over 8,500 substances isolated from microbial sources, and close to 100,000 prepared by chemical modification of the native material. Well-known classes of antibiotics are the penicillins, cephalosporins, and tetracyclines, while other microbial products include immunosuppressive, antiparasitic, and antifungal agents. Until the development of SCUBA (Self-Contained Underwater Breathing Apparatus), the exploration of the marine environment was virtually impossible, with the result that few marine natural products of medicinal value have been developed to date. That, however, is changing rapidly, and more thorough investigation of this area is yielding an increasing number of novel active substances. . .

RECENT NCI DISCOVERIES

A total of 54,000 extracts, derived from all natural product sources, have been submitted for anti-HIV screening since about 1986. To date, over 35,000 plant samples have been collected by the NCI contractors, and over 25,000 have been extracted to yield more than 50,000 plant extracts. Over 25,000 of these plant extracts have been tested in the anti-HIV screen, and about 2,700 have exhibited some intro activity; of these, close to 2,400 are aqueous extracts, and in the majority of cases the activity has been attributed to the presence of ubiquitous types of chemicals, such as polysaccharides and tannins. Such compounds are not a current NCI focus for drug development and typically are eliminated early in the discovery process. Therefore, the number of extracts undergoing active investigation is much smaller.

A number of novel in vitro active anti-HIV agents have been isolated and selected for preclinical development. The dimeric alkaloid, michellamine B, has been isolated from the leaves of a tropical vine collected in the rain forest regions of southwestern Cameroon. Michellamine B shows in vitro activity against both the HIV-1 and HIV-2, and is in advanced preclinical development. Preliminary surveys of the occurrence and abundance of the species, as well as cultivation experiments, have been carried out by Missouri Botanical Garden through its contract with the NCI. Surveys thus far indicate that its range and abundance are very limited, but fallen leaves collected from the forest floor have been shown to contain reasonable quantities of michellamine B; the collection of these leaves has obviated the large-scale harvest of fresh leaves, and avoided possible endangerment of the wild species. Fallen leaf collections will provide sufficient michellamine B to complete preclinical studies, but the NCI is proceeding with feasibility studies of the cultivation of the plant through contract mechanisms. The collections and cultivation experiments are being performed with the full participation of Cameroon authorities and scientists, as well as through close collaboration with the World Wide Fund for Nature, which is coordinating conservation projects in the Korup region of Cameroon. Thus far, no other related species have shown significant anti-HIV activity.

Calanolide A is a novel coumarin isolated from the leaves and twigs of a tree collected in the rain forest regions of Sarawak, Malaysia. Calanolide A shows potent intro activity against HIV-1 and several resistant strains of the virus, but not against HIV-2, and is in early preclinical development. Recollections of plant material of the original plant species from the same general location have shown a range of test results varying from reasonable activity to total lack of activity. It is apparent that the production of calanolide A is dependent on various factors, possibly including the immediate growth environment and the time of harvest. Thus far, calanolide A has not been detected in any of the recollections, and the original source tree cannot be located. Careful taxonomic and chemotaxonomic studies of this species are being performed by the UIC, under contract to and in collaboration with the NCI and scientists from Sarawak. A survey of related species has shown that the latex of another species collected in the same region yields the related compound, costatolide, which has significant in vitro anti-HIV activity, though being somewhat less active than calanolide A. Costatolide and a derivative have also been approved for preclinical development. The latex contains high yields of costatolide, and would be an excellent renewable source of the compound, should it advance to clinical development. In addition, the synthesis of calanolide A has recently been reported.

A novel chemical compound, conocurvone, has been isolated from a plant species endemic to Western Australia; this plant was originally collected for the NCI program by the USDA in 1981. Conocurvone exhibits potent in vitro activity against HIV-1 and is in early preclinical development. Conocurvone has been synthesized from a simpler chemical which can also be isolated from the plant, and in addition, other simpler analogs have been synthesized and shown to possess equivalent in vitro anti-HIV activity. The development of conocurvone or related compounds will be undertaken in close collaboration with Australian scientists, and surveys of the occurrence and abundance of the source plant and related species are being carried out by the Western Australian Department of Conservation and Land Management.

Another potential anti-HIV agent, prostratin, has been isolated from the stemwood of a Western Samoan tree. This tree is used in Western Samoa for the treatment of a variety of diseases, including yellow fever, and an extract of the stemwood was provided by Dr. Paul Cox of Brigham Young University. The prostratin belongs to the phorbol class of compounds which frequently exhibit significant tumor promoting properties, it does not appear to be associated with tumor promotion, and has been selected for early preclinical development.

Of the approximately 30,000 extracts tested so far in the intro human cancer cell line screen, which started after the anti-HIV screen, a very small percentage (< 1.0 percent) have shown some degree of selective cytotoxicity. Interesting, novel patterns of differential cytotoxicity have been observed, and while some have been associated with known classes of compounds, others appear to be new leads which are being investigated further. Two natural products currently approved for preclinical development are halomon, isolated from a red algae collected in the Philippines, and halichondrin B, isolated from a species of marine sponge found in the western pacific ocean. The procurement of materials for future development is underway. . .

NOTES & QUESTIONS

1. Scientists continue to examine numerous plants as they search for a cure for AIDS. A University of California, Irvine scientist has identified a Bolivian plant that contains a chemical that prevents the AIDS virus from reproducing and infecting healthy cells, though a decade of testing may be needed to determine whether the chemical can actually be used against AIDS in humans. The Centers for Disease Prevention and Control report that "[h]erbs have been used extensively in hopes of improving immune response and reducing symptoms. Aloe vera, St. Johnswort, echinacea, licorice, and ginseng are just a few of the herbs used to treat HIV/AIDS." CDC, *Fact Sheet: HIV/AIDS and Alternative Therapies* http://www.aegis.com/pubs/cdc fact sheets/1994/cdc94033.html. To date, however, the cure for AIDS remains undiscovered.

Besides helping in the fight against AIDS, plants and animals are an important source of drugs and other medical treatments. Numerous exotic plants have yielded live-saving drugs. "Bark from the white willow gave us salicin, an ancient version of aspirin; the Grecian foxglove provided digoxin, a cardiac medication; bear bile is the origin of ursodiol, a gallstone dissolver; deadly nightshade led to atropine, an eye dilator and anti-inflammatory; the velvet bean produced L-dopa, a treatment for Parkinson's disease; and everyone knows the story of penicillin, the bacteria slayer discovered accidentally in a mold." CHARLES C. MANN & MARK L. PLUMMER, NOAH'S CHOICE: THE FUTURE OF ENDANGERED SPECIES 120–21 (1995). Animals, fish, amphibians and insects possess medical value as well. *See* THE ENDANGERED SPECIES COALITION, THE ENDANGERED SPECIES ACT: A COMMITMENT WORTH KEEPING 10 (1995) (citing the medical benefits of bats, crustaceans, mollusks, insects, and snakes); Myers, *supra*, at 265 (describing how frogs can provide antitoxins and pain killers, an octopus produces a substance that relieves hypertension, and insects secrete substances similar to hormones). "Coral reef products include anti-inflammatory, antiviral, and anti-tumor compounds isolated from a variety of invertebrates." BEATTIE & EHRLICH, *supra*, at 202–204. The leaves of the desert yellowhead—a plant found in only one location in Fremont County, Wyoming—"contain a chemical that produces a mild numbing sensation in the human mouth when even tiny portions are tasted. This could indicate potential medicinal qualities that could prove attractive to pharmaceutical companies. . ." Endangered and Threatened Wildlife and Plants: Listing the Desert Yellowhead as Threatened, 67 Fed. Reg. 11442, 11445 (2002). Traditional medicines are especially dependent upon products derived from plants, animals, and other natural sources. Herbal medicines are becoming increasingly popular in the United States and other developed countries as well. And we are only beginning to study most species to learn if they possess any medical value. *See Endangered Species Act: Washington, DC-Part II: Oversight Hearing Before the Task Force on Endangered Species Act of the Comm. on Resources, House of Representatives*, 104th Cong. 35 (1995) (testimony of Dr. Kevin H. Browngoehl, Biodiversity Committee, National Physicians for the Environment) (stating that "[o]nly 5 percent of our flowering plant species have been studied chemically with any thoroughness to look for their medicinal value"); Mann & Plummer, *supra*, at 121–22 (observing that "biologists frequently liken the world's biodiversity to a library in which the vast majority of books has never been read. . . Reading the books in the species library once will not be enough. . . Each generation will profit from reading them over and over again.").

Biodiversity contributes to human health in other ways as well. A wide variety of animals serve as medical models: sharks rarely develop tumors, armadillos acquire leprosy, the large optic nerves of horseshoe crabs enable the study of human vision, and the failure of bears to lose bone mass might help address osteoporosis. Conversely, the absence of biodiversity can have lethal consequences for humans. A reduction in the predators of the deer mouse in the southwestern United States resulted in a population surge in the mice that caused a respiratory syndrome epidemic that killed 13 people in 1993. For additional information about such medical issues, see Biodiversity and Human Health (Francesa Grifo & Joshua Rosenthal eds. 1997); and Francesco T. Grifo & Eric Chivian, *The Implications of Biodiversity Loss for Human Health*, in THE LIVING PLANET IN CRISIS: BIODIVERSITY SCIENCE AND POLICY 197–208 (Joel Crancraft & Francesca T. Grifo eds. 1999).

2. Biodiversity offers many benefits beyond medicines and human health. Congress has explained that "species of fish, wildlife, and plants are of aesthetic, ecological, educational, historical, recreational, and scientific value to the Nation and its people." 16 U.S.C. § 1531(a)(3). These are all utilitarian justifications for protecting endangered species of wildlife and plants. The benefits are impressive:

- *Food*—People eat animals and plants, and not much else. This gives tasty or nutritious animals and plants real economic value. Today "the constant infusion of genes from wild plant species adds approximately $1 billion per year to U.S. agricultural production." *Washington ESA Hearing Part II, supra*, at 175 (statement of the National Wildlife Federation). Producing food provides jobs for millions of Americans. If an edible species disappears, so do the food and the jobs they provide. Thus some members of the Pacific Northwest's salmon industry are among the ESA's biggest supporters. Moreover, genetic diversity within species has helped increase the yields of many agricultural crops.

- *Aesthetics, tourism and recreation*—People enjoy visiting, photographing, painting, and just looking at wildlife. The aesthetic value of a beautiful animal or plant often produces a tangible economic value in the form of ecotourism. Grizzly bears attract millions of people to Yellowstone and Glacier National Parks annually. Whales bring visitors to California, Hawaii, and New England. Tourists travel to numerous areas to visit bald eagles. These visits produce substantial economic value. The FWS recently reported that the 76 million Americans who watched, photographed and fed birds and other wildlife in 1991 spent $18.1 billion on those activities. *See* James D. Caudill, U.S. Fish and Wildlife Service, 1991 Economic Impacts of Nonconsumptive Wildlife-Related Recreation 6–7 (1997). Another report calculated that birdwatching alone is a $15 billion dollar business annually. These general economic benefits also result from endangered species in particular. Whooping cranes and other wildlife generate $5 million annually to the economy of the area surrounding the Aransas National Wildlife Refuge in Texas. A rancher in the Texas Hill Country earned

$14,000 from groups that came to see the endangered golden-cheeked warbler and black-capped vireo. Developing countries with a wealth of biodiversity benefit from increasing ecotourism, such as the $87 million in revenues that Costa Rica's protected areas account for annually. The aesthetic appeal of many ecosystems and endangered species extends to those who never see such an ecosystem or species in the wild, or who never will.

Biodiversity possesses other utilitarian values, too. Much clothing is made from natural fibers. Bioremediation employs bacteria and other organisms to fight oil spills and remove other forms of pollution. Copper production is facilitated by the use of bacteria to extract metals. The trees, animals and other life that form a natural landscape give many people a sense of place that contributes to their well being. Various plants and animals have served as a blueprint for human efforts to develop robotics, fire and smoke detectors, air conditioning, and energy. Biodiversity provides raw materials for the biotechnology industry. All of these benefits are cataloged in ANDREW BEATTIE & PAUL EHRLICH, WILD SOLUTIONS: HOW BIODIVERSITY IS MONEY IN THE BANK (2001); National Research Council, Perspectives on Biodiversity 43–67 (1999); YVONNE BASKIN, THE WORK OF NATURE: HOW THE DIVERSITY OF LIFE SUSTAINS US (1997).

Yet biodiversity can be a two-edged sword. Is the unknown monkey in the Amazon rainforest the source of the cure for AIDS, or is it the bearer of the next AIDS virus? Species that stray outside of their natural habitats can have deadly consequences for people and biodiversity alike, as demonstrated by the effects of the smallpox virus on Native Americans and by the devastation wrought on native Hawaiian wildlife by goats, sheep, and mosquitos that were introduced (sometimes intentionally, sometimes not) by western settlers. National Geographic published the journal of a nature photographer whose assignment at a new Bolivian national park led him to encounter toxic moths, stinging black ants, burrowing maggots, and a sand fly whose bite spread flesh-eating parasites that created a wound requiring surgery and 21 days of intravenous treatment with an antimony compound. *See* Joel Sartore, *Bugging Out*, NAT'L GEO., Mar. 2000, at 24–29. Moreover, not all species or ecosystems are equal in providing benefits to humanity. People depend upon about two dozen species for most of their food, but even considering that another 3,000 plant species may be a source of food, that still leaves many species with no nutritional value for humans. Efforts to identify plants and animals with medicinal uses have identified far more "useless" species than helpful ones. Beauty may be in the eye of the beholder, but if we are willing to designate certain areas as worthy of special protection because of their unique features, why not make such distinctions among plants and animals? Tourists make such choices daily: whatever abstract arguments can be made about their aesthetic appeal, the wildlife of the Everglades National Park attracts far more visitors than most local nature preserves. Charles Mann and Mark Plummer have thus concluded that "biodiversity as a whole has overwhelming utilitarian value, but most individual species do not." MANN & PLUMMER, *supra*, at 133. Indeed, they suggest that "the entire discussion of utilitarian value, though often invoked as a reason to conserve biodiversity, is a red herring." *Id.* at 134. Are they right?

Sandra Postel & Stephen Carpenter, *Freshwater Ecosystem Services*

NATURE'S SERVICES: SOCIETAL DEPENDENCE ON NATURAL ECOSYSTEMS (Gretchen Daily ed. 1997). Pages 195–207.

It is no coincidence that early human civilizations sprang from river valleys and floodplains. Sufficient quantities of freshwater have underpinned the advancement of human societies since their beginning. Today, we rely on the solar-powered hydrological cycle not only for water supplies, but also for a wide range of goods and life-support services, many of which are hidden and easy to take for granted.

Only a small portion of earth's water wealth consists of liquid water that is fresh enough to drink, grow crops, and satisfy other human needs. Of the total volume of water on the planet (an estimated 1,386,000,000 cubic kilometers, or km^3), only 2.5 percent is fresh—and two-thirds of that is locked in glaciers and ice caps. Merely 0.77 percent of all water is held in lakes, rivers, wetlands, underground aquifers, soil pores, plant life, and the atmosphere.

Of particular importance to the sustenance of earth's biological richness is precipitation on land, an estimated 110,000 km^3 per year. This water is made available year after year by the hydrological cycle and constitutes the total terrestrial renewable freshwater supply. Natural systems, such as forests, grasslands, and rivers, as well as many human-dominated landscapes, such as croplands and pasture, depend upon this rainfall and are finely tuned to natural precipitation patterns.

In some sense, this water is infinitely valuable, since without it landbased life as we know it would disappear. In this chapter, however, we focus not on the entire hydrological cycle, but on the benefits to the human enterprise provided by freshwater systems—primarily, rivers, lakes, aquifers, and wetlands. We attempt to estimate the total value of selected goods and services provided by these systems and, where data exist, offer some estimates of marginal values as well.

The benefits provided by freshwater systems fall into three broad categories: (1) the supply of water for drinking, irrigation, and other purposes; (2) the supply of goods other than water, such as fish and waterfowl; and (3) the supply of nonextractive or "instream" benefits, such as recreation, transportation, and flood control. . .

Water Supply Services

Once precipitation falls on land, it divides into two parts—evapotranspiration (representing the water supply for all nonirrigated vegetation) and runoff (overland flow back toward the sea via rivers, streams, and under ground aquifers). Through their role in the hydrological cycle, rivers, lakes, and underground aquifers provide a renewable source of freshwater for the human economy to tap. They are the principal source of freshwater for irrigation, households, industries, and other uses that require the removal of water from its natural channels.

Human demands for this water have increased rapidly in recent decades as a result of population growth, changes in diet, and higher levels of material consumption: withdrawals or extractions of water from the aquatic environment have more than tripled since 1950. Today, the volume of water removed from rivers, lakes, and aquifers for human activities worldwide totals some 4,430 km³ per year. Because accessing this water typically requires the construction of dams, reservoirs, canals, groundwater wells, and other infrastructure, there is a direct and tangible economic cost associated with it; this water supply service is not totally free. However, the full value of the service comes to light by considering the cost of replacing natural sources of freshwater with the next best alternative.

Unlike oil, coal, or tin, for which substitutes exist, freshwater is largely nonsubstitutable. The next best alternative is water processed by technological desalination—the removal of salt from seawater, the function performed naturally by the hydrological cycle. Worldwide, desalination accounts for less than 0.1 percent of total water use. It is a highly energy-intensive process and therefore an expensive supply option. The cost of desalination is in the neighborhood of $1–2 per cubic meter (m³)—four to eight times more than the average cost of urban water supplies today, and at least 10–20 times what most farmers currently pay. Not surprisingly, some 60 percent of the world's desalting capacity is in the Persian Gulf, where fossil energy sources are abundant and freshwater is scarce. Through desalination, countries in this region have essentially been turning oil into water to satisfy drinking and other household need. . .

Supply of Goods Other Than Water

In addition to supplying water, aquatic ecosystems provide many other goods of value to the human economy. Among the most important are fish waterfowl, shellfish, and pelts.

The global freshwater fishery harvest offers a lower-bound estimate of the commercial value of freshwater fish. The annual harvest in 1989–91 was about fourteen million tons, and was valued at some $8.2 billion. This figure does not include the values of the distribution economy or other components of the total economic impact of fishing.

Perhaps surprisingly, the value of sport fisheries often exceeds that of commercial fisheries—in some areas by one hundred-fold or more. Sport fishing is a substantial recreational pursuit in the United States. In 1991 thirty-one million anglers fished an average of fourteen days each in the United States. Expenditures—including equipment, travel costs, etc.—totaled about $16 billion. The full economic impacts of freshwater angling, however, are far larger than direct expenditures. These impacts include changes in income or employment resulting from angling, spending on intermediate goods and services by firms that benefit directly from angling and the economies supported by those firms. In the United States alone, the total economic output of freshwater fishing in 1991 was approximately $46 billion.

Waterfowl hunting in the United States in 1991 involved approx. 3 million hunters who, on average, spent about seven days each hunting migratory ducks and geese. Expenditures for these activities totaled $670 million. This figure underestimates the total economic value of waterfowl hunting, however, because it does not include secondary economic impacts.

Although the total global value of fish, waterfowl, and other goods extracted from freshwater systems cannot be estimated from available data, it certainly exceeds $100 billion per year and may be several times that amount. Moreover, the marginal value of these benefits is increasing in many places, as more people desire to spend time and money on these outdoor activities.

A wide variety of human activities threaten to diminish the benefits derived from living resources extracted from aquatic ecosystems. Overexploitation threatens to permanently diminish fish stocks. Toxic pollutants can render fish and other aquatic organisms unsafe to eat or reduce their productivity. Eutrophication, which can be caused by erosion, sewage inputs, or loss of riparian ecosystems, is correlated with undesirable shifts in fish communities. And to the extent that exotic species are introduced to develop sport fisheries, unexpected costs may result—such as collapse of native fish stocks and the spread of disease—that offset the benefits of the new fishery.

Nonextractive or Instream Benefits

Freshwater provides a host of services to humanity without ever leaving its natural channel or the aquatic system of which it is a part. These are the services most easily taken for granted, because they are provided with minimal or no investment or action on our part. They are also the services most rapidly being lost, since water and land management decisions frequently do not adequately value them or take them into account.

Most instream benefits have strong "public good" characteristics that make it difficult to capture their full value in the marketplace. For example, rivers, lakes, and reservoirs can provide environmental and recreational benefits to many people simultaneously (known in the economics lexicon as "nonrivalry in consumption"). It is also frequently difficult or impossible to exclude anyone from enjoying the benefits of public good resources, whether they pay for that enjoyment or not (known as "nonexcludability").

The value of at least some instream services provided by aquatic systems depends on cultural and societal factors, which makes it impossible to derive an estimate of their total global value. Recreational uses, for example, may be valued highly in wealthy countries but very little in poor countries, where people do not have as much free time or money to enjoy leisure activities. By contrast flood-recession farmers, fishers, and pastoralists may value certain instream services more than the rich, because they depend directly on them for their livelihoods. The value placed on protection of habitat for fish, birds, and other wildlife also may vary with the cultural and economic setting in which the aquatic habitat resides. What follows is a discussion of a few of the nonextractive or instream benefits provided by freshwater systems, along with some estimates of their value— either by way of rough global figures, or by regional or local examples.

Pollution Dilution

In late 1994 and early 1995, an estimated forty thousand migratory birds died at a reservoir in central Mexico. Scientists identified the cause to be an extremely high concentration of untreated human sewage in the water body, which allowed botulism bacteria to spread and poison the food eaten by ducks and other migratory waterfowl. During the months when most of the birds died, the reservoir reportedly consisted almost entirely of raw sewage. Given the vast quantities of sewage produced by the world's 5.7 billion people, such incidents might be commonplace were it not for a key environmental service performed by freshwater systems: the dilution of pollutants.

Freshwater remaining in its natural channels helps keep water quality parameters at levels safe for fish, other aquatic organisms, and people. Today, some 1.2 billion people—about one out of every three in the developing world—lack access to safe supplies of drinking water, and 1.7 billion lack adequate sanitation services. As a result, water-borne diseases are primary killers of the world's poorest. The number of deaths due to unsafe water and inadequate sanitation—which include at least 2 million children each year—would be far higher were it not for the dilution of pollution by freshwater systems.

The old adage "Dilution is the solution to pollution" described the basic approach to pollution control up until about 1970, when, in response to pollution episodes like the Cuyahoga River catching fire in the United States, laws began to be passed requiring that cities and industries treat their waste before releasing it into the environment. Large sums were spent to restore and protect water quality. Virtually all countries, however, still depend heavily upon the diluting capacity of natural waters. Even in the OECD countries, domestic wastewater treatment is estimated to cover only about 60 percent of the population. Information for developing countries is sparse, but treatment coverage is certainly far lower. Moreover, few regions control for farm runoff and other dispersed pollution sources that add substantial quantities of sediment, pesticides, and fertilizers to water bodies. Dilution alone is certainly not sufficient to protect water quality or human health where pollution is highly concentrated or toxic or where people lack access to safe drinking water supplies or adequate sanitation. But without the dilution function, things would be much worse.

One way of gauging the value of dilution as an instream service is to estimate what it would cost to remove all nutrients and contaminants from wastewater technologically. . . The combined cost of $150 billion/year likely underestimates the total value of the dilution function, because a portion of agricultural drainage water would also require treatment to remove nitrates, pesticides, and other contaminants, a cost we do not attempt to estimate here.

Society already pays some of this price because pollution loads often exceed what nature can absorb, process, or dilute. But were the natural dilution service to be completely absent, the economic costs of keeping water pollution at harmless or tolerable levels would rise greatly. The risk today is that as increasing quantities of water are diverted from rivers and other water bodies to satisfy rising water demands, less water remains instream to provide this important ecosystem service. Decisions to divert water from its natural channels need to take into account the increased treatment costs that may be incurred as a result, as well as the potential costs to downstream water users of lower-quality water.

Transportation

In many parts of the world, inland waterways offer convenient and relatively expensive pathways for the transport of goods from one place to another. One way of valuing this instream service would be to estimate the cost of the next best alternative means of freight transportation in each area where navigation is used, and then to calculate the total cost-savings from navigation—an extremely difficult task since the next best alternative and its cost would vary from place to place. An easier approach is to examine the revenue derived from transportation by freshwater, averaged over all types of goods transported, exclusive of taxes. (Ideally, we should subtract from such figures the cost of maintaining navigation channels in order to arrive at a more accurate value of the ecosystem service, but we do not do that here.) In the United States, such revenues total $360 billion per year, and in Western Europe they total $169 billion per year.

Unfortunately, consistent or reliable figures for transportation revenues are not available for Asia, Africa, or South America. However, the major rivers of these continents are important arteries for commerce. In China, for example, waterways accounted for 9 percent of the cargo shipped in 1988.

Thus, the combined revenue derived from transportation by water in the United States and Western Europe—$529 billion per year—provides a lower-bound estimate of the value of this instream service. The additional value from water transport in other geographic areas, along with the benefit of waterways for human travel (which is not included in these revenue figures), would raise the total value of this important instream service considerably. These transportation benefits are placed at risk by river diversions that reduce flows to levels too low to support navigation, by land-use practices that result in siltation of waterways, and by other activities that impair the use of freshwater systems for shipping.

Recreation

Freshwater systems provide numerous and varied opportunities for recreation—including swimming, sports fishing, kayaking, canoeing, and rafting. Like most other instream benefits, these recreational services have "public good" characteristics that make it difficult to capture their full value in the marketplace. In countries such as the United States, where enjoyment of the outdoors is on the rise, a large group of people benefit from these recreational services, but the total value of their enjoyment is difficult to measure. There is no charge levied or donation made that fully captures their collective willingness to pay. . .

Instream recreational uses of water also generate substantial additional benefits to local economies in the form of recreation-related expenditures, such as boating, fishing, and camping equipment. One study, for example, found that boaters on a twenty-mile stretch of the Wisconsin River spurred more than $800,000 in sales by local businesses during the summer season. Such sales are a key source of livelihood for small towns and Native American reservations in the western United States. . .

[A]t least during low-flow periods, the marginal value of water for instream recreational uses appears to be equal to or greater than the marginal value of water used in a substantial portion of irrigated agriculture in the western United States. The key policy message is similar to that for pollution dilution: Were these instream recreational values properly taken into account, fewer diversions for offstream uses would be economically justified. And a corollary: If water markets were able to operate more freely and purchases of water for instream recreational uses were more feasible, water would likely shift out of agriculture to the protection of instream recreational services.

Provision of Habitat

The supply of vital habitat by aquatic ecosystems depends greatly upon the dynamic connection between water and land, physical processes such as water and sediment flows, and a host of biophysical conditions such as water quality, temperature, and food web relationships. Freshwater ecosystems contain abundant life, including 41 percent of the world's known fish species and most of the world's endangered fish species. Decades of large-scale water engineering have disrupted many critical ecosystem functions and processes, with consequences that are just beginning to be recognized.

The provision of habitat in many large river systems, for example, depends critically on the annual flood. Floodplains are not only highly productive biologically, they offer a variety of aquatic habitats, including backwaters, marshes, and lakes. During a flood, many aquatic organisms leave the river channel to make use of these floodplain habitats as spawning, breeding, and nursery grounds. As floodwaters recede, young fish, water-fowl, and other organisms get funneled back into the main channel, along with nutrients and organic matter from the floodplain. In turn, the floodwaters deposit a new supply of sediment that enhances the floodplain's fertility. In this way, so called "flood pulses" provide critical habitat and increase the productivity of both the floodplain and the main river channel. Examples of large river-floodplain ecosystems that are world renowned for their wildlife and other habitat benefits include the Gran Pantanal of the Paraguay River in South America, which alone harbors 600 species of fish, 650 species of birds, and 80 species of mammals; the Sudd swamps on the White Nile in Sudan; and the Okavango River wetlands in Botswana.

In addition, the timing, volume, and quality of water flowing in its natural channel greatly affect the supply of habitat for fish and other aquatic organisms. Migrating fish species, for instance, may require certain minimum flow volumes at particular points in their life cycle. And many species have specific temperature, water quality, and other needs that must be met if they are to survive in a given river system.

The value of natural river, lake, and wetland systems as habitat for fish, waterfowl, and wildlife is even harder to estimate than recreational values, since the beneficiaries and benefits are much less clear and direct. In some cases, these values become visible only when they are lost or destroyed. In the Aral Sea basin in Central Asia, for instance, what was once the world's fourth largest inland lake has lost two-thirds of its volume because of excessive river diversions for irrigated agriculture. Some 20 of the 24 native fish species have disappeared, and the fish catch, which totaled approx. 40,000 tons a year in the 1950s and supported 60,000 jobs, has dropped to zero.

Wetlands have shrunk by 85 percent, which, combined with high levels of agricultural chemical pollution, has greatly reduced waterfowl populations. In the delta of the Syr Dar'ya River—one of the Aral Sea's two major sources of inflow—the number of nesting bird species has dropped from an estimated 173 to 38. This region illustrates vividly how economic and social decline may follow close on the heels of ecological destruction.

In the western United States, the emergence of active water markets combined with growing public interest in preserving fish species, bird populations, and wildlife generally has begun to attach some market values to the critical habitat supplied by aquatic ecosystems. During 1994, there were nineteen reported water transactions in the western United States that had the purpose of securing more water for aquatic habitats, especially rivers and wetlands. A sampling of such transactions during recent years [illustrates that] the value of water for habitat protection in the western United States, as with the value of instream water for recreation, appears to equal or exceed that for some offstream uses, particularly in agriculture.

Option, Bequest, and Existence Values

Because of freshwater's central role in maintaining uniquely beautiful natural areas, critical habitat, or highly valued recreational sites, "nonuser" values of water can be substantial. Estimating people's willingness to pay to preserve the option of enjoying a site in the future (option value), to ensure that descendants will be able to enjoy a site (bequest values), or simply to know that a site will continue to exist (existence values) is not easy. These values are important, however, particularly when irreversible decisions are to be made, such as constructing a dam that will flood a beautiful mountain canyon, or channeling through a wetland that will permanently destroy wildlife habitat. According to Colby, "existence, bequest and option values ranging from $40-$80 per year per non-user household have been documented for stream systems in Wyoming, Colorado, and Alaska." It is estimated that the total (user and non-user) benefits of preserving Mono Lake levels amount to about $40 per California household, 80 percent of which is attributed to option, bequest, and existence values.

NOTES & QUESTIONS

1. Gretchen Daily defines ecosystem services as "the conditions and processes through which natural ecosystems, and the species that make them up, sustain and fulfill human life." Gretchen C. Daily, *Introduction: What Are Ecosystem Services?*, in NATURE'S SERVICES: SOCIETAL DEPENDENCE ON NATURAL ECOSYSTEMS 3 (Gretchen C. Daily ed. 1997). In other words, ecosystems are valuable because they serve us—the people who live in those ecosystems. The contributions of freshwater ecosystems are complemented by the services provided by other kinds of ecosystems. Forests prevent erosion that causes flooding, sedimentation that interferes with hydroelectric dams and coral reefs, and the depletion of the ozone layer with its attendant exposure to harmful ultraviolet sun rays. Oceans distribute chemical and biological materials, detoxify or sequester wastes, and host abundant fisheries. Grasslands conserve soils, maintain the genetic library, and maintain the composition of the atmosphere. Soils moderate the climate, support plants, and dispose of dead organic matter. Specific insects pollinate specific plants, so if the diversity of insects declines, the diversity of plant life will decline, too. Natural predators, parasites, and pathogens operate to control pests that threaten agricultural crops. For more examples and analysis of the services that ecosystems provide, see the other chapters in Nature's Services, and the collection of articles contained in 20 STAN. ENVTL. L.J. 309 (2001). We explore the topic further in Chapter 7.

2. The value of ecosystem services is exceedingly difficult to measure. The most obvious measure is the cost of providing the services via alternative means. How expensive would it be to stop the flooding that forests prevent, to replicate the recreational opportunities afforded by wetlands, or to dispose of wastes that the soil naturally processes? Such questions have yielded dramatically different figures when economists have attempted to calculate their answers. The values of using an ecosystem, though, are actually the least difficult to determine. Ecosystems also afford many nonuse values, including the intangible benefit that many people experience simply by knowing that the ecosystem exists. Economists have constructed numerous studies for measuring those values, including a contingent valuation approach that asks people how much they would be willing to spend to preserve a resource. Any means of measurement is controversial, yet all agree that the value of ecosystems extends beyond the types of commodities whose economic value the market quantifies. Such challenges to any effort to measure the value of ecosystem services are analyzed in NATURAL RESEARCH COUNCIL, *supra*, at 87–115; Dominic Moran & David Pearce, *The Economic Consequences of Biodiversity Loss*, in CRACRAFT & GRIFO, *supra* at 217–29; Lawrence H. Goulder & Donald Kennedy, *Valuing Ecosystem Services: Philosophical Bases and Empirical Methods*, in DAILY, *supra*, at 23–47; and Robert Costanza & Carl Folke, *Valuing Ecosystem Services with Efficiency, Fairness, and Sustainability as Goals*, in DAILY, *supra*, at 49–68.

3. Suppose that we could obtain all of these services—plus all of our medicinal, food, clothing, recreational and other utilitarian needs—from a handful of species and ecosystems. Why would we need a diversity of species and ecosystems if we could satisfy all of our needs with just a few species and ecosystems? The law continues to struggle with the importance of diversity in a number of contexts, including affirmative action, broadcasting, political parties, language, and agriculture. *See* Jim Chen, *Diversity in a Different Dimension: Evolutionary Theory and Affirmative Action's Destiny*, 59 OHIO ST. L. J. 811, 834–62 (1998). Indeed, "diversity as an affirmative goal of civil society and of government, has gained broad acceptance in America only very recently and only after a very long struggle with the forces favoring ethnic homogeneity, forces that have prevailed in virtually all other societies at all other times." Peter H. Schuck, *The Perceived Values of Diversity, Then and Now*, 22 CARDOZO L. REV. 1915 (2001). The diversity of human cultures throughout the world has received growing attention as globalization and other developments threaten the existence of many native cultures. Several writers have even analogized biodiversity and cultural diversity. *See* NOSS & COOPERRIDER, *supra*, at 13–14; Kieran Suckling, *A House on Fire: Linking the Biological and Linguistic Diversity Crises*, 6 ANIMAL L. 193 (2000). Diversity is usually seen as a virtue in those settings, though the role of the law in achieving diversity is often controversial. There are times, though, where diversity is irrelevant or actually undesirable. Dan Perlman and Glenn Adelson have grouped the importance of the diversity of the features of their conservation biology students as follows:

- "Features in which we seek diversity"—academic background, nationality, home culture, gender, year in college, and leaves of absence.
- "Features in which we ignore diversity"—blood type, hair color, right or left handedness, and musical ability.
- "Features in which we actively avoid diversity"—general intelligence, writing ability, interest in subject, and commitment to class.

DAN L. PERLMAN & GLENN ADELSON, BIODIVERSITY: EXPLORING VALUES AND PRIORITIES IN CONSERVATION 53 (1997). To take another example, consider the infamous response that Senator Roman Hruska offered to those who questioned the abilities of Supreme Court nominee G. Harold Carswell: "Even if he was mediocre, there are a lot of mediocre judges and people and lawyers. They are entitled to a little representation, aren't they, and a little chance?" 116 CONG. REC. 7498 (1970). What makes a diversity of genes, species, and ecosystems more important than a diversity of intelligence among the students in the classroom or the Justices on the United States Supreme Court?

Or suppose that we could obtain all of these services through human efforts rather than through natural means. Would there be any reason for preferring the services provided by ecosystems instead of services that we would provide ourselves?

Bruce Babbitt, *Between the Flood and the Rainbow: Our Covenant to Protect the Whole of Creation*

2 ANIMAL LAW 1 (1996).

I began 1995 with one of the more memorable events of my lifetime. It took place in the heart of Yellowstone National Park during the first week of January, a time when a layer of deep, pure snow blanketed the first protected landscape in America. But for all its beauty, the last sixty years had rendered this landscape an incomplete ecosystem. By the 1930s, government-paid hunters had systematically eradicated the predator at the top of the food chain: the American grey wolf. I was there on that day, knee deep in the snow, because I had been given the honor of carrying the first wolves back into that landscape. Through the work of conservation laws, I was there to restore the natural cycle—to make Yellowstone complete.

The first wolf was an Alpha female. After I set her down in the transition area, where she would later mate and bear wild pups, I looked through the grate into the green eyes of this magnificent creature within a spectacular landscape. I was profoundly moved by the elevating nature of America's conservation laws—laws with the power to make creation whole. Upon returning to Washington, I witnessed a new Congress wielding a power of a different kind.

Attack on Water, Land, and Creatures

. . . [M]ore than any of our environmental laws, the act they have most aggressively singled out for elimination—one that made Yellowstone complete—is the Endangered Species Act (ESA). Never mind that this Act is working, having saved ninety-nine percent of all listed species. Never mind that it effectively protects hundreds of plants and animals, from grizzly bears to whooping cranes to greenback cutthroat trout. Never mind that it is doing so while costing each American sixteen cents per year. Although the new Congress may list some species as endangered, they can find absolutely no reason to protect all species in general. Who cares, they ask, if the spotted owl goes extinct? We won't miss it or, for that matter, the Texas blind salamander or the kangaroo rat. That goes double for the fairy shrimp, the burying beetle, the Delhi sands flower-loving fly, and the virgin spine dace. If they get in our way, and humans drive some creatures to extinction, that is just too bad. This is a fairly accurate summary of how the new majority in Congress has expressed its opinion of the ESA.

The Values of Children

Fortunately, there are other Americans who have expressed their opinion on this issue. I recently read an account of a Los Angeles "Eco-Expo," where children were invited to write down their answers to a basic question: "Why save endangered species?" One child, Gabriel, answered, "Because God gave us the animals." Travis and Gina wrote, "Because we love them." A third answered, "Because we'll be lonely without them." Still another wrote, "Because they're a part of our life. If we didn't have them, it would not be a complete world. The Lord put them on the earth to be enjoyed, not destroyed."

In my lifetime I have heard many political, agricultural, scientific, medical, and ecological reasons for saving endangered species. In fact, I have hired biologists and ecologists for just that purpose. All their reasons have to do with providing humans with potential cures for disease, yielding humans new strains of drought-resistant crops, offering humans bioremediation of oil spills, or thousands of other justifications for why species are useful to humans. However, none of their reasons moved me like those of the children. These children are using plain words to express a complex notion that has either been lost, forgotten, or never learned by some members of Congress and, indeed, by many of us. The children expressed the moral and spiritual imperative that there may be a higher purpose inherent in creation, one demanding our respect and our stewardship quite apart from whether a particular species is or ever will be of material use to mankind. They see in creation what our adult political leaders refuse to acknowledge. They express an answer that can be reduced to one word: values.

A Sacred Blue Mountain

I remember when I was their age as a child growing up in a small town in northern Arizona. I learned my religious values through a church that kept silent on our moral obligation to nature. By its silence, the church implicitly sanctioned the prevailing view of the earth as something to be used and disposed of however we saw fit, without any higher obligation. In all the years that I attended services, there was never any reference nor any link to our natural heritage or to the spiritual meaning of the land surrounding us. However, outside that church, I always had a nagging instinct that the vast landscape was somehow sacred and holy. It was connected to me in a sense that my religious training ignored.

At the edge of my home town, a great blue mountain called the San Francisco Peaks soars up out of the desert to a snowy summit, snagging clouds on its crest, changing color with the seasons. It was always a mystical, evocative presence in our daily lives. To me, that mountain, named by Spanish missionaries for Saint Francis, remains a manifestation of the presence of our Creator. That I was not alone in this view was something I had to discover through a very different religion, because the Hopi Indians lived on the opposite side of the blue mountain in small pueblos on the high mesas that stretch away toward the north. It was a young Hopi friend who taught me that the blue mountain was truly a sacred place.

One Sunday morning in June, my friend led me out to the mesa top villages where I watched as the Kachina filed into the plaza, arriving from the snowy heights of the mountain and bringing blessings from another world. Another time, he took me to the ceremonials where the priests of the snake clan chanted for rain and then released live rattlesnakes to carry their prayers to the spirits deep within the earth. Later, I went with my friend to a bubbling spring, deep in the Grand Canyon, lined with pahoes—

the prayer feathers—where his ancestors had emerged from another world to populate this earth. By the end of that summer, I came to deeply and irrevocably believe that the land, the blue mountain, and all the plants and animals in the natural world together are a direct reflection of divinity.

Genesis and the Deluge

That awakening made me acutely aware of a poverty amidst my own rich religious tradition. I felt I had to either embrace a borrowed culture, or turn back and have a second look at my own. While priests then, as now, were not too fond of people rummaging about in the Bible to draw their own meanings, I chose to do so, asking, "Is there nothing in our Western, Judeo-Christian tradition that speaks to our natural heritage and the sacredness of that blue mountain? Is there nothing that can connect me to the surrounding Creation?" There are those who argue that there is not. There are those industrial apologists who, when asked about Judeo-Christian values relating to the environment, reply that the material world, including the environment, is just an incidental fact of no significance in the relation between us and our Creator. They cite the first verses of Genesis, concluding that God gave Adam and his descendants the absolute, unqualified right to "subdue" the earth and gave man "dominion over the fish of the sea, over the fowl of the air, and over every living thing that moveth upon the earth."[1] God, they assert, put the earth here for the disposal of man in whatever manner he sees fit. However, if they read a few verses further, they would discover in the account of the Deluge that the Bible conveys a far different message about our relation to God and to the earth. In Genesis, God commanded Noah to take into the ark two by two and seven by seven of every living thing in creation, the clean and the unclean.[2] God did not specify that Noah should limit the ark to two charismatic species, two good for hunting, two species that might provide some cure down the road, and two that draw crowds to the city zoo. He specified the whole of creation. When the waters receded and the dove flew off to dry land, God set all of the creatures free, commanding them to multiply upon the earth.[3] Then, in the words of the covenant with Noah, "when the rainbow appears in the clouds, I will see it and remember the everlasting covenant between me and all living things on earth."[4] We are thus instructed that this everlasting covenant was made to protect the whole of creation, not for the exclusive use and disposition of mankind, but for the purposes of the Creator.

Now, we all know that the commandment to protect creation in all its diversity does not come to us with detailed operating instructions. It is left to us to translate a moral imperative into a way of life and into public policy. Compelled by this ancient command, modern America turned to the national legislature which forged our collective moral imperative into one landmark law—the Endangered Species Act of 1973.

---

[1]   Genesis 1:24.

[2]   Genesis 6:20, 7:2–3.

[3]   Genesis 8:17.

[4]   Genesis 9:12–16.

. . . Whenever I confront some of these bills that are routinely introduced—bills sometimes openly written by industrial lobbyists; bills that systematically attempt to eviscerate the Endangered Species Act-I take refuge and inspiration from the simple written answers of those children at the Los Angeles expo. However, I sometimes wonder if children are the only ones who express religious values when talking about endangered species. I wonder if anyone else in America is trying to restore an ounce of humility to mankind, reminding our political leaders that the earth is a sacred precinct designed by and for the purpose of the Creator.

I recently got my answer. I read letter after letter from five different religious orders, representing tens of millions of churchgoers, all opposing a House bill to weaken the Endangered Species Act. They opposed it not for technical or scientific or agricultural or medicinal reasons, but for spiritual reasons. I was moved not only by how such diverse faiths could reach so pure an agreement against this bill, but by the common language and terms with which they opposed it—language that echoed the voices of the children. Suddenly, I understood exactly why some members of Congress react with such unrestrained fear and loathing towards the Endangered Species Act. I understood why they tried to ban all those letters from the Congressional Record. I understand why they are so deeply disturbed by the prospect of religious values entering the national debate, because if they heard that command of our Creator—if they truly listened to His instructions to be responsible stewards—then their entire framework of human rationalizations for tearing apart the Act would unravel. Those religious values remain at the heart of the Endangered Species Act. They make themselves manifest through the green eyes of the grey wolf, through the call of the whooping crane, through the splash of the Pacific salmon, and through the voices of America's children. We are living between the flood and the rainbow—between the threats to creation on the one side and God's covenant to protect life on the other. Why should we save endangered species? Let us answer this question with one voice, the voice of the child at that expo, who scrawled her answer at the very bottom of the sheet: "Because we can."

NOTES & QUESTIONS

1. The limitations of the utilitarian arguments for preserving endangered species have led many to consider the moral, ethical, and religious arguments for protecting biodiversity. "It is our duty as citizens of God's world to honor the plant and animal kingdom God created," according to the Democratic members of the House Committee on Resources. Committee on Resources Democrats, Endangered Species Act 4 (Apr. 2005), *available at* http://resourcescommittee. house.gov/democrats/backgrounders/ESA2.pdf. The Democratic House members add that "[i]f there is intelligent design or a plan to God's work, human beings are to conserve the fabric God has woven so that future generations may witness the beauty created." *Id.* at 1. Consider, too, the position of the Evangelical Environmental Network (EEN), an evangelical Protestant group whose lobbying and nationwide advertising campaign regarding the ESA gained widespread attention. The EEN believes that "[a] species should be preserved because it has been created by God." Thus the EEN "oppose[s] any Congressional action that would weaken, hamper, reduce or end the protection, recovery and preservation of God's creatures, including their habitats, especially as accomplished under the Endangered Species Act." Likewise, Rabbi David Saperstein testified before a House ESA task force that "[e]very species is sacred."

The story of Noah features prominently in the positions of Secretary Babbitt and other religious defenses of the ESA. God "did not specify that Noah should limit the ark to two charismatic species, two good for hunting, two species that might provide some cure down the road, and, say, two that draw crowds to the city zoo." Noah invested much time, money and resources in building the ark and collecting all of the species. The resulting covenant between God and Noah "was made to protect the whole of creation, not for the exclusive use and disposition of mankind, but for the purposes of the Creator." Some have even suggested that the story implies that "God was more concerned about preserving animal species than sinful people." Moreover, the flood confronted by Noah has been compared to the flood of people and pollution that threatens biodiversity today. These and more lessons learned from Noah continue to inform wildlife protection thousands of years after the story was recorded. *See generally* John Copeland Nagle, *Playing Noah*, 82 MINN. L. REV. 1171, 1216–33 (1998).

Calls to imitate Noah have met with opposition. Idaho Representative Helen Chenoweth spoke at length against the incorporation of personal beliefs into laws that punish those who do not share those beliefs. *See* 142 CONG. REC. H1002-05 (daily ed. Jan. 31, 1996) (objecting to Secretary Babbitt's speech, characterizing environmentalism as a religion, and concluding that "this religious vision is not shared by every American and no American should be forced to promote a religious vision contrary to their own beliefs"); *see also* 134 CONG. REC. S9759 (daily ed. July 25, 1988) (statement of Sen. Symms) (criticizing the ESA as an effort to change moral attitudes by "the sheer brute force of Government"). Those seeking to avoid a duty to protect every endangered species are more likely to turn to other parts of the scriptures. Genesis records that God entrusted man with dominion over the earth, a notoriously difficult passage for environmentalists. *See Gen.* 1:26 ("Then God said . . . 'let [man] have dominion over the fish of the sea, over the birds of the air, and over the cattle, over all the earth and over every creeping thing that creeps on the earth' "); *Gen.* 1:28 (commanding man to "fill the earth and subdue it; have dominion over the fish of the sea, over the birds of the air, and over every living thing that moves on the earth"). Thus former Interior Secretary Manuel Lujan cited the dominion command to justify actions that could result in the loss of a species. California Representative William Dannemeyer complained that the ESA "has reversed" God's grant of dominion so that "[a]nimals today are more important than people." Oregon Representative Wes Cooley expressed his belief that "we are going against God" by protecting endangered species, adding that "maybe we might be the higher creatures of God's creation."

But many insist that the dominion of which Genesis speaks should not be understood as a license for humans to do whatever they want to the world for whatever purpose they happen to have in mind. The word "dominion" is used elsewhere in the scriptures to refer to a peaceful rule designed to serve those living subject to it. Even under this understanding, though, the biblical commands conflict with ethical theories that treat people and other species in an identical fashion. Thus the claim of "speciesism"—a discriminatory preference for the human species over all other species—has been levelled against Christian environmentalists and others who acknowledge a higher ethical position for humanity. *See, e.g.*, Peter Singer, Animal Liberation (2d ed. 1990). The balance between human needs and the needs of animals will be set differently by someone seeking to adhere to the biblical account and by someone seeking to treat all species (including humans) alike.

2. For a judicial recognition of these themes, consider this statement of Judge Biery in a case presenting a challenge to the FWS's approval of a habitat conservation plan for three endangered invertebrate species that are dependent upon the Edward Aquifer in Texas:

> [This] case compels us to think about our responsibility as stewards of the earth which bore and sustains us. For those of Western religious beliefs, the author of the creation story teaches that we "have dominion over the fish of the sea, and over the fowl of the air, and over every living thing that moveth upon the earth." But "dominion" does not mean "destruction," and our elected representatives have passed the Endangered Species Act standing for that proposition. At about the time our political ancestors were writing the Magna Carta, St. Francis of Assisi implicitly foresaw the need for protective legislation when he wrote:
>
>> By our own fault we have lost the beautiful relationship which we once had with all . . . creation. . . Give us the grace to see all animals as gifts from [God] and to treat them with respect for they are [God's] creation.
>
> In a perfect world, the lion would lie down with the lamb; and we would live in peace with each other and in harmony with the land. It is not; lions still eat lambs; and we do not. Instead of a community of neighborhoods, we are becoming a segregated collection of consuming Haves served by minimum wage Have-nots whose festering envy will someday manifest itself. While ancient Rome had its bread and circuses, we have our air conditioned malls and arenas to satisfy the appetites of American materialism and entertainment. The reaping and reckoning in public health and quality of life which will come to our children and grandchildren will echo from what we incrementally sow into their environment and whether we come to an epiphany of the interdependence and interrelatedness played out in the mystery of the dance called life.

Center for Biological Diversity v. United States Fish & Wildlife Serv., 202 F.Supp.2d 594, 596–97 (W.D. Tex. 2002). Nonetheless, Judge Biery concluded that the FWS had satisfied its obligations under the ESA, so he reluctantly put aside his personal beliefs and enforced the law.

3. Would different moral, ethical, or religious perspectives lead to different conclusions about protecting biodiversity? Secretary Babbitt referred to the imperative to protect rare wildlife that flows from the Native American spiritual tradition. As one writer has explained:

> The attitude of Indians toward the natural environment was basically what we would call spiritual or religious, although religion for them was not separated from the rest of life. . . The Indians saw themselves as one

with nature. All of their traditions agree on this. Nature is the larger whole of which mankind is only a part. People stand within the natural world, not separate from it; and are dependent on it, not dominant over it. All living things are one, and the people are joined with trees, predators and prey, rocks and rain in a vast, powerful, interrelationship. . . Because of this deep kinship, Indians accorded to every form of life the right to live, perpetuate its species, and follow the way of its own being as a conscious fellow creature. Animals were treated with the same consideration and respect as human beings.

J. DONALD HUGHES, AMERICAN INDIAN ECOLOGY 14–17 (1983). Four northwestern tribes expressed those beliefs when they responded to the disappearance of salmon from the Columbia River. The tribes explained that their unwritten laws "begin with the recognition of nature's bounty as a gift from the Creator, that everything in nature has a purpose, and that human society has a need to harmonize itself with the structures and rhythms of nature. When the first salmon comes up the river, the human world stops to honor the returning spirit of the salmon." COLUMBIA RIVER INTERTRIBAL FISH COMMISSION, THE TRIBAL VISION FOR THE FUTURE OF THE COLUMBIA RIVER BASIN & HOW TO ACHIEVE IT 2 (1999), *available at* http://www.critfc.org/legal/vision.pdf. As with Christian teachings, though, the extent to which Native Americans have acted consistently with these principles has been questioned, as discussed below at pages 139–40.

Animal rights ideas offer another alternative. The premise of animal rights arguments is that each living creature is important not because of its importance to people (as with utilitarian arguments) or because of its importance to God (as with many religious arguments), but because of its intrinsic importance. The physical and mental characteristics that more developed animals share with humans are emphasized in advocating similar legal rights for animals. Such claims have met limited success in a legal system that has long regarded animals and plants as human property or at least unworthy of the legal protections afforded people. The case for extending rights to animals is made in STEVEN M. WISE, RATTLING THE CAGE: TOWARD LEGAL RIGHTS FOR ANIMALS (2000), while the current legal treatment of animals is described in PAMELA D. FRASCH ET AL., ANIMAL LAW (2000).

What other religious or moral arguments would support efforts to prevent species from going extinct? Do any of those arguments suggest that the preservation of a species may give way to other considerations in some circumstances? More generally, is it appropriate to rely upon any such contested theories? Is it possible *not* to rely on such theories?

C. THREATS TO BIODIVERSITY

Determination of Endangered Status for Five Freshwater Mussels and Threatened Status for Two Freshwater Mussels From the Eastern Gulf Slope Drainages of Alabama, Florida, and Georgia

United States Fish and Wildlife Service, 1998.
63 Federal Register 12664.

The fat threeridge, shinyrayed pocketbook, Gulf moccasinshell, Ochlockonee moccasinshell, oval pigtoe, Chipola slabshell, and purple bankclimber are freshwater mussels of the family Unionidae found only in eastern Gulf Slope streams draining the Apalachicolan Region, defined as streams from the Escambia to the Suwannee river systems, and occurring in southeast Alabama, southwest Georgia, and north Florida. The Apalachicolan Region is known for its high level of endemicity, harboring approximately 30 species of endemic (found only in the region) mussels. The Region drains primarily the Coastal Plain Physiographic Province. Only the headwaters of the Flint and Chattahoochee rivers, in the Apalachicola-Chattahoochee-Flint (ACF) River system, occur above the Fall Line in the Piedmont Physiographic Province in west-central Georgia.

The purple bankclimber

The decline of some of the species included in this rule was evident decades ago. The fat threeridge, oval pigtoe, Chipola slabshell, and purple bankclimber were considered rare, but locally abundant, in the 1950's. The Gulf moccasinshell, oval pigtoe, and purple bankclimber were recognized in a list of rare species in 1970, and the fat threeridge was added to the list of regionally rare mussels a year later.

. . . Freshwater mussel adults are filter-feeders, positioning themselves in substrates to facilitate siphoning of the water column for oxygen and food. Their food includes primarily detritus, plankton, and other microorganisms.

As a group, freshwater mussels are extremely long-lived, with life spans of up to 130 years for certain species. Life spans of these seven species are unknown. Based on the longevity of a congener of the fat threeridge (the threeridge [*Amblema plicata*]); the longevity of thick-shelled species, and the large size attained by the fat threeridge and purple bankclimber, the latter two species probably have long lifespans. . .

Summary of Factors Affecting the Species

. . . A species may be determined to be an endangered or threatened species due to one or more of the five factors described in section 4(a)(1) [of the Endangered Species Act]. These factors and their application to the fat threeridge (*Amblema neislerii*), shinyrayed pocketbook (*Lampsilis subangulata*), Gulf moccasinshell (*Medionidus penicillatus*), Ochlockonee moccasinshell (*Medionidus simpsonianus*), oval pigtoe (*Pleurobema pyriforme*), Chipola slabshell (*Elliptio chipolaensis*), and purple bankclimber (*Elliptoideus sloatianus*) are as follows.

A. The Present or Threatened Destruction, Modification, or Curtailment of its Habitat or Range

Historically, mussel faunas in the United States have declined extensively as an unintended consequence of human development. The mussel fauna in much of the Apalachicolan Region has been negatively impacted by impoundments, siltation, channelization, and by water pollution. The cumulative effect of these factors on the aquatic ecosystems of the ACF River basin has not been systematically evaluated; an ongoing USGS National Water Quality Assessment is currently addressing this task.

Impoundments have permanently altered a significant portion of the ACF River system, which has 16 mainstem impoundments. Impoundments affect mussels by altering current, substrate, and water chemistry, factors which are important to riverine mussels. Lack of mussel recruitment in impoundments may be due to loss of glochidia in the substrate, attacks on glochidia by microorganisms, or the juveniles' inability to survive in silt.

The Chattahoochee River has 13 dams, including three locks and dams along its lower half; the lower mainstem is inundated for approximately 400 km (248 mi). An additional 85 km (53 mi) of mainstem habitat are impounded upstream of Atlanta, making approximately 485 km (301 mi) of the mainstem's 700 km (434 mi) total length (69 percent) impounded. The lower portions of many tributaries were permanently flooded because of these reservoirs, including a known site for the shinyrayed pocketbook in Walter F. George Reservoir.

. . . Many regional streams have increased turbidity levels due to siltation. These seven mussels probably attract host fishes with visual cues. Such a reproductive strategy depends on clear water. Turbidity is a limiting factor impeding sight-feeding fishes, and may have contributed to the decline of these seven species.

Light to moderate levels of siltation are common in many Apalachicolan Region streams with populations of these seven species, while heavy siltation has occurred in the Piedmont, which is well known for its highly erodible soils. Most of the topsoil in the Piedmont was eroded by 1935. Clench attributed the decline of the rich mussel fauna of the Chattahoochee River to erosion from intensive farming before the Civil War. The steep slopes characteristic of the Fall Line Hills and the Piedmont result in higher erosion rates than slopes on more level lands.

Couch et al. indicated that all parts of the ACF Basin have been subject to alteration of forest cover. They attributed severe historical erosion and sedimentation in the Blue Ridge Province to mining and logging. The Service believes that while deforestation historically represented a threat to these mussels, current silvicultural activities following best management practices are compatible with the continued existence of the species.

Because of their sedentary characteristics, mussels are extremely vulnerable to toxic effluents. There are discharges from 137 municipal waste water treatment facilities in the ACF River basin. Although the quality of effluents has improved since the 1980's due to improved waste water treatment and a 1990 phosphate detergent ban in Georgia, two-thirds of the 938 stream miles in the Georgia portion of the ACF River basin do not meet the designated water use classifications under the requirements of the Clean Water Act.

Agricultural influences include nutrient enrichment from confined feeding of poultry and livestock (primarily in the Piedmont Province), and inputs of pesticides and fertilizers from row crop agriculture (primarily in the Coastal Plain).

An estimated 3.6 billion liters (0.95 billion gallons) of chemical-laden rinse, stripping, cleaning, and plating solutions were discharged through a short canal into the Flint River from 1955 to 1977 at a Department of Defense facility in Albany, Georgia. The Service believes the long-term release of this effluent likely had, and may continue to have, a chronic toxic effect on Flint River mussel populations. The canal and other portions of the facility are a Superfund site.

Abandoned battery salvage operations affect water quality in the Chipola River. Concentrations of heavy metals (e.g., chromium and cadmium) in Asian clams and sediments increased in samples taken downstream from two operations. Dead Lake, on the lower mainstem, was considered a contaminant sink. Chromium was found at levels known to be toxic to mussels in sediment samples from Dead Lake downstream. A large population of the fat threeridge has been extirpated in Dead Lake, possibly from such contamination.

Residential development in Georgia is resulting in the conversion of farmland to subdivisions in areas relatively distant from the cities of Albany, Atlanta, and Columbus. Development and land clearing increases siltation from erosion, runoff and transport of pollutants from stormwater, and municipal waste water facility effluents. Lenat and Crawford found that in Piedmont drainages, urban catchments had higher maximum average concentrations of heavy metals than agricultural or forested catchments. Urban waterways may harbor human-produced contaminants in concentrations sufficient to significantly affect fish health.

Additional water supply impoundments may be planned to satisfy expanding urban and suburban demand. Any impoundments on streams that support these species may have impacts on their long-term survival. Impoundments on streams that do not harbor these species could be designed in ways to minimize or eliminate potential impacts to these mussels and their habitat downstream. Future impoundments, particularly in the metropolitan Atlanta area, could impact stream habitats where small populations of the shinyrayed pocketbook, Gulf moccasinshell, and oval pigtoe exist.

In-stream and near-stream gravel mining has occurred in various portions of the Apalachicolan Region. Jenkinson recorded the shinyrayed pocketbook, oval pigtoe, Gulf moccasinshell, and ten other species in Little Uchee Creek, a tributary of the Chattahoochee River in Alabama. The creek had supported in-stream gravel mining; only a few shell fragments were found at Jenkinson's site in the status survey, although living shinyrayed pocketbooks were found at another site in Little Uchee Creek. Gravel mining operations in the Chattahoochee River do not pose a threat to these mussels since no populations exist there now. However, where in-stream gravel operations are conducted in the vicinity of populations of these species, mussels may be displaced, crushed, or covered by bottom materials.

Some artifact and fossil collectors have used suction dredges to scour benthic habitats in the ACF system. This can destroy mussel habitat at the collection site and resuspend silt, impacting downstream areas. In a study on the effects of suction dredging for gold on stream invertebrates, Harvey concluded that impacts from suction dredges can be expected to be more severe in streams with softer substrates (e.g., sand, gravel), as is typical for most Apalachicolan Region streams.

Many of the impacts discussed above occurred in the past as unintended consequences of human development in the Apalachicolan Region. Improved understanding of these consequences has led to regulatory (e.g., the Clean Water Act) and voluntary measures (e.g., best management practices for agriculture and silviculture) and improved land use practices that are generally compatible with the continued existence of these mussels. Nonetheless, the seven mussel species currently are highly restricted in numbers and distribution and show little evidence of recovering from historic habitat losses.

B. Overutilization for Commercial, Recreational, Scientific, or Educational Purposes

The threeridge (a relative of the fat threeridge) and the washboard (Megalonaias nervosa), which is superficially similar to both the fat three-ridge and purple bankclimber, are heavily utilized as sources of shell for nuclei in the cultured pearl industry. The Service has been informed by commercial shell buyers that shells from the ACF River system are of poor quality. However, shell material from this area may be used as "filler" for higher quality material from elsewhere. In the 1980's, the price of shell increased, resulting in increased competition for the harvesting of shell beds in the Apalachicolan Region.

Biological supply companies have used the Flint River and possibly the Ochlockonee River as sources for large mussel specimens, including the purple bankclimber and possibly the fat threeridge, to sell to academic institutions for use in laboratory studies. The practice of dissecting mussels in introductory laboratory courses is no longer widespread, and the threat posed to large species such as the fat threeridge and purple bankclimber is probably decreasing.

Nonetheless, harvest of the fat threeridge and purple bankclimber for these purposes could decimate their remaining populations. The increasing rarity of these mussels potentially makes them more appealing to shell collectors. Revealing specific stream reaches harboring these species could pose a threat from collectors. . .

C. Disease or Predation

Diseases of mussels are virtually unknown; this factor is not currently known to affect these seven species.

Juvenile and adult mussels may serve as prey for various animals, mostly fishes, turtles, birds, and mammals. The muskrat has been implicated in potentially jeopardizing recovery of federally listed mussels. Although muskrats are not common within the range of these species, Piedmont populations of the shinyrayed pocketbook, Gulf moccasinshell, and oval pigtoe in the upper Flint River system may be subject to some degree of muskrat predation. . .

E. Other Natural or Manmade Factors Affecting Its Continued Existence

Because of slow growth and relative immobility, mussel recolonization of impacted river reaches is a lengthy process, achieved by dispersal of newly metamorphosed juveniles via infected host fish, passive adult movement downstream, and active migration or passive movement downstream of small individuals. Establishment of self-sustaining populations requires decades of immigration and recruitment, even for common species that may occur in high densities. A mussel species should be considered stable only when active population recruitment is demonstrated and a significant number of viable populations exists.

The exotic Asian clam (*Corbicula fluminea*) has invaded all of the rivers where these seven mussels occur. First reported from the Apalachicolan Region about 1960, this species may compete with native mussels for nutrients and space. Densities of Asian clams are sometimes high in Apalachicolan Region streams, with estimates ranging from approximately 100/m (9/ft) square to over 2,100/m (195/ft) square. In some streams, the substrate has changed from homogenous silty sand or sand to one with a gravel-like component comprised of huge numbers of live and dead Asian clams.

. . . Another introduced bivalve, the zebra mussel (*Dreissena polymorpha*), has caused the extirpation of numerous native mussel populations and may pose a threat to these mussels in the future. Introduced into the Great Lakes in the late 1980's, this exotic species has been rapidly expanding its range in the South, but has not been reported yet from Apalachicolan Region streams.

The complex life cycle of mussels increases the probability that weak links in their life history will preclude successful reproduction and recruitment. Egg formation and fertilization are critical phases in the life history, because many mussels fail to form eggs or fertilization is incomplete. Fertilization success has been shown to be strongly correlated with spatial aggregation; excessively dispersed populations may have poor success. The need for specific fish hosts and the difficulty in recolonizing areas where mussels have been decimated are other life history attributes which make them vulnerable.

These seven species have been rendered vulnerable to extinction due to significant habitat loss, range restriction, and population fragmentation and size reduction. Most of their populations have been extirpated from the Piedmont portion of their historical ranges, four of five species are extirpated from Alabama, and none of the species remain in the Chattahoochee River. The restricted distribution of these seven species also makes localized populations susceptible to catastrophic events and collection.

NOTES & QUESTIONS

1. Why are these mussels threatened with extinction? What actions would help prevent the mussels from becoming extinct?

2. Habitat destruction is the greatest threat to the survival of most endangered species. What is destroying the habitat of the mussels and so many other species? What can be done to preserve that habitat? What are the possible consequences of protecting the habitat of plants and wildlife?

3. The other threats faced by the seven Gulf Slope mussels confront numerous other species as well. Pollution raises a concern for many fish and aquatic species that depend upon clean water for their survival. Nor are the seven Gulf

Slope mussels alone in having to compete with the zebra mussel, an exotic species that has wreaked havoc in the United States. As environmental historian J.R. McNeill describes:

> The zebra mussel is a striped mollusc, native to the Black and Caspian Seas. It hitched a ride to the Great Lakes in ballast water in 1985 or 1986. By 1996 it had colonized all the Great Lakes and the St. Lawrence, Illinois, Ohio, Tennessee, Arkansas, and most of the Mississippi Rivers. The zebra mussel filters water to feed and removes numerous pollutants and algae, leaving cleaner and clearer water wherever it goes. Preferring hard, smooth surfaces, it delighted in the industrial infrastructure of the Great Lakes region, building thick colonies that sank navigational buoys and clogged water intakes on factories, power plants, and municipal water filtration systems. By the early 1990s it had temporarily shut down a Ford Motor plant, a Michigan town's water power supply, and cost the United States about a billion dollars a year. In dollar terms it threatened to become the most costly invader in U.S. history, a distinction previously held by the boll weevil.

J.R. McNEILL, SOMETHING NEW UNDER THE SUN: AN ENVIRONMENTAL HISTORY OF THE TWENTIETH-CENTURY WORLD 259 (2000). The broader problem presented by invasive species is described in Invasive Species in a Changing World (Harold A. Mooney & Richard J. Hobbs eds. 2000). More generally, the FWS recently explained that "[i]ntroduced species are one of the primary threats contributing to species' extinction and are one of the most serious threats to native aquatic species, especially in the Southwest. It is estimated that approximately 50,000 non-native species have been introduced into the United States. While some of these introductions have been beneficial, many have caused dramatic declines in populations of native plants and animals." Listing Roswell springsnail, Koster's springsnail, Noel's amphipod, and Pecos assimeinea as Endangered With Critical Habitat, 70 Fed. Reg. 46304, 46313 (2005).

Concern that the seven Gulf Slope mussels will be sought because of their rarity demonstrates a much broader threat to many species. The Fish & Wildlife Service routinely refuses to indicate where an endangered plant species is located precisely because of the fear that collectors will take the plants at the site. Such purposeful exploitation has resulted in the demise of many kinds of species. Writing in 1913, conservationist William T. Hornaday (about whom more later at 864) insisted that "[i]t is high time for the whole civilized world to know that many of the most beautiful and remarkable birds of the world are now being exterminated to furnish millinery ornaments for women's wear." WILLIAM T. HORNADAY, OUR VANISHING WILD LIFE: ITS EXTERMINATION AND PRESERVATION 114 (1913). Yet over eighty years later, the Tibetan antelope faces a nearly identical threat. Scarves and shawls made from the wool from the antelope (known as "shatoosh") "sell for US$1,000 to $5,000 and more, and have become the rage among the rich, famous, and fashionable." Over $100,000 worth of shatoosh shawls were sold in one evening during a benefit for the Memorial Sloan-Kettering Cancer Center held at New York City's Mayfair Hotel. But shatoosh can only be obtained by killing the wild and shy antelope, often by poachers using automatic weapons against entire herds. Awareness of the rapid disappearance of the Tibetan antelope has yielded both legal sanctions against poachers and societal stigma against consumers, but the animal remains threatened by the underground trade in shatoosh. *See* Judy Mills, *Fash-*

ion Statement Spells Death for Tibetan Antelope, available at http://
www.worldwildlife.org/news/pubs/shahtoosh/shahtoosh3.pdf; Susan Saulny,
Shawls Sold at Charity Event: So Soft and So Illegal, N.Y. TIMES, Jan. 3, 2001,
§ B, at 2.

Other species face threats not encountered by the seven Gulf Slope mussels. Bighorn sheep, black-footed ferrets, and other animals are often the accidental victims of collisions with motor vehicles. And sometimes the threat results from natural causes rather than human activities. The Karner blue butterfly, for example, depends upon a specific kind of ecosystem that itself is constantly changing. Floods, droughts, hurricanes, and other natural disasters can cause species to disappear. There are also some instances where one species threatens the survival of another rare species. In southern California, the kit fox—a candidate for listing under the ESA— preys upon the endangered kangaroo rat, which itself eats certain endangered plants.

4. It was long believed that no species that ever lived on the earth could ever go extinct. Thomas Jefferson, for example, wrote that "[s]uch is the economy of nature, that no instance can be produced of her having permitted any one race of her animals to become extinct; of her having formed any link in her great work so weak as to be broken." THOMAS JEFFERSON, NOTES ON THE STATE OF VIRGINIA 54 (1955 ed.). During the nineteenth century, scientists gradually realized that species could—and had—gone extinct. *See generally* MARK V. BARROW, JR., NATURE'S GHOSTS: CONFRONTING EXTINCTION FROM THE AGE OF JEFFERSON TO THE AGE OF ECOLOGY (2009). The International Union for Conservation of Nature (IUCN) estimates that 784 species have disappeared from the earth since 1500. IUCN, Extinctions in Recent Time, http://data.iucn.org/dbtw-wpd/html/Red%20List%202004/completed/Section3.html. *See also* STEIN, KUTNER & ADAMS, *supra*, at 323–35 (listing the animals and plants extinctions in the United States); NILES ELDREDGE, LIFE IN THE BALANCE: HUMANITY AND THE BIODIVERSITY CRISIS 195–207 (1998) (listing all of the animal species throughout the world that have gone extinct since 1600); World Conservation Monitoring Centre, *supra*, at 206–26 (listing animal species extinct since circa 1600 and extinct higher plant taxa). The IUCN reports that 27 species that become extinct between 1984 and 2004, including the golden toad of Costa Rica, the St. Helena Olive tree, and two Hawaiian songbirds. Their demise was preceded by species such as the dodo, great auk, red gazelle of northern Africa, Steller's sea cow, Bavarian pine-vole, pink-headed duck of India, Caribbean monk seal, desert rat-kangaroo of central Australia, and Carolina parakeet. Many of those species are pictured and the reasons for their extinction are described in TIM FLANNERY & PETER SCHOUTEN, A GAP IN NATURE: DISCOVERING THE WORLD'S EXTINCT ANIMALS (2001).

The passenger pigeon provides the most dramatic extinction story in American history. The passenger pigeon flew about 60 miles per hour, was a prodigious breeder, and received its name because its migrations were so spectacular. It was the most common bird in North America as recently as two centuries ago—it represented as many as four of every ten birds on the continent—with flocks containing up to two billion birds extending from Florida to Arkansas in the winter and New York to northern Canada in the summer. Then it was shot to death. Passenger pigeons were viewed as a pest by farmers precisely because of their massive numbers, they were sold for meat in city markets, and they were hunted simply for sport. In the 1860s, John James Audubon described how an approaching flock of passenger pigeons was so large that it blocked his view of the sun, but after the flock encountered the hunters, "[t]he pigeons were picked up and piled in heaps, until each had as many as he could dispose of, when the hogs were let loose to feed on the remainder." The advent of the breech-loading shotgun around 1870 led to even more frenzied hunting, including a competition that was won by a hunter who killed 30,000 pigeons. Within twenty years, the survival of the species was doubtful, and the last wild bird was killed in Ohio in 1900. Martha, the last passenger pigeon, died in her cage in the Cincinnati Zoo in 1914. Her stuffed remains are now on view in the Smithsonian's National Museum of Natural History in Washington. *See* BAR-ROW, *supra*, at 96-100; TIM FLANNERY, THE ETERNAL FRONTIER: AN ECOLOGICAL HISTORY OF NORTH AMERICA AND ITS PEOPLES 312–15 (2001).

Of course, extinction is not an exclusively modern phenomenon. *Jurassic Park* notwithstanding, dinosaurs have long since departed the earth. Indeed, mass extinctions occurred late in each of five geologic periods. That leads some observers to argue that there is no extinction crisis today because extinction is simply a fact of natural life. Most scientists, though, believe that the rate of extinction is much higher today than it has ever been. E.O. Wilson estimates that 27,000 species become extinct each year. The calculation of how many species have gone extinct is easier for species that are well known or live in places that are well known, whereas many obscure species in remote areas can go extinct without anyone knowing that they had existed.

The Passenger Pigeon

Audubon's painting of a male and female passenger pigeon

It can even be difficult to know whether a particular species is extinct. Like other efforts to prove a negative, it is nearly impossible to know for certain whether a species no longer exists in the wild. For example, the first edition of this book confidently remarked that the ivory-billed woodpecker had been declared extinct in 2000. But to the surprise and delight of scientists and the general public alike, in April 2005 it was announced that the ivory-billed woodpecker was rediscovered in the Big Woods of Arkansas. The last confirmed sighting of the bird in North America had occurred in 1944, though there had been rumored sightings since then. The presumed demise of the bird had been described in several recent books, including PHILIP HOOSE, THE RACE TO SAVE THE LORD GOD BIRD (2004), and JEROME A. JACKSON, IN SEARCH OF THE IVORY BILLED WOODPECKER (2004). Then a lone kayaker reported that he saw a bird while paddling through the bottomland swamp forest of the Big Woods, and a team of experts from Cornell University and the Nature Conservancy confirmed that the bird survived there. But seven years have passed since the bird was seen, and now we are again uncertain whether it still survives. Other examples include the Tasmanian tiger, which some people insist survives deep within the western Tasmanian forests even though it was last seen in the wild in the 1930's; the New Zealand Storm Petrel, a bird that was not seen between the nineteenth century and 2003; and the Borneo River shark, which was thought to be extinct for nearly a century until Malaysian fishermen caught one in 1997. The list of species protected by the ESA today includes numerous other species that were thought extinct for decades before they were rediscovered.

5. Ecosystems have declined in recent years as well. A 1995 report prepared for the National Biological Service within the U.S. Department of the Interior attempted to collect the many studies of individual ecosystems that are threatened in the United States and around the world. According to that report, ecosystems that have completely disappeared include coastal rocky headland in New Hampshire, bluegrass savanna-woodland in Kentucky, and coastal strand in San Diego County. Another group of ecosystems have suffered greater than 99% losses, including oak savanna in the midwest, native grasslands in California, basin big sagebrush in Idaho's Snake River plain, European primary forests, and prairies in Illinois, Texas, and elsewhere. *See* Reed F. Noss, Edward T. LaRoe III & J. Michael Scott, *Endangered Ecosystems of the United States: A Preliminary Assessment of Loss and Degradation*, 28 BIOLOGICAL REP. 1, 37–49 (1995), *available at* http://biology.usgs.gov/pubs/ecosys.htm.

The Fund for Animals v. Norton

United States District Court for the Southern District of New York, 2005.
365 F.Supp.2d 394.

■ CASTEL, DISTRICT JUDGE:

The double-crested cormorant (Phalacrocorax auritus) is a water bird native to North America. It is a fish-eating bird with a hooked bill, turquoise eyes, a long tail, dark brown in color with two white crests of feathers that appear on its head during breeding season. . . According to the

United States Fish and Wildlife Service (the "Agency," "Fish and Wildlife Service" or "FWS"), the double-crested cormorant is one of 38 cormorant species worldwide, and one of six found in North America. Double-crested cormorants often live in flocks, and are sometimes confused with geese or loons. Prior to 1970, the cormorant population was jeopardized by DDT and other organochlorine contaminants. The population recovered during the 1970s and 1980s, but its growth rate slowed during the 1990s. It is not a species protected by the Endangered Species Act, 16 U.S.C. § 1531, et seq. The estimated population of the bird is about 2 million.

As the population expanded and the birds became more visible, fishermen and others complained that the birds were responsible for declining fish stocks. Cormorants also were drawn to the live fish raised in aquaculture facilities for human consumption. Migratory Bird Permits; Regulation for Double-Crested Cormorant Management, 68 Fed. Reg. 58,022, 58,026 (Oct. 8, 2003). Specifically, the cormorants have proved detrimental to commercial catfish farms located near the Mississippi Delta. The birds' eating habits prompted the aquaculture industry to seek curbs on the cormorant population.[5]

The Fish and Wildlife Service is the federal agency with primary responsibility for the regulation of migratory birds. Its authority to regulate the double-crested cormorant arises from the Migratory Bird Treaty Act ("MBTA"), 16 U.S.C. § 703 et seq., which implements bilateral conventions that the United States signed with Great Britain, Mexico, Japan and Russia. The double-crested cormorant received federal protection under the 1972 amendment to the Convention for the Protection of Migratory Birds and Game Mammals, Feb. 7, 1936, United States-Mexico, 50 Stat. 1311, T.S. No. 912. Under the statute's terms, protected birds may not be "taken" except as authorized by regulations implementing the MBTA. 16 U.S.C. § 703. According to 50 C.F.R. § 10.12: "Take means to pursue, hunt, shoot, wound, kill, trap, capture, or collect, or attempt to pursue, hunt, shoot, wound, kill, trap, capture, or collect."

In an attempt to address complaints about the double-crested cormorant's deleterious effects on aquaculture, the FWS adopted the Aquaculture Depredation Order ("ADO") in 1998. 50 C.F.R. § 21.47. Depredation is defined as "an act of plundering, despoiling, or making inroads." WEBSTER'S THIRD INT'L DICTIONARY UNABRIDGED (2002). The ADO permits landowners, operators and tenants of aquaculture facilities to utilize firearms to take double-crested cormorants when the birds are found committing or about to commit acts of depredation on the aquaculture stock. 50 C.F.R. § 21.47. It also permits the killing of double-crested cormorants only within the boundaries of aquaculture facilities in thirteen states. 50 C.F.R. § 21.47(c)(1).[6]

---

[5] Aquaculture is defined as "the raising or fattening of fish in enclosed ponds." WEBSTER'S THIRD INT'L DICTIONARY UNABRIDGED (2002).

[6] The ADO applies to Alabama, Arkansas, Florida, Georgia, Kentucky, Louisiana, Minnesota, Mississippi, North Carolina, Oklahoma, South Carolina, Tennessee and Texas. 50 C.F.R. § 21.47(b).

Subsequent to the ADO's issuance, the Fish and Wildlife Service continued to receive complaints about the cormorant population. By 1999, the regional offices of the Fish and Wildlife Service received an increasing number of applications for cormorant depredation permits unrelated to aquaculture, at which time FWS began to explore additional methods to control the cormorant population. In addition to decrying the birds' effects on aquaculture, the complaints received by FWS claimed that the cormorants were destroying vegetation, causing erosion, displacing other bird species and reducing sport fish populations. In November 1999, the Fish and Wildlife Service issued a Notice of Intent to develop a national management plan and to prepare an Environmental Impact Statement ("EIS") to consider different methods of addressing complaints over cormorant activities without unduly depleting the bird's population. The Fish and Wildlife Service received public comments in response to the Notice of Intent, which included submissions that were both supportive and critical of widespread efforts to limit the cormorant population.

A so-called "Cormorant Team" formed for the purpose of evaluating methods of managing the cormorant population. The team was comprised of staff from the Fish and Wildlife Service's Division of Migratory Birds Management, migratory bird staffers from the FWS's regional offices, in consultation with representatives of the Animal and Plant Health Inspection Service's ("APHIS") Wildlife Services division. As of October 2000, the Cormorant Team considered several population-management alternatives, including, but not limited to, the following: (1) no damage control; (2) nonlethal management; (3) maintaining the then-existing system by pursuing no action; (4) increased lethal control, possibly via an expanded depredation order; (5) coordinated statewide management; (6) allowing for sport-hunting; and (7) "rescindment of MBTA protection."

In August 2001, the FWS's Division of Migratory Birds issued a draft Environmental Impact Statement ("Draft EIS") to the Fish and Wildlife Service's regional offices. (FWS at 2729–2891) An EIS is required by statute. 42 U.S.C. § 4332(2)(C). In the Draft EIS, the FWS set forth the proposed action of issuing a "Public Resource Depredation Order" (the "Order" or "PRDO") that would allow state and federal wildlife agencies "greater flexibility and timeliness in dealing with [double-crested cormorant]-related public resource conflicts, while maintaining Federal oversight of [double-crested cormorant] populations.". . . On March 17, 2003, the Fish and Wildlife Service published a proposed rule adopting the PRDO. 68 Fed. Reg. 12,653. It surveyed the procedural history of the FWS's efforts to control the double-crested cormorant population, as well as the bird's geographic distribution throughout North America. As one of its premises, the proposed rule stated that cormorants posed a specific threat to artificial, highly managed fish populations, and that their impact on other fish populations varied across regions. The proposed rule also asserted that other bird species may be negatively affected by the burgeoning double-crested cormorant population, that its highly acidic guano destroyed vegetation, and that it was responsible for $25 million of lost catfish production annually. . .

The Fish and Wildlife Service received nearly 10,000 public comments, approximately 85 percent of which expressed opposition to the proposed rule. The FWS ascribes the level of opposition to organized e-mail and letter-writing campaigns. According to the plaintiffs, the comments submitted in response to the proposed rule were submitted by "scientists, ornithological organizations, [and] environmental organizations," and largely argued that the rule "was an extreme over-reaction" that risked lasting damage to double-crested cormorants and other species, and represented an overly broad grant of authority to states. Along with the public comments received by the Cormorant Team, the proposed rule triggered sometimes-pointed disagreements within the Fish and Wildlife Service itself. . .

A final rule issued on October 8, 2003. 50 C.F.R. § 21.48; 68 Fed. Reg. at 58,035. In the Record of Decision implementing the new rule, the FWS noted that "public involvement occurred throughout the [environmental impact statement] and rulemaking process. From 1999 to 2003, we held 22 public meetings over the course of 10 months of total public comment." The Record of Decision stated that the final rule had been adopted because it was environmentally sound, cost effective, and flexible enough to satisfy different management needs around the country, and did not threaten long-term sustainability of the double-crested cormorants or other natural resources. "It will provide a net benefit to fish, wildlife, and plants by allowing agencies to control [double-crested cormorants] to protect these resources from damages." 68 Fed. Reg. at 58,034. . .

The final rule governs the taking of double-crested cormorants on land and in the freshwater of 24 states. It reads in part:

> This depredation order authorizes State fish and wildlife agencies, Federally recognized Tribes, and State Directors of [APHIS's Wildlife Service Program] to prevent depredations on the public resources of fish (including hatchery stock at Federal, State, and Tribal facilities), wildlife, plants, and their habitats by taking without a permit double-crested cormorants found committing or about to commit, such depredations.

50 C.F.R. § 21.48(c)(1). The rule provides that non-lethal control methods should first be attempted as a means of population control. 50 C.F.R. § 21.48(d)(1). Thereafter, double-crested cormorants "may be taken only by means of egg oiling, egg and nest destruction, cervical dislocation, firearms, and CO[2] asphyxiation." 50 C.F.R. § 21.48(d)(2). The rule specifies acceptable forms of shotgun shot and egg-oiling substances. Id. "Nothing in this depredation order authorizes the take of any migratory bird species other than double-crested cormorants." 50 C.F.R. § 21.48(d)(7). The rule also included measures intended to protect bird species such as the anhinga, the neotropic cormorant, the piping plover, the interior least tern, the wood stork and the bald eagle from any impact from the rule's implementation. 50 C.F.R. § 21.48(d)(7), (8). Any agency whose single control action would kill more than 10 percent of a breeding colony is bound by pre-clearance procedures. 50 C.F.R. § 21.48(d)(9)(i), (12). In addition to adopting the PRDO, the FWS also amended the ADO to allow the take of double-

crested cormorants at their winter roost sites. In the Final EIS, the defendants estimate that the annual take of double-crested cormorants will total 159,635 birds, out of a total continental population of approximately two million. Approximately eight percent of the bird's total population will be taken each year. The plaintiffs are comprised of organizations that work on behalf of the protection and preservation of native wild animals, and include individual persons located throughout the United States who describe themselves as avid bird watchers and photographers.

. . . Plaintiffs challenge the PRDO, codified at 50 C.F.R. § 21.48, for its alleged failure to comply with the Migratory Bird Treaty Act, 16 U.S.C. §§ 703 et seq., the Fish and Wildlife Service's own implementing regulations, 50 C.F.R. § 21 et seq., the Endangered Species Act, 16 U.S.C. § 1531 et seq., the National Environmental Policy Act, 42 U.S.C. § 4321 et seq., and the Administrative Procedure Act, 5 U.S.C. § 706. [The court rejected each of the challenges to the PRDO].

NOTES & QUESTIONS

1. What "belongs" in the Mississippi Delta: cormorants, catfish, or both? Why should the law favor the catfish over the cormorants?

2. Aquaculture is just one of the innumerable ways in which people have modified ecosystems. Nearly half of the land in the United States is used for agriculture, which intentionally prefers one set of species instead of others. Increasingly, agricultural activities have relied upon a shrinking number of species, raising concerns about genetic diversity. Also, farmers and ranchers go to great lengths and incur great expense to eliminate unwanted species. Farmers spent over $200 billion in 2001 on products that are designed to remove the species that we judge to be "pests."

In fact, humans have long had a much more dramatic impact upon the landscape. Consider two dramatic examples on opposite sides of the world. China has spent millennia redirecting water to facilitate irrigated rice production and channeling watercourses so that goods and people could be transported to where they were needed. Such human manipulation of hydrology yielded a landscape that was quite different from the naturally occurring environment, but the forces of nature were always fighting back against the human constraints. During the sixteenth century, for example, China restructured the lower Yellow River at enormous cost, and with only temporary success. As one historian writes:

> The same skill in water control that had contributed so greatly to the development of the Chinese economy in ancient, medieval, and even in the early part of the late-imperial times, slowly fashioned a straight-jacket that in the end hindered any easy reinvention of the economic structure. Neither water nor suitable terrain was available for further profitable hydraulic expansion. . . Deadliest of all, hydrological systems kept twisting free from the grip of human would-be mastery, drying out, silting up, flooding over, or changing their channels. . . No other society reshaped its hydraulic landscape with such sustained energy as did the Chinese, nor on such a scale, but the dialectic of longterm interaction with the environ-

ment transformed what had been a one-time strength into a source of weakness.

MARK ELVIN, THE RETREAT OF THE ELEPHANTS: AN ENVIRONMENTAL HISTORY OF CHINA 164 (2004). China continues to struggle with its water, building the massive and controversial Three Gorges Dam to control flooding on the Yangtze River, and with equally questionable plans to divert the abundant freshwater from its southeastern provinces nearly one thousand miles north to the parched capital city of Beijing. Moving to the western hemisphere, some scientists question whether today's Amazonian forest, "[f]ar from being the timeless, million-year-old wilderness portrayed on calendars," is instead "the product of a historical interaction between the environment and human beings" who burned trees, channeled water, and otherwise modified the landscape to suit their needs. CHARLES C. MANN, 1491: NEW REVELATIONS OF THE AMERICAS BEFORE COLUMBUS 285 (2005). "Faced with an ecological problem" of poor soils, "the Indians fixed it" by carefully burning trees to add nutrients to the soil. "Rather than adapt to Nature, they created it." *Id.* at 311. The scope and effect of such human activities in the Amazon, China, and elsewhere has led some writers to question whether there is any such thing as a "natural" ecosystem at all. *See, e.g.*, NEIL EVERNDEN, THE SOCIAL CREATION OF NATURE 132 (1992) (concluding that " 'Nature' is a perilous device, all too easily employed in the quest to dominate others"). How would you respond to them?

At the same time, ecosystems are constantly changing even absent human intervention. In September 2005, Hurricane Katrina damaged sixteen National Wildlife Refuges, eliminating half of the 13,000 acres of land in the Breton National Wildlife Refuge in coastal Louisiana, and destroying much of the habitat of the endangered Alabama beach mouse. *See* Allison A. Freeman, *Hurricane Slammed 16 Refuges, Destroying Habitat for Three Species*, LAND LETTER, Sept. 12, 2005. Unimpeded by fire, weather, or disease, a forest can grow taller and taller and thus support a much different collection of accompanying species. Animals move from one place to another, establishing new populations that alter the dynamics of the community that existed before their arrival. Plants populate new areas, too, thanks to wind, water, and animals that carry seeds to increasingly distant locations. How can we distinguish between natural processes and "threats" to an ecosystem? For example, given the movement of many species, what does it mean to say that a species is "invasive?" Should it matter whether people were involved—directly or indirectly—in the spread of the species? Biologist David Lodge and philosopher Kristin Shrader-Frechette offer scientific, public policy, and ethical qualifications to the suggestion that all species invasions are created equal:

- "First, although humans are, of course, as natural as any other species, in recent centuries human influence has increased far more dramatically than that of any other species."

- "Second, rational disagreement exists about the temporal benchmarks for ecological conservation or restoration," with scientists debating whether the arrival of Europeans in North America is an appropriate point of comparison.

- "Third, some writers . . . presuppose that whatever is natural (e.g., species invasions) is morally acceptable, an example of the naturalistic fallacy. This presupposition is obviously false, as murder, auto accidents, and species extinctions are all natural or normal, but clearly they are neither moral or acceptable."

Lodge and Shrader-Frechette assert that "an ethically defensible conclusion is that both native species and nonindigenous species should be managed with respect to what is both humanly and ecologically desirable." David M. Lodge & Kristin Shrader-Frechette, *Nonindigenous Species: Ecological Explanation, Environmental Ethics, and Public Policy*, 17 CONSERVATION BIOLOGY 1, 3 (2003). So what is humanly and ecologically desirable?

CHAPTER 3

HOW TO PROTECT BIODIVERSITY

Chapter Outline:
A. Ways of Protecting Biodiversity
B. Private Actions to Protect Biodiversity
C. Constitutional Restraints on Government Regulation of Biodiversity
D. State Law Protection of Biodiversity
E. Tribal Protection of Biodiversity

Biodiversity can be protected in many ways by many people. The threats to particular species or ecosystems often dictate the strategies that are best designed to protect biodiversity. The management of land to promote the natural life that is found there is a popular measure because it addresses the destruction of habitat that affects so many plants and animals. Different actions may be required to combat other threats, including the elimination of pollution, the removal of exotic species, and the regulation of hunting or collecting. If a species is nearing extinction, then more aggressive measures such as captive breeding and the reintroduction of the species into other habitats may become necessary.

Who should take those actions is often more contested than the determination of the appropriate action itself. The threshold issue is to decide whether the imperative to protect biodiversity in a given instance must be augmented by a legal duty. Private individuals and institutions play a significant role in the effort to save ecosystems and species alike, yet such efforts are typically complemented by government actions as well. Sometimes the government—and the laws it enforces—relies upon carrots to encourage the preservation of biodiversity, while at other times resort is made to sticks to compel such preservation, with predictable responses from those who are affected by the law's commands. And the decision to enlist the government in the preservation of biodiversity raises the question of which government should enact such laws: municipal or county governments, states, the United States, or a collection of concerned nations throughout the world.

Most of the attention on recent actions intended to protect biodiversity focuses on two kinds of responses: in the United States, federal regulation of activities that interfere with biodiversity; and internationally, the development of treaties that regulate conduct adverse to biodiversity. The role of the federal government and actions of the international community will be explored in much more detail in Parts 3 and 4 of this book. But there are many other options. This chapter examines the role of private actors, states, and Native American tribes in preserving biodiversity. First, though, this chapter surveys the types of actions that can be taken to protect ecosystems, species, and other aspects of biodiversity. The two questions that arise throughout these materials are which actors are best suited to protect biodiversity in certain instances, and what kinds of actions are likely to be most effective in achieving that end.

A. WAYS OF PROTECTING BIODIVERSITY

Defenders of Wildlife v. Salazar

United States Court of Appeals for the District of Columbia Circuit, 2011.
651 F.3d 112.

■ GRIFFITH, CIRCUIT JUDGE.

As required by the National Wildlife Refuge System Improvement Act, the U.S. Fish and Wildlife Service and the National Park Service devised a plan to manage the elk and bison populations in the National Elk Refuge and Grand Teton National Park. Part of this plan includes ending the longstanding agency practice of feeding these animals during the winter. The Defenders of Wildlife challenge the plan because it fails to include a time certain for ending the practice. The district court rejected the challenge, and, for the reasons set forth below, we affirm its judgment.

I.

The National Wildlife Refuge System includes over 550 refuges and 150 million acres of protected land. The Department of the Interior, acting through the U.S. Fish and Wildlife Service, manages these properties pursuant to the National Wildlife Refuge Administration Act, Pub. L. No. 89-669, 80 Stat. 926 (1966), as amended by the National Wildlife Refuge System Improvement Act ("Improvement Act"), Pub L. No. 105-57, 111 Stat. 1252 (1997) (codified at 16 U.S.C. §§ 668dd-668ee).

The National Elk Refuge is part of that system. Located just north of Jackson, Wyoming, and adjacent to Grand Teton National Park, the Refuge was established in 1912 when Congress designated 2000 acres in Jackson Hole as a "winter game (elk) reserve." Act of Aug. 10, 1912, Pub. L. No. 62-261, 37 Stat. 293 (codified as amended at 16 U.S.C. § 673). The Refuge is now a 24,700-acre expanse that the Secretary holds "for the grazing of, and as a refuge for, American elk and other big game animals." 16 U.S.C. § 673a. Its landscape consists of meadows, marshes, streams, ponds, and open fields across a valley floor that includes sagebrush and rock outcroppings, all set against the majestic backdrop of the Teton and Gros Ventre mountain ranges. Lucky wayfarers may spot wolves, grizzly bears, trumpeter swans, and any number of the area's magnificent ungulates, including bison, bighorn sheep, pronghorn, mule deer, and, of course, elk. The National Elk Refuge's eponymous herd comprises one of the largest concentrations of elk in North America. It goes without saying that these elk are of considerable ecological, economic, and cultural value.

The National Elk Refuge

Around the turn of the last century, a series of severe winters in Wyoming strained the elk populations and spurred the good people of Jackson to save the elk by feeding them. When Congress created the Refuge in 1912, the federal government continued this practice, which the parties refer to as supplemental feeding. For roughly seventy days each winter, approximately 7000 elk and 1000 bison are drawn daily to the federal trough.

In recent years, it has become apparent that this practice, though born of benevolence, causes significant problems. According to the Department of the Interior, supplemental feeding leads to a seasonal concentration of elk and bison that is "an unnatural situation that has contributed to . . . an increased risk of potentially major outbreaks of exotic diseases . . . [and] damage to and loss of habitat." Final Bison and Elk Management Plan and Environmental Impact Statement for the National Elk Refuge / Grand Teton National Park / John D. Rockefeller, Jr., Memorial Parkway 9 (Feb. 1, 2007) [hereinafter February 2007 Management Plan and EIS]. This risk poses an existential threat to the elk and bison and puts the very purpose of the Refuge at jeopardy. *See id.* (noting that the risk of diseases posed by increased concentrations of the animals has "the greatest potential to hinder . . . [the] purposes . . . [of] the National Elk Refuge").

One major problem is brucellosis—also known as "Bangs disease, undulant fever, and contagious abortion,"—which causes an infected female to abort her first calf, leaving behind contaminated fetal tissue on the ground capable of transmitting the disease to other animals. Brucellosis rates within normal Wyoming elk herds are approximately two percent, but rates among elk that frequent the Refuge feeding lines have averaged around seventeen percent in recent years. Another major problem, chronic wasting disease (CWD), is the elk version of mad cow disease: Like its bovine counterpart, CWD assaults the central nervous system, causing brain lesions, behavioral changes, a loss of body condition, and ultimately death. CWD is caused by abnormal, non-living proteins known as prions that persist in the soil where infected animals graze, even after intensive efforts to remove them. Statistical sampling suggests that in open, elk-hunt areas in Wyoming, the prevalence of CWD in elk averages around four percent. But in confined areas—like those created by the feed lines—the prevalence can exceed ninety percent. CWD is not yet prevalent in the Refuge, but if that changes, "environmental contamination will become a major concern due to the disease's ability to persist in the environment for a long period of time."

All agree that supplemental feeding increases the risk of such diseases. Without supplemental feeding, the elk would gather in smaller groups, meaning that one sick elk would infect only the handful of others around it. But because the feeding lines bring so many together, the disease of one can quickly become that of many, if not all.

Spurred by a district court order requiring reassessment of the winter feeding operation, *see* Fund for Animals v. Clark, 27 F. Supp. 2d 8, 12-15 (D.D.C. 1998), the Fish and Wildlife Service teamed with the National Park Service, also part of the Department of the Interior, to prepare a management plan for the elk and bison populations. The agencies analyzed six alternatives for managing the herds over the next fifteen years. These plans ran the gamut from maintaining the status quo to ending the practice of supplemental feeding within five years.

In April 2007, the agencies settled on an approach that would, over time, create conditions that would allow the elk and bison to survive the winter without supplemental feeding and, in the meantime, manage the risk of contagion until the practice ended. In essence, their plan seeks to restore natural forage that will allow the animals to sustain themselves during wintertime without the help of supplemental feeding. Bison and Elk Management Plan: National Elk Refuge and Grand Teton National Park 129-34 (Apr. 2007) [hereinafter April 2007 Management Plan]. For example, it provides for substantial reductions in the numbers of elk and bison, primarily through short-term increases in hunting, so that their populations will be closer to levels that would have existed had there never been a practice of supplemental feeding. The plan also seeks to reduce disease transmission by rotating feed sites, spreading feed in long lines, separating elk and bison from neighboring livestock, providing increased CWD monitoring, and allowing Wyoming to vaccinate the herds. Ultimately, over a fifteen-year period, "[a]s habitat and population objectives are achieved, [the agencies will aim to] decrease reliance on intensive supplemental winter feeding, including complete transition to free-standing forage if and when several established criteria are met, including support from the Wyoming Game and Fish Department and the public."

Before adopting this approach, the agencies considered and rejected the petitioners' preferred alternative, which would have committed the Secretary to ending supplemental feeding within five years. As described in their brief, the agencies recognized that this alternative "would provide some advantages in terms of habitat benefits, a lower prevalence of brucellosis over the long term, and a lower risk for the spread of chronic wasting disease." Appellees' Br. 19 (citing Record of Decision, Final Bison and Elk Management Plan and Environmental Impact Statement: National Elk Refuge and Grand Teton National Park 10 (Apr. 2007) [hereinafter Record of Decision]). But they also found that "[this alternative] would likely result in an increase in elk mortality from starvation, predation, and disease related to poor body condition, particularly in severe winters." This in turn would lead to a "long-term decrease in elk hunting and viewing opportunities in the Refuge, with attendant impacts on the area economy, and could cause elk herd numbers to fall below [the Wyoming Game and Fish Department's] statewide objective in some years." The agencies concluded that their preferred plan "[is more] consistent with regional herd management objectives, better balances divergent stakeholder interests, builds upon success on the ground, and enables managers to adapt to new information and changing conditions," all while preparing the animals for the eventual cessation of supplemental feeding and providing most of the benefits offered by the petitioners' preferred alternative. On the issue of when to end supplemental feeding, the agencies stressed that although they are committed to abandoning the practice, they would "not preclude the use of supplemental feeding or other management tools as [they] work to resolve the bison and elk management issues . . . [N]or [would they] make predictions about how fast [they could] implement the phased approach for improving forage, reducing the [elk and bison populations], and reducing the need for supplemental feed . . . When the biological, social, and political conditions enable [them] to consider a phase-out of feeding, [the plan's] adaptive framework provides [the agencies] with that flexibility." In essence, the agencies determined that a deadline for ceasing supplemental feeding would be unduly restrictive in light of the many variables and concerns that need to be accounted for in managing the Refuge.

The Defenders of Wildlife, the Jackson Hole Conservation Alliance, the National Wildlife Refuge Association, the Greater Yellowstone Coalition, and the Wyoming Outdoor Council (collectively, the Defenders) filed suit in the district court, challenging the Secretary's plan under the Administrative Procedure Act. They argue the plan's failure to commit to a deadline for ending supplemental feeding was arbitrary and capricious given the Secretary's duty under the Improvement Act to "provide for the conservation of . . . wildlife" and "ensure that the biological integrity, diversity, and environmental health of the [wildlife refuge system] are maintained." 16 U.S.C. § 668dd(a)(4)(A)-(B). The district court granted summary judgment for the agencies, reasoning that the plan accounted for and managed the dangers of supplemental feeding and also created a program for phasing out the practice over a fifteen-year period. Defenders of Wildlife v. Salazar, 698 F. Supp. 2d 141, 147–48 (D.D.C. 2010). The Defenders of Wildlife filed a timely appeal, and we take jurisdiction pursuant to 28 U.S.C. § 1291.

We review the district court's grant of summary judgment de novo. Under the Administrative Procedure Act, we set aside agency action that is "arbitrary, capricious, an abuse of discretion, or otherwise not in accordance with law." 5 U.S.C. § 706(2)(A). Our review focuses on whether the agency examined the relevant data, articulated a satisfactory explanation for its action, based its decision on the relevant factors, and committed no clear error of judgment.

II.

The parties agree that supplemental feeding poses serious risks for the elk and bison in the Refuge. The only question this case presents is whether it was arbitrary and capricious for the Secretary to transition away from supplemental feeding without committing himself to ending the practice on a particular date.

The Defenders argue it was, inasmuch as the very purpose of the National Wildlife Refuge System, as set out in the Improvement Act, "is to administer a national network of lands and waters for the conservation, management, and where appropriate, restoration of the fish, wildlife, and plant resources and their habitats within the United States for the benefit of present and future generations of Americans." 16 U.S.C. § 668dd(a)(2). To that end, the Defenders point out, the Act mandates that the Secretary manage refuges to "provide for the *conservation* of fish, wildlife, and plants, and their habitats within the System" and to "ensure that the *biological integrity, diversity, and environmental health* of the System are maintained for the benefit of present and future generations of Americans." *Id.* § 668dd(a)(4)(A), (B) (emphases added). The Act also instructs the Secretary to "sustain and, where appropriate, restore and enhance, healthy populations of fish, wildlife, and plants utilizing . . . methods and procedures associated with modern scientific resource programs." *Id.* § 668ee(4). The Defenders argue that the Secretary's plan is unlawful because it does not fix a definite time for ending supplemental feeding, even though the agencies have acknowledged that the dangers posed by this practice imperil explicit statutory objectives. Underlying this statutory argument is some common sense: the whole point of a National Elk *Refuge* is to provide a sanctuary in which populations of healthy, reproducing elk can be sustained. *See* 16 U.S.C. § 673a (creating a "refuge" for the elk). The Refuge can hardly provide such a sanctuary if, every winter, elk and bison are drawn by the siren song of human-provided food to what becomes, through the act of gathering, a miasmic zone of life-threatening diseases.

The Defenders acknowledge that the Improvement Act also requires the Secretary to consider other factors such as the importance of recreation on refuge lands and cooperation with state officials in pursuing the objectives of the Act. *See id.* § 668dd(4)(I), (M). They argue, however, that such considerations may be pursued only when "compatible" or "consistent with" the conservation mission of the System and the purposes of each refuge. *See id.* § 668dd(a)(3)(B), (e)(3). Reading the several provisions of the Act that emphasize the importance of wildlife conservation together with the general purpose of the National Wildlife Refuge System, the Defenders contend that the agencies' top priority in managing the Refuge must be conservation, and other considerations must not hinder that objective.

For their part, the Secretary and Wyoming (intervening as a defendant-appellee in this case) argue that the Improvement Act confers upon the Secretary broad managerial discretion in how to pursue the Act's objectives. They concede that conservation is the overarching objective, but argue that it cannot be the sole consideration. After all, the Act lists fourteen factors that the Secretary "shall" consider in administering the System, including, among others, "ensur[ing] effective coordination, interaction, and cooperation" with adjoining landowners and State fish and wildlife agencies in pursuit of the objectives of the Act. *Id.* § 668dd(a)(4)(E).

Given the discretion afforded him, the Secretary argues that the agencies reasonably determined that the plan is consistent with the objectives of the Act and the purposes of the Refuge. The plan addresses the risk of diseases by (1) increasing natural forage and decreasing the herd sizes, which will work in tandem to create conditions under which supplemental feeding can be stopped without unduly increasing the risk of starvation, (2) monitoring and managing the diseases that accompany gathering at the feed lines, and (3) progressively reducing reliance on supplemental feeding when certain criteria have been met.

There is no doubt that unmitigated continuation of supplemental feeding would undermine the conservation purpose of the National Wildlife Refuge System. But we cannot conclude that the agencies acted unlawfully by adopting a plan that contained no deadline for ending the practice, and that is the only issue before us. The record amply demonstrates that the agencies collected the relevant data, identified the dangers posed by supplemental feeding, and adopted a plan to mitigate those dangers. That they also determined that the many objectives of the Act, including conservation, could best be met without implementation of a fixed deadline for stopping supplemental feeding was not arbitrary or capricious.

The district court was right that the plan "might well have been unreasonable had the agencies categorically refused to phase out the winter feeding program in spite of all the evidence in the record about the dangers of supplemental feeding." But they did no such thing. Instead, they selected an approach that is geared toward ending the practice over time while maintaining the flexibility needed to respond to facts on the ground. The Defenders are understandably concerned that this flexibility could be used to continue the practice indefinitely. But the agencies must proceed in a manner that is consistent with the science and accounts for the risks posed by supplemental feeding. There is nothing the agencies have said or done that causes us to doubt that they will. It is highly significant and indeed dispositive to us, as it was to the district court, that the agencies are committed to ending supplemental feeding. We do not know precisely how they will proceed, and that makes it impossible, at this stage, to declare that their plan is arbitrary and capricious simply because it does not specify a particular date by which the practice will cease. Should the agencies act unreasonably in establishing criteria for the transition or in otherwise carrying out the plan, that will be a different issue for another panel.

III.

The Defenders also argue that the plan unlawfully gives the Wyoming Fish and Game Department a veto over whether supplemental feeding will end. They point to language in the plan stating that the agencies will seek to "decrease reliance on intensive supplemental winter feeding, including complete transition to free-standing forage *if and when several established criteria are met, including support from the Wyoming Game and Fish Department* and the public."

Regardless of how we might have read this language in the first instance, the Secretary has assured us in his briefs and at oral argument that the language confers no veto. *See* Appellees' Br. 34 (characterizing the disputed provision as "aspirational" rather than a grant of any power to Wyoming); Wyoming's Br. 28 n.6 (also agreeing that Wyoming does not have a veto); *cf.* Wyoming v. United States, 279 F.3d 1214, 1234 (10th Cir. 2002) ("[F]ederal management and regulation of federal wildlife refuges preempts state management and regulation of such refuges . . . where state management and regulation stand as an obstacle to the accomplishment of the full purposes and objectives of the Federal Government."). We take the Secretary at his word that Wyoming has no veto over the Secretary's duty to end a practice that is concededly at odds with the long-term health of the elk and bison in the Refuge.

IV.

For the foregoing reasons, the district court's judgment is

Affirmed.

NOTES & QUESTIONS

1. Why do we need an elk "refuge?" Why is it necessary to *manage* such a refuge, instead of simply letting nature take its course? How should the FWS and the Park Service manage the National Elk Refuge given the issues described in the case?

2. In 2011, the National Elk Refuge provided supplemental feeding for 100 days, beginning on January 6. In 2012, supplemental feeding did not begin until February 2 because of greater forage production during the previous summer and below average snow cover in January. National Elk Refuge Manager Steve Kallin explained that the refuge's "overall goal is to reduce the reliance on supplemental feeding." U.S. Fish & Wildlife Service, Press Release, National Elk Refuge Announces Supplemental Feeding Start Date, Jan. 31, 2012. Is that statement consistent with the D.C. Circuit's decision?

3. The importance of land to the preservation of biodiversity is easily explained: habitat destruction is the greatest threat to ecosystems and individual species, but most habitat destruction occurs only with the approval of the landowner. A shopping center cannot displace a wetland, for example, if the landowner does not want to build a shopping center there. Thus a landowner can do much to protect biodiversity simply by managing the land with that goal in mind. The challenge, then, is to persuade landowners that the protection of biodiversity is a worthy goal.

According to Bradley Karkkainen,

> There is a broad, though not universal, consensus within the scientific community that a biodiversity conservation strategy should be built on the foundation of a system of biological reserves containing relatively undisturbed habitats for diverse communities of species, linked where possible by a network of wildlife migration corridors. It is also widely agreed that, other things being equal, large reserves are preferable to small ones. This preference exists for several reasons. First, reserves large enough to protect naturally functioning ecosystems containing viable populations of resident species protect far more biodiversity—at the genetic, species, and ecosystem levels—at a far lower cost than do species-by-species management strategies. These reserves are also generally cheaper to acquire and maintain per unit of protected area than a series of smaller reserves of comparable total size. Second, some species, especially large mammals, have large home ranges, low natural growth rates, and low population densities, and therefore require large areas of protected habitat. Third, larger protected areas can generally support larger and more genetically diverse populations and "metapopulations," thus supporting genetic diversity within species and reducing the risk of extinction from human or natural disturbances, invasion by exotics, predation, disease, demographic events, or genetic depression. Fourth, other things being equal, larger protected areas are less likely to suffer from adverse "edge effects," including both human and natural disturbances from adjacent unprotected lands.

Bradley C. Karkkainen, *Biodiversity and Land,* 83 CORNELL LAW REVIEW 1, 10–14, 103–04 (1997). The identification of the most biologically valuable lands has centered on the hotspots concept developed by ecologist Norman Myers. Conservation International describes the biodiversity hotspots as "the richest and most threatened reservoirs of plant and animal life on earth." Conservation International, Biodiversity Hotspots, available at http://www.biodiversityhotspots.org/xp/Hotspots. The organization concludes that "the amount of biodiversity contained in hotspots is extremely high," so "[u]nless we succeed in conserving this small fraction of the planet's land area, we will lose more than half of our natural heritage—regardless how successful conservation is outside of the hotspots." RUSSELL MITTERMEIER ET AL., HOTSPOTS REVISITED: EARTH'S BIOLOGICALLY RICHEST AND MOST ENDANGERED TERRESTRIAL ECOREGIONS 68 (2004). Several recent studies have listed hotspots around the world, as mentioned above at pages 424–25.

4. There are, of course, millions of landowners. The largest landowner in the United States is the federal government, which owns about 650 million acres, or nearly one-third of the land in the nation. Federal ownership is especially prevalent in the western states, where the government owns 83% of the land in Nevada and more than half of the land in four other states. The management of federal land is divided among numerous agencies, each of which has different priorities in managing the land. They include:

- the FWS, which administers the National Wildlife Refuge system that includes 535 national wildlife refuges totaling 96 million acres, with the purposes of individual refuges ranging from protecting migratory bird habitat and elk refuges to "vast Alaskan holdings [that] may come closer than any other category of federal lands to constituting genuine biodiversity reserves" (and whose statutory responsibilities with respect to biodiversity are described in more detail in chapter 7);
- the National Park Service, which contains 376 national parks, monuments, and other areas comprised of 84 million acres that "contribute less to biological diversity than might be expected;"
- the Bureau of Land Management (BLM), which manages the most land (264 million acres), primarily in the west, that was never reserved for a special purpose but which is "relatively rich in biodiversity" (and whose statutory responsibilities with respect to biodiversity are described in more detail in chapter 9); and
- the Forest Service, which oversees 192 million acres of national forests throughout the nation (and whose statutory responsibilities with respect to biodiversity are described in more detail in chapter 8).

Each agency must abide by different statutes that regulate what kinds of activities can occur on each type of land, with the importance of biodiversity varying significantly in each statute. The result is that "wildlife conservation is not a commanding force in federal land management. It is one of several management objectives on all the major federal land classifications. . . It is not the exclusive, or even the dominant, goal on any lands but the national wildlife refuges." MICHAEL J. BEAN & MELANIE J. ROWLAND, THE EVOLUTION OF NATIONAL WILDLIFE LAW 278 (3d ed. 1997). The statutes governing each agency are complemented by statutes such as the National Environmental Policy Act (NEPA) and the ESA (about which much more in Part II of this book) that require federal agencies to account for environmental values, and biodiversity in particular, when making land use decisions.

5. One might expect that the more than 100 million acres of national wilderness areas would serve as a key home for much biodiversity. The Wilderness Act of 1964 empowers Congress to designate wilderness areas "where the earth and its community of life are untrammeled by man, where man himself is a visitor who does not remain." 16 U.S.C. § 1131(c). A leading management treatise explains the benefit that wilderness areas provide for biodiversity as follows:

> Wilderness ecosystems have long been revered as places where nature is allowed to run free, unhindered by human activity. Their often-large size, relatively intact biota, and high water and air quality have made them important places for ecosystem study. Wilderness areas are among the last places where large predators still roam and may be among the last places where evolutionary forces still operate without significant human impacts. In general, wilderness ecosystems have been found to be among the healthiest systems left in the United States, befitting their role, in Aldo

Leopold's words, as a "base datum of normality" for a "science of land health."

Jerry F. Franklin & Gregory H. Aplet, Wilderness Ecosystems, in WILDERNESS MANAGEMENT: STEWARDSHIP AND PROTECTION OF RESOURCES AND VALUES 263 (3d ed. 2002). The biodiversity value of the Wilderness Act is illustrated by The Wilderness Society v. FWS, 353 F.3d 1051 (9th Cir. 2003) (en banc), which involved a program to benefit Alaska's commercial fishing operations by adding hatchery-reared salmon to Tustumena Lake in the Kenai National Wilderness Area. Environmentalists objected that hatchery fish could compromise the genetic diversity of the native salmon. The court held 11–0 that the program constituted a commercial enterprise that was prohibited by the Wilderness Act. But not everyone is impressed with the ability of designated wilderness areas to protect biodiversity. "Only 19 of 261 ecosystems in the United States are represented" in wilderness areas, Michael McCloskey, *Changing Views of What the Wilderness System is All About*, 76 DENVER U. L. REV. 369, 373 (1999), and Reed Noss has complained that the wilderness system "does a poor job" of protecting biodiversity. *Id.* (quoting Noss). Additionally, while Karkkainen and other observers champion buffer zones, Congress has explicitly rejected that concept with respect to wilderness areas. *See, e.g.*, James Peak Wilderness and Protection Area Act, 107 Pub. L. No. 216, § 7(a), 116 Stat. 1055, 1060 (2002) (providing that the establishment of a new wilderness area in Colorado "shall not create or imply the creation of protective perimeters or buffer zones around any wilderness area"). To remedy some of these deficiencies, Dave Foreman has proposed an elaborate "rewilding" of North America that selects, designs, and manages wilderness areas with biodiversity in mind. *See* DAVE FOREMAN, REWILDING NORTH AMERICA 168–217 (2004).

6. Federal land ownership is not static. The federal government transfers some lands to private parties and state and local governments even as it acquires other lands. Federal acquisition of land holds special promise for the protection of biodiversity. As Professor Karkkainen observes, "in some areas—Hawaii, Florida, Texas, parts of the southeast, and high-population coastal areas generally—where combinations of rare, unique, or especially fragile ecosystems combine with intense development pressure to create a heightened threat of species and ecosystem extinction, targeted federal acquisitions of the last remaining habitat fragments may be the last best hope for conserving biodiversity." *Id.* at 51. But coastal property in rapidly developing areas is expensive, too. A number of federal programs empower the government to purchase lands of special biological value, including section 5 of the ESA and the Land and Water Conservation Fund (LWCF). Critics complain, however, that those programs are chronically underfunded.

7. Besides the federal government, many other actors own land that contains abundant biodiversity. Increasingly, state and local governments are purchasing land in order to conserve the biodiversity it contains. Thus the State of Illinois spent $21 million to obtain property that contained great blue heron rookeries and other wildlife once the Supreme Court held in Solid Waste Agency of Northern Cook County v. U.S. Army Corps of Engineers, 531 U.S. 159 (2001), that federal Clean Water Act regulations could not prevent local governments from using the site to store its municipal wastes. Nature reserves also play a prominent role in the efforts of many other countries to protect biodiversity, as detailed in chapter 13. And many private landowners seek to protect biodiversity around the world. These actions range from the decisions of individual land-owners to attract and sustain a diverse range of flora and fauna on their property to the purposeful efforts of international groups to acquire land that is especially noted for its biodiversity. (The work of the Nature Conservancy, the largest organization focused on the acquisition of lands for biodiversity, is described below).

National Audubon Society v. Hester
United States Court of Appeals for the District of Columbia Circuit, 1986.
801 F.2d 405.

■ EDWARDS, STARR and SILBERMAN, CIRCUIT JUDGES.

■ PER CURIAM

The California condor, the largest winged inhabitant of North America, has been decimated to the point where only twenty-six members of the species remain in existence. At the time this controversy began, all but six of the birds were kept in zoos in Los Angeles and San Diego as part of a breeding program designed to avert extinction of the species. This lawsuit arises from the U.S. Fish & Wildlife Service's decision to bring the remaining condors in from the wild. The district court granted plaintiff National Audubon Society's request for a preliminary injunction barring the Service from carrying out this decision. Because we believe that the agency's decision constituted a reasoned exercise of its discretion in fulfilling its statutory mandate, we reverse.

I.

In recent years, the Wildlife Service's energies have been engaged in inauspicious efforts to stem the condor flock's steady decline. In 1979, working in tandem with public and private groups (including the plaintiff), the Service developed a "Condor Recovery Plan." This plan had two principal elements: extensive tracking and study of wild birds, and the commencement of a captive propagation program. At the time, it was hoped that better information about the birds' lifestyle (and causes of death), together with enhanced breeding in capacity, could save the condor. The mortality rate among wild birds, however, proved to be alarming: in the winter of 1984–85, six of the then fifteen wild condors vanished. A common cause of death was believed to be lead poisoning following the birds' feeding on the carcasses of animals shot by hunters (the condor is a member of the vulture family).

After considering a wide range of scientific opinion, the Wildlife Service issued an Environmental Assessment in October, 1985 setting forth seven alternative courses of action for condor preservation. The option chosen by the agency combined capture of birds whose genes were poorly represented among the captive flock, maintenance of a small wild flock, and eventual release of young birds bred in captivity. This choice struck a balance between the competing considerations at stake (as well as the contending views of biologists and naturalists): on the one hand, bringing in the remaining wild condors would minimize mortality and increase the genetic diversity of the captive flock; on the other hand, preservation of a wild flock would provide "guide birds" available to lead captive-bred condors ultimately released, facilitate the improvement of techniques of protecting the birds, and prevent the erosion of public support for preserving the condors' habitat.

The California condor

Shortly after this report was released, however, troubling news began reaching the Wildlife Service. One of the birds scheduled to remain in the wild appeared to be courting one of the birds slated for capture. Second, due to apparent zoo mismanagement, the young condors selected for release into the wilderness in the next year had grown too tame. And, most importantly, one condor inhabiting an area regarded as very safe, where "clean" carcasses were provided for the birds, nonetheless came down with lead poisoning (and has since died). In late December, the agency reversed its earlier decision and announced that all remaining wild birds would now be brought in. The federal Council on Environmental Quality certified that an emergency existed and that immediate documentation of the environmental effects of this decision was unnecessary. In any event, on December 23 the Service issued an "Addendum" to its October Environmental Assessment explaining the reasons why the agency now believed a different plan of action was called for.

This lawsuit followed. Audubon claimed that the Wildlife Service's action violated the Administrative Procedure Act (APA), 5 U.S.C. § 701 *et seq.* (1982), the Endangered Species Act (ESA), 16 U.S.C. § 1531 *et seq.* (1982), and the National Environmental Policy Act (NEPA), 42 U.S.C. § 4321 *et seq.* (1982), and moved for a preliminary injunction barring the capture of the wild condors. The district court granted Audubon's motion, finding that the plaintiff had demonstrated a likelihood of success on the merits and a balance of hardships in its favor. *See* 627 F. Supp. 1419 (D.D.C.1986). While acknowledging that a "reviewing court must be wary of substituting its own judgment for that of the agency," *id.* at 1422 (citing Citizens to Preserve Overton Park, Inc. v. Volpe, 401 U.S. 402, 416 (1971)), the district court nevertheless concluded that the agency's decision was fatally flawed. The court opined that the Wildlife Service had exhibited insufficient analysis and explanation of its departure from past policy. In the court's view, this change of policy amounted to arbitrary and capricious action in violation of the above-mentioned statutes and threatened irreparably to harm the plaintiff's interests.

II.

This court customarily reviews a district court's grant of preliminary equitable relief under the deferential abuse of discretion standard. A preliminary injunction premised upon an erroneous view of the law, however, is not insulated from appellate review. In this case, the district court's decision appears to have rested entirely on its view that the Wildlife Service had failed to justify its change of policy; the court relied upon this point not only in determining the plaintiff's likelihood of success on the merits, but also in concluding that the "balance of harms" favored Audubon. Since we believe, contrary to the district court, that the agency fully considered all appropriate courses of action and adequately explained its policy choice, we cannot uphold the district court's decision.

Although the district court relied upon the ESA and NEPA as well as the Administrative Procedure Act, it is clear that those statutes essentially place the same demands on agency decisionmakers as does the APA. Under the ESA, an agency's determination that its action will not threaten endangered species is to be set aside only if arbitrary and capricious. Under NEPA, agencies must prepare an Environmental Impact Statement (EIS) whenever proposed major federal action will significantly affect the quality of the human environment, see 42 U.S.C. § 4332(2)(C) (1982); an agency's decision not to prepare an EIS—because the proposed action will not significantly affect the environment—may be overturned, again, only if arbitrary and capricious. The question for reviewing courts is not whether an agency decision is "correct," but rather whether the decision reflects sufficient attention to environmental concerns and is adequately reasoned and explained. The ESA and NEPA were intended to ensure that agencies, in discharging their various functions, do not blithely disregard the environmental effects of their decisions; it is obvious, then, that judicial review of agency decisionmaking is at its most deferential where, as here, the agency action is based solely upon environmental considerations—where the challenge to agency action simply represents a quarrel with the agency's means of pursuing a universally desired end.

We believe the Wildlife Service's decision to capture the remaining wild condors was manifestly defensible. That decision represented a reevaluation by the responsible agency of the costs and benefits associated with the existence of captive and wild condor flocks. Contrary to the plaintiff's assertion, the decision was not markedly at odds with previous policy. In its October Environmental Assessment, while endorsing the maintenance of a small wild flock, the Service had recognized that there were weighty arguments to the contrary and that the question was close; it noted that "if the condor population appears to continue steadily downward after implementation of this option, we stand ready to reevaluate the taking into captivity of all, or a significant portion of, the remaining [wild] population." This is, in part, precisely what happened: the agency reconsidered its policy after learning of recent developments, including the lead poisoning suffered by a bird inhabiting what was thought to be one of the safest locations. The Wildlife Service simply exercised its discretion to "adapt [its] rules and policies to the demands of changing circumstances." Permian Basin Area Rate Cases, 390 U.S. 747, 784 (1968). The district court, however, concluded that the factual developments supporting the agency's change of course were not "new"—that they had been known at an earlier stage, when the agency reaffirmed its commitment to preserving a wild flock. The flaw in this reasoning is that in a case like this one there is no particular significance attached to the exact date that factual information reaches any official of an agency. It takes time for information to be disseminated from the lower echelons of agency staff to the agency's decisionmakers, and still more time for the decisionmakers to appraise the policy implications of that information.

More fundamentally, agencies are entitled to alter their policies " 'with or without a change in circumstances,' " so long as they satisfactorily explain why they have done so. Motor Vehicle Mfrs. Ass'n v. State Farm Mut. Auto. Ins. Co., 463 U.S. 29, 57 (1983) (quoting Greater Boston Television Corp. v. FCC, 444 F.2d 841, 852 (D.C.Cir.1970), cert. denied, 403 U.S. 923 (1971)) (emphasis added). We have little problem concluding that the Wildlife Service met its burden of justifying its change of course. The agency's October Environmental Assessment thoroughly surveyed the competing factors at stake and examined the desirability of seven alternative courses of action. Its December Addendum incorporated the earlier document's reasoning and additionally set forth the agency's reasons for preferring a different option than before. The Service's documentation may have been succinct, but nonetheless adequately discloses the concerns underlying the agency's decision and demonstrates that that decision rests on a rational basis. That much being so, our inquiry is at an end: NEPA's "mandate to the agencies is essentially procedural. . . It is to insure a fully informed and well-considered decision, not necessarily a decision [federal judges] would have reached had they been members of the decisionmaking unit of the agency." Vermont Yankee Nuclear Power Co. v. NRDC, 435 U.S. 519, 558 (1978). The decision of the district court is therefore REVERSED.

NOTES & QUESTIONS

1. The legal case for the removal of the last condors from the wild was aided by an associate solicitor at the Department of the Interior, Gail Norton. In April 2001, as Secretary of the Interior Norton released five captively-bred condors into the wilderness along California's Big Sur Coast. During the intervening fifteen years, the number of California condors grew from 24 to 184. Three facilities—the San Diego Wild Animal Park, the Los Angeles Zoo, and the World Center for Birds of Prey in Boise—have worked to breed the condors in captivity. The first condors were released back into the wild in 1992, and the wild population of condors reached 137 in California and 73 in Arizona by 2011 (along with a captive population of 180). The goal of the recovery program is to establish two separate wild populations comprised by 150 condors (and 15 breeding pairs) each. *See generally* FWS, Hopper Mountain National Wildlife Refuge, California Condor Recovery Program, http://www.fws.gov/hoppermountain/CACORecoveryProgram/CACondorRecoveryProgram.html.

The captive breeding of the condors has been a success, but the birds still face numerous challenges in the wild. Numerous condors died from contact with electrical power lines, so young captive condors are taught to avoid perching on such lines. Condors have also been poisoned by feeding on carrion laced with lead shotgun pellets, a danger that can be avoided by non-toxic—but more expensive—bullets. Coyotes killed two condors, ravens and golden eagles threaten condor eggs, and two condors drowned. Still other condors have moved dangerously close to humans whose homes now occupy the ancestral nesting sites of the condors.

The ongoing challenges facing the condors prompted one writer to ask, "What is the good of captive breeding if the birds are reintroduced to a habitat that still threatens their extinction? How long can human nursemaids guard against their missteps in the vast outdoors?" Michael K. Burns, *Rare Condors Return to Wild*, BALTIMORE SUN, July 18, 2001, at 2A. Holly Doremus responds that active human management will often remain part of the protection of biodiversity:

> [A] strict hands-off strategy is inconsistent with the protection of species, ecosystems, or natural processes. No place in the United States remains entirely unaffected by human actions. Ongoing management efforts are often necessary to compensate for the effect of past actions, or current actions outside the designated reserves. Competition with or predation by alien species, for example, is one of the leading threats to domestic biodiversity. Once introduced, alien species often spread rapidly and are difficult, if not impossible, to remove. Protecting native species from the threat of such exotics requires ongoing management. Intensive management may also be required to substitute for changes in historic fire regimes, predation levels, and other elements of the biophysical environment. Given the extensive changes in background conditions, ecologists tell us that most areas dedicated to the preservation of nature cannot simply be left to their own devices, but will require active human management.

Holly Doremus, *The Rhetoric and the Reality of Nature Protection: Toward a New Discourse*, 57 WASH. & LEE. L. REV. 11, 56–57 (2000). Note, too, that the effort to save the California condor has cost over $25 million. For current information about the status of the condors, visit the San Diego Wild Animal Park's site "Condor Ridge" at www.sandiegozoo.org/wap/ex condor ridge.html, the Los Angeles Zoo's "California Condor Conservation" site at www.lazoo.org/condorall/index.html.

2. Zoos play an active role in preserving biodiversity. The San Diego Wild Animal Park hosts a "Condor Ridge" exhibit that displays condors along with other native wildlife, such as black-footed ferrets and desert bighorn sheep. The exhibit has two purposes: to educate the public about the condor and endangered species generally, and to allow older condors to train younger condors so that they can be released in to the wild. *See* Jane Hendron, *Return to the Wild*, 25 ENDANGERED SPECIES BULLETIN 10 (May/June 2000). Other zoos feature species from more distant homes. The recovery of the Virgin Islands boa—the subject of an ESA dispute described below at pages 214–215 is led by the Toledo Zoo. A variety of zoos have conducted captive breeding programs for such endangered species as black-footed ferrets, Hawaiian geese, Mongolian wild horses, and giant pandas. More generally, the American Zoo and Aquarium Association has established a program of Species Survival Plans (SSP). "Each SSP carefully manages the breeding of a species in order to maintain a healthy and self-sustaining captive population that is both genetically diverse and demographically stable. Beyond this, SSPs include a variety of other cooperative conservation activities, such as research, public education, reintroduction, and field projects. Currently, the American Zoo and Aquarium Association oversees more than 300 SSPs, American Zoo and Aquarium Association, *Species Survival Plan (SSP) Programs,* http://www.aza.org/species-survival-plan-program/. The Center for Plant Conservation promotes a similar program to conserve and restore America's native plants, including a National Collection of Endangered Plants that houses more than 700 rare plants in institutions throughout the United States.

The relationship of zoos to the conservation of biodiversity can be problematic. David Hancocks, the director of the Open Range Zoo in Werribee, Australia, sees zoos as presenting "a perpetual dichotomy, which is the reverence that humans hold for Nature while simultaneously seeking to dominate it and smother its very wildness." He asserts that "[k]eeping wild animals in captivity warrants stronger justification than the setting for a social gathering" for "a family day out." He sees zoos as having a tremendous opportunity for teaching about biodiversity, but he laments that such a role has been largely neglected. Hancocks also questions the AZA's work by observing "SSP is more accurately an acronym for a Self Supporting Program for zoos." And Hancocks calls for greater attention to the native biodiversity that exists near each zoo, citing the example of the San Diego zoos that are working to protect the condor and other species:

> Visitors to the San Diego Zoo can hear messages about the threat of tiger extinction and nod their head in concern, then drive north to the San Diego Wild Animal Park and hear messages about the depradation of elephants by poaching and comfort themselves by agreeing that they will never purchase ivory. The road they will have traveled between these sister zoos will have carried them through a region in which virtually every

square inch of native chaparral habitat has been destroyed. It has been replaced by suburban sprawl and monoculture farms. Southern California contains one-fourth of all plant species known in the United States, half of them found nowhere else in the world, and it is one of the most endangered ecosystems on Earth. Yet there will be no hint from these Southern California zoos revealing this problem. It is too uncomfortably close to home.

DAVID HANCOCKS, A DIFFERENT NATURE: THE PARADOXICAL WORLD OF ZOOS AND THEIR UNCERTAIN FUTURE xvii, 6, 170–71 (2001). How can zoos that are interested in preserving biodiversity respond to Hancocks? What is the appropriate role for zoos in conserving biodiversity?

3. The condor case demonstrates that the captive breeding of endangered species can be especially controversial. Hancocks complains that captive breeding "has nothing to do with conservation of biological diversity" because biodiversity is not "a thing, like a tiger, that can be saved and put on display." *Id.* at 159. The FWS and NMFS agree that "[c]ontrolled propagation is not a substitute for addressing factors responsible for an endangered or threatened species' decline," but they see a role for such breeding programs nonetheless. The FWS praised the role of captive breeding in saving three species of African antelopes in 2005. "Captive breeding," explained the agency, "has provided the founder stock necessary for reintroduction, maintenance of otherwise potentially lost bloodlines, and opportunities for research. The scimitar-horned oryx is possibly extinct in the wild and therefore, but for captive breeding, the species might be extinct." Final Rule to List the Scimitar-Horned Oryx, Addax, and Dama Gazelle as Endangered, 70 Fed. Reg. 52319, 52322 (2005). More generally, the official policy published by the FWS and the NMFS states that "the controlled propagation of threatened and endangered species" ordinarily will be employed only if 14 criteria are satisfied: (1) measures to save the species in the wild are inadequate, (2) captive breeding is coordinated with efforts to provide secure and suitable habitat for the species, (3) an official recovery strategy recommends captive breeding, (4) the potential ecological and genetic effects of the removal of individuals from the wild are considered, (5) sound scientific principles to conserve genetic variation and species integrity support captive breeding, (6) a genetics management plan is developed, (7) all known precautions against the spread of diseases and parasites into the environment are taken, (8) the escape or accidental introduction of individuals outside their historic range is prevented, (9) more than one location is used, (10) other appropriate organizations and individuals are involved, (11) information needs and accepted protocols and standards are satisfied, (12) a commitment to funding is secured in advance, (13) captive breeding is tied to development of a reintroduction plan, and (14) regulations implementing the Endangered Species Act, Marine Mammal Protection Act, Animal Welfare Act, Lacey Act, Fish and Wildlife Act of 1956, and the Services' procedures relative to NEPA are followed. Policy Regarding Controlled Propagation of Species Listed Under the Endangered Species Act, 65 Fed. Reg. 59,616, 59,619–21 (2000). Is captive breeding appropriate in those circumstances? Is it appropriate even if those criteria are not satisfied?

Would satisfaction of those criteria also justify the cloning of an endangered species? In November 2000, the world's first cloned endangered species— an ox-like gaur that is native to southeast Asia—was born to an Iowa cow, but the baby gaur only lived two days. The scientists who cloned the gaur also described plans to clone the African bongo antelope, the Sumatran tiger, and the giant panda, and to reincarnate the recently extinct bucardo mountain goat of Spain. They defend cloning both as "a way to preserve and propagate endangered species that reproduce poorly in zoos until their habitats can be restored and they can be reintroduced into the wild," and as a means for enabling "researchers to introduce new genes back into the gene pool of a species that has few remaining animals." Robert P. Lanza, Betsy L. Dresser & Philip Damiani, *Cloning Noah's Ark: Biotechnology Might Offer the Best Way to Keep Some Endangered Species From Disappearing From the Planet*, SCIENTIFIC AMERICAN, Nov. 2000. It has even been suggested that long extinct animals such as the woolly mammoth could be recreated thanks to modern scientific breakthroughs. *See* Corey A. Salsberg, *Resurrecting the Woolly Mammoth: Science, Law, Ethics, Politics, and Religion*, 2000 STAN. TECH. L. REV. 1. At the same time, the possibility of cloning of humans has generated tremendous controversy, as evidenced by the approval of the Human Cloning Prohibition Act of 2001 by the U.S. House of Representatives in August 2001. Should the cloning of endangered species face the same objections as the cloning of humans?

4. Would biodiversity be satisfactorily protected if every species could be kept alive in zoos and every ecosystem could be contained in nature preserves? Holly Doremus argues that "none of the congressionally listed values of species can be fully protected in captivity." She explains:

> The esthetic benefits of wild and captive animals, for example, are quite different. Wild creatures, unconfined and uncontrolled by any human volition, inspire awe and wonder that captive animals cannot match. A bald eagle soaring above a river choked with spawning salmon offers a far richer esthetic experience than a caged eagle feasting on canned fish. A butterfly pinned to a display card, although beautiful and easy to view at leisure, cannot approach the beauty of one glimpsed passing on the wing, or perched on a native flower. Captivity similarly diminishes the recreational value of species. The joy of wildlife-based recreation derives in large part from the quarry's lack of domestication. The thrill of the chase, the skill and knowledge it demands, are more important than the photograph or trophy it produces. Captive species, divorced from any natural ecosystem, have no ecological value. They provide only pale echoes of the educational and scientific value of species in their natural habitats. Even historic value is reduced by captivity. The bison that today roam free in Yellowstone National Park offer a far closer link to the continent's history than their semi-domesticated predecessors. . . Wildness, understood as unpredictability or freedom from human control, imparts an aura that cannot be duplicated by captive species. That aura attracts and inspires us. It makes us care about wild places and wild creatures, and leads us to believe they merit special protection. Without wildness, the level of human concern for other species would be reduced.

Holly Doremus, *Restoring Endangered Species: The Importance of Being Wild*, 23 HARV. ENVTL. L. REV. 1, 12–13 (1999). Is there a contrary argument that would support the preservation of certain species only in zoos or elsewhere in captivity?

In another article, Professor Doremus asserts that biodiversity protection should encompass "the ordinary" as well as those species and ecosystems that we view as special. Holly Doremus, *Biodiversity and the Challenge of Saving the Ordinary*, 38 IDAHO L. REV. 325 (2002). Doremus observes that "[h]istorically, efforts to protect nature in the United States have focused on the places and things we recognize as special." *Id.* at 325. But, she insists, focusing upon such special instances of biodiversity has failed to protect biodiversity in general, it limits our efforts to a small part of biodiversity, and it sets nature apart from our daily lives. How could the protection of "ordinary" biodiversity become a greater priority?

B. PRIVATE ACTIONS TO PROTECT BIODIVERSITY

Testimony of Steven J. McCormick, *Tax Code Issues and Land Conservation: Hearing Before the Senate Finance Committee*

United States Senate, 2005.

Mr. Chairman, Senator Baucus and members of the Committee, thank you for the opportunity to present the views of The Nature Conservancy at this hearing on tax incentives for land conservation and on your report on our organization and our conservation practices. I am Steve McCormick, the President and CEO of The Nature Conservancy.

The Nature Conservancy is an international, nonprofit organization dedicated to the conservation of biological diversity. Our mission is to preserve the plants, animals and natural communities that represent the diversity of life on Earth by protecting the lands and waters they need to survive. Our on-the-ground conservation work is carried out in all 50 states and in 27 foreign countries and is supported by approximately one million individual members. We have helped conserve nearly 15 million acres of land in the United States and Canada and more than 102 million acres with local partner organizations globally.

The Conservancy owns and manages approximately 1,400 preserves throughout the United States—the largest private system of nature sanctuaries in the world. We recognize, however, that our mission cannot be achieved by core protected areas alone.

Therefore, our projects increasingly seek to accommodate compatible human uses, and especially in the developing world, to address sustained human well-being.

The past two years have been a challenging time for The Nature Conservancy.

Having just run the triple gauntlet of a newspaper series, a Senate committee investigation and an IRS audit, I want of all my colleagues at the Conservancy to know how proud I am of the way they have responded to the challenge. Thousands and thousands of actions and transactions conducted by the people in our organization over the past decade have been held up to the closest scrutiny and, based on that examination, I am confident in saying that all of our work is, and has been, in compliance with the applicable laws and regulations and motivated by the sincerest commitment to our mission. Not everything we tried has succeeded and on occasion we made mistakes, but all of our work was done in good faith. . .

The Importance of Land and Easement Donations as Conservation Tools

The subject of your hearing this morning, the federal tax incentives encouraging the donation of conservation lands and easements, is of vital importance to the environmental health of our country. I would dare say that, today, conservation easements are the principal tool that is advancing the cause of environmental protection in the United States. Our nation experienced a very public revolution in its view of the natural environment in the 1970s and Congress responded with a series of laws from the Clean Air and Clean Water Acts to the Endangered Species and the Fisheries Management and Conservation Acts. The government agencies and regulatory programs they launched allowed us to make significant progress improving the quality of our environment through the early 1990s. But in the minds of many, that approach seems to have reached the limit of its effectiveness and for the last decade and a half the nation has been searching for new tools that are market-based and landowner-friendly.

A second environmental revolution is underway right now, and conservation easements are a principal tool in that work. Easements are one of the most powerful and effective means available for the conservation of private lands and the biodiversity they support. Easements are successfully protecting millions of acres of wildlife habitat, natural areas and a way of life for many farming and ranching families in the United States and many other countries.

A conservation easement is a restriction placed on a piece of property to protect its ecological or open-space values. It is a voluntary, legally-binding agreement that limits certain types of uses or prevents development from taking place in perpetuity. The easement is an agreement between a landowner, who voluntarily agrees to donate or sell certain rights associated with his or her property (such as the right to subdivide and develop) to a private organization or public agency that agrees to hold the landowner's promise not to exercise those rights.

As public policy is becoming more sensitive to the rights of private property owners, and we appreciate the need to provide financial incentives for the contribution they make through their wildlife stewardship practices, the many attractive features of conservation easements as a public policy tool are clear. Under conservation easements:

—Property remains privately owned and landowners often continue to live on the property;

—Many types of private land use, such as farming, ranching and timber harvesting, can continue;

—The land can remain productive, generating jobs and tax revenues to support local government services; and

—The tax benefits are a flexible financial incentive for good stewardship that a landowner can tailor to meet his or her own needs.

There has been dramatic growth in the use of easements as a conservation tool since the beginning of the 1990s. This growth is supported by the tax incentives that Congress, under the leadership of this Committee, has thoughtfully enacted, by the support of similar incentives in the tax laws of many states and by the success that easements have realized in practice.

—There are now more than 1200 land trusts in the United States and more than 600 accept and manage easements as one of their activities;

—As of 2000, local and regional land trusts had protected nearly 2.6 million acres of lands through easements—a fivefold increase since 1990; and

—Between January 1997 and June 2003, the easement holdings of The Nature Conservancy grew from 645,000 acres to more than 2 million acres.

The Nature Conservancy is an organization dedicated to the protection of biodiversity pursuing its work by protecting the lands and waters that provide habitat for the plants and wildlife that share our Earth. We are a charity. We do that work using the tools that this Committee has enacted. We want you to know how very important the tax incentives for conservation land and easement donations are to the future environmental health of our nation. They are the foundation for a second generation of environmental protection—a new era of biodiversity conservation on private lands is underway because of these incentives.

The Nature Conservancy's Mission and Method

How do we apply these tools in our work?

The Nature Conservancy was first incorporated as a nonprofit organization in 1951 and has grown to be the world's largest private land conservation and biodiversity protection organization with operations in all 50 states and 27 other countries. The Conservancy launched the first biological inventory of the United States in 1970 that became the basis for the Natural Heritage data system now maintained in each state and has been a leader in the science of biodiversity protection ever since.

The Conservancy takes a systematic, science-based approach to identifying sites for protection. Called Conservation by Design, this approach begins by identifying distinct divisions in the natural landscape defined by climate, geography and species—known as ecoregions. For each ecoregion, the Conservancy identifies a portfolio of high priority sites—those places that collectively capture the biological diversity of the region.

The Conservancy then develops customized conservation strategies, ranging from outright acquisition, to environmental education, to working in partnership with private landowners to ensure lasting protection of these target sites.

The following principles describe The Nature Conservancy's approach to land conservation:

—The Nature Conservancy works collaboratively with partners— communities, businesses, government agencies, multilateral institutions, individuals and other nonprofit organizations.

—We employ the best available scientific information and practices to guide our conservation actions.

—We pursue non-confrontational, pragmatic, market-based solutions to conservation challenges.

—We tailor our conservation strategies and tools to local circumstances.

—We work across landscapes and seascapes at a scale large enough to conserve ecological processes and to ensure that protected lands and waters retain their ecological integrity.

—We work with willing sellers and donors, both public and private, to protect plants and wildlife through purchases, gifts, exchanges, conservation easements and management agreements and partnerships.

—Outside the United States, we work with government agencies and like-minded partner organizations to provide scientific information, infrastructure, community development, professional training and long-term resources.

The Conservancy has protected nearly 15 million acres of wildlife habitat in the United States. Some of these lands are in the more than 1,400 preserves owned and managed by the Conservancy. Other protected lands have been left in private ownership with permanent conservation easements or transferred to government agencies for management.

The Conservancy is a decentralized organization with its conservation activities focused in chapters in each of the 50 states and more than 400 offices around the world. The Conservancy employs more than 3,000 people, including 700 scientists engaged every day in research and management activities to improve habitat functions at high priority sites.

The work of the Conservancy is legally governed and guided by a 21-member national Board of Directors. The Conservancy also benefits from more than 1,500 unpaid, volunteer trustees who provide leadership and guidance to our programs.

The Conservancy has grown to be the largest conservation organization and one of the largest charities in the United States with assets of more than $3 billion (reflecting primarily the value of the land we own and manage) and a 2003 budget of nearly $350 million. By far, the most significant source of support and revenue to the Conservancy comes from its approximately one million members and other individual supporters. In fiscal year 2004, individuals contributed 64 percent and foundations 22 percent to the Conservancy's donated revenue. Business donations were 6 percent of our contributions and 8 percent came from other sources. In addition to gifts, the Conservancy receives funding from a wide variety of sources including government grants, investment income, and contracts.

Recently, the Conservancy launched a series of five initiatives reflecting the principal threats to important wildlife habitat at our sites including programs to address invasive species, global climate change, impairment of freshwater quality, threats to marine life, and the alteration of natural fire regimes.

For several decades the Conservancy has worked closely with federal, state and local government agencies to assist them in acquiring key conservation lands for the benefit of the public. These projects help public agencies meet their mandate to conserve key natural resources and wildlife habitat. These projects also significantly help advance the Conservancy's mission. The Conservancy has had in place for nearly a decade a specific written policy of "no net profit" on sales of conservation lands to governmental entities. Over the years, the Conservancy has spent substantially more on land sales and associated costs on land transactions with the government than it has received in return. The Nature Conservancy's work has resulted in gains not only for the natural world but for communities, private landowners and the public:

—In Maine's Katahdin Forest, our conservation approach led to the protection of core wilderness surrounded by ecologically compatible timber harvesting—and the preservation of local forestry jobs.

—In the Malpai Borderlands of New Mexico, Arizona and Mexico, it led to the creation of a public-private partnership that has effectively protected 800,000 acres from development and helped re-establish the natural fire regime across huge swaths of public and private lands.

—In the Blackfoot Valley of Montana, the Conservancy accepted the state's first conservation easement on 1,800 acres in the mid-1970s. Today, more than 50 river miles and 85,000 acres in the Blackfoot are covered by easements and it is one of the most intact landscapes in all of Montana.

—In Northwest Florida, The Nature Conservancy, the Department of Defense and the State of Florida have joined in a formal partnership to protect a 100-mile corridor of forest, rivers and wetlands that will buffer military bases and military flight paths while preserving the plant and animal life of these undeveloped lands. The first conservation easement fostered by this partnership, for more than 18,000 acres on the Nukose Plantation, was purchased in February 2005.

—And, in the Big Woods of Arkansas, as we all have recently learned, The Nature Conservancy's conservation approach led to the protection of essential habitat for the ivory-billed woodpecker, heretofore presumed extinct. There, more than 20 years ago, The Nature Conservancy began working with duck hunters, legislators and state and federal agencies to conserve rapidly disappearing bottomland hardwood forest—the shelter and lifeline into the 21st century for this extraordinary bird on the brink of extinction.

We are proud of this record. . .

NOTES & QUESTIONS

1. What advantages are there to relying upon privately owned easements for protecting biodiversity? Are there any disadvantages?

2. Like any organization, the Nature Conservancy is not without its detractors. Mr. McCormick testified in response to the controversy resulting from a three-part series of articles that the Washington Post published in May 2003 about the Nature Conservancy, whose headquarters are located in nearby Arlington, Virginia. The articles suggested that the Nature Conservancy has become too close to its corporate supporters and too willing to sacrifice particular pieces of ecologically valuable land in order to obtain the broader benefits of financial contributions and public support. The organization adopted reforms in response to many of these criticisms, and it has proposed several changes in the tax laws to ensure that conservation easements are appropriately valued. *See* The Nature Conservancy, Final Report: Conservation Working Group 27 (2004) (outlining fourteen recommendations for "ensuring the long term integrity of conservation easements as a very useful tool in achieving . . . our mission of protecting habitat for the diversity of plant and animal species"); *see also* The Nature Conservancy's web site at http://nature.org/.

The Nature Conservancy is the largest group committed to acquiring land to protect biodiversity, but it is not the only such organization. And even without an organization, individual landowners can play a significant role with respect to particular places or species. Tom Aley, for example, is a "recognized cave specialist and expert karst hydrogeologist" who owns the cave in southwestern Missouri that is the only known home to the Tumbling Creek cavesnail, which was listed as endangered on an emergency basis in December 2001. *See* Listing the Tumbling Creek Cavesnail as Endangered, 66 Fed. Reg. 66803, 66804, 66806 (2001).

3. Private groups have been particularly creative in soliciting funding for their conservation work. For example, Defenders of Wildlife has encouraged individuals to fund the ongoing work to protect wolves, the Arctic National Wildlife Refuge, and other biodiversity by donating the rebate that they received as a result of the 2001 federal income tax break legislation. Many organizations encourage private efforts to protect biodiversity by allowing individuals to "adopt" a particular rare animal. The National Zoo sponsors an "Adopt a Species" program that provides you with a photograph of "your" animal or plant (chosen from among dozens of species) and other benefits in exchange for a monetary contribution toward the preservation of that species. Defenders of Wildlife offers a choice of a bear, dolphin, polar bear, sea otter, snowy owl, whale, or wolf for adoption. The Adopt-A-Manatee program offers an adoption certificate, photo, biography of "your" manatee and other materials to those who pay an annual membership fee used to protect endangered Florida manatees. Overseas, the Chengdu Giant Panda Breeding and Research Center sponsors a more ambitious program for the preservation of pandas. *See Taiwan Pop Singers Adopt Two Chengdu Giant Pandas*, XINHUA NEWS AGENCY, Oct. 12, 1998 (reporting that two entertainers paid $5,000 to adopt two pandas and that most of those who adopt pandas travel to visit them each year). The Nature Conservancy allows individuals to adopt an acre of wildlife habitat.

Private groups have also encouraged the preservation of biodiversity by compensating those who suffer losses caused by an endangered animal. The most notable program is sponsored by the Defenders of Wildlife, which pays ranchers whose livestock is killed by rare wolves. Since 1987, the organization has paid over $206,000 to 179 ranchers who lost a total of 249 cattle, 545 sheep and 28 other animals to attacks by wolves. *See* The Bailey Wolf Foundation Wolf Compensation Trust: Payments to Ranchers from Defenders' Wolf Compensation Program, *available at* http://www.defenders.org/wildlife/wolf/wolfcomp.pdf.

Besides giving money or land, private groups and individuals have worked in other ways to protect endangered species. For example, businesses have allowed their employees to take time off to remove invasive vegetation that threatens the habitat of rare wildlife. Ranchers allowed researchers working to save the California condor to use their property free of charge. Members of a Florida Boy Scout troop worked with National Wildlife Federation volunteers to collect melaleuca leaf weevils so that the insects could be released elsewhere in the Picayune State Forest to feed on Australian melaleuca trees that were destroying the habitat of Florida panthers. What other actions can private parties take to protect endangered species?

4. Notwithstanding all of these efforts, few believe that private actions alone will be sufficient to preserve biodiversity. Why?

Lujan v. Defenders of Wildlife

Supreme Court of the United States, 1992.
504 U.S. 555.

■ JUSTICE SCALIA delivered the opinion of the Court with respect to Parts I, II, III-A, and IV, and an opinion with respect to Part III-B, in which THE CHIEF JUSTICE, JUSTICE WHITE, and JUSTICE THOMAS join.

This case involves a challenge to a rule promulgated by the Secretary of the Interior interpreting § 7 of the Endangered Species Act of 1973 (ESA), 87 Stat. 892, as amended, 16 U.S.C. § 1536, in such fashion as to render it applicable only to actions within the United States or on the high seas. The preliminary issue, and the only one we reach, is whether respondents here, plaintiffs below, have standing to seek judicial review of the rule.

I.

The ESA, 87 Stat. 884, as amended, 16 U.S.C. § 1531 *et seq.*, seeks to protect species of animals against threats to their continuing existence caused by man. *See generally* TVA v. Hill, 437 U.S. 153 (1978). The ESA instructs the Secretary of the Interior to promulgate by regulation a list of those species which are either endangered or threatened under enumerated criteria, and to define the critical habitat of these species. 16 U.S.C. §§ 1533, 1536. Section 7(a)(2) of the Act then provides, in pertinent part:

"Each Federal agency shall, in consultation with and with the assistance of the Secretary [of the Interior], insure that any action authorized, funded, or carried out by such agency . . . is not likely to jeopardize the continued existence of any endangered species or threatened species or result in the destruction or adverse modification of habitat of such species which is determined by the Secretary, after consultation as appropriate with affected States, to be critical." 16 U.S.C. § 1536(a)(2).

In 1978, the Fish and Wildlife Service (FWS) and the National Marine Fisheries Service (NMFS), on behalf of the Secretary of the Interior and the Secretary of Commerce respectively, promulgated a joint regulation stating that the obligations imposed by § 7(a)(2) extend to actions taken in foreign nations. The next year, however, the Interior Department began to reexamine its position. A revised joint regulation, reinterpreting § 7(a)(2) to require consultation only for actions taken in the United States or on the high seas, was proposed in 1983, and promulgated in 1986, 51 Fed. Reg. 19926; 50 CFR 402.01 (1991).

Shortly thereafter, respondents, organizations dedicated to wildlife conservation and other environmental causes, filed this action against the Secretary of the Interior, seeking a declaratory judgment that the new regulation is in error as to the geographic scope of § 7(a)(2) and an injunction requiring the Secretary to promulgate a new regulation restoring the initial interpretation. [The Eighth Circuit rejected the Secretary's motion to dismiss the case for lack of standing]. . .

Over the years, our cases have established that the irreducible constitutional minimum of standing contains three elements. First, the plaintiff must have suffered an "injury in fact"—an invasion of a legally protected interest which is (a) concrete and particularized, and (b) "actual or imminent, not 'conjectural' or 'hypothetical.' " Second, there must be a causal connection between the injury and the conduct complained of—the injury has to be "fairly . . . trace[able] to the challenged action of the defendant, and not . . . the result [of] the independent action of some third party not before the court." Third, it must be "likely," as opposed to merely "speculative," that the injury will be "redressed by a favorable decision.". . .

III.

We think the Court of Appeals failed to apply the foregoing principles in denying the Secretary's motion for summary judgment. Respondents had not made the requisite demonstration of (at least) injury and redressability.

A.

Respondents' claim to injury is that the lack of consultation with respect to certain funded activities abroad "increas[es] the rate of extinction of endangered and threatened species." Of course, the desire to use or observe an animal species, even for purely esthetic purposes, is undeniably a cognizable interest for purpose of standing. "But the 'injury in fact' test requires more than an injury to a cognizable interest. It requires that the party seeking review be himself among the injured." To survive the Secretary's summary judgment motion, respondents had to submit affidavits or other evidence showing, through specific facts, not only that listed species were in fact being threatened by funded activities abroad, but also that one or more of respondents' members would thereby be "directly" affected apart from their " 'special interest' in the subject."

With respect to this aspect of the case, the Court of Appeals focused on the affidavits of two Defenders' members—Joyce Kelly and Amy Skilbred. Ms. Kelly stated that she traveled to Egypt in 1986 and "observed the traditional habitat of the endangered nile crocodile there and intend[s] to do so again, and hope[s] to observe the crocodile directly," and that she "will suffer harm in fact as the result of [the] American . . . role . . . in overseeing the rehabilitation of the Aswan High Dam on the Nile . . . and [in] developing . . . Egypt's . . . Master Water Plan." Ms. Skilbred averred that she traveled to Sri Lanka in 1981 and "observed the habitat" of "endangered species such as the Asian elephant and the leopard" at what is now the site of the Mahaweli project funded by the Agency for International Development (AID), although she "was unable to see any of the endangered species"; "this development project," she continued, "will seriously reduce endangered, threatened, and endemic species habitat including areas that I visited . . . [, which] may severely shorten the future of these species"; that threat, she concluded, harmed her because she "intend[s] to return to Sri Lanka in the future and hope[s] to be more fortunate in spotting at least the endangered elephant and leopard." When Ms. Skilbred was asked at a subsequent deposition if and when she had any plans to return to Sri Lanka, she reiterated that "I intend to go back to Sri Lanka," but confessed that she had no current plans: "I don't know [when]. There is a civil war going on right now. I don't know. Not next year, I will say. In the future."

We shall assume for the sake of argument that these affidavits contain facts showing that certain agency-funded projects threaten listed species—though that is questionable. They plainly contain no facts, however, showing how damage to the species will produce "imminent" injury to Mses. Kelly and Skilbred. That the women "had visited" the areas of the projects before the projects commenced proves nothing. As we have said in a related context, " 'Past exposure to illegal conduct does not in itself show a present case or controversy regarding injunctive relief . . . if unaccompanied by any continuing, present adverse effects.' " And the affiants' profession of an "intent" to return to the places they had visited before—where they will presumably, this time, be deprived of the opportunity to observe animals of the endangered species—is simply not enough. Such "some day" intentions—without any description of concrete plans, or indeed even any specification of when the some day will be—do not support a finding of the "actual or imminent" injury that our cases require.

Besides relying upon the Kelly and Skilbred affidavits, respondents propose a series of novel standing theories. The first, inelegantly styled "ecosystem nexus," proposes that any person who uses any part of a "contiguous ecosystem" adversely affected by a funded activity has standing even if the activity is located a great distance away. This approach, as the Court of Appeals correctly observed, is inconsistent with our opinion in [Lujan v. National Wildlife Federation, 497 U.S. 871 (1990)], which held that a plaintiff claiming injury from environmental damage must use the area affected by the challenged activity and not an area roughly "in the vicinity" of it. It makes no difference that the general-purpose section of the ESA states that the Act was intended in part "to provide a means whereby the ecosystems upon which endangered species and threatened species depend may be conserved," 16 U.S.C. § 1531(b). To say that the Act protects ecosystems is not to say that the Act creates (if it were possible) rights of action in persons who have not been injured in fact, that is, persons who use portions of an ecosystem not perceptibly affected by the unlawful action in question.

Respondents' other theories are called, alas, the "animal nexus" approach, whereby anyone who has an interest in studying or seeing the endangered animals anywhere on the globe has standing; and the "vocational nexus" approach, under which anyone with a professional interest in such animals can sue. Under these theories, anyone who goes to see Asian elephants in the Bronx Zoo, and anyone who is a keeper of Asian elephants in the Bronx Zoo, has standing to sue because the Director of the Agency for International Development (AID) did not consult with the Secretary regarding the AID-funded project in Sri Lanka. This is beyond all reason. Standing is not "an ingenious academic exercise in the conceivable," but as we have said requires, at the summary judgment stage, a factual showing of perceptible harm. It is clear that the person who observes or works with a particular animal threatened by a federal decision is facing perceptible harm, since the very subject of his interest will no longer exist. It is even plausible—though it goes to the outermost limit of plausibility—to think that a person who observes or works with animals of a particular species in the very area of the world where that species is threatened by a federal decision is facing such harm, since some animals that might have been the subject of his interest will no longer exist, see Japan Whaling Assn. v. American Cetacean Society, 478 U.S. 221, 231, n. 4 (1986). It goes beyond the limit, however, and into pure speculation and fantasy, to say that anyone who observes or works with an endangered species, anywhere in the world, is appreciably harmed by a single project affecting some portion of that species with which he has no more specific connection.

B.

Besides failing to show injury, respondents failed to demonstrate redressability. Instead of attacking the separate decisions to fund particular projects allegedly causing them harm, respondents chose to challenge a more generalized level of Government action (rules regarding consultation), the invalidation of which would affect all overseas projects. This programmatic approach has obvious practical advantages, but also obvious difficulties insofar as proof of causation or redressability is concerned. As we have said in another context, "suits challenging, not specifically identifiable Government violations of law, but the particular programs agencies establish to carry out their legal obligations . . . [are], even when premised on allegations of several instances of violations of law, . . . rarely if ever appropriate for federal-court adjudication."

The most obvious problem in the present case is redressability. Since the agencies funding the projects were not parties to the case, the District Court could accord relief only against the Secretary: He could be ordered to revise his regulation to require consultation for foreign projects. But this would not remedy respondents' alleged injury unless the funding agencies were bound by the Secretary's regulation, which is very much an open question. Whereas in other contexts the ESA is quite explicit as to the Secretary's controlling authority, see, e.g., 16 U.S.C. § 1533(a)(1) ("The Secretary shall" promulgate regulations determining endangered species); § 1535(d)(1) ("The Secretary is authorized to provide financial assistance to any State"), with respect to consultation the initiative, and hence arguably the initial responsibility for determining statutory necessity, lies with the agencies, see § 1536(a)(2) ("Each Federal agency shall, in consultation with and with the assistance of the Secretary, insure that any" funded action is not likely to jeopardize endangered or threatened species) (emphasis added). When the Secretary promulgated the regulation at issue here, he thought it was binding on the agencies, see 51 Fed. Reg. 19928 (1986). The Solicitor General, however, has repudiated that position here, and the agencies themselves apparently deny the Secretary's authority. (During the period when the Secretary took the view that § 7(a)(2) did apply abroad, AID and FWS engaged in a running controversy over whether consultation was required with respect to the Mahaweli project, AID insisting that consultation applied only to domestic actions.). . .

A further impediment to redressability is the fact that the agencies generally supply only a fraction of the funding for a foreign project. AID, for example, has provided less than 10% of the funding for the Mahaweli project. Respondents have produced nothing to indicate that the projects they have named will either be suspended, or do less harm to listed species, if that fraction is eliminated. . . [I]t is entirely conjectural whether the nonagency activity that affects respondents will be altered or affected by the agency activity they seek to achieve. There is no standing.

NOTES & QUESTIONS

1. Disputes concerning biodiversity feature prominently in the Supreme Court's standing jurisprudence. See, e.g., Bennett v. Spear, 520 U.S. 154 (1997) (granting standing to irrigation districts to challenge a biological opinion issued pursuant to the ESA); Lujan v. National Wildlife Federation, 497 U.S. 871 (1990) (denying standing to the National Wildlife Federation to challenge the Bureau of Land Management's proposal to reclassify certain federal lands); Sierra Club v. Morton, 405 U.S. 727 (1972) (denying standing to the Sierra Club to challenge a proposed Disney ski resort in a national game refuge). Why does the

Constitution—and the Court—restrict who may bring suit to object to governmental decisions? Was Justice Blackmun right to imply that the Court's decision implied that plaintiffs raising environmental claims were being subjected to more rigorous standing requirements? *See Defenders of Wildlife*, 504 U.S. at 595 (Blackmun, J., dissenting). Or was Justice Scalia right to suggest in another part of his opinion that "[t]o permit Congress to convert the undifferentiated public interest in executive officers' compliance with the law into an 'individual right' vindicable in the courts is to permit Congress to transfer from the President to the courts the Chief Executive's most important constitutional duty, to 'take Care that the Laws be faithfully executed,' Art. II, § 3." *Id.* at 577.

2. Private individuals and organizations can bring suit to enforce the terms of the ESA by virtue of the act's citizen suit provision. That provision, and the similar provisions in nearly every federal environmental law, gives private parties a role in implementing the law. Generally, the federal government's FWS (or the NMFS) plays the lead role in enforcing the ESA, but Congress created the citizen suit provision to provide an alternative means of seeking compliance with the statute's demands. Likewise, many state biodiversity statutes contain analogous provisions. *See* Susan George, William J. Snape III & Rina Rodriguez, *The Public inAction: Using State Citizen Suit Statutes to Protect Biodiversity*, 6 U. BALT. J. ENVTL. L. 1 (1997). Of course, a citizen suit provision can also be employed by developers, agricultural interests, and other organizations that are concerned about how the law is being applied. As you read through the cases in this book, note whether the plaintiff was a governmental official or agency, an environmental or trade organization, or a private individual, and consider why it was the government or a private party that brought a particular lawsuit.

3. Another alternative is for the affected creatures to bring suit to protect themselves. The reported decisions include many lead plaintiffs such as the loggerhead turtle, the northern spotted owl, the marbled murrelet, and the Mt. Graham red squirrel. Whether such animals are entitled to sue is questionable. An early article written by Christopher Stone argued that trees should have standing to sue in court, *see* Christopher Stone, *Should Trees Have Standing: Toward Legal Rights for Natural Objects*, 45 S. CAL. L. REV. 450 (1972), a theory that Justice Douglas adopted in *Sierra Club v. Morton*, 405 U.S. at 742 (Douglas, J., dissenting), but which failed to attract the support of the rest of the Court. More recent commentators still insist that animals can, or at least should, be entitled to sue. *See* Cass R. Sunstein, *Standing for Animals (With Notes on Animal Rights)*, 47 U.C.L.A. L. REV. 1333, 1335 (2000) (concluding that "Congress can accord standing to animals if it chooses to do so"). But the Ninth Circuit recently held that the ESA does not empower species to bring suit on their own behalf because "animals are the protected rather than the protectors" under the ESA. Cetacean Community v. Bush, 386 F.3d 1169, 1177–78 (9th Cir. 2004). Should animals be allowed to sue for themselves? If so, who should be entitled to represent them?

4. Filing a lawsuit is just one of the ways in which private parties can invoke the law to protect biodiversity. Individuals and environmental groups often lobby legislators to enact laws conducive to biodiversity. Agency officials solicit and consider public comments on such decisions as the listing of a species as endangered and the proper management plan for national forests. Moreover, many laws are designed to provide information about the environmental consequences of a governmental action to any interested parties. The National Environmental Policy Act itself cannot block a federal project even if an environmental impact statement (EIS) identifies threats to an ecosystem or a species, but the information gained from an EIS can be used by private organizations and individuals to apply political pressure against that project.

C. CONSTITUTIONAL RESTRAINTS ON GOVERNMENT REGULATION OF BIODIVERSITY

Palazzolo v. Rhode Island

Supreme Court of the United States, 2001.
533 U.S. 606.

■ JUSTICE KENNEDY delivered the opinion of the Court.

Petitioner Anthony Palazzolo owns a waterfront parcel of land in the town of Westerly, Rhode Island. Almost all of the property is designated as coastal wetlands under Rhode Island law. After petitioner's development proposals were rejected by respondent Rhode Island Coastal Resources Management Council (Council), he sued in state court, asserting the Council's application of its wetlands regulations took the property without compensation in violation of the Takings Clause of the Fifth Amendment, binding upon the State through the Due Process Clause of the Fourteenth Amendment. Petitioner sought review in this Court, contending the Supreme Court of Rhode Island erred in rejecting his takings claim. We granted certiorari.

I

The town of Westerly is on an edge of the Rhode Island coastline. The town's western border is the Pawcatuck River, which at that point is the boundary between Rhode Island and Connecticut. Situated on land purchased from the Narragansett Indian Tribe, the town was incorporated in 1669 and had a precarious, though colorful, early history. Both Connecticut and Massachusetts contested the boundaries—and indeed the validity—of Rhode Island's royal charter; and Westerly's proximity to Connecticut invited encroachments during these jurisdictional squabbles. *See* M. BEST, THE TOWN THAT SAVED A STATE—WESTERLY 60–83 (1943); *see also* W. MCLAUGHLIN, RHODE ISLAND: A BICENTENNIAL HISTORY 39–57 (1978). When the borders of the Rhode Island Colony were settled by compact in 1728, the town's development was more orderly, and with some historical distinction. For instance, Watch Hill Point, the peninsula at the southwestern tip of the town, was of strategic importance in the Revolutionary War and the War of 1812. *See* Best, *supra*, at 190; F. DENISON, WESTERLY AND ITS WITNESSES 118–119 (1878).

In later times Westerly's coastal location had a new significance: It became a popular vacation and seaside destination. One of the town's historians gave this happy account:

"After the Civil War the rapid growth of manufacture and expansion of trade had created a spending class on pleasure bent, and Westerly had superior attractions to offer, surf bathing on ocean beaches, quieter bathing in salt and fresh water ponds, fishing, annual sail and later motor boat races. The broad beaches of clean white sand dip gently toward the sea; there are no odorous marshes at low tide, no railroad belches smoke, and the climate is unrivalled on the coast, that of Newport only excepted. In the phenomenal heat wave of 1881 ocean resorts from northern New England to southern New Jersey sweltered as the thermometer climbed to 95 and 104 degrees, while Watch Hill enjoyed a comfortable 80. When Providence to the north runs a temperature of 90, the mercury in this favored spot remains at 77." BEST, *supra*, at 192.

Westerly today has about 20,000 year-round residents, and thousands of summer visitors come to enjoy its beaches and coastal advantages.

One of the more popular attractions is Misquamicut State Beach, a lengthy expanse of coastline facing Block Island Sound and beyond to the Atlantic Ocean. The primary point of access to the beach is Atlantic Avenue, a well-traveled 3-mile stretch of road running along the coastline within the town's limits. At its western end, Atlantic Avenue is something of a commercial strip, with restaurants, hotels, arcades, and other typical seashore businesses. The pattern of development becomes more residential as the road winds eastward onto a narrow spine of land bordered to the south by the beach and the ocean, and to the north by Winnapaug Pond, an intertidal inlet often used by residents for boating, fishing, and shellfishing.

In 1959 petitioner, a lifelong Westerly resident, decided to invest in three undeveloped, adjoining parcels along this eastern stretch of Atlantic Avenue. To the north, the property faces, and borders upon, Winnapaug Pond; the south of the property faces Atlantic Avenue and the beachfront homes abutting it on the other side, and beyond that the dunes and the beach. To purchase and hold the property, petitioner and associates formed Shore Gardens, Inc. (SGI). After SGI purchased the property petitioner bought out his associates and became the sole shareholder. In the first decade of SGI's ownership of the property the corporation submitted a plat to the town subdividing the property into 80 lots; and it engaged in various transactions that left it with 74 lots, which together encompassed about 20 acres. During the same period SGI also made initial attempts to develop the property and submitted intermittent applications to state agencies to fill substantial portions of the parcel. Most of the property was then, as it is now, salt marsh subject to tidal flooding. The wet ground and permeable soil would require considerable fill—as much as six feet in some places—before significant structures could be built. SGI's proposal, submitted in 1962 to the Rhode Island Division of Harbors and Rivers (DHR), sought to dredge from Winnapaug Pond and fill the entire property. The application was denied for lack of essential information. A second, similar proposal followed a year later. A third application, submitted in 1966 while the second application was pending, proposed more limited filling of the land for use as a private beach club. These latter two applications were referred to the Rhode Island Department of Natural Resources, which indicated initial assent. The agency later withdrew approval, however, citing adverse environmental impacts. SGI did not contest the ruling.

No further attempts to develop the property were made for over a decade. Two intervening events, however, become important to the issues presented. First, in 1971, Rhode Island enacted legislation creating the Council, an agency charged with the duty of protecting the State's coastal properties. 1971 R. I. Pub. Laws ch. 279, § 1 *et seq.* Regulations promulgated by the Council designated salt marshes like those on SGI's property as protected "coastal wetlands," Rhode Island Coastal Resources Management Program (CRMP) § 210.3 (as amended, June 28, 1983), on which development is limited to a great extent. Second, in 1978 SGI's corporate charter was revoked for failure to pay corporate income taxes; and title to the property passed, by operation of state law, to petitioner as the corporation's sole shareholder.

In 1983 petitioner, now the owner, renewed the efforts to develop the property. An application to the Council, resembling the 1962 submission, requested permission to construct a wooden bulkhead along the shore of Winnapaug Pond and to fill the entire marsh land area. The Council rejected the application, noting it was "vague and inadequate for a project of this size and nature." The agency also found that "the proposed activities will have significant impacts upon the waters and wetlands of Winnapaug Pond," and concluded that "the proposed alteration . . . will conflict with the Coastal Resources Management Plan presently in effect." Petitioner did not appeal the agency's determination.

Petitioner went back to the drawing board, this time hiring counsel and preparing a more specific and limited proposal for use of the property. The new application, submitted to the Council in 1985, echoed the 1966 request to build a private beach club. The details do not tend to inspire the reader with an idyllic coastal image, for the proposal was to fill 11 acres of the property with gravel to accommodate "50 cars with boat trailers, a dumpster, port-a-johns, picnic tables, barbecue pits of concrete, and other trash receptacles."

The application fared no better with the Council than previous ones. Under the agency's regulations, a landowner wishing to fill salt marsh on Winnapaug Pond needed a "special exception" from the Council. In a short opinion the Council said the beach club proposal conflicted with the regulatory standard for a special exception. To secure a special exception the proposed activity must serve "a compelling public purpose which provides benefits to the public as a whole as opposed to individual or private interests." CRMP § 130A(1). This time petitioner appealed the decision to the Rhode Island courts, challenging the Council's conclusion as contrary to principles of state administrative law. The Council's decision was affirmed.

Petitioner filed an inverse condemnation action in Rhode Island Superior Court, asserting that the State's wetlands regulations, as applied by the Council to his parcel, had taken the property without compensation in violation of the Fifth and Fourteenth Amendments. The suit alleged the Council's action deprived him of "all economically beneficial use" of his property, resulting in a total taking requiring compensation under Lucas v. South Carolina Coastal Council, 505 U.S. 1003 (1992). He sought damages in the amount of $3,150,000, a figure derived from an appraiser's estimate as to the value of a 74-lot residential subdivision. The State countered with a host of defenses. After a bench trial, a justice of the Superior Court ruled against petitioner. . . The Rhode Island Supreme Court affirmed. 746 A.2d 707 (2000). . .

II

The Takings Clause of the Fifth Amendment, applicable to the States through the Fourteenth Amendment, Chicago, B. & Q. R. Co. v. Chicago, 166 U.S. 226 (1897), prohibits the government from taking private property for public use without just compensation. The clearest sort of taking occurs when the government encroaches upon or occupies private land for its own proposed use. Our cases establish that even a minimal "permanent physical occupation of real property" requires compensation under the Clause. Loretto v. Teleprompter Manhattan CATV Corp., 458 U.S. 419, 427 (1982). In Pennsylvania Coal Co. v. Mahon, 260 U.S. 393 (1922), the Court recognized that there will be instances when government actions do not encroach upon or occupy the property yet still affect and limit its use to such an extent that a taking occurs. In Justice Holmes' well-known, if less than self-defining, formulation, "while property may be regulated to a certain extent, if a regulation goes too far it will be recognized as a taking." Id. at 415.

Since Mahon, we have given some, but not too specific, guidance to courts confronted with deciding whether a particular government action goes too far and effects a regulatory taking. First, we have observed, with certain qualifications, that a regulation which "denies all economically beneficial or productive use of land" will require compensation under the Takings Clause. Lucas, 505 U.S. at 1015; see also id. at 1035 (KENNEDY, J., concurring); Agins v. City of Tiburon, 447 U.S. 255, 261 (1980). Where a regulation places limitations on land that fall short of eliminating all economically beneficial use, a taking nonetheless may have occurred, depending on a complex of factors including the regulation's economic effect on the landowner, the extent to which the regulation interferes with reasonable investment-backed expectations, and the character of the government action. [Penn Central Transportation Co. v. New York City, 438 U.S. 104, 124 (1978)]. These inquiries are informed by the purpose of the Takings Clause, which is to prevent the government from "forcing some people alone to bear public burdens which, in all fairness and justice, should be borne by the public as a whole." Armstrong v. United States, 364 U.S. 40, 49 (1960).

Petitioner seeks compensation under these principles. . .

III

. . . [The Rhode Island Supreme Court] held that all economically beneficial use was not deprived because the uplands portion of the property can
still be improved. On this point, we agree with the court's decision. Petitioner accepts the Council's contention and the state trial court's finding
that his parcel retains $200,000 in development value under the State's
wetlands regulations. He asserts, nonetheless, that he has suffered a total
taking and contends the Council cannot sidestep the holding in *Lucas* "by
the simple expedient of leaving a landowner a few crumbs of value."

Assuming a taking is otherwise established, a State may not evade the
duty to compensate on the premise that the landowner is left with a token
interest. This is not the situation of the landowner in this case, however. A
regulation permitting a landowner to build a substantial residence on an
18-acre parcel does not leave the property "economically idle." *Lucas, supra,*
at 1019.

In his brief submitted to us petitioner attempts to revive this part of
his claim by reframing it. He argues, for the first time, that the upland parcel is distinct from the wetlands portions, so he should be permitted to assert a deprivation limited to the latter. This contention asks us to examine
the difficult, persisting question of what is the proper denominator in the
takings fraction. *See* Michelman, *Property, Utility, and Fairness: Comments
on the Ethical Foundations of "Just Compensation Law"*, 80 HARV. L. REV.
1165, 1192 (1967). Some of our cases indicate that the extent of deprivation
effected by a regulatory action is measured against the value of the parcel
as a whole, *see, e.g.*, Keystone Bituminous Coal Assn. v. DeBenedictis, 480
U.S. 470, 497 (1987); but we have at times expressed discomfort with the
logic of this rule, *see Lucas, supra*, at 1016–1017, n. 7, a sentiment echoed
by some commentators, *see, e.g.*, Epstein, *Takings: Descent and Resurrection*, 1987 SUP. CT. REV. 1, 16–17 (1987); Fee, *Unearthing the Denominator
inRegulatory Takings Claims*, 61 U. CHI. L. REV. 1535 (1994). Whatever the
merits of these criticisms, we will not explore the point here. Petitioner did
not press the argument in the state courts, and the issue was not presented
in the petition for certiorari. The case comes to us on the premise that petitioner's entire parcel serves as the basis for his takings claim, and, so
framed, the total deprivation argument fails

*   *   *

For the reasons we have discussed, the State Supreme Court erred in
finding petitioner's claims were unripe and in ruling that acquisition of title after the effective date of the regulations barred the takings claims. The
court did not err in finding that petitioner failed to establish a deprivation
of all economic value, for it is undisputed that the parcel retains significant
worth for construction of a residence. The claims under the *Penn Central*
analysis were not examined, and for this purpose the case should be remanded.

The judgment of the Rhode Island Supreme Court is affirmed in part and reversed in part, and the case is remanded for further proceedings not inconsistent with this opinion.

It is so ordered.

NOTES AND QUESTIONS

1. Does the fifth amendment demand that Anthony Palazzolo be compensated for his loss? On remand, the Rhode Island Superior Court answered "no." *See* Palazzolo v. State, 2005 WL 1645974 (R.I. Super. Ct. 2005). The court observed that the "size and shallow depth" of the pond adjacent to Palazzolo's land "make it a particularly fragile ecosystem." *Id.* at *12. Moreover, "filling of the Palazzolo site would result in 12% less salt marsh and a reduction of pollutant and nitrogen filtering by the pond's salt marsh ecosystem. . . Loss of the marsh filtering effect, together with the loss of wildlife habitat which would occur if [Palazzolo's] planned subdivision was constructed, was previously found by this Superior Court to constitute a nuisance." *Id.* at *13. The U.S. Supreme Court's decision in *Lucas* had held that the takings clause does not require compensation to a property owner when the government acts to abate a nuisance because an owner never has a property right to engage in a nuisance in the first instance. In any event, the Superior Court added that "the sale of the single, approved house lot would generate gross income to Palazzolo in the amount of approximately $200,000, a modest return on investment." *Id.* at *58. Palazzolo declined to appeal, but he was unconvinced. "The state stole my land, let's put it that way. . . They have staffs of lawyers. They are tough to beat." Peter B. Lord, *Westerly Wetlands Dispute Finally Over*, PROVIDENCE JOURNAL, Sept. 14, 2005.

2. Justice Kennedy mentioned but did not resolve the denominator problem, which considers the proper comparison between the size of a property owner's land and the amount of land affected by government regulation. Two biodiversity cases arising out of the Federal Circuit are especially noteworthy on that point because that the Federal Circuit is the lower federal court with jurisdiction over many takings claims. Loveladies Harbor, Inc. v. United States, 28 F.3d 1171 (Fed. Cir. 1994), involved a developer that acquired 250 acres of wetlands on Long Beach Island in Ocean County, New Jersey in 1958. It developed 199 acres before the enactment of wetlands regulations of the federal Clean Water Act (CWA) in 1972. Loveladies then needed to obtain permission from both the New Jersey Department of Environmental Protection (NJDEP) and the Army Corps of Engineers in order to fill 50 acres in order to develop the 51 acre parcel for residential use. During its negotiations with NJDEP, Loveladies agreed to develop only 12.5 of the 51 acres. NJDEP issued a state permit, but it then exercised its authority under the CWA to veto the federal permit. The Federal Circuit upheld a compensation award of $2,658,000 plus interest. Whether there had been a partial or total loss of economic use depended on the denominator problem, *i.e.*, identifying the specific property that was affected by the permit denial. In other words, is the test the effect of the imposition on the value of just the 12.5 acres, or is it the effect of the imposition on the total value of, say, the original 250 acres, or on some other size unit? The court declined to state a fixed rule, finding instead that the trial court's conclusion that land developed or sold before the regulatory environment existed should not be included in the denominator was not clearly erroneous. In particular, the exclusion of the 38.5 acres which had essentially been promised to New Jersey in exchange for the NJDEP permit was logical because whatever value that land had now belonged to the state and not to Loveladies. The relevant property for the takings analysis was thus the 12.5 acres. And the court held that the 99% diminution of the value of the parcel—from $2,658,000 before the permit denial to $12,500 afterward—constituted the denial of all economically feasible use within the meaning of *Lucas*.

Then, in Seiber v. United States, 364 F.3d 1356 (Fed. Cir. 2004), Marsha and Alvin Seiber wanted cut the timber on 40 of their 200 acres in Linn County, Oregon. In July 2000, the FWS denied an ESA incidental take permit to allow, because the application did not adequately mitigate the impact on nearby threatened northern spotted owls. In June 2002, the FWS informed the Seibers that a permit was no longer necessary because "the area will no longer be likely to attract and maintain spotted owls." *Id.* at 1362. The Seibers alleged that the government had taken their property for two years. The Federal Circuit disagreed. With respect to the denominator problem, the court rejected the suggestion that each individual tree could serve as the appropriate denominator—a test that would require compensation whenever a property owner is prohibited from cutting down a single tree. The court also held that there had not been a temporary physical occupation for the denial of "the right to exclude others (i.e., the spotted owls)." *Id.* at 1366.

3. The only successful takings claims against biodiversity protection have involved water. *See* Tulare Lake Basin Water Storage Dist. v. United States, 49 Fed. Cl. 313 (2001) (holding that water use restrictions imposed to protect the endangered delta smelt and winter-run Chinook salmon worked a taking of the contractual water rights held by two county water districts); *see also* Casitas Municipal Water Dist. v. United States, 543 F.3d 1276 (Fed. Cir. 2008) (2-1 decision reversing summary judgment for the government on a takings claim involving the diversion of irrigation water to conserve the West Coast steelhead trout). Why is it easier to prove that government regulation has taken your water than your land?

4. Property rights advocates have publicized a number of "horror stories" about individuals who suffered economic losses because of government regulation designed to protect biodiversity. One of the most sympathetic stories concerns Margaret Rector, who purchased land outside of Austin, Texas in 1973 as an investment for retirement. When she sought to realize her investment two decades later, she discovered that it was "virtually impossible to find a buyer for a tract of land that has been labelled habitat of the golden-cheeked warbler." Endangered Species Act Implementation: Hearing Before the House Committee on Resources, 104th Cong., 2d Sess. 14–15 (1996). She complained that "I'm 74 years old. I want the money so I can go to a nice rest home. . . I think it is unfair for me to bear the burden when the bird belongs to everyone." Ralph Haurwitz, *Who Pays? Warbler Stokes Debate: Landowner Sees Retirement Money Fly Away on Endangered Songbird's Wings*, AUSTIN AMERICAN STATESMAN, Sept. 26, 1994, at A25. Many of the other so-called "horror stories," though, are questioned by supporters of the ESA. *See* Michael Allan Wolf, *Overtaking The Fifth Amendment: The Legislative Backlash Against Environmentalism*, 6 FORDHAM ENVTL. LAW J. 637 (1995).

Such stories have led to claims that fairness dictates that landowners be paid if the presence of an endangered species makes their land less valuable. when Nebraska Senator Chuck Hagel introduced his proposed Private Property Fairness Act of 1999, he explained that "if the Government condemns part of a farm to build a highway, it has to pay the farmer for the value of his land. But if the Government requires that same farmer [to] stop growing crops on that same land in order to protect endangered species or conserve wetlands, the farmer gets no compensation." 145 CONG. REC. S734 (daily ed. Jan. 20, 1999). Likewise, Professor Barton Thompson argues that "both incentive and fairness considerations militate in favor of at least partial compensation to landowners injured by the imposition of section 9's constraint on habitat modification." He explains:

> Absent any compensation under section 9, some landowners will destroy the habitat value of their land in order to escape ESA regulation—unnecessarily wasting valuable societal resources to annihilate the very public good that the ESA seeks to preserve. Others will refrain from creating or improving habitat. So long as the listing of a species remains a prerequisite of section 9 regulation, a no compensation rule will also encourage property owners to oppose new listings of endangered species, undermining all recovery efforts for those species. A no compensation rule biases those species-recovery efforts that do occur toward property-focused efforts and, because property owners vary among themselves in the political power they enjoy, distorts which property is used for habitat preservation and which landowners bear the burden of preservation. Finally, a no compensation rule is inequitable. The ESA's impact on particular parcels of land depends not on the behavior of the landowner or even on his ability to finance public services, but on the happenstance of where the remaining habitat of an endangered species is.

Barton H. Thompson, Jr., *The Endangered Species Act: A Case Study in Takings & Incentives*, 49 STAN. L. REV. 305, 375 (1997).

Are Professor Thompson and Senator Hagel right? Should landowners be entitled to compensation if the presence of an endangered species limits their ability to use their land? Is Palazzolo deserving of compensation? Is Rector? If so, who should pay them?

5. Dean William Treanor has advocated narrowly focused takings legislation that seeks to compensate those most harshly affected by government regulation. He proposes to compensate landowners when "unanticipated regulations destroy a significant portion of the total assets of a property owner." William Michael Treanor, *The Armstrong Principle, the Narratives of Takings, and Compensation Statutes*, 38 WM. & MARY. L. REV. 1151, 1155 (1997). The three qualifications insure that someone who was aware of applicable government regulation or who is a repeat player who loses on one investment but gains on others need not be compensated. Compensation is provided, though, to the small landowners who could lose their life's savings, the individuals most deserving of compensation and those whose predicament has informed much of the current debate. How is that test different from the constitutional formula announced in *Lucas* and applied in *Palazzolo*? Would Palazzolo receive compensation under the bill or under Dean Treanor's proposal? Would Rector?

Rancho Viejo, LLC v. Norton

United States Court of Appeals for the District of Columbia Circuit, 2003.
323 F.3d 1062.

GARLAND, CIRCUIT JUDGE: Rancho Viejo is a real estate development company that wishes to construct a 202-acre housing development in San Diego County, California. The United States Fish and Wildlife Service determined that Rancho Viejo's construction plan was likely to jeopardize the continued existence of the arroyo southwestern toad, which the Secretary of the Interior has listed as an endangered species since 1994. Rather than accept an alternative plan proposed by the Service, Rancho Viejo filed suit challenging the application of the Endangered Species Act, 16 U.S.C. §§ 1531 *et seq.*, to its project as an unconstitutional exercise of federal authority under the Commerce Clause. The district court dismissed the suit. We conclude that this case is governed by our prior decision in *National Association of Home Builders v. Babbitt*, 130 F.3d 1041 (D.C. Cir. 1997), and therefore affirm. . .

In *NAHB*, this circuit applied *Lopez* in a case challenging the application of the ESA to a construction project in an area that contained the habitat of the Delhi Sands Flower-Loving Fly. . . A majority of the *NAHB* court held that the take provision of ESA § 9, and its application to the facts of that case, constituted a valid exercise of Congress' commerce power. 130 F.3d at 1042, 1057 (Wald, J.); *id.* at 1057 (Henderson, J., concurring). The court found that application of the ESA fell within the third *Lopez* category, concluding that the regulated activity "substantially affects" interstate commerce. In so holding, the majority agreed upon two rationales: (1) "the loss of biodiversity itself has a substantial effect on our ecosystem and likewise on interstate commerce"; and (2) "the Department's protection of the flies regulates and substantially affects commercial development activity which is plainly interstate." *Id.* at 1058 (Henderson, J., concurring); *see id.* at 1046 n.3, 1056 (Wald, J.). Examining those two rationales within the context of [United States v. Lopez, 514 U.S. 549 (1995)], the *NAHB* court concluded that application of the ESA to the county's proposed construction project was constitutional. *Id.* at 1042, 1057 (Wald, J.); *id.* at 1057 (Henderson, J., concurring). Because the second *NAHB* rationale readily resolves this case, it is the focus of the balance of our discussion.[1] . . .

The fourth *Lopez* factor is whether the relationship between the regulated activity and interstate commerce is too attenuated to be regarded as substantial. Although Rancho Viejo avers that the effect on interstate

---

[1] In focusing on the second *NAHB* rationale, we do not mean to discredit the first. Nor do we mean to discredit rationales that other circuits have relied upon in upholding endangered species legislation. We simply have no need to consider those other rationales to dispose of the case before us. *See, e.g., Gibbs v. Babbitt*, 214 F.3d 483, 497 (4th Cir. 2000) ("The protection of the red wolf on both federal and private land substantially affects interstate commerce through tourism, trade, scientific research, and other potential economic activities."); *United States v. Bramble*, 103 F.3d 1475, 1477, 1481 (9th Cir. 1996) (upholding the Bald and Golden Eagle Protection Act's prohibition on the possession of eagle feathers, see 16 U.S.C. § 668(a), because "extinction of the eagle would substantially affect interstate commerce by foreclosing any possibility of several types of commercial activity," including "future commerce in eagles," "future interstate travel for the purpose of ... studying eagles," "or future commerce in beneficial products derived ... from analysis of their genetic material").

commerce of preserving endangered species is too tenuous to satisfy this test, it does not argue that the effect of commercial construction projects is similarly attenuated. Because the rationale upon which we rely focuses on the activity that the federal government seeks to regulate in this case (the construction of Rancho Viejo's housing development), and because we are required to accord congressional legislation a "presumption of constitutionality," [United States v. *Morrison*, 529 U.S. 598, 607 (2000)], plaintiff's failure to demonstrate (or even to argue) that its project and those like it are without substantial interstate effect is fatal to its cause.

This conclusion is not diminished by the fact that the arroyo toad, like the Flower-Loving Fly, does not travel outside of California, or that Rancho Viejo's development, like the San Bernardino hospital, is located wholly within the state. *See NAHB*, 130 F.3d at 1043–44 (Wald, J.) (noting that the fly has an eight-mile radius, limited to California alone). As Judge Henderson said in *NAHB*, the regulation of commercial land development, quite "apart from the characteristics or range of the specific endangered species involved, has a plain and substantial effect on interstate commerce." *Id.* at 1059. There, "the regulation related to both the proposed redesigned traffic intersection and the hospital it [was] intended to serve, each of which had an obvious connection with interstate commerce." *Id.* (Henderson, J., concurring); *accord id.* at 1048, 1056 (Wald, J.). Here, Rancho Viejo's 202-acre project, located near a major interstate highway, is likewise one that "is presumably being constructed using materials and people from outside the state and which will attract" construction workers and purchasers "from both inside and outside the state." *Id.* at 1048 (Wald, J.).[2] . . .

Rancho Viejo does not seriously dispute that *NAHB* is indistinguishable from this case. Rather, plaintiff argues that, as a result of subsequent Supreme Court decisions in *United States v. Morrison*, 529 U.S. 598 (2000), and *Solid Waste Agency v. United States Army Corps of Eng'rs* ("*SWANCC*"), 531 U.S. 159 (2001), *NAHB* is no longer "good law.". . . Rancho Viejo contends that Morrison stands for the proposition that whether the regulated activity is economic is not simply a factor in the analysis, but instead is outcome determinative: that noneconomic activity, whatever its effect on interstate commerce, cannot be regulated under the Commerce Clause. Although plaintiff acknowledges that *Morrison* expressly "declined to 'adopt a categorical rule against aggregating the effects of any noneconomic activity' because a categorical rule was unnecessary to the outcome of that case," it argues that the Court "came pretty close" to adopting such a rule. Because the arroyo toad is not itself "the subject of commercial activity," Rancho Viejo argues that regulation of the toad fails *Morrison's* (and *Lopez's*) first factor.

---

[2] Application of the ESA to habitat degradation has a further impact on interstate commerce by removing the incentives for states "to adopt lower standards of endangered species protection in order to attract development," thereby preventing a destructive "race to the bottom." *NAHB*, 130 F.3d at 1054–56 (Wald, J.).

But how close the Court came to embracing plaintiff's view is irrelevant to the disposition of this appeal, because the ESA *regulates takings, not toads. Morrison* instructs that "the proper inquiry" is whether the challenge is to "*a regulation of activity* that substantially affects interstate commerce." 529 U.S. at 609 (emphasis added). Similarly, SWANCC declares that what is required is an evaluation of "*the precise object or activity* that, in the aggregate, substantially affects interstate commerce." 531 U.S. at 173 (emphasis added). When, as directed, we turn our attention to the precise activity that is regulated in this case, there is no question but that it is economic in nature.

That regulated activity is Rancho Viejo's planned commercial development, not the arroyo toad that it threatens. The ESA does not purport to tell toads what they may or may not do. Rather, section 9 limits the taking of listed species, and its prohibitions and corresponding penalties apply to the persons who do the taking, not to the species that are taken. *See* 16 U.S.C. § 1538(a)(1), (a)(1)(B) (making it "unlawful *for any person . . . to take* any such species") (emphasis added); *id.* § 1540 (providing civil and criminal penalties for "any person who knowingly violates" the ESA). In this case, the prohibited taking is accomplished by commercial construction, and the unlawful taker is Rancho Viejo. . .

Finally, Rancho Viejo draws our attention to *Morrison's* declaration that "the Constitution requires a distinction between what is truly national and what is truly local." 529 U.S. at 617–18. Plaintiff argues that the ESA represents an unlawful assertion of congressional power over local land use decisions, which it describes as an area of traditional state regulation. The ESA, however, does not constitute a general regulation of land use. Far from encroaching upon territory that has traditionally been the domain of state and local government, the ESA represents a national response to a specific problem of "truly national" concern.

In making these points, we can do little to improve upon the Fourth Circuit's opinion in *Gibbs*, which upheld, as a valid exercise of federal power under the Commerce Clause, an FWS regulation that limited the taking of red wolves. 214 F.3d at 487. As Chief Judge Wilkinson explained, regulation of the taking of endangered species "does not involve an 'area of traditional state concern,' one to which 'States lay claim by right of history and expertise.' "*Id.* at 499 (quoting Lopez, 514 U.S. at 580, 583 (Kennedy, J., concurring)). Rather, as the Supreme Court acknowledged in *Minnesota v. Mille Lacs Band of Chippewa Indians*, "although States have important interests in regulating wildlife and natural resources within their borders, this authority is shared with the Federal Government when the Federal Government exercises one of its enumerated constitutional powers." 526 U.S. 172, 204 (1999). Moreover, while "states and localities possess broad regulatory and zoning authority over land within their jurisdictions, . . . it is well established . . . that Congress can regulate even private land use for environmental and wildlife conservation." *Gibbs*, 214 F.3d at 500. Tracing a hundred-year history of congressional involvement in natural resource conservation, Chief Judge Wilkinson concluded that "it is clear from our laws and precedent that federal regulation of endangered wildlife does not trench impermissibly upon state powers." *Id.* at 500–01.

The Fourth Circuit also recognized the national scope of the problem posed by species conservation. Citing the ESA's legislative history, the court noted Congress' concern that " 'protection of endangered species is not a matter that can be handled in the absence of coherent national and international policies: the results of a series of unconnected and disorganized policies and programs by various states might well be confusion compounded.' "*Gibbs*, 214 F.3d at 502 (quoting H.R. REP. NO. 93–412, at 7 (1973)). As the *Gibbs* court explained: "States may decide to forego or limit conservation efforts in order to lower these costs, and other states may be forced to follow suit in order to compete." Id. at 501. Our court has recognized this problem as well. *See NAHB*, 130 F.3d at 1055 (Wald, J.) (noting that states may be "motivated to adopt lower standards of endangered species protection in order to attract development"). And the Supreme Court, as the Fourth Circuit observed, "has held that Congress may take cognizance of this dynamic and arrest the 'race to the bottom' in order to prevent interstate competition whose overall effect would damage the quality of the national environment." *Gibbs*, 214 F.3d at 501 (citing *Hodel v. Virginia Surface Mining & Reclamation Ass'n*, 452 U.S. 264 (1981)).

For these reasons, the protection of endangered species cannot fairly be described as a power "which the Founders denied the National Government and reposed in the States." *Morrison*, 529 U.S. at 618. Rather, "the preservation of endangered species is historically a federal function," *Gibbs*, 214 F.3d at 505, and invalidating this application of the ESA "would call into question the historic power of the federal government to preserve scarce resources in one locality for the future benefit of all Americans," *id.* at 492. We therefore agree with Chief Judge Wilkinson that to sustain challenges of this nature "would require courts to move abruptly from preserving traditional state roles to dismantling historic federal ones." *Id.* at 504. . .

GINSBURG, CHIEF JUDGE, concurring: Although I do not disagree with anything in the opinion of the court, I write separately because I do not believe our opinion makes clear, as the Supreme Court requires, that there is a logical stopping point to our rationale for upholding the constitutionality of the exercise of the Congress's power under the Commerce Clause here challenged. . . In this case I think it clear that our rationale for concluding the take of the arroyo toad affects interstate commerce does indeed have a logical stopping point, though it goes unremarked in the opinion of the court. Our rationale is that, with respect to a species that is not an article in interstate commerce and does not affect interstate commerce, a take can be regulated if—but only if—the take itself substantially affects interstate commerce. The large-scale residential development that is the take in this case clearly does affect interstate commerce. Just as important, however, the lone hiker in the woods, or the homeowner who moves dirt in order to landscape his property, though he takes the toad, does not affect interstate commerce. . .

NOTES AND QUESTIONS

1. The D.C. Circuit voted 8–2 not to rehear the case en banc. In dissent, Judge—and now Chief Justice—Roberts observed that "[t]he panel's approach in this case leads to the result that regulating the taking of a hapless toad that, for reasons of its own, lives its entire life in California constitutes regulating 'Commerce . . . among the several states.' U.S. Const. Art I, § 8, cl. 3." Rancho Viejo, LLC v. Norton, 334 F.3d 1158, 1160 (D.C. Cir. 2003) (Roberts, J., dissenting from denial of rehearing en banc). He insisted that the panel wrongly asked "whether the challenged *regulation* substantially affects interstate commerce, rather than whether the *activity* being regulated does so." *Id.* Judge Roberts believed that the proper query was whether "the incidental taking of arroyo toads can be said to be interstate commerce," *id.*, not whether the proposed development constituted interstate commerce. What is the difference? Which focus is correct? Earlier, in *NAHB*, three judges reached different conclusions because they asked three different questions. Judge Wald asked whether there was a sufficient relationship between *endangered species* and interstate commerce. Judge Henderson asked whether there was a relationship between the *hospital* and interstate commerce. Judge Sentelle asked whether there was a relationship between the *fly* and interstate commerce. Who asked the right question? *See* John Copeland Nagle, *The Commerce Clause Meets the Delhi Sands Flower-Loving Fly*, 97 MICH. L. REV. 174 (1998).

2. The court emphasized that the housing development proposed by Rancho Viejo possessed numerous connections to interstate commerce. But the arroyo southwestern toad is also threatened by off-road vehicles (ORVs) that "cause extensive damage to the shallow pools in which arroyo toads breed," children that collect the toads while on camping trips, accidental road kill at nighttime, and "[l]ight and noise pollution from adjacent developments." Determination of Endangered Status for the Arroyo Southwestern Toad, 59 Fed. Reg. 64859, 64862–64 (1994). Could Congress regulate any or all of those activities?

3. The commerce clause issue has also arisen in the context of federal efforts to protect wetlands. In footnote 2, Judge Garland cited Solid Waste Agency of Northern Cook County v. U.S. Army Corps of Engineers, 531 U.S. 159 (2001), which questioned the extent to which Congress may rely upon the commerce clause to protect wetlands that are home to migratory birds. (*SWANCC* and the scope of federal regulation of wetlands is explored in more detail in chapter 10.) If the courts decide that certain applications of federal law exceeds the scope of the commerce clause, are there any other sources of federal power to protect endangered species that live in only one state? And why should it matter whether a species or wetland occurs in more than one state, anyway?

4. The supremacy clause of the U.S. Constitution presents the flip side of the commerce clause issue. The supremacy clause provides that federal law "shall be the supreme Law of the Land." U.S. Const., Art. VI, cl. 2. The preemption doctrine builds upon the supremacy clause to forbid state actions that contradict federal law. For example, in UFO Chuting of Hawaii, Inc. v. Young, 327 F.Supp.2d 1220 (D. Hawaii 2004), a parasailing business challenged a state statute banned parasailing in certain waters around Maui between December 15 and May 15. The statute was designed to protect whales, though it addressed water safety, visual pollution, and noise pollution as well. The parasailing business argued that the statute was preempted by the federal Marine

Mammal Protection Act (MMPA), which prohibits state laws "relating to the taking of any . . . marine mammal" unless the state had obtained authority to conserve that species, which Hawaii had not done here. 16 U.S.C. § 1379(a). Another provision of the MMPA expressly authorizes anyone to come within 100 yards of a humpback whale. The federal district court held that both of the MMPA's provisions preempted Hawaii's parasailing ban.

D. STATE LAW PROTECTION OF BIODIVERSITY

Barrett v. New York

Court of Appeals of New York, 1917.
220 N.Y. 423, 116 N.E. 99.

■ ANDREWS, J.

At one time beaver were very numerous in this state. So important were they commercially that they were represented upon the seal of the New Netherlands and upon that of the colony as well as upon the seals of New Amsterdam and of New York.

Because of their value they were relentlessly killed, and by the year 1900 they were practically exterminated. But some fifteen animals were left, scattered through the southern portion of Franklin county.

In that year the legislature undertook to afford them complete protection, and there has been no open season for beaver since the enactment of chapter 20 of the Laws of 1900.

In 1904 it was further provided that "No person shall molest or disturb any wild beaver or the dams, houses, homes or abiding places of same." (Laws 1904, ch. 674, section 1.) This is still the law, although in 1912 the forest, fish and game commission was authorized to permit protected animals which had become destructive to public or private property to be taken and disposed of. (Laws 1912, ch. 318.)

By the act of 1904 $500 was appropriated for the purchase of wild beaver to restock the Adirondacks, and in 1906 $1,000 more was appropriated for the same purpose. The commission, after purchasing the animals, was authorized to liberate them.

Under this authority twenty-one beaver have been purchased and freed by the commission. Of these four were placed upon Eagle creek, an inlet of the Fourth Lake of the Fulton Chain. There they seem to have remained and increased.

Beaver are naturally destructive to certain kinds of forest trees. During the fall and winter they live upon the bark of the twigs and smaller branches of poplar, birch and alder. To obtain a supply they fell even trees of large size, cut the smaller branches into suitable lengths and pull or float them to their houses. All this it must be assumed was known by the legislature as early as 1900.

The claimants own a valuable tract of woodland upon Fourth Lake bounded in the rear by Eagle creek. The land was held by them for building sites and was suitable for that purpose. Much of its attractiveness depended upon the forest grown upon it. In this forest were a number of poplar trees. In 1912 and during two or three years prior thereto 198 of these poplars were felled by beaver. Others were girdled and destroyed. The Board of Claims has found, upon evidence that fairly justifies the inference, that this destruction was caused by the four beaver liberated on Eagle creek and their descendants, and that the claimants have been damaged in the sum of $1,900. An award was made to them for that sum and this award has been affirmed by the Appellate Division.

To sustain it the respondents rely upon three propositions. It is said, first, that the state may not protect such an animal as the beaver which is known to be destructive; second, that the provision of the law of 1904 with regard to the molestation of beaver prohibits the claimants from protecting their property and is, therefore, an unreasonable exercise of the police power; and, *third*, that the state was in actual physical possession of the beaver placed on Eagle creek and that its act in freeing them, knowing their natural propensity to destroy trees, makes the state liable for the damage done by them.

We cannot agree with either of these propositions.

As to the first, the general right of the government to protect wild animals is too well established to be now called in question. Their ownership is in the state in its sovereign capacity, for the benefit of all the people. Their preservation is a matter of public interest. They are a species of natural wealth which without special protection would be destroyed. Everywhere and at all times governments have assumed the right to prescribe how and when they may be taken or killed. As early as 1705 New York passed such an act as to deer. (Colonial Laws, vol. 1, p. 585.) A series of statutes has followed protecting more or less completely game, birds and fish.

"The protection and preservation of game has been secured by law in all civilized countries, and may be justified on many grounds. * * * The measures best adapted to this end are for the legislature to determine, and courts cannot review its discretion. If the regulations operate, in any respect, unjustly or oppressively, the proper remedy must be applied by that body." (Phelps v. Racey, 60 N. Y. 10, 14.)

Wherever protection is accorded harm may be done to the individual. Deer or moose may browse on his crops; mink or skunks kill his chickens; robins eat his cherries. In certain cases the legislature may be mistaken in its belief that more good than harm is occasioned. But this is clearly a matter which is confided to its discretion. It exercises a governmental function for the benefit of the public at large and no one can complain of the incidental injuries that may result.

It is sought to draw a distinction between such animals and birds as have ordinarily received protection and beaver on the ground that the latter are unusually destructive and that to preserve them is an unreasonable exercise of the power of the state.

The state may exercise the police power "wherever the public interests demand it, and in this particular a large discretion is necessarily vested in the legislature to determine, not only what the interests of the public require, but what measures are necessary for the protection of such interests. To justify the state in thus interposing its authority in behalf of the public, it must appear, *first*, that the interests of the public generally, as distinguished from those of a particular class, require such interference; and, *second*, that the means are reasonably necessary for the accomplishment of the purpose, and not unduly oppressive upon individuals." (Lawton v. Steele, 152 U.S. 133, 136.)

The police power is not to be limited to guarding merely the physical or material interests of the citizen. His moral, intellectual and spiritual needs may also be considered. The eagle is preserved, not for its use but for its beauty.

The same thing may be said of the beaver. They are one of the most valuable of the fur-bearing animals of the state. They may be used for food. But apart from these considerations their habits and customs, their curious instincts and intelligence place them in a class by themselves. Observation of the animals at work or play is a source of never-failing interest and instruction. If they are to be preserved experience has taught us that protection is required. If they cause more damage than deer or moose, the degree of the mischief done by them is not so much greater or so different as to require the application of a special rule. If the preservation of the former does not unduly oppress individuals, neither does the latter.

In the determination of what is a reasonable exercise of the powers of the government, the acts of other governments under similar circumstances have some bearing. In Wyoming, Utah, North Dakota, Wisconsin, Maine, Colorado and Vermont beaver are absolutely protected. In Michigan they are protected except between November 1st and May 15th of each year. In South Dakota except between November 15th and April 2d. In Quebec for a number of years there was no open season. Lately there has been an open season for a short time in the autumn.

We, therefore, reach the conclusion that in protecting beaver the legislature did not exceed its powers. Nor did it so do in prohibiting their molestation. It is possible that were the interpretation given by the respondents to this section right a different result might follow. If the claimants, finding beaver destroying their property, might not drive them away, then possibly their rights would be infringed. In Aldrich v. Wright (53 N. H. 398) it was said in an elaborate opinion, although this question we do not decide, that a farmer might shoot mink even in the closed season should he find them threatening his geese.

But such an interpretation is too rigid and narrow. The claimants might have fenced their land without violation of the statute. They might have driven the beaver away, were they injuring their property. The prohibition against disturbing dams or houses built on or adjoining watercourses is no greater or different exercise of power from that assumed by the legislature when it prohibits the destruction of the nests and eggs of wild birds even when the latter are found upon private property.

The object is to protect the beaver. That object as we decide is within the power of the state. The destruction of dams and houses will result in driving away the beaver. The prohibition of such acts, being an apt means to the end desired, is not so unreasonable as to be beyond the legislative power.

We hold, therefore, that the acts referred to are constitutional. But had we reached a different conclusion the respondents would not be aided. We know of no principle of law under which the state becomes liable because of the adoption of an unconstitutional statute. Such a statute is no protection to officers assuming to proceed under its authority. The state itself, if it permits such a claim to be enforced against it, may become liable for what they do. But the statute itself is void. No one need obey it. If no affirmative act is done under its supposed authority neither the state nor its officers are liable, because the citizen chooses to obey where he need not have done so.

Somewhat different considerations apply to the act of the state in purchasing and liberating beaver.

The attempt to introduce life into a new environment does not always result happily. The rabbit in Australia—the mongoose in the West Indies have become pests. The English sparrow is no longer welcome. Certain of our most troublesome weeds are foreign flowers.

Yet governments have made such experiments in the belief that the public good would be promoted. Sometimes they have been mistaken. Again the attempt has succeeded. The English pheasant is a valuable addition to our stock of birds. But whether a success or failure the attempt is well within governmental powers.

If this is so with regard to foreign life, still more is it true with regard to animals native to the state, still existing here, when the intent is to increase the stock upon what the Constitution declares shall remain forever wild forest lands. If the state may provide for the increase of beaver by prohibiting their destruction it is difficult to see why it may not attain the same result by removing colonies to a more favorable locality or by replacing those destroyed by fresh importations.

Nor are the cases cited by the respondents controlling. It is true that one who keeps wild animals in captivity must see to it at his peril that they do no damage to others. But it is not true that whenever an individual is liable for a certain act the state is liable for the same act. In liberating these beaver the state was acting as a government. As a trustee for the people and as their representative it was doing what it thought best for the interests of the public at large. Under such circumstances we cannot hold that the rule of such cases as those cited is applicable.

We reach the conclusion that no recovery can be had under this claim. It is assumed, both by the respondents and by the appellant, that the Board of Claims had jurisdiction to determine the questions involved. That we do not discuss.

The judgment of the Appellate Division and the determination of the Board of Claims must be reversed and the claim dismissed, with costs in Appellate Division and in this court.

NOTES & QUESTIONS

1. The saga of the beaver illustrates how states responded to the first indications of a crisis regarding biodiversity. Beaver were plentiful when the first European settlers arrived in America. Over the next several centuries, French, English and Native American trappers aggressively hunted beavers to the extent that the beavers began to disappear. Shepard Krech III picks up the story at that point:

> By the late nineteenth century, the beaver harvest was 10 percent of its level one century before, and beavers were scarce or locally extinct in North America. They disappeared from New Jersey by 1820 and New Hampshire by 1865. By 1890, they were rare or absent in Pennsylvania, Wisconsin, Minnesota, most of New York, many parts of Quebec and Ontario, and elsewhere.

> Concerned legislators passed laws designed to halt the destruction of beavers as they had with deer. Men and women active in the conservation movement that formed in the last three decades of the nineteenth century were appalled at the eradication of buffaloes, passenger pigeons, and other wildlife including beavers. New conservationists spoke of a "mad rush at the counter for fur and psuedo-fur" and the fashion for fur as a "craze." In the twentieth century, conservation sentiments and regulations had taken a stronger hold and for beavers, the tide turned. . . In the first two decades of the twentieth century, restocking programs were instituted widely in the United States and Canada. Together with stringent laws restricting trapping, the programs succeeded—to the extent that within just a few years in the Adirondacks, where beavers had been extinct, New York's Conservation Commission called them "interesting but destructive," responsible for flooding highways and railroads. This success brought renewed trapping during fur booms in the 1920s and 1940s. Soon most states again allowed beaver trapping and the annual harvest in North America climbed to hundreds of thousands of pelts.

> Like white-tailed deer, beavers survived to recover much of their former range. . . Beavers recovered as a consequence of trapping restrictions, restocking, changes in fashion, and conservation. In the 1990s, antifur lobbies and changing fashions have cast trapping as a pariah profession, leaving beaver populations unchecked. Anthropomorphized, beavers are loved

in the abstract—until like deer their unbridled populations explode into suburban cultural landscapes as pests, attracting headlines like "Busy Beavers Gnaw on Suburban Nerves" and "Besieged by Beavers in Rural New York." As the millennium approaches, these "annoying overachievers" once again are busily and eagerly altering every conceivable habitat in North America.

SHEPARD KRECH III, THE ECOLOGICAL INDIAN: MYTH AND HISTORY 178–79 (1999).

2. The *Barrett* court held that the protection of wildlife is within the state's police power. Historically, states played the leading role in regulating wildlife within their borders. Geer v. Connecticut, 161 U.S. 519 (1896), is the leading case establishing the primacy of states with respect to wildlife. In *Geer*, the defendant was convicted for violating a state law prohibiting the possession of game birds with the intent to transfer them out of state. Geer charged that the exclusive congressional power to regulate interstate commerce rendered the Connecticut law unconstitutional. The Supreme Court disagreed, with Justice White explaining that states had the right "to control and regulate the common property in game . . . as a trust for the benefit of the people." *Id.* at 528–29. *Geer* came to stand for the proposition that the states owned the wildlife within their borders. To some, it also indicated that *only* the states could regulate wildlife, so that the federal government lacked the constitutional power to do so. That claim was soon called into question when Congress enacted the Lacey Act in 1900, it further eroded when the Court upheld the Migratory Bird Act of 1913 as a valid exercise of the federal treaty power in Missouri v. Holland, 252 U.S. 416 (1920), and it has grown even more difficult to sustain in the aftermath of several Court decisions since the 1970s that have found that various federal wildlife statutes are authorized by either the congressional power to regulate interstate commerce or to regulate the property of the United States. *See generally* BEAN & ROWLAND, *supra*, at 15–27 (reviewing the federal constitutional authority to regulate wildlife).

3. The defendant in *Barrett* also demanded that the state compensate him for the damage that the beavers caused to his property. Why did Judge Andrews reject that claim? Did the state government cause the injury suffered by the landowner? *Cf.* Palsgraf v. Long Island R. Co., 162 N.E. 99, 101 (1928) (Andrews, J., dissenting) (insisting that the railroad was the proximate cause of Mrs. Palsgraf's injuries). Damage done by wildlife protected—or even introduced—by the government continues to give rise to claims for compensation. *See* Christy v. Hodel, 857 F.2d 1324 (9th Cir.1988) (holding that the federal government did not take a Montana rancher's property when a grizzly bear killed his livestock), *cert. denied*, 490 U.S. 1114 (1989); State v. Sour Mountain Realty, Inc., 276 A.D.2d 8, 17–18 (N.Y.App.Div.2000) (holding that the state did not take a quarry owner's property when it prohibited the landowner from removing protected rattlesnakes).

Bolsa Chica Land Trust v. The Superior Court of San Diego County

Court of Appeal of California, Fourth Appellate District, Division One, 1999.
71 Cal.App.4th 493, 83 Cal.Rptr.2d 850.

■ BENKE, J.

This case concerns development plans for a large tract of land in southern Orange County known as Bolsa Chica. Although the California Coastal Commission (Commission) approved a local coastal program (LCP) for Bolsa Chica, the trial court found defects in the program and remanded it to Commission for further proceedings. In this court both the opponents and proponents of the LCP contend that the trial court erred.

The opponents of the LCP contend the trial court erred in finding a planned relocation of a bird habitat was permissible under the Coastal Act. The proponents of the LCP contend the trial court erred in preventing residential development of a wetlands area and in requiring preservation of a pond that would have been eliminated under the LCP in order to make room for a street widening. The proponents also attack the trial court's award of attorney fees to the opponents of the LCP.

We find the trial court erred with respect to relocation of the bird habitat. The Coastal Act does not permit destruction of an environmentally sensitive habitat area (ESHA) simply because the destruction is mitigated offsite. At the very least, there must be some showing the destruction is needed to serve some other environmental or economic interest recognized by the act.

Factual Background

Bolsa Chica is a 1,588-acre area of undeveloped wetlands and coastal mesas. Urban development surrounds Bolsa Chica on three sides. On the fourth side is the Pacific Ocean, separated from Bolsa Chica by a narrow strip of beach, coastal dunes and coastal bluffs.

Approximately 1,300 acres of Bolsa Chica consist of lowlands ranging from fully submerged saltwater in Bolsa Bay to areas of freshwater and saltwater wetlands and islands of slightly raised dry lands used by local wildlife for nesting and foraging. However, a large part of the lowlands is devoted to an active oil field and at one time the area was farmed.

The lowlands are flanked by two mesas, the Bolsa Chica Mesa on the north and the Huntington Mesa on the south. The Bolsa Chica Mesa consists of 215 acres of uplands hosting a variety of habitat areas. Although much of Huntington Mesa is developed, a long narrow undeveloped strip of the mesa abutting the lowlands is the planned site of a public park.

In 1973 the State of California acquired 310 contiguous acres of the Bolsa Chica lowlands in settlement of a dispute over its ownership of several separate lowland parcels and the existence of a public trust easement over other lowland areas.

In 1985 the County of Orange and Commission approved a land use plan for Bolsa Chica which contemplated fairly intense development. The 1985 plan allowed development of 5,700 residential units, a 75-acre marina and a 600-foot-wide navigable ocean channel and breakwater.

By 1988 substantial concerns had been raised with respect to the environmental impacts of the proposed marina and navigable ocean channel. Accordingly, a developer which owned a large portion of Bolsa Chica, a group of concerned citizens, the State Lands Commission, the County of Orange and the City of Huntington Beach formed the Bolsa Chica Planning Coalition (coalition). The coalition in turn developed an LCP for Bolsa Chica which substantially reduced the intensity of development. The coalition's LCP was eventually adopted by the Orange County Board of Supervisors. Commission approved the LCP with suggested modifications which were adopted by the board of supervisors.

As approved by Commission, the LCP eliminated the planned marina and navigable ocean channel, eliminated 3 major roads, reduced residential development from a total of 5,700 homes to 2,500 homes on Bolsa Chica Mesa and 900 homes in the lowlands and expanded planned open space and wetlands restoration to 1,300 acres.

The material features of the LCP which are in dispute here are: the replacement of a degraded eucalyptus grove on Bolsa Chica Mesa with a new raptor habitat consisting of nesting poles, native trees and other native vegetation on Huntington Mesa at the sight of the planned public park; the residential development in the lowland area which the LCP permits as a means of financing restoration of substantially degraded wetlands; and the elimination of Warner Pond on Bolsa Chica Mesa in order to accommodate the widening of Warner Avenue.

Throughout the approval process several interested parties and public interest groups, including the Bolsa Chica Land Trust, Huntington Beach Tomorrow, Shoshone-Gabrieleno Nation, Sierra Club and Surfrider Foundation (collectively the trust) objected to these and other portions of the LCP. . .

IV. Eucalyptus Grove

A. History and Condition of the Grove

The LCP would permit residential development over five acres of a six-and-one-half-acre eucalyptus grove on Bolsa Chica Mesa. The five acres where development would be permitted is owned by Koll; the remainder of the grove is owned by the state.

The eucalyptus grove is not native to the area and was planted almost 100 years ago by a hunting club which owned large portions of Bolsa Chica.

Since the time of its planting, the original 20-acre grove has diminished considerably because of development in the area and the lack of any effort to preserve it. Indeed, although the eucalyptus grove was nine and two-tenths acres large as recently as 1989, it had shrunk to no more than six and one-half acres by 1994 and portions of it were under severe stress. According to expert testimony submitted to Commission, the grove is probably shrinking because of increased salinity in the soil.

Notwithstanding its current diminished and deteriorating condition, Commission identified the grove as an ESHA within the meaning of Public Resources Code section 30107.5. The ESHA identification was based on the fact the grove provided the only significant locally available roosting and nesting habitat for birds of prey (raptors) in the Bolsa Chica area. At least 11 species of raptors have been identified as utilizing the site, including the white-tailed kite, marsh hawk, sharp skinned hawk, Cooper's hawk and osprey. According to Commission, a number of the raptors are dependent upon the adjacent lowland wetlands for food and the eucalyptus grove provides an ideal nearby lookout location as well as a refuge and nesting site.

B. Section 30240

Under the Coastal Act, Commission is required to protect the coastal zone's delicately balanced ecosystem. (§ 30001, subds. (a)-(c), 30001.5, subd. (a); City of San Diego v. California Coastal Com. (1981) 119 Cal. App. 3d 228, 233 [174 Cal. Rptr. 5]; Sierra Club v. California Coastal Com. (1993) 12 Cal. App. 4th 602, 611 [15 Cal. Rptr. 2d 779].) Thus in reviewing all programs and projects governed by the Coastal Act, Commission must consider the effect of proposed development on the environment of the coast.

In terms of the general protection the Coastal Act provides for the coastal environment, we have analogized it to the California Environmental Quality Act (CEQA) (§ 21000–21174). (Coastal Southwest Dev. Corp. v. California Coastal Zone Conservation Com. (1976) 55 Cal. App. 3d 525, 537 127 Cal. Rptr. 775].) We have found that under both the Coastal Act and CEQA: " 'The courts are enjoined to construe the statute liberally in light of its beneficent purposes. The highest priority must be given to environmental consideration in interpreting the statute.' "*Ibid.*)

In addition to the protection afforded by the requirement that Commission consider the environmental impact of all its decisions, the Coastal Act provides heightened protection to ESHA's. Section 30107.5 identifies an ESHA as "any area in which plant or animal life or their habitats are either rare or especially valuable because of their special nature or role in an ecosystem and which could be easily disturbed or degraded by human activities and developments." "The consequences of ESHA status are delineated in section 30240: '(a) Environmentally sensitive habitat areas shall be protected against any significant disruption of habitat values, and only uses dependent on those resources shall be allowed within those areas. [P] (b) Development in areas adjacent to environmentally sensitive habitat areas and parks and recreation areas shall be sited and designed to prevent impacts which would significantly degrade those areas, and shall be compatible with continuance of those habitat and recreation areas.' Thus development in ESHA areas themselves is limited to uses dependent on those resources, and development in adjacent areas must carefully safeguard their preservation."

Commission found that residential development in the eucalyptus grove was permissible under section 30240 because the LCP required that an alternate raptor habitat be developed on Huntington Mesa. Commission reasoned that section 30240 only requires that "habitat values" be protected and that given the deteriorating condition of the grove, creation of a new raptor habitat on Huntington Mesa was the best way to promote the "habitat values" of the eucalyptus grove.

The reasoning Commission employed is seductive but, in the end, unpersuasive. First, contrary to Koll's argument, we are not required to give great weight to the interpretation of section 30240 set forth by Commission in its findings approving the LCP... Secondly, the language of section 30240 does not permit a process by which the habitat values of an ESHA can be isolated and then recreated in another location. Rather, a literal reading of the statute protects the area of an ESHA from uses which threaten the habitat values which exist in the ESHA. Importantly, while the obvious goal of section 30240 is to protect habitat values, the express terms of the statute do not provide that protection by treating those values as intangibles which can be moved from place to place to suit the needs of development. Rather, the terms of the statute protect habitat values by placing strict limits on the uses which may occur in an ESHA and by carefully controlling the manner uses in the area around the ESHA are developed.

Thirdly, contrary to Commission's reasoning, section 30240 does not permit its restrictions to be ignored based on the threatened or deteriorating condition of a particular ESHA. We do not doubt that in deciding whether a particular area is an ESHA within the meaning of section 30107.5, Commission may consider, among other matters, its viability. However, where, as is the case here, Commission has decided that an area is an ESHA, section 30240 does not itself provide Commission power to alter its strict limitations. There is simply no reference in section 30240 which can be interpreted as diminishing the level of protection an ESHA receives based on its viability. Rather, under the statutory scheme, ESHA's, whether they are pristine and growing or fouled and threatened, receive uniform treatment and protection.

In this regard we agree with the trust that Commission's interpretation of section 30240 would pose a threat to ESHA's. As the trust points out, if, even though an ESHA meets the requirements of section 30107.5, application of section 30240's otherwise strict limitations also depends on the relative viability of an ESHA, developers will be encouraged to find threats and hazards to all ESHA's located in economically inconvenient locations. The pursuit of such hazards would in turn only promote the isolation and transfer of ESHA habitat values to more economically convenient locations. Such a system of isolation and transfer based on economic convenience would of course be completely contrary to the goal of the Coastal Act, which is to protect all coastal zone resources and provide heightened protection to ESHA's.

In short, while compromise and balancing in light of existing conditions is appropriate and indeed encouraged under other applicable portions of the Coastal Act, the power to balance and compromise conflicting interests cannot be found in section 30240.

C. Section 30007.5

Koll argues that even if transfer of habitat values was not permissible under section 30240, such a transfer was permissible under the provisions of section 30007.5 and our holding in [Sierra Club v. California Coastal Comm'n, 19 Cal.App.4th 547, 23 Cal.Rptr.2d 534 (1993) (*Batiquitos Lagoon*)]. Section 30007.5 states: "The Legislature further finds and recognizes that conflicts may occur between one or more policies of the [Coastal Act]. The Legislature therefore declares that in carrying out the provisions of this division such conflicts be resolved in a manner which on balance is the most protective of significant coastal resources. In this context, the Legislature declares that broader policies which, for example, serve to concentrate development in close proximity to urban and employment centers may be more protective, overall, than specific wildlife habitat and other similar resource policies."

In *Batiquitos Lagoon* we were confronted with "the conflicting interests of fish and fowl." Each interest was protected by a specific provision of the Coastal Act: The fish were protected by section 30230 which directed that marine resources be preserved and, where feasible, restored; the fowl were protected by the requirement of section 30233, subdivision (b), that the very substantial dredging needed to restore the fish habitat avoid significant disruption of the bird habitat. We found that under section 30007.5, Commission could resolve these conflicting policy interests by favoring long-term restoration of the fish habitat over the short-term, but significant, disruption of the bird habitat.

Here, in contrast to the situation in *Batiquitos Lagoon*, the record at this point will not support application of the balancing power provided by section 30007.5. Unlike the record in that case, here our review of the proceedings before Commission does not disclose any policy or interest which directly conflicts with application of section 30240 to the eucalyptus grove.

Although the Coastal Act itself recognizes the value and need for residential development, nothing in the record or the briefs of the parties suggests there is such an acute need for development of residential housing in and around the eucalyptus grove that it cannot be accommodated elsewhere. Rather, the only articulated interests which the proposed transfer of the "habitat values" serves is Commission's expressed desire to preserve the raptor habitat values over the long term and Commission's subsidiary interest in replacing nonnative eucalyptus with native vegetation. However, as the trust points out, there is no evidence in the record that destruction of the grove is a prerequisite to creation of the proposed Huntington Mesa habitat. In the absence of evidence as to why preservation of the raptor habitat at its current location is unworkable, we cannot reasonably conclude that any genuine conflict between long-term and short-term goals exists.

In sum then the trial court erred in sustaining that portion of the LCP which permitted development of the eucalyptus grove.

[The court also upheld the Commission's conclusion that neither residential development in the wetlands nor destruction of the pond is permissible].

NOTES & QUESTIONS

1. Many states have their own statutes protecting the rare wildlife and plants within their borders. Some of those laws offer protections similar to those provided by the federal laws such as the Endangered Species Act. The Defenders of Wildlife have published a comprehensive analysis of the effectiveness of state laws protecting endangered species. *See* SUSAN GEORGE, WILLIAM J. SNAPE III & MICHAEL SENATORE, STATE ENDANGERED SPECIES ACTS: PAST, PRESENT AND FUTURE, *available at* www.defenders.org/pubs/sesa01.html. According to that study, 45 states have some kind of legislation that requires the protection of endangered species. (The exceptions are Alabama, Arkansas, Utah, West Virginia, and Wyoming). The report concludes, however, that "most acts easily fall far short of what is needed to adequately protect a state's imperiled species." Specifically, the report identifies shortcomings in the procedures by which species are listed, the protection of critical habitat, the conduct prohibited by the laws, recovery plans, and the penalty and enforcement provisions. The state listing procedures are often similar to the federal ESA (which is described below in chapter 4), with a handful of exceptions such as New Jersey's provision that listing is optional, the Virginia provision that plants and insects need not be listed if that is not "in the best interest of man," and the Maine and Montana provisions that final listing decisions are made by the legislature. The critical habitat provisions are more troubling: "Only six states have provisions requiring critical habitat designation and they are rarely used." States also differ from the federal ESA in failing to prohibit the destruction of the habitat of a listed species. While the U.S. Supreme Court has held that the federal prohibition on the "take" of an endangered species can apply to some habitat destruction (as discussed below at pages 279–86, only in Massachusetts is the destruction of habitat a prohibited "take" of the species. Instead, most state laws prohibit hunting, capturing, or otherwise actually injuring a listed species. Recovery plans are similarly absent from most state acts, again unlike the federal ESA's requirement that the Fish & Wildlife Service prepare a plan detailing the steps that are needed to help each listed species recover from the brink of extinction. Finally, the report finds that "most states suffer from a lack of proper enforcement" of their endangered species laws, including the omission of a citizen suit provision

that would allow concerned individuals to seek to enforce the provisions of the law themselves.

Other kinds of state statutes aid in the preservation of biodiversity, too. A survey conducted in 2003 reviewed the ways in which state land use planning enabling laws and growth management laws address concerns about biodiversity. *See* Linda Breggin & Susan George, *Planning for Biodiversity: Sources of Authority in State Land Use Laws*, 81 VA. ENVTL. L. J. 81 (2003). The survey found that "[a]ll of the growth management laws and many of the land use planning enabling laws contain provisions that provide localities with the authority or duty to consider biodiversity-related factors and concepts. Such factors include, but are not limited to, local comprehensive plan requirements for natural resources, open space, wildlife habitat, and critical and sensitive areas." *Id.* at 120–21. A 2004 study by the Environmental Law Institute identified eight guidelines for local governments seeking to regulate land use in a manner that preserves biodiversity: "(1) maintain large areas of contiguous habitat and avoid fragmenting those areas; (2) maintain meaningful connections between habitat areas; (3) protect rare landscape elements, sensitive areas, and associated species; (4) allow natural patterns of disturbance to continue in order to maintain diversity and resilience of habitat types; (5) minimize the introduction and spread of non-native species and favor native plants and animals; (6) minimize human introduction of nutrients, chemicals, and pollutants; (7) avoid land uses that deplete natural resources over a broad area; and (8) compensate for adverse effects of development on natural processes." JAMES M. MCELFISH, JR., NATURE-FRIENDLY ORDINANCES 10 (2003). Can such land use laws play a greater role in preserving biodiversity?

2. There may be other ways of using state law to protect biodiversity besides state statutes. The public trust doctrine offers one approach. *See* Ralph W. Johnson & William C. Galloway, *Can the Public Trust Doctrine Prevent Extinctions?*, in BIODIVERSITY AND THE LAW 157–64 (William J. Snape III ed. 1996). Nuisance law might provide another alternative. Recall that a public nuisance is "an unreasonable interference with a right common to the general public." Restatement (Second) Torts § 821B. An interference is "unreasonable" if it significantly interferes with public health, safety, comfort or convenience, if it is illegal, or if it is continuing or long-lasting and known to have a significant effect. *Id.* One author has argued that public nuisance actions may be used to protect biodiversity because "[a] healthy and viable population of native wildlife is arguably a public right." Siobhan O'Keeffe, *Using Public Nuisance Law to Protect Wildlife*, 6 BUFF. ENVT'L. L.J. 85 (1998). But Richard Epstein counters that "common law actions for trespass and nuisance are forlorn in the context of habitat preservation, because so much of the modification and destruction of habitat targeted by the ESA typically comes from ordinary husbandry of land: the clearing of trees, the construction of houses, the diversion of waters for drink and irrigation (subject to its own distinctive rules), and the like. It would take a stunning reversal of hundreds of years of legal history if these activities, generally productive, were now, for the first time, castigated by the common law as generally harmful." Richard A. Epstein, *Habitat Preservation: A Property Rights Perspective*, in WHO OWNS THE ENVIRONMENT? 229 (Peter J. Hill & Roger E. Meiners eds. 1998).

West v. State

Supreme Court of Alaska, 2010.
248 P.3d 689.

■ CHRISTEN, JUSTICE.

. . . Controlling predator populations to increase prey populations is a practice with a long and sometimes controversial history in Alaska.[3] Following World War II, the federal government began a far-reaching predator control program that used poison baiting and aerial hunting to control wolf populations throughout Alaska. After statehood, the use of poison baiting was prohibited in Alaska but aerial wolf hunting was not. Concerns over aerial wolf hunting and the use of snares continued in the 1990s, as did the controversy over predator control.[4]

Alaska's constitution incorporates principles of natural resource management that serve as the foundation for the management of Alaska's wildlife. Alaska was the first state to have a constitutional article devoted to natural resources, and it is the only state to have a constitutional provision addressing the principle of sustained yield. Alaska's sustained yield clause—article VIII, section 4—provides that:

[f]ish, forests, wildlife, grasslands, and all other replenishable resources belonging to the State shall be utilized, developed, and maintained on the sustained yield principle, subject to preferences among beneficial uses.

Alaska Statute 16.05.255 is an implementing statute for Alaska's sustained yield clause. In 1994, the Alaska legislature amended AS 16.05.255 to incorporate new principles of intensive management aimed at increasing big game prey populations in areas where the Board determines human consumptive use is preferred. Alaska's intensive management statute requires that the Board adopt regulations "to provide for intensive management programs to restore the abundance or productivity of identified big game prey populations as necessary to achieve human consumptive use goals." The changes to AS 16.05.255 set the stage for the current dispute because the amended statute provides for "control of predation" in areas where the Board determines intensive management is required.

---

[3]   Some anthropologists believe that, long before European contact, indigenous people in Alaska sought to reduce predator populations, particularly wolf populations, in order to increase their harvest of prey species. *See* COMM. ON MGMT. OF WOLF AND BEAR POPULATIONS IN ALASKA, NATIONAL RESEARCH COUNCIL, WOLVES, BEARS, AND THEIR PREY IN ALASKA: BIOLOGICAL AND SOCIAL CHALLENGES IN WILDLIFE MANAGEMENT 27-28 (1997).

[4]   A 1996 public initiative banned aerial and land-and-shoot wolf hunting except by state employees when a biological emergency was declared in a specific geographical area. In 1999 the legislature expanded the grounds for authorizing a wolf control program, including to increase prey populations. *See* AS 16.05.783. The following year, the legislature passed a statute that would have allowed the general public to engage in land-and-shoot wolf hunting in areas where a wolf control program was authorized, but the statute was overturned by public referendum several months later. A 2008 public initiative sought to reimpose strict limits on authorizing predator control programs, but it was defeated.

When the legislature adopted the intensive management statute in 1994, it expressed a clear policy that "providing for high levels of harvest for human consumptive use *in accordance with the sustained yield principle* is the highest and best use of identified big game prey populations in most areas of the state." In 1998 AS 16.05.255 was again amended, this time, to include an explicit requirement that intensive game management be "consistent with sustained yield," which the legislature defined as "the achievement and maintenance in perpetuity of the ability to support a high level of human harvest of game, subject to preferences among beneficial uses, on an annual or periodic basis."

Until 2006, the Board's general regulatory framework for predator control of wolves and bears [required] that the Board consider "sound wildlife management principles *based upon sustained yield*" for all predator control plans. [The Board eliminated that requirement in 2006, and Defenders of Wildlife and The Alaska Wildlife Alliance brought suit to challenge the change.]

IV. DISCUSSION

Defenders and West argue that the constitutional and statutory principles of sustained yield apply to predators and that the Board did not apply sustained yield when it adopted its 2006 predator control plans. The State counters that it has no constitutional or statutory duty to apply sustained yield to wolves and bears in predator control areas, but that it nonetheless did so. We first consider whether Alaska's sustained yield clause and intensive management statute require that the Board apply principles of sustained yield when it adopts predator control plans. Because we conclude that the Board is bound by both a constitutional and statutory duty to do so, we next consider whether Defenders and West have met their burden of demonstrating that the Board's 2006 predator control plans are invalid under Alaska's sustained yield clause and intensive management statute. Ultimately, we uphold the 2006 plans because Defenders and West failed to meet this burden.

A. The Sustained Yield Clause Applies To Predator Control.

The superior court concluded that Alaska's sustained yield clause applies to predators, including bears and wolves, but that "the management of wildlife resources may constitutionally include a selection between predator and prey populations." We apply our independent judgment to questions of constitutional interpretation and interpret Alaska's constitution "according to reason, practicality, and common sense, taking into account the plain meaning and purpose of the law as well as the intent of the drafters."

1. The sustained yield clause does not distinguish between predator and prey populations.

When we interpret the Alaska Constitution, "[u]nless the context suggests otherwise, words are to be given their natural, obvious[,] and ordinary meaning." The text of Alaska's sustained yield clause provides that "[f]ish, forests, *wildlife,* grasslands, and all other replenishable resources belonging to the State shall be utilized, developed, and maintained on the sustained yield principle." According to a plain text reading of this clause, the sustained yield principle applies to all "wildlife." The natural, obvious, and ordinary meaning of the term "wildlife" suggests that the drafters of our constitution intended a broad application of the sustained yield principle encompassing all wild animals, including wolves and bears.

The definition of "sustained yield principle" provided to the constitutional delegates by the Resources Committee of the Constitutional Convention is also helpful to our inquiry:

> As to forests, timber volume, rate of growth, and acreage of timber type can be determined with some degree of accuracy. For fish, for wildlife, and for some other replenishable resources such as huckleberries, as an example, it is difficult or even impossible to measure accurately the factors by which a calculated sustained yield could be determined. Yet the term "sustained yield principle" is used in connection with management of such resources. When so used it denotes conscious application insofar as practicable of principles of management intended to sustain the yield of the resource being managed. That broad meaning is the meaning of the term as used in the Article.

This explanation explicitly states that the term "sustained yield" as used in Alaska's constitution has a "broad meaning." In addition, the statement that the sustained yield principle is used in connection with the management of fish, wildlife—and even huckleberries—suggests a broad application of this principle.

. . . Our inquiry here is aided by the "Report to the People of Alaska" prepared by the Alaska Constitutional Convention delegates in the period leading up to the ratification vote. This report informed the voters that:

> The [natural resources] article's primary purpose is to balance maximum use of natural resources with their continued availability to future generations. In keeping with that purpose, all replenishable resources are to be administered, insofar as practicable, on the sustained yield principle. This includes fish, forests, wildlife and grasslands, among others. [35]

The description in the Report to the People of Alaska, like the plain meaning of the sustained yield clause itself, does not suggest any distinction between predator and prey for purposes of applying sustained yield.

We find nothing in the plain language of the sustained yield clause suggesting that a distinction should be drawn between predator and prey populations for purposes of applying the sustained yield principle, and there is no such distinction in the descriptions of "sustained yield" supplied by the delegates who drafted the constitution or to the voters who ratified it. We have acknowledged that "the framers of Alaska's constitution intended the sustained yield clause to play a meaningful role in resource management," and we hold today that the sustained yield clause in Alaska's constitution applies to both predator and prey populations, including populations of wolves and bears.

2. The sustained yield clause permits the State to establish preferences among beneficial uses.

Having held that the sustained yield clause applies to predator populations, we must also consider whether the sustained yield clause permits the Board to give preference to populations of moose and caribou over populations of wolves and bears through the use of intensive management practices.

The starting point of this analysis is again the text of the sustained yield clause itself, which provides "wildlife . . . shall be utilized, developed, and maintained on the sustained yield principle, *subject to preferences among beneficial uses.*" The qualifier that makes sustained yield "subject to preferences among beneficial uses" suggests that the legislature and the Board have some discretion to establish management priorities for Alaska's wildlife. Such a construction is consistent with the constitutional history of the sustained yield clause. As we noted in *Native Village of Elim v. State,* "the primary emphasis of the framers' discussions and the glossary's definition of sustained yield is on the flexibility of the sustained yield requirement and its status as a guiding principle rather than a concrete, predefined process." This is reflected in the Report to the People of Alaska distributed before ratification of Alaska's constitution, which explains that "all replenishable resources are to be administered, *insofar as practicable,* on the sustained yield principle." The glossary definition of "sustained yield" provided by the Resources Committee of the Constitutional Convention contains similar language: "[the term sustained yield principle] denotes conscious application *insofar as practicable* of principles of management intended to sustain the yield of the resource being managed."

Based upon the text and constitutional history of the sustained yield clause, the State argues that "it allows for some uses, and therefore some resources, to be preferred over others." And Defenders recognize that "[w]hile [the sustained yield clause] requires that all wildlife, including predators, be managed for sustained yield, that does not mean the sustained yield principle precludes 'predator control' in appropriate circumstances." We agree with both these statements and affirm the superior court's ruling "that the management of wildlife resources may constitutionally include a selection between predator and prey populations."

B. The Statutory Principle Of Sustained Yield In Alaska's Intensive Management Statute Applies To The Board's Management Of Predator Populations.

Consistent with the State's position, the superior court found it "unambiguous" that the sustained yield principle in Alaska's intensive management statute—AS 16.05.255—applies only within the context of the Board's management of moose and caribou populations and is inapplicable to the Board's management of predator populations. Defenders counter that the statutory principle of sustained yield, like the constitutional principle, does not distinguish between predator and prey populations. "The interpretation of a statute is a question of law to which we apply our independent judgment"; we interpret statutes "according to reason, practicality, and common sense, considering the meaning of the statute's language, its legislative history, and its purpose."

Alaska's intensive management statute states that "[t]he Board of Game shall adopt regulations to provide for *intensive management* programs to restore the abundance or productivity of identified big game prey populations as necessary to achieve human consumptive use goals of the board." The statute also provides definitions for key terms. "Intensive management" is defined as "management of an identified big game prey population consistent with *sustained yield* through active management measures to enhance, extend, and develop the population to maintain high levels or provide for higher levels of human harvest, including control of predation." "Sustained yield" is defined by the statute as "the achievement and maintenance in perpetuity of the ability to support a high level of human harvest of game, subject to preferences among beneficial uses, on an annual or periodic basis."

Substituting the meaning of the defined terms into *subsection (e)* of the statute produces the following legislative mandate for intensive management:

The Board of Game shall adopt regulations to provide for [management of an identified big game prey population consistent with [the achievement and maintenance in perpetuity of the ability to support a high level of human harvest of *game,* subject to preferences among beneficial uses]] to restore the abundance or productivity of identified big game prey populations as necessary to achieve human consumptive use goals of the board.

From this language it follows that whether or not the statutory principle of sustained yield distinguishes between predator and prey populations depends on the meaning of the word "game." Alaska Statute 16.05.940(19) defines "game" as "any species of bird, reptile, and mammal," suggesting that intensive management must be consistent with a principle of sustained yield which encompasses all animals, including both predator and prey populations.

The State does not provide an alternative construction based upon the statute's language, but argues that Defenders' construction "turns [the] intensive management law into a nonsensical, unworkable mess" by applying the sustained yield principle to predators. According to the State, application of sustained yield to predators requires that the State simultaneously maximize the populations of predators and their prey. We disagree. The language of this implementing legislation does not result in the absurd results the State warns against because the statutory principle of sustained yield, like its constitutional counterpart, contains the qualifier that sustained yield is "subject to preferences among beneficial uses." [48]

Based upon the text of Alaska's intensive management statute, as well as the principle that a statutory construction that is consistent with constitutional principles is preferred over one that is inconsistent, we hold that the principle of sustained yield set forth in Alaska's intensive management statute applies to predator populations but that the management of wildlife resources may include a selection between predator and prey populations.

C. Defenders And West Failed To Meet Their Burden To Prove That The Board's 2006 Predator Control Plans Violate Principles Of Sustained Yield.

Having held that both the constitutional and statutory principles of sustained yield apply to wolf and bear populations, we now consider the contention that the Board failed to apply principles of sustained yield to its 2006 predator control plans. The superior court ruled that "to the extent that [the State's existing management of the predator populations] was challenged by any Plaintiff" it does "not violate th[e] constitutional mandate" of Alaska's sustained yield clause. The court did not reach the question of whether the Board's 2006 plans are consistent with the statutory principle of sustained yield because it determined the statutory mandate did not apply to predators. Appellant and cross-appellants had the burden of demonstrating the invalidity of the Board's 2006 predator control plans. To survive summary judgment, they were required to establish that a genuine issue of material fact was in dispute.

Defenders acknowledge that the sustained yield principle does not preclude predator control in appropriate circumstances, but Defenders contend that the Board did not consider or apply the sustained yield principle to wolves and bears when it adopted its 2006 predator control plans. Defenders argue that we should decline to infer that the Board applied sustained yield when there is no mention or discussion of applying sustained yield to wolf and bear populations in either the Board's predator control plans or in the administrative record. Defenders also argue that the Board's repeal of the express sustained yield requirements . . . along with the statement in its bear management policy that "[g]enerally, bear hunting will be conducted on a sustained yield basis, except in areas where a bear predation control program is authorized" demonstrates that the Board chose *not* to apply sustained yield to wolf and bear populations.

The State argues the Board was not required to apply sustained yield to wolf and bear populations in its predator control plans. Nonetheless, the State maintains that the Board's plans and the supporting administrative record illustrate the conscious application of sustained yield principles, although that term is not used explicitly.

In considering whether the Board actually applied principles of sustained yield when it adopted its 2006 predator control plans, we first examine the language of the plans themselves and observe that the plans do not expressly mention the sustained yield mandate. But the regulation adopting the 2006 plans . . . sets management objectives for the wolf and bear populations in each predator control area, establishes procedures for tracking when predator populations are in danger of falling below the management objectives, and requires that the Board suspend predator control activities and close hunting and trapping seasons when necessary to ensure that minimum population objectives are met. The regulation also sets specific geographic boundaries for predator control areas and includes sunset provisions establishing expiration dates for the Board's authority to engage in predator control.

The regulations also contain numerous statements relating to the continuation and maintenance of wolf and bear populations within predator control areas. For example, the regulations state "it is the intent of this plan to maintain wolves as part of the natural ecosystem within the geographical area described for this plan." In balancing the goal of "substantially reduc[ing] wolf numbers compared to the pre-control level in order to relieve predation pressure on moose and allow for improved recruitment to the moose population" with the goal of "maintain[ing] wolves as part of the natural ecosystem" within the predator control area, the regulation sets a minimum wolf population objective for each plan in order to "ensure that wolves persist within the plan area." The predator control regulation also states that "if wolf predation control efforts continue and the wolf population is reduced according to the wolf population and harvest objectives, the wolf population will be maintained at [the control population objective] for several years, but once the moose population increases and wolf control efforts are discontinued, the wolf population will increase in response to the increased prey base." Even where the regulation sets an objective of reducing black and brown bear populations to "the lowest level possible" within the bear control area in GMU 19(D)-East, the regulation states that "because the [bear control area] is a relatively small geographic area, removing black [and brown] bears from within it will have only a minor effect on the black [and brown] bear population[s] in Unit 19(D)-East overall."

The predator control regulation also provides for continued harvest of wolves and bears for human consumption as an integral component of the predator control plans, setting "annual harvest objective[s]" for wolves and bears in the predator control areas and acknowledging that "some hunters and trappers will continue to pursue wolves . . . regardless of same-day-airborne wolf control efforts."

We also find it significant that while the Board eliminated the regulatory requirements set forth in sections .110 and .115—including the express requirement that it consider sustained yield—it appears that the Board nonetheless adopted its 2006 predator control plans to be consistent with these requirements. The subsection headings in the Board's predator control plans closely mirror the requirements of subsections .110(b) and .115(b), and the content of the predator control plans reflects the substantive requirements of subsections .110(d) and .115(c).

A review of the administrative record demonstrates that the Board considered a great deal of information about how the long-term viability and sustainability of wolf and bear populations would be impacted by predator control efforts. Most significantly with respect to wolf control, the

Board heard testimony from ADF&G biologists that wolf populations would recover to, or even exceed, pre-control levels within three to five years after wolf control ends. And while testimony relating to bears suggested that bear recovery would take longer given the lower reproductive and immigration rates of bears, ADF&G biologists did not suggest that the long-term viability or sustainability of bear populations would be put at risk by the 2006 bear control plans.

Based on our review of the record, we are unpersuaded by Defenders' argument that the Board failed to apply sustained yield altogether. Failing to show that the Board did not apply sustained yield at all, Defenders' burden was to show that the Board's application of sustained yield to predator populations lacked a reasonable basis, was arbitrary or capricious, or failed to consider important factors by showing, for example, that the Board used incorrect estimates of populations, or because harvest levels were set too high. Defenders did not contend that the Board acted arbitrarily in applying sustained yield principles to its 2006 plans; it focused entirely on its claim that the Board failed to apply the sustained yield principles at all. Defenders did express concern over whether the Board's minimum population objectives "will be large enough to permit a yield, sustained or otherwise, now or in the future" but Defenders did not elaborate or support this concern with evidence. Because the Board is entitled to deference in areas where it has special expertise, such as application of sustained yield, Defenders bore a significant burden in demonstrating that it acted in an arbitrary manner. On this record, we must conclude that Defenders failed to meet their burden, and that the superior court properly declined to vacate the 2006 predator control regulations on those grounds.

In reaching this decision, we expressly reject the Board's position that the application of sustained yield to wolf and bear populations in predator control areas is discretionary and based only on its policy view that these "highly valued resources" should be "maintained as healthy and necessary components of our ecosystems," rather than any constitutional or statutory mandate. It is the Board's constitutional and statutory duty to apply principles of sustained yield when it adopts predator control plans; this is not a policy question subject to Board discretion.

NOTES & QUESTIONS

1. Alaska is not the only state to struggle with predator control. For many years, state and federal officials systematically sought to eliminate wolves, bears, mountain lions, and other predators because they preyed on livestock and game species that people wanted to hunt. The federal government even exterminated predators from national parks. *See* ALSTON CHASE, PLAYING GOD IN YELLOWSTONE: THE DESTRUCTION OF AMERICA'S FIRST NATIONAL PARK (1987). Today wildlife management recognizes the critical role that predators play in the natural functioning of an ecosystem. Many (though not all) predators are now protected by the federal Endangered Species Act, so hunting and other forms of predator control of such listed predators is prohibited. States retain their traditional authority to manage the wildlife within their borders so long as they are not protected by the ESA or another federal law. Thus Idaho, Mon-

tana, and Wyoming resumed their management of wolf populations once the wolves that were reintroduced to the Yellowstone ecosystem in 1995 were delisted from the ESA once their population recovered in 2011. See Endangered and Threatened Wildlife and Plants; Removal of the Gray Wolf in Wyoming From the Federal List of Endangered and Threatened Wildlife and Removal of the Wyoming Wolf Population's Status as an Experimental Population, pt. II, 76 Fed. Reg. 61782 (2011).

2. Like Alaska, numerous state constitutions address wildlife management and environmental protection more generally. Most of those provisions have not been viewed as creating any judicially enforceable individual rights, one decision suggests a broader role for such provisions. *See* Montana Environmental Information Center v. Department of Envtl. Quality, 988 P.2d 1236 (Mont.1999) (holding that Montana's constitutional right to a clean and healthful environment mandates that a state statute permitting certain water pollution must satisfy strict scrutiny).

Could constitutional provisions play a greater role with respect to biodiversity? Rodger Schlickeisen, the president of Defenders of Wildlife, has argued that the federal constitution should be amended to include a provision protecting biodiversity. His proposed amendment would state:

> The living resources in the United States are the common property of all the people, including generations yet to come. All persons and their progeny have an inalienable, enforceable right to the benefits of those resources for themselves and their posterity. The United States and every state shall assure that use of those resources is sustainable and that they are conserved and maintained for the benefit of all the people.

Rodger Schlickeisen, *The Argument for a Constitutional Amendment to Protect Living Nature*, in BIODIVERSITY AND THE LAW 234 (William J. Snape III ed. 1996). What is the advantage of including the protection of biodiversity within the constitution? Are there any disadvantages? What laws or actions would be unconstitutional under Schlickeisen's proposed amendment? For an argument against constitutional provisions addressing environmental rights, *see* J.B. Ruhl, *The Metrics of Constitutional Amendments: And Why Proposed Environmental Quality Amendments Don't Measure Up*, 74 NOTRE DAME L. REV. 245 (1999).

3. One of the factors that the federal Endangered Species Act considers when deciding to list a species is the adequacy of the existing regulatory mechanisms available for the protection of the species. *See* ESA § 4(a)(1)(C). This analysis considers both federal and state laws, and thus offers a helpful means of comparing the protection offered by the federal government versus individual states. For example, the listing notice for the seven southeastern mussels indicated that Alabama has commercial harvest guidelines for mussels, Florida imposed a moratorium on the commercial mussel harvest in 1996, and Georgia law places numerous restrictions on the collection of mussels, but that such restrictions are difficult to enforce. See Endangered and Threatened Wildlife and Plants; Determination of Endangered Status for Five Freshwater Mussels and Threatened Status for Two Freshwater Mussels from the Eastern Gulf Slope Drainages of Alabama, Florida, and Georgia, 63 Fed. Reg. 12,664,

12,682–12,683 (1998). The federal ESA, by contrast, prohibits a much larger range of conduct.

Consider also the Fish and Wildlife Service's analysis of the state laws available to protect the population of the Arkansas River shiner (ARS) that lives in three rivers crossing four states. The agency explained:

> Federal and state laws and regulations can protect the ARS and its habitat to some extent. The State of Kansas lists the ARS as a State endangered species. The [Kansas Department of Wildlife and Parks] has designated portions of the mainstem Cimarron, Arkansas, South Fork Ninnescah, and Ninnescah rivers as critical habitat for the shiner. A permit is also required by the State of Kansas for public actions that have the potential to destroy listed individuals or their critical habitat. Subject activities include any publicly funded or State or federally assisted action, or any action requiring a permit from any other State or Federal agency. Violation of the permit constitutes an unlawful taking, a Class A misdemeanor, and is punishable by a maximum fine of $2,500 and confinement for a period not to exceed 1 year. Kansas does not permit the commercial harvest of bait fish from rivers and streams.

> The State of New Mexico lists the ARS as a State endangered species. This listing prohibits the taking of the ARS without a valid scientific collecting permit but does not provide habitat protection. The State of Oklahoma lists the ARS as a State threatened species, but like New Mexico, this listing does not provide habitat protection. The States of Arkansas and Texas provide no special protection for the species or its habitat.

> While Kansas, New Mexico, and Oklahoma protect the ARS from take and/or possession, only Kansas addresses the problem of habitat destruction or modification. Only New Mexico provides significant protection from the potential introduction of non-native, competitive species. Licensed commercial bait dealers in New Mexico may sell bait minnows only within the drainage where they have been collected and cannot sell any State-listed fish species.

> The Kansas legislature can identify a minimum desirable streamflow for a stream as part of the Kansas Water Plan. The Chief Engineer is then required to withhold from appropriation the amount of water necessary to establish and maintain the minimum streamflow. New Mexico and Oklahoma water law does not include provisions for acquisition of instream water rights for protection of fish and wildlife and their habitats. However, Oklahoma indirectly provides some protection of instream uses, primarily by withholding appropriations for flows available less than 35 percent of the time. . .

> The status and threats to the ARS reflect, in part, the inability of these laws and regulations to adequately protect and provide for the conservation of the ARS. Even listing as threatened or endangered by the States of Kansas, New Mexico, and Oklahoma has not reversed the decline of this species.

Endangered and Threatened Wildlife and Plants; Final Rule to List the Arkansas River Basin Population of the Arkansas River Shiner (*Notropis girardi*) as Threatened, 63 Fed. Reg. 64,772, 64,795 (1998).

5. Many environmentalists insist that states are incapable of protecting biodiversity. One concern is that many species live in more than one state, thereby complicating the efforts of any particular state to preserve the species. Another contention posits that states have a disincentive to protect endangered species. As quoted earlier in this chapter, "states are motivated to adopt lower standards of endangered species protection in order to attract development." National Association of Home Builders v. Babbitt, 130 F.3d 1041 (D.C.Cir.1997), *cert. denied*, 524 U.S. 937 (1998). Are those fears well-founded? Are there any ways in which states actually have a greater incentive than the federal government to protect biodiversity?

E. TRIBAL PROTECTION OF BIODIVERSITY

The Northern Arapahoe Tribe v. Hodel

United States Court of Appeals for the Tenth Circuit, 1987.
808 F.2d 741.

■ SEYMOUR, CIRCUIT JUDGE.

The Northern Arapahoe and Shoshone Tribes jointly inhabit the Wind River Indian Reservation in western Wyoming. At the request of the Shoshone Tribe (the Shoshone), the Secretary of the Interior promulgated regulations establishing a game code regulating hunting on the reservation. The Arapahoe Tribe (the Arapahoe) sued the Secretary and other federal officials, seeking declaratory and injunctive relief to prevent enforcement of the regulations. The Shoshone intervened in the litigation as a defendant. The court held a two-day hearing on the request for a preliminary injunction. It thereafter entered an order denying the Arapahoe request for temporary relief and, at the same time and without prior notice, deciding the case on the merits and denying a permanent injunction.

On appeal, the Arapahoe contend that the district court's denial of a permanent injunction should be reversed because the Secretary has no authority to regulate hunting on the reservation and because the Secretary violated the Administrative Procedure Act. Alternatively, they assert that the trial court erred in consolidating the preliminary injunction hearing with a trial on the merits without prior notice, and ask that the case be remanded for trial. We affirm in part, reverse in part, and remand for further proceedings.

I.

BACKGROUND

The Wind River Indian Reservation was established in 1868 pursuant to the Treaty of Fort Bridger, which set aside territory "for the absolute and undisturbed use and occupation of the Shoshonee Indians . . . , and for such other friendly tribes or individual Indians as from time to time they may be willing, with the consent of the United States, to admit amongst them." Treaty between the United States of America and the Eastern Band of Shoshonees and the Bannack Tribe of Indians, July 3, 1868, 15 Stat. 673, 674 (the Treaty). Ten years after signing the Treaty, the United States broke this covenant when it brought a band of Northern Arapahoe onto the reservation under military escort. The Arapahoe had been allies of the Sioux, who were antagonistic toward the Shoshone. Despite the Shoshone's continual and vigorous efforts to have the Arapahoe removed, the United States failed to respond, dealing instead with the two tribes as lawful occupants and equals. The Shoshone ultimately were compensated for the taking of part of the reservation in an amount equal to one-half the value of the land, including the timber and mineral resources.

Today, both tribes inhabit the reservation. According to the superintendent of the Wind River Indian Agency, the combined adult population of the tribes is approximately 5,900. Each tribe governs itself separately by vote of the tribal membership at general council meetings or by vote of its elected business council. A joint business council of representatives from both tribes deals with certain matters of common interest.

The reservation itself encompasses nearly 1.9 million acres and ranges in altitude from 4,200 to over 13,000 feet. This topographical diversity provides habitat for a variety of wildlife, from waterfowl to big and small game. Only enrolled members of the tribes may hunt on the reservation. For the Shoshone and the Arapahoe, hunting is a traditional activity and a source of food.

Over the years, the tribes have submitted the issue of tribal game codes to their general memberships for decision. They have managed reservation wildlife both jointly and separately. In 1948 they enacted a joint game code, but abolished it five years later. Since that time, the only joint regulations have been prohibitions against waste, spotlighting, and the selling or trading of game meat.

In 1977 the tribes expressed concern for game management and called for a study of reservation wildlife. The joint business council passed Resolution No. 3923, which provided:

"WHEREAS: The Joint Shoshone and Arapahoe Business Council is aware of the potential of the wildlife habitat available and increasing game herds on the Wind River Indian Reservation, and

WHEREAS: A sound wildlife program is based on high-quality habitat and proper management of wildlife species, and

WHEREAS: Lack of management and protection of wildlife in the past and unrestricted harvest of wildlife species have occurred,

NOW, THEREFORE BE IT RESOLVED, that the US Fish and Wildlife Service be requested to establish a wildlife biologist position in Lander to assist in collecting data to protect habitat and wildlife, and to manage and insure the optimum potential of wildlife species on the Wind River Indian Reservation now, and for the future."

Pursuant to the joint resolution, the United States Fish and Wildlife Service (FWS) undertook a series of habitat and species studies. FWS reported its findings in various separate reports from 1980 to 1982 and in a comprehensive report in 1982 entitled "A Plan for the Management of Wildlife on the Wind River Reservation" (the 1982 Report). The 1982 Report concluded that the tribes' concern about dwindling herds was justified, and recommended management of all wildlife, particularly big game.[5] In December 1983 and February 1984 FWS conducted aerial big game surveys. Richard Baldes, project leader at the Lander FWS office, testified about the results of these surveys: "The information that we collected is the same. The herds are still going down, and we have serious problems. It hasn't changed. It just strengthened what we were saying before."

The tribes disagreed on the proper course of action in light of the conclusions of the FWS studies. In 1980, two years before the publication of the comprehensive 1982 Report, the Shoshone enacted a game code to govern the tribe's own members, which the Arapahoe General Council subsequently rejected as too restrictive. The Shoshone asked the Secretary to impose a moratorium on all hunting on the reservation until the two tribes could agree on a game code. The Associate Solicitor of Indian Affairs declined to intervene, opting instead to encourage the tribes to resolve the matter. In June 1983 the Arapahoe membership again considered enactment of a game code, but voted to table the issue.

At various times during the spring and fall of 1983, officials from the Bureau of Indian Affairs (BIA) met with the tribes both jointly and separately and expressed their concern about the need for a game code. The biggest meeting was held in September in Billings, attended by representatives from both tribes, their attorneys, and BIA officials from Washington and the regional office. At that meeting, BIA officials discussed the possibility that the federal government would have to issue regulations in order to fulfill its trust responsibility. The Arapahoe tribal council asked for more time, indicating that it would try to establish a code by January 1984.

The hard winter of 1983–1984 forced many of the big game herds to seek shelter and forage in the lower elevations of the reservation. This movement made big game vulnerable to hunters, particularly those with snowmobiles and four-wheel drive vehicles. Reports of a "massive elk kill" in December 1983 prompted wide publicity and a plea from the chairmen of the Shoshone and Arapahoe business councils for tribal members to exercise restraint in the hunting of big game.

The Arapahoe failed to enact a game code by January 1984, its preferred target date. Meetings among the tribes and BIA officials continued through the spring. The Arapahoe membership voted in May not to

---

[5] The regulations promulgated by the Secretary define big game as "any one of the following species of animals: elk, mule deer, whitetail deer, bighorn sheep, moose, antelope, black and grizzly bear, and mountain lion." 25 C.F.R. § 244.2 (1986).

enact a game code. After meeting further with both tribes in July, BIA officials informed them it would accede to the Shoshone request to impose federal regulations.

On October 5 the BIA published an interim rule entitled "Wind River Reservation Game Code," which is the subject of this lawsuit. *See* 49 Fed. Reg. 39,308 (1984) (codified at 25 C.F.R. pt. 244 (1986)). The game code was designed to establish "a controlled wildlife hunting program on the Wind River Reservation in order to conserve, protect and increase the existing wildlife in the reservation area.". . . By its terms, the game code will remain in effect only until the tribes jointly enact a game code. *See* 25 C.F.R. § 244.1(a).

The game code provides that in 1984 the Wind River Agency Superintendent, an employee of the BIA, would establish the hunting seasons, define the hunting areas, set permit fees, and establish season limits for all wildlife. In subsequent years, the superintendent is to make those determinations before each June 1 after consulting with the tribes. In 1984, all enrolled members who wished to hunt were required to purchase a permit at a cost of $5.00, as well as big game tags at $1.00 per species. The only big game that could legally be harvested were elk, antlered deer, and buck antelope, and those only during specific hunting seasons. Hunting of bighorn sheep, moose, black bear, and mountain lion was prohibited. Other rules were established for hunting or trapping furbearing animals, upland game, and waterfowl. Substantial civil and criminal penalties and forfeitures may be imposed for violations of the regulations. After the game code was implemented, the Wind River Agency Superintendent obtained equipment and employed five federal enforcement agents.

On October 23, 1984, shortly after the regulations were imposed, the Arapahoe filed this action for declaratory and injunctive relief and moved for a temporary restraining order (TRO) to prevent enforcement of the game code. The Shoshone moved to intervene and opposed the issuance of temporary or preliminary relief. On October 24 and 25 the district court held hearings on the motion for a TRO. The Arapahoe filed fifty identical affidavits from members of the tribe, each averring that the affiant had hunted regularly on the reservation for a number of years, that he planned to hunt during the fall, that he hunted only for food, and that enforcement of the regulations would leave him and his family without an adequate food supply. The Arapahoe relied entirely on these affidavits at the hearing, presenting no other evidence.

The Government offered the testimony of two witnesses. Richard Baldes of FWS stated his opinion that the regulation was necessary to protect the reservation's game resources. He testified that, if hunting continued at its present rate, moose and bighorn sheep might become extinct or endangered on the reservation. He further stated that, while prong horn antelope and mule deer were in danger of being eliminated from the reservation if hunting continued at past rates, elimination probably would not occur for several years. Baldes also stated that management of furbearing animals was neither necessary nor a concern of the tribes. Lavern William

Collier, Wind River Agency superintendent, testified that since implementation of the code, 103 permits had been sold, no violations had been found, and hunting had been somewhat light. In response to the allegations by Arapahoe tribal members that the regulation would leave them without sufficient food, Collier testified that each enrolled Arapahoe member received a $235 monthly allotment derived from the reservation's assets and that various food and assistance programs were available to needy families.

[The district court denied the Arapahoe motion for a temporary restraining order, and the Arapahoe appealed.]

II.

REGULATION OF HUNTING ON THE WIND RIVER RESERVATION

. . . The Arapahoe contend that the Secretary lacks any authority to regulate on-reservation hunting by Indians and that, even if he has such authority in exigent circumstances, the fact-finding below was inadequate to determine that the wildlife on the reservation have been hunted "to a point of endangerment or extinction." The Secretary and the Shoshone maintain that, in the absence of a jointly-adopted tribal game code, the Secretary has authority to regulate hunting on the reservation pursuant to his responsibility as trustee in accordance with the Treaty and his general authority under 25 U.S.C. §§ 2 and 9 (1982).

A. The Rights of Both Tribes to Hunt and Fish

As an initial matter, the Shoshone claim that they possess exclusive treaty rights to hunt and fish on the reservation and that the Arapahoe have no such special rights. Although the Treaty does not expressly mention hunting or fishing rights, these rights were included by implication in the setting aside of the reservation for the Shoshone's "absolute and undisturbed use and occupation," Treaty of July 3, 1868, 15 Stat. 673, 674. The Shoshone contend that their treaty rights to hunt and fish were neither lost nor diminished by the congressional and executive acts recognizing the settlement of the Arapahoe on the reservation, and that the Arapahoe cannot claim treaty rights to hunt and fish by virtue of their coexistence on the reservation. The Shoshone further submit that, although they were compensated for the Arapahoe presence on the reservation in an amount equal to one-half the value of the land including timber and mineral resources, they were never compensated for the loss of their exclusive treaty rights to hunt and fish.

We are not persuaded. The very principles of Indian law which dictate that the Shoshone have hunting and fishing rights notwithstanding the lack of an express treaty provision dictate that the Arapahoe have equivalent rights. The Arapahoe have rights to the reservation derived from their status as occupants of the land confirmed by congressional and executive acts. The rights to hunt and fish are part of the tribes' larger rights of possession. Whether by treaty or by congressional and executive acts, the Shoshone and the Arapahoe have equal rights to hunt on the reservation.

B. Authority of the Secretary

Actions of the Secretary and those under his authority are subject to judicial review under principles of administrative law. Furthermore, in Indian matters, as in other areas, federal executive officials are limited to the authority conferred on them by Congress. "The rulemaking power granted to an administrative agency . . . is not the power to make law. Rather, it is 'the power to adopt regulations to carry into effect the will of Congress. . .' " Santa Fe Industries, Inc. v. Green, 430 U.S. 462, 472 (1977) (quoting Ernst & Ernst v. Hochfelder, 425 U.S. 185, 213–14 (1976)). We thus must determine if the Secretary has been granted authority sufficient to support his enactment of the regulations.

The district court found that "historically, the Shoshone and Northern Arapahoe Tribes now occupying the Wind River Reservation have been free to self-regulate the hunting activities of tribal members on the reservation." The Government does not dispute that the primary authority to regulate hunting lies with the tribes, consistent with their sovereignty over the reservation land and resources. The narrower question presented in this appeal is whether authority exists for the Secretary, at the request of one of the tribes, to adopt interim hunting regulations as a necessary conservation measure to protect endangered wildlife and game on the reservation.

1. 25 U.S.C. §§ 2 and 9.

Congress has delegated to the Secretary broad authority to manage Indian affairs, *see* 25 U.S.C. § 2, and to promulgate regulations relating to Indian affairs, *see id.* § 9. Sections 2 and 9, however, do not vest the Secretary with general regulatory authority. Section 2 delegates the general management of Indian affairs and relations to the Secretary of the Interior and Commissioner of Indian Affairs. The language of section 9 vests authority "for carrying into effect the various provisions of any act relating to Indian affairs." 25 U.S.C. § 9. Given the language of the statute and the fact that hunting on the reservation has historically been a matter of tribal self-regulation, we are reluctant to hold that sections 2 and 9 by themselves could support the regulations. For the reasons set out below, however, we conclude that Sections 2 and 9 together with the Treaty, construed in accordance with the special relationship between the United States and Indian tribes, provide the necessary authority for the Secretary to enact these regulations.

2. The Relationship Between the Federal Government and Indian Tribes

The United States has a unique relationship with Indian tribes "derived from [their] separate constitutional status," and their existence as quasi-sovereign governments. Drawing upon the concept of a protectorate or alliance relationship founded upon agreement by treaty, Chief Justice John Marshall described Indian tribes as "domestic dependent nations" which "look to our government for protection." Cherokee Nation v. Georgia, 30 U.S. (5 Pet.) 1, 17 (1831); *see* Worcester v. Georgia, 31 U.S. (6 Pet.) 515, 551–52 (1832). The Supreme Court has recognized "the undisputed existence of a general trust relationship between the United States and the Indian people." United States v. Mitchell, 463 U.S. 206 (1983). "This principle has long dominated the Government's dealings with Indians." *Id.*

3. The Treaty and the Trust Responsibility

The Treaty of 1868 was intended to preserve for the Shoshone a reservation land base with sufficient resources to supply the needs of the Indian people who settled thereon. In the Treaty, the Government undertook the responsibility to protect the persons and property of the Shoshone from wrongdoers "among the whites, or among other people subject to the authority of the United States." Treaty of July 3, 1868, 15 Stat. 673. The right to hunt on the reservation is held in common by both tribes, and one tribe cannot claim that right to a point of endangering the resource in derogation of the other tribe's rights. Under the Treaty, the Government has the right upon request of the Shoshone to protect the resources guaranteed the Shoshone by treaty from misappropriation by third parties. The Government's right extends to preventing overuse by the Arapahoe of their shared right when that overuse endangers the resource and threatens to divest the Shoshone of their right. Because the right to the resource is shared, however, federal regulation of hunting on the reservation must accommodate the rights of both tribes.

When viewed in light of the trust responsibility and the Shoshone's specific request for regulation, the Treaty along with 2 U.S.C. §§ 2 and 9 support the Secretary's authority to establish an interim game code on the reservation when there exists a risk of extinction or endangerment of the wildlife. If the facts support such a risk, the Secretary may implement reasonable interim measures so long as the tribes fail to enact their own game code.

[The court also rejected several procedural objections to the Game Code, and remanded for a trial on the merits.]

NOTES & QUESTIONS

1. The interim game code was finalized with minor modifications soon after the Tenth Circuit's decision. *See* Wind River Reservation Game Code, 52 Fed. Reg. 23805 (1987).

2. Native Americans have an excellent reputation for their treatment of biodiversity. The romanticized version of the relationship of Native Americans to their natural surroundings asserts that "[w]hen Indians alone cared for the American earth, this continent was clothed in a green robe of forests, unbroken grasslands, and useful desert plants, filled with an abundance of wildlife." J. DONALD HUGHES, AMERICAN INDIAN ECOLOGY 1–2 (1983). The continuing concern that Native Americans have for biodiversity is evidenced by stories of the restoration of wetlands and other degraded habitats and by efforts to facilitate the recovery of disappearing species of trout and wolves. Native Americans often possess information about native wildlife and vegetation that conservation biologists have not yet uncovered. *See generally* BIODIVERSITY AND NATIVE AMERICA (Paul E. Minnis & Wayne J. Elisens eds. 2000) (collection of essays exploring how Native Americans have addressed biodiversity).

But not every observer sees a consistent pattern of regard for wildlife and plants. Consider two different accounts of the native treatment of buffalo in the nineteenth century. On one view, "[t]he Plains hunters expressed their thanks for the gifts of the buffalo by killing only as many as they needed and by using every part of the animals." *Id.* at 7. By contrast, other scholars describe "Indians who ate only the buffalo's tongue, only the fetus, or only the hump, or who abandoned bulls because they preferred cows." Krech, *supra*, at 142. Many of the current disputes are the result of the tribal view of wildlife and plants as essential resources for their physical and cultural survival. That attitude has prompted conflicts between tribes and contemporary environmentalists on several issues. *See, e.g.*, Cook Inlet Beluga Whale v. Daley, 156 F.Supp.2d 16, 18, 20 (D.D.C. 2001) (describing how Native American hunting of about 77 Cook Inlet Beluga whales annually is "the single most significant factor in the population decline" of the whale). Native American hunting practices have evoked complaints from those who want to prohibit hunting of certain species, or to prohibit hunting altogether. The desperate economic conditions that exist on many Indian reservations have prompted some tribes to authorize development activities opposed by many environmentalists. And, as discussed at pages 260–68, Native American religious ceremonies sometimes employ parts of bald eagles, panthers, and other species that are now protected by federal and state law. In each instance, the tribal way of life has presented challenges to today's conceptions about the preservation of biodiversity.

3. Indian tribes enjoy a unique relationship to each state and to the United States as a whole. Early in the nineteenth century, Chief Justice John Marshall explained that Indian tribes are sovereign nations that are subject to the higher power of the federal government. *See* Worcester v. Georgia, 31 U.S. (6 Pet.) 515 (1832); Cherokee Nation v. Georgia, 30 U.S. (5 Pet.) 1 (1831). The sovereign status of Indian tribes led the federal government to enter into numerous treaties with individual tribes throughout the nineteenth century. Like the Treaty of Fort Bridger at issue in *The Northern Arapahoe Tribe*, many of those treaties provided that the tribes ceded most of their lands in exchange for rights to use the lands that the tribes retained. As Sandra Zellmer explains, "These retained lands are critical to tribal sovereignty and, indeed, the very survival of tribes as distinct cultural and political communities." Sandra B. Zellmer, *Indian Lands as Critical Habitat for Indian Nations and Endangered Species: Tribal Survival and Sovereignty Come First*, 43 S.D. L. REV. 381 (1998).

The relative rights of tribes, the federal government, and the state government regarding wildlife continues to generate substantial litigation. *See, e.g.*, Minnesota v. Mille Lacs Band of Chippewa Indians, 526 U.S. 172 (1999) (holding 5–4 that the Chippewa Indians still retain hunting, fishing, and gathering rights guaranteed by a 1837 treaty with the United States); BEAN & ROWLAND, *supra*, at 450–64 (analyzing state authority to regulate hunting and fishing by Native Americans on reservation lands and off reservation lands, federal authority to regulate Native American hunting and fishing, and tribal regulation of hunting and fishing by non-Indians on reservation lands). In particular, there is a tension between federal efforts to protect biodiversity the sovereignty enjoyed by tribes. Notwithstanding the *Billie* case reprinted below at page 260, it is still uncertain whether the ESA abrogates treaties affording tribal hunting and fishing rights when endangered species are at stake. Another controversy involves the designation of tribal lands as the critical habitat of a species pursuant to the ESA. Professor Zellmer contends that critical habitat "designation flies in the face of the United States' solemn promises to preserve tribal homelands for the undisturbed use of Indian nations and to protect tribal sovereignty from external incursions." Zellmer, *supra*, at 382. For the federal government's view of how the Indian ESA affects tribes, visit U.S. Fish & Wildlife Service, Working with Tribes: Overview, http://www.fws.gov/endangered/what-we-do/tribes-overview.html.

4. In 2012, the FWS announced its intention to empower the Confederated Salish and Kootenai Tribes (CSKT) to manage the National Bison Range Complex in northwestern Montana. According to the FWS, the benefits of the proposed arrangement include "closer cooperation with its professional peers employed by the CSKT Division of Fish, Wildlife, Conservation and Recreation, who have extensive scientific knowledge, significant traditional ecological knowledge, and a long and successful history of conserving, managing, and restoring the fish, wildlife, and habitat resources of the Flathead Reservation" and furthering and supporting tribal self-governance. Notice of Intent to Prepare an Environmental Assessment Regarding the Interest of the Confederated Salish and Kootenai Tribes to enter into an Annual Funding Agreement with the Department of the Interior, U. S. Fish and Wildlife Service, for the Operation and Management of Programs at the National Bison Range Complex, 77 Fed. Reg. (forthcoming 2012). But the Public Employees for Environmental Responsibility object that the plan "would improperly contract out major federal functions without adequate oversight to protect taxpayer." PEER, Press release, New Plan for Outsourcing National Bison Range to Tribe — Tribal Takeover Resembles Agreement Invalidated by Federal Court in 2010 (May 15, 2012). Should we encourage or discourage tribal management of biodiversity on federal public lands?

PART 2

THE ENDANGERED SPECIES ACT

CHAPTER 4 Identifying Which Species to Protect

CHAPTER 5 Federal Government Responsibilities

CHAPTER 6 The Take Prohibition

The Endangered Species Act is the most revered and reviled of federal environmental laws. Its champions praise it for saving the bald eagle from extinction, for blocking many misconceived development projects, and for providing a tool to protect ecosystems ranging from the southern California coast to the majestic forests of Pacific northwest. Its detractors accuse it of sacrificing timber jobs for obscure owls, nearly completed dams for tiny fish, and small farmers for unknown rodents. The basis for these claims lies in the unparalleled stringency of the ESA's provisions. Most other environmental statutes contain numerous opportunities for environmental interests to be balanced against other human needs. The ESA, by contrast, has long been viewed as requiring efforts "to halt and reverse the trend toward species extinction, *whatever the cost.*" Tennessee Valley Authority v. Hill, 437 U.S. 153, 184 (1978) (emphasis added). There are some who question whether the ESA is really so intransigent, *see* Oliver A. Houck, *The Endangered Species Act and Its Implementation by the U.S. Departments of Interior and Commerce*, 64 U. COLO. L. REV. 277, 292 (1993) (asserting that the actual implementation of the ESA is much more relaxed), but the fact that environmentalists turn to the ESA to save whole ecosystems when other laws fail suggests that the common impression of the ESA is well founded.

The ESA was the culmination of nearly a century of legislation to protect rare wildlife. Most of the early statutes were enacted by states, consistent with Supreme Court's view that the states owned all of the wildlife within their borders. *See* Geer v. Connecticut, 161 U.S. 519 (1896). But the problem of extinctions soon gained national attention. John Lacey, a member of Congress from Iowa, worried that the passenger pigeon, "formerly in this country in flocks of millions, has entirely disappeared from the face of the earth." So in 1900, Congress passed the Lacey Act— the first federal wildlife statute—to aid state wildlife preservation efforts by making it a federal crime to transport across state lines any wildlife killed in violation of state law. But the law did not prevent the passenger pigeon from going extinct when the last bird died in the Cincinnati Zoo in 1914, nor did it save the Carolina parakeet, the heath hen, and a growing number of other species once found in the United States.

The whooping crane is often credited with motivating federal efforts to devise a program to save rare wildlife from extinction. At one time, the whooping crane lived throughout the middle of the United States and in Canada, but fewer than thirty survived by the 1940's. The seemingly imminent demise of the whooping crane prompted federal officials, the Canadian government, and the National Audubon Society to begin the first concerted attempt to save a particular species from extinction. Still, it was not until 1966 that Congress enacted the first federal statute aimed at saving vanishing wildlife and plants. The Endangered Species Preservation Act, Pub. L. No. 89–669, 80 Stat. 926 (1966), directed the Secretary of the Interior to use existing land acquisition authorities to purchase the habitat of native fish and wildlife that were threatened with extinction, and it instructed the Secretary to "encourage other Federal agencies to utilize, where practicable, their authorities" to further the preservation effort. Congress expanded the effort three years later with the Endangered Species Conservation Act of 1969, Pub. L. No. 91–135, 83 Stat. 275 (1969), which authorized the creation of a list of species "threatened with worldwide extinction" and prohibited the importation of most such species into the United States. Yet even then the concept of an "endangered species" was so new that the term itself did not appear in a federal court decision until 1973—and then it was used to describe not an animal on the brink of extinction, but the Internal Revenue Code. *See* Dennis v. Commissioner, 473 F.2d 274, 286 (5th Cir.1973).

Almost immediately, the 1969 law was criticized for not going far enough. The law did not prohibit the hunting or collecting or killing of a listed species, it did not regulate conduct that destroyed the habitat of a species, and it did not offer any protection at all to plants. Throughout 1972 and 1973, Congress considered a range of proposed bills that would provide much more powerful protections for any wildlife or plant species that was facing extinction. But the debate in Congress always referred to bald eagles, grizzly bears, whooping cranes, alligators, whales, and other prominent species now described as "charismatic megafauna." Few members of Congress wanted to be seen as opposed to such popular animals, and few were. The Senate approved its bill 92–0, and after several minor changes, the final bill passed the House 355–4. So on December 28, 1973, President Nixon signed the Endangered Species Act, Pub. L. No. 93–205, 87 Stat. 884 (1973) (codified at 16 U.S.C. §§ 1531-1544)—what we have known since as the ESA.

The first reported case under the new law involved a water dispute between cattle ranchers in Nevada and the endangered Devil's Hole pupfish. *See* United States v. Cappaert, 508 F.2d 313 (9th Cir.1974). Shortly thereafter, though, another case emerged that has colored the perception of the

ESA ever since. Much to the chagrin of the United States Fish & Wildlife Service (FWS) and many of the members of Congress who had just voted for the ESA, the listing of the snail darter as endangered resulted in a Supreme Court decision holding that the nearly completed Tellico Dam could not be finished because the resulting reservoir would wipe out the fish. (The case—*Tennessee Valley Authority v. Hill*—is reprinted below at page 228). That decision caused Congress to amend the statute, albeit in a relatively modest fashion. Several other amendments occurred in 1982, but since then the law has remained virtually unchanged.

The congressional failure to amend the law is not for want of trying. During the early 1990s, environmentalists pressed to expand the coverage of the ESA to include whole ecosystems that were imperilled by human developments or other causes. Conversely, the ESA was blamed for causing economic dislocation throughout the Pacific northwest as a result of the listing of the northern spotted owl. The first sustained effort to reform—or gut, depending on your perspective—the ESA occurred in 1994. Speaker of the House Newt Gingrich established an ESA task force that held hearings across the country in areas that had chafed under the restrictions of the law. Landowners and developers told horror stories of widows losing their life's savings when the presence of an endangered songbird prevented them from building on their land and of farmers facing federal prosecutions for attempting to prevent fires in a manner that harmed endangered kangaroo rats. Several bills were introduced to amend the ESA by requiring more rigorous scientific evidence before a species could be listed, helping private landowners who confront a listed species on their property, and speeding recovery efforts so that a species could be delisted. The bills stalled in the face of a certain presidential veto and pressure from environmentalists, religious leaders, moderate eastern politicians, and others who were intent on saving rare wildlife.[1] The process repeated itself again in 2005, when the House of Representatives approved the Threatened and Endangered Species Act of 2005 (TESRA), which would overhaul the recovery planning process, repeal the ESA's critical habitat provisions, provide additional incentives for private actions to conserve protected species, and most controversially, mandate government compensation of landowners who are adversely affected by the ESA's land use regulations. The Senate deferred action on any ESA amendments until 2006.

As amended, the ESA has ten sections. The statute's principal provisions are as follows:

§ 2—congressional findings and purposes of the law

§ 3—definitions of key statutory terms

§ 4—procedures for listing a species as "endangered" or "threatened"

---

[1] For an account describing perhaps the unlikeliest foe of the proposed changes to the ESA, *see* Michael J. Bean, *The Gingrich That Saved the ESA*, ENVTL. FORUM, at 26–32 (1999).

§ 5—authority to purchase land to conserve wildlife and plants, not just listed species

§ 6—means of encouraging federal cooperation with state preservation efforts

§ 7—duties imposed on federal agencies to conserve listed species and not to jeopardize the continued existence of a species or its critical habitat

§ 8—means of encouraging cooperation with the efforts of foreign governments to preserve listed species

§ 9—prohibition on killing, harming, smuggling, or any other "taking" of any endangered species

§ 10—permits and exceptions from the prohibitions in section 9

§ 11—enforcement mechanisms and penalties for violating the law

§ 18—Secretary of the Interior's duty to provide an annual report to Congress on the cost of measures to preserve each listed species

The ESA charges the Secretary of the Interior with the primary responsibility for implementing the act with respect to most kinds of species. The Secretary, in turn, has delegated that authority to the United States Fish & Wildlife Service (FWS), an agency within the Department of the Interior. An exception to that structure exists for marine species, which are under the jurisdiction of the Secretary of Commerce, who has delegated that statutory authority to the National Marine Fisheries Service (NMFS)(also known as "NOAA-Fisheries"). Thus, the FWS and the NMFS are the federal agencies with the most responsibility for enforcing the ESA, though the law also calls upon all federal agencies to support that effort (as described in chapter 5).

The following three chapters examine the three major issues raised by the ESA. Chapter 4 explains and analyzes the procedure for identifying which species are "endangered" or "threatened" and thus entitled to the statute's protections. Chapter 5 addresses the duties that the ESA imposes on the FWS and other federal agencies. Chapter 6 details the increasingly controversial provisions that restrict the actions of private individuals, corporate developers, and state and local governments alike. The concluding section of this Part evaluates the success of the ESA and considers the statute's future.

There are, of course, many extremely helpful sources of information about the ESA. The provisions of the law are detailed in STANFORD ENVIRONMENTAL LAW SOCIETY, THE ENDANGERED SPECIES ACT (2001); MICHAEL J. BEAN & MELANIE J. ROWLAND, THE EVOLUTION OF NATIONAL WILDLIFE LAW 198–276 (3d ed. 1997); and RICHARD LITTELL, ENDANGERED SPECIES AND OTHER PROTECTED SPECIES: FEDERAL LAW AND REGULATION (1992). Current information about the law, lists of protected species, and succinct explanations of the ESA's provisions are available at the FWS's web site at http://www.fws.gov/endangered. REBUILDING THE ARK: NEW PERSPECTIVES

ON ENDANGERED SPECIES REFORM (Jonathan Adler ed., 2011); and THE ENDANGERED SPECIES ACT AT THIRTY (Dale D. Goble, J. Michael Scott & Frank W. Davis eds. 2006), provide insightful collections of essays on the working of the law and possible reforms. For more popular accounts of the ESA and its implementation, see JOE ROMAN, LISTED: DISPATCHES FROM AMERICA'S ENDANGERED SPECIES ACT (2011); CHARLES C. MANN & MARK L. PLUMMER, NOAH'S CHOICE: THE FUTURE OF ENDANGERED SPECIES (1995).

CHAPTER 4

IDENTIFYING WHICH SPECIES TO PROTECT

Chapter Outline:
A. Identifying Species
B. Identifying Threats to Species
C. The Listing Decision Process
D. Case Study: The Black-Tailed Prairie Dog

The title of the ESA provides an accurate description of the scope of the law. The law only applies to a species that is "endangered" or "threatened." The ESA offers no help to deer and cardinals and dolphins because they are not endangered or threatened with extinction, so a landowner can "take" a deer without threat of federal sanction. More importantly, the ESA protects only those species that have been formally listed as endangered or threatened. The ESA operates to protect species only once they are formally listed, no matter how endangered they may be in fact.

The ESA's other limitation is that it applies to species, not to individual animals or entire ecosystems. The demise of a popular animal such as Ling-Ling, the panda who lived in Washington's National Zoo, can be cause for sadness, but the ESA's sole concern is about the survival of the panda as a species. The only exceptions to the focus on a whole species involve the ESA's protection of "subspecies" and of separate populations of a species. Similarly, while increased understanding of the importance of ecosystems has prompted numerous calls for an endangered ecosystems act, no such statute has yet emerged from Congress.

Section 4 of the ESA describes the procedure by which a species is designated as "endangered" or "threatened." The procedure has been criticized in recent years both by landowners and developers who believe that many species are listed without adequate scientific studies, and by environmentalists who complain that the federal government has moved much too slowly to add disappearing species to the list. The controversy about the listing process even resulted in a temporary moratorium on the listing of any new species during most of 1995 and the beginning of 1996. The moratorium was supposed to have enabled Congress to address the problems with the listing process, but the absence of a sufficient consensus about which changes were appropriate has left the listing process unchanged since the last congressional amendments to section 4 in 1982.

A. IDENTIFYING SPECIES

United States v. Guthrie

United States Court of Appeals for the Eleventh Circuit, 1995.
50 F.3d 936.

■ CARNES, CIRCUIT JUDGE:

[In 1990, Robert Waites Guthrie asked an undercover agent working for the U.S. Department of the Interior whether the agent could obtain any Alabama red-bellied turtles, a species that had been listed as endangered in 1987. Guthrie explained that he planned to buy up the remaining wild of Alabama red-bellied turtles that lived in the wild, and then apply for a government grant to reintroduce the turtles into the wild from his own private stock. Guthrie was charged with illegally taking, possessing, selling and transporting the turtles in violation of the ESA. He moved to dismiss the charge alleging that the Alabama red-bellied turtle is a hybrid, and thus it was improperly listed as a "species" under the ESA. Guthrie asked the court to authorize a DNA study to determine whether the turtle was a hybrid or a pure species. When the district court refused, Guthrie entered a conditional guilty plea that preserved his right to appeal the court's ruling on the species question. The district court sentenced Guthrie to thirteen months in prison with three years supervised release, and it ordered him to pay $150 in special assessments and $5,000 as a fine or as a donation to the state or federal government efforts to preserve the Alabama red-bellied turtle.]

The Alabama red-bellied turtle

The Secretary of the Interior ("the Secretary") has authority under the ESA to promulgate a list of endangered and threatened species to be protected under the Act. *See* 16 U.S.C.A. § 1533 (1985).[1] The ESA defines "endangered species" as "any species which is in danger of extinction throughout all or a significant portion of its range," 16 U.S.C.A. § 1532(6) (1985), and "threatened species" as "any species which is likely to become an endangered species within the foreseeable future throughout all or a significant portion of its range." 16 U.S.C.A. § 1532(20) (1985). In July 1986, the Secretary proposed listing the Alabama red-bellied turtle as a threatened species. 51 Fed. Reg. 24,727 (1986). Eleven months later, he adopted a regulation listing the turtle as an endangered species. 52 Fed. Reg. 22,939 (1987). During the process, the Secretary changed the status of the turtle from threatened to endangered, and he did so in response to one of the public comments received in support of the turtle's protection. Neither Guthrie nor anyone else submitted any public comments opposed to listing the turtle.

The ESA provides a petition process for agency review, *see* 16 U.S.C.A. § 1533(b)(3)(A) (1985 & Supp.1994), and it also authorizes citizen suits to challenge whether the Secretary has met his duties under the act. 16 U.S.C.A. § 1540(g) (1985). In the seven years since the regulation listing the Alabama red-bellied turtle as an endangered species was adopted, neither Guthrie nor anyone else has attempted to have the regulation reviewed by either of these authorized means. Instead, having willfully violated the regulation, Guthrie now seeks to collaterally attack its validity in this criminal proceeding. Guthrie's sole defense to the charge that his conduct violated the ESA is that the Alabama red-bellied turtle is not a species, that the Secretary therefore lacked the authority to list it as an endangered species, and that as a result, the ESA does not entitle the Alabama red-bellied turtle to protection.

. . . Guthrie did not seek to change the agency regulation. He chose to violate the law. We will not reward that choice by allowing him to bypass the agency and receive judicial review of the regulation in light of the new DNA study. Instead, Guthrie at most is entitled to the same review he would have received had he sought direct review of the agency regulation at the time it was promulgated. Such review is limited to the evidence before the agency at that time. . .

On direct review of the Secretary's decision to list the Alabama red-bellied turtle as an endangered species, we would hold that decision unlawful only if we found it to be "arbitrary, capricious, an abuse of discretion, or otherwise not in accordance with law." This arbitrary and capricious standard applies to the Secretary's finding that "the Alabama red-bellied turtle is considered to be a valid species." Having reviewed the sources and studies

---

[1] The Secretary of the Interior shares authority with the Secretary of Commerce, with each being authorized to list different animals. *See* 16 U.S.C.A. § 1532 (1985). With the general exception of marine animals, most species (including the Alabama red-bellied turtle) fall within the authority of the Secretary of the Interior, who has delegated that authority to the Fish and Wildlife Service. *See* 48 Fed. Reg. 29,990, 29,997 (1983); *see also* 50 C.F.R. § 402.01(b) (1993); Reorganization Plan No. 4 of 1970, *reprinted in* 1970 U.S.C.C.A.N. at 6326. Because the Fish and Wildlife Service is part of the Department of the Interior and thus under the Secretary's control, for simplicity's sake we refer to the Secretary, even though the Fish and Wildlife Service actually took the administrative actions in question.

cited by the Secretary in support of this finding, we conclude that the Secretary did not act arbitrarily or capriciously when he found the Alabama red-bellied turtle to be a valid species.

In its proposed regulation, the Secretary acknowledged that "the taxonomic status of this turtle has been questioned . . . and questions still remain regarding its relationships with other members of the *Pseudemys rubriventris* group, specifically the Florida red-bellied turtle. . ." The Secretary then cited two texts by the same herpetologist questioning the taxonomic status of the species. In the final regulation, the Secretary listed six other texts in support of his finding that the Alabama red-bellied turtle is nevertheless a valid species. The eight texts cited by the Secretary reflect the scientific history behind the Secretary's conclusion that the Alabama red-bellied turtle is a separate species.

The Alabama red-bellied turtle was first classified as a species with the name "Pseudemys alabamensis" by a herpetologist named Baur in 1893. In the 1930s, another herpetologist named Archie Carr authored an article and a book questioning whether the Alabama red-bellied turtle was a species. In the article, Carr concluded that Pseudemys alabamensis was not a species but likely "a mutant occurring in [Pseudemys] mobiliensis and suwanniensis." In the book, Carr catalogued the morphological traits of several species from the floridana group of turtles before stating that "it seems nearly certain that another Gulf coast turtle known to herpetologists for the last fifty years as P. alabamensis, and characterized by having a deep notch and toothlike cusps at the tip of the upper jaw, is really just a variant form that occurs with apparently equal frequency among [two different subspecies of turtle in the family Emydidae]."

Five years after his book was published, Carr changed his position in an article he co-authored with John W. Crenshaw, Jr. Carr and Crenshaw explained that in reaching his earlier conclusion that the Alabama red-bellied turtle was not a species, Carr had examined specimens of the turtle from New Orleans, Mobile, and Crystal River in Florida, and had observed that they exhibited characteristics of other turtles in those areas. Carr and Crenshaw then distinguished the Alabama red-bellied turtle from Pseudemys floridana based on different morphological characteristics from the ones Carr had noted previously, especially the presence of head markings in the shape of a pre-frontal arrow. The herpetologists also suggested that at least one of Carr's Crystal River turtles may have been misidentified. They concluded that the Alabama red-bellied turtle was indeed a separate species, despite its apparent intergradation with two different groups of emydid turtles.

Since Carr and Crenshaw's publication, the authors of five other books and studies cited by the Secretary have agreed that the Alabama red-bellied turtle, Pseudemys alabamensis, deserves separate species status. Some of these scientists have concurred in this status even while noting that unresolved taxonomic questions remain.

The final study relied upon by the Secretary was published just two years before the Secretary's decision. It reclassifies some of the turtle specimens labeled Pseudemys alabamensis by Carr and Crenshaw, and finds that the Alabama red-bellied turtle is a "valid species" that "is endemic to Alabama." After trapping twelve rivers and the lakes on one island, Dobie found Alabama red-bellied turtles only along the Mobile River system, suggesting that earlier studies which found the Alabama red-bellied turtle as widely spread as Texas and Florida had misidentified the examined turtles. Dobie and the later sources thus re-affirmed the resurrected species status of Pseudemys alabamensis, the Alabama red-bellied turtle.

Given scientific support from numerous herpetologists, the Secretary did not act arbitrarily or capriciously when he listed the Alabama red-bellied turtle as an endangered species. This circuit is "highly deferential" to an agency's consideration of the factors relevant to its decision. The Secretary noted that the Alabama red-bellied turtle's status had indeed been questioned in the past, and thus he did not "entirely fail[ ] to consider an important aspect of the problem." Nor was the Secretary's finding "so implausible that it could not be ascribed to a difference in view or the product of agency expertise." Having examined the articles, studies, and books relied upon by the Secretary when he concluded that the Alabama red-bellied turtle is a separate taxonomic species, we are satisfied that, despite the absence of total agreement within the scientific community, his finding is entirely reasonable. It certainly is not arbitrary or capricious.

NOTES & QUESTIONS

1. How is the Alabama red-bellied turtle different from other turtles? Do those differences support the conclusion that the turtle is a separate species? Are those differences sufficient to support efforts to keep the turtle from going extinct?

2. The Alabama red-bellied turtle is the official reptile of Alabama. *See* Ala. Code § 1–2–25 (1999). Should that suffice to justify protection of the turtle, whether or not it is faced with the threat of extinction? *Cf.* 42 U.S.C. § 9605(a)(8)(B) (authorizing each state to select one hazardous waste site for inclusion on a list of the highest priority cleanup sites throughout the United States, regardless of whether the state's site is actually as contaminated as other sites that are placed on the list based on a scientific assessment of their hazardousness).

3. *Guthrie* is not the only instance in which the question of what constitutes a species has been contested. The Arizona leatherflower, for example, was once regarded as a separate species because its leaflet lobes were wider and its leaves were more spread out than its nearest relative, but the FWS removed the flower from consideration for listing under the ESA once a new scientific study showed that there were no clear differences between the two flowers. *See* Notice of Reclassification of a Candidate Taxon: *Clematis Hirsutisima var. Arizonica* (Arizona Leatherflower), 63 Fed. Reg. 1418 (1998). It is even possible that a plant or animal can be removed from the list of species protected by the ESA if the FWS determines that it is no longer a distinct species. *See* Final Rule To Remove the Idaho Springsnail (Pyrgulopsis (=Fontelicella) idahoensis)

From the List of Endangered and Threatened Wildlife, 72 Fed. Reg. 43560 (2012).

The FWS must make such determinations without any statutory definition of what constitutes a "species." The standard scientific taxonomy dates from eighteenth century Swedish botanist Carl Linnaeus, who developed a hierarchy that now progresses from kingdom to phylum to class to order to family to genus to species. The Alabama red-bellied turtle, for example, is a member of the animal kingdom, the reptilia class, the Testudines order, the Emydidae family, the Pseudemys genus, and the alabamensis species—with the latter two designations comprising the Latin name of the species, *Pseudemys alabamensis*. What that neat formula omits is any indication of what features support the characterization of the Alabama red-bellied turtle as a distinct species from, say, the Florida red-bellied turtle or the Alabama map turtle. As explained in chapter 2, the prevailing explanation adheres to the definition of a species offered by Harvard evolutionary biologist Ernst Mayr: "A species is a reproductive community of populations, reproductively isolated from other populations, that occupies a specific niche in nature." ERNST MAYR, THE GROWTH OF BIOLOGICAL THOUGHT 273 (1982). But that approach still leaves ample room for debate about the nature of a "community of populations," the meaning of reproductive isolation, and the scope of the relevant niche in nature. As Professor Kevin Hill has written, "Ambiguity is inherent in the taxonomic classification of endangered species." Kevin D. Hill, *What Do We Mean By Species?*, 20 B.C. ENVTL. AFF. L. REV. 239, 257 (1993). Even accounting for that ambiguity, Hill faults "the drafters of the ESA and frequently the Fish and Wildlife Service" because they "seem to have a very simplistic view of what constitutes a species. Quite often, under the Act, species are treated as discrete entities under a traditional typological approach emphasizing physical characteristics. Thus, a species is defined if it has a particular kind of shape, size, color, or other attribute. The purpose of many endangered species programs was to preserve this particular snapshot of present day characteristics, ignoring the changes caused by evolutionary adaptation." *Id.* at 253. As an alternative, two biologists have recently suggested that "[t]he best approach to arriving at a biologically accurate definition of 'species' is to use a hierarchy of species concepts to compare diversity across all taxonomic groups and not to limit recognition of species to groupings identifiable by humans using one particular technique." Anna L. George & Richard L. Mayden, *Species Concepts and the Endangered Species Act: How a Valid Biological Definition of Species Enhances the Legal Protection of Biodiversity*, 45 NAT. RESOURCES J. 369, 369 (2005).

Hybrids present an especially acute definitional problem. A hybrid occurs when two different species combine to reproduce, notwithstanding the reproductive isolation inherent in the very understanding of a species. Robert Guthrie argued that the Alabama red-bellied turtle was actually a hybrid, but the FWS disagreed. The FWS has deleted a plant from the list of endangered species when new scientific information indicated that the plant is a hybrid rather than a distinct species. *See, e.g.*, Final Rule to Remove the Plant "*Echinocereus lloydii*" (Lloyd's Hedgehog Cactus) from the Federal List of Endangered and Threatened Plant, 64 Fed. Reg. 33796 (1999) (concluding that a cactus that had been listed as endangered in 1979 was actually a hybrid rather than a distinct species, and thus removing the cactus from the ESA's list of protected species). But it remains uncertain whether the ESA protects another kind of hybrid: the offspring of an endangered species and another species, such as Florida panthers that have mated with captive panthers from South America. *See* LITTELL, *supra*, at 21.

4. The ESA protects nearly every kind of species that biologists recognize. Section 3(16) indicates that the Act applies to "fish or wildlife or plants." "Fish or wildlife," in turn, "means any member of the animal kingdom, including without limitation any mammal, fish, bird . . . amphibian, reptile, mollusk, crustacean, arthropod or other invertebrate." ESA § 3(8). And "[t]he term plant means any member of the plant kingdom." ESA § 14. The only exception to the universal coverage of the ESA concerns "a species of the Class Insecta determined by the Secretary to constitute a pest whose protection under the provisions of this chapter would present an overwhelming and overriding risk to man." ESA § 3(6); 50 C.F.R. § 424.02(k).

As of July 2012, exactly 2,000 species are listed under the ESA. There are 1,629 endangered species and 371 threatened species. The list of endangered or threatened species includes 761 flowering plants, 361 mammals, 309 birds, 161 fish, 118 reptiles, 78 clams, 66 insects, 40 snails, 34 amphibians, 29 ferns and allies, 22 crustaceans, 12 arachnids, five conifers and cycads, and two lichens. 1,394 of those species live in the United States; the balance live in other countries throughout the world. Within the United States, Hawaii has the most species with 380, followed by California (313) Alabama (126), Florida (118), and Tennessee (100). Only ten listed species are found in North Dakota. For the latest totals, *see* the FWS web site at http://ecos.fws.gov/tess_public/.

5. The ESA defines "species" to include "any subspecies of fish or wildlife or plants." 16 U.S.C. § 1532(16). "Subspecies" is undefined in the statute and imprecisely defined elsewhere. *See, e.g.*, EDWARD O. WILSON, THE DIVERSITY OF LIFE 406 (1992) (definition of a "subspecies" is "[s]ubdivision of a species. Usually defined narrowly as a geographical race: a population or series of populations occupying a discrete range and differing genetically from other geographical races of the same species."). The protection of subspecies has potentially sweeping consequences. The Delhi Sands Flower-Loving Fly is a subspecies; so is the northern spotted owl whose listing resulted in tremendous controversies in the Pacific northwest.

Why protect subspecies? That question elicited contrasting responses during the 1995 congressional hearings on the ESA. Opponents of the listing of subspecies argued that they need not be protected unless their survival was essential to the survival of the species as a whole. At a minimum, they argued, "[t]he sub-species or sub-sub-species of kangaroo rat should not receive the same treatment as the California condor." *Endangered Species Act-Vancouver, Washington: Hearing Before the Task Force on Endangered Species of the House Resources Comm.*, 104th Cong., 1st Sess. 65 (1995) (testimony of Barbara Tilly, Chairman, Chelan County Public Utility District Board of Commissioners). Secretary of the Interior Bruce Babbitt answered that "[s]hould a subspecies begin to decline, this may be a warning that the species as a whole may be in danger," and that an early response to that trend can improve the likelihood and decrease the cost of protection efforts. He added that the existence of genetically distinct subspecies "improve the ability of the species as a whole to survive." *Endangered Species Act: Washington, DC-Part III: Hearing Before the*

Task Force on Endangered Species of the House Resources Comm., 104th Cong., 1st Sess. 261–62 (1995).

6. The ESA also protects populations of a vertebrate species—but not an invertebrate or a plant—that is endangered in one place but not in another. *See* ESA § 3(16) (defining "species" to include "any distinct population segment of any species of vertebrate fish or wildlife that interbreeds when mature"). The FWS has listed so-called "distinct population segments" of a species if the population (1) is isolated from other members of the species, (2) occupies an ecosystem that is danger of destruction throughout much of its historical distribution, (3) is the only occurrence of the species in the United States, or (4) lives within different political jurisdictions that provide varying degrees of protection. Thus the FWS listed the population of the Canada lynx that lives in the contiguous United States from New Hampshire to Montana despite the presence of many lynx in Alaska and Canada. The agency explained that the lynx population "in the contiguous United States may be considered biologically and ecologically significant simply because of the climatic, vegetational, and ecological differences between lynx habitat in the contiguous United States and that in northern latitudes in Canada and Alaska." Determination of Threatened Status for the Contiguous U.S. Distinct Population Segment of the Canada Lynx and Related Rule, 65 Fed. Reg. 16052, 16060 (2000). By contrast, the FWS rejected a petition to list the American black bear in Nevada as a distinct population segment, finding that "[t]he American black bear in Nevada is not found to be markedly separate from other American black bear populations because it is not physically separate from other adjacent populations due to various kinds of barriers, it is not genetically different and does not demonstrate physiological or behavioral differences, nor does it occur in ecological settings in Nevada that are dissimilar from other areas occupied by the American black bear." 90-Day Finding on a Petition To List a Distinct Population Segment of the American Black Bear in Nevada as Endangered or Threatened, 77 Fed. Reg. 39670, 39673 (2012).

Or consider the FWS's 2000 decision to list anadromous Atlantic salmon in the Gulf of Maine as a distinct population segment. "Atlantic salmon from fish farms fill seafood coolers in supermarkets, but wild strains have disappeared from old American haunts," including several rivers in Maine. Andrew C. Revkin, *Maine Salmon Are a Breed Apart, Panel Reports*, N.Y. TIMES, Jan. 8, 2002, at A17. The status of the salmon in Maine is further complicated by the mixing of the original wild populations with salmon stocks that were added to the river beginning in the 1870's and by salmon that escaped from fish farms. The FWS concluded that "[t]he conservation of the populations of the Gulf of Maine population segment is essential because these Atlantic salmon represent the remaining genetic legacy of ancestral populations that were locally adapted to the rivers and streams of the region that formerly extended from the Housatonic River in Connecticut to the headwaters of the Aroostook River in Maine." Final Endangered Status for a Distinct Population Segment of Anadromous Atlantic Salmon (*Salmo salar*) in the Gulf of Maine, 65 Fed. Reg. 69459, 69460 (2000). A report released by the National Academy of Sciences in 2004 confirmed the genetic distinctiveness of salmon in Maine. *See* NATIONAL ACADEMY OF SCIENCES, ATLANTIC SALMON IN MAINE 5 (2004), *available at* http://fermat.nap.edu/books/0309091357/html/5.html.

Ultimately, the determination of a "distinct population segment" requires both scientific evidence and a normative basis for interpreting that evidence. Thus, as Ryan Kelly explains, "[t]he tools of population genetics offer an unsurpassed means of generating information that bears directly on an ESA determination, such as the degree to which populations are demographically separated, how large their populations might be or might have been in the past, and to identify populations or individuals that carry the genetic diversity that is the grist of evolution and resilience." Ryan P. Kelly, *The Use of Population Genetics in Endangered Species Act Listing Decisions*, 37 ECOLOGY L. Q. 1108, 1127 (2010). But, Kelly adds, "the complexity of genetic analysis carries the danger of obscuring a decisionmaking process designed to be transparent." *Id.*

The listing of distinct population segments also elicits many of the same criticisms and defenses as the listing of subspecies. Or, to put it another way, consider why the law allows the bald eagle to be listed as endangered in the lower 48 states even though there have always been many bald eagles living in Alaska. Michael Bean offers one answer when he states that "[a]voiding local extirpation of a species is desirable not only because a series of local extirpations frequently leads to endangerment of the species as a whole, but also because of the ecological, recreational, aesthetic, and other values populations provide in their localities." Bean, *supra*, at 200. By contrast, when federal officials threatened to remove a beaver that had been eating the cherry trees surrounding Washington's Tidal Basin, Idaho's Representative Helen Chenoweth mockingly suggested that "[t]his distinct population segment of the Rodentia family must be saved." 145 CONG. REC. H1840 (daily ed. Apr. 12, 1999).

Two attorneys have argued that "[d]espite the warnings of potential abuse and the congressional mandate that the 'distinct population segment' concept be used sparingly, federal agencies have nonetheless used the DPS concept to substantially increase [Evolutionary Significant Units] ESU listings," especially among the salmon species in the Pacific northwest. Leslie Marshall Lewallen & Russell C. Brooks, Alsea Valley Alliance v. Evans *and the Meaning of "Species" Under the Endangered Species Act: A Return to Congressional Intent*, 25 ENVTL. L. 731, 742 (2002). The courts are beginning to have more occasions to review the listing of a distinct population segment of a species. *See, e.g.*, Northwest Ecosystem Alliance v. United States Fish & Wildlife Serv., 475 F.3d 1136 (9th Cir. 2007) (upholding the FWS's decision not to list western gray squirrels in Washington state as a distinct population segment); National Association of Home Builders v. Norton, 340 F.3d 835 (9th Cir. 2003) (holding that the FWS failed to explain why the tiny population of ferruginous pygmy-owls that lives in Arizona was "significant" for the species as a whole).

B. IDENTIFYING THREATS TO SPECIES

Final Rule to List the Illinois Cave Amphipod as Endangered

United States Fish and Wildlife Service, 1998.
63 Fed. Reg. 46900.

[The Illinois cave amphipod, *Gammarus acherondytes*, lives in the dark zone of streams in six cave systems in central Illinois. An amphipod is a scavenger that feeds on dead animal and plant matter or the thin bacterial film covering most of the submerged surfaces in their aquatic habitat. The Illinois cave amphipod is distinguished from other amphipods by its light gray-blue color, its small kidney-shaped eyes, and the size of one of its two antennas that stretches nearly half the length of its less than an inch-long body.]

. . . The cave streams from which this species is historically known are each fed by a distinct watershed or recharge area; and there are no known interconnections between them, or with other cave systems. Two of the six caves may become hydrologically connected during extremely high rainfall over short periods of time. Thus, it is believed that there is virtually no opportunity for this species to become distributed to other cave systems via natural pathways.

The Illinois cave amphipod

There are few data or adequate survey techniques on which to base population, productivity, or trend estimates for this species. Sampling for cave fauna is difficult at best, and the challenges of surveying are compounded by the relatively small size of this species and the difficulty of researchers to distinguish it from other similar amphipods in the field. Thus, survey data are not sufficient to accurately record numbers of this small subterranean invertebrate; however, they do demonstrate a reduction in its range and the number of extant populations. . .

The most recent and extensive sampling effort was in 1995 in which the Illinois Natural History Survey (INHS) investigated 25 caves in the Illinois Sinkhole Plain and confirmed the presence of the species in only 3 of the original 6 cave systems, all in Monroe County. The species was not found in any additional caves. In 1995, 56 specimens were taken from Illinois Caverns, 19 specimens from Fogelpole Cave, and 2 specimens from a third, privately owned cave. The species appears to be extirpated from the two caves where no specimens were collected in 1965 or 1986. Its status in a sixth cave is currently unknown because the cave entrance has been closed by the landowner, thus the cave has not been re-surveyed since 1965. Due to the extensive searches by INHS, it is possible, but unlikely, that there are populations in other caves in the Illinois Sinkhole Plain. The INHS made an intensive effort to collect in all small side rivulets and drip pools in the 25 caves it sampled and believes that the collection results reasonably reflect the relative abundance of the species in cave streams of the Sinkhole Plain.

. . . The Service received comments [on its proposal to list the Illinois cave amphipod as an endangered species] from 27 individuals and organizations during the comment periods; some parties provided more than one comment letter. Eight commenters supported the proposal. Twelve parties expressed concern over the possible effect the listing may have on their area of interest (agriculture or cave visitation), and several offered rebuttals to the Service's rationale but did not directly oppose the proposal. Four commenters expressed opposition to the proposal.

. . . Issue 3: The Service lacks the scientific data to justify listing this species since there has been inadequate sampling conducted: one cave in which the species historically occurred could not even be surveyed.

Service Response: The Service believes that the sampling efforts conducted in 1993 and 1995 were by far the most intensive and extensive to date, and were appropriate to demonstrate the decline in the species' range with a high degree of certainty. In 1995 the [Illinois Natural History Survey] sampled 25 caves in the Illinois Sinkhole Plain and found *Gammarus acherondytes* in only 3 caves. In 1 cave that historically contained *G. acherondytes*, for example, a total of 561 amphipods from other species were collected without collecting any *G. acherondytes*. In a second cave that historically contained the species, 673 amphipods were collected without taking any *G. acherondytes*. If it is present in either of these caves, it would have to be extremely rare, constituting less than 2 individuals per 1000 amphipods sampled. By comparison, *G. acherondytes* appeared in higher numbers in much smaller amphipod samples in Fogelpole Cave (at a rate of more than 50 individuals per 1000 sampled) and Illinois Caverns (at a rate of about 250 individuals per 1000 sampled). If the species is present in significant numbers in the other 2 caves, it should have been readily collected in mainstream samples at the level of sampling intensity that was carried out in the 1993 and 1995 surveys. More intensive collecting, in which thousands of amphipod specimens are taken from each cave for later identification, might be inappropriate and probably unhealthy for the cave community. Such intensive collecting might decimate or extirpate an amphipod species whose numbers already are extremely low. Although survey data cannot unequivocally prove that the species is extirpated from any cave, they demonstrate that the most optimistic scenario is that the species is extremely rare, and its numbers have decreased since the surveys done prior to 1993.

The Service recognizes that the species may still occur in the one cave whose entrance has been closed by the landowner, and we have not made the assumption that it has been extirpated from that location. However, even if it does still occur there, the data indicate that the species' range has decreased from six caves to three or four.

Issue 4: Recent sampling efforts have yielded more specimens than previous efforts, indicating that species numbers may actually be increasing.

Service Response: The Service acknowledges a remote possibility that the species may be found in other cave streams in the sinkhole plain. There is also a chance that it may be found in other locations within Fogelpole Cave and Illinois Caverns. However, the Service believes the sampling effort that was expended looking for this species is more than adequate and reasonably reflects the relative abundance and diminishing distribution of the species in cave streams of the sinkhole plain. The Service does intend to keep looking for this species in other locations, however.

With regard to estimating the actual population of this species, the Service acknowledges that it is not likely to ever achieve that goal, regardless of the amount of effort put into surveys. The nature of this species and its habitat make it difficult, at best, to survey for it. Furthermore, the current identification technique for the species requires that it be sacrificed. It would be counter productive to sacrifice substantial numbers of an extremely rare species in order to obtain a more precise population estimate.

However, obtaining an accurate estimate of species numbers is not necessary for the Service to determine that the species warrants protection under the Act. What must be demonstrated is that its range has been significantly reduced and the threats to the species continue and can reasonably be expected to result in a further decline. An accurate population estimate also is not necessary to establish and achieve recovery goals for the species. Recovery can be achieved by protecting the quality of its habitat and by restoring stable and viable populations to the caves from which it has been extirpated. Once listed, the amphipod's relative abundance and population trend will be monitored safely using standard scientific methods.

Peer Review

In accordance with policy promulgated July 1, 1994, the Service solicited the expert opinions of independent specialists regarding pertinent scientific or commercial data relating to the supportive biological and ecological information for species under consideration for listing. The purpose of such review is to ensure listing decisions are based on scientifically sound data, assumptions, and analyses, including input of appropriate experts and specialists.

Following the publication of the listing proposal, the Service solicited the comments of two biologists having recognized expertise in invertebrate zoology and one individual having recognized expertise in karst hydrology and underground environments and requested their review of the available data concerning the Illinois cave amphipod. In order to ensure an unbiased examination of the data, the Service selected individuals who had only minor or no involvement in previous discussions on the possible listing of the species.

Comments were received from all three peer reviewers within the comment period. The two biological reviewers concurred with the Service on factors relating to the taxonomic, biological, and ecological information and concurred with the proposal to list the Illinois cave amphipod as an endangered species. The karst hydrologist provided additional clarification of the importance of oxygen depletion as the primary mechanism by which the species is being harmed. That reviewer also concurred that the Illinois cave amphipod is in danger of extinction in the foreseeable future.

Summary of Factors Affecting the Species

Section 4 of the Act and regulations promulgated to implement the listing provisions of the Act set forth the procedures for adding species to the Federal lists. A species may be determined to be threatened or endangered due to one or more of the five factors described in section 4(a)(1). These factors and their application to the Illinois cave amphipod (*Gammarus acherondytes*) of are as follows:

A. The Present or Threatened Destruction, Modification, or Curtailment of Its Habitat or Range

The degradation of habitat through the contamination of groundwater is believed to be the primary threat to the Illinois cave amphipod. . . There are several sources of groundwater contamination affecting the amphipod's habitat: (1) the application of agricultural chemicals, evidence of which has been found in spring and well water samples in Monroe County; (2) bacterial contamination from human and animal wastes, which finds its way to subsurface water via septic systems, the direct discharge of sewage waste into sinkholes, or from livestock feedlots; (3) the application of residential pesticides and fertilizers; and (4) the accidental or intentional dumping of a toxic substance into a sinkhole. . .

B. Overutilization for Commercial, Recreational, Scientific, or Educational Purposes

Overexploitation or scientific collecting are not believed to be factors affecting the species' continued existence at this time, but the Federal listing will prohibit unauthorized collection of individuals of the species. Exact numbers are unknown, but at a minimum 139 specimens have been collected from 6 caves over a 55-year period. Protection from collection may become important because collectors may seek the species once it becomes listed.

C. Disease or Predation

The importance of these factors is presently unknown.

D. The Inadequacy of Existing Regulatory Mechanisms

This species currently has no protection under Federal law. The Federal Cave Resources Protection Act of 1988 seeks to secure, protect, and preserve significant caves on Federal lands for the perpetual use, enjoyment, and benefit of all people. However, at this time, the Cave Resources Protection Act provides no protection to any caves containing, or potentially containing, Illinois cave amphipods, because none of the caves are on or under Federal land or are located in the immediate vicinity of Federal ownership. Therefore, these caves are ineligible for Federal protection under the Cave Resources Protection Act.

The Illinois cave amphipod is listed as an endangered species under the Illinois Endangered Species Protection Act. As such, it is protected from direct taking (*i.e.*, injury or mortality) regardless of whether it is on public or private land. However, "take" under State law does not include indirect harm through such mechanisms as habitat alteration. As long as the actions of private landowners are otherwise in compliance with the law, actions which destroy or degrade habitat for this species are allowed under Illinois law. . .

As mentioned under Factor A of this section, several of the entrances to caves containing the species are dedicated as Illinois Nature Preserves which is the strongest land protection mechanism in Illinois. Such dedication restricts future uses of the land, in perpetuity, for the purpose of preserving the site in its natural state. The removal of biota from the site is prohibited except by permit and for scientific purposes only. Allowable uses of the site are limited to nonconsumptive, nondestructive activities. The landowner may decide whether to allow public access to the site, and management is accomplished in accordance with a master management plan prepared jointly by the Illinois Nature Preserves Commission and the landowner. Dedicated properties cannot be subdivided, and the dedication instrument is attached to the deed and recorded.

Ownership or protection of cave entrances does not necessarily ensure protection of the caves' environment, particularly water quality. Water quality is largely a function of land use in the cave stream recharge areas on the land surface, and the vast majority of the watersheds of all caves containing the amphipod is in private ownership, and land use is primarily agriculture. Recharge areas may be several square miles in size, and runoff and seepage from thousands of acres of agricultural land may be funneled into one cave system, thus increasing the magnitude of any toxic hazard posed by the use of agricultural chemicals. . . Current State and local regulations are inadequate for protecting water quality in a sensitive geological formation like karst. St. Clair and Monroe counties are rapidly developing as residential communities for the St. Louis, Missouri, Metropolitan Area with most home sites being served by individual wells and septic systems. Septic systems may not perform as designed, and, in some cases, septic effluent drains directly into sinkholes. Studies have shown that there is no general housing density zoning in karst terrain that assures that groundwater quality will be protected when septic systems are used. The more houses there are in a spring or cave stream recharge area, the greater the chance that some of them will introduce contaminants into the groundwater system, and the greater the chance that one or more of the septic field systems will constitute a major source of groundwater contamination.

E. Other Natural or Manmade Factors Affecting Its Continued Existence

Because of the low numbers of the Illinois cave amphipod and a highly restricted range, even the loss of a few individuals to natural events may be significant to the species' survival. As a group, aquatic amphipods have adapted to the extremes of natural events such as spring floods or high water discharges following rainstorms and, no doubt, some individuals are washed out of the cave environment during such events. Because the species is extant in only three or four cave systems within a relatively small geographic area, it is conceivable that a heavy spring snowmelt or rainstorm could cause a flushing of all systems at one time significantly affecting each population.

The risk of extinction due to the threats to the Illinois cave amphipod (*Gammarus acherondytes*) posed by the above factors is exacerbated by the small number of low density populations that remain. Although *Gammarus acherondytes* was always rare, the current population densities are likely much lower (due to the previously identified threats) than historical levels. Despite any adaptations to conditions which result in rarity, habitat loss and degradation increase a species' vulnerability to extinction. Environmental variation, whether random or predictable, naturally causes fluctuations in populations. However, populations with small numbers are more likely to fluctuate below the minimum viable population (*i.e.*, the minimum number of individuals needed for a population to survive). If population levels stay below this minimum size, an inevitable, and often irreversible, slide toward extinction will occur. Small populations are also more susceptible to inbreeding depression and genetic drift. Populations subjected to either of these problems usually have low genetic diversity, which reduces fertility and survivorship. Lastly, chance variation in age and sex ratios can affect birth and death rates. Changes to demographics may lead to death rates exceeding the birth rates, and when this occurs in small populations there is a higher risk of extinction.

The Service has carefully assessed the best scientific and commercial information available regarding the past, present, and future threats faced by this species in determining to make this rule final. Based on this evaluation, the preferred action is to list the Illinois cave amphipod as endangered. . .

NOTES & QUESTIONS

1. Is the Illinois cave amphipod in danger of becoming extinct? How do we know? The agency admits that it will probably never be able to estimate the actual population of the species. Moreover, the agency agrees that natural causes play some role in the disappearance of the Illinois cave amphipod, and that the precise effect of various human activities is not entirely understood.

Note, too, that the agency acknowledges that the amphipod was always *rare*. How can we distinguish between a species that is rare and a species that is endangered?

2. Why did the FWS list the Illinois cave amphipod as endangered instead of as threatened? A species is endangered if it "is in danger of extinction," whereas a species is threatened if it "is likely to become an endangered species in the foreseeable future." ESA § 3(6), 3(20). Congress included the "threatened" category "not only as a means of giving some protection to species before they become endangered, but also as a means of gradually reducing the level of protection for previously endangered species that had been successfully 'restored' to the point at which the strong protective measures for that category were no longer necessary." BEAN, *supra*, at 201. There are only a few practical consequences between the two categories. The restrictions on "taking" a species (discussed in chapter 6) automatically apply to endangered species, but their application to threatened species is within the discretion of the FWS. Most of the time the agency simply extends the takings prohibitions to threatened species, but in an increasing number of controversial cases the agency has developed somewhat less stringent prohibitions for threatened species. Another difference between endangered and threatened species lies in the greater penalties that the ESA imposes on those who violate the law with respect to an endangered species.

3. The ESA defines "endangered species" as "any species which is in danger of extinction *throughout all or a significant portion of its range*." 16 U.S.C. § 1532(6) (emphasis added); see also 16 U.S.C. § 1532(20) (defining "threatened species" as "any species which is likely to become an endangered species within the foreseeable future *throughout all or a significant portion of its range*") (emphasis added). The statute thus anticipates that a species may be in danger of disappearing from one area, but it is nonetheless outside the scope of the ESA unless that are comprises a "significant portion of its range." In December 2011, the FWS and NOAA proposed to define "significant portion of its range" for the first time. *See* Draft Policy on Interpretation of the Phrase "Significant Portion of Its Range" in the Endangered Species Act's Definitions of "Endangered Species" and "Threatened Species", 76 Fed. Reg. 76987 (2011). The agencies proposed the following interpretations:

Significant: A portion of the range of a species is "significant" if its contribution to the viability of the species is so important that without that portion, the species would be in danger of extinction.

Range: The range of a species is considered to be the general geographical area within which that species can be found at the time FWS or NMFS makes any particular status determination. This range includes those areas used throughout all or part of the species' life cycle, even if they are not used regularly (e.g., seasonal habitats). Lost historical range is relevant to the analysis of the status of the species, but it cannot constitute a significant portion of a species' range.

Id. at 77002. A number of conservation groups have objected to the proposal, characterizing it as too narrow in light of the purposes of the ESA and the principles of conservation biology.

4. As the Illinois cave amphipod cave listing explains, ESA section 4(a)(1) lists five factors that the FWS must consider when determining if a species is endangered or threatened. Suppose three of those factors suggest that a species is endangered, but two do not? The statute does not say how the FWS should balance the factors, and the FWS has simply considered the factors in the process of making a holistic decision about the status of a species. The deference afforded by the courts to the FWS means that it is difficult to overturn the agency's decision. And perhaps that is as it should be. Alternatively, should the FWS – or the ESA itself – adopt quantitative criteria that specific precisely size of the population, or the rate of population decline, that a species must experience in order to qualify as endangered or threatened? *See* Kalyani Robbins, *Strength in Numbers: Setting Quantitative Criteria for Listing Species Under the Endangered Species Act*, 27 UCLA J. ENVTL. L. & POL'Y 1 (2009).

5. Four of the statutory factors require consideration of the actual threats to the species. The fifth factor—"the inadequacy of existing regulatory mechanisms"—examines the protection that the species already enjoys under federal, state, local, or foreign law. This factor presumes that a species need not be listed under the ESA if alternative legal measures are sufficient to prevent the species from becoming extinct. The FWS determined that the Federal Cave Resources Protection Act of 1988 and the Illinois Endangered Species Protection Act failed to provide that assurance for the Illinois cave amphipod. In other instances, governing authorities have strengthened the protections for a species in response to the threat that it might be listed under the ESA.

Most recently, the FWS declined to list the dunes sagebrush lizard because of the conservation measures adopted by New Mexico and Texas. *See* Withdrawal of the Proposed Rule to List Dunes Sagebrush Lizard, 77 Fed. Reg. 36872 (2012). The lizard lives "within the Permian Basin, which is one of the most productive oil and gas producing areas in the western United States." *Id.* at 36887. The potential conflict between preserving the lizard and oil and gas development caused local members of Congress to introduce legislation that would have exempted the lizard from the ESA. *See* 158 CONG. REC. S2174 (daily ed. Mar. 28, 2012) (amendment introduced by Sen. Corwyn to amend the ESA to "not apply to the sand dune lizard"); *see also* 157 CONG. REC. H5557 (daily ed. July 26, 2011) (statement of Rep. Pearce) (reporting that his constituents asked, "They couldn't kill our jobs with a lizard, could they?"). While Congress was debating, governmental authorities in New Mexico and Texas worked to develop a variety of conservation initiatives. The FWS found that "83 percent of the dunes sagebrush lizard's habitat was enrolled in the New Mexico Conservation Agreements," 77 Fed. Reg. at 36884-36885, while "[t]he Texas Conservation Plan focuses on the avoidance of activities within lizard habitat that would further degrade habitat, reclamation of lizard habitat to reduce fragmentation, and, due to the presence of mesquite in Texas habitat, removal of mesquite that is encroaching into shinnery oak dunes." *Id.* at 36885. The FWS

determined that the conservation efforts have a high certainty of being implemented. Our reasons for concluding that our level of certainty is high are that the level of enrollment is high, the mechanism and authorities for collecting funds are in place, the process for allocating funds to support reclamation work and research in lizard habitat is in place, the monitoring and documentation of compliance with the conservation measures are in place, and monthly and annual reports are complete, and all parties have the legal authorities to carry out their responsibilities under the New Mexico Conservation Agreements.

Id. at 36886; *see also id.* (finding that "the [Texas] conservation effort will be effective at eliminating or reducing threats to the species, because it first avoids habitat and if necessary, limits development within suitable and occupied habitat as a priority, and it also improves and strives to restore habitat and reduces fragmentation").

The law governing whether the FWS or the NMFS may consider conservation agreements in deciding not to list a species—and if so, under what conditions—is mixed. The agencies themselves have indicated that whether such actions can make an ESA listing unnecessary depends upon the certainty that the conservation effort will be implemented and the certainty that the effort will be effective. That general approach is instructive, but not all courts follow it. To cite three examples, one court precluded reliance upon conservation measures to save the bull trout that were speculative or unavailable for public scrutiny. *See* Friends of the Wild Swan, Inc. v. United States Fish & Wildlife Serv., 945 F.Supp. 1388 (D.Or.1996). Another court held that listing could not be avoided by a candidate conservation agreement for the slickspot peppergrass that provided only a 64% likelihood that the plant would not become extinct within one hundred years. *See* Center for Biological Diversity v. FWS, 351 F.Supp.2d 1137 (D. Colo. 2004). The latest decision held that "[t]he absence of detail about lease provisions" which the FWS had found would assure the protection of Graham's penstemon from oil and gas development "precludes a meaningful determination of whether such provisions adequately protect the species." Center for Native Ecosystems v. FWS, 795 F. Supp. 2d 1199, 1209 (D. Colo. 2011).

6. The ESA provides that science should be the determinative factor in deciding whether to list a species as endangered or threatened. *See* ESA § 4(b)(1)(A) (stating that the Secretary of the Interior's decision whether to list a species must be made "solely on the basis of the best scientific and commercial data available at the time the decision is made"). The problem posed in this circumstance—and in many others—is how to respond to scientific uncertainty regarding the status of a species. The ESA does not require the government or the party requesting the listing of a species to conduct any research concerning the status of a species. Instead, the listing decision must be made with whatever scientific information is available. Thus the state studies of the Illinois cave amphipod provided the primary source of data on which the FWS relied in concluding that the amphipod was endangered.

The quality of the scientific evidence supporting ESA listing decisions has been controversial in recent years. The complaints about the reliability and sufficiency of the evidence regarding the Illinois cave amphipod are similar to those voiced in many other listing decisions. Conservationists accused the FWS of manipulating scientific evidence to avoid listing species during the Bush Administration; developers have turned the tables and accused the FWS of relying on poor science when listing species during the Obama Administration. Sometime the problem is not whether the science is good or bad, but rather the fact that the science is susceptible to competing – and equally valid – interpretations. In a controversy about the status of the Preble's jumping mouse in Colorado, "different scientists took different positions based on the outcomes of their studies, but few recognized that at the heart of the disagreement was a difference of opinion about which risks were more problematic." Eric Biber, *Which Science? Whose Science?*, 79 U. CHI. L. REV. 471, 529 (2012).

The courts have rejected all attempts to require additional scientific research prior to the determination of whether a species should be listed. When a federal district court ordered the FWS to conduct an actual count of the number of Queen Charlotte goshawks to determine whether the bird should be listed, the court of appeals reversed because the ESA provides that the listing decision must "be made solely on the basis of the best scientific and commercial data available," so "the district court was without authority to order the Secretary to conduct an independent population count of the birds." Southwest Center for Biological Diversity v. Babbitt, 215 F.3d 58 (D.C.Cir.2000). Nor is the inadequacy of the existing data a sufficient cause for delay. In Defenders of Wildlife v. Babbitt, 958 F.Supp. 670 (D.D.C.1997), the FWS had concluded that listing the Canada lynx was unwarranted because there was not "any conclusive evidence of the biological vulnerability or real threats to the species in the 48 contiguous states." The court overturned that decision because the ESA "contains no requirement that the evidence be conclusive in order for a species to be listed." *Id.* at 679. Indeed, the FWS must proceed with its listing determination even if the best available scientific evidence is inherently flawed. *See* Defenders of Wildlife v. Babbitt, 1999 WL 33537981 at *14 (S.D.Cal.1999) (upholding the FWS's use of questionable scat count data when listing the flat-tailed horned lizard).

7. In an effort to dispel the concerns about the adequacy of the scientific evidence used to list species, the FWS and the NMFS have adopted a scientific peer review policy that promises to "[s]olicit the expert opinions of three appropriate and independent specialists regarding pertinent scientific or commercial data and assumptions relating to the taxonomy, population models, and supportive biological and ecological information for species under consideration for listing." Notice of Interagency Cooperative Policy for Peer Review in Endangered Species Act Activities, 59 Fed. Reg. 34270 (1994). The Illinois cave amphipod listing briefly describes the results of such peer review. Nonetheless, some members of Congress continue to insist that the listing process must be informed by better science. One proposed bill would have required the FWS to determine that any petition to list a species to contain the following information:

- scientific documentation from a published scientific source that the fish or wildlife or plant that is the subject of the petition is a species;
- a description of all available data on the historical and current range, population, and distribution of the species, an explanation of the methodology used to collect the data, and an identification of the location where the data can be reviewed;
- scientific evidence that the population of the species is declining or has declined from historic population levels and beyond normal population fluctuations for the species;
- an appraisal of the available data on the threats to the species or the cause of its decline;

- an identification of the information contained or referred to in the petition that has been peer-reviewed or field-tested;

- a bibliography of scientific literature on the species, if any, in support of the petition;

- the qualifications of any person cited in the petition as an expert on the species or the status of the species; and

- at least one study or credible expert opinion, by a person who is not affiliated with the petitioner, to support the action requested in the petition.

H.R. 3160, 106th Cong., 2d Sess. § 101 (2000). What effect might those standards have on listing decisions? Is it correct to suggest, as one opponent charges, that such requirements are "simply an attempt to use science to make the listing process more difficult?"

A. 8. There is one way in which a species can be protected by the ESA even though it is neither endangered nor threatened. If a species is so similar in appearance to another listed species that protection of the listed species requires protection of the similar species, too, then the similar species can be listed even though it is not endangered or threatened itself. *See* ESA § 4(e). For example, when the Fish and Wildlife Service listed the pallid sturgeon as endangered, it also listed the more common shovelnose sturgeon in areas where both fish are found because the two fish look alike. A group of fishermen challenged the listing of the shovelnose sturgeon because it meant that they would no longer be able to catch the fish. The court upheld the listing because "the evidence that fishermen and fish biologists have trouble distinguishing between the species is relevant because it shows that even people with greater familiarity and expertise than the enforcement personnel cannot always tell the difference between shovelnose and pallid sturgeon." Illinois Commercial Fishing Ass'n v. Salazar, 2012 WL 2114816, *17 (D.D.C. 2012). Thus far, relatively few species have been listed because they are similar in appearance to another protected species.

C. THE LISTING DECISION PROCESS

Northern Spotted Owl v. Hodel

United States District Court for the Western District of Washington, 1988.
716 F.Supp. 479.

■ ZILLY, DISTRICT JUDGE

A number of environmental organizations bring this action against the United States Fish & Wildlife Service ("Service") and others, alleging that the Service's decision not to list the northern spotted owl as endangered or threatened under the Endangered Species Act of 1973, as amended, 16 U.S.C. § 1531 *et seq.* ("ESA" or "the Act"), was arbitrary and capricious or contrary to law.

Since the 1970s the northern spotted owl has received much scientific attention, beginning with comprehensive studies of its natural history by

Dr. Eric Forsman, whose most significant discovery was the close association between spotted owls and old-growth forests. This discovery raised concerns because the majority of remaining old-growth owl habitat is on public land available for harvest.

In January 1987, plaintiff Greenworld, pursuant to Sec. 4(b)(3) of the ESA, petitioned the Service to list the northern spotted owl as endangered. In August 1987, 29 conservation organizations filed a second petition to list the owl as endangered both in the Olympic Peninsula in Washington and in the Oregon Coast Range, and as threatened throughout the rest of its range.

The ESA directs the Secretary of the Interior to determine whether any species have become endangered or threatened[2] due to habitat destruction, overutilization, disease or predation, or other natural or manmade factors. 16 U.S.C. § 1533(a)(1).[3] The Act was amended in 1982 to ensure that the decision whether to list a species as endangered or threatened was based solely on an evaluation of the biological risks faced by the species, to the exclusion of all other factors. *See* Conf. Report 97–835, 97th Cong. 2d Sess. (Sept. 17, 1982) at 19, *reprinted in* 1982 U.S. Code Cong. & Admin. News 2860.

The Service's role in deciding whether to list the northern spotted owl as endangered or threatened is to assess the technical and scientific data in the administrative record against the relevant listing criteria in section 4(a)(1) and then to exercise its own expert discretion in reaching its decision.

In July 1987, the Service announced that it would initiate a status review of the spotted owl and requested public comment. The Service assembled a group of Service biologists, including Dr. Mark Shaffer, its staff expert on population viability, to conduct the review. The Service charged Dr. Shaffer with analyzing current scientific information on the owl. Dr. Shaffer concluded that:

> the most reasonable interpretation of current data and knowledge indicate continued old growth harvesting is likely to lead to the extinc-

---

[2]   The ESA defines an "endangered species" as "any species which is in danger of extinction throughout all or a significant portion of its range...." 16 U.S.C. § 1532(6). A "threatened species" is "any species which is likely to become an endangered species within the foreseeable future throughout all or a significant portion of its range." 16 U.S.C. § 1532(20).

[3]   Section 4(a)(1) ... provides that:

> The Secretary [of Interior in the case of terrestrial species] shall ... determine whether any species is an endangered species or a threatened species because of any of the following factors:
>
>   (A) the present or threatened destruction, modification, or curtailment of its habitat or range;
>
>   (B) overutilization for commercial, recreational, scientific, or educational purposes;
>
>   (C) disease or predation;
>
>   (D) the inadequacy of existing regulatory mechanisms; or
>
>   (E) other natural or manmade factors affecting its continued existence.

tion of the subspecies in the foreseeable future which argues strongly for listing the subspecies as threatened or endangered at this time.

The Service invited a peer review of Dr. Shaffer's analysis by a number of U.S. experts on population viability, all of whom agreed with Dr. Shaffer's prognosis for the owl, although each had some criticisms of his work.

The Service's decision is contained in its 1987 Status Review of the owl ("Status Review") and summarized in its Finding on Greenworld's petition ("Finding"). The Status Review was completed on December 14, 1987, and on December 17 the Service announced that listing the owl as endangered under the Act was not warranted at that time.[4] 52 Fed. Reg. 48552, 48554 (Dec. 23, 1987). This suit followed. Both sides now move for summary judgment on the administrative record before the Court. . .

This Court reviews the Service's action under the "arbitrary and capricious" standard of the Administrative Procedure Act ("APA"). This standard is narrow and presumes the agency action is valid, but it does not shield agency action from a "thorough, probing, in-depth review." Courts must not "rubber-stamp the agency decision as correct."

Rather, the reviewing court must assure itself that the agency decision was "based on a consideration of the relevant factors. . ." Moreover, it must engage in a "substantial inquiry" into the facts, one that is "searching and careful." This is particularly true in highly technical cases. . .

> Agency action is arbitrary and capricious where the agency has failed to "articulate a satisfactory explanation for its action including a 'rational connection between the facts found and the choice made.' "

The Status Review and the Finding to the listing petition offer little insight into how the Service found that the owl currently has a viable population. Although the Status Review cites extensive empirical data and lists various conclusions, it fails to provide any analysis. The Service asserts that it is entitled to make its own decision, yet it provides no explanation for its findings. An agency must set forth clearly the grounds on which it acted. Judicial deference to agency expertise is proper, but the Court will not do so blindly. The Court finds that the Service has not set forth the grounds for its decision against listing the owl.

The Service's documents also lack any expert analysis supporting its conclusion. Rather, the expert opinion is entirely to the contrary. The only reference in the Status Review to an actual opinion that the owl does not face a significant likelihood of extinction is a mischaracterization of a conclusion of Dr. Mark Boyce:

---

[4]   The Service's Finding provides as follows:

A finding is made that a proposed listing of the northern spotted owl is not warranted at this time. Due to the need for population trend information and other biological data, priority given by the Service to this species for further research and monitoring will continue to be high. Interagency agreements and Service initiatives support continued conservation efforts.

Boyce in his analysis of the draft preferred alternative conclusions that there is a low probability that the spotted owls will go extinct. He does point out that population fragmentation appears to impose the greatest risks to extinction. . .

Dr. Boyce responded to the Service:

I did not conclude that the Spotted Owl enjoys a low probability of extinction, and I would be very disappointed if efforts to preserve the Spotted Owl were in any way thwarted by a misinterpretation of something I wrote.

Numerous other experts on population viability contributed to or reviewed drafts of the Status Review, or otherwise assessed spotted owl viability. Some were employed by the Service; others were independent. None concluded that the northern spotted owl is not at risk of extinction. For example, as noted above, Dr. Shaffer evaluated the current data and knowledge and determined that continued logging of old growth likely would lead to the extinction of the owl in the foreseeable future. This risk, he concluded, argued strongly for immediate listing of the subspecies as threatened or endangered.

The Service invited a peer review of Dr. Shaffer's analysis. Drs. Michael Soule, Bruce Wilcox, and Daniel Goodman, three leading U.S. experts on population viability, reviewed and agreed completely with Dr. Shaffer's prognosis for the owl.

For example, Dr. Soule, the acknowledged founder of the discipline of "conservation biology" (the study of species extinction), concluded:

I completely concur with your conclusions, and the methods by which you reached them. The more one hears about *Strix occidentalis caurina*, the more concern one feels. Problems with the data base and in the models notwithstanding, and politics notwithstanding, I just can't see how a responsible biologist could reach any other conclusion than yours.

The Court will reject conclusory assertions of agency "expertise" where the agency spurns unrebutted expert opinions without itself offering a credible alternative explanation. Here, the Service disregarded all the expert opinion on population viability, including that of its own expert, that the owl is facing extinction, and instead merely asserted its expertise in support of its conclusions.

The Service has failed to provide its own or other expert analysis supporting its conclusions. Such analysis is necessary to establish a rational connection between the evidence presented and the Service's decision. Accordingly, the United States Fish and Wildlife Service's decision not to list at this time the northern spotted owl as endangered or threatened under the Endangered Species Act was arbitrary and capricious and contrary to law.

The Court further finds that it is not possible from the record to determine that the Service considered the related issue of whether the northern spotted owl is a threatened species. This failure of the Service to review and make an express finding on the issue of threatened status is also arbitrary and capricious and contrary to law.

In deference to the Service's expertise and its role under the Endangered Species Act, the Court remands this matter to the Service, which has 90 days from the date of this order to provide an analysis for its decision that listing the northern spotted owl as threatened or endangered is not currently warranted. Further, the Service is ordered to supplement its Status Review and petition Finding consistent with this Court's ruling.

NOTES & QUESTIONS

1. Why was the FWS so reluctant to list the northern spotted owl under the ESA? Why were many environmental groups so eager to list the owl? Note that the FWS listed the northern spotted owl as a threatened species in 1990, and its listing began an extensive effort to preserve the owl that continues to this day. *See* FWS, A Northern Spotted Owl Chronology, http://www.fws.gov/oregonfwo/ExternalAffairs/News/Documents/NSO.Timeline.9-8-10.pdf.

2. The ESA contains two procedures for the consideration of whether a species should be listed. The FWS or the NMFS can initiate the process itself based on information collected by agency scientists, as the FWS did for the Illinois cave amphipod and many other species. Alternately, any interested person may petition the appropriate agency to list a species, as illustrated by the thirty environmental groups that petitioned the FWS to list the northern spotted owl in 1987. The same substantive standards apply to the agency's subsequent determination of whether the species is endangered, threatened, or neither.

In 1982, Congress amended section 4 to establish a specific schedule for the evaluation of petitions to list a species. To the maximum extent practical, the agency must determine whether the petition presents substantial evidence that listing is warranted within 90 days after the petition is filed. The agency then has 12 months to decide whether listing is warranted, unwarranted, or warranted but precluded by higher agency priorities. Once the agency proposes to list the species, it must reach a final decision within 12 months (with a possible six month extension). During that time, the public has 60 days after the proposal to submit comments on the proposed listing, and a public hearing will be held if requested within 45 days of the proposal. At the end of the 12 months, the agency will either list the species or decide to withdraw the proposal to list the species.

Judicial review of any final decision regarding a species is available to any party who can establish standing to sue. Judicial review is also available if the agency fails to make a decision within the statutory period. The courts have generally been sympathetic to the FWS when it fails to act within the statutory deadlines, but they have ordered the agency to comply nonetheless. *See, e.g.,* Biodiversity Legal Foundation v. Badgley, 1999 WL 1042567 (D.Or.1999) (establishing a tight compliance schedule for findings that were over three years overdue); Biodiversity Legal Foundation v. Babbitt, 63 F.Supp. 2d 31

(D.D.C.1999) (ordering the FWS to act on a 1997 petition to list the Baird's sparrow). Conversely, the courts have been unwilling to void a decision to list a species when the FWS acted beyond the statutory period. *See* Idaho Farm Bureau Fed'n v. Babbitt, 58 F.3d 1392 (9th Cir.1995); Endangered Species Comm. of the Bldg. Ind. Ass'n of Southern Cal. v. Babbitt, 852 F.Supp. 32 (D.D.C.1994).

3. Conservation groups, individuals, and others take advantage of the petition process. In recent years, the Center for Biological Diversity (CBD) has embraced the ESA's listing petitions with special zeal. *See* CBD, Listing Petitions, http://www.biologicaldiversity.org/publications/petitions/listing/index.html (providing links to dozens of petitions submitted by the CBD). The CBD and WildEarth Guardians have introduced a new innovation to the listing process by petitioning to list hundreds of species at a time. *See* CBD, Petition to List 404 Aquatic, Riparian and Wetland Species From The Southeastern United States as Threatened or Endangered Under the Endangered Species Act (Apr. 20, 2010), http://www.biologicaldiversity.org/programs/biodiversity/1000_species/the_southeast_freshwater_extinction_crisis/pdfs/SE_Petition.pdf; A Petition to List 206 Critically Imperiled or Imperiled Species in the Mountain-Prairie Region of the United States as Threatened or Endangered Under the Endangered Species Act, 16 U.S.C. §§ 1531 et seq. (July 24, 2007), http://www.wildearthguardians.org/site/DocServer/petition_protection-206-species-r6_7-24-07.pdf?docID=1522&AddInterest=1103; A Petition to List All Critically Imperiled or Imperiled Species in the Southwest United States as Threatened or Endangered Under the Endangered Species Act, 16 U.S.C. §§ 1531 et seq.(June 18, 2007), http://www.wildearthguardians.org/site/DocServer/petition_protection-475-species_6-21-07.pdf?docID=1442&AddInterest=1103.

The FWS has embraced the listing of multiple species at the same time when those species are part of the same ecosystem. The agency defended that approach when it listed 45 plants, two birds, and one picture-wing fly species that live on the Hawaiian island of Kauai:

> On the island of Kauai, as on most of the Hawaiian Islands, native species that occur in the same habitat types (ecosystems) depend on many of the same biological features and on the successful functioning of that ecosystem to survive. We have therefore organized the species addressed in this final rule by common ecosystem. Although the listing determination for each species is analyzed separately, we have organized the specific analysis for each species within the context of the broader ecosystem in which it occurs to avoid redundancy. In addition, native species that share ecosystems often face a suite of common threat factors that require similar management actions to reduce or eliminate those threats. Effective management of these threat factors often requires implementation of conservation actions at the ecosystem scale to enhance or restore critical ecological processes and provide for long-term viability of those species in their native environment. Thus, by taking this approach, we hope to not only organize this final rule effectively, but also to more effectively focus conservation management efforts on the common threats that occur across these ecosystems, restore ecosystem function for the recovery of each species, and provide conservation benefits for associated native species, thereby potentially precluding the need to list other species under the Act that occur in these shared ecosystems.

Determination of Endangered Status for 48 Species on Kauai and Designation of Critical Habitat, 75 Fed. Reg. 18960, 18961 (2010).

4. The listings of the northern spotted owl, the Illinois cave amphipod, and numerous other species were opposed by local residents and developers who feared listing the species under the ESA would adversely effect commercial, recreational, and other activities. The ESA, however, precludes consideration of such factors when deciding whether to list a species. Instead, the ESA insists that the determination of endangered or threatened status is a purely scientific question, and that the effects of a listing can be considered at other points once a species is listed.

Why should scientific data alone determine whether a species should be listed? Professor Holly Doremus has argued that "the closed, technocratic decisionmaking process in the scientific community . . . is inappropriate in the endangered species context because the relevant scientific questions are both intractable and closely intertwined with controversial value choices." Instead, she suggests, Congress "should separate the scientific aspects of listing determinations from the value judgments, including which groups should be considered for protection, what level of extinction risk is tolerable, and what the time line for evaluating extinction risks should be." Holly Doremus, *Listing Decisions Under the Endangered Species Act: Why Better Science Isn't Always Better Policy*, 75 WASH. U. L. Q. 1029, 1036, 1153 (1997).

Or consider another alternative. When the FWS publishes a final rule listing a species as endangered or threatened, it indicates how many public comments supported the proposed listing and how many opposed it. The votes recorded on several recent listing proposals are as follows:

	Yes	No
Blackburn's sphinx moth	5	0
Flatwoods salamander	39	136
Kauai cave wolf spider & Kauai cave amphipod	3	2
Lake Erie water snakes	89	7
Pecos sunflower	7	7
Preble's meadow jumping mouse	35	86
Rough popcornflower	3	3
San Bernardino kangaroo rat	29	14
Sierra Nevada population of the California bighorn sheep	37	2
St. Andrew beach mouse	2	3
Topeka shiner	92	80

Do these results suggest that the Flatwoods salamander, Preble's meadow jumping mouse, and St. Andrew beach mouse should not be listed? How about the Pecos sunflower and the rough popcornflower? Should the listing of a species under the ESA depend upon a popular vote? If not, why solicit comments from the general public on a listing proposal?

Western Watersheds Project v. United States Fish & Wildlife Service

United States District Court for the District of Idaho, 2012.
2012 WL 369168.

■ WINMILL, CHIEF UNITED STATES DISTRICT JUDGE.

The sage grouse is being squeezed. Its western range is consumed by wildfires; its eastern range is trampled by oil and gas drilling. The resulting fragmented habitat isolates and weakens populations, causing a dramatic decline in the species.

Alarmed by these trends, the Fish and Wildlife Service (FWS) decided that listing of the sage grouse was warranted under the Endangered Species Act. At the same time, however, the FWS declined to begin drafting rules to protect the birds because the agency has a limited budget and many other species were in worse condition.

This toothless finding - declaring that the sage grouse deserves protection but doing nothing about it - is known as a "warranted-but-precluded" finding. Critics claim that the agency has used this category as a dumping ground for politically-charged species, calling it "an ER waiting room strewn with the corpses of those species who were forced to wait too long." Kalyani Robbins, *Strength in Numbers: Setting Quantitative Criteria for Listing Species Under the Endangered Species Act*, 27 UCLA J. ENVTL. L. & POL'Y 1 (2009).

Indeed, the backlog at the agency was challenged by environmental groups. Some of those groups reached a settlement with the FWS, committing the agency to a timetable to reduce the backlog. Specifically with regard to the sage grouse, the FWS agreed to remove the bird from its "warranted-but-precluded" limbo by 2015.

Plaintiff WWP, however, did not enter into that settlement, and continues to litigate here, seeking a faster resolution for the sage grouse. For reasons explained below, the Court rejects arguments that WWP is barred from proceeding with this lawsuit because it is somehow bound by a settlement that it did not sign.

WWP asks the Court to reverse the FWS's warranted-but-precluded decision for the sage grouse, and to order the agency to prepare listing rules for the sage grouse within 90 days. WWP is challenging the "precluded" portion of the "warranted-but-precluded" decision, focusing on a key finding by the Director of the FWS that the threats to the sage grouse were merely "moderate" rather than "high". This finding, which WWP alleges was based on politics rather than science, essentially guaranteed that the listing would be "precluded."

Before making this finding, the FWS Director had received a recommendation from FWS Regional Director Steve Guertin that the listing be "warranted-but-precluded." Guertin's recommendation ignored his agency's own guidelines, contained no scientific analysis, and featured off-hand comments about the various political interests at play in the case. Given that political meddling has already resulted in one reversal in this case, the Court was frankly astonished at Guertin's cavalier recommendation.

It was not until after Guertin made his recommendation that the agency's scientists supplied the necessary scientific analysis to the Director. This sequence of events raises a red flag of warning: Did the agency scientists "bend" the science to justify Guertin's recommendation? To answer this question, the Court engaged in an especially thorough review of the record. It contains evidence that (1) sage grouse populations in some areas are stable, (2) substantial habitat exists in many parts of the range, and (3) 96% of all populations will remain above effective population sizes over the next 30 years. All of this supports the finding of the Director that the threat level is moderate.

However, the record also contains substantial contrary evidence which indicates that the threats to the sage grouse are high and immediate. The science is thus not conclusive on the threat level—it does not lead inevitably to a threat level finding that fits precisely within the bureaucratic designations of "high" or "moderate." Given this, the Director had to exercise his discretion to make a difficult decision. In reviewing that decision, the Court is prohibited by law from substituting its own judgment for that of the Director, but must instead defer to that decision so long as it is not arbitrary or capricious.

The initial recommendation of Regional Director Guertin was clearly arbitrary and capricious, since it was offered before receiving any scientific input. But the subsequent decision of the Director was based on sound science and cured the significant deficiencies of the recommendation. The Court therefore upholds the Director's decision that the threat level to the sage grouse falls into the moderate category.

The Director also had to certify that the FWS is making expeditious progress on its ESA duties in order to place the sage grouse in the warranted-but-precluded category. Congress originally intended that this category be used sparingly and that it not become a bottomless pit where controversial species are dumped and forgotten. There are now over 250 species in this category, and the average time spent there is about 19 years. Species have gone extinct while waiting for listing rules. By no common sense measure of the word "expeditious" has the FWS made expeditious progress in its ESA duties. While the FWS blames these delays on a lack of funding by Congress, some of the agency's financial woes are self-inflicted. In the past, the FWS's parent agency - the Interior Department - has refused to seek sufficient funds from Congress and has actively sought caps on ESA spending.

Nevertheless, as discussed above, the FWS has recently committed to reducing the backlog, and has made specific commitments regarding the sage grouse. These commitments are the only reason the Court will uphold the agency's certification that it is making expeditious progress. If those commitments prove unreliable, the Court will quickly revisit its findings here upon prompting from any party.

Despite troubling aspects of the FWS decision process, the Court ultimately finds that the Director's decision to place the sage grouse in the warranted-but-precluded category is not arbitrary or capricious.

NOTES & QUESTIONS

1. The question of priorities exists because Congress has never appropriated enough funds to perform all of the tasks imposed by the ESA and it is unlikely to do so in the future. How should the FWS determine which listing actions have the greatest priority? Should the agency treat all species equally? Is saving some species more important than others? If the agency is forced to choose among species, what criteria should it use to do so?

2. There were 231 species that were formal candidates for listing under the ESA as of July 2012. The FWS defines a candidate species as "plants and animals for which the [FWS] has sufficient information on their biological status and threats to propose them as endangered or threatened under the [ESA], but for which development of a proposed listing regulation is precluded by other higher priority listing activities," while the NMFS uses a slightly broader definition that includes species whose status is of concern but for which more information is needed. A species remains a candidate until the agency has the time and resources to conduct the determination of whether the species should be listed under the ESA. The status of each species is reevaluated annually.

The protections of the ESA do not apply to candidate species. The combination of the threat of legal regulation resulting from a listing and the absence of any regulation prior to listing has caused some individuals to attempt to eliminate a species before it is protected. For example, a developer bulldozed one of the three remaining populations of the San Diego mesa mint just days before the plant was listed, and some western landowners expedited their extermination of black-tailed prairie dogs once that species was identified as a potential addition to the list of species covered by the ESA.

3. The FWS can avoid such strategies by listing a species on an emergency basis. Section 4(b)(7) of the ESA allows the FWS to immediately list any fish, wildlife or plant species for 240 days when there is an "emergency posing a significant risk to the well-being of" the species. These emergencies have included unauthorized county road construction that threatened the survival of the bull trout in Nevada's Jarbridge River, rapid development amidst the breeding sites of the California tiger salamander, and hungry mountain lions feeding on the California bighorn sheep in the Sierra Nevada mountains. The leading case involving an emergency listing—City of Las Vegas v. Lujan, 891 F.2d 927 (D.C.Cir.1989)—upheld the FWS's protection of the Mojave Desert population of the desert tortoise pursuant to a more deferential standard of judicial review appropriate given the exigencies of the situation. The FWS must then decide whether to list a species on a permanent basis by the end of the 240 days following an emergency listing.

Emergency listings are uncommon. According to Professor Francesca Ortiz, there were only sixteen such listings between 1980 and 1999. She finds this surprising for three reasons:

> First, Congress specifically indicated that emergency listings should be used "less cautiously," in a "shoot first and ask . . . questions later" fashion, to prevent a significant risk to the well-being of candidate species. . . Second, the evidentiary standard for emergency listings is less exacting than that for normal listings, suggesting that in appropriate cases, implementation of an emergency rule would be easily justified. Finally, the FWS is not financially incapacitated with regard to emergency listings, which have been given the highest priority under each listing priority guidance issued since the moratorium.

Francesca Ortiz, *Candidate Conservation Agreements as a Devolutionary Response to Extinction*, 33 GA. L. REV. 413, 459 (1999). Perhaps the FWS heeded Professor Ortiz's advice, for the agency listed five species on an emergency basis in the first two years after her article was published. Even so, why does the FWS exercise its emergency listing power so infrequently?

4. Congress has authorized the FWS to establish priorities among the agency's various responsibilities under the ESA. The agency's guidelines give emergency listings highest priority, the processing of final decisions on proposed listings second priority, resolving the status of candidate species third priority, and processing petitions fourth priority. *See* Final Listing Priority Guidance for Fiscal Year 2000, 64 Fed. Reg. 57114 (1999). The Tenth Circuit rejected a challenge to an earlier version of those guidelines, reasoning that "the Service must retain the ability to order and prioritize its work, particularly when provided with limited resources, in order to adequately fulfill its mission." Biodiversity Legal Foundation v. Babbitt, 146 F.3d 1249, 1255 (10th Cir.1998).

5. In 1995, Congress enacted—and President Clinton reluctantly signed—a moratorium on the listing of any additional species as endangered or threatened. The proponents of the moratorium wanted to fix the problems that they perceived with the ESA before additional species became subject to its coverage, and they hoped that the contested issues regarding the reform of the ESA could be resolved while the moratorium was in place. Opponents of the moratorium complained that it would simply require additional efforts to save species in the future once they had become even more endangered. Indeed, one environmentalist characterized the moratorium as "one of the most shortsighted, mean-spirited, and counterproductive legislative actions in recent years." *Lifting of Moratorium on ESA Listings: Hearing Before the House Comm. On Resources*, 105th Cong., 2d Sess. 129 (1996) (statement of Eric R. Glitzenstein, Fund for Animals). The courts refused to intervene. In the *Environmental Defense Center v. Babbitt* decision cited in the bull trout case, the Ninth Circuit held that the listing duties imposed by the ESA remained in effect, but lack of funding to perform that duty precluded the Fish and Wildlife Service from taking any action on previous proposal to list the California red-legged frog. By contrast, when the agency was subject to a prior court order to designate critical habitat for the marbled murrelet, the lack of funds did not excuse the agency from proceeding with such a designation. *See* Marbled Murrelet v. Babbitt, 918 F.Supp. 318 (W.D.Wash.1996). Congress allowed President Clinton to lift the moratorium in the spring of 1996, and he did so immediately.

But funding difficulties continued to plague the listing process after the moratorium was lifted. In November 2000, the FWS announced that it would not be able to work on any listing proposals for the remaining ten months of its fiscal year because of court orders directing the agency to process critical habitat designation requests. "We just don't have the staff or the funding necessary to do anything that isn't ordered by a court," the FWS explained, but the Center for Biological Diversity accused the FWS of "playing serious politics, and the loser is America's endangered wildlife." *Wildlife Service Says Lawsuits Delaying Additions to Endangered List*, WASH. POST, Nov. 24, 2000, at A5. By August 2001, though, the FWS, the Center for Biological Diversity, and other interested groups reached an agreement pursuant to which the agency moved to list 29 species while the environmental groups refrained from litigating to obtain critical habitat designations. The compromise gained widespread acclaim, though the *New York Times* editorialized that "it would have never been necessary if, over the years, Congress had provided Interior with the resources it needed to enforce the act in a systematic, timely way." *A Victory for Endangered Species*, N.Y. TIMES, Sept. 3, 2001, at A14. The suggestion that more money would cure the problem is disputed by Utah Representative James Hansen, who has complained that "we continue to throw money at the ESA in the hope that somehow funding might recover species. This approach will not work." 145 CONG. REC. H3061 (daily ed. May 12, 1999).

6. Listing is not supposed to be forever. The goal of the ESA is to help a species recover so that it is no longer in danger of extinction and no longer in need of the law's protections. Toward that end, the FWS can delist a species when it is no longer endangered or threatened according to the same five criteria set forth in section 4(a)(1) that are used to determine whether a species should be listed in the first place. We describe the desliting process and its implications at the end of this chapter.

D. CASE STUDY: THE BLACK-TAILED PRAIRIE DOG

Imagine that you are the Director of the FWS. The National Wildlife Federation (NWF) petitioned the FWS to list the blacktailed prairie dog under the ESA, both on a permanent and on an emergency basis. The Secretary of the Interior—your boss—has asked you to prepare a memorandum responding to the NWF's petition to list the blacktailed prairie dog under the ESA. In particular, he wants your opinion on the following matters: (1) whether the black-tailed prairie dog satisfies the statutory and regulatory criteria for listing under the ESA, (2) the legal obligations that would be imposed on the FWS if the black-tailed prairie dog is listed, (3) the legal obligations that would be imposed on other federal agencies if the black-tailed prairie dog is listed, (4) the legal obligations that would be imposed on private parties and on state and local governments if the black-tailed prairie dog is listed, and (5) how to respond to the policy arguments raised by the supporters and the opponents of the petition, wholly apart from the legal requirements of the ESA. You have gathered the following information.

The black-tailed prairie dog is shaped like a football, is colored brown except for its black-tailed tail, and is actually a burrowing ground squirrel that is labeled a dog because of its barking call. It is one of five species of prairie dogs in North America: the Mexican prairie dog is listed as endangered under the ESA and the Utah prairie dog is listed as threatened, while the white-tailed prairie dog and the Gunnison prairie dog are both abundant and are not listed. The black-tailed prairie dog can be found on plains and plateaus from southern Saskatchewan to northern Mexico. Of the nearly ten million black-tailed prairie dogs in the United States, half live in South Dakota, the next largest populations live in Montana and Wyoming, and the rest of the animals live in Colorado, Kansas, Nebraska, New Mexico, North Dakota, Oklahoma, and Texas.

Black-tailed prairie dogs live in towns comprised of thousands of individual animals. Those towns (also known as colonies) are a boon to nearby wildlife and to the entire short-grass prairie ecosystem. More kinds of birds and other mammals live in areas inhabited by prairie dogs than in adjacent parts of the prairie. The tunnels that the prairie dogs dig are also used by snakes, birds and the other mammals that live in the prairie. And the black-tailed prairie dog is prey for black-footed ferrets (which are listed as endangered under the ESA), mountain plovers (which the FWS has proposed to list as threatened), swift foxes (a candidate for ESA listing), burrowing owls, bobcats, badgers, and hawks. The black-footed ferret nearly became extinct because of the decline of the prairie dogs, and efforts to reintroduce the ferret into the wild are hampered by the lack of suitable sites containing prairie dog colonies. Similarly, mountain plovers depend upon large colonies of prairie dogs to reduce vegetation and thus create nesting sites for the birds.

At one time, about 1.5 billion black-tailed prairie dogs lived on about 100 million acres of habitat in North America. The animals thrived in huge colonies that extended more than one hundred miles and contained more than one million individual animals. Today, the number of black-tailed prairie dogs has dropped to about ten million, and the FWS estimates that only about 768,000 acres of habitat remain. Of that remaining land, 45% is privately owned, 30% is on Native American tribal reservations, 15% is federally owned, and 10% is state owned. The black-tailed prairie dog colonies that survive are often small, fragmented, and surrounded by lands that are unsuitable for expansion. The two largest colonies, numbering about one million animals each, are found in the Badlands National Park in South Dakota and in Custer National Forest in rural southeastern Montana. The three smallest colonies contain less than five hundred animals each: one survives on federal land in central Wyoming that is used by private ranchers for cattle grazing but which is managed by the Bureau of Land Management (BLM), another exists on BLM land just outside of Yellowstone National Park, and the third lives on the fringes of Denver on privately owned lands that are in the path of that city's recent housing boom.

The causes of the decline in the population of the black-tailed prairie dog are:

- Habitat destruction—Less than one percent of the original prairie dog habitat remains intact. Most of what was once the prairie dog's habitat is now used to grow crops. Today colonies of prairie dogs are often too small and widespread to support viable populations or to allow for critical movement between populations.

- Poison—Ranchers regard prairie dogs as pests akin to hazardous substances. Millions of prairie dogs have been killed by the application of poisons to the habitat and food of the animals. Poisoning wiped out the entire population of black-tailed prairie dogs that once lived in Arizona.

- Recreational shooting—Prairie dogs are used as targets by hunters throughout the west. Some rural communities host prairie dog shooting contests with cash prizes for those who kill the most animals in a day.

- Disease—Prairie dogs have no known immunities to Sylvatic plague, a disease spread among squirrels and other rodents by fleas. Whole colonies of prairie dogs have been killed by the disease. Only South Dakota has remained untouched by the disease thus far. On the other hand, prairie dogs are reported to transmit the plague to other animals and to humans.

All of the states in which the black-tailed prairie dog lives mandate or encourage the extermination of prairie dogs because they regard the animal as a pest. For example, a 1927 Colorado statute provides that "prairie dogs are such a grave menace to the agricultural and livestock industries that the state is directed to take immediate action to control, suppress and eradicate such rodents in the areas infested by them." South Dakota requires private landowners to keep prairie dogs at least one hundred yards from neighboring property or otherwise pay for their control. The federal government has long had the same view of prairie dogs. The United States Department of Agriculture (USDA) issues permits for the poisoning of 200,000 acres of prairie dog colonies annually. Nonetheless, attitudes toward prairie dogs are beginning to change. In 1998, the Forest Service banned the shooting of prairie dogs on 9,000 acres in the Buffalo Gap National Grassland in southwestern South Dakota, an area where hunters have killed hundred of thousands of prairie dogs and where only 200,000 remain. Earlier this year, the BLM called for a voluntary moratorium on prairie dog shooting in the area immediately adjacent to Yellowstone National Park. Since the NWF petitioned for the listing of the black-tailed prairie dog, several state agencies, trade associations, tribal governments and private landowners have begun to meet with the NWF to discuss ways of protecting the prairie dog and prairie ecosystems while respecting the concerns of local residents.

The NWF says that these facts support the listing of the black-tailed prairie dog under the ESA. Further, the NWF has petitioned for an emergency listing as well. Besides the facts already recounted, the NWF cites three additional reasons why an emergency listing is appropriate: (1) the number of events organized for the shooting of prairie dogs has risen from 200 to 600 in just the past three years, (2) the Denver metropolitan area is experiencing a housing construction boom that is expected to replace 100,000 acres of prairie dog habitat with residential subdivisions this year, and (3) the very act of asking that the black-tailed prairie dog be listed under the ESA is likely to encourage ranchers to wipe out as many of the animals as they can before it becomes illegal to do so.

Not surprisingly, the effort to extend the protections of the ESA to black-tailed prairie dogs has been extremely controversial. The FWS has received 3,300 comments on the petition, with 60% favoring the listing and 40% opposing it. Other environmentalists have joined the NWF in extolling the virtues of the prairie dog as a crucial component of the rapidly disappearing prairie ecosystems. But the proposed listing of the black-tailed prairie dog has many opponents.

Ranchers see prairie dogs as pests of the worst kind. Cattle, horses and ranchers themselves break their legs in the holes dug by prairie dogs. Also, ranchers have long complained that prairie dogs compete with cattle for grass to eat, though environmentalists insist that there is little overlap between the plants eaten by cattle and the plants eaten by prairie dogs. It is difficult for ranchers to believe that prairie dogs are becoming rare when they spend millions of dollars annually to get rid of them, and when they see the animals reproduce so quickly. The additional costs that prairie dogs impose on ranchers come at a time when many western ranchers are struggling to survive amidst falling livestock prices and when many rural western communities are economically depressed.

Hunters love prairie dogs. Forty thousand people belong to the Varmint Hunters Association, which specializes in hunting prairie dogs. Another group, the Varmint Militia, prides itself in "defending farmers from the true invaders: the prairie dogs." Some outfitters charge $350 per day to conduct prairie dog hunts. Other hunters participate in prairie dog killing contests. For example, the tiny town of Lucla, Colorado sponsors a contest that draws over one hundred hunters who pay $100 each for the privilege of taking shoot at prairie dogs. One Lucla contest produced 3,000 dead prairie dogs, $7,000 in prizes, and $3,000 for the town's budget. Alas, in 1997 the Colorado Wildlife Commission limited the number of prairie dogs that could be killed to five per day. Even so, hunters are opposed by numerous animal rights groups that object to any killing of prairie dogs.

Developers object to prairie dogs. The dangers presented by having so many animals and their tunnels near human homes have forced many developers to use vacuums and hoses to force prairie dogs from their tunnels so the animals can be moved elsewhere. But developers are most concerned about the effects of federal protection of prairie dogs. The Colorado Home Builders Association (CAHB) predicts that housing construction in the Denver area will grind to a halt if black-tailed prairie dogs are protected under the ESA. The CAHB is unmoved by assurances that many construction activities may be allowed if a special ESA "take" rule is issued if the species is listed as threatened instead of as endangered. Moreover, the CAHB notes that many residential developments must include golf courses to be economically viable, but prairie dogs can destroy a golf course by their tunneling. Not only could the ESA prohibit a golf course from taking steps designed to control prairie dogs, but the animals could inadvertently suffer from the toxic effects of pesticides and fertilizers used to maintain a course.

The military is suspicious of the consequences of listing the blacktailed prairie dog under the ESA. Prairie dog colonies keep appearing on Army bases in areas that have been used as a target range for the testing of new weapons. Air Force bases have struggled to maintain dirt landing strips on land where prairie dogs continue to build new holes and tunnels. The military also has a general concern about the disruptive effect that protecting wildlife can have on the military's primary defense mission.

State and local officials perceive the proposed listing of the prairie dog as yet another effort by Washington bureaucrats to wrest land use control from westerners. Colorado's Representative Schaffer reports that when a member of his staff called the FWS for information on the black-tailed prairie dog, an agency official asked "is that some kind of hunting dog or something?" Officials in Baca County recently persuaded the Colorado state legislature to ban the importation of prairie dogs into any county where they are not welcomed by local residents. Throughout the west, most local officials contend that prairie dogs are not worthy of any protection, but if such protection is necessary, then it should be provided on a local basis because county and town officials are most familiar with the habits of prairie dogs and the steps that would be needed to save them. Native American officials are more sympathetic to the plight of the prairie dog, but they, too, worry about the intrusive effects of federal regulation of tribal reservations and the effects of the ESA in particular.

Finally, and perhaps most surprisingly, Japanese pet owners object to any federal regulation of prairie dogs. Every year thousands of prairie dogs are exported from the United States to Japan, where the animals are sold in pet stores for several hundred dollars each. Pat Storer, the author of "Prairie Dog Pets," explains that "the Japanese are crazy about small animals because they are good luck to them." Some members of the Japanese Prairie Dog Association even place dirt on the top of their buildings so that prairie dogs can establish colonies there. But prairie dogs cannot be kept as pets in most U.S. states because the animals are considered wildlife.

CHAPTER 5

FEDERAL GOVERNMENT RESPONSIBILITIES

Chapter Outline:

Once a species has been listed as endangered or threatened, the substantive obligations of the Endangered Species Act (ESA) come into play. The ESA imposes a variety of duties and prohibitions on government and private parties. The responsibilities of the federal government will be detailed in this chapter; the responsibilities applicable to others—including private parties and state and local governments—will be described in chapter 6.

The substantive commands of the ESA for the federal government can be divided into two groups. The first set of commands apply to the agency that is responsible for the species once it is listed. This is usually the Fish & Wildlife Service (FWS), though the National Marine Fisheries Service (NMFS) will be the responsible agency for marine mammals and fish listed under the ESA. The second set of commands apply to *all* federal agencies. Those commands are often difficult to enforce because they require an agency to protect biodiversity even when such protection conflicts with the agency's primary statutory responsibility to, for example, promote military readiness or respond to natural disasters.

A. LISTING AGENCY RESPONSIBILITIES UNDER THE ESA

The ESA's substantive provisions are designed to eliminate the danger of extinction which led to the listing of the species. The listing agency—the FWS or the NMFS—is charged with the responsibility for finding a way to remove the species from the brink of extinction, and thus, from the ESA's list. The statute directs the agency to take two steps toward that goal upon the listing of the species. First, the ESA provides for the listing of the "critical habitat" of the species at the same time that the species itself is listed as endangered or threatened. Second, the ESA requires the agency to prepare a "recovery plan" that explains the measures that will be necessary to bring the species back from the brink of extinction. Neither provision, however, has performed the kind of invaluable role that the original supporters of the ESA had hoped, and the appropriate roles of the designation of critical habitat and recovery plans continue to be debated as changes to the ESA are being considered.

1. DESIGNATION OF CRITICAL HABITAT

Natural Resources Defense Council v. United States Department of the Interior

United States Court of Appeals for the Ninth Circuit, 1997.
113 F.3d 1121.

■ PREGERSON, CIRCUIT JUDGE:

This case presents the question whether the defendants violated the Endangered Species Act by failing to designate critical habitat for the coastal California gnatcatcher... The coastal California gnatcatcher is a songbird unique to coastal southern California and northern Baja California. The gnatcatcher's survival depends upon certain subassociations of coastal sage scrub, a type of habitat that has been severely depleted by agricultural and urban development. Approximately 2500 pairs of gnatcatchers survive in southern California today.

The California gnatcatcher

On March 30, 1993, the U.S. Fish and Wildlife Service listed the gnatcatcher under the Endangered Species Act as a "threatened species." Under section 4 of the Act, the listing of a threatened species must be accompanied by the concurrent designation of critical habitat for that species "to the maximum extent prudent and determinable." The designation of critical habitat in turn triggers the protections of section 7 of the Act. Section 7 requires that federal agencies consult with the Secretary of the Interior (the

"Secretary") to ensure that actions authorized, funded, or carried out by federal agencies do not harm critical habitat.

At the time of the gnatcatcher's listing as a threatened species, the Service found that coastal sage scrub habitat loss posed "a significant threat to the continued existence of the coastal California gnatcatcher." Nevertheless, the Service concluded that critical habitat designation would not be "prudent" within the meaning of section 4 for two reasons. First, the Service claimed that the public identification of critical habitat would increase the risk that landowners might deliberately destroy gnatcatcher habitat. Second, the Service claimed that critical habitat designation "would not appreciably benefit" the gnatcatcher because most gnatcatcher habitat is found on private lands to which section 7's consultation requirement does not apply. . .

The Service's Failure to Designate Critical Habitat

Section 4 of the Act requires that the gnatcatcher's listing as a threatened species be accompanied by concurrent designation of critical habitat "*to the maximum extent prudent* and determinable":

> The Secretary, by regulation promulgated in accordance with subsection (b) of this section and *to the maximum extent prudent* and determinable—
>
> (A) shall, concurrently with making a determination under paragraph
>
> (1) that a species is an endangered species or a threatened species, designate any habitat of such species which is then considered to be critical habitat; and
>
> (B) may, from time-to-time thereafter as appropriate, revise such designation.

16 U.S.C. § 1533(a)(3) (emphasis added).

The Act itself does not define the term "prudent." The Service has defined what would *not* be prudent, however, in the regulations promulgated under the Act. According to the regulations, critical habitat designation is not prudent "when one or both of the following situations exist":

> (i) The species is threatened by taking or other human activity, and identification of critical habitat can be expected to *increase the degree of such threat to the species*, or
>
> (ii) Such designation of critical habitat *would not be beneficial to the species*.

50 C.F.R. § 424.12(a)(1)(I)-(ii) (1995) (emphasis added).

When the Service published the gnatcatcher's final listing as a threatened species, the Service stated that critical habitat designation would not be prudent under either prong of the regulatory definition. The final listing fails to show, however, that the Service adequately "considered the relevant factors and articulated a rational connection between the facts found and the choice made". . .

A. Increased Threat to the Species

The Service's first reason for declining to designate critical habitat was that designation would increase the degree of threat to the gnatcatcher. The final listing referred to eleven cases in which landowners or developers had destroyed gnatcatcher sites; in two of these cases, habitat was destroyed after the Service notified local authorities that gnatcatchers were present at a proposed development site. On the basis of this history, the Service concluded that because the publication of critical habitat descriptions and maps would enable more landowners to identify gnatcatcher sites, designating critical habitat "would likely make the species more vulnerable to [prohibited takings] activities."

This "increased threat" rationale fails to balance the pros and cons of designation as Congress expressly required under section 4 of the Act. Section 4(b)(2) states that the Secretary may only exclude portions of habitat from critical habitat designation "if he determines that the benefits of such exclusion *outweigh the benefits* of specifying such area as part of the critical habitat." 16 U.S.C. § 1533(b)(2) (emphasis added). In addition, the Service itself has said that it will forgo habitat designation as a matter of prudence only "in those cases in which the possible adverse consequences would *outweigh the benefits* of designation." 49 Fed. Reg. 38900, 38903 (1984) (emphasis added).

In this case, the Service never weighed the benefits of designation against the risks of designation. The final listing decision cited only eleven cases of habitat destruction, out of 400,000 acres of gnatcatcher habitat. The listing did not explain how such evidence shows that designation would cause more landowners to destroy, rather than protect, gnatcatcher sites. The absence of such an explanation is particularly troubling given that the record shows these areas had already been surveyed extensively in other gnatcatcher or coastal sage scrub studies published prior to the date of final listing.

By failing to balance the relative threat of coastal sage scrub takings both with and without critical habitat designation, the Service failed to consider all relevant factors. . . The Service's reliance on the "increased threat" exception to section 4 designation was therefore improper.

B. No Benefit to the Species

The Service's second reason for declining to designate habitat was that designation "would not appreciably benefit the species." According to the Service's final listing decision, most populations of gnatcatchers are found on private lands to which section 7's consultation requirement would not apply. The final listing decision suggests that designation may only be deemed "beneficial to the species" and therefore "prudent" if it would result in the application of section 7 to "the *majority* of land-use activities occurring within critical habitat."

By rewriting its "beneficial to the species" test for prudence into a "beneficial to *most* of the species" requirement, the Service expands the narrow statutory exception for imprudent designations into a broad exemption for imperfect designations. This expansive construction of the "no benefit" prong to the imprudence exception is inconsistent with clear congressional intent.

The fact that Congress intended the imprudence exception to be a narrow one is clear from the legislative history, which reads in part:

> The committee intends that in most situations the Secretary will . . . designate critical habitat at the same time that a species is listed as either endangered or threatened. *It is only in rare circumstances where the specification of critical habitat concurrently with the listing would not be beneficial to the species.*

H.R. Rep. No. 95–1625 at 17 (1978), *reprinted in* 1978 U.S.C.C.A.N. 9453, 9467 (emphasis added). *See also* Enos v. Marsh, 769 F.2d 1363, 1371 (9th Cir.1985) (holding that the Secretary "may only fail to designate critical habitat under *rare* circumstances") (emphasis added); Northern Spotted Owl v. Lujan, 758 F. Supp. 621, 626 (W.D.Wash.1991) ("This legislative history leaves little room for doubt regarding the intent of Congress: The designation of critical habitat is to coincide with the final listing decision absent *extraordinary* circumstances") (emphasis added).

By expanding the imprudence exception to encompass all cases in which designation would fail to control "*the majority* of land-use activities occurring within critical habitat," the Service contravenes the clear congressional intent that the imprudence exception be a rare exception. Since "the court, as well as the agency, must give effect to the unambiguously expressed intent of Congress," we reject the Service's suggestion that designation is only necessary where it would protect the majority of species habitat.

In the present case, the Service found that of approximately 400,000 acres of gnatcatcher habitat, over 80,000 acres were publicly-owned and therefore subject to section 7 requirements. Other privately-owned lands would also be subject to section 7 requirements if their use involved any form of federal agency authorization or action.

The Service does not explain why a designation that would benefit such a large portion of critical habitat is not "beneficial to the species" within the plain meaning of the regulations and "prudent" within the clear meaning of the statute. Accordingly, we conclude that the Service's "no benefit" argument fails to "articulate[ ] a rational connection between the facts found and the choice made". . . The Service's reliance on the "no benefit" exception to section 4 designation was therefore improper.

C. Less Benefit to the Species

In addition to the above two rationales which were stated in the final listing, the defendants now offer a third argument in defense of the Service's failure to designate critical habitat. The defendants contend that a "far superior" means of protecting gnatcatcher habitat is provided by the state-run "comprehensive habitat management program" created under California's Natural Communities Conservation Program ("NCCP"). The Service has endorsed the NCCP as a "special rule" for gnatcatcher protection under section 4(d) of the Act, 16 U.S.C. § 1533(d).

Regulations under the Act provide that "the reasons for not designating critical habitat will be stated in the publication of proposed and final rules listing a species." 50 C.F.R. § 424.12(a). The NCCP alternative was not identified in the Service's proposed or final listings as a reason not to designate critical habitat. Therefore, this argument is not properly before us for consideration.

Even if we were to consider the NCCP alternative, however, the existence of such an alternative would not justify the Service's failure to designate critical habitat. The Act provides that designation of critical habitat is necessary except when designation would not be "prudent" or "determinable." The Service's regulations define *"not* prudent" as "increasing the degree of [takings] threat to the species" or *"not* . . . beneficial to the species." 50 C.F.R. § 424.12(a)(1)(I)-(ii) (emphasis added). Neither the Act nor the implementing regulations sanctions nondesignation of habitat when designation would be merely less beneficial to the species than another type of protection.

In any event, the NCCP alternative cannot be viewed as a functional substitute for critical habitat designation. Critical habitat designation triggers mandatory consultation requirements for federal agency actions involving critical habitat. The NCCP alternative, in contrast, is a purely voluntary program that applies only to non-federal land-use activities. The Service itself recognized at the time of its final listing decision that "no substantive protection of the coastal California gnatcatcher is currently provided by city/county enrollments [in the NCCP]." Accordingly, we reject the defendants' post hoc invocation of the NCCP to justify the Service's failure to designate critical habitat. . .

■ O'SCANNLAIN, CIRCUIT JUDGE, dissenting:

. . . The majority states that a determination of whether a designation would be prudent must include weighing the benefits of designation against its risks. Our cases do not support this conclusion, however; they generally require only that the agency follow a rational decision-making process. . . That point aside, however, I believe that a fair reading of the Service's decision reveals that it did in fact conduct precisely the balancing test called for by the majority when it concluded that designation may cause the intentional destruction of habitat by private landowners, but would produce little benefit since most of the habitat is not on publicly-owned land. It is worth quoting the Service at length:

> [S]ome landowners or project developers have brushed or graded sites occupied by gnatcatchers prior to regulatory agency review or the issuance of a grading permit. In some instances, gnatcatcher habitat was destroyed shortly after the Service notified a local regulatory agency that a draft environmental review document for a proposed housing development failed to disclose the presence of gnatcatchers onsite. On the basis of these kinds of activities, *the Service finds that publication of critical habitat descriptions and maps would likely make the species more vulnerable* to [prohibited] activities. . .
>
> Most populations of the coastal California gnatcatcher in the United States are found on private lands where Federal involvement in land-use activities does not generally occur. Additional protection resulting from critical habitat designation is achieved through the section 7 consultation process. *Since section 7 would not apply to the majority of land-use activities occurring within critical habitat, its designation would not appreciably benefit the species.*

58 Fed. Reg. 16742, 16756 (1993) (emphasis added). In my view, applying the majority's balancing requirement, the Service indeed weighed the benefits and risks of designation and came to a rational, defensible conclusion that designation was not prudent. . .

The second situation in which designation would not be prudent exists when "such designation of critical habitat would not be beneficial to the species." 50 C.F.R. § 424.12(a)(1)(ii) (1996). . . In my view, the majority takes too narrow a view of the phrase "beneficial to the species." The question should not be whether any member of the species would be better off by a slender margin, but whether the species as a whole would benefit from the designation. Even though the gnatcatchers in most of the habitat would not benefit, reasons the majority, some of the gnatcatchers would benefit, and hence designation would be beneficial for the species. The problem with this argument is that it overlooks the Service's expert opinion, to which we are required to defer, that designation may harm the gnatcatchers when landowners intentionally destroy the habitat. Even though individual pockets of gnatcatchers may benefit, the species as a whole may not.

NOTES & QUESTIONS

1. One of the congressional purposes in enacting the ESA was "to provide a means whereby the ecosystems upon which endangered species and threatened species depend may be conserved." ESA § 2(b), 16 U.S.C. § 1531(b). How can that goal be accomplished? How could the designation of critical habitat help accomplish that goal? For an illustration of how the ESA's various provisions, including the designation of critical habitat, "can protect imperilled ecosystems far more effectively than is commonly thought," see William Snape III et al., *Protecting Ecosystems Under the Endangered Species Act: The Sonoran Desert Example*, 41 WASHBURN L. REV. 14, 15 (2001).

2. Most of the substantive provisions of the ESA focus on the species itself, rather than the habitat of a species. There are only a few provisions that specifically aim to protect habitat. Section 5 of the ESA authorizes the government to purchase land that serves as the habitat of an endangered or threatened species. Section 9 of the ESA has been interpreted to prohibit certain private or governmental actions that adversely affect the habitat of a species. *See* Babbitt v. Sweet Home Chapter of Communities for a Great Oregon, 515 U.S. 687 (1995). The gnatcatcher case illustrates the means by which the ESA designates the "critical habitat" of a species pursuant to ESA section 4.

The ESA defines "critical habitat" as "the specific areas within the geographical area occupied by the species, at the time it is listed .. on which are found those physical and biological features (I) essential to the conservation of the species and (II) which may require special management considerations or protections." ESA § 3(5)(i); *see also* ESA § 3(5)(ii) (adding that critical habitat can also include areas outside the current range of a listed species if the Secretary determines that "such areas are essential for the conservation of the species"). If critical habitat is designated, the only regulatory consequence is that ESA section 7 requires all federal agencies to insure that none of their actions "result in the destruction or adverse modification" of the designated critical habitat of a species. The most famous example of that prohibition is Tennessee Valley Authority v. Hill, 437 U.S. 153 (1978), which blocked the completion of the Tellico Dam because the resulting impoundment would have destroyed the endangered snail darter's critical habitat. The designation of critical habitat has no effect on the activities of private parties or state governments unless they are seeking federal funding or a federal permit that triggers the section 7 scrutiny. Moreover, the prohibition on federal actions that destroy or modify critical habitat usually overlaps the restrictions imposed by section 9's ban on the "take" of a protected species. Yet the official designation of critical habitat has been controversial. Why?

3. The designation of critical habitat is to occur at the same time that the listing agency determines that a species is endangered or threatened. The court in the gnatcatcher case expected that the agency would decline to designate critical habitat only in "rare" circumstances. In fact, it is much more common for the agency *not* to designate the critical habitat of a species. As of July 2012, critical habitat had been designated for 616 species, which is 44% of the listed species that live in the United States.

Plants pose a particular problem for the designation of critical habitat. Rare plants are attractive to collectors, and plants are stationary, so identifying where rare plants can be found is often counterproductive. For example, when declining to designate critical habitat for the San Diego thornmint and three other southern Californian plants, the Fish and Wildlife Service explained:

> Landowners may mistakenly believe that critical habitat designation will be an obstacle to development and impose restrictions on their use of their property. Unfortunately, inaccurate and misleading statements reported through widely popular medium available worldwide, are the types of misinformation that can and have led private landowners to believe that critical habitat designations prohibit them from

making use of their private land when, in fact, they face potential constraints only if they need a Federal permit or receive Federal funding to conduct specific activities on their lands... A designation of critical habitat on private lands could actually encourage habitat destruction by private landowners to rid themselves of the perceived endangered species problem. Listed plants have limited protection under the Act, particularly on private lands... Thus, a private landowner concerned about perceived land management conflicts resulting from a critical habitat designation covering his property would likely face no legal consequences if the landowner removed the listed species or destroyed its habitat. For example, in the spring of 1998, a Los Angeles area developer buried one of the only three populations of the endangered *Astragalus brautonii* in defiance of efforts under the [California Environmental Quality Act] to negotiate mitigation for the species. The designation of critical habitat involves the publication of habitat descriptions and mapped locations of the species in the Federal Register, increasing the likelihood of potential search and removal activities at specific sites.

Determination of Endangered or Threatened Status for Four Plants from Southwestern California and Baja California, Mexico, 63 Fed. Reg. 54938, 54951–52 (1998). Are these explanations for resisting the designation of the critical habitat of endangered plants persuasive?

4. As the gnatcatcher case illustrates, the ESA requires the designation of critical habitat "to the maximum extent prudent and determinable." ESA § 4(a)(3). There have not been too many instances when the listed agency has refused to designate critical habitat because it was indeterminable. Critical habitat is not determinable if there is inadequate information about biological needs of the species or the impacts of a designation. 50 C.F.R § 424.12(a)(2). The courts have been wary of the instances in which the FWS has claimed that critical habitat is not determinable. *See* Northern Spotted Owl v. Lujan, 758 F.Supp. 621 (W.D.Wash.1991) (holding that the failure to provide any reason for concluding that the critical habitat of the northern spotted owl was not determinable was arbitrary and capricious); Colorado Wildlife Federation v. FWS, 36 E.R.C. (BNA) 1409 (D.Colo. 1992) (holding that the agency's fear of designating too large an area as critical habitat because of the inadequacy of current information violated the statutory directive to make the determination based on whatever information was presently available).

The most common reason for failing to designate critical habitat is that such a designation is not "prudent." Beginning in April 1996, the FWS has determined that it would not be prudent to designate critical habitat in 228 out of 256 cases. But the Ninth Circuit's decision rejecting the agency's broad understanding of when a critical habitat designation is not prudent produced different results. On remand, the FWS designated over 500,000 acres in five southern California counties as the critical habitat of the California gnatcatcher. Final Determination of Critical Habitat for the Coastal California Gnatcatcher, 65 Fed. Reg. 63680 (2000). The FWS designated public and private land alike, omitting only those areas that were already protected by a habitat conservation plan. The Ninth Circuit's decision also prompted the FWS to reverse its original determination and conclude that it would be prudent to designate critical habitat for ten newly listed plants on Maui, Molokai, Lanai and Kahoolawe. *See* Final Endangered Status for 10 Plant Taxa from Maui Nui, HA, 64 Fed. Reg. 48307, 48319 (1999). More recently, when the FWS determined that the designation of critical habitat for the jaguar in Arizona was not prudent because of the small number of jaguars there and the greater importance of protecting habitat in Central America, a court held that the agency "failed to articulate a rational basis for invoking the exceedingly rare imprudence exception." Center for Biological Diversity v. Kempthorne, 607 F. Supp. 2d. 1078, 1091 (D. Ariz. 2009).

5. An area can be excluded from the designated critical habitat if the benefits of exclusion outweigh the benefits of inclusion, unless the failure to designate the area as critical habitat will result in the extinction of the species. In conducting that balance, the ESA directs the listing agency to consider "the economic impact, and any other relevant impact, of specifying any particular area as critical habitat." 16 U.S.C. § 1533(b)(2). What result should such balancing yield in the gnatcatcher case? The California gnatcatcher has sparked a serious conflict in land use in southern California. The gnatcatcher's habitat is on land along the Pacific coast around Los Angeles and San Diego—precisely the land that developers, companies, and homeowners desire for their own uses. Some of that land costs as much as $200,000 per lot. Does that mean that the economic impact of designating the gnatcatcher's critical habitat should outweigh any benefit from a designation?

And how should one calculate the economic impact attributable to the designation of critical habitat? The FWS has insisted that any economic impact of the listing of the species should not count toward the determination of the economic impact of designating critical habitat. Thus, for example, any economic losses that landowners suffer because the listing of the California gnatcatcher prevents them from clearing sage scrub from their property would not be relevant in calculating the economic impact of designating that land as the gnatcatcher's critical habitat. That baseline approach greatly reduced the likelihood that the costs of designating critical habitat would outweigh the benefits. But in New Mexico Cattle Growers Association v. FWS, 248 F.3d 1277 (10th Cir. 2001), the court held that the statutory language of the ESA requires FWS to consider "all of the economic impact of the [critical habitat designation], regardless of whether those impacts are caused co-extensively by any other agency action (such as listing) and even if those impacts would remain in the absence of the" designation. *Id.* at 1283. Applying that approach, what would the FWS need to investigate to decide whether the economic impacts of designating certain land as the critical habitat of the California gnatcatcher outweigh the benefits?

6. The efforts of all of the interested parties to reach an agreement about how to comply with the ESA's protection of the gnatcatcher while also allowing development in the area are detailed in Charles C. Mann & Mark L.

Plummer, *California v. Gnatcatcher*, Audubon, Jan.-Feb. 1995, at 38; and Dwight Holing, *The Coastal Scrub Solution*, Nature Conservancy, July/August 1997, at 16. More recently, the gnatcatcher has been the subject of the California Natural Communities Conservation Program, a regional Habitat Conservation Plan (HCP) of the type discussed in chapter 6.

Gifford Pinchot Task Force v. United States Fish & Wildlife Service

United States Court of Appeals for the Ninth Circuit, 2004.
378 F.3d 1059.

■ GOULD, CIRCUIT JUDGE:

This is a record review case in which the Appellants, an assortment of environmental organizations, challenge six biological opinions (BiOps) issued by the United States Fish and Wildlife Service (USFWS or FWS) pursuant to the Endangered Species Act (ESA), 16 U.S.C. § 1531 *et seq.* The BiOps in question allowed for timber harvests in specified Northwest forests and also authorized incidental "takes" of the Northern spotted owl (spotted owl), a threatened species under the ESA. . .

[T]he federal government adopted a comprehensive forest management plan for the entire range of the spotted owl known as the "Northwest Forest Plan." The NFP survived litigation, *see Seattle Audubon Soc'y v. Moseley*, 80 F.3d 1401 (9th Cir. 1996), and currently controls the use of the forests at the heart of this challenge. Relevant to this appeal, the NFP allocated the forests into "late successional reserves" (LSRs), "matrix" lands, and "adaptive management areas," with different harvesting rules applied to each area. The LSR allows less harvesting than matrix lands. An interagency analysis of the NFP found that it would provide for stable and well-distributed owl populations, though owl populations were projected to decline in the short-term. The NFP was subject to a Section 7 consultation and the resulting BiOp concerning this broad forest plan found no jeopardy or adverse modification. Because the NFP covered such a wide area, from Northern Washington to Northern California, involving virtually all of the federal government's forested land in this expansive area, the NFP BiOp explicitly declined to address the unique impacts of any particular action or implementation of the NFP. The NFP BiOp did not authorize incidental takes, deferring such consideration instead to future BiOps that would address specific projects.

Since the government approval of the NFP, the FWS has issued at least 298 BiOps and incidental take statements for spotted owls in the lands covered by the NFP. A total of 1080 incidental takes of spotted owls have been authorized, and 82,000 acres of spotted owl habitat have been removed, downgraded, or degraded. Six representative BiOps are the subject of this litigation. [The district court granted summary judgment for the FWS]. . .

We . . . turn to the critical habitat portion of the challenged BiOps. It is here that the picture is complicated by error and, on our analysis, becomes less rosy for the FWS.

1

Appellants first argue that the FWS's interpretation of "adverse modification," 50 C.F.R. § 402.02, is unlawful. ESA Section 7 consultations require that in every biological opinion, the consulting agency (here the FWS) ensure that the proposed action "is not likely to jeopardize the continued existence of" an endangered or threatened species and that the federal action will not result in the "destruction or adverse modification" of the designated "critical habitat" of the listed species. 16 U.S.C. § 1536(a)(2).

The FWS, in turn, defined "destruction or adverse modification" as:

> [A] direct or indirect alteration that appreciably diminishes the value of critical habitat for both the survival and recovery of a listed species. Such alterations include, but are not limited to, alterations adversely modifying any of those physical or biological features that were the basis for determining the habitat to be critical.

50 C.F.R. § 402.02. This regulation requires a close reading to grasp its import. Appellants argue that the regulatory definition sets the bar too high because the adverse modification threshold is not triggered by a proposed action until there is an appreciable diminishment of the value of critical habitat for both survival and recovery.[6]

We agree. Here, the FWS has interpreted "destruction or adverse modification" as changes to the critical habitat "that appreciably diminish[] the value of critical habitat for *both* the survival *and* recovery of a listed species." 50 C.F.R. § 402.02 (emphases added). This regulatory definition explicitly requires appreciable diminishment of the critical habitat necessary for survival before the "destruction or adverse modification" standard could ever be met. Because it is logical and inevitable that a species requires more critical habitat for recovery than is necessary for the species survival, the regulation's singular focus becomes "survival." Given this literal understanding of the regulation's express definition of "adverse modification," we consider whether that definition is a permissible interpretation of the ESA.

To answer that question, there is no need to go beyond *Chevron*'s first step in analyzing the permissibility of the regulation; the regulatory definition of "adverse modification" contradicts Congress's express command. As the Fifth and Tenth Circuits have already recognized, the regulatory definition reads the "recovery" goal out of the adverse modification inquiry; a proposed action "adversely modifies" critical habitat if, and only if, the value of the critical habitat for *survival* is appreciably diminished. *See N.M. Cattle Growers Ass'n v. United States Fish and Wildlife Serv.*, 248 F.3d 1277, 1283

---

[6] This claim, which challenges the FWS regulation, is reviewed under the familiar *Chevron U.S.A., Inc. v. Natural Resources Defense Council, Inc.*, 467 U.S. 837 (1984), framework.

& n.2 (10th Cir. 2001); *Sierra Club v. United States Fish and Wildlife Serv.*, 245 F.3d 434, 441–42 (5th Cir. 2001). The FWS could authorize the complete elimination of critical habitat necessary only for recovery, and so long as the smaller amount of critical habitat necessary for survival is not appreciably diminished, then no "destruction or adverse modification," as defined by the regulation, has taken place. This cannot be right. If the FWS follows its own regulation, then it is obligated to be indifferent to, if not to ignore, the recovery goal of critical habitat.

The agency's controlling regulation on critical habitat thus offends the ESA because the ESA was enacted not merely to forestall the extinction of species (i.e., promote a species survival), but to allow a species to recover to the point where it may be delisted. *See* 16 U.S.C. § 1532(3) (defining conservation as all methods that can be employed to "bring any endangered species or threatened species to the point at which the measures provided pursuant to this [Act] are no longer necessary"); *Sierra Club*, 245 F.3d at 438. The ESA also defines critical habitat as including "the specific areas . . . occupied by the species . . . which are . . . essential to the *conservation* of the species" and the "specific areas outside the geographical area occupied by the species . . . that . . . are essential for the *conservation* of the species. . ." 16 U.S.C. § 1532(5)(A) (emphases added). By these definitions, it is clear that Congress intended that conservation and survival be two different (though complementary) goals of the ESA. *See* 16 U.S.C. § 1533(f)(1) ("The Secretary shall develop and implement plans . . . for the *conservation* and *survival* of endangered species and threatened species.") (emphasis added). Clearly, then, the purpose of establishing "critical habitat" is for the government to carve out territory that is not only necessary for the species' survival but also essential for the species' recovery.

Congress, by its own language, viewed conservation and survival as distinct, though complementary, goals, and the requirement to preserve critical habitat is designed to promote both conservation and survival. Congress said that "destruction or adverse modification" could occur when sufficient critical habitat is lost so as to threaten a species' recovery even if there remains sufficient critical habitat for the species' survival. The regulation, by contrast, finds that adverse modification to critical habitat can only occur when there is so much critical habitat lost that a species' very survival is threatened. The agency's interpretation would drastically narrow the scope of protection commanded by Congress under the ESA. To define "destruction or adverse modification" of critical habitat to occur only when there is appreciable diminishment of the value of the critical habitat for both survival *and* conservation fails to provide protection of habitat when necessary only for species' recovery. The narrowing construction implemented by the regulation is regrettably, but blatantly, contradictory to Congress' express command. Where Congress in its statutory language required "or," the agency in its regulatory definition substituted "and." This is not merely a technical glitch, but rather a failure of the regulation to implement Congressional will. . .

That the agency was operating under a regulation that we now hold was impermissible has an inescapable bearing on the requisite showing of whether the FWS considered recovery in its critical habitat inquiry. Here, the Supreme Court demands that we afford the agency a presumption of regularity. In other words, the FWS must be presumed to have followed the adverse modification regulation. Thus, when analyzing the BiOps' critical habitat analysis, we must presume, unless rebutted by evidence in the record, that the FWS followed its definition of adverse modification and thereby ignored the evaluation of whether adequate critical habitat would remain to ensure species recovery. . .

[The court reviewed each of the BiOps and concluded that the role of critical habitat in facilitating the recovery of the owls was either neglected or cursory, so the flaws in the agency's regulation did not constitute a harmless error].

2

. . . Appellants claim that the critical habitat analysis relies, in part, on alternative habitat in the LSRs and that such reliance on the LSR to compensate for a loss of critical habitat is unlawful. The FWS responds that the LSR is not used as a substitute, but as a mutually overlapping regime. The rule that designated the critical habitat for the spotted owl specifically provided that adverse modification analysis should take into account consistency with other conservation plans.

There is little doubt that there is overlap and complementation between critical habitat areas and LSRs. In our view, however, Appellants have the better of the argument as to why LSRs cannot stand in for critical habitat within the meaning of the ESA. First, the plain language of the ESA requires that the adverse modification inquiry examine a given project's effect on critical habitat, that is, the land specifically designated by the Secretary of Interior for that purpose. 16 U.S.C. § 1536(a)(2). The purpose of designating "critical habitat" is to set aside certain areas as "essential" for the survival and recovery of the threatened species. 16 U.S.C. § 1532(5). To create critical habitat, there is extensive study, detailed analysis, and ultimately notice and comment rule-making. Once designated, critical habitat receives its legal protection because it is subject to the exact Section 7 consultations at issue in this case. If we allow the survival and recovery benefits derived from a parallel habitat conservation project (the NFP and its LSRs) that is not designated critical habitat to stand in for the loss of designated critical habitat in the adverse modification analysis, we would impair Congress' unmistakable aim that critical habitat analysis focus on the actual critical habitat. We would also be approving a transition away from ESA protections to mere compliance with the broader but perhaps less rigorous NFP. Compliance with the NFP, as important as it is, does not in itself generate the same protection for habitat as Section 7 compliance. Congressional intent is clear, and existing or potential conservation measures outside of the critical habitat cannot properly be a substitute for the maintenance of critical habitat that is required by Section 7.

This conclusion, which is borne out by analysis of the ESA, is mandated by the Supreme Court. *See TVA v. Hill*, 437 U.S. 153, 171–72 (1978) (holding that the potential to transplant the endangered snail darter to suitable habitat does not circumvent the ESA's bar on destruction of critical habitat). Suitable alternative habitat, here LSRs, is no substitute for designated critical habitat. If it were, then the Court in *TVA* would have allowed the completion of the Tellico Dam and simply required that the snail darter be moved to the suitable alternative habitat. However, the Court held that the ESA's plain language precluded such a result. *Id.* In our case, the result is the same: That the spotted owl has suitable alternative habitat (e.g., non-critical habitat LSRs) has, strictly speaking, no bearing on whether there is adverse modification of critical habitat.

If the FWS wants to change the boundaries of the critical habitat, it might do so if permitted by law after notice and comment procedures. But it cannot rely on a conservation program that has the same goal as critical habitat to change the boundaries of the spotted owl's critical habitat. Congress told the FWS to designate critical habitat and ensure that the designated critical habitat is not adversely modified. It matters not if there is worthwhile and possibly suitable habitat outside of the designated "critical habitat;" what mattered to Congress, and what must matter to the agency, is to protect against loss or degradation of the designated "critical habitat" itself. We hold that the agency's finding that loss of critical habitat was not an "adverse modification" because of the existence of suitable external habitat is arbitrary and capricious and is contrary to law. . .

NOTES & QUESTIONS

1. How does the FWS's understanding of critical habitat differ from the court's? Which understanding is most consistent with the statute?

2. The meaning of *Gifford Pinchot Task Force* was contested in Butte Environmental Council v. U.S. Army Corps of Engineers, 607 F.3d 570 (9th Cir. 2010). There the Army Corps of Engineers issued a permit for the construction of a business park, but environmental objected that the project would adversely modify the critical habitat of the endangered vernal pool fairy shrimp, vernal pool tadpole shrimp, and slender Orcutt grass. The court responded that *Gifford Pinchot*, "did not alter the rule that an "adverse modification" occurs only when there is "a direct or indirect alteration that *appreciably diminishes* the value of critical habitat." 50 C.F.R. § 402.02 (emphasis added)." 607 F.3d at 582. And "[a]n area of a species' critical habitat can be destroyed without appreciably diminishing the value of the species' critical habitat overall." *Id.* The fact that "the project would affect only a very small percentage of the total critical habitat" of the three species supported the finding that the no "adverse modification" finding. *Id.*

3. The designation of critical habitat is limited by the resources available to the FWS. Thus, when sued for not designating critical habitat for 245 recently listed Hawaiian plants, the agency responded that "if the FWS must complete prudency determinations for all 245 plants by 2000, it will need to suspend all other listing activity" in that region. Conservation Council for Hawai'i v. Babbitt, 24 F.Supp.2d 1074, 1078 (D.Hawai'i 1998). The environmental plaintiffs

pointed out, though, that the agency had received all of the funds that it had requested from Congress. The court fashioned a compromise that required the agency to publish proposed rules regarding the designation of critical habitat for 100 of the plants by November 30, 2000, with the remaining plants to be addressed by April 30, 2002. Also, the court deferred to the agency's decision to consider plants in the same Hawaiian ecosystem first, rather than accepting the environmentalists's suggestion to first consider those plants most directly affected by federal actions. Additional examples of how courts have responded to the FWS's resource limitations with respect to designating critical habitat include Forest Guardians v. Babbitt, 164 F.3d 1261 (10th Cir.1998) (holding that the Secretary of the Interior failed to perform his statutory duty to designate the critical habitat of the Rio Grande silvery minnow, and that claims of impossibility because of resource limitations were premature); Center for Biological Diversity v. FWS, 350 F.Supp.2d 23 (D.D.C. 2004) (advising that "[t]he Court cannot meaningfully assess whether the agency has efficiently used the resources available to it simply by taking the agency at its word"); and Biodiversity Legal Foundation v. Norton, 285 F.Supp.2d 1 (D.D.C. 2003) (giving the agency sixty days to adopt a schedule for designating critical habitat for the Cape Sable seaside sparrow, one of the most endangered birds in the United States).

The FWS insists that its limited resources should not be devoted to critical habitat designations. "Imagine an emergency room where lawsuits force the doctors to treat sprained ankles while patients with heart attacks expire in the waiting room and you've got a good picture of our endangered species program right now," explained Assistant Secretary of the Interior for Fish and Wildlife and Parks Craig Manson in May 2003. In an accompanying statement addressing a series of questions and answers concerning critical habitat, FWS explained that "the average cost of designating critical habitat for a species is approximately $400,000," or twice the cost of listing a new species. The agency also offered this question and answer:

Why hasn't the Interior Department asked for enough funds from Congress to do all the designations?

The President's FY 2004 budget request for listing totals nearly $12.3 million, an amount that, if approved by Congress, is almost double the $6.2 million appropriated in FY 2000 and a 35 percent increase over FY 2003. However, no matter how much funding was provided, it would take many years to complete this process. The real question is whether the benefits of critical habitat warrant the large expenditures that would be required were it to be designated for all listed species.

What is the answer to the latter question? John Kostyack of the National Wildlife Federation testified before Congress in April 2003 that "the ESA's requirement to designate and protect a listed species' critical habitat is among the most important of the ESA's habitat protection provisions" for three reasons: (1) the identification of which habitat is critical for the survival of a species "helps educate people about the natural world they inhabit, and more importantly, helps to ensure that key habitats are not destroyed out of sheer ignorance;" (2) critical habitat includes "all habitats needed for recovery," not just the areas currently inhabited by a species; and (3) critical habitat designation triggers the section 7 prohibition on federal agency actions that are likely to result in the "destruction or adverse modification" of critical habitat. Does that answer the "real question" posed by the FWS? And is that really the *real* question? For an argument that "critical habitat absolutely must add value beyond listing and that this value is in the form of a greater focus on recovery of the species," see Kalyani Robbins, *Recovery of an Endangered Provision: Untangling and Reviving Critical Habitat Under the Endangered Species Act*, 58 BUFFALO L. REV. 2095 (2010).

4. Congress amended the critical habitat provisions of the ESA in the 2004 Defense Department appropriations bill, which allows the FWS to decline to include military lands in critical habitat designations if the harm to national security outweighs the conservation benefit, or if the Interior Department determines that approved resource management plans will adequately protect the species. Pursuant to that provision, the FWS excluded thousands of acres from the critical habitat of the Riverside fairy shrimp and the arroyo toad, and it declined to designate any critical habitat for the Lane Mountain milk-vetch. *See* Endangered and Threatened Wildlife and Plants; Designation of Critical Habitat for the Riverside Fairy Shrimp, Part II, 70 Fed. Reg. 19154 (2005); Endangered and Threatened Wildlife and Plants; Final Designation of Critical Habitat for the Arroyo Toad (Bufo californicus), Part II, 70 Fed. Reg. 19562 (2005); Endangered and Threatened Wildlife and Plants; Designation of Critical Habitat for Astragalus jaegerianus (Lane Mountain milk-vetch), Part V, 70 Fed. Reg. 18220 (2005).

2. DEVELOPMENT OF RECOVERY PLANS

Strahan v. Linnon

United States District Court for the District of Massachusetts, 1997.
967 F.Supp. 581.

■ WOODLOCK, DISTRICT JUDGE

[The Northern Right whale, the Humpback whale, and other endangered marine mammals live in the Atlantic Ocean off the coast of New England. The United States Coast Guard operates in the same area, and on several occasions its vessels struck and killed a whale. Therefore, the Coast Guard initiated formal consultations with the National Marine Fisheries Service (NMFS) regarding the effect of the Coast Guard's operations on the endangered whales and other mammals. Not satisfied with the results of those consultations, Max Strahan filed a citizen suit alleging, *inter alia*, that the NMFS had failed to prepare a recovery plan pursuant to ESA § 4 for several of the endangered species, and that the recovery plans that did exist for other species did not comply with the ESA's requirements.]

The plaintiff . . . alleges that NMFS has violated § 4(f) of the ESA because it has not "developed and implemented plans for the conservation and survival of endangered species and threatened species. . ." 16 U.S.C. § 1533(f). Plaintiff makes two separate arguments with respect to NMFS's recovery plans. First, he contends that NMFS has violated the ESA because it has not developed any recovery plans for the Blue, Sei, Fin, or Minke whales, but only the Right and Humpback whales. The plaintiff then alleges that the existing Right whale recovery plan is insufficient because it does not "incorporate implementable site-specific management actions necessary to achieve the plan's goal" and because it does not "establish a realistic recovery goal." The Amended Complaint further alleges that the existing plan has not been revised.

With respect to the claim that NMFS has violated § 4(f) because it has not developed recovery plans for federally protected whales other than Right and Humpback whales, the defendants respond that the there are no time limits in § 4(f) within which the Secretary must develop, implement, or revise a recovery plan. I am persuaded by the defendants' argument. *See* Oregon Natural Resource Council v. Turner, 863 F. Supp. 1277, 1282–83 (D.Or.1994). The court observed:

> Congress recognized that the development of recovery plans for listed species would take significant time and resources. It therefore provided in the ESA that the Secretary could establish a priority system for developing and implementing such plans. This priority system allows the Secretary broad discretion to allocate scare resources to those species that he or she determines would most likely benefit from development of a recovery plan. Unlike other requirements under the ESA, such as the designation of critical habitat, the statute places no time constraints on the development of recovery plans. *See* 16 U.S.C. § 1533(f).[7]

Accordingly, the Secretary has developed a priority system for developing such recovery plans. *See* 55 Fed. Reg. 24296. I find, therefore, that the fact that NMFS has not issued recovery plans for Sei, Blue, and Fin whales[8] does not constitute a violation of § 4(f).

The plaintiff also asserts that the recovery plans that do exist, are deficient and thus violative of the statute. He claims that "as a general matter, [the recovery plan] does not contain objective, scientific, measurable criteria." More specifically, the plaintiff contends that the plan "fails to include ... an annual census, a population viability analysis, modeling of ship-whale interactions, risk analysis, and interim numerical goals." The defendants assert that the discretionary nature of a recovery plan also applies to the plan's content and that "it is not necessary for a recovery plan to be an exhaustively detailed document."

Case law instructs that the defendants are correct in their assertion that the content of recovery plans is discretionary. For example, in Fund for

---

[7] I am also persuaded, therefore, that there are no stringent time requirements for revising a recovery plan. The plaintiff argues, nevertheless, that NMFS itself determined that the Recovery Plan should be revised every three years for the first fifteen years and every five years thereafter. At oral argument, plaintiff argued that such revision was, therefore, nondiscretionary. The relevant language in the Recovery Plan states that "three-year intervals [for updating the Plan] are recommended." This is clearly the language of discretion. Moreover, inasmuch as 16 U.S.C. § 1533(f) requires NMFS to report to Congress "on the status of efforts to develop and implement recovery plans," the defendants represented at oral argument that the 1996 report was forthcoming. Considering these factors, I find the plaintiff's allegation with respect to revision to be meritless.

[8] The plaintiff includes Minke whales in his list. Minke whales, however, are not listed as an endangered or threatened species under the ESA.

Animals, Inc. v. Rice, 85 F.3d 535 (11th Cir.1996), the plaintiffs' argument relied on the assumption that "Recovery Plan[s] [are] document[s] with the force of law." *Id.* at 547. The court rejected that characterization stating that "section 4(f) makes it plain that recovery plans are for guidance purposes only." *Id.* Similarly, the court in Morrill v. Lujan, 802 F. Supp. 424, 433 (S.D.Ala.1992), found that "the contents of [recovery] plans are discretionary." While it is true that § 4(f) "does not permit an agency unbridled discretion," and "imposes a clear duty on the agency to fulfill the statutory command to the extent that it is feasible or possible," Fund for Animals v. Babbitt, 903 F. Supp. 96, 107 (D.D.C.1995), the requirement does not mean that the agency can be forced to include specific measures in its recovery plan. In fact, all that is required in a recovery plan is "the identification of management actions necessary to achieve the Plan's goals for the conservation and survival of the species." *Id.* at 108.

In any event, the evidence does not support that the measures suggested by the plaintiff are "necessary to achieve the plan's goal for the conservation and survival of the species." 16 U.S.C. § 1533(f)(B)(ii). And in fact, some of the measures advocated by the plaintiff are currently being implemented by NMFS [such as a population study]. Experts in the field plainly have different opinions as to what measures should be taken most effectively to promote conservation efforts for Right whales. It is also plain, however . . . that NMFS has considered the alternatives suggested by the plaintiff. The fact that NMFS did not adopt precisely the recommended measures in its recovery plan, does not make that plan deficient. Indeed, especially when expert, scientific judgments are involved, the court must afford the agency's decision a great deal of deference.

Last, I find that the recovery plan does contain "objective, measurable criteria," § 4(f)(1)(B)(ii), and "a description of site-specific management actions," § 4(f)(1)(B)(i). In terms of "objective, measurable criteria," the recovery plan states that the recovery goal is 7000 animals. The plaintiff argues that this goal is unrealistic and meaningless without a provision for interim goals. I find nothing in § 4(f) that mandates such interim goals. I also find that the Recovery Plan satisfies the "site-specific" requirement. The term "site-specific" has been interpreted to refer to geographical areas, requiring that the agency "in designing management actions, consider the distinct needs of separate ecosystems or recovery zones occupied by a threatened or endangered species." *Fund for Animals,* 903 F. Supp. at 106. The Recovery Plan meets this requirement because it considers the separate needs of the northern Atlantic population and the northern Pacific population. Additionally, the plan also addresses the different habitats of Northern Right whales at different times of year and contains measures specifically directed at each habitat. I find that the Recovery Plan is not arbitrary and capricious.

The plaintiff argues that even if the Recovery Plan is not arbitrary and capricious, NMFS has still violated the ESA because it has not implemented the plan. To support this contention, the plaintiff lists certain goals limned in the Recovery Plan that are not yet in effect. While it appears that some of the Recovery Plan's goals have not been implemented, *e.g.*, "appropriate seasonal or geographic regulations for the use of certain fishing gear in" the Bay of Fundy and the Southern Nova Scotia Shelf, I find plaintiff's allegations to be largely unfounded and needlessly technical. For example, the plaintiff states that no regulations on whale-watch vessels exist today. In February, 1997, however, NMFS issued a rule restricting all vessels and aircraft from approaching Right whales at a distance closer than 500 yards. Moreover, while the plaintiff asserts that "NMFS still has not located the unknown wintering area it alleges exists," [a government expert] avers that the research enabling NMFS to "find the unknown summer nursery and wintering grounds" is ongoing. After considering these efforts, I find that NMFS is taking steps to implement its Recovery Plan and that no ESA violation exists. . .

NOTES & QUESTIONS

1. On appeal, the First Circuit affirmed in an unpublished opinion and rejected the challenges to the recovery plan "essentially for the reasons stated by the district court." *See* Strahan v. Linnon, 187 F.3d 623 (1st Cir.1998).

2. Does the recovery plan for the whales satisfy the goals of the ESA? What actions would be necessary to be absolutely certain that the whales will not become extinct? Obviously, Max Strahan believes that far more needs to be done to save the whales, but his approach has alienated many environmentalists. *See* Carey Goldberg, *A Boston Firebrand Alienates His Allies Even as He Saves Whales*, N.Y. TIMES, Jan. 23, 1999, at A9 (reporting that Strahan has been barred from the New England Aquarium after ranting at visitors about whale-watching cruises and from government offices where he has made workers cry, and that he has been arrested 130 times).

3. Section 4 of the ESA directs the Secretary of the Interior to "develop and implement [recovery plans] for the conservation and survival of endangered and threatened species . . . unless he finds that such a plan will not promote the conservation of the species." ESA § 4(f), 16 U.S.C. § 1533(f). The FWS does not develop a recovery plan for a species if (1) the species is thought to be extinct, (2) state management plans serve as an adequate substitute, or (3) ecosystem initiatives addressing the recovery of multiple species exist. The law further describes how to establish priorities among species for recovery plans and what must be included in a recovery plan. To the maximum extent practicable, priority is to be given to listed species "that are most likely to benefit from such plans, particularly those species that are, or may be, in conflict with construction or other development projects or other forms of economic activity." ESA § 4(f)(1)(A), 16 U.S.C. § 1533(f)(1)(A). Taxonomic classification is not to be considered in establishing such priorities. The contents of a recovery plan—again, to the maximum extent practicable—must include (1) "a description of such site-specific management actions as may be necessary to achieve the plan's goal for the conservation and survival of the species," (2) "objective, measurable criteria which, when met, would result in a determination . . . that the species be removed from the list" of endangered or threatened species; and (3) "estimates of the time required and cost to carry out those measures needed to achieve the plan's goal and to achieve intermediate steps toward that goal." ESA § 4(f)(1)(B), 16 U.S.C. § 1533(f)(1)(B). Public comments on a proposed recovery plan must be considered, and the Secretary must report to Congress every two years regarding the status of efforts to develop recovery plans and the status of species for which plans have been developed. ESA § 4(f)(1)(C), (D), 16 U.S.C. § 1533(f)(1)(C), (D).

4. Recovery plans were in place for 1,139 species as of July 2012. Some kinds of species—such as snails, clams, and ferns and other plants— are much more likely to have a recovery plan than other kinds of species, such as mammals. *See* John Copeland Nagle, *Playing Noah*, 82 MINN. L. REV. 1171, 1200 n.114 (1998) (indicating that recovery plans existed for 80% of arachnids, 78% of snails, 71% of ferns and certain other plants, 69% of clams, 62% of fishes, 58% of flowering plants, 57% of insects, 44% of amphibians, 33% of crustaceans, 27% of reptiles, 26% of birds, 25% of conifers, and 12% of mammals as of July 1991). Why are endangered and threatened snails so likely to have a recovery plan, but listed mammals are not?

5. Judicial review of the content and implementation of recovery plans has been deferential to the agency. One notable exception is The Fund for Animals v. Babbitt, 903 F.Supp. 96 (D.D.C.1995), where the court rejected many objections to the recovery plan for the grizzly bear, but the court ordered the agency to reconsider the plan because it failed to adequately address some of the threats to the grizzlies and because it failed to justify a population target that was lower than what the environmentalists sought. More typical is Morrill v. Lujan, 802 F.Supp. 424, 433 (S.D.Ala.1992), where the court stated that the contents of a recovery plan are discretionary, and therefore refused to order the Fish and Wildlife Service to protect an area occupied by the endangered Perdido Key beach mouse but where a lounge was being built. Should the courts take a more active role in managing the recovery process?

Recovery Plan for Five Plants from Monterey County, California

U.S. Fish & Wildlife Service, Pacific Region, 2004.

EXECUTIVE SUMMARY

Current Species Status: This recovery plan addresses five plants that occur in Monterey County, California. *Astragalus tener* var. *titi*, *Piperia yadonii, Trifolium trichocalyx*, and *Potentilla hickmanii* are listed as endangered, and *Cupressus goveniana* ssp. *goveniana* is listed as threatened.

- *Astragalus tener* var. *titi* (coastal dunes milk-vetch) occurs in 11 scattered patches within 1 population separated by 17-Mile Drive on the western edge of the Monterey Peninsula. The land is owned by the Pebble Beach Company and the Monterey Peninsula Country Club. approximately 4,000 individuals were counted within 11 patches of this 1 remaining population during 1995. Fewer than 200 plants remained in a protective enclosure on the west side of 17-Mile Drive in 1999 with none of these plants flowering in 2000.

- *Piperia yadonii* (Yadon's piperia) is centrally distributed within large undeveloped tracts of *Pinus radiata* (Monterey pine) forest. Its range extends from the Los Lomos area near the Santa Cruz County border in the north to approximately 25 kilometers (15 miles) south of the Monterey Peninsula near Palo Colorado Canyon, where it occurs in maritime chaparral habitat.

- *Potentilla hickmanii* (Hickman's potentilla) currently occurs within Monterey pine forest on the Monterey Peninsula, and at one site in San Mateo County. Fewer than 40 plants were found in 1999 at the Monterey Peninsula location. Between 2,000 and 3,000 individuals were found during 1995 and 1996 in San Mateo County.

- *Trifolium trichocalyx* (Monterey clover) is known from only one area (Huckleberry Hill) covering approximately 16 hectares (40 acres) on property owned by the Pebble Beach Company on the Monterey Peninsula. During 1996, two locations in the Huckleberry Hill area with a total of 22 plants were located.

- *Cupressus goveniana* ssp. *goveniana* (Gowen cypress) is currently found in only two stands. The largest stand (Del Monte Forest) is near Huckleberry Hill on the west side of the Monterey Peninsula and covers approximately 40 hectares (100 acres) on lands owned by the Pebble Beach Company and the Del Monte Forest Foundation. The second stand (Point Lobos) occurs approximately 10 kilometers (6 miles) south of the Huckleberry Hill stand on the north side of Gibson Creek inland of the Point Lobos Peninsula. The property is owned by the California Department of Parks and Recreation and is approximately 16 to 32 hectares (40 to 80 acres).

Habitat Requirements and Limiting Factors: All five plant taxa are found primarily along the coast of northern Monterey County, California. *Potentilla hickmanii* also occurs in San Mateo County and has historically occurred in Sonoma County. *Astragalus tener* var. *titi* has historically occurred in both Los Angeles and San Diego Counties.

Astragalus tener var. *titi* occurs on sandy soil within 30 meters (100 feet) of the ocean surf zone. *Piperia yadonii* and *Cupressus goveniana* ssp. *goveniana* occur in Monterey pine forest and in maritime chaparral habitats. *Trifolium trichocalyx* is found in openings that occur within Monterey pine forest. *Potentilla hickmanii* is found in a meadow community of grasses and herbs. These five plant taxa are threatened by one or more of the following factors: alteration, destruction, and fragmentation of habitat resulting from urban development and recreational activities (*i.e.*, golf course development and ongoing maintenance, equestrian activities, etc.); competition with nonnative plant species; herbivory from native or nonnative species; random naturally occurring variation in population characteristics; and disruption of natural fire cycles due to fire suppression associated with increasing residential development around and within occupied habitat.

Recovery Objectives: Our objective is to recover these species sufficiently to delist *Cupressus goveniana* ssp. *goveniana*, and to reclassify *Astragalus tener* var. *titi*, *Piperia yadonii*, *Potentilla hickmanii*, and *Trifo-*

lium trichocalyx to threatened status. The biology of the latter four species is not yet well enough known to set delisting as an objective of this plan.

Recovery Criteria:

Downlisting criteria for *Astragalus tener* var. *titi*, *Piperia yadonii*, *Potentilla hickmanii*, and *Trifolium trichocalyx* are summarized below. Delisting criteria should be provided for these species in future revisions of this recovery plan when additional information about their biology is available.

- Provide permanent protection of habitat presently occupied by the species and the surrounding ecosystem upon which they depend. Include longterm commitments to conserve the species and provide funding for longterm management.

- In protected habitat, provide successful control of invasive, nonnative plants and successful management of other threats, including but not limited to snails, deer, pedestrians, recreation, and fire suppression activities. Management success must be demonstrated through at least 12 years (based on a 12-year weather cycle) of biological monitoring. This amount of time (and possibly more) is needed to observe management effectiveness, making adjustments as necessary.

- Develop management strategies based on life-history research and quantification of species' responses to vegetation management.

- Conduct successful reintroductions or establishment of populations of *Astragalus tener* var. *titi*, *Potentilla hickmanii*, and *Trifolium trichocalyx*.

- Conduct monitoring that demonstrates long-term viability of existing populations, including successful recruitment and reproduction.

- Establish seed banks for the taxa at a recognized institution. Delisting criteria for *Cupressus goveniana* ssp. *goveniana* include:

- Monitoring of both populations over at least 10 years shows long-term reproductive success, and protected habitat is of adequate size to support ecosystem function and allow population expansion.

- Monitoring shows successful recruitment has caused an increase in population size in both populations.

- A prescribed burn plan or successful alternative management strategy is implemented.

- A seed bank is established at a recognized institution.

Actions Needed:

1. Secure and protect existing populations and habitat on private or unprotected lands through willing landowners.

2. Manage lands to control or eliminate threats to the plants and their habitat.

3. Conduct research to document life history characteristics and plants' responses to vegetation management.

4. Survey for additional populations and suitable habitat for reintroduction or reestablishment and establish new populations.

5. Develop management strategies and monitor populations to determine effectiveness of management.

6. Coordinate recovery actions with other listed species or species of concern.

7. Develop and implement a public outreach program.

8. Reevaluate recovery criteria and revise recovery plan in the future based on Actions 1 through 7.

Recovery Costs: $1,645,000 over the next 12 years, with costs yet to be determined for securing and protecting lands, and for assurance of successful implementation of additional populations of *Astragalus tener* var. *titi*, *Potentilla hickmanii*, and *Trifolium trichocalyx*. Funding opportunities and management would need to be developed between landowners, regulatory agencies, nonprofit organizations, and other interested parties.

Date of Recovery: Meeting the recovery objective for *Astragalus tener* var. *titi*, *Piperia yadonii*, *Potentilla hickmanii*, and *Trifolium trichocalyx* (whose current objectives are downlisting to threatened status) depends on 1) how soon habitat can be secured and monitoring programs begin; 2) assurances that ecosystem and community processes of surrounding habitat are maintained; and 3) establishment of additional populations of *A. tener* var. *titi*, *P. hickmanii*, and *T. trichocalyx* that are successfully reproducing. At least 12 years (based on a 12-year weathercycle) of monitoring would be needed to assure that site management benefits these plants. If the recovery criteria have been met by 2016, these species may be considered for downlisting.

For *Cupressus goveniana* ssp. *goveniana*, the speed with which delisting objectives can be met depends on determining effective means of managing secured areas and improving the surrounding habitat, and monitoring to determine whether successful recruitment has caused an increase in the overall size of both populations. Twelve years of monitoring or more may be needed to assure that site management is appropriate. If the recovery criteria have been met by 2016, this species may be considered for delisting.

NOTES & QUESTIONS

1. Is the recovery plan likely to result in the preservation of these five plants? What other steps could be taken to preserve them?

2. How should the plan be implemented? Consider that the detailed account in the plan that seeks to "provide species information to the public through outreach programs." The plan suggests "an informational public outreach program" that would include "[i]nformation brochures, roadside kiosks (*e.g.*, displays that discuss the benefits of not mowing or spraying vegetation around sensitive species), and other materials (*e.g.*, videos, slide presentations, Pebble Beach website, ideas for possible deer control measures)." The plan further encourages landowners "to landscape with local native plant species. Information should be provided to them that describe the benefits of establishing effective buffer areas between secured areas and intensely used residential or recreational areas. These 'restored' areas could also serve as demonstration gardens to increase the public's knowledge and appreciation for the local landscape and unique habitat of this area."

3. Does the recovery plan satisfy the requirements of ESA § 4? More generally, do the requirements of section 4 assure that a species will recover from the danger of extinction? The role of recovery planning has been the subject of numerous recent reform proposals. H.R. 960, introduced by Representative Miller in 1999, would (1) expand recovery plans to include species that have not yet been listed as endangered or threatened but which are under consideration for listing, (2) require each affected federal agency to prepare specific implementation plans involving their relationship with a protected species, and (3) include in each recovery plan a list of activities that would be prohibited by the substantive commands of the ESA. Another bill introduced by Senator Kempthorne in 1997 would have established fixed deadlines for the preparation of recovery plans, required the plans to include specific numerical targets, and given states a greater role in the preparation of the plans. Which of these ideas would improve the role that recovery plans play in the ESA?

4. The recovery plan for the five Monterey County plants estimates that its implementation will cost $1,645,000 over the next 12 years. That cost, remember, is for only five of the species protected by the ESA. A 1994 study indicated that it would cost nearly $900 million to implement the recovery plans existing at that time, while the Fish and Wildlife Service had requested only $84 million to implement them. *See* NATIONAL WILDERNESS INSTITUTE, GOING BROKE? COSTS OF THE ENDANGERED SPECIES ACT AS REVEALED IN ENDANGERED SPECIES RECOVERY PLANS 1 (1994). The FWS has cautioned, though, that the cost estimates contained in recovery plans overstate the true cost of achieving the recovery goal for a species. Additionally, the recovery plan for the five Monterey County plants contains the following disclaimer:

> Disclaimer: Recovery plans delineate reasonable actions that are believed to be required to recover and/or protect listed species. We, the U.S. Fish and Wildlife Service, publish recovery plans, sometimes preparing them with the assistance of recovery teams, contractors, State agencies, and other affected and interested parties. Recovery teams serve as independent advisors to us. Plans are reviewed by the public and submitted to additional peer review before they are adopted by us. Objectives of the recovery

plan will be attained and necessary funds made available subject to budgetary and other constraints affecting the parties involved, as well as the need to address other priorities. Recovery plans do not obligate cooperating or other parties to undertake specific tasks, and may not represent the views nor the official positions or approval of any individuals or agencies involved in the recovery plan formulation, other than our own. They represent our official position *only* after they have been signed by the Director, Regional Director, or California/Nevada Operations Manager as approved. Approved recovery plans are subject to modification as dictated by new findings, changes in species status, and the completion of recovery actions.

Is that description consistent with the statutory provisions governing recovery plans?

5. ESA section 18 requires the FWS to provide Congress with an annual report "accounting on a species-by-species basis of all reasonably identifiable . . . expenditures made [by the federal and state governments] primarily for the conservation of endangered or threatened species pursuant to this Act." The report for fiscal year 2010 documented $1,360,790,593 spent federal agencies and $87,947,941 by states. FWS, Federal and State Endangered and Threatened Species Expenditures, at 5 (Fiscal Year 2010), http://www.fws.gov/endangered/ esa-library/pdf/2010.EXP.FINAL.pdf. More than $51 million was spent on the Snake River chinook salmon, and 19 of the next 25 species on the list were also fish. The only non-fish species in the top 26 were the red-cockaded woodpecker, two populations of the Steller sea lion, the desert tortoise, the northern spotted owl, and the right whale. *Id.* at 68. The purple cat's paw and the west Pacific Ocean population of gray whales brought up the bottom of the list with only $100 of expenditures each. *Id.* at 92. What explains the vast disparity in expenditures?

Establishment of a Nonessential Experimental Population of the Mexican Gray Wolf in Arizona and New Mexico

United States Fish and Wildlife Service, 1998.
63 Fed. Reg. 1752.

Background

Legislative

The Endangered Species Act Amendments of 1982, created section 10(j), providing for the designation of specific populations of listed species as "experimental populations." Under previous authorities of the Act, the Service was permitted to re-establish (reintroduce) populations of a listed species into unoccupied portions of its historic range for conservation and recovery purposes. However, local opposition to reintroduction efforts, stemming from concerns by some about potential restrictions, and prohibitions on Federal and private activities contained in sections 7 and 9 of the Act, reduced the effectiveness of reintroduction as a conservation and recovery tool.

Under section 10(j), a population of a listed species re-established outside its current range but within its probable historic range may be designated as "experimental" at the discretion of the Secretary of the Interior (Secretary). Reintroduction of the experimental population must further the conservation of the listed species. An experimental population must be separate geographically from nonexperimental populations of the same species. Designation of a population as experimental increases the Service's management flexibility.

Additional management flexibility exists if the Secretary finds the experimental population to be "nonessential" to the continued existence of the species. For purposes of section 7 [except section 7(a)(1), which requires Federal agencies to use their authorities to conserve listed species], nonessential experimental populations located outside national wildlife refuge or national park lands are treated as if they are proposed for listing. This means that Federal agencies are under an obligation to confer, as opposed to consult (required for a listed species), on any actions authorized, funded, or carried out by them that are likely to jeopardize the continued existence of the species. Nonessential experimental populations located on national wildlife refuge or national park lands are treated as threatened, and formal consultation may be required. Activities undertaken on private or tribal lands are not affected by section 7 of the Act unless they are authorized, funded, or carried out by a Federal agency.

Individual animals used in establishing an experimental population can be removed from a source population if their removal is not likely to jeopardize the continued existence of the species, and a permit has been issued in accordance with 50 C.F.R. part 17.22.

The Mexican gray wolf was listed as an endangered subspecies on April 28, 1976. The gray wolf species in North America south of Canada was listed as endangered on March 9, 1978, except in Minnesota where it was listed as threatened. This listing of the species as a whole continued to recognize valid biological subspecies for purposes of research and conservation.

Biological

This final experimental population rule addresses the Mexican gray wolf (*Canis lupus baileyi*), an endangered subspecies of gray wolf that was extirpated from the southwestern United States by 1970. The gray wolf species (*C. lupus*) is native to most of North America north of Mexico City. An exception is in the southeastern United States, which was occupied by the red wolf species *(C. rufus)*. The gray wolf occupied areas that supported populations of hoofed mammals (ungulates), its major food source.

The Mexican gray wolf historically occurred over much of New Mexico, Arizona, Texas, and northern Mexico, mostly in or near forested, mountainous terrain. Numbering in the thousands before European settlement, the "lobo" declined rapidly when its reputation as a livestock killer led to concerted eradication efforts. Other factors contributing to its decline were commercial and recreational hunting and trapping, killing of wolves by game managers on the theory that more game animals would be available for hunters, habitat alteration, and human safety concerns (although no documentation exists of Mexican wolf attacks on humans).

The subspecies is now considered extirpated from its historic range in the southwestern United States because no wild wolf has been confirmed since 1970. Occasional sightings of "wolves" continue to be reported from U.S. locations, but none have been confirmed. Ongoing field research has not confirmed that wolves remain in Mexico. . .

Recovery Efforts

The *Mexican Wolf Recovery Plan* was adopted by the Directors of the Service and the Mexican Direccion General de la Fauna Silvestre in 1982. Its objective is to conserve and ensure survival of the subspecies by maintaining a captive breeding program and re-establishing a viable, self-sustaining population of at least 100 Mexican wolves in a 5,000 square mile area within the subspecies' historic range. The plan guides recovery efforts for the subspecies, laying out a series of recommended actions. The recovery plan is currently being revised; the Service expects to release a draft for public review in 1998. The revised plan will more precisely define population levels at which the Mexican wolf can be downlisted to "threatened" status and removed from protection under the Act (i.e., delisted).

A captive breeding program was initiated with the capture of five wild Mexican wolves between 1977 and 1980, from Durango and Chihuahua, Mexico. Three of these animals (two males and a female that was pregnant when captured) produced offspring, founding the "certified" captive lineage. Two additional captive populations were determined in July 1995 to be pure Mexican wolves—each has two founders. The captive population included 148 animals as of January 1997–119 are held at 25 facilities in the United States and 29 at five facilities in Mexico.

[In 1992, the Service began planning for the reintroduction of the Mexican wolves. The Service held 14 public meetings and three public hearings, prepared an environmental impact statement, and received comments on the EIS from about 18,000 people. After consulting with state and local governments, other federal agencies, private landowners, native American tribes, and technical experts, the Service issued a proposed rule to reintroduce the Mexican wolves in 1996. Four additional public meetings were held in the affected area. Then in April 1997, the Service announced its intention to reintroduce captive-raised Mexican wolves as a designated non-essential experimental population in eastern Arizona within the designated Blue Range Wolf Recovery Area. The Service added that it would reintroduce wolves into the White Sands Wolf Recovery Area, the designated back-up area, if that becomes necessary for the recovery of the wolves and feasible.]

Mexican Wolf Recovery Areas

. . . The two wolf recovery areas are within the Mexican wolf's probable historic range. The Mexican wolf is considered extinct in the wild in the United States. Thus, both areas are geographically separate from any known, naturally-occurring, nonexperimental populations of wild wolves.

[T]his rule establishes a larger Mexican Wolf Experimental Population Area, which also is geographically separate from any known, naturally-occurring nonexperimental populations of wild wolves. The Service is not proposing to re-establish Mexican wolves throughout this larger area. The purpose of designating an experimental population area is to establish that any member of the re-established Mexican wolf population found in this larger area is a member of the nonessential experimental population, and subject to the provisions of this rule including, but not limited to, its capture and return to the designated recovery area(s). . .

Management of the Reintroduced Population

The nonessential experimental designation enables the Service to develop measures for management of the population that are less restrictive than the mandatory prohibitions that protect species with "endangered" status. This includes allowing limited "take" of individual wolves under narrowly defined circumstances. Management flexibility is needed to make reintroduction compatible with current and planned human activities, such as livestock grazing and hunting. It is also critical to obtaining needed State, Tribal, local, and private cooperation. The Service believes this flexibility will improve the likelihood of success.

Reintroduction will occur under management plans that allow dispersal by the new wolf populations beyond the primary recovery zones where they will be released into the secondary recovery zones of the designated wolf recovery area(s). The Service and cooperating agencies will not allow the wolves to establish territories on public lands wholly outside these wolf recovery area boundaries. With landowner consent, the Service also would prevent wolf colonization of private or tribal lands outside the designated recovery area(s).

No measures are expected to be needed to isolate the experimental population from naturally occurring populations because no Mexican wolves are known to occur anywhere in the wild. The Service has ensured that no population of naturally-occurring wild wolves exists within the recovery areas. Surveys for wolf signs in these areas have been conducted, and no naturally occurring population has been documented. No naturally occurring population of Mexican wolves has been documented in Mexico following four years of survey efforts there. Therefore, based on the best available information, the Service concludes that future natural migration of wild wolves into the experimental population area is not possible.

Findings Regarding Reintroduction

The Service finds that . . . the reintroduced experimental population is likely to become established and survive in the wild within the Mexican gray wolf's probable historic range. The Service projects that this reintroduction will achieve the recovery goal of at least 100 wolves occupying 5,000 square miles. The Blue Range Wolf Recovery Area comprises 6,854 square miles of which about 95% is National Forest.

Some members of the experimental population are expected to die during the reintroduction efforts after removal from the captive population. The Service finds that even if the entire experimental population died, this would not appreciably reduce the prospects for future survival of the subspecies in the wild. That is, the captive population could produce more surplus wolves and future reintroductions still would be feasible if the reasons for the initial failure are understood. The individual Mexican wolves selected for release will be as genetically redundant with other members of the captive population as possible, thus minimizing any adverse effects on the genetic integrity of the remaining captive population. . . The United States captive population of Mexican wolves has approximately doubled in the last 3 years, demonstrating the captive population's reproductive potential to replace reintroduced wolves that die. In view of all these safeguards the Service finds that the reintroduced population would not be "essential" under 50 C.F.R. § 17.81(c)(2).

The Service finds that release of the experimental population will further the conservation of the subspecies and of the gray wolf species as a whole. Currently, no populations or individuals of the Mexican gray wolf subspecies are known to exist anywhere in the wild. No wild populations of the gray wolf species are known to exist in the United States south of Washington, Idaho, Wyoming, North Dakota, Minnesota, Wisconsin, and Michigan. Therefore, based on the best available information, the Service finds that the re-established population would be completely geographically separate from any extant wild populations or individual gray wolves and that future migration of wild Mexican wolves into the experimental population area is not possible. The Mexican wolf is the most southerly and the most genetically distinct of the North American gray wolf subspecies. It is the rarest gray wolf subspecies and has been given the highest recovery priority for gray wolves worldwide by the Wolf Specialist Group of the World Conservation Union (IUCN).

. . . Designation of the released wolves as nonessential experimental is considered necessary to obtain needed State, Tribal, local, and private cooperation. This designation also allows for management flexibility to mitigate negative impacts, such as livestock depredation. Without such flexibility, intentional illegal killing of wolves likely would harm the prospects for success.

Potential for Conflict With Federal and Other Activities

As indicated, considerable management flexibility has been incorporated into the final experimental population rule to reduce potential conflicts between wolves and the activities of governmental agencies, livestock operators, hunters, and others. No major conflicts with current management of Federal, State, private, or Tribal lands are anticipated. Mexican wolves are not expected to be adversely affected by most of the current land uses in the designated wolf recovery areas. However, temporary restrictions on human activities may be imposed around release sites, active dens, and rendezvous sites.

Also, the U.S. Department of Agriculture, Animal and Plant Health Inspection Service, Wildlife Services (WS) division will discontinue use of M–44's and choking-type snares in "occupied Mexican wolf range." Other predator control activities may be restricted or modified pursuant to a cooperative management agreement or a conference between the WS and the Service.

The Service and other authorized agencies may harass, take, remove, or translocate Mexican wolves under certain circumstances described in detail in this rule. Private citizens also are given broad authority to harass Mexican wolves for purposes of scaring them away from people, buildings, facilities, pets, and livestock. They may kill or injure them in defense of human life or when wolves are in the act of attacking their livestock (if certain conditions are met). In addition, ranchers can seek compensation from a private fund if depredation on their livestock occurs.

No formal consultation under section 7 of the Act would be required regarding potential impacts of land uses on nonessential experimental Mexican wolves. Any harm to wolves resulting solely from habitat modification caused by authorized uses of public lands that are not in violation of the temporary restriction provisions or other provisions regarding take or harassment would be a legal take under this rule. Any habitat modification occurring on private or tribal lands would not constitute illegal take. Based on evidence from other areas, the Service does not believe that wolf recovery requires major changes to currently authorized land uses. The main management goals are to protect wolves from disturbance during vulnerable periods, minimize illegal take, and remove individuals from the wild population that depredate livestock or otherwise cause significant problems.

The Service does not intend to change the "nonessential experimental" designation to "essential experimental," "threatened," or "endangered" and the Service does not intend to designate critical habitat for the Mexican wolf. Critical habitat cannot be designated under the nonessential experimental classification, 16 U.S.C. 1539(j)(2)(C)(ii). The Service foresees no likely situation which would result in such changes in the future. . .

Summary of Public Participation

In June 1996, public open house meetings and formal public hearings were held in El Paso, Texas; Alamogordo and Silver City, New Mexico; and Springerville, Arizona. About 166 people attended these meetings and had an opportunity to speak with agency representatives and submit oral and written comments. Oral testimony was presented by 49 people at the hearings, and 150 people submitted written comments on the proposed rule. We received a petition supporting full endangered status for reintroduced Mexican wolves signed by 32 people; and a petition opposing the reintroduction of Mexican wolves signed by 91 people. In addition, many comments on the [draft] EIS were specific to the draft proposed rule or related management considerations. These comments also were considered in this revision of the proposed rule. . .

NOTES & QUESTIONS

1. On March 30, 1998, the first Mexican wolves were released in the Apache National Forest in eastern Arizona. By the end of the year, five wolves had been shot and killed, one was missing and presumed dead, and three were recaptured for their own protection, leaving only two wolves in the wild. The first wolf pup born in the wild in half a century was missing and presumed dead, too. One of the wolves was shot by a camper who believed his family was in danger when the wolf attacked his dog. Environmentalists criticized the camper for taking his dogs into wolf country and for not leaving with his family after their first encounter with the wolf. The government decided not to prosecute the camper. A reward of $50,000 was offered by the government, environmental groups, and Michael Blake (the author of "Dances With Wolves") for information regarding those who killed the other wolves, but even the offer of a reward had been controversial. *See* E.J. Montini, *Of Wolves and Men and Money*, ARIZ. REP., Nov. 2, 1998, at B1 (interviewing a man who noted that only $12,000 had been raised as a reward for his son's unsolved murder).

Fifty-eight Mexican wolves were estimated to live in the recovery area in 2011 (32 in Arizona, 26 in New Mexico. Meanwhile, 88 wolves died in the area between 1998 and 2011. Illegal shootings killed 43 of the wolves, 14 died in vehicle collisions, and the remainder died of natural, unknown, or other causes. A three-year review of the program conducted in 2001 concluded that "[t]he ultimate factor determining population viability for wolves is human attitude." The review also advised that the small size of the recovery zone established for the wolves, the FWS's insistence that the wolves remain in that area, and an insufficient target population of 100 wolves were the primary factors that "hinder the recovery of a self-sustaining and viable wolf population." PAUL C. PAQUET, MEXICAN WOLF RECOVERY: THREE-YEAR PROGRAM REVIEW AND ASSESSMENT 60–61 (2001). For updates on the progress of the reintroduction effort, *see* the FWS website at http://www.fws.gov/southwest/es/mexicanwolf/MWRP.cfm.

2. Wolves have long been controversial in the United States. As one environmental leader observed, "When Europeans reached this continent, they brought with them thousand of years of accumulated prejudice against the wolf. Widely expressed in mythology and in folk takes from Aesop's fables to The Three Little Pigs and Little Red Riding Hood, it easily overpowered the Native American view of the wolf as a respected fellow creature in the web of life." Rodger Schlickeisen, *A Positive Turn for Man and Nature; Wolf Reintroduction Marks True Progress,* ARIZ. REP., Jan. 26, 1998, at B5. Wolves were killed by the tens of thousands—with government support or by government agents—from the mid-nineteenth century until about 1920, by which time wolves were nearly eradicated from the entire country. The attitude toward wolves today is much more divided. Many ranchers and westerners retain the traditional fear of wolves, while others are fascinated by wolves, including tourists who flock to hear wolves howl in areas where wolves are more common. *See generally* WOLVES AND HUMAN COMMUNITIES: BIOLOGY, POLITICS, AND ETHICS (Virginia A. Sharpe, Bryan G. Norton & Strachan Donnelly eds. 2001) (collecting essays on the relationship of wolves to their ecosystems and to people).

The divisive attitude toward wolves has taken on increased importance amidst the federal government's efforts to reintroduce them. The FWS has experienced mixed results in reintroducing wolves to two other places besides the Mexican wolves in Arizona and New Mexico. In 1987, the FWS reintroduced red wolves as an experimental population in the Alligator National Wildlife Refuge in northeastern North Carolina. There were about 66 wolves there by 2011. *See* FWS, Red Wolf Recovery Program, http://www.fws.gov/redwolf/index.html. The FWS experienced such remarkable success in reintroducing wolves to Yellowstone National Park that the wolves there were delisted from the ESA in 2012, as we discuss in the last section of this chapter. The ESA also delisted the western Great Lakes population of gray wolves in 2011 after the species recovered without recourse to reintroducing any animals. *See* Revising the Listing of the Gray Wolf (Canis lupus) in the Western Great Lakes, 76 Fed. Reg. 81666 (2011).

3. Almost by definition, a species that has become endangered no longer lives in many areas where it once could be found. Efforts to save the species often seek to reintroduce it to areas from which it has disappeared, or even to areas where it never lived but which offer suitable habitat. The list of species that have been reintroduced into former or new habitat since the enactment of the ESA includes California condors, grizzly bears, black-footed ferrets, peregrine falcons, and many others. Many other recovery plans—including the plan for the five Monterey County plants—list reintroduction as a possible step toward the preservation of a species. But a 1994 study of 145 reintroduction efforts involving 115 species concluded that only sixteen had produced populations that were sustaining themselves in the wild, and that only half of those species had been endangered. *See* Mark Derr, *As Rescue Plan for Threatened Species, Breeding Programs Falter,* N.Y. TIMES, Jan. 19, 1999, at F1. The reintroduction of the red wolf into the Great Smoky Mountains National Park was abandoned in 1998 when government officials removed the remaining wolves because the wolves could not find enough prey to survive. Reintroduction efforts face other criticisms as well. They are costly: reintroduction of the condor, wolf and black-footed ferret alone have cost a total of more than $50 million. They are dependent upon adequate habitat, and so face the same challenges as existing populations of wild species in the face of human development. And they can be controversial among local residents, as illustrated by the reaction of Arizona ranchers to the reintroduction of the Mexican wolf and the reaction of many Idaho residents to proposed grizzly bear reintroductions.

4. How far should we go in reintroducing species to places where they once lived? Should we reintroduce species to places where they never lived, but which contain suitable habitat? Consider the following contrast: "North America lost most of its large vertebrate species—its megafauna— some 13,000 years ago at the end of the Pleistocene. And now Africa's large mammals are dying, stranded on a continent where wars are waging over scarce resources." The solution proposed by Cornell University biologist Josh Donlan is to introduce African cheetahs, African elephants, and lions to private property in the United States. "Free-roaming, managed cheetahs in the southwestern United States could save the fastest carnivore from extinction, restore what must have been strong interactions with pronghorn, and facilitate ecotourism as an economic alternative for ranchers." Elephants "might suppress the woody plants that threaten western grasslands," while the introduction of African lions "while challenging, has clear aesthetic and economic benefits." Donlan adds that "[t]he third state in our vision for Pleistocene re-wilding would entail one or more 'ecological history parks,' covering vast areas of economically depressed part of the Great Plains." Josh Donlan et al., *Re-wilding North America*, NATURE, Aug. 18, 2005, at 913–14. Do you think the remaining residents of, say, western Nebraska would welcome this kind of economic development?

5. In 1982, Congress added section 10(j) to the ESA. That provision authorizes the Secretary to release an experimental population of an endangered or threatened species if the Secretary determines that such a release will further the conservation of the species. The purpose of section 10(j) is to promote the recovery of a species in a manner that encourages the cooperation of other federal agencies and private landowners. Any experimental population must be kept wholly separate from nonexperimental populations of the same species, *see* ESA § 10(j)(1), 16 U.S.C. § 1539(j)(1), and an experimental population is automatically listed as a separate threatened species. ESA § 10(j)(2)(C), 16 U.S.C. § 1539(j)(2)(C). Because it is a threatened species, the Secretary may decide to issue a special rule imposing somewhat more relaxed restrictions on private landowners than those ordinarily provided by section 9 of the ESA. Additionally, section 10(j) requires the Secretary to determine whether the experimental population "is essential to the continued existence" of the species. ESA § 10(j)(2)(B), 16 U.S.C. § 1539(j)(2)(B). If the population is not essential to the survival of the species, then section 7 of the ESA (concerning the duties of federal agencies) does not apply unless the species is in a National Park or a National Wildlife Refuge. ESA § 10(j)(2)(C), 16 U.S.C. § 1539(j)(2)(C).

The FWS prefers to reintroduce species as experimental and not essential pursuant to section 10(j). In response to a public comment regarding the Mexican wolf reintroduction, the agency explained:

> The "experimental nonessential" terminology in section 10(j) of the Act is confusing. It does not mean that the animal is not near extinction and it does not mean the reintroduction is just an experiment. It is a classification designed to make the reintroduction and management of endangered species more flexible and responsive to public concerns to improve the likelihood of successfully recovering the species.

63 Fed. Reg. at 1757. That flexibility is important to the agency because it allows the crafting of special rules favored by local residents and by other federal agencies and because it permits the agency to more actively manage the rein-

FEDERAL GOVERNMENT RESPONSIBILITIES

troduced population. But that flexibility has its costs. Professor Holly Doremus has criticized the FWS for effectively eliminating the statutory distinction between essential and nonessential experimental populations by reading the law so that no population is ever deemed essential to the survival of the species. More broadly, she argues that "adoption of special rules permitting incidental and deliberate take of introduced populations is a choice to restrict the wildness of those populations." She explains that "species must be protected as wild creatures, rather than merely as biological entities," and that "none of the congressionally listed values of species can be fully protected in captivity." She adds that animals are wild only "if they enjoy natural autonomy, that is if their natural instincts determine such basic choices as where they sleep, what they eat, and how they select a mate." Holly Doremus, *Restoring Endangered Species: The Importance of Being Wild*, 23 HARV. ENVTL. L. REV. 1, 10–16, 38–47 (1999). Is Professor Doremus right about the importance of preserving biodiversity in its wild, natural state? Why isn't the ESA satisfied if species are preserved in zoos? And how can purposeful human efforts to reintroduce a species be reconciled with the wildness of a species? Should the FWS impose the same restrictions on private and government activity that the ESA imposes on naturally occurring populations of a listed species? Are the Mexican wolves truly wild if government employees use food to steer the pack in another direction?

Section 10(j)'s requirement that an experimental population be wholly separate from any existing population of the species has generated challenges to high profile reintroduction efforts. *See* Forest Guardians v. U.S. Fish & Wildlife Serv., 611 F.3d 692, 710 (10th Cir. 2010) (holding "that substantial evidence in the record supports the FWS's conclusion that no wild population of [Aplomado] Falcons in New Mexico would prevent the release of captive-bred Falcons into that area as part of a nonessential experimental population"); United States v. McKittrick, 142 F.3d 1170 (9th Cir.1998) (upholding the reintroduction of wolves to Yellowstone because the occasional appearance of a few native wolves did not constitute a "population" that overlapped with the reintroduction population); *accord id.* at 1179 (O'Scannlain, J., concurring) ("A single straggler does not a population make.").

B. RESPONSIBILITIES OF ALL FEDERAL AGENCIES UNDER THE ESA

Congress has charged the FWS (and in some circumstances, the NMFS) with the responsibility for taking the lead on federal efforts to protect species listed as endangered or threatened under the ESA. While the FWS leads, other federal agencies are supposed to follow. The ESA requires all federal agencies to consider the effects of their activities on listed species. That means that a Federal Highway Administration interstate project, an Air Force missile range, and a Corps of Engineers river dredging project must all account for any listed species that they might affect. In particular, the ESA imposes an affirmative duty and a negative duty on federal agencies. The affirmative duty directs all agencies to conserve listed species. The negative duty prohibits federal agencies from jeopardizing the continued existence of a listed species or adversely affecting the designated critical habitat of a species. (Federal agencies must also comply with the ESA's prohibition against taking a listed species, but that provision is discussed in chapter 6 because it applies to governmental and private parties alike). The jeopardy prohibition has received much more attention than the conservation duty to date, but there are indications that the conservation duty could begin to become a more prominent feature of the act.

1. THE CONSERVATION DUTY

The Hawksbill Sea Turtle v. Federal Emergency Management Agency

United States District Court for the District of the Virgin Islands, 1998.
11 F.Supp.2d 529.

■ BROTMAN, DISTRICT JUDGE, Sitting by Designation.

[In September 1995, Hurricane Marilyn swept through St. Thomas in the U.S. Virgin Islands, killing eleven people and displacing hundreds of others from their homes. Several months afterward, the Federal Emergency Management Agency (FEMA) provided funds to the Virgin Island Housing Authority for the construction of a temporary housing shelter project to house the low-income residents who were still homeless as a result of the hurricane. The project was to consist of prefabricated buildings that could house up to 800 people and that would be dismantled after the emergency abated. The site of the project, though, was near the habitat of three listed species: the endangered Virgin Island Tree Boa, a secretive snake that lives only on the eastern portion of St. Thomas; the endangered Hawksbill Sea Turtle, which lives in coral reefs off of St. Thomas and other islands; and the threatened Green Sea Turtle. FEMA worked with local officials in the Virgin Islands to prepare a "Tree Boa Mitigation Plan" that directed construction personnel to hand clear the area before heavy machinery was operated at the site. FEMA also took steps to assure that the construction activities would not degrade water quality to the detriment of the turtles. Finding these steps unsatisfactory, a group of residents who lived in the area of the proposed emergency housing project sued to block construction alleging, *inter alia*, that FEMA failed to comply with the conservation duties of the ESA.]

Plaintiffs allege that Defendants violated their Section 7(a)(1) duties to conserve the Tree Boa and the Sea Turtles. Section 7(a)(1) provides in pertinent part that:

The Secretary [of the Interior] shall review other programs administered by him and utilize such programs in furtherance of the purposes of this chapter. All other Federal agencies shall, in consultation with and with the assistance of the Secretary, utilize their authorities in furtherance of the purposes of this chapter by carrying out programs for the conservation[9] of endangered species and threatened species listed pursuant to section 1533 of this title.

---

[9] The term "conservation" means "the use of all methods and procedures which are necessary to bring any endangered species or threatened species to the point at which the measures provided pursuant to this chapter are no longer necessary. Such methods and proce-

16 U.S.C. § 1536(a)(1) (footnote added). Plaintiffs claim that Defendants' violated their Section 7(a)(1) conservation duties by constructing a housing project that would have a harmful effect on the Tree Boa and the Sea Turtles. They also aver that Defendants failed "to take the affirmative steps required by the ESA to conserve" the species.

This Court finds Plaintiffs' Section 7(a)(1) claims without merit. "Conservation plans under [Section] 7(a)(1) are 'voluntary measures that the federal agency has the discretion to undertake' and 'the [ESA] does not mandate particular actions be taken by Federal Agencies to implement [Section] 7(a)(1).' " Strahan v. Linnon, 967 F. Supp. 581, 596 (D.Mass. 1997) (quoting 51 Fed. Reg. 19926, 19931, 19934). "Agencies have 'some discretion in ascertaining how best to fulfill the mandate to conserve under section 7(a)(1).' " J. B. Ruhl, *Section 7(a)(1) of the "New" Endangered Species Act: Rediscovering and Redefining the Untapped Power of Federal Agencies' Duty to Conserve Species*, 25 Envtl. L. 1107, 1132 (1995) (quoting Pyramid Lake Paiute Tribe of Indians v. United States Dep't of the Navy, 898 F.2d 1410 (9th Cir.1990)). "Reasonable people could disagree as to the proper level of activism required by an agency under the ESA. The court will not substitute its judgment for the agency's in deciding as a general matter that the totality of defendant's actions taken to protect threatened and endangered species were insufficient." Defenders of Wildlife v. Administrator, Environmental Protection Agency, 688 F. Supp. 1334, 1352 (D.Minn.1988), *aff'd in part and rev'd in part on other grounds*, 882 F.2d 1294 (8th Cir.1989). Defendants have provided evidence that they have adopted various, specifically targeted mitigation measures in an attempt to conserve the Tree Boa and the marine environment in Vessup Bay. On the other hand, Plaintiffs have not specified any conservation measures that Defendants have failed to take. Given Plaintiffs failure to specify alternative conservation measures, this Court must conclude that the Defendants' actions as a whole did not constitute an arbitrary and capricious failure to conserve threatened and endangered species. *See Strahan*, 967 F. Supp. at 595–96 (finding Section 7(a)(1) argument unpersuasive because plaintiff "has not demonstrated . . . specific measures that are necessary to prevent the loss of any 'endangered species' in addition to those adopted by the agency)."

NOTES & QUESTIONS

1. The "temporary" housing project at issue in *Hawksbill Turtle* was two and a half years old by the time the district court decided the case. In April 1998, the governor of the Virgin Islands ordered a stay of eviction of the families remaining in the project until alternative housing was arranged. FEMA advised the FWS of the delay, but FWS did not find any additional threat to the listed species so long as the plans to relocate the remaining families proceeded.

---

dures include, but are not limited to, all activities associated with scientific resources management such as research, census, law enforcement, habitat acquisition and maintenance, propagation, live trapping, and transplantation, and, in the extraordinary case where population pressures within a given ecosystem cannot be otherwise relieved, may include regulated taking." 16 U.S.C. § 1532(3).

2. The conservation duty has been interpreted narrowly by most other courts. *See, e.g.,* Pyramid Lake Paiute Tribe of Indians v. U.S. Department of the Navy, 898 F.2d 1410 (9th Cir.1990) (holding that the Navy did not violate section 7(a)(1) when it took water from the Truckee River to suppress dust that interfered with flight training despite the possible adverse effect on endangered fish living in Pyramid Lake resulting from the reduction in the lake's water level); Strahan v. Linnon, 966 F.Supp. 111 (D.Mass.1997) (rejecting the claim that the Coast Guard violated section 7(a)(1) by refusing to impose speed limits and other constraints on vessels operating in waters containing the Northern Right whale and other endangered marine species); Center for Marine Conservation v. Brown, 917 F.Supp. 1128, 1149–50 (S.D.Tex.1996) (concluding that the federal agencies responsible for regulating fishery resources did not violate section 7(a)(1) when they refused to take additional steps to protect endangered sea turtles from commercial shrimping operations); National Wildlife Fed'n v. Hodel, 1985 WL 186671 (E.D.Cal.1985) (holding that FWS did not violate section 7(a)(1) when it permitted the use of lead shot in hunting migratory birds); *but see* Florida Key Deer v. Stickney, 864 F.Supp. 1222 (S.D.Fla. 1994) (finding that FEMA violated section 7(a)(1) when it failed to undertake *any* actions to protect the endangered Florida Key deer); Defenders of Wildlife v. Andrus, 428 F.Supp. 167 (D.D.C.1977) (holding that the FWS violated section 7(a)(1) when it failed to consider whether permitting hunting during twilight would result in protected birds being shot by mistake).

The Fifth Circuit, has adopted a much more sweeping understanding of the conservation duty. In Sierra Club v. Glickman, 156 F.3d 606 (5th Cir.1998), the court held that the Department of Agriculture failed to comply with section 7(a)(1) when it declined to take actions necessary to prevent the contamination of the Edwards Aquifer in central Texas. The Edwards Aquifer provides water to irrigate millions of dollars worth of crops, but the aquifer is also home to the Texas blind salamander and four other endangered species. The court held that the Sierra Club had standing to challenge the effects of the USDA's actions on the listed species because the court interpreted section 7(a)(1) as follows:

> At first blush, this section appears to suggest that federal agencies have only a generalized duty to confer and develop programs for the benefit of endangered and threatened species—*i.e.*, not with respect to any particular species... When read in the context of the ESA as a whole, however, we find that the agencies' duties under § 7(a)(1) are much more specific and particular... By imposing a duty on all federal agencies to use "all methods and procedures which are necessary to bring *any* endangered species or threatened species to the point at which the measures provided pursuant to this chapter are no longer necessary," 16 U.S.C. § 1532(2) (emphasis added), Congress was clearly concerned with the conservation of each endangered and threatened species. To read the command of § 7(a)(1) to mean that the agencies have only a generalized duty would ignore the plain meaning of the statute.

The court rejected the USDA's argument that it had complied with the conservation duty because the endangered species in the Edwards Aquifer had enjoyed incidental benefits from USDA programs carried out for other purposes. USDA did not work with FWS, as required by section 7(a)(1), and USDA's efforts were inadequate in any event.

Similarly, a federal district court in Florida enjoined FEMA from issuing national flood insurance in the state in part because the agency "failed to implement any conservation plan with respect to [the Florida Key deer and eight other listed species] as required by ESA § 7(a)(1)." Florida Key Deer v. Brown, 364 F.Supp.2d 1345, 1361 (S.D. Fla. 2005). The agency had argued that it complied with section 7(a)(1) by providing "incentive credits to communities that develop and implement habitat conservation plans," *id.* at 1360, but the county that hosted the species was ineligible for such credits. The court cited the Fifth Circuit's decision in *Sierra Club v. Glickman* in holding that section 7(a)(1) imposes "a specific, rather than a generalized duty to conserve species." *Id.* at 1361.

3. Suppose that a recovery plan for a species encourages the removal of exotic plants from the area inhabited by the species. The land is owned by the Army, which uses it for infantry training exercises that seek to simulate the lush, tropical vegetation in other parts of the world where it might one day need to deploy. Does the conservation duty require the Army to follow the guidance of the recovery plan?

4. In an article on section 7(a)(1) that is cited in *Hawksbill Turtle*, one of us has observed that federal agencies "may possibly cultivate, channel, and control the potentially broad application of that duty to conserve in ways not possible under the core programs, thereby expanding the effectiveness of section 7(a)(1) without attracting the same backlash the core programs have suffered." Three features of section 7(a)(1) illustrate "this dual virtue of breadth and flexibility." First, "unlike jeopardy consultations under section 7(a)(2), the duty to conserve species under section 7(a)(1) applies to federal programs and not merely to federal actions." The difference is that while the jeopardy provision only applies on a case-by-case basis as individual problems arise, the conservation duty can be applied to entire federal agency "authorities" that can be used to implement species conservation "programs." Second, "unlike conservation plans under section 10(a)(1) and jeopardy consultations under section 7(a)(2), the duty to conserve species under section 7(a)(1) applies independent of take and jeopardy findings." Much of the controversy surrounding the take and jeopardy provisions results from the sometimes dramatic consequences for a proposed project of a finding that the project takes an endangered species or jeopardizes the continued existence of the species as a whole. Section 7(a)(1) avoids such dire results by encouraging efforts to protect listed species that operate independently of an agency or private party's desire to pursue a particular project. Third, "the duty to conserve species under section 7(a)(1), like jeopardy consultations under section 7(a)(2), applies to endangered and threatened animals and plants." Plants and threatened species receive limited protection under the ESA's take and jeopardy provisions, despite the significant values associated with many plants and despite the law's objective of preventing a threatened species from actually becoming endangered. The conservation duty offers a means by which plants and threatened species can be protected by all federal agencies. If the conservation duty is this appealing, then why has it not received more attention?

2. THE DUTY TO AVOID CAUSING JEOPARDY

Karuk Tribe of California v. United States Forest Service

United States Court of Appeals for the Ninth Circuit, 2012.
681 F.3d 1006.

■ W. FLETCHER, CIRCUIT JUDGE:

We consider whether the U.S. Forest Service must consult with appropriate federal wildlife agencies under *Section 7* of the Endangered Species Act ("ESA") before allowing mining activities to proceed under a Notice of Intent ("NOI") in critical habitat of a listed species. The ESA requires consultation with the Fish and Wildlife Service or the NOAA Fisheries Service for any "agency action" that "may affect" a listed species or its critical habitat. 16 U.S.C. § 1536(a)(2); 50 C.F.R. § 402.14(a). There are two substantive questions before us.

The first is whether the Forest Service's approval of four NOIs to conduct mining in the Klamath National Forest is "agency action" within the meaning of *Section 7*. Under our established case law, there is "agency action" whenever an agency makes an affirmative, discretionary decision about whether, or under what conditions, to allow private activity to proceed. The record in this case shows that Forest Service District Rangers made affirmative, discretionary decisions about whether, and under what conditions, to allow mining to proceed under the NOIs.

The second is whether the approved mining activities "may affect" a listed species or its critical habitat. Forest Service regulations require a NOI for all proposed mining activities that "might cause" disturbance of surface resources, which include fisheries and wildlife habitat. 36 C.F.R. §§ 228.4(a), 228.8(e). In this case, the Forest Service approved mining activities in and along the Klamath River, which is critical habitat for threatened coho salmon. The record shows that the mining activities approved under NOIs satisfy the "may affect" standard.

We therefore hold that the Forest Service violated the ESA by not consulting with the appropriate wildlife agencies before approving NOIs to conduct mining activities in coho salmon critical habitat within the Klamath National Forest.

I. Background

The Karuk Tribe has inhabited what is now northern California since time immemorial. The Klamath River originates in southeastern Oregon, runs through northern California, and empties into the Pacific Ocean about forty miles south of the California-Oregon border. In northern California, the Klamath River passes through the Six Rivers and Klamath National Forests. The Klamath River system is home to several species of fish, including coho salmon. Coho salmon in the Klamath River system were listed as "threatened" under the ESA in 1997. The Klamath River system and adjacent streamside riparian zones were designated as critical habitat for coho salmon in 1999. The Karuk Tribe depends on coho salmon in the Klamath River system for cultural, religious, and subsistence uses.

The rivers and streams of the Klamath River system also contain gold. Commercial gold mining in and around the rivers and streams of California was halted long ago due, in part, to extreme environmental harm caused by large-scale placer mining. *See generally* People v. Gold Run Ditch & Mining Co., 4 P. 1152 (Cal. 1884) (affirming injunction against hydraulic gold mining because of impacts on downstream rivers); GREEN VERSUS GOLD: SOURCES IN CALIFORNIA'S ENVIRONMENTAL HISTORY 101-40 (Carolyn Merchant ed., 1998) (describing environmental impacts of the California Gold Rush). However, small-scale recreational mining has continued. Some recreational miners "pan" for gold by hand, examining one pan of sand and gravel at a time. Some conduct "motorized sluicing" by pumping water onto streambanks to process excavated rocks, gravel, and sand in a sluice box. As the material flows through the box, a small amount of the heavier material, including gold, is slowed by "riffles" and is then captured in the bottom of the box. The remaining material runs through the box and is deposited in a tailings pile. Finally, some recreational miners conduct mechanical "suction dredging" within the streams themselves. These miners use gasoline-powered engines to suck streambed material up through flexible intake hoses that are typically four or five inches in diameter. The streambed material is deposited into a floating sluice box, and the excess is discharged in a tailings pile in or beside the stream. Dredging depths are usually about five feet, but can be as great as twelve feet.

The Karuk Tribe contends that these mining activities adversely affect fish, including coho salmon, in the Klamath River system. The Tribe challenges the Forest Service's approval of four NOIs to conduct mining activities in coho salmon critical habitat in the Klamath National Forest, without first consulting with federal wildlife agencies pursuant to *Section 7 of the ESA*.

A. Mining Regulations

Under the General Mining Law of 1872, a private citizen may enter public lands for the purpose of prospecting and mining. 30 U.S.C. § 22. The Organic Administration Act of 1897 extended the Mining Law to the National Forest system but authorized the Secretary of Agriculture to regulate mining activities in the National Forests to protect the forest lands from destruction and depredation. 16 U.S.C. §§ 482, 551. The Act specified that prospectors and miners entering federal forest lands "must comply with the rules and regulations covering such national forests." *Id.* § 478. We have repeatedly upheld the Forest Service's authority to impose reasonable environmental regulations on mining activities in National Forests, so long as they do not prohibit or impermissibly encroach on legitimate mining uses.

In 1974, the Forest Service promulgated regulations to minimize the adverse environmental impacts of mining activities in *National Forests*. The regulations establish three different categories of mining, based on whether the proposed activities "will not cause," "might cause," or "will likely cause" significant disturbance of surface resources, which include fisheries and wildlife habitat. The first category, *de minimis* mining activities that "will not cause" significant disturbance of surface resources, may proceed without notifying the Forest Service or obtaining the agency's approval or authorization. The third category, mining activities that "will likely cause" significant disturbance of surface resources, may not proceed until the Forest Service approves a Plan of Operations ("Plan") submitted by the miner. A Plan requires relatively detailed information, including "the approximate location and size of areas where surface resources will be disturbed" and "measures to be taken to meet the requirements for environmental protection." Within 30 days of receiving a Plan, or 90 days if necessary, the Forest Service must approve the proposed Plan or notify the miner of any additional environmental conditions necessary to meet the purpose of the regulations.

At issue in this appeal is the middle category of mining activities: those that "might cause" disturbance of surface resources. Forest Service mining regulations require that any person proposing such activities must submit a Notice of Intent to operate, or NOI, to the appropriate District Ranger. A NOI is less detailed than a Plan. It need only contain information "sufficient to identify the area involved, the nature of the proposed operations, the route of access to the area of operations and the method of transport." Within 15 days of receiving a NOI, the District Ranger must notify the miner whether a Plan is required. . .

B. 2004 Mining Season

Before the start of the 2004 mining season, representatives of the Karuk Tribe expressed concern to the Forest Service about the effects of suction dredge mining on fisheries in the Klamath River system. The District Ranger for the Happy Camp District of the Klamath National Forest, Alan Vandiver, responded by organizing meetings that included Tribal leaders, miners, and district officials. Vandiver also consulted with Forest Service biologists Bill Bemis and Jon Grunbaum. . . [Eventually, Vandiver approved a number of NOIs, and the tribe sued the Forest Service for allegedly violating the ESA, the National Environmental Policy Act, and the National Forest Management Act. The district court rejected the tribe's claims, and a Ninth Circuit panel affirmed that decision 2-1. The Ninth Circuit then agreed to rehear the case en banc.]

Consultation Under the Endangered Species Act

We have described *Section 7* as the "heart of the ESA." W. Watersheds Project v. Kraayenbrink, 632 F.3d 472, 495 (9th Cir. 2011). *Section 7* requires federal agencies to ensure that none of their activities, including the granting of licenses and permits, will jeopardize the continued existence of listed species or adversely modify a species' critical habitat.

Section 7 imposes on all agencies a duty to consult with either the Fish and Wildlife Service or the NOAA Fisheries Service before engaging in any discretionary action that may affect a listed species or critical habitat. Turtle Island Restoration Network v. Nat'l Marine Fisheries Serv., 340 F.3d 969, 974 (9th Cir. 2003). The purpose of consultation is to obtain the expert opinion of wildlife agencies to determine whether the action is likely to jeopardize a listed species or adversely modify its critical habitat and, if so, to identify reasonable and prudent alternatives that will avoid the action's unfavorable impacts. *Id.* The consultation requirement reflects "a conscious decision by Congress to give endangered species priority over the 'primary missions' of federal agencies." Tenn. Valley Auth. v. Hill, 437 U.S. 153, 185 (1978).

Section 7(a)(2) of the ESA provides:

Each Federal agency shall, in consultation with and with the assistance of the Secretary, insure that any action authorized, funded, or carried out by such agency (hereinafter in this section referred to as an *"agency action"*) is not likely to jeopardize the continued existence of any endangered species or threatened species or result in the destruction or adverse modification of [critical] habitat of such species . . .

16 U.S.C. § 1536(a)(2) (emphasis added).

Regulations implementing *Section 7* provide:

Each Federal agency shall review its actions at the earliest possible time to determine whether any action *may affect* listed species or critical habitat. If such a determination is made, formal consultation is required . . .

50 C.F.R. § 402.14(a) (emphasis added).

We discuss the "agency action" and "may affect" requirements in turn.

1. Agency Action

Section 7 of the ESA defines agency action as "any action authorized, funded, or carried out by [a federal] agency." The ESA implementing regulations provide:

Action means all activities or programs of any kind authorized, funded, or carried out, in whole or in part, by Federal agencies in the United States or upon the high seas. Examples include, but are not limited to: (a) actions intended to conserve listed species or their habitat; (b) the promulgation of regulations; (c) the granting of licenses, contracts, leases, easements, rights-of-way, permits, or grants-in-aid; or (d) actions directly or indirectly causing modifications to the land, water, or air.

50 C.F.R. § 402.02. There is "little doubt" that Congress intended agency action to have a broad definition in the ESA, and we have followed the Supreme Court's lead by interpreting its plain meaning "in conformance with Congress's clear intent." Pac. Rivers Council v. Thomas, 30 F.3d 1050, 1054-55 (9th Cir. 1994) (citing *Tenn. Valley Auth.*, 437 U.S. at 173).

The ESA implementing regulations limit Section 7's application to "'actions in which there is discretionary Federal involvement or control.'" Nat'l Ass'n of Home Builders v. Defenders of Wildlife, 551 U.S. 644, 666 (2007) (quoting 50 C.F.R. § 402.03). The Supreme Court explained that this limitation harmonizes the ESA consultation requirement with other statutory mandates that leave an agency no discretion to consider the protection of listed species. *Home Builders*, 551 U.S. at 665-66.

Our "agency action" inquiry is two-fold. First, we ask whether a federal agency affirmatively authorized, funded, or carried out the underlying activity. Second, we determine whether the agency had some discretion to influence or change the activity for the benefit of a protected species.

a. Affirmative Authorization

We have repeatedly held that the ESA's use of the term "agency action" is to be construed broadly. Examples of agency actions triggering Section 7 consultation include the renewal of existing water contracts, Natural Res. Def. Council v. Houston, 146 F.3d 1118, 1125 (9th Cir. 1998), the creation of interim management strategies, Lane Cnty. Audubon Soc'y v. Jamison, 958 F.2d 290, 293-94 (9th Cir. 1992), and the ongoing construction and operation of a federal dam, *Tenn. Valley Auth.,* 437 U.S. at 173-74. We have also required consultation for federal agencies' authorization of private activities, such as the approval and registration of pesticides, Wash. Toxics Coal. v. Envtl. Prot. Agency, 413 F.3d 1024, 1031-33 (9th Cir. 2005), and the issuance of permits allowing fishing on the high seas, *Turtle Island,* 340 F.3d at 974.

An agency must consult under *Section 7* only when it makes an "affirmative" act or authorization. Where private activity is proceeding pursuant to a vested right or to a previously issued license, an agency has no duty to consult under *Section 7* if it takes no further affirmative action regarding the activity. Similarly, where no federal authorization is required for private-party activities, an agency's informal proffer of advice to the private party is not "agency action" requiring consultation.

Here, the Forest Service's mining regulations and actions demonstrate that the agency affirmatively authorized private mining activities when it approved the four challenged NOIs. By regulation, the Forest Service must authorize mining activities before they may proceed under a NOI. The regulations require that a miner submit a NOI for *proposed* mining activities. By contrast, a miner conducting *de minimis* mining activities, such as gold panning or mineral sampling, may proceed without submitting anything to, or receiving anything from, the Forest Service. When a miner submits a NOI, the regulations also require that the Forest Service inform the miner within 15 days whether the mining may proceed under the NOI or whether he must prepare a Plan of Operations instead. In other words, when a miner proposes to conduct mining operations under a NOI, the Forest Service either affirmatively authorizes the mining under the NOI or rejects the NOI and requires a Plan instead. . .

The Forest Service and the Miners contend that the underlying mining activities are authorized by the General Mining Law, rather than by the agency's approval of the NOIs. But private activities can and do have more than one source of authority, and more than one source of restrictions on that authority. *See* 50 C.F.R. § 402.02 (agency "action" under the ESA includes all private activities authorized "in part" by a federal agency). The Mining Law and the Organic Act give miners "a statutory right, not mere privilege," to enter the National Forests for mining purposes, but Congress has subjected that right to environmental regulation. The Forest Service concedes that its approval of a Plan of Operations "authorizes" mining activities and constitutes an "agency action" under the ESA, even though the Mining Law presumably "authorized" those activities as well. The same logic extends to the agency's approval of a NOI.

The Forest Service contends that approval of a NOI is merely a decision not to regulate the proposed mining activities. But the test under the ESA is whether the agency *authorizes*, funds, or carries out the activity, at least in part. 50 C.F.R. § 402.02 (emphasis added). As shown above, the Forest Service authorizes mining activities when it approves a NOI and affirmatively decides to allow the mining to proceed. Moreover, the record in this case demonstrates that the Forest Service controls mining activities through the NOI process, whether or not such control qualifies a NOI as a "regulatory instrument." As discussed below, the Forest Service formulated precise criteria for the protection of coho salmon, communicated those criteria to prospective miners, and approved the miners' activities under a NOI only if they strictly conformed their mining to the specified criteria. The Forest Service also monitored the miners' compliance with those criteria. . .

In sum, the Forest Service's approval of the four challenged NOIs constituted agency action under *Section 7 of the ESA*.

b. Discretionary Involvement or Control

The ESA implementing regulations provide that *Section 7* applies only to actions "in which there is discretionary Federal involvement or control." 50 C.F.R. § 402.03. There is no duty to consult for actions "that an agency is *required* by statute to undertake once certain specified triggering events have occurred." *Home Builders,* 551 U.S. at 669 (emphasis in original); *id. at 672-73* (no duty to consult where Clean Water Act required Environmental Protection Agency ("EPA") to transfer regulatory authority to a state upon satisfaction of nine specified criteria). However, to avoid the consultation obligation, an agency's competing statutory mandate must require that it perform specific nondiscretionary acts rather than achieve broad goals. An agency "cannot escape its obligation to comply with the ESA merely because it is bound to comply with another statute that has consistent, complementary objectives." The competing statutory objective need only leave the agency "some discretion."

To trigger the ESA consultation requirement, the discretionary control retained by the federal agency also must have the capacity to inure to the benefit of a protected species. The relevant question is whether the agency *could* influence a private activity to benefit a listed species, not whether it *must* do so.

Here, the Forest Service's mining regulations and actions demonstrate that the decision whether to approve a NOI is a discretionary determination through which the agency can influence private mining activities to benefit listed species. . . The agency's exercise of discretion under the mining regulations also may influence the mining activities to protect a listed species. The overriding purpose of the regulations is "to minimize [the] adverse environmental impacts" of mining activities on federal forest lands. The touchstone of the agency's discretionary determination is the likelihood that mining activities will cause significant disturbance of surface resources, which include fisheries and wildlife habitat. Thus, the Forest Service can exercise its discretion to benefit a listed species by approving or disapproving NOIs based on whether the proposed mining activities satisfy particular habitat protection criteria. The agency can reject a NOI and require that the prospective miner instead submit a Plan of Operations, under which the Forest Service can impose additional habitat protection conditions.

The record in this case reveals at least three ways in which the Forest Service exercised discretion when deciding whether, and under what conditions, to approve NOIs for mining activities in the Klamath and Six Rivers National Forests.

First, the Forest Service exercised discretion by formulating criteria for the protection of coho salmon habitat. . . Second, the Forest Service exercised discretion by refusing to approve a detailed NOI submitted by the New 49'ers for mining activities in the Orleans District of the Six Rivers National Forest. . . Third, the Forest Service exercised discretion when it applied different criteria for the protection of fisheries habitat in different districts of the Klamath National Forest.

Under our established case law, there is "agency action" sufficient to trigger the ESA consultation duty whenever an agency makes an affirmative, discretionary decision about whether, or under what conditions, to allow private activity to proceed. As to all four NOIs challenged in this appeal, the Forest Service made an affirmative, discretionary decision whether to allow private mining activities to proceed under specified habitat protection criteria. Accordingly, we hold that the Forest Service's approval of the NOIs constituted discretionary agency action within the meaning of *Section 7 of the ESA.*

2. May Affect Listed Species or Critical Habitat

An agency has a duty to consult under *Section 7 of the ESA* for any discretionary agency action that "may affect" a listed species or designated critical habitat. An agency may avoid the consultation requirement only if it determines that its action will have "no effect" on a listed species or critical habitat. Once an agency has determined that its action "may affect" a listed species or critical habitat, the agency must consult, either formally or informally, with the appropriate expert wildlife agency. If the wildlife agency determines during informal consultation that the proposed action is "not likely to adversely affect any listed species or critical habitat," formal consultation is not required and the process ends. Thus, actions that have any chance of affecting listed species or critical habitat—even if it is later determined that the actions are "not likely" to do so—require at least some consultation under the ESA.

We have previously explained that "may affect" is a "relatively low" threshold for triggering consultation. Cal. ex rel. Lockyer v. U.S. Dep't of Agric., 575 F.3d 999, 1018 (9th Cir. 2009). "*Any possible effect*, whether beneficial, benign, adverse or of an undetermined character,"" triggers the requirement. *Id.* at 1018-19 (quoting 51 Fed. Reg. 19,926, 19,949 (June 3, 1986)*)* (emphasis in *Lockyer*). The Secretaries of Commerce and the Interior have explained that "[t]he threshold for formal consultation must be set sufficiently low to allow Federal agencies to satisfy their duty to 'insure'" that their actions do not jeopardize listed species or adversely modify critical habitat. 51 Fed. Reg. at 19,949.

Whether the mining activities approved by the Forest Service in this case "may affect" critical habitat of a listed species can almost be resolved as a textual matter. By definition, mining activities that require a NOI "might cause" disturbance of surface resources. "Surface resources" include underwater fisheries habitat. The Forest Service approved NOIs to conduct mining activities in and along the Klamath River system, which is designated critical habitat for listed coho salmon. If the phrase "might cause" disturbance of fisheries habitat is given an ordinary meaning, it follows almost automatically that mining pursuant to the approved NOIs "may affect" critical habitat of the coho salmon. Indeed, the Forest Service does not dispute that the mining activities in the Klamath River system "may affect" the listed coho salmon and its critical habitat.

The Miners, however, contend that the record is "devoid of any evidence" that the mining activities may affect coho salmon. The Miners make two arguments in support of their contention. . . First, the Miners argue that there is no evidence "that even a single member of any listed species would be 'taken' by reason" of the mining activities approved in the NOIs. "Take" has a particular definition under the ESA. 16 U.S.C. § 1532(19) ("The term 'take' means to harass, harm, pursue, hunt, shoot, wound, kill, trap, capture, or collect, or to attempt to engage in any such conduct."); *see also* 50 C.F.R. § 17.3 (further defining "harm" and "harass"). Whether mining activities effectuate a "taking" under *Section 9 of the ESA* is a distinct inquiry from whether they "may affect" a species or its critical habitat under *Section 7*. The Miners also fault the Tribe for failing to identify "so much as a single endangered fish or fish egg ever injured by this [mining] activity." But where, as here, a plaintiff alleges a procedural violation under *Section 7 of the ESA*, as opposed to a substantive violation under *Section 9*, the plaintiff need not prove that a listed species has in fact been injured. The plaintiff need only show, as the Tribe has done here, that the challenged action "may affect" a listed species or its critical habitat.

Second, the Miners argue that Vandiver's consultation with Forest Service biologists, and the resulting habitat protection criteria, "assured" that there would be "no impact whatsoever on listed species." This argument cuts against, rather than in favor of, the Miners. The fact that District Ranger Vandiver formulated criteria to mitigate effects of suction dredging on coho salmon habitat does not mean that the "may affect" standard was not met. Indeed, that Vandiver consulted with Forest Service biologists in an attempt to reduce a possible adverse impact on coho salmon and their habitat suggests exactly the opposite. . .

We conclude that the mining activities approved by the Forest Service in this case "may affect" the listed coho salmon and its critical habitat. Indeed, as a textual matter, mining activities in designated critical habitat that require approval under a NOI likely satisfy the low threshold triggering the duty to consult under the ESA.

3. Burden on the Forest Service

The burden imposed by the consultation requirement need not be great. Consultation under the ESA may be formal or informal. Formal consultation requires preparation of a biological opinion detailing how the agency action affects listed species or their critical habitat, but informal consultation need be nothing more than discussions and correspondence with the appropriate wildlife agency. If the wildlife agency agrees during informal consultation that the agency action "is not likely to adversely affect listed species or critical habitat," formal consultation is not required and the process ends. Thus, whereas approval of a Plan of Operations—for mining activities that "will likely cause significant disturbance of surface resources"—may often require formal consultation and preparation of a biological opinion, informal consultation may often suffice for approval of a NOI. . .

M. SMITH, Circuit Judge, with whom KOZINSKI, Chief Judge, joins, and with whom IKUTA and MURGUIA, Circuit Judges, join as to Parts I through VI, dissenting:

. . . Until today, it was well-established that a regulatory agency's "'inaction' is not 'action'" that triggers the Endangered Species Act's (ESA) arduous interagency consultation process. W. Watersheds Project v. Matejko, 468 F.3d 1099, 1108 (9th Cir. 2006). Yet the majority now flouts this crystal-clear and common sense precedent, and for the first time holds that an agency's decision *not to act* forces it into a bureaucratic morass. . .

The majority asserts that the Forest Service's *decision* not to require a Plan of Action for the mining activities described in a Notice of Intent constitutes an *implicit authorization* of those mining activities, therefore equating the Forest Service's "decision" with an agency "authorization" under the ESA.

The Forest Service never contemplated such a result. The Forest Service's explanation of its mining regulations establishes that a Notice of Intent is used as an information-gathering tool, not an application for a mining permit. Consistent with the Forest Service's interpretations, the Ranger's response to a Notice of Intent is analogous to the Notice of Intent itself, and provides merely notice of the agency's review decision. It is not a permit, and does not impose regulations on private conduct as does a Plan of Operations. The Forest Service interprets the Notice of Intent as . . . "a *simple notification procedure*" that would

> "assist prospectors in determining whether their operations would or would not require the filing of an operating plan. Needless uncertainties and expense in time and money in filing unnecessary operating plans could be avoided thereby . . . [The 1974 notice-and-comment rulemaking] record makes it clear that *a notice of intent to operate was not intended to be a regulatory instrument; it simply was meant to be a notice* given to the Forest Service by an operator which describes the operator's plan to conduct operations on [National Forest Service] lands. Further, this record demonstrates that the intended trigger for a notice of intent to operate is reasonable uncertainty on the part of the operator as to the significance of the potential effects of the proposed operations. In such a circumstance, *the early alert provided by a notice of intent to operate* would advance the interests of both the Forest Service and the operator by *facilitating resolution of the question,* "Is submission and approval of a plan of operations required before the operator can commence proposed operations?"

[Clarification as to When a Notice of Intent To Operate and/or Plan of Operation Is Needed for Locatable Mineral Operations on National Forest System Lands, 70 Fed. Reg. 32,713, at 32,728 (June 6, 2005) (emphasis added)].

Under the Forest Service's regulations, a Notice of Intent is exactly what its name implies: a *notice* from the miner, not a *permit* or *license* issued by the agency. It is merely a precautionary agency notification procedure, which is at most a preliminary step prior to agency action being taken.

Precedent distinguishing "action" from "inaction"

Our precedent establishes that there is a significant difference between a *decision not to act* and an *affirmative authorization*. These cases distinguish between "agency action" and "agency inaction," and illustrate the meaning of the operative regulation's reference to "licenses," "permits," and the like. 50 C.F.R. § 402.02 (2004). In the pertinent cases involving "agency action," the agency takes an *affirmative step* that allows private conduct to take place; without the agency's affirmative action (such as issuing a permit, license, or contract), the private conduct could not occur.[5] In the pertinent cases involving agency *inaction*, private conduct may take place until the agency takes affirmative steps to intervene. The relevant case law requires us to identify the default position: if the agency does

nothing, can the private activity take place? If the activity can proceed regardless of whether the agency takes any actions, then the activity does not
involve the agency's "granting of licenses, contracts, leases, easements,
rights-of-way, permits, or grants-in-aid" as required for "agency action" under the regulations. *Id.* . .

VII. Brave New World

Abandon all hope, ye who enter here.

— Dante Alighieri, THE DIVINE COMEDY, Inferno Canto III

I cannot conclude my dissent without considering the impact of the
majority's decision in this case, and others like it, which, in my view, flout
our precedents and undermine the rule of law. In doing so, I intend no personal disrespect or offense to any of my colleagues. My intent is solely to
illuminate the downside of our actions in such environmental cases.

By rendering the Forest Service impotent to meaningfully address low
impact mining, the majority effectively shuts down the entire suction
dredge mining industry in the states within our jurisdiction. The informal
Notice of Intent process allows projects to proceed within a few weeks. In
contrast, ESA interagency consultation requires a formal biological assessment and conferences, and can delay projects for months or years. Although the ESA generally requires agencies to complete consultations within ninety days, 16 U.S.C. § 1536(b), the agencies frequently miss their
deadlines due to personnel shortages. One study found that nearly 40 percent of U.S. Fish and Wildlife Service ESA consultations were untimely,
with some taking two or three years. Government Accountability Office,
*More Federal Management Attention is Needed to Improve the Consultation
Process*, March 2004. Moreover, formal consultation comes at great costs to
the private applicants, often requiring them to hire outside experts because
the agency is backlogged. Most miners affected by this decision will have
neither the resources nor the patience to pursue a consultation with the
EPA; they will simply give up, and curse the Ninth Circuit.

As a result, a number of people will lose their jobs and the businesses
that have invested in the equipment used in the relevant mining activities
will lose much of their value. In 2008, California issued about 3,500 permits for such mining, and 18 percent of those miners received "a significant
portion of income" from the dredging. *See* Justin Scheck, *California Sifts
Gold Claims*, THE WALL STREET JOURNAL, April 29, 2012. The gold mining
operation in this case, the New 49ers, organizes recreational weekend gold-
mining excursions. The majority's opinion effectively forces these people to
await the lengthy and costly ESA consultation process if they wish to pursue their mining activities, or simply ignore the process, at their peril. . .

No legislature or regulatory agency would enact sweeping rules that
create such economic chaos, shutter entire industries, and cause thousands
of people to lose their jobs. That is because the legislative and executive
branches are directly accountable to the people through elections, and its

members know they would be removed swiftly from office were they to enact such rules. In contrast, in order to preserve the vitally important principle of judicial independence, we are not politically accountable. However,
because of our lack of public accountability, our job is constitutionally confined to *interpreting* laws, not *creating* them out of whole cloth. Unfortunately, I believe the record is clear that our court has strayed with lamen-
table frequency from its constitutionally limited role . . . when it comes to
construing environmental law. When we do so, I fear that we undermine
public support for the independence of the judiciary, and cause many to
despair of the promise of the rule of law.

     I respectfully dissent.

NOTES & QUESTIONS

1. Why does Judge Fletcher think that the Forest Service needs to consult with
the FWS regarding possible impacts on endangered species whenever the Forest Service issues a NOI? Why does Judge Smith think that consultation is unnecessary at that time? What decisions could the Forest Service make regarding mining in national forests that would not require consultation according to
Judge Fletcher? What decisions could the Forest Service make that would require consultation according to Judge Smith? What, after all, is the purpose of
section 7's consultation requirement?

2. Suppose that a federal highway project is proposed for Las Vegas, the fastest
growing city in the United States. Scores of other commercial, residential, and
road projects are under consideration, about to begin construction, or already
being built. Some of these projects are supported or authorized by federal agencies; others are state, local or private projects with no federal nexus. The area is
also home to the endangered desert tortoise and a number of other listed species and species under consideration for listing. In determining the effect of the
federal highway project, must the cumulative impact of all of the other projects
be considered, or only some of them? Must the impact on species that are not
listed be considered?

3. What happens if the federal agency action changes or additional information
is learned about a species—or a new species is listed—after the consultation is
completed? The FWS regulations provide that an agency must reopen consultation when (1) the amount or extent of a taking specified in a incidental take
statement is exceeded, (2) new information reveals effects of the action that
may affect listed species or critical habitat in a manner or to an extent not previously considered, (3) the identified action is subsequently modified in a manner that causes an effect to the listed species or critical habitat that was not
considered in the biological opinion, or (4) a new species is listed or critical habitat designated that may be affected by the identified action. 50 C.F.R. § 402.16.
The application of the regulations is illustrated by Sierra Club v. Marsh, 816
F.2d 1376 (9th Cir.1987), where the Army Corps of Engineers agreed as a result of a consultation with the FWS to purchase 200 acres of land to protect two
endangered birds that could be affected by a Corps highway and flood control
project. When the land proved to be difficult to obtain, the Corps continued
work on the project but refused to reinitiate consultation with the FWS. The
court held that the Corps could not proceed with the project until it further

consulted with the FWS or it acquired the land because of the "institutionalized caution mandated by section 7 of the ESA."

4. Judge Smith, joined by Chief Judge Kozinski, claims that the majority's interpretation of the ESA is ill-founded because "[n]o legislature or regulatory agency would enact sweeping rules that create such economic chaos, shutter entire industries, and cause thousands of people to lose their jobs." Can you think of any examples of a legislature or regulatory agency enacting such rules? If such rules are to be enacted, who should enact them?

5. Judge Smith also claims that the Ninth Circuit's entire ESA jurisprudence – indeed, its whole environmental jurisprudence – is flawed. He is not the only one to make that argument, which has inspired repeated attempts to divide the Ninth Circuit in a way that separates presumably pro-environmental Californians from those in other western states who are more skeptical of federal environmental regulation. None of those efforts have come close to succeeding. But unlike the Ninth Circuit, the Supreme Court has been seemingly hostile to the broad application of the ESA, *see* J.B. Ruhl, *The Endangered Species Act's Fall from Grace in the Supreme Court*, 36 HARV. ENVTL. L. REV. 487 (2012)—with the dramatic exception of the following case.

Tennessee Valley Authority v. Hill

Supreme Court of the United States, 1978.
437 U.S. 153.

■ MR. CHIEF JUSTICE BURGER delivered the opinion of the Court.

The questions presented in this case are (a) whether the Endangered Species Act of 1973 requires a court to enjoin the operation of a virtually completed federal dam—which had been authorized prior to 1973—when, pursuant to authority vested in him by Congress, the Secretary of the Interior has determined that operation of the dam would eradicate an endangered species; and (b) whether continued congressional appropriations for the dam after 1973 constituted an implied repeal of the Endangered Species Act, at least as to the particular dam.

I

The Little Tennessee River originates in the mountains of northern Georgia and flows through the national forest lands of North Carolina into Tennessee, where it converges with the Big Tennessee River near Knoxville. The lower 33 miles of the Little Tennessee takes the river's clear, free-flowing waters through an area of great natural beauty. Among other environmental amenities, this stretch of river is said to contain abundant trout. Considerable historical importance attaches to the areas immediately adjacent to this portion of the Little Tennessee's banks. To the south of the river's edge lies Fort Loudon, established in 1756 as England's southwestern outpost in the French and Indian War. Nearby are also the ancient sites of several native American villages, the archeological stores of which are to a large extent unexplored. These include the Cherokee towns of Echota and Tennase, the former being the sacred capital of the Cherokee Nation as early as the 16th century and the latter providing the linguistic basis from which the State of Tennessee derives its name.

In this area of the Little Tennessee River the Tennessee Valley Authority, a wholly owned public corporation of the United States, began constructing the Tellico Dam and Reservoir Project in 1967, shortly after Congress appropriated initial funds for its development. Tellico is a multipurpose regional development project designed principally to stimulate shoreline development, generate sufficient electric current to heat 20,000 homes, and provide flatwater recreation and flood control, as well as improve economic conditions in "an area characterized by underutilization of human resources and outmigration of young people." Of particular relevance to this case is one aspect of the project, a dam which TVA determined to place on the Little Tennessee, a short distance from where the river's waters meet with the Big Tennessee. When fully operational, the dam would impound water covering some 16,500 acres—much of which represents valuable and productive farmland—thereby converting the river's shallow, fast-flowing waters into a deep reservoir over 30 miles in length.

The Tellico Dam has never opened, however, despite the fact that construction has been virtually completed and the dam is essentially ready for operation. Although Congress has appropriated monies for Tellico every year since 1967, progress was delayed, and ultimately stopped, by a tangle of lawsuits and administrative proceedings. After unsuccessfully urging TVA to consider alternatives to damming the Little Tennessee, local citizens and national conservation groups brought suit in the District Court, claiming that the project did not conform to the requirements of the National Environmental Policy Act of 1969 (NEPA). After finding TVA to be in violation of NEPA, the District Court enjoined the dam's completion pending the filing of an appropriate environmental impact statement. The injunction remained in effect until late 1973, when the District Court concluded that TVA's final environmental impact statement for Tellico was in compliance with the law.

A few months prior to the District Court's decision dissolving the NEPA injunction, a discovery was made in the waters of the Little Tennessee which would profoundly affect the Tellico Project. Exploring the area around Coytee Springs, which is about seven miles from the mouth of the river, a University of Tennessee ichthyologist, Dr. David A. Etnier, found a previously unknown species of perch, the snail darter, or Percina (Imostoma) tanasi. This three-inch, tannish-colored fish, whose numbers are estimated to be in the range of 10,000 to 15,000, would soon engage the attention of environmentalists, the TVA, the Department of the Interior, the Congress of the United States, and ultimately the federal courts, as a new and additional basis to halt construction of the dam.

Until recently the finding of a new species of animal life would hardly generate a cause celebre. This is particularly so in the case of darters, of which there are approximately 130 known species, 8 to 10 of these having been identified only in the last five years.[10] The moving force behind the snail darter's sudden fame came some four months after its discovery, when the Congress passed the Endangered Species Act of 1973 (Act). This legislation, among other things, authorizes the Secretary of the Interior to declare species of animal life "endangered" and to identify the "critical habitat" of these creatures. When a species or its habitat is so listed, the following portion of the Act—relevant here—becomes effective:

> "The Secretary [of the Interior] shall review other programs administered by him and utilize such programs in furtherance of the purposes of this chapter. All other Federal departments and agencies shall, in consultation with and with the assistance of the Secretary, utilize their authorities in furtherance of the purposes of this chapter by carrying out programs for the conservation of endangered species and threatened species listed pursuant to section 1533 of this title and *by taking such action necessary to insure that actions authorized, funded, or carried out by them do not jeopardize the continued existence of such endangered species and threatened species or result in the destruction or modification of habitat of such species* which is determined by the Secretary, after consultation as appropriate with the affected States, to be critical." 16 U.S.C. § 1536 (1976 ed.) (emphasis added).

In January 1975, the respondents in this case and others petitioned the Secretary of the Interior to list the snail darter as an endangered species. After receiving comments from various interested parties, including TVA and the State of Tennessee, the Secretary formally listed the snail darter as an endangered species on October 8, 1975. In so acting, it was noted that "the snail darter is a living entity which is genetically distinct and reproductively isolated from other fishes." More important for the purposes of this case, the Secretary determined that the snail darter apparently lives only in that portion of the Little Tennessee River which would be completely inundated by the reservoir created as a consequence of the Tellico Dam's completion.[11] The Secretary went on to explain the significance of the dam to the habitat of the snail darter:

> "[The] snail darter occurs only in the swifter portions of shoals over clean gravel substrate in cool, low-turbidity water. Food of the snail darter is almost exclusively snails which require a clean gravel substrate for their survival. *The proposed impoundment of water behind the proposed Tellico Dam would result in total destruction of the snail darter's habitat.*" (emphasis added).

---

[10] In Tennessee alone there are 85 to 90 species of darters, of which upward to 45 live in the Tennessee River system. New species of darters are being constantly discovered and classified—at the rate of about one per year. This is a difficult task for even trained ichthyologists since species of darters are often hard to differentiate from one another.

[11] Searches by TVA in more than 60 watercourses have failed to find other populations of snail darters. The Secretary has noted that "more than 1,000 collections in recent years and additional earlier collections from central and east Tennessee have not revealed the presence of the snail darter outside the Little Tennessee River." It is estimated, however, that the snail darter's range once extended throughout the upper main Tennessee River and the lower portions of its major tributaries above Chattanooga—all of which are now the sites of dam impoundments.

Subsequent to this determination, the Secretary declared the area of the Little Tennessee which would be affected by the Tellico Dam to be the "critical habitat" of the snail darter. [TVA tried to find an alternative river to which it could relocate the snail darters, but those efforts failed. TVA continued to seek congressional funding for the dam, which Congress and President Carter approved in a December 1975 appropriations bill containing funds for the continued construction of the dam. In February 1976, a University of Tennessee law student named Hiram Hill sued TVA to enjoin the completion of the dam based on section 7 of the ESA. The district court refused to issue an injunction, but the Sixth Circuit reversed an ordered a permanent injunction against the construction of the Tellico Dam. TVA officials testified before congressional committees at several times during the course of the litigation, and each time the committee stated its understanding that the dam should be completed notwithstanding the ESA.]

II

We begin with the premise that operation of the Tellico Dam will either eradicate the known population of snail darters or destroy their critical habitat. Petitioner does not now seriously dispute this fact. In any event, under § 4 (a)(1) of the Act, the Secretary of the Interior is vested with exclusive authority to determine whether a species such as the snail darter is "endangered" or "threatened" and to ascertain the factors which have led to such a precarious existence. By § 4(d) Congress has authorized—indeed commanded—the Secretary to "issue such regulations as he deems necessary and advisable to provide for the conservation of such species." As we have seen, the Secretary promulgated regulations which declared the snail darter an endangered species whose critical habitat would be destroyed by creation of the Tellico Reservoir. Doubtless petitioner would prefer not to have these regulations on the books, but there is no suggestion that the Secretary exceeded his authority or abused his discretion in issuing the regulations. Indeed, no judicial review of the Secretary's determinations has ever been sought and hence the validity of his actions are not open to review in this Court.

(A)

It may seem curious to some that the survival of a relatively small number of three-inch fish among all the countless millions of species extant would require the permanent halting of a virtually completed dam for which Congress has expended more than $100 million. The paradox is not minimized by the fact that Congress continued to appropriate large sums of public money for the project, even after congressional Appropriations Committees were apprised of its apparent impact upon the survival of the snail darter. We conclude, however, that the explicit provisions of the Endangered Species Act require precisely that result.

One would be hard pressed to find a statutory provision whose terms were any plainer than those in § 7 of the Endangered Species Act. Its very words affirmatively command all federal agencies "to *insure* that actions *authorized, funded, or carried out* by them do not *jeopardize* the continued existence" of an endangered species or "*result* in the destruction or modification of habitat of such species. . ." 16 U. S. C. § 1536 (1976 ed.). (Emphasis added.) This language admits of no exception. Nonetheless, petitioner urges, as do the dissenters, that the Act cannot reasonably be interpreted as applying to a federal project which was well under way when Congress passed the Endangered Species Act of 1973. To sustain that position, however, we would be forced to ignore the ordinary meaning of plain language. It has not been shown, for example, how TVA can close the gates of the Tellico Dam without "carrying out" an action that has been "authorized" and "funded" by a federal agency. Nor can we understand how such action will "*insure*" that the snail darter's habitat is not disrupted. Accepting the Secretary's determinations, as we must, it is clear that TVA's proposed operation of the dam will have precisely the opposite effect, namely the eradication of an endangered species.

Concededly, this view of the Act will produce results requiring the sacrifice of the anticipated benefits of the project and of many millions of dollars in public funds. But examination of the language, history, and structure of the legislation under review here indicates beyond doubt that Congress intended endangered species to be afforded the highest of priorities. . .

The legislative proceedings in 1973 are, in fact, replete with expressions of concern over the risk that might lie in the loss of any endangered species. . . Congress was concerned about the unknown uses that endangered species might have and about the unforeseeable place such creatures may have in the chain of life on this planet.

In shaping legislation to deal with the problem thus presented, Congress started from the finding that "[the] two major causes of extinction are hunting and destruction of natural habitat." Of these twin threats, Congress was informed that the greatest was destruction of natural habitats. Witnesses recommended, among other things, that Congress require all land-managing agencies "to avoid damaging critical habitat for endangered species and to take positive steps to improve such habitat." Virtually every bill introduced in Congress during the 1973 session responded to this concern by incorporating language similar, if not identical, to that found in the present § 7 of the Act. These provisions were designed, in the words of an administration witness, "for the first time [to] *prohibit* [a] federal agency from taking action which does jeopardize the status of endangered species," furthermore, the proposed bills would "[direct] all . . . Federal agencies to utilize their authorities for carrying out programs for the protection of endangered animals." (Emphasis added.)

As it was finally passed, the Endangered Species Act of 1973 represented the most comprehensive legislation for the preservation of endangered species ever enacted by any nation. Its stated purposes were "to provide a means whereby the ecosystems upon which endangered species and threatened species depend may be conserved," and "to provide a program for the conservation of such . . . species. . ." In furtherance of these goals, Congress expressly stated in § 2 (c) that "all Federal departments and agencies *shall* seek *to conserve endangered species* and threatened species. . ." (Emphasis added.) Lest there be any ambiguity as to the meaning of this statutory directive, the Act specifically defined "conserve" as meaning "to use and the use of *all methods and procedures which are necessary* to bring *any endangered species* or threatened species to the point at which the measures provided pursuant to this chapter are no longer necessary." (Emphasis added.) Aside from § 7, other provisions indicated the seriousness with which Congress viewed this issue: Virtually all dealings with endangered species, including taking, possession, transportation, and sale, were prohibited, except in extremely narrow circumstances. The Secretary was also given extensive power to develop regulations and programs for the preservation of endangered and threatened species. Citizen involvement was encouraged by the Act, with provisions allowing interested persons to petition the Secretary to list a species as endangered or threatened, and bring civil suits in United States district courts to force compliance with any provision of the Act.

Section 7 of the Act, which of course is relied upon by respondents in this case, provides a particularly good gauge of congressional intent. As we have seen, this provision had its genesis in the Endangered Species Act of 1966, but that legislation qualified the obligation of federal agencies by stating that they should seek to preserve endangered species only *"insofar as is practicable and consistent with [their] primary purposes. . ."* Likewise, every bill introduced in 1973 contained a qualification similar to that found in the earlier statutes. Exemplary of these was the administration bill, H. R. 4758, which in § 2(b) would direct federal agencies to use their authorities to further the ends of the Act *"insofar as is practicable and consistent with [their] primary purposes. . ."* (Emphasis added.) Explaining the idea behind this language, an administration spokesman told Congress that it "would further signal to all . . . agencies of the Government that this is the *first priority, consistent with their primary objectives."* (Emphasis added.) This type of language did not go unnoticed by those advocating strong endangered species legislation. A representative of the Sierra Club, for example, attacked the use of the phrase "consistent with the primary purpose" in proposed H. R. 4758, cautioning that the qualification "could be construed to be a declaration of congressional policy that other agency purposes are necessarily more important than protection of endangered species and would always prevail if conflict were to occur."

What is very significant in this sequence is that the final version of the 1973 Act carefully omitted all of the reservations described above. . . It is against this legislative background that we must measure TVA's claim that the Act was not intended to stop operation of a project which, like Tellico Dam, was near completion when an endangered species was discovered in its path. While there is no discussion in the legislative history of precisely this problem, the totality of congressional action makes it abundantly clear that the result we reach today is wholly in accord with both the words of the statute and the intent of Congress. The plain intent of Congress in enacting this statute was to halt and reverse the trend toward species extinction, whatever the cost. This is reflected not only in the stated policies of the Act, but in literally every section of the statute. All persons, including federal agencies, are specifically instructed not to "take" endangered species, meaning that no one is "to harass, harm, pursue, hunt, shoot, wound, kill, trap, capture, or collect" such life forms. Agencies in particular are directed by §§ 2(c) and 3(2) of the Act to "use . . . *all methods* and procedures which are necessary" to preserve endangered species. (emphasis added). In addition, the legislative history undergirding § 7 reveals an explicit congressional decision to require agencies to afford first priority to the declared national policy of saving endangered species. The pointed omission of the type of qualifying language previously included in endangered species legislation reveals a conscious decision by Congress to give endangered species priority over the "primary missions" of federal agencies.

It is not for us to speculate, much less act, on whether Congress would have altered its stance had the specific events of this case been anticipated. In any event, we discern no hint in the deliberations of Congress relating to the 1973 Act that would compel a different result than we reach here. Indeed, the repeated expressions of congressional concern over what it saw as the potentially enormous danger presented by the eradication of any endangered species suggest how the balance would have been struck had the issue been presented to Congress in 1973.

Furthermore, it is clear Congress foresaw that § 7 would, on occasion, require agencies to alter ongoing projects in order to fulfill the goals of the Act. Congressman Dingell's discussion of Air Force practice bombing, for instance, obviously pinpoints a particular activity—intimately related to the national defense—which a major federal department would be obliged to alter in deference to the strictures of § 7. . . One might dispute the applicability of these examples to the Tellico Dam by saying that in this case the burden on the public through the loss of millions of unrecoverable dollars would greatly outweigh the loss of the snail darter. But neither the Endangered Species Act nor Art. III of the Constitution provides federal courts with authority to make such fine utilitarian calculations. On the contrary, the plain language of the Act, buttressed by its legislative history, shows clearly that Congress viewed the value of endangered species as "incalculable." Quite obviously, it would be difficult for a court to balance the loss of a sum certain—even $100 million—against a congressionally declared "incalculable" value, even assuming we had the power to engage in such a weighing process, which we emphatically do not. . .

Notwithstanding Congress' expression of intent in 1973, we are urged to find that the continuing appropriations for Tellico Dam constitute an implied repeal of the 1973 Act, at least insofar as it applies to the Tellico Project. In support of this view, TVA points to the statements found in various House and Senate Appropriations Committees' Reports; as described in Part I, *supra*, those Reports generally reflected the attitude of the *Committees* either that the Act did not apply to Tellico or that the dam should be completed regardless of the provisions of the Act. Since we are unwilling to assume that these latter Committee statements constituted advice to ignore the provisions of a duly enacted law, we assume that these Committees believed that the Act simply was not applicable in this situation. But even under this interpretation of the Committees' actions, we are unable to conclude that the Act has been in any respect amended or repealed. There is nothing in the appropriations measures, as passed, which states that the Tellico Project was to be completed irrespective of the requirements of the Endangered Species Act. These appropriations, in fact, represented relatively minor components of the lump-sum amounts for the entire TVA budget. To find a repeal of the Endangered Species Act under these circumstances would surely do violence to the " 'cardinal rule . . . that repeals by implication are not favored.' " . . . The doctrine disfavoring repeals by implication "applies with full vigor when . . . the subsequent legislation is an appropriations measure." . . . Perhaps mindful of the fact that it is "swimming upstream" against a strong current of well-established precedent, TVA argues for an exception to the rule against implied repealers in a circumstance where, as here, Appropriations Committees have expressly stated their "understanding" that the earlier legislation would not prohibit the proposed expenditure. We cannot accept such a proposition. Expressions of committees dealing with requests for appropriations cannot be equated with statutes enacted by Congress, particularly not in the circumstances presented by this case. First, the Appropriations Committees had no jurisdiction over the subject of endangered species, much less did they conduct the type of extensive hearings which preceded passage of the earlier Endangered Species Acts, especially the 1973 Act. . . Second, there is no indication that Congress as a whole was aware of TVA's position, although the Appropriations Committees apparently agreed with petitioner's views.

(B)

Having determined that there is an irreconcilable conflict between operation of the Tellico Dam and the explicit provisions of § 7 of the Endangered Species Act, we must now consider what remedy, if any, is appropriate. It is correct, of course, that a federal judge sitting as a chancellor is not mechanically obligated to grant an injunction for every violation of law. . . As a general matter it may be said that "[since] all or almost all equitable remedies are discretionary, the balancing of equities and hardships is appropriate in almost any case as a guide to the chancellor's discretion." . . . But these principles take a court only so far. Our system of government is, after all, a tripartite one, with each branch having certain defined functions delegated to it by the Constitution. While "[it] is emphatically the province and duty of the judicial department to say what the law is," Marbury v. Madison, 1 Cranch 137, 177 (1803), it is equally—and emphatically—the exclusive province of the Congress not only to formulate legislative policies and mandate programs and projects, but also to establish their relative priority for the Nation. Once Congress, exercising its delegated powers, has decided the order of priorities in a given area, it is for the Executive to administer the laws and for the courts to enforce them when enforcement is sought. Here we are urged to view the Endangered Species Act "reasonably," and hence shape a remedy "that accords with some modicum of common sense and the public weal." But is that our function? We have no expert knowledge on the subject of endangered species, much less do we have a mandate from the people to strike a balance of equities on the side of the Tellico Dam. Congress has spoken in the plainest of words, making it abundantly clear that the balance has been struck in favor of affording endangered species the highest of priorities, thereby adopting a policy which it described as "institutionalized caution." Our individual appraisal of the wisdom or unwisdom of a particular course consciously selected by the Congress is to be put aside in the process of interpreting a statute. Once the meaning of an enactment is discerned and its constitutionality determined, the judicial process comes to an end. We do not sit as a committee of review, nor are we vested with the power of veto. The lines ascribed to Sir Thomas More by Robert Bolt are not without relevance here:

> "The law, Roper, the law. I know what's legal, not what's right. And I'll stick to what's legal. . . I'm not God. The currents and eddies of right and wrong, which you find such plain-sailing, I can't navigate, I'm no voyager. But in the thickets of the law, oh there I'm a forester. . . What would you do? Cut a great road through the law to get after the Devil? . . . And when the last law was down, and the Devil turned round on you—where would you hide, Roper, the laws all being flat? . . . This country's planted thick with laws from coast to coast— Man's laws, not God's—and if you cut them down . . . d'you really think you could stand upright in the winds that would below then? . . . Yes, I'd give the Devil benefit of law, for my own safety's sake." R. Bolt, A Man for All Seasons, Act I, p. 147 (Three Plays, Heinemann ed. 1967).

We agree with the Court of Appeals that in our constitutional system the commitment to the separation of powers is too fundamental for us to pre-empt congressional action by judicially decreeing what accords with "common sense and the public weal." Our Constitution vests such responsibilities in the political branches.

■ MR. JUSTICE POWELL, with whom MR. JUSTICE BLACKMUN joins, dissenting.

The Court today holds that § 7 of the Endangered Species Act requires a federal court, for the purpose of protecting an endangered species or its habitat, to enjoin permanently the operation of any federal project, whether completed or substantially completed. This decision casts a long shadow over the operation of even the most important projects, serving vital needs of society and national defense, whenever it is determined that continued operation would threaten extinction of an endangered species or its habitat. This result is said to be required by the "plain intent of Congress" as well as by the language of the statute.

In my view § 7 cannot reasonably be interpreted as applying to a project that is completed or substantially completed when its threat to an endangered species is discovered. Nor can I believe that Congress could have intended this Act to produce the "absurd result"—in the words of the District Court—of this case. If it were clear from the language of the Act and its legislative history that Congress intended to authorize this result, this Court would be compelled to enforce it. It is not our province to rectify policy or political judgments by the Legislative Branch, however egregiously they may disserve the public interest. But where the statutory language and legislative history, as in this case, need not be construed to reach such a result, I view it as the duty of this Court to adopt a permissible construction that accords with some modicum of common sense and the public weal.

... I have little doubt that Congress will amend the Endangered Species Act to prevent the grave consequences made possible by today's decision. Few, if any, Members of that body will wish to defend an interpretation of the Act that requires the waste of at least $53 million, and denies the people of the Tennessee Valley area the benefits of the reservoir that Congress intended to confer. There will be little sentiment to leave this dam standing before an empty reservoir, serving no purpose other than a conversation piece for incredulous tourists.

But more far reaching than the adverse effect on the people of this economically depressed area is the continuing threat to the operation of every federal project, no matter how important to the Nation. If Congress acts expeditiously, as may be anticipated, the Court's decision probably will have no lasting adverse consequences. But I had not thought it to be the province of this Court to force Congress into otherwise unnecessary action by interpreting a statute to produce a result no one intended.

■ [JUSTICE REHNQUIST dissented because he concluded that the district court's refusal to issue an injunction was not an abuse of discretion]

NOTES & QUESTIONS

1. In 1979, six years after voting for the ESA, Tennessee Senator Howard Baker described the snail darter as "the bold perverter of the Endangered Species Act." 125 CONG. REC. 23867 (1979). Was he right?

2. What would happen if the snail darter was discovered just *after* the dam was completed, but before the darter's habitat was destroyed? Would TVA have to tear down the dam? At oral argument, when Justice Powell asked Zygmunt Plater—Hiram Hill's professor at the University of Tennessee and counsel for those opposing the dam—whether the ESA would require the removal of Arizona's Grand Coulee Dam if an endangered species was found there, Plater answered "yes." In fact, the ESA has never been applied to require the destruction or removal of an existing structure. Recently, though, environmentalists have been pressing to remove some of the dams on the Columbia River system in the Pacific Northwest in order to protect several endangered species of salmon. *See* Michael C. Blumm et al., *Saving Snake River Water and Salmon Simultaneously: The Biological, Economic, and Legal Case for Breaching the Lower Snake River Dams, Lowering the John Day Reservoir, and Restoring Natural River Flows*, 28 ENVTL. L. 997 (1998).

If the TVA had succeeded in its efforts to relocate the snail darter to any river, would that have been an acceptable solution?

3. Section 7's jeopardy provision has been employed to block other notable projects. For example, one of the first ESA decisions, National Wildlife Federation

v. Coleman, 529 F.2d 359 (5th Cir.), *cert. denied*, 429 U.S. 979 (1976), enjoined construction of a segment of Interstate 10 in Mississippi because of the highway's impact on the endangered Mississippi sandhill crane. Also, in Roosevelt Campobello International Park Commission v. EPA, 684 F.2d 1041 (1st Cir.1982), the court overturned EPA's issuance of a permit to build an oil refinery along the coast of Maine because EPA failed to adequately study the likelihood of an oil spill that would jeopardize the continued existence of several endangered whales.

Perhaps the most dramatic jeopardy finding occurred in April 2001 when the FWS and NMFS advised the Federal Bureau of Reclamation that its annual operating plan for the Klamath Reclamation Project would jeopardize the continued existence of the endangered Lost River sucker, the shortnose sucker, and the Southern Oregon/Northern California Coast coho salmon. Congress authorized the irrigation project as part of its effort to encourage the settlement of previously arid parts of Oregon. By 2001, though, farmers relying upon irrigation water competed with the suckers and salmon living in the Klamath River, bald eagles preying upon waterfowl in the Lower Klamath National Wildlife Refuge, and members of the Klamath and Yurok Tribes who revered the suckers and who possessed treaty rights to the rivers. Then a drought was predicted for 2001. An ESA section 7 consultation between FWS, NMFS, and the Bureau of Reclamation resulted in a biological opinion that the Bureau's plans to provide irrigation water from the project would jeopardize the suckers and the salmon, so the Bureau issued a revised plan that denied water to most of the farmers who had historically relied upon it. The farmers and their irrigation district then sought an injunction against that revised plan for the Klamath Reclamation Project. The district court denied the injunction because the balance of hardships did not tip sufficiently in favor of the plaintiffs: while there was "no question that farmers who rely upon irrigation water and their communities will suffer severe economic hardship" from the plan, the court cited *TVA v. Hill* as evidence that "[t]hreats to the continued existence of endangered and threatened species constitute ultimate harm." Kandra v. United States, 145 F.Supp.2d 1192, 1200–01 (D.Or.2001).

The jeopardy finding and the court's refusal to enjoin the revised plan triggered civil unrest in Oregon throughout the summer of 2001. Farmers watched as their crops died during the record drought. In early July, "100 to 150 people formed a human chain and shielded men who cut off the headgate's lock using a diamond-bladed chainsaw and a cutting torch, sending water from the Upper Klamath Lake into the canal." *Farmers Force Open Canal in Fight with U.S. Over Water*, N.Y. TIMES, July 6, 2001, at A10. The irrigation canal's headgates were opened three more times in a symbolic protest against the lack of irrigation water. The protestors withdrew after the September 11 terrorist attacks, but the controversy gained a racial edge when three men were arrested in December for driving through the town of Chiloquin, Oregon while firing shotguns and deriding Native Americans as "sucker lovers." And then the premise for the dispute was called into question when the National Academy of Sciences reported in February 2002 that the provision of water to the endangered suckers and salmon instead of the farmers did not yield any appreciable benefit to the fish. *See* NATIONAL ACADEMY OF SCIENCES, SCIENTIFIC EVALUATION OF THE BIOLOGICAL OPINIONS ON ENDANGERED AND THREATENED FISHES IN THE KLAMATH RIVER BASIN: INTERIM REPORT (2002).

Looking back on the dispute concerning the Klamath River, Holly Doremus and Dan Tarlock identify "the root cause" as "too many demands competing for too little water." They conclude that "[s]cience alone cannot determine how water should be allocated among those competing demands. It is a mistake to demand that scientists identify the magic point at which agricultural water withdrawals can be precisely balanced with environmental protection. . . Instead, policymakers should understand that they are dealing with a clash of cultures, and must make value choices. Society must choose between farming and fish, or find a way to accommodate both." Holly Doremus & A. Dan Tarlock, *Fish, Farms, and the Clash of Cultures in the Klamath Basin*, 30 ECOLOGY L.Q. 279, 349 (2003). Marcilynn Burke offers another perspective on the dispute, arguing that the political rhetoric accompanying the Klamath controversy "lures it audience into a world where costs eclipse benefits, conjecture prevails over sound science, and species protection abrogates private property rights." Marcilynn A. Burke, *Klamath Farmers and Cappucino Cowboys: The Rhetoric of the Endangered Species Act and Why It (Still) Matters*, 14 DUKE ENVTL. L. & POL'Y F. 441, 520 (2004). Nor are such disputes between endangered fish (and other species) and competing users of water limited to the Pacific Northwest. Similar controversies arose in 2003 involving the Missouri and Rio Grande Rivers. *See* Rio Grande Silvery Minnow v. Keys, 333 F.3d 1109 (10th Cir. 2003) (holding that the Bureau of Reclamation has the discretion to reduce the delivery of water for irrigation in order to satisfy section 7 of the ESA); American Rivers v. United States Army Corps of Engineers, 271 F.Supp.2d 230 (D.D.C. 2003) (enjoining the Corps from managing its operations along the Missouri River in a way that would jeopardize the least tern, piping plover, and pallid sturgeon); Sandra B. Zellmer, *A New Corps of Discovery for Missouri River Management*, 83 NEB. L. REV. 305 (2004).

4. Professor Oliver Houck counters that the vast majority of section 7 consultations result in no jeopardy findings. His 1993 study determined that fewer than .02% of all consultations have resulted in the termination of the project in question. "No major public activity, nor any major federally-permitted activity was blocked" in any of the 99 FWS jeopardy opinions issued between 1987 and 1992 that Houck examined. Indeed, he argues that FWS has wrongly avoided the invocation of the jeopardy provision by narrowly viewing the agency action at issue, by failing to apply section 7 to federal projects overseas, by conflating jeopardy and critical habitat, and by improperly declining to list species in the first place. *See* Oliver A. Houck, *The Endangered Species Act and Its Implementation By the U.S. Departments of Interior and Commerce*, 64 U. Colo. L. Rev. 277, 317–26 (1993). Daniel Rohlf reached a similar conclusion when he asserted that "the concept of jeopardy often amounts to little more than a vague threat employed by FWS and NMFS to negotiate relatively minor modifications to federal and non-federal actions." Daniel J. Rohlf, *Jeopardy Under the Endangered Species Act: Playing a Game Protected Species Can't Win*, 41 WASHBURN L. REV. 114, 115 (2001).

5. The Supreme Court's decision in *TVA v. Hill* was not the end of the fight between the Tellico Dam and the snail darter. Later in 1978, Congress responded by adding a provision to the ESA that established an Endangered Species Committee empowered to waive the jeopardy prohibition in appropriate circumstances. This committee—commonly known as the "God Squad" because of its power to determine the fate of a species on the brink of extinction—is comprised of seven federal officials and one individual selected by the President from each of the states involved. The exemption process may be triggered by a request from the federal agency proposing the action, the governor of the state in which the action will occur, or a private applicant for federal permit or license that results in a jeopardy finding. The committee is empowered to waive the prohibitions of section 7 (and also section 9, whose provisions are discussed in chapter 6) only if at least five of its members determine that (1) there are no reasonable and prudent alternatives to the federal agency action, (2) the benefits of the agency action clearly outweigh alternatives that would protect the species, (3) the agency action is of national or regional significance, and (4) no irreversible or irretrievable commitment of resources are made prior to the committee's ruling. *See* ESA § 7(e).

Not surprisingly, the God Squad made its debut when TVA requested a waiver for the Tellico Dam. More surprisingly, in January 1979 the committee unanimously rejected the request. As Secretary of the Interior Cecil Andrus stated, "Frankly, I hate to see the snail darter get the credit for stopping a project that was ill-conceived and uneconomical in the first place."

The subtle approach having failed, congressional supporters of the Tellico Dam responded by adding a provision to the 1980 Interior appropriations bill that exempted the dam from *all* federal laws. The House approved the bill without debate, then it passed the Senate by a narrow 48–44 margin. President Carter opposed the exemption for the dam, but he signed the bill anyway because of the other things that it contained.

The fight against the dam had one last gasp. The congressional waiver protected the dam from any federal statutory requirements, but it did not—and probably could not—bar constitutional objections to the dam. A group of Native Americans claimed that the dam would result in flooding of their sacred sites and would thus violate their first amendment right to the free exercise of their religion. The courts said no. *See* Sequoyah v. Tennessee Valley Auth., 480 F.Supp. 608 (E.D.Tenn.1979), *cert. denied*, 449 U.S. 953 (1980).

Finally, on November 29, 1979, the Tellico Dam was completed and the Little Tennessee River was impounded. Again, the consequences were not at all expected. The economic development forecast by the supporters of the dam never quite materialized. An early proposal would have located a hazardous waste facility near the newly created reservoir, but instead a retirement community known as Tellico Village developed at the site. On the other hand, the snail darter did not become extinct. Nearly one year after the dam was completed, the same scientist who had discovered the snail darter on the Little Tennessee River in 1973 found other populations of snail darters in four other rivers in Tennessee whose conditions were not supposed to have been acceptable for the fish. Apparently the snail darters did not know that, though, and they survive in such abundance that the species was downlisted from endangered to threatened in 1984.

The saga of the snail darter and the Tellico Dam is told in CHARLES C. MANN & MARK L. PLUMMER, NOAH'S CHOICE: THE FUTURE OF ENDANGERED SPECIES 147–175 (1995); WILLIAM B. WHEELER & MICHAEL J. MCDONALD, TVA AND THE TELLICO DAM, 1936–1979 (1986); Zygmunt Plater, *In the Wake of the Snail*

Darter: An Environmental Law Paradigm and Its Consequences, 19 U. MICH. J. L. REF. 19 (1986).

6. Congress designed the Endangered Species Committee with the snail darter in mind, but the committee remains a permanent fixture in the ESA. It has been employed infrequently. Only a handful of applications have been made to invoke the committee to waive a jeopardy finding, and only twice has the committee agreed to do so. The first instance occurred in 1979, when the committee approved a settlement that allowed the operation of Nebraska's Greyrocks Dam and Reservoir consistent with the needs of the endangered whooping crane. The committee granted its second waiver in 1992 when it exempted 13 out of a requested 44 proposed Oregon timber sales despite the presence of the northern spotted owl, but a court decision questioning the committee's procedures and the advent of the Clinton Administration resulted in the timber sales never actually occurring. The exemption process has not been invoked since then, though there has been speculation that the listing of several species of salmon in the Pacific Northwest could trigger a request for an exemption if a federal water project is found to jeopardize the salmon. Most recently, the irrigation districts denied water pursuant to the jeopardy finding described above in note 3 sought to obtain an exemption in the summer of 2001, but Interior Secretary Gale Norton concluded that the districts were not among the parties empowered by the statute to invoke the exemption process.

Arizona Cattle Growers' Association v. United States Fish & Wildlife Service

United States Court of Appeals for the Ninth Circuit, 2001.
273 F.3d 1229.

■ WARDLAW, CIRCUIT JUDGE:

At issue in these consolidated cross-appeals is whether the United States Fish and Wildlife Service's provision of Incidental Take Statements pursuant to the Endangered Species Act was arbitrary and capricious under Section 706 of the Administrative Procedure Act. In separate actions, the Arizona Cattle Growers' Association ("ACGA") challenged the Incidental Take Statements set forth in the Biological Opinions issued by the Fish and Wildlife Service in consultation with the Bureau of Land Management (ACGA I) and the United States Forest Service (ACGA II) in response to ACGA's application for cattle grazing permits in Southeastern Arizona. In the district courts, each of the Incidental Take Statements was set aside, with one exception, as arbitrary and capricious actions by the Fish and Wildlife Service, due to insufficient evidence of a take.

We hold, based on the legislative history, case law, prior agency representations, and the plain language of the Endangered Species Act, that an Incidental Take Statement must be predicated on a finding of an incidental take. Further, the Fish and Wildlife Service acted in an arbitrary and capricious manner by issuing Incidental Take Statements imposing terms and conditions on land use permits, where there either was no evidence that the endangered species existed on the land or no evidence that a take would occur if the permit were issued. We also find that it was arbitrary and capricious for the Fish and Wildlife Service to issue terms and conditions so vague as to preclude compliance therewith.

I. Background

[*ACGA*] involved he BLM's livestock grazing program, which covered 288 separate grazing allotments on nearly 1.6 acres of land. The FWS issued a Biological Opinion concluding that the livestock grazing program was not likely to jeopardize the continued existence of any listed species nor was it likely to result in destruction or adverse modification of the designated or proposed critical habitat. Nonetheless, the FWS issued Incidental Take Statements for various species of fish and wildlife listed or proposed as endangered. In *ACGA II*, ACGA challenged Incidental Take Statements set forth in another Biological Opinion issued by the Fish and Wildlife Service that concerns livestock grazing on public lands administered by the United States Forest Service. The Fish and Wildlife Service examined 962 allotments, determining that grazing would have no effect on listed species for 619 of those allotments and cause no adverse effects for 321 of the remaining allotments, leaving 22 allotments. These allotments were each roughly 30,000 acres, but several of the allotments were significantly larger. In its Biological Opinion, the Fish and Wildlife Service concluded that ongoing grazing activities on 21 out of the 22 allotments at issue would not jeopardize the continued existence of any protected species or result in the destruction or adverse modification of any critical habitat. It determined, however, that ongoing grazing activities would incidentally take members of one or more protected species in each of the 22 allotments, and it issued Incidental Take Statements for each of those allotments. In both cases, the Arizona Cattle Growers' Association (ACGA) challenged the need for, and contents of, the Incidental Take Statements. The district court held that the FWS acted arbitrarily and capriciously by issuing Incidental Take Statements where it was not reasonably certain that the take of a listed species would occur. The court found that such a take would occur only at the Cow Flat Allotment, and it upheld only that Incidental Take Statement.

. . . Section 7 of the Act imposes an affirmative duty to prevent violations of Section 9 upon federal agencies, such as the Bureau of Land Management and the U.S. Forest Service. 16 U.S.C. § 1536(a)(2). This affirmative duty extends to "any action authorized, funded, or carried out by such agency," including authorizing grazing permits on land owned by the federal government. *Id.*

To determine whether an "action may affect listed species or critical habitat," the agency may be required to create a Biological Assessment that "evaluates the potential effects of the action on listed and proposed species and . . . critical habitat and determines whether any such species or habitat are likely to be adversely affected by the action." 50 C.F.R. § 402.12. If the agency finds evidence of an adverse impact on any issued species, it must initiate formal consultation with the Fish and Wildlife Service. 50 C.F.R. § 402.14.

If formal consultation is necessary, the Fish and Wildlife Service will issue a Biological Opinion, summarizing the relevant findings and determining whether the proposed action is likely to jeopardize the continued existence of the species. 16 U.S.C. § 1536(b). If so, the Biological Opinion must list any "reasonable and prudent alternatives" that, if followed, would not jeopardize the continued existence of the species. 16 U.S.C. § 1536(b)(3)(A); 50 C.F.R. § 402.14.

Additionally, the Fish and Wildlife Service must specify whether any "incidental taking" of protected species will occur, specifically "any taking otherwise prohibited, if such taking is incidental to, and not the purpose of, the carrying out of an otherwise lawful activity." 16 U.S.C. § 1536(b)(4); 50 C.F.R. § 17.3. Its determination that an incidental taking will result leads to the publication of the "Incidental Take Statement," identifying areas where members of the particular species are at risk. Contained in the Incidental Take Statement is an advisory opinion which:

(i) specifies the impact of such incidental taking on the species,

(ii) specifies those reasonable and prudent measures that the Secretary considers necessary or appropriate to minimize such impact [and] . . .

(iv) sets forth the terms and conditions . . . that must be complied with by the Federal agency or applicant . . . or both, to implement the measures specified under clause (ii).

16 U.S.C. § 1536(b)(4) (subsection (iii) omitted).

Significantly, the Incidental Take Statement functions as a safe harbor provision immunizing persons from Section 9 liability and penalties for takings committed during activities that are otherwise lawful and in compliance with its terms and conditions. 16 U.S.C. § 1536(o). Any such incidental taking "shall not be considered to be a prohibited taking of the species concerned." *Id.* Although the action agency is "technically free to disregard the Biological Opinion and proceed with its proposed action . . . it does so at its own peril." [Bennett v. Spear, 520 U.S. 154, 170 (1997)]. Consequently, if the terms and conditions of the Incidental Take Statement are disregarded and a taking does occur, the action agency or the applicant may be subject to potentially severe civil and criminal penalties under Section 9.

V. Determining When the Fish and Wildlife Service Must Issue an Incidental Take Statement

The Fish and Wildlife Service contends that the district courts erred in scrutinizing its decision to issue Incidental Take Statements because it is statutorily required pursuant to the ESA to "issue an ITS in all nojeopardy determinations." In particular, it contests the *ACGA I* court's requirement that it provide evidence of a listed species' existence on the land and the *ACGA II* court's holding that issuing an Incidental Take Statement is "appropriate only when a take has occurred or is reasonably certain to occur."

The Fish and Wildlife Service argues that both standards establish "an inappropriate and high burden of proof" and that it should be permitted to issue an Incidental Take Statement whenever there is any possibility, no matter how small, that a listed species will be taken. As we believe that Congress has spoken to the precise question at issue, we must reject the agency's interpretation of the ESA as contrary to clear congressional intent. . .

The Fish and Wildlife Service argues that the plain language of the statute and implementing regulations "expressly direct" it to issue an Incidental Take Statement in every case. Section 7(b)(4) of the ESA provides:

If after consultation under subsection (a)(2) of this section, the Secretary concludes that—

> (A) the agency action will not violate such subsection, or offers reasonable and prudent alternatives which the Secretary believes would not violate such subsection;
>
> (B) the taking of an endangered species or a threatened species incidental to the agency action will not violate such subsection; and
>
> (C) if an endangered species or threatened species of a marine mammal is involved, the taking is authorized pursuant to section 1371(a)(5) of this title;
>
> the Secretary shall provide the Federal agency and the applicant concerned, if any, with a written statement that—
>
> (i) specifies the impact of such incidental taking on the species,. . .

16 U.S.C. § 1536(b)(4). The Fish and Wildlife Service relies on the statutory provision directing the Secretary to provide "a written statement that . . . specifies the impact of such incidental taking on the species." *Id.* . .

When read in context, it is clear that the issuance of the Incidental Take Statement is subject to the finding of the factors enumerated in the ESA. The statute explicitly provides that the written statement is subject to the consultation and the Secretary's conclusions. A contrary interpretation would render meaningless the clause stating that the Incidental Take Statement will specify "the impact of *such* incidental taking." 16 U.S.C. § 1536(b)(4)(C)(i) (emphasis added). We therefore agree with ACGA that the plain language of the ESA does not dictate that the Fish and Wildlife Service must issue an Incidental Take Statement irrespective of whether any incidental takings will occur. *See* Nat'l Wildlife Fed'n v. Nat'l Park Serv., 669 F. Supp. 384, 389–90 (D.Wyo.1987) (holding that a careful reading of § 1536(b) supports the defendants' contention that an Incidental Take Statement is not required if no incidental takings are foreseen). . . Accordingly, we hold that absent rare circumstances such as those involving migratory species, it is arbitrary and capricious to issue an Incidental Take

Statement when the Fish and Wildlife Service has no rational basis to conclude that a take will occur incident to the otherwise lawful activity.

VI. Review of the Incidental Take Statements under the Arbitrary and Capricious Standard Pursuant to the APA

Because we reject the Fish and Wildlife Service's interpretation of the ESA and hold that it is not required to provide an Incidental Take Statement whenever it issues a Biological Opinion, we must now examine each Incidental Take Statement at issue under Section 706. 5 U.S.C. § 706. . .

A. ACGA I

1. The Razorback Sucker

In the Biological Opinion issued in response to ACGA's first request for land use permits, the Fish and Wildlife Service concluded that the direct effects of cattle grazing are infrequent to the razorback sucker, a moderately sized fish listed as endangered in November 1991. Although once abundant in the project area, the Fish and Wildlife Service admitted that there have been no reported sightings of the razorback sucker in the area since 1991 and that "effects of the livestock grazing program on individual fish or fish populations probably occur infrequently." Nevertheless, the Fish and Wildlife Service issued an Incidental Take Statement for the fish, anticipating take as a result of the direct effects of grazing in the project area, the construction of fences, the construction and existence of stock tanks for non-native fish, as well as other "activities in the watershed." Because the Fish and Wildlife Service could not directly quantify the level of incidental take, it determined that authorized take would be exceeded if range conditions in the allotment deteriorated and cattle grazing could not be ruled out as a cause of the deterioration.

Despite the lack of evidence that the razorback sucker exists on the allotment in question, the Fish and Wildlife Service argues that it should be able to issue an Incidental Take Statement based upon prospective harm. While we recognize the importance of a prospective orientation, the regulations mandate a separate procedure for reinitiating consultation if different evidence is later developed:

Reinitiation of formal consultation is required and shall be requested by the Federal agency or by the Service, where discretionary Federal involvement or control over the action has been retained or is authorized by law and:

(a) If the amount or extent of taking specified in the incidental take statement is exceeded;

(b) If new information reveals effects of the action that may affect listed species or critical habitat in a manner or to an extent not previously considered;

(c) If the identified action is subsequently modified in a manner that causes an effect to the listed species or critical habitat that was not considered in the biological opinion; or

(d) If a new species is listed or critical habitat designated that may be affected by the identified action.

50 C.F.R. § 402.16. Additionally, the ESA provides for the designation of critical habitat outside the geographic area currently occupied by the species when "such areas are essential for the conservation of the species." 16 U.S.C. § 1532(5)(A)(ii). Absent this procedure, however, there is no evidence that Congress intended to allow the Fish and Wildlife Service to regulate any parcel of land that is merely capable of supporting a protected species.

The only additional evidence that the Fish and Wildlife Service offers to justify its decision is that "small numbers of the juvenile fish . . . likely survived" in an unsuccessful attempt to repopulate the project area between 1981–1987. This speculative evidence, without more, is woefully insufficient to meet the standards imposed by the governing statute. *See* 50 C.F.R. § 402.14(g)(8) ("In formulating its biological opinion . . . the Service will use the best scientific and commercial data available. . ."). Likewise, the Fish and Wildlife Service failed to present evidence that an indirect taking would occur absent the existence of the species on the property. Although habitat modification resulting in actual killing or injury may constitute a taking, the Fish and Wildlife Service has presented only speculative evidence that habitat modification, brought about by livestock grazing, may impact the razorback sucker. The agency has a very low bar to meet, but it must at least attain it. It would be improper to force ACGA to prove that the species does not exist on the permitted area, as the Fish and Wildlife Service urges, both because it would require ACGA to meet the burden statutorily imposed on the agency, and because it would be requiring it to prove a negative.

Based on a careful review of the record, we find that it is arbitrary and capricious to issue an Incidental Take Statement for the razorback sucker when the Fish and Wildlife Service's speculation that the species exists on the property is not supported by the record. We agree with the district court's ruling that the Fish and Wildlife Service failed to establish an incidental taking because it did not have evidence that the razorback sucker even exists anywhere in the area. Where the agency purports to impose conditions on the lawful use of that land without showing that the species exists on it, it acts beyond its authority in violation of 5 U.S.C. § 706.

2. The Cactus Ferruginous Pygmy-owl

As with the razorback sucker, the record does not support a claim that the cactus ferruginous pygmy-owl exists in the area of the allotment in question, and the Fish and Wildlife Service thus acted in an arbitrary and capricious manner in issuing an Incidental Take Statement for that species. . .

B. The ACGA II Consultation

1. The Issuance of Incidental Take Statements

[For similar reasons, the court held that the Incidental Take Statements issued for four other allotments were arbitrary and capricious as well.]

The loach minnow

E. The Cow Flat Allotment (loach minnow and spikedace)

According to the Biological Opinion, the Blue River passes through or adjacent to approximately 3.5 miles of the Cow Flat Allotment, made up of 22,592 acres in the Apache-Sitgreaves National Forest. Surveys conducted in 1994, 1995, and 1996 found loach minnow throughout the Blue River. The Fish and Wildlife Service concluded that the segment of the Blue River that passes through or adjacent to the Cow Flat Allotment is considered occupied loach minnow habitat.

Having determined that loach minnow exist on the allotment, Fish and Wildlife Service determined that the loach minnow are vulnerable to direct harms resulting from cattle crossings, such as trampling. Moreover, because the fish use the spaces between large substrates for resting and spawning, sedimentation resulting from grazing in pastures that settles in these spaces can adversely affect loach minnow habitat. The Biological Opinion determines that this indirect effect, along with the direct crushing of loach minnow eggs and the reduction in food availability, will result in take of the loach minnow. The Incidental Take Statement, however, does not directly quantify the incidental takings of loach minnow and determines that such takings "will be difficult to detect." Defining the incidental take in terms of habitat characteristics, the Fish and Wildlife Service found that take will be exceeded if several conditions are not met. One such condition was if "ecological conditions do not improve under the proposed livestock management" plan.

We agree with the district court that the issuance of the Cow Flat Incidental Take Statement was not arbitrary and capricious. Unlike the other allotments in question, the Fish and Wildlife Service provided evidence that the listed species exist on the land in question and that the cattle have access to the endangered species' habitat. Accordingly, the Fish and Wildlife Service could reasonably conclude that the loach minnow could be harmed when the livestock entered the river. Additionally, the Fish and Wildlife Service provided extensive site-specific information that discussed not only the topography of the relevant allotment, but the indirect effects of grazing on the species due to the topography. The specificity of the Service's data, as well as the articulated causal connections between the activity and the "actual killing or injury" of a protected species distinguishes the Fish and Wildlife Service's treatment of this allotment from the other allotments at issue in the two consultations. Thus, we hold that because the Fish and Wildlife Service articulated a rational connection between harm to the species and the land grazing activities at issue, the issuance of the Incidental Take Statements for the Cow Flat Allotment was not arbitrary and capricious.

2. The Anticipated Take Provisions

We now turn to the question whether the Service acted arbitrarily and capriciously by failing to properly specify the amount of anticipated take in the Incidental Take Statement for the Cow Flat Allotment and by failing to provide a clear standard for determining when the authorized level of take has been exceeded. The district court upheld the Cow Flat take provision, including its conditions on the land use, issued by the Fish and Wildlife Service, finding that it was rationally connected to the proposed action of cattle grazing and thus did not violate the arbitrary and capricious standard.

In general, Incidental Take Statements set forth a "trigger" that, when reached, results in an unacceptable level of incidental take, invalidating the safe harbor provision, and requiring the parties to reinitiate consultation. Ideally, this "trigger" should be a specific number. *See, e.g.*, Mausolf v. Babbitt, 125 F.3d 661 (8th Cir.1997) (snowmobiling activity may take no more than two wolves); Fund for Animals v. Rice, 85 F.3d 535 (11th Cir.1996) (municipal landfill may take fifty-two snakes during construction and an additional two snakes per year thereafter); Mt. Graham Red Squirrel v. Madigan, 954 F.2d 1441 (9th Cir.1992) (telescope construction may take six red squirrels per year); Ctr. for Marine Conservation v. Brown, 917 F. Supp. 1128 (S.D.Tex.1996) (shrimping operation may take four hawksbill turtles, four leatherback turtles, ten Kemp's ridley turtles, ten green turtles, or 370 loggerhead turtles). Here, however, the "trigger" took the form of several conditions. We must therefore determine whether the linking of the level of permissible take to the conditions set forth in the various Incidental Take Statements was arbitrary and capricious.

ACGA argues that the Incidental Take Statements fail to specify the amount or extent of authorized take with the required degree of exactness. Specifically, ACGA objected to the first condition:

The service concludes that incidental take of loach minnow from the proposed action will be considered to be exceeded if any of the following conditions are met:

[Condition 1] Ecological conditions do not improve under the proposed livestock management. Improving conditions can be defined through improvements in watershed, soil condition, trend and condition of rangelands (e.g., vegetative litter, plant vigor, and native species diversity), riparian conditions (e.g., vegetative and geomorphologic: bank, terrace, and flood plain conditions), and stream channel conditions (e.g., channel profile, embeddedness, water temperature, and base flow) within the natural capabilities of the landscape in all pastures on the allotment within the Blue River watershed.

We have never held that a numerical limit is required. Indeed, we have upheld Incidental Take Statements that used a combination of numbers and estimates. *See* Ramsey v. Kantor, 96 F.3d 434, 441 n. 12 (9th Cir.1996) (utilizing both harvesting rates and estimated numbers of fish to reach a permitted take); Southwest Ctr. for Biological Diversity v. U.S. Bureau of Reclamation, 6 F. Supp. 2d 1119 (D.Ariz.1997) (concluding that an Incidental Take Statement that indexes the permissible take to successful completion of the reasonable and prudent measures as well as the terms and conditions is valid); Pac. Northwest Generating Coop. v. Brown, 822 F. Supp. 1479, 1510 (D.Or.1993) (ruling that an Incidental Take Statement that defines the allotted take in percentage terms is valid).

Moreover, while Congress indicated its preference for a numerical value, it anticipated situations in which impact could not be contemplated in terms of a precise number. *See* H.R. Rep. No. 97–567, at 27 (1982) ("The Committee does not intend that the Secretary will, in every instance, interpret the word impact to be a precise number. Where possible, the impact should be specified in terms of a numerical limitation."); *see also* 50 C.F.R. § 402.14 (defining impact as "the amount or extent, of such incidental taking on the species."). In the absence of a specific numerical value, however, the Fish and Wildlife Service must establish that no such numerical value could be practically obtained.

We agree with the *ACGA II* court's conclusion that, "the use of ecological conditions as a surrogate for defining the amount or extent of incidental take is reasonable so long as these conditions are linked to the take of the protected species." Indeed, this finding is consistent with the Fish and Wildlife Service's Section 7 Consultation Handbook:

When preparing an incidental take statement, a specific number (for some species, expressed as an amount or extent, e.g., all turtle nests not found and moved by the approved relocation technique) or level of disturbance to habitat must be described. Take can be expressed also as a change in habitat characteristics affecting the species (e.g., for an aquatic species, changes in water temperature or chemistry, flows, or sediment loads) where data or information exists which links such changes to the take of the listed species. In some situations, the species itself or the effect on the species may be difficult to detect. However, some detectable measure of effect should be provided . . . If a sufficient causal link is demonstrated (i.e., the number of burrows affected or a quantitative loss of cover, food, water quality, or symbionts), then this can establish a measure of the impact on the species or its habitat and provide the yardstick for reinitiation.

Final ESA Section 7 Consultation Handbook, March 1998 at 4–47 to 4–48. By "causal link" we do not mean that the Fish and Wildlife Service must demonstrate a specific number of takings; only that it must establish a link between the activity and the taking of species before setting forth specific conditions.

ACGA argues that it is entitled to more certainty than "vague and undetectable criteria such as changes in a 22,000 acre allotment's 'ecological condition.' " In response, the Fish and Wildlife Service argues that "the [Incidental Take Statement] provides for those studies necessary to provide the quantification of impacts which the Cattle Growers claim is lacking."

We disagree with the government's position. The Incidental Take Statements at issue here do not sufficiently discuss the causal connection between Condition 1 and the taking of the species at issue. Based on the Incidental Take Statement, if "ecological conditions do not improve," takings will occur. This vague analysis, however, cannot be what Congress contemplated when it anticipated that surrogate indices might be used in place of specific numbers. Moreover, whether there has been compliance with this vague directive is within the unfettered discretion of the Fish and Wildlife Service, leaving no method by which the applicant or the action agency can gauge their performance. Finally, Condition 1 leaves ACGA and the United States Forest Service responsible for the general ecological improvement of the approximately 22,000 acres that comprise the Cow Flat Allotment.

Based upon the lack of an articulated, rational connection between Condition 1 and the taking of species, as well as the vagueness of the condition itself, we hold that its implementation was arbitrary and capricious. The terms of an Incidental Take Statement do not operate in a vacuum. To the contrary, they are integral parts of the statutory scheme, determining, among other things, when consultation must be reinitiated.

Thus, even though the Fish and Wildlife Service was not arbitrary and capricious in issuing Incidental Take Statements for the Cow Flat Allotment, its failure to properly specify the amount of anticipated take and to provide a clear standard for determining when the authorized level of take has been exceeded is arbitrary and capricious. As with the Incidental Take Statements for the other allotments, we therefore conclude that the issuance of the Cow Flat Allotment Incidental Take Statement was arbitrary and capricious.

VII. Conclusion

For the foregoing reasons, the decision of the ACGA I district court is AFFIRMED, and the decision of the ACGA II district court is AFFIRMED in part, and REVERSED in part.

NOTES & QUESTIONS

1. Why did the FWS think that it could use the ESA to condition the grazing of cattle on federal land even though no species would be jeopardized by the grazing? Should it have that power? For a review of the effects of grazing on grassland ecosystems and the law governing the use of federal lands, see chapter 9.

2. Both section 7 and section 9 of the ESA limit the "take" of endangered species. The FWS argued in *Arizona Cattle Growers Association* that "take" should have a broader meaning in section 7 because of the protective nature of that provision. The court disagreed because "[i]nterpreting the statutes in the manner urged by the Fish and Wildlife Service could effectively stop the proposed cattle grazing entirely. Such a broad interpretation would allow the Fish and Wildlife Service to engage in widespread land regulation even where no Section 9 liability could be imposed." *Id.* at 1240. Should the FWS be empowered to conduct such regulation? That is precisely what many landowners dislike about section 9 of the ESA, as detailed in chapter 6. Section 9, moreover, states a firm prohibition, whereas the agencies or ranchers here could ignore the conditions contained in the incidental take statements. But the court dismissed that possibility as merely theoretical because "Biological Opinions exert a 'powerful coercive effect' in shaping the policies of the federal agencies whose actions are at issue." *Id.* (citing *Bennett*, 520 U.S. at 169).

Gifford Pinchot Task Force v. FWS, 378 F.3d 1059 (9th Cir. 2004), further demonstrates the relationship between the consultation duty, the jeopardy provision, and the take prohibition. The FWS issued six biological opinions that authorized the incidental take of over one thousand northern spotted owls on national forest land. The Ninth Circuit agreed that the FWS could predict species jeopardy based upon habitat degradation, rather than having to measure the effects on the owls themselves. But the court invalidated the FWS's regulation interpreting section 7 to prohibit "changes to the critical habitat that appreciably diminish[] the value of critical habitat for *both* the survival *and* recovery of a listed species." *Id.* at 1069 (quoting 50 C.F.R. § 402.02). According to the court, "the purpose of establishing 'critical habitat' is for the government to carve out territory that is not only necessary for the species' survival but also essential for the species's recovery." *Id.* at 1070. In other words, providing land for the survival of a species is not enough; critical habitat must be available for the recovery of a species, too.

3. What changes in the incidental take statement for the Cow Flat allotment would be sufficiently precise to satisfy the court's concerns?

4. The court cited the agency consultation handbook that FWS prepared with the NMFS to explain the details of how section 7 consultations should proceed. *See* FWS & NMFS, Endangered Species Consultation Handbook: Procedures for Consultation and Conference Activities Under Section 7 of the Endangered Species Act (March 1998), available at http://endangered.fws.gov/consultations/

s7hndbk/toc-glos.pdf. The handbook was prepared for the scientists and officials working for both agencies, but it is an excellent source of information about the consultation process for all concerned parties (and students!). The handbook highlights four aspects of the consultation process: (1) the use of *sound science* as an "overriding factor" in making all determinations under section 7; (2) the need for *flexibility and innovation*, with biologists encouraged to "be creative in problem solving and look for ways to conserve listed species while still accommodating project goals;" (3) coordination with state agencies and affected tribal governments; and (4) efforts to "streamline consultation processes" and thus *shorten timeframes* "without giving up any protection for listed species/designated critical habitats or the use and review of the best available information." *Id.* at 25–26.

The handbook also offers the following "thoughts . . . as an expression of the philosophy guiding section 7 work":

- The biology comes first. Know the facts; state the case; and provide supporting documentation. Keep in mind the FWS's ecosystem approach to conservation of endangered and threatened species.

- Base the determination of *jeopardy/no jeopardy* on a careful analysis of the best available scientific and commercial data. Never determine the conclusion of a biological opinion before completing the analysis of the best available data.

- Clarity and conciseness are extremely important. They make consultation documents more understandable to everyone. A biological opinion should clearly explain the proposed project, its impacts on the affected species, and the Services' recommendations. It should be written so the general public could trace the path of logic to the biological conclusion and complete enough to withstand the rigors of a legal review.

- Strong interpersonal skills serve section 7 biologists well. Establishing a positive working relationship with action agencies enhances the Services' ability to do the job successfully. Remember, you are trying to assist the agency in meeting their section 7 responsibilities under the Act.

- Present a positive image as a representative of your Service.

- Section 7 consultation is a cooperative process. The Services do not have all the answers. Actively seek the views of the action agency and its designated representatives, and involve them in your opinion preparation, especially in the development of reasonable and prudent alternatives, reasonable and prudent measures, terms and conditions to minimize the impacts of incidental take, and conservation recommendations.

- Use all aspects of section 7, especially opportunities for informal consultation where solutions can be worked out prior to the structured process mandated by formal consultation. Be creative, and make the process work to the species' advantage.

- It is important to be consistent throughout a species' range when implementing section 7. Be flexible but not inconsistent. Study the law, the regulations and this handbook. Know the authorities and be flexible when it is prudent, but always stand firm for maintaining the substantive standards of section 7.

- Take advantage of professional support within and outside the Services. For example, the FWS Division of Engineering can provide valuable technical review of development proposals. Attorneys in the Regional and field offices of the FWS Solicitor/NMFS General Counsel can offer advice on section 7 regulations and the latitude within which to conduct consultation. Similarly, the Services' law enforcement personnel may be able to answer questions about direct or incidental take.

- Strive to solve problems locally.

- An effective section 7 biologist is a good teacher and a good student. Seek every opportunity to teach the section 7 process within and outside the Services in an informative and non-threatening way. Learn all you can about other Services' programs, Federal action agency's mandates and procedures, and State/tribal/private agency's/client's needs and expectations.

Id. at 1–2 to 1–3. Were those suggestions heeded in *Arizona Cattle Growers' Association*? What other suggestions would you offer to the scientists who are responsible for preparing biological opinions and enforcing section 7?

5. For an illustration of the contents of an actual biological opinion, consider the opinion that FWS provided to the federal Bureau of Prisons (BOP). In August 2001, BOP initiated consultation with FWS concerning a proposed new federal penitentiary to be built in Tucson. BOP's biological assessment indicated that the prison may affect the endangered Pima pineapple cactus but not the cactus ferruginous pygmy-owl or the lesser long-nosed bat. After consultation between the agencies, FWS provided its biological opinion in March 2002. The opinion contained six sections. First, it described the proposed action to build the minimum security prison on 631 acres in southern Tucson and the conservation measures proposed by BOP to minimize any adverse effects on the Pima pineapple cactus and its habitat. Second, it described the status of the cactus, including its listing as endangered in 1993, a scientific account of the life of the cactus, a positive report on the population of the cactus, the habitat and distribution of the cactus in the Sonoran desert scrub and semidesert grasslands of Arizona, and the effects of urbanization, farming, and exotic species on the survival of the cactus. ("Very little is known," the opinion explains, "regarding the effects of low to moderate levels of livestock grazing on Pima pineapple cactus distribution.") Third, the opinion describes the "environmental baseline": the condition of the land at the site of the proposed prison, the presence of the cactus on certain parts of the site, and the general suitability of the land for the cactus. Fourth, the opinion details the effects of the proposed action, notably the development of 200 acres of cactus habitat, and the BOP's proposal to set aside another 200 acres of land south of the construction zone where nearly 80% of the cactus plants had been found. Fifth, the opinion explained that the cumulative effects of other actions in the area included continuing private development with little or no federal nexus. Based on all of these factors, the opinion's conclusion stated that "the proposed action is not likely to jeopardize the continued existence of Pima pineapple cactus." FWS based that conclusion on the 200 acres that BOP had agreed to set aside as a permanent conservation area for the cactus, plus BOP's ongoing monitoring of the cactus.

The letter that FWS sent to BOP contained three additional sections. It said that no incidental take statement is needed. It recommended two actions to fulfill the conservation duty imposed by ESA section 7(a)(1): working with the Arizona-Sonora Desert Museum when relocating cactus to the conservation area, and expanding the conservation area to include an extra 231 acres that connect to other parcels of cactus habitat. The letter finished by noting the circumstances in which the BOP would need to reinitiate consultation under section 7.

CHAPTER 6

THE TAKE PROHIBITION

Chapter Outline:
A. Poaching, Smuggling, and Direct Takings of a Listed Species
B. Habitat Destruction and Indirect Taking of Endangered Species
    1. The Scope of the Take Prohibition
    2. Authorizing Incidental Take of Protected Species
    3. The Debate Over the ESA

Despite all of the land that it owns and all of its responsibilities, the efforts of the federal government alone cannot save most endangered species. Most listed species live on at least some privately owned land, and many of the threats to particular species are attributable to the actions of state and local governments and private individuals. The ESA addresses the conduct of all public and private parties in section 9. That provision makes it illegal to "import," "export," "possess," "transport," or "take" a listed species, just to list a few of the verbs contained in the law. ESA § 9(a)(1). In other words, the ESA prohibits the smuggling of a listed fish or wildlife species—dead or alive—into the United States, and it prohibits poaching or killing of such a species. (By contrast, these provisions of section 9 do not apply to plants.)

But section 9 applies to other conduct, too. "Take" is defined to include "to harass, harm, pursue, hunt, shoot, wound, kill, trap, capture, or collect, or to attempt to engage in any such conduct." ESA § 3(18). Those terms, in turn, open the possibility that the unintentional destruction of the habitat of a listed species runs afoul of the law. The extension of the ESA to private developers and landowners whose actions adversely impact the habitat of a species has resulted in most of the controversy surrounding the law in recent years. Private landowners object that while the discovery of gold or oil makes a property owner rich, the discovery of a rare animal or bird on one's property threatens bankruptcy if that blocks the landowner from using the property. Yet the preservation of habitat is essential for the survival of biodiversity, especially given that habitat destruction is the primary cause of the decline of most endangered species.

The ongoing debate about the application of the ESA to these and other scenarios has produced a rich body of legal and scientific literature. The controversies that have developed in the course of the application of section 9 have also led to regulatory changes, proposed legislation, and other ideas regarding the best way to prevent species from going extinct. The response to these developments says much about the seriousness with which we take the ESA's stated purpose of "provid[ing] a means whereby the ecosystems upon which endangered species and threatened species depend may be conserved." ESA § 2(c)(1).

A. POACHING, SMUGGLING AND DIRECT TAKINGS OF A LISTED SPECIES

You may not shoot an endangered species. Nor may you "harass, harm, pursue, hunt . . . wound, kill, trap, capture, or collect" an endangered species. ESA § 3(19). Most of these verbs connote some kind of direct action that targets a particular animal, bird, fish, or other protected species. Whether that is all that those terms connote has been a source of great controversy—answered in the negative by the FWS and the Supreme Court as discussed below at page 275—but there has never been any doubt about the illegality of shooting, hunting, killing or otherwise directly harming an endangered species. The statute also makes it plain that one cannot "possess, sell, deliver, carry, transport, or ship" any illegally taken species, ESA § 9(a)(1)(D); or "deliver, receive, carry, transport, or ship" any species in interstate or foreign commerce, ESA § 9(1)(E); or import, export, or sell any species, ESA § 9(1)(A), (F).

But people do it anyway. Bald eagles are shot, butterflies are collected, and rhinoceros horns are imported in violation of the law. The greatest challenge in most of those instances is to catch the perpetrators. Once caught, the appropriate sanction quickly becomes the crucial issue. Sometimes, though, a defendant accused of illegally taking an endangered species asserts a defense or other privilege that would allow his or her action. Those cases say much about the nature of the prohibition on taking an endangered species and the zeal with which it is applied.

United States v. Clavette

United States Court of Appeals for the Ninth Circuit, 1998.
135 F.3d 1308.

■ REAVLEY, CIRCUIT JUDGE:

This is an appeal from the conviction of Paul Clavette for killing a grizzly bear in violation of the Endangered Species Act, 16 U.S.C. §§ 1538(a)(1)(G) and 1540(b)(1). We affirm.

I. Background

On September 20, 1995, U.S. Fish and Wildlife Service Special Agent Tim Eicher began investigating the killing of a grizzly bear at a campsite southwest of Big Sky, Montana. At the campsite, Eicher discovered two pine trees with a pole suspended by rope between them. This was a "meat pole," used for stringing up and skinning large game animals. Underneath it, Eicher found traces of moose blood and hair, indicating that a moose had recently been dressed there. Eicher found the dead grizzly bear approximately 170 yards away, lying in a large pool of blood. The bear had been shot at least four times. Looking for bullets or spent shell casings, Eicher searched a conical area extending about 25 yards beyond the bear toward the campsite; he found one .7 mm casing by the meat pole and two bullets, one buried about two inches in the dirt at the base of a tree near the bear, and one on the surface of the ground next to the pool of the bear's blood.

Eicher located two bowhunters who had stopped at the campsite on September 17, 1995, to visit with an Oregon man skinning a freshly killed moose. The man seemed to be in a hurry and did not say anything about confronting or killing a grizzly. He did ask the bowhunters what would happen to someone who shot a grizzly bear. The bowhunters told him he had better be prepared to prove it was in self-defense.

Through these bowhunters and Montana hunting license records, Eicher identified the defendant, Paul Clavette, as the man at the campsite on September 17, 1995. Agents of the U.S. Fish and Wildlife Service in Portland, Oregon, obtained and executed a search warrant in defendant's home on November 2, 1995. During the course of that search, and after full *Miranda* warnings, Clavette admitted to killing the grizzly, claiming that it was in self-defense.

After a bench trial, the district court found Clavette guilty of illegally killing a grizzly bear. Clavette was sentenced to three years' probation. Additionally, Clavette was ordered to pay a fine of $2,000 and restitution of $6,250 to the United States Fish & Wildlife Service. . .

III. SUFFICIENCY OF THE EVIDENCE

Because Clavette moved to dismiss at the close of the Government's case-in-chief, the sufficiency of the evidence is reviewed *de novo*. If any reasonable person could have found each of the essential elements of the offense charged beyond a reasonable doubt, the evidence is sufficient to convict.

To find Clavette guilty of knowingly taking an endangered species, the Government must prove, beyond a reasonable doubt, that: (1) Clavette knowingly killed a bear; (2) the bear was a grizzly; (3) Clavette had no permit from the United States Fish & Wildlife Service to kill a grizzly bear; and (4) Clavette did not act in self-defense or in the defense of others. Pursuant to the regulations, a grizzly bear may be taken in self-defense or defense of others, but any such taking must be reported within five days to the U.S. Fish and Wildlife Service.[1]

There is no dispute that Clavette knowingly killed a grizzly bear without first obtaining a permit from the Fish & Wildlife Service. The only issue at trial was whether he acted in self-defense or in defense of his wife. Because Clavette presented evidence that he acted in self-defense, the Government must disprove self-defense beyond a reasonable doubt.

Clavette and his wife changed their story multiple times. Clavette initially described his trip to Montana to Agent Earl Kisler as follows. Clavette said that as he was skinning a moose he had killed, he sensed something was wrong. He looked up and saw a seven-or eight-foot bear standing on its hind legs about 25 yards away from him, across a creek that ran past the campsite. He made noises to try to drive the bear away and

---

[1]   50 C.F.R. § 17.40(b)(i)(B) (1996).

fired a warning shot with his .7 mm rifle. Then, Clavette said, the bear began to circle the campsite, and Clavette was sure it was going to come forward. He told Kisler that he was terrified. Clavette's wife had retreated into the pickup truck. Clavette stated that when the bear was 40 to 75 yards away from the campsite, he shot it. The first shot hit the bear on the left side and appeared to paralyze its hindquarters, but it kept struggling, trying to get up, and so he emptied his rifle into it, reloaded, and fired more rounds into the bear.

Clavette later stated that there were two bears, although his wife still said that there had been one bear. Then, at trial, Clavette's wife testified that not only were there two bears, but that the second one charged her husband at a dead run. When asked why she had not mentioned two bears before, she explained that only one bear was shot. Clavette himself testified at trial that he had in fact told Agent Kisler about the second bear during their first discussion; Clavette surmised that it must have slipped their minds. He also testified that the second bear charged straight at him and that he crippled it with his first shot at 33 yards. Clavette said he saw the bear spin 180 degrees and dig with its front paws, trying to move away from him. The bear looked as if it was paralyzed in its hindquarters but actually ran another hundred yards away from him, without bleeding, so as to die in the spot where the bear was found by the agents.

Although he could not identify the order in which the shots occurred, Keith Aune, a wildlife laboratory supervisor for the Montana Department of Fish, Wildlife and Parks, testified that the shots Clavette described were inconsistent with his own observations and measurements gathered during the necropsy. No entry wounds appeared on the head, chest or front legs, as would be expected if the bear had been approaching at high speed; all the entry wounds were in the rear portion. The stories were also inconsistent with the physical evidence found by Agent Eicher at the site.

Given the physical evidence and the inconsistencies in the Clavettes' stories, a reasonable person could have found beyond a reasonable doubt that Clavette had not killed the bear in self-defense.

NOTES & QUESTIONS

1. ESA section 11 provides that no civil or criminal penalty "shall be imposed if it can be shown by a preponderance of the evidence that the defendant committed an act based on a good faith belief that he was acting to protect himself or herself, a member of his or her family, or any other individual from bodily harm, from any endangered or threatened species." ESA §§ 11(a)(3), (b)(3), 16 U.S.C. §§ 1540(a)(3), (b)(3). Suppose that Clavette had shot and wounded a grizzly as it charged him, then stood over the bear and fired six more shots into the bear as it lay motionless on the ground. Or suppose that Clavette killed a grizzly that was attacking his dog. Would he succeed in arguing self-defense?

Idaho Representative Helen Chenoweth objected to efforts to expand the range of the grizzly bear for the following reasons:

The grizzly bear . . . is a huge and dangerous animal, and that is a huge and dangerous problem for us. The grizzly bear is, by its nature, a large predatory mammal that, provoked or unprovoked, can move very quickly to viciously attack a human or an animal . . . . An adult grizzly can weigh as much as 450 pounds. It can run up to 40 miles an hour over irregular terrain. It has a keen sense of hearing and an even keener sense of smell. The teeth are large and very, very sturdy, especially the canines, and although they are not particularly sharp, the power of the jaw muscles allow them to readily penetrate deep into soft tissues and to fracture facial bones and bones of the hand and forearm with ease. . . The resulting trauma is characteristically a result of punctures with sheering, tearing, and crushing force. Claws on the front pads can be as long as human fingers and can produce significant soft tissue damage in a scraping maneuver that results in deep parallel gashes. The bear paw is capable of delivering powerful forces, resulting in significant blunt trauma, particularly to the head and the neck region, the rib cage and the abdomen.

. . . [T]he Fish and Wildlife Service is planning for about one human injury that could result in death due to the grizzly every single year. . . [N]ot one human death or injury resulting from a grizzly bear attack is acceptable to this Congressman. In fact, it should not be accepted by anyone who values human life.

143 CONG. REC. H5909 (daily ed. July 28, 1997).

2. While self-defense or defense of others is permissible under the ESA, defense of property is not. In Christy v. Hodel, 857 F.2d 1324 (9th Cir.1988), *cert. denied*, 490 U.S. 1114 (1989), a rancher was fined $2,500 for killing a grizzly bear that had attacked his sheep on a nightly basis. The court upheld the fine and rejected the rancher's argument that the government has effectively taken his property without providing just compensation. The Supreme Court declined to review the case over the dissent of Justice White, who stated that "perhaps a government edict barring one from resisting the loss of one's property is the constitutional equivalent of an edict taking such property in the first place." He then suggested that the situation was analogous to "the government decid[ing] (in lieu of the food stamp program) to enact a law barring grocery store owners from 'harassing, harming, or pursuing' people who wish to take food off grocery shelves without paying for it." 490 U.S. at 1115–16. Would it matter if the government had introduced the grizzly into the area in the first place? Or suppose that the government prohibited a landowner from building a fence that would keep the grizzly bear outside his or her property? *Cf.* New York v. Sour Mtn. Realty, 703 N.Y.S.2d 854 (N.Y.Sup.Ct.1999) (applying state law to enjoin a mining company from constructing a fence that would prevent timber rattlesnakes from traveling across the company's property).

3. There are two instances in which a species listed under the ESA may not receive the protection afforded by the take prohibition of section 9. First, the take prohibition does not apply to endangered or threatened plants. Instead, it is illegal to "remove, cut, dig up, or damage or destroy" any listed plant "in knowing violation of any law or regulation of any state or in the course of any violation of a state criminal trespass law." ESA § 9(a)(2)(B). There are no reported cases involving this provision, which makes plants dependent upon state law for their protection from collectors, vandals and others on private and state lands. On federal lands, it is illegal to take possession of any listed plant or to "maliciously damage or destroy any such species." *Id.* It is also illegal to engage in any commerce involving an endangered or threatened plant.

Professor Jeffrey Rachlinski reports that most states do not protect endangered plants, and most of those that do offer only minimal protection. He concludes that "plants that depend on private property for their habitat do not fare well, and they fare much worse in those states that do not restrict private landowners." Jeffrey J. Rachlinski, *Protecting Endangered Plants Without Regulating Private Landowners: The Case of Endangered Plants*, 8 CORNELL J. L. PUB. POL'Y 1, 3 (1998). Why would Congress fail to protect plants in the same way that it protects fish and wildlife species? And why do states offer limited protections, too?

The second instance in which a species is not automatically protected by the take prohibition of section 9 occurs if the species is listed as threatened instead of endangered. Section 9 excludes threatened species from its scope, but section 4 authorizes the Secretary of the Interior to extend those provisions to threatened species or to otherwise "issue such regulations as he deems necessary and advisable to provide for the conservation" of threatened species. ESA § 4(d). In 1978, the Secretary issued regulations that extend the provisions of section 9 to all threatened species. 50 C.F.R. § 17.31(a). Increasingly, though, the FWS and the NMFS are promulgating rules establishing special provisions regarding the application of the take prohibition to threatened species. These rules are designed to minimize the impact on landowners and other parties caused by the take prohibition while still offering substantial protection to the threatened species. For example, the NMFS has lifted the take prohibition of section 9 for certain threatened salmon and steelhead for a party who is otherwise participating in a program that protects the species. Such programs include fishery management activities, hatchery and genetic management programs, habitat restoration activities, properly screened water diversion devices, ongoing scientific research, and certain forest management activities. Final Rule Governing Take of 14 Threatened Salmon and Steelhead Evolutionary Significant Units (ESUs), 65 Fed. Reg. 42422 (2000).

United States v. Billie

United States District Court for the Southern District of Florida, 1987.
667 F.Supp. 1485.

■ PAINE, DISTRICT JUDGE.

On April 14, 1987, James Billie was charged in a two count information with the taking and subsequent possession, carrying, and transportation of a Florida panther, in violation of the Endangered Species Act, 16 U.S.C. § 1531 *et seq.* (1982) (the Act); *see id.* §§ 1538(a)(1)(B), 1538(a)(1)(D), 1540(b)(1). The *felis concolor coryi* or Florida panther is a particular subspecies of panther listed as "endangered" pursuant to the Act. The defendant is a member and chairman of the Seminole Indian Tribe, which has approximately 1,700 enrolled members. All of the acts complained of in the information were committed in December 1983 on the Big Cypress Seminole Indian Reservation in the Southern District of Florida.

Applicability of Endangered Species Act to Seminole Indian Reservations

Billie first moves to dismiss the information on the ground the Act does not apply to non-commercial hunting on the Seminole Indian Reservations. He argues that the Act evinces no Congressional intent to abrogate or modify his traditional right to hunt and fish on the reservation. The Government disagrees, maintaining that the Act is a reasonable, necessary, and nondiscriminatory conservation statute which has limited Indian rights to take or possess species to the extent those rights are inconsistent with the Act. In United States v. Dion, 476 U.S. 734 (1986), the Supreme Court expressly left unresolved the question whether the Act abrogates Indian hunting rights. . .

A. The Endangered Species Act

The Supreme Court has described the Endangered Species Act as "the most comprehensive legislation for the preservation of endangered species ever enacted by any nation." Tennessee Valley Authority v. Hill, 437 U.S. 153, 180 (1978). . . The Florida panther, whose historic range is listed as in the United States from Louisiana and Arizona east to South Carolina and Florida, has been listed as endangered since 1967. 50 C.F.R. § 17.11 (1986).

The Act's prohibitions are set forth in 16 U.S.C. § 1538. Included within these prohibitions are the taking of any endangered species within the United States, the possession of any illegally taken endangered species, and the sale or offer for sale of any endangered species in interstate or foreign commerce. Civil and criminal penalties may be imposed for violations of the Act. Id. § 1540.

Congress has drawn several extraordinarily narrow exceptions to the Act's prohibitions. Indians, Aleuts, or Eskimos who are Alaskan Natives residing in Alaska and, in some circumstances other non-native permanent residents of Alaskan native villages, may take endangered or threatened species, but only if the taking is primarily for subsistence purposes and only subject to such regulations as the Secretary may issue upon his determination that such takings materially and negatively affect the species. Id. § 1539(e). In addition, the Secretary may permit otherwise prohibited acts for scientific purposes, to enhance the propagation or survival of the affected species, or when the taking is incidental to carrying out an otherwise lawful activity. Such permits may be issued only on the basis of stringent statutory procedures designed to assure that any adverse impact on the particular species will be minimized. Id. § 1539(a).

B. Hunting Rights on the Seminole Indian Reservations

The Seminole Indian Reservations were established pursuant to an Executive Order by which certain lands were "set aside as a reservation for the Seminole Indians in southern Florida."[2] Although the Executive Order

---

[2] During the nineteenth century, the United States entered into numerous treaties with the Seminoles in attempts to end the Seminole Indian Wars, to convince the Seminoles to settle west of the Mississippi, and to settle land disputes between the Seminole and other tribes

does not expressly mention hunting and fishing rights, those rights were included by implication in the setting aside of the lands as an Indian reservation. The Seminoles' rights to hunt and fish are part of their larger rights of possession.

Although the Congress is empowered to abrogate Indian rights, its intent to do so must be clear and plain. . . Billie maintains that the Act and its legislative history lack the evidence of congressional intent necessary to abrogate his hunting rights.

C. The Scope of the Right

Before the court can determine whether the Seminoles' rights have been abrogated, however, it must assess the scope of those rights. As a general rule, treaties with the Indians should be interpreted as the Indians themselves would have understood them. The Supreme Court has stated that Indian treaties "cannot be interpreted in isolation but must be read in light of the common notions of the day and the assumptions of those who drafted them." Oliphant v. Suquamish Indian Tribe, 435 U.S. 191, 206 (1978).

When the Seminole reservations were set aside in 1911, the Florida panther was not endangered. The court has received no evidence showing that in 1911 either the Seminoles or the United States imagined that the Florida panther would be nearly extinct in 1987. Given this historical setting, and as the Government aptly points out in its memorandum, it is inconceivable that the Seminoles would have demanded, and the United States would have conceded, a right to hunt on the lands in question free from regulation by the federal sovereign.

The Supreme Court has confirmed that Indian treaty rights do not extend to the point of extinction. . . Indian rights to hunt and fish are not absolute. Where conservation measures are necessary to protect endangered wildlife, the Government can intervene on behalf of other federal interests. The migratory nature of the Florida panther gives Indians, the states, and the federal Government a common interest in the preservation of the species. Where the actions of one group can frustrate the others' efforts at conservation, reasonable, nondiscriminatory measures may be required to ensure the species' continued existence.

The Endangered Species Act is such a measure. Its general comprehensiveness, its nonexclusion of Indians, and the limited exceptions for certain Alaskan natives, demonstrate that Congress considered Indian interests, balanced them against conservation needs, and defined the extent to which Indians would be permitted to take protected wildlife. . . The narrow Alaskan exception, the inclusion of Indians within the Act's definition of "person," the Act's general comprehensiveness, and the evidence that the House committee desired to prohibit Indians from hunting and fishing pro-

that did move west. Not all Seminoles moved west, however. In 1911, President Taft signed an Executive Order No. 1379, creating a reservation for those Seminoles remaining in Florida.

tected species all provide "clear evidence that Congress actually considered the conflict between its intended action on the one hand and Indian treaty rights on the other, and chose to resolve that conflict by abrogating" the Indian rights. *Dion*, 106 S. Ct. at 2220.

In summary, this court's conclusion that the Endangered Species Act applies to hunting by Indians on the Seminole reservations is based on both the character of their hunting rights and on the Act's abrogation of those rights. On-reservation hunting rights are not absolute when a species such as the Florida panther is in danger of extinction. To the extent that evidence of congressional abrogation of these rights is required, that standard has been met. When Congress passed "the most comprehensive legislation for the preservation of endangered species ever enacted by any nation," *Tennessee Valley Authority*, 437 U.S. at 180, and empowered the Secretary of the Interior to classify a species as "in danger of extinction," 16 U.S.C. § 1532(6), it could not have intended that the Indians would have the unfettered right to kill the last handful of Florida panthers. . .

Religious Freedom

Billie last contends that the possession charge violates his right to freedom of religion under the First Amendment. He argues that the Act is overbroad either on its face or as applied to him because, unlike the Bald Eagle Protection Act, 16 U.S.C. § 668 *et seq.* (1982), it does not authorize the Secretary to permit the possession of the species for Indian religious purposes. Thus, according to the defendant, the Act is invalid because it sweeps within its ambit his constitutionally-protected practices.

A. Facial Overbreadth

A statute is overbroad on its face if it is unconstitutional in every application or if it seeks to prohibit such a broad range of protected conduct that it is unconstitutionally overbroad. The mere fact that some impermissible applications of a statute are conceivable, however, does not render it overbroad. . . The Endangered Species Act represents the legislature's attempt to achieve the laudable goal of protecting this country's vulnerable wildlife. The possible constitutional applications of the Act are too numerous to conceive. The possibility that it might be unconstitutionally applied to certain religious practices does not render it void on its face where the remainder of the statute covers a whole range of easily identifiable and constitutionally proscribable conduct. Billie, therefore, must demonstrate that the Act is unconstitutional as applied to him.

B. Overbreadth as Applied

Not all burdens on religion are unconstitutional. The Free Exercise Clause "embraces two concepts,—freedom to believe and freedom to act. The first is absolute but, in the nature of things, the second cannot be. Conduct remains subject to regulation for the protection of society." Cantwell v. Connecticut, 310 U.S. 296, 303–04 (1940). . . Before the court balances competing governmental and religious interests, the governmental action must pass two threshold tests. First, the law must regulate conduct rather than belief. Second, the law must have both a secular purpose and a secular effect. The Endangered Species Act passes both of these tests. The Act regulates conduct, not belief, and is facially neutral in its application. In purpose and effect, the Act protects endangered and threatened wildlife.

The court next "faces the difficult task of balancing governmental interests against the impugned religious interest." The stated purposes of the Act are "to provide a means whereby the ecosystems upon which endangered species and threatened species depend may be conserved" and "to provide a program for the conservation of such endangered species and threatened species." 16 U.S.C. § 1531(b). Congress recognized that the "two major causes of extinction" are hunting and destruction of natural habitat. S. Rep. No. 93–307, 93d Cong., 1st Sess. 300, *reprinted in* 1973 U.S. Code Cong. & Admin. News 2989, 2990. In its judgment, the need for strong endangered species efforts was more than aesthetic. It found that many species facing extinction "perform vital biological services to maintain a balance of nature within their environments" and that biological diversity among species was essential for scientific purposes.

The Florida panther was one of the first species protected under the 1966 Endangered Species Preservation Act, the predecessor to the present Endangered Species Act, when it was listed as threatened with extinction. At the evidentiary hearing, the Government presented testimony that population levels are extremely critical. David Wesley, field supervisor of the Jacksonville Office of Endangered Species of the United States Fish and Wildlife Service, estimated that approximately twenty to fifty Florida panthers remain in the wild. A 1985 Interior Department memorandum discussed the species which would probably be most affected were Indians allowed to take endangered and threatened species for religious purposes. The Florida panther was listed as one of those species. The memorandum stated that, although the *coryi* was listed in 1967 as endangered in Louisiana and Arkansas east to South Carolina and Florida, the species now appears to be confined to southern Florida. . .

The evidence presented by the Government, considered along with the Endangered Species Act and its legislative history, establishes that the governmental interest in protecting the Florida panther on the Seminole Indian Reservations is compelling. Considering the small number of remaining *coryi* and their regular presence on Indian land in South Florida, the cost to the Government of altering its conservation efforts would also be substantial. The governmental interest presented in this case would be substantially harmed by a decision allowing Indians to hunt and possess *coryi* free from regulation on Indian reservations. . .

According to Seminole tradition, the panther was the first choice of the creator to enter the earth. In Miccosukee, the panther is called *cowachobee*. Buffalo Jim, a Seminole medicine man, testified that panther claws are good for cramps and different ailments. Jim Shore, general counsel to the Seminole tribal council, testified that panther parts are an important part of a medicine man's bundle. It is commonly known that panther claws and tails are used for different ailments, and a medicine man should have them on hand in case they are needed to minister to a particular illness. Sonny Billie, a Seminole and Miccosukee medicine man, testified that the panther is an "important" animal for a medicine man, because they are difficult to find, and a person has to be lucky to kill one. Sonny Billie also stated that panther claws provide "number one" relief from muscle cramps, which cannot be treated as well without the panther part.

The defendant testified that he was initiated into the practice of Seminole medicine in 1983. Although he can practice medicine, he considers himself a "beginner" and will not have the title of medicine man until he has done many deeds or perhaps achieved his first successful operation or healing. The defendant testified that he had no thoughts regarding what he would do with the panther carcass after he shot it until the morning on which it was seized. At that time, it occurred to Billie that he could give it as a gift to a medicine man in order to humble himself. In bestowing such a high honor, Billie hoped that he would be able to learn more medicine.

. . . Billie has not adequately shown that the possession of panther parts is regular and material to an important religious ceremony or ritual. Although there was testimony that panther parts are important to healing, after having viewed the witnesses, the court is not convinced that panther parts are critical or essential. Sonny Billie stated that panther parts are preferable. They do not appear to be indispensable, however. Furthermore, no evidence was submitted that the *coryi* is the only kind of panther found in Florida today. This lack of evidence gives rise to the inference that other subspecies of panther may be available for Indian religious use and demonstrates Billie's failure to show the gravity of the cost to his religious interest imposed by the Government activity.

Considering the foregoing, the court finds that the evidence has not adequately shown that Billie's religious interest in possessing panther parts[3] should outweigh the compelling governmental interest in protecting the Florida panther.

[The court also rejected Billie's claim that he did not "knowingly" take an endangered species, holding that the government did not have to prove that Billie knew that the panther that he shot belonged to the protected subspecies, nor did the government have to prove that Billie knew that it was illegal to kill an endangered species on an Indian reservation.]

---

[3] For the first time in his reply memorandum, Billie raises the argument that outlawing possession of *coryi* parts without an exception for Indian religious use if the possession has not been involved in the taking does not serve the compelling governmental purpose of prohibiting the killing of the species. The court is not persuaded. In drafting the Endangered Species Act, Congress made possession, carrying, or transportation of protected species a crime in itself. This demonstrates that Congress believed that preventing protected species from being killed is not the only means to rescue it from endangerment. The court also notes Sonny Billie's testimony that the parts of a panther found dead would not be good enough for use by a medicine man, because there would have to be something wrong with that panther. This testimony tends to show a link between hunting *coryi* and possessing their parts. Congress foresaw such a connection when it drafted the Endangered Species Act.

NOTES & QUESTIONS

1. James Billie gained national attention for killing—and then barbequing—a Florida panther in 1983. He reported that the panther tasted "like a cross between a manatee and bald eagle." Efforts to prosecute him failed despite the federal district court's denial of his motion to dismiss the claims in the decision reprinted above. A federal prosecution ended in a mistrial, a state prosecution resulted in an acquittal because the jury questioned whether than animal was a pure Florida panther, and then federal authorities dropped their charges. Billie asked the government for the return of the panther hide and skull which had been used as evidence, but that request was denied because the ESA prohibits the possession of such items. Six years later, Billie was fined $2,000, placed on two years probation, and banned from hunting outside of Seminole tribal reservation after he illegally shot elk in an Idaho national forest.

Billie has been described as "arguably the leading pioneer of Indian gaming in America." Sean Rowe, *Big Chief Moneybags: Part CEO, Part Shaman, Seminole Leader James Billie Has His Tribe Charging Toward Economic Independence*, MIAMI NEW TIMES, Mar. 26, 1998. Billie also operates the tribe's Billie Swamp Safari, where three Florida panthers are on display, and where he lost a finger while wrestling with an alligator. *See* http://www.seminoletribe.com/safari/. He served as the Seminole tribal chairman until he was forced out in 2001 amidst charges of financial mismanagement and sexual harassment. *See* Tanya Weingberg, *After 22 Years, Seminole Leader's World Crumbling*, SUN-SENTINEL (Ft. Lauderdale, Fla.), June 10, 2001, at 1B.

2. As discussed in chapter 2, the relationship between Native Americans and the preservation of biodiversity presents a number of difficult problems. Many Native Americans rely upon certain animals, birds and plants for their very subsistence, including food, clothing and shelter. Also, the religious traditions of many tribes rely upon particular animals. Some federal statutes—including the Bald Eagle Act—provide some exceptions from their provisions in recognition of the special needs of Native Americans, but the ESA and other statutes do not. Thus a number of conflicts have occurred between the dictates of the law and the historic practices of tribes and their members. *See generally* MICHAEL J. BEAN & MELANIE J. ROWLAND, THE EVOLUTION OF NATIONAL WILDLIFE LAW 449–67 (3d ed. 1997) (chapter on wildlife and Native Americans).

The ESA does contain an exception for Eskimos and other Alaskan natives who take an endangered or threatened species "primarily for subsistence purposes." ESA § 10(e)(1), 16 U.S.C. § 1539(e)(1). The Secretary of the Interior can regulate the time during which such takings take place if the species are "materially and negatively affect[ed]" by the actions of the Alaskan natives. ESA § 10(e)(4), 16 U.S.C. § 1539(e)(4). Native Hawaiians do not enjoy such treatment, and an equal protection objection to the ESA for failing to extend the exception to Native Hawaiians was unsuccessful. *See* United States v. Nuesca, 945 F.2d 254 (9th Cir.1991).

Should cultural differences result in special treatment under the ESA? Which differences matter? In United States v. Tomono, 143 F.3d 1401 (11th Cir.1998), a Japanese operator of a commercial reptile import and export business was convicted for bringing sixty turtles into the United States in violation of the Lacey Act. The district court reduced his sentence because he did not realize the seriousness of the offense under U.S. law and because of the special role that the turtles play in Japan, where they are quite common. The court of appeals reversed 2–1, concluding that the circumstances of the case were not sufficiently unusual to justify a reduction on the sentence.

3. The Florida panther plays a prominent role in Seminole medicinal practices. Other endangered species are used in traditional Asian medicine. For example, Chinese medicine uses tiger bones (for arthritis and rheumatism), rhino horns (for fevers), and bear gall bladders. Chinese pharmaceutical factories use 1,400 pounds of rhino horns annually, the product of about 650 rhinos. The ESA does not provide an exception for the use of listed (or the parts of listed species) in medicinal practices, but such practices persist, even in the United States. The Fish & Wildlife Service placed advertisements in the Asian language media in Los Angeles that encouraged the use of alternatives to endangered species in Chinese medicine after noting that six of nine Asian product stores visited in the city carried rhino and tiger-based products. *See* Peter Y. Hong, *Remedy to Extinction; Education Effort Targets Use of Tiger, Rhino Parts in Asian Medicines*, L.A. TIMES, Oct. 20, 1995, at B3. Whether such efforts will succeed remains unclear. A 1998 report concluded that "both Hong Kong Chinese and Chinese-Americans have little knowledge of the ingredients in the [traditional Chinese medicines (TCM)] they use, and little interest in obtaining that knowledge before using such products." SAMUEL LEE ET AL., A WORLD APART? ATTITUDES TOWARD TRADITIONAL CHINESE MEDICINE AND ENDANGERED SPECIES IN HONG KONG AND THE UNITED STATES 8 (1998), *available at* http://www.traffic.org/tcm/ChineseMedicine.pdf.

4. Like most other courts, *Billie* rejected the claim that application of the ESA violated the rights of Native Americans to practice their religion. Tribal reliance upon the first amendment's free exercise clause is unlikely to work given the Supreme Court's decision in Employment Division v. Smith, 494 U.S. 872 (1990), that the application of a neutral and generally applicable statute does not violate the first amendment. Congress enacted the Religious Freedom Restoration Act (RFRA) to expand the scope of rights to exercise religion, but most Native American claims that the ESA infringes on the rights stated by RFRA have failed, too. *See* United States v. Sandia, 188 F.3d 1215, 1218 (10th Cir.1999) (explaining that "a defendant may not claim First Amendment or RFRA protection for the taking and possession of a protected bird when he subsequently sells it for pure commercial gain"); United States v. Lundquist, 932 F.Supp. 1237 (D.Or. 1996) (holding that RFRA did not provide a defense to a Native American charged with possessing bald eagle feathers); United States v. Jim, 888 F.Supp. 1058 (D.Or.1995) (denying a RFRA challenge to the conviction of a Native American who killed twelve bald eagles); *but see* United States v. Gonzales, 957 F.Supp. 1225 (D.N.M.1997) (upholding a RFRA challenge to the criminal prosecution of a Native American who shot a bald eagle for use in a religious ceremony). RFRA no longer limits the actions of states, *see* City of Boerne v. Flores, 521 U.S. 507 (1997), but the applicability of the statute to *federal* government actions may well remain intact. *See* In re Young, 141 F.3d 854 (8th Cir.1998).

United States v. Winnie

United States Court of Appeals for the Seventh Circuit, 1996.
97 F.3d 975.

■ EVANS, CIRCUIT JUDGE.

Gail Winnie of Harshaw, Wisconsin, was a member of a party that went on a monthlong hunting safari in Africa in 1981. During the safari a cheetah was shot and killed. The cheetah was imported into the United States and found its way into Winnie's home where its skin and skull were mounted and displayed on a basement wall. Eleven years later, in 1992, federal and state wildlife agents descended on Winnie and seized the mounted cheetah, which they claimed he possessed in violation of law.

Three years after the seizure Winnie was charged with a federal misdemeanor—unlawfully possessing a cheetah (it's a good thing its common name is so simple, for a cheetah's formal name is Acinonyx jubatus) traded in contravention of the Convention in International Trade in Endangered Species of Wild Fauna and Flora as prohibited by the Endangered Species Act, 16 U.S.C. § 1538(c)(1).

Winnie possessed the cheetah (at least what was left of it after it was shot) continuously from 1981. But because all elements of the offense were present in 1981, Winnie says the government waited too long to file its charge. It had to act, he said, by 1986. Because he was not charged within five years, Winnie claimed the prosecution was too stale to proceed. Nonsense, said the government. The possession of an illegally imported endangered species is a continuing offense which only stops when the possession stops. Winnie's possession ended in 1992, says the government, so the charge here was filed with plenty of time to spare. The district court bought the government's view, and when Winnie's motion to dismiss came up short he entered a guilty plea to the charge (his penalty; six months probation and a $500 fine), preserving his right to argue his statute of limitations defense on this appeal.

In criminal law, the purpose of a statute of limitations is to limit prosecutions to a fixed period of time after the commission of an offense. The limitation protects individuals from having to defend against stale charges. It also encourages law enforcement officials to move promptly when investigating suspected criminal activity. The "continuing offense" doctrine, which enlarges the permissible time period for bringing criminal charges, is, therefore, applied in only limited circumstances. . .

We think Winnie's defense must fail without even considering the continuing offense doctrine. The only relevant facts necessary to this appeal are not in dispute. Winnie admits continued possession of the cheetah from 1981 to 1992. His contention that the offense was "committed" in 1981 when he first took possession of the animal is contrary to the plain language of the statute, part of which makes it a crime "to possess" protected wildlife. Winnie's analysis would require a conclusion that the crime defined by Congress was "to take possession of" illegally traded wildlife, which Winnie did in 1981, rather than "to possess" wildlife, which he did through 1992. Congress did not define the crime that way. The statute of limitations thus did not begin to run until Winnie ceased possessing the cheetah. It was only then that he stopped violating the law.

The cheetah was contraband, just like heroin, and the passage of time never made its possession legal. Otherwise, someone like Winnie could hide a cheetah hide for five years and then display it (or even wear it) with impunity. That scenario was not what Congress had in mind when it prohibited the possession of endangered species. So we need not venture into the thicket of the continuing offense doctrine. Winnie was violating the law on the day the cheetah was seized, and the judgment of the district court is affirmed.

■ RIPPLE, CIRCUIT JUDGE.

I concur in the result.

NOTES & QUESTIONS

1. The statute of limitations issue arises, of course, when an item made from protected wildlife is discovered many years after it was obtained. How do you suppose that federal and state authorities learned of the cheetah eleven years after the animal was shot? Why did Congress criminalize possession of the remains of a dead animal? How does the wrongfulness of possessing a cheetah skin compare to possessing drugs or weapons?

2. ESA section 9(a)(e) makes it illegal to "possess, receive, carry, transport, or ship in interstate or foreign commerce, by any means whatsoever and in the course of a commercial activity" any species that is taken illegally. The law, however, allows the Secretary of the Interior to permit the possession of a species in certain circumstances. They include the progeny of listed raptors that were held prior to the 1978, articles that are more than 100 years old that were made from a listed species, the possession of a species that was obtained before it was listed, and the possession of a species within one year after it was listed where the owner would suffer undue economic hardship from the application of the ESA's prohibitions. *See* ESA § 10(b), (e), (f), & (h); LITTELL, *supra*, at 65–70.

More commonly, a permit may be obtained to take or possess a species "for scientific purposes or to enhance the propagation or survival of the affected species." ESA § 10(a)(1)(A). The FWS considers a number of factors when evaluating a scientific permit request, including the reason for taking a species from the wild, the impact on the existing wild populations, and the likelihood that the action would reduce the threat to the species. *See* 50 C.F.R. § 17.22(a)(2). This provision enables zoos to obtain and keep a listed species with the government's permission, provided that the zoo is working for the survival of the species. Zoos have become crucial to efforts to save endangered species because they facilitate research into a species and because they work to propagate the species in captivity so that it can be returned to the wild. For example, the Toledo Zoo leads the effort to save the Virgin Islands Tree Boa—discussed above at page 218—through a captive breeding program that has generated over one hundred new snakes. For a description of the work of zoos and aquariums in supporting the captive breeding of endangered species ranging from the Kanab ambersnail to the razorback sucker, *see* Mike Demlong, *Beyond Captive Propagation*, 24 ENDANGERED SPECIES BULLETIN 22 (1999), *available at* http://endangered.fws.gov/ESB/99/05-06/22-24.pdf.

3. A knowing violation of the ESA can also result in a $50,000 fine and one year's imprisonment. *See* ESA § 11(b)(1). The law further provides for the forfeiture of any items illegally possessed or imported—as illustrated by the following case—and the revocation of various hunting, fishing and other permits. But the actual sanctions in most endangered species cases are far more modest. Winnie was fined $500 and placed on six months probation for illegally possessing the cheetah skin. Is that an appropriate penalty? It is the same fine that was imposed on Adriano Teobadlelli, an Italian tourist who was caught with over 250 rare butterflies that he had collected in several western national parks. Another butterfly poacher was fined $3,000 and given three years probation for his role in illegally capturing 2,200 butterflies—some of which were endangered species—after a judge rejected a plea agreement that would have required the defendant to serve time in prison.

United States v. One Handbag of Crocodilus Species

United States District Court for the Eastern District of New York, 1994.
856 F.Supp. 128.

■ HURLEY, DISTRICT JUDGE

[The United States brought a forfeiture action to obtain 55 handbags and two belts made from the yacare—an endangered subspecies of crocodile—and other listed crocodiles and reptiles. The government alleged that the goods were imported into the United States by J.S. Suarez, Inc. in violation of section 11(e)(4)(A) of the ESA. That provision states that "all fish or wildlife or plants taken, possessed, sold, purchased, offered or sale or purchase, transported, delivered, received, carried, shipped, exported, or imported contrary to the provisions of [the ESA], any regulation made pursuant thereto, or any permit or certificate issued hereunder shall be subject to forfeiture to the United States." 16 U.S.C. § 1540(e)(4)(A).]

The claimant maintains that the forfeiture of his merchandise for allegedly containing yacare is a denial of due process, because that subspecies of caiman is not identifiable with reasonable certainty. The Court has already rejected, at least in part, the premises for the present argument by concluding that an expert is capable of identifying products made of yacare with reasonable certainty. However, there are apparently a limited number of such experts, and it may well be that businesspersons in the trade rarely possess the requisite expertise.

Presumably this problem is not limited to commerce in certain caiman skins. Difficulty in identification of many endangered species is to be expected due to the rarity of the product involved, coupled with the fact that trade in the product is prohibited. Such being the case, it appears that few persons would have had an opportunity to gain familiarity with the animal. The situation is further complicated when the endangered wildlife is, as in the present case, but one of a number of subspecies which share similar physical characteristics, so that only experts can draw critical distinctions.

Yacare caimens along the Paraguay River in southern Brazil

Does such difficulty in identification render enforcement of the Endangered Species Act, and concomitant forfeiture actions, violative of the due process clause of the 5th amendment? In this Court's view, the answer to that question is "no." Initially, it should be noted that if the claimant's argument was accepted, it would be virtually impossible to protect endangered species; paradoxically, the degree of difficulty typically would escalate as the number of a protected species in existence declined.

Moreover, and by way of analogy, in the criminal law there are certain crimes that are *malum prohibitum*. In such instances, society has decided that the legislative goal sought to be realized outweighs the unfairness that might befall an individual who unintentionally violates the law. Similarly, those who traffic in products involving endangered species run the risk of having the product forfeited, even if compliance with the law is sometimes difficult because of identification problems. Whether the rationale for this result is based upon the fact that the target of the action is the *res*, and not the person having an interest in the *res*, or whether it is based upon a balancing of the competing interests involved, the result is the same.

In sum, this Court rejects the argument that the identification difficulties associated with yacare render the statutory scheme to protect such animals unconstitutional as violative of due process. . .

Claimant argues that he is an "innocent owner," thereby insulating his merchandise from forfeiture. Having reviewed the respective positions of the parties, however, as well as the relevant case law, the Court concludes that a good faith defense is not available in a forfeiture proceeding based on violations of the Endangered Species Act. As one court has persuasively explained,

> [T]he application of strict liability in wildlife forfeiture actions is necessary to effect Congressional intent. To permit an importer to recover the property because he or she lacks culpability would lend support to the continued commercial traffic of the forbidden wildlife. Additionally, a foreseeable consequence would be to discourage diligent inquiry by the importer, allowing him or her to plead ignorance in the face of an import violation. Furthermore, it is not unreasonable to expect the importer to protect his or her interest by placing the risk of non-compliance on the supplier in negotiating the sales agreement.

United States v. 1,000 Raw Skins of Caiman Crocodilus Yacare, No. CV-88-3476, 1991 WL 41774, at *4 (E.D.N.Y. Mar.14, 1991); *see also* United States v. 2,507 Live Canary Winged Parakeets, 689 F. Supp. 1106, 1117 (S.D.Fla. 1988) ("The Court is of the opinion that the defense of 'innocent owner' is not available in actions under the Lacey Act. . . The Act provides for forfeiture of the fish, wildlife and plants on a *strict liability basis*, because the merchandise is, in effect, contraband.") (emphasis in original); United States v. Proceeds From The Sale of Approximately 15,538 Panulirus Argus Lobster Tails, 834 F. Supp. 385 (S.D.Fla.1993). *But see* United States v. 3,210 Crusted Sides of Caiman Crocodilus Yacare, 636 F. Supp. 1281, 1286–87 (S.D.Fla.1986) (court assumed, without analysis, that an innocent owner defense was available in wildlife forfeiture proceeding, but held that defense was unavailable to claimant in that case); Carpenter v. Andrus, 485 F. Supp. 320 (D. Del. 1980) (where owner did not intend to ship leopard hide to United States, but shipping agent accidentally brought the hide into the country, court held that owner was wholly innocent of wrongdoing and denied government's forfeiture application).

Moreover, the Court notes that, as a forfeiture proceeding under the Endangered Species Act, the present case is not one in which some type of nexus has to be established between the property subject to forfeiture and the conduct sought to be controlled, such as those instances in which the government seeks to have currency forfeited as traceable to illegal trafficking in narcotics. Here, the two items are the same: the endangered species is the contraband. Under such circumstances, and given the language of the relevant statutes and the rationale underlying their enactment, a "good faith" or "innocent purchaser" defense is not available in the present case.

Even if, *arguendo*, a claimant's non-culpability is a defense, it should be noted that the Court has significant reservations about Mr. Suarez's innocence. On several prior occasions, he and the same supplier imported products into the United States, including yacare, in violation of the Endangered Species Act. Given the previous illegality, claimant may not close his eyes to the likelihood of a repeat occurrence. Simply relying on that supplier for compliance with the law, as Mr. Suarez testified he did, is not sufficient to trigger a good faith defense, assuming that such a defense exists in this type of forfeiture proceeding.

NOTES & QUESTIONS

1. How can someone tell if the crocodile handbag that they are buying was made from a protected subspecies like the yacare or from an unprotected subspecies? It is even more difficult to know whether other products are produced from endangered species. That, however, is no defense under the law. *See* Delbay Pharmaceuticals v. Department of Commerce, 409 F.Supp. 637 (D.D.C.1976) (prohibiting the sale of a prescription drug made from a substance derived from the endangered sperm whale).

2. Is forfeiture an appropriate remedy in endangered species cases? Suppose that the government sought forfeiture from a woman who bought a yacare handbag from J.S. Suarez? Note that "[u]pon returning to the United States, unwary tourists are . . . forced to surrender their foreign purchases of articles like fur coats and hats, leather pocketbooks, rugs, ivory carvings, or religious statutes." Littell, *supra*, at 42 (citing administrative cases).

3. In 2000, the FWS reclassified the Yacare caiman as threatened. At the same time, the FWS issued a special rule permitting strictly regulated trade in the caiman in order "to promote the conservation of the yacare caiman by ensuring proper management of the commercially harvested caiman species in the range countries and, through implementation of trade controls . . . to reduce commingling of caiman specimens." Reclassification of Yacare Caiman in South America From Endangered to Threatened, and the Listing of Two Other Caiman Species as Threatened by Reason of Similarity of Appearance, 65 Fed. Reg. 25867 (2000). Why did the FWS allow any trade in the species?

4. Smuggling remains a great threat to many endangered species. Assistant Attorney General Lois Schiffer described the government's successful prosecution of a smuggling ring in Madagascar that used local residents to collect Madagascan tree boas and rare radiated and spider tortoises (each of which is listed under the ESA) and then transported the animals to the United States where reptile dealers could sell them at a 10,000% mark-up on the price paid to collectors. Lois J. Schiffer & Timothy J. Dowling, *Government Works! Case Studies in Environmental Protection*, 32 CREIGHTON L. REV. 781, 784 (1999). The World Wildlife Fund's "Traffic North America" newsletter provides an update on smuggling activities, including a recent report on several cases involving the seizure of large amounts of sea turtle eggs that were smuggled into the United States. *Illegal Egg Trade Threatens Sea Turtles*, 2 TRAFFIC NORTH AMERICA 1 (1999), *available at* http://www.worldwildlife.org/trade/traffic.cfm. Such imports are illegal under the federal Lacey Act and the international Convention on International Trade in Endangered Species of Wild Fauna and Flora (CITES), as well as the ESA. Additional materials on the threat that smuggling and other illegal activities pose to endangered species around the world is contained in chapter 14.

B. HABITAT DESTRUCTION AND INDIRECT TAKING OF ENDANGERED SPECIES

Half of the species listed under the ESA have at least 80% of their habitat on private lands. As detailed in chapter 2, habitat destruction presents the greatest threat to the survival of species in the United States and throughout the world. The drafters of the ESA recognized as much when they stated that the purpose of the law is "to provide a means whereby the ecosystems upon which endangered species and threatened species depend may be conserved." ESA § 2(b). Yet the ESA does not contain a provision that protects all of the habitats of all listed species from destruction or other harms. Instead, the ESA addresses habitat destruction through several different kinds of provisions. Section 4 authorizes the FWS to designate the critical habitat of a species, as described above at pages 185–200. Section 5 directs appropriate federal agencies to acquire land used as habitat by listed species. Most controversially, the take prohibition of section 9 can be read to encompass the modification of the habitat of an endangered species, as discussed in the *Sweet Home* case below.

Besides habitat destruction, a variety of other indirect actions can harm a species. The contested cases have featured disoriented baby sea turtles attracted to beachfront lights, grizzly bears feasting on grain spilled on railroad tracks as another train looms, and the fear that bald eagles would be poisoned by lead shot used to kill deer. Federal, state and local governments often find themselves accused of injuring listed species by failing to take actions necessary to protect them from a variety of threats.

But private parties have been the most critical of the restrictions imposed by the ESA. The extension of the ESA to certain kinds of habitat destruction and other activities that indirectly harm a species has prompted a lively theoretical debate and numerous calls for legislative reform. The same actions that environmentalists view as critical for the survival of a species are often denounced as overzealous government interference with private landowners. The provisions of the ESA itself are at issue in this debate, which shows no signs of ending any time soon.

1. THE SCOPE OF THE TAKE PROHIBITION

Babbitt v. Sweet Home Chapter of Communities for a Great Oregon

Supreme Court of the United States, 1995.
515 U.S. 687.

■ JUSTICE STEVENS delivered the opinion of the Court.

The Endangered Species Act of 1973 (ESA or Act), contains a variety of protections designed to save from extinction species that the Secretary of the Interior designates as endangered or threatened. Section 9 of the Act makes it unlawful for any person to "take" any endangered or threatened species. The Secretary has promulgated a regulation that defines the statute's prohibition on takings to include "significant habitat modification or degradation where it actually kills or injures wildlife." This case presents the question whether the Secretary exceeded his authority under the Act by promulgating that regulation.

I

Section 9(a)(1) of the Endangered Species Act provides the following protection for endangered species:

Except as provided in sections 1535(g)(2) and 1539 of this title, with respect to any endangered species of fish or wildlife listed pursuant to section 1533 of this title it is unlawful for any person subject to the jurisdiction of the United States to . . . (B) take any such species within the United States or the territorial sea of the United States[.]

Section 3(19) of the Act defines the statutory term "take": "The term 'take' means to harass, harm, pursue, hunt, shoot, wound, kill, trap, capture, or collect, or to attempt to engage in any such conduct." The Act does not further define the terms it uses to define "take." The Interior Department regulations that implement the statute, however, define the statutory term "harm": "Harm in the definition of 'take' in the Act means an act which actually kills or injures wildlife. Such act may include significant habitat modification or degradation where it actually kills or injures wildlife by significantly impairing essential behavioral patterns, including breeding, feeding, or sheltering." This regulation has been in place since 1975.[4]

A limitation on the § 9 "take" prohibition appears in § 10(a)(1)(B) of the Act, which Congress added by amendment in 1982. That section authorizes the Secretary to grant a permit for any taking otherwise prohibited by § 9(a)(1)(B) "if such taking is incidental to, and not the purpose of, the carrying out of an otherwise lawful activity."

. . . Respondents in this action are small landowners, logging companies, and families dependent on the forest products industries in the Pacific Northwest and in the Southeast, and organizations that represent their interests. They brought this declaratory judgment action against petitioners, the Secretary of the Interior and the Director of the Fish and Wildlife Service, in the United States District Court for the District of Columbia to challenge the statutory validity of the Secretary's regulation defining "harm," particularly the inclusion of habitat modification and degradation in the definition. Respondents challenged the regulation on its face. Their complaint alleged that application of the "harm" regulation to the red-cockaded woodpecker, an endangered species, and the northern spotted owl, a threatened species, had injured them economically.

Respondents advanced three arguments to support their submission that Congress did not intend the word "take" in § 9 to include habitat modification, as the Secretary's "harm" regulation provides. First, they correctly noted that language in the Senate's original version of the ESA would have defined "take" to include "destruction, modification, or curtailment of [the] habitat or range" of fish or wildlife, but the Senate deleted that language from the bill before enacting it. Second, respondents argued that Congress

---

[4]   The Secretary, through the Director of the Fish and Wildlife Service, originally promulgated the regulation in 1975 and amended it in 1981 to emphasize that actual death or injury of a protected animal is necessary for a violation.

intended the Act's express authorization for the Federal Government to buy private land in order to prevent habitat degradation in § 5 to be the exclusive check against habitat modification on private property. Third, because the Senate added the term "harm" to the definition of "take" in a floor amendment without debate, respondents argued that the court should not interpret the term so expansively as to include habitat modification.

[The District Court upheld the regulation. On appeal, the D.C. Circuit first upheld the regulation 2–1, but on rehearing the court struck down the regulation 2–1 after Judge Williams changed his mind.]

II

Because this case was decided on motions for summary judgment, we may appropriately make certain factual assumptions in order to frame the legal issue. First, we assume respondents have no desire to harm either the red-cockaded woodpecker or the spotted owl; they merely wish to continue logging activities that would be entirely proper if not prohibited by the ESA. On the other hand, we must assume arguendo that those activities will have the effect, even though unintended, of detrimentally changing the natural habitat of both listed species and that, as a consequence, members of those species will be killed or injured. Under respondents' view of the law, the Secretary's only means of forestalling that grave result—even when the actor knows it is certain to occur—is to use his § 5 authority to purchase the lands on which the survival of the species depends. The Secretary, on the other hand, submits that the § 9 prohibition on takings, which Congress defined to include "harm," places on respondents a duty to avoid harm that habitat alteration will cause the birds unless respondents first obtain a permit pursuant to § 10.

The text of the Act provides three reasons for concluding that the Secretary's interpretation is reasonable. First, an ordinary understanding of the word "harm" supports it. The dictionary definition of the verb form of "harm" is "to cause hurt or damage to: injure." In the context of the ESA, that definition naturally encompasses habitat modification that results in actual injury or death to members of an endangered or threatened species.

Respondents argue that the Secretary should have limited the purview of "harm" to direct applications of force against protected species, but the dictionary definition does not include the word "directly" or suggest in any way that only direct or willful action that leads to injury constitutes "harm."[5] Moreover, unless the statutory term "harm" encompasses indirect

---

[5] Respondents and the dissent emphasize what they portray as the "established meaning" of "take" in the sense of a "wildlife take," a meaning respondents argue extends only to "the effort to exercise dominion over some creature, and the concrete effect of [sic] that creature." This limitation ill serves the statutory text, which forbids not taking "some creature" but "tak[ing] any [endangered] species"—a formidable task for even the most rapacious feudal lord. More importantly, Congress explicitly defined the operative term "take" in the ESA, no matter how much the dissent wishes otherwise, thereby obviating the need for us to probe its meaning as we must probe the meaning of the undefined subsidiary term "harm." Finally, Congress' definition of "take" includes several words—most obviously "harass," "pursue," and "wound," in addition to "harm" itself—that fit respondents' and the dissent's definition of "take" no better than does "significant habitat modification or degradation."

as well as direct injuries, the word has no meaning that does not duplicate the meaning of other words that § 3 uses to define "take." A reluctance to treat statutory terms as surplusage supports the reasonableness of the Secretary's interpretation.[6]

Second, the broad purpose of the ESA supports the Secretary's decision to extend protection against activities that cause the precise harms Congress enacted the statute to avoid. In *TVA v. Hill*, 437 U.S. 153 (1978), we described the Act as "the most comprehensive legislation for the preservation of endangered species ever enacted by any nation." Whereas predecessor statutes enacted in 1966 and 1969 had not contained any sweeping prohibition against the taking of endangered species except on federal lands, the 1973 Act applied to all land in the United States and to the Nation's territorial seas. As stated in § 2 of the Act, among its central purposes is "to provide a means whereby the ecosystems upon which endangered species and threatened species depend may be conserved. . ."

Respondents advance strong arguments that activities that cause minimal or unforeseeable harm will not violate the Act as construed in the "harm" regulation. Respondents, however, present a facial challenge to the regulation. Thus, they ask us to invalidate the Secretary's understanding of "harm" in every circumstance, even when an actor knows that an activity, such as draining a pond, would actually result in the extinction of a listed species by destroying its habitat. Given Congress' clear expression of the ESA's broad purpose to protect endangered and threatened wildlife, the Secretary's definition of "harm" is reasonable.

Third, the fact that Congress in 1982 authorized the Secretary to issue permits for takings that § 9(a)(1)(B) would otherwise prohibit, "if such taking is incidental to, and not the purpose of, the carrying out of an otherwise lawful activity," strongly suggests that Congress understood § 9(a)(1)(B) to prohibit indirect as well as deliberate takings. The permit process requires the applicant to prepare a "conservation plan" that specifies how he intends to "minimize and mitigate" the "impact" of his activity on endangered and threatened species, making clear that Congress had in mind foreseeable rather than merely accidental effects on listed species. No one could seriously request an "incidental" take permit to avert § 9 liability for direct, deliberate action against a member of an endangered or threatened species, but respondents would read "harm" so narrowly that the permit procedure would have little more than that absurd purpose. "When Congress acts to amend a statute, we presume it intends its amendment to have real and substantial effect." Congress' addition of the § 10 permit provision supports

---

[6] In contrast, if the statutory term "harm" encompasses such indirect means of killing and injuring wildlife as habitat modification, the other terms listed in § 3—"harass," "pursue," "hunt," "shoot," "wound," "kill," "trap," "capture," and "collect"— generally retain independent meanings. Most of those terms refer to deliberate actions more frequently than does "harm," and they therefore do not duplicate the sense of indirect causation that "harm" adds to the statute. In addition, most of the other words in the definition describe either actions from which habitat modification does not usually result (e.g., "pursue," "harass") or effects to which activities that modify habitat do not usually lead (e.g., "trap," "collect"). To the extent the Secretary's definition of "harm" may have applications that overlap with other words in the definition, that overlap reflects the broad purpose of the Act.

the Secretary's conclusion that activities not intended to harm an endangered species, such as habitat modification, may constitute unlawful takings under the ESA unless the Secretary permits them.

The Court of Appeals made three errors in asserting that "harm" must refer to a direct application of force because the words around it do.[7] First, the court's premise was flawed. Several of the words that accompany "harm" in the § 3 definition of "take," especially "harass," "pursue," "wound," and "kill," refer to actions or effects that do not require direct applications of force. Second, to the extent the court read a requirement of intent or purpose into the words used to define "take," it ignored § 9's express provision that a "knowing" action is enough to violate the Act. Third, the court employed *noscitur a sociis* to give "harm" essentially the same function as other words in the definition, thereby denying it independent meaning. The canon, to the contrary, counsels that a word "gathers meaning from the words around it." The statutory context of "harm" suggests that Congress meant that term to serve a particular function in the ESA, consistent with but distinct from the functions of the other verbs used to define "take." The Secretary's interpretation of "harm" to include indirectly injuring endangered animals through habitat modification permissibly interprets "harm" to have "a character of its own not to be submerged by its association."

Nor does the Act's inclusion of the § 5 land acquisition authority and the § 7 directive to federal agencies to avoid destruction or adverse modification of critical habitat alter our conclusion. Respondents' argument that the Government lacks any incentive to purchase land under § 5 when it can simply prohibit takings under § 9 ignores the practical considerations that attend enforcement of the ESA. Purchasing habitat lands may well cost the Government less in many circumstances than pursuing civil or criminal penalties. In addition, the § 5 procedure allows for protection of habitat before the seller's activity has harmed any endangered animal, whereas the Government cannot enforce the § 9 prohibition until an animal has actually been killed or injured. The Secretary may also find the § 5 authority useful for preventing modification of land that is not yet but may in the future become habitat for an endangered or threatened species. The § 7 directive applies only to the Federal Government, whereas the § 9 prohibition applies to "any person." Section 7 imposes a broad, affirmative duty to avoid adverse habitat modifications that § 9 does not replicate, and § 7 does not limit its admonition to habitat modification that "actually kills or injures wildlife." Conversely, § 7 contains limitations that § 9 does not, applying only to actions "likely to jeopardize the continued existence of any endan-

---

[7]   The dissent makes no effort to defend the Court of Appeals' reading of the statutory definition as requiring a direct application of force. Instead, it tries to impose on § 9 a limitation of liability to "affirmative conduct intentionally directed against a particular animal or animals." Under the dissent's interpretation of the Act, a developer could drain a pond, knowing that the act would extinguish an endangered species of turtles, without even proposing a conservation plan or applying for a permit under § 9(a)(1)(B); unless the developer was motivated by a desire "to get at a turtle," no statutory taking could occur. Because such conduct would not constitute a taking at common law, the dissent would shield it from § 9 liability, even though the words "kill" and "harm" in the statutory definition could apply to such deliberate conduct....

gered species or threatened species," and to modifications of habitat that has been designated "critical" pursuant to § 4. Any overlap that § 5 or § 7 may have with § 9 in particular cases is unexceptional, and simply reflects the broad purpose of the Act set out in § 2 and acknowledged in *TVA v. Hill.*

We need not decide whether the statutory definition of "take" compels the Secretary's interpretation of "harm," because our conclusions that Congress did not unambiguously manifest its intent to adopt respondents' view and that the Secretary's interpretation is reasonable suffice to decide this case. *See generally Chevron U.S.A. Inc. v. Natural Resources Defense Council, Inc.,* 467 U.S. 837 (1984). The latitude the ESA gives the Secretary in enforcing the statute, together with the degree of regulatory expertise necessary to its enforcement, establishes that we owe some degree of deference to the Secretary's reasonable interpretation. *See* Breyer, *Judicial Review of Questions of Law and Policy,* 38 ADMIN. L. REV. 363, 373 (1986).

III

Our conclusion that the Secretary's definition of "harm" rests on a permissible construction of the ESA gains further support from the legislative history of the statute... The Senate Report stressed that " '[t]ake' is defined . . . in the broadest possible manner to include every conceivable way in which a person can 'take' or attempt to 'take' any fish or wildlife." The House Report stated that "the broadest possible terms" were used to define restrictions on takings . . . [By contrast, the fact that a proposed endangered species bill included "the destruction, modification, or curtailment of [the] habitat or range of fish and wildlife" does not indicate the take prohibition that was ultimately adopted excludes habitat protection. Additionally, "the history of the 1982 amendment that gave the Secretary authority to grant permits for 'incidental' takings provides further support for his reading of the Act. The House Report expressly states that '[b]y use of the word "incidental" the Committee intends to cover situations in which it is known that a taking will occur if the other activity is engaged in but such taking is incidental to, and not the purpose of, the activity.' "]

IV

When it enacted the ESA, Congress delegated broad administrative and interpretive power to the Secretary. The task of defining and listing endangered and threatened species requires an expertise and attention to detail that exceeds the normal province of Congress. Fashioning appropriate standards for issuing permits under § 10 for takings that would otherwise violate § 9 necessarily requires the exercise of broad discretion. The proper interpretation of a term such as "harm" involves a complex policy choice. When Congress has entrusted the Secretary with broad discretion, we are especially reluctant to substitute our views of wise policy for his. *See Chevron,* 467 U.S. at 865–866. In this case, that reluctance accords with our conclusion, based on the text, structure, and legislative history of the ESA, that the Secretary reasonably construed the intent of Congress when he defined "harm" to include "significant habitat modification or degradation that actually kills or injures wildlife."

In the elaboration and enforcement of the ESA, the Secretary and all persons who must comply with the law will confront difficult questions of proximity and degree; for, as all recognize, the Act encompasses a vast range of economic and social enterprises and endeavors. These questions must be addressed in the usual course of the law, through case-by-case resolution and adjudication.

■ JUSTICE O'CONNOR, concurring.

My agreement with the Court is founded on two understandings. First, the challenged regulation is limited to significant habitat modification that causes actual, as opposed to hypothetical or speculative, death or injury to identifiable protected animals. Second, even setting aside difficult questions of scienter, the regulation's application is limited by ordinary principles of proximate causation, which introduce notions of foreseeability. These limitations, in my view, call into question *Palila v. Hawaii Dept. of Land and Natural Resources*, 852 F.2d 1106 (C.A.9 1988) (*Palila II*), and with it, many of the applications derided by the dissent. Because there is no need to strike a regulation on a facial challenge out of concern that it is susceptible of erroneous application, however, and because there are many habitat-related circumstances in which the regulation might validly apply, I join the opinion of the Court. . .

■ JUSTICE SCALIA, with whom THE CHIEF JUSTICE and JUSTICE THOMAS join, dissenting.

I think it unmistakably clear that the legislation at issue here (1) forbade the hunting and killing of endangered animals, and (2) provided federal lands and federal funds for the acquisition of private lands, to preserve the habitat of endangered animals. The Court's holding that the hunting and killing prohibition incidentally preserves habitat on private lands imposes unfairness to the point of financial ruin—not just upon the rich, but upon the simplest farmer who finds his land conscripted to national zoological use. I respectfully dissent.

I

. . . The regulation has three features which . . . do not comport with the statute. First, it interprets the statute to prohibit habitat modification that is no more than the cause-in-fact of death or injury to wildlife. Any "significant habitat modification" that in fact produces that result by "impairing essential behavioral patterns" is made unlawful, regardless of whether that result is intended or even foreseeable, and no matter how long the chain of causality between modification and injury. *See, e.g.,* Palila v. Hawaii Dept. of Land and Natural Resources (Palila II), 852 F.2d 1106, 1108–1109 (CA9 1988) (sheep grazing constituted "taking" of palila birds, since although sheep do not destroy full-grown mamane trees, they do destroy mamane seedlings, which will not grow to full-grown trees, on which the palila feeds and nests).

Second, the regulation does not require an "act": the Secretary's officially stated position is that an omission will do. . . The third and most important unlawful feature of the regulation is that it encompasses injury inflicted, not only upon individual animals, but upon populations of the protected species. "Injury" in the regulation includes "significantly impairing essential behavioral patterns, including breeding." Impairment of breeding does not "injure" living creatures; it prevents them from propagating, thus "injuring" a population of animals which would otherwise have maintained or increased its numbers. What the face of the regulation shows, the Secretary's official pronouncements confirm. The Final Redefinition of "Harm" accompanying publication of the regulation said that "harm" is not limited to "direct physical injury to an individual member of the wildlife species," and refers to "injury to a population.". . .

II

The Court [argues that] "the broad purpose of the [Act] supports the Secretary's decision to extend protection against activities that cause the precise harms Congress enacted the statute to avoid." I thought we had renounced the vice of "simplistically . . . assum[ing] that whatever furthers the statute's primary objective must be the law." . . . Second, the Court maintains that the legislative history of the 1973 Act supports the Secretary's definition. Even if legislative history were a legitimate and reliable tool of interpretation (which I shall assume in order to rebut the Court's claim); and even if it could appropriately be resorted to when the enacted text is as clear as this, here it shows quite the opposite of what the Court says. I shall not pause to discuss the Court's reliance on such statements in the Committee Reports as " '[t]ake' is defined . . . in the broadest possible manner to include every conceivable way in which a person can 'take' or attempt to 'take' any fish or wildlife." This sort of empty flourish—to the effect that "this statute means what it means all the way"—counts for little even when enacted into the law itself. . . Both the Senate and House floor managers of the bill explained it in terms which leave no doubt that the problem of habitat destruction on private lands was to be solved principally by the land acquisition program of § 1534, while § 1538 solved a different problem altogether—the problem of takings . . . Habitat modification and takings, in other words, were viewed as different problems, addressed by different provisions of the Act. . .

III

In response to the points made in this dissent, the Court's opinion stresses two points, neither of which is supported by the regulation, and so cannot validly be used to uphold it. First, the Court and the concurrence suggest that the regulation should be read to contain a requirement of proximate causation or foreseeability, principally because the statute does—and "[n]othing in the regulation purports to weaken those requirements [of the statute]." I quite agree that the statute contains such a limitation, because the verbs of purpose in § 1538(a)(1)(B) denote action directed at animals. But the Court has rejected that reading. The critical premise on which it has upheld the regulation is that, despite the weight of the other words in § 1538(a)(1)(B), "the statutory term 'harm' encompasses indirect as well as direct injuries." Consequently, unless there is some strange category of causation that is indirect and yet also proximate, the Court has already rejected its own basis for finding a proximate-cause limitation in the regulation. In fact "proximate" causation simply means "direct" causation.

. . . The regulation says (it is worth repeating) that "harm" means (1) an act which (2) actually kills or injures wildlife. If that does not dispense with a proximate-cause requirement, I do not know what language would. And changing the regulation by judicial invention, even to achieve compliance with the statute, is not permissible.

The second point the Court stresses in its response seems to me a belated mending of its hold. It apparently concedes that the statute requires injury to particular animals rather than merely to populations of animals. The Court then rejects my contention that the regulation ignores this requirement, since, it says, "every term in the regulation's definition of 'harm' is subservient to the phrase 'an act which actually kills or injures wildlife.' " As I have pointed out, this reading is incompatible with the regulation's specification of impairment of "breeding" as one of the modes of "kill[ing] or injur[ing] wildlife."[8]

. . . The Endangered Species Act is a carefully considered piece of legislation that forbids all persons to hunt or harm endangered animals, but

---

[8] Justice O'Connor supposes that an "impairment of breeding" intrinsically injures an animal because "[t]o make it impossible for an animal to reproduce is to impair its most essential physical functions and to render that animal, and its genetic material, biologically obsolete." This imaginative construction does achieve the result of extending "impairment of breeding" to individual animals; but only at the expense of also expanding "injury" to include elements beyond physical harm to individual animals. For surely the only harm to the individual animal from impairment of that "essential function" is not the failure of issue (which harms only the issue), but the psychic harm of perceiving that it will leave this world with no issue (assuming, of course, that the animal in question, perhaps an endangered species of slug, is capable of such painful sentiments). If it includes that psychic harm, then why not the psychic harm of not being able to frolic about—so that the draining of a pond used for an endangered animal's recreation, but in no way essential to its survival, would be prohibited by the Act? That the concurrence is driven to such a dubious redoubt is an argument for, not against, the proposition that "injury" in the regulation includes injury to populations of animals. Even more so with the concurrence's alternative explanation: that "impairment of breeding" refers to nothing more than concrete injuries inflicted by the habitat modification on the animal who does the breeding, such as "physical complications [suffered] during gestation." Quite obviously, if "impairment of breeding" meant such physical harm to an individual animal, it would not have had to be mentioned. The concurrence entangles itself in a dilemma while attempting to explain the Secretary's commentary to the harm regulation, which stated that "harm" is not limited to "direct physical injury to an individual member of the wildlife species." The concurrence denies that this means that the regulation does not require injury to particular animals, because "one could just as easily emphasize the word 'direct' in this sentence as the word 'individual.' " One could; but if the concurrence does, it thereby refutes its separate attempt to exclude indirect causation from the regulation's coverage. The regulation, after emerging from the concurrence's analysis, has acquired both a proximate-cause limitation and a particular-animals limitation—precisely the one meaning that the Secretary's quoted declaration will not allow, whichever part of it is emphasized.

places upon the public at large, rather than upon fortuitously accountable individual landowners, the cost of preserving the habitat of endangered species. There is neither textual support for, nor even evidence of congressional consideration of, the radically different disposition contained in the regulation that the Court sustains. For these reasons, I respectfully dissent.

NOTES & QUESTIONS

1. So who is right? Does one "take" an endangered species when one adversely affects its habitat? Did the Congress that enacted the ESA in 1973 intend for section 9 to apply to habitat modification? Or did that Congress plan to protect habitat through other provisions in the act? Does the addition of section 10's incidental take provision in 1982 suggest that "take" must be read to include habitat modification?

2. Justice O'Connor's concurrence indicates that she questions the application of the take prohibition in *Palila II*. The palila is a six-inch bird that lives in mamane and naio forests on the slopes of Mauna Kea on the island of Hawai'i. That area is also home to the Mauna Kea Game Management Area, where the state introduced wild goats and sheep to facilitate game hunting, an otherwise rare commodity in Hawaii. The goats and the sheep were eating the seedlings, leaves, stems, and sprouts of the mamane and naio trees on which the palila depended for its survival. In *Palila I*, the courts held that the state's act of permitting the goats and the sheep to live in the area constituted a take of the palila. Palila v. Hawaii Dep't of Land & Natural Resources, 471 F.Supp. 985 (D.Haw.1979), *aff'd*, 639 F.2d 495 (9th Cir.1981). *Palila II* reached a similar conclusion regarding the state's introduction of mouflon sheep into the same area, sheep that were prized by hunters but which fed on the mamane trees. Palila v. Hawaii Dep't of Land & Natural Resources, 649 F.Supp. 1070 (D.Haw.1986), *aff'd*, 852 F.2d 1106 (9th Cir.1988). The fact that the goats and sheep were destroying the habitat on which the palila depended led the courts to find a take in both cases, even though there was no evidence of an actual injury to any individual palila and even though the numbers of palilas had not dropped. Subsequently, the state's resulting "[u]ngulate eradication efforts have become so successful that hunters frequently cannot find any sheep to shoot" in the game area. Palila v. Hawaii Dep't of Land & Natural Resources, 73 F.Supp.2d 1181, 1184 (D.Haw.1999). A group of frustrated hunters then moved to dissolve the court's orders, but the court held that the balance of the equities favored the species because "mouflon sheep can always be reintroduced on Mauna Kea," whereas "[p]alila once extinct are gone forever." *Id.* at 1187.

3. As the Court understands the regulation, which of the following activities constitute a prohibited "take" of an endangered species?

> a. A train spilled grain alongside the railroad tracks, thus attracting hungry grizzly bears to the area. Environmentalists claim that both the failure to remove the grain and the railroad's ongoing operations constitute a take. National Wildlife Fed'n v. Burlington N. R.R., 23 F.3d 1508 (9th Cir.1994).

> b. A Tucson school district wants to build a new high school on part of a 73 acre site. A pygmy-owl has been seen on the north part of the property,

outside the area where the school will be built but near the construction activities and where the student parking lot will be located. Defenders of Wildlife v. Bernal, 204 F.3d 920 (9th Cir.2000).

c. An irrigation district pumps water from the Sacramento River. Salmon are killed when they crash into a fish screen that was installed by the state wildlife agency, but the district claims that it has not committed a prohibited take because it did not install the fish screen that is killing the fish. United States v. Glenn-Colusa Irrigation Dist., 788 F.Supp. 1126 (E.D.Cal.1992).

d. Dewitt DeWeese wants to build a lounge on ten acres of his land on Perdido Key north of Florida's Highway 182. The critical habitat of the Perdido Key Beach mouse occupies 88 acres south of the highway. A biologist contends that the lounge would result in three different prohibited takes of the mouse because (1) construction activities might actually kill or injure some mice, even though no mouse has been seen on DeWeese's property; (2) the project will degrade the habitat of the mouse; or (3) the lounge will attract cats that will prey upon the mouse. Morrill v. Lujan, 802 F.Supp. 424 (S.D.Ala.1992).

e. A timber company wants to clear cut 93 acres of its old growth forest land. A pair of spotted owls forages on the land, but also on similar forest on neighboring property as well. United States v. West Coast Forest Resources Ltd. Partnership, 2000 WL 298707 (D.Or. 2000).

Alternately, consider the following hypothetical case. A river with a typical flow of ten cubic-feet per second (cfs) is subject to traditional western prior appropriation rules. Smith has the right to withdraw four cfs dating from 1900, Jones has had the right to four cfs since 1930, and Williams obtained a right to withdraw one cfs in 1990. Then the FWS listed a fish that is native to the river as endangered, and the fish needs two cfs to survive. Who has what right to the water? *See* James R. Rasband, *Priority, Probability, and Proximate Cause: Lessons from Tort Law About Imposing ESA Responsibility for Wildlife Harm on Water Users and Other Joint Habitat Modifiers*, 33 ENVTL. L. 595 (2003) (posing and analyzing the hypothetical).

4. The application of the take prohibition to habitat modification has prompted several constitutional challenges. As discussed in chapter 3, several federal appeals courts have rejected claims that the take prohibition exceeds the power of Congress to regulate interstate commerce, but the issue has yet to be decided by the Supreme Court. Likewise, numerous landowners have argued that the take prohibition has resulted in a taking for which they are entitled just compensation. These claims have failed, too, with one exception: Tulare Lake Basin Water Storage Dist. v. United States, 49 Fed. Cl. 313 (2001), which held that water use restrictions imposed to protect the endangered delta smelt and winter-run chinook salmon worked a taking of the contractual water rights held by two county water districts. Why have the courts found so few regulatory takings resulting from the ESA?

5. The FWS has tried to respond to the uncertainty that continues to surround the precise scope of the ESA's take prohibition in the aftermath of *Sweet Home*. Whenever it lists a new species, the agency specifies which activities would constitute a take and which would not. For example, when it listed two snails in Alabama as endangered, the FWS advised that it would not view the following activities as a prohibited take: existing permitted discharges into the snail's habitat; typical agricultural and silvicultural practices carried out in compliance with existing state and federal regulations and best management practices; development and construction activities designed and implemented according to state and local water quality regulations; existing recreational activities such as swimming, wading, canoeing, and fishing; and the use of pesticides and herbicides in accordance with the label restrictions within the species' watersheds. But the agency warned that other activities could result in a take, including unauthorized collection or capture of the snails; dredging, channelization, the withdrawal of water, and other unauthorized destruction or alteration of the habitat of the snails; the violation of any discharge or water withdrawal permit; and illegal discharge or dumping of toxic chemicals or other pollutants into waters supporting the snails. Endangered Status for the Armored Snail and Slender Campeloma, 65 Fed. Reg. 10033, 10038 (2000). Is that guidance consistent with *Sweet Home*? Is it likely to be helpful to local residents and landowners? Note that the agency's advice is nonbinding, but the agency promises to answer questions about the application of the take prohibition to particular activities.

United States v. Town of Plymouth, Massachusetts

United States District Court for the District of Massachusetts, 1998.
6 F.Supp.2d 81.

■ SARIS, UNITED STATES DISTRICT JUDGE.

[The piping plover is a small shorebird that nests on sandy coastal beaches from North Carolina to Newfoundland. The 1,200 breeding pairs that live along the Atlantic Coast in the United States are listed as threatened under the ESA. Over one-third of those breeding pairs nest along beaches in Massachusetts. The piping plovers nest on the beaches in Massachusetts from mid-March through May, and the chicks remain there until they are able to fly by late July or early August. Piping plover chicks are particularly vulnerable to off-road vehicles (ORVs) because the chicks leave their nests within hours of hatching and wander some distance along the beach and adjacent areas. The chicks can move quickly, but sometimes when vehicles approach they stand motionless in an attempt to blend into the sand. Thus Dr. Scott Melvin, a rare species zoologist with the Massachusetts Division of Fisheries and Wildlife, documented 25 piping plover chicks and two adults that were found dead in ORV tire ruts on the upper beach in Massachusetts and New York between 1989 and 1997. Dr. Melvin also described how ORVs destroy beach habitat that would be suitable for piping plovers and how ORVs disrupt feeding by scaring chicks and burying insects and other food that would otherwise be available to the piping plovers.

Plymouth Long Beach is 2.8 miles long and is used by both piping plovers and ORVs. Most of the beach is owned by the town of Plymouth, while the remainder is home to eighteen private residences. The town permits ORVs and other vehicles to travel on the beach from 4:00 a.m. until 9:00 p.m daily. The town sold between 1,100 and 2,700 ORV permits in the years from 1991 through 1997, with up to 325 vehicles allowed on the beach at one time. When it became aware of the threat to the piping plovers, the town's park division issued guidelines for protecting the birds, and John Crane—a park division employee who served as the town's natural resources officer (NRO)—worked to install fencing and take other actions to prevent ORVs from harming the birds. Those efforts failed, however, because of opposition from ORV users and pressure from town officials. On June 13, 1996, Crane sought to close the beach while four piping plover chicks were hatched from their eggs, but the town's selectmen refused to do so and one of the chicks was found dead in a vehicle track later that same day. On August 5, 1997, irate local residents packed a town meeting concerning the proposed closure of the beach. People wanted to "take our beach back" from the "bird watchers," the crowd booed supporters of the plan to protect the piping plovers, and Crane was hung in effigy. Crane was fired one month later. Later in 1997, Fish and Wildlife Service officials recommended that the town take certain actions to protect the birds, but the town rejected those recommendations in January 1998. The federal government then brought suit against the town and sought a preliminary injunction to prohibit use of the beach by ORVs unless the town were to take numerous specified actions to guard the piping plovers.]

"In ruling on a motion for preliminary injunction, a district court is charged with considering: (1) the likelihood of success on the merits; (2) the potential for irreparable harm if the injunction is denied; (3) the balance of relevant impositions, i.e., the hardship to the nonmovant if enjoined as contrasted with the hardship to the movant if no injunction issues; and (4) the effect (if any) of the court's ruling on the public interest." Strahan v. Coxe, 127 F.3d 155, 160 (1st Cir.1997). "Under the ESA, however, the balancing and public interest prongs have been answered by Congress' determination that the 'balance of the hardships and the public interest tips heavily in favor of protected species'." Id. (quoting National Wildlife Fed'n v. Burlington Northern R.R., 23 F.3d 1508, 1510 (9th Cir.1994)). Examination of the language, history and structure of Section 7 of the ESA indicates "beyond doubt that Congress intended endangered species to be afforded the highest of priorities." Tennessee Valley Authority v. Hill, 437 U.S. 153, 174 (1978) (holding that Congress had foreclosed the exercise of the usual discretion possessed by a court of equity); see also Sierra Club v. Marsh, 816 F.2d 1376, 1383 (9th Cir.1987) (holding that the courts may not use equity's scales to strike a difference balance).

1. The ESA

. . . A " 'take' is construed in the broadest possible manner to include every conceivable way in which a person can 'take' or attempt to 'take' any fish or wildlife." Strahan, 127 F.3d at 162 (quoting S. Rep. No. 93–307, at 7 (1973)); see also Babbitt v. Sweet Home Chapter of Communities for a Great Oregon, 515 U.S. 687, 703–04 (1995) (same). Moreover, the ESA's prohibitions contemplate both the actions of individuals who directly take a species and those of a third party authorized by the government to engage in activity resulting in a taking. See 16 U.S.C. § 1538(g) ("It is unlawful for any person . . . to attempt to commit, solicit another to commit, or cause to be committed, any offense" prohibited by the ESA); *see also Strahan*, 127 F.3d at 163 (holding that "the statute not only prohibits the acts of those parties that directly exact the taking, but also bans those acts of a third party that bring about the acts exacting a taking").

The piping plover

The ESA specifically authorizes the Attorney General, acting on behalf of the United States, to "seek to enjoin any person who is alleged to be in violation of any provision of this chapter or regulation issued under authority thereof." 16 U.S.C. § 1540(e)(6). In order for the United States to prove a likelihood of success on the merits, it must demonstrate that the Town of Plymouth has caused, through action or inaction, the illegal taking of the piping plover on Plymouth Long Beach or that future takes will occur if management of the beach continues on its present course. Proof of a taking requires a showing "that the alleged activity has actually harmed the species or if continued will actually, as opposed to potentially, cause harm to the species." American Bald Eagle v. Bhatti, 9 F.3d 163, 166 (1st Cir.1993) (citing cases); *see also Strahan*, 939 127 F.3d at 162. A movant can make a showing of actual harm by proving that significant modification or damage to the habitat of an endangered or threatened species is likely to occur so as to injure that species. In *TVA v. Hill*, the Supreme Court stated that "some" may find it "curious" that an endangered three-inch fish, the snail darter, could stop a $100 million dam under the ESA, but that "the explicit provisions of the [ESA] require precisely that result." *Id.* at 172–73. Similarly, here a 2.5 inch piping plover can stop a behemoth ORV if the government proves a taking under the ESA.

2. Proof of Harm

The Service has proved a likelihood of success on its claim that current management practices with respect to ORV access to Plymouth Long Beach have actually harmed piping plovers and will continue to cause harm to the species if they remain unchecked. Plymouth's persistent refusal over the last five years to undertake adequate and timely precautionary measures on the initiative of those town officials responsible for management of the beach creates a likelihood that piping plover chicks will be killed and disturbed and that the nesting and feeding habitat will be adversely modified during the upcoming breeding season.

The Town points out that Plymouth Long Beach has experienced an increase in the number of nesting pairs of piping plovers from one in 1991 to nine in 1997, and that the piping plover population is "flourishing" under the Town's "upgraded" management of the beach under the 1992 Plan. Douglass Gray, the Superintendent of Parks and Forestry, claims he is empowered by the by-laws to limit the number of vehicles and by the 1998 Protocol to create "vehicle-free zones for nonessential vehicles where unfledged (flightless) piping plover chicks are present." I do not doubt the good faith or diligence of those employees entrusted with managing Long Beach and with monitoring the piping plover. However, as a matter of unwritten policy and practice, these employees do not have the authority on their own to take necessary measures to create adequate vehicle-free buffer zones.

Rather, there is compelling evidence that certain selectmen and at least one town manager have failed in the past to take prompt measures to close the beach to ORVs to protect nests and unfledged piping plover chicks and have instead declined to authorize a beach closing until state or federal officials intervened and recommended the closures in writing. Moreover, the lack of authority vested in the NRO to close the beach on his own volition to protect piping plovers and the absence of mandatory requirements in the 1998 Protocol with respect to minimum buffer zones for unfledged chicks have restricted the NRO's ability to prevent takes.

This failure to act quickly and decisively resulted, in all probability, in the June 13, 1996 taking of the plover chick. While the Town maintains that no conclusions can be drawn about the cause of the death of the recently hatched plover—observed healthy in the morning and found dead in vehicle tracks just hours later—the reasonable inference to be drawn in this whodunit is that the chick was killed by an ORV. Although the Selectmen perceive Long Beach as a multipurpose beach where ORV users and piping plovers can happily co-exist, the expert evidence proves that the large vehicle-free zones are essential to protect this threatened species from takes, and will often be inconsistent with ORV use during the summer months.

Based on the transcript and videotape of the August 5, 1997 hearing before the Board of Selectmen; the hostility of many residents to "bird watchers;" the roasting of Town Counsel and the Town Manager, who were attempting to work with state and federal authorities; the firing of John

Crane, who was doing his best to comply with the federal and state guidelines; and the decision to rescind the Memorandum of Agreement, I conclude that the Selectmen will not authorize the Town Manager or NRO to take appropriate measures to protect the piping plover from "takes" as required by law. The long-standing intransigence of town officials persuades me that without an injunction, the town officials will not act to protect plovers when the pressure from ORV owners intensifies.

Accordingly, I adopt in large part the proposed preliminary relief recommended by the Service based on the Service guidelines and the affidavits of Dr. Melvin and Ms. Von Oettingen, each of whom point out that the Town of Plymouth stands apart from all private and municipally owned beaches in Massachusetts and other New England states in its failure to manage ORV use in accordance with the Service guidelines.

Because the 1992 Plan ceases to be effective on September 25, 1998, I am hopeful that the Town will work with appropriate state and federal officials to reach an acceptable beach management plan which will make the attached court order no longer necessary. Although I have adopted the Service's proposed order verbatim in most respects, I have modified the government's proposed order in the following ways. First, I do not require the Town to report to a Service employee, but instead give it the authority to implement the order itself. If there are violations of the order, the Service may move for contempt sanctions. I expect that there will be adequate consultation so that this will not be necessary. Second, I did not adopt the government's requested definition of "essential" vehicles because it was unclear to me whether residents of Long Beach have other access to their homes. Third, I leave it up to the Town to regulate pets, kites, and fireworks, as there is no evidence that in the past these activities have caused any "takes" or were improperly managed. Fourth, I did leave in the requirement of monitoring by a biologist, but do not expect the Town to hire someone new for this position if a current employee already has adequate training and expertise to do the job; the Town may make another proposal if a biologist is unnecessary. Finally, although there are mandatory buffer zones, the Service suggested that there should be flexibility to permit ORV access where not inconsistent with the breeding, nesting, and feeding needs of the piping plovers. In consultation with state and/or federal officials, the Town may take reasonable measures consistent with the needs of the piping plovers so long as any deviations from the order are reported to the Service and logged. The order requires the Town and the Service to provide full written reports at the end of the summer to ensure compliance.

The order expires in one year unless the Service demonstrates good cause to continue it based on the actions of the Town.

NOTES & QUESTIONS

1. Judge Saris issued her decision in the battle between the piping plover and ORV users for Plymouth's beach on May 15, 1998. Four days later, the town's selectmen voted 4–1 to comply with the judge's order rather than appealing. The lone dissenter—Selectman Linda Teagan—remarked that she "[c]ontinued to be baffled by a federal judge basically concluding that the oldest town in the United States is unable to govern itself." John O'Keefe, *Plover Dispute Comes to Head; Vehicle Restriction Effective Today*, THE PATRIOT LEDGER (Quincy, Mass.), May 19, 1998, at 5S. The first piping plover chicks hatched on May 23, and the ban on vehicle traffic went into effect. By the end of the summer, the FWS was complimenting the town for doing "a terrific job managing the beach." John O'Keefe, *Off-Road Vehicle Limits May Be Lifted*, THE PATRIOT LEDGER (Quincy, Mass.), July 24, 1998, at 13S. Twenty of the thirty chicks that hatched on Plymouth's beach in 1998 survived. The casualties resulted not from ORVs, but from storms, malnourishment, and predators. Indeed, foxes were the primary reason why only three of the chicks hatched in 1999 lived long enough to fly, even though there were 12 nesting pairs on the beach that summer. The threats that foxes, skunks, crows and other predators posed to piping plovers on nearby beaches caused the Fish and Wildlife Service to summon a sharpshooter to kill a coyote suspected of damaging plover nests, and it prompted speculation that increased enforcement of local dog leash laws would be required by the ESA.

2. The piping plover is one of the few species protected by the ESA that has provoked controversy among residents of the northeastern United States. Besides the dispute in Plymouth, efforts to protect piping plovers have been responsible for modifying Fourth of July fireworks celebrations in Connecticut and slowing beachfront development on Long Island. *See* John Rather, *On Resort Shores, It's People vs. Plovers*, N.Y. TIMES, June 21, 1998, sec. 14LI, at 3; *see also Spielberg Seeks Access to Bluff Point*, N.Y. TIMES, Mar. 15, 1997, at 28 (describing concerns about the possible impact on piping plovers of trucks using a Long Island beach to film the movie *Amistad*). The piping plover also features in the dispute about the management of off-road vehicles in Cape Hatteras National Seashore in North Carolina, as illustrated in Chapter 13. By contrast, most of the controversies about the ESA have involved the Pacific Northwest, southern California, other western states, Texas and Florida. Not surprisingly, support for the ESA is greatest in the northeast while endangered species protections are much more divisive in the west. Imagine, though, what actions could have been contested—and which species could have been saved—if Congress had enacted the ESA in 1800.

3. Colorado Representative Dan Schaeffer has objected to what he views as the litigious radical wing of the environmental movement because of its willingness to employ the ESA's take prohibition to block certain activities. He offered two examples: "In Massachusetts, environmentalists sued the state for merely licensing fishermen who used certain kinds of lobster traps because the traps actually worked. In Florida, one radical environmental group sued in the name of the Loggerhead Turtles because they believed aggressive local actions to curb beach-front lighting were not aggressive enough." 144 CONG. REC. E2362 (daily ed. Dec. 21, 1998).

Like *Town of Plymouth*, both of the cases mentioned by Representative Schaeffer involve the application of the ESA's take prohibition to the government's failure to regulate private conduct that harms an endangered species. In Strahan v. Coxe, 127 F.3d 155 (1st Cir.1997), the First Circuit held that the Massachusetts state agency responsible for regulating fishing violated the ESA's take prohibition when it issued permits to fishermen whose nets entangled endangered Northern Right whales. Similarly, in Loggerhead Turtle v.

County Council of Volusia County, Florida, 148 F.3d 1231 (11th Cir.1998), *cert. denied*, 526 U.S. 1081 (1999), the court held that the defenders of the turtle made a sufficient causal showing to establish standing to contend the county violated the take prohibition when it failed to regulate lighting in homes and businesses along the beach because the lights confuse newly-hatched sea turtles and make them more susceptible to predators and less likely to reach the safety of the water. On remand, however, the district court held that the county's new lighting regulations did not constitute a take because they were designed to help the turtle, and because the county could not be held liable for the unwillingness of private individuals to abide by the regulations. Loggerhead Turtle v. County Council of Volusia County, Fla., 92 F.Supp.2d 1296 (M.D.Fla.2000). Another example (not mentioned by Representative Schaeffer) occurred in Defenders of Wildlife v. Administrator, Environmental Protection Agency, 882 F.2d 1294 (8th Cir.1989), where the court held that EPA's licensing of pesticides that were ultimately ingested by black-footed ferrets constituted a prohibited take. Remember, too, that Hawaii violated the take prohibition when it managed state lands for hunting sheep and goats that injured the habitat of the palila. *See supra* at page 292.

Do such cases satisfy the understanding of the take prohibition articulated in *Sweet Home*? Should state or local officials be held liable for failing to regulate conduct that harms a species? *See* Shannon Petersen, *Endangered Species in the Urban Jungle: How the ESA Will Reshape American Cities*, 19 STAN. ENVTL. L. J. 423, 439 (2000) (arguing that *Town of Plymouth*, *Strahan*, and *Loggerhead Turtle* were wrongly decided because (1) "state and local regulatory regimes governing private activities cannot be the proximate cause of an illegal take," (2) "the Tenth Amendment prohibits the federal government from coercing local governments to implement the ESA," and (3) "the doctrine of sovereign immunity should protect state and local governments from ESA citizen suits in some limited situations"). How should local officials respond to residents who ask why they can no longer use ORVs on the beach or turn on their lights at night? *See also* J.B. Ruhl, *State and Local Government Vicarious Liability Under the ESA*, 16 NATURAL RESOURCES & ENV'T 70 (2001).

4. *Town of Plymouth* also illustrates the issuance of injunctive relief for future violations of the take prohibition. In Forest Conservation Council v. Rosboro Lumber Company, 50 F.3d 781, 784 (9th Cir.1995), the Ninth Circuit held that "a showing of imminent threat to injury to wildlife suffices" to support an injunction against a future take. In so holding, the court rejected the claim that the regulatory requirement of an "actual" injury was limited to a part or present injury. The court reaffirmed that conclusion in Marbled Murrelet v. Babbitt, 83 F.3d 1060, 1064–65 (9th Cir.1996), rejecting the assertion that the Supreme Court's decision in *Sweet Home* compelled a different result. In both cases the court concluded that injunctions were available against logging that threatened to take endangered birds. A district court has since read the Ninth Circuit test to allow for an injunction in a future take case if the plaintiff proves that (1) the endangered species is located on the property at issue, and (2) the defendant's activities are reasonably certain to constitute a threat of imminent harm to the species. Applying that test, a district court refused to enjoin a private campground project because the two endangered species— the San Francisco garter snake and the red-legged frog—were not present on all parts of the land in question and because the campground and its ancillary activities were not reasonably likely to harm the species. *See* Coastside Habitat Coalition v. Prime Properties, Inc., 1998 WL 231024 (N.D.Cal.1998).

5. Blackburn's sphinx moth is Hawaii's largest native insect, with a wingspan of five inches. Its natural host plants are a shrub named the popolo and a tree named the aiea, which the moths rely upon for food and shelter. Many other host plants for the moth are not native to Hawaii, including eggplant, tomatoes, Jimson weed, tree tobacco, and *Nicotiana tabacum*—commonly known as commercial tobacco.

Blackburn's sphinx moth

The moth is named after the Reverend Thomas Blackburn, a missionary who collected the first specimens in the nineteenth century. Hawaii's landscape has undergone extreme alteration since that time as a result of ranching, agricultural development, the deliberate introduction of alien animals and plants, and tourism. Much of the state's native wildlife and plants have suffered from these events, as illustrated by the fact that Hawaii has more federally listed endangered species than any other state.

The moth was thought to be extinct after an unsuccessful attempt to relocate the species in the late 1970s. In 1984, several moths were found on private and state land on Maui, part of which is within a nature reserve but part of which is used by the national guard for military training. Then two more moths were found on another part of Maui in 1992. This second population was feeding on commercial tobacco on private land that contained none of the native plants favored by the moth. Four more small populations of the moth have been found since then: two on Maui, one on Kahoolawe, and one on the island of Hawaii. These newest populations, numbering less than ten moths each, live in areas where there are few or no aiea trees and few or no commercial tobacco plants, so they rely upon the other host plants listed above instead. The small numbers of these populations and the ongoing threats to all of them persuaded the United States Fish & Wildlife Service to list Blackburn's sphinx moth as endangered on February 1, 2000.

The cultivation of tobacco faces increasing government regulation. The United States Department of Agriculture (USDA) pays millions of dollars to farmers who are willing to switch from growing commercial tobacco to growing other crops instead. The Hawaii legislature recently imposed a $2.00 tax on each package of cigarettes sold in the state. And Hyatt just announced plans to purchase thousands of acres on Maui that are used to grow tobacco—including the land where the two moths were found in 1992 and where a small population of the moths still lives today—and to build a new beachfront resort on that land instead.

Philip Morris, Incorporated, R.J. Reynolds Tobacco Company, and the Gallins Vending Company (a leading seller of cigarette vending machines) worry that the decrease in commercial tobacco cultivation on Maui will harm their businesses. They have brought suit in federal district court alleging that the USDA subsidies, the Hawaiian state cigarette tax, and the Hyatt resort proposal all violate the ESA because they will adversely affect the commercial tobacco plants used by some Blackburn's sphinx moths for food and for shelter. Do any of the three challenged actions violate any provisions of the ESA?

2. AUTHORIZING INCIDENTAL TAKE OF PROTECTED SPECIES

Friends of Endangered Species, Inc. v. Jantzen

United States Court of Appeals for the Ninth Circuit, 1985.
760 F.2d 976.

■ PREGERSON, CIRCUIT JUDGE:

[In 1975, Visitacion Associates and the Crocker Land Company purchased about 3,000 acres of land on San Bruno Mountain. The owners proposed to build a large residential and commercial development, but they scaled back their plans after environmentalists objected because the land was so rich in wildlife. The U.S. Fish and Wildlife Service then discovered that the endangered Mission Blue butterfly lived on the mountain, and that the butterfly's existence would be seriously threatened by the development. In response, the San Bruno Mountain Steering Committee was formed by the landowners and other prospective developers, environmentalists, and representatives of state and local government agencies. The Committee developed a Habitat Conservation Plan that would preserve 81% of the open space on the mountain as wildlife habitat and require landowners to pay $60,000 annually to finance a permanent habitat conservation program in exchange for permission to proceed with the modified development. To satisfy the ESA, the parties applied for a permit pursuant to ESA section 10(a) that would allow the incidental taking of the endangered Mission Blue butterflies, San Bruno Elfin butterflies, and San Francisco garter snakes in the course of the development. FWS issued the permit, but Friends of Endangered Species, Inc. filed suit alleging that the development violated the ESA and the National Environmental Policy Act (NEPA).

The district court granted summary judgment for the FWS, and Friends of Endangered Species appealed.]

. . . Section 10(a) of the ESA allows the Service to permit an applicant to engage in an otherwise prohibited "taking" of an endangered species under certain circumstances. The applicant first must submit a comprehensive conservation plan. The Service then must scrutinize the plan and find, after affording opportunity for public comment, that: (1) the proposed taking of an endangered species will be "incidental" to an otherwise lawful activity; (2) the permit applicant will minimize and mitigate the impacts of the taking "to the maximum extent practicable"; (3) the applicant has insured adequate funding for its conservation plan; and (4) the taking will not appreciably reduce the likelihood of the survival of the species. Appellant challenges the sufficiency of the Permit findings relating to the second and fourth of these section 10(a) requirements.

1. The field study adequately supported the Service's findings that "the taking will not appreciably reduce the likelihood of the survival of the species."

The Service went beyond the statutory requirement and concluded that the Permit, coupled with the Plan, was likely to enhance the survival of the Mission Blue butterfly.

Appellant contends that the Service's determination that issuing the permit would not reduce the likelihood of the Mission Blue butterfly's survival was arbitrary and capricious because of alleged scientific shortcomings in the Biological Study upon which the decision was based. Specifically, appellant argues that low recapture rates and allegedly mistaken recaptures by the field crew in the mark-release-recapture phase of the field study invalidated the Study's conclusions, and that the Service abused its discretion in relying upon such data to approve the Permit. With respect to this contention, appellant fails to raise a genuine issue of material fact.

As the district court determined, the legislative history to section 10(a)'s 1982 amendments suggests that Congress viewed appellees' conduct in the present case as the paradigm approach to compliance with section 10(a):

> *In some cases, the overall effect of a project can be beneficial to a species, even though some incidental taking may occur. An example is the development of some 3000 dwelling units on San Bruno Mountain near San Francisco.* This site is also habitat for three endangered butterflies . . . *Absent the development of this project these butterfly recovery actions may well have never been developed.* The proposed amendment should lead to resolution of potential conflicts between endangered species and the actions of private developers, while at the same time encouraging these developers to become more actively involved in the conservation of these species.

S. Rep. No. 97–418, 97th Cong., 2d Sess. 10 (1982) (emphasis added). The House Conference Report indicates, in stronger terms than the Senate Report, that the Service acted properly in relying upon the Biological Study to comply with section 10(a):

> Because the San Bruno Mountain plan is the model for this long term permit and because the adequacy of similar conservation plans should be measured against the San Bruno plan, the Committee believes that the elements of this plan should be clearly understood. . .
>
> Prior to developing the conservation plan, the County of San Mateo conducted an independent exhaustive biological study which determined the location of the butterflies. . . The biological study was conducted over a two year period and at one point involved 50 field personnel.

The San Bruno Mountain Conservation Plan is based on this extensive biological study.

H.R. REP. 97–835, 97th Cong., 2d Sess. 31–32 (1982).

In addition, appellant failed to bring many of these purported field data "errors" and "inconsistencies" to the attention of the Service until after the district court denied appellant's motion for summary judgment. Clearly, the Service did not act arbitrarily in failing to consider criticisms not presented to it before issuing the Permit. Review of the reasonableness of an agency's consideration of environmental factors is "limited . . . by the time at which the decision was made."

The Service did, however, extensively solicit and consider expert and public comments on the Biological Study before issuing the Permit. And, the Biological Study itself acknowledged methodological limitations.

Thus, there is no evidence that the Service issued the Permit either in ignorance or deliberate disregard of the Biological Study's limitations. Moreover, the Service responded in good faith in its Permit Findings to the criticisms which it sought out and received concerning the Biological Study, and acted reasonably in relying upon the Biological Study to conclude that the Plan would not reduce the likelihood of survival of the Mission Blue butterfly. Again, the Service cannot be said to have acted arbitrarily by not responding to criticisms not received when it approved the Permit.

We also consider it relevant that the Permit was expressly made subject to revocation and reconsideration based upon data that might be revealed from the continuing monitoring called for under the Plan. Thus, the Service complied with section 10(a)'s mandate by determining that "the incidental taking" of the Mission Blue would enhance the survival of the species. In light of the clear declaration of legislative intent and the Service's efforts to consider all criticisms of the Biological Study before relying upon it, we hold that the district court was correct in concluding that there were no genuine issues of material fact that would preclude it from determining that the Service did not act arbitrarily or capriciously in relying on the Biological Study.

2. The Service did not act arbitrarily or capriciously in concluding that the Plan complied with section 10(a)'s requirement to minimize and mitigate the impact of the taking upon endangered species.

The Plan at issue contains various measures to "minimize and mitigate" the impact of the project upon the Mission Blue butterfly. The Plan and the Agreement provide for the permanent protection of 86% of the Mission Blue's habitat. Moreover, funding for the Plan would yield $60,000 annually, which would be used to halt the apparent incursion of brush and gorse into the habitat and permit the re-establishment of grasslands for the butterfly.

In addition to provisions to halt advancing brush and gorse, the Plan contains continuing and comprehensive restrictions on land development and significant financial incentives. Regardless of whether brush and gorse continue to spread, these additional mitigating measures should play a significant role in enhancing the protection of endangered species on the Mountain.

Appellant also contends that the Saddle Area of the Mountain, now publicly owned for parkland and consisting of 75% brush, should be substituted for one of the grassland parcels currently proposed for development. Appellant suggests that this Saddle Area alternative would more effectively mitigate the Plan's effects. The [environmental impact report/environmental assessment (EIR/EA)] authors considered and rejected this Saddle Area development alternative. They concluded, among other things, that development of the Saddle Area would have secondary impacts including a biological impact greater than that produced by the Saddle's proposed use as a county park. The Saddle Area allegedly contains unique wetlands and endangered plants, and its development could meet with stiff environmental opposition.

Thus, the district court correctly concluded that there is simply no genuine factual dispute as to whether the Service acted arbitrarily or unreasonably in determining that the Plan complied with section 10(a)'s mitigation requirement.

3. Appellant does not raise a genuine issue of material fact in alleging that the Service failed to comply with section 7(a)(2) of the ESA.

Section 7(a)(2) of the ESA states:

Each Federal agency shall . . . insure that any action authorized, funded, or carried out by such agency . . . is not likely to jeopardize the continued existence of any endangered species or threatened species or result in the destruction or adverse modification of habitat of such species which is determined by the Secretary . . . to be critical. . . In fulfilling [these] requirements . . . each agency shall use the best scientific and commercial data available.

An action would "jeopardize" a species if it "reasonably would be expected to reduce the reproduction, numbers, or distribution of a listed species to such an extent as to appreciably reduce the likelihood of the survival and recovery of that species in the wild."

Pursuant to section 7(a)(2), the Service determined that the Permit would not likely jeopardize the continued existence of the Mission Blue butterfly. In so determining, the Service relied upon a variety of information including the Biological Study, the Plan, the Agreement, the EIR/EA, public comments received on the Permit Application, peer reviews of the Biological Study, and file materials on the Mission Blue butterfly.

Appellant erroneously contends that these sources did not represent the best scientific data available because of "the uncontroverted evidence from [the two experts upon whom it relies] revealing major mistakes in the field study."

Again, the low recapture rate realized in the mark-release-recapture phase of the Biological Study was a limitation that the Study itself and the Service acknowledged. And, several peer reviews took note of the limitations inherent in low mark-release-recapture rates. Thus, the Service was aware of all relevant limitations on the Biological Study and the field data, and the Service addressed those limitations in its Permit Findings. During the administrative process, appellant and its two experts did not direct the Service to any better available data. Moreover, the Service considered whatever data and other materials appellants provided. "The issue for review is whether the [agency's] decision was based on a consideration of the relevant factors and whether there has been a clear error of judgment." There is no genuine issue of material fact to dispute the district court's determination that the Service did not act unreasonably or capriciously, or in violation of section 7(a)(2), by considering all the data it received in the present case.

[The court also held that the FWS complied with the requirements of NEPA].

NOTES & QUESTIONS

1. The upshot of the habitat conservation plan (HCP) is that some of the butterfly's habitat is protected while the developers are permitted to build amidst other parts of butterfly's habitat. Why would the government agree to that deal? Why would the developer? Note that since the HCP went into effect, 800 housing units have been built on the San Bruno Mountain, while developers and homeowners have paid $70,000 annually to remove non-native plants, replant native species, and monitor the activities of the butterflies. A 1999 study concluded that "[a]t best, the HCP has been a wash. The development has not drastically decreased the population of endangered species on the mountain, but the restoration projects have not dramatically raised the numbers either." Marcus E. Walton, *San Bruno Ecology Faces Threat of Urban Sprawl*, SAN JOSE

MERCURY NEWS, June 16, 1999. Most recently, the FWS and the nearby City of Brisbane agreed to spend a total of over one million dollars to purchase a part of the mountain that provides ten percent of the habitat of the callippe silverspot butterfly.

2. Section 10(a)(1)(B), which was part of the 1982 amendments to the ESA, authorizes the FWS to permit an "incidental take" of a listed species. An incidental take is an action that constitutes a "take" within ESA section 9, but the take is "incidental to, and not the purpose of, the carrying out of an otherwise lawful activity." Michael Bean and Melanie Rowland assert that "this provision likely increased the Secretary's leverage over activities that incidentally take endangered species because it substituted a flexible regulatory authority for a threat of prosecution that few found credible." BEAN & ROWLAND, *supra*, at 234. That leverage, however, does face some limits. In Arizona Cattle Growers' Association v. FWS, 273 F.3d 1229 (9th Cir.2001), reprinted above at page 242, the court held that the FWS could not issue an incidental take permit that imposed conditions on federal grazing permits where there was no evidence that the grazing would result in a take of an endangered species in the first place.

3. More recent cases have tended to continue the deference to the FWS's application of the standards for granting an incidental take permit pursuant to a HCP. For example, in Center for Biological Diversity v. FWS, 202 F.Supp.2d 594 (W.D. Tex. 2002), the court produced a lengthy opinion expressing significant concerns about the wisdom of a proposed shopping development near San Antonio, but the court concluded that the FWS had not acted arbitrarily or capriciously in determining that the developer satisfied the statutory requirements for an incidental take permit. A district court did invalidate the Natomas Basin HCP designed to protect habitat and facilitate development around Sacramento, *see* National Wildlife Fed'n v. Babbitt, 128 F.Supp.2d 1274 (E.D. Cal. 2000) (reprinted below in chapter 13), but the court later approved a revised HCP that remedied the earlier problems. *See* National Wildlife Fed'n v. Norton, 2005 WL 2175874 (E.D. Cal. 2005).

4. The developer in *Jantzen* produced the first HCP, and it received the first incidental take permit. Despite the enactment of section 10(a)(1)(B), only three HCPs were adopted between 1982 and 1989. Then the number of HCPs boomed. By September 1995, over 100 HCPs had been approved and about 200 were in various stages of development. (For a summary of each of the approved plans, visit the FWS's HCP database at http://ecos.fws.gov/conserv plans/public.jsp.) So why have HCPs become so popular, especially compared to the lack of interest in them throughout the 1980s?

Wisconsin Statewide Karner Blue Butterfly Habitat Conservation Plan and Environmental Impact Statement

Wisconsin Department of Natural Resources, 1999.
http://dnr.wi.gov/org/land/forestry/hcptext/pdfs/Executive/Summary.pdf

EXECUTIVE SUMMARY

Background

This summary provides a synopsis of the *Wisconsin Statewide Karner Blue Butterfly Habitat Conservation Plan* (HCP) and the associated environmental impact statement (EIS). These two documents have been combined into a single document, with the HCP comprising Chapters I and II of the EIS and several appendices. This approach was taken so that those parties wishing to focus only on the proposed habitat conservation activities can easily extract that material from the overall document.

The HCP is an integral part of an application to the U.S. Fish and Wildlife Service (USFWS) for a statewide incidental take permit covering the federally endangered Karner blue butterfly (*Lycaeides melissa samuelis*). The Wisconsin Department of Natural Resources (DNR) is applying for the permit in collaboration with 26 other private and public partners. The partners are proposing the HCP as a resource management strategy to assure the long-term sustainability of Karner blue butterfly habitat and the persistence of Karner blue butterflies on the Wisconsin landscape.

In addition to the partners, development of the HCP relied heavily on people representing various associations and organizations. These organizations have contributed extensive and continuous time and effort to the process and include groups such as the Sierra Club, the Wisconsin Audubon Council and the Wisconsin Woodland Owners Association. It is anticipated that these organizations, and others, will play an important role in HCP implementation and Karner blue butterfly conservation in Wisconsin.

The HCP describes broad-scale land conservation and outreach/education strategies. Efforts are focused on conservation both in the Karner blue butterfly's high potential habitat area and across the Karner blue butterfly's Wisconsin range, with implementation relying heavily on adaptive management principles. The efficacy of the plan is tied to partner commitments (outlined in legally-binding conservation agreements with the DNR) and a hierarchy of monitoring systems developed to assure the anticipated, positive results of proposed actions.

While the HCP specifically addresses only one species, the Karner blue butterfly, its focus on habitat management is designed to benefit numerous other species that rely on the rare habitats in which the butterfly occurs. Through a state consultation process, implementation of the HCP will factor in considerations for other species listed under the Wisconsin endangered species laws.

The HCP was prepared by the DNR in collaboration with the partners and other participants. Because preparation, approval and implementation of the HCP are actions requiring environmental review, the DNR and the USFWS agreed to prepare a single environmental document (i.e. the EIS) that would comply with the requirements of both the Wisconsin and National Environmental Policy Acts (WEPA and NEPA), as well as other state and federal regulations. Both WEPA and NEPA are intended to help public officials make decisions that are based on an understanding of environmental consequences and to take actions that protect, restore and enhance the environment. Preparation of a joint document is encouraged under both WEPA and NEPA, thereby reducing paperwork and best using limited public resources, while ensuring broad public involvement.

The innovative approach to endangered resources conservation proposed in the HCP is designed to move regulated communities beyond compliance and into efforts to proactively apply conservation measures on the land while engaging in normal land management activities. The U.S. Congress, in establishing the incidental take permit provisions of the Endangered Species Act, expressed the hope that the provision would encourage creative partnerships between the public and private sectors and among governmental agencies in the interest of species and habitat conservation, as well as provide a framework to permit cooperation between the public and private sectors. Those goals are accomplished by the HCP, an effort that arose out of and has been developed through a solid and diverse grassroots effort.

The Karner blue butterfly

The greatest numbers of Karner blue butterflies and some of the best Karner blue butterfly habitat currently occur in Wisconsin. Karner blue butterflies have been extirpated from Ontario, Maine, Pennsylvania, Massachusetts, New Jersey, Ohio and Iowa; appear to be extirpated in Illinois;

and persist in only remnant populations in Minnesota, Indiana, New York and New Hampshire. Because of these disappearances and the relative abundance of this species' populations in Wisconsin and Michigan, Wisconsin plays an important role in protecting Karner blue butterflies.

The Karner Blue Butterfly in Wisconsin

Wisconsin supports the largest and most widespread Karner blue butterfly populations worldwide. More than 270 Karner blue butterfly occurrences are known from 23 counties. Most of the occurrences can be grouped in about fifteen large population areas, and most of the larger populations are found on sizable contiguous acreages in central and northwest Wisconsin. . .

Karner blue butterflies are found in close association with wild lupine (*Lupinus perennis*), the only known host plant for their larvae. Natural habitats that Karner blue butterflies occupy include sandy pine and oak barrens, pine prairies, oak savannas and some lake shore dunes. Current Karner blue butterfly habitat in Wisconsin includes abandoned agricultural fields, mowed utility and road rights-of-way, managed forest lands, military training areas and bombing ranges and managed barrens. Potential habitat at the specific site level can only occur where conditions exist to support wild lupine. Given the knowledge of certain ecological criteria relative to Karner blue butterflies such as the distribution of wild lupine, general soils information and climatic parameters, potential habitat is predictable. . .

The Need for a Statewide Conservation Effort

While many extant Karner blue butterfly populations occur on public lands, it has become increasingly clear to conservation interests that species conservation cannot occur on public lands alone. There are simply not enough acres in public ownership to provide long-term stewardship. In addition, species like the Karner blue butterfly depend on active land management which results in the perpetuation of particular habitat types.

The amount of conservation that can be accomplished on private lands for which there are economic goals depends on landowner flexibility in time, space and financial strategy. In principle, the most intensive conservation measures for Karner blue butterflies are concentrated on public lands. However, the role of private lands cannot be underestimated. Large scale, multi-level conservation is best accomplished with statewide planning in which the participants accept various levels of responsibility for plan implementation. The *Wisconsin Statewide Karner Blue Butterfly HCP* was formulated with this concept in mind.

The HCP partners envision a *statewide* conservation effort that gains and incorporates the support of landowners and land users throughout Wisconsin. As the applicant for the incidental take permit, the DNR will administer the permit with the cooperation of all the partners, as well as other participants and cooperators. Regardless of their individual roles, each HCP partner has shown the capability and resolve to make significant contributions to the conservation effort through management practices, through public outreach, education and assistance programs, or through both management practices and public outreach and education. The 27 partners own or manage nearly two million acres of land in the state and have agreed to manage their lands in the Karner blue butterfly's high potential range with conservation considerations. Individual partner roles and commitments for both management and outreach are described in each individual partner's conservation agreement ("Species and Habitat Conservation Agreement") with the DNR, in the HCP, or in the DNR's Implementing Agreement with the USFWS.

The Karner blue butterfly is adapted to barrens and other early successional habitats. Because the persistence of these habitats is disturbance-dependent, an important aspect of this HCP is to provide for land management regimes that assure a balance between habitat gain from disturbance and habitat loss from vegetational succession. Stopping land management activities which provide desirable disturbance would be detrimental to maintaining this balance. A conventional "do not touch" regulatory approach, therefore, is inappropriate for the particular considerations presented in the conservation of the Karner blue butterfly. Such an approach would discourage, in many cases, the maintenance of habitat and conservation of the species. Consequently, this statewide conservation program may be distinct in its approach and application.

As applied to statewide landowner involvement in conservation, a participation strategy has been developed to provide incentives for conservation through cooperative partnerships. It includes a review mechanism to ensure that implementation does not adversely affect the species in the long-term. Although outreach is intended to reach any and all parties with the potential to become involved in Karner blue butterfly conservation, geographical areas and activities associated with the greatest potential will be given greater outreach emphasis. For example, broad general efforts will be made statewide and greater efforts will be made in the Karner blue butterfly's high potential range. The participation strategy also includes a notification system designed to inform landowners and users, where possible and feasible, of the opportunities presented under this HCP. Implementation of this strategy is intended to be at the county level, as much as possible, using county and town communication mechanisms and providing information and assistance locally.

Conservation Strategies

Insect conservation efforts are based on different premises than traditional vertebrate conservation efforts. The Karner blue butterfly, like most insect species, has adapted to survive by producing relatively large numbers of eggs and large populations, with short individual lifespans and frequent generation turnovers. Most of the Karner blue butterfly's life is spent in the egg and larval stages. Natural mortality rates during these immature life stages are much greater than mortality rates observed for vertebrate animals. The survival strategy of the Karner blue butterfly centers on the success of overall populations rather than individual organisms. To ac-

commodate this strategy, a focus on habitat conservation and the maintenance of populations—rather than individuals—is key to butterfly preservation.

The long-term viability of Karner blue butterfly populations depends
on habitat disturbance. Without periodic disturbance, natural woody succession shades out wild lupine and nectar plants and can passively eliminate Karner blue butterfly populations. Creation of new habitat to replace
habitat lost to succession is therefore necessary. This reality underscores
the need for managing landscapes for a dynamic, shifting mosaic of habitat
and populations. Fortunately, many land management activities, such as
those used in forest management and utility right-of-way maintenance,
provide such disturbances.

There are two approaches being proposed in the HCP. . .

Management with consideration for Karner blue butterflies. This management category represents lands owned or managed by partners on
which consideration for the Karner blue butterfly and its habitat will be
incorporated into land management activities. Partners have committed to
management with consideration for Karner blue butterflies on 227,492
acres in the Karner blue butterfly's high potential range. *The long term biological goal on these lands is that Karner blue butterfly habitat gains be
equal to or exceed losses occurring through natural succession or otherwise.*

Management to feature, protect or enhance Karner blue butterflies. This
management category represents lands that are owned or managed by
partners on which one of the primary management goals is to feature the
Karner blue butterfly habitat or the broader barrens community that includes it. Partners have committed 37,725 acres in the Karner blue butterfly's high potential range to this level of focus. As with the management
with consideration category, *the long term biological goal on these lands is
that butterfly habitat gains be equal to or exceed losses occurring through
natural succession or otherwise. Additional measures are taken however, to
promote viable Karner blue butterfly populations despite potential economic
costs.*

Overall, the partners own and maintain 2.03 million acres in Wisconsin. Of these 2.03 million acres, 265,217 acres in the high·potential range
will be subject to the management categories described above. Incorporating conservation into management activities on lands in the high potential
range focuses efforts where they can have the most conservation benefit
(the high potential range includes the Karner blue butterfly's documented
range, as well as a significant buffer around known Karner blue butterfly
occurrences).

Land Management Activities Affecting Karner Blue Butterfly

The partners engage in a variety of activities on the lands they own
and manage. These activities have been grouped into five categories for the
purposes of developing conservation strategies:

Forest Management
- Timber harvesting
- Stand improvement
- Prescribed fire
- Forest roads
- Forest regeneration

Barrens, Prairie and Savanna Management
- Prescribed fire

- Mechanical treatment
- Herbicide treatment

- Native plant propagation

- Grazing

Recreational Management
- Intensive construction
- Less intensive construction
- Maintenance
- Public use

Transportation Management
- Road development
- Road maintenance
- Vegetation control

Utility Right-of-Way Management
- Construction of electric transmission lines
- Operations and maintenance of electric transmission lines
- Vegetation control
- Construction of new pipelines and underground transmission lines
- Operations and maintenance of pipelines

Participation Strategy and Additional Conservation Measures

    ... The strategy seeks to incorporate conservation into the working landscape. The HCP is built upon the extensive land ownership and conservation commitments of the 27 partners identified in this HCP, but seeks to go beyond those partners to include the assistance and participation of other landowners, nonprofit groups, environmental and industrial organizations and a variety of governmental units.

    The HCP, with its biological approach, focuses efforts on geographic areas and activities which provide the highest potential to safeguard or enhance Karner blue butterfly habitat. The strategy goes beyond the initial 27 partners and seeks to reach all landowners and users, but will vary in approach and process. The HCP's inclusion strategy therefore includes:

    1. A category of non-voluntary participants that must formally apply for partnership to the DNR and receive a Certificate of Inclusion from the USFWS, because of the value their land and activities provide to conservation of the species;

    2. An opportunity for voluntary participants that receive incidental take permit coverage, without further process, so as to encourage land management activities that may benefit the species;

    3. An extensive public outreach and education plan to reach all landowners and land users, and others, to describe the effort and encourage their cooperation and participation in this conservation effort; and

4. A review of the participation strategy after three years of implementation to determine its effectiveness, with the option of modifying it should it prove to need changes to provide the anticipated conservation.

Through this HCP, the partnership intends to achieve the endangered species conservation goals while protecting the economic interests of non-federal landowners through this increasing partnership statewide. Strategies that support Karner blue butterfly conservation included in the HCP are as follows:

> *Outreach and Education. Efforts will be made to create awareness by potential mandatory participants, such as county and town highway departments, railroads, electric utilities and others. HCP partners will also encourage Karner blue butterfly conservation by those in the voluntary segment, such as the small private landowners and those in the agricultural community.*

> *Federal Recovery. In 1994, the USFWS appointed a federal recovery team for the Karner blue butterfly, which at the time of this writing has produced a working draft recovery plan. Representatives of three Wisconsin Statewide Karner Blue Butterfly HCP partners participated in the development of the draft recovery plan: the DNR, Consolidated Papers, Inc. and Georgia-Pacific Corporation.*

Two Wisconsin HCP Partners, the DNR and The Nature Conservancy, intend to participate in federal recovery efforts, as funding allows. In addition, Jackson and Eau Claire County Forests (also HCP partners), will consider participating in recovery, pending approval by their respective county boards.

Adaptive Management

The long-term viability of Karner blue butterfly populations depends on habitat disturbance. Without periodic disturbance, natural woody succession shades out wild lupine and nectar plants, eliminating Karner blue butterfly habitat. Given this reality, the absence of management activities that create beneficial disturbances is ultimately detrimental to Karner blue butterflies. Halting on-going management activities to wait until all unanswered questions about Karner blue butterflies are answered is impractical. Therefore, this HCP will be implemented using adaptive management.

Adaptive management is a formal, structured approach to dealing with uncertainty in natural resources management, using the experience of management and the results of research as an on-going feedback loop for continuous improvement. Adaptive approaches to management recognize that the answers to all management questions are not known and that the information necessary to formulate answers is often unavailable. Adaptive management also includes, by definition, a commitment to change management practices when determined appropriate. The HCP partners have committed to using adaptive management.

The adaptive management approach, in part, relies on the management activities and practices that are already in place and for which there is no existing data or obvious reasons that suggest a need for change. This approach allows for up-front conservation measures to be used during routine operations and as management practices are implemented on the landscape. However, under this approach, carefully designed monitoring and research procedures are initiated to determine if there are any effects of the management practices.

Research. Several Karner blue butterfly research efforts are already underway or have recently been completed. A summary of each activity is included in the HCP:

- Effects of Herbicides on the Development of Karner Blue Butterfly Eggs and Larvae Development
- Effects of Herbicide on Seed Germination (wild lupine) and Development
- Effects of Herbicide Application on Lupine and Select Nectar Plants
- Dispersal Research (Karner blue butterflies)

NOTES & QUESTIONS

1. The Karner blue butterfly was the first insect listed under the ESA. Wisconsin's HCP website provides updated information on the efforts to protect the butterfly, along with the Karner Blue Butterfly Hot Line—(877) 4KARNER—which you can call to listen to a "flight status" report or to report sightings of the butterflies. *See* http://dnr.wi.gov/org/land/forestry/karner/. Black River Falls, Wisconsin, hosts a Karner Blue Butterfly Festival each year in early July, featuring the unlikely combination of a tour of the butterfly's local habitat, a pet costume contest, and the coronation of the Karner Butterfly Princess. Besides the Wisconsin population, the largest number of butterflies now live near Albany, New York (including a sizeable population amidst the runways of the Saratoga County Airport) and in the Indiana Dunes National Lakeshore along Lake Michigan near the steel mills of Gary, Indiana.

2. Consider how much more ambitious the habitat conservation plan (HCP) for the Karner blue butterfly is than the HCP for the Mission blue butterfly. The Karner blue butterfly HCP encompasses 260,000 acres of land throughout central Wisconsin, whereas the Mission blue butterfly plan covers less than 3,000 acres. The Wisconsin HCP reflects the dramatic increase in the scope of HCPs in recent years. The most prominent efforts to develop HCPs that cover entire regions exist in southern California and around Austin, Texas. *See, e.g.*, Mann & Plummer, *supra*, at 178–211 (describing the efforts to develop a HCP in Austin); Marc J. Ebbin, *Southern California Habitat Conservation: Is the Southern California Approach to Conservation Succeeding?*, 24 ECOLOGY L.Q. 695 (1997). Over 20 million acres are now covered by HCPs.

The increased scope of HCPs also extends to the number of species. Unlike the Karner blue butterfly plan, many HCPs apply to lots of different species. For example, two of the California plans protect 63 and 47 species, respectively. Additionally, many plans apply to species that have not yet been listed under the ESA.

3. Interior Secretary Bruce Babbitt trumpeted the development of HCPs as evidence of the success of the ESA. When he signed the Karner blue butterfly HCP, he described it as "the first comprehensive statewide Habitat Conservation Plan and the most inclusive agreement of its kind in the country. . . It is an excellent example of how the flexibility of the Endangered Species Act can promote regional habitat conservation planning by states and local governments and is a model for what other states and their partners might consider." More generally, Babbitt described HCPs as "one of the vanguards in a Quiet Revolution in American conservation," adding that "I know these plans work. Businesses know they work. Individual citizens know they work." U.S. Fish & Wildlife Service, *Habitat Conservation Plans: The Quiet Revolution* 5 (1998), *available at* http://endangered.fws.gov/hcp/Quiet/03-09.pdf.

Environmentalists are more skeptical. They complain that HCPs are being developed without adequate scientific guidance. They further charge that the FWS is abandoning the safeguards that are supposed to characterize HCPs in its rush to approve more plans. Many of the recent HCPs, they say, are inadequately funded and monitored. They conclude that many HCPs are "habitat giveaways" that cater to the interests of developers rather than furthering the purposes of the ESA. *See, e.g.*, Patrick Parenteau, *Rearranging The Deck Chairs: Endangered Species Act Reforms in an Era Of Mass Extinction.* 22 WM. & MARY ENVTL. L. & POL'Y REV. 227; John Kostyack, *"Surprise!"*, 15 ENVTL. FORUM 19 (1998).

Some environmental organizations have cautiously approved of HCPs, but only provided that steps are taken to make the plans more protective of the species they are designed to preserve. The National Wildlife Federation (NWF) advocates the inclusion of five additional safeguards in the HCP process: (1) clarify that HCPs must be consistent with an overall recovery strategy before approving them, (2) allow greater participation by concerned citizens and independent scientists, (3) encourage conservation strategies that prevent the need to list species, (4) provide regulatory assurances only when a credible adaptive management strategy is in place, and (5) ensure that HCPs are adequately funded to ensure that they are an effective strategy for conserving biodiversity. National Wildlife Federation, *Habitat Conservation Plans: Safeguards Are Needed to Ensure that the Endangered Species Act's Recovery Goal is Not Undermined*, http://www.nwf.org/endangered/hcp/hcpsaf.html. What objections might landowners raise to any of those recommendations? What other actions would improve the HCP process?

For more on the debate about HCPs, see REED F. NOSS, MICHAEL A. O'CONNELL & DENNIS D. MURPHY, THE SCIENCE OF CONSERVATION PLANNING: HABITAT CONSERVATION UNDER THE ENDANGERED SPECIES ACT (1997); *Symposium on Habitat Conservation Plans: Reshaping Habitat Conservation Plans For Species Recovery*, 27 ENVTL. L. 755 (1997); National Wildlife Federation, *Habitat Conservation Plans: The New Movement in Endangered Species Protection*, http://www.nwf.org/endangered/hcp/index.html; National Audubon Society, *Report of the National Audubon Society Task Force on Habitat Conservation Plans*, http://www.audubon.org/campaign/esa/hcp-report.html.

4. The development of a HCP may include reliance upon conservation banking. "A conservation bank is like a biological bank account," explains the FWS, in which lands that are managed for endangered or otherwise rare species may be sold "to developers or others who need to compensate for the environmental impacts of their projects." FWS, Conservation Banking: Incentives for Stewardship (July 2005), *available at* http://www.fws.gov/endangered/landowner/banking.7.05.pdf. For example, recall the new conservation bank that has been established for the preservation of the Delhi Sands Flower-Loving Fly, as discussed in chapter 1. The idea of conservation banking developed in the context of wetlands preservation, so we will discuss it in greater detail in chapter 10.

5. The attractiveness of HCPs to private landowners further increased as a result of the "No Surprises" rule adopted by the FWS, the NMFS, and NOAA. *See* Habitat Conservation Plan Assurances ("No Surprises") Rule, 63 Fed. Reg. 8859 (1998). According to that rule, "[o]nce an HCP permit has been issued and its terms and conditions are being fully complied with, the permittee may remain secure regarding the agreed upon cost of conservation and mitigation. If the status of a species addressed under an HCP unexpectedly worsens because of unforeseen circumstances, the primary obligation for implementing additional conservation measures would be the responsibility of the Federal government, other government agencies, or other non-Federal landowners who have not yet developed an HCP." *Id.* at 8867.

Many environmentalists object to the "No Surprises" rule. They contend that the dynamic nature of ecosystems makes it impossible to predict the needs of a species or the pressures on a species that will occur in future years. The FWS counters that the government is committed to doing whatever it takes to protect a species if the commitments embodied in a HCP prove to be inadequate. It also defends the scientific basis for its plans and its record of monitoring compliance with HCPs. And it emphasizes that the Congress that adopted the HCP provision in 1982 believed that "property owners should be provided economic and regulatory certainty regarding the overall cost of species conservation and mitigation, provided that the affected species were adequately covered by a properly functioning HCP, and the permittee was properly implementing the HCP and complying with the terms and conditions of the HCP permit in good faith." *No Surprises Rule*, 63 Fed. Reg. at 8860 (citing H.R. Rep. No. 835, 97th Cong., 2d Sess. 29 (1982)). The no surprises rule was temporarily enjoined because of procedural flaws in its publication, but the FWS remedied those errors and the rule remains in effect. *Cf.* Spirit of the Sage Council v. Norton, 411 F.3d 225 (D.C. Cir. 2005) (describing the history of the rule and holding that further challenges to it were moot).

6. The "No Surprises" Rule is only one example of recent efforts to reduce the regulatory impact of the ESA on private parties. The FWS has adopted several regulatory reforms designed to encourage private landowners to protect biodiversity. A safe harbor agreement lifts the restrictions of the ESA from a private landowner whose voluntary habitat creation, restoration or improvement attracts a new species to the land. "For example," under the Safe Harbor Agreement that FWS drafted for the Karner blue butterfly in September 2005, "if two Karner blue butterfly family groups are present when the baseline is established and the population grows by three family groups over the next decade, the landowner is responsible only for the two family groups, not five, should he or she change land management goals." News Release, FWS, Public Input Sought on Plan to Conserve Endangered Butterfly in Northern Indiana (Sept. 22, 2005). Another regulatory device known as a candidate conservation agreement offers a similar promise of reduced ESA regulation to a landowner who takes agreed upon steps to conserve the habitat of a species that has not yet been listed under the ESA. For a discussion of each mechanism, *see* Darcy H. Kishida, Note, *Safe Harbor Agreements Under the Endangered Species Act: Are They Right for Hawai'i?*, 23 HAWAI'I L. REV. 507 (2001); Francesca Ortiz, *Candidate Conservation Agreements as a Devolutionary Response to Extinction*, 33 GA. L. REV. 413 (1999); J.B. Ruhl, *The Endangered Species Act and Private Property: A Matter of Timing and Location*, 8 CORNELL J.L. & PUB. POL'Y 37 (1998).

7. Are there other ways to encourage private landowners to manage their land in a way to protects biodiversity besides the ESA's prohibition on adversely affecting the habitat of a species? Section 9 operates as a stick to force landowners not to harm an endangered species. Conversely, there is a broad consensus that the law should offer landowners and others affected by the ESA a carrot as well. TESRA, the ESA reform bill enacted by the House in 2005, contains numerous provisions designed to provide incentives for private landowners to protect endangered species. The National Wildlife Federation has proposed that several tax and financial incentives be extended to landowners and that technical and financial assistance be offered to small private landowners, states, tribes, and local communities. *See* National Wildlife Federation, *Support Landowner Incentives to Promote Endangered Species Conservation*, http://www.nwf.org/endangered/hcp/lndinc.html. And as Texas Governor (and presidential candidate), George W. Bush advocated a landowner incentive program that would provide matching grants to states for use in helping private landowners protect rare species while engaging in traditional land management practices. He would also establish a private stewardship grant program to fund for private conservation initiatives. What other incentives should be offered to private landowners and others so that they will act to protect endangered species? *See generally* John F. Turner & Jason C. Rylander, *The Private Lands Challenge: Integrating Biodiversity Conservation and Private Property*, in PRIVATE PROPERTY AND THE ENDANGERED SPECIES ACT: SAVING HABITATS, PROTECTING HOMES 116–23 (Jason F. Shogren ed. 1998) (describing possible incentive programs).

3. THE DEBATE OVER THE ESA

Removal of Echinacea tennesseensis (Tennessee Purple Coneflower) From the Federal List of Endangered and Threatened Plants

United States Fish and Wildlife Service, 2011.
76 Federal Register 46632.

Section 12 of the Act directed the Secretary of the Smithsonian Institution to prepare a report on those plants considered to be endangered, threatened, or extinct. On July 1, 1975, the Service published a notice in the Federal Register *(40 FR 27824)* accepting the Smithsonian report as a petition to list taxa named therein under section 4(c)(2) [now 4(b)(3)] of the Act and announced our intention to review the status of those plants. *Echinacea tennesseensis* was included in that report *(40 FR 27873)*. . . On June 16, 1976, we published a proposed rule in the Federal Register *(41 FR 24524)* to designate approximately 1,700 vascular plant species, including

Echinacea tennesseensis, as endangered under section 4 of the Act. On June 6, 1979, we published a final rule in the Federal Register *(44 FR 32604)* designating *E. tennesseensis* as endangered. The final rule identified the following threats to *E. tennesseensis:* Loss of habitat due to residential and recreational development; collection of the species for commercial or recreational purposes; grazing; no State law protecting rare plants in Tennessee; and succession of cedar glade communities in which *E. tennesseensis* occurred. . .

A member of the sunflower family (Asteraceae), *Echinacea tennesseensis* is a perennial herb with a long, fusiform (*i.e.,* thickened toward the middle and tapered towards either end), blackened root. In late summer, the species bears showy purple flower heads on one-to-many hairy branches. Linear to lance-shaped leaves up to 20 centimeters (cm; 8 inches (in.)) long and 1.5 cm (0.6 in.) wide arise from the base of *E. tennesseensis* and are beset with coarse hairs, especially along the margins. The ray flowers (*i.e.,* petals surrounding the darker purple flowers of the central disc) are pink to purple and spread horizontally or arch slightly forward from the disc to a length of 2–4 cm (0.8–1.8 in.). . .

When *Echinacea tennesseensis* was listed as endangered in 1979, it was known only from three locations, one each in Davidson, Rutherford, and Wilson Counties. When the species' recovery plan was completed in 1989, there were five extant populations ranging in size from approximately 3,700 to 89,000 plants and consisting of one to three colonies each. The recovery plan defined a population as a group of colonies in which the probability of gene exchange through cross pollination is high, and a colony was

defined as all *E. tennesseensis* plants found at a single site that are separated from other plants within the population by unsuitable habitat. While
analysis of genetic variability within *E. tennesseensis* did not reveal high
levels of differentiation among these populations, recovery efforts have
been implemented and tracked with respect to these geographically defined
populations. The geographic distribution of these populations and the colonies they are comprised of was updated in a status survey of *E.
tennesseensis* by TDEC to include all known colonies at that time, including
those from a sixth population introduced into glades at the Stones River
National Battlefield. For the purposes of this rule, we have followed these
population delineations and have assigned most colonies that have been
discovered since the status survey was completed to the geographically
closest population.

The six *Echinacea tennesseensis* populations occur within an approximately 400 square kilometer (km<2>; 154 square miles (mi<2>)) area and
include between 2 and 11 colonies each. In 2005, TDEC and the Service
confirmed the presence of *E. tennesseensis* at 36 colonies and counted the
number of flowering stems in each. Fifteen of these are natural colonies,
and 21 of the 36 colonies have been established through introductions for
the purpose of recovering *E. tennesseensis*. Three of these introduced colonies constitute the sixth population that was established at a Designated
State Natural Area (DSNA) in the Stones River National Battlefield in
Rutherford County. We do not consider 2 of the 21 introduced colonies as
contributing to recovery and do not include them in our analysis of the current status of *E. tennesseensis* for reasons explained in the Recovery section
of this rule. An additional introduced colony that was not monitored during
2005, but for which TDEC maintains an element occurrence record, brings
the number of introduced colonies we consider here to 20 and the total
number of colonies considered for this rulemaking to 35. . .

We have carefully assessed the best scientific and commercial information available regarding the threats faced by *Echinacea tennesseensis* in
developing this rule. As identified above, site protection and habitat management efforts by TDEC, working cooperatively with TDF, TNC, COE, the
Service, and private landowners, has reduced habitat loss from residential
and recreational development so that it is no longer a threat. Potential effects of ORV use, illegal and otherwise, in habitats containing colonies of *E.
tennesseensis* remain. While disturbance from ORV use has been observed
in the past and remains unaddressed at four colonies on publicly and privately owned lands harboring *E. tennesseensis,* these four colonies accounted for only 2 percent of the species' total distribution in 2005. Most of the
largest colonies are located in DSNAs and are protected from this threat by
fences or other barriers that TDEC has constructed and maintained. At the
time the 1989 recovery plan was written, there were five extant populations ranging in size from approximately 3,700 to 89,000 plants and consisting of one to three colonies each. There was an estimated total of
146,000 individual plants in 1989. Recovery efforts have secured habitat for
19 colonies that are self-sustaining and distributed among six geographically defined populations. These 19 secured colonies accounted for 88,773

flowering stems in 2005, or approximately 83 percent of the flowering stems observed; whereas, colonies that we do not consider secure accounted for 18,576 flowering stems, or approximately 17 percent of the flowering stems observed. The number of secured plants and colonies is adequate to ensure that Factor A is no longer a threat to the species overall. Thus, destruction and modification of habitat from ORV use is not a threat to the species throughout all its range now or into the foreseeable future.

The final rule that listed *Echinacea tennesseensis* as endangered identified the overuse of this species for commercial or scientific (*i.e.,* medicinal) purposes as a potential threat to this species. This threat has not materialized, and we do not believe it will in the future due to the emphasis on use of three other species from the genus *Echinacea* for this purpose. Neither do livestock grazing, as identified in the listing rule, nor browse by herbivores threaten *E. tennesseensis.*

The State of Tennessee enacted the Rare Plant Protection Act of 1985, addressing the inadequacy of existing regulatory mechanisms for protecting this species at the time it was listed. Should the State of Tennessee remove *Echinacea tennesseensis* from its List of Endangered Plants, we believe that the protected status of the lands where the 19 secure colonies currently exist will continue to provide adequate regulatory protection for those colonies. Also, TDEC's program for managing vegetation succession and other threats to cedar glade habitats on DSNAs inhabited by *E. tennesseensis* and their cooperative efforts with TDF, Tennessee State Parks, and COE to manage threats in habitats where colonies exist on properties under their jurisdictions have been effective in maintaining habitats in the absence of disturbances from ORV activity. . .

Based on biological evidence and historical factors discussed above in relation to the potential threat of climate change, and the fact that we have no evidence that climate changes observed to date have had any adverse impact on *Echinacea tennesseensis* or its habitat, we do not believe that climate change is a threat to *E. tennesseensis* now or within the foreseeable future.

With respect to *Echinacea tennesseensis,* we have sufficient evidence (see Summary of Factors Affecting the Species section above) to show that all of the threats identified at or since the time of listing are no longer significant threats to the species, and are not likely to become threats in the foreseeable future. We believe that the 19 secure, self-sustaining colonies distributed among six populations are secure for the foreseeable future from the threats currently affecting the species and those identified at the time of listing. These 19 colonies are located on protected conservation lands, the long-term management of which we believe precludes threats due to residential or recreational development and succession of cedar glade communities for the foreseeable future. Based on the analysis above and given the reduction in threats, *Echinacea tennesseensis* does not currently meet the Act's definition of endangered in that it is not in danger of extinction throughout all of its range, nor the definition of threatened in that it is not likely to become endangered in the foreseeable future throughout all its range. . .

NOTES & QUESTIONS

1. Are you confident that the Tennessee purple cornflower is no longer in danger of extinction? How did it recover?

2. As of July 2012, 53 species have been delisted. Of those 53, just fewer than half had recovered so they are no longer in danger of extinction. The recovered species include such high-profile animals as the American alligator, the bald eagle, the American peregrine falcon, the brown pelican, the gray wolf, and three species of kangaroos. Eleven of the remaining species were delisted because of new information about the species, six were delisted because of taxonomical changes, and ten were delisted because they are believed to be extinct. The list of delisted species is available at http://ecos.fws.gov/tess_public/pub/delistingReport.jsp.

3. The protections of the ESA no longer apply once a species is delisted. That is why the delisting of the gray wolves that had been reintroduced into Yellowstone National Park became so controversial. Wolves were reintroduced into Yellowstone and nearby central Idaho in 1995 after years of public debate and administrative review. The wolves quickly thrived in their old habitat, and they reached the numerical and distributional recovery goals by 2000. The FWS then moved to delist the wolves there. That idea provoked both widespread support among the local residents who blamed the wolves for reduced opportunity to hunt elk and immediate concern among conservationists who worried that the wolves would again be hunted in oblivion without the protection of the ESA. Thus, as the Ninth Circuit explained in 2012, "Over the last decade, the United States Fish and Wildlife Service ("FWS") has repeatedly attempted to remove all or parts of the distinct population of gray wolves in the northern Rocky Mountains from the protections of the ESA. These efforts have been struck down by the courts for violating the ESA." Alliance for the Wild Rockies v. Salazar, 672 F.3d 1170, 1171 (9th Cir. 2012). Then Congress intervened by passing a rider to a 2011 appropriations bill that ordered the delisting of the wolves, a move that the courts upheld against a separation of powers challenge. *See id.* (citing Department of Defense and Full-Year Continuing Appropriations Act of 2011, Pub. L. 112-10, 125 Stat. 38, § 1713 (2011)). Idaho, Montana, and Wyoming have all approved limited hunting of wolves.

4. Delisting, and what happens before and after it, provokes substantial controversy regarding the lessons for the overall effectiveness of the ESA. The political controversy surrounding the ESA was summarized during the competing presentations at a December 2011 congressional hearing provocatively entitled "The Endangered Species Act: How Litigation is Costing Jobs and Impeding True Recovery Efforts." The witnesses variously described the ESA as:

- "failing badly" and "[i]nstead of focusing on recovering endangered species, there are groups that use the ESA as a way to bring lawsuits against the government and block job-creating projects" (Rep. Doc Hastings);

- growing "out of an emerging consensus that the protection of both charismatic animals and other lesser-known species, once deemed valueless, is necessary if we are to succeed in protecting not only the species we find charismatic, but also the ecosystems on which they, and ultimately we, depend" that generates litigation "merely [as] a tool to increase compliance with the law" (James Tutchton, General Counsel of WildEarth Guardians);

- "as a sword to tear down the American economy, drive up food, energy and housing costs and wear down and take out rural communities and counties" (Wyoming rancher & attorney Karen Budd-Falen);

- "successfully implemented with only rare resort to the courts. While the Ac tputs endangered species concerns squarely on the table when decisions about projects that could affect them are made, in the vast majority of situations, those concerns are accommodated with modest adjustments, little disruption, and no litigation." (U.C. Hastings College of Law Professor John Leshy);

- "punish[ing] those whose property contains land that might be used as habitat by endangered and threatened species. The statute's success rate is dismal, at best–few species that are classified as endangered or threatened ever return to recovered, healthy populations. Further, expansive and inflexible Endangered Species Act regulation by federal agencies often frustrates innovative local and state conservation efforts, with the result being greater conflict and less compromise." (Brandon Middleton, staff attorney with the Pacific Legal Foundation); and

- "deliver[ing] remarkable successes. Since Congress passed this landmark conservation law in 1973, the ESA has prevented the extinction of hundreds of imperiled species across the nation and has promoted the recovery of many others – like the bald eagle, the very symbol of our Nation's strength." (FWS Director Dan Ashe).

The Endangered Species Act: How Litigation is Costing Jobs and Impeding True Recovery Efforts: Hearing Before the House Natural Resources Comm., 112th Cong., 1st Sess (2011), http://naturalresources.house.gov/Calendar/EventSingle.aspx?EventID=270315.

So has the ESA succeeded or not? The ESA itself contains the most obvious way of evaluating its effectiveness. The text of the statute identifies three purposes, so the initial inquiry is to ascertain whether the law has achieved those purposes. The ESA first says that it is "to provide a means whereby the ecosystems upon which endangered species and threatened species depend may be conserved." ESA § 2(b). This is central purpose of the ESA according to many observers. Judging by that criteria, the law has been rather unsuccessful. The ESA's provisions related to ecosystem preservation have been the target of complaints voiced by supporters and opponents of the law alike, as the materials describing the designation of critical habitat (in chapter 5) and the application of the take prohibition (in chapter 6) illustrate. In 2008, the West Virginia northern flying squirrel became the first species to be removed from the ESA's list of protected species based upon the restoration of the species' habitat. *See* Endangered and Threatened Wildlife and Plants; Final Rule Removing the Virginia Northern Flying Squirrel (Glaucomys sabrinus fuscus) from the Federal List of Endangered and Threatened Wildlife, 73 Fed. Reg. 50226, 50241 (2008). Much ecosystem preservation that has occurred since the enactment of the ESA in 1973 is the result of actions outside the scope of the ESA. Other federal laws (such as the National Forest Act, the National Park Service's Organic Act, and even pollution control statutes such as the Clean Air Act and the Clean Water Act) have been responsible for significant ecosystem preservation. State laws have protected many other ecosystems. And private organizations such as the Nature Conservancy account for a significant proportion of protected ecosystems. Even so, the habitat of most listed species is shrinking. So it is difficult to conclude that the ESA has achieved its first purpose.

The ESA's second stated purpose is "to provide a program for the conservation of such endangered species and threatened species." ESA § 2(b). *See also* National Ass'n of Home Builders v. Defenders of Wildlife, 127 S. Ct. 2518, 2526 (2007) (stating that the ESA "is intended to protect and conserve endangered and threatened species and their habitats"); Bennett v. Spear, 520 U.S. 154, 175 (1997) (describing "species preservation" as the "overarching purpose" of the ESA). The law has created such a program, and in that strict sense it has accomplished that purpose. Whether that program actually succeeds in conserving endangered and threatened species is a different question. To answer it, one could look at whether endangered and threatened species have been "conserved." The ESA defines "conservation" as "the point at which the measures provided pursuant to this Act are no longer necessary." ESA § 3(3). Put differently, the ESA is intended to help species recover. That has not happened, for the vast majority of the listed species are still endangered or threatened with extinction.

But some contest that understanding of the purpose of the law. Holly Doremus and Joel Pagel have argued that "[d]elistings are not an appropriate measure of the extent to which the ESA is fulfilling the goal of protecting species." Holly Doremus & Joel Pagel, *Why Listing May Be Forever: Perspectives on Delisting Under the U.S. Endangered Species Act*, 15 CONSERVATION BIOLOGY 1258, 1260 (2001). Doremus and Pagel go even further, "expect[ing] that the majority of currently listed species . . . will need the protection of the ESA in perpetutity. Far from demonstrating the shortcomings of the ESA, we believe that this fact emphasizes the ESA's unique role in species conservation." Doremus & Pagel, *supra*, at 1261

The third statutory purpose of the ESA is "to take such steps as may be appropriate to achieve the purposes of the treaties and conventions set forth in subsection (a) of this section." ESA § 2(b). The "treaties and conventions set forth in subsection (a)" are "(A) migratory bird treaties with Canada and Mexico; (B) the Migratory and Endangered Bird Treaty with Japan; (C) the Convention on Nature Protection and Wildlife Preservation in the Western Hemisphere; (D) the International Convention for the Northwest Atlantic Fisheries; (E) the International Convention for the High Seas Fisheries of the North Pacific Ocean; (F) the Convention on International Trade in Endangered Species of Wild Fauna and Flora; and (G) other international agreements." ESA § 2(a)(4). Those laws, in turn, recite a variety of appeals for conservation, preservation, and protection of various species located in certain parts of the world.

The fact that the ESA states only three purposes has not prevented others from attributing additional purposes to the law. The most common claim is that the purpose of the ESA is to prevent species from going extinct. Happily, only nine listed species have gone extinct. That record yields the further claim "the Endangered Species Act has worked so well" because 99% "of the species that have been put on the Endangered Species List have avoided extinction." *Threatened And Endangered Species Recovery Act of 2005: Hearing on H.R. 3824 Before the House Comm. on Res.*, 109th Cong. 23 (2005) (statement of Sen. Clinton). Moreover, several of the initially-listed species may have already been extinct by the time they were listed under the law. *See, e.g.*, Final Rule to Remove the Caribbean Monk Seal from the Federal List of Endangered and Threatened Wildlife, 73 Fed. Reg. 63900 (2008) (delisting a species that was last sighted in 1952, fifteen years before it was among the first species listed in 1967). We still do not know the status of one famous species – the ivory-billed woodpecker – that was listed as endangered in 1973, declared extinct by impressive scientific authorities around 2000, and then reappeared – or perhaps not – in 2002. The balance of the 2,000 listed species remains alive.

Or perhaps it is too soon to tell whether the ESA has succeed. In 2012, the Center for Biological Diversity "compared the *actual* recovery rate of 110 species with the *projected* recovery rate in their federal recovery plans." Kieran Suckling, Noah Greenwald & Tierra Curry, On Time, On Target: How the Endangered Species Act Is Saving America's Wildlife 1 (2012), http://www.esasuccess.org/pdfs/110_REPORT.pdf. The study found that "species recovered in 25 years, while their recovery plan predicted 23 years." *Id.* Further some of the species that have yet to be listed long enough to reach their recovery goals have already experienced rapid increases in numbers including a 8,280% increase in black-footed ferrets and a 22,312% increase in El Segundo blue butterflies.

The ESA fares well under some understandings of its purpose, and not so well under other understandings. Yet that is not the end of the debate. Many supporters of the law admit that it has not achieved its goals, but they blame other factors instead of the ESA itself. The failure to fund or enforce the ESA's requirements is a common complaint of those who defend the ESA against its perceived shortcomings. By contrast, many opponents of the law admit that it has achieved some of its goals, but they worry that it has done so at too great a cost.

How do you evaluate the effectiveness of the ESA? What could be done to improve it? Just remember that as the political debate continues with no apparent end in sight, the actual application of the law depends on the administrative and judicial decisions that are described in this part, and on how affected parties employ the law in traditional and innovative ways.

PART 3

MANAGING ECOSYSTEM DIVERSITY

CHAPTER 7

INTRODUCTION TO ECOSYSTEM MANAGEMENT LAW

Chapter Outline:

The term "ecosystem management law" includes three components, each of which poses its own set of challenges. First, we must develop some sense of the underlying subject matter—ecosystems. What are they? Where are they? What happens in them? What threatens to disrupt them? In their purest form these are questions of *science*, of the discipline of ecology. But in this case we seek the answers to these questions in order to develop *policy*, that of ecosystem management. Given what we know about ecosystems, what are we trying to accomplish when we think of managing them? How will we know whether we have succeeded? Who gets to decide these questions? As difficult as it is to hash out these policy questions, the third challenge requires that we reduce the decisions to *law*, that is, to legal script. What is the legal definition of an ecosystem? What legal process must be followed for implementing and challenging policy decisions? How will courts review agency decisions implementing ecosystem management policy? Consensus on these questions, as well as the pertinent questions of science and policy, is the extreme exception. This chapter thus delves deeper into the questions surrounding these three components of ecosystem management law in order to provide an overview of the core issues the law faces in the particular ecosystem settings taken up in the remaining chapters of this part of the text.

Before going there, however, some thought must be given to the question, why have *any* law of ecosystem management? The Endangered Species Act (ESA) may funnel ecosystem protection concerns through a species-specific focus, but why isn't that sufficient to address whatever concerns we have about ecosystems? The answer has much to do with endangered species and much not to do with them. The connection to endangered species is obvious: with habitat loss as the leading cause of endangered status, conservation of the ecosystems within which endangered species exist will be vital to their recovery. Clearly, however, any hope of limiting future additions to the list of endangered species will depend on a habitat conservation policy that is at least in part decoupled from the ESA—that is, which does not require the presence of an endangered species to trigger a response. Moreover, humans may value, and thus wish to manage, ecosystems for reasons completely apart from any concern about species. Even the desire to use an ecosystem primarily for human benefit, such as for timber production or water purification, implies some need for management.

Still, that there may be some potential purposes for ecosystem management law does not answer the question of whether we *need* ecosystem management law now. Other than ecosystems within which endangered species exist, which we could reasonably assume can be managed through the authority of the ESA, is there an "ecosystem problem" in the United States? Most ecologists working in the field agree there is, based on any plausible definition of ecosystem. Groundbreaking work on the state of the nation's ecosystems appeared in 1995 through the work of Reed Noss and fellow researchers in a report for the National Biological Service of the U.S. Department of the Interior, *see* REED F. NOSS ET AL., BIOLOGICAL REPORT 28, ENDANGERED ECOSYSTEMS OF THE UNITED STATES: A PRELIMINARY ASSESSMENT OF LOSS AND DEGRADATION (1995), *available at* http://biology.usgs.gov/pubs/ecosys.htm, and in a report prepared for the Defenders of Wildlife, *see* REED F. NOSS AND ROBERT L. PETERS, ENDANGERED ECOSYSTEMS: A REPORT ON AMERICA'S VANISHING HABITAT AND WILDLIFE (1995), *available at* http://www.defenders.org/pubs/eco00.html. Noss and his colleagues explained that "ecosystems can be lost or impoverished in basically two ways. The most obvious kind of loss is quantitative—the conversion of a native prairie to a corn field or to a parking lot... The second kind of loss is qualitative and involves a change or degradation in the structure, function, or composition of an ecosystem." Their work assessed ecosystem status in the United States across these two scales. On a national level, the magnitude of quantitative and qualitative ecosystem decline since prior to European settlement is significant. Some indicia of the level of loss and degradation include:

- 177 million acres of wetlands lost—a loss of more than 50 percent
- 25 million acres of ancient forests lost in the Northwest—a 90 percent loss
- 22 million acres of native grassland lost in California
- 360,000 miles of roads in national forests
- 270 million acres of public lands affected by grazing

The study concluded that the overall risk to ecosystems is extreme in seven southeastern states, Texas, California, and Hawaii, high in 25 states, and moderate in only 15 states. Twenty-one ecosystems rank as the nation's most endangered, listed here in descending order based on extent of decline, present area (rarity), imminence of threat, and number of federally listed threatened and endangered species associated with each type:

- South Florida landscape
- Southern Appalachian sprucefir forest
- Longleaf pine forest and savanna
- Eastern grassland, savanna and barrens
- California native grassland
- Coastal communities in conterminous 48 states
- Southwestern riparian forest
- Hawaiian dry forest
- Large streams and rivers in conterminous 48 states
- Cave and karst systems
- California riparian forest and wetland
- Florida scrub
- Old-growth eastern deciduous forest
- Old-growth forests of Pacific Northwest
- Old-growth red and white pine forest of Great Lakes states
- Old-growth ponderosa pine forest
- Midwestern wetlands
- Southern forested wetlands

Several recent comprehensive studies point generally in the same direction as Noss's groundbreaking report. For example, in 2002 the nonpartisan Heinz Center for Science, Economics and the Environment released *The State of the Nation's Ecosystems*, which was far and away the most comprehensive, detailed, useful guide to the topic available at the time. The Heinz Center then updated the report in 2008. Much to your authors' satisfaction, the report examines ecosystem conditions in 6 categories closely aligned with the structure of this part of your casebook: coasts and oceans, farmlands, forests, fresh waters, grasslands and shrublands, and urban and suburban areas. The study developed numerous indicators of conditions and trends for each ecosystem type. The most telling finding, however, is that data are simply not widely available to make complete assessments of the indicators for each type of ecosystem. Where available data were sufficient to draw conclusions, the report's findings are in line with those Noss reached: nitrate loads in U.S. rivers, wetlands, and estuaries are sharply on the rise; chemical contamination in all our nation's waters is alarmingly high; over a third of native species are "vulnerable," with half of those "imperiled" or "critically imperiled;" agricultural production is rising; and so on.

Dovetailing closely with the Heinz Center's report, the U.S. Environmental Protection Agency issued its *Report on the Environment* as a draft available for public comment in 2003 and in final report form in 2008. The report, available with updates at http://www.epa.gov/roe/, describes the agency's efforts to engage in the research initiative necessary to develop ecological conditions indicators. Using the Heinz Center's ecosystem categories, EPA grouped the necessary indicator research into six fields: landscape conditions; biotic conditions; ecological processes; chemical and physical characteristics; hydrology and geomorphology; and natural disturbance regimes. Beyond this descriptive explanation, however, EPA reached no concrete findings on ecological conditions.

The problem of ecosystem decline is by no means confined to the United States. One of the most comprehensive, methodical, long-range of efforts to quantify losses of biodiversity was reported in 2004 based on a comparison at the national scale of populations and regional extinctions of birds, butterflies, and vascular plants from Britain. Through various public and private monitoring and survey programs operated over the past several decades in Britain at thousands of sites, a large database of historical trends grew more available over time. A team of researches meticulously studied the data and found losses across the board, with an especially precipitous loss of butterflies. *See* J.A. Thomas et al., *Comparative Losses of British Butterflies, Birds, and Plants and the Global Extinction Crisis*, 303 SCIENCE 1879 (2004).

More broadly, the World Wildlife Fund issued its *Living Planet Report* in 2002, updated in 2010, finding sustained decline in world ecosystem integrity. The report, available with updates at http://wwf.panda.org/about_our_earth/all_publications/living_planet_report/, examines trends on the state of forest, freshwater, and marine ecosystems from around the world and assembles a database to measure the "living planet index," finding a 37 percent decline in the condition of these resources since 1970. At the same time, WWF's index of "world ecological footprint," which measure's human use of renewable natural resources such as cropland, fisheries, grazing land, forest, energy resources, and freshwater, found an 80 percent rise in use from 1961 to 1999. WWF concluded that current human use of renewable natural resources is 20 percent above the Earth's biological capacity, meaning that we are dipping into the natural capital base to make up the difference. Obviously, just as for a personal bank account, that cannot go on indefinitely. Surely WWF's data and conclusions will be debated, but it is difficult to dispute the fundamental message it and the other recent reports convey—that we must pay close attention to the balance between ecosystem integrity and human resource uses.

That theme also dominated in the March 2005 release of the Millennium Ecosystem Assessment (MEA) Synthesis Report. The MEA was a project of the United Nations taking place over a five-year period and involving many scientists and policy experts from around the world focusing on the state of global ecosystems and, specifically, how changes in those ecosystems affect human well-being. The MEA reached four principal findings:

- Over the past 50 years, humans have changed ecosystems more rapidly and extensively than in any comparable period of time in human history, largely to meet rapidly growing demands for food, fresh water, timber, fiber and fuel. This has resulted in a substantial and largely irreversible loss in the diversity of life on Earth.

- The changes that have been made to ecosystems have contributed to substantial net gains in human well-being and economic development, but these gains have been achieved at growing costs in the form of the degradation of many ecosystem services, increased risks of nonlinear changes, and the exacerbation of poverty for some groups of people. These problems, unless addressed, will substantially diminish the benefits that future generations obtain from ecosystems.

- The degradation of ecosystem services could grow significantly worse during the first half of this century and is a barrier to achieving the Millennium Development Goals.

- The challenge of reversing the degradation of ecosystems while meeting increasing demands for their services can be partially met under some scenarios that the MA has considered but these involve significant changes in policies, institutions and practices, that are not currently under way. Many options exist to conserve or enhance specific ecosystem services in ways that reduce negative tradeoffs or that provide positive synergies with other ecosystem services.

MILLENNIUM ECOSYSTEM ASSESSMENT, ECOSYSTEMS AND HUMAN WELL-BEING: SYNTHESIS 1 (2005).

Of course, the presence of many imperiled ecosystems throughout much of the United States does not lead inexorably to a particular design for the law of ecosystem management. People offer many different explanations of the causes of ecosystem decline, and thus what should be done about it in law. Indeed, the design of comprehensive ecosystem management law is a question that has been pondered seriously only since the early 1990s.

The absence of a unified, national ecosystem management statute thus presents both opportunities and obstacles to the development of ecosystem management law. The many federal and state laws dealing explicitly or potentially with facets of ecosystem management allow for experimentation and flexibility in dealing with the challenge of forging policy in varied natural settings. Like ecosystems, ecosystem management law must be diverse, dynamic, and evolving. On the other hand, important overarching issues of ecosystem management may require common understanding and uniform treatment throughout the nation, which is complicated when the law is fractured into many statutes administered by many political units. To assist in the examination of how these laws are or are not evolving toward the ecosystem management theme, this chapter provides a foundational understanding of the three core issues: What is an ecosystem? What is ecosystem management? And what is ecosystem management law?

A. WHAT IS AN ECOSYSTEM?

Like the term "biodiversity," the term "ecosystem" is simply a human invention used to represent what we perceive to be happening in nature. *Eco* represents ecology; *systems* are assemblages of parts forming a complex or unitary whole. What we have in mind with *ecosystems*, therefore, is the sense that the physical and biological parts of nature—water, air, species, etc.—assemble into complex, interacting wholes. From there, however, agreement on what constitutes an ecosystem, particularly for purposes of formulating ecosystem management law, is elusive. A good working definition can be found in a regulation the United States Forest Service adopted in 2012 for forest ecosystem management planning:

> *Ecosystem.* A spatially explicit, relatively homogeneous unit of the Earth that includes all interacting organisms and elements of the abiotic environment within its boundaries. An ecosystem is commonly described in terms of its:
>
> (1) Composition. Major vegetation types, rare communities, aquatic systems, and riparian systems.
>
> (2) Structure. Vertical and horizontal distribution of vegetation, stream habitat complexity, and riparian habitat elements.
>
> (3) Function. Ecological processes such as stream flows, nutrient cycling, and disturbance regimes.
>
> (4) Connectivity. Habitats that exist for breeding, feeding, or movement of wildlife and fish within species home ranges or migration areas.

36 C.F.R. 219.19 (2012).

Some definitions—and many have been offered—are quite broader. Testifying before Congress as Secretary of the Interior, Bruce Babbitt once observed that "an ecosystem is in the eye of the beholder." That may be true for purposes of conceptualizing ecosystems, but that will not suffice for making ecosystem management *law*.

The challenge, therefore, is in defining the concept of ecosystem in such a way as to provide a metric for formulating management objectives and promoting the development of policy and law. There is no obvious spatial or functional unit to select. As the Fish and Wildlife Service has observed, an ecosystem could reasonably be defined as anything "from a drop of water to the North American continent to the entire biosphere." U.S. FISH AND WILDLIFE SERVICE, AN ECOSYSTEM MANAGEMENT APPROACH TO FISH AND WILDLIFE CONSERVATION: AN APPROACH TO MORE EFFECTIVELY CONSERVE THE NATION'S BIODIVERSITY 6 (1994). Some critics have used this trait to question the wisdom of attempting to forge policy and law around any concept that is so amorphous. Sound natural resources policy, they say, requires the ability to designate unambiguous ecosystem boundaries on maps, so that the jurisdiction and application of government authority can be clearly delineated. *See* ALLAN K. FITZSIMMONS, DEFENDING ILLUSIONS: FEDERAL PROTECTION OF ECOSYSTEMS 34–39 (1999). On the other hand, few people would mistake the Everglades for the Rocky Mountains, suggesting that there are some unambiguous distinguishing characteristics with which to work after all. Nevertheless, the demand for a metric of ecosystems that is not only scientifically accurate, but also politically and legally viable, cannot be ignored.

The law of ecosystem management thus will require some sort of framework for delineating and describing the ecosystems being managed. In these materials we explore five different approaches for that purpose. First, we must have some way of identifying where the ecosystem is located. One approach is to use *geographic units*, such as an island, a forest, or a lake. Several federal agencies have sliced up the ecosystem landscape using this approach, as in the U.S Fish and Wildlife Service's map of watershed-based ecosystem geography, available at http://www.fws.gov/offices/ecounits.html.

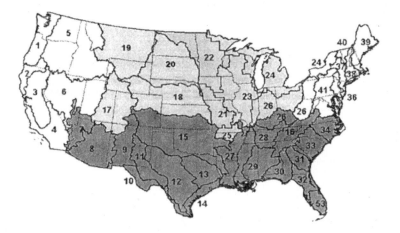

The United States Fish and Wildlife Service has identified and defined boundaries for 53 ecosystem units in the contiguous states according to watershed geography units.
U.S. FWS

But there are other ways to slice up the landscape, as the U.S. Environmental Protection Agency has suggested with its "Large Ecosystem" map:

USEPA Watershed Information Network Water Atlas

As these maps illustrate, moreover, the geography of ecosystems does not always correspond to the way the political and social landscape is divided. We may want to describe ecosystems, therefore, according to *management units*, such as a park, a county, or a farm. Once we have identified where the ecosystem is located, we are likely to be interested in what is happening within and to its physical and biological systems. In this sense, ecosystems consist of *functional units*, such as nutrient cycles, energy transfers, and chemical processes. These functional processes support the biodiversity found in the ecosystem, and for some people the primary goal of ecosystem management is to ensure the continued integrity of the processes that maximize biodiversity. The processes in some ecosystems, however, are managed for other purposes. A private timber forest, for example, is managed to maximize the *commodity units* of timber value. A public water supply company, by contrast, might manage the forest in the watershed of its water supply reservoir to take advantage of the *ecosystem service units* of water purification.

These five ways of thinking about ecosystems are not mutually exclusive, but neither are they entirely compatible. Management units such as parks may contain all of a geographic ecosystem unit, or only part of several units. Functional processes in ecosystems often transcend both geographic and management boundaries. Managing a forest for the commodity value of the timber may result, incidentally, in maximizing some ecosystem service values beneficial to human populations, but may sacrifice some functional processes beneficial to biodiversity. In different settings, there may be scientific and policy-based advantages and disadvantages to emphasizing one or a particular combination of the five approaches in the law of ecosystem management. The following materials explore the challenges that await the law of ecosystem management as it searches for the appropriate mix of these approaches to defining ecosystems in different contexts.

1. SCIENTIFIC PERSPECTIVES

John M. Blair, Scott L. Collins & Alan K. Knapp, *Ecosystems As Functional Units in Nature*
14 Natural Resources & Environment 150 (2000).

In the last two decades or so, the word "ecosystem" has become increasingly used by the media and in nonscientific public and private sectors to denote some portion of the natural world, ranging in size and scope from a rotting log to the entire planet on which life as we know it exists. It also has become associated with environmental issues, and with certain land use practices and management approaches (e.g., ecosystem management). This variable and sometimes vague use of the term ecosystem has led to some confusion regarding the meaning of this important ecological concept. Our objectives in this essay are to define the ecosystem concept and briefly describe ecosystem ecology as a scientific discipline. We then provide some examples of ecosystem research and how human activities can impact ecosystems. Finally, we link ecosystem research to the recently conceived concept of ecosystem management and discuss the potential for using knowledge of how ecosystems function to achieve desired management goals.

The ecosystem concept has been used in many contexts. In the scientific realm, the term ecosystem is used most often to describe a relatively discrete unit of nature, such as a lake, a grassland, or a forested mountain valley. Such a view is consistent with much current ecosystem-based research in which the units of study are often well-delineated watersheds, or catchment basins, which are areas defined by topographic features and a common hydrologic drainage. Ecosystem research also includes studies of processes within these entities, such as the flow of energy from plants to consumers (e.g., animals, fungi, bacteria), or the processes determining the amount of soil nitrogen available for use by plants. Research concerned with these processes is a cornerstone of ecosystem science, but such research is not necessarily constrained by a need for ecosystems with distinct physical boundaries. A third use of the ecosystem concept is based on the application of principles derived from ecosystem ecology to achieve certain management goals. An example of this usage would be the Greater Yellowstone Ecosystem that includes Yellowstone and Grand Teton National Parks, surrounding public and private lands, human settlements, and multiple types of other land use. Thus the ecosystem concept can apply to the description and study of a distinct entity, such as a grassland or forested watershed; a process or collection of processes, such as nitrogen cycling; or a management unit like the Greater Yellowstone Ecosystem. Use of the ecosystem concept in all of these contexts is appropriate, when defined explicitly.

Ecosystem ecology as a scientific discipline has relatively recent origins. Although the term ecosystem was coined in 1935 by the British ecologist Arthur Tansley, ecosystem ecology did not begin to flourish as a scientific discipline until the 1960s. Several factors, including an influx of new funding for ecological research, an increase in academic positions at universities, the development of computer technology, and an increased awareness of the effects of human activities on the environment, combined to enhance the development of ecosystem ecology as an important new area of ecological study. Together, these factors enhanced the growth of ecosystem science in the U.S. and the relevance of this discipline for addressing important environmental issues. Indeed, ecosystem science was one of the first of ecological disciplines to explicitly include the impact of human populations and activities as part of its comprehensive research agenda.

Just What Is an Ecosystem?

An ecosystem can be described in simple terms as a biological community (all of the organisms in a given area) plus its abiotic (nonliving) environment. In fact, the word ecosystem was first used by Tansley to describe natural systems in a way that encompassed all of the living organisms occurring in a given area and the physical environment with which they interact. In this sense, the ecosystem is the first level in the traditional hierarchical arrangement of biological systems. It explicitly includes both living organisms and the abiotic environment as integral parts of a single system. This is one reason that ecosystem studies often focus on quantifying transfer of energy and materials between living organisms and the physical environment.

Tansley originally described the ecosystem as part of a continuum of physical systems in nature, and in fact the concept of "system" and much of the language used to describe ecosystem structure and function are borrowed from physics. In very general terms, a system is any collection of components, interacting in an organized manner to form a unit, through which may flow materials, energy and information. An ecosystem is a particular kind of system, defined by Eugene P. Odum, a leading proponent of ecosystem ecology, as any unit in nature that includes all the organisms that function together in a given area and their abiotic environment, interacting so that energy flows lead to biotic structure and material cycles. ODUM, BASIC ECOLOGY (1983).

The definition above implies that ecosystems occupy a given area, and that they therefore have boundaries (at least conceptually). Indeed, some ecosystems have fairly obvious, distinct boundaries (a lake, an urban forest, a distinct watershed); but more often the boundaries of an ecosystem are much less distinct and may be user-defined. The concept of the ecosystem as a real physical entity sometimes presents problems, especially in terrestrial habitats, where it is often difficult to say where one ecosystem ends and another begins. Further, boundaries which might be appropriate for quantifying hydrologic fluxes or nutrient budgets may not apply to more mobile or migratory organisms. However, the difficulty in defining precise boundaries does not negate the value of the ecosystem concept, and many ecosystem ecologists simply define their ecosystems based on the area under study. Indeed the same difficulties in defining precise boundaries apply to natural populations and communities; yet these organizational levels are widely accepted and used by ecologists and provide the basis for many management-related decisions.

A Process–Based View of Ecosystems

An alternate way of viewing an ecosystem is based on the processes that comprise ecosystem functioning. These processes include productivity, energy flow among trophic levels, decomposition, and nutrient cycling. In this way, an ecosystem can be defined based on the collection of processes required to continue normal functioning, as opposed to the physical boundaries within which those processes operate. Defining what constitutes "normal" functioning is a critical issue, with important implications for preserving and managing ecosystems. Some early proponents of the ecosystem concept viewed ecosystems as highly integrated collections of organisms which would achieve a stable equilibrium (the "balance of nature") in the absence of outside disturbances. However, this view has largely been replaced by a non-equilibrium perspective in which disturbances are seen as natural phenomena. Thus, defining a natural disturbance regime and the boundaries of ecosystem functioning are challenges for both ecosystem scientists and ecosystem managers.

Ecosystems function by processing energy and materials, operating under certain internal constraints or rules and producing certain outputs. Systems, by definition, have boundaries that delimit them from their surroundings, or their environment. An important aspect of ecosystems, however, is that they are "open" systems with respect to both materials and energy. They are subject to an input environment (beyond the system boundaries), which includes inputs of energy (e.g., sunlight) and materials (e.g., water and nutrients). These inputs can cause changes in the internal components of an ecosystem (compartments called state variables) over time. The interactions of inputs and state variables affect ecosystem processes and result in ecosystem outputs, or an output environment. For example, inputs of water and carbon dioxide in combination with state variables such as soil nutrients and plants leads to primary productivity—an ecosystem process—that may be consumed by grazers and transported to another ecosystem. Inputs that play a major role in altering ecosystem components and outputs are also referred to as forcing functions. For example, sunlight, water and nutrients are important forcing functions that affect the structure and functioning of most ecosystems. Natural disturbances, such as periodic fires or hurricanes, also play a role in affecting ecosystem structure and function. It is also important to note that the open nature of ecosystems means that the output environment of one ecosystem becomes part of the input environment of another. Thus, flows of material and energy link ecosystems in the biosphere.

Although ecosystems are open with respect to flows of both energy and materials, the behaviors of energy and materials, once they are in ecosystems, fundamentally differ. Energy transformations are essentially one-way flows, and thus energy cannot be recycled or reused within an ecosystem. Nutrients, however, can circulate or cycle within an ecosystem, and the flow of nutrients among different compartments is referred to as nutrient cycling. Nutrients include substances such as phosphorus, nitrogen, potassium, and calcium that are required by living organisms. Because the flows of chemical nutrients typically involve both biological (organic) and geological (inorganic) pools, nutrient cycles also are referred to as biogeochemical cycles. Ecosystem ecologists are often interested in describing and quantifying the storage and movement of nutrients among these pools, as well as understanding the factors that regulate these patterns of movement. This is important from both theoretical and practical perspectives. Unwanted, and unintended, changes in nutrient cycles can have profound consequences for environmental quality and human populations (e.g., groundwater contamination, acid rain, global climate change, eutrophication of lakes).

Ecosystem management

As our understanding of the processes occurring within and among ecosystem components increases, ecosystem management may provide a viable strategy for sustainable use of natural resources. For this to be realized, knowledge of the inputs, processes and cycles, and outputs of a managed ecosystem is required. This may be most feasible in clearly defined ecosystems, . . . where the natural boundaries are relatively well defined and encompass most of the major components necessary for ecosystem functioning. Ecosystem management of less well delineated or more fragmented ecosystems (e.g., a forest fragment surrounded by agricultural fields) will be far more challenging because of the increased interactions with surrounding ecosystems and the potential for greater movement of materials and organisms from the surrounding landscape into and out of the ecosystem of interest.

Such challenges should not be viewed as impediments to ecosystem management, however. The benefits of ecosystem versus species-level management are numerous. Attempts to manage species as entities isolated from their biotic and abiotic environment (the ecosystem) are doomed to failure and the costs associated with the loss of ecosystem services due to mismanagement can be astounding. Clearly, the open nature of ecosystems and their lack of discrete boundaries should not be used as excuses for failing to design policies to manage them. Our legal system is replete with regulations that cross boundaries (e.g., interstate laws) and regulate processes and phenomena that are not discrete entities (e.g., air quality).

The ecosystem concept is often applied to well-defined and relatively small geographic entities in nature, where the input and outflow of energy and materials is reasonably well delineated. The main goal of ecosystem ecology as a research discipline is to understand, in detail, the processes of energy capture and the conversion of matter (e.g., nitrogen, carbon) and energy (e.g., sunlight) from one state to another within ecosystems, and the rules that govern these processes. The ecosystem concept, however, can also be applied to systems in nature that are less clearly bounded, including larger geographic areas that often contain several smaller ecosystems in whole or in part. These ecosystems may be more difficult to manage, unless management is scaled to definable subunits. This explains, perhaps, why ecosystem management is better developed in some ecosystems (forested watersheds) than others (coastal ocean areas, large rivers). In fact, it may be more difficult to apply ecosystem management approaches to large ecosystems that interact in many complex ways with the surrounding landscape, as is the case with coastal estuaries. Perhaps that is why many of the most difficult and unpredictable environmental problems (e.g., outbreaks of the toxic marine dinoflagellate *Pfeisteria*) occur in such complex, open systems. The challenges associated with ecosystem management highlight the importance of basic research in ecosystem ecology for understanding how ecosystems work at many different spatial scales. Ecosystem components represent the basic building blocks of complex food webs, of which humans are a part, and ecosystem processes provide many services upon which humans rely. As the impacts of human activities on ecosystem structure and function increase through time, a better understanding of the workings of both natural and managed ecosystems can be combined with predictive models to help manage ecosystems in a sustainable way.

NOTES & QUESTIONS

1. One problem in using geographic units to define ecosystem boundaries is that there is more than ample disagreement over which unit to use. The principal units discussed in the scientific literature are watersheds, biomes, and ecoregions. Their working definitions are:

> watershed: The entire topographic region within which apparent surface water runoff drains to a specific point on a stream or to a body of water such as a lake or bay.

> biome: A major regional community of plants and animals with similar life forms and environmental conditions. It is the largest geographical biotic unit, named after the dominant type of life form, such as rain forest, grassland, or coral reef.

> ecoregion: Regions of relative homogeneity of biotic, abiotic, terrestrial, and aquatic ecological components (e.g., physiography, soils, vegetation, geology, climate, and land use) within which the mosaic of characteristics is holistically different than adjacent regions.

None of these is fully satisfying for purposes of defining ecosystem boundaries. Watersheds are hard to define in flat and arid areas. Ecoregions can require sophisticated data and mapping analysis to delineate. Biomes can be large areas containing many watershed and ecoregions. *See generally* G. E. Griffith et al., *Ecoregions, Watersheds, Basins, and HUCs: How State and Federal Agencies Frame Water Quality*, 54 JOURNAL OF SOIL AND WATER CONSERVATION 666 (1999); James M. Omernik & Robert G. Bailey, *Distinguishing Between Watersheds and Ecoregions*, 33 JOURNAL OF THE AMERICAN WATER RESOURCES ASSOCIATION 935 (1997); M. LYNNE CORN, CONGRESSIONAL RESEARCH SERVICE REPORT FOR CONGRESS, ECOSYSTEMS, BIOMES, AND WATERSHEDS: DEFINITIONS AND USE, 93–655 ENR (1993). Some commentators argue that all three units must be used in combination to effectively manage ecosystems, while others argue that doing so will impede the formation of coherent ecosystem management policy, thus one unit should be adopted as the dominant unit. *Com pare* Griffith et al., *supra*, and Omernik and Bailey, *supra* (use combinations of units), *with* J. B. Ruhl, *The (Political) Science of Watershed Management in the Ecosystem Age*, 35 JOURNAL OF THE AMERICAN WATER RESOURCES ASSOCIATION 519 (1999) (adopt watersheds as the dominant unit). What do you think?

2. Although it seems unremarkable today to think of ecosystems in process-based terms, Blair et al. explain that this was not always the conventional wisdom, with many ecologists propounding a stable-equilibrium theory of ecosystem evolution. The classic depiction of this "balance of nature" model was the so-called "climax" or "peak" forest in which species succession had run its course and the final stage of forest biomass development had been reached, to remain in this state in perpetuity barring catastrophic disturbance. But recent studies have shown that the maximal biomass phase reached during succession in forests cannot be maintained in the long term even in the absence of catastrophic disturbances. Rather, retrogressive succession takes hold with gradual changes in litter decomposition rates, phosphorous release from litter, and decomposer microbe activity. The forest begins to experience gradual reductions in productivity, biomass, nutrient availability, and soil processing as a result. Although the retrogressive succession processes remain poorly understood, their presence is unmistakable, providing additional support for the shift from the equilibrium to the non-equilibrium conception of ecosystems. *See* David A. Wardle, et al., *Ecosystem Properties and Forest Decline in Contrasting Long-Term Chronosequences*, 305 SCIENCE 509 (2004).

3. As Blair et al. suggest, most scientific definitions of ecosystems, once they go beyond the obvious statement that ecosystems are interacting collections of biological and physical parts, focus on the *process* characteristics of an ecosystem as a means of defining its boundaries. It is what happens in an ecosystem that makes it more than just the sum of its parts or a set of lines on a map. Consider, however, whether this manner of describing ecosystems provides a politically and legally useful metric. How would you draft the *legal* definition of "ecosystem functions" or "ecosystem processes" in such a way as to describe clearly for agencies, courts, and citizens where the ecosystems are?

4. At the dawn of its ecosystem management policy development, the Department of Interior's Bureau of Land Management outlined the ecosystem functions it believes should be managed on federal public rangeland, which is located primarily in states west of the Mississippi and leased extensively to private ranchers for grazing cattle and sheep. *See* 60 Fed. Reg. 9894 (Feb. 22, 1995). Some of the function-management objectives the agency specified include:

> Maintaining or promoting adequate amounts of vegetative ground cover, including standing plant material and litter, to support infiltration, maintain soil moisture storage, and stabilize soils.

> Maintaining or promoting subsurface soil conditions that support permeability rates appropriate to climate and soils.

> Maintaining, improving or restoring riparian-wetland functions including energy dissipation, sediment capture, groundwater recharge, and stream bank stability.

Maintaining or promoting stream channel morphology (e.g., gradient, width/depth ratio, channel roughness and sinuosity) and functions appropriate to climate and landform.

Maintaining or promoting the appropriate kinds and amounts of soil organisms, plants and animals to support the hydrologic cycle, nutrient cycle, and energy flow.

Do these adequately translate Blair's description of ecosystem functions into administrative standards capable of being easily understood and implemented without difficult interpretation? How would an agency, or an interest group watching over the agency's management decisions, conclude whether a decision the agency made maintains, degrades, or promotes any of these specified functions? The history and status of the public rangeland rule is discussed in more detail in Chapter 9.

5. Blair et al. contend that "the benefits of ecosystem versus species-level management are numerous." Do you agree? What implications does this view have for the future of the Endangered Species Act in the formation of ecosystem management law? Should an ecosystem approach replace or supplement the species approach of the ESA? Most conservation biologists, not surprisingly, argue that both approaches are needed. As Noss et al. argue:

Ecosystem conservation offers several advantages over a species-by-species approach for the protection of biodiversity: it directly addresses the primary cause of many species declines (habitat destruction), it offers a meaningful surrogate to surveying every species, and it provides a cost-effective means for simultaneous conservation and recovery of groups of species. The species-by-species approach—although extremely important to our efforts of saving biodiversity—is inefficient. . . As the public becomes more familiar with the evidence that entire ecosystems or groups of species have declined and that saving individual species under the Endangered Species Act of 1973 does not solve all conservation problems and does not necessarily prevent the need for future listings, the rationale for ecosystem management becomes more apparent.

REED F. NOSS ET AL., BIOLOGICAL REPORT 28, ENDANGERED ECOSYSTEMS OF THE UNITED STATES: A PRELIMINARY ASSESSMENT OF LOSS AND DEGRADATION 6 (1995).

6. Sir Arthur George Tansley (1871–1955), mentioned in Blair's article as the founder of the concept of ecosystems, was educated at Highgate School, University College, London, and Trinity College, Cambridge. He returned to University College as assistant to Professor F. W. Oliver until 1906, when he moved to Cambridge as a lecturer. In 1901 he founded the *New Phytologist*, an influential botanical journal which he continued to edit for thirty years. Tansley took a prominent part in the development of plant ecology in Britain. He was instrumental in founding the British Ecological Society in 1913, and edited its *Journal of Ecology* for many years. In 1927 he was appointed Sherardian Professor of Botany at Oxford from which he retired with the title of Professor Emeritus in 1937. His classic book *The British Islands and their Vegetation* appeared in

1939. The last fifteen years of his life were largely devoted to working for nature conservation in Britain, a subject which had long been of concern to him. He was knighted in 1950 while serving as the first chairman of the Nature Conservancy.

7. Tansley's contemporary in the United States, Barrington Moore, described the dawn of ecology sciences in the 1920 inaugural issue of *Ecology*, the American counterpart to Britain's *Journal of Ecology*:

> There have been three stages in the development of the biological sciences: first, a period of general work, when Darwin, Agassiz and others amassed and gave their knowledge of such natural phenomena as could be studied with the limited methods at hand; next, men specialized in different branches, and gradually built up the biological sciences which we know today; and now has begun the third or synthetic stage. Since the biological field has been reconnoitered and divided into its logical parts, it becomes possible to see the interrelations and to bring these related parts more closely together. Many sciences have been developed to the point where, although the field has not yet been fully covered, contact and cooperation with related sciences are essential to full development. Ecology represents the third phase.

Barrington Moore, *The Scope of Ecology*, 1 ECOLOGY 3 (1920). Although the "methods at hand" for scientific discourse have progressed tremendously since Moore wrote those words, principally through the computer and satellite and other remote sensing technologies, his theme of interdisciplinary synthesis remains at the forefront of the biological sciences. *See* Edward O. Wilson, Consilience: The Unity of Knowledge (1998).

2. POLICY PERSPECTIVES

The system of metrics chosen for defining ecosystems should have scientific validity, but it also has much to do with the underlying question of policy objective. For example, one concern some people have with the view of ecosystems as functional process units in nature is that it can lead to a primarily biocentric approach to ecosystem management—i.e., we should manage ecosystems above all else to preserve natural ecosystem functions where and as they operate. Of course, for many people that is precisely the approach that is needed to rebut the anthropocentric view of nature as primarily a source of commodities humans can sever from nature and use to serve human needs, such as lumber, minerals, and water. Given their vastly different objectives, a commodity-based view of ecosystems is likely to adopt a much different metric for ecosystem management than will a preservation-based view. This form of economy versus environment debate has plagued environmental law for decades. As Senator Hatfield suggested when he introduced the Ecosystem Management Act of 1994 (reproduced *infra*), developing ecosystem management policy will require that we "look beyond the polarized positions of 'economic growth' and 'environmental protection' which have crippled our system of land management planning and implementation in recent years." 141 CONG. REC. S 320 (Jan. 4, 1995).

The functional view of ecosystems, however, does not necessarily align with only a biocentric set of policy objectives for resources management. Likewise, even a commodity-oriented view of ecosystems must acknowledge that ecosystem functions are essential to the goal of continued delivery of an ecosystem's market-valued goods. But the functions themselves also provide economic value to humans in the form of *ecosystem services*. These include:

- mitigation of droughts and floods
- purification of air and water
- generation and preservation of soils and renewal of their fertility
- detoxification and decomposition of wastes
- pollination of crops and natural vegetation
- dispersal of seeds
- cycling and movement of nutrients
- control of the vast majority of potential agricultural pests
- maintenance of biodiversity
- protection of coastal shores from erosion by waves
- protection from the sun's harmful ultraviolet rays
- partial stabilization of climate
- moderation of weather extremes and their impacts

Estimates of the value of these services to humans are staggering at the global scale. In 1997, the economist Robert Costanza and a team of researchers gained headline news when they published an article in *Nature* magazine estimating the global value of ecosystm services at over $33 trillion. In the book on the topic published later that year, NATURE'S SERVICES: SOCIETAL DEPENDENCE ON NATURAL ECOSYSTEMS (Gretchen Daily ed., 1997), the biologist Gretchen Daily and other authors from the fields of ecology and economics fused decades worth of path-breaking research and scholarship on the economic value *to humans* of ecosystem functions.

There being no more unambiguous yardstick of value than money, legal scholars quickly adapted the concept of ecosystem services as an answer to the quest for a scientifically *and* politically viable metric for defining ecosystems and the objectives of ecosystem management. For example, in his review of *Nature's Services*, the first part of which is excerpted below (the remaining parts are reproduced *infra*), law professor James Salzman provided a framework for beginning to think of ecosystem functions in anthropo*metric*, and thus potentially more policy-viable, terms:

James Salzman, *Valuing Ecosystem Services*

24 Ecology Law Quarterly 887 (1997).

INTRODUCTION

Beneath the Arizona desert sun on September 26, 1991, amid reporters and flashing cameras, eight men and women entered a huge glass-enclosed structure and sealed shut the outer door. Their 3.15 acre miniature world, called Biosphere II, was designed to re-create the conditions of the earth (modestly named Biosphere I). Built at a cost of over $200 million, Biosphere II boasted a self-sustaining environment complete with rain forest, ocean, marsh, savanna, and desert habitats. The eight "Bionauts" intended to remain inside for two years. Within sixteen months, however, oxygen levels had plummeted thirty-three percent, nitrous oxide levels had increased 160-fold, ants and vines had overrun the vegetation, and nineteen of the twenty-five vertebrate species and all the pollinators had gone extinct. Eden did not last long.

What went wrong? With a multimillion dollar budget, the designers of Biosphere II had sought to recreate the level of basic services that support life itself—services such as purification of air and water, pest control, renewal of soil fertility, climate regulation, pollination of crops and vegetation, and waste detoxification and decomposition. Together, these are known as "ecosystem services," taken for granted yet absolutely essential to our existence, as the inhabitants of Biosphere II ruefully learned. Created by the interactions of living organisms with their environment, ecosystem services provide both the conditions and processes that sustain human life. Despite their obvious importance to our wellbeing, recognition of ecosystem services and the roles they play rarely enters policy debates or public discussion.

The general ignorance of ecosystem services is partly the result of modern society's dissociation between computers, cars and clothing on the one hand and biodiversity, nutrient cycling, and pollination on the other. It is perhaps not surprising that many children, when asked where milk comes from will reply without hesitation, "from the grocery store." The primary reason that ecosystem services are taken for granted, however, is that they are free. We explicitly value and place dollar figures on "ecosystem goods" such as timber and fish. Yet the services underpinning these goods generally have no market value—not because they are worthless, but rather because there is no market to capture and express their value directly.

Perhaps the most fundamental policy challenge facing ecosystem protection is that of valuation—how to translate an ecosystem's value into common units for assessment of development alternatives. The tough decisions revolve not around whether protecting ecosystems is a good thing but, rather, how much we should protect and at what cost. For example, how would the flood control and water purification services of a particular forest be diminished by the clearcutting or selective logging of 10%, 20% or 30% of its area? At what point does the ecosystem's net value to humans diminish, and by how much? Can the degradation of these services (in addition to ecosystem goods) be accurately measured? And, if so, how can partial loss of these services be balanced against benefits provided by development or pollution?

One might argue that ecosystem services cannot be evaluated, but this is clearly incorrect. We implicitly assess the value of these services every time we choose to protect or degrade the environment. The fundamental question is whether our implicit valuation of ecosystem services is accurate, and if not, what should be done about it. Indeed, studies such as *Nature's Services* indicate that our valuations are grossly and systematically understated. This essay explores the importance—and the challenges—of integrating ecosystem services research with the law. The potential is exciting, for a focus on ecosystem services would significantly change the way we understand and apply environmental law.

I. ECOSYSTEM SERVICES

Nature's Services addresses two basic questions: what services do natural ecosystems provide society, and what is a first approximation of their monetary value? Separate chapters describe the range of services and physical benefits provided by climate, biodiversity, soil, pollinators, pest control, the major biomes (oceans, freshwater, forests, and grasslands), and offer case studies of ecosystem services whose values are particularly well-known. The authors do not attempt to measure non-use values such as aesthetic or existence values, arguing that such work has already been done elsewhere. Instead, the authors determine lower-bound estimates of monetary value, using replacement costs where possible. Such information, it is hoped, will provide a basis for better incorporation of ecosystem services in decisionmaking.

The chapter on soil provides a useful example of the book's specific findings. More than a clump of dirt, soil is a complex matrix of organic and inorganic constituents transformed by numerous tiny organisms. The level of biological activity within soil is staggering. Under a square meter of pasture soil in Denmark, scientists identified over 50,000 worms, 48,000 small insects, and ten million nematodes. This living soil provides six ecosystem services: buffering and moderation of the hydrological cycle (so precipitation may be soaked up and metered out rather than rushing off the land in flash floods); physical support for plants; retention and delivery of nutrients to plants; disposal of wastes and dead organic matter; renewal of soil fertility; and regulation of the major element cycles. What are these services worth in the aggregate?

Take, for example, soil's service of providing nitrogen to plants. Nitrogen is supplied to plants through both nitrogen-fixing organisms and recycling of nutrients in the soil. As mentioned above, the authors rely primarily on replacement costs to estimate the value of ecosystem services. If nitrogen were provided by commercial fertilizer rather than natural processes, the lowest-cost estimate for its use on crops in the U.S. would be $45 billion, the figure for all land plants $320 billion. Most of the services identified in the book, however, such as breaking down dead organic material, are not valued in dollars because no technical substitutes are available.

Overall, *Nature's Services* reaches four conclusions. First, the services that ecosystems provide are both wide-ranging and critical. The question, "where would we be without ecosystem services?" is nonsensical, for we simply would not exist without them. Second, as Biosphere II's failure showed, the substitute technologies for most ecosystem services are either prohibitively expensive or nonexistent. Massive hydroponic gardening in the absence of soil is at least conceivable, if unfeasible. Substitutes for climate regulation are neither conceivable nor feasible. Third, our overall understanding of ecosystem services—the contributions of individual species, threshold effects, synergies, etc.—is poor. Finally, even taking into account the inevitable imprecision of such valuation exercises, ecosystem services have extraordinarily high values. A recent study in the journal *Nature* estimated their aggregate value at between $16–54 trillion per year. The global GNP is $18 trillion.

Whether such a total estimate is precisely accurate is beside the point. The sheer magnitude of their dollar figures dictates that ecosystem services cannot be treated as merely add-on considerations. Nor can they be shunted aside as soft numbers (as often occurs with scenic beauty or existence value) when assessing the impacts of development or pollution. Tastes may differ over beauty, but they are in universal accord over fertile soil. If the goal of ecologists is to wake people up with big numbers, *Nature's Services* delivers. But are these numbers a convertible currency?

The greatest shortcoming of *Nature's Services*, one openly admitted by its authors, is the macro-scale of the analysis. The fact that pollinators annually provide Americans up to $1.6 billion of service or that soil fertility is worth $45 billion is important to know for general policy direction, but that fact does not help to inform specific land-use or pollution permitting decisions. One cannot divide the $45 billion value of soil fertility by the nation's total agricultural acreage to determine the value of the services of five acres of land threatened by development. Thus, the greatest need for ecosystem service valuation is at the margins. Few policy decisions, thankfully, will involve obliterating an ecosystem service. Rather, policy decisions tend to be incremental. What is the extent of degradation to these services at various points along a continuum of impacts? Given the complexity of ecosystem services, the responses are almost certainly nonlinear.

This problem, the assessment and valuation of services at the margin, is at once the most useful and most difficult challenge for economists and ecologists. *Nature's Services* establishes the range of ecosystem services and their great significance. The next step is to pick up where the book leaves off and identify how ecosystem services should be explicitly considered in real-life decisions, for ecosystem services are rarely, if ever, considered in current agency cost-benefit analyses.

NOTES & QUESTIONS

1. Ecosystem services are often categorized according to the kinds of roles they play in nature and in benefitting humans. A good working definition using this approach can be found in the United States Forest Service's regulation for forest ecosystem management planning:

Ecosystem services. Benefits people obtain from ecosystems, including:

(1) *Provisioning services,* such as clean air and fresh water, as well as energy, fuel, forage, fiber, and minerals;

(2) *Regulating services,* such as long term storage of carbon; climate regulation; water filtration, purification, and storage; soil stabilization; flood control; and disease regulation;

(3) *Supporting services,* such as pollination, seed dispersal, soil formation, and nutrient cycling; and

(4) *Cultural services,* such as educational, aesthetic, spiritual, and cultural heritage values, as well as recreational experiences and tourism opportunities.

36 C.F.R. 219.19 (2012).

2. The concept of ecosystem services suggests that even an individual tree provides some service value to humans—that it provides economic utility other than its commodity value as cut timber. Salzman suggests that the challenge facing efforts to make the ecosystem services concept a policy-viable tool is that it is much easier to determine a single tree's commodity value than its service value. In short, the theory and methodology of valuing ecosystem services at micro levels are far behind the abilities of the market to generate commodity values. On the other hand, we know with certainty that ecosystem values are extremely high at macro levels. Is knowing that enough to justify moving ahead with ecosystem service values as a policy-shaping tool before we refine the microeconomic understanding? For a comprehensive review of the theory and literature on the ecology, geography, and economics of ecosystem services, see J.B. Ruhl, Steven E. Kraft, and Christopher L. Lant, The Law and Policy of Ecosystem Services (2007).

3. As an example of the macro/micro scale problem of ecosystem service valuation, one of the classic examples of ecosystem services is pollination of crops by wild honeybees and other pollinators. Studies from organic watermelon farms in California's Central Valley show that a variety of wild bees from nearby oak woods and chaparral provided sufficient crop pollination to make hiring of domesticated honeybee services unnecessary. Of course, wild bees need wild places in which to live, so one cost of developing the oak woods and chaparral for other uses is the loss of the "free" pollination services of wild bees for nearby farms. *See Bees Bear Fruit—For Free,* Nature Conservancy, Summer 2003, at 14. But although we know that, overall, wild bees provide a valuable service because we can identify the cost of hiring domesticated honeybee services, how could the value of this service be quantified on a per-acre of wild habitat basis? And how would we determine which farms suffer the costs of losing these services when the wild habitat is developed? Answers to those questions can be found from research studying the effects of proximity to forest habitat for wild pollinators on the productivity of coffee trees on coffee plantations in Costa Rica. The field studies found that trees close to such habitat were 20 percent more productive than trees far away from such habitat because they receive more pollinator visits and also enjoy a greater variety of pollinator species. This translated into $62,000 in additional annual revenue for a typical plantation. The value of the wild habitat were it transformed into grazing land (which local property owners consider a "high" value use of the land) would be about

$24,000 per year for the typical parcel needed to generate these pollination benefits. Domesticated pollination services are not generally available for hire. Clearly, then, coffee plantations near these forest habitats are reaping an ecosystem service-based use of the land that is capable of being valued in hard dollar terms and compared to a commodity-based use of the land. What policy should we adopt given this new knowledge? Consider these possible alternative approaches:

- Do nothing, relying on basic market forces to drive the coffee plantation owners to buy out the forest land owners given the higher value they derive from the land versus the current owners derive by converting the land to grazing.

- Use "command and control" regulation to limit the ability of the forest land owners to convert their lands into grazing or other uses that eliminate the forest habitat.

- Tax coffee sales at wholesale or at export to generate public funds to buy out the forest lands and create preserves that provide not only the pollination services, but other services the coffee plantation owners might not value and thus might not consider in deciding whether to buy out the forest lands.

4. Dailey's and Costanza's work on ecosystem service valuation opened up a sizable rift among ecologists, many of whom argue that it is immoral to attempt to assign anthropometric values to biometric processes. On the one hand, many ecologists contend that it is morally wrong to value the ecological attributes of a resource, as valuation implies that these attributes are only of relative and not absolute importance. Even under an anthropocentric view, they would contend that ecological considerations, such as the maintenance of ecological integrity, are of such fundamental importance to future generations of people that they should never be compromised no matter how large any assessment of the economic benefits of changing an ecosystem may be. On the other hand, respond Costanza, Daily, and others advocating ecosystem service valuation, both as a society and as individuals we make choices and tradeoffs about ecosystems every day. These choices necessarily imply valuations. To say that we shouldn't try to perform more precise, quantifiable valuation of ecosystems is to simply deny these tradeoffs are already occurring, and are occurring in the absence of reliable data. Who has the better argument?

B. WHAT IS ECOSYSTEM MANAGEMENT?

As we refine our understanding of ecosystems and design a politically and legally viable set of units for representing what they are and what they mean to us, the next threshold question on the way to formulating a law of ecosystem management is deciding the specific management goals and methods. After all, ideally the law will simply put the goals and methods into motion. Thus, at the most fundamental level:

Ecosystem management is management driven by explicit goals, executed by policies, protocols, and practices, and made adaptable by monitoring and research based on our best understanding of the ecological interactions and processes necessary to sustain ecosystem composition, structure, and function.

Norman L. Christensen, *The Report of the Ecological Society of America Committee on the Scientific Basis for Ecosystem Management*, 6 ECOLOGICAL APPLICATIONS 665 (1996). Of course, this only begs the question: What are the goals, policies, protocols, and practices of ecosystem management?

Indeed, there is yet a threshold question to consider before debating goals and methods. Assuming we have agreed on where an ecosystem is and whether to use natural function preservation, commodity extraction value, service delivery value, or some combination thereof as the yardstick of ecosystem management, the initial management challenge is in devising the policy metrics with which to define ecosystem management goals and measure the performance of the policies and practices used to achieve them. The specification of metrics, goals, and methods, in that order, thus are the three central challenges to devising a coherent ecosystem management policy.

1. METRICS SELECTION

As challenging as it is to manage a business, the goal is usually quite straightforward (make a profit) and the method, at least in theory, can be textbook simple (sell more product). There is also no shortage of readily available measurements for expressing business goals and measuring performance. Business and economic performance indicators abound, and management can use them to make strategic decisions about employment, capital expenditure, product line expansion, and so on. Market forces ruthlessly weed out bad decisions and reward the good ones. Every newspaper has pages of business and economic data available to investors. CEO employment packages now routinely use one or a combination of precisely measurable performance indicators to set compensation and bonuses. In short, although figuring out how to boost profits can be quite a challenge, knowing where profits stand is not.

Ecosystem management does not have it so easy. To be sure, an ecosystem managed purely for its commodity value units (e.g., a farm, a fishery, a timber forest) can take advantage of business management performance indicators, but management for other purposes becomes far more complicated to evaluate. For example, if we were to prescribe "no net loss of habitat" as the goal for management of a large park or forest, what would that mean? We could use acres as the yardstick for determining net position over time. But we know that not all habitat is created equal—that some habitat is "better" than other habitat. Merely keeping the number of acres constant could lead to a significant degradation of habitat quality over time. So, we could use total habitat quality as the index and forget about counting acres. But quality based on what? Quality for rodents? For birds? High quality bird habitat may make low quality rodent habitat, so which species wins? And how do we quantify habitat quality in any event? We could avoid those questions altogether by focusing on ecosystem processes as the measure of habitat, as in no net loss of ecosystem processes. This would leave it to whatever happens under those processes to decide what the habitat looks like and which species occupy it. While this seems to be the direction most ecosystem management literature takes, it simply raises a different set of questions about measurement, such as which processes to count and how to count them.

Alas, ecosystem management law cannot get very far off the ground until these very basic questions are answered. It is relatively easy to describe ecosystem processes and declare abstract goals for them, such as "protect," "maintain," or "restore," but those are not legally viable concepts until agencies, courts, and interest groups have a common language for determining whether management decisions comply with the law. Returning to Professor Salzman's review of *Nature's Services*, we see that achieving agreement on this fundamental metrics selection issue for ecosystem management, in this case taking the ecosystem services perspective of ecosystems, is no mean feat:

James Salzman, Valuing Ecosystem Services
24 Ecology Law Quarterly 887 (1997).

II. Valuing Ecosystems

So how does one value an ecosystem? Assume our object of study is a wetland along the banks of the Potomac. The first step lies in defining the ecosystem's contribution to human wellbeing. An ecosystem may be characterized by its physical features (site-specific characteristics such as landscape context, vegetation type, salinity), its goods (vegetation, fish), its services (nutrient cycling, water retention) or its amenities (recreation, birdwatching). These four aspects may not be complementary. For example, one could manage a wetland for cranberry production at the expense of primary productivity and services. Furthermore, the location of the system will be a critical factor of its net utility because location determines the distribution of goods and services. An ecosystem's carbon sequestration and biodiversity will be valuable even if distant from human populations, but its role in pollination and flood control likely will not. Thus two identical ecosystems may have very different values depending on their landscape context.

Economists classify these characteristics using four categories. The most obvious category includes consumable ecosystem goods such as cranberries and crabs that are exchanged in markets and easily priced (direct market uses). Activities such as hiking and fishing (direct non-market uses) as well as more intangible existence and option values (non-market, non-use) are not exchanged in markets. As a result, their values must be determined indirectly by shadow pricing techniques such as hedonic pricing, travel-cost methodologies, or contingent valuation. Ecosystem services are categorized as indirect non-market uses, for while they provide clear benefits to humans they are neither directly "consumed" nor exchanged in markets. These are also classic public goods because their use cannot be exclusively controlled.

Currently, there are three challenges to incorporating benefits of ecosystem services more directly into decisionmaking: identifying services on a local scale, measuring the value of these services, and projecting their future value. First, ecologists must understand the services provided by a specific ecosystem. For example, wetlands provide an important service in nutrient trapping, which retards and prevents eutrophication. The capacity to trap nutrients depends on the biophysical capacity of the site (e.g., its vegetation, benthic community, size, slope) and on the in-flow from adjacent water sources. Data on these factors can be provided in great detail. One can make empirically sound predictions that actions on a gross scale, such as clearcutting, will affect nutrient flows and services, or that a loss of populations reduces ecosystem resiliency. In aggregate, such knowledge can provide policy guidance in warning against extreme actions. But in most cases, our scientific knowledge is inadequate to predict with any certainty how specific local actions affecting these factors will impact the local ecosystem services themselves.

This lack of knowledge is due both to the lack of relevant data and to the multivariate complexity of the task. Analysis of how ecosystems provide services has proceeded slowly because ecosystem level experiments are difficult, costly, and lengthy. More important, research to date has focused much more on understanding ecosystem processes than determining ecosystem services, and how an ecosystem works is not the same as the services it provides. This focus has been reinforced, and partly driven, by regulatory requirements. Federal and state wetland regulations assess the adequacy of wetland mitigation on the basis of the site's functional capacity, not on the basis of the services actually provided and their extant benefits to humans. For this reason alone, publications such as *Nature's Services* are valuable: they increase awareness of the need to shift the focus of ecological research toward provision of services.

As noted above, an ecosystem's benefit to humans is not a straightforward biophysical measure, for identical ecosystems in different locations will have very different values. The value of a wetland's nutrient trapping service, for instance, depends on the location of its out-flow. Does it flow to shellfish beds (high value) or a fast-flowing ocean current (low value)? In valuing each ecosystem service, and indirectly the "cost" of its diminution, substitutes become important. Will the threatened service be replaced by other natural processes? Is it redundant or scarce? To what extent can technology overcome or mitigate these harms? If the loss of a service is important and nonlinear, when will it become asymptotically more valuable approaching the point of collapse? None of these questions can be answered without intricate, localized knowledge of the ecosystem service itself.

Despite these difficulties, let us assume we understand fully the ecosystem service and have determined its current value. Even then, we face a third challenge when we try to determine in dollars the future stream of services flowing from the current biophysical features and landscape of the ecosystem. This figure is important because the net present value of most proposed actions that will degrade an ecosystem, such as shopping mall developments, take into account future streams of income. To ensure a full accounting of costs and benefits, the future "income" flow of the ecosystem service should be factored into its current value as well, since that value may change over time due to land-use patterns, weather, pollution, etc. How then does one link a site's current ecological characteristics with future ecosystem services?

[T]here is no clear method yet for valuing or measuring ecosystem services, much less future services. Differing expectations also contribute to the disparity. In the environmental context, uncertain values are often set at zero. In contrast, when assessing corporate acquisitions, financial analysts routinely provide credible values greater than zero. Uncertainty is an accepted part of the profession. Finally, the lack of information plays a role. Making accurate projections of ecosystem services (or future stock prices) requires a great deal of robust data. Yet basic research and regulatory compliance have focused far more on the biophysical capacities of ecosystems than on their services. Moreover, information on ecosystem services is expensive to collect because the benefits of ecosystem services are a public good. Since there is no financial gain from "investing" in services (unlike with IBM's stock) there is no secondary market generating relevant data.

The combination of methodological difficulty, inherent complexity, and lack of data makes placing absolute dollar figures on local ecosystem services unfeasible in many cases. At the same time, the current research and regulatory focus on ecosystems' biophysical measures is too removed from valuation of services. Is there a middle ground to inform decisionmakers?

Wall Street and IBM's stock price may provide some guidance. As noted above, many of the sources on which analysts rely to value stocks are not, in fact, monetary. They are composite indicators such as market strength, consumer confidence, and housing starts. Similarly, some of the most advanced work in wetlands valuation is now focusing on nonmonetary indicators. This research area combines traditional biophysical measures (i.e., the capacity to provide ecosystem services and goods) with landscape context to determine the opportunity and impact of providing these services to people. Such indicators do not provide dollar figures for ecosystem services, but they do provide more accurate bases for assessing relative qualities of different ecosystems.

NOTES & QUESTIONS

1. The installment of Salzman's article used in this section pinpoints why it is that we can more easily determine a tree's commodity value than its service value: unlike commodities such as lumber, ecosystem services are indirect non-market uses, for while they provide clear benefits to humans they are neither directly "consumed" nor exchanged in markets, and their use cannot be exclusively controlled. But is that necessarily the case? Could ecosystem services be made a form of private property that owners could withhold or remove from distribution? If so, a direct use market in ecosystem services would arise as the beneficiaries of the service values pay to have them restored. Salzman's point, of course, is that it is difficult to withhold the service of, say, air purification. Some ecosystem services, however, can be withheld or removed by property owners, such as water purification from riparian vegetation. But who "owns" those services? And why is there presently no market in them?

2. Another problem with ecosystem services that Salzman's work reveals is that it may be too expensive, given current knowledge, to measure the metric. Measuring ecosystem service value delivery at local levels takes time and extensive, expensive research. Less elegant, less precise, but far less expensive metrics thus threaten to crowd out ecosystem service values as the measure of policy performance. In the context of wetland conservation, for example, a cheap, fast, and easy way to measure policy performance is to count acres of wetlands under a "no net loss" policy goal. Measuring wetland process integrity is far more difficult, and measuring wetland service value delivery is yet more difficult. Not surprisingly, therefore, actual wetlands conservation policy stuck closely to acres as the currency well into the 1990s before more functional approaches were employed. *See* J. B. Ruhl & R. Juge Gregg, *Integrating Ecosystem Services Into Environmental Law: A Case Study of Wetlands Mitigation Banking*, 20 STANFORD ENVTL. L. J. 365 (2001).

3. Hence the dilemma: we know that ecosystem functions provide services that are valuable to humans, but we do not know how either (1) efficiently to measure those values or (2) efficiently to exchange the values in markets even if we could measure them. So when a landowner decides to convert riparian vegetation areas to other uses such as crop production or suburban housing, what metric *are* we supposed to use in order to weigh the ecosystem effects of that decision?

4. Does this metrics selection problem explain why the species-by-species approach of the Endangered Species Act remains essentially the default approach for much of what we call ecosystem management, particularly on nonpublic lands? In effect, can we use endangered species as the metrics for much of ecosystem management policy?

2. GOAL SELECTION

Almost every definition offered of ecosystem management includes some normative goals-statement dimension. Indeed, the very notion of ecosystem management generally invokes debate cast in normative terms. At one extreme, some people decry ecosystem management *on any basis* as an unwarranted human interference with nature. This "nature knows best" and "leave only footprints" camp follows the preservation principle of "nondestruction, noninterference, and generally, nonmeddling." Tom Regan, *The Nature and Possibility of an Environmental Ethic*, 3 ENVIRONMENTAL ETHICS 31 (1981). Wildness is their metric, and "many who value wildness, although unable to say exactly what it is, are nonetheless positive that less management is better management." Peter Alpert, *Incarnating Ecosystem Management*, 9 CONSERVATION BIOLOGY 952 (1995). For them, therefore, ecosystem management is an unwarranted intrusion on the wildness of ecosystems.

Others, however, condemn ecosystem management as an unwarranted intrusion on private property rights. Allan K. Fitzsimmons, for example, has argued that ecosystem management, "if fully implemented, would greatly intrude on the property rights of all Americans." ALLAN K. FITZSIMMONS, DEFENDING ILLUSIONS 16 (1999). It is a form of "national land use planning wherein nature protection takes precedence over improvements in human wellbeing." *Id.* For him and others of this view, therefore, ecosystem management is a form of "nature worship," overly biocentric in perspective and relying too heavily on management of private land to achieve its goals.

Yet another view, this one in support of an active framework of ecosystem management, is that it is a form of beneficial interference, designed usually to undo or impede all or many of the results of past human destructive interference, and based on some sense of what the ecosystem's "natural" conditions should be. As the environmental ethicist Mark Michael has pointed out, "to claim that a human action interferes with an ecosystem or species is to say nothing more than that its presence or occurrence makes a difference in terms of what happens to the ecosystem or species." Mark A. Michael, *How to Interfere With Nature*, 23 ENVIRONMENTAL ETHICS 135 (2001). Interference, in other words, is simply a causal state; whether the effects are desirable is a different matter. And, as Michael posits, the effects of properly designed interference, even in the eyes of the most ardent preservationist, may be healthy for the ecosystem.

The latter view, of course, is what justifies publishing the remainder of this part of the text! There will be no law of ecosystem management under extreme versions of the wildness principle or the property rights principle, except by default. Moreover, given the rather unavoidable realities that humans are on the planet and that part of the planet consists of private property, some exploration of how to manage the whole package of ecosystems, humans, and property seems worth undertaking.

Yet with that threshold normative debate out of the way for our immediate pedagogical purposes (to be taken up again *infra*), only more numerous and complicated normative debates are opened. In short, what are the goals of a "beneficial interference" framework of ecosystem management? While consensus on that question remains elusive, the following landmark article by Edward Grumbine has become a reference point for virtually every person who has made a stab at an answer.

R. Edward Grumbine, *What Is Ecosystem Management?*
8 Conservation Biology 27 (1994).

Introduction

Deep in a mixed conifer forest on the east side of the Washington Cascades, a U.S. Forest Service silviculturalist, responding to a college student's query, suggests that ecosystem management means snag retention and management of coarse woody debris on clear cut units.

In northern Florida on a US. Department of Defense reservation, a team of biologists and managers struggles with the design of a fire management plan in longleaf pine (Pinus palustris) forests that mimics natural disturbance regimes while minimizing the risk of burning adjacent private lands.

To avert what he calls "national train wrecks," Interior Secretary Bruce Babbitt announces that the Clinton Administration plans to shift federal policy away from a single species approach to one that looks "at entire ecosystems."

Commenting on a draft federal framework for the Greater Yellowstone Ecosystem that proposes increased interagency cooperation, a lawyer claims that "Congress does not intend that national forests should be managed like national parks" and that there exists no need to create ecosystem management.

Other observers in the Greater Yellowstone region contend that an ecosystem approach could provide just the holistic management necessary for sustaining resources in a complex ecological/political landscape.

What is ecosystem management?

The above vignettes portray but a few of the various interpretations of ecosystem management that can be found in the conservation biology, resource management, and popular literature. Since the ecosystem approach is relatively new, and still unformed, this is not surprising. As any concept evolves, debates over definition, fundamental principles, and policy implications proceed apace. Yet the discussion surrounding ecosystem management is not merely academic. Nor is it limited to those scientists, resources professionals, and policymakers who work directly with federal management issues. The debate is raising profound questions for most people who are concerned with the continuing loss of biodiversity at all scales and across many administrative boundaries and ownerships. Along with defining the ecosystem management approach as a new policy framework there appears to be a parallel process of redefining the fundamental role of humans in nature.

Dominant Themes of Ecosystem Management

Ecosystem management has not been uniformly defined or consistently applied by federal or state management agencies. Yet consensus is developing, at least within the academic literature. Using standard keyword search techniques focused on "ecosystem management," "ecosystem health," "biodiversity" "management," "adaptive management," etc., I surveyed papers published on ecosystem management in peer reviewed journals (Conservation Biology, Environmental Management, Ecological Applications, Society and Natural Resources etc.) up through June 1993 to determine where agreement exists on the subject. Articles came from a broad spectrum of disciplines including conservation biology, resource management, and public policy. I also reviewed books with substantive accounts of ecosystem management, lay environmental publications, and several federal and state-level documents that discuss ecosystem level policymaking.

Ten dominant themes of ecosystem management emerged from my review. Dominant themes were those attributes that authors identified explicitly as critical to the definition, implementation, or overall comprehension of ecosystem management. The ten dominant themes emerged repeatedly throughout the literature. I believe the following themes faithfully represent areas of agreement.

1. **Hierarchical Context.** A focus on any one level of the biodiversity hierarchy (genes, species, populations, ecosystems, landscapes) is not sufficient. When working on a problem at any one level or scale, managers must seek the connections between all levels. This is often described as a "systems" perspective.

2. **Ecological Boundaries.** Management requires working across administrative/political boundaries (i.e., national forests, national parks) and defining ecological boundaries at appropriate scales.

3. **Ecological Integrity**. Norton defines managing for ecological integrity as protecting total native diversity (species, populations, ecosystems) and the ecological patterns and processes that maintain that diversity. Most authors discuss this as conservation of viable populations of native species, maintaining natural disturbance regimes, reintroduction of native, extirpated species, representation of ecosystems across natural ranges of variation, etc.

4. **Data Collection.** Ecosystem management requires more research and data collection (i.e., habitat inventory/classification, disturbance regime dynamics, baseline species and population assessment) as well as better management and use of existing data.

5. **Monitoring.** Managers must track the results of their actions so that success or failure may be evaluated quantitatively. Monitoring creates an ongoing feedback loop of useful information.

6. **Adaptive Management.** Adaptive management assumes that scientific knowledge is provisional and focuses on management as a learning process or continuous experiment where incorporating the results of previous actions allows managers to remain flexible and adapt to uncertainty.

7. **Interagency Cooperation.** Using ecological boundaries requires cooperation between federal, state, and local management agencies as well as private parties. Managers must team to work together and integrate conflicting legal mandates and management goals.

8. **Organizational Change.** Implementing ecosystem management requires changes in the structure of land management agencies and the way they operate. These may range from the simple (forming an interagency committee) to the complex (changing professional norms, altering power relationships).

9. **Humans Embedded In Nature.** People cannot be separated from nature. Humans are fundamental influences on ecological patterns and processes and are in turn affected by them.

10. **Values.** Regardless of the role of scientific knowledge, human values play a dominant role in ecosystem management goals.

These ten dominant themes form the basis of a working definition: *Ecosystem management integrates scientific knowledge of ecological relationships within a complex sociopolitical and values framework toward the general goal of protecting native ecosystem integrity over the long term.*

Ecosystem Management Goals

Most of the authors cited in this review agree that setting clear goals is crucial to the success of ecosystem management. Within the overall goal of sustaining ecological integrity, five specific goals were frequently endorsed:

1. Maintain viable populations of all native species in situ.

2. Represent, within protected areas, all native ecosystem types across their natural range of variation.

3. Maintain evolutionary and ecological processes (i.e., disturbance regimes, hydrological processes, nutrient cycles, etc.).

4. Manage over periods of time long enough to maintain the evolutionary potential of species and ecosystems.

5. Accommodate human use and occupancy within these constraints.

The first four of these goals are value statements derived from current scientific knowledge that aim to reduce (and eventually eliminate) the biodiversity crisis. The fifth goal acknowledges the vital (if problematic) role that people have to play in all aspects of the ecosystem management debate.

These fundamental goals provide a striking contrast to the goals of traditional resource management. Though different agencies operate under a variety of federal and state mandates, current resource management in the U.S. is based on maximizing production of goods and services, whether these involve number of board feet (commodities) or wilderness recreational visitor days (amenities). Managers and lawmakers have always been careful to speak of "balance" and "sustained yield" but this language is obfuscatory—balance has never been defined in any U.S. environmental law and sustained yield has often been confused with sustainability.

If ecosystem management is to take hold and flourish, the relationship between the new goal of protecting ecological integrity and the old standard of providing goods and services for humans must be reconciled. Much of the oft-complained "fuzziness" or lack of precision surrounding ecosystem management derives from alternative views on this point. Kessler et al., for example, suggest that ecosystem management represents a further evolution of multiple use, sustained yield policy where managers "must not diminish the importance of products and services, but instead treat them within a broader ecological and social context." These authors envision ecosystem-level management as an expansion of focus from particular resource outputs to the ecosystem as "life support system [for humans]." Kessler et al. fail to see that expanding the scale of concern by itself does not address the fact that there are certain ecological limits in any system which constrain human use. Ecological integrity as expressed by the five specific goals explicitly considers all resource use as a managerial artifact that may flow sustainably from natural systems only if basic ecosystem patterns and processes are maintained.

Echoing Kessler et al., the most detailed Forest Service working definition of ecosystem management exemplifies lack of clarity over the key policy problem of defining ecosystem management goals. The report defines the philosophy of ecosystem management as sustaining "the patterns and processes of ecosystems for the benefit of future generations, while providing goods and services for each generation." The study characterizes the main limiting factors to ecosystem management as defining societal expectations, integrating these expectations with the sustainable capabilities of ecosystems, and filling information gaps in baseline data describing historical ecosystem variability and disturbance regimes. The Forest Service prescribes adaptive management as a process to blend ecosystem sustainability and human concerns. Specific solutions offered, however, are problematic. If societal goals conflict with ecosystem sustainability, cost/benefit analyses are offered as the standard for solutions. Adaptive management is described as an ongoing experiment yet "landscapes can be restored," managers are said to already be capable of mimicking natural disturbance regimes successfully, and there is speculation that future experiments may reveal new sustainable ecosystem states that may differ from evolutionary and historical states. In short, the Forest Service defines the goals of ecosystem management narrowly within the old resource management paradigm ("for the benefit of future generations") and seeks to operationalize this goal within a positivistic scientific framework. These characterizations of ecosystem management are also found in the other government policy documents in this review.

As several analysts point out, however, it takes more than scientific knowledge to reframe successfully complex policy problems. Knowledge of organizational structure and behavior as well as the policy process itself are equally important. Yet none of the five government treatments of the ecosystem management concept reviewed here mention substantive organizational change, nor do they discuss the policy process as it is defined by policy scientists. This emphasis on science is an artifact of the training and professional norms of the major group writing about ecosystem management—scientists. But defining ecosystem management goals is also a political process; those authors advocating a new vision of ecological integrity are more often employed independently or in academia. Authors affiliated with government agencies tend to support the Forest Service version of ecosystem management. As policy analyst Tim Clark (personal communication) has pointed out, " 'the ecosystem management debate' is really a complex, competitive, conflictual social process about whose values will dominate, it is not about science."

Management goals are statements of values—certain outcomes are selected over others. Choosing the management goal of maintaining ecological integrity along with the five specific goals may be debated, but in the academic and popular literature there is general agreement that maintaining ecosystem integrity should take precedence over any other management goal. This may be due partially to the fact that, given the rate and scale of environmental deterioration along with our profound scientific ignorance of ecological patterns aid processes, we are in no position to make judgments about what ecosystem elements to favor in our management efforts. An increasing number of people also believe that humans do not have any privileged ethical standing from which to arbitrate these types of questions.

Conclusion

History tells us that change does not always come easily, peacefully, or in a planned manner. Implementing the short-term scientific aspects of ecosystem management is daunting enough. For the moment, however, ecosystem management provides our best opportunity to describe, understand, and fit in with nature. We know that the risk of extinction increases under certain conditions, that wildfires cannot long be suppressed without significant successional consequences, that political power must somehow become less centralized, that whales and spiders must also be allowed to vote. We are also coming to realize that resourcism has for so long prevented us from putting our ecological knowledge to work that we are facing the limits of life on Earth for many species. Where once we thought endangered species were the problem, we now face the loss of entire ecosystems.

Ecosystem management, at root, is an invitation, a call to restorative action that promises a healthy future for the entire biotic enterprise. The choice is ours—a world where the gap between people and nature grows to an incomprehensible chasm, or a world of damaged but recoverable ecological integrity where the operative word is hope.

NOTES & QUESTIONS

1. The unmistakable unifying theme of Grumbine's treatment of ecosystem management is "the general goal of protecting native ecosystem integrity over the long term." Is it self-evident what a "native ecosystem" is, or what its "integrity" involves? Is Grumbine suggesting that any ecosystem management approach necessarily must adopt this as its goal to be considered true ecosystem management, or simply that the weight of academic literature at the time—around the mid-1990s—had identified this as the goal? Could ecosystem management chart protection of something other than "native ecosystem integrity" as its goal and still be ecosystem management? If so, what would that goal be?

2. Adhering to his "native ecosystem integrity" model, Grumbine criticizes Kessler et al. for positing as the goal of ecosystem management protecting "the patterns and processes of ecosystems for the benefit of future generations, while providing goods and services for each generation." Grumbine suggests that this is an overly anthropocentric perspective and the wrong "philosophy" of ecosystem management. How different are Grumbine's and Kessler's philosophies of ecosystem management? With which do you agree more?

3. The disagreement between Grumbine's and Kessler's approaches was covered thoroughly in Thomas R. Stanley Jr., *Ecosystem Management and the Arrogance of Humanism*, 9 CONSERVATION BIOLOGY 255 (1995). The debate permeated early ecosystem management theory and practice. Compare these two early definitions of ecosystem management:

> A collaborative process that strives to reconcile the promotion of economic opportunities and livable communities with the conservation of ecological integrity and biodiversity. THE KEYSTONE NATIONAL POLICY DIALOGUE ON ECOSYSTEM MANAGEMENT 6 (1996).

> Management of natural resources using systemwide concepts to ensure that all plants and animals in ecosystems are maintained at viable levels in native habitats and basic ecosystem processes are perpetuated indefinitely. U.S. FISH AND WILDLIFE SERVICE, AN ECOSYSTEM APPROACH TO FISH AND WILDLIFE CONSERVATION 4 (1994).

Are these close in theme? Which is closer to Grumbine? To Kessler? Does lack of agreement over the basic objectives of ecosystem management suggest that fundamental normative decisions have yet to be made about ecosystem management policy?

4. Consider the Grumbine-Kessler debate in terms of the five ecosystem unit frameworks discussed in the previous section of the text—geographic, management, functions, commodities, and services. What mix of these comes closest to capturing Grumbine's philosophy of ecosystem management? Kessler's? Are they much different? Would any particular mix of units preclude using Grumbine's vision of ecosystem management policy, or Kessler's?

5. Grumbine also suggests the need for taking a "systems approach" to ecosystem management, which he defined as requiring that "when working on a problem at any one level or scale, managers must seek the connections between all levels." Notice that the U.S. Fish and Wildlife Service's definition of ecosystem management quoted in Note 3 above also relies on "management of natural resources using systemwide concepts." What are "systemwide" concepts? In large part these references are to the system component of eco*system*, and to the development in the discipline of ecology of a greater understanding and appreciation of the complex, adaptive, dynamic nature of ecological settings. As noted previously, while once thought of as reaching constant equilibrium states, as in so-called climax forests, today's understanding of ecosystems is that they are governed by forces of short-term disturbance (e.g., fire, flood, and drought) and long-term change (e.g., decline of one species, gradual change in climate), and that what was taken as "equilibrium" and "the balance of nature" is actually a state of constant and resilient adaptation at a *system* level to these perturbations. As one of the leaders of this "new ecology" put it:

Throughout the 20th century, most theoretical and empirical research attempted to understand the structure and dynamics of populations, communities, and ecosystems by identifying their components and studying their relations in isolation from the complicating influences of larger systems. This research strategy was successful in elucidating fundamental ecological processes: response to stresses of extreme abiotic conditions; limiting resources of food, water, and inorganic nutrients; and the biotic interactions of competition, mutualism, predation, parasitism, and disease. It was less successful in revealing the complex patterns of temporal and spatial variation in abundance, distribution, and diversity of species or the complicated roles of species in ecosystems. By the 1980s, it was becoming apparent that more holistic, synthetic approaches were needed. To understand realistically complex ecological systems, it is necessary to study how the components affect and are affected by the larger, more complicated systems within which they are located.

James H. Brown et al., *Complex Species Interactions and the Dynamics of Ecological Systems: Long-Term Experiments*, 293 SCIENCE 643 (2001). Legal scholars picked up quickly on these emerging scientific models to consider the effect of systems-based ecology on our overall approach to environmental law and policy. *See, e.g.,* Symposium, *Beyond the Balance of Nature: Environmental Law Faces the New Ecology*, 7 DUKE ENVTL. L. J. 1 (1996); Symposium, *Ecology and the Law*, 69 CHICAGO-KENT L. REV. 847 (1994); Jonathan Baert Wiener, *Law and the New Ecology: Evolution, Categories, and Consequences*, 22 ECOLOGY L. Q. 325 (1995).

6. Just as the "old ecology" had its model of equilibrium and nature in balance, so too must the "new ecology" develop models of complex ecosystem dynamics. *See* Norman L. Christiansen et al., *The Report of the Ecological Society of America Committee on the Scientific Basis for Ecosystem Management*, 6 ECOLOGICAL APPLICATIONS 665 (1996) ("Ecosystem management should be rooted in the best current models of ecosystem functioning."). But modeling equilibrium is easier than modeling disequilibrium. The effort requires access to vast repositories of data and sophisticated computational capacity. The scientific community argued that substantial progress would be needed on both fronts in order to implement ecosystem management. *See* James S. Clark et al., *Ecological Forecasts: An Emerging Imperative*, 293 SCIENCE 657 (2001).

7. Grumbine later took stock of the development of ecosystem management policy after his landmark article, in R.E. Grumbine, *Reflections on "What is Ecosystem Management,"* 11 CONSERVATION BIOLOGY 41 (1997), and concluded based on interviews and a literature review that "many [resource] managers and academics believe that the 10 themes described in 'What is Ecosystem Management' remain useful as a framework for specific applications of EM. No major additions or subtractions have been proposed, though much new information has come into light."

8. If Grumbine is correct that his version of ecosystem management continues to make sense to most resource managers and academics in terms of policy goals selection, is it also important to know whether it has a sound scientific basis? A committee of the Ecological Society of America considered that issue early in the history of ecosystem management thinking, concluding that there is a good match between the current scientific understanding of ecosystems dynamics and the ecosystem management approach Grumbine outlined, particularly in light of the threats to ecosystem integrity researchers have begun to identify. *See* Norman L. Christiansen et al., *The Report of the Ecological Society of America Committee on the Scientific Basis for Ecosystem Management*, 6 ECOLOGICAL APPLICATIONS 665 (1996).

10. When all is said and done, is Grumbine's vision of ecosystem management—indeed, *any* vision of ecosystem management—just a fantasy? Is it really possible to accomplish most, or even a few, of what Grumbine suggests are the core goals of ecosystem management? At least one commentator believes not, suggesting that all forms of ecosystem management rely unrealistically on the ability of humans, through policy and technology, to manipulate ecological conditions. Under this view

> the assumptions underlying ecosystem management are presumptuous and false. Ecosystem management cannot deliver what it has promised, and to deny this is to set a destructive course destined to fail. . . As currently espoused, ecosystem management is a magical theory . . . that promises the impossible—that we can have our cake and eat it too. Worse, however, it addresses only the symptoms of the problem and not the problem itself. The problem is not how to maintain current levels of resource output while also maintaining ecosystem integrity; the problem is how to control population growth and constrain resource consumption.

Thomas R. Stanley, Jr., *Ecosystem Management and the Arrogance of Humanism*, 9 CONSERVATION BIOLOGY 255 (1995). If true, the Grumbine-Kessler debate is rather moot. Naturally, however, your authors hope you will forge ahead in these materials even if Stanley has you convinced that ecosystem management is a mirage!

11. Define nature. What is it? Where is it? Can nature exist where ecosystem management has tread? Can you define nature without reference to humans? Try it! For more, see Steven Vogel, *Environmental Philosophy after the End of Nature*, 24 ENVTL. ETHICS 23 (2002), and BILL MCKIBBEN, THE END OF NATURE (1989).

12. Global climate change will throw a bit of a monkey wrench into ecosystem management goal selection, particularly under Grumbine's "native ecosystem integrity" model. Climate change could make the concept of natural conditions difficult to integrate into management decisions, as ecologists now warn of a no-analog future—ecological variability unprecedented in the history of ecology, riddled with nonlinear feedback and feed-forward loops, previously unknown emergent properties, and new thresholds of irreversible change. Matthew C. Fitzpatrick & William W. Hargrove, *The Projection of Species Distribution Models and the Problem of Non-Analog Climate*, 18 BIODIVERSITY & CONSERVATION 2255, 2255 (2009) ("By 2100, a quarter or more of the Earth's land surface may experience climatic conditions that have no modern analog . . ."); Douglas Fox, *Back to the No-Analog Future?*, 316 SCIENCE 823, 823 (2007) ("[I]f the climate changes over the next 100 years as current models predict, surviving species throughout much of Earth's land area . . . are likely to be reshuffled into novel ecosystems unknown today."); Douglas Fox, *When Worlds Collide*, CON-SERVATION, Jan.–Mar. 2007, at 28 (arguing that it is likely that the world will enter into a no-analog future within 100–200 years). What should be the management goal for ecosystems undergoing such transition? For more discussion of this and other climate change issues, see Chapters 17–19.

3. METHOD SELECTION

As described by Grumbine, ecosystem management refers to a set of policy *goals* directed at ensuring the sustainability of natural resource qualities within ecologically functional units. Grumbine mentions another concept, "adaptive management," as a set of policy *tools* intended to move decision making from a process of incremental trial and error to one of experimentation using continuous monitoring, assessment, and recalibration. Ecosystem management and adaptive management are not interchangeable, but are nearly inseparable. Successful ecosystem management usually requires a heavy dose of adaptive management, and using adaptive management in natural resources conservation contexts generally leads to expressing goals in term of ecosystem management. As the General Accounting Office summarized in its early assessment of the status of ecosystem management in federal agencies:

> Just as ecosystems are continually changing over time, so, too, will the understanding of their ecology and, by implication, the management choices based on this understanding. Scientists and policy analysts generally recognize that their understanding of how different ecosystems function and change and how they are affected by human activities is incomplete. For this reason, they see a need for continually researching, monitoring, and evaluating the ecological conditions of ecosystems and, where necessary, modifying management on the basis of new information to better accommodate socioeconomic considerations while ensuring the minimum or desired ecological conditions are being achieved.

> This process, sometimes known as "adaptive management," has been identified as a requirement for ecosystem management by . . . the federal interagency team tasked to examine ecosystem management in the old-growth forests of the Pacific Northwest. It is also reflected in the administration's principle to "use monitoring and assessment and the best science available." Thus, applying this principle will require (1) continually researching, monitoring, and assessing ecological conditions as well as the effects of activities on ecosystems and (2) modifying prior management choices on the basis of this new information. This . . . underscores the continuing, iterative nature of ecosystem management.

GENERAL ACCOUNTING OFFICE, ECOSYSTEM MANAGEMENT: ADDITIONAL ACTIONS NEEDED TO TEST A PROMISING APPROACH (AUGUST 1994).

Adaptive management theory traces its origins to C. S. "Buzz" Holling's seminal book, *Adaptive Environmental Assessment and Manage-*

ment, published in 1978. During the two decades following the book's publication, Holling's basic framework for adaptive management found followers in environmental policy and law circles, eventually becoming one of the coordinating principles for ecosystem management implementation in many contexts today. When the term "adaptive management" rolls off people's tongues with reference to ecosystem management policy, they mean essentially what Holling outlined over 30 years ago, but the concept is often described in terms too brief to be meaningful. It is worth examining what Holling had in mind in some detail.

Holling edited *Adaptive Environmental Assessment and Management* while at the Institute of Animal Resource Ecology at the University of British Columbia. He and a team of hand-picked scientists met over a period of two years to hammer out an alternative to conventional environmental assessment methods, such as the Environmental Impact Statement (EIS) process of the National Environmental Policy Act (NEPA) (discussed later in this chapter). The group perceived the EIS and similar assessment methods as involving "fixed review of an independently designed policy" which over time would "inhibit laudable economic enterprises as well as violate critical environmental constraints." They called their alternative "adaptive management and policy design, which integrates environmental with economic and social understanding at the very beginning of the design process, in a sequence of steps during the design phase and after implementation."

The team introduced adaptive management first by debunking twelve principles—what they called myths—which they contended formed the premises of conventional environmental assessment theory. These statements, in other words, define what adaptive management theory explicitly *rejects*. Four of these myths centered around the premises of environmental management policy:

Myth 1   The central goal for design is to produce policies and developments that result in stable social, economic, and environmental behavior.

Myth 2   Development programs are fixed sets of actions that will not involve extensive modification, revision, or additional investment after the development occurs.

Myth 3   Policies should be designed on the basis of economic and social goals with environmental concerns added subsequently as constraints during a review process.

Myth 4   Environmental concerns can be dealt with appropriately only by changing institutional constraints.

To these the group added eight myths relating to the premises underlying conventional approaches to environmental assessment:

Myth 5   Environmental assessment should consider all possible impacts of the proposed development.

Myth 6   Each new assessment is unique. There are few relevant background principles, information, or even comparable past cases.

Myth 7   Comprehensive "state of the system" surveys (species lists, soil conditions, and the like) are a necessary step in environmental assessment.

Myth 8   Detailed descriptive studies of the present condition of system parts can be integrated by systems analysis to provide overall understanding and predictions of systems impact.

Myth 9   Any good scientific study contributes to better decision making.

Myth 10   Physical boundaries based on watershed area or political jurisdictions can provide sensible limits for impact investigations.

Myth 11   Systems analysis will allow effective elections of the best alternative from several proposed plans and programs.

Myth 12   Ecological evaluation and impact assessment aim to eliminate uncertainty regarding the consequences of proposed development.

One does not have to agree that all these "myths" are flatly wrong and misguided, or even that they undergird EIS and similar assessment methods, in order to appreciate the alternative view adaptive management theory introduced. Holling's group found the 12 conventional tenets of resource management at odds with four basic properties of ecological systems. First, although the parts of ecological systems are connected, not all parts are strongly or intimately connected with all other parts. It cannot possibly be the case, for example, that every species in an ecosystem depends for its survival on the survival of every other species. The connections within ecosystems are themselves selective and variable, meaning what should be measured will depend on our understanding of the way the system as a whole works. Second, events are not uniform over space, meaning that impacts of development do not gradually dilute with distance from the development. In particular, induced effects of developments such as pipelines and water reservoirs may be of greatest magnitude at distant points. Third, ecological systems exhibit multi-equilibrium states between which the system may move for unpredictable reasons, in unpredictable manners, and at unpredictable times. Small variations in conditions such as temperature, nutrient content, or species composition can "flip" ecosystems into vastly different behavioral states, sometimes well after the event that started the reaction. The upshot is that the unexpected can happen, and it will be difficult to predict when, where, and to what degree. Finally, Holling's group observed that because ecosystems are not static but in continual change, environmental quality is not achieved by eliminating change. Flood, fire, heat, cold, drought, and storm continually test ecosystems, enhancing resilience through system "self-correction." Efforts to suppress change are thus not only futile, but counterproductive.

Ecologists today generally agree that these four properties define important characteristics of ecosystems. Holling's point was that environmental assessment methods thus ought to take these four properties into account, and that the twelve "myths" of conventional environmental assessment theory are unsuitable premises for doing so. In their place, Holling's adaptive management theory builds on eight key premises:

1. Since everything is not intimately connected to everything else, there is no need to measure everything. There is a need, however, to determine the significant connections.

2. Structural features (e.g., size distribution, age, who connects to whom) are more important to measure than numbers.

3. Changes in one variable (e.g., a population) can have unexpected impacts on variables at the same place but several connections away.

4. Events at one place can reemerge as impacts at distant places.

5. Monitoring of the wrong variable can seem to indicate no change even when drastic change is imminent.

6. Impacts are not necessarily immediate and gradual; they can appear abruptly some time after the event.

7. Variability of ecological systems, including occasional major disruptions, provides a kind of self-monitoring system that maintains resilience. Policies that reduce variability in space or time, even in an effort to improve environmental "quality," should always be questioned.

8. Many existing impact assessment methods (e.g., cost-benefit analysis, input-output, cross-impact matrices, linear models, discounting) assume none of the above occurs or, at least, that none is important.

So the central question Holling's group confronted was: If none of the existing assessment methods takes these critically important premises into account, what kind of assessment protocol would? Their answer was the creation of the adaptive management method, which they formed through integration of several key design features and process steps:

1. Environmental dimensions should be introduced at the very beginning of the development or policy design process and should be integrated as equal partners with the economic and social dimensions.

2. Thereafter, in the design phase, there should be periods of intense, focused innovation involving significant outside constituencies, followed by periods of stable consolidation.

3. Part of the design should include benefits attached to increasing information on unknown or partially known social, economic, and environmental effect. Information can be given a value just as jobs, income, and profit can.

4. Some of the experiments designed to produce information can be part of an integrated research plan, but others should be designed into the actual management activities. Managers as well as scientists learn from change.

5. An equally integral part of the design are the monitoring and remedial mechanisms. They should not simply be post hoc additions after implementation.

6. In the design of those mechanisms there should be careful analysis of the economic tradeoffs between structures and policies that presume that the unexpected can be designed into insignificance and less capital intensive mechanisms that monitor and ameliorate the unexpected.

Although it is seldom described with the preceding level of detail, when most people today use the term adaptive management they mean what was laid out in Holling's seminal work. As a result, adaptive management has been joined at the hips with ecosystem management as the tool with which to implement the policy.

NOTES & QUESTIONS

1. As ecosystem management theory was gaining its footings in the mid-1990s, a general consensus quickly formed among resource managers and academics that adaptive management is the only practical way to implement ecosystem management. *See* Ronald D. Brunner and Tim W. Clark, *A Practice-Based Approach to Ecosystem Management*, 11 CONSERVATION BIOLOGY 48 (1997); Paul L. Ringold et al., *Adaptive Management Design for Ecosystem Management*, 6 ECOLOGICAL APPLICATIONS 745 (1996); Anne E. Heissenbuttel, *Ecosystem Management—Principles for Practical Application*, 6 ECOLOGICAL APPLICATIONS 730 (1996). Indeed, the Ecological Society of America's comprehensive study of ecosystem management treated the use of adaptive management methods as a given. *See* Norman L. Christensen et al., *The Report of the Ecological Society of America Committee on the Scientific Basis for Ecosystem Management*, 6 ECOLOGICAL APPLICATIONS 665 (1996). Not surprisingly, prescribing adaptive management thus has by now become standard fare in policy statements. *See, e.g.*, Exec. Order No. 13,508, 74 Fed. Reg. 23,099, 23,101–03 (May 12, 2009) (directing the EPA to draft pollution-control strategies for the Chesapeake Bay watershed that are "based on sound science and reflect adaptive management principles," while also directing the Departments of the Interior and Commerce to use "adaptive management to plan, monitor, evaluate, and adjust environmental management actions" in the Chesapeake Bay watershed).

2. Adaptive management is hungry for information. Besides raw data about ecosystems, the kinds of information policy makers could integrate into adaptive management decisions are quite varied. The Environmental Protection Agency, for example, has been focusing on developing ecological risk assessment methods that focus on measuring "endpoint" values of attributes of ecological entities, such as mass deaths, survival rates, wetland area, and aquatic habitat structure, upon which to base management decisions about what steps to manage future ecological risks. *See* U.S. EPA, Generic Assessment Endpoints for Ecological Risk Assessments (2002). Another important body of information will be the cost-effectiveness experience of different management options, and thus economic evaluations must enter into the picture. *See* Kenneth F.D. Hughey et al., *Integrating Economics into Priority Setting and Evaluation in Conservation Management*, 17 CONSERVATION BIOLOGY 93 (2003). The wealth of information from these and other sources can be represented through the powerful tool of Geographic Information Systems, which maps and allows manipulation and correlation of "layers" of information on landscape scales— e.g., correlating rainfall, habitat canopy cover, invasive species management measures, and population distribution of target species in one mapping system—so as to more fully inform management decisions. *See* Karen V. Root et al., *A Multispecies Approach to Ecological Valuation and Conservation*, 17 CONSERVATION BIOLOGY 196 (2003). In short, enabling adaptive management as the method for ecosystem management will require a massive influx of information sources that can only be accomplished through concerted efforts across the board at local, state, national, and private levels.

3. Given its demand for constant flow of information, can we afford adaptive management—is it *financially* viable? Who will pay for the continuous stream of monitoring, measuring, modeling, and assessing that adaptive management contemplates? Are you concerned that if we adopt adaptive management as the method for implementing ecosystem management, but then under-fund the process itself, we risk making irreparably damaging decisions? *See* D. James Baker, *What Do Ecosystem Management and the Current Budget Mean for Federally Supported Environmental Research?*, 6 ECOLOGICAL APPLICATIONS 712 (1996).

4. Perhaps adaptive management is the only *practical* way to implement ecosystem management, but, even assuming we could afford to implement it properly, is adaptive management as Holling describes it *politically* feasible? Holling himself has recognized that adaptive management requires flexible institutions, as in "ones where signals of change are detected and reacted to as a self-correcting process." C.S. Holling, *Surprise for Science, Resilience for Ecosystems, and Incentives for People*, 6 ECOLOGICAL APPLICATIONS 733 (1996). But how, politically and legally, would this "self-correcting process" be constructed within resource management agencies? Will the public have a right to participate in the "self-correction process," and how will judicial review be conducted of the "self-correction process" decisions? Is our political context willing to give agencies the discretion they would need to engage in constant "self-correction" free of legislative, judicial, and citizen oversight and challenge? As Grumbine has observed, agencies "have not often been rewarded for flexibility, openness, and their willingness to experiment, monitor, and adapt." *Reflections on "What is Ecosystem Management*," 11 CONSERVATION BIOLOGY 41 (1997). Why is that so? On this score, consider the following commentary:

J.B. Ruhl, *The Disconnect Between Environmental Assessment and Adaptive Management*
36 Trends 1 (July/Aug. 2005).

Environmental lawyers increasingly are finding themselves having to retool their skills to fit the new set of policy challenges, such as sprawl, invasive species, habitat loss, terrorism, and climate change. The first wave of environmental laws addressed concerns characterized by discrete sources and technological solutions: Smokestacks, discharge pipes, and landfills were the bread and butter of environmental law from the early 1970s through the millennium. These concerns, however, were the low-hanging fruit.

By contrast, problems such as invasive species and habitat loss are characterized by a multitude of dispersed sources, unclear causal relations, and vast geographic scales that do not respond well to "command-and-control" regulatory techniques. Rather, they have prompted the so-called second generation of policy instruments, such as market-based trading programs, information disclosure requirements, ecosystem management and performance track incentives. It is thought by some that decentralization better matches the complex nature of these problems and their underlying causes.

Proposals for using these new policy tools usually depend on an implementation method known as *adaptive management*. For example, several federal agencies asked the National Academy of Sciences' National Research Council to explore how to improve resource agency decision making in the Klamath River Basin, which straddles southern Oregon and northern California. The study recommended using adaptive management and outlined its eight essential steps: (1) define the problem; (2) determine management goals and objectives; (3) determine the resource baseline; (4) develop conceptual models; (5) select future restoration actions; (6) implement management actions; (7) monitor ecosystem response and (8) evaluate restoration efforts and proposals for remedial actions. *See* National Research Council, Endangered and Threatened Fishes in the Klamath River Basin: Causes of Decline and Strategies for Recovery 332–35 (2004).

The committee's description of the last step illustrates how much adaptive management depends on a continuous monitoring-adjustment cycle of decision making:

> After implementation of specific restoration activities and procedures, the status of the ecosystem is regularly and systematically reassessed and described. Comparison of the new state with the baseline state is a measure of progress toward objectives. The evaluation process feeds directly into adaptive management by informing the implementation team and leading to testing of management hypotheses, new simulations, and proposals for adjustments in management experiments or development of wholly new experiments or management strategies. Adaptive management is an approach to resources management in which policy choices are made incrementally. As each choice is made, data on the effects of these choices are collected and analyzed in order to assess whether to retain, reverse, or otherwise alter the policy choice.

Id. at 335.

Most environmental lawyers, however, will see a problem right away for the prospects of the adaptive management approach. To put it bluntly, the structure and culture of environmental law have evolved over the last thirty years to become what Professors Sidney Shapiro and Rob Glicksman call a "front-end" system of decision making that has little tolerance for flexibility and experimentation.

The central premise of environmental decision making is that through expert agency policy analysis, thrashing public notice and comment, and hard look judicial review, we can predict what is going to happen in the future, make a decision about what to do, and not have to look back. To be sure, many environmental regulation programs anticipate change, such as requiring permit renewals and land management plan revisions after prescribed periods.

However, each such juncture is treated as if the agency is starting over in the process, necessitating another front-loaded decision making process. In short, it has become monumentally difficult for agencies to adjust their decisions without gearing up the full-blown decision making apparatus.

The backbone of this system of policy administration is the *environmental assessment*, the process through which agencies describe a proposed action and predict its future effects for purposes of facilitating a fully informed decision. Although usually associated with the well-known Environmental Impact Statement (EIS) procedure of the National Environmental Policy Act (NEPA), which requires all federal agencies to prepare an environmental assessment for all "major federal actions significantly affecting the quality of the human environment," 42 U.S.C. 4332(2)(C), many other federal and state environmental programs depend on the assumption that agency can comprehensively and accurately assess the effects of a proposed action and its alternatives.

For example, the Endangered Species Act (ESA) requires that permit applicants submit a "conservation plan," known as a Habitat Conservation Plan (HCP), to the U.S. Fish and Wildlife Service predicting the impacts of the proposed land use activity on protected species and explaining why alternatives were rejected. 16 U.S.C. 1539(a)(2)(A).

The problem is that agencies are trapped between a rock and a hard place when it comes to practicing environmental assessment *and* adaptive management. On the one hand, they are under pressure to integrate adaptive management into decision making. Recently, for example, a White House task force on NEPA reform advocated the need for adaptive management in the implementation of environmental impact assessments. *See* THE NEPA TASK FORCE, REPORT TO THE COUNCIL ON ENVIRONMENTAL QUALITY, MODERNIZING NEPA IMPLEMENTATION 45–46 (2003).

Responding to that call, the Department of the Interior revised its NEPA implementation regulations to make adaptive management an explicit goal of environmental assessment practice. *See* 69 Fed. Reg. 10866 (Mar. 8, 2004). Similarly, the Fish and Wildlife Service announced it will administer the HCP program using adaptive management as a means to "examine alternative strategies for meeting measurable biological goals and objectives through research and/or monitoring, and then, if necessary, to adjust future conservation management actions according to what is learned." 64 Fed. Reg. 11485, 11486–87 (Mar. 9, 1999).

On the other hand, because the front-end apparatus of environmental regulation remains firmly in place, whenever an agency actually practices adaptive management it faces a substantial risk of being sued for failure to comply with environmental assessment procedures. Litigation abounds over the type of environmental assessment that an agency must conduct to make or change a decision and whether a particular assessment adequately covers the necessary elements. Each adaptive move an agency makes thus raises the chance of claims an environmental assessment was required or that the assessment conducted was incomplete.

If the past is any indication, interest groups and courts relentlessly will peck away at adaptive agency behavior, using all the armament conventional administrative law puts at their disposal. Ironically, efforts by an agency to cover itself by preparing litigation-proof environmental assessments for every adaptive decision adjustment necessarily with thwart the agency's ability to make the adjustments in the first place.

A stunning example of this predicament comes from the litigation over the U.S. Army Corps of Engineers' (Corps) management of the Missouri River navigation and flow regime system. *See In re Operation of the Missouri River System Litigation*, 363 F.Supp.2d 1145 (D. Minn. 2004). Although the court in one phase of the litigation rejected Missouri's claim that the Corps had violated NEPA's environmental review provisions when it adopted an adaptive management approach, the Corps' "victory" sowed the seeds of a long future in court:

> Missouri maintains that the adaptive management approach violates NEPA because it permits the Corps to circumvent the NEPA process when policy choices are modified. Missouri takes issue with the potential flow changes that the Corps may undertake in the future. Missouri fails to point to any evidence that indicates that the Corps intends to avoid its NEPA obligations buy implementing this adaptive management approach. To the contrary, the Corps acknowledges that in the event a major policy change results, the Corps will be required to comply with NEPA. Absent evidence that the adaptive management process actually results in the Corps' evasion of NEPA obligations, the Court declines to declare this approach invalid.

Id. at 14.

In other words, the Corps did not err in law by adopting adaptive management as its implementation method; rather, it erred in sensibility by doing so because that opened the door to litigation over whether each policy adjustment triggers NEPA. If the Corps seeks to reduce that risk by preparing ironclad environmental assessments, it is less likely to practice effective adaptive management. If the Corps emphasizes effective adaptive management, each adaptive adjustment exposes it to litigation risks over environmental assessment compliance. The message to agencies thus is to assess or to adapt, but don't be foolish enough to try doing both.

Agencies should not be relieved of environmental assessment practices. Rather, the method and role of environmental assessment must change.

It's simply not possible to assess all there is to know about problems like invasive species and predict the responses of the problem to different policy options. We must accept the reality that sprawl, habitat loss, climate change, terrorism, and invasive species are here to stay. Hence, we must abandon the notion that the "record of decision" closes the books on environmental assessment and decision making.

To anyone convinced of the potential of adaptive management, it is nonsensical that NEPA does not require an agency to monitor the effects of an action *after* its EIS is completed, just in case the EIS was wrong. For adaptive management to work, the assessment process and the decision process must be continuous, simultaneous, and connected. Less emphasis must be placed on "the EIS" and more on long-term monitoring and the framework for decision adjustment. If anything, an environmental assessment ought to establish the basis for practicing adaptive management.

The concern is whether legislatures, agencies, interest groups, and courts will be able to let go of the front-end decision making system to which they have all become acculturated so that NEPA and other environmental assessment procedures can grow into their second generation. If they can't, the disconnect between environmental assessment and adaptive management will persist and the future of adaptive management will be bleak.

NOTES & QUESTIONS

1. Notwithstanding the risks identified in the foregoing commentary, the Corps of Engineers' basic adaptive management approach withstood judicial scrutiny when the Eighth Circuit ruled that a full supplemental EIS was not necessary to support flow adjustments made in 2006 to account for an annual "spring rise" to benefit endangered species. *See* In re Operation of the Missouri River System Litigation, 516 F.3d 688 (8th Cir. 2008).

2. For a discussion of the law of adaptive management, including how agencies define it, how they practice it, and what courts think of it, see J.B. Ruhl & Robert Fischman, *Adaptive Management in the Courts*, 95 MINN. LAW REV. 424 (2010). The authors find that "from theory to policy to practice, at each step forward in the emergence of adaptive management something has been lost in the translation. The end product is something we call 'a/m-lite,' a watered-down version of the theory that resembles ad hoc contingency planning more than it does planned 'learning while doing.' This gap between theory and practice leads to profound disparities between how agencies justify decisions and how adaptive management in practice arrives at the courthouse doorsteps." Based on their review of all judicial opinions addressing agency adaptive management practices, they conclude that "although courts genuinely and often enthusiastically endorse adaptive management theoretically, they frequently are underwhelmed by how agencies implement adaptive management in the field." For other legal commentary on adaptive management, see Mary Jane Angelo, *Stumbling Toward Success: A Story of Adaptive Law and Ecological Resilience*,

87 NEB. L. REV. 950, 951–52 (2009) (detailing the theory of adaptive management through a case study based in Florida); Alejandro Esteban Camacho, *Can Regulation Evolve? Lessons from a Study in Maladaptive Management*, 55 UCLA L. REV. 293, 294–99 (2007) (critiquing the use of adaptive management in the ESA); Holly Doremus, *Adaptive Management, the Endangered Species Act, and the Institutional Challenges of "New Age" Environmental Protection*, 41 WASHBURN L.J. 50, 50–52 (2001) (identifying challenges for adaptive management in the administration of the ESA); Robert L. Glicksman, *Ecosystem Resilience to Disruptions Linked to Global Climate Change: An Adaptive Approach to Federal Land Management*, 87 NEB. L. REV. 833, 871 (2009) (proposing the broad use of adaptive management in public land management); Bradley C. Karkkainen, *Panarchy and Adaptive Change: Around the Loop and Back Again*, 7 MINN. J. L. SCI. & TECH. 59, 70–71 (2005) (examining the theory of active adaptive management); J.B. Ruhl, *Regulation by Adaptive Management— Is It Possible?*, 7 MINN. J. L. SCI. & TECH. 21, 33–34 (2005) (identifying disconnects between adaptive management and conventional administrative procedure).

3. Notwithstanding its demands on agency resources and its incompatibility with conventional administrative law practices, most legal commentary recognizes the need for adaptive management in responding to global climate change, particularly in the ecosystem management context, given how difficult it will be to use conventional impact assessment methods to predict the path of ecosystem disruption. See Alejandro Camacho, *Adapting Governance to Climate Change: Managing Uncertainty through a Learning Infrastructure*, 59 Emory L.J. 1 (2009), Robin Kundis Craig, *"Stationarity is Dead"—Long Live Transformation: Five Principles for Climate Change Adaptation Law*, 34 HARV. ENVTL. L. REV. 9 (2010); Holly Doremus, *Adapting to Climate Change Through Law that Bends Without Breaking*, 2 SAN DIEGO J. OF CLIMATE & ENERGY L. 45 (2010); Robert L. Glicksman, *Ecosystem Resilience to Disruptions Linked to Global Climate Change: An Adaptive Approach to Federal Land Management*, 87 KAN. L. REV. 833 (2009); J.B. Ruhl, *Climate Change Adaptation and the Structural Transformation of Environmental Law*, 40 ENVTL. L. 363, 365-71 (2010). For more on the use of adaptive management in response to climate change, see Chapter 19.

4. Draft a legal definition of adaptive management—one that could be inserted in a new law instructing a federal resource management agency how to implement ecosystem management. Does your definition address the concerns discussed above about political viability and the temptation for agencies to practice a/m lite?

C. WHAT IS ECOSYSTEM MANAGEMENT LAW?

As law professor Robert Keiter observed at the dawn of the ecosystem management movement, "until Congress speaks, ecosystem management can only claim a tenuous legitimacy, which also leaves the concept undefined for legal purposes." Robert Keiter, *Toward Legitimizing Ecosystem Management on the Public Domain*, 6 ECOLOGICAL APPLICATIONS 727 (1996). He elaborated:

An antagonistic and recalcitrant Congress can impede and even reverse agency policies with which it disagrees. Congressional funding for key ecosystem initiatives can be stopped through appropriations riders without full debate over the merits of the policy. Administrative regulations that are not statutorily mandated can always be revised by a subsequent, unsympathetic administration, just as policies lacking congressional support can be abandoned or reformulated. And courts inclined to defer to legislative or administrative discretion are unlikely to intervene in the absence of an express ecosystem mandate.

Yet the prospect of enacting a comprehensive, mandate-stating national ecosystem management law in the foreseeable future is essentially nil. The last bill to attempt anything close to that goal was introduced in Congress in 1994 and quickly died. That bill was not very ambitious. It did not even define ecosystem management! Rather, it would have established a federal commission to study how to coordinate an ecosystem management approach for federal land management policy. Nevertheless, the bill's sponsor, Senator Hatfield, introduced the bill with an impassioned plea for Congress to do *something* about ecosystem management, and the bill did contain the seeds of an ecosystem management approach:

Ecosystem Management Act of 1995 (S. 2189)

141 CONG. REC. S320 (daily ed. Jan. 4, 1995.).

MR. HATFIELD. Mr. President, the last proposal I will introduce today relates to ecosystem management and watershed protection. These are the "buzz words" for a new generation of land management philosophies and techniques. A number of federal land management agencies are now working to implement ecosystem management on a landscape levels, including the Bureau of Land Management, the Forest Service and the Bureau of Reclamation.

Unfortunately, we as legislators and appropriators understand little about this new and innovative land management technique. Each federal government agency, state agency, interest group and Congress-person has his or her own idea of what ecosystem management means for the people and ecology of their particular state or region. As appropriators, we are required to fund these actions with little more than faith that the agencies' recommendations are based on sound science and a firm understanding of the needs of ecosystems and the people who live there.

Numerous additional questions surround not only the integrity but the functionality of the ecosystem management boat we have already launched. For example, what is ecosystem management, how should it be implemented and who should be implementing it? How does the ecosystem oriented work of the federal agencies, states, municipalities, counties, and interest groups mesh? And is the existing structure of our government agencies adequate to meet the requirements of managing land across which state and county lines have been drawn? Finally, with a decreasing resource production receipt base, how shall we pay for ecosystem management? Direct federal appropriations? Consolidation of federal, state, local and private funds? And if we determine how to pay for ecosystem management, who coordinates collection of these funds and how are they distributed?

I do not disagree with the theory that holistic, coordinated management of our natural resources is necessary. On the contrary, I and many of my Senate colleagues are prepared to move in that direction. It makes eminent sense to manage resources by the natural evolution of river basins and watersheds rather than according to the artificial boundaries established by counties, states and nations. Nevertheless, as our nation's funding resources become more scarce and our government agencies, states, localities and private interests seek to coordinate their ecosystem restoration efforts, Congress and the Executive Branch need to avail themselves of the best information in order to make educated, informed decisions about how ecosystem management will affect our nation's people, environment and federal budget.

To help answer these questions, I am introducing legislation today to create an Ecosystem Management Study Commission. The Commission will submit a report to Congress 1 year after enactment which: defines ecosystem management; identifies constraints and opportunities for coordinated ecosystem planning; examines existing laws and Federal agency budgets to determine whether any changes are necessary to facilitate ecosystem management; identifies incentives, such as trust funds, to encourage parties to engage in the development of ecosystem management strategies; and identifies, through case studies representing different regions of the United States, opportunities for and constraints on ecosystem management.

It is time to look beyond the polarized positions of "economic growth" and "environmental protection" which have crippled our system of land management planning and implementation in recent years. Instead we must work toward the creation of cooperative, regionally-based, incentive-driven planning for the management of our water, air, land and fish and wildlife resources in perpetuity.

S. 93 Be it enacted by the Senate and House of Representatives of the United States of America in Congress assembled,

SECTION 1. SHORT TITLE.

This Act may be cited as the "Ecosystem Management Act of 1995."

SEC. 2. ECOSYSTEM MANAGEMENT.

(a) Definitions. Section 103 of the Federal Land Policy and Management Act of 1976 (43 U.S.C. 1702) is amended by adding at the end the following new subsections:

"(r) The term 'systems approach', with respect to an ecosystem, means an interdisciplinary scientific method of analyzing the ecosystem as a whole that takes into account the interconnections of the ecosystem."

(b) Ecosystem Management. Title II of the Federal Land Policy and Management Act of 1976 (43 U.S.C. 1711 et seq.) is amended by adding at the end the following new sections:

"ECOSYSTEM MANAGEMENT

Sec. 216. It is the policy of the Federal Government to carry out ecosystem management with respect to public lands in accordance with the following principles:

(1) Human populations form an integral part of ecosystems.

(2) It is important to address human needs in the context of other environmental attributes

(A) in recognition of the dependency of human economies on viable ecosystems; and

(B) in order to ensure diverse, healthy, productive, and sustainable ecosystems.

(3) A systems approach to ecosystem management furthers the goal of conserving biodiversity.

(4) Ecosystem management provides for the following:

(A) The promotion of the stewardship of natural resources.

(B) The formation of partnerships of public and private interests to achieve shared goals for the stewardship of natural resources.

(C) The promotion of public participation in decisions and activities related to the stewardship of natural resources.

(D) The use of the best available scientific knowledge and technology to achieve the stewardship of natural resources.

(E) The establishment of cooperative planning and management activities to protect and manage ecosystems that cross jurisdictional boundaries.

(F) The implementation of cooperative, coordinated planning activities among Federal, tribal, State, local, and private landowners."

"ECOSYSTEM MANAGEMENT COMMISSION

Sec. 217. (a) Establishment. There is established an Ecosystem Management Commission (referred to in this section as the 'Commission').

(b) Purposes of the Commission. The purposes of the Commission are as follows:

(1) To advise the Secretary and Congress concerning policies relating to ecosystem management on public lands.

(2) To examine opportunities for and constraints on achieving cooperative and coordinated ecosystem management strategies that provide for cooperation between the Federal Government and Indian tribes, States and political subdivisions of States, and private landowners to incorporate a multijurisdictional approach to ecosystem management.

*   *   *

(e) Duties of the Commission. The duties of the Commission are as follows:

(1) To conduct studies to accomplish the following:

(A) To develop, in a manner consistent with section 216, a definition of the term 'ecosystem management'.

(B) To identify appropriate geographic scales for coordinated ecosystem-based planning.

(C) To identify, with respect to the Federal Government, the governments of Indian tribes, States and political subdivisions of States, and private landowners, constraints on, and opportunities for, ecosystem management in order to facilitate the coordination of planning activities for ecosystem management among the governments and private landowners.

(D) To identify strategies for implementing ecosystem management that recognize the following:

(i) The role of human populations in the operation of ecosystems.

(ii) The dependency of human populations on sustainable ecosystems for the production of goods and the provision of services.

(E) To examine this Act, and each other Federal law or policy that directly or indirectly affects the management of public lands, including Federal lands that have been withdrawn from the public domain, to determine whether any legislation or changes to administrative policies, practices, or procedures are necessary to facilitate ecosystem management by the Federal Government in accordance with section 216."

NOTES & QUESTIONS

1. Senator Hatfield's bill reduced ecosystem management to six core topics of policy development:

- stewardship of natural resources
- partnerships of public and private interests
- public participation in decisions and activities
- use of the best available scientific knowledge and technology
- cooperative planning and management activities across jurisdictional boundaries
- cooperative, coordinated planning activities among Federal, tribal, State, local, and private landowners

Do these correspond well with Grumbine's suggested approach to ecosystem management outlined *supra*? Are there other key topics that must be considered?

2. Rather than defining ecosystem management, Senator Hatfield's bill defined the "systems approach" and emphasized its importance to developing an effective ecosystem management policy. Senator Hatfield defined systems approach as "an interdisciplinary scientific method of analyzing the ecosystem as a whole that takes into account the interconnections of the ecosystem." Recall that Grumbine's work on ecosystem management also acknowledged the importance of taking this kind of approach, which he defined as requiring that "when working on a problem at any one level or scale, managers must seek the connections between all levels." Also, Holling's theory of adaptive management, detailed *supra*, is based on the conception of ecosystems as dynamic systems. Was Senator Hatfield's reference to the "systems approach" thus an endorsement of Grumbine's and Hollings' approach to ecosystem management?

3. Senator Hatfield's proposed law would have required the Ecosystem Management Commission to define ecosystem management consistent with the systems approach and the six specified policy components. Assume you are a member of the Commission. What definition would you propose?

4. Note the reference in the bill to "the dependency of human populations on sustainable ecosystems for the production of goods and the provision of services." Are the "services" to which the bill refers the same as the "ecosystem services" Salzman, Costanza, and Daily propose as a unit of ecosystem measurement? What other "services" could the bill have had in mind?

1. CHANGING THE FOCUS OF EXISTING LAWS

Must ecosystem management wait for Congress or state legislatures to endorse it? The existing array of environmental laws presents an opportunity to forge ecosystem management through reinvention rather than invention. Indeed, the guru of government reinvention during the 1990s, Vice President Al Gore, suggested just this approach in his September 1993 National Performance Review, in which he directed federal environmental agencies to develop "a proactive approach to ensuring a sustainable economy and a sustainable environment through ecosystem management."

Recall, however, Professor Keiter's description of the ways in which any such effort can be thwarted: new administrations may change course; legislatures may enact new law to preempt the direction of reinvention; courts may find existing law does not authorize where reinvention has led. One way to conceptualize these possibilities is to think of existing law as defining a box of "policy space." Statutory text rarely defines the policy options in such a way that the box is extremely small. Agencies charged with implementing the statute thus often have plenty of space within which to develop alternative policies. Indeed, often the box is sufficiently large that we don't know how large it is until a court finds that an agency has adopted a policy that falls outside the box. Of course, at any time the legislature could alter the dimensions of the box through statutory amendments, putting the point in space representing the current administrative policy position outside or inside of the new box.

The Clinton Administration's call for reinvention of environmental policy through ecosystem management thus was an effort to move within the policy space box from one point—the point where previous administrations had left policy—to another. The materials in this section chart the administration's initial efforts in that regard, taking place primarily in the time period from 1995 through 2000. Keiter's point, of course, is clearly put front and center by the events of politics and law since that time: new administrations; shifting leaderships Congress; and time for courts to test whether ecosystem management violates the boxes of existing law. For example, soon after taking office, the George W. Bush Administration announced that it would revisit many of the rulemakings the Clinton Administration made in furtherance of ecosystem management, and thereafter the Obama Administration in turn revisited changes the Bush Administration had made (see Chapters 8-11 for examples).

In general, though, fields of law and policy tend to evolve and entrench over time—it becomes harder to change the box of policy space and to move around within it. Court interpretations of statutes become not news but rather long-held precedent. Legislatures become less willing, or able, to re-open statutes hashed out in the past. Administrations come and go with less effect on the course of long-term policy. Occasionally, of course, there is chaos in the form of new jurisprudence or a wave of "reform" fever in legislatures or agencies. By and large, however, ecosystem management law is simply too young to have reached this point. For purposes of law and policy, it began yesterday, and is still finding its feet. It is useful, therefore, to examine its origins, for they continue to have a profound influence on its future.

a. EARLY ASSESSMENTS

Soon after Senator Hatfield introduced his bill, House Natural Resources Committee Chair Rep. George Miller instructed the Congressional Research Service (CRS) and the Government Accounting Office (GAO) to examine what federal agencies were doing to move toward ecosystem management. After surveying and examining the work of a group of federal agencies that had formed an Interagency Ecosystem Management Coordinating Group (IEMCG), CRS and GOA concluded as follows:

Congressional Research Service, *Ecosystem Management: Federal Agency Activities*
(April 19, 1994).

Many Federal agencies appear to be very aggressive in redirecting current efforts or initiating ecosystem management activities. These efforts and activities are diverse in scale, focus, institutional relationships, goals, and accomplishments. When they are viewed together, two themes seem most common. One is improved communication and coordination. Improvement is based on building new partnerships, sharing information, and reaching agreements or definitions for key terms and data collection. The second is trying to improve the condition of resources, which some are calling protection of biodiversity. These efforts might grow out of working to protect individual species and their habitats, restoring ecological processes and ecosystem services, or restoring degraded resources in an area. Agencies have listed many examples of these approaches in these summaries.

The current focus seems centered on the communication and coordination aspects of ecosystem management, perhaps because results here are visible far more quickly than for significant changes in resources. Improved resource conditions are decades away in many cases, even if ecosystems are managed in a scientifically sound and programmatically consistent manner. And these improved conditions are hard to measure, because ecosystems involve so many interrelated components, but the crucial variable is the health of the overall system rather than any single component. The [Interagency Ecosystem Management Coordinating Group] plays a key role in these efforts by supporting activities to improve communication and coordination and to change resource conditions. In a recent brochure, its listed efforts included:

- forming committees and working groups to address the complex of issues arising as agencies adopt ecosystem management;
- facilitating the standardization of data sharing techniques and ecosystem mapping techniques;
- establishing general implementation guidelines on ecosystem management for assimilation by participating agencies;
- identifying training needs and instituting collaborative training programs;
- adopting a Memorandum of Understanding among participating agencies to formally establish the Coordination Group and its role;
- serving as a resource to ensure each agency is current with ongoing research and information including legislative concerns;
- facilitating the adoption of standard terminology for participating agencies to use in ecosystem management and relevant aspects of research and operation;
- maintaining an education and outreach component; and
- encouraging existing and new partnerships for management on an ecosystem basis on a multiagency basis.

These papers also illustrate the wide variety of missions by reporting agencies. The agencies responsible for Federal lands and the resources on those lands have a very different mix of efforts than the agencies that deal with resources that are primarily on private lands. Some agencies deal more with the tools of resource analysis and with the development of resource information while others are more interested in the actual management of resources. These differences in missions are cause for a remarkable diversity in the approaches taken, in the reasons for interest in ecosystem management, and in the ways that agencies have integrated these efforts with ongoing activities and approaches to problem solving or resource management.

The intensity of the effort is also striking. All these agencies are devoting significant resources, both staff and financial, to this effort at a time of budget constraints and Federal downsizing. But the benefits of this approach, as they are defining it, seem to outweigh any costs, assuming successful implementation. Equally striking is the faith that the many government employees who participated in this demonstration appear to place in an ecosystem approach as a more rational way of serving the public good. One of the more difficult challenges for these agencies will be to maintain this intensity in continuing to work together successfully toward a consistent approach over time and in the face of changes in priorities, authorizations, and appropriations from year to year.

General Accounting Office, *Ecosystem Management: Additional Actions Needed to Test a Promising Approach*
(August 1994).

Purpose

Even though many laws have been enacted to protect individual natural resources—air, water, soils, plants, and animals, including forests, rangelands, threatened and endangered species, wetlands, and wilderness areas—ecological conditions on many federal lands have declined. As a result of these declines and the recognition that some historic levels of natural resource-commodity production and other natural resource uses cannot be sustained indefinitely; federal land managers have had to substantially decrease production of some renewable commodities, such as timber, and other uses, such as recreational activities, on some land units. These reductions have, in some instances, disrupted local economies and communities, contributing to intractable conflicts between ecological and economic values and concerns.

Since the late 1980s, many federal agency officials, scientists, and natural resource policy analysts have advocated a new, broader approach to managing the nation's lands and natural resources called "ecosystem management." This approach recognizes that plant and animal communities are interdependent and interact with their physical environment (soil, water, and air) to form distinct ecological units called ecosystems that span federal and nonfederal lands. In response to congressional requests, GAO identified (1) the status of federal initiatives to implement ecosystem management, (2) additional actions required to implement this approach, and (3) barriers to governmentwide implementation.

Results in Brief

Over the past 2 years, all four of the primary federal land management agencies have independently announced that they are implementing or will implement an ecosystem approach to managing their lands and natural resources, and each has been working to develop its own strategy primarily within its existing framework of laws and land units. In addition, the administration is proposing in its fiscal year 1995 budget, among other things, to fund the initial stage of a governmentwide approach to ecosystem management, including four ecosystem management pilot projects. It is also considering various principles for its governmentwide approach, including managing along ecological rather than political or administrative boundaries.

Implementing the initial stage of a governmentwide approach to ecosystem management will require clarifying the policy goal for ecosystem management and taking certain practical steps to apply the principles being considered by the administration. These steps include (1) delineating ecosystems, (2) understanding their ecologies, (3) making management choices, and (4) adapting management on the basis of new information. In taking these steps, the federal government will have to make difficult policy decisions about how it can best fulfill its stewardship responsibilities.

The administration's initiatives to implement ecosystem management governmentwide face several significant barriers. For example, although ecosystem management will require greater reliance on ecological and socioeconomic data, the available data collected independently by various agencies for different purposes, are often noncomparable, and insufficient, and scientific understanding of ecosystems is far from complete. While ecosystem management will require unparalleled coordination among federal agencies, disparate missions and planning requirements set forth in federal land management statutes and regulations hamper such efforts. And although ecosystem management will require collaboration and consensus-building among federal and nonfederal parties within most ecosystems, incentives, authorities, interests, and limitations embedded in the larger national land and natural resource use framework—many beyond the ability of the federal land management agencies individually or collectively to control or affect—constrain these parties' efforts to work together effectively.

NOTES & QUESTIONS

1. Do the CRS and GAO reports differ significantly in overall perspective on the progress of ecosystem management policy in the federal agencies at the time of their assessments? Doesn't CRS seem more positive in its comments? For example, CRS marvels at the "remarkable diversity in the approaches taken," whereas GAO expresses the concern that "while ecosystem management will require unparalleled coordination among federal agencies, disparate missions and planning requirements set forth in federal land management statutes and regulations hamper such efforts." Looking back over the materials in the prior sections of this Chapter, which of the two reports strikes you as more attuned to the issues that Blair raises about ecosystem functions, that Grumbine discusses in his exposition on ecosystem management policy, and that Holling's team revealed in their work on adaptive management?

2. The GAO refers to the "four . . . primary federal and management agencies." These agencies administer vast expanses of federally-owned land and natural resources. Three are within the Department of the Interior: the Bureau of Land Management (264 million acres); the National Park Service (84 million acres); and the United States Fish and Wildlife Service (96 million acres). The fourth agency is the United States Forest Service, a branch of the Department of Agriculture, which oversees 192 million acres of national forests and grasslands. As the GAO points out, how these agencies decide to manage their combined total of over 630 million acres of federal land has played and will continue to play a prominent role in the development of ecosystem management law.

b. INITIAL EFFORTS

As the CRS and GAO reports clearly demonstrate, notwithstanding the congressional endorsement Professor Keiter contends will be necessary for moving ecosystem management from de facto to de jure status, there is room for steering the ship of existing environmental law toward ecosystem management. It matters, of course, what basic objectives have been set, currencies selected, and management goals and methods installed. But as those policy decisions are made, even existing law can be used to put them into action.

In that regard, the laws that could be part of the reshaping movement toward ecosystem management can be thought of as falling into five categories. One set of laws has general conservation of environmental quality as the principle focus already, but the laws lack explicit reference to ecosystem management as a conservation objective. The Endangered Species Act is an example.

A second set of laws, including most prominently the National Environmental Policy Act, uses impact assessment procedures as an opportunity to improve government decision making. If impact assessment were to be defined to include ecosystem-level impacts, these law could focus attention on the need for ecosystem management.

Another set of laws, typified by the Clean Water Act and Clean Air Act, has pollution control as the central subject matter and protection of public health as the primary concern. Improving environmental quality is an additional objective of many of these laws, but it is not accomplished in the statutory schemes through anything like ecosystem management.

A fourth type of law consists of those concerned primarily with management of defined public land or resource units, such as forests, parks, or fisheries. This variety of laws provides the most promising foundation from which to build an ecosystem management approach, as the laws already have ecosystem units or functions as their core organizing principle. Many of these laws, however, were enacted before ecosystem management became a dominant policy theme, and thus the degree to which it can be incorporated for the future is uncertain. Moreover, these laws are limited in operative effect to public (primarily federal) lands.

Finally, the body of law with perhaps the most influence over how land is used has long been local land use controls such as zoning and growth management. While the emphasis of zoning has been form and function, and growth management has emerged largely in response to the nuisances of urban sprawl, there is no reason why local land use laws could not move toward ecosystem management as an additional objective. Yet, being local in nature and subject ultimately to state authority, the question is whether state and local political will are primed to do so.

As the following materials suggest, therefore, each of these five types of laws presents opportunities and challenges for development of a law of ecosystem management.

(1) Environmental Conservation Laws

How far has ecosystem management come? How much does existing law box it in? If any existing statute provides the test case for asking those questions, it is the Endangered Species Act. As noted in the opening to this Part of the text, the ESA proclaims that one of its purposes is "to provide a means whereby the ecosystems upon which endangered species and threatened species depend may be conserved." 16 U.S.C. § 1531(b). More than any other federal statute, the agencies charged with administering the ESA, the U.S. Fish and Wildlife Service (FWS) and the National Marine Fisheries Service (NMFS), embraced ecosystem management and attempted to make it the dominant theme of law and policy. Did they succeed?

To examine that question, one of your authors has proposed a set of questions designed to test how far "big" policy ideas have advanced toward formulation as hard law to apply. The seven "degrees of relevance" through which concepts such as ecosystem management progress from mere idea to law are:

level one:	The idea has become widely expressed through a generally accepted norm statement.
level two:	Advocating the opposite of the norm is no longer a tenable policy position.
level three:	The charge of acting contrary to the norm no longer can be left unaddressed.
level four:	Failure affirmatively to portray an action as being consistent with the norm is seen as a significant deficiency.
level five:	Important governmental authorities have established the norm as an explicit policy goal.
level six:	Proposed actions are being denied or delayed on the basis of perceived failure to facilitate the norm.
level seven:	The norm is fully transformed into law to apply.

The materials presented thus far in this chapter go a long way toward establishing that ecosystem management has in general passed at least as far as the fourth level—ecosystem management has been associated with specified normative goals and, while pockets of resistance exist, it has become a dominant theme of academic and policy dialogue. But is it *law*? Is it relevant *to lawyers*? The following excerpt picks up the analysis of that question, based on the status of ecosystem management in 2000, at the fifth level:

J. B. Ruhl, *Ecosystem Management, The Endangered Species Act, and the Seven Degrees of Relevance*

14 Natural Resources & Environment 156 (2000).

Level 5: Have important governmental authorities established the norm as an explicit policy goal? Has anyone employed by FWS or NMFS *not* heard of ecosystem management? The story of these two agencies' aggressive, and at times bold, effort to infuse the ESA with ecosystem management policy begins in March 1994 with FWS's publication of *An Ecosystem Approach to Fish and Wildlife Conservation: An Approach to More Effectively Conserve the Nation's Biodiversity* (March 1994). The agency portrayed this policy document as its road map for applying "the concept of managing and protecting ecosystems to everything the Service does." *Id.* at 5. The agency thereby explicitly endorsed the emerging body of conservation biology literature and research advocating that biological diversity—the variety and number and distribution of species across the earth—is the primary index of the health of the environment, and that the way to sustain that diversity is through protection and management of whole ecosystems. Each species is part of a dynamic, co-adapted assemblage of species dependent on and interacting with their surrounding habitat. It is that total package that must be managed, not just some of the bits and pieces. To do so, FWS has divided the country into watershed-based planning units representing major ecosystems of the nation, around which it will orient implementation of its various regulatory authorities. FWS announced through this publication that, where it can, it will attempt to use its powers to manage on the ecosystem level, for protection of the ecosystem dynamics, and thereby promote conservation of all the assembled species and environmental qualities. The agency promised that specific ecosystem-based reform measures for the ESA would follow.

FWS soon lived up to its promise through other initiatives, and often hand-in-hand with NMFS. Shortly after FWS published the general "Ecosystem Approach" agenda, FWS and NMFS adopted two significant policies designed to take the new focus on ecosystem dynamics straight to the ESA. The magic behind the agencies' approach was the realization that whereas the agencies do not have the discretion to transform the ESA into an ecosystem protection statute—the Act is fundamentally species-by-species in its orientation—nothing in the statute prevents the agencies from considering ecosystem factors in making species-specific decisions. Thus, in July 1994 the agencies announced that they would "promote healthy ecosystems through activities undertaken by the Service under authority of the Endangered Species Act." Notice of Interagency Cooperative Policy for the Ecosystem Approach to the Endangered Species Act, 59 Fed. Reg. 34273 (July 1, 1994). The agencies declared that henceforth they would incorporate ecosystem-level considerations into species listings and recovery planning under section 4 of the Act and for interagency cooperation under section 7. The agencies thus will "develop and implement recovery plans for communities or ecosystems where multiple listed and candidate species occur." *Id.* That policy recognizes that, in many ways, all the species are in the same boat, and our efforts to bring about their recovery must be approached with that reality in mind. Even more specifically, FWS and NMFS announced in a separate policy that the "method to be used for recovery plan preparation shall be based on several factors, including the range or ecosystem of the species," *id.*, and that recovery planning teams would be assembled with the species' ecosystem in mind. An expert in the biology of a species, for example, may not be an expert in the ecosystem functions that have been degraded and pose the threat to the species. If recovering the species requires repairing the ecosystem, the recovery planning effort must use expertise from both disciplines.

FWS and NMFS have acted to cement their ecosystem management policies for the ESA in a number of subsequent publications and announcements. For example, in 1997 the two agencies jointly published a policy statement emphasizing how the emerging ecosystem management approach would guide their ESA implementation in a variety of specific programs. *See Making the ESA Work Better: Implementing the 10 Point Plan . . . and Beyond* (June 1997). More recently, the [then] Director of FWS proclaimed that she has "challenged the agency to pioneer the practical implementation of an ecosystem approach," citing habitat conservation plan permits as a focal point for the ESA in that respect, and she invited the scientific community to join that endeavor. *See* Jamie Rappaport Clark, *The Ecosystem Approach from a Practical Point of View*, 13 CONSERVATION BIOLOGY 679 (1999). Through the efforts of FWS and NMFS, therefore, ecosystem management has become a new defining model for how the ESA will be implemented as a matter of official *policy*.

Level 6: Are proposed actions being denied or necessary authorization delayed on the basis of perceived failure to facilitate the norm? Notwithstanding all the momentum behind ecosystem management in the scientific literature, in the rhetoric of environmental and preservation groups, and in the official policies of FWS, NMFS, and other federal, state, local, and tribal agencies . . ., the practically-minded lawyer will still want to know what his or her burden of proof is—i.e., will anything about the ecosystem management dimension of a proposed project make or break the project's approval. An attorney hired to oppose a project will want to know this just as much as the attorney hired to advocate on behalf of the project. In the long run, all the rah-rah support for ecosystem management means very little in the right here, right now context in which real-world lawyers operate if it does not have the capacity directly and overtly to change their clients' outcomes.

In the ESA setting, this question focuses attention on the fact that nothing in the ESA advances ecosystem management beyond an implied consequence of the stated purpose of conserving ecosystems upon which protected species rely. Rather, virtually everything that counts under the

ESA is species specific: *species* are listed and their critical habitat designated under section 4; federal agencies must conserve listed *species* under section 7(a)(1); federal agencies must avoid jeopardizing *species* and destroying *species*' critical habitat under section 7(a)(2); all persons must avoid taking animal *species* under section 9; permits may be granted for incidental take of listed *species* under section 10. Hence, FWS and NMFS are left to channel all their ecosystem management policy into a law that is species-specific in implementation, a tactic they know can go only so far before it is open to attack as *ultra vires*. For example, the agencies declined recently to develop a policy of designating and listing distinct breeding populations based on the importance of the population to its ecosystem. The adopted policy observed that "despite its orientation toward conservation of ecosystems, the Services do not believe that the Act provides authority to recognize a potential [population] as significant on the basis of the importance of its role in the ecosystem in which it occurs." *Policy on Recognition of Distinct Vertebrate Population Segments Under the Endangered Species Act*, 61 Fed. Reg. 4722, 4723 (1996).

Does this mean ecosystem management can make no difference to outcomes under the ESA? Not at all. But it does mean that it is difficult to know when it will make a difference, as it is difficult for the agencies to pin up or down decisions directly on ecosystem management goals and criteria. Some actions are easier in this respect, such as grouping species listings when the species are found in the same ecosystem, or developing recovery plans designed around ecosystem restoration. In those cases the nexus between ecosystem and the ESA action is often direct—i.e., a significant component in the explanation for the species' decline and a key factor in designing the species' recovery.

Level 7: Is the norm fully transformed into law to apply? Even under the harm rule, FWS and NMFS must have a listed endangered animal species relying on the ecosystem to provide the necessary leverage to shape the ESA's species-specific and project-specific outcome with ecosystem management policy. The most die-hard ecosystem management advocate thus must concede that ecosystem management has not attained the status of law to apply under the ESA. Although its policy star is rising, ecosystem management remains in the background of the ESA. No ecosystem management rules are to be found in the agencies' ESA regulations. No citizen suits are brought for violation of ecosystem management. No court has enjoined a development project because it impedes ecosystem management. The ESA's species-specific focus will limit ecosystem management in this respect at every turn, preventing it from becoming more than a driving policy force in species-specific legal actions. But perhaps that is not much of a distinction to the practically-minded real-world lawyer interested more in the outcome than in how one gets there. As FWS increasingly uses the harm rule as a surrogate for ecosystem management, it matters less and less that ecosystem management itself is not in the black letter law.

Indeed, the greatest challenge to a lawyer is when an idea has made it to Level 6—where it affects legal outcomes—and is stuck there, for in that

setting the lawyer knows there is lawyering to be done to deal with the issue but the lawyer cannot point to clear legal standards to guide clients, to
argue to agencies, and to appeal to courts. Despite all the efforts of FWS
and NMFS to push ecosystem management to the forefront, and despite all
the scientific journal and law review articles advocating ecosystem management, this is, I am afraid, where ecosystem management is stuck under
the ESA, and it will remain so in the absence of legislative reform.

NOTES & QUESTIONS

1. Given this view of the ESA, shaped largely by its species-by-species approach, is it possible that the ESA may eventually hinder rather than support
the formulation of ecosystem management law? The point of the article seems
to be that ecosystem management law fundamentally *cannot* be based on a species-by-species focus, so eventually the authority of the ESA to bring about ecosystem management will run out, as will, therefore, its effectiveness in achieving the goals of ecosystem management. Do you agree? How would you change
the ESA to eliminate these concerns? For more on this theme, see Jacqueline
Lesley Brown, *Preserving Species: The Endangered Species Act Versus Ecosystem Management Regime, Ecological and Political Considerations, and Recommendations for Reform*, 12 JOURNAL OF ENVTL. L. & LITIG. 151 (1997).

2. How close did FWS and NMFS under the Clinton Administration come to
crossing their line of authority? Assume you had been hired by an industry
trade group to challenge FWS and NMFS ecosystem management policy on the
ground that it violates the ESA. What arguments would you have made?

(2) Environmental Assessment Laws

Grumbine's approach to ecosystem management outlined previously in
this chapter relies heavily on the adaptive management process of monitoring, modeling, assessing, and adjusting. Holling forged that process in response to what he saw as the shortcomings of conventional environmental
assessment procedures in use in the 1970s. The genesis of those procedures
was the National Environmental Policy Act (NEPA) and its infamous "Environmental Impact Statement" procedure. Although Holling roundly criticized the assumptions and methods of the EIS process and his substitute of
adaptive management has been widely endorsed as the only way to go in
ecosystem management, NEPA continues to have its supporters as a tool
for promoting ecosystem management. *See* Dinah Bear, *The Promise of
NEPA*, in BIODIVERSITY AND THE LAW 178 (William Snape III ed., 1996). As
the following excerpt reveals, however, the promise of NEPA in this regard
may be quite dim.

David R. Hodas, *NEPA, Ecosystem Management and Environmental Accounting*

14 Natural Resources & Environment 185 (2000).

If law were to reorient our analytical framework so that each decision
were to include, to the greatest extent possible, adverse environmental consequences, we could institutionalize a process of making sound ecosystem

management decisions. One law that was supposedly designed to break decisionmaking out of its narrow, economically focused box was the National Environmental Policy Act (NEPA), 42 U.S.C. §§ 4321-4370d. Predicated on the idea that governmental decisions should not be made without full consideration of adverse environmental implications of the decisions, NEPA suggests that the more environmentally realistic our expectations, the greater the opportunity to reduce poverty, increase wealth, and diminish environmental degradation. Unfortunately, NEPA does not advance the cause of sound ecosystem management or the related concept of sustainable development, but, as will become apparent, allows decisions affecting ecosystem development to be whitewashed with a thin coat of "apparent" soundness or sustainability. In other words, NEPA, as it has evolved, lets us feel comforted by the illusion that our decisions are environmentally sensitive; as a society we willingly pretend that environmental impact statements are important, thorough, reliable analyses, when in most cases they are mere formalities based on data and predictions made by people who have no accountability for error.

Enacted January 1, 1970, NEPA was the first environmental law of the modern environmental age, and is now the model for a law that has been adopted worldwide. Although it does not use the phrase ecosystem management or sustainable development in its text, the purpose of NEPA was to achieve that which is now referred to as sustainable development, namely, " . . . [t]o declare a national policy which will encourage productive and enjoyable harmony between man and his environment; to promote efforts which will prevent or eliminate damage to the environment and biosphere and stimulate the health and welfare of man." *Id.* at § 4321. To implement this policy, Congress directed that agencies "insure that presently unquantified environmental amenities and values . . . be given appropriate consideration in decisionmaking along with economic and technical considerations;" and that they "include in every recommendation or report on proposals for legislation and other major federal actions significantly affecting the quality of the human environment, a detailed statement . . . on . . . the environmental impact of the proposed action." *Id.* at § 4332(2)(B), (C).

As with most new requirements, compliance with the new beast known as the environmental impact statement (EIS) requirement was slow. Although NEPA § 102 requires that each federal agency must prepare an EIS when making a decision that could significantly affect the human environment, many agencies, particularly those with a mandate to promote development projects, such as the Atomic Energy Commission, vigorously resisted. In response, the early litigation under NEPA, such as *Calvert Cliffs' Coordinating Comm., Inc. v. U.S. Atomic Energy Comm'n*, 449 F.2d 1109 (D.C.Cir.1971), addressed the fundamental failure of the agency to include environmental impacts in its evaluation and approval of licenses to construct nuclear power plants. In that now famous decision, the court declared that "Congress did not intend [NEPA] to be . . . a paper tiger," and ruled that all agencies of the federal government "must—to the fullest extent possible under its statutory obligations—consider alternatives to its actions which would reduce environmental damage." After it became clear that NEPA applied broadly to all agencies of the government, the litigation shifted to more lawyerly gamesmanship in which agencies tried to avoid significant environmental evaluation by narrowly defining the statutory requirements so that hard issues might not be subject to the EIS mandate.

The early litigation that arose under NEPA fell into two large categories: threshold questions and adequacy questions. In cases raising threshold questions, agencies asserted that no EIS was needed because one of the elements of the statute's requirement ("proposals . . . for . . . major federal action significantly affecting the quality of the human environment") for an EIS was not present. The second category addressed whether the EIS adequately evaluated the adverse environmental consequences of a project, as well as alternatives that could avoid or mitigate the harm. In 1978, the President's Council on Environmental Quality (CEQ) promulgated regulations, 40 C.F.R. parts 1500–1508, that substantially standardized the way that federal agencies approach the NEPA process.

The courts, however, significantly narrowed the practical impact of the mandate that agencies think deeply about the environmental consequences of their actions, that they seriously explore alternatives, and that they consider the larger, long-term picture of accommodating development with ecological soundness, even though these requirements remain in the words of NEPA and the CEQ regulations. In a series of decisions, the U.S. Supreme Court has bleached out the meaning of NEPA and the CEQ regulations by its "crabbed interpretation of NEPA" and its dismissal of the goals of NEPA in § 101(b) as "largely rhetorical." Lynton Caldwell, *NEPA Revisited: A Call for a Constitutional Amendment*, THE ENVIRONMENTAL FORUM, Nov.-Dec. 1989, at 18.

The Supreme Court's Evisceration of NEPA

Since the late 1970s, the Supreme Court has been unwilling to read the substantive goals of NEPA into its interpretations, especially when major government policy issues were at stake. It did this, in part, by narrowing the remedies it would permit under NEPA. First, in *Kleppe v. Sierra Club*, 427 U.S. 390 (1976), the Court, defined "proposal" in the most narrow, legalistic sense possible, on the theory that an agency could avoid preparing an EIS so long as it was only contemplating action. . . According to the Court, an EIS need not be prepared until the eleventh hour: "the moment at which an agency must have a final statement ready is the time at which it makes a recommendation or report on a proposal for federal action." *Id.* at 405–06. . . By looking at NEPA solely as a procedural requirement devoid of any substantive value, the Court signaled its hostility toward NEPA's advancement of any of its sustainable development goals, even in a requirement as minor as allowing courts to order agencies to begin early preparation of EISs.

Shortly after its *Kleppe* decision, the Court narrowed the vision called for by NEPA. In *Vermont Yankee Nuclear Power v. NRDC*, 435 U.S. 519 (1978), public interest groups challenged the issuance of a nuclear power plant construction license on the grounds, *inter alia*, that the agency had failed to consider alternative sources of electricity, including energy conservation. The Court in *Vermont Yankee* stated explicitly that although NEPA established "significant substantive goals for the Nation," the duties it imposed on agencies was "essentially procedural."

Just two years after *Vermont Yankee*, the Court announced summarily that an agency was "free under NEPA to reject an alternative acknowledged to be environmentally preferable solely on the ground that any change in [plans] would cause delay." *Strycker's Bay Neighborhood Council v. Karlen*, 444 U.S. 223, 230 (1980) (Marshall, J., dissenting). As a result, NEPA does not require an agency either to develop or implement a plan to mitigate environmental damage, so long as the agency considers mitigation in general terms as an option; nor does NEPA require an agency to perform a "worst-case analysis" to assess the effects of catastrophe. *Robertson v. Methow Valley Citizens Council*, 490 U.S. 332 (1989).

Thus, NEPA now merely requires a relatively narrow document that accompanies files reflecting foregone conclusions. At best, NEPA may marginally improve narrow decisions affecting the environment, but NEPA does not provide even marginal ecological or sustainable security. Unfortunately, NEPA, the most widely copied environmental law in the world, now provides the means to thoroughly wallpaper serious structural flaws in our decisions, so that decisions appear to be sustainable when in reality they are no more than mirages of environmental concern.

NEPA's tragic devolution can be traced to the lack of any criteria to measure conduct and to hold actors accountable for their decisions. The lack of post-EIS review and monitoring not only makes the promises of mitigation hollow, but decisionmakers and project advocates have also learned the short-term lessons of NEPA litigation in meeting NEPA's technical requirements without hindering a project by asking important questions. This short-term approach results in no post-project monitoring and deprives us of the feedback needed to improve future decisions. Under the current law, project proponents know there is no consequence from underestimating adverse environmental effects. Because there is no liability for inaccuracy, there is no need for post-project review that would check the accuracy of the predictions.

NOTES & QUESTIONS

1. Professor Hodas's rather gloomy view of NEPA's usefulness in ecosystem management illustrates one of the difficulties of trying to stretch existing environmental laws into ecosystem management laws—the preexisting "box" of judicial interpretations that may limit how far the stretching can go. But the Supreme Court is not the only potential source of the watering down of NEPA of which Professor Hodas complains. For example, the Defenders of Wildlife released a report in 2003 examining the positions taken by the Bush Administration in 172 different NEPA cases. *See* WILLIAM A. SNAPE AND JOHN M. CARTER III, WEAKENING THE NATIONAL ENVIRONMENTAL POLICY ACT (Defenders of Wildlife, 2003). The report contended that the federal government's position in 94 of these cases was "NEPA-hostile," meaning they would have weakened the requirements of NEPA, of which the government lost 73 cases. By contrast, the government prevailed in 75 of the 78 cases in which it took a "NEPA-consistent" position. Other evidence of the Bush Administration's attempts to take NEPA is a new direction appeared from the Council of Environmental Quality's creation of a NEPA Task Force to examine areas for potential reform. *See* 67 Fed. Reg. 45510 (July 9, 2002). The prospect of NEPA reform—a topic not opened at this level for over a decade—sent jitters through many environmental groups. But the Task Force's report, delivered to CEQ in September 2003, proposed no broad reforms to the scope or jurisdiction of NEPA, although the Task Force's support for "streamlining" NEPA procedures for environmental evaluation of low-impact activities opens the door to reduced analytical vigor and information disclosure in some settings. For more perspectives on the potential impact of the Task Force's recommendations, see Bradley C. Karkkainen, *Whither NEPA?*, 12 N.Y.U. ENVTL. L.J. 333 (2004).

3. Complying with NEPA's assessment and documentation procedure is the responsibility of the federal agency proposing the action, which raises concerns as to the objectivity of the process. The U.S. Environmental Protection Agency provides some level of independent review under its authority, found in the Clean Air Act, to review and comment on the environmental impacts of "any matter relating to duties and responsibilities granted" to EPA under federal law, and to refer to the White House Council on Environmental Quality any proposed action EPA finds "is unsatisfactory from the standpoint of public health or welfare or environmental quality." 42 U.S.C. 7609(a). EPA uses this authority to review and comment on NEPA EISs it and other agencies prepare, and in the late 1990s released a guidance designed to focus its NEPA review efforts on the degree to which the EIS reflects consideration of the impact the proposed action will have on biodiversity conservation and ecosystem functions. *See* USEPA, CONSIDERING ECOLOGICAL PROCESSES IN ENVIRONMENTAL IMPACTS ASSESSMENTS (1999). The guidance, which built on previous guidance documents that focused the use of terrestrial environment and habitat evaluations in NEPA reviews, explicitly adopted conservation biology as the review framework and specifies ten ecosystem processes that its NEPA reviewers should consider when assessing the impact of proposed actions. While EPA cannot mandate that other federal agencies adopt conservation biology or an ecosystem processes approach to their NEPA duties, the fact that EPA can use those frameworks in its NEPA review authority is likely to help promote the development of ecological economics as a discipline and to develop substantive measurements of ecological processes. *See generally* Robert L. Fischman, *EPA's NEPA Duties and Ecosystem Services*, 20 STAN. ENVTL. L.J. 497 (2001).

(3) Pollution Control Laws

The U.S. Environmental Protection Agency (EPA) is the nation's leading pollution control authority, administering dozens of statutes designed to control industrial, municipal, agricultural, and other sources of environmental media pollutants. EPA's primary media-specific pollution control authorities include the Clean Water Act (water pollution), Clean Air Act (air pollution), Resources Conservation Recovery Act (solid and hazardous waste), Comprehensive Environmental Response, Compensation, and Liability Act (contaminated media remediation), Federal Insecticide, Rodenticide, and Fungicides Act (pesticides), and Toxic Substances Control Act (chemicals). Many conventional courses and casebooks on environmental law use a "tour" of these EPA authorities as their core subject matter. But EPA's administration of its pollution control authorities has not been particularly focused on ecosystem-level concerns. Indeed, the laws themselves for the most part do not build explicitly on such an approach. Rather, technology-based and health-based standards are the chief concern of EPA as it regulates discrete sources of air, water, and soil pollution. The authority to regulate based on environmental quality performance that does exist in some of EPA's statutes had been largely untapped through the 1980s. With the emergence of ecosystem management as a broad federal policy objective in the 1990s, however, the agency began to focus on that latent potential. First, in a vision statement issued late in the George H. Bush Administration, REDUCING RISK: SETTING PRIORITIES AND STRATEGIES FOR ENVIRONMENTAL PROTECTION (1990), EPA concluded that it "has paid too little attention to natural ecosystems" and that its "response to human health risks as compared to ecological risks is inappropriate." *Id.* at 9. This new sentiment led to the following more developed policy statement:

U.S. Environmental Protection Agency, *Ecosystem Protection Workgroup, Toward a Place-Driven Approach: The Edgewater Consensus on an EPA Strategy for Ecosystem Protection*
(March 15, 1994 Draft).

Background

To date, EPA has accomplished a great deal, addressing many major sources of pollution to the nation's air, water and land. Yet, even as we resolve the more obvious problems, scientists discover other environmental stresses that threaten our ecological resources and general wellbeing. Evidence of these problems can be seen in the decline of the salmon populations in the Pacific Northwest and the oyster stock in the Chesapeake Bay, the decline in migratory bird populations, and degraded coral reef systems.

The causes of these problems are as varied as human activity itself: the way we farm, work, travel, and spend our leisure hours. Although many federal, state, and local regulations address these problems, past efforts have been as fragmented as our authorizing statutes. Because EPA has concentrated on issuing permits, establishing pollutant limits, and setting national standards, the Agency has not paid enough attention to the overall environmental health of specific ecosystems. In short, EPA has been "program-driven" rather than "place-driven."

Recently, we have realized that, even if we had perfect compliance with all our authorities, we could not assure the reversal of disturbing environmental trends. We must collaborate with other federal, state, and local agencies, as well as private partners to reverse those trends and achieve our ultimate goal of healthy, sustainable ecosystems that provide us with food, shelter, clean air, clean water and a multitude of other goods and services. We therefore should move toward a goal of ecosystem protection.

Goal of Ecosystem Protection

The goal of EPA's ecosystem protection approach is to help improve the Agency's ability to protect, maintain, and restore the ecological integrity of the nation's lands and waters (which includes the health of humans, as well as plant and animal species) by moving toward a place-driven focus. This approach will integrate environmental management with human needs, consider long-term ecosystem health, and highlight the positive correlations between economic prosperity and environmental wellbeing. An ecosystem protection approach will create a framework within which to discuss numerous other issues facing the Agency and our country, such as environmental justice, unfunded mandates, flexibility, state capacity, sustainable development, use of science and data, and measuring environmental results.

The Edgewater Consensus

On March 5, 1994, EPA's Ecosystem Protection Workgroup met in Edgewater, Maryland to develop a strategy for realizing that goal. The Workgroup described a vision for reorienting the Agency toward a "placedriven" orientation; that is, the work of the Agency would be driven by the environmental needs of communities and ecosystems. For any given "place," EPA would establish a process for determining long-term ecological, economic, and social needs and would reorient its work to meet those needs. Although this approach is being demonstrated in a number of places, the Workgroup envisioned that, over time, the entire country would benefit from this approach. To realize that vision, the Workgroup determined that systems must be established to move toward a place-driven approach that would:

1. establish a process (with appropriate partners) for picking places, and for

- developing steps for implementing ecosystem protection that:
- identifies environmental goals and indicators;
- identifies ways to support sustainable development and communities
- develops and implements a joint action plan based on sound science; and,
- measures progress and adapts management to new information over time;

2. coordinates different programs within our Agency, and collaborates with our external partners and defines roles and responsibilities at each identified place; and,

3. identifies tools and support that could be provided at a national level.

Critical Success Factors

Three critical success factors exist for EPA to make ecosystem protection a reality. First, government activities must be driven by the issues faced by particular ecosystems and the economies founded upon them. The protection of ecosystems cannot be viewed by the Agency as a separate task existing on the margins of environmental protection, or as a special initiative imposed from above. The issues threatening the sustainability of ecosystems must drive the Agency's agenda, and policy, planning, budgeting, and information systems must be developed accordingly. This will involve "changing the unit of work" from piecemeal program mandates to the imperatives of a specific place. It will require EPA to devise programs that respond to the needs of specific geographic areas, not simply statutory mandates. Success will be achieved with greater integration and teamwork among environmental and natural resource agencies, and commerce, trade, and economic development programs.

Second, the ecosystem approach requires coordinated, integrated action by federal, state, tribal, and local agencies; between government and private enterprises (e.g., NGOs and industry); and, most importantly, between government and the people for whom services are being offered and provided. Environmental problems are almost always beyond the purview of any one program or organization. EPA is committed to working more effectively in an interagency, intergovernmental process. EPA will enlist the support of a spectrum of participants in the priority-setting and decisionmaking processes. EPA will increase it efforts to support the ecosystem protection efforts of states and local agencies that have recently proliferated throughout the country.

Third, information is a key to empowerment that moves communities to action. The availability of quality information on the resources to be protected is essential and, in many cases, is primarily available at the local level. Whereas the traditional approach spawned rules for an agency to follow, ecosystem protection, restoration and management at EPA will be dedicated to strategically responding to the best information on the needs of the resource and adapting management over time based on careful monitoring and new information. This means we will improve and integrate the information we gather and make it more accessible through the Agency's information systems, and forge a much stronger link between the Agency's scientific community and the information technology community, so that work is aligned with the needs of protecting entire ecosystems. EPA will also provide leadership in conducting public education and outreach programs to explain the importance of ecosystem protection to the public.

Making it Happen

Recognizing that we must move to a place-driven approach, the Edgewater Conference identified existing barriers to progress. These barriers include a lack of information on specific ecosystems; inadequate ecological endpoints for specific places; staff lacking a focus toward which to orient their work; historical single-media focus on programs and not places; the

Agency's lack of a central system for planning, budgeting, and accountability; and staff not trained or hired for the right skills.

To address the critical success factors and barriers discussed above, the Agency will respond on several paths. We will align our policy, regulatory, institutional, and administrative infrastructure to support ecosystem protection; we will develop information and tools to facilitate the approach; and we will reorient the Agency's culture to facilitate a place-driven approach. We also will promote our ecosystem protection activities within and outside the Agency and measure our success as we proceed.

NOTES & QUESTIONS

1. Recall Grumbine's goal for ecosystem management of protecting "native ecological integrity." The EPA said its goal for ecosystem management is "to protect, maintain, and restore the ecological integrity of the nation's lands and waters (which includes the health of humans, as well as plant and animal species)." Are these consistent? Assume that we could, for any particular ecosystem, identify its "native ecological integrity" and measure how close its current condition is to that state. Would using the EPA's goal justify attempting to restore the ecosystem to that native state? Would using the EPA's goal justify a decision *not* to restore the ecosystem to that native state?

2. Soon after *Edgewater Consensus* the EPA produced an inventory of ongoing projects that presented some ecosystem focus component, though admitting that very few involved comprehensive ecosystem assessment or management. *See* USEPA, A PHASE I INVENTORY OF CURRENT EPA EFFORTS TO PROTECT ECOSYSTEMS (1995), available at http://www.epa.gov/docs/ecoplaces. The projects took place at many levels. Examples included:

large scale:	Great Lakes Program; Colorado River Program; Gulf of Mexico Program; Pacific Northwest Forest Plan; Prairie Pothole Region Ecosystem Assessment
local scale:	Merrimack River, N.H.; Lake Champlain, N.Y.; Tampa Bay, Fla.; Corpus Christi Bay, Tex.; Malibu Creek, Haw.
multi-site:	Wetlands Restoration Research Project; Pacific Salmon Habitat Recovery Project; Clean Lakes Program

Even by 1995, these projects blanketed most of the United States:

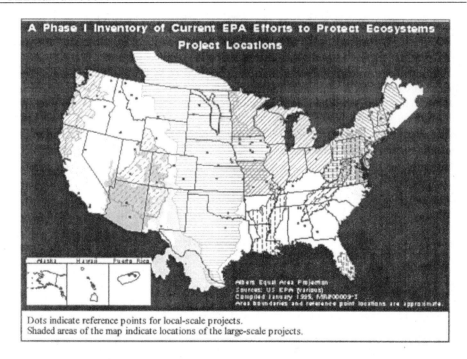

Dots indicate reference points for local-scale projects.
Shaded areas of the map indicate locations of the large-scale projects.

3. To follow through with the general theme of the *Edgewater Consensus*, the EPA identified the provisions in its media-specific pollution control authorities that could be shaped toward ecosystem management, mainly by linking EPA's primary regulatory authority with its coordinate species protection responsibilities under the Endangered Species Act. *See* Environmental Law Institute (for EPA), Using Pollution Control Authorities to Protect Threatened and Endangered Species and Reduce Ecological Risk. Rather than using endangered species as its metric for incorporating ecosystem management, could the EPA have used ecosystem services? For such a proposal, suggesting that there is indeed room for the EPA to use ecosystem services for direct implementation of statutory authorities or as the performance measure, see J.B. Ruhl, *Ecosystem Services and the Clean Water Act: Strategies for Fitting New Science into Old Law*, 40 ENVTL. L. 1381 (2010). Regardless of which metric it might use, however, the EPA still has not developed a comprehensive proposal for redrafting its pollution control regulations into an ecosystem management regime.

4. The states play a large role in implementation of pollution control authorities, both through administration of state pollution control laws and through a process by which the EPA delegates to states the authority to implement federal law. During the 1990s, over a dozen states moved their pollution control authorities increasingly toward ecosystem management goals, principally through watershed-based initiatives. *See* R. Steven Brown and Karen Marshall, *Ecosystem Management in State Government*, 6 ECOLOGICAL APPLICATIONS 712 (1995); Jessica Bennett, *State Biodiversity Planning*, THE ENVTL. FORUM, July/August 1998, at 19. For example, even before the EPA undertook its ecosystem management initiative, the Florida Department of Environmental Protection (FDEP) undertook a similar effort to reorient its pollution control (and other) authorities with ecosystem management as a coordinating purpose. In legislation consolidating several state environmental and resources agencies into the unified FDEP, the Florida legislature and Governor Lawton Chiles required

FDEP to develop and implement measures to "protect the functions of entire ecological systems through the enhanced coordination of public land acquisition, regulatory, and planning programs." FDEP convened an Ecosystem Management Work Group to develop means of using ecosystem management to fulfill that legislative directive. In the series of reports that emanated from the Work Group, FDEP outlined an approach for integrating ecosystem management into its existing authorities, including principally its pollution control authorities, that relied heavily on the principles R.E. Grumbine laid out in his landmark article *What Is Ecosystem Management?*, which is reproduced in the previous section of this book. *See* Florida DEP, Beginning Ecosystem Management (1994); Florida DEP, Ecosystem Management At Work in Florida (1998); *see generally* Mike Batts, *Ecosystem Management in Florida—A Case Study*, 20 NOVA L. REV. 743 (1996). Still, like EPA's Edgewater Consensus, FDEP's vision lacked concrete legislative and regulatory proposals, and the effort became largely moribund with the change of administrations in the Governor's office.

(4) Public Land and Resource Management Laws

The Congressional Research Service and General Accounting Office assessments of ecosystem management policy that open this section of the text focus on four federal public land management agencies: The U.S. Fish and Wildlife Service; the National Park Service; the Bureau of Land Management; and the U.S. Forest Service. The Property Clause of the U.S. Constitution provides that "Congress shall have power to dispose of and make all needful Rules and Regulations respecting the Territory or other Property belonging to the United States." U.S. const. Art IV, § 3, cl. 2. The Supreme Court has held that this authority provides Congress essentially unfettered power to regulate actions and to protect the resources on federal public land. *See* Kleppe v. New Mexico, 426 U.S. 529 (1976); *see generally* Peter A. Appel, *The Power of Congress "Without Limitation": The Property Clause and Federal Regulation of Private Property*, 86 MINN. L. REV. 1 (2001) (providing an exhaustive review of the Property Clause power). So, if Congress wished to make ecosystem management the law for all federal public land, it could. But we know it hasn't. The following excerpt explores initial efforts by federal land management agencies to use existing public land and resource management authorities to implement ecosystem management in the absence of congressional initiative.

Rebecca W. Thomson, *"Ecosystem Management"— Great Idea, But What Is It, Will It Work, and Who Will Pay?*

9 Natural Resources & Environment 42 (Winter 1995).

Existing Law and Litigation

Ecosystem management's *potential* significance is enormous—if incorporated into agency practice and law, it could act as an overlay over *all environmental laws*. Generally, federal land management and environmental laws are not organized around either biodiversity or ecosystem concepts. The public lands (30 percent of the land mass of the United States) are essentially divided up along jurisdictional boundaries between four public land agencies: Bureau of Land Management (BLM), Forest Service, Fish and Wildlife Service (FWS), and Park Service. The legal mandates of these agencies are largely directed to different purposes—the Forest Service and BLM lands are to be managed for multiple uses, including commodity production (trees, grass, and minerals), while the Park Service and FWS lands mainly serve conservation goals. Traditionally, the scientists who worked in each agency were trained to accomplish the agency's primary mandate with little interdisciplinary exchange.

In 1993, the White House Office on Environmental Policy (White House Task Force) established an Interagency Ecosystem Management Task Force to focus the administration's ecosystem management efforts. The administration's fiscal year 1995 budget includes $700 million for ecosystem management initiatives, over 70 percent of which will fund four "pilot ecosystem management projects" in the Pacific Northwest, Prince William Sound, the Everglades, and the Anacostia River in the District of Columbia.

The White House Task Force has also developed "draft" principles that would guide federal implementation of ecosystem management:

- Manage along ecological, rather than political or administrative boundaries.
- Ensure coordination among federal agencies and increased collaboration with state, local, and tribal governments; the public; and Congress.
- Use monitoring, assessment, and the best science available.
- Consider all natural and human components and their interactions.

Independently, the four public land agencies have also begun to move toward ecosystem management. Most notable, for the amount of controversy it engendered, was the Department of the Interior (DOI) proposal for [a National Biological Survey (NBS)] to inventory the nation's natural resources. DOI Secretary Bruce Babbitt described the NBS as a "very basic instrument for getting at these basic issues of inventory classification . . . to get, at least, a first cut of how we relate to these ecosystems." After property rights proponents stalled the NBS legislation in Congress, DOI implemented the NBS administratively in November 1993 by using existing funding, authority, and personnel.

On December 14, 1993, BLM issued a report on ecosystem management that contains its three principles: (1) sustaining the productivity and diversity of *viable ecological processes and functions*; (2) adopting an interdisciplinary approach to land management in which *program advocacy will yield to ecosystem advocacy*; and (3) basing management on long-term horizons and goals. FWS issued a report in March 1994 describing how to apply ecosystem management to fish and wildlife conservation. FWS has developed a map of fifty-two ecosystems, based on watersheds, in 50 states and, most significantly, reinforced its February 1992 policy decision to take a multispecies approach (rather than a species-by-species approach) to protecting plants and animals. To that end, FWS will list *groups* of species in a particular area to move to protection of ecosystems upon which several species depend. The National Park Service established an ecosystem working group and plans to promote comprehensive regional ecosystem restoration and management throughout the park system.

In 1989, the Forest Service announced "New Perspectives for Managing the National Forest System." The Forest Service stated that it would move from a multiple-use management approach—where forest land is viewed as a "place to produce commodities and amenities"—to an ecological vision in which living systems on the land "have importance beyond traditional commodity and amenity uses." Kessler, *New Perspectives for Sustainable Natural Resource Management*, 2 ECOLOGICAL APPLICATIONS 221, 222 (1992).

Accordingly, in 1992, the chief of the Forest Service announced a commitment to the use of ecosystem management to "blend[ ] the needs of people and environmental values in such a way that the national forests and grasslands represent diverse, healthy, productive, and sustainable ecosystems." Significantly, at the same time, the Forest Service announced its intent to reduce clear-cutting as a standard commercial timber harvest practice by over 70 percent from its 1988 level.

A Forest Service report describes four fundamental principles that guide its approach to ecosystem management: the use of an ecological approach to multiple-use management; application of the best scientific knowledge and technologies to decisionmaking; encouragement of partnerships with state agencies and private landholders; and the promotion of grass-roots participation in the planning process. FOREST SERVICE, A NATIONAL FRAMEWORK: ECOSYSTEM MANAGEMENT (1994). And, on June 13, 1994, Chief Thomas told regional foresters in a letter that "new forest plan standards and guidelines and program levels will be fully based on and carried out in accordance with the evolving concepts of ecosystem management."

The Forest Service announced its intent to revise its forest planning regulations, 36 C.F.R. § 219, to incorporate ecosystem management in accord with its four principles. These proposed rules have been slated for publication since August 1994, but apparently are on hold until the White House Task Force sorts out its administration-wide ecosystem management efforts.

The Forest Service also holds the distinction of implementing one of the most high-profile efforts at ecosystem management—the Federal Ecosystem Management Assessment Team (FEMAT) created to "solve" the spotted owl/timber crisis through ecosystem management. The President's 1993 Timber Summit directed this team of scientists to recommend an alternative based on analysis of biological and socioeconomic science that would balance the need for a healthy ecosystem with the needs of timber dependent communities in the Pacific Northwest. However, "Option 9,"

FEMAT's preferred alternative that calls for a 70 percent reduction in timber harvests, immediately resulted in suits from both the environmentalists and timber interests.

The Barriers and the Future

[T]he fundamental barrier to implementing ecosystem management identified by GAO is the failure of the White House Task Force to address and answer the tough public policy question of "who wins" in a conflict between socioeconomic needs and ecosystem health. The Report argues that a "healthy" ecosystem should take priority and buttresses its argument with references to NEPA. The Report also notes that the principles developed by BLM and FWS "leave no doubt" that greater priority will have to be given to maintaining or restoring minimum levels of ecosystem integrity "over unsustainable commodity production and other uses." How the White House Task Force will address this politically sensitive policy issue is not known at this time. If FEMAT is any example, it looks like the ecosystem "wins."

The hurdles described by the GAO report will not be easily cleared. Nonetheless, there is a great deal of momentum from many disparate groups to adopt ecosystem management. Agencies praise ecosystem management as having the potential to resolve the multiple, piecemeal battles over individual species or commodity uses. Timber industry groups have expressed guarded optimism about ecosystem management, for its inclusion of human needs, reliance on sound science, adaptive management, and emphasis on a cooperative, open process. Environmentalists, though they fear that the inclusion of human concerns and consensus building will invite compromises detrimental to the environment, are supportive of management seemingly directed to "healthy" ecosystems rather than only commodities production. As the CRS report aptly noted, "there is not enough agreement on the meaning of the concept to hinder its popularity."

Senator Hatfield asked how ecosystem management should be defined, implemented, and funded. Without really knowing the answers to any of these questions, the federal government is forging ahead. What we do know, is that for the near future, the policy of ecosystem management will be yet another overlay on top of existing environmental and public land law and processes.

NOTES & QUESTIONS

1. Thompson refers to different "mandates" Congress has given the different federal public land agencies. It is important to recognize that there are many different units of federal public lands—parks, refuges, forests, recreation areas, etc.—serving many different purposes. There is, in other words, no single unifying federal land policy. Rather, different units of federal land are managed according to one of three principal types of mandate. *Multiple use* lands are managed to optimize a bundle of prescribed uses. *Dominant use* lands have a primary use specified, but may accommodate other uses so long as the primary use is not impeded. *Single use* lands have, as the name suggests, just one prescribed use. The vast majority of federal land is subject to a multiple use mandate of one form or another, and usually some of the uses involve an intensive human use, such as timber production, grazing, recreation, or mineral extraction, while others are more consistent with the goals of ecosystem management, such as wildlife conservation. Congress usually leaves the agencies a fairly large policy space "box," meaning a wide variety of options is available to the agency. Nevertheless, given constant oversight by Congress, industry, conservation groups, and the public in general, the perpetual challenge federal land agencies face under multiple use mandates is to balance the multiple uses, particularly balancing the intense human uses against the resource conservation uses.

2. Thompson's perspective clearly is that by adopting ecosystem management principles, federal agencies are changing the balance of multiple uses, or even functionally transforming multiple use lands into dominant use lands under the ecosystem management "overlay." This raises the question, explored in detail in the remaining chapters of Part III, as to whether the agencies have reached the outer edges of the "box"—that is, have taken ecosystem management beyond their existing legal authority.

3. Thompson mentions another federal agency, the National Biological Service, now known as the Biological Resources Division (BRD) of the Ecosystems Bureau of the Department of the Interior's U.S. Geological Survey (USGS). The BRD is a biogeographical research agency, not a public land management agency. The BRD's roots actually go back to 1885, when Congress allocated funds to the Division of Entomology of the U.S. Department of Agriculture to conduct biological studies of birds in their environment. The program was expanded to include mammals the next year, and in 1890 the funding language referred specifically to investigations of species' geographic distributions. The Division was elevated to Bureau status in 1905, and for the next three decades the Bureau of Biological Survey conducted numerous important studies. In 1939 the Bureau was transferred to the Department of Interior as part of the Fish and Wildlife Service, where it remained until 1993. That year, the Department of Interior consolidated the biological research components of all of its various branches into the newly organized National Biological Survey, which was designed to operate as a nonadvocacy biological science research program. As Thompson explains, funding for creation of a new branch of the Department was controversial in Congress, and in 1995 Secretary Bruce Babbitt administratively moved the program to operate within the Department's existing USGS and renamed it the National Biological Service. Congress later renamed and funded the agency as the Biological Resources Division of the USGS. One of its primary missions, besides providing biological research capacity to all of the Department's branches, was to coordinate the nation's ongoing National Biological Information Infrastructure (NBII) that emerged from the recommendations of Vice President Gore's 1997 National Performance Review of federal agencies. In 2011, however, funding shortages led USGS to terminate the NBII. For current information on the BRD and the Ecosystems Bureau of the USGS, see http://ecosystems.usgs.gov/. For background on its precursor agencies, see Milton Friend, *Conservation Landmarks: Bureau of Biological Survey and National Biological Service*, in NATIONAL BIOLOGICAL SERVICE, DEPARTMENT OF THE INTERIOR, OUR LIVING RESOURCES 7 (1995); O. J. Reichman and H. Ronald Pulliam, *The Scientific Basis for Ecosystem Management*, 6 ECOLOGICAL APPLICA-

TIONS 694 (1996). Why do you suppose funding for a science-oriented, nonregulatory biological research agency was controversial in Congress?

4. Federal lands are held in a wide variety of forms of conservation. A partial listing of the different federal land units and their basic authorities shows this tremendous variation:

UNIT	AUTHORITY	AGENCY
Bureau of Land Management Land	Taylor Grazing Act, 43 U.S.C. 315—316o; Federal Land Policy and Management Act, 43 U.S.C. 1701—1782	BLM
Game and Bird Preserves	Game and Bird Preserves Act, 16 U.S.C. 671—698t	various
National Conservation Recreation Area	Refuge Recreation Act, 16 U.S.C. 460k	Dept. of Interior
National Forest	Forest Service Administration Act, 16 U.S.C. 473—478, 479—482; National Forest Management Act, 16 U.S.C. 1600—1614	Forest Service
National Grassland	Bankhead-Jones Farm Tenant Act, 7 U.S.C. 1000—1013; National Forest Management Act, 16 U.S.C. 1600—1614	Forest Service
National Lakeshore	National Park Service Act, 16 U.S.C. 1—18f-1	Park Service
National Marine Sanctuary	Marine Protection, Research, and Sanctuaries Act, 16 U.S.C. 1431—1445a	Dept. of Commerce
National Monument	Antiquities Act, 16 U.S.C. 431; National Park Service Act, 16 U.S.C. 1—18f-1	Park Service
National Park	National Park Service Act, 16 U.S.C. 1—18f-1	Park Service
National Preserve	National Park Service Act, 16 U.S.C. 1—18f-1	Park Service
National Recreation Area	various	various
National Scenic Trail	National Trail Systems Act, 16 U.S.C. 1241—1251	various
National Wildlife Refuge	National Wildlife Refuge Administration Act, 16 U.S.C. 668dd—668ee	FWS
Primitive Area	Wilderness Act, 16 U.S.C. 1131—1138	Forest Service
Wild and Scenic River	Wild and Scenic Rivers Act, 16 U.S.C. 1271—1287	various
Wilderness Area	Wilderness Act, 16 U.S.C. 1131—1136	various

5. As is explained in more detail in Chapter 9, federal public land management policy has gone through many phases. Initially, federal policy was to dispose of federal holdings, transferring them through a multitude of programs into private hands for settlement and resource development. As the public domain diminished increasingly over the 1800s, an era of "withdrawal and reservation" took hold in the late 1800s under which the federal government retained dominion over public lands and managed them under an increasing diversity of designations such as those described in the previous note. As Rebecca Thompson points out, with still almost one-third of the nation's land mass in federal hands, the formulation of public land management policy is of tremendous importance to many communities who depend on one or another use of the land. Over time, especially since the 1960s, the trend has unmistakably been to deemphasize resource extractive uses and to lean more toward recreational and conservation uses. Indeed, Thompson's central argument is that the rise of "ecosystem management" as a policy mantra signifies the dominance of conservation in federal public lands management.

6. For an excellent and concise history of federal public land policies, see Paul Smyth, *Conservation and Preservation of Federal Public Resources: A History*, NATURAL RESOURCES & ENVIRONMENT, Fall 2002, at 77. A thorough analysis of trends in federal public land management law is found at CAROL HARDY VINCENT ET AL., CONGRESSIONAL RESEARCH SERVICE REPORT FOR CONGRESS: FEDERAL LAND MANAGEMENT AGENCIES: BACKGROUND ON LAND AND RESOURCE MANAGEMENT (Feb. 27, 2001).

(5) Local Land Use Laws

Habitat loss on non-federal lands is the leading cause of species decline in the United States. *See* William Stolzenberg, *Habitat Is Where It's At*, NATURE CONSERVANCY, Nov.-Dec. 1997, at 6. Although under five percent of the nation's land mass is "built up" in the urban sense, conversion of undeveloped and agricultural land to urban uses nonetheless is associated with species and ecosystem decline in many areas, leading to "hot spots" of concern. *See* A.P. Dobson et al., *Geographic Distribution of Endangered Species in the United States*, 275 SCIENCE 550 (1997); T. Adler, *Mapping Out Endangered Species' Hot Spots*, 150 SCIENCE NEWS 101 (1996). Much of that land development activity is subject to regulation through local land use controls such as zoning and growth management. Traditionally, however, cities and counties have not used their land use authorities to effectuate any meaningful ecosystem-level conservation policy. Local governments face several constraints to doing so. First, their boundaries often are too limited to provide effective management of ecosystem-level conditions. Second, fiscal concerns may deter one local government from investing in protecting ecosystems that transcend political boundaries, lest neighboring localities "free ride" by forgoing similar investments or, worse, scoop up the businesses and industry that may no longer be welcome in the locality that exercises ecosystem management. These boundary and fiscal concerns could be solved through regional cooperation, but that requires divesting local control over issues or even succumbing to preemptive regional and state government authority.

On the other hand, local governments have often exhibited a distaste for federal control of matters that are profoundly local in impact. And ecosystem management is, in the end, profoundly local in impact given its focus on landscape-level implementation. There is, moreover, little question that local governments could exercise considerable power in the field of eco-system management. *See* A. Dan Tarlock, *Local Government Protection of Biodiversity: What Is Its Niche?*, 60 U. CHI. L. REV. 555 (1993). There is also the concern that the federal government at some point will exhaust its authority to implement ecosystem management when it affects decisions that are fundamentally within the scope of local land use authority. The federalism of ecosystem management at the landscape level is thus quite complex. *See* A. Dan Tarlock, *Federalism Without Preemption: A Case Study in Bioregionalism*, 27 PAC. L. J. 1629 (1996). As one observer summed up during the heady days of ecosystem management's emergence in the 1990s:

> Supposing local governments have the incentives, either through federal and state encouragement or from the bottom up, to tackle critical issues of biodiversity protection, what tools are likely to be at their disposal? There is a wide web of real and potential legal authorities in contemporary American local government law with which to address some of the problems of resource use and ecosystem management. Some of these authorities require institutional and doctrinal innovations; that is, they require a change in local government law to better serve the aims of ecosystem management. At the same time, other sources of local government authority are currently serviceable. While other demands and exigencies may make these innovations undesirable, there are good reasons to consider the potential of local institutions and local government law to grapple with the needs of modern ecosystems.

Daniel B. Rodriguez, *The Role of Legal Innovation In Ecosystem Management: Perspectives from American Local Government Law*, 24 ECOLOGY L. Q. 745, 755 (1997). Local governments thus find themselves in one sense in much the same position as the federal and state governments: some authority already exists to shape an ecosystem management policy, but legal reform would be required to do so comprehensively.

2. DESIGNING NEW LAW TO APPLY

As you may have noticed by now, thus far the law of ecosystem management has failed to take hold widely in concrete legal forms—in "hard law" that can be applied to discrete factual settings. This section explores the approach legislation might take in so doing and then turns to another source of law previously ignored—the common law.

a. LEGISLATIVE DIRECTIONS

In the absence of a comprehensive substantive ecosystem management legislation, federal and state agencies have tried to recraft specific conservation, impact assessment, pollution control, and land management laws into ecosystem management tools by administratively-led policy initiatives. But, as the case of the ESA demonstrates, that approach can only go so far before the connection between the text of the statutes involved and explicit policy adoption of ecosystem management goals becomes too tenuous to withstand challenge. At some point, in other words, Congress and the state legislatures, if they become committed to ecosystem management in a particular setting, will need to design substantive statutory authority for explicit adoption of ecosystem management goals under the relevant laws. The final segment of Professor Salzman's review of *Nature's Services* provides a vision of how substantially amended or entirely new laws could be designed to fulfill a greater ecosystem management purpose, in this case with the objective of ecosystem service delivery values in mind as the common policy theme:

James Salzman, *Valuing Ecosystem Services*

24 Ecology Law Quarterly 887 (1997).

III. ECOSYSTEM SERVICES AND THE LAW

In addition to its ecological and economic analyses, *Nature's Services* is fascinating because it recognizes a key role for ecosystem services in environmental law and policy. In fact, as potential symbiotic partners, both environmental law and research on ecosystem services have much to offer: together, they provide a new way to view environmental law, beyond command-and-control mandates and single-species protections.

How can environmental law promote our understanding of ecosystem services? It can do so through the creation of information markets that drive scientific research. Our understanding of groundwater chemistry and hydrology has increased tremendously in recent years, due primarily to markets created for this information as a result of CERCLA actions. Potentially responsible parties require a sophisticated understanding of local groundwater conditions to design the most efficient remediation strategies, and now-wealthy consulting businesses have arisen to meet these needs. Indeed, the role of regulation in creating secondary information markets is an important pillar of economics of information theory.

Ecosystem services have real value, yet they are not understood well enough to be valued monetarily. Could current regulations spur the creation of secondary information markets without the liability hammer of CERCLA? To a large extent, current wetlands regulations have already created information markets for wetlands vegetation and hydrology data. A great deal more is known today than just ten years ago, largely because the assessment models used to comply with wetlands regulations have focused on biophysical characteristics. But such emphasis is misplaced if ecosystem services are as valuable as current research indicates.

If government officials explicitly required significant data on ecosystem services for natural resource damage assessments and environmental impact statements, then a secondary information market likely would develop. Some regulations have begun to make these demands in the areas of groundwater hydrology and wetlands vegetation.... If ecosystem services are significantly undervalued, and such undervaluation therefore leads to misallocation of resources, then the use of regulations to create a profitable secondary market in ecosystem service data and indicators could prove an efficient intervention for improved management of resources.

What does ecosystem service research offer in return to environmental law? [One possibility] is specificity of indicators. For some services, benefits are too diffuse and monetary valuation is no more than a guess. Here, the law can use indicators of ecosystem services as a surrogate for economic value. While ecosystem management has become a catchword in government, a recent study by Professor Oliver Houck indicates serious shortcomings. He makes a strong case that, despite the trumpeting of an ecosystem approach to conservation, "[e]cosystem management, as currently promoted, is politics with a strong flavor of law-avoidance." He argues that the only effective legal standards to ensure protection of an ecosystem rely on assessments of keystone or indicator species:

> Why is it that indicator species work? Granted, they are by no means perfect surrogates for ecosystems and, granted again, the proof of their requirements can be complex and demanding for scientists operating at the far edge of data and predictability and trained to conclude nothing until all possible alternative hypotheses, however remote, have been disproved. Nonetheless, indicators work because, in the end, they produce specifics.

Robust, quantified indicators of ecosystem services could serve a similar role, providing an additional legal standard on which to base ecosystem management strategies. Much as the [National Forest Management Act] currently requires conservation of indicator species as a surrogate measure for ecosystem health, one could imagine a legal standard requiring maintenance of a specified, measurable level of local ecosystem services. Thus indicators assessing water flow into and out of a wetland might, for example, include dynamic measures of water retention, nutrient trapping, or water quality. These indicators, at least on the local level, could mandate management of ecosystems based on functional standards, i.e., maintaining the provision of baseline levels of services. Moreover, the direct benefit to humans of such conservation actions would be more obvious than the current focus on indicator species.

Perhaps the greatest value that increased understanding of ecosystem services offers to environmental policy, however, is its persuasive argument that biodiversity and habitat protection provide important benefits in ways not normally considered. Wheeling out the rosy periwinkle and charismatic megafauna every time the Endangered Species Act or wetlands protections come under threat goes only so far. *Nature's Services* takes a different, potentially more effective tack, calling for explicit recognition of ecosystem services because of the direct, tangible benefits they provide. Such recognition could provide a more integrated and compelling basis for action than those suggested by a focus on single-species or biodiversity protection for the simple reason that the impacts of these services on humans are more immediate and undeniably important. Indeed, a focus on ecosystem services has the potential to unify disparate parts of environmental law, linking the conservation goals in laws such as the Endangered Species Act and

National Forest Management Act more closely with the human health goals in seemingly unconnected laws such as the Clean Air Act and Safe Drinking Water Act.

These developments in environmental law are at once speculative and foreseeable consequences of future research on the production and delivery of ecosystem services. The study of ecosystem services is a new and very promising area of interdisciplinary research with the potential to create a significant shift in how we address environmental protection. Just as *Nature's Services* provides a valuable bridge linking ecologists and economists to policymakers, so, too, is it important for environmental lawyers to engage themselves in this research effort, both to explore the role ecosystem services should play in the law's development and to influence the direction of research so that the services provided by nature may be accorded their proper value.

NOTES & QUESTIONS

1. How would you implement Salzman's vision of using ecosystem services as the organizing principle of ecosystem management law? Along with a team of biologists and economists, Salzman later outlined a proposal for the creation of Ecosystem Service Districts (ESDs) and empowering them with land use and taxing authority to gather information about ecosystem services, assess their flow through the environment and economy, and manage their use and distribution. *See* Geoffrey Heal et al., *Protecting Natural Capital Through Ecosystem Service Districts*, 20 STAN. ENVTL. L.J. 333 (2001). Naturally this would involve some shifting of power from political units arranged more along political boundaries, such as counties, to units arranged more in line with environmentally relevant boundaries, such as watersheds. Do you think ESDs could be both a politically and environmentally viable arrangement?

2. The article on ESDs discussed in the note above appears in an issue of the *Stanford Environmental Law Journal* devoted entirely to the concept of ecosystem services. *See* Symposium, 20 STAN. ENVTL. L. J. 309 (2001). The *Journal* hosted a conference in 2000 at which economists, ecologists, lawyers, and representatives from industry, government, and nongovernmental organizations discussed the viability of ecosystem services as a foundation for the formation of ecosystem management and environmental policy generally. A second similar conference, held at the Florida State University Law School in 2006, took a closer look at how ecosystem services concepts had been integrated into legal contexts. *See* Symposium, J. LAND USE & ENVTL. L. 157 (2007). Consider some of the questions debated at the two conferences: How viable do you find the concept of ecosystem services as a core principle for purposes of developing ecosystem management law? Should any new law of ecosystem management use it as a core principle? If not, around what core principles would you fashion new hard law to apply in ecosystem management?

3. In his preamble to the Ecosystem Management Act of 1994 (excerpted above at the beginning of this part of the chapter), Senator Hatfield asks a series of questions about ecosystem management law and policy:

- What is ecosystem management, how should it be implemented and who should be implementing it?

- How does the ecosystem oriented work of the federal agencies, states, municipalities, counties, and interest groups mesh?

- And is the existing structure of our government agencies adequate to meet the requirements of managing land across which state and county lines have been drawn?

- Finally, with a decreasing resource production receipt base, how shall we pay for ecosystem management? Direct federal appropriations? Consolidation of federal, state, local and private funds?

- And if we determine how to pay for ecosystem management, who coordinates collection of these funds and how are they distributed?

After studying and discussing the materials presented thus far in this chapter, do you feel any more comfortable than Senator Hatfield apparently did that we have good answers to these questions? Do we need good answers to these questions in order to formulate good ecosystem management law and policy?

4. In his strident attack on the ecosystem management movement, *Defending Illusions: Federal Protection of Ecosystems*, Allan K. Fitzsimmons seized on Senator Hatfield's questions as the reason why any effort to steer existing law toward ecosystem management or to forge altogether new law is misguided. His overall take on ecosystem management as it was emerging during the 1990s in the Clinton Administration:

> Empowering the federal government to manage and protect ecosystems across the country is bad public policy. Advocates of ecosystem arguments use sectarian arguments built on false claims of pending environmental doom. They cloak themselves in a garment woven from ill-defined scientific buzzwords that are valueless for the purpose of guiding government decision making. They employ religious arguments that confuse the Creator with creation. New paradigmists would lessen human liberty and improvements in human well-being through assaults on constitutionally protected property rights. They would establish a vast new centralized bureaucracy to manage land use throughout the nation, using a maze of rules and regulations that would greatly surpass in complexity and cost any set of environmental regulations previously seen in the United States.

DEFENDING ILLUSIONS, *supra*, at 251. Do you find these qualities in the materials included in this chapter that advocate use of ecosystem management? Does Grumbine, for example, base his description of ecosystem management on "false claims of pending environmental doom"? Is Holling's adaptive management method "woven from ill-defined scientific buzzwords" and "valueless for the purpose of guiding government decision making"? Is Salzman's work on ecosystem services proposing "assaults on constitutionally protected property rights"? Have the Environmental Protection Agency and Fish and Wildlife Service ever mentioned the Creator or creation in any of their materials on ecosystem management that you have reviewed? To whom *is* Fitzsimmons referring?

5. The concept of ecosystem services is beginning to take hold in concrete legal contexts. For example, the 2008 Farm Bill directed the Secretary of Agriculture to "establish technical guidelines that outline science-based methods to measure the environmental services benefits from conservation and land management...in order to facilitate the participation of farmers, ranchers, and forest landowners in emerging environmental services markets." In December 2008 the Secretary established an Office of Ecosystem Services and Markets to carry out this task. Also in 2008, the Corps of Engineers and EPA adopted final regulations to introduce ecosystem services into the Clean Water Act Section 404 wetlands compensatory mitigation decisionmaking standards for the first time by requiring that "compensatory mitigation should be located . . . where it is most likely to successfully replace lost functions and services." 33 C.F.R. 332.3(b)(1). In 2010, the Department of Agriculture used the concept of ecosystem services to define grassland functions for purposes of conservation funding, explaining that grassland services "domestic animal productivity, biological productivity, plant and animal richness and diversity, fish and wildlife habitat (including habitat for pollinators and native insects), water quality and quantity benefits, aesthetics, open space, and recreation." 7 C.F.R. 1415.3. Do these strike you as appropriate applications of the concept?

6. Perhaps most significantly for the role of ecosystem services in decision making, in 2011 the President's Council of Advisors on Science and Technology (PCAST) issued a broad set of recommendations on using ecosystem services for law and policy in SUSTAINING ENVIRONMENTAL CAPITAL: PROTECTING SOCIETY AND THE ECONOMY (July 2011). PCAST summed up its thoughts as follows:

> In the report we transmit here, PCAST's Working Group on Biodiversity Preservation and Ecosystem Sustainability addressed the needs and opportunities in relation to both of these dimensions of the capacity of governments—and especially the U.S. Federal government—to fulfill more effectively their responsibility in relation to the protection of environmental capital and ecosystem services. The Working Group's recommendations, which we endorse, involve a three-pronged effort encompassing ways to make better use of existing knowledge, to support the generation of essential new knowledge, and to expand the use of informatics. We here boil down those recommendations to the following six key points.
>
> **1. The U.S. government should institute and fund a Quadrennial Ecosystems Services Trends (QuEST) Assessment.** QuEST should provide an integrated, comprehensive assessment of the condition of U.S. ecosystems; predictions concerning trends in ecosystem change; syntheses of research findings on how ecosystem structure and condition are linked to the ecosystem functions that contribute to societally important ecosystem services; and characterization of challenges to the sustainability of benefit flows from ecosystems, together with ways to make policy responses to these challenges more effective. The QuEST assessment should draw and build upon the wide variety of ongoing monitoring programs, previously conducted and ongoing assessments of narrower scope, and the expanded monitoring and species-discovery efforts for which we also call in this Report. And, it should be closely coordinated with the quadrennial National Climate Assessment mandated by the Global Change Research Act of 1990.
>
> **2. The U.S. Department of State, in coordination with the Office of Science and Technology Policy (OSTP), should take a leading role in the development of the Intergovernmental Science-Policy Plat-**

form on Biodiversity and Ecosystem Services (IPBES). The goal of IPBES is regular, thematic, global assessments of biosphere change, as well as preliminary assessments of emerging issues. The U.S. contribution to IPBES should be derived from and coordinated with the U.S. QuEST Assessment described above. Long-term oversight of this effort could be assigned to the Committee on International Science, Engineering, and Technology of the National Science and Technology Council (NSTC), the Sustainability Task Force of the NSTC's Committee on Environment, Natural, Resources, and Sustainability (CENRS), or a working group created between the Department of State and CENRS.

3. Federal agencies that implement biodiversity and ecosystem conservation programs should prioritize expenditures based on cost efficiency. Federal agencies collectively currently spend more than $10 billion annually on ecosystem restoration activities, land and easement purchases, and incentive payments, activities aimed primarily at conserving biodiversity or protecting and restoring ecosystem services within the United States. While additional funding for these conservation investments is warranted, much more careful targeting could achieve greater environmental benefits at the same cost. The Council on Environmental Quality (CEQ) should assist in this effort by reviewing conservation programs and identifying those that should be subject to this recommendation (e.g., Title 2 Farm Bill payments, mitigation payments, etc.).

4. Federal agencies with responsibilities relating to ecosystems and their services (e.g., EPA, NOAA, DOI, USDA) should be tasked with improving their capabilities to develop valuations for the ecosystem services affected by their decision-making and factoring the results into analyses that inform their major planning and management decisions. This will entail expanding current efforts on ecosystem-service valuation in EPA, USDA, and other agencies, as well as generating new knowledge about the ecosystem-service impacts (in both physical and value terms) of activities taking place on both public and private lands. The Office of Management and Budget (OMB), OSTP, and CEQ should ensure that the methodologies are developed collaboratively across agencies.

5. CENRS should identify the most important data gaps within existing biodiversity inventories and Federal and regional ecological monitoring systems, and clarify priorities and agency roles and funding for filling these. Further, OSTP and CEQ, with the help of NSTC, should encourage and coordinate cross-scale and cross-agency collaboration in monitoring. There are a number of key areas in which such collaboration in monitoring could rapidly improve the information base available for ecosystem assessment and management. Among other dimensions of such collaboration, recommendations should be developed for integrating the existing monitoring networks with the help of state-of-the art informatics.

6. NSTC should establish an Ecoinformatics-based Open Resources and Machine Accessibility (EcoINFORMA) initiative. This initiative would maximize financial savings by enabling integration and utilization of current knowledge (held by many different agencies) to inform decisions while facilitating the gathering of new essential knowledge. EcoINFORMA is needed to ensure that Federal agency data relevant to biodiversity and ecosystems, as well as the socio-economic and geophysical data required in support of ecosystem valuation and decision-support, are published in machine-readable, interoperable format to facilitate research engagement by public, private, academic, and other stakeholders, and to support policy- and decision-making at Federal, state, and local levels. In support of EcoINFORMA, OMB should enforce existing requirements that Federal agencies publish data related to biodiversity preservation and ecosystem services within one year of collection. EcoINFORMA should interact with international biodiversity and ecosystem information systems in the development of globally accepted biodiversity and ecosystem information standards, and should seek out and encourage partnerships with the private and academic sectors to develop innovative tools for data integration, analysis, visualization, and decision making.

What do you think of these recommendations? Are they likely to receive the funding necessary to implement them effectively? What law and policy frameworks would likely flow from doing so?

b. A ROLE FOR THE COMMON LAW?

J.B. Ruhl, *Ecosystem Services and the Common Law of "The Fragile Land System"*

20 Natural Resources & Environment 3 (Fall 2005).

[There is almost universal support for the proposition that] the source, the very backbone of the wave of federal pollution control laws the federal government enacted in the 1970s, was the common law of nuisance. And many observers also agree that there has been a profound shift of emphasis in environmental policy from controlling smokestacks and discharge pipes to managing ecosystem-wide phenomena such as habitat loss, invasive species, and nutrient-laden runoff—what today goes under the umbrella term of ecosystem management.

What is missing from this more recent focus on ecosystems and their sensitivity to human insult, however, is any notion that legislative initiatives might find some guidance in the framework of the common law. How is it that the common law of nuisance is regarded as the genesis of pollution control law, but for the law of ecosystem management it is as if the common law never happened?

Ecosystem management finds itself in [a] fragmented and stalled condition because, unlike the antipollution legislation, it had no common law foundation on which to build its structure and legitimacy. Perhaps out of arrogance, or ignorance, or the failure fully to appreciate the importance of the common law to antipollution legislation, ecosystem management legislation tried to leapfrog its common law formative stage, and it has gained little traction as a result. The question is whether the common law can overcome its reputation as having little meaningful to add to the field and backfill a foundation for the public law of ecosystem management. There is a basis for hope in this regard.

The Common Law of Ecosystem Services

Many commentators before me have advanced the case that the common law is profoundly adaptive. *See* J.B. Ruhl, *Complexity Theory as a Paradigm for the Dynamical Law-and-Society System*, 45 DUKE L.J. 849, 916–20 (1996). We know industrialization has harmed our ecosystems, that federal legislation does not hold all the answers, and that the ecological frontier, if anything, is vanishing. And we know much more today than we did thirty years ago about ecosystem services. As Justice Scalia acknowledged in [*Lucas v. South Carolina Coastal Commission*, 505 U.S. 1003 (1992)], "changed circumstances *or new knowledge* may make what was previously permissible [under common law] no longer so." 505 U.S. at 1031 (emphasis added). Hence, there is no reason why the common law cannot make an adaptive move to fill some of the gap in ecosystem management which, as discussed in the previous section, federal legislation has left open and is not likely to fill without help.

So, what would be the organizing principles for the evolution of a common law doctrine of ecosystem management? It is too easy to propose that the common law simply reverse direction and place a "green thumb on the scales of justice" in favor of protecting ecosystems in general. Nor will it be as easy as simply pointing out the objectives of ecosystem management and inviting the common law to have at it. There has to be a concrete theme to motivate the interest and action of private litigants and the courts, and that theme must have dimensions fitting within the basic contours of common law doctrine and institutions. This includes articulating a coherent statement of rights and liabilities that are susceptible to analysis through commonly understood and applied principles of proof of breach, injury, and causation, as well as a remedial system that provides efficient and equitable outcomes. In other words, the approach has to be legally practical.

Unfortunately, the discipline of ecosystem management is for the most part brimming with themes that are decidedly impractical for these purposes. Its organizing principles include conserving biodiversity, restoring naturalness, providing safe harbor for native species, and the implementation technique of adaptive management. Impressive sounding as these terms may be, they are square pegs to the common law's round holes.

By contrast, the ecosystem services branch of ecosystem management holds great promise for the common law. Most of ecosystem management is devoted to keeping ecosystem functions healthy for the sake of ecosystems, whereas the study of ecosystem services is devoted to articulating which ecosystem functions provide service values to humans that would be costly, but clearly necessary or desirable, to replace were they to degrade in quantity or quality. Moreover, because ecosystem services are the product of ecosystem functions, and ecosystem functions are the product of ecosystem structure, it follows as a matter of economic theory that the relevant ecosystem structure is no less than the "natural capital" necessary for providing economically valuable services to humans. And this new focus in ecology is producing a rapidly mounting body of research attaching real numbers to ecosystem service values at local and regional scales.

Recently, for example, researchers studying pollination services in Costa Rica demonstrated that the conversion of land from forest to grazing uses reduces the local populations of wild pollinator species enough to diminish productivity of nearby coffee plantations by more than 20 percent, resulting in a loss of $64,000 annually for a typical plantation. *See* T.H. Ricketts, *Tropical Forest Fragments Enhance Pollinator Activity in Nearby Coffee Crops*, 18 CONSERVATION BIOLOGY 1262 (2003). On a larger scale, more than twenty years ago law professor Oliver Houck demonstrated that the loss of coastal wetlands in Louisiana was costing the state billions of dollars in lost service values. *See* Oliver Houck, *Land Loss in Coastal Louisiana: Causes, Consequences, and Remedies*, 58 TULANE L. REV. 3 (1983). The idea took some time to catch on, but Louisiana recently embarked on an "Americas Wetland" campaign to call attention to its vanishing coastal wetlands, including a major push to gain federal assistance by noting the economic consequences of having its "working coastline" of oil rigs, ports, fishing villages, and New Orleans casinos flooded by the combination of rising sea levels and falling coastline levels. *See America's Wetland Campaign*, W. Ecosystem services are not about just birds and bees—they are about money, and lots of it.

Armed with that core set of principles, it is remarkable how straightforward an exercise it is to outline a set of common law rights and liabilities that put ecosystem services into play as the essential fabric of a new stage in the development of environmental common law. Every law student learns the black letter doctrine of nuisance: one commits a nuisance when his or her use of land unreasonably interferes with another person's reasonable use and enjoyment of his or her interest in land. Lawyers through the ages have had no problem agreeing that odors from a pigsty, or fumes from a copper smelting plant, or chemical pollution of a lake or stream are within the ballpark of nuisance so defined. Why should matters be any different when one person's use of land severs the flow of economically valuable ecosystem services to another person's use of land?

Nuisance law is quite a thicket on the question of what is unreasonable, but that is both the beauty and the frustration of the common law. It is made for this kind of balancing inquiry, which Justice Scalia described as an "analysis of, among other things, the degree of harm to public lands and resources, or adjacent private property, posed by the [landowner's] proposed activities, the social value of the [landowner's] activities and their suitability to the locality in question, and the relative ease with which the alleged harm can be avoided through measures taken by the [landowner] and the government (or adjacent landowners) alike." 505 U.S. at 1031 (citations omitted).

To be sure, it is not expected that every loss of natural capital should be or would be branded unreasonable under this test. Some natural capital is more critical than most, in that its degradation or destruction leads to significant economic injury on other lands. But given that we increasingly know where natural capital is located, where the ecosystem services it produces flow, and the value of those services at benefited properties, there is no reason why nuisance law in both its public and private stripes could not sort through questions about whether the destruction of natural capital in discrete cases is reasonable or not.

Not far from where I live and teach in Florida, for example, one can see quite palpable evidence of the importance of coastal dunes to the mitigation of hurricane storm surge damage at inland locations. There is a staggering difference in outcome between inland areas shielded by intact dunes and those inland of coastal development that did not retain dunes. On a far more devastating scale, surely the media coverage of Katrina, which repeatedly made the point that damage in New Orleans would have been mitigated had the coastal wetlands not been so severely degraded, has focused the nation's mind on the economic importance of ecosystem services. Under Justice Scalia's version of the nuisance balancing test, the harm to the public resources and private property resulting from the impaired dune and wetland systems unquestionably was severe, likely far outweighing the social utility of development that destroyed the resources, and the owners of prior intact dune and wetland areas were in the best position to avoid the harm. Were those resources thus critical natural capital, the destruction of which was unreasonable in relation to the expectations of inland property owners whose homes and businesses are now in splinters?

It is my belief that the common law is equipped to answer that question and others like it. The fact that it has not until now attempted to do so does not mean that it cannot, or will not have the opportunity, or simply is against all notion of it. The only missing ingredient until now has been the storehouse of knowledge ecologists and economists are building about the value of ecosystem services. This is precisely the kind of new knowledge Justice Scalia confirmed in *Lucas* can transform the common law and "make what was previously permissible no longer so." 505 U.S. at 1031. As sovereigns and landowners become aware of this new knowledge and begin to appreciate the cost imposed to them when others sever the flow of ecosystem services to their lands, they *will* sue in public and private nuisance actions. Indeed, such a claim recently was initiated with respect to the losses suffered in Katrina, alleging that those responsible for the disruption of wetland processes are also responsible for the economic losses that followed. *See* Barasich v. Columbia Gulf Transmission Co., Civ. A. No. 05–4161 (E.D. La. Complaint filed Sept. 13, 2005). And when lawyers and experts use this new knowledge to demonstrate to courts the cause of the injury and the value of the services lost, the courts *will* award damages, injunctions, and other relief. And it will all seem quite mundane, because there will be nothing about it that is out of the ordinary for the common law.

NOTES & QUESTIONS

1. Going beyond the suggestion that the common law has been overlooked in the development of ecosystem management law is the argument that common law institutions have *deliberately* pursued anti-environmental policies to facilitate other interests such as the protection of property rights and promoting economic uses of land. Evidence for this view was comprehensively assembled by law professor John Sprankling in *The Anti-Wilderness Bias in American Property Law*, 63 U. CHI. L. REV. 519 (1996), in which he systematically surveys property law doctrines such as waste, adverse possession, trespass, and nuisance, and argues that they were and remain "tilted toward wilderness destruction" in order "to encourage the agrarian development" of the nation. *Id.* at 521. He points out, for example, that American law abandoned the British version of the waste doctrine, which banned forest clearing for cultivation, and replaced it with the view that clearing for cultivation was "good husbandry." *Id.* at 534–35. And American trespass law developed in many states so as to tolerate, if not to endorse, open grazing of livestock on the unenclosed lands of another landowner. *Id.* at 548–49. These and other examples of his thesis, Sprankling argued, flowed from the abundance of wilderness America enjoyed relative to England, the need to build an economy, and the exalted position in which Americans generally place private property rights. He concluded that, "all other things being equal, the property law system tends to resolve disputes by preferring wilderness destruction to wilderness preservation." *Id.* at 520.

2. Whether the common law has been benign or hostile with respect to ecosystems as it is being leap-frogged by legislative and administrative initiatives, how realistic do you think it is to hope for the evolution of the common law suggested in the article? Is it more likely that judges will pick up the ball than Congress and state legislatures?

3. Assuming that property owner A could demonstrate that an adjacent property owner B's destruction of natural capital on B's property has directly impaired the use and enjoyment of A's property, and that A could credibly quantify the injury, what policy reasons would one make for arguing that the common law should *not* recognize that as cognizable in a claim for nuisance or some other form of common law action?

D. CASE STUDY: NATIONAL WILDLIFE REFUGE SYSTEM POLICY

The National Wildlife Refuge System is "a national network of lands and waters for the conservation, management, [and] appropriate restoration of the fish, wildlife, and plant resources and their habitats within the United States for the benefit of present and future generations of Americans." 16 U.S.C. § 668dd(a)(2). The system today comprises over 535 refuges and related wildlife conservation units. It covers 96 million acres of federal public land in total—an area larger than the National Park System—and including a wide variety of ecosystem types. Every state has at least one national refuge. Current administration of these refuge lands through the Department of the Interior's U.S. Fish and Wildlife Service (FWS) is controlled principally under the terms of the National Wildlife Refuge System Administration Act of 1966, as amended by the National Wildlife Refuge System Improvement Act of 1997. But the history of national wildlife refuges begins far prior to those laws.

The first instance of setting aside federal public land specifically for wildlife protection came in 1869 when Congress protected the Pribilof Islands in Alaska as a reserve for the northern fur seal. Later initiatives led to national parks and national forests, but not until 1903, when President Theodore Roosevelt used a presidential proclamation to set aside the three-acre Pelican Island in south Florida as a place for wildlife protection, were any lands designated as a wildlife refuge. Quickly thereafter, many other islands were given the same status, and eventually Congress and the Executive began routinely to establish wildlife refuges throughout the nation. The enactment of the Migratory Bird Treaty Act in 1918 fueled the process given the Federal government's new role in migratory bird protection, which was carried out often through Executive Order designating bird refuges.

To bring some order to the hodgepodge of refuges established through the collection of legislative and executive actions, FWS published a "Refuge Manual" in 1942 to guide individual refuge managers. Nevertheless, by the 1960s, although tens of millions of acres had been placed in refuge status, the ad hoc process of establishing refuge units and purposes resulted in numerous, uncoordinated establishing acts and executive orders and no coherent management standards, leading one commentator to describe it as the National "Bunch" of Wildlife Refuges. *See* Cam Tredennick, *The National Wildlife System Improvement Act of 1997: Defining the National Wildlife Refuge System for the Twenty-First Century*, 12 FORDHAM ENVTL. L. J. 41, 46 (2000).

Congress made a stab at bringing order to the program in the Refuge Recreation Act of 1962, which allowed refuge managers to prohibit forms of recreation on refuge land that are not directly related to the primary purposes of the refuge *unless* such uses would not interfere with those primary purposes. This "noninterference" standard provided a systemwide test for a set of allowable uses, in this case recreational uses, but in the end only compounded the management confusion by failing to provide meaningful clarifying standards for determining when interference was present.

The 1966 legislation was a more concerted effort to manage the various refuge units as a single coordinated network, and thus can be regarded as an organic act for the refuge program, or at least the beginnings thereof. The 1966 legislation consolidated the various refuge units into a unified "system." The legislation failed to provide specific guidelines and directives for administration and management of areas in the system, but did authorize the Secretary to "permit the use of any area within the System for any purpose, including but not limited to hunting, fishing, public recreation and accommodations, and access whenever he determines that such uses are compatible with the major purposes for which such areas were established." 16 U.S.C. § 668dd(d)(1). This so-called "compatibility" standard placed refuge lands in the "dominant use" model of public lands management—i.e., although multiple uses are allowed, protection of wildlife dominates over the others. Beyond that, however, the statute did not define compatibility or attach specific planning or substantive duties to it.

The FWS defined compatibility in its refuge manual to mean that a use "does not materially interfere with or detract from the purpose(s) for which the refuge was established." This not especially demanding or clarifying standard helped little to avoid inconsistent applications of the compatibility requirement across the System. But a series of events moved the Congress ever closer to additional legislative intervention on the subject. First, the District of Columbia federal district court held that refuge managers bear the burden of proving that a secondary use is "incidental to, compatible with and does not interfere with the primary purpose of a refuge." Defenders of Wildlife v. Andrus, 11 Env't Rep. Cas. (BNA) 2098, 2101 (D.D.C. 1978); see also Defenders of Wildlife v. Andrus, 455 F.Supp. 446 (D.D.C. 1978). This placed pressure on the agency to articulate and defend tests for compatibility. Then, declining migratory bird populations in the 1980s prompted Congress to direct the General Accounting Office (GAO) to study refuge management practices. GAO's report was less than glowing to say the least, criticizing FWS for allowing numerous harmful secondary uses. See U.S. General Accounting Office, National Wildlife Refuges: Continuing Problems with Incompatible Uses Call for Bold Action, GAO/T-RCED-89-196 (1989). Several years later FWS settled a lawsuit brought in 1992 that tracked the GAO report in challenging numerous secondary use decisions at specific refuges around the nation. FWS agreed to review each secondary use and continue only those deemed compatible with the refuge. National Audubon Society v. Babbitt, No. C92-1641 (W.D. Wash) (settlement agreement filed Oct. 22, 1993).

By this time support had grown in Congress, led by Senator Bob Graham of Florida, for a legislative overhaul of the program. But Senator Graham's bills failed sufficiently to protect hunting and fishing as refuge uses in the eyes of those interest groups, and thus failed to pass. See, e.g., S. 823, 103d Cong., 1st Sess. (1993). The Clinton Administration then thwarted efforts to enact legislation that would have strengthened the prominence of hunting and fishing uses in refuges, and in 1996 President Clinton adopted an Executive Order specifically making wildlife conservation the primary purpose of the entire National Wildlife Refuge System, relegating hunting, fishing, and other "wildlife-dependent public uses" to subordinate use priority. See Executive Order No. 12,996, 61 Fed. Reg. 13647 (March 28, 1996). This opened the door to the 1997 legislation.

The 1997 legislation endorsed many facets of the Executive Order, focusing in particular on articulating the compatibility standard by incorporating detailed planning and substantive duties for the agency. The legislation defined "compatible use" to mean "a wildlife-dependent recreational use or any other use of a refuge that, in the sound professional judgment of the Director, will not materially interfere with or detract from fulfillment of the mission of the System or the purposes of the refuge." 16 U.S.C. § 668ee(1). The mission of the System, and thus the defining dominant use, is conservation of wildlife, plants, and their habitats. Id. § 668dd(a)(2). To the extent they are compatible with that dominant use, wildlife-dependent human uses, which Congress defined to include hunting and fishing as well as less intrusive activities such as photography and observation, are the highest priority for human uses. *Id.* § 668dd(a)(4)(D). Other "general public uses," such as grazing and oil exploration, are allowed only where they are deemed appropriate and where they are compatible not only with the wildlife protection purpose, but also all higher-priority human uses. The tiered use structure can be summarized as follows:

priority of use	type of use
dominant	conservation of wildlife, plants, and their habitats (System mission) plus specific purposes for which the particular Refuge was created
first subordinate	a wildlife-dependent recreational use, such as hunting, fishing, photography, and observation, or any other use of the Refuge that, in the sound professional judgment of the Director, will not materially interfere with or detract from fulfillment of the mission of the System or the purposes of the Refuge
second subordinate	general public uses, such as grazing and oil exploration, but only where they are deemed appropriate and where they are compatible not only with the System and Refuge purposes, but also all higher-priority human uses

FWS issued policies outlining how it will permit wildlife-dependent and other general public uses in refuge lands. *See* 66 Fed. Reg. 3668 (Jan. 16, 2001). With respect to the *dominant* mission of wildlife conservation, the 1997 legislation added the directive that the agency "ensure that the biological integrity, diversity, and environmental health of the System are maintained." *Id.* § 668dd(a)(4)(B). In October 2000, USFWS issued a draft policy for implementing this core directive, which, not surprisingly, incorporated many principles of ecosystem management and adaptive management. The agency summarized its proposal as follows:

We (U.S. Fish and Wildlife Service) propose to establish an internal policy to guide personnel of the National Wildlife Refuge System (Refuge System) in implementing the clause of the National Wildlife Refuge System Improvement Act of 1997 (Refuge Improvement Act) that calls for maintaining the "biological integrity, diversity, and environmental health" of the Refuge System. The holistic integration of these three qualities constitutes ecological integrity. The concept of ecological integrity requires a frame of reference for natural conditions. Our frame of reference extends from 800 AD to 1800 AD. The former date marked the beginning of an ecological transformation associated with higher temperatures; the latter approximates the advent of the industrial era, including drastic and widespread habitat loss. In areas where pre-industrial European settlement was particularly intensive, however, our frame of reference may be shorter. Natural conditions also include those that would have persisted or evolved to the present time if European settlement and industrialization had not occurred. At each refuge, we ascertain natural conditions, assess current conditions, and strive to decrease the difference. However, we are especially concerned with ecological integrity of the Refuge System as a whole, which can conflict with the maintenance of ecological integrity at individual refuges. In some cases, we may compromise the ecological integrity of a refuge for the sake of maintaining a higher level of ecological integrity at the Refuge System scale.

Department of the Interior, Draft Policy on Maintaining the Ecological Integrity of the National Wildlife Refuge System Fish and Wildlife Service, 65 Fed. Reg. 61356 (October 17, 2000).

To summarize, the agency outlined a three-step process to be carried out at each Refuge in order to fulfill the Systemwide mandate of protecting biological integrity, diversity, and environmental health:

Step 1   determine the natural conditions of the Refuge that existed in the time frame of 800 to 1800 AD
Step 2   determine the current conditions of the Refuge and any extent to which they deviate from natural conditions
Step 3   design management actions that will eliminate the deviation of current conditions from natural conditions

This proposed approach received sharp criticism in the public comment process, motivating the agency to recraft certain terms and conditions in the final policy. Many of these criticisms resonate in the general themes described in the preceding section as running through the law of ecosystem management. Consider how FWS responded to these issues and criticisms in arriving at a final policy.

Department of the Interior, *Policy on Maintaining the Biological Integrity, Diversity, and Environmental Health of the National Wildlife Refuge System*
66 Fed. Reg. 3810 (Jan. 16, 2001).

The proposed policy was derived from Section 5(a)(4)(B) of the Refuge Improvement Act that the Secretary of the Interior "ensure that the biological integrity, diversity, and environmental health of the System are maintained * * *" The policy presented in this notice is a final policy that has been modified after consideration of public comment. The finalized policy will constitute part 601 Chapter 3 of the Fish and Wildlife Service Manual.

Purpose of This Policy

The purpose of the policy is to provide guidance for maintaining, and restoring where appropriate, the biological integrity, diversity, and environmental health of the National Wildlife Refuge System.

Response to Comments Received

The combined comment periods totaled 60 days. We received 106 comments from the following sources: Nongovernmental organizations (36); State agencies or commissions (31); Federal agencies or facilities (9); local or county governmental agencies (3); and individuals (24). The key points raised by these comments fell into 10 general categories:

— Creation of the term "ecological integrity" and its definition:

— Definition of the term "natural conditions" and application of the concept in management;

— Impact of the policy on the ongoing refuge management activities;

— Impact of the policy on recreational use of refuges, primarily hunting and fishing;

— Concern that the policy would not meet specific refuge purpose(s) in favor of the System mission or some other management direction;

— Concern that the policy might adversely affect private property rights of refuge neighbors, and does not adequately recognize the State interests in how we manage refuges;

— Confusion regarding management for biological integrity, diversity, and environmental health at various landscape scales;

— Concern that the policy contains too many exceptions;

— General support either for the entire policy or significant elements of it; and

— A collection of other issues.

Issue 1: The Term "Ecological Integrity"

Comment: Most of the commenters (9 of 14) who cited this term stated that it went beyond the Refuge Improvement Act by creating a term that was not contained in the law or legislative history. Another stated it provided managers too much latitude to threaten private landowners. Still others stated it was too academic and basically unnecessary to meet the requirements of the Refuge Improvement Act. One commenter supported the term but stated the definition needed further refinement pursuant to scientific literature and that we should provide more guidance as to how to measure it.

Response: We never intended for the term "ecological integrity" to be more than a convenient means of referencing the terms biological integrity, diversity and environmental health. We agree, however, that as we used the term throughout the policy it appeared to take on meaning beyond the reference to the three terms. We abandoned the term in the final policy and substitute its appearance with the three specific terms as they appear in the law.

Issue 2: The Definition of the Term "Natural Conditions" and Its Application in Management

Fifty-nine of 106 commenters made specific references to the definition of natural conditions. Of these, 14 generally favored the concept and the remainder expressed concern about the concept and/or its application in management. An additional 9 commenters indicated general support for the policy overall, thus indicating support for the concept as well. However, even the 14 commenters who specifically endorsed the concept did so with various qualifications or suggestions. Overall, the commenters raised the following concerns:

Comment: A reference period is unnecessary, since the Refuge Improvement Act merely requires us to maintain the biological integrity, diversity, and environmental health necessary to meet refuge purposes.

Response: We believe the use of a reference point is pivotal to compliance with the mandate of the Refuge Improvement Act to ensure the maintenance of biological diversity, integrity, and environmental health. To implement the Refuge Improvement Act mandate, we needed definitions for the three terms. We believe a reference period is a critical element in these definitions and thus critical to the assessment of current habitat and wildlife conditions. In using the term "natural conditions" relative to a specific period (i.e., 800 to 1800 AD), we chose an approach with scientific underpinnings. Our intent in using the period was not to suggest a return to some particular community or habitat but, in fact, to reference something within the historic range of variability as found within that time frame. Notwithstanding, the way the draft policy presents this concept clearly created a catalyst for controversy among reviewers, and while nine commenters supported the concept with some variation, the great majority expressed strong concern. Thus, we agree that the term "natural conditions" and the implications for management in the framework we have described should be removed from the policy. Instead, we adopted the more general and open-ended term, "historic conditions," which we refer to as the condition of the landscape in a particular area before the onset of significant, human-caused change. See final policy Section 3.12. On that basis, we refined the definitions of biological integrity and environmental health to mean composition, structure and functioning of ecosystems "comparable to historic conditions." The intent is to emphasize not a particular point in time, but the range of ecosystem processes and functions that we believe would have occurred historically.

Issue 3: Implications for Refuge Purposes and System Mission

Comment: One commenter felt that the Ecological Integrity Policy and Refuge Improvement Act should take precedence over, or replace refuge purpose(s).

Response: The fulfillment of refuge purpose(s) is a nondiscretionary statutory duty of the Service. However, the law also requires that we ensure that the biological integrity, diversity, and environmental health of the System is maintained, and therefore, this is an additional duty which we must fulfill as we endeavor to achieve refuge purpose(s) and System mission.

Issue 4: Impacts on Public Use, Especially Hunting and Fishing

We received 34 letters that addressed the relationship between the draft policy and its relationship to public uses on refuges and public use as mandated under the Refuge Improvement Act.

Comment: More than half of these letters (17) were concerned that the policy, as drafted, would interfere with or eliminate hunting and fishing on refuges while another 13 letters were concerned that this policy would affect or find all public uses incompatible with ecological integrity.

Response: We did not write the draft policy with the intent or direction to eliminate hunting, fishing, or other priority public uses recognized by the Refuge Improvement Act. This draft policy rarely mentions public use, but where it does, the purpose is for refuge managers to consider impacts on wildlife and habitat (i.e., biological integrity, diversity, and environmental health) when implementing public uses. The authority for this draft policy is the Refuge Improvement Act, which also clearly identifies hunting and fishing as priority public uses. Section 2.(6) of the Refuge Improvement Act states, "When managed in accordance with principles of sound fish and wildlife management and administration, fishing [and] hunting in national wildlife refuges have been and are expected to continue to be generally compatible uses."

Comment: A few letters thought that hunting, fishing and trapping should not be permitted on refuges because they interfere with ecological integrity, while one letter wanted "trapping" added to Section 3.14 where hunting and fishing are encouraged in cooperation with State fish and wildlife management agencies.

Response: The six priority wildlife-dependent uses are given special status by the Refuge Improvement Act, which specifically recognizes hunting, fishing, wildlife observation, photography, interpretation, and environmental education. Refuges must facilitate these uses when compatible. The Refuge Improvement Act does not similarly recognize trapping.

Issue 5: Implications for States and Other Partnerships

Comment: Various States commented that the policy should place emphasis on cooperation and coordination with States in the management of wildlife populations on refuges.

Response: Strong partnerships with the respective States are an essential part of all refuge planning and management, including the maintenance of biological integrity, diversity, and environmental health of refuges. We encourage and expect managers to forge effective partnerships with States through cooperation and coordination in the management of wildlife habitats and populations found on refuges. We have changed the language in the final policy, Section 3.14, to more clearly state this expectation.

Issue 6: Implications for Private Property Rights

Comment: Several commenters were concerned that the policy was not mindful of the property rights of others and encouraged managers to seek resolutions to problems injuring resources on refuges through litigation.

Response: We changed Section 3.20 of the final policy to emphasize that the preferred course of action for managers in cases of injury to refuge resources from outside sources is first to seek cooperative resolution to such conflicts through neighborly discussion, negotiation, and consultation. This includes working with State or local agencies and other third party interests to seek solutions of mutual satisfaction. The revised policy offers several steps for a manager to take in this regard. Ultimately, however, and with full respect of private property rights, we recognize our responsibility to protect the property and resources of the American public, and state the responsibility to do so.

Issue 7: Implications for Wildlife and Habitat Management on Refuges

Comment: We received many comments which expressed concern about the role of active management on refuges under the proposed policy. These comments noted that active management is often necessary to achieve refuge purpose(s). Some felt management for natural conditions basically implied an absence of management and would, therefore, conflict with achieving refuge purpose(s). Comments also noted that numerous refuges are located in highly altered landscapes where active management is needed to maintain wildlife values of the refuge. A few comments identified that active management actions are required to maintain desirable wildlife populations where habitats surrounding the refuge have been degraded.

Response: We acknowledge that active management is often critically important to achieve refuge purpose(s). We also acknowledge that at some refuges very intensive management actions are required to maintain high densities of some wildlife species. We will continue active management where needed. However, we will evaluate management practices on all refuges to ensure that we take appropriate management action to achieve refuge purpose(s), while at the same time addressing the guidelines identified in the final policy.

Issue 8: Implications of Policy at Different Landscape Scales

Comment: There were 12 letters that raised issues of scale and the definitions and references to landscapes.

Response: Use of the term "local landscape" in the draft policy caused some confusion among these commenters. We intended the term to describe the refuge and its immediate surroundings. In the final policy, we dropped the "landscape" part of the term and use "local scale" or "refuge scale" to refer to a refuge and the area around it.

The text of the final policy follows:

3.3 What Is the Biological Integrity, Diversity, and Environmental Health Policy?

The policy is an additional directive for refuge managers to follow while achieving refuge purpose(s) and System mission. It provides for the consideration and protection of the broad spectrum of fish, wildlife, and habitat resources found on refuges and associated ecosystems. Further, it provides refuge managers with an evaluation process to analyze their refuge and recommend the best management direction to prevent further degradation of environmental conditions; and where appropriate and in concert with refuge purposes and System mission, restore lost or severely degraded components.

3.4 What Are the Objectives of This Policy?

A. Describe the relationships among refuge purposes, System mission, and maintaining biological integrity, diversity, and environmental health.

B. Provide guidelines for determining what conditions constitute biological integrity, diversity, and environmental health.

C. Provide guidelines for maintaining existing levels of biological integrity, diversity, and environmental health.

D. Provide guidelines for determining how and when it is appropriate to restore lost elements of biological integrity, diversity, and environmental health.

E. Provide guidelines to follow in dealing with external threats to biological integrity, diversity, and environmental health.

3.6 What Do These Terms Mean?

A. Biological diversity. The variety of life and its processes, including the variety of living organisms, the genetic differences among them, and communities and ecosystems in which they occur.

B. Biological integrity. Biotic composition, structure, and functioning at genetic, organism, and community levels comparable with historic conditions, including the natural biological processes that shape genomes, organisms, and communities.

C. Environmental health. Composition, structure, and functioning of soil, water, air, and other abiotic features comparable with historic conditions, including the natural abiotic processes that shape the environment.

D. Historic conditions. Composition, structure, and functioning of ecosystems resulting from natural processes that we believe, based on sound professional judgment, were present prior to substantial human related changes to the landscape.

E. Native. With respect to a particular ecosystem, a species that, other than as a result of an introduction, historically occurred or currently occurs in that ecosystem.

3.7 What Are the Principles Underlying This Policy?

A. Wildlife First

The Refuge Administration Act, as amended, clearly establishes that wildlife conservation is the singular National Wildlife Refuge System mission. House Report 105–106 accompanying the National Wildlife Refuge System Improvement Act of 1997 states " * * * the fundamental mission of our System is wildlife conservation: wildlife and wildlife conservation must come first." Biological integrity, diversity, and environmental health are critical components of wildlife conservation.

B. Accomplishing Refuge Purposes and Maintaining Biological Integrity, Diversity, Environmental Health of the System

The Refuge Administration Act states that each refuge will be managed to fulfill refuge purpose(s) as well as to help fulfill the System mission, and we will accomplish these purpose(s) and our mission by ensuring that the biological integrity, diversity, and environmental health of each refuge is maintained, and where appropriate, restored. We base our decisions on sound professional judgment.

C. Biological Integrity, Diversity, and Environmental Health in a Landscape Context

Biological integrity, diversity, and environmental health can be described at various landscape scales from refuge to ecosystem, national, and international. Each landscape scale has a measure of biological integrity, diversity, and environmental health dependent on how the existing habitats, ecosystem processes, and wildlife populations have been altered in comparison to historic conditions.

D. Maintenance and Restoration of Biological Integrity, Diversity, Environmental Health

We will, first and foremost, maintain existing levels of biological integrity, diversity, and environmental health at the refuge scale. Secondarily, we will restore lost or severely degraded elements of integrity, diversity, environmental health at the refuge scale and other appropriate landscape scales where it is feasible and supports achievement of refuge purpose(s) and System mission.

E. Wildlife and Habitat Management

Management, ranging from preservation to active manipulation of habitats and populations, is necessary to maintain biological integrity, diversity, and environmental health. We favor management that restores or mimics natural ecosystem processes or function to achieve refuge purpose(s). Some refuges may differ from the frequency and timing of natural processes in order to meet refuge purpose(s) or address biological integrity, diversity, and environmental health at larger landscape scales.

F. Sound Professional Judgment

Refuge managers will use sound professional judgment when implementing this policy primarily during the comprehensive conservation planning process to determine: The relationship between refuge purpose(s) and biological integrity, diversity, and environmental health; what conditions constitute biological integrity, diversity, and environmental health; how to maintain existing levels of all three; and, how and when to appropriately restore lost elements of all three. These determinations are inherently complex. Sound professional judgment incorporates field experience, knowledge of refuge resources, refuge role within an ecosystem, applicable laws, and best available science including consultation with others both inside and outside the Service.

G. Public Use

The priority wildlife-dependent public uses, established by the National Wildlife Refuge System Improvement Act of 1997, are not in conflict with this policy when determined to be compatible. The directives of this policy do not generally entail exclusion of visitors or elimination of public use structures, e.g., boardwalks and observation towers. However, maintenance and/or restoration of biological integrity, diversity, and environmental health may require spatial or temporal zoning of public use programs and associated infrastructures. General success in maintaining or restoring biological integrity, diversity, and environmental health will produce higher quality opportunities for wildlife-dependent public use.

3.9 How Do We Implement This Policy?

The Director, Regional Directors, Regional Chiefs, and Refuge Managers will carry out their responsibilities specified in Section 3.8 of this chapter. In addition, refuge managers will carry out the following tasks.

A. Identify the refuge purpose(s), legislative responsibilities, refuge role within the ecosystem and System mission.

B. Assess the current status of biological integrity, diversity, and environmental health through baseline vegetation, population surveys and studies, and any other necessary environmental studies.

C. Assess historic conditions and compare them to current conditions. This will provide a benchmark of comparison for the relative intactness of ecosystems' functions and processes. This assessment should include the opportunities and limitations to maintaining and restoring biological integrity, diversity, and environmental health.

D. Consider the refuge's importance to refuge, ecosystem, national, and international landscape scales of biological integrity, diversity, and environmental health. Also, identify the refuge's roles and responsibilities within the Regional and System administrative levels.

E. Consider the relationships among refuge purpose(s) and biological integrity, diversity and environmental health, and resolve conflicts among them.

G. Through the comprehensive conservation planning process, interim management planning, or compatibility reviews, determine the appropriate management direction to maintain and, where appropriate, restore, biological integrity, diversity, and environmental health, while achieving refuge purpose(s).

H. Evaluate the effectiveness of our management by comparing results to desired outcomes. If the results of our management strategies are unsatisfactory, assess the causes of failure and adapt our strategies accordingly.

NOTES & QUESTIONS

1. Overall, how different is the final policy from the proposed policy? Does the final policy remove agency discretion that may have existed under the proposed policy? Can you think of a decision with respect to management of a particular refuge that could have been made under the proposed policy but cannot be made under the final policy? For the argument that the FWS implementation policies for the 1997 statute are not sufficiently clear to guide management of non-wildlife dependent uses, see Michael J. Brennan and Leah A. Kukowski, *Managing the Wildlife Refuge System: Is Anything Compatible Anymore?*, 20 NATURAL RESOURCES & ENV'T 51 (Fall 2005).

2. More to the point, is there any meaningful difference between the "natural conditions" concept as outlined in the proposed policy and the "historic conditions" concept adopted in the final policy? The basic three-step process the agency outlined in the proposed rule is the same in the final rule, except the concept of historical conditions replaces that of natural conditions. Can you envision any set of circumstances in which a manager of a particular refuge would be legally constrained by the historic conditions policy but would not have been under the natural conditions policy? Do you suppose those who criticized the natural conditions policy are satisfied with the agency's final historic conditions policy? Does either concept have relevance in the no-analog future of climate change?

3. Can you articulate the difference between "ecological integrity" and the combination of "biological integrity, diversity, and environmental health?" What particular refuge management action could be accomplished under the former but not the latter? Do you believe the agency's response that it intended the ecological integrity term to serve merely as shorthand for the longer statutory list of three objectives, or do you think the agency had some ulterior motive?

4. What is "sound professional judgment," and how will we know when the agency has failed to apply it? The 1997 refuge system legislation defined it to mean "a finding, determination or decision that is consistent with principles of sound fish and wildlife management and administration, available science and resources, and adherence to the requirements of this act and other applicable laws." 16 U.S.C. § 668ee(3). Does that help? Is this just another way of saying the agency should be left free to exercise adaptive management as best as it can? But if so, does this not also illustrate the difficulty of legislative, judicial, and citizen oversight of adaptive management? It is difficult for the legislature to define ahead of time what is and is not sound judgment in the exercise of adaptive management, because the challenges of adaptive management arise unpredictably. Citizens who contest agency decisions thus bear the burden of proving them to be "unsound," which courts are loathe to find in the absence of strong evidence that the agency acted no less than arbitrarily.

5. Is the process FWS outlines for refuge management consistent with adaptive management theory?

6. Why are hunting and fishing allowed on *wildlife refuges*? Ironically, hunting has been perhaps the best friend of wildlife refuges. Under the Migratory Bird Conservation Stamp Act of 1929, 16 U.S.C. §§ 715-715r, and the Migratory Bird Hunting Stamp Act of 1934, 16 U.S.C. §§ 718-718h, all waterfowl hunters must purchase a federal waterfowl "stamp" and attach it to their state hunting licenses. FWS deposits revenue from the stamp sales into the Migratory Bird Conservation Fund, which funds acquisition of refuge lands. This source of funding has contributed to all or part of the lands acquisition of over 345 refuges. *See* Migratory Bird Conservation Commission, U.S. Fish and Wildlife Service, Report for the Fiscal Year 1999 (2000). This steady source of funding, however, has "almost assured a refuge system keyed principally to the production of migratory waterfowl." Michael J. Bean and Melanie J. Rowland, The Evolution of National Wildlife Law 284 (3d ed., 1997).

7. What private property rights are threatened by the proposed or final policy for management of public wildlife refuge lands? How might the exercise of private property rights threaten public wildlife refuge interests?

8. On June 26, 2006, the Fish and Wildlife Service issued three additional new policies implementing the 1997 legislation. *See* 71 Fed. Reg. 36,404; 71 Fed. Reg. 36,408; and 71 Fed. Reg. 36,418 (2006). In a thorough review of their contents, Professor Robert Fischman concludes that the new policies deserve "high marks for creativity, fidelity to the 1997 Refuge Improvement Act, and promoting ecological integrity," but that they "stumble badly in their emphasis on the individual refuge purposes, which tend to focus more on traditional fish and game concerns than on the newer 1997 systemic mission." Robert L. Fischman, *From Words to Action: The Impact and Legal Status of the 2006 National Wildlife Refuge System Management Policies*, 26 STAN. ENVTL. L.J. 77 (2007). It is also worth noting that, contrary to the experience with most other Clinton Administration policy initiatives, the 2006 Bush Administration policies incorporated most of the foundation of their respective draft proposals that were issued five years earlier in the waning days of the Clinton Administration. *See* 66 Fed. Reg. 3668; 66 Fed. Reg. 3673; and 66 Fed. Reg. 3708 (1999).

9. Professor Fischman has compiled what is surely the most thorough and insightful examinations of the legal dimensions of the National Wildlife Refuge System. See ROBERT L. FISCHMAN, THE NATIONAL WILDLIFE REFUGES: COORDINATING A CONSERVATION SYSTEM THROUGH LAW (Island Press, 2003); Robert L. Fischman, *From Words to Action: The Impact and Legal Status of the 2006 National Wildlife Refuge System Management Policies*, 26 STAN. ENVTL. L. J. 77 (2007); Robert L. Fischman, *The Significance of the National Wildlife Refuge System in the Development of U.S. Conservation Policy*, 21 J. LAND USE & ENVTL. L. 1 (2005); Robert L. Fischman, *The National Wildlife Refuge System and the Hallmarks of Modern Organic Legislation*, 29 ECOLOGY L.Q. 457 (2002). Also, a compendium of articles examines the refuge biodiversity issue in Symposium, *Managing Biological Integrity, Diversity, and Health in the National Wildlife Refuges*, 44 NATURAL RESOURCES J. 931 (2004).

10. We used the wildlife refuge system as the case study for the introductory chapter on ecosystem management law because, unlike many other federal land conservation units, it cuts across many ecosystem types, thus forcing a more generic management approach. The remaining chapters of this part of the text divide the materials by ecosystem type, and other federal land conservation units correspond more closely to that division (e.g., National Forests with the forest ecosystems materials; BLM Land and National Grasslands with the grasslands ecosystems materials). The wildlife refuge policy presents a template of the issues and controversies explored in these chapters in more particularized and often more intensified settings. As has the refuge policy debate, those controversies often focus on the issue of use versus restoration, and on what, precisely, restoration means. For a broad take on the concept of restoration in environmental law, see Alyson C. Flournoy, *Restoration Rx: An Evaluation and Prescription*, 42 ARIZONA L. REV. 187 (2000).

11. If climate change threatens to disrupt ecosystems over the next several centuries, is the goal of managing a refuge for a specific purpose viable? Is the concept of ecosystem restoration on refuge land and elsewhere moot?

CHAPTER 8

FOREST ECOSYSTEMS

A. BIODIVERSITY AND FOREST ECOSYSTEMS

Nearly half the forests that once covered the earth are gone. Notwithstanding the loss of biodiversity values suffered as a result of that depletion of forest resources, forests today provide our planet's largest terrestrial storehouse of biodiversity, covering 27 percent of the ice-free land surface of the earth. How the earth's forest resources are managed in the future—in particular, whether the rate of loss can be slowed or even reversed—thus will play an important role in biodiversity conservation at the global level.

In addition to storing biodiversity resources, forests provide critical ecosystem services such as shelter for countless species, protection of soils from rainfall erosion, flood control, carbon sequestration, and water filtration. Of course, humans value forests also for purely economic reasons, namely for lumber, paper, and fuel production. About 55 percent of the wood cut today is used for fuel (primarily in India, China, Brazil, Indonesia, and Nigeria), with the remainder going to production for lumber, paper, and other industrial products (primarily in the United States, Canada, and Russia). Forest lands have also been valuable to humans for conversion to other uses, principally agriculture, urban development, and recreational uses. One of the challenges for management of forests thus has been how to take into account the biodiversity storage and ecosystem service values of forests when making decisions about how to take advantage of their more direct economic values.

If the biodiversity and ecosystem service values of forest parcels could be precisely monetized, so that their losses could be factored into forest management decisions in direct economic terms, timber and paper production or conversion of forested areas to urban development may make much less economic sense in many settings. Even though we lack the technical and financial resources to perform this sort of perfect monetization, the knowledge that forest ecosystems deliver significant value to humans suggests that forest management decisions could factor those values into the decision making process in some manner. Yet only a few countries have begun to consider the biodiversity storage and ecosystem service values of forests as core decision making criteria. In the last two decades of heightened global awareness of biodiversity losses, total global forest losses experienced in that period would cover an area larger than Mexico. Global deforestation is concentrated in poor nations, with devastating effects. For example, Haiti has lost over 90 percent of its tree cover in the last five decades, resulting in massive erosion of farmland, silting of lakes and rivers, and contamination of drinking water supplies. Still, forests cover more than one quarter of the earth's land area (excluding Antarctica and Greenland), with the largest holdings in Russia, Brazil, Canada, the United States, China, Indonesia, and the Democratic Republic of the Congo, in that order.

Even in countries that have in recent decades halted or reversed forests losses, such as the United States, biodiversity values in forested areas are generally on the decline. In many countries the primary forest stands have been largely depleted and production is mostly from secondary stands or tree plantations. In the United States, for example, about 46 percent of the land was forested at the time of European settlement, and about 32 percent is today, but virtually none of the original trees—the so-called old growth forests—remain today (indeed, many were lost even before European settlement). The biodiversity values of the secondary stands and managed plantations that replaced them, which do not count in most studies as deforested acres, are generally less than for primary stands. Moreover, the biodiversity capacity of many standing forests has been imperiled by industrial and agricultural pollution of air and water, invasive species introduced through inadvertent or purposeful human import, raging wildfires caused, ironically, by fuel buildup resulting from prior fire suppression, and other results of human management decisions both within and external to forests. And as overall forest health declines, natural threats such as insects and disease become more acute. For example, over 90 million acres of standing forests in the United States are threatened by seven major pests and diseases.

Thus, although headlines focus on loss of the tropical rainforests to agriculture and timber extraction, the United States has been no stranger to forest resource depletion and continues to suffer serious declines in health of its remaining forest stands. Our nation's appetite for wood is voracious: we consume one fourth of the world's industrial timber; ten percent of the world's industrial timber is used in the U.S. construction industry, mostly for home building; we produce 30 percent of the world's paper. These demands have taken their toll on American forests. Today, about 33 percent of the U.S. land area—747 million acres—is forest lands, but that is two-thirds of our forested area in 1600. More than 75 percent of the 307 million acres lost to other uses were converted in the 19th century, mostly to agricultural uses and mostly in the Midwest and lower Mississippi Valley. The net area of forested land has remained relatively stable since 1920, as the introduction of mechanized farm machines reduced the need to devote cropland to growing feed for farm draft animals. In short, we have little need for converting more forest land into farmland. Yet only a small fraction of what remains of our forested lands is primary old growth forest.

About two-thirds of the nation's remaining forested lands are classified as timberland suitable for production of lumber, paper, and other industrial goods. The federal government owns and manages about one-third of U.S. forested land. The rest is owned by nonfederal public agencies, forest industry firms, farmers, and some 6 million other private individuals. Forest lands, types, and ownership patterns are distributed unevenly. North Dakota, for example, is only one percent forested land, while Maine has the largest proportion at 89 percent. Most of the privately owned forest land is east of the Mississippi River, while most forest land to the west is publicly owned. Most hardwood timber stock is in the east; western timber is mostly softwood. Private forest lands in the eastern states, particularly plantation forests in the southeast, will be our nation's primary source of timber in this century. This diversity of distribution, ownership, and type of forest lands makes formation of a national management policy for our forest ecosystems a difficult political and scientific undertaking.

NOTES & QUESTIONS

1. The marketplace assigns values to timber products and non-forest uses of forested land, but often overlooks the value of ecosystem services that standing forests provide. *See* Robert Bonnie et al.*, Counting the Cost of Deforestation*, 288 Science 1763 (2000). Norman Myers lists among the ecosystem services forests supply with real value to humans: landscape stabilization; soil nutrient cycling; water flow regulation; energy balance; siltation removal; sunlight reflectance (albedo), atmospheric moisture regulation; and a host of others. *See* Norman Myers, *The World's Forests and Their Ecosystem Services*, in Nature's Services: Societal Dependence on Natural Ecosystems 215–26 (Gretchen Daily ed. 1997). Assigning monetized values to these services is difficult, but rough estimates can be derived in numerous contexts from real-world examples, and they are staggering in magnitude. *See id.* at 226–28. For example, if a forest buffer could reduce pollution of a fishery from upland runoff, one could consider the added fishery yield as a value gained from the forest, and the cost of duplicating that effect through technological means as an avoided cost. While leaving the forest buffer in that use may impose an opportunity cost in terms of foregone development of that land to "higher" uses, ought not the cost-benefit calculus include the values gained and costs avoided as a result of the forest's delivery of the identified services to other economically valuable land and resource uses? On the other hand, the value of cut timber is subject to fairly precise quantification, whereas the ecosystem service values of standing timber are not. Should the cost-benefit decision making be required to use both valuation components given that one side suffers from far inferior measurement accuracy?

2. A related problem in deciding how to value timber as cut versus as uncut is the lack of knowledge we have about the long term effects of cutting timber on overall ecosystem integrity and productivity. The value of cut timber may be precisely quantifiable, but that market value does not account for potential loss of ecological and economic productivity the removal of timber imposes. For example, cutting roads into tropical forests has been shown to begin a process of forest transformation that fundamentally reduces the forest's value even in terms of cut timber, and the long term effects on forest ecosystem service dynamics are even more severe. *See* Claude Gascon, *Receding Forest Edges and Vanishing Reserves*, 288 SCIENCE 1356 (2000). Timber harvesting also has been shown to have devastating long term effects on timber resources through increased fire risk, and on other commercial activities, such as seed harvesting, through the depletion of vegetative diversity. *See* Gary Hartshorn & Nora Bynum, *Tropical Rainforest Synergies*, 286 SCIENCE 2093 (2000). Even putting aside the question whether ecosystem service values can be sufficiently quantified to include in forest management decision making, does research such as this suggest we should be less confident that we know the true value of cut timber?

3. Some argue that, regardless of whether it focuses narrowly on market value or broadly to include ecosystem service value, ecosystem *productivity* should not be used as the criterion in deciding how to manage a forest ecosystem. Rather, in this alternative view, ecosystem *restoration* is the correct policy goal. But restoration to what condition? This question has triggered a burning debate among ecologists. *See* Keith Kloor, *Returning America's Forests to Their "Natural" Roots*, 287 SCIENCE 573 (2000). While acting as Secretary of the Interior, Bruce Babbitt suggested that ecosystem restoration means returning lands "to a presettlement equilibrium." In conventional use this means prior to European settlement, but some ecologists contend that Native Americans were significantly shaping and altering the land, particularly through fire manipulation and clearing on forested lands, well before European settlers arrived. For a thorough account this debate, see CHARLES C. MANN, 1491: NEW REVELATIONS OF THE AMERICAS BEFORE COLUMBUS (2005). Regardless of who is right, though, picking any particular date for restoration also fails to account for a variety of naturally-induced factors, such as drought, fire, temperature swings, that caused long term variations in healthy forest ecosystems. Trying to "lock" a forest ecosystem into a particular equilibrium state in which it existed in the past thus may not truly restore it to some privileged set of presettlement conditions. Instead, some ecologists advocate working to rehabilitate an "ailing" forest back into its natural "envelope of variability." Others eschew any notion of stasis and advocate use of past conditions simply as reference points designed to guide in the restoration of a "natural flux" in "dynamic processes" such as fire, flood, predation, and regeneration. Clearly, there is a lack of agreement among scientists as to where and how to do forest restoration, how much to use the past as the guide, and which past to use. And if the scientists can't agree, what should the policy-makers do?

4. Nearly half of the world's vascular plant species and one-third of the vertebrate species are endemic to 25 "hotspots" of biodiversity covering a total of less than two percent of the planet's land mass. *See* Thomas Brooks et al., *Habitat*

Loss and Extinction in the Hotspots of Biodiversity, 16 CONSERVATION BIOLOGY 909 (2002). Managing this two percent of the world's landmass, in other words, dictates the fate of a substantial portion of the planet's plant and vertebrate species. Globally, however, these hotspots have lost on average over 70 percent of their original geographic range, and many continue to decline. Strongly associated with forest ecosystems, two of these hotspots appear in the United States, in southern Florida and along California's Pacific coast. Should ecosystem management policy pay special attention to these two hotspot locations? Given scarce resources, should we devote ourselves disproportionately to these areas, even if it means resources in other ecosystems suffer?

5. Edward Cook, a paleoecologist at Columbia University, led an effort to find remnants of native forests in the eastern United States, where many ecologists believed all the native forests were decimated by 1830. He and other researchers have made some remarkable finds by looking in unusual places. They have found 2000-year old bald cypresses in the nooks of North Carolina swamps, 1000-year old white cedars on inaccessible slopes in Ontario, and 400-year old longleaf pines on an Air Force base in Florida. The common theme is that these trees were bypassed by early timber harvests because of inaccessibility, and have been ignored since then by the modern landowners. These ancient trees are proving to be valuable sources for measuring historical climate trends and tracing the effects of modern climate change. Measures are underway in many states and on federal public lands to identify and protect these treasures. *See* Kevin Krajick, *Methuselahs in Our Midst*, 302 SCIENCE 768 (2003).

B. PRIMER ON THE LAW OF FORESTS

1. HISTORICAL BACKGROUND

Although the early North American colonists found a virtually boundless supply of forests, it was not long before the common practice of setting fire to forests as a means of opening the land to other uses became regarded as economically wasteful and environmentally unsound. For example, a 1626 ordinance of the Plymouth Colony in Massachusetts banned setting of open forest fires on the ground that an inconvenience might result from a depletion of the timber supply, and much later a North Carolina act of 1777 proscribed unlawful firing of the woods as being extremely prejudicial to the soil. By the early eighteenth century many colonial governments also forbade unnecessary cutting of timber on common lands, and shortly after the Revolutionary War concluded Massachusetts enacted a law requiring licenses for removal of large white pines from state lands.

The newly formed national government entered the forest policy scene quickly after the war as a result of repeated pirate attacks on American merchant vessels. Congress, realizing the need for a national navy, also realized the need for a national timber supply to build the navy's ships. By an act of February 25, 1799, 1 Stat. 622, Congress appropriated money to purchase a timber supply, which later was used to acquire Grover's and Blackbeard's Islands off the coast of Georgia to secure about 2000 acres of prime timber property. Later, after the navy proved instrumental to victory against the British in the War of 1812, an act of March 1, 1817, 3 Stat. 347, authorized the Secretary of the Navy to select vacant and unappropriated tracts on federal lands with prime timber resources and recommend that the President reserve them from sale.

Timber policy through 1850 thus was defined largely by ad hoc state laws regulating open fires and federal reservation of timber supplies on federal lands to meet the navy's shipbuilding needs. Reports of widespread theft of timber from federal, state, and private lands suggest that these laws were difficult to enforce. The development of iron shipbuilding technology in the mid-1800s, moreover, led Congress to return most of its naval timber reserves to the public domain, meaning they were once again open for sale. The federal and state land settlement policies of the 1800s then surged the transfer of title to federal and state lands from public to private ownership by sale, homestead laws, railroad laws, and other means, shifting most eastern forest lands to private hands by the late 1800s.

The first glimmer of forest conservation policy was lit when the American Forestry Congress of 1882, meeting in Cincinnati, created the American Forestry Association to cooperate with the federal and state governments toward formulating a definite policy for managing public forest lands. In the following two decades, several states created state-level forestry agencies to regulate fires, encourage timber culture, and, in some cases, promote forest conservation, preservation, and extension. While in most cases the motivating force behind these laws was security of timber supply, laws such as one New York enacted in 1885, Session Laws, N.Y., 1885 ch. 283, p. 482, were among the first truly comprehensive forest management policies in America. The New York law established a system for designating, maintaining, and protecting state forests, complete with a state forest commission, wardens, forest inspectors, foresters, and other staff.

Federal policy witnessed a similar trend after the 1873 meeting of the American Society for the Advancement of Science appointed a committee to present to Congress a plan for the extension and preservation of forests, providing the impetus for a flurry of additional studies and proposals and even several federal laws promoting timber culture and the collection of forest statistics. The seeds of today's Forest Service also were planted in the Department of Agriculture through creation of the Division of Forestry, which began with one employee and an annual budget of $2000. By the late 1800s, though, federal forest policy remained a complete muddle—while promoting the extension of forest lands by subsidized plantings and other culture programs, albeit often in areas not suited to trees of any kind, the federal government was at the same time disposing of vast tracts of prime forest lands into private possession.

To resolve this inconsistency, a rider provision to the 1891 General Revision Act, known as the Forest Reserve Act of 1891, authorized the President to establish forest reservations on federal lands. *See* Act of March 3, 1891, ch. 561, § 26 Stat. 1095, 1103 (repealed 1976). Not all the federal lands had yet been given away or sold, and Presidents Harrison and Cleveland withdrew extensive areas in the Western states from sale or entry and declared them national forest reserves. But much remained uncertain:

Western interests were quite bitter over the turn of events, there was debate over the actual authority of the president under the 1891 law, and
there were no monies appropriated to manage what by 1896 amounted to
millions of acres of national forests. Congress resolved the situation with
the passage of the Forest Service Organic Act of 1897, 30 Stat. 11, 34–35
(Organic Act), which ratified the presidential reservations and authorized
administration of the national forests, then called forest reserves, through
a federal agency.

The Organic Act marks the beginning of the development of comprehensive federal forest policy and administration. Although it made no mention of biodiversity, ecosystems, or even wildlife, it provided that the national forests should be established "to improve and protect the forest within the boundaries, or for the purposes of securing favorable water flows,
and to furnish a continuous supply of timber for the use and necessities of
citizens of the United States." 15 U.S.C. § 473. For the latter purpose, the
Organic Act authorized the Department of the Interior, then after 1905 the
Forest Service in the Department of Agriculture, to

> cause to be designated and appraised so much of the dead, matured or
> large growth trees found upon such national forests as may be compat-
> ible with the utilization of the forests thereon, and may sell the
> same. . . Such timber, before being sold, shall be marked and designat-
> ed, and shall be cut and removed under the supervision of some person
> appointed for that purpose by the Secretary. . .

Gifford Pinchot, who became head of the Forestry Service in 1898, envisioned the national forests as primarily a timber supply resource, and for
nearly seventy years the Forest Service interpreted the Organic Act as allowing widespread extraction of timber. Indeed, after World War II, housing construction demands placed tremendous new pressure on the nation's
timber supply, and on the Forest Service. Clearcutting became a common
practice on private forest lands, thus depleting private timber supplies and
causing the timber industry to pressure the Forest Service to increase the
yield from national forests. The agency met this demand, but by doing so
fueled a conflict between timber harvesting and another demand that
boomed after the war—recreation. As clearcutting became common in the
national forests, so too did the previously uncommon instance of public criticism of Forest Service decisions.

Congress nevertheless gave the Forest Service basically a free hand in
all such matters of national forest policy, intervening only once to enact the
Multiple Use and Sustained Yield Act of 1960 (MUSY). MUSY expanded
the purposes of national forest management from water flows and timber
supply to include "outdoor recreation, range, timber, watershed, and wildlife and fish purposes." 16 U.S.C. § 528. Recognizing that "some land will be
used for less than all the resources," MUSY required that the five multiple
uses, which Congress deliberately named in alphabetical order, be treated
as co-equal and managed "with consideration being given to the relative
values of the various resources." *Id.* The statute described the core mandate
of multiple use as meaning

The management of all the various renewable surface resources of the national forests so that they are utilized in the combination that will best meet the needs of the American people; making the most judicious use of the land for some or all these resources or related services over areas large enough to provide sufficient latitude for periodic adjustments in use to conform to changing needs and conditions. . .

Id. § 531.

Conservation and recreation interests opposed the legislation while the agency and timber industry actively supported it. Critics of the Forest Service charged that the agency had elevated timber extraction above the other uses and exercised widespread clearcutting without due regard to the Organic Act, and would continue to do both under MUSY. Indeed, for all practical purposes MUSY codified precisely the policy discretion the agency sought (and argued it had even without MUSY). After MUSY, the law of national forests explicitly recognized the breadth of the agency's discretion. While courts demanded that the agency give "due consideration" to each of the multiple use components, *see* Parker v. United States, 307 F.Supp. 685 (D.Colo.1969), in the final analysis most courts agreed that "the decision as to the proper mix of uses within any particular area is left to the sound discretion and expertise of the Forest Service." Sierra Club v. Hardin, 325 F.Supp. 99, 123 (D. Alaska 1971). MUSY's multiple use mandate was essentially rendered directionless, leaving it to the agency to decide where to go and providing no meaningful legislative or judicial check on the path chosen.

As Congress and the courts continued to afford the Forest Service wide latitude in setting policy after MUSY, the agency began experimenting with planning as a way to resolve multiple use conflicts, requiring each national forest to develop a land use plan. Yet the agency used the end products as a vehicle to portray its policy of clearcutting as not merely a capitulation to the powerful timber industry, but the result a rational, scientifically sound policy decision making process. Neither congressional appropriations nor agency will would have supported any other outcome, thus leaving the growing recreational and conservation interests on the outside of the forest.

The first chink in this armor came in 1964 with passage of the Wilderness Act. 16 U.S.C. §§ 1131–36. Since 1929 the Forest Service had regulations in place in one form or another for designating "primitive," "wilderness," and "wild" areas to be removed from timber harvesting and other resource extraction uses. Although this administrative policy had produced over 2 million mainly roadless acres of preserve acres and was well within the agency's discretion before and after MUSY became part of national forest law, the agency could not satisfy conservationists that the agency would retain such designations in the face of increased demand for timber. After all, it would have been well within the agency's discretion and financial capability to withdraw the protected status, build roads, and open the lands to harvesting. After a decade of lobbying, these interests finally succeeded in convincing Congress to pass the Wilderness Act, in which the Forest

Service was forced to place the protected lands into "The National Wilderness System" of wilderness and pristine lands, and thus out of the path of the timber industry. And although the Wilderness Act left MUSY untouched for the remaining lands under Forest Service control, the new law required the agency to examine the eligibility of certain roadless national forest lands to be added to the National Wilderness System, a process that has embroiled the agency ever since and is discussed in more detail later in this chapter.

An incremental step toward wrestling the agency under control came with the Forest and Rangelands Renewable Resources Planning Act of 1974, Pub. L. No. 93–378, 88 Stat. 476. This law required the Forest Service to prepare a system-wide five-year plan for the national forests, known as the Renewable Resources Program, but also directed the agency to develop "land and resource management plans for units of the National Forest System." Yet the statute provided no direction as to procedure or content of such plans, leaving the agency in a position to continue the forest plan process it had already devised as a means of supporting the clearcutting program.

The next significant blow came in 1975, as the clearcutting age came to a screeching halt when the court in West Virginia Division of Izaak Walton League v. Butz, 522 F.2d 945 (4th Cir.1975), used plain English meanings to interpret the Organic Act's "designated," "marked," "dead," "mature," and "large" terms to prohibit widespread clearcutting in most circumstances. The court simply noted that the Organic Act referred only to "dead, matured, or large growth" trees as eligible for harvesting, and that the statute required the Forest Service to designate and mark the trees before removal. MUSY did not alter that basic starting point, so, the court concluded, clearcutting is illegal. In modern terms, this simply did not "compute" for the agency or the industry. As environmental groups seized the moment and filed suits around the nation to extend the Fourth Circuit's reasoning, the Forest Service and timber industry immediately sought congressional action to clear up what the agency could and could not do with respect to timber extraction policy.

What the agency sought and fully expected it would receive was legislative nullification of the court's opinion, but by this time criticism of the Forest Service had crept into Congress, focused initially through the so-called Bolle Report, commissioned by Senator Lee Metcalf of Montana, and the Church Commission hearings held in 1971 before the Senate Subcommittee on Public Lands of the Committee on Interior and Insular Affairs. At the request of Senator Metcalf, Arnold Bolle led a team of academics from the University of Montana in 1970 to study Forest Service practices. Their report, entitled *A University View of the Forest Service*, was sharply critical of the Forest Service's land management practices, concluding that the agency overemphasized timber production and thus undermined the multiple use mandate. At the Church Commission hearings the next year, numerous distinguished witnesses testified in those hearings as to the environmental harm Forest Service policies had caused. Amidst the emerging broad attention to environmental affairs that took hold in Congress during the early 1970s, this testimony proved critical in convincing Congress that the agency required more explicit direction. The result was the National Forest Management Act of 1976 (NFMA), Pub. L. No. 94–588, 90 Stat 2949, codified at 16 U.S.C. §§ 1601–14.

Adding to rather than replacing the Organic Act and MUSY, the NFMA prescribed a set of substantive standards and planning requirements for the Forest Service, the details of which are explored in the principal cases included in this chapter. Generally it restricts timber harvests to only those national forest lands where "soil, slope, or other watershed conditions will not be irreversibly damaged" and which could "be adequately restocked within five years after harvest." 16 U.S.C. § 1604(g)(3)(E). In particular, clearcutting and other even-aged management techniques are specifically addressed and restricted by standards which, while loose, were more than had appeared in law previously. *Id.* § 1604(g)(3)(F). Also, making NFMA relevant to the scope of this text, the statute requires the Forest Service to "provide for diversity of plant and animal communities." *Id.* § 1604(g)(3)(B). These and other standards are to be coordinated for each national forest though individual "land and resources management plans" that require public input and are subject to judicial review. *Id.* §§ 1601–1604. Hence, although it is not without its detractors, the NFMA unquestionably charted a new direction for national forest policy, one in which, for the first time in Forest Service history, biodiversity values had to be taken into account.

2. CURRENT SCENE

Although the NFMA provided vastly more detail to guide Forest Service policy than had the Organic Act and MUSY, it left many more questions than it answered. A rich history of litigation helps fill in the details of such issues as where timber can be harvested under the "irreversible damage" standard, when clearcutting is allowed, and whether forest plans have been properly compiled. In this chapter we focus on the "diversity of plant and animal communities" standard in particular, showing how it has been the subject of varying judicial and administrative interpretations and had emerged by the close of the century as a potential force of change in future Forest Service policy.

There are other laws, of course, that play an important role in forest management, both within national forests and on state, local, and private forest lands. In the years preceding enactment of NFMA, Congress passed a flurry of other environmental laws, many with general application to federal agencies and some with general application to the public at large. Although the impact of these laws on forest management was not immediately apparent or felt substantially in the 1970s and 1980s, by the early 1990s it had become clear, primarily through citizen initiated litigation, that a web of federal environmental laws profoundly affects forest management decisions taken by federal, state, local, and even private forest managers. Indeed, as the materials in this chapter illustrate, in many circumstances statutes such as the Endangered Species Act, the National Environmental Policy Act, and the Clean Water Act have had a far more prescriptive effect on Forest Service policy than have the agency's trio of primary statutes— the Organic Act, MUSY, and NFMA. Their effect on state, local, and private forest lands has been no less substantial.

NOTES & QUESTIONS

1. Why have national forests? If the Forest Service identifies an area of federally-owned forest as most suitable for timber harvesting, why not auction the land—not just the timber—for sale to timber companies? If another area is deemed best suited to recreation, why not sell it to the Disney Corporation? Having paid for the land, won't these private interests have more incentive to manage it appropriately than does the federal government? Indeed, rather than having the federal government decide what use is suitable for particular parcels of forest, wouldn't a better way to determine "highest and best use" be to let the market decide through open auctions? Won't the successful bidder have the most incentive to manage the land in such a way as to maximize its realization of highest and best use, thus maximizing total social wealth? These are not idle questions. For decades federal land policy was one of disposition, not permanent retention. Only recently has the principal issue of federal land management become one of use rather than to whom to dispose and when. *See* GEORGE C. COGGINS ET AL., FEDERAL PUBLIC LAND AND RESOURCES LAW 39–148 (4th ed. 2001). And serious questions still are raised about the wisdom of the permanent retention approach. Some economists, for example, advocate privatizing the national forests to end many of the management issues that plague the Forest Service by replacing the incentives of negative-sum political dynamics with those of positive-sum private entrepreneurship. *See* RICHARD L. STROUP & JOHN A. BADEN, NATURAL RESOURCES: BUREAUCRATIC MYTHS AND ENVIRONMENTAL MANAGEMENT 118–27 (1983). As you delve into the materials on public forest lands, keep in mind that alternative ownership frameworks exist and consider whether they offer superior avenues to ecological management of forested lands.

2. Why have a Forest Service? Consider that the Forest Service has a workforce of over 30,000 employees. The agency is divided into 9 regions, within which are distributed 155 national forests, which together are comprised of a total of more than 600 ranger districts ranging in size from 50,000 to 1 million acres. Each district has a staff of 10 to 100 people. Overseeing the whole structure is the Chief, who reports directly to the USDA's Under Secretary for Natural Resources and Environment. Even if we maintain federal public lands as "national forests," are there alternatives we might consider for implementing national objectives for those lands other than through a large, centralized, hierarchical federal agency? Indeed, Professor Robert Nelson has characterized the Forest Service as bloated, anachronistic, and lacking a coherent vision, choosing instead to hop from one fashionable environmental solution to the next—most recently ecosystem management. He advocates abolishing the agency and replacing it with a decentralized system to manage protection of our national forests. *See* ROBERT NELSON, A BURNING ISSUE: A CASE FOR ABOLISHING THE U.S. FOREST SERVICE (2000). Other observers propose models that retain a role for the Forest Service in setting national forest management policy, but vesting greater power in local and private decision making bodies. *See* ROGER A. SEDJO,

THE NATIONAL FORESTS: FOR WHOM AND FOR WHAT?, PERC Policy Series No.
PS-23 (2001). Indeed, in 1987 New Zealand, which at one time managed its national forests under a system explicitly modeled after the Forest Service, replaced its centralized agency with a system of dominant-use management by a
conservation agency and a state-owned forestry corporation. *See* Robert L.
Fischman and Richard L. Nagle, *Corporatisation: Implementing a Forest Management Reform in New Zealand*, 16 ECOLOGY L.Q. 719 (1989). For a spectrum
of views about the role of national forests and the Forest Service, see A VISION
FOR THE U.S. FOREST SERVICE (Roger A. Sedjo ed., 2000). For a comprehensive
study finding that the Forest Service operates without a credible system to
evaluate its performance and the results achieved from its annual $5 billion
budget expenditures, see U.S. GENERAL ACCOUNTING OFFICE, FOREST SERVICE:
LITTLE PROGRESS ON PERFORMANCE ACCOUNTABILITY UNLESS MANAGEMENT AD-
DRESSES KEY CHALLENGES (June 2, 2003).

3. Given that, for now and the foreseeable future, we do have national forests
and a Forest Service, a few words are merited about the mechanics of one of the
agency's principal functions—selling timber. Timber sale contracts are governed by a blend of traditional contract law and statutory and regulatory provisions that alter normal rules of contract interpretation in some circumstances.
The Forest Service must publicly advertise all sales, providing information
about the quality and age of the timber and methods of bidding and payment.
Bidding must be conducted through open and fair competition. The timber sale
contract must incorporate the successful bidder's plan of operation designed to
ensure orderly harvesting of the timber consistent with the NFMA. At the end
of the contract term—usually ten years—the purchaser must replant and take
measures to reduce erosion. Rules of contract modification and termination,
particularly in the context of changing environmental constraints, have often
been tested in the courts. *See* Everett Plywood Corp. v. United States, 651 F.2d
723 (Ct.Cl.1981); Scott Timber Co. v. United States, 40 Fed.Cl. 492 (1998). For
more on the timber sale contracting process, Thomas R. Lundquist, *Providing
the Timber Supply from National Forest Lands*, 5 NATURAL RESOURCES & ENV'T
6 (Winter 1991). The Forest Service's multiple-use mandate also requires it to
administer rules for mineral resource extraction on national forest lands. *See*
Lyle K. Rising, *Public Land and National Forest Access for Mining*, 5 NATURAL
RESOURCES & ENV'T 16 (Winter 1991); Jan G. Laitos, *Oil and Gas Leasing on
Forest Service Lands*, 5 NATURAL RESOURCES & ENV'T 23 (1991).

4. The early history of federal and state forest policy is thoroughly explored in
J. CAMERON, THE DEVELOPMENT OF GOVERNMENTAL FOREST CONTROL IN THE
UNITED STATES (1972); J. P. KINNEY, THE DEVELOPMENT OF FOREST LAW IN
AMERICA (1917); and James L. Huffman, *A History of Forest Policy in the Unit-
ed States*, 8 ENVTL. L. 239 (1978). Excellent summaries of Forest Service poli-
cies prior to, leading to, and after the enactment of NFMA are found in
MICHAEL J. BEAN & MELANIE J. ROWLAND, THE EVOLUTION OF NATIONAL WILD-
LIFE LAW 340–56 (3rd ed.1997); Lawrence Ruth, *Conservation on the Cusp: The
Reformation of National Forest Policy in the Sierra Nevada*, 18 J. ENVTL. L. 1
(2000); Federico Cheever, *Four Failed Forest Standards: What We Can Learn
From the History of the National Forest Management Act's Substantive Timber
Management Provisions*, 77 OR. L. REV. 601 (1998); and Oliver A. Houck, *On the
Law of Biodiversity and Ecosystem Management*, 81 MINN. L. REV. 869, 883–

929 (1997). The history of forests and of forest policy is also covered extensively by the Forest History Society. *See* http://www.foresthistory.org.

C. BIODIVERSITY MANAGEMENT IN FOREST ECOSYSTEMS

As the foregoing history of forest law suggests, two difficult sets of issues have plagued U.S. forest policy at all levels of government in recent decades: how much to take into account the biodiversity storage and ecosystem service values of forests in forest management decisions, and how to formulate a national forest policy given the diverse geography of ownership of forested lands. The two sets of issues are, of course, interrelated, as public agencies will have more discretion in establishing a biodiversity-ecosystem values policy for lands they own than for lands that are privately owned.

1. PUBLIC LANDS: NATIONAL FORESTS AND THE BIODIVERSITY MANDATE

As the nation's largest single owner of forest lands, the federal government's decisions about forest management have lasting effects on the biodiversity and ecosystem values of our nation's forests. Of the federal land management agencies, the U.S. Forest Service controls the largest holding of federal forests—192 million acres of land in 42 states, the Virgin Islands, and Puerto Rico—through its jurisdiction over the National Forest System. The system is composed of 155 national forests, 20 national grasslands, and various other lands under the jurisdiction of the Secretary of Agriculture (the Secretary). The vast majority of the national forests acres are located west of Texas and the Great Plains states, though some other states have significant holdings.

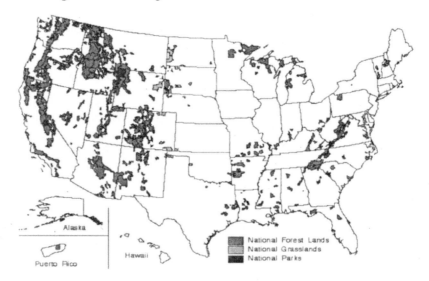

National Forest lands are located predominantly in the western states and Appalachian Mountains
U.S. Forest Service

According to the combined mandates of the Multiple-Use Sustained-Yield Act (MUSY) and the National Forest Management Act (NFMA), the National Forest System lands are to be managed for a variety of uses on a sustained-yield basis to ensure a continued supply of products and services in perpetuity. (Further detail on the MUSY and NFMA mandates is provided in the first principal case presented below). Exactly what that management mandate means has been the subject of intense debate in Congress, the Forest Service, and the courts. The NFMA injects a biodiversity factor into the mix of overlapping and conflicting goals the Forest Service serves, requiring that the agency

> provide for diversity of plant and animal communities based on the suitability and capability of the specific land area in order to meet overall multiple-use objectives, and within the multiple-use objectives of a land management plan adopted pursuant to this section, provide, where appropriate, to the degree practicable, for steps to be taken to preserve the diversity of tree species similar to that existing in the region controlled by the plan.

16 U.S.C. § 1604(g)(3)(B). The Forest Service has implemented that statutory provision, complete with all its escape valves, qualifiers, and sources of discretion, through its regulation at 36 C.F.R. pt. 219.

Pursuant to that regulation, the diversity mandate, as well as all the other concerns the Forest Service must consider under its multiple use mandate, is factored into each national forest's land and resource management plan, or LRMP. Preparation of an LRMP is the first step in resource allocation within a national forest. In the case of timber harvesting, the LRMP outlines where, when, and under what conditions harvesting generally can occur. The Forest Service then authorizes harvesting in particular locations by selecting a timber sale area and preparing an environmental assessment subject to public review and comment. The agency must consider the environmental consequences of each sale and must determine that a decision to sell in a particular area complies with the LRMP. Only then can the agency award a timber harvest contract.

During the 1990s in particular, environmental groups pressed hard on the Forest Service to emphasize this biodiversity side of the agency's forest management mandate and de-emphasize the use of national forests for timber extraction. The groups initiated litigation challenging numerous LRMPs resulting in the trilogy of influential cases presented in this section, through which they tried to force the agency to (1) use a new brand of science known as conservation biology as the guiding light for all forest management decisions; (2) manage forests to ensure the long-term viability of sensitive species above all else; and (3) perform rigorous population viability analyses for forest species before making forest management decisions. Although the suits largely failed in achieving the intended overhaul of Forest Service policy by judicial decree, the effort scored some modest successes in some courts and the relentless pressure the groups placed on the agency, coupled with recommendations from independent experts, had by the end of the decade produced a proposal for change by the agency under the heading of "ecological sustainability." The agency later explained what it believed this to mean:

> The concept of sustainability has become an internationally recognized objective for land and resource stewardship. In 1987, the Brundtland Commission Report (The World Commission on Environment and Development) articulated in "Our Common Future" the need for intergenerational equity in natural resource management. The Commission defined sustainability as meeting the needs of the present without compromising the ability of future generations to meet their own needs. During the last twenty years, the world has increasingly come to recognize that the functioning of ecological systems is a necessary prerequisite for strong productive economies, enduring human communities, and the values people seek from wildlands.
>
> Similarly, the Forest Service and scientific community have developed the concepts of ecosystem management and adaptive management. Scientific advances and improved ecological understanding support an approach under which forests and grasslands are managed as ecosystems rather than focusing solely on single species or commodity output. Indeed, ecosystem management places greater emphasis on assessing and managing broad landscapes and sustaining ecological processes. Ecosystem management focuses on the cumulative effects of activities over time and over larger parts of the landscape. Planning and management under ecosystem management also acknowledge the dynamic nature of ecological systems, the significance of natural processes, and the uncertainty and inherent variability of natural systems. Ecosystem management calls for more effective monitoring of management actions and their effects to facilitate adaptive management, which encourages changes in management emphasis and direction as new, scientific information is developed. In accord with ecosystem management, regional ecosystem assessments have become the foundation for more comprehensive planning, sometimes involving multiple forests and other public land management units. . .
>
> Taken together, ecosystem management, scientific reviews, and collaboration enable the Forest Service to identify key scientific and public issues and to target its limited resources on trying to resolve those issues at the most appropriate time and geographic scale. Based on these changes in the state of scientific and technical knowledge, the Forest Service's extensive experience, and a series of systematic reviews, the Forest Service has concluded that 36 CFR part 219 must be revised in order to better reflect current knowledge and practices and to better meet the conservation challenges of the future. Indeed, while the 1982 planning rule was appropriate for developing the first round of plans from scratch, it is no longer well suited for implementing the NFMA or responding to the ecological, social, and economic issues currently facing the national forests and grasslands.

65 Fed. Reg. 67514 (Nov. 7, 2000).

Alas, as the following materials reveal, pinning down exactly what sustainability means in regulatory text and in judicial review proceedings has proven difficult for the agency at best.

a. CONSERVATION BIOLOGY SCIENCE

In Chapter 7 of the text we explored the three critical decisions for formulation of ecosystem management policy: (1) choosing the framework for describing ecosystems; (2) selecting a metric for describing policy goals and performance; and (3) adopting a method for implementing the policy goals and measuring policy success. The following case focuses on step one, illustrating how what is at one level purely a matter of scientific discourse—the ecosystem biology principles used in forest management—has profound implications for the Forest Service's multiple use policy decisions.

Sierra Club v. Marita

United States Court of Appeals for the Seventh Circuit, 1995.
46 F.3d 606.

■ FLAUM, CIRCUIT JUDGE.

Plaintiffs Sierra Club, Wisconsin Forest Conservation Task Force, and Wisconsin Audubon Council, Inc. (collectively, "Sierra Club") brought suit against defendant United States Forest Service ("Service") seeking to enjoin timber harvesting, road construction or reconstruction, and the creation of wildlife openings at two national forests in northern Wisconsin. The Sierra Club claimed that the Service violated a number of environmental statutes and regulations in developing forest management plans for the two national forests by failing to consider properly certain ecological principles of biological diversity. The district court determined that the plaintiffs' claims were justiciable but then granted the Service summary judgment on the merits of those claims. We affirm.

I.

The National Forest Management Act ("NFMA") requires the Secretary of Agriculture, who is responsible for the Forest Service, to develop "land and resource management plans" to guide the maintenance and use of resources within national forests. 16 U.S.C. §§ 1601–1604. In developing these plans the Secretary must determine the environmental impact these plans will have and discuss alternative plans, pursuant to the National Environmental Policy Act ("NEPA"), 42 U.S.C. § 4321 et seq. The Secretary must also consider the "multiple use and sustained yield of the several products and services obtained" from the forests, pursuant to the Multiple-Use Sustained Yield Act ("MUSYA"), 16 U.S.C. §§ 528–531. The process for developing plans is quite elaborate. The Service must develop its management plans in conjunction with coordinated planning by a specially-designated interdisciplinary team, extensive public participation and comment, and related efforts of other federal agencies, state and local governments, and Indian tribes. 36 C.F.R. §§ 219.4–219.7. Directors at all levels of the Service participate in the planning process for a given national forest.

The Forest Supervisor, who is responsible for one particular forest, initially appoints and then supervises the interdisciplinary team in order to help develop a plan and coordinate public participation. The Supervisor and team then develop a draft plan and draft environmental impact statement ("EIS"), which is presented to the public for comment. 36 C.F.R. §§ 219.10(a), 219.10(b). After a period of comment and revision, a final plan and final EIS are sent to the Regional Forester, who directs one of four national forest regions, for review. If the Regional Forester approves them, she issues both along with a Record of Decision ("ROD") explaining her reasoning. 36 C.F.R. § 219.10(c). An approved plan and final EIS may be appealed to the Forest Service Chief ("Chief") as a final administrative decision. 36 C.F.R. §§ 219.10(d), 211.18.

The final plan is a large document, complete with glossary and appendices, dividing a forest into "management areas" and stipulating how resources in each of these areas will be administered. The plans are ordinarily to be revised on a ten-year cycle, or at least once every fifteen years. 36 C.F.R. § 219.10(g). The present case concerns management plans developed for two forests: Nicolet National Forest ("Nicolet") and Chequamegon (She-WA-me-gon) National Forest ("Chequamegon"). Nicolet spreads over 973,000 acres, of which 655,000 acres are National Forest Land, in northeastern Wisconsin, while Chequamegon encompasses 845,000 publicly-owned acres in northwestern and north-central Wisconsin. Collectively, the Nicolet and the Chequamegon contain hundreds of lakes and streams, thousands of miles of roads and trails, and serve a wide variety of uses, including hiking, skiing, snowmobiling, logging, fishing, hunting, sightseeing, and scientific research. The forests are important for both the tourism and the forest product industries in northern Wisconsin.

Until the mid-1800s, both the Nicolet and Chequamegon were old-growth forests consisting primarily of northern hardwoods. Pine logging around 1900, hardwood logging in the 1920s, and forest fires (caused by clear cutting) significantly affected the landscape. Government replanting and forest-fire control efforts beginning in the 1930s have reclaimed much of the land as forest. The forests now contain a mixture of trees that markedly differs from the forests' pre-1800 "natural" conditions but is also more diverse in terms of tree type and age.

A scenic view from the Chequamegon-Nicolet National Forest

[In the late 1970s and early 1980s, the Nicolet and Chequamegon Forest Supervisors and interdisciplinary teams each began drafting a forest management plan for their respective forests. These plans were expected to guide forest management for ten to fifteen years beginning in 1986. The Regional Forester issued final drafts of both plans on August 11, 1986, as well as final environmental impact statements (FEIS) and RODs explaining the final planning decisions. The Sierra Club brought an action against the Service in the district court on April 2, 1990, over the Nicolet plan and on October 10, 1990, over the Chequamegon plan. Suing under the Administrative Procedure Act (APA), 5 U.S.C. § 701–06, the Sierra Club argued in both cases that the Service had acted arbitrarily or capriciously in developing these forest management plans and FEISs.]

The Sierra Club's primary contention concerned the Service's failure to employ the science of conservation biology, which failure led it to violate a number of statutes and regulations regarding diversity in national forests. Conservation biology, the Sierra Club asserted, predicts that biological diversity can only be maintained if a given habitat is sufficiently large so that populations within that habitat will remain viable in the event of disturbances. Accordingly, dividing up large tracts of forest into a patchwork of different habitats, as the Nicolet and Chequamegon plans did, would not sustain the diversity within these patches unless each patch were sufficiently large so as to extend across an entire landscape or regional ecosystem. Hence, the Sierra Club reasoned, the Service did not fulfill its mandates under the NFMA, NEPA and MUSYA to consider and promote biological diversity within the Nicolet and the Chequamegon.

II.

[The court determined that the Sierra Club had standing to challenge the plans and that the claims were ripe for judicial review]

III.

   The Sierra Club claims that the Service violated the NFMA and NEPA by using scientifically unsupported techniques to address diversity concerns in its management plans and by arbitrarily disregarding certain principles of conservation biology in developing those plans. The Sierra Club asserts that the Service abdicated its duty to take a "hard look" at the environmental impact of its decisions on biological diversity in the forests on the erroneous contentions that the Sierra Club's proposed theories and predictions were "uncertain" in application and that the Service's own methodology was more than adequate to meet all statutory requirements. According to the Sierra Club, the Service, rather than address the important ecological issues the plaintiffs raised, stuck its head in the sand. The result, the Sierra Club argues, was a plan with "predictions about diversity directly at odds with the prevailing scientific literature."

   Several statutes and regulations mandate consideration of diversity in preparing forest management plans. Section 6(g) of the NFMA, the primary statute at issue, directs the Secretary of Agriculture in preparing a forest management plan to, among other things,

> provide for diversity of plant and animal communities based on the suitability and capability of the specific land area in order to meet overall multiple-use objectives, and within the multiple-use objectives of a land management plan adopted pursuant to this section, provide, where appropriate, to the degree practicable, for steps to be taken to preserve the diversity of tree species similar to that existing in the region controlled by the plan[.]

16 U.S.C. § 1604(g)(3)(B).

   A number of regulations guide the application of this statute. The most general one stipulates that:

> Forest planning shall provide for diversity of plant and animal communities and tree species consistent with the overall multiple-use objectives of the planning area. Such diversity shall be considered throughout the planning process. Inventories shall include quantitative data making possible the evaluation of diversity in terms of its prior and present condition. For each planning alternative, the interdisciplinary team shall consider how diversity will be affected by various mixes of resource outputs and uses, including proposed management practices.

36 C.F.R. § 219.26. Another regulation addresses the substantive goals of the plan:

> Management prescriptions, where appropriate and to the extent practicable, shall preserve and enhance the diversity of plant and animal communities, including endemic and desirable naturalized plant and animal species, so that it is at least as great as that which would be

expected in a natural forest and the diversity of tree species similar to that existing in the planning area. Reductions in diversity of plant and animal communities and tree species from that which would be expected in a natural forest, or from that similar to the existing diversity in the planning area, may be prescribed only where needed to meet overall multiple-use objectives. . .

36 C.F.R. § 219.27(g); see also 36 C.F.R. § 219.27(a)(5) (requiring that all management prescriptions "provide for and maintain diversity of plant and animal communities to meet overall multiple-use objectives"). Diversity is defined for the purposes of these regulations as "[t]he distribution and abundance of different plant and animal communities and species within the area covered by a land and resource management plan." 36 C.F.R. § 219.3.

Regulations implementing the NFMA with regard to the management of fish and wildlife resources are more specific still. First,

[f]ish and wildlife habitat shall be managed to maintain viable populations of existing native and desired non-native vertebrate species in the planning area. . . In order to ensure that viable populations will be maintained, habitat must be provided to support, at least, a minimum number of reproductive individuals and that habitat must be well distributed so that those individuals can interact with others in the planning area.

36 C.F.R. § 219.19. In order to perceive the effects of management on these species, the Service must monitor the populations of specially selected "management indicator species" ("MIS"). 36 C.F.R. § 219.19(a)(1). The selection of MIS must include, where appropriate, "endangered and threatened plant and animal species" identified on state and federal lists for the area; species with "special habitat needs that may be influenced significantly by planned management programs; species commonly hunted, fished or trapped, non-game species of special interest; and additional . . . species selected because their population changes are believed to indicate the effects of management activities on other species . . . or on water quality." Id.

The NFMA diversity statute does not provide much guidance as to its execution; "it is difficult to discern any concrete legal standards on the face of the provision." . . . However, "when the section is read in light of the historical context and overall purposes of the NFMA, as well as the legislative history of the section, it is evident that section 6(g)(3)(B) requires Forest Service planners to treat the wildlife resource as a controlling, co-equal factor in forest management and, in particular, as a substantive limitation on timber production."

The Sierra Club argues that the diversity statute and regulations . . . required the Service to consider and apply certain principles of conservation biology in developing the forest plan. These principles, the Sierra Club asserts, dictate that diversity is not comprehensible solely through analysis of the numbers of plants and animals and the variety of species in a given area. Rather, diversity also requires an understanding of the relationships between differing landscape patterns and among various habitats. That understanding, the Sierra Club says, has led to the prediction that the size of a habitat—the "patch size"—tends to affect directly the survival of the habitat and the diversity of plant and animal species within that habitat.

A basic generalization of conservation biology is that smaller patches of habitat will not support life as well as one larger patch of that habitat, even if the total area of the smaller patches equals the total area of the large patch. This generalization derives from a number of observations and predictions. First, whereas a large-scale disturbance will wipe out many populations in a smaller patch, those in a larger patch have a better chance of survival. Second, smaller patches are subject to destruction through "edge effects." Edge effects occur when one habitat's environment suffers because it is surrounded by different type of habitat. Given basic geometry, among other factors, the smaller the patch size of the surrounded habitat, the greater the chance that a surrounding habitat will invade and devastate the surrounded habitat. Third, the more isolated similar habitats are from one another, the less chance organisms can migrate from one habitat to another in the event of a local disturbance. Consequently, fewer organisms will survive such a disturbance and diversity will decline. This third factor is known as the theory of "island biogeography." Thus, the mere fact that a given area contains diverse habitats does not ensure diversity at all; a "fragmented forest" is a recipe for ecological trouble. On the basis of these submissions, the Sierra Club desires us to rule that to perform a legally adequate hard look at the environmental consequences of landscape manipulation across the hundreds of thousands of hectares of a National Forest, a federal agency must apply in some reasonable fashion the ecological principles identified by well accepted conservation biology. Species-by-species techniques are simply no longer enough. Ecology must be applied in the analysis, and it will be used as a criterion for the substantive results.

As a way of putting conservation biology into practice, the Sierra Club suggested that large blocks of land (at least 30,000 to 50,000 acres per block), so-called "Diversity Maintenance Areas" ("DMAs"), be set aside in each of the forests. The Sierra Club proposed and mapped three DMAs for the Nicolet and two for the Chequamegon. In these areas, which would have included about 25% of each forest, habitats were to be undisturbed by new roads, timber sales, or wildlife openings. Neither forest plan, however, ultimately contained a DMA; the Chequamegon Forest Supervisor initially did include two DMAs, but the Regional Forester removed them from the final Chequamegon plan.

The Sierra Club contends that the Service ignored its submissions, noting that the FEISs and RODs for both the Nicolet and the Chequamegon are devoid of reference to population dynamics, species turnover, patch size, recolonization problems, fragmentation problems, edge effects, and island biogeography. According to the Sierra Club, the Service simply disregarded extensive documentary and expert testimony, including over 100 articles and 13 affidavits, supporting the Sierra Club's assertions and thereby shirked its legal duties.

The Service replies that it correctly considered the implications of conservation biology for both the Nicolet and Chequamegon and appropriately declined to apply the science. The Service asserts that it duly noted the "concern [of the Sierra Club and others] that fragmentation of the . . . forest canopy through timber harvesting and road building is detrimental to certain plant and animal species." The Service decided that the theory had "not been applied to forest management in the Lake States" and that the subject was worthy of further study. However, the Service found in both cases that while the theories of conservation biology in general and of island biogeography in particular were "of interest, . . . there is not sufficient justification at this time to make research of the theory a Forest Service priority." Given its otherwise extensive analysis of diversity, as well as the deference owed its interpretation of applicable statutory and regulatory requirements, the Service contends that it clearly met all the "diversity" obligations imposed on it.

IV.

The case now turns to whether the Service was required to apply conservation biology in its analysis and whether the Service otherwise complied with its statutory mandates and regulatory prescriptions regarding diversity in national forests. We hold that the Service met all legal requirements in addressing the concerns the Sierra Club raises.

The Sierra Club's arguments regarding the inadequacy of the Service's plans and FEISs can be distilled into five basic allegations, each of which we address in turn. First, the Sierra Club asserts that the law "treats ecosystems and ecological relationships as a separately cognizable issue from the species by species concepts driving game and timber issues." The Sierra Club relies on the NFMA's diversity language to argue that the NFMA treats diversity in two distinct respects: diversity of plant and animal communities and diversity of tree species. See 16 U.S.C. § 1604(g)(3)(B). The Sierra Club also points to NEPA's stipulations that environmental policy should focus on the "interrelations of all components of the natural environment," 42 U.S.C. § 4331, and regulations which require an EIS to include an analysis of "ecological" effects. See 40 C.F.R. § 1508.8. The Sierra Club concludes from these statutes and regulations that the Service was obligated to apply an ecological approach to forest management and failed to do so. In the Sierra Club's view, MISs and population viability analyses present only half the picture, a picture that the addition of conservation biology would make complete.

The Sierra Club errs in these assertions because it sees requirements in the NFMA and NEPA that simply do not exist. The drafters of the NFMA diversity regulations themselves recognized that diversity was a complex term and declined to adopt any particular means or methodology of providing for diversity. We agree with the district court that "[i]n view of the committee's decision not to prescribe a particular methodology and its failure to mention the principles that plaintiffs claim were by then well established, the court cannot fairly read those principles into the NFMA. . ." Thus, conservation biology is not a necessary element of diversity analysis insofar as the regulations do not dictate that the service analyze diversity in any specific way.

Furthermore, the Sierra Club has overstated its case by claiming that MIS and population viability analyses do not gauge the diversity of ecological communities as required by the regulations. Except for those species to be monitored because they themselves are in danger, species are chosen to be on an MIS list precisely because they will indicate the effects management practices are having on a broader ecological community. Indeed, even if all that the Sierra Club has asserted about forest fragmentation and patch size and edge effects is true, an MIS should to some degree indicate their impact on diversity. While the NFMA would not permit the Service to limit its choices to either enhancing diversity or protecting a particular species, see Seattle Audubon Society v. Evans, 952 F.2d 297, 301–02 (9th Cir.1991), such is not the case here. The Sierra Club may have wished the Service to analyze diversity in a different way, but we cannot conclude on the basis of the records before us that the Service's methodology arbitrarily or capriciously neglected the diversity of ecological communities in the two forests.

In a second and related argument, the Sierra Club submits that the substantive law of diversity necessitated the set-aside of large, unfragmented habitats to protect at least some old-growth forest communities. The Sierra Club points out that 36 C.F.R. § 219.27(g) requires that "where appropriate and to the extent practicable" the Service "shall preserve and enhance the diversity of plant and animal communities . . . so that it is at least as great as that which would be expected in a natural forest. . ." Furthermore, "[r]eductions in diversity of plant and animal communities and tree species from that which would be expected in a natural forest or from that similar to the existing diversity in the planning area[ ] may be prescribed only where needed to meet overall multiple-use objectives." Id. Diversity, the Sierra Club asserts, requires the Service to maintain a range of different, ecologically viable communities. Because it is simply not possible to ensure the survival of any old-growth forest communities without these large, undisturbed patches of land, the Service has therefore reduced diversity. The Service was thus bound to protect and enhance the natural forest or explain why other forest uses prevented the Service from doing so. The Sierra Club believes the Service did neither.

The Sierra Club asserts that the diversity regulations require a certain procedure and that because the substantive result of the Service's choices will produce, in the Sierra Club's view, results adverse to "natural forest" diversity, the Service has violated its mandate. However, as the Service points out, the regulations do not actually require the promotion of "natural forest" diversity but rather the promotion of diversity at least as great as that found in a natural forest. The Service maintains that it did provide for such diversity in the ways discussed above. Additionally, the Service did consider the maintenance of some old-growth forest, even though the Sierra Club disputes that the Service's efforts will have any positive effects. And to the extent the Service's final choice did not promote "natural diversity" above all else, the Service acted well within its regulatory discretion.

V.

The creation of a forest plan requires the Forest Service to make tradeoffs among competing interests. The NFMA's diversity provisions do substantively limit the Forest Service's ability to sacrifice diversity in those trades, and NEPA does require that decisions regarding diversity comply with certain procedural requirements. However, the Service neither ignored nor abused those limits in the present case. Thus, while the Sierra Club did have standing to challenge the choices made by the Service, the Service made those choices within the boundaries of the applicable statutes and regulations.

For the foregoing reasons, we affirm the decisions of the district court.

NOTES & QUESTIONS

1. The *Marita* court suggests that the Forest Service enjoys considerable discretion in selecting its scientific methodology, but is science really what was at issue? One commentator, critical in general of Forest Service policy with respect to biodiversity protection, has pointed cases like *Marita* as evidence that the Forest Service "has avoided judicial decisions that would restrict its discretion—by crafting an issue as one of scientific methodology over substantive choice, thereby taking advantage of the arbitrary and capricious standard of review." Greg D. Corbin, *The United States Forests Service's Response to Biodiversity Science*, 29 ENVTL. L. 377, 400 (1999). But why shouldn't the agency seek to avoid judicial decisions that would restrict its discretion? As in many administrative law settings, the combination of Congress delegating broad discretion to the Forest Service with the practice of judicial deference to administrative implementation of that discretion makes for a double-edged sword.

2. The same commentator argues that *Marita* "allows the Forest Service to . . . insulate itself from scientific advances in the name of uncertainty." *Id.* at 406. In the same vein, another commentator has described the Forest Service as engaging in a "science charade" that effectively prevents courts from applying "hard look" judicial review. *See* Sara A. Clark, *Taking a Hard Look at Agency Science: Can the Courts Ever Succeed?*, 36 ECOLOGY L.Q. 317 (2009). Assuming an agency has discretion to choose the methodology to implement a substantive statutory mandate, when is a "scientific advance" so untested that for the agency to adopt it would be arbitrary and capricious, versus being sufficiently tested to allow the agency to adopt it or not, versus becoming so dominant in the field that the agency *must* adopt it to the exclusion of all other scientific views?

3. Since *Marita*, has conservation biology so much further "advanced" that the Forest Service now has no choice but to adopt it—has conservation biology become the *only* science of ecosystem management? At the time *Marita* was decided, conservation biology as a distinct discipline was relatively young, emerging as a coherent methodology in the mid-1980s. Since then, it has quickly become a leading force in ecosystem management policy. Yet, as you might have picked up in the *Marita* opinion, disciples of conservation biology make no bones about it being an agenda-driven discipline focused on preserving biodiversity. *See* Curt Meine et al., *"A Mission-Driven Discipline": The Growth of Conservation Biology*, 20 CONSERVATION BIOLOGY 631 (2006). Are you concerned that the science of conservation biology is part political science? Should the Forest Service adopt such a methodology? With its heavy emphasis on preservation of large contiguous tracts of habitat, moreover, is conservation biology well-suited to the multiple use mandate under which the Forest Service operates? But if conservation biology becomes or has become the dominant scientific perspective in ecosystem management, how could the Forest Service justify not adopting it? For an overview of conservation biology accessible to the non-scientist, see RICHARD B. PRIMACK, A PRIMER OF CONSERVATION BIOLOGY (2000).

b. INDICATOR SPECIES

Regardless of whether the Forest Service chooses conservation biology or some other brand of biology as the guiding scientific perspective for ecosystem management, it must identify metrics for formulating policy goals and measuring the success of its multiple use decisions. The agency has done so historically by designating particular species as the metric and basing conservation decisions around them, on the premise that by conserving these species the ecosystems within which they exist (and thus the other species in those ecosystems) will be adequately conserved. Though the name given to this metric has changed over time, the selection of the species has become a critical decision in national forest planning, making it subject to tremendous pressure and debate.

Oregon Natural Resources Council v. Lowe
United States Court of Appeals for the Ninth Circuit, 1997.
109 F.3d 521.

PER CURIAM.

OVERVIEW

Appellants Oregon Natural Resources Council ("ONRC") and other environmental groups filed this action against the United States Forest Service, alleging that the Forest Service failed to comply with the National Forest Management Act ("NFMA") and the National Environmental Policy Act ("NEPA") in developing and amending the Winema National Forest Land and Resource Management Plan ("LRMP" or "Forest Plan").

FACTUAL AND PROCEDURAL BACKGROUND

In this suit, the ONRC challenges two Forest Service planning decisions relating to the management of old growth forests on the Winema National Forest, located in south-central Oregon. It challenges the Winema LRMP and Amendment 3 to that plan. Both the LRMP and Amendment 3 were developed pursuant to section 6(a) of the NFMA, which directs the

Secretary of the Forest Service to develop, maintain, and revise resource plans for units of the National Forest Service. 16 U.S.C. § 1604(a) . . .

The Winema proposed Forest Plan and DEIS were published in December 1987 for a 100-day public review and comment period. On the basis of comments received regarding the DEIS and proposed plan, the Forest Service issued a final Forest Plan and an FEIS in 1990. The Winema Forest Plan breaks the forest into a number of Management Areas ("MAs"), which are characterized by different types of forest and objectives for use. One of these, MA7, is devoted to the provision and maintenance of old growth forest and old growth associated species. The Forest Service designated five [Management Indicator Species (MIS)] associated with old growth forest, which were to be managed so as to ensure general species viability in MA7: the pileated woodpecker, northern goshawk, three-toed woodpecker, pine marten, and northern spotted owl.

The ONRC and other plaintiffs administratively appealed both the LRMP and Amendment 3. The Chief of the Forest Service denied both appeals. Having exhausted its administrative remedies, the ONRC and six other organizations filed this suit in the district court on September 9, 1992. They alleged that the LRMP and Amendment 3 failed to insure viable populations of old growth associated wildlife, failed to identify adequate old growth MIS, and failed to comply with NEPA. The Thomas Lumber Company and others intervened as defendants. Both the ONRC and the Forest Service moved for summary judgment.

On September 28, 1993, the district court entered a final judgment granting the Forest Service's motion and denying the ONRC's motion, and dismissing the ONRC's complaint. Oregon Natural Resources Council v. Lowe, 836 F.Supp. 727 (D.Or.1993).

ANALYSIS

I. ONRC's Claims Under the NFMA

B. Failure to Designate the White-Headed Woodpecker as an MIS

The ONRC argues that in failing to designate the white-headed woodpecker as an MIS, the Forest Service acted arbitrarily and capriciously and left "the most critical and imperiled forest type," old growth ponderosa pine, entirely unprotected. In support of this argument, the ONRC points to an October 1989 letter to the Forest Service Supervisor from a group of Forest Service biologists, including one sent from the Winema National Forest, which concluded that the only animals closely associated with old growth ponderosa pine were the flammulated owl and the white-headed woodpecker. The ONRC also notes that both the Klamath Tribe and the Oregon Department of Fish and Wildlife ("ODFW") criticized the Forest Service's failure to designate the white-headed woodpecker as an MIS in comments on the draft EIS.

The Forest Service argues that the white-headed woodpecker is adequately protected by the [minimum management requirements (MMRs)] for pileated woodpeckers and goshawks and by the forest-wide standards for cavity nesters such as snag retention requirements. Further, it asserts that although neither the pileated woodpecker nor the goshawk are closely associated with old-growth ponderosa pine, there is enough overlap between the habitats of the whiteheaded woodpecker and the goshawk and pileated woodpecker that the Winema LRMP provides adequate protection for the whiteheaded woodpecker. Because the ONRC has not shown that these justifications are arbitrary and capricious, we hold that the Forest Service did not violate the NFMA in failing to designate the whiteheaded woodpecker as an MIS in the LRMP . . .

NOTES & QUESTIONS

1. Why did the plaintiffs want yet another MIS for the forest? At some point, does loading up on the number of MIS defeat the purpose of MIS concept? On the other hand, their argument was that a significant forest resource—old growth ponderosa pine—had no adequate dedicated MIS. Are you satisfied by the Forest Service's argument that habitat overlap between the species would serve that purpose?

2. The concept of "indicator species," central to each of the cases in this section, does not find uniform approval among researchers. Indicator species are "organisms whose presence is used to mirror environmental conditions or biological phenomena too difficult, inconvenient, or expensive to measure directly." Jorund Rolstad et al., *Use of Indicator Species to Assess Forest Continuity: A Critique*, 16 CONSERVATION BIOLOGY 253 (2002). But a significant body of research suggests that using selected species to formulate forest management decisions may not always be using the best "mirror." Other indicator values, such as historical forest structure, may be more accurate for assessing forest sustainability over the long run. Moreover, a significant debate has opened up among researchers about the dynamics of species relationships and the reliability of indicator species. The theory behind indicator species is based on a conflict model of species dynamics, with indicator species often being those in the role of predator keeping other foundation species in check. But this model may underestimate the role of facilitative species—species whose behavior boosts the success of others. They may be just as important as predators, making it less clear which, if any, species can be used as the "mirror" for such complex interactions. Indeed, when species facilitation is taken into consideration, many features of the current models of ecosystem dynamics come into question. *See* Ben Shouse, *Conflict over Cooperation*, 299 SCIENCE 644 (2003). What should ecosystem management law do with this emerging information?

c.   IMPACT ASSESSMENT METHOD

Once the Forest Service has designated the metric species for an area of national forest, the rules require it to develop a method of measuring the status of the species in order to develop and evaluate its multiple use planning. Here again we find ample room for debate over the appropriate method. Indeed, the following two decisions illustrate how the courts have grappled with their role in judicial review of the agency's chosen methodology.

Although the second decision overrules the substance of the first, we ask you to read both to gain an appreciation of the underlying tensions in national forest management playing out through the courts.

Ecology Center, Inc. v. Austin

United States Court of Appeals for the Ninth Circuit, 2005.
430 F.3d 1057.

■ FLETCHER, CIRCUIT JUDGE.

Ecology Center, Inc. ("Ecology Center") challenges the United States Forest Service's ("Forest Service" or "Service") Lolo National Forest Post Burn Project ("Project"), which was designed in the aftermath of the 2000 wildfires on the Lolo National Forest ("LNF"). Ecology Center raises a number of procedural and substantive claims under the . . . National Forest Management Act ("NFMA"). We have jurisdiction pursuant to 28 U.S.C. § 1291. Because we find that the Forest Service's decision to permit logging in critical old-growth forest and post-fire habitats was arbitrary and capricious, we reverse the grant of summary judgment to the Service and remand.

I

In 2000, wildfires burned approximately 74,000 acres on the Lolo National Forest. While the fires caused considerable damage to the forest, they also created habitat for species that are dependent upon post-fire habitats, such as the black-backed woodpecker.

In response to the 2000 fires, the Forest Service began developing the Lolo National Forest Post Burn Project and preparing the requisite Environmental Impact Statement ("EIS"). The Forest Service considered four alternatives in detail, including a "no action alternative." In July 2002, the Forest Service selected a slightly modified version of "Alternative Number Five" for the Project. This alternative involves, *inter alia,* commercial thinning of small diameter timber and prescribed burning in old-growth forest stands, as well as salvage logging of burned and insect killed timber in various areas of the forest.

Ecology Center objects to the Forest Service's decision to permit commercial logging in old-growth forest stands, raising concerns about the impact of such logging on the viability of species that are dependent upon old-growth habitat, such as the pileated woodpecker and the northern goshawk. Similarly, Ecology Center questions the Service's impact analysis of salvage logging in post-fire habitat, particularly with respect to the black-backed woodpecker, a sensitive species.

II

A. "Treatment" of Old-Growth Habitat

The Project involves what the Forest Service characterizes as rehabilitative "treatment" of old-growth (and potential old-growth) forest stands;

this treatment entails the thinning of old-growth stands via commercial logging and prescribed burning. The Forest Service cites a number of studies that indicate such treatment is necessary to correct uncharacteristic forest development resulting from years of fire suppression. The Service also points out that the treatment is designed to leave most of the desirable old-growth trees in place and to improve their health.

Ecology Center highlights the scientific uncertainty and debate regarding the necessity, design, and long-term effects of such old-growth treatment. In particular, Ecology Center alleges that the treatment of old-growth forest harms species that are dependent upon old-growth habitat. For example, Ecology Center claims that, even if treatment leaves most old-growth trees in place, it removes or alters other essential elements within old-growth habitat and disturbs bird species currently nesting or foraging within targeted stands. Although treatment may be designed to restore old-growth to "historic conditions," Ecology Center points out this can be a misleading concept: for example, information regarding historic conditions is incomplete; altering particular sections of forest in order to achieve "historic" conditions may not make sense when the forest as a whole has already been fundamentally changed; many variables can affect treatment outcomes; and the treatment process is qualitatively different from the "natural" or "historic" processes it is intended to mimic.

While Ecology Center does not offer proof that the proposed treatment causes the harms it fears, the Service does not offer proof that the proposed treatment benefits—or at least does not harm—old-growth dependent species. Ecology Center argues that because the Forest Service has not assessed the effects of old-growth treatment on dependent species, the Service cannot be reasonably certain that treating old-growth is consistent with NFMA's substantive mandate to ensure species diversity and viability. As a result, especially given the scientific uncertainty surrounding the treatment of old-growth stands, the Forest Service's decision to treat additional old-growth stands was arbitrary and capricious.

Although the Forest Service points to a report which notes that two species of woodpecker were observed foraging in treated old-growth forest, it does not otherwise dispute the charge that it has not directly monitored the impact of treating old-growth on dependent species. Instead, the Service maintains that it need not do so because (1) it has observed the short-term effects of thinning old-growth stands via commercial logging and prescribed burning on forest composition, (2) it has reason to believe that certain old-growth dependent species would prefer the post-treatment composition of old-growth forest stands, and (3) its assumption that treatment does not harm old-growth dependent species is therefore reasonable. The Service further argues that we must defer to its methodological choices regarding what to monitor and how to assess the impact of old-growth treatment.

An agency's choice of methodology is entitled to deference. *See, e.g., Salmon River Concerned Citizens v. Robertson,* 32 F.3d 1346, 1359 (9th Cir.1994). However, there are circumstances under which an agency's choice of methodology, and any decision predicated on that methodology, are arbitrary and capricious. For example, we have held that in order to comply with NFMA, the Forest Service must demonstrate the reliability of its scientific methodology. Here...the Forest Service's conclusion that treating old-growth forest is beneficial to dependent species is predicated on an unverified hypothesis. While the Service's predictions may be correct, the Service has not yet taken the time to test its theory with any "on the ground analysis," despite the fact that it has already treated old-growth forest elsewhere and therefore has had the opportunity to do so. Just as it would be arbitrary and capricious for a pharmaceutical company to market a drug to the general population without first conducting a clinical trial to verify that the drug is safe and effective, it is arbitrary and capricious for the Forest Service to irreversibly "treat" more and more old-growth forest without first determining that such treatment is safe and effective for dependent species. This is not a case in which the Forest Service is asking for the opportunity to verify its theory of the benefits of old-growth treatment. Rather, the Service is asking us to grant it the license to continue treating old-growth forests while excusing it from ever having to verify that such treatment is not harmful.

Although the Service concedes that the opinions of well-qualified experts vary with respect to the appropriateness of management activities in old-growth areas, it also argues that it must have the "discretion to rely on the reasonable opinions of its own qualified experts even if, as an original matter, a court might find contrary views more persuasive." *Marsh v. Oregon Natural Resources Council,* 490 U.S. 360, 378 (1989). However, this is not a case in which different experts have studied the effects of commercial thinning and prescribed burning in old-growth forests and reached different conclusions. Here, experts have differing hypotheses regarding the effects that treating old-growth has on dependent species, yet the Forest Service proposes to continue treating old-growth without first taking the time to observe what those effects actually are. In light of its responsibilities under NFMA, this is arbitrary and capricious.

The Lands Council v. McNair

United States Court of Appeals for the Ninth Circuit, 2008.
537 F.3d 981.

■ MILAN D. SMITH, JR., CIRCUIT JUDGE.

We took this case en banc to clarify some of our environmental jurisprudence with respect to our review of the actions of the United States Forest Service.

The Lands Council and Wild West Institute (collectively, Lands Council) moved for a preliminary injunction to halt the Mission Brush Project (the Project), which called for the selective logging of 3,829 acres of forest in the Idaho Panhandle National Forest (IPNF). As the basis for the preliminary injunction, Lands Council claimed that Ranotta McNair and the United States Forest Service (collectively, the Forest Service), failed to comply with the National Forest Management Act (NFMA), 16 U.S.C. § 1600 *et seq.,* the National Environmental Policy Act (NEPA), 42 U.S.C. § 4231 *et seq.,* and the Administrative Procedure Act (APA), 5 U.S.C. § 701 *et seq.,* in developing and implementing the Project.

Boundary County, City of Bonners Ferry, City of Moyie Springs, Everhart Logging, Inc., and Regehr Logging, Inc. (collectively, Intervenors) intervened on behalf of the Forest Service. The district court denied Lands Council's motion for a preliminary injunction. A three-judge panel of this court reversed the district court's decision and remanded for entry of a preliminary injunction in *Lands Council v. McNair,* 494 F.3d 771 (9th Cir.2007). We vacate that decision and affirm the district court.

FACTUAL AND PROCEDURAL BACKGROUND

A. Mission Brush Area

The Mission Brush Area (or Project Area) encompasses approximately 31,350 acres and is located in the northeastern portion of the Bonners Ferry Ranger District. Approximately 16,550 acres of the Project Area are National Forest System lands, which are home to a variety of species (or their habitats), including the northern gray wolf, Canada lynx, grizzly bear, black-backed woodpecker, flammulated owl, fisher, western toad, pileated woodpecker, and the white-tailed deer. The Project Area is also home to old-growth trees.

The current structure and composition of the forest in the Project Area differs significantly from the forest's historic composition. While the Project Area previously consisted of relatively open ponderosa pine and Douglas-fir stands, today it is crowded with stands of shade-tolerant, younger Douglas-firs and other mid-to-late-successional species. The suppression of naturally occurring fires, past logging practices, and disease are primarily responsible for this shift in forest composition.

The increased density of trees has proven deleterious to the old-growth trees and the Project Area's ecology. First, old-growth trees need relatively open conditions to survive and maintain their growth rates. Second, the increased density is causing a decline in the health and vigor of all trees because they must compete for moisture, sunlight, and nutrients, and the densely clustered trees are less tolerant of insects and disease. Third, dense, dry forests are at risk for large, stand-replacing fires, due to the build-up of fuels. Lastly, wildlife species that prefer a relatively open forest composition with more old-growth trees have suffered a decline in habitat.

B. Mission Brush Project

The Forest Service proposed the Project, in part, to restore the forest to its historic composition, which, in the Forest Service's assessment, is more likely to be sustainable over time. But this is not the Project's only objective. According to the Supplemental Final Environmental Impact Statement (SFEIS) that the Forest Service issued in April 2006, the overall "objectives of the project are to begin restoring forest health and wildlife habitat, improv[e] water quality and overall aquatic habitat by reducing sediment and the risk of sediment reaching streams, and provid[e] recreation opportunities that meet the varied desires of the public and the agency while reducing negative effects to the ecosystem." The Project proposes to accomplish these varied objectives through a number of actions, such as improving roads that presently contribute to sediment in the watersheds, decommissioning roads posing a great risk of contributing to sediment, ensuring that the Project Area has acceptable toilets and wheelchair accessible pathways to toilets, installing a boat ramp and fishing dock, and improving trails.

After considering multiple approaches on how best to accomplish the Project's goals with respect to forest composition, including one no-action alternative, the Forest Service chose to implement a modified version of Alternative 2. In relevant part, Alternative 2 calls for silvicultural treatments on 3,829 acres of forest, fuels treatments on 3,698 acres, and ecosystem burns without harvest on 238 acres. The silvicultural treatments proposed include commercial thinning, regeneration cuts, and sanitation salvage harvesting.

As a part of the Project, the Forest Service plans to treat 277 acres of dry-site old-growth stands in order to increase the overall quality of dry-site old-growth stands and scattered old-growth Douglas-fir, and to improve and maintain trees that could be old-growth in the future. Despite its plans to perform treatments within old-growth stands, the Project will not involve harvesting allocated old-growth trees. The Forest Service represented in the SFEIS that the allocated old-growth in the IPNF has not been harvested for several years, and that its "focus is on maintaining [existing] old growth stands . . . and allocating additional stands for future old growth as they mature." In those units containing old-growth trees, the Forest Service has identified those non-old-growth trees it plans to harvest.

The Project is expected to generate 23.5 million board feet of timber, which has been, or will be, sold pursuant to three timber sale contracts: the Brushy Mission Sale, the Haller Down Sale, and the Mission Fly By Sale. The Forest Service sold the Brushy Mission Sale to Everhart Logging, and the Haller Down Sale to Regehr Logging. The Forest Service received no bids for the Mission Fly By Sale, which contains all but fourteen of the old-growth acres that are part of the Haller Down Sale. Though logging under the Brushy Mission and Haller Down sales has already begun, the injunction imposed by the district court pursuant to the three-judge panel opinion in *Lands Council*, 494 F.3d 771, prohibits the Forest Service from logging in the fourteen acres of old-growth in the Haller Down Sale. The same injunction imposes other restrictions on the Forest Service, including a prohibition on taking any action in the area encompassed by the Mission Fly By Sale.

C. Procedural History

In late 2002, the Forest Service decided to undertake management activities in the Mission and Brush Creek areas. In 2003, the Forest Service issued a draft Environmental Impact Statement (EIS). After receiving public comments, the Forest Service released its final EIS and Record of Decision (ROD) in June 2004. Lands Council appealed the ROD. The Forest Service upheld the Project, but ordered the preparation of a supplemental EIS in light of this court's decision in *Lands Council v. Powell (Lands Council I),* 379 F.3d 738 (9th Cir.2004), *amended by* 395 F.3d 1019 (9th Cir.2005), which addressed the management of National Forest System lands in the IPNF in connection with a different Forest Service project. The Forest Service subsequently released a supplemental draft EIS for public comment, and issued the SFEIS and ROD in April 2006. Lands Council and other environmental groups filed an administrative appeal, which the Forest Service denied in July 2006. In October 2006, Lands Council filed this action and moved for a preliminary injunction.

DISCUSSION

Lands Council argues that, in developing the Project, the Forest Service violated the NFMA in two ways: (1) by failing to demonstrate the reliability of the scientific methodology underlying its analysis of the Project's effect on wildlife, (specifically the flammulated owl and its habitat),[FN4] and (2) by not complying with Standard 10(b) of the IPNF Forest Plan, which requires the Forest Service to maintain at least ten percent old-growth throughout the forest. Lands Council also argues that the Forest Service violated NEPA because, in Lands Council's view, the Forest Service did not adequately address the uncertainty concerning its proposed treatment as a strategy to maintain species viability.

In essence, Lands Council asks this court to act as a panel of scientists that instructs the Forest Service how to validate its hypotheses regarding wildlife viability, chooses among scientific studies in determining whether the Forest Service has complied with the underlying Forest Plan, and orders the agency to explain every possible scientific uncertainty. As we will explain, this is not a proper role for a federal appellate court. But Lands Council's arguments illustrate how, in recent years, our environmental jurisprudence has, at times, shifted away from the appropriate standard of review and could be read to suggest that this court should play such a role.

Below, we address each of Lands Council's arguments. We first discuss the language and purpose of the NFMA and how, in *Ecology Center, Inc. v. Austin,* 430 F.3d 1057 (9th Cir.2005), we misconstrued what the NFMA requires of the Forest Service. We then turn to whether the Forest Service met the NFMA's requirements in this case; specifically, we consider the sufficiency of the Forest Service's analysis of the Project's effect on the flammulated owl and its habitat....

We are mindful, of course, that important environmental resources are at stake in cases such as this, and we strongly reaffirm that the Forest Service must fully comply with the requirements of the NFMA and NEPA. We conclude that the Forest Service has complied with those requirements in this case, and we affirm the district court's denial of Lands Council's request for a preliminary injunction.

A. The National Forest Management Act

1. Statutory Language And Purpose

The NFMA sets forth the statutory framework and specifies the procedural and substantive requirements under which the Forest Service is to manage National Forest System lands. Procedurally, the NFMA requires the Forest Service to develop a forest plan for each unit of the National Forest System. 16 U.S.C. § 1604(a). In developing and maintaining each plan, the Forest Service is required to use "a systematic interdisciplinary approach to achieve integrated consideration of physical, biological, economic, and other sciences." *Id.* § 1604(b). After a forest plan is developed, all subsequent agency action, including site-specific plans such as the Mission Brush Project, must comply with the NFMA and be consistent with the governing forest plan. *Id.* § 1604(i); *see Idaho Sporting Cong., Inc. v. Rittenhouse,* 305 F.3d 957, 962 (9th Cir.2002) ("[A]ll management activities undertaken by the Forest Service must comply with the forest plan, which in turn must comply with the Forest Act." (citing *Inland Empire Pub. Lands Council v. U.S. Forest Serv.,* 88 F.3d 754, 757 (9th Cir.1996))).

Substantively, the NFMA requires the Secretary of Agriculture to develop guidelines "to achieve the goals of the Program," including:

[P]rovid[ing] for diversity of plant and animal communities based on the suitability and capability of the specific land area in order to meet overall multiple-use objectives, and within the multiple-use objectives of a land management plan adopted pursuant to this section, provide, where appropriate, to the degree practicable, for steps to be taken to preserve the diversity of tree species similar to that existing in the region controlled by the plan . . .

The Project also must be consistent with the IPNF Forest Plan's provisions regarding wildlife viability. *See* 16 U.S.C. § 1604(i). In the IPNF Forest Plan, the Forest Service designated the flammulated owl, the only species at issue in this appeal, as a sensitive species. The IPNF Forest Plan requires the Forest Service to "[m]anage the habitat of species listed in the Regional Sensitive Species List to prevent further declines in populations which could lead to federal listing under the Endangered Species Act."

Congress has consistently acknowledged that the Forest Service must balance competing demands in managing National Forest System lands. Indeed, since Congress' early regulation of the national forests, it has never been the case that "the national forests were . . . to be 'set aside for nonuse.' " *United States v. New Mexico,* 438 U.S. 696, 716 n. 23, 98 S.Ct. 3012, 57 L.Ed.2d 1052 (1978) (citing 30 Cong. Rec. 966 (1897) (statement of Rep. McRae)). For example, in the Organic Administration Act of June 4, 1897, passed less than a decade after Congress began regulating the national forests, Congress identified two purposes for which it would reserve a national forest at that time: "[to] secur[e] favorable conditions of water flows, and to furnish a continuous supply of timber." *Id.* at 707-08, 98 S.Ct. 3012 (quoting 16 U.S.C. § 475 (1976)).

Congress' current vision of national forest uses, a broader view than Congress articulated in 1897, is expressed in the Multiple-Use Sustained Yield Act of 1960, 16 U.S.C. § § 528-31, which states that "[i]t is the policy of the Congress that the national forests are established and shall be administered for outdoor recreation, range, timber, watershed, and wildlife and fish purposes." *Id.* § 528. The NFMA references 16 U.S.C. § § 528-531 and requires that plans developed for units of the National Forest System "provide for multiple use and sustained yield of the products and services obtained therefrom . . . and [must] include coordination of outdoor recreation, range, timber, watershed, wildlife and fish, and wilderness[.]" *Id.* § 1604(e)(1). Thus, the NFMA is explicit that wildlife viability is not the Forest Service's only consideration when developing site-specific plans for National Forest System lands.

2. We Overrule Ecology Center

Lands Council argues that the Forest Service violated the NFMA because it has not demonstrated the reliability of the scientific methodology underlying its analysis of the effect of the Project's proposed treatment on the flammulated owl and its habitat. Relying primarily on *Ecology Center,* Lands Council specifically contends that the Forest Service erred by not verifying its prediction regarding the effect of treatment on old-growth species' habitat with observation or on-the-ground analysis. We disagree, and hereby overrule *Ecology Center.* We also hold that the district court did not abuse its discretion in concluding that Lands Council is unlikely to succeed on the merits of this claim.

In *Ecology Center,* we applied an on-the-ground analysis requirement to our review of the Lolo National Forest Post Burn Project, in which the Forest Service proposed logging in old-growth forest and post-fire habitats. 430 F.3d at 1060. We held that in order to comply with the NFMA, the Forest Service was required to conduct on-the-ground analysis to verify its soil quality analysis and to establish the reliability of its hypothesis that "treating old-growth forest is beneficial to dependent species." *Id.* at 1064, 1070-71.

Ecology Center even suggests that such an analysis must be on-site, meaning *in the location of the proposed action.* There, we rejected the Forest Service's argument that its on-the-ground soil analysis was "sufficiently reliable because it utilized data from areas with ecological characteristics similar to the proposed harvest units." *Id.* at 1070. We noted that, as in *Lands Council I,* the Forest Service had not tested "much of *the activity area.*" *Id.*

We made three key errors in *Ecology Center.* First, we read the holding of *Lands Council I* too broadly. Second, we created a requirement not found in any relevant statute or regulation. And, third, we defied well-established law concerning the deference we owe to agencies and their methodological choices. Today, we correct those errors.

In *Lands Council I*, we expressly limited our holding that "on-site spot verification" was required for soil analysis to "the circumstances of [that] case." 395 F.3d at 1036. But in *Ecology Center,* we expanded the on-the-ground analysis requirement beyond the facts of *Lands Council I*, and even beyond the context of soil analysis. In holding that the Forest Service violated the NFMA by not verifying its hypothesis that treating old-growth forest is beneficial to dependent species with on-the-ground analysis, *Ecology Center* established a far-reaching rule that the Forest Service must always verify its methodology with on-the-ground analysis, regardless of the context. 430 F.3d at 1064. We accept the description in *Lands Council I* that it was "limited to the circumstances of [that] case," and hold that it does not impose a categorical requirement of on-the-ground analysis or observation for soil analysis, or any other type of analysis.

The Forest Service is at liberty, of course, to use on-the-ground analysis if it deems it appropriate or necessary, but it is not required to do so....The NFMA unquestionably requires the Forest Service to "provide for diversity of plant and animal communities . . . in order to meet overall multiple-use objectives." 16 U.S.C. § 1604(g)(3)(B). Similarly, the IPNF Forest Plan requires the Forest Service to "[m]anage the habitat of species listed in the Regional Sensitive Species List to prevent further declines in populations which could lead to federal listing under the Endangered Species Act." IPNF Forest Plan, *supra,* at II-28. However, despite imposing these substantive requirements on the Forest Service, neither the NFMA and its regulations [FN6] nor the IPNF Forest Plan specify precisely how the Forest Service must demonstrate that its site-specific plans adequately provide for wildlife viability.

Granting the Forest Service the latitude to decide how best to demonstrate that its plans will provide for wildlife viability comports with our reluctance to require an agency to show us, by any particular means, that it has met the requirements of the NFMA every time it proposes action....Thus, we defer to the Forest Service as to what evidence is, or is not, necessary to support wildlife viability analyses.

Were we to grant less deference to the agency, we would be ignoring the APA's arbitrary and capricious standard of review. Essentially, we assessed the quality and detail of on-site analysis and made "fine-grained judgments of its worth." It is not our proper role to conduct such an assessment....Instead, our proper role is simply to ensure that the Forest Service made no "clear error of judgment" that would render its action "arbitrary and capricious." *See Marsh v. Or. Natural Res. Council,* 490 U.S. 360, 378 (1989). To do so, we look to the evidence the Forest Service has provided to support its conclusions, along with other materials in the record, to ensure that the Service has not, for instance, "relied on factors which Congress has not intended it to consider, entirely failed to consider an important aspect of the problem, offered an explanation for its decision that runs counter to the evidence before the agency, or [an explanation that] is so implausible that it could not be ascribed to a difference in view or the product of agency expertise." *Motor Vehicle Mfrs. Assn., Inc. v. State*

Farm Mut. Auto. Ins. Co., 463 U.S. 29, 43 (1983); *see Lands Council I,* 395 F.3d at 1026.

This approach respects our law that requires us to defer to an agency's determination in an area involving a "high level of technical expertise." *See Selkirk Conservation Alliance v. Forsgren,* 336 F.3d 944, 954 (9th Cir.2003) (quoting *Marsh,* 490 U.S. at 377-78, 109 S.Ct. 1851). We are to be "most deferential" when the agency is "making predictions, within its [area of] special expertise, at the frontiers of science." *Forest Guardians v. U.S. Forest Serv.,* 329 F.3d 1089, 1099 (9th Cir.2003) (citations omitted).

Thus, as non-scientists, we decline to impose bright-line rules on the Forest Service regarding particular means that it must take in every case to show us that it has met the NFMA's requirements. Rather, we hold that the Forest Service must support its conclusions that a project meets the requirements of the NFMA and relevant Forest Plan with studies that the agency, in its expertise, deems reliable. The Forest Service must explain the conclusions it has drawn from its chosen methodology, and the reasons it considers the underlying evidence to be reliable. We will conclude that the Forest Service acts arbitrarily and capriciously only when the record plainly demonstrates that the Forest Service made a clear error in judgment in concluding that a project meets the requirements of the NFMA and relevant Forest Plan.

For these reasons, we overrule *Ecology Center* and affirm that *Lands Council I's* requirement of on-the ground analysis was limited to the circumstances of that particular case.

3. Reliability of the Forest Service's Analysis Concerning The Effects Of Treating Old-Growth Habitat On The Flammulated Owl

Today, as we have in the past, we approve, based on the record before us, of the Forest Service's use of the amount of suitable habitat for a particular species as a proxy for the viability of that species. We therefore find "eminently reasonable" the Forest Service's conclusion that the Project will maintain a viable population of flammulated owls because it will not decrease suitable flammulated owl habitat in the short-term and will promote the long-term viability of suitable flammulated owl habitat.

To always require a particular type of proof that a project would maintain a species' population in a specific area would inhibit the Forest Service from conducting projects in the National Forests. We decline to constrain the Forest Service in this fashion. Were we to do so, we may well be complicit in frustrating one or more of the other objectives the Forest Service must also try to achieve as it manages National Forest System lands.

Of course, a reviewing court still must ensure that the Forest Service's use of "habitat as a proxy" is not arbitrary and capricious. We therefore hold that when the Forest Service decides, in its expertise, that habitat is a reliable proxy for species' viability in a particular case, the Forest Service nevertheless must both describe the quantity and quality of habitat that is necessary to sustain the viability of the species in question and explain its methodology for measuring this habitat. We will defer to its decision to use habitat as a proxy unless the Forest Service makes a "clear error of judgment" that renders its decision arbitrary and capricious.

On the basis of the studies provided by the Forest Service and the Forest Service's reasonable assumption that maintaining suitable habitat for the flammulated owl will also maintain a viable population of flammulated owls, we conclude that the district court did not abuse its discretion in deciding that Lands Council is not likely to succeed on this aspect of its NFMA claim.

NOTES & QUESTIONS

1. Was *Ecology Center* an aberrant mistake, or a needed correction? How different would Forest Service policy, and judicial review of Forest Service decisions, be had *Ecology Center* stood as the applicable standard of review?

2. Based on all the cases excerpted in this section, from *Marita* to *McNair*, what *is* the Forest Service's substantive duty under the MUSY and NFMA with respect to biodiversity and ecosystem management, and how much latitude does the agency have in choosing the method of implementing that duty? If the agency had settled each case by agreeing to do everything the plaintiffs argued was necessary to comply with the statutes and regulations, could timber industry interests have challenged the agency's action as arbitrary and capricious? Indeed, the outcomes in the cases are of little surprise, as one would be hard-pressed to read the MUSY and NFMA as making clear choices about which science to use, which species to designate as indicator species, and how to measure species viability. Who should make these decisions, Congress, the Forest Service, or the courts?

3. Why all the fuss? How much difference does it make? In other words, how altered would the Forest Service's planning process and decision making outcomes be for the national forests if it (1) had to apply conservation biology; (2) had to adopt more indicator species; and (3) had to conduct "on the ground" population surveys to evaluate indicator species viability? Clearly, the plaintiffs in the cases believe the difference would be substantial, and apparently so did the Forest Service given how steadfastly it opposed the plaintiffs' arguments. But what would be the bottom line impact on Forest Service decisions for national forests?

4. The extensive discretion the Forest Service enjoys in the courts is neither an accident nor a recent phenomenon. As a leading expert in national forest law and policy explains, Gifford Pinchot, the progenitor of the national forests and first leader of the Forest Service, worked hard to steer Congress toward a statutory text for the Organic Act that appeared on its surface to impose mandates, but which had no depth of content or sense of direction. In other words, "Pinchot received *carte blanche*." *See* Federico Cheever, *The United States Forest Service and National Park Service: Paradoxical Mandates, Powerful Founders, and the Rise and Fall of Agency Discretion*, 74 DENV. U. L. REV. 625, 638 (1997). Congress since then has resisted efforts to enact prescriptive reform legislation, instead expanding the multiple use mandate through the MUSY and adding planning layers through the NFMA.

5. As Professor Cheever further explains, the inherent tension in national forest policy between use and protection of biodiversity also was by design, as Pinchot extended the offer of a protection mandate to soften the use mandate that was his central goal in shaping the Organic Act. *See id.* at 631–35. A wealthy man used to acting as a strong leader, Pinchot used the Forest Service's wall of discretion to build agency prestige and pride. But over time the combination of multiple use mandate and extensive discretion became the agency's downfall. The environmental protection movement of the 1970s forged a powerful set of interest groups who clamored for more emphasis of the protection mandate. The agency thus was pulled between its use and protection mandates more forcefully than it had been in the past, though how to strike the balance was no more clear even after the NFMA was enacted. Gradually, each of the multiple uses became increasingly associated with strong interest groups demanding that their use be the dominant use. The agency's discretion then became more a burden than a benefit, for the open-ended statutes "allow those of us interested in public land management to project our vision and values onto the language Congress used to instruct [the agency]. This almost insures that some significant part of the interested public will believe that the [agency's] conduct is not only wrong but illegal." *Id.* at 629. It is no surprise that after decades of such battering from both sides, Forest Service prestige and morale have eroded. Indeed, in his assessment of the Forest Service, Michael Mortimer likens the agency's situation to that of purgatory, saddled with vague goal-setting laws that give it almost unbridled discretion but leave it "wallowing about, unable to define a consistent path or to stay on a path . . . in the rush to embrace management philosophies that may appease its varying critics." Michael J. Mortimer, *The Delegation of Law-Making Authority to the United States Forest Service: Implications for the Struggle for National Forest Management*, 54 ADMIN. L. 907, 914 (2002). He suggests that Congress either provide more definitive guidance to the agency or, if it lacks the political will to do so, consider the more radical approach of abolishing the agency and replacing it with a new institutional structure. In either case, it seems that the discretion Pinchot worked so hard to gain for the agency has become its curse.

6. For further background on NFMA jurisprudence, see Federico Cheever, *Four Failed Forest Standards: What We Can Learn From the History of the National Forest Management Act's Substantive Timber Management Provisions*, 77 OR. L. REV. 601 (1998); Greg D. Corbin, *The United States Forests Service's Response to Biodiversity Science*, 29 ENVTL. L. 377 (1999); Michael A. Padilla, *The Mouse that Roared: How National Forest Management Act Diversity of Species Requirement is Changing Public Timber Harvesting*, 15 UCLA J. ENVTL. L. & PUB. POL'Y 113 (1996–97); Jack Tuholske and Beth Brennan, *The National Forest Management Act: Judicial Interpretation of a Substantive Environmental Statute*, 15 PUB. LAND. L. REV. 53 (1994); Julie A. Weis, *Eliminating the National Forest management Act's Diversity Requirement as a Substantive Standard*, 27 ENVTL. L. 641 (1997); Charles F. Wilkinson, *The National Forest Management Act: The Twenty Years Behind and Twenty Years Ahead*, 68 U. COLO. L. REV. 659 (1997).

7. The materials in this text focus primarily on the biodiversity and ecosystem management aspects of the different legal regimes considered. For a broad overview of the full scope of the NFMA, see *The National Forest Management Act: Law of the Forest in the Year 2000*, 21 J. LAND, RES., & ENVTL. L. 151 (2001). For a thorough description of all that the Forest Service must cover in its land and resource management plans for national forests, see Michael J. Gippert and Vincent L. DeWitte, *The Nature of Land and Resource Management Planning Under the National Forest Management Act*, 3 ENVTL. L. 149 (1996).

d. ECOLOGICAL SUSTAINABILITY

As noted above, the Ninth Circuit's NFMA jurisprudence has largely stymied the environmental groups' efforts to overhaul Forest Service policy toward biodiversity and ecosystem values through judicial interpretation of the agency's regulations. Congress during this period was by no means friendly to the groups' positions either, which left only direct pressure on the agency itself as a means to effect change. Ironically, it was there, after decades of fighting in the courts, that the groups had had the most visible success by the close of the 1990s. With the help of the auspicious sounding Committee of Scientists, many of the policies the environmental groups had been pursuing in court surfaced in the form of a proposed regulation and a proposed strategic plan the Forest Service published late in 1999, then a final rule the agency adopted late in 2000, just prior to the transition from the Clinton administration to the George W. Bush Administration. This effort, however, was just the beginning of a controversial and erratic evolution of rule proposals that continues to this day. To give you a sense of the substantive components of the agency's approach, what follows are excerpts giving a flavor of what the auspicious sounding Committee of Scientists recommended to the agency in 1999 and what the agency most recently adopted as its planning rule in 2012.

Committee of Scientists, Sustaining the People's Lands: Recommendations for Stewardship of the National Forests and Grasslands Into the Next Century
March 15, 1999.

CHAPTER SIX

Implementing the Laws and Policies Governing the National Forests and Grasslands in the Context of Sustainability

The previous chapters have developed a framework for management of the national forests and grasslands to achieve ecological, economic, and social sustainability. In this chapter, we apply the concepts from those chapters in suggesting planning principles for implementing the environmental laws and policies under which the Forest Service operates: the National Forest Management Act, Multiple-Use Sustained-Yield Act, Organic Act, Endangered Species Act, Clean Water Act, Clean Air Act, and related legislation. We use the suite of legislation that influences the management of the national forests and grasslands, rather than focus solely on the National Forest Management Act, in keeping with our overall goal of assisting in the development of an integrated planning process.

The Committee recognizes that its role is not to dictate specific management approaches for the Forest Service but to provide advice that the Secretary and Chief may act on as they deem appropriate. Nonetheless, the Committee recognizes that such concepts as focal species, ecological integrity, and the use of scientific information may involve technical issues and that the Committee thus has an obligation to the Secretary and the Chief to provide some insight on how this framework for ecological sustainability might be converted from concept to application. Therefore, while our approach has not been field-tested, the Committee has drafted the following regulatory language, that, we believe, provides a useful approach to this issue.

Committee's Proposed Regulation on Ecological Sustainability

36 CFR Sec. 219. Ecological Sustainability.

A. Goals. Nature provides many goods, services, and values to humans. These ecological benefits occur as two, major, interdependent forms: the variety of native plants and animals and the products of ecological systems, such as clean water, air, and fertile soil. The most fundamental goal of the National Forest System is to maintain and restore ecological sustainability, the long-term maintenance of the diversity of native plant and animal communities and the productive capacity of ecological systems. Ecological sustainability is the foundation of national forest stewardship and makes it possible for the national forests and grasslands to provide a wide variety of benefits to present and future generations.

B. Diversity. Ecosystems are inherently dynamic; changes regularly result from natural events, such as floods, fires, or insect outbreaks. Human intervention, such as through forest cutting and water diversions, is often substantial. Thus, because species must have the capability and opportunity to respond adaptively to changes in their environment, species diversity and ecological processes can only be sustained if the essential elements of the natural dynamics of ecosystems are recognized and accommodated when human intervention occurs. Planners and managers must apply the best available scientific information and analysis so that the diversity and adaptive capability of ecosystems will be maintained and restored.

1. Levels of diversity. Ecological diversity must be considered at three hierarchical levels: ecosystems, species, and genes, all of which are necessary parts of a strategy to sustain species values and ecological goods and services.

2. Use of surrogate approaches. Ecological diversity is expressed at a variety of spatial and temporal scales. Explicitly describing and managing all elements of diversity and their interconnections within a single assessment or planning effort is beyond the capacity of the agency. Thus, plan-

ners must identify surrogate approaches that rely on a subset of ecological measurements that are sensitive to management and indicative of overall diversity. Although all three levels of diversity are essential to providing ecological sustainability, the most developed scientific knowledge and assessment strategies relevant to broad-scale resource management occur at the ecosystem (especially landscape scales) and species levels. Accordingly, this section primarily addresses ecosystem and species diversity.

C. Ecosystem Diversity. The first step in providing for ecological sustainability is to sustain the variety and functions of ecosystems across multiple spatial scales, from microsites to large landscapes, to maintain the diversity of native plant and animal communities and the productive capacity of ecological systems.

1. Management standards: ecological integrity. The decisions of resource managers must be based upon the best available scientific information and analysis to provide for conditions that support ecological integrity sufficient to meet the goals of this section. The ecological integrity of an ecosystem can be defined as the completeness of the composition, structure, and processes that are characteristic of the native states of that system. . . Ecological integrity should be analyzed at appropriate spatial and temporal scales and consider the cumulative effects of human and natural disturbances.

2. Assessment and planning. Measures of ecosystems integrity shall be developed in regional assessments based on scientific principles and knowledge of local conditions. As natural forests and grasslands may comprise only a portion of the landscape under consideration, coordination with other landowners and institutions concerning probable future conditions is critical.

3. Validation. The assumption that coarse-filter elements can serve as a basis of sustaining native species diversity shall be validated through monitoring and research. The best available scientific information and analysis shall be used to assess this assumption in a timely manner.

D. Species Diversity. A second step in providing for ecological sustainability is to sustain the diversity of native plant and animal communities through maintaining and restoring the viability of the species that comprise them. The goal of this section is to provide the ecological conditions needed to protect and, as necessary, restore the viability of native species.

1. Focal species. The primary obligation in the selection of focal species is to provide for the diversity of native species. However, since it is not feasible to assess the viability of all species, this section will employ focal species to provide for plant and animal diversity. The status of a single species, or group of species, such as a functional guild of species, can convey information about the status of the larger ecological system in which it resides or about the integrity of specific habitat or ecosystem processes. Regional assessments shall select an appropriate number of focal species.

2. Management standards: species viability. The decisions of resource managers must be based upon the best available scientific information and analysis to provide ecological conditions needed to protect and, as necessary, restore the viability of focal species and of threatened, endangered, and sensitive species. A viable species is defined as consisting of self-sustaining populations that are well distributed throughout the species' range.

3. Validation. The assumption that focal species are providing reliable information about the status and trend of species not being directly monitored shall be validated through monitoring and research. The best available scientific information and analysis shall be used to assess this assumption in a timely fashion.

E. Implementation. The determinations required regarding ecosystem integrity and species viability shall be made at the appropriate planning level. Decisions at each level must be consistent with such determinations for wide-ranging species are best made at the regional scale. Planners and managers must then demonstrate consistency with this determination in all subsequent decisions made at finer scales of planning, including the project level.

F. Monitoring. Effective monitoring is a critical aspect of achieving ecological sustainability. The monitoring program must select indicators of ecosystem integrity and species viability, develop methods for measuring such indicators, designate critical indicator values that would trigger changes in management practices, obtain data to determine whether such critical values are being approached, and interpret those data in relation to past and potential management decisions. If analysis and assessment concludes that some critical values are being approached, then the appropriate plan must be reevaluated to determine whether amendments are necessary to comply with the provisions of this section.

NOTES & QUESTIONS

1. How closely does the approach the Committee recommended track themes in Grumbine's vision of ecosystem management, Holling's theory of adaptive management, and the foundations of conservation biology outlined in the *Marita* case? If the congressionally convened representatives of science adopt or reject those principles, must the Forest Service follow their lead?

2. The genesis of the planning rule overhaul effort was an informal policy directive known as "New Perspectives in Forestry," which launched a public relations effort designed to convey the agency's approach to biodiversity protection planning. *See* Harold Salawasser, *New Perspectives for Sustaining Diversity in the U.S. National Forest Ecosystems*, 5 CONSERVATION BIOLOGY 567, 567–69 (1991). But "New Perspectives" was quickly, and rightly, criticized as primarily a presentation of vague policy goals with little practical effect. *See* Oliver Houck, *On the Law of Biodiversity and Ecosystem Management*, 81 MINN. L. REV. 869, 923 (1997). By the early 1990s the agency was faced with the reality that the time was due for an overhaul of its 1982 rule.

3. Congress created the Committee when it enacted the NFMA in 1976 to guide the Forest Service in drafting regulations to implement the Act. *See* 16 U.S.C. § 1604(h)(1). The original seven-member Committee met in eighteen public meetings around the country by the end of 1978 and issued a final report in late 1979. *See Final Report of the Committee of Scientists*, 44 Fed. Reg. 26599 (1979). The Forest Service adopted substantially the Committee's recommendations in September 1979, and reconvened the Committee to assist in the 1982 amendments to the rules. At every stage in this process, the Committee emphasized the importance of science, the central role the diversity protection mandate must play, and the need for specificity. *See* Oliver Houck, *On the Law of Biodiversity and Ecosystem Management*, 81 MINN. L. REV. 869, 887–89 (1997). In an effort to replicate these good experiences, and no doubt seeing the writing on the wall, Agriculture Secretary Dan Glickman appointed a second Committee in 1997 to make recommendations for improving the forest planning process. The thirteen-member Committee of experts was racked by disputes over how much of a role to give ecological goals and how much of a role science should play in shaping policy. *See* Charles C. Mann & Mark L. Plummer, *Call for "Sustainability" In Forests Sparks a Fire*, 283 SCIENCE 1996 (1999). After several drafts, in 1999 the second Committee issued the report excerpted above. Law professor Charles Wilkinson, a member of the second Committee, provides a synopsis of its deliberations and a summary of its perspectives in *A Case Study in the Intersection of Law and Science: The 1999 Report of the Committee of Scientists*, 42 ARIZ. L. REV. 307 (2000).

Much activity transpired on the planning rule—or more accurately, planning *rules*—after the Committee issued its report, as changing political administrations engaged in a battle of contrasting visions. A brief history of the back-and-forth is provided in the following excerpt from one of the litigation matters that evolved along the way, Citizens for Better Forestry v USDA, 632 F.Supp.2d 968 (N.D. Cal. 2009):

In 2000, the USDA amended the 1982 Rule. The USDA did not prepare an EIS in connection with the 2000 Rule, but it did prepare an EA. The EA found that the amendment had no significant impact on the environment.

The 2000 Rule modified its predecessor in a number of ways. First, it relaxed the species "viability" requirement by providing that "[p]lan decisions affecting species diversity must provide for ecological conditions that . . . provide a high *likelihood* that those conditions are capable of supporting over time the viability of . . . species well distributed throughout their ranges within the plan area." *National Forest System Land and Resource Management Planning*, 65 Fed. Reg. 67,514, 67,575 (Nov. 9, 2000) (amending 36 C.F.R. § 219.20(b)(2)) (emphasis added). The 1982 Rule had more stringently required that the USDA "insure" continued species existence. 47 Fed. Reg. at 43,038. The 2000 Rule also eliminated the requirement of developing and issuing "regional guides" to maintain regional consistency in forest management. *See* 65 Fed. Reg. at 67, 527. It further eliminated many of the "minimum specific management requirements." For example, in comments submitted in response to the draft 2000 Rule, the Environmental Protection Agency ("EPA") observed that "while [the 1982 Rule] contain[s] specific limits on clear cutting [of trees], the proposed [2000 Rule] would require only that individual forest plans 'provide standards and guidelines for timber harvest and regeneration methods,' " and asked "[h]ow will the proposed [2000 Rule] ensure requirements necessary for sustainability?"

Finally, the 2000 Plan Development Rule eliminated the post-decision appeal process of 36 C.F.R. pt. 217, and replaced it with a pre-decision "objection" process. 65 Fed. Reg. at 67,568 (removing 36 C.F.R. pt. 217); *id.* at 67,578 79 (creating 36 C.F.R. § 219.32). Under this new process, members of the public wishing to object to an amendment or revision of an LRMP have 30 days from the date an EIS is made available to do so. *See id.* Thus, this process can occur before the finalization of the planned amendment if the EIS is published more than 30 days before the amended LRMP becomes final. Citizens and other environmental groups sued the USDA, challenging the substance of the 2000 Rule as contrary to the provisions of the NFMA and alleging that, in promulgating the Rule, the agency failed to adhere to procedures mandated by NEPA and the ESA. After the lawsuit was filed, the USDA announced its intention to revise the new rule. The parties agreed to stay Citizens' substantive challenges, but proceeded with the procedural challenges. The district court granted summary judgment against Citizens on the procedural claims, finding that they were not justiciable for lack of standing and ripeness. The Ninth Circuit reversed the district court on appeal and remanded the case for further proceedings. [The litigation] was dismissed pursuant to stipulation after remand.

In 2002, the USDA proposed amending the 2000 Rule. In its notice of proposed rulemaking, it found that, "[a]lthough the 2000 rule was intended to simplify and streamline the development and amendment of land and resource management plans, . . . the 2000 rule [was] neither straightforward nor easy to implement" and "did not clarify the programmatic nature of land and resource management planning." *National Forest System Land and Resource Management Planning,* 67 Fed. Reg. 72,770, 72,770 (Dec. 6, 2002). The proposed rule purported to retain "many of the basic concepts in the 2000 rule, namely sustainability, public involvement and collaboration, use of science, and monitoring and evaluation," but "attempted to substantially improve these aspects of the 2000 rule by eliminating unnecessary procedural detail, clarifying intended results, and streamlining procedural requirements consistent with agency staffing, funding, and skill levels." *Id.* at 72772.

The USDA did not publish the final version of the rule it proposed in 2002 until 2005. *National Forest System Land Management Planning,* 70 Fed. Reg. 1023 (Jan. 5, 2005). It did not conduct an EIS or an EA, asserting that the rule fell within a previously declared "categorical exclusion" to

NEPA's requirements. A categorical exclusion is "a category of actions which do not individually or cumulatively have a significant effect on the human environment and which have been found to have no such effect in procedures adopted by a Federal agency . . . and for which, therefore, neither an environmental assessment nor an environmental impact statement is required." 40 C.F.R. § 1508.4. In the USDA's view, the 2005 Rule fell within an existing categorical exclusion that applied to "rules, regulations, or policies to establish Service-wide administrative procedures, program processes, or instruction." 70 Fed. Reg. at 1054. In addition, the USDA did not consult with the Fish and Wildlife Service (FWS) or the National Marine Fisheries Service (NMFS) to determine whether the 2005 rule would have an adverse effect on any endangered or threatened species.

Citizens and other environmental groups again sued the USDA, claiming procedural violations of NEPA and the ESA. In *Citizens for Better Forestry v. United States Department of Agriculture* (*Citizens II*), 481 F.Supp.2d 1059 (N.D.Cal.2007), the district court granted summary judgment in part against the USDA, finding that: 1) the agency had violated the Administrative Procedure Act by promulgating the 2005 Rule – a self-described "paradigm shift" from earlier rules, including the rule proposed in 2002 – without first providing notice of the changes and allowing the public to submit comments; 2) the agency had violated NEPA by applying the categorical exclusion and failing to prepare either an EA or an EIS; 3) the agency had violated the ESA by failing to engage in consultations with other federal agencies or to publish a biological assessment (BA). The court enjoined the USDA from putting the 2005 rule into effect until the agency complied with these statutes.

In 2007, the USDA re-published the 2005 rule along with a draft EIS and sought public comment. *National Forest System Land Management Planning*, 72 Fed. Reg. 48,514 (Aug. 23, 2007). The agency published the final version of the EIS and the rule in 2008. *National Forest System Land Management Planning*, 73 Fed. Reg. 21,468 (April 21, 2008). The final version differs in some respects from the proposal, but adheres to the same basic approach to forest plan development. The EIS was undertaken in an effort to comply with the district court's decision in *Citizens II* and concluded, as the USDA had concluded previously, that the proposed rule would have no direct or indirect impact on the environment because the rule was programmatic in nature and did not, in itself, effect any predictable changes in the management of specific National Forest sites. In an effort to comply with the ESA, the USDA also published a BA in connection with the rule's promulgation. The BA concluded, similarly to the EIS, that the Rule would not have a direct or indirect effect on species protected by the Act.

The *Citizens* court invalidated the 2008 rule on procedural grounds, and the agency reinstated the 2000 rule given that it was the last version of the planning rule not invalidated by a court. *See* 74 Fed. Reg. 67062. The agency then published a proposed rule in 2010, yet again moving in an entirely new direction, *see* 76 Fed. Reg. 8480, and then promulgated the final rule excerpted below in 2012.

As the most recent iteration in the planning rule saga, we are focusing your attention on the 2012 rule and sparing you the burden of delving into the substance of the 2000, 2005, and 2008 rules. Our objective is not to have you track the precise language of combating versions of the rule through time—indeed, like its predecessors the 2012 rule might not withstand judicial review (as of this writing it is immersed in litigation), congressional action, or a future administration—but rather to make you aware of the agency's effort to pin down exactly what it means by ecological sustainability and how it has struggled to translate that into regulatory text. But be prepared—even with our rather aggressive editing, the excerpt is lengthy. And get used to that, as anyone wishing to practice in the field of ecosystem management must get used to the challenge of wading through many pages of dense regulatory text.

U.S. Forest Service, Department of Agriculture, *National Forest System Land and Resource Management Planning; Final Rule*

U.S. Forest Service, 2012.
77 Fed. Reg. 21162.

The mission of the Forest Service is to sustain the health, diversity, and productivity of the Nation's forests and grasslands to meet the needs of present and future generations. Responsible officials for each national forest, grassland, and prairie will follow the direction of the planning rule to develop, amend, or revise their land management plans.

The new planning rule provides a process for planning that is adaptive and science-based, engages the public, and is designed to be efficient, effective, and within the Agency's ability to implement. It meets the requirements under the National Forest Management Act (NFMA), the Multiple-Use Sustained-Yield Act (MUSYA), and the Endangered Species Act, as well as all other legal requirements. It was also developed to ensure that plans are consistent with and complement existing, related Agency policies that guide management of resources on the National Forest System (NFS), such as the Climate Change Scorecard, the Watershed Condition Framework, and the Sustainable Recreation Framework.

The planning rule framework includes three phases: Assessment, plan development/amendment/revision, and monitoring. The framework supports an integrated approach to the management of resources and uses, incorporates the landscape-scale context for management, and will help the Agency to adapt to changing conditions and improve management based on new information and monitoring. It is intended to provide the flexibility to respond to the various social, economic, and ecologic needs across a very diverse system, while including a consistent set of process and content requirements for NFS land management plans. The Department anticipates that the Agency will use the framework to keep plans current and respond to changing conditions and new information over time.

The planning rule requires the use of best available scientific information to inform planning and plan decisions. It also emphasizes providing meaningful opportunities for public participation early and throughout the planning process, increases the transparency of decision-making, and provides a platform for the Agency to work with the public and across boundaries with other land managers to identify and share information and inform planning.

The final planning rule reflects key themes expressed by members of the public, as well as experience gained through the Agency's 30-year history with land management planning. It is intended to create a more efficient and effective planning process and provide an adaptive framework for planning.

This final planning rule requires that land management plans provide for ecological sustainability and contribute to social and economic sustainability, using public input and the best available scientific information to inform plan decisions. The rule contains a strong emphasis on protecting and enhancing water resources, restoring land and water ecosystems, and providing ecological conditions to support the diversity of plant and animal communities, while providing for ecosystem services and multiple uses.

The 1982 planning rule procedures have guided the development, amendment, and revision of all existing Forest Service land management plans. However, since 1982 much has changed in our understanding of land management planning. The body of science that informs land management planning in areas such as conservation biology and ecology has advanced considerably, along with our understanding of the values and benefits of NFS lands, and the challenges and stressors that may impact them.

Because planning under the procedures of the 1982 rule is often time consuming and cumbersome, it has been a challenge for responsible officials to keep plans current. Instead of amending plans as conditions on the ground change, responsible officials often wait and make changes all at once during the required revision process. The result can be a drawn-out, difficult, and costly revision process. Much of the planning under the 1982 rule procedures focused on writing plans that would mitigate negative environmental impacts. The protective measures in the 1982 rule were important, but the focus of land management has changed since then and the Agency needs plans that do more than mitigate harm. The Agency needs a planning process that leads to plans that contribute to ecological, social, and economic sustainability to protect resources on the unit and maintain the flow of goods and services from NFS lands on the unit over time.

The instability created by ... past planning rule efforts has caused delays in planning and confused the public. At the same time, the vastly different context for management and improved understanding of science and sustainability that have evolved over the past three decades have created a need for an updated planning rule that will help the Agency respond to new challenges in meeting management objectives for NFS lands.

This final rule is intended to ensure that plans respond to the requirements of land management that the Agency faces today, including the need to provide sustainable benefits, services, and uses, including recreation; the need for forest restoration and conservation, watershed protection, and wildlife conservation; and the need for sound resource management under changing conditions. The new rule sets forth a process that is adaptive, science-based, collaborative, and within the Agency's capability to carry out on all NFS units. Finally, the new rule is designed to make planning more efficient and effective.

*   *   *

B PART 219—PLANNING

Subpart A—National Forest System Land Management Planning

§ 219.1 Purpose and applicability.

(c) The purpose of this part is to guide the collaborative and science-based development, amendment, and revision of land management plans that promote the ecological integrity of national forests and grasslands and other administrative units of the NFS. Plans will guide management of NFS lands so that they are ecologically sustainable and contribute to social and economic sustainability; consist of ecosystems and watersheds with ecological integrity and diverse plant and animal communities; and have the capacity to provide people and communities with ecosystem services and multiple uses that provide a range of social, economic, and ecological benefits for the present and into the future. These benefits include clean air and water; habitat for fish, wildlife, and plant communities; and opportunities for recreational, spiritual, educational, and cultural benefits.

§ 219.2 Levels of planning and responsible officials.

Forest Service planning occurs at different organizational levels and geographic scales. Planning occurs at three levels—national strategic planning, NFS unit planning, and project or activity planning.

(a) National strategic planning. The Chief of the Forest Service is responsible for national planning, such as preparation of the Forest Service strategic plan required under the Government Performance and Results Modernization Act of 2010 (5 U.S.C. 306; 31 U.S.C. 1115-1125; 31 U.S.C. 9703-9704), which is integrated with the requirements of the Forest and Rangeland Renewable Resources Planning Act of 1974, as amended by the NFMA. The strategic plan establishes goals, objectives, performance measures, and strategies for management of the NFS, as well as the other Forest Service mission areas: Research and Development, State and Private Forestry, and International Programs.

(b) National Forest System unit planning. (1) NFS unit planning results in the development, amendment, or revision of a land management plan. A land management plan provides a framework for integrated resource management and for guiding project and activity decisionmaking on a national forest, grassland, prairie, or other administrative unit. A plan reflects the unit's expected distinctive roles and contributions to the local area, region, and Nation, and the roles for which the plan area is best suited, considering the Agency's mission, the unit's unique capabilities, and the resources and management of other lands in the vicinity. Through the adaptive planning cycle set forth in this subpart, a plan can be changed to reflect new information and changing conditions.

(2) A plan does not authorize projects or activities or commit the Forest Service to take action. A plan may constrain the Agency from authorizing or carrying out projects and activities, or the manner in which they may occur. Projects and activities must be consistent with the plan (§ 219.15). A plan does not regulate uses by the public, but a project or activity decision that regulates a use by the public under 36 CFR Part 261, Subpart B, may be made contemporaneously with the approval of a plan, plan amendment, or plan revision. Plans should not repeat laws, regulations, or program management policies, practices, and procedures that are in the Forest Service Directive System.

§ 219.3 Role of science in planning.

The responsible official shall use the best available scientific information to inform the planning process required by this subpart. In doing so, the responsible official shall determine what information is the most accurate, reliable, and relevant to the issues being considered. The responsible official shall document how the best available scientific information was used to inform the assessment, the plan decision, and the monitoring program as required in §§ 219.6(a)(3) and 219.14(a)(4). Such documentation must: Identify what information was determined to be the best available scientific information, explain the basis for that determination, and explain how the information was applied to the issues considered.

§ 219.5 Planning framework.

(a) Planning for a national forest, grassland, prairie, or other comparable administrative unit of the NFS is an iterative process that includes assessment (§ 219.6); developing, amending, or revising a plan (§§ 219.7 and 219.13); and monitoring (§ 219.12). These three phases of the framework are complementary and may overlap. The intent of this framework is to create a responsive planning process that informs integrated resource management and allows the Forest Service to adapt to changing conditions, including climate change, and improve management based on new information and monitoring.

(1) Assessment. Assessments rapidly evaluate existing information about relevant ecological, economic, and social conditions, trends, and sustainability and their relationship to the land management plan within the context of the broader landscape. The responsible official shall consider and evaluate existing and possible future conditions and trends of the plan ar-

ea, and assess the sustainability of social, economic, and ecological systems within the plan area, in the context of the broader landscape (§ 219.6).

(2) Plan development, plan amendment, or plan revision.

(i) The process for developing or revising a plan includes: Assessment, preliminary identification of the need to change the plan based on the assessment, development of a proposed plan, consideration of the environmental effects of the proposal, providing an opportunity to comment on the proposed plan, providing an opportunity to object before the proposal is approved, and, finally, approval of the plan or plan revision. A new plan or plan revision requires preparation of an environmental impact statement.

(ii) The process for amending a plan includes: Preliminary identification of the need to change the plan, development of a proposed amendment, consideration of the environmental effects of the proposal, providing an opportunity to comment on the proposed amendment, providing an opportunity to object before the proposal is approved, and, finally, approval of the plan amendment. The appropriate NEPA documentation for an amendment may be an environmental impact statement, an environmental assessment, or a categorical exclusion, depending upon the scope and scale of the amendment and its likely effects.

(3) Monitoring. Monitoring is continuous and provides feedback for the planning cycle by testing relevant assumptions, tracking relevant conditions over time, and measuring management effectiveness (§ 219.12). The monitoring program includes plan-level and broader-scale monitoring. The plan-level monitoring program is informed by the assessment phase; developed during plan development, plan amendment, or plan revision; and implemented after plan decision. The regional forester develops broader-scale monitoring strategies. Biennial monitoring evaluation reports document whether a change to the plan or change to the monitoring program is warranted based on new information, whether a new assessment may be needed, or whether there is no need for change at that time.

(b) Interdisciplinary team(s). The responsible official shall establish an interdisciplinary team or teams to prepare assessments; new plans, plan amendments, and plan revisions; and plan monitoring programs.

§ 219.6 Assessment.

The responsible official has the discretion to determine the scope, scale, and timing of an assessment described in § 219.5(a)(1), subject to the requirements of this section.

(a) Process for plan development or revision assessments. An assessment must be completed for the development of a new plan or for a plan revision. The responsible official shall:

(1) Identify and consider relevant existing information contained in governmental or non-governmental assessments, plans, monitoring reports, studies, and other sources of relevant information. Such sources of information may include State forest assessments and strategies, the Resources Planning Act assessment, ecoregional assessments, non-governmental reports, State comprehensive outdoor recreation plans, community wildfire protection plans, public transportation plans, State wildlife data and action plans, and relevant Agency or interagency reports, resource plans or assessments. Relevant private information, including relevant land management plans and local knowledge, will be considered if publicly available or voluntarily provided.

(2) Coordinate with or provide opportunities for the regional forester, agency staff from State and Private Forestry and Research and Development, federally recognized Indian Tribes and Alaska Native Corporations, other governmental and non-governmental parties, and the public to provide existing information for the assessment.

(3) Document the assessment in a report available to the public. The report should document information needs relevant to the topics of paragraph (b) of this section. Document in the report how the best available scientific information was used to inform the assessment (§ 219.3). Include the report in the planning record (§ 219.14).

(b) Content of the assessment for plan development or revision. In the assessment for plan development or revision, the responsible official shall identify and evaluate existing information relevant to the plan area for the following:

(1) Terrestrial ecosystems, aquatic ecosystems, and watersheds;

(2) Air, soil, and water resources and quality;

(3) System drivers, including dominant ecological processes, disturbance regimes, and stressors, such as natural succession, wildland fire, invasive species, and climate change; and the ability of terrestrial and aquatic ecosystems on the plan area to adapt to change;

(4) Baseline assessment of carbon stocks;

(5) Threatened, endangered, proposed and candidate species, and potential species of conservation concern present in the plan area;

(6) Social, cultural, and economic conditions;

(7) Benefits people obtain from the NFS planning area (ecosystem services);

(8) Multiple uses and their contributions to local, regional, and national economies;

(9) Recreation settings, opportunities and access, and scenic character;

(10) Renewable and nonrenewable energy and mineral resources;

(11) Infrastructure, such as recreational facilities and transportation and utility corridors;

(12) Areas of tribal importance;

13) Cultural and historic resources and uses;

(14) Land status and ownership, use, and access patterns; and

(15) Existing designated areas located in the plan area including wilderness and wild and scenic rivers and potential need and opportunity for additional designated areas.

(c) Plan amendment assessments. Where the responsible official determines that a new assessment is needed to inform an amendment, the responsible official has the discretion to determine the scope, scale, process, and content for the assessment depending on the topic or topics to be addressed.

§ 219.7 New plan development or plan revision.

e) Plan components. Plan components guide future project and activity decisionmaking. The plan must indicate whether specific plan components apply to the entire plan area, to specific management areas or geographic areas, or to other areas as identified in the plan.

(1) Required plan components. Every plan must include the following plan components:

(i) Desired conditions. A desired condition is a description of specific social, economic, and/or ecological characteristics of the plan area, or a portion of the plan area, toward which management of the land and resources should be directed. Desired conditions must be described in terms that are specific enough to allow progress toward their achievement to be determined, but do not include completion dates.

(ii) Objectives. An objective is a concise, measurable, and time-specific statement of a desired rate of progress toward a desired condition or conditions. Objectives should be based on reasonably foreseeable budgets.

(iii) Standards. A standard is a mandatory constraint on project and activity decisionmaking, established to help achieve or maintain the desired condition or conditions, to avoid or mitigate undesirable effects, or to meet applicable legal requirements.

(iv) Guidelines. A guideline is a constraint on project and activity decisionmaking that allows for departure from its terms, so long as the purpose of the guideline is met. (§ 219.15(d)(3)). Guidelines are established to help achieve or maintain a desired condition or conditions, to avoid or mitigate undesirable effects, or to meet applicable legal requirements.

(v) Suitability of lands. Specific lands within a plan area will be identified as suitable for various multiple uses or activities based on the desired conditions applicable to those lands. The plan will also identify lands within the plan area as not suitable for uses that are not compatible with desired conditions for those lands. The suitability of lands need not be identified for every use or activity. Suitability identifications may be made after consideration of historic uses and of issues that have arisen in the planning process. Every plan must identify those lands that are not suitable for timber production (§ 219.11).

(3) Requirements for the set of plan components. The set of plan components must meet the requirements set forth in this part for sustainability (§ 219.8), plant and animal diversity (§ 219.9), multiple use (§ 219.10), and timber (§ 219.11).

§ 219.8 Sustainability.

The plan must provide for social, economic, and ecological sustainability within Forest Service authority and consistent with the inherent capability of the plan area, as follows:

(a) Ecological sustainability. (1) Ecosystem Integrity. The plan must include plan components, including standards or guidelines, to maintain or restore the ecological integrity of terrestrial and aquatic ecosystems and watersheds in the plan area, including plan components to maintain or restore structure, function, composition, and connectivity, taking into account:

(i) Interdependence of terrestrial and aquatic ecosystems in the plan area.

ii) Contributions of the plan area to ecological conditions within the broader landscape influenced by the plan area.

iii) Conditions in the broader landscape that may influence the sustainability of resources and ecosystems within the plan area.

iv) System drivers, including dominant ecological processes, disturbance regimes, and stressors, such as natural succession, wildland fire, invasive species, and climate change; and the ability of terrestrial and aquatic ecosystems on the plan area to adapt to change.

v) Wildland fire and opportunities to restore fire adapted ecosystems.

vi) Opportunities for landscape scale restoration.

(2) Air, soil, and water. The plan must include plan components, including standards or guidelines, to maintain or restore:

(i) Air quality.

ii) Soils and soil productivity, including guidance to reduce soil erosion and sedimentation.

iii) Water quality.

iv) Water resources in the plan area, including lakes, streams, and wetlands; ground water; public water supplies; sole source aquifers; source water protection areas; and other sources of drinking water (including guidance to prevent or mitigate detrimental changes in quantity, quality, and availability).

(3) Riparian areas. (i) The plan must include plan components, including standards or guidelines, to maintain or restore the ecological integrity of riparian areas in the plan area, including plan components to maintain or restore structure, function, composition, and connectivity, taking into account:

(A) Water temperature and chemical composition;

(B) Blockages (uncharacteristic and characteristic) of water courses;

(C) Deposits of sediment;

(D) Aquatic and terrestrial habitats;

(E) Ecological connectivity;

(F) Restoration needs; and

(G) Floodplain values and risk of flood loss.

(ii) Plans must establish width(s) for riparian management zones around all lakes, perennial and intermittent streams, and open water wetlands, within which the plan components required by paragraph (a)(3)(i) of this section will apply, giving special attention to land and vegetation for approximately 100 feet from the edges of all perennial streams and lakes.

(A) Riparian management zone width(s) may vary based on ecological or geomorphic factors or type of water body; and will apply unless replaced by a site-specific delineation of the riparian area.

(B) Plan components must ensure that no management practices causing detrimental changes in water temperature or chemical composition, blockages of water courses, or deposits of sediment that seriously and adversely affect water conditions or fish habitat shall be permitted within the riparian management zones or the site-specific delineated riparian areas.

(4) Best management practices for water quality. The Chief shall establish requirements for national best management practices for water quality in the Forest Service Directive System. Plan components must ensure implementation of these practices.

(b) Social and economic sustainability. The plan must include plan components, including standards or guidelines, to guide the plan area's contribution to social and economic sustainability, taking into account:

(1) Social, cultural, and economic conditions relevant to the area influenced by the plan;

(2) Sustainable recreation; including recreation settings, opportunities, and access; and scenic character;

(3) Multiple uses that contribute to local, regional, and national economies in a sustainable manner;

(4) Ecosystem services;

(5) Cultural and historic resources and uses; and

(6) Opportunities to connect people with nature.

§ 219.9 Diversity of plant and animal communities.

This section adopts a complementary ecosystem and species-specific approach to maintaining the diversity of plant and animal communities and the persistence of native species in the plan area. Compliance with the ecosystem requirements of paragraph (a) is intended to provide the ecological conditions to both maintain the diversity of plant and animal communities and support the persistence of most native species in the plan area. Compliance with the requirements of paragraph (b) is intended to provide for additional ecological conditions not otherwise provided by compliance with paragraph (a) for individual species as set forth in paragraph (b). The plan must provide for the diversity of plant and animal communities, within Forest Service authority and consistent with the inherent capability of the plan area, as follows:

(a) Ecosystem plan components. (1) Ecosystem integrity. As required by § 219.8(a), the plan must include plan components, including standards or guidelines, to maintain or restore the ecological integrity of terrestrial and aquatic ecosystems and watersheds in the plan area, including plan components to maintain or restore their structure, function, composition, and connectivity.

(2) Ecosystem diversity. The plan must include plan components, including standards or guidelines, to maintain or restore the diversity of ecosystems and habitat types throughout the plan area. In doing so, the plan must include plan components to maintain or restore:

(i) Key characteristics associated with terrestrial and aquatic ecosystem types;

ii) Rare aquatic and terrestrial plant and animal communities; and

iii) The diversity of native tree species similar to that existing in the plan area.

(b) Additional, species-specific plan components. (1) The responsible official shall determine whether or not the plan components required by paragraph (a) of this section provide the ecological conditions necessary to: contribute to the recovery of federally listed threatened and endangered species, conserve proposed and candidate species, and maintain a viable population of each species of conservation concern within the plan area. If the responsible official determines that the plan components required in paragraph (a) are insufficient to provide such ecological conditions, then additional, species-specific plan components, including standards or guidelines, must be included in the plan to provide such ecological conditions in the plan area.

(2) If the responsible official determines that it is beyond the authority of the Forest Service or not within the inherent capability of the plan area to maintain or restore the ecological conditions to maintain a viable population of a species of conservation concern in the plan area, then the responsible official shall:

(i) Document the basis for that determination (§ 219.14(a)); and

ii) Include plan components, including standards or guidelines, to maintain or restore ecological conditions within the plan area to contribute to maintaining a viable population of the species within its range. In providing such plan components, the responsible official shall coordinate to the extent practicable with other Federal, State, Tribal, and private land managers having management authority over lands relevant to that population.

(c) Species of conservation concern. For purposes of this subpart, a species of conservation concern is a species, other than federally recognized threatened, endangered, proposed, or candidate species, that is known to occur in the plan area and for which the regional forester has determined that the best available scientific information indicates substantial concern about the species' capability to persist over the long-term in the plan area.

§ 219.10 Multiple use.

While meeting the requirements of §§ 219.8 and 219.9, the plan must provide for ecosystem services and multiple uses, including outdoor recreation, range, timber, watershed, wildlife, and fish, within Forest Service authority and the inherent capability of the plan area as follows:

(a) Integrated resource management for multiple use. The plan must include plan components, including standards or guidelines, for integrated resource management to provide for ecosystem services and multiple uses in the plan area. When developing plan components for integrated resource management, to the extent relevant to the plan area and the public participation process and the requirements of §§ 219.7, 219.8, 219.9, and 219.11, the responsible official shall consider:

(1) Aesthetic values, air quality, cultural and heritage resources, ecosystem services, fish and wildlife species, forage, geologic features, grazing and rangelands, habitat and habitat connectivity, recreation settings and opportunities, riparian areas, scenery, soil, surface and subsurface water quality, timber, trails, vegetation, viewsheds, wilderness, and other relevant resources and uses.

(2) Renewable and nonrenewable energy and mineral resources.

3) Appropriate placement and sustainable management of infrastructure, such as recreational facilities and transportation and utility corridors.

(4) Opportunities to coordinate with neighboring landowners to link open spaces and take into account joint management objectives where feasible and appropriate.

(5) Habitat conditions, subject to the requirements of § 219.9, for wildlife, fish, and plants commonly enjoyed and used by the public; for hunting, fishing, trapping, gathering, observing, subsistence, and other activities (in collaboration with federally recognized Tribes, Alaska Native Corporations, other Federal agencies, and State and local governments).

(6) Land status and ownership, use, and access patterns relevant to the plan area.

(7) Reasonably foreseeable risks to ecological, social, and economic sustainability.

(8) System drivers, including dominant ecological processes, disturbance regimes, and stressors, such as natural succession, wildland fire, invasive species, and climate change; and the ability of the terrestrial and aquatic ecosystems on the plan area to adapt to change (§ 219.8);

(9) Public water supplies and associated water quality.

(10) Opportunities to connect people with nature.

(b) Requirements for plan components for a new plan or plan revision. (1) The plan must include plan components, including standards or guidelines, to provide for:

(i) Sustainable recreation; including recreation settings, opportunities, and access; and scenic character. Recreation opportunities may include non-motorized, motorized, developed, and dispersed recreation on land, water, and in the air.

ii) Protection of cultural and historic resources.

iii) Management of areas of tribal importance.

iv) Protection of congressionally designated wilderness areas as well as management of areas recommended for wilderness designation to protect and maintain the ecological and social characteristics that provide the basis for their suitability for wilderness designation.

v) Protection of designated wild and scenic rivers as well as management of rivers found eligible or determined suitable for the National Wild and Scenic River system to protect the values that provide the basis for their suitability for inclusion in the system.

vi) Appropriate management of other designated areas or recommended designated areas in the plan area, including research natural areas.

(2) Other plan components for integrated resource management to provide for multiple use as necessary.

§ 219.12 Monitoring.

(a) Plan monitoring program. (1) The responsible official shall develop a monitoring program for the plan area and include it in the plan. Monitoring information should enable the responsible official to determine if a change in plan components or other plan content that guide management of resources on the plan area may be needed. The development of the plan monitoring program must be coordinated with the regional forester and Forest Service State and Private Forestry and Research and Development. Responsible officials for two or more administrative units may jointly develop their plan monitoring programs.

(2) The plan monitoring program sets out the plan monitoring questions and associated indicators. Monitoring questions and associated indicators must be designed to inform the management of resources on the plan area, including by testing relevant assumptions, tracking relevant changes, and measuring management effectiveness and progress toward achieving or maintaining the plan's desired conditions or objectives. Questions and indicators should be based on one or more desired conditions, objectives, or other plan components in the plan, but not every plan component needs to have a corresponding monitoring question.

(3) The plan monitoring program should be coordinated and integrated with relevant broader-scale monitoring strategies (paragraph (b) of this section) to ensure that monitoring is complementary and efficient, and that information is gathered at scales appropriate to the monitoring questions. (5) Each plan monitoring program must contain one or more monitoring questions and associated indicators addressing each of the following:

(i) The status of select watershed conditions.

(ii) The status of select ecological conditions including key characteristics of terrestrial and aquatic ecosystems.

(iii) The status of focal species to assess the ecological conditions required under § 219.9.

(iv) The status of a select set of the ecological conditions required under § 219.9 to contribute to the recovery of federally listed threatened and endangered species, conserve proposed and candidate species, and maintain a viable population of each species of conservation concern.

(v) The status of visitor use, visitor satisfaction, and progress toward meeting recreation objectives.

(vi) Measurable changes on the plan area related to climate change and other stressors that may be affecting the plan area.

(vii) Progress toward meeting the desired conditions and objectives in the plan, including for providing multiple use opportunities.

(viii) The effects of each management system to determine that they do not substantially and permanently impair the productivity of the land (16 U.S.C. 1604(g)(3)(C)).

(6) A range of monitoring techniques may be used to carry out the monitoring requirements in paragraph (a)(5) of this section.

(7) This section does not apply to projects or activities. Project and activity monitoring may be used to gather information for the plan monitoring program, and information gathered through plan monitoring may be used to inform development of projects or activities. But, the monitoring requirements of this section are not a prerequisite for making a decision to carry out a project or activity.

(b) Broader-scale monitoring strategies. (1) The regional forester shall develop a broader-scale monitoring strategy for plan monitoring questions that can best be answered at a geographic scale broader than one plan area.

(2) When developing a monitoring strategy, the regional forester shall coordinate with the relevant responsible officials, Forest Service State and Private Forestry and Research and Development, partners, and the public. Two or more regional foresters may jointly develop broader-scale monitoring strategies.

(3) Each regional forester shall ensure that the broader-scale monitoring strategy is within the financial and technical capabilities of the region and complements other ongoing monitoring efforts.

(4) Projects and activities may be carried out under plans developed, amended, or revised under this part before the regional forester has developed a broader-scale monitoring strategy.

(c) Timing and process for developing the plan monitoring program and broader-scale strategies.

1) The responsible official shall develop the plan monitoring program as part of the planning process for a new plan development or plan revision. Where a plan's monitoring program has been developed under the provisions of a prior planning regulation and the unit has not initiated plan revision under this part, the responsible official shall modify the plan monitoring program within 4 years of the effective date of this part, or as soon as practicable, to meet the requirements of this section.

(2) The regional forester shall develop a broader-scale monitoring strategy as soon as practicable.

(3) To the extent practicable, appropriate, and relevant to the monitoring questions in the plan monitoring program, plan monitoring programs and broader-scale strategies must be designed to take into account:

(i) Existing national and regional inventory, monitoring, and research programs of the Agency, including from the NFS, State and Private Forestry, and Research and Development, and of other governmental and non-governmental entities;

ii) Opportunities to design and carry out multi-party monitoring with other Forest Service units, Federal, State or local government agencies, scientists, partners, and members of the public; and

iii) Opportunities to design and carry out monitoring with federally recognized Indian Tribes and Alaska Native Corporations.

(d) Biennial evaluation of the monitoring information. (1) The responsible official shall conduct a biennial evaluation of new information gathered through the plan monitoring program and relevant information from the broader-scale strategy, and shall issue a written report of the evaluation and make it available to the public.

(i) The first monitoring evaluation for a plan or plan revision developed in accordance with this subpart must be completed no later than 2 years from the effective date of plan decision.

ii) Where the monitoring program developed under the provisions of a prior planning regulation has been modified to meet the requirements of paragraph (c)(1) of this section, the first monitoring evaluation must be completed no later than 2 years from the date the change takes effect.

(iii) The monitoring evaluation report may be postponed for 1 year in case of exigencies, but notice of the postponement must be provided to the public prior to the date the report is due for that year (§ 219.16(c)(6)).

(2) The monitoring evaluation report must indicate whether or not a change to the plan, management activities, or the monitoring program, or a new assessment, may be warranted based on the new information. The

monitoring evaluation report must be used to inform adaptive management of the plan area.

(3) The monitoring evaluation report may be incorporated into other planning documents if the responsible official has initiated a plan revision or relevant amendment.

(4) The monitoring evaluation report is not a decision document representing final Agency action, and is not subject to the objection provisions of subpart B.

§ 219.19 Definitions.

Connectivity. Ecological conditions that exist at several spatial and temporal scales that provide landscape linkages that permit the exchange of flow, sediments, and nutrients; the daily and seasonal movements of animals within home ranges; the dispersal and genetic interchange between populations; and the long distance range shifts of species, such as in response to climate change.

Conservation. The protection, preservation, management, or restoration of natural environments, ecological communities, and species.

Disturbance. Any relatively discrete event in time that disrupts ecosystem, watershed, community, or species population structure and/or function and changes resources, substrate availability, or the physical environment.

Disturbance regime. A description of the characteristic types of disturbance on a given landscape; the frequency, severity, and size distribution of these characteristic disturbance types; and their interactions.

Ecological conditions. The biological and physical environment that can affect the diversity of plant and animal communities, the persistence of native species, and the productive capacity of ecological systems. Ecological conditions include habitat and other influences on species and the environment. Examples of ecological conditions include the abundance and distribution of aquatic and terrestrial habitats, connectivity, roads and other structural developments, human uses, and invasive species.

Ecological integrity. The quality or condition of an ecosystem when its dominant ecological characteristics (for example, composition, structure, function, connectivity, and species composition and diversity) occur within the natural range of variation and can withstand and recover from most perturbations imposed by natural environmental dynamics or human influence.

Ecosystem. A spatially explicit, relatively homogeneous unit of the Earth that includes all interacting organisms and elements of the abiotic environment within its boundaries. An ecosystem is commonly described in terms of its:

(1) Composition. The biological elements within the different levels of biological organization, from genes and species to communities and ecosystems.

(2) Structure. The organization and physical arrangement of biological elements such as, snags and down woody debris, vertical and horizontal distribution of vegetation, stream habitat complexity, landscape pattern, and connectivity.

(3) Function. Ecological processes that sustain composition and structure, such as energy flow, nutrient cycling and retention, soil development and retention, predation and herbivory, and natural disturbances such as wind, fire, and floods.

Ecosystem services. Benefits people obtain from ecosystems, including:

(1) Provisioning services, such as clean air and fresh water, energy, fuel, forage, fiber, and minerals;

(2) Regulating services, such as long term storage of carbon; climate regulation; water filtration, purification, and storage; soil stabilization; flood control; and disease regulation;

(3) Supporting services, such as pollination, seed dispersal, soil formation, and nutrient cycling; and

(4) Cultural services, such as educational, aesthetic, spiritual and cultural heritage values, recreational experiences and tourism opportunities.

Focal species. A small subset of species whose status permits inference to the integrity of the larger ecological system to which it belongs and provides meaningful information regarding the effectiveness of the plan in maintaining or restoring the ecological conditions to maintain the diversity of plant and animal communities in the plan area. Focal species would be commonly selected on the basis of their functional role in ecosystems.

Native species. An organism that was historically or is present in a particular ecosystem as a result of natural migratory or evolutionary processes; and not as a result of an accidental or deliberate introduction into that ecosystem. An organism's presence and evolution (adaptation) in an area are determined by climate, soil, and other biotic and abiotic factors.

Restoration. The process of assisting the recovery of an ecosystem that has been degraded, damaged, or destroyed. Ecological restoration focuses on reestablishing the composition, structure, pattern, and ecological processes necessary to facilitate terrestrial and aquatic ecosystems sustainability, resilience, and health under current and future conditions.

Sustainability. The capability to meet the needs of the present generation without compromising the ability of future generations to meet their needs. For purposes of this part, "ecological sustainability" refers to the capability of ecosystems to maintain ecological integrity; "economic sustainability" refers to the capability of society to produce and consume or otherwise benefit from goods and services including contributions to jobs and market and nonmarket benefits; and "social sustainability" refers to the capability of society to support the network of relationships, traditions, culture, and activities that connect people to the land and to one another, and support vibrant communities.

NOTES & QUESTIONS

1. Looking at the 2012 rule holistically, are the Committee of Scientists and the Forest Service on the same page? How has the agency advanced or departed from the Committee's vision? Has it essentially adopted conservation biology as its ecosystem management method? If so, could timber and other resource interests successfully challenge that change in policy from the days of *Marita*?

2. The previous question assumes that the Forest Service's holistic vision of ecosystem management in the 2012 rule is comprehensible. Summarize in 25 words or less what you believe that vision is. One of the more vocal critics of ecosystem management law and policy has suggested that the entire planning rule reform effort from the time of the Committee's report has been an exercise in administrative obfuscation:

> To summarize, the FS seeks to oversee the national forest system in order to sustain undefined conditions on undefined landscape units that exist in limitless numbers in undefined locations and that are dynamic and constantly changing over time and space in unclear ways.

ALLAN K. FITZSIMMONS, DEFENDING ILLUSIONS: FEDERAL PROTECTION OF ECOSYSTEMS 185 (1999). Does that accurately sum it up—is the 2012 rule essentially a means for securing more agency discretion, or is the agency's vision more specific and grounded?

3. Let's unpack the 2012 rule into some of its more important components and get down to the brass tacks:

> In the provision on the role of science (219.3), are you comfortable with its description of "best available science"?

> Does the assess/monitor/revise approach of the planning framework provision (219.5), with elaborations on assessment (219.6) and monitoring (219.12) implement adaptive management the way Holling outlined it?

> Does the new and revised plans provision (219.7) lay out a clear method for setting goals, metrics, and methods?

> Does the provision on sustainability (219.8) clearly describe how the Forest Service will use sustainability and ecosystem integrity as metrics?

> To what extent will the addition of climate change as one of the ecosystem integrity drivers (219.8(a)) change Forest Service discretion? Does it undermine other provisions for using native species as a metric (see the definition of ecosystem integrity in 219.19)?

Has the provision on diversity (219.9) provided adequate details to implement the statutory requirements?

Will the addition of ecosystem services as a multiple use metric (219.10) broaden or limit Forest Service discretion?

What else in the 2012 rule either raises or resolves concerns you have about national forest policy?

4. As you will learn as you become more exposed to regulatory law, one of the most important sections of a statute is the definitions provision. We have excerpted some of the key definitions. Based on the introductory materials in Chapter 7 and what you have learned thus far about forest ecosystem management, would you change any of the definitions? Has the Forest Service added to or limited its scope of discretion by adopting these definitions?

5. If the approach outlined in the Forest Service's 2012 proposed rule had been in effect since the early 1990s, would the rule have *required* the agency to use conservation biology science? Would the Forest Service have been *required* to designate the white-headed woodpecker? And would the Forest Service have been *required* to conduct on the ground population surveys to satisfy the viability analysis requirement? Examine the standards of review the courts applied to those issues. If the answer is that the 2012 rule would not have required the agency to act differently then, what has the rule changed?

6. Is the agency's focus on ecosystem sustainability a departure from the multiple use mandate of MUSY? Based on this response to comments on the Bush Administration's 2005 rule, which also leaned heavily on the sustainability concept, the agency seems to think it has authority to follow the new approach:

> Comment: Multiple-Use Sustained-Yield Act (MUSYA). Some respondents pointed out that "multiple use" is part of the law and "ecosystem management" is not. Active forest management, they asserted, is necessary for forest health, maintaining biological diversity, and sustaining wildlife populations. These respondents requested that the final rule uphold what they believe are the active forest management principles mandated by the MUSYA. Further, they stated that timber harvesting is a goal of the MUSYA. They asked that the Forest Service provide a high-level sustained yield of renewable timber resources.

> Some respondents requested that the Forest Service comply with MUSYA by managing lands according to what they call its "wood, water, wildlife, range, and recreation" formula. Others stated that the 2002 proposed rule violates the MUSYA requirement that NFS lands be used to best meet the needs of the American people. These respondents requested that emphasis be placed on recreation, aesthetics, air and water quality, species habitat, and ecosystem integrity, rather than natural resource development.

> Response: The final rule is faithful to NFMA, which requires the use of the MUSYA to provide the substantive basis for forest planning. [S]ustainability embodies these Congressional mandates. The interrelated and interdependent elements of sustainability are social, economic, and ecological as described in § 219.10. The final rule sets the stage for a plan-

ning process that can be responsive to the desires and needs of both present and future generations of the Americans for the multiple uses of NFS lands. The final rule does not make choices among the multiple uses; it describes the processes by which those choices will be made as a preliminary step during development of plans. Later, the plan provides guidance for projects and activities.

If what the agency says is true about how ecosystem sustainability fits into the MUSY and NFMA mandates, has it left itself any room for turning back from pursuing ecosystem sustainability? Would it violate the statutes were the agency to follow a "wood, water, wildlife, range, and recreation" formula?

7. Do we really know what is ecologically sustainable? Particularly in developing nations and areas of the United States where local populations depend on forests for economic well-being, are there income-producing uses of forests that are economically and ecologically sustainable? In many cases we won't know what is sustainable for a long time. For example, a major part of the rainforest economy in Brazil has been Brazil nut harvesting, and this was thought to be a sustainable way to prevent more destructive activities such as ranching. After 25 years of studying the practice, however, wildlife biologist Carlos Peres discovered that nut harvesting has been taken to ecologically unsustainable extremes—there are no nuts left on the ground to regenerate new Brazil nut trees. Peres advocates harvest quotas and rotating "no take" zones to allow new trees to take hold in the forest. Other researchers worry that it may take more invasive measures, such as clearing areas to open up sunlight to young trees, to ensure the survival of the Brazil nut tree. Either way, few people saw this coming. *See* Erik Stokstad, *Too Much Crunching on Rainforest Nuts*, 302 SCIENCE 2049 (2003). What other unanticipated consequences lurk behind today's prescriptions for sustainable uses of forest resources?

Note on the Endangered Species Act in National Forests and the Northwest Forest Plan

As the principal cases and regulations covered in this section illustrate, at the heart of Forest Service ecosystem management practice are *planning* and *assessment*. The NFMA, through land resource management plans, and the National Environmental Policy Act (NEPA), through environmental assessments and impact statements, impose significant process duties on the agency and result in countless written forest plans and environmental impact assessments. The Forest Service's recent forest planning rule promulgation illustrates that the agency's movement toward ecosystem management builds on that core, expanding planning and assessment deep into the agency's environmental decision making process. In the final analysis, however, planning and assessment duties do not dictate substantive outcomes, and a multiple use mandate remains the background for all of the agency's planning focus.

Dissatisfied with the agency's environmental policy direction, and often turned away at the courthouse when making their case as a challenge to agency planning and assessment under the NFMA and NEPA, advocates of an "environment-first" policy for the national forest have seized on the Endangered Species Act (ESA) as a way to cut through the multiple use muddle. The listing as endangered of two remarkably unadaptable species of birds—the Northern Spotted Owl and the Marbled Murrelet—played center stage in court battles that raged across western forests in the 1990s, and yet a third bird—the Red Cockaded Woodpecker—served that position in southeastern forests. With the additional listing of several endangered runs of salmon in rivers of the Pacific Northwest running through the heart of several national forests, it is no exaggeration to suggest that by the end of the 1990s the ESA had brought the Forest Service to its knees.

The reason the ESA could prove so effective for the environmental advocates, in precisely the settings where the NFMA and NEPA had not, has to do with the ESA's fundamentally different structure. The ESA is anything but a multiple use planning statute. As the materials in Chapter 5 explain, federal agencies face numerous substantive constraints under the ESA which they cannot plan around or balance with countervailing policy objectives. Section 9(a)(1) of the ESA prohibits any person, including federal agencies, from taking a protected species, which can include destruction of the species' habitat. *See* Babbitt v. Sweet Home Chapter of Communities for a Great Oregon, 515 U.S. 687 (1995). Section 7(a)(2) of the ESA prohibits federal agencies from jeopardizing the continued existence of protected species through actions the agency carries out, funds, or authorizes, which includes the "granting of licenses, contracts, easements, rights-of-way, permits, or grants-in-aid." 50 C.F.R. 402.02. This "no jeopardy" constraint is one of the most unyielding provisions of environmental law. *See* Tennessee Valley Authority v. Hill, 437 U.S. 153 (1978).

Timber management plans and timber sale contracts fall squarely into these two regulatory proscriptions. Notwithstanding that a timber sale contract and all the Forest Service's planning leading up to it may comply in all procedural and substantive respects with the NFMA and NEPA, the ESA adds an additional layer of requirements that fall outside the agency's multiple use mandate and planning discretion. In short, if the harvesting authorized in a timber sale contract may result in take of a listed species, the Forest Service must defend its decision to let the contract under not only the NFMA and NEPA, but also the ESA. *See* Murray Feldman, *National Forest Management under the Endangered Species Act*, NAT. RESOURCES & ENV'T, Winter 1995, at 32.

Beginning in the 1980s, environmental advocates started using this added factor of the ESA to challenge Forest Service decisions about specific projects in national forests. *See, e.g.*, Thomas v. Peterson, 753 F.2d 754 (9th Cir.1985) (challenge to construction of road in Nez Perce National Forest in Idaho). Following some success in that setting, ESA cases began taking on broader forest management planning decisions in particular forests, such as the decision to use even-aged timber management. *See* Sierra Club v. Yeutter, 926 F.2d 429 (5th Cir.1991). By the early1990s, the focus of the ESA litigation effort had expanded to challenging large-scale programmatic decisions regarding entire national forest plans and even national forest management policies affecting large regions and many national forests. *See, e.g.*, Resources Ltd., Inc. v. Robertson, 35 F.3d 1300 (9th Cir.1993) (challenge to forest plan for the Flathead National Forest). The grand slam came in a series of cases enjoining timber sales in the range of the spotted owl for failure to satisfy the procedures for fulfilling the "no jeopardy" restriction of the ESA. *See, e.g.*, Seattle Audubon Soc'y v. Espy, 998 F.2d 699 (9th Cir.1993).

With the stakes this high, the Clinton Administration responded in 1993 with the Northwest Forest Plan (NWFP), an ecosystem management planning process designed to produce land management plans for 24.5 million acres in nineteen national forests covering the range of owl habitat. Against challenges from environmental and industry groups, the federal courts upheld FEMAT's compromise. *See* Seattle Audubon Society v. Lyons, 871 F.Supp. 1291 (W.D.Wash.1994), *aff'd*, 80 F.3d 1401 (9th Cir.1996). A similar effort followed in owl habitat further to the south, in the national forests throughout California's Sierra Nevada region, through an effort known as the Sierra Nevada Ecosystem Project (SNEP). *See* Dave Owen, *Prescriptive Laws, Uncertain Science, and Political Stories: Forest Management in the Sierra Nevada*, 29 ECOLOGY L.Q. 747 (2002); Lawrence Ruth, *Conservation on the Cusp: The Reformation of National Forest Policy in the Sierra Nevada*, 18 J. ENVTL L. 1, 58–81 (1999–2000). Simultaneously, President Clinton directed the Forest Service to develop a plan for national forests in the Columbia River Basin to avoid the same conflicts in salmon habitat that prompted the need for the NFP in owl country. Suits involving the salmon had already had an impact on timber sales in some forests, so the writing was on the wall that attacks on a more programmatic level were to come. *See* Pacific Rivers Council v. Robertson, 854 F.Supp. 713 (D.Or.1993), *aff'd in part, rev'd in part*, 30 F.3d 1050 (9th Cir.1994) (enjoining timber sales while ESA compliance procedures for salmon were underway). The agency's resulting Interior Columbia Basin Ecosystem Management Project (ICBEMP) eventually reached over 70 million acres of federal lands including thirty-two national forests. *See also* Susan Bucknum, *The U.S. Commitment to Agenda 21: Chapter 11 Combating Deforestation—The Ecosystem Management Approach*, 8 DUKE ENVTL. L. & POL'Y F. 305, 332–42 (1998) (summarizing other regional applications).

Nevertheless, few observers of national forest policy are surprised that the NWFP and ICBEMP spawned more litigation than they avoided. Indeed, the ESA continues to play a central role in national forest policy in the affected areas, with courts maintaining the role of policing timber sales, forest plans, and national forest policy in general. While it has by no means entirely displaced the multiple-use mandate, the ESA's single-use focus has squeezed its way into national forest policy, in many cases completely overshadowing and controlling the NFMA multiple use planning and NEPA environmental impact assessment processes. Indeed, there is strong evidence that the effect of the NWFP has been to reduce logging rates in the region far below projections the Clinton Administration made at the time the plan was instituted. Annual timber harvests in the northern California-Oregon-Washington region were about 4 billion board feet (it takes 10,000 board feet to build a modest single-family home) in the 1980s and were projected to fall to 1 billion board feet under the NWFP. Logging rates in the region, however, have fallen to under 400 million board feet.

Consider, for example, how the NWFP controls Forest Service planning decisions. One of the key components of the NWFP is the Aquatic Conservation Strategy (ACS), a comprehensive plan designed to maintain and restore the ecological health of the waterways in the federal forests. There are four components to the ACS: (1) key watersheds (the best aquatic habitat, or hydrologically important areas), (2) riparian reserves (buffer zones along streams, lakes, wetlands and mudslide risks), (3) watershed analysis (to document existing and desired watershed conditions), and (4) watershed restoration (a long-term program to restore aquatic ecosystems and watershed health). The ACS also has binding standards and guidelines that restrict certain activities within areas designated as riparian reserves or key watersheds. Additionally, ACS has nine objectives designed to maintain or restore properly functioning aquatic habitats.

When a timber sale or other project is proposed for the NFP region, it is initially subject to the Forest Service's internal planning process under the NFMA. The Forest Service then creates a team of biologists and other resource management specialists to incorporate the NFP requirements, including ACS standards and guidelines. A biologist on the team uses a Matrix of Pathways and Indicators (the "MPI") and a checklist developed by The National Marine Fisheries Service (NMFS) to assess the project's effect on listed species. The MPI and checklist help the biologist to analyze 18 different habitat indicators and determine whether they are properly functioning, at risk, or not properly functioning. The biologists also determine whether the proposed action is likely to restore, maintain, or degrade the indicator. Projects that receive either zero or only one degrade checkmark are considered "not likely to adversely affect" listed species.

Those projects determined "likely [to] adversely affect" listed species, i.e., those that received one or more degrade checkmarks, are referred to a Level 1 Team. This team is made up of biologists from various agencies. It reviews the proposed project for ACS consistency. The team can suggest changes in the plan to bring it into ACS compliance.

If the Level 1 Team agrees that the project complies with ACS, it then forwards the project to the NMFS for formal consultation. Otherwise, the team elevates the review to a Level 2 Team, and the project undergoes the same review process. Failure to reach a consensus elevates the project to a Level 3 Team. Once one of these three teams approves the project, it goes to NMFS for ESA consultation. The NMFS must review the project pursuant to Section 7 of ESA, which, as described in Chapter 5 of your text, requires federal agencies to "insure that any action authorized, funded, or carried out by such agency . . . is not likely to jeopardize the continued existence of" any species listed as threatened or endangered under the ESA. 16 U.S.C. § 1536(a)(2). Finally, NMFS issues a Biological Opinion for Forest Service use in going forward. See Pacific Coast Federation of Fishermen's Associations v. NMFS, 253 F.3d 1137 (9th Cir. 2001). Efforts by the Bush Administration to weaken this "survey and manage" approach were overturned in the courts, see Conservation Northwest v. Rey, 674 F. Supp. 2d 1232 (W.D. Wash. 2009), and the Obama Administration has neither appealed the decision nor initiated similar reforms. For all practical purposes, therefore, the Clinton Administration's version of the NWFP remains in effect.

Drawing from this history and current experience, Professor Oliver Houck suggests that the ESA has thus served to "convene the meeting and draw a bottom line. It has acted as the therapist for conduct we all knew was harmful and had limits, but could not bring ourselves to admit was a problem, much less begin to solve." Oliver Houck, *On the Law of Biodiversity and Ecosystem Management*, 81 MINN. L. REV. 869, 959 (1997). But along with this "muscle" comes fewer policy options and more litigation to enforce the "bottom line," leading another commentator to suggest that the ESA has "reduced agencies' flexibility to deal with forest health in the integrated fashion that ecosystem management envisioned." Rebecca W. Watson, *Ecosystem Management in the Northwest: "Is Everybody Happy?"*, 14 NATURAL RESOURCES & ENV'T 173, 178 (2000).

Has the ESA become the tail wagging the NFMA dog? Is the tradeoff between regulatory muscle and policy flexibility inevitable? If not, how are the two harmonized? If the tradeoff is inevitable, which approach serves ecosystem management objectives more effectively over the long run? For the view that the hybrid NFMA-ESA model of the NWFP represents the most advanced example of ecosystem-scale adaptive management, see Bernard T Bormann et al., *Adaptive Management of Forest Ecosystems: Did Some Rubber Hit the Road?*, 57 BIOSCIENCE 186 (2007). Do you agree? For broad histories and assessments of the NWFP and the ACS, see Jack Ward Thomas et al., *The Northwest Forest Plan: Origins, Components, Implementation Experience, and Suggestions for Change*, 20 CONSERVATION BIOLOGY 277 (2006); Gordon Reeves et al., *The Aquatic Conservation Strategy of the Northwest Forest Plan*, 20 CONSERVATION BIOLOGY 319 (2006).

Note on Roads and Roadless Areas in National Forests

Most of the preceding discussion of ecosystem management in national forests has focused on how the Forest Service has adapted its timber harvest policies to changes in law and administrative goals. Yet the multiple-use mandate means, of course, that activities other than timber harvesting will take place in national forests with frequency. Hardrock mining, energy resource extraction, grazing, water uses, recreation, and conservation are among the other uses competing for access to national forest lands, and must necessarily be a component of any national forest plan based on an ecosystem management philosophy. Construction and maintenance of roads in national forests is a critical infrastructure issue that dictates in large part which of these uses can claim a stake in the multiple-use competition for a given area of national forest.

The Forest Service maintains over 370,000 miles of roads in national forests, which carry 9000 Forest Service vehicles, 15,000 timber harvest vehicles, and 1.7 million vehicles involved in recreation each day. Yet vast areas of national forests have long been legally off limits to roads—lands designated as wilderness under the Wilderness Act of 1964 and subsequent congressional designations amount today to 35 million acres within which roads, motor vehicles, motorized equipment, and mechanical transport are prohibited. 43 U.S.C. § 1133. Rather, the roads debate has focused on the much larger area of national forest lands—over 58 million acres, or 31 percent of the national forest lands—that are not legally off limits to roads as designated wilderness areas, but have yet to be opened to road access. Over 33 million of those acres consist of blocks of over 5000 acres of contiguous, undisturbed forest land, eight million acres of which are classified as suitable for timber production. In short, there is a lot of land potentially up for grabs in the national forests, the fate of which depends on whether new roads are constructed into their presently undisturbed interiors.

Debate over these so-called "de facto wilderness" lands has been brewing for decades. In 1967, the Forest Service engaged in a Roadless Area Review and Evaluation (RARE I) to evaluate the suitability of roadless areas for wilderness designation. RARE I inventoried the 5000-acre blocks of roadless non-wilderness lands, but accomplished little more. Litigation over the fate of the inventoried roadless areas resulted in an injunction against timber harvesting until the Forest Service could complete environmental impact review under NEPA. *See* Wyoming Outdoor Coordinating Council v. Butz, 484 F.2d 1244 (10th Cir.1973). The Forest Service published an EIS on the inventoried areas in 1973, selecting about 12 million acres for further study as potential wilderness areas. In 1977, the new Administration geared up another study, known as RARE II, which defined the divide between non-wilderness and potential wilderness areas for over 60 million identified acres of national forests. Subsequent litigation again successfully enjoined the Forest Service from changing the character of designated non-wilderness areas without NEPA review. *See* California v. Block, 690 F.2d 753 (9th Cir.1982). After that blow, the Forest Service began a new review, known unoriginally as RARE III. In 1984, however, Congress intervened in the seemingly endless series of RAREs with 19 bills designating a total of nine million acres as wilderness protected under the Wilderness Act. This nevertheless left unclear the status of tens of millions of roadless areas RARE II had designated as nonwilderness, as well as those areas RARE II had designated as potential wilderness but which Congress had not so declared. *See, e.g.,* Smith v. United States Forest Service, 33 F.3d 1072 (9th Cir.1994) (holding that Forest Service must consider character of area as 5000-acre roadless area in EIS authorizing timber sale).

In 1998, the Forest Service sought once again to bring closure to the roadless area issue by proposing to temporarily suspend road construction and reconstruction in the roadless areas while devising a new policy for their future. Following a series of agency proposals and presidential directives, the Forest Service promulgated a final rule on January 11, 2001 designed "to protect and conserve inventoried roadless areas on the National Forest System lands." 66 Fed. Reg. 3244 (Jan. 12, 2001). The agency identified eight key values and amenities the roadless areas convey more strongly and efficiently than other lands in the national forests:

- High quality or undisturbed soil, water, and air.
- Sources of public drinking water.
- Diversity of plant and animal communities.
- Habitat for threatened, endangered, proposed, candidate, and sensitive species and for those species dependent on large, undisturbed areas of land.
- A place for primitive, semi-primitive non-motorized, and semi-primitive motorized classes of dispersed recreation (e.g., mountain bikes).
- Reference landscapes for research.
- Natural appearing landscape with high scenic value.
- Traditional cultural properties and sacred sites.

To protect these values, the rule prohibited new road construction and reconstruction in inventoried roadless areas on national forest lands, except in limited circumstances. The rule also substantially restricted cutting, sale, and removal of timber in inventoried roadless areas.

The rule and its timing—less than ten days before the inauguration of President George W. Bush—engendered tremendous controversy, with many Republican lawmakers vowing to fight it in every possible forum. Not surprisingly, the timber industry declared the rule the beginning of the industry's demise and filed litigation to block the rule. In May 2001, a federal district court in Idaho preliminarily enjoined USDA from implementing the roadless area rule because the agency failed to follow necessary procedures for environmental impact assessment and public participation. *See* Kootenai Tribe of Idaho v. Veneman (D. Id.), and Idaho v. U.S. Forest Service (D. Id.). Although the Bush administration had previously stated its commitment to the overall objective of conservation in the roadless areas, the Forest Service had already begun a process of revisiting the rule. *See* 66 Fed. Reg. 8899 (Feb. 5, 2001) (delaying effective date of the rule by 60 days, until May 12, 2001). The court's injunction accelerated that process: in July 2001, the agency announced that it "is studying whether to amend the Roadless Area Conservation Rule . . . or to provide further administrative protections" and invited public comment on that decision. *See* 66 Fed. Reg. 35918 (July 10, 2001). Thereafter, in August and December 2001 the agency promulgated for public comment a series of "interim directives" governing roadless areas, both of which signaled that a retreat from the Clinton Administration rule was likely. *See* 66 Fed. Reg. 44590 (Aug. 1, 2001); 66 Fed. Reg. 65796 (Dec. 20, 2001). In a stunning turn of events, however, on December 12, 2002, in an appeal brought by the environmental group intervenors (the Forest Service declined to appeal), the Ninth Circuit Court of Appeals nullified the trial court's injunction issued against the roadless area rule in the *Kootenai Tribe* case. *See* Kootenai Tribe of Idaho v. Veneman, 313 F.3d 1094 (9th Cir. 2002). The court found that the Forest Service had adequately performed environmental review and public input process for the rule, and the Ninth Circuit denied en banc reconsideration of that decision in April 2003, issuing a mandate to the lower court to vacate its injunction.

By no means was that the end of the matter. Although no longer enjoined, the Forest Service displayed no intention of actually implementing the rule, instead continuing with its initiative to review and revise the rule. On July 15, 2003, as part of a settlement of litigation challenging application of the roadless rule in Alaska, the agency issued a proposed rule exempting Alaska's 16.8 million-acre Tongass National Forest from the roadless program. *See* 68 Fed. Reg. 41865 (July 15, 2003). The agency received over 300,000 comments on that proposal by the September 2, 2003 public comment deadline. The Bush Administration continued to develop plans for the roadless rule in general.

Meanwhile, with the injunction no longer effective, the *Kootenai Tribe* case and seven others like it that had been stayed during the injunction period once again became active litigation. The principal issues involved in the cases were whether the rule would create "de facto" wilderness, which arguably is beyond the agency's authority given that Congress retained exclusive authority to designate wilderness in the Wilderness Act, and, if the agency does have that authority, whether it could impose the roadless area restrictions immediately for all affected areas rather than having to do so through formal amendment to each of the national forests' plans. In July 2003, one day before the Forest Service's proposed rules on the Tongass National Forest were published in the *Federal Register*, a federal district court in Wyoming enjoined enforcement of the rule on the grounds that the agency failed properly to conduct National Environmental Policy Act analyses and exceeded its authority by using the NFMA roadless initiative to create de facto wilderness. *See* Wyoming v. U.S. Department of Agriculture, 277 F. Supp. 2d 1197 (D. Wyo. 2003). The United States declined to appeal the order, but the intervenor environmental groups did. *See* Wyoming Outdoor Council v. Wyoming, 2004 WL 1763083 (10th Cir.). In November, 2003, however, the United States argued in an amicus brief to the Tenth Circuit that the environmental groups lack standing to appeal when the United States elected not to, which the court ultimately found persuasive. *See* Wyoming v. U.S. Department of Agriculture, 414 F.3d 1207 (10th Cir. 2005)). And one month later the Administration promulgated a final rule exempting parts of the Tongass National Forest from the roadless policy. *See* 68 Fed. Reg. 75136 (Dec. 30, 2003).

As it stood at the beginning of 2004, therefore, the roadless rule was *de jure* enjoined from enforcement in Wyoming, was *de facto* a dead letter within the Bush Administration, and was being challenged across the landscape in litigation. Then, in July 2004, the Bush Administration proposed its version of a roadless policy, under which states would have to petition to the Forest Service to place roadless areas into protected status. *See* 69 Fed. Reg. 42636 (July 16, 2003). The agency adopted what it called a State Petitions Rule version of the roadless policy in May 2005. 70 Fed. Reg. 25,654 (May 13, 2005). It explained the basic thrust of the new rule as follows:

> USDA is committed to conserving and managing inventoried roadless areas and considers these areas an important component of the NFS. The Department believes that revising 36 CFR part 294 by adopting a new rule that establishes a State petitioning process that will allow State-specific consideration of the needs of these areas is an appropriate solution to address the challenges of inventoried roadless area management on NFS lands.

> States affected by the roadless rule have been keenly interested in inventoried roadless area management, especially the Western States where most of the agency's inventoried roadless areas are located. Collaborating and cooperating with States on the long-term strategy for the conservation and management or inventoried roadless areas on NFS lands allows for the recognition of local situations and resolutions of unique resource management challenges within a specific State. Collaboration with others who have strong interest in the conservation and management of inventoried roadless areas also helps ensure balanced management decisions that maintain the most important characteristics and values of those areas.

> The State petitions under this final rule must include specific information and recommendations on the management requirements for individual inventoried roadless areas within that particular State. If an inventoried roadless area boundary extends into another State, the petitioning Governor should coordinate with the Governor of the adjacent State. Petitions must be submitted to the Secretary of Agriculture within 18 months of the effective date of this final rule. Petitions will be evaluated, and if accepted, the Secretary would initiate subsequent

rulemaking for inventoried roadless area conservation and management within that State. The Department's general petitioning process for the approval, amendment or repeal of rules (7 CFR 1.28) will remain available after expiration of the 18-month petitioning period.

The Secretary has decided to establish a national advisory committee to provide advice and recommendations on the implementation of this State-specific petition for rulemaking process (§ 294.15). This committee is being established in response to comments received that roadless area management has national aspects that need to be considered. This point is well taken and a national advisory committee can fulfill this function. The advisory committee will consist of members who represent diverse national organizations interested in the conservation and management of National Forest System inventoried roadless areas.

Needless to say, the State Petitions Rule triggered a flurry of legal activity. The Forest Service summarized the subsequent events in a notice for a petition by the State of Idaho regarding the roadless areas in that state.

The Tenth Circuit Court of Appeals held that the appeal [from the district court decision in the *Wyoming* case] was moot after promulgation of the State Petitions Rule [and] dismissed the appeal and vacated the district court decision. In May 2005, the states of California, New Mexico, Washington, and Oregon, as well as a coalition of environmental groups, challenged the State Petitions Rule in the Northern District of California. On September 20, 2006, the District Court set aside the State Petitions Rule and reinstated the Roadless Rule. The California court's order triggered the State of Wyoming to seek reinstatement by the Wyoming District Court of the vacated 2003 injunction against the original Roadless Rule. The State of Wyoming also filed a new complaint, again challenging the Roadless Rule.

On June 23, 2005, the State of Idaho announced it would submit a petition pursuant to the State Petitions Rule, requesting specific regulatory protections and certain management flexibility for the 9.3 million acres of NFS inventoried roadless areas in Idaho. As part of that announcement, the State invited affected county commissioners to develop specific recommendations for the NFS inventoried roadless areas in their respective counties. Additionally, over 50 public meetings were held and the general public was encouraged to send individual comments directly to the Governor's office for consideration.

Idaho's petition was submitted to the Secretary of Agriculture for consideration on September 20, 2006. When the State Petitions Rule was injoined, Idaho submitted a petition on October 5, 2006, under section 553(e) of the Administrative Procedure Act and Department regulations at 7 CFR 1.28 which allow an interested person the opportunity to petition for the issuance, amendment, or repeal of a rule.

The Roadless Area Conservation National Advisory Committee reviewed the Idaho petition on November 29 and 30, 2006, in Washington, DC. Governor James Risch, on behalf of the State of Idaho discussed his views on the scope and intent of the petition during the first day of the meeting. The Committee also heard comments from other State and Forest Service officials, and members of the public. On December 19, 2006, the Committee issued a unanimous consensus-based recommendation that the Secretary direct the Forest Service, with the State of Idaho as a cooperating agency, to proceed with rulemaking. On December 22, 2006, the Secretary accepted the petition based on the Advisory Committee's review and report and directed the Forest Service to initiate rulemaking.

72 Fed. Reg. 17816 (Apr. 10, 2007). The Forest Service finalized the Idaho rule, which applies to 9.3 million acres in that state, in 2008. *See* 73 Fed. Reg. 61,456 (Oct. 16, 2008).

As noted in the excerpt, the State Petitions Rule was struck down in Lockyer v. U.S. Department of Agriculture, 459 F. Supp. 2d 874 (N.D. Cal. 2006), on the basis that the Forest Service had changed course without "explaining why it had concluded that the protections of the Roadless Rule were no longer necessary for the reasons it had previously laid out in detail." The Forest Service had pointed to no changed circumstances, but merely asserted that the State Petitions Rule was a "better means." Also, the court faulted the agency for failing to conduct adequate reviews of the rule under the National Environmental policy Act and Endangered Species Act. The court thus ordered the agency to reinstate the Clinton Administration's original Roadless Rule.

Not to be outdone, in August 2008 the Wyoming federal court reinstated its injunction against the Clinton Administration's 2001 rule, stating it was "extremely perplexed over how the California court resurrected the Clinton roadless rule." *See* Wyoming v. USDA, 570 F. Supp. 2d 1309 (D. Wyo. 2008). Hence, at the end of 2008, two different versions of the roadless rule were in place, in different parts of the country, both of which were tied up in litigation, and the Idaho rule was embroiled in litigation as well.

Since then, matters have gotten somewhat clearer. First, the Ninth Circuit affirmed the lower court decision rejecting the State Petitions Rule. *See* California ex rel. Lockyer v. U.S. Dep't of Agric., 575 F.3d 999 (9th Cir.2009). Over in the Tenth circuit, an Idaho federal district court upheld the Idaho rule in 2011, *see* Jayne v. Rey, 780 F. Supp. 2d 1099 (D. Idaho 2011), but then, in a turn of events, the Tenth Circuit overturned the Wyoming decision and sided with the Ninth Circuit in rejecting the State Petitions Rule, *see* Wyoming v USDA, 661 F.3d 1209 (10th Cir. 2011), which puts into question the Idaho court's decision. This is where matters stand as of this writing.

What do you think of the roadless policy dispute—which approach strikes you as better? Are you concerned that the Clinton Administration rule, which appears to be restored as the law of the land—except possibly in Idaho—allows the Forest Service to dictate wilderness policy outside of the framework contemplated in the Wilderness Act? Was the Bush Administration's State Petitions Rule, which empowered states to be the driving force, warranted by calls to decentralize decision making for national forests? How much power should the states have in deciding the management of national forest roadless areas in their boundaries?

Note on Fire Control in National Forests

One ecosystem management issue that cuts across all forest ownership regimes, but is utterly confounded by the patchwork of modern forest land ownership patterns, is fire. The importance of fire to forest ecosystem dynamics is indisputable. A variety of natural causes of fire, particularly lightning, lead to a disturbance regime of periodic fires to which forest ecosystems adapt and, eventually, upon which they come to depend. For example, the heat from such fires releases seeds in many pine species without burning them, and it clears out underbrush vegetation to control species distribution. Forest ecosystems respond to these periodic fires through a balance between understory and forest crown vegetation that keep fires generally closer to the surface and thus not a threat to the majority of biomass in the forest.

Few ecosystems demonstrate this dynamic balancing role fire plays better than the longleaf pine woodlands of the American southland. For 5000 years, the vast longleaf pine woodlands stretched for over 90 million acres from southern New Jersey in a crescent across the southeast to Texas. Fire both opened the forest to young longleafs and then suppressed understory growth once the pines were established. So uncluttered was the forest floor, European settlers spoke of driving wagons through this vast forest without need of roads. But they also relished the pines for the solid lumber they produced, gradually replacing the forests with agricultural and, later, urban land uses. Today, only 3 percent of the original longleaf pine forest remains, with only 10,000 acres representing true "old growth" longleaf pine forest. Not surprisingly, species endemic to or substantially dependent on the longleaf pine forest also declined.

One such species, the red-cockaded woodpecker, was in sufficiently poor shape as to warrant listing under the Endangered Species Act. That listing led to judicial rulings that sharply curtailed logging in the bird's habitat, yet the species showed little if any improvement even with that protection. With local economies suffering from the loss of timber harvest revenue—one Florida county deep in woodpecker country saw annual tax revenues from timber sales drop from $5000,000 to $50,000 in eight years—many people began to question the efficacy of the logging restrictions. Then, researchers began to uncover the complex role fire plays in the species' sustainability. The woodpecker builds nests only in the softer wood of older pine trees, trees at least 90 years old, with the longleaf as its favorite variety. Sparing such trees from harvest, however, is not necessarily the solution. To maintain dominance in the forest, longleaf pines depended on periodic fires to clear out the underbrush while they built a shadowy canopy high in the forest story. Fire suppression and uncoordinated controlled burns failed to supply this important clearing effect, stunting the growth of new pines. Researchers such as Fran James at Florida State University thus have begun studying which prescribed fire and timber management practices best duplicate the "fire ecology" of the longleaf pine forest. Ironically, they have found that both more fire *and* more timber harvests in combination may produce the best results for biological diversity in the forest. Their findings were unequivocal, and led environmental groups in the area to agree that controlled timber harvests followed by controlled fires are needed in order to restore the longleaf forest and to recover the woodpecker. *See* Bruce Ritchie, *Trees Trimmed to Clear Way for Birds*, Tallahassee Democrat, July 6, 2003, at 1A.

Native Americans and early European settlers understood fire's role in forest and grassland ecosystems, using it to manage vegetative regimes to serve their purposes, usually for agricultural clearing and game management. Where human populations were relatively sparse and agriculture was not yet intensively developed, these fire *manipulation* techniques posed little threat either to forest ecosystems or to human settlements. *See* U.S Forest Service, Faces of Fire (1998).

With increased urbanization and conversion of land to agricultural uses, forest fires increasingly became a threat to human lives and property. In 1910, for example, fires in Idaho and Montana swept through millions of acres, killing dozens of firefighters and destroying extensive private holdings. Thus was born the national policy of fire *suppression*. Fires in forests were to be stopped at all costs, as quickly as possible. Icons of popular culture such as Bambi and Smokey the Bear instilled a "fire is bad" mentality in the public, and the job of forest managers was to keep fire at bay.

The problem with fire suppression, however, is that it does not always work and, indeed, can make matters worse for humans and ecosystems in many settings. As fire suppression policies entered forest ecosystems adapted to natural fire regimes, it disrupted the balance of forest floor litter, undergrowth, and mature crown growth in the forest regime. The fuel available for fires when they started was far more abundant as a result, making suppression that much more difficult. In short, over time the fire suppression policy fueled catastrophic wildfire conditions. But allowing natural fire regimes to return to forested lands was not a viable option near urbanized areas or, for that matter, in forests that were used for timber harvesting, recreation, and other human uses. Indeed, even in remote forests designated for wilderness, the understory is often so developed from decades of fire suppression that any fire is likely to rage catastrophically and potentially alter basic ecosystem dynamics permanently.

The answer to this dilemma was the policy of fire *prescription*, or prescribed burns. Prescribed burning involves intentional setting of fire under planned and controlled conditions to meet specified management objectives, such as heat release and removal of understory fuel. The National Park Service adopted prescribed burning as its fire management policy in 1967, followed in 1978 by the Forest Service, and then in 1995 by a unified policy for all federal land management agencies. *See* National Park Service et al., Wildland and Prescribed Fire Management Policy Implementation Procedures Reference Guide (1998). Many state governments adopted prescribed burn policies as well, including measures to provide private landowners limited liability protection for prescribed burns if proper procedures are followed. Florida, for example, describes prescribed burning as "a land management tool that benefits the safety of the public, the environment, and the economy of the state," and protects certified burners that follow specified prescribed burn procedures from common law negligence and nuisance liabilities. *See, e.g.,* Florida Prescribed Burning Act of 1990, Fla. Stat. § 590. On the other hand, there is no liability, common law or otherwise, for failing to conduct prescribed burning. *See* Department of Transportation v. Whiteco Metrocom, 1999 WL 1486516 (Fla. Div. Admin. Hrgs.).

Prescribed burning has proven to be no panacea, however, as escaped fire is always a concern and even well-managed prescribed fires pose inconveniences to nearby human populations. Moreover, prescribed fire policies could not be implemented in all forests quickly enough to counter the buildup of understory fuel, creating the risk that prescribed burns simply could not be adequately controlled and might trigger more intensive wildfires. Indeed, the years after prescribed burning was adopted as official national and state policy have included some of the worst fire years on record. In 1998, 2000 wildfires raged across Florida, burning 500,000 acres to a crisp. And in 2000, the nation suffered 123,000 fires, burning a total of more than 8 million acres, and the federal government alone spent over $2 billion fighting them. The most visible of wildfires in many years occurred in May 2000, when a prescribed burn set in the Bandelier National Monument in New Mexico escaped into the Santa Fe National Forest and triggered a wildfire that burned 17,000 acres and destroyed 380 structures in the Los Alamos area. *See Cerro Grande Fire, 2000: Hearings Before the Senate Committee on Energy and Natural Resources* 106th Cong., 2d. Sess. (2000).

With over 11,000 communities located precariously close to federal lands considered at risk of wildland fire, it seemed an appropriate time to develop a more concerted national fire management policy for forest and range lands. President Clinton and Congress thus directed the Secretaries of Interior and Agriculture to work with the states to develop a comprehensive approach to the management of wildland fires, hazardous fire conditions, and ecosystem restoration for federal and adjacent state, tribal, and private forest lands. *See* Pub. L. 106–291 (2000). The agencies soon developed a National Fire Plan with four key principles: (1) improve prevention and suppression; (2) reduce hazardous fuels; (3) restore fire adapted ecosystems; and (4) promote community assistance. *See* U.S. Forest Service et al., A Collaborative Approach for Reducing Wildland Fire Risks to Communities and the Environment: 10-Year Comprehensive Strategy (Aug. 2001).

Alas, notwithstanding this degree of preparation and planning, 2002 was the worst fire year on record—6.9 million acres, most of it in the west and much of it approaching the so-called "wildland-urban interface," was scorched in raging infernos. In the aftermath, a new culprit was identified by the Bush Administration and many others as the cause—environmental regulations and litigation. Regulations and the litigation opportunities they spawn, went the argument, slowed efforts to remove or thin fuel from the forests most in need of fire management. Indeed, in December 2002 the Bush administration made eliminating the "costly delays" of administrative appeals and the "red tape" associated with National Environmental Policy Act reviews the new fire management policy in its new Healthy Forests Initiative (HFI), the goal being to streamline and expedite approvals of fuel reduction and habitat restoration projects. In a move that shocked many in the environmental preservation interest groups, however, Secretary of Interior Gale Norton then appointed Allan Fitzsimmons as the Interior Department's Wildlands Fuels Coordinator in charge of implementing the HFI, the same Allan Fitzsimmons whose strident criticisms of ecosystem management are quoted frequently in this text!

HFI supporters argued that its approach finds scientific support in forest research, such as studies of ponderosa pine forests conducted by Wally Covington of Northern Arizona University, who advocates extensive cutting to reduce fuel density. Indeed, there is almost universal agreement that high biomass accumulations from dead and dying trees, dense undergrowth, and stands of small trees contribute to larger, more intense fires as well as to pest problems and lower biodiversity. *See* Congressional Research Service, Forest Ecosystem Health: An Overview, CRS Report RS20822 (Feb. 21, 2001). Covington argued, however, that the HFI was too vague, failed to differentiate between forest types, and lacked a forest restoration mission, though he did criticize "environmental obstructionists" for impeding forest thinning projects. *See Arizona Ecologist Puts Stamp on Forest Restoration Debate*, 297 Science 2194 (2002). Indeed, he argued that the HFI, with the improvements he suggested, should be extended to more acres than even the Bush Administration proposed. *See* Robert F. Service, *Critics Say New Law Is a Bit Thin on Science*, 302 Science 1879 (2003).

The HFI quickly found support in Congress, where a bill to codify the expedited environmental review procedures for prescribed burn and timber thinning projects worked its way through the House Resources Committee and Agriculture Committee. At about the same time the bill was advanced from those committees, however, the General Accounting Office released a comprehensive study showing that, in fact, very few prescribed burn or timber thinning projects had experienced delays attributable to environmental review or regulation, thus removing any empirical basis for the "red tape" premise of the bill and the HFI. *See* U.S. General Accounting Office, Information on Forest Service Decisions Involving Fuels Reduction Activities, GAO-03-689R (May 14, 2003). The Bush administration nevertheless finalized rules putting the HFI into action in June 2003, see 68 Fed. Reg. 33,794 (June 5, 2003) (NEPA categorical exclusions); 68 Fed. Reg. 33,814 (June 5, 2003) (streamlined administrative procedures and appeals), which environmental groups promptly challenged.

Then the 2003 fire season put an end to debate over the HFI, at least in Congress. It was one of the worst on record, surpassing 2002 in many areas. California lost more acres of grassland and forest to fire than in any year in its history—989,000 acres, as well as 4,800 structures destroyed and 22 people killed. The prevalence of fire near urban areas led several states to tighten building codes and clear buffer zones as a preventative measure. Even insurance companies entered the scene, informing policyholders to take preventative measures and comply with new ordinances or lose coverage. Congress responded by passing HFI legislation, the Healthy Forests Restoration Act of 2003, which President Bush signed on December 3, 2003. A few days later the Fish and Wildlife Service and National Marine Fisheries Service finalized rules permitting the Forest Service and other agencies responsible for implementing the National Fire Plan to conduct internal consultations under the Endangered Species Act for projects carried out under the HFI. *See* Joint Counterpart Endangered Species Act Section 7 Consultation Regulations, 68 Fed. Reg. 68254 (Dec. 8, 2003). And by early January 2004 the Forest Service had adopted rules imposing strictly demarcated administrative review procedures for groups or individuals objecting to forest-thinning projects authorized under the HFI.

Hence in just over one year the HFI had gone from nascent proposal to becoming firmly entrenched as the nation's new fire management policy. The Forest Service thinned 1.6 million acres of national forest lands in fiscal year 2003 under the HFI, with 3.7 million acres targeted for fiscal year 2004. The Bush Administration requested $760 million to run the HFI in fiscal year 2005—the full amount authorized under the legislation—and projected that it would take 10 years to accomplish the HFI's forest-thinning goal of 80 to 90 million acres and begin to reap its postulated ecological benefits. As these projections were made, the 2004 fire season at midsummer was the worst on record, with 4.5 million acres burned in over 40,000 fires through July 20. In the next 30 days, another 12,000 fires burned 1.5 million additional acres.

Critics of the HFI dubbed it the "no tree left behind" program, and some of the agencies' more aggressive procedural reforms were overturned in the courts. *See* Sierra club v. Bosworth, 510 F.#d 1016 (9th Cir. 2007) (rejecting the NEPA categorical exclusions). During the Obama Administration, the emphasis has turned to fostering multi-jurisdictional efforts to restore "fire resilient landscapes" and foster "fire adapted communities." The Federal Land Assistance, Management, and Enhancement Act of 2009, more commonly known as the FLAME Act, directed the Secretaries of the Interior and Agriculture to submit jointly to Congress a cohesive wildfire management strategy. In June 2012, the agencies issued a strategy they promoted as an "all-lands, all-hands" approach to addressing wildland fire issues that is far more reminiscent of the National Fire Plan than the HFI. See NATIONAL COHESIVE WILDLAND FIRE MANAGEMENT & STRATEGY PLAN, PHASE II NATIONAL REPORT, *available at* http://www.forestsandrangelands.gov/strategy/documents/reports/phase2/CSPh aseIIReport_FINAL20120524.pdf. Although fuel reduction remains a part of this cohesive strategy, the aggressive timber removal approach of the HFI is no longer the nation's centerpiece of national fire policy. Regardless, wildland fires remain a serious concern—as of this writing in 2012 record-setting forest fires in Colorado threatened many communities and forests.

If you were in charge of designing a national fire policy, what would you recommend for management of fire in a public forest that is near an urban community and experiences high levels of understory fuels as a result of decades of fire suppression? Continue fire suppression? Take a chance on prescribed burns? Manually remove or thin the understory? What about the policy for a forest far from urbanized and rural land uses, but popular with recreational users? Would you let it "go natural" entirely?

Note on Ecosystem Management in State-Owned Forest Lands

The materials in this section of the chapter focus on federal administration of forest policy in national forests. As the previous historical overview explained, however, many states have also had a long history of administering forest policy on state-owned lands. Lest we leave the impression that state forest policies are unimportant to the question of how to describe the law of forest ecosystem management, a few words on state-owned forest lands are merited here.

All states have established agencies charged with duties similar to those of the Forest Service, and many states own substantial areas of land designated as state forests or devoted to similar purposes. In total, state and local governments own almost 70 million acres of forest land, or 8.75 percent of total national forested land. While this pales by comparison to federal and private holdings, much of the state and local forest lands provide valuable recreational opportunities or were acquired specifically to preserve sensitive resources.

Most states, however, have adopted forest management policies that put their forest management agencies in the same predicament as the Forest Service—having to satisfy a multiple-use mandate on public lands while responding to the increased focus on ecosystem management for protection of biodiversity. Florida, for example, maintains a state forest system covering over 830,000 acres in 36 state forests, as well as significant additional public land holdings devoted to forestry management. The Division of Forestry, an arm of the Florida Department of Agriculture and Consumer Services, oversees these lands under the following mandate:

> The Division of Forestry shall provide direction for the multiple-use management of forest lands owned by the state; serve as the lead management agency for state-owned land primarily suited for forest resource management; and provide to other state agencies having land management responsibilities technical guidance and management plan development for managing the forest resources on state-owned lands managed for other objectives. Multiple-use purposes shall include, but is not limited to, water-resource protection, forest-ecosystems protection, natural-resource-based low-impact recreation, and sustainable timber management for forest products.

Fla. Stat. 589.04(3). Other state agencies with oversight of Florida's state public lands must prepare a multiple-use analysis for tracts over 1000 acres, which must assess

> the feasibility of managing timber resources on the parcel for resource conservation and revenue generation purposes through a stewardship ethic that embraces sustainable forest management practices if the lead resource agency determines that the timber resource management is not in conflict with the primary objectives of the parcel. For purposes of this section, practicing sustainable forest management means meeting the needs of the present without compromising the ability of future generations to meet their own needs by practicing a land stewardship ethic which integrates the reforestation, managing, growing, nurturing, and harvesting of trees for useful products with the conservation of soil, air and water quality, wildlife and fish habitat, and aesthetics.

Fla. Stat. 253.036. Do these provisions give a clearer mandate to the Division of Forestry than the MUSY and NFMA give the Forest Service? Does the Florida Division of Forestry enjoy less discretion in determining how to implement the "stewardship ethic" than does the Forest Service in its implementation of the NFMA's biodiversity principle?

2. PRIVATE LANDS: INTEGRATED APPROACHES

Private lands make up over 57 percent of forest cover and 73 percent of the nation's timberland forests, divided among over six million owners. In eastern states the ratio between public and private forests is even more unbalanced. Florida, for example, has 830,000 acres in state forests and another two million acres of public lands devoted to forest management, but over 13 million acres, or *90 percent* of the state's forested land and 42 percent of the state's *total* land area, is privately-owned timberland. Although the lion's share of that land is held by nonindustrial private forest (NIPF) landowners, the forest industry controls about one-third. Forestry is among the state's major agricultural industries, contributing over $8 billion to the state economy annually. The leading product is nothing glamorous—plywood.

Clearly, private forest lands in states such as Florida present tremendous potential as economic and environmental resources. Yet there is no national forest management law other than the rules governing forests on federal public lands. The question, therefore, is how to integrate private forest lands into a coordinated forest ecosystem management policy without running directly into the same multi-objective problems faced on public lands.

An example comes from the Chesapeake Bay. In June 2000, Maryland, Pennsylvania, Virginia, the District of Columbia, the Chesapeake Bay Commission, and several federal agencies entered into a renewed Chesapeake Bay Agreement, a multi-government compact designed to manage the resources of the Chesapeake Bay and its watershed of 64,000 square miles. The first Bay Agreement, signed in 1983, was "a huge step forward in the restoration of the Bay. It brought together the principal leaders in the watershed, committed them to action, and created an organized structure dedicated to the systematic and scientific analysis of the Bay's problems and the refinement of a science-based, consensus driven plan for the Chesapeake's cleanup." Harry R. Hughes & Thomas W. Burke, Jr., *The Cleanup of the Chesapeake Bay: A Test of Political Will*, NAT. RESOURCES & ENV'T, Fall 1996, at 30, 31. A second agreement, signed in 1986, was more specific and established a set of goals in six areas: living resources, water quality, population, public information, public access, and governance. The second agreement also adopted measurable performance standards and placed political responsibility, and authority, in the hands of the elected leaders of the state signatories. *See id.* at 31–33. The new Chesapeake Bay Agreement adds to that structure, among other things, a commitment to take actions that will "promote the expansion and connection of the contiguous forests" in the Bay watershed.

Forests remain the primary land cover in the Bay watershed, covering 24.1 million acres of the watershed's 41.2 million acres in the three signatory states. Over 80 percent of that forested area is in private ownership. The parcel size of the forested land is decreasing over time, NIPF ownership is increasing, and the patches of forest are increasingly surrounded by urban land uses. Clearly, therefore, any effort to expand and connect contiguous forests must enlist the cooperation of a multitude of private forest land owners or be doomed to failure. The question is, how?

To answer that question, the Environmental Law Institute (ELI) laid out a multi-faceted plan of integrated policy approaches for forest management in the Chesapeake Bay watershed. *See* ENVTL. L. INST., FORESTS FOR

THE BAY (2000). Like many proposals evaluating options in similar circumstances around the nation, ELI gravitated to five basic policy tools: (1) tax reform; (2) voluntary conservation programs; (3) land and development rights acquisition; (4) targeted subsidies and incentives; and (5) conventional regulation. Each of these tools, and the more recent development of certification programs, offers many options, and finding the right configuration for each and blend of all for private forest land conservation will prove to be at least as challenging as has been the experience for designing public forest policy. *See* Barton H. Thompson, Jr., *Conservation Options: Toward a Greater Private Role*, 21 VIRGINIA ENVTL. L.J. 245 (2001–2002); Lee P. Breckenridge, *Reweaving the Landscape: The Institutional Challenges of Ecosystem Management for Lands in Private Ownership*, 19 VT. L. REV., 363 (1995) (covering the northern forests of New England and New York). Consider how ELI and others have proposed using these tools in the private forest land context.

Tax Reform. Forests and forest lands are taxed at federal, state, and local levels in a variety of ways that do not always favor conservation and stewardship goals. For example, a small private commercial timber operation faces several tax policies that run counter to conservation goals:

- Federal capital gains taxes penalize investment in growing and holding older growth timber resources, because the taxed inventory value increases over time with no revenue yield until the timber is cut.

- Annual local property taxes, while lower in most states than for developed land, impose a carrying cost on land value that places pressure on the landowner to generate revenues through timber harvests.

See CONSTANCE BEST AND LAURIE A. WASHBURN, AMERICA'S PRIVATE FORESTS 109–112 (2001). Reversing these and other tax policy perversions is a chief goal of private forest conservation advocates. Indeed, the three Chesapeake Bay states have programs in place to reduce the property tax burden on private forest land owners who meet certain conditions. For example, Maryland's Forest Conservation Management Agreement program allows land owners to agree not to develop forest land for nonforest uses for 15 years and thereby freeze property valuation assessments at $100/acre for the duration of the agreement term. Md. Code Ann., Tax-Property 8–209. Many other states have similar property tax reduction programs. *See* FORESTS FOR THE BAY, *supra*, at 16–20.

While removing these tax barriers would go a long way toward relieving anti-conservation pressures, ELI and others have proposed using incentive-based tax policy to *promote* private forest land conservation, such as tax deductions or credits for investment in replantings and forest management practices. Virginia, for example, allows a state income tax credit for owners of forest land who forego timber harvesting along rivers and streams. Va. Code 58.1–512. The federal tax code also allows a blend of tax credits and deductions for qualifying reforestation expenses. Internal Revenue Code 631(b). ELI recommends that such programs link the tax benefits to preparation of and adherence to forest management plans, the costs of which would also benefit from a tax credit. *See* FORESTS FOR THE BAY, *supra*, at 20–26.

Voluntary Conservation Programs. Tax policy reform may remove disincentives and create incentives for conservation of privately-owned forest land, but in neither case does it direct the land owner's behavior. Other government and private programs also attempt to lead private landowners in the direction of selected forest conservation goals without commanding them to do so. Many of these programs are designed to link landowners and timber operators with viable markets, or to increase efficiency through cooperative efforts. For example, the Maine Low Impact Forestry Project consists of loggers, foresters, and land owners practicing and promoting low impact forestry who have cooperatively worked to develop and access markets for sustainably harvested forest products. *See* http://www.acadia.net/hcpc/. Similar sustainable forestry cooperatives operate in a number of states. *See* FORESTS FOR THE BAY, *supra*, at 75–80. Many forest products companies provide free forest management advice to assist NIPFs located within the relevant "woodshed" supplying mills and other manufacturing centers in forest management planning. Large organizations of NIPFs and other commercial forest operations, such as the American Forest Foundation and the National Woodland Owners Association, also provide valuable repositories of information about forest management practices and offer regular educational programs. *See* AMERICA'S PRIVATE FORESTS, *supra*, at 146–48.

Timber and Wood Product Certification Programs. An emerging non-governmental voluntary program that taps more overtly into market forces involves efforts to "certify" timber and finished wood products as ecologically "friendly." This is part of a larger trend in which businesses commit to meet environmental standards set by an independent certifying body, banking on the consuming public to pay premiums for the positive effects associated with purchase of certified products. *See* Gordon R. Alphonso et al., *Fire, Wood, and Water: Trends in Forest Management Requirements*, 18 NATURAL RESOURCES & ENV'T 18 (2003); Errol Meidenger: *The New Environmental Law: Forest Certification*, 10 BUFFALO ENVTL. L.J. 211 (2002–03); Errol E. Meidenger, *Environmental Certification Programs and Environmental Law: Closer than You May Think*, 31 ENVTL. L. REP. (Envtl. L. Inst.) 10162 (2001). For forest products, the Forest Stewardship Council (FSC) is an international, non-profit, non-governmental organization founded in 1993 to act as the certifying body. The FSC has issued its Principles and Criteria for Forest Management, a set of certification standards developed by highly respected individuals representing FSC's expertise in environmental, economic, and social factors involving forests and forest management. *See* http://www.fscus.org. Criteria 6.3 states that "Ecological functions and values shall remain intact, enhanced, or restored." Using this and other criteria, FSC approves regional certification standards tailored to the type of forests in the region and accredits certifiers to work in that region. Two FSC accredited certification organizations, SmartWood and Scientific Certification Systems, are located in the United States and have issued management certificates to forest operations with combined forest holdings of more than 4.8 million acres. Forest products coming from FSC certified timber operations, which is determined through "chain-of-custody" certification, can carry the FSC product label. A similar program was the American Forest and Paper Association's Sustainable Forest Initiative, now known as the Better Practices,

Better Planet program, the ultimate goal of which is to have 100 percent of the loggers supplying material to the Association's member companies verify their adherence to a set of sustainable forestry standards and principles. *See* http://www.afandpa.org/Sustainability. Other programs like these are described in FORESTS FOR THE BAY, *supra*, at 67–69. Some conservation biologists remain skeptical, however, of the efficacy of these programs toward promotion of their version on ecosystem management. *See* Conservation Forum, *Timber Certification*, 15 CONSERVATION BIOLOGY 308 (2001) (collection of articles critiquing timber certification programs).

Land and Development Rights Acquisition. One of the more obvious policy options for ecosystem management in private forest lands is to convert them to public forest lands through direct acquisition by the government. For example, the Forest Service administers the Forest Legacy Program, through which state foresters can receive generous federal funding matches for acquisition of "environmentally important forest areas that are threatened by conversion to nonforest uses." 16 U.S.C. § 2103(c). *See* http://www.fs.fed.us/loa/coop. The Chesapeake Bay Agreement states all have state funded programs for acquisition of threatened forest land as well. *See* FORESTS FOR THE BAY, *supra*, at 32–36. Maryland's Rural Legacy program, for example, has acquired woodlands for the protection of watersheds, streams, and wetlands. *See* http://www.dnr.state.md.us/rurallegacy.html.

A variant of direct acquisition is the purchase of a conservation easement that limits the landowner's development options for the land. It may not be economically or socially desirable, or environmentally necessary, to move all or most of a region's private timber land into public preserve status. Where private forestry practices are consistent with ecosystem management objectives, the main conservation threat may be the potential for conversion to urban nonforest uses. Buying those development rights through purchase of conservation easements allows the landowner to retain ownership and continue deriving economically productive use of the land, but precludes the potential for deleterious future uses. Such conservation easement payments can also be conditioned on the landowner's use of prescribed sustainable forest practices, thus enhancing the value of continued forest use of the land. *See* FORESTS FOR THE BAY, *supra*, at 38–39.

Either of the direct acquisition or conservation easement options can be accomplished by private entities as well, or through cooperation of public governments and private organizations. Indeed, the largest conservation easement in U.S. history was announced in 1999, when the Pingree family agreed to sell development rights to over 760,000 acres of forest land in northern Maine to the New England Forestry Foundation. The Foundation raised $28 million in private funding over the next two years to finance the acquisition, and closed the deal in March 2001. The Pingrees, which had amassed a reputation for environmentally sensitive timber management, retained the right to continue limited timber harvests pursuant to guidelines spelled out in the easement, and the public retained recreational access to much of the land (a longstanding Maine custom), but conversion to nonforest uses was taken off the table through the purchase of the development rights. *See* http://www.neforestry.org. The cumulative impact of numerous smaller state and local land trusts also should not be overlooked. Over 1700 land trusts are members of the Land Trust Alliance, which provides support to its members through training, lobbying, and legal publications. LTA has grown to that number from 880 in 1990, and today its members protect over 6.3 million acres, almost one million of which are timberlands. Over 70 percent of all land trust lands protect some forest resources in addition to wetlands, grasslands, and other resources.

Targeted Subsidies and Incentives. An extrapolation of the tax incentive policies discussed above is the use of more aggressive subsidy and incentive funding options designed to promote forest conservation. The Forest Service's Forest Stewardship Program, for example, provides technical support through state foresters to landowners who develop Forest Stewardship Plans designed to manage private forests for timber, wildlife, watersheds, and other benefits. 16 U.S.C. § 2103a. Cost-sharing support for development and implementation of the plans is available through the Forest Service's Stewardship Incentive Program. 16 U.S.C. § 1603b. *See* http://www.fs.fed.us/loa/coop. The Chesapeake Bay Agreement states and many other states offer more generous incentives for reforestation and riparian forest preservation. *See* FORESTS FOR THE BAY, *supra*, at 46–49. The California Forest Improvement Program, for example, provides cost-share assistance to private forest landowners (20–5000 acres) to develop management plans, replant, improve timber stands, improve fish and wildlife habitat, and engage in forest conservation management practices. *See* http://www.fire.ca.gov/ResourceManagement/CFIP.asp.

In addition to endorsing the Bush Administrations Healthy Forests Initiative (see *supra*), Title V of the Healthy Forest Restoration Act created the Healthy Forests Reserve Program to provide financial assistance to private forest owners with endangered, threatened, or rare species on their lands. The funds provide cost-sharing for habitat restoration and compensation for reductions in land value associated with conservation easements. Title V directs the USDA, which administers the program through the Natural Resources Conservation Service, to establish the Healthy Forests Reserve Program to acquire short-and long-term agreements and easements on private land to promote the recovery of endangered species, improve biodiversity, and enhance carbon sequestration. The legislation:

- Directs the Secretary of Agriculture, in consultation with the Secretaries of the Interior and Commerce, to designate rare forest ecosystems that are eligible for the reserve program
- Specifies lands eligible for enrollment and lists eligibility and enrollment requirements for program participants, including enrollment priorities for land with threatened and endangered species
- Allows lands to be enrolled based on a 10-year cost-share agreement, a 30-year easement, or an easement of not more than 99 years
- Specifies a maximum enrollment of 2 million acres

- Requires the Secretary to consider the cost effectiveness of each agreement and its restoration plans to maximize the environmental benefits per dollar expended

Voluntary Public-Private Partnerships. Another trend in private forest management, strongly pursued by Bush Administration, involves quasi-contractual ecosystem management partnerships between public agencies and private forestland owners. Rather than paying the landowner to conserve habitat or species, or providing technical assistance, or acquiring public interest in the land, this approach outlines practices the landowner will follow and which the landowner also will allow the conservation agency to implement on the private lands. A major example of such an arrangement is the May 2004 agreement the U.S. Fish and Wildlife Service entered into with International Paper Company to conduct ecological surveys and conservation projects on 5.5 million acres of land IP owns in nine Southeastern states over a 10-year agreement period. According to the parties, the "Aquatic Resources Conservation and Management Partnership Agreement" was the first comprehensive agreement that the U.S. Fish and Wildlife Service has signed with a corporation to foster conservation of aquatic species, habitats and ecosystems. The cooperative conservation actions called for in the agreement include:

- Identifying areas on International Paper land to survey for presence of imperiled aquatic species where they might occur but have not yet been detected

- Implementing and measuring the effectiveness of Best Management Practices to protect water quality during forest operations

- Supporting propagation programs for imperiled aquatic species

- Re-introducing imperiled aquatic species within International Paper forestlands where there is suitable habitat

- Publicly promoting awareness of the needs of these species

Conventional Regulation. All of the policy options discussed above rely on some relatively passive mechanism—the market, peer pressure, financial incentives—to lead private forest land owners toward ecosystem management goals the government or some private entity has selected. The most obvious option available for ecosystem management in private forest contexts, however, is plain vanilla government regulation. Federal laws such as the Endangered Species Act and Clean Water Act clearly have significant regulatory effects on private forest lands. *See* Jan S. Pauw & James R. Johnston, *Habitat Planning Under the ESA on Commercial Forestlands*, 16 NATURAL RESOURCES & ENVIRONMENT 102 (2001). Other than through the incidental effects of such environmental conservation or pollution control laws, however, there is no body of federal forestry law for private lands. By contrast, Maryland's Forest Conservation Act, Md. Code Ann., Nat. Res., 5–1601 et seq., requires each unit of local government having planning and zoning authority to adopt a forest conservation program applicable to subdivision developments. Plans must provide for forest retention and reforestation generally, and for forest retention in sensitive areas. Most states, however, do not have nearly as aggressive regulation of development activities as does Maryland, although the combination of land use, zoning, and environmental quality regulatory authorities in many states provides a foundation for such regulation. *See* FORESTS FOR THE BAY, *supra*, at 83–99.

Some states also regulate beyond the question of conversion of forest land to nonforest uses by regulating forestry practices on private lands. The variety of approaches, however, is remarkable. Within the Chesapeake Bay Agreement states, for example, Virginia and Pennsylvania have no law directly covering private forest management and harvesting, while Maryland has enacted a relatively comprehensive effort in its Forest Conservancy District Law. Md. Code Ann., Nat. Res. 5–601 et seq. The Maryland law allows the state to "administer forest conservation practices on privately owned forest land" through rules implemented by appointed forest conservancy district boards. *See* FORESTS FOR THE BAY, *supra*, at 61–64. Moreover, like the federal system, most states have environmental protection laws that incidentally regulate forestry practices. *See id.* at 64–67. The multiple-use dilemma that plagues public forest land policy is absent from this private forestry regulation context of course, but the challenge of prescribing and proscribing private forestry practices is nonetheless a complex policy undertaking.

NOTES & QUESTIONS

1. How confident are you that ecosystem management goals like those Grumbine and other conservation biologists have prescribed can be achieved through the non-regulatory tools discussed above? Virginia is an example of a state that has traditionally had pressing private forest issues, little regulatory authority on the books, and a moderate commitment to voluntary and incentive programs. To more effectively address the goals of the Chesapeake Bay Agreement, should Virginia (a) increase regulation of private forestry and conversion of forest land to nonforest uses, or (b) increase subsidies and incentives, or (c) increase both but to a lesser degree?

2. Assuming you were charged with drafting a state law to comprehensively regulate private forestry practices and conversion of forest land to nonforest uses, how useful would you find the Forest Service's recent series of policy initiatives as a guide for what to do with respect to private lands? Would you ban new roads in forested areas? Would you require private landowners to restore private forests to some reference point of ecological composition or process integrity?

3. In your law, how useful would the ecosystem services concept be to designing regulations or subsidies and incentives? Whom would you vest with ownership of the services? The public? The forest owner? The recipient of the service values? What would you do with the ecosystem service "property" rights once you assigned ownership? Could they be traded, sold, and banked?

4. For more information on the Chesapeake Bay Program, primarily its aquatic resources, see Chapter 11. For additional discussion of the various regulatory and other policy tools available to advance private forest ecosystem management, see Robert L. Fischman, *Stumbling to Johannesburg: The United States' Haphazard Progress Toward Sustainable Forestry Law*, 32 ENVTL. L. REP. (Envtl. L. Inst.) 10291, 10299–10305 (2002).

5. The provincial government of British Columbia in Canada adopted legislation in 2004, known as the Forest and Range Practices Act, to streamline approval steps for logging in private forests, but would require companies to develop and implement comprehensive forest stewardship plans. Plans must state results and strategies that will address risks associated with terrain hazards and cumulative impacts in designated watersheds. Companies that commit to innovative measures designed to promote forest values beyond the requirements of regulatory measures benefit from streamlined regulatory processes, while companies that violate the regulatory minimum standards face stiffer penalties. For more on this comprehensive regulation of private forest lands, see http://www.gov.bc.ca/for.

6. Perhaps the most incendiary private forest use issue in decades, the so-called Headwaters Forest controversy in California, revolved around the threat of a regulatory takings claim. The Pacific Lumber Company (PALCO) owned the largest remaining stand of privately-owned, old-growth redwoods in the world, including some trees well over 2000 years old. Charles Hurwitz, the CEO of PALCO's parent company MAXAAM, made it clear that to PALCO the 3,500-acre stand of redwoods was essentially a valuable crop ready for harvest. To ardent environmentalist groups, however, the trees held nearly religious values. They argued that PALCO had no right to log the forest given the spiritual value of the redwoods. As habitat for the endangered marbled murrelet, a small bird, the Endangered Species Act (ESA) held the chain saws at bay. But PALCO, which had holdings of over 210,000 acres of redwood forest land on which it hoped to harvest, used the takings issue as its leverage in the affair through an inverse condemnation lawsuit it filed against the United States. A long, arduous series of negotiations between PALCO, the U.S. Department of Interior, and the State of California brokered a deal involving the $380 million purchase of 7,500 acres of PALCO's land, including the old growth stands, and the issuance of an ESA permit to conduct harvesting on PALCO's remaining lands under specified conservation conditions. The environmental advocacy groups were incensed, working tirelessly to block the deal, and PALCO and Interior ran into many last-minute negotiation impasses, but on March 1, 1999, the deal was finalized. On July 22, 2003, however, Humboldt County Superior Court Visiting Judge John J. Golden found the procedures state agencies used to implement the Headwaters agreements were "extensively flawed," agreeing with plaintiffs Environmental Protection Information Center and the Sierra Club that PALCO's permits must be vacated. *See* Environmental Protection Information Center v. California Department of Forestry and Fire Protection, No. 99–445 (2003). Later, however, the judge tempered the effect of the ruling by enjoining only new timber harvesting permits and allowing logging under plans submitted prior to the July ruling.

Putting aside their status as endangered species habitat, did PALCO have the right to remove these 2000-year old trees from the face of the planet? If so, would any of the policy tools discussed in this section, other than outright acquisition, have been useful in dissuading PALCO from doing so? Assuming, as PALCO asserted, that the commercial timber value of the disputed redwoods was well over the $380 million purchase price, did the government use the ESA to take the land for less than the just compensation it would have had to pay under an exercise of eminent domain? For two sharply contrasting insider views of these and other questions swirling in Headwaters Forest controversy, see Gideon Kanner, *Redwoods, Junk Bonds, and Tools of Cosa Nostra: A Visit to the Dark Side of the Headwaters Controversy*, 30 Envtl. Law Reporter (ELI) 10756 (2000) (attorney for PALCO in the takings litigation); David J. Hayes, *Saving the Headwaters Forest: A Jewel That Nearly Slipped Away*, 30 Envtl. Law Reporter (ELI) 10131 (2000) (attorney for Interior in the acquisition negotiation).

D. Case Study: The Shawnee National Forest in Southern Illinois

The Shawnee National Forest in southern Illinois is a 268,000-acre patch-work national forest which, like many in the eastern United States, the national government purchased when agricultural uses failed and soil erosion was a serious problem. In pre-European settlement times the Shawnee area was covered predominantly with a thriving hardwood forest and open glades or barrens communities. Early settlers cleared the forest to make way for croplands, but the combination of erosion of poor soils and agricultural market failures during the Depression wiped out the hardscrabbled farming communities. The federal government purchased many abandoned and marginal tracts of land in the 1930s and planted short-leaf pines to control soil erosion and to establish a timber source. President Roosevelt designated the Shawnee National Forest in 1939.

Today the Shawnee protects at least seven federally-listed endangered species and provides numerous outdoor recreation opportunities. But it is not what it once was. The planted pine forest, though thriving and covering 16 percent of the forest, provides only a fraction of the habitat value and species diversity the pre-settlement hardwood forest provided. The Forest Service thus devised an "ecological restoration program" to return approximately 10,000 acres of the Shawnee to pre-settlement hardwood and mixed hardwood/pine forest conditions. By allowing timber companies to selectively cut pines, the Forest Service hoped to open the forest canopy sufficient to promote hardwood growth and, eventually, to support a hardwood forest of superior ecological value than the existing pine forest.

A scenic view from cliffs overlooking the Shawneee National Forest
U.S. Forest Service

One area the Forest Service chose for the project, however, had grown dear to many environmental activists, not to mention many pine forest species. Known as the Bell Smith Springs area, it is filled with deep untouched pine stands, crystal clear streams, and miles of peaceful walking trails. Species don't know which trees are supposed to be where, and so over the years since the planting of the pines, species that favor pine ecosystems had made Bell Smith Springs their home. This group of species, anchored by a small bird known as the pine warbler, was known as the "pine warbler guild." The Forest Service did not dispute that removal of the pines would severely affect the pine warbler guild, most likely extirpating the species from the Bell Smith Springs area. As one Friends of Bell Smith Springs activist put it, "if they take those trees out now, it will set the area back 60 years," which was, ironically, precisely the agency's objective. Notwithstanding the agency's strong case that the hoped-for hardwood forest would supply higher biodiversity, activists fought hard to protect what they facetiously called the "offending pines."

The central portion of the Shawnee National Forest showing the Bell Smith Springs area and the division between federal land (dark) and non-federal land (light).

NOTES & QUESTIONS

1. Using the NMFA cases and the relevant Forest Service statutes and regulations discussed in this chapter, what would you tell the Friends of Bell Smith Springs when they seek your advice on how to proceed in a lawsuit seeking to enjoin the agency's restoration plan timber cuts? Do they have a chance? What are their best arguments?

2. Now put yourself in the role of the Forest Service's attorney. How can the agency portray its plan so as to minimize vulnerability to the activists' case? In the end, although the Forest Service has a substantive duty to protect biodiversity, is its discretion so broad that it has the power to choose *which version* of biodiversity it protects?

3. Are your answers affected by the additional fact that Forest Service had designated the pine warbler as a management indicator species for pine forest areas in the Shawnee National Forest? If so, is it also important to know whether the pine warbler is a native or non-native species in the forest? How long does a species have to be "in" a forest for it to be "native" to that forest?

4. Does the description of conservation biology in *Marita* suggest an approach a conservation biologist would take to the Forest Service's "ecological restoration program" for the Shawnee? Can you tell whether the Forest Service's scientists were practicing conservation biology when they proposed the forest "restoration" program for the Shawnee? How important is it to your answer to any of these questions that the pine forest itself was not native to the Bell Smith Springs area, but rather was introduced following agricultural clearing of the pre-settlement hardwood forest? How long do the pines have to be in the forest before they are no longer "offending" but rather the ecosystem to protect?

5. Consider how the courts that decided these questions ruled. The litigation, Glisson v. U.S. Forest Service, 138 F.3d 1181 (7th Cir.1998), *aff'g* 876 F.Supp.

1016 (S.D. Ill. 1993), culminated in this opinion by Chief Judge Posner of the Seventh Circuit:

> Before us is an appeal from a grant of summary judgment to the Forest Service in a suit to enjoin an "ecological restoration" project in a 10,500 acre tract ("Opportunity Area 6") of the Shawnee National Forest in southern Illinois. The litigation has a long history unnecessary to recount, as the issues presented by the appeal are narrow ones. The first concerns the Service's compliance with a federal regulation that requires it "to maintain viable populations of existing native" species. 36 C.F.R. § 219.19. The project, although designed to promote a variety of fauna and flora native to the area, will have adverse effects on shortleaf pines and pine warblers. The Forest Service, however, interprets the word "native" in the regulation to mean "native to the project area," that is, to OA6, rather than native to the state or even to the national forest; and it interprets "native" to mean existing in a "natural" state in the area rather than introduced by man in recent times. On the basis of these interpretations, the Service held that the regulation does not bar the restoration project. The pines, which in turn provide a habitat for the warblers, were first planted in OA6 during the 1930s and 1940s, and that is too recent to satisfy the Service's conception of what it means for a plant or animal to be "native" to an area.

> An agency is entitled to broad latitude in interpreting its regulations. E.g., Thomas Jefferson University v. Shalala, 512 U.S. 504, 512 (1994); Arkansas v. Oklahoma, 503 U.S. 91, 112 (1992); Lyng v. Payne, 476 U.S. 926, 939 (1986). Since the regulation in question contains no definition of "native," we are required to uphold the Forest Service's interpretation unless it is unreasonable. E.g., Thomas Jefferson University v. Shalala, supra, 512 U.S. at 512; Bradvica v. INS, 128 F.3d 1009, 1014 (7th Cir.1997). It is not.

Does this outcome surprise you? Recall that this is the same court that decided *Marita*.

6. Would either the Committee of Scientists' proposal or the Forest Service's 2012 rule have required a different ruling in the *Glisson* case?

7. The map of the central portion of the Shawnee National Forest reproduced above shows how federal and non-federal lands co-exist in close proximity, with non-federal lands often "intruding" on the integrity of the national forest (and vice-versa!). Assume that private lands jut into portions of the Shawnee pine forest area in which the Forest Service would like to see its "ecological restoration project" take hold. The private lands contain thriving pine forest habitat which, because of its adjacency to the project area, could impede the effects of the project within the Shawnee. The Forest Service cannot include those private lands in the timber leases designed to cull pine trees. What can the agency do to avoid having private land management activities thwart the effects of the project within the national forest?

8. Private and state lands virtually slice the Shawnee National Forest in half. Does this geographic distribution of land ownership constrain Forest Service decision options for the Shawnee? What techniques could federal or state law use to coerce or provide incentives for owners of private forested lands near the Shawnee to "cooperate" with Forest Service policy goals for the national forest?

9. For a history of the formation of the Shawnee National Forest from the depleted agricultural lands of southern Illinois, see http://www.fs.usda.gov/Internet/FSE_DOCUMENTS/stelprdb5092992.pdf

CHAPTER 9

GRASSLAND ECOSYSTEMS

A. BIODIVERSITY AND GRASSLAND ECOSYSTEMS

The Great Plains of North America comprise more than 500 million acres of grasslands or former grasslands west of the 100th meridian, extending from central Alberta, Canada, to the Texas panhandle. Grasslands are composed of a rich complex of grasses and forbs—few trees or shrubs are found in intact grasslands. Most grasslands are also associated with low moisture and seasonal extremes in temperature. Two general varieties exist in the world: temperate grasslands are found primarily in North America, Europe, and in the plains of Asia; savanna grasslands dominate in the hotter climates of South America, Africa, and the Australian Outback. In the United States, grasslands east of the continental divide reaching to western Indiana and Kansas were dominated by tall, mixed, and shortgrass prairie (French for meadow), with the more arid lands being in the "rain shadow" of the Rocky Mountains. West of the continental divide were found the sagebrush grasslands of such Intermountain West states as Wyoming, Montana, Colorado, and New Mexico.

Much of the world's temperate grassland areas are well-suited to agriculture and have been converted to row crops or pasture. Some of this continent's prairie grasslands are among the world's best agricultural lands. In 1820, for example, at least 60 percent of Illinois' land area was high quality grassland of one type or another. Today, 99.99 percent of that habitat is gone, most of it converted to crop production, making the state known as the Prairie State a bit of an imposter. Worse, the remaining areas of original Illinois grasslands—just over 2000 acres in all—are fragmented into over 200 remnants, four out of five of which are smaller than ten acres and one third of which are smaller than one acre—a size too small to function as a self-sustaining ecosystem. Most of these remnant sites are not protected as dedicated preserves. *See* ILLINOIS DEPARTMENT OF ENERGY AND NATURAL RESOURCES, THE CHANGING ILLINOIS ENVIRONMENT: CRITICAL TRENDS (1994).

To be sure, manipulation of grasslands began well before European settlers introduced large-scale agriculture, as Native Americans set many fires throughout the central grasslands, possibly to manage grassland species composition and to prevent establishment of forests, but also possibly simply to improve travel corridors or as an act of warfare. Later, as European settlers suppressed fire, species composition moved in the other direction—toward woody plants and other species introduced from adjacent forests that were unchecked by periodic fires, natural or otherwise. Today, less than one percent of the original grasslands of the American Great Plains are undisturbed by human activities. Much of the area that is used for rangeland is owned and administered by the federal government through the Department of Interior's Bureau of Land Management (BLM). Most of the private land is irrigated for agricultural uses. In short, no person who walked the land of the Great Plains in 1800 would recognize what is there today as a grassland.

The combination of agricultural encroachment, fire suppression, and elimination of keystone species such as bison and prairie dogs (see Chapter 4) has led to a general decline in native grassland biodiversity in the United States. Native grassland birds are among the most imperiled avian species in North America. Three bird species once common on Illinois prairies are completely extirpated from the state. Native prairie fishes have also experienced losses as impoundments on rivers and streams have altered habitat and fragmented populations. Even insects are finding it hard to adapt—the Karner blue butterfly, native to northern Illinois, had not been seen in the state for over a century until a single sighting event in 1992.

There is promise in efforts to rehabilitate grassland ecosystems, however. The Great Plains comprise 20 percent of the land area of the lower 48 states, but house only two percent of the nation's population. The rural nature of the area provides opportunities for land acquisition and restoration efforts. On the other hand, the rural population, though sparse, is committed to its lifestyle, and that lifestyle relies largely on access to large stretches of land. Efforts to acquire or regulate areas for grassland ecosystem management may threaten the economic and cultural viability of these rural communities. As the materials in this chapter attest, the history and future of land management on the Great Plains thus involves much controversy.

NOTES & QUESTIONS

1. The degree to which Native Americans altered North American grassland ecosystems prior to European settlement is controversial. *See* CHARLES C. MANN, 1491: NEW REVELATIONS OF THE AMERICAS BEFORE COLUMBUS (2005). There is a raging debate among ecological historians as to the impact early human inhabitants of the continent had on the surrounding flora and fauna. Was it the deadly Clovis point, used expertly by early native hunters? Or was it climate change, natural fire regimes, or species competition? And while there is ample evidence of Native American manipulation of vegetative regimes through fire, how widespread was it, and how lasting were its effects? In particular, paleoecologists disagree as to causes of the rapid extinction of the rich array of megafauna that were found on the continent around the time the first human migrations to North America are believed to have occurred (about 13,000 years ago). *See* Matt McGlone, *The Hunters Did It*, 335 SCIENCE 1452 (2012) (rejecting natural fire and climate change as causes and arguing hunting alone was the major factor); Christopher Johnson, *Megafuanal Decline and Fall*, 326 SCIENCE 1072 (2009) (explaining different theories); Martyn Murray, *Overkill and Sustainable Use*, 299 SCIENCE 1851 (2003) (discussing evidence of unsustainable hunting); Richard A. Kerr, *Megafauna Died from Big Kill, Not Big Chill*, 300 SCIENCE 885 (2003) (discussing research suggesting that humans arrived in North America just before the time of the megafauna collapse, and that the collapse preceded the era of massive climate change beginning 10,000 years ago); Vance Holliday, *Where Have All the Mammoth Gone?*, 300 SCIENCE 1373 (2003) (reviewing and questioning recent studies); *Did Human Hunting Cause Mass Extinction?*, 294 SCIENCE 1459 (2001) (series of letters debating the question). In any event, there is little debate that the largest set of impacts on the Great Plains has been the post-European settlement introductions of widespread irrigated agriculture, intensive domestic cattle and sheep grazing, and concerted fire suppression. Background on the ongoing degrading condition of North American grasslands attributable to these factors is available in U.S. DEPT. OF INTERIOR, OUR LIVING RESOURCES 295–307 (1995), and WORLD RESOURCES INST., PEOPLE AND ECOSYSTEMS 119–135 (2000). For epic accounts of the ecological history of our continent, including the interaction of early human inhabitants and their surroundings, see TIM FLANNERY, THE ETERNAL FRONTIER: AN ECOLOGICAL HISTORY OF NORTH AMERICA AND ITS PEOPLES (2001); DAVID S. WILCOVE, THE CONDOR'S SHADOW: THE LOSS AND RECOVERY OF WILDLIFE IN AMERICA (1999). An excellent history of the social, physical, and ecological conditions associated with grazing on the American rangelands is found in DEBRA L. DONAHUE, THE WESTERN RANGE REVISITED 1–160 (1999).

2. One reason to focus on grazing policy as the medium for studying the law of grassland ecosystems is that the impact of grazing on the environment is a matter of degree. Grazing is simply one form of "herbivory," which is a natural process in any ecosystem where flora and fauna co-exist. A leaf-chewing grasshopper is an herbivore. The now extinct megafauna of the pre-human continent were herbivores. Herbivory contributes to nutrient cycling, species control, and other natural ecosystem processes. Grazing by large ungulate (hooved) species plays an important role in maintaining soil composition and mediating vegetative species abundance. So, is grazing of cattle and sheep a "natural" ecosystem process? That depends on how it is conducted. By most ecological accounts, it has been conducted too intensively on many of our nation's public lands to sustain the conditions believed to be necessary to support a thriving grassland ecosystem. Overstocking the lands (placing too many cattle or sheep in an area at once) or overgrazing the lands (allowing the stock to graze an area too much) can lead to extensive trampling and compaction of soil, deposition of urine and feces, devegetation, and introduction of nonnative grasses and weeds. Yet, many ranching interests, and even a fair number of range ecologists, maintain that there is a level of grazing that is sustainable ecologically. The challenge for grassland ecosystem management policy is finding that level. For detailed, albeit contrasting, accounts of the impacts grazing has on grassland ecosystems, compare Thomas L. Fleischner, *Ecological Costs of Livestock Grazing in Western North America*, 8 CONSERVATION BIOLOGY 629 (1994) (grazing is detrimental), with Jaymee T. Marty, *Effects of Cattle Grazing on Diversity in*

Ephemeral Wetlands, 19 CONSERVATION BIOLOGY 1626 (2005) (grazing helps maintain species diversity); James H. Brown & William McDonald, *Livestock Grazing and Conservation on Southwest Rangelands*, 9 CONSERVATION BIOLOGY 1644 (1995) (grazing is not detrimental); *see also* William Stolzenberg, *Good Cow, Bad Cow*, NATURE CONSERVANCY, July/Aug. 2000, at 12. Whatever the effects of early Native American and modern grazing practices may be, it is clear that grasslands offer significant ecosystem service values, including sequestering carbon, methane, and nitrogen and, of most direct value, reducing soil erosion, and that improperly managed cultivation and grazing can significantly reduce the ability of grasslands to deliver those values. *See* Osvaldo E. Sala & Jose M. Paruelo, *Ecosystem Services in Grasslands*, in NATURE'S SERVICES 237 (Gretchen C. Daily ed., 1997).

B. PRIMER ON THE LAW OF GRASSLANDS

1. HISTORICAL BACKGROUND

The importance of history, both social and legal, to the development of ecosystem management law could not be more plainly illustrated than through the lens of the following United States Supreme Court opinion. Before addressing the subtle merits of a challenge to "Rangeland Reform" regulations the Bureau of Land Management (BLM) adopted for administration of public rangelands (discussed *infra*), the Court described the unfolding of the federal law of rangelands and its gradual movement toward an ecosystem management model.

This history has witnessed the evolution of two themes headed on a collision course. The first involves the definition of grazing privileges on the 176 million acres of public rangelands BLM administers in the western states (excluding Alaska), 90 percent of which are approved for livestock grazing by private ranching operations. The second involves the ecological condition of the rangelands and the degree to which BLM approval of grazing levels takes those conditions into account.

While grazing on public lands has always been a privilege and nothing more in the strict legal sense, a culture of property rights emerged around those privileges based on how BLM administered them and on how ranchers used them. To understand how this transpired, read carefully the Court's description of the "grazing preference" method of rangeland grazing privilege allocation and the related concepts of "base property" and "suspended Animal Unit Months." As the Court describes how this history unfolded, track also the Court's description of the ecological condition of the rangelands through time.

Public Lands Council v. Babbitt

Supreme Court of the United States, 2000.
529 U.S. 728.

■ JUSTICE BREYER delivered the opinion of the Court.

This case requires us to interpret several provisions of the 1934 Taylor Grazing Act, 48 Stat. 1269, 43 U.S.C. § 315 et seq. The Petitioners claim that each of three grazing regulations, 43 CFR §§ 4100.0–5, 4110.1(a), and 4120.3–2 (1998), exceeds the authority that this statute grants the Secretary of the Interior. We disagree and hold that the three regulations do not violate the Act.

I

We begin with a brief description of the Act's background, provisions, and related administrative practice.

A

The Taylor Grazing Act's enactment in 1934 marked a turning point in the history of the western rangelands, the vast, dry grasslands and desert that stretch from western Nebraska, Kansas, and Texas to the Sierra Nevada. Ranchers once freely grazed livestock on the publicly owned range as their herds moved from place to place, searching for grass and water. But the population growth that followed the Civil War eventually doomed that unregulated economic freedom.

A new era began in 1867 with the first successful long drive of cattle north from Texas. Cowboys began regularly driving large herds of grazing cattle each year through thousands of miles of federal lands to railheads like Abilene, Kansas. From there or other towns along the rail line, trains carried live cattle to newly opened eastern markets. The long drives initially brought high profits, which attracted more ranchers and more cattle to the land once home only to Indian tribes and buffalo. Indeed, an early-1880's boom in the cattle market saw the number of cattle grazing the Great Plains grow well beyond 7 million.

But more cattle meant more competition for ever-scarcer water and grass. And that competition was intensified by the arrival of sheep in the 1870's. Many believed that sheep were destroying the range, killing fragile grass plants by cropping them too closely. The increased competition for forage, along with droughts, blizzards, and growth in homesteading, all aggravated natural forage scarcity. This led, in turn, to overgrazing, diminished profits, and hostility among forage competitors—to the point where violence and "wars" broke out, between cattle and sheep ranchers, between ranchers and homesteaders, and between those who fenced and those who cut fences to protect an open range. These circumstances led to calls for a law to regulate the land that once was free.

The calls began as early as 1878 when the legendary southwestern explorer, Major John Wesley Powell, fearing water monopoly, wrote that ordinary homesteading laws would not work and pressed Congress to enact "a general law . . . to provide for the organization of pasturage districts." Report on the Lands of the Arid Region of the United States, H. Exec. Doc. No. 73, 45th Cong., 2d Sess., 28 (1878). From the end of the 19th century on, Members of Congress regularly introduced legislation of this kind, often with Presidential support. In 1907, President Theodore Roosevelt reiterated Powell's request and urged Congress to pass laws that would "provide for Government control of the public pasture lands of the West." S. Doc. No. 310, 59th Cong., 2d Sess., 5 (1907). But political opposition to federal regulation was strong. President Roosevelt attributed that opposition to "those who do not make their homes on the land, but who own wandering bands of sheep that are driven hither and thither to eat out the land and render it worthless for the real home maker"; along with "the men who have already obtained control of great areas of the public land . . . who object . . . because it will break the control that these few big men now have over the lands which they do not actually own." Ibid. Whatever the opposition's source, bills reflecting Powell's approach did not become law until 1934.

By the 1930's, opposition to federal regulation of the federal range had significantly diminished. Population growth, forage competition, and inadequate range control all began to have consequences both serious and apparent. With a horrifying drought came dawns without day as dust storms swept the range. The devastating storms of the Dust Bowl were in the words of one Senator "the most tragic, the most impressive lobbyist, that ha[s] ever come to this Capitol." 79 Cong. Rec. 6013 (1935). Congress acted; and on June 28, 1934, President Franklin Roosevelt signed the Taylor Grazing Act into law.

B

The Taylor Act seeks to "promote the highest use of the public lands." 43 U.S.C. § 315. Its specific goals are to "stop injury" to the lands from "overgrazing and soil deterioration," to "provide for their use, improvement and development," and "to stabilize the livestock industry dependent on the public range." 48 Stat. 1269. The Act grants the Secretary of the Interior authority to divide the public range lands into grazing districts, to specify the amount of grazing permitted in each district, to issue leases or permits "to graze livestock," and to charge "reasonable fees" for use of the land. 43 U.S.C. §§ 315, 315a, 315b. It specifies that preference in respect to grazing permits "shall be given . . . to those within or near" a grazing district "who are landowners engaged in the livestock business, bona fide occupants or settlers, or owners of water or water rights." § 315b. And, as particularly relevant here, it adds:

"So far as consistent with the purposes and provisions of this subchapter, grazing privileges recognized and acknowledged shall be adequately safeguarded, but the creation of a grazing district or the issuance of a permit . . . shall not create any right, title, interest, or estate in or to the lands." Ibid.

C

The Taylor Act delegated to the Interior Department an enormous administrative task. To administer the Act, the Department needed to determine the bounds of the public range, create grazing districts, determine their grazing capacity, and divide that capacity among applicants. It soon set bounds encompassing more than 140 million acres, and by 1936 the Department had created 37 grazing districts. The Secretary then created district advisory boards made up of local ranchers and called on them for further help. Limited department resources and the enormity of the administrative task made the boards the effective governing and administrative body of each grazing district.

By 1937 the Department had set the basic rules for allocation of grazing privileges. Those rules recognized that many ranchers had long maintained herds on their own private lands during part of the year, while allowing their herds to graze farther afield on public land at other times. The rules consequently gave a first preference to owners of stock who also owned "base property," i.e., private land (or water rights) sufficient to support their herds, and who had grazed the public range during the five years just prior to the Taylor act's enactment. They gave a second preference to other owners of nearby "base" property lacking prior use. Ibid. And they gave a third preference to stock owners without base property, like the nomadic sheep herder. Ibid. Since lower preference categories divided capacity left over after satisfaction of all higher preference claims, this system, in effect, awarded grazing privileges to owners of land or water.

As grazing allocations were determined, the Department would issue a permit measuring grazing privileges in terms of "animal unit months" (AUMs), i.e., the right to obtain the forage needed to sustain one cow (or five sheep) for one month. Permits were valid for up to 10 years and usually renewed, as suggested by the Act. See 43 U.S.C. § 315b; Public Land Law Review Commission, One Third of the Nation's Land 109 (1970). But the conditions placed on permits reflected the leasehold nature of grazing privileges; consistent with the fact that Congress had made the Secretary the landlord of the public range and basically made the grant of grazing privileges discretionary. The grazing regulations in effect from 1938 to the present day made clear that the Department retained the power to modify, fail to renew, or cancel a permit or lease for various reasons.

First, the Secretary could cancel permits if, for example, the permit holder persistently overgrazed the public lands, lost control of the base property, failed to use the permit, or failed to comply with the Range Code. Second, the Secretary, consistent first with 43 U.S.C. § 315f, and later the land use planning mandated by 43 U.S.C. § 1712, was authorized to reclassify and withdraw land from grazing altogether and devote it to a more valuable or suitable use. Third, in the event of range depletion, the Secretary maintained a separate authority, not to take areas of land out of grazing use altogether as above, but to reduce the amount of grazing allowed on that land, by suspending AUMs of grazing privileges "in whole or in part," and "for such time as necessary."

Indeed, the Department so often reduced individual permit AUM allocations under this last authority that by 1964 the regulations had introduced the notion of "active AUMs," i.e., the AUMs that a permit initially granted minus the AUMs that the department had "suspended" due to diminished range capacity. Thus, three ranchers who had initially received, say, 3,000, 2,000, and 1,000 AUMs respectively, might find that they could use only two-thirds of that number because a 33% reduction in the district's grazing capacity had led the Department to "suspend" one-third of each allocation. The "active/suspended" system assured each rancher, however, that any capacity-related reduction would take place proportionately among permit holders, see 43 CFR § 4111.4-2(a)(3) (1964), and that the Department would try to restore grazing privileges proportionately should the district's capacity later increase, see § 4111.4–1.

In practice, active grazing on the public range declined dramatically and steadily (from about 18 million to about 10 million AUMs between 1953 and 1998)... Despite the reductions in grazing, and some improvements following the passage of the Taylor act, the range remained in what many considered an unsatisfactory condition. In 1962, a congressionally mandated survey found only 16.6% of the range in excellent or good condition, 53.1% in fair condition, and 30.3% in poor condition. Department of Interior Ann. Rep. 62 (1962). And in 1978 Congress itself determined that "vast segments of the public rangelands are . . . in an unsatisfactory condition." 92 Stat. 1803 (codified as 43 U.S.C. § 1901(a)(1)).

D

In the 1960's, as the range failed to recover, the Secretary of the Interior increased grazing fees by more than 50% (from 19 cents to 30 cents per AUM/year), thereby helping to capture a little more of the economic costs that grazing imposed upon the land. And in 1976, Congress enacted a new law, the Federal Land Policy and Management Act of 1976 (FLPMA), 90 Stat. 2744, 43 U.S.C. § 1701 et seq., which instructed the Interior Department to develop districtwide land use plans based upon concepts of "multiple use" (use for various purposes, such as recreation, range, timber, minerals, watershed, wildlife and fish, and natural and scenic, scientific, and historical usage), § 1702(c), and "sustained yield" (regular renewable resource output maintained in perpetuity), § 1702(h). The FLPMA strengthened the Department's existing authority to remove or add land from grazing use, allowing such modification pursuant to a land use plan, §§ 1712, 1714, while specifying that existing grazing permit holders would retain a "first priority" for renewal so long as the land use plan continued to make land "available for domestic livestock grazing." § 1752(c).

In 1978, the Department's grazing regulations were, in turn, substantially amended to comply with the new law. See 43 Fed. Reg. 29067. As relevant here, the 1978 regulations tied permit renewal and validity to the land use planning process, giving the Secretary the power to cancel, suspend, or modify grazing permits due to increases or decreases in grazing forage or acreage made available pursuant to land planning.

That same year Congress again increased grazing fees for the period 1979 to 1986. See Public Rangelands Improvement Act of 1978, 43 U.S.C. § 1905. However neither of the two Acts from the 1970's significantly modified the particular provisions of the Taylor Act at issue in this case.

NOTES & QUESTIONS

1. What led to the emergence of the property rights culture in BLM grazing administration? The short answer is that it grew from the early decision to link grazing preferences to tracts of land through the "base property" concept. Preferences for grazing privileges, expressed as Animal Unit Months (AUMs), fluctuated according to BLM's decisions about the impact of total grazing on the relevant rangeland unit, but did so proportionately among all affected ranchers and without ever having the so-called "suspended AUMs" expire. Ranchers, over time, began treating their preferences, including suspended AUMs, as one of the sticks in their bundle of property rights associated with their base property. As one of the leading experts on grazing law explains, "preference for grazing privileges, then, was given to lands and not people. Because the preference right virtually guaranteed perpetual renewal of the 10-year grazing permits, the permits came to be treated by the market as appurtenances to base properties, with the market price of the base property, and its assessed value for mortgage purposes, reflecting the value of the permit." Joseph M. Feller, *Back to the Present: The Supreme Court Refuses to Move Public Range Law Backward, But Will the BLM Move Public Range Law Forward?*, 31 ENVTL. L. REP. (ENVTL. L. INST.) 10021 (2001). As we shall see in the remaining materials, however, the property rights status of the grazing preferences was far less stable than many ranching interests believed.

2. If ranchers using public rangelands don't have a property interest in their grazing preferences, what *do* they own, other than their livestock and private ranch holdings? That question was central in an arduously long litigation brought by ranching interests in Nye County, Nevada, whose grazing permits BLM had suspended and cancelled. They argued that the BLM's actions took several property interests without just compensation as required by the Fifth Amendment to the U.S. Constitution. In its final opinion in the case, the Court of Federal Claims explained that ranchers: (1) have no property interest under state or federal law in the surface estate of the federal lands on which their grazing allotments applied, and thus suffered no taking in that respect as a result of the reduced grazing allotments, but (2) do have vested rights in certain water rights and rights of way that were perfected according to state and federal law, and thus could suffer takings of those interests as a result of BLM's actions. *See* Hage v. United States, 51 Fed.Cl. 570 (2002). Since then, however, the Federal Circuit has held that water rights carry with them no protected interest in grazing, and thus BLM's denial of grazing privileges also does not take any vested water rights. *See* Colvin Cattle Co., Inc. v. United States, 468 F.3d 803 (Fed. Cir. 2006).

3. Much like the history of national forest law discussed in Chapter 8, federal rangeland law evolved through three major statutes representing three phases of development. First, BLM's organic statute, the Taylor Grazing Act (TGA), provided the basic authority for BLM to administer grazing privileges, with some attention to environmental impact. Next, the Federal Lands Planning and Management Act (FLPMA) emphasized BLM's multiple-use mandate and overlaid a more sophisticated planning regime on BLM's administration of grazing. Finally, the Public Rangelands Improvement Act (PRIA) tweaked the system toward a greater focus on economic and ecological factors. For more extensive histories of these three primary BLM laws and related legal developments, see George Cameron Coggins & Margaret Lindeberg-Johnson, *The Law of Public Rangeland management II: The Commons and the Taylor Act*, 13 ENVTL. L. 1 (1982); George Cameron Coggins, *The Law of Public Rangeland Management IV: FLPMA, PRIA, and the Multiple Use Mandate*, 14 ENVTL. L. 1 (1983).

2. CURRENT SCENE

The controversy in *Public Lands Council v. Babbitt* was over the effect Rangeland Reform regulations the Bureau of Land Management (BLM) adopted in 1995 would have on BLM's public grazing preferences allocation system by altering the historically entrenched "property" status of the privileges. Elsewhere in the new Rangeland Reform rules, BLM also changed its criteria for adjusting the quantity of allotments based on newly-formulated ecological factors. Known as the Fundamentals of Rangeland Health regulations, these criteria laid out a new ecosystem management focus and made subtle but nonetheless potentially far-reaching changes to the way BLM allocates grazing rights. In its preamble to the final adoption of the 1995 rules, BLM provided its take on the ecological condition of the rangelands and its justification of both the need and authority for legal reform directed at improving those conditions.

Department of the Interior, Bureau of Land Management, *Department Hearings and Appeals Procedures; Cooperative Relations; Grazing Administration—Exclusive of Alaska*

Bureau of Land Management, 1995.
60 Federal Register 9894.

SUMMARY: This final rule amends the regulations that govern how the Secretary of the Interior, through the Bureau of Land Management (BLM), administers livestock grazing. This rule applies to all lands on which BLM administers livestock grazing. This rule also amends the Department of the Interior's appeals regulations pertaining to livestock grazing to provide consistency with administrative remedies provided for in the grazing regulations, increases public participation in the management of the public grazing lands, and amends the regulations on cooperative relations to reflect changes in the organization of certain advisory committees. The changes will improve the management of the Nation's public rangeland resources.

Numerous comments addressed the overall rulemaking. These comments asserted several central themes which crosscut different sections of the rulemaking. Accordingly, BLM has decided to address these central issues in this portion of the preamble. Within the context of such discussion, particular sections of the proposed and final rules will be referred to as necessary. Nevertheless, in these responses, BLM focuses upon central issues that were of concern to commenters throughout the proposal.

Some commenters took the position that general rangeland improvement is unnecessary. Their view was that current legislation, regulations, and procedures provide enough latitude and capability for the government to administer the public rangelands properly, therefore there is no justification for designing and implementing the rangeland improvement program. They stated that the initiative should be dropped or abandoned immediately. They asserted that the government has not shown that the proposal will benefit the western range and many of the elements of the rule are more appropriately dealt with in manuals, instruction memos, and policy guidance.

In addition, the comment was often made that the National Research Council study commissioned by the National Academy of Sciences reports that the conditions of rangeland health in the West are largely unknown. If the conditions are unknown, stated the commenters, it is impossible to demonstrate a need for the proposed rule. Some commenters stated that the entire proposal and EIS were politically driven and did not relate to the resource protection issues of public land administration.

The Department believes that there is a need for changes in public rangeland grazing administration. The Department has been collecting data on the condition of the rangelands for over 60 years. The Department does have considerable information on all BLM lands, based on these years of data collection, although the same level of detailed knowledge may not be available on every allotment. The information available is sufficient to identify trends in rangeland health across the western rangelands.

The status and trends of the western rangelands upon passage of the Public Rangelands Improvement Act (PRIA) in 1978 indicated that western rangelands were producing below their potential and that rangelands would remain in unsatisfactory condition or decline further unless the unsatisfactory conditions could be addressed and corrected by intensive public rangelands maintenance, management and improvement. Congress articulated its view in PRIA that such unsatisfactory conditions on public rangeland present a risk for soil loss, siltation, desertification, water loss, loss of wildlife and fish habitat, loss of forage for livestock and other grazing animals, degradation of water quality, flood danger, and threats to local economies. In addition, BLM National Public Lands Advisory Council recommended in 1992 that "* * * foremost consideration needs to be given to protecting the basic components of soil, water and vegetation. Without assurances for the future well-being of these basic natural resources, there is little to squabble about."

BLM's research has concluded that in the long term under current management practices 22 million acres of BLM uplands would be functioning but susceptible to degradation, and about 20 million acres would be nonfunctioning. The vegetation in some areas would change because of overgrazing, fire, or drought. Conditions would be worse in riparian and wetland areas. The overall trends would be a slow, steady, long-term decline in conditions. Approximately 466,000 acres of riparian areas (43 percent of the total) on BLM land would be functioning but susceptible to degradation, and 219,000 acres (21 percent) would be nonfunctioning. . . These studies show that without some changes in the current program conditions in critical riparian areas would continue to decline.

Some commenters asserted that rangeland improvement is unnecessary because it will not improve the condition of the public rangelands. The Department disagrees. Commenters argued that few permittees or lessees are poor stewards of the public rangelands. They stated that the program will alienate many conscientious ranchers. The commenters asserted that the agencies and public may lose the service and support of these users in maintaining and improving the conditions of the public rangelands, and that rangeland conditions are likely to degrade. Therefore, they claimed, the initiative should be abandoned. However, the Department believes that improving administration of public rangelands will improve their condition, which will benefit all uses, including livestock grazing. . .

The standards and guidelines in the final rule are aimed at improving the ecological health of the rangelands. . . The Department recognizes that the majority of public land grazing permittees and lessees are conscientious stewards. However, it also notes that line managers need clear authority and guidance to help correct problems in grazing use and to improve the degraded condition of some areas expeditiously. This program is intended to facilitate cooperation between BLM employees and public land users in making those improvements. Also, by making BLM and Forest Service management more similar, it will be easier for permittees and lessees to comply with land use requirements. Good stewards will not be adversely affected by this initiative and will have an opportunity to work with the Department to sustain the economic vigor of their industry while maintaining or improving the ecological health of the public lands. The Department recognizes that it is in the best interests of the users, the public, and BLM to cooperate in meeting these objectives.

A number of comments questioned whether the proposed amendments to the grazing rule conflict directly with TGA, FLPMA, PRIA and other related Federal laws. The BLM's main statutory authorities for regulating grazing on the public lands are TGA, FLPMA and PRIA. In TGA Congress directed the Secretary to bring order to the management of the public rangelands and improve range conditions.

Specifically, Section 2 of TGA provides:

The Secretary of the Interior shall make provision for the protection, administration, regulation, and improvement of such grazing districts * * * and he shall make such rules and regulations * * * and do any and all things necessary to accomplish the purposes of this Act * * * namely to regulate their occupancy and use, to preserve the land and its resources from destruction or unnecessary injury, to provide for the orderly use, improvement, and development of the range.

The TGA authorizes the Secretary to, among other things, establish fees, issue permits and leases and prescribe terms and conditions for them, issue range improvement permits, and provide for local hearings on appeals. The emphasis on disposal of Federal lands changed with the Classification and Multiple Use Act in 1964 and FLPMA in 1976. In FLPMA Congress articulated the national policy that "the public lands be retained in Federal ownership." 43 U.S.C. § 1701. FLPMA also directs that land management be on the basis of multiple use and sustained yield, thus clarifying that other uses of public lands are equally appropriate. FLPMA did not repeal TGA, but did provide additional management direction. For example, section 402 of FLPMA provides that grazing permits and leases shall be:

> [S]ubject to such terms and conditions the Secretary concerned deems appropriate and consistent with the governing law, including, but not limited to the authority of the Secretary concerned to cancel, suspend, or modify a grazing permit or lease for any violation of a grazing regulation or of any term or condition of such grazing permit or lease.

In 1978 Congress again focused on the public rangelands when it passed PRIA. In Section 2 of that Act Congress found that "vast segments" of the public rangelands were "producing less than their potential for livestock, wildlife habitat, recreation, forage and water and soil conservation benefits," and so were considered to be in an unsatisfactory condition. Congress went on in Section 2 to reaffirm a national commitment to "manage, maintain and improve the condition of the public rangelands so that they become as productive as feasible for all rangeland values." The Department has concluded that the amendments to the grazing rule are within the statutory authority granted by Congress to the Secretary to administer the public lands under TGA, FLPMA, PRIA, and related acts.

NOTES & QUESTIONS

1. BLM unequivocally stated that the Fundamentals of Rangeland Health and their associated standards and guidelines set forth in the 1995 final rule were aimed at improving the *ecological health* of the rangelands. Before delving further into what BLM thinks ecological health entails, are you convinced from BLM's description of the state of the rangelands that they were ecologically unhealthy? Based on its account of history, did the Supreme Court in *Public Lands Council v. Babbitt* seem convinced?

2. BLM described the majority of ranching interests using BLM lands as "conscientious stewards" and notes that "good stewards will not be adversely affected by this initiative." But if they majority of the ranchers are good stewards, why the need for rules to improve the ecological health of the rangelands?

3. As it did for other public land agency rules adopted in the Clinton Administration, the George W. Bush Administration signaled its intent comprehensively to revisit BLM's 1995 rule. In March 2003, BLM issued a request for public comment on the 1995 rule in connection with an advance notice of proposed rulemaking. *See* 68 Fed. Reg. 9964 (Mar. 3, 2003). The notice suggested that BLM would consider virtually all substantive features of the 1995 rule as open for review. BLM conducted public meetings on the 1995 rule and requested input on the open-ended objective of how to "encourage partnerships in public land stewardship and establish new options for BLM and rangeland users in the administration and management of public lands." BLM accepted public comments through May 2, 2003, and published a proposed rule on December 8, 2003. *See* 68 Fed. Reg. 68452 (Dec. 8, 2003). As discussed later in this Chapter, however, the effort to unwind what the Clinton Administration had done ultimately failed in the courts.

4. The BLM is responsible for managing 264 million acres of land—about one-eighth of the land in the United States—and about 300 million additional acres of subsurface mineral resources. The agency is also responsible for wildfire management and suppression on 388 million acres. Most of the lands the BLM manages are located in the western United States, including Alaska, and are dominated by extensive grasslands, forests, high mountains, arctic tundra, and deserts. The BLM manages a wide variety of resources and uses, including energy and minerals; timber; forage; wild horse and burro populations; fish and wildlife habitat; wilderness areas; archaeological, paleontological, and historical sites; and other natural heritage values.

Public Lands Managed by the Bureau of Land Management (BLM)

The BLM's roots go back to the Land Ordinance of 1785 and the Northwest Ordinance of 1787. These laws provided for the survey and settlement of the lands that the original 13 colonies ceded to the Federal government after the War of Independence. As additional lands were acquired by the United States from Spain, France, and other countries, Congress directed that they be explored, surveyed, and made available for settlement. In 1812, Congress established the General Land Office in the Department of the Treasury to oversee the disposition of these Federal lands. As the 19th century progressed and the Nation's land base expanded further west, Congress encouraged the settlement of the land by enacting a wide variety of laws, including the Homesteading Laws and the Mining Law of 1872. These statutes served one of the major policy goals of the young country—settlement of the Western territories. With the exception of the Mining Law of 1872 and the Desert Land Act of 1877 (which was amended), all have since been repealed or superseded by other statutes.

The late 19th century marked a shift in Federal land management priorities with the creation of the first national parks, forests, and wildlife refuges. By withdrawing these lands from settlement, Congress signaled a shift in the policy goals served by the public lands. Instead of using them to promote settlement, Congress decided that they should be retained in public ownership because of their other resource values.

In the early 20th century, Congress directed the Executive Branch to manage activities on the remaining public lands—the lands now known as BLM Lands—not already devoted to a specific purpose such as park or refuge. The Mineral Leasing Act of 1920 allowed leasing, exploration, and production of selected commodities such as coal, oil, gas, and sodium to take place on these public lands. The Taylor Grazing Act of 1934 established the U.S. Grazing Service to manage grazing on the public rangelands. In 1946, the Grazing Service was merged with the General Land Office to form the Bureau of Land Management within the Department of the Interior. When the BLM was initially created, there were over 2,000 unrelated and often conflicting laws for managing the public lands. The BLM had no unified legislative mandate until Congress enacted the Federal Land Policy and Management Act of 1976 (FLPMA). As noted in *Public Lands Council v. Babbitt*, FLPMA declared that the lands known today as the BLM lands would remain in public ownership and directed the agency to implement "multiple use" management, defined as "management of the public lands and their various resource values so that they are utilized in the combination that will best meet the present and future needs of the American people." 43 U.S.C. § 1702(c). For what is unquestionably the most comprehensive history of the BLM itself, see JAMIE SKILLEN, THE NATION'S LARGEST LANDOWNER: THE BUREAU OF LAND MANAGEMENT IN THE AMERICAN WEST (2009).

5. Maybe the problem is not the ranchers, but BLM, or, more specifically, public lands operated under a multiple-use mandate. Wouldn't the "health" of the public rangelands be most improved if they were sold to the highest bidder? It is unlikely that a private rancher would degrade lands he or she owns by overgrazing. And if the highest bidder were a land conservation trust, it would hardly need BLM to help it manage the land for grassland values. The lands least suited to grazing or grassland conservation may go to recreational, mining, or urban uses. So what? How, as a matter of national policy that "best meet[s] the present and future needs of the American people," is it preferable to have BLM manage these lands, given that it has done so in a manner that, by its own description, is *neither* economically efficient *nor* ecologically sound? For contrasting views on this topic, *compare* Charles H. Callison, *The Fallacies of Privatization*, 25 ENVIRONMENT 18 (Oct. 1983), *with* John Baden and Laura Rosen, *The Environmental Justification*, 25 ENVIRONMENT 7 (Oct. 1983), and Delores T. Martin, *Divestiture and the Creation of Property Rights in Public Lands: A Comment*, 2 CATO JOURNAL 687 (1992).

6. BLM also administers lands Congress has designated as National Conservation Areas. Ten such NCAs exist, covering a total of about 3 million acres, each with its own designation legislation and set of prescribed purposes and allowed uses. In most cases Congress has stated conservation purposes for the NCAs.

But while some NCAs allow only uses that will further the primary purposes for which the NCA is established, others specifically allow uses such as motorized vehicles, hunting, and even grazing. BLM has not adopted a uniform set of management procedures or standards for NCAs. *See* Andy Kerr & Mark Salvo, *Bureau of Land Management National Conservation Areas: Legitimate Conservation or Satan's Spawn?*, 20 J. ENVTL. L. 67 (2002).

7. BLM is also responsible for administering about 700 million acres of subsurface mineral rights perfected on federal public lands pursuant to the General Mining Law of 1872. *See* 30 U.S.C. §§ 22–47. The Mining Law grants free access to individuals and companies to prospect for mineral on these lands and to stake claims upon discovery of a deposit. A claim gives the holder the right to develop the minerals and may be "patented" for nominal fees ($2.50 to $5.00 per acre) to convey full title to the surface and mineral rights. This system has been roundly criticized by environmental conservation groups as lacking environmental and fiscal rationale, and has been vocally supported by the mining industry as supporting the development of an economically important resource. BLM's administration of Mining Law claims on BLM lands, including for environmental protection purposes, is carried out under the Federal Land Policy and Management Act of 1976, 43 U.S.C. §§ 1701 et seq., which BLM implements pursuant to regulations found at 43 C.F.R. subpart 3809, known as the "3809 regulations."

8. As with the other ecosystem types covered the chapters in Part III of the text, grassland ecosystem management, particularly on federal public lands, has become a battleground for the Endangered Species Act. In particular, climate change and renewable energy policies have focused attention on the impacts of using grasslands for large-scale solar power generation. We cover this policy debate in Chapter 19.

C. BIODIVERSITY MANAGEMENT IN GRASSLAND ECOSYSTEMS

As the preceding materials suggest, by far the most influential force in national grassland management policy is the Department of Interior's Bureau of Land Management (BLM). To a far lesser extent the U.S. Forest Service, through the 10 million-acre National Grasslands program, and the U.S. Fish and Wildlife Service, through its management of the National Wildlife Refuge System, also have a hand in grassland management policy. And the substantial amount of private lands in the Great Plains used largely for irrigated agriculture presents another opportunity for development of national, state, and local grassland management policy. The following materials provide background on each of those fronts of grassland ecosystem management.

1. BLM'S RANGELAND MANAGEMENT POLICIES

a. THE FUNDAMENTALS OF RANGELAND HEALTH

We now come to the substantive provisions of the Rangeland Reform rules BLM adopted in 1995 that triggered *Public Lands Council v. Babbitt* and which represented BLM's turn toward ecosystem management. Recall that we have traced the development of two themes in BLM grazing policy: (1) describing the status of grazing preferences as property rights or personal privileges; and (2) the regulation of grazing allotments pursuant to ecological factors. The materials in this section bring closure to the history of those two themes (at least for the time being), first through the BLM's description of its ecosystem management criteria, and then through the Supreme Court's endorsement of BLM's new way of describing grazing preferences.

In its Fundamentals of Rangeland Health and Standards and Guidelines for Grazing Administration, BLM took explicit steps toward use of ecosystem management principles in the determination of range grazing levels. The rules established nationally uniform "fundamentals" and then require the adoption by field offices of the agency of state and local "standards and guidelines" consistent with the national criteria. BLM's field level decisions, moreover, are to be made in consultation with Resource Advisory Councils (RACs) composed of people representing a variety of interests, including grazing interests, environmental interests, and state and local political interests.

Department of the Interior, Bureau of Land Management, *Department Hearings and Appeals Procedures; Cooperative Relations; Grazing Administration—Exclusive of Alaska*

Bureau of Land Management, 1995.
60 Federal Register 9894.

Subpart 4180—Fundamentals of Rangeland Health and Standards and Guidelines for Grazing Administration

Section 4180.1, The fundamentals of rangeland health (titled National Requirements for Grazing Administration in the proposed rule) for grazing administration, are added to establish fundamental requirements for achieving functional, healthy public rangelands. These fundamentals address the necessary physical components of functional watersheds, ecological processes required for healthy biotic communities, water quality standards, and habitat for threatened or endangered species or other species of special interest.

Where it is determined that existing grazing management needs to be modified to ensure that the conditions of healthy rangelands set forth in § 4180.1, Fundamentals of rangeland health, are met or significant progress is being made to meet the fundamentals, the authorized officer must take appropriate action as soon as practical, but not later than the start of the next grazing season. This may include actions such as reducing livestock stocking rates, adjusting the season or duration of livestock use, or modifying or relocating range improvements.

Section 4180.2, Standards and guidelines for grazing administration, is added to direct that standards and guidelines will be developed for an entire State or for an area encompassing portions of more than one State, except where the geophysical or vegetal character of an area is unique and the health of the rangelands will not be ensured by using standards and guidelines developed for a larger geographical area. The geographical area covered will be determined by BLM State Directors in consultation with affected RACs. Once standards and guidelines are in effect, the authorized officer shall take appropriate action as soon as practical, but not later than the start of the next grazing year upon determining that existing grazing management practices are significant factors in failing to ensure significant progress toward the fulfillment of the standards and toward conformance with the guidelines. The preparation of standards and guidelines will involve public participation and consultation with RACs, Indian tribes, and Federal agencies responsible for the management of lands within the affected area.

Section 4180.2(d) lists factors that, at a minimum, must be addressed in the development of State or regional standards. The guiding principles for the development of standards pertain to the factors needed to help achieve rangeland health. More specifically, the factors relate to watershed function, threatened or endangered species and candidate species, habitat for native plant and animal populations, water quality and the distribution of nutrients and energy flow. Section 4180.2(e) lists guiding principles to be addressed in the development of guidelines.

Subpart 4180—Fundamentals of Rangeland Health and Standards and Guidelines for Grazing Administration

§ 4180.1 Fundamentals of rangeland health.

The authorized officer shall take appropriate action under subparts 4110, 4120, 4130, and 4160 of this part as soon as practicable but not later than the start of the next grazing year upon determining that existing grazing management needs to be modified to ensure that the following conditions exist.

(a) Watersheds are in, or are making significant progress toward, properly functioning physical condition, including their upland, riparian-wetland, and aquatic components; soil and plant conditions support infiltration, soil moisture storage, and the release of water that are in balance with climate and landform and maintain or improve water quality, water quantity, and timing and duration of flow.

(b) Ecological processes, including the hydrologic cycle, nutrient cycle, and energy flow, are maintained, or there is significant progress toward their attainment, in order to support healthy biotic populations and communities.

(c) Water quality complies with State water quality standards and achieves, or is making significant progress toward achieving, established BLM management objectives such as meeting wildlife needs.

(d) Habitats are, or are making significant progress toward being, restored or maintained for Federal threatened and endangered species, Federal Proposed, Category 1 and 2 Federal candidate and other special status species.

§ 4180.2 Standards and guidelines for grazing administration.

(a) The Bureau of Land Management State Director, in consultation with the affected resource advisory councils where they exist, will identify the geographical area for which standards and guidelines are developed. Standards and guidelines will be developed for an entire state, or an area encompassing portions of more than 1 state, unless the Bureau of Land Management State Director, in consultation with the resource advisory councils, determines that the characteristics of an area are unique, and the rangelands within the area could not be adequately protected using standards and guidelines developed on a broader geographical scale.

(b) The Bureau of Land Management State Director, in consultation with affected Bureau of Land Management resource advisory councils, shall develop and amend State or regional standards and guidelines. The Bureau of Land Management State Director will also coordinate with Indian tribes, other State and Federal land management agencies responsible for the management of lands and resources within the region or area under consideration, and the public in the development of State or regional standards and guidelines.

(c) The authorized officer shall take appropriate action as soon as practicable but not later than the start of the next grazing year upon determining that existing grazing management practices or levels of grazing use on public lands are significant factors in failing to achieve the standards and conform with the guidelines that are made effective under this section. . .

(d) At a minimum, State or regional standards developed under paragraphs

(a) and (b) of this section must address the following:

(1) Watershed function;

(2) Nutrient cycling and energy flow;

(3) Water quality;

(4) Habitat for endangered, threatened, proposed, Candidate 1 or 2, or special status species; and

(5) Habitat quality for native plant and animal populations and communities.

(e) At a minimum, State or regional guidelines developed under paragraphs

(a) and (b) of this section must address the following:

(1) Maintaining or promoting adequate amounts of vegetative ground cover, including standing plant material and litter, to support infiltration, maintain soil moisture storage, and stabilize soils;

(2) Maintaining or promoting subsurface soil conditions that support permeability rates appropriate to climate and soils;

(3) Maintaining, improving or restoring riparian-wetland functions including energy dissipation, sediment capture, groundwater recharge, and stream bank stability;

(4) Maintaining or promoting stream channel morphology (e.g., gradient, width/depth ratio, channel roughness and sinuosity) and functions appropriate to climate and landform;

(5) Maintaining or promoting the appropriate kinds and amounts of soil organisms, plants and animals to support the hydrologic cycle, nutrient cycle, and energy flow;

(6) Promoting the opportunity for seedling establishment of appropriate plant species when climatic conditions and space allow;

(7) Maintaining, restoring or enhancing water quality to meet management objectives, such as meeting wildlife needs;

(8) Restoring, maintaining or enhancing habitats to assist in the recovery of Federal threatened and endangered species;

(9) Restoring, maintaining or enhancing habitats of Federal Proposed, Category 1 and 2 Federal candidate, and other special status species to promote their conservation;

(10) Maintaining or promoting the physical and biological conditions to sustain native populations and communities;

(11) Emphasizing native species in the support of ecological function; and

(12) Incorporating the use of non-native plant species only in those situations in which native species are not available in sufficient quantities or are incapable of maintaining or achieving properly functioning conditions and biological health.

NOTES & QUESTIONS

1. Consider the 12 criteria the state and regional guidelines must address under section 4180.2(e) of BLM's rule. Compare them to Grumbine's list of ingredients in his 1994 description of ecosystem management, *What Is Ecosystem Management?*, reproduced in Chapter 7. Does BLM's list seem complete? Does it seem reasonable to expect the BLM to be able to satisfy the criteria throughout its public land domain?

2. The obvious implication of BLM's rule is that ecological criteria will be used to determine grazing levels. As a leading grazing law expert explains, ranchers thus feared "that the BLM, acting in response to concerns raised by environ-mentalists or other public land users, will use its land planning process to sub-stantially reduce authorized grazing levels, and possibly eliminate grazing al-together in some areas, in order to favor competing interests such as preserva-tion and improvement of wildlife habitat, enhancement of recreational oppor-tunities, or protection of the natural character of wilderness areas." Joseph M. Feller, *Back to the Present: The Supreme Court Refuses to Move Public Range Law Backward, But Will the BLM Move Public Range Law Forward?*, 31 ENVTL. L. REP. (Envtl. L. Inst.) 10021 (2001). Do you think the BLM's rules could support such an effort? Will they *necessarily* lead to such a result? How much discretion does BLM retain under the new rules?

3. To evaluate the effect of the Fundamentals of Rangeland Health rule in terms of its potential to change grazing allotment decision outcomes, fill in the following chart. The chart uses the three components of ecosystem manage-ment policy articulated in Chapter 7 as a way of identifying differences in ap-proach between the pre-and post-rule policies. Use the two excerpts from *Public Lands Council v. Babbitt* to guide your description of BLM's "before 1995 rule" policy approaches.

	Metrics	**Goals**	**Methods**
Before 1995 rule			
After 1995 rule			

4. Are you convinced that BLM has the legal authority under the three relevant statutes to manage the rangelands based on improving their ecological health?

5. Before adopting its 1995 rule, BLM had issued two policy statements that pointed clearly in the direction of an ecological health focus. First, in 1994 the agency published *Ecosystem Management in the BLM: From Concept to Com-mitment*, wherein it defined nine operating principles of ecosystem manage-ment. Two of the nine principles included "sustain the productivity and diversi-ty of ecological systems" and "minimize or repair impacts to the land." The agency also advocated using the adaptive management methods described in Chapter 7. Later that year, the agency released its *Blueprint for the Future*, in which it stated its policy focus would include "becoming more aware of the sta-tus, trend, and overall health of the land." These precursors to the 1995 rule laid the groundwork for the ecological health focus of the rule. *See also* Michael P. Dombeck, *Thinking Like a Mountain: BLM's Approach to Ecosystem Man-agement*, 6 ECOLOGICAL APPLICATIONS 699 (1996) (Director of BLM).

6. Some commenters asserted that various sections of BLM's proposed rule, which was substantially the same as the final rule, raised the possibility of a "taking" of private property rights without "just compensation" as required by the Fifth Amendment. BLM pointed out that, as a threshold matter, the United States Constitution gives Congress the "Power to dispose of and make all need-ful Rules and Regulations respecting the Territory or other Property belonging to the United States." Article IV, § 3, cl. 2. This power includes authority to control the use and occupancy of Federal lands, to protect them from trespass and injury and to prescribe the conditions upon which others may obtain rights in them. *See* Utah Power & Light Co. v. United States, 243 U.S. 389, 405 (1917). BLM also pointed to the series of laws through which Congress has delegated primary responsibility and authority to manage livestock grazing on public lands to the Secretary, acting through BLM. The basic laws, again, are the Taylor Grazing Act, Federal Land Planning and Management Act, and the Public Rangelands Improvement Act. As BLM explained:

> In authorizing the issuance of grazing permits in TGA, Congress expressly provided that the "issuance of a permit * * * shall not create any right, title, interest, or estate in or to the [public] lands." 43 U.S.C. § 315b. In FLPMA, Congress authorized the Secretary to "cancel, suspend, or modify a grazing permit or lease, in whole or in part, pursuant to the terms and conditions" of the permit or lease. 43 U.S.C. § 1752(a). The same section also authorizes the Secretary to "cancel or suspend a grazing permit or lease for any violation of a grazing rule or of any term or condition of such permit or lease." These statutes are implemented by BLM's regulations at 43 CFR Part 4100 et seq., including the amendments adopted here.

> The Fifth Amendment to the United States Constitution provides in relevant part that no person shall be denied property without due process of law, and no private property shall be taken for public use, without just compensation. This Amendment protects private property. Because Congress made clear in TGA that grazing permits create no private property interest in public lands, the Fifth Amendment's protection is not implicated. The Courts have long held that no taking of private property occurs in the course of lawful administration and regulation of Federal grazing lands because the grazing permit represents a benefit or privilege bestowed by the Federal government upon a private individual and not a compensable property interest under the Fifth Amendment.

> Thus, an authorized officer's decision to change permitted use (§ 4110.3), decrease permitted use (§ 4110.3–2), implement a reduction in permitted use (§ 4110.3–3), decrease land acreage (§ 4110.4–2), approve an AMP (§ 4120.2), or approve a cooperative range improvement agreement (§ 4120.3–2) does not give rise to a takings claim.

> Some commenters asserted that permittees and lessees should be compensated for any indirect adverse impact that cancellation, nonrenewal, suspension or modification of grazing permits might have on the permittee's base property. While base property is private property protected by the Fifth Amendment, the United States Supreme Court, in an opinion by Chief Justice Rehnquist, specifically considered and rejected the argument that the increment of value added to a private ranch by a public land grazing permit is a compensable property interest, United States v. Fuller, 409 U.S. 488 (1973).

> Even if, in other words, cancellation, nonrenewal, suspension, or changes in the terms and conditions of a grazing permit might have some negative effect on the value of the base property, the Supreme Court has made clear this is not a "taking."

Does this resolve the matter to your satisfaction?

7. Why allow *any* grazing of cattle and sheep in public lands that were formerly grasslands? Many people are surprised to learn that, while grazing is authorized on most of the western lands under BLM's jurisdiction, (1) the livestock produced from those lands accounts for a small fraction of the nation's beef supply; (2) the direct and indirect ranching economies associated with public land grazing, including down to the coffee shops where the ranchers meet, is insignificant to the national economy; and (3) revenues from the grazing fees BLM charges fail to cover even the agency's costs of administration. *See* THOMAS M. POWER, LOST LANDSCAPES AND FAILED ECONOMIES (1996); U.S. DEPARTMENT OF THE INTERIOR, RANGELAND REFORM § 94, DRAFT AND FINAL ENVIRONMENTAL IMPACT STATEMENTS (1994 & 1995); GENERAL ACCOUNTING OFFICE, RANGELAND MANAGEMENT: BLM'S HOT DESERT GRAZING PROGRAM MERITS RECONSIDERATION (Nov. 1991). As currently administered, therefore, BLM's grazing program thus is both economically and ecologically a losing proposition on a national level. Why squander these irreplaceable and diminishing national public resources on such an activity? Why indeed, asked Professor Deb Donahue, in her recent book calling for an end to grazing on the public rangelands, *The Western Range Revisited: Removing Livestock from Public Lands to Conserve Native Biodiversity*. Focusing on the more arid rangelands where the negative impact of grazing is even more pronounced, she argues that "management of public lands to produce livestock is vulnerable to challenge on several grounds. It is "out of sync" with changed public values and demands, with policies currently expressed in federal law, and with historical legislative and popular intent regarding use of public rangelands. Moreover, it is beyond cavil that for decades neither ranchers nor land managers have understood range ecology; as a consequence, rangelands that never should have been grazed were, and continue to be, used by domestic livestock." *See also* Debra L. Donahue, *Justice for the Earth in the Twenty-First Century*, 1 WYO. L. REV. 373 (2001) (summarizing her thesis). This unquestionably is a controversial position for anyone to take. What made it all the more so for Professor Donahue is that she is on the law faculty at the University of Wyoming, one of the more cattle-friendly states in the nation. The reaction was predictable: letters to the editor condemning Donahue filled Wyoming's newspapers; the Wyoming Senate entertained legislation to close the law school; livestock interests demanded an investigation and an overhaul of faculty selection procedures; and the University's president proclaimed the institution's official position of "support for those industries—including production agriculture—that have brought this state from its status as a territory in 1886 to its promise in the new millennium." *See* Tom Kenworthy, *A Discouraging Word in Tome on the Range*, USA TODAY, Mar. 3, 2000, at 3A. Ironically, the fallout of the 1999 publication of her book brought her thesis national media attention. Regardless of what you think of her idea, could BLM adopt her recommendation and still comply with its regulations and authorizing statutes? Given what you know about the state of the rangelands and the causes thereof, *must* BLM adopt her proposal? How, using the statutory and regulatory text, would you construct the legal argument leading to Professor Donahue's policy recommendation?

8. In the final analysis, the 1995 Fundamentals of Rangeland Health regulations only opened the door to ecosystem management. They did not preclude or mandate grazing anywhere within BLM's domain. How BLM planned to implement them would be the real test of their effect. For contemporaneous assessments of the rules and their prospects for implementation, *see* Karl N. Arruda and Christopher Watson, *The Rise and Fall of Grazing Reform*, 32 LAND & WATER L. REV. 413 (1997); Joseph H. Feller, *Til the Cows Come Home: The Fatal Flaw in the Clinton Administration's Public Lands Grazing Policy*, 25 ENVTL. L. 703 (1995); Todd M. Olinger, *Public Rangeland Reform: New Prospects for Collaboration and Local Control Using the Resource Advisory Councils*, 69 U. COLO. L. REV. 633 (1998); Bruce M. Pendery, *Reforming Livestock Grazing on the Public Domain: Ecosystem Management-Based Standards and Guidelines Blaze a New Path for Range Management*, 27 ENVTL. L. 513 (1997).

9. In the introduction to *Public Lands Council v. Babbitt* at the beginning of the section on the history of grasslands law, we asked you to read carefully the Court's description of the grazing preference allotment system. Nothing in BLM's Fundamentals of Rangeland Health criteria altered the way that system operates. But implementing the ecosystem management focus of the new rule may have been difficult had the precise status of the preferences remained fuzzy. Read on to see how BLM brought the preference system terminology into the age of ecosystem management.

Public Lands Council v. Babbitt

Supreme Court of the United States, 2000.
529 U.S. 728.

■ JUSTICE BREYER delivered the opinion of the Court.

[The first portion of the opinion, providing the historical background of the Taylor Grazing Act and the subsequent law of grazing on BLM's federal public lands, is reproduced at the beginning of this chapter.]

This case arises out of a 1995 set of Interior Department amendments to the federal grazing regulations. 60 Fed. Reg. 9894 (1995) (Final Rule). The amendments represent a stated effort to "accelerate restoration" of the rangeland, make the rangeland management program "more compatible with ecosystem management," "streamline certain administrative functions," and "obtain for the public fair and reasonable compensation for the grazing of livestock on public lands." 58 Fed. Reg. 43208 (1993) (Proposed Rule). The amendments in final form emphasize individual "stewardship" of the public land by increasing the accountability of grazing permit holders; broaden membership on the district advisory boards; change certain title rules; and change administrative rules and practice of the Bureau of Land Management to bring them into closer conformity with related Forest Service management practices. See 60 Fed. Reg. 9900–9906 (1995).

Petitioners Public Lands Council and other nonprofit ranching-related organizations with members who hold grazing permits brought this lawsuit against the Secretary and other defendants in Federal District Court, challenging 10 of the new regulations. The court found 4 of 10 unlawful. 929 F.Supp. 1436, 1450–1451 (D.Wyo.1996). The Court of Appeals reversed the District Court in part, upholding three of the four. 167 F.3d 1287, 1289 (C.A.10 1999). Those three (which we shall describe further below) (1) change the definition of "grazing preference"; (2) permit those who are not "engaged in the livestock business" to qualify for grazing permits; and (3) grant the United States title to all future "permanent" range improvements. One judge on the court of appeals dissented in respect to the Secretary's authority to promulgate the first and the third regulations. See 167 F.3d, at 1309–1318. We granted certiorari to consider the ranchers' claim that these three regulatory changes exceed the authority that the Taylor act grants the Secretary.

II

A

The ranchers attack the new "grazing preference" regulations first and foremost. Their attack relies upon the provision in the Taylor act stating that "grazing privileges recognized and acknowledged shall be adequately safeguarded. . ." 43 U.S.C. § 315b. Before 1995 the regulations defined the term "grazing preference" in terms of the AUM-denominated amount of grazing privileges that a permit granted. The regulations then defined "grazing preference" as "the total number of animal unit months of livestock grazing on public lands apportioned and attached to base property owned or controlled by a permittee or lessee." 43 CFR § 4100.0–5 (1994).

The 1995 regulations changed this definition, however, so that it now no longer refers to grazing privileges "apportioned," nor does it speak in terms of AUMs. The new definition defines "grazing preference" as "a superior or priority position against others for the purpose of receiving a grazing permit or lease. This priority is attached to base property owned or controlled by the permittee or lessee." 43 CFR § 4100.0–5 (1995).

The new definition "omits reference to a specified quantity of forage." 60 Fed. Reg. 9921 (1995). It refers only to a priority, not to a specific number of AUMs attached to a base property. But at the same time the new regulations add a new term, "permitted use," which the Secretary defines as "the forage allocated by, or under the guidance of, an applicable land use plan for livestock grazing in an allotment under a permit or lease and is expressed in AUMs." 43 CFR § 4100.0–5 (1995).

This new "permitted use," like the old "grazing preference," is defined in terms of allocated rights, and it refers to AUMs. But this new term as defined refers, not to a rancher's forage priority, but to forage "allocated by, or under the guidance of an applicable land use plan." Ibid. (emphasis added). And therein lies the ranchers' concern.

The ranchers refer us to the administrative history of Taylor Act regulations, much of which we set forth in Part I. In the ranchers' view, history has created expectations in respect to the security of "grazing privileges"; they have relied upon those expectations; and the statute requires the Secretary to "safeguar[d]" that reliance. Supported by various farm credit associations, they argue that defining their privileges in relation to land use plans will undermine that security. They say that the content of land use plans is difficult to predict and easily changed. Fearing that the resulting uncertainty will discourage lenders from taking mortgages on ranches as security for their loans, they conclude that the new regulations threaten the stability, and possibly the economic viability, of their ranches, and thus fail to "safeguard" the "grazing privileges" that Department regulations previously "recognized and acknowledged." Brief for Petitioners 22–23.

We are not persuaded by the ranchers' argument for three basic reasons. First, the statute qualifies the duty to "safeguard" by referring directly to the Act's various goals and the Secretary's efforts to implement them. The full subsection says:

"So far as consistent with the purposes and provisions of this subchapter, grazing privileges recognized and acknowledged shall be adequately safeguarded, but the creation of a grazing district or the issuance of a permit pursuant to the provisions of this subchapter shall not create any right, title, interest or estate in or to the lands." 43 U.S.C. § 315b (emphasis added).

The words "so far as consistent with the purposes . . . of this subchapter" and the warning that "issuance of a permit" creates no "right, title, interest or estate" make clear that the ranchers' interest in permit stability cannot be absolute; and that the Secretary is free reasonably to determine just how, and the extent to which, "grazing privileges" shall be safeguarded, in light of the Act's basic purposes. Of course, those purposes include "stabiliz[ing] the livestock industry," but they also include "stop[ping] injury to the public grazing lands by preventing overgrazing and soil deterioration," and "provid[ing] for th[e] orderly use, improvement, and development" of the public range. 48 Stat. 1269; see supra, at 1819.

Moreover, Congress itself has directed development of land use plans, and their use in the allocation process, in order to preserve, improve, and develop the public rangelands. See 43 U.S.C. §§ 1701(a)(2), 1712. That being so, it is difficult to see how a definitional change that simply refers to the use of such plans could violate the Taylor Act by itself, without more. Given the broad discretionary powers that the Taylor Act grants the Secretary, we must read that Act as here granting the Secretary at least ordinary administrative leeway to assess "safeguard[ing]" in terms of the Act's other purposes and provisions. Cf. §§ 315, 315a (authorizing Secretary to establish grazing districts "in his discretion" (emphasis added), and to "make provision for protection, administration, regulation, and improvement of such grazing districts").

Second, the pre-1995 AUM system that the ranchers seek to "safeguard" did not offer them anything like absolute security—not even in respect to the proportionate shares of grazing land privileges that the "active/suspended" system suggested. As discussed above, the Secretary has long had the power to reduce an individual permit's AUMs or cancel the permit if the permit holder did not use the grazing privileges, did not use the base property, or violated the Range Code. See supra, at 1820 (collecting CFR citations 1938–1998). And the Secretary has always had the statutory authority under the Taylor act and later FLMPA to reclassify and withdraw range land from grazing use, see 43 U.S.C. § 315f (authorizing Secretary, "in his discretion, to examine and classify any lands . . . which are more valuable or suitable for the production of agricultural crops . . . or any other use than [grazing]"); §§ 1712, 1752(c) (authorizing renewal of permits "so long as the lands . . . remain available for domestic livestock grazing in accordance with land use plans" (emphasis added)). The Secretary has consistently reserved the authority to cancel or modify grazing permits accordingly. See supra, at 1820–1821 (collecting CFR citations). Given these well-established pre-1995 Secretarial powers to cancel, modify, or decline to review individual permits, including the power to do so pursuant to the adoption of a land use plan, the ranchers' diminishment-of-security point is at best a matter of degree.

Third, the new definitional regulations by themselves do not automatically bring about a self-executing change that would significantly diminish the security of granted grazing privileges. The Department has said that the new definitions do "not cancel preference," and that any change is "merely a clarification of terminology." 60 Fed. Reg. 9922 (1995). It now assures us through the Solicitor General that the definitional changes "preserve all elements of preference" and "merely clarify the regulations within the statutory framework." See Brief in Opposition 13, 14.

The Secretary did consider making a more sweeping change by eliminating the concept of "suspended use"; a change that might have more reasonably prompted the ranchers' concerns. But after receiving comments, he changed his mind. See 59 Fed. Reg. 14323 (1994). The Department has instead said that "suspended" AUMs will "continue to be recognized and have a priority for additional grazing use within the allotment. Suspended use provides an important accounting of past grazing use for the ranching community and is an insignificant administrative workload to the agency." Bureau of Land Management, Rangeland Reform § 94: Final Environmental Impact Statement 144 (1994).

Of course, the new definitions seem to tie grazing privileges to land-use plans more explicitly than did the old. But, as we have pointed out, the Secretary has since 1976 had the authority to use land use plans to determine the amount of permissible grazing, 43 U.S.C. § 1712. The Secretary also points out that since development of land use plans began nearly 20 years ago, "all BLM lands in the lower 48 states are covered by land use plans," and "all grazing permits in those States have now been issued or renewed in accordance with such plans, or must now conform to them." Brief for United States 26. Yet the ranchers have not provided us with a single example in which interaction of plan and permit has jeopardized or might yet jeopardize permit security. An amicus brief filed by a group of Farm Credit Institutions says that the definitional change will "threate[n]" their "lending policies." Brief for Farm Credit Institutions as Amicus Curiae 3. But they do not explain why that is so, nor do they state that the new definitions will, in fact, lead them to stop lending to ranchers.

We recognize that a particular land use plan could change pre-existing grazing allocation in a particular district. And that change might arguably lead to a denial of grazing privileges that the pre-1995 regulations would have provided. But the affected permit holder remains free to challenge such an individual effect on grazing privileges, and the courts remain free to determine its lawfulness in context. We here consider only whether the changes in the definitions by themselves violate the Taylor act's requirement that recognized grazing privileges be "adequately safeguarded." Given the leeway that the statute confers upon the Secretary, the less-than-absolute pre-1995 security that permit holders enjoyed, and the relatively small differences that the new definitions create, we conclude that the new definitions do not violate that law.

NOTES & QUESTIONS

1. Have you pieced together what made this portion of BLM's 1995 rule controversial? Consider this summary by an expert in grazing law:

> The Rangeland Reform amendments sought to clear away some of the mythological haze associated with "suspended" AUMs and with the use of the term "preference" over the previous two decades. In order to clarify that the preferences established under the Taylor Act determine only who is permitted to place livestock on the range and not how many cattle or sheep are allowed, the new regulations define "grazing preference" to mean simply "a superior priority position against others for the purpose of receiving a grazing permit or lease." To emphasize that number of livestock is a resource management issue governed by BLM's land use plans, the amendments added a new regulatory term, "permitted use," defined as "the forage allocated by, or under the guidance of, an applicable land use plan for livestock grazing in an allotment under a permit or lease."

> To further clarify that grazing permittees have no permanent entitlement to graze a particular number of livestock, the Rangeland Reform Amendments prospectively discontinued, for the most part, the terminology of "suspending" rather than reducing grazing privileges when a permit is scaled down.

Joseph M. Feller, *Back to the Present: The Supreme Court Refuses to Move Public Range Law Backward, but Will the BLM Move Public Range Law Forward?*, 31 ENVTL. L. REP. (Envtl. L. Inst.) 10021 (2001). Couple these changes with the new Fundamentals of Rangeland Health rules, which emphasized ecological factors in the determination of grazing levels, and one had the recipe for ecosystem management on BLM lands. For contemporaneous accounts on this theme, see Steven C. Forrest, *Creating New Opportunities for Ecosystem Restoration on Public Lands: An Analysis of the Potential for Bureau of Land Management Lands*, 23 PUBLIC LAND & RESOURCES L. REV. 21 (2002); Erik Schlenker-Goodrich, *Moving Beyond Public Lands Council v. Babbitt: Land Use Planning and the Range Resource*, 16 J. ENVTL. L. & LITIG. 139 (2001). For the counterview, that Public Lands Council v. Babbitt was wrongly decided and expanded BLM authority beyond congressional intent, see Julie Andersen, *Public Lands Council v. Babbitt: Herding Ranchers Off Public Land?*, 2000 BYU L. REV. 1273.

2. Of course, emphasizing ecosystem factors does not bring them to fruition. The Court in *Public Lands Council* states that a particular land use plan could lead to a denial of grazing privileges that the pre-1995 regulations would have provided. How, substantively and procedurally, would the 1995 rule make that possible?

3. As the Court also noted, the adoption of the "permitted use" definition to describe what grazing privileges really are did not change what they had been all along—privileges, not property rights. Yet BLM must have felt it was important to make that clear through the new definition as a means of facilitating its ecosystem management policy and the Fundamentals of Rangeland Health. What if grazing privileges *were* constitutionally protected property rights? Could BLM have applied its Fundamentals of Rangeland Health criteria to determine grazing levels?

4. For the suggestion that permit fees be reformed so as to reflect true market values, and thereby also promote better rangeland health, see Michelle M. Campana, *Public Lands Grazing Fee Reform: Welfare Cowboys and Rolex Ranchers Wrangling with the New West*, 10 N.Y.U. ENVTL. L.J. 403 (2002). Indeed, in March 2003 the Center for Biological Diversity filed suit against the Forest Service, which allows grazing in some public lands under its jurisdiction, alleging that the agency charges fees that are illegally below market rates. The federal grazing fee is $1.35 per month for each cow/calf pair—about the cost of feeding a pet hamster. According to the suit, this subsidy amounts to a taxpayer cost of $500 million-$1 billion per year in the form of unrecouped administrative and mitigation costs. BLM has never adopted a market based fee system. Should it?

––––––––––––––

Just as the Supreme Court was upholding the 1995 regulations, the BLM under the George W. Bush Administration was not hiding its plans to change the course of rangeland reform. A sweeping account of the agency's efforts in this regard can be found in Scott Nicoll, *The Death of Rangeland Reform*, 21 J. ENVTL. LAW AND LITIGATION 47 (2006). The central target was the 1995 rule. The following opinion from the Tenth Circuit recounts the history of the BLM's promulgation of amendments that in the court's opinion would have had significant environmental impacts. We excerpt the portion of the opinion focusing on that aspect of the rules and why the court concluded that the agency failed to comply with the environmental impact assessment process of the National Environmental Policy Act.

Western Watersheds Project v. Kraayenbrink

United States Court of Appeals for the Ninth Circuit, 2011.
632 F.3d 472.

■ PAEZ, CIRCUIT JUDGE.

The Bureau of Land Management (BLM) is the federal agency charged with overseeing livestock grazing on over 160 million acres of public land in the western United States. Pursuant to the BLM's authority under the Taylor Grazing Act of 1934, 43 U.S.C. § 315 *et seq.,* the BLM has adopted regulations that implement its grazing management responsibilities. *See* 43 C.F.R. § 4100 *et seq.*

On July 12, 2006, the Secretary of the Interior proposed eighteen amendments to the BLM's grazing regulations (collectively the 2006 Regulations). *See* 71 Fed. Reg. 39,402. The stated purpose of the proposed amendments was to improve the working relationships with permittees and lessees (i.e. ranchers), to protect the health of rangelands, and to increase the administrative efficiency and effectiveness of the BLM grazing management program. *See id.* at 39,402, 39,403; *see also* Proposed Revisions to Grazing Regulations for the Public Lands, Final Impact Statement (Final EIS) at ES-5, 4-38. Among other changes, the proposed amendments decreased public involvement in public lands management, put new limitations on the BLM's enforcement powers, and increased ranchers' ownership rights to improvements and water on public lands.

Western Watersheds Project and Maughan *et al.* (collectively Plaintiffs) challenged the new amendments on procedural and substantive grounds. Plaintiffs argued that the BLM violated the National Environmental Policy Act (NEPA) by failing to take the required "hard look" at the environmental effects of the revised regulations; failed to consult with the United States Fish & Wildlife Service (FWS) as required by the Endangered Species Act (ESA); and violated the Federal Land Policy and Management Act (FLPMA) in promulgating the 2006 Regulations.

Shortly after the suit was filed, Public Lands Council and the American Farm Bureau Federation (collectively Intervenors) – two organizations that represent the interests of ranchers in the western states – intervened on behalf of the BLM to defend the proposed amendments. In June 2007, the district court granted summary judgment to Plaintiffs and enjoined enforcement of the proposed regulations. *W. Watersheds Project v. Kraayenbrink,* 538 F.Supp.2d 1302, 1324 (D. Idaho 2008).

The BLM and Intervenors separately appealed. In December 2008, the BLM filed a motion to dismiss the agency's appeal, which we granted, and the BLM no longer seeks to challenge the district court's judgment or defend the proposed amendments. Intervenors maintain their appeal. Plaintiffs challenge Intervenors' standing to defend the 2006 Regulations without the BLM as a party to this appeal. Indeed, the BLM filed an amicus brief in support of Plaintiffs' standing challenge. Intervenors counter that not only do they have standing but Plaintiffs lack standing and their claims are not ripe. We conclude that both parties have standing and that Plaintiffs' claims are ripe.

Because we agree with the district court that the BLM violated NEPA and the ESA in adopting the 2006 amendments, we affirm the court's grant of summary judgment to Plaintiffs as to these claims. We also affirm the district court's permanent injunction enjoining the BLM regulations as set forth in the Federal Register of July 12, 2006, amending 43 C.F.R. Part 4100 *et seq.* Because the district court erred when it failed to consider Plaintiffs' FLPMA claim under the framework and with the deference set forth in *Chevron U.S.A., Inc. v. Natural Resources Defense Council, Inc.,* 467 U.S. 837, 842–43 (1984), we vacate the district court's grant of summary judgment in favor of Plaintiffs on this claim and remand it for further consideration.

The 2006 Regulatory Changes

In 2002, the Secretary of the Interior began efforts once again to amend the regulations governing BLM's oversight of livestock grazing on public lands. The BLM developed a list of proposed changes and assembled an interdisciplinary team of experts to review them.

In July 2002, the BLM interdisciplinary team reported that the proposed "changes [that limit public participation] conflict with the spirit of the Secretary's 4 C's [communication, consultation, cooperation, and conservation] because they explicitly allow for excluding a segment of the population [i.e. the non-ranching public] who would otherwise choose to publicly participate." The report further explained that "[r]estricting public participation will ultimately lead to poorer land management decisions . . . [and] environmental harm, without necessarily sustaining or improving economic conditions." The BLM, however, made no substantial changes to the proposed changes and published them in December 2003 for comment. *See* 68 Fed.Reg. 68,453.

Following the public comment period, a second interdisciplinary BLM team reviewed the proposed amendments. That team was led by an official from the BLM's Washington D.C. office and included a fisheries biologist, a wildlife biologist, a hydrologist, a soils scientist, and other specialists in economics, fire, recreation, wild horses, and archeology. In November 2003, the second BLM interdisciplinary team issued its report titled the Administrative Review Copy Draft EIS (ARC-DEIS). The ARC-DEIS criticized the new regulations, concluding that if put into effect the changes will cause "a slow long-term adverse effect on wildlife and biological diversity in general."

In December 2003, undeterred, the BLM proceeded to publish the proposed regulations and seek public comment. The BLM assembled a third interdisciplinary team to write the Final EIS. The Final EIS team made substantial changes to the ARC-DEIS and deleted without comment the ARC-DEIS's conclusion that the proposed changes would have adverse impacts on wildlife, biological diversity, and riparian habitats. By March 2006, the BLM issued the Final EIS and Addendum, and in July 2006, the BLM issued its Final Rule and Record of Decision, adopting the proposed changes (i.e. the 2006 Regulations).

The 2006 Regulations make several major modifications to the 1995 Regulations. Generally, the proposed amendments make changes that fall into three broad categories: (1) public input in public rangelands management; (2) the BLM's environmental enforcement powers; and (3) permittee's and lessee's (i.e. ranchers) ownership rights on public grazing lands. We explain the changes with respect to each broad category in turn.

1. Public input in public rangelands management

The 2006 Regulations both narrow the definition of "interested public" and remove the requirement that the BLM consult, cooperate, and coordinate with the "interested public" with respect to various management decisions. 43 C.F.R. § 4100.0-5. Under the 1995 Regulations, an individual, group, or organization that submitted a written request to the BLM to be involved in the decision-making process regarding a specific allotment would be put on a list of "interested public" and would receive notice of issues concerning that allotment. 43 C.F.R. § 4300.0-5 (1995). Under the 2006 Regulations, if the individual, group, or organization receives notice but does not comment, it will be dropped from the "interested public" list. *See* 43 C.F.R. § 4300.0-5.

Furthermore, under the 2006 Regulations, the BLM is no longer required to involve interested members of the public when issuing or renewing an individual grazing permit. *Id.* § 4130.2(b). Instead, the BLM must only "consult, cooperate, and coordinate" with "affected permittees and lessees, and the state." *Id.* The 2006 Regulations similarly remove the requirement to consult with the interested public on the following decisions, all of which required consultation under the 1995 Regulations: modifications to the terms in grazing permits, *id.* § 4130.3-3(a); adjustments to allotment boundaries, *id.* § 4110.2-4; changes in active use, *id.* § 4110.3-3(a); emergency allotment closures, *id.* § 4110.3-3(b); and issuance of temporary nonrenewable grazing permits and leases, *id.* § 4130.6-2(a).

2. Environmental enforcement on public rangelands

The 1995 Regulations required the BLM to take corrective actions upon finding either a violation of the Fundamentals of Rangeland Health ecological criteria that, pursuant to the 1995 Regulations, all public lands had to meet, or the Standards and Guidelines for Grazing Administration (Standards and Guidelines). 43 C.F.R. §§ 4180.1, 4180.2(c) (1995). The 2006 Regulations eliminate [enforcement of] the Fundamentals of Rangeland Health, leaving only the Standards and Guidelines as enforceable standards. 43 C.F.R. § 4180.2(c)(1).

Upon discovery of a violation of either the Fundamentals of Rangeland Health or the Standards and Guidelines, the 1995 Regulations required the BLM to take corrective action "as soon as practicable but not later than the start of the next grazing year." 43 C.F.R. § 4180.1 (1995). The 2006 Regulations extend the time for the BLM to take corrective measures to 24 months. 43 C.F.R. § 4180.2(c)(1)(i).

The 2006 Regulations also increase the amount of monitoring required before the BLM can enforce the Standards and Guidelines. Prior to initiating an enforcement proceeding, the 2006 Regulations require that the BLM gather baseline monitoring data to determine "that existing grazing management practices or levels of grazing use on public lands are significant factors in failing to achieve the standards and conform with the guidelines" and only multi-year BLM data (not all available data as provided in the

1995 Regulations) may be considered. *Id.* § 4180.2(c)(1). In short, under the 2006 Regulations, the BLM cannot rely upon other sources for data and must gather monitoring data for each allotment prior to determining whether a rancher has violated the Standards and Guidelines and initiating corrective measures.

The 2006 Regulations also include a novel "phase-in" provision whereby the BLM is required to phase-in grazing reductions of over ten percent over a five-year period. *Id.* § 4110.3-3(a)(1).

3. Permittee and lessee ownership rights

Under the 2006 Regulations, as under the previous 1995 Regulations, the BLM may enter into cooperative range improvement agreements with a person, organization, or other government entity for the installation, use, maintenance, and/or modification of permanent range improvements or rangeland developments. Under the 1995 Regulations, however, the United States retained full title to any permanent range improvements. Under the 2006 Regulations, the private cooperator and the United States share title to permanent range improvements. *Compare* 43 C.F.R. § 4120.3-2 (1995), *with* 43 C.F.R. § 4120.3-2.

With respect to water rights, under the 1995 Regulations, to the extent allowed by state law, the right to any water on public lands was held by the United States. 43 C.F.R. § 4120.3-9 (1995). Under the 2006 Regulations, to the extent permitted by state law, permittees, not the United States, acquire and hold water rights on public lands. 43 C.F.R. § 4120.3-9.

In summary, the proposed amendments reduce public oversight of federal grazing management, eliminate the Fundamentals of Rangeland Health as enforceable standards, allow the BLM additional time to respond to failing allotments, increase monitoring requirements, and cede ownership rights to permanent rangeland structures and water from the United States to private ranchers.

National Environmental Policy Act

In passing NEPA, Congress "recogniz[ed] the profound impact of man's activity on the interrelations of all components of the natural environment" and set out "to create and maintain conditions under which man and nature can exist in productive harmony." 42 U.S.C. § 4331(a). To bring federal action in line with Congress' goals and to foster environmentally informed decision-making by federal agencies, NEPA "establishes 'action-forcing' procedures that require agencies to take a 'hard look' at environmental consequences." *Metcalf v. Daley,* 214 F.3d 1135, 1141 (9th Cir.2000) (quoting *Robertson v. Methow Valley Citizens Council,* 490 U.S. 332, 348, 109 S.Ct. 1835, 104 L.Ed.2d 351 (1989)). Foremost among those procedures is the preparation of an environmental impact statement (EIS).

Agencies considering "major Federal actions significantly affecting the quality of the human environment" are required to prepare an EIS. 42

U.S.C. § 4332(C). The EIS "shall provide full and fair discussion of [the] significant environmental impacts" of the proposed action. 40 C.F.R. § 1502.1. That discussion serves two purposes:

First, it ensures that the agency, in reaching its decision, will have available, and will carefully consider, detailed information concerning significant environmental impacts. Second, it guarantees that the relevant information will be made available to the larger audience that may also play a role in both the decisionmaking process and the implementation of that decision.

Dep't of Transp. v. Pub. Citizen, 541 U.S. 752, 768, 124 S.Ct. 2204, 159 L.Ed.2d 60 (2004) (internal quotation marks, brackets, and citation omitted). By focusing agency and public attention on the environmental effects of proposed agency action, "NEPA ensures that the agency will not act on incomplete information, only to regret its decision after it is too late to correct." *Marsh v. Or. Natural Res. Council*, 490 U.S. 360, 371, 109 S.Ct. 1851, 104 L.Ed.2d 377 (1989).

Here, the BLM prepared a Final EIS in which it concluded that the proposed 2006 Regulations and related changes to the management of grazing on public rangelands would not have significant environmental effects. Plaintiffs challenge the BLM's no effect finding and argue that it is arbitrary and capricious. Specifically, Plaintiffs argue that the BLM (1) failed to take a "hard look" at the environmental consequences of the proposed changes and to respond adequately to concerns and criticisms raised by the agency's own experts, FWS, and other agencies; (2) failed to consider adequately the combined effects of the regulatory changes; and (3) failed to offer a reasoned explanation for why the BLM was changing its grazing management policies, particularly given that the BLM seeks to reduce public participation and roll back environmental protections. We address the three NEPA challenges in turn.

Plaintiffs' first claim is that the BLM failed to take a "hard look" at the environmental consequences of the proposed regulatory changes, and that the BLM's approval of the 2006 Regulations was, therefore, arbitrary and capricious. We review the regulatory changes together in considering whether the BLM violated NEPA.

An agency considering "major federal actions significantly affecting the quality of the human environment" has an obligation under NEPA to prepare an EIS that in "form, content and preparation foster[s] both informed decision-making and informed public participation." *Native Ecosystems Council v. United States*, 418 F.3d 953, 958 n. 4, 960 (9th Cir.2005) (internal quotation marks omitted). The "hard look" "must be taken objectively and in good faith, not as an exercise in form over substance, and not as a subterfuge designed to rationalize a decision already made," *Metcalf*, 214 F.3d at 1142, and the final EIS must include a "discussion of adverse impacts that does not improperly minimize negative side effects." *Earth Island Inst. v. U.S. Forest Serv.*, 442 F.3d 1147, 1159 (9th Cir.2006), *abrogated on other grounds by Winter v. Natural Res. Defense Council, Inc.*, 555

U.S. 7, 129 S.Ct. 365, 375, 172 L.Ed.2d 249 (2008). "Accurate scientific analysis, expert agency comments, and public scrutiny are essential to implementing NEPA." 40 C.F.R. § 1500.1(b). "[G]eneral statements about possible effects and some risk do not constitute a hard look absent a justification regarding why more definitive information could not be provided." *Blue Mountains Biodiversity Project v. Blackwood,* 161 F.3d 1208, 1213 (9th Cir.1998) (internal quotation marks omitted).

Here, the BLM failed to address concerns raised by its own experts, FWS, the EPA, and state agencies. For example, the BLM offered no reasoned analysis whatsoever in support of its conclusion – which is in direct conflict with the conclusion of its own experts and sister agency, FWS – that there will be no environmental effect caused by both the across-the-board reduction in public involvement in management of grazing on public lands and the elimination of public input into particular management decisions. Similarly, the BLM never seriously considered the concerns raised by FWS and the California Department of Fish and Game among others that the 2006 Regulations weaken the ability of the BLM to manage rangelands in a timely fashion. As FWS explained in its comment, "in the west, environmental, and therefore, vegetation changes happen stochastically, rapidly, and often involve extremes," and "it is important for BLM range professionals to respond immediately and to the extent necessary to avoid a change in range condition from which it may take decades to recover." The BLM's Final EIS also does not address the consequences of increased construction and private water rights on public rangeland, despite concerns expressed by its own expert scientists that the "present ability of BLM to hold water rights to benefit wildlife, particularly fish has been significant."

Instead of a serious response to FWS's concerns and an analysis and consideration of the various delays and impediments in the BLM's stewardship of public rangelands, as required by NEPA, the Final EIS downplays the environmental impacts of the 2006 Regulations. The BLM, invoking notions of efficiency, justifies the reduction in public participation and the elimination of the Fundamentals of Rangeland Health as enforceable standards by stating that the 2006 Regulations are "anticipated to improve the efficiency and effectiveness" of grazing administration. The Final EIS does not address the environmental consequences of a mandatory five-year delay in implementing reductions of ten percent or greater in active use on a permittee's grazing land, but rather speculates that this delay would "often result[ ] in improved cooperative relations and management between BLM and the permittee or lessee."

While diplomacy with permittees or lessees of public rangelands is certainly a worthy goal, it is no substitute for the BLM's obligations to comply with NEPA and to conduct a studied review and response to concerns about the environmental implications of major agency action. While we recognize that NEPA is a procedural statute, which "exists to ensure a process, not to mandate particular results," *Native Ecosystems Council v. Tidwell,* 599 F.3d 926, 936 (9th Cir.2010), part of the procedure required is that an agency in its Final EIS address "any responsible opposing view which was not adequately discussed in the draft statement and shall indicate the agency's response to the issues raised." 40 C.F.R. § 1502.9(b). "This disclosure requirement obligates the agency to make available to the public high quality information, including accurate scientific analysis, expert agency comments and public scrutiny, before decisions are made and actions are taken." *Center for Biological Diversity v. U.S. Forest Serv.*, 349 F.3d 1157, 1167 (9th Cir.2003) (citing 40 C.F.R. § 1500.1(b)). When an agency, such as the BLM, submits proposed regulatory changes for public comment and then offers no meaningful response to serious and considered comments by experts, that agency renders the procedural requirement meaningless and the EIS an exercise in "form over substance." *See Metcalf*, 214 F.3d at 1142.

Here, the BLM gave short shrift to a deluge of concerns from its own experts, FWS, the EPA, and state agencies; the BLM neither responded to their considered comments "objectively and in good faith" nor made responsive changes to the proposed regulations. *Id.* "[P]ublic scrutiny [is] essential to implementing NEPA," 40 C.F.R. § 1500.1(b), and the BLM was required to "assess and consider . . . both individually and collectively" the public comments received during the NEPA process and to respond to such in its Final EIS. *Id.* § 1503.4(a); *see Center for Biological Diversity,* 349 F.3d at 1167 (holding that the agency in that case violated NEPA when it failed "to disclose and discuss responsible opposing scientific viewpoints in the final statement"). We therefore conclude that the BLM violated NEPA by failing to take a "hard look" at the environmental consequences of the proposed regulatory amendments.

Finally, we note that the Final EIS offers no reasoned explanation for the BLM's change of policy from the 1995 Regulations. "[A]n agency changing its course by rescinding a rule is obligated to supply a reasoned analysis for the change beyond that which may be required when an agency does not act in the first instance." *Motor Vehicle Mfrs. Ass'n v. State Farm Mut. Auto. Ins. Co.,* 463 U.S. 29, 42, 103 S.Ct. 2856, 77 L.Ed.2d 443 (1983).

The Supreme Court has said, in considering an agency's decision to change its regulatory policy, "[i]f Congress established a presumption from which judicial review should start, that presumption . . . is . . . *against* changes in current policy that are not justified by the rulemaking record." *Id.* at 42, 103 S.Ct. 2856 (emphasis in original). "[T]he agency must examine the relevant data and articulate a satisfactory explanation for its action including a rational connection between the facts found and the choice made." *Id.* at 43, 103 S.Ct. 2856 (internal quotation marks and citation omitted).

Here, the BLM decreased its regulatory authority over rangeland management, decreased the role of the public in overseeing that management, and granted permittees and lessees increased ownership rights. These changes are inconsistent with the 1995 Regulations and discordant with the lessons learned from the history of rangeland management in the west, which has been moving towards multiple use management and increased public participation.

Therefore, we conclude that the BLM has failed to take a "hard look" at the environmental impacts of the 2006 Regulations as required by NEPA, and its conclusion in the Final EIS that the proposed action would have no significant environmental impact is arbitrary and capricious under the APA. We affirm the district court's grant of summary judgment to Plaintiffs.

NOTES & QUESTIONS

1. Where was the BLM? As the appellate court points out, the government decided to drop its appeal of the lower court's injunction, leaving the ranching and environmental groups to fight it out. Why? Look at the timeline.

2. NEPA imposes procedural duties on federal agencies to examine and assess the environmental impacts of their actions, but it imposes no substantive standards on agencies once they have made that assessment. In other words, had the BLM's Final EIS acknowledged the concerns some of the agency's experts and outside interests had raised, it would have complied with NEPA. Why was the agency so reluctant to do so?

3. How much public participation should there be in BLM's grazing decisions? The agency offered the following rationale for the restrictions on public input the 2006 rules would impose:

> In adopting these changes, BLM has attempted to balance the important role of the interested public with the need for prompt decisionmaking on day-to-day management issues. Thousands of these decisions are made annually by BLM. Actions are guided by broader decisions (such as allotment management plans) and monitoring and other reports as to which the interested public will continue to have an opportunity to review and provide input. In addition, prior to considering any on-the-ground action, BLM must determine whether the proposed action conforms to the applicable land use plan. If a proposed action does not conform to the land use plan, a land use plan amendment must be completed before BLM can further consider the proposed action. The public is assured involvement in the land use planning process.
>
> We expect the changes in the definition and role of the interested public in the grazing program to improve administrative efficiency and lead to more timely decision making. It is BLM's expectation that this increased efficiency and faster reaction time will ultimately benefit overall rangeland health. Also note that these changes do not affect public participation opportunities available through the NEPA environmental analysis process, in administrative appeals of grazing decisions, or, to the extent practicable, in the preparation of reports and evaluations.

71 Fed. Reg. at 39414-15. Do you find these arguments convincing? Some BLM employees involved in the rulemaking evidently did not, but others did. When there is internal conflict within an agency, who decides the agency's final position? Was it proper for the court to reject the agency's final position about the environmental effects of this change in process, essentially siding with agency employees who were in the minority?

4. Another significant amendment the 2006 rules made was dropping the fundamentals of rangeland health as directly enforceable. The agency offered this rationale for doing so:

> Although the 1995 rule established requirements for "appropriate action" when either the fundamentals or established standards and guidelines were not being met due to existing grazing, we believe requiring "appropriate action" in both circumstances is unnecessary and inefficient. Standards and guidelines have been developed in conformance with the fundamentals...[T]he standards and guidelines provide specific measures for achieving healthy rangelands within the framework of the broad fundamentals. Therefore, a duplicate administrative mechanism to require "appropriate action" under the fundamentals is unnecessary. Further, as previously noted, the fundamentals are broad concepts that describe healthy rangelands. Because the standards and guidelines are more specific, they lend themselves to determining whether the ecosystem functions and processes as described by the fundamentals are in fact occurring, and to communicating achievement status in a way that the fundamentals do not. For this same reason, the standards also lend themselves to enforcement in a way that the fundamentals do not. Finally, we believe that removing the "appropriate action" requirement under the fundamentals will better enable authorized officers to focus on the implementation of the standards and guidelines, which we in turn expect to result in more efficient implementation of decisions that will maintain healthy rangelands.

71 Fed. Reg. at 39412-13. The agency accurately describes the way in which the fundamentals and the standards operate—the standards must incorporate the fundamentals in more specific regional and state grazing applications. How then does enforcing only the standards as direct mandates have an adverse environmental impact? On the other hand, why, if the standards incorporate the fundamentals, was the agency so interested in dropping the fundamentals as directly enforceable?

5. What grazing rules apply after *Western Watersheds*? As the court noted, the government dropped its appeal. The court affirmed the injunction of the 2006 rules based on procedural violations of NEPA. If the agency does not "fix" its NEPA deficiencies, will it effectively have repealed the 2006 amendments without public notice and comment? Does this give you some insight to the question posed above in Note 1?

Note on Grazing Preference "Buyouts"

Western grazing interests often advance strong property rights positions in support of their use of private and public lands. Ironically, however, one of the property rights they do not support—indeed, which they strenuously oppose—is the right *not* to graze livestock on public land. Notwithstanding the purely voluntary nature of the decision not to graze, it is one that has triggered a firestorm across the western grasslands.

So-called livestock grazing "buyouts," which involve the voluntary relinquishment of grazing permits for market value, have become an increasingly popular approach for environmental groups wishing to avoid confrontation in the courthouse. The Grand Canyon Trust actively forged this idea, negotiating directly with willing ranchers to structure agreements in which the rancher is either compensated for relinquishing grazing privileges to BLM, or is paid for transferring the grazing preferences to the Trust's non-profit grazing corporation. Many ranchers found this arrangement financially attractive, and the Trust retired all or substantially all of the Animal Unit Months (AUM) allotments on hundreds of thousands of acres. Its first such project resulted in the retirement of grazing from 55,000 acres around the Horseshoe Canyon section of Canyonlands National Park. Having visited the site personally, your authors can attest to the dramatic ecological transformation that has occurred from the removal of cattle from the land since 1996. Other market-based major retirement efforts achieving similar results include the Defenders of Wildlife's purchase of domestic sheep grazing permits in grizzly bear habitat of the Caribou-Targhee National Forest, and the National Wildlife Federation's retirement of a 2,400-acre lease in the Gallatin National forest near Yellowstone National Park.

Alas, free-market environmentalism, it turns out, is not such a good fit with the Taylor Grazing Act. The TGA requires BLM to establish grazing districts comprised of public lands "chiefly valuable for grazing and raising forage crops." 43 U.S.C. 315. It also requires that permittees be "stock owners." 43 U.S.C. 315b. Grazing permits usually have a term of ten years, and each year the permit holder submits an annual grazing application stating how many active (not suspended) AUMs will be grazed that year. For many years prior to the 1995 rules, BLM routinely approved "nonuse" application by permit holders intending to conserve natural resources, though it required an annual determination that there was a need to continue to rest the public lands from more intensive uses. These temporary nonuse approvals often continued to be granted for many years, which may have provided an approximate but tenuous equivalent to permanent retirement.

Grazers opposed to indefinite "temporary" nonuse successfully challenged the practice through administrative litigation, however, and in response the 1995 rules limited the practice of temporary nonuse but also established long term "conservation use" as an authorized active use of grazing permits. The rules required that temporary nonuse could continue for no more than three consecutive years, or else the unused active AUMs could be transferred to another grazer. The conservation use permit, however, allowed market-based buyouts of grazing permits and permanent retirement of some or all of the grazing privileges without requiring BLM to find an ongoing need to rest the land.

The conservation use rule was successfully challenged before the Tenth Circuit in the *PLC v. Babbitt* litigation, with the court finding that it was "an impermissible exercise of the Secretary's authority under section three of the TGA because land that he has designated as 'chiefly valuable for grazing livestock' will be completely excluded from grazing even though range conditions could be good enough to support grazing." PLC v. Babbitt, 167 F.3d 1287, 1308 (10th Cir. 1999). The United States did not appeal that aspect of the case to the Supreme Court. In the waning days of the Babbitt Administration, however, the DOI Solicitor issued an opinion that the Federal Land Planning and Management Act and Public Rangeland Improvement Act give BLM sufficient authority to accept voluntarily relinquished grazing permits based on a plain vanilla "multiple use" decision that the lands should be devoted to uses other than grazing. *See* Memorandum from the Solicitor of the U.S. Department of the Interior to Director of the Bureau of Land Management (Jan. 19, 2001). The opinion did not address the TGA provisions directly and, like many such decisions of the Clinton Administration, it was issued the day before President Bush took control of the White House.

Not surprisingly, in October 2002 the new Interior Solicitor superseded the prior opinion by adding the requirement that BLM could accept a proposed relinquishment of grazing on land within a grazing district only if it finds under the TGA land use planning process that the lands are no longer chiefly valuable for grazing and raising forage crops. *See* Solicitor's Opinion M-37,008, Memorandum from the Solicitor of the U.S. Department of the Interior to Secretary of the U.S. Department of the Interior (Oct. 4, 2002). According to the new opinion, any such decision must be supported in the land use planning record of decision, and it is subject to reconsideration, modification, or reversal in subsequent TGA land use planning cycles. The agency's 2006 rangeland rule amendments then removed "conservation use" from the definition of "active use." *See* 43 C.F.R. 4100.0-5.

These legal developments have left grazing permit buyouts on precarious terms. A willing conservation organization and rancher could approach BLM to urge that the land use plan for a grazing district find the particular land no longer suitable for grazing, or suitable for a vastly reduced AUM allotment, but that would require administrative findings and be open to later reconsideration and challenge. Alternatively, BLM could grant a request to reduce the AUMs allotted to particular grazing permits to levels acceptable to the conservation group, but this still requires administrative findings that are open to subsequent reconsideration and challenge. The last alternative is for BLM to approve temporary nonuse of grazing permits, but for any long-term conservation impact the agency would have to ignore the three-year limit, which would subject the permit to administrative challenge by others. In short, there is no legally airtight mechanism for achieving the long-term conservation goals of grazing permit buyouts on BLM lands. Efforts to address the problem in Congress, most recently a bill filed in 2011 that would allow a third party to pay a rancher a generous set fee to retire active AUMs, have failed.

Why do you suppose grazing interests, who hold property rights so dear, are so opposed to voluntary, free-market agreements to retire grazing privileges? So long as all the permit holders who wish to graze may do so at levels they desire, what beef do they have with permit holders who wish not to graze, or to graze at what they believe to be ecologically sound levels? Even if the grazers would like to graze more land than they currently do, what complaint do they have if others outbid them in the market for the permits to do so and then retire the grazing preferences? For more information about the buyouts issue, see David G. Alderson, *Buyouts and Conservation Permits: A Market Approach to Address the Federal Land Grazing Problem*, 12 N.Y.U. ENVTL. L.J. 903 (2005).

b. WILDERNESS STUDY AREAS

One of the most controversial matters BLM has faced involves the agency's effort to withdraw approximately 2.6 million acres of BLM in Utah from possible consideration for wilderness status. Section 603 of FLPMA,

43 U.S.C. 1782, directs BLM to evaluate the suitability of federal lands for congressional designation of roadless, primarily natural recreational areas as wilderness under the Wilderness Act of 1964. In 1991, toward the close of the George H. Bush Administration, BLM determined that 22.8 million acres satisfy the criteria, of which Congress designated close to 7 million for protection as wilderness and continues to study the remainder. The Clinton Administration, purportedly acting on concerns that the prior administration's Section 603 designations were based on outdated or faulty data, reopened the process and eventually identified more Section 603 acres, including the 2.6 million Utah acres in question, as qualifying for congressional designation.

In 1996, Utah sued BLM challenging the procedural and substantive validity of the new findings. Although the state prevailed in federal district court, the Tenth Circuit dismissed most of Utah's claims in 1998, remanding the case to the lower court where it laid moribund for some years. Then the Clinton Administration, once again in its wee hours of tenure, issued a guidance document for managing the wilderness identification process known informally as the *Wilderness Handbook*. Utah later amended its litigation to challenge that guidance and BLM, under the new George W. Bush Administration, settled the litigation by agreeing to rescind the guidance, to withdraw the 2.6 million Utah acres from identification, and to limit restricted uses to areas already designated as WSAs. *See* Utah v. Norton, No. 96–870B (D. Utah) (settlement filed Apr. 11, 2003). Failing to convince the courts to reopen the settlement, environmentalists decried the Bush Administration's narrow view of Section 603 as invented for political reasons, though there clearly has been gamesmanship on both sides of the political fence on the question of how and when to implement Section 603. For a more detailed blow-by-blow account of this episode, see Tom Turner, *Unsettling Development*, THE ENVTL. FORUM, Jan./Feb. 2004, at 32.

By now the following should be of no surprise to you: In December 2010 the Obama Administration yet again reversed course, effectively nullifying the Bush Administration settlement when Secretary of the Interior Ken Salazar issued Secretarial Order 3310 requiring that when making decisions on projects that may impair the wilderness characteristics of lands that have not been "inventoried and analyzed in a land use planning process conducted in accordance with this Order" but appear to have wilderness characteristics, the BLM must conduct an inventory of the lands to determine if they have wilderness characteristics. If the inventory reveals lands with wilderness characteristics that may be impaired, the BLM is required to consider the effects of the proposed project and mitigation measures through a National Environmental Policy Act (NEPA) review process. A number of western legislators immediately decried this new Wild Lands policy and called for its withdrawal. As of this writing the new policy remains in effect.

The following case, involving BLM lands in Utah that were recommended for wilderness status, focuses on the substantive aspects of the Section 603 program.

Norton v. Southern Utah Wilderness Alliance

Supreme Court of the United States, 2004.
542 U.S. 55.

■ SCALIA, J., delivered the opinion for a unanimous Court.

In this case, we must decide whether the authority of a federal court under the Administrative Procedure Act (APA) to "compel agency action unlawfully withheld or unreasonably delayed," 5 U.S.C. § 706(1), extends to the review of the United States Bureau of Land Management's stewardship of public lands under certain statutory provisions and its own planning documents.

I

Almost half the State of Utah, about 23 million acres, is federal land administered by the Bureau of Land Management (BLM), an agency within the Department of Interior. For nearly 30 years, BLM's management of public lands has been governed by the Federal Land Policy and Management Act of 1976 (FLPMA), 90 Stat. 2744, 43 U.S.C. § 1701 *et seq.*, which "established a policy in favor of retaining public lands for multiple use management." *Lujan v. National Wildlife Federation,* 497 U.S. 871, 877, 110 S.Ct. 3177, 111 L.Ed.2d 695 (1990). "Multiple use management" is a deceptively simple term that describes the enormously complicated task of striking a balance among the many competing uses to which land can be put, "including, but not limited to, recreation, range, timber, minerals, watershed, wildlife and fish, and [uses serving] natural scenic, scientific and historical values." 43 U.S.C. § 1702(c). A second management goal, "sustained yield," requires BLM to control depleting uses over time, so as to ensure a high level of valuable uses in the future. § 1702(h). To these ends, FLPMA establishes a dual regime of inventory and planning. Sections 1711 and 1712, respectively, provide for a comprehensive, ongoing inventory of federal lands, and for a land use planning process that "project[s]" "present and future use," § 1701(a)(2), given the lands' inventoried characteristics.

Of course not all uses are compatible. Congress made the judgment that some lands should be set aside as wilderness at the expense of commercial and recreational uses. A pre-FLPMA enactment, the Wilderness Act of 1964, 78 Stat. 890, provides that designated wilderness areas, subject to certain exceptions, "shall [have] no commercial enterprise and no permanent road," no motorized vehicles, and no manmade structures. 16 U.S.C. § 1133(c). The designation of a wilderness area can be made only by Act of Congress, see 43 U.S.C. § 1782(b).

Pursuant to § 1782, the Secretary of the Interior has identified so-called "wilderness study areas" (WSAs), roadless lands of 5,000 acres or more that possess "wilderness characteristics," as determined in the Secretary's land inventory. § 1782(a); see 16 U.S.C. § 1131(c). As the name suggests, WSAs (as well as certain wild lands identified prior to the passage of FLPMA) have been subjected to further examination and public comment in order to evaluate their suitability for designation as wilderness. In 1991, out of 3.3 million acres in Utah that had been identified for study, 2 million were recommended as suitable for wilderness designation. 1 U.S. Dept. of Interior, BLM, Utah Statewide Wilderness Study Report 3 (Oct. 1991). This recommendation was forwarded to Congress, which has not yet acted upon it. Until Congress acts one way or the other, FLPMA provides that "the Secretary shall continue to manage such lands . . . in a manner so as not to impair the suitability of such areas for preservation as wilderness." 43 U.S.C. § 1782(c). This nonimpairment mandate applies to all WSAs identified under § 1782, including lands considered unsuitable by the Secretary. See §§ 1782(a), (b); App. 64 (BLM Interim Management Policy for Lands Under Wilderness Review).

Aside from identification of WSAs, the main tool that BLM employs to balance wilderness protection against other uses is a land use plan-what BLM regulations call a "resource management plan." 43 CFR § 1601.0-5(k) (2003). Land use plans, adopted after notice and comment, are "designed to guide and control future management actions," § 1601.0–2. See 43 U.S.C. § 1712; 43 CFR § 1610.2 (2003). Generally, a land use plan describes, for a particular area, allowable uses, goals for future condition of the land, and specific next steps. § 1601.0-5(k). Under FLPMA, "[t]he Secretary shall manage the public lands under principles of multiple use and sustained yield, in accordance with the land use plans . . . when they are available." 43 U.S.C. § 1732(a).

Protection of wilderness has come into increasing conflict with another element of multiple use, recreational use of so-called off-road vehicles (ORVs), which include vehicles primarily designed for off-road use, such as lightweight, four-wheel "all-terrain vehicles," and vehicles capable of such use, such as sport utility vehicles. See 43 CFR § 8340.0-5(a) (2003). According to the United States Forest Service's most recent estimates, some 42 million Americans participate in off-road travel each year, more than double the number two decades ago. H. Cordell, Outdoor Recreation for 21st Century America 40 (2004). United States sales of all-terrain vehicles alone have roughly doubled in the past five years, reaching almost 900,000 in 2003. The use of ORVs on federal land has negative environmental consequences, including soil disruption and compaction, harassment of animals, and annoyance of wilderness lovers. Thus, BLM faces a classic land use dilemma of sharply inconsistent uses, in a context of scarce resources and congressional silence with respect to wilderness designation.

In 1999, respondents Southern Utah Wilderness Alliance and other organizations (collectively SUWA) filed this action in the United States District Court for Utah against petitioners BLM, its Director, and the Secretary. In its second amended complaint, SUWA sought declaratory and injunctive relief for BLM's failure to act to protect public lands in Utah from damage caused by ORV use. SUWA made three claims that are relevant here: (1) that BLM had violated its nonimpairment obligation under § 1782(a) by allowing degradation in certain WSAs; (2) that BLM had failed to implement provisions in its land use plans relating to ORV use; (3) that BLM had failed to take a "hard look" at whether, pursuant to the National

Environmental Policy Act of 1969 (NEPA), 83 Stat. 852, 42 U.S.C. § 4321 *et seq.*, it should undertake supplemental environmental analyses for areas in which ORV use had increased. SUWA contended that it could sue to remedy these three failures to act pursuant to the APA's provision of a cause of action to "compel agency action unlawfully withheld or unreasonably delayed." 5 U.S.C. § 706(1).

The District Court entered a dismissal with respect to the three claims. A divided panel of the Tenth Circuit reversed. 301 F.3d 1217 (2002). The majority acknowledged that under § 706(1), "federal courts may order agencies to act only where the agency fails to carry out a mandatory, nondiscretionary duty." *Id.*, at 1226. It concluded, however, that BLM's nonimpairment obligation was just such a duty, and therefore BLM could be compelled to comply. Under similar reasoning, it reversed the dismissal with respect to the land use plan claim; and likewise reversed dismissal of the NEPA claim. We granted certiorari.

II

All three claims at issue here involve assertions that BLM failed to take action with respect to ORV use that it was required to take. Failures to act are sometimes remediable under the APA, but not always. We begin by considering what limits the APA places upon judicial review of agency inaction. [The Court emphasized that "the only agency action that can be compelled under the APA is action legally *required.* This limitation appears in § 706(1)'s authorization for courts to 'compel agency action *unlawfully* withheld.' . . . Thus, a claim under § 706(1) can proceed only where a plaintiff asserts that an agency failed to take a *discrete* agency action that it is *required to take.*"]

III

A

With these principles in mind, we turn to SUWA's first claim, that by permitting ORV use in certain [Wilderness Study Areas (WSAs)], BLM violated its mandate to "continue to manage [WSAs] . . . in a manner so as not to impair the suitability of such areas for preservation as wilderness," 43 U.S.C. § 1782(c). SUWA relies not only upon § 1782(c) but also upon a provision of BLM's Interim Management Policy for Lands Under Wilderness Review, which interprets the nonimpairment mandate to require BLM to manage WSAs so as to prevent them from being "degraded so far, compared with the area's values for other purposes, as to significantly constrain the Congress's prerogative to either designate [it] as wilderness or release it for other uses."

Section 1782(c) is mandatory as to the object to be achieved, but it leaves BLM a great deal of discretion in deciding how to achieve it. It assuredly does not mandate, with the clarity necessary to support judicial action under § 706(1), the total exclusion of ORV use.

SUWA argues that § 1782 *does* contain a categorical imperative, namely the command to comply with the nonimpairment mandate. It contends that a federal court could simply enter a general order compelling compliance with that mandate, without suggesting any particular manner of compliance. It relies upon the language from the Attorney General's Manual quoted earlier, that a court can "take action upon a matter, without directing how [the agency] shall act," and upon language in a case cited by the Manual noting that "mandamus will lie . . . even though the act required involves the exercise of judgment and discretion." *Safeway Stores v. Brown,* 138 F.2d 278, 280 (Emerg.Ct.App.1943). The action referred to in these excerpts, however, is *discrete* agency action, as we have discussed above. General deficiencies in compliance, unlike the failure to issue a ruling that was discussed in *Safeway Stores,* lack the specificity requisite for agency action.

The principal purpose of the APA limitations we have discussed—and of the traditional limitations upon mandamus from which they were derived—is to protect agencies from undue judicial interference with their lawful discretion, and to avoid judicial entanglement in abstract policy disagreements which courts lack both expertise and information to resolve. If courts were empowered to enter general orders compelling compliance with broad statutory mandates, they would necessarily be empowered, as well, to determine whether compliance was achieved—which would mean that it would ultimately become the task of the supervising court, rather than the agency, to work out compliance with the broad statutory mandate, injecting the judge into day-to-day agency management. To take just a few examples from federal resources management, a plaintiff might allege that the Secretary had failed to "manage wild free-roaming horses and burros in a manner that is designed to achieve and maintain a thriving natural ecological balance," or to "manage the [New Orleans Jazz National] [H]istorical [P]ark in such a manner as will preserve and perpetuate knowledge and understanding of the history of jazz," or to "manage the [Steens Mountain] Cooperative Management and Protection Area for the benefit of present and future generations." 16 U.S.C. §§ 1333(a), 410bbb-2(a)(1), 460nnn-12(b). The prospect of pervasive oversight by federal courts over the manner and pace of agency compliance with such congressional directives is not contemplated by the APA.

NOTES & QUESTIONS

1. If the wilderness study area provision is "mandatory as to the object to be achieved," but the status of the agency's success is unreviewable because the statute "leaves BLM a great deal of discretion in deciding how to achieve it," how will anyone know whether the "object to be achieved" has been achieved? Is this a question generally for adaptive management in application?

2. The Court seems to suggest that the mandatory statutory duty—i.e., to "continue to manage [WSAs] . . . in a manner so as not to impair the suitability of such areas for preservation as wilderness,"—is simply too broad to allow judicial review. Do you agree? What kind of tests could a court devise for assessing agency performance under this standard, recognizing that judicial review must be based on the record and accord substantial deference to agency decisions?

c. BLM'S PLANNING REQUIREMENTS

In addition to the substantive provisions of its organic statutes, BLM is subject to planning requirements found principally in Federal Land Planning and Management Act (FLPMA). The following cases illustrate the steps BLM must take to satisfy its FLPMA planning obligations and the effect of the land use plans it produces.

Norton v. Southern Utah Wilderness Alliance

Supreme Court of the United States, 2004.
542 U.S. 55.

[The introductory portions of the case are reproduced in the previous section of the text.]

IV

SUWA's second claim is that BLM failed to comply with certain provisions in its land use plans, thus contravening the requirement that "[t]he Secretary shall manage the public lands . . . in accordance with the land use plans . . . when they are available." 43 U.S.C. § 1732(a); see also 43 CFR § 1610.5-3(a) (2003) ("All future resource management authorizations and actions . . . and subsequent more detailed or specific planning, shall conform to the approved plan"). The relevant count in SUWA's second amended complaint alleged that BLM had violated a variety of commitments in its land use plans, but over the course of the litigation these have been reduced to two, one relating to the 1991 resource management plan for the San Rafael area, and the other to various aspects of the 1990 ORV implementation plan for the Henry Mountains area.

The actions contemplated by the first of these alleged commitments (completion of a route designation plan in the San Rafael area), and by one aspect of the second (creation of "use supervision files" for designated areas in the Henry Mountains area) have already been completed, and these claims are therefore moot. There remains the claim, with respect to the Henry Mountains plan, that "in light of damage from ORVs in the Factory Butte area," a sub-area of Henry Mountains open to ORV use, "the [plan] obligated BLM to conduct an intensive ORV monitoring program." This claim is based upon the plan's statement that the Factory Butte area "will be monitored and closed if warranted." SUWA does not contest BLM's assertion in the court below that informal monitoring has taken place for some years, but it demands continuing implementation of a monitoring *program.* By this it apparently means to insist upon adherence to the plan's general discussion of "Use Supervision and Monitoring" in designated areas, which (in addition to calling for the use supervision files that have already been created) provides that "[r]esource damage will be documented and recommendations made for corrective action," "[m]onitoring in open areas will focus on determining damage which may necessitate a change in designation," and "emphasis on use supervision will be placed on [limited and closed areas]." SUWA acknowledges that a monitoring program has recently been *commenced*. In light, however, of the continuing action that existence of a "program" contemplates, and in light of BLM's contention that the program cannot be compelled under § 706(1), this claim cannot be considered moot.

The statutory directive that BLM manage "in accordance with" land use plans, and the regulatory requirement that authorizations and actions "conform to" those plans, prevent BLM from taking actions inconsistent with the provisions of a land use plan. Unless and until the plan is amended, such actions can be set aside as contrary to law pursuant to 5 U.S.C. § 706(2). The claim presently under discussion, however, would have us go further, and conclude that a statement in a plan that BLM "will" take this, that, or the other action, is a binding commitment that can be compelled under § 706(1). In our view it is not-at least absent clear indication of binding commitment in the terms of the plan.

FLPMA describes land use plans as tools by which "present and future use is *projected*." 43 U.S.C. § 1701(a)(2) (emphasis added). The implementing regulations make clear that land use plans are a preliminary step in the overall process of managing public lands-"designed to guide and control future management actions and the development of subsequent, more detailed and limited scope plans for resources and uses." 43 CFR § 1601.0–2 (2003). The statute and regulations confirm that a land use plan is not ordinarily the medium for affirmative decisions that implement the agency's "project[ions]." Title 43 U.S.C. § 1712(e) provides that "[t]he Secretary may issue management decisions to implement land use plans"—the decisions, that is, are distinct from the plan itself. Picking up the same theme, the regulation defining a land use plan declares that a plan "is not a final implementation decision on actions which require further specific plans, process steps, or decisions under specific provisions of law and regulations." 43 CFR § 1601.0-5(k) (2003). The BLM's Land Use Planning Handbook specifies that land use plans are normally not used to make site-specific implementation decisions. See Handbook II–2.

Plans also receive a different agency review process from implementation decisions. Appeal to the Department's Board of Land Appeals is available for "a specific action being proposed to implement some portion of a resource management plan or amendment." 43 CFR § 1610.5-3(b). However, the Board, which reviews "decisions rendered by Departmental officials relating to . . . [t]he use and disposition of public lands and their resources," § 4.1(b)(3)(i), does not review the approval of a plan, since it regards a plan as a policy determination, not an implementation decision. See, *e.g., Wilderness Society,* 109 I.B.L.A. 175, 178 (1989); *Wilderness Society,* 90 I.B.L.A. 221, 224 (1986); see also Handbook II-2, IV-3. Plans are protested to the BLM director, not appealed.

The San Rafael plan provides an apt illustration of the immense scope of projected activity that a land use plan can embrace. Over 100 pages in length, it presents a comprehensive management framework for 1.5 million acres of BLM-administered land. Twenty categories of resource management are separately discussed, including mineral extraction, wilderness protection, livestock grazing, preservation of cultural resources, and recreation. The plan lays out an ambitious agenda for the preparation of additional, more detailed plans and specific next steps for implementation. Its introduction notes that "[a]n [ORV] implementation plan is scheduled to be prepared within 1 year following approval of the [San Rafael plan]." San Rafael Plan 9. Similarly "scheduled for preparation" are activity plans for certain environmentally sensitive areas, "along with allotment management plans, habitat management plans, a fire management plan, recreation management plans . . ., cultural resource management plans for selected sites, watershed activity plans, and the wild and scenic river management plan." *Ibid.* The projected schedule set forth in the plan shows "[a]nticipated [i]mplementation" of some future plans within one year, others within three years, and still others, such as certain recreation and cultural resource management plans, at a pace of "one study per fiscal year." *Id.,* at 95–102.

Quite unlike a specific statutory command requiring an agency to promulgate regulations by a certain date, a land use plan is generally a statement of priorities; it guides and constrains actions, but does not (at least in the usual case) prescribe them. It would be unreasonable to think that either Congress or the agency intended otherwise, since land use plans nationwide would commit the agency to actions far in the future, for which funds have not yet been appropriated. Some plans make explicit that implementation of their programmatic content is subject to budgetary constraints. While the Henry Mountains plan does not contain such a specification, we think it must reasonably be implied. A statement by BLM about what it plans to do, at some point, provided it has the funds and there are not more pressing priorities, cannot be plucked out of context and made a basis for suit under § 706(1).

Of course, an action called for in a plan may be compelled when the plan merely reiterates duties the agency is already obligated to perform, or perhaps when language in the plan itself creates a commitment binding on the agency. But allowing general enforcement of plan terms would lead to pervasive interference with BLM's own ordering of priorities. For example, a judicial decree compelling immediate preparation of all of the detailed plans called for in the San Rafael plan would divert BLM's energies from other projects throughout the country that are in fact more pressing. And while such a decree might please the environmental plaintiffs in the present case, it would ultimately operate to the detriment of sound environmental management. Its predictable consequence would be much vaguer plans from BLM in the future-making coordination with other agencies more difficult, and depriving the public of important information concerning the agency's long-range intentions.

We therefore hold that the Henry Mountains plan's statements to the effect that BLM will conduct "use supervision and monitoring" in designated areas-like other "will do" projections of agency action set forth in land use plans-are not a legally binding commitment enforceable under § 706(1). That being so, we find it unnecessary to consider whether the action envisioned by the statements is sufficiently discrete to be amenable to compulsion under the APA.

NOTES & QUESTIONS

1. Is the effect of the Court's decision more likely or less likely to encourage BLM to engage in adaptive management in and through its land use plans? Is a strong citizen standing right—allowing intervention to litigate over agency compliance with even minute details of the land use plan—more likely or less likely to encourage BLM to engage in adaptive management in and through its land use plans?

2. If plans were legally binding commitments requiring the agency to follow terms going above and beyond the statutory minimum, citizens could sue to challenge agency compliance with any such terms, and courts would engage in "hard look" judicial review. In that environment, would agencies be more likely or less likely to include such terms?

3. For a critique of *SUWA*, suggesting that, contrary to the theme of the previous two notes, strong citizen standing and broad judicial review will improve environmental conditions, see Miyoko Sakashita, *Supreme Court Eschews Agency's Failure to Protect Wilderness in Redrock Country*, 32 ECOLOGY L.Q. 391 (2005). For the view that *SUWA* undermines federal public land management generally, by giving land managers a roadmap for insulating a wide swath of actions and inactions from judicial review, see Michael C. Blumm and Sherry L. Bosset, Norton v. SUWA *and the Unraveling of Federal Public Land Planning*, 18 DUKE ENVTL. L. & POL'Y FORUM 105 (2007). What is your take on the effects of *SUWA* on federal public land management?

National Wildlife Federation v. Bureau of Land Management

Interior Board of Land Appeals, 1997.
140 IBLA 85.

■ Opinion by DEPUTY CHIEF ADMINISTRATIVE JUDGE HARRIS.

On December 20, 1993, District Chief Administrative Law Judge John R. Rampton, Jr., issued a Decision involving appeals relating to grazing in the Comb Wash Allotment in southeastern Utah. In his Decision, Judge Rampton precluded BLM from allowing any further grazing of cattle on certain public lands in the allotment, specifically five canyons (Arch, Mule, Fish Creek, Owl Creek, and Road Canyons), pending compliance with the environmental review mandate of section 102(2)(C) of the National Environmental Policy Act of 1969 (NEPA), as amended, 42 U.S.C. § 4332(2)(C) (1994), and the requirements of sections 302(a) and 309(e) of the Federal Land Policy and Management Act of 1976 (FLPMA), 43 U.S.C. §§ 1732(a) and 1739(e) (1994), for consideration of principles of "multiple use" and public participation.

The American Farm Bureau Federation (AFBF) and Utah Farm Bureau Federation (UFBF), the Ute Mountain Ute Indian Tribe (Tribe), and BLM each filed appeals from that Decision. Together with its notice of appeal, the Tribe filed a petition for stay. Neither of the other Appellants sought a stay. National Wildlife Federation, Southern Utah Wilderness Alliance, and Joseph M. Feller (collectively referred to as NWF) filed a document, inter alia, opposing the petition for stay and requesting that the Decision be put into full force and effect.

In a Decision dated March 1, 1994, the Board denied the petition for stay and granted the request to put Judge Rampton's Decision into effect, pursuant to 43 C.F.R. § 4.477(b) (1994), thereby prohibiting grazing in the canyons pending resolution of the appeals on their merits. National Wildlife Federation v. BLM, 128 IBLA 231 (1994). In a subsequent Decision, the Board granted a motion to dismiss the appeal of AFBF, but granted AFBF amicus curiae status. National Wildlife Federation v. BLM, 129 IBLA 124 (1994).

I. Factual and Procedural Background

The Comb Wash Allotment encompasses nearly 72,000 acres, of which approximately 63,000 acres are public lands, the remainder being state and private. The allotment is located southwest of Blanding, Utah, and northwest of Bluff, Utah. Within the allotment boundaries is the geographic feature from which the allotment derives its name, Comb Wash, a narrow valley that runs north-south just west of the Comb Ridge for about 20 miles. Draining into Comb Wash from the west are five canyons, Arch, Mule, Fish Creek, Owl Creek, and Road, sections of which, ranging from approximately 4 to 7 miles in length, are also within the allotment boundaries. The canyon bottoms are narrow, generally less than a half-mile wide and in places no more than 200 yards wide. The canyons encompass about 7,000 acres, or 10 percent of the allotment land. Each canyon contains a perennial or ephemeral stream, with an associated riparian area. The canyons provide recreational opportunities for camping, hiking, photography, sightseeing, and the viewing of archaeological sites, including many remnants of the ancient Anasazi culture.

The White Mesa Community, whose members are enrolled to the Tribe, owns the White Mesa Cattle Company, which conducts grazing operations on the allotment. The Comb Wash Allotment is one of six allotments on approximately 250,000 acres of public and national forest lands used by the White Mesa Community for its grazing operations. From 1987 to 1991, the White Mesa Community employed about four tribal members per year in its grazing operations. Despite limited employment opportunities for tribal members, the operation provides income for the White Mesa Community, which the community uses to make home repairs for senior citizens, purchase clothing for school children, and maintain a small store.

In 1966, BLM established an active grazing preference of 3,796 animal unit months (AUM's) for BLM-administered public lands in the allotment for the annual grazing season from October 16 to May 31. That preference allowed 506 cattle to graze the allotment. Prior to 1985, the number of cattle using the canyons was unknown because cattle were allowed to graze the entire allotment, including the canyon areas, during the annual 7 ½ month grazing season.

In May 1986, BLM issued a draft resource management plan (RMP) and environmental impact statement (EIS) to establish general management standards and guidelines concerning grazing and other permitted resource uses of the 1.8 million acres of public land in its San Juan Resource Area. In developing that document, BLM grouped the Comb Wash Allotment with other allotments for purposes of considering the environmental consequences of alternative grazing management plans for the resource area. In September 1987, BLM issued a proposed RMP and final EIS (FEIS) for the resource area. Following another comment period, BLM reissued the proposed RMP in April 1989. However, prior to reissuance, on February 20, 1989, the San Juan Resource Area Manager issued a 10-year grazing permit to the Tribe for the Comb Wash Allotment authorizing grazing in the amount of 3,791 AUM's. The Utah State Director, BLM, approved the RMP in a March 18, 1991, Record of Decision and Rangeland Program Summary.

During the development of the RMP, BLM changed its grazing scheme for the Comb Wash Allotment. In the fall of 1986, it began to manage the canyon areas, as well as other land in the allotment, as separate pastures, regulating the movement of cattle among the pastures by the use of existing or newly-constructed fences. The BLM authorized the Tribe to drive cattle into the canyons and hold them there for a month at a time with fences constructed across the canyon mouths. It also began to monitor forage utilization. It established trend study plots and established objectives for increasing the frequency of key plant species in the allotment. However, none of those study plots was in the canyons or in any riparian area on the Comb Wash Allotment. Following a number of years of monitoring, BLM found that key species in the study plots had not changed or had decreased in frequency. In response to that finding, BLM adjusted its objectives downward to reflect the status quo in 1991.

The BLM developed a plan for a 4-year grazing cycle for the allotment in order to improve the vegetation and in response to increased recreational use of the canyons. The features of that plan were that the season of use would be changed so that the canyons would be grazed only during the dormant season, from November 1 to the middle of March; only 50 cattle would be grazed in each canyon for a period of only 1 month; at least one canyon would be rested every fourth or fifth year; pastures outside the canyons would be grazed each year in an alternating pattern of spring grazing for two seasons followed by winter grazing for two seasons; and forage utilization in the canyons would be limited to 40 percent and outside the canyons to 50 percent in spring and 60 percent in the winter.

The BLM never formally adopted the 4-year grazing cycle, but it nevertheless implemented the plan through annual grazing authorizations with the 1990–91 season being the first year of the cycle. However, BLM did not adhere strictly to the features of the system. There was evidence at the hearing of the authorization of more than 50 cattle to graze in certain canyons, scheduling grazing in a canyon that was to be rested, and overutilization of certain key species in certain canyons.

The annual grazing authorizations, two of which were challenged in this case, were issued by the San Juan Resource Area Manager, Edward Scherick, who believed he had discretion under the RMP to determine whether grazing should take place in the canyons. However, in exercising that discretion, he relied exclusively on the recommendations provided to him by Paul Curtis, the San Juan Resource Area range conservationist. Scherick did not conduct any independent analysis of the effects of grazing on other resources. He testified that he always accepted Curtis' recommendations concerning grazing.

Curtis stated that it had been decided in the RMP that the canyons were available for livestock use. He came to that conclusion because the RMP did not preclude grazing in the Comb Wash Allotment. However, he acknowledged that he did not know if there was specific information in the RMP about the impacts of grazing in the canyons.

Curtis testified that he "monitor[s] the grazing in the San Juan resource area, and presently that covers approximately two million acres. And I deal with the biggest percent of that two million acres, and approximately 66 different allotments and 66 different permittees, give or take a few." Given the scope of his duties, it is not surprising that Curtis stated that he did not have the time or personnel to conduct the necessary monitoring in the canyons. Under those circumstances, he is generally left to rely on the permittee to adhere to the grazing schedule in the Comb Wash Allotment. He stated: "I try to call them, you know, periodically to make sure that things are going close to right." It is clear from the record that things did not always go right. . .

IV. Discussion

B. FLPMA Violation

The issue for resolution is whether Judge Rampton properly held that BLM violated FLPMA. After citing section 302(a) of FLPMA, 43 U.S.C. § 1732(a) (1994), which requires the Secretary to "manage the public lands under principles of multiple use and sustained yield," Judge Rampton quoted the FLPMA definition of "multiple use." That term is defined as the management of the public lands and their various resource values so that they are utilized in the combination that will best meet the present and future needs of the American people; * * * the use of some land for less than all of the resources; a combination of balanced and diverse resource uses that takes into account the long-term needs of future generations for renewable and non-renewable resources, including, but not limited to, recreation, range, timber, minerals, watershed, wildlife and fish, and natural scenic, scientific and historical values; * * * with consideration given to the relative values of the resources and not necessarily to the combination of uses that will give the greatest economic return or greatest unit production. 43 U.S.C. § 1702(c) (1994). He then cited a statement by the court in Sierra Club v. Butz, 3 Envtl. L. Rep. 20,292, 20,293 (9th Cir.1973), that the multiple-use principle "requires that the values in question be informedly and rationally taken into balance." He concluded that an agency is required to engage in such a balancing test in order to determine whether a proposed activity is in the public interest.

However, in applying those standards to the facts in this case, Judge Rampton held that "BLM violated FLPMA by failing to make a reasoned and informed decision that the benefits of grazing the canyons outweigh the costs." It is with this highlighted language that all Appellants disagree, asserting that FLPMA does not require an economic cost/benefits analysis.

It is not clear that Judge Rampton intended that BLM engage in an economic cost/benefits analysis. A reading of his Decision at pages 23–25 discloses that the sentence quoted above is the only place in his Decision where he uses the word "costs," other than in the heading to the discussion. Later in his Decision when he is addressing the appropriate relief for the various violations, he describes the violation as the failure to make a reasoned and informed decision to graze the canyons in violation of FLPMA. He mentions neither costs nor benefits. He described the appropriate relief, as follows: "Because BLM may choose to prohibit grazing in the canyons in the future, BLM is not compelled to make a reasoned and informed decision that grazing the canyons is in the public interest. However, until a decision is made, BLM is prohibited from allowing grazing in the canyons." Again, no mention is made of benefits and costs.

To the extent Judge Rampton's Decision may be construed as requiring an economic cost/benefit analysis, it is modified to make it clear that no such analysis is required.

On appeal, BLM makes no argument that it satisfied FLPMA's multiple-use mandate in authorizing grazing in the canyons. Instead, it agrees that the actions it takes, including authorizing grazing on the public lands, are required to be "in the public interest," but it asserts that if Judge Rampton intended to impose a "specific public interest determination," such as is found in section 206(a) of FLPMA, 43 U.S.C. § 1716(a) (1994), dealing with exchanges, "he has clearly overstepped his authority." It contends that "FLPMA simply does not require a specific public interest finding in the grazing context."

We agree with BLM that FLPMA does not require a "specific" public interest determination for grazing. However, FLPMA's multiple-use mandate requires that BLM balance competing resource values to ensure that public lands are managed in the manner "that will best meet the present and future needs of the American people." 43 U.S.C. § 1702(c) (1994). Indeed, all parties agree that BLM must conduct some form of balancing of competing resource values in order to comply with the statute. Counsel for BLM states that "we agree that all BLM decisions should be in the public interest as that interest is defined by Congress in law * * *." The UFBF also recognizes that "[c]learly, management for multiple use does require a balancing and review of the relative resource values." The Tribe also "does not dispute that under FLPMA the BLM must give consideration to the relative values of the resources in the Comb Wash canyons. Moreover, we agree that those values must be rationally considered." And NWF concurs that "BLM must informedly and rationally balance competing values."

What is important in this case, and what we affirm, is Judge Rampton's finding that BLM violated FLPMA, because it failed to engage in any reasoned or informed decisionmaking process concerning grazing in the canyons in the allotment. That process must show that BLM has balanced competing resource values to ensure that the public lands in the canyons are managed in the manner that will best meet the present and future needs of the American people.

NOTES & QUESTIONS

1. The *NWF v. BLM* case illustrates the important role of administrative litigation in environmental law, and for matters within the jurisdiction of the Department of the Interior (DOI) in particular. Within DOI's Office of the Secretary resides the Office of Hearings and Appeals (OHA). OHA is the Secretary's delegated representative for matters subject to secretarial review, which comprises a wide variety of topics in the case of DOI. OHA is divided into a Hearings Division and three standing appeals boards, one of which is the Interior Board of Land Appeals (IBLA) involved in *NWF v. BLM*. IBLA is the largest of the appeals boards and has jurisdiction over the variety of public lands issues within the jurisdiction of such agencies as BLM and the Fish and Wildlife Service. When DOI agencies such as BLM make decisions, an appeal to the Secretary generally can involve, first, a hearing before an Administrative Law Judge (ALJ) of the OHA Hearings Division, and then an appeal to IBLA, the decision of which is final agency action for purposes of judicial review. The rules of jurisdiction and procedure are, however, quite complex and depend on the subject matter and underlying administrative circumstances. No lawyer wishing to practice ecosystem management law can avoid having to wade through these and other procedural and substantive niceties of administrative law. For a thorough explanation of the IBLA and administrative litigation in DOI generally, see Michael C. Hickey, *Litigation Before the Department of the Interior*, 11 NAT. RESOURCES & ENV'T 20 (Summer 1996).

2. FLPMA requires BLM to make grazing decisions that "will best meet the present and future needs of the American people." 43 U.S.C. § 1702(c). IBLA's interpretation of that provision in *NWF v. BLM* is DOI's final interpretation of the statute. What, then, did IBLA require BLM to do to satisfy the statutory standard? It is clear, at least, what IBLA believes this provision does *not* require. First, it rejected the argument that FLPMA requires any sort of "economic cost/benefit analysis." IBLA also rejected the argument that FLPMA requires "a 'specific' public interest determination." Why are neither of those two analyses required in order for an agency to make decisions that "best meet the present and future needs of the American people?" Don't a weighing of cost and benefit consequences and an analysis of impacts to competing public interests seem relevant inquiries to any effort to make such a decision? Does IBLA satisfy you that FLPMA does not require these detailed analysis? What would the

BLM decision making process, and litigation over BLM grazing decisions, look like if BLM had to compile detailed cost-benefit and public interest analyses?

3. The IBLA interpreted FLPMA at least to require that BLM demonstrate that it engaged in a "reasoned [and] informed decisionmaking process concerning grazing in the . . . allotment," a process, IBLA explains, that "must show that BLM has balanced competing resource values to ensure that the public lands . . . are managed in the manner that will best meet the present and future needs of the American people." Does that clarify things for you? Does this standard *require* that BLM adopt ecosystem management principles? Does it *allow* BLM to do so?

4. Weren't the San Juan Resource Area Manager, Edward Scherick, and his field conservationist assistant, Paul Curtis, practicing adaptive management as that method of ecosystem management is described in Chapter 7? Scherick believed he had discretion to determine whether grazing should take place in the canyons, and he relied on the recommendations Curtis provided to him based on his field investigations and discussions with ranchers. To be sure, Curtis did not have the resources to conduct his assessments as thoroughly as he (or IBLA) would have liked, but isn't the basic understanding Scherick and Curtis had of their discretion, and the manner in which they executed it, what adaptive management theory has in mind?

Note on Forest Service Management of the National Grasslands System

The United States acquired most of the Great Plains from France with the Louisiana Purchase of 1803. Until the late 1860s, the Great Plains region remained a true "frontier." But the Homestead Act of 1862 brought almost six million settlers by 1890, many of whom tried to replace grass with crops more beneficial to economic aspirations. The settlers soon discovered, however, that while these vast grasslands were productive in wet years, they were also subject to serious drought and bitter winters. Plowed land exposed topsoil to incessant dry winds. Above parts of Oklahoma, Texas, Wyoming, Nebraska, Kansas, Colorado and the Dakotas, dust clouds rose to over 20,000 feet. Ten-foot drifts of fine soil particles piled up, burying fences and closing roads. During the same time, bison were largely eliminated by westward expansion. Ranchers filled the large open ranges of the plains with cattle and sheep. By the early 1930s, the broad midsection of America was in trouble, not only because of the Dust Bowls, but because the Great Depression was reaching its economic depths.

Emergency measures taken to provide relief to the farmers and settlers included the National Industrial Recovery Act of 1933 and the Emergency Relief Appropriations Act of 1935, which allowed the federal government to purchase and restore damaged lands and to resettle destitute families. Under the direction of the Department of Agriculture's Soil Conservation Service, the purchased lands were rehabilitated and enrolled in Land Utilization Projects for use as summer pasture lands by the farms and ranches that had withstood the economic and agricultural collapse of the prior decade.

From these roots, one hundred years after the Homestead Act, the National Grasslands were born when on June 23, 1960, the Secretary of Agriculture designated 3.8 million acres of the Land Utilization Project lands as the new National Grasslands System. Today, there are 20 National Grasslands, 17 of which are located in the Great Plains region east of the Rockies (the other three are in California, Oregon, and Idaho). The Little Missouri National Grassland in North Dakota is the biggest with 1,028,051 acres. The smallest National Grassland is McClelland Creek in Texas with 1,449 acres. Biological resources on national grasslands can be rich. For example, the Comanche National Grassland has approximately 275 different species of birds and the longest dinosaur track-way in the world.

The Department of Agriculture's Forest Service manages the National Grasslands System for sustainable multiple uses as part of and under the same legal authorities applicable to the National Forest System. These laws, and the complex legal issues arising under them, are the focus of Chapter 8 of the text. The multiple use mandate leads, indeed, to multiple uses. For example, the Caddo and southwestern LBJ National Grasslands in Texas, which are within a four-hour drive of four million people, provide forage for more than 1,584 head of cattle on 3,050 acres of improved pasture and 19,600 acres of native pasture. The largest coal producing mine in the world (Thunder Basin) is on the Thunder Basin National Grassland in Wyoming.

Entry to the Cimarron National Grassland in Kansas

Only a few cases involve Forest Service management of national grasslands, *see, e.g.*, Sharps v. U.S. Forest Service, 823 F.Supp. 668 (D.S.D. 1993), and no specialized doctrine has been applied. For a more complete understanding of National Grassland System management, therefore, refer to the public lands forest ecosystem law materials in Chapter 8 of the text. *See also* Coby C. Dolan, *The National Grasslands and Disappearing Biodiversity: Can the Prairie Dog Save Us From an Ecological Desert?*, 29 ENVTL. L. 213 (1999).

2. RESTORING GRASSLAND ECOSYSTEMS ON PRIVATE LANDS

Ted Turner, the founder of CNN, is one of North America's largest private individual landowners by acreage. Is he turning his 1.9 million acres of personal land holdings into telecommunications centers and shopping malls? Quite the opposite. Turner is an ecosystem management dream come true for the grasslands of the far western states. On over 15 of his huge ranches throughout Montana, New Mexico, South Dakota, Nebraska, and Kansas, Turner is tearing down barbed wired fences, replacing cattle and sheep with buffalo, reintroducing fire-based vegetation management, restocking streams and rivers with native trout, raising and releasing endangered wolves, and doing just about everything else many ecologists say BLM ought to be doing on the public rangeland.

Before you get inspired to join in Turner's private grassland restoration effort, however, consider that just one of the ranches he has acquired, the 580,000-acre Vermejo Park Ranch in New Mexico, cost him over $80 million. So, what can be done to expand private grassland ecosystem restoration efforts short of winning the lottery? Congress has grappled with that question recently, searching for a model that treads lightly on property rights but yields some meaningful ecological results. One approach suggested in connection with debate over farm policy has been to initiate a program for purchase of easements on private property that would allow the owner to continue use of the land (usually for agricultural purposes, given where most land suitable for grassland restoration is located) in return for instituting a program of grassland conservation measures. The following is an example of such a program Congress adopted in connection with adoption of the 2002 the Farm Bill:

Farm Security and Rural Investment Act of 2002
H.R. 2646 (2002).
Subtitle E—Grassland Reserve.

SEC. 2401. GRASSLAND RESERVE PROGRAM.

Chapter 2 of the Food Security Act of 1985 (as amended by section 2001) is amended by adding at the end the following:

Subchapter C—Grassland Reserve Program

SEC. 1238N. GRASSLAND RESERVE PROGRAM.

(a) ESTABLISHMENT—The Secretary shall establish a grassland reserve program (referred to in this subchapter as the "program") to assist owners in restoring and conserving eligible land described in subsection (c).

(b) ENROLLMENT CONDITIONS—

(1) MAXIMUM ENROLLMENT—The total number of acres enrolled in the program shall not exceed 2,000,000 acres of restored or improved grassland, rangeland, and pastureland.

(2) METHODS OF ENROLLMENT—

(A) IN GENERAL—Except as provided in subparagraph (B), the Secretary shall enroll in the program from a willing owner not less than 40 contiguous acres of land through the use of—

(i) a 10-year, 15-year, or 20-year rental agreement;

(ii)(I) a 30-year rental agreement or permanent or 30-year easement; or (II) in a State that imposes a maximum duration for easements, an easement for the maximum duration allowed under State law. * * *

(c) ELIGIBLE LAND—Land shall be eligible to be enrolled in the program if the Secretary determines that the land is private land that is—

(1) grassland, land that contains forbs, or shrubland (including improved rangeland and pastureland); or

(2) land that—

(A) is located in an area that has been historically dominated by grassland, forbs, or shrubland; and

(B) has potential to serve as habitat for animal or plant populations of significant ecological value if the land is—

(i) retained in the current use of the land; or

(ii) restored to a natural condition; * * *

SEC. 1238O. REQUIREMENTS RELATING TO EASEMENTS AND AGREEMENTS.

(a) REQUIREMENTS OF LANDOWNER—

(1) IN GENERAL—To be eligible to enroll land in the program through the grant of an easement, the owner of the land shall enter into an agreement with the Secretary—

(A) to grant an easement that applies to the land to the Secretary;

(B) to create and record an appropriate deed restriction in accordance with applicable State law to reflect the easement;

(C) to provide a written statement of consent to the easement signed by persons holding a security interest or any vested interest in the land;

(D) to provide proof of unencumbered title to the underlying fee interest in the land that is the subject of the easement; and

(E) to comply with the terms of the easement and restoration agreement.

(2) AGREEMENTS—To be eligible to enroll land in the program under an agreement, the owner or operator of the land shall agree—

(A) to comply with the terms of the agreement (including any related restoration agreements); and

(B) to the suspension of any existing cropland base and allotment history for the land under a program administered by the Secretary.

(b) TERMS OF EASEMENT OR RENTAL AGREEMENT—An easement or rental agreement under subsection (a) shall—

(1) permit—

(A) common grazing practices, including maintenance and necessary cultural practices, on the land in a manner that is consistent with maintaining the viability of grassland, forb, and shrub species common to that locality;

(B) subject to appropriate restrictions during the nesting season for birds in the local area that are in significant decline or are conserved in accordance with Federal or State law, as determined by the Natural Resources Conservation Service State conservationist, haying, mowing, or harvesting for seed production; and

(C) fire rehabilitation and construction of fire breaks and fences (including placement of the posts necessary for fences);

(2) prohibit—

(A) the production of crops (other than hay), fruit trees, vineyards, or any other agricultural commodity that requires breaking the soil surface; and

(B) except as permitted under this subsection or subsection (d), the conduct of any other activity that would disturb the surface of the land covered by the easement or rental agreement; and

(3) include such additional provisions as the Secretary determines are appropriate to carry out or facilitate the administration of this subchapter.

(c) EVALUATION AND RANKING OF EASEMENT AND RENTAL AGREEMENT APPLICATIONS—

(1) IN GENERAL—The Secretary shall establish criteria to evaluate and rank applications for easements and rental agreements under this subchapter.

(2) CONSIDERATIONS—In establishing the criteria, the Secretary shall emphasize support for—

(A) grazing operations;

(B) plant and animal biodiversity; and

(C) grassland, land that contains forbs, and shrubland under the greatest threat of conversion.

(d) RESTORATION AGREEMENTS—

(1) IN GENERAL—The Secretary shall prescribe the terms of a restoration agreement by which grassland, land that contains forbs, or shrubland that is subject to an easement or rental agreement entered into under the program shall be restored.

(2) REQUIREMENTS—The restoration agreement shall describe the respective duties of the owner and the Secretary (including the Federal share of restoration payments and technical assistance).

SEC. 1238P. DUTIES OF SECRETARY.

(a) IN GENERAL—In return for the granting of an easement, or the execution of a rental agreement, by an owner under this subchapter, the Secretary shall, in accordance with this section—

(1) make easement or rental agreement payments to the owner in accordance with subsection (b); and

(2) make payments to the owner for the Federal share of the cost of restoration in accordance with subsection (c).

(b) PAYMENTS—

(1) EASEMENT PAYMENTS—

(A) AMOUNT—In return for the granting of an easement by an owner under this subchapter, the Secretary shall make easement payments to the owner in an amount equal to—

(i) in the case of a permanent easement, the fair market value of the land less the grazing value of the land encumbered by the easement; and

(ii) in the case of a 30-year easement or an easement for the maximum duration allowed under applicable State law, 30 percent of the fair market value of the land less the grazing value of the land for the period during which the land is encumbered by the easement. * * *

(c) FEDERAL SHARE OF RESTORATION—The Secretary shall make payments to an owner under this section of not more than—

(1) in the case of grassland, land that contains forbs, or shrubland that has never been cultivated, 90 percent of the costs of carrying out measures and practices necessary to restore functions and values of that land; or

(2) in the case of restored grassland, land that contains forbs, or shrubland, 75 percent of those costs.

SEC. 1238Q. DELEGATION TO PRIVATE ORGANIZATIONS.

(a) IN GENERAL—The Secretary may permit a private conservation or land trust organization (referred to in this section as a "private organization") or a State agency to hold and enforce an easement under this subchapter, in lieu of the Secretary, subject to the right of the Secretary to conduct periodic inspections and enforce the easement, if—

(1) the Secretary determines that granting the permission will promote protection of grassland, land that contains forbs, and shrubland;

(2) the owner authorizes the private organization or State agency to hold and enforce the easement; and

(3) the private organization or State agency agrees to assume the costs incurred in administering and enforcing the easement, including the costs of restoration or rehabilitation of the land as specified by the owner and the private organization or State agency.

NOTES & QUESTIONS

1. In March 2006, USDA issued final rules to implement the Grassland Reserve Program. *See* 71 Fed. Reg. 11139 (Mar. 6, 2006). The agency decided to distribute funds through states based on the number of grazing operations in each state, the acres of grassland under threat of conversion, and the biodiversity index of those lands. Pursuant to compliance and monitoring provisions Congress adopted in 2008 for all conservation programs, USDA adopted additional implementing regulations in 2010. *See* 75 Fed. Reg. 73912 (Nov. 29, 2010).

2. The Natural Resources Conservation Service (NRCS), formerly the Soil Conservation Service, is the USDA division that focuses primarily on conservation practices on private lands. Soil conservation divisions of the USDA were formed in response to the Dust Bowl catastrophe of the mid-1930's. The agency's first chief, Hugh Hammond Bennett, convinced the Congress that soil erosion was a national threat; that a permanent agency was needed within the USDA to call landowners' attention to their land stewardship opportunities and responsibilities; and that nationwide coordination between federal agencies and local communities was needed to help farmers and ranchers conserve their land. Today, more than six decades later, NRCS is USDA's lead conservation agency, partnering with state and federal agencies, NRCS Earth Team volunteers, agricultural and environmental groups, professional societies, and the nation's 3,000 local soil and water conservation districts that are at the heart of the NRCS conservation delivery system. Most NRCS employees serve in USDA's network of local, county-based offices. The rest are at state, regional, and national offices, providing technology, policy, and administrative support. NRCS employees have technical expertise and field experience in many scientific and technical specialties, including soil science, soil conservation, agronomy, biology, agroecology, range conservation, forestry, engineering, geology, hydrology, cultural resources, and economics. Nearly three-fourths of the technical assistance provided by the agency goes to helping farmers and ranchers develop conservation systems uniquely suited to their land and individual ways of doing business. The agency also provides assistance to rural and urban communities to reduce erosion, conserve and protect water, and solve other resource problems. Based on this description, do you find that NRCS is an appropriate agency to implement the Grassland Reserve Program? For more on the agency, see www.nrcs.usda.gov.

3. Note that the easement agreements executed under the Grasslands Reserve Program would permit "grazing on the land in a manner that is consistent with maintaining the viability of natural grass, shrub, forb, and wildlife species indigenous to that locality." Based on the readings in the previous sections of this chapter, are you comfortable that BLM or the Forest Service has determined what satisfies that criterion on public rangelands? Do you anticipate that NRCS would apply a different approach in the context of easements on private lands? Can you, in 50 words or less, draft a regulation defining what conditions should satisfy this criterion in that context?

4. NRCS is also required to "prescribe the terms of a restoration agreement by which grassland that is subject to an easement or rental agreement entered into under the program shall be restored." To what extent should NRCS do so by general regulation versus through specific, tailormade provisions of each easement? Notice that the legislation does not define "restored." If this type of legislative provision were adopted, should NRCS provide a definition in general regulations, or leave the concept undefined, to be worked out on a case-by-case basis? What should be the ecological reference point for knowing when a grassland has been restored? NRDC regulations define "restoration" as "implementing any conservation practice, system of practices, or activities to restore functions and values of grasslands and shrublands. The restoration may reestablish grassland functions and values on degraded land, or on land that has been converted to another use." 7 C.F.R. 1415.3. The agency in turn defines "functions" as "ecosystem services provided, including domestic animal productivity, biological productivity, plant and animal richness and diversity, fish and wildlife habitat (including habitat for pollinators and native insects), water quality and quantity benefits, aesthetics, open space, and recreation. *Id.* Does the incorporation of ecosystem services as the reference provide a clear standard?

5. The Grassland Reserve Program allows NRCS to permit a private conservation or land trust organization to hold and enforce an easement in lieu of the Secretary. Several land conservation organizations have placed stunning grasslands into permanent preservation status. The Nature Conservancy, for example, acquired the 42-square-mile Zumwalt Prairie Preserve in eastern Oregon, home to a rich diversity of bunchgrasses, and a 25,000-acre tallgrass prairie preserve in Minnesota, part of the organization's larger tallgrass prairie preserve project, that is home to a variety of rare birds, flowers, and native grasses. What do you think about having NRCS turn over management and enforcement of its grassland preserves to organizations like The Nature Conservancy?

6. NRCS engages in private grassland conservation outreach through its participation with state resource agencies and private agricultural interests in the Grazing Lands Conservation Initiative (GLCI), which is designed to deliver technical, educational, and related assistance to owners of private grazing lands through a voluntary "Prescribed Grazing" program. Based on the premise that grazing can be a component of ecosystem management in grassland settings, GLCI focuses its program on improved grazing management through soil conservation methods, invasive weed controls, drought preparation and other water conservation practices, and wildlife habitat protection.

D. CASE STUDY: THE LITTLE DARBY PRAIRIE NATIONAL WILDLIFE REFUGE

Another federal public land management agency with a hand in grassland ecosystem management is the U.S. Fish and Wildlife Service (FWS), which administers the 93 million-acre National Wildlife Refuge System (see Chapter 7, Part D). The difference between BLM and the Forest Service on the one hand, and FWS on the other, is that FWS generally has to acquire new land suitable for grassland restoration to add to its refuge land inventory, whereas BLM and the Forest Service are devising ecosystem management policies for lands already under their jurisdiction (albeit under the horribly complex multiple-use mandate). As the following examples show, FWS has had some warm and some cold receptions when it has pulled into town with grassland restoration as the goal of establishing new refuge lands.

———————————

U.S. Fish and Wildlife Service, Region 3, *Midwest* *Celebrates Its Newest National Prairie Refuge* *Public Invited To Dedication*
Friday, Aug. 10, 2001 at 4 p.m.

Today, less than one percent of the northern tallgrass prairie, which once blanketed the upper Midwest, still remains. Once stretching from horizon to horizon, this native prairie now exists only in scattered patches tucked away in pasture corners or atop rock-strewn rises. These parcels—forgotten, neglected or accidental survivors—are the tracts that Ron Cole, a U.S. Fish and Wildlife Service manager, wants to protect before they disappear forever. His ultimate goal: to protect up to 77,000 acres of native tallgrass prairie in Minnesota and Iowa, half through protective easements and half through outright purchase from willing sellers. On Aug. 10, he'll purchase his first tract of land for the new Northern Tallgrass Prairie National Wildlife Refuge, a 360-acre tract near Luverne, Minn. It will be the first step in an effort which may take decades to reach fruition.

"We're going to celebrate," Cole said. "This is a very important first step for the new refuge. It's taken several years of hard work by refuge staff, our Service realty folks, our local Friends of Prairie group, The Nature Conservancy, and the Brandenburg Prairie Foundation, to make this first acquisition for the refuge a reality."

The public celebration of the new Northern Tallgrass Prairie NWR will kick-off at 4:00 p.m. on Friday, Aug. 10, on the site of the new prairie tract near Luverne, Minn. Transportation to the site will be provided by the Luverne Chamber of Commerce—buses will depart from Luverne High School shortly before 4:00 p.m. Following the dedication, participants are invited to a reception at the Brandenburg Gallery in Luverne, followed by dinner and a slide show of prairie images presented by internationally-renowned photographer Jim Brandenburg. Contact the Chamber for more information at 507/283–4061.

Cole notes the National Wildlife Refuge System will be celebrating its centennial anniversary in 2003 and sees the establishment of the Northern Tallgrass Prairie refuge as a timely, and fitting, gesture. "A hundred years ago, the prairie took care of us; this rich soil has fed generations of Americans." he said. "Now it's time for us to take care of the prairie, at least a small part of what's left."

Things were not nearly as rosy for the Fish and Wildlife Service on the other side of the Great Lakes, in Ohio, where the proposed Little Darby Prairie National Wildlife Refuge met vociferous local landowner opposition and has been ground into a state of political limbo. FWS explained the rationale for the refuge as follows:

U.S. Fish & Wildlife Service, *Notice of Intent to Prepare an Environmental Impact Statement (EIS) for the Proposed Establishment of the Little Darby National Wildlife Refuge*

U.S. Fish & Wildlife Service, 2000.
65 Fed. Reg. 36711.

Purpose of Action.

The general purpose of the refuge would be "for the development, advancement, management, conservation, and protection of fish and wildlife resources" (Fish and Wildlife Act of 1956). More specifically, the Service's interests include preservation and restoration of Federal threatened and endangered species and migratory birds and their habitats in the Little Darby Creek Watershed, ensuring that the overall Darby Creek watershed biodiversity and Federal wildlife trust resources are protected and enhanced, while providing opportunities for wildlife-dependent public uses consistent with preservation and restoration of the natural resources.

Need for Action

Big and Little Darby Creeks, located 20 miles west of downtown Columbus, are the major streams in a 580-square mile watershed encompassing portions of 6 counties in central Ohio. The Darby watershed is one of the healthiest aquatic systems of its size in the Midwest and is ranked among the top five warm freshwater habitats in Ohio by the Ohio Environmental Protection Agency. Land use in the drainage basin has historically been agriculture, with appropriately 80 percent of the land area in fields, row-cropped, in a corn-soybean rotation. The project area was the location of the easternmost extension of the mid-continent tallgrass prairie. The following eight points help explain the need to preserve this area:

(1) Existing and threatened conversion of the watershed, from agriculture to urban land uses, presents an increased risk to the health of this aquatic system.

(2) Scientists (Ohio EPA surveys) place the number of fish species in the Darby Creek System at 94 and 60v in the Little Darby Creek sub watershed. The number of mollusk species, including the federally endangered Northern riffle shell and the Northern club shell, is 35 (Dr. Tom Watters). They are reported to be declining.

(3) There are 3 federally endangered, 1 threatened, 1 candidate, and 10 monitored species confirmed in the original project area or likely to be in the original project area.

(4) Collectively, 44 species are designated as being state threatened or endangered throughout the watershed. Another 36 species are identified as potentially threatened or of special interest in the state. A total of 38 (24 percent) species listed in the Service's regional conservation priorities would be affected potentially by the project as proposed in the draft Environmental Assessment.

(5) While the Refuge project area encompasses only 14–15 percent of the entire Little Darby Creek Watershed, it includes almost 50 percent of all stream miles and important aquatic habitat that is in the watershed.

(6) The Ohio Department of Natural Resources, the National Park Service and the Nature Conservancy have all given special designations to the Big Darby and Little Darby Creeks. The Nature Conservancy identified this watershed as one of the "Last Great Places" in the Western Hemisphere.

(7) A 1996 report (Swanson, D.) found that the population trend in Ohio for 10 species of nongame grassland migratory birds exhibited declines in populations from 30 to 84 percent.

(8) The Service's Regional Wetlands Concept Plan, November 1990, identified the Big Darby Creek Watershed that includes Little Darby Creek as, "One of the last remaining watersheds in Ohio with excellent biological diversity." Under threat from development for water use and

urban development, the area was listed as a potential wetland acquisition site.

The only party held over the Darby refuge, however, was a September 2000 rally of several hundred angry people in London, Ohio, protesting the federal government's proposed "land grab." Here is an example of the local reaction to the Darby refuge:

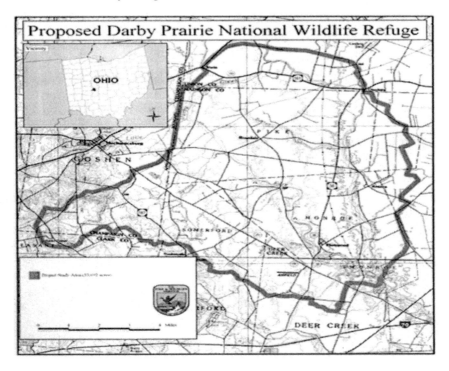

Stewards of the Darby (SOD) and Citizens Against Refuge Proposal (CARP), Declaration: "Our Land Is Our Responsibility"

We, the residents of the area publicized as the "Darby Prairie National Wildlife Refuge Study Area" want our voices heard! We, who live and work in this farming community, believe the impact to area businesses would jeopardize their very existence. The Madison County Auditor's Office projects the affected region generates $300 per acre, which turns over 6–7 times (in buying power) before leaving the community. This translates into a potential deficit of $90 million dollars to our area businesses.

The State Forest Department manages and protects 7.1 million acres of forest land in Ohio, for the benefit of all Ohio citizens. One hundred eighty one thousand acres of State-owned forest land are available for multiple benefits, including wildlife, recreation, timber products, and soil and water protection. In addition, there are 72 State Parks in Ohio where the public can interact with nature at its leisure. With this great abundance of parks and wildlife areas, all supported by our tax dollars, is there really a need for more public land?

Actual area land auctions show that a 500-acre farm is worth $1.5 million dollars. To this initial cost, add a reasonably priced home at a cost of $85,000, and minimal equipment at approximately $641,000, and the combined start-up cost totals $2.226 MILLION DOLLARS. After committing to an investment of such magnitude, why would our astute, agriculturally-and family-minded farmers want to sell?

In the case of the proposed Darby Prairie National Wildlife Refuge, most of the 53,692 acres is land that has been acquired by our farmers over many generations. This "ownership endurance" enables us to continue our conservation-accredited farming skills, thus growing with our investments. At an average of 4.5 persons per home, this equates to the possible residential displacement of over 7,500 people from the Study Area alone, with a loss of approximately 4,000 taxpayers to the community. We have a proven track record of providing Americans with a diversity of products in the global marketplace, with a combination of wheat, corn, and soybeans; there would be a loss of over 3 million bushels of grain from the Study Area!

With well over 50,000 acres lost to food production, how many nonfarmers would be willing to relinquish their combined homes and yards to replace the fertile soil that presently feeds so many, that would be permanently lost by the introduction of a National Wildlife Refuge? At some point, we will no longer have the abundance of high-quality, reasonably priced food that we now take for granted at our supermarkets.

The growing of food to nourish our citizens is certainly as much a consideration as re-establishing a tall grass prairie. Eating is not going to go out of style, and we are not willingly going to yield our bountiful land to either developers or Federal Agencies who say they are "protecting us" from development.

Those of us who have been entrusted with the privilege of caring for the land, know well the proper care and nurturing required to maintain, protect and preserve our farmlands, and sustain a well-established wildlife habitat through conservation management. With an eye to the future, and the experience of almost two hundred years, we know that Our Land Is Our Responsibility!

NOTES & QUESTIONS

1. What explains the starkly different reactions to the Northern Tallgrass Prairie refuge and the Little Darby refuge? Both, clearly, are worthwhile projects from an ecological perspective. Neither involved regulation of private land, relying instead on federal acquisition at fair market value. Is the difference that the Darby refuge was proposed in an area heavily dominated by agricultural land uses and in a state that has little previous FWS land management presence, whereas the Northern Tallgrass Prairie refuge was proposed in a state with a long history of national wildlife refuge presence? Perhaps the farming community in Ohio is simply fearful of what a new federal land presence will mean to its future. Yet the Darby refuge proposal definitively pointed out that:

- The federal government will not use condemnation powers to acquire refuge land, relying on willing sellers at negotiated prices.

- The refuge would make revenue sharing payments to the county to make up for lost tax revenues.

- The refuge cannot regulate agricultural practices on non-refuge lands.

- The refuge, at its largest proposed extent, would retire only 50,000 of the area's 860,000 acres of active farmland.

So, what were the farmers in the Darby refuge area afraid of? Is it really credible for them to have posed national food scarcity as a reason not to support the refuge? Or was the main issue one of the preservation of their culture, their way of living? Was that element truly at risk as a result of the Darby proposal? If so, how would you account for that in refuge design and management?

2. As noted previously in the chapter, most of the nation's original prairie lands have been converted to agricultural uses, mostly on public lands but much on private lands as well, as the Darby refuge story attests. This suggests that most land suitable for grassland restoration will be in or near agricultural lands. Hence, can grassland restoration, and grasslands ecosystem management generally, get very far without coming to grips with the agriculture question, that is, the question of what to do with the agricultural interests affected by grassland restoration? Efforts to restore grasslands in agriculture-intensive areas, such as Deborah Donahue's call for an end to grazing on public lands and the Darby refuge proposal, meet stiff local, agriculturally-based opposition, but often receive broad national support and the ringing endorsement of ecologists. Should local agricultural interests be given a "veto" over national resource goals such as grassland ecosystem restoration? Should national goals such as grassland restoration take priority over local community preferences? For an insightful and thought-provoking survey of the cultural and psychological biases many rural communities have against conservation efforts initiated by government and "outsider" environmental groups, see Christopher S. Elmendorf, *Ideas, Incentives, Gifts, and Governance: Toward Conservation Stewardship of Private Land, In Cultural and Psychological Perspective*, 2003 U. ILL. L. REV. 423.

3. Instead of purchasing lands for the Darby refuge, couldn't FWS have purchased easements and allow continued limited agricultural uses on the refuge lands? Indeed, FWS proposed doing so for a ring of land around the central refuge preserve land, stating that it preferred to see the lands bounding the central preserve remain in agricultural uses as opposed to being converted to urban uses. But could the entire refuge be handled in this manner, as is the approach of the Grassland Reserve bill discussed in the previous section of the chapter? What concerns would you have in doing so?

4. Given the degree of local opposition, should FWS have given up on the Darby refuge, or was it time for the farmers to make way for the return of the grasslands? In the end, the farmers won. On March 12, 2002, Craig Manson, Assistant Secretary of the Interior for Fish and Wildlife, sent letters to U.S. Representatives Deborah Pryce and David Hobson informing them that "conservation of the agricultural and natural resources of the Darby watershed is important," and that "the strong interest expressed in protecting the rural nature of this area indicates it is best that all levels of government work with local citizens to find a preferred approach to conserving those resources." The refuge proposal, he wrote, would be officially withdrawn. Apparently, it was not the preferred approach after all.

CHAPTER 10

FRESHWATER ECOSYSTEMS

A. BIODIVERSITY AND FRESHWATER ECOSYSTEMS

The water in all of Earth's rivers, lakes, and wetlands makes up just 0.01 percent of the world's water and only one percent of the earth's surface. Fortunately, the United States has bountiful supplies of freshwater resources: 3.6 million miles of rivers and streams, 41 million acres of lakes, 275 million acres of wetlands, and 33 trillion gallons of groundwater. These resources provide tremendous value to biodiversity conservation, as well as to human economies. Globally, for example, over 12 percent of all wildlife species live in freshwater ecosystems, and most other species depend on freshwater resources in some way for their survival. Wetlands, in particular, harbor many species and provide valuable shoreline protection, inland flood control, and sediment and chemical filtration services. Humans use freshwater resources to generate over 20 percent of the world's electricity through hydropower, to irrigate 40 percent of the world's crops, and to supply 12 percent of the world's fish consumption. A person in the United States on average uses two gallons of water brushing teeth, 25–50 gallons for a shower, and 20 gallons to wash dishes by hand (but only 9–12 gallons in an automatic dishwasher). It takes 1800 gallons to refine one barrel of crude oil and 24 gallons to make one pound of plastic. Half of the population of the United States, and virtually all its rural population, depends on groundwater for its drinking water supply.

How well are we managing these freshwater resources for humans and nature? Wherever that question is asked, on whatever scale it is posed, the answer boils down to two interrelated but distinct issues: quantity and quality. Freshwater ecosystems depend, obviously, on water to function. And where a sufficient quantity of water is present to allow functions to transpire naturally, very often the quality of the water will be a factor in determining whether those functions actually do so.

On the quantity issue, much depends on location. The United States uses over 500,000 gallons of water per person, per year. That sounds like a lot to most people. Nationally, however, our renewable water supply is 4 times the amount withdrawn and 15 times the amount actually consumed. So why all the headlines about water shortages? The answer is that this pattern of use and replenishment is not uniform geographically or temporally. Many areas of our nation are close to or beyond their physical capacity to supply suitable water to meet human and environmental needs. This condition is particularly acute in the West and Southwest, where low water renewal plus high water consumption have combined to spell economic and ecological trouble in recent decades. Ironically, irrigated agriculture, which consumes four times as much freshwater as all other uses in the nation combined, is concentrated in the 19 western states and is subsidized extensively through federal reclamation projects. Among the 17 states in which withdrawal of groundwater exceeded one billion gallons per day in 2000, in only two, Florida and New York, did withdrawals for public water supply surpass withdrawals for irrigation. Ten of the states were in the West. U.S. GEOLOGICAL SURVEY, ESTIMATED USE OF WATER IN THE UNITED STATES IN 2000, USGS CIRCULAR 1268, Table 4 (March 2004).

1990 TOTAL WATER WITHDRAWALS
(excluding power)

A topographic representation of water withdrawals, showing
disproportionate removal of water from freshwater systems in the western
states, primarily as a result of irrigated agriculture.
U.S. Geological Survey

A recent comprehensive study of water in the West suggests that rising global temperatures will dramatically alter water conditions in the region. The Western states have experienced an average rise in temperatures of 0.8°C since the 1950s. Even modestly higher winter temperatures are likely to reduce snowpack that is vital to water supply in the Western states— spring snowmelt makes up 75 percent of all water in streams throughout the West. Ironically, higher spring temperatures will increase the melting rate of what snow does fall, posing an increased risk of spring floods as peak snowmelts occur earlier. And higher summer temperatures will increase evaporation from reservoirs and lead to more forest fires. *See* Robert F. Service, *As the West Goes Dry*, 303 SCIENCE 1124 (2004).

Already starved for water and anticipating an even more arid future, fast-growing Western cities are scrambling for secure water supplies. Las Vegas has investigated a $2 billion network of wells and pipes that would suck water from deep wells across rural Nevada. El Paso is purchasing vast lands to its east to provide a future well field site, and also has considered a $500 million pipeline to reach water wells in distant Dell Valley. Colorado Springs is planning a 43-mile, $900 million pipeline to the Arkansas River to support 40 more years of growth. (These pale in comparison, though, to a proposal in Spain to spend $4.5 billion to pipe water from the soggy north to the arid southern coastal regions where tourism fuels demand.)

But water scarcity is increasingly becoming a serious economic and environmental issue for states east of the Mississippi River as well. Georgia, Alabama, and Florida, for example, have been locked in battle for decades over the distribution of water in the Apalachicola-Chattahoochee-Flint River basin, which many ecologists consider one of the world's most stunning and imperiled hot spots of biodiversity (more on the "ACF" in Part D of this chapter). In times of drought, which often last for years, these and similar water battles become more heated, but also only more difficult to resolve. In short, water quantity is becoming an ecosystem management issue in many parts of the United States as human consumption and ecosystem needs are increasingly in competition.

The functions of freshwater ecosystems are not limited to the water itself. The *habitat* that freshwater resources support can be reduced in quantity without impairing the quantity of *water* available in the system. Perhaps no topic has presented this dimension of the water resources quantity issue as the history and status of the nation's wetlands—areas such as swamps, bogs, marshes, and other areas saturated by surface or ground water sufficiently to support vegetation adapted for saturated soil conditions (more on these qualities later). Wetlands can be broadly divided into two categories: coastal wetlands and inland wetlands. Coastal wetlands are mostly marshes and swamps that are flooded by the tides. Non-tidal inland wetlands include wetlands along rivers and lakes, as well as isolated wetlands that are not directly connected to a major body of water but which are nonetheless valuable ecological resources. An important example of the latter variety is the "prairie pothole," which provides habitat for about half of the U.S. waterfowl population. Among the most biologically productive of land types, wetlands cover approximately 4 to 6 percent of the Earth's land surface. Their high productivity results from the essential characteristic of a wetland: an area that is flooded part of the time but not all of the time. This flooding ensures that the wetlands have ample supplies of water, minerals, or both. In addition to their high biological productivity, wetlands are important habitat for birds, fish, and other species. Wetlands are also important cleansing mechanisms for preventing pollutants from farms and other activities from running off and degrading water quality in rivers, lakes, and streams.

At the time of European settlement, the area that is today the coterminous United States had approximately 221 million acres of wetlands. Today about 105 million acres remain in these lower 48 states. Six states have lost over 85 percent of their wetlands, and 22 have lost more than 50 percent. None of the lower 48 states has lost less than 20 percent of its original wetlands. Florida has lost the most acres of wetlands—9.3 million acres—though it also is the state with the most remaining acres of wetlands, other than Alaska. Alaska adds 170 million acres of wetlands to the total, only a small fraction of which have been lost in the last 200 years.

Most of this history of loss is attributable to drainage of wetlands for conversion to agriculture, a practice that began in earnest with the earliest European settlers and was the official federal and state policy throughout most of the 1800s. Wetlands were considered undesirable, swampy, mosquito-infested wastelands that truly were wasted if not converted to some better use, usually agriculture but increasingly for urban development. This attitude prevailed well into the 1900s. Consider Gene Zion's 1957 children's book, *Dear Garbage Man*, which tells the supposedly happy story of how garbage should be used:

That night as the city slept, the tugboats chugged and whistled softly as they pulled the barges down the river. The trash and ashes they carried would be used to fill in swampland. Then parks and playgrounds would be built there.

And many such parks and playgrounds were built. But as the ecological value of wetlands was increasingly understood and appreciated, protection of wetlands became a major public policy objective by the mid-1970s. That trend, plus the gradual decline in conversion of land to agricultural uses significantly dampened the rate of wetland losses. During the 1990s, we lost on average only about 58,500 acres annually to a combination of urban development (30%), agriculture (26%), forestry (23%), and rural development (21%), which is a dramatic reduction from the previous decade. A recent assessment of wetland status estimates there are 107.7 million acres of wetlands in the coterminous United States, the vast majority of which are freshwater wetlands. *See* U.S. FISH AND WILDLIFE SERVICE, STATUS AND TRENDS OF WETLANDS IN THE COTERMINOUS UNITED STATES 1998–2004 (2006). Also, the report suggests that the tide has turned on wetland losses, with an estimated net gain of over 190,000 acres since 1998. This assertion was controversial, however, as included as wetlands for purposes of the net gain are artificial freshwater ponds such as farm stock ponds, golf course ponds, and urban stormwater control ponds, which as a category increased by 700,000 acres since 1998. If those artificial wetlands were not counted, there would have been a net loss of wetlands. Some state studies have shown continuing net losses of wetlands as well, particularly through conversion to suburban development. See Janat C. Morlan et al., *Oregon Study Finds Continued Loss of Freshwater Wetlands*, NATIONAL WETLANDS NEWSL., May-June 2011, at 11.

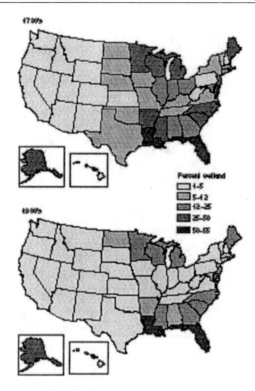

*Percentage of the areas of each state occupied by wetlands in the 1780's
(top map) and the 1980's.(bottom map).*
U.S. Geological Survey, Biological Resources Division, Status and Trends of the
Nation's Biological Resources (1999)

Water and habitat quantity in rivers, streams, lakes, and wetlands is
one primary metric of freshwater ecosystem management policy. The other
is water quality. A variety of factors can impair water quality for human
and ecological uses. The chief threats to ecological processes include low
dissolved oxygen, excessive nutrients, unsuitable temperature, sediment
and siltation, bacteria and other pathogens, toxic organic chemicals and
dissolved metals, unsuitable acidity levels, and loss or degradation of habitat. All of these factors continue to pose threats to our nation's waters,
though in many areas the magnitude of the threat has decreased measurably after decades of concerted water quality protection regulation.

The U.S. Environmental Protection Agency periodically prepares comprehensive assessments of national water quality, evaluating data on a
significant portion of our nation's freshwater ecosystems. *See, e.g.,* USEPA,
OFFICE OF WATER, ATLAS OF AMERICA'S POLLUTED WATERS (May 2000);
USEPA, OFFICE OF WATER, NATIONAL WATER QUALITY INVENTORY: 1994
REPORT TO CONGRESS (Dec. 1995). For rivers and streams, EPA in 1995
evaluated data for 17 percent of total river miles, finding 36 percent of that
portion to be impaired. For lakes, ponds, and reservoirs, EPA surveyed data for 42 percent of total surface acres, finding 37 percent of those waters to
be impaired. The leading source of water quality impairment in both categories of water bodies, by far, was agriculture, which is a significant source
of nutrients, sediment, and pathogens. EPA also assessed available data on

wetland quality, finding sediment, flow alterations, and habitat alterations as leading threats to habitat quality, with agriculture, again, the leading source of those threats. Results from EPA's 2000 National Water Quality Inventory showed no improvements: 39 percent of assessed river miles and 45 percent of lakes, ponds, and reservoirs were found to be polluted, with pesticides and nutrients in agricultural runoff the leading source of pollution in both categories. *See* USEPA, OFFICE OF WATER, NATIONAL WATER QUALITY INVENTORY: 2000 REPORT (2002).

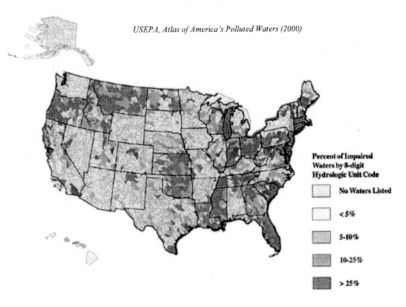

USEPA, Atlas of America's Polluted Waters (2000)

Percent of Impaired Waters by 8-digit Hydrologic Unit Code

No Waters Listed

<5%

5-10%

10-25%

>25%

Another alarming trend is the detection of a wider array of household chemicals in freshwater systems. For example, a study from Johns Hopkins University detected the presence of a triclocarbon, common antibacterial agent used in consumer soaps and detergents, at relatively alarming levels in several streams in Maryland. Sources include municipal wastewater treatment plant discharges and sewer system leaks. Although over a million pounds of the agent are produced and used in consumer products each year since the 1950s, virtually nothing is known about its fate and behavior in the environment. *See* Susan Bruninga, *Antibacterial Agent Used in Soap, Detergent Reported Found in Maryland Streams, Rivers*, 35 Env't Rep. (BNA) 1829 (2004).

Water quality and water quantity are intricately related factors in overall functioning of freshwater ecosystems. For example, the National Academy of Science's National Research Council concluded that higher spring flows and lower summer flows—i.e., a flow regime closer to natural conditions—are necessary along the Missouri River in order to reverse the widespread degradation that ecosystem has suffered in recent decades. *See* NATIONAL ACADEMY OF SCIENTISTS/NATIONAL RESEARCH COUNCIL, THE MISSOURI RIVER ECOSYSTEM: EXPLORING THE PROSPECTS FOR RECOVERY (2002). The Missouri River has dozens of dams and levees controlling water flow, and has over 735 miles "channelized" to promote barge navigation. As a result, over 3 million acres of riparian habitat have been substantially degraded. Farmers, however, are fearful that high spring flows will flood croplands, and barge operators contend low summer flows will stall barge traffic. And the U.S. Army Corps of Engineers, which maintains navigability of the river, and the U.S. Fish and Wildlife Service, which oversees habitat quality, have disagreed hotly over how to manage the flow regime. Clearly, the quantity and timing of river flows have much to do with both the ecological and the economic values a river delivers.

Indeed, dams are perhaps the human-induced change that has had the most adverse overall impact on freshwater ecosystems, largely because they affect both quantity and quality. Large dams—those over 15 meters high—now impound over 14 percent of the freshwater runoff in the world. Over 60 percent of the globe's major rivers are fractured, often significantly, by dams. While dams increase surface area of reservoirs, they also enable larger withdrawal of water from the system. For example, most of the world's irrigation is made possible by dams. Also, the interruption of water and silt flow that dams cause, combined with the disruption of thermal conditions caused by their altered outflow water temperatures, has wreaked ecological havoc on almost every dammed river system.

The impact of these and other degradations of freshwater ecosystems on biodiversity is palpable: in the United States, 37 percent of freshwater fish species, 67 percent of mussel species, 51 percent of crayfish species, and 40 percent of amphibian species are considered threatened, endangered, or extinct. Overall, therefore, while much progress has been made on both the quantity and quality fronts for freshwater ecosystems, much room for improvement remains.

NOTES & QUESTIONS

1. Filling wetlands for playgrounds has obvious impacts to wetland resources, and further losses attributable to such obvious causes can be easily halted. But more often the causes of wetlands degradation are complex and not easily solved. For example, the nation's two large wetlands complexes, the Everglades in Florida and the Mississippi River Delta in Louisiana, face demise from contrasting and seemingly intractable conditions. The Everglades are a naturally low-lying freshwater system that is suffering from nutrient overload caused by agricultural and urban runoff that is "plugged up" by canals and dikes restricting outflow from the system. Efforts to "replumb" the system and control nutrient inflow hold some promise, but at the expensive price tag of over $10 billion. *See* Mary Doyle and Donald E. Jodrey, *Everglades Restoration: Forging New Law in Allocating Water for the Environment*, 8 ENVTL. LAWYER 255 (2002); Alfred Light, *Ecosystem Management in the Everglades*, 14 NATURAL RESOURCES & ENV'T 166 (2000). The Delta wetlands, twice the size of the Everglades, are actually starving for nutrients as the nutrient-rich Mississippi outflow has been diked and channeled so as to send the water out into the Gulf of Mexico well beyond the reach of Delta wetlands. And the Delta is sinking—actually, slumping outward and downward into the Gulf—due to geologic faults that run throughout the area. The Delta now loses over 60 square kilometers of wetlands annually. Louisiana embarked on an "Americas Wetland" campaign to call attention to its vanishing coastal wetlands, including a major push to gain federal assistance by noting the economic consequences of having its

"working coastline" of oil rigs, ports, fishing villages, and New Orleans casinos flooded by the combination of rising sea levels and falling coastline levels. *See America's Wetland Campaign*, www.americaswetland.com. Plans to reverse these losses, known as Coast 2050, were expected cost over $14 billion to implement. *See Louisiana's Vanishing Wetlands: Going, Going . . .*, 289 SCIENCE 1860 (2000). Clearly, after Hurricane Katrina in 2005, the need for restoration is even more acute and widely appreciated, and the price tag is no doubt much higher (we provide further discussion of the effects of Hurricane Katrina in the materials on the Mississippi Delta in Chapter 11).

2. Not all nations turned the corner on appreciation of wetlands as soon as did the United States. In 1983, for example, Romanian dictator Nicolae Ceausescu decreed that the Romanian portion of the Danube River delta, one of the largest wetland complexes in Europe, would be diked and converted to agricultural and other land uses. His regime managed to transform 15 percent of the delta into marginal cropland—the delta's soil is too salty to support viable agriculture—before his government's fall saved not only Romania's future, but also the delta's. After the overthrow of Ceausescu, the new government proclaimed a policy of restoring and protecting the delta that appeared to have meaningful results. *See* Karen F. Schmidt, *A True-Blue Vision for the Danube*, 294 SCIENCE 1444 (2001).

3. The impact of climate change on freshwater resources depends on changes in the amount of rainfall, as well as when and where it occurs, which scientists are unable to forecast with precision under current models of climate change dynamics. Some studies suggest that the influence of human population increases will place far greater stress on the adequacy of freshwater supply than will climate change. *See* Union of Concerned Scientists and the Ecological Society of America, Confronting Climate Change in the Gulf Coast Region (2001), *available at* http://www.ucsusa.org. But when climate change is added to the scenario, many parts of the world that have never or rarely been concerned with water availability, including the eastern United States, could experience dramatic increases in water supply stress. *See* Charles J. Vorosmarty et al., *Global Water Resources: Vulnerability from Climate Change and Population Growth*, 289 SCIENCE 284 (2000).

4. For more information on the extent and value of freshwater resources, see Sandra Postel and Stephen Carpenter, *Freshwater Ecosystem Services, in* Nature's Services: Societal Dependence on Natural Ecosystems (Gretchen C. Daily ed., 1997) (excerpted in Chapter 1); Nels Johnson et al., *Managing Water for People and Nature*, 292 SCIENCE 1071 (2001), as well as the material excerpted in Chapter 2 of this text. For detailed statistical presentation of water use in the United States, see U.S. GEOLOGICAL SURVEY, ESTIMATED USE OF WATER IN THE UNITED STATES IN 1990: TOTAL WATER USE. For additional information on the history of wetland losses in the United States, see THOMAS E. DAHL AND GREGORY J. ALLORD, TECHNICAL ASPECTS OF WETLANDS, HISTORY OF WETLANDS IN THE COTERMINOUS UNITED STATES, U.S. GEOLOGICAL SURVEY WATER SUPPLY PAPER 2425 (1997); RALPH E. HEIMLICH, WETLANDS AND AGRICULTURE: PRIVATE INTERESTS AND PUBLIC BENEFITS, USDA AGRICULTURAL ECONOMIC REPORT NO. 765 (Sept. 1998); JONATHAN TOLMAN, GAINING MORE GROUND: ANALYSIS OF WETLAND TRENDS IN THE UNITED STATES (Competitive Enterprise Inst. 1994).

B. PRIMER ON THE LAW OF FRESHWATER RESOURCES

The law of freshwater resources—of groundwater, lakes, rivers, wetlands, and their watersheds—is an incredible patchwork of federal, state, and local initiatives. The major force in that body of law, and our major focus in this chapter, is the Federal Water Pollution Control Act, also known by the name of its 1972 amendatory legislation, the Clean Water Act. A brief description of the history of that law and its current policy direction follows.

1. HISTORICAL BACKGROUND

In a recent case involving the jurisdictional limits of the Clean Water Act with respect to wetlands, the U.S. Supreme Court took the occasion to explore the legislative history of that statute. Because he disagreed with the majority's interpretation of congressional intent, Justice Stevens, writing for the dissenting Justices, delved even more deeply into the history of federal regulation of water resources. His opinion provides an eloquent capsule history of that topic. (The portions of the opinions in the case addressing the jurisdictional limits of the Clean Water Act are reproduced *infra*.)

Solid Waste Agency of Northern Cook County v. United States Army Corps of Engineers

Supreme Court of the United States, 2001.
531 U.S. 159.

■ JUSTICE STEVENS, with whom JUSTICE SOUTER, JUSTICE GINSBURG, and JUSTICE BREYER join, dissenting.

*   *   *

Federal regulation of the Nation's waters began in the 19th century with efforts targeted exclusively at "promot[ing] water transportation and commerce." Kalen, Commerce to Conservation: The Call for a National Water Policy and the Evolution of Federal Jurisdiction Over Wetlands, 69 N.D.L.Rev. 873, 877 (1993). This goal was pursued through the various Rivers and Harbors Acts, the most comprehensive of which was the RHA of 1899. Section 13 of the 1899 RHA, commonly known as the Refuse Act, prohibited the discharge of "refuse" into any "navigable water" or its tributaries, as well as the deposit of "refuse" on the bank of a navigable water "whereby navigation shall or may be impeded or obstructed" without first obtaining a permit from the Secretary of the Army. 30 Stat. 1152.

During the middle of the 20th century, the goals of federal water regulation began to shift away from an exclusive focus on protecting navigability and toward a concern for preventing environmental degradation. This awakening of interest in the use of federal power to protect the aquatic environment was helped along by efforts to reinterpret § 13 of the RHA in order to apply its permit requirement to industrial discharges into navigable waters, even when such discharges did nothing to impede navigability. See, e.g., United States v. Republic Steel Corp., 362 U.S. 482, 490–491

(1960) (noting that the term "refuse" in § 13 was broad enough to include industrial waste). Seeds of this nascent concern with pollution control can also be found in the [Federal Water Pollution Control Act (FWPCA)], which was first enacted in 1948 and then incrementally expanded in the following years.

The FWPCA of 1948 applied only to "interstate waters." § 10(e), 62 Stat. 1161. Subsequently, it was harmonized with the Rivers and Harbors Act such that—like the earlier statute—the FWPCA defined its jurisdiction with reference to "navigable waters." Pub.L. 89–753, § 211, 80 Stat. 1252. None of these early versions of the FWPCA could fairly be described as establishing a comprehensive approach to the problem, but they did contain within themselves several of the elements that would later be employed in the [Clean Water Act (CWA)]. Milwaukee v. Illinois, 451 U.S. 304, 318, n. 10 (1981) (Rehnquist, J.) (Congress intended to do something "quite different" in the 1972 Act); 2 W. Rodgers, Environmental Law: Air and Water § 4.1, pp. 10–11 (1986) (describing the early versions of the FWPCA).

The shift in the focus of federal water regulation from protecting navigability toward environmental protection reached a dramatic climax in 1972, with the passage of the CWA. The Act, which was passed as an amendment to the existing FWPCA, was universally described by its supporters as the first truly comprehensive federal water pollution legislation. The "major purpose" of the CWA was "to establish a comprehensive long-range policy for the elimination of water pollution." S.Rep. No. 92–414, p. 95 (1971), reprinted in 2 Legislative History of the Water Pollution Control Act Amendments of 1972 (Committee Print compiled for the Senate Committee on Public Works by the Library of Congress), Ser. No. 93–1, p. 1511 (1971) (hereinafter Leg. Hist.) (emphasis added). And "[n]o Congressman's remarks on the legislation were complete without reference to [its] 'comprehensive' nature. . ." Milwaukee v. Illinois, 451 U.S. 304, 318 (1981) (Rehnquist, J.). A House sponsor described the bill as "the most comprehensive and far-reaching water pollution bill we have ever drafted," 1 Leg. Hist. 369 (Rep. Mizell), and Senator Randolph, Chairman of the Committee on Public Works, stated: "It is perhaps the most comprehensive legislation that the Congress of the United States has ever developed in this particular field of the environment." Id., at 1269. This Court was therefore undoubtedly correct when it described the 1972 amendments as establishing "a comprehensive program for controlling and abating water pollution." Train v. City of New York, 420 U.S. 35, 37 (1975).

Section 404 of the CWA resembles § 13 of the RHA, but, unlike the earlier statute, the primary purpose of which is the maintenance of navigability, § 404 was principally intended as a pollution control measure. A comparison of the contents of the RHA and the 1972 Act vividly illustrates the fundamental difference between the purposes of the two provisions. The earlier statute contains pages of detailed appropriations for improvements in specific navigation facilities, 30 Stat. 1121–1149, for studies concerning the feasibility of a canal across the Isthmus of Panama, id., at 1150, and for surveys of the advisability of harbor improvements at numerous other locations, id., at 1155–1161. Tellingly, § 13, which broadly prohibits the discharge of refuse into navigable waters, contains an exception for refuse "flowing from streets and sewers . . . in a liquid state." Id., at 1152.

The 1972 Act, in contrast, appropriated large sums of money for research and related programs for water pollution control, 86 Stat. 816–833, and for the construction of water treatment works, id., at 833–844. Strikingly absent from its declaration of "goals and policy" is any reference to avoiding or removing obstructions to navigation. Instead, the principal objective of the Act, as stated by Congress in § 101, was "to restore and maintain the chemical, physical, and biological integrity of the Nation's waters." 33 U.S.C. § 1251. Congress therefore directed federal agencies in § 102 to "develop comprehensive programs for preventing, reducing, or eliminating the pollution of the navigable waters and ground waters and improving the sanitary condition of surface and underground waters." 33 U.S.C. § 1252. The CWA commands federal agencies to give "due regard," not to the interest of unobstructed navigation, but rather to "improvements which are necessary to conserve such waters for the protection and propagation of fish and aquatic life and wildlife [and] recreational purposes." Ibid.

Because of the statute's ambitious and comprehensive goals, it was, of course, necessary to expand its jurisdictional scope. Thus, although Congress opted to carry over the traditional jurisdictional term "navigable waters" from the RHA and prior versions of the FWPCA, it broadened the definition of that term to encompass all "waters of the United States." § 1362(7). Indeed, the 1972 conferees arrived at the final formulation by specifically deleting the word "navigable" from the definition that had originally appeared in the House version of the Act.

2. CURRENT SCENE

Justice Stevens' dissenting opinion in *SWANCC* traces the transformation of federal water resources policy from its focus on protection of navigation to its modern focus on water quality. Yet, his opinion does not reveal the aspect of federal water quality policy that has plagued it in terms of effectiveness in ecosystem management—the distinction between "point source" and "nonpoint source" pollution and the disparate regulatory treatment the two categories receive.

Under the CWA, a point source is a discharge of regulated pollutants from "any discernable, confined and discrete conveyance, including but not limited to any pipe, ditch, channel, tunnel, conduit, well, discrete fissure, container, rolling stock, concentrated animal feeding operation, or vessel or other floating craft, from which pollutants are or may be discharged." 33 U.S.C. § 1362(14). As all-encompassing as this definition seems, it misses a huge component of water pollution sources. First, by exclusion, any regulated pollutant not so discharged is a so-called nonpoint source of pollution. This includes, significantly, overland runoff from rain and snowmelt that is not collected in storm sewers. Second, by definition, most agricultural pollution, including irrigation return flows carried, believe it or not, *in ditches and pipes*, is not point source pollution. *See* 33 U.S.C. § 1362(14). Therein lies the problem: As noted previously, EPA has identified agricultural pollution as the leading cause of impairment to our nation's rivers, lakes, and wetlands, and not far behind in all of those cases is urban runoff. In other words, today's leading causes of impairment to freshwater resources are the two significant sources of water pollution that are *not* regulated as point sources under the CWA.

So how has federal law managed these nonpoint sources? Not much. Efforts to address nonpoint source water pollution in the CWA and other statutes have been feeble, unfocused, and underfunded. Section 208 of the CWA requires states to develop areawide waste treatment management plans that include a process for identifying nonpoint sources and establishing feasible control measures. *See* 33 U.S.C. § 1288(a). With high expectations for this program, Congress used it as the rationale for moving irrigation return flows from the point source side of the CWA to the nonpoint source side of the CWA. *See* S. Rep. No. 370, at 35 (1977), *reprinted in* 1977 U.S.C.C.A.N. 4326, 4360 ("All such sources, regardless of the manner in which the flow was applied to the agricultural lands, and regardless of the discrete nature of the entry point, are more appropriately treated under the requirements of section 208"). Similarly, in the 1987 amendments, Congress added section 319 to the statute to require states to prepare "state assessment reports" that identify waters that cannot reasonably be expected to meet water quality standards because of nonpoint source pollution. 33 U.S.C. § 1329(a). States must prepare "state management programs" prescribing the "best management practices" to control sources of nonpoint pollution. When EPA approves a state's assessment reports and the management plans, the state is eligible for financial assistance to implement its programs.

In the absence of any concrete, enforceable federal blueprint for addressing nonpoint source pollution, the efficacy of the section 208 and section 319 programs depended largely on state initiative to develop new approaches. It is little surprise, then, that neither section 208 nor section 319 led anywhere meaningful. An EPA Federal Advisory Committee summed up the weakness of the section 208 and 319 programs by explaining that "EPA had no 'hammer' provision for states not adopting programs and no ability to establish a program if a State chose not to." EPA TMDL Federal Advisory Committee, Discussion Paper, Nonpoint Source-Only Waters 5 (1997).

Congress thus took a more aggressive step in section 6217 of the Coastal Zone Act Reauthorization Amendments of 1990. Pub. L. No. 101–508, Title VI, § 6217 (1990). This legislation amended the Coastal Zone Management Act (CZMA) (discussed more fully in Chapter 11) to add a requirement that any state with a federally approved coastal zone management program must develop a Coastal Nonpoint Pollution Program subject to federal review and approval. States must identify land uses leading to nonpoint pollution and develop measures to apply "best available nonpoint pollution control practices, technologies, processes, siting criteria, operating methods, or other alternatives." 16 U.S.C. § 1455b(g)(5). When EPA and the National Oceanic and Atmospheric Administration approve a state's Coastal Nonpoint Pollution Program, the federal government agrees not to fund, authorize, or carry out projects inconsistent with the state's plan. *Id.* 1455b(k). For coastal states, this requirement can serve as an impetus for more aggressive regulation of nonpoint source pollution generally, though funding assistance from the federal government is woefully short of the expected cost of Coastal Nonpoint Pollution Program plan preparation and implementation for the states (for example, the appropriation for fiscal year 1998 was $12 million).

By the mid-1990s, therefore, it had become clear that the primary objective of ecosystem management for freshwater resources had to be getting a handle on nonpoint source water pollution, but that significant obstacles would need to be overcome, not the least of which is the gaping hole in the CWA. Congress remained essentially inert on such matters through the 1990s. Thus, on October 18, 1997, during the Clean Water Act's 25th Anniversary celebration, then Vice President Gore requested that the Secretary of Agriculture and the Administrator of the United States Environmental Protection Agency (EPA), in consultation with affected federal agencies, devise an action plan to address enhanced protection from public health threats posed by water pollution; more effective control of polluted runoff; and promotion of water quality protection on a watershed basis. The result, the *Clean Water Action Plan: Restoring and Protecting America's Waters* (CWAP), outlined an ambitious agenda for coordinating existing federal water conservation authorities toward, among other things, ecosystem management. A principal focus of this component of the CWAP agenda was bringing nonpoint source pollution more fully within the federal water policy umbrella, but its scope also extended to wetland conservation policy and the broader ambition of developing a watershed-based framework for resource management.

The Bush Administration developed a new water quality plan in 2003 known as the *500-Day Water Quality Plan: Twice as Clean by 2015* (Dec. 2003). The six major strategies charted in the plan were: clean and safe drinking water; beaches safe for swimming; gain one million acres of wetlands; cut polluted waters in half; safe and sustainable water and wastewater infrastructure; and regional collaboration to solve multijurisdictional problems. Later that year the Administration unveiled its five-year *EPA Strategic Plan 2003–08*, the "water elements" of which outline six desired accomplishments: increasing the amount of water safe to drink; increasing the amount of fish and shellfish safe to consume; increasing the amount of waters safe for swimming; restore polluted watersheds; improve conditions in coastal ecosystems; and increase net wetlands by 400,000 acres. Some of the planned measures focused on the central problem of nonpoint sources. For example, in October 2003 EPA published a new set of guidelines for nonpoint source program grants to states under CWA section 319. *See* 68 Fed. Reg. 60653 (Oct. 23, 2003). A significant focus of the grant program was on the implementation of state watershed management plans. These plans were intended to provide an analytical framework for assessing sources of pollution and estimating the amount of pollutant reduction necessary on a watershed basis.

The Obama Administration announced its signature water policy in April 2011. *See* http://www.whitehouse.gov/administration/eop/ceq/ initiatives/clean-water. Known as the *Clean Water Framework*, it pursues several objectives:

Promoting Innovative Partnerships. Federal agencies are partnering with states, tribes, local governments and diverse stakeholders on innovative approaches to restore urban waters, promote sustainable water supplies, and develop new incentives for farmers to protect clean water.

Enhancing Communities and Economies by Restoring Important Water Bodies. The Obama Administration is dedicating unprecedented attention to restoring iconic places like the Chesapeake Bay, California Bay-Delta, Great Lakes, Gulf of Mexico and Everglades, investing in action and helping states, local governments and stakeholders find pollution control solutions that are tailored to their specific needs.

Innovating for More Water-Efficient Communities. The Administration is working with policymakers, consumers, farmers and businesses to save water – and save money – through 21st century water management policies and technology.

Ensuring Clean Water to Protect Public Health. The Obama Administration is aggressively pursuing new ways to protect public health by reducing contaminants in Americans' drinking water. This includes action to update drinking water standards, protect drinking water sources, modernize the tools available to communities to meet their clean water requirements, and provide affordable clean water services in rural communities.

Enhancing Use and Enjoyment of our Waters. The Administration is promoting stewardship of America's waters through innovative programs and partnerships. These efforts include expanding access to waterways for recreation, protecting rural landscapes, and promoting public access to private lands for hunting, fishing and other recreational activities.

Updating the Nation's Water Policies. The Administration is strengthening protection of America's waters and American communities. This includes action to modernize water resources guidelines, and update Federal guidance on where the Clean Water Act applies nationwide. The draft guidance from U.S. EPA and the U.S. Army Corps of Engineers, which is open for 60 days of public comment, will protect waters that many communities depend upon for drinking, swimming, and fishing, and provide clearer, more predictable guidelines for determining which water bodies are protected from pollution under the Clean Water Act.

Supporting Science to Solve Water Problems. The Administration is using the latest science and research to improve water policies and programs and identify and address emerging pollution challenges.

NOTES & QUESTIONS

1. In addition to the several programs discussed in the text that were initiated specifically to address nonpoint source pollution, over 30 other federal programs deal with nonpoint source pollution in some way or another. Many of these programs provide funding assistance and incentives to states or private actors to improve nonpoint source pollution management—for example, to improve farm runoff control practices. Some of the programs address actions on federal lands, where the solution is more amenable to direct regulation of private actors or altering federal agency action. Overall, the federal government spends over $3 billion per year implementing this array of programs, with EPA, USDA, and the Department of the Interior as the lead agencies. For an overview of the programs, see U.S. GENERAL ACCOUNTING OFFICE, FEDERAL ROLE IN ADDRESSING—AND CONTRIBUTING TO—NONPOINT SOURCE POLLUTION, GAO/RCED-99-45 (Feb. 1999).

2. Knowing what we now know about their impact on freshwater ecosystems, why hasn't Congress regulated nonpoint sources more aggressively? One factor is that they are fundamentally different from point sources in terms of amenability to regulation. Point sources such as chemical plants and wastewater treatment facilities generally are highly regulated enterprises. They discharge water pollutants in discrete, easily monitored locations and events. The discharge is usually a byproduct or waste of a technological process that can be altered with technological solutions. Regulation of point sources, in other words, is primarily a technology issue, not a land use issue. Most categories of nonpoint sources, by contrast, are diffuse and diverse land uses. Take farms for example. There are one million farms in the United States today, using over 900 million acres for crop and livestock production. Differences in weather, soil, and other local factors lead to tremendous diversity of farming practices around the nation. While modern farming is more technologically intensive than in the past, it is still primarily a local land use practice, and the federal government has traditionally been reluctant to regulate local land uses directly. Still, given how significant the nonpoint source pollution problem is, does it surprise you that Congress has responded how it has?

3. Perhaps it is understandable that Congress has not tried to undertake comprehensive nation-wide regulation of nonpoint sources such as farms. Have the states closed that gap? Generally, not much, at least not until recently. Most states followed the federal lead and focus regulatory clout almost entirely on point sources. Some states had authorities in place that could, arguably, be used to regulate nonpoint sources, but many did not use them in any concerted effort to do so. And the few states that ventured into more aggressive regulation of nonpoint sources generally left the worst offender—farms—relatively untouched. See Environmental Law Institute, Enforceable State Mechanisms for the Control of Nonpoint Source Water Pollution (1997); Environmental Law Institute, Almanac of Enforceable State Laws to Control Nonpoint Source Water Pollution (1998); James M. McElfish, State Enforcement Authorities for Polluted Runoff, 28 ENVTL. L. REP. (ELI) 10,181 (1998). More recently, however,

several states have received federal approval of a Nonpoint Source Pollution Control Program under Section 6217 of the Coastal Zone Management Act discussed above. In July 2000, California became the first state to receive such approval. Its 400-page, state-wide plan addressed nonpoint source pollution from agriculture, forestry, urban areas, marinas, and other sources over a 15-year planning horizon. It contemplates an initial period of voluntary improvement by each source category followed by aggressive regulation and enforcement if improvements are not brought about voluntarily. California also plans to use state implementation of a controversial federal program—the total maximum daily load program—as the cornerstone of nonpoint source management, including agricultural nonpoint source pollution (the so-called TMDL program is the subject of the materials in the next section of the text). It may be, therefore, that states will use the opportunity of compiling their coastal nonpoint source plans to reverse the trend of general neglect of nonpoint source pollution. A thorough survey of state authorities covering nonpoint source pollution can be found at ROBIN KUNDIS CRAIG & SCHLY NOTO, STATE NONPOINT SOURCE CONTROL PROGRAMS FOR AGRICULTURE: A LOOK AT AGRICULTURAL CERTAINTY (2012).

4. For an excellent history of the social, economic, and legal events leading up to the passage of the FWPCA, see William L. Andreen, *The Evolution of Water Pollution Control in the United States—State, Local, and Federal Efforts, 1789–1972: Part I*, 22 STAN. ENVTL. L. J. 145 (2003), and *Part II*, 22 STAN. ENVTL. L. J. 215 (2003).

Note on Water Rights

Two core and interrelated issues drive ecosystem management in freshwater ecosystems—water quality and water quantity. As ecosystem management policies increasingly demand authority over both of those domains, they have run head on into what in many parts of the nation is dearer than diamonds—water rights. Congress understood the potential for this collision at the dawn of the environmental legislation movement in the early 1970, advising that one policy of the Endangered Species Act was "that Federal agencies shall cooperate with State and local agencies to resolve water resource issues in concert with conservation of endangered species." 16 U.S.C. 1531(c)(2). Alas, as many of the cases and materials in this chapter attest, that has been easier said than done. Before delving into those sources, therefore, some background on water rights will be useful.

Generally speaking, freshwater is far scarcer in supply west of the nation's 100th meridian, which has led to the development of two different, but equally rich, bodies of water law. Water in its natural watercourses is in all the states owned by the states as a public resource, but *use* of the water is what matters, and the states have developed highly articulated legal regimes for distributing that right.

In the East, where water is more plentiful, surface water has traditionally been allocated under the common law "riparian rights" system, under which water is treated essentially as common property of all owners of land underlying or bordering the water body, known as riparian lands. Under strict riparian rules, only riparian land may use the water, and the water may be used only on and for the riparian land, though for obvious reasons (e.g., public water supplies) many states have altered that rule to allow specified offsite uses. Also, although the amount of water that may be used was in early versions of the system limited such that the landowner had to leave the "natural flow" of the watercourse unimpaired, conventional riparian rights systems are based on a "reasonable use" standard that allows some reduction in natural flow so long as other riparian owners are not harmed. What constitutes a reasonable use depends on a variety of factors such as the purpose of the use, suitability of the use to the watercourse, its economic and social values, and the extent of harm to others. To summarize, several general characteristics define the classic riparian rights system:

1. riparian rights are of equal priority;

2. the right is not quantified, but rather extends to the amount of water which can be reasonably and beneficially used on the riparian parcel;

3. riparian rights are correlative, so that during times of water shortage, the riparian proprietors share the shortage;

4. water may be used only upon that portion of the riparian parcel which is within the watershed of the water source;

5. the riparian right does not extend to seasonal storage of water;

6. the riparian right is part of the riparian land and cannot be transferred for use on other lands;

7. a riparian right is not lost by non-use; and

8. the riparian rights remain with the land when riparian lands are sold, but parcels which are severed from the adjacent water source lose their riparian rights unless the rights are reserved by deed.

The conventional riparian rights system, based as it is on the balancing test applied for reasonable use, can lead to significant uncertainty as to the quantity of water to which each riparian is entitled and how to resolve disputes between them. The on-site use requirement can also constrain economic development. In general, moreover, as a common property system it leaves water flows generally unregulated and unplanned. Most of the eastern states, therefore, have moved to a permit allocation system which, while preferring riparian uses, focuses primarily on the purpose of the use and facilitates a more orderly monitoring and enforcement of approved uses. About half of the eastern states have adopted this system, often referred to as "regulated riparianism." *See* Joseph W. Dellapenna, *The Law of Water Allocation in the Southeastern States at the Opening of the Twenty-First Century*, 2 U. ARK. LITTLE ROCK L. REV. 9, 33 (2002).

As for groundwater, the eastern states follow several different doctrines. The so-called "rule of capture" or "absolute ownership" allows landowners to withdraw unlimited supplies of groundwater from beneath the surface regardless of the consequences for other landowners drawing from the same source. Some states temper this under the doctrine of "correlative rights," which allows use only in proportion to the relative size of the surface estate unless using more would not injure other users from the same source. And about a third of the eastern states have adopted a "reasonable use" rule that recognizes proper beneficial uses, such as domestic supply, irrigation, and mining, and allows withdrawal so long as no injury is caused to other beneficial uses relying on the same source. As has happened with surface water, however, most of the eastern states have adopted a more formal permitting system for groundwater uses that approves and monitors withdrawals. Agricultural uses are, even in these permit system states, usually exempt or minimally covered.

Although water in the east was a plentiful resource well into the twentieth century, a growing population has demanded ever more supply, agriculture in the east has increased the use of irrigation as insurance against drought, and environmental concerns have made water quantity an important factor in the management of water quality and wildlife habitat. *See* Steven T. Miano and Michael E. Crane, *Eastern Water Law: Historical Perspectives and Emerging Trends*, 18 NATURAL RESOURCES & ENV'T 14 (Fall 2003). Hence, no longer is it the case that "water is for fightin'" only in the West. As this chapter's case study of the Apalachicola-Chattahoochee-Flint River basin in Georgia and Florida reveals (see section D), these days the East is no stranger to people warring over water.

In the West, where water supply has always been scarce and unreliable, allocation of surface and groundwater supplies generally follows an "appropriative rights" system that implements a rule of "first in time, first in right." Four core principles guide this system:

1. water in its natural course is the property of the public and is not subject to private ownership;

2. a vested right to use the water may be acquired by appropriation and application to a beneficial use;

3. the person first in time is first in right; and

4. beneficial use is the basis, measure, and limit of the right.

What matters under this approach, in other words, is appropriation of water to a beneficial use, which defines a user's allocation from the particular stream. The time of appropriation is of the utmost importance, with the "senior" appropriators who put water in a stream to use earlier than "junior" users having a priority when water supplies are short. In dry periods, therefore, the senior user takes as much as his or her allocation allows, the next most senior user comes next, and so on until the supply is exhausted, meaning some junior users may have no water at all.

Although it makes water rights more predictable than does the riparian system (which is why the western states abandoned riparianism early in their settlement), there are flaws in the appropriative rights system as well. For example, senior uses may not be the most economically useful or efficient, but will nonetheless trump socially superior uses in dry periods. The risk associated with junior rights also can deter investment in watersheds that have unreliable supplies. New users may be able to purchase rights from senior users, but many states severely restrict inter-watershed transfers of water. Also, because senior users must maintain their beneficial use to keep their rights intact, the appropriative system does not reward water conservation. In many watersheds, moreover, the quantity of appropriated rights and the quantity of water supply were sometimes far from certain, a problem many states address through an "adjudication" process requiring users to prove their seniority and amount of beneficial use in a multi-party proceeding that results in each user's rights being established through an "adjudicated right."

The appropriative rights system has evolved with many different nuances among the western states. For example, some states prioritize beneficial uses, usually with domestic and agricultural uses receiving the highest priority. And some states recognize limited riparian rights. But one of the most controversial issues has been how to ensure that, for recreational and wildlife purposes, some minimum amount of water remains undiverted and not consumed, known as "instream flow." The catch has been that the conventional appropriation system requires a beneficial use *and* a diversion. Some state courts have recognized instream flow as a beneficial use not requiring a diversion. *See, e.g.*, Nevada v. Morros, 766 P.2d 263 (Nev. 1988). Most states, however, handle this through statutes allowing public agencies to "reserve" instream flow under prescribed conditions and procedures. Some states also are beginning to allow nongovernmental entities to lease instream flows. Only New Mexico has neither a statute nor clear case law on the question. An excellent summary of state instream flow law is found at Jesse A. Boyd, *Hip Deep: A Survey of State Instream Flow Law from the Rocky Mountains to the Pacific Ocean*, 43 NATURAL RESOURCES J. 1151 (2003). An excellent summary of state instream flow law is found at Jesse A. Boyd, *Hip Deep: A Survey of State Instream Flow Law from the Rocky Mountains to the Pacific Ocean*, 43 NATURAL RESOURCES J. 1151 (2003). For an in-depth look at Oregon's innovative approaches to instream flows, see Janet Neuman et al., *Sometimes a Great Notion, Oregon's Instream Flow Experiments*, 36 ENVTL. L. 1125 (2006).

Groundwater rights are even more varied among the western states, ranging from a pure "rule of capture," to a rule of "correlative rights" assigning rights in an aquifer relative to surface area of the land, to a rule of "reasonable use," to a system basically the same as the surface water appropriative rights approach. The bottom line in all cases, though, is that the various systems define water use rights—rights that can transferred, sold, abandoned, and, importantly, which if taken by the government can give rise to a claim for just compensation. An excellent state-by-state overview of the surface and groundwater law for the western states is found at Bureau of Land Management, *Western States Water Laws*, http://www.blm.gov/nstc/WaterLaws/abstract1.html.

There are two important additional layers to western water law. One, the doctrine of "reserved rights," results from the fact that the federal government owns so much land in the West. Under this doctrine, the federal government acts as a public trustee to ensure adequate water supplies for federal public land purposes. Whenever federal land is withdrawn from general public domain for a specific use, such as a national park or an Indian reservation, water arising on or flowing across the land is reserved in sufficient quantity to accomplish in a reasonable manner the present *and future* purposes. As the Supreme Court explained in Winters v. United States, 207 U.S. 564 (1908), this reserved right vests at the time of the reservation of the lands, regardless of when the water is put to use, and is superior to all subsequent appropriated rights. This has caused significant disruption of "settled" water rights in states where Indian reservations have in recent years sought to quantify their reserved rights long after numerous other users—junior to the federal reserved right—thought they had secured a water supply through their place in line.

The federal government also plays a leading role in the second wrinkle— the history of "reclamation" in the arid West. One of the major authorities of the Bureau of Reclamation (BOR), an agency of the Department of the Interior, has been to manage and allocate water for the promotion of agriculture and settlement in the western states. Starting with the Reclamation Act of 1902, 43 U.S.C. § 371 *et seq.*, the idea was to have the BOR reclaim arid lands in certain states through irrigation projects and then open those lands to entry by homesteaders. This required the federal agency to secure water rights under state law, and then to distribute irrigation water through contractual arrangements with irrigation districts and individual farmers. This project led over time to a convoluted, but deeply embedded, system of water distribution throughout many parts of the West, upon which vast investments of public and private capital have been based to this day.

This summary of water law is a standard story told in countless law books and articles, taken as a given by courts and law practitioners around the nation, and considered sacrosanct by those who believe they hold precious water rights. Enter ecosystem management. Simply put, the demands of federal environmental laws such as the Endangered Species Act, Clean Water Act, and National Environmental Policy Act, as well as of their numerous state counterparts, include demands not only on water quality, but also on water *quantity*. The substantive and procedural dictates of this growing body of law have rocked settled expectations about water use in many states, putting water rights under a microscope.

C. BIODIVERSITY MANAGEMENT IN FRESHWATER ECOSYSTEMS

We have divided the discussion of the law of freshwater ecosystem management into four topics: (1) groundwater; (2) lakes and rivers; (3) wetlands; and (4) watersheds. We have two reasons for taking this approach. One was simple convenience—the legal framework follows essentially the same approach. The other reason, however, was to emphasize the complexity of the task. When asked to describe a freshwater ecosystem—where it begins and ends, what is in it, what influences it—the simplest unit is a lake or river. They have geographically-defined and well-known boundaries. Clearly, however, there is interaction across these lines—lakes and rivers, for example, are influenced by events outside their boundaries, even from areas infrequently or never inundated by the water body surface that defines the lake or river. Groundwater sources feed into and are fed by lakes and rivers, for example. Another significant influence is from the quantity and quality of adjacent wetlands, which purify water entering the lake or river and provide habitat and nutrients for the wildlife associated with the lake or river. But we cannot stop even there. A lake or river feels influences from well beyond the geographic line where wetlands end and dry uplands begin. Any lake or river has its watershed, from which it draws water, nutrients, sediments, and other inputs vital to the processes of the water body itself.

So what should be the focus of freshwater ecosystem management policy? Should we set the scale at the larger, holistic watershed level, or at the smaller, more easily managed scale of individual lakes and rivers? Should the approach be regulatory or incentive-based? Should we focus on national concerns through federal initiatives, or keep things local? Given the patchwork of federal, state, and local laws having to do with conservation of water quality and water quantity, the answer, thus far, has been a little bit of everything. The following materials provide a taste of the major initiatives in that regard. We leave it to you to decide whether anything coherent has emerged from them that we can call the law of freshwater ecosystem management.

1. GROUNDWATER

Cappaert v. United States
United States Supreme Court, 1976.
426 U.S. 128.

■ BURGER, C.J.

The question presented in this litigation is whether the reservation of Devil's Hole as a national monument reserved federal water rights in unappropriated water.

Devil's Hole is a deep limestone cavern in Nevada. Approximately 50 feet below the opening of the cavern is a pool 65 feet long, 10 feet wide, and at least 200 feet deep, although its actual depth is unknown. The pool is a remnant of the prehistoric Death Valley Lake System and is situated on land owned by the United States since the Treaty of Guadalupe Hidalgo in 1848, 9 Stat. 922. By the Proclamation of January 17, 1952, President Truman withdrew from the public domain a 40-acre tract of land surrounding Devil's Hole, making it a detached component of the Death Valley National Monument. Proclamation No. 2961, 3 CFR 147 (1949–1953 Comp.). The Proclamation was issued under the American Antiquities Preservation Act, 34 Stat. 225, 16 U.S.C. § 431, which authorizes the President to declare as national monuments "objects of historic or scientific interest that are situated upon the lands owned or controlled by the Government of the United States . . ."

The 1952 Proclamation notes that Death Valley was set aside as a national monument "for the preservation of the unusual features of scenic, scientific, and educational interest therein contained." The Proclamation also notes that Devil's Hole is near Death Valley and contains a "remarkable underground pool." Additional preambulary statements in the Proclamation explain why Devil's Hole was being added to the Death Valley National Monument:

"WHEREAS the said pool is a unique subsurface remnant of the pre-historic chain of lakes which in Pleistocene times formed the Death Valley Lake System, and is unusual among caverns in that it is a solution area in distinctly striated limestone, while also owing its formation in part to fault action; and

"WHEREAS the geologic evidence that this subterranean pool is an integral part of the hydrographic history of the Death Valley region is further confirmed by the presence in this pool of a peculiar race of desert fish, and zoologists have demonstrated that this race of fish, which is found nowhere else in the world, evolved only after the gradual drying up of the Death Valley Lake System isolated this fish population from the original ancestral stock that in Pleistocene times was common to the entire region; and

"WHEREAS the said pool is of such outstanding scientific importance that it should be given special protection, and such protection can be best afforded by making the said forty-acre tract containing the pool a part of the said monument. . ."

The Proclamation provides that Devil's Hole should be supervised, managed, and directed by the National Park Service, Department of the Interior. Devil's Hole is fenced off, and only limited access is allowed by the Park Service.

View of Devil's Hole (National
Park Service)

The Cappaert petitioners own a 12,000-acre ranch near Devil's Hole,
4,000 acres of which are used for growing Bermuda grass, alfalfa, wheat,
and barley; 1,700 to 1,800 head of cattle are grazed. The ranch represents
an investment of more than $7 million; it employs more than 80 people
with an annual payroll of more than $340,000.

In 1968 the Cappaerts began pumping groundwater on their ranch on
land 2 1/2 miles from Devil's Hole; they were the first to appropriate
groundwater. The groundwater comes from an underground basin or aquifer which is also the source of the water in Devil's Hole. After the
Cappaerts began pumping from the wells near Devil's Hole, which they do
from March to October, the summer water level of the pool in Devil's Hole
began to decrease. Since 1962 the level of water in Devil's Hole has been
measured with reference to a copper washer installed on one of the walls of
the hole by the United States Geological Survey. Until 1968, the water level, with seasonable variations, had been stable at 1.2 feet below the copper
marker. In 1969 the water level in Devil's Hole was 2.3 feet below the copper washer; in 1970, 3.17 feet; in 1971, 3.48 feet; and, in 1972, 3.93 feet.

When the water is at the lowest levels, a large portion of a rock shelf in
Devil's Hole is above water. However, when the water level is at 3.0 feet
below the marker or higher, most of the rock shelf is below water, enabling

algae to grow on it. This in turn enables the desert fish (Cyprinodon diabolis, commonly known as Devil's Hole pupfish), referred to in President Truman's Proclamation, to spawn in the spring. As the rock shelf becomes exposed, the spawning area is decreased, reducing the ability of the fish to spawn in sufficient quantities to prevent extinction.

In April 1970 the Cappaerts, pursuant to Nevada law, Nev.Rev.Stat. s 533.325 (1973), applied to the State Engineer, Roland D. Westergard, for permits to change the use of water from several of their wells. Although the United States was not a party to that proceeding and was never served, employees of the National Park Service learned of the Cappaerts' application through a public notice published pursuant to Nevada law. An official of the National Park Service filed a protest as did a private firm. Nevada law permits interested persons to protest an application for a permit; the protest may be considered by the State Engineer at a hearing. A hearing was conducted on December 16, 1970, and a field solicitor of the Department of the Interior appeared on behalf of the National Park Service. He presented documentary and testimonial evidence, informing the State Engineer that because of the declining water level of Devil's Hole the United States had commissioned a study to determine whether the wells on the Cappaerts' land were hydrologically connected to Devil's Hole and, if so, which of those wells could be pumped safely and which should be limited to prevent lowering of the water level in Devil's Hole. The Park Service field solicitor requested either that the Cappaerts' application be denied or that decision on the application be postponed until the studies were completed.

The State Engineer declined to postpone decision. At the conclusion of the hearing he stated that there was no recorded federal water right with respect to Devil's Hole, that the testimony indicated that the Cappaerts' pumping would not unreasonably lower the water table or adversely affect existing water rights, and that the permit would be granted since further economic development of the Cappaerts' land would be in the public interest. In his oral ruling the State Engineer stated in part that "the protest to the applications that are the subject of this hearing are overruled and the applications will be issued subject to existing rights." The National Park Service did not appeal.

In August 1971 the United States sought an injunction in the United States District Court for the District of Nevada to limit, except for domestic purposes, the Cappaerts' pumping from six specific wells and from specific locations near Devil's Hole. The complaint alleged that the United States, in establishing Devil's Hole as part of Death Valley National Monument, reserved the unappropriated waters appurtenant to the land to the extent necessary for the requirements and purposes of the reservation. The complaint further alleged that the Cappaerts had no perfected water rights as of the date of the reservation. The United States asserted that pumping from certain of the Cappaerts' wells had lowered the water level in Devil's Hole, that the lower water level was threatening the survival of a unique species of fish, and that irreparable harm would follow if the pumping were not enjoined. On June 2, 1972, the United States filed an amended complaint, adding two other specified wells to the list of those to be enjoined.

The Cappaerts answered, admitting that their wells draw water from the same underlying sources supplying Devil's Hole, but denying that the reservation of Devil's Hole reserved any water rights for the United States. The Cappaerts alleged that the United States was estopped from enjoining use of water under land which it had exchanged with the Cappaerts. The State of Nevada intervened on behalf of the State Engineer as a party defendant but raised no affirmative defenses.

On June 5, 1973, the District Court, by Chief Judge Roger D. Foley, entered a preliminary injunction limiting pumping from designated wells so as to return the level of Devil's Hole to not more than 3.0 feet below the marker. Detailed findings of fact were made and the District Judge then appointed a Special Master to establish specific pumping limits for the wells and to monitor the level of the water at Devil's Hole. The District Court found that the water from certain of the wells was hydrologically connected to Devil's Hole, that the Cappaerts were pumping heavily from those wells, and that that pumping had lowered the water level in Devil's Hole. The court also found that the pumping could be regulated to stabilize the water level at Devil's Hole and that neither establishing an artificial shelf nor transplanting the fish was a feasible alternative that would preserve the species. The District Court further found that if the injunction did not issue "there is grave danger that the Devil's Hole pupfish may be destroyed, resulting in irreparable injury to the United States." 375 F.Supp., 456, 460 (1974).

The District Court then held that in establishing Devil's Hole as a national monument, the President reserved appurtenant, unappropriated waters necessary to the purpose of the reservation; the purpose included preservation of the pool and the pupfish in it. The District Court also held that the federal water rights antedated those of the Cappaerts, that the United States was not estopped, and that the public interest required granting the injunction. On April 9, 1974, the District Court entered its findings of fact and conclusions of law substantially unchanged in a final decree permanently enjoining pumping that lowers the level of the water below the 3.0-foot level. 375 F.Supp. 456 (1974).

The Court of Appeals for the Ninth Circuit affirmed, 508 F.2d 313 (1974), in a thorough opinion by Senior District Judge Gus J. Solomon, sitting by designation, holding that the implied-reservation-of-water doctrine applied to groundwater as well as to surface water. The Court of Appeals held that "(t)he fundamental purpose of the reservation of the Devil's Hole pool was to assure that the pool would not suffer changes from its condition at the time the Proclamation was issued in 1952. . ." Id., at 318. The Court of Appeals further held that neither the Cappaerts nor their successors in interest had any water rights in 1952, nor was the United States estopped from asserting its water rights by exchanging land with the Cappaerts. In answer to contentions raised by the intervenor Nevada, the Court of Appeals held that "the United States is not bound by state water laws when it reserves land from the public domain," Id., at 320, and does not need to take steps to perfect its rights with the State; that the District Court had concurrent jurisdiction with the state courts to resolve this claim; and, that the state administrative procedures granting the Cappaerts' permit did not bar resolution of the United States' suit in Federal District Court.

We granted certiorari to consider the scope of the implied-reservation-of-water-rights doctrine.

I

Reserved-Water-Rights Doctrine

This Court has long held that when the Federal Government withdraws its land from the public domain and reserves it for a federal purpose, the Government, by implication, reserves appurtenant water then unappropriated to the extent needed to accomplish the purpose of the reservation. In so doing the United States acquires a reserved right in unappropriated water which vests on the date of the reservation and is superior to the rights of future appropriators. Reservation of water rights is empowered by the Commerce Clause, Art. I, § 8, which permits federal regulation of navigable streams, and the Property Clause, Art. IV, § 3, which permits federal regulation of federal lands. The doctrine applies to Indian reservations and other federal enclaves, encompassing water rights in navigable and nonnavigable streams. Colorado River Water Cons. Dist. v. United States, 424 U.S. 800, 805 (1976); United States v. District Court for Eagle County, 401 U.S. 520, 522–523(1971); Arizona v. California, 373 U.S. 546, 601 (1963); FPC v. Oregon, 349 U.S. 435 (1955); United States v. Powers, 305 U.S. 527 (1939); Winters v. United States, 207 U.S. 564 (1908).

Nevada argues that the cases establishing the doctrine of federally reserved water rights articulate an equitable doctrine calling for a balancing of competing interests. However, an examination of those cases shows they do not analyze the doctrine in terms of a balancing test. For example, in Winters v. United States, supra, the Court did not mention the use made of the water by the upstream landowners in sustaining an injunction barring their diversions of the water. The "Statement of the Case" in *Winters* notes that the upstream users were homesteaders who had invested heavily in dams to divert the water to irrigate their land, not an unimportant interest. The Court held that when the Federal Government reserves land, by implication it reserves water rights sufficient to accomplish the purposes of the reservation.

In determining whether there is a federally reserved water right implicit in a federal reservation of public land, the issue is whether the Government intended to reserve unappropriated and thus available water. Intent is inferred if the previously unappropriated waters are necessary to accomplish the purposes for which the reservation was created. Both the District Court and the Court of Appeals held that the 1952 Proclamation expressed an intention to reserve unappropriated water, and we agree. The Proclamation discussed the pool in Devil's Hole in four of the five preambles and recited that the "pool . . . should be given special protection." Since a pool is a body of water, the protection contemplated is meaningful only if the water remains; the water right reserved by the 1952 Proclamation was thus explicit, not implied.

The implied-reservation-of-water-rights doctrine, however, reserves only that amount of water necessary to fulfill the purpose of the reservation, no more. Here the purpose of reserving Devil's Hole Monument is preservation of the pool. Devil's Hole was reserved "for the preservation of the unusual features of scenic, scientific, and educational interest." The Proclamation notes that the pool contains "a peculiar race of desert fish . . . which is found nowhere else in the world" and that the "pool is of . . . outstanding scientific importance. . ." The pool need only be preserved, consistent with the intention expressed in the Proclamation, to the extent necessary to preserve its scientific interest. The fish are one of the features of scientific interest. The preamble noting the scientific interest of the pool follows the preamble describing the fish as unique; the Proclamation must be read in its entirety. Thus, as the District Court has correctly determined, the level of the pool may be permitted to drop to the extent that the drop does not impair the scientific value of the pool as the natural habitat of the species sought to be preserved. The District Court thus tailored its injunction, very appropriately, to minimal need, curtailing pumping only to the extent necessary to preserve an adequate water level at Devil's Hole, thus implementing the stated objectives of the Proclamation.

Petitioners argue that even if the intent of the 1952 Proclamation were to maintain the pool, the American Antiquities Preservation Act did not give the President authority to reserve a pool. Under that Act, according to the Cappaert petitioners, the President may reserve federal lands only to protect archeologic sites. However, the language of the Act which authorizes the President to proclaim as national monuments "historic landmarks, historic and prehistoric structures, and other objects of historic or scientific interest that are situated upon the lands owned or controlled by the Government" is not so limited. The pool in Devil's Hole and its rare inhabitants are "objects of historic or scientific interest." See generally Cameron v. United States, 252 U.S. 450, 455–456, 40 S.Ct. 410, 411, 64 L.Ed. 659, 661 (1920).

II

Groundwater

No cases of this Court have applied the doctrine of implied reservation of water rights to groundwater. Nevada argues that the implied-reservation doctrine is limited to surface water. Here, however, the water in the pool is surface water. The federal water rights were being depleted because, as the evidence showed, the "(g)roundwater and surface water are physically interrelated as integral parts of the hydrologic cycle." C. Corker, Groundwater Law, Management and Administration, National Water Commission Legal Study No. 6, p. xxiv (1971). Here the Cappaerts are causing the water level in Devil's Hole to drop by their heavy pumping. See Corker, supra; see also Water Policies for the Future Final Report to the President and to the Congress of the United States by the National Water Commission 233 (1973). It appears that Nevada itself may recognize the potential interrelationship between surface and groundwater since Nevada applies the law of prior appropriation to both. See generally F. Trelease, Water Law Resource Use and Environmental Protection 457–552 (2d ed. 1974); C. Meyers & A. Tarlock, Water Resource Management 553–634 (1971). Thus, since the implied-reservation-of-water-rights doctrine is based on the necessity of water for the purpose of the federal reservation, we hold that the United States can protect its water from subsequent diversion, whether the diversion is of surface or groundwater.

We hold, therefore, that as of 1952 when the United States reserved Devil's Hole, it acquired by reservation water rights in unappropriated appurtenant water sufficient to maintain the level of the pool to preserve its scientific value and thereby implement Proclamation No. 2961. Accordingly, the judgment of the Court of Appeals is Affirmed.

NOTES & QUESTIONS

1. The historical discussion presented at the beginning of this section reviews laws governing water quality in lakes, rivers, and wetlands, but as *Cappaert* demonstrates, groundwater is very much a factor in the surface water hydrological system and ecology. Yet, even more so than for nonpoint source pollution, the Clean Water Act leaves management and regulation of groundwater pollution to the states. Some courts have held that the regulatory arm of the CWA—the NPDES permit program—covers discharges of pollutants to groundwater that is hydrologically connected to jurisdictional surface waters. *See, e.g.,* Idaho Rural Council v. Bosma, 143 F.Supp.2d 1169 (D. Idaho 2001); Sierra Club v. Colorado Refining Co., 838 F. Supp. 1428 (D. Colo.1993). Most courts, however, have held that the statute does not reach that far, *see, e.g.,* Village of Oconomowoc Lake v. Dayton Hudson Corp., 24 F.3d 962 (7th Cir.1994); Exxon Corp. v. Train, 554 F.2d 1310 (5th Cir.1977), and no court has applied the CWA to isolated groundwater. *See generally* Jason R. Jones, *The Clean Water Act: Groundwater Regulation and the National Pollutant Discharge Elimination System,* 8 DICKINSON J. ENVTL. LAW & POLICY 93 (1999).

2. Some states, however, regulate to protect groundwater quality more comprehensively. In the central Texas "Hill Country" around San Antonio and Austin, for example, the Edwards Aquifer is a highly productive karst (limestone) aquifer providing a bountiful and valuable source of high-quality water for residential and industrial purposes. It is the principal water supply for San Antonio and a major source of agricultural irrigation water in counties farther west. Through natural spring openings, the aquifer also supplies water to many surface streams and rivers that are home to a host of endangered aquatic species. Given the importance of this resource to the state, the Texas Natural Resources Conservation Commission and its predecessor agencies have for many years regulated development over the aquifer's recharge zone to prevent intrusion of pollutants and contaminants. *See* 30 Tex. Admin. Code ch. 213. In addition, Texas took the controversial step of regulating withdrawals from the aquifer. Landowners previously were entitled, under the so-called "rule of capture," to use whatever groundwater they could withdraw from the aquifer free of quantitative regulation. The Edwards Aquifer Authority Act of 1993 required land-owners to document historical uses and seek a permit from the Edwards Aquifer Authority to continue withdrawals, subject to additional restrictions. *See* 31 Tex. Admin. Code chs. 701–711, *available at* http://www.edwardsaquifer.org/. For histories of these developments, see Todd H. Votteler, *Raiders of the Lost Aquifer? Or, the Beginning of the End to Fifty Years of Conflict over the Texas Edwards Aquifer*, 15 TULANE ENVTL. L.J. 257 (2002); Gregory Ellis and Jace A. Houston, *Senate Bill 2: "Step Two" Towards Effective Water Resource Management and Development for Texas*, 32 ST. BAR OF TEXAS ENVTL. L.J. 53 (2002). For an excellent series of case studies on groundwater regulation and the effects of unrestricted pumping, see ROBERT GLENNON, WATER FOLLIES: GROUNDWATER PUMPING AND THE FATE OF AMERICA'S FRESH WATERS (2002).

3. One growing use of groundwater resources is the bottling of water for consumption in individual serving sizes. By most estimates, Americans presently consume about six billion gallons of bottled water annually, which represents sales revenues of about $8 billion. These numbers have been increasing at about 12 percent per year over the past decade, making it the fastest growing segment of the beverage industry. Reasons usually cited for this trend are the population's increased awareness of the positive health effects of water ingestion coupled with the convenience and perceived superior purity and taste of bottled water compared to tap water. Americans, of course, did not discover bottled water, so while our trend seems significant to us, which it is, on a global scale it is overshadowed. Consider these statistics:

- The worldwide market for bottled water is over $35 billion annually.
- Americans spend over $11,000 on bottled water per minute.
- North America accounts for only 20% of worldwide bottled water consumption, with Western Europe at 45%. Eastern Europe and the Pacific Rim combine for another 20%. Thus, the growing populations of Asia, Africa, and Latin America today account for only 15% of worldwide consumption.
- Rates of consumption are rising more rapidly in the Pacific Rim and Asian nations than in North America and Western Europe.
- The price of bottled water, about one dollar per 12oz bottle, is 500–1000 times the price of tap water in most markets.
- Production costs of the water in bottled water are under a dime per gallon. The significant production costs of bottled water are the bottles, bottling, transportation, and marketing.
- Although several worldwide marketers of bottled water are in operation (e.g., Danone, Nestle/Perrier, and, increasingly, Coca-Cola and PepsiCo), 75% of the world market is controlled by local firms.
- Over 1.5 billion people worldwide have no access to safe drinking water from taps, and over 12 million people die each year from diseases brought on by unsanitary water.

Following on the heels of this trend has been an increasing concern by many observers that bottling of water presents serious adverse environmental effects. Chief among these are the demand bottling of water places on local water supply resources, the resources consumed and pollution generated in the production of plastic bottles and shipping of the bottled water, and the waste management problems of discarded plastic bottles. There have also been public health concerns expressed regarding the possible uneven quality of bottled water. Consider these statistics:

- Over 75% of bottled water sold in the U.S. finds a protected spring or well as its source. The rest is bottled from purified tap water.

- Most large bottlers have many sources (e.g., Nestle/Perrier collects water from over 75 springs in the U.S.), and thus most bottled water is consumed within markets that are relatively local to the source. Worldwide, 75% of bottled water is consumed in the same region it is produced.

- Nevertheless, transportation of bottled water does contribute to pollution emissions, and must be accounted for to make an accurate assessment of the overall balance of effects.

- Polyethylene terephthalate (PET) is the plastic of choice for the bottles. Producing a kilo of PET consumes petroleum products and, ironically in the case of PET for water bottles, requires 17.5 gallons of water. The production process results in emissions of sulfur oxides, hydrocarbons, carbon monoxide, nitrogen oxide, and carbon dioxide. Over 1.5 million tons of PET are used each year to contain bottled water.

- 14 billion water bottles were sold in the U.S. in 2002. Estimates are that 90 percent were discarded rather than recycled, albeit in many cases perhaps after some level of reuse (filling from taps or filtered taps). PET is essentially non-biodegradable.

- Compared to glass and aluminum, however, PET provides a superior bottle container in terms of weight, breakage, production emissions, reuse rate, recycling rate, and solid waste disposal rate.

Bottled water thus presents a mixed bag: it is a healthy trend, but it uses ecologically sensitive resources; overall its production and consumption in plastic containers are sources of environmental degradation, but in some categories are less so than for other beverages and container types. For more on the topic, see Tara Boldt-Van Rooy, *"Bottling Up" Our Natural Resources: The Fight over Bottled Water Extraction in the United States*, 18 J. LAND USE & ENVTL. L. 267 (2003).

2. LAKES AND RIVERS

a. CLEAN WATER ACT

The CWA is a lengthy and involved statute. To aid in understanding such a comprehensive piece of legislation, the following is a brief outline of its major provisions. The operation and implementation of these provisions will be discussed in further detail in the sections that follow.

§ 101 *Goals.* Declares the national goals of the CWA to create fishable/swimmable waters by 1983 and the elimination of pollutant discharges into navigable waters by 1985. While neither of these deadlines were met, these goals continue to be the thrust of the CWA. 33 U.S.C. § 1251.

§ 301 *Effluent Limitations.* Prohibits "the discharge of any pollutant by any person" except as in compliance with law. "The discharge of any pollutant" is defined in § 502 as the addition of any pollutant to navigable waters from any point source or to the waters of the ocean or contiguous zone from any source other than a vessel. This section also imposes effluent limitations on discharges of pollutants which vary depending on the nature of the pollutant discharged and the type of water body into which the pollutant is discharged. 33 U.S.C. § 1311.

§ 302 *Water Quality Related to Effluent Limitations.* Authorizes the establishment of more stringent effluent limitations for any discharge of pollutants from a point source or group of point sources that would otherwise interfere with the attainment or maintenance of the water quality in a specific portion of the navigable waters. 33 U.S.C. § 1312.

§ 303 *State Water Quality Standards & Total Maximum Daily Loads (TMDLs).* Requires states to establish water quality criteria and water quality standards, subject to EPA approval, which identify waters where water quality standards may not be met, or are not being met, and to establish TMDLs for specific pollutants for those waters. These standards are to be reviewed every three years. If EPA does not approve the standard, EPA shall set its own standard for the water body. 33 U.S.C. § 1313.

§ 304 *Federal Water Quality Guidelines and Criteria.* Requires EPA to establish water quality criteria for effluent limitations, pretreatment programs, and provides for administration of the NPDES permit program. 33 U.S.C. § 1314.

§ 306 *New Source Performance Standards.* Requires EPA to establish national standards for new sources of pollutant discharges which reflect the best demonstrated control technology. 33 U.S.C. § 1316.

§ 307 *Toxic and Pretreatment Effluent Standards.* Requires dischargers of toxic pollutants to meet established effluent limits reflecting the best economically available control technologies and directs EPA to establish pretreatment standards to prevent discharges from interfering with POTWs. 33 U.S.C. § 1317.

§ 309 *Enforcement.* Authorizes compliance orders, civil actions, criminal penalties, and administrative penalties as enforcement options for violations of the CWA. 33 U.S.C. § 1319.

§ 319 *Nonpoint Source Management Provisions.* Requires states and tribes to identify water bodies that cannot meet water quality standards due to discharges from nonpoint sources and to identify the responsible sources and create a plan to control such sources. 33 U.S.C. § 1329.

§ 401 *State Water Quality Certification.* Requires applicants for federal licenses and permits to obtain certification from the state within which the discharge will occur that it will not interfere with the state's efforts in achieving water quality standards. 33 U.S.C. § 1341.

§ 402 *NPDES Permit Program.* Establishes the National Pollutant Discharge Elimination System permit program, which may be administered by the states or tribes through delegation from EPA. This is known by many as the centerpiece of the CWA, and was specifically designed to address many of the weaknesses of earlier water pollution legislation. 33 U.S.C. § 1342.

§ 404 *Permits for Dredged or Fill Materials.* Requires permits to be obtained through the Army Corps of Engineers for the disposal of dredged or fill material into navigable waters unless it occurs as part of "normal" farming operations or as part of the maintenance of dams or other water control structures. 33 U.S.C. § 1344.

§ 505 *Citizen Suits.* Creates standing for citizens to bring suit against anyone who violates an effluent standard or order and also against EPA for failure to perform any nondiscretionary duty. 33 U.S.C. 1365.

(1) NPDES Permits

Congress enacted the Clean Water Act (CWA) in 1972. Its stated objective was "to restore and maintain the chemical, physical, and biological integrity of the Nation's waters." 33 U.S.C. § 1251. To serve those ends, the CWA prohibits "the discharge of any pollutant by any person" unless done in compliance with some provision of the Act. *Id.* § 1311(a). One such provision establishes the National Pollutant Discharge Elimination System, or NPDES, permit program. *Id.* § 1342. Generally speaking, the NPDES program requires dischargers to obtain permits that place limits on the type and quantity of pollutants that can be released into the nation's waters. The Act defines the phrase "discharge of a pollutant" to mean "any addition of any pollutant to navigable waters from any point source." *Id.* § 1362(12). A "point source," in turn, is defined as "any discernible, confined and discrete conveyance," such as a pipe, ditch, channel, or tunnel, "from which pollutants are or may be discharged." *Id.* § 1362(14). The Supreme Court has provided some illumination on what these terms mean in an ecosystem-scale setting.

South Florida Water Management District v. Miccosukee Tribe of Indians

Supreme Court of the United States, 2004.
541 U.S. 95.

■ O'CONNOR, J.

Petitioner South Florida Water Management District operates a pumping facility that transfers water from a canal into a reservoir a short distance away. Respondents Miccosukee Tribe of Indians and the Friends of the Everglades brought a citizen suit under the Clean Water Act contending that the pumping facility is required to obtain a discharge permit under the National Pollutant Discharge Elimination System. The District Court agreed and granted summary judgment to respondents. A panel of the United States Court of Appeals for the Eleventh Circuit affirmed. Both the District Court and the Eleventh Circuit rested their holdings on the predicate determination that the canal and reservoir are two distinct water bodies. For the reasons explained below, we vacate and remand for further development of the factual record as to the accuracy of that determination.

I

A

The Central and South Florida Flood Control Project (Project) consists of a vast array of levees, canals, pumps, and water impoundment areas in the land between south Florida's coastal hills and the Everglades. Historically, that land was itself part of the Everglades, and its surface and groundwater flowed south in a uniform and unchanneled sheet. Starting in the early 1900's, however, the State began to build canals to drain the wetlands and make them suitable for cultivation. These canals proved to be a source of trouble; they lowered the water table, allowing salt water to intrude upon coastal wells, and they proved incapable of controlling flooding. Congress established the Project in 1948 to address these problems. It gave the United States Army Corps of Engineers the task of constructing a comprehensive network of levees, water storage areas, pumps, and canal improvements that would serve several simultaneous purposes, including flood protection, water conservation, and drainage. These improvements fundamentally altered the hydrology of the Everglades, changing the natural sheet flow of ground and surface water. The local sponsor and day-to-day operator of the Project is the South Florida Water Management District (District).

Five discrete elements of the Project are at issue in this case. One is a canal called "C-11." C-11 collects groundwater and rainwater from a 104 square-mile area in south central Broward County. App. 110. The area drained by C-11 includes urban, agricultural, and residential development, and is home to 136,000 people. At the western terminus of C-11 is the second Project element at issue here: a large pump station known as "S-9." When the water level in C-11 rises above a set level, S-9 begins operating and pumps water out of the canal. The water does not travel far. Sixty feet away, the pump station empties the water into a large undeveloped wetland area called "WCA-3," the third element of the Project we consider here. WCA-3 is the largest of several "water conservation areas" that are remnants of the original South Florida Everglades. The District impounds water in these areas to conserve fresh water that might otherwise flow directly to the ocean, and to preserve wetlands habitat. *Id.,* at 112.

Using pump stations like S-9, the District maintains the water table in WCA-3 at a level significantly higher than that in the developed lands drained by the C-11 canal to the east. Absent human intervention, that water would simply flow back east, where it would rejoin the waters of the canal and flood the populated areas of the C-11 basin. That return flow is prevented, or, more accurately, slowed, by levees that hold back the surface waters of WCA-3. Two of those levees, L-33 and L-37, are the final two elements of the Project at issue here. The combined effect of L-33 and L-37, C-11, and S-9 is artificially to separate the C-11 basin from WCA-3; left to nature, the two areas would be a single wetland covered in an undifferentiated body of surface and ground water flowing slowly southward.

B

As the above description illustrates, the Project has wrought largescale hydrologic and environmental change in South Florida, some deliberate and some accidental. Its most obvious environmental impact has been the conversion of what were once wetlands into areas suitable for human use. But the Project also has affected those areas that remain wetland ecosystems.

Rain on the western side of the L-33 and L-37 levees falls into the wetland ecosystem of WCA-3. Rain on the eastern side of the levees, on the other hand, falls on agricultural, urban, and residential land. Before it enters the C-11 canal, whether directly as surface runoff or indirectly as groundwater, that rainwater absorbs contaminants produced by human activities. The water in C-11 therefore differs chemically from that in WCA-3. Of particular interest here, C-11 water contains elevated levels of phosphorous, which is found in fertilizers used by farmers in the C-11 basin. When water from C-11 is pumped across the levees, the phosphorous it contains alters the balance of WCA-3's ecosystem (which is naturally low in phosphorous) and stimulates the growth of algae and plants foreign to the Everglades ecosystem.

The phosphorous-related impacts of the Project are well known and have received a great deal of attention from state and federal authorities for more than 20 years. A number of initiatives are currently under way to reduce these impacts and thereby restore the ecological integrity of the Everglades. Respondents Miccosukee Tribe of Indians and the Friends of the Everglades (hereinafter simply Tribe), impatient with the pace of this progress, brought this Clean Water Act suit in the United States District Court for the Southern District of Florida. They sought, among other things, to enjoin the operation of S-9 and, in turn, the conveyance of water from C-11 into WCA-3.

C

Congress enacted the Clean Water Act (Act) in 1972. Its stated objective was "to restore and maintain the chemical, physical, and biological integrity of the Nation's waters." 86 Stat. 816, 33 U.S.C. § 1251. To serve those ends, the Act prohibits "the discharge of any pollutant by any person" unless done in compliance with some provision of the Act. § 1311(a). The provision relevant to this case, § 1342, establishes the National Pollutant Discharge Elimination System, or NPDES. Generally speaking, the NPDES requires dischargers to obtain permits that place limits on the type and quantity of pollutants that can be released into the Nation's waters. The Act defines the phrase " 'discharge of a pollutant' " to mean "any addition of any pollutant to navigable waters from any point source." § 1362(12). A " 'point source,' " in turn, is defined as "any discernible, confined and discrete conveyance," such as a pipe, ditch, channel, or tunnel, "from which pollutants are or may be discharged." § 1362(14).

According to the Tribe, the District cannot operate S-9 without an NPDES permit because the pump station moves phosphorous-laden water from C-11 into WCA-3. The District does not dispute that phosphorous is a pollutant, or that C-11 and WCA-3 are "navigable waters" within the meaning of the Act. The question, it contends, is whether the operation of the S-9 pump constitutes the "discharge of [a] pollutant" within the meaning of the Act.

The parties filed cross-motions for summary judgment on the issue of whether S-9 requires an NPDES permit. The District Court granted the Tribe's motion, reasoning as follows:

"In this case an addition of pollutants exists because undisputedly water containing pollutants is being discharged through S-9 from C-11 waters into the Everglades, both of which are separate bodies of United States water with different quality levels. They are two separate bodies of water because the transfer of water or its contents from C-11 into the Everglades would not occur naturally."

The Court of Appeals affirmed. It reasoned first that "in determining whether pollutants are added to navigable waters for purposes of the [Act], the receiving body of water is the relevant body of navigable water." 280 F.3d 1364, 1368 (C.A.11 2002). After concluding that pollutants were indeed being added to WCA-3, the court then asked whether that addition of pollutants was from a "point source," so as to trigger the NPDES permitting requirement. To answer that question, it explained:

"[F]or an addition of pollutants to be from a point source, the relevant inquiry is whether—but for the point source—the pollutants would have been added to the receiving body of water. We, therefore, conclude that an addition from a point source occurs if a point source is the cause-in-fact of the release of pollutants into navigable waters."

"When a point source changes the natural flow of a body of water which contains pollutants and causes that water to flow into another distinct body of navigable water into which it would not have otherwise flowed, that point source is the cause-in-fact of the discharge of pollutants."

Because it believed that the water in the C-11 canal would not flow into WCA-3 without the operation of the S-9 pump station, the Court of Appeals concluded that S-9 was the cause-in-fact of the addition of pollutants to WCA-3. It accordingly affirmed the District Court's grant of summary judgment, and held that the S-9 pump station requires an NPDES permit. We granted certiorari.

II

The District and the Federal Government, as *amicus,* advance three separate arguments, any of which would, if accepted, lead to the conclusion that the S-9 pump station does not require a point source discharge permit under the NPDES program. Two of these arguments involve the application of disputed contentions of law to agreed-upon facts, while the third involves the application of agreed-upon law to disputed facts. For reasons explained below, we decline at this time to resolve all of the parties' legal disagreements, and instead remand for further proceedings regarding their factual dispute.

A

In its opening brief on the merits, the District argued that the NPDES program applies to a point source "only when a pollutant originates from the point source," and not when pollutants originating elsewhere merely pass through the point source. Brief for Petitioner 20. This argument mirrors the question presented in the District's petition for certiorari: "Whether the pumping of water by a state water management agency that adds nothing to the water being pumped constitutes an 'addition' of a pollutant 'from' a point source triggering the need for a National Pollutant Discharge Elimination System permit under the Clean Water Act." Although the Government rejects the District's legal position, it and the Tribe agree with the factual proposition that S-9 does not itself add any pollutants to the water it conveys into WCA-3.

This initial argument is untenable, and even the District appears to have abandoned it in its reply brief. A point source is, by definition, a "discernible, confined, and discrete *conveyance.*" § 1362(14) (emphasis added). That definition makes plain that a point source need not be the original source of the pollutant; it need only convey the pollutant to "navigable waters," which are, in turn, defined as "the waters of the United States." § 1362(7). Tellingly, the examples of "point sources" listed by the Act include pipes, ditches, tunnels, and conduits, objects that do not themselves generate pollutants but merely transport them. § 1362(14). In addition, one of the Act's primary goals was to impose NPDES permitting requirements on municipal wastewater treatment plants. See, *e.g.,* § 1311(b)(1)(B) (establishing a compliance schedule for publicly owned treatment works). But under the District's interpretation of the Act, the NPDES program would not cover such plants, because they treat and discharge pollutants added to water by others. We therefore reject the District's proposed reading of the definition of " 'discharge of a pollutant' " contained in § 1362(12). That definition includes within its reach point sources that do not themselves generate pollutants.

B

Having answered the precise question on which we granted certiorari, we turn to a second argument, advanced primarily by the Government as *amicus curiae* in merits briefing and at oral argument. For purposes of determining whether there has been "any addition of any pollutant to navigable waters from any point source," the Government contends that all the water bodies that fall within the Act's definition of " 'navigable waters' " (that is, all "the waters of the United States, including the territorial seas," § 1362(7)) should be viewed unitarily for purposes of NPDES permitting requirements. Because the Act requires NPDES permits only when there is an addition of a pollutant "to navigable waters," the Government's approach would lead to the conclusion that such permits are *not* required when water from one navigable water body is discharged, unaltered, into another navigable water body. That would be true even if one water body were polluted and the other pristine, and the two would not otherwise mix. Under this "unitary waters" approach, the S-9 pump station would not need an NPDES permit.

1

The "unitary waters" argument focuses on the Act's definition of a pollutant discharge as "any addition of any pollutant to navigable waters from any point source." § 1362(12). The Government contends that the absence of the word "any" prior to the phrase "navigable waters" in § 1362(12) signals Congress' understanding that NPDES permits would not be required for pollution caused by the engineered transfer of one "navigable water" into another. It argues that Congress intended that such pollution instead would be addressed through local nonpoint source pollution programs. Section 1314(f)(2)(F), which concerns nonpoint sources, directs the Environmental Protection Agency (EPA) to give States information on the evaluation and control of "pollution resulting from changes in the movement, flow, or circulation of any navigable waters or ground waters, including changes caused by the construction of dams, levees, channels, causeways, or flow diversion facilities."

We note, however, that § 1314(f)(2)(F) does not explicitly exempt nonpoint pollution sources from the NPDES program if they *also* fall within the "point source" definition. And several NPDES provisions might be read to suggest a view contrary to the unitary waters approach. For example, under the Act, a State may set individualized ambient water quality standards by taking into consideration "the designated uses of the navigable waters involved." 33 U.S.C. § 1313(c)(2)(A). Those water quality standards, in turn, directly affect local NPDES permits; if standard permit conditions fail to achieve the water quality goals for a given water body, the State must determine the total pollutant load that the water body can sustain and then allocate that load among the permit holders who discharge to the water body. § 1313(d). This approach suggests that the Act protects individual water bodies as well as the "waters of the United States" as a whole.

The Government also suggests that we adopt the "unitary waters" approach out of deference to a longstanding EPA view that the process of "transporting, impounding, and releasing navigable waters" cannot constitute an " 'addition' " of pollutants to " 'the waters of the United States.' " But the Government does not identify any administrative documents in which EPA has espoused that position. Indeed, an *amicus* brief filed by several former EPA officials argues that the agency once reached the opposite conclusion. See Brief for Former Administrator Carol M. Browner et al. as *Amici Curiae* 17 (citing *In re Riverside Irrigation Dist.*, 1975 WL 23864 (Ofc. Gen. Coun., June 27, 1975) (irrigation ditches that discharge to navigable waters require NPDES permits even if they themselves qualify as navigable waters)).

The "unitary waters" approach could also conflict with current NPDES regulations. For example, 40 CFR § 122.45(g)(4) (2003) allows an industrial water user to obtain "intake credit" for pollutants present in water that it withdraws from navigable waters. When the permit holder discharges the water after use, it does not have to remove pollutants that were in the water before it was withdrawn. There is a caveat, however: EPA extends such credit "only if the discharger demonstrates that the intake water is drawn from the same body of water into which the discharge is made." The NPDES program thus appears to address the movement of pollutants among water bodies, at least at times.

Finally, the Government and numerous *amici* warn that affirming the Court of Appeals in this case would have significant practical consequences. If we read the Act to require an NPDES permit for every engineered diversion of one navigable water into another, thousands of new permits might have to be issued, particularly by western States, whose water supply networks often rely on engineered transfers among various natural water bodies. See Brief for Colorado et al. as *Amici Curiae* 2–4. Many of those diversions might also require expensive treatment to meet water quality criteria. It may be that construing the NPDES program to cover such transfers would therefore raise the costs of water distribution prohibitively, and violate Congress' specific instruction that "the authority of each State to allocate quantities of water within its jurisdiction shall not be superseded, abrogated or otherwise impaired" by the Act. § 1251(g). On the other hand, it may be that such permitting authority is necessary to protect water quality, and that the States or EPA could control regulatory costs by issuing general permits to point sources associated with water distribution programs. See 40 CFR §§ 122.28, 123.25 (2003). Indeed, that is the position of the one State that *has* interpreted the Act to cover interbasin water transfers. See Brief for Pennsylvania Department of Environmental Protection as *Amicus Curiae* 11–18.

2

Because WCA-3 and C-11 are both "navigable waters," adopting the "unitary waters" approach would lead to the conclusion that the District may operate S-9 without an NPDES permit. But despite its relevance here, neither the District nor the Government raised the unitary waters approach before the Court of Appeals or in their briefs respecting the petition for certiorari. (The District adopted the position as its own in its reply brief on the merits.) Indeed, we are not aware of any reported case that examines the unitary waters argument in precisely the form that the Government now presents it. As a result, we decline to resolve it here. Because we find it necessary to vacate the judgment of the Court of Appeals with respect to a third argument presented by the District, the unitary waters argument will be open to the parties on remand.

C

In the courts below, as here, the District contended that the C-11 canal and WCA-3 impoundment area are not distinct water bodies at all, but instead are two hydrologically indistinguishable parts of a single water body. The Government agrees with the District on this point, claiming that because the C-11 canal and WCA-3 "share a unique, intimately related, hydrological association," they "can appropriately be viewed, for purposes of Section 402 of the Clean Water Act, as parts of a single body of water." The Tribe does not dispute that if C-11 and WCA-3 are simply two parts of the same water body, pumping water from one into the other cannot constitute an "addition" of pollutants. As the Second Circuit put it in *Trout Unlimited,*"[i]f one takes a ladle of soup from a pot, lifts it above the pot, and pours it back into the pot, one has not 'added' soup or anything else to the pot." 273 F.3d, at 492. What the Tribe disputes is the accuracy of the District's factual premise; according to the Tribe, C-11 and WCA-3 are two pots of soup, not one.

The record does contain information supporting the District's view of the facts. Although C-11 and WCA-3 are divided from one another by the L-33 and L-37 levees, that line appears to be an uncertain one. Because Everglades soil is extremely porous, water flows easily between ground and surface waters, so much so that "[g]round and surface waters are essentially the same thing." C-11 and WCA-3, of course, share a common underlying aquifer. Moreover, the L-33 and L-37 levees continually leak, allowing water to escape from WCA-3. This means not only that any boundary between C-11 and WCA-3 is indistinct, but also that there is some significant mingling of the two waters; the record reveals that even without use of the S-9 pump station, water travels as both seepage and groundwater flow between the water conservation area and the C-11 basin.

The parties also disagree about how the relationship between S-9 and WCA-3 should be assessed. At oral argument, counsel for the Tribe focused on the differing "biological or ecosystem characteristics" of the respective waters, while counsel for the District emphasizes the close hydrological connections between the two. Despite these disputes, the District Court granted summary judgment to the Tribe. It applied a test that neither party defends; it determined that C-11 and WCA-3 are distinct "because the transfer of water or its contents from C-11 into the Everglades would not occur naturally." The Court of Appeals for the Eleventh Circuit endorsed this test. 280 F.3d, at 1368.

We do not decide here whether the District Court's test is adequate for determining whether C-11 and WCA-3 are distinct. Instead, we hold only that the District Court applied its test prematurely. Summary judgment is appropriate only where there is no genuine issue of material fact. See *Celotex Corp. v. Catrett,* 477 U.S. 317, 106 S.Ct. 2548, 91 L.Ed.2d 265 (1986). The record before us leads us to believe that some factual issues remain unresolved. The District Court certainly was correct to characterize the flow through the S-9 pump station as a nonnatural one, propelled as it is by diesel-fired motors against the pull of gravity. And it also appears true that if S-9 were shut down, the water in the C-11 canal might for a brief time flow *east,* rather than west, as it now does. But the effects of shutting down the pump might extend beyond that. The limited record before us suggests that if S-9 were shut down, the area drained by C-11 would flood quite quickly. See 280 F.3d, at 1366 ("Without the operation of the S-9 pump station, the populated western portion of Broward County would flood within days"). That flooding might mean that C-11 would no longer be a "distinct body of navigable water," *id.,* at 1368, but part of a larger water body extending over WCA-3 and the C-11 basin. It also might call into question the Eleventh Circuit's conclusion that S-9 is the cause in fact of phosphorous addition to WCA-3. Nothing in the record suggests that the District Court considered these issues when it granted summary judgment. Indeed, in ordering later emergency relief from its own injunction against the operation of the S-9 pump station, the court admitted that it had not previously understood that shutting down S-9 would " 'literally ope[n] the flood gates.' " *Id.,* at 1371.

We find that further development of the record is necessary to resolve the dispute over the validity of the distinction between C-11 and WCA-3. After reviewing the full record, it is possible that the District Court will conclude that C-11 and WCA-3 are not meaningfully distinct water bodies. If it does so, then the S-9 pump station will not need an NPDES permit. In addition, the Government's broader "unitary waters" argument is open to the District on remand. Accordingly, the judgment of the United States Court of Appeals for the Eleventh Circuit is vacated, and the case is remanded for further proceedings consistent with this opinion.

NOTES & QUESTIONS

1. From the perspective of advancing ecosystem management goals, does the "unitary waters" argument make any sense? As the Court pointed out, if the unitary waters approach were adopted, it would mean no NPDES permit would be needed for transfers of water between waterbodies "even if one water body were polluted and the other pristine, and the two would not otherwise mix." Why would Congress require a permit to discharge pollutants from a point source into one discrete waterbody, but not to transfer the polluted water from that waterbody to another?

2. On the other hand, if it were to be determined that C-11 and WCA-3 are "two hydrologically indistinguishable parts of a single water body," would there be any reason to require an NPDES permit for transfers of water between the two? Consider that the basis for the claim that the two *surface water* areas are

hydrologically connected is that the Everglades soils are porous and that *groundwater* connects the two areas. Is it necessarily the case that if ground-water flows from one area to he other, so too does the pollutant load of the sur-face waters? In other words, ecologically speaking, is the transfer of water be-tween the two areas by pumping surface water from one into the other the same as the transfer by groundwater flow? If not, then wouldn't the pumping extend the zone of polluted waters within the hydrologically connected system? Was this inquiry part of the remand to the lower courts?

3. Although the setting of the Everglades may suggest that *Miccosukee Tribe* is an exotic and unique case, in fact the transfer of water from one water body to another is fairly common in many parts of the country, particularly in the West, as a water supply management technique. Daunted by the prospect of having to regulate all such discharges, EPA initially issued a guidance docu-ment in 2005 and then a proposed rule in 2006, both of which defined "water transfer" as "an activity that conveys waters of the United States to another water of the United States without subjecting the water to intervening indus-trial, municipal, or commercial use" and took the position that such water transfers are not regulated under the CWA. *See* 71 Fed. Reg. 32887 (June 7, 2006). But in Friends of the Everglades v. South Florida Water Management District, 2006 WL 3635465 (S.D. Fla. 2006), a federal district court found that water transfers between distinct water bodies that result in the addition of a pollutant to the receiving navigable water body are subject to CWA jurisdiction and require a permit. The Second Circuit reached the same result in Catskill Mountains Chapter of Trout Unlimited v. City of New York, 451 F.3d 77 (2d Cir. 2006). Then, in 2008, EPA issued its final National Pollutant Discharge Elimination System (NPDES) Water Transfers Rule, in which it maintained its position in the proposed rule that water transfers not subject to intervening industrial, municipal, or commercial use are not regulated under the CWA. *See* 73 Fed. Reg. 33697 (June 13, 2008) (codified at 40 C.F.R. pt. 122).

The final EPA Water Transfers Rule was then applied for the first time in the continuing saga of the *Miccosukee Tribe* case. Prior to EPA's enactment of the rule, the district court had held on remand from the Supreme Court that the water bodies at issue in the case were "meaningfully distinct," and that be-cause the pumping station introduced pollutants from the canal to the lake, it caused "an addition" of pollutants to the lake and required an NPDES permit. Soon after the district court's decision, EPA finalized the rule. On appeal, the Eleventh Circuit accepted the lower court's conclusion that the water bodies were meaningfully distinct, noted that all existing case law was contrary to the defendant's "unitary waters" theory, but nevertheless reversed the lower court's holding that an NPDES permit was required because it found EPA's Water Transfers Rule to be a reasonable construction of the CWA and deferred to EPA's interpretation. Friends of the Everglades v. South Florida Water Man-agement Dist., 570 F.3d 1210 (11th Cir. 2009). Later in 2009, however, the Obama Administration announced it would reconsider the Bush-era Water Transfers Rule, though as of this writing it has issued no proposed revisions.

4. Section 401 of the Clean Water Act requires state approval of any activity, including federal approval of NPDES permits and other environmental per-mits, which may result in any discharge into navigable waters. 33 U.S.C. § 1331. The purpose of this so-called "401 certification" process is to ensure fed-eral agencies to not carry out or authorize activities that will impede the states

in achieving their water quality standards. The scope of the requirement is quite broad. Recently, for example, the Supreme Court ruled that the Federal Energy Regulatory Commission must obtain 401 certification for renewal of hydropower dam licenses, on the ground that the passage of water from the reservoir, through the dam, and then into the stream is a discharge within the meaning of Section 401. *See* S.D. Warren Co. v. Maine Board of Environmental Protection, 547 U.S. 370 (2006).

(2) The Total Maximum Daily Load Program

Given the relative impotence of CWA programs designed specifically for nonpoint sources, EPA looked elsewhere in the 1990s for a hook upon which to hang the nonpoint source program hat. It found it, not entirely voluntarily, in a previously little-noticed program of the CWA known as total maximum daily loads (TMDL).

The TMDL program is a bridge between the two primary CWA programs for water pollution control. One program is the National Pollutant Discharge Elimination Permit System (NPDES), discussed in the previous section, through which regulated point sources obtain permits to discharge water pollutants pursuant to nationally-uniform, technology-based discharge limits that are devised for each major industry. The other major branch of the CWA is the Water Quality Standards (WQS) program, under which states designate ambient water quality goals and criteria to arrive at expressions of maximum tolerable contaminant concentrations in a waterbody. In essence, the TMDL program answers the question of what happens when a particular WQS for a waterbody is not met even though all the NPDES-regulated discharges into the waterbody are complying with the most stringent technology-based limits applicable to the relevant industries. Under Section 303 of the CWA, states must identify the designated uses of each water body in the state (e.g., recreational purposes, propagation of fish and wildlife, public water supplies) and then create "water quality criteria" designed to protect the designated use. Water quality criteria quantitatively describe the physical, chemical, and biological characteristics of waters necessary to support the designated uses. State water criteria generally are based on federal water quality criteria EPA promulgates under Section 304(a) for more than 150 pollutants. The federal criteria are not enforceable standards but are instead guidance states can use to determine appropriate numerical criteria for water bodies in the state.

The combination of designated uses and water quality criteria result in WQSs, which are limits on the ambient concentration of pollutants in particular classes of waters. For example, a standard may state that the level of arsenic in a stream for used to support certain fish cannot exceed 0.2 milligrams per liter. States must review their WQSs every three years and must submit the standards to EPA for review, modification, and approval. States have been slow to enact WQSs and often have adopted "narrative" standards that do not create numerical limits on the ambient concentrations of pollutants. Without numerical limits, of course, it is difficult to use WQSs to impose additional limitations on pollutant discharges to water bodies.

Section 303(d) of the CWA requires each state to identify and establish a priority ranking for water bodies for which effluent limitations are insufficient to attain and maintain applicable WQSs. For those "impaired waters," states must establish and submit to EPA for approval the total maximum daily load (TMDL) for those pollutants identified by EPA as suitable for TMDL calculation. If a state fails to submit the necessary TMDLs, EPA must establish a list of impaired water bodies and TMDLs for the state. A TMDL sets the total amount of a particular pollutant that a segment of water may receive from point sources, nonpoint sources, and background sources without exceeding applicable water quality criteria, allocates allowable pollutant loads among the sources contributing the pollutant to that water body, and provides the basis for attaining or maintaining the WQS.

States were very slow to submit lists of impaired waters to EPA and even slower in developing TMDLs. The task is huge—tens of thousands of water segments are reported as impaired nationwide for multiple pollutants. The difficulty in developing TMDLs is a lack of necessary data, technological support, and cost. A 1996 EPA study found the costs of preparing a TMDL can reach $1 million and those costs today are significantly more. The slow progress of TMDLs is also a function of the fact that EPA essentially ignored the TMDL program for decades, focusing instead on developing technology-based effluent standards. Numerous citizen lawsuits beginning in the 1990s resulted in EPA coming under court order to establish TMDLs in dozens of states and EPA attempting to overhaul its TMDL regulatory program. Proposed regulatory changes met with significant resistance, particularly regulations expressly applying the TMDL rules to water bodies impaired solely by nonpoint sources of pollution and EPA action creating its own list of impaired waters for states that refused to list waters as impaired if the pollutants were exclusively from nonpoint sources.

Despite these problems, the TMDL program is a significant bridge between the NPDES Program and the WQS Program. In essence, the TMDL program answers the question of what happens when a particular WQS for a waterbody is not met even though all the NPDES-regulated discharges into the waterbody are complying with the most stringent technology-based limits applicable to the relevant industries. Because NPDES limits are based on end-of-the-pipe effluent concentrations, and WQSs are based on ambient conditions in the entire waterbody, no obvious connection exists by which to adjust the NPDES discharges. The TMDL program is designed to produce that connection, albeit in ways that are far less than obvious. The following materials provide additional detail on the WQS and TMDL programs and demonstrate how even they may be ineffective in the long run for dealing with nonpoint source pollution.

Pronsolino v. Nastri

United States Court of Appeals for the Ninth Circuit, 2002.
291 F.3d 1123.

■ BERZON, CIRCUIT JUDGE.

The United States Environmental Protection Agency ("EPA") required California to identify the Garcia River as a water body with insufficient pollution controls and, as required for waters so identified, to set so-called "total maximum daily loads" ("TMDLs")—the significance of which we explain later—for pollution entering the river. Appellants challenge the EPA's authority under the Clean Water Act ("CWA" or the "Act") § 303(d), 33 U.S.C. § 1313(d), to apply the pertinent identification and TMDL requirements to the Garcia River. The district court rejected this challenge, and we do as well.

CWA 303(d) requires the states to identify and compile a list of waters for which certain effluent limitations are not stringent enough to implement the applicable water quality standards for such waters. 303(d)(1)(A). Effluent limitations pertain only to point sources of pollution; point sources of pollution are those from a discrete conveyance, such as a pipe or tunnel. Nonpoint sources of pollution are non-discrete sources; sediment run-off from timber harvesting, for example, derives from a nonpoint source. The Garcia River is polluted only by nonpoint sources. Therefore, neither the effluent limitations referenced in 303(d) nor any other effluent limitations apply to the pollutants entering the Garcia River.

The precise statutory question before us is whether the phrase "are not stringent enough" triggers the identification requirement both for waters as to which effluent limitations apply but do not suffice to attain water quality standards and for waters as to which effluent limitations do not apply at all to the pollution sources impairing the water. We answer this question in the affirmative, a conclusion which triggers the application of the statutory TMDL requirement to waters such as the Garcia River.

I. STATUTORY BACKGROUND

Resolution of the statutory interpretation question before us, discrete though it is, requires a familiarity with the history, the structure, and, alas, the jargon of the federal water pollution laws. Natural Res. Def. Council v. EPA, 915 F.2d 1314, 1316 (9th Cir.1990). We therefore begin with a brief overview of the Act.

A. The Major Goals and Concepts of the CWA

Congress enacted the CWA in 1972, amending earlier federal water pollution laws that had proven ineffective. EPA v. California, 426 U.S. 200, 202 (1976). Prior to 1972, federal water pollution laws relied on "water quality standards specifying the acceptable levels of pollution in a States interstate navigable waters as the primary mechanism . . . for the control of water pollution." Id. The pre-1972 laws did not, however, provide concrete direction concerning how those standards were to be met in the foreseeable future.

In enacting sweeping revisions to the nation's water pollution laws in 1972, Congress began from the premise that the focus on the tolerable effects rather than the preventable causes of pollution constituted a major shortcoming in the pre 1972 laws. Oregon Natural Desert Assoc. v. Dombeck, 172 F.3d 1092, 1096 (9th Cir.1998) (quoting EPA v. State Water Resources Control Board, 426 U.S. 200, 202–03 (1976)). The 1972 Act therefore sought to target primarily the preventable causes of pollution, by emphasizing the use of technological controls. Id.; Oregon Natural Res. Council v. United States Forest Serv., 834 F.2d 842, 849 (9th Cir.1987).

At the same time, Congress decidedly did not in 1972 give up on the broader goal of attaining acceptable water quality. CWA § 101(a), 33 U.S.C. § 1251(a). Rather, the new statute recognized that even with the application of the mandated technological controls on point source discharges, water bodies still might not meet state-set water quality standards, Natural Res. Def. Council, 915 F.2d at 1316–17, and therefore put in place mechanisms other than direct federal regulation of point sources designed to "restore and maintain the chemical, physical, and biological integrity of the Nation's waters." 101(a).

In so doing, the CWA uses distinctly different methods to control pollution released from point sources and those that are traceable to nonpoint sources. Oregon Natural Res. Council, 834 F.2d at 849. The Act directly mandates technological controls to limit the pollution point sources may discharge into a body of water. Dombeck, 172 F.3d at 1096. On the other hand, the Act "provides no direct mechanism to control nonpoint source pollution but rather uses the 'threat and promise' of federal grants to the states to accomplish this task," id. at 1907 (citations omitted), thereby "recogniz[ing], preserv[ing], and protect[ing] the primary responsibilities and rights of States to prevent, reduce, and eliminate pollution, [and] to plan the development and use . . . of land and water resources. . ." § 101(b).

B. The Structure of CWA 303, 33 U.S.C. 1313

1. Water Quality Standards

Section 303 is central to the Act's carrot-and-stick approach to attaining acceptable water quality without direct federal regulation of nonpoint sources of pollution. Entitled Water Quality Standards and Implementation Plans, the provision begins by spelling out the statutory requirements for water quality standards: "Water quality standards" specify a water body's "designated uses" and "water quality criteria," taking into account the water's "use and value for public water supplies, propagation of fish and wildlife, recreational purposes, and agricultural, industrial, and other purposes. . ." § 303(c)(2). The states are required to set water quality standards for all waters within their boundaries regardless of the sources of the pollution entering the waters. If a state does not set water quality standards, or the

EPA determines that the state's standards do not meet the requirements of the Act, the EPA promulgates standards for the state. §§ 303(b), (c)(3)-(4).

2. Section 303(d): "Identification of Areas with Insufficient Controls; Maximum Daily Load"

Section 303(d)(1)(A) requires each state to identify as "areas with insufficient controls" "those waters within its boundaries for which the effluent limitations required by section [301(b)(1)(A)] and section [301(b)(1)(B)] of this title are not stringent enough to implement any water quality standard applicable to such waters." Id. The CWA defines "effluent limitations" as restrictions on pollutants "discharged from point sources." CWA § 502(11), 33 U.S.C. § 1362(11). Section 301(b)(1)(A) mandates application of the "best practicable control technology" effluent limitations for most point source discharges, while § 301(b)(1)(B) mandates application of effluent limitations adopted specifically for secondary treatment at publicly owned treatment works. § 301(b)(1), 33 U.S.C. § 1311(b)(1).

For waters identified pursuant to § 303(d)(1)(A)(the § 303(d)(1) list), the states must establish the "total maximum daily load" ("TMDL") for pollutants identified by the EPA as suitable for TMDL calculation. § 303(d)(1)(C). "A TMDL defines the specified maximum amount of a pollutant which can be discharged or 'loaded' into the waters at issue from all combined sources." Dioxin/Organochlorine Center v. Clarke, 57 F.3d 1517, 1520 (9th Cir.1995). The TMDL "shall be established at a level necessary to implement the applicable water quality standards. . ." § 303(d)(1)(C).

Section 303(d)(2), in turn, requires each state to submit its § 303(d)(1) list and TMDLs to the EPA for its approval or disapproval. If the EPA approves the list and TMDLs, the state must incorporate the list and TMDLs into its continuing planning process, the requirements for which are set forth in § 303(e). § 303(d)(2). If the EPA disapproves either the § 303(d)(1) list or any TMDLs, the EPA must itself put together the missing document or documents. Id. The state then incorporates any EPA-set list or TMDL into the states continuing planning process. Id.

Each state must also identify all waters not placed on its § 303(d)(1) list (the " '303(d)(3) list' ") and "estimate" TMDLs for pollutants in those waters. § 303(d)(3). There is no requirement that the EPA approve the § 303(d)(3) lists or the TMDLs estimated for those waters. Id.

The EPA in regulations has made more concrete the statutory requirements. Those regulations, in summary, define "water quality limited segment[s]"—those waters that must be included on the § 303(d)(1) list—as "[a]ny segment where it is known that water quality does not meet applicable water quality standards, and/or is not expected to meet applicable water quality standards, even after the application of the technology-based effluent limitations required by sections 301(b) and § 306 [33 U.S.C. § 1316]." 40 C.F.R. § 130.2(j) (2000). The regulations then divide TMDLs into two types: "load allocations," for nonpoint source pollution, and "wasteload allocations," for point source pollution. § 130.2(g)-(i); see also pp. 7919, infra. Under the regulations, states must identify those waters on the § 303(d)(1) lists as "still requiring TMDLs" if any required effluent limitation or other pollution control requirement (including those for nonpoint source pollution) will not bring the water into compliance with water quality standards. § 130.7(b) (2000).

3. Continuing Planning Process

The final pertinent section of § 303, § 303(e), requiring each state to have a continuing planning process, gives some operational force to the prior information-gathering provisions. The EPA may approve a state's continuing planning process only if it "will result in plans for all navigable waters within such State" that include, inter alia, effluent limitations, TMDLs, areawide waste management plans for nonpoint sources of pollution, and plans for "adequate implementation, including schedules of compliance, for revised or new water quality standards." § 303(e)(3).

The upshot of this intricate scheme is that the CWA leaves to the states the responsibility of developing plans to achieve water quality standards if the statutorily-mandated point source controls will not alone suffice, while providing federal funding to aid in the implementation of the state plans. See *Dombeck*, 172 F.3d at 1097; § 303(e); see also § 319(h), 33 U.S.C. § 1329(h) (providing for grants to states to combat nonpoint source pollution). TMDLs are primarily informational tools that allow the states to proceed from the identification of waters requiring additional planning to the required plans. See Alaska Center for the Environment v. Browner, 20 F.3d 981, 984–85 (9th Cir.1994). As such, TMDLs serve as a link in an implementation chain that includes federally-regulated point source controls, state or local plans for point and nonpoint source pollution reduction, and assessment of the impact of such measures on water quality, all to the end of attaining water quality goals for the nation's waters.

II. FACTUAL AND PROCEDURAL BACKGROUND

A. The Garcia River TMDL

In 1992, California submitted to the EPA a list of waters pursuant to § 303(d)(1)(A). Pursuant to § 303(d)(2), the EPA disapproved California's 1992 list because it omitted seventeen water segments that did not meet the water quality standards set by California for those segments. Sixteen of the seventeen water segments, including the Garcia River, were impaired only by nonpoint sources of pollution. After California rejected an opportunity to amend its § 303(d)(1) list to include the seventeen sub-standard segments, the EPA, again acting pursuant to § 303(d)(2), established a new § 303(d)(1) list for California, including those segments on it. California retained the seventeen segments on its 1994, 1996, and 1998 § 303(d)(1) lists.

California did not, however, establish TMDLs for the segments added by the EPA. Environmental and fishermen's groups sued the EPA in 1995 to require the EPA to establish TMDLs for the seventeen segments, and in a March 1997 consent decree the EPA agreed to do so. See *Pacific Coast Fishermens Assocs. v. Marcus*, No. 95–4474. According to the terms of the consent decree, the EPA set March 18, 1998, as the deadline for the establishment of a TMDL for the Garcia River. When California missed the deadline despite having initiated public comment on a draft TMDL and having prepared a draft implementation plan, the EPA established a TMDL for the Garcia River. The EPA's TMDL differed only slightly from the states' draft TMDL.

The Garcia River TMDL for sediment is 552 tons per square mile per year, a sixty percent reduction from historical loadings. The TMDL allocates portions of the total yearly load among the following categories of nonpoint source pollution: a) "mass wasting" associated with roads; b) "mass wasting" associated with timber-harvesting; c) erosion related to road surfaces; and d) erosion related to road and skid trail crossings.

B. The Appellants

In 1960, appellants Betty and Guido Pronsolino purchased approximately 800 acres of heavily logged timber land in the Garcia River watershed. In 1998, after re-growth of the forest, the Pronsolinos applied for a harvesting permit from the California Department of Forestry ("Forestry").

In order to comply with the Garcia River TMDL, Forestry and/or the state's Regional Water Quality Control Board required, among other things, that the Pronsolinos' harvesting provide for mitigation of 90% of controllable road-related sediment run-off and contain prohibitions on removing certain trees and on harvesting from mid-October until May 1. The Pronsolino's forester estimates that a large tree restriction will cost the Pronsolinos $750,000.

Larry Mailliard, a member of the Mendocino County Farm Bureau, submitted a draft harvesting permit on February 4, 1998, for a portion of his property in the Garcia River watershed. Forestry granted a final version of the permit after incorporation of a 60.3% reduction of sediment loading, a requirement included to comply with the Garcia River TMDL. Mr. Mailliard's forester estimates that the additional restrictions imposed to comply with the Garcia River TMDL will cost Mr. Mailliard $10,602,000.

Bill Barr, another member of the Mendocino County Farm Bureau, also applied for a harvesting permit in 1998 for his property located within the Garcia River watershed. Forestry granted the permit after incorporation of restrictions similar to those included in the Pronsolino's permit. A forester states that these additional restrictions, included to comply with the TMDL, will cost Mr. Barr at least $962,000.

III. ANALYSIS

B. Plain Meaning and Structural Issues

1. The Competing Interpretations

Section 303(d)(1)(A) requires listing and calculation of TMDLs for "those waters within [the states] boundaries for which the effluent limitations required by section [301(b)(1)(A)] and section [301(b)(1)(B)] of this title are not stringent enough to implement any water quality standard applicable to such waters." § 303(d) (emphasis added). The precise statutory question before us is whether, as the Pronsolinos maintain, the term "not stringent enough to implement . . . water quality standard[s]" as used in § 303(d)(1)(A) must be interpreted to mean both that application of effluent limitations will not achieve water quality standards and that the waters at issue are subject to effluent limitations. As only waters with point source pollution are subject to effluent limitations, such an interpretation would exclude from the § 303(d) listing and TMDL requirements waters impaired only by nonpoint sources of pollution.

The EPA, as noted, interprets "not stringent enough to implement . . . water quality standard[s]" to mean "not adequate" or "not sufficient . . . to implement any water quality standard," and does not read the statute as implicitly containing a limitation to waters initially covered by effluent limitations. According to the EPA, if the use of effluent limitations will not implement applicable water quality standards, the water falls within § 303(d)(1)(A) regardless of whether it is point or nonpoint sources, or a combination of the two, that continue to pollute the water.

2. The Language and Structure of § 303(d)

Whether or not the appellants' suggested interpretation is entirely implausible, it is at least considerably weaker than the EPA's competing construction. The Pronsolinos' version necessarily relies upon: (1) understanding "stringent enough" to mean "strict enough" rather than "thorough going enough" or "adequate" or "sufficient"; (2) reading the phrase "not stringent enough" in isolation, rather than with reference to the stated goal of implementing "any water quality standard applicable to such waters." Where the answer to the question "not stringent enough for what?" is "to implement any [applicable] water quality standard," the meaning of "stringent" should be determined by looking forward to the broad goal to be attained, not backwards at the inadequate effluent limitations. One might comment, for example, about a teacher that her standards requiring good spelling were not stringent enough to assure good writing, as her students still used bad grammar and poor logic. Based on the language of the contested phrase alone, then, the more sensible conclusion is that the § 303(d)(1) list must contain any waters for which the particular effluent limitations will not be adequate to attain the statute's water quality goals.

Nothing in § 303(d)(1)(A) distinguishes the treatment of point sources and nonpoint sources as such; the only reference is to the "effluent limitations required by" § 301(b)(1). So if the effluent limitations required by § 301(b)(1) are "as a matter of law" "not stringent enough" to achieve the applicable water quality standards for waters impaired by point sources not subject to those requirements, then they are also "not stringent enough" to achieve applicable water quality standards for other waters not subject to those requirements, in this instance because they are impacted only by nonpoint sources.

3. The Statutory Scheme as a Whole

The Pronsolinos' objection to this view of § 303(d) . . . is, in essence, that the CWA as a whole distinguishes between the regulatory schemes applicable to point and non-point sources, so we must assume such a distinction in applying §§ 303(d)(1)(A) and (C). We would hesitate in any case to read into a discrete statutory provision something that is not there because it is contained elsewhere in the statute. But here, the premise is wrong: There is no such general division throughout the CWA.

Point sources are treated differently from nonpoint sources for many purposes under the statute, but not all. In particular, there is no such distinction with regard to the basic purpose for which the § 303(d) list and TMDLs are compiled, the eventual attainment of state-defined water quality standards. Water quality standards reflect a state's designated uses for a water body and do not depend in any way upon the source of pollution. See § 303(a)-(c).

True, there are, as the Pronsolinos point out, two sections of the statute as amended, § 208 and § 319, that set requirements exclusively for nonpoint sources of pollution. But the structural inference we are asked to draw from those specialized sections—that no other provisions of the Act set requirements for waters polluted by nonpoint sources—simply does not follow. Absent some irreconcilable contradiction between the requirements contained in §§ 208 and 319, on the one hand, and the listing and TMDL requirements of § 303(d), on the other, both apply.

There is no such contradiction. Section 208 provides for federal grants to encourage the development of state areawide waste treatment management plans for areas with substantial water quality problems, § 208(a), (f), and requires that those plans include a process for identifying and controlling non-point source pollution "to the extent feasible." § 208(b)(2)(F). Section 319, added to the CWA in 1987, directs states to adopt "nonpoint source management programs;" provides grants for nonpoint source pollution reduction; and requires states to submit a report to the EPA that "identifies those navigable waters within the State which, without additional action to control nonpoint sources of pollution, cannot reasonably be expected to attain or maintain applicable water quality standards or the goals and requirements of this chapter." § 319(a)(1)(A). This report must also describe state programs for reducing nonpoint source pollution and the process "to reduce, to the maximum extent practicable, the level of pollution" resulting from particular categories of nonpoint source pollution. § 319(a)(1)(C), (D).

The CWA is replete with multiple listing and planning requirements applicable to the same waterways (quite confusingly so, indeed), so no inference can be drawn from the overlap alone. See, e.g., § 208(b); § 303(d)(1)(A), (d)(1)(B), (d)(3), (e); CWA § 304(*l*), 33 U.S.C. § 1314(*l*); CWA § 314, 33 U.S.C. § 1324(a); § 319(a). Nor are we willing to draw the more discrete inference that the § 303(d) listing and TMDL requirements cannot apply to nonpoint source pollutants because the planning requirements imposed by § 208 and § 319 are qualified ones—"to the extent feasible" and "to the maximum extent practicable"—while the § 303(d) requirements are unbending. For one thing, the water quality standards set under § 303 are functional and may permit more pollution than it is "feasible" or "practicable" to eliminate, depending upon the intended use of a particular waterway. For another, with or without TMDLs, the § 303(e) plans for attaining water quality standards must, without qualification, account for elimination of nonpoint source pollution to the extent necessary to meet those standards. § 303(e)(3)(F).

The various reporting requirements that apply to nonpoint source pollution are no more impermissibly redundant than are the planning requirements. Congress specifically provided that in preparing the § 319 report, states may rely on information from § 303(e), which incorporates the TMDLs. § 319(a)(2). Moreover, states must produce a § 319 report only once, but must update the § 303(d)(1) list periodically. § 319; § 303(d)(2). Also, the § 319 report requires the identification of a plan to reduce nonpoint source pollution, without regard to the attainment of water quality standards, while the plans generated using the § 303(d)(1) lists and TMDLs are guided by the goal of achieving those standards. § 319; § 303(d), (e).

Essentially, § 319 encourages the states to institute an approach to the elimination of nonpoint source pollution similar to the federally-mandated effluent controls contained in the CWA, while § 303 encompasses a water quality based approach applicable to all sources of water pollution. As various sections of the Act encourage different, and complementary, state schemes for cleaning up nonpoint source pollution in the nation's waterways, there is no basis for reading any of those sections—including § 303(d)—out of the statute.

There is one final aspect of the Act's structure that bears consideration because it supports the EPA's interpretation of § 303(d): The list required by § 303(d)(1)(A) requires that waters be listed if they are impaired by a combination of point sources and nonpoint sources; the language admits of no other reading. Section 303(d)(1)(C), in turn, directs that TMDLs shall be established at a level necessary to implement the applicable water quality standards. . . Id. (emphasis added). So, at least in blended waters, TMDLs must be calculated with regard to nonpoint sources of pollution; otherwise, it would be impossible "to implement the applicable water quality standards," which do not differentiate sources of pollution. This court has so recognized. *Browner*, 20 F.3d at 985 ("Congress and the EPA have already determined that establishing TMDLs is an effective tool for achieving water quality standards in waters impacted by non-point source pollution.").

Nothing in the statutory structure—or purpose—suggests that Congress meant to distinguish, as to § 303(d)(1) lists and TMDLs, between waters with one insignificant point source and substantial nonpoint source pollution and waters with only nonpoint source pollution. Such a distinction would, for no apparent reason, require the states or the EPA to monitor waters to determine whether a point source had been added or removed, and to adjust the § 303(d)(1) list and establish TMDLs accordingly. There is no statutory basis for concluding that Congress intended such an irrational regime.

Looking at the statute as a whole, we conclude that the EPA's interpretation of § 303(d) is not only entirely reasonable but considerably more convincing than the one offered by the plaintiffs in this case.

C. Federalism Concerns

The Pronsolinos finally contend that, by establishing TMDLs for waters impaired only by nonpoint source pollution, the EPA has upset the balance of federal-state control established in the CWA by intruding into the state's traditional control over land use. See Solid Waste Agency of Northern Cook County v. United States Army Corps of Eng'rs, 531 U.S. 159, 172–73 (2001). That is not the case.

The Garcia River TMDL identifies the maximum load of pollutants that can enter the Garcia River from certain broad categories of nonpoint sources if the river is to attain water quality standards. It does not specify the load of pollutants that may be received from particular parcels of land or describe what measures the state should take to implement the TMDL. Instead, the TMDL expressly recognizes that "implementation and monitoring" "are state responsibilities" and notes that, for this reason, the EPA did not include implementation or monitoring plans within the TMDL.

Moreover, § 303(e) requires—separately from the § 303(d)(1) listing and TMDL requirements—that each state include in its continuing planning process "adequate implementation, including schedules of compliance, for revised or new water quality standards" "for all navigable waters within such State." § 303(e)(3). The Garcia River TMDL thus serves as an informational tool for the creation of the state's implementation plan, independently—and explicitly—required by Congress.

California chose both if and how it would implement the Garcia River TMDL. States must implement TMDLs only to the extent that they seek to avoid losing federal grant money; there is no pertinent statutory provision otherwise requiring implementation of § 303 plans or providing for their enforcement. See CWA § 309, 33 U.S.C. § 1319; CWA § 505, 33 U.S.C. 1365.

IV. CONCLUSION

For all the reasons we have surveyed, the CWA is best read to include in the § 303(d) listing and TMDLs requirements waters impaired only by nonpoint sources of pollution. . . . We therefore hold that the EPA did not exceed its statutory authority in identifying the Garcia River pursuant to § 303(d)(1)(A) and establishing the Garcia River TMDL, even though the river is polluted only by nonpoint sources of pollution.

NOTES & QUESTIONS

1. The TMDL process outlined in *Pronsolino*, in essence, is the following:

- States identify specific waters where problems exist or are expected as a result of point *and/or nonpoint* sources.

- States allocate pollutant loadings among point *and nonpoint* sources contributing to the impairment, and EPA approves State actions or acts in lieu of the State if necessary.

- Point *and nonpoint* sources then reduce pollutants to achieve the pollutant loadings established by the TMDL through a wide variety of Federal, State, Tribal, and local authorities, programs, and initiatives.

As it relates to nonpoint source pollution, then, application of the TMDL program breaks down into three discrete questions. First, can impairment resulting entirely or mostly from nonpoint sources be considered when deciding whether a water body must be listed as impaired for purposes of section 303? Second, if a water body impaired in part by nonpoint sources can be listed, can a TMDL waste load allocation be made that includes nonpoint sources contributing to impairment of the water body? Finally, if a TMDL waste load allocation can be made to nonpoint sources, how can it be enforced against them? *Pronsolino* is seen by many as a victory on the first two issues for advocates of using the TMDL program as the hook for controlling nonpoint source pollution. Plaintiffs argued that EPA lacked authority to require TMDLs for waters of the Garcia River in Northern California impaired solely by nonpoint sources of pollution due to sediment from soil erosion caused by timber harvesting along the river's banks. The court disagreed, ruling that EPA has authority to require states to list waters receiving only nonpoint source pollutants on a state's Section 303(d) list and subsequently to prepare TMDLs for the listed waters.

2. But what about the third question—enforcement of the TMDL against nonpoint sources? Here *Pronsolino* is less helpful to those who would use the TMDL program as the basis of nonpoint source regulation. The court observed that EPA could not regulate land use because that matter was reserved for the states. The court further concluded that, although section 303(e) of the CWA requires states to include TMDLs such as the Garcia River sediment TMDL in their continuing planning processes, California is free to decide whether to implement the TMDL by regulating nonpoint sources such as farms and timber operations through its land use practices, and is free to risk possible loss of federal environmental grant funds if it decides not to implement the TMDL. So where does that leave matters? Do you think most states will accept the invitation to regulate nonpoint sources? Or will they bite the bullet, leave their nonpoint sources alone, and forego federal monies? Will it depend on who the nonpoint sources are? And, if the states do refuse to go after the nonpoint sources, what happens to the TMDL?

3. In an effort to entice states into including nonpoint sources in their TMDL implementation programs, in the late 1990s EPA ingeniously (some said deviously) unveiled a plan to take advantage of the point source side of the TMDL program as leverage for the nonpoint source side. Point sources, of course, have long been subject to direct technology-based regulation under the CWA NPDES permitting program. Nonpoint sources have not. It is reasonable to assume, therefore, that the marginal cost of satisfying TMDL waste load allocations— i.e., the cost of reducing a unit of pollutant load— will be more for point sources than it will for nonpoint sources. Hence, as an alternative to direct regulation of nonpoint sources, EPA suggested that states could allow NPDES dischargers to pay for nonpoint source dischargers' reductions in discharge loads and thereby avoid additional load restrictions in their NPDES permits. *See* Revisions to the Water Quality Planning and Management Regulation and Revisions to the National Pollutant Discharge Elimination System Program in Support of Revisions to the Water Quality Planning and Management Regulation, 65 Fed. Reg. 4365 (2000) (amending various provisions of 40 C.F.R. pts. 9, 122, 123, 124, 130). Provided the state can demonstrate with reasonable assurance that the nonpoint source load reduction measures will actually lead to load reductions, such trading can take advantage of the disparity in marginal cost of load unit of reduction—i.e., point sources could actually save money by paying for nonpoint source reductions. Of course, this approach won't work for waters impaired entirely by nonpoint sources, such as those involved in *Pronsolino*.

4. There is far from universal agreement, however, that EPA has the authority the *Pronsolino* court believes it does. The history of EPA's efforts to establish its position in this regard is a story in bizarre politics, though one many would regard as politics as usual. In 1999, EPA published proposed revisions to its TMDL regulations that would have brought the program squarely in line with *Pronsolino* and the strategy for nonpoint sources the court endorsed. *See* 64 Fed. Reg. 46,057 (1999); 64 Fed. Reg. 46,011 (1999); *see generally* Lisa E. Roberts, *Is the Gun Loaded This Time? EPA's Proposed Revisions to the Total Maximum Daily Load Program*, 6 ENVTL. LAWYER 635 (2000). These proposals immediately attracted controversy. EPA received over 34,000 comments on the proposed rules. Farming groups initiated litigation challenging EPA's authority to implement the TMDL program so as to assign allocations to nonpoint sources. *See* American Farm Bureau Federation v. Browner, Nos. 00–1320 and consolidated cases (D.C. Cir). The National Governors Association immediately sought federal legislation to add funding and flexibility to the TMDL program. Some members of Congress also questioned EPA's authority in this regard and took measures to block implementation of the final rules. Indeed, prior to EPA's promulgation of the final rules, Congress adopted a rider to the 2001 Military Construction/Supplemental Appropriations bill (the bill dealt with funding of U.S. Forces in Kosovo and of Columbian anti-drug efforts) that prevented EPA not only from enforcing new TMDL rules before fiscal year 2002, but also from even finishing its work on the proposed rules and adopting them as final. In a political gambit to thwart Congress, EPA adopted the final rules, which retain most of the relevant structure of the proposed rules, before President Clinton signed the appropriations bill restricting the agency from doing so. *See* Revisions to the Water Quality Planning and Management Regulation and Revisions to the National Pollutant Discharge Elimination System Program in Support of Revisions to the Water Quality Planning and Management Regulation, 65 Fed. Reg. 4365 (2000) (amending various provisions of 40 C.F.R. pts. 9, 122, 123, 124, 130). In other words, the rules went on the books, but were "not effective until 30 days after the date that Congress allows EPA to implement this regulation." 65 Fed. Reg. at 53586.

5. Soon after that, of course, a new administration took command of EPA. In July 2001, one year after the final rules were "adopted," the Bush administration announced that it would further delay implementation of the rules so that it may reconsider them in light of concerns raised by stakeholders, with spring 2002 as a projected target date for proposing any changes to the rules. *See* 66 Fed. Reg. 41,817 (2001). The court in American Farm Bureau Federation v. Browner then stayed the challenge to the "old" rules pending issuance of any revised rules. With the 2000 TMDL rule in a state of limbo, the Bush administration began exploring alternative approaches. In the summer of 2001, EPA began developing a new concept it called the "TMDL/Watershed" rule, and later that year conducted five public "listening sessions" around the country to receive input on the basic approach of linking TMDLs to a broader watershed-based implementation program that would use watershed assessment scales, rely heavily on state implementation plans, and promote pollutant trading between emission sources. In June 2002 EPA announced that it was drafting the new rule and would propose it by the end of that year. That didn't happen, but a draft rule was "leaked" in April 2003 and in March 2003 EPA did take the step of formally withdrawing the 2000 TMDL rule. *See* 69 Fed. Reg. 13608 (Mar. 19, 2003).

6. As of this writing EPA still has not proposed any form of a watershed-based TMDL rule. In other words, as of 2012, the TMDL regulations that apply are those adopted in 1985 and amended in 1992. *See* 40 C.F.R. Part 130. Since 2003, gloss on the program has come primarily through EPA guidance, and like its predecessors the Obama Administration has focused its guidance efforts on crafting a watershed-based approach. *See* http://water.epa.gov/lawsregs/lawsguidance/cwa/tmdl/guidance.cfm.

7. Assume TMDL rules eventually put into effect retain the basic features EPA adopted in July 1999, and do apply to nonpoint sources at least as far as *Pronsolino* says they do. To what extent could the TMDL program become a useful tool in the ecosystem management effort? The events leading up to *Pronsolino* suggest that states will be reluctant to take on regulation of agricultural interests; costs of TMDL calculation, not to mention implementation, are staggering; local land use decisions are highly complex and must be coordinated with state TMDL decisions; and so on. Some concerns with the TMDL program are physical: TMDLs may be very difficult to accomplish in small watersheds; TMDLs are too narrow in focus, failing to take into account habitat quality and water quantity issues; and nonpoint source pollution often is caused in part by physical environment conditions beyond the control of regulators or dischargers. *See generally* Jory Ruggiero, *Toward a Law of the Land: The Clean Water Act as a Mandate for the Implementation of an Ecosystem Approach to Land Management*, 20 PUBLIC LAND & RESOURCES L.J. 31 (1999). For a contrary view based on the experience of TMDL implementation in Texas, see Margaret Hoffman, *Integrating TMDLs into Watershed-Based Water Quality Management*, 31 ST. BAR OF TEXAS ENVTL. L.J. 193 (2001).

8. Another action Congress took after EPA proposed its TMDL rule in 2000 was to commission the National Research Council (an arm of the National Academy of Sciences) to evaluate the scientific basis of the rule and the TMDL program in general. The Council's report concluded, among other things, that the TMDL program narrowly focuses on pollutant loads, whereas habitat degradation and stream channel modifications should play a key role in any water quality restoration program. Also, consistent with much of the literature on ecosystem management, the Council recommended that the TMDL program employ adaptive management techniques so that TMDLs can evolve as better data are collected and assessed. *See* National Academy of Sciences/National Research Council, Assessing the TMDL Approach to Water Quality Management (2001). How would you design adaptive management techniques for the TMDL program?

9. The *Pronsolino* court noted that, because EPA has no authority to regulate nonpoint sources directly, the only leverage EPA really has over states that refuse to regulate nonpoint sources is withdrawing federal environmental grant funds. As the court explained, while this is not federal regulation, the withdrawal effects may be too severe for states that have become dependent on the federal dollars to help run state environmental programs. They may knuckle under, as the court put it, and apply the federal program uncritically and contrary to other legitimate state policy objectives. What do you think of this technique of "federalizing" environmental policy? For an overview of how Congress can use the spending power to influence state environmental policy, see Denis Binder, *The Spending Clause as a Positive Source of Environmental Protection: A Primer*, 4 CHAPMAN L. REV. 147 (2001).

10. The *Pronsolino* opinion drives the cost point home by attaching some whopping compliance cost figures to individual landowner contexts in California—in some cases to the tune of millions of dollars each. Why is it so expensive to reduce pollutant loads from their lands? Is it that their forestry and other land management practices were so bad, or is it simply that controlling nonpoint source pollution is so difficult? If it will cost landowners tens of millions of dollars to comply with TMDLs in just this small watershed, imagine the total national price tag for controlling nonpoint source pollution! Is it worth it? Should the cost be borne entirely by the private landowners?

11. To throw even more confusion into the picture, in 2011 a Ninth Circuit panel issued an opinion ruling that, contrary to 30 years of EPA and judicial understanding, stormwater runoff from logging roads like those involved in *Pronsolino* actually is subject to regulation as *point source* pollution because the runoff is collected in systems of ditches, channels, and culverts before discharge. *See* NEDC v. Brown, 640 F.3d 1063 (9th Cir. 2011). The Supreme Court agreed in 2012 to review the case, and as of this writing has not issued an opinion. It remains to be seen whether this startling new interpretation withstands the Court's scrutiny, and in any event the Court's ruling could present important guidelines for differentiating point and nonpoint sources.

12. Because the TMDL program depends on Water Quality Standards (WQS) program as the driver of impairment determinations and then, for waters that are impaired, the TMDL load allocation process, the rise of the TMDL program has focused greater attention on the WQS program. One of the most controversial WQS issues in this regard has been the EPA's efforts to require states to establish quantitative numeric standards for nutrients, primarily nitrogen and phosphorus. The vast majority of states have established what are known as narrative standards for nutrients in waterbodies—qualitative descriptions of water quality such as Florida's declaration that "in no case shall nutrient concentrations of body of water be altered so as to cause an imbalance in natural populations of flora or fauna." By comparison, numeric standards stated in measurable parts per million or billion are more definitive and thus more amenable to impairment determinations and TMDL load allocations and enforcement. For many waterbodies, however, the primary source of nutrient pollution is nonpoint source flows from agriculture, which means any effort to move in the direction of numeric standards and TMDL program enforcement is in for a battle. Nowhere has this been more the case than for Florida, where EPA and the state have been locked in contentious litigation and negotiations over EPA's court-ordered demand that the state adopt numeric nutrient standards. *See* Florida Wildlife Federation v. Jackson, 2009 WL 5217062 (N.D. Fla. Dec. 30, 2009). EPA finalized regulations for the state in 2010. *See* 75 Fed. Reg. 75762 (Dec. 6, 2010). Since then EPA and the state have been in litigation over EPA's rule and gone back and forth over requests for retractions and extensions, although the state did by November 2011 adopt standards meeting EPA approval, though not that of environmental groups. When numeric nutrient standards go into effect, the next shoe to drop, and the next battleground, will be over how the TMDL program is thrown into action. To follow EPA's nutrient standard effort for Florida, see http://water.epa.gov/lawsregs/rulesregs/florida_index.cfm. Florida's responses can be followed at http://www.dep.state.fl.us/water/wqssp/nutrients.

13. For history on the rise of the TMDL program and the false start of the watershed-based rulemaking, particularly as it relates to nonpoint sources, see OLIVER A. HOUCK, THE CLEAN WATER ACT TMDL PROGRAM: LAW, POLICY, AND IMPLEMENTATION (Envtl. L. Inst. 1999); Robert W. Adler, *Controlling Nonpoint Source Pollution: Is Help on the Way (From the Courts or EPA?)*, 31 ENVTL. L. REP. (ELI) 10270 (2001); Sarah Birkeland, *EPA's TMDL Program*, 28 ECOLOGY L.Q. 297 (2001); James Boyd, *The New Face of the Clean Water Act: A Critical Review of EPA's New TMDL Rules*, 11 DUKE ENVTL. L. & POL'Y F. 39 (2000).

b. WILD AND SCENIC RIVERS

As an ecosystem management tool, the TMDL program may be too powerful an authority channeled into too narrow a mandate. An alternative approach would be a broader mandate—protect the overall integrity of the river or the lake—within a more flexible regulatory framework. One model of such a program is the Wild and Scenic Rivers Act of 1968 (WSRA), 16 U.S.C. § 1271–1287. Enacted in advance of the flurry of environmental legislation that began in the 1970s, WSRA protects "free-flowing" rivers that possess "outstandingly remarkable value." 16 U.S.C. § 1271. The designation and boundary delineation of such rivers is made by Congress on its own initiative, by congressional approval of a federal agency nomination, or by a state with the approval of the Secretary of the Interior.

WSRA classifies designated rivers into three categories based on their degree of naturalness (i.e., lack of evidence of human influence): wild, scenic, and recreational. Depending on the classification of a designated river, different management mandates apply, to be implemented by the appropriate federal or state agency. The responsible agency must prepare a management plan designed to implement its duty to "protect and enhance the values which caused [the river] to be included in said system without, insofar as is consistent therewith, limiting other uses that do not substantially interfere with public use and enjoyment of those values." *Id.* 1281(a). WSRA thus is organized around the functions of designating, classifying, managing, and protecting free-flowing rivers for their identified outstanding resource values.

WSRA has led to designation and classification of substantial river miles. The U.S. Forest Service manages 76 rivers under WSRA, amounting to over 4000 river miles, and the Bureau of Land Management covers almost 2000 river miles in 15 rivers. Over 170 rivers and over 11,000 river miles in all are within the WSRA system. Only recently, however, has the force of WSRA's management mandates been felt in ways that limit land use options and thus could be included as a potent component of ecosystem management policy. The cases in what is known as the "Oregon Trilogy" recognized WSRA's "protect and enhance" standard as an enforceable mandate. *See* Oregon Natural Desert Association v. Green, 953 F.Supp. 1133 (D.Or.1997); National Wildlife Federation v. Cosgriffe, 21 F.Supp.2d 1211 (D.Or.1998); Oregon Natural Desert Association v. Singleton, 47 F.Supp.2d 1182 (D.Or. 1998). The following case provides an epilogue to the trilogy.

Oregon Natural Desert Association v. Singleton

United States District Court for the District of Oregon, 1999.
75 F.Supp.2d 1139.

■ REDDEN, DISTRICT JUDGE.

This is an action brought by environmental groups (collectively "ONDA"), against the Bureau of Land Management ("BLM") and three individuals. Oregon Cattlemen's Association appears as an intervenor-defendant. ONDA challenges the BLM's management of the Main, West Little, and North Fork Owyhee River corridors, alleging that the BLM failed to prepare an environmental impact statement ("EIS") analyzing the effect of cattle grazing on the area, as required by the National Environmental Policy Act ("NEPA"), 42 U.S.C. §§ 4321-4370a, and that its management plan violates the BLM's mandate under the Wild and Scenic Rivers Act ("WSRA"), 16 U.S.C. §§ 1271–1284.

Findings of Fact

Background

In 1984, Congress designated 120 miles of the Main Owyhee River as a federal wild and scenic river pursuant to the WSRA. In the Oregon Omnibus Wild and Scenic Rivers Act of 1988, Pub.L. 100–557, codified at 16 U.S.C. § 1274(a)(91), Congress added 57 miles of the West Little Owyhee and nine miles of the North Fork Owyhee to the national wild and scenic rivers system. Congress classified all three segments as "wild." A wild river area is defined under the WSRA as "free of impoundments and generally inaccessible except by trail, with watersheds or shorelines essentially primitive and waters unpolluted." 16 U.S.C. § 1273(b). The "wild" classification is the most restrictive of three possible classifications. Id.

Section 3 of the WSRA required the BLM to issue a "comprehensive management plan" to "provide for the protection of the river values" within three fiscal years after designation. 16 U.S.C. § 1274(d)(1). The WSRA requires that the plan "address resource protection, development of lands and facilities, user capacities, and other management practices necessary or desirable to achieve the purposes of this chapter." 16 U.S.C. § 1264(d)(1).

Conditions in the river corridor at plan implementation

In September 1991, the BLM issued a final management plan ("the Plan"). The Plan identified five outstandingly remarkable values ("ORVs") on the Main Owyhee: scenery, geology, recreation, wildlife, and cultural. The ORVs identified for the West Little and North Fork Owyhee included recreation, scenery and wildlife. The Plan did not designate botanical or fishery ORVs, but characterized vegetation as a "key component of the visual resource, important to watershed values, wildlife habitat, and a vital part of the natural setting for recreation."

Although cattle had been grazing the river corridor for many years at the time the Plan was written and implemented, the BLM recognized that in some of the river areas accessible to livestock, cattle grazing had created substantial negative effects. Cattle are grazed on 67 miles of the 186-mile river system, and the BLM found that 18 of these miles constituted "areas of livestock concern," i.e., showed noticeable negative effects created by grazing. The areas most affected by livestock grazing were trail crossings and "water gaps," the places where livestock come to the river to drink.

The Environmental Assessment ("EA") issued with the Plan noted that areas within at least seven of 11 grazing allotments and one trail area showed negative effects from livestock grazing, and that these negative effects had a direct impact on the scenic, recreational, and watershed ORVs of the Owyhee Rivers.

The BLM's range management objectives for the river corridor

Section 1281(a) of the WSRA specifies the management duties of the federal agency charged with managing the designated river:

> Each component of the national wild and scenic rivers system shall be administered in such manner as to protect and enhance the values which caused it to be included in said system without, insofar as is consistent therewith, limiting other uses that do not substantially interfere with public use and enjoyment of these values. In such administration primary emphasis shall be given to protecting its esthetic, scenic, historic, archeologic, and scientific features. Management plans for any such component may establish varying degrees of intensity for its protection and development, based on the special attributes of the area.

16 U.S.C. § 1281(a).

The Plan promulgated by the BLM specified the following objectives for range management:

Maintain or improve the vegetative cover of key species and the visual aspect of native perennial plants, within the soil and vegetative capabilities of ecological sites, in the corridor by 1999. Maintain proper utilization of key species. Minimize livestock impacts on vegetation and soils, within the river corridor, at water gaps/trail crossings, on uplands, and in riparian areas. Minimize livestock/recreation conflicts at water gaps/trail crossings by 1999.

The Plan's first management prescription for grazing was to "[i]nventory the river corridors to determine riparian areas and potentials." The inventory was necessary because the BLM did not at the time the Plan was written have baseline data on the level of grazing that had occurred at the time the rivers were designated or that was occurring at the time the Plan was being written.

However, Mr. Taylor [of BLM] testified at the evidentiary hearing on September 13, 1999, that this inventory has not been done, and will not be done unless and until a funding request is granted. If the funding becomes available, the inventory is scheduled to begin in 2001.

To achieve its goal of "maintaining or improving" vegetation, the Plan established three "utilization" standards: livestock could not consume more than 40% of the annual growth of "key grass species" in upland areas except for certain winter allotments, where 50% consumption was permitted, and livestock could not consume more than 30% of the annual growth of "current years leaders" for willows in riparian areas.

However, at the time the standards were set, the BLM had done no utilization studies for riparian areas. It appears from the Plan and other parts of the administrative record that the 30, 40 and 50% utilization standards represented the grazing levels in existence at the time the Plan was being written.

The Plan further provided that

[h]erbaceous riparian vegetation will be managed to insure a properly functioning riparian system. Management may include restrictions on use levels, seasons or where feasible and compatible exclusionary fencing. Key sites will be monitored and use levels and/or management may be revised, on a case by case basis, through the allotment evaluation process. Any changes in use levels and or management must ensure plan objectives are being met. Water gaps and trail crossings will be managed so that vegetative cover does not decrease and, if possible, increases. Alternate sources of water, fencing and improved herding practices will be utilized where possible to reduce or eliminate livestock impacts at water gaps and trail crossings. Primary focus will be given to areas where camping/livestock conflicts exist.

Grazing impacts since promulgation of the Plan

The BLM asserts that since the Plan was promulgated, the overall impact of grazing on the river corridor has decreased, and four of the areas of concern have improved.

Mr. Taylor testified that [an] indicator of improved conditions in the river corridor was the BLM's recent finding of attainment of Properly Functioning Condition of Riparian Areas on 146.5 miles of the river areas (93%), with 6.8 miles (4.4%) functioning at risk. According to the BLM, "properly functioning riparian condition" means that adequate vegetation, landform, or large woody debris is present to:

1) dissipate stream energy associated with high waterflows, thereby reducing erosion and improving water quality;

2) filter sediment, capture bedload, and aid floodplain development;

3) improve flood-water retention and ground-water recharge;

4) develop root masses that stabilize streambanks against cutting action;

5) develop diverse ponding and channel characteristics to provide the habitat and the water depth, duration, and temperature necessary for fish production, waterfowl breeding, and other uses; and

6) support greater biodiversity.

Only 67 miles of the 186-mile river system are accessible to livestock. The evidence does not reveal how many of those 67 miles are encompassed within the 146.5 miles found to be properly functioning, how many are within the 39.5 miles still to be assessed, and how many are included in the 6.8 miles which are functioning at risk. (The areas of concern identified in 1993 comprise about 18 miles). The attainment of properly functioning condition in 146.5 miles, without more, does not provide the court with any basis for determining the condition of the areas of concern.

In August 1999, Katie Fite, a biologist who had been active in bringing conditions in Deary Pasture to the BLM's attention, wrote a letter to Mr. Taylor describing her observations of areas around the West Little Owyhee in July 1999, and enclosed photographs of some of those areas. Her observations included:

1. Trampled creek banks and signs of heavy grazing at Jackson Creek.

2. Severely damaged springs and seeps near the Anderson Crossing road, with livestock having completely "stripped the vegetation and pounded it into a mass of mud." Ms. Fite also noted that livestock were "wallowing well above their knees in the slime that passed for water here."

3. Salt located in several places near wet meadows and springs along the main road between Antelope Creek and Anderson Crossing, near Exchange Spring, and within 20 feet of a running spring.

4. Cattle defecating in the water, trampling stream banks, and grazing heavily upstream of Anderson Crossing.

Even the intervenor's expert witness, Gar Lorain, has opined that hot springs or other springs "could have unique [plant] species subject to fairly heavy grazing. These areas should be fenced to protect their unique characteristics." Declaration of Gar Lorain, Exhibit 2, p. 2. However, there is no indication that the BLM has responded to these observations with any reduction in the number of grazing animals or modification of grazing practices.

Conclusions of Law

The WSRA states the policy of the United States that certain designated rivers which possess "outstandingly remarkable scenic, recreational, geologic, fish and wildlife, historic, cultural or other similar values," shall be "preserved in free-flowing condition" and that the rivers and their immediate environments be "protected for the benefit and enjoyment of present and future generations." 16 U.S.C. § 1271.

Although the BLM asserts that its grazing management practices have generated improvements in the areas of concern first identified in 1993, the court concludes that the assertion is unsubstantiated by objective evidence except for the closure of Deary Pasture. Perhaps the most troubling evidence is Mr. Taylor's testimony that the numbers of animals and the seasons of use have remained completely unchanged since implementation of the Plan, except when grazing permits have been increased to exploit good water years.

The BLM's finding that most of the river corridor is in properly functioning riparian condition is not probative with respect to improvement in the areas of concern because the percentages provide no specific information about areas of concern. Other data gathered since 1993—the surveys of the West Little Owyhee, for example—consistently indicate heavy cattle grazing and erosion.

The Plan provided that restrictions on levels and seasons of use would be implemented where necessary to ensure that utilization standards were met, riparian vegetation was in a properly functioning condition, and livestock impacts on vegetation and soils within the river corridor, at water gaps and trail crossings were minimized so that vegetative cover would not decrease and, if possible, would increase. See, e.g., AR Tab 178, p. 30–31. None of this has been done. Mr. Taylor testified that the BLM has neither made changes to seasons of use nor reduced the number of AUMs permitted for any of the allotments since the Plan was implemented. In fact, Mr. Taylor admitted that the BLM has actually increased the number of AUMs in some allotments, because greater than anticipated rainfall had yielded more vegetation. The court is troubled by this indication that the BLM regards beneficial natural events as justifications for increased grazing, rather than as opportunities for recovery and enhancement of natural resources.

The Public Interest and the Balance of Equities

Factors favoring closure of the areas of concern

The WSRA charges the BLM with administering "each component of the national wild and scenic rivers system" in a manner which will "protect and enhance the values which caused it to be included in said system." 16 U.S.C. § 1281(a). In that administration, "primary emphasis shall be given to protecting its esthetic, scenic, historic, archeologic, and scientific features." Id.

The values and special attributes of each river segment are enumerated in the 1993 Plan. Recreation values on the Main Owyhee include rafting, drift boating, kayaking, hiking, photography, nature study, fishing, hunting, camping, and rockhounding. The West Little river segment offers very high quality primitive recreation experiences, including off-trail backpacking, swimming, hiking, wildlife viewing, and hunting. The North Fork Owyhee offers very high quality backpacking opportunities, early season expert level kayaking, hiking, hunting, camping, wildlife viewing and photography.

The scenic values of the Owyhee River include its dramatic landforms, whitewater, and slow-moving pools. The West Little Owyhee is characterized by canyons, flat sagebrush plateaus, and secluded pools confined by sheer rock walls; between the pools are reaches that flow as riffles or rapids during periods of high water, and become sandy or gravelly dry beaches in the dry, hot summer months. The North Fork of the Owyhee combines canyon bottoms overshadowed by steep canyon walls with flat high sagebrush desert.

Over 200 species of wildlife are found in the river canyons and the sagebrush desert on the rims. Birds include nesting raptors such as hawks, kestrel, falcon, and golden and bald eagles; game birds such as partridge, quail, mourning dove and sage grouse; waterfowl; and song birds. Mammal species include California bighorn sheep, mule deer, wild horses, pronghorn antelope, mountain lion, bobcat, coyote, badger, beaver, otter, muskrat, marmot, raccoon, porcupine and rabbit.

Several plant species within the canyonlands are classified as federal or state sensitive species or are on "watch lists." The preservation of all of these features is in the public interest.

Congress has classified the three river segments as "wild," the most restrictive of three WSRA classifications. A wild river area is defined under the WSRA as "free of impoundments and generally inaccessible except by trail, with watersheds or shorelines essentially primitive and waters unpol-

luted." 16 U.S.C. § 1273(b). The public interest also includes the public policy stated by Congress of preserving these rivers in as pristine and unpolluted a condition as possible.

It has been almost seven years since the BLM recognized that cattle
grazing was creating noticeable negative effects on the rivers' values in
some parts of the corridor. The BLM found that grazing conflicted with recreational values where livestock congregated, grazed and defecated around
campsites; that the visual impact of livestock trailing and grazing affected
scenic and recreation values; and that the ecological condition of upland
and riparian areas was being degraded by livestock grazing, trampling and
defecation. The BLM designated specific areas of concern in 1993, and stated its goal of managing those areas so as to maintain or improve the vegetative cover of key species and the visual aspect of native perennial plants,
ensure proper utilization of key species, minimize livestock impact on vegetation and soils, and reduce livestock/recreation conflicts.

Although the BLM asserts that it has met these objectives, the evidence shows that, with the exception of the areas around Deary Pasture,
grazing in the areas of concern has been neither reduced nor otherwise
regulated. The same observations of heavy grazing, trampling, and bank
erosion reported in 1993 have continued well into 1999. The persistent degradation of these areas, and the BLM's apparent inability to manage cattle
grazing in a manner which would repair and restore the areas of concern
has serious negative consequences for the recreational, scenic and ecological values of the designated rivers. These negative effects have existed for
many years and there is no indication that they will change significantly in
the future.

Economic impact on permittees of closing areas of concern

The grazing allotments within the river corridor enable private cattle
and sheep ranchers to graze their livestock on publicly-owned land, typically at below-market rates. Although the parties dispute the dollars involved,
it is uncontroverted that grazing permits constitute a public subsidy to
livestock operators, sometimes a substantial one. The court notes that grazing privileges on publicly-owned land are not property rights, and the government is under no obligation either to provide or to continue them.

At present, the total AUMs for the 19 grazing allotments and 58
ranching operations in the river corridor are approximately 104,000. Closure of the areas of concern would represent a loss of 26,976 AUMs, or
about 26% of the total in the river corridor.

Economic impact on Malheur County of closing areas of concern

According to the government's evidence, the total personal income in
Malheur County is $491 million. According to a study by plaintiffs' expert
witness Hans Radtke, an agricultural economist, the total income generated by the livestock industry in Malheur County is approximately $30 mil-
lion a year—about 6% of the county's total personal income. The intervenor

disputes this amount, arguing that agriculture and agriculture-related businesses generate about $92 million per year. Neither the government nor the intervenor has submitted evidence on the economic consequences to the affected permittees of closing the areas of concern. However, according to figures submitted by the plaintiffs, which neither the government nor the intervenor disputes, the maximum amount of personal income lost to Malheur County by eliminating 26,976 AUMs would be $692,204—approximately .023% of the county's total livestock income, using Radtke's $30 million figure. Because neither the government nor the intervenor has provided the court with evidence on prospective income loss to livestock-related businesses caused by the elimination of 26,976 AUMs, I make no finding on the economic impact to livestock-related businesses within Malheur County.

The public interest in requiring the BLM to implement the Congressional mandate contained in the WSRA is manifest, as is the public's interest in preserving and enhancing the extraordinary values of the Owyhee Rivers. The continued degradation of the areas of concern within the river corridor constitutes irreparable harm, and there are no legal remedies available to redress this harm. While a 25% reduction in subsidized grazing privileges will have an adverse economic effect on some of the individual permit holders, its overall effect on the county's economy is negligible.

For these reasons, the public interest and the balance of equities require the issuance of an injunction directing the BLM to exclude the areas of concern from any further grazing by domestic livestock.

NOTES & QUESTIONS

1. In deciding whether to enjoin BLM from issuing AUMs in the disputed areas, the court determined that while the reduction in subsidized grazing privileges would have an adverse economic effect on some of the individual permit holders, its overall effect on the county's economy would be negligible. What if the economic impact on the county would have been substantial? Does that matter under WSRA? Should it?

2. WSRA defines "outstanding resource values" as including not only "scenic, recreational, geologic, fish and wildlife, historic, [and] cultural" values, but also "other similar" values as well. 16 U.S.C. § 1271. In their guidelines for administration of the program, the Departments of Interior and Agriculture have clarified that ecological values are ORVs. *See* 47 Fed. Reg. 39,454, 39,455–57 (Sept. 7, 1982).

3. Given its limitation to free-flowing rivers, it should be no surprise that a principal objective of WSRA is to keep designated rivers in that condition. Section 7 of WSRA thus prohibits the Federal Energy Regulatory Commission, an agency within the Department of Energy that oversees nongovernmental hydroelectric projects and dams, from licensing any such project "on or directly affecting" a WSRA river. 16 U.S.C. § 1278(a). All federal agencies are prohibited from assisting any water project that would have a "direct and adverse effect on the values for which such river was established." *Id.*

4. As the Oregon trilogy demonstrates, WSRA's "protect and enhance" mandate goes well beyond limiting dams. Section 10 and 12 of WSRA outline the duties of federal river corridor management agencies and of federal agencies administering lands adjacent to the river corridor, respectively. Section 10 requires the federal land management agency with jurisdiction over the land through which the river flows to prepare the river management plan and constrain its land management actions pursuant to the protect and enhance mandate. The Departments of Interior and Agriculture interpret this section as codifying a "nondegradation and enhancement policy" that applies to all designated rivers regardless of classification. 47 Fed. Reg. 39,454, 39,458 (Sept. 7, 1982). Section 12 then extends the protect and enhance mandate, and thus the nondegradation and enhancement policy, to "any lands which include, border upon, or are adjacent to" the designated river. Federal agencies with jurisdiction over such lands, which may include agencies other than the river corridor management agency, need not prepare WSRA management plans, but must incorporate WSRA management purposes into all policies, regulations, contracts, and other actions that affect the designated river. *See* Wilderness Society v. Tyrrel, 918 F.2d 813 (9th Cir. 1990). In short, WSRA preempts the multiple-use regime under which most federal land management agencies operate, vaulting preservation to a dominant-use status for designated rivers. For further background on these aspects of the WSRA program, see Charlton H. Bonham, *The Wild and Scenic Rivers Act and the Oregon Trilogy*, 21 PUBLIC LANDS & RESOURCES L. REV. 109 (2000); Sally K. Fairfax et al., *Federalism and the Wild and Scenic Rivers Act: Now You See It, Now You Don't*, 59 WASH. L. REV. 417 (1984); Peter M. K. Frost, *Protecting and Enhancing Wild and Scenic Rivers In the West*, 29 IDAHO L. REV. 313 (1992–93). For a thorough review of the broad scope and history of WSRA law and policy, see Murray Feldman et al., *Learning to Manage Our National Wild and Scenic Rivers System*, 20 NATURAL RESOURCES & ENV'T 10 (Fall 2005).

5. Why would a state seek designation of a Wild and Scenic River in its borders? The state must first so designate the river under state law, then it must petition the Secretary of the Interior for federal designation. If the river is designated, the state must manage nonfederal lands within the designation boundary consistent with WSRA's mandate at no cost to the federal government. So what's in it for the state? Indeed, several counties in California asked that question when, in June 1980, Governor Jerry Brown petitioned the Department of Interior to designate five river segments in northern California as WSRA rivers. The counties within which the river segments were located challenged the designations and managed, until the wee hours of the Carter Administration, to secure judicial injunctions against final approval by Secretary of Interior Cecil Andrus. The Ninth Circuit lifted the injunction in time for Andrus to sign the designations—his last official act in office—and the Ninth Circuit later rejected the merits of the counties' challenge to the final designations. *See* Del Norte County v. United States, 732 F.2d 1462 (9th Cir. 1984). What do you suppose were the counties' reasons for challenging the designations, and why would the Governor have petitioned for designation despite the counties' opposition?

6. Only free-flowing rivers, of which few remain, can be designated for protection under the regulatory reach of the Wild and Scenic Rivers Act. In 1997, the Clinton Administration launched a non-regulatory program to coordinate protection and restoration of a limited number of "American Heritage Rivers" (AHR). *See* Exec. Order 13061, 62 Fed. Reg. 48,860 (Sept. 11, 1997). This American Heritage Rivers Initiative was designed to promote the environmental, economic, and cultural aspects of rivers and their river communities. In 1997, local communities, acting in coordination with their state, local, and tribal governments, nominated rivers for inclusion in the AHR program, and Vice President Gore announced the first batch of 14 AHRs in July 1998. A federal interagency task force then determined how existing environmental, economic, and cultural programs could best be refocused to benefit each AHR and its local community. Each AHR is assigned a federal employee to serve as "River Navigator" to help implement AHR management plans and act as a liaison to federal agencies. Federal agencies are responsible for matching AHR community needs with available federal resources within their respective jurisdictions, including pollution control, greenway and alternative transportation facilities, historic structure restoration, biological resources inventories, and similar efforts. Although critics of the program derided it as a step along the perilous road to federal regulation of private and local land uses, in fact the AHR Initiative remained entirely non-regulatory and was continued by the Bush and Obama Administrations. For further background on the program, see Thomas Downs, *American Heritage Rivers Initiative: A Harbinger of Future White House Environmental Policy?*, 29 ENVTL. L. REP. (ELI) 10065 (1999), and for updated information, including a "state of the river" report for each AHR, see EPA's web site, American Heritage Rivers, http://water.epa.gov/type/watersheds/named/heritage.

7. WSRA protects rivers that are free-flowing, and the AHR Initiative is non-regulatory in scope. Neither program, therefore, gets to the nub of the most controversial topic in riverine ecosystem management—dams. Dam building in the 20th century was practically a national pastime, and certainly a national policy. Over 75,000 public and private dams (over six feet high) have been erected on this nation's rivers, impeding over 600,000 miles of flowing water. As we have for the filling of wetlands, have we turned the corner on building dams? Most likely we have. There appears to be a broad consensus in federal and state policy that, as Bruce Babbitt quipped in the later years of his tenure as Secretary of Interior, we overdid it with dams. But the far thornier question is whether to remove existing dams to restore the free-flowing qualities of impounded waterways. Dams provide tremendous economic values to local and distant populations, including hydroelectric power, irrigation water, and recreation. But they fundamentally alter the ecosystem dynamics of the imprisoned waterway, and they can be as deadly as any predator to fish that are trapped behind them, or swept over spillways to their death, or pureed in power-generating turbine blades.

8. If dams are so bad for aquatic ecosystems, why not get rid of them? Indeed, during the Clinton Administration Secretary of Interior Bruce Babbitt pushed the politics of dam removal front and center with his infamous "dam-busting tour" of 1998, and the Endangered Species Act listings of numerous runs of salmon in Pacific Northwest rivers, and of sturgeon in the Missouri River, have forced federal dam managers, principally the Bureau of Reclamation and the Army Corps of Engineers, to consider dam removal as a serious policy option. *See* Richard A. Lovett, *As Salmon Stage Disappearing Act, Dams May Too*, 284 SCIENCE 574 (1999). In 2003 the Heinz Center for Science, Economics and the

Environment issued two major reports on dams and dam removal. *See* Heinz Center for Science, Economics and the Environment, Dam Removal: Science and Decision Making (William L. Graf ed., 2003); Heinz Center for Science, Economics and the Environment Dam Removal Research: Status and Prospects (William L. Graf ed., 2003). The reports are filled with facts and historical accounts of dams in the United States, and provide a thorough investigation of the consequences of dam removal. The matter moved from theory to reality when, on February 23, 2004, Army divers set off 600 pounds of plastic explosives to breach the 94-year old Embry Dam on the Rappahannock River in Fredericksburg, Virginia. Built to produce hydropower, the dam had not been used for that purpose since the 1960s. After removal is complete, it will make the Rappahannock the longest free-flowing river in the Chesapeake Bay watershed and will reopen hundreds of miles of river to migratory fish for the first time since 1854. In 2004 the American Rivers conservation organization reported that about 60 other dams were slated for removal in 14 states around the nation by different governmental and private operators. They ranged from old grist mill dams to inactive hydropower dams. A representative example is a small powerhouse dam on the Elwah River in Washington, removed in 2011 to, it is hoped, restore salmon access to the upper reaches of the river. *See Will Busting Dams Boost Salmon?*, 334 SCIENCE 888 (2011).

Yet the trend in the United States toward dam removal—or at least not building new dams—is not being followed in general around the world. A study of the global effects of dams reports that over half of the world's large river systems are substantially affected by dams. *See* Christer Nilsson, *Fragmentation and Flow Regulation of the World's Large River Systems*, 308 SCIENCE 405 (2005). By 2000 there were over 45,000 large dams in more than 150 countries, and each year hundreds more are being built. The world's largest dam is the Three-Gorges Dam in China, which rests in the middle of one of the world's richest biodiversity hotspots. The dam's reservoir watershed area is larger than Switzerland, and the reservoir area itself is over 1000 square kilometers. Dozens of former mountaintops are now islands, leading some scientists to describe it as the most spectacular "grand-scale habitat fragmentation" in modern times. *See* Jianguo Wu et al., *Three-Gorges Dam—Experiment in Habitat Fragmentation?*, 300 SCIENCE 1293 (2003). Few issues will more squarely test riverine ecosystem management policy than how national, state, and local interests deal with dam removal in the next decade. For a concise history of national policy on dams from its building phase to the current movement toward removal, see Christine A. Klein, *Dam Policy: The Emerging Paradigm of Restoration*, 31 Envtl. L. Rep. (ELI) 10486 (2001); Christine A. Klein, *On Dams and Democracy*, 78 OREGON L. REV. 641 (1999).

3. WETLANDS

As previously described, wetland losses, while slowing dramatically in recent years, have been widespread in the history of this nation. The ecological values lost to the legacy of draining and filling are immeasurable, as are the habitat values that continue to be delivered from the 270 million acres of wetlands we still have in place. So, how should we manage those remaining resources?

A threshold question we inevitably confront along the way to reaching that management issue is where, exactly, are these wetlands, and which of them are subject to federal, state, or local regulatory authority? That question has befuddled federal policy for decades. Section 404 of the Clean Water Act establishes the primary federal program for answering those questions of boundary and application. Section 404 is jointly administered by the U.S. Army Corps of Engineers (Corps), with primary responsibility for implementing a permitting program regulating discharges of "fill" material into waters of the United States, including wetlands, and by the Environmental Protection Agency (EPA), which has authority to define environmental guidelines the Corps must follow. The materials in this section explain how these two agencies have dealt with the problem of defining where and how this program serves to define the core of our national wetland ecosystem management policy.

a. BOUNDARIES

The term "wetland" implies the existence of "dryland" and thus a geographic limit to the ecosystem unit identified for management under Section 404 of the CWA. Identifying where wet ends and dry begins under Section 404, however, has not been as simple as it may seem. Indeed, wetness is not the exclusively dispositive factor.

The relevant provisions of the Clean Water Act originated in the Federal Water Pollution Control Act Amendments of 1972, 86 Stat. 816, and have remained essentially unchanged since that time. Under Sections 301 and 502 of the Act, 33 U.S.C. §§ 1311 and 1362, any discharge of dredged or fill materials into "navigable waters"—defined as the "waters of the United States"—is forbidden unless authorized by a permit issued by the Corps of Engineers pursuant to Section 404, 33 U.S.C. § 1344. After initially construing the Act to cover only waters navigable in fact, in 1975 the Corps issued interim final regulations redefining "the waters of the United States" to include not only actually navigable waters but also tributaries of such waters, interstate waters and their tributaries, and nonnavigable intrastate waters whose use or misuse could affect interstate commerce. *See* 40 Fed. Reg. 31320 (1975). The Corps also construed the Act to cover all "freshwater wetlands" that were adjacent to other covered waters. A "freshwater wetland" was defined as an area that is "periodically inundated" and is "normally characterized by the prevalence of vegetation that requires saturated soil conditions for growth and reproduction." 33 CFR § 209.120(d)(2)(h) (1976). In 1977, the Corps refined its definition of wetlands by eliminating the reference to periodic inundation and making other minor changes. The 1977 definition read as follows:

> The term "wetlands" means those areas that are inundated or saturated by surface or ground water at a frequency and duration sufficient to support, and that under normal circumstances do support, a prevalence of vegetation typically adapted for life in saturated soil conditions. Wetlands generally include swamps, marshes, bogs and similar areas. 33 CFR § 323.2(c) (1978).

In 1982, the 1977 regulations were replaced by substantively identical regulations that remain in force today.

In 1985, the Supreme Court addressed whether the provision extending jurisdiction to "adjacent" wetlands was consistent with the scope of federal jurisdiction established under the Clean Water Act. *See* United States v. Riverside Bayview Homes, Inc., 474 U.S. 121 (1985). The Court held that it was:

> The regulation extends the Corps' authority under § 404 to all wetlands adjacent to navigable or interstate waters and their tributaries. Wetlands, in turn, are defined as lands that are "inundated or saturated by surface or ground water at a frequency and duration sufficient to support, and that under normal circumstances do support, a prevalence of vegetation typically adapted for life in saturated soil conditions." 33 CFR § 323.2(c) (1985). The plain language of the regulation refutes the Court of Appeals' conclusion that inundation or "frequent flooding" by the adjacent body of water is a sine qua non of a wetland under the regulation. Indeed, the regulation could hardly state more clearly that saturation by either surface or ground water is sufficient to bring an area within the category of wetlands, provided that the saturation is sufficient to and does support wetland vegetation.

> *   *   *

> We cannot say that the Corps' conclusion that adjacent wetlands are inseparably bound up with the "waters" of the United States—based as it is on the Corps' and EPA's technical expertise—is unreasonable. In view of the breadth of federal regulatory authority contemplated by the Act itself and the inherent difficulties of defining precise bounds to regulable waters, the Corps' ecological judgment about the relationship between waters and their adjacent wetlands provides an adequate basis for a legal judgment that adjacent wetlands may be defined as waters under the Act.

Relative calm remained until Solid Waste Agency of Northern Cook County v. United States Army Corps of Engineers, 531 U.S. 159 (2001) (*SWANCC*), in which the Court addressed whether Section 404 also properly was being applied to "isolated" wetlands—wetlands neither adjacent to nor hydrologically connected to navigable waters but that serve as a habitat for migratory birds (the "migratory bird rule"). At issue whether a proper reading of CWA supported the migratory bird rule, and, if so, whether the existence of migratory birds was sufficient to give Congress the authority to regulate such intrastate, isolated wetlands under the Commerce Clause in the first place. The Court addressed the statutory issue (whether the CWA supported the migratory bird rule) but not the constitutional issue. Over a blistering dissent (part of which is reproduced above), the majority held these wetlands to be beyond what Congress intended to be within the scope of Section 404:

This is not the first time we have been called upon to evaluate the meaning of § 404(a). In United States v. Riverside Bayview Homes, Inc., 474 U.S. 121 (1985), we held that the Corps had § 404(a) jurisdiction over wetlands that actually abutted on a navigable waterway. In so doing, we noted that the term "navigable" is of "limited import" and that Congress evidenced its intent to "regulate at least some waters that would not be deemed 'navigable' under the classical understanding of that term." Id., at 133. But our holding was based in large measure upon Congress' unequivocal acquiescence to, and approval of, the Corps' regulations interpreting the CWA to cover wetlands adjacent to navigable waters. See id., at 135–139. We found that Congress' concern for the protection of water quality and aquatic ecosystems indicated its intent to regulate wetlands "inseparably bound up with the 'waters' of the United States." Id., at 134.

It was the significant nexus between the wetlands and "navigable waters" that informed our reading of the CWA in *Riverside Bayview Homes*. Indeed, we did not "express any opinion" on the "question of the authority of the Corps to regulate discharges of fill material into wetlands that are not adjacent to bodies of open water. . ." Id., at 131–132, n. 8, 106 S.Ct. 455. In order to rule for respondents here, we would have to hold that the jurisdiction of the Corps extends to ponds that are not adjacent to open water. But we conclude that the text of the statute will not allow this.

We . . . decline respondents' invitation to take what they see as the next ineluctable step after *Riverside Bayview Homes*: holding that isolated ponds, some only seasonal, wholly located within two Illinois counties, fall under § 404(a)'s definition of "navigable waters" because they serve as habitat for migratory birds. As counsel for respondents conceded at oral argument, such a ruling would assume that "the use of the word navigable in the statute . . . does not have any independent significance." We cannot agree that Congress' separate definitional use of the phrase "waters of the United States" constitutes a basis for reading the term "navigable waters" out of the statute. We said in *Riverside Bayview Homes* that the word "navigable" in the statute was of "limited effect" and went on to hold that § 404(a) extended to nonnavigable wetlands adjacent to open waters. But it is one thing to give a word limited effect and quite another to give it no effect whatever. The term "navigable" has at least the import of showing us what Congress had in mind as its authority for enacting the CWA: its traditional jurisdiction over waters that were or had been navigable in fact or which could reasonably be so made.

The lower federal courts were quick to apply *SWANCC* in a variety of circumstances with the effect of cutting off federal jurisdiction over isolated waters. *See, e.g.*, Rice v. Harken Exploration Co., 250 F.3d 264 (5th Cir. 2001) (construing *SWANCC* to mean that the CWA applies only to a "body of water that is actually navigable or is adjacent to an open body of navigable water"); United States v. Newdunn, 195 F. Supp. 2d 751 (E.D. Va. 2002)

(Corps had no jurisdiction over 38 acres of wetlands in the absence of proof of connection to navigable waters); United States v. Rapanos, 190 F. Supp. 2d 1011 (E.D. Mich. 2002) (dismissing criminal prosecution for unauthorized filling of wetlands because Corps did not prove area was navigable or an adjacent water). Over time, however, lower court opinions after *SWANCC* scattered around the apparently fine lines dividing jurisdictional and non-jurisdictional waters with no apparent resolution. The Fifth Circuit's *Harken* decision and later decision in In re Needham, 354 F.3d 340 (5th Cir. 2003), represented the broadest construction of *SWANCC*, with the Fourth and Ninth Circuits interpreting *SWANCC* more narrowly. *See* United States v. Deaton, 332 F.3d 698 (4th Cir. 2003); Treacy v. Newdunn Associates, 344 F.3d 407 (4th Cir. 2003); United States v. Rapanos, 339 F.3d 447 (6th Cir. 2003); Headwaters Inc. v. Talent Irrigation District, 243 F.3d 526 (9th Cir. 2001). *See also* Stan Millan, *Clean Water Act Waters Have a Beginning, But Do They Have an End?*, 35 Env't Rep. (BNA) 964 (2004); Joan Mulhern and Michael Lozeau, *Federal Agencies: In Brief, Follow Your Own Counsel*, National Wetlands Newsletter, July–Aug. 2003, at 9; Mark A Ryan, *CWA Jurisdiction Four Years After* SWANCC, NATURAL RESOURCES & ENV'T, Fall 2005, at 63.

As these cases piled up in the lower federal courts, EPA and the Corps wrestled with how to interpret *SWANCC*. On January 10, 2003, EPA and the Corps issued a guidance document taking a fairly broad view of the holding in *SWANCC*, leading to a narrow view of federal power to regulate wetlands. The guidance instructed Corps regional offices that "field staff should not assert CWA jurisdiction over isolated waters that are both intrastate and non-navigable," where the sole basis available for asserting CWA jurisdiction rests on any of the factors listed in the "Migratory Bird Rule." The guidance also outlined the uncertainty ostensibly left by *SWANCC* and its lower court progeny over questions such as whether the other interstate commerce criteria in the Corps' regulations (e.g., use of waters by interstate travelers) would justify assertion of jurisdiction over intrastate, non-navigable waters, and whether *SWANCC* affects jurisdiction over tributaries that are neither navigable nor immediately adjacent to navigable waters. To resolve some of those posited ambiguities, the agencies also jointly issued an Advance Notice of Proposed Rulemaking to "further the public interest by clarifying what waters are subject to CWA jurisdiction." 68 Fed. Reg. 1991 (Jan. 15, 2003) (attaching the guidance document as Appendix A). Almost one year and 135,000 public comments later, however, the agencies decided in December 2003 to rescind the notice, but to keep the guidance in place. Most of the comments were form cards or short e-mails urging the agencies not to codify the broad reading of *SWANCC* suggested in the guidance document. The belief that the agencies might do just that was confirmed when, a few weeks before the rescission announcement, a draft rule "leaked" to the *Los Angeles Times* revealed that the agencies were planning to propose a rule that would resolve the ambiguous cases by erring on the side of limiting federal jurisdiction. For some accounts of this continuing saga, see Robert R.M. Verchick, *Toward Normative Rules for Agency Interpretation: Defining Jurisdiction Under the Clean Water Act*, 55 ALA. L. REV. 845 (2004); Sheila Deely and Mark Latham, *The*

Federal Wetlands Program: A Regulatory Program Run Amuck, 34 Env't Rep. (BNA) 966 (2003); *The Public Speaks Out: Comments from the Federal Docket*, National Wetlands Newsletter, July–Aug 2003, at 13. An instructive study also can be found in GENERAL ACCOUNTING OFFICE, WATERS AND WETLANDS: CORPS OF ENGINEERS NEEDS TO EVALUATE ITS DISTRICT PRACTICES IN DETERMINING JURISDICTION (2004), which not surprisingly found that more consistency and greater transparency is needed throughout the Corps in the determination of when to assert jurisdiction.

Then along came Rapanos v. United States, 547 U.S. 715 (2006), which resolved two consolidated cases from the Sixth Circuit. In one case, the United States brought an enforcement action alleging that property owners and their affiliated businesses deposited fill materials into wetlands without a permit, in violation of the CWA. In the other, property owners were denied a permit to deposit fill material in a wetland approximately one mile from a lake and, after exhausting their administrative appeals, they filed suit. The wetland areas in both cases thus were neither obviously isolated from, nor obviously adjacent to, navigable waters. In both cases, the district court found that there was federal regulatory jurisdiction over the sites in question, and the Sixth Circuit affirmed. The Supreme Court consolidated the cases and granted certiorari to decide whether the wetlands were "waters of the United States" under the CWA, and, if so, whether it is within Congress's authority under the Commerce Clause to regulate such intrastate, isolated wetlands. As in *SWANCC*, the Court in *Rapanos* did not reach the constitutional question but instead based its decision solely on an interpretation of the CWA. However, as the following post-*Rapanos* decision from the Sixth Circuit explains, the Court's 4–1–4 decision did little to clarify the law in this area.

United States v. Cundiff

United States Court of Appeals for the Sixth Circuit, 2009.
555 F.3d 200.

■ MARTIN, CIRCUIT JUDGE.

After eight years of failed negotiations and ignored orders, the United States sued George Rudy Cundiff (who goes by Rudy) and his son, Christopher Seth Cundiff (who goes by Seth), seeking injunctive relief and civil penalties against them for discharging "pollutants" into "waters of the United States" without a permit in violation of the Clean Water Act. 33 U.S.C. § 1362. The district court granted summary judgment for the government, imposed injunctive relief in the form of a restoration plan for the Cundiffs' wetlands, and imposed a civil penalty of $225,000. All but $25,000 of that penalty was suspended, however, provided that the Cundiffs implemented the restoration plan. The district court also dismissed the Cundiffs' array of statutory, common law, and constitutional counterclaims. While the original appeal in this case was pending, the Supreme Court issued its splintered ruling in Rapanos v. United States, 547 U.S. 715 (2006), which defined the Act's jurisdiction over "waters of the United States." In light of Rapanos, we returned the case to the district court to reconsider whether jurisdiction was proper over the Cundiffs' wetlands. The district court determined that it was because the Cundiffs' wetlands were in fact waters of the United States, and the Cundiffs appealed. We affirm the district court on all grounds.

I.

Defendants Rudy and Seth Cundiff own two adjacent tracts of land in Muhlenberg County, Kentucky. Their properties together sit next to Pond and Caney Creeks, which are tributaries of the Green River. The Green River, in turn, flows into the Ohio River. In 1990, Rudy Cundiff bought the southern tract, which contains roughly eighty-five acres of wetlands and an upland area where his house sits. When Rudy bought it, portions of the wetlands contained exceptionally acidic orangish to reddish colored water that had drained out of an abandoned coal mine located on a neighbor's nearby property. As a result, locals referred to the Cundiffs' property as a putrid eyesore, and this stagnant, discolored water caused the wetlands to become a festering mosquito haven-though the Cundiffs knew all this when they bought it. Shortly after his purchase, Cundiff began excavating drainage ditches and clearing trees to make the wetlands suitable for farming.

In October 1991, federal officials from the Army Corps of Engineers and state officials from the Kentucky Division of Water observed ditches, artificially filled wetlands, and mechanically cleared land on the wetlands. The Corps suspected possible Clean Water Act violations. Rudy had failed to obtain a section 404 permit as required for such dredging and filling activities, . . . Consequently, the Corps sent him a cease-and-desist letter "specifically prohibiting any further activity involving the placement of excavated or fill material into these jurisdictional wetlands" without a federal permit.

Federal and state officials then began meeting with Cundiff in 1992, though they reached no agreement. Instead, he insisted on converting the wetlands into farmland and continued to drain and clear the property. The Corps referred the matter to the Environmental Protection Agency. Over the next several years, Cundiff continued his draining and ditch digging activities, simply ignoring whatever government directives came his way. In 1997 he planted wheat on the southern tract, and government officials observed downed trees in that area. The EPA issued an Order of Compliance informing him that he had violated the Clean Water Act by depositing fill material into waters of the United States without authorization, and it directed him to "immediately cease participating in or causing any additional discharges" of pollutants.

In 1998 Rudy's son, Seth, purchased a tract of land located north of Rudy's which contains roughly 103 acres of wetlands. (Seth leases this property back to Rudy for the exact amount of the mortgage payment.) Rudy quickly began excavating and clearing that property as well, activity of which Seth was aware. In October 1998, officials from the EPA informed Rudy Cundiff that he needed a permit for this work too. Rudy-somewhat surprisingly-said that, though he knew he needed a permit, he thought the Corps would never grant him one so he planned on digging his ditches anyway. He eventually completed a two-hundred foot ditch through the wetlands that extended all the way to Caney Creek, . . . In 1999, Kentucky officials told Cundiff that he was destroying wetlands without a permit in violation of state law (he ignored this too), and the EPA issued additional Orders of Compliance to both Rudy and Seth Cundiff requiring them to cease their excavation activities and to restore the unauthorized ditches by refilling them. The Cundiffs responded to these orders as they had to the others.

III.

Congress enacted the Clean Water Act in 1972 "to restore and maintain the chemical, physical, and biological integrity of the Nation's waters." 33 U.S.C. § 1251(a). Section 301(a) of the Act prohibits "the discharge of any pollutant by any person" except in compliance with the Act. 33 U.S.C. § 1311(a). "[D]ischarge of any pollutant" is broadly defined to mean "any addition of any pollutant to navigable waters from any point source." 33 U.S.C. § 1362(12)(A). In turn, "pollutant" is defined to include not only traditional contaminants, but also solids such as "dredged spoil, . . . rock, sand [and] cellar dirt." 33 U.S.C. § 1362(6). The Act defines "navigable waters" to mean "the waters of the United States, including the territorial seas." 33 U.S.C. § 1362(7).

The Act also sets up two permit schemes. Section 404(a) authorizes the Secretary of the Army (through the United States Army Corps of Engineers), or a state with an approved program, to issue permits "for the discharge of dredged or fill material into the navigable waters at specified disposal sites." 33 U.S.C. § 1344(a). Section 402 authorizes the Environmental Protection Agency (or a state with an approved program) to issue a National Pollutant Discharge Elimination System (NPDES) permit for the discharge of pollutants other than dredged or fill material. 33 U.S.C. § 1342. The Corps and the EPA share responsibility for implementing and enforcing Section 404. See, e.g., 33 U.S.C. § 1344(b)-(c).

Although at one time the term "navigable waters" included only waters that were navigable in fact, The Daniel Ball, 77 U.S. (10 Wall.) 557, 563, 19 L.Ed. 999 (1870), "navigable waters" is a defined term in the Act that expressly includes all "waters of the United States." 33 U.S.C. § 1362(7). The Supreme Court has repeatedly recognized that, with this definition, Congress "evidently intended to repudiate limits that had been placed on federal regulation by earlier water pollution control statutes and to exercise its powers under the Commerce Clause to regulate at least some waters that would not be deemed 'navigable' under the classical understanding of that term." United States v. Riverside Bayview Homes, Inc., 474 U.S. 121, 133, 106 S.Ct. 455, 88 L.Ed.2d 419 (1985). As a result, the Corps and EPA have put out substantively equivalent regulatory definitions of "waters of the United States," compare 33 C.F.R. § 328.3(a), with 40 C.F.R. § 230.3(s), that define it to encompass not only traditional navigable waters of the kind susceptible to use in interstate commerce, but also tributaries of traditional navigable waters and wetlands adjacent to covered waters. See 33 C.F.R. § 328.3(a)(1), 328(3)(a)(5), 328(a)(7).

A. Are the Wetlands "Waters of the United States"?

1. Rapanos

Rapanos involved two consolidated cases in which the Act had been applied to actual or proposed discharges of pollutants into wetlands adjacent to nonnavigable tributaries of traditional navigable waters. 547 U.S. at 729-30. Although there was no single majority opinion, all the Justices agreed that the statutory phrase "waters of the United States" encompasses some waters not navigable in the traditional sense. See id. at 731 (Scalia, J., plurality opinion); id. at 767-68, 126 S.Ct. 2208 (Kennedy, J., concurring in the judgment); id. at 793, 126 S.Ct. 2208 (Stevens, J., dissenting). The four-Justice plurality interpreted the Act to cover "relatively permanent, standing, or continuously flowing bodies of water," 547 U.S. at 739, that are connected to traditional navigable waters, id. at 742, as well as wetlands with a continuous surface connection to such water bodies. Id. at 732 n. 5 (observing that the Act's reference to "relatively permanent" waters "d[id] not necessarily exclude streams, rivers, or lakes that might dry up in extraordinary circumstances, such as drought," or "seasonal rivers, which contain continuous flow during some months of the year but no flow during dry months").

Justice Kennedy, writing only for himself, interpreted the term to cover wetlands that "possess a 'significant nexus' to waters that are or were navigable in fact or that could reasonably be so made." Id. at 759, 126 S.Ct. 2208 (Kennedy, J., concurring in the judgment) (quoting Solid Waste Agency v. United States Army Corps. of Eng'rs., 531 U.S. 159 (2001)). He explained:

> [W]etlands possess the requisite nexus, and thus come within the statutory phrase "navigable waters," if the wetlands, either alone or in combination with similarly situated lands in the region, significantly affect the chemical, physical, and biological integrity of other covered waters more readily understood as "navigable." When, in contrast, wetlands' effects on water quality are speculative or insubstantial, they fall outside the zone fairly encompassed by the statutory term "navigable waters."

Id. at 780. And Justice Kennedy, relying on Riverside Bayview, concluded that the Corps' assertion of jurisdiction over "wetlands adjacent to navigable-in-fact waters" may be met "by showing adjacency alone." Id. On the other hand, where the wetlands are adjacent to nonnavigable tributaries, "[a]bsent more specific regulations," Justice Kennedy would require the government to "establish a significant nexus on a case-by-case basis." Id. He therefore concurred in the judgment vacating the lower court's decision and voted to remand the case for more fact-finding on whether the government could prove the existence of a significant nexus between the wetlands and nearby navigable-in-fact waters.

The dissenters, with Justice Stevens writing, would have upheld the determination that the wetlands at issue were "waters of the United

States" as a reasonable agency interpretation of the Act under Chevron U.S.A. Inc. v. Natural Resources Defense Council, Inc., 467 U.S. 837 (1984). In the dissenters' view, any "significant nexus" requirement-insofar as the Act contained one-would be "categorically satisfied as to wetlands adjacent to navigable waters or their tributaries." Rapanos, 547 U.S. at 807-08.

Parsing any one of Rapanos's lengthy and technical statutory exegeses is taxing, but the real difficulty comes in determining which-if any-of the three main opinions lower courts should look to for guidance. As the Chief Justice observed: "It is unfortunate that no opinion commands a majority of the Court on precisely how to read Congress' limits on the reach of the Clean Water Act. Lower courts and regulated entities will now have to feel their way on a case-by-case basis." Id. at 758 (Roberts, C.J., concurring) (citing Grutter v. Bollinger, 539 U.S. 306, 325 (2003), and Marks v. United States, 430 U.S. 188 (1977)). The dissent, for its part, offered its view of what lower courts should do:

In these cases, however, while both the plurality and Justice Kennedy agree that there must be a remand for further proceedings, their respective opinions define different tests to be applied on remand. Given that all four Justices who have joined this opinion would uphold the Corps' jurisdiction in both of these cases-and in all other cases in which either the plurality's or Justice Kennedy's test is satisfied-on remand each of the judgments should be reinstated if either of those tests is met.

Rapanos, 547 U.S. at 810 (emphasis added). Fortunately, as the following section explains, jurisdiction is proper here under each of the primary Rapanos opinions and therefore we do not have to decide here, once and for all, which test controls in all future cases.

2. Marks-meets-Rapanos

In Marks v. United States, the Supreme Court instructed that "[w]hen a fragmented Court decides a case and no single rationale explaining the result enjoys the assent of five Justices, the holding of the Court may be viewed as that position taken by those Members who concurred in the judgments on the narrowest grounds." 430 U.S. at 193 (quoting Gregg v. Georgia, 428 U.S. 153, 169 n. 15 (1976) (opinion of Stewart, Powell, and Stevens, JJ.)). But all is not always so rosy. The Supreme Court has oft-noted Marks' limitations, stating that it is "more easily stated than applied to the various opinions supporting the result," Grutter, 539 U.S. at 325, and that "[i]t does not seem useful to pursue the Marks inquiry to the utmost logical possibility when it has so obviously baffled and divided the lower courts that have considered it," Nichols v. United States, 511 U.S. 738, 745 (1994) (quotations omitted).

In its short life, Rapanos has indeed satisfied any "bafflement" requirement. The first court to decide what opinion was controlling decided to ignore all of them and instead opted for earlier circuit precedent which it felt was clearer and more readily applied. United States v. Chevron Pipe Line Co., 437 F.Supp.2d 605, 613 (N.D. Tex. 2006). The Courts of Appeals have not fared much better. The Ninth Circuit has stated that Justice Kennedy's test applies in most instances, Northern California River Watch v. City of Healdsburg, 496 F.3d 993, 1000 (9th Cir. 2007), while the Eleventh Circuit has held that the Act's coverage may be established only under his test. United States v. Robison, 505 F.3d 1208, 1219-22 (11th Cir. 2007). By contrast, the First and the Seventh Circuits, though differing somewhat in their analyses, have followed Justice Stevens' advice and held that the Act confers jurisdiction whenever either Justice Kennedy's or the plurality's test is met. United States v. Johnson, 467 F.3d 56, 60-66 (1st Cir. 2006); United States v. Gerke Excavating, Inc., 464 F.3d 723, 725 (7th Cir. 2006). This is the approach the district court here followed, largely in reliance on the First Circuit's thoughtful reasoning.

Taken literally, Marks instructs lower courts to choose the "narrowest" concurring opinion and to ignore dissents. Marks, 430 U.S. at 193. But what does "narrowest" mean? Marks considered an earlier Supreme Court obscenity decision, A Book Named "John Cleland's Memoirs of a Woman of Pleasure" v. Attorney General of Massachusetts, 383 U.S. 413 (1966), where the Court split on whether a particular work was protected by the First Amendment. In Marks, the Court determined that the Memoirs plurality's standard controlled because, while two Justices would have held that the First Amendment applies equally to all materials-whether obscene, hardcore, or Grated, id. at 433, (Douglas, J., concurring); id. at 421 (Black, J., concurring)-the plurality would have afforded protection only to non-obscene materials, id. at 419-20, and therefore that concurring opinion was doctrinally the "narrowest."

The so-called Marks rule in fact derived from the Court's earlier opinion in Gregg v. Georgia, 428 U.S. 153, 96 S.Ct. 2909 (1976). Gregg had interpreted Furman v. Georgia, 408 U.S. 238 (1972), in which a majority found that Georgia's death penalty scheme was unconstitutional. Two Justices believed that the death penalty was per se unconstitutional, while three others merely stated that it was unconstitutional as then administered in Georgia. So the Gregg Court stated that "[s]ince five Justices wrote separately in support of the judgments in Furman, the holding of the Court may be viewed as that position taken by those Members who concurred in the judgments on the narrowest grounds. . ." 428 U.S. at 169 n. 15.

As these cases indicate-and contrary to assertions by the Cundiffs and their amici-Marks does not imply that the "narrowest" Rapanos opinion is whichever one restricts jurisdiction the most. But it also makes little sense for the "narrowest" opinion to be the one that restricts jurisdiction the least, as the government's amici allege; the ability to glean what substantive value judgments are buried within concurring, plurality, and single-Justice opinions would require something like divination to be performed accurately. Instead, "narrowest" opinion refers to the one which relies on the "least" doctrinally "far-reaching-common ground" among the Justices in the majority: it is the concurring opinion that offers the least change to the law. See Johnson v. Bd. of Regents of the Univ. Of Ga., 263 F.3d 1234, 1247 (11th Cir.2001); Johnson, 467 F.3d at 63. In both Memoirs and Furman the controlling opinion was less doctrinally sweeping. The Memoirs controlling opinion did not agree that obscenity laws per se violated the Constitution, and the Furman controlling opinion did not agree that the death penalty was per se unconstitutional.

Yet problems await. For cases like Furman and Memoirs, Marks' application is straightforward. But when "one opinion supporting the judgment does not fit entirely within a broader circle drawn by the others, Marks is problematic." King v. Palmer, 950 F.2d 771, 782 (D.C.Cir.1991) (en banc). Specifically, "Marks is workable-one opinion can be meaningfully regarded as 'narrower' than another-only when one opinion is a logical subset of other, broader opinions." Id. at 781. Where no standard put forth in a concurring opinion is a logical subset of another concurring opinion (or opinions) that, together, would equal five votes, Marks breaks down.

Enter Rapanos. Although "in most cases in which [Justice Kennedy] concludes that there is no federal authority he will command five votes (himself plus the four Justices in the Rapanos plurality)," in other cases Justice Kennedy "would vote against federal authority only to be outvoted 8-to-1 (the four dissenting Justices plus the members of the Rapanos plurality) because there was a slight surface hydrological connection." Gerke, 464 F.3d at 725. Indeed, there is quite little common ground between Justice Kennedy's and the plurality's conceptions of jurisdiction under the Act, and both flatly reject the other's view. See Rapanos, 547 U.S. at 756 (Scalia, J., plurality opinion) ("[Justice Kennedy's] test simply rewrites the statute."); id. at 778, (Kennedy, J., concurring) ("[T]he plurality reads nonexistent requirements into the Act.").

Thus, because Rapanos is not easily reconciled with Marks, the question becomes what to do. Fortunately, we need not reconcile Rapanos with Marks. Here, jurisdiction is proper under both Justice Kennedy's and the plurality's tests (and thus also the dissent's). Recently, this Court addressed an analogous situation:

3. Jurisdiction is proper under both tests

Justice Kennedy's test. Under this test, the Clean Water Act applies to wetlands that "possess a significant nexus to waters that are or were navigable in fact or that could reasonably be so made." Rapanos, 547 U.S. at 758. This nexus exists "if the wetlands, either alone or in combination with similarly situated lands in the region, significantly affect the chemical, physical, and biological integrity of other covered waters more readily understood as navigable." Id. at 755. By contrast, "[w]hen ... wetlands' effects on water quality are speculative or insubstantial, they fall outside the zone fairly encompassed by the statutory terms 'navigable waters.'" Id. This standard must be met on a case-by-case basis. Id.

The district court found that the Cundiffs' wetlands have a significant nexus with the navigable-in-fact Green River, via Pond and Caney Creeks, which are tributaries of that river. The court credited the government's expert who testified that the wetlands perform significant ecological functions in relation to the Green River and the two creeks, including: temporary and long-term water storage, filtering of the acid runoff and sediment from the nearby mine, and providing an important habitat for plants and wildlife. And the court found that the Cundiffs' alterations-unauthorized ditch digging, the mechanical clearing of land, and the dredging of material and using it as filler-have undermined the wetlands' ability to store water which, in turn, has affected the frequency and extent of flooding, and increased the flood peaks in the Green River. Thus, it has "impact[ed] navigation, crop production in bottomlands, downstream bank erosion, and sedimentation." The district court further credited another government expert's testimony who stated that Rudy Cundiff's ditch digging had created channels so that the acid mine runoff would largely bypass his wetlands and instead flow more directly into Pond and Caney Creek and thus the Green River. It found that these channels cause "direct and significant impacts to navigation (via sediment accumulation in the Green River) and to aquatic food webs . . . that are not adapted to thrive in acid waters and/or sediment-choked environments." The record supports this conclusion and the district court found that the government's witnesses were credible, and so we cannot say that its conclusion was clearly erroneous.

The Cundiffs do not really dispute these findings. Instead, they assert that a "significant nexus" may only be proved by "laboratory analysis" of soil samples, water samples, or through other tests. Though no doubt a district court could find such evidence persuasive, the Cundiffs point to nothing-no expert opinion, no research report or article, and nothing in any of the various Rapanos opinions-to indicate that this is the sole method by which a significant nexus may be proved such that the district court's finding was inherently improper. So the district court properly concluded that the government passed Justice Kennedy's test.

The Plurality's test. Under this standard, the government must make two showings to establish jurisdiction: "First, that the adjacent channel contains a 'wate[r] of the United States,' (i.e., a relatively permanent body of water connected to traditional interstate navigable waters); and second, that the wetland has a continuous surface connection with that water, making it difficult to determine where the 'water' ends and the 'wetland' begins." Rapanos, 547 U.S. at 742.

The first question is whether the adjacent property contains a "water of the United States." The district court held that jurisdiction was proper under the plurality's standard because the South Channel (located on the northern tract of the wetlands), and Pond and Caney Creeks were all "relatively permanent bodies of water connected to a traditional interstate navigable water, the Green River." Regarding the South Channel, the district court found that the water flows through the channel into Pond Creek for all but a few weeks a year, the two creeks are open waterbodies with significant flowing water, and that both flow into the Green River. (Pond Creek itself is navigable in part.) So the first prong of the plurality's test is met.

The second question is whether the wetlands possess a "continuous surface connection" with the Green River and its tributaries. The Cundiffs argue that, because the wetlands are at a different elevation level than the two creeks and it is not readily apparent that water perpetually flows between them, there is no continuous surface connection. The district court, observing that Riverside Bayview stated that it is often ambiguous where the transition between water and dry land exactly exists, 474 U.S. at 132, 135 n. 9, disagreed and held that a continuous surface connection existed. Specifically, the Court observed that the inquiry was whether it was ambiguous where land stopped and water began, because otherwise the plurality's recognition of these gradual transitions would be "completely eviscerat[ed]."

We agree; the Cundiffs' argument proves too much. Although the term "continuous surface connection" clearly requires surface flow, it does not mean that only perpetually flowing creeks satisfy the plurality's test. Indeed, the Rapanos plurality, in tipping its hat to Riverside Bayview, fashioned its test to determine when wetlands were "waters of the United States," and therefore implicitly recognized that wetlands are neither navigable-in-fact nor even literally bodies of water. Instead, wetlands are merely "inundated or saturated" soil that can "support . . . under normal circumstances . . . a prevalence of vegetation typically adapted for life in saturated soil conditions." 33 C.F.R. § 328.3(b). In other words, the plurality's test requires a topical flow of water between a navigable-in-fact waterway or its tributary with a wetland, and that connection requires some kind of dampness such that polluting a wetland would have a proportionate effect on the traditional waterway. If the Cundiffs' restrictive version of the plurality's test was accurate, then the plurality could have saved itself time and effort by saying that wetlands could never be "waters of the United States" and overruled Riverside Bayview's holding to the contrary. It did not do that; instead, the plurality went through a lengthy analysis and therefore the standard is broader than the Cundiffs assert.

Further undermining their argument is the fact that the district court took note of the South Channel, which provides a largely uninterrupted permanent surface water flow between the wetlands and traditional waterways. The district court also found that the existence of additional (and substantial) surface connections between the wetlands and permanent water bodies "during storm events, bank full periods, and/or ordinary high flows" provides additional evidence of a continuous surface connection. Finally, Cundiff personally went a long way towards creating a continuous surface connection when he dug or excavated ditches to enhance the acid mine drainage into the creeks and away from his wetlands; in determining whether the Act confers jurisdiction, it does not make a difference whether the channel by which water flows from a wetland to a navigable-in-fact waterway or its tributary was manmade or formed naturally. Thus, we affirm the district court's determination that the Act confers jurisdiction over the Cundiffs' wetlands because both tests are met.

NOTES & QUESTIONS

1. Before going to the legal merits of *Rapanos* and its aftermath, it is important to consider what was put at stake ecologically and administratively. Ecologically, EPA estimated during the litigation that if the petitioners' position—the position adopted in Justice Scalia's plurality opinion—were to prevail, roughly 30 percent of all streams and associated wetlands in the United States outside of Alaska, about 20 million acres in all, would have been pushed outside of Section 404 jurisdiction. While this figure was debated, it was clear to all interests that *Rapanos*, depending on how it was implemented, could significantly shrink what the federal government previously asserted to be under Section 404. Moreover, as an administrative matter Justice Kennedy's highly fact-intensive "significant nexus" test suggested that the Corps would face daunting resource demands in order to prove the existence of such conditions. Indeed, litigation initiated not long after *Rapanos* led ultimately to the Fourth Circuit kicking back a Corps permit denial to the agency on the ground that it had not adequately established the factual presence of a significant nexus. *See* Precon Development Corp. v U.S. Army Corps of Engineers, 633 F.3d 278 (4th Cir. 2011). Beyond Section 404, moreover, *Rapanos* threw into doubt how to implement other programs under the statute, such as the TMDL program, that use the term "waters of the United States" to define the scope of federal jurisdiction. *See* Symposium, Rapanos v. United States, 22 NATURAL RESOURCES & ENV'T (Summer 2007). Hence, determining which test to apply and how to apply it presented substantial consequences.

2. Given the potential impact of *Rapanos* in these two respects, legal eyes quickly turned to the interpretation of the odd 4-1-4 opinion and resolution of the multitude of questions it praises. Congress has produced no solutions as of this writing. Surprised? Most courts have adopted the view that the Corps may assert jurisdiction so long as either the plurality's test or Justice Kennedy's test is satisfied. *See* Richard E. Glaze, Jr., Rapanos *Guidance III: Waters Revisited*, 42 Envtl. L. Rep. 10118 (2012) (providing a survey of the cases). But that does not answer *how* to apply the tests. It took the Corps and EPA until June 5, 2007, a year after the Court's decision, to develop guidance for agency determinations of jurisdictional wetlands consistent with *Rapanos*. *See* Clean Water Act Jurisdiction Following the U.S. Supreme Court's Decision in Rapanos v. United States and Carabell v. United States, 72 Fed. Reg. 31,824 (June 8, 2007). The guidance essentially adopted Justice Kennedy's case-by-case "significant nexus" approach, but in so doing it was not clear how much clarification the guidance delivered—it was 12 pages long, not including several complex decision flow charts and a seven-page "key questions" document explaining the 12-page guidance. The 2007 guidance was highly controversial, with criticism coming primarily from environmental groups claiming it took too narrow a view. Under the Obama Administration, the agencies took another stab at draft guidance in 2011, this time adopting the "either/or" approach the courts have gravitated around but, say many landowner interests, implementing the "significant nexus" test so as to extend jurisdiction far more broadly than did the 2007 guidance. *See* Draft Guidance on Identifying Waters Protected by the Clean Water Act, 76 Fed. Reg. 24479 (May 2, 2011). As of this writing, the agencies have not issued a final version of the guidance. For a detailed and thoughtful analysis of the draft guidance, see Glaze, *supra*.

3. In connection with the 2011 draft guidance discussed in the previous note, in April 2011 the EPA issued an economic analysis of the impacts of adopting the draft guidance. The analysis is notable for its extensive discussion and integration of ecosystem services as part of the economic impact criteria. *See* Potential

Indirect Economic Impacts and Benefits Associated with Guidance Clarifying the Scope of Clean Water Act Jurisdiction (Apr. 27, 2011).

4. The controversy and confusion surrounding *Rapanos* have tended to overshadow the importance of *Riverside Bayview* and *SWANCC* to questions of ecosystem management. Acting far ahead if its time, the *Riverside Bayview* Court gave great deference to the Corps' "ecological judgment" about the "ecological integrity" of the wetland resource. But 15 years later, when deep in the midst of the ecosystem movement, the Court gave little deference at all to the Corps in *SWANCC*. The more pertinent *legal* question, of course, is whether the difference between "adjacent" and "isolated" wetlands is a meaningful difference under the Clean Water Act. The *Riverside Bayview* Court found it was reasonable, in the adjacent wetland context, that the Corps "concluded that wetlands adjacent to lakes, rivers, streams, and other bodies of water may function as integral parts of the aquatic environment even when the moisture creating the wetlands does not find its source in the adjacent bodies of water." In the isolated wetland context involved in *SWANCC*, by contrast, the majority opinion devoted no attention whatsoever to the ecological role of the wetland resource in deciding that the CWA does not reach that far. Is that because isolated wetlands do not "function as integral parts of the aquatic environment." Did Congress think that? Did the Corps? Did the Court? Or, even if isolated wetlands are integral parts of aquatic ecosystems, is the problem that they are not part of the legally-relevant aquatic ecosystem—the kind Congress had in mind in the CWA? Indeed, perhaps the real question ought to be not whether *SWANCC* unjustifiably cut off federal jurisdiction at the line between adjacent and isolated wetlands, but whether *Riverside Bayview* unjustifiably extended the line beyond surface waters to adjacent wetlands. Was *Riverside Bayview* correctly decided in this regard? Did Congress *really* mean to cover adjacent wetlands?

5. As important as isolated wetlands may be ecologically, wasn't the *SWANCC* majority correct that the ecological processes that make isolated wetlands valuable are not the same as those that make adjacent wetlands valuable? The *Riverside Bayview* Court did, after all, focus specifically on hydrological process connections—specifically, the connections between adjacent wetlands and waters that are unquestionably within the scope of federal authority. Those connections do not exist in the case of isolated wetlands. Clearly, these distinctions are real *ecologically*. The majority and dissent in *SWANCC* simply differed over how relevant Congress thought that ecological distinction was *legally*.

6. An implicit message of *SWANCC* was that states are free to regulate isolated wetlands, to fill in whatever gap in coverage the opinion opened. Many observers quickly reacted to *SWANCC*, however, as if political and economic constraints would prevent states from taking such action, and thus derided the decision as exposing isolated wetlands to rampant destruction. *See, e.g.,* Jon Kusler, *The SWANCC Decision and the States—Fill in the Gaps or Declare Open Season?*, 23 National Wetlands Newsletter 9 (Mar.-Apr. 2001). The concern that *SWANCC* opened a gap in states without their own wetlands protection programs seemed well founded when, not long after the opinion, anecdotal reports from around that nation suggested that land developers were moving to fill wetlands. *See* Traci Wilson, *Developers Rush to Build In Wetlands After Ruling*, USA TODAY, Dec. 6, 2002, at 15A. But in fact, many states responded to *SWANCC* by enacting or recommending the enactment of relatively aggressive regulatory programs to protect isolated wetlands now beyond the reach of the federal government. *See* Michael Gerhardt, *The Curious Flight of the Migratory Bird Rule*, 31 Envtl. L. Rep. (ELI) 10079 (2001); *New and Revised State Wetland Regulations Take Effect Across the County*, 23 National Wetlands Newsletter 18 (Sept.-Oct. 2001). Hence the concern that states would not fill the gap seems mostly unfounded, though one can always debate whether they have gone far enough fast enough. For a series of articles presenting positive reviews of state and local efforts in Wisconsin, Illinois, Virginia, and Indiana, see Symposium, *SWANCC and the States*, National Wetlands Newsletter, July-Aug. 2002, at 1. For gloomier assessments of state and local progress, see Turner Odell, *On Soggy Ground—State Protection for Isolated Wetlands*, National Wetlands Newsletter, Sept.-Oct. 2003, at 7; Bowden Quinn, *Indiana's New Wetland Legislation: Threat to Isolated Wetlands . . .*, National Wetlands Newsletter, May-June 2004, at 1. You can find descriptions of all the state wetlands regulation programs that "fill the gap" through the Association of State Wetland Managers, www.aswm.org.

7. As controversial as was the statutory interpretation the majority reached in *SWANCC*, most Court-watchers agreed that an equally important aspect of the case was the majority's constitutionally-based concern that the regulation of isolated wetlands would result in a "significant impingement of the States' traditional and primary power over land and water use." The majority did not go so far as to base its decision on the constitutional footing, but did warn that

> permitting respondents to claim federal jurisdiction over ponds and mudflats falling within the "Migratory Bird Rule" would result in a significant impingement of the States' traditional and primary power over land and water use. See, e.g., Hess v. Port Authority Trans–Hudson Corporation, 513 U.S. 30, 44 (1994) ("[R]egulation of land use [is] a function traditionally performed by local governments"). Rather than expressing a desire to readjust the federal-state balance in this manner, Congress chose to "recognize, preserve, and protect the primary responsibilities and rights of States . . . to plan the development and use . . . of land and water resources. . ." 33 U.S.C. § 1251(b). We thus read the statute as written to avoid the significant constitutional and federalism questions raised by respondents' interpretation, and therefore reject the request for administrative deference.

The Migratory Bird Rule had long been a target of such Commerce Clause challenges, with mixed results in the lower courts. *See* Hoffman Homes v. Administrator, 999 F.2d 256 (7th Cir.1993) (upholding the rule but finding insufficient evidence of the presence of migratory birds); Leslie Salt Co. v. United States, 55 F.3d 1388 (9th Cir. 1995) (upholding the rule); United States v. Wilson, 133 F.3d 251 (4th Cir.1997) (rejecting federal authority to regulate isolated wetlands that merely "could affect" interstate commerce). The setting thus was ripe for Supreme Court treatment of the issue after the Court's somewhat revolutionary Commerce Clause decision in United States v. Lopez, 514 U.S. 549 (1995), the first decision in over 60 years in which the court struck down federal legislation as exceeding Congress's authority to regulate interstate commerce. *See* Jonathan H. Adler, *Wetlands, Waterfowl, and the Menace of Mr. Wilson: Commerce Clause Jurisprudence and the Limits of Federal Wetland Regulation*, 29 ENVTL. L. 1 (1999). The Court's *dicta* in SWANCC appears to have endorsed the view that there is, indeed, a limit to how far Congress can regulate to protect wetlands, and that isolated wetlands are too far afield. *See*

Jonathan Adler, *The Ducks Stop Here? The Environmental Challenge to Federalism*, 9 SUPREME COURT ECONOMIC REV. 205 (2001). But how far do you think the Court believes this concern reaches?

Recall, for example, the endangered Delhi Sands Flower-Loving Fly that introduces this text in Chapter 1. Its habitat certainly is as isolated as the waters in *SWANCC*, and the Endangered Species Act restrictions its listing imposed on surrounding government and commercial development surely appears to be a form of land use control. The split D.C. Circuit opinion rejecting the Commerce Clause challenges to those regulations, National Association of Home Builders v. Babbitt, 130 F.3d 1041 (D.C. Cir. 1997) (discussed in Chapters 1 and 6), preceded the Supreme Court's decision in *SWANCC*. Did the court of appeals get it wrong? If so, what does that mean for the Endangered Species Act, and for the implementation of ecosystem management law and policy in general? The converse question is also a puzzle: If private activities affecting isolated wetlands and the Delhi Sands Flower-Loving Fly are within Congress' power to regulate, what isn't? Would there be any stopping federal ecosystem management law and policy from permeating every nook and cranny of local and private land use decision making? Would *anything* be beyond the purview of federal ecosystem management?

8. There are a number of federal programs relating to wetlands protection that will withstand any future Commerce Clause scrutiny of Section 404 because they are non-regulatory in scope and based on a source of federal authority other than the power to regulate interstate commerce, such as the spending power. For example, the so-called Swampbuster Program withdraws agricultural subsidies from farmers that plant commodity crops (corn, wheat, soybeans, etc.) on lands converted from wetlands lands after 1985. 16 U.S.C. § 3821. The subsidy restriction does not apply to normal farming operations in wetlands, such as rice production, or to draining for non-crop uses such as cranberry farming or raising poultry. Because it involves withdrawal of subsidies to induce compliance with its goals, rather than regulation, the dicta in *SWANCC* regarding the limits of Congress's Commerce Clause authority should pose no threat to Swampbuster. *See* United States v. Dierckman, 201 F.3d 915 (7th Cir.2000) (finding Swampbuster is based on Congress's spending power, not its interstate commerce power). Several other nationwide agriculture programs, including the Wetland Reserve Program and the Conservation Reserve Program, are geared specifically to provide subsidies to qualifying farmers who retire wetlands from agricultural uses, and thus should also withstand scrutiny under the evolving Commerce Clause jurisprudence. While these programs have their own inherent limits, they have proven valuable for wetland conservation policy and are always at the forefront of Congress' Farm Bill deliberations. *See* Roger L. Pederson, *Farms and Wetlands Benefit from Farm Bill Conservation Measures*, 23 National Wetlands Newsletter 9 (Sept.-Oct. 2001). Other wetland programs depend for their authority on the power of the federal government to regulate itself. For example, the Fish and Wildlife Coordination Act requires that federal agencies, when considering whether to construct or finance water resources development projects, give equal consideration to wildlife conservation, including wetlands habitat impacts, as they give to other purposes of proposed projects. 16 U.S.C. § 661. For a description of these and over a dozen more federal programs that directly or indirectly establish wetlands conservation policy, see U.S. GAO, Wetlands Overview: Federal and State Policies, Legislation, and Programs, GAO/RCED-92-79FS (Nov. 1991).

9. In *Riverside Bayview* the Court made short-shrift of the "spurious" argument that the requirement that a developer seek a Corps permit under CWA Section 404 before filling jurisdictional wetlands constitutes a taking of property. For a thorough discussion of the background and status of the regulatory takings issue in the wetlands regulation context, see Robert Meltz, *Wetlands Regulation and the Law of Regulatory Takings*, 30 Envtl. L. Rep. (ELI) 10468 (2000); Robert Meltz, *Wetland Regulation and the Law of Property Rights "Takings,"* 23 National Wetlands Newsletter (ELI) 1 (May-June 2001).

10. Unlike federal public land units such as national forests (discussed in Chapter 8), where boundaries are sharply drawn lines on a map, ecosystem management for wetlands does not lend itself well to definition of the relevant ecosystem by discrete management unit. Congress chose to take a geographic unit approach in Section 404, but that approach inevitably leads to the kind of jurisdictional line drawing the Court has grappled with in *Riverside Bayview*, *SWANCC*, and *Rapanos*. Can you think of another way of defining "wetlands" for ecosystem management purposes that avoids this problem?

b. REGULATED DISCHARGES

Riverside Bayview Homes, *SWANCC*, and *Rapanos* involve the question of the *geographic* boundary of federal regulatory jurisdiction over wetlands. Another boundary is erected by the definition of *activities* subject to that jurisdiction. Even where an area indisputably is a surface water or an adjacent wetland subject to federal control, the activity taking place within the wetlands must fit the parameters of Section 404 for the regulatory program to attach. This activity-based limit on the Section 404 program has also proved significant and controversial. For example, in 1997 the D.C. Circuit held that mechanized drainage, excavation, and channelization of wetlands is not subject to Section 404 merely because of the "incidental fallback" of dirt and debris from the machine parts. *See* National Mining Association v. Army Corps of Engineers, 145 F.3d 1399 (D.C. Cir. 1998). The Corps had previously taken the position, in the so-called "Tulloch Rule" (named after one of the cases leading to its development), that incidental fall back does trigger Section 404 and that, since it is virtually impossible to conduct mechanized activities in wetlands without some incidental fallback, such activities necessarily require permits. 58 Fed. Reg. 45,008 (Aug. 25, 1993). After the D.C. Circuit opinion in *National Mining Association*, the Corps revised its rules to impose only a rebuttable presumption that such activities require permits. The presumption is removed if "project-specific evidence shows that the activity results in only incidental fallback." 66 Fed. Reg. 4550, 4575 (Jan. 17, 2001). New litigation ensued over that interpretation, which resulted in the following decision:

National Association of Home Builders v. U.S. Army Corps of Engineers

United States District Court for the District of Columbia, 2007.
2007 WL 259944.

■ ROBERTSON, DISTRICT JUDGE

Plaintiffs challenge a regulation jointly issued by the Army Corps of Engineers and the Environmental Protection Agency that governs when the use of "mechanized earth-moving equipment" results in the discharge of "dredged or fill material" and is thus subject to a permitting regime administered by the Corps. Plaintiffs contend that the agencies have exceeded their authority under the Clean Water Act, the Administrative Procedure Act, and the Tenth Amendment. In an earlier order, I dismissed these claims as unripe. 311 F. Supp. 2d 91 (2004). That decision was reversed, 370 U.S. App. D.C. 137, 440 F.3d 459 (2006), and the case was remanded for determination of the parties' cross-motions for summary judgment.

BACKGROUND

Section 301 of the Clean Water Act (CWA) prohibits the "discharge of any pollutant" unless pursuant to a permit. 33 U.S.C. § 1311(a). The statute defines a "discharge" as the "addition of any pollutant to navigable waters from any point source." *Id.* § 1362(12). Under Section 404(a) of the CWA, the Corps is authorized to issue permits for the discharge of "dredged or fill material" into the waters of the United States. *Id.* § 1344(a). The Corps, in turn, requires such permits. 33 C.F.R. § 323.3(a).

This suit is the most recent manifestation of a longstanding legal dispute about just what constitutes the discharge of dredged material. Between 1986 and 1993, the Corps defined the discharge of dredged material as "any addition of dredged material into the waters of the United States" while expressly excluding "*de minimis*, incidental soil movement occurring during normal dredging operations." Final Rule for Regulatory Programs of the Corps of Engineers, 51 Fed. Reg. 41,206, 41,232 (Nov. 13, 1986) (to be codified at 33 C.F.R. § 323.2(d)). In 1993, however, the Corps issued a new rule that eliminated the *de minimis* exception. This rule, promulgated as part of a settlement agreement in *California Wildlife Federation v. Tulloch*, Civ. No. C90–713–CIV–5–BO (E.D.N.C. 1996), became known as the "Tulloch Rule" or "*Tulloch I*." It defined the discharge of dredged material as "any addition of dredged material into, including redeposit of dredged material within, the waters of the United States." Clean Water Act Regulatory Programs, 58 Fed. Reg. 45,008, 45,035 (Aug. 25, 1993)(to be codified at 33 C.F.R. § 323.2(d)(1) and 40 C.F.R. § 232.2(1))(emphasis added).

Industry trade associations challenged the expanded definition. The district court invalidated the regulation. *American Mining Cong. v. United States Army Corps of Engineers*, 951 F. Supp. 267 (D.D.C. 1997) (Harris, J.). The Court of Appeals affirmed, *National Mining Association v. United States Army Corps of Engineers*, 330 U.S. App. D.C. 329, 145 F.3d 1399 (D.C. Cir. 1998), agreeing with plaintiffs and the district court that "the straightforward statutory term 'addition' cannot reasonably be said to encompass the situation in which material is removed from the waters of the United States and a small portion of it happens to fall back." *Id.* at 1404. Because incidental fallback represents a "net withdrawal, not an addition, of material," *id.*, the Court held, it is not a discharge and cannot be regulated. The Court of Appeals was careful, however, to make clear that it was not prohibiting the regulation of any redeposit, but only incidental fallback:

> [W]e do not hold that the Corps may not legally regulate some forms of redeposit under its § 404 permitting authority. We hold only that by asserting jurisdiction over "any redeposit," including incidental fallback, the Tulloch Rule outruns the Corps's statutory authority. Since the [CWA] sets out no bright line between incidental fallback on the one hand and regulable redeposits on the other, a reasoned attempt by the agencies to draw such a line would merit considerable deference. But the Tulloch Rule makes no effort to draw such a line, and indeed its overriding purpose appears to be to expand the Corps's permitting authority to encompass incidental fallback and, as a result, a wide range of activities that cannot remotely be said to "add" anything.

Id. at 1405.

In 2000, the Corps and EPA proposed a new rule, which would have amended the definition by adding the following language:

> A discharge of dredged material shall be presumed to result from mechanized landclearing, ditching, channelization, in-stream mining, or other mechanized excavation activity in waters of the United States. This presumption is rebutted if the party proposing such an activity demonstrates that only incidental fallback will result from its activity.

Further Revisions to the Clean Water Act Regulatory Definition of "Discharge of Dredged Material," 65 Fed. Reg. 50,108, 50,117 (Aug. 16, 2000)(to be codified at 33 C.F.R. § 323.2(d)(2) and 40 C.F.R. § 232.2(1)). After receiving comments, in January 2001 the Corps and EPA issued their final rule, commonly known as *Tulloch II*. It states:

> The Corps and EPA regard the use of mechanized earth-moving equipment to conduct landclearing, ditching, channelization, in-stream mining or other earth-moving activity in the waters of the United States as resulting in a discharge of dredged material unless project-specific evidence shows that the activity results in only incidental fallback. This paragraph does not and is not intended to shift any burden in any administrative or judicial proceeding under the CWA.

66 Fed. Reg. 4550, 4575 (codified at 33 C.F.R. § 323.2(d)(2)(i) and 40 C.F.R. § 232.2(2)(i)). In addition, the agencies added a provision defining incidental fallback:

> Incidental fallback is the redeposit of small volumes of dredged material that is incidental to excavation activity in waters of the United States when such material falls back to substantially the same place as the initial removal. Examples of incidental fallback include soil that is disturbed when dirt is shoveled and the back-spill that comes off a bucket when such small volume of soil or dirt falls into substantially the same place from which it was initially removed.

Id. (codified at 33 C.F.R. § 323.2(d)(2)(ii) and 40 C.F.R. § 232.2(2)(ii)).

On February 6, 2001, plaintiffs filed this suit, challenging both provisions. My view, that the case was not fit for review, because "both the court and the agencies would benefit from letting the questions presented here 'arise in some more concrete and final form,'" 311 F. Supp. 2d at 97–98 (quoting *State Farm Mut. Auto Ins. Co. v. Dole*, 255 U.S. App. D.C. 398, 802 F.2d 474, 479 (D.C. Cir. 1986)), was rejected, a panel of the Court of Appeals having concluded that "the legality *vel non* of the two challenged features will not change from case to case or become clearer in a concrete setting."

ANALYSIS

Following the Court of Appeals' ruling on *Tulloch I*, Judge Harris warned the agencies against "parsing the language of [prior] decisions . . . to render a narrow definition of incidental fallback that is inconsistent with an objective and good faith reading of those decisions." *American Mining Cong. v. Army Corps of Eng.*, 120 F. Supp. 2d 23, 31 (D.D.C. 2000) (Harris, J.). Yet by defining incidental fallback partly in terms of volume, the EPA and the Corps appear to have done exactly what they were warned not to do.

Although the decisions of this court and the Court of Appeals have described incidental fallback in terms of volume, neither court has gone so far as to require that the volume of fallback be small. Conceivably, the operator of a shovel removing 500 tons of dirt could accidentally drop all 500 tons back to the earth without redepositing anything. In determining whether fallback is incidental—i.e., not an addition within the meaning of the Clean Water Act—the volume of material being handled is irrelevant. The difference between incidental fallback and redeposit is better understood in terms of two other factors: (1) the time the material is held before being dropped to earth and (2) the distance between the place where the material is collected and the place where it is dropped. In striking down *Tulloch I* because of its failure to exclude activities resulting only in incidental fallback, Judge Silberman stated:

> [T]he word addition carries both a temporal and geographic ambiguity. If the material that would otherwise fall back were moved some distance away and then dropped, it very well might constitute an "addition." Or if it were held from some time and then dropped back in the same spot, it might also constitute an "addition."

145 F.3d at 1410 (Silberman, J., concurring). Although *Tulloch II* addresses the "geographic ambiguity" raised by Judge Silberman—material must fall back to "substantially the same place as the initial removal"—it makes no reference to the amount of time that the material is held before it is dropped. For that reason, and because it improperly includes a volume requirement, the rule must be rewritten.

As the Corps rewrites its definition of incidental fallback, it should also reconsider its statement that it "regards" the use of mechanized earth-moving equipment as resulting in a discharge of dredged material unless project-specific evidence shows otherwise. That statement, followed by the coy explanation that it "is not intended to shift any burden," 66 Fed. Reg. at 4575, essentially reflects a degree of official recalcitrance that is unworthy of the Corps.

The Court of Appeals, in striking down *Tulloch I*, recognized the difficult task of distinguishing incidental fallback, which cannot be regulated under the Clean Water Act, from other redeposits, which can. Because the Act sets out "no bright line" separating one from the other, the court suggested that "a reasoned attempt by the agencies to draw such a line would merit considerable deference." The agencies, however, have made no such attempt. Although the agencies contend that a bright-line rule would not be "feasible or defensible," the Court of Appeals has made clear, and the government has acknowledged, that not all uses of mechanized earth-moving equipment may be regulated. The agencies cannot require "project-specific evidence" from projects over which they have no regulatory authority.

Because the *Tulloch II* rule violates the Clean Water Act, it is invalid. Therefore, plaintiffs' motion for summary judgment will be granted, and the Corps and EPA will be enjoined from enforcing and applying the rule. An appropriate order accompanies this memorandum.

NOTES & QUESTIONS

1. The *Home Builders* court lays out two parameters the Corps must use to develop a bright line test—distance between place of removal and place of redeposit and holding time—and one parameter that is off limits—volume. How would you go about advising the Corps to develop such a regulation? Should the rule state a specific distance and time?

2. The court also chided the Corps for its "coy" move of establishing a rebuttable presumption that all use of mechanized earth-moving equipment results in a discharge of dredged material unless project-specific evidence shows otherwise. When bright jurisdictional lines do not exist in statutes and regulations, or even when they do, if they are not easy to verify in the field, who should bear the burden of proving whether jurisdiction attaches to a particular place and activity? Under the Endangered Species Act, for example, the government bears the burden of proving habitat is occupied by a protected species and that an activity in that habitat has caused actual death or injury to the species. *See* Babbitt v. Sweet Home Chapter of Communities for a Great Oregon, 515 U.S. 687 (1995); Arizona Cattle Growers' Association v. United States Fish and

Wildlife Service, 273 F.3d 1229 (9th Cir. 2001); Defenders of Wildlife v. Bernal, 204 F.3d 920 (9th Cir. 2000).

3. Why is the Corps trying to regulate as close as possible to "incidental fallback" as the courts will let it? Consider what will happen if the Corps drafts a rule consistent with the *Home Builders* court's guidelines: volume of earth removed does not matter. Conducted properly, "mechanized earth moving" thus can escape regulation under Section 404 while accomplishing what a landowner engaging in the practice is hoping for—opening channels to drain the wetland and convert the entire area to non-jurisdictional upland. Once a wetland, not always a wetland.

4. A similar and equally controversial activity with unclear jurisdictional implications was "deep ripping," which is a form of "plowing" using extremely long plow prongs to open wetlands up to drainage. But the Ninth Circuit ruled that Section 404 covers this practice, *see* Borden Ranch Partnership v. U.S. Army Corps of Engineers, 261 F.3d 810 (9th Cir. 2001), and the Supreme Court, in a split 4–4 per curiam decision, upheld the Ninth Circuit's opinion. *See* Borden Ranch Partnership v. U.S. Army Corps of Engineers, 537 U.S. 99 (2002). What is the difference between "mechanized earth moving" and "deep ripping" in terms of whether either results in "fill" of a wetland area?

5. In Coeur Alaska, Inc. v. Southeast Alaska Conservation Council, 129 S. Ct. 2485 (2009), the plaintiff mining company sought to pipe a slurry of 210,000 gallons of process wastewater and 1,440 tons of tailings each day to the bottom of Lower Slate Lake, which would fill the lake with solids and destroy all aquatic life. Upon conclusion of the mining operations, Coeur Alaska proposed to cap the tailings with four inches of native material and restore and expand the lake.

Since the lake was a water of the United States, Coeur Alaska needed a permit to discharge the slurry. But did it need a Section 404 Permit from the Army Corps (subject to EPA veto) or did it need a permit under CWA 402 from EPA subject to effluent limitations? In 2002, the Corps and EPA promulgated a regulation that defined fill material to include "tailing or similar mining-related materials." Still, the regulation failed to identify whether the fill material, that was subject to the Army Corps jurisdiction, needed to meet performance standards. In a 2004 internal memorandum written by Diana Regas, the Director of EPA's Office of Wetlands, Oceans and Watersheds during the Bush administration, Ms. Regas declared that EPA's performance standards did not apply to discharges of fill material. Based on this information, Coeur Alaska sought a discharge permit from the Army Corps rather than EPA. The Army Corps determined that any environmental damage would be temporary and issued the permit. SEACC challenged the permit decision and won at the 9th Circuit, but lost before the Supreme Court which upheld the permit. In a 6-3 decision, the Court found that the "because Congress has not 'directly spoken' to the 'precise question' of whether an EPA performance standard applies to discharges of fill material, the statute alone does not resolve the case." Since the statute did not provide the answer, the Court attempted to determine congressional intent but could not find any. Next, the Court looked to agency regulations, but found them to be ambiguous. The Court then turned to the 2004 internal EPA memorandum that the performance standards do not apply to fill material. The Court declared that the memo did qualify for Chevron deference but found that it "presents a reasonable interpretation of the regulatory regime" and thus the Court deferred to the interpretation because it is not "plainly erroneous or inconsistent with the regulation[s]." So long as one federal agency (the Army Corps) is regulating the discharge at issue, why was it so important to the environmental group challenging the permit to have another federal agency (EPA) to regulate the discharge? Even if the two agencies have different views on certain permitting matters, isn't that solved by the CWA giving EPA veto authority over Army Corps permits?

c. PERMITTING AND MITIGATION

When actions in areas within the federal side of the Section 404 line meet the action-based parameters of Section 404—i.e., result in a nonexempt discharge of fill material into federal jurisdictional wetlands—they trigger the procedures and standards of the Section 404 permitting program. Although the Corps of Engineers is the lead federal agency for these purposes, as explained in more detail below several other federal agencies are involved in the process:

> **Corps of Engineers**: makes site-specific wetland delineations; promulgates nationwide and regional general permits; makes decisions on individual permits; takes enforcement actions; promulgates regulations to implement these programs.

> **EPA**: issues standards under CWA section 404(b)(1) governing the environmental criteria for location of fill locations; can veto Corps permits based on environmental criteria.

> **U.S. Fish and Wildlife Service**: reviews and comments on Corps permit applications pursuant to the Fish and Wildlife Coordination Act, 16 U.S.C. §§ 661-666c; may elevate disputes with the local Corps offices over permit issuance decisions to Corps Headquarters.

> **National Oceanic and Atmospheric Administration**: reviews and comments on Corps permit applications and may also elevate local permit decisions.

The CWA provides several exemptions from permit requirements for activities in areas that otherwise might fit the parameters. For example, routine, ongoing farming operations are exempt from permitting, as are many maintenance activities for dikes, berms, dams, and bridges. *See* 33 U.S.C. § 1344(f)(1); 33 C.F.R. § 323.4. These exemptions do not allow new farming or construction in wetlands, however.

Activities requiring permits might qualify for one of the Corps' Nationwide Permits. These are so-called general permits, or permits by rule, that apply to specified low-impact activities with little or no application and review process. *See* 33 U.S.C. § 1344(c); 33 C.F.R. pt. 330. The Corps must find that activities covered by such permits generally will have minimal adverse impacts, separately and cumulatively. Some of the general permits require pre-discharge notifications to allow the Corps, on a case-by-case basis, to review impacts and deny the benefit of the general permit. The Corps may issue general permits on a regional and local basis as well.

Activities not qualifying for exemption or a general permit must undergo the Corps individual permit review process. *See* 33 C.F.R. pt. 325. An important facet of this program are the EPA's guidelines, issued pursuant to CWA Section 404(b)(1), governing where the Corps may specify sites for disposal of fill material. *See* 33 U.S.C. § 1344(b)(1). The criteria, which are binding on the Corps, include such factors as the effects on wildlife, on ecosystem diversity, productivity and stability, and on shorelines and beaches. *See* 40 C.F.R. pt. 230. EPA has used the guidelines to impose an "alternatives" analysis on Corps decisions, under which disposals in wetlands that are not associated with "water-dependent" activities are presumed to have financially practicable alternatives that are less environmentally damaging. *Id.* § 230.10(a).

For proposed disposals that meet EPA's environmental criteria and alternatives test, the Corps conducts a "public interest" analysis involving a wide variety of factors covering economic, environmental, and social interests. *See* 33 C.F.R. pt. 320. The Corps also submits the application to review by several other federal agencies through interagency consultation required under CWA Section 404(q), though recommendations derived from this process do not bind the Corps. Even the states get involved, as the Corps must obtain the state's certification that issuance of the permit will not cause a violation of state water quality standards developed pursuant to the CWA. *See* 33 U.S.C. § 1341(c). Lastly, although it has been used infrequently, EPA may veto Corps issuance of a permit if EPA concludes it would have "unacceptable adverse effect on . . . shellfish beds and fishery areas . . . wildlife, or recreational areas." 33 U.S.C. § 1344(c).

The premise of any permit program, of course, is that *some* of the regulated activity will be allowed. But under what conditions, and at what cost to the both the regulated entity and the affected ecosystem? As the following materials illustrate, the Corps and EPA have grappled with these questions for many years under the Section 404 program, and have recently gravitated to innovative approaches such as "regional permits" and "mitigation banking" that are designed to allow both sides of the equation to get most of what they need, if not all of what they want. See what you think of both the design and implementation of such "second generation" regulatory efforts to achieve a "win-win" ecosystem management policy.

(1) Regional Permitting

Sierra Club v. United States Army Corps of Engineers

United States District Court for the Middle District of Florida, 2005.
399 F. Supp. 2d 1335.

■ CORRIGAN, DISTRICT JUDGE.

I. Background

On June 30, 2004, defendant United States Army Corps of Engineers issued SAJ-86, a regional general permit, which contemplates development of 48,150 acres in Northwest Florida in the Lake Powell, Choctawhatchee Bay and West Bay watersheds along the U.S. Highway 98 corridor, an area which has been used since the 1920s for the intense production of pine trees. Intervenor St. Joe Company owns more than 75% of the acreage covered by the regional general permit. SAJ-86 allows the discharge of dredged and fill materials into wetlands to support the construction of thousands of homes and other residential, commercial, recreational and institutional projects. SAJ-86 contemplates that development will only be allowed on 30% of the area covered by the permit. No more than 20% of the wetlands in any one of 19 different geographic sub-basins may be destroyed and no more than 1500 total acres of wetlands may be destroyed within the entire 48, 150 acre parcel. SAJ-86 also includes detailed plans to mitigate for lost wetlands by preservation, restoration and enhancement of other wetlands both within and outside the permit area. By statute, this regional general permit, SAJ-86, expires in five years and may be revoked or modified. 33 U.S.C. § 1344(e)(2).

Under SAJ-86, developers and others seeking to build within the permit area apply to the Corps' District Engineer who may authorize individual projects upon finding them to be compliant with the terms of SAJ-86. Without the issuance of this regional general permit, those seeking to build in the permit area would have to apply to the Corps for an "individual permit," which process includes opportunity for public review and input regarding the specific details of each individual development project, a feature which is not a component of individual project authorization under SAJ-86. Notwithstanding the existence of SAJ-86, however, a party may still apply for an individual permit to dredge and fill within the regional permit area.

In April and May of 2005 the plaintiffs filed complaints against the Corps and two Corps officials challenging the Corps' authority to issue the SAJ-86 permit on grounds that it violates the Clean Water Act of 1977, 33 U.S.C. § 1251 *et seq.* ("CWA"), and the National Environmental Policy Act, 42 U.S.C. § 4321 *et seq.* ("NEPA").

III. Discussion

To secure a preliminary injunction, a party must establish that "(1) it has a substantial likelihood of success on the merits; (2) irreparable injury will be suffered unless the injunction issues; (3) the threatened injury to the movant outweighs whatever damage the proposed injunction may cause the opposing party; and (4) if issued, the injunction would not be adverse to the public interest." *Siegel v. LePore,* 234 F.3d 1163, 1176 (11th Cir.2000) (citations omitted).

A. Likelihood of success

Plaintiffs claim that issuance of SAJ-86 was arbitrary, capricious, an abuse of discretion or otherwise not in accordance with the law because it violates several provisions of both the CWA and NEPA as well as Corps regulations and guidelines for enforcement of these Acts. To secure a preliminary injunction, plaintiffs must demonstrate a substantial likelihood of showing that the Corps' issuance of SAJ-86 violated any one of the relevant provisions of either Act or the attendant regulations, as alleged in their complaints. While the Court will address the parties' other contentions in its Final Order, for the reasons discussed below, the Court finds plaintiffs have demonstrated a substantial likelihood of showing that the issuance of SAJ-86 fails to comply with the statutory requirements for issuance of a general permit under the CWA; therefore, plaintiffs have also demonstrated a substantial likelihood of showing that the Corps' decision to issue the permit was "arbitrary, capricious, an abuse of discretion or otherwise not in accordance with the law" within the meaning of the Administrative Procedure Act, 5 U.S.C. § 706(2)(A).

1. CWA General Permitting Scheme

Congress enacted the CWA "to restore and maintain the chemical, physical and biological integrity of the Nation's waters." 33 U.S.C. § 1251(a). Under the CWA statutory scheme, a party must secure an individual permit (a section 404(a) permit) from the Corps before discharging dredged or fill material into navigable waters unless the discharge of dredged or fill material is already authorized under the terms of a general permit. 33 U.S.C. § 1344. Section 404(e) of the CWA (33 U.S.C. § 1344(e)) authorizes the Corps to issue a general permit "for any category of activities involving discharges of dredged or fill material" where "the activities [covered by the general permit] are similar in nature, will cause only minimal adverse environmental effects when performed separately, and will have only minimal cumulative adverse effects on the environment." 33 U.S.C. § 1344(e)(1). General permits may be issued on a regional, statewide or nationwide basis. *Id.*

Unlike individual permits, which cover a single project and which are each vetted through a public input process, general permits, like SAJ-86, render *specific* project review and public input unnecessary, although the public has opportunity for input into the Corps' decision whether to issue a general permit. Once a general permit has issued, the Corps, acting under a more relaxed review process, issues authorizations for proposed individual projects within the general permit area that comply with the general permit terms. Notably, neither plaintiff alleges that any irregularities occurred with the *process* of SAJ-86's issuance (meaning plaintiffs are not challenging whether required findings were made or whether notice was given or whether hearings were held). Rather, as discussed below, plaintiffs claim the terms of SAJ-86 do not comply with the requirements for issuance of a general permit under 33 U.S.C. § 1344(e) and that the Corps has therefore acted outside its lawful authority in issuing SAJ-86.

As stated, Congress has directed that the Corps may "issue general permits . . . for any category of activities involving discharges of dredged or fill material if the Secretary determines that the activities in such category: (1) are similar in nature, (2) will cause only minimal adverse environmental effects when performed separately, and (3) will have only minimal cumulative adverse effect on the environment." 33 U.S.C. § 1344(e).

a. Similar in Nature

The CWA authorizes the Corps to issue a general permit for any category of activities which are "similar in nature." 33 U.S.C. § 1344(e). SAJ-86 "applies to the discharges of dredged or fill material into non-tidal waters of the United States for[:]

> the construction of residential, commercial, recreational and institutional projects, including building foundations, building pads and attendant features that are necessary for the use and maintenance of the structures. Attendant features may include, but are not limited to, roads, parking lots, garages, yards, utility lines, and stormwater management facilities. Residential developments include multiple and single unit developments. Examples of commercial developments include retail stores, light industrial facilities, restaurants, business parks, and shopping centers. Examples of recreational facilities include playgrounds, playing fields, golf courses, hiking trails, bike paths, horse paths, stables, nature centers, and campgrounds. Examples of institutional developments include schools, fire stations, government office buildings, judicial buildings, public works buildings, libraries, hospitals and places of worship."

> Although the permit itself does not describe how these activities are similar in nature, in response to a public comment which challenged the proposed permit on the ground that it failed to conform with this CWA statutory requirement, the Corps stated that these activities are "similar in nature" because they are all components of "suburban development."

The phrase "similar in nature" is not further defined in the statute. Neither the parties nor the Court's own limited review has unveiled any legislative history bearing on the meaning of this term. However, we know from the plain language that Congress has intended that the activities authorized by a general permit be "similar." Few reported cases discuss the meaning of "similar in nature." One is *Alaska Center for the Environment v. West,* 157 F.3d 680 (9th Cir.1998), in which five general permits were challenged, one that applied to residential buildings under 50 feet high; one to residential streets no more than 75 feet wide; one to public and private institutions and businesses authorized by a municipal code, excluding underground storage tanks and prohibiting particular pollutants; one to industrial developments for the production of inert materials, with a variety of restrictions; and one to particular environmental enhancement projects. 157 F.3d at 681, 683. In determining whether the ranges of activities authorized under each permit were similar in nature, the court addressed issues such as whether the residential building general permit was overly broad in failing to distinguish between single and two-family dwellings. *Id.* at 684. In contrast to the specific and circumscribed general permits in *Alaska Center,* here, the Court is not looking to find meaning between such "fine distinctions"—rather, in this case, the Court looks to the statute to see if it provides an answer to congressional intent on the question of whether the rather expansive list of activities authorized by SAJ-86 are "similar in nature."

In SAJ-86, the Corps has authorized the discharge of dredged or fill material to support the construction of activities ranging from horse stables to public works buildings, from light industrial facilities to multiple unit residential developments, from restaurants to roads, and from hospitals to utility lines, all under the rubric of "suburban development." Moreover, as noted above, SAJ-86 states that activities such as these are just *examples* of what might be authorized under the broad categories of "construction of residential, commercial, recreational and institutional projects." At argument, the Corps was unable to articulate an activity that might not be authorized under this permit other than heavy industrial facilities, though even this activity might arguably fall within the definition of commercial development and is therefore not necessarily outside the bounds of the permit.

Alaska Center stands in contrast to this case. Here, on its face, the panoply of development activities authorized by SAJ-86 can only be defined as "similar in nature" if that phrase is robbed of all its meaning, a result inconsistent with Congress' decision to limit the scope of general permits.

Even the Corps' lone effort to describe the "similarity" of the allowable activity under SAJ-86, that is, that it all relates to "suburban development," is belied by the fact that every activity listed in the permit could also be a feature of, for example, "urban development" or, for that matter, "development." This is even assuming that a broad catch-all description such as "suburban development" is sufficient to meet the "similarity in nature" parameters under the CWA, a proposition as to which the Court is in serious doubt. *Cf., Wyoming Outdoor Council v. U.S. Army Corps of Engineers,* 351 F.Supp.2d 1232, 1257–58 (D.Wyo.2005) (citing *Alaska Center* and finding Corps complied with CWA by issuing one general permit for surveys, roads, well pads, utilities, reservoirs, erosion control, hazardous waste cleanup, and mitigation to support oil and gas production in Wyoming). The Corps forthrightly says it has never before used a regional general permit in this way; preliminarily, the Court finds the plaintiffs have shown a substantial likelihood of proving that it may not do so. Plaintiffs have therefore demonstrated a substantial likelihood that the Corps has issued a general permit that fails to comply with the CWA requirement that a general permit issue only for activities which are similar in nature.

b. Separate and Cumulative Adverse Environmental Effects

The CWA authorizes the Corps to issue a general permit for activities which "will cause only minimal adverse effects when performed separately, and will have only minimal cumulative adverse effect on the environment." 33 U.S.C. § 1344(e). As noted above, SAJ-86 authorizes a wide range of activities. The permit does, however, place a 20% limit on the percentage of wetlands which may be destroyed within any of the 19 sub-basins in the permit area and further limits the total area of high quality wetlands which can be destroyed to 125 acres, and only for purposes of road and bridge crossings. The permit contains a complex scheme of compensatory mitigation and conservation meant to replace some of the lost wetlands in the permit area, although the permit contemplates that at least some of the mitigation may take place outside the geographic area covered by SAJ-86. There is no particular limit on the separate environmental effect of any single project (provided no one project exceeds the 20% limit for the total destruction of wetlands in the sub-basin in which the project is located) and any mitigation to be required for a specific project is determined during the post-permit pre-authorization stage.

The Corps acknowledges that "[r]egulated activities that would be authorized" under SAJ-86 "would include the placement of fill in regulated wetlands for the construction of residential, commercial, recreational and institutional projects, *possibly including* multiple and single unit residential developments, retail stores, light industrial facilities, restaurants, business parks, shopping centers, playgrounds, playing fields, golf courses, stables, nature centers, campgrounds, schools, fire stations, government office buildings, judicial buildings, public works buildings, libraries, hospitals, and places of worship, roads, bridges, and utility line installation" and further acknowledges that "[t]he construction and operation of these various developments . . . *would have direct, indirect, and cumulative impacts on onsite wetlands and waters;* but no direct and only minimal indirect impact on aquatic resources outside the [SAJ-86] project area, which include wetlands and receiving waterbodies." Thus, the Corps contemplates that the authorized activities will have environmental impacts—the question here is whether these impacts will be separately and cumulatively minimal, as required by statute for issuance of a general permit.

The Corps argues that . . . SAJ-86 caps the limits of the environmental impacts to wetlands at 20% for the permitted region, thus ensuring that the effects will be minimal. However, the CWA requires that both the cumulative and the separate environmental effects be minimal and it does not limit the consideration to wetlands impact only. SAJ-86 allows an extremely broad range of as yet undetermined development activities. Because the Corps has not defined with any precision the number and type of activities that may be authorized by SAJ-86, it cannot assess the separate impact of any particular activity (which impact may well differ depending on the activity) that may later be authorized under the permit.

The Court finds . . . that SAJ-86 violates the statutory requirement that the Corps reach a final determination of minimal environmental impact *before,* not *after,* issuance of a general permit. Because the activities to be authorized by SAJ-86 and their separate and cumulative adverse environmental effects was not and could not be determined at the time the permit issued but rather are assessed during a post-permit process when a project is brought to the Corps for authorization, the Court preliminarily finds that the permitting scheme of SAJ-86 does not comply with the statutory requirements of the CWA. Plaintiffs have therefore demonstrated a substantial likelihood that the Corps has issued a general permit that fails to comply with the statutory requirements that the permit only regulate activities which will cause minimal adverse environmental effects both separately and cumulatively.

[The court then held, under the other factors for preliminary injunction, that the balance of interests weighed in favor of granting injunctive relief]

IV. Conclusion

Both the Corps and St. Joe espouse their good faith in utilizing a regional general permit to bring a cohesive environmental approach to the inevitable development of a large tract in Northwest Florida, rather than a less effective piecemeal approach under the individual permitting process. However, it is not the Court's function to determine the public policy wisdom of this endeavor, only to decide whether it meets the requirements of existing law. Preliminarily, I conclude it does not.

NOTES & QUESTIONS

1. The St. Joe regional general permit was lauded by the Corps and the Florida Department of Environmental Protection as a shining example of ecosystem management. The St. Joe Company, which owns over 900,000 acres of Florida, has plans to move its huge timber holdings along Florida's Gulf Coast Panhandle into land development. The company entered into the regional general permit with the Corps and an "Ecosystem Management Agreement" with the state, the net effect of which was to authorize St. Joe's development in a 31,000-acre area in return for securing eight conservation areas totaling over 12,000 acres and restoring two mitigation areas totaling over 7,600 acres. The effect of the conservation units was to create a 25-mile wildlife habitat corridor connecting several existing state conservation areas and protecting one of the state's most pristine coastal lakes. St. Joe would receive streamlined federal and state permitting for its development projects, subject to conditions stated in the two instruments. The state announced the arrangement with much fanfare:

> The Department of Environmental Protection (DEP) today reached a highly protective, comprehensive agreement with The St. Joe Company to save wetlands and conserve 20,760 acres along the Florida Panhandle. The Ecosystem Management Agreement requires The St. Joe Company to go above and beyond standard environmental requirements to protect natural areas in a region known for its biological diversity. The agreement will benefit Bay and Walton counties.

> "This agreement provides unparalleled wetlands protection," said DEP's Northwest District Director Mary Jean Yon. "By taking a regional approach and working closely with our federal partners, we are able to preserve sensitive natural resources and achieve more protection for Florida's environment."

The plan, known as an Ecosystem Management Agreement, covers more than 31,350 acres of St. Joe owned property stretching from West Bay to Choctawhatchee Bay. Three years ago, DEP and the federal government urged St. Joe to take a comprehensive, regional approach to conservation and development that would provide for predictable community growth while affording greater protection to natural lands along the Emerald Coast.

DEP Secretary David B. Struhs praised the Department staff for convincing St. Joe to enter into the agreement. "Florida's environmental team has secured a commitment that will better protect the resources that matter most. This will avoid traditional piecemeal development that would be insensitive to our desire to protect the entire landscape."

"This serves as a national example of responsible growth," said newly appointed DEP Secretary Colleen Castille. "Not only does the agreement allow the region's economy to grow, it does so in a way that safeguards important water resources and protects the quality of life of those that live and work in Northwest Florida."

As part of the agreement, St. Joe is setting aside thousands of acres of high quality habitat for preservation. The conservation areas create a two-pronged "Bay to Bay" wildlife corridor linking public land from Choctawhatchee Bay to St. Andrew Bay and preserving the ecological integrity of two of Northwest Florida's most rapidly developing watersheds.

See http://www.dep.state.fl.us/secretary/news/2004/feb/0225.htm.

2. The Florida DEP explained that "An Ecosystem Management Agreement is an alternative to traditional permitting that provides a comprehensive, coordinated approach to regional development and provides greater environmental benefits. Use of a binding Ecosystem Management Agreement is voluntary and detailed in Section 403.0752, Florida Statutes. To enter into an Ecosystem Management Agreement, the applicant must demonstrate that a net ecosystem benefit will result over and above the environmental standards required by traditional permitting." Consider the two possible scenarios the agencies had before them. Under the traditional permitting approach, St. Joe might have sold off or developed chunks of its holdings piecemeal over time, requiring the agencies to process perhaps scores of individual permits and negotiate terms of development with perhaps as many different landowners. Under the alternative approach they took, by contrast, they were able to negotiate terms of development with a single entity, St. Joe, which then bound all of the development projects St. Joe or its purchasers might initiate. Clearly, the agencies prefer the alternative approach, having urged St. Joe to use it, and St. Joe seems to have fought hard to secure it.

3. So what was the problem with SAJ-86? Was it simply too general, having lumped too many activities together as "similar" and having left too much in the air regarding cumulative impacts? Yet, how specific is it reasonable to expect a permit of this magnitude to be? The individual permitting approach has the advantage of allowing the agencies to examine a well-defined development plan and its impacts simultaneously, whereas the alternative approach demands a bit of forecasting and tolerance for adjustment "on the fly." But indi-

vidual permitting risks having the impact analysis lose track of the big picture
of regional development impacts, whereas the very point of alternative permitting is to take a comprehensive regional planning approach. Traditional permitting is inefficient, but alternative permitting is imprecise. Is ecosystem
management simply not well suited for either kind of environmental permitting? How would you administer a permitting program such as Section 404 in
such a way as to promote ecosystem management goals?

4. In November 2006, the court in the SAJ–86 permit case vacated its preliminary injunction and found "by the slimmest of margins that the Corps' issuance
of regional general permit SAJ–86 does not violate the statutory and regulatory
requirements of either the CWA or NEPA." Sierra Club v. U.S. Army Corps of
Engineers, 464 F. Supp. 2d 1171 (M.D. Fla. 2006). The court was clearly not
overwhelmed by the Corps' position, but in a lengthy opinion sympathized with
the fact that "the Corps was faced here with an unprecedented situation in trying to regulate a relatively homogeneous, contiguous 48,150 acre parcel owned
largely by one entity, with wetlands interspersed throughout. It has responded
to this unique scenario with SAJ–86, which represents a non-traditional use of
the Corps' permitting authority under the Clean Water Act, a use which the
Court finds is at, but not beyond, the outer limits of that authority." As an example of how close the court felt the case was, on the question of "similar in
nature" the judge explained that he was "barely" satisfied by the Corps' argument that the category of activities involved in the permit met that requirement:

> The Corps argued that all activities in the long list of permitted land uses
> are all components of suburban development and the special and general
> conditions of the permit ensure that only suburban development activities
> would meet the permit terms. The Corps also states that the uniform to-
> pography and undeveloped character of the geographic region covered by
> this permit combined with the limits to the developable area within each
> sub-basin further ensures that activities associated with other types of de-
> velopment (such as urban development) would not be authorized by this
> permit. The Corps explains that its objective in proposing this permit was
> to guide the inevitable suburban growth that was about to take place
> along the U.S. Highway 98 corridor in a manner which maximized protec-
> tion of the wetlands. The only mechanism to do this, explains the Corps, is
> through a general permit which captures the various types of development
> activities the potential permit seekers would likely propose. The Corps
> further notes that its finding in this regard is reasonable because past
> permits, such as NWP 39 and SAJ–74 had similarly categorized activities.
> Thus, the Corps claims, in this unique circumstance, issuing a general
> permit for a range of activities that encompass all the features of subur-
> ban development was a reasonable interpretation of the statute it is
> charged with administering.

Are you also satisfied by these arguments, even if only barely? Given the
rocky start the Corps and Florida DEP had with ecosystem management in this
case, how eager do you think they and other agencies will be to experiment
with ecosystem management in other regulatory settings? Should they count on
being sued? What can they do to improve their outcomes—to demonstrate by
more than the slimmest of margins that ecosystem management is an appropriate set of goals and methods to implement under existing laws?

(2) Mitigating Banking

J.B. Ruhl & R. Juge Gregg, *Integrating Ecosystem Services Into Environmental Law: A Case Study of Wetlands Mitigation Banking*

20 Stanford Environmental Law Journal 365 (2001).

I. Introduction

The federal wetland mitigation banking experience, a habitat trading program that has been in existence for over a decade, presents an opportunity for examining how ecosystem service values could be integrated into existing environmental law frameworks. In wetlands mitigation banking, a "bank" of wetlands habitat is created, restored, or preserved and then made available to developers of wetlands habitat who must "buy" habitat mitigation as a condition of federal government approval for development in wetland areas. Wetlands provide extensive and important services to human populations, including flood control and water quality improvement. If environmental law protects ecosystem services, evidence to that effect should exist in the structure and performance of the wetlands banking program. In particular, a program allowing what essentially amounts to trading of wetlands—exchanging acres destroyed in one location for acres created or improved elsewhere—ought to take into account the service values of the wetlands being traded. This article tests that hypothesis, exploring both the legal authority and the actual practice that exists in wetlands mitigation banking with respect to accounting for ecosystem service values that wetlands provide.

The genesis of wetlands mitigation banking was the revelation of widespread evidence that various forms of mitigation for wetlands losses used in the 1980s were not adequately protecting environmental values. During the 1990s, government and industry moved toward the banking program as a cornerstone of wetlands mitigation. This movement presented an opportunity to introduce greater emphasis on service values in the goals of mitigation. Indeed, there are now several specific regulatory provisions within the wetlands regulation and mitigation program that are particularly suited to incorporating ecosystem service values into the regulatory decision making process. Yet, while the existing legal framework of wetlands banking clearly accommodates integration of ecosystem service values with little or no changes to regulatory text, nothing in the regulations explicitly requires or encourages that approach generally. In short, the authority to integrate ecosystem service concerns into the wetlands mitigation banking program is implicit, but implementation in any broad, deliberate policy form remains only a latent potential.

II. Law and Policy Background

Section 311 of the Clean Water Act (CWA) prohibits "the discharge of any pollutant by any person," which, because of the way those terms are defined, also prohibits filling of wetlands. Nevertheless, section 404(a) of the statute authorizes the Secretary of the Army, through the Army Corps of Engineers (the Corps), to "issue permits for the discharge of dredged or fill material in the navigable waters of the United States at specified disposal sites." Pursuant to section 404(b)(1) of the CWA, the Environmental Protection Agency (EPA) must promulgate substantive permitting standards, known as the "404(b)(1) Guidelines," which the Corps must follow in administering the permit program. Thus, under the CWA, wetlands may be filled only if a permit is granted in accordance with the 404(b)(1) guidelines. These permits, known ubiquitously as "404 permits," "wetland permits," or "Corps permits," have become the cornerstone for federal protection of wetland resources. The permitting program, however, admits of many exceptions and nuances making it less than straightforward to determine whether a permit is required for a particular fill activity, and how to get one. Many routine land development activities do, however, require and receive a 404 permit. And along the way, permit applicants and the agencies often confront the issue of "mitigation" as one of the conditions the developer must satisfy in order to obtain the permit.

The Corps' guidelines for administering wetlands mitigation require it to review 404 permit applications using a preference "sequencing" approach. The first preference is to require the applicant to avoid filling wetland resources; the second preference is to require minimization of adverse impacts that cannot reasonably be avoided; and the least desirable preference is to require the developer to provide compensatory mitigation for those unavoidable adverse impacts that remain after all minimization measures have been exercised. The least desirable option, compensatory mitigation, is the basis for wetlands trading.

Both EPA and the Corps traditionally have preferred on-site to off-site locations for the compensatory mitigation activity, and have preferred in-kind mitigation to mitigation that uses a substantially different type of wetland. Regardless of location, EPA and the Corps prefer measures that restore prior wetland areas as the highest form of mitigation, followed by enhancement of low-quality wetlands, then creation of new wetlands, and, least favored of all, preservation of existing wetlands. To take an extreme example, if compensatory mitigation is deemed appropriate for a project involving fill of mangrove swamp wetlands in Florida, on-site restoration of an area of prior mangrove swamp wetlands would be a favored mitigation strategy, whereas off-site preservation of existing cranberry bog wetlands in Maine would be least favored.

Notwithstanding its official status as the least-favored alternative in the agencies' sequencing pecking order, compensatory mitigation has been used frequently in the 404 program. Compensatory mitigation frees up highly valued wetlands for more comprehensive and flexible development. While attractive for these purposes, the project-by-project compensatory mitigation approach has been widely regarded as having failed miserably in terms of environmental protection. Whether mitigation was accomplished onsite or near-site, the piecemeal approach complicated the Corps' ability to articulate mitigation performance standards, monitor success, and enforce conditions; not surprisingly, the success rate for this approach suffered as a result.

In light of these problems, during the late 1980s the Corps and EPA started shifting compensatory activities increasingly from on-site to off-site mitigation, thus opening the door to the wetlands mitigation banking technique. This approach, its proponents argued, would prove advantageous both in terms of economic efficiency and ecological integrity, aggregating small wetlands threatened by development into larger restored wetlands in a different location. It is defined generally as "a system in which the creation, enhancement, restoration, or preservation of wetlands is recognized by a regulatory agency as generating compensation credits allowing the future development of other wetland sites." In its most basic form, wetlands mitigation banking allows a developer to protect wetlands at one site in advance of development and then draw down the resulting bank of mitigation "credits" as development is implemented and wetlands at another site are filled. Indeed, the concept has progressed beyond this personal bank model. Today, large commercial and public wetlands banks, not tied to a particular development, sell mitigation piecemeal to third-party developers in need of compensatory mitigation.

III. The Potential Role for Ecosystem Service Valuation

As the preceding discussion suggests, there are three legal instruments that directly address wetlands mitigation banking. First, under the Clean Water Act section 404(b)(1), Congress delegated to EPA the responsibility for issuing regulations governing the location of wetlands fill-sites to ensure adequate environmental protection. These regulations are known as the "404(b)(1) Guidelines." Second, in 1990, the United States Army Corps of Engineers (Corps) and the EPA signed a memorandum of agreement, known as the "Mitigation Guidance," clarifying the role each plays in wetlands mitigation under the 404(b)(1) Guidelines. And finally, as promised in the Mitigation Guidance, several agencies issued a guidance document in 1995 detailing operation of a wetlands mitigation bank, known as the "Banking Guidance."

This section discusses how these three instruments could be used to integrate consideration of ecosystem service values into wetland mitigation banking decision making with little or no change to regulatory text. For now, however, the authority to do so remains only implicit, leaving any more comprehensive and deliberate integration of ecosystem services in the wetlands mitigation banking program a latent potential.

A. *404(b)(1) Guidelines*

The 404(b)(1) Guidelines provide extensive descriptions of wetlands values that the Corps should consider in assessing potential mitigation requirements. These guidelines are the reference point for both the Mitigation Guidance and the Banking Guidance, and provide clear regulatory authority to consider ecosystem service values such as those derived from the water purification and recreational opportunities that wetlands provide.

Subparts D through F of the Guidelines focus on the negative effects of disrupting wetlands, identifying the functions and values that may be lost due to the discharge of dredged or fill materials. Subpart F, entitled "Potential Effects on Human Use Characteristics," focuses exclusively on wetlands functions used for the benefit of humans; it thus deals most directly with values and functions that can be considered ecosystem services. Subpart F identifies five general human uses that are potentially impacted by wetlands development: (1) municipal and private water supplies; (2) recreational and commercial fisheries; (3) water-related recreation; (4) aesthetics; and (5) parks. For each category, the Guidelines chronicle specific impacts that such developments could have on wetlands values.

Subparts D through F thus acknowledge that certain human activities influence wetland functioning, and Subpart F explains how humans benefit from wetland functioning. The scope of Subpart F does not cover the full range of service values associated with wetlands; for example, it fails to address the value to humans of such functions as sedimentation control, nutrient cycling, flood control, and energy fixation. The tone and content of the section clearly indicates, though, that EPA's authority under section 404(b)(1) includes protection of wetland service values generally.

B. *The Mitigation Guidance*

Initially, the Corps and EPA "clashed over the proper role of mitigation in the . . . permitting process." However, the Mitigation Guidance that the two agencies adopted in 1990 clarified the role of wetlands mitigation under the 404(b)(1) Guidelines. The Mitigation Guidance divides mitigation into three phases—avoidance, minimization, and compensatory mitigation—and required that those phases be conducted sequentially. Thus, the Corps "first makes a determination that potential impacts have been avoided to the maximum extent practicable . . .;" if there are any "remaining unavoidable impacts," the Corps is to mitigate them "to the extent appropriate and practicable by requiring steps to [2] minimize impacts, and . . . [3] compensate for aquatic resource values." Mitigation banking is an option only if the third phase, compensatory mitigation, is reached. The Mitigation Guidance explicitly endorses mitigation banking as a form of compensatory mitigation and promised additional guidance on the subject. With respect to compensatory mitigation generally, the Mitigation Guidance requires that it be used "for unavoidable adverse impacts which remain after all appropriate and practicable minimization has been required;" expresses preferences for on-site mitigation and for wetlands restoration (as opposed to wetlands creation); and requires that "functional values" be examined. Thus, the Mitigation Guidance simply requires that functional value be examined and compensation provided—preferably onsite—for unavoidable adverse impacts.

The declaration of purpose is strong but the tactics to achieve it are not well-defined. Under the Mitigation Guidance, the Corps "*will strive* to achieve a goal of no overall net loss of values and functions." The methodologies used to determine whether this goal is being met are, however, only broadly described. The Mitigation Guidance simply advocates that "qualified professionals" tailor generally recognized assessment techniques to each site, constrained only by the requirement that they "consider" the ecological functions listed in the 401(b)(1) Guidelines.

According to the Mitigation Guidance, "mitigation should provide, at a minimum, one for one functional replacement (i.e., no net loss of values), with an adequate margin of safety." Nevertheless, because determining functional replacement may be difficult, "in the absence of more definitive information on the functions and values of specific wetlands sites, a minimum of one-to-one acreage replacement may be used as a reasonable surrogate for no net loss of functions and values." Thus, the Mitigation Guidance purports to require a margin of safety that ensures a one-to-one functional replacement, but if information is uncertain—as it usually will be—the Mitigation Guidance only requires a more easily quantified and nonfunctional one-to-one acreage replacement.

The Mitigation Guidance pays homage to the idea of "functions and values" in numerous instances. It commits the agencies to "strive to achieve a goal of no overall net loss of [wetlands] values and function" and purports to base "[t]he determination of what level of mitigation constitutes 'appropriate' mitigation . . . solely on the values and functions of the aquatic resource that will be impacted." The Mitigation Guidance's attempts at quantitative valuation repeatedly focus on wetlands values and function, but it never defines these essential terms.

C. *The Banking Guidance*

In 1995, five United States agencies published the Banking Guidance, as promised in the Mitigation Guidance, in order to detail the use and operation of mitigation banks. The document's introduction declares that the "objective of a mitigation bank is to provide for *the replacement of the chemical, physical, and biological functions of wetlands and other aquatic resources which are lost* as a result of authorized impacts." This perspective is later broadened to acknowledge that "[t]he overall goal of a mitigation bank is to provide *economically efficient and flexible mitigation opportunities*, while fully compensating for wetland and other aquatic resource losses in a manner that contributes to the long-term ecological functioning of the watershed within which the bank is to be located." The Banking Guidance thus qualifies the goal of replacing ecological functioning by acknowledging economic realities.

The Banking Guidance describes the intricacies of creating a wetlands mitigation bank, but, like the Mitigation Guidance, is vague on what exactly is being "banked." Also like the Mitigation Guidance, the document relies heavily on the term "function." For example, site selection requires agencies to "give careful consideration to the ecological suitability of a site for achieving the goal and objectives of a bank, i.e., that it possess the physical, chemical and biological characteristics to support establishment of the desired aquatic resources and functions." Similarly, credit for wetland preservation is contingent upon the "functions" provided or augmented by the preserved land, and "credit may be given for the inclusion of upland areas occurring within a bank only to the degree that such features increase the overall ecological functioning of the bank."

Because the crediting and debiting procedure forms the heart of a wetlands mitigation bank, the determination of what will be counted as "currency" is crucial. The Banking Guidance focuses initially on the use of "aquatic functions" as its banking currency—a currency that is easily "exchanged" or translated into service values. But the Banking Guidance then follows the lead of the Mitigation Guidance and allows acreage to be a surrogate measure if functional assessment is impractical. The Banking Guidance then takes one more step back from its vision and allows any "appropriate functional assessment methodology . . . acceptable to all signatories" to be used to quantify credits. Once again, therefore, the official guidance provides an opportunity, but not a requirement, to rely on ecosystem indicators as the assessment methodology.

D. *Conclusion: Implicit Authority but No Explicit Requirement*

Each of the three cornerstone policies supporting wetlands mitigation banking supports integrating greater use of ecosystem services in the wetlands mitigation banking decision making process. Certainly nothing in the 404(b)(1) Guidelines, the Mitigation Guidance, or the Banking Guidance precludes the use of ecosystem service factors. The emphasis in each of the sources of authority on wetlands functions opens the door to more focused attention to the service values of those functions. Nevertheless, the functions emphasis falls short of explicit adoption of ecosystem services as a central or even relevant factor in wetlands mitigation banking decisions. At best, therefore, the current legal framework of wetlands mitigation banking establishes the implicit authority, but no explicit requirement, for the consideration of ecosystem services.

Given the current state of affairs, there is little promise for the integration of ecosystem service valuation methods into wetlands mitigation banking until methods of wetland assessment are significantly improved. In the absence of widely available, readily applied methods for calculating and comparing ecosystem service values of the wetlands being traded, the Corps will likely put constraints on trading markets to compensate for ecosystem function losses not recognized by acre-based methods. These constraints significantly undercut the market and information advantages ecosystem service valuation would impart to wetlands mitigation banking in general, thus further reducing any incentive to apply such methods.

Hence, unless some way is developed to capture the ecosystem service value of wetlands without costly, time-consuming, and complicated valuation methods—e.g., by measurement of readily determinable indicators of ecosystem service value—wetlands mitigation banking is likely to rely most heavily on acre-based and narrow function-based methods and highly regulated "markets" for trades. Nevertheless, if such assessment methods can be developed, . . . the authority to require their use is implicit in the existing legal framework of the section 404 program. By using these new assessment methods, the wetlands mitigation banking program would surely come closer to meeting its environmental protection objectives.

The basic premise of the wetlands mitigation banking program is that wetlands values are fungible and transportable within certain limits, and thus can be traded back and forth between locations in defined geographic areas with no net loss to overall wetlands values. Soon into the history of the program, however, commentators began questioning the premises of mitigation banking on two levels, not only for wetlands banking but for any habitat mitigation compensation program. First, as discussed in the preceding excerpt, so long as the measure of "value" remains bundled into relatively crude units such as wetland acres, the premise of fungibility seems suspect, thus placing the equivalency of trades beyond meaningful evaluation. Second, as the unit of valuation becomes more refined, thus making trade equivalence more measurable, the transportability of value becomes more questionable. For example, if very accurate measures of wetland ecosystem service values could be used, it would become apparent that wetland mitigation banking moves those values from one community to another community with virtually no public participation in the decision. Why, just because a developer and the mitigation banker agree, should wetlands policy endorse, indeed promote, such ecosystem service transfers? *See* James Salzman and J.B. Ruhl, *Currencies and the Commodification of Environmental Law*, 53 STAN. L. REV. 607 (2000).

Indeed, a number of scientific studies suggested that the failure of the fungibility premise was a profound defect in the wetlands mitigation banking program as implemented. In June 2001, the National Research Council, an arm of the National Academy of Sciences, concluded that compensatory wetlands mitigation is an abject failure. *See* National Academy of Sciences/National Research Council, Compensating for Wetland Losses Under the Clean Water Act (June 2001). For one thing, the Corps does a poor job, according to the report, accounting for the acre-for-acre trades, meaning even on an acre counting basis the program is losing "value." But more problematic is that acres of "enhanced" or "recreated" wetlands generally are not as functionally valuable as the acres that are lost to development. Fungibility, in other words, is not being met either on an acre basis or on a functions basis. *See also* R. Eugene Turner et al., *Count It by Acre or Function— Mitigation Adds Up to Net Loss of Wetlands*, National Wetlands Newsletter, Nov.-Dec. 2001, at 5; Chesapeake Bay Foundation, Maryland Nontidal Wetland Mitigation: A Progress Report (1997). After publication of the NRC report, the Corps of Engineers issued a defense of its program in the form of a guidance document, *see* U.S. Army Corps of Engineers, Regulatory Guidance Letter No. 01–1 (Oct. 31, 2001), which numerous environmental advocacy organizations immediately condemned as "arrogant" and evidence of an "anything goes approach," and which even some congressional and Bush Administration interests found alarmingly premature given the Corps' lack of coordination with EPA. *See* National Wildlife Federation et al., Press Release, Conservation Community Outraged by Army Corps of

Engineers' Reversal on Wetlands Policy (Nov. 6, 2001); *EPA, NMFS Slam Corps RGL on Wetlands Mitigation*, Endangered Species and Wetlands Report, Mar. 2002, at 13; *Corps Releases Mitigation Guidance*, National Wetlands Newsletter, Nov.-Dec. 2001, at 21; *Army Corps Urged by House Chairman to Withdraw Guidance, Seek EPA Comment*, 32 Env't Rep. (BNA) 2404 (2001). But the Corps soon began to change its tune. In December 2002, the Bush Administration issued the *National Wetlands Mitigation Action Plan* (Dec. 24, 2002) and a *Regulatory Guidance Letter on Compensatory Mitigation* (Dec. 27, 2002). The *Action Plan* listed action items that agencies will undertake to improve the effectiveness of the process of restoring wetlands affected by actions regulated under federal water quality laws. Prominent action items include integrating compensatory mitigation into a watershed context and clarifying performance standards for mitigation projects. The *Regulatory Guidance Letter* emphasized monitoring, long term management, financial aid, and a focus on functional quality to promote the success of restored compensatory wetland mitigation projects. The two initiatives immediately attracted supporters and critics. *Compare* John Goodin et al., *Mitigation Guidance and Action Plan Make Improvements, Outline Future*, National Wetlands Newsletter, Mar.-Apr. 2003, at 3 (lauding the initiatives), with Julie Sibbing, *Mitigation Guidance or Mitigation Myth*, National Wetlands Newsletter, Jan.-Feb. 2003, at 9 (criticizing the initiatives).

The second fundamental premise of wetland mitigation banking—transportability—also came under fire. One study of wetland banking in Florida found that wetland banking trades, even within the same watershed, produced "a transfer of wetlands from highly urbanized, high-population density areas to more rural low-population areas." *See* Dennis M. King & Luke W. Herbert, *The Fungibility of Wetlands*, 19 National Wetlands Newsletter, 10, 11 (Sept.-Oct. 1997). In similar research one of your authors has conducted, findings are that wetland mitigation bank sites are on average well over 15 miles from the associated development projects that purchase credits, and that population densities are on average about 10 times higher around the development projects compared to the area around the banks. *See* J.B. Ruhl and James Salzman, *The Effects of Wetland Mitigation Banking on People*, 28 National Wetlands Newsletter 1 (Mar.-Apr. 2006). And other studies have questioned the merits of the assumption that trading many small isolated wetlands for a large, contiguous wetland necessarily improves the ecological value of the wetlands. Many species actually are adapted to using complexes of many small, detached wetlands given greater variability of conditions, insurance against total loss in natural disasters, and source-sink population dynamics that may not operate in a contiguous wetland of equal total size. *See* Raymond D. Semlitsch, *Size Does Matter: The Value of Small Isolated Wetlands*, 22 National Wetlands Newsletter 5 (Jan.-Feb. 2000). So, moving wetlands around, even if total acreage and functions are held constant, may prove detrimental to some human populations as well as to some plant and wildlife species.

A number of state and federal studies of wetland mitigation confirmed much of what the National Research Council found in its 2001 report regarding the success of off-site wetlands mitigation. The Washington Department of Ecology found that of 24 randomly selected mitigation sites, only 13 percent adequately compensated for the loss of wetlands while over 50 percent were minimally successful. Washington Department of Ecology, Washington State Wetland Mitigation Evaluation Study (2002). Similarly, New Jersey found that, notwithstanding a requirement of a 2-to-1 compensation-to-loss ratio, only 78 percent of the freshwater wetland acres lost had been replaced with even one acre of compensation—i.e., a 122 percent shortfall. New Jersey Department of Environmental Protection, Creating Indicators of Wetland Status (Quantity and Quality): Freshwater Wetland Mitigation in New Jersey (2002). Finally, the New England District of the Corps found that in the six states under its jurisdiction, only 17 percent of mitigation projects were considered to be adequate functional replacements for the impacted wetlands. U.S. Army Corps of Engineers, New England District, Success of Corps-Required Wetland Mitigation In New England (2003). Most of the mitigation sites studied in these reports, however, were smaller mitigation projects associated with individual development permits, not full-scale mitigation banking projects. And one reason each report offers for the poor performance is that lack of administrative resources to monitor all the smaller projects. Administrative efficiency is one of the advantages usually posited for larger bank projects.

Congress eventually became interested in the administration of mitigation under Section 404, and in 2005 the Corps and EPA also began an initiative to consolidate the various rules and polices governing mitigation decisions. Ultimately, in April 2008, the U.S. Army Corps of Engineers and EPA issued new regulations regarding wetland mitigation. The regulations, which replaced the Mitigation Guidance and Banking Guidance, establish a "watershed approach" for mitigation projects to address situations where loss cannot be avoided or minimized and thus compensation is required. The regulations create a hierarchy of approaches, with mitigation banks ranked highest, followed by "in-lieu" fees which are paid to nonprofit organizations, and permittee-conducted site mitigation being ranked lowest. 73 Fed. Reg. 19594 (April 10, 2008) (codified at 33 C.F.R. §§ 332.1 to 332.8 (Corps regulations); 40 C.F.R. §§ 230.91 to 230.98 (EPA regulations)). The rule also focuses on the need to place a high priority on compensatory mitigation compliance and provides principles for establishing ecological performance standards and criteria to ensure success of mitigation projects and to "take into account regional variations in aquatic resource characteristics, functions, and services." 73 Fed. Reg. at 19601.

Notably, the 2008 rule move in the direction Ruhl and Gregg advocated, defining "services," for the first time, as "the benefits that human populations receive from functions that occur in ecosystems." Although this represented the first time the Corps placed ecosystem service values in regulatory text, the proposed rule does not carry them far in regulatory implementation. The preamble to the rule mentions ecosystem services dozens of times in a long and emphatic defense of integrating the concept into the mitigation program, but the rule itself leaves much to be determined about how the agencies will do so. The rule explains that "in general, the required compensatory mitigation should be located within the same watershed as the impact site, and should be located where it is most likely to successfully replace lost functions and services." 73 Fed. Reg. at 19673. On the question of offsite mitigation such as through banks, the rule states that "locational factors (e.g., hydrology, surrounding land use) are important to the success of compensatory mitigation for impacted habitat functions and may lead to siting of such mitigation away from the project area. However, consideration should also be given to functions and services (e.g., water quality, flood control, shoreline protection) that will likely need to be addressed at or near the areas impacted by the permitted impacts." *Id.* at 19674. To fulfill these requirements, "district engineers may require on- site, off-site, or a combination of on-site and off-site compensatory mitigation to replace permitted losses of aquatic resource functions and services." *Id.* at 19673. Yet, while recognizing the problem identified in Ruhl and Salzman's study of Florida wetland mitigation banking, the rule does not provide concrete criteria, metrics, or procedures for following through with this mandate—there are absolutely no implementation details in the regulation, suggesting the Corps will provide them later in guidance. Thus far, however, the Corps has issued no such guidance.

NOTES & QUESTIONS

1. Based on the foregoing description, do you consider wetlands mitigation banking an ecosystem management policy? How would you articulate it as such? Try doing so using the three design components of ecosystem management policy articulated in Chapter 7:

	Metric	Goals	Methods
Wetlands Mitigation Banking			

2. Numerous studies illustrate that wetlands provide significant service values in more than the obvious way of flood control. For example, in warmer agricultural regions one of the major risks of crop freeze comes from the heat-radiation effect—heat radiating away from the ground on dry winter nights rapidly lowers soil temperatures and freezes the moist root zone. Wetlands impede this effect by moisturizing the atmosphere, which can then better trap heat, and because the water in saturated soil retains heat better than dry soil. Based on an intense heat-radiation freeze event in 1993 that cost South Florida vegetable and sugar cane growers $300 in lost crops, researchers at the U.S. Geological Survey developed models to contrast the heat-radiation effects that would be expected to occur with and without wetlands present in the region under similar circumstances. They found that most of the region would have stayed in the mid to upper 30s, avoiding a freeze, and other areas would have experienced a freeze of substantially shorter duration and thus less crop damage. *See* Curtis Marshall et al., *Crop Freezes and Land Use Change in Florida*, 426 NATURE 29 (2003).

3. Only recently have reliable data become available for determining the share of wetlands mitigation attributable to mitigation banks. Almost 15 years after its inception, the Corps has finally established a database for tracking wetlands mitigation banks and trades. *See* Steven Martin and Robert Brumbaugh, *Entering a New Era: What Will RIBITS Tell Us About Mitigation Banking?*, NATIONAL WETLANDS NEWSLETTER, May-June 2011, at 16. Both the Corps and the Environmental Law Institute have previously found that banking accounts for over 30 percent of all mitigation under Section 404. In-lieu fee payments account for just over 8 percent, and the remaining mitigation is satisfied through direct on-site or off-site actions by permittees. *See* JESSICA WILSON AND JARED THOMPSON, 2005 STATUS REPORT ON COMPENSATORY MITIGATION IN THE UNITED STATES (Environmental Law Institute 2006); U.S. ARMY CORPS OF ENGINEERS, DRAFT ENVIRONMENTAL ASSESSMENT FOR PROPOSED COMPENSATORY MITIGATION REGULATION (Mar. 13, 2006). For comprehensive overviews of wetland values and valuation methods, see James Boyd and Lisa Wainger, *Measuring Ecosystem Service Benefits for Wetland Mitigation*, National Wetlands Newsletter, Nov.-Dec. 2002, at 1; Charles Andrew Cole and James G. Kooser, *HGM: Hidden, Gone, Missing?*, NATIONAL WETLANDS NEWSLETTER, Mar.-Apr. 2002, at 1; PAUL F. SCODARI, MEASURING THE BENEFITS OF FEDERAL WETLAND PROGRAMS (ENVTL. L. INST. 1997); Special Issue, *The Values of Wetlands; Landscape and Institutional Perspectives*, 35 ECOLOGICAL ECONOMICS 1 (2000). For a thorough description of the history and operation of wetlands mitigation banking programs, see ENVIRONMENTAL LAW INSTITUTE, BANKS AND FEES: THE STATUS OF OFF-SITE WETLAND MITIGATION IN THE UNITED STATES (2002); ENVIRONMENTAL LAW INST., WETLAND MITIGATION BANKING (1993).

4. How would you advise the Corps to implement the ecosystem services provision of its 2008 rule?

4. WATERSHEDS

Wouldn't it be reasonable to expect a federal statute known as the Watershed Protection and Flood Prevention Act to spell out and implement a comprehensive national framework for, say, watershed protection and flood prevention? Alas, statutes often have grandiose names with very little substance to back it up. The federal statute that goes by that name, *see* 16 U.S.C. § 1001 et seq., could hardly be characterized as a watershed-based initiative. It starts by recognizing that "[e]rosion, floodwater, and sediment damages in the watersheds of the rivers and streams of the United States, causing loss of life and damage to property, constitute a menace to the national welfare." Yet the statute does little more than direct the Department of Agriculture to cooperate and cost-share with state and local governments "for the purpose of preventing such damages, of furthering the conservation, development, utilization, and disposal of water, and the conservation and utilization of land and thereby preserving, protecting, and improving the Nation's land and water resources and the quality of the environment."

It is reassuring that the environmental protection slipped in there at the end, though it is less than clear how "development, utilization, and disposal of water, and the . . . utilization of land" will serve that objective. Suffice it to say that there is no national comprehensive legislation defining and implementing a "watershed approach." But can a coherent national policy on the topic be pieced together? We turn to the following materials to see. They are organized into three components: (1) the basic overarching theme of watershed management; (2) the variety of approaches for implementing that theme; and (3) the experience with particular applications of watershed-level ecosystem management.

a. THEME

William E. Taylor & Mark Gerath, *The Watershed Protection Approach: Is the Promise About to Be Realized?*

11 Natural Resources & Environment 16 (Fall 1996).

The concept of managing water resources and protecting water quality on a geographical or watershed basis has been evolving since the late 1800s. Only in the last few years, however, have water resource and protection organizations, both public and private, begun to focus seriously on a watershed approach to address remaining water quality problems. Until recently, water quality regulation and management focused on control of point source dischargers of pollutants. Technology and water quality-based effluent limitations on point sources, in conjunction with implementation of antibacksliding and antidegradation requirements, have resulted in a substantial reduction in point source pollutant loadings to waters and consequent upgrading of many receiving waters.

To achieve further cost-effective improvements in water quality, water resource managers recognize that they must now focus on a more comprehensive approach to water quality management, including continued control of point source discharges as well as control of nonpoint source discharges, preservation of habitat, and ground water protection and flow.

This article gives a brief history of watershed protection efforts and an analysis of why the watershed approach makes technical sense.

Historical Development of the Watershed Protection Approach

For several decades, agencies such as the Army Corps of Engineers, the Soil Conservation Service (now known as the Natural Resources Conservation Service) and the Federal Energy Regulatory Commission (FERC) have funded and approved water resource projects designed to achieve multiple objectives which in turn required watershed-based planning and management. Early federal initiatives typically involved basinwide projects for flood control, municipal water supply, irrigation, hydroelectric power generation, recreation, and water quality improvement as part of a single project.

Section 3 of the 1917 Newland Act, 33 U.S.C. § 701 (1988) (repealed 1994), gave the Corps authority to undertake a comprehensive study of watersheds for flood control improvements. The Corps reports served as the basis for most river planning documents for the next several decades. Early basinwide plans tended to address water resource development rather than quality and focus on structural solutions rather than nonstructural pollution control-based planning. In the early 1960s, the focus of water resources management turned from a large basinwide economic development approach to a more regional development and water quality protection approach.

The Water Resources Planning Act of 1965 (WRPA), 42 U.S.C. § 1962 (1988 & Supp. V. 1993), evolved from several years of congressional review of river basin management plans. The WRPA recognized water pollution as a major national concern and attempted to coordinate federal programs to address both water quantity and quality. It did not result in significant change in national water policy, however, because Congress was unwilling to put regulatory teeth into the law or to cede any authority to local or regional basin entities.

The Federal Water Pollution Control Act of 1972, Pub. L. No. 92–500, 86 Stat. 816 (1972) (Clean Water Act or CWA), provided the United States Environmental Protection Agency (EPA) with authority and funding mechanisms specifically directed to watershed protection. The Clean Water Act's principal purpose was the restoration and maintenance of the "chemical, physical and biological integrity of the nation's waters." Section 102(a) of the Act directed EPA, in cooperation with other federal agencies, states and dischargers, to "prepare or develop comprehensive plans for preventing, reducing or eliminating pollution in navigable waters and ground waters." Section 102(c) and (d) provided federal grants for states to develop comprehensive water control plans consistent with the basin planning process under the Water Resources Planning Act. Section 208 of the CWA required states to develop "area wide waste treatment management plans" including land use-based pollution sources.

Despite all the available CWA statutory authority to begin watershed protection, implementation of these provisions has been limited because EPA and states initially focused on point source dischargers under section 402 of the CWA, the National Pollutant Discharge Elimination System (NPDES) permit program. The Water Quality Act of 1987, P.L. 100–4 (Feb. 4, 1987), added more specific planning-based approaches to the Clean Water Act, including section 319, which specifically required states to develop watershed-based approaches to polluted nonpoint source runoff. In addition, Section 320 established the national estuary program which adopts the planning and implementation of water quality management activities for an estuary's entire drainage area. Currently, there are twenty-eight approved national estuary projects.

Since the 1987 amendments to the Clean Water Act, states and federal agencies have begun to embrace watershed protection approaches seriously. A 1993 watershed management conference drew well over 1,000 participants from state and federal water resource agencies as well as other public and private organizations. The proceedings from that conference have served as a guide for many states implementing watershed protection approaches and for EPA's development of its watershed protection guidance.

In a series of guidance documents published within the last year, EPA has finally begun to define and establish a framework for implementing a watershed protection approach.

What Is the Watershed Protection Approach and Does It Make Technical Sense?

Although each watershed will have different aquatic resources, pollutant loadings, land uses and regulatory programs, it is possible to define a watershed protection approach. In its latest guidance, *Watershed Approach Framework* (Final Draft May 15, 1996), EPA defined a watershed approach as a "coordinating framework for environmental management that focuses public and private sector efforts to address the highest priority problems within hydrologically-defined geographic areas, taking into consideration both ground and surface water flow." The goals are to protect and restore aquatic ecosystems and to protect human health. To be successful, the approach must include consideration of all environmental concerns, including protection of critical habitats, such as wetlands within the watershed, in addition to protection of surface and ground waters.

Much of the momentum behind the watershed approach derives from its very clear advantages for enhancing water quality. Water quality and quantity within a receiving water are affected by the sum of human activities and environmental processes in the hydrologic basin. It makes sense to coordinate water quality management in recognition of the sum of activities. . . For example, the simple act of synchronizing wastewater discharge permits within a basin helps the permitting agency coordinate its data collection and modeling while more readily considering the combined impacts of the various dischargers and background loadings. The logical extension of this technique is the explicit consideration and management of nonpoint sources of pollutants and water consumption within the basin. The alternative approach of considering each pollutant source in isolation is not only less efficient, but also not suitable for assessing the full range of potential pollutant loads and necessary control measures.

While the watershed approach provides significant technical advantages, it can be very difficult to administer. The watershed approach is by its nature more complex than either traditional technology or water quality-based permitting. Full implementation of the watershed approach requires an understanding of: (1) the sources of each important pollutant throughout the basin; (2) the source and frequency of different rates of water flow through the system; and (3) how pollution control strategies are likely to affect the loadings and/or flows. For many pollutants (e.g., nutrients or short-lived toxics), it is desirable to understand the rate of pollutant loss from the system to avoid overestimation of loadings. The sitespecific chemistry (e.g., bioavailability and toxicity) of the pollutant may bear consideration to develop effluent limitations appropriate for the specific watershed. Finally, it may be necessary to consider two critical flow periods: the low flow events traditionally examined in wasteload allocations at which point source effluents tend to dominate, and wet weather events during which nonpoint source pollutant loadings increase. Thus, permitting agencies face a data collection effort with significant spatial and temporal demands.

A key element of most watershed protection strategies is the use of mathematical modeling to estimate water quality. A narrowly focused point source permitting approach often allowed the discharge to be considered in isolation, and background receiving water concentration was usually assumed rather than measured. The watershed approach puts all contaminant sources on an equal footing and requires a relatively sophisticated model to track all the loadings, dilutions, and attenuation mechanisms.

Another complexity associated with the watershed approach is the issue of regulatory jurisdiction. The watershed approach, by its very nature, recognizes watershed boundaries but it must also acknowledge political ones. Many significant loadings (e.g., mercury from atmospheric deposition and nutrients from septic tanks) come from diffuse and remote (from a regulatory and geographical sense) sources. Controlling these types of sources will likely require new regulatory initiatives such as evaluation and regulation of air emissions for long-distance and long-term impacts. Conversely, many of the critical issues in watershed management are under local or regional control. For example, control of development, with simultaneous control of water consumption, runoff, and septic loadings, is generally local. To be successful, watershed management must motivate local officials and taxpayers to consider impacts across jurisdictional and geographical lines.

As discussed above, a key premise of the watershed approach is that nonpoint sources can and will be controlled on a basis similar to point source dischargers. This assumption is questionable. The agencies charged with regulating water quality through the NPDES program have little or no authority over many important nonpoint sources. This regulatory gap was the subject of a recent debate within EPA regarding trading of point source and nonpoint source pollutants. The EPA Office of Enforcement, recognizing EPA's tenuous ability to regulate many nonpoint sources, wants to hold the point source discharger responsible for the performance of the nonpoint source controls. On the other hand, the Office of Water, wishing to facilitate trading, wants to minimize the point source discharger's responsibility following the trade.

While pollutant trading is relatively well established under the Clean Air Act, it is more complicated under the watershed approach because the location and timing of the relevant loadings within the watershed greatly affect the results. It may be necessary, for example, to assure that the partners in a trade affect the water quality within the same river reaches. EPA is currently developing an effluent trading guidance document to clarify how such trades may be accomplished and credited.

Complexities such as jurisdictional questions and pollutant trading associated with watershed protection have led and will continue to lead to a proliferation of different approaches. Most states are rapidly moving to a watershed based approach and many hundreds of citizen groups are becoming directly involved in those efforts. EPA has published a number of watershed protection guidance documents in the last year and maintains a site on the World Wide Web to discuss the approaches different states are adopting. EPA has even established a Watershed Academy to educate state managers on watershed protection strategies.

The need and benefits of the watershed approach are becoming increasingly clear. Local, state and federal agencies are beginning to use any regulatory mandates available to them to further the watershed approach. Efforts are underway to reorganize regulatory agencies, to revamp the data collection and permitting processes, and to involve stakeholders to an unprecedented degree. In many cases, the state agencies and even the citizen watershed groups are out in front of EPA as the case studies below illustrate. Water pollution control agencies agree that the low-hanging fruit has been picked on the water pollution control tree. The watershed approach, despite its complexity, is a cost-effective means to provide the next highest level of water quality.

NOTES & QUESTIONS

1. Taylor and Gerath adopt an EPA definition of "the watershed approach" that calls for a "coordinating framework for environmental management that focuses public and private sector efforts to address the highest priority problems within hydrologically-defined geographic areas, taking into consideration both ground and surface water flow." Putting aside, for the moment, the rather open-ended nature of that definition, many other commentators have agreed with the core premise of adopting the hydrologically-defined geographic area of a watershed as the unit of water resources ecosystem management policy. This approach, they posit, fairly closely ties the unit to the "problem-shed" within which the relevant socioeconomic and environmental dynamics play out. *See* J.B. Ruhl, et al., *Proposal for a Model State Watershed Management Act*, 33 ENVTL. L. 929 (2003) (excerpted later in this chapter); A. Dan Tarlock, *The Potential Role of Local Governments in Watershed Management*, 32 ENVTL. L. REP. (ELI) 11273 (2002); Joe Cannon, *Choices and Institutions in Watershed Management*, 25 WM. & MARY ENVTL. L. & POLICY REV. 379 (2000); William Goldfarb, *Watershed Management: Slogan or Solution*, 21 B.C. ENVTL. AFF. L. REV. 483 (1994); A. Dan Tarlock, *Reconnecting Property Rights to Watersheds*, 25 WM. & MARY ENVTL. L. & POLICY REV. 69 (2000).

2. Notwithstanding their general endorsement of the watershed-based approach in theory, most of these same authors, and many like them, would also agree with Professor Goldfarb's general assessment that "analysis of the concept's historical evolution and current applications discloses that it lacks specific descriptive or operational meaning. There are also significant theoretical problems in defining and applying watershed management." Goldfarb, *supra*, at 504. The devil, in other words, is in the details. For example, while there is general concurrence that a watershed-based approach is most likely the best, if not the necessary, approach to take for addressing nonpoint source pollution, few agree on how to do it. Basic design issues have to be hammered out before the watershed approach becomes more than a theory. Thus, in his epic exploration of the details of the watershed approach, Robert Adler identifies five core design issues for resolution, which can be summarized as follows:

- *scale*: What is the appropriate scale? Are programs that cover broadly defined regions more appropriate than those on a smaller scale? What is the right unit of watershed for watershed-based approaches, taking into account the tension that exists between appropriate ecological considerations and necessary political realities?

- *boundary*: What are appropriate boundaries? Should aquatic ecosystem restoration and protection programs be organized according to natural, rather than political boundaries. Should programs be based on watersheds? Ducksheds? Forestsheds? Bearsheds? How can we reconcile the overlapping nature of the physical boundaries of watersheds, the ecological boundaries that may be more open and complex, and existing political and decision making boundaries?

- *control*: Simply, who's in charge? Is the watershed approach a "bottom-up" or "top-down" political process? Is it a federal concern or a state concern? How does public participation enter the decision making process?

- *mission*: What is the fundamental mission of watershed programs? Will watershed management be primarily procedural, as in serving a coordination function, or substantive, as in imposing regulatory standards and constraints?

- *consistency*: How consistent need be, and can be, the various national and regional watershed approaches? To what extent does consistency limit flexibility to adapt to varying ecological factors?

See Robert W. Adler, *Addressing Barriers to Watershed Protection*, 25 ENVTL. L. 973, 1088–1104 (1995); Robert W. Adler, *Model Watershed Protection*, 18 NATIONAL WETLANDS NEWSLETTER 7, 8 (July-Aug. 1996). As you review the remaining materials in this section illustrating various approaches and applications of the watershed approach, consider how coherently they articulate answers to Adler's five factors.

b. APPROACHES

Department of Agriculture, Department of Commerce, Department of Defense, Department of Energy, Department of the Interior, Environmental Protection Agency, Tennessee Valley Authority, Army Corps of Engineers, *Unified Federal Policy for a Watershed Approach to Federal Land and Resource Management*

65 Federal Register 62566 (Oct. 8, 2000).

Background

More than 800 million acres of the Nation's land are managed by Federal agencies. These public lands contain significant physical and biological resources and are important to millions of Americans for multiple uses, such as drinking water, irrigation, transportation, recreation, and wildlife habitat. Federal land managers are responsible for protecting and restoring these resources.

The objective of the Federal Water Pollution Control Act of 1972, as amended, which is commonly referred to as the Clean Water Act, is to "restore and maintain the chemical, physical and biological integrity of the Nation's waters." Although Federal agencies are working to implement the applicable requirements of the Clean Water Act, further progress is needed both to prevent degradation of high quality waters and sensitive aquatic ecosystems and to accelerate the restoration of degraded water resources. This policy provides a foundation to help ensure that Federal land and resource management activities meet these goals and that the Federal government serves as a model for water quality stewardship.

Unified Federal Policy for a Watershed Approach to Federal Land and Resource Management

Introduction

Federal agencies manage large amounts of public lands throughout the country. To protect water quality and aquatic ecosystems on these public lands, Federal agencies have developed the following policy to reduce water pollution from Federal activities and foster a unified, watershed-based approach to Federal land and resource management. This policy is intended to accelerate Federal progress towards achieving the goals of the Clean Water Act (Federal Water Pollution Control Act of 1972, 33 U.S.C. § 1251 et seq.). This policy applies only to Federal lands and resources and does not affect water rights laws, procedures, or regulations. This policy does not supersede or otherwise affect existing State or Tribal authority under the Clean Water Act. The Federal agencies also acknowledge that, in international waters, the watershed approach is subject to the international treaties and agreements affecting those waters.

I. Policy Goals

We, the Federal agencies who have signed this policy, are committed to managing the Federal lands, resources, and facilities in our care as models of good stewardship and effective watershed management.

We recognize that State, Tribal, and local programs for watershed protection and improvement are currently underway and producing positive results. We also recognize the success of locally led, voluntary, watershed groups in planning and implementing water quality improvement actions. This policy seeks to build upon those existing efforts and expand cooperation among Federal, Tribal, State and local partners. This policy will enhance these programs by improving consistency among Federal agency watershed protection programs. We acknowledge that those Federal agencies without established programs will face an additional challenge to implement this policy and that the pace and level of implementation will vary by agency.

The following policy has two goals: (1) Use a watershed approach to prevent and reduce pollution of surface and ground waters resulting from Federal land and resource management activities; and (2) Accomplish this in a unified and cost-effective manner.

To develop a unified Federal policy that meets these two goals, we incorporated the following guiding principles:

A. Use a consistent and scientific approach to manage Federal lands and resources and to assess, protect, and restore watersheds.

B. Identify specific watersheds in which to focus our funding and personnel and accelerate improvements in water quality, aquatic habitat, and watershed conditions.

C. Use the results of watershed assessments to guide planning and management activities in accordance with applicable authorities and procedures.

D. Work closely with States, Tribes, local governments, private landowners, and stakeholders to implement this policy.

E. Meet our Clean Water Act responsibility to comply with applicable Federal, State, Tribal, interstate, and local water quality requirements to the same extent as non-governmental entities.

F. Take steps to help ensure that Federal land and resource management actions are consistent with applicable Federal, State, Tribal, and local government water quality management programs.

II. Agency Objectives

To accomplish these policy goals, we propose to use existing funding, personnel, and authorities to pursue the following objectives. All agencies will implement this policy as individual agency laws, missions, funding, and fiscal and budgetary authorities permit.

A. We will develop a science-based approach to watershed assessment for Federal lands. Watershed assessment information will become part of the basis for identifying management opportunities and priorities and for developing alternatives to protect or restore watersheds.

1. We will develop consistent procedures for delineating, assessing, and classifying watersheds.

2. We will conduct assessments of watersheds that have significant Federal lands and resources.

B. We will use a watershed management approach when protecting and restoring watersheds.

1. We will work collaboratively to identify priority watersheds.

2. Using existing legal authorities, we will develop a process and guidelines for identifying and designating waters or watersheds on Federal lands that may have significant human health, public use, or aquatic ecosystem values and a need for special protection.

3. We will implement pollution prevention and controls, consistent with applicable legal authorities.

4. We will improve watershed conditions through restoration and adaptive management. We will strive to work with States, Tribes, local governments, private landowners, and interested stakeholders to improve the condition of priority watersheds. Changes in management strategies and restoration efforts will focus on watersheds where Federal land and resource management activities can meaningfully influence surface and ground water quality and aquatic resources.

5. We will base watershed management on scientific principles and methods. We will use scientific information from research and management experience in designing and implementing watershed planning and management programs, and setting management goals (e.g., desired conditions). To expand current knowledge, we will collaborate to identify research needs and contribute to or sponsor research, as appropriate.

6. We will identify and incorporate watershed management goals into our planning, programs, and actions. We will periodically review and amend, as appropriate, policies and management plans for Federal lands and resources to meet goals for watershed protection and improvement. We will incorporate adaptive management principles into our programs. Our watershed goals will seek to minimize adverse water quality impacts due to ongoing and future management programs, minimize impairment of current or future uses, and restore watersheds where applicable State and Tribal water quality requirements under the Clean Water Act are not achieved due to activities occurring on Federal lands.

7. We will help Tribes and States develop science-based total maximum daily loads (TMDLs). We will assist and support State and Tribal efforts to develop and implement TMDLs in watersheds with significant Federal land and resource management activities. We will provide technical assistance, tools, and expertise. We will use TMDL results in watershed planning and subsequent resource management activities to meet applicable State and Tribal water quality requirements under the Clean Water Act.

Glossary of Terms

These definitions are intended only to help you understand the policy better, and do not change the meanings of terms defined by law or regulation.

Adaptive management: A type of natural resource management in which decisions are made as part of an ongoing science-based process. Adaptive management involves testing, monitoring, and evaluating applied strategies, and incorporating new knowledge into management approaches that are based on scientific findings and the needs of society. Results are used to modify management policy, strategies, and practices.

Watershed: A geographic area of land, water, and biota within the confines of a drainage divide. The total area above a given point of a water body that contributes flow to that point.

Watershed approach: A framework to guide watershed management that: (1) uses watershed assessments to determine existing and reference conditions; (2) incorporates assessment results into resource management planning; and (3) fosters collaboration with all landowners in the watershed. The framework considers both ground and surface water flow within a hydrologically defined geographical area.

Watershed assessment: An analysis and interpretation of the physical and landscape characteristics of a watershed using scientific principles to describe watershed conditions as they affect water quality and aquatic resources. Initial watershed assessments will be conducted using existing data, where available. Data gaps may suggest the collection of additional data.

Watershed condition: The state of the watershed based on physical and biogeochemical characteristics and processes (e.g., hydrologic, geomorphic, landscape, topographic, vegetative cover, and aquatic habitat), water flow characteristics and processes (e.g., volume and timing), and water quality characteristics and processes (e.g., chemical, physical, and biological), as it affects water quality and water resources.

U.S. EPA, Office of Water, *Draft Framework for Watershed-Based Trading*

(May 1996).

EXECUTIVE SUMMARY

Why Is EPA Publishing This Framework Now?

In response to President Clinton's *Reinventing Environmental Regulation* (March 1995), EPA is strongly promoting the use of watershed-based trading. Trading is an innovative way for water quality agencies and community stakeholders to develop common-sense, cost-effective solutions for water quality problems in their watersheds. Community stakeholders include states and water quality agencies, local governments, point source dischargers, contributors to nonpoint source pollution, citizen groups, other federal agencies, and the public at large. Trading can allow communities to grow and prosper while retaining their commitment to water quality.

The bulk of this framework discusses effluent trading in watersheds. Remaining sections discuss transactions that, while not technically fulfilling the definition of "effluent" trades, do involve the exchange of valued water quality or other ecological improvements between partners responding to market initiatives. This document therefore includes activities such as trades within a facility (intra-plant trading) and wetland mitigation banking.

Trading and Water Quality

Trading is not a retreat from Clean Water Act (CWA) goals. It can be a more efficient, market-driven approach to meet those goals. EPA supports only trades that meet existing CWA water quality requirements.

Similarly, support for trading does not represent any change in EPA's traditional enforcement responsibilities under the CWA. EPA encourages innovation in meeting water quality goals but will not depart from its enforcement and compliance responsibilities under the CWA. Trades that depend on fundamental chance in EPA's enforcement and compliance responsibilities will not be allowed.

EPA encourages trades that will result in desired pollution controls at appropriate locations and scales. Water quality standards must be met throughout watersheds. A buyer cannot arrange for reductions from a downstream discharger if violations of water quality standards would result. Generally, trades will shift additional load reductions to upstream sources. Thus, discharges will be reduced in the area between the sources.

Trading Provides Flexibility

Trading provides watershed managers with opportunities to facilitate implementing loading reductions in a way that maximizes water quality and ecological improvements. Managers can encourage trades that result in desired pollution controls, preferred reduction locations, and optimal scales for effective efforts.

Trading can fully use the flexibility of existing regulatory programs. The following examples illustrate this flexibility and demonstrate how trading can contribute to the cost-effectiveness of meeting water quality objectives.

Trading Encourages Environmental Benefits

Regardless of who trades and how, the common goal of trading is achieving water quality objectives, including water quality standards, more cost-effectively. Some communities will use trading to meet their waterbodies' designated uses at a lower cost than the cost without trading. Other communities will use trading to expand a waterbody's designated uses for the same amount they would have spent preserving fewer uses without trading. Communities can also use trading to maintain water quality in the face of proposed new discharges.

In particular, trading offers significant opportunities to expand non-point source pollution reductions beyond current levels. Point/nonpoint and nonpoint/nonpoint trading can facilitate nonpoint source reductions where they otherwise would not have occurred. In so doing, it can help address one of the sources of water pollution that is most persistent and difficult to reduce (economically, technically, and politically).

Beyond implementing trades, the process communities go through when they consider a trading option moves them toward more complete management approaches and more effective environmental protection. Identifying trading opportunities involves examining all pollution sources at once when evaluating technical and financial capabilities to achieve loading reductions. This brings regulated and unregulated sources together with other watershed stakeholders and engages them in a partnership to solve water quality problems.

Economic Benefits of Trading

One of the most immediately visible benefits of trading is the money some sources save while meeting pollution control responsibilities. Sources that "sell" loading reductions can also benefit financially and can invest proceeds in research and development, for example, or use them to offset other costs.

These economic benefits reach beyond dischargers to consumers and communities. Trading can keep municipal wastewater treatment or storm-water utility charges from increasing as quickly or by as much as they might without trading. Trading also can keep costs to consumers down as industry and business save on pollution control costs.

Who Might Trade?

Many sources or contributors to water pollution might consider trading. Point source dischargers, nonpoint sources, and indirect dischargers may all participate in trades.

Point sources are direct dischargers that introduce pollutants into waters of the United States. Examples of point sources include [publicly owned treatment works (POTWs)], private wastewater treatment facilities, industrial dischargers, federal facilities that discharge pollutants. active and inactive mining operations, aquaculture operations, and municipal stormwater outfalls (generally communities with populations over 100,000). Point sources are regulated under the National Pollutant Discharge Elimination System (NPDES) established under section 402 of the CWA. Many point source dischargers are required to comply with national discharge standards developed for industrial categories.

Indirect dischargers are industrial or commercial (i.e., nonresidential) dischargers that discharge pollutants to a POTW. Many indirect dischargers "pretreat" their wastewater prior to releasing effluent to POTW collection systems. Pretreatment includes pollution prevention and waste minimization practices, as well as on-site and off-site pollution control technology. Indirect dischargers are regulated under certain circumstances by POTWs according to CWA requirements. Many indirect dischargers also comply with national discharge standards developed for industrial categories.

Nonpoint sources are more diffuse, conveying pollution via erosion, runoff, and snowmelt to surface waters. Nonpoint sources also pollute groundwater via infiltration; this pollution can sometimes reach surface waters. Nonpoint sources include agriculture, silviculture, urban development, construction, land disposal, and modification of flow and channel structure. The CWA does not require federal controls for nonpoint sources. Instead, it requires that states, with EPA funding and technical support, develop and implement programs to control nonpoint sources.

Five Types of Trading in a Watershed Context

Generally, the term "trading" describes any agreement between parties contributing to water quality problems on the same waterbody that alters the allocation of pollutant reduction responsibilities among the sources. Such agreements also may include third parties, such as state agencies, local agencies, or brokerage entities. This framework groups trades into five categories:

1. **Point/Point Source Trading:** a point source(s) arranges for another point source(s) to undertake greater-than-required reductions in pollutant discharge in lieu of reducing its own level of pollutant discharge, beyond the minimum technology-based discharge standards, to achieve water quality objectives more cost-effectively.

2. **Intra-plant Trading:** a point source allocates pollutant discharges among its outfalls in a cost-effective manner, provided that the combined permitted discharge with trading is no greater than the combined permitted discharge without trading and discharge from each outfall complies with the requirements necessary to meet applicable water quality standards.

3. **Pretreatment Trading:** an indirect industrial source(s) that discharges to a POTW arranges for greater-than-required reductions in pollutant discharge by other indirect sources in lieu of upgrading its own pretreatment beyond the minimum technology-based discharge standards, to achieve water quality goals more cost-effectively.

4. **Point/Nonpoint Source Trading:** a point source(s) arranges for control of pollutants from nonpoint source(s) to undertake greater-than-required pollutant reductions in lieu of upgrading its own treatment beyond the minimum technology-based discharge standards, to achieve water quality objectives more cost effectively.

5. **Nonpoint/Nonpoint Source Trading:** a nonpoint source(s) arranges for more cost-effective control of other nonpoint sources in lieu

of installing or upgrading its own control or implement pollution prevention practices.

These categorizations are broad and might not reflect all possible trading combinations. As communities gain experience with trading and as EPA improves its understanding of the opportunities afforded by watershed-based decision making, the Agency will provide information about additional forms of trading.

Trading Arrangements

Trading arrangements can take many different forms. There are varying degrees of complexity related to the number of partners involved, the pollutant or reduction traded, and the form of the trade. Trading programs that involve point sources or indirect discharges require EPA's preapproval of trades.

Under trading arrangements, the total pollutant reduction must be the same or greater than what would be achieved if no trade occurred. A "buyer" and "seller" agree to a trade in which the buyer compensates the seller to reduce pollutant loads. Buyers purchase pollutant reductions at a lower cost than what they would spend to achieve the reductions themselves. Sellers provide pollutant reductions and may receive compensation.

Sources may negotiate trades bilaterally or may trade within the context of an organized program. Sources may negotiate prices or exchange rates for loading reductions themselves, or they may face those established by a market. A buyer and seller may be the only parties to trading, or third parties—public or private—may become involved.

NOTES & QUESTIONS

1. Using Adler's proposed set of five factors that define watershed-based programs (see previous section), fill in this table to describe and compare the two programs outlined in the preceding agency policy statements:

	Unified Federal Land Management Policy	EPA Watershed Trading Policy
scale		
boundary		
control		
mission		
consistency		

Do either of the policies provide sufficient detail to allow you clearly to articulate how it approaches each of these design factors? If so, are watershed-based approaches really as hard to assemble as Adler and others suggest? If, on the other hand, you had difficulty expressing how the policies address these design issues, does that suggest the watershed-based approach as a general matter has limited utility? Could the policy statements be more clearly articulated? What language or other editing, *specifically*, would you recommend for doing so?

2. Now that you've described the basic design parameters of the two programs, can you articulate them as ecosystem management policies? Try doing so using the three components of ecosystem management policy articulated in Chapter 7:

	Metric	*Goal*	*Method*
Unified Federal Land Management Policy			
EPA Watershed Trading Policy			

Again, do the policy statements allow you to describe the underlying ecosystem management frameworks with sufficient clarity? Do the ecosystem management frameworks of the two policies differ substantially?

3. The Unified Federal Policy says that the signatory agencies will manage federal lands using a science-based watershed management approach. What does "science-based" mean, and what other approaches does it preclude? Who makes decisions using a "science-based" approach? Scientists? Is the public not a part of a "science-based" approach? Would you be comfortable leaving federal land management policy decisions exclusively to scientists? What if the scientists can't agree?

4. The watershed-based trading program EPA described is known as a "cap and trade" program, because government regulation of some form limits the available "commodity" being traded in order to create scarcity, and thus the incentive to trade. This is an inherent necessity in pollutant trading programs, for in the absence of a cap, pollutant dischargers would have no incentive to trade. It may sound straightforward, but as Richard E. Ayers has outlined, a number of difficult design questions confront efforts to institute such cap and trade programs. *See* Richard E. Ayers, *Expanding the Use of Environmental Trading Programs into New Areas of Environmental Regulation*, 18 Pace Envtl. L. Rev. 87,106–112 (2000). In summary, these are:

- *Determining the scope and geographical extent of the market.* Usually this means corresponding the trading "shed" to the resource unit in question, such as a watershed, but this can cause complications when the resource shed is very small (few traders) or large (lack of control over geographic distribution of trades).

- *Determining the geographic relationship between parties.* There may be areas within the resource shed that are of critical environmental value and thus off limits to trading. Or there may be directional issues within the resource shed, such as water flow, that influence who may trade what with whom. And, for a variety of reasons, trading could lead to "hot spots," areas where far more buying than selling of rights to pollute occurs, which could disproportionately expose the local human populations or ecological resources to adverse effects.

- *Determining the types of pollution sources permitted to be traded.* For example, if the concern in a watershed is nutrient pollution, which pollutants can be cross-traded, and between whom? There are many kinds and sources of nitrogen-based nutrients. As the trading unit becomes more universal, the scarcity of tradable units falls.

- *Determining a baseline.* A cap and trade program, to be effective, must ensure that the cap is lower than existing discharges. Determining this baseline of existing levels of emissions is an essential first step.

- *Determining the allocation of emission rights.* Unlike programs based on auctioning of emission rights or taxing use of rights, cap and trade programs require a mechanism of initially allocating the emission units being traded. This could be based on past emission levels of each trader, or past emission efficiency (e.g., units of pollutants emitted per unit of production).

- *Determining the method of quality assurance.* How will we know, as trading takes place, that emission rights that are "retired" or "moved" as part of a trade are actually retired or not emitted by both parties?

How well does the watershed-based trading policy EPA outlined in 1996 address these determinations?

5. The Clinton Administration conceived of both the Clean Water Action Plan, from which the watershed-based trading policy was spawned, and the Unified Federal Policy late in its tenure. The Bush Administration barely acknowledged their existence, but aggressively pursued watershed-based water policy. Examples include:

- In December 2002 EPA issued a memorandum to its water program staff entitled *A Renewed Commitment to Watershed Management.* This general policy overview commits the agency to "the watershed approach" through tighter program integration, more funding of state and local capacity, and fostering innovative approaches. *See* Memorandum from G. Tracy Meehan, III, Assistant Administrator to Office Directors Re Committing EPA's Water Programs to Advancing the Watershed Approach (Dec. 3, 2002).

- In January 2003 EPA issued a new Water Quality Trading Policy describing effluent trading as "a voluntary, incentive-based approach that can offer greater efficiency in restoring or protecting water bodies." U.S. EPA, Water Quality Trading Policy (2003); 68 Fed. Reg. 1608 (Jan. 13, 2003). Like its predecessor excerpted in the text, the new policy takes a strong watershed-based focus. In December 2003 Clean Water Services of Hillsboro, a wastewater utility in the suburbs of Portland, was the first entity to receive a permit under the policy, consolidating four separate facility permits and an urban runoff permit into one that also allows for trading of effluent pollution credits between the facilities. For a series of commentaries on the 2003 policy, see The Forum, *Emissions Trading Moves to Water, But It's Not as Simple,* The Environmental Forum, Mar.-Apr. 2003, at 62.

- In December 2003 EPA issued a policy moving the NPDES permitting system toward the watershed-based approach. *See* U.S. EPA, Watershed-Based National Pollutant Discharge Elimination System (NPDES) Permitting Implementation Guidance (Dec. 17, 2003). The focus of the guidance is to develop a framework for coordinating multiple NPDES source permits within a defined watershed.

- In November 2004 EPA and the Corps of Engineers entered into an agreement to coordinate both agencies' watershed-based efforts. *See* U.S. EPA and U.S. Department of the Army, Partnership Agreement for Watershed Management (Nov. 19, 2004).

- In October 2005 EPA released its Handbook for Developing Watershed Plans to Restore and Protect Our Waters, designed as a roadmap for federal, state, and local governments to assemble and implement watershed planning initiatives, in particular for complying with Clean Water Act NPDES permitting and TMDL requirements (both of which are discussed in section C.2 of this section of the text).

Endorsing these sources and the Clinton-era policies, the Obama Administration continued to pursue a watershed focus. *See* http://water.epa.gov/type/watersheds/approach.cfm. No comprehensive watershed-based legislation has surfaced from Congress, however. In the absence of such legislation, how far can agencies go with the watershed-based approach?

6. States have also begun to adopt watershed-based programs. Vermont adopted legislation in 2004 (H. 785) requiring its Agency of Natural Resources to develop remediation plans for the state's 17 watersheds impaired by stormwater runoff. New Mexico adopted legislation in 2003 (H.B. 910) requiring its Energy, Minerals, and Natural Resources Department to develop a strategy to restore the natural ecology of watersheds in the state. For a review of these other state efforts, see U.S. EPA, OFFICE OF WATER, A REVIEW OF STATEWIDE WATERSHED MANAGEMENT APPROACHES-FINAL REPORT (Apr. 2002). By and large, however, state initiatives follow no particular model. As the following article suggests, perhaps state watershed planning should begin with a coherent approach to the institutional arrangements necessary for establishing both political legitimacy and meaningful authority.

J.B. Ruhl, Christopher Lant, Tim Loftus, Steven Kraft, Jane Adams, & Leslie Duram, *Proposal for a Model State Watershed Management Act*

33 Environmental Law 929 (2003).

I. INTRODUCTION

The progress of watershed management stands at a fork in the political road. It is widely agreed that implementing watershed management, to the extent it grows in importance as an organizing policy foundation, is complicated by the mismatch between watershed boundaries and conventional political boundaries. Finding the right "fit" between the two realms presents difficult choices when constructing political institutions. On the one hand, as we increasingly understand that the "problemshed" of most water quality and water quantity issues corresponds more closely to geographically delineated watersheds, proposals for new watershed-based political structures have grown more focused. On the other hand, many local government authorities have extended beyond their traditional role as land-use regulators into environmental protection and resource conservation, giving many watershed management advocates hope that existing local political structures may play a central role in shaping and implementing watershed management policy. Watershed management, it seems, is as much a political science as it is a physical science.

The connection between the physical and political dynamics of watersheds has become increasingly apparent. Decades ago researchers demonstrated that land-use patterns within watersheds have a dominant influence on the hydrologic regime, water quality, and physical habitat of streams and rivers, and on the ecological interactions that take place in the aquatic ecosystem. More recently, researchers have targeted restoring the physical integrity of rivers while using a watershed framework across a wide range of geographic environments, focusing on facilitating the dynamics of rivers as the key to reversing the rapid decline of aquatic ecosystems in the United States. In short, watershed-based problems—including river fragmentation from the construction of dams, the loss of riverine wetlands, and the separation of river channels from floodplains through levees— demand watershed-based solutions.

Accordingly, the need for watershed-based land-use and resource management has gradually been integrated into concrete policy objectives. The idea itself is not new by any means, and numerous historical antecedents to watershed-based policy frameworks exist, but none are as comprehensive as what we are witnessing today. It is not surprising, therefore, that the National Research Council recently concluded that "[m]any factors are converging to cause citizens, scientists, resource managers, and government decisionmakers to look increasingly to watershed management as an approach for addressing a wide range of water-related problems."

Nevertheless, while the need for a watershed-based approach has become a basic tenet of policy, it is not nearly as clear how to match political structures to the problem so defined. The EPA has established the Watershed Management Council, comprised of representatives from the agency's headquarters and regional offices, to integrate the watershed into the agency's planning and policy apparatus. But the initiative contemplates no explicit federal, state, or local governance structure for watershed management. Indeed, EPA observes that there can be many variations in the specific approaches states use to implement programs on a watershed basis and thus declines to suggest a particular watershed management model, leaving it instead for the states to implement the approaches they find work best for them. Yet, while we applaud EPA's movement toward the watershed approach, we are concerned with the agency's apparent indifference to the absence of a model for the development of state watershed management law.

Being far from indifferent about the matter, in this Article we take the step of proposing a framework for a model state watershed management law. Our model law establishes a three-tiered governance structure within which the authority, expertise, and accountability for watershed-based decision making are carefully distributed so as to balance the physical and political realities of watersheds and watershed management. In Part II of this Article we lay out what we believe are the critical design parameters for any legal framework intended to implement the watershed management approach across large geographic scales. In Part III we explain our reasons for proposing a model state enabling law rather than either a comprehensive federal regulatory law or a model local ordinance. In Part IV we outline the basic theoretical underpinnings of the approach we have taken in our model state law. Part V then outlines the key features of the model law, providing annotated explanations of and justifications for its critical components.

II. DESIGN PARAMETERS FOR WATERSHED MANAGEMENT LAW

The objective of treating watershed-based problems through watershed-based political institutions raises many foundational issues. In particular, three themes emerge as critical to the discussion of watershed-based political structures. First, watersheds, even where they can be clearly delineated, come in many sizes, and their different scales often are "nested" in hierarchies of relatedness. In a large riverine system, for example, the cumulative impacts of land-use actions taken in countless small tributary watersheds may have profound impacts in the river mainstem and estuary. Seasonal hypoxia in the northern Gulf of Mexico offers a striking example of such cumulative impacts. Hence, one core issue of watershed management is the scale at which to design watershed-based political institutions and how the related nature of different physical scales can be reflected in political boundaries.

Second, even using watershed-based political boundaries, water quality and water quantity issues cannot always be described and addressed though intrashed features, or even through exclusively water-based features. Air pollution from sources within or even beyond a watershed's boundary may profoundly affect its water quality, and water supply demands from local or distant populations can impair water availability in a watershed. Yet as the political unit's scope of authority increases both in geographic extent and in subject matter, the institution's legitimacy to effect change at local levels may be more difficult to establish and maintain. Accordingly, once their boundaries are delineated, what is the appropriate geographic and substantive scope of authority for watershed-based political units?

Finally, as watershed-based political institutions would serve limited purposes, conventional political entities such as cities and counties would surely continue to exist for many other purposes. Presumably, however, some of the authority previously enjoyed by various existing political entities would be transferred to or shared by the new watershed-based institutional structure. Thus, watershed management policy must confront the question of how watershed-based political institutions will be "overlain" on the existing political framework such that these divisions of authority are clear and respected. Our study of the issue has led us to conclude that several overarching institutional design goals should shape the approach taken to answering these three foundational questions. The institutional design goals are as follows:

1) The institutional structure for watershed management must enjoy the type of power and authority generally associated with centralized administrative governments, such as the federal or state governments, but must also be capable of establishing democratically based legitimacy at regional and local levels where many regulatory actions are implemented. This requires going beyond federal or state laws enabling local districts to take action. Rather, much like watersheds themselves, a nested hierarchy of interrelated federal, state, and local governmental authorities will be necessary.

2) The institutional structure must have the authority and the responsibility to manage watershed issues "holistically" on a system level. This requires, at a minimum, some form and level of authority over surface and ground water, over water quality and water quantity, and over key physical and biological effects on aquatic ecosystems such as flood control, soil conservation, wetlands conservation, fisheries, recreation, stream entrenchment, dams, reservoirs, pollutant sources, and land uses with significant watershed impacts.

3) The institutional structure must rely on more than voluntary governance and voluntary compliance with specified standards and goals. In particular, where implementation relies on local units of governance, accountability must be lodged at the local level. The full range of financing mechanisms should be made available (e.g., taxes, fees, surcharges, bonds) and the full range of compliance instruments should be capable of being used effectively as appropriate (e.g., regulatory, market-based, incentives, reporting and information requirements, planning requirements, voluntary).

4) The institutional structure must have the capacity—the budget, staff, and expertise—to carry out complex scientific, economic, and social analysis functions, as well as the responsibility to make policy and regulatory decisions through public, transparent procedures based on the record of best available evidence it generates through its capacities.

5) The institutional structure should be generalizable across watershed types, scales, and political units, and the information gathering capacity and protocols should be standardized so as to allow sharing of information vertically (e.g., within a state from local to higher levels) and horizontally (e.g., between local districts and between states).

Our proposed framework for a model state watershed management law is intended to make these five design goals operational. A critical premise of our approach, to which we turn in the next section, is that doing this requires a comprehensive and coordinated effort led by the states—that is, not the federal or local governments—and implemented at several levels of governance within each state.

III. The Need For A State-Level Watershed Management Initiative

Many of our nation's environmental policy concerns have been addressed through comprehensive federal regulatory laws, such as the Clean Water Act and Clean Air Act, that rely heavily on nationally prescribed standards and centralized regulatory and policy decision making. While states often play a large role in administration and enforcement of these federal statutes, federal authority is paramount and local autonomy is minimal. These laws have unquestionably led to tremendous gains in environmental quality, but their model is seldom offered as the solution to issues most frequently cited as the challenges of the future for environmental policy, such as diffuse nonpoint source water pollution from urban and agricultural land uses.

Indeed, several factors strongly suggest that a comprehensive federal regulatory law is not the most effective or efficient vehicle for carrying out the policy challenges our design parameters present. First, watersheds vary across many dimensions throughout the national landscape and respond primarily to local land-use and water-use actions. It is difficult to envision a set of nationally uniform standards, such as the approach taken in the Clean Water Act and Clean Air Act, for managing them that could be efficiently implemented. Second, support for centralized regulation of natural resources, in general, has eroded the desire for more state and local control of key land-use decisions has intensified. A federal regulatory statute governing watershed management would thus risk failure to establish legitimacy at local levels.

On the other hand, we would not suggest that the federal government remove itself entirely from the objective of influencing state and local watershed management initiatives. Federal law can be useful as a motivator for state action without intruding on basic design choices. There undoubtedly are some national objectives for watershed management (*e.g.*, to address nonpoint source pollution; to conserve endangered species), which, while not lending themselves to nationally uniform standards, may nonetheless justify federal support for states that satisfy the national concerns as they become increasingly and more formally involved in watershed management within their boundaries. A federal watershed initiative could express broad national goals and standards and establish a mechanism for states to submit their respective watershed management programs for federal approval, offering in return federal financial support for design and implementation as well as the commitment that federal agencies will not carry out, fund, or authorize actions inconsistent with the state plan. At the very least, the federal government can and ought to maintain an important role as a source of scientific data and research that has broad usefulness to state-based watershed institutions and as an environmental engineering contractor. At the most, however, the federal government might consider ways to influence state policy through a statute, like the CZMA, that provides cooperative support for state action. Full-blown command-and-control style federal regulation imposing watershed management is not advised.

For different reasons, but equally as compelling, effective watershed management regimes cannot rely exclusively on the initiative of local governance, particularly if channeled through conventional local political entities. Even putting aside the lack of match between conventional local political boundaries and watersheds, local governments face several constraints to effective watershed management. First, while most state political systems allow considerable local authority—certainly enough to establish watershed ordinances—management of transboundary effects often lies outside their authority or is able to be undertaken only through burdensome interlocal coordination procedures. Second, many watershed management issues will present difficult political choices with potentially significant economic consequences, and local governments, particularly those constituted by popular election, may be reluctant to make economic sacrifices not being made by others. Finally, even with most local governments committed to watershed management, it is doubtful that all could afford the intensive scientific, social, and economic data gathering and analysis necessary to carry it out effectively. Small rural counties, for example, are already hard-pressed to support water quality requirements of the Safe Drinking Water Act. It is not surprising, therefore, that soil and water conservation districts, which in many states are elected and have political boundaries corresponding to county borders, have generally failed to live up to their promise of comprehensively managing soil and water quality issues. The emerging generation of "place-based" resource management proposals, while stressing local autonomy, should strive to avoid repeating that history.

Hence, on the one hand there is good reason to believe that the federal government should not attempt to initiate a sweeping federal regulatory scheme for national watershed management. On the other hand, watershed-based management cannot effectively rely exclusively on the initiative and authority of local governance. States, therefore, will have to carry the primary burden of designing and empowering the institutional structure for watershed management. Nevertheless, several of our design parameters also suggest that states should design their internal political frameworks around a hierarchy of physical watershed units, and should consider ways to achieve interstate coordination of their respective watershed management efforts. One advantage of initiating watershed management at the state level is to accommodate watershed policy diversity across states and within states. By sharing the same basic governance framework states can more freely exchange data and experience and thus work in a more coordinated and efficient pattern to solve both intrastate and interstate watershed problems. Developing a model framework for a state watershed management law is thus an appropriate exercise.

IV. KEY FEATURES OF THE MODEL STATE WATERSHED MANAGEMENT ACT

Our model framework for a state watershed management law draws on the experience of several states in the related fields of land-use controls and water quality management, as well as on our jointly-coordinated research in Illinois focusing on the locally perceived legitimacy of watershed planning and on the responsiveness of landowners and landscapes to differing policy environments. Several states, such as Florida, have adopted multitiered approaches to these problems of land-use planning and resource allocation. For example, Florida's land-use planning programs rely on local governments to prepare comprehensive land-use plans, which are then weighed against a set of state land-use standards for consistency with state goals. Some land-use projects also are evaluated for their regional impact— i.e., impact that extends beyond political boundaries. Therefore Florida uses a blend of different scales of authority (state, regional, and local) and sources of legitimacy (elected and appointed) in a variety of land-use and resource management contexts, and in some cases has designed political units around the resource problem rather than the reverse. Many other states have attempted to develop land-use regimes that integrate state, regional, and local planning.

Washington's Watershed Planning Act, which is based on local geographic areas known as Water Resource Inventory Areas, and Oregon's Watershed Health Program, which operates in part through Watershed Councils, provide examples of states entering the watershed management realm with this kind of integrated, hierarchical approach. Similarly, Florida uses a regional approach to manage many of its water quality and allocation issues, through its several Water Quality Management Districts, each of which is defined by regional watershed boundaries. Overall, however, most states purporting to adopt statewide watershed management approaches omit important water resource authorities from the program, such as wetlands protection, coastal land-use regulation, water quality standards, and even nonpoint source pollution control, and fail to link watershed management with local planning and zoning decisions.

Borrowing, combining, and enhancing a number of features from these examples, we have designed a multitiered approach that can distribute funding, authority, and other resources in a way that addresses many of the design parameters discussed above. In particular, our approach aims to establish legitimacy for watershed management at the local level while not sacrificing broader state and regional concerns. The framework relies on creating and coordinating institutions at three levels of government, including: 1) the state watershed management agency, 2) appointed regional watershed coordination districts, and 3) elected local watershed management councils. Each level of government must prepare a watershed management plan for its respective scale of focus. In the case of the regional and local entities, the plan must be consistent with the plan that is vertically above it in the tiered system. The state agency would continue to direct policy for matters of statewide concern, including developing a state watershed management plan, but would delegate most watershed management policy development, implementation, and enforcement authority to the regional districts. The regional districts would develop regional plans to implement the state plan, and would be the locus of most planning and policy expertise. They would have staffs including engineers, biologists, economists, hydrologic modelers, information specialists, conservation experts, and lawyers. Yet the regional districts would still rely in large part on the elected local councils for final policy development, implementation, and enforcement.

To fulfill this role, the local councils must be more than mere "special districts" (lest they wither the way many other special district initiatives have), and more than conventional local governments. The local councils would be organized around watershed-based boundaries and held account-able to state and regional interests through the requirement that their local plans be consistent with the regional (and thus state) plans. Perhaps even more importantly, local councils would coordinate the review of all land-use decisions by other existing state and local authorities, such as state high-way agencies and municipal and county zoning authorities, for consistency with the state, regional, and local watershed management plans. This would extend the policy reach of watershed planning beyond the direct management of water resources.

This framework allows our institutional structure to match the physi-cal realities of watersheds in both the vertical and horizontal dimensions. The vertical integration of local, regional, and state planning and regulato-ry authority matches the nested hierarchies of watershed scales. The abil-ity at each level of this structure to examine the horizontal impacts the de-cisions of other governmental authorities have on watershed resources matches the dynamics of watershed processes at each physical scale. Ac-counting for each of these dimensions in the institutional design is neces-sary for successful implementation of watershed management, but none of these features is sufficient alone.

V. THE PROPOSED INSTITUTIONAL FRAMEWORK

Using the three-tiered institutional structure described above, we pro-pose distributing watershed management responsibility and authority as follows:

A. *State Watershed Management Agency*

Every state has a state agency responsible for developing law and poli-cy for the protection of water quality. Many states also have a state agency or set of institutions responsible for water allocation. Under our proposal, the two functions would be consolidated into a single state agency or divi-sion referred to as the State Watershed Management Agency. This agency would continue to serve as the original authority for statewide water quali-ty and quantity regulation, and would implement federal laws, such as the Clean Water Act is water quality standards and impaired water lists. Un-der the state watershed law, however, the agency would also be required to:

1) Prepare a State Watershed Management Plan specifying the goals for watershed management in the state.

2) Delegate responsibility to Regional Watershed Coordination Agen-cies (RWCA) for implementing programs that affect "matters primarily of

regional or local watershed significance." Matters of primarily regional or local watershed significance would be defined in the statute to include: 1) rules and decisions specified in the statute and 2) any other types of rules or decisions that the State Watershed Management Agency prescribes by rule.

3) Include in its deliberations on statewide decisions and rules within its authority any information and comments supplied by RWCAs.

4) Review the Regional Watershed Management Plans for compliance with the State Watershed Management Plan and provide corrective elements in case a plan is deficient.

5) Review and comment on the actions of all other state and regional agencies that are deemed to have "substantial watershed effects." Substantial watershed effects are any effects the State Watershed Management Agency concludes could substantially interfere with the State Watershed Management Plan, any Regional Watershed Management Plan, or any Local Watershed Management Plan.

B. *Regional Watershed Coordination Agencies*

The Regional Watershed Coordination Agencies (RWCAs) will be organized based to the extent practicable on the 222 subregional hydrological units the United States Geological Survey (USGS) has defined for the nation, as constrained by state boundaries. RWCA will be appointed boards with significant staff and budgets. Because they will take over many functions previously managed by the state agency, their budgets will be state appropriated. Each RWCA will do the following:

1) Establish the Local Watershed Management Council boundaries as it deems appropriate, but to the maximum extent practicable according to the 2150 USGS watershed cataloging units.

2) Establish a Regional Watershed Management Plan (RWMP) demonstrating how it will satisfy compliance with a) all federal and state laws governing water quality and quantity, and b) the State Watershed Management Plan.

3) Decide all matters of primarily regional watershed significance that are prescribed in the statute or by the State Watershed Management Agency.

4) Review Local Watershed Management Plans and develop one for any Local Watershed Management Council that fails to meet the State Watershed Management Plan and Regional Watershed Management Plan criteria.

5) Define Special Watershed Areas.

6) Define the criteria for land-use and water project developments to be classified as a Development of Regional Watershed Impact.

7) Review local government land-use and water project decisions that are either a) in Special Watershed Areas or b) for a Development of Regional Watershed Impact, and impose the conditions it deems necessary to ensure compliance with the Regional Watershed Management Plan.

8) Hear appeals from local governments and citizens of Local Watershed Management Council decisions on local government land-use and water project development matters, including whether a project is in a Special Watershed Area or is a Development of Regional Watershed Impact.

9) Provide the scientific, economic, and social-data gathering and analysis capacity for implementation of the Regional Watershed Management Plan and the various Local Watershed Management Plans within its jurisdiction.

10) Notify the State Watershed Management Agency of any state agency or regional agency action it believes may substantially interfere with the Regional Watershed Management Plan.

11) Serve as the primary points of contact for the state with federal agencies, such as the Army Corps of Engineers, with respect to past, present, and future civil and environmental development projects that may have a substantive impact on the achievement of the Regional Watershed Management Plan.

C. *Local Watershed Management Councils*

The Local Watershed Management Councils would be generally elected local governmental bodies. They would have the following authorities and responsibilities:

1) Prepare a Local Watershed Management Plan demonstrating how the Council will achieve compliance with the Regional Watershed Management Plan.

2) Review all local government land-use and water project development applications. Local governments, defined to include municipalities, counties, and other special entities such as irrigation districts and soil conservation districts with jurisdiction extending to all or part of the Council's area, would be required to provide advance notice of their proposed actions and decisions to the Council. The Council then would either a) find the matter has no significant local watershed, regional watershed, or Special Watershed Area impacts and take no action; b) for those matters the Council deems to have the potential for significant local watershed impacts, provide the conditions the Council deems necessary to ensure compliance with the Local Watershed Management Plan to local governments; or c) for those matters the Council deems to be located in Special Watershed Areas or to constitute a Development of Regional Watershed Impact, refer the matter to the Regional Watershed Management District.

3) To acquire (including by eminent domain) and manage lands it deems important to local watershed management and fulfillment of the Local Watershed Management Plan.

4) To finance its operations through property taxes, recreational-user fees, water-utility fees, and development-permit fees, including fees levied as a surcharge, and through bonds.

5) To notify the State Watershed Management Agency of any state or regional agency action it believes may substantially interfere with the Local Watershed Management Plan.

6) To develop processes for citizen volunteers to participate in the development of Local Watershed Management Plans through planning forums undertaken at the sub-basin level as delineated by the Council.

VI. CONCLUSION

The challenges of water resource management in the United States traditionally have been water resource development, structural flood control, and centralized treatment of drinking water and wastewater. Increasingly, however, the focus is shifting to the management of land uses to prevent polluted runoff and groundwater contamination, the restoration of the physical integrity of rivers to reverse declines in aquatic ecosystems, and the promotion and protection of environmental services those ecosystems could potentially produce. This shift in goals also requires a shift in institutional structure from a system of congressional appropriations for cost-sharing of largely federalized civil and environmental engineering projects to a system of watershed-based, state-facilitated, locally led planning and management of economic incentives. In most states, unfortunately, these institutions do not exist in a form that has the political power and local legitimacy necessary to accomplish these goals.

In this Article we have proposed a structure for such institutions that is amenable to wide application among the fifty states and is guided by the political and other considerations required to meet twenty-first century challenges in water resources management. We acknowledge that, in many states, the proposal would add to the "layers" of governmental structure, and for that reason will not be politically popular. These layers, however, are designed to match politics with the physical reality of one of our nation's most important resources—water. We believe the layers are worth considering. Every jurisdiction, state or national, that has seriously undertaken watershed management implementation has arrived at the same conclusion.

We welcome comments on the proposal at this stage, as we plan to undertake the task of putting meat on its bones by drafting its specific provisions.

NOTES & QUESTIONS

1. Can you think of a governance framework that would be both capable of implementation at only one level of government—federal, state, or local—and effective at watershed management? The article proposes that states create a multi-layered governance system which, because of its uniformity among states, could in theory facilitate coordination and funding at the federal level. But is it simply too complicated? Is it politically feasible? Perhaps the fact that no state has adopted such a plan suggests not.

2. For comparison purposes, review the three different governance frameworks in use in the three estuarine management programs covered in Chapter 11. Do any resemble the framework suggested here for freshwater watersheds? Do you think the framework suggested here could be useful in the multi-state estuary setting?

c. ECOSYSTEM MANAGEMENT APPLICATIONS

Barton H. Thompson, Jr., *Markets for Nature*
25 William & Mary Environmental Law & Policy Review 261 (2000).

I. Introduction: Regulatory Markets versus Markets for Nature

The environment is a good in more than one sense of the word. The environment is beneficent to humanity, nurturing us, entertaining us, enlightening us, and providing us with the foundations of life—air, water, food, and a sustaining climate. To many, the environment reflects innate virtue as either God's handiwork or the aesthetic consequence of elegant physical laws. For these reasons, there is also human demand for protecting, sustaining, and enjoying the environment. The environment, in short, is also an economic "good." Although we are used to receiving for free many of the services and amenities provided by the environment, those services and amenities have value to us for which we would each be willing to pay some sum. "Natural" resources such as water, petroleum, and fish are already economic commodities, but as a consequence of their consumptive values. The values provided by a preserved nature raise the possibility that market systems also can support efforts to protect watersheds and other natural ecosystems. Markets for nature hold out the promise of a third rail, along with regulation and education, for preservation efforts.

III. Ecosystem Service Markets: Preserving Watersheds

Healthy ecosystems provide a variety of commercially valuable services that we take largely for granted because, for millennia, we have received the services free of charge. Such services include partial stabilization of climate, detoxification and decomposition of wastes, air purification, generation and renewal of soil and soil fertility, crop pollination, and pest control. Because many of these services are extremely valuable, efforts to preserve ecosystems may be able to capitalize on the value to bring in additional funding. The key is to find institutions or individuals who benefit from these ecosystem services and are willing to invest in their preservation.

In the twentieth century, a growing number of water suppliers turned to technological solutions such as filtration and disinfection to address water quality problems. Technological solutions, however, are often extremely expensive. Moreover, technology alone may not provide safe drinking water, as demonstrated by outbreaks of serious illnesses like cryptospiridiosis in cities that filter and disinfect their water supplies. Technological solutions also can have negative side effects in terms of both aesthetics (e.g., the taste of chlorine in drinking water) and health (e.g., the possible carcinogenicity of chlorine by-products). The abandonment of reservoirs because technological approaches could not keep pace with land development and thus pollution provides perhaps the most vivid illustration of the limitations of technological solutions and the critical importance of protecting watershed lands.

In theory, water suppliers can try to protect watershed lands through either regulation or the acquisition of property interests. In practice, many water suppliers have found acquisition more effective than regulation for several reasons. First, regulations are often difficult to enforce effectively, particularly where the watershed is in a political jurisdiction distant from the water supplier. Second, local communities typically fight significant regulatory efforts by distant water users.

A. Acquisitions Motivated by Watershed Services

Investment by water suppliers, cities, and others in the ecosystem services provided by riparian land is not hypothetical. In perhaps the best known example, New York City has chosen to invest over a quarter of a billion dollars in the acquisition and preservation of up to 350,000 acres of land in the Catskill watershed. Regulations under the federal Safe Drinking Water Act require water suppliers to filter their water unless the supplier can demonstrate that it has taken other steps, including protection of the watershed, that will adequately protect its customers from the risks of contamination. As noted earlier, filtration can be very expensive and is not always effective. New York City obtained an exemption from the filtration requirement by not only acquiring sensitive watershed lands, but funding watershed-based efforts to minimize pollution from farming and development, paying to improve sewage facilities in the watershed, and updating and extending its regulation of watershed activities to effectively police septic systems and other local sources of pollution. New York City estimates that the total cost of its entire watershed-protection program through 2010 will be about $1.5 billion, far less than the $4–8 billion cost of constructing a filtration plant (which would also entail annual operating costs of about $300 million).

New York City's efforts to preserve watershed land are not unique. Water companies have long acquired land in their watersheds to protect the quality of their drinking water. On average, water companies in the United States own only about two percent of the land in their watersheds.

In some portions of the nation, however, water suppliers control a much higher percentage, including most of the remaining open space.

Renewed emphasis on drinking water quality, including the federal Environmental Protection Agency's filtration regulations, are today driving additional land acquisition. In the late 1990's, more than 140 cities were considering watershed conservation in an effort to ensure safe drinking water for their customers. In 1998, Seattle increased its ownership of land in the South Fork Tolt River watershed from about 30 to 70 percent through a land exchange with the Weyerhaeuser Company; previously Seattle had acquired close to 100 percent land ownership in the Cedar River watershed, its other major water source, through land exchanges with the federal government. Portland, Maine is actively purchasing land within 1,000 feet of its main reservoir and tributaries. Salt Lake City assesses its water customers a small additional monthly fee to pay for land preservation in the city's Provo River watershed. Charlotte-Mecklenburg Utilities, in North Carolina, uses a portion of its capital improvement budget each year to acquire watershed lands. In a joint interstate effort, New Jersey and New York have purchased over 17,000 acres of land in Sterling Forest, the watershed for almost a quarter of New Jersey's population. Both Syracuse, New York and Rochester, Minnesota have embarked on programs to protect the cities' water supplies by paying riparian farmers to establish buffer zones along key water bodies. Rather than protecting riparian land from any development, some water suppliers have used easements, leases, or other financial incentive programs to minimize the size of the footprint that local activities impose on the land.

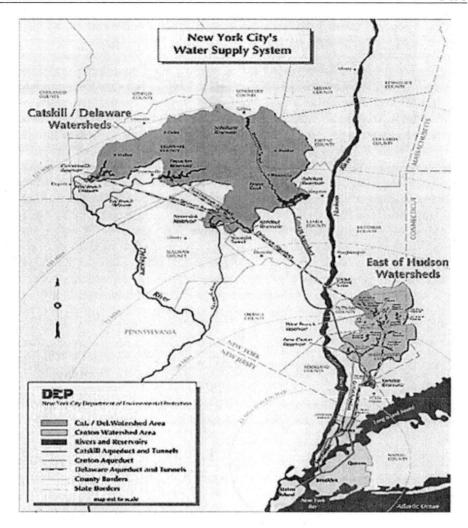

Fewer examples exist of cities or others investing in watershed preservation for flood control purposes, but interest is growing in such "soft" solutions to flood damage. With funding from a voter-approved initiative, California's Napa County plans to spend $160 million to acquire 500 acres of flood plain; the county expects that the acquisition will significantly reduce flood damages, which totaled $500 million in the last four decades of the twentieth century. Local governments near Boston acquired rights to 8,000 acres of wetlands capable of holding some 50,000 acres of water during potential flood periods, rather than building a $100 million system of dams and levees or bearing continued flood damages averaging $17 million annually. Littleton, Colorado, acquired over 600 acres of land for both flood control and park purposes.

B. Potential Barriers to Capitalizing on Ecosystem Services

One should have a healthy dose of skepticism regarding how often water companies, local governments, and other entities will find it worthwhile to preserve watershed lands. A number of the situations where water suppliers have chosen to preserve watershed lands, for example, involve unique settings that are not likely to be widely duplicated. New York City, for example, was able to escape building a multi-billion dollar filtration plant not simply because it planned to acquire riparian property, but also because it promised to engage in extensive regulation, both mandatory and voluntary, of the watershed. New York City could do this because of its historic regulatory authority over activities in the watershed; many cities will lack this power and find it difficult to obtain such authority over the almost certain opposition of local governments. But the opportunity to enlist cities, water suppliers, and others in the preservation of watersheds is significant enough to justify examining how public policies either support or undermine incentives to invest in ecosystem services.

One approach . . . would be the creation of a special watershed district empowered to tax individuals or entities benefiting from the watershed services and to use the revenues to acquire watershed lands or take other protective actions. Local communities have long used special districts as a means to overcome collective action problems in the provision of services with public good qualities. Farmers, for example, have formed irrigation districts to import and distribute water supplies and pest control districts to exterminate crop-threatening insects. Residents of flood-prone areas have formed flood control districts to finance dams and other engineering control measures. Local communities have formed school districts to provide public education. Each of these various districts is governed by a board of directors, generally elected by the affected population, which decides which measures to take and how to apportion the total cost among the local population, and then implements the measures and collects the necessary funds. The concept of a watershed services district would simply take this tried-and-true approach, which has been used to date primarily to finance engineering solutions to problems, and use it to ensure adequate provision of natural services.

NOTES & QUESTIONS

1. Why was the New York City watershed management experience Thompson describes so successful? Consider the previous discussion of Professor Adler's five design parameters of watershed-based policy—scale, boundary, control, mission, and consistency. Were any of these poorly defined in the New York City case? For further background on the New York City drinking water watershed program, see Symposium, *The New York City Watershed in the 21st Century*, 22 Fordham Envtl. L.J. 417 (2001); Michael C. Finnegan, *New York City's Watershed Agreement: A Lesson in Sharing Responsibility*, 14 Pace Envtl. L. Rev. 577 (1997). In particular, at least one commentary on the program suggests it was not all quite as easy as Thompson suggests, and that without the specter of regulation, it would not have succeeded. *See* Mark Sagoff, *A Billion-Dollar Misunderstanding*, PERC Reports (June 2005).

2. Thompson suggests that a local "watershed services district" governance unit model would simply apply the tried-and-true approach taken in many other local management contexts. How simple would this be? Many local district governments, such as flood control districts, irrigation districts, and soil conservation districts, face the challenge of calculating a relevant policy metric. Irrigation districts distribute irrigation water and thus have to determine a price for units of water. How would a watershed services district specify the unit for determining how much different taxpayers within its jurisdiction benefit from the watershed services it manages. To the extent that actual watershed ecosystem service values are beyond monetary calculation, would acres of property suffice as a surrogate? Property values? How would you draft a state watershed services district enabling statute?

Pacific Coast Federation of Fishermen's Associations, Inc. v. National Marine Fisheries Service

United States Court of Appeals for the Ninth Circuit, 2001.
253 F.3d 1137.

■ GOODWIN, CIRCUIT JUDGE:

Six environmental organizations sued the National Marine Fisheries Service ("NMFS") for declaratory and injunctive relief to challenge four biological opinions which had the effect of clearing the way for 23 proposed timber sales in the Umpqua River watershed in southwestern Oregon. The district court granted substantial relief and the defendant agency, together with intervening timber operators, appeal.

The Pacific Coast Federation of Fishermen's Associations, Inc. and five other organizations representing fishermen and environmental concerns are collectively referred to as "Pacific Coast." Their principal claim is that the "no jeopardy" opinions issued by NMFS filed in Seattle, where the agency has its regional headquarters, were arbitrary and inadequately supported by the "best available science" as required by the Endangered Species Act ("ESA"). At the heart of the controversy is the impact of proposed timber sales on the Umpqua River cutthroat trout and the Oregon Coast coho salmon. Douglas Timber Operators ("DTO") and the Northwest Forestry Association were allowed to enter the cases as defendant-intervenors. The cases have been consolidated for this appeal.

Pacific Coast alleged that NMFS acted arbitrarily and capriciously in reaching the conclusion that the proposed timber sales are not likely to jeopardize the continued existence of the listed species. The district court found that NMFS had acted arbitrarily and capriciously by assessing Aquatic Conservation Strategy ("ACS") compliance only at the watershed level, by failing to evaluate short-term degradations, and by failing to fully and sufficiently incorporate the watershed analysis consistently with the "best available science" requirements set by the ESA. The district court granted summary judgment in favor of Pacific Coast.

The NMFS issued four biological opinions stating that 23 timber sales in the Umpqua River Basin were not likely to jeopardize the continued existence of the Umpqua cutthroat trout and the Oregon Coast coho salmon. The proposed sales are within the range of the northern spotted owl, and therefore fall within the region covered by the Northwest Forest Plan

("NFP"). The United States Forest Service ("USFS") and the BLM adopted the NFP in 1994. The plan was designed to provide a comprehensive management program for 24.5 million acres of federal forest lands throughout the range of the spotted owl. See Seattle Audubon Society v. Lyons, 871 F.Supp. 1291, 1304 (W.D.Wash.1994), aff'd 80 F.3d 1401 (9th Cir.1996). One of the key components of the NFP is the ACS, a comprehensive plan designed to maintain and restore the ecological health of the waterways in the federal forests.

There are four components to the ACS: (1) key watersheds (the best aquatic habitat, or hydrologic ally important areas), (2) riparian reserves (buffer zones along streams, lakes, wetlands and mudslide risks), (3) watershed analysis (to document existing and desired watershed conditions), and (4) watershed restoration (a long-term program to restore aquatic ecosystems and watershed health). The ACS also has binding standards and guidelines that restrict certain activities within areas designated as riparian reserves or key watersheds. Additionally, ACS has nine objectives designed to maintain or restore properly functioning aquatic habitats.

Pacific Coast argued, and the district court agreed, that NMFS acted arbitrarily and capriciously by ... ignoring site-specific project effects and limiting its ACS compliance analysis to the watershed scale ...

WATERSHED SCALE ACS CONSISTENCY

In determining ACS consistency for the 23 timber projects challenged in this case, NMFS analyzed the projects' consistency with ACS at the watershed level. A watershed ... generally covers between 20 to 200 square miles of land. This equates to between 12,800 and 128,000 acres. The largest watershed considered with reference to projects at issue here is 350 square miles, or 224,000 acres. By contrast, a project site generally covers only a few sections (square miles) or fractions of sections. The NMFS conducts its analysis of the program by assessing the affects of any project level degradation on the entire watershed. Any degradation that cannot be measured at the watershed level is considered to be consistent with both ACS standards and objectives and therefore warrants a "no jeopardy" finding.

Pacific Coast contends that the watershed measure effectively masks all project level degradation. This argument raises two questions: (1) whether, because a 128 acre project represents only 1% to 0.1% of a watershed, any degradation would be perceptible at the watershed level; and (2) whether any effect was given to the cumulative degradation in an ACS.
* * *

The NMFS contends that the proper level to evaluate ACS consistency is the watershed, because NFP and ACS are aimed at maintaining and restoring millions of acres of forest lands. Given that overall protection of forest and water resources is the concern of both NFP and ACS, it does not follow that NMFS is free to ignore site degradations because they are too small to affect the accomplishment of that goal at the watershed scale. For some purposes, the watershed scale may be correct, but NFP does not provide support for so limiting NMFS review. The purpose of ACS is to maintain and restore ecosystem health at watershed and landscape scales to protect habitat for fish and other riparian-dependent species and resources and restore currently degraded habitats. This general mission statement in NFP does not prevent project site degradation and does nothing to restore habitat over broad landscapes if it ignores the cumulative effect of individual projects on small tributaries within watersheds. The agency also must determine "how the proposed project or management action maintains the existing condition or moves it within the range of natural variability." The NMFS relies on this requirement to show that consistency will be attained at the watershed level. However, it is unclear whether NMFS performed an analysis of the cumulative effect of small degradations over a whole watershed. Pacific Coast asserts that NMFS did not consider cumulative effect. The NMFS had an opportunity to place in the record evidence demonstrating that it considered cumulative effect. We find nothing to show that it did. Appropriate analysis of ACS compliance is undertaken at both the watershed and project levels.

Its disregard of projects with a relatively small area of impact but that carried a high risk of degradation when multiplied by many projects and continued over a long time period is the major flaw in NMFS study. Without aggregation, the large spatial scale appears to be calculated to ignore the effects of individual sites and projects. Unless the effects of individual projects are aggregated to ensure that their cumulative effects are perceived and measured in future ESA consultations, it is difficult to have any confidence in a wide regional no-jeopardy opinion. . . If the effects of individual projects are diluted to insignificance and not aggregated, then Pacific Coast is correct in asserting that NMFS's assessment of ACS consistency at the watershed level is tantamount to assuming that no project will ever lead to jeopardy of a listed species.

NOTES & QUESTIONS

1. What was the problem with NMFS using a watershed-based approach to assess the impact of timber leases in *Pacific Coast Federation*? Did BLM use the wrong watersheds? Did it use watersheds that were too large, or too small? Should it not have used watersheds at all? Does the case suggest a flaw in the "watershed approach" generally? In March 2004, apparently to offset the effects of *Pacific Coast Federation*, the Forest Service and Bureau of Land Management announced a change to the Aquatic Conservation Strategy that would clarify it is to be applied on a broad, watershed-based scale. The federal district court found that the 2004 amendments violated NEPA and the ESA for inadequately accounting for impacts to the environment and endangered species. *See* Pacific Coast Federation of Fishermen's Associations v. National Marine Fisheries Services, 482 F. Supp. 2d 1248 (W.D. Wash. 2007). Later in 2007, the federal government withdrew its appeal of the decision in the Ninth Circuit.

2. The challenge for the agencies in *Pacific Coast Federation* was to devise a system for identifying when project-specific actions would jeopardize the continued existence of the protected species. This is simply one form of a problem that plagues environmental law—how to measure, account for, and respond to the cumulative effects of many independent actions, none of which has substantial effects in isolation. Using ecosystem-level units of impact assessment, such as watersheds, may make us more cognizant of the impact of cumulative effects on large scales, but, as *Pacific Coast Federation* suggests, doing so does not necessarily answer or simplify the challenge of knowing how to manage the many small actions that lead to those accumulated impacts. Indeed, the system the agencies adopted in *Pacific Coast Federation* avoided many management issues because it screened out most of the project-specific actions from closer evaluation by assessing impacts on the watershed only on a project-by-project basis—i.e., without evaluating cumulative effects.

3. By contrast, the very heart of environmental impact assessment under the National Environmental Policy Act (NEPA) is to evaluate cumulative effects. NEPA requires federal agencies, before they make a final decision on major actions they propose to carry out, fund, or authorize, to prepare a detailed statement of the environmental impact of the proposed action, known as an environmental impact statement (EIS). 42 U.S.C. § 4332(C). Regulations the Council of Environmental Quality (CEQ) has promulgated to implement NEPA, and which are binding on other federal agencies as they fulfill their NEPA duties, require agencies to consider the cumulative impacts of "connected actions" and "cumulative actions" in the same EIS. "Connected actions" are actions that "automatically trigger other actions which may require environmental impact statements," or "cannot or will not proceed unless other actions are taken previously or simultaneously," or "are independent parts of a larger action and depend on the larger action for their justification." 40 C.F.R. § 1508.25(a)(1). "Cumulative actions" are actions "which when viewed together with other proposed actions have cumulatively significant impacts." *Id.* § 1508.25(a)(2). And "cumulative impacts" are "the impact on the environment which results from the incremental impact of the action when added to other past, present, and reasonably foreseeable future actions regardless of what agency (Federal or non-Federal) or person undertakes such other actions." *Id.* § 1508.7. Thus, even when a proposed major federal action may have insignificant effects on the environment standing alone, NEPA would require assessment of the cumulative effects of the proposed action plus the effects of any connected or cumulative actions. Is this the kind of approach the *Pacific Coast Federation* court is demanding the agencies take? Is it the kind of approach that should be used in all "watershed-based" ecosystem management?

D. Cᴀsᴇ Sᴛᴜᴅʏ: Tʜᴇ Aᴘᴀʟᴀᴄʜɪᴄᴏʟᴀ-Cʜᴀᴛᴛᴀʜᴏᴏᴄʜᴇᴇ-Fʟɪɴᴛ Rɪᴠᴇʀ Bᴀsɪɴ Wᴀᴛᴇʀ Wᴀʀs

The old adage, *whisky is for drinking and water is for fighting*, has long defined history in the American West. But in these days, it applies just as well east of the Mississippi.

Deep in the North Georgia hills, just a few hundred feet off the southernmost reaches of the Appalachian Trail, a small mountain brook marks the headwaters of the Chattahoochee River. As it meanders its way out of the Chattahoochee National Forest, through the quaint Bavarian style town of Helen, the water soon empties into Lake Lanier, a huge reservoir north of Atlanta impounded in the 1940s by the U.S. Army Corps of Engineers' Buford Dam. Below the dam, cooled water spills out and works its way toward Atlanta, brushing by just north of that major southeastern city and then drifting westward toward Alabama. At West Point Lake Dam, the river veers more sharply southward and becomes the boundary between Alabama and Georgia. It passes by Columbus, Georgia on its east bank, then later the Alabama plantation town of Eufaula. At Sneads, Alabama, where Lake Seminole is impounded, it joins the Flint River, which has its origins near the south side of Atlanta, and crosses into Florida. There it becomes the Apalachicola River, a ribbon of water slicing across the Florida panhandle and emptying into the Gulf of Mexico at Apalachicola. This collection of rivers, over 750 river miles in all, makes up the Apalachicola-Flint-Chattahoochee River system, known by shorthand as "the ACF."

The ACF is the lifeblood of one of the richest, most biologically diverse estuaries in the world—Apalachicola Bay. Life is so good in the Bay, its oysters grow faster than anywhere on earth (the Bay supplies 10 percent of the nation's oysters) and many species of fish found in the Gulf spend part their lives there. The Nature Conservancy lists the Bay as one of its hottest of biodiversity hotspots in the world. The Apalachicola River itself, plus its floodplain of over 180,000 acres, is home to one of the highest diversities of freshwater fish, amphibians, and crayfish in the nation.

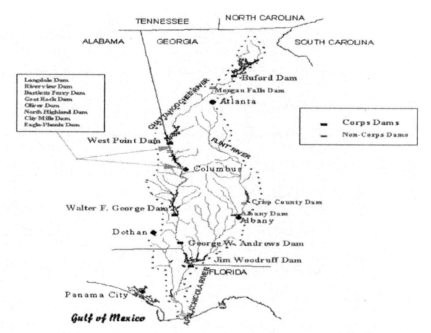

Apalachicola-Chattahoochee-Flint River Basin

Since the 1940s, however, biodiversity has had a tough competitor—humans, or, more specifically, dams. Under congressional mandate, the Corps of Engineers began "taming" the Chattahoochee with a series of major dams designed to impound water to meet a variety of human needs. The ready supply of water proved irresistible to residential and industrial development throughout the region. Population growth in the ACF basin boomed, concentrated in Atlanta. The area became one of the hottest regional economies in the nation. A hotspot of biodiversity and of economic vitality—the ACF had it all.

But trouble was on the horizon. A series of record droughts in the 1980s illustrated the limits of ACF water. In 1989, Georgia and the Corps proposed diverting more water from the Corps' impoundments to quench Atlanta's thirst. Georgia then applied to the Corps to add yet another major impoundment in the state—this one on the Tallapoosa River just five miles from where it crosses into Alabama. Alabama, fearing that less water flowing into the state and along its boundary with Georgia would mean less potential for its own economic growth, immediately brought litigation to halt both plans under a variety of federal laws, most prominently the National Environmental Policy Act. Florida, fearing less water emptying into Apalachicola Bay could damage the Bay ecosystem and the oyster and recreational fishing industries it supports, soon joined the fray.

Western states have resolved their many interstate water allocation battles in three ways: (1) litigation before the U.S. Supreme Court under its original jurisdiction; (2) congressional allocation; and (3) interstate compacts approved by Congress. Because water disputes of any substantial magnitude have been rare in the east, these methods have been seriously field tested in eastern settings only a few times, and not at all in recent history. But the ACF dispute was sizing up to be a biggie, with serious potential to head to the Supreme Court if the states could not agree. To avoid that high stakes proposition, in 1992 the three states entered into negotiations that led to a 1997 interstate compact to negotiate some more. *See* Pub. L. No. 105–104, 111 Stat. 2219 (1997) (unlike the only other eastern compact, the Delaware River Compact between Pennsylvania, Delaware, New York, New Jersey, and the federal government, the ACF compact includes the federal government as a participating, non-voting member, but it can exercise a veto power over what the states propose).

The negotiations were protracted, focusing on each state's model of river flow conditions experienced under an array of climate and population projections. Unable to reach quick consensus, the states extended their self-imposed deadlines numerous times, hired respected mediators, and employed the best legal and technical experts money can buy, but to no avail. After several years of negotiation under the compact, which was basically a compact to negotiate, the states failed to reach a consensus on the proper allocation and threw in the towel in late 2003. Georgia wanted to retain rights sufficient to serve its vast urban and agricultural demands in times of drought, whereas Florida demanded that ecological flow regimes be retained on behalf of Apalachicola Bay. *See* Letter to Editor of Tallahassee Democrat from David Struhs, Secretary, Florida Department of Environmental Protection, *Unwilling to Accept Agreement that Relied on Minimum Flow*, TALLAHASSEE DEMOCRAT, Sept. 7, 2003, at 4E ("In the end, Florida was unwilling to accept an agreement that relied on the minimum flow").

Clearly, the politics of the ACF are as complex as is its ecosystem. The social and economic fabric of the ACF watershed illustrates why. Consider just a sample of who wants a piece of the ACF—that is, besides the ecosystem itself:

Atlanta Drinking and Industrial Water Suppliers: Located not far downstream of Lake Lanier, the Atlanta metropolitan area population has grown from 1 million in 1950 to over 4.0 million today. With groundwater supplying less than 2 percent of the water for Atlanta area residents and businesses, they have turned to Lake Lanier and the Chattahoochee. Overall, more than 2.5 million Atlanta area residents rely on water from the river or Lake Lanier for their domestic water supply. Local water supply authorities draw over 130 million gallons per day from the lake and over 275 million gallons per day from the river to supply residents and industry. To serve expected population and industrial growth, Atlanta planning officials would like to raise those figures to 297 and 408 million gallons per day, respectively, in the next 20 years. But over 65 percent of all that withdrawn water is returned to the river, albeit as treated wastewater, and the Atlanta area must maintain a healthy downstream flow in the river below the city—over 480 million gallons a day—to dilute the wastewater in order to meet Clean Water Act standards. So the impact of Atlanta on minimum daily water flow at the other end of the watershed is muted to a substantial degree, though, as you will see, many Florida interests don't see it that way.

Electric Power Utilities: Beginning in the 1930s, hydropower generated from dams has been an important source of electricity throughout the Southeastern United States. The Chattahoochee and Flint Rivers contribute substantially to this relatively inexpensive source of power. The U.S. Army Corps of Engineers operates several federal dams on the Chattahoochee, together supplying power to over 80,000 homes in the Southeast. The Georgia Power Company also operates dams on the Chattahoochee and Flint Rivers. Because they can come "on line" very quickly after water is diverted through their turbines, hydropower plants offer an extremely efficient way of meeting peak power demands, such as on hot summer afternoons. Fossil fuel plants take much longer to stoke up and wind down their turbines in response to demand fluctuations. But the hydropower turbines don't spin if the water doesn't flow, thus pitting the power plants in direct competition with upstream water diversions such as those going to Atlanta water supply companies, and with recreational interests that advocate more water storage in the reservoirs.

Shipping Industry. During the early 1800s, riverboat shipping traffic on the ACF system was a thriving industry, making the Port of Apalachicola one of the transportation centers of the Southeast. Cotton, timber, honey, and turpentine were the main goods shipped. But rail shipping proved a potent competitor, and riverboat shipping along the ACF river declined steadily in the latter part of the century and was negligible by the early 1900s. Improved dredging by the Corps, required by federal legislation in 1945, and the introduction of large barges that could compete more effectively against rail and truck shipping, returned some vitality to the ACF shipping industry in the mid-1900s. Fertilizer, coal, and agricultural products became the commodities of choice for shipping up and down the ACF. But the Corps needed to keep the river channel dredged and river levels sufficiently high in order to accommodate the deeper draft barges. One means of doing so, which the Corps has used since the early 1990s when drought conditions became more common, is to release water from upstream reservoirs in slugs to raise the river levels at times when barge traffic is present. Still, even with these "navigation windows," the narrow ACF makes a poor venue for barges, allowing a tug to push only two at a time. Barge trips dropped from 204 in 1993 to 47 in 1999. Meanwhile, the Corps spends $4.5 million per year to dredge the channel and $2.5 million to operate the locks. That's right, over $7 million annually for 45 or so barge trips. You do the math! In addition, the dredging unquestionably damages the river ecosystem, and the pulses of water spill fish into floodplain pools that become isolated after the water quickly subsides, dooming the trapped fish. A May 2000 release to allow two barges to navigate up the river stranded thousands of fish in this manner. The slow-filling Lake Lanier is still recovering from the consequences of that release episode.

Farm Irrigation. The 26 southwest Georgia counties are dominated by agricultural economies, generating $1.6 billion in agricultural product revenue annually. These agricultural operations also used 325 million gallons of water per day, mostly for crop irrigation, and are projected to use 570 million gallons per day by 2050. Most of the irrigation water is drawn not from lakes or rivers, but rather from the Floridan Aquifer, a huge, highly productive limestone aquifer stretching from southern Georgia well into Florida. The relation between withdrawals from the aquifer and the chief surface water resource in the area, the Flint River, is not fully understood. But the impact of irrigation on the ACF system in general was sufficiently clear to prompt the Georgia legislature to pass legislation in 2000 authorizing payments to farmers who draw directly from the river to stop irrigating. Regulation of agricultural water conservation practices nonetheless remains a touchy issue in these parts.

Lake Recreation Economies. In addition to supplying residential and industrial water to urban Atlanta, Lake Lanier has become the city's playground. At 38,500 tree-rimmed surface acres, Lake Lanier is a boater's and retiree's heaven. Its shores are dotted with marinas, million dollar homes, resort hotels, and golf courses. Houseboats as long as 120 feet are not uncommon. Its recreational economy generates billions of dollars in revenue. All of this depends, however, on there being water in Lake Lanier. Yet the water level was 9 feet below normal in the summer of 2001, leaving boat docks high and dry, mangling boat propellers in never before seen shallows, and scarring the "lake appeal" of sprawling estate homes. If the dam gates were closed today and rainfall were to return to normal, it would take three months to return to normal levels. Since neither of those events seems likely to happen anytime soon, Lake Lanier recreational interests have to fight with all the other interests for every drop. The same is true of local economies built on the recreational amenities offered by the other major impoundments along the Chattahoochee. The question is whether these recreational economies, which depend on keeping water stored in reservoirs built to serve *the river*, are becoming the tails wagging the dog.

The Bay Fishing Industry. At the opposite end of the ACF watershed from Lake Lanier, 544 miles from the headwaters of the Chattahoochee, lies the Apalachicola Bay, home to the most productive oyster beds in the nation and the center of a highly productive estuary. A small but sustainable oyster and fishing industry has been based in Apalachicola for decades. But it is a far cry from the estates of Lake Lanier—most oyster harvesters and fishermen live week to week in fairly hard-scrabble circumstances. Their very livelihood depends on one thing above all else—water flowing out of the mouth of the Apalachicola River. But not just any flow. It has to be the right amount at the right time—the so-called natural flow regime. This demand is not a human invention. The life cycle of oysters and the value of the estuary as nursery habitat for shrimp, mullet, flounder, red snapper, and grouper depend on a fluctuating supply of freshwater throughout the year. By and large, that's all many of the Florida interests want from the ACF system—water at the end of the pipe the way nature intended it to be delivered. Franklin County, through which the Apalachicola River flows, has no aspirations of withdrawing water to launch another Atlanta. There is but one traffic light in the entire county! For those leading this modest lifestyle, however, whether what they think is a modest request can be met has become a major concern.

Any western water war presents an equally diverse set of interests. What makes the ACF truly a new type of water dispute—one not experienced even in the west, is that one of the states, in this case Florida, is in the mix primarily to advance an *ecological* dimension. To be sure, environmental factors have entered into the positions states have taken elsewhere in water allocation disputes, but primarily as a means of supporting the proposed economically-driven split of water quantity. Florida's ecologically-based position presents not only a quantity component, but also a qualitative factor in terms of the natural flow regime. This feature truly is new to the universe of interstate water disputes. As one observer concluded:

> the "natural flow regime" approach to allocation proposed by Florida elevates environmental concerns to a new level in water quantity disputes. As a practical matter, the protection of Apalachicola Bay and its oysters represents a significant economic incentive for Florida's position, but the environmental elements are unmistakable. In any event, the water wars have made their way east, and they represent a new and complicated issue on the horizon of water law.

C. Grady Moore, *Water Wars: Interstate Water Allocation in the Southeast*, 14 NATURAL RESOURCES & ENV'T 5 (1999).

NOTES & QUESTIONS

1. Put yourself in the following circumstances, changing which ACF stakeholder has hired you, and consider what you would propose:

- You have been hired by all the stakeholders as a group to mediate a solution among them.

- You have been hired to negotiate in the mediation for one of the stakeholders.

- You have been hired by one of the stakeholders to draft federal and state legislation that best ensures its needs are met and to lobby for its adoption.

- You have been hired by one of the stakeholders to lobby the Corps of Engineers to convince it to act in your client's best interests.

- You are an aide to the governor of one of the states involved—Georgia, Alabama, or Florida—asked to outline the best overall position for the state to take in negotiations with the other states.

2. What is the relevant ecosystem for tackling any of the assignments outlined in the previous note? Is it the entire ACF watershed? Should particular stretches of the system—say, the segments between dams—be considered separately? Are farmers who draw from the Floridan aquifer in south Georgia in or out of the ecosystem?

If the three states continue to fail to agree on water allocation in the ACF system, they could take their fight to the U.S. Supreme Court. If the dispute over ACF water were to reach the Supreme Court, the Court would decide the issue using the federal common law doctrine of equitable apportionment. The Constitution assigns the Supreme Court original jurisdiction over disputes between the states. U.S. Const. art. III, sec. 2, cl. 2. Because the states have adopted a range of legal regimes for dealing with intrastate water rights, none of which takes into account impact on other states, the Court has developed federal common law principles for dividing the water when interstate disputes arise. *See* Hinderlider v. La Plata River & Cherry Creek Ditch Co., 304 U.S. 92 (1938). The basic theme of the Court's approach is to divide the interstate water so as to balance benefits and injury with a sense of fairness to both states. This doctrine of equitable apportionment takes into account not only each state's respective water law, but also economic impacts, climate conditions, available water use conservation measures, and the overall impact of diversions on existing uses. The Court appoints a Special Master to engage in this multi-factored analysis, then reviews the Special Master's recommendations. The doctrine has long been employed in the west, *see, e.g.*, Kansas v. Colorado, 206 U.S. 46 (1907), and has occasionally been used to resolve disputes between eastern states, *see e.g.*, Connecticut v. Massachusetts, 282 U.S. 660 (1931). But no case has presented issues quite like those the ACF case would pose. Usually the Court is called upon to decree an annual amount or minimum flow to which each state is entitled. In the ACF case, however, Florida presumably would claim that, primarily for ecological reasons (albeit with incidental economic impacts), upstream states must deliver a particular "natural" flow regime that fluctuates throughout the year.

Although the Court's equitable apportionment jurisprudence certainly leaves room for incorporating ecological factors into the analysis, the precedents do not suggest how the Court would do so. The Court has, however, ruled that the doctrine applies not only to water, but to allocation of resources that run within interstate waters, such as anadromous fish. *See* Idaho v. Oregon, 462 U.S. 1017 (1983). And the Court has held that the doctrine imposes on states "an affirmative duty . . . to take reasonable steps to conserve and even to augment natural resources within their borders for the benefit of other States." *Id.* at 1025. Yet, when downstream states claim injury from upstream diversions, the Court generally requires the downstream state to "prove by clear and convincing evidence some real and substantial injury or damage." *See id.* at 1027; Missouri v. Illinois, 200 U.S. 496, 521 (1906) (first holding that the doctrine requires a showing that the injury is of "serious magnitude clearly and fully proved").

NOTES & QUESTIONS

1. If the Supreme Court were asked to divide ACF water between the states, to what extent would the concept of ecosystem services (discussed in Chapter 2) be useful in the Court's determination? After all, isn't that why Florida wants ACF water—for the services it provides to Apalachicola Bay?

2. If the Court can equitably apportion a river's water and the fish that travel in it, couldn't the Court also equitably apportion the ecosystem services the water delivers? For an argument that the Court should take into account ecosystem services in its equitable apportionment of interstate waters, see J.B. Ruhl, *Equitable Apportionment of Ecosystem Services: New Water Law for a New Water Age*, 19 J. LAND USE & ENVTL. L. 47 (2003). For a suggestion of such an approach for international water apportionment, see A. Dan Tarlock, *Safeguarding International River Ecosystems in Times of Scarcity*, 3 U. DENVER WATER L. REV. 231 (2000).

3. And as a general matter, should the doctrine of equitable apportionment be expanded to allow, or even to require, that interstate river disputes be resolved according to an *ecologically* equitable apportionment?

Of course, there is another path down which the ACF dispute could venture, and has. Ever heard of *Lamsilis subangulata*? Better known, to a few people at least, as shinyrayed pocketbook, it is one of the mussels found in the ACF system that has been listed as an endangered species under the Endangered Species Act. Threats to the endangered mussel species living in the ACF include excessive nutrient levels from agriculture, siltation from land deforestation, toxic runoff from industry, loss of habitat to reservoir inundation, decreased water flow due to diversions, and competition from invasive species. The threats are quite evident, as none of the species is found in the Chattahoochee today. Another listed species found in the

ACF, the threatened Gulf sturgeon, is also dependent on the natural flow regime. Is the Endangered Species Act thus a mechanism for interstate water allocation between the battling states? Florida thought so, but a court took a different perspective in the case that follows.

Alabama v. United States Army Corps of Engineers

United States District Court for the Northern District of Alabama, 2006.
441 F. Supp. 2d 1123.

■ BOWDRE, DISTRICT JUDGE.

I. INTRODUCTION

This case is before the court on Florida's Renewed Motion for Temporary Restraining Order to Protect Threatened and Endangered Mussels. In this Motion, Florida requests that the court order the U.S. Army Corps of Engineers ("the Corps") to maintain water releases of 6,300 cubic feet per second ("cfs") from the Jim Woodruff Lock and Dam until September 5, 2006, when the U.S. Fish and Wildlife Service issues its biological opinion.

II. BACKGROUND

A. The ACF System and the Jim Woodruff Lock and Dam.

The Chattahoochee River flows from the mountains of North Georgia across the state, runs along the border between Alabama and Georgia, then joins with the Flint River at the Florida–Georgia border to form the Apalachicola River. From there, the river flows into the Apalachicola Bay and the Gulf of Mexico. Those three rivers, their tributaries, and the associated drainage area form the Apalachicola–Chattahoochee–Flint ("ACF") Basin.

The Corps operates a number of federal reservoir projects within the ACF Basin, including Jim Woodruff Dam (Lake Seminole), George W. Andrews Dam and Lake, Walter F. George Dam and Lake, West Point Dam and Lake, and Buford Dam (Lake Sidney Lanier). Congress authorized these reservoirs to operate for multiple project purposes such as flood control, hydropower generation, and navigation. Florida's Motion focuses on the alleged adverse impacts of the Corps' ACF Basin operations on the threatened and endangered species in the Apalachicola River downstream from the Jim Woodruff Lock and Dam ("Woodruff Dam").

B. The Threatened and Endangered ACF Species ("ACF Species.")

Four federally-listed threatened and endangered species are present in the Apalachicola River downstream from Woodruff Dam: the threatened Gulf sturgeon, the endangered fat threeridge mussel, the threatened purple bankclimber mussel, and the threatened Chipola slabshell mussel. Florida contends that, since 1990, the Corps has operated the reservoirs upstream from Woodruff Dam in a manner that favors upstream recreational and non-authorized uses to the detriment of the downstream ACF species. Specifically, Florida argues that the Corps retains water in upstream reservoirs and fails to satisfy the interim flow needs of the ACF species during periods of low flow conditions, such as those currently experienced.

Because of the current drought, discharges into the Apalachicola River from Woodruff dam, and the corresponding water levels in the Apalachicola basin, have steadily declined since June 1, 2006. The mussels in the Apalachicola River are slow moving, and, while capable of moving to deeper water refuges for short distances, they generally cannot escape the adverse conditions they currently are experiencing in side channels and sloughs along the river. Particularly dramatic flow reductions, as have been previously experienced in the Apalachicola River, quickly sever the connection between the main river channel and occupied mussel habitats outside the main channel before mussels can relocate, resulting in stranding and death due to heat, predation, and dessication. As a result, hundreds, if not thousands of dead and dying mussels were observed in the Apalachicola River during field visits between June 12 and 14, 2006. Among the dead and dying mussels were members of two species protected under the ESA: the threatened purple bankclimber and the endangered fat threeridge. These mussels are the ACF species at issue for purposes of this memorandum opinion.

C. The Endangered Species Act ("ESA").

Florida contends that the Corps is violating the ESA by killing the threatened and endangered mussels living in the Apalachicola River downstream of Woodruff Dam. The ESA protects threatened and endangered species in two ways relevant to this case. First, § 7 requires federal agencies to consult with the U.S. Fish and Wildlife Service ("FWS") to ensure that their actions do not "jeopardize the continued existence" of any protected species or result in the "destruction or adverse modification" of "critical habitat." *See* 16 U.S.C. § 1536(a)(2) (2005). Under this section, an agency proposing an action must first determine whether the action "may affect" listed species. 50 C.F.R. § 402.11 (2005). If the agency determines that its actions "may affect" a protected species or its habitat, then the agency must generally enter into consultation with FWS. *See* 16 U.S.C. § 1536(a)(2) (2005).

The ESA regulations provide for two forms of consultation—informal and formal. Informal consultation is "an optional process that includes all discussions, correspondence, etc., between the Service and the Federal agency . . . designed to assist the Federal agency in determining whether formal consultation is required." *Id.* at § 402.13(a) (2005). If, on the other hand, the agency determines during informal consultation that its action is likely to adversely affect protected species or critical habitat, then the agency *must* request initiation of formal consultation with the appropriate service. *See Id.* at 402.14(a) & (b) (2005).

By regulation, formal consultation concludes "within 90 days after its initiation" unless extended by mutual consent of FWS and the action agency. *Id.* at § 402.14(e) (2005). FWS then has 45 days from the completion of formal consultation to deliver a "biological opinion" to the action agency. *Id.*

The regulations thus provide FWS with no less than 135 days from the initiation of formal consultation to deliver a biological opinion.

The biological opinion provides FWS' assessment as to whether the action is "likely to jeopardize the continued existence of listed species or result in the destruction or adverse modification of critical habitat." *Id.* at § 402.14(h)(3). In the event the biological opinion includes a "jeopardy opinion," the opinion must also include "reasonable and prudent alternatives," if any, to mitigate the effects of agency action. *Id.*

The second method relevant to this case by which the ESA protects threatened and endangered species is through § 9. Section 9 prohibits the "take" of protected species by federal agencies or private individuals. *See* 16 U.S.C. § 1538(a)(1)(B). The ESA defines "take" to mean "to harass, harm, pursue, hunt, shoot, wound, kill, trap, capture, or collect." 16 U.S.C. § 1532(19) (2005). The term "harass" is further defined as

an intentional or negligent act which creates the likelihood of injury to wildlife by annoying it to such an extent as to significantly disrupt normal behavior patterns which include, but are not limited to breeding, feeding, or sheltering.

50 C.F.R. § 17.3. The term "harm" means

[a]n act which actually kills or injures wildlife. Such act may include significant habitat modification or degradation where it actually kills or injures wildlife by significantly impairing essential behavior patterns, including breeding, feeding or sheltering.

Id.

Florida argues that the Corps can kill threatened and endangered mussels only pursuant to an Incidental Take Statement. An Incidental Take Statement can be obtained through the successful completion of formal consultation. *See* 16 U.S.C. § 1536(b)(4) and (*o*); 50 C.F.R. § 402.14(I). The Statement permits some "incidental take" of protected species that "result[s] from, but are not the purpose of, carrying out an otherwise lawful activity conducted by the Federal agency." 50 C.F.R. § 402.02; *see also* 16 U.S.C. § 1536(b)(4). The Statement specifies the impact the agency action will have on the species, sets forth "reasonable and prudent measures" to alleviate the anticipated adverse impact, and establishes "terms and conditions" necessary for the implementation of the measures. 16 U.S.C. § 1536(b)(4); *see also* 50 C.F.R. § 402.14(i)(ii). Pursuant to the ESA, a take that complies with an Incidental Take Statement is a lawful take. *See* 16 U.S.C. § 1536(*o*)(2). However, because the Corps has not completed formal consultation with FWS and does not possess an Incidental Take Statement, Florida contends that the Corps' river operations violate the ESA by causing a prohibited take and warrant immediate injunctive relief. Florida requests that the court order the Corps to maintain releases of 6,300 cubic feet per second ("cfs") from Woodruff Dam until September 5, 2006—the date that the biological opinion from FWS is scheduled to be issued.

D. ESA consultation and the Interim Operations Plan.

For some undefined period of time, the Corps and FWS have been engaged in informal discussions over the operation of the ACF basin reservoirs. Pursuant to its obligations under § 7 of the ESA, the Corps initiated formal consultation with FWS on March 7, 2006. FWS is scheduled to complete its consultation and issue a biological opinion on September 5, 2006. Until the biological opinion is issued, the Corps intends to implement—and, in fact, has been following—an Interim Operations Plan ("IOP"). The IOP incorporates a sliding scale water release schedule that is triggered by basin inflow to the ACF System. For the time period relevant to this Motion, the IOP provides for releases from Woodruff Dam in the following quantities:

Basin Inflow (cfs)	Releases from Woodruff Dam (cfs)
37,400 or greater	at least 37,400
8,000 to 37,399	greater than or equal to 70% to 90% of basin inflow; but no less than 8,000
less than 8,000	at least basin inflow; but no less than 5,000

Further, the plan establishes down ramping rates that correspond to the releases from Woodruff Dam. These rates attempt to limit the stranding of mussels that have limited mobility. The schedule for maximum down ramping rates is as follows:

Release Range	Maximum Fall Rate (feet/day) measured at Chattahoochee gauge
Exceeds 18,000 cfs	0.5 to 1.0 ft/day
8,000 to 17,999 cfs	0.25 to 0.5 ft/day
less than 8,000 cfs	0.25 ft/day or less

E. Procedural background.

On January 31, 2006, Florida filed a Motion for Preliminary Injunction on its ESA claim, primarily to protect the Gulf Sturgeon. In its Motion, Florida sought injunctive relief to compel the Corps to comply with the ESA when operating reservoirs in the ACF Basin. In response to Florida's Motion, the Corps initiated formal consultation with FWS pursuant to § 7 of the ESA. In its consultation request, the Corps acknowledged that "impacts to protected mussels may potentially occur whenever flows are less than 8,000 cfs".

After allowing the parties to fully brief the issues, and pursuant to the hearing conducted on April 14, 2006, the court denied Florida's Motion because Florida did not show a substantial likelihood of success on the merits or an irreparable injury. However, the court expressly stated that if the Corps took future action that resulted in an irreparable injury under the ESA, Florida was permitted to again seek injunctive relief.

Thereafter, on June 21, 2006, Florida filed a Motion for Temporary Restraining Order to Protect Threatened and Endangered Mussels. In this Motion, Florida argued that the IOP, as implemented, resulted in an unlawful take of the ACF species, specifically the endangered and threatened mussels. Florida supported its Motion with evidence that the Corps' implementation of the IOP and allowing precipitous drops in flows stranded hundred of mussels and resulted in the deaths of numerous protected mussels. Accordingly, on June 22, 2006, the court granted Florida's Motion and ordered the Corps to deviate from the IOP and maintain releases of 8,000 cfs from Woodruff Dam. The court then set the case for a hearing the next day.

Pursuant to the June 23, 2006 hearing, and a tentative agreement reached by the parties at the court's urging, the court revised its temporary restraining order and lowered the required release from Woodruff to 7,000 cfs. Over the next seven days, as the parties negotiated a settlement, the court lowered the releases at Woodruff Dam from 7,000 cfs to 6,000 cfs. Ultimately, on June 30, 2006, the parties entered into an Interim Settlement Agreement. This historic Agreement created an environmental storage pool in the ACF System that Florida could access to ensure that flows from Woodruff were maintained at an average of 6,000 cfs. The court approved the Interim Settlement Agreement and vacated its temporary restraining order.

Currently, the ACF Basin is experiencing a severe drought, with basin inflows recently measured below 2,500 cfs. Moreover, the Interim Settlement Agreement expired on July 24, 2006. Accordingly, the Corps reverted back to the IOP and gradually ramped down releases from Woodruff Dam to 5,000 cfs. As a result, Florida filed this Motion for Temporary Restraining Order, requesting a minimum flow of 6,300 cfs in the Apalachicola River until the Corps and FWS complete their formal consultation. The court permitted the parties to submit briefs and evidence in support of their respective positions, and heard oral arguments on July 24, 2006. A portion of the evidence submitted for purposes of this Motion was the same evidence submitted during Florida's previous Motion for Temporary Restraining Order. However, a substantial quantity of new evidence was introduced for purposes of this Motion. The most important new evidence came from the declaration and oral testimony of Ms. Gail Carmody, the local Field Supervisor for the FWS.

[The court ruled that Florida complied with the ESA's 60–day citizen suit notice requirement, and that the proper standard for preliminary injunctive relief to apply in this case is the traditional four-prong test, but with the recognition of the balancing of equities and the determination of public good already made by Congress in enacting the ESA.]

<h1 style="text-align:center">V. DISCUSSION</h1>

Having determined that the traditional 4–prong test applies, with special deference to be given to Congressional balancing of equities in favor of an endangered species, the court must apply that standard to determine whether Florida's request for an injunction should be granted. Georgia and ARC raise some procedural challenges to Florida's motion. The court need not consider those challenges in light of the determination that Florida has not met its burden to establish that the Corps' IOP is responsible for the alleged take of the protected mussels and that the take will result in irreparable harm before the FWS issues its biological opinion on September 5, 2006.

A. Likelihood of success on the merits.

Florida bears the burden of establishing that it has a substantial likelihood of success on the merits of its claim. In this case, Florida must establish that the IOP under which the Corps currently operates is causing a prohibited take of the endangered mussels in the Apalachicola River basin in violation of § 9 of the ESA. No one disputes that protected mussels are dying by the hundreds, that more will die at 5,000 cfs, and that their habitat is being modified by the decreased flows so that they are facing death, harm and harassment. Thus, the court finds that a take has occurred as that term is defined by 16 U.S.C. § 1532(19) and 50 C.F.R. § 17.3. If that take is caused by a "person," that take is prohibited by 16 U.S.C. § 1538(a)(1)(B). Florida, however, has not demonstrated "but for" causation between the Corps' actions in implementing the IOP and the take of these mussels. *See Babbitt v. Sweet Home Chapter of Communities for a Great Or.,* 515 U.S. 687, 700, n. 13 (1995) ("but for" causation required for a takings claim); *Cold Mountain v. Garber,* 375 F.3d 884, 890 (9th Cir.2004) (affirming summary judgment because plaintiffs failed to establish a causal link between the challenged activity and the alleged "taking"); *Loggerhead Turtle v. County Council of Volusia County, Fla.,* 92 F. Supp. 2d 1296, 1306–07 (M.D. Fla. 2000) (plaintiff failed to establish that the challenged ordinance caused the takings).

Florida cites the Declaration of Gail Carmody, filed by the Corps on July 14, 2006 as showing that the IOP results in a take. Ms. Carmody is the Field Supervisor for the Northwest Florida Ecological Services Field Office of the Southeastern Region of the U.S. Fish and Wildlife Services, an agency of the Department of Interior. She bears responsibility for administration of § 7 of the ESA, including consultation with federal agencies, such as the Corps, when their actions might affect endangered species; issuance of biological opinions concerning the effect of those activities on the species; and devising reasonable and prudent alternatives to avoid the likelihood of jeopardizing the continued existence of the species.

The FWS has been engaged in informal then formal consultation with the Corps concerning the IOP and its possible effects on the protected species within the ACF basin. At the request of the court, the Corps obtained Ms. Carmody's declaration containing the preliminary conclusions of the

FWS, and Ms. Carmody appeared at the hearing on the TRO so the court could benefit from her expertise.

All parties to this dispute point to portions of Ms. Carmody's declaration to support whatever position they assert. Although the entire report provides important historical background and current analysis of the plight of the protected mussels, the most significant statement is paragraph 6(g), where Ms. Carmody states: "[b]ased on the preliminary conclusions listed above, we anticipate that the Service's Biological Opinion will find that the IOP is likely to result in incidental take of the listed mussels, but is not likely to jeopardize their continued existence." Florida relies on the first part—that the IOP is likely to result in incidental take—to support its argument that the Corps has and is continuing to violate § 9's prohibition of any take. Not surprisingly, the Corps cites the second part—that the IOP is not likely to jeopardize the continued existence of the mussels—as support of its position of no take, or alternatively, that it will not cause irreparable harm.

At the hearing, Ms. Carmody explained FWS's position. She confirmed that adverse effects caused by the IOP are likely to result in a take, but that the combination of all the adverse effects will not likely jeopardize the future existence of the species as a whole. However, she did clarify that when she refers to a "take" she is using that term within the context of § 7 and not § 9.

The court recognizes that the standard for a prohibited take under § 9 differs from the standard that the FWS must apply in evaluating an incidental take pursuant to § 7. Section 9 prohibits the "take" of any endangered species. *See* 16 U.S.C. § 1538(a)(1)(B). Section 7 requires a federal agency, such as the Corps, to insure that its action "is not likely to jeopardize the continued existence of any endangered species or threatened species or result in the destruction or adverse modification of habitat of such species. . ." 16 U.S.C. § 1536(a)(2) (2005). This section further requires consultation with the FWS and provides for the granting of an exemption for certain activities that jeopardize endangered or threatened species or adversely alter the habitat of these species. *Id.; see also* 16 U.S.C. § 1536(h).

In *Loggerhead Turtle v. County Council of Volusia County, Fla.,* the court noted:

> It is irrelevant for the purposes of the Act whether the "taking" at issue involves a critical habitat or not. Moreover, the Act does not distinguish between a taking of the whole species or only one member of the species. *Any taking and every taking*—even of a single individual of the protected species—is prohibited by the Act. *See* 16 U.S.C. § 1538. Hence the future threat of a even [sic] single taking is sufficient to invoke the authority of the Act. *See Swan View Coalition, Inc. v. Turner,* 824 F. Supp. 923, 938 (D. Mont. 1992) (threatened extinction is not necessary for a finding of harm under the Endangered Species Act).

896 F.Supp. 1170, 1180 (M.D. Fla. 1995) (emphasis in original). Florida argues that this court should follow the declaration of the court in *Loggerhead Turtle* and hold that the loss of even one mussel constitutes an impermissible take in this case. The court need not reach this disputed point because, even assuming the loss of any mussels qualifies as a take, Florida has not established the necessary causal link between the actions of the Corps and the harm to the mussels. As the Corps asserts, not every take violates the ESA. Section 9 prohibits takes by "any person." 16 U.S.C. § 1538(a)(1)(B). Takes that result from acts of nature do not fall within the prohibition of § 9 and cannot be blamed on the Corps. *See* 16 U.S.C. § 1532(19).

Florida urges this court to find that the Corps' choice as to the amount of water to retain upstream in storage verses the amount to release downstream to support protected mussels violates the anti-taking provision of the ESA. The court is not convinced that the predicament faced by these protected mussels rests at the feet of the Corps. Instead, the weight of evidence points to other causes for the exposure of the mussels and harm to their habitat. No one disputes that the ACF basin suffers from severe drought conditions. Evidence from FWS indicates that drought conditions have become more severe than droughts were in the years prior to the constructing of dams on these affected rivers. While the presence of these dams may have contributed in some ways to the effects of this year's drought, Florida offered no evidence on this point. Because of decreased rainfall and increased evaporation, the amount of water available in the ACF basin has fallen sharply. The court cannot hold the Corps responsible for the absence of rain.

Given these facts, and the lack of evidence to establish a causal connection between any take of the mussels and actions by the Corps, Florida fails to meet its burden of establishing a substantial likelihood of success on the merits.

[The court also found Florida failed to meet the standards for irreparable harm and balancing of equities]

VI. CONCLUSION

In summary, the court finds that Florida's proof falls short of establishing that the actions by the Corps in implementing the IOP have caused or will cause a take of the protected mussels in the Apalachicola River basin. The Corps cannot control the weather, nor can it be held responsible for the effects of the weather on the mussels' habitat. The Corps, in consultation with FWS, faces the unenviable task of balancing the competing demands for the dwindling amounts of water in the reservoirs it manages. Providing more water for the mussels than nature has herself demonstrates that the Corps takes seriously its responsibility to ensure that its actions do not jeopardize the continued existence of these mussels....Having found that Florida failed to show that the Corps' actions caused an unlawful "take" of federally protected species, the court finds that Florida's Renewed Motion for Temporary Restraining Order is due to be DENIED.

NOTES & QUESTIONS

1. Stating the obvious in the physical sense, the court in the ACF case observed that it cannot hold the Corps responsible for the absence of rain. But is it consistent with the ESA to characterize the Corps as being *completely* outside the chain of causation of take?

2. What are the implications of the court's ruling that "takes that result from acts of nature do not fall within the prohibition of § 9 and cannot be blamed on the Corps." What is *natural* about the ACF? The Corps manages water flows on the Chattahoochee River through its four massive reservoirs, meaning the Apalachicola River receives for the most part only what the Corps releases. If the drought persisted, is the Corps ever responsible under the court's rationale for managing the river flows in favor of the mussels? What if Florida could show that the drought is being caused in part by global climate change resulting in part from anthropogenic releases of greenhouse cases? Would anyone be responsible for takes in those circumstances, or would those takes still be the result of "acts of nature" and thus outside the scope of the ESA?

3. In connection with the balancing of equities prong of analysis not reproduced above, the court found influential the argument that while the release of more water from the upstream reservoirs would benefit the mussels in the short term, the long term effect of drawing down water from Lake Lanier could be more deleterious to the actual survival of the mussel species "because using the reserves now would mean that less water will be available in the future to combat the effects of this drought should it continue as anticipated." When would this ever *not* be a possibility? At what point does the balance tip in favor of taking immediate action to avoid take notwithstanding the effect this may have on the reserve of water available for the future? Given this and the perplexing questions raised in the previous notes, does it strike you that the ESA is an effective mechanism for allocating water between states?

The ACF water war heated up to multiple boiling points after the district court's ruling in the ESA case:

July 2006. Judge Bowdre ordered the three states into mediated negotiation.

August 2006. A U.S. Geological Survey report examined water level drops over the past half century that have caused drier conditions in wetlands and adjacent river flood plains. Florida claimed the study supports its argument that Apalachicola River water levels have declined more than previously thought.

September 2006. The Fish and Wildlife Service finally issues its biological opinion concluding that the Corps' 5000 cfs minimum flow plan will not jeopardize the mussels' continued existence, and Florida and Alabama immediately file suit challenging the opinion.

October 2006. The Corps announced it will update the 50–year–old management manuals used to regulate the ACF. The old manuals may not accurately reflect the growth along the rivers and the current water needs of towns, industries and recreational lakes.

November 2006. The Corps began public meetings on water releases from Lake Lanier as part of its preparation of an environmental impact statement on proposed water storage contracts. The impact statement is mandated by a settlement the Corps reached that year (without Florida's knowledge) with Alabama power users in a suit alleging that increased delivery of water to Atlanta would increase the cost of hydro-power to them.

January 2007. The three states extended their confidential mediated negotiations ordered by Judge Bowdre through January, the second such extension. Also, the Georgia House of Representatives passed Ga. H.R. 56, a unanimous resolution asking Congress to raise allowed lake levels in the Corps reservoirs.

February 2007. The states requested another extension.

March 2007. Having played out in four different federal district courts over almost two decades, a federal panel of judges consolidated four active ACF lawsuits and appointed U.S. District Judge Paul A. Magnuson, who handled arguments several years ago over water management issues on the Missouri River, to preside over the case.

October 2007. Georgia's congressional delegation submits bills in the Senate and House which would amend the ESA to allow the Corps or a Governor to suspend operation of the ESA upon finding a drought is endangering public health, safety, or welfare.

October 2007 – January 2008. While preparing for litigation in the consolidated proceeding, the three states negotiated further, to no avail.

February 2008. In Southeastern Federal Power Customers v. Geren, 514 F.3d 1316 (D.C. Cir. 2008), the D.C. Circuit Court of Appeals ruled that the Corps exceeded its statutory authority by entering into the 2006 settlement agreement that required the Corps to reallocate some of the storage in Lake Lanier to water supply.

April 2008. The Corps issued an operating plan and submitted it to the Fish and Wildlife Service for consultation under the Endangered Species Act.

March 2009. The Corps issued a legal opinion saying it has statutory authority to meet metro Atlanta's water needs.

Then, in July 2009, Judge Magnuson issued his first major ruling from the consolidated proceedings, deciding to the surprise of many—and to the dismay of the Corps and Georgia—that the Corps does *not* have statutory authority to provide drinking water to Atlanta from Lake Lanier and giving Atlanta three years to either obtain congressional authorization for such purposes or find alternative sources of water. In re Tri-State Water Rights Litigation, 639 F.Supp.2d 1308 (M.D. Fla. 2009). The decision did not reach the issues raised under the ESA, NEPA, and other environmental laws, leaving them for a second phase of the case, but does close with the following observation about water policy in the United States:

> Too often, state, local, and even national government actors do not consider the long-term consequences of their decisions. Local governments allow unchecked growth because it increases tax revenue, but these same governments do not sufficiently plan for the resources such unchecked growth will require. Nor do individual citizens consider frequently enough their consumption of our scarce resources, absent a crisis situation such as that experienced in the ACF basin in the last few years. The problems faced in the ACF basin will continue to be repeated throughout this country, as the population grows and more undeveloped land is developed. Only by cooperating, planning, and conserving can we avoid the situations that gave rise to this litigation.

In another astounding turn of events, however, in 2011 the Eleventh Circuit relieved Atlanta of the pressure cooker Judge Magnuson's order created, reversing the lower court's findings that the applicable reservoir management statutes precluded delivery of water for municipal drinking supplies and giving the Corps one year to devise a plan for doing so. *See* In re MDL – 1824 Tri-State Water Rights Litigation, 644 F.3d 1160 (11th Cir. 2011). The Supreme Court declined to hear Florida's request for review in 2012.

As it stood at the end of 2012, therefore, Georgia appeared to hold the cards with respect to the question of whether the Corps' reservoir management authority allows it to deliver water to Atlanta, but the environmental law issues remained unresolved. If you were an advisor to the Governor of Georgia, what would you suggest as the state's next step? How about for the Governor of Florida?

CHAPTER 11

COASTAL AND MARINE ECOSYSTEMS

Chapter Outline:

A. BIODIVERSITY IN COASTAL AND MARINE ECOSYSTEMS

Coastal and marine ecosystems, which cover over 70 percent of the earth's surface, pose the irony of being both highly productive in terms of goods and services provided *to* humans, and highly sensitive to the assaults caused *by* humans. Both conditions are the result of the sheer complexity of the matrix of ecological factors we call the coastal zone—the beaches, bays, estuaries, tidelands, reefs, and other features that form the transition between terrestrial ecosystems and the open ocean. The complex ecosystem dynamics of the coastal zone involve immense inputs of water, nutrients, and sediments from terrestrial and freshwater sources, plus cold, nutrient-rich seawater from upwelling currents that run along the continental shelves. The result is an ecological mixing bowl that, combined with the open ocean, accounts by some estimates for over two-thirds of global ecological goods and services. Yet, because the mixing bowl depends on continued inputs from land and sea, human activities in those regions have profound effects on the coastal zone recipe. By all measures humans have altered

754

that recipe dramatically, the only question being whether we have also done so irreversibly.

Anyone who has walked along a shoreline will appreciate the sheer diversity of life and ecological processes found where land meets sea. Estimates are that this thin ribbon of land and water accounts for over one-third of the earth's ecological goods and services, making it by far the most productive ecosystem type per acre. The coastal zones of the United States (excluding Alaska) include 34,000 square miles of estuaries and almost 60,000 miles of ocean shoreline. Estuaries, where freshwater from rivers and streams meets salty seawater, are vitally important to birds, mammals, fish, shellfish and other wildlife. They support habitat for 75 percent of our nation's commercial fish stocks and 75 percent of the listed threatened and endangered birds and mammals. In particular, the wetlands and other land areas ringing the aquatic component of estuaries help to filter pollution and sediment from upland runoff, stabilize the shoreline, provide flood control, and support highly productive plant life and other habitat. Indeed, in terms of net primary production per acre, coastal mangrove forests are perhaps the most productive ecosystem on the planet. Other important systems in the coastal zone include seagrass and algae beds, kelp forests, tidal marshes, and coral reefs.

By comparison, the open ocean is not nearly as productive as the coastal zone ecosystems, but it is far from the void it was once thought to be. United States jurisdiction extends to more than 2.2 million nautical square miles of ocean. Ocean waters over the U.S. continental shelf have always played an important role in fishery harvests. The deep ocean has been far less explored, but is increasingly understood to support a considerable array of pelagic (living in the vertical water column) and benthic (living on the ocean floor) marine life. The ocean itself is also crucially important to overall global health, serving as a sort of planetary biological pump regulating numerous ecological conditions. It is a vast sink for global carbon and nutrients, and its deep currents modulate global weather patterns.

As productive and important to global functioning as it is, the complex of coastal and marine ecosystems is nonetheless under substantial assault by human land-based and water-based activities. Many people fail to appreciate the connections between their land-based actions and the health of coastal and marine ecosystems, and most also are largely unaware of the impacts of water-based industries on coastal and marine resources.

Coastal areas are among the most popular places to live and locate industry in the United States. The coastal zone, defined for demographic purposes as all areas within 50 miles of shoreline, constitutes 17% of the U.S. land area, but is inhabited by more than 53% of the nation's population. Coastal populations continue to grow, a trend that could result in three-quarters of the U.S. population's living in the coastal zone by as soon as 2020. Current estimates by the federal government are that 163 million people lived in coastal watershed counties in the United States in 2010, which is an increase of 40 million since 1980, and that the number will increase to 180 million by 2020. This continuing pressure to develop the coastal zone has resulted in significant conversion of habitat, particularly of coastal wetlands and seagrass beds. But the impacts of land-based development on coastal ecosystems go far beyond direct habitat losses. In its comprehensive report on the issue, *Protecting the Oceans from Land-based Activities*, the United Nations Environment Program explains that by altering runoff flow regimes and coastal land barrier effects, coastal development accelerates erosion of shorelines. Also, urban land uses in the coastal zone, as well as agricultural land uses there and far inland, contribute to runoff of sediment, nutrient, and other pollutants into coastal ecosystems, and direct discharge of treated sewage and industrial effluent visibly impairs coastal waters. For example, the U.S. Environmental Protection Agency's *1994 National Water Quality Inventory*, its first comprehensive take of the issue, rated nutrients and bacteria as the primary pollutants that are impairing estuaries, with urban runoff, sewage plants, agriculture, and industry discharges, in that order, as the leading sources. Even land-based air pollution, given the ocean's efficiency at absorbing atmospheric chemicals, is increasingly becoming a concern in the marine environment.

Water-based industries have taken their toll on coastal and marine ecosystems as well. The shipping industry discharges and spills millions of tons of oil per year. The cruise ship industry, a worldwide fleet of more than 200 ships carrying over 10 million passengers annually, is a major discharger of "graywater" (galley and bath water), "blackwater" (human wastes), and ballast water. *See* Aaron Courtney et al., *Multijurisdictional Regulation of Cruise Ship Discharges*, 19 NATURAL RESOURCES & ENV'T 50 (Summer 2004). For a comprehensive study of marine pollution from sources including sewage treatment plants, industrial facilities, ships, and at-sea dumping of sewage sludge and garbage, see DONALD F. BOESCH, MARINE POLLUTION IN THE UNITED STATES (2001) (science report prepared for the Pew Oceans Commission), *available at* http://www.pewtrusts.org/our_work_report_detail.aspx?id=30035. The fishing industry, which experienced massive capitalization and technological advances in the 1970s and 1980s, is at risk of fishing itself out of existence. Of 200 marine stocks of fish harvested worldwide, the U.S. National Oceanographic and Atmospheric Administration (NOAA) considers at least a third to be below estimated long term sustainable levels, and a survey by the American Fisheries Society identifies more than 80 North American marine fish species considered at risk of extinction. As one might expect, these are comprised largely of high trophic level species that grow slowly, mature late in life, and reproduce less frequently—generally, the fish humans like to eat for food and prize as recreational trophy catches.

So how bad is it? Is it all doom and gloom? Can the impacts be reversed? The fact is that we don't know. The first study ever to comprehensively examine the effects of human actions on coastal ecosystems since the rise of modern *homo sapiens* suggests that long time lags exist between cause and effect and that the effects usually are larger than ever imagined. *See* Jeremy B. C. Jackson et al., *Historical Overfishing and the Recent Collapse of Coastal Ecosystems*, 293 SCIENCE 629 (2001). The researchers concluded that historical overfishing exceeds pollution, habitat loss, and climate change as the leading factor in this story. As overfishing directly removes members of complex food chains, cascade effects through the food chains are substantial but may take decades or longer to play out. Long after a species at a particular trophic level is decimated, others may perish simply as a result of the new food chain dynamic. There is also mounting evidence, however, that marine species are suffering increased disease as the stresses of pollution and ocean warming decrease host resistance and improve conditions for opportunistic parasites and other disease vectors. *See* C.D. Harvell et al., *Emerging Marine Diseases—Climate Links and Anthropogenic Factors*, 285 SCIENCE 1505 (1999). No one knows whether these and other effects are preordained to become worse given what has happened up to now, or whether they could be reversed by action, perhaps drastic action, taken immediately.

Indeed, some may argue the situation is not that grim. Although many of our coastal waters are threatened by the assaults mentioned above, many remain in good condition. Many local economies and industries depend on healthy coastal and marine ecosystems, and thus have an incentive to protect them.

Perhaps the policy measures discussed in the remainder of this chapter already have turned the tide of degradation. There is evidence in both directions. In its first comprehensive report on the issue, EPA described the ecological and environmental conditions of the nation's coastal waters, showing a mixed bag. *See* USEPA, OFFICE OF WATER, CLEAN WATER ACTION PLAN: NATIONAL COASTAL CONDITION REPORT (2002). EPA summarized its findings as follows:

> Existing data show that the overall condition of the U.S. coastal waters as fair to poor, varying from region to region and that 44% of estuarine areas in the U.S. are impaired for human use or aquatic life use. To determine the overall condition of the Nation's estuaries, EPA measured seven coastal condition indicators, including water clarity, dissolved oxygen, sediments, benthos, fish contamination, coastal wetlands loss, and eutrophication. These indicators were rated in estuaries in each region of the country (northeastern, southeastern, Gulf of Mexico, west coast, and Great Lakes regions). The condition of each resource was rated as good, fair, or poor. The indicators were combined to describe the overall coastal condition for each of the region.

> The northeastern estuaries, Gulf of Mexico and the Great Lakes are in fair to poor ecological condition, while southeastern and west coast estuaries are in fair ecological condition. Water clarity is good in west coast and northeastern estuaries, but fair in the Gulf of Mexico, southeastern estuaries, and the Great Lakes. Dissolved oxygen conditions are generally good and sediment contaminant conditions are generally poor throughout the estuaries and Great Lakes of the United States. Eutrophication in coastal waters is increasing throughout much of the United States and results in poor eutrophic conditions in the Gulf of

Mexico, west coast and northeastern estuaries and in fair to good conditions in the remaining estuaries of the continental United States.

Living resources are in fair condition in estuaries throughout the United States, although small changes in water quality could cause this condition to worsen and result in a poor rating. Living resources in the Great Lakes, northeastern estuaries, Gulf of Mexico and the west coast are currently in poor condition. Contaminant concentrations in fish tissues are low throughout the estuarine waters of the United States with exceptions in selected northeastern estuaries, Gulf of Mexico estuaries and the Great Lakes. Fish consumption advisories exist throughout the Gulf of Mexico and northeastern coastal areas, although these advisories largely pertain to offshore species (e.g., king mackerel).

USEPA, OFFICE OF WATER, FACT SHEET NATIONAL COASTAL CONDITION REPORT (2001), *available at* http://water.epa.gov/type/oceb/assessmonitor/nccr/.

- A decade later, EPA released its fourth such report, summarizing its findings as follows:

- Overall condition of the Nation's coastal waters was fair from 2003 to 2006.

- The three indices that showed the poorest conditions throughout the U.S. were coastal habitat condition, sediment quality, and benthic condition.

- Southeastern Alaska and American Samoa received the highest overall condition scores (5=Good).

- The Great Lakes received the lowest overall condition score (2.2=Fair to poor).

- Comparison of the condition scores shows that overall condition in U.S. coastal waters has improved slightly since NCCR I.

USEPA, Office of Water, Fact Sheet National Coastal Condition Report IV (2012), *available at* http://water.epa.gov/type/oceb/assessmonitor/nccr/. EPA also provided the following "score card" showing the bottom line for each coastal region of the United States:

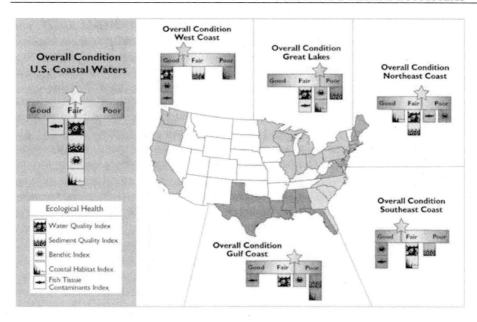

NOTES & QUESTIONS

1. What is your "take away" message from EPA's conclusions? With conditions having improved over the past decade, how concerned should we be about the need for yet more ecosystem management law for coastal and marine settings? How much should we be willing to invest to restore all coastal factors to good condition?

2. In the late 1990s, a group of marine scientists responded to growing concerns about the depletion of marine diversity by forming an effort to conduct a census of marine species. With $20 million in seed funding by the Alfred P. Sloan Foundation, in May 2000 the Census of Marine Life (CoML) officially began this initiative, which has involved more than 300 scientists from 53 countries and is planned to last a decade. In October 2003, after having spent $70 million of what is expected to be a $1 billion price tag before it is complete, the CoML released its first set of findings, known as the "baseline" report. *See* THE UN-KNOWN OCEAN: BASELINE REPORT OF THE CoML 2003 (Oct. 16, 2003), *available at* www.coml.org/baseline/Baseline Report 101603.pdf. The report noted that scientists had already named more than 210,000 marine species before the CoML began, but that the CoML has already assembled information on 25,000 additional species so far. The CoML released its final report in 2010, documenting the discovery of tens of thousands of new species and the high degree of both the interconnectedness and the degradation of their environments. *See* FIRST CENSUS OF MARINE LIFE 2010: HIGHLIGHTS OF A DECADE OF DISCOVERY (2010), *available at* http://www.coml.org/press-releases-2010.

3. Among the many sources of stress in marine environments, one not usually thought of is increased human-induced ocean noise. Seismic surveys, the whine of motors, test explosives blasts, Navy sonar systems, and a host of other intrusions have made a cacophony out of some coastal and ocean waters. Marine mammal researchers are increasingly concerned that these unnatural noises may disrupt the hearing of whales and other marine mammals, *see* David Malakoff, *A Roaring Debate Over Ocean Noise*, 291 SCIENCE 576 (2001), and litigation has been initiated to challenge some noise-producing activities for alleged failure adequately to take those effects into account. Finding agency violations of the Endangered Species Act, Marine Mammals Protection Act, and the National Environmental Policy Act, the court in Natural Resources Defense Council v. Evans, 279 F.Supp.2d 1129 (N.D. Cal. 2003), enjoined the U.S. Navy from testing low frequency active sonar (LFAS) systems in ocean waters inhabited by whales, dolphins, seals, and other marine mammals. The Navy and the plaintiff environmental protection interest groups later agreed to terms under which testing could take place in specified waters subject to guidelines. Later, however, the same court refused to preliminarily enjoin private testing of a high-frequency whale-detecting sonar system designed to help the military and commercial ships avoid hitting whales. *See* Australians for Animals v. Evans, 301 F.Supp.2d 1114 (N.D. Cal. 2004). For background on these events, see John M. Van Dyke, *More Bad News for the Whales*, 19 NATURAL RESOURCES & ENV'T 20 (Summer 2004). *See also* Hawaii County Green Party v. Clinton, 124 F.Supp.2d 1173 (D. Haw. 2000) (dismissing suit challenging Navy development and deployment of low-frequency active sonar defense system). Litigation over sonar training raged on, however, with courts imposing restrictions on Navy training. *See* NRDC v. Winter, 530 F. Supp. 2d 1110 (C.D. Cal. 2008), *aff'd* 518 F.3d 704 (9th Cir. 2008). In Winter v. NRDC, 129 S.Ct. 365 (2008), the Supreme Court vacated the Ninth Circuit's preliminary injunction requiring additional mitigation measures for sonar training exercises, finding the lower courts had applied too lenient a standard for award of preliminary injunctive relief and that the balance of equities tipped strongly in the Navy's favor. In August 2008, the Navy then settled the outstanding litigation, agreeing to specified mitigation measures.

4. Ecosystem management policies in coastal and marine settings have generally followed one of two approaches: the Integrated Coastal Management (ICM) approach and the Large Marine Ecosystem Management (LME) approach. *See* Roger B. Griffis and Katharine W. Kimball, *Ecosystem Approaches to Coastal and Ocean Stewardship*, 6 ECOLOGICAL APPLICATIONS 708 (1996). ICM techniques focus on coordinating the policy and governance process for a defined eco-region along issue-specific lines. LME, the more science-driven of the two approaches, defines large-scale hydrographic regimes within which management decisions are focused on thematic rather than species-specific objectives. The two methods are not mutually exclusive; indeed, combined they recognize what others have stated as a fundamental reality of ecosystem management—that it is both a political and a scientific endeavor.

5. We've organized this chapter into subcategories of ecosystems such as beaches, coastal waters, estuaries, and bays. These are, at best, rough geographic divisions that bear only limited ecological validity. A subset of the field of oceanography is, essentially, geography for marine ecologists, and at its more advanced levels includes ecological divisions far more detailed than we undertake here. For a lucid account of the field, see ALAN LONGHURST, ECOLOGICAL GEOGRAPHY OF THE SEA (1998).

B. PRIMER ON THE LAW OF COASTAL AND MARINE ECOSYSTEMS

Like the law of the other ecosystems treated in this part of the text, the law of coastal and marine ecosystems evolved initially as an adjunct to the development of property rights and in response to the demands of resource extraction industries. Only recently has anything approaching an ecosystem management model surfaced in this body of laws, and it has done so far less coherently than for the terrestrial and freshwater ecosystems studied in other chapters.

1. Historical Background

The law of coastal and marine ecosystems has unfolded against a context of property and resource ownership that is more complicated than for terrestrial environments. The general framework in force in the United States today, subject to nuances and exceptions not studied here, is as follows: the private owner of land in the coastal zone owns seaward only to the mean high tide water line; the states control the waters (and lands below them) from that point seaward for three miles; federal jurisdiction begins at that point and extends outward another nine miles to the edge of the internationally-recognized 12-mile limit of the territorial sea, and then still farther, albeit for more limited purposes, to the edge of the 200-mile Exclusive Economic Zone. It has not always been so, however, as international law long held that national jurisdiction ended at a three-mile territorial sea limit. All ocean resources beyond that point were a common-pool resource for which open access by all nations was the default rule, subject to modification by international law. The federal government thus was largely excluded from a meaningful role in coastal and marine ecosystem management law—the states dominated along the coastal zone, including the nation's then 3-mile territorial sea, and beyond that only international law could regulate anyone's actions.

That traditional set of affairs was rocked in the 1970s by several developments. Domestically, of course, generic environmental laws such as the Clean Water Act, Clean Air Act, and Endangered Species Act increased federal power everywhere, including the coastal zone. But another new federal law came on line during that period to address coastal issues in particular. The Coastal Zone Management Act of 1972 (CZMA), 16 U.S.C. § 1451–65, established a cooperative venture between the federal and coastal state governments whereby states that agree to regulate coastal development, pursuant to nationally-prescribed goals, receive federal funding and a federal commitment not to act inconsistent with the state's coastal management program. The federal government thereby entered into the coastal arena without upsetting the dominant role states had historically enjoyed.

Just as the CZMA was beginning its tenure, the culmination of movement in the international law forum led to enactment of the other principal federal marine ecosystem legislation, the Magnuson-Stevens Fishery Conservation and Management Act of 1976 (Magnuson-Stevens Act), 16 U.S.C.

§ 1801–1882. The roots of this new law, however, stretched far back in time. President Truman dealt the first blow to the traditional international rule of open access when he declared in 1945 that the United States would exercise regulatory control over "conservation zones in those areas of the high seas contiguous to the coast of the United States wherein fishing activities have been or in the future may be developed and maintained on a substantial scale." Presidential Proclamation No. 2667, 10 Fed. Reg. 12303 (1945). In 1964 Congress enacted the Bartlett Act, Pub. L. No. 88–308, 78 Stat. 194 (1964) (repealed 1977), to prohibit foreign vessel fishing in the United States' territorial sea. The Contiguous Fisheries Zone Act, Pub. L. No. 88–308, 78 Stat. 194 (1964) (repealed 1977), followed in 1966 to formally adopt a 9-mile wide "contiguous zone" beginning at the outer limit of the states' 3-mile territorial sea, but the law established no governance framework for the area beyond state waters. Most other nations made similar or more extensive claims, but by the 1970s most nations were still dissatisfied with the international law of fisheries management generally. Because of the lack of enforcement provisions in most of the bilateral and multilateral international fishing agreements that had been hammered out, open access remained the *de facto* rule of law. Work thus began in the United Nations 1974 Law of the Sea Conference to develop a uniform rule of a 12-mile territorial sea and a 200-mile fishery conservation zone.

Displeased with the Conference's progress on this issue, in 1976 the United States enacted the Magnuson-Stevens Act, unilaterally declaring exclusive fisheries jurisdiction in the 200-mile fishery conservation zone and certain portions of the continental shelf beyond that, and establishing a dominant federal role for governance in the new jurisdiction. Several years later the Law of the Sea Conference settled on the respective 12-mile and 200-mile limits, and President Reagan renamed the fisheries zone the Exclusive Economic Zone (EEZ). Thus the present jurisdictional configuration was not in place, with all the terminology applicable today, until 1982. This explains the rather late start the federal government got in managing coastal and marine fishery resources.

Somewhat like the CZMA in its reliance on shared local and federal roles, the Magnuson-Stevens Act establishes eight Regional Fishery Management Councils to design and implement fisheries management plans that meet nationally-prescribed goals. Also like the CZMA, the Magnuson-Stevens Act did not intrude significantly on the traditional powers of the states to regulate fishing in their coastal waters.

Since their original enactment, both the CZMA and the Magnuson-Stevens Act have received significant amendments the effect of which, arguably, has been to move them closer to the ecosystem management approach. The CZMA was amended in 1990 by the Coastal Zone Act Reauthorization Amendments (CZARA), Pub. L. No. 101–508, tit. VI, subtit. C, 104 Stat. 1388 (1990). Section 6217 of CZARA added a special provision to the CZMA dealing with coastal nonpoint source pollution. *See* 16 U.S.C. § 1455b. The Section 6217 program, as it is often called, requires states with coastal management programs to also develop a coastal nonpoint pollution control program to retain federal funding. CZARA thus moved the CZMA beyond its original focus on development in coastal areas, to recognizing the important indirect effects of land-based activities on the coastal zone. Similarly, the Magnuson-Stevens Act was substantially amended twice, first through the Sustainable Fisheries Act of 1996 (SFA) and again in 2007 under a collection of provisions strengthening catch limits. The SFA amendments expanded federal authority to identify, respond to, and regulate overfishing, required fishery management plans for the first time to identify "essential fish habitat," and added to the national criteria by which fishery plans are measured. The amendments thus recognized that fishery management will usually involve not only regulation of harvests, but also conservation of habitat. After their amendments, therefore, both the CZMA and the Magnuson-Stevens Act incorporate the more holistic approach characteristic of ecosystem management. The details of both laws, as amended, as well as a host of related laws and initiatives, are covered in later sections of this chapter.

Although they may provide a foundation, neither the CZMA nor the Magnuson-Stevens Act can fairly be described as having had comprehensive ecosystem management foremost in mind at their inception. The subsequent amendments to both laws added tidbits of ecosystem focus, but still, by 1990 we lacked a comprehensive national ecosystem management policy for coastal and marine ecosystems. Responding to this gap, and in concert with its overall push to reorient environmental policy toward ecosystem management, the Clinton Administration initiated several ecosystem management initiatives for the coastal and marine settings. The EPA took its watershed approach, developed initially for freshwater ecosystems, seaward in its *Coastal Watershed Protection Strategy*. The U.S. National Oceanographic and Atmospheric Administration (NOAA) teamed up with a group of conservation organizations known as Restore America's Estuaries to develop a *National Strategy to Restore Estuarine Habitat*, a collaborative effort of federal, state, scientific, and community leaders to develop estuary restoration methods and goals. *See* Steve Emmett-Mattox, *Restoration at the Edge—A National Strategy for America's Estuaries*, 23 NATIONAL WETLANDS NEWSLETTER 7 (July-Aug. 2001). Indeed, this effort actually resulted in something tangible—in 2000 the Estuary Restoration Act was enacted to coordinate estuary restoration plans and to fund $275 million in federal money toward estuary restoration over the next 5 years. *See* 33 U.S.C. § 2901; Pub. L. No. 106–457. NOAA also developed final regulations to guide Regional Fishery Management Councils in the identification of essential fish habitat under the Sustainable Fisheries Act amendments to the Magnuson-Stevens Act. *See* 67 Fed. Reg. 2343 (Jan. 17, 2002) (amending 50 C.F.R. part 600). Under authority of an Executive Order President Clinton issued in 2000, NOAA also began directing a coordinated program to assemble and manage Marine Protected Areas—sanctuaries and other preserves designed to replicate in the marine ecosystem what wilderness and other preserve designations accomplish on land. Finally, EPA and NOAA together oversee review and approval of the state Coastal Nonpoint Pollution Control Programs, as required by section 6217 of the CZARA (discussed above).

2. Current Scene

Two important developments that have prompted recent significant changes in our national oceans policy were the release of major policy studies by the U.S. Commission on Ocean Policy and the Pew Charitable Trust's Oceans Commission. Both of these studies had their roots in the United Nations' 1998 ocean policy conference, known as the "Year of the Ocean," at which President Clinton charged NOAA with the task of studying ways to strengthen federal ocean policy. In early 1999, Congress introduced the Oceans Act of 1999, S. 959, 106th Cong. (1999), to establish a National Ocean Council to do much the same thing NOAA was undertaking. NOAA released its report, *Turning to the Sea: America's Ocean Future*, later in 1999, which prompted the administration to form another study task force, this time comprised of the White House Council on Environmental Quality and National Security Council. Meanwhile, Congress had progressed little on the Oceans Act. Hoping to sidestep the political stagnation, the Pew Charitable Trusts initiated its own independent study of national ocean policy in June 2000, and shortly thereafter Congress passed a watered-down version of the Oceans Act aimed primarily at convening the study by the Commission on Ocean Policy. *See* Pub. L. No. 106–256, 114 Stat. 644.

The Commission on Ocean Policy issued a "mid-term" report in September 2002 to apprise Congress of its progress and the preliminary findings drawn from a series of regional public meetings and site visits. *See* U.S. Commission on Ocean Policy, Developing a National Ocean Policy (Sept. 2002). The opening passage of the report provides the gist of the findings: "The oceans are in trouble. Our coasts are in trouble. Our marine resources are in trouble . . . all, perhaps, in serious trouble." *Id.* at 1. While drawing no definitive findings or conclusions, the Commission did identify several key drivers in the declining state of marine and costal resources: (1) rise in coastal population and pollution; (2) overfishing; (3) long-term and abrupt climate change; (4) deterioration of conditions in the Arctic Ocean; (5) the decline of coral and other sensitive resources; (6) the impact of land-based actions; and (7) a confusing, disjointed legal regime. *See id.* at 1–2.

The next study product was the June 2003 report of the Pew Oceans Commission, *America's Living Oceans: Charting a Course for Sea Change*. Central to the Pew report was its focus on bringing an ecosystem management approach to national oceans policy through three broad recommended governance changes: (1) creating an independent oceans agency; (2) better coordination and streamlining of federal management; and (3) creating regional interagency councils to develop multi-state watershed management plans. Specific topics and recommendations made in the report cover the wide spectrum of topics addressed in this chapter of the book. Among other proposals, the Commission recommended:

- Creating a national system of marine reserves in which extractive use of any resource or destruction of any habitat is flatly prohibited;

- Aggressive public acquisition of critical habitat areas in wetlands, estuaries, beaches, dunes, and islands;

- Basing fisheries management on historical, ecologically-based stock levels rather than sustainable commercial yields;

- Developing nonpoint discharge controls for nutrient runoff from inland uses such as agriculture and for toxic chemical in urban runoff;

- Developing more comprehensive controls for inland point sources of pollution such as concentrated animal feeding operations and industrial operations;

- Regulating cruise ship wastewater discharges;

- Regulating ballast water discharges, a leading source of transport of invasive aquatic species;

- Regulating the aquaculture industry to control waste discharges, disease control, and its impacts on land use and wild species; and

- Strengthening coastal land use planning, including reforming federal programs and subsidies that contribute to rapid coastal development.

Over a year later, on September 20, 2004, the U.S. Commission on Ocean Policy issued its final report, *An Ocean Blueprint for the 21st Century*. Like the Pew report, the U.S. Commission identified a wide array of marine resource policy concerns and made over 200 specific recommendations, most of which resemble the thrust of those made in the Pew Commission report. Ecosystem management and governance reform were at the heart of the U.S. Commission's recommendations, as it proposed a National Ocean Policy Framework built on (1) legislation to establish a National Ocean Council; (2) a focus on regional approaches to resource management; and (3) better coordination of federal agency actions and consolidation of their authorities. The National Ocean Council would be an advisory body to the President based in a new White House Office of Ocean Policy and comprised of cabinet secretaries and directors of departments and independent agencies with authorities over coastal and marine resources. The National Ocean Council would develop national ocean management goals, develop a regional framework for ocean governance, and create and coordinate regional ocean councils that would develop and implement regional ocean and coastal management plans consistent with the national goals. The report also recommended that Congress approve an organic statute strengthening and defining the role of NOAA to allow it to execute its many ocean- and coastal-related responsibilities.

The U.S. Commission on Ocean Policy report is available at http://www.oceancommission.gov/documents. The Pew Oceans Commission report is available at http://www.pewoceans.org/oceans/index.asp. For background on these events, see Donna R. Christie, *Implementing an Ecosystem-Approach to Ocean Management: An Assessment of Current Regional Governance Models*, 16 DUKE ENVTL. LAW AND POLICY F. 117 (2006); Linda M.B. Paul, *The 2003 Pew Oceans Commission Report: Law, Policy, and Governance*, 19 NATURAL RESOURCES & ENVIRONMENT 10 (Summer 2004); Ken Gish and Eric Laschever, *The President's Ocean Commission: Progress Toward a New Ocean Policy*, 19 NATURAL RESOURCES & ENVIRONMENT 17 (Summer 2004).

As impressive as the two reports were, implementing them has been slow and difficult. President Bush responded to the U.S. Commission report with his *U.S. Ocean Action Plan*, released on December 17, 2004, in which he called for, among other actions, establishment of a Cabinet-level committee on ocean policy, use of market-based instruments for fishery management, local strategies for coral reef protection, regional coordination of Gulf of Mexico management, and passage of an organic act for NOAA. By executive order he established the Executive Office Committee on Ocean Policy on December 17, 2004. Congress responded with bills focusing primarily on the proposed White House coordination office and a strengthened authority for NOAA. However, although the Magnuson-Stevens Act was amended in 2007 by the Magnuson-Stevens Fishery Conservation and Management Reauthorization Act of 2006. Pub. Law No. 109-479 (2007) (discussed later in this Chapter), no comprehensive oceans policy legislation advanced beyond committee approval in the Bush Administration.

President Obama took a similar approach. First, in 2009 he convened the Interagency Ocean Policy Task Force composed of 24 senior-level officials from executive departments, agencies, and offices across the Federal government and led by the Chair of the Council on Environmental Quality (CEQ). The President charged the Task Force with developing recommendations to enhance our ability to maintain healthy, resilient, and sustainable ocean, coasts, and Great Lakes resources for the benefit of present and future generations. The Task force completed its recommendations in July 2011.   *See*   http://www.whitehouse.gov/administration/eop/ceq/initiatives/ oceans. Acting on the Task Force recommendations, President Obama issued the following Executive Order endorsing the key premises and recommendations of the U.S. Commission.

Executive Order 13547, Stewardship of the Ocean, Our Coasts, and the Great Lakes
The President of the United States, 2010.
75 Federal Register 43023.

By the authority vested in me as President by the Constitution and the laws of the United States of America, it is hereby ordered as follows:

Section 1. Purpose. The ocean, our coasts, and the Great Lakes provide jobs, food, energy resources, ecological services, recreation, and tourism opportunities, and play critical roles in our Nation's transportation, economy, and trade, as well as the global mobility of our Armed Forces and the maintenance of international peace and security. The Deepwater Horizon oil spill in the Gulf of Mexico and resulting environmental crisis is a stark reminder of how vulnerable our marine environments are, and how much communities and the Nation rely on healthy and resilient ocean and coastal ecosystems. America's stewardship of the ocean, our coasts, and the Great Lakes is intrinsically linked to environmental sustainability, human health and well-being, national prosperity, adaptation to climate and other environmental changes, social justice, international diplomacy, and national and homeland security.

This order adopts the recommendations of the Interagency Ocean Policy Task Force, except where otherwise provided in this order, and directs executive agencies to implement those recommendations under the guidance of a National Ocean Council. Based on those recommendations, this order establishes a national policy to ensure the protection, maintenance, and restoration of the health of ocean, coastal, and Great Lakes ecosystems and resources, enhance the sustainability of ocean and coastal economies, preserve our maritime heritage, support sustainable uses and access, provide for adaptive management to enhance our understanding of and capacity to respond to climate change and ocean acidification, and coordinate with our national security and foreign policy interests.

This order also provides for the development of coastal and marine spatial plans that build upon and improve existing Federal, State, tribal, local, and regional decisionmaking and planning processes. These regional plans will enable a more integrated, comprehensive, ecosystem-based, flexible, and proactive approach to planning and managing sustainable multiple uses across sectors and improve the conservation of the ocean, our coasts, and the Great Lakes.

Sec. 2. Policy. (a) To achieve an America whose stewardship ensures that the ocean, our coasts, and the Great Lakes are healthy and resilient, safe and productive, and understood and treasured so as to promote the well-being, prosperity, and security of present and future generations, it is the policy of the United States to:

- (i) protect, maintain, and restore the health and biological diversity of ocean, coastal, and Great Lakes ecosystems and resources;

- (ii) improve the resiliency of ocean, coastal, and Great Lakes ecosystems, communities, and economies;

- (iii) bolster the conservation and sustainable uses of land in ways that will improve the health of ocean, coastal, and Great Lakes ecosystems;

- (iv) use the best available science and knowledge to inform decisions affecting the ocean, our coasts, and the Great Lakes, and enhance humanity's capacity to understand, respond, and adapt to a changing global environment;

- (v) support sustainable, safe, secure, and productive access to, and uses of the ocean, our coasts, and the Great Lakes;

- (vi) respect and preserve our Nation's maritime heritage, including our social, cultural, recreational, and historical values;

- (vii) exercise rights and jurisdiction and perform duties in accordance with applicable international law, including respect for and preservation of navigational rights and freedoms, which are essential for the global economy and international peace and security;

- (viii) increase scientific understanding of ocean, coastal, and Great Lakes ecosystems as part of the global interconnected systems of air, land, ice, and water, including their relationships to humans and their activities;

- (ix) improve our understanding and awareness of changing environmental conditions, trends, and their causes, and of human activities taking place in ocean, coastal, and Great Lakes waters; and

- (x) foster a public understanding of the value of the ocean, our coasts, and the Great Lakes to build a foundation for improved stewardship.

(b) The United States shall promote this policy by:

- ensuring a comprehensive and collaborative framework for the stewardship of the ocean, our coasts, and the Great Lakes that facilitates cohesive actions across the Federal Government, as well as participation of State, tribal, and local authorities, regional governance structures, nongovernmental organizations, the public, and the private sector;

- (ii) cooperating and exercising leadership at the international level;

- (iii) pursuing the United States' accession to the Law of the Sea Convention; and

- (iv) supporting ocean stewardship in a fiscally responsible manner.

Sec. 4. Establishment of National Ocean Council. (a) There is hereby established the National Ocean Council (Council).

(b) The Council shall consist of the following:

- the Chair of the Council on Environmental Quality and the Director of the Office of Science and Technology Policy, who shall be the Co-Chairs of the Council;

- (ii) the Secretaries of State, Defense, the Interior, Agriculture, Health and Human Services, Commerce, Labor, Transportation, Energy, and Homeland Security, the Attorney General, the Administrator of the Environmental Protection Agency, the Director of the Office of Management and Budget, the Under Secretary of Commerce for Oceans and Atmosphere (Administrator of the National Oceanic and Atmospheric Administration), the Administrator of the National Aeronautics and Space Administration, the Director of National Intelligence, the Director of the National Science Foundation, and the Chairman of the Joint Chiefs of Staff;

- (iii) the National Security Advisor and the Assistants to the President for Homeland Security and Counterterrorism, Domestic Policy, Energy and Climate Change, and Economic Policy;

- (iv) an employee of the Federal Government designated by the Vice President; and

- (v) such other officers or employees of the Federal Government as the Co-Chairs of the Council may from time to time designate.

Sec. 5. Functions of the Council.

To implement the policy set forth in section 2 of this order, the Council shall provide appropriate direction to ensure that executive departments', agencies', or offices' decisions and actions affecting the ocean, our coasts, and the Great Lakes will be guided by the stewardship principles and national priority objectives set forth in the Final Recommendations, to the extent consistent with applicable law. The Council shall base its decisions on the consensus of its members. With respect to those matters in which consensus cannot be reached, the National Security Advisor shall coordinate with the Co-Chairs and, as appropriate, the Assistants to the President for Energy and Climate Change, and Economic Policy, and the employee of the United States designated by the Vice President, subject to the limitations set forth in section 9 of this order, to present the disputed issue or issues for decision by the President.

Sec. 6. Agency Responsibilities. (a) All executive departments, agencies, and offices that are members of the Council and any other executive department, agency, or office whose actions affect the ocean, our coasts, and the Great Lakes shall, to the fullest extent consistent with applicable law:

- (i) take such action as necessary to implement the policy set forth in section 2 of this order and the stewardship principles and national priority objectives as set forth in the Final Recommendations and subsequent guidance from the Council; and

- (ii) participate in the process for coastal and marine spatial planning and comply with Council certified coastal and marine spatial plans, as described in the Final Recommendations and subsequent guidance from the Council.

(b) Each executive department, agency, and office that is required to take actions under this order shall prepare and make publicly available an annual report including a concise description of actions taken by the agency in the previous calendar year to implement the order, a description of written comments by persons or organizations regarding the agency's compliance with this order, and the agency's response to such comments.

(c) Each executive department, agency, and office that is required to take actions under this order shall coordinate and contribute resources, as appropriate, to assist in establishing a common information management system as defined in the Final Recommendations and shall be held accountable for managing its own information assets by keeping them current, easily accessible, and consistent with Federal standards.

(d) To the extent permitted by law, executive departments, agencies, and offices shall provide the Council such information, support, and assistance as the Council, through the Co-Chairs, may request.

Sec. 7. Governance Coordinating Committee. The Council shall establish a Governance Coordinating Committee that shall consist of 18 officials from State, tribal, and local governments in accordance with the Final Recommendations. The Committee may establish subcommittees chaired by representatives of the Governance Coordinating Committee. These subcommittees may include additional representatives from State, tribal, and local governments, as appropriate to provide for greater collaboration and diversity of views.

Pursuant to the Executive Order, the National Ocean Council released a draft implementation plan in 2010 outlining these key national priority objectives:

Ecosystem-Based Management: Adopt ecosystem-based management as a foundational principle for the comprehensive management of the ocean, our coasts, and the Great Lakes.

Inform Decisions and Improve Understanding: Increase knowledge to continually inform and improve management and policy decisions and the capacity to respond to change and challenges. Better educate the public through formal and informal programs about the ocean, our coasts, and the Great Lakes.

Observations, Mapping, and Infrastructure: Strengthen and integrate Federal and non-Federal ocean observing systems, sensors, data collection platforms, data management, and mapping capabilities into a national system, and integrate that system into international observation efforts.

Coordinate and Support: Better coordinate and support Federal, State, Tribal, local, and regional management of the ocean, our coasts, and the Great Lakes. Improve coordination and integration across the Federal Government and, as appropriate, engage with the international community.

Regional Ecosystem Protection and Restoration: Establish and implement an integrated ecosystem protection and restoration strategy that is science-based and aligns conservation and restoration goals at the Federal, State, Tribal, local, and regional levels.

Resiliency and Adaptation to Climate Change and Ocean Acidification: Strengthen resiliency of coastal communities and marine and Great Lakes environments and their abilities to adapt to climate change impacts and ocean acidification.

Water Quality and Sustainable Practices on Land: Enhance water quality in the ocean, along our coasts, and in the Great Lakes by promoting and implementing sustainable practices on land.

Changing Conditions in the Arctic: Address environmental stewardship needs in the Arctic Ocean and adjacent coastal areas in the face of climate-induced and other environmental changes.

Coastal and Marine Spatial Planning: Implement comprehensive, integrated, ecosystem-based coastal and marine spatial planning and management in the United States.

NATIONAL OCEAN COUNCIL, DRAFT NATIONAL OCEAN POLICY IMPLEMENTATION PLAN (2010), *available at* http://www.whitehouse.gov/administration/eop/oceans/implementationplan. Public comment periods on the draft plan extended into 2012 and as of this writing the Commission has taken no further action.

Finally, no mention of coastal and marine policy can leave out the 2010 *Deepwater Horizon* oil spill in the Gulf of Mexico. More a story of regulatory failure and corporate neglect than one of ecosystem management policy—there was none—the spill focused attention on the Gulf ecosystem and the need for a more comprehensive approach. To move in that direction, President Obama convened a multi-jurisdictional Gulf Coast Ecosystem Restoration Task Force and charged it to prepare a Strategy that proposes a Gulf Coast ecosystem restoration agenda, including goals for ecosystem restoration, development of a set of performance indicators to track progress, and means of coordinating intergovernmental restoration efforts guided by shared priorities. *See* Executive Order 13544, 75 Fed. Reg. 62313 (Oct. 5, 2010). The Task Force issued its strategy document in 2011 calling for greater coordination as well using civil penalties from enforcement litigation to fund restoration efforts. *See* Gulf of Mexico Regional Ecosystem Restoration Strategy (2011), *available at* http://www.restorethegulf.gov. The Task Force's work, however, is focused primarily on restoration, not ongoing management, and the Executive Order, like all such proclamations, establishes no new legal authority.

NOTES & QUESTIONS

1. As you work though the materials in this chapter, consider that most of the legal framework for ocean and coastal management stems from laws that are decades old. How easy will it be to fulfill the National Ocean Council's vision working from that collection of statutes? Identify specific bottlenecks for moving in that direction, as well as specific means of facilitation.

2. We have a U.S. Forest Service to oversee comprehensive management of public national forests (see Chapter 8) and a Bureau of Land Management to oversee comprehensive management of federal public range lands (see chapter 9). The closest federal equivalent for coasts and oceans is the National Oceanographic and Atmospheric Administration (NOAA), a division of the Department of Commerce. NOAA's strategic plan assigns responsibility for much of its research and conservation of the ocean's living marine resources to the National Marine Fisheries Service (NMFS), also known as NOAA Fisheries. NMFS implements six statutes pertinent to coastal and marine ecosystem management: the Magnuson-Stevens Fishery Conservation and Management Act, which regulates fisheries within the U.S. Exclusive Economic Zone (see this chapter); the Endangered Species Act, which protects threatened or endangered species (see Part II); the Marine Mammal Protection Act, which regulates the taking or harassment of marine mammals (see this chapter); the Lacey Act, which prohibits fishery transactions that violate state, federal, American tribal, or foreign laws; the Fish and Wildlife Coordination Act, which authorizes NMFS to collect fisheries data and to advise other agencies on environmental decisions affecting living marine resources; and the Agricultural Marketing Act, which authorizes a voluntary seafood inspection program. NMFS implements these programs principally through several divisions: the Sustainable Fisheries Division, the Protected Resources Division, and the Habitat Conservation Division.

Elsewhere within NOAA, the National Ocean Service's Office of Ocean and Coastal Resource Management (OCRM) implements two additional laws that are integral to coastal and marine ecosystem management, both of which are covered in this chapter: the Coastal Zone Management Act and the Marine Protection, Research, and Sanctuaries Act. Through this authority OCRM administers 21 Estuarine National Research Preserves and 12 National Marine Sanctuaries, and is the federal representative in 29 state coastal management plans covering over 99 percent of the nation's coastlines. Overall, therefore, NOAA's combined responsibilities bring it close to being the coastal and marine equivalent of the major federal land management agencies.

3. Notwithstanding the scope of NOAA's role in coastal and marine resources management, as both the Pew Oceans Commission and the U.S. Commission on Ocean Policy observed, ecosystem management of coastal and marine resources remains difficult so long as the law is in such disarray. "Not a system at all, U.S. ocean policy is a hodgepodge of individual laws that has grown by accretion over the years, often in response to crisis. More than 140 federal laws pertain to the oceans and coasts. Collectively, these statutes involve at least six departments of the federal government and dozens of federal agencies in the day-to-day management of our ocean and coastal resources." PEW OCEANS

COMMISSION, AMERICA'S LIVING OCEANS: CHARTING A COURSE FOR SEA CHANGE 14 (2003). *See also* U.S. Commission on Ocean Policy, An Ocean Blueprint for the 21st Century App. 6 (2004) (providing a thorough historical review of U.S. ocean and coastal laws); Robin Kundis Craig, *Regulation of U.S. Marine Resources: An Overview of the Current Complexity*, 19 NATURAL RESOURCES & ENV'T 3 (Summer 2004) (providing background on the existing regulatory framework). To bring some sense of order to this chaotic system, both studies strongly advocated legal reform to provide a more centralized and coherent governance regime for coastal and marine resources.

4. Does the National Ocean Council President Obama established move us in that direction? If so, does President Obama have the authority to do so unilaterally, as he did? Congressman Doc Hastings (R-Wash), then Chair of the House committee on Natural resources, did not think so, questioning the President's authority, the funding for the Council's work, and its impacts on jobs and the economy. *See Hastings Says Ocean Policy Oversteps Authority, Seeks Answers from White House*, 42 Env't Rep. 2418 (2011).

5. State ownership of and jurisdiction over the coastal zone was long assumed a right of statehood for the original states as successors to the King's interests in tidelands and the adjacent seas, and for later admitted states based on the doctrine of equal footing, which provides that states admitted into the Union after adoption of the Constitution are entitled to the same rights as the original states in their tidal waters and submerged lands. *See* Pollard's Lessee v. Hagan, 44 U.S. 212 (1845). It was widely assumed that this sovereignty extended not only to the states' inland submerged lands, but also to their claimed three-mile band of coastal waters. State constitutions and statutes treated this arrangement as uncontroversial well into the 20th century, as did the federal government and, it appeared, the United States Supreme Court. This seemingly settled state of affairs was thrown asunder in United States v. California, 332 U.S. 19 (1947), and United States v. Texas, 339 U.S. 707 (1950), wherein the Court held that it was in fact the federal government that had established claim to the three-mile territorial sea and thus had paramount rights to the entire continental shelf, including the minerals in the seabeds beneath what previously had been assumed to be these states' three-mile territorial seas. The states, in other words, had no title or interest in the territorial sea or its submerged lands off their respective coasts after all. This ruling, understandably, caused great controversy. After some congressional jockeying with President Truman over terms, the United States ceded these rights back to the states under the Submerged Lands Act of 1953, while retaining its navigation rights and the rights to regulate within its constitutional scope of power over interstate commerce, navigation, national defense, and international affairs. *See* 43 U.S.C. §§ 1301–1315. Then, to make the extent of federal power and jurisdiction clear, Congress adopted the Outer Continental Shelf Lands Act, mentioned in the previous note, to establish federal ownership and management of the submerged lands seaward of the three-mile state coastal jurisdiction line. As a nuance to this strange jurisdictional history, the Submerged Lands Act allowed states to make claims beyond the three-mile line based on historical claims. The Supreme Court later determined that the historic boundaries of Texas (based on its claims as an independent nation) and Florida (based on congressional approval of its constitution) along the Gulf of Mexico extended three marine leagues (about 10 miles) from the coast. *See* United States v. Florida, 363

U.S. 121 (1960); United States v. Louisiana, 363 U.S. 1 (1960). The final turn of events was the successful suit the United States brought in 1975 against the Atlantic Coast states to extend to those states the reasoning of *United States v. California.*, i.e., that their rights to territorial seas flowed not as a right of statehood, but from the federal government's cession of its paramount rights under the Submerged Lands Act. *See* United States v. Maine, 420 U.S. 515 (1975).

6. As messy as the history of international, national, and state boundary lines has been, the boundary between private and public land ownership along the coast can also be just as complicated. As a general rule, the states, either by original statehood or the equal footing doctrine, have title to lands subject to the ebb and flow of the tides on the basis that they are not capable of private development and that their general uses, such as navigation and fishing, are public in nature. *See* Shively v. Bowlby, 152 U.S. 1 (1894). And, as a general rule, most states follow the federal rule that the state owns these lands seaward of the mean high tide of all high tides. *See* Borax Consolidated v. City of Los Angeles, 296 U.S. 10 (1935). But if tidelands were conveyed into private hands by the United States prior to statehood, or were conveyed by other nations prior to acquisition by the United States through cession or treaty, the private landowner may have a claim seaward of the high tide line, though such grants are narrowly construed. And some states take the position that they do not own tidelands that are not under waters navigable in fact. *See, e.g.,* Lee v. Williams, 711 So.2d 57 (Fla. 5th Dist. Ct. App. 1998) (Florida includes only tidelands under navigable waters as sovereign lands). As for attempts by states to convey tidelands and other submerged lands they own into private hands, see the discussion of the Public Trust Doctrine later in this chapter.

7. Some states have implemented coastal conservation measures going far beyond anything required in federal law. Indeed, South Carolina took such aggressive measures to protect beaches that it wound up in the U.S. Supreme Court. In 1988, the state enacted its Beachfront Management Act, which had the direct effect of barring a beach lot owner, who had purchased his lots before the new law was enacted, from erecting any permanent structures on his property. At the time, the legislation provided for no waivers or permits. A landowner alleged that the state had taken his property without just compensation in violation of the Fifth Amendment. The Supreme Court held that, because the state had denied all economically or beneficial use of all the land in question, it had effected a regulatory taking unless, in the state courts' view, the new law functionally did no more than codify the state's background common law nuisance restrictions on the land. *See* Lucas v. South Carolina Coastal Council, 505 U.S. 1003 (1992). For a discussion of South Carolina's beach conservation efforts before and after the *Lucas* case, see Douglas T. Kendall, *Preserving South Carolina's Beaches: The Role of Local Planning in Managing Growth in Coastal South Carolina*, 1 S.C. ENVTL. L.J. 61 (2000).

8. Coastal states also have a long history of regulating recreational and commercial fishing in their waters. Ironically, this is what recently landed Massachusetts in hot water under the Endangered Species Act. The state established a licensing program for commercial gillnets and lobster pots. The state's licensees, however, fished in waters also occupied by right whales, an endangered species protected under the ESA. Because the use of the licensed gear was associated with whale deaths, a federal appellate court found that the state could be held liable for taking the whales in violation of the ESA because its licenses were a "but for" causative factor in the illegal takes. *See* Strahan v. Coxe, 127 F.3d 155 (1st Cir. 1997). What incentive does such vicarious liability present to states considering whether to regulate fishing in their waters?

9. This chapter focuses primarily on the handful of federal laws and initiatives that can be cobbled together into an ecosystem management framework for coastal and marine ecosystems. For a comprehensive survey of the numerous other federal and state laws that apply to some degree or another to coastal and marine ecosystem issues, see OCEAN AND COASTAL LAW AND POLICY (Donald C. Bauer et al. eds., ABA Press 2008) (twenty chapters covering the full scope of ocean and coastal law); U.S. COMMISSION ON OCEAN POLICY, AN OCEAN BLUE-PRINT FOR THE 21ST CENTURY App. 6 (2004) (providing a thorough historical review of U.S. ocean and coastal laws); Robin Kundis Craig, *Regulation of U.S. Marine Resources: An Overview of the Current Complexity*, 19 NATURAL RESOURCES & ENV'T 3 (Summer 2004) (providing background on the existing regulatory framework); W.M. von Zharen, *Ocean Ecosystem Stewardship*, 23 WM. & MARY ENVTL. LAW AND POLICY FORUM 1, 2–27 (1998).

C. BIODIVERSITY MANAGEMENT IN COASTAL AND MARINE ECOSYSTEMS

Because of its wide geographic spread, the United States enjoys a vast diversity of marine ecosystems in five major regions: Northeast, Southeast, Alaska, Pacific coast, and western Pacific oceanic. While each of these regions presents familiar components of marine ecosystems—beaches, tidelands, estuaries, continental shelf waters, and open ocean—each is distinct given the broad array of climate and geography our nation spans. There may be a common set of problems, including beach erosion, nonpoint source pollution, and overfishing, but solutions will vary by location. The topic of coastal and marine ecosystem management thus is a large umbrella under which many laws and polices will fit.

So what *is* ecosystem-based management for the coastal and marine environments? Recently a group of scientists and policy experts interested in oceans policy addressed that question in a white paper calling for concerted action to implement the recommendations of the U.S. Commission on Ocean Policy. *See* Communication Process for Science and the Sea, Scientific Consensus Statement on Marine Ecosystem-Based Management (Mar. 21, 2005) Their answer, which was specifically adopted by the National Ocean Commission:

> Ecosystem-based management is an integrated approach to management that considers the entire ecosystem, including humans. The goal of ecosystem-based management is to maintain an ecosystem in a healthy, productive and resilient condition so that it can provide the services humans want and need. Ecosystem-based management differs from current approaches that usually focus on a single species, sector, activity or concern; it considers the cumulative impacts of different sectors. Specifically, ecosystem-based management:

- emphasizes the protection of ecosystem structure, functioning, and key processes;

- is place-based in focusing on a specific ecosystem and the range of activities affecting it;

- explicitly accounts for the interconnectedness within systems, recognizing the importance of interactions between many target species or key services and other non-target species;

- acknowledges interconnectedness among systems, such as between air, land and sea; and

- integrates ecological, social, economic, and institutional perspectives, recognizing their strong interdependences.

Consider the extent to which the laws, regulations, and judicial outcomes covered in the text satisfy these criteria. We have chosen a rather obvious, geographically-focused approach for organizing the materials you will study—start at the coastline and work out to the open seas. By and large, this also happens to be approach the applicable legal framework takes. It is, of course, a flawed approach, as the coastal and marine environment comprises one of the most open set of ecosystem dynamics imaginable. Indeed, even what happens well inland of the coastline, in terrestrial and freshwater ecosystems, can have a profound influence on coastal and marine systems. Hence, as you review the following materials, consider how the legal framework (and thus future editions of this text) might be reconceived to more effectively achieve a coherent policy of coastal and marine ecosystem management.

1. BEACHES AND COASTAL LANDS

The Coastal Zone Management Act (CZMA), 16 U.S.C. §§ 1451–1465, is the nation's primary foundation for beach and coastal area conservation. The CZMA authorizes the Department of Commerce to administer a federal grant program to encourage coastal states to develop and implement coastal zone management programs for the purpose of protecting, developing, and enhancing coastal zone resources, which include wetlands, flood plains, estuaries, beaches, dunes, barrier islands, coral reefs, and fish and wildlife and their habitat. The coastal states include any bordering an ocean or the Gulf of Mexico, Long Island Sound, or the Great Lakes. The coastal zone within these states includes coastal waters and adjacent shorelands in proximity to the shoreline. It includes islands, transitional and intertidal areas, salt marshes, wetlands, and beaches. *Id.* § 1453(1). The objectives of the grant program and related CZMA provisions are to improve the management of the coastal zone resources within those states, which necessarily includes managing private and public land development actions in the coastal zone.

Two features set the CZMA apart from many other federal natural resource management laws. First, it relies heavily on states to implement national policy through state-designed land management decision making frameworks. Second, it obligates federal agencies to implement their respective actions in a manner consistent with state coastal management programs. The result is a form of ecosystem management that is quite decentralized but which reaches a broad array of actors and actions.

a. STATE LAND MANAGEMENT FRAMEWORKS

One of the congressional findings supporting the CZMA was that

The key to more effective protection and use of the land and water resources of the coastal zone is to encourage the states to exercise their full authority over the lands and waters in the coastal zone by assisting the states, in cooperation with Federal and local governments and other vitally affected interests, in developing land and water use programs for the coastal zone, including unified policies, criteria, standards, methods, and processes for dealing with land and water use decisions of more than local significance.

16 U.S.C. § 1451(i). The CZMA thus outlines a national policy on coastal zone management, but allows states to devise their own plans for fulfilling those goals and to use state law to implement them. To receive federal approval, which triggers the requirement of federal agency consistency (discussed in the next section), a state coastal management program must describe "permissible land uses and water uses within the coastal zone" and "the means by which the state proposes to exert control over the land uses and water uses . . . including a list of relevant State constitutional provisions, laws, regulations, and judicial decisions." *Id.* § 1455(d)(2). This legal framework must provide for "adequate consideration of the national interest involved in planning for, and managing the coastal zone, including the siting of facilities . . . which are of greater than local significance," *id.* § 1455(d)(8), and it must include "procedures whereby specific areas may be designated for the purpose of preserving or restoring them for their conservation, recreational, ecological, historical, or esthetic values." *Id.* § 1455(d)(9).

So long as the national goals are satisfactorily addressed, the states have considerable latitude in the design of their land use management frameworks. The CZMA lays out three general schemes from which the states can choose: (1) local implementation of the state plan and state-promulgated standards, subject to state review; (2) direct state regulation; and (3) state review of state and local decisions for consistency with the state plan. The intensity of land use regulation can vary under any of these approaches, and some states go well beyond the minimum necessary scope of regulation to implement the CZMA's national goals, albeit others do not. The following case provides an example of a state coastal management program that takes the more aggressive approach.

Kirkorowicz v. California Coastal Commission

Court of Appeal, Fourth District, Division 1, California, 2000.
100 Cal. Rptr. 2d 124.

WORK, J.

FACTUAL AND PROCEDURAL BACKGROUND

The Kirkorowiczes' 21.47 acre property consists of three separate legal parcels. It is irregularly shaped, zoned rural/residential permitting one single-family residential unit per parcel and private stables by right, and located in the Olivenhain community of the City of Encinitas (City). This periodically flooded property lies north of San Elijo Lagoon Preserve within the 100-year floodplain of the Escondido Creek, which forms its eastern boundary. Consistent with the Encinitas General Plan Policies, which encourage equestrian activities in the floodplain, the Kirkorowiczes currently board horses on their property using corrals and fences.

In 1994, the Kirkorowiczes applied to City for a [City Development Permit (CDP)] to board a maximum of 42 horses and to construct an approximately 1,728 square foot enclosed stable, a storage area for supplies and manure, a driveway and a car/horse trailer turnaround area. The proposal included a 27,000 square foot building pad to be created by placing 8,700 cubic yards of fill on the site. City hired biologist Vincent N. Scheidt to evaluate the permit application, to survey the biological resources and to determine whether the proposal would impact wetlands. In a series of reports between October 1995 and July 1996, Scheidt determined that parts of the project were proposed to be developed in wetlands; concluded the project would have a direct, minor impact on marginal wetland habitat areas; identified the wetlands plant species found onsite; mapped the wetlands onsite; and concluded the project would result in a direct loss of .44 acre of jurisdictional wetlands, but that the potentially significant loss was mitigable. On behalf of the Kirkorowiczes, John W. Brown, senior biologist with Dudek & Associates, visited the site in March 1996 and concluded that using United States Army Corps of Engineers' standards for determining jurisdictional wetlands, "wetland hydrology is absent from this portion [the locus of the proposed fill] of the site." However, the Kirkorowiczes' habitat mitigation plan conceded that project implementation would permanently impact .44 acre of very low-quality wetland. Given the historical use of the property as grazing land, the wetlands resource was described as "degraded" in the environmental documentation.

The original project site plan proposed two driveways. Due to the horizontal curve along Manchester Avenue and the obstruction of visibility due to the dirt embankment on Manchester Avenue across from the project site, the original driveway design did not meet City standards for safe stopping sight distance. Consequently, the project was revised to place a single driveway at the southerly end of the building pad that met sight-line requirements for safe ingress from and egress to Manchester Avenue. During City review, the Kirkorowiczes agreed to reduce the proposed wetlands fill and move the pad area closer to the northern boundary to minimize possible wetlands and visual impacts. Later, before the Commission, they further agreed to reduce the area of wetlands impact to .35 acre.

On January 9, 1997, the City Planning Commission (CPC) approved the project, concluding the project would not impose any significant environmental impact that would not be reduced to a level below significant by the required mitigation measures established by the EIA. The San Elijo Lagoon Conservancy, a local preservation group, appealed the CPC's decision to the City Council. On May 14, the City Council approved the project and the issuance of a CDP for construction of the 1,728 square foot stable facility to board up to 39 horses, involving placement of approximately 8,700 cubic yards of fill in approximately .44 acre of wetlands within the 100-year floodplain. On June 2, the matter was appealed to the Commission. On April 8, 1998, by a vote of nine to zero, the Commission followed its staff's recommendation and denied the project as inconsistent with City's certified [Local Comprehensive Plan (LCP)] regarding floodplain development (Land Use Policy 8.2 of the Land Use Plan (LUP)) and protection of wetlands (LUP Resource Management Element Policy 10.6). Specifically, the staff concluded the proposed fill of wetlands to accommodate vehicle access and a turnaround is not permitted under the LCP and that other alternatives to provide safe access to the site and avoid filling the wetlands had not been adequately explored.

The Kirkorowiczes' petition for a writ of administrative mandamus challenged the Commission's decision on several grounds. However, by the time of the hearing on May 7, 1999, the parties agreed that in light of this court's decision in Bolsa Chica Land Trust v. Superior Court (1999) 71 Cal.App.4th 493, 83 Cal.Rptr.2d 850, the Kirkorowiczes' intended construction of a stable under an implied historic use exception was no longer permitted in the wetlands and thus their argument focused on whether their project would affect jurisdictional wetlands. In granting the petition, the trial court declared:

> In this matter, it appears to the Court that the Coastal Commission conducted its proceedings operating under the presumption that the subject property was a protected wetland. However, after having reviewed the administrative record, the Court finds that there is not substantial evidence to support a finding that the Kirkorowicz' property is a protected wetland as contemplated by the Coastal Act, § 30121 and the City's Local Coastal Program Policy 10.6. Accordingly, absent substantial evidence to support the conclusion that the property involves a wetland, the decision denying the CDP was erroneous.

On July 19, 1999, the judgment issuing the peremptory writ was filed, directing the Commission to set aside its April 8, 1998 decision denying the CDP, to rehear the matter and to determine whether there are protected wetlands on the Kirkorowiczes' property. The Commission timely appealed.

THE STANDARD OF REVIEW

Because this matter came to the trial court on a petition for a writ of mandate under Code of Civil Procedure section 1094.5, that court was required to determine whether substantial evidence supported the Commission's findings and whether those findings supported its decision. * * * In determining whether substantial evidence supports the Commission's decision, we look to the "whole" administrative record and consider all relevant evidence, including that evidence which detracts from the decision. Although this task involves some weighing to fairly estimate the worth of the evidence, that limited weighing does not constitute independent review where the court substitutes its own findings and inferences for that of the Commission. Rather, it is for the Commission to weigh the preponderance of conflicting evidence, as we may reverse its decision only if, based on the evidence before it, a reasonable person could not have reached the conclusion reached by it.

THE RECORD CONTAINS SUBSTANTIAL EVIDENCE THAT WETLANDS EXIST ON THE KIRKOROWICZES' PROPOSED PROJECT SITE

Emphasizing wetlands are areas within the coastal zone that may be covered periodically or permanently with shallow water and are characterized by hydric soils and/or hydrophytes, the Commission contends the administrative record contains substantial evidence there are wetlands on the Kirkorowiczes' property. It asserts the area in which the Kirkorowiczes intend to put their driveway and turnaround is covered periodically with shallow water, is marked by the presence of hydrophytes, and was identified by City's consulting biologist as wetlands. In response, the Kirkorowiczes echo their plea below that in light of our decision in Bolsa Chica Land Trust v. Superior Court, supra, "absolutely prohibiting" the Commission from approving any encroachment into wetlands, except for the enumerated uses permitted by section 30233, it is incumbent upon the Commission to take a much closer look at what, in fact, constitutes protected wetlands and thus their case requires reevaluation. They assert that the occasionally wet area on their property is not remotely of the character the Coastal Act was intended to protect. Rather, they contend the Act was intended to protect areas predominantly much wetter than the area in dispute. They argue the periodic coverage of an area with water is not determinative of whether property constitutes a wetland; the wet areas on their property are not part of a marine environment; the mere presence of some hydrophytes is not determinative; and there is no substantial evidence of wetlands hydrology or hydric soils on their property.

The Coastal Act defines "wetland" in section 30121 as "lands within the coastal zone which may be covered periodically or permanently with shallow water and include saltwater marshes, freshwater marshes, open or closed brackish water marshes, swamps, mudflats, and fens." Although the Commission relies on the cited definition to identify "wetlands," by necessity it has expanded the definition, given the highly variable environmental conditions along the California coast rendering some wetlands not readily identifiable by simple means. In its expanded definition, the Commission includes [in guidelines] those lands where "saturation with water is the dominant factor determining the nature of soil development and the types of plant and animal communities living in the soil and on its surface." Consequently, the Commission's regulations further describe wetlands as "land where the water table is at, near, or above the land surface long enough to promote the formation of hydric soils or to support the growth of hydrophytes . . ." (Cal.Code Regs., tit. 14, § 13577(b)(1)), thus recognizing "the presence or absence of hydrophites [sic] and hydric soils are the most useful, but not exclusive, criteria to determine whether a particular parcel is a 'wetland.' " The Commission explains:

> "channels, lakes, reservoirs, bays, estuaries, lagoons, marshes, and the lands underlying and adjoining such waters, whether permanently or intermittently submerged, to the extent that such waters and lands support and contain significant fish, wildlife, recreational, aesthetic, or scientific resources." (§ 5812, subd. (a).)

Our review of the administrative record convinces us that substantial evidence supports the Commission's finding that protected wetlands exist on the Kirkorowiczes' property. Guided by the foregoing broad definition of wetlands, substantial evidence shows the proposed site requiring fill is periodically covered with shallow water and is replete with hydrophytes, and that it specifically has been identified by City's consulting biologist, Scheidt, as wetlands. Preliminarily, located within the 100-year floodplain of the Escondido Creek, the testimonial and photographic evidence shows the development area is periodically covered with shallow water, as even moderate rain causes the area to become submerged and flooded. In fact, since 1982, the Kirkorowiczes' property has been flooded to an extreme depth on an average of two to three times a year, and on countless other occasions has been significantly impacted by average rainfall regardless whether occurring during a wet or dry season. Another professional biologist confirmed this "obvious" inundation lasting for some time each year. Secondly, the record is replete with evidence of the presence of hydrophytes in the development area. The development site involves two broadly overlapping plant communities: ruderal, non-native, mostly upland vegetation associated with intensive agricultural or equestrian site usage, and very low-quality, but mostly native, floodplain fringe wetlands vegetation in areas which are subject to longer periods of hydration during the rainy season. Consulting biologist Scheidt inventoried the flora and fauna he observed and classified the species based on their primary habitat. Of the 42 species of flora he recorded, 18 were wetland species. Four of these species are included in the Commission's representative list of wetland species in its Interpretive Guideline. A third-party professional biologist who conducted a field site inspection concluded the site to be a high-quality functional wetland habitat dominated by these wetland species. Scheidt concluded that a portion of the property proposed for development supported areas of jurisdictional wetlands, relying primarily on the presence or absence of indicator wetland plant species. He noted: "All wetland areas, even those in a heavily disturbed state, are considered significant biological resources in so far as they have a potential to buffer adjacent, higher quality areas. In this case, much higher quality wetland habitat is present to the south beyond the limits of the proposed site development area."

Emphasizing their property constitutes marginal degraded wetlands at best and is not designated as an environmentally sensitive habitat area (ESHA), the Kirkorowiczes argue it is of no environmental consequence and thus not worthy of protection. To the contrary, the Coastal Act by its definition of wetland (§ 30121) does not distinguish between wetlands according to their quality. Indeed, section 30233 limits development in all wetlands without reference to their quality. This is so because of the dramatic loss of over 90 percent of historical wetlands in California and their critical function in the ecosystem. * * * Simply stated, in determining whether a wetland is protected under the Coastal Act and the LCP, the quality of the wetland is essentially legally irrelevant. As City's biologist Scheidt explained, "[a]ll wetland areas, even those in a heavily disturbed state, are considered significant biological resources in so far as they have a potential to buffer adjacent, higher quality areas. In this case, much higher quality wetland habitat is present to the south beyond the limits of the proposed site development area." The logic of this argument is apparent, for the failure to preserve and protect degraded or disturbed wetlands buffering adjacent higher quality wetlands will inevitably jeopardize, compromise and eventually erode the latter.

The judgment is reversed. The Commission is entitled to costs on appeal.

NOTES & QUESTIONS

1. The Kirkorowiczes argued that, based on their poor quality, "the wet areas on their property are not part of a marine environment." What marine environment did they have in mind, of which these wet areas were not a part, and of what environment were they a part? What if they had shown that the areas, while often wet, had no hydrologic connection to coastal waters? Under the CZMA, the coastal zone extends inland from the shoreline "only to the extent necessary to control shorelands, the uses of which have a direct and significant impact on the coastal waters, and to control those geographic areas which are likely to be affected by or vulnerable to sea level rise." 16 U.S.C. § 1453(1). Did the Kirkorowiczes' land fit that standard?

2. As our appreciation of the connectedness of ecosystems advances, defining the inland limits of the coastal zone according to the "extent necessary to control shorelands" standard could lead to some interesting results. Hawaii's coastal zone, for example, has long included the entire state, albeit for rather obvious reasons. Most states use either a defined distance (e.g., in California, the 1000-yard wide strip adjoining the coast), or a politically-defined boundary (e.g., in North Carolina, all land in a county bounded by the coast). Where would an *ecologically*-defined line be drawn in your state?

3. Even accepting that the regulated areas of the Kirkorowiczes' property were properly within the state's defined coastal zone *and* a part of the marine environment, does it make sense to construct a coastal ecosystem management program in which, as the court put it, "the quality of the wetland is essentially legally irrelevant." In other words, should biological quality make *no* difference? It undoubtedly is true, as the state argued, that "wetland areas . . . in a heavily disturbed state have a potential to buffer adjacent, higher quality areas," but does that make them "significant biological resources" worthy of the same level of protection as the higher quality areas?

4. Of the 35 states and territories eligible for CZMA participation, many embraced the CZMA quickly and moved toward rapid adoption of coastal programs for federal approval, with 25 reaching that point by 1980. In the "recalcitrant" states, however, issues arose about the wisdom and desirability of adding yet an additional layer of land use control, particularly one motivated by federal initiative. Indeed, Florida went so far as to enact a law, known as the "no-nothing-new bill," requiring that any CZMA program the state environmental agency submitted for federal approval be based exclusively on existing state laws and regulations. This precipitated a rather long and bruising battle in the early 1980s between the Florida legislature, the Governor's office, and the federal NOAA to hash out a plan all parties could accept. The federal government saw Florida, with a coastline second in magnitude only to Alaska, as a vital member in the CZMA club. The Florida legislature wanted no new regulations. The end result was a compromise in which existing law and policy were reconfigured, along with nonstatutory initiatives, to create a plan the federal government could respectably declare a step forward, but which did not step forward with new regulatory teeth. *See* Daniel O. O'Connell, *Florida's Struggle for Approval Under the Coastal Zone Management Act*, 25 NATURAL RESOURCES J. 61 (1985). Some states were even more resistant to the idea of joining the CZMA club than Florida—Texas, Georgia, and Ohio did not enter the program until after 1995, and Illinois was the last coastal state to enter the program, in 2012. A description of the national program and the state programs is available at http://coastalmanagement.noaa.gov/mystate/welcome.html.

5. As previously noted, Section 6217 of the Coastal Zone Act Reauthorization Amendments (CZARA), Pub. L. 101–508, tit. VI, subtit. C, 104 Stat. 1388 (1990), added a special provision to the CZMA dealing with coastal nonpoint source pollution. *See* 16 U.S.C. § 1455b. The Section 6217 program, as it is often called, requires states and territories with coastal zone management programs to also develop a Coastal Nonpoint Pollution Control Program to retain federal funding under the CZMA. In its CNPCP, a state or territory is to describe how it will implement nonpoint source pollution "management measures" that conform to criteria NOAA and the EPA have specified in a series of guidances for six categories of *inland* land uses: agriculture, forestry, urbanization, marinas and boating, hydromodification, and wetland and riparian areas. *See* U.S. EPA, GUIDANCE SPECIFYING MANAGEMENT MEASURES FOR SOURCES OF NONPOINT POLLUTION IN COASTAL WATERS (1993).

Rather than focusing on water quality, the statute and the agencies' specified management measures focus primarily on control technology and specification of "best management" practices, *see* 16 U.S.C. § 1455b(g)(5), and states may adopt the management measures that are appropriate given local physical and political conditions. This approach was intended to avoid difficult issues of causation—i.e., linking specific nonpoint sources to specific water quality impacts—and to avoid creating yet another unwieldy and expensive water quality improvement program. Yet, as they were in response to the original CZMA coastal plan process (see previous note), many states resented the new planning and management step as both and unfunded mandate and yet another layer of federally-induced regulation of local land use, in this case pushing yet further inland in focus.

Repeated threats by coastal states to leave the CZMA program and attacks on the program in Congress, while unavailing, eventually led EPA and NOAA to appease the states by adding greater flexibility to the program at the administrative level. By July 1996, all 29 states with approved CZMA coastal zone programs had submitted CNPCP proposals and the process of negotiation with the federal agencies was in full swing. For more information on the Section 6217 program, including the relevant implementing regulations and interpretive guidances, see U.S. EPA, *Coastal Nonpoint Source Pollution Control Program*, http://www.epa.gov/OWOW/NPS/coastnps.html, and NOAA, *Coastal Nonpoint Pollution Control Program*, http://coastalmanagement.noaa.gov/nonpoint/welcome.html/. For a critique of Section 6217, see Andrew Solomon, *Section 6217 of the Coastal Zone Act Reauthorization Amendments of 1990: Is there Any Point?*, 31 ENVTL. L. 151 (2001). Solomon argues that the voluntary nature of the CZMA generally, plus the rather faint threat of withdrawing CZMA funding for failure to compile a CNPCP, has positioned states to exercise leverage over EPA and NOAA to force them to make the CNPCP too flexible and undemanding.

b. FEDERAL AGENCY CONSISTENCY

Why would a state, even if it wishes to manage its coastal resources comprehensively, bother with subjecting its state coastal management program (CMP) to federal review and approval under the CZMA? The answer, obviously, is that the CZMA dangles some additional carrots. First, federal grants are available for implementation of an approved coastal management program. 16 U.S.C. § 1455(a). More importantly, and the subject of the following case, is that approval of a state CMP triggers the requirement that federal agencies ensure that activities they carry out, fund, or authorize in the coastal zone are "carried out in a manner which is consistent to the maximum extent practicable with the enforceable policies of approved state management programs." *Id.* § 1456(c)(2). After working with state CMP managers and making any appropriate changes to the proposed action, federal agencies and applicants provide a consistency statement to the CMP, along with supporting information. A state CMP reviews the federal action to determine if the proposed action will be consistent with the CMP. These federal consistency reviews are the responsibility of the lead state CMP agency. As the following case demonstrates, this state consistency review power can significantly influence federal agency action.

California Coastal Commission v. United States

United States District Court for the Southern District of California, 1998.
5 F. Supp. 2d 1106.

■ MILLER, DISTRICT JUDGE.

Plaintiff California Coastal Commission seeks a preliminary injunction against defendants United States of America, Department of the Navy, and Secretary of the Navy enjoining the disposal of dredged material from the San Diego Bay previously designated for coastal beach replenishment. This dredging of the bay is part of a homeporting project by which the Navy will base a Nimitz class aircraft carrier. Defendants oppose the motion for a preliminary injunction. After careful consideration of all the pleadings, parties' arguments and applicable law, the court rules as follows:

BACKGROUND

This case deals with the fundamental federal policy of conforming a federal coastal project to meet the dictates, to "the maximum extent possible," of state coastal management plans. This federal policy is codified in federal legislation known as the Coastal Zone Management Act (CZMA) 16 U.S.C. §§ 1451, 1456(c)(1).

Plaintiff California Coastal Commission (Commission) is the state agency responsible for review of federal agency projects for consistency with the federally approved California Coastal Management Program (CMP). The Commission reviewed and approved the Homeporting project of defendants United States of America, Department of the Navy, and Secretary of the Navy (collectively, the Navy) which included the dredging of portions of the San Diego Bay and the use of dredged sandy material for beach replenishment along certain San Diego coastal communities. In 1995, the Navy submitted Consistency Determination (CD) 95–95 which discussed the specifics of the dredging and disposal of the sandy material. Specifically, CD 95–95 called for the deposit of approximately 7.9 million cubic yards of material to Imperial Beach, Mission Beach, Del Mar and Oceanside to replenish areas affected by erosion. Additionally, 2 million cubic yards of other material not suitable for replenishment was to be disposed of in the ocean itself at site LA-5 approximately 4.5 miles off the coast of Point Loma. The remaining material, unsuitable for ocean disposal, would be confined to a new wharf structure at NASNI.

On November 16, 1995 the Commission concurred with CD 95–95 and the Navy commenced its dredging project in September, 1997. Shortly thereafter, live ordnance and munitions were discovered in the dredged material deposited on the beach.

In October, 1997 the Navy requested that the Commission concur with modifications to the project which would permit the disposal of 2.5 million cubic yards of dredged material earlier designated for beach replenishment at the LA-5 site. The Navy contends it requested the modifications in order to continue dredging while a long term solution was found. According to the Navy, an interruption of the dredging would result in excessive dredging expenses and a possible delay in the Homeporting project. On October 17, 1997 the Navy submitted a new CD (CD-140-97) which proposed that all remaining sediment be dumped into the ocean at LA-5 and that some inner channel materials be used for beach replenishment. The Navy asserts that CD 140–97 called for the use of a 3 inch ordnance grate to screen out larger ordnance in the outer channel. The Navy recognized however, that it did not know the exact size of the ordnance in the outer channel and the possibility existed that some of the ordnance was too small to be sifted through the grate. Thus, the Navy could not guarantee that all ordnance would be removed through its grating system proposed in CD 140–97.

The Commission objected to CD 140–97 stating that the amended project was not consistent with the requirement of the Coastal Zone Management Act (CZMA) that a project conform to a state coastal management plan to the maximum extent possible, that alternatives were available which would permit the Navy to complete the dredging as originally planned, and that the Navy had failed to document the cost of alternatives.

On November 19, 1997 the Navy sought and received a permit modification from the U.S. Army Corps of Engineers (Corps) which authorized the Navy to dispose of the remaining materials at LA-5. This modification was issued pursuant to § 404 of the Clean Water Act 33 U.S.C. § 1344(CWA) which gives the Corps authority to regulate the Navy's dredging and disposal operations for the project. The Corps approved this modification without Commission concurrence which the Navy contends thereby became unnecessary. On November 19, 1997 the Navy sent a letter to the Commission indicating that the Navy intended to continue dredging and disposal of previously designated beach replenishment at the LA-5 site without the Commission's concurrence. The Navy also indicated that it planned to "fully investigate beach nourishment options for placement of sand from the Homeporting project in coordination with the California Coastal Commission."

The Commission now moves for a preliminary injunction enjoining the Navy from further dredging and disposal of beach replenishment until the alternatives outlined in the Harris Report, CD 161–97 and other reports generated by the Commission are explored. The Commission submits the Navy is in violation of the CZMA as it has not demonstrated that the disposal of all material at the LA-5 site is consistent to the maximum extent practicable with the state's CMP under the CZMA. Further the Commission argues that the Navy has never demonstrated, as required by state and federal law, that alternatives to ocean dumping or other mitigation measures are unfeasible or impracticable. The Commission believes that injunctive relief is appropriate as the public will suffer irreparable injury from the continued dredging and disposal of beach replenishment which would otherwise be irretrievably lost. The Commission submits it is likely to ultimately succeed on the merits of its claim.

The Navy opposes the motion stating that the provisions of the CMP are not applicable as the ordnance laden material is not suitable for beach replenishment, that consistency with the CMP does not require the Navy to violate other applicable federal or state laws (in this case § 404 of the CWA) and that the discovery of ordnance was an unforeseeable event which, under the CZMA, allows the Navy to deviate from the CMP. Additionally, the Navy argues that a preliminary injunction would impose a great hardship on the Navy and that the Commission has failed to establish the likelihood of success or that the balance of hardships tips in its favor.

DISCUSSION

Federal agencies seeking to engage in project activity in a coastal zone must comply with the requirements of the CZMA. 16 U.S.C. § 1456(c)(1), (2). Section 307(c)(1)(A) of the CZMA states, in pertinent part:

> Each federal agency activity within or outside the coastal zone that affects any land or water use or natural resource of the coastal zone shall be carried out in a manner which is consistent to the maximum extent practicable with the enforceable policies of approved state management programs.

A federal agency is required to submit a "consistency determination" (as previously discussed "CD") to the state no later than 90 days before the proposed activity indicating that the federal activity would likely affect the coastal zone. 15 C.F.R. § 930.34.

The California Coastal Act (CCA) addresses the federal activity in this case. Under § 30233(a) of the CCA:

> [t]he diking, filling, or dredging of open coastal waters . . . shall be permitted where there is no feasible less environmentally damaging alternative, and where feasible mitigation measures have been provided to minimize adverse environmental effects.

Section 30233(b) of the CCA further provides that:

> [d]redging and spoils disposal shall be planned and carried out to avoid significant disruption to marine and wildlife habitats and water circulation. Dredge spoils suitable for beach replenishment should be transported for such purposes to appropriate beaches or into suitable longshore current systems.

There is no private right of action under the CZMA itself. City and County of San Francisco v. United States, 443 F.Supp. 1116, 1127 (N.D.Cal.1977), aff'd, 615 F.2d 498 (9th Cir.1980). Judicial review of a federal agency action under the CZMA is obtained through the Administrative Procedure Act (APA). 5 U.S.C. §§ 701–706. However, in a case such as this where Congress has provided in the CZMA more than one method in achieving the Act's purpose of protecting the nation's coastal zones, the principles of equitable discretion should be applied. Weinberger v. Romero-Barcelo, 456 U.S. 305, 315–318 (1982). Accord Friends of the Earth v. U.S. Navy, 841 F.2d 927, 934–935 (9th Cir.1988).

INJUNCTIVE RELIEF

The threshold issue in the analysis of whether the Commission should be afforded equitable injunctive relief is what is the standard this court should employ for judicial review. The Navy urges this court to apply a deferential standard by which the Navy's determination to dump dredged materials previous designated for beach replenishment must be upheld unless it was "arbitrary, capricious, an abuse of discretion, or otherwise not in accordance with the law." 5 U.S.C. § 706(2)(A). The Navy argues application of this narrow standard must result in affirmance of its action under the following rationale: The Navy, in effect, has the exclusive right to determine whether the sediments in question are "suitable for beach replenishment," the sediments as they exist in their pre-dredge state are not suitable for beach replenishment purposes, within the meaning of Cal.Pub.Res.C § 30233, because of the presence of ordnance and munitions, and, therefore, disposal of these materials into deep ocean water complies with the CZMA and CCA. The Navy then concludes that because there is sufficient evidence (existence of ordnance and munitions) to support its conclusion, this court must defer.

Initially, as mentioned above, the deferential standard of review should not apply in this case. The Ninth Circuit has recognized that traditional equitable discretion should be applied in determining whether the Navy has complied with the requirement of the CZMA that a homeporting project conform to the relevant state coastal management plan. See Friends of the Earth v. U.S. Navy, supra, 841 F.2d 927 (9th Cir.1988). The CZMA was enacted by Congress to clearly encourage the wise use of coastal resources through adoption of state coastal plans. Traditional judicial review subserves that stated legislative intent.

Preliminary injunctive relief is available if the party meets one of two tests: (1) a combination of probable success and the possibility of irreparable harm, or (2) the party raises serious questions and the balance of hardship tips in its favor. Arcamuzi v. Continental Air Lines, Inc., 819 F.2d 935, 937 (9th Cir.1987). "These two formulations represent two points on a sliding scale in which the required degree of irreparable harm increases as the probability of success decreases." Id. Under both formulations, however, the party must demonstrate a "fair chance of success on the merits" and a "significant threat of irreparable injury." Id.

Likelihood of Success on the Merits

The Commission argues that the Navy cannot show, as required under the CCA, that no less environmentally damaging alternative exists or that feasible mitigation measures have been provided to minimize adverse environmental effects. Specifically, the Navy has submitted only CD 140–97 for consideration, has withdrawn CD 161–97, and has never submitted other analyses, including the Harris Report. Thus, the Navy's position that no feasible alternative exists other than to waste a valuable resource is predicated upon an incomplete factual record and unilateral determinations made by the Navy without the benefit of Commission input. On this record, the Navy has not shown that the dredging and disposal is consistent to the maximum extent practicable with the enforceable policies of approved state management programs in violation of the CZMA.

The Navy's position that it considered a reasonable range of alternatives as required under § 30233(a) of the CCA which it addressed in CD 140–97 and CD 161–97 simply does not answer the question. The Navy acknowledges in its pleadings and oral argument it "remains willing to negotiate a reasonable solution" to offshore dumping. This position presupposes there may indeed be a feasible alternative to wasting this valuable beach replenishment resource. Until pending alternatives have at least been considered by both parties, it is illogical to conclude that offshore dumping is consistent with the CCA to the maximum extent possible. Finally, this portion of the analysis does not depend on whether the discovery of ordnance was an unforeseen event which warrants deviation from the CCA. As long as a reasonable alternative to dumping may be found with further expeditious study by the parties this factor is not material.

The Navy's contention that it has submitted feasible, less environmentally damaging alternatives and has provided certain measures to mitigate the adverse environmental effects all in compliance with the CCA and CZMA, is not borne out by the record. Specifically, the Navy's alternatives are contained in CD 161–97 and other analyses [including one known as the Harris Report] which have either been withdrawn from consideration by the Navy or never submitted in final form to the Commission. The Navy cannot meritoriously argue that these alternatives contained in the CD 161–97 or the subsequent analyses are properly before the Commission at this time and therefore in compliance with the CCA or CZMA. Therefore, as the Navy has failed to demonstrate that it has complied with the requirements of the CZMA and CCA and has failed to allege an acceptable exemption from these requirements, the court finds that on the present record the Commission would likely succeed on the merits of its case against the Navy for disposing of beach replenishment materials off the coast of California in a manner inconsistent with the federal and state law.

Irreparable Harm and the Balancing of Hardships

Legitimate considerations of irreparable harm and hardship balance in favor of the Commission. One or more viable alternatives to ocean dumping of a valuable natural resource may presently exist and be quickly identified through further expeditious study and good faith negotiation by the parties. A reasonable additional period of time should be afforded for that contingency. Any offshore dumping of this resource during this period of study represents an irretrievable loss which such study and negotiation could prove to be an unnecessary and costly waste.

Any excess dredging fees to be paid by the Navy, as well as any short term delay in the completion of dredging operations for this homeporting project are more than counterbalanced by the need to allow an additional period of expedited study and negotiation by the parties during which offshore dumping operations cease. Thus, a preliminary injunction is granted enjoining the Navy from disposing at LA-5 or any other offshore dumping site dredging material previously designated for beach replenishment purposes. This preliminary injunction is conditioned upon the Commission's expeditious study of proposed alternatives to offshore dumping, including those set forth in the Harris Report, and the good faith of the parties to negotiate a resolution which is the stated goal of both sides. The court reserves jurisdiction to modify or dissolve this preliminary injunction upon shortened notice.

NOTES & QUESTIONS

1. What was the Navy supposed to do with the sand? Would *you* like to walk along a beach that had been "renourished" with the Navy's sand? Of course, all the court held is that the Navy had not yet met its burden of proving no less damaging alternative to ocean dumping exists. But how far would the Navy have to go to prove this? For example, what if, at great expense, the Navy could clean the sand of munitions? Would the CZMA require that it do so?

2. The court explains that the CZMA consistency determination requires a finding that "that no less environmentally damaging alternative exists or that feasible mitigation measures have been provided to minimize adverse environmental effects." The Commission and the court, however, focused not on the ecological impact of disposal of the sand on the *ocean* ecosystem, but on the loss of the dredged sand itself, which both portrayed as a valuable *beach* ecology resource that should not be wasted. The Commission and the court thus appear to take as a given that using the sand for what is known as beach "restoration" or "nourishment" is ecologically superior to dumping it in the ocean. Even putting aside the presence of munitions in the sand, is it clear that beach nourishment is such a good thing ecologically, not to mention economically?

As for cost, beach nourishment projects can carry hefty price tags. Federal spending on beach nourishment, which carries a state or local match requirement, continues at high levels. Total federal spending on beach restoration over the last 75 years comes in at almost $4 billion, about two-thirds of which has gone to New Jersey, Florida, and New York. *See* Dennis Cauchon, *Beach Protection: A Tale of Two Cities in Va.*, USA TODAY, Nov. 10, 2003, at 4A. One amazingly expensive program involved nourishing the beaches from Sandy Hook to Barnegat Inlet in New Jersey, to the tune of $1.16 billion, but dozens of local projects have topped $150 million in cost, much of it federally subsidized. *See Surf's Up. So Is Costly Bid to Shield "Sand Castles,"* USA Today, Apr. 9, 2001, at 12A.

Ecologically, beach nourishment can disrupt subaerial zone habitat by altering temperature and compaction conditions, and can alter wave and runoff conditions important to adjacent shallow subtidal habitat. Of particular concern, for example, is the effect it has on turtle eggs as nests are buried deeper and compacted, as well as on the ability of the female turtles to reach areas of the beach above tidal influence to lay the eggs. *See* U.S. Fish and Wildlife Service, Life History and Environmental Requirements of Loggerhead Turtles (1988); National Academy of Sciences, Decline of the Sea Turtles: Cause and Prevention (1990); Sarah L. Minton et al., *The Effect of Beach Nourishment with Aragonite Versus Silicate Sand on Beach Temperature and Loggerhead Sea Turtle Nesting Success*, 13 J. COASTAL RESOURCES 904 (1997).

Florida, with the second longest coastline of the states and the second largest share of federal beach restoration funding, is a natural hot zone for controversy over beach nourishment. It is home to one of the earliest lawsuits challenging beach nourishment. *See* American Littoral Society v. Herndon, 720 F.Supp. 942 (S.D. Fla. 1988). Today, over half of the state's coastline is eroding, much of it at rates the state describes as "critical," meaning "a level of erosion which threatens substantial development, recreational, cultural, or environmental interests." *See* Florida Department of Environmental Protection, *Beach Erosion Control Program*, http://www.dep.state.fl.us/beaches/programs/bcherosn.htm. The state has adopted an extensive set of regulatory controls and approval criteria for beach nourishment proposals, requiring the state resources agency to consider causes and economic effects of shoreline erosion, costs of nourishment, ecological impacts of nourishment, and alternative erosion management strategies. *See* Fla. Stat. Ann. 161.161. Nonetheless, beach nourishment projects meeting the criteria have in any event illustrated the tenuous nature of the investment. In Escambia County, where Pensacola is situated, the county government initiated a $20 million effort to pump 4 million cubic yards from offshore waters to an 8.2 mile stretch of beach. Critics of the plan argued that the sand was likely to wash away in the next hurricane, of which there is no shortage in the region. They were proven right in 2004, and again in 2005, and again in....

For an extensive study of both the economy and the ecology of beach nourishment, searching for ways to balance the economic benefits and the ecological consequences, see NATIONAL ACADEMY OF SCIENCES, BEACH NOURISHMENT AND PROTECTION (1995), *available at* http://books.nap.edu/books/0309052904/html/index.html. The Academy concluded that beach nourishment is a viable shore protection technique and means for restoring lost recreational assets, but that it must be carefully designed, implemented, and monitored through multidisciplinary methods.

3. Before you make up your mind about beach nourishment, consider the ecosystem services beaches provide and the value of maintaining beach structure, even if done through beach nourishment. As the mid-Atlantic coast's experience with Hurricane Isabel in 2003 illustrates, coastal communities that have invested (with federal support) in beach nourishment projects usually sustain far less damage inland than do areas where beach erosion has not been addressed. Residents in Virginia Beach, which a few years before had imported enough sand to widen the beach by 300 feet, four feet deep, were able to watch the wind and rain from the boardwalk. By contrast, the oceanfront communities that sustained the most damage, Kitty Hawk and Nags Head in North Carolina, had not yet initiated beach nourishment projects by the time the storm struck. *See* Dennis Cauchon, *Beach Protection: A Tale of Two Cities in Va.*, USA TODAY, Nov. 10, 2003, at 4A. It is no surprise, therefore, that Broward County, on Florida's Atlantic Coast, once estimated that rnourishment of its beaches, costing in the tens of millions of dollars, protects $4 billion in upland property, structures, and infrastructure in that county alone—a stunning example of the value of the storm surge mitigation service beaches provide. *See* Broward County, Florida, *Beach Renourishment Program*, http://www.broward.org/BeachRenourishment/Pages/Default.aspx. Clearly, it is not merely beachfront property owners who are receiving a public subsidy from beach nourishment.

4. Although the previous point begs the question of how wise it is to allow so much development in coastal counties in the first place, the ecosystem service value of intact beach and dune systems to inland landowners is plainly nothing to ignore in the formulation of ecosystem management policy. Indeed, in an ironic twist of fate, landowners along the Gulf Coast areas hit hardest by the 2004 hurricanes had several years beforehand bemoaned the development restrictions imposed through the Endangered Species Act because of the presence of a small endangered mouse in the area's remaining dune habitat. After Hurricane Ivan, however, it turned out that the development projects that were forced inland of the preserved mouse habitat fared much better than development that had come previously and without much attention to maintaining the dunes. " 'Thank God for the beach mouse,' said a University of South Alabama civil engineer to the Birmingham News. 'The developers hate the thing, but it saved their developments.' " Oliver Houck, *Ivan and the Mouse*, NEW ORLEANS TIMES PICAYUNE, Oct. 3, 2004, at B-7.

5. One significant limitation on the state consistency review power flows from the CZMA exclusion from the coastal zone of any "lands the use of which is by law subject solely to the discretion of or which is held in trust by the Federal Government." 16 U.S.C. § 1453(1). The Supreme Court has held, however, that states may nonetheless exercise direct environmental regulation over non-federal activities occurring on federal lands. *See* California Coastal Commission v. Granite Rock Company, 480 U.S. 572 (1987). In *Granite Rock*, the state imposed environmental conditions on mining operations the company proposed to carry out on national forest lands pursuant to Forest Service regulations. The company argued that the exclusion of federal lands in the CZMA from the coastal zone preempted the state from imposing the environmental conditions, but the Court held that "even if all federal lands are excluded from the CZMA definition of coastal zone the CZMA does not automatically preempt all state regulation of activities on federal land." *Id.* at 593. Hence, although the state could not use CZMA consistency review to limit the mining activities, it could use its police power authority directly to impose environmental conditions on the company's mining operations.

6. The consistency requirement is becoming an increasingly influential component of land use regulation in the coastal zone. For example, in United States v. San Juan Bay Marina, 239 F.3d 400 (1st Cir. 2001), the court upheld a Corps of Engineers order requiring the developer of a marina to remove a large dock platform that had been erected without a consistency certification by Puerto Rico. Similarly, in Mountain Rhythm Resources v. FERC, 302 F.3d 958 (9th Cir. 2002), the court upheld the Federal Energy Regulatory Commission's denial of hydroelectric generation permits on the ground that the State of Washington had not provided a consistency certification.

On the other hand, courts have also made it clear that the CZMA, which does not include a citizen suit provision expressly allowing citizens to challenge land uses on the ground that the consistency requirement is not satisfied, also provides no implied cause of action for citizen enforcement. *See* Serrano-Lopez v. Cooper, 193 F.Supp.2d 424 (D.P.R. 2002). Moreover, the Secretary of the Interior may override a state's denial of consistency certification if he or she finds that the "activity is consistent with the objectives of [the CZMA]" or is "otherwise necessary in the interest of national security." 16 U.S.C. § 1456(c)(3)(A). Indeed, if a state successfully challenges the Secretary's override decision in federal court, the statute also allows the President to override the court's decision "if the President determines that the activity is in the paramount interest of the United States." *Id.* § 1456(c)(1)(B). So for example, the limitations on the enforcement of the consistency certification may play an important role in how federal, state, and tribal interests contest decisions such as whether to open the Arctic National Wildlife Refuge to exploration and extraction of oil and other resources. *See* Jeffrey H. Wood, *Protecting Native Coastal Ecosystems: CZMA and Alaska's Coastal Plain*, 19 NATURAL RESOURCES & ENV'T 57 (Summer 2004).

7. An approach similar to the CZMA's consistency step, but perhaps delivering more punch, is used in the Coastal Barrier Resources Act of 1982 (CBRA), 16 U.S.C. §§ 3501–3510, as substantially amended by the Coastal Barrier Improvement Act of 1990, Pub. L. 101–591 (1990), and administered by the Department of the Interior. CBRA establishes the Coastal Barrier Resources System (CBRS), consisting of undeveloped coastal barriers—natural formations that protect landward aquatic habitats from the direct forces of waves, tides, and windand other identified coastal areas. Included in the classification of coastal barriers are the following:

Bay Barriers—barriers that enclose a pond or marsh by connecting two headlands.

Tombolos—sand or gravel beaches that connect islands to each other or to the mainland

Barrier Spits—barriers which are attached to the mainland at one end and extend into the open water

Barrier Islands—barriers completely detached from the mainland

Dune or Beach Barriers—wide sandy beaches with dunes or hills

Fringing Mangroves—bands of mangrove trees along tropical/subtropical shores.

The CBRA recognizes that these features are unique landscapes that serve as a protective barrier against the forces of wind and tidal actions caused by coastal storms. In addition, coastal barriers provide a protective habitat for a variety of aquatic species. Thus, Congress declared three important goals to be met through the statute: (1) minimize loss of human life by discouraging development in high-risk areas; (2) reduce wasteful expenditure of Federal resources; and (3) protect the natural resources associated with coastal barriers.

Congress initially defined the CBRS as a collection of specific undeveloped coastal barriers along the Atlantic and Gulf of Mexico coasts, later expanding it to include additional areas along the Atlantic and Gulf coasts, the Great Lakes, Puerto Rico, and the U.S. Virgin Islands. Over 1,200 miles of shoreline, comprising approximately 1.3 million acres, make up the 560 units included today within the CBRS.

Unlike the CZMA, inclusion of a unit in the system is initiated by a federal decision, though the Interior Department consults with states and will consider voluntary state inclusion of state or local lands into the system. Under the statute, with limited exceptions no new federal expenditures or direct or indirect financial assistance may be used for any purpose within the system, including construction, improvement, or purchase of structures, roads, and boat facilities, and the stabilization of shoreline areas. Thus, for example, federal flood insurance under the National Flood Insurance Program is not available for structures located in the CBRS. While this approach does not induce state-led management of coastal resources, the prevalence of federal funding of land use activities in coastal areas (e.g., flood insurance and beach renourishment) suggests that the withdrawal of such funding in CBRS areas could have significant effects on land use.

Indeed, the U.S. Fish and Wildlife Service estimated in 2002 that the Coastal Barrier Resources Act will was on track to save the federal government $1.3 billion in infrastructure subsidies and disaster relief costs by 2010. Included in this estimate were reductions in federal subsidy of insurance, road building, wastewater facilities, water facilities, bridge and jetty construction, beach restoration, and structure reconstruction. Nevertheless, the agency observed that "the spending examined in this study comprises only a small fraction of the myriad of funding sources that encourage development along our nation's coasts," and that "where the economic incentive for development is extremely high, the Act's funding limitations can be overcome." USFWS, The Coastal Barrier Resources Act: Harnessing the Power of Market Forces to Conserve America's Coasts and Save Taxpayers' Money, http://www.fws.gov/habitat conservation/TaxpayerSavingsfromCBRA.pdf. For a comprehensive overview of the CBRA program, see the USFWS website at http://www.fws.gov/CBRA/.

Note on the Public Trust Doctrine

Virtually all of the ecosystem management materials covered in this text are based in federal, state, or local legislative initiatives. Does the common law have any role to play in coastal ecosystem management? Generally, the answer has been no. Nothing approaching a judicial doctrine of ecosystem management emerges from them.

One common law principle that many scholars have argued could defy this trend is known as the Public Trust Doctrine. The name is impressive, suggesting great possibilities. Indeed, in his landmark 1970 article, inspiring many since then to envision a Public Trust Doctrine motivating broad goals of natural resources conservation, Professor Joseph Sax outlined an ambitious agenda for just those purposes. *See* Joseph L. Sax, *The Public Trust Doctrine In Natural Resource Law: Effective Judicial Intervention*, 68 MICH. L. REV. 471 (1970). Sax argued that "[o]f all the concepts known to American law, only the public trust doctrine seems to have the breadth and substantive content which might make it useful as a tool of general application for citizens seeking to develop a comprehensive legal approach to resource management problems." *Id.* at 474. Forty years later, however, this vision remains largely unfulfilled hope. Why?

The Public Trust Doctrine traces its roots to the Institutes of Justinian in Roman Law, which declared that there are three things common to all people: (1) air; (2) running water; and (3) the sea and its shores. Along with the Romans, this principle invaded England and became part of its common law, which the states imported with minor variations after the American Revolution. While the British version held that tidelands were held by the King for the benefit of all English subjects, the American version replaced the crown with the states, and the courts became the doctrine's chief enforcer.

The scope of the trust imposed by the Public Trust Doctrine can be thought of in several dimensions. First, it has a geographic reach that must be defined. In the American version, this has generally meant all lands subject to the ebb and flow of the tide, and all waters navigable in fact, such as rivers, lakes, ponds, and streams. Next, the uses that the trust protects and prohibits must be defined. In American jurisprudence, fishing, commerce, and navigation are core protected uses, with other uses such as boating, swimming, anchoring, and general recreation being recognized as well in most states. Uses inconsistent with those protected values may be prohibited—that is, even if the state wishes to facilitate such incompatible uses, it may be restrained from doing so. Finally, the Public Trust Doctrine carries with it restrictions on the alienation of public trust lands to private interests when to do so would undermine the protected public uses. Clearly, these are dimensions in which ecosystem management operates as well, so the thought of linking the Public Trust Doctrine with ecosystem management is by no means far-fetched.

A series of nineteenth century U.S. Supreme Court cases, focused principally on the scope of property rights associated with statehood, breathed apparent life into these parameters of the Public Trust Doctrine. First, in Martin v. Waddell's Lessee, 41 U.S. (16 Pet.) 367 (1842), the Court applied the doctrine in a case involving resolution of title to tidelands and tidal rivers. Next, in The Daniel Ball, 77 U.S. (10 Wall.) 557 (1870), the Court held that "[t]hose rivers must be regarded as public navigable rivers in law which are navigable in fact." But, as Professor Sax described it, the lodestar case of the Public Trust Doctrine, at least for purposes of thinking about it as a tool of resource conservation, came in the Court's 1892 opinion in Illinois Central Railroad Co. v. Illinois, 146 U.S. 387 (1892). The Court held that Illinois could not sell fee interests in the land under Chicago Harbor to private developers because

> the State holds the title to the lands under the navigable waters. . . It is a title held in trust for the people of the State that they can enjoy the navigation of the waters, carry on commerce over them, and have liberty of fishing therein freed from the obstruction or interference of private parties.

Id. at 452. Almost 100 years later, the Court reiterated the principle using similar terms in Phillips Petroleum Co. v. Mississippi, 484 U.S. 469, 476 (1988) ("our cases firmly establish that the States, upon entering the Union, were given ownership over all the lands beneath the waters subject to the tides' influence"). Yet, that about sums up the Public Trust Doctrine as far as the U.S. Supreme Court is concerned—the states may not alienate fee title in tidelands, shores, and other public trust lands in violation of the Public Trust Doctrine. Suffice it to say that the Court has not championed Professor Sax's vision of doing more with the doctrine, limiting its jurisprudence largely to questions of who owns what, and much less so to the federalism question of what a state may do with public trust lands acquired as a matter of statehood.

The *Phillips Petroleum* decision did remind us, however, that "[i]t has been long established that the individual states have the authority to define the limits of the lands held in public trust." *Id.* at 475. As it is fundamentally a state law doctrine, therefore, many state courts have opined on the scope of the Public Trust Doctrine as well, some with a vigor not found in the U.S. Supreme Court jurisprudence. One famous case from California, regarding the diversion of water from Mono Lake, ruled that "[t]he state has an affirmative duty to take the public trust into account in the planning and allocation of water resources, and to protect public trust uses whenever feasible." National Audubon Soc'y v. Superior Court of Alpine County, 658 P.2d 709 (Cal. 1983). This and other state cases like it, however, are mindful of the "publicness" of public trust lands, emphasizing uses such as navigation, fishing, and recreation, and not necessarily preservation or even active conservation. Even in the Mono Lake case, for example, the court held that in exercising the public trust "the state must bear in mind its duty as trustee to consider the effect of the taking [of water] on the public trust, and to preserve, so far as consistent with the public interest, the *uses* protected by the trust." *Id.*

Even in the states, therefore, the Public Trust Doctrine has had its chief impact as an arbiter of property rights and, thereby, as a tool mainly to facilitate public access to and use of tidelands and beaches. It has by no means been transformed into a judicial ecosystem management program in any state. It is true that an occasional state case suggests an ecologically-oriented purpose to the doctrine. Perhaps the most noted case in this regard is from Wisconsin, in which the court found that the doctrine required that wetland areas be limited to uses consistent with natural conditions. *See* Just v. Marinette County, 201 N.W.2d 761 (Wis.1972). Several more recent cases are variations on that theme. *See e.g.*, Selkirk-Priest Basin Association v. Idaho ex rel. Andrus, 899 P.2d 949 (Idaho 1995) (doctrine allows environmental group standing to challenge timber sales on ground that sedimentation could injure fish spawning grounds); Vander Bloemen v. Wisconsin Department of Natural Resources, 551 N.W.2d 869 (Wis.App.1996) (doctrine extends to protection of lakeside ecology). For a thorough update of these and other state law cases on the application of the Public Trust Doctrine in ecosystem management contexts, see Arnold L. Lum, *How Goes the Public Trust Doctrine: Is the Common Law Shaping Environmental Policy?*, 18 NATURAL RESOURCES & ENV'T 73 (Fall 2003). Lum covers state cases extending the trust duties to public natural resources other than navigable waters, such as groundwater, parks, and extending the trust uses to recreational and ecological uses. On the other hand, he notes that not all state cases result in expansion of the doctrine's scope, e.g., Rettkowski v. Department of Ecology, 858 P.2d 232 (Wash. 1993) (does not apply to groundwater), and that few state courts have endorsed breach of trust claims against state agencies, such as the claim brought in California's 1983 Mono Lake case discussed in the text (page 663). Lum concludes that the force of the Public Trust Doctrine in ecosystem management law is "growing," though by how much and how fast he does not estimate. *See also* Robin Kundis Craig, *A Comparative Guide to the Western States' Public Trust Doctrines – Public Values, Private Rights, and the Evolution Toward an Ecological Public Trust*, 37 ECOLOGY L.Q. 1 (2010). By and large, however, the state courts have declined to mobilize Professor Sax's vision of the Public Trust Doctrine as a means of effective and broad judicial intervention in resource management policy. There is, simply put, no general ecosystem management duty to be found in the judiciary's version of the Public Trust Doctrine.

And what of the *federal* version of the Public Trust Doctrine? It amounts to little, according to Professor Eric Pearson. He observes that federal courts have virtually never applied any form of public trust duties to federal government use and regulation of public lands and resources. *See* Eric Pearson, *The*

Public Trust Doctrine in Federal Law, 24 J. LAND, RESOURCES & ENVTL. L. 173 (2004). As he points out, the seminal case describing the federal government's public trust duties, Light v. United States, 220 U.S. 523 (1911), ruled that "it is not for the courts to say how that trust shall be administered. That is for Congress to determine. The courts cannot compel it to set aside lands for settlement; or to suffer them to be used for agricultural purposes; nor interfere when, in the exercise of its discretion, Congress establishes a forest reserve for what it decides to be national and public purposes." *Id.* at 537. As Professor Pearson observes, therefore, "the public trust doctrine in state law empowers the judicial branch to overturn substantive choices made by political branches of government. The public trust doctrine in federal law works to the opposite end. In federal law, the doctrine empowers the political branches of government to implement substantive choices despite objections in the judicial branch. Night, meet day." Pearson, *supra* at 176–77. What could be the justification for this legal dichotomy? Whatever the reason, to the extent it persists, it suggests that the federal version of the Public Trust Doctrine, given the federal government's vast land holdings, is even less likely to shape ecosystem management law than is the state version.

Ironically, what has given the Public Trust Doctrine a bit of a boost recently is the aftermath of recent developments in the U.S. Supreme Court's takings jurisprudence. Several courts have found that the restrictions associated with the Public Trust Doctrine are part of the background principles of state property law for purposes of evaluating regulatory takings claims as outlined in Lucas v. South Carolina Coastal Council, 505 U.S. 1003 (1992). In McQueen v. South Carolina Coastal Council, 580 S.E.2d 116 (S.C. 2003), the South Carolina Supreme Court found no regulatory taking occurred when the state denied McQueen a permit to install bulkheads and fill in the tidelands situated behind it for purposes of developing residential housing units. The tideland area had been above the high water mark within the lots when purchased in the 1960s, but through McQueen's neglect of the property the shoreline eroded and much of the property became "critical area saltwater wetlands," which the state regulates closely. McQueen alleged the state committed a regulatory taking of the property when it denied the development permit, but the court observed that the tideland area appeared on the property as a result of the forces of nature and McQueen's lack of vigilance, and hence "the tidelands included on the McQueen's lots are public trust property subject to control of the state." As a result, "McQueen's ownership rights do not include the right to backfill or place bulkheads on public trust land and the state need not compensate him for the denial of the permits to do what he cannot otherwise do."

Similarly, the Ninth Circuit held that the State of Washington has always incorporated the Public Trust Doctrine in its property law and thus the restrictions associated with it run with the title to land. The City of Seattle's denial of a permit to develop shoreline property on Elliott Bay did not take the landowner's property, therefore, because the Public Trust Doctrine already attached to the property and would have restricted the state from approving the permits. *See* Esplanade Properties, LLC v. City of Seattle, 307 F.3d 978 (9th Cir. 2002). Yet, as much as these cases remind us that the Public Trust Doctrine inheres in the title to private property, they address only what the state may accomplish through public legislation—they do not give affirmative force to the doctrine itself as a direct agent of ecosystem management.

By contrast, since Professor Sax's seminal work, many environmental law scholars have charted and claimed all sorts of ecosystem management goals for the Public Trust Doctrine. Of course, doing so requires that one or more of the doctrine's parameters be expanded beyond present judicial interpretations. So, for example, courts could extend the geographic scope to encompass regulation of private lands adjacent to public trust lands, or they could add ecosystem dynamics to the protected "uses." The doctrine might even be transformed from its current status as a restriction on state power to alienate public trust lands or to allow incompatible uses, to one imposing an affirmative *duty* of ecosystem management. For examples of these and other academically posited stretchings of the doctrine, see JACK H. ARCHER ET AL., THE PUBLIC TRUST DOCTRINE AND THE MANAGEMENT OF AMERICA'S COASTS (1994); Jack H. Archer and Terrance W. Stone, *The Interaction of the Public Trust and the "Takings" Doctrines: Protecting Wetlands and Critical Coastal Areas*, 20 VERMONT L. REV. 81 (1995); Robin Kundis Craig, *Mobil Oil Exploration, Environmental Protection, and Contract Repudiation: It's Time to Recognize the Public Trust in the Outer Continental Shelf*, 30 Envtl. L. Rep. (Envtl. L. Inst.) 11104 (2000); Ralph W. Johnson and William C. Galloway, *Can the Public Trust Doctrine Prevent Extinctions?*, in BIODIVERSITY AND THE LAW 157 (William J. Snape III ed., 1996).

What explains the chasm between the judicial and the academic visions of the Public Trust Doctrine? What keeps academics coming back to the Public Trust Doctrine, asking ever more of it, but repels judges from taking it farther? One rather obvious possibility is that, not long after Professor Sax suggested how its latent power could be tapped, the legislative revolution of the 1970s unfolded to bring one after the other of comprehensive environmental laws into being. In short, who needs the Public Trust Doctrine? By comparison to the targeted legislative agenda that brought on line the Clean Water Act, Coastal Zone Management Act, National Forest Management Act, Endangered Species Act, and other resource management laws spawned in that era and which remain the workhorses of ecosystem management today, the Public Trust Doctrine seems, like many common law doctrines, hopelessly open-ended, amorphous, and unwieldy. Perhaps, in addition to seeing no critical need to go down the road Sax mapped, courts see trouble ahead were they tempted to start the journey.

Indeed, in a countercurrent to the Saxian vision, Professor Richard Lazarus and a few other academics with impeccable "green" credentials have argued that the Public Trust Doctrine, if shaped as Sax wanted, could actually be antithetical to proactive and innovative environmental and resource management. *See* Richard J. Lazarus, *Changing Conceptions of Property and Sovereignty in Natural Resources: Questioning the Public Trust Doctrine*, 71 IOWA L. REV. 631 (1986); Richard Delgado, *Our Better Natures: A Revisionist View of Joseph Sax's Public Trust Theory of Environmental Protection, and Some Dark Thoughts on the Possibility of Law Reform*, 44 VAND. L. REV. 1209 (1991). For one thing, they argued, it places too much reliance on a judiciary that is not always in tune with what the academic vision of the Public Trust Doctrine appears to want have happen. The growth of the police power state, its authorities grown and channeled since World War II into a huge administrative law apparatus, seem a far better prospect for carrying out an environmentalist agenda. And, they point out, at its core the Public Trust Doctrine is about property rights in the form of public rights to *use* the environment of public trust lands. Like any trust, the purpose of the public trust lands is not merely to preserve their corpus, but to put them to public use. The administrative law version of ecosystem management is potentially more flexible—its course charted by congressional and agency will—and thus may not lead to a regime biased toward use versus preservation (though, for the most part, "multiple use" doctrine is the rule for public lands managed outside of the scope of the Public Trust Doctrine).

In any event, whatever it is, and whatever the wisdom of the Saxian vision of it, the Public Trust Doctrine is not a font of ecosystem management law as it stands today. True, that could change, but any movement in that regard does not appear on the horizon. Yet, hope for Public Trust Doctrine's place in the larger picture of resource management will not seem to go away. It is, as Professor Carol Rose put it, an "arresting phrase" with tremendous rhetorical power to remind us of why we might think of something like ecosystem management. *See* Carol M. Rose, *Joseph Sax and the Idea of the Public Trust*, 25 ECOLOGY L.Q. 351 (1998). It is also, as Professor Charles Wilkinson observed, decidedly enduring and pan-cultural, owing its roots to Roman law laid down centuries ago and coming to us via British common law. *See* Charles F. Wilkinson, *The Headwaters of the Public Trust: Some Thoughts on the Source and Scope of the Traditional Doctrine*, 19 ENVTL. L. 425 (1989). We think of this note, therefore, as a placeholder for potential expansion of the topic in future editions of this text, though it may just as likely become a candidate for paring down.

2. ESTUARIES

Estuaries, also known as bays, lagoons, harbors, inlets, or sounds, are partially enclosed bodies of water formed where freshwater from rivers and streams flows into the ocean, mixing with the salty sea water. The defining feature of an estuary is the mixing of fresh and salt water. Estuaries and the lands surrounding them are places of transition from land to sea, and from fresh to salt water. Although influenced by the tides, estuaries are protected from the full force of ocean waves, winds, and storms by the dunes, reefs, barrier islands, and other features that define an estuary's seaward boundary.

Biologically, the tidal, sheltered waters of estuaries support unique communities of plants and animals, specially adapted for life at the margin of the sea. Because many different habitat types are found in and around estuarine environments, they are among the most diverse, complex, and productive on earth, creating more organic matter each year than comparably-sized areas of forest, grassland, or agricultural land.

With over 50 percent of the nation's population living within 50 miles of the sea, it is no wonder that estuaries are also of tremendous economic value. Tourism, fisheries, and other commercial activities thrive on the wealth of natural resources estuaries supply. Because estuaries offer protected coastal waters, they also are used extensively as harbors and ports vital for shipping, transportation, and industry. The EPA has quantified some of these economic values:

Estuaries provide habitat for more than 75% of America's commercial fish catch, and for 80–90% of the recreational fish catch. Estuarine-dependent fisheries are among the most valuable within regions and across the nation, worth more than $1.9 billion in 1990, excluding Alaska.

Nationwide, commercial and recreational fishing, boating, tourism, and other coastal industries provide more than 28 million jobs. Commercial shipping alone employed more than 50,000 people as of January, 1997.

There are 25,500 recreational facilities along the U.S. coasts—almost 44,000 square miles of outdoor public recreation areas. The average American spends 10 recreational days on the coast each year. In 1993 more than 180 million Americans visited ocean and bay beaches—nearly 70% of the U.S. population. Coastal recreation and tourism generate $8 to $12 billion annually.

In just one estuarine system—Massachusetts and Cape Cod Bays—commercial and recreational fishing generate about $240 million per year. In that same estuary, tourism and beach-going generate $1.5 billion per year, and shipping and marinas generate $1.86 billion per year.

See USEPA, Office of Water and Watersheds, *About Estuaries, available at* http://www.epa.gov/owow/estuaries/about1.htm.

Notwithstanding the important ecosystem values estuaries deliver to humans, human-induced impairment of estuarine resources is particularly acute in many areas of the nation. On the list of sources of impairment: nutrients from agriculture, sewage treatment, septic tanks, and residential yards; pathogens from released sewage, agricultural manure, medical waste, boat waste, and urban runoff; habitat alteration from transportation, residential, commercial, and agricultural development; and toxins from industrial pollution, urban runoff, and agricultural pesticides; and introduced species. In its comprehensive study of these conditions in states bordering the Gulf of Mexico, the EPA found the most troubling trend to be declining wetland habitat, with Gulf states having lost 41 to 54 percent of historic estuarine wetlands during the last 200 years. *See* USEPA, THE ECOLOGICAL CONDITION OF ESTUARIES IN THE GULF OF MEXICO (July 1999), *available at* http://www.epa.gov/ged/gulf.htm. Other conditions are varied throughout the states, with EPA issuing a "report card" on 11 ecological indicators for each showing some indicators in the "good-no problem" category for most states, while the score for others in some states was as low as "poor-severe problem." Texas and Louisiana showed particularly serious concerns with nutrients; Alabama and Mississippi rated good to fair on most indicators; Florida was representative of the Gulf as a whole.

The law of estuaries is as complex as are their ecological and economic features. Estuaries are, not surprisingly, included within the definition of coastal waters under the Coastal Zone Management Act and thus are fully within the scope of state coastal management programs as described in the previous section of this chapter. *See* 16 U.S.C. § 1453(3) (referring to "sounds, bays, lagoons, bayous, ponds, *and estuaries*"). Ecosystem management for estuarine resources is also embodied in a more focused manner in the Clean Water Act's National Estuary Program (NEP) and in several programs devoted to some of the nation's largest estuaries.

a. THE NATIONAL ESTUARY PROGRAM

Like the Coastal Zone Management Act, covered in the previous section, the National Estuary Program (NEP) targets a broad range of issues going far beyond just water quality, and it engages state and local governments and communities in the land and resource management process. The following article provides an excellent overview of the NEP.

Matthew W. Bowden, *An Overview of the National Estuary Program*
11 Natural Resources & Environment 35 (Fall 1996).

After more than three decades of environmental regulation aimed at specific media and individual activities, a trend is developing toward a broader, more holistic approach to environmental management. Today's buzzword and the first guiding principle in the U.S. Environmental Protection Agency's (EPA) new Five Year Strategic Plan is "ecosystem protection." Watersheds are one of the most widely accepted types of ecosystems, and a little-known watershed management program called the National Estuary Program (NEP) is at the forefront of EPA's recent focus on ecosystem protection.

The addition of section 320 to the Clean Water Act (CWA), 33 U.S.C. § 1330, in 1987 established the NEP... Rather than taking the traditional command-and-control regulatory approach, the NEP seeks to involve all affected stakeholders in the process of identifying an estuary's problems and developing management measures to solve those problems... [T]he NEP's final work product is not enforceable regulation. Rather, the ultimate goal of the NEP is to prepare a comprehensive management plan for estuaries selected for the program. Although such plans are not binding regulation, they represent an influential joint statement of public policy by federal and state governments and affected stakeholders on how the estuary should be managed. As such, management plans can foster changes in existing regulation and development of new approaches to protecting estuarine resources.

Nomination and Funding of Estuary Programs

Under section 320 of the CWA, the governor of a state may nominate an estuary within the state to the NEP by submitting an application to EPA. If the nomination is accepted, EPA convenes a "Management Conference" to begin assessing the condition of the estuary. After identifying the estuary's problems, the Management Conference begins work on a management plan. EPA provides 75 percent of the funding for the Management

Conference, while state and local governments or other nonfederal sources supply the remaining 25 percent.

Management Conference Participation and Organization

Once an estuary is accepted in the NEP, EPA and the state governor select members of a Management Conference to carry out the program. Section 320 of the CWA provides that the Management Conference must include representatives of all states located in the estuarine zone, agencies and local governments having jurisdiction over any significant part of an estuary, affected industries, educational institutions, and the general public. As a general rule, most Management Conferences consist of four committees: a Policy Committee, a Management Committee, a Science/Technical Advisory Committee, and a Citizen Advisory Committee.

The Policy Committee is the governing body of the Management Conference. Members of this committee normally include high-level representatives from EPA, key state agencies, and local governments. The Policy Committee may also include representatives from business, industry, and environmental groups. The Policy Committee sets goals, objectives and priorities and provides overall direction for the conference. It usually selects members of the other three committees and must ultimately approve a management plan for the estuary.

The Citizen Advisory Committee serves as the main voice of the stakeholders in the estuary and its watershed. Representatives of business and industry, associations, environmental and civic groups, farming and fishing groups, educators, and other affected and interested citizens on this committee communicate the concerns of the public and the regulated community to the Management Conference. The Citizen Advisory Committee also helps inform the public about the activities and work product of the Management Conference.

EPA promotes the NEP as a model of collective decisionmaking among various stakeholders with competing interests. The Management Conference is designed to foster collaborative decision making and consensus building around conflicting interests. Ideally, the Management Conference structure encourages open discussion and compromise that produce widespread support for the actions needed to restore and protect the estuary.

Duties of the Management Conference

Section 320(b) of the CWA directs the Management Conference to perform the following:

- assess trends in the estuary's water quality, natural resources, and uses;

- identify environmental problems by collecting and analyzing relevant data;

- determine relationships between pollutant loadings to changes in water quality and natural resources;

- develop a Comprehensive Conservation and Management Plan to restore and maintain the estuary;

- develop plans for coordinated implementation of the management plan by federal, state, and local regulatory agencies;

- monitor effectiveness of the management plan; and

- review all federal assistance programs and development projects to determine their consistency with the management plan.

These responsibilities reveal that the NEP is primarily a study and planning program. However, the Management Conference will address impacts on the estuary from a wide variety of human activities that occur across a large geographic area.

[T]he Management Conference must identify the environmental problems throughout this area and seek to link these problems with their probable causes. EPA defines this as the "characterization" process. This process involves analysis of existing information and knowledge on the condition of the estuary, its problems, the probable causes of these problems, and any apparent trends. Existing sources of information on estuaries are usually quite extensive, including research initiatives and EPA or state environmental databases, research on fisheries and coastal habitats from the National Oceanic and Atmospheric Administration or the state wildlife agency, and research and data from other federal and state agencies, academic institutions, and the private sector.

Comprehensive Conservation and Management Plan

After completing the characterization process, the Management Conference will begin work on a Comprehensive Conservation Management Plan (CCMP) for the estuary. CCMPs are not direct, enforceable regulation. This important detail prompted one witness testifying before a House subcommittee to describe the NEP as a program which "may encourage those states with good intentions to gum away. The teeth, however, are lacking." HOUSE MERCHANT MARINE AND FISHERIES COMMITTEE, COASTAL WATERS IN JEOPARDY, H.R. DOC. NO. 38, 101st Cong., 1st Sess. at 27 (1989) (quoting testimony of Oliver A. Houck, Professor of Law, Tulane University on September 28, 1988).

While this may be true to some extent, when properly developed, CCMPs represent a blueprint for restoring and protecting an estuary. They contain numerous recommendations for regulatory changes based on available scientific data. Consequently, CCMPs can serve as an important catalyst for changing a host of existing regulations and adopting new regulations necessary to accomplish its goals. If implemented, these recommendations would have a significant impact on the various stakeholders who live and operate in the watershed.

EPA guidance requires that CCMPs contain five main components. First and foremost, a CCMP must contain proposed solutions for the priority problems identified by the Management Conference. Although some CCMPs contain innovative solutions to identified problems, most proposed solutions consist of recommendations for more stringent and comprehensive controls and enforcement in existing regulatory regimes.

The second part of a CCMP is a plan for implementing its specific recommendations. Accordingly, CCMPs include strategies for obtaining and maintaining support in the public and private sectors for recommended initiatives. These strategies generally involve coordinating and focusing various government agencies on the goals of the CCMP and developing political support in the private sector and regulated communities to accomplish these goals.

The third element of a CCMP is a plan for financing the various recommended corrective actions. Invariably, solutions proposed by CCMPs are extremely expensive and implementation costs can run into the tens of millions of dollars. Financing can come from various sources. Federal funding is available from the CWA's State Revolving Fund and nonpoint source program along with several other EPA programs. However, state and local sources will incur most of the costs for implementing CCMP recommendations. This often requires tax increases or imposition of costs on the public, property owners, businesses and industries, and other citizens directly affected by increased regulation.

The fourth component of a CCMP is a plan for monitoring the effectiveness of implementation of proposed solutions. Monitoring is needed to determine whether management actions are having their intended impact and whether they should be modified in any way. Monitoring also helps assess the success of the CCMP.

The fifth and last part of a CCMP is the federal consistency review. The Management Conference must review all federal financial assistance programs and federal development projects to determine their consistency with the CCMP. If federal programs or projects conflict with the CCMP, they may require modification. Consequently, in addition to fostering numerous regulatory changes, CCMPs can have a significant impact on federal activities within the study area.

Within 120 days after completion of the CCMP and after providing for public review and comment, EPA must approve the plan if it satisfies the requirements of the NEP and if the state governor concurs. Section 320 of the CWA states that, "upon approval of a [CCMP], such plan *shall be implemented.*" 33 U.S.C. § 1330(f)(2) (emphasis added). Although there are no authorities construing the ultimate effect of this mandate, the language is quite strong and implies, at a minimum, that federal agencies must do everything in their power to implement a CCMP. This would also include making any necessary changes in federal programs and projects to ensure that federal activities in the study area are consistent with the CCMP.

The NEP is a watershed-based management approach to protecting our nation's estuaries. Acceptance into the NEP leads to a comprehensive evaluation of all the problems in a given estuary and the development of strategies to address the most serious problems threatening the long-term health of the estuary. Public participation in this effort is one of the conceptual cornerstones of the NEP, although meaningful participation by the public may not be fully realized in all cases. Management plans created under the NEP do not have the force of law, but they can and do motivate federal, state and local regulators into action.

NOTES & QUESTIONS

1. Through its CCMP device, the NEP takes the same approach as is taken under the Coastal Zone Management Act through Coastal Management Program, described in the previous section of this chapter. The article describes the CCMP as a blueprint for management of the estuary's ecological and economic resources, but notes the potential force of the federal action "consistency" review step in putting that blueprint into action. As the materials on the Coastal Zone Management Act explore, a consistency review step can indeed alter federal agency actions. But is it strong enough to serve as the primary ecosystem management instrument for estuaries? Or, as Professor Houck put it in his congressional testimony cited in the article, is the NEP, even with the consistency review step, all gums and no teeth?

2. The management challenge facing the NEP is compounded by the rather open ecological features of an estuary. As the transition from land to sea and freshwater to marine water, what jurisdictional boundary makes the most ecological sense for the NEP? Clearly, what happens in an estuary will depend in large part on what happens in the rivers leading to it, which leads in turn to the upland watersheds of those rivers. *See* USEPA, *Coastal Watersheds*, http://www.epa.gov/owow/oceans/factsheets/fact1.html (summarizing the impacts of land based activities on coastal watersheds). As shown in the figure below, the watersheds of the estuaries that are in the NEP cover a lot of ground, with many extending through several states. The effects of inland and upriver actions land and resource uses on estuaries can be quite complex and varied between estuaries. For example, a recent study of global estuaries found that, overall, human land uses have increased the amount of sediment load to rivers because of increased erosion, but that in many cases the actual flux of sediment into estuaries has been reduced because of reservoirs. *See* James P.M. Syvitski et al., *Impact of Humans on the Flux of Terrestrial Sediment to the Global Coastal Ocean*, 303 SCIENCE 376 (2005). The result is that some estuaries, such as the Mississippi River Delta, are starved of sediment flux, while others, such as the Chesapeake Bay, have too much sediment flowing into them. Is the NEP, as described above, equipped to manage on that scale of ecosystem dynamics? *See* Randall B. Wilburn, *Mediate Water Quality Problems on a Watershed Basis? Done That, What's Next?*, 31 ST. BAR OF TEXAS ENVTL. L.J. 151, 155–161 (2001). Does the coastal nonpoint pollution program, added to the Coastal Zone Management Act through section 6217 of the Coastal Zone Act

Reauthorization Amendments (described in the previous section of this chapter), provide scope and depth of regulation where the NEP might not?

Watersheds of National Estuaries

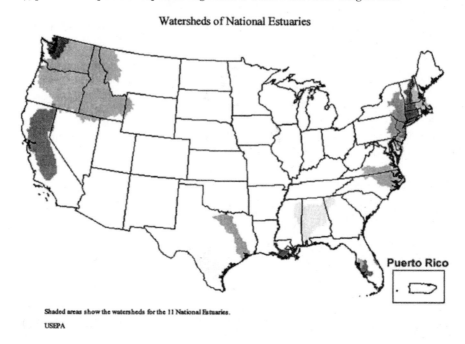

Shaded areas show the watersheds for the 11 National Estuaries.

USEPA

3. What goes up must come down. To further complicate matters, consider that each estuary's inland watershed shown in the previous figure is influenced by an "airshed" which, as shown in the next figure, can cover a much larger area. While not as well-defined as a watershed, airsheds represent prevailing atmospheric patterns that circulate and carry particulate and gaseous matter within the roughly-defined airshed boundary. They are defined more formally as the area responsible for emitting 75 percent of the air pollution reaching a body of water. Because different pollutants behave differently in the atmosphere, the airshed for different pollutants will vary. Air pollutants such as oxidized nitrogen thus may be emitted far outside the boundary of a watershed but within the airshed that covers the watershed. This and other pollutants thus may settle within the watershed and, if they dissolve in water or bind with soils that erode into water, may eventually enter the estuary. The nitrogen added through this process of atmospheric deposition acts as a nutrient within the estuarine ecosystems, and, like all good things, there can be too much of nutrients (see the discussion of "hypoxia" later in this chapter). Indeed, studies show that well over 20 percent of the total nitrogen entering some estuarine watersheds comes through atmospheric deposition. For example, vehicle exhaust has been shown to contribute as much as 30 percent of the nitrogen entering the Chesapeake Bay ecosystem (still less than the 40 percent attributable to agricultural wastes entering through surface waters). *See Vehicle Exhaust Said to Be Responsible for Much of Nitrogen in Chesapeake Bay*, 38 Env't Rep. 1710 (2007). Other pollutants that can enter and severely affect estuaries through atmospheric deposition include mercury, sulfur gases, and heavy metals.

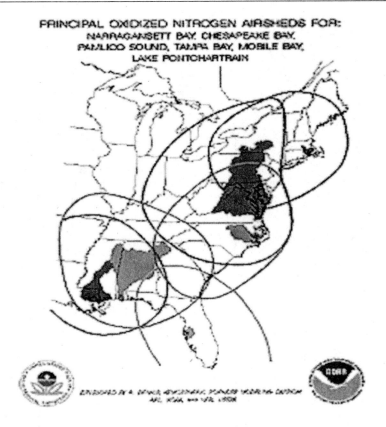

4. Section 315 of the Coastal Zone Management Act, 16 U.S.C. § 1461, establishes the National Estuarine Research Reserve System (NEERS). As stated in the program's implementing regulations, 15 C.F.R. § 921.1, the NEERS has the following mission:

> the establishment and management, through Federal-state cooperation, of a national system of estuarine research reserves representative of the various regions and estuarine types in the United States. National Estuarine Research Reserves are established to provide opportunities for long-term research, education, and interpretation.

The NERRS was established by the CZMA to help address the problem of current and potential degradation of coastal resources brought about by increasing and competing demands for these resources. Prior to establishment of the NERRS, the management of estuarine resources was inadequate, and scientific understanding of estuarine processes necessary for improving management was increasing slowly and without national coordination. There were no ready mechanisms to detect trends in estuarine conditions, or to provide information on these trends, the overall significance of estuaries, and possible solutions to the growing problems. The NERRS is portrayed as one part of the solution for maintaining healthy coastal resources. NERRS research, education, and resource stewardship programs are tools that can help fill gaps in knowledge, and guide decision-making so that our estuaries can sustain multiple uses over the long term. Accordingly, the goals of NEERS are to:

- Ensure a stable environment for research through long-term protection of National Estuarine Research Reserve resources;

- Address coastal management issues identified as significant through coordinated estuarine research within the System;

- Enhance public awareness and understanding of estuarine areas and

- Promote Federal, state, public and private use of one or more Reserves within the System when such entities conduct estuarine research; and

- Conduct and coordinate estuarine research within the System, gathering and making available information necessary for improved understanding and management of estuarine areas.

15 C.F.R. § 921.1(b). Currently, the NEERS includes 28 reserves distributed in 22 states and covering a total of 1 million acres. For more information on the NEERS program, see http://www.nerrs.noaa.gov/.

b. THREE MAJOR ESTUARINE SYSTEMS

(1) The Chesapeake Bay

The nation's largest estuary, the Chesapeake Bay, is not part of the National Estuary Program, but rather is managed through a multi-jurisdictional cooperative agreement between the federal government and several states that is administered as the Chesapeake Bay Program. Indeed, the Chesapeake Bay Program, initiated in 1983 through the first Chesapeake Bay Agreement, was the model for the National Estuary Program. The major difference is that the Chesapeake Bay Program is a multi-party agreement in which the member states have agreed to adopt watershed level regulation of land use and environmental quality to meet the ecological performance goals set for the estuary. The following materials describe how this agreement came into being, its evolution, and the ecological impact the program has had.

The Chesapeake Bay watershed encompasses 66,387 square miles. Its year 2000 population is estimated to be 15,594,241. Major populated places include: Baltimore, MD; Washington, DC; Norfolk, VA; Richmond, VA; Arlington, VA.

Chesapeake Bay Program (2002).

Harry R. Hughes & Thomas W. Burke, Jr., *The Cleanup of the Nation's Largest Estuary: A Test of Political Will*

11 Natural Resources & Environment 30 (Fall 1996).

The Chesapeake Bay's largest tributary, the Susquehanna River, rises in Cooperstown, New York, a sleepy little village more famous for its Baseball Hall of Fame than for being the headwaters of North America's largest estuary. At Havre de Grace, Maryland, 240 miles south of Cooperstown, the Susquehanna is released from its banks and blossoms into the Chesapeake Bay, famous for other joys of summer—blue crabs, rockfish, sailboats, sunshine, and Silver Queen corn. Two hundred miles south of Havre de Grace, past the ports of Baltimore, Cambridge, Newport News, and Norfolk, are the lighthouses of Cape Charles and Cape Henry, Virginia, the twin towers that mark the Bay's end and the beginning of the open Atlantic Ocean.

Over 64,000 square miles of land between Cooperstown, New York, and Cape Charles, Virginia, drain into the Chesapeake Bay through her tributaries. This estuary, where fresh water from these vast river networks and salt water from the Atlantic mix, boasts over 2,700 different species of plants and animals, more than any other similar area on the North American continent. Rivers like the Susquehanna, which drains central Pennsylvania, and the Potomac, whose hundreds of tributaries drain parts of Maryland, Virginia, West Virginia, and Pennsylvania, bring a mixture of good and bad to the Bay. In Maryland, smaller rivers like the Patuxent, Patapasco, Choptank, Chester, Sassafras, and Severn also carry fresh water down to the Bay, but like the larger rivers, they too transport other "cargo"—nitrogen, phosphorous, sediment, and toxic chemicals. In Virginia, the Rappahannock, James, and Elizabeth Rivers empty similar loads into the Bay.

The British call the Thames River "liquid history." America too has its liquid history, and much of it runs into the Chesapeake Bay. Antietam Creek, Bull Run, the Shenandoah and Appomattox Rivers conjure images of blue and grey warriors, struggling to assert their definition of freedom. The canals that link the Chesapeake with the Delaware River and the Ohio River speak to us of an even earlier time, when "way out West" meant places just over the Appalachians. St. Mary's City (Maryland's first capitol), Annapolis (the nation's first capitol) and Richmond (the Confederate States' only capitol) all owe their existence to "their" rivers, the Potomac, Severn, and James.

Today, 13 million people in six states and the District of Columbia call the Chesapeake's watershed home. That number will climb to 15 million by the year 2020. Two major ports, wide-ranging basic and high-value manufacturing, hi-tech, bio-tech and information processing businesses are a part of the Bay area's economy. The U.S. Naval Academy and scores of other colleges and universities, as well as the "business" of government are headquartered in this region. A highly developed tourism industry depends on the Bay while grain, chickens, fruit, vegetables, tobacco, dairy cattle and beef make agriculture the number one economic enterprise of the region and its largest single land use. The economy and use of the Bay, therefore, is as diverse as its biology.

Looking Back

The Chesapeake Bay of the eighteenth and nineteenth centuries was a prolific food source with abundant oysters, fish, and waterfowl beyond imagination. The Bay was also an avenue of commerce. The Baltimore clipper and paddle-wheel steamboat opened many rivers, streams, and creeks to trade and commerce. Little towns, isolated from one another and hard to reach by road or rail, became connected at the wharf. Baltimore became the hub of the watershed, drawing in seafood, crops, and raw materials, and sending out finished goods and, as the second busiest port of entry after New York City, immigrants.

But the industrialization of the region brought a new use for the Bay—garbage disposal. From foundries, factories, and farms, waste material was dumped in the Bay "free of charge." We built factories beside the rivers and streams for fuel-free power and then used the same waterways as ready-made sewers without concern for the long-term health of the resource. The Bay has suffered at our hands. By 1850, over 50 percent of Maryland forests had been cut down. The deep-water ports of Bladensburg, Port Tobacco, and Joppatown were closed to navigation by 1830 due to siltation and runoff. Where ocean-going ships once loaded cargo for England and European ports, only canoes and dories could navigate by the end of the War of 1812. The Bay yielded oyster harvests in excess of 20 million bushels a year in the 1880s, but only a mere fraction (approximately 1 percent) of the historic harvest is available today. Overfishing and impoundments which block spawning runs have reduced the shad population in the Bay to 10 percent of its historic level.

By the 1940s and 1950s, the cumulative impact of historic abuses and the surging effect of the population explosion in war-driven Washington, D.C., Baltimore and Newport News, finally began to overwhelm the Bay.

In 1972, Hurricane Agnes did heavy damage to bay grasses, and they did not recover. Scientists began to realize that poor water quality inhibited bay grass recovery and growth. Large areas of the Bay were suffering from anoxia (no dissolved oxygen) or hypoxia (little dissolved oxygen) and toxics were a persistent problem, especially in major industrial areas—Baltimore Harbor, the waters around Norfolk, and the Anacostia River in the District of Columbia.

A new environmental group, the Chesapeake Bay Foundation, began to sound the alarm and rally people with the cry, "Save the Bay." At the same time, the Alliance for the Chesapeake dedicated itself to bringing together government, business and environmentalists in a cooperative spirit to solve common problems.

Maryland's U.S. Senator Charles "Mac" Mathias called on the U.S. Environmental Protection Agency to study the Bay to determine the causes of its decline and offer suggestions for the Bay's recovery. That study, funded in 1976 and completed in 1983, provided the scientific foundation for action, including several scientific breakthroughs. The first and most important discovery was that excess nutrients (phosphorus and nitrogen) were significantly responsible for the water quality decline. These nutrients (from sewage treatment plant outfalls, farm fields and feed lots and suburban lawns and construction sites) over-enrich algae in the Bay, which then multiplies so fast and thick that it blocks sunlight from bay grasses, killing them. Bay grasses are the "nursery" areas for small fish and crabs and a critical food source for many types of waterfowl. To compound the problem, when this algae dies, it uses up the available oxygen in the water as it decomposes, seriously limiting the water's ability to sustain aquatic life or even to assimilate pollution.

Another technical breakthrough involved modeling the way the Bay works, at first with a scaled-down physical model that spread out over two acres, and later with Cray supercomputers. With the help of the computers, the models aided in determining the flow dynamics of the Bay and helped pinpoint where nutrients were coming from and how land use affects water quality in the Bay.

It is important to understand that the Chesapeake does not "drain" out into the Atlantic. For the most part, what goes in, stays in. Further, the ratio of watershed land to water—how many acres of land drain into so many acres of water—is almost 17 to 1 for the Chesapeake Bay. For comparison, the Great Lakes ratio is only 7 to 1 and the Mediterranean Sea ratio is 1 to 1. In the Chesapeake watershed, actions on land have profound effects in the water.

But inactions on land can also profoundly affect the water. When preliminary EPA study findings began to be reported, it was clear that we could not wait or let this report sit on a shelf, gathering dust. We had to take action. We began by working with citizen groups, city and county governments, and neighboring states. Both Governor Thornburg of Pennsylvania and Governor Dalton of Virginia overcame longstanding "institutional" and geographic biases against a coalition where, "someone might tell them what to do." Additionally, Pennsylvania had to confront the "it doesn't affect me" syndrome to form the beginnings of a cooperative partnership. Broad grassroots support also was building, and a new coalition of federal agencies, state and local governments, and scientists was named the "Chesapeake Bay Program." Its mission was to understand the reasons behind the Bay's decline and to begin to implement recovery measures.

By 1983, our early work paid off and the working coalition of federal agencies, state and local governments, and citizens had progressed to the point where a formal declaration, in the form of a "Chesapeake Bay Agreement," was signed by the leaders of the six interests most involved with the Bay—the U.S. EPA, signing on behalf of all federal agencies; the State of Maryland; the Commonwealths of Virginia and Pennsylvania; the District of Columbia; and the Chesapeake Bay Commission, an alliance of state legislators from Maryland, Virginia, and Pennsylvania.

This agreement, although short, was a huge step forward in the restoration of the Bay. It brought together the principal leaders in the watershed, committed them to action, and created an organized structure dedicated to the systematic and scientific analysis of the Bay's problems and the refinement of a science-based, consensus-driven plan for the Chesapeake's cleanup.

The 1987 Chesapeake Bay Agreement

In 1987, a second Chesapeake Bay Agreement was signed by the same six parties who signed the original compact. This agreement, longer and more specific, set out goals, objectives, and commitments in six areas:

1. Living Resources: Providing for restoration and protection of the Bay's living resources, their habitats and ecological relationships was the goal established in the first area of this new agreement. The agreement declared the Bay's living resources to be the ultimate measure of the restoration's progress. The health and abundance of benthos, fish, shellfish, plants, and waterfowl would signal the cleanup's success.

2. Water Quality: To "[r]educe and control point and non-point sources of pollution to attain the water quality condition necessary to support the Living Resources of the Bay," was the objective in the second area. But how clean should the Bay be to support these living resources? And which living resources? Before any decisions could be made, scientists and Bay manag-

ers first had to determine the water quality levels necessary to support all the varied forms of life in the Bay. This investigation is ongoing.

3. Population Growth and Development: "Plan for and manage the adverse environmental effects of human population growth and land development in the Chesapeake Bay watershed." Growth devours forest and farm land, wetlands and shoreline as well as local governments' budgets to build new infrastructure. But a strong economy finances environmental action. Balancing population growth and economic development with environmental concerns and the restoration of the Chesapeake Bay is a difficult task.

4. Public Information, Education and Participation: "Promote general understanding among citizens . . . the problems facing the Bay and policies and programs designed to help it. Foster individual responsibility and stewardship of the Bay's resources." Action follows consensus. Public understanding and public participation allow people to make informed decisions and provide the political support for tough choices.

5. Public Access: "Promote increased opportunities for public appreciation and enjoyment of the Bay and its tributaries." If people cannot use the Bay, why should they support its restoration? With 95 percent of the Bay's shoreline privately owned, encouraging use and the concept of personal stewardship is a key to success.

6. Governance: "Support and enhance the present comprehensive efforts and perpetuation of commitments necessary to ensure long-term results." Laws and regulations are necessary to effect the Bay cleanup, but continuity of management and steady commitment also are important.

Politically, the 1987 Chesapeake Bay Agreement put the responsibility for success directly on the elected leaders of the Bay states. The Bay cleanup was now "officially" part of executive and legislative agendas. The agreement also provided a yardstick for measuring success. With over fifty separate commitments, watchdog groups and concerned citizens could measure success and levels of dedication to Bay restoration by the number of commitments fulfilled.

For Bay managers and scientists, the 1987 agreement provided goals. The most important was the 40 percent reduction in *controllable* nitrogen and phosphorus loadings to the Bay by the year 2000. This commitment precipitated significant action at the state and local levels, in the agriculture industry, and in the business arena, including the construction and upgrade of wastewater treatment plants, and new ways for farmers to plow, manage herds, control manure, and harvest crops. The agreement also affected changes in growth management regulations and even in the process for building highways and housing developments.

The agreement called for management plans for dozens of species of fish and shellfish (crabs, oysters, rockfish, white and yellow perch, bluefish, American shad), wildfowl and tidal and nontidal wetlands. The signatories agreed to eliminate blockages to spawning fish trying to swim upstream. To date, the Bay states have invested millions of dollars in fish ladders, fish elevators, and removal of stream blockages, thereby freeing hundreds of miles of stream and river for migration of shad, rockfish, and perch. Projects like the fish "elevator" at the Conowingo Dam on the Susquehanna River, and the destruction of small dams and creation of fish ladders on the James River are helping many species make a comeback.

Finally, the 1987 Bay Agreement created an extensive state and federal infrastructure dedicated to the Chesapeake's restoration and operated on a consensus basis. All of the signatories have committed significant state resources. Maryland, for instance, has spent an average of $80 million a year on direct Chesapeake Bay activities, augmented by $20 million a year in federal support since 1987. Local governments and business have shouldered their share of the responsibility by implementing new regulations and ordinances, adhering to higher permit levels and by spending money directly on Bay-saving construction. The Bay cleanup has even become an international model for multijurisdictional cooperation and success. Visitors from China, Japan, Russia, Europe, South America, and Africa make pilgrimages to the Bay to discover the recipe for the Bay cleanup's success. They are interested in finding out how three states, the District of Columbia, over fifty federal agencies, and more than 2,000 local governments develop and cooperatively implement a broad-based array of programs without laws mandating coordination or cooperation.

What must be done for the Bay now seems clear:

- Assume individual responsibility for the Bay. We all must understand that what we do, whether at home or in the workplace, affects the environment and waters like the Chesapeake Bay. In the Bay watershed, helping people recognize and adopt an ethic of personal stewardship is at the top of the "how to save the Bay" list.

- Reach the nitrogen and phosphorus reduction goals as close to the year 2000 as possible. Government actions, legislation, personal habits, and business practices all should be geared toward cutting the input of nutrients to local waterways and the Bay.

- Manage growth to protect the economy and preserve the ecology. A healthy economy and a healthy Bay are not mutually exclusive. Law and regulation should not be crafted at the expense of either.

A few years ago, there was a Chesapeake Bay education campaign that used a large arrowhead, pointing to the drain of a bathroom sink, the tailpipe of a car, the edge of a farm field, the smokestack of a power plant or factory, a shower drain, suburban lawn, boat holding tank, storm drain, dam, suburban development or city. It said, "The Bay Starts Here!" The idea, of course, was simple. The Bay, and the Bay cleanup, starts with us. It begins at our doorsteps, in our homes and offices and where we play or relax, whether that is on the water, on the golf links or in our own backyards.

In the final analysis, the challenge to preserve and protect the Chesapeake is not a test of how clever our scientists are or how smart sewage treatment plant engineers can be. It is, rather, a test of our political will, a measure of our strength of commitment. We know what the problems are. We know what needs to be done to fix them. The test is whether we will, not whether we can.

NOTES & QUESTIONS

1. The governance structure of the Chesapeake Bay Agreement is quite unusual, and may explain both why it appears to be effective and why it may be difficult to generalize for ecosystem management. As Professor Jon Cannon has postulated, multi-jurisdictional collaborative resource management programs such as this present three types of transaction costs: the costs of gathering information relevant to the management goals (information costs); the costs of negotiating, monitoring, and enforcing the agreement (coordination costs); and the costs of controlling strategic behavior by participants, such as free-riding, that may impeded cooperation (strategic costs). *See* Jon Cannon, *Choices and Institutions in Watershed Management*, 25 WM. & MARY ENVTL. L. & POLICY REV. 379, 394 (2000). The Chesapeake Bay Program has achieved a rather complex, decentralized, but nonetheless efficient structure for controlling these costs. The ultimate decision making body for the Agreement is the Executive Council, which consists of the Governors of Virginia, Maryland, and Pennsylvania, the Administrator of the USEPA, the Mayor of the District of Columbia, and the Chair of the Chesapeake Bay Commission. The Executive Council draws on the work of many advisory committees, but most of its decisions are implemented through the Chesapeake Bay Commission, an appointed advisory body composed of state legislators, agency heads, and citizen representatives. The Commission works to implement the Executive Council's decisions through legislative and administrative initiatives. Cannon argues that this structure works because management of the Bay involves a relatively small number of jurisdictions with a relatively high number of shared concerns and goals given the configuration of the states and the physical characteristics of the Bay. In particular, typical upstream versus downstream issues often posed in watershed contexts are not as acute in the Bay. The Chesapeake Bay Program, therefore, may suggest a governance model that cannot efficiently be transported to other resource management contexts because of physical and ecological constraints.

2. As the foregoing history illustrates, over time a primary concern of the Chesapeake Bay Program has become controlling the nitrogen and phosphorous inputs into the estuary. The 1987 agreement had expressed the goal of 40 percent reduction of nitrogen and phosphorous entering the mainstem of the Bay. The agreement also stated that the parties would "reduce and control point and nonpoint sources of pollution to attain the water quality condition necessary to support the living resources of the Chesapeake Bay." Based on modeling and monitoring in the years that followed, the parties to the agreement determined that the program had paid insufficient attention to the quality of the Bay's *tributaries*, where most spawning grounds and essential habitat are found, and needed to intensify its focus on nonpoint sources of nutrients, particularly from agriculture. In 1992, therefore, the parties amended the agreement to require development of tributary-specific strategies aimed primarily at nonpoint

sources of nitrogen and phosphorous. *See* Chesapeake Bay Agreement: 1992 Amendments (Aug. 12, 1992).

3. Some conditions in the Chesapeake Bay began to improve after the 1992 amendments focused efforts on tributaries (see previous note), but many did not. Blue crab populations continued declining, bay grass acreage increased slightly, and oyster populations rebounded only marginally. Most importantly, the nitrogen and phosphorous reduction goals, while seemingly within reach, were not met, and rising population and urbanization suggested that more concerted efforts would be required not only to gain on the remaining increment, but to avoid losing ground. On June 28, 2000, therefore, the program parties adopted a new and more far-reaching agreement, known as Chesapeake 2000, with the effect of greatly increasing the program's attention to comprehensive management of the watershed lands. Chesapeake 2000 outlined 93 commitments detailing protection and restoration goals in 5 main categories: (1) living resource protection and restoration; (2) vital habitat protection and restoration; (3) water quality protection and restoration; (4) sound land use control; and (5) stewardship and community engagement. Among the commitments were to:

- increase the number of native oysters tenfold by 2010

- restore blue crabs by establishing harvest targets

- reduce the loss rate of farmland and forest land to urban development by 30 percent by 2012

- permanently preserve from development 20 percent of the lands in the watershed by 2010

The focus on preserving forested land added an important new dimension to the program, recognizing the watershed-based link between terrestrial ecosystems and coastal estuary ecosystems. This focus appeared to gain ground on the problem. Riparian forest buffers along streambanks have increased substantially already, to over 120,000 miles—about 60 percent of all streambank miles in the watershed. Almost 7 million acres of land in the watershed are preserved from development. Gradually, therefore, the Chesapeake Bay Program evolved from its inception in 1983, when the principal focus was the Bay, to including tributaries and, later still, the watershed lands as co-equal partners in the management challenge.

4. The Chesapeake Bay Program participants also entered into three agreements in December 2001 to mitigate the effects of stormwater runoff. One agreement committed the Program to developing and demonstrating innovative stormwater control methods and technologies that local governments and private landowners can employ. Another agreement committed several Program participants to working to achieve 50 restoration targets for one of the major watersheds in the system, the Anacostia River watershed. The final agreement, called "Building for the Bay," enlisted several cooperating organizations, including the National Association of Home Builders, to help the Program promote voluntary adoption of 22 principles that reduce the environmental effects of residential and commercial development "through employment of site design practices which restore natural hydrology, retain rainwater onsite, reduce reliance on constructed conveyances, and otherwise prevent the erosion and scouring of natural streambeds."

5. Notwithstanding the expanded focus on tributaries, nutrients, forests, and stormwater outlined in the previous notes, conditions in the Bay continued to slide in many respects. In its *2004 State of the Bay Report*, the Chesapeake Bay Foundation, a non-governmental organization, rated the conditions in the Bay a 27 out of 100, with 100 representing the pristine conditions Captain John Smith described in his accounts of his explorations in the early 1600s. *See* Chesapeake Bay Foundation, 2004 State of the Bay Report (2004). The major threat, according to the group, was excessive nitrogen and phosphorous nutrient levels, which lead to reduced dissolved oxygen necessary for aquatic life. In 2003 the states in the Chesapeake Bay Program agreed to take measures to reduce the flow of nutrient-laden sediment load into the estuary, as well as to focus on land use practices that are sources of nutrient load to soils and rivers, such as agriculture, municipal waste treatment, and residential fertilizers. The Chesapeake Bay Program's 2004 status report, however, concluded that the Bay shows "mixed trends." *See* Chesapeake Bay Program, The State of the Chesapeake Bay and its Watershed (2004). Then a U.S. Government Accountability Office study of the program issued in 2005 concluded that the program is using an implementation process that "has led to negative trends being downplayed and a rosier picture of the bay's health being reported than may have been warranted." U.S. GOVERNMENT ACCOUNTABILITY OFFICE, CHESAPEAKE BAY PROGRAM: IMPROVED STRATEGIES ARE NEEDED TO BETTER ASSESS, REPORT, AND MANAGE RESTORATION PROGRESS, GAO-06-96 (Oct. 2005). Could this explain why the political workings of the program participants appeared relatively friendly? That did not last much longer.

———

By 2005 it was clear more was going to be needed to meet the Chesapeake Bay Program goals. That something more became the Clean Water Act's Total Maximum Daily Load (TMDL) program. The mechanics of the TMDL program, administered by the EPA, are covered in Chapter 10. It is often portrayed as a means of establishing a "pollution diet" for a water body. The Chesapeake Bay, however, is quite a large water body, and the idea of establishing a TMDL for nitrogen and phosphorous in a region so dominated by urban and agricultural sources of those pollutants threw the Chesapeake Bay Program into a political buzzsaw. Ultimately, the EPA managed to promulgate a TMDL for the Bay in 2010. This brief summary of the history reveals how difficult that process was and how all-encompassing the TMDL is.

US EPA, *Chesapeake Bay Total Maximum Daily Load for Nitrogen, Phosphorus and Sediment*
December 29, 2010.

The U.S. Environmental Protection Agency (EPA) has established the Chesapeake Bay Total Maximum Daily Load (TMDL), a historic and comprehensive "pollution diet" with rigorous accountability measures to initiate sweeping actions to restore clean water in the Chesapeake Bay and the region's streams, creeks and rivers.

Despite extensive restoration efforts during the past 25 years, the TMDL was prompted by insufficient progress and continued poor water quality in the Chesapeake Bay and its tidal tributaries. The TMDL is required under the federal Clean Water Act and responds to consent decrees in Virginia and the District of Columbia from the late 1990s. It is also a keystone commitment of a federal strategy to meet President Barack Obama's Executive Order to restore and protect the Bay.

The TMDL – the largest ever developed by EPA – identifies the necessary pollution reductions of nitrogen, phosphorus and sediment across Delaware, Maryland, New York, Pennsylvania, Virginia, West Virginia and the District of Columbia and sets pollution limits necessary to meet applicable water quality standards in the Bay and its tidal rivers and embayments. Specifically, the TMDL sets Bay watershed limits of 185.9 million pounds of nitrogen, 12.5 million pounds of phosphorus and 6.45 billion pounds of sediment per year – a 25 percent reduction in nitrogen, 24 percent reduction in phosphorus and 20 percent reduction in sediment. These pollution limits are further divided by jurisdiction and major river basin based on state-of-the-art modeling tools, extensive monitoring data, peer-reviewed science and close interaction with jurisdiction partners.

The TMDL is designed to ensure that all pollution control measures needed to fully restore the Bay and its tidal rivers are in place by 2025, with at least 60 percent of the actions completed by 2017. The TMDL is supported by rigorous accountability measures to ensure cleanup commitments are met, including short-and long-term benchmarks, a tracking and accountability system for jurisdiction activities, and federal contingency actions that can be employed if necessary to spur progress. Watershed Implementation Plans (WIPs), which detail how and when the six Bay states and the District of Columbia will meet pollution allocations, played a central role in shaping the TMDL.

Most of the draft WIPs submitted by the jurisdictions in September 2010 did not sufficiently identify programs needed to reduce pollution or provide assurance the programs could be implemented. As a result, the draft TMDL issued September 24, 2010 contained moderate- to high-level backstop measures to tighten controls on federally permitted point sources of pollution.

A 45-day public comment period on the draft TMDL was held from September 24 to November 8, 2010. During that time, EPA held 18 public meetings in all seven Bay watershed jurisdictions, which were attended by about 2,500 citizens. EPA received more than 14,000 public comments and, where appropriate, incorporated responses to those comments in developing the final TMDL.

After states submitted the draft WIPs, EPA worked closely with each jurisdiction to revise and strengthen its plan. Because of this cooperative work and state leadership, the final WIPs were significantly improved. Examples of specific improvements include:

Regulated point sources and non-regulated nonpoint sources of nitrogen, phosphorus, and sediment are fully considered and evaluated separately in terms of their relative contributions to water quality impairment of the Chesapeake Bay's tidal waters.

Committing to more stringent nitrogen and phosphorus limits at wastewater treatment plants, including on the James River in Virginia. (Virginia, New York, Delaware)

Pursuing state legislation to fund wastewater treatment plant upgrades, urban stormwater management and agricultural programs. (Maryland, Virginia, West Virginia)

Implementing a progressive stormwater permit to reduce pollution. (District of Columbia)

Dramatically increasing enforcement and compliance of state requirements for agriculture. (Pennsylvania)

Committing state funding to develop and implement state-of-the-art technologies for converting animal manure to energy for farms. (Pennsylvania)

Considering implementation of mandatory programs for agriculture by 2013 if pollution reductions fall behind schedule. (Delaware, Maryland, Virginia)

These improvements enabled EPA to reduce and remove most federal backstops, leaving a few targeted backstops and a plan for enhanced oversight and contingency actions to ensure progress. As a result, the final TMDL is shaped in large part by the jurisdictions' plans to reduce pollution, which was a long-standing priority for EPA and why the agency always provided the jurisdictions with flexibility to determine how to reduce pollution in the most efficient, cost-effective and acceptable manner.

Now the focus shifts to the jurisdictions' implementation of the WIP policies and programs that will reduce pollution on-the-ground and in-the-water. EPA will conduct oversight of WIP implementation and jurisdictions' progress toward meeting two-year milestones. If progress is insufficient, EPA is committed to take appropriate contingency actions including targeted compliance and enforcement activities, expansion of requirements to obtain NPDES permit coverage for currently unregulated sources, revision of the TMDL allocations and additional controls on federally permitted sources of pollution, such as wastewater treatment plants, large animal agriculture operations and municipal stormwater systems.

In 2011, while the jurisdictions continue to implement their WIPs, they will begin development of Phase II WIPs, designed to engage local governments, watershed organizations, conservation districts, citizens and other key stakeholders in reducing water pollution.

Most of the Chesapeake Bay and its tidal waters are listed as impaired because of excess nitrogen, phosphorus and sediment. These pollutants cause algae blooms that consume oxygen and create "dead zones" where fish and shellfish cannot survive, block sunlight that is needed for underwater Bay grasses, and smother aquatic life on the bottom. The high levels of nitrogen, phosphorus and sediment enter the water from agricultural operations, urban and suburban stormwater runoff, wastewater facilities, air pollution and other sources, including onsite septic systems. Despite some reductions in pollution during the past 25 years of restoration due to efforts by federal, state and local governments; non-governmental organizations; and stakeholders in the agriculture, urban/suburban stormwater, and wastewater sectors, there has been insufficient progress toward meeting the water quality goals for the Chesapeake Bay and its tidal waters.

More than 40,000 TMDLs have been completed across the United States, but the Chesapeake Bay TMDL will be the largest and most complex thus far – it is designed to achieve significant reductions in nitrogen, phosphorus and sediment pollution throughout a 64,000-square-mile watershed that includes the District of Columbia and large sections of six states. The TMDL is actually a combination of 92 smaller TMDLs for individual Chesapeake Bay tidal segments and includes pollution limits that are sufficient to meet state water quality standards for dissolved oxygen, water clarity, underwater Bay grasses and chlorophyll-a, an indicator of algae levels (Figure ES-1). It is important to note that the pollution controls employed to meet the TMDL will also have significant benefits for water quality in tens of thousands of streams, creeks, lakes and rivers throughout the region.

Since 2000, the seven jurisdictions in the Chesapeake Bay watershed (Delaware, District of Columbia, Maryland, New York, Pennsylvania, Virginia, and West Virginia), EPA and the Chesapeake Bay Commission, which are partners in the Chesapeake Bay Program, have been planning for a Chesapeake Bay TMDL.

Since September 2005, the seven jurisdictions have been actively involved in decision-making to develop the TMDL. During the October 2007 meeting of the Chesapeake Bay Program's Principals' Staff Committee, the Bay watershed jurisdictions and EPA agreed that EPA would establish the multi-state TMDL. Since 2008, EPA has sent official letters to the jurisdictions detailing all facets of the TMDL, including: nitrogen, phosphorus and sediment allocations; schedules for developing the TMDL and pollution reduction plans; EPA's expectations and evaluation criteria for jurisdiction plans to meet the TMDL pollution limits; reasonable assurance for controlling nonpoint source pollution; and backstop actions that EPA could take to ensure progress.

The TMDL also resolves commitments made in a number of consent decrees, Memos of Understanding, the Chesapeake Bay Foundation settlement agreement of 2010, and settlement agreements dating back to the late 1990s that address certain tidal waters identified as impaired in the District of Columbia, Delaware, Maryland and Virginia.

NOTES & QUESTIONS

1. The basic approach of the Bay TMDL is to (1) require reductions of nitrogen entering the Bay by 25 percent, phosphorous by 24 percent, and sediment by 20 percent; (2) divide the Bay-wide caps by jurisdictions and then by major river basins; (3) require the states from there to allocate loads for point sources such as municipal wastes and non-point sources such as agriculture; (4) require the states to demonstrate how they will achieve the reductions through Watershed Implementation Plans; and (5) have EPA step in to develop load allocations and regulations if a state fails to do so. EPA portrayed this approach as deferring to the states. Are you surprised that the states did not see it that way?

2. As is explained in Chapter 10, EPA may not use the TMDL program to directly regulate nonpoint sources of water pollution, such as farm runoff, but states can do so under their respective authorities. Agricultural interests have sued to block the Bay TMDL, arguing it exceeds EPA's authority by forcing the states to regulate nonpoint sources. *See* Am. Farm Bureau v EPA, No. 1:11-CV 00067 (M.D. Pa.). For insight on the kind of arguments they are raising, see the discussion of the TMDL program in Chapter 10.

3. On May 12, 2009, President Obama issued Executive Order 13508 to address protection and restoration of the Chesapeake Bay, proclaiming "a renewed commitment" on the part of the federal government toward the goal of improved Bay quality. *See* 74 Fed. Reg. 23099 (May 12, 2009). The order directs a host of federal agencies to develop a strategy "for the implementation of adaptive management principles," to make decisions for management of the Bay that "reflect adaptive management principles," and to use "adaptive management to plan, monitor, evaluate, and adjust environmental management actions." Nowhere does the order provide more detail about what "adaptive management principles" entail.

(2) The Bay-Delta

The West Coast version of the Chesapeake Bay Program, in terms of scope and ambition, is the San Francisco Bay/Sacramento-San Joaquin Delta Estuary Plan (Bay-Delta Plan). By contrast, however, the Bay-Delta Plan management framework is structurally far more complex than is the case for the Chesapeake Bay Program. The Bay-Delta Estuary is one of the largest ecosystems for fish and wildlife habitat and production in the United States, and is the largest on the West Coast. Efforts to manage it comprehensively began in 1960s with a series of decisions by the California State Water Rights Board, predecessor to the current State Water Resources Control Board (SWRCB), affecting water rights in the federal Central Valley Project (CVP) and the State Water Projects (SWP), both of which influence the Bay-Delta. The state also enacted the Porter-Cologne Water Quality Control Act of 1969, Cal. Water Code §§ 13000 et seq., which established the SWRCB and a group of Regional Water Quality Control Boards whose charge was to develop water quality control plans for their respective regions of the state. These plans are to define beneficial uses of water rights, water quality objectives, and a program of implementation.

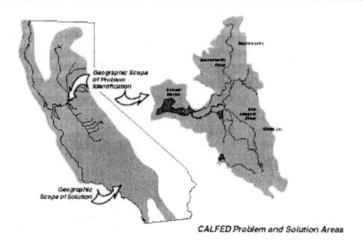

CALFED 1999

CALFED Problem and Solution Areas

During the 1970s and 1980s, the state and federal governments became increasingly concerned that the impaired flow conditions and increasing salinity of water in the Bay-Delta basin were degrading the ecosystem. In 1994, the Governor's Water Policy Council and the federal government's Federal Ecosystem Directorate, known collectively as CALFED, entered into a framework agreement to focus on coordination of water quality standards, water project operations, and ecosystem resources. The following case explores the Byzantine history of events leading to the formation of CALFED in its ecological, land use, and political contexts. Notice how much of that ecology, land use, and politics revolves around what the Court calls California's most precious resource—water.

In re Bay–Delta Programmatic Environmental Impact Report Coordinated Proceedings

Court of Appeal of California, Third Appellate District, 2005.
133 Cal. App. 4th 154, 34 Cal. Rptr. 3d 696.

■ HULL, J.

In response to concerns over the decline of water quality and the ecology of the San Francisco Bay and the Sacramento-San Joaquin Delta (Delta) and concerns over recurrent shortages of water for beneficial uses, 18 state and federal agencies with management or regulatory responsibility over the Bay-Delta formed CALFED to devise a long-range plan to address those concerns. After many years of study and analysis, including significant public participation, CALFED adopted a program (the CALFED Program or Program) to be administered over the next 30 years, which includes measures for improving the Bay-Delta ecosystem, water quality and quantity, and Delta levee stability. On August 28, 2000, the Secretary of the California Resources Agency certified the final Programmatic Environmental Impact Statement/Environmental Impact Report (PEIS/R) and CALFED adopted the Record of Decision (ROD) for the Program in accordance with the National Environmental Policy Act of 1969 (42 U.S.C. § 4321 et seq.) and the California Environmental Quality Act (CEQA) (Pub. Resources Code, § 21000 et seq.).

Appellants, who include the California Farm Bureau Federation (Farm Bureau), the Central Delta Water Agency (CDWA) and the Regional Council of Rural Counties (RCRC), filed petitions for writ of mandate challenging the PEIS/R under CEQA and asserting various non-CEQA claims based on actions taken or anticipated under the Program. The trial court found the PEIS/R satisfactory under CEQA and dismissed the non-CEQA claims as either premature or not properly stated.

Appellants challenge the trial court's rulings on a number of grounds. Among other things, they contend the PEIS/R does not contain a sufficient discussion of adverse environmental impacts.

Facts and Proceedings

I

Introduction

Although the central focus of the CALFED Program is the environmental health of the Bay-Delta estuary, the problems that exist in that area cannot be divorced from the more generalized problems of water quality, quantity, and allocation that have long been a fact of life in the State of California (State).

The CALFED Program is the latest attempt to break the impasse among the various interest groups competing for water in California. One of the intractable problems the Program seeks to address is the disparity between the amount of water needed to satisfy the demands and desires of the State's various beneficial users and the amount of water available for such use. Historically, the resolution of the physical fact of water scarcity in California has focused almost exclusively on the development and augmentation of water supplies. In the best tradition of the old West, water scarcity was viewed as something to be conquered rather than managed. Substantial amounts of public resources were invested in the construction and operation of vast storage and conveyance facilities.

Those days are over. Limits of the developed water supply in the State are being reached, and there is fierce competition for what remains. It is now recognized that each new project to harness greater amounts of water comes at a price beyond the cost of construction and maintenance. A new water reservoir or conveyance facility may mean the destruction of many acres of farmland or wildlife habitat. Water diverted from a stream or other watercourse to some beneficial use may mean less water passing to the sea through which fish migrate or a reduction in the natural barrier to saltwater intrusion. Water allocated to one area of the State may mean less water available for another area.

Another problem the Program seeks to resolve is the inequality between water availability and water demand in the different regions of the State. At the risk of oversimplification, this problem is primarily one of supply exceeding demand in the northern regions coupled with the opposite condition in the central and southern regions. This is not just a matter of reallocation. Water taken from one area to convert a desert in another area into a productive agricultural community may retard development in the area of origin.

To aid in our examination of the CALFED Program and the issues raised in these coordinated proceedings, we first place the Program in its proper geographic and historic context. The Program is not an isolated effort to restore the ecological health of the Bay-Delta or to resolve conflicts among the State's water users. The problems giving rise to CALFED have lasted for decades, and the Program is the latest, and certainly the most comprehensive and ambitious, attempt to provide relief to those dependent on this State's limited water resources.

III

Geographic Setting

The Delta is a maze of tributaries, sloughs, and islands covering over 738,000 acres in five counties. The legal boundary of the Delta is roughly triangular, with the three vertices being Sacramento in the north, Vernalis in the south and Pittsburg in the west. The Bay-Delta estuary includes California's two largest rivers, the Sacramento, which flows into the Delta from the north, and the San Joaquin, which flows into the Delta from the south. Water that accumulates in these rivers flows through the Delta and, if not diverted elsewhere, into Suisun Bay. From there it continues to the San Francisco Bay and on to the Pacific Ocean.

The Delta originally consisted of overflow and seasonally inundated land. Today, this area is crisscrossed by the Sacramento and San Joaquin Rivers and many meandering sloughs, creating over 50 islands protected by levees that, along with the adjacent mainland, contain highly productive farmland. The Delta also contains major transportation networks, towns, homes and businesses. Because this area is drying out due to exposure to sun and wind by farming, it has been sinking at an annual rate of two to five inches, faster than any other place on earth. Islands that were at sea level a century ago are now as much as twenty to thirty feet below sea level and protected by old and increasingly precarious levees.

The Delta is the hub for distribution of water emptying into the Bay-Delta estuary to other regions in the State, including the Central Valley and Southern California. Average annual precipitation in California is approximately 24 inches. However, this amount varies from area to area, with a low of almost nothing in the southern desert regions and a high of 100 inches in the mountainous north coast regions. Sixty percent of the precipitation that falls over the State eventually evaporates or is transpired by trees and other vegetation. The rest, approximately 71 million acre-feet, ends up as runoff that gathers in streams and other watercourses. Half of this runoff flows through the Delta.

California's Central Valley stretches nearly 500 miles from Redding in the north to Bakersfield in the south, and more than a hundred miles from the Sierra Nevada in the east to the coastal ranges in the west. Average annual precipitation in the Central Valley ranges from five inches in the south to more than 30 inches in the north, with more than three-fourths of this precipitation occurring between December and April. The water flow of the Sacramento and San Joaquin Rivers is also seasonal, with rains and melting snow creating high flow in the spring and early summer.

The Central Valley has been described as "[a] phenomenally rich and broad alluvial plain" watered by streams draining the Sierra Nevada in the east and the coastal ranges in the west. However, precipitation in the area comes mostly after the end of the crop-growing season. Originally, the Central Valley floor had approximately 922,000 acres of riparian vegetation supported by a watershed of more than 40,000 square miles. The Sacramento River alone was bordered by up to 500,000 acres of riparian forest. But transformation of the Central Valley into the nation's leading agricultural area has resulted in the loss of 99 percent of native grasses, 89 percent of riparian woodlands, and 95 percent of wetlands in this area.

III

Population Growth and Water Projects

The first settlers to the San Francisco area encountered scant fresh water supplies, and these proved inadequate to meet the boom of the later gold rush era. After some early efforts to enlist private enterprise to meet the city's water needs, the city turned its attention to public water projects and distant water supplies. The city eventually settled on the Tuolumne River—which drains a large portion of the Sierra Nevada, including the Hetch Hetchy Valley 170 miles to the east—for its water. In 1901, San Francisco filed for rights to Tuolumne River water. However, due to intense opposition, the project did not move forward until 1913. Eventually, a dam was built, creating the Hetch Hetchy Reservoir. San Francisco began importing water from the Tuolumne River in 1923 and a similar project was undertaken later to import water from the Mokulumne River to areas on the east side of the San Francisco Bay. This water began flowing in 1930.

Early residents of Southern California struggled with problems of drought and limited water supply. When available above-ground sources were exhausted, wells were drilled to tap groundwater sources. By 1905, the population of Los Angeles had grown to 220,000. By 1920, the population was 576,000 and, during the next decade, it doubled to over a million. During this period, groundwater use in Southern California reduced artesian wells from 2,500 to 22.

Faced with the necessity of importing water to the area to meet the needs of its growing population, Los Angeles began searching for new water sources. Shortly after 1900, it began acquiring land in the Owens Valley, 238 miles north on the eastern slope of the Sierra Nevada, in order to gain control of the water supply in the area. The city eventually acquired 97 percent of the available privately held land in Inyo and Mono Counties. In 1908, Los Angeles commenced construction of an aqueduct to bring Owens Valley water to Southern California. This project was completed and water began flowing in 1913.

Soon thereafter, Los Angeles began looking further north to Mono Lake as a source of additional water to meet its growing needs. Mono Lake is the second largest lake in the State and sits at the base of the Sierra Nevada near the east entrance to Yosemite National Park. In 1940, the Division of Water Resources, the predecessor of the State Water Resources Control Board (SWRCB), granted Los Angeles a permit to appropriate water from four fresh water streams that emptied into Mono Lake. The city constructed facilities to divert about half of this flow into the existing Owens Valley Aqueduct. In 1970, the city completed a second aqueduct from Owens Valley and thereafter began diverting nearly the entire flow of these four streams. Until these diversions were curtailed by court action, the level of Mono Lake had dropped considerably and the surface area had receded by one-third.

Not long after completion of the first phase of the Owens Valley project, Los Angeles explored the feasibility of importing water from the Colorado River. In 1928, the Metropolitan Water District of Southern California (Metropolitan) was created for the purpose of combining the financial resources of cities and communities in Southern California to bring water to the area. Metropolitan constructed the Colorado River Aqueduct to bring in water from the Colorado River. This water began flowing in 1941. An offshoot of the Colorado River Aqueduct, the San Diego Aqueduct, was also constructed to supply Colorado River water to San Diego County.

Because of the interstate and international nature of the Colorado River, California's rights to its water, as well as those of several other states and Mexico, are governed by a series of agreements, treaties, laws, and court decisions. Under these legal constraints, California is limited in a normal year to 4.4 million acre-feet of Colorado River water plus no more than half of any surplus water available. Of this amount, agricultural users receive 3.8 million acre-feet, with the balance going to urban users.

Historically, California has used more than its normal-year entitlement of Colorado River water. This has been made possible through underuse by Arizona and Nevada and the availability of surplus water. However, because both Arizona and Nevada are approaching full use of their respective apportionments, the United States Secretary of the Interior has directed California to devise a plan to live within its 4.4 million acre-feet entitlement.

The Central Valley has undergone dramatic change since the first settlement of California. During those early years, winter rains and spring runoff brought annual floods that soaked half a million acres of tule swamps in the valley. Seasonal flooding caused serious damage to farms and cities along the Sacramento and San Joaquin Rivers. Early attempts at coordinated flood control in this area began in 1911. In that year, the Legislature created a State Reclamation Board and vested it with all authority over protective works in the Sacramento River Valley. In conjunction with the U.S. Army Corp of Engineers, the Reclamation Board implemented a valley-wide plan, the Sacramento Flood Control Project, to establish a network of levees and bypasses to prevent flooding.

Later efforts were made to adopt a comprehensive plan for the entire Central Valley. These efforts culminated in the Central Valley Project (CVP), which was approved by the State Legislature in 1933. (Stats. 1933, ch. 1042, p. 2643; Wat. Code, § 11100 et seq.) The CVP is the nation's largest water reclamation project, with total reservoir capacity of more than 8.5 million acre-feet in its principal dams. The CVP is also the State's largest water supplier, delivering approximately 7.3 million acre-feet of water to over 250 water contractors, primarily for agricultural use.

Operation of the CVP involves impounding the natural flow of the San Joaquin River at Friant Dam and diverting the water through the Friant-Kern Canal to the southern reaches of the San Joaquin Valley. The other major aspect of the CVP involves impounding the waters of the Sacramento River at Shasta Dam. The water allowed to flow past Shasta Dam in the Sacramento River is augmented by water brought through a tunnel from the Trinity River and from reservoirs formed by Folsom and Nimbus Dams on the American River. This water eventually flows into the Delta. About 30 miles south of Sacramento, the Delta Cross Channel regulates the flow of water through the Delta to the Tracy Pumping Plant. There, it is lifted into the Delta Mendota Canal through which it flows to the Mendota Pool and eventually replaces the natural flow of the San Joaquin River.

Although the CVP was originally a State project, the lingering effects of the Great Depression made it impossible for the State to sell bonds for it and the federal government took control of the project. The United States Bureau of Reclamation (USBOR) operates the CVP pursuant to appropriative water rights granted by the SWRCB. Construction of the CVP began in 1937, with first water delivery in 1940.

Operation of the CVP helped to transform agriculture in the Central Valley. Agriculture is one of the foundations of this State's prosperity, providing employment for one in 10 Californians and a variety and quantity of foodstuffs that both feed the nation and provide a significant source of exports. In 1889, the State's 14,000 farmers irrigated approximately one million acres of farmland between Stockton and Bakersfield. By 1981, the number of acres in agricultural production had risen to 9.7 million. More recently, the amount of agricultural land in the State has declined. From 1982 to 1992, more than a million acres of farmland were lost to other uses. Between 1994 and 1996, another 65,827 acres of irrigated farmland were lost, and this trend is expected to continue.

Despite recent reductions in farmland, agriculture remains by far the largest user of the State's developed water supply, with the CVP supplying 30 percent of the amount used by agriculture.

From 1940 to 1970, the population of Los Angeles doubled to 3 million, and the populations of Los Angeles, Orange, Ventura and San Diego Counties increased two and one-half times, to 10 million. When Colorado River water began flowing into the State in 1941, the amount of water available to Southern California exceeded local needs. The member communities of Metropolitan did not begin using all of the water brought into the State from the Colorado River until the 1960's.

In 1951, the SWRCB reported that " '[t]he greatest challenge' facing the state . . . was 'redistribution of the water supply from areas of surplus to areas of deficiency.' " That year, the Legislature authorized construction of the State Water Project (SWP), another large water storage and delivery system. However, it was not until 1959, when the Legislature passed the California Water Resources Development Bond Act (the Burns-Porter Act) (Wat. Code, § 12930 et seq.) authorizing $1.75 billion in bonds, and the electorate approved the bonds the following year, that construction of the SWP began.

Discussions leading to approval of the SWP were marked by a good deal of acrimony between northern and southern California interests. Southern Californians objected to the project because of area-of-origin laws that were enacted in the early 1930's in conjunction with the CVP. Those laws protect the future water needs of users in areas where water originates. Southern Californians did not want to pay for the SWP without assurances that northern Californians would not later prevent delivery of water based on superior water rights. Northern Californians objected to the project because they did not want to give up water that might someday be needed for future development. Northern Californians argued that people should come to the water, not vice versa.

The Burns-Porter Act was approved despite nearly unanimous opposition by legislators from the northern part of the state. To satisfy northern concerns, the Legislature enacted the Delta Protection Act (Wat. Code, §§ 12200–12220), which recognizes the unique "salinity intrusion" problems of the Delta and provides "for the protection, conservation, development, control and use of the waters in the Delta for the public good." (Wat. Code, § 12200.) To placate the south, area-of-origin laws were amended to provide that water supply contracts entered into pursuant to the SWP could not be abrogated while bonds to pay for the project are outstanding. Some of those bonds are not scheduled to be paid off until 2029.

Delivery of SWP water began in 1971. The SWP supplies water to users from San Francisco to Southern California, serving approximately two-thirds of all Californians. Metropolitan is by far the SWP's largest contractor, receiving about half of all water delivered. Seventy percent of SWP urban water users are in Southern California. However, because of the various other sources of water available to Southern California, including Owens Valley and the Colorado River, Southern California water requirements did not catch up with available SWP water until 1988.

As growth, and hence water consumption, has increased in the northern parts of the State in recent years, less water has been flowing into the Delta and, consequently, saltwater intrusion from the San Francisco Bay has increased. During periods of low flow and drought, saltwater advanced far enough inland to be drawn into pumps sending water to the south. In 1965, the Interagency Delta Committee released a plan for a 43-mile-long "Peripheral Canal" beginning on the Sacramento River 15 miles below Sacramento, running along the eastern edge of the Delta, and ending at State and federal pumping plants near Tracy. This canal was designed to allow water diversion into the Delta for salinity control while permitting delivery of higher quality water to the south.

Battle raged over the peripheral canal until 1980, when the Legislature passed a bill to authorize construction. Voting on the bill was generally along north-south lines, with northern legislators opposed. Voters also approved Proposition 8, providing added protection to the Delta. However, in 1982, the voters approved a referendum reversing the canal and the Delta protection legislation. Subsequent attempts to resurrect the canal project have failed.

The availability of sufficient water to meet the State's growing needs continued to be a problem in the 1980's and 1990's. This problem was exacerbated by a persistent drought that occurred between 1987 and 1992. In 1991, DWR organized a drought water bank to allow for large-scale water transfers to relieve shortages.

IV

Ecological Conditions

The expansion of agriculture, population increases and the side effects of the various water projects have taken a toll on the State's natural environment. The State has been called an " 'epicenter of extinction,' " with at least 73 native species lost forever. Transformation of the Central Valley has resulted in the loss of nearly all native grasses, riparian woodlands, and wetlands. Only about 18 percent of the Central Valley's original salmon spawning habitat remains. Upstream water development, depletion of natural flows and the export of water from the Delta have changed seasonal patterns of inflow, reduced annual outflow and muted the natural variability of flows into and through the Delta.

Seven hundred thousand acres of overflow and seasonally inundated land in the Delta have been converted to agricultural or urban uses. As discussed earlier, flood control activities and land development in the late 1800's and early 1900's created leveed Delta islands and the loss of wetlands, thereby reducing habitat for wetland wildlife species. Wetland losses in the Delta have also reduced the available area for biological conversion of nutrients necessary for wetland wildlife. Many of the remaining Delta stream sections have been dredged or channelized to improve navigation, increase stream conveyance during periods of flood, and facilitate water export.

The construction of levees in the Delta has also resulted in the loss of sloughs, which provide warmer, highly productive habitat for seasonal spawning, rearing, and foraging for many aquatic organisms, as well as important organic carbon productivity for all habitats of the Bay-Delta. Floodplains that once provided seasonal habitat for fish and wildlife as well as sediment and nutrients for flooded lands have been all but eliminated.

In addition to the conversion of natural habitat to agricultural, urban or flood control uses, the pumping of water from the Delta for use elsewhere has had a significant negative impact on ecological functions. Tidal aquatic habitats that link wetlands with open-water habitats are used as foraging and resting places for shorebirds, wading birds, and waterfowl. Resident and migratory fish use such habitats for spawning, rearing, foraging, and escape cover. However, when natural freshwater outflows through the Bay-Delta decrease due to water exports, the tidal aquatic habitats are compressed and move upstream into areas unsuitable for nursery habitat and the creation of new tidal marshes. The diversion of Bay-Delta water also harms the ecosystem by drawing fish into the pumps or into the vicinity of predators. The Resources Agency has reported that more than 300 unscreened diversions on the upper Sacramento River alone cause up to 10 million juvenile salmonids to be pulled into the pumps annually, resulting in the loss of 100,000 adult fish.

Although agriculture sometimes provides important habitat for birds and other animals, it can also cause considerable environmental harm. (Ruhl, *Farms, Their Environmental Harms, and Environmental Law* (2000) 27 Ecology L.Q. 263, 275 (hereafter Ruhl).) Farms often pollute ground and surface water, replace wildlife habitat, erode soils, contribute sediment to lakes and rivers, and deplete water resources. The Central Valley is home to two-thirds of the State's dairies, and their cows create a considerable amount of waste. Creeks in the Central Valley often contain 200 times more ammonia than the level poisonous for fish. And cows are not the only source of farming waste. Chicken manure contains twice as much phosphorous as human waste. In 1991, the SWRCB identified agriculture as the contributor of over 58 percent of the pollution in the State's rivers.

Due to the many adverse environmental impacts described above, two fish species, the winter run salmon and the Delta smelt, had been listed under the Endangered Species Act by the spring of 1993. Petitions to list other species had also been filed. These listings soon resulted in the imposition of restrictions on the operations of the CVP and SWP, thereby significantly affecting the amount of water exported from the Delta.

VI

CALFED

In June 1994, 18 state and federal agencies with management or regulatory authority over the Bay-Delta signed an agreement (the Framework Agreement) to coordinate their activities in three areas: (1) operating the SWP and CVP to accommodate environmental mandates; (2) establishing water quality standards; and (3) developing a long-term strategy for managing the Delta.

In December 1994, the CALFED agencies signed a Statement of Principles for the Bay-Delta Standards (the Bay-Delta Accord) setting interim Bay-Delta water quality standards and water project constraints for the following three years. These standards were later extended until no later than September 15, 2000. To protect water quality, the Bay-Delta Accord called for additional fresh water flows through the Delta of 0.4 million acre-feet in years of normal rainfall and 1.1 million acre-feet in critically dry years. To provide a measure of protection for water supplies to beneficial users, the Bay-Delta Accord provided that any additional water needs arising from further listings under the Endangered Species Act would be met by water purchases financed by the federal government.

The Bay-Delta Accord also included a commitment to develop and fund nonflow-related ecosystem restoration projects, commonly referred to as "Category III" projects, to address "unscreened water diversions, waste discharges, water pollution prevention, fishery impacts due to harvest and poaching, land-derived salts, exotic species, fish barriers, channel alterations, riparian wetland loss, and other causes of estuarine habitat degradation." The Bay-Delta Accord incorporated salinity standards, significant reductions in Delta exports during the critical spring period, increases in San Joaquin River flows, reductions in export pumping, restrictions on the take of endangered species, real-time operation of Delta pumps so that pumping is reduced when necessary for environmental protection but increased when environmentally safe, and a $180 million fund to improve habitat conditions through upstream restoration.

As a direct result of the Framework Agreement and the Bay-Delta Accord, the CALFED agencies launched the CALFED Program, an unprecedented effort to build a framework for managing California's most precious natural resource: water. The Program is divided into three phases. Phase I is concerned with identifying Bay-Delta problems, developing a mission statement and guiding principles, and devising preliminary solution alternatives. During phase II, a preferred program alternative is identified, environmental documents created, and a plan for the first seven years of development devised. Phase III involves implementation of the Program.

NOTES & QUESTIONS

1. To implement the Bay-Delta Plan, a clear definition of the problems had to be addressed and a range of solution alternatives developed. Also, to comply with the National Environmental Policy Act (NEPA) and the California Environmental Quality Act (CEQA), a program level or first-tier environmental impact statement (EIS) and environmental impact report (EIR) had to be prepared to identify impacts associated with the various alternatives. Then, as specific projects were contemplated within the Bay-Delta Plan area, project-level or second-tier EIS/EIR documents were to prepared for each element of the selected solution. The adequacy of these EIS and EIR documents was challenged in several cases, including *Bay-Delta*. The *Bay-Delta* court ultimately found that the EIR specifically found the conversion of agricultural land was an adverse impact of the program. The EIR's cumulative impacts analysis took into consideration impacts to agriculture and satisfied the good faith disclosure obligation. The EIR did not provide, however, any basis for the estimates of water that would be made available from willing sellers among the various rivers. Nor did the EIR identify what new storage was contemplated. In light of the overarching importance of water to the success of the program, merely listing potential sources of water, indicating that the ultimate source determination would be made later, and deferring CEQA analysis of the need to provide water to the program violated the EIR's basic informational purpose. The court also ruled that EIR also should have included an alternative that assumed reduced water exports from one region, but a mitigation measure calling for a proportional replacement of agricultural lands was not necessary to the EIR.

2. The four primary objectives of the Bay-Delta Plan were the overall objectives for each of the key program areas it created: water quality, ecosystem quality, water supply, and vulnerability of Delta functions. Secondary objectives within each of these areas tied back to the primary objectives:

- Provide good water quality for all beneficial uses;

- Improve and increase aquatic and terrestrial habitats and improve ecological functions in the Bay-Delta to support sustainable populations of diverse and valuable plant and animal species;

- Reduce the mismatch between Bay-Delta water supplies and current and projected beneficial uses dependent on the Bay-Delta system;

- Reduce the risk to land use and associated economic activities, water supply, infrastructure, and the ecosystem from catastrophic breaching of Delta levees.

3. Unlike the Chesapeake Bay Program, the scope of CALFED's work was within one state, but within that more limited scope almost two dozen federal and state agencies had some regulatory or management responsibility for some aspect of the Bay-Delta, and all had a seat on the CALFED Policy Group. Each agency assigned staff to CALFED; however, CALFED was not itself an agency. Rather, CALFED, in essence, was a forum through which the agencies coordinated and evaluated their actions. Each agency implemented elements of the Bay-Delta Plan that were consistent with and within the scope of its respective statutory responsibility.

Notwithstanding this cumbersome structure, within five years of the Bay-Delta Plan approval the CALFED participants had achieved progress toward implementation. In the first phase of implementation CALFED members developed a range of alternatives, consisting of hundreds of actions. The Program conducted meetings and workshops to obtain public input, prepared a Notice of Intent and Notice of Preparation pursuant to NEPA and CEQA, and held public scoping sessions to determine the focus and content of the EIS/EIR. The first phase concluded in September 1996 with the development of a range of alternatives for achieving long-term solutions to the problems of the Bay-Delta estuary.

During Phase II, the Program conducted a comprehensive program-wide environmental review process. A draft programmatic EIS/EIR and interim Phase II Report identifying three draft alternatives, each outlining many different specific projects and actions, and program plans was released on March 16, 1998. The release of the documents was followed by a 105-day public comment period. On June 25, 1999, CALFED again released a draft programmatic EIS/EIR followed by a 90 day comment period. The final programmatic EIS/EIR was released July 21, 2000, followed on August 28, 2000, by the Record of Decision (ROD) and Implementation Memorandum of Understanding (MOU) between the CALFED participants. *See* http://calfed.ca.gov/adobe_pdf/rod.

The ROD completed Phase II, and the MOU began Phase III-implementation of the preferred alternative. The first seven years of Phase III were referred to as Stage 1, and were designed to lay the foundation for the following years. Site-specific, detailed environmental review will occur during this phase prior to the implementation of each proposed action.

4. Implementation of the CALFED Bay-Delta Plan was expected to take 30 years. Projects covered areas such as water supply reliability, ecosystem restoration and watershed management, water quality controls, levee systems, scientific research, and basic program management. At some point along the way, it was envisioned that CALFED may actually have been transformed, by concurrent federal and state legislation, into some form of joint governance mechanism closer in framework to the Chesapeake Bay Program. The question, as with the Chesapeake Bay Program, was how to balance state and federal sovereignty with the joint project's mission in such a way as to control information, coordination, and strategic costs.

5. California adopted a new state governance framework for CALFED in 2003, known as the California Bay-Delta Authority (CBDA), and President Bush renewed federal endorsement of the program in 2004. Yet in December 2005 the CBDA recommended to Governor Schwarzenegger that he dissolve the entity and transfer its powers to the California Water Commission. By almost all accounts, the CBDA was underfunded and overtaxed in terms of its role in coordinating state involvement in CALFED. Indeed, notwithstanding its apparent early progress, by 2005 CALFED was looking in disarray. The situation in the Bay-Delta began to deteriorate in epic proportions. An assessment in *Science* magazine was that "the hub of California's freshwater system is plagued by crashing fisheries, high demand, invasive species, and pollution—and a major earthquake there could devastate the state's drinking water and agriculture. *Delta Blues, California Style*, 317 SCIENCE 442, 442 (2007).

6. The Endangered Species Act also became a main driver of controversy and change. A key decision, one of many from a complex web of litigation, was *Nat-*

ural Resources Defense Council v. Kempthorne, 506 F. Supp. 2d 322 (E.D. Cal. 2007), in which the court evidenced little tolerance for the FWS' failure to consider climate change in a consultation report.

> [T]he climate change issue was not meaningfully discussed in the biological opinion, making it impossible to determine whether the information was rationally discounted because of its inconclusive nature, or arbitrarily ignored . . . The BiOp does not gauge the potential effect of various climate change scenarios on Delta hydrology. Assuming, *arguendo*, a lawful adaptive management approach, there is no discussion when and how climate change impacts will be addressed, whether existing take limits will remain, and the probable impacts on CVP-SWP operations. FWS acted arbitrarily and capriciously by failing to address the issue of climate change in the BiOp.

If things aren't going well, one strategy is to start over. This is essentially what happened to CALFED. Through events too complex to detail here, CALFED morphed into yet another planning effort. Consider from this brief history and summary of the new effort whether what arose from CALFED's ashes shows more promise.

Delta Stewardship Council, *Final Staff Draft of the Delta Plan*
May 2012.

Finding the right balance of these competing needs and demands on the Delta has bedeviled California policy makers for decades. Regulators clash with water system operators; stakeholders often take each other to court, and Delta residents fear that the solutions will alter their way of life and land.

A New Path Forward

Creation of the CALFED Bay-Delta Program in 1995 was supposed to bring everyone together and it did, for a short time, until State and federal budgets were cut and hard decisions ultimately were deferred. In the aftermath, a gubernatorial Delta Vision Task Force in 2008 declared that Delta problems could not be solved in isolation – they were inextricably linked to statewide water supply, habitat, and flood management programs – and that stronger governance and accountability were a must. In response, the Legislature, water agencies, and environmental groups throughout the state united in an unprecedented manner in 2009 to pass a series of water-related measures that included the Delta Reform Act.

The Delta Reform Act established coequal goals of a more reliable water supply for California and protecting, restoring, and enhancing the Delta ecosystem as overarching State policy. Furthermore, the Act notably required that Californians reduce their reliance on the Delta. Subsequently, Congress passed legislation requiring federal agencies to abide by the coequal goals as well, thus setting a new course for water management in the state.

In a nod to lessons learned from CALFED, the Act created the Delta Stewardship Council (Council) with the authority and responsibility to develop a legally enforceable Delta Plan, and to ensure that actions by State and local agencies in the Delta are consistent with the Plan. It was directed to adequately incorporate the best available science and adaptive management principles in order to improve decision making and reduce stakeholder conflict. The Council also was empowered to coordinate and collaborate across the myriad governmental agencies that have responsibility for some aspect of the Delta. In this way, the Delta Reform Act signaled that business-as-usual is over.

After more than 2 years, nearly a hundred public meetings, and after reviewing thousands of public comments, the resulting Delta Plan relies on a mix of legally enforceable policies and essential recommendations to prioritize actions and strategies for improved water management, ecosystem restoration, and levee maintenance. It also restricts actions that may cause harm, and provides regulatory guidance for all significant plans, projects, and programs in the Delta.

Successful implementation of the Delta Plan depends not only on the Council, but also on coordinated actions by other government agencies—federal, State, and local—and the stakeholders to which they are responsible. Through this Delta Plan, the Council details an open and transparent interagency structure for decision making that fosters communication among scientists: local, State, and federal decision makers; and stakeholders. Future plan iterations will build on successes as well as lessons learned in order to achieve the coequal goals.

Lessons from the Delta Plan Process

Act Now and Invest Sustainably

We have been studying the problems of our water supply and the declining Delta ecosystem for decades. Near-term actions must move forward while long-term conveyance, storage, and ecosystem solutions are brought to completion. We also must consistently invest in the Delta ecosystem and in California's water supplies. Boom and bust funding will occur, but steady and reliable funding must be found to sustain needed scientific advancement and infrastructure improvements to achieve the coequal goals.

Improve Water Supply Reliability

This is a responsibility shared by all Californians, who must treat water as a precious and scarce natural resource that must be used as efficiently as possible. We must make a strategic combination of State and regional investments that enable California to avoid environmental conflicts and better match water use to the amount of water that is available. New surface and groundwater storage is necessary to manage the timing of water for people and for fish, and successful completion of the Bay Delta Conservation Plan (BDCP) is essential to finding the right balance for the ecosystem and exports from the Delta.

Commit to Delta Ecosystem Restoration

Restoring the functionality of the Delta ecosystem also is a responsibility shared by all Californians. We must preserve land for future habitat restoration, and we must immediately begin restoration efforts in priority areas. In the Delta, we must change the way we move water so that it better protects the health and viability of native species. To do this, minimum flows must be established for the Delta and its major tributaries as part of a comprehensive effort to address all ecosystem stressors.

Protect the Delta's Unique Values

The Delta serves many demands but its unique sense of place must not be lost in that service. The inherent high flood risk in the Delta mandates that agriculture and natural resource land uses are the most appropriate, but we also must protect Legacy Communities and a mix of economic and recreational activities.

What the Delta Plan Does

The Delta Plan seeks to first declining water reliability and environmental conditions related to the Delta ecosystem, and ultimately improve them. Additionally, it seeks to reduce flood risk, improve water quality, and protect the Delta's unique values. Generally speaking, these are long-term goals to reverse or reduce increasing long-term environmental impacts due to inaction.

In the Delta Reform Act, the Legislature outlined a process for what it called "covered actions," projects, plans, or programs over which the Council would have jurisdiction. In addition, the Legislature gave the Council the authority to hold hearings and make recommendations.

Through its policies and recommendations, the Delta Plan:

- Increases California's water supply reliability by calling for more regional water supply development and setting a deadline for successful completion of the BDCP, which is intended to improve water conveyance through the Delta and improve habitat for threatened and endangered species.

- Consistent with the longstanding water rights in California, it also reduces reliance on the Delta watershed by recommending that all local agencies implement local plans to diversify water supplies and improve efficiency.

- Protects and enhances the Delta ecosystem by identifying and protecting high-priority restoration areas and setting a deadline for the State Water Resources Control Board to support the coequal goals by updating flow standards for the major rivers and tributaries of the Delta. It also reduces Delta ecosystem stressors through a suite of specific recommendations to address such problems as pollution and invasive species.

- Protects and enhances the Delta as a place by recognizing that all actions must be achieved in a manner that protects and enhances the values and unique but "evolving" characteristics of the Delta. The Delta Plan defines a role for local input in decision making about major projects and minimizes interference with local land use planning. It also supports designation as a National Heritage Area and encourages economic development through agriculture and recreation.

- Improves water quality by prioritizing State and regional actions to deal with high-priority Delta-specific water quality problems.

- Reduces risk by requiring new development in and around the Delta to have adequate flood protection, protects and preserves floodplains, and promotes setback levees to increase habitat and reduce flood damage.

- Sets an example by using the "best available science" and adaptive management and requires that others do the same so that projects can move forward in a way that is efficient and allows decision making in the face of uncertain conditions.

The Delta of 2100 likely will be very different from the Delta of today. Some of the changes will be intentional or predictable, and others will be unintended and surprising. Changes are likely or expected to result from population growth, climate change and sea level rise, land subsidence, and earthquakes—most beyond human ability or willingness to control. Human-made changes in land use and water use are also expected to continue.

All of this will involve tradeoffs, between competing—in some cases mutually exclusive—values, goals, and objectives. The Delta Plan seeks to ensure that these decisions are made in a timely and open manner, based on best available information and science as a predictor of the future. Thus the Legislature required that the Delta Plan be updated every 5 years, and each plan is intended to build on an evolving base of knowledge, directing near- and mid-term actions, and preserving and protecting longer-term opportunities as yet unknown.

NOTES & QUESTIONS

1. The Delta Stewardship Council claims that "business as usual" is over. From the report's general summary, what is the new business model? How different is it from CALFED's?

2. As mentioned above, over time the Endangered Species Act, covered extensively in Part II of the text, has increasingly played a role in shaping the Bay-Delta ecosystem management program. Indeed, some might say the ESA now dominates Bay-Delta policy. To follow how the ESA is influencing the Bay-Delta policies through what is known as the Bay Delta Conservation Plan, see http://baydeltaconservationplan.com/Home.aspx.

(3) The Mississippi River Delta

Between the Chesapeake Bay and the Bay-Delta, on the nation's "third coast," sits the Mississippi River Delta and its coastal wetlands. The catastrophic events of Hurricane Katrina in 2005 revealed the importance of those wetlands to the protection of inland areas from storm surge and flooding and what damage might have been avoided had those wetlands not been severely degraded by decades of water diversion and energy development. The following case traces the history of those pre-Katrina disturbances and the efforts of federal and state agencies to reverse them.

Avenal v. State
Supreme Court of Louisiana, 2004.
886 So.2d 1085.

■ VICTORY, J.

In this case, oyster fishermen holding oyster leases in the Breton Sound area claim they suffered a compensable taking under La. Const. Art. I, § 4 as a result of the State of Louisiana's operation of the Caernarvon Freshwater Diversion Structure ("Caernarvon"), which altered salinity levels in the waters covering the oyster fishermen's leases. After a review of the record and the applicable law, we reverse the judgments of the lower courts and hold that the vast majority of the oyster fishermen are not entitled to compensation under La. Const. Art. I, § 4 because their leases contain clauses holding the State harmless from any loss or damage resulting from this coastal diversion project.

FACTS AND PROCEDURAL HISTORY

Following the flood of 1927, the United States Army Corps of Engineers (the "Corps") expanded the Mississippi River levee system to confine the river to prevent further major floods. Before the levees were built, naturally occurring floods deposited millions of tons of sediments into the marshlands, which allowed marshland and other grasses to grow; without those nutrient-rich sediments, the plants that hold surrounding soils in place disappear and the land turns to open water. In the last fifty years, hundreds of square miles of wetlands along the Louisiana coast have disappeared and scientists have estimated that between thirty-five and forty-five square miles of coastal wetlands are lost each year.

Another effect of the levee system was on the salinity of the water. The coastal waters of Louisiana have historically provided excellent conditions for oyster growth, because the freshwater from the Mississippi River and smaller coastal streams mix with the saltwater of the Gulf of Mexico, creating an ideal ecosystem for oyster cultivation. By keeping fresh water out of the wetlands that surrounded the Mississippi River in the Breton Sound Basin, the levees unexpectedly raised the salinity of the waters covering those wetlands and this change in salinity fostered new oyster growth in the landward region of the basin that had previously been too fresh to sustain oyster growth. However, the changes in salinity that made some previously unproductive waters productive also ruined some oyster grounds that had been extremely productive before the levees were created.

These effects were recognized in the 1950s, and the state and federal governments began planning to divert freshwater from the Mississippi River into adjacent marshlands to address these problems. According to a 1959 memorandum issued by the U.S. Fish and Wildlife Service to the Corps, certain man-made and natural causes, over time, had increased the salinity level of the sub-delta marshlands below New Orleans, thereby adversely affecting fish and wildlife, including oysters, waterfowl, and fur animals. This investigation was prompted, in part, by requests from local groups, including the oyster industry, which attended a public hearing in New Orleans on April 25, 1955, concerning the need for freshwater diversions. After finding "a marked reduction [in oyster yield] per unit area" over time, the U.S. Fish and Wildlife Service concluded in the 1959 memorandum that "[i]ntroduction of fresh water to reestablish natural patterns of salinity and alluviation and increase fertility would provide the most effective method of restoring fish and wildlife production." The 1959 memorandum identified four separate areas in Plaquemines Parish as freshwater diversion sites, two of which were located on the west side of the Mississippi, Areas No. 1 and 3, and two on the east side, Areas 2 and 4. The diversion structures were to be designed to benefit both public seed grounds and privately held water-bottom leases obtained from the state for oyster leasing. Between 1968 and 1969, the Corps met with local interests, including the Louisiana Department of Wildlife and Fisheries ("DWF") and the Plaquemines Parish Commission Council, to discuss proposed locations for the diversion structures authorized by Congress. During Corps-sponsored public hearings held in 1968, the Corps proposed Caernarvon as the situs of the freshwater diversion structure for Area No. 4 to be located on the east side of the Mississippi.

The 1959 memorandum described the entire area covering Area 4 as "usually too fresh to support an oyster industry. . ." The memorandum stated that the pollution resulting from Caernarvon's discharge of silt would "not be a problem in Area No. 4 as in other areas because an oyster fishery is not present." Thus, the 1959 memorandum confirmed that Area No. 4, where Caernarvon would alter salinity levels in the water, coincided with the area of Breton Sound Basin that had been shown to be outside the productive oyster zone as of 1960.

During the 1970s, as land continued to erode and disappear further and further inshore, the zone favorable for oyster growth continued to move landward, due to saline changes. This landward salinity movement spawned an oyster community in the marshlands in the northwest portion of the Breton Sound Basin, which had previously been too fresh to sustain such growth. While creating new oyster grounds, the inland movement of salinity had the deleterious effect of rendering unusable large areas of previously productive oyster grounds, including the public seed grounds. Between 1978 and 1982, the Corps and relevant state and local agencies continued to discuss the construction of a freshwater diversion structure at Caernarvon at informal meetings. On January 21, 1982, the State submitted a letter to the Corps, announcing its intent to participate in the Caernarvon project, and the Corps and the Louisiana Department of Natural Resources (the "DNR") issued a joint public notice about the project.

In 1984, the Corps prepared an environmental impact statement suggesting locations of large salinity concentrations (isohalines) at three areas along the southeast Louisiana coast to enhance fisheries and to combat coastal erosion. To create optimal salinity regimes, the environmental impact statement proposed the construction of three freshwater diversion structures in the three areas: (1) the Bonnet Carre Spillway in the Lake Ponchartrain Basin; (2) the Davis Pond Freshwater Diversion Structure in the Barataria Basin; and (3) the Caernarvon Freshwater Diversion Structure in the Breton Basin near Braithwaite, Louisiana. The Caernarvon project, in particular, was designed to abate saltwater intrusion and marine tidal invasion, while promoting coastal restoration and enhancing fisheries and wildlife in the basin. At a July 31, 1984, public hearing, the President of the Louisiana Oyster Dealers and Growers indicated his support for both the Caernarvon project and freshwater diversion structures generally.

On October 30, 1986, Congress authorized the funds for construction of Caernarvon, and the State entered into a formal cooperation agreement with the Corps on June 10, 1987. The agreement recognized Caernarvon as one of the four sites originally authorized by the Flood Control Act of 1965. In anticipation of the operation of Caernarvon, in 1989, DWF inserted a clause in its lease form, requiring that the State be indemnified and held harmless for any claims related to coastal restoration.

Construction commenced at the Caernarvon site on June 7, 1988, and was completed in February 1991. The official Caernarvon dedication was held on April 12, 1991. Caernarvon operates based on gravity and hydrostatic pressure from the river and consists of five culverts equipped with gates that can be raised or lowered to regulate the rate of flow from the river. Caernarvon was initially tested from an operational standpoint in August 1991, but could not be operated in accordance with its intended flow regime at that time since the entire Breton Sound area had been heavily impacted in early 1991 by heavy rains, resulting runoff, and the high river conditions which had overflowed the Mississippi's east bank directly into Breton Sound at the Bohemia Spillway. Caernarvon became operational in September of 1991 in accordance with the recommended flow rates, and this achieved some, but not all of the intended effects of the project. As a result, the CIAC eventually voted to significantly increase the flows of the Caernarvon project in 1993, resulting in a greater freshening of Breton Sound. While this greatly improved oyster production on the public seed grounds, it reduced the salinity of the water covering the private oyster leases north of the public seed grounds and closer to the structure, where plaintiffs' leases are located. In 1996, the CIAC voted to decrease the flow to the original flow regime and has since monitored conditions, increasing or decreasing the flow in order to keep the annual average salinity within the . . . target area or isohaline (area of equal salinity concentration).

On March 29, 1994, plaintiffs filed the instant class action suit on behalf of all persons holding oyster leases on state-owned water bottoms in Breton Sound, asserting that their oyster leases were destroyed or damaged because of the intrusion of freshwater from the Mississippi River by the Caernarvon project. The plaintiffs' oyster leases are located in Breton Sound, east of Caernarvon and west of the public seed grounds; further east of the public seed grounds is the Gulf of Mexico. There are approximately 204 oyster leases involved in this class action. Plaintiffs asserted that the State's action of lowering the salinity levels of the water in Breton Sound below that necessary to support oyster cultivation "has resulted in a permanent and substantial interference with plaintiffs' use and enjoyment of their land amounting to a taking of an interest in [their] property rights without compensation in violation of Article I, § 4 of the Louisiana Constitution. . ."

After an eight-day jury trial on the merits, the jury returned a verdict in favor of the five class representatives, finding that "the state has taken actions which have taken or damaged the [plaintiffs'] right to property." The jury determined that $21,345.00 per damaged acre would adequately compensate plaintiffs Duplessis, Skansi, Fox, and Fox Oyster Company for their losses, while $1,000.00 per acre would adequately compensate Avenal. The trial court, in accordance with the jury's verdict, rendered judgment awarding Avenal $826,000.00; Duplessis $5,442,975.00; Fox $20,235,060.00; Fox Oyster Company $16,200,885.00; and Skansi $5,571,045.00. The court awarded the remaining class members similarly situated to Avenal and those similarly situated to the four other class representatives their respective damages, which included 63,000 acres of oyster leases resulting in an award of over $1,000,000,000.00. In addition to compensatory damages, the court awarded plaintiffs attorneys' fees and court costs. The trial court denied all post-trial motions. The DNR filed an application for supervisory writs seeking review of the trial court's denial of its motion for new trial and its refusal to abide by the court of appeal's December 15, 2000 ruling that the trial court either grant or deny the motion for partial summary judgment on the hold harmless clauses at least ten days prior to trial. The court of appeal declined to exercise its supervisory jurisdiction, ruling that the DNR's writ application should be consolidated with its pending appeal. *Avenal v. State,* 01–0542 (La.App. 4 Cir. 5/22/01).

A divided five-judge panel affirmed the trial court judgment. *Avenal v. State Dept. of Natural Resources,* 01–0843 (La.App. 4 Cir. 10/15/03), 858 So.2d 697. Although the plaintiffs did not prove at trial the amount of oyster production on their leases before and after Caernarvon, and some leaseholders admitted that their leases had never produced oysters, the court of appeal held that "so long as plaintiffs proved *generally* that their leases were productive before [Caernarvon] came on line, and that they were not productive after [Caernarvon] came on line, and that [Caernarvon] caused the loss of oyster productivity. . ." the plaintiffs were entitled to recover. *Id.* at 704 (emphasis added). In addition, the court of appeal increased the award to the lead plaintiff Avenal to over $17,000,000 because he is "a well-established oyster fisherman," and there was no proper basis for Avenal to be treated differently than the other plaintiffs, despite the fact that he had acquired some of his leases at the same time the present suit was filed. *Id.* at 703, n. 4.

We granted the DNR's writ application to determine whether plaintiffs are entitled to compensation under La. Const. Art. I, § 4 as a result of the State's operation of Caernarvon, which altered salinity levels in the waters covering the oyster fishermen's leases. *Avenal v. State,* 03–3521 (La.1/30/04), 864 So.2d 638.

DISCUSSION

The Oyster Statutes

The leasing of state-owned water bottoms to private parties for the purpose of oyster farming is governed exclusively by a specific statutory scheme. According to this statutory scheme, the State owns "all oysters and other shellfish and parts thereof grown [on the State's water bottoms], either naturally or cultivated, and all oysters in the shells after they are caught and taken therefrom . . . except as provided in R.S. 56:4." La. R.S. 56:3. Further, the State owns all water bottoms "bordering on or connecting with the Gulf of Mexico within the territory or jurisdiction of the State," and the State may not alienate these water bottoms. La. R.S. 56:3; La. Const. art. VII, § 14 (2004); Art. IX, § 3 (2004). However, in order to foster, cultivate, and protect the Louisiana oyster industry, the State has statutorily authorized the issuance of oyster leases to private parties.

The property rights of an oyster lessee are defined in La. R.S. 56:423 as follows:

A. A lessee shall enjoy the exclusive use of the water bottoms leased and of all oysters and cultch grown or placed thereon, subject to the restrictions and regulations of this subpart.

B. (1) A lessee of oyster beds or grounds who has obtained, recorded and marked his lease in compliance with the law shall have the right to maintain an action for damages against any person, partnership, corporation or other entity causing wrongful or negligent injury or damage to the beds or grounds under lease to such lessee.

In exchange for this exclusive use of state resources, a lessee pays the State two dollars per acre for plots up to 2,500 acres (formerly 1,000 acres). La. R.S. 56:423(A); La. R.S. 56:432 (2003); Act 449 of 2003. The leaseholder can unilaterally terminate his lease at any time by notice or by simply ceasing rental payments. If the DWF unilaterally terminates a lease and takes it back to create new seed grounds, DWF must compensate the leaseholder but only for "oysters, seed oysters, and other improvements." La. R.S.

56:434(B) (1991). La. R.S. 56:428(A) also allows the State to forego giving an oyster lessee the first right of renewal under his lease upon a determination that the lease is not capable of supporting oyster populations.

The Hold Harmless Clauses

The vast majority of the leases in this case, except for 12 of the approximately 204 leases alleged by the named plaintiffs to have been "taken" by Caernarvon, contain hold harmless clauses which legally and validly hold the State harmless from any damages suffered by the oyster fishermen by the operation of this coastal diversion project. As explained below, we hold that the these oyster fishermen's takings claims are precluded by virtue of these hold harmless clauses.

In 1989, when DWF became concerned that Caernarvon would alter the salinity levels in the waters covering the oyster leases in Breton Sound, DNR objected to the issuance of oyster leases in Breton Sound or elsewhere in the vicinity of planned coastal restoration projects. However, a compromise was confected by then Chairman of the Louisiana Coastal Restoration Policy Committee, Manual Fernandez, to allow oyster leases to issue as long as they contained a hold harmless and indemnity clause in favor of the state. Thus, instead of not issuing any more leases on the basis that these leases would not be capable of supporting oyster populations under the authority of La. R.S. 56:428(A), DWF inserted a hold harmless clause into all leases issued after 1989, which cover 140 of the 204 leases in this case. It was only with this clause that the oyster leases were allowed to issue, which was solely for the benefit of the oyster industry. This 1989 hold harmless clause stated:

> This lessee hereby agrees to hold and save the State of Louisiana, its agents or employees, free and harmless from any claims for loss or damages to rights arising under this lease, from diversions of fresh water or sediment, depositing of dredged or other materials or any other actions, taken for the purpose of management, preservation, enhancement, creation or restoration of coastal wetlands, water bottoms or related renewable resources; said damages to include, but not to be limited to, oyster mortality, oyster disease, damage to oyster beds or decreased oyster production, due to siltation, pollution or other causes.

All leases issued between 1989 and 1995 contain the same clause while leases issued from July 1995 to the present contain even more detailed indemnity clauses, namely the Coastal Wetlands Restoration Advisory Clause and the Allocation of Risk and Liability, and Indemnity Clause. These clauses were inserted into the leases given the fact that several suits had been filed as of 1995 by various oyster leaseholders alleging damages as a result of freshwater diversion structures (including this suit), and more were expected. These clauses were also in accordance with Legislative amendments in 1995 to the existing coastal restoration statutes requiring that the State be held harmless regarding coastal restoration in an effort to promote coastal restoration for the good of the public.

All leases issued from July 1995 to present contain the Coastal Wetlands Advisory Clause and the Allocation of Risk and Liability and Indemnity Clause, which include 53 of the approximately 64 leases remaining in this case.

In spite of the undisputed fact that the language of the 1989 clause is clear on its face and explicitly releases the State from any liability to the oyster fishermen due to this diversion project, the court of appeal found that our prior decision in *Jurisich v. Jenkins,* 99–0076 (La.10/19/99), 749 So.2d 597, dictates the conclusion that the "unilateral insertion" of the 1989 hold harmless clauses are "legally invalid." 858 So.2d at 706. As to the post-1995 hold harmless clauses, the court of appeal recognized a 2000 statutory amendment that purportedly permitted the State to insert indemnity clauses into oyster leases, 2000 La. Acts No. 107, and that applied to oyster leases renewed or extended after July 1, 1995, but did not consider the validity of the post-1995 indemnity provisions because it found that none of the leases at issue in this case were dated after July 1, 1995. These holdings are erroneous, as *Jurisich* does not compel the conclusion that the types of indemnity provisions in plaintiffs' leases are legally invalid, and the evidence presented clearly showed that 53 leases were renewed between 1996 and 1998 that contained the more detailed indemnity clause.

The issue in *Jurisich* was whether the DWF could refuse to renew oyster leases unless the oyster lessees agreed to the inclusion of a "navigation and oil field activity clause," which made the oyster leases "subservient to navigation, maintenance of navigation, and all normal, usual and permissible mineral and oil field activity which has been sanctioned by the State of Louisiana through a prior existing lease, permit, or contract." While the State had included other clauses in the leases at issue in that case, including the Coastal Wetlands Advisory Clause and the Allocation of Risk and Liability and Indemnity Clause, the Court expressly did not address the validity of these clauses. 749 So.2d at 599, 605 n. 8. Indeed, following an application for rehearing, this Court emphasized that "its discussion of the authority of the Secretary [of the DWF] and its ultimate holding were restricted to the inclusion of the navigation and oil field activity clause." *Id.* at 610. Accordingly, we expressly reserved the issue of whether that holding could be extended to other types of indemnity clauses, including in particular, the 1996 clauses at issue in this case.

Jurisich recognized that the statutory laws relative to the leasing of water bottoms for oyster production differ from the provisions that govern ordinary conventional leases addressed in Title IX of Book II of the Civil Code, La. C.C. arts. 2668, *et seq. Jurisich, supra* at 600 (citing *Vujnovich v. Louisiana Wildlife and Fisheries Commission,* 376 So.2d 330 (La.App. 4 Cir.1979)). The Court found that the discretion the DWF has to renew an oyster lease is therefore limited by a determination of the lease's capability of supporting oyster populations under La. R.S. 56:428(A), and that legislative, or statutory, authority was necessary for an expansion of that authority. *Id.* at 601. The Court found that the legislative authority found in La. R.S. 56:425(C), which provides that "the [DWF] may make such stipulations in the leases made by him as he deems necessary and proper to develop the industry; however, these stipulations must be consistent with the provisions of this Subpart," did not grant the DWF authority to include the navigation and oil field activity clause.

[Among several reasons for holding against the state,] the Court in *Jurisich* rejected DWF's argument that the public trust doctrine allowed them to insert the clause into the leases. *Id.* at 604–06. La. Const. art. IX, § 1 provides, in pertinent part:

> The natural resources of the state, including air and water, and the healthful, scenic, historic, and esthetic quality of the environment shall be protected, conserved, and replenished insofar as possible and consistent with the health, safety, and welfare of the people. The legislature shall enact laws to implement this policy.

The *Jurisich* court noted that this Court in *Save Ourselves, Inc. v. Louisiana Environmental Control Com'n,* 452 So.2d 1152, 1157 (La.1984), has interpreted that article as follows:

> This is a rule of reasonableness which requires an agency or official, before granting approval of proposed action affecting the environment, to determine that adverse environmental impacts have been minimized or avoided as much as possible consistently with the public welfare. Thus, the constitution does not establish environmental protection as an exclusive goal, but requires a balancing process in which environmental costs and benefits must be given full and careful consideration along with economic, social and other factors.

Id. at 604–605. In *Jurisich,* as the stipulated purpose of the clause at issue, i.e., to protect oil and gas companies from claims by oyster lessees was clearly not mandated by the public trust doctrine, the Court rejected the DWF's argument in that regard. *Id.* Further, as the Constitution vests primary responsibility for implementing the public trust in the State legislature, the clause could not stand because it was contrary to state legislation. The Court also specifically noted that "[i]n reaching this conclusion on the application of the public trust doctrine, we note that our determination is made in the context of the Secretary's duty to develop the oyster industry and is *only* made relative to the inclusion of the navigation and oil field activity clause, the only clause in the oyster lease now before us." *Id.* at 605 n. 8.

We find that the implementation of the Caernarvon coastal diversion project fits precisely within the public trust doctrine. The public resource at issue is our very coastline, the loss of which is occurring at an alarming rate. The risks involved are not just environmental, but involve the health, safety, and welfare of our people, as coastal erosion removes an important barrier between large populations and ever-threatening hurricanes and storms. Left unchecked, it will result in the loss of the very land on which Louisianians reside and work, not to mention the loss of businesses that rely on the coastal region as a transportation infrastructure vital to the region's industry and commerce. The State simply cannot allow coastal erosion to continue; the redistribution of existing productive oyster beds to other areas must be tolerated under the public trust doctrine in furtherance of this goal. *See* La. C.C. art. 450 and Comment (b) (stating that navigable water bodies are "public things that belong to the State," and that such property is "dedicated to public use, and held as a public trust, for public uses.").

For all of the above reasons, the decision in *Jurisich* is clearly distinguishable from the case at bar, and does not make the hold harmless clauses inserted in 193 of the approximately 204 leases as early as 1989 legally invalid. We find that they are legally valid and clearly enforceable under the authority granted the DWF in La. R.S. 56:425(C).

Thus, the named plaintiffs holding 192–193 of the approximately 204 leases in this case do not have valid takings claims because the indemnity clauses in their leases hold the state harmless from any and all claims for loss or damage to their rights under the leases caused by this coastal diversion project. However, the named plaintiffs introduced into evidence 12 leases that are dated prior to 1989. Thus, because these lessees' takings claims are not precluded by virtue of any indemnity clauses, we must continue this analysis, which is applicable only to these remaining 12 leases.

[The court further held the state's actions did not take property rights associated with the oyster leases under the Louisiana Constitution or United States Constitution, and that to the extent any of the oyster fishermen's lease rights under the 12 leases not containing hold harmless clauses were "damaged," such damage claims were prescribed two years from the completion and acceptance of Caernarvon] For the reasons expressed herein, the judgments of the lower courts are reversed and plaintiffs' claims are dismissed.

NOTES & QUESTIONS

1. In his concurring opinion in *Avenal*, Justice Weimer of the Louisiana Supreme Court assembled some information about the magnitude of the economic losses the state faces as a result of the coastal erosion:

> The plight of Louisiana's coast and its wetlands warrants national concern.
>
> Many factors, some natural, some due to human intervention, are converging to result in the loss of Louisiana's wetlands and the concomitant alteration of its coast. Louisiana, because of its many bays and sounds, has the longest coastline (15,000 miles) of any state and 41 percent of the nation's wetlands. The losses are alarming and devastating.
>
> The rate of coastal land loss in Louisiana has reached catastrophic proportions. Within the last 50 years, land loss rates have exceeded 40 square miles per year, and in the 1990's the rate has been estimated to be between 25 and 35 square miles each year. This loss represents 80% of the coastal wetland loss in the entire continental United States.

The reasons for wetland loss are complex and vary across the state. Since the scale of the problem was recognized and quantified in the 1970's, much has been learned about the factors that cause marshes to change to open water and that result in barrier island fragmentation and submergence. The effects of natural processes like subsidence and storms have combined with human actions at large and small scales to produce a system on the verge of collapse.

System collapse threatens the continued productivity of Louisiana's bountiful coastal ecosystems, the economic viability of its industries, and the safety of its residents. If recent loss rates continue into the future, even taking into account current restoration efforts, then by 2050 coastal Louisiana will lose more than 630,000 additional acres of coastal marshes, swamps, and islands. The loss could be greater, especially if worst-case scenario projections of sea-level rise are realized, but in some places there is nothing left to lose.

Along with the loss of acreage goes the loss of the various functions and values associated with the wetlands: commercial harvests of fisheries, furbearers, and alligators; recreational fishing and hunting, and ecotourism; habitats for threatened and endangered species; water quality improvement; navigation corridors and port facilities; flood control, including buffering hurricane storm surges; and the intangible value of land settled centuries ago and passed down through generations. The public use value of this loss is estimated to be in excess of $37 billion by 2050, but the losses associated with cultures and heritage are immeasurable.

For a comprehensive report on the loss of coastal wetlands in the Mississippi Delta even before Hurricane Katrina in 2005, see NATIONAL RESEARCH COUNCIL, DRAWING LOUISIANA'S NEW MAP: ADDRESSING LAND LOSS IN COASTAL LOUISIANA (2005).

2. Note the important role the Public Trust Doctrine plays in *Avenal*, providing the central justification for the hold harmless clauses. As discussed previously in this chapter, this application of the doctrine falls squarely within its geographic bull's eye—navigable waters—and rests not only on environmental factors but, as the court puts it, the state's general welfare. Does *Avenal* suggest a more expansive use of the doctrine in the future of coastal and estuarine resource protection?

3. The damages awarded to the oyster farmers in the lower courts were staggering—over $1 billion. Had the Louisiana Supreme Court upheld the award, what effect might that have had on future efforts to "replumb" the Delta?

4. The *Avenal* opinion seems to have been prescient given the aftermath of Hurricane Katrina. According to the U.S. Geological Survey, satellite imagery indicates that Hurricane Katrina caused substantial marsh loss in St. Bernard and Plaquemines parishes. This land loss potentially further reduces southeastern Louisiana's natural protection from future storms. Louisiana already had previously lost about 1,900 square miles of coastal land, primarily marshes, since the 1930s. Scientists estimate that the effects of Katrina transformed more than 30 square miles of marsh around the upper portion of Breton Sound to open water, or 20 to 26 percent of this 133-square mile area. What is the appropriate response to these losses, and to calls to restore wetlands throughout the region? What if restoring ecological integrity to the wetlands would require forgoing rebuilding parts of New Orleans such as St. Bernard Parish? For a range of views addressing that and other post-Katrina questions, see ENVIRONMENTAL LAW INSTITUTE, AFTER THE STORM: RESTORING AMERICA'S GULF COAST WETLANDS (2006).

Note on Hypoxia in Coastal Waters

The increasing focus on nonpoint source pollution in the National Estuary Program, the Chesapeake Bay Program, and the Bay-Delta Plan stems from the alarming phenomenon of hypoxia conditions that is becoming more frequent and widespread in estuarine settings. *See* Robert J. Diaz and Rutger Rosenberg, *Spreading Dead Zones and Consequences for Marine Ecosystems*, 321 SCIENCE 926 (2008) (summary of global hypoxic zones and their impacts). Hypoxia means an absence of oxygen reaching living tissues. In coastal waters, it is characterized by low levels of dissolved oxygen, so that not enough oxygen is available to support fish and other aquatic species. Hypoxia results from too much of a good thing—nutrients. Nutrients, obviously, are necessary to aquatic environments at some level. But if nutrients entering the system exceed the capacity of the food web to assimilate them, the accelerated production of organic matter, manifested in the massive algae blooms that induce hypoxia, begins to choke the system with its own waste—the process known as eutrophication. The increased primary productivity leads to increased flux of organic matter to the bottom, causing bottom water hypoxia, altered energy flow, and stresses to fisheries resources. Particularly vulnerable are benthic (bottom level) species such as crabs and lobsters that are unable to migrate quickly enough to escape the toxic conditions.

Dead crab following acute hypoxia conditions
in the Gulf of Mexico (USEPA 2002)

While hypoxia occurs in the Chesapeake Bay, Bay-Delta, and other of our nation's estuaries, nowhere in the United States is the hypoxia problem more of a concern than where the Mississippi River empties into the Gulf of Mexico. There the hypoxic zone has reached a size larger than the state of New Jersey—an 8000 square mile area running from the Mississippi Delta to the Texas-Louisiana border. It is most acute there during the summer months, when the weather is warm and the Gulf is especially calm, because of a lack of any "churning" of the layers of fresh and salt water. When this stratification of the water column occurs, the lower saltwater layer becomes cut off from the resupply of oxygen from fresh surface waters. This is when the rich nutrient content of the Mississippi River water becomes a liability to the system. The nutrients encourage the growth of algae, and as other aquatic organisms feast on the algae blooms that generate large amounts of fecal matter. This abundance of organic waste sinks to the saltier depths where it decomposes, using what remains of the available oxygen and creating a hypoxic zone. This condition can persist well into autumn, until storms and other high winds begin to churn the water layers and bring much-needed oxygen back to the bottom.

Some level of hypoxia events is natural in many estuarine ecosystems as annual floods flush high levels of naturally-occurring nutrients into the marine system. The largest recorded hypoxic zone in the Gulf at the time, for example, was after the massive floods on the Mississippi in 1993—it neared 8,000 square miles, an area as large as the entire Chesapeake Bay. But increasingly, hypoxia conditions are more persistent, occur more frequently, and affect larger areas even in relatively dry years. Some reasons include stream channelization, which moves nutrient flow faster downriver, and the loss of riparian buffers that impede flow of nutrients from land into streams. But the core of the problem is simply too much nutrient loading—about 40 percent higher today than the average loads experienced during 1955–1970. The excess supply of nutrients that accounts for the surge in hypoxia conditions may come from a wide range of sources: runoff from developed land, atmospheric deposition, soil erosion, and agricultural fertilizers. Sewage and industrial discharges can also contribute nutrients. Of all these causes, nitrogen runoff from agriculture has been implicated as both the most significant contributor of excess nutrients and the most difficult problem to solve. *See* Dan Ferber, *Keeping the Stygian Waters at Bay*, 291 SCIENCE 968 (2001). In fairness, though, recent research suggests that phosphorous from urban runoff is a significant contributor, leading many to suggest that a "dual nutrient approach" is needed, though by no means does that simplify things.

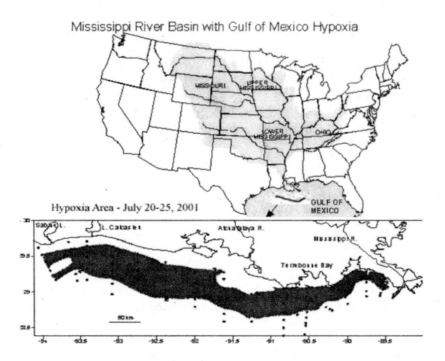

In recognition of the growing and alarming nature of the hypoxia problem, Congress in late 1998 passed the Harmful Algal Bloom and Hypoxia Research and Control Act of 1998. *See* Pub. L. No. 105–383, Title VI., § 604. During the fall of 1997, the Clinton Administration had formed the multi-agency Mississippi River/Gulf of Mexico Watershed Nutrient Task Force to research Gulf hypoxia in conjunction with the White House Office of Science and Technology Policy's Committee on Environment and Natural Resources. The 1998 law required the Task Force to submit a scientific assessment of Gulf hypoxia and a plan for reducing, controlling, and mitigating its effects. After voluminous comments on a draft plan (see 65 Fed. Reg. 42690 (July 2000)), in January 2001, in one of its last official acts, the Clinton Administration released the Task Force's report. *See* ACTION PLAN FOR REDUCING, MITIGATING, AND CONTROLLING HYPOXIA IN THE NORTHERN GULF OF MEXICO (Jan. 2001), *available at* http://www.epa.gov/msbasin/actionplan.htm.

The 2001 Action Plan focused on two primary approaches: (1) reduce nitrogen loads to streams and rivers in the Mississippi River Basin, and (2) restore and enhance denitrification and nitrogen retention within the Basin. These prescriptions seemed both obvious and easier said than done. The magnitude of the management challenge Gulf hypoxia poses is staggering. The Basin covers 1.2 million square miles. The river pours 612,000 cubic feet per second into the Gulf of Mexico. Over 12 million people live just in the 125 counties that directly border the Mississippi River itself. In other words, geographically, physically, and demographically, this is a monster-sized problem.

Accordingly, the 2001 Action Plan's finding and recommendations were rather sweeping in scope. The Task Force endorsed an "adaptive management" approach like the framework outlined in Chapter 7 of this text, and it identified what it believes will be the important indicators of implementation and results, such as riparian acres preserved. But overall, the tone was visionary far more than it was detailed. Representative are the following remarks:

> There are no simple solutions that will reduce hypoxia in the Gulf. An optimal approach would take advantage of the full range of possible actions to reduce nutrient loads and increase nitrogen retention and denitrification. This should proceed within a framework that encourages adaptive management and accomplishes this in a cost-effective manner. While reduction of nitrogen is the principal focus of this framework, many of the actions needed to reduce nitrogen loads will complement and enhance existing efforts to restore water quality throughout the basin. With additional assistance, this national effort to reduce Gulf hypoxia will be implemented within the existing array of State and Federal laws, programs, and private initiatives.

> The tools provided by the Clean Water Act, and the programs established under the last several Farm Bills, the Coastal Wetlands Planning, Protection, and Restoration Act, and Water Resources Development Acts, are critical to implementing this plan. Because nutrient overenrichment is a widespread problem, these existing national programs and initiatives incorporate specific elements intended to reduce nutrient loadings to surface waters and to foster restoration of natural habitats capable of removing nutrients from waters. They include the following:

> - encouraging nonpoint source pollutant reductions under the Clean Water Act, the Farm Bill, Coastal Zone Amendments and Reauthorization Act, and State cost-sharing programs;

> - implementation of the Environmental Quality Incentives Program (EQIP) to assist grain and livestock producers in reducing excessive nutrients' movement to water resources;

> - implementation of the Conservation Reserve Program, Wetlands Reserve Program, Corps of Engineers Environmental Restoration Programs, and Agricultural Extension Education Programs to promote restoration and enhancement of natural systems for nitrogen retention and denitrification;

> - implementation of nutrient management through State and Tribal efforts to implement watershed-based approaches to water quality management, including monitoring and assessing waters, adoption of water quality standards, which include nutrient criteria, developing total maximum daily loads (TMDLs), and implementing point source controls for nutrients through the National Pollutant Discharge Elimination System (NPDES);

> - promoting public-private partnerships to restore buffers;

> - promoting cost-effective flood control alternatives and implementing projects under the Coastal Wetlands Planning, Protection, and

Restoration Act that result in nitrogen removal from the Mississippi and Atchafalaya Rivers;

- supporting actions by non-water quality State and Tribal agencies, private landowners, and agricultural and other industries to reduce nitrogen loadings to the basin; and

- providing voluntary incentives for nitrogen reductions from point and nonpoint sources.

ACTION PLAN at 9–10.

Nothing too specific to be found there. Moreover, as described in Chapter 10 of this text, many of the "tools" the 2001 Action Plan said are already provided by the Clean Water Act and other programs to manage hypoxia have, for the most part, already proven to be ineffective for controlling nonpoint source runoff, particularly from agriculture. For more on that problem, see Sarah White, *Gulf Hypoxia: Can A Legal Remedy Breathe Life Into The Oxygen Depleted Waters?*, 5 DRAKE J. OF AGRICULTURAL LAW 519 (2000).

The Harmful Algal Bloom and Hypoxia Amendments Act of 2004, Pub L. No. 108–456, then authorized continuing research on hypoxia and requires the federal agencies to cooperate more closely with local authorities in assessing causes and solutions. Since the original legislation in 1998, research sponsored by the U.S. Environmental Protection Agency led to conclusions taking some of the spotlight off of the nitrogen in agricultural runoff as the major contributor to excess nutrient load, placing increased emphasis instead on the phosphorous component in municipal wastewater treatment discharges. Agriculture industry interests seized on early results of the research to call for more studies and delay of the 2001 Action Plan. *See* Dan Ferber, *Dead Zone Fix Not a Dead Issue*, 305 SCIENCE 1557 (2004).

The Task Force then released its updated Action Plan in 2008. *See* MISSISSIPPI RIVER BASIN & GULF OF MEXICO HYPOXIA TASK FORCE, Gulf Hypoxia Action Plan 2008 9 (2008), *available at* http://water.epa.gov/type/watersheds/named/msbasin/actionplan.cfm. Consisting of representatives from six different federal agencies and agencies from ten different states from the 31-state watershed, the Task Force recognized that "implementation of the Action Plan will require a significant commitment from the Federal agencies and State and local governments," thus necessitating "a reassessment of the roles and responsibilities assigned to Federal agencies, the States, Tribes, and the Sub-Basin Committees." *Id.* at 5. The 2008 Action Plan also recognizes that "no single approach to nutrient reduction would be effective in every state." *Id.* at 32. Instead, the 2008 Action Plan advises using a mix of instruments including incentives, technical assistance, planning, research, education, land conservation, and voluntary and mandatory best management practices. The 2008 Action Plan also emphasizes collaboration with nutrient sources, including companies developing technology to reduce nutrient emissions from farms and industrial facilities. A major theme of the 2008 Action Plan is that "States and Federal agencies must coordinate efforts across organizations and programs and use adaptive management to modify the strategies as new information and innovative solutions are acquired." *Id.* at 17. State sub-basin committees have "worked to coordinate actions in the sub-basin states" and "have opened the discussion to include many stakeholders not represented on the Task Force, including additional basin states, state agencies, and interested parties and organizations." *Id.* Next step agenda items include to "coordinate, consolidate, and improve access to date collected by State and Federal agencies" and to "track progress on the actions to reduce nitrogen and phosphorous by producing an annual report on federal and state program nutrient reduction activities and results." *Id.* at 50. Do these measures sound more promising than the steps outlined in the 2001 Action Plan?

Overall, Gulf hypoxia, like many of the problems examined in this text, remains a known and accelerating ecological dilemma with no concrete solution in sight. This is not the case elsewhere, however, as some other nations have confronted hypoxia with more deliberate and forceful measures. In Denmark, for example, a massive lobster die-off in 1986 in the Kattegat straight heightened public awareness and demands for action. Denmark enacted tighter restrictions on farmers, making them account for all manure and commercial fertilizer applications, and forced wastewater treatment plants to reduce phosphorous emissions. The government also began an aggressive program of buying and restoring riparian lands and paying farmers to plant winter wheat to soak up soil nitrogen. The combination of approaches appears to be working, as phosphorous loads have decreased by 80 percent and algae growth appears to have been stunted. *See* John S. MacNeil, *Off Denmark, A Drawn-Out War Against Hypoxia*, 291 SCIENCE 969 (2001). Could these measures be replicated in the United States? Why haven't they been? What measures, with any reasonable chance of success *and* of being implemented, would you recommend for the United States?

3. LIVING RESOURCES

As our focus moves from the coastline outward to the continental shelf and open seas, ecosystem management concerns also shift from an emphasis on the impacts of land-based activities to one emphasizing the importance of water-based activities. The activity of primary concern is the harvesting of living resources, more commonly known as fishing. To be sure, other activities on the continental shelf, such as oil and mineral exploration and pollution from vessels, have had significant marine resource impacts, but *no* activity by any stretch of the imagination has had as profound an impact on the ocean ecosystem as has fishing. Ecosystem management in that setting has relied primarily on the two techniques covered in this section—management of fisheries and protection of marine areas through preserves.

a. FISHERIES MANAGEMENT

It was, at one time, unthinkable that we could exhaust the ocean's vast living resources. Today, the question is whether we are on an irreversible path toward their virtual depletion. And there appears to be no end to our voracious appetite for fish and other marine food sources. Although humans account for the largest take of fish from the oceans, seabirds are not far behind. Estimates are that the world's 700 million seabirds take over 70 million tons of fish from marine environments annually, with the Macaroni penguin leading the pack at over 11 million tons. *See* Constance Holden, *Fishy Figure*, 303 SCIENCE 1287 (2004). It is unlikely, however, that control of seabird appetites will prove to be a fruitful ecosystem management policy. We can, however, think about controlling how humans take the sea's bounty. And take we do. Humans consumed 71.7 million tons of fish, crustaceans, and molluscs in 1990, and 93.8 million tons in 1997—a one-third increase in 7 years. This rise in consumption, mirrored by a rise in harvesting production, might suggest that the ocean's resources are indeed limitless, but that is far from the truth. Increasingly, fishing operations (and thus human consumption) are depleting "higher" food chain species and relying more and more on "lower" species. And, as fishing is more often than not indiscriminate in terms of target species, a tremendous amount of unwanted species, known as "bycatch," is simply discarded, usually dead, back into the ocean. The result is that today estimates are that at least 50 major world fish stocks are "fully exploited," meaning they can withstand no increase in harvests and remain sustainable, and at least 25 percent are overfished or depleted. *See* U.N. Food and Agriculture Organization, State of the World Fisheries and Aquaculture-SOPHIA 2000 (2001), *available at* www.fao.org. The bottom line is that the fishing industry, if it intends to remain economically viable, must face significant self—or externally—imposed regulation. The following excerpt provides a concise explanation of how matters have evolved from the state of bounty to one of scarcity.

United Nations Food and Agriculture Organization, *Code of Conduct for Responsible Fisheries*
(October 31, 1995).

Preface

From ancient times, fishing has been a major source of food for humanity and a provider of employment and economic benefits to those engaged in this activity. The wealth of aquatic resources was assumed to be an unlimited gift of nature. However, with increased knowledge and the dynamic development of fisheries after the second world war, this myth has faded in face of the realization that aquatic resources, although renewable, are not infinite and need to be properly managed, if their contribution to the nutritional, economic and social well-being of the growing world's population is to be sustained.

The widespread introduction in the mid-seventies of exclusive economic zones (EEZs) and the adoption in 1982, after long deliberations, of the United Nations Convention on the Law of the Sea provided a new framework for the better management of marine resources. The new legal regime of the ocean gave coastal States rights and responsibilities for the management and use of fishery resources within their EEZs which embrace some 90 percent of the world's marine fisheries. Such extended national jurisdiction was a necessary but insufficient step toward the efficient management and sustainable development of fisheries. Many coastal States continued to face serious challenges as, lacking experience and financial and physical resources, they sought to extract greater benefits from the fisheries within their EEZs.

In recent years, world fisheries have become a market-driven, dynamically developing sector of the food industry and coastal States have striven to take advantage of their new opportunities by investing in modern fishing fleets and processing factories in response to growing international demand for fish and fishery products. By the late 1980s it became clear, however, that fisheries resources could no longer sustain such rapid and often uncontrolled exploitation and development, and that new approaches to fisheries management embracing conservation and environmental considerations were urgently needed. The situation was aggravated by the realization that unregulated fisheries on the high seas, in some cases involving straddling and highly migratory fish species, which occur within and outside EEZs, were becoming a matter of increasing concern.

NOTES & QUESTIONS

1. Substantive provisions of the Code are reproduced later in this section. For thorough accounts of how the trends discussed in the Code of Conduct preamble have evolved in the United States, and how legal and policy frameworks have been constructed in response, see MICHAEL L. WEBER, FROM ABUNDANCE TO SCARCITY: A HISTORY OF U.S. MARINE FISHERIES POLICY (2002); SUSAN HANNA ET AL., FISHING GROUNDS 23–35 (2000); MICHAEL J. BEAN & MELANIE J. ROWLAND, THE EVOLUTION OF NATIONAL WILDLIFE LAW 148–151 (1997); Eldon V.C. Greenberg, *Ocean Fisheries*, in ENVIRONMENTAL LAW: FROM RESOURCES TO RECOVERY 260–274 (Celia Campbell-Mohn et al. eds, 1993).

2. Overfishing can have profound effects on ecosystem dynamics well beyond the depletion of target and bycatch species populations, yet often these impacts are indirect and delayed in nature. For example, researchers are piecing together an explanation for the collapse of kelp forests off the Alaskan coast that begins with the impacts of whaling practices from 50 years ago. After World War II, whaling in Pacific waters steadily decimated the great whale species populations. As a result, Orcas, or killer whales, had to "fish down" the food chain, turning to other species as prey. Their initial target was sea lions. As sea lions faced the twin threat of Orcas, as well as human overfishing of their own prey fish species, their populations also began to dwindle. Orcas next turned to sea otters to fill the gap. As sea otters took the brunt, their food of choice, sea urchins, began to explode in numbers. And what is the sea urchin's staple? Kelp. Thus, the effects of whaling over 50 years ago set in motion an ecological reverberation effect that only recently has manifested itself in depleted kelp forests. *See* Jay Withgott, *A Whale of a Chain Reaction*, 295 SCIENCE 1457 (2002). Does this potential for complex, time-delayed ecological cascades suggest any particular approach to fisheries management? Consider as you review the following materials whether any of the legal frameworks covered could prevent this story from being repeated for other ecological contexts of the coastal and marine environment.

(1) Regulating Fish Harvests

The United States, obviously, falls squarely within the challenge the U.N. Food and Agriculture Organization outlined in its 1995 Code of Conduct. At the core of our response is the Magnuson-Stevens Fishery Conservation and Management Act (Magnuson-Stevens Act), 16 U.S.C. §§ 1801–1882, as amended by the Sustainable Fisheries Act (SFA), Pub. L. No. 104–297, 110 Stat. 3559 (1996), which provides the primary statutory framework for the protection and management of the nation's marine fishery resources. It establishes eight Regional Fishery Management Councils (Councils), each of which has the authority and responsibility to govern conservation and management of the fisheries under its geographical jurisdiction. *See* 16 U.S.C. § 1852. The Councils perform this function by developing and implementing fishery management plans (FMPs) and amendments thereto. After a Council develops an FMP, the National Marine Fisheries Service (NMFS) and/or the National Ocean and Atmospheric Administration (NOAA), acting on behalf of the Secretary of Commerce, evaluate the FMP and determine whether it complies with the Magnuson-Stevens Act and other applicable law. The Secretary of Commerce may then approve, disapprove, or partially approve the FMP. *See id.* § 1854.

The approval of an FMP requires several steps: (1) an initial review of the FMP to ensure its consistency with the Magnuson-Stevens Act and other applicable law; (2) the publishing of the FMP in the Federal Register, followed by the commencement of a 60-day public comment period; and (3) the approval, disapproval, or partial approval of the FMP within 30 days of the end of the comment period. The Secretary may not adopt an FMP recommended by a Council if that FMP violates any of the ten "National Standards" for FMPs established by the Magnuson-Stevens Act, as amended. These are described as follows:

> Any fishery management plan prepared, and any regulation promulgated to implement any such plan, pursuant to this title shall be consistent with the following national standards for fishery conservation and management:
>
> (1) Conservation and management measures shall prevent overfishing while achieving, on a continuing basis, the optimum yield from each fishery for the United States fishing industry.
>
> (2) Conservation and management measures shall be based upon the best scientific information available.
>
> (3) To the extent practicable, an individual stock of fish shall be managed as a unit throughout its range, and interrelated stocks of fish shall be managed as a unit or in close coordination.
>
> (4) Conservation and management measures shall not discriminate between residents of different States. If it becomes necessary to allocate or assign fishing privileges among various United States fishermen, such allocation shall be (A) fair and equitable to all such fishermen; (B)

reasonably calculated to promote conservation; and (C) carried out in such manner that no particular individual, corporation, or other entity acquires an excessive share of such privileges.

(5) Conservation and management measures shall, where practicable, consider efficiency in the utilization of fishery resources; except that no such measure shall have economic allocation as its sole purpose.

(6) Conservation and management measures shall take into account and allow for variations among, and contingencies in, fisheries, fishery resources, and catches.

(7) Conservation and management measures shall, where practicable, minimize costs and avoid unnecessary duplication.

(8) Conservation and management measures shall, consistent with the conservation requirements of this Act (including the prevention of overfishing and rebuilding of overfished stocks), take into account the importance of fishery resources to fishing communities in order to (A) provide for the sustained participation of such communities, and (B) to the extent practicable, minimize adverse economic impacts on such communities.

(9) Conservation and management measures shall, to the extent practicable, (A) minimize bycatch and (B) to the extent bycatch cannot be avoided, minimize the mortality of such bycatch.

(10) Conservation and management measures shall, to the extent practicable, promote the safety of human life at sea.

16 U.S.C. §§ 1853(a)(1)-(10). In addition, the Secretary may propose federal management measures if such measures become necessary and the relevant Council failed to propose an appropriate measure within a reasonable amount of time. *See id.* at § 1854(c)(1). After the Secretary approves an FMP, the relevant Council implements it through a "framework adjustment." *See* 50 C.F.R. § 648.90.

In 1996, Congress enacted the Sustainable Fisheries Act (SFA) in order to further protect fishery stocks, many of which had become severely depleted by the mid-1980s. The SFA strengthened the Magnuson-Stevens Act by requiring NMFS and the Councils (1) to prevent overfishing and rebuild depleted fish populations, and (2) to report, assess, and minimize bycatch. The statute defines "overfishing" as the "rate or level of fishing mortality that jeopardizes the capacity of a fishery to produce the maximum sustainable yield on a continuing basis." 16 U.S.C. § 1802(29). The SFA regulates fishing mortality rates (F) with reference to this maximum sustainable yield (MSY), which is defined by regulation as "the largest long-term average catch or yield that can be taken from a stock or stock complex under prevailing ecological and environmental conditions." 50 C.F.R. § 600.310(c)(1)(i). Hence, as one legislator put it, the SFA "essentially says we can only catch that portion of the fish that represents interest.

This is called the maximum sustainable yield. Without touching the principal fish; that being the critical population necessary to replenish the stock year after year, we will continue to have fish." 141 Cong. Rec. H10232 (daily ed. Oct. 18, 1995) (statement of Rep. Wayne Gilchrest, House Subcommittee on Fisheries Conservation, Wildlife and Oceans).

In addition, however, the SFA also required that all fishery management plans rebuild depleted fish populations within a period "as short as possible," but "not to exceed ten years." 16 U.S.C. § 1854(e)(4)(A). The SFA thus not only prohibited all fishing at levels exceeding MSY, but also required fish populations to be rebuilt to a biomass level (B) that "allows the fishery to produce MSY on a continuing basis." *See id.* §§ 1802(28)-(29). The SFA imposed an October 11, 1998 deadline on all Councils to develop the necessary rules and regulations to comply with this and other provisions of the statute, and imposes a statutory duty on NMFS to ensure that the Councils do so. *See id.* § 1854(c)(1).

The Magnuson-Stevens Act was amended again in 2007 by the Magnuson-Stevens Fishery Conservation and Management Reauthorization Act of 2006. Pub. Law No. 109-479 (2007). Although mild by comparison to some of the reform proposals that were in play, key measures added the following:

- A deadline to end over-fishing by 2010 for currently overfished stocks and by 2011 for all stocks.

- Facilitating the use of market-based "limited-access privilege" programs such as ITQs (discussed below)

- Enhanced enforcement provisions.

- Requiring a regionally based registry for recreational fishermen.

- Authorizing the Secretary to provide assistance to the Regional Fishery Management Councils for development of regional ecosystem pilot programs.

- Establishing Community Based Restoration Programs that utilize public-private partnerships to restore fishery and coastal habitat, in line with the President's Cooperative Conservation Agenda.

The following materials assess the Magnuson-Stevens Act from three perspectives. First, we present two cases illustrating the type of disputes that arise under the Act and how the courts approach them. Second, we provide a critique of conventional fisheries management regulation from an economist and a legal scholar. Finally, we present the central substantive provisions of the FAO Code of Conduct to allow evaluation of the extent to which the United States has fulfilled the Code's vision.

Coastal Conservation Commission v. Gutierrez

United States District Court for the Middle District of Florida, 2005.
2005 WL 2850325.

■ STEELE, J.

The Gulf of Mexico is home to a variety of ecologically and commercially important fish species, including groupers, snappers, tilefishes, jacks, sea basses, porgies, wrasses, triggerfishes, and grunts. Both recreational and commercial anglers fish for grouper within the grouper fishery in the Gulf of Mexico. The grouper complex includes seventeen species of groupers, including, goliath, dwarf sand perch, sand perch, misty, snowy, yellow edge, nasa, Warsaw, speckled hind, black, gag, red, yellow-fin, scamp, yellow mouth, rock hind, and red hind groupers. Red grouper is primarily fished off the west coast of Florida from Panama City, Florida to the Florida Keys, with a heavy concentration in the Tampa, Florida area southward.

On July 25, 2005, the Secretary of the United States Department of Commerce (the Secretary), in conjunction with the National Oceanic and Atmospheric Administration (NOAA) and the National Marine Fisheries Service (NMFS) (collectively defendants), published an interim Rule to Reduce the Recreational Harvest of Gulf of Mexico Red Grouper, Rule No. 62605 (the Interim Rule). The Interim Rule reduced the red grouper bag limit from two fish per person to one fish per person, reduced to aggregate grouper bag limit from five fish per person to three fish, and closed recreational fishing for all grouper species in the Gulf of Mexico Exclusive Economic Zone ("Gulf of Mexico EEZ") for November and December, 2005. Meetings of the Gulf Council concerning a final draft Red Grouper Regulatory Amendment for the recreational sector are currently scheduled for November, 2005.

In these consolidated civil actions, plaintiffs seek declaratory and injunctive relief pursuant to the Magnuson-Stevens Fishery Conservation and Management Act, as amended in 1996 by the Sustainable Fisheries Act, 16 U.S.C. § 1801 *et seq.* ("Magnuson-Stevens Act"), the National Environmental Policy Act, 42 U.S.C. § 4321 *et seq.* ("NEPA"), and the Administrative Procedures Act, 5 U.S.C. §§ 701–706 ("APA") to preclude the lower aggregate grouper bag limit and the two month closure. All parties filed cross motions for summary judgment, and the Court heard oral argument on October 27, 2005.

I.

In 1976 Congress found, *inter alia,* that fish off the coasts of the United States were a valuable and renewable natural resource, but that certain stocks of fish had declined or could decline to the point where their survival was threatened. 16 U.S.C. § 1801(a)(1), (2). Congress also found that commercial and recreational fishing constituted a major source of employment which contributed significantly to the national economy, and that fishery resources were finite but renewable. 16 U.S.C. § 1801(a)(3), (5). Further, Congress found that a national program for the conservation and management of fishery resources was necessary to prevent overfishing, to rebuild overfished stocks, to insure conservation, to facilitate long-term protection of essential fish habitats, and to realize the full potential of the country's fishery resources. 16 U.S.C. § 1801(a)(6).

Based on these findings, Congress enacted the Magnuson-Stevens Act (the Act). The purposes of the Act included to "conserve and manage the fishery resources found off the coasts of the United States," 16 U.S.C. § 1801(b)(1); to promote domestic commercial and recreational fishing under sound conservation and management principles, 16 U.S.C. § 1801(b)(3); to provide for the preparation and implementation of fishery management plans, in accordance with national standards, which would achieve and maintain, on a continuing basis, the optimum yield for each fishery, 16 U.S.C. § 1801(b)(4); and to establish Regional Fishery Management Councils to be stewards of fishery resources through the preparation, monitoring, and revision of fishery management plans (FMP), 16 U.S.C. § 1801(b)(5). The Act as amended created eight Regional Fishery Management Councils. 16 U.S.C. § 1852(a). The Councils develop fishery management plans and plan amendments for each fishery requiring conservation and management; conduct public hearings concerning the development of fishery management plans and amendments and the administration and implementation of the Act; submit proposed plans and amendments to the Secretary, 16 U.S.C. § 1852(h); and submit proposed regulations to the Secretary. 16 U.S.C. § 1853(c).

The relevant Council in this case is the Gulf of Mexico Fishery Management Council (the Gulf Council). The Gulf Council manages fishery resources off the coasts of Texas, Louisiana, Mississippi, Alabama and Florida. The Gulf Council's jurisdiction to manage fishery resources in the Gulf of Mexico extends from the outer limits of the state territorial waters (about nine miles) to 200 nautical miles seaward.

The fishery management plans or amendments must be consistent with ten national standards promulgated by the Magnuson-Stevens Act, 16 U.S.C. § 1851(a), must satisfy fourteen other specific criteria, 16 U.S.C. § 1853(a)(1)-(14), and may address twelve other components, 16 U.S.C. § 1853(b)(1)-(12). The Secretary reviews each proposed plan or amendment, and either approves, disapproves, or partially approves it after complying with certain procedural requirements. 16 U.S.C. § 1854(a). If approved, the Secretary promulgates regulations to implement the plan or amendment, which have the force and effect of law. 16 U.S.C. §§ 1854(b)(3) and 1855(d). The Secretary is also given authority to prepare fishery management plans or amendments under certain circumstances. 16 U.S.C. § 1854(c).

The Act further vested the Secretary with the authority to ask Councils to take action and to develop and implement rebuilding plans for overfished fish species. 16 U.S.C. § 1854(e). Additionally, the Act conferred authority on the Secretary to promulgate short-term emergency rules and interim measures needed to reduce overfishing. "If the Secretary finds that an emergency exists or that interim measures are needed to reduce overfishing for any fishery, he may promulgate emergency regulations or interim measures necessary to address the emergency or overfishing without regard to whether a fishery management plan exists for such fishery." 16 U.S.C. § 1855(c)(1). These are intended to be relatively short-term, stopgap measures. 16 U.S.C. § 1855(c)(3)(B).

II.

In June 1983, the Secretary approved the Gulf of Mexico Fishery Management Plan for Reef Fish Resources ("Reef Fish FMP") submitted by the Gulf Council for management of the grouper complex (and others) in the Gulf of Mexico, and the plan was implemented in November, 1984. (AR 321). The primary objectives of the Reef Fish FMP were to rebuild overfished reef fish stocks to stable population levels and to manage access to the reef fish fishery. A major revision of the Reef Fish FMP was implemented in 1990 (id.), and the NMFS implemented the Reef Fish FMP through a series of amendments and regulations providing for such things as the imposition of limitations on fishing equipment, data reporting requirements, quotas and bag limits, seasonal and size limitations, and a permitting system.

Stock assessments for the red grouper were conducted in 1991, 1993, and 1999. In October, 2000, the NMFS determined that the red grouper stock was overfished and undergoing overfishing. This finding was based primarily on the results of the 1999 stock assessment, which assessed the red grouper stock as of 1997. Under the Act, the Gulf Council had one year to submit a plan to the NMFS to end overfishing and rebuild the red grouper stock. 16 U.S.C. § 1854(c). For various reasons the Gulf Council missed the October, 2001 deadline, and on September 27, 2002, the Secretary submitted a proposed Secretarial Amendment 1 to the Reef Fish Fishery Management Plan.

A subsequent 2002 assessment found that while red grouper were overfished in 1997, the red grouper stock was in an improved condition by 2001 and was no longer considered overfished. However, red grouper was not yet at the biomass level capable of producing maximum sustainable yield (MSY) on a continuing basis.

On May 8, 2004, a revised Secretarial Amendment 1 was promulgated. After summarizing the 2002 assessment that red grouper was no longer overfished but was not at a sufficient biomass level, it stated "measures to reduce overfishing and a rebuilding plan are still needed to restore the stock to the level in 10 years or less." A secondary purpose of Secretarial Amendment 1 was "to evaluate and control the impact of the red grouper rebuilding plan on other species," specifically gag grouper, deep-water grouper, and tilefish. NMFS adopted the revised Secretarial Amendment 1 on May 28, 2004.

On June 15, 2004, the NMFS published its final rule to implement Secretarial Amendment 1 to the Reef Fish FMP. The Secretarial Amendment 1, effective July 15, 2004, imposed bag limits for recreational anglers (two per day for red grouper and five aggregate grouper per day per angler), set a total allowable catch ("TAC") of 6.56 million pounds gutted weight, allocated 5.31 million pounds to the commercial sector, and established a ten year rebuilding plan for red grouper. The remaining 1.25 million pounds gutted weight of the TAC was allocated to the recreational sector. Since Secretarial Amendment 1 was specific to red grouper, anglers still had flexibility to fish for other grouper and reef fish species.

During its March 9–10, 2005, meeting, the Gulf Council reviewed red grouper landings and concluded that, without additional regulations, recreational red grouper landings in 2005 were likely to exceed the recreational target level, as they had in 2003 and 2004. Recreational red grouper landings for 2003 were slightly over target, but landings for 2004 were over the target level by almost 2.5 times. As a result, the Gulf Council passed a motion giving the NMFS the authority through emergency or interim rule to bring the recreational red grouper fishing within their target catch levels in Secretarial Amendment 1 for the year 2005.

After additional research was conducted and collected, NOAA requested approval of an interim rule. The stated purpose of the Interim Rule was to "reduce the likelihood that overfishing for red grouper will occur in 2005." NOAA also noted that failure to seek such an interim rule to reduce the 2005 recreational red grouper harvest to target catch levels would likely result in litigation from the commercial sector, which had stayed within its red grouper harvest target catch levels.

On July 25, 2005, NMFS published the Interim Rule in the Federal Register. The Interim Rule reduced the red grouper bag limit from two fish per person per day to one fish per person per day, reduced the aggregate grouper bag limit from five fish per person to three fish, and closed recreational fishing for all grouper species in Gulf of Mexico for November and December, 2005.

On August 17, 2005, plaintiff Coastal Conservation Association filed its four-count Complaint seeking declaratory and injunctive relief as to the aggregate bag limits and the closure (but not the red grouper bag limits). On August 24, 2005, plaintiff Fishing Rights Alliance filed its Complaint seeking similar relief. The Court has consolidated the two cases upon plaintiffs' request.

III.

All parties agree on the standard of review to be utilized by the Court. The Magnuson-Stevens Act adopts portions of the standard of review set forth in the Administrative Procedures Act. 16 U.S.C. § 1855(f)(1)(B), (2). The Court's review is limited to the administrative record, and in this case the applicable review standard is whether the agency action is arbitrary, capricious, an abuse of discretion, or otherwise not in accordance with law. 5 U.S.C. § 706(2)(A); *Midwater Trawlers Coop. v. Department of Commerce*, 393 F.3d 994, 1002 (9th Cir.2004). Under the arbitrary and capricious standard, the reviewing court "gives deference to the agency decision by reviewing for clear error, and by refraining from substituting its own judgment for that of the agency. However, the court must also look beyond the scope of the decision itself to the relevant factors that the agency considered." *Sierra Club v. United States Army Corps. of Eng'rs,* 295 F.3d 1209, 1216 (11th Cir.2002) (citations omitted). A regulation will be found arbitrary and capricious "if the agency has relied on factors which Congress has not intended it to consider, entirely failed to consider an important aspect of the problem, offered an explanation for its decision that runs counter to the evidence before the agency, or is so implausible that it could not be ascribed to a difference in view or the product of agency expertise." *Southern Offshore Fishing Ass'n v. Daley,* 995 F.Supp. 1411, 1425 (M.D.Fla.1998) (quoting *Motor Vehicle Mfrs. Ass'n of U.S. v. State Farm Mut. Auto. Ins.,* 463 U.S. 29, 43, 103 S.Ct. 2856, 77 L.Ed.2d 443 (1983)).

IV.

A. Count One: Finding of Red Grouper Overfishing

In Count One of the Complaints, plaintiffs seek a declaratory judgment that defendants violated the Magnuson-Stevens Act and the Administrative Procedures Act by adopting the Interim Rule without a finding of either an emergency or of overfishing of red grouper in the Gulf of Mexico EEZ.

It is clear from th[e] statutory scheme that there must be a determination of overfishing by the Secretary before an interim measure may be promulgated. The Magnuson-Stevens Act defines the terms "overfishing" and "overfished" to mean "a rate or level of fishing mortality that jeopardizes the capacity of a fishery to produce the maximum sustainable yield on a continuing basis." 16 U.S.C. 1802(29).

The Administrative Record, however, establishes that the Secretary made the required finding of overfishing. The Federal Register publication of the Interim Rule summarized the background of the matter, including the 2002 stock assessment which found that the red grouper stock was no longer overfished, but had not yet reached a biomass level that was capable of producing maximum sustainable yield on a continuing basis. The publication continued that the Gulf Council had concluded that a reduction in recreational red grouper landings "is needed to end overfishing in 2005." Additionally, the publication stated: "The purpose of this temporary rule is to reduce the likelihood of overfishing red grouper, while minimizing biological impacts on gag and other groupers that could result from shifts in effort due to red grouper management actions." The Court concludes that this is a sufficient finding for the Secretary to implement interim measures pursuant to 16 U.S.C. § 1855(c). Judgment will therefore be entered in favor of defendants as to Count One.

B. Count Two: Interim Rule Overbroad

In Count Two of the Complaints, plaintiffs seek a declaratory judgment that defendants violated the Magnuson-Stevens Act and the Administrative Procedures Act by adopting an overbroad Interim Rule which does not conform with 16 U.S.C. § 1855(c). Count Two asserts that there was no determination that sixteen of the seventeen species of grouper are overfished, yet the Interim Rule prohibits fishing within the entire grouper fishery for two months and limits the aggregate bag limit for grouper. Count Two contends that the Interim rule is therefore arbitrary, capricious, contrary to law, and an abuse of agency discretion.

The Interim Rule was intended to reduce overfishing of red grouper in the Gulf of Mexico and to minimize the potential adverse impacts on other grouper stocks that could result from a shift in fishing effort from red grouper to other grouper species. (AR 1633–34). The Secretary made the finding of overfishing of red grouper, as discussed above. The Administrative Record, however, clearly establishes that the entire grouper fishery was never determined to be overfished or undergoing overfishing. Indeed, the record establishes the contrary with regard to some species of grouper. The limitation and closure as to other grouper species goes beyond the request made by the Gulf Council to promulgate an interim measure to bring the catch levels of red grouper into line with the Secretarial Amendment 1 requirements. Even when there is a temporary closure of the commercial fishery because the red grouper limits have been reached, fishing is not banned for all grouper species. The statute does not allow the Secretary to institute interim measures as to the other grouper species unless there has been a finding that the other grouper species are overfished. Such a measure may be appropriate in an amendment to a fishery management plan after completion of the procedural requirements imposed by the statutes and regulations. It cannot, however, be implemented as an interim measure without findings of overfishing as to the other grouper species. Such findings are lacking in this case.

Defendants argue that the pertinent national standards require the Interim Rule to include a two-month closure and bag limits for the entire grouper complex. The Court disagrees. The Secretary has consistently treated red grouper as a distinct stock of fish by conducting separate stock assessments of red grouper. The Secretary previously precluded any landings of two grouper species, goliath and nasa, yet the Secretary did not feel compelled by any national standard to limit or close fishing as to other grouper species in order to further these restrictions. Secretarial Amendment 1 stated that one of the benefits of the amendment was that it gave fishermen the flexibility to fish for other species of grouper. The Court finds that the two-month closure of the entire grouper complex and the aggregate grouper bag limit were not necessary to satisfy any of the ten national standards.

The Court concludes that, on this Administrative Record, the extension of the Interim Rule remedies beyond red grouper was arbitrary, capricious, an abuse of discretion, and not in accordance with 16 U.S.C. § 1855(c)(1). Therefore, judgment will be entered in favor of plaintiffs as to Count Two.

C. Count Three: Best Scientific Evidence

In Count Three of the Complaints, plaintiffs seek a declaratory judgment that defendants violated the Magnuson-Stevens Act and the Administrative Procedures Act by adopting an Interim Rule which was not based upon the best scientific evidence available. Specifically, Count [Three] asserts that there was no scientific data to establish, support or confirm that overfishing of red grouper in the recreational fishery was occurring sufficient to trigger the interim rule provision of 16 U.S.C. § 1855(c). For this reason, Count Three contends that the Interim rule is arbitrary, capricious, contrary to law, and an abuse of agency discretion.

It is Congressional policy to assure that the national fishery conservation and management program utilizes and is based upon the best scientific information available. 16 U.S.C. § 1801(c)(3). The Magnuson-Stevens Act also requires that "[c]onservation and management measures shall be based upon the best scientific information available." 16 U.S.C. § 1851(a)(2); *see also Midwater Trawlers Coop.,* 393 F.3d at 1003. "The fact that scientific information concerning a fishery is incomplete does not prevent [regulation]." *Midwater Trawlers Coop.,* 393 F.3d at 1003 (quoting 50 C.F.R. § 600.315(b)); *see also Blue Water Fisherman's Ass'n v. Mineta,* 122 F.Supp.2d 150, 166 (D.D.C.2000). "By specifying that decisions be based on the best scientific information *available,* the Magnuson-Stevens Act recognizes that such information may not be exact or totally complete." *Midwater Trawlers Coop.,* 393 F.3d at 1003 (emphasis in original).

Defendants assert that "NMFS properly relied on the available [Marine Recreational Fisheries Statistics Survey ('MRFSS')] estimates of recreational red grouper catches." (Doc. #32, p. 14). The MRFSS uses telephone surveys to estimate fishing effort in the recreational fishing industry. For shore mode and private/rental boat fishing, effort is estimated from data collected in a random survey of coastal residents. (*Id.*). For party/charter boat fishing, effort is estimated from a random survey of charter vessel operators. (*Id.*). While NMFS determined that "MRFSS 2004 red grouper catch and harvest estimates are considered sound and the best available[,]" several recreational anglers and the red grouper recreational fishing associations questioned the validity of the 2004 landing estimates and the MRFSS method itself.

Secretarial Amendment 1 demonstrates that characterizing a fishery as overfished is a matter of experience and expertise as well as "scientific evidence." Secretarial Amendment 1 stated:

> Additionally, it should be noted that the increasing stock size seen in recent years appears to be due in large part to increased recruitment [reproduction] entering the fishery. Recruitment is variable, and variation in recruitment is difficult to predict. This creates the real possibility that setting a TAC at any given level may be acceptable for one year under current standards, and unacceptable in another. The result is a stock that varies between being fished within acceptable limits one year, and being overfished in another. This is one of the benefits of

moving to a strategy based on OY [optimum yield] rather than MSY [maximum sustainable yield]. Annual fluctuations in recruitment would be much less likely to result in an overfishing situation under an OY management strategy.

Secretarial Amendment 1 also noted that red groupers are protogynous hermaphrodites (they initially mature as females and then transition to males), and that the effect of this on the stock's susceptibility to overfishing is not well understood. Additionally, Secretarial Amendment 1 noted that the fishery was currently being influenced by the strong 1996 red grouper year-class, and would likely continue to be influenced for the next three years. (AR 355). Further, Secretarial Amendment 1 also specifically discussed how the selection of red grouper biological reference points and stock status determination criteria impacts whether a stock is considered overfished.

Having reviewed at length the entire administrative record, especially that relating directly to the Interim Rule, the Court concludes that the best available scientific evidence was used to promulgate the Interim Rule. Therefore, judgment will be entered in favor of defendants as to Count Three.

NOTES & QUESTIONS

1. What reasons might NMFS have had for imposing recreational fishing bans and catch limits on the entire grouper complex? One reason may have to do with the practicalities of fishing—i.e., that recreational fishers might have difficulty distinguishing between the species, or would have difficulty fishing in such a manner as to exclude red grouper from their possible catch. It might also be the case that there are ecological reasons for the strategy. For example, perhaps fishing for any species of grouper has an adverse impact on the habitat or other environmental conditions for all groupers. In either case, if the goal is to rebuild the red grouper stock, wouldn't it make sense to extend the catch limit to the entire complex? Why, then, does the statutory scheme require a finding of overfishing for each species?

2. The court's discussion of the "best scientific information available" standard is consistent with the way that phrase has been interpreted in the Endangered Species Act—i.e., so as to allow regulatory action on the basis of the agency's professional judgment when working with incomplete scientific data. *See* J.B. Ruhl, *The Battle Over Endangered Species Act Methodology*, 34 ENVTL. L. 555 (2004). Is there any practical way ecosystem management can be implemented without such an approach? If you believe more conclusive scientific evidence should be required before an agency can take action such as banning recreational fishing of a species, how would you express the standard in written statutory text?

Natural Resources Defense Council, Inc. v. Daley

United States Court of Appeals for the District of Columbia Circuit, 2000.
209 F.3d 747.

■ EDWARDS, CHIEF JUDGE:

Paralichthys dentatus, or summer flounder, a commercially valuable species of flounder, dwells off the Atlantic coast and are harvested primarily between May and October from North Carolina to Maine. The summer flounder fishery is an "overfished" fishery, in the process of recovering from severe depletion prevalent during the late 1980s and early 1990s. The Secretary of Commerce, advised by the National Marine Fisheries Service ("the Service"), the principal appellee in this case, annually sets a fishing quota limiting each year's summer flounder catch, pursuant to the Magnuson-Stevens Fishery Conservation and Management Act ("the Fishery Act"), 16 U.S.C. §§ 1801–1883 (1994 & Supp. IV 1998). This case involves appellants' challenge to the Service's quota for the 1999 summer flounder harvest.

Before the District Court, appellants alleged that the 1999 quota did not provide sufficient assurance that it would meet the conservation goals of the Fishery Act and attendant regulations. Appellants also claimed that the Service's conclusion that the quota had no significant environmental impact was based on an inadequate environmental assessment, thereby violating the National Environmental Policy Act ("NEPA"). On crossmotions for summary judgment, the District Court granted judgment in favor of appellees. See Natural Resources Defense Council, Inc. v. Daley, 62 F.Supp.2d 102 (D.D.C.1999).

We reverse the District Court and remand the case to the Service for further proceedings consistent with this opinion. The 1999 quota, when adopted, had a documented 18% likelihood of meeting the statute's conservation goals. We hold that, under the Fishery Act, the disputed quota is insufficient to meet Congress' mandate to the Service to prevent overfishing and to assure that specific conservation goals are met. We also hold that the Service's proposal to supplement the quota with other purportedly protective measures does not satisfactorily ameliorate the quota's glaring deficiencies. Because of our disposition on these grounds, we have no need to reach appellants' NEPA claims.

I. BACKGROUND

A. Regulatory Background

The Fishery Act was enacted to establish a federal-regional partnership to manage fishery resources. Under the statute, there are eight Regional Fishery Management Councils "to exercise sound judgment in the stewardship of fishery resources." 16 U.S.C. §§ 1801(b)(5), 1852(a) (Supp. IV 1998). Management Councils propose and monitor fishery management plans "which will achieve and maintain, on a continuing basis, the optimum yield from each fishery." Id. § 1801(b)(4) (1994). Management Councils submit management plans to the Secretary of Commerce (functionally the Service), who may then adopt them through notice and comment rule-making. See id. § 1854(a) (Supp. IV 1998). An "optimum yield" under the statute is defined as the "maximum sustainable yield from the fishery." Id. § 1802(28)(B) (Supp. IV 1998). If a fishery is "overfished," the management plan must "provide[ ] for rebuilding to a level consistent with" the maximum sustainable yield. Id. § 1802(28)(C). A fishery is "overfished" if the rate of fishing mortality "jeopardizes the capacity of a fishery to produce the maximum sustainable yield on a continuing basis." Id. § 1802(29).

The Service defines overfishing and optimum yield according to the fishing mortality rate ("F"). F represents that part of a fish species' total mortality rate that is attributable to harvesting by humans, whether through capture or discard. Fish are "discarded" for many reasons, including, for example, when they are the wrong species, undersized, or not valuable enough. Values for F can range anywhere from 0 to over 2, and only indirectly represent the amount of fish captured by industry. For instance, an F of 1.4 means that about 20% of all summer flounder that are alive at year 1 will be alive at year 2. There is a specific F, termed "F submax," that is defined as that fishing mortality rate that will maximize the harvest of a single class of fish over its entire life span. Overfishing is fishing in excess of F submax. Therefore, the basic goal of a management plan is to achieve F submax, thereby preventing overfishing and assuring optimum yield.

B. The Summer Flounder Fishing Quota

From a commercial standpoint, the summer flounder is one of the most important species of flounder in the United States. All parties agree that the summer flounder fishery is "overfished" and has been for some time. The Mid-Atlantic Fishery Management Council ("MAFMC"), covering New York, New Jersey, Delaware, Pennsylvania, Maryland, Virginia, and North Carolina, developed the original summer flounder management plan with the assistance of two other regional Management Councils and the Atlantic States Marine Fisheries Commission ("the Commission"), a consortium of 15 coastal states and the District of Columbia. The Service approved the original management plan in 1988; however, the Service has amended the plan several times. At the time relevant to the instant case, the plan was designed to achieve a fishing mortality rate equal to F submax by 1998.

Pursuant to the management plan, the Service must set a quota each year fixing the total weight of summer flounder that may be harvested by commercial and recreational fishers. This quota is referred to as the "total allowable landings" for the year, or "TAL." The Service allocates 60% of the TAL to commercial fisheries and 40% of the quota to recreational fisheries, and states receive allocations based upon their share of the summer flounder fishery. States may subdivide their allocated commercial quota between "incidental" and "directed" catch. Directed fisheries intentionally harvest summer flounder. Fishers who catch juvenile flounder, or who are part of the directed fishery for another species and catch summer flounder unintentionally, have harvested incidental catch.

The TAL must meet several requirements. It must be consistent with the 10 national standards of fishery conservation and management set out in the Fishery Act. See 16 U.S.C. § 1851(a)(1)-(10) (1994 & Supp. IV 1998). Most relevant to the instant case, the quota must embody conservation measures that "shall prevent overfishing while achieving, on a continuing basis, the optimum yield from each fishery for the United States fishing industry." Id. § 1851(a)(1) (1994). The quota must also be "consistent with" the fishery management plan. See id. § 1854(b)(1). Finally, under the applicable regulations, the Regional Administrator of the Service must annually adopt a final rule "implement[ing] the measures necessary to assure that the applicable specified F will not be exceeded." 50 C.F.R. § 648.100(c) (1999). The "applicable specified F" is also referred to as the "target F."

There is a relatively direct relationship between the TAL and the likelihood of achieving the target F. In general, the higher the TAL, the less likely a plan is to achieve the target F. In other words, the lower the target F, the lower the TAL must be to attain the target F. The basic dispute between the parties concerns whether the 1999 TAL provides a sufficient guarantee that the target F for summer flounder will be achieved.

For 1999, the summer flounder fishery management plan mandated a target F equivalent to F submax, which was 0.24. The Summer Flounder Monitoring Committee, a MAFMC committee, had recommended a TAL of 14.645 million pounds, while MAFMC had recommended a TAL of 20.20 million pounds. The Service rejected MAFMC's recommendation as "unacceptably risk-prone" for several reasons: (1) it had an "unacceptably low probability" of 3% of achieving the target F; (2) it had a 50% probability of achieving an F of 0.36, which was "significantly higher" than the target F; (3) the proposal relied on unpredictable data; and (4) MAFMC had "yet to specify a harvest level that has achieved the annual target F." Fisheries of the Northeastern United States; Summer Flounder, Scup, and Black Sea Bass Fisheries, 63 Fed.Reg. 56,135, 56,136 (1998) (to be codified at 50 C.F.R. pt. 648) (proposed Oct. 21, 1998) ("Proposed TAL"). The Service also rejected the Summer Flounder Monitoring Committee's recommendation of a 14.645 million pound TAL. Although the Committee's recommendation had a 50% chance of achieving the target F, the Service rejected the proposal without any meaningful explanation.

On October 21, 1998, the Service proposed a TAL of 18.52 million pounds. See id. All parties agree that, at most, the Service's proposal afforded only an 18% likelihood of achieving the target F. The Service also proposed an incidental catch restriction "to address discards in this fishery that should further reduce the overall mortality." Id. This measure provided that, within the commercial fishery, 32.7% of the allocated quota be committed to incidental catch. In the end, then, the Service proposed a TAL of 7.41 million pounds for recreational harvest, 7.47 million pounds for directed commercial harvesting, and 3.64 million pounds for incidental commercial catch, for a total of 18.52 million pounds. See id. The Service also considered recent changes in minimum mesh size. On this point, the Service noted that, while MAFMC felt that the "recently adopted mesh provision requiring 5.5 inch" mesh throughout the net would "substantially reduce discard and discard mortality," the alleged benefits of mesh had yet to be verified by anyone. Id.

Between the time of proposal of the 1999 TAL and its adoption, the Service concluded that it did not have the authority to impose any incidental catch restrictions on the states. Therefore, the Service merely recommended that the states adopt the incidental catch proposal, making the proposal entirely voluntary. The Commission, the body representing 15 coastal states and the District of Columbia, also declined to command the states to adopt the proposal. According to an advisor to the Service's Assistant Administrator for Fisheries, this development "result[ed] in an unknown but probably substantial reduction in the likelihood that [MAFMC's] rebuilding schedule will be achieved," and he therefore recommended that the Service adopt the Summer Flounder Monitoring Committee's recommended 14.645 million pound TAL.

The Service rejected this recommendation and, on December 31, 1998, issued the final TAL, adopting its initial proposal. The Service acknowledged that the Summer Flounder Monitoring Committee's recommended quota had a 50% chance of achieving the target F, while the Service's TAL had only an 18% chance of achieving the target F. See Fisheries of the Northeastern United States; Summer Flounder, Scup, and Black Sea Bass Fisheries, 63 Fed.Reg. 72,203, 72,203–04 (1998) (codified at 50 C.F.R. pt. 648) ("Final TAL"). The Service also recognized that the incidental catch provisions were entirely voluntary. See id. at 72,204. The Service simply recommended that states adopt the additional incidental catch provisions "[t]o improve the probability of achieving the target [F]." Id. Nowhere did the Service analyze the effect on fishing mortality of shifting from a mandatory to a voluntary incidental catch provision.

The Service responded to comments that the TAL did not sufficiently assure achievement of the target F by stating that: (1) the TAL had a higher probability of meeting the target F than MAFMC's 20.2 million pound recommendation; and (2) the incidental catch recommendations "would improve the likelihood that the target fishing mortality rate would be attained." Id. at 72,206. In response to other comments, the Service suggested that the 5.5 inch minimum mesh provision might ameliorate other mortality concerns, but acknowledged that the requirement had not been in effect long enough to determine its efficacy. See id. at 72,208.

Appellants filed suit in District Court on January 29, 1999, seeking, inter alia, (1) a declaratory judgment that defendants violated the Fishery Act, the Administrative Procedure Act ("APA"), and NEPA, and (2) remand to the agency to impose a new summer flounder TAL. The District Court upheld the Service's adoption of the 18.52 million pound TAL, deferring to the agency under Chevron U.S.A. Inc. v. Natural Resources Defense Council, Inc., 467 U.S. 837, 104 S.Ct. 2778, 81 L.Ed.2d 694 (1984). The District Court first determined that §§ 1851 (a)(1) and (a)(8) in the Fishery Act evinced competing interests between advancing conservation and minimizing adverse economic effects and that Congress offered no insight as to how to balance these concerns. See Natural Resources Defense Council, 62 F.Supp.2d at 106–07. In addition, the trial court found that the Fishery Act expressed no clear intent as to the particular level of certainty a TAL must guarantee to be consistent with 16 U.S.C. § 1851(a)(1). See id. at 107. Given these perceived ambiguities, the District Court deferred to the Service pursuant to Chevron Step Two. This appeal followed.

II. ANALYSIS

As we recently held in Associated Builders & Contractors, Inc. v. Herman, 166 F.3d 1248 (D.C.Cir.1999), [i]n a case like the instant one, in which the District Court reviewed an agency action under the [APA], we review the administrative action directly. See Troy Corp. v. Browner, 120 F.3d 277, 281 (D.C.Cir.1997); Gas Appliance Mfrs. v. Department of Energy, 998 F.2d 1041, 1045 (D.C.Cir.1993). In other words, we accord no particular deference to the judgment of the District Court. See Gas Appliance Mfrs., 998 F.2d at 1045. Rather, on an independent review of the record, we will uphold [the agency's] decision unless we find it to be "arbitrary, capricious, an abuse of discretion, or otherwise not in accordance with law." 5 U.S.C. § 706(2)(A) (1994). Id. at 1254.

As for the Service's disputed interpretations of the Fishery Act, we are guided by the Supreme Court's seminal decision in Chevron U.S.A., Inc., [467 U.S. at 837], [which] governs review of agency interpretation of a statute which the agency administers. Under the first step of Chevron, the reviewing court "must first exhaust the 'traditional tools of statutory construction' to determine whether Congress has spoken to the precise question at issue." Natural Resources Defense Council, Inc. v. Browner, 57 F.3d 1122, 1125 (D.C.Cir.1995) (quoting Chevron, 467 U.S. at 843 n. 9. * * * If, however, "the statute is silent or ambiguous with respect to the specific issue," Chevron, 467 U.S. at 843, Congress has not spoken clearly, and a permissible agency interpretation of the statute merits judicial deference. Id. Bell Atlantic Telephone Companies v. FCC, 131 F.3d 1044, 1047 (D.C.Cir.1997). Although agencies are entitled to deferential review under Chevron Step Two, our judicial function is neither rote nor meaningless: [W]e will defer to [an agency's] interpretation[ ] if [it is] reasonable and consistent with the statutory purpose and legislative history. * * * This case presents a situation in which the Service's quota for the 1999 summer flounder harvest so completely diverges from any realistic meaning of the Fishery Act that it cannot survive scrutiny under Chevron Step Two.

As an initial matter, we reject the District Court's suggestion that there is a conflict between the Fishery Act's expressed commitments to conservation and to mitigating adverse economic impacts. Compare 16 U.S.C. § 1851(a)(1) (directing agency to "prevent overfishing" and ensure "the optimum yield from each fishery"); with id. § 1851(a)(8) (directing agency to "minimize adverse economic impacts" on fishing communities). The Government concedes, and we agree, that, under the Fishery Act, the Service must give priority to conservation measures. It is only when two different plans achieve similar conservation measures that the Service takes into consideration adverse economic consequences. This is confirmed both by the statute's plain language and the regulations issued pursuant to the statute. See id. § 1851(a)(8) (requiring fishery management plans, "consistent with the conservation requirements of this chapter," to take into account the effect of management plans on fishing communities); 50 C.F.R. § 600.345(b)(1) (1999) ("[W]here two alternatives achieve similar conservation goals, the alternative that . . . minimizes the adverse impacts on [fishing] communities would be the preferred alternative.").

The real issue in this case is whether the 1999 TAL satisfied the conservation goals of the Fishery Act, the management plan, and the Service's regulations. In considering this question, it is important to recall that the Service operates under constraints from three different sources. First, the statute requires the Service to act both to "prevent overfishing" and to attain "optimum yield." 16 U.S.C. § 1851(a)(1). Overfishing is commonly understood as fishing that results in an F in excess of F submax. Since F submax for 1999 was equivalent to 0.24, this constraint required the Service to issue regulations to prevent F from exceeding 0.24. Second, any quota must be "consistent with" the fishery management plan adopted by the Service. See id. § 1854(b)(1). In this case the fishery management plan called for an F of 0.24. Therefore, the quota had be to "consistent with" achieving that F. Third, the Service is required to adopt a quota "necessary to assure that the applicable specified F will not be exceeded." 50 C.F.R. § 648.100(c). The "applicable specified F" for 1999 was F submax, or 0.24.

All of these constraints, then, collapse into an inquiry as to whether the Service's quota was "consistent with" and at the level "necessary to assure" the achievement of an F of 0.24, and whether it reasonably could be expected to "prevent" an F greater than 0.24. In other words, the question is whether the quota, as approved, sufficiently ensured that it would achieve an F of 0.24. Appellants argue that the quota violates applicable standards under both *Chevron* Step One and *Chevron* Step Two. Because we find appellants' *Chevron* Step Two arguments convincing, we have no need to reach their alternative argument that the Service violated NEPA by relying on an inadequate environmental assessment in promulgating the final rule.

Appellants' *Chevron* Step One "plain meaning" argument is virtually indistinguishable from their *Chevron* Step Two reasonableness argument. Appellants acknowledge that the statutory terms "assure," "prevent," and "consistent with" do not mandate a precise quota figure. However, appellants contend that a TAL with only an 18% likelihood of achieving the target F is so inherently unreasonable that it defies the plain meaning of the statute. This is an appealing argument on the facts of this case, because, as we explain below, the Service's action is largely incomprehensible when one considers the principal purposes of the Fishery Act. Nonetheless, we still view this case as governed by *Chevron* Step Two. The statute does not prescribe a precise quota figure, so there is no plain meaning on this point. Rather, we must look to see whether the agency's disputed action reflects a reasonable and permissible construction of the statute. In light of what the statute does require, short of a specific quota figure, it is clear here that the Service's position fails the test of *Chevron* Step Two.

The 1999 quota is unreasonable, plain and simple. Government counsel conceded at oral argument that, to meet its statutory and regulatory mandate, the Service must have a "fairly high level of confidence that the quota it recommends will not result in an F greater than [the target F]." Fishermen's Dock Coop., Inc. v. Brown, 75 F.3d 164, 169–70 (4th Cir.1996). We agree. We also hold that, at the very least, this means that "to assure" the achievement of the target F, to "prevent overfishing," and to "be consistent with" the fishery management plan, the TAL must have had at least a 50% chance of attaining an F of 0.24. This is not a surprising result, because in related contexts, the Service has articulated precisely this standard. See National Marine Fisheries Service, Final Fishery Management Plan for Atlantic Tunas, Swordfish and Sharks, Vol. I, at 288, reprinted in J.A. 382 (April 1999) (concluding that the Service should choose management measures that have "at least a 50-percent confidence in target reference points," and when choosing between two alternatives with a greater than 50% probability, should choose the higher "unless there are strong reasons to do otherwise").

The disputed 1999 TAL had at most an 18% likelihood of achieving the target F. Viewed differently, it had at least an 82% chance of resulting in an F greater than the target F. Only in Superman Comics' Bizarro world, where reality is turned upside down, could the Service reasonably conclude that a measure that is at least four times as likely to fail as to succeed offers a "fairly high level of confidence."

As we noted at the outset of this opinion, the Service's quota for the 1999 summer flounder harvest so completely "diverges from any realistic meaning" of the Fishery Act that it cannot survive scrutiny under *Chevron* Step Two. See GTE Serv. Corp., 205 F.3d at 421. The Service resists this result by suggesting that we owe deference to the agency's "scientific" judgments. See Br. for Appellees at 33. While this may be so, we do not hear cases merely to rubber stamp agency actions. To play that role would be "tantamount to abdicating the judiciary's responsibility under the Administrative Procedure Act." A.L. Pharma, Inc. v. Shalala, 62 F.3d 1484, 1491 (D.C.Cir.1995). The Service cannot rely on "reminders that its scientific determinations are entitled to deference" in the absence of reasoned analysis "to 'cogently explain' " why its additional recommended measures satisfied the Fishery Act's requirements. Id. at 1492 (quoting Motor Vehicle Mfrs. Ass'n, Inc. v. State Farm Mut. Auto. Ins. Co., 463 U.S. 29, 48, 103 S.Ct. 2856, 77 L.Ed.2d 443 (1983)). Indeed, we can divine no scientific judgment upon which the Service concluded that its measures would satisfy its statutory mandate.

Here, the adopted quota guaranteed only an 18% probability of achieving the principal conservation goal of the summer flounder fishery management plan. The Service offered neither analysis nor data to support its claim that the two additional measures aside from the quota would in-

crease that assurance beyond the at-least-50% likelihood required by statute and regulation.

NOTES & QUESTIONS

1. As the *NRDC v. Daley* case makes abundantly clear, fisheries biology, as a
branch of applied ecology, has focused on a quest for the perfect fish harvest
optimization "algorithm," and the result has been a regulatory structure that is
expressed through highly technical, quasi-mathematical concepts such as F, F
submax, and TAL. As the ecologist P.A. Larkin suggested several decades ago,
this approach opens the door to the fundamental question: What shall be opti-
mized? *See* P.A. Larkin, *Fisheries Management—An Essay for Ecologists*, 9 Annual Review of Ecology and Systematics 57 (1978). As Larkin explained then,
traditional fisheries biologists sought to optimize maximum sustained yield.
Later, attention turned to maximum sustained economic return, and then, with
the Magnuson-Stevens Act, to an optimum sustained yield approach. But the
expansion of EEZs to 200-miles invited many countries to pursue "variations of
long-standing policies that place fisheries matters in a much broader context of
economic and political optimization. The field is wide open for modeling extravaganzas which may expose the consequences of virtually any proposed course of
action; and the recipes for action that emerge will be the logical consequences of
the predisposing assumptions." *Id.* at 69. Is there any evidence in *NRDC v. Daley* that the "optimization" that had taken place for the summer flounder was
more political than biological in focus? Put another way, how is that, as the
court put it, we wound up with a management regime for the summer flounder
straight out of Superman Comics' Bizarro world?

2. The "modeling extravaganzas" of which P.A. Larkin wrote suggest a science-
policy interface that depends on confidence that (1) the models are sound; (2)
the scientific information used in the models is reliable; and (3) the policy decision makers actually follow the model results. For example, as the *NRDC v.
Daley* court described it, that case "collapse[d] into an inquiry as to whether the
Service's quota was 'consistent with' and at the level 'necessary to assure' the
achievement of an F of 0.24, and whether it reasonably could be expected to
'prevent' an F greater than 0.24." How confident are you that we can reliably
determine what F is? How confident are you that, if we know F for a species,
NMFS and the Regional Councils will implement quotas that will achieve F?

3. The Stanford Fisheries Policy Project examined these questions based on a
survey of 25 years of historical records from 11 U.S. fisheries. *See The Use of
Science in U.S. Fisheries*, http://fisheries.stanford.edu. The lead researchers
published a report of their findings in 2003. *See* Josh Eagle & Barton H.
Thompson, Jr., *Answering Lord Perry's Question: Dissecting Regulatory Overfishing*, 46 OCEAN & COASTAL MANAGEMENT 649 (2003). The foundation for
their inquiry was a question a member of the British House of Lords, Lord Perry of Walton, asked in 1995 about the perpetual failure in fishery policy:

> There seem to be three factors to account for it: first, the scientific advice
> that is given; secondly, how far that advice is accepted by politicians who
> set the [total allowable take] and quotas; and, thirdly, whether the fisher-
> men obey the regulations. Which of these are the most at fault at the mo-
> ment?

They conclude that overfishing is the result of a collection of causes, with the dominant cause varying by fishery. The causes include illegal fishing, deliberate political management decisions not in line with scientific evidence, excessively precise scientific standards that are beyond the capacity of management systems to administer, poorly designed regulatory frameworks that actually promote overfishing, failure to account for bycatch as fish landings, and lack of enforcement. The answer to Lord Perry's question, in other words, is all of the above. Is this evidence of "political optimization" or simply lack of understanding?

4. With so much dysfunctional about the current U.S. fishing policy regime, it is no surprise that the focus of policy reform proposals increasingly is the Regional Councils. One commentator goes so far as to suggest that "one possible solution is to remove all decisions, other than allocation choices, from Fishery Management Councils," and to transfer all decision making authority about stock depletion and management plans to NOAA-Fisheries. Councils would simply recommend how to allocate catch between and within commercial and recreational fishing. *See* Marianne Cufone, *Will There Always Be Fish in the Sea? The U.S. Fishery Management Process*, 19 NATURAL RESOURCES & ENV'T 28, 34–35 (Summer 2004); *see also* Donna R. Christie, *Living Marine Resources Management: A Proposal for Integration of United States Management Regimes*, 34 ENVTL. L. 107, 173 (2004) (similar proposal). Would this go to the heart of Lord Perry's question, or simply rearrange the deck chairs? Thus far the researchers have found that the fishery quotas Regional Councils set often fall above or below the range recommended by the scientists advising the Councils. It remains to be seen whether the 2007 amendments correct that over time.

5. There is also a growing sentiment that the problems in U.S. fishery management go beyond the Regional Councils or the other causes cited by Eagle and Thompson, but rather have to do fundamentally with the species-specific, catch-based focus of the Magnuson-Stevens Act framework. The premise of the program, in other words, is that the fate of a particular species can be manipulated by regulating the catch of that particular species—nothing else matters. By now, we hope, you should be skeptical of any such premise, as it is no more accurate in the ocean as it is for terrestrial or freshwater species management. Researchers are finding, for example, that the stock of striped bass in the Chesapeake Bay depends on the stock of their primary food source, the Atlantic menhaden. The menhaden is an oily, bony fish, practically inedible to humans but a primary source of cattle feed and cat food. *See* H. Bruce Franklin, The Most Important Fish in the Sea: Menhaden and America (2007). The menhaden fishery, with no quota set under the Magnuson-Stevens Act, uses spotter planes to locate schools and direct catch boats to their precise location. It is an effective fishing method, so effective that it has depleted the bass population by depleting its major source of forage. *See* CHESAPEAKE BAY ECOLOGICAL FOUNDATION, CHESAPEAKE BAY FORAGE BASE COLLAPSE AND INTERACTIONS OF STRIPED BASS & ATLANTIC MENHADEN (2003), *available at* http://www.chesbay.org/articles/7.asp.

In a sign that the two species are intertwined, bass interests blame menhaden interests for wiping out the bass food, and menhaden interests blame the bass for eating too many menhaden. In response, NOAA-Fisheries is pushing for the fisheries in the Chesapeake Bay to adopt an ecosystem-based approach that relies on managing the interconnected ecosystem rather than individual species. Yet this ecosystem-based approach, strongly recommended for broad adoption by the Pew Commission on Oceans and the President's Commission on Ocean Policy, remains a somewhat fuzzy proposal. At its core, ecosystem-based fishery management must "delineate all marine habitats utilized by humans in the context of vulnerability to fishing-induced and other human impacts, identify the potential irreversibility of those impacts, and elucidate habitats critical to species for vital population processes." E.K. Pikitch et al., *Ecosystem-Based Fishery Management*, 305 SCIENCE 346 (2004). Also, community and system level standards are necessary, which may require evolution from species-specific standards, to standards based on suites of related species (such as the menhaden and bass), to broad ecosystem-based standards. All of this, of course, will depend on a flow of data into decision makers that would dwarf the current data volume delivered to and used by Regional Councils today. Moreover, because it has never been done before, ecosystem-based fishery management will depend on adaptive management techniques to test proposals and develop better methods over time. Everyone agrees that ecosystem based fishery management is necessary, but nobody has figured out how to do it or pay for it. As one researcher working on the menhaden issue summed it up, "if we don't do ecosystem-based, we may as well give up. . . But it's part getting the data and part the will, since no one has done this before. A lot is on the line." Michelle Boorstein, *Marine Conservation Hits Bumpy Waters*, TALLAHASSEE DEMOCRAT, Dec. 5, 2004, at 4A (quoting Dave Loewensteiner).

On the other hand, the Ecosystem Principles Advisory Panel Congress established in 1996 through the Sustainable Fisheries Act observed that "ecosystem based fisheries management does not require that we understand all things about all components of the ecosystem." Ecosystems Principles Advisory Panel, Ecosystem Based Fisheries Management, A Report to Congress 10 (1999). So the question is, when do we know enough to make ecosystem-based decisions with confidence? For more on the topic and proposals, see Donna R. Christie, *Living Marine Resources Management: A Proposal for Integration of United States Management Regimes*, 34 ENVTL. L. 107, 135–40, 168–70 (2004).

6. Those political and policy issues aside, the basic legal grist of the Magnuson-Stevens Act boils down to issues like that presented in *NRDC v. Daley*. At the very least, therefore, F, TAL, and their related acronyms do provide fact-based inquiries for the law to apply. The *NRDC v. Daley* court explained how these legal hooks operate on three levels:

> First, the statute requires the Service to act both to "prevent overfishing" and to attain "optimum yield." 16 U.S.C. § 1851(a)(1). Overfishing is commonly understood as fishing that results in an F in excess of F submax. Second, any quota must be "consistent with" the fishery management plan adopted by the Service. See id. § 1854(b)(1). In this case the fishery management plan called for an F of 0.24. Third, the Service is required to adopt a quota "necessary to assure that the applicable specified F will not be exceeded." 50 C.F.R. § 648.100(c). The "applicable specified F" for 1999 was F submax, or 0.24.

As Professor Oliver Houck has argued, without these legal hooks there may be little hope of producing anything but political optimization in domestic fisheries management. *See* Oliver A. Houck, *On the Law of Biodiversity and Ecosystem Management*, 81 MINN. L. REV. 869, 949–53 (1997). Does *NRDC v. Daley* suggest to you that there is an adequate legal backstop to prevent fisheries management from falling into that trap?

7. What do you think of the court's interpretation in *NRDC v. Daley* that "under the Fishery Act, the Service must give priority to conservation measures. It is only when two different plans achieve similar conservation measures that the Service takes into consideration adverse economic consequences." NMFS has interpreted the statute this way. *See* 50 C.F.R. § 600.345(b). Do you agree with the court's and the agency's interpretation of the statute? Do you agree with their interpretation as a matter of policy in general? If this is true, couldn't the agency ensure that it will never have to take into account adverse economic consequences simply by characterizing different management plans as achieving dissimilar conservation measures? Several courts have grappled with these issues. One found, quite to the contrary of *NRDC v. Daley*, that NMFS failed adequately to evaluate the economic impact of summer flounder quotas on North Carolina fishing operations, characterizing the quota as "a buzzsaw to mow down whole fishing communities in order to save some fish." North Carolina Fisheries Ass'n v. Daley, 27 F.Supp.2d 650, 667 (E.D.Va.1998). A thorough summary of these and other cases on the topic is found in Kristen M. Fletcher, *When Economic Analysis and Conservation Clash: Challenges to Economic Analysis in Fisheries Management*, 31 ENVTL. L. REP. (ELI) 1168 (2001).

Shi-Ling Hsu & James E. Wilen, *Ecosystem Management and the 1996 Sustainable Fisheries Act*

24 Ecology Law Quarterly 799 (1997).

The record of fisheries conservation in the U.S. since the [Magnuson-Stevens Fisheries Conservation and Management Act (FCMA)] is checkered. In some regions, councils have been able to insulate the scientific determination of optimum yield from the intensely acrimonious decisions about which groups using what kinds of gear should catch the fish. In other regions, however, councils have not overcome industry pressures to increase harvest targets, sometimes justified by directives that weaken the mandate to set clear biological targets with vague admonitions to consider economic or social factors. In some regions, managers have been unable even to gather rudimentary data necessary to begin managing fisheries, such as landings records.

This . . . highlights one of the most significant failures of fisheries conservation under the FCMA: the failure to contain entry and capacity growth in fisheries. As economists have warned for forty years, fishing capacity in open access fisheries tends to be directly proportional to their profitability. If no authority regulates the fish stocks, too many vessels end up chasing too few fish, which can lead to a complete collapse of the fishery. Regulators may be able to maintain a healthy biomass by employing management measures like shortened seasons to limit harvests to sustainable levels. However, because such measures encourage overcapitalization, as in the halibut case where the whole fleet geared up to fish a five day season, they create significant economic waste. The original FCMA avoided addressing the inevitability of overcapitalization and left this responsibility to the regional councils, where political pressures to leave fisheries open to all entrants were most strongly expressed. As a result of this, most of the fisheries in the U.S. are vastly overcapitalized. Short seasons govern even those in good shape biologically, leading to relatively poorer quality fish, and encouraging fishing with methods that emphasize volume and induce bycatch, discarding, and other forms of waste.

THE 1996 SUSTAINABLE FISHERIES ACT

The 1996 Sustainable Fisheries Act (the "SFA"), which amended the 1976 Magnuson Act, reflects another step in fine tuning the fisheries regulatory apparatus established under the original act. At the same time, the SFA, like the original act, is clearly the outcome of political logrolling, tradeoffs, and compromises among disparate groups with different agendas. The policy impacts, achieved by a negotiation process that included input from conservation organizations and fishing industry representatives, are by no means inconsequential, but they should not be taken for a systemic overhaul of fisheries management.

Stamps of conservation groups are imprinted upon numerous provisions of the SFA. Perhaps the most significant change the SFA effected is the removal of some discretion regarding "overfished" fisheries. If the Secretary of Commerce (the "Secretary") determines that a fishery is "overfished," she is required to immediately notify the appropriate regional fishery management council and give the council one year to develop a fishery management plan that ends overfishing and rebuilds the stock of fish. If the regional council fails to develop a plan within one year, the Secretary is required to prepare a plan within nine months. The plan to end overfishing must do so within a time frame that is "as short as possible, taking into account the status and biology of any overfished stock of fish . . . and the interaction of the overfished stock of fish within the marine ecosystem," but must generally be accomplished in less than ten years. The regional council developing the fishery management plan is still responsible for specifying "objective and measurable criteria for identifying when the fishery . . . is overfished." The SFA also establishes new requirements regarding bycatch—fish that fishermen catch incidentally when fishing for another species. Fishery management plans under the SFA must be consistent not only with the seven national standards described above, but also with the three additional ones specified by the SFA, including one that requires plans to minimize bycatch or minimize the mortality from bycatch. Further, the first national standard, mandating that management achieve the "optimum yield" from each fishery, previously defined as "maximum sustainable yield . . . as modified by any relevant economic, social, or ecological factor," has been altered to allow only that maximum yield be reduced by any such relevant factors. This prevents councils from raising allowable harvests in response to local pressure for larger allocations.

THE OVERCAPITALIZATION PROBLEM

While the SFA contains some notable conservation advances, it does little to address the most fundamental cause of overfishing and waste—the chronic overcapitalization of fishing industries. The technological resourcefulness of fishermen has historically made a mockery of the most stringent and carefully crafted command and control regulations aimed at reducing fishing effort. For example, reductions in season lengths have encouraged fishermen to build bigger, faster vessels with more short-term harvesting capacity, necessitating further reductions in season lengths. Limitations or restrictions on gear types or capacity (e.g., net size regulations) have invited substitution of other inputs that partially thwart the regulations' original purpose, leading to further attempts by regulators to contain fishing technology's impact on overall harvest levels. Even in cases where limited entry programs have been instituted to freeze capacity and prevent further entry by new boats, there has been a need for additional measures to control capacity as fishermen have continued to increase individual vessel capacity on existing boats. In fact, measures that constrain fishing capital growth by fiat focus only on the symptom of the problem and not on the cause, which is the open access nature of the resource.

A few fisheries have adopted a measure that attacks the fundamental property rights problem: individual fishermen quotas (IFQs). IFQs grant rights to harvest a given percentage of the biologically determined total annual allowable catch. They are, in effect, a property right to the potential harvest. As a result, they change the incentives fishermen face in a radical way. Under IFQs, a fisherman does not need to build a bigger boat to outfish his competitors before regulators close the season; he may fish whenever it is efficient to do so during the season. While IFQs have only been adopted in three fisheries in the U.S., they have been adopted in over fifty fisheries worldwide.

The impacts of IFQs on fisheries are a remarkable counterpoint to the status quo in traditional fisheries managed by closed seasons and gear restrictions. IFQs have reversed the race to overcapitalize, because they encourage fishermen to downsize and adopt fishing practices more suitable to producing higher valued products year-round. Reduced overcapitalization offers many benefits. First, the product itself improves, as fish formerly frozen because of short seasons are available fresh throughout the year. Second, fishermen begin to act as stakeholders of the resource, since detrimental actions more clearly impact their own potential revenues. This is an important byproduct since fishermen and regulators tend to view most modern regulated fisheries as an adversarial struggle. Finally, in fisheries where there were formerly significant amounts of bycatch and discards, fishermen reduce waste, particularly if bycatch is included in their quota.

NOTES & QUESTIONS

1. When Individual Fishing Quotas (IFQs) are made transferable, they are referred to as Individual Transferable Quotas (ITQs). The point of IFQs, as the authors of the article explain, is to reduce the motivation each individual fish-

ing operation has to race to maximize its individual harvest share of a fishery-wide quota. The IFQ relieves the pressure to invest in technology to compete in the race. The point of transforming IFQs into ITQs, then, is to allow a market in IFQs that will direct the quotas to the most efficient fishing operations. The result is that the holders of ITQs should be the fishing operations that have most efficiently balanced investment in technology and intensity of fishing against the yield. Yet, as elegant as the economic theory sounds, not everyone is enamored of IFQs or ITQs. One commentator argues that they are subject to three structural flaws. First, they require an initial allocation of individual quotas that becomes entrenched economically in the form of reliance, and the quotas are thus politically difficult to change later in the light of better scientific evidence about appropriate harvest levels. Second, they impose a heavy information burden in order to set the initial quotas at reliable levels. Finally, they produce the possibility of "hot spots" as quotas may be exercised, particularly under ITQ systems, in concentrated areas and times. *See* Sharon R. Siegel, *Applying the Habitat Conservation Model to Fisheries Management: A Proposal for a Modified Fisheries Planning Requirement*, 25 COLUM. J. ENVTL. L. 141, 151–54 (2000). But aren't these three problems evident, perhaps far more than the authors of article suggest, in conventional fishery-wide quota systems? How can ecosystem management policies be crafted that avoid or mitigate these three phenomena? For an additional perspective on overcapitalization in the fishing industry and the role ITQs in particular could play, see Robert J. McManus, *America's Saltwater Fisheries: So Few Fish, So Many Fishermen*, 9 NATURAL RESOURCES & ENV'T 13 (Spring 1995).

2. The IFQ and ITQ instruments are examples of the broader set of market-based tools known as "catch shares," all of which focus on the relationship between the success of fisheries management and the economic structure of property rights in the fisheries themselves. Researchers have compiled compelling evidence that these approaches are highly effective in stemming the collapse of fisheries. *See* Christopher Costello et al., *Can Catch Shares Prevent Fisheries Collapse*, 321 SCIENCE 1678 (2008). Open access regimes, in which exclusivity of fishing rights does not exist or is poorly enforced, seem inevitably to lead to counter-productive "racing" and over-capitalization behavior. Far more effectively than fishery-wide quotas, catch shares provide the right economic incentives to their holders to conserve fishing effort and capital.

3. What of the Native American fisheries? Did they not prosper despite a lack of poorly defined private property rights? This conventional lore may in fact be at odds with the historical record. For example, evidence suggests that the tribes of the Pacific Northwest maintained thriving salmon fisheries for thousands of years prior to European settlement by relying on a complex, but strictly enforced, system of exclusive tribal rights to different salmon streams. In essence, they developed tribal catch shares long before any economic theory supported the case for doing so. *See* D. Bruce Johnsen, *Customary Law, Scientific Knowledge, and Fisheries Management among Northwest Coast Tribes*, 10 N.Y.U. ENVTL. L.J. 1 (2001). On the other hand, there is also evidence that as long as 25,000 years ago coastal human communities were exploiting fish and shellfish populations sufficiently to put measurable stress on coastal ecosystems and species assemblies. The depletion of cod, once an abundant keystone species of the North Atlantic, began about 3500 years ago. *See* Torben C. Rick and Jon M. Erlandson, *Coastal Exploitation*, 325 SCIENCE 952 (2009).

4. Despite the continued debate over the economic and environment effects of individual fishing quotas, transferable or not, they continue to gain prominence in policy. As mentioned in the opening to the Chapter, President Bush's December 2003 *U.S. Ocean Action Plan* advocated greater use of market-based fisheries management tools such as individual quotas and several Regional Councils began contemplating or implementing individual quotas for specific species. Then the Magnuson-Stevens Fishery Conservation and Management Reauthorization Act of 2006 included two significant and complementary new provisions that contributed to NOAA's current focus on catch shares. The first provision required the establishment of a mechanism for specifying annual catch limits (ACL) in most fisheries by 2011. The ACLs place a firm cap on fisheries removals at a level such that overfishing will not occur. Accountability measures were required to accompany the ACL mechanisms. The second provision was the elaboration of criteria and guidance authorizing a program of limited access privileges (LAP) to help rebuild overfished stocks, reduce overcapacity if it exists, and promote safety, fishery conservation and management, and social and economic benefits. NOAA issued a catch share policy implementing these provisions at the end of 2010, and today catch share programs are currently used in 15 fisheries managed by six regional fishery management councils, with additional programs in development. *See* NOAA Office of Sustainable Fisheries, *Catch Shares*, http://www.nmfs.noaa.gov/sfa/domes_fish/catchshare/index.htm.

United Nations Food and Agriculture Organization, *Code of Conduct for Responsible Fisheries*

(October 31, 1995).

Preface

[The opening paragraphs of the Preface are reproduced earlier in the chapter.]

The Committee on Fisheries (COFI) at its Nineteenth Session in March 1991 called for the development of new concepts which would lead to responsible, sustained fisheries. Subsequently, the International Conference on Responsible Fishing, held in 1992 in Canc□n (Mexico) further requested FAO to prepare an international Code of Conduct to address these concerns. The outcome of this Conference, particularly the Declaration of Canc□n, was an important contribution to the 1992 United Nations Conference on Environment and Development (UNCED), in particular its Agenda 21. Subsequently, the United Nations Conference on Straddling Fish Stocks and Highly Migratory Fish Stocks was convened, to which FAO provided important technical back-up. In November 1993, the Agreement to Promote Compliance with International Conservation and Management Measures by Fishing Vessels on the High Seas was adopted at the Twenty-seventh Session of the FAO Conference (Annex 1).

Noting these and other important developments in world fisheries, the FAO Governing Bodies recommended the formulation of a global Code of Conduct for Responsible Fisheries which would be consistent with these instruments and, in a non-mandatory manner, establish principles and standards applicable to the conservation, management and development of all fisheries. The Code, which was unanimously adopted on 31 October 1995 by the FAO Conference, provides a necessary framework for national and international efforts to ensure sustainable exploitation of aquatic living resources in harmony with the environment.

This Code sets out principles and international standards of behaviour for responsible practices with a view to ensuring the effective conservation, management and development of living aquatic resources, with due respect for the ecosystem and biodiversity. The Code recognises the nutritional, economic, social, environmental and cultural importance of fisheries, and the interests of all those concerned with the fishery sector. The Code takes into account the biological characteristics of the resources and their environment and the interests of consumers and other users. States and all those involved in fisheries are encouraged to apply the Code and give effect to it.

Article 1—Nature and Scope of the Code

1.1 This Code is voluntary. However, certain parts of it are based on relevant rules of international law, including those reflected in the United Nations Convention on the Law of the Sea of 10 December 1982.* * *1.3 The Code provides principles and standards applicable to the conservation, management and development of all fisheries. It also covers the capture, processing and trade of fish and fishery products, fishing operations, aquaculture, fisheries research and the integration of fisheries into coastal area management. * * *

Article 2—Objectives of the Code

The objectives of the Code are to:

a. establish principles, in accordance with the relevant rules of international law, for responsible fishing and fisheries activities, taking into account all their relevant biological, technological, economic, social, environmental and commercial aspects;

b. establish principles and criteria for the elaboration and implementation of national policies for responsible conservation of fisheries resources and fisheries management and development;

c. serve as an instrument of reference to help States to establish or to improve the legal and institutional framework required for the exercise of responsible fisheries and in the formulation and implementation of appropriate measures;

d. provide guidance which may be used where appropriate in the formulation and implementation of international agreements and other legal instruments, both binding and voluntary;

e. facilitate and promote technical, financial and other cooperation in conservation of fisheries resources and fisheries management and development;

f. promote the contribution of fisheries to food security and food quality, giving priority to the nutritional needs of local communities;

g. promote protection of living aquatic resources and their environments and coastal areas;

h. promote the trade of fish and fishery products in conformity with relevant international rules and avoid the use of measures that constitute hidden barriers to such trade;

i. promote research on fisheries as well as on associated ecosystems and relevant environmental factors; and

j. provide standards of conduct for all persons involved in the fisheries sector

Article 6—General Principles

6.1 States and users of living aquatic resources should conserve aquatic ecosystems. The right to fish carries with it the obligation to do so in a responsible manner so as to ensure effective conservation and management of the living aquatic resources.

6.2 Fisheries management should promote the maintenance of the quality, diversity and availability of fishery resources in sufficient quantities for present and future generations in the context of food security, poverty alleviation and sustainable development. Management measures should not only ensure the conservation of target species but also of species belonging to the same ecosystem or associated with or dependent upon the target species.

6.3 States should prevent overfishing and excess fishing capacity and should implement management measures to ensure that fishing effort is commensurate with the productive capacity of the fishery resources and their sustainable utilization. States should take measures to rehabilitate populations as far as possible and when appropriate.

6.4 Conservation and management decisions for fisheries should be based on the best scientific evidence available, also taking into account traditional knowledge of the resources and their habitat, as well as relevant environmental, economic and social factors. . .

6.5 States and subregional and regional fisheries management organizations should apply a precautionary approach widely to conservation, management and exploitation of living aquatic resources in order to protect them and preserve the aquatic environment, taking account of the best scientific evidence available. The absence of adequate scientific information should not be used as a reason for postponing or failing to take measures to conserve target species, associated or dependent species and non-target species and their environment.* * *

6.8 All critical fisheries habitats in marine and fresh water ecosystems, such as wetlands, mangroves, reefs, lagoons, nursery and spawning areas, should be protected and rehabilitated as far as possible and where necessary. Particular effort should be made to protect such habitats from destruction, degradation, pollution and other significant impacts resulting from human activities that threaten the health and viability of the fishery resources.

6.9 States should ensure that their fisheries' interests, including the need for conservation of the resources, are taken into account in the multiple uses of the coastal zone and are integrated into coastal area management, planning and development.* * *

6.19 States should consider aquaculture, including culture-based fisheries, as a means to promote diversification of income and diet. In so doing, States should ensure that resources are used responsibly and adverse impacts on the environment and on local communities are minimized.

Article 7—Fisheries Management

7.1 General

7.1.1 States and all those engaged in fisheries management should, through an appropriate policy, legal and institutional framework, adopt measures for the long-term conservation and sustainable use of fisheries resources. Conservation and management measures, whether at local, national, subregional or regional levels, should be based on the best scientific evidence available and be designed to ensure the long-term sustainability of fishery resources at levels which promote the objective of their optimum utilization and maintain their availability for present and future generations; short term considerations should not compromise these objectives. * * *

7.1.3 For transboundary fish stocks, straddling fish stocks, highly migratory fish stocks and high seas fish stocks, where these are exploited by two or more States, the States concerned, including the relevant coastal States in the case of straddling and highly migratory stocks, should cooperate to ensure effective conservation and management of the resources. This should be achieved, where appropriate, through the establishment of a bilateral, subregional or regional fisheries organization or arrangement.* * *

7.5 Precautionary approach

7.5.1 States should apply the precautionary approach widely to conservation, management and exploitation of living aquatic resources in order to protect them and preserve the aquatic environment. The absence of adequate scientific information should not be used as a reason for postponing or failing to take conservation and management measures. 7.5.2 In implementing the precautionary approach, States should take into account, inter alia, uncertainties relating to the size and productivity of the stocks, reference points, stock condition in relation to such reference points, levels and distribution of fishing mortality and the impact of fishing activities, including discards, on non-target and associated or dependent species, as well as environmental and socio-economic conditions. 7.5.3 States and subregional or regional fisheries management organizations and arrangements should, on the basis of the best scientific evidence available, inter alia, determine:

a. stock specific target reference points, and, at the same time, the action to be taken if they are exceeded; and

b. stock-specific limit reference points, and, at the same time, the action to be taken if they are exceeded; when a limit reference point is approached, measures should be taken to ensure that it will not be exceeded.

7.5.4 In the case of new or exploratory fisheries, States should adopt as soon as possible cautious conservation and management measures, including, inter alia, catch limits and effort limits. Such measures should remain in force until there are sufficient data to allow assessment of the impact of the fisheries on the long-term sustainability of the stocks, whereupon conservation and management measures based on that assessment should be implemented. The latter measures should, if appropriate, allow for the gradual development of the fisheries.

NOTES & QUESTIONS

1. The Code of Conduct certainly says all the right things when it comes to fisheries management. But will it just be another in the long line of international environmental policy documents that said all the right things and, because of deficient international enforcement provisions, have had no meaningful impact? The FAO points to numerous bilateral, subregional, and regional actions inspired by the Code of Conduct. See FAO Fisheries Department, Code of Conduct for Responsible Fisheries, http://www.fao.org/fi/agreem/codecond/codecond.asp.

These too, however, may suffer from lack of adequate enforcement mechanisms or political will. Ultimately, the real test may be whether the Code of Conduct shapes domestic law reform. How well does U.S. fisheries law fare when tested against the Code of Conduct principles? What specific legal reforms would you institute to bring our law closer to the international ideal?

2. The basic jurisdictional conundrum of fisheries management is covered in extensive detail in Donna R. Christie, It Don't Come EEZ: The Failure and Future of Coastal State Fisheries Management, 14 J. OF TRANSNATIONAL LAW & POLICY, 1 (2004). Professor Christie argues that "the premise that coastal state jurisdiction over marine living resources to 200 miles offshore would prevent overexploitation of marine fisheries has proved to be flawed." Id. at 34. With the 200-mile EEZ being no panacea, to where should policy turn. She argues that the policies outlined in the FAO Code of Conduct and the United Nations' Agenda 21 would, if integrated into the domestic policies of coastal states, fulfill the promise of the 200-mile EEZ approach. The problem, of course, is that

"none of these documents are binding . . . and at this point cannot be characterized as customary international law creating international minimum standards
for EEZ management." *Id.* at 35.

3. Article 7.5 of the Code of Conduct endorses state adoption of what has come
to be known as the Precautionary Principle, which has become a bedrock of international environmental law and of many domestic legal regimes as well,
most notably that of Germany. At its core, the Precautionary Principle counsels
that scientific uncertainty should not be used to justify taking economically
appealing actions with potentially adverse environmental consequences. Stated
more proactively, scientific uncertainty ought not preclude regulation of economic activity if it is feared (but not necessarily known) that the environmental
consequences could be significant. In more concrete terms, the Precautionary
Principle suggests using cost-benefit analysis cautiously, as it is subject to
ends-driven manipulation, and emphasizing interdisciplinary, long-term, risk
averse approaches to decision making. *See* PERSPECTIVES ON THE PRECAUTION-
ARY PRINCIPLE (Ronnie Harding and Elizabeth Fisher eds., 1999); PROTECTING
PUBLIC HEALTH & THE ENVIRONMENT: IMPLEMENTING THE PRECAUTIONARY
PRINCIPLE (Carolyn Raffensperger and Joel Tickner eds., 1999). Beyond this,
little meat fills out the bones of the Precautionary Principle. It is found as almost a premise of many international policies such as the Code of Conduct. But
with no realistic proposition of enforcement in that realm, it remains largely a
principle and not a mandate at the international level. Many scientists and
legal scholars, therefore, are working feverishly to provide more definition to
the Precautionary Principle in a variety of domestic law contexts where enforcement can be more directly achieved.

Still, is the Precautionary Principle nonetheless comprised of too amorphous and potentially unstable a set of precepts to put forth as the foundation
of domestic fisheries management law? The Code of Conduct, for example,
leaves many open-ended questions unanswered in its call for member states to

> adopt as soon as possible cautious conservation and management
> measures, including, inter alia, catch limits and effort limits. Such
> measures should remain in force until there are sufficient data to allow
> assessment of the impact of the fisheries on the long-term sustainability of
> the stocks, whereupon conservation and management measures based on
> that assessment should be implemented. The latter measures should, if
> appropriate, allow for the gradual development of the fisheries.

How cautious is cautious enough? What is sufficient data? When is
long term sustainability achieved? How gradually should emerging fisheries be developed to be sufficiently precautionary? Some commentators contend that U.S. fisheries law does not go far enough explicitly to implement
the Precautionary Principle, yet they offer little concrete description of legal text that would do so and answer questions like these. *See, e.g.,* Michele
Territo, *The Precautionary Principle in Marine Fisheries Conservation and
the U.S. Sustainable Fisheries Act of 1996*, 24 VERMONT L. REV. 1351
(2000). One commentator goes so far as to argue that "to restore the severely depleted global stocks, countries must cede their national sovereignties
to international bodies and jurists must enforce the precautionary principle." Thomas A. Telesca, *Sovereignty or the Precautionary Principle: Which*

Will Save Our Fish?, 12 SOUTHEASTERN ENVTL. L.J. 23 (2003). Do you agree that such extreme measures are necessary, and if so, how likely are they to materialize? Other commentators focus on domestic policy, suggesting that the Sustainable Fisheries Act of 1996 "includes a precautionary approach to fisheries management in the U.S. Exclusive Enterprise Zone." Richard G. Hildreth, M. Casey Jarman, and Maggie Langlas, *Roles for the Precautionary Approach in U.S. Marine Resources Management*, 19 NATURAL RESOURCES & ENV'T 64 (Summer 2004). Clearly, however, there is no binding doctrine of international law requiring application of the precautionary principle in coastal nations' domestic fishery policies, and, as Professor Donna Christie points out, as for U.S. domestic policy there is no specific reference to the precautionary approach or the precautionary principle in the Sustainable Fisheries Act or implementing regulations. Why has the precautionary principle failed to gain traction as a binding legal principle? Do you believe our domestic law inadequately reflects the Precautionary Principle? What *specific* legal provisions would you draft to improve our precautionary performance?

4. How different are the three approaches to fisheries management covered in this section: the species-wide harvest limits applied under the conventional Fisheries Management Plan framework; the market-based approach of tradable Individual Fishing Quotas; and the U.N.'s Code of Conduct principles? Using the framework for evaluation of ecosystem management programs developed in Chapter 7 of this text, compare the three approaches:

	Metric	**Goals**	**Methods**
Conventional Fishery Management Plans			
Tradable Individual Fishing Quota			
U.N. Code of Conduct			

Note on Aquaculture

Article 6.19 of the Code of Conduct promotes use of aquaculture, which entails the controlled propagation of aquatic species for commercial, recreational, or public uses. Aquaculture already is a big business in the United States, accounting for almost $1 billion in production revenue. The epicenter of the industry is in the southeastern states, which account for two-third of production revenue, and the principal product is food fish, primarily catfish, trout, and salmon. *See* U.S. Department of Agriculture, National Agricultural Statistics Service, 1998 Census of Agriculture, *available at* http://www.nass.gov/census/census97/aquaculture.

Why isn't aquaculture the perfect answer to overfishing of wild species? The problem is that aquaculture presents its own set of environmental impacts, some quite alarming in potential. One concern is that fish may be farmed in areas where they are not native species, meaning that escaped eggs or fry have the potential to invade and disrupt local ecological dynamics. *See* Rosamond L. Naylor et al., *Aquaculture—A Gateway for Exotic Species*, 294 SCIENCE 1655 (2001). Even where they are local, farmed fish may have been genetically altered, such that intermingling with native species can alter population gene resources. Also, like terrestrial farms, fish farms take up space, often displacing valuable natural coastal habitat. And, also like some terrestrial farms, fish farming concentrates animal waste, parasites, and disease and discharges them into local ecosystems. *See* REBECCA J. GOLDBURG, MATTHEW S. ELLIOTT, AND ROSAMOND L. NAYLOR, MARINE AQUACULTURE IN THE UNITED STATES (2001) (science report prepared for the Pew Oceans Commission), *available at* http://www.pewtrusts.org/pdf/env pew oceans aquaculture.pdf; James S. Dana, *Aquaculture Production and Biodiversity Conservation*, 59 BIOSCIENCE 27 (2009); Martin Krkosek et al., *Declining Wild Salmon Populations in Relation to Parasites from Farm Salmon*, 318 SCIENCE 1772 (2007); Rosamond L. Naylor et al., *Effect of Aquaculture on World Fish Supplies*, 405 NATURE 1017 (2000). Ironically, one of the primary concerns with aquaculture is that many fish farms use fish feed made from processed wild fish. We are, in other words, zealously fishing one species in the wild to feed another in captivity. *See* REBECCA GOLDBERG ET AL., PEW OCEANS COMMISSION, MARINE AQUACULTURE IN THE UNITED STATES: ENVIRONMENTAL IMPACTS AND POLICY OPTIONS (2001). Some farmed species continue to require 5 kilograms of wild fish meal to produce 1 kilogram of product, thus fueling claims that aquaculture is a net drain on marine biomass. The diversion of this wild feed to farming also diverts it from the supply available to wild marine predator species. But people really started paying attention to the costs and benefits of farmed fish when a comprehensive study definitively showed that farmed salmon have higher levels of polychlorinated biphenyls and other pollutants than do wild-caught salmon. *See* Ronald A. Hites et al., *Global Assessment of Organic Contaminants in Farmed Salmon*, 303 SCIENCE 226 (2004). Does the Code of Conduct adequately warn of and balance these adverse consequences in its promotion of aquaculture?

Despite these environmental warnings, the sky-rocketing rise of the aquaculture industry continues to be a lead story of fisheries policy. And many other countries are investing more heavily in aquaculture than the United States. According to the 2010 United Nations Food and Agriculture Organization report on *The State of World Fisheries and Aquaculture*, the United States ranks 13th in total aquaculture production behind China, India, Viet Nam, Indonesia, Thailand, Bangladesh, Norway, Chile, the Philippines, Japan, Egypt, and Myanmar. Indeed, the United States imports significant volumes of marine aquaculture products from these and other countries, resulting in an annual seafood trade deficit of well over $10 billion. Aquaculture now supplies one-third of the seafood humans consume.

In the United States, consumption of farmed seafood is dominated by shrimp and salmon. Professor Josh Eagle describes farmed salmon as a " 'super-commodity,' a uniform product available fresh and on demand around the globe." Josh Eagle et al., *Why Farm Salmon Outcompete Fishery Salmon*, 28 MARINE POLICY 259 (2004). Naturally, the ability to produce a sustained and secure supply of nutritious seafood is an important domestic and international policy goal, and aquaculture clearly is moving us closer in that direction. But Eagle contends that "the sharp increase in the production of fresh, farm salmon has rearranged the economic and political landscape of the fishing industry." *Id.* at 259. Alaska, the source of over half of the world's salmon as recently as 1980, now supplies only 15 percent, with most of the rest coming from net-pen farms along the coasts of Norway, Scotland, Chile, and Canada (Alaska bans salmon farming). Eagle contends that the United States has responded primarily through subsidies to the Alaska salmon fishing industry rather than through regulatory reform that could make the industry more competitive. And even the subsidies are insufficient to make the Alaskan industry price competitive. For example, your Tennessee-based author can obtain fresh, wild-caught Copper River King salmon from Alaska on demand during its season, but the price is twice that of fresh farmed salmon from Chile.

In the United States, regulation of aquaculture remains in its fledgling stages, described by many as "muddled and incoherent." Thomas R. Head, III, *Fishy Business—Regulating Aquaculture Operations in the United States*, 18 NATURAL RESOURCES & ENV'T 21 (Summer 2003); *see also* Graham M. Wilson, *A Day on the Fish Farm: FDA and the Regulation of Aquaculture*, 23 VA. ENVTL. L. REV. 351 (2004); Ann Powers, *Farming the Ocean*, NATURAL RESOURCES & ENV'T, Fall 2007, at 45. The aquaculture industry in the U.S. remains focused primarily on freshwater species such as catfish and tilapia, and thus relies mainly on pond and flow-through "raceway" operations rather than open water net pens used for salmon and other marine species. Until recently, most regulation of the industry had been "soft," relying on voluntary compliance with loosely defined best management practices. The U.S. Environmental Protection Agency had for many years designated certain aquaculture operations as concentrated aquatic animal production (CAAP) facilities based on thresholds of production and feed quantity, making them subject to regulation of point source discharges under the Clean Water Act (see Chapter 10 of the main text), but it had not promulgated effluent standards for such operations. One legal uncertainty was whether the CWA could apply at all to fish waste discharges from CAAPs, given that the focus of the statute is on human and industrial waste. *See* APHETI v. Taylor Resources, Inc., 299 F.3d 1007 (9th Cir. 2002) (mussel waste from mussel-harvesting operation that did not add food or chemicals to the water were not discharges subject to the CWA); *but see* U.S. PIRG v. Stolt Sea Farming Inc., 301 F.Supp.2d 46 (D. Me.2004) (salmon farm is subject to CWA because of introduction of chemicals, feed, and antibiotics and because of salmon release of diseases, viruses, parasites, and waste).

As a result of litigation over the lack of standards, in 2004 EPA promulgated effluent standards for CAAPs which regulate the discharge of nutrients, solids, and other chemicals directly to waters of the United States from flow-through, recirculating, and net pen systems. *See* 69 Fed. Reg. 51892 (Aug. 23, 2004). EPA defined CAAPs as aquaculture operations that produce over 100,000 pounds of product per year and estimated that approximately 245 of the 4,200 aquaculture operations in the nation will be subject to the rule. The rule requires that all regulated CAAP facilities:

- Prevent discharge of drugs and pesticides that have been spilled and minimize discharges of excess feed.

- Regularly maintain production and wastewater treatment systems.

- Keep records on numbers and weights of animals, amounts of feed, and frequency of cleaning, inspections, maintenance, and repairs.

- Train staff to prevent and respond to spills and to properly operate and maintain production and wastewater treatment systems.

- Report the use of experimental animal drugs or drugs that are not used in accordance with label requirements.

- Report failure of or damage to a containment system.

- Develop, maintain, and certify a Best Management Practice plan that describes how the facility will meet the requirements.

The rule requires flow-through and recirculating discharge facilities to minimize the discharge of solids such as uneaten feed, settled solids, and animal carcasses. For open water systems the rule requires the facilities to:

- Use active feed monitoring and management strategies to allow only the least possible uneaten feed to accumulate beneath the nets.

- Properly dispose of feed bags, packaging materials, waste rope, and netting.

- Limit as much as possible wastewater discharges resulting from the transport or harvest of the animals.

- Prevent the discharge of dead animals in the wastewater.

How effective do these restrictions strike you in combating the problems associated with aquaculture? For EPA's summary and collection of the laws and regulations applicable to aquaculture, see http://www.epa.gov/oecaagct/anaqulaw.html.

On June 9, 2011, NOAA released its first set of national aquaculture policy for operations in federal *coastal* waters. NOAA designed the policy to establish a framework to allow sustainable domestic aquaculture to contribute to the U.S. seafood supply, support coastal communities and important commercial and recreational fisheries, and help to restore species and habitat. NOAA identified nine actions for Regional Fisheries Councils to promote science-based management of aquaculture consistent with natural resources protection and collaboration among resource users and management agencies. Priorities include the following:

- making timely management decisions based on the best available science

- continuing to advance aquaculture science;

- ensuring aquaculture decisions protect wild species and healthy coastal and ocean ecosystems;

- developing aquaculture in locations compatible with other uses;

- working with partners domestically and internationally;

- and promoting a level playing field for U.S. aquaculture businesses engaged in international trade.

See
http://www.nmfs.noaa.gov/aquaculture/policy/2011_policies_homepage.html.
NOAA's policy, however, does not address the major freshwater sector of aquaculture in the United States. Moreover, Regional Fisheries Councils manage fishing, whereas aquaculture is farming. Does the United States need a dedicated legal regime for aquaculture?

(2) Protecting Fish Habitat

Prior to the Sustainable Fisheries Act of 1996 (SFA), the primary focus of fishery management under the Magnuson-Stevens Act had been on regulating fish harvests. The quality of fish habitat, however, is undeniably a significant factor in fishery harvest sustainability. Thus, the SFA introduced a new component to federal regulation of fisheries management—the Essential Fish Habitat (EFH) program.

The statutory provisions for EFH are quite streamlined, establishing two core programs supported by a relatively tame regulatory authority:

16 U.S.C. § 1855

(b) FISH HABITAT.—

(1) (A) The Secretary shall, within 6 months of the date of enactment of the Sustainable Fisheries Act, establish by regulation guidelines to assist the Councils in the description and identification of essential fish habitat in fishery management plans (including adverse impacts on such habitat) and in the consideration of actions to ensure the conservation and enhancement of such habitat.* * *

(2) Each Federal agency shall consult with the Secretary with respect to any action authorized, funded, or undertaken, or proposed to be authorized, funded, or undertaken, by such agency that may adversely affect any essential fish habitat identified under this Act.* * *

(4) (A) If the Secretary receives information from a Council or Federal or State agency or determines from other sources that an action authorized, funded, or undertaken, or proposed to be authorized, funded, or undertaken, by any State or Federal agency would adversely affect any essential fish habitat identified under this Act, the Secretary shall recommend to such agency measures that can be taken by such agency to conserve such habitat.

The National Marine Fisheries Service (NMFS) has promulgated a series of comprehensive regulations to implement these EFH provisions. The agency adopted a proposed rule in early 1997, *see* 62 Fed. Reg. 19723 (Apr. 23, 1997), and an interim final rule late that year, *see* 62 Fed. Reg. 66531 (Dec. 19, 1997), all the while soliciting and integrating public comment into a final rule making. The agency's regulatory efforts culminated in January 2002 with promulgation of a comprehensive final rule, excerpts of which are reproduced below. Under the final NMFS regulations, the basic scheme for EFH follows the SFA's two-staged process of EFH identification followed by federal agency consultation that leads to, at most, voluntary recommendations for EFH management.

First, Regional Fishery Management Councils (Councils) must identify in their Fishery Management Plans (FMPs) the EFH for each life stage of each managed species in the fishery management unit. Councils must identify as EFH those habitats that are necessary to the species for spawning, breeding, feeding, or growth to maturity. Councils must describe EFH in text and must provide maps of the geographic locations of EFH or the geographic boundaries within which EFH for each species and life stage is found. Councils also can identify EFH that is especially important ecologically or particularly vulnerable to degradation as "habitat areas of particular concern" (HAPC) to help provide additional focus for conservation efforts. HAPC status, however, carries with it no additional substantive protections or procedural safeguards. Councils must evaluate the potential adverse effects of fishing activities on EFH and must include in FMPs management measures that minimize adverse effects to the extent practicable. Councils must identify other nonfishing activities that may adversely affect EFH and recommend actions to reduce or eliminate these effects.

Once EFH is identified, NMFS and the Councils must implement the EFH coordination, consultation, and recommendation requirements of the Magnuson-Stevens Act. NMFS will make available descriptions and maps of EFH to promote EFH conservation and enhancement. The regulations encourage Federal agencies to use existing environmental review procedures to fulfill the requirement to consult with NMFS on actions they fund, carry out, or authorize that may adversely affect EFH, and the regulations contain procedures for abbreviated or expanded consultation in cases where no other environmental review process is available. Consultations may conducted at a programmatic and/or project-specific level. In cases where adverse effects from a type of actions will be minimal, both individually and cumulatively, a General Concurrence procedure further simplifies the consultation requirements. The regulations encourage coordination between NMFS and the Councils in the development of nonbinding EFH Conservation Recommendations to federal or state agencies for actions that would adversely affect EFH. Federal agencies must respond in writing within 30 days of receiving EFH Conservation Recommendations from NMFS. If the action agency's decision is inconsistent with the NMFS's EFH Conservation Recommendations, the agency must explain its reasoning and NMFS may request further review of the decision.

NMFS's rule making was not without controversy. Although the EFH program is not nearly as imposing as the framework the Endangered Species Act establishes for protection of species and their habitat, some fishing industry interests were concerned that NMFS may go too far in regulation, while many conservation groups were concerned that NMFS may fail to give EFH any teeth at all. Some of the more interesting and controversial provisions of the rule are presented in the following excerpt.

Department of Commerce, *National Marine Fisheries Service, Magnuson-Stevens Act Provisions; Essential Fish Habitat (EFH)*

National Marine Fisheries Service, 2002.
67 Federal Register 2343.

SUMMARY: NMFS issues this final rule to revise the regulations implementing the essential fish habitat (EFH) provisions of the Magnuson-Stevens Fishery Conservation and Management Act (Magnuson-Stevens Act). This rule establishes guidelines to assist the Regional Fishery Management Councils (Councils) and the Secretary of Commerce (Secretary) in the description and identification of EFH in fishery management plans (FMPs), the identification of adverse effects to EFH, and the identification of actions required to conserve and enhance EFH. These regulations also detail procedures the Secretary (acting through NMFS), other Federal agencies, and the Councils will use to coordinate, consult, or provide recommendations on Federal and state actions that may adversely affect EFH. The intended effect of the rule is to promote the protection, conservation, and enhancement of EFH. NMFS amends 50 CFR part 600 as follows:

§ 600.10 Definitions

Essential fish habitat (EFH) means those waters and substrate necessary to fish for spawning, breeding, feeding, or growth to maturity. . . "necessary" means the habitat required to support a sustainable fishery and the managed species' contribution to a healthy ecosystem;

Subpart J—Essential Fish Habitat (EFH)

§ 6000.810 Definitions and word usage

Habitat areas of particular concern means those areas of EFH identified pursuant to § 600.812(a)(8). Healthy ecosystem means an ecosystem where ecological productive capacity is maintained, diversity of the flora and fauna is preserved, and the ecosystem retains the ability to regulate itself. Such an ecosystem should be similar to comparable, undisturbed ecosystems with regard to standing crop, productivity, nutrient dynamics, trophic structure, species richness, stability, resilience, contamination levels, and the frequency of diseased organisms.

§ 600.815 Contents of Fishery Management Plans

(a) Mandatory contents—

(1) Description and identification of EFH—

(i) Overview. FMPs must describe and identify EFH in text that clearly states the habitats are habitat types determined to be EFH for each life stage of the managed species. FMPs should explain the physical, biological, and chemical characteristics of EFH and, if known, how these characteristics influence the use of EFH by the species/life stage. FMPs must identify the specific geographic location or extent of habitats described as EFH. FMPs must include maps of the geographic locations of EFH or the geographic boundaries within which EFH for each species and life stage is found.* * *

(iv) EFH determination

(C) If a species is overfished and habitat loss or degradation may be contributing to the species being identified as overfished, all habitats currently used by the species may be considered essential in addition to certain historic habitats that are necessary to support rebuilding the fishery and for which restoration is technologically and economically feasible. Once the fishery is no longer considered overfished, the EFH identification should be reviewed and amended, if appropriate.

(D) Areas described as EFH will normally be greater than or equal to aquatic areas that have been identified as "critical habitat" for any managed species listed as threatened or endangered under the Endangered Species Act.

(E) Ecological relationships among species and between the species and their habitat require, where possible, that an ecosystem approach be used in determining the EFH of a managed species. EFH must be designated for each managed species, but where appropriate, may be designated for assemblages of species or life stages that have similar habitat needs and requirements. If grouping species or using species assemblages for the purpose of designation EFH, FMPs must include a justification and scientific rationale. The extent of the EFH should be based on the judgment of the Secretary and the appropriate Council(s) regarding the quantity and quality of habitat that are necessary to maintain a sustainable fishery and the managed species' contribution to a healthy ecosystem.* * *

(2) *Fishing activities that may adversely affect EFH*

(ii) *Minimizing adverse effects.* Each FMP must minimize to the extent practicable adverse effects from fishing on EFH, including EFH designated under other Federal FMPs. Councils must act to prevent, mitigate, or minimize any adverse effects from fishing, to the extent practicable, if there is evidence that a fishing activity adversely affects EFH in a manner that is more than minimal and not temporary in nature. . .

(iii) *Practicability.* In determining whether it is practicable to minimize an adverse effect from fishing, Councils should consider the nature and extent of the adverse effect on EFH and the long and short-term costs and benefits of potential management measures to EFH, associated fisheries, and the nation, consistent with national standard

7. In determining whether management measures are practicable, Councils are not required to perform formal cost/benefit analysis.

(iv) *Options for managing adverse effects from fishing.* Fishery management options may include, but are not limited to:

(A) *Fishing equipment restrictions...*

(B) *Time/area closures...*

(C) *Harvest limits...*

(4) *Non-fishing related activities that may adversely affect EFH.* FMPs must identify activities other than fishing that may adversely affect EFH. Broad categories of such activities include, but are not limited to: dredging, filling, excavation, mining, impoundment, discharge, water diversions, thermal additions, actions that contribute to non-point source pollution and sedimentation, introduction of potentially hazardous materials, introduction of exotic species, and the conversion of aquatic habitat that may eliminate, diminish, or disrupt the functions of EFH. For each activity, the FMP should describe known and potential adverse effects to EFH.* * *

(7) *Prey species.* Loss of prey may be an adverse effect on EFH and managed species because the presence of prey makes waters and substrate function as feeding habitat, and the definition of EFH includes waters and substrate necessary to fish for feeding. Therefore, actions that reduce the availability of major prey species, either through direct harm or capture, or through adverse impacts to the prey species, may be considered adverse effects on EFH if such actions reduce the quality of EFH. FMPs should list the major prey species for the species in the fishery management unit and discuss the location of prey species' habitat. Adverse effects on prey species and their habitats may result from fishing and non-fishing activities.

(8) *Identification of habitat areas of particular concern.* FMPs should identify specific types or areas of habitat within EFH as habitat areas of particular concern based on one or more of the following considerations:

(i) The importance of the ecological function provided by the habitat.

(ii) The extent to which the habitat is sensitive to human-induced environmental degradation.

(iii) Whether, and to what extent, development activities are, or will be, stressing the habitual type.

(iv) The rarity of the habitat type.

Subpart KBEFH Coordination, Consultation, and Recommendations

§ 600.905 Purpose, scope, and NMFS/Council cooperation.

(a) *Purpose.* These procedures address the coordination, consultation, an recommendation requirements of sections 305(b)(1)(D) and 305(b)(2-4) of the Magnuson-Stevens Act. The purpose of these procedures is to promote the protection of EFH in the review of Federal and state actions that may adversely affect EFH.

(b) *Scope.* Section 305(b)(1)(D) of the Magnuson-Stevens Act requires the Secretary to coordinate with, and provide information to, other Federal agencies regarding the conservation and enhancement of EFH. Section 305(b)(2) requires all Federal agencies to consult with the Secretary on all actions or proposed actions authorized, funded, or undertaken by the agency that may adversely affect EFH. Sections 305(b)(3) and (4) direct the Secretary and the Councils to provide comments and EFH Conservation Recommendations to Federal or state agencies on actions that affect EFH. Such recommendations may include measures to avoid, minimize, mitigate, or otherwise offset adverse effects on EFH resulting from actions authorized, funded, or undertaken by that agency. Section 305(b)(4)(B) requires Federal agencies to respond in writing to such comments.

NOTES & QUESTIONS

1. NMFS clearly adopted a watershed-based approach to EFH management and conservation. Consider how it handled the charge that in so doing it acted outside its statutory authority:

> Comments on Using an Ecosystem or Watershed Approach to Resource Management

> Comment A: A number of commenters representing non-fishing interest state that the Magnuson-Stevens Act does not authorize a risk-averse or ecosystem approach to EFH. These commenters thought that the focus should be limited to fish species and not ecosystem principles.

> Response A: NMFS provided a detailed response to this comment in the preamble to the interim final rule at 62 FR 66532–66533, and the response remains the same. In summary, the Magnuson-Stevens Act provides authority for the link between EFH and the managed species' contribution to a healthy ecosystem in a number of places. Ecosystem concepts are common in the statutory definitions of "fishery resources," "conservation and management," and "optimum." The fact that the Magnuson-Stevens Act directs the Councils to address the degradation and loss of EFH from both fishing and non-fishing activities through conservation and enhancement measures further reflects support for the ecosystem-based management of marine and anadromous fisheries. Ecosystem management encourages sustainable resource use and recognized the uncertainties inherent in management and the need to make risk-averse decisions. This regulation embraces those concepts and urges Councils to seek

environmental sustainability in fishery management, within the current statutorily prescribed fishery management framework (i.e., management by FMPs).

67 Fed. Reg. 2349.

This response resembles the approach other resource management agencies have taken when responding to similar "ultra vires" claims lodged against their adoption of ecosystem management principles. Because few federal laws explicitly authorize ecosystem management as a policy model or goal, agencies are left to wedging it into existing laws through open ended statutory terms that are sufficiently flexible to encompass ecosystem management principles. A statutorily-specified resource "sustainability" goal, in particular, is amenable as administratively-devised justifications for ecosystem management. Should agencies be allowed to graft ecosystem management onto existing laws that clearly were passed without explicit congressional intent endorsing its underlying principles? Can an agency interpret sustainability to mean one thing at one time (e.g., sustained economic yield) and later to mean quite another thing (e.g., sustained ecosystem dynamics) with no change in the statute? Of course, NMFS can point to the Sustainable Fisheries Act as a legislative endorsement of some change in approach, but was it an endorsement of ecosystem management? For more on this theme, see Lee Banaka and Dennis Nixon, *Essential Fish Habitat and Coastal Zone Management: Business As Usual Under the Magnuson-Stevens Act?*, 30 GOLDEN GATE U. L. REV. 969 (2000).

2. Many fisheries biologists argue that conventional fisheries management policy for too long ignored the obvious connection between habitat and fishery. The dogma of catch limits and time/place limits does absolutely nothing to advance habitat conservation, yet, according to some research, investment in habitat conservation, particularly of coastal and inland wetlands, could yield greater fishery performance results at less cost. *See* Special Focus Issue: *Wetland Dependent Fisheries*, 22 NATIONAL WETLANDS NEWSLETTER 1 (Nov.-Dec. 2000). Will the EFH program take advantage of that connection? *See* 67 Fed. Reg. 2347 (affirming EFH can include wetland areas).

3. As fruitful as wetland conservation may be to fisheries performance, haven't we seen time and again that land-based upland activities can profoundly degrade coastal and estuarine resources? EFH, however, is defined as including only waters and substrate, *see* 16 U.S.C. § 1802(10), thus precluding designation of upland areas as EFH. By contrast, designation of critical habitat for species listed under the Endangered Species Act can include areas outside the species' occupied range. *See* 16 U.S.C 1532(5)(A). Why did Congress not take the same approach for EFH? For comparison of the EFH and ESA programs on this and other scores, see Kim Diana Connolly, *An Introduction to the Essential Fish Habitat (EFH) Consultation Process for the South Atlantic Region*, 11 SOUTHEASTERN ENVTL. L.J. 1 (2002); Kristen M. Fletcher and Sharonne E. O'Shea, *Essential Fish Habitat: Does Calling it Essential Make it So?*, 30 ENVTL. L. 1 (2000). Notwithstanding that EFH cannot include upland areas, can activities on upland areas that affect EFH areas be subjected to EFH consultation procedures? How would you make the argument under the statute and regulations that such an approach could be taken? If you have studied the Endangered species Act in this or another course, compare the EFH program to the ESA's critical habitat program. Which covers more species? Which has more regulatory clout? Which has been more effective for species conservation?

4. One of the more controversial aspects of the EFH program is the focus NMFS has put on non-fishing activities. Fishing may deplete fish, but generally without affecting the physical or biological components of habitat. Yet fishing techniques can have dramatic impacts on fish habitat in some contexts. In particular, there is mounting evidence that trawling, which drags large nets across the ocean floor, has scraped large areas clean of all functional habitat. *See* David Malakoff, *Papers Posit Grave Impact of Trawling*, 282 SCIENCE 2168 (1988). NMFS has recognized that trawling's "mobile fishing gear" can reduce the structural complexity of fish habitat, making it more difficult for fish to hide from their predators and interfering with benthic (bottom) ecosystem processes. *See* NMFS, Essential Fish Habitat: FAQs (Jan. 2002).

Note on the Marine Mammal Protection Act

The focus of the preceding materials has been on fish species—the biologically-relevant jurisdictional limit of the Magnuson-Stevens Act. But as debate over fishery management emerged as a serious legislative initiative in the 1970s, support also built for an initiative directed at conservation of marine mammals. Many scientists and conservationists portrayed marine mammals as not only ecologically important, but also ethically entitled to protection given their apparent intelligence and social behavior. Although a patchwork of federal and state laws provided some level of protection to a limited array of marine mammals, this approach proved to be neither coordinated nor effective. A number of highly publicized stories—such as the slaughter of harp seal pups in Canada, the hunting of several whale species to near extinction, and the killing of dolphins and porpoises as bycatch from industrialized tuna fishing operations—brought the problem into sharp focus. By the early 1970s, the calls had grown quite loud in support of broader federal protective measures for all marine mammals. The Marine Mammal Protection Act of 1972 (MMPA), 16 USC §§ 1361-1421h, is designed to provide such comprehensive levels of protection to this other valuable form of living marine resources.

The primary goal of the MMPA is to "maintain the health and stability of the marine ecosystem," which the statute links to a marine mammal's "optimum sustainable population keeping in mind the carrying capacity of the habitat." 16 U.S.C. § 1361(6). At the core of the statute, therefore, is this notion of an optimal sustainable population, defined as "the number of animals which will result in the maximum productivity of the population or the species, keeping in mind the carrying capacity of the habitat and the health of the ecosystem of which they form a constituent element." *Id.* § 1362(9). To achieve this ideal for marine mammal species, the original enactment established a blanket moratorium on "take" of marine mammals, *id.* § 1372 (a), defining take, much as Congress did later in the Endangered Species Act, to include such acts as killing, capturing, harming, and harassing. *Id.* § 1362(12). This moratorium, however, excluded certain activities, the most significant of which was "incidental taking" of marine mammals in the course of commercial fishing operations—i.e., bycatch of marine mammals. *Id.* § 1371(a)(2). Congress added this exemption in response to concerns that after years of little or no protection, imposing the blanket taking moratorium on commercial fishing for all marine mammal species could seriously disrupt the industry. Thus, instead of being subject to the blanket moratorium, commercial fishing operations were required to obtain permits from the Department of Commerce, acting through the National Marine Fisheries Service (NMFS) in consultation with the independent Marine Mammal Commission, to authorize such bycatch takes.

NMFS implemented the commercial fishing incidental take program through permits designed to allow takes only of "nondepleted" marine mammal stocks. The initial goal of the permit program, moreover, was to reach "zero mortality" through the adoption of practicable fishing techniques. In practice, however, the permit program was rather laxly administered, and no clear statutory standard allowed conservationists to invoke rigorous judicial review. Amendments in 1981 and 1984 attempted to reach compromises, focusing in particular on the tuna-dolphin problem, but in general the framework remained unsatisfying to both fishing and conservation interests through the 1980s.

This uneasy state of affairs was rocked in 1988 when, in Kokechik Fishermen's Association v. Secretary of Commerce, 839 F.2d 795 (D.C. Cir. 1988), the D.C. Circuit held that NMFS had improperly implemented the incidental take permit system because it had failed to ensure that the authorized commercial fishing operations would not also result in takings of depleted stocks or of stocks whose status had not been determined. The case had been brought by Alaskan subsistence salmon fishing interests challenging NMFS's issuance of a general incidental take permit to Japanese operations in the Pacific Northwest, which had authorized take of over 6000 Dall's porpoises over a three-year period. But the plaintiffs got more than they bargained for. Given how indiscriminate commercial fishing is in terms of ability to screen out particular bycatch species, other fisheries in U.S. waters that had the benefit of general or "small scale" incidental take permits were in the same boat, so to speak, as the Japanese salmon fishing operations. Strict application of Kokechik would have required in practical terms either shutting down most domestic commercial fishing or abandoning the MMPA.

To avoid having to make that choice, and to buy time to design an alternative, Congress in 1988 established a five-year exemption from the incidental take permit requirement for vessels that allowed NMFS to station observers aboard to study more closely the impacts of fishing on marine mammals. 16 U.S.C. § 1383a. Along with the Regional Fisheries Management Councils and the Marine Mammal Commission, NMFS was required to develop a proposal based on its study that would more effectively manage the interaction between marine mammals and commercial fishing. The agencies submitted their proposal on January 1, 1992, which fishing and conservation interests alike criticized as based on insufficient evidence. The fishing and conservation interests crafted a joint counterproposal, which NMFS in turn criticized as administratively impracticable. The battle eventually led to the adoption of sweeping amendments to the MMPA in 1994. See Pub. L. No. 103–238, 108 Stat. 532 (1994).

One of the key changes the amendments made was to replace the incidental take permit requirement with a program for establishing "Take Reduction Plans" and related regulatory authorities. Under this approach, NMFS must prepare and periodically revise stock assessment reports for all marine mammals that reside in U.S. waters, including population estimates, productivity rates, mortality rates, geographic range, and estimated "potential biological removal" (PBR)—the maximum number of animals, excluding natural mortality, that the stock can withstand losing without affecting its ability to reach and maintain an optimal sustainable population level. 16 U.S.C. § 1386. Any stock for which human-caused mortality exceeds the PBR, as well as any stock designated as depleted under the MMPA or as endangered or threatened under the Endangered Species Act, is designated a "strategic stock." *Id.* § 1362(19). If NMFS determines that a fishery's operations frequently or occasionally cause mortality or serious injury to a strategic stock, the relevant fishing and conservation interests must work with NMFS to develop a Take Reduction Plan. *Id.* § 1387(f). The plan must have as its short-term goal to reduce mortality to PBR levels, and as its five-year goal to reduce fishing impacts to "insignificant levels approaching a zero mortality and serious injury rate." *Id.* § 1387(f)(2). NMFS is authorized in the plans to adopt time, place, gear, and technique restrictions on fishing operations in order to achieve PBR. If the fishery complies with the plan, it has complied with the MMPA incidental take prohibition.

As some commentators have observed, the 1994 amendments moved the MMPA away from the original "presumption of sacredness," under which all marine mammals received blanket protection from take in the absence of an incidental take permit, to a regime closer to the sustainable yield approach of the Magnuson-Stevens Act (and many other public resource management laws discussed in other chapters of this text). *See* George A. Chmael II et al., *The 1994 Amendments to the Marine Mammal Protection Act*, 9 NATURAL RESOURCES & ENV'T 18 (Spring 1995). Other commentators have noted the apparently intentional ambiguities Congress has sprinkled into the statute that vex attempts to pin down congressional intent. For example, the statute states that "[w]henever consistent with" the primary objective of maintaining the health and stability of the marine ecosystem, "it should be the goal to obtain an optimum sustainable population," yet it is not clear under any provision of the statute when achieving optimum sustainable population would be inconsistent with the health and stability of the marine ecosystem. *See* MICHAEL J. BEAN & MELANIE J. ROWLAND, THE EVOLUTION OF NATIONAL WILDLIFE LAW 135–36 (3d ed. 1997).

Also, although the greater focus the 1994 amendments brought to stock assessment may suggest endorsement of an ecosystem management approach to marine mammal habitat and ecosystem components—after all, that is the statute's expressed purpose—the statute never has required any formal ecosystem management framework. The statute repeatedly defines terms, such as optimum sustainable population, with the suggestion that it is "keeping in mind the carrying capacity of the habitat," but that is where habitat is kept-in mind only. The 1994 amendments also introduced several ecosystem study and monitoring programs, but no authority to manage habitat or other ecosystem components. *See* Susan C. Alker, *The Marine Mammal Protection Act: Refocusing the Approach to Conservation*, 44 UCLA L. REV. 527 (1996). Overall, then, the MMPA stands as yet another example of how identifying the "law" of ecosystem management is often really an exercise in piecing together bits of legislation into incomplete, but sometimes effective, programs of regulation and conservation.

b. MARINE PROTECTED AREAS

One ecosystem management approach we have seen used frequently in terrestrial settings is preservation of the ecological status quo, at least as nearly as possible, through creation of refuges, wilderness areas, and other land reserves. The Marine Protection, Research, and Sanctuaries Act of 1972 (MPRSA), 16 U.S.C. §§ 1431-1447(f), provides the analogous authority for coastal and marine ecosystems. The MPRSA authorizes the Secretary of Commerce, acting through the National Ocean Service (NOS), to "designate any discrete area of the marine environment as a national marine sanctuary and promulgate regulations implementing the designation." *Id.* § 1433(a). The factors NOS must use in determining sanctuary status include "the area's natural resource and ecological qualities, including its contribution to biological productivity, maintenance of ecosystem structure, . . . and the biogeographic representation of the site." *Id.* § 1433(b)(1)(A). Extensive consultation and notice requirements attach to the sanctuary designation process, requiring NOS to notify affected federal, state, and local entities, prepare an environmental assessment, and complete public notice and comment. *See id.* § 1434.

Once designated, national marine sanctuaries are generally managed for limited multiple uses such as recreation, education, commercial fishing, and shipping, though resource uses such as fishing are subject to regulation. *Id.* § 1431. Regulations thus vary by sanctuary, but, overall, NOS must facilitate public and private uses of the resources within sanctuaries "to the extent compatible with the primary objective of resource protection." *Id.* § 1431(b)(2). Also, federal agencies must consult with NOS regarding actions they undertake, inside or outside the sanctuary, that are likely to "destroy, cause the loss of, or injure any sanctuary resource." *Id.* § 1434(d)(1)(A). NOS can recommend "reasonable and prudent alternatives" to the action, and the action agency must justify any departure from them through a written statement. *Id.* § 1434(d).

The most potentially controversial exercise of conservation authority in sanctuaries involves the power NOS has to restrict commercial fishing. But NOS is limited in this respect by a cumbersome process and difficult statutory burdens. Regional Fishing Councils established under the Magnuson-Stevens Act (see this chapter, *supra*) are entitled to decide whether fishing regulations are needed in a sanctuary and, if so, to draft them. A Council's decision "shall be accepted and issued as proposed regulations by the Secretary unless the Secretary finds that the Council's action fails to fulfill the purposes and policies of this chapter and the goals and objectives of the proposed designation." *Id.* § 1434(a)(5). That burden, plus the agency's obligation to facilitate sanctuary resource use, make it unlikely that NOS will employ its regulatory authority in a way that restricts commercial fishery access beyond the Councils' wishes. Indeed, most litigation over NOS regulations has involved restrictions on recreational pursuits such as diving and personal watercraft, with courts generally upholding the restrictions as within the agency's authority. *See* Craft v. National Park Service, 34 F.3d 918 (9th Cir.1994) (diving); Personal Watercraft Industry Association v. Department of Commerce, 48 F.3d 540 (D.C. Cir.1995) (small craft use); United States v. Fisher, 22 F.3d 262 (11th Cir.1994) (salvage collectors).

Through its Office of the National Marine Sanctuaries, NOS now administers over a dozen national marine sanctuaries located throughout the Pacific and Atlantic coasts, the Gulf of Mexico, Hawaii, and other United States territories. They range in size from the one-quarter square mile Fagatele Bay sanctuary in American Samoa, to the 5,300 square-mile Monteray Bay sanctuary on the California coast. The total protected area is nearly 18,000 square miles. NOS has issued consolidated regulations for the sanctuary system, see 15 C.F.R. part 922, and descriptions of the program and the various sanctuaries are available at the NOS website, National Marine Sanctuaries, http://www.sanctuaries.nos.noaa.gov.

Although many observers laud its objectives, few rave about the National Marine Sanctuary program's accomplishments. The designation process has proven cumbersome and politically handicapped, and meaningful conservation is not guaranteed for a designated sanctuary in any event. *See* David Owen, *The Disappointing History of the National Marine Sanctuaries Act*, N.Y.U. ENVTL. L.J. 711 (2003); MICHAEL J. BEAN AND MELANIE J. ROWLAND, THE EVOLUTION OF NATIONAL WILDLIFE LAW 338–40 (3rd ed. 1997). Hence, in order to expand on the ideal of marine sanctuaries embodied in the National Marine Sanctuaries program, in May 2000 President Clinton issued the following Executive Order to coordinate a system "Marine Protected Areas" (MPA) that would include the sanctuaries and any other marine area protected under related federal laws. The term "marine protected area" has been in use for over two decades, and the practice of establishing marine protected areas has been around for centuries. A marine protected area has come to mean different things to different people, based primarily on the level of protection provided by the MPA. Some see MPAs as sheltered or reserved areas where little, if any, use or human disturbance should be permitted. Others see them as specially managed areas designed to enhance multiple uses such as recreation, fishing, and mineral exploration. Consider how President Clinton defined the term and outlined its management implications in his 2000 Executive Order:

Executive Order 13158, Marine Protected Areas
The President of the United States, 2000.
65 Federal Register 34909.

By the authority vested in me as President by the Constitution and the laws of the United States of America and in furtherance of the purposes of the National Marine Sanctuaries Act (16 U.S.C. 1431 et seq.), National Wildlife Refuge System Administration Act of 1966 (16 U.S.C. 668dd-ee), National Park Service Organic Act (16 U.S.C. 1 et seq.), National Historic Preservation Act (16 U.S.C. 470 et seq.), Wilderness Act (16 U.S.C. 1131 et seq.), Magnuson-Stevens Fishery Conservation and Management Act (16 U.S.C. 1801 et seq.), Coastal Zone Management Act (16 U.S.C. 1451 et seq.), Endangered Species Act of 1973 (16 U.S.C. 1531 et seq.), Marine Mammal Protection Act (16 U.S.C. 1362 et seq.), Clean Water Act of 1977

(33 U.S.C. 1251 et seq.), National Environmental Policy Act, as amended (42 U.S.C. 4321 et seq.), Outer Continental Shelf Lands Act (42 U.S.C. 1331 et seq.), and other pertinent statutes, it is ordered as follows:

Section 1. Purpose. This Executive Order will help protect the significant natural and cultural resources within the marine environment for the benefit of present and future generations by strengthening and expanding the Nation's system of marine protected areas (MPAs). An expanded and strengthened comprehensive system of marine protected areas throughout the marine environment would enhance the conservation of our Nation's natural and cultural marine heritage and the ecologically and economically sustainable use of the marine environment for future generations. To this end, the purpose of this order is to, consistent with domestic and international law: (a) strengthen the management, protection, and conservation of existing marine protected areas and establish new or expanded MPAs; (b) develop a scientifically based, comprehensive national system of MPAs representing diverse U.S. marine ecosystems, and the Nation's natural and cultural resources; and (c) avoid causing harm to MPAs through federally conducted, approved, or funded activities.

Sec. 2. Definitions. For the purposes of this order: (a) "Marine protected area" means any area of the marine environment that has been reserved by Federal, State, territorial, tribal, or local laws or regulations to provide lasting protection for part or all of the natural and cultural resources therein.

(b) "Marine environment" means those areas of coastal and ocean waters, the Great Lakes and their connecting waters, and submerged lands thereunder, over which the United States exercises jurisdiction, consistent with international law.

(c) The term "United States" includes the several States, the District of Columbia, the Commonwealth of Puerto Rico, the Virgin Islands of the United States, American Samoa, Guam, and the Commonwealth of the Northern Mariana Islands.

Sec. 3. MPA Establishment, Protection, and Management. Each Federal agency whose authorities provide for the establishment or management of MPAs shall take appropriate actions to enhance or expand protection of existing MPAs and establish or recommend, as appropriate, new MPAs. Agencies implementing this section shall consult with the agencies identified in subsection 4(a) of this order, consistent with existing requirements.

Sec. 4. National System of MPAs. (a) To the extent permitted by law and subject to the availability of appropriations, the Department of Commerce and the Department of the Interior, in consultation with the Department of Defense, the Department of State, the United States Agency for International Development, the Department of Transportation, the Environmental Protection Agency, the National Science Foundation, and other pertinent Federal agencies shall develop a national system of MPAs.

They shall coordinate and share information, tools, and strategies, and provide guidance to enable and encourage the use of the following in the exercise of each agency's respective authorities to further enhance and expand protection of existing MPAs and to establish or recommend new MPAs, as appropriate:

(1) science-based identification and prioritization of natural and cultural resources for additional protection;

(2) integrated assessments of ecological linkages among MPAs, including ecological reserves in which consumptive uses of resources are prohibited, to provide synergistic benefits;

(3) a biological assessment of the minimum area where consumptive uses would be prohibited that is necessary to preserve representative habitats in different geographic areas of the marine environment;

(4) an assessment of threats and gaps in levels of protection currently afforded to natural and cultural resources, as appropriate;

(5) practical, science-based criteria and protocols for monitoring and evaluating the effectiveness of MPAs;

(6) identification of emerging threats and user conflicts affecting MPAs and appropriate, practical, and equitable management solutions, including effective enforcement strategies, to eliminate or reduce such threats and conflicts;

(7) assessment of the economic effects of the preferred management solutions; and

(8) identification of opportunities to improve linkages with, and technical assistance to, international marine protected area programs.

*   *   *

(f) To better protect beaches, coasts, and the marine environment from pollution, the Environmental Protection Agency (EPA), relying upon existing Clean Water Act authorities, shall expeditiously propose new sciencebased regulations, as necessary, to ensure appropriate levels of protection for the marine environment. Such regulations may include the identification of areas that warrant additional pollution protections and the enhancement of marine water quality standards. The EPA shall consult with the Federal agencies identified in subsection 4(a) of this order, States, territories, tribes, and the public in the development of such new regulations.

Sec. 5. Agency Responsibilities. Each Federal agency whose actions affect the natural or cultural resources that are protected by an MPA shall identify such actions. To the extent permitted by law and to the maximum extent practicable, each Federal agency, in taking such actions, shall avoid harm to the natural and cultural resources that are protected by an MPA.

In implementing this section, each Federal agency shall refer to the MPAs identified under subsection 4(d) of this order.

Sec. 6. Accountability. Each Federal agency that is required to take actions under this order shall prepare and make public annually a concise description of actions taken by it in the previous year to implement the order, including a description of written comments by any person or organization stating that the agency has not complied with this order and a response to such comments by the agency.

* * *

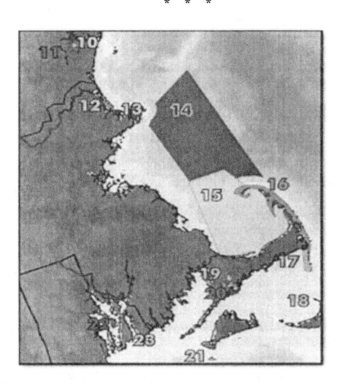

Marine Protected Areas off the Cape Cod coast: (10) Great Bay National Wildlife Refuge (11) Great B ay National Estuarine Research Reserve (12) Parker River National Wildlife Refuge (13) Thacher Island National W ildlife Refuge (14) Gerry E. Studds Stellwagen Bank National Marine Sanctuary (15) Cape Cod Bay Northern Right Whal e Critical Habitat (16) Cape Cod National Seashore (17) Monomoy National Wildlife Refuge (18) Nantucket Nationa l Wildlife Refuge (19) Mashpee National Wildlife Refuge (20) Waquoit Bay National Estuarine Research Reserve (2 1) Nomans Land Island National Wildlife Refuge (22) Narragansett Bay National Estuarine Research Reserve (23) Sachuest Point National Wildlife Refuge (Marine Protected Areas Initiative, 2002)

NOTES & QUESTIONS

1. Do MPAs work? It is, after all, rather difficult to contain fish through lines drawn on a map of the ocean. There is mounting evidence, however, that marine preserves do serve as sinks for recovering fish stocks. In Florida waters, for example, sport anglers have landed a disproportionate number of world and state record trophy fish from waters adjacent to a 60-square mile area near Cape Canaveral that was closed to access in 1962 for security reasons. Some researches believe the closed area—the functional equivalent of a reserve—provided sheltered nursery habitat for the surrounding areas. Similar results are being recorded near other marine preserve areas around the world. *See*

Callum M. Roberts et al., *Effects of Marine Preserves on Adjacent Fisheries*, 294 SCIENCE 1920 (2001). But there is substantial disagreement over the reliability of these findings. Many other researchers and interested parties attribute the purported effects of the Florida and other "no take" areas to other causes, such as overall increases in regulation, unusually superior habitat regimes, ecological change, and experimental bias. *See Marine Reserves and Fisheries Management*, 295 SCIENCE 1233 (2002). The scientists, in other words, don't agree, largely because "the science behind marine protected areas is still in its infancy." Ove Hoegh-Guldberg, *Complexities of Coral Reef Recovery*, 311 SCIENCE 42 (2006) (discussing effects of MPAs on predator-prey balance). What should ecosystem management *policy* do in that case? For further thoughts on this question in light of the uncertainty about the effectiveness of MPAs and the controversial nature of MPA management, see NATIONAL ACADEMY OF SCIENCES/NATIONAL RESEARCH COUNCIL, MARINE PROTECTED AREAS: TOOLS FOR SUSTAINING OCEAN ECOSYSTEMS (2001).

2. Not all MPAs prohibit human activities as comprehensively as does the Florida research site involved in the reserve productivity study discussed in the previous note. As in terrestrial public lands settings, the management norm for most MPAs is closer to a multiple use mandate rather than an ideal of wilderness. How effective is a multiple-use model, particularly one that allows commercial and recreational fishing, in meeting the objective of biodiversity conservation in MPA areas?

Indeed, the nation's first MPA provides an example of the range of possibilities that are available under the MPA approach and the limitations associated with different approaches. About 70 miles west of Key West in Florida lie the Dry Tortugas—seven small coral and sand islands Ponce de Leon charted in 1513 and named after their dry, yet turtle-abundant, environs. They were well known in the 17th and 18th centuries as a haven for pirates attacking merchant ships in the Gulf of Mexico. Well into the 20th century, their remote location and inhospitable (for humans) environment had left them largely pristine, home to more than 400 species of reef fish, lush corals, seabird rookeries, and crystal clear waters. In 1935, they became the Dry Tortugas National Monument, and in 1990 most of the surrounding waters were included in the Florida Keys National Marine Sanctuary. In 1992, the entire area also was included in the Dry Tortugas National Park, within which commercial fishing was banned.

Yet, notwithstanding its long history of MPA status and inclusion in overlapping national sanctuary and park programs, the Dry Tortugas ecosystem faced numerous stresses, most notably from recreational fishing. Modern fishing and boating technology has made the Dry Tortugas well within reach of recreational boating and sport fishing from the Keys and Florida's lower Gulf Coast. For example, the National Park had 18,000 visitors in 1984, and over 84,000 in 1999. The sizes of individual fish being taken from the area were falling substantially below healthy species averages, suggesting a path toward overfished status. With the threat of fishing primarily in mind, the Florida Keys National Marine Sanctuary and Protection Act of 1990 allowed the Sanctuary managers to use "zoning" as a means of designating limited uses for different areas. In July 1997, the Sanctuary instituted a comprehensive network of zones, including a series of 23 "no-take" areas covering only one percent of the Sanctuary area, but over 65 percent of the shallow reef habitat. A much larger no-take preserve had been proposed in 1994, but was dropped from the final plan in response to heated opposition from commercial and recreational fishing operations, divers, and other recreational interests used to moving about and using the Sanctuary with relatively little impediment.

The Sanctuary managers regrouped, however, and in 1998 formed a multi-stakeholder planning initiative, known as Tortugas 2000, to study the resurrection of the large ecological reserve concept. In May 1999, the working group approved a proposal that represented consensus between fishing and conservation interests. The plan called for a 151-square nautical mile Tortugas Ecological Reserve split into two sections: Tortugas North, which protects extensive coral resources and in which diving and snorkeling using mooring buoys (no anchoring) will be allowed by permit; and Tortugas South, which protects important fish resources and in which only research is allowed. Florida approved the inclusion of state waters in the reserve in April 2001, and in July 2001 the National Ocean Service issued its formal approval. Later that month, the Department of the Interior carved out a no-take Research Natural Area from a portion of the national park adjacent to the sanctuary, pushing the total no-take reserve area to almost 200 square nautical miles.

3. What do you take from the fact that fishery resources in the Dry Tortugas continued to decline for decades after the initial designation of the area as an MPA in 1935, primarily from recreational fishing? Does this suggest that the MPA approach must make frequent and significant use of permanent no-take reserves in order to be truly effective as an ecosystem management instrument? How should the process of identification of the need for and location of no-take areas be carried out, and who should be involved? Indeed, the debate over MPAs focuses less on whether they provide *any* benefit and more on questions such as how much of a benefit they produce, whether they are worth the cost to other interests, primarily subsistence fishing and recreational fishing, and whether their advocates have built a risk of unfulfilled expectations. The truth is that, while we know MPAs on balance are good for marine habitat and marine species, without a concerted research and monitoring initiative we won't know enough about them to answer these tougher policy questions. *See* Ray Hilborn et al., *When Can Marine Reserves Improve Fisheries Management?*, 47 OCEAN & COASTAL MANAGEMENT 197 (2004). Of course, we can't study the effects of marine reserves without establishing at least some of them, which is why researchers have called for designation of a larger network of MPAs and a program for monitoring inside and outside of their boundaries to help inform decisions about size, shape, and allowable uses of future MPAs. *See* STEPHEN R. PALUMBI, MARINE RESERVES: A TOOL FOR ECOSYSTEM MANAGEMENT AND CONSERVATION (2003) (science report prepared for the Pew Oceans Commission).

4. Upon taking office the Bush Administration announced, through the Secretary of Commerce, that it had decided to continue federal development of the MPA program. Statement by Secretary of Commerce Donald L. Evans Regarding Executive Order 13158, Marine Protected Areas (June 4, 2001). Indeed, in June 2006 President Bush created the world's largest MPA by designating a 140,000 square mile area of the Northwestern Hawai'ian Islands. *See* Proclamation 8031, 71 Fed. Reg. 36441 (June 26, 2006). In cooperation with the Department of the Interior and working closely with other organizations, the Department of Commerce, through the National Oceanic and Atmospheric Administration (NOAA), created the Marine Protected Areas Center (MPA Center) to coordinate the effort to implement the Executive Order, develop a framework for a national system of MPAs, and provide Federal, State, territorial, tribal, and local governments with the information, technologies, and strategies to support the system. *See* U.S. Departments of Commerce and the Interior, *The National MPA Initiative*, available at http://mpa.gov. The MPA Center has published final criteria for creating an inventory of areas that will be the basis of the future designations of MPAs. 70 Fed. Reg. 3512 (Jan. 25, 2005). The inventory process can be followed at MPA Center, *Inventory of Sites-Status of the Inventory*, http://www.mpa.gov/inventory/status.html. By the end of the Bush Administration NOAA had assembled an impressive guiding document for national MPA policy. *See* FRAMEWORK FOR THE NATIONAL SYSTEM OF MARINE PROTECTED AREAS OF THE UNITED STATES OF AMERICA (2008). The Obama administration also continued to adhere to the 2000 policy.

5. One vocal critic of the MPA program is the Recreational Fishing Alliance (RFA), which lobbies intensely on behalf of fishery conservation, and particularly in opposition to the effects of commercial fishing, but also objects to protective measures that restrict what it contends are the relatively minor impacts of recreational fishing. The RFA argues as follows with respect to MPAs:

> Designed correctly, MPAs can be useful for fishery conservation/management purposes as a part of a fishery management plan and could be implemented with the endorsement of the recreational fishing community if they accommodate the following:
>
> (A) There must be a clear identification of the conservation problem. Traditional management practices (gear restrictions, quotas, bag limits, closed seasons etc.) have been evaluated and do not provide sufficient conservation and management remedies to the affected stocks of fish;
>
> (B) The proposal for a specifically-identified MPA must include measurable criteria to determine the conservation benefit to the affected stocks of fish and contain economic impact information on how the proposed actions would affect fishermen;
>
> (C) The proposal also should allow for other types of recreational fishing, such as trolling for pelagic species, that would not have an impact on demersal stocks of concern, as an example.
>
> (D) Any closed areas within a MPA should be established with a sunset provision. On that date-certain, the zones will automatically reopen unless there is scientific proof that the closure should remain in effect and those findings are communicated to the public through a process integrating substantial public review and comment;
>
> (E) The plan provides a timetable for periodic review of the continued need for any closed area at least once every three years and an estimated timeline for removing the closure;
>
> (F) The closed area is no larger than that which is supported by the best available scientific information;

(G) The fishery management measures are part of a fishery management plan as required by the Magnuson-Stevens Act as amended by the proposed Freedom to Fish Act.

See Recreational Fishing Alliance, RFA Position Paper on MPAs, *available at* http://www.savefish.com/mpaprop.html.

The debate between MPA advocates and recreational fishing interests intensified dramatically as MPAs sunk deeper into policy preferences. One of the central figures in the controversy has been Felicia Coleman, a researcher at Florida State University, whose research has revealed that recreational fishing is having a significant adverse effect on fisheries. *See* David Grimm, *Sportfishers on the Hook for Dwindling U.S. Fish Stocks*, 305 SCIENCE 1235 (2004). Recreational fishing interests blame commercial fishing as the culprit, but as Coleman puts it, "it doesn't matter whose hook is in the water." Indeed, recreational fishing, according to Coleman, represents the major human threat for some marine fish species. She has become a strong advocate of no-take MPAs for species such as the grouper. Researchers at FSU have identified an area 50 miles south of Apalachicola Bay on Florida's Gulf Coast (see the Case Study in Chapter 10) where grouper aggregate and spawn at 15 different sites along an ancient submerged coral reef ridge. Much to the chagrin of fishing interests, who know the sites well, the area has been designated a no-take MPA to protect the grouper. *See* Parker Neils, *Tasting the No-Take Tonic*, 13 FLORIDA STATE UNIVERSITY RESEARCH IN REVIEW 18 (Summer 2003).

Some MPA advocates have suggested that Coleman's work will help rebuff the "Freedom to Fish" movement, which has relied heavily on the claim that recreational fishing has small impacts compared to commercial fishing. But Freedom to Fish legislation, which would restrict MPAs using the conditions outlined in the main text, remains a popular item in Congress and state legislatures. *See* State Environmental Resource Center, *Freedom to Fish Acts*, http://www.serconline.org/freedomFish.html. One condition the legislation would impose is to prohibit states from closing waters to fishing unless "there is a clear indication that recreational fishing is the cause of a specific conservation problem." Coleman's work certainly points in that direction for some species, though it has been hotly contested by recreational fishing interests. *See The Recreational Fisher's Perspective*, 307 SCIENCE 1560 (2005) (series of letters to the editor).

Using the framework for ecosystem management policy analysis developed in Chapter 7 of this book, compare the MPA ecosystem management frameworks as described in the Executive Order and MPA Initiative versus the criteria outlined in the RFA proposal:

	Metric	**Goals**	**Methods**
Executive Order			
RFA Proposal			

6. Protection from overfishing is the purpose usually associated with an MPA, but other water-based actions can prove difficult to manage without using an MPA approach. In the case of the Florida manatee, for example, the chief threat to the species' survival is boating. The species is cold-intolerant, relatively slow swimming, and spends much of its time near the surface foraging on marine vegetation. These traits put it right in the path of one of Floridians' favorite pastimes—boating. Over 800,000 vessels are registered in the State of Florida, with an additional 400,000 vessels registered in other states regularly using Florida waters. Not surprisingly, the leading non-natural cause of manatee deaths today is collision with boats and boat propellers, primarily in seven Florida counties. Although enforcement of "speed zones" can help alleviate fatal boat collisions, federal and state agencies have limited resources to patrol all of Florida's waters. Thus, Florida agencies and the U.S. Fish and Wildlife Service, exercising its authority under the Endangered Species Act and Marine Mammals Protection Act, have established a network of "manatee refuges," where boating is highly regulated, and "manatee sanctuaries," where all waterborne activity is regulated. *See, e.g.*, USFWS, Manatee Protection Areas in Florida, 67 Fed. Reg. 680 (Jan. 7, 2002) (designating two new manatee refuge areas totaling more than 1500 surface acres). Should boating in Florida's waters be more severely restricted to protect the manatee? Should the total number of registered boats be capped? Should large areas of coastal waters be posted as completely off limits to boating?

7. The states are becoming more aggressive in the use of MPAs. In California, for example, the Marine Life Protection Act (MLPA), requires that the Department of Fish and Game develop a plan for establishing networks of marine protected areas in California waters to protect habitats and preserve ecosystem integrity, among other things. *See* California Fish & Game Code, §§ 2850–2863. Sponsored by the Natural Resources Defense Council, the legislation was supported by conservation, diving, scientific and educational groups. The purpose of the MLPA is to improve the array of MPAs existing in California waters through the adoption of a Marine Life Protection Program and a comprehensive MPA Master Plan. The MLPA states that "marine life reserves" (defined as no-take areas) are essential elements of an MPA system because they "protect habitat and ecosystems, conserve biological diversity, provide a sanctuary for fish and other sea life, enhance recreational and educational opportunities, provide a reference point against which scientists can measure changes elsewhere in the marine environment, and may help rebuild depleted fisheries." The Master Plan requires that recommendations be made for a preferred alternative network of MPAs with "an improved marine life reserve component." The MLPA further states that "it is necessary to modify the existing collection of MPAs to ensure that they are designed and managed according to clear, conservation-based goals and guidelines that take full advantage of the multiple benefits that can be derived from the establishment of marine life reserves." The six goals are:

> To protect the natural diversity and abundance of marine life, and the structure, function, and integrity of marine ecosystems.
>
> To help sustain, conserve, and protect marine life populations, including those of economic value, and rebuild those that are depleted.
>
> To improve recreational, educational, and study opportunities provided by marine ecosystems that are subject to minimal human disturbance, and to manage these uses in a manner consistent with protecting biodiversity.

To protect marine natural heritage, including protection of representative and unique marine life habitats in California waters for their intrinsic value.

To ensure that California's MPAs have clearly defined objectives, effective management measures, and adequate enforcement, and are based on sound scientific guidelines.

To ensure that the state's MPAs are designed and managed, to the extent possible, as a network.

Id. § 2853(b). These goals were used as guiding principles in the development of the process used by a Master Plan Team to formulate recommendations of networks of MPAs. California's implementation of the MLPA got off to a rocky start. *See Science Meets Politics Off California's Coast*, 327 SCIENCE 1574 (2010). In 2004 the state announced an "indefinite postponement" for lack of funding. A private foundation, the Resources Legacy Fund Foundation, then offered the state $2 million toward MLPA implementation. This led ultimately to Fish and Game Commission approval in 2007 of an 85-square mile MPA system, with more MPA areas instituted since then. To stay current on developments under the MLPA, see http://www.dfg.ca.gov/mlpa.

8. In Illinois Central Railroad Co. v. Illinois, 146 U.S. 387 (1892), the seminal Public Trust Doctrine case (discussed previously in this chapter), the Supreme Court noted that one purpose of the doctrine is to require that states provide their citizens, among other things, "the liberty of fishing" in navigable waters. What if a state decides to exclude a specified area from fishing in order to promote ecological values? Focusing on Florida, which has begun to do just this through its marine preserve initiatives, Professor Donna Christie has argued that the "public trust doctrine does not establish any apparent priority among conflicting public trust uses," and thus "Florida's public trust doctrine is not a limitation on the use of marine reserves; the state must protect a broad array of public interests and uses in navigable waters. The state has the authority to regulate public trust uses to minimize conflicts and assure the protection of waters and wildlife that are fundamental to the enjoyment of all other public trust uses." *See* Donna R. Christie, *Marine Reserves, the Public Trust Doctrine, and Intergenerational Equity*, 19 LAND USE & ENVTL. L. 427, 434 (2004); see also Katryna D. Bevis, *Stopping the Silver Bullet: How Recreational Fishermen Can Use the Public Trust Doctrine to Prevent the Creation of Marine Reserves*, 13 SOUTHEASTERN ENVTL. L.J. 171 (2005).

9. For a concise overview of MPAs in the U.S., see Robin Kundis Craig, *Fishers, Divers, Scientists, Lawyers, and Marine Protected Areas; The US Experience in Protecting Coral Reefs*, 5 TOURISM IN MARINE ENVIRONMENTS 89 (2009). The literature on MPAs has shifted from portraying them as the marine analogy to wilderness to thinking of them as a form of community-based collaborative zoning. *See* N.A. Sloan, *History and Application of the Wilderness Concept in Marine Conservation*, 16 CONSERVATION BIOLOGY 294 (2002) (suggesting that the wilderness concept "carries too much terrestrial preservationist baggage" to be useful in the marine conservation context); Denise Antolini, *Marine Reserves in Hawaii: A New Call for Community Stewardship*, 19 NATURAL RESOURCES & ENV'T 36 (Summer 2004); Jeff Brax, *Zoning the Oceans: Using the National Marine Sanctuaries Act and the Antiquities Act to Establish Marine Protection Ar-*

eas and Marine Reserves in America, 29 ECOLOGY L.Q. 71 (2002). As one commentator has put it, "designing modern marine reserves demands a deft touch," which may explain why a growing number of scientists and policy makers are turning to the tools of urban land use planning for designing marine reserves that are both politically viable and ecologically effective. David Malakoff, *Picturing the Perfect Preserve*, 296 SCIENCE 245 (2002).

10. If you had a limited budget to place 10 new MPAs into being, where would you put them? Would it make sense to place them in areas of highest biodiversity? Of highest threat to human-induced degradation? Of lowest cost? There is an extensive effort in "bio-geography" underway to make the case that "hot spots" of biodiversity are where we should put our money for the most bang from the buck. *See* Callum M. Roberts, *Marine Biodiversity Hotspots and Conservation Priorities for Tropical Reefs*, 295 SCIENCE 1280 (2002). The argument is that by focusing financial and regulatory effort on making these areas no-take MPAs, we yield the greatest protection of the greatest concentration of biodiversity at the most efficient level of effort. Given the harsh unlikelihood that the entire marine environment will ever attain no-take MPA status, isn't this a sensible second-best alternative for those interested in maximizing the impact of MPAs?

11. All told, only about one percent of the coastal and ocean waters within U.S. jurisdiction qualify as an MPA, and of that only ten percent receives the highest level of protection—a no-take prohibition of all fishing and other resource extraction activities. Is this tool of ecosystem management, used frequently in terrestrial settings, simply underused in the coastal and marine ecosystem context? Why hasn't it been used more?

12. Another land management unit along our coastlines is the National Seashore, of which there are ten. Unlike MPAs, the National Seashores generally contemplate more recreational uses—indeed, they are managed by the National Park Service. We present a case study of the kind of disputes this recreational focus fuels at the conclusion of Chapter 13.

D. CASE STUDY: THE PLIGHT OF THE WHITE MARLIN

One of the most problematic management issues in marine and coastal settings involves what are known as highly migratory fish (HMS), which include tuna species, marlin, oceanic sharks, sailfishes, and swordfish. See 16 U.S.C. § 1802(2) (provision of the Magnuson-Stevens Act defining HMS). These fish roam the oceans with no respect for political boundaries— researchers in 2005 tracked one great white shark swimming from Africa to Australia and back, a distance of 12,000 miles. They are top-level predators in the marine food chain. They are also highly prized by humans for food and as sporting trophies, causing many HMS populations to decline precipitously. *See* Julia K. Baum, *Collapse and Conservation of Shark Populations in the Northwest Atlantic*, 299 SCIENCE 389 (2003) (all shark species in the region have declined at least 50 percent since 1970). In this case study we examine the challenge domestic ecosystem management policy faces in conserving these species, an issue that has been rocked to the core by the developments surrounding a popular sporting fish—the White Marlin.

The marlin's predicament can be summarized as follows: marlins like to eat tuna; humans also like to eat tuna; when humans hunt tuna, marlins are the collateral damage. The method of choice for humans to hunt tuna is the pelagic longline gear rig. The gear consists of a mainline, often miles long, suspended in the water column by floats and from which up to several thousand baited hooks are attached on leaders called gangions. The lines remain in the water for a day or so, and then they are reeled in and the caught tuna are removed from the hooks one-by-one. This method, however, is not especially discriminating—in addition to tuna, longline fishing also hooks sea birds, marine mammals, and billfish such as marlins. This so-called "bycatch" usually is not retained, either for economic or regulatory reasons, but it is nonetheless usually very much dead.

Commercial longline fishing bycatch is without question the leading cause of white marlin mortality. U.S commercial fishing operations killed 40.8 metric tons of white marlin as bycatch in 2001, mostly from the longline fishery bycatch (by contrast, recreational fishing landed 0.2 metric tons). Decades of this and other fishing pressures on white marlins throughout Atlantic waters decimated the population. Things have gotten even worse since the data NMFS used in its listing petition finding. By the beginning of 2000, the biomass of white marlin had been driven to an estimated 13 percent of the sustainable level (MSY, as described earlier in this chapter) and it continues to decline. The sustainable fishing level rose to roughly 8 times the MSY level by 2000. As a result, the white marlin population approached the point of recruitment failure—the population level below which there are too few adult breeders to replace the population even under the best of circumstances. If that rate of decline had continued, the tipping point would eventually be passed irreversibly and the marlin would become extinct. Some biologists estimated this would occur in less than five years unless something was done—that something being listing the species as endangered under the Endangered Species Act (ESA). Here we see how that strategy has turned out.

Department of Commerce, National Marine Fisheries Service (NMFS), *90-Day Finding for a Petition to List Atlantic White Marlin*

National Marine Fisheries Service, 2001.
66 Fed. Reg. 65676.

On September 4, 2001, NMFS received a petition from the Biodiversity Legal Foundation and James R. Chambers requesting NMFS to list the Atlantic white marlin (*Tetrapturus albidus*) as threatened or endangered throughout its range, and to designate critical habitat under the ESA. The petition contained a detailed description of the species, including the present legal status; taxonomy and physical appearance; ecological and fisheries importance; distribution; physical and biological characteristics of its habitat and ecosystem relationships; population status and trends; and factors contributing to the population's decline. Potential threats identified in the petition include: (1) overutilization for commercial purposes; (2) inadequacy of existing regulatory mechanisms; (3) predation; and (4) other natural or man-made factors affecting the species' continued existence. The petitioners also included information regarding how the species would benefit from being listed under the ESA, cited references and provided appendices in support of the petition.

Under the ESA, a listing determination can address a species, subspecies, or a distinct population segment (DPS) of a species (16 U.S.C. 1532 (16)). The petitioners requested that NMFS list Atlantic white marlin throughout its entire range. They are found in warm waters throughout tropical and temperate portions of the Atlantic Ocean and its adjacent seas (Caribbean, Mediterranean and Gulf of Mexico). A highly migratory pelagic species, they are found predominantly in the open ocean over deep water, near the surface in the vicinity of major ocean currents where their prey is concentrated. Their food resources include small fishes and invertebrates such as squid that can be swallowed whole.

The petitioners provided a detailed narrative justification for their petitioned action, describing past and present numbers and distribution of Atlantic white marlin. Information regarding its status was provided for the entire range of the species. The petition was accompanied by appropriate supporting documentation, including the most recent stock assessment for this species.

In 1997, the Atlantic white marlin was listed as overfished under the Magnuson-Stevens Fishery Conservation and Management Act (16 U.S.C. 1801 et seq.). In April 1999, NMFS published Amendment 1 to the Atlantic Billfish Fishery Management Plan, which included rebuilding programs and measures to reduce bycatch and bycatch mortality for Atlantic billfish, including white marlin. The International Commission for the Conservation of Atlantic Tunas (ICCAT), responsible for management of tunas and tuna-like fishes of the Atlantic Ocean also considers the Atlantic white marlin to be overfished. Several binding recommendations have been adopted by ICCAT over the last few years to reduce landings and improve data and monitoring. The most recent recommendation in November 2000 included a two-phase rebuilding plan involving further landing reductions and the development of more rebuilding measures after the next stock assessments in 2002.

The petitioners assert that existing protection for Atlantic white marlin at both the national and international level is inadequate to conserve the species or prevent its slide to extinction. The population's decline has been documented thoroughly by ICCAT's scientific advisors, the Standing Committee for Research and Statistics (SCRS). According to the petitioners, the primary cause of the Atlantic white marlin decline is due to bycatch in the international swordfish and tuna fisheries. The most recent stock assessment conducted in July of 2000 (SCRS/00/23) indicates that by the end of 1999: (1) the total Atlantic stock biomass had declined to less than 15 percent of its maximum sustainable yield level; (2) fishing mortality was estimated to be at least seven times higher than the sustainable level; (3) overfishing has taken place for over three decades; and (4) the stock is less productive than previously estimated, with a maximum sustainable yield smaller than 1,300 metric tons. The population's abundance was last at its long-term sustainable level in 1980. Reduction in prey species availability may also be a threat to the species, with two of its important prey species, Atlantic bluefish and squid, listed as overfished under the Magnuson-Stevens Act (16 U.S.C. 1801 et seq.).

Petition Finding

Based on the above information and the criteria specified in 50 CFR 424.14 (b)(2), NMFS finds that the petitioner presents substantial scientific and commercial information indicating that a listing of Atlantic white marlin may be warranted. Under section 4 (b)(3)(A) of the ESA, this finding requires that NMFS commence a status review on Atlantic white marlin. NMFS is now initiating this review. Within one year of the receipt of the petition (by September 3, 2002), a finding will be made as to whether listing the Atlantic population of the white marlin as threatened or endangered is warranted, as required by section 4 (b)(3)(B) of the ESA. If warranted, NMFS will publish a proposed rule and take public comment before developing and publishing a final rule.

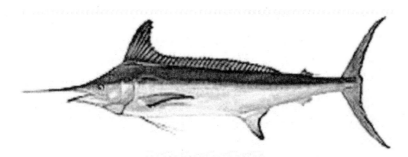

The White Marlin

Events since the initial petition "may be warranted" finding were a bit of a see-saw. On September 9, 2002, the NMFS announced that it had rejected the petition to list the Atlantic white marlin. *See* 67 Fed. Reg. 57240 (Sept. 9, 2002). The agency agreed with the status review team (1) there is no evidence of range curtailment or habitat degradation to suggest that white marlin are at risk of extinction; (2) while overutilization is occurring and the Atlantic white marlin population is declining, the stock is not in danger of imminent extinction; (3) there is no evidence that competition, predation, or disease are affecting the Atlantic white marlin population in ways that would contribute to risk of extinction; (4) since the U.S. currently accounts for approximately 5 percent of total reported catch of white marlin, domestic management measures including the Magnuson-Stevens Act, Atlantic Tunas Convention Act, and possibly the ESA are not adequate to protect this species from continued decline. Under current management measures, the stock will likely continue to decline, but not to high risk levels; and (5) no other natural or manmade factors affecting white marlin's continued existence were identified.

In January 2004, the Center for Biological Diversity and Turtle Island Restoration Network filed an action in federal district court challenging the agency's decision. One year later, the parties, which by then had expanded to include commercial and recreational fishing associations, settled the lawsuit. Under the terms of the settlement, NMFS agreed to reassess the status of the white marlin after the International Commission for the Conservation of Atlantic Tunas conducts its own assessment of the stock, scheduled for no later than 2007. NMFS also agreed to study the need for more areas closed to longline fishing in domestic waters. The fate of the white marlin, both legally and biologically, thus remains to be determined.

At the conclusion of those studies, in early January 2008 during the waning days of the Bush Administration, the FWS announced that it had concluded the white marlin did not warrant ESA listing. *See* 73 Fed. Reg. 843 (Jan. 4, 2008). Going beyond its earlier findings, the agency concluded that the species was overfished but, due in large part to management efforts ICCAT had adopted, the species was stable or even increasing in population for the foreseeable future. The white marlin thus remains in a legal gray zone—overexploited to the point of requiring conservation management actions, but not sufficiently in trouble to warrant ESA protection.

Regardless of its ESA status, the white marlin reveals the complexity of coastal and marine ecosystems, and thus the challenge of any effort to manage them. The white marlin is a long-lived, top-level predator fish that lives in the open ocean and travels long distances following schools of mackerel, tuna, dolphin fish, and squid. It is one of the lions of the ocean; yet, its behavioral characteristics have spelled trouble for its continued survival.

So, short of ESA listing, what can the United States do through domestic law to help ensure the white marlin does not slide back into precipitous decline? More to the point, what does ecosystem management have to offer as a domestic policy instrument to help avoid white marlin extinction? In fact, the United States did take some decisive action. As noted in the petition finding, in 1997 NMFS declared the white marlin an overfished species under the Magnuson-Stevens Act (described earlier in this chapter). NMFS has instituted limited "time/area" closures of areas to longline fishing in a few areas of domestic waters, *see* NMFS, Atlantic Highly Migratory Species-Pelagic Longline Fishing, 65 Fed. Reg. 47213 (Sept. 1, 2000) (codified at 50 C.F.R. pt. 635), and it prohibited commercial harvests of white marlin in all U.S. waters. Bycatch, however, is not considered commercial harvest, and that is the major problem for the marlin. Moreover, marlin, like other HMS fish, regularly travel outside U.S. waters, where only international agreements can restrict fishing harvests.

As NMFS explained, in international waters the International Commission for the Conservation of Atlantic Tunas (ICCAT) is responsible for management of tunas and tuna-like fishes of the Atlantic Ocean and adjacent seas. The organization was established in 1969, at a Conference of Plenipotentiaries, which prepared and adopted the International Convention for the Conservation of Atlantic Tunas in Rio de Janeiro, Brazil, in 1966. (For a history of ICCAT and related international regimes for HMS, see Karen L. Smith, *Highly Migratory Fish Species: Can International and Domestic Law Save the North Atlantic Swordfish?*, 21 New Eng. L. Rev. 10 (1999).) The Convention established exclusive jurisdiction in ICCAT as the only fisheries organization that can undertake the range of work required for the study and management of tunas and tuna-like fishes in the Atlantic, which include about 30 species of direct concern. Such studies include research on biometry, ecology, and oceanography, with a principal focus on the effects of fishing on stock abundance. The Commission's work requires the collection and analysis of statistical information relative to current conditions and trends of the fishery resources in the Convention area. The Commission also undertakes work in the compilation of data for other fish species that are caught during tuna fishing (bycatch) in the Convention area, and which are not investigated by another international fishery organization—e.g., the white marlin.

Not everyone is pleased with ICCAT's work—it is known in some circles as the "International Commission to Catch All Tunas." Yet ICCAT also considers the white marlin to be overfished and adopted some restrictions on landings. ICCAT has not, however, banned commercial harvests in international waters. Tuna fishing operations from many other nations thus are free keep their white marlin and other "bycatch" for commercial use, or to discard it. It is difficult, therefore, for U.S. domestic regulation to manage the fishing-based mortality rate for the white marlin and other HMS fish.

In addition to the commercial longline tuna fishing industry, another major player in the white marlin's future is the recreational fishing industry, represented by organizations such as The Billfish Foundation and the Recreational Fishing Alliance. Few fish are more prized among sport fishermen than the white marlin. At the 23rd Annual White Marlin Open held in 1996, the world's largest billfishing tournament with over 235 boats entering, the winner landed a 73.5 pound marlin and for that won a prize of $401,140. *See World Fishing Firsts at White Marlin Open*, www.beachnet.com/wmopen.html. The competition often has total prize money of well over $1 million, with the white marlin category receiving a large cut.

Overall, recreational billfish anglers spend more than $2 billion annually on their sport. The NMFS estimates that, whereas the total economic activity generated by commercial fishing is roughly $27 billion annually, the recreational fishing industry generates over $100 billion of economic impact. *See* NMFS, 2001 Stock Assessment and Fishery Evaluation for Atlantic Highly Migratory Species (2001). For obvious reasons, therefore, the recreational fishing industry was keenly interested in how NMFS treated the white marlin listing petition. Indeed, when NMFS announced it would not list the species, White Marlin Open founder and director Jim Motsko proclaimed, "Needless to say, we're very happy....I feel like we dodged another bullet." Shawn J. Soper, *NMFS Study Finds White Marlin Not Endangered*, OCEAN CITY DISPATCH, Jan. 11, 2008.

A prize-winning white marlin.

To be sure, listing of the white marlin as endangered under the ESA would be a drastic approach to management of the species in domestic waters. As the materials in Part II of this text explain, bycatch of white marlin would be considered "incidental take" of the species for which a permit would be required. Recreational fishing for white marlin would be flatly prohibited, and recreational fishing for other species with the incidental potential to land a marlin would be regulated.

But what are the alternatives? Is there any option short of ESA listing and rigorous enforcement of the incidental take prohibition that will ensure the white marlin does not slide back into decline, and does any option (even ESA listing) really solve the problem that, as an HMS, U.S. law cannot truly manage the white marlin's ecosystem? Consider how these other approaches fare under those criteria:

1. Ban longline tuna fishing at all times in all domestic waters, but leave recreational and other commercial tuna harvesting methods alone.

2. Develop longline fishing bycatch reduction methods and enforce them through stiff fines and by posting NMFS observers or video mon-

itoring systems (VMS) aboard longline tuna fishing vessels. (For more on VMS methods see Blue Water Fisherman's Association v. Mineta, 122 F.Supp.2d 150 (D.D.C.2000), and NMFS, Notice of Reconsideration of VMS Requirements, 66 Fed. Reg. 1907 (Jan. 10, 2001).)

3. Avoid direct banning or regulation of longline tuna fishing as in (1) and (2), but impose a significant per fish white marlin "bycatch fee" that would be enforced through counts made by onboard observers or VMS.

4. Buy out the domestic longline tuna fishing fleet and ban any new longline tuna fishing vessels from operating within domestic waters. (For an example of a buyout proposal see The Atlantic Highly Migratory Species Act of 2001, H.R. 1367, 107th Cong. (2001).)

5. Establish a chain of white marlin Marine Protected Area preserves within domestic waters, within which no commercial or recreational fishing for tuna or billfish is allowed.

6. Establish a voluntary tuna fishing certification program for domestic and foreign vessels that use verified bycatch reduction methods, and institute a massive public education campaign centering around "Marvin the Marlin" in an effort to convince consumers to eat only "marlin friendly" tuna—i.e., tuna processed only from certified vessels' harvests.

7. Levy a tax on the tuna processing industry or on retail sales of tuna, and use the revenue to finance a white marlin recovery effort that would include any or all of options (2) through (6).

What would the petitioner, Mr. Chambers, have to say about each of these proposals? How about the commercial fishing industry? How about the recreational fishing industry? Sport fishing boat manufacturers? The tuna processing industry? Consumers?

Of course, another interested party is NMFS, which could have been in the unusual position of potentially managing the white marlin through two different statutory programs administered through two different divisions of the agency. The NMFS Highly Migratory Species Division, which is part of the NMFS Office of Sustainable Fisheries, administers the Magnuson-Stevens Act for the white marlin and other HMS. See http://www.nmfs.noaa.gov/sfa. The decision whether to list an HMS under the ESA, however, is assigned to the Endangered Species Division of the NMFS Office of Protected Resources. See http://www.nmfs.noaa.gov/pr/index.htm. Assume you are the NMFS HMS Division employee tasked with managing the white marlin. How would you react to potential ESA listing and what action would you take to influence the outcome? Assume you are the NMFS ESA Division employee tasked with reviewing the ESA listing criteria. How would you interact with the employees of the HMS Division?

Considering that this is a chapter on ecosystem management, does it also strike you as odd that none of the proposals outlined above involves management of an *ecosystem*? In other words, they all involve efforts to reduce the direct take of white marlins. Is there any way to address the plight of the white marlin through habitat management? Isn't that the fundamental challenge for recovering highly migratory fish species—i.e., that it's not about the habitat? So, is the white marlin really a problem in ecosystem management? On the other hand, as a top-level predator in its domain, the white marlin surely is an important facet of the relevant ecosystem, and thus its demise can be expected to alter the dynamics thereof.

Does it seem an odd twist of fate that a fish worth over $400,000 as a trophy prize for recreational fishers was being driven to extinction because it is scrap to tuna fishing operations? Perhaps the species appreciates the irony—at the 2012 White Marlin Open, only one marlin bothered to take the bait. *See White Marlin Aren't Biting at Ocean City Tornament*, http://wamu.org/news/12/08/10/white_marlin_arent_biting_at_ocean_city_tourna ment.

CHAPTER 12

FRAGILE ECOSYSTEMS

Chapter Outline:
A. Arctic Ecosystems
B. Desert Ecosystems
C. Island Ecosystems
D. Coral Reef Ecosystems

In *Lucas v. South Carolina Coastal Council,* 505 U.S. 1003 (1992), the Supreme Court held that a regulatory taking occurs when government regulation deprives land of all economically beneficial use. An exception to this categorical treatment, however, exists when "background principles" of state nuisance and property law would have in any event restricted the property owner from the use subsequently restricted by regulation. In such circumstances, the crucial question is what constitutes such a background principle. Concurring, Justice Kennedy insisted that "[c]oastal property may present such unique concerns for a fragile land system that the State can go further in regulating its development and use than the common law of nuisance might otherwise permit." *Id.* at 825. So what is a "fragile land system?" This chapter offers four examples of fragile ecosystems which may necessitate a special approach to management.

A. ARCTIC ECOSYSTEMS

"The popular perception of the Arctic is of a vast, unchanging and timeless wilderness, undisturbed by humans, in which harsh environments challenge the ability of plants, animals and people to survive and flourish. In fact the Arctic has constantly undergone changes, life has flourished there and human impacts may have caused dramatic landscape changes even early within the last 10,000 years." Mark Nuttall & Terry V. Callaghan, *Introduction,* in THE ARCTIC: ENVIRONMENT, PEOPLE, POLICY xxv (Mark Nuttall & Terry V. Callaghan eds. 2000). The Arctic features a variety of spectacular ecosystems, ranging from the coastal Arctic plains to the delicate tundra to marine environments teeming with marine mammals and fish. Generally, fewer species live within most parts of the Arctic than in similarly sized places elsewhere. On the other hand, bald eagles, grizzly bears, and other species that have been endangered in other parts of the United States are found in massive abundance in the Arctic. And just as the number of species is relatively small, the human population is much lower in the Arctic than in nearly any other place that we have studied.

A small group of nations border the Arctic. Those nations, in order of the extent of their contact with the Arctic, are Russia, Canada, the United States (though only Alaska), Denmark (which is sovereign over Greenland), Iceland, and the very northern parts of Norway, Sweden and Finland. The environmental challenges are similar—though not the same—throughout the Arctic, but the governing legal systems vary quite dramatically. Compare that legal regime to the one governing Antarctica, which has similar environmental issues but which has been treated as the sovereign territory of no single nation pursuant to a 1959 treaty. We will focus upon the manner in which the United States manages the Arctic ecosystems in Alaska here, for the diversity of terrestrial and marine environments presents ample challenges for the understanding of how the law treats this harsh but stunning environment.

National Parks & Conservation Association v. Babbitt

United States Court of Appeals for the Ninth Circuit, 2001.

241 F.3d 722.

■ REINHARDT, CIRCUIT JUDGE.

Glacier Bay National Park and Preserve is a place of "unrivaled scenic and geological values associated with natural landscapes" and "wildlife species of inestimable value to the citizens." The Bay was proclaimed a national monument in 1925 and a national park in 1980. UNESCO designated Glacier Bay an international biosphere reserve in 1986 and a world heritage site in 1992.

Not surprisingly, many people wish to visit the park. As there are no roads to Glacier Bay, most tourists arrive by boat. To be more specific, most—approximately 80% of the park's visitors—arrive on large, thousand-passenger cruise ships. In 1996 the National Park Service (Parks Service) commenced implementation of a plan that increased the number of times cruise ships could enter Glacier Bay each summer season immediately by 30% and overall by 72% if certain conditions were met. In its environmental assessments, the Parks Service acknowledged that this plan would expose the park's wildlife to increased multiple vessel encounters, noise pollution, air pollution, and an increased risk of vessel collisions and oil spills. The Parks Service also acknowledged that it did not know how serious these dangers to the environment were, or whether other dangers existed at all. Nevertheless, declaring that its plan would have "no significant impact" on the environment, the Parks Service put it into effect without preparing an environmental impact statement (EIS).

The plaintiff National Park and Conservation Association (NPCA), a nonprofit citizen organization, alleges that the Parks Service's failure to prepare an EIS violated the National Environmental Policy Act (NEPA), 42 U.S.C. § 4321 *et seq.* It seeks an order requiring the Parks Service to prepare an EIS and enjoining implementation of the plan pending its completion. The district court ruled that an EIS was not required because the Parks Service had made its findings after adequately "canvassing the existing knowledge base." We reverse the district court's ruling and remand with instructions to enjoin the plan's increases in vessel traffic, including any portion already put into effect, until the Parks Service has completed an EIS.

FACTUAL AND PROCEDURAL HISTORY

There may be no place on Earth more spectacular than the Glacier Bay. Located in the Alaskan panhandle, surrounded by snow-capped mountain ranges, Glacier Bay extends sixty miles inland and encompasses ten deep fjords, four of which contain actively calving tidewater glaciers, and approximately 940 square miles of "pristine" marine waters. The air quality, though fragile, is still unspoiled and permits those fortunate enough to be visitors a crisp, clear view of the Bay with its glacier faces as well as the opportunity to breathe the fresh and invigorating air. The park is the habitat for an extraordinary array of wildlife. On the land, pioneer plant communities grow in areas recently exposed by receding glaciers. Moose, wolves, and black and brown bears roam the park's spruce and hemlock rain forest. Bald eagles, kittiwakes, murrelets, and other seabirds nest along the shore; sea otters, harbor seals, Steller sea lions, harbor and Dall's porpoises, minke, killer, and humpback whales reside in the bay.

Glacier Bay National Park

The Steller sea lion and the humpback whale, two of the marine mammal species that inhabit Glacier Bay, are imperiled. The Steller sea lion was listed as a threatened species under the Endangered Species Act (ESA), 16 U.S.C. 1531 et seq., in 1990. The worldwide population of the species declined by as much as 48% in the thirty years prior to 1992. Glacier Bay has several "haul-out" sites where hundreds of Steller sea lions gather. The humpback whale, "the most gamesome and lighthearted of all the whales," Herman Melville, *Moby Dick,* 123 (Harrison Hayford & Hershel Parker, eds., W.W. Norton & Co. 1967) (1851), has been listed as an endangered species since the enactment of the ESA in 1973. Until a moratorium was instituted in 1965, commercial whaling decimated the worldwide population of humpback whales. Today only 10,000 to 12,000 remain. A subpopulation of humpbacks spends the summer feeding season in southeast Alaska, including the waters of Glacier Bay; other humpbacks remain there throughout the year.

Watercraft—cruise ships, tour boats, charter boats, and private boats— provide primary access to Glacier Bay's attractions. Approximately

80% of the park's visitors are cruise ship passengers. According to the Parks Service's environmental assessment, the "key attraction of the visit to Glacier Bay . . . [is] the glaciers at the head of the West Arm [of the Bay.] [They] are larger, more active, and considered by the [cruise-ship] companies to offer a more spectacular experience." The ships linger at the glaciers from between fifteen minutes to an hour and provide a large, high viewing platform from which to witness the crack and crash of the great ice masses as they cast off huge shards of floating ice. Although the ships' height permits an unobstructed view of the park's geologic features, it limits close views of the wildlife and vegetation that form such a significant feature of the park.

Between 1968 and 1978, vessel traffic in Glacier Bay increased dramatically. In 1978 the U.S. National Marine Fisheries Service (Fisheries Service) . . . recommended that the Parks Service regulate the number of vessels entering Glacier Bay; restrict vessels from approaching and pursuing whales; and conduct studies on whale feeding behavior, the effect of vessels on whale behavior, and the acoustic environment.

The Parks Service soon thereafter promulgated regulations governing the entry and activity of cruise ships and other vessels in Glacier Bay. The regulations provided that only two cruise ships could enter the bay each day, with a maximum of 89 cruise ship entries between June 1 and August 31. Smaller boats, designated "private/pleasure craft," were limited to twenty-one entries per day with a seasonal maximum of 538 entries. Vessels were prohibited from intentionally positioning themselves within a quarter of a nautical mile of a whale or attempting to pursue a whale. Within "designated whale waters," vessels had to operate at a constant speed of ten knots or less and follow a mid-channel course. [Over the next fifteen years, the Park Service allowed an increasing number of vessels to enter Glacier Bay. Then, in] September 1992 the Parks Service completed an internal draft of a new VMP that proposed to increase the then current level of cruise ship entries in Glacier Bay by an additional 72%. . . As mandated by NEPA, the Parks Service investigated whether a substantial cruise-ship increase would significantly affect the environment in Glacier Bay. In May 1995 the Parks Service issued a combined proposed VMP and environmental assessment (EA). An EA is a document that, under NEPA, (1) provides "sufficient evidence and analysis for determining whether to prepare an environmental impact statement or a finding of no significant impact;" (2) aids an agency's compliance with NEPA when no EIS is necessary; and (3) facilitates preparation of an EIS when one is necessary. 40 C.F.R. § 1508.9(a). An EA is a "less formal and less rigorous" document than an EIS.

The combined VMP/EA . . . described and assessed six alternative approaches for managing vessels in Glacier Bay, ranging from Alternative Four's reduction in vessel traffic by between 14% and 22%, to Alternative One's maintenance of the status quo, to Alternative Five's increase of cruise ship entries by 72%. Notwithstanding the environmental problems it recognized, the Parks Service expressed its preference for Alternative Five.

This alternative maintained the limit of two cruise ship entries per day, but increased the total number of seasonal entries from 107 to 184. It did not increase seasonal entries for other vessels.

The Parks Service conducted six public hearings on the VMP. The Parks Service received approximately 450 comments, approximately 85% of which opposed Alternative Five and favored Alternative Four. The Sierra Club, the Alaska Wildlife Alliance, and the plaintiff NPCA spoke out against Alternative Five at the hearings, and submitted expert opinion and evidence in opposition to the Parks Service's findings. On March 20, 1996, the Parks Service announced its decision to implement a modified version of Alternative Five as its new VMP. Under this modified plan, the seasonal entry quota for cruise ships would increase by 30% for 1996 and 1997, and by as much as 72% thereafter if certain conditions were met. Also, the entry quotas for charter boats and private/pleasure craft would increase by 8% and 15%, respectively. An accompanying revised EA, titled "Impacts of the Modified Alternative," discussed the effects of the new VMP on threatened and endangered marine mammals, other marine mammals, birds, and the human environment, including air quality. . .

[NPCA filed suit challenging the Park Service's Finding of No Significant Impact (FONSI) with respect to the VMP, and the district court granted the government's motion for summary judgment].

ANALYSIS

I. THE PARKS SERVICE VIOLATED NEPA. . .

C. Uncertainty

An agency must generally prepare an EIS if the environmental effects of a proposed agency action are highly uncertain. Preparation of an EIS is mandated where uncertainty may be resolved by further collection of data, or where the collection of such data may prevent "speculation on potential . . . effects. The purpose of an EIS is to obviate the need for speculation by insuring that available data are gathered and analyzed prior to the implementation of the proposed action." *Sierra Club [v. United States Forest Serv.,* 843 F.2d 1190, 1195 (9th Cir. 1988)].

Here, scientific evidence presented in the Parks Service's own studies revealed very definite environmental effects. The uncertainty was over the intensity of those effects. The FONSI reported increased daily and seasonal exposure of humpback whales and other denizens of the Bay to underwater noise (and predicted a range of adverse behavioral responses), "traffic effects" (including increased risk of collision, affecting whales, harbor seals, sea otters, murrelets, and molting waterfowl), and increased risk of oil pollution for all animal life in the Park. An increase in cruise ships would also "result in more violations of state air quality standards for cruise ship stack emissions." Among the specific effects set forth in the VMP/EA upon which the FONSI was based were that increased vessel entry into the Bay would: subject stellar sea lions to additional disturbance; increase the escape patterns of various types of whales; potentially increase mortality rates and change the social patterns of the harbor seal; preclude sea otters from colonizing the upper Bay; and increase disturbance of feeding murrelets, other seabird nesting colonies, and bald eagles.

The EA describes the intensity or practical consequences of these effects, individually and collectively, as "unknown." The uncertainty manifested through the EA stems from two sources: an absence of information about the practical effect of increased traffic on the Bay and its inhabitants; and a failure to present adequate proposals to offset environmental damage through mitigation measures. . . [The EA] states that "little is known about the effects of the [cruise ship] disturbance" on steller sea lions; "the effect of increased levels of disturbance" on Glacier Bay's cetacean populations is "unknown"; and "the degree of increase [in oil spills as a result of increased traffic] is unknown." It also states that the effect of noise and air pollution on murrelets, bald eagles, and waterfowls remains "unknown" because unstudied. Moreover, the extent to which air pollution will diminish the beauty and quality of the natural environment is also unknown. The Parks Service's EA does, however, establish both that such information may be obtainable and that it would be of substantial assistance in the evaluation of the environmental impact of the planned vessel increase. The EA proposes a park research and monitoring program to "fill information needs, and understand the effects of vessel traffic on air quality, marine mammals [and] birds . . . to assist in the prediction, assessment, and management of potential effects on the human, marine, and coastal environments of Glacier Bay resulting from human use of the environment with particular emphasis on traffic." That is precisely the information and understanding that is required *before* a decision that may have a significant adverse impact on the environment is made, and precisely why an EIS must be prepared in this case.

The Parks Service proposes to increase the risk of harm to the environment and then perform its studies. It has in fact already implemented the first part of its VMP. This approach has the process exactly backwards. Before one brings about a potentially significant and irreversible change to the environment, an EIS must be prepared that sufficiently explores the intensity of the environmental effects it acknowledges. A part of the preparation process here could well be to conduct the studies that the Park Service recognizes are needed. That might be done here by performing the studies of the current vessel traffic and extrapolating or projecting the effects of the proposed increase. Ultimately, the Park Service may develop other means for obtaining the information it currently lacks. The point is, however, that the "hard look" must be taken before, not after, the environmentally-threatening actions are put into effect. . .

The second source of uncertainty is the Parks Service's ability to offset the environmental impact of the increase in vessel traffic through its proposed mitigation measures. An agency's decision to forego issuing an EIS may be justified in some circumstances by the adoption of such measures. . . There is a paucity of analytic data to support the Parks Service's conclusion that the mitigation measures would be adequate in light of the potential environmental harms. . . The Parks Service first described its proposed mitigation measures in the initial EA. That document reflects the uncertainty that exists as to whether the mitigation measures would work: moreover, it is unclear from that document whether the measures are sufficiently related to the effects they are designed to cure. The Parks Service simply noted, for example, that mitigation measures *"could* mitigate some potential effects to humpbacks in concentrated whale-use areas"; *"could* reduce whale/vessel collisions and reduce the noise emanating from the ships"; "special-use-area closures and restrictions implemented under . . . alternative [five] *may* off-set some of the expected disturbance." Air pollution measures "would *be expected* to contribute to a reduction in cruise ship stack emissions *over time."* Further, the service stated that it:

> intends to institute a comprehensive research and monitoring program to fill informational needs and quantity the effects of vessel traffic on air quality, marine mammals, birds and visitor-use enjoyment. The monitoring program, developed within one year of the record of decision, will stipulate research and protection actions [Parks Service] will undertake to ensure that environmental effects do not exceed acceptable levels . . .

The final EA was similarly uncertain with respect to the proposed measures' effects. It recognized that a 10-knot speed restriction to offset the increased vessel traffic might disturb the creatures in the park, but that "very little is known about the effects of the disturbance." The EA also stated that the increase in seasonal entries *"could* reduce whale/vessel collisions and reduce the noise level emanating from the ships . . ., follow-up research and monitoring will be essential to define humpback whale use patterns in Glacier Bay resulting from this alternative"; and that "requiring cruise ships to implement oil-spill response plans *could* mitigate the effects of oil spills." As for air pollution, "the magnitude of increased violations would presumably be reduced over time." There is no indication, however, as to how long any such reduction might take or how great a reduction might ultimately be accomplished. In short, there is no evidence that the mitigation measures would significantly combat the mostly "unknown" or inadequately known effects of the increase in vessel traffic. The EA's speculative and conclusory statements are insufficient to demonstrate that the mitigation measures would render the environmental impact so minor as to not warrant an EIS. . .

[The court also held that NPCA had made the requisite showing that the preparation of an EIS is mandated by the "controversy," as well as by the "uncertainty," factor of the intensity provision. 40 C.F.R. § 1508.27(b).]

II. INJUNCTIVE RELIEF

NPCA asks this court to "reverse the District Court and remand the case with instructions to enjoin further implementation of the 1996 Vessel Management Plan until a full Environmental Impact Statement is prepared." To determine whether injunctive relief is appropriate, "even in the context of environmental litigation," we apply "the traditional balance of harms analysis." *Forest Conservation Council v. United States Forest Serv.,* 66 F.3d 1489, 1496 (9th Cir. 1995) (citations omitted); *see also Amoco Prod. Co. v. Village of Gambell,* 480 U.S. 531, 541, 542 (1987) (holding that unless Congress directed otherwise, "a court must balance the competing claims of injury" in determining whether injunctive relief is appropriate). "Environmental injury, by its nature, can seldom be adequately remedied by money damages and is often permanent or at least of long duration, i.e., irreparable," *Amoco Prod. Co.,* 480 U.S. at 545. When the "proposed project may significantly degrade some human environmental factor," injunctive relief is appropriate. *Alaska Wilderness Recreation & Tourism Assoc. v. Morrison,* 67 F.3d 723, 732 (9th Cir.1995).

NPCA has made the requisite showing for injunctive relief. As we concluded in Section I, an EIS is required. We so held because of the significant adverse impact on the environment that might result from the implementation of the VMP. Where an EIS is required, allowing a potentially environmentally damaging project to proceed prior to its preparation runs contrary to the very purpose of the statutory requirement. Here, the Parks Service has already undertaken a 30% increase in cruise-ship traffic preliminary to a seventy-two percent increase. The potential effects of its action extend beyond the endangered marine mammal population to the rest of the wildlife at Glacier Bay, as well as the Park's air quality. Kittiwakes, murrelet, eagles, sea otters, seals, sea lions, porpoises, and killer and minke whales, as well as the better known humpbacks, are affected. Until an EIS is prepared and the effects of increased vessel traffic on the inhabitants and air quality of Glacier Bay are properly examined, there is a sufficient possibility of environmental harm that the VMP may not be implemented.

Westours argues that the damage to its business should be considered when addressing injunctive relief, that its financial losses outweigh the potential damage to the environment, and that NPCA "is not entitled to an injunction against the 32 seasonal cruise ship entries" that the Parks Service authorized for the 2000–2004 seasons. As a general rule, only the federal government may be a defendant in a NEPA action. An exception may be made in the remedial phase of a case where the contractual rights of the applicant are affected by the proposed remedy. Here, Westours was permitted to intervene, and appears before us as a party-defendant. Westours has asserted financial damages premised upon its contracts of carriage. Its loss of anticipated revenues, however, does not outweigh the potential irreparable damage to the environment. Moreover, neither Westours nor those of its passengers who may be unable to view Glacier Bay at the time they originally planned have cause to claim surprise as a result of any injunction. The plaintiffs filed their objections to the plan approximately five years ago and just one year later sought an injunction. If the passengers who booked cruises on any "excess" tours were not warned by Westours of the pending litigation, their interests were not well served by that company. Thus, while Westours has standing to object to our grant of injunctive relief, its evidence fails to tilt the balance of harms in its favor.

CONCLUSION

Much of the briefing and argument in this appeal has focused on the impact of the VMP on the imperilled humpback whale population. However, a variety of other non-human inhabitants of the Park—bald eagles, kittiwakes, murrelets, sea otters, harbor seals, Steller sea lions, harbor and Dall's porpoises, minke, and killer whales—are, as the EA reflects, affected, and the already fragile air quality is as well. The existence of adverse effects is not uncertain. What is uncertain is the extent of the likely environmental injury, and the impact of the proposed mitigation measures. The Parks Service's own experts, whose integrity the government commended at oral argument, admitted both the likelihood of certain harms to the environment of Glacier Bay and their uncertainty about the likelihood of other harms. In giving insufficient respect to their experts' evaluation of harm, declaring that no significant environmental effects were likely, and implementing the vessel traffic increase without complying with the requirements of NEPA, the Parks Service's decision-makers made a "clear error of judgment." *Marsh v. Or. Natural Res. Council,* 490 U.S. 360, 378 (1989).

Glacier Bay Park is too precious an ecosystem for the Parks Service to ignore significant risks to its diverse inhabitants and its fragile atmosphere. We reverse the decision below and remand with instructions that the district court issue an injunction enjoining the granting of permits to vessels pursuant to the 1996 increase in vessel entry quotas pending the Parks Service's completion of an EIS. . .

NOTES & QUESTIONS

1. In response to the Ninth Circuit's decision, Congress enacted legislation approving the 1996 increases in cruise vessel entries into Glacier Bay, pending the completion of an EIS. The EIS completed by the Park Service in 2003 identified six alternative courses of action. The Park Service preferred the alternative that maintained most of the existing vessel regulations, while the "environmentally preferred alternative" would have reduced cruise ship visits to Glacier Bay by 33%. "Many of the environmental effects of vessel traffic would be similar among the six alternatives," according to the EIS, and "most adverse effects would occur in proportion to vessel numbers, speed, and distribution, including air emissions and disturbance of wildlife and visitors." NATIONAL PARK SERVICE, GLACIER BAY NATIONAL PARK AND PRESERVE, ALASKA, VESSEL QUOTAS AND OPERATING REQUIREMENTS FINAL ENVIRONMENTAL IMPACT STATEMENT 31 (2003). A fuller view of the ecosystems and wildlife of Glacier Bay and how they are managed is provided by the national park's web site at http://www.nps.gov/glba/pphtml/naturalfeatures.html.

2. Alaska has long mesmerized wilderness enthusiasts. The United States bought Alaska in 1867, ending a century and a half of Russian control. Within twelve years, John Muir arrived there for the first of seven visits. "For Muir," writes one historian, "Alaska was the epitome of nature's perfection." STEPHEN HAYCOX, ALASKA: AN AMERICAN COLONY 273–312 (2002). Muir was also the first American to popularize the beauties of Glacier Bay. More generally, he proclaimed that "[t]o the lover of pure wildness Alaska is one of the most wonderful countries in the world." A 1901 *National Geographic* article agreed that "[t]he scenery of Alaska is so much grander than anything else of its kind in the world, that, once beheld, all other scenery becomes flat and insipid." Henry Gannett, *The General Geography of Alaska*, 12 NATIONAL GEOGRAPHIC 182, 196 (1901). As early as 1937, Wilderness Activist Bob Marshall asked Congress to "keep northern Alaska largely a wilderness." Robert Marshall, *Comments on the Report of Alaska's Recreational Resources Committee*, Alaska—Its Resources and Development, House Doc. No. 485, 75th Cong., 3d Sess, App. B, at 213. Then, "[b]eginning in the 1950s, and increasing in the subsequent two decades, a flood of publicity called attention to the values of wild Alaska." Roderick Frazier Nash, Wilderness in the American Mind 275 (4th ed. 2001). Justice William O. Douglas, for example, asserted in 1965 that "Alaska represents one last opportunity to preserve vast wilderness areas intact." WILLIAM O. DOUGLAS, A WILDERNESS BILL OF RIGHTS 134 (1965). Roderick Nash explains that "[t]he image of Alaska that emerges from the accounts of recreationseekers and environmentalists is that of a wilderness mecca, a qualitatively wilder country that any that exists or, perhaps, ever existed in the lower forty-eight states." NASH, *supra*, at 293. Nash cites the state's harsh climate and the fact that only about five percent of its land is "considered fit for agriculture and grazing." *Id.* at 274. Alaska remains the least populated state, and many of its lands are both wild and still owned by the federal government, which has yielded ongoing battles to determine the appropriate status and management of those lands.

3. The State of Alaska has been at the vanguard of efforts to regulate the pollution resulting from cruise ships. Alaska's Commercial Passenger Vessel Environmental Compliance Program (CPVEC), established in 2001, regulates and monitors discharges from vessels. The discharge of untreated sewage is prohibited, and the discharge of treated sewage—sometimes called "gray water"— must satisfy designated scientific and regulatory standards. According to the Alaska Department of Environmental Conservation, eleven compliance letters were sent to large cruise ships for violating the applicable fecal coliform standard or sampling requirements in 2003 and 2004. CPVEC also addresses air pollution from cruise ships, requiring that visible emissions from vessel smoke stacks be no greater than 20% opacity.

4. On March 24, 1989, the *Exxon Valdez* ran aground on Bligh Reef in Prince William Sound. Eleven million of the ship's 53 million gallons of oil spilled into the water. The precise toll on the marine wildlife will never be known, but the best estimate is that spill killed 250,000 seabirds, 2,800 sea otters, 300 harbor seals, 250 bald eagles, up to 22 killer whales, and billions of salmon and herring eggs. Exxon paid nearly one billion dollars to settle the criminal and civil suits brought by the federal and state governments. Part of that settlement compensated for "natural resources damages" caused by the spill. Such damages are authorized by CERCLA, which is more commonly employed to remedy the threats that hazardous wastes pose to public health, but which also contains a provision authorizing natural resource damages. *See* 42 U.S.C. § 9607(f)(1). The governments also relied upon section 311(f)(5) of the federal Clean Water Act, which provides that "[t]he President, or the authorized representative of any State, shall act on behalf of the public as trustee of the natural resources to recover for the costs of replacing or restoring such resources. Sums recovered shall be used to restore, rehabilitate, or acquire the equivalent of such natural resources by the appropriate agencies of the Federal Government, or the State government." 33 U.S.C. § 1321(f)(5). Summary of Injuries to Natural Resources as a Result of the *Exxon Valdez* Spill, 56 Fed. Reg. 14,687, 14,688 (1991), documents the injuries suffered by the wildlife for which the federal government served as a trustee. Natural resource damages are also available via the Oil Pollution Act, which Congress enacted in 1990 in response to the *Exxon Valdez* spill. *See* 33 U.S.C. § 2701–2761.

National Research Council, *The Bering Sea Ecosystem*

National Academy Press, 1996.

Executive Summary

The Bering Sea, a semi-enclosed northern extension of the North Pacific Ocean, contains a tremendous variety of biological resources, including at least 450 species of fish, crustaceans, and mollusks; 50 species of seabirds; and 25 species of marine mammals. The plentiful fish and game of the Bering Sea have supported the lives and livelihoods of people on both the Asian and the North American continents since prehistoric times. As the world's demand for furs and whale oil grew in the eighteenth and nineteenth centuries, exploitation of the Bering Sea's bountiful living resources began on a commercial scale. During the twentieth century, international markets turned to the Bering Sea for its seafood resources. Today, approximately 25 species of fish, crustaceans, and mollusks of the Bering Sea are considered important commercially.

Despite a variety of recent protections for marine mammals, birds, and fish resources afforded by laws of the United States and Russia and a number of international agreements, some species of the Bering Sea and adjacent regions have undergone large and sometimes sudden population fluctuations. For example, Steller sea lions have declined by 50 to 80 percent, and northern fur seal pups on the Pribilof Islands (the major Bering Sea rookeries) declined by 50 percent between the 1950s and 1980s. In parts of the Gulf of Alaska, harbor seal populations have dropped by as much as 90 percent since the 1970s. Populations of seabirds such as common murres, thick-billed murres, and red-legged and black-legged kittiwakes have also declined significantly in some areas such as the Pribilof Islands and the eastern Aleutians. Large changes in the abundance of a number of shellfish and fish populations over the past 30 years—including some large increases—have occurred as well. . .

CHANGES IN THE BERING SEA ECOSYSTEM

Both natural environmental fluctuations and human activities have caused biological changes in the Bering Sea ecosystem. Fish populations and other components of the ecosystem appear to react to many different environmental variables in the atmosphere and ocean. Overall, the committee concludes that climate-driven variability in the Bering Sea ecosystem is significant, occurs at many different time scales, and appears to affect many ecosystem components. It appears that climate has caused relatively rapid shifts in the organization of this marine ecosystem—most recently in the late 1970s—and that changes over periods of decades may have larger effects than those over yearly periods.

Human-induced change in the ecosystem is also significant. Fishing and hunting of marine mammals by Aleuts and Eskimos have occurred for hundreds of years at least; intensive exploitation of Bering Sea marine resources by the United States, Russia, Japan, and other nations began in the eighteenth century and increased in the nineteenth and twentieth centuries. Exploitation by indigenous peoples affected the abundance and community structures of marine resources, especially close to shore, and, coupled with natural fluctuations, led to occasional food shortages. The more extensive exploitation of the region's resources by Russia, the United States, Japan, and European nations that began in the eighteenth century led to more severe local food shortages and even starvation among the indigenous peoples.

Intensive exploitation of Bering Sea resources continued until the expansion of exclusive economic zones in the 1970s, when overall exploitation rates in U.S. waters began to decline. Intense fishing continued in international waters (e.g., the "donut hole"), but in recent years that has been reduced or eliminated as well. Information on exploitation rates in the western Bering Sea since the dissolution of the Soviet Union in 1991 is very unreliable, but anecdotal information suggests that exploitation rates are unsustainably high, especially near shore.

Large-scale, intensive exploitation of whales occurred during the 1950s, 1960s, and early 1970s in many parts of the Bering Sea and Gulf of Alaska. During this period, trawl fisheries severely reduced populations of eastern Bering Sea shelf flatfishes and slope rockfishes. Eastern Bering Sea pollock abundance increased in the late 1960s, perhaps as a result of an increase in the amount of food made available by the reduction in whales and other fishes, and the trawl fisheries switched their primary focus to pollock, where it has remained to the present.

As a result of environmental changes and human exploitation of the ecosystem, the eastern Bering Sea fish assemblage probably became pollock-dominated in the late 1960s and early 1970s, and a similar shift probably occurred in the western Bering Sea as well. In addition, both eastern Bering Sea king crab and herring were reduced significantly, perhaps by fishing, in the 1960s and early 1970s. King crab populations and their fisheries increased in the early 1970s, and then collapsed again in the early 1980s. Several eastern Bering Sea finfish populations grew rapidly in the late 1970s and early 1980s while one flatfish species and a number of forage species appear to have declined significantly.

Super-imposed on all of this are the changes in Bering Sea and Gulf of Alaska seabird and mammal populations. Fluctuations in seabird populations vary across the region, apparently depending on local environmental and ecological conditions. The pinnipeds (seals, sea lions, and walruses) present a different picture, with more uniform changes. Juvenile and adult female fur seals declined in the Pribilof Islands from the mid-1970s to the early 1980s and then subsequently stabilized. Harbor seals in the Gulf of Alaska declined rapidly in the late 1970s and have remained low. The trend in the number of Steller sea lions is uncertain before the 1970s, but declines were first noted in the eastern Aleutians in the early 1970s and then continued in the central and western Aleutians and western Gulf of Alaska during the 1980s. These declines appear to be related to a lack of adequate food, with juveniles probably affected most severely.

CAUSE AND EFFECT IN THE BERING SEA: THE CASCADE HYPOTHESIS

The most likely explanation of events over the past few decades in the Bering Sea ecosystem is that a combination of changes in the physical environment acted in concert with human exploitation of predators (whales, other fish) to cause pollock to dominate the ecosystem. The increase of adult pollock and other predatory fishes in the past 20 years might also be responsible for keeping the forage fishes relatively scarce. As a result, sortie forage fishes that have higher nutritional value than pollock became less available to some marine mammals and birds, leading to their decline. This food shortage might have been exacerbated by fishing for pollock that was concentrated in space and time, which might have removed them from some areas for long enough to cause difficulties to marine mammals and birds, especially juveniles.

Although the committee concludes that such a "cascade hypothesis" is the most likely explanation of events over the past 50 years, other explanations of these changes might develop as research progresses. There is no evidence that any human activity other than fishing and whaling has had any significant effect on the Bering Sea ecosystem, although more evidence concerning the effects of various pollutants would be of interest.

This scenario does not lead to the conclusion that overfishing of pollock over the past 25 years—often blamed for some of the changes in the Bering Sea—is directly (or even indirectly) responsible for recent declines of mammals and birds. As a result, it is unlikely that reduction of the total rate of exploitation of pollock would halt or reverse the declines in the short term. It is more likely, although by no means certain, that marine mammals and birds have been affected by the distribution in space and time of fishing effort on pollock, and thus that they would be helped by a broader distribution of fishing effort in space and time, especially in areas where they are known to feed.

It is also hard to predict the effects of protecting other marine mammals. It seems extremely unlikely that the productivity of the Bering Sea ecosystem can sustain current rates of human exploitation as well as the large populations of all marine mammal and bird species that existed before human exploitation—especially modern exploitation—began. Over the long term, fishing competes to some degree with at least some top-level predators. Therefore, if the goal of management is to have as many top-level predators as possible (not a common management goal), then it seems that ultimately fishing will have to be reduced. Note that "fishing" includes subsistence, recreational, and various kinds of commercial fishing, all of whose effects need to be dealt with.

Finally, it will be difficult for human management to cause a large, complex marine ecosystem to achieve and maintain a desirable balance. Some of the changes that have occurred might be irreversible over normal human time frames (100 years or less). This difficulty emphasizes the need for an adaptive approach to management and the need for good, long-term data on physical and biological phenomena . . ..

RECOMMENDATIONS

Research Recommendations

- **Adopt a broader ecosystem perspective for both scientific research and management of Bering Sea resources.**

- **Adopt an adaptive or experimental approach to management actions concerning the Bering Sea ecosystem.**

- **Conduct research on the structure of the Bering Sea ecosystem, including the nature and causes of the dynamics of pollock populations in the northeastern Pacific and Bering Sea over the past 50 years. . .**

  - **Conduct research on how well the management and institutions of the Bering Sea are structured to address problems and provide appropriate management solutions.**

Management and Institutional Recommendations

The committee identified four basic problems that need to be solved to achieve proper management of the Bering Sea ecosystem: the lack of knowledge and inherent limitations on understanding and predictability, incomplete specification of management objectives, lack of appropriate domestic institutional structures through which to make and implement coordinated management decisions on either side of the Bering Sea, and the limited ability to coordinate domestic management with users and management agencies of other nations. The committee recommends the following steps to address these problems:

- **Improve the coordination of the many institutional structures that make management decisions concerning resource use in the Bering Sea.**

- **Coordinate the philosophy and objectives of laws dealing with management in the Bering Sea ecosystem.**

- **Improve processes and institutions to coordinate the implementation of major federal acts relating to re-**

source use in the ecosystem, and federal-state and international management.

- **Develop a research program to increase understanding of the Bering Sea ecosystem (keeping international issues and cooperation in mind), to fulfill the research needs identified by the committee to help future policy makers solve both short-term management and longer-term ecological problems.**

Recommendation to Reverse Declines in Marine Mammals and Birds

The concentrated fishing for pollock in some places at specific times probably reduces the availability of food for marine mammals and birds, especially juveniles. Thus one step that might help improve the food supply for and reverse declines in marine mammals and birds would be to distribute fishing over wider areas and over longer periods. This management strategy is unlikely to have any adverse effects. Note that this is a call for broadening the distribution of fishing, not a recommendation to increase total catches; in fact, some areas should probably be closed to fishing to protect specific fish, bird, and mammal populations. This leads to the recommendation below. As with all management actions, this strategy should be followed on an adaptive basis.

- **Broaden the distribution of fishing effort in space and time, especially for pollock.**

THE FUTURE

The Bering Sea ecosystem, like all ecosystems, has been affected by natural fluctuations since time immemorial. Like most ecosystems, it has been affected by human activities since prehistory, but especially within the past 200 years as commercial exploitation developed. Thus, the recent changes that we see today should not be thought of as perturbations of a "pristine" ecosystem, but as part of a pattern of change affected by a complex array of natural and human influences.

The complexity of the influences on the ecosystem makes understanding and management difficult, but some things are clear. First, environmental change will continue to occur in the future. Second, significant human exploitation of a single species can affect not only that species but many other species as well. In other words, there are connections among ecosystem components. Finally, the total productivity of the ecosystem has a limit, which means that human use of living resources will affect the ecosystem to some degree. Those three conclusions imply that unexpected events will continue in the future and that they will be larger as living resources are more heavily exploited. It also follows that actions with respect to single species will have complex consequences that will be hard to predict. Simply changing exploitation rates on a single species—pollock, for example—is unlikely to have easily predictable effects on other ecosystem components—marine mammals, for example.

To operate successfully within this complex system, management strategies must be developed based on long-term data on physical and biological phenomena and must be adapted as we learn more about the structure and functioning of the ecosystem. A better understanding of institutional and socioeconomic factors will also be needed. Finding a balance between human uses of the region's many resources and maintaining other desired aspects of the ecosystem, such as high productivity of marine mammals or a particular composition of fish communities, will be an ongoing challenge.

NOTES & QUESTIONS

1. Is the Council's cascade hypothesis the likely cause for the demise of the Bering Sea ecosystem? Consider the conclusion that the Fish & Wildlife Service reached when it listed the northern sea otter populations in the Aleutians as threatened in 2005: "The weight of evidence of available information suggests that predation by killer whales (*Orcinus orca*) may be the most likely cause of the sea otter decline in the Aleutian Islands." The agency explained that theory as follows:

> The hypothesis that killer whales may be the principal cause of the sea otter decline suggests that there may have been significant changes in the Bering Sea ecosystem. For the past several decades, harbor seals (*Phoca vitulina*) and Steller sea lions (*Eumetopias jubatus*), the preferred prey species of transient, marine mammal-eating killer whales, have been in decline throughout the western north Pacific... Estes *et al.* hypothesized that killer whales may have responded to declines in their preferred prey species, harbor seals and Stellar sea lions, by broadening their prey base to include sea otters. While the cause of sea lion and harbor seal declines is the subject of much debate, it is possible that changes in composition and abundance of forage fish as a result of climatic changes and/or commercial fishing practices may be contributing factors.
>
> It also recently has been hypothesized that the substantial reduction of large whales from the North Pacific Ocean as a result of post-World War II industrial whaling may be the ultimate cause of the decline of several species of marine mammals in the north Pacific. Killer whales are considered to be the foremost natural predator of large whales. By the early 1970's, the biomass of large whales had been reduced by 95 percent, a result attributed to commercial harvesting. This reduction may have caused killer whales to begin feeding more intensively on smaller coastal marine mammals such as sea lions and harbor seals. As those species became increasing rare, the killer whales that preyed on them may have expanded their diet to include the even smaller and calorically less profitable, sea otter. The information supporting this theory is still under review. Although the proximate cause of the current sea otter decline may be predation by killer whales, the ultimate cause remains unknown.

Determination of Threatened Status for the Southwest Alaska Distinct Population Segment of the Northern Sea Otter (Enhydra lutris kenyoni), 70 Fed. Reg. 46366, 46382 (2005). What explanation is most plausible? Will the Council's recommendations arrest or reverse the decline of the ecosystem? What other actions would be appropriate?

2. The Bering Sea is named after Captain Vitus Bering, a Danish explorer who led the Russian voyages into the area during the early eighteenth century. Bering was accompanied in 1742 by the German naturalist Georg Wilhem Steller, who managed to affix his name to numerous species during his relatively brief visit to Alaskan waters. *See, e.g.,* Endangered and Threatened Wildlife and Plants; Threatened Status for the Alaska Breeding Population of the Steller's Eider, 62 Fed. Reg. 31748 (1997); Sherry Marie Cote, Note, *The Manatee: Facing Imminent Extinction*, 9 FLA. J. INT'L L. 189, 192 (1994) (observing that a species of manatee known as Steller's sea cow "was exterminated by Russian hunters in the Bering Sea in 1768").

The Steller sea lion has received the most attention in recent years. Steller sea lions stretch up to eleven feet long and weigh up to a ton. Mating animals gather to form rookeries on isolated islands or rocky shorelines, while the remaining animals remain on haulouts. The species was listed as threatened in 1990 after experiencing a 80% decline from its 240,000 population in the 1950's, and then the western population was listed as endangered in 1997. A 2003 National Resource Council study advised that "[t]he causes of the decline of the western stock have been the subject of much speculation and debate despite numerous analyses and many detailed reports. There is no widely accepted answer to the question of why the Steller sea lion population is declining. What might otherwise be an obscure ecological mystery has become an issue of great regional and even national interest because of the regulatory implications for management of the large commercial fisheries in the North Pacific. These fisheries target many of the same fish species that comprise the prey based for Steller sea lions." NATIONAL RESEARCH COUNCIL, DECLINE OF THE STELLER SEA LION IN ALASKAN WATERS: UNTANGLING FOOD WEBS AND FISHING NETS (2003). The conflict between the Steller sea lions and commercial fishery interests escalated in July 2000 when a federal district court held that fishing in the Aleutian Islands was jeopardizing Steller's sea lions, and therefore ordered the National Marine Fisheries Service (NMFS) to ban such fishing within the sea lion's critical habitat. *See* Greenpeace v. NMFS, 106 F.Supp.2d 1066 (W.D. Wash. 2000). That decision " 'made it hard to be an environmentalist in western Alaska.' " It "hit the industry hard" because "[b]oats had to go farther out to get the pollock, reducing the freshness of their catch. Instead of getting fish less than 40 hours old, you get fish 60 to 80 hours old," explained the manager of one of the fish processing plants. " 'You can't do much with that. You can't make filets. Roe quality is diminished.' " And "[t]he ban infuriated fishermen and Alaska Senator Ted Stevens, who claimed that it had little scientific basis. Stevens inserted language into an appropriations bill that granted a year to come up with a more palatable plan—today a hodgepodge of protected zones ranging from 10 to 20 miles—and he earmarked more than 40 million dollars for new research to find the cause of the sea lions' decline." Joel K. Bourne, Jr., *Alaska's Wild Archipelago*, NATIONAL GEOGRAPHIC, Aug. 2003, at 78. The *National Geographic* story neglected to mention that the appropriations rider crafted by Senator Stevens also provided $30 million in disaster relief assistance to coastal Alaskan communities that had suffered from the fishery restrictions, as well as providing $20 million to the National Research Council to conduct its report of the decline of the Steller sea lion. *See* Consolidated Appropriations Act of 2001, Pub. L. No. 106–554, § 209(d)(e), 114 Stat. 2763 (2000).

Native Village of Point Hope v. Salazar
United States Court of Appeals for the Ninth Circuit, 2012.
680 F.3d 1123.

■ IKUTA, CIRCUIT JUDGE.

In these expedited petitions for review, we consider the allegations of Native Village of Point Hope et al. and Inupiat Community of the Arctic Slope (collectively, "petitioners") that the Bureau of Ocean Energy Management (BOEM) failed to discharge its obligations under the Outer Continental Shelf Lands Act (OCSLA) in approving Shell Offshore Inc.'s plan for exploratory oil drilling in the Beaufort Sea. We have jurisdiction pursuant to 43 U.S.C. § 1349(c), and we deny the petitions.

I

This case is the latest chapter in a long-running saga beginning back in April 2002, when the Minerals Management Service (MMS) established a five-year lease sale schedule for the outer continental shelf of Alaska. Alaska Wilderness League v. Kempthorne, 548 F.3d 815, 817-18 (9th Cir 2008), *vacated*, 559 F.3d 916 (9th Cir. 2009), *dismissed as moot sub nom.* Alaska Wilderness League v. Salazar, 571 F.3d 859 (9th Cir. 2009). Indeed, this is the third time the government has appeared before us to defend its approval of Shell's exploration plan against challenges by many of these same petitioners. We begin by describing the legal framework and factual background for these challenges.

A

In enacting the Outer Continental Shelf Lands Act (OCSLA), 43 U.S.C. §§ 1331-1356a, Congress authorized the Secretary of the Interior to lease portions of the outer continental shelf to qualified bidders for the purpose of exploring and developing its oil and gas reserves. Under OCSLA, the Secretary begins by holding a lease sale to identify qualified bidders. Becoming the successful bidder in a lease-sale auction is merely the first step. Before undertaking exploration activities in the leased area, the winning bidder must obtain the Secretary's approval of an exploration plan, and obtain many other permits and approvals.[1] If, after completing such exploration activities, the leaseholder concludes there is potential for developing oil and gas reserves on the leased area, the leaseholder must obtain approval of a development and production plan, as well as obtaining a new round of permits and approvals before pursuing development of the leased area.

---

[1] The required permits include *inter alia* an approval of an oil spill response plan under the Clean Water Act, a National Pollutant Discharge and Elimination System (NPDES) permit under the Clean Water Act, a dredge-and-fill permit under the Clean Water Act, an air quality permit under the Clean Air Act, a permit to drill, and a range of state approvals.

Only the exploration plan stage and the leaseholder's obligations under OCSLA are at issue here. In general, the applicable regulations require the leaseholder to submit specified information about its proposed exploration plan. Within thirty days of the leaseholder's submission or last modification of the exploration plan, the Secretary "shall approve" the plan if it is consistent with OCSLA, its implementing regulations, and the applicable lease, unless the Secretary determines that the proposed activity "would probably cause serious harm or damage to life . . ., to property, to any mineral . . ., to the national security or defense, or to the marine, coastal, or human environment," and that "such proposed activity cannot be modified to avoid such condition."

While OCSLA focuses on development of the outer continental shelf, the Clean Water Act § 311, as amended by the Oil Pollution Act of 1990, focuses on the prevention of and response to oil spills. *See* 33 U.S.C. § 1321. Among other things, § 311 requires a leaseholder to submit an oil spill response plan, which is "a plan for responding, to the maximum extent practicable, to a worst case discharge, and to a substantial threat of such a discharge, of oil or a hazardous substance." Offshore facilities "may not handle, store, or transport oil unless" the leaseholder's oil spill response plan "has been approved by the President" and the "facility is operating in compliance with the plan."

At the time Shell began its leasing and exploration efforts, MMS was in charge of conducting lease sales, reviewing exploration plans under OCSLA, and approving oil spill response plans under § 311 of the Clean Water Act. Following the Deepwater Horizon oil spill in the Gulf of Mexico in early 2010, the Secretary divided MMS's responsibilities among three new regulatory entities in order to separate the "three distinct and conflicting missions" of (1) promoting resource development, (2) enforcing safety regulations, and (3) maximizing revenues from offshore operations. In the reorganization, the Secretary made BOEM responsible for managing the development of offshore resources, including approving a leaseholder's exploration plan under OCSLA and conducting an environmental analysis of that plan under the National Environmental Policy Act (NEPA). The Secretary made the Bureau of Safety and Environmental Enforcement (BSEE) responsible for enforcement of safety and environmental functions, including the oil spill response plan requirements in 30 C.F.R. pt. 254. As the regulatory process now stands, BOEM and BSEE are independent entities with separate responsibilities.

B

Although a winning bidder in the Beaufort Sea lease sale in 2003, Shell has yet to commence exploration activities. [After years of administrative review and litigation,] BOEM approved Shell's revised exploration plans subject to eleven conditions. Conditions 8 and 9 require Shell to make certain technical demonstrations concerning its oil spill response capabilities to BSEE before beginning exploratory drilling operations. BSEE approved Shell's revised oil spill response plan on March 28, 2012.

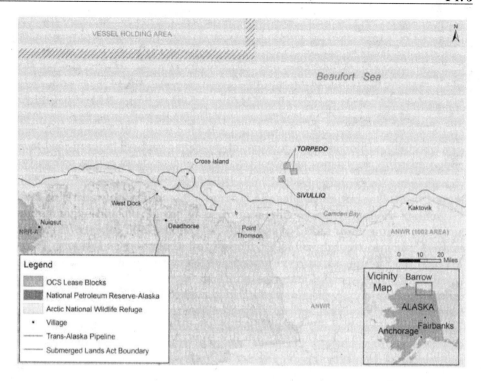

In these expedited petitions, petitioners challenge BOEM's approval of Shell's revised exploration plan. Petitioners claim that BOEM erred in approving the plan for three reasons. First, they claim that Shell's revised exploration plan did not meet the informational standards set by OCSLA and the regulations, because (1) it failed to reference an approved oil spill response plan as required by 30 C.F.R. § 550.219(a) and (2) did not contain an adequate description of Shell's well-capping stack and containment system as required by 30 C.F.R. § 550.213(d). Second, they claim that BOEM erred by failing to reconcile conflicting evidence regarding the feasibility of well-capping technology and the amount of time it takes to drill a relief well in the event of a well blowout and oil spill. Finally, they claim that BOEM erred by approving the revised exploration plan subject to conditions.

II

... BOEM's approval of an exploration plan is a final agency action subject to review under § 706 of the Administrative Procedure Act (APA). Under this standard, we may set aside BOEM's approval only if it is "arbitrary, capricious, an abuse of discretion, or otherwise not in accordance with law." 5 U.S.C. § 706(2)(A). Review under the arbitrary and capricious standard is deferential. We will not vacate an agency's decision unless it has "relied on factors Congress did not intend it to consider, entirely failed to consider an important aspect of the problem, or offered an explanation [for that decision] that runs counter to the evidence before the agency or is so implausible that it could not be ascribed to a difference in view or the product of agency expertise." Lands Council v. McNair, 537 F.3d 981, 987 (9th Cir. 2008) (en banc) (internal quotation marks omitted) (quoting *Earth*

Island Inst. v. U.S. Forest Serv., 442 F.3d 1147, 1157 (9th Cir. 2006), overruled on other grounds as recognized by Am. Trucking Ass'ns v. City of L.A., 559 F.3d 1046, 1052 (9th Cir. 2009)). We have emphasized that deference to the agency's decisions "is especially warranted when 'reviewing the agency's technical analysis and judgments, based on an evaluation of complex scientific data within the agency's technical expertise.'" Ctr. for Biological Diversity v. Kempthorne, 588 F.3d 701, 707 (9th Cir. 2009) (quoting Envtl. Def. Ctr., Inc. v. EPA, 344 F.3d 832, 869 (9th Cir. 2003)). . .

While OCSLA gives appellate courts jurisdiction over challenges to BOEM's approval of an exploration plan, BSEE's decisions regarding oil spill prevention, response, and liability are committed to a separate review process in the district court. We have interpreted *§ 1321(n)* as a grant of exclusive original jurisdiction to the district court to review an oil spill response plan.

We . . . turn to petitioners' argument that BOEM erred in approving the exploration plan because the agency did not explain how it reconciled inconsistencies in Shell's 2011 plan regarding the feasibility of the proposed well-capping stack and containment system and the time for drilling a relief well.

A

Petitioners first argue that BOEM erred in not explaining how it reconciled Shell's statements in its pre-2011 oil spill response plans that "proven technology is not available" for well capping and "well capping would not be an effective option for regaining well control while operating from a moored vessel," with its statement in the 2011 exploration plan that "subsea capping equipment and containment capabilities . . . would be implemented if all other kick control methods fail." We disagree.

First, there is no statutory or regulatory requirement that BOEM include a statement identifying and reconciling inconsistent positions taken by a permit applicant. Nor does BOEM's failure to do so make its approval of the exploration plan arbitrary and capricious under the APA. While an agency must present an adequate explanation for a decision that contradicts the agency's previous decision, BOEM did not adopt Shell's past statements, and therefore the agency is not taking an inconsistent position. Rather, it is Shell, not BOEM, that reassessed the feasibility of a well-capping stack and containment system in light of new information, namely that "[w]ell capping techniques have improved, especially since [their] frequent application during the Iraq-Kuwait conflict in the early 1990s, and the recent Macondo [Deepwater Horizon oil spill] incident." Because OCSLA requires industries to adopt the best available and safest technology, which would include technological advances, Shell's reassessment is consistent with the regulatory scheme.

More important, BOEM's failure to expressly address Shell's changed position on well-capping technology does not cast doubt on BOEM's decision that the activities in the exploration plan will not "probably cause serious harm or damage to life (including fish and other aquatic life), to property, ... or to the marine, coastal, or human environment." First, the well-capping stack and containment system challenged by petitioners is not the sole means identified in the exploration plan for responding to a well blow-out and oil spill. Rather, Shell has several response tools at its disposal, including surface control options and relief well capabilities. As BOEM reasonably concluded, "Shell's proposed subsurface collection system will be an added tool for responding to a potential well control incident where fluids flow and will increase response preparedness, but is not necessary or required to comply with" the regulations. Second, BOEM's conclusion that well-capping technology is now feasible in the Arctic is supported by substantial evidence in the record. BOEM found that "[s]ubsea containment technology has been successfully used in the past," including by Shell at the NaKika and Mars sites and by British Petroleum during the Deepwater Horizon spill, and that "most major components for such a system are available and have been field tested." Whether well-capping technology is now feasible in the Arctic is a technical issue that lies squarely within the agency's scientific expertise and, therefore, is accorded great deference by a reviewing court. Accordingly, we conclude that the inconsistency in Shell's prior statements does not invalidate BOEM's approval of Shell's current exploration plan.

B

We apply similar reasoning to petitioners' contention that BOEM acted arbitrarily and capriciously when it approved the exploration plan without reconciling evidence in the record that runs contrary to Shell's estimate of the time necessary to drill a relief well. Petitioners argue that Shell's estimate for the time it will take to drill the planned production wells is far longer than its estimate for the time it will take to drill an emergency relief well, and they further argue that Shell "failed to provide the agency any rational explanation for why it expects to drill a relief well so much faster."

We reject petitioners' contention that BOEM acted arbitrarily by failing to state on the record how it reconciled these different estimates. As noted above, there is no requirement that BOEM do so. Moreover, BOEM's decision to rely on Shell's time estimate for drilling relief wells was "supported by substantial evidence on the record considered as a whole" and is therefore "conclusive." 43 U.S.C. § 1349(c)(6). The well control plan submitted as a part of Shell's exploration plan explained that it would take a shorter time to drill relief wells than to drill exploratory wells because "[r]elief well drilling is rapid," relief wells "intercept a deep blowout at some point above the total vertical depth," which saves time, and in an emergency situation "all available resources are quickly accessed and funneled into drilling the relief well and killing the blowout as quickly as possible." BOEM's conclusion that Shell provided a realistic estimate of the time it would take to drill a relief well is a technical issue that lies squarely within the agency's scientific expertise and is therefore entitled to "great deference."

V

Finally, we consider petitioners' argument that BOEM acted arbitrarily by approving Shell's exploration plan on the condition that Shell provide additional information about the "procedures for deployment, installation[,] and operation of the system under anticipated environmental conditions." This argument likewise fails. As noted above, BOEM must approve an exploration plan that is consistent with OCSLA and its implementing regulations unless the proposed activity will "probably cause serious harm or damage to life (including fish and other aquatic life), to property, . . . or to the marine, coastal, or human environment." 43 U.S.C. §§ 1334(a)(2)(A)(i), 1340(c)(1); *see also* 30 C.F.R. § 550.233. BOEM takes the position that after approving a plan, it may still "require [the applicant] to meet certain conditions, including those to provide monitoring information." 30 C.F.R. § 550.233(b)(1). According to BOEM, its approval here followed this path: BOEM concluded that Shell's exploration plan complied with applicable requirements and would not cause serious harm or damage to the environment, but nevertheless required Shell to provide further documentation of its well-capping stack and containment system, as well as to meet certain additional conditions. This interpretation by BOEM of its own regulations is controlling unless plainly erroneous or inconsistent with the regulation. Further, the conditions at issue here, which require Shell to seek additional authorizations before commencing drilling, are consistent with the statutory scheme's requirement that a leaseholder with an approved exploration plan obtain a permit to drill and other approvals that "conform to the activities described in detail in [the] approved [exploration plan]" before conducting exploration activities. 30 C.F.R. § 550.281; *see also* 43 U.S.C. § 1340(d). For these reasons, petitioners' argument that BOEM impermissibly conditioned its approval is without merit.

VI

The Secretary's recent division of MMS's responsibilities between BSEE and BOEM makes it clear that BOEM's duty here is limited. Within the thirty days provided by statute, BOEM had to determine whether Shell's exploration plan complied with OCSLA's requirements and would not "probably cause serious harm or damage" to life, property or the human, marine, or coastal environment. 43 U.S.C. §§ 1334(a)(2)(A)(i), 1340(c)(1); *see also* 30 C.F.R. §§ 550.202, 550.233. Here, BOEM's decision that Shell's exploration plan complied with OCSLA's requirements is entitled to deference and is supported by the record as a whole. We deny the expedited petitions.

NOTES & QUESTIONS

1. Oil spills are a major concern in the Arctic because of the fragile nature of the ecosystem there. A 2012 Center for Biological Diversity report stated:

> For thousands of years, America's Arctic has been home to vibrant human communities that depend on healthy, functioning ecosystems to support their subsistence way of life. The Arctic Ocean provides vital habitat for

many of our nation's most iconic wildlife species—polar bears, walruses, ice seals, bowhead whales, beluga whales, eiders and more. And, ever more critically, the Arctic helps regulate the planet's rapidly changing weather and climate.

Today, this national treasure is in peril as plans to drill for oil in the Arctic's remote and undeveloped seas move forward. Despite an acknowledged lack of basic scientific information and the inability to respond to or clean up a spill, the Department of the Interior and other federal entities are considering final approvals for exploration drilling in the Arctic. Here are the reasons to delay drilling this summer:

- Hazardous conditions: The Arctic Ocean is prone to hurricane-force storms, 20-foot swells, pervasive sea ice, frigid temperatures, heavy fog and wind, and seasonal darkness. These severe conditions can complicate and hamper drilling and response to problems — risking oil spills, human lives and wildlife.

- No oil spill response: An oil spill in the remote, ice-choked waters of the Arctic would be impossible to clean up. Even the Deepwater Horizon oil spill spewed for months with a tremendous toll in the relatively calm waters of the Gulf of Mexico. The Coast Guard has noted that it lacks oil spill response capabilities in the Arctic. The nearest Coast Guard facilities are nearly 1,000 miles away, and there is no port in the Arctic capable of serving large response vessels. Claims that 95 percent of oil

- spilled could be cleaned up cannot be trusted; indeed, only only 3 percent was cleaned up in the Gulf in 2010, and only 8 percent was cleaned up after the Exxon Valdez spill.

- Sensitive wildlife: The Arctic is home to polar bears, walruses, and ice seals that are entirely dependent on sea ice for their survival. These animals are already threatened with extinction by climate change that's melting away their habitat. Ocean drilling increases activities that will disturb sensitive wildlife. Additionally, the fossil fuels under the Arctic Ocean should be left untapped — as well as the massive amount of greenhouse gasses that it holds—as we pursue a clean energy future. Drilling in the Arctic Ocean promises to make it ever more difficult to return to atmospheric levels of carbon dioxide that scientists tell us are needed to prevent some of the worst consequences of global warming.

Center for Biological Diversity, Arctic Ocean Drilling: Risking Oil Spills, Human Life, and Wildlife, http://www.biologicaldiversity.org/programs/public_lands/energy/dirty_energy_development/oil_and_gas/arctic/pdfs/ArcticOil DrillingFactsheet.pdf.

The EIS prepared for Shell's drilling proposal described the marine mammals within Shell's proposed action area as follows:

Table 9   The stock, habitat, and estimated abundance of marine mammals occurring within the Proposed Action area.

Species	Stock	Habitat	Estimated Abundance	Analyzed further?
Beluga Whale	Eastern Chukchi Sea	Open leads and polynyas, coastal areas, ice edges	3,710	Yes, due to relative abundance
Beluga Whale	Beaufort Sea	Open leads and polynyas, coastal areas, ice edges	32,453	Yes, due to relative abundance
Narwhal		Offshore, ice edge, heavy pack ice, open leads	86,000, Rare in Chukchi/Beaufort	No, due to relative abundance
Killer Whale	Offshore	Open-water	Not estimated, but rare in Chukchi/Beaufort	No, due to relative abundance
Harbor Porpoise	Bering Sea	Coastal waters <100m depth, Chukchi only	40,039, Rare in Chukchi/Beaufort	No, due to relative abundance
Bowhead Whale	Western Arctic	Ice edge, polynyas and leads, open-water	9,472	Yes, endangered species
Gray Whale	Eastern North Pacific	Open and coastal waters	17,752, Rare in Chukchi/Beaufort	No, due to relative abundance
Fin Whale	Northeast Pacific	Open-water	5,700, Rare in Chukchi/Beaufort	Yes, endangered species
Minke Whale	Alaska	Open-water	Rare in Chukchi/Beaufort	No, due to relative abundance
Humpback Whale	Central North Pacific	Open-water	5,833, Rare in Chukchi/Beaufort	Yes, endangered species
Bearded Seal	Alaskan Arctic	Pack ice and open-water	30,000	Yes, proposed for listing
Spotted Seal	Alaska	Pack ice, ice edge and coastal habitat	59,214	Yes, due to relative abundance
Ringed Seal	Alaska	Shorefast and pack ice	249,000	Yes, proposed for listing
Ribbon Seal	Alaska	Open-water and pack ice	49,000, Rare in Chukchi/Beaufort	No, due to relative abundance
Pacific Walrus	Chukchi/ Bering	Pack ice and coastal haulouts	129,000, Rare in Chukchi/Beaufort	No, due to relative abundance
Polar Bear	Southern Beaufort Sea	Coastal, barrier islands, pack ice	1,526	Yes, threatened species
Polar Bear	Northern Beaufort Sea	Coastal, barrier islands, pack ice	1,200	Yes, threatened species
Polar Bear	Chukchi/ Bering	Coastal, barrier islands, pack ice	2,000	Yes, threatened species

Note: Species listed under the Endangered Species Act are analyzed further; rare or uncommon species are not analyzed further.

Source: Allen and Angliss, 2010.

U.S. Dep't of the Interior, Bureau of Ocean Energy Management, Regulation & Enforcement, Alaska OCS Region, Beaufort Sea Planning Area Environmental Assessment 58 (Aug. 2011), http://www.boem.gov/uploadedFiles/BOEM/Oil_and_Gas_Energy_Program/Plans/Regional_Plans/Alaska_Exploration_Plans/2012_Shell_Beaufort_EP/EA_Shell2012CamdenBay.pdf.

The lease that BOEM thus contains a number of stipulations regarding wildlife in the area of the proposed drilling. For example, to guard against the possibility that endangered Steller's eiders would become disoriented by lighted vessels and structures in open-waters, Shell "must adhere to lighting requirements for all exploration or delineation structures so as to minimize the likelihood that migrating spectacled or Steller's eiders would strike these structures. Lessees are required to implement lighting requirements aimed at minimizing the radiation of light outward from exploration/delineation structures to minimize the likelihood that spectacled or Steller's eiders would strike those structures." *Id.* at 31. Further, "Shell's proposed activities include a mid-drilling-season suspension of activities beginning August 25 to avoid conflicts with the fall subsistence bowhead whale hunts of the villages of Kaktovik and Nuiqsut." *Id.* at 11. More generally, the EIS continues, "[d]espite the extremely low likelihood of a large oil-spill occurring during exploration, Shell has designed its response program for a regional capability of responding to a range of spill volumes that increase from small operational spills up to and including a Worst Case Discharge (WCD) scenario from an exploration well blowout, as required under 30 CFR 254.47. Shell's program is based on a WCD scenario that meets the response planning requirements of the State of Alaska and Federal oil-spill-planning regulations." *Id.* at 134. The EIS proceeds to detail the steps that Shell proposes to take to avoid an oil spill and to respond to a spill if one occurs. The EA also includes a lengthy section responding to the lessons of the Deepwater Horizon accident in the Gulf of Mexico.

Shell's plans thus convinced BOEM to approve its proposed drilling activities. Are you satisfied that Shell's drilling plans should be approved? Is there any basis for denying approval under the law? Should Congress intervene in the dispute one way or the other?

2. Drilling for oil is controversial throughout the Arctic, but nowhere more so than the Arctic National Wildlife Refuge (ANWR). Fred Seaton, the Secretary of the Interior for President Eishenhower, established the Arctic National Wildlife Range in December 1960 "[f]or the purpose of preserving unique wildlife, wilderness and recreational values." F.R. Doc. 60–11510 (Dec. 8, 1960). The ANWR website adds that "[a] prominent reason for the establishment of the Arctic Refuge was the fact that this single protected area encompasses an unbroken continuum of arctic and subarctic ecosystems." The website further explains that ANWR "is inhabited by 45 species of land and marine mammals, ranging from the pygmy shrew to the bowhead whale. Best known are the polar, grizzly, and black bear; wolf, wolverine, Dall sheep, moose, muskox, and the animals that has come to symbolize the area's wildness, the free-roaming caribou." The Porcupine caribou herd contains 123,000 animals and migrates 400 miles between its summer and winter ranges; the 27,000 animals of the Central Arctic herd travel 120 miles between ranges. But ANWR is also the apparent site of some of the largest oil deposits in the United States. President Bush insists that "[a]dvanced new technologies allow entrepreneurs to find oil and to extract it in ways that leave nature undisturbed... In Arctic sites, like ANWR, we can build roads on ice that literally melt away when summer comes and the drilling stops to protect wildlife." The President's Radio Address, 1 Pub. Papers 550, 551 (May 21, 2001). Much of the debate about ANWR presents wholly contradictory portrayals of the refuge and the possible effects of oil development. Opponents of drilling see ANWR as a pristine wilderness where the abundant wildlife would disappear upon any human influence. Proponents of drilling see ANWR as a bleak and uninhabited place whose wildlife could easily adapt to the presence of environmentally friendly drilling operations. The status quo favors the opponents of drilling because the existing law prohibits oil development.

3. Most of ANWR is not formally designated as a wilderness area pursuant to the Wilderness Act, but that would change if proposed federal legislation becomes law. Representative Edward Markey contends that "[w]e have an opportunity to preserve the Arctic Refuge as the magnificent wilderness the way God made it... President Eisenhower and [former Representative] Mo Udall had the vision to protect a remote but very special piece of wilderness for future generations. It is now our responsibility to stop those who would tear down this legacy. This legislation would, at long last, complete the job they began." 151

Cong. Rec. E159 (daily ed. Feb. 2, 2005) (statement of Rep. Markey). Would you vote for Representative Markey's bill?

4. Who should be able to decide how to manage Alaskan ecosystems? During the April 2005 debate over ANWR, Senator Roth proclaimed that "[t]hese are pristine lands that belong to all of us." 146 CONG. REC. S2206 (daily ed. Apr. 5, 2005) (statement of Sen. Roth). Alaskans bristle at such language. They insist that they should have a greater say in what happens on Alaskan lands than residents of other parts of the country, especially in distant Washington, D.C. How would you respond to them?

The fate of ANWR would not necessarily be clearer if it were left to the native peoples. During the April 2005 debate, Senator Feinstein relied upon the Gwich'in people's opposition to drilling, while Senator Akaka stressed that the local Inupiats support drilling. Both peoples are native to the area, but he Gwich'in are subsistence caribou hunters, while the Inupiat have embraced embraced oil development as a means to improve their standard of living. "To most Gwich'in, the Inupiat are motivated by greed, and have sold out their traditional culture for the lure of oil dollars; to many Inupiat, the Gwich'in are hopeless romantics, living voluntarily in squalor to cling to a way of life that is bound to disappear." Scott Wallace, *ANWR: The Great Divide*, SMITHSONIAN, Oct. 2005, at 51.

5. Native Alaskans have long enjoyed an intimate relationship with the wildlife and ecosystems where they live. "Alaska Natives have relied on marine mammals for their food, handicrafts, and culture for centuries. They have successfully managed their use of marine mammals, assuring that no more is taken than is needed. Working with their governing tribes, Alaska Natives have created marine mammal commissions and organizations to protect these uses, and to formalize Native management." *The Marine Mammal Protection Act of 1972, as Amended: Hearing Before Subcomm. On Fisheries, Wildlife and Oceans of the House Resources Comm.*, 10th Cong., 2d Sess. (Apr. 6, 2000) (testimony of Caleb Pungowiyi Chairman, MMPA Reauthorization Comm., Indigenous Peoples Council for Marine Mammals). That understanding is recognized in several laws governing biodiversity. ANILCA authorizes subsistence activities on wilderness lands, as mentioned in the previous note. The ESA exempts Native Alaskans who commit an otherwise unlawful "take" for subsistence purposes. *See* 16 U.S.C. § 1539(e). The Marine Mammal Protection Act contains a similar exemption. *See* 16 U.S.C. § 1371. But the application of such provisions can be controversial. For example, when the FWS proposed to list the Aleutian population of sea otters under the ESA, it received comments asserting that the subsistence harvest was contributing to the decline of the otters. The agency responded that "[t]he best available scientific information does not indicate that the subsistence harvest has had a major impact on the southwest Alaska DPS of the northern sea otter," but it added that regulation could become warranted if the population continued to decline. Determination of Threatened Status for the Southwest Alaska Distinct Population Segment of the Northern Sea Otter (Enhydra lutris kenyoni), 70 Fed. Reg. 46366, 46376 (2005).

6. Alaska did not become a state until January 1959. Its "very low population, enormously high percentage of federal lands, and lack of any provisions made over the years ... for resolving Alaska Native land ownership claims" explained the long wait for statehood even more than the area's geographic separation of the lower 48 states. WALTER R. BORNEMAN, ALASKA: SAGA OF A BOLD LAND 395 (2003). Sparsely populated lands thus played a central role in the state's evolution. The federal statehood legislation promised that over one hundred million acres—or 28% of the state— would be given to the new state government, but precisely which land would be handed over to the state and the status of native land claims was both left unresolved. Twelve years passed before Congress approved the Alaska Native Claims Settlement Act (ANCSA), which provided forty million acres and nearly one billion dollars for twelve regional corporations established for native Alaskans throughout the state. *See* 43 U.S.C. §§ 1603(b), 1605(a), 1611. Meanwhile, state officials and development interests battled environmentalists and federal officials in Washington to resolve the status of the bulk of the federal lands in the state. Finally, in December 1980, a lame duck Congress approved the Alaska National Interest Lands Conservation Act (ANILCA). ANILCA afforded federal protection to vast amounts of land, provided for the transfer of other land to the state and to native corporations, and directed studies with respect to the status of additional lands. The statute created ten new national parks and expanded three others, established nine wildlife refuges and expanded seven others, designated 26 wild and scenic rivers, and produced various new conservation areas and national monuments.

ANILCA also designated 56.7 million acres of wilderness lands, thus doubling the size of the national wilderness preservation system in one fell swoop. But the precise relationship between ANILCA's wilderness provisions and the provisions of the Wilderness Act remains unclear. Section 707 of ANILCA states that "except as otherwise expressly provided for in this Act, wilderness designated by this Act shall be administered in accordance with applicable provisions of the Wilderness Act governing areas designated by that Act as wilderness." *See* ANILCA § 707. ANILCA allows for subsistence activities, mineral assessment, access to inholdings, sport hunting and fishing, and motorized access for traditional activities in wilderness areas. *See* ANILCA § 811 (subsistence activities); *id.* at 1010 (mineral assessment); *id.* § 1109 (existing rights of access); *id.* § 1110(a) (access for traditional activities); *id.* § 1110(b) (access to inholdings); *id.* § 1313 (hunting and fishing). The extent of such activities, and the extent to which they can be regulated, is still contested.

Izembek National Wildlife Refuge, *Land Exchange/Road Corridor Draft Environmental Impact Statement, Executive Summary*

U.S. Fish & Wildlife Service, 2011.

ES-1.1 Introduction

In the *Omnibus Public Land Management Act of 2009* (Public Law 111-11, Title VI, Subtitle E) (Act), Congress authorized the Secretary of the Interior to exchange lands within the Izembek National Wildlife Refuge for lands owned by the State of Alaska and the King Cove Corporation for the purpose of constructing a single lane gravel road between the communities of King Cove and Cold Bay, Alaska if it is in the public interest. In the Act, Congress directed the Secretary of the Interior to prepare an Environmental Impact Statement (EIS) in accordance with the terms of the Act and the *National Environmental Policy Act of 1969* (NEPA), as amended (42 USC

4321 et. seq.), and its implementing regulations (40 CFR Parts 1500-1508). Congress specified that the EIS must analyze the land exchange, potential road construction and operation, and a specific road corridor through the Izembek National Wildlife Refuge and the Izembek Wilderness that is to be identified in consultation with the State of Alaska, the City of King Cove, and the Agdaagux Tribe of King Cove (Section 6402(b)(2)). Upon completion of the EIS, the Act requires the Secretary of Interior to determine whether the proposed land exchange and road is in the public interest.

If determined to be in the public interest, the land exchange would enable construction and operation of a single lane gravel road between the communities of King Cove and Cold Bay, Alaska, that would provide King Cove residents road access to the Cold Bay Airport. Congress responded to continuing concerns about reliable access for health and safety purposes on the part of the King Cove Corporation, the City of King Cove, the Aleutians East Borough, and the Agdaagux Tribe of King Cove. . .

ES-1.2 Proposed Action

The proposed action is the exchange of land between the federal government, the State of Alaska, and the King Cove Corporation for the purpose of constructing and operating a single lane gravel road between the communities of King Cove and Cold Bay, Alaska. As provided in the Act, the road "shall be used primarily for health and safety purposes, (including access to and from the Cold Bay Airport) and only for noncommercial purposes." The use of taxis, commercial vans for public transportation, and shared rides is exempted from the prohibition on commercial uses of the road.

Congress identified the federal and non-federal lands involved in the exchange and provided guidance regarding the administration of the exchanged lands . . .

- Approximately 206 acres of federal land (surface and subsurface estate) of the Izembek

- National Wildlife Refuge would be conveyed to the State under the land exchange. The final acreage to be exchanged would be determined by the width and location of the road corridor including safety turnouts as determined in each of the road alternatives considered. The boundary of the Izembek Wilderness would be modified to exclude the road corridor. . .

- Approximately 1,600 acres (surface and subsurface estate) within the Alaska Maritime National Wildlife Refuge on Sitkinak Island, including land withdrawn for use by the U.S. Coast Guard (Coast Guard) and approximately 170 acres of refuge-managed land would be transferred to the State.

- Approximately 43,093 acres of land owned by the State of Alaska, adjacent to the North Creek and Pavlof Units of the Alaska Peninsula National Wildlife Refuge, would be conveyed to the United States (U.S.) and added to the Alaska Peninsula National Wildlife Refuge as wilderness. . .

- Approximately 13,300 acres of land owned by King Cove Corporation . . . would be conveyed to the U.S. and added to the Izembek National Wildlife Refuge. The Kinzarof Lagoon parcel would also be added to Izembek Wilderness. As a part of the exchange, the King Cove Corporation would also relinquish its selection of 5,430 acres in Izembek Wilderness (selected lands) on the east side of Cold Bay made under the terms of the *Alaska Native Claims Settlement Act* (ANCSA).

The Act directed that the exchange could not be finalized before the parcel of state land located in Kinzarof Lagoon had been designated as part of the State of Alaska Izembek State Game Refuge. The Alaska Legislature passed and the Governor signed the *Izembek State Game Refuge Land Exchange Bill* into law (HB 210 Chapter 119 SLA 10) satisfying this requirement.

The proposed road corridor would connect the road terminus at the Northeast Hovercraft Terminal, approved in the King Cove Access Project EIS (2003 EIS) (USACE 2003), which is approximately 22 miles north of the City of King Cove, with the existing Cold Bay road system. Two road corridor alternatives are evaluated in this EIS. Both were developed in consultation with the State, the City of King Cove, and the Agdaagux Tribe of King Cove as required by Section 6402 (b)(2) of the Act. The proposed road corridor would be approximately 19.4 to 21.6 miles long and 100 feet wide. The proposed routes would cross Izembek National Wildlife Refuge (including Izembek Wilderness) and lands owned by the King Cove Corporation. . . If the Secretary of the Interior finds that a land exchange is in the public interest, an enforceable mitigation plan for road design and construction as required in Section 6043(e) will be developed as a part of the land exchange process, building upon mitigation measures identified as part of this EIS, with provisions to avoid wildlife and fish impacts and to mitigate wetlands loss.

Should the land exchange be found in the public interest but a construction permit is not authorized, or upon expiration of congressional legislative authority, the land exchange would be void, and federal and nonfederal lands would remain in, or would be returned to, the ownership status prior to the exchange (Section 6406 of the Act). In general, the Act's legislative authority expires 7 years from the date of the Act, unless a construction permit has been issued. Upon issuance of a construction permit, legislative authority would be extended for 5 additional years.

ES-1.3 Purpose and Need

The purpose of the proposed land exchange, as provided in the Act, is to transfer to the State of Alaska all right, title, and interest to a road corridor that would allow the construction, operation, and maintenance of a single lane gravel road between the communities of King Cove and Cold Bay, Alaska. The proposed road is to be used primarily to address health and safety issues, including reliable access to and from the Cold Bay Airport, and only for noncommercial purposes.

If the Secretary of the Interior finds that a land exchange and construction of the proposed road is in the public interest, then the applicant (not currently defined, but likely to be the State of Alaska) would submit an application to the Corps which would then determine compliance with the *Clean Water Act* Section 404 (b) (1) Guidelines. . . The basic project purpose is to provide a transportation system between the City of King Cove and the Cold Bay Airport. The overall project purpose is to construct a long term, safe, and reliable year round transportation system between the cities of King Cove and Cold Bay.

Objectives to be achieved by the proposed action include:

- Providing a safe, reliable, affordable transportation system between the City of King Cove and the airport in Cold Bay, Alaska;

- Addressing health and safety issues for King Cove residents, including timely emergency medical evacuations when needed and improved access to health care services not available in King Cove through access to the Cold Bay Airport;

- Balancing the needs of the communities, the national wildlife refuges (including wilderness), and ecosystem functions in the area;

- Transferring the minimum federal acreage necessary for the proposed road corridor;

- Developing an environmentally sensitive project design to minimize impact to wildlife, fish, plants, and their habitats, subsistence uses, wilderness character, and wetlands; and

- Selecting a road corridor that makes use of existing trails and roads to the maximum extent practicable.

NOTES & QUESTIONS

1. Should the Secretary of the Interior approve the road? Before you decide, consider the arguments of its supporters and its opponents. As described in the draft EIS, the residents of King's Cove articulate three justifications for the road:

- Health and safety: "Residents of the City of King Cove emphasize that access to the Cold Bay Airport is essential. Safe and reliable transportation to advanced medical care, including emergency medical care, is not available. They state that the proposed land exchange and construction of a road to the airport in Cold Bay will establish a safe and reliable land connection between the communities and provide access to advanced and emergency medical care." Id. at ES-6;

- Quality of life: "Residents of the City of King Cove state that improved access to the Cold Bay Airport would enhance their quality of life by providing reliable access the Cold Bay Airport, and from there to Anchorage and Seattle for health care services, including emergency medical evacuations when needed... Road access would provide peace of mind, particularly during extended periods of inclement weather that prevent marine and air travel. In addition, access to the Cold Bay Airport would provide the students, school board, borough assembly members, and medical service providers residing in King Cove with enhanced opportunities to travel out of their community. Residents would be able to meet with government officials in Anchorage and Juneau more reliably and to visit extended families living in other communities." Id. at ES-6 – ES-7.

- Affordable transportation: "Air transportation is limited by weather, availability of aircraft, and the topographic constraints of the King Cove Airport. Similar to other rural communities in Alaska, flights to and from the King Cove Airport are sometimes delayed or cancelled due to weather. Cost can be an issue for King Cove residents, not all of whom can afford air fares for a family flying back and forth between the communities of King Cove and Cold Bay, or the associated lodging costs when a continuing flight out of Cold Bay is missed or when weather prevents getting back to King Cove from Cold Bay on a return trip." Id. at ES-7.

But the National Wildlife Refuge Association (NWRA) objects to the proposed road:

- Constructing a road through the Izembek National Wildlife Refuge would have numerous negative impacts on wildlife and would degrade the critical wetlands habitat and wilderness quality of the refuge. It would devastate the exceptional refuge habitat vital to over half a million migratory birds, as well as brown bear, caribou, red fox, sea otters, and other wildlife. Almost the entire population of emperor geese and 98% of the Pacific brant population, as well as threatened Steller's eiders and tundra swans, depend on the Izembek National Wildlife Refuge.

- The isthmus where the road would be constructed is extremely narrow; standing in the center, one can easily see both the Izembek Lagoon to the north and the Kinzarof Lagoon to the south. Pacific brant gorge on the eelgrass beds of Izembek Lagoon before their non-stop journey to wintering grounds in Mexico. Birds and wildlife, such as brown bears, travel between the two lagoons, sometimes more than once a day, in search of food revealed by receding tides. Caribou use the isthmus as a wintering ground and a pathway when traveling to and from wintering grounds beyond the refuge. Brown bear make extensive use of the area for denning.

- Road construction, traffic, and maintenance could cause irreversible harm to the eelgrass beds and wetlands vital to many migratory birds. Passing vehicles would flush birds, wasting their valuable energy as they try to build up enough strength and resources for their migration.

A road through this isthmus would also disrupt wildlife movement and result in increased mortalities.

- The very wilderness character of the refuge is at stake. By definition, wilderness is where humans leave no mark. This precedent could open the door for other destructive practices on wilderness areas.

National Wildlife Refuge Ass'n, The Road to Nowhere: Gravel Road Full of Potholes for Wildlife and Taxpayers, at 4, http://www.refugeassociation.org/new-pdf-files/Izembek_report09.pdf. The NWRA adds that Congress already solved the problem by funding medical and airport improvements and by authorizing the hovercraft in 1998.

2. So should the Secretary of the Interior find that the proposed road is "in the public interest," or not? What factors are most important in determining the public interest? Why would Congress ask the Secretary of the Interior to make that decision, instead of relying on the ordinary process governing the management of national wildlife refuges, or alternately, Congress legislating to require or prohibit the road itself?

B. DESERT ECOSYSTEMS

Although they teem deceptively with abundant biodiversity, deserts are not especially resilient ecosystems. Tank tracks from World War II training exercises remain clearly visible in parts of the Mojave desert, and the devastation of the Gulf War on Kuwait's desert lands, despoiled by over 250 million gallons of oil that Iraqi troops intentionally released (20 times more than the *Exxon Valdez* spill), will take over $1 billion and several decades to restore to some semblance of functional health. *See* Ben Shouse, *Kuwait Unveils Plan to Treat Festering Desert Wound*, 293 Science 1410 (2001). And restoration is a term that can be used only loosely in desert settings. In the deserts of the American West, perhaps the most important ecological component is a thin veneer of life known as biological soil crust. The crusts are composed primarily of cyanobacteria (a type of blue-green algae) as well as lichens, mosses, microfungi, bacteria, and green algae. Some of these organisms protect themselves from sharp sand by secreting sticky mucilage around their cells, which over time builds up and binds the biological crust layer to underlying soils. This "gluing" effect provides important protection for the soils from wind and water erosion. Also, the biological matter in the crust absorbs up to ten times its volume in water, providing water retention and erosion reduction during rainfalls. The crusts, however, are usually no more than one-eight of an inch thick, and are no match for vehicle tires, cattle hooves, or even the soles of a hiker's shoes. Once the crust is crushed, nitrogen fixation is impaired, erosion becomes more acute, and dust covers surrounding crust areas. Under the best conditions, the affected crust may return to its healthy state in five years, 20 years if rainfall is high in the area, and 250 years if the area is particularly dry. *See* USGS, Biological Soil Crusts (2002). Moreover, in his studies of western ghost towns, Robert Webb of the U.S. Geological Survey has found that while vegetative communities have been established over a century after boom towns turned bust, the species composition is significantly different in many areas. Hardy, long-lived species such as creosote have been replaced by fast-breeding, short-lived plants like cheese-bush. *See* Kathryn Brown, *Ghost Towns Tell Tales of Ecological Boom and Bust*, 290 Science 35 (2000).

In a modern day version of this story, consider how the court in the following opinion describes and addresses the effects of off-road vehicles (ORV) on a portion of California desert. As ORV use became increasingly popular, both President Nixon and President Carter acted to control their presence on federal public lands through Executive Orders. *See* Exec. Order 11644, 37 Fed. Reg. 2877 (Feb. 8, 1972); Exec. Order 11989, 42 Fed. Reg. 26959 (May 25, 1977). Congress also addressed the issue of ORV use on Bureau of Land Management lands in the Federal Land Planning and Management Act. The case involves the manner in which the agency implemented these authorities in a particularly sensitive desert area.

Sierra Club v. Clark
United States Court of Appeals for the Ninth Circuit, 1985.
22 ERC 1748, 15 Envtl. L. Rep. 20,319.

■ POOLE, CIRCUIT JUDGE:

Plaintiffs Sierra Club, Desert Protective Council and California Native Plant Society ("Sierra Club") filed this action seeking judicial review under the Administrative Procedure Act, 5 U.S.C. § 706(1), of the failure of defendants Secretary of the Interior, Director of the Bureau of Land Management ("BLM"), and California State Director of BLM ("Secretary") to close Dove Springs Canyon to off road vehicle ("ORV") use. Sierra Club appeals from the district court's denial of their motion for summary judgment, and the grant of the Secretary's cross-motion for summary judgment. We affirm.

FACTS

Dove Springs Canyon is located in the California Desert Conservation Area ("Desert Area"), established in 1976, 43 U.S.C.§ 1781, under the Federal Land Policy Management Act ("the Act"), 43 U.S.C. § 1701 et seq. The Desert Area covers approximately 25 million acres in southeastern California, approximately 12.1 million of which are administered by the BLM. Dove Springs Canyon is comprised of approximately 5500 acres; 3000 acres are designated "open" for unrestricted use of ORVs.

Dove Springs Canyon possesses abundant and diverse flora and fauna. Over 250 species of plants, 24 species of reptiles, and 30 species of birds are found there. It also offers good habitat for the Mojave ground squirrel, the desert kit fox, and the burrowing owl. Because the rich and varied biota is unusual for an area of such low elevation in the Mojave Desert, the Canyon was once frequented by birdwatchers and naturalists, as well as hikers and fossil hunters.

CH. 12 FRAGILE ECOSYSTEMS 955

Recreational ORV usage of Dove Springs Canyon began in 1965 and became progressively heavier in the ensuing years. By 1971, the Canyon was being used intensively by ORV enthusiasts. It became especially popular because the site's diverse terrain, coupled with relatively easy access, provides outstanding hill-climbing opportunities. By 1979, up to 200 vehicles used the Canyon on a typical weekend; over 500 vehicles used it on a holiday weekend. In 1973, the BLM adopted its Interim Critical Management Program for Recreational Vehicle Use on the California Desert ("Interim Program") which designated Dove Springs Canyon as an ORV Open Area, permitting recreational vehicle travel in the area without restriction.

Extensive ORV usage has been accompanied by severe environmental damage in the form of major surface erosion, soil compaction, and heavy loss of vegetation. The visual aesthetics have markedly declined. The character of the Canyon has been so severely altered that the Canyon is now used almost exclusively for ORV activities.

In July of 1980 Sierra Club petitioned the Secretary of the Interior to close Dove Springs Canyon to ORV use under the authority of Executive Order No. 11644, as amended by Executive Order No. 11989, and 43 C.F.R.§ 8341.2 because of "substantial adverse effects" on the vegetation, soil and wildlife in the Canyon. The Secretary responded that the matter would be addressed in the California Desert Conservation Plan and Final Environmental Impact Statement ("the Final Plan").

The Final Plan approved by the Secretary in December 1980 maintained unrestricted ORV use in Dove Springs of 3000 of the 5500 acres. Sierra Club filed this action on January 6, 1981, alleging that the Secretary's failure to close Dove Springs violated Executive Order No. 11644, as amended by Executive Order No. 11989, and 43 C.F.R. § 8341.2; 43 U.S.C. § 1732(b), which requires the Secretary to prevent "unnecessary or undue degradation of the lands;" and 43 U.S.C. §§ 1781(b) and (d), which require the Secretary to maintain and conserve resources of the Desert Area under principles of "multiple use and sustained yield." Sierra Club sought declaratory relief and a writ of mandate compelling closure. . .

ANALYSIS

The district court ruled that the plaintiffs' complaint was an attack upon the Canyon's initial designation as an "ORV freeplay area" in the Final Plan, and refused to address plaintiffs' contention that the Executive Orders and the Regulation required closure of the area after the Final Plan was adopted. . . The district court also ruled that the Secretary's and BLM's exercise of discretion under the Act in designating the Canyon as open mooted the plaintiffs' claim. The plaintiffs in the district court and on appeal contend, however, that the closure standard contained in the Executive Orders and the Regulation applies independently of the designation process. The plain meaning of the provisions supports their view.

The Regulation provides:

> Notwithstanding the consultation provisions of § 8342.2(a), where the authorized officer determines that off-road vehicles are causing or will cause considerable adverse effects . . . the authorized officer shall immediately close the areas or trails affected. . . Such closures will not prevent designation . . ., but these lands shall not be opened to the type(s) of off-road vehicle to which it was closed unless the authorized officer determines that the adverse effects have been eliminated and measures implemented to prevent recurrence.

43 C.F.R. § 8341.2(a). This provision creates a separate duty to close without regard to the designation process; it does not automatically become inoperative once the Secretary exercises his discretion to designate the land.

The district court erred in its analysis and conclusion that the Secretary's designation mooted the Sierra Club's claims. Nevertheless, we do not reverse the district court on account of this error because we must affirm if the record fairly presents any basis for affirmance. On appeal from a grant of summary judgment, we review the record de novo, using the same standard as the district court under Fed.R.Civ.P. 56(c). Because we have decided that the closure standard of the Executive Orders and the Regulation applies independently of the designation of the land as open under the Act, the issue before us is whether the damage to Dove Springs Canyon amounts to "considerable adverse effects" which require the Canyon's closure. The parties agree that there is no genuine issue as to the extent of the damage to the Canyon, and therefore resolution of this issue depends upon whether the Secretary's interpretation of this phrase or that of the Sierra Club is to control.

Traditionally, an agency's interpretation of its own regulation is entitled to a high degree of deference if it is not unreasonable. The Secretary interprets "considerable adverse effect" to require determining what is "considerable" in the context of the Desert Area as a whole, not merely on a parcel-by-parcel basis. The Secretary contends such a broad interpretation is necessary and is consistent with 43 U.S.C. § 1781(a)(4) which expresses a congressional judgment that ORV use is to be permitted "where appropriate." . . .

Sierra Club argues that . . . the Secretary's interpretation should not be adopted because it is unreasonable. Sierra Club insists that the sacrifice of any area to permanent resource damage is not justified under the multiple use management mandate of 43 U.S.C.§ 1702(c) that requires multiple use "without permanent impairment of the productivity of the land and the quality of the environment." In further support of its position Sierra Club adverts to the requirement in the Act that the Secretary prevent "unnecessary and undue degradation" of the public lands, 43 U.S.C. § 1732(b). In addition, Sierra Club contends, when Congress established the Desert Area it intended the Secretary to fashion a multiple use and sustained yield management plan "to conserve [the California desert] resources for future generations, and to provide present and future use and enjoyment, particularly outdoor recreational uses, including the use, where appropriate, of off-road recreational vehicles." 43 U.S.C.§ 1781(a)(4). Sierra Club argues that it is unreasonable for the Secretary to find ORV use "appropriate" when that use violates principles of sustained yield, substantially impairs productivity of renewable resources and is inconsistent with maintenance of environmental quality.

We can appreciate the earnestness and force of Sierra Club's position, and if we could write on a clean slate, would prefer a view which would disallow the virtual sacrifice of a priceless natural area in order to accommodate a special recreational activity. But we are not free to ignore the mandate which Congress wrote into the Act. Sierra Club's interpretation of the regulation would inevitably result in the total prohibition of ORV use because it is doubtful that any discrete area could withstand unrestricted ORV use without considerable adverse effects. However appealing might be such a resolution of the environmental dilemma, Congress has found that ORV use, damaging as it may be, is to be provided "where appropriate." It left determination of appropriateness largely up to the Secretary in an area of sharp conflict. If there is to be a change it must come by way of Congressional reconsideration. The Secretary's interpretation that this legislative determination calls for accommodation of ORV usage in the administrative plan, we must conclude, is not unreasonable and we are constrained to let it stand.

*   *   *

Under the California Desert Conservation Area Plan, approximately 4 percent (485,000 acres) of the total acreage is now open to unrestricted ORV use. Dove Springs itself constitutes only 0.025 percent of BLM administered lands in the Desert Area. Although all parties recognize that the environmental impact of ORV use at Dove Springs is severe, the Secretary's determination that these effects were not "considerable" in the context of the Desert Area as a whole is not arbitrary, capricious, or an abuse of the broad discretion committed to him by an obliging Congress.

NOTES AND QUESTIONS

1. *Sierra Club v. Clark* illustrates the difficulty of managing particularly fragile areas that lie within larger public land management units, especially when the amorphous "multiple use" mandate applies. Dove Springs Canyon, at 5500 acres, was a minuscule fraction of the Desert Area's 25 million acres. It provided, however, a concentration of biodiversity that was particularly susceptible to damage from a concentration of ORV usage. The BLM strategy for implementing the multiple use mandate seems to have been to concentrate ORV use into contained areas such as the Canyon and write them off from a conservation perspective, leaving the remaining areas free for different management objectives. While this spelled doom for Dove Springs Canyon, was it an appropriate strategy for management of the Desert Area as a whole? Assuming that some ORV use must be allowed in the Desert Area—after all, Congress decreed as much—how would you have managed the distribution of ORV areas? Should they be allowed at moderate levels everywhere, or at intensive levels in special areas only? Should areas of intensive use be periodically rotated throughout the Desert Area, so as to allow recovery in used areas over time?

2. The court's reasoning was that BLM was within its discretion to define "considerable adverse effects" such that the numerator was the 3000 acres of Dove Springs Canyon open to ORV use, but the denominator was the entire Desert Area's 25 million acres. Does that make sense? Will any area under, say, 10,000 acres that is opened to concentrated ORV use ever affect the entire Desert Area so substantially as to trigger the "considerable adverse effects" standard under this approach? On the other hand, where would ORV use ever be allowed if the test were to focus only on the area where ORV "freeplay" use is concentrated? That approach might lead to decisions that spread ORV use out over larger areas, so as to make the effects more diffuse and thus less likely to be "considerable." Which outcome would you prefer? Do you have an alternative approach to recommend?

3. The ORV battles have continued to rage in desert settings. For example, ongoing litigation in *Center for Biological Diversity v. Bureau of Land Management* challenges decisions by the Department of the Interior to open 50,000 acres of the Algodonales Dunes in the Imperial Sand Dunes Recreation Area to ORVs. And one desert ORV case recently reached the United States Supreme Court, which ruled that an environmental group had no remedy in an action challenging BLM's decision to allow ORVs onto wilderness study areas in Utah. The Court held that the claims challenged programmatic decisions rather than discrete agency actions, and thus were not within the scope of judicial review under the Administrative Procedure Act, and that because the decisions had already been made in the agency's land use plans, there was no new agency decision that could have triggered the need for more impact review under the National Environmental Policy Act. *See* Norton v. Southern Utah Wilderness Alliance, 542 U.S. 55 (2004) (discussed in Chapter 9).

Western Watersheds Project v. Salazar

United States District Court for the Central District of California, 2011.
2011 U.S. Dist. LEXIS 151556.

■ GEE, UNITED STATES DISTRICT JUDGE.

. . . The Ivanpah Solar Electric Generating System ("ISEGS") is a 370-megawatt solar concentrating thermal power plant currently under construction on BLM-administered land in the Mojave Desert. It is located 4.5 miles southwest of Primm, Nevada and 0.5 miles west of the Primm Valley Golf Club, beyond which lies the Ivanpah Dry Lake. BLM, *California Desert Conservation Area Plan Amendment / Final Environmental Impact Statement for Ivanpah Solar Electric Generating System* ("FEIS") 3-26 to 3-27 (July 2010). The project is being developed in three phases: Ivanpah unit 1 will occupy approximately 914 acres and generate 120 megawatts of electricity. Ivanpah units 2 and 3 are each designed to provide 125 megawatts of electricity and will occupy approximately 1,097 and 1,227 acres, respectively. All three phases will share an administration building, an operation and maintenance building, and a substation that will be located between Ivanpah 1 and 2. The total project area, including roads, natural gas, water, transmission lines, and construction staging areas, will occupy approximately 3,471 acres (5.4 square miles).

The project is comprised of fields of heliostat mirrors focusing solar energy on boilers located in central power towers. FEIS at 1-2. Each mirror will track the sun throughout the day and reflect solar energy onto the receiver boiler. Each of the three Ivanpah units will have one 459-foot tower. Ivanpah 1 and 2 will have up to 55,000 heliostats, while Ivanpah 3 will have approximately 63,500 heliostats. Each of the three power plants will contain a power block with a steam turbine generator. Generator interconnection lines will tie each power plant into Southern California Edison's transmission grid via a new Ivanpah substation.

An 8-foot tall chain-link security fence topped with barbed wire will surround the site. The project also includes a tortoise barrier fence that will be installed to a depth of 12 inches and extending 22 to 24 inches above the ground. The tortoise fence will be integrated with the security fence. Construction will be performed in accordance with certain plans and mitigation measures to avoid or minimize adverse impacts on the environment, including a raven management plan, a desert tortoise translocation/relocation plan, an application for incidental take permit, and a biological assessment ("BA"). . .

Figure 3.3
Ivanpah Solar Electric Generating System - Visual Simulation view from Benson Mine / Mojave Preserve

U.S. BUREAU OF LAND MANAGEMENT and CALIFORNIA ENERGY COMMISSION, SITING, TRANSMISSION AND ENVIRONMENTAL PROTECTION DIVISION, OCTOBER 2009
SOURCE: Data Response Set 2C #1.48 Figure DR 1.47-3

The Ivanpah Valley And The Desert Tortoise

The desert tortoise is listed as a threatened species under the ESA. Its range covers the Mojave Desert region of Nevada, California, and Utah, and the Sonoran Desert region of Arizona and Northern Mexico. The Ivanpah Valley supports part of the tortoise's Mojave population. Throughout their range, desert tortoise populations have declined. Urbanization, agricultural development, military training, recreational use, mining, and livestock grazing have caused the loss and degradation of their habitat. Increased predation by common ravens, collection by humans for pets or consumption, collisions with vehicles on paved and unpaved roads, and mortality resulting from diseases are also factors.

The principal strategy for the desert tortoise's recovery and delisting is the FWS desert tortoise recovery plan. As part of the recovery plan, the FWS designated "critical habitat," *i.e.*, areas "essential to the conservation of the species" that "may require special management considerations or protection," 16 U.S.C. § 1532, in the Mojave desert region. The ISEGS project is not located within a designated critical habitat for any species, but it is approximately five miles north of the Ivanpah Critical Habitat Unit for the desert tortoise.

Although the FWS tortoise recovery plan provides that land managers should "focus the most aggressive recovery efforts towards tortoise conservation areas," it also emphasizes that "land managers should strive to limit the loss of desert tortoise habitat outside conservation areas as much as possible." It recognizes that "activities occurring on lands beyond the boundaries of existing tortoise conservation areas can affect tortoise populations as well as the effectiveness of conservation actions occurring within the conservation area boundaries."

Desert tortoises are distributed throughout the Ivanpah Valley except in the dry lakes and developed areas. The Ivanpah Valley provides excellent quality tortoise habitat and supports some of the highest population densities in the East Mojave. The ISEGS project is located within the Northeastern Mojave Recovery Unit. The project area coincides with a high-quality habitat for the desert tortoise with low levels of disturbance and high plant species diversity. The population in the project area is unique "because it is the highest elevation at which this species is known to reside in the state."

Whether BLM Satisfied NEPA's "Hard Look" Requirement

[BLM published a draft EIS in November 2009, a supplemental draft EIS in April 2010, and the final EIS in 2011. After reviewing the public comments, including comments submitted by the plaintiff here, BLM "issued a determination of NEPA adequacy concluding that the existing NEPA documentation (the draft EIS, supplemental draft EIS, and FEIS) were adequate "[e]ven though some on-the-ground information has developed" because the "impacts to the desert tortoise and the means to mitigate those impacts that were identified in the NEPA process are the same as those previously identified" and thus "additional public involvement is not necessary." The plaintiffs seek to enjoin further work on the project until BLM complies with NEPA.]

a. The FEIS' Description Of The Existing Tortoise Populations

Plaintiff argues that the FEIS is inadequate to meet NEPA's "hard look" standard because it "grossly understates the tortoise population on the Project site, precluding an accurate assessment of the Project's impacts." Based on FWS data from a 2009 survey in the North Ivanpah Valley, the FEIS posits that "up to 50 tortoises may reside in the project area." Plaintiff, in its comments on the FEIS, criticized this estimate for lack of "further documentation" and because "[n]o clarification is given as to whether this is an estimated number of adult tortoises or includes desert tortoises of all age classes." Plaintiff maintains that the revised tortoise estimates in the 2011 biological opinion prove his criticisms of BLM's tortoise count to be correct. . .

BLM properly focused its analysis on the impact that the ISEGS project would have on the desert tortoise population as a whole. *See* Envtl. Prot. Info. Ctr. v. U.S. Forest Serv., 451 F.3d 1005, 1010 (9th Cir. 2006) ("NEPA regulations direct the agency to consider the degree of adverse effect on a species, not the impact on individuals of that species."). A complete and accurate assessment of "population viability in terms of actual population size, population trends, or the population dynamics of other species" may be helpful to the Court's analysis, but is not required. Inland Empire Pub. Lands Council v. U.S. Forest Serv., 88 F.3d 754, 761 n.8 (9th Cir. 1996).

Thus, Plaintiff's assertion that "statements regarding tortoise populations" in the FEIS "are wholly unqualified and make no mention of any possible shortcomings" is incorrect. Plaintiff criticizes the FEIS for failing to indicate that its population estimates excluded juvenile tortoises and tortoise eggs. In fact, the FEIS acknowledged that tortoise densities in the northern Ivanpah Valley "were typically less than 50 *adults* per square mile" during the 1990s" (emphasis added). This corresponds to the FEIS estimate, based on FWS survey data from the northern Ivanpah Valley, that "up to 50 tortoises may reside in the project area." The exclusion of sub-adult tortoises was reasonable given the "difficulty in locating juvenile desert tortoises and eggs" and the fact that 95-98% of tortoises "die prior to reaching reproductive age."

Finally, Plaintiff asserts that previous tortoise counts were inaccurate as they were conducted during a "strong drought year when tortoises tend to remain in their burrows" and locating them "is known to be problematic." Plaintiff overlooks that the 2010 biological opinion "include[d] a correction factor for surveys conducted during drought years." Although in hindsight the correction factor was too conservative as "2007 was one of the driest years on record", an agency "is entitled to rely on reasonable assumptions in its environmental analyses," and here the assumption was not plainly erroneous.

As BLM adequately considered the impacts of the project on the desert tortoise habitat and species, an underestimation of population size within the project area is understandable given the uncertainties in producing such an estimate. Plaintiff is unlikely to succeed on this claim.

b. Analysis Of Habitat Connectivity And Fragmentation Impacts

Plaintiff contends that the FEIS fails to analyze the ISEGS project's impacts on connectivity between desert tortoise habitats and fragmentation of occupied habitat into smaller, isolated populations. draft EIS cited loss of connectivity among the indirect effects of the ISEGS project and stated that this impact was "discussed in more detail below", although no such discussion followed. The draft EIS also noted that the project would "fragment and degrade adjacent habitat" and that this impact would "directly and adversely affect habitat for a threatened species (the desert tortoise), and would likely be highly controversial" but did not attempt to quantify the fragmentation effects. Plaintiff pointed out these shortcomings in its comments on the draft EIS. The FEIS does not differ materially from the draft EIS in these respects and does not directly address Plaintiff's comments.

The FEIS discusses habitat fragmentation and connectivity impacts only generally and without any discussion of their negative impacts on the tortoise as required by NEPA. Such "general statements about 'possible' effects and 'some risk' do not constitute a 'hard look' absent a justification regarding why more definitive information could not be provided."

BLM disputes that it was required to expand on its analysis of fragmentation and connectivity impacts in the FEIS. It maintains that Plaintiff "need[s] to demonstrate a likely effect on the tortoise population as a whole, not merely a potential impact on individual animals" and that "the 2010 and 2011 [biological opinions] demonstrate[] that there is unlikely to be any such population effects." Although an agency may integrate by reference other documents into the EIS, the "incorporated material shall be cited in the statement and its content briefly described." 40 C.F.R. § 1502.21. As the FEIS was issued before either the 2010 or 2011 biological opinions, BLM's reliance on them as a *post hoc* justification are inappropriate. An agency may not rely on supplemental reports "to present information and analysis that it was required, but . . . failed to include in its original NEPA documents." BLM offers no justification for its failure to analyze the issue of habitat fragmentation and connectivity impacts in any greater depth.

BrightSource's similar extrinsic evidence suggesting that connectivity and fragmentation effects do not jeopardize the desert tortoise population as a whole—while relevant to the irreparable harm analysis—does not justify the FEIS' failure to perform this type of analysis at all.

Plaintiff raises a serious question as to whether BLM violated NEPA by engaging in a cursory discussion of habitat connectivity and fragmentation without analyzing the potential impacts of habitat fragmentation on the Mojave population of the desert tortoise.

c. Assessment Of Translocation Impacts

Plaintiff next asserts that the FEIS fails to take a "hard look" at the translocation plan's impact on the desert tortoise because it does not quantify the actual risks posed to the tortoises during the translocation but merely refers to general statements about possible effects. In addition, Plaintiff maintains that BLM inadequately examined the risk that disease will spread among tortoise populations during translocation.

The translocation of desert tortoises currently living in the ISEGS project area to other sites is one of the mitigation measures discussed in the FEIS. Although "[m]itigation must 'be discussed in sufficient detail to ensure that environmental consequences have been fairly evaluated,'" an EIS "need not contain a 'complete mitigation plan' that is 'actually formulated and adopted.'"

Recognizing that translocation has "inherent risks and could [itself] result in direct effects such as mortality, injury, or harassment of desert tortoises," the FEIS discusses translocation at length. In December 2008, FWS provided BrightSource with guidelines for developing a translocation plan. BrightSource submitted its initial draft translocation plan in March 2009. Following comments from FWS, the California Energy Commission ("CEC"), and the California Department of Fish and Game ("CDFG"), BrightSource submitted a revised draft translocation plan in May 2009 that changed the proposed translocation areas. FWS, CEC, and CDFG provided further feedback in July 2009.

In response, BrightSource conducted surveys in the four potential translocation sites for desert tortoise and vegetation. Based on the results of these surveys, BLM and FWS determined that the proposed translocation sites "fulfill expectations regarding assessment of habitat quality." Three of the four proposed translocation sites exhibited "excellent desert tortoise habitat potential, ranking as 0.9 on a scale of 1.0." The ranking was based on a United States Geological Survey model of desert tortoise habitat potential that encompassed variables related to soil, landscape, climate, and biotic factors.

Based on comments from the public, BLM and FWS, in conjunction with state agencies, developed additional translocation guidelines for renewable energy projects. FWS modified its disease testing protocols such that tortoises "must be tested and assessed as free of disease before they are released into the translocation area." Based on this guidance, BLM developed its translocation strategy.

Plaintiff hypothesizes that "translocated healthy tortoises may displace diseased resident tortoises who would thereby spread disease ever farther." Such a "ripple" effect is unlikely. Following BrightSource's survey, its consultants concluded that "the density of desert tortoises in the proposed translocation area [i]s low and translocation of animals from the ISEGS site to this area would not overburden the resident population." BLM and FWS deemed the survey results "satisfactory." Moreover, in August 2010 FWS developed a revised set of translocation guidelines, "which is expected to be more protective than the translocation plan as discussed in [the FEIS]" because it "require[s] disease testing and health assessments for tortoises being moved *and for tortoises in the resident population of the receiving area.*"

Based on the discussion in the FEIS, it does not appear that Defendants developed the translocation strategy in an arbitrary and capricious manner. Consequently, Plaintiff is unlikely to succeed on its claim that they inadequately assessed translocation impacts.

d. Analysis Of Cumulative Impacts

Plaintiff also disputes the adequacy of BLM's cumulative impact analysis. Specifically, it contends that the agency did not discuss the cumulative impact of the tortoise translocation strategy and the envisioned DesertXpress railway. DesertXpress is a proposed high-speed railway that would run between Victorville, California, and Las Vegas, Nevada. . .

Here, the 56-page cumulative impacts analysis in the FEIS appears copacetic. It contains a chart of 14 existing projects in the Ivanpah Valley and 17 future foreseeable projects, including a brief description of each project, its current status, and a summary of resources that it would potentially affect. The FEIS offers a more detailed discussion of the features and impacts of six "reasonably foreseeable future projects that could contribute cumulative impacts to those of the ISEGS," including the DesertXpress railway. It then provides a thorough analysis of the cumulative impacts posed by the proposed ISEGS project, its two main alternatives, and the "no action" alternative, considering 18 different factors, including biological resources. . .

e. Analysis Of The Impact On Special Status Birds

Plaintiff's next basis for asserting that BLM failed to take a "hard look" at the impact of the ISEGS project concerns special-status birds. Plaintiff points out that there "are numerous species of rare and special-status birds that frequent the Ivanpah Valley and Project site, including many migratory birds like the golden eagle."

[T]he FEIS took a sufficiently hard look at the ISEGS project's effect on special status birds. To the extent Plaintiff maintains that the FEIS should have *explicitly* addressed the impact on the Mexican whip-poor-will and hepatic tanager, BLM had no obligation to exhaustively chronicle every conceivable effect on every special status bird. The [Migratory Bird Treaty Act (MBTA)] alone protects more than 1,000 species of migratory birds. *See* 50 C.F.R. § 10.13(c). . . BLM's discussion of the general impacts on migratory birds and specific impacts on representative MBTA species, including those found on the project site, is sufficient to comply with NEPA.

[The court also held that BLM was not required to issue a supplemental EIS or to consider the impact of a nearby power transmission line project, and BLM adequately defined the public purpose and need for the ISEGS project].

6. Whether BLM Properly Dismissed The Proposed Alternatives

NEPA regulations require the agency, in considering a proposed project, to "[r]igorously explore and objectively evaluate all reasonable alternatives, and for alternatives which were eliminated from detailed study, briefly discuss the reasons for their having been eliminated." 40 C.F.R. § 1502.14. Analysis of alternatives to a proposed federal action "is the heart" of an EIS. An EIS "should present the environmental impacts of the proposal and the alternatives in comparative form, thus sharply defining the issues and providing a clear basis for choice among options by the decisionmaker and the public." To adequately consider alternatives to the proposed project, BLM "must look at every reasonable alternative within the range dictated by the nature and scope of the proposal."

An EIS is inadequate if there are any "reasonable but unexamined alternatives." An alternative that is consistent with the policy goals of the project and is potentially feasible must be analyzed in depth and not "preliminarily eliminated." Conversely, an alternative does not need to be analyzed if that alternative is unreasonable. A proposed alternative is unreasonable if it is inconsistent with the purpose of the project. That the proposed project is preferable to an alternative does not relieve an agency of its duty to analyze the alternative; so long as the alternative is reasonable, it must be examined.

Here, BLM developed and evaluated 25 alternatives to the proposed project. It found only three of these alternatives "to be both feasible and have the potential to result in lesser impacts": (1) the selected "Mitigated Ivanpah 3" alternative, which will use fewer heliostats and reduce the total acreage of the ISEGS project; (2) a "Modified I-15" alternative, which would have moved the project location to the south, required less acreage and grading, and had less of an impact on the desert tortoise and vegetation; and (3) the "No Action" alternative. Plaintiff claims that BLM violated NEPA by not considering the alternatives of siting the ISEGS project on the Ivanpah Dry Lake or on private land.

a. The Ivanpah Dry Lake Alternative

BLM considered and rejected the Ivanpah Dry Lake bed alternative, finding that while it "would eliminate impacts to vegetation and tortoises," it "would not be economically feasible, and would be inconsistent with current management objectives for non-motorized recreation on the Dry Lake bed." The Ivanpah Dry Lake alternative would be economically and likely technically infeasible because, notwithstanding its name, the lake bed floods, "sometimes more than once per year." The lake bed "usually remains flooded for a period of weeks or months," during which "vehicles cannot drive on the Dry Lake bed surface." Although the Ivanpah Dry Lake could theoretically be diked to prevent flooding, "this would likely be economically prohibitive, and would also not protect the facility against direct rainfall." Additionally, placement of the ISEGS project on the Dry Lake would conflict with BLM management objectives for the lake, which is currently designated "for nonmotorized open-space recreational activities."

The choice of alternatives in an FEIS that an agency chooses to analyze is governed by the "rule of reason." A lake bed prone to flooding for weeks or months at a time is not consistent with the ISEGS project's purpose of operating an electrical generating facility. The Ivanpah Dry Lake alternative was not reasonable and thus was properly dismissed. Plaintiff is unlikely to prevail on its claim that BLM should have considered the Dry Lake alternative in greater detail.

b. The Private Land Alternative

BrightSource evaluated three private land alternatives: Harper Lake, Lucerne Valley, and Rabbit Lake. Only the Harper Lake site had sufficient land for a 400 megawatt facility with the configuration of the ISEGS project, but one of the major land owners at the Harper Lake site "requested too much money to make the site economically feasible." BLM eliminated the private land alternatives because "its implementation is remote and speculative" and "would depend upon the ability of a developer to acquire multiple, contiguous private land holdings covering a large area, which is not likely to be feasible." In addition, the Harper Lake alternative "was considered to be time consuming."

The Harper Lake private land alternative was infeasible and inconsistent with the project's purpose. The large landholder who would not sell necessary land at an economically viable price prevented the project from moving forward. Even if BrightSource eventually could have settled on a non-prohibitive purchase agreement with each individual landholder, through a land swap or otherwise, the process would have been time consuming. Expediting the development of alternative energy projects was one of BLM's explicit purposes.

Accordingly, BLM did not dismiss the Harper Lake alternative improperly. Plaintiff fails to show a likelihood of success on this claim.

B. Plaintiff's Likelihood Of Irreparable Harm

In order to prevail on a preliminary injunction motion, a litigant must "demonstrate that irreparable injury is *likely* in the absence of an injunction." Winter [v. Natural Res. Def. Council, Inc., 555 U.S. 7, 22 (2008)]. "[E]nvironmental injury, by its nature, can seldom be adequately remedied by money damages and is often permanent or at least of long duration, *i.e.*, irreparable." An organization's actual injury may include its members' loss of their ability to "view, experience, and utilize" wilderness areas in their undisturbed state. . .

The harm to the population at the proposed site brought about by the loss of thousands of acres of desert habitat is itself a sufficient irreparable injury to warrant equitable relief. The fact that Plaintiff's members may be able to enjoy the desert tortoise in its habitat elsewhere is of little consequence.

In evaluating the *likelihood* of irreparable harm, the Court is mindful of the "significant overlap" with the merits in a NEPA case. As a procedural statute, NEPA does not guarantee any particular outcome. Thus, the likelihood of injury depends, at least in part, on the implicit assumption that further review may cause the agency to change its decision. Generally, this is a reasonable assumption. Here, it is not.

Plaintiff's only claim that raises serious questions on the merits is its assertion that BLM failed to fully analyze connectivity and fragmentation impacts. The 2011 biological opinion indicates that the ISEGS impact on connectivity and fragmentation will be minimal. Historically, desert tortoise "population connectivity in the Northeastern Mojave Recovery Unit and Ivanpah Valley was constrained through geographic and topographic bottlenecks." In the area west of I-15 where the ISEGS project is located, the tortoise population "is likely isolated and suffering from demographic stochasticity and genetic deterioration because of *existing* barriers that greatly reduce the potential for movement." Although the ISEGS project would exacerbate these stresses on the local tortoise population west of I-15, "populations to the west and east of ISEGS would still largely be connected." Ultimately, the 2011 biological opinion concludes that the "negative effect on population stability within some local portions of Ivanpah Valley that are close to the project site" will not "affect a large enough portion of the population to affect substantially the overall population trend within the recovery unit or range wide."

Because the current record demonstrates that overall connectivity fragmentation and connectivity impacts will be modest, it is unlikely that further review by BLM will cause it to change its decision. For this reason, Plaintiff cannot demonstrate that it will likely sustain irreparable injury if construction proceeds as planned.

C. The Balance Of Equities

Plaintiff must show "that the balance of equities tips in [its] favor." As an injunction is a matter of equitable discretion, the Court must assign weight to particular harms. Economic harm, including jobs and the value of a project to the local community, may be weighed against environmental impacts. "[C]ourts must always carefully balance the competing claims of injury" and carefully scrutinize the written record, including expert testimony, regarding the harm posed by the project.

The Government avers that the ISEGS project "will benefit the nation, the State of California, and San Bernardino County by stimulating employment, enhancing energy security, reducing greenhouse gas emission, and providing other economic benefits." It asserts that the project will provide "approximately $350 million over the 30-year life of the project in tax revenue annually in property taxes for San Bernardino County" and will employ approximately 1,000 workers "at peak construction activity." During the life of the ISEGS facility, it will require sixty employees.

CURE argues in its *amicus* brief that the ISEGS project will employ "hundreds of skilled workers at a time when good jobs are in very short supply. The Ivanpah project will "employ highly trained workers, including pipefitters, electricians, boilermakers and ironworkers for four years, and will provide approximately $197 million in construction payroll, at an average salary of $50 per hour (including benefits)." As of July 13, 2011, there were approximately 420 construction workers employed at the ISEGS site, and that number is expected to grow to approximately 1,400 workers by Spring of 2012. The project has provided joint labor-management training opportunities for apprentices from certified training programs, funded by labor unions, and has also provided counseling and training opportunities for military veterans through the Helmets to Hardhats program of the AFL-CIO.

The timing of the implementation of the ISEGS project "is critical to its ultimate success" because delay would "frustrate the federal and state public policies" underlying ISEGS funding "and the incentives the project would qualify for." The project has been financed by several different "mutually dependent" sources of funding, including a $1.3 billion loan commitment from the United States Department of Energy, $600 million in federal tax grants, bridge loans from the Federal Financing Bank, and equity capital from BrightSource, NRG Solar, and Google, Inc.

A delay in construction activities could jeopardize project funding. BrightSource has entered into power purchase contracts with Southern California Edison and PG&E, which require the three ISEGS units to come on line by July 1, 2013, September 30, 2013, and December 31, 2013, respectively. If these deadlines are not met, BrightSource will pay "penalties of over $30,000 per day" and will ultimately be exposed "to the loss of millions of dollars in development security." BrightSource would also be exposed to increased construction costs associated with remobilizing workers and equipment that "could easily exceed $2 million." BrightSource estimates that any delay in construction would incur costs amounting to approximately $125,000 per day. A delay in the project would also place California's two largest utilities at risk of failing to meet their obligations under California's Global Warming Solutions Act of 2006 and the California Renewables Portfolio Standard.

. . . Plaintiff has known the basis for its claims regarding the adequacy of the connectivity and fragmentation analyses since October 2010. Plaintiff waited while construction began, then stopped, only to begin again before finally seeking an injunction more than eight months later—after BrightSource had spent more than $712 million constructing the project. Even if the unique facts of this case do not support denying injunctive relief on laches alone, Plaintiff's substantial delay is one factor weighing against it.

The potential harm faced by Plaintiff—the loss of an opportunity to preserve more than five square miles of high quality desert tortoise habitat—is certainly not trivial. Nonetheless, this represents less than one-tenth of one percent of the estimated 6,400 square miles of desert habitat in the Northeastern Mojave recovery unit. In contrast, several important factors weigh against injunctive relief: (1) this project is expected to contribute to state and federal goals for the increased use of renewable energy and the reduction of greenhouse gas emissions; (2) BrightSource has already expended more than $712 million constructing the project to date; (3) the project's success includes a substantial socioeconomic impact upon hundreds of workers and state revenues; and (4) Plaintiff delayed in bringing its motion for a preliminary injunction until after the project was well underway. Thus, the balance of equities tips against an injunction.

D. The Public Interest

Plaintiff must additionally show that an injunction is in the public interest in order to prevail on its motion. *Winter*, 555 U.S. at 20. "[C]areful consideration of environmental impacts before major federal projects go forward" may be in the public interest. In considering a motion for an injunction under NEPA, however, where the ultimate claim is that the defendants must adequately prepare an EIS, an injunction should not be granted when there is a strong public interest weighing against the injunction.

BLM emphasizes that the ISEGS project advances the stated policy of Congress and the President to facilitate and promote the development of renewable energy resources. This policy is designed to "increase domestic energy production, provide alternatives to traditional energy resources, and enhance the energy security of the United States." The project additionally furthers BLM's goal of confronting "[t]he realities of climate change" and changing "how we manage the land, water, fish and wildlife, and cultural heritage and tribal lands and resources we oversee."

The Governor of California argues that the ISEGS project is also of critical importance in advancing California's long-standing commitment to the reduction of the use of fossil fuels. The Ivanpah project is of importance to California's Renewable Portfolio Standard ("RPS"), signed into law in April 2011. RPS requires "all retail sellers of electricity to serve 33 percent of their load with renewable energy by 2020." The California Air Resources Board has estimated that the RPS goal of 33 percent renewable will reduce greenhouse gas emissions from the state by at least 12 million electric tons and will reduce air pollutants and contaminants, providing positive health benefits.

Plaintiff does not contest the importance of energy security or renewable energy to public policy. Instead, Plaintiff argues that the Ivanpah project is not necessary to serve those policies, and that there are superior and more cost effective means to develop renewable energy and enhance energy security. Plaintiff also cites the policies of the Governor, who, in conjunction with the CEC and in furtherance of its goal of bringing 12,000 megawatts of local renewable energy on line, has focused on "local solar PV, not industrial-scale projects that require massive federal financial support to get built." According to the Governor, however, the state has adopted a "multi-prong development approach," which it has determined to be the only method by which it can achieve its aggressive goals for renewable energy. The CEC itself found that "[d]istributed solar must be viewed as a partner, not a competitor or replacement for utility scale solar."

The Ninth Circuit has "recognized the public interest in careful consideration of environmental impacts before major federal projects go forward," and has "held that suspending such projects until that consideration occurs 'comports with the public interest.'" Nonetheless, weighing the competing public interests at stake, the Court finds that the balance tips sharply against an injunction. Plaintiff's sole response to the need for the development of renewable energy is that rooftop photovoltaic energy would be more cost efficient. Defendants point out that the need for a greater volume of energy to meet state-mandated energy goals cannot be met by such energy sources alone. Plaintiff's dispute with Defendants in this regard amounts to a policy disagreement. It is a policy fight that Plaintiff lost when state and federal executives and legislatures enunciated goals and adopted measures relating to renewable energy in support of their current positions. It is not this Court's role to substitute its own policy judgments for those of the legislature or an agency charged with overseeing matters within its expertise.

Although Plaintiff has raised "serious questions" regarding the adequacy of certain aspects of the FEIS, at this juncture, the existence of "serious questions" does not excuse Plaintiff's failure to show the other three elements necessary for injunctive relief. Therefore, Plaintiff is not entitled to a preliminary injunction.

NOTES & QUESTIONS

1. Solar energy is championed by many environmentalists who see it as a nonpolluting, carbon-free source of energy. The court's opinion notes some of the recent federal and state laws designed to encourage the development of solar energy. But solar energy has negative environmental impacts, too. Besides harming rare desert tortoises, the construction of large solar energy facilities can impact other kinds of desert biodiversity, important scenic views in an otherwise desolate landscape, and consume significant quantities of the desert's limited supply of water. Several federal agencies are working together on a programmatic EIS that addresses solar energy development on public lands. *See* Solar Energy Development Programmatic EIS Information Center, http://solareis.anl.gov/. Each solar energy proposal on federal lands is also subject to individualized NEPA review and must comply with all relevant statutes, including the ESA.

2. The Mojave Desert would seem to be the ideal place to site a solar energy facility. Indded, as California Governor Arnold Schwarzenegger once remarked, "if we cannot solar power plants in the Mojave Desert, I don't know where the hell we can put it." But the Mojave symbolizes different things to different people. It was long regarded a barren wasteland that was inhospitable to human presence as temperatures soared as high as 134 degrees. That is perhaps still the most common view today as most people see the Mojave as they drive across it from Los Angeles to Las Vegas. By the late nineteenth century, though, some people saw the Mojave as a resource to be exploited by miners, ranchers, military installations, and other settlers. Most recently, numerous writers and travelers have extolled the scenic value of the desert, prompting Congress to consider preserving the desert landscape. Nevada Senator Harry Reid has rhapsodized "[t]here is no place on the Earth that has better scenery than" the Mojave Desert. 140 CONG. REC. 7117 (1994) (statement of Sen. Reid). Heeding Senator Reid's advice, Congress enacted the California Desert Protection Act (CDPA) of 1994, which seeks to protect the desert by establishing the Mojave National Preserve, Death Valley National Park, Joshua Tree National Park, and dozens of new wilderness areas. *See generally* ELISABETH M. HAMIN, MOJAVE LANDS: INTERPRETIVE PLANNING AND THE NATIONAL PRESERVE 32-35 (2003). *See generally* ELISABETH M. HAMIN, MOJAVE LANDS: INTERPRETIVE PLANNING AND THE NATIONAL PRESERVE 32-35 (2003); John Copeland Nagle, *See the Mojave!*, 89 OR. L. REV. 1357 (2011). Many of the activists who pushed for the establishment of those national parks and wilderness areas dislike the idea of large, industrial facilities being constructed in the desert that they worked so hard to protect.

So, to answer Governor Schwarzenegger's question, if we don't build solar energy facilities in the Mojave, where should we build them? Are any of the alternatives examined in the EIS and discussed in the court's opinion more attractive? Where else could we collect solar energy?

3. The FWS issued the revised recovery plan for the desert tortoise in May 2011. The plan acknowledges the challenges presented by the sudden interest in the tortoise's habitat for solar energy:

> [When Plan revision began we did not anticipate the extent to which the landscape of desert ecosystems in the Pacific Southwest might become modified as a result of the nation's renewable energy priorities (since 2009, an emphasis on renewable energy has resulted in a large increase in the number of proposed utility-scale projects within the range of the desert tortoise in California)... Implementation of a number of the recommended Recovery Actions, as articulated throughout the Plan, would make progress towards reducing threats associated with energy development:
>
> - *Recovery Action 2.1, Conserve intact desert tortoise habitat* - Recommends that solar project facilities be sited outside Desert Wildlife Management Areas and Areas of Critical Environmental Concern, as well as the development of a cumulative impacts assessment to identify mitigation measures for this type of activity.
>
> - *Recovery Action 2.9, Secure lands/habitat for conservation* - Recommends conserving sensitive areas that would connect functional habitat or improve management capability of surrounding areas, such as inholdings within tortoise conservation areas that may be open to renewable energy development.

- *Recovery Action 2.11, Connect functional habitat* - Recommends connecting blocks of desert tortoise habitat, such as tortoise conservation areas, in order to maintain gene flow between populations.

- *Recovery Action 4.3, Track changes in the quantity and quality of desert tortoise habitat* - Recommends quantifying the loss or restoration of habitat as it relates to potential energy and other projects.

- *Recovery Action 5.5, Determine the importance of corridors and physical barriers to desert tortoise distribution and gene flow* - This action, in part, would determine the effects of corridors and barriers like energy development, on desert tortoise movement and recovery."

U.S. Fish & Wildlife Service, Revised Recovery Plan for the Mojave Population of the Desert Tortoise (Gopherus agassizii), at 3-4 (2001).

4. The court described the analysis of the Ivanpah project's impact on desert tortoises as follows:

> BLM initiated consultation with FWS on December 7, 2009. As a result of that consultation, FWS issued a biological opinion on October 1, 2010. The biological opinion concluded that the ISEGS project was likely to result in the deaths of some desert tortoises but was unlikely to jeopardize the desert tortoise's continued existence on account of mitigation measures that BrightSource would use and because the desert tortoise population located on the ISEGS site was insignificant in comparison to the total population. The biological opinion also included an incidental take statement governing the taking of desert tortoises during the ISEGS project.

> In October 2010, BLM issued a record of decision, which approved decisions to: (1) "amend the CDCA Plan to include the ISEGS facility as an approved power generation location under the Energy Production and Utility Corridors Element of the CDCA Plan"; and (2) "grant four [right-of-way] authorizations for the selected Mitigated Ivanpah 3 Alternative, and to close certain routes of travel within the project site." On March 2, 2011, BLM issued two notices to proceed, which authorized perimeter security and tortoise fencing for Ivanpah 2 and Ivanpah 3.

> On April 15, 2011, BLM issued a suspension decision to halt work because the incidental take limit set by the biological opinion and incidental take statement had been reached and in some categories exceeded. On April 19, 2011, BLM issued a revised biological assessment for the ISEGS project as part of a reinitiated consultation with FWS to ensure ESA compliance. The revised biological assessment reflected four changes to the original biological assessment: (1) a higher than expected number of tortoises on the project site; (2) changes to the desert tortoise translocation strategy and area; (3) changes to the desert tortoise handling procedures; and (4) identification of a specific mitigation measure to install culverts and fencing along the Yates Well Road.

> FWS issued a second biological opinion on June 10, 2011, which estimated that the ISEGS project would result in the taking, by mortality or injury, of between 405 and 1,136 desert tortoises, the majority of which would be

small tortoises or eggs. Few, if any, of the tortoises would be larger than 160 millimeters. The 2011 biological opinion required a series of mitigation measures to reduce the impact of the ISEGS project on the desert tortoise and imposed new terms and conditions on the project, including requirements to reinitiate consultation with FWS should a specified number of tortoises be killed by ISEGS project activity.

Western Watersheds Project, 2011 U.S. Dist. LEXIS 151556, at *11 - *13. Is the death of 1,136 desert tortoises acceptable? Is it the cost that we need to pay to obtain more renewable energy? More generally, should we be more willing to allow solar energy development to harm biodiversity than, for example, a coal plant or ORV users (as in *Sierra Club v. Clark*)? Does the ESA or other federal law allow such a preference for "green" projects?

Cabeza Prieta National Wildlife Refuge Comprehensive Conservation Plan, Wilderness Stewardship Plan & Environmental Impact Statement

United States Fish & Wildlife Service, 2006.
http://library.fws.gov/CCPs/cabezaprieta_final06.pdf.

PURPOSE AND NEED FOR PLAN ACTIONS

The refuge plays a critical role in the recovery and protection of rare and sensitive species such as the desert bighorn sheep and the federally endangered Sonoran pronghorn, as well as the conservation of a diversity of desert wildlife within the Sonoran Desert. Cabeza Prieta NWR, which contains the largest refuge wilderness outside of Alaska, presents issues related to appropriate levels of intervention for wildlife management in designated wilderness that have national significance for the Service. A CCP establishes refuge Goals, Objectives and Management Strategies. These planned actions are all designed to assist the refuge in achieving its formal purposes and the Mission of the National Wildlife Refuge System. This document proposes the implementation of a wide array of actions that lead to achievement of such purposes and mission.

Cabeza Prieta NWR was:

> . . . reserved and set apart for the conservation and development of natural wildlife resources, and for the protection and improvement of public grazing lands and natural forage resources. . . Provided, however, that all the forage resources in excess of that required to maintain a balanced wildlife population within this range or preserve should be available for livestock. . . (Executive Order 8038 January 25, 1939)

Title III of the Arizona Desert Wilderness Act of 1990 supplemented the refuge purposes with an additional refuge purpose; the protection of the wilderness resource on 325,270 hectares (803,418 acres) in accordance with the Wilderness Act of 1964.

A CCP also sets guidelines for management of refuge resources, describes the desired outcomes for the next 15 years, and encourages refuge management in concert with an overall ecosystem approach. The CCP development process provides a forum for public participation relative to the type, extent, and compatibility of uses on refuges. As a majority of the refuge is designated wilderness, this plan addresses administrative needs for wilderness and serves as the refuge's Wilderness Stewardship Plan.

REFUGE VISION STATEMENT

1.8.1 At Cabeza Prieta National Wildlife Refuge, wildlife conservation comes first.

Cabeza Prieta National Wildlife Refuge is dedicated first and foremost to conservation of wildlife and habitats. Situated on the international border, and located in the heart of the Sonoran Desert, the refuge is unlike any other wild place in the Western Hemisphere. More than 90 percent of this unit of the National Wildlife Refuge System has been officially designated a Wilderness Area by Congress. The refuge's high diversity of plant and animal species and varied geology make it an important component of the Sonoran Desert ecosystem. The Service's role at the refuge is to protect native wildlife and plant populations within the greater Sonoran Desert ecosystem.

1.8.2 Proactive management is important to the recovery and conservation of endangered species

The refuge plays a continuing role in the protection and recovery of threatened and endangered species, including the Sonoran pronghorn and the lesser long-nosed bat. The refuge is a critical resource for the recovery of the Sonoran pronghorn, an endangered sub-species of American pronghorn limited to two small remnant populations in the United States and Mexico. The refuge comprises nearly half the range of the U.S. population, and is central to its recovery. Cooperatively with partners, especially the Arizona Game and Fish Department (AGFD), the refuge will continue its commitment to biological data gathering, monitoring, and analysis so that current natural resource management questions can be answered and the future of threatened and endangered species such as the pronghorn will be more secure.

1.8.3 Refuge wilderness resources are protected for posterity

The refuge, with its vast wilderness including Sonoran Desert habitat, is permanently protected as a component of the National Wilderness Preservation System. Protection of the existing landscape and management of the refuge's wildlife populations are top priorities. Desert bighorn sheep are recognized as a wilderness resource, as well as a species basic to the original purpose of the refuge. Conservation of this species, and other native species, will require a cooperative effort between the refuge and its partners, especially with the AGFD, using the best available science, established practices and new approaches and techniques based on the most current research.

1.8.4 The beauty and solitude of the refuge will continue to be enjoyed by visitors.

The refuge is, and will remain, a place where visitors can enjoy the magnificence of the Sonoran Desert and experience wilderness solitude rarely found elsewhere in the Southwest. Refuge interpretive programs will continue to educate visitors and area residents about the unique resources of the Sonoran Desert and the mission of the refuge and the National Wildlife Refuge System. Visitors to the refuge; whether enjoying an extended backpacking trip, a day's drive on the Camino del Diablo, or an informational session at the visitor center; are drawn to its beauty and untrammeled wilderness character. These traits will be protected through Service management and administration.

1.8.5 The refuge embraces cooperative working relationships with partners.

The refuge values its relationships with other natural resource agencies, tribal governments, non-governmental organizations, and local communities in accomplishing the refuge purposes and the National Wildlife Refuge System mission. Local communities will continue to identify and promote the region as a tourist destination. The unique resources and natural beauty of the refuge will continue to draw visitors. Refuge outreach and visitor services programs will continue to enhance the area's attraction to visitors from around the nation and foreign countries. The refuge will continue to be an ideal site for cooperative scientific study and research leading to the conservation of

REFUGE MANAGEMENT DIRECTION: GOALS AND GUIDING PRINCIPLES

The following four goals are proposed for Cabeza Prieta NWR. They are consistent with the refuge purpose, the Refuge System mission and goals, the National Wildlife Refuge System Administration Act of 1996, as amended, Service policy, the Wilderness Act of 1964, the Arizona Desert Wilderness Act of 1990, and the Service's Gila/Salt/Verde Ecosystem Team goals. The goals are to be considered as integrated goals containing elements of each, rather than being mutually exclusive of each other. Specific objectives to be achieved to realize these goals, as well as implementation strategies for each objective have been developed. The objectives and strategies for implementing Alternative 4, the preferred alternative, are presented in Appendix M. Management actions proposed in support of the goals are described in Chapter 2, Alternatives.

1.9.1 Wildlife and Habitat Management

Protect, maintain, enhance, and/or restore the diversity and abundance of wildlife species and ecological communities of the Sonoran desert represented at Cabeza Prieta NWR.

- Intact habitats are key to viable wildlife populations.

- The refuge must integrate its responsibilities for trust species and biodiversity to meet Refuge System and ecosystem goals.

- Management should mimic, where possible, natural processes.

- The refuge needs sound scientific data in order to evaluate management options and prioritize activities.

1.9.2 Wilderness Stewardship

Protect and conserve refuge wilderness employing strategies of wildlife and plant conservation that will conserve, maintain and where possible, restore the wilderness character of Cabeza Prieta NWR.

1.9.3 Visitor Services Management

Provide visitors with compatible, high quality wildlife-dependent recreational and educational experiences designed to foster better appreciation, understanding, and protection of the plant, animal and wilderness resources.

- Compatible wildlife-dependent recreation and education are appropriate public uses with priority given to hunting, fishing, wildlife observation, wildlife photography, environmental interpretation, and education.

- Visitors find national wildlife refuges welcoming, safe, and accessible with a variety of opportunities to enjoy and appreciate America's legacy of wildlife.

- The heritage and future of the Refuge System is intertwined with the support of concerned citizens.

1.9.4 Cultural Resources Management

Protect, maintain, and interpret cultural and historic resources on Cabeza Prieta NWR, in cooperation with Tribal governments and the State of Arizona to benefit present and future generations.

- Comply with Section 106 of the National Historic Preservation Act and enforce the Archeological Resources Protection Act to protect sites and objects from construction impacts or illegal activities.

- Archeological research proposals will be in compliance with the Archeological Resources Protection Act and will undergo formal review by regional recognized tribes.

- The location of sites will not be disclosed.

- Report site and object discoveries and report specific site maintenance, stabilization, and protection needs to the Service's Regional Office.

- Observe and honor the provisions of the American Indian Religious Freedom Act and Executive Order 13007 to guarantee access by tribal members to sacred sites and to traditional cultural properties.

- Limit archives and collections to the minimal amounts essential for Refuge record keeping and for basic public interpretation. All other collections will be housed in public repositories and may become candidates for repatriation to regionally recognized tribes. . .

MANAGEMENT ALTERNATIVES

ALTERNATIVE 1: NO ACTION ALTERNATIVE (CURRENT MANAGEMENT)

This alternative describes the current management activities at the refuge. These programs and activities would continue if none of the action alternatives (Alternatives 2 through 5) were adopted. Management activities are focused on recovery of the endangered Sonoran pronghorn, maintaining the populations of desert bighorn sheep, monitoring nongame wildlife species, monitoring and controlling invasive species, protecting wilderness character, and providing visitors with quality wildlife-dependent recreational experiences that are compatible with the refuge purposes. . .

ALTERNATIVE 2: MINIMUM INTERVENTION

This alternative features an approach to refuge management that minimizes active intervention on ecological processes, particularly within the refuge wilderness areas. Other than management activities required for Sonoran pronghorn or other endangered species recovery, the refuge will not haul water in wilderness; develop new, or redevelop existing, wildlife waters; or otherwise attempt to support wildlife populations greater than those that refuge natural resources and precipitation support in the context of existing decimating factors. These factors include changes in native vegetation due to past over-grazing by domestic livestock, introduction of exotic plants and animal species, fragmentation of the habitats of wide ranging species and introduction of diseases from domestic livestock. Desert bighorn sheep hunting and use of pack and saddle stock would not be allowed under this alternative. . .

ALTERNATIVE 3: RESTRAINED INTERVENTION

This alternative emphasizes preserving the refuge's wilderness character. It focuses on restoring the natural conditions and self-sustaining ecosystem processes that will support healthy populations of native species. This alternative assumes that permanent, artificial structures and installations, no matter how well camouflaged, are inappropriate in wilderness. This alternative will support wildlife populations primarily with naturally occurring precipitation; supplemental water will be provided to developed waters as an infrequent measure during periods of extreme drought, rather than as a response to summertime desert conditions. While not embracing aggressive manipulation of habitats and processes, this alternative recommends some habitat manipulation to restore endangered species and would take additional steps, if necessary, to protect them. By restoring degraded portions of the habitat (e.g. by establishing wildlife corridors in non-wilderness) the wilderness itself can maintain its wildness and be free from man's control. This alternative also favors increased habitat management outside of wilderness and working aggressively with adjacent landowners and other partners to reduce active management in the wilderness. . .

ALTERNATIVE 4 (PREFERRED ALTERNATIVE): ACTIVE MANAGE-
    MENT

This alternative emphasizes maintaining the refuge's wildlife populations through the continued provision of developed waters. Assumptions central to this alternative's approach include the following. Habitat fragmentation and human development around perennial sources of water have restricted access to alternate sources of water and forage previously used by wide-ranging resident wildlife during times of drought stress on the refuge. Habitat degradation by past overgrazing impacts the quality of forage and increases the density of woody shrubs. Many diseases introduced by domestic livestock persist in refuge wildlife populations. In view of these assumptions, provision of developed waters to refuge wildlife is considered essential to maintaining natural population densities of large, wide-ranging species such as desert bighorn sheep and Sonoran pronghorn. In the context of providing reliable waters for wildlife, the refuge will continue to investigate and implement measures to reduce and eventually eliminate the need to haul water in wilderness. This Alternative is most similar to the No Action Scenario, but offers a more active approach to the achieving the refuge's purposes, goals and objectives. . .

ALTERNATIVE 5: MAXIMUM EFFORT

This alternative emphasizes active management aimed at increasing the size of the refuge desert bighorn sheep population and also enhancing the refuge visitor experience. An assumption basic to this alternative is that desert bighorn abundance was historically much greater in the region prior to habitat fragmentation, groundwater withdrawals, surface water diversion, over hunting and the introduction of diseases carried by domestic livestock. In view of this assumption, a population goal established for desert bighorn sheep reflects the densities observed in the better stocked existing habitats with developed water sources in the region today. This density is considered a component of refuge wilderness character. . .

Table 2.9: Summary comparison of the management alternatives organized by planning issues identified in scoping (Section 1.12)					
Issue	Alternative 1. No Action	Alternative 2	Alternative 3	Alternative 4 Preferred alternative	Alternative 5
Wildlife & Habitat Management					
Managing Healthy Ecosystems	Climate monitoring Some wildlife monitoring Buffelgrass and trespass livestock control	Same as No Action	Same as No Action plus additional wildlife monitoring, remote sensed change detection analysis, development of wild plant nursery	Same as No Action plus additional wildlife monitoring, beyond that of Alternative 3, remote sensed change detection analysis.	Same as No Action plus greatest intensity of wildlife monitoring of any alternative, remote sensed change detection analysis
Endangered Species	Implement Sonoran pronghorn recovery. Protect lesser long nosed bat roost with fence	Same as No Action	Same as No Action, except that water is supplied to charcos only during extreme drought	Same as No Action, plus installation of a gate at entrance to lesser long nosed bat roost if unauthorized access becomes a problem.	Same as Alternative 4 program plus annual Sonoran pronghorn population surveys.
Desert Bighorn Sheep	Population surveys every three years 15 developed waters maintained and supplied Study of sheep water use No numerical population goal Annual hunts	Population surveys every three years 14 developed waters in wilderness dismantled Study of sheep water use Population goal of 100-200 sheep No hunts	Population surveys every three years Developed waters supplied only during extreme drought Sheep water use study Population goal of 250 to 300 sheep No hunts during drought years	Population surveys every three years 15 developed waters maintained, supplied and upgraded Sheep water use study Population goal of 500 to 700 sheep Annual hunts	Population surveys every three years Developed waters maintained, supplied, upgraded and supplemented Sheep water use study Population goal of 900 to 1,200 sheep Annual hunts
Predators	Coyote control as prescribed by Sonoran pronghorn recovery plan	Same as No Action	Same as No Action, plus collaring studies of coyote and mountain lion	Same as Alternative 3 plus control of mountain lions if studies indicate	Same as Alternative 4

NOTES & QUESTIONS

1. Why does the FWS prefer management Alternative 4? How is that alternative different from the other alternatives?

2. Active management of wildlife in the desert requires attention to water. In Alternative 4. the FWS EIS blithely explains that the "refuge will continue to investigate and implement measures to reduce and eventually eliminate the need to haul water in wilderness. The FWS discusses the need for water at greater length later in the EIS:

> Five types of water developments are found on the refuge: buried reservoirs with collection points and drinking troughs, runoff tanks (modified tinajas), charcos, wells with drinking troughs, and storage tanks with drinking troughs. Buried reservoirs are typically constructed of one or more 1,780-liter (470-gallon) pipes connected to water collection points in natural drainage courses and wildlife drinking troughs. Buried tanks are covered with native soil and have very little visual impact on the surroundings. Runoff tanks mimic natural tinajas and are the next most natural looking structures. They are created by either blasting holes in rock or building small dams in mountain washes. A few hold water throughout the season. Charcos are dugout ponds also locally called repressos. An area is bulldozed and lined to hold water. The charcos dry up during the driest time of year. Fiberglass tanks and drinkers were added to charcos and other sites to augment water in dry months. These structures include a water reservoir of some type connected to a drinker, or trough regulated by a float valve, and require hauling water once or twice each year. Most of the wells are located outside of wilderness. They were developed for livestock when grazing was permitted and now feed drinkers for wildlife. Most are located in pronghorn habitat, but levels of use by pronghorn are poorly understood, although refuge photography by motion triggered cameras verifies use of several developed waters by Sonoran pronghorn..

There are 22 developed waters on the refuge in Sonoran pronghorn habitat. . . . A determination to haul water is based upon observation of water levels by AGFD personnel during weekly aerial reconnaissance, observations by refuge staff conducting field work near the waters, and best judgment of refuge staff considering precipitation and temperature.

Id. at 44-45.

But the Wilderness Act constrains the ability of the FWS to affirmatively provide water for wildlife in those parts of the refuge. In Wilderness Watch, Inc. v. U.S. Fish & Wildlife Serv., 629 F.3d 1024 (9th Cir. 2010) – decided four years after the FWS completed its plan for Cabeza Prieta NWR—the court held that the conservation of desert bighorn sheep in Arizona's Kofa National Wildlife Refuge was consistent with the Wilderness Act, but the court then held that the FWS had failed to demonstrate that the installation of two water structures to aid the sheep was "necessary" to meet the "minimum requirements" for conserving the sheep, as demanded by the Wilderness Act. Judge Bybee dissented from that conclusion because "'[t]he dominant wildlife and habitat management theme for the Kofa . . . has been the preservation of the desert bighorn sheep species'" and "water is, and historically has been, critical to conserving bighorn populations in the Kofa, and any proposal that does not take account of the herds' need for additional water sources is unlikely to succeed." Id. at 1040, 1053 (Bybee, J., dissenting)

3. The Cabeza Prieta National Wildlife Refuge is situated along a remote stretch of Arizona's border with Mexico. That location means that wildlife management must compete with illegal immigration and drug violence. The refuge's plan recognizes that "[i]n recent years undocumented alien (UDA) traffic in and around the refuge has increased significantly, apparently in response to increased law enforcement in urban areas." Cabeza Prieta National Wildlife Refuge Comprehensive Conservation Plan, Wilderness Stewardship Plan & Environmental Impact Statement, *supra*, at 53. Some members of Congress worry that illegal immigration threatens the wildlife that the refuge is intended to protect. *See* 157 CONG. REC. 3540 (daily ed. June 6, 2011) (statement of Mr. Lummis) ("This is madness. If you want to protect the species and ecosystems along the border, then secure the border."); 156 CONG. REC. 5694 (daily ed. July 19, 2010) (statement of Mr. Poe of Texas) (observing that "the Sonoran Pronghorn antelope is in danger of extinction, so government "envirocrats" have prohibited Border Patrol from entering some wildlife areas on the range where the antelope play in Arizona. . . The antelope protectors have stopped construction of seven Border Patrol observation towers they feel are too intrusive for the antelope. Never mind the Border Patrol can protect the antelope and secure the border as well."). Nearby, "'[v]iolence on the [Buenos Aires National Wildlife] Refuge associated with smugglers and border bandits" has forced the closure of 3,500 acres within the refuge since 2006. FWS, Closure of Refuge Lands Adjacent to Border: Buenos Aires National Wildlife Refuge, http://www.fws.gov/southwest/refuges/arizona/buenosaires/PDFs/Closure.pdf..

Congress have given the Secretary of Homeland Security "the authority to waive all legal requirements such Secretary, in such Secretary's sole discretion, determines necessary to ensure expeditious construction of the barriers and roads" along the border." REAL ID Act § 102(c), 8 U.S.C. § 1103 note. *See also* Defenders of Wildlife v. Chertoff, 527 F. Supp. 2d 119 (D.D.C. 2007) (rejecting a challenge to the Secretary's exercise of that authority), *cert. denied*, 554 U.S. 918 (2008). In June 2012, the House of Representatives approved legislation that would prohibit the Secretaries of Interior and Agriculture from impeding or restricting activities of U.S. Customs and Border Protection on land under their respective jurisdiction within 100 miles of an international U.S. border. *See* H.R. 2578, 112 Cong., 2d Sess., tit. IX (2012). The bill would block the application of the ESA, NEPA, and other federal environmental laws that could interfere with border security efforts.

Environmentalists, by contrast, worry that border security efforts will harm biodiversity by restricting the ability of animals to freely migrate across the border. The construction of fences along the border could prevent permissible animal migrations as well as illegal human immigration. "Due to its limited ability to jump, fences have become an obstacle for the [Sonoran] pronghorns." Tara M. Sanchez, Note, *Waving Good-bye to Environmental Laws along the Arizona Borderlands:* Defenders of Wildlife v. Chertoff, 16 MO. ENVTL. L. & POL'Y REV. 281, 298 (2009). Similarly, "[t]he reemergence of [jaguars] in the United States is the result of a migratory corridor used by the jaguars to move between the United States and Mexico. The fencing and road projects are destined to cut off this migration." *Id. See also* Anne Minard, *U.S. Immigration Law Could Harm Desert Animals, Critics Say*, NATIONAL GEOGRAPHIC, Mar. 31, 2006, http://news.nationalgeographic.com/news/2006/03/0331_060331_desert_fence.html.

C. ISLAND ECOSYSTEMS

Islands are both hot spots of biodiversity and the site of dramatic losses of biodiversity. Hawai'i, our nation's island state, leads all others in listed endangered species. Madagascar is famous for its collection of endemic species, as is the much smaller Galapogos Island in the Pacific Ocean. Socotra Island offers an example of a less well known island that is rich with biodiversity. Socorta is located off the coast of Yemen is considered among the top 10 islands in the number of endemic species. Its native species, which include the oddly shaped Socotran boab and the viciously sharp dragon's blood tree, have long had to deal with feral goats. Ironically, however, the fragile ecosystems were protected for decades by the presence of a secretive Soviet military base on the island, which ruled out any chance of commercial development. With the base gone, proposals are in the works for five-star resorts, marinas, golf courses, and other trappings of luxury island development. Advocate for the island's 40,000 local inhabitants, most living in poverty, argue in favor of a softer ecotourism development strategy. *See A Bid to Save the "Galapagos of the Indian Ocean,"* 303 SCIENCE 1753 (2004). More generally, island comprise 3% of the world's surface but host as much as 20% of all plant, reptile, and bird species.

A recent draft report identified four reasons why islands are essential to the conservation of biodiversity. First, many island species are endemic to their particular location. Second, many seabirds, sea turtles, and marine mammals depend upon islands for breeding and nesting. Third, many (though certainly not all) islands have few or no people living on them, thereby avoiding conflicts with human activities. Fourth, species that have adapted to life on islands can avoid the problems of habitat fragmentation that plague many species living within larger continental ecosystems. "In summary, by restoring and protecting islands, functioning ecosystems can be maintained without large expenditures for land acquisition or management, or significant contact with local human populations." U.S. DEPARTMENT OF INTERIOR & STATE OF HAWAI'I, LEHUA ISLAND ECOSYSTEM RESTORATION PROJECT: DRAFT ENVIRONMENTAL ASSESSMENT 2 (2005). Given these advantages, do islands need special protection from development pressures? Should development be banned in some circumstances, or is the staggering economic potential of island development sufficient to justify turning their ecosystems from fragile to human-dominated?

Morimoto v. Board of Land and Natural Resources

Supreme Court of Hawai'i, 2005.
113 P.3d 172.

■ ACOBA, J.

 . . . This appeal concerns [the Board of Land and Natural Resources's (BLNR)] decision to grant a conservation district use permit (CDUP) for a project to upgrade State Highway 200, also known as Saddle Road, to a two-lane highway that would comply with the design of the American Association of State Highway and Transportation Officials for rural arterials and accommodate an expected increase in traffic flow along the highway. A CDUP was required because the project proposed a realignment route, referred to as PTA-1, that would traverse 206.70 acres of conservation district lands. PTA-1 was selected from amongst a list of alternative routes after Appellees [Hawai'i State Department of Transportation and the Federal Highway Administration (FHA)] and other government agencies completed an environmental impact statement (EIS) to comply with the National Environmental Policy Act, 42 U.S.C. §§ 4321-4370f, and Hawaii Revised Statutes (HRS) chapter 343. The EIS incorporated a July 27, 1998 biological opinion (BO) issued by the United States Fish and Wildlife Service (FWS). The opinion represented a culmination of interagency consultation as required under section 7 of the Endangered Species Act (ESA), 16 U.S.C. § 1536. Appellees had initiated section 7 consultation by requesting that FWS provide them with information on any "listed species" or critical habitat within the project area. Based upon the list of species provided by FWS, Appellees then conducted biological inventory surveys. A biological assessment (BA), which addressed potential impacts of the realignment project on the listed species, was prepared by Appellees.

Seven of the endangered/threatened species evaluated in the BA are relevant to this appeal. Specifically, the BA established that (1) moderate numbers of the Hawaiian Hoary Bat (peapea) were observed, (2) a single Palila (finch-billed honeycreeper) was detected, although three other sightings were previously documented, (3) no Akiaplau were observed, but two sightings were previously documented, (4) Nn used the area on a regular and incidental basis, (5) during breeding season, the Dark-rumped Petrel (Uau) was seen flying over the area, (6) two populations of Silene hawaiiensis (a sprawling shrub known to exist only on the Island of

Hawai'i) were located in the area, and (7) there was a possibility that the Hawaiian Hawk (Io) would use the area for nesting, although none was detected. Based upon these findings, the BA concluded that (1) it would be "unlikely" that the realignment project would have a deleterious impact on the Hawaiian Hoary Bat and the Nn, (2) fire posed a threat to the Akiaplau, Palila, and Silene hawaiiensis, and (3) lighting used in the project might disorient the Dark-rumped Petrel.

The BO issued by FWS, largely based upon the information in the BA, observed that two of the species, the Palila and Silene hawaiiensis, required specific attention. Thus, the BO included a detailed plan to offset damage to Palila critical habitat and minimize effects on the species. To mitigate the approximately 100 acres of Palila critical habitat taken up by the construction of PTA-1, the plan called for, inter alia, the acquisition and management of approximately 10,000 acres for Palila habitat restoration and an attempt to reintroduce the Palila to areas within their historic range where they had not resided. Appellees, BLNR, and other agencies signed a memorandum of understanding (MOU) to implement the Palila mitigation plan. With respect to the Silene hawaiiensis, the proposed alignment path was moved south to avoid a population of seventy plants.

The BO also incorporated the following additional mitigation measures, which FWS considered to be part of the proposed project: (1) lighting restrictions to avoid potential downing of the Dark-rumped Petrels; (2) a plan for minimizing fire hazards; and (3) with respect to the Hawaiian Hawk, "nest searches" by a qualified ornithologist prior to the onset of construction and, in the event an "active nest" is detected, the halting of the project within one kilometer of the nest and the initiation of consultation with FWS. Ultimately, the BO concluded as follows:

> After reviewing the current status of the Palila and its critical habitat and the current status of Silene hawaiiensis, the environmental baseline of the species in the action area, and the effects of the proposed Saddle Road Realignment and Improvement Project, including the cumulative effects, it is [FWS's] biological opinion that the Saddle Road Realignment and Improvement Project is not likely to jeopardize the continued existence of the Palila or Silene hawaiiensis and is not likely to adversely modify Palila critical habitat. These findings are based in large part on the conservation measures built into the project by [FHA]. . . [FWS] believes that the mitigation measures built into the project design by [FHA] will offset the modifications being made to Palila critical habitat and enhance the likelihood of survival and recovery of the Palila.

In October 1999, at the close of the EIS process and section 7 consultation, FHA issued a record of decision (ROD) that (1) confirmed PTA-1 as the selected route and (2) legally bound Appellees to implement the mitigation commitments delineated in the EIS and the BO. The ROD also required Appellees to incorporate the mitigation commitments into all construction contract documents. The mitigation plan in the ROD received wide support from scientific, regulatory agency, and environmental communities, and segments of the local community. [BLNR granted a CDUP to the Appellees, and after the circuit court affirmed that decision, then Dr. Daniel Morimoto and Kats Yamada appealed to this court.]

VIII.

. . .Morimoto contends that consideration of mitigation measures was error because the BLNR failed "to specify the impact[,] . . . to specify the diminution[,] . . . to address other endangered species[, and] . . . engaged in new rule-making." Relatedly, Yamada asserts . . . that the entire area must be protected from the project. He remonstrates that (1) Appellees were not aware of Asplenium fragile, (2) findings 115–141 only deal with the Palila mitigation plan and "the criteria [of the HAR] requires examining the impact to the existing natural resources[,]" (3) there was no demonstrative evidence presented that the use met the criteria in HAR 13-5-20(c), (4) the survey was limited to the PTA-1 corridor and not to the surrounding area, (5) one-hundred acres of habitat lands are being removed from the other eight endangered and threatened species but there are no mitigation land being proposed for those species.

A.

As to Morimoto's first and second and Yamada's second concerns, we have said, supra, that, in the circumstances of this case, BLNR must consider proposed ameliorative steps in evaluating the substantial adverse impact criterion. Contrary to Morimoto's argument, the findings regarding Palila mitigation are responsive to the perceived impact of the realignment project upon the species. BLNR found, in finding no. 117, that "a small portion of Palila critical habitat . . . must be used" for the project. Finding no. 120 noted that "no Palila have resided in the portion of the Palila critical habitat located in the environs of PTA-1 (PTA Training Areas 1–4) for decades." Finally, finding no. 121, expressly referencing impacts, recognized that Appellees have "made legally binding commitments in the ROD to undertake significant mitigative steps to offset any potential impacts on Palila critical habitat." These findings, in addition to other findings that explain Appellees' mitigation commitments, dispel Appellants' argument that BLNR did not consider the impact or the effect of measures to "diminish" the impact of the project upon the Palila.

B.

As to other endangered or threatened species, Morimoto's third and Yamada's first, second, third, and fifth concerns, the court determined that "although some listed species were not specifically mentioned in the BLNR findings of fact, evidence presented would support specific findings that they will not suffer a substantial adverse impact as a result of the construction of PTA-1." Based upon a review of the record, including the BA, BO, and ROD, the court was ultimately correct in concluding that substantial evidence existed to support the finding that these species would not suffer substantial adverse impact.

In finding no. 102, BLNR stated that, "in general, the extensive mitigation commitments enumerated in the ROD will ensure that the Saddle Road improvement project, including the construction of PTA-1, will have no substantial adverse impacts on any rare or listed species, and in fact will improve the current environmental situation." Thus, even though BLNR did not render specific findings as to each species, it did examine the mitigation commitments in the ROD to arrive at the conclusion that the project would not have a substantial adverse impact on listed or rare species.

1.

We note, in that regard, that the BA and BO expressly addressed seven of the nine species identified by Appellants according to the list provided to them by FWS. Specifically, the BA noted the detection of moderate numbers of the Hawaiian Hoary Bat, the detection of a lone Palila and three other documented sightings, two documented sightings of Akiaplau, regular incidental usage of the PTA-1 area by Nn, the overflying of the Dark-rumped Petrel during breeding season, two populations of Silene hawaiiensis, and the possible nesting of the Hawaiian Hawk, although none were detected. The BA concluded it would be "unlikely" that the realignment project would have a deleterious impact on the Hawaiian Hoary Bat and the Nn, but that fire posed a threat to the Akiaplau, Palila, and Silene hawaiiensis. In response, the ROD requires that a fire ecologist be contracted to develop a comprehensive fire management plan to reduce the risk of fire in the vicinity of PTA-1. To avoid harm to a population of seventy Silene hawaiiensis plants within PTA-1, the proposed path was moved south of the population. As for the Dark-rumped Petrel, which returns to its nesting colony after dark, the BA noted that the major threat to these birds would be disorientation by light. Thus, the BO required that no construction or unshielded equipment maintenance be permitted after dark during breeding season and that this prohibition be incorporated into the construction contract documents.

With respect to the Hawaiian Hawk, even though none of these birds were detected during the surveys, the BA noted a potential impact upon the species if a nest was located near the construction corridor. Thus, the BA called for a "nest search" by a qualified ornithologist prior to the onset of construction and, in the event an active nest was detected during construction, the BO mandated that construction halt within one kilometer of the nest until consultation with FWS could take place.

2.

Appellees identified two species—the Asplenium fragile and the Pueo— as not being surveyed or addressed in the BA and BO. However, the record suggests that these species do not exist in PTA-1. Reginald David, who prepared the BA, testified that Asplenium fragile, an endangered plant species, was not found within PTA-1 and was not addressed in the BO. Yamada relied on Rare Plants of Pohakuloa Training Area by Robert B. Shaw to establish the existence of the Asplenium fragile in the project area. Lena Schnell, a natural resources specialist at Pohakuloa Training

Area, testified that the species exists in the area, but that she was "not exactly certain where." She also stated that she did not use Shaw's maps to conduct botanical surveys. The only evidence of a Pueo sighting came from the testimonies of Yamada and Dr. Harvey Chan, who, while on a hunting excursion, saw an owl cross the road in front of their truck. Thus, the fact that the BA or BO did not report on the Asplenium fragile or Pueo would not affect BLNR's ultimate decision regarding substantial adverse impact of the project. Based on the record, substantial evidence existed to support a finding that the species concerned would not suffer substantial adverse impact.

IX.

As to Argument 5, Yamada declares that an adequate survey for endangered species was not conducted. Appellants point to the testimony of David and a representation made in the EIS. David did testify that his survey of the avian and mammalian species was limited to the corridor "where the road goes." The final EIS stated that "Species inventories were conducted by means of 100-percent pedestrian surveys within the 60-m wide corridor."

However, as Appellees point out, David also testified that the surveys on which the BA, BO, and ROD are based considered the entire area of the project, not just the roadway. For instance, David testified that his survey team "went outside the alignment and searched all areas of likely habitat, rocky outcroppings, rain cuts in valleys and any promising looking areas that given their many years of experience they would expect to find remnant endangered species in." Upon examination of the BA, BO, and ROD, it does not appear that the surveys were limited to a sixty-meter wide area where the road would traverse but, rather, that the area surrounding PTA-1 was surveyed. As BLNR noted in findings 86 and 87, which were not disputed, "the bulk of the listed species" were found in *"the area surrounding PTA-1"* and the survey covered PTA Training Areas 22 and 23, which are "located on the western and southern portions of PTA, *distant from the route selected for the proposed PTA-1 realignment."* (Emphases added.)

X.

. . .Morimoto takes issue with finding no. 137, which states that "the Palila Mitigation Plan does not require that Palila actually be reintroduced/translocated into areas where they do not presently reside. The Mitigation Plan merely requires that the effort be made." Morimoto argues that "effort alone can never become the standard for the proper care and preservation of our conservation land and endangered species. With mere effort alone, the applicant cannot demonstrate benefit to the Palila."

However, despite the fact that translocation may not be successful, BLNR found, in finding no. 137, that if the effort to translocate "does not ultimately appear successful, *other approaches will be tried."* (Emphasis added.) Morimoto does argue that the approaches are not defined. But the mitigation plan involves more than translocation. In finding no. 138, BLNR found that the "project will not harm, and in fact will benefit the Palila, by restoring degraded areas of Palila habitat[,] ... [and] *re-establishing mamane forest on parts of its former range.*" (Emphasis added.) The plan calls for the re-vegetation of approximately 10,000 acres of mamane forest. Thus, even though translocation of the Palila may not succeed, there is substantial evidence that the Palila will benefit in other ways, supporting BLNR's finding that the project will not harm the species. The finding, therefore, that the Saddle Road realignment would not cause substantial adverse impact to any rare or listed species was not clearly erroneous. . .

NOTES & QUESTIONS

1. Saddle Road is the only road through the interior of the island of Hawai'i, gaining its name by connecting the island's two highest points. The Lonely Planet travel guide reports that Saddle Road "is 50 miles long and has no gas stations or other facilities along the way." Moreover, "most rental car contracts prohibit travel on the Saddle Rd." GLENDA BENDURE & NED FRIARY, HAWAII: A TRAVEL SURVIVAL KIT 309 (1st ed. 1990). A news report described Saddle Road as "dangerous and deteriorating." Kevin Dayton, *New Road in Works Since 1961 Ready for Traffic on Big Island*, HONOLULU ADVERTISER, Sept. 22, 2004, at 1B. The fact that a short stretch of highway could affect seven protected species gives you a sense of Hawai'i's remarkable biodiversity. All of Hawai'i's forest birds and 80% of its plants are endemic to the islands. Those species occupy a surprising variety of ecosystems; describe Hawai'i's ecosystems. But many of those species are threatened with extinction. Hawai'i has 317 species listed as endangered or threatened under the ESA, more than any other state. Most of those species—273, to be precise—are plants.

2. The palila is a relatively large yellow, gray, and white finch. It is the best known of the many native Hawaiian honeycreepers the once filled the forests of the islands. It was listed as endangered in 1967, and the 3,000 remaining birds are restricted to the west slope of Mauna Key on the island of Hawai'i, occupying about five percent of their historical range. The bird's fate has generated extensive litigation in the federal courts, even eliciting comments from the Supreme Court. That litigation has centered on the effect of the feral—*i.e.*, wild—pigs, sheep, and goats that now roam the forests of Hawai'i. Consider the discussion of those feral animals provided by the FWS when it listed ten Maui plants as endangered in 1998:

> Animals such as pigs, goats, axis deer, and cattle were introduced either by the early Hawaiians or more recently by European settlers for food and/or commercial ranching activities. Over the 200 years following their introduction, their numbers increased and the adverse impacts of feral ungulates on native vegetation have become increasingly apparent. Beyond the direct effect of trampling and grazing native plants, feral ungulates have contributed significantly to the heavy erosion still taking place on most of the main Hawaiian islands.
>
> Pigs, originally native to Europe, Africa, and Asia, were introduced to Hawaii by the Polynesian ancestors of Hawaiians, and later by western immigrants. The pigs escaped domestication and invaded primarily wet and mesic forests of Kauai, Oahu, Molokai, Maui, and Hawaii. . . While forag-

ing, pigs root and trample the forest floor, encouraging the establishment of alien plants in the newly disturbed soil. Pigs also disseminate alien plant seeds through their feces and on their bodies, accelerating the spread of alien plants through native forests. Pigs facilitate the spread of *Psidium cattleianum* (strawberry guava) and *Schinus terebinthifolius* (Christmas berry). . .

Goats, native to the Middle East and India, were first successfully introduced to the Hawaiian Islands in 1792. Feral goats now occupy a wide variety of habitats from lowland dry forests to montane grasslands on Kauai, Oahu, Molokai, Maui, and Hawaii, where they consume native vegetation, trample roots and seedlings, accelerate erosion, and promote the invasion of alien plants. . .

Final Endangered Status for 10 Plant Taxa from Maui Nui, HA, 64 Fed. Reg. 48307, 48315 (1999).

The feral animals are accused of threatening the native birds as well as the native plants. In the litigation concerning the palila, the goats and the sheep were eating the seedlings, leaves, stems, and sprouts of the mamane and naio trees on which the palila depended for its survival. In *Palila I*, the courts held that the state's act of permitting the goats and the sheep to live in the area constituted a take of the palila. Palila v. Hawaii Dep't of Land & Natural Resources, 471 F.Supp. 985 (D. Haw. 1979), *aff'd*, 639 F.2d 495 (9th Cir. 1981). *Palila II* reached a similar conclusion regarding the state's introduction of mouflon sheep into the same area, sheep that were prized by hunters but which fed on the mamane trees. Palila v. Hawaii Dep't of Land & Natural Resources, 649 F.Supp. 1070 (D. Haw. 1986), *aff'd*, 852 F.2d 1106 (9th Cir. 1988). The fact that the goats and sheep were destroying the habitat on which the palila depended led the courts to find a take in both cases, even though there was no evidence of an actual injury to any individual palila and even though the numbers of palilas had not dropped. Subsequently, the state's resulting "[u]ngulate eradication efforts have become so successful that hunters frequently cannot find any sheep to shoot" in the game area. Palila v. Hawaii Dep't of Land & Natural Resources, 73 F.Supp.2d 1181, 1184 (D. Haw. 1999). A group of frustrated hunters then moved to dissolve the court's orders, but the court held that the balance of the equities favored the species because "mouflon sheep can always be reintroduced on Mauna Kea," whereas "[p]alila once extinct are gone forever." *Id.* at 1187.

But "[w]hether the feral pig properly qualifies as an alien species in Hawaii is a matter of heated cultural debate." ALAN BURDICK, OUT OF EDEN: AN ODYSSEY OF ECOLOGICAL INVASION 106 (2005). "In the natural landscape of native Hawaii, no animal is more central than the pig. It is a key figure in the Hawaiian creation myth as a source of food and ritual." *Id.* at 114. Not surprisingly, efforts to eliminate the pigs and other feral animals have been controversial among some native Hawaiians. Moreover, there is even an alternative biological theory which posits that the pigs might actually help the native ecology. *See id.* at 142–43 (describing the theory "that removing pigs from open woodlands serves only to increase the density of the rat population; the grasses grow taller, the rats take refuge from owls and other predators, their numbers soar, and they ravage the succulent native plants"). Whatever the explanation, scientists from the United States Geological Service's Pacific Island Ecosystems Research Center have noted that "despite improving habitat conditions, the palila has not increased in numbers." Paul Banko et al., *Developing Techniques for Palila Restoration*, *available at* http://biology.usgs.gov.pierc/PLBankoPage1. htm.

3. Hawai'i was once an independent nation, and its native people have a long and storied history. Nonetheless, native Hawaiians do not enjoy the same exemptions that the law gives to native Alaskans engaged in traditional activities. For example, when two native Hawaiians challenged their convictions for killing endangered green sea turtles and a Hawaiian monk seal, the Ninth Circuit refused to find a statutory or constitutional justification for exempting them from the requirements of the ESA. "Whatever may be the subsistence needs of the arctic hunters," the court explained, "native Hawaiians are not similarly circumstanced to native Alaskans" because "native Hawaiians, as a group, [do not] depend upon the hunting of endangered and threatened species for subsistence." United States v. Nuesca, 945 F.2d 254, 257 (9th Cir. 1991).

4. The land at issue in *Morimoto* is part of the nearly half of the state's land that is zoned for conservation. Hawai'i's statewide zoning scheme divides all land in the state into urban, agricultural, rural, or conservation districts. The BLNR is responsible for determining permissible uses of conservation lands and considering permit applications. The substantial role assigned to the state agency in determining appropriate uses of land reflects Hawai'i's unique history of land. "The theory of private ownership of land was a foreign concept in Hawaiian history. Initially, all Hawaiian land was owned collectively by the people of Hawaii and held in trust for their benefit by the King." Napeahi v. Wilson, 987 F.Supp. 1288 (D.Haw. 1996). Then King Kamehameha III oversaw the "Great Hahele," an 1840 reform by which land was divided between the king, the government, and private parties. Over the next century, land ownership became concentrated in a few, wealthy individuals and organizations. In 1967—seven years after becoming a state—the Hawai'i legislature enacted a Land Reform Act that created a mechanism to transfer title to existing lessees. Since then, Hawai'i's extensive regulation of private land ownership has yielded two United States Supreme Court decisions rejecting takings claims against the state government. *See* Lingle v. Chevron U.S.A., Inc., 544 U.S. 528 (2005) (rejecting a takings claim against a cap on the rent charged to gasoline stations); Hawaii Housing Authority v. Midkiff, 467 U.S. 229 (1984) (holding that an application of the Land Reform Act satisfied the fifth amendment's public use requirement).

National Parks & Conservation Association v. U. S. Department of Transportation

United States Court of Appeals for the Ninth Circuit, 2000.
222 F.3d 677.

■ KOZINSKI, CIRCUIT JUDGE:

National Parks and Conservation Association and Malama Pono (collectively National Parks) are environmental organizations that petition for review of the Federal Aviation Administration's (FAA) approval of the expansion of Kahului Airport in Maui. National Parks contend that the FAA violated the National Environmental Policy Act (NEPA), 42 U.S.C. § 4321 *et seq.*, by failing to analyze the impact of the expansion on the introduction of alien, or non-indigenous, species into Maui. National Parks further contend that the FAA violated the Airport and Airway Improvement Act, 49 U.S.C. § 47106(c)(1)(C), and section 4(f) of the Transportation Act, 49 U.S.C. § 303(c), both of which govern the impact of transportation projects on the environment.

I

Kahului is Hawaii's second largest airport after Honolulu International. In addition to inter-island traffic, Kahului serves flights from the mainland United States and, less frequently, Canada. Kahului's main runway can accommodate the arrival of any size airplane, but is too short for large carriers to take off with a full load of passengers, cargo and fuel. Such aircraft must either fly with a partial load or stop for refueling in Honolulu. To accommodate rising demand, the Hawaii Department of Transportation (HDOT) and the FAA plan to repave and strengthen the runway, extend it from 7,000 to 9,600 feet and make related infrastructure improvements. The centerpiece of the project is the runway extension, which would allow fully loaded large carriers to depart Kahului nonstop.[1]

National Parks contend that the runway extension will lead to more flights arriving at Kahului, thus introducing dangerous alien species into Maui. Alien species—a problem in Maui since the first Polynesian settlers arrived 1,500 years ago—are non-native animals, insects and plants introduced into the island by air or sea. Some of these new arrivals—primarily disease-carrying organisms and insects such as fruit flies—can become pests that damage crops, livestock and scenic areas. National Parks express special concern for nearby Haleakala National Park, the last intact habitat for a number of native species.

Because the project is a major federal action that affects the environment, *see* 42 U.S.C. § 4332, the FAA and HDOT drafted an Environmental Impact Statement (EIS), held hearings and solicited public and agency input. In response to widespread concern over alien species, the FAA convened a Biological Assessment Technical Panel consisting of experts from federal and state agencies, Maui County and private organizations. The resulting Biological Assessment reviewed the project, surveyed the alien species problem on Maui and proposed mitigation measures, though it acknowledged that "no one can predict which alien species might be introduced into Maui and/or Hawaii due to the Proposed Project." Biological Assessment (BA) at 9–1. In addition, the Fish and Wildlife Service (FWS) prepared a Biological Opinion pursuant to the Endangered Species Act, 16 U.S.C. § 1536(a)(2), that found the project was "not likely to jeopardize the continued existence of any endangered, threatened, or proposed endan-

---

[1] Since this petition for review was filed, the Governor of Hawaii has canceled plans for the runway extension. *See, e.g.*, Claudine San Nicolas, *Governor Halts Kahului Runway-Extension Plan, Ending 10-Year Controversy*, Maui News, Feb. 9, 2000. The FAA's approval of the project, however, remains in effect. Because the extension could still go forward based on the Environmental Impact Statement at issue in this case, National Parks' challenge continues to present a live controversy.

gered species on Maui." These documents were incorporated into the Final EIS, along with a report titled "The Threat of Alien Species to Natural Areas of Maui," an extensive bibliography, numerous independent studies of the project and responses to public comments.

Based on this documentation, the Final EIS concluded that "the impact of the Proposed Project on [the] alien species introduction rate is, in and by itself, insignificant. However, the introduction of alien species is an existing statewide problem and therefore, the potential impact of the Proposed Project on the introduction rate of alien species, would be considered a *significant cumulative* impact." FEIS § 3.11.3.3.

II

Our review of an EIS under NEPA is extremely limited. We evaluate the EIS simply to determine whether it "contains a reasonably thorough discussion of the significant aspects of the probable environmental consequences" of a challenged action. *Oregon Envtl. Council* v. *Kunzman*, 817 F.2d 484, 492 (9th Cir. 1987) (internal quotation marks omitted). We need not agree with the agency's conclusions; we must approve the EIS if we are satisfied that the EIS process fostered informed decision-making and public participation. *See Idaho Conservation League* v. *Mumma*, 956 F.2d 1508, 1519 (9th Cir. 1992). If we determine that the agency took a "hard look" at a project's environmental consequences, our review is at an end. *Id.*

Given the volume of information in the EIS that addresses alien species, National Parks can hardly claim the FAA ignored the problem. Instead, they argue that, had the FAA taken a harder look, it would have concluded that the project's alien species impact will be significant. Their claim hinges on two variables, the rise in international arrivals and the risk that such flights might carry dangerous alien species.

The EIS is replete with data regarding the project's impact on international arrivals. The very first table of the Biological Assessment estimates that 50 foreign flights will land at Kahului this year, all from Vancouver. *See* BA Table 1–1. With the runway extension, this figure is expected to grow to 1,200 yearly flights—1,100 from Japan and 100 from Vancouver— over the course of a decade.[2] But this increase—just three flights per day— pales in comparison to the total number of arrivals. Kahului currently serves 35,500 flights, a figure that is projected to rise to 40,350 in 2010 if the extension is built. International arrivals, then, will account for only 3% of the total air traffic at Kahului.

Even this modest increase, however, is not assured. As we have noted, airport demand projections are little more than guesses that depend on economic conditions, airline routing decisions and other variables. *See City of Los Angeles* v. *Federal Aviation Admin.*, 138 F.3d 806, 807–08 & n.2 (9th Cir. 1998). The figures for Kahului are no exception. One independent

---

[2] National Parks are primarily concerned with arrivals from Japan, as flights from a new port of origin carry a heightened risk of alien species introduction.

study contained in the EIS found that tourism and airline executives expected *"no or little lasting long-term growth-inducing impact"* from the runway extension. Another study noted that Hilo Airport on the Big Island has had a 9,800 foot runway for nearly 30 years, but lack of demand led to the phase out of all direct overseas flights. Currently, demand from Asia is so low that three Asian carriers have ended service to Honolulu due to economic and strategic considerations. When it comes to airport runways, it is not necessarily true that " 'if you build it, they will come.' " *City of Los Angeles*, 138 F.3d at 807.

Moreover, evidence in the EIS demonstrates that international arrivals could grow even if the runway is not extended. Kahului can already serve international flights, and cannot discriminate against a foreign carrier that wishes to establish a direct route. If service to Kahului becomes economically attractive, foreign flights could arrive in Maui regardless of the extension. After all, planes don't need to stop in Honolulu to *land* at Kahului; if direct arrivals became profitable, a carrier could fly directly to Maui, but include a layover in Honolulu upon departure. Additionally, factors such as lighter aircraft or other technological advances could allow fully loaded planes to depart nonstop, even on the shorter runway.

The EIS also contains extensive discussion of the fact that the alien species impact of the project is highly uncertain. Foreign flights account for only 13% of the total number of animals, insects and plants introduced into Hawaii.[3] Of this relatively small influx, it is impossible to determine which species will be introduced at Kahului, or whether they will be dangerous. National Parks cannot identify a single species that will become established as a result of the project, nor can they pinpoint a particular resource that will be adversely impacted. Moreover, new alien species may not be harmful; since the 1970's, for example, 20 species of alien invertebrates per year have become established in Hawaii, only three of which have turned out to be economic pests. . .

No such harmful species has been identified here, and possible environmental damage, if any, is purely speculative. It was therefore appropriate for the EIS to focus on broad mitigation measures to combat all types of alien species that might arrive at Kahului. The detailed mitigation plan outlined in the EIS includes traveler education videos, training of airport personnel and hiring of Arrival Inspectors. In addition, the project calls for a new air cargo building that would prevent escape of insects during inspection. After completion of the EIS, the FAA supplemented these measures with an Alien Species Action Plan that incorporates suggestions made by the National Parks Service and the public during the review process. For example, the Action Plan establishes an Alien Species Prevention Team to conduct risk management assessments and monitor data on inbound flights. The FAA conditioned its approval of the project on the implementation of the mitigation measures in the Alien Species Action Plan. . .

---

[3]   Domestic air traffic accounts for 27% of introduced species; first class mail, 23%; air and sea cargo, 18%; military vessels, 13%; and private boats and planes, 6%.

In sum, National Parks seek too much from the EIS. While they may disagree with the FAA's substantive conclusions as to the alien species impact of the project, NEPA does not guarantee substantive results. So long as the agency has made an informed decision, we cannot intervene. The discussion in the EIS is reasonably thorough, and we are satisfied that the FAA has made an informed decision. Because the EIS contains the requisite hard look at the alien species problem, it satisfies NEPA. . .

III

For section 4(f) of the Transportation Act to apply, the project must "use" Haleakala National Park, a property protected by the Act. *See* 49 U.S.C. § 303(c). National Parks argue that the potential impact of alien species is a sufficient use of the Park to trigger section 4(f). But "use" turns on whether the action "substantially impairs the value of the site in terms of its prior significance and enjoyment." *Adler* v. *Lewis*, 675 F.2d 1085, 1092 (9th Cir. 1982). National Parks cannot demonstrate that the runway extension will so increase the rate of alien species introduction as to substantially impair Haleakala's economic or environmental value. The FAA's determination that the runway extension would not use the Park was not arbitrary or capricious.

Nor does approval of the project violate the Airport and Airway Improvement Act of 1982, 49 U.S.C. 47106(c)(1)(C), under which the FAA may not approve an airport development project that has "a significant adverse effect on natural resources" without first ensuring that "every reasonable step has been taken to minimize the adverse effect." AAIA § 509(b)(5). The only "reasonable step" National Parks identify as missing—funding for the mitigation measures—does not have to be finalized for the FAA to approve the project.

W. FLETCHER, dissenting. . . The central flaw in the Final EIS is that the FAA failed to admit or analyze the likely environmental consequences of increased non-stop overseas arrivals resulting from the proposed runway extension. The FAA is free to conclude that the likely benefits of the extension outweigh the likely adverse environmental consequences, but it cannot arrive at that conclusion without first adequately admitting and analyzing those risks. Because of the demonstrable insufficiency of the Final EIS, I find it impossible to agree with the majority's conclusion that the FAA took a "hard look" at the likely environmental consequences of its proposed action.

II

The Final EIS concludes that the proposed project will have no impact on the introduction rate of alien species. . . The FAA proposes the runway extension at Kahului Airport because fully-loaded, fully-fueled non-stop overseas flights cannot take off from the present runway. As a physical matter, non-stop overseas arrivals can land on the present runway, but as an economic matter, many such arrivals—particularly those from Asia—are not profitable unless they are combined with non-stop overseas departures by those same airplanes. Thus, while the proposed runway extension will permit fully-loaded, fully-fueled aircraft to leave Maui on non-stop overseas flights, the practical and environmentally significant impact of the extension is that many non-stop overseas *arrivals* will become economically feasible for the first time.

Yet, according to the FAA, the significance of the runway extension is the departures it will permit, not the arrivals it will produce: "Although the existing 7,000-foot-long runway adequately serves domestic and international aircraft *arriving* at Maui, these arrivals do not and will not require the proposed extension to maintain service to Maui. Conversely, the existing runway is not long enough and does not have adequate pavement strength to accommodate *departing*, non-stop flights fully loaded[.]" *Id.* at 4 (emphasis in original). This statement accurately conveys the purpose of the extension, but that purpose cannot be the basis for an analysis of its environmental consequences. . .

III

The most critical issue . . . is the increased non-stop arrivals from Asia. There have been non-stop arrivals from North America to Maui for a number of years, but there have been virtually no non-stop arrivals from Asia. Because they are new, non-stop arrivals from Asia pose by far the greatest danger of introducing new alien species. According to Table 1–1 [of the Biological Assessment], the proposed project will produce an increase in the yearly non-stop arrivals from Asia from 0 to 1,100. . .

Even if one assumes that there will be no overall increase in non-stop overseas flights from Asia to the Hawaiian islands and that non-stop overseas flights originally bound for Oahu will instead land in Maui, the increased arrivals on Maui are significant. One might think that, if the only result of the extension is to shift non-stop Asian overseas arrivals from Oahu to Maui, the overall impact on the Hawaiian islands, considered as a whole, would remain the same. But this is not the case. The environment immediately around Kahului airport and on Maui generally is more hospitable to alien species than the environment immediately surrounding the Honolulu airport and on Oahu generally. The more hospitable, and therefore more vulnerable, environment on Maui results from several factors. First, the prevailing trade winds on Maui blow from the Kahului airport toward adjacent sugar cane fields and wetlands, whereas the prevailing winds on Oahu blow from the Honolulu airport toward the ocean. Second, the Kahului airport is immediately adjacent to hospitable environments for alien species, such as cane fields and wetlands, whereas the Honolulu airport is isolated from hospitable environments by expanses of concrete. Third, due to its greater elevations and greater geographical diversity, Maui has a much larger number of hospitable environmental niches than does Oahu. It is therefore possible that some alien species that could never establish themselves on Oahu could easily do so on Maui. Finally, even if we indulge the counter-factual assumption that the two islands are equal in their vulnerability to introduction of alien species, the Biological Assessment concluded that "opening Maui to more direct overseas flights [in addition to Oahu] doubles the potential area available for colonization."

The Biological Assessment states in its conclusion that "*if* the present aircraft flights are one of the pathways for alien species introduction into Hawaii, and *if* the Proposed Project results in more direct flights to Maui from the mainland U.S. and, in the future, from Asia, the Proposed Project could potentially increase the risk of alien species being introduced." BA § 9.1 (emphasis added). This conclusion fails to face up to the information the FAA has in its possession. The two clauses introduced by "if" purport to state hypothetical propositions. The first is not the least bit hypothetical. The FAA *knows* that aircraft flights are "one of the pathways for alien species introductions into Hawaii" and the FAA *knows* that this is particularly true for non-stop overseas flights. The second is hypothetical in the sense that it is a prediction rather than a fact, but the FAA itself has projected that the airport extension is likely to result in "more direct flights to Maui from the mainland U.S. and, in the future, from Asia," including 1,100 non-stop flights per year from Asia where none exist today. . .

IV

None of this matters to the majority. They conclude that the FAA's flight projections are unreliable. They write that "it is not necessarily true that 'if you build it, they will come,' " *supra* at 8878 (quoting *City of Los Angeles v. FAA*, 138 F.3d 806, 807 (9th Cir. 1998)), and that "airport demand projections are notoriously unreliable," *id.* at 8881 (citing *City of Los Angeles*, 138 F.3d at 807–08 & n.2). They conclude that plaintiffs "seek too much from the EIS." *Id.* And they conclude that "the discussion in the EIS is reasonably thorough, and we are satisfied that the FAA has made an informed decision." *Id.* . . . As Judge Kozinski recognized in *City of Los Angeles*, airport demand projections are peculiarly within the expertise of the FAA. He should give as much deference to the FAA's projections in this case as he gave to such projections in *City of Los Angeles*. The FAA's projections of increased non-stop overseas arrivals may not be perfectly accurate, but they are entitled to more than an ad hoc rejection based on the "common sense" of the majority of this panel.

I do not agree with the majority that the plaintiffs in this case "seek too much." They ask only that the FAA honestly confront the knowledge they have in their possession. I also do not agree that the discussion in the EIS of the critical issue—the threat of introduction of alien species by non-stop overseas arrivals—is "reasonably thorough." It is virtually non-existent, and what little discussion exists is dishonest.

Finally, while it is possible that the FAA has made an "informed decision," we cannot know that this is so. For all we can judge, the FAA may have analyzed alien species introductions resulting from arriving overseas flights as part of its internal decision-making process. But if such an analysis was made, the FAA should have put it in the EIS where it belongs.

V

NEPA is a purely procedural statute. It does not require that an agency reach any particular decision in approving or disapproving a project. It does require, however, that the agency prepare a Final EIS that evaluates carefully and honestly the likely environmental consequences of a proposed action. The FAA has failed to perform its duty. Rather than taking a hard look at the possible environmental consequences, the FAA has deliberately averted its eyes from a well known environmental problem and from the potential consequences of its proposed action.

In failing to perform its duty under NEPA, the FAA has short-changed the political process Congress had in mind when it required the preparation of environmental impact statements. Because the FAA has failed in its duty, and because the majority of this panel has acquiesced in that failure, we will never know what decision a properly informed political process would have produced.

NOTES & QUESTIONS

1. The feral animals that threaten the palila and the other species on the island of Hawai'i were brought there by purposeful human action. By contrast, the expansion of the Kahului Airport threatened to result in the unintentional introduction of new species to Maui. Should it matter how a species arrives in a new location?

2. Invasive species threaten the survival of much of Hawai'i's native biodiversity. For example, fourteen Hawaiian plants were listed under the ESA in 1996 because they were "threatened by competition with one or more alien plant taxa," including strawberry guava, Christmas berry, thimbleberry, silk oak, molasses grass, Hilo grass, common guava, and Maui pamakani. Consider just one of those invasive species. Strawberry guava, "an invasive shrub or small tree native to tropical America, has become widely naturalized on all of the main Hawaiian islands, forming dense strands that exclude other plant species in disturbed areas. This alien plant grows primarily in mesic and wet habitats and is dispersed mainly be feral pigs and fruit-eating birds. Strawberry guava is considered to be one of the greatest alien plant threats to Hawaiian rain forests. . ." Determination of Endangered or Threatened Status for Fourteen Plant Taxa From the Hawaiian Islands, 61 Fed. Reg. 53108, 53110, 53119 (1996). Additional examples were offered by Dr. Lloyd Loope of the Pacific Island Ecosystems Research Center, whose list of six recently introduced pests that are especially damaging included (1) Erythrina gall wasp, which arrived from Africa via Taiwan and now threatens the "survival of wiliwili, until now one of the few abundant endemic tree species in remnant areas of lowland dry areas of Hawaii;" (2) 'Ohi', a rust disease, which arrived in April 2005 with "a plant shipment from Florida or perhaps a foreign country somewhere in the neotropics" and already threatens native Hawaiian forests; (3) nettle caterpillar, a new arrival from Taiwan that attacks palms and can produce anaphylactic shock in humans; (4) little fire ant, which blinds mammals "perhaps by stinging their corneas" and is spread by logging; (5) scale insect of hala, which attacks the hala that "is common to abundant in many Hawaiian coastal ecosystems and an extremely important plant species for native Hawaiians, who

have traditionally used it for cordage, thatching, healing, decoration, etc."; (6) and cycad scale or sago palm scale, which traveled from Thailand to Florida to Hawai'i, and now threatens trees both there and now in Guam. *Invasive Species: Hearing Before the National Parks Subcomm. of the Senate Energy and Natural Resources Comm.*, 109th Cong., 1st Sess. (Aug. 9, 2005) (testimony of Dr. Lloyd Loope, Research Scientist USGS, Pacific Island Ecosystems Research Center).

3. How should the law respond to such invasive species? The ESA provides one mechanism, but by definition it only applies once the native species are headed toward extinction. NEPA offers another alternative. Before the Ninth Circuit decided that an EIS was not required, several state and federal agencies created the Kahului Airport Pest Risk Assessment (KARA) which "involved intensive inspections of checked and carry-on-baggage by inspectors and detector dog teams; inspections of aircraft cabins and cargo holds of mainland flights; and 100% inspections of agricultural products shipped by air cargo." The head of the Hawai'i Department of Agriculture's Plant Quarantine Branch told a congressional hearing in 2005 that an inspection of 1,897 commercial direct overseas flights containing 399,463 passengers and crew found only eleven undeclared agricultural items in passenger baggage. By contrast, "[c]argo was identified as a high-risk pathway for the entry of pests into Maui," with 279 different species intercepted, including 125 that were not known to occur in Hawai'i. *Invasive Species: Hearing Before the National Parks Subcomm. of the Senate Energy and Natural Resources Comm.*, 109th Cong., 1st Sess. (Aug. 9, 2005) (testimony of Dr. Neil J. Reimer).

The proposed Hawaii Invasive Species Prevention Act would state "the sense of Congress that there exists a need for improved and better coordinated control, interdiction, and eradication of invasive species and diseases on the part of the United States and other interested parties to prevent the introduction or spread of invasive species or diseases in Hawaii." H.R. 3469, 109th Cong., 1st Sess., § 4(a) (2005). The substantive provisions of the law would prohibit federal agencies from taking any actions "that would likely cause or promote the introduction or spread of invasive species and diseases in Hawaii," *id.* § 4(c); and authorize quarantines to prevent the introduction of invasive species, *id.* § 5(a). What other provisions would you add to such an act?

4. Hawai'i is hardly the only island ecosystem to suffer from the adverse effects of invasive species. Perhaps the most troublesome invader of the Pacific islands has been the brown tree snake. The scope of the threat posed by the snake and the response to it are illustrated in the FWS's explanation of why it could delist the Tinian monarch pursuant to the ESA. Tinian is a small island in the Commonwealth of the Northern Mariana Islands (CNMI), an American possession located three islands north of Guam. The monarch is a small forest bird that was listed as endangered in 1970, but recovered to become the second most abundant bird species on the island. Nonetheless, the FWS the possibility that the brown tree snake could arrive in Tinian prompted the FWS to observe that "if an incipient population of brown tree snakes is discovered on Tinian, then the monarch and all other birds on Tinian would again be in clear danger of extinction." Final Rule to Remove the Tinian Monarch from the Federal List of Endangered and Threatened Wildlife, 69 Fed. Reg. 56367, 56369 (2004). The FWS then elaborated on the response to the threat posed by the brown tree snake to the Tinian monarch:

The brown tree snake climbs exceptionally well and forages opportunistically on a wide variety of vertebrates, including birds and their eggs, reptiles, and mammals. On Guam, predation by the brown tree snake decimated the avifauna, causing the local extirpation or complete extinction of 10 of the 13 native forest bird species on the island. It has few competitors and no known predators in the Marianas, and can reach population densities of up to 80 to 120 snakes per hectare (32 to 48 snakes per acre). Declines in bird populations on Guam occurred extremely rapidly once the brown tree snake became established.

While there have been reports of possible brown tree snakes on Tinian, the brown tree snake is not known to be established on Tinian, and the monarch is not known to be affected by brown tree snake predation. Nevertheless, we recognize that effective methods for interdiction, monitoring, and control of incipient populations of brown tree snakes must be implemented on all islands in the Marianas, including Tinian. Moreover, implementation of brown tree snake interdiction is not dependent on the listing status of the Tinian monarch.

On Tinian, where there are no native snakes, there have been at least seven reports of snakes some of which probably were brown tree snakes. Brown tree snakes potentially could reach Tinian from Guam, where the snake is established, or from Saipan, which is now thought to have an incipient population of brown tree snakes. Several measures have been taken on Guam, Saipan, and Tinian in an attempt to decrease the possibility of brown tree snakes spreading among the Mariana Islands. The U.S. Department of the Interior Office of Insular Affairs (OIA), U.S. Department of Defense (DOD), U.S. Department of Agriculture Wildlife Services (USDA), the Service, the Government of Guam, the CNMI, and the State of Hawaii are working together regionally to control brown tree snakes, particularly around transport centers. The OIA and DOD have and continue to actively fund research into methods of controlling snakes on Guam, in part to reduce the threat of introduction to other Pacific islands. Both the CNMI Division of Fish and Wildlife (DFW) and Guam Department of Aquatic and Wildlife Resources conduct brown tree snake public awareness educational campaigns consisting of school presentations, news releases, workshops, and poster/pamphlet distribution, and the CNMI maintains a snake reporting hotline. . .

On Guam, high-risk cargo leaving by air and sea currently undergoes inspection for brown tree snakes by dog teams from USDA Wildlife Services, under contract from the DOD and OIA. Inspections on Guam are as effective as possible using existing techniques; however, inspections are voluntary, compliance by shippers with quarantine procedures is variable, and USDA Wildlife Services has no regulatory authority to require inspections.

All construction companies operating in the CNMI must have a snake control plan, and the Governor of the CNMI signed a directive for the Ports Authority and related agencies to work with the CNMI DFW to develop effective snake interdiction strategies. The CNMI also conducts training for its DFW and Quarantine personnel with the U.S. Geological Survey Biological Resources Discipline and USDA Wildlife Services on Guam at least two to three times per year.

On Saipan, the CNMI Quarantine Division operates a sniffer dog program that consists of two handlers and two dogs that check incoming cargo for brown tree snakes. The efficacy of these inspections needs verification, however, and the level of staffing is inadequate for the volume of goods shipped via air and sea. Outgoing cargo on Saipan currently does not undergo any inspection for brown tree snakes. Construction was completed recently on a brown tree snake barrier and quarantine area designed to facilitate inspection of high-risk cargo at the commercial port on Saipan. The 3000-square-meter (32,400-square-foot) area within the barrier will be monitored for brown tree snakes with dogs and traps. Although the efficacy of this barrier has not yet been tested, it was designed and is expected to enhance brown tree snake interdiction.

On Tinian, a dog and handler have been used to inspect incoming cargo, but as on Saipan, the efficacy of these inspections has not been verified. In June of 2004, the Service obligated funds to construct a brown tree snake barrier and quarantine yard at the commercial port on Tinian. We expect the barrier will be completed in 12 to 18 months. This barrier will be similar to the barrier on Saipan, and will facilitate inspection of high-risk cargo and is expected to enhance brown tree snake interdiction.

In 2004, section 101 of the Sikes Improvement Act of 1997 (Sikes Act, 16 U.S.C. 670a) was amended by adding subsection (g), sometimes termed the "invasives pilot project for Guam," which states that the Secretary of Defense shall, to the maximum extent practicable and conducive to military readiness, incorporate in Integrated Natural Resource Management Plans (INRMP) for military installations on Guam the management, control, and eradication of invasive species that are not native to the ecosystem of the military installation, and the introduction of which may cause harm to military readiness, the environment, or human health and safety, and that the Secretary of Defense shall carry out this subsection in consultation with the Secretary of the Interior. . . The Navy has also reaffirmed their commitment to continuing brown tree snake interdiction in the CNMI in general, and Tinian specifically; "Military cargo originating on Guam undergoes brown tree snake inspection prior to loading and again when offloaded on Tinian. During the past decade of DoD and USDA WS cooperation in brown tree snake control and interdiction, there has been no reported brown tree snakes found in military cargo shipped from Guam to the CNMI. Our existing control and interdiction efforts are working to significantly reduce the probability of the accidental introduction of the brown tree snake in military cargo from Guam to CNMI."

Id. Most recently, Congress enacted the Brown Tree Snake Control and Eradication Act of 2004, Pub. L. No. 108–384, 118 Stat. 2221, which authorized funding for research and interdiction, established quarantine protocols, prohibited the mailing of brown tree snakes, and created a technical working group to address the threats posed by the snake.

Estate of Edgar E. Sims, Jr. v. Department of Environmental Protection

Office of Administrative Law, State of New Jersey, 1994.
95 N.J.A.R.2d (EPE) 6.

INITIAL DECISION AND FINAL AGENCY DECISION

■ KANE, ALJ:

STATEMENT OF THE CASE AND PROCEDURAL HISTORY

Pursuant to N.J.A.C. 7:7EB3.21, the respondent classified property owned by the petitioner as a "bay island". The petitioner disagreed with this determination claiming instead that the property known as Rum Point, is part of the barrier island of the City of Brigantine, located immediately north of Atlantic City, New Jersey. On May 3, 1993, this matter was transmitted to the Office of Administrative Law (OAL) to be heard as a contested case pursuant to N.J.S.A. 52:14BB1 to B15 and N.J.S.A. 52:14FB1 to B13. The hearing was conducted at the Atlantic City OAL, 1201 Bacharach Boulevard, Atlantic City, New Jersey on April 25, 26 and May 2, 3, 11 and 17, 1994. The record was held open until June 29, 1994 in order to permit the filing of post-hearing briefs. An initial decision was rendered on August 5, 1994.

ISSUES

1. Whether evidence submitted in support of the summary statement to N.J.A.C. 7:7EB3.21, should be excluded from the consideration of what constitutes a bay island.

2. Whether the respondent properly classified Rum Point as a bay island pursuant to the criteria set forth at N.J.A.C. 7:7EB3.21.

INTRODUCTION

Over 22,000 years ago the coast line of New Jersey began 75 miles east of its current location. As the ice age concluded and the ice packs receded northward and began to melt, the ocean levels began to rise over 400 feet which had the effect of causing the coast line to recede westwardly.

As the ocean, over thousands of years, continued to consume the land mass, barrier islands and bay islands were formed and destroyed. These dramatic geologic changes have, within historic time, resulted in the formation of the barrier island and back bay system known as the New Jersey coast.

Located in Atlantic County, the barrier islands of Brigantine and Absecon Island were formed. Absecon Island contains New Jersey's gambling mecca, Atlantic City, while Brigantine Island lies to the north immediately across Absecon Channel. The dramatic geologic changes which formed Brigantine and Absecon Islands also resulted in the formation of Rum

Point, which is located in the Absecon Channel between these two barrier islands.

Absecon Island and Brigantine Island are connected by State Route 87 which leaves Absecon Island in the vicinity of Harrah's Hotel Casino and Trump Castle Hotel Casino, proceeds northward across Absecon Channel, and first makes land fall on the island of Rum Point. Petitioner claims that, geologically, Rum Point is part of the Brigantine barrier island system while the respondent has classified Rum Point as a bay island pursuant to N.J.A.C. 7:7EB3.21.

Whether Rum Point is classified as a bay island or part of the barrier island of Brigantine significantly impacts on the type, location, and extent of development which would be permitted on Rum Point.

LOCATION OF RUM POINT

Rum Point is located at the confluence of St. George's Thorofare and Absecon Channel, one mile west of where Absecon Channel meets the Atlantic Ocean, between the barrier islands of Absecon and Brigantine. Rum Point is one of the stepping stone islands utilized by the causeway which links Absecon Island with Brigantine Island. State Route 87 leaves Absecon Island in the vicinity of Harrah's Hotel Casino and Trump Castle Hotel Casino, commonly known as the Marina District. The causeway proceeds over Absecon Channel making land fall on Rum Point.

Petitioner's property consists of less than eight acres of undeveloped uplands surrounded on three sides by a large expanse of coastal wetlands, a small beach, and tidal waterways. The fourth side abuts the causeway which acts as a boundary line between the portion of Rum Point owned by the petitioner and the remainder of the island owned by Resorts International Hotel Casino. The entire island is known as Rum Point; however, for the purposes of this opinion, Rum Point will refer to that tract of land owned by the petitioner.

Prior to 1926, access to Brigantine Island was gained through a ferry between Absecon Island and Brigantine Island in the same location as the current causeway or Brigantine Bridge, also named the Haneman Memorial Bridge. Between 1926 and 1927, when the bridge was built between the two barrier islands, a causeway was built on fill across Rum Point, Boot Island and onto Brigantine Island. This causeway had the effect of linking the islands of Rum Point and Boot Island with the barrier island. . .

With the elimination of the ferry service in 1926–1927, and the completion of the causeway between the two barrier islands, Brigantine began to grow rapidly in both commercial and residential development. Within the last 25 years, the lack of available developable land on Brigantine Island subsequently increased the pressure to develop uplands on Boot Island and a narrow band of uplands adjacent to the causeway. This area quickly filled with single family residences and small condominium complexes.

The causeway transversing Rum Point is undeveloped due largely to the unavailability of uplands. Tidal waters and some coastal wetlands abut the filled area which serves as the basis for the causeway. Large pieces of concrete rubble have been placed adjacent to the causeway in several areas facing St. George's Thorofare in order to reinforce the causeway and prevent soil erosion caused by wave action. To this date, the Rum Point property has remained undeveloped.

FINDINGS OF FACT AND CONCLUSIONS OF LAW

Since purchasing the property prior to his death in 1986, Edgar Sims, Jr., and since that point, his estate, have had numerous meetings and discussions with the respondent concerning the classification of Rum Point as a bay island. Finally, by letter dated October 30, 1992 DEP confirmed its classification of Rum Point as a bay island which in turn triggered the within appeal.

The conclusion that Rum Point was a bay island was based upon materials submitted by the petitioner and the definition of bay island set forth at N.J.A.C. 7:7EB3.21 including the rationale statement accompanying the bay island rule, including the USGS map of the site. The October 30, 1992 letter stated specifically:

> Rum Point remains today an undeveloped parcel of land surrounded by tidal waters with the exception of the right-of-way of Route 87 and its accompanying underpass. The property is adjacent to highly sensitive areas. Extensive wetlands surrounds the uplands portion of the site which serves as a year round haven for numerous animal species on a year round and seasonal basis. An exceptionally good shellfish habitat is found throughout the Absecon inlet, St. George's and Panama Thorofares and the Department has taken great care to protect and foster this valuable natural resource.

> Rum Point is also subject to storm inundation and tidal flooding and classified by the Federal Emergency Management Act as a "V"-Zone. Route 87 is the only storm evacuation route for residents of the City of Brigantine. Any development which would contribute greater numbers of vehicles to the already strained evacuation capacity of the road system is unacceptable.

The definition of a Bay Island set forth in N.J.A.C. 7:7EB3.21 states:

> Bay Island are islands or filled areas surrounded by tidal waters, wetlands, beaches or dunes, lying between the mainland and barrier islands.

Petitioner contends that the DEP overstepped its bounds when it classified Rum Point as a bay island because it utilized factors and criteria not contained within the plain language of N.J.A.C. 7:7EB3.21. Respondent counters that in addition to the language set forth in N.J.A.C. 7:7EB3.21, its decision to classify Rum Point as a bay island was augmented by a consideration of the factors set forth in the rule's summary statement which accompanied the rule at 22 N.J. Register 1188(a).

This statement details certain factors concerning environmental impact when classifying a tract of land. This rule rationale statement states:

> New Jersey Bay Islands are for the most part inaccessible and undeveloped. Many of these islands are former wetlands where upland areas have been created by past filling, particularly with dredge spoils. Many are suitable for future dredge spoil disposal. They are adjacent to areas with high environmental sensitivity, particularly wetlands, intertidal flats, tidal waterways, shellfish beds, and endangered and threatened wildlife habitats. Development of the islands would pose a great threat to these natural resources and habitat. The majority of, if not all, bay islands are valuable wildlife habitats or have the potential to become habitat through the implementation of management techniques. Their value, in part, stems from their isolation from human activity as compared to the intense development and beach usage of oceanfront barrier islands. For example, sandy areas are used by beach nesting birds such as least tern, black skimmer, and piping plover, and vegetated areas are used by colonial nesting birds such as heron and noncolonial birds such as the marsh hawk. Bay islands are also subject to flooding and by virtue of their location function as bridges between the mainland and barrier islands. If developed, these islands would pose added storm evacuation problems. They are usually distant from public services, and therefore unsuitable for development. . .

In summary, bay islands have historically remained undeveloped and their importance for the maintenance of wildlife habitat requires that development be limited to only areas that are already developed. . .

[Finding that the island in question met the criteria prescribed in the regulation and its rationale statement, the Administrative Law Judge initially held for the Department, and on administrative appeal of that ruling the Department issued the following final decision.]

FINAL AGENCY DECISION

■ SHINN, COMMISSIONER:

. . . Rum Point meets the regulatory definition of a bay island. First, the ALJ found, "an examination of the most recent topographical maps demonstrates that Rum Point is located between the barrier island of Brigantine and the mainland." He further found that "the construction of the causeway linking Rum Point to the barrier island did not alter its essential characteristic and nature as that of a bay island which is part of a flood delta complex." Although petitioner argues in one of its exceptions that Rum Point is located between two barrier islands and not between a barrier island and the mainland, it does not follow that because Rum Point lies between two barrier islands (Absecon and Brigantine), it does not also lie between a barrier island and the mainland. This circumstance satisfies one condition of the definition set forth in N.J.A.C. 7:7EB3.21(a). Rum Point is also surrounded by tidal water, wetlands, beaches and dunes, except where the constructed causeway links it to Boot Island. Thus, the second condition of the definition is met since that definition expressly provided at the time of decision that the presence of a causeway is to be discounted.

NOTES AND QUESTIONS

1. New Jersey's approach seems to have been to let development dominate on barrier islands and conservation dominate on bay islands. As the case illustrates, this approach makes the status of a particular island all important and, apparently, worth fighting over. But why the sharp distinction? Is it because bay islands are inherently more ecologically valuable than barrier islands? Nothing in the opinion suggests that is the case. Is it because barrier islands are inherently more valuable for development than bay islands? Mr. Sims apparently found bay island development economically viable. So why establish an ecosystem management regime that depends so crucially on this distinction?

2. A barrier island is a thin sliver of sand separated from the mainland by a wide bay and marsh system. Barrier islands rim the Texas, Florida, and Alabama coasts on the Gulf of Mexico as well the Atlantic coasts of New Jersey, Delaware, Maryland, North Carolina, and South Carolina. One study found that in 100 coastal counties, towns located on barrier islands approved construction of 54,000 homes in 1998, worth over $6.5 billion in home construction value alone. *See Boom on the Beach*, USA TODAY, July 27, 2000, at 4A. Home lot prices for choice oceanfront real estate regularly exceed $1 million. Commercial real estate prices are soaring as well (the two-bedroom condominium unit one of your authors frequents in Destin, one of 30 units in the building, is available for $650,000!).

What will all these people mean for the barrier island ecosystems? Islands, for obvious reasons, present unusual ecosystem dynamics. Isolated from the mainland and one another, their assemblage of species often depends on chance and accident, such as how finches reached the Galapagos Islands. This makes island ecosystems particularly vulnerable to disruption from natural disaster and invasive species, both of which have been exacerbated by human impact. Development in island habitat reduces ecosystem resilience to natural flood and storm events and exposes island species to higher risks of extirpation. *See* Thomas Brooks and Michael Leonard Smith, *Caribbean Catastrophes*, 294 SCIENCE 1469 (2001). Non-native species introduced deliberately or unintentionally by human action can come to dominate an island ecosystem food web within decades. *See* Erik Stokstad, *Parasitic Wasps Invade Hawaiian Ecosystem*, 293 SCIENCE 1241 (2001). Beyond these dramatic potential effects, the sheer presence of so much humanity in island settings poses tremendous growth management problems. In the Florida Keys, for example, sewage effluent poses a significant threat to island resources. Sydney T. Bacchus, *Knowledge of Groundwater Responses*, 18 ENDANGERED SPECIES UPDATE 79 (2001).

3. One of the classic experiments in ecology took place in the 1970s when two ecologists who helped spearhead the discipline of island biogeography, Daniel Simberloff and E.O. Wilson, fumigated several islands in the Florida Keys in an effort to relate species diversity to geographic area. Several ecologists had been exploring the concept that species diversity increases in a function relationship with increases in geographic area and independent of habitat diversity within the area. Thus, it was thought, islands may experience dramatic changes in species composition after a hurricane sweeps prior occupants off the surface, but the total number of species that reappear will be the same as before, and the equilibrium level of species will be a function of the size of the island, not the habitat composition on the island. If this "size matters" theory were true, it could help guide not just island ecosystem management, but the design of any sort of terrestrial or aquatic preserve. By wiping out all the species on an island, Simberloff and Wilson could follow the emergence of a new species assemblage and test the species-area hypothesis. Indeed, their experiment turned out just as the theory predicted, and many ecologists since then have worked to test and refine the theory. For an account of the experiment and its impact on island ecology, see CHARLES C. MANN AND MARK L. PLUMMER, NOAH'S CHOICE: THE FUTURE OF ENDANGERED SPECIES 53–81 (1996).

4. Mountains are the "sky islands" of terrestrial settings, presenting many of the same ecosystem dynamics as do their aquatic cousins— isolation, pronounced exposure to extreme natural events, and delicate balances of biodiversity. This feature is seldom as pronounced as it is in the "archipelago" of mountain ranges running from southern Arizona and New Mexico into the Mexican states of Sonora and Chihuahua. Research has found that these mountains, while containing discrete biodiversity complexes, also interact through the migration of species using riparian habitat travel corridors between the ridge tops. As these riparian corridors have become increasingly fragmented from urban, agricultural, and recreational development, however, the biota distribution in the various mountains has shown increasing levels of mountain-specific endemism. Like aquatic islands, in other words, the mountain sky islands are profoundly influenced by what happens between them, in the larger landscape context, and thus preserving just the mountains is not sufficient to conserve their ecosystem dynamics. *See* Peter Warshall, *Southwestern Sky Island Ecosystems*, in NATIONAL BIOLOGICAL SERVICE, OUR LIVING RESOURCES 318 (1995).

And like the Arctic, climate change appears to be taking its toll on high-mountain ecosystems. Researchers are finding that the lowest elevation at which freezing occurs in mid-latitude mountains has climbed 150 meters since 1970. This means that habitat for species adapted to high-mountain tundra conditions have to stay higher up in the mountains. Of course, that strategy can only last for so long—the species on any particular mountain are stranded when the freeze line inches above the top of the mountain, and are in dire straights long before then as their domain shrinks and species adapted to warmer settings work their way higher up the slopes. Already the numbers of hardy pikas (tough but cute cousins of the rabbit) and cold-loving plants are crashing in their native high-mountain settings. *See All Downhill from Here?*, 303 SCIENCE 1600 (2004).

5. Is island ecosystem management, whether of the aquatic or terrestrial variety, largely a question of managing what takes place elsewhere?

D. CORAL REEF ECOSYSTEMS

The world's coral reefs cover only about 113,720 square miles—less than 0.1 percent of the globe's ocean area—but are second only to tropical rain forests in plant and animal diversity. Coral reefs house over one-fourth of all marine life. Even more so than rain forests, however, coral reefs are extremely sensitive to environmental disturbance. Even slight variations in temperature, light, salinity, oxygen, and nutrient load can fundamentally alter coral reef dynamics. Thus, unlike rain forests, coral reefs are small islands of fragility sprinkled throughout the huge, dominant ocean ecosystem. Variations in conditions that the ocean as a whole may shrug off thus can have devastating consequences for ecosystems. *See* U.S. EPA, Office of Water and Watersheds, *Coral Reefs and Your Coastal Watershed*, http://www.epa.gov/owow/oceans/factshhets/fact4.html.

Indeed, it is estimated that over 25 percent of the world's coral reefs are severely damaged. About half of those losses are attributed to direct and indirect human pressures, such as coastal development, waste dumping, oil spills, nonpoint source pollution, overfishing, and coral mining. The remainder is attributable to temperature-induced "bleaching," which results when the algae that inhabit the coral polyps die or are expelled due to stress. *See* Craig Quirolo, *Coral Disease and Monitoring in the Florida Keys*, 19 ENDANGERED SPECIES UPDATE 15 (2002).

The Florida coral reef tract, which is the third largest in the world after the Great Barrier Reef in Australia and the Belize reef, is by no means immune to these problems. The same is true of the United States' other reef systems, off of the Virgin Islands and the Hawaiian Islands. But managing coral reefs independently of the surrounding ocean waters is, of course, impossible. Coral is stationary. Given this constraint, how should ecosystem management of our nation's coral reefs proceed?

Establishment of the Virgin Islands Coral Reef National Monument

Presidential Proclamation 7399.
66 Fed. Reg. 7364 (January 22, 2001).

By the President of the United States of America

A Proclamation

The Virgin Islands Coral Reef National Monument, in the submerged lands off the island of St. John in the U.S. Virgin Islands, contains all the elements of a Caribbean tropical marine ecosystem. This designation furthers the protection of the scientific objects included in the Virgin Islands National Park, created in 1956 and expanded in 1962. The biological communities of the monument live in a fragile, interdependent relationship and include habitats essential for sustaining and enhancing the tropical marine ecosystem: mangroves, sea grass beds, coral reefs, octocoral hardbottom, sand communities, shallow mud and fine sediment habitat, and algal plains. The fishery habitats, deeper coral reefs, octocoral hardbottom, and algal plains of the monument are all objects of scientific interest and essential to the long-term sustenance of the tropical marine ecosystem.

* * *

As part of this important ecosystem, the monument contains biological objects including several threatened and endangered species, which forage, breed, nest, rest, or calve in the waters. Humpback whales, pilot whales, four species of dolphins, brown pelicans, roseate terns, least terns, and the hawksbill, leatherback, and green sea turtles all use portions of the monument. Countless species of reef fish, invertebrates, and plants utilize these submerged lands during their lives, and over 25 species of sea birds feed in the waters. Between the nearshore nursery habitats and the shelf edge spawning sites in the monument are habitats that play essential roles during specific developmental stages of reef-associated species, including spawning migrations of many reef fish species and crustaceans.

The submerged monument lands within Hurricane Hole include the most extensive and well-developed mangrove habitat on St. John. The Hurricane Hole area is an important nursery area for reef associated fish and invertebrates, instrumental in maintaining water quality by filtering and trapping sediment and debris in fresh water runoff from the fast land, and essential to the overall functioning and productivity of regional fisheries. Numerous coral reef-associated species, including the spiny lobster, queen conch, and Nassau grouper, transform from planktonic larvae to bottom-dwelling juveniles in the shallow nearshore habitats of Hurricane Hole. As they mature, they move offshore and take up residence in the deeper coral patch reefs, octocoral hardbottom, and algal plains of the submerged monument lands to the south and north of St. John. The monument lands south of St. John are predominantly deep algal plains with scattered areas of raised hard bottom. The algal plains include communities of mostly red and calcareous algae with canopies as much as half a meter high. The raised hard bottom is sparsely colonized with corals, sponges, gorgonians, and other invertebrates, thus providing shelter for lobster, groupers, and snappers as well as spawning sites for some reef fish species. These algal plains and raised hard bottom areas link the shallow water reef, sea grass, and mangrove communities with the deep water shelf and shelf edge communities of fish and invertebrates.

Section 2 of the Act of June 8, 1906 (34 Stat. 225, 16 U.S.C. 431), authorizes the President, in his discretion, to declare by public proclamation historic landmarks, historic and prehistoric structures, and other objects of historic or scientific interest that are situated upon the lands owned or controlled by the Government of the United States to be national monuments, and to reserve as a part thereof parcels of land, the limits of which in all cases shall be confined to the smallest area compatible with the proper care and management of the objects to be protected.

WHEREAS it appears that it would be in the public interest to reserve such lands as a national monument to be known as the Virgin Islands Coral Reef National Monument:

NOW, THEREFORE, I, WILLIAM J. CLINTON, President of the United States of America, by the authority vested in me by section 2 of the Act of June 8, 1906 (34 Stat. 225, 16 U.S.C. 431), do proclaim that there are hereby set apart and reserved as the Virgin Islands Coral Reef National Monument, for the purpose of protecting the objects identified above, all lands and interests in lands owned or controlled by the United States within the boundaries of the area described on the map entitled "Virgin Islands Coral Reef National Monument" attached to and forming a part of this proclamation. The Federal land and interests in land reserved consist of approximately 12,708 marine acres, which is the smallest area compatible with the proper care and management of the objects to be protected.

All Federal lands and interests in lands within the boundaries of this monument are hereby appropriated and withdrawn from all forms of entry, location, selection, sale, or leasing or other disposition under the public land laws, including but not limited to withdrawal from location, entry, and patent under the mining laws, and from disposition under all laws relating to mineral and geothermal leasing, other than by exchange that furthers the protective purposes of the monument. For the purpose of protecting the objects identified above, the Secretary shall prohibit all boat anchoring, except for emergency or authorized administrative purposes.

For the purposes of protecting the objects identified above, the Secretary shall prohibit all extractive uses, except that the Secretary may issue permits for bait fishing at Hurricane Hole and for blue runner (hard nose) line fishing in the area south of St. John, to the extent that such fishing is consistent with the protection of the objects identified in this proclamation.

Lands and interests in lands within the monument not owned or controlled by the United States shall be reserved as a part of the monument upon acquisition of title or control thereto by the United States.

The Secretary of the Interior shall manage the monument through the National Park Service, pursuant to applicable legal authorities, to implement the purposes of this proclamation. The National Park Service will manage the monument in a manner consistent with international law.

The Secretary of the Interior shall prepare a management plan, including the management of vessels in the monument, within 3 years, which addresses any further specific actions necessary to protect the objects identified in this proclamation.

The establishment of this monument is subject to valid existing rights. Nothing in this proclamation shall be deemed to revoke any existing withdrawal, reservation, or appropriation; however, the national monument shall be the dominant reservation.

Warning is hereby given to all unauthorized persons not to appropriate, injure, destroy, or remove any feature of this monument and not to locate or settle upon any of the lands thereof.

IN WITNESS WHEREOF, I have hereunto set my hand this seventeenth day of January, in the year of our Lord two thousand one, and of the Independence of the United States of America the two hundred and twenty-fifth.

WILLIAM J. CLINTON

NOTES AND QUESTIONS

1. The Coral Reef Task Force approach represents an effort to identify a fragile ecosystem type and apply concerted conservation measures to it wherever it occurs. A similar effort has been initiated at the international level through the International Coral Reef Initiative, which now has over 90 member countries. *See* http://www.environnement.gouv.fr/icri/index.html. The designation of the Virgin Islands Coral Reef National Monument represents an effort to identify a discrete example of the fragile ecosystem type and direct focused conservation measures toward it. President Clinton established a similar coral preserve when he designated a 200-kilometer-long necklace of islands northwest of Hawai'i as the Northwestern Hawaiian Islands Coral Reef Ecosystem Reserve. *See* Exec. Order 13178, 65 Fed. Reg. 76903 (Dec. 7, 2000). Through both approaches direct injury internal to the coral reefs from anchoring, fishing, and mineral extraction can be addressed, but in neither case can the conservation regime insulate the coral reef from degradation of surrounding marine resources from pollution, temperature warming, fishing, and other external forces of injury. How much promise do these approaches, separately or combined, thus hold for coral reef conservation?

2. To drive the previous point home, the greatest single threat to coral reefs likely is global warming, something neither the Coral Reef Task Force nor special protection status can competently address. Coral is white. The color in corals is supplied by microscopic algae that inhabit the coral in a symbiotic relationship. Warm water temperatures can stress the corals, causing them to expel the algae and thus lose their color and in many cases die out. This phenomenon, known as "bleaching," is being recorded as unprecedented levels worldwide, and is considered a more prominent threat to coral than is pollution or any other source of degradation. *See Warmer Waters More Deadly to Coral Reefs than Pollution*, 290 SCIENCE 682 (2000). Then there is the problem of dust, from Africa. That's right, researchers believe that great dust storms in Africa spread dust westward across the Atlantic Ocean to be deposited over coral rich waters in the Caribbean Sea. The dusts introduce pathogens and nutrients into surrounding waters, apparently damaging corals even in remote, otherwise undisturbed areas. See John C. Ryan, *Dust in the Wind: Fallout from Africa May Be Killing Coral Reefs an Ocean Away*, WORLD-WATCH, Jan.-Feb. 2002, at 32. Obviously, these are not the kind of injuries that can be controlled by designating a coral reef for special protection.

3. Considerable and growing attention has been devoted to the status of coral reef system in United States waters over the past several years. In September 2002, NOAA's U.S. Coral Reef Task Force issued the first comprehensive study of our reefs, *The State of Coral Reef Ecosystems of the United States and Pacific Freely Associated States*, which provides a baseline assessment of 13 major systems. The report concludes that while some systems are in good shape, reefs near urbanizing areas are degrading rapidly, and it advises that we know too little about reef structure and functions to make reliable assessments of options for recovering them. In conjunction with that finding, the task force also issued *A Coral Reef Action Strategy* outlining 13 goals for responding to coral reef degradation. The top goals are to map and thoroughly assess all U.S. coral reefs, with others being to use Marine Protected Areas more strategically and to reduce impacts from pollution, fishing, and other coastal uses. Dissatisfied with the depth of NOAA's assessment, two major groups of scientists released their own evaluations of coral reef status, these being far gloomier than NOAA's. *See* J.M. Pandolfi, et al., *Are U.S. Coral Reefs on the Slippery Slope to Slime?*, 307 Science 1725 (2005); T.P. Hughes, et al., *Climate Change, Human Impacts, and the Resilience of Coral Reefs*, 301 SCIENCE 929 (2003). These in turn led some other scientists to claim the new assessments were too dismal. *See Reassessing U.S. Coral Reefs*, 308 SCIENCE 1740 (2005) (series of letters).

4. President Clinton established the Virgin Islands Coral Reef National Monument pursuant to his authority under the Antiquities Act of 1906, which states in virtually its entirety as follows:

> The President of the United States is authorized, in his discretion, to declare by public proclamation historic landmarks, historic and prehistoric structures, and other objects of historic or scientific interest that are situated upon the lands owned or controlled by the Government of the United States to be national monuments, and may reserve as a part thereof parcels of land, the limits of which in all cases shall be confined to the smallest area compatible with the proper care and management of the objects to be protected. When such objects are situated upon a tract covered by a bona fide unperfected claim or held in private ownership, the tract, or so much thereof as may be necessary for the proper care and management of the object, may be relinquished to the Government, and the Secretary of the Interior is authorized to accept the relinquishment of such tracts in behalf of the Government of the United States.

16 U.S.C. 431. The Antiquities Act has more frequently been used to designate special protection sites in terrestrial ecosystems. Indeed, presidential decrees under the Antiquities Act were responsible for designation of significant protected areas within the Grand Canyon, Glacier Bay, Death Valley, and Carlsbad Caverns. But President Clinton caused considerable controversy when, acting on a strategy then Secretary of Interior Bruce Babbitt devised, late in his tenure he designated vast areas of federal public lands in western states as national monuments. (He designated the Virgin Islands reef monument on his last day in office.) Because the Antiquities Act allows the Executive to do so without Congress's involvement, and then to restrict land uses within the designated area, this was seen by many in Congress, the state and local governments, and the private landowner community as an end run way of injecting enhanced conservation measures into public lands otherwise subject to the "multiple use" management mandate, but by many others as the only viable way of establishing ecosystem management regimes in those lands given Republican control of Congress. We never said ecosystem management isn't political! For much more background on the recent use of the Antiquities Act, see Sandra Zellmer, *A Preservation Paradox: Political Prestidigitation and an Enduring Resource of Wildness*, 34 ENVTL. L. 1015 (2004); Mark Squillace, *The Monumental Legacy of the Antiquities Act of 1906*, 37 GA. L. REV. 473 (2003); Christine A. Klein, *Preserving Monumental Landscapes Under the Antiquities*

Act, 87 CORNELL L. REV.1333 (2002); James R. Rasband, *Moving Forward: The Future of the Antiquities Act*, 21 J. LAND RESOURCES & ENVTL. L. 619 (2001); Justin James Quigley, *Grand-Staircase Escalante National Monument: Preservation or Politics*, 19 J. LAND, RESOURCES, AND ENVT'L L. 55 (1999); Sanjay Ranchod, *The Clinton National Monuments, Protecting Ecosystems With the Antiquities Act*, 25 HARV. ENVT'L L. REV. 535 (2001).

NOAA Coral Reef Conservation Program Goals & Objectives 2010-2015

NOAA Coral Reef Conservation Program, 2009.

NOAA's Coral Reef Conservation Program (CRCP or Program) was established in 2000 to help fulfill NOAA's responsibilities under the Coral Reef Conservation Act of 2000 (CRCA) and Presidential Executive Order 13089 on Coral Reef Protection. The mission of the CRCP is to protect, conserve and restore coral reef resources by maintaining healthy ecosystem function. The CRCP addresses strategic coral reef management needs in a targeted, costeffective, and efficient manner.

The CRCP is an overarching program between NOAA line offices working on coral reef issues, including the National Ocean Service, the National Marine Fisheries Service, the Office of Oceanic and Atmospheric Research, and the National Environmental Satellite, Data and Information Service. In strong partnership with managers of coral reef areas, the CRCP works to provide the best available science and conservation tools to reduce harm to, and restore the condition of, coral reefs, including deep-sea corals.

The CRCP funds and conducts conservation activities for the benefit of the Nation's coral reefs. Areas of focus include the seven primary jurisdictions containing coral reefs: American Samoa, the Commonwealth of the Northern Mariana Islands (CNMI), Florida, Guam, Hawai`i, Puerto Rico, and the U.S. Virgin Islands (USVI). The Program also conducts activities in the northern Gulf of Mexico, Navassa Island, and the Pacific Remote Island Areas (PRIA). The Program further funds conservation activities internationally, including in the Coral Triangle, Micronesia, and the wider Caribbean regions, among others. The Program also works to protect and conserve deep-sea coral ecosystems found off the east and west coasts of the United States. . .

Beginning in the fiscal year 2010, the CRCP is concentrating its efforts to understand and address the top three recognized global threats to coral reef ecosystems: impacts from climate change, fishing, and from land-based sources of pollution.

Climate change threatens all coral reef ecosystems around the globe through increased mass coral bleaching and disease, sea level rise, and increased storm activity. In addition, increasing atmospheric carbon dioxide is already reducing calcification rates in some reef-building and reef-associated organisms by altering sea water chemistry including decreasing pH (a process referred as "ocean acidification"). In the long term, failure to address the impacts of rising temperatures and ocean acidification could limit the effectiveness of other management efforts.

Fishing in coral reef areas, when ecologically unsustainable, can lead to the depletion of key functional groups of reef species, with cascading impacts on coral reef habitats and associated species and ecosystems. Some fishing practices physically damage coral reefs and associated habitats.

Impacts from land-based sources of pollution (such as agriculture, coastal development, road construction, and oil and chemical spills) on coral reef ecosystems include increased sedimentation, eutrophication (nutrient loading that can lead to algal blooms which reduce oxygen in the water), toxins, and pathogen introduction. These pollutants and related synergistic effects can cause disease and mortality in sensitive species, disrupt critical ecological functions, change the foodweb and impede growth, reproduction, and larval settlement of corals. . .

NOTES & QUESTIONS

1. How can NOAA address the three threats to coral reefs that it identifies in its report?

2. NOAA describes the CRCP as "a cross-cutting program that brings together expertise from a wide array of NOAA programs and offices." Its specific activities include:

- CRCP funds and equips reef conservation activities by NOAA and its partners in the seven US states and jurisdictions containing coral reefs (American Samoa, the Commonwealth of the Northern Mariana Islands, Florida, Guam, Hawai`i, Puerto Rico, and the US Virgin Islands), uninhabited islands including the Northwestern Hawaiian Islands and Pacific Remote Island Areas, and internationally, including the Pacific Freely Associated States.

- The program provides coral reef managers, scientists, and other users worldwide with information and forecasts of coral bleaching events using sea surface temperature data from satellites.

- Citizens and government officials acting locally are our partners in improving coral reef health globally. CRCP provides information that empowers our public partners to act; for example, informative signs in coastal areas and distributing educational information to coastal businesses and the public.

- Coral Reef Conservation Grants Programs – Between 2002 and 2009, NOAA awarded a total of over $50 million in matching grants for coral conservation projects.

- Coral Reef Conservation Fund, administered by the National Fish and Wildlife Foundation, builds public-private partnerships and leveraged NOAA's $4.7 million into more than $12 million for 140 projects in 28 countries.

- CRCP serves as the Secretariat for the US Coral Reef Task Force, which includes leaders of 12 Federal agencies, seven US states and jurisdictions, and three Freely Associated States.

NOAA Coral Reef Conservation Program, How We Work, http:// coralreef.noaa.gov/aboutcrcp/howwework/#activities. The CRRP was established pursuant to the Coral Reef Conservation Act of 2000, 16 U.S.C. 64016409, which calls for a national coral reef action strategy and authorizes financial assistance for coral reef preservation projects, but which does not give NOAA any regulatory authority over activities that harm coral reefs. Moreover, the Act "subordinated coral reef protection and the creation of coral reef MPAs - which would help promote tourism - to other United States ocean policies, including fishing." Robin Kundis Craig, *Coral Reefs, Fishing, and Tourism: Tensions in U.S. Ocean Law and Policy Reform*, 27 STAN. ENVTL. L. J. 3, 27 (2008).

3. Thus far, the Endangered Species Act has played at most an indirect role in preserving coral reef ecosystems. In 2006, though, the FWS listed elkhorn and staghorn corals as threatened species. (A third species, fused-staghorn coral, was determined to be a hybrid that was ineligible for listing under the ESA). Both corals live throughout the Caribbean Sea. Disease is the "single largest cause of both elkhorn and staghorn coral mortality and decline," though scientists are uncertain about the number or identity of the diseases affecting the corals. Other threats include global warming, elevated nutrients, sedimentation, African dust, breakage, and pollution. *See* Final Listing Determination for Elkhorn Coral and Staghorn Coral, 71 Fed. Reg. 26852 (2006). What actions should be taken to help these corals to recover?

CHAPTER 13

HUMAN-DOMINATED ECOSYSTEMS

Chapter Outline:
A. Urban Areas
B. Agricultural Lands
C. Recreational Areas

The biologist Stephen Palumbi described what is increasingly the reality for ecosystem management policy development: "Human impact on the global biosphere now controls many major facets of ecosystem function." Stephen R. Palumbi, *Humans as the World's Greatest Evolutionary Force*, 293 SCIENCE 1786 (2001). This naked truth is hard for many environmental advocates to accept. For them, it suggests that we ought to throw in the towel. For many others, however, it is nothing less than a call to arms for ecosystem management. In this section we consider the consequences of human domination in several ecosystem settings, and explore some ways of addressing their future.

A. URBAN AREAS

Urban America hardly needs an introduction. It seems to be everywhere, and growing incessantly in what is known derisively as "sprawl." But in fact the urban, built-up environment accounts for a small fraction—well under 10 percent—of our nation's land mass; it's just that it is such a visible and fast-changing domain that makes it so front and center in the environmental policy debate. Also, urbanization has tended to be selective in terms of type of setting, favoring coasts, lakes, mountains, and other areas where, it so happens, so much of ecosystem management policy seems to be focused. Urbanization thus has become a central theme in ecosystem management circles.

Far from being ecological wastelands, however, there is life in the city. A new breed of urban ecologists are finding exceedingly diverse and complex web of life in distinctly urbanized locations. Metropolitan Phoenix, for example, has over 75 species of bees, 200 species of birds, and hundreds of insect species documented within its area housing 2.8 million people. As one astute ecologist concluded, Phoenix is not moving or shrinking, so we ought to consider ways of designing urban development there and elsewhere to foster urban ecosystem richness. *See* Keith Kloor, *A Surprising Tale of Life in the City*, 286 SCIENCE 663 (1999). On the other hand, ought not "sprawl" be prevented from further intruding into what is now relatively undisturbed habitat? Is there a way of knowing where urban "ecosystems" should flourish and where they should be contained? In the following materials, we explore these issues by examining frameworks for assessing and managing the impact of urban development on ecosystems.

Heffernan v. Missoula City Council

Supreme Court of Montana, 2011.
255 P.3d 80.

■ NELSON, JUSTICE.

In December 2007, the Missoula City Council approved zoning and a preliminary plat for a 37-lot subdivision known as Sonata Park. . . The proposed Sonata Park subdivision is located on the north side of Missoula in an area of the city known as Rattlesnake Valley. . . Rattlesnake Valley lies at the southern end of the 82-square-mile Rattlesnake Watershed. Rattlesnake Creek begins near McLeod Peak (17 miles to the north) and proceeds in a southerly direction, ultimately flowing into the Clark Fork River on the east side of downtown Missoula. The creek has been an important source of water for Missoula residents. A water system was established in Rattlesnake Valley in the 1870s, and an intake dam was built in 1901. Montana Power Company operated the system from 1930 to 1979. In an effort to protect its investment in the water supply, Montana Power purchased most of the private lands above the intake dam in 1934 and 1935, which in turn helped to reduce contamination of potable water by domestic animals. As a result, the upper portion of Rattlesnake Valley was mostly limited to resource management and recreational use, and development occurred primarily in the lower (southern) six square miles of the valley. That area has evolved over the last century from a sparsely settled rural community to a set of interconnected residential neighborhoods.

Rattlesnake Valley serves as the gateway to the Rattlesnake National Recreation Area and Wilderness, which was established by act of Congress in 1980. The valley also is an important habitat for numerous big game animals, including elk, white-tailed deer, mule deer, black bear, mountain lions, and mountain goats. Two areas in the valley serve as critical winter/spring range for big game, and the remaining open hillsides provide winter feeding areas for deer and elk. In addition, bald eagles, beaver, and blue heron have been sighted frequently in the area around the intake dam.

The City annexed nearly 1,500 acres of Rattlesnake Valley in 1989, including the land on which Muth-Hillberry proposes to develop Sonata Park. The City adopted interim zoning for the area, but the zoning expired in 1992 and the land became unzoned. Between 1989 and 1992, the City also purchased 418 acres of land in the middle valley for the purpose of preserving the acquired area as open space. This land encompasses hillsides and a creek corridor and is valuable for wildlife habitat and recreational uses such as walking, biking, jogging, horseback riding, and cross-country skiing. . .

There is a long tradition of coordinated planning endeavors between Missoula County and the City of Missoula, particularly in the Missoula urban area. In 1961, the Missoula City-County Planning Board completed a master plan for the area. In 1975, the City and County collaborated again to create two sets of land-use planning guidelines, one for the Missoula urban area and the other for rural areas. These guidelines were broad in scope and general in application. To address the unique characteristics of individual areas and provide more specific guidance for particular regions, the County and the City adopted various neighborhood plans over the years. These plans were subsequently added as amendments to the general growth policies.

One such neighborhood plan is the Rattlesnake Valley Comprehensive Plan, which applies to a 12-square-mile area of the Rattlesnake Valley consisting of County land and City land. . .The County and the City adopted the Rattlesnake Valley plan in 1988 and then adopted an updated version of it in 1995. The County and the City incorporated the 1995 version into the Missoula County Growth Policy in 2002, and reaffirmed it four years later in an update to the Missoula County Growth Policy. The 1995 version of the Rattlesnake Valley plan "thus continue[s] to have full force and effect."

The Rattlesnake Valley plan was drafted through a public planning process. The 1995 update itself received extensive public review, including five public hearings. Numerous citizens participated in the process. By its terms, the plan is intended "to reduce the problems associated with unplanned and uncoordinated growth." The plan is a "policy document" which provides the City, the County, other agencies and districts, and citizens with "a coordinated guide for change over a long period of time." It addresses a number of questions that had been "the focus of much community discussion for several years," including which areas are best suited for future development, which areas are best suited to remain relatively unchanged, and what role and responsibilities Rattlesnake Valley shares as part of the larger Missoula community. The plan lists various goals and guiding principles under the categories of air and water quality, open space and natural resources, transportation, and neighborhood character and quality of life. The plan then lists the recommended policies and actions with respect to each of these categories.

On the subject of land use, the plan explains that Rattlesnake Valley ranges from rural to urban. The upper valley is comprised of heavily forested lands and limited residential development, including some small-scale ranches. The middle valley contains some established neighborhoods, with densities ranging from two to six dwelling units per acre. But more than half of this area is sparsely settled or used as pasture land. The lower valley is occupied primarily by residential construction. This area contains the highest densities in the valley (six to eight dwelling units per acre) and is closest to services and existing roadway and pedestrian networks.

Given these features, the plan does not recommend one development density threshold for the entire valley. Rather, it states that "development should be at a scale which is compatible with the development patterns of existing Rattlesnake neighborhoods and the natural ecosystem which underlies and surrounds the entire study area." To that end, the plan recommends different densities for different parts of the valley. The desired densities range from six to eight dwelling units per one acre (in the very southern portion of the valley) to one dwelling unit per five to ten acres (on the west and east hillsides). Of relevance to the present case, the Sonata Park land—consisting of 34.08 acres on the west hillside—straddles two density zones: one dwelling unit per five to ten acres, and one dwelling unit per two acres. This translates to seven or eight units on the 34.08 acres. The plan states that "[a]ll subdivision, zoning and rezoning requests should substantially comply with the land use recommendations of this Plan."

[In 2006, Muth-Hillberry proposed to develop Sonata Park as a 41-lot subdivision. The Missoula Office of Planning and Grants (OPG), however, determined that such development was not consistent with the densities recommended in the Rattlesnake Valley plan. Muth-Hillberry then submitted a revised plan for a 37-lot subdivision, which the city council approved subject to 34 listed conditions. The project's neighbors sued to overturn the city's rezoning decision, which the district court did because the city "failed to substantially comply with the density recommendations, and with many other recommendations, of the Rattlesnake Plan."

Issue 4. Was the City's decision on Sonata Park arbitrary, capricious, or unlawful?

. . . The stipulated record fully supports the District Court's conclusion that the City did not substantially comply with the Rattlesnake Valley plan. Indeed, many of the city officials involved in approving Muth-Hillberry's application were openly contemptuous of the plan. Some second-guessed its goals and recommendations, others downplayed its relevance, and one bluntly characterized growth policies in general as a "waste of time." OPG cautioned at the outset that the subdivision, as proposed, could have deleterious effects on the neighborhood. Neighbors and two members of the City Council pointed out repeatedly that the subdivision did not honor the plan. Nevertheless, the City Council granted approval under the rationale that the City is growing and Rattlesnake Valley is not exempt—regardless of what the neighborhood plan might recommend.

The City's findings of fact and conclusions of law bear this out. By law, the City was required to be "guided by and give consideration to" the general policy and pattern of development set out in the Rattlesnake Valley plan. Yet, there are numerous components of the plan that the City did not give *any* consideration to in its findings and conclusions. Moreover, while the City states that it did "consider" other parts of the plan, there is little indication that the City was "guided by" them. . .

Three [of the] goals stated in the plan are land preservation, wildlife protection, and protection of natural resources, including wildlife corridors and habitat. In this regard, there is a woody draw running east-west through Sonata Park. It is a "significant natural feature" and "an important wildlife corridor" between the North Hills open space and Rattlesnake Creek. The Sonata Park project, however, will put a road across the corridor and generate hundreds of vehicle trips per day. Furthermore, the plan calls for providing connections between neighborhoods to parks, opens spaces, churches, commercial areas, and schools. The City purports to accommodate this goal by requiring Muth-Hillberry to dedicate a 20-foot-wide public pedestrian easement through the woody draw. In addition, to meet the "parkland dedication" requirement of its own subdivision regulations, the City approved a 16-acre common area—within which the woody draw is located. As the District Court noted, however, the City cannot use the woody draw to satisfy all three goals of providing a wildlife corridor, a public thoroughfare, and parkland. For one thing, the area is supposed to "remain undisturbed to facilitate wildlife movement through the area." Moreover, there are riparian resources within the woody draw, and locating a public easement through what purports to be the common area, the wildlife corridor, and the riparian-protection zone conflicts with the goals of the Rattlesnake Valley plan. As the court observed, "The common area cannot be all things."

. . . Finally, Muth-Hillberry attacks the Rattlesnake Valley plan for recommending too low of a density for Sonata Park and criticizes Neighbors for "refus[ing] to accept their fair share of the exploding growth in the City." Yet, while Muth-Hillberry may disagree with the Rattlesnake Valley plan, that is not grounds to flout it. As we have said, "changes in the [growth policy] may well be dictated by changed circumstances occurring after the adoption of the plan. If this is so, the correct procedure is to amend the [growth policy] rather than to erode [it] by simply refusing to adhere to its guidelines."

The City reaffirmed the Rattlesnake Valley plan in 2006, and it thus continues "to have full force and effect" as part of the City's growth policy. Yet, notwithstanding that growth policy, the City approved a development which, as the District Court observed, exists on a scale that is incompatible with the development patterns of the neighborhoods in the area and especially with the natural ecosystem that underlies the area. While it is not necessary for the Sonata Park zoning to be "consistent with every goal and objective expressed" in the Rattlesnake Valley plan, it is necessary for the zoning to substantially comply with the plan. It does not, as established by the stipulated record and the City's findings of fact and conclusions of law. . .

NOTES & QUESTIONS

1. Missoula provides just one example of the conflict between expanding human developments and biodiversity. More generally, a 2005 EPA report explained:

> Direct environmental impacts of current development patterns include habitat loss and fragmentation, and degradation of water resources and water quality. Building on undeveloped land destroys and fragments habitat and thus displaces or eliminates wildlife communities. The construction of impervious surfaces such as roads and rooftops leads to the degradation of water quality by increasing runoff volume, altering regular stream flow and watershed hydrology, reducing groundwater discharge,

and increasing stream sedimentation and water acidity. A 1-acre parking lot produces a runoff volume almost 16 times as large as the runoff volume produced by an undeveloped meadow. Development claimed more than half of the wetlands in the lower 48 states between the late 1700s and the mid-1980s.

EPA, OUR BUILT AND NATURAL ENVIRONMENTS: A TECHNICAL REVIEW OF THE INTERACTIONS BETWEEN LAND USE, TRANSPORTATION, AND ENVIRONMENTAL QUALITY II (2001). "Another impact—one that frequently follows the destruction and/or degradation of habitat—is the invasion of non-native species. Disturbed habitat is readily invaded by exotic plants." *Id.* at 13. Many observers believe that the effect of such sprawling developments is the leading threat to biodiversity in the United States.

So what is "sprawl" and why is it occurring? Is sprawl bad? Who says? If it is so bad, why is it happening? Are the people who are moving out into the previously rural areas being deceived by developers eager to sell homes, or duped by local politicians greedy for tax dollars, or guided to ruin by some invisible force against their will? Indeed, the public distaste for sprawl seems matched only by its appetite for it. And many commentators come to sprawl's defense, questioning the calls for regulation. For example, Gregg Easterbrook reveals the irony of the anti-sprawl movement with his observation that "the ideal restaurant would have terrific food, moderate prices, and would be unpopular, so lines would never inconvenience diners. Legislatures could make restaurants less crowded by, say, mandating that some tables be kept vacant even when customers are queued. Those already seated would surely benefit. But others would stew over being denied service, while business and jobs would be lost." Gregg Easterbrook, *The Case for Sprawl*, NEW REPUBLIC, Mar. 15, 1999. And Nicole Garnett has noted that voters frequently approve local sprawl initiatives but defeat statewide ones, suggesting that the reason is that voters realize that they cannot escape the restrictions of state growth controls nearly as easily as they can local rules. People want just the right amount of sprawl, in other words, and want to retain local control over exactly how much that is. *See* Nicole Stelle Garnett, *Trouble Preserving Paradise?*, 87 CORNELL L. REV. 158 (2001). At bottom, then, sprawl occurs because people value the many personal benefits of living in previously rural areas, even as they recognize the adverse environmental consequences of doing so. Clearly, that is a tradeoff the anti-sprawl movement deems unwise, but who is to decide?

3. Critics of sprawl suggest that the alternative, referred to hopefully as "smart growth," should be a tighter urban envelope facilitated through polices favoring urban redevelopment, infill (using unused urban pockets), and denser development patterns. Is it necessarily the case that a denser, more contained pattern of urban development is a desirable ecosystem management policy? Conservation biologists appear to assume that is the case, but as one researcher has pointed out, we actually know very little about urban ecosystems. Most of the foundations of ecosystem management are built on conservation biologists' studies of landscapes that are relatively undisturbed by human presence. Do we know enough about urban ecosystems to choose the optimum urban development pattern? *See* James R. Miller and Richard J. Hobbs, *Conservation Where People Live and Work*, 16 CONSERVATION BIOLOGY 330 (2002).

Ferry County v. Concerned Friends of Ferry County, 123 P.3d 102 (Wash. 2005), illustrates the application of growth controls as a means of preserving biodiversity. Washington enacted a Growth Management Act (GMA) in 1990 and 1991 because of concerns about sprawl in the Seattle metropolitan area. Ferry County is home to only 7,300 people in northeastern Washington who have the lowest income in the state. Even so, the county opted to become subject to the GMA in order to obtain financial assistance from the state. The GMA requires each participating county to designate "critical areas," including fish and wildlife habitat conservation areas, and then to adopt regulations upon development in those areas. Ferry County's 2000 comprehensive plan listed two endangered, threatened, or sensitive species (ETS)—the bald eagle and the lynx—whereas the state's Department of Fish & Wildlife has recommended that the county also list the ferruginous hawk, peregrine falcon, sandhill crane, upland sandpiper, American white pelican, pygmy rabbit, gray wolf, woodland caribou, and bull trout. The county had relied upon the expertise of Dr. Donald McKnight, a retired Alaskan biologist who consulted various books and talked to a local biologist, but the Western Washington Growth Management Hearings Board held that the county's decision failed to satisfy the statutory mandate to rely upon the "best available science" (BAS), a term that is undefined in the GMA. The Washington Supreme Court agreed, concluding that "[t]he information used to support the county's listing does not pass the smell test for BAS regardless of how it is defined. Far from rising to the level of BAS, the information obtained through Dr. McKnight's methods more greatly resembles nonscientific information, and his conclusions are more similar to speculation or surmise, which the requirement of BAS seeks to prevent." *Id.* at 108. Dissenting, Justice Johnson insisted that "[a] system controlled by state agencies directly conflicts with the GMA's declaration of a 'broad range of discretion that may be exercised by counties and cities consistent with the requirements . . . and goals of [the GMA].' " *Id.* at 119 (quoting RCW 36.70A.3201). Justice Johnson also observed that the county's decision to participate in the GMA cannot be revoked. *Id.* at 115.

4. Like any piece of land, different individuals will assign different values to undisturbed habitat. If the ecological value of areas under development pressure is high, why don't those who value it so much in its undeveloped state purchase it? Well, they do. Private, non-profit land trusts directed at securing ecosystem resources in and around urban land uses have exploded in number, finances, and acquisitions in recent years. Over 1,200 such entities exist, boasting a total of over 1 million members. As described in Chapter 3, large land conservation organizations such as the Nature Conservancy, Ducks Unlimited, and the Trust for Public Land are national in scope and have large paid staffs. By contrast, most land trusts are staffed by volunteers and local in focus. Operating primarily by acquisition of fee simple title and conservation easements, these smaller land trusts have conserved over 5 million acres of habitat in the United States. *See* Jean Hocker, *Land Trusts: Key Elements in the Struggle Against Sprawl*, 15 NATURAL RESOURCES & ENV'T 244 (2001). Land trusts benefit from the generous tax consequences land donors receive for land contribution, suggesting that tax policy can play an important role in ecosystem management. *See* Nancy A. McLaughlin, *The Role of Land Trusts in Biodiversity Conservation on Private Lands*, 38 IDAHO L. REV. 453 (2002). For more information on land trusts, see the Land Trust Alliance's home page at http://www.lta.org.

5. Humans are not always the winners in conflicts between sprawling development and biodiversity. The expansion of human settlement into new lands often results in increased encounters between people and the animals that have long lived there. For example, the growth of Boulder, Colorado toward the front range of the Rocky Mountains produced numerous contacts between mountain lions and suburban residents, and more ominously, their pets. *See* David Baron, The Beast in the Garden: The True Story of a Predator's Deadly Return to Suburban America (2004) . Mountain lions have attacked and people engaged in recreational activities on the edge of sprawling development outside of Los Angeles. Overseas, India has experienced a growing number of fatal conflicts between tigers and the residents of that country's sprawling cities. How can biodiversity management respond to this problem?

Utahns for Better Transportation v. United States Department of Transportation

United States Court of Appeals for the Tenth Circuit, 2002.
305 F.3d 1152.

■ Kelly, Circuit Judge.

. . . The Great Salt Lake ("GSL") and the wetlands surrounding its shoreline serve as an important habitat for a variety of birds, reptiles, amphibians, and mammals, some of which are endangered. The wetlands of the GSL account for 75 percent of all wetlands in the State of Utah, whose total land area consists of only 1.5 percent wetlands. The shores of the GSL are internationally important because they are a link of the Pacific Flyway for migratory waterfowl and a link of the Western Hemisphere Shorebird Reserve Network ("WHSRN"). Some two to five million birds use the GSL yearly and 90 percent of that use is concentrated in the eastern shore.

By the year 2020, population and travel demand in the five counties along the eastern shore of the GSL is anticipated to increase by 60 percent and 69 percent, respectively. To prepare the transportation infrastructure to meet this future demand, Utah's state, local, and regional officials have developed a three-part plan collectively called "Shared Solution." The plan calls for improving and expanding Interstate 15, expanding transit, and constructing the Legacy Parkway. The Legacy Parkway is to be a four-lane, divided, limited access, state-funded highway. As currently proposed, it is to be 330 feet wide consisting of four lanes, a 65.6-foot median, a 59-foot berm and utility corridor, and a 13.1-foot pedestrian/equestrian/bike trail. It is to start near Salt Lake City ("SLC"), run north along the eastern portion of the GSL, and end fourteen miles later by connecting with US 89.

Because the Legacy Parkway will connect to the interstate highway system and will require filling in 114 acres of wetland, it must receive approval from the Federal Highway Administration ("FHWA") and a § 404(b) permit from the U.S. Army Corps of Engineers ("COE"). . . On January 9, 2001, the COE released its Record of Decision ("ROD") issuing the § 404(b) permit to [the Utah Department of Transportation ("UDOT")]; and, on October 31, 2000, the FHWA issued its ROD approving UDOT's request for additions and modifications of access points to the interstate highway system. . . On appeal, Appellants contend that the COE violated the CWA in issuing a permit for the Legacy Parkway where less environmentally damaging "practicable alternatives" existed to the configuration and alignment of the highway. . .

Statutory Overview

. . .Section 404 of the Clean Water Act ("CWA"), 33 U.S.C. § 1344, prohibits the filling or dredging of wetlands without first receiving a § 404(b) permit from the COE. 33 U.S.C. § 1344 (a), (d). A permit may not be issued if (i) there is a practicable alternative which would have less adverse impact and does not have other significant adverse environmental consequences, (ii) the discharge will result in significant degradation, (iii) the discharge does not include all appropriate and practicable measures to minimize potential harm, or (iv) there does not exist sufficient information to make a reasonable judgment as to whether the proposed discharge will comply with the COE's Guidelines for permit issuance. 40 C.F.R. § 230.12(a)(3)(i-iv). For non-water dependent projects, it is presumed that a practicable alternative exists and the burden to clearly demonstrate otherwise is on the applicant. Id. § 230.10(a)(3); Resource Inv's, Inc. v. United States Army Corps of Eng'rs, 151 F.3d 1162, 1167 (9th Cir. 1998). "Practicable" is defined at 40 C.F.R. § 230.10(a)(2) as "available and capable of being done after taking into consideration cost, existing technology, and logistics in light of overall project purposes." The presumption for a non-water dependent project that a practicable alternative exists is not an automatic bar on issuance of a permit, but it does require that an applicant make a persuasive showing concerning the lack of alternatives. Sylvester v. United States Army Corps of Eng'rs, 882 F.2d 407, 409 (9th Cir. 1989) (internal citation omitted). Finally, a permit may not be issued "unless appropriate and practicable steps have been taken which will minimize potential adverse impacts of the discharge on the aquatic ecosystem." 40 C.F.R. § 230.10(d). . .

Analysis

[The court concluded in Part I of its opinion that the federal agencies failed to comply with the informational requirements of the National Environmental Policy Act (NEPA)].

II. CWA

A. D & RG Regional Alignment

The Appellants contend that the Federal Agencies applied the wrong legal standards in rejecting the D & RG alternative. Under CWA, the test is not whether a proposed project is "better" than an alternative with less wetlands impact because it would cost less and have less impact on existing and future development. The test is whether the alternative with less wetlands impact is "impracticable," and the burden is on the Applicant UDOT, with independent verification by the COE, to provide detailed, clear and convincing information *proving* impracticability.

While the Appellants are correct that CWA requires that the least damaging alternative be selected unless impracticable, they are quoting from the DEIS and the FEIS which are governed by NEPA, not CWA. NEPA does not require the selection of the least damaging practicable alternative. NEPA only requires that the Agencies "rigorously explore and objectively evaluate all reasonable alternatives, and for alternatives which were eliminated from detailed study, briefly discuss the reasons for their having been eliminated." 40 C.F.R. § 1502.14(a). NEPA prescribes the necessary process, but does not mandate a particular result. Therefore, failure to select the better alternative is not a violation of NEPA.

CWA prevents the COE from issuing a § 404(b) permit if there is a less damaging practicable alternative. 40 C.F.R. § 230.10(a). Practicable is defined as "available and capable of being done after taking into consideration cost, existing technology, and logistics in light of overall project purposes." 40 C.F.R. § 230.3(q). In its ROD, the COE found the D & RG Alignment to be infeasible because of its high cost and high impact on existing development. Merriam-Webster's Collegiate Dictionary defines infeasible as impracticable. Id. at 618 (9th ed. 1991). Therefore, the Appellants are incorrect in saying that the Federal Agencies applied the wrong legal standard in rejecting the D & RG alternative.

The Appellants further argue that even if the impracticable test was applied, it was not met. We can set aside the COE's action only if we find that the COE abused its discretion, or acted arbitrarily, capriciously, or contrary to law. 5 U.S.C. § 706(2)(A). Impact on existing development would appear to fall within both the cost and the logistics portion of the practicable definition. For reasons discussed at I.A., we find that the COE violated its own regulations by failing to verify the cost estimates provided by the Applicant. Thus, the high cost rationale is inadequate to uphold the COE's permit decision.

Turning to the other justification, while there is evidence that the D & RG Alignment is more highly developed relative to the GSL Alignment, that evidence simply does not adequately address whether the D & RG's impact on existing development would be so high that it would be impracticable. The burden of proof to demonstrate compliance with the § 404(b) permit Guidelines rests with the applicant; where insufficient information is provided to determine compliance, the Guidelines require that no permit be issued. Issuance of the permit with insufficient information concerning the D & RG Alignment was arbitrary and capricious.

B. Narrower Right of Way

The Appellants urge that the COE violated CWA by applying the wrong legal test in eliminating a narrower ROW as an alternative. Instead of requiring the Applicant to demonstrate clearly that a narrower configuration was impracticable, the COE justified the width of the ROW by explaining why the amenities would be desirable to various interests. The COE argues it reasonably concluded that a narrower ROW was not a feasible stand-alone alternative, and appropriately considered environmental, safety, and community concerns as appropriate elements of the project under review.

1. Median Width

The Appellees allege that a median of less than 65.6 feet is not a practicable alternative. The Evaluating Officer concluded in the § 404(b)(1) Evaluation Report that a narrower median was not practicable based on the following considerations: (1) the visual impact of unsightly concrete barriers; (2) the hazard created by concrete barrier required in narrower medians; (3) the water quality mitigation function of the vegetated median; (4) the public preference for a parkway type facility that requires a median; (5) failure to include the median would be inconsistent with the mitigation proposed in the FEIS; and (6) failure to include the median would be inconsistent with the land use plans of local governments which have included the project as a parkway-type facility.

However, on the next page, the Officer's Roadway Requirements list contains the following quotes: "Note: Median width also necessary to accommodate possible addition of two lanes in the median shown in FEIS, Volume 1, section 2.2.1." Although the existence of less environmentally damaging practicable alternatives must be determined in the present, the Officer's acknowledgment that the median width is also necessary for the future addition of two lanes undercuts his conclusion that anything less than a 65.6-foot median is impracticable for this four lane highway.

Regardless, the Officer's safety reason is amorphous and brought into question by his Note. It is not clear whether a median of less than 65.6 feet requires concrete barriers or only medians narrower than the average require concrete barriers. The width under which concrete barriers are required is not quantified. Additionally, Section 2.2.1 of the FEIS states:

> There would be ample space for the addition of two lanes in the median. The median between the northbound and southbound lanes would serve as a vegetated buffer to filter runoff and minimize concentrated discharges. These vegetated medians would have to be maintained to satisfy water quality certification requirements. If replacing these vegetated medians with additional highway lanes is ever proposed, environmental clearances would be necessary and replacement of the water quality functions of the vegetated medians would be required.

This quote from the FEIS and the "Note" from the Evaluation Report indicate that there are methods of water quality control other than a large vegetated median. There is no evidence that the COE considered whether a substitute water quality control method was practicable in the context of a narrower median—the state water quality certification incorporating the large vegetated median was obtained after the § 404(b) permit was issued and appears to be a function of a four lane highway with a 65.6 foot median.

As to the other reasons, the Officer justified the wider configuration by explaining why a package including several amenities would be desirable to various interests. The CWA test is not, however, whether features of a proposal would make a more desirable project. Rather the Applicant and the COE are obligated to determine the feasibility of the least environmentally damaging alternatives that serve the basic project purpose. If such an alternative exists—like a highway configuration that is much narrower because it dispenses with the amenities—then the CWA compels that the alternative be considered and selected unless proven impracticable. UDOT's stated purpose here was to meet the 2020 travel demand for the I-15 North Corridor and the amenities are irrelevant to meeting that purpose. We, therefore, conclude that the COE failed to assess rationally whether a narrower median is practicable, thereby rendering the issuance of the permit arbitrary and capricious on this basis.

2. Trail

In the § 404(b)(1) Evaluation, the Officer stated that the following issues were considered concerning the trail portion of the project when project features were analyzed to determine if a narrower ROW was practicable: (1) meetings were held with trail interests in which it was determined that there was a need for a trail system in the Legacy Parkway to continue the Jordan River trails; (2) the 1998 MIS stated that there was a need for a pathway system for pedestrians, bicycle-riders, and equestrians in the study area; (3) many people expressed the belief that a trail system was needed for use as an alternative means of transportation; (4) failure to include a trail in the project would be inconsistent with decisions made during and in response to the NEPA process; (5) failure to include the trail would eliminate a benefit that has been identified as needed in the context of public interest; and (6) failure to include the trail would be inconsistent with the local land use plans for the majority of cities in the study area. I Aplee. App. at 109. CWA does not permit the discharge of fill material if there is a practicable alternative which would have a less adverse impact. 40 C.F.R. § 230.10(a). As discussed before, an alternative is practicable if it is "available and capable of being done after taking into consideration cost, existing technology and logistics in light of overall project purposes." Id. § 230.10(a)(2). The project purpose of the Legacy Parkway has been repeatedly identified as meeting the 2020 transportation needs of the North Corridor. The Evaluating Officer identified one of the functions of the trails as providing an alternative means of transportation. The COE reasonably concluded that removing the trails was not practicable in light of the project's overall purpose of meeting the transportation needs of the Northern Corridor in 2020, thus, the issuance of the permit is not arbitrary and capricious on this basis.

3. Berm and Utility Corridor

Although the Evaluating Engineer wrote that the berm portion of the project was considered when a narrower ROW was analyzed for practicability, no reason is given in the COE's ROD, § 404(b)(1) Evaluation Report or permit for why a ROW without a berm and utility corridor was not practicable. Reasons were only given for why a ROW without trails or a median was impracticable. Additionally, no explanation is given for why the ROW must be 330 feet for the entire 14 miles of the Legacy Parkway since the berm which is to be 33.1 feet is to run for only 3.2 miles.

The CWA does not permit the discharge of fill material if there is a practicable alternative which would have a less adverse impact. 40 C.F.R. § 230.10(a). "Practicable" is considered in light of the overall project purpose. Id. § 230.10(a)(2). As noted supra II.B.2, the project purpose of the Legacy Parkway has been repeatedly identified as meeting the 2020 transportation needs of the North Corridor. The Appellees have not cited to any place in the administrative record where providing a future utility corridor was included in the project purpose of the Legacy Parkway. Consequently, we consider the future utility corridor to be merely incidental to the Applicant's basic purpose. The failure of the COE to consider whether a ROW without a future utility corridor would be impracticable and the failure of the COE to provide any reasoning for why a ROW without a berm would be impracticable renders issuance of the permit arbitrary and capricious on this basis.

C. "Mass Transit" Alternative

We find that all sub-issues under Appellant's Mass Transit Alternative issue are waived for failure to adequately brief as to violations of CWA. The Appellants argue only the inadequacies of the FEIS which is governed by NEPA. They make no mention of the COE's ROD, § 404(b) Evaluation Report, or § 404(b) permit which are governed by CWA. They cite only to regulations pursuant to NEPA. The Appellants' entire argument as to CWA on the mass transit alternative issue is that "the District Court's holding eviscerates the alternatives analysis required . . . by the CWA," and "the omission of the assumptions and supportive information underlying the Federal Agencies' transit analysis violates NEPA and the CWA." We, therefore, deem this issue waived.

D. Reducing Travel Demand and Alternative Land Use Scenario Alternative

The Appellants allege that CWA was violated by COE's failure to consider reducing travel demand through alternative land use scenarios alone and in combination with public transit as a practicable alternative. The regulations passed pursuant to CWA defines a practicable alternative as "available and capable of being done after taking into consideration cost, existing technology and logistics in light of overall project purposes." 40 C.F.R. § 230.3(q). The COE found that an alternative land use scenario was not reasonable based on the fact that all of the record evidence demonstrates that the local governments in the study area are not implementing the type of coordinated planning and restrictive zoning that would be required to achieve the type of land use proposed by the Appellants. We find the COE's conclusion to be reasonable and issuance of the permit was not arbitrary and capricious on this basis.

E. Cumulative Effects of Six Lanes

The Appellants assert that CWA was violated by the COE's failure to consider the cumulative impact of a future expansion of Legacy from four lanes to six. Cumulative effects attributable to the filling of wetlands must be predicted to the extent reasonable and practicable. 40 C.F.R. § 230.11(g)(2). The permitting authority is to collect and solicit information about the cumulative impacts on the wetlands, and this information is to be documented and considered during the decision-making process concerning the evaluation of the permit application. Id. Cumulative impacts are identified as the changes in wetlands that are attributable to the collective effect of a number of individual discharges or fills of material. 40 C.F.R. § 230.11(g)(1). Although we are told that the definition of cumulative impacts given in the NEPA regulations are to be used uniformly throughout the federal government, 40 C.F.R. § 1508.1, the CWA regulations appear to define "cumulative impacts" in a different and more narrow way. Given our conclusion in Part I.C. that NEPA was not violated by the failure of the FEIS to consider the cumulative impact of a possible expansion of the Legacy to six lanes and the narrower definition for cumulative impact in the CWA regulations, we find that the decision to issue the permit was not arbitrary and capricious on this basis.

F. Failure to Consider Land Use Impacts; Failure to Consider Impacts on Salt Lake City; Failure to Consider Growth and Land Use Impacts on Areas North of the Legacy Parkway

No mention is made of CWA in the portion of Appellants' brief dedicated to these issues. Therefore, we deem the issues waived for failure to brief as to the alleged CWA violation.

G. Failure to Consider Impacts to Wetlands

A § 404(b) permit cannot be issued if the proposed discharge will result in significant degradation of the aquatic ecosystem or if there is insufficient information to make a reasonable judgment as to whether the discharge will result in significant degradation. 40 C.F.R. §§ 230.12(a)(3)(ii), (iv). Effects contributing to significant degradation include significant adverse effects of the discharge on wildlife, special aquatic sites, stages of aquatic life and other wildlife dependent on aquatic ecosystems, and aquatic ecosystem diversity, productivity, and stability. 40 C.F.R. § 230.10(c)

The regulations pursuant to the CWA require the permitting authority to determine in writing the potential short-term or long-term effects of a proposed discharge on the physical, chemical, and biological components of the aquatic environment. 40 C.F.R. § 230.11. Such factual determinations are to be used in deciding whether a discharge will result in significant degradation and, therefore, the applicant cannot receive a permit. Impacts that should be considered in making the factual determinations and in making the finding of compliance or non-compliance include: major potential impacts on threatened or endangered species, 40 C.F.R. § 230.30(b); loss or change of breeding or nesting areas, escape cover, travel corridors, and preferred food sources for resident and transient wildlife species associated with the aquatic ecosystem, 40 C.F.R. § 230.32(b); impacts to sanctuaries and refuges which disrupt breeding, spawning, migratory movements or other critical life requirements of resident or transient fish and wildlife resources, 40 C.F.R. § 230.40(b)(1); impacts to wetlands that are likely to damage or destroy habitat and adversely affect the biological productivity of the wetlands' ecosystem, 40 C.F.R. § 230.41(b)(3).

The Appellants contend that the COE violated CWA by its "unbelievably cursory" analysis of impacts to wetlands. The Appellants have ignored the COE's analysis in its ROD and its Permit which were released on the same day as the § 404(b)(1) Evaluation Report. I Aplee. App. at 38, 124. Even assuming without deciding that the wetlands analysis in the § 404(b)(1) Evaluation Report is cursory, the wetlands analysis of all three documents is adequate to support the COE decision.

Appellants also assert that CWA was violated by the Agencies': (1) failure to classify wetlands into subcategories as required by HGM protocols; (2) failure to take actual field data for developing the functional profile; (3) assuming that land use changes within 1000 feet predicted the wetlands' level of functionality; and (4) use of the Everglades HGM Regional Guidebook. For substantially the same reasons given in Parts I.I.1.-I.I.4, we find that the COE did not act arbitrarily and capriciously in issuing the permit on this basis.

H. Failure to Consider Impacts to Wildlife

The Appellants note that the COE's wildlife impact analysis, like the FEIS, was limited to consideration of impacts within 1000 feet of the project despite the CWA regulation's requirement that written factual findings be made on the potential short-term or long-term effects of the proposed discharge on threatened and endangered species, nesting areas, escape cover, travel corridors, and preferred food sources for resident and transient wildlife species associated with the aquatic ecosystem, and sanctuaries and refuges. For substantially the same reasons give in I.J., and also because practicable alternatives cannot be ignored because of mitigation potential, we hold that the COE acted arbitrarily and capriciously in granting the permit on this basis.

I. Air Quality Impacts

No mention is made of CWA in the portion of Appellants' brief dedicated to this issue. Therefore, we deem this issue waived for failure to brief as to the alleged CWA violation.

Conclusion

We affirm in part and reverse and remand in part. . . We conclude that the COE's issuing of the § 404(b) permit was arbitrary and capricious on the following grounds: issuing a permit with insufficient information to determine whether the D & RG Regional Alignment was a practicable alternative, infra II.A, failure to consider whether a narrower median was a practicable alternative, infra II.B.1, failure to consider whether a ROW without a future utility corridor or berm was a practicable alternative, infra II. B.3, and failure to consider the impacts to wildlife, infra II.H

NOTES & QUESTIONS

1. Can roads and biodiversity coexist? The effects of roads upon biodiversity include accidents that "kill an estimated 1 million vertebrates per day in the United States," the alternation or prevention of species movement, and the expansion of the range of some species that can now "penetrate deeply into undisturbed habitats." Elizabeth A. Johnson & Michael W. Klemens, *The Impacts of Sprawl on Biodiversity*, in NATURE IN FRAGMENTS: THE LEGACY OF SPRAWL 23 (Elizabeth A. Johnson & Michawel W. Klemmens, eds. 2005). Additionally, "[t]he environmental consequences of vehicle travel and dependency include degradation of air quality, greenhouse gas emissions and increased threat of global climate change, and noise"—each of which threatens numerous species and ecosystems. EPA, OUR BUILT AND NATURAL ENVIRONMENTS: A TECHNICAL REVIEW OF THE INTERACTIONS BETWEEN LAND USE, TRANSPORTATION, AND ENVIRONMENTAL QUALITY ii (2001).

2. What else could Salt Lake City to do satisfy its transportation demands? What else could it do to protect its biodiversity? Three years after the Tenth Circuit's decision, and after ten months of negotiations, the parties settled their dispute. The settlement bars large trucks on the Legacy Parkway, prohibits billboards, mandates special noise-reducing pavement, imposes a 55 miles per hour speed limit, adds 121 acres to an existing wetland and wildlife preserve near the road, directs appropriate landscaping, and requires $2.5 million in state funds to study a rapid transit study by 2008—all in exchange for approval to construct the highway. *See* Tripp Baltz, *Settlement, Legislative Action Clears Way for Highway to Be Built Near Great Salt Lake*, 225 BNA DAILY ENV'T REP. A-10 (Nov. 23, 2005). Is that a fair settlement? Does it properly accommodate the needs of both biodiversity and transportation?

National Wildlife Federation v. Babbitt

United States District Court for the Eastern District of California, 2000.
128 F. Supp. 2d 1274.

■ LEVI, DISTRICT JUDGE.

Plaintiffs challenge the United States Fish and Wildlife Service's issuance of an incidental take permit to allow development in the Natomas Basin, a 53,000 acre tract of largely undeveloped land stretching to the North of the City of Sacramento. The Natomas Basin contains habitat of the Giant Garter Snake, a threatened species under the federal Endangered Species Act, and the Swainson's hawk, a threatened species under the California Endangered Species Act. The parties now bring cross-motions for summary judgment.

I. Background and Procedural History

A. The Natomas Basin

The Natomas Basin ("Basin") is a low-lying region of predominately agricultural lands in the Sacramento Valley consisting of approximately 53,000 acres. The Basin is part of a larger flood plain known as the American Basin, and is situated at the northern end of the City of Sacramento ("City"). Approximately 22% of the area of the Basin is within the City limits, with the remainder to the north, in the jurisdiction of Sacramento and Sutter Counties. Because the area was subject until recently to frequent flooding, the Basin has remained relatively immune from development despite its proximity to a growing metropolitan region. The Basin provides habitat or potential habitat for a number of species listed as endangered or threatened under federal or state law. Of the 11,387 acres of the Basin that lie within the City, approximately 30% has been developed, while roughly 55% is in crop land and 15% is vacant or in its natural state. The land containing natural vegetation is primarily located along irrigation canals, drainage ditches, pastures, and uncultivated fields.

In 1986, heavy spring rains caused significant flood damage in the Sacramento area. In response, the Army Corps of Engineers ("Corps") undertook a study of proposals to improve flood control measures. This study culminated in the Corps' issuance, in 1991, of the "American River Watershed Investigation Feasibility Report" ("Feasibility Report"). The Feasibility Report proposed to provide 200 year flood protection through construction of the Auburn Dam and a series of levee improvements.

The United States Fish and Wildlife Service ("the Service") reacted to the Corps' proposal with concern, noting the importance of the Basin to waterfowl using the Pacific Flyway for migration and to certain native species listed as endangered or threatened under federal or state law. The Service issued a report in 1991, the "American River Watershed Investigation, Natomas Area," ("1991 Report"), that examined the "indirect impacts" from development likely to result from flood control in the Basin. The 1991 Report considered a 41,000 acre subarea of the Basin that provided upland or wetland habitat and concluded that nearly the entire area—39,200 acres— would be developed if a 200 year flood control plan were implemented. The 1991 Report found that the biological effects of this degree of urbanization in the Basin would be a dramatic loss of wildlife habitat.

The 1991 Report contained an extensive discussion of potential means of mitigating for the urbanization that would follow upon flood control. The 1991 Report recommended that an area totaling 17,650 acres in the Natomas Area be acquired and managed as a wetland/upland complex, to offset the expected loss of 22,717 acres of such habitat. Excluding acquisition costs, the 1991 Report anticipated the nonrecurring cost for development of acquired lands into habitat at approximately $171,675,000Cover $9700 per acre. In addition, the Report estimated annual management costs of $8,825,000, or $500 per acre.

In 1991, the Sacramento Area Flood Control Authority ("SAFCA") began the process of applying for an incidental take permit ("ITP") under § 10 of the Endangered Species Act ("ESA"), 16 U.S.C. §§ 1531 et seq. * * *

In 1993, the Service listed the Giant Garter Snake ("GGS") as a threatened species under the ESA. The listing notice identified 13 distinct populations of the GGS, of which the American Basin population was one of the largest. See 58 Fed.Reg. 54053 (Oct. 20, 1993). The Natomas Basin population is a subpopulation of the American Basin population of the GGS. After the listing of the GGS, "interest renewed . . . in developing a habitat conservation plan." In January 1994, the Natomas Basin Habitat Conservation Plan Working Group ("Working Group") was formed, and began development of a habitat conservation plan ("Plan," or "HCP"),[1] as required to qualify for an ITP. The Working Group was comprised of "representatives of land owners of a large proportion of the affected area."

* * *

B. The Final HCP

The Natomas Basin HCP is intended "to promote biological conservation along with economic development and the continuation of agriculture within the Natomas Basin." The HCP lists 26 species that are "potentially subject to take," and which are to "be included in the state and federal permits issued in accordance with the Plan." The proposed permit authorizes incidental take resulting from urban development, as well as any incidental take that may occur through rice-farming or result from management of the Plan's reserve lands. The HCP was developed as a regional conservation plan for the entire Natomas Basin, and was intended for use in connection with ITP applications for each of the municipalities and water companies with interests in the Basin . . .

The Plan is administered by the Natomas Basin Conservancy ("NBC") which has the responsibility to establish and oversee "a concerted Basinwide program for acquiring and managing mitigation lands on behalf of the permittees. Specifically, the NBC will be responsible for collecting and managing mitigation fees required by the City and Counties, for using the fees to establish mitigation lands, and for managing the mitigation lands for the benefit of the covered species." The Plan provides for a Technical Advisory Committee ("TAC"), comprised of representatives from the Service, the California Department of Fish and Game, and any permittee, as well as outside experts, "to advise the NBC in implementing" the HCP.

---

[1] Section 10 of the ESA allows the Secretary to issue an incidental take permit ("ITP"), authorizing its holder to take some members of protected species when such taking is incidental to carrying out an otherwise lawful activity. See 16 U.S.C. § 1539(a). To obtain an ITP, an applicant must develop and submit an HCP, which specifies (1) the likely impact from the proposed takings; (2) the steps the applicant will take to minimize and mitigate such impacts and the funding available for such mitigation; (3) alternative actions considered, and the reasons for not selecting them; and (4) such other measures as the Secretary may require as necessary or appropriate for the purposes of the plan. See 16 U.S.C. § 1539(a)(2)(A); see also Part II.A, infra.

The Plan calls upon the NBC to assemble connected 400 acre blocks of reserve lands—with one block of at least 2500 acres—for the benefit of the Giant Garter Snake and to protect Swainson's hawk habitat and nesting areas. The HCP states that "to the maximum extent practicable, the [Natomas Basin] HCP will ensure that habitat acquisition will be provided in advance of habitat conversion resulting from urban development in the Natomas Basin." Funding for land acquisition, however, is derived from the collection of mitigation fees for development. Thus, with regard to the phasing of land acquisition, the HCP actually requires only that, after an initial acquisition of 400 acres, which is to be made "as soon as possible," "no more than one year shall elapse between receipt of a fee and expenditure of that fee in the purchase or other acquisition of mitigation land."

The Plan is based on certain key principles and assumptions. First, the Plan assumes that only 17,500 acres of Basin land will be developed over the 50 year life of the permit, and that a substantial proportion of the undeveloped land will remain in agriculture, particularly rice, which is believed to have unique value as habitat for the GGS. The Plan's conclusion that a ratio of .5 acres of reserve lands for each 1 acre of developed land will ensure the biological needs of the protected species is based on the assumption that a considerable portion of the undeveloped and agricultural lands in the Basin will remain undeveloped, thereby augmenting the habitat value of the reserve lands. Second, the Plan pursues a regional approach to conservation. Whereas without the Plan, individual landowners could pursue separate permit applications, or develop their land without securing an ITP, the HCP is intended to provide a consolidated approach under which resources may be pooled and conservation lands may be purchased throughout the Basin. Third, the HCP treats all Basin lands as fungible, as equally valuable habitat. Thus, the HCP requires developers to "mitigate" for the anticipated take of individuals or habitat by payment of a fee for each acre developed. Rather than differentiating among lands according to their value as habitat for protected species, the HCP requires all landowners within the Permit area to pay a mitigation fee for developing their land, regardless of whether any particular parcel has or lacks habitat value. Depending on one's point of view, this uniform treatment is either a strength or a weakness of the Plan. It is a strength because mitigation fees are to be collected on all acreage and are used "to set aside 0.5 acres of habitat land for each 1.0 acres of gross development that occurs in the Basin."[2] It is a potential weakness because the Plan does not attempt to identify, prior to intensified development under the ITP, particular parcels for acquisition as reserves, based upon the importance of those parcels as habitat, but simply specifies acquisition criteria, and leaves specific reserve acquisition to the future decisionmaking of the NBC.

---

[2]   The initial base fee was set at $2240 per acre developed, of which $1829 was allocated for acquisition of land, $142 for restoration, enhancement and monitoring, $150 for administration of operation and monitoring, $75 for an operations and monitoring endowment, and $44 for administration of fee collection. Because these figures represent the amount collected for each acre developed, the amount available for each acre of mitigation land is twice the given figures. For example, the HCP assumes that land can be acquired for $1829 x 2, or $3658 per acre, and sets aside $142 x 2, or $284 per acre for restoration, enhancement, and monitoring.

Finally, the Plan is based upon what it calls "adaptive management." The Plan recognizes that the current state of knowledge as to the conservation needs of protected species is imperfect, and that its assumptions as to the amount, location, and pace of development in the Basin and as to the adequacy of the mitigation fee to accommodate increased expenses may prove inaccurate. The Plan addresses these uncertainties through its "adaptive management" provisions, which permit the Plan's conservation strategy to be adjusted based on new information. The HCP's conservation program can be modified under the adaptive management provisions if: (1) new information results from ongoing research on the GGS or other covered species; (2) recovery strategies under Fish and Wildlife Service recovery plans for the GGS or the Swainson's hawk differ from the measures contemplated by the HCP; (3) certain of the HCP's mitigation measures are shown through monitoring to require modification; or (4) the HCP's required minimum block sizes for reserve lands are shown to require revision. The Plan anticipates that the NBC will make discretionary decisions in future years based upon new information. The NBC will decide, for example, which lands to purchase, depending on a variety of future considerations difficult now to predict, and whether to change the mix of in and out of Basin reserve lands and agricultural as opposed to marsh reserve lands.

*　*　*

IV. Endangered Species Act Claims

The nub of plaintiffs' challenge to the HCP concerns its strategy of adaptive management. Plaintiffs object that in the face of incomplete information as to a number of important issues—including the conservation needs of the covered species, the likely location and pace of development in the Basin, and the preferred location and availability of reserves— the Plan does not undertake studies to develop better information, but simply creates a structure and describes a process for reaching and adjusting decisions in the future based on developing information. Plaintiffs contend that many of the Service's findings are arbitrary because of the uncertainty inherent in the HCP's deferred decisionmaking scheme. * * *

With miscellaneous exceptions, plaintiffs' ESA claims fall into two categories. First, plaintiffs challenge as arbitrary the Service's findings as to the adequacy of the Plan's provisions, particularly those related to funding and mitigation; second, plaintiffs contend that the Service's findings regarding the biological effects of the Plan on covered species are arbitrary and capricious. As explained below, under the APA's deferential standard of review, the Service's findings largely pass muster with respect to the Plan as a whole; however, with respect to the City's Permit, the Service's findings do not. Many of the provisions of the HCP are based on the assumption that all of the land-use agencies with jurisdiction over parts of the Basin will become permittees. Similarly, the Service's findings are plainly geared toward the regional nature of the HCP, and do not adequately reckon with the local nature of the Permit or analyze what would happen if the City's lands were developed under the HCP, while the lands outside the City limits were developed piecemeal, by individual landowners, outside the HCP and the protections provided by the HCP. The importance of this point is most obvious with respect to the funding mechanism, which relies on future fee increases to fund current increases in land acquisition costs. Because reserve land acquisition lags behind the development that funds it, the funding mechanism must play catch up, passing increased costs on to the next developer. The Plan can cope with increased expenses for mitigation, monitoring, and the like, only so long as there exists a ready supply of land to be developed under the HCP. The biological findings, too, are based on inadequate consideration of the tension between the regional Plan and the local Permit. The record contains no particularized analysis of the importance of the City's lands as habitat, and no consideration of how the species will fare if the City's lands are developed under the Plan and some or all of the remainder of the Basin is fully developed outside the HCP. Similarly, although the 1997 Biological Opinion concedes that large blocks of reserve lands may not be possible if only the City is a permittee, there is no analysis of the consequences—particularly for the GGS—of abandoning the goal of large connected blocks of reserve lands.

NOTES & QUESTIONS

1. The central flaw the court identifies is not that the Natomas Basin plan fails to satisfy the criteria of the Endangered Species Act, but that its manner of implementation rests on the faulty premise that Sacramento could begin to issue development approvals under the plan without the other local government jurisdictions in the Natomas Basin having sought to enter the conservation program. Obviously, Sacramento can't force other jurisdictions to enter into the plan, but since the plan is based on Basinwide habitat assumptions, the court ruled that Sacramento cannot act as if those jurisdictions have entered the plan. This result illustrates the difficulty and importance of intergovernmental cooperation at the local level when ecosystem management goals are not embedded in federal or state law. *See* James W. Spensley, *Using Intergovernmental Agreements to Manage Growth*, 15 NATURAL RESOURCES & ENV'T 240 (2001).

2. The Natomas Basin plan pegged the cost at $2,240 per acre of developed land. Of course, the costs will be passed on to the end consumer, such as the residential home buyer. How would you feel if, upon purchasing a home for, say, $200,000, you learned that $2,500 of that cost was devoted to habitat conservation taking place thirty miles away? Have you contributed that much to habitat conservation efforts in cash donations this year? Over the past five years? In your lifetime?

3. For that matter, is it equitable to place the cost of urban ecosystem management on *new* development? The Natomas Basin plan relied on a fee on new development to fund its $170 million land acquisition and $8 million annual operations costs. But new development in the Basin did not cause the area's endangered species problem. Past development did that. Existing developed land also would benefit not only from the ecological values of the newly protected lands, but also from the market impact of increased scarcity of developable land and costs of development. If you believe it is appropriate to charge $2,240 for each acre of new development in the Basin, ought not owners of acres of *ex-*

isting developed land be assessed an equal fee? How successful would a candidate for local office be running on such a platform? Are there other ways of allocating some of the cost of urban land development to existing land uses or some surrogate?

4. After the court's decision, the city and the county prepared a revised Natomas Basin HCP authorizing the development of 15,517 acres of land. The FWS approved the new HCP in 2003. This time, though, the district court upheld the HCP, finding that the agency had adequately considered all of the issues that it had neglected in the original plan. *See* National Wildlife Fed'n v. Norton, 2005 WL 2175874 (E.D. Cal.2005).

Detroit River International Wildlife Refuge Comprehensive Conservation Plan

United States Fish & Wildlife Service, 2005.
http://www.fws.gov/midwest/planning/detroitriver/finalCCP/DetroitRiver_finalCCP.pdf

The Detroit River has long served the United States and Canada as a vital transportation corridor and center for industries that helped forge the economies of both nations. But the river and its ecosystem have paid a tremendous price for human progress. Indeed, in our mind and in reality, most of what was natural in and around the Detroit River is gone. Yet special places exist alongside the concrete, steel, and groomed gardens of this vast metropolitan area; the beginnings of North America's first International Wildlife Refuge. A place where wildlife can come first.

What could be the future of this fledgling refuge in the midst of millions of people? We try to answer that question in this Comprehensive Conservation Plan. We will describe the creation of the Refuge, the historical and current conditions of the area, and a vision for its future.

A positive view for the future of the Detroit River and Lake Erie Western Basin reflects an abiding faith in nature. One possible view would have been to look at what has been lost, wring our hands, and give up. Another possible view is to recognize what is left and what can recover, value it, and work for its conservation. The multitude of partners that are making the Detroit River International Wildlife Refuge a reality have chosen the second view.

Our view is influenced by the recognition of wildlife's persistence. Despite almost complete conversion of the riverbank to concrete and steel, despite elimination of more than 95 percent of the coastal wetlands, despite decades of industrial pollution, the lower Detroit River remains a globally significant area for congregating waterfowl, especially diving ducks. Sport fishing, once in dire trouble, has become a foundation for a growing tourism economy.

We intend to help make the Detroit River ecosystem a safer place for fish, wildlife, and people. We intend to work with others on both sides of the border to conserve, re-establish and improve natural areas in the ecosystem. In this plan we describe our intended actions for the next 15 years. . .

Refuge Purposes

The Detroit River International Wildlife Refuge was established by an Act of Congress, which became Public Law 107-91 on December 21, 2001. Section 4 of the Act states the following purposes for the new Detroit River International Wildlife Refuge:

- To protect the remaining high-quality fish and wildlife habitats of the Detroit River before they are lost to further development and to restore and enhance degraded wildlife habitats associated with the Detroit River.

- To assist in international efforts to conserve, enhance, and restore the native aquatic and terrestrial community characteristics of the Detroit River (including associated fish, wildlife, and plant species) both in the United States and Canada.

- To facilitate partnerships among the United States Fish and Wildlife Service, Canadian national and provincial authorities, State and local governments, local communities in the United States and in Canada, conservation organizations, and other non-Federal entities to promote public awareness of the resources of the Detroit River.

Wyandotte National Wildlife Refuge was established by an Act of Congress known as Public Law 87-119, 75 Stat. 243, 87th Congress, H.R. 1182, dated August 3, 1961: . . . "to be maintained as a refuge and breeding place for migratory birds and other wildlife. . ." Mud Island was added to Wyandotte NWR in January 2001 using the authority to accept donations of real property contained in the Fish and Wildlife Act of 1956 (16 U.S.C. 742f).

The islands and shoals of the former Wyandotte NWR retain their original legislative purposes as well as gaining new ones from the 2001 legislation.

Refuge Vision

A draft vision for the Detroit River International Wildlife Refuge was produced during a public comprehensive conservation plan workshop held in October 2002. Workshop participants first reviewed a vision statement for the Lower Detroit River developed in 2001 as part of a broad-scale partnership of Federal, provincial, and local governments, conservation groups, and industry representatives.

Vision Statement for Lower Detroit River Ecosystem (2001)

"In 10 years the Lower Detroit River Ecosystem will be an international conservation region where the health and diversity of wildlife and fish are sustained through protection of existing significant habitats and rehabilitation of degraded ones, and where the resulting ecological, recreational, economic, educational and 'quality of life' benefits are sustained for present and future generations."

Draft Vision Statement for the Detroit River International Wildlife Refuge

"The Detroit River International Wildlife Refuge, including the Detroit River and Western Lake Erie Basin, will be a conservation region where a clean environment fosters the health and diversity of wildlife, fish, and plant resources through protection, creation of new habitats, management, and restoration of natural communities and habitats on public and private lands. Through effective management and partnering, the Refuge will provide outstanding opportunities for "quality of life" benefits such as hunting, fishing, wildlife observation and environmental education, as well as ecological, economic, and cultural benefits, for present and future generations."

Purpose and Need For the Plan

This comprehensive conservation plan, or CCP, identifies the role the Refuge will play in supporting the mission of the National Wildlife Refuge System and provides guidance for Refuge management. The plan articulates management goals for the next 15 years and specifies objectives and strategies that will achieve those goals. Several legislative mandates within the National Wildlife Refuge System Improvement Act of 1997 have guided the development of this plan. These mandates include:

- Wildlife has first priority in the management of refuges.

- Wildlife-dependent recreation activities of hunting, fishing, wildlife observation, wildlife photography, environmental education and interpretation are the priority public uses of the National Wildlife Refuge System. These uses will be facilitated when they do not interfere with our ability to fulfill the Refuge's purposes or the mission of the National Wildlife Refuge System.

- Other uses of the Refuge will only be allowed when they are determined to be appropriate and compatible with the Refuge purposes and mission of the National Wildlife Refuge System.

This CCP will enhance the management of the Detroit River International Wildlife Refuge by:

- Providing a clear statement of direction for future management of the Refuge.

- Giving Refuge neighbors, visitors, and the general public an understanding of the Service's management actions on and around the Refuge.

- Ensuring that the Refuge's management actions and programs are consistent with the mandates of the National Wildlife Refuge System.

- Ensuring that Refuge management is consistent with federal, state and county plans.

- Establishing continuity in Refuge management.

- Providing a basis for the development of budget requests on the Refuge's operation, maintenance, and capital improvement needs.

Habitat Restoration and Management

Detroit River: Numerous efforts are under way along the Detroit River to restore and manage natural shorelines, riparian wetlands, and island habitats.

Nearly the entire U.S. shoreline, with the exception of the Humbug Marsh, has been engineered with concrete bulkheads or armor rock to halt erosion. This type of armoring provides little or no habitats for aquatic plants, fish or wildlife. Recently, several sites have received treatments using more natural materials for bank stabilization. Examples of this "soft engineering" of shorelines can be found at some Trenton street ends, the Solutia site on the Trenton Channel and on BASF Corporation lands.

Lake Erie Shoreline: The western Lake Erie shoreline is subject to erosion and flooding during periods of high lake water and storm events. Several barrier islands that once protected coastal marshes and beaches have been severely eroded in recent decades. Rock dikes and breakwater structures have been constructed at several communities and marinas. Some large structures have allowed for the restoration of coastal marshes and/or management of water impoundments. A large barrier reef-like structure at Pointe Mouillee has been constructed along the shoreline to recreate the protection afforded by eroded barrier islands. The Pointe Mouillee Confined Disposal Facility is a 3-mile-long structure constructed to contain dredgings from the Detroit River and the Lake Erie Shipping Channel. The lake water barriers created by the disposal facility permit the management of water levels and emergent vegetation on several impoundments of the Pointe Mouillee State Game Area.

Exotic Species Control

Invasive species of current concern within the approved boundary of the Refuge, in order of priority, are common reed (*Phragmites australis/communis*), purple loosestrife (*Lythrum salicaria*), and reed canary grass (*Phalaris canariensis*). Phragmites, purple loosestrife and reed canary grass have invaded wetland, prairie and upland habitats. Several management techniques have been used to reduce encroachment of these non-desirable plant species, including mowing, burning, water level manipulation, plowing, and chemical and biological controls.

Common reed is an aggressive nuisance plant that has infested many areas of southeast Michigan. If this plant goes unchecked it will threaten the biological diversity that was once provided by natural wetlands. An aggressive approach needs to be made to stop further encroachment of this invasive weed. Not only do phragmites shade out native plant species, but the dense rhizomes and shoot litter also prevent more desirable plants from establishing.

One biological control that has been successful against purple loosestrife has been the release of Galerucella beetles. Beetles have been released at Pointe Mouillee State Game Area, Celeron Island, Stony Island and Grosse Ille with good results in reducing purple loosestrife. These beetles are natural predators of purple loosestrife in their original habitats of Europe and Asia. In most cases, native species such as cattail, bulrushes, and nut sedges come through and establish themselves after purple loosestrife stands are eradicated. Continuation and expansion of the beetle program will be important as the Detroit River IWR expands.

Private Lands Partnerships

Partners for Fish and Wildlife is a voluntary program that focuses on restoring and enhancing wetlands, grasslands, stream corridors and instream habitats on private lands to provide wildlife, fisheries, water quality and recreational benefits for private landowners.

Through the Partners Program, the Service focuses on improving habitat for federal trust resources: migratory birds, federally-listed endangered or threatened species, and interjurisdictional fish. In Michigan, restoration of wetlands has been, and remains, the primary focus for the Partners Program. The program also includes restoration of grasslands, stream channels, riparian corridors, and specific habitats used by federally listed endangered or threatened species. Since this program began in Michigan in 1988, more than 1,500 projects have been completed.

The Partners Program within the counties surrounding the Refuge is currently administered by Service staff located in the East Lansing Field Office, Ottawa NWR and Shiawassee NWR. When Partners Program staff are added to the Refuge, a Management District will be created which may include Wayne and Monroe counties and surrounding counties that are within the watersheds of the Detroit River, St. Clair River and Lake Erie.

Wetland restorations are generally focused where previous agricultural drainage provides an opportunity to restore hydrology, or put the wet back into altered wetlands. Restorations are designed to re-establish shallow water wetlands, those less than 3 feet deep, containing a mixture of open water and vegetated areas. The program does not create excavated farm ponds and does not alter existing natural, undisturbed wetlands.

Grasslands provide a buffer around wetland areas and nesting cover for some waterfowl and a number of declining grassland birds, such as Bobolinks. The Partners Program is working with its partners in Michigan to promote the establishment of mixed stands of warm-season grasses and native wild flowers. Grasslands 20 to 40 acres in size and larger help provide adequate cover and food throughout the year for a variety of migratory birds, pheasants, and other wildlife.

Projects are funded by the Service with cost-share assistance provided by conservation organizations, other governmental agencies, and landowners. Project construction is often completed at little or no cost to the landowner. Landowners are required to sign an agreement to leave the project in place on their property a minimum of 10 years.

Farm Services Administration Conservation Easements: The Service assists the Farm Service Agency in identifying important wetland and floodplain resources on government foreclosed farm properties. Once these resources have been identified, the Farm Services Administration conserves the areas through perpetual easements and transfers the management responsibility to the Service. Properties with recorded easements are then sold to the private sector. Easement areas managed by the Service become part of the National Wildlife Refuge System.

Currently 161 conservation easements in Michigan are managed by three national wildlife refuges. The 50 counties of southern Michigan have 133 easements totaling 5,213 acres, of which Ottawa NWR and Shiawassee NWR manage 18 and 115 tracts, respectively. Shiawassee NWR manages the most conservation easements in the Service's eight-state Great Lakes/Big Rivers Region. There are currently 158 landowners on these 115 tracts that need to be contacted annually.

When biological and/or enforcement staff are added to the Refuge, a Management District will be created which may include Wayne and Monroe Counties and surrounding counties that are within the watersheds of the Detroit River, St. Clair River and Lake Erie. At that time, a portion of the current conservation easement responsibilities of Shiawassee and Ottawa NWRs may be transferred to the Detroit River IWR. In addition, the Refuge may become involved in the acquisition and management of Waterfowl Production Areas in southeast Michigan.

Waterfowl Production Areas: Waterfowl Production Areas (WPAs) conserve wetlands and grasslands critical to waterfowl and other wildlife. These public lands, managed by the U.S. Fish and Wildlife Service, are part of the National Wildlife Refuge System. The WPA Program was authorized by Congress in 1958 to safeguard natural wetlands that were rapidly being destroyed by agriculture drainage, housing developments and other commercial land use practices.

In southern Michigan there are currently three WPAs: the 160-acre Schlee WPA in Jackson County, the 77-acre Kinney WPA in Van Buren County, and the 95-acre Schoonover WPA in Lenawee County. All three areas are managed as a mixture of wetlands and grasslands to provide quality nesting and brood-rearing habitat for waterfowl and a variety of migratory songbirds. All of the WPAs are open for public use, including hunting and other wildlife dependent activities such as wildlife observation, photography, and environmental education.

Currently, the Service and Michigan DNR are proposing to reinitiate the 1980 WPA Program and expand the current state Wetland Management District from 14 counties to 48 counties across southern Michigan.

NOTES & QUESTIONS

1. What is the value of establishing and managing a national wildlife refuge in Detroit? Could a wildlife refuge be created in *any* urban area?

2. Much of the plan seeks to restore the land within the refuge to . . . what? Should the refuge reflect what the area was like before Detroit grew into a large urban area? Or what it was like while the urban area was thriving? Or something altogether different?

3. As the human population of Detroit shrinks, the wildlife population has grown. Coyotes, foxes, pheasants, and turkeys have all moved into areas of the city that have been abandoned by former human residents. *See generally* Peggy Walsh-Sarnecki, *Leaving the Wild Behind*, DETROIT FREE PRESS, Oct. 10, 2011, at A3. What can these natural processes tell us about our efforts at ecosystem management?

Chicago Wilderness and Its Biodiversity Recovery Plan

http://www.chicagowilderness.org/files/3413/3034/7640/biodiversity_recovery_plan.pdf

Executive Summary Chicago Wilderness and Its Biodiversity Recovery Plan

1.1

Introduction

1.1.1 Chicago Wilderness: who we are, what we are accomplishing.

"Chicago Wilderness" refers to nature and to the people and institutions that protect it. Chicago Wilderness is 200,000 acres of protected conservation land—some of the largest and best surviving woodlands, wetlands, and prairies in the Midwest. It is also the much larger matrix of public and private lands of many kinds that support nature in the region along with the people who protect and live compatibly with it.

Native Americans were part of the natural ecosystem here for thousands of years. Today, thousands of volunteers and hundreds of scientists, land managers, educators, and others are crucial to the survival of our natural ecosystems, as is the "Chicago Wilderness" work of the 88 member organizations. The geographic area covered by the Chicago Wilderness region includes northeastern Illinois, northwestern Indiana, and southeastern Wisconsin. The coalition's membership includes local governments, state and federal agencies, centers for research and education, and conservation organizations.

The boundaries of the Chicago Wilderness region capture a spectacular concentration of rare ecosystem types. These ecosystems harbor a high diversity of species, including a large number of those listed as threatened or endangered in the states of Illinois, Indiana, and Wisconsin. Indeed, outside of the Chicago Wilderness region, levels of diversity drop off sharply. Boundaries of the watersheds containing the natural communities helped to define the region, as did the large concentration of natural preserves in the metropolitan area. . .

*   *   *

1.2

The vision

For the past 200 years, the south end of Lake Michigan has been the setting of a classic drama. While building its economic and cultural wealth, Chicago, one of the nation's largest metropolises, has partially preserved the natural communities that had developed here since the retreat of the last glacier, approximately 10,000 years ago. As the metropolis continues to expand, its natural riches decline. Hence the vision:

To establish a broad policy of beneficial coexistence in which the region's natural heritage is preserved, improved, and expanded even as the metropolis grows. . .

1.3 Key findings and recommendations

The Biodiversity Recovery Plan contains a number of recommended actions at varied levels of detail and importance. Some of the more important ones are indicated below, either verbatim or in summary form, with chapter references.

1.3.1 Manage more land to protect and restore biodiversity.

Much of the region's legally protected land is not yet being effectively managed to preserve remnant native communities. Until recently, it was thought that most types of natural areas, if left alone, would preserve themselves. Studies have increasingly shown that the quality of our natural communities, including those protected by public ownership, is steadily degrading because natural processes have been interrupted and/or because of invasive or overly abundant species. The continuing degradation of existing preserves is a major threat to sustaining and enhancing biodiversity.

Ecological management practices are available to deal with these problems. Limited management is underway in certain forest preserves and parks and on some privately held lands. But current levels of management are, in most instances, far from adequate. *Therefore, this plan assigns the highest priority to establishing and maintaining the proper management of natural communities.*

- More resources need to be applied to the management of protected lands in the region. The shortage of dollars to manage lands and waters for biodiversity represents a major threat to the region's natural communities. In addition to the high-quality sites being managed today, medium-and lower-quality sites, particularly those containing higher-priority community types, need management efforts.

- State-of-the-art management practices should be applied more broadly to protected lands. This will require more qualified personnel, both volunteer and paid, than are presently available. Land managers should apply a diversity of management practices in order to sustain natural communities.

- The expanded and more effective use of volunteers in land management, monitoring, and stewardship will be essential for maintaining the health of conservation lands.

- The use of prescribed fire needs to be greatly expanded. A regional training program should be developed for crew members and burn leaders. Outreach programs should be used to educate local governments in the use of prescribed fire in managing natural ecosystems. State agencies need to craft air-quality regulations that foster the expanded use of prescribed burns. Finally, a variety of burn strategies is needed. A single management regime, such as burning at the same intensity and same time each year, is unlikely to sustain biological diversity.

- Planning for the management of natural communities should be carried out on a countywide or regional scale, allowing a diversity of management strategies and effects. For example, wetland management should be coordinated on a regional basis to assure that birds have appropriate habitat within the region regardless of local fluctuations in wetland conditions.

1.3.2 Preserve more land with existing or potential benefits for biodiversity.

The Chicago region currently contains 200,000 acres of protected land in national parks, state parks, regional forest preserves, and open spaces owned and maintained by park districts, private institutions, and corporations. All of these lands contain important natural communities or else serve as buffers, protecting and supporting the natural areas. Over the past few years, local preservation agencies have steadily acquired land for a variety of purposes and they expect to acquire more in the years ahead. *This plan recommends that a high priority be given to identifying and preserving important but unprotected natural communities, especially those threatened by development, and to protecting areas that can function as large blocks of natural habitat though restoration and management. The plan recommends that these areas be preserved where possible by the expansion of public preserves, by the public acquisition of large new sites, or by the actions of qualified private owners.*

- Public and private agencies should act immediately to preserve those high-quality natural areas in the region that remain unprotected. High-quality remnants, even if small, are important reservoirs of genetic material for maintaining regional biodiversity. Emphasis should be on those community types of higher priority as outlined in this plan.

- Chicago Wilderness and the regions' land-owning agencies should develop a priority list of areas needing protection based on regional priorities for biodiversity conservation.

- Federal, state, and local funding for land acquisition by county forest preserve and conservation districts and by other preservation agencies should be expanded with the preservation of biodiversity as a priority. Recognizing that public funds are limited, biodiversity conservation efforts should to the greatest extent possible also support the multiple-use missions of public agencies.

- In Illinois, the state's imposition of property-tax caps makes the funding of further acquisition and management more problematic. Local governments should seek to pass referenda as necessary to obtain the re venues needed to achieve this plan.

- State governments should increase funding to open space grants programs, both for their own lands and for lands to be acquired by county forest preserve and conservation districts, park districts, and other eligible jurisdictions.

- Increased federal funding for preserving conservation land is a critical need. High priority should be given to applications by states and local governments that address critical needs for conserving biodiversity as outlined in this plan.

- Land-acquisition plans of public agencies should give consideration to the presence of endangered and threatened species.

- The granting of protective easements and other protective measures by private landowners for natural areas and buffer zones is an important tool for biodiversity protection and will increase in significance as acquisition of public lands becomes more difficult. More training and resources for the use of these techniques are needed.

1.3.3 Protect high-quality streams and mitigation of harmful activities to conserve aquatic biodiversity.

One of the most significant negative impacts of human settlement on the Chicago region's natural environment has been on streams, rivers, lakes, and wetlands. Draining and filling of wetlands, channelizing of streams, increases in storm-water runoff due to expanding impervious surfaces and resultant changes in the frequency and extent of floods, changes in groundwater levels, and the introduction of wastes, chemical products, and eroded soils into all of the region's water bodies have had disastrous consequences for virtually all forms of aquatic life.

As urbanization continues, programs, policies, and regulations to manage water resources should be developed and implemented with an eye to sustaining natural communities. The effectiveness of our efforts to manage water resources should be measured, in part, by the number and variety of native species found in aquatic habitats throughout the region.

- The highest priority for biodiversity conservation is to maintain the quality of the remaining high-quality streams and lakes, those that support high numbers of native and threatened species.

- State and local public agencies should protect high-quality streams and lakes through proper watershed planning and management, including plans for storm water management.

- Local agencies should promote natural drainage, create buffer strips and greenways along streams, and create or restore streamside wetlands. Attention should be given to changes in groundwater levels for terrestrial communities and wetlands.

- Local agencies and private landowners should consider restoring streams to their natural meandering courses, restoring riffles and other elements of stream habitat, and using bioengineering solutions to control streambank erosion.

- Local agencies should avoid new or expanded wastewater discharges into high-quality streams. Alternatives include routing flows to regional facilities, using land treatment, and using constructed wetlands for improving treated effluent before discharging to streams.

- Many dams in the region impede the movement of fish and other aquatic life up and down the waterway. Consequently, high-quality streams sometimes abruptly deteriorate above or below a dam. Where dams are not needed for water supply, flood control, or recreation, removal or modification with structures that effectively permit the passage of aquatic species would help to conserve biodiversity.

1.3.4 Continue and expand research and monitoring.

While land managers use the best current knowledge about the management needs of natural communities and species, there is always opportunity and need to improve management techniques and learn more about the complexity of ecosystems and their functioning. Management and monitoring activities need to be organized so that they help evaluate the effectiveness of current techniques, and research projects need to be designed to answer questions relevant to management. There are distinct differences between research, monitoring, and inventory, yet if these activities are linked together in meaningful ways, the results can immediately be put to use by conservation practitioners and thus can improve biodiversity management. Management within an experimental framework, making use of results in future management decisions, is referred to as adaptive management. *Developing and implementing a regional monitoring program and pursuing a prioritized research agenda will provide significant contributions to conservation of biodiversity.*

- Compile a prioritized list of research needs. Support research projects that will help Chicago Wilderness scientists and land managers to better understand presettlement landscape conditions and processes, current landscape conditions and processes, the best techniques to restore communities to improved ecological health, and requirements for sustaining biodiversity over the long-term. . .

- Compile a thorough literature review of previous studies regarding management of natural communities and conservation of biodiversity relevant to efforts in Chicago Wilderness.

- Develop better links with academia and promote more research projects within the Chicago Wilderness region. This could be achieved through a number of approaches, including setting up a central location of priority research needs as a resource for graduate students. Another suggestion is to promote the Chicago Wilderness region as a research station. This would help students to identify appropriate sites and experts, as well as to receive permits.

- Develop and implement a regional monitoring protocol that emphasizes adaptive management for making progress toward selected management goals.

1.3.5 Apply both public and private resources more extensively and effectively to inform the region's citizens of their natural heritage and what must be done to protect it.

A precondition to the success of any important public endeavor is the understanding and support of a significant portion of the public. The topic of sustaining biodiversity, including an understanding of its importance to current and future generations, is just beginning to be taught in schools and conveyed through the local media. Many communities are not being reached through these efforts and even citizens who already have a strong environmental ethic are often unaware of the richness of our regional biodiversity and of local restoration successes.

[The report] lays out two types of communications actions aimed at addressing the challenge described above. The long-term goals are necessary to build long-term capacity and understanding in the region, while the short-term goals address immediate issues of communication and public relations.

- Ensure that every student graduating from a school in the Chicago Wilderness region is "biodiversity-iterate."

- Make topics relating to biodiversity and Chicago Wilderness a focus of local colleges and universities.

- Increase the number of communities receiving nonschool-based biodiversity education programs.

- Gain a better understanding of the views of a broader segment of the Chicago-area population on restoration.

- Improve the public's understanding of the role of management in natural areas and communicate documented benefits of local restoration efforts, particularly those of most value to humans.

- Foster local grassroots communication and provide more opportunities for citizens to get involved in the decision-making process. Work with user groups affected by restoration efforts on issues of common concern.

- Improve the credibility and public perception of the people involved in restoration efforts.

- Engage advocacy organizations in our efforts. Put a structure in place to respond quickly to issues of perception as they arise.

- Assess the current state of biodiversity knowledge held by key decision-makers such as elected officials and their staff, land managers, and planners. Create programs to address their needs for biodiversity education .

1.3.6 Adopt local and regional development policies that reflect the need to restore and maintain biodiversity.

In the course of regulating private development and expanding the public infrastructure in the three-state region, public officials have the opportunity to preserve and enhance biodiversity. This can be accomplished through the inclusion of biodiversity objectives within state, regional, and local plans and laws or ordinances governing the urban and suburban development processes.

- Counties and municipalities should amend their comprehensive plans, zoning ordinances, and other regulations to incorporate relevant recommendations contained in this plan.

- The Illinois EPA should establish a process for reviewing and approving the expansion of wastewater service areas that takes into consideration the impacts on the total natural environment within affected watersheds.

- State agencies responsible for major transportation infrastructure should incorporate biodiversity principles into their planning and implementation decisions. Further, when a state infrastructure investment such as a toll road or major airport is likely to trigger substantial residential, commercial, or industrial development, impacted state agencies and local governments should be required to enter enforceable agreements minimizing adverse environmental impacts including the loss of biodiversity.

- Support the Regional Greenways Plan for northeastern Illinois and the Natural Areas Plan for southwestern Wisconsin. These plans identify actions to protect and manage critical habitats for plants and animals and generally improve ecosystems. They complement and support the objectives of this Recovery Plan.

- Participate in the discussions of the Campaign for Sensible Growth and Metropolis 2020. The Campaign promotes principles of economic development, redevelopment, and open space preservation. Metropolis 2020 has proposed actions to help the region develop in a manner that will protect its economic vitality, while maintaining its high quality of life.

- Support implementation of regional growth strategies by the Northeastern Illinois Planning Commission, the Southeastern Wisconsin Regional Planning Commission, and the Northwest Indiana Regional Planning Commission, insofar as these plans seek to reduce the region's excessive rate of land consumption, preserve important open spaces, and promote improved water quality.

NOTES & QUESTIONS

1. How does the Chicago Wilderness plan seek to preserve biodiversity in the area? Is it likely to succeed? Who will object to it? What alternatives are there to the plan?

2. According to the FWS, which provides $600,000 annually to the Chicago Wilderness project, "[o]ver 200 collaborative projects that address priorities set by the teams have been funded. These projects include native prairie gardens in the urban center, large wetland restorations in suburban forest preserves, development of education and outreach materials, green infrastructure planning, and ecological research and monitoring. In addition to funded projects, many more projects have been launched by members who came together through the partnership." FWS further reports that Chicago Wilderness "has gained national and international attention as a model for conservation in metropolitan areas, which is vitally important as we move further toward an urban and suburban society." The U.S. Fish & Wildlife Service's Involvement with Chicago Wilderness: People and Nature in the Urban Environment, *available at* http://www.fws.gov/midwest/chicago/cwfactsheet.htm. Chicago Wilderness is one of seven model programs touted by a recent study of state and regional biodiversity conservation planning. The other programs are the Florida Ecological Network Project, which has mapped priority habitats in order to guide public funding and local land-use decisions; the Oregon Biodiversity Project, which emphasizes private incentives for private landowners; the Massachusetts Biomap, which operates as a tool to establish priorities for land protection; the New Jersey Landscape Project, which seeks to move beyond to piecemeal protection of patches of habitat; the Willamette Basin Conservation Strategy, which advises affected public and private stakeholders on a strategy for preserving priority conservation areas; and the Sonoran Desert Conservation Plan, which identifies both conservation and development reserves and seeks to direct Tucson's growth toward those areas with the least natural, historic, and cultural values. *See* Jessica Wilkinson, Sara Vickerman & Jeff Lerner, *Conserving Biodiversity Through State and Regional Planning*, in NATURE IN FRAGMENTS: THE LEGACY OF SPRAWL 298–306 (Elizabeth A. Johnson & Michawel W. Klemmens, eds. 2005). Which of these approaches is most likely to succeed?

B. AGRICULTURAL LANDS

For farmers and ranchers, for people who make a living on the land, every day is Earth Day. There's no better stewards of the land than people who rely on the productivity of the land. And we can work with our farmers and ranchers to help improve the environment.

President Bush offered this perspective on farming in America when he signed the 2002 Farm Bill on May 13, 2002. Our nation's farm policy has for decades rested, and continues to rest, on this bedrock premise—that farmers are the "best stewards of the land" because they depend on the land's productivity for their livelihood. But consider what farming means to the ecosystems within and around the farmed lands. First, any pre-farm undisturbed habitat is removed. About 900 million acres of the United States—45 percent of the nation's land mass—have experienced this transformation and remain in agricultural uses today. Next, while the number of environmentally conscious farmers is strong and growing, in most cases farming tills soil, irrigates, fertilizes, applies pesticides, plants monoculture crops or grazes domesticated livestock, removes the commodity product and starts the process over again. Finally, farming practices generally rely on the ability to move excess fertilizer, animal waste, and pesticides off of the farm land, and onto surrounding lands and waters.

The end result is that farming American-style leads to massive soil erosion, depletion of surface and underground water supplies, pollution of air and water with nutrients, pesticides, and sediments, and depletion of soil resources. A few facts and figures drive this picture home:

- 930 million acres of habitat have been converted to farming uses

- 25 percent of all cropland has become highly erodible

- 2 billion tons of soil are eroded annually from farms by wind and water

- 331 million tons of eroded farm soils empty each year into the Gulf of Mexico alone

- 55 million acres of cropland are irrigated

- 48 million acres of cropland have become saline, most due to irrigation

- 750 million pounds of pesticides are released annually into surface and ground waters

- farms produce 200 times as much animal waste as the nation's human waste

- Maryland's 300 million chickens produce 720 million pounds of waste annually

- farm runoff releases 1.16 million tons of phosphorous into the nation's waters each year

- farm runoff releases 4.65 million tons of nitrogen into the nation's waters each year

- ammonia from hog waste releases 179 million pounds of nitrogen into the atmosphere each year in North Carolina alone

See J.B. Ruhl, *Farms, Their Environmental Harms, and Environmental Law*, 27 ECOLOGY L.Q. 263 (2000). Not surprisingly, the EPA has determined that runoff from agriculture is the leading cause of impairment of lakes, rivers, and wetlands in our nation's waters. *See* OFFICE OF WATER, U.S. EPA, NATIONAL WATER QUALITY INVENTORY 1994 REPORT TO CONGRESS (1994).

The policy response to this unusual form of ecological "stewardship" has not been what one might imagine. Unlike other polluting industries, most of which have been target of command-and-control style federal and state regulation since the 1970s, farming has enjoyed extensive exemptions from environmental regulation. The policy for most industries is that the polluter pays—that is, the polluter must assume the costs of internalizing the social costs of the polluting activity. Instead, the environmental policy for agriculture has been to pay farmers to avoid causing environmental harms. The following article provides an excellent history and overview of how that irony came about and the possible future directions in which it is headed.

Christopher R. Kelley and James A. Lodoen, *Federal Farm Program Conservation Initiatives: Past, Present, and Future*

9 Natural Resources & Env't 17 (Winter 1995).

In testimony before Congress during the 1990 farm bill debate, the U.S. Department of Agriculture's Assistant Secretary for Economics, Dr. Bruce Gardner, rhetorically asked "Why do we need a conservation title in the farm bill?" His response captured the long-standing ambivalence over conservation's role in federal farm policy:

The purpose [of a conservation title] is to maintain the environment for farmers and the rest of us and to maintain the productive capacity of agriculture for future generations. At the same time we have to keep in mind the overall objective of farm policy, to promote an economically healthy agriculture and an internationally competitive one, and moreover, we have to achieve these objectives at the minimum possible cost to the taxpayer.

Conservation Issues and Agricultural Practices and Oversight on the Forestry Title of the 1990 Farm Bill: Hearings Before the Subcomm. on Conservation and Forestry of the Senate Comm. on Agriculture, Nutrition, and Forestry, 101st Cong., 1st & 2d Sess. 469 (pt. XI) (1990). As Dr. Gardner recognized, the "overall objective" of federal farm policy is to improve the agricultural economy. From its New Deal beginnings, farm policy has been primarily designed to stabilize commodity prices and to support farm income. Stated bluntly, "[federal] farm policy should be taken for what it is, namely, industrial policy with some economic benefits for farmers and their industrial partners." WILLIAM P. BROWNE, SACRED COWS AND HOT POTATOES: AGRARIAN MYTHS IN AGRICULTURAL POLICY 35 (1992).

Federal farm policy has been ambivalent toward conservation initiatives. On the one hand, sound conservation practices can produce short-and long-term economic benefits. On the other hand, the natural resources capital on which agriculture is based has not been the primary concern of those who have guided federal farm policy for the last sixty years. Instead, farmers' wealth relative to the wealth of the nonfarm population has mattered most. Nevertheless, conservation and the federal farm programs have been linked in varying degrees throughout the programs' history, although this linkage has not been inspired by an unadulterated desire to conserve natural resources. Rather, conservation initiatives have largely served to garner political support or otherwise to assist in achieving a given program's primary economic objectives.

If the past is prologue, the economic well-being of the agricultural sector will continue to be the predominant concern of federal farm policy for the foreseeable future. Conservation, however, is likely to assume a greater role for at least two reasons. First, agriculture is coming under greater environmental scrutiny. Examination of the farm programs' impact on the environment is giving credence to the contention that "[m]any farmers in these programs manage their farms to maximize present and future program benefits, sometimes at the expense of environmental quality." NAT'L RESEARCH COUNCIL, ALTERNATIVE AGRICULTURE 10 (1989) (Alternative Agriculture). As a result, Congress can be expected to continue to respond to concerns about the environmental impact of farm policy. Second, budgetary constraints and international competition will accelerate the trend toward market-oriented policies, thus diminishing the programs' traditional role in supply management. At the same time, the economic consequences of ending income transfers to farmers, particularly the decline in land values that may result, are likely to discourage an abrupt halt to income transfers. Paying farmers for adopting conservation practices is likely to expand, perhaps ultimately replacing other current mechanisms for supporting farm income, albeit with reduced fiscal outlays.

Conservation's past and present role in the federal commodity programs—the flagships of federal farm policy—and the future of conservation initiatives are examined here. In the process, one fact emerges as inescapable—just as farming alters the natural environment, federal farm programs are not environmentally neutral. They produce both harm and good, with the final accounting being a matter of perspective and debate. The debate's scale is not insignificant for there is considerable support for the proposition that the farm programs have done more harm than good to the environment.

Inauspicious Beginnings

The earliest significant linkage of conservation with federal farm policy was short-lived. As the nation entered the Great Depression, the farm sector was suffering from low income, surplus crops, and eroded cropland. Farming employed about 20 percent of the civilian labor force and accounted for almost 8 percent of the gross national product. Improving the farm economy, therefore, was viewed as an important first step in restoring the nation's economy. *See* Kristen Allen & Barbara J. Elliott, *The Current Debate and Economic Rationale for U.S. Agricultural Policy in* U.S. AGRICULTURE IN A GLOBAL SETTING: AN AGENDA FOR THE FUTURE 9, 17–18 (M. Ann Tutwiler ed., 1988). Prior to enactment of the first New Deal farm legislation, national land-use planning and the retirement of submarginal lands from crop production was debated as a way to improve the farm economy. Conservation, however, was not the only goal of those urging land-use planning—"a fervent desire to avoid imposing controls on individual farmers' operations also prompted its promotion." Harold F. Breimyer, *Agricultural Philosophies and Policies in the New Deal*, 68 MINN. L. REV. 333, 338 (1983).

In the Agricultural Adjustment Act of 1933, the New Deal's first farm legislation, production controls prevailed over land-use planning as the mechanism for improving commodity prices. The use of conservation as a tool to promote economic interests had not been forgotten, however. When the 1933 Act's production controls and funding mechanism were declared unconstitutional in *United States v. Butler*, 297 U.S. 1 (1936), Congress responded less than two months later with the Soil Conservation and Domestic Allotment Act of 1936.

The 1936 Act paid participating farmers to plant "soil-building" grasses and legumes, instead of "soil-depleting" commodities such as corn and cotton. In so doing, it inaugurated the idea of making "green payments" to farmers, a concept still in currency today. Nevertheless, the Act's fundamental economic objectives were revealed by the classification of wheat, then in surplus, as "soil depleting" despite its soil-conserving characteristics. Moreover, although soil conservation improved, the legislation did little to stabilize commodity production and improve farm income. Consequently, Congress once again turned to production controls and enacted the

Agricultural Adjustment Act of 1938. After surviving constitutional challenges in *Mulford v. Smith*, 307 U.S. 38 (1939), and *Wickard v. Filburn*, 317 U.S. 111 (1942), the 1938 Act became the cornerstone of today's commodity programs.

Originally intended as temporary measures, the commodity programs begun by the Agricultural Adjustment Act of 1938 have survived for six decades. During these years, they have weathered considerable criticism. While some of this criticism reflects a fundamental disagreement with government intervention in the farm economy, other criticism has been more focused. For example, commodity traders and handlers have challenged the trade-distorting effects of government-supported prices and the loss of production through acreage reduction programs. Consumers and taxpayers have questioned the programs' marketplace and government costs. Farmers have criticized the programs' failure to improve prices and the increasing complexity of the program rules. Finally, environmentalists have asserted that the basic mechanisms used to support commodity prices and farm income have had negative environmental consequences.

Because some environmentalists have indicted the basic mechanisms used by the programs, an understanding of this criticism requires an understanding of the incentives and disincentives the programs create. In turn, this dictates examining what the federal commodity programs do.

The Role of the Federal Commodity Programs

The commodity programs have two primary functions—price support and income support. Commodity prices are supported through nonrecourse loans. The loans are made post-production, usually for a nine-month term. The loan rate established for each price-supported commodity effectively sets the commodity's market price floor because producers can forfeit the crop securing the loan to the government in lieu of repaying the loan. In addition to establishing a market price floor, nonrecourse loans provide individual farmers with capital at a time when market prices typically are at their lowest, thus providing a direct incentive for participation. Nonrecourse loans also tend to spread marketings throughout the year. *See generally* J.W. Looney, *The Changing Focus of Government Regulation of Agriculture in the United States*, 44 MERCER L. REV. 763, 781–89 (1993).

Nonrecourse loans are dwarfed in economic significance by deficiency payments, the primary form of farm income support. Deficiency payments are direct income transfers to participating producers of feed grains (corn, sorghum, oats, and barley), wheat, rice, and upland cotton. 7 U.S.C. §§ 1444f(c), 1445b-2(c), 1441-2(c), 1444-2(c). Deficiency payments use the concept of "target prices," a per-unit sum deemed by Congress to cover the commodity's cost of production. Payments are based on the difference between the commodity's "target price" and the commodity's averaged market price or the commodity's loan rate, whichever difference is less. If the averaged market price exceeds the target price, no deficiency payments are made.

Commodity programs are annual programs, and program enrollment is voluntary. To participate in a commodity's deficiency program, farmers may have to set aside land, idling it from production. Under this "production adjustment" requirement, known as the acreage reduction program (ARP), the idled land must be dedicated to a conservation use, also known as the acreage conservation reserve.

The annual decision to participate is usually based on economic considerations. When an ARP is in effect, the decision turns on whether the projected market price will justify setting aside the required acreage. In most years for most program crops, the overwhelming majority of eligible acreage is enrolled. Because enrollment reduces financial risks, program participation is often required by lenders.

The deficiency payment rate for each commodity is a per-unit rate. Payments are made on "program production," a calculation that involves multiplying a farm's "permitted acres" for a commodity by that farm's yield for the commodity. Prior to 1985, program yields were subject to adjustment based on actual production. Average yields were frozen in 1985, however, and have not been adjusted since.

A farm's permitted acres for a commodity are the crop acreage base minus the ARP acreage if an ARP is in effect. Only the production on a farm's "crop acreage base" for each particular commodity is eligible for deficiency payments. Crop acreage bases are calculated on a five-year moving average. If, for example, a farmer planted less corn in a particular year, the farm's corn acreage base would be reduced in subsequent years. Recapturing lost base takes time because a producer cannot increase a program crop's acreage base above its existing level without losing that year's eligibility for payments on all program crops.

* * *

Commodity Programs' Effect on Conservation

Federal farm policy is marked by contradictions and unintended consequences. Some of the contradictions are obvious. For example, "[s]et asides are designed to control supplies and increase market prices, but price supports induce farmers to increase supply, and by so doing, to depress market prices." ROBBIN A. SHOEMAKER, A MODEL OF PARTICIPATION IN U.S. FARM PROGRAMS 14 (U.S. Dep't of Agric., Econ. Res. Serv., Tech. Bull. No. 1819, Aug. 1993). The contradictions also extend to other agricultural sectors. Policies that increase feed grain prices, for example, disfavor livestock farmers who feed grain to their livestock. The environment, in particular, is buffeted by contradictory incentives and disincentives, producing results that were probably never intended.

The most fundamental criticism made by environmentalists against the commodity programs is that the availability of deficiency payments encourages farmers to plant program crops in continuous cycles to preserve crops' acreage bases. The environmental consequences of this incentive have been summarized as follows:

> The farm programs support crops that tend to require high agrichemical inputs and are associated with high rates of soil erosion. Other lesserosive and less-agrichemical-dependent crops receive little government support. The programs reward farmers for specializing in program crops year after year, resulting in further soil depletion and pest problems, which in turn lead to a greater need for agrichemical inputs. The programs tend to discourage farmers from planting other crops and from using more diversified crop rotations.

U.S. GEN. ACCOUNTING OFFICE, ALTERNATIVE AGRICULTURE: FEDERAL INCENTIVES AND FARMERS' OPTIONS 3 (Pub. No. PEMD-90-12, Feb. 1990).

*   *   *

In addition to reducing the incentives for engaging in monocultural production, recent program rules have created disincentives to converting highly erodible land and wetland to cropland. Also, highly erodible land in production must be farmed in accordance with an approved conservation plan beginning in 1995. The highly erodible land and wetland conservation provisions are commonly known as "sodbuster" and "swampbuster," respectively. Of the two, the swampbuster provisions have elicited greater attention.

Under the swampbuster provisions, a person is ineligible for any benefits administered through the U.S. Department of Agriculture (USDA) if

> [1] [t]he person produces an agricultural commodity on wetland that was converted after December 23, 1985; or

> [2] [a]fter November 28, 1990, the person converts a wetland by draining, dredging, filling, leveling or other means for the purpose, or to have the effect, of making the production of an agricultural commodity possible.

16 U.S.C. § 3821(a), (b). The first of these two "triggers" was enacted in the Food Security Act of 1985 (FSA); the second in the Food, Agriculture, Conservation, and Trade Act of 1990 (FACTA). Under the FSA, a wetland could be converted with impunity (but for a possible Clean Water Act § 404 violation) so long as an agricultural commodity was not produced. FACTA closed that "loophole" by making the triggering event the conversion of the wetland. Also, under the FSA, benefits were denied only for the crop year in which the agricultural commodity was produced. 16 U.S.C. § 3821(a)(1)B(3). Violations of FACTA result in ineligibility for benefits for the crop year in which the conversion occurred and for all subsequent crop years until the converted wetland is restored. 16 U.S.C. § 3821(b).

Wetlands may still be farmed under natural conditions, such as a drought, provided the action of the person farming the wetland "does not permanently alter or destroy natural wetland characteristics." 16 U.S.C. § 3822(b)(1)(D). This means that no action can be taken to increase the effects on the water regime beyond that which existed on such land before December 23, 1985, unless it is determined that the effect on remaining wetland values would be minimal. 7 C.F.R. § 12.33(a).

There are numerous exemptions from ineligibility under the swampbuster provisions. 16 U.S.C. § 3822(b). In addition to these exemptions, the loss of USDA benefits may be avoided by restoration of a wetland that had been converted prior to December 23, 1985. This "mitigation through restoration of another converted wetland" provision is available if the wetland that was converted was either frequently cropped or converted between December 23, 1985, and November 28, 1990. 16 U.S.C. § 3822(f).

* * *

For some environmentalists the disincentives imposed by the sodbuster and swampbuster provisions are not sufficient to make farm programs a net gain for the environment for they only add "another layer of regulation without altering the more fundamental incentives imbedded in the structure of agricultural policies." Paul Faeth, Paying the Farm Bill: U.S. Agricultural Policy and the Transition to Sustainable Agriculture 3 (1991). Others bemoan the fact that the provisions apply only to program participants, while objecting to the government's near total nonenforcement of the swampbuster provisions. Anthony N. Turrini, *Swampbuster: A Report from the Front*, 24 IND. L. REV. 1507, 1511 (1991) ("[f]ortunately for wetlands . . . most producers participate in federal farm programs."). Still others find in the conservation provisions' combination of directives and exemptions a continuation of the congressional "ambivalence in creating an aggressive environmental program for agriculture. . ." Linda A. Malone, *Reflections on the Jeffersonian Ideal of an Agrarian Democracy and the Emergence of an Agricultural and Environmental Ethic in the 1990 Farm Bill*, 12 STAN. ENV'TL L. REV. 3, 46 (1993).

The Future

Although they are not a part of the basic commodity programs, the Conservation Reserve Program (CRP) and the Wetland Reserve Program (WRP) may provide a rough guide for the direction of federal farm policy. Under the CRP, farmers are paid to take highly erodible land out of production for an extended period, usually ten years. 16 U.S.C. §§ 3831–3836. Under the WRP, wetlands are removed from production through permanent or thirty-year easements. 16 U.S.C. §§ 3837-3837f. Both programs have had their critics, but the basic concept of paying farmers to further environmental goals generally has been well-received by farmers and environmentalists.

Paying farmers to behave in an environmentally responsible manner offers an alternative to command-and-control regulations based on the "polluter pays" principle. The concept, often described as "green payments," has been suggested as a substitute for deficiency payments. As such, income transfers to farmers would cease to be linked to production as they are to-day. Instead, the payments would be "coupled" to conservation practices. *See* Tim Osburn, *U.S. Conservation Policy—What's Ahead?*, AGRIC. OUT-LOOK, Nov. 1993, at 36.

While attractive to many farmers and environmentalists, green pay-ments present a number of political problems. The most fundamental prob-lem is that the favored recipients of green payments are not likely to be the same farmers favored by current income transfers. Because current income transfers are coupled with production, larger producers are favored. In ad-dition, current programs favor producers in the Midwest, particularly in the upper and lower Great Plains. Green payments, on the other hand, are likely to be parceled out where the environmental problems are most acute and nearest to population centers, resulting in a shifting of payments to both coasts and to major watersheds.

In addition, green payments do not present the ideal mechanism for redirecting payments to the small family farmer whose maintenance is of-ten the rallying cry and justification for income transfers to agriculture. If, for example, green payments are "means tested" so that they are received by only those farmers who are less financially secure relative to other farmers and the nonfarm population, the environmental benefits may be diluted. To the extent environmentalists deplore the environmental harms resulting from large-scale, industrial agriculture, an argument could be made that the financial incentives should be directed toward reforming the behavior of those who farm the most land, thus putting the smaller farmer at a disadvantage.

Finally, there is no certainty that green payments would result in suf-ficient income to satisfy farmers. An idea attracting considerable attention in the 1995 farm bill debate is a program that would guarantee a farmer's per-acre return for a given crop at a prescribed level. *See* Joy Harwood, *Streamlining Farm Policy: The Revenue Guarantee Approach*, AGRIC. OUT-LOOK, Apr. 1994, at 24. The notion that farmers' revenue should be guaran-teed serves as a reminder that farm policy is economic policy.

In all likelihood, federal farm policy will remain an inconsistent and contradictory collection of economic incentives and disincentives. At the same time, conservation initiatives will expand, but only gradually. Re-calling that price and income support has formed the core of federal farm policy for six decades, the redirection of that policy will more likely be evo-lutionary rather than revolutionary.

Wildlife Habitat Incentive Program

United States Department of Agriculture, Commodity Credit Corporation, 2010.
7 C.F.R. Pt. 636.

§ 636.1 Applicability.

(a) The purpose of the Wildlife Habitat Incentive Program (WHIP) is to help participants develop fish and wildlife habitat on private agricultural land, nonindustrial private forest land (NIPF), and Indian land.

(b) The regulations in this part set forth the requirements for WHIP.

(c) The Chief, Natural Resources Conservation Service (NRCS), may implement WHIP in any of the 50 States, District of Columbia, Puerto Rico, Guam, the Virgin Islands of the United States, American Samoa, and the Commonwealth of the Northern Mariana Islands. . .

§ 636.4 Program requirements.

(a) To participate in WHIP, an applicant must:

(1) Be in compliance with the highly erodible and wetland conservation provisions found in 7 CFR part 12;

(2) Be in compliance with the terms of all other USDA-administered conservation program contracts to which the participant is a party;

(3) Develop and agree to comply with a WHIP plan of operations and O&M agreement, as described in § 636.8;

(4) Enter into a cost-share agreement for the development of fish and wildlife habitat as described in § 636.9;

(5) Provide NRCS with written evidence of ownership or legal control of land for the term of the proposed cost-share agreement, including the O&M agreement. An exception may be made by the Chief in the case of land allotted by the Bureau of Indian Affairs (BIA) or Indian land where there is sufficient assurance of control;

(6) Agree to provide all information to NRCS determined to be necessary to assess the merits of a proposed project and to monitor cost-share agreement compliance;

(7) Agree to grant to NRCS or its representatives access to the land for purposes related to application, assessment, monitoring, enforcement, verification of certifications, or other actions required to implement this part;

(8) Provide a list of all members of the legal entity and embedded entities along with members' tax identification numbers and percentage interest in the entity. Where applicable, American Indians, Alaska Natives, and Pacific Islanders may use another unique identification number for each individual eligible for payment;

(9) With regard to cost-share agreements with individual Indians or Indians represented by the BIA, payments exceeding the payment limitation may be made to the tribal participant if a BIA or tribal official certifies in writing that no one individual, directly or indirectly, will receive more than the payment limitation. The BIA or tribal entity must also provide annually, a listing of individuals and payments made, by tax identification number or other unique identification number, during the previous year for calculation of overall payment limitations. The tribal entity must also produce, at the request of NRCS, proof of payments made to the person or legal entity that incurred costs related to conservation activity implementation;

(10) Supply information, as required by NRCS, to determine eligibility for the program including, but not limited to, information to verify the applicant's status as a limited resource farmer or rancher or beginning farmer or rancher and payment eligibility as established by 7 CFR part 1400, Adjusted Gross Income (AGI);

(11) With regard to any participant that utilizes a unique identification number as an alternative to a tax identification number, the participant will utilize only that identifier for any and all other WHIP cost-share agreements to which the participant is a party. Violators will be considered to have provided fraudulent representation and are subject to § 636.13; and

(12) Comply with applicable registration and reporting requirements of the Federal Funding Accountability and Transparency Act of 2006 (Pub. L. 109-282, as amended) and 2 CFR parts 25 and 170.

(b) Eligible land includes:

(1) Private agricultural land;

(2) NIPF;

(3) Indian land; and

(4) Trust land owned in fee title by a State, including an agency or subdivision of a State, when such trust land is held under a long-term lease by a person or nongovernmental entity and when the Chief determines that (i) by the nature of the lease, such land is tantamount to private agricultural land; (ii) the duration of the lease is at least the length of any WHIP agreement; and (iii) no funds under the WHIP program are paid to a governmental entity.

(c) *Ineligible land.* NRCS will not provide cost-share assistance with respect to land:

(1) Enrolled in a program where fish and wildlife habitat objectives have been sufficiently achieved, as determined by NRCS;

(2) With onsite or offsite conditions which NRCS determines would undermine the benefits of the habitat development or otherwise reduce its value;

(3) On which habitat for threatened or endangered species, as defined in section 3 of the ESA, *16 U.S.C. 1532*, would be adversely affected; or

(4) That is owned in fee title by an agency of the United States, other than:

(i) Land held in trust for Indian tribes, and

(ii) Lands owned in fee title by a State, including an agency or subdivision of a State or a unit of government except as provided in § 636.4(b)(4).

§ 636.5 National priorities.

(a) The following national priorities will be used in WHIP implementation:

(1) Promote the restoration of declining or important native fish and wildlife habitats;

(2) Protect, restore, develop, or enhance fish and wildlife habitat to benefit at-risk species;

(3) Reduce the impacts of invasive species on fish and wildlife habitats;

(4) Protect, restore, develop, or enhance declining or important aquatic wildlife species' habitats; and

(5) Protect, restore, develop, or enhance important migration and other movement corridors for wildlife.

(b) NRCS, with advice of other Federal agencies, will undertake periodic reviews of the national priorities and the effects of program delivery at the State, tribal, and local levels to adapt the program to address emerging resource issues. NRCS will:

(1) Use the national priorities to guide the allocation of WHIP funds to the State offices;

(2) Use the national priorities in conjunction with State, tribal, and local priorities to assist with prioritization and selection of WHIP applications; and

(3) Periodically review and update the national priorities utilizing input from the public, Indian tribes, and affected stakeholders to ensure that the program continues to address priority resource concerns.

§ 636.6 Establishing priority for enrollment in WHIP.

(a) NRCS, in consultation with Federal and State agencies, tribal, and conservation partners, may identify priorities for enrollment in WHIP that will complement the goals and objectives of relevant fish and wildlife conservation initiatives at the State, regional, tribal land, or national levels. In response to national, tribal, regional, or State fish and wildlife habitat concerns, the Chief may focus program implementation in any given year to specific geographic areas or to address specific habitat development needs.

(b) The State Conservationist, with recommendations from the State Technical Committee and Tribal Conservation Advisory Council (for tribal land), may give priority to WHIP projects that will address unique habitats or special geographic areas identified in the State. Subsequent cost-share agreement offers that would complement previous cost-share agreements due to geographic proximity of the lands involved or other relationships may receive priority consideration for participation.

(c) NRCS will evaluate the applications and make enrollment decisions based on the fish and wildlife habitat need using some or all of the following criteria:

(1) Contribution to resolving an identified habitat concern of national, tribal, regional, or State importance including at-risk species;

(2) Relationship to any established wildlife or conservation priority areas;

(3) Duration of benefits to be obtained from the habitat development practices;

(4) Self-sustaining nature of the habitat development practices;

(5) Availability of other partnership matching funds or reduced funding request by the person applying for participation;

(6) Estimated costs of fish and wildlife habitat development activities;

(7) Other factors determined appropriate by NRCS to meet the objectives of the program; and

(8) Willingness of the applicant to complete all conservation improvements during the first 2 years of the WHIP cost-share agreement.

NOTES & QUESTIONS

1. According to the USDA's Commodity Credit Corporation,

> WHIP is a voluntary program administered by NRCS using the funds and authorities of the CCC. WHIP is available in any of the 50 States, District of Columbia, Puerto Rico, Guam, the Virgin Islands of the United States, American Samoa, and the Commonwealth of the Northern Mariana Is-

lands. Through WHIP, NRCS provides technical and financial assistance to participants to develop upland, wetland, and aquatic wildlife habitat, as well as fish and wildlife habitat on other areas and to develop habitat for at-risk species, including threatened and endangered species. NRCS first allocated funds for WHIP in 1997. Over the life of the program, NRCS has entered into over 29,000 cost-share agreements that cover over 4.7 million acres.

WHIP was originally authorized under section 387 of the Federal Agriculture Improvement and Reform Act of 1996 (Pub. L. 104-127). In 1997, NRCS published regulations to implement WHIP at 7 CFR part 636. Section 2502 of the Farm Security and Rural Investment Act of 2002 (Pub. L. 107-171) repealed the original WHIP authority and established a new WHIP under section 1240N of the Food Security Act of 1985, as amended. Section 2602 of the 2008 Act made further changes to WHIP.

Wildlife Habitat Incentive Program, 75 Fed. Reg. 71325 (2010). The WHIP program has funded such activities as the removal of undesirable woody species from forest land, planting in critical areas, spraying herbicide on undesirable vegetation, and restoration of oak savanna, tall grass prairie, and other ecosystems. What factors will determine whether the WHIP program is a success?

2. The farm bills that are periodically enacted by Congress contain several other provisions designed to encourage the conservation of agricultural lands. For example, nearly 30 million acres of agricultural land enrolled in the Conservation Reserve Program (CRP), most of which are planted in grasses and thus offer significant wildlife habitat resources. The FWS has cited the CRP for helping numerous species to avoid listing under the ESA. *See, e.g.,* Partial 90-Day Finding on a Petition To List 404 Species in the Southeastern United States as Threatened or Endangered With Critical Habitat, 76 Fed. Reg. 6220, 62272 (2011) (finding that listing of the spotted darter is not warranted); 90-Day Finding on a Petition to List the Straight Snowfly and Idaho Snowfly as Endangered, 76 Fed. Reg. 46238 (2011) (finding that the listing of two Idaho snowflies is not warranted). But studies have shown that farmers will exit the CRP program on expiration of their contracts if crop prices make land more valuable in production. The CRP is, after all, primarily designed to provide another form of economic support to the agricultural community. So what is the CRP: ecosystem management, economic management, or both? *See* Arthur W. Allen, *Agricultural Ecosystems*, in NATIONAL BIOLOGICAL SERVICE, OUR LIVING RESOURCES 423 (1995).

3. If programs like the CRP, WRP, and EQIP make sense to you as a tool of ecosystem management, should they be expanded into other economic sectors? Should we pay residential subdivision developers, golf courses, and ski areas to set aside more land for habitat? Of course, we don't do that as a general rule, and it is unlikely we ever will, but why not?

4. So far, the ESA has played a modest role on farm lands, but a recent effort in Washington could change that. The Douglas County Multi-Species Habitat Conservation Plan is being drafted by multiple stakeholders in Douglas County, a rural area in eastern Washington. "The areas' wheat farms, ranches, and orchards provide decent habitat for sagebrush-dependent species like sage grouse, sharp-tailed grouse, shrike, burrowing owls, and Brewer's sparrows."

Natalie M Henry, *Eastern Wash. HCP Seeks to Preserve Farms as Habitat*, LAND LETTER, Nov. 10, 2005. Four local species— pygmy rabbits, bull trout, spring chinook, and summer steelhead—are listed under the ESA. The proposed HCP would encourage farmers "to do things a little more sloppily when it comes to farming but to the benefit of the species," according to a local official. *Id.* "For example, the plan will ask farmers to wait during mating season until late morning, when grouse are usually finished with their mating rituals, before going out on the land." *Id.*

In re Freshwater Wetlands Protection Act Rules

Supreme Court of New Jersey, 2004.
852 A.2d 167.

■ CHIEF JUSTICE PORITZ delivered the opinion of the Court.

This case raises questions in respect of the validity of General Permit 23 (GP23), N.J.A.C. 7:7A-5.23, adopted by the New Jersey Department of Environmental Protection (DEP) in 1999. Appellants[3] claim that GP23, which permits the limited expansion of existing cranberry growing operations in the Pinelands National Reserve, violates provisions of the Federal Water Pollution Control Act Amendments of 1972, commonly known as the Clean Water Act (CWA), 33 U.S.C.A. § 1344, the Freshwater Wetlands Protection Act (FWPA), N.J.S.A. 13:9B-1 to-30, and the State's Surface Water Quality Standards (SWQS), N.J.A.C. 7:9B-1.1 et seq. A unanimous panel of the Appellate Division rejected appellants' challenge in its entirety. *In re Freshwater Wetlands Prot. Act Rules, Statewide General Permit, Cranberry Expansion, Promulgated by the New Jersey Dep't of Envtl. Prot. (In re FWPA)*, 798 A.2d 634 (2002). We . . . now affirm.

I.

This Court previously has had occasion to discuss the "unique ecological, economic, and cultural features of the New Jersey Pine Barrens, or Pinelands." *Gardner v. New Jersey Pinelands Comm'n*, 593 A.2d 251 (1991). *Gardner* described the pinelands and discussed the purpose of the regulatory programs designed to protect them:

> A "wilderness" of pine-oak forests and wild and scenic rivers, the Pinelands harbors a "wide variety of rare, threatened and endangered plant and animal species," and encompasses "many other significant and unique ecological, historical, recreational, and other resources." The region overlies the vast, seventeen-trillion gallon Cohansey aquifer, "one of the largest virtually untapped sources of pure water in the world." There has been very little development in the Pinelands; there are no major retail centers, and developed property comprises only one or two percent of the land in most areas. Agriculture in the Pinelands,

---

[3]   Appellants are a coalition of environmental organizations that includes the American Littoral Society, Environmental Defense, National Wildlife Federation, New Jersey Audubon Society, New Jersey Environmental Federation, New Jersey Environmental Lobby, New Jersey Public Interest Research Group Citizen Lobby, Inc., Sierra Club-New Jersey Chapter, and Pinelands Preservation Alliance.

especially the cultivation of cranberries and blueberries is particularly important both nationally and locally.

In recent years, anxiety over the loss of farming and the fragile ecology of the Pinelands has produced increasingly stringent federal and state regulation. . . The New Jersey Pinelands Protection Act (Act), L. 1979, c. 111; *N.J.S.A.* 13:18A-1 to 29, declares that its goals are, among others, to protect, preserve, continue, and expand agriculture and horticulture and to discourage piecemeal and scattered development within the Pinelands.

[*Id.* at 199–200 (citations omitted).]

In this case, we focus on the unique role of cranberry agriculture in the history of the pinelands and the methods used to produce the fruit.

A.

Cranberry Agriculture in New Jersey

The high water table and sandy, acidic soils of the pinelands render the cultivation of most field crops difficult. Those same ingredients, however, are essential to the growth of the cranberry. Due to a confluence of favorable ecological and climatological variables, farmers have been harvesting cranberries in the pinelands for almost two centuries. *See* 30 N.J.R. 3721 (Oct. 19, 1998) (noting cranberries have been harvested in pinelands since early 1800s).

By the early 1900s, cranberry production was the region's principle industry. In the 1930s, approximately 13,000 acres of the pinelands were dedicated to cranberry agriculture. More recently, market conditions and other factors have conspired to reduce the number of cranberry growing operations and the amount of acreage in production. Thus, in 1999, there were approximately forty-seven active operations in the pinelands, whereas the amount of acreage in production has fluctuated between 3100 and 4000 acres. Nat'l Agric. Statistical Serv., U.S. Dep't of Agric., *2001 National Rankings, Cranberries* (2001), available at http://www.nass.usda.gov/nj; Nat'l Agric. Statistical Serv.; U.S. Dep't of Agric., *Cranberry Statistics by State and U.S., Total Acres Harvested, 1990–2000* (2000), available at http://www.nass.usda.gov/nj. Despite that decline, the State is the third-largest producer of cranberries in the country, behind only Massachusetts and Wisconsin, and the value of the 1999 harvest was approximately $7.4 million.

Although cultivation techniques have improved considerably over the years, one factor continues to dictate the location of cranberry growing operations: the fruit requires easy access to large amounts of clean water, at least 227 gallons per minute per acre of cranberry bog. Through an extensive network of reservoirs, dikes and canals, farmers use the water "to flood the bogs in winter and early spring to protect against frost, to flood the bogs during harvest, and to irrigate the bogs during the summer." Most cranberry operations are situated in wetland areas where water is readily available. Indeed, the fruit is classified by the United States Army Corps of Engineers (Corps) and United States Fish and Wildlife Service as a "wetland crop species" that "must be grown in wetlands or areas altered to create a wetlands environment." U.S. Army Corps of Engr's, *Regulatory Guidance Letter 92–2*, 57 Fed. Reg. 32523, 32524 (July 22, 1992) (citing U.S. Fish & Wildlife Serv., *1988 National List of Plant Species that Occur in Wetlands* (1989)).

Finding suitable wetland locations for cranberry operations is only the first step. Converting the wetlands for use as a cranberry bog requires removal of the indigenous vegetation and excavation of the soil to a depth of up to three feet. After the dikes and other water control structures are built, a layer of organic soil is placed on the bottom of the bog. The soil is covered with between one and two feet of sand and, finally, the cranberry vines are planted. A newly constructed bog can take more than three years to produce its first crop.

B.

Regulatory Environment

Building or expanding a cranberry growing operation in a wetland implicates a complex permitting scheme. Under the CWA, generally parties seeking to discharge dredged or fill material into wetlands may do so only if they have secured a "section 404" permit from the United States Army Corps of Engineers. 33 U.S.C.A. § 1344(a). The CWA, however, specifically allows states to assume permitting authority for waters within their jurisdictions so long as the state program is at least as stringent as the federal 404 program. In 1987, the New Jersey Legislature enacted the FWPA, N.J.S.A. 13:9B-1 to-30, to satisfy federal assumption requirements, although it was not until March 2, 1994, that the State's application was approved. 40 C.F.R. § 233.71; see N.J.S.A. 13:9B-2; Oliver A. Houck & Michael Rolland, *Federalism in Wetlands Regulation: A Consideration of Delegation of Clean Water Act Section 404 and Related Programs to the States*, 54 Md. L. Rev. 1242, 1276–79 (1995) (detailing New Jersey's efforts to assume permitting authority).

An applicant seeking to engage in regulated activities in State open waters or wetlands must apply for and secure either a general or an individual permit from the DEP. As the name implies, individual permits are project-related and are required for activities that will have substantial wetlands impacts. General permits, such as GP23, are designed to streamline the permitting process for certain activities that have only a minimal impact, individually and cumulatively, on the environment. N.J.S.A. 13:9B-23c. . . [D]raft general permits proposed by the State must be forwarded to the EPA Regional Administrator, who may approve or interpose objections that, if not resolved to the Regional Administrator's satisfaction, will prevent the adoption of the permit. 40 C.F.R. § 233.50(a), (d); N.J.A.C. 7:7A-12.2(j).

C.

General Permit 23

. . .GP23 authorizes the limited expansion of existing cranberry growing operations (as defined at N.J.A.C. 7:7A-5.23(a)), located in the pinelands. A GP23 authorization can only be used to create new bogs and attendant water control infrastructure, not the construction of storage facilities or housing. N.J.A.C. 7:7A-5.23(b). Although individual operators may theoretically expand up to fifty acres (ten acres a year for each year) during the five-year life of the permit, *id.* at (h)(1), a statewide cap of 300 acres "limits the growers' activities in the aggregate." *In re FWPA, supra,* 351 N.J. Super. at 372 (citing N.J.A.C. 7:7A-5.23(i)). . . Under GP23 as adopted, only eighty acres of forested wetlands may be disturbed during the life of the general permit, N.J.A.C. 7:7A-5.23(i)3, and, of these eighty acres, only twenty-five may be AWC wetlands. Id. at (i)4. In addition, individual operators may not disturb more than ten acres of forested wetlands, only four of which can be AWC wetlands. *Id.* at (h)2, (h)3. Indeed, the final permit requires that the loss or disturbance of AWC wetlands must be compensated at a one-to-one ratio. *Id.* at (n)2. The DEP Commissioner (Commissioner) must determine yearly whether "the pace of impacts under is proportional to the pace of [AWC] restoration efforts." *Id.* at (q). If the pace of impacts exceeds the pace of restoration, DEP must temporarily "stop issuing authorizations under [the permit]." *Id.* at (q)2. . .

II.

. . .*N.J.S.A.* 13:9B-6b states:

Activities in areas under the jurisdiction of the Pinelands Commission pursuant to [the Pinelands Protection Act, N.J.S.A. 13:18A-1 to-29] shall not require a freshwater wetlands permit, or be subject to transition area requirements established in this act, *except that the discharge of dredged or fill material shall require a permit* issued under the provisions of the Federal Act, *or under an individual or general permit program administered by the State under the provisions of the Federal Act and applicable State laws,* provided that the Pinelands Commission may provide for more stringent regulation of activities in and around freshwater wetland areas within its jurisdiction. [(Emphasis added).]. . .

Appellants argue . . . that N.J.S.A. 13:9B-13a mandates compulsory mitigation for all "adverse environmental impacts" attributable to activities requiring a general permit or an individual permit. In their view, neither one-to-one mitigation for all AWC impacts, nor the GP23 "no net loss" provision, provides sufficient mitigation under the statute. Conversely, DEP maintains that it may adopt General Permits "that do not require mitigation, except as necessary to ensure that a General Permit will not cause more than minimal impacts on a cumulative or individual basis." See 31 N.J.R. 2969 (Oct. 4, 1999). DEP points out that, nonetheless, it retains discretionary authority to impose mitigation requirements or other special conditions as part of an individual General Permit authorization when such requirements are necessary to insure compliance with the FWPA or the CWA.

As with any administrative regulation, we begin with the settled principle that GP23 must be "accorded a presumption of validity." *New Jersey State League of Municipalities v. Dep't of Cmty. Affairs*, 729 A.2d 21 (N.J.1999); *In re Township of Warren*, 622 A.2d 1257 (1993). . . In this case, DEP interprets N.J.A.C. 7:7A-5.23(g) to require any loss of wetlands caused by activities authorized under GP23 to "be compensated for on a one-to-one ratio." See N.J.A.C. 7:7A-5.23(g); 31 N.J.R. 1566 (June 21, 1999). Appellants contend that the mitigation requirements of N.J.S.A. 13:9B-13 and its implementing regulations, N.J.A.C. 7:7A-15.1 et seq., can be met only through the "creation or restoration of wetlands to compensate for any damage done pursuant to [GP23]" at a one-to-one ratio for all wetland impacts, including disturbances. Thus, the issue is joined over the mitigation requirements, if any, for disturbances to, as opposed to loss of wetlands caused by activities permitted under GP23.

N.J.S.A. 13:9B-13 states in pertinent part:

a. The department shall require as a condition of a freshwater wetlands permit that all appropriate measures have been carried out to mitigate adverse environmental impacts, restore vegetation, habitats, and land and water features, prevent sedimentation and erosion, minimize the area of freshwater wetlands disturbance and insure compliance with the Federal Act and implementing regulations.

b. The department *may require* the creation or restoration of an area of freshwater wetlands of equal ecological value to those which will be lost,. . .

[(Emphasis added).]

Again, the statutory language is clear. Although Section 13(a) requires "all appropriate measures" by way of mitigation, restoration and minimization of "adverse environmental impacts" and "wetland disturbances," Section 13(b) is permissive and states only that the DEP "may require creation or restoration" of wetlands of equal value and, then, only when wetlands have been "lost" through a permitted activity. Moreover, a review of the legislative history supports DEP's assertion that the creation or restoration of wetlands to compensate for adverse impacts attributable to a permitted activity is by no means mandatory, but merely a weapon in DEP's larger mitigation arsenal. *See* Senate Energy and Environment Committee, *Statement to Senate Committee Substitute for Assembly Committee Substitute for Assembly Bills 2342 and 2499*, at 4 (June 25, 1987) (noting "this bill *authorizes* the department to require the creation or restoration of wetlands to compensate for any wetlands destroyed as a result of a project in a freshwater wetland permitted by the department") (emphasis added).

Finally, we recognize that the FWPA covers more types of wetlands activities than does the CWA. That DEP has the power to control activities in New Jersey wetlands that are not covered under federal law does not, however, lead to a conclusion that more stringent mitigation requirements than those found in GP23 are mandated when the express language of the statute states otherwise. We find, therefore, that the mitigation provisions of GP23 are consistent with the FWPA. . .

IV.

A.

Surface Water Quality Standards

The state surface water quality standards, N.J.S.A. 58:10A-4c, N.J.A.C. 7:9B-1.1 et seq., are an important part of an integrated federal and state regulatory program adopted to fulfill the goals of the CWA. 33 U.S.C.A. § 1313; *PUD No. 1 v. Washington Dep't of Ecology*, 511 U.S. 700, 704–05 (1994); *see E.I. du Pont de Nemours & Co. v. Train*, 430 U.S. 112, 116–21 (1977) (describing broader statutory scheme enacted by Congress "to achieve the goal of eliminating all discharges of pollutants into the Nation's waters"). . . In 1987, the CWA was amended to require the SWQS to include an "antidegradation policy," 33 U.S.C.A. § 1313(d)(4)(B); 40 C.F.R. § 131.12(a), to "ensure that 'existing instream water uses and the level of water quality necessary to protect the existing uses shall be maintained and preserved.' " *Jefferson County, supra*, 511 U.S. at 705 (quoting 40 C.F.R. § 131.12(a)(1) (1993)). Like FWPA permits (which must be as stringent as their federal analog), the State antidegradation policy must be at least as stringent as the federal program, 40 C.F.R. §§ 131.6(d), 131.12, and is subject to EPA approval. 33 U.S.C.A. § 1313(c)(3); 40 C.F.R. § 131.5. In [*In re Issuance of a Permit by the Department of Environmental Protection to Ciba-Geigy* Corp, 576 A.2d 784 (N.J. 1990)], we explained that under the state policy, N.J.A.C. 7:9B-1.5(d), "no irreversible changes may be made to existing water quality that would impair or preclude attainment of the designated uses of a waterway."

To effectuate that mandate, New Jersey has established four categories of state waters that receive differing levels of protection from discharges affecting existing water quality. The waters of the pinelands are designated either FW1 or PL, N.J.A.C. 7:9B-1.4, and classified as "Outstanding National Resource Waters of the State." Those waters are considered "nondegradation waters," N.J.A.C. 7:9B-1.5(d)(4), and are afforded the highest level of protection from changes in existing water quality. 40 C.F.R. § 131.12(a)(3); N.J.A.C. 7:9B-1.5(d). Under the state antidegradation policy, "*no changes* shall be allowed in waters which constitute an outstanding National or State resource or in waters that may affect these outstanding resource waters." N.J.A.C. 7:9B-1.5(d)4 (emphasis added); see 40 C.F.R. § 131.12(a)(3) ("Where high quality waters constitute an outstanding National resource, such as the waters of National and State parks and wildlife refuges and waters of exceptional recreational or ecological significance, that water quality shall be maintained and protected."). Similarly, "for

Pinelands waters, the Department shall not approve any activity which alone or in combination with any other activities, might cause changes, other than toward natural water quality, in the existing surface water quality characteristics." N.J.A.C. 7:9B-1.5(d)(6).

B.

GP23 and the Antidegradation Policy

Appellants' remaining claim is that DEP adopted GP23 without consideration of the state's antidegradation policy thereby violating the SWQS. In their view, that failure renders GP23 invalid. They acknowledge that the SWQS contain a provision that states: "The [antidegradation] policy is not intended to interfere with water control in the operation of cranberry bogs or blueberry production," N.J.A.C. 7:9B-1.5(d)(6)(ii)(1), but contend that that provision was meant to exempt review of water flows, *i.e.*, quantity, and not the chemical content of the water. *Cf. Jefferson County, supra,* 511 U.S. at 718–20 (1994) (holding State of Washington could condition required CWA project certification on quantity of water removed).

The question before the Court, then, is whether the exemption provided in N.J.A.C. 7:9B-1.5(d)(6)(ii)(1) shields GP23 from antidegradation review. The Appellate Division accepted DEP's interpretation that the rule is applicable both to the quality and the quantity of water used in cranberry growing operations. Reduced to its simplest form, the question whether antidegradation review is required involves dueling interpretations of arguably ambiguous regulatory language.

Appellants rely on the United States Supreme Court decision in *Jefferson County, supra,* to support their argument that N.J.A.C. 7:9B-1.5(d)(6)(ii)(1) "only deals with the flow and volume of water." In *Jefferson County,* the Supreme Court . . . determined that states "*may* include minimum stream flow requirements" in a § 401 water quality certification "insofar as necessary to enforce a designated use contained in a state water quality standard." *Id.* at 723 (emphasis added).

It is a substantial jump from a holding that water flows may be regulated by the states under their antidegradation policies to the claim that the exemption for water control in cranberry and blueberry production found in N.J.A.C. 7:9B-1.5(d)(6)(ii)(1) applies *only* to water flows and *not* water quality. (One might ask why blueberries that are not grown in bogs would be included in an exemption that only dealt with water flows.) Moreover, an examination of the Water Pollution Control Act and its implementing regulations reveals that agricultural uses are shielded by statute and by rule from many of the requirements of the Act. As pointed out by the Appellate Division, N.J.S.A. 58:10A-6(d)(8) specifically provides DEP with the authority to exempt from NJPDES permitting requirements "discharges resulting from agriculture, including aquaculture, activities." *In re FWPA, supra,* 351 N.J. Super. at 383. In line with that grant of statutory authority, DEP has broadly exempted from those requirements "any introduction of pollutants from nonpoint source agricultural and silvicultural activities, including runoff from orchards, cultivated crops, pastures, range lands, and forest lands" and "return flows from irrigated agriculture." N.J.A.C. 7:14A-2.5(a)(4), (5).

Most important, "cranberry bog water supply and other agricultural uses" are included among the designated uses of PL, or pinelands waters. N.J.A.C. 7:9B-1.12(b). A broad reading of the exemption is consistent therefore with the goals of the SWQS—to maintain and protect the existing uses of the waters of this State. N.J.A.C. 7:9B-1.5(d)(2); see N.J.A.C. 7:9B-1.5(a)(2) ("It is the policy of the State . . . to enhance the domestic, municipal, recreational, industrial, agricultural and other reasonable uses of the State's waters."). Given the favored status accorded both agriculture generally (by the Water Pollution Control Act) and cranberry agriculture in particular (by the Pinelands Protection Act), DEP's broad interpretation of the N.J.A.C. 7:9B-1.5(d)(6)(ii)(1) exemption is reasonable. . . We find that the state antidegradation policy has not been violated by the adoption of GP23.

JUSTICE ZAZZALI, concurring:

. . .I am persuaded that appellants' interpretation of N.J.A.C. 7:9B-1.5(d)(6)(ii)(1) better serves the express intent of New Jersey's antidegradation policy to give pinelands waters the highest level of protection from changes in water quality. . . Notwithstanding my preference for appellants' reading of the regulation, I recognize that "our task is not to decide which among several competing interpretations best serves the regulatory purpose." *Thomas Jefferson Univ. v. Shalala*, 512 U.S. 504, 512 (1994). I therefore reluctantly concur in the Court's opinion. If DEP has erred, as I believe it has, it is the Legislature that must take corrective action.

NOTES & QUESTIONS

1. Environmental law has been reluctant to regulate most farming operations. "Some laws, while not expressly exempting or even mentioning farms, are structured in such a way that farms escape most if not all of the regulatory impact. Other laws expressly exempt farms from regulatory programs that would otherwise clearly apply to them." J.B. Ruhl, *Farms, Their Environmental Harms, and Environmental Law*, 27 ECOLOGY L.Q. 263, 293 (2000). How does the New Jersey Supreme Court's decision fit into this understanding? Why are farming operations treated differently from other activities that affect wetlands or other ecosystems?

2. In June 2012, the Environmental Law Institute (ELI) issued a report entitled "Subsidies With Responsibilities: Placing Stewardship and Disclosure Conditions on Government Payments to Large-Scale Commodity Crop Operations." The report found that "[t]here is no reason to believe that environmental harm is intended, or that agricultural producers are uninterested in conservation. Indeed, many agricultural operations implement stewardship practices that can and do mitigate environmental damage. Yet pollution resulting from commodity crop production—in particular, nutrient pollution—remains a significant, national problem that must be more effectively addressed." Id. at 7. ELI's two recommendations for addressing the problem are (1) "large-scale commodity crop operations that opt to receive any form of federal farm subsidy, including federally subsidized crop insurance, assume responsibility for implementing a set of baseline stewardship measures to reduce pollution," and (2) "large-scale commodity crop operations that opt to receive any form of federal farm subsidy, including federally subsidized crop insurance, assume responsibility for publicly disclosing information about their application of fertilizers." Id. at 9. Is Congress likely to adopt those recommendations, despite the historic reluctance to regulate pollution from agricultural activities? Can you propose any other recommendations that would reduce agricultural pollution and its effects on biodiversity?

3. Perhaps the most familiar narrative in the history of environmental law focused upon the harms that farming practices can cause to biodiversity. In *Silent Spring*, Rachel Carson warned that DDT and the other chemicals that had been praised for facilitating the post-World War II agricultural revolution were also killing birds, fish, and wildlife while threatening human health in new and insidious ways. Carson's book elaborated upon earlier fears that DDT was destroying wildlife populations, notably wiping out bald eagle and peregrine falcon populations by thinning their eggs. Congress responded by enacting the Federal Insecticide, Fungicide, Rodenticide Act (FIFRA), which attempts to achieve the benefits gained by the appropriate use of a pesticide while prohibiting "unreasonable adverse effects on the environment." 7 U.S.C. § 136a(c)(5)(C). The heart of FIFRA is to mandate the registration and labeling of pesticides. The registration provisions are designed to ensure that a pesticide is only used in the amount, method, purposes, and places in which it is effective. Labeling, in turn, both instructs farmers in the proper application of a particular pesticide and warns of the dangers of being exposed to the pesticide. In short, the goal of the regulatory exercise is kill the pests while leaving the wildlife that we prefer unharmed.

C. RECREATIONAL AREAS

Americans love the outdoors. Indeed, we may be loving it to death. Golfing, skiing, fishing, scuba diving, camping, rafting, mountain biking, hiking, jet skiing, horseback riding, hunting, snowmobiling, and other outdoor recreations expose their enthusiasts to the splendor of nature, no doubt committing millions of people to conservation values, but at what cost to the ecosystems within which these activities take place? Recall, for example, the devastation offroad vehicle recreation use caused the desert canyon in the *Sierra Club v. Clark* case covered in chapter 12's section on desert ecosystems. The court there noted that extensive recreational usage had caused severe environmental damage in the form of major surface erosion, soil compaction, and heavy loss of vegetation. Is this kind of intense recreation a serious challenge to ecosystem management?

That question has been posed with increasing frequency on public lands, where the gradual withdrawal of public forests, lakes, grasslands, and other resources from commercial extractive uses has, ironically, opened the door to different kind of conflict. Past conflicts, many of which are recounted in earlier chapters in this text, focused on the ecological cost of logging, mining, and other traditional industries that dominated on public lands under the "multiple use" policy. For both economic and political reasons, however, those uses are in sharp decline, leading to increased commercial opportunity in the form of recreation and tourism. For example, the Forest Service estimates that of the national forests system's $130 billion annual contribution to the national economy, over $100 billion is attributable to recreation in the system's 23,000 recreation sites, 133,000 miles of trails, and 380,000 miles of roads.

But recreation is not ecologically cost-free. Mountain bikes rut out trails; snowmobile engines emit pollutants; and horses pollute in obvious ways. One or two of each a day may not be a problem along a mountain trail, but recreational usage on public lands has skyrocketed in the past decade, with no end in sight. It is not clear that the host ecosystems can withstand larger and larger onslaughts of tourists and recreationists without suffering injury to fundamental ecosystem dynamics. Indeed, even the personal experience of "being in the woods" has changed. The solitary hiker and canoeist is now hardly visible among the waves of mountain bikes and traffic jams of rubber rafts found in many public parks. To the traditionalist, fun in the wild has been trampled by wild fun. Thus, as Professor Jan Laitos and Thomas Carr have observed, "the looming conflict in public land use will be between two former allies—recreation and preservation interests. Such a conflict is particularly likely to arise between low-impact, human-powered recreational users (preservationists) and high-impact, motorized recreational users (recreationists)." Jan G. Laitos & Thomas A. Carr, *The Transformation on Public Lands*, 26 ECOLOGY L.Q. 140 (1999).

Mausolf v. Babbitt

United States Court of Appeals for the Eighth Circuit, 1997.
125 F.3d 661.

■ BOWMAN, J. The Voyageurs Region National Park Association and other conservation groups (collectively, "the Association") appeal from the decision of the District Court granting summary judgment to the Minnesota United Snowmobilers Association, Jeffrey Mausolf, and other individual snowmobiling enthusiasts ("the Snowmobilers"), who sued the Secretary of the Interior and other governmental defendants seeking to enjoin the enforcement of restrictions on snowmobiling in Voyageurs National Park ("the Park"). See Mausolf v. Babbitt, 913 F. Supp. 1334 (D. Minn. 1996). We postponed issuing our decision in this case based on counsels' representations at oral argument that the parties hoped to negotiate a settlement. It appears, however, that the parties have been unable to reach an agreement, necessitating our resolution of this matter. We reverse.

I.

Establishment of Voyageurs National Park was authorized in 1971. See Pub. L. 91–661, 84 Stat. 1970 (codified as amended at 16 U.S.C. §§ 160-160k (1994)). Snowmobiling, which had been engaged in freely both prior to and after the Park's establishment, continued pending the results of wildlife-impact studies conducted by the National Park Service (NPS). Although snowmobiling generally is prohibited in national parks, see 36 C.F.R. § 2.18(c) (1996), the Voyageurs Park enabling legislation authorized the Secretary of the Interior to permit snowmobiling in the Park. See 16 U.S.C. § 160h (1994) ("The Secretary may, when planning for development of the park, include appropriate provisions for (1) winter sports, including the use of snowmobiles. . .") In 1991, the NPS issued regulations, pursuant to statutory authority granted by Congress, see, e.g., 16 U.S.C. § 3 (1994), based on the results of a series of environmental-and wildlife-impact reports, allowing snowmobiling on nearly all of the Park's lake surfaces and on certain overland trails and portage routes. See 36 C.F.R. § 7.33(b). These regulations also specifically authorize the superintendent of Voyageurs National Park to close portions of the Park temporarily after "taking into consideration . . . wildlife management, . . . and park management objectives." Id. § 7.33(b)(3). . .

In August 1991, the NPS . . . proposed a draft wilderness plan which reduced the Park areas available for overland snowmobiling but permitted the activity on major lakes, some designated portage routes, and the Chain of Lakes Trail. The NPS made this recommendation after concluding that snowmobiling on overland trails might adversely impact the gray wolf population. The NPS then requested a "biological opinion" from the Fish and Wildlife Service (FWS) concerning the effects, if any, of the proposed action on gray wolf, bald eagle, and other animal populations in the Park. In March 1992, the FWS concluded that the NPS's proposed wilderness plan would not jeopardize the animals' survival or adversely affect their critical habitats. However, the FWS acknowledged that snowmobiler disruption of wolves while hunting prey, although likely insignificant in isolation, could lead to cumulatively significant negative effects if the disruptions were frequent. The FWS directed that the NPS close specific trails, lakeshores, and lakes to snowmobiles and other motorized vehicles, including areas that had been exempted from closure under the NPS's originally submitted wilderness plan.

Thereafter, in December 1992, Park officials issued an order closing sixteen of the Park's lake bays and certain shoreline areas to snowmobiling pursuant to authority granted under 36 C.F.R. § 7.33(b)(3) (authorizing temporary closure of lake surfaces for wildlife-management purposes). This order, which was renewed in 1993 and 1994, reduced the Park areas available for snowmobiling. In 1994, the FWS supplemented its biological opinion, stating that the lakeshore closures were designed to minimize the harm, harassment, and taking of gray wolves. The FWS, expressing its intent to reduce adverse human/wolf contact, explained that while snowmobiles themselves do not adversely impact the gray wolf, the vehicles provide access to remote wolf-habitat areas for individuals who could intentionally or unwittingly harm the species or its individual members. Five "incidents that constitute take by the harassment or harming of gray wolves," and "numerous additional reports of harassment of gray wolves, . . . most of which are anecdotal and not well documented," were cited by the FWS as support for the closures. The FWS revised its initial incidental take statement, reducing the permissible number of incidental takings of gray wolves from six wolves to two wolves per year.

In January 1994, the Snowmobilers sued the Secretary of the Interior and other governmental defendants claiming that the FWS's biological opinion did not support the closures ultimately ordered, and that the closures were therefore arbitrary, capricious, and in violation of the Endangered Species Act, 16 U.S.C. §§ 1531–1544 (1994) (ESA), and the Administrative Procedure Act, 5 U.S.C. §§ 701–706 (1994) (APA)...

Snowmobiling is a prohibited activity in national parks except where the NPS has promulgated special regulations designating areas open to snowmobiling, and even then it is allowed only where such "use is consistent with ... park management objectives, and will not disturb wildlife or damage park resources." 36 C.F.R. § 2.18(c). Congress endowed the Secretary of the Interior with discretion to permit snowmobiling in Voyageurs National Park when statutes establishing the Park were enacted: "The Secretary may, when planning for development of the park, include appropriate provisions for (1) winter sports, including the use of snowmobiles. . ." 16 U.S.C. § 160h (1994). Consistent with the NPS's responsibility to manage and regulate Park resources, the NPS has been given wide latitude to make management decisions regarding the type and scope of activities permitted on Park property...

The regulations designating routes for snowmobiling within the Park specifically grant the Park Superintendent the discretion temporarily to close routes and lake surfaces to snowmobiling after taking into consideration, among other factors, park management objectives. The 1992 Park closure order, on its face, declares that the order was issued "under the authority of Title 36, Code of Federal Regulations, Chapter 1, Section 7.33(b)(3)." This order was renewed in 1993, and in 1994, again under the authority granted the Superintendent under § 7.33(b)(3) to mandate temporary closures to effectuate park management objectives.

The Snowmobilers argue that the challenged Park closures are outside the Superintendent's authority under § 7.33(b)(3) because there is no stated time limit on the closure order. However, these orders are issued as temporary, annual directives that must be reviewed and either renewed or repealed through yearly compendiums establishing the management goals for the Park. Nothing in the language of the closure order indicates that it is intended to operate as a permanent closure and, because the orders are issued annually, the closures will be reviewed and either renewed or modified on a yearly basis. Before the District Court enjoined enforcement of the closure order, the NPS, in conjunction with the FWS, was conducting just such a review to determine the benefits, if any, the closures have had on the wolf population and to determine whether the closures should be maintained, modified, or rescinded. Consistent with its past practice, we hold that, under 36 C.F.R. § 7.33(b)(3), the NPS must conduct, at minimum, an annual review if snowmobile trails are to be closed "temporarily" and such decisions must be supported by the record. The annual closure order is not outside the Superintendent's authority for lack of a specific time limit.

As we have previously noted, agency actions are entitled to a great deal of deference and a "reviewing court may not set aside an agency rule that is rational, based on consideration of the relevant factors and within the scope of the authority delegated to the agency by the statute." Motor Vehicle Mfrs. Ass'n v. State Farm Mut. Auto. Ins. Co., 463 U.S. 29, 42 (1983). A reviewing court "may not substitute its own construction of a statutory provision for a reasonable interpretation made by the administrator of an agency." Id. at 43. This is not to say that the Superintendent's discretion to order Park closures is without limit. It must be exercised with an eye toward promoting specific regulatory objectives such as "protection of environmental or scenic values" or "protection of natural or cultural resources," 36 C.F.R. § 1.5(a), and it is subject to the arbitrary-and-capricious standard of review. Whether an agency's action is arbitrary and capricious depends on whether "the agency has . . . offered an explanation for its decision that runs counter to the evidence before the agency, or is so implausible that it could not be ascribed to a difference in view or the product of agency expertise." Motor Vehicle Mfrs. Ass'n, 463 U.S. at 43.

Applying this standard to the Park closure order, we cannot say that the NPS's decision is arbitrary and capricious. The evidence in the administrative record, while not overwhelming, is sufficient to provide a rational foundation on which the NPS could base its closure order. The NPS issued its closure order under authority granted by § 7.33(b)(3) to close portions of the Park temporarily in order to further management objectives—including preservation and protection of wildlife. This conclusion was reached after consultation with the FWS and was based on biological opinions and incidental take statements issued by that agency. These reports are contained in the administrative record and establish that the closures may prevent some incidental takings of gray wolves.

In its 1992 biological opinion, the FWS noted that the use of snowmobiles in areas of concentrated gray wolf activity "has been observed to cause the temporary disruption of gray wolf [feeding] activity." While the FWS concluded that this type of disruption was insignificant in isolation, it determined that continued disruption of feeding activity by snowmobiles could have significant, negative cumulative effects on individual wolves, especially during severe winters when prey availability dwindles. In its 1994 supplement to this biological opinion, the FWS noted that "several cases of harassment and harming of gray [wolves] have been reported within the Park in past years," and that "in each documented case, access was gained to gray wolf habitat by motorized vehicle." The FWS concluded that "the problem lies with providing human access to gray wolf habitat that would not be provided without motorized vehicles." A number of specific incidents are recounted, along with anecdotal evidence that harassment of gray wolves is not "an unheard of event." While this evidence is not definitive, it does provide a rational basis on which the NPS could have concluded that the Park closures were a reasonable solution to the problem of gray wolf harassment.

The absence of definitive, irrefutable evidence in the record to establish the adverse connection between snowmobiling and incidental taking of gray wolves is not fatal to the NPS's closure order, since a reviewing court "will uphold a decision of less than ideal clarity if the agency's path may reasonably be discerned." We conclude that the evidence in the administrative record on which the NPS based its decision to order the Park closures was sufficient to justify the determination and that the action was not arbitrary or capricious.

Because the administrative record supports the closures as measures taken to protect wildlife under 36 C.F.R. § 7.33(b)(3), and under other regulatory provisions, see 36 C.F.R. §§ 1.5, 2.18, we reverse the judgment of the District Court and direct that judgment be entered in favor of the federal defendants and the intervenors.

NOTES & QUESTIONS

1. In *Mausolf*, the court upheld a government decision that pleased one group (environmentalists) while disappointing another (recreationists). Before it do so, though, the court held in an earlier ruling that the concerned environmental groups could formally intervene in the litigation. The district court had denied the motion to intervene because it concluded that the government could adequately represent the concerns of the environmentalists, but the Eighth Circuit disagreed:

> The Snowmobilers insist that the Government, like the Association, is interested in protecting wildlife and in upholding environmental regulations. This is true; it does not, however, answer the Association's objection that this interest is not adequately represented by the Government in this case. Unlike the Association, the Government is "obliged to represent . . . all of its citizens." When managing and regulating public lands, to avoid what economists call the "tragedy of the commons," the Government must inevitably favor certain uses over others. The Park was established for both recreational and conservationist purposes. Voyageurs National Park Act, 16 U.S.C. § 160 et seq. These purposes will sometimes, unavoidably, conflict, and even the Government cannot always adequately represent conflicting interests at the same time. In this case, the Government's interest in promoting recreational activity and tourism in the Park, an interest many citizens share, may be adverse to the Association's conservation interests, interests also shared by many.

Mausolf v. Babbitt, 85 F.3d 1295, 1303–04 (8th Cir. 1996). How do the government's responsibilities differ from other landowners? How should it avert the tragedy of the commons?

2. Snowmobiling is also a contested issue in Yellowstone National Park. Established on March 1, 1872, Yellowstone was the first national park and was included as one of the original parks under the Park Service's jurisdiction in the Organic Act. Indeed, Yellowstone is the first and oldest national park in the world. Preserved within its boundaries are Old Faithful Geyser and over 10,000 hot springs and geysers, the majority of the planet's total. Yellowstone is also home of the grizzly bear, wolf, and free-ranging herds of bison and elk, the park's 2.2 million acres form the core of the Greater Yellowstone Ecosystem, one of the largest intact temperate zone ecosystems remaining on the planet.

Yellowstone was designated an International Biosphere Reserve on October 26, 1976, and a World Heritage Site on September 8, 1978.

Yellowstone is a popular spot for tourists, too. Over 2.7 million recreation visits were made to the park in 2001 (the record is over 3.1 million in 1992). About 140,000 visits are made to the park during an average winter, most prominently for snowmobiling. Take it from your authors, snowmobiling is *a lot* of fun. But besides being speedy and noisy, snowmobiles also pollute heavily. The two-stroke engines used on older snowmobiles are woefully inefficient, burning less than half of the fuel and dumping the rest into the environment. Such a snowmobile emits more than 100 times as much pollution as a car in the same amount of running time. Given these characteristics, it is no wonder that the growing concentration of snowmobiling in Yellowstone led eventually to an air pollution problem. In 2002, for example, the Park Service provided employees in certain areas of the park with respirators to combat poor air quality attributable to snowmobiles. The Park Service estimates that snowmobiles produce up to 68 percent of Yellowstone's carbon monoxide pollution and 90 percent of the hydrocarbon emissions. *See* NATIONAL PARK SERVICE, AIR QUALITY CONCERNS RELATED TO SNOWMOBILE USAGE IN NATIONAL PARKS (2000).

So should snowmobiles be allowed in Yellowstone and other national parks? Environmental protection interests argue that mass transit snow coaches can deliver people into the park's winter wonderland efficiently and with far less ecological impact. Snowmobile interests defend their "right" of personal access and argue that technological improvements in snowmobile performance can solve the problem. This conflict has festered since the 1990s, with policy flip-flops and rhetorical assaults characteristic of the many other ecosystem management issues studied in this text. The National Park Service, Congress, and the courts have produced conflicting plans and decisions governing the permissible number and type of snowmobiles and when and where they can be ridden. *See generally* Wyoming v. United States DOI, 674 F.3d 12 (10th Cir. 2012) (summarizing the procedural history); MICHAEL J. YOCHIM, YELLOWSTONE AND THE SNOWMOBILE: LOCKING HORNS OVER NATIONAL PARK USE (2009). A final resolution to the dispute is nowhere in sight.

Florida Marine Contractors v. Williams

United States District Court for the Middle District of Florida, 2005.
378 F. Supp. 2d 1353.

■ MOODY, DISTRICT JUDGE.

This case involves the scope of the Marine Mammal Protection Act, 16 U.S.C. § 1361 *et seq.* (the "Act"), and specifically whether the environmental protections contained therein apply to recreational docks built on Florida's inland waterways. Plaintiffs are land owners, marine contractors, and a marine contractors' industry association seeking permits (on their own behalf or on the behalf of others) to construct docks and other similar structures (hereafter "docks") on Florida's inland waterways that are inhabited by Florida manatees. These docks will be used by property owners for recreational purposes, including the operation of recreational motorboats from the docks to other nearby bodies of water and the docking of these motorboats when they are not in use.

Plaintiffs applied for building permits for the docks with the appropriate state authorities, who forwarded the applications to the U.S. Army Corps of Engineers ("Corps") for federal permitting pursuant to Section 404 of the Clean Water Act, 33 U.S.C. § 1344. Because the Corps determined that the issuance of the permits might threaten the West Indian manatee, commonly known as the Florida manatee, it consulted with the Fish and Wildlife Service (the "Service") in accordance with Section 7 of the Endangered Species Act, 16 U.S.C. § 1536, and the regulations promulgated thereunder. The Service, in turn, had to determine whether the issuance of the permits was prohibited by Section 1371(a)(5)(A) of the Act since "an endangered species or threatened species of a marine mammal was involved." *See* 16 U.S.C. § 1536(b)(4)(C); 16 U.S.C. § 1362(6)(defining "marine mammal" as including members of the order Sirenia); 50 C.F.R. § 23.23 (identifying the West Indian manatee as a member of the order Sirenia).

After studying the proposed construction plans at each proposed site, the Service concluded that the building and intended use of the docks would result in the "incidental taking" of the Florida manatee. Additionally, the Service reasoned that the construction of the docks and the operation of motorboats to and from these structures would have more than a "negligible impact" on the Florida manatee species, due to the absence of necessary precautions such as speed zones, sign postings, and enforcement that would protect the manatees in the area from being harmed. The Service concluded, therefore, that Plaintiffs' permit applications should be denied. *See* 16 U.S.C. § 1371(a)(5)(A) (authorizing the issuance of permits to U.S. citizens permitting recreational activities that would cause the incidental taking of protected marine mammals only if the Service finds, *inter alia,* that the "total of such taking . . . will have a negligible impact on such species").

Plaintiffs filed this action pursuant to the Administrative Procedures Act, 5 U.S.C. §§ 706, after being notified that their permit applications were denied. This statute authorizes federal courts to review a federal agency's interpretation of a federal statute. Plaintiffs do not challenge the Service's findings that the issuance of the permits ultimately would have more than a negligible impact on the Florida manatees inhabiting the creeks, rivers and other internal waters where the docks would be built. Plaintiffs' sole contention, rather, is that the Act does not apply to residential docks built on Florida's inland waters, and, therefore, the Service unlawfully applied the Act's provisions to deny their permit applications. Because the dispute is exclusively one of statutory construction, the parties agree that the case should be resolved based on their respective motions for summary judgment.

II. Marine Mammal Protection Act

The Act was passed by Congress to protect marine mammal species and population stocks that are or may be "in danger of extinction or depletion as a result of man's activities." 16 U.S.C. § 1361(1). *Section 1361* enumerates the congressional findings on which Congress relied in passing the Act, and announces the policies intended to be served by its enactment. The aim of Congress was to prevent marine mammals from "diminishing beyond the point at which they cease to be a significant functioning element in the ecosystem of which they are a part, and . . . below their optimum sustainable population." 16 U.S.C. § 1361(2). In furtherance of this purpose, Congress declared that "efforts should be made to protect essential habitats, including the rookeries, mating grounds, and areas of similar significance for each species. . . from the adverse effect of man's actions." *Id.* Having found that "marine mammals [are] resources of great international significance, esthetic and recreational as well as economic," Congress also declared that "they should be protected and encouraged to develop to the greatest extent feasible commensurate with sound policies of resource management . . . [and] it should be the goal to obtain an optimum sustainable population keeping in mind the carrying capacity of the habitat." 16 U.S.C. § 1361(6).

Congress used several methods to further these objectives. First, Congress declared in *Section 1371* that "there shall be a moratorium on the taking and importation of marine mammals and marine mammal products, commencing on the effective date of this chapter, during which time no permit may be issued for the taking of any marine mammal . . ." By "moratorium," Congress meant "a complete cessation" of the taking of marine mammals. 16 U.S.C. § 1362(8).

Section 1371 contains a number of exceptions to and exemptions from this general moratorium, allowing the issuance of permits under certain limited circumstances for scientific research; for the taking of marine mammals "incidentally in the course of commercial fishing operations;" for takings that are "in accord with sound principles of resource protection and conservation as provided in the purposes and policies" set forth in *Section 1361*; and under circumstances where the "incidental, but not intentional, taking by citizens. . .of small numbers of marine mammals. . . will have a negligible impact on such species or stock. . ." 16 U.S.C. §§ 1371(a)(1), (a)(2), (a)(3)(A) and (a)(5)(A).

Exemptions from the moratorium are given to Alaskan natives, persons acting in self defense and in defense of property, "Good Samaritans," and for citizens employed on foreign fishing vessels operating outside the "United States exclusive economic zone." 16 U.S.C. §§ 1371(a)(4)(A), (b), (c), (d) and (e). Apart from these enumerated exceptions and exemptions, *Section 1371* does not contain any limitations on the scope of the moratorium, geographic or otherwise.

In addition to the moratorium set forth in *Section 1371*, Congress enacted *Section 1372* which makes it "unlawful" for persons to take any marine mammal. *Section 1372* generally prohibits the taking, possession, transportation, sale, exportation or importation of any marine mammal or marine mammal product. *See generally* 16 U.S.C. § 1372. Unlike *Section 1371*, the provisions in *Section 1372* address the geographic scope of the prohibitions. For example, *Section 1372(a)(1)* makes it unlawful for "any person . . . vessel or other conveyance subject to the jurisdiction of the United States to take any marine mammal on the high seas." The provisions of *Section 1372(a)(2)(A)* make it unlawful for "any person or vessel or other conveyance to take any marine mammal in waters or on lands under the jurisdiction of the United States." *Section 1372(a)(2)(B)* prohibit persons from "using any port, harbor, or other place under the jurisdiction of the United States to take or import marine mammals or marine mammal products."

Congress also included in the Act a grant of exclusive jurisdiction over the conservation and management of marine mammals to the federal government. 16 U.S.C. § 1379. Under *Section 1379(a)*, Congress usurped state authority over the regulation of marine mammals by prohibiting the States from enforcing or attempting to enforce "any State law or regulation relating to the taking of any species . . . of marine mammal within the State." *Section 1379(b)* allows for the conditional transfer of the federal government's authority to a State that has developed its own program "consistent with the purposes, policies and goals" of the Act. 16 U.S.C. § 1379(b)(1)(A). These transfers can occur if the State's management and conservation program "does not permit the taking of the species unless and until the State has determined . . . that the species is at its optimum sustainable population" and the State's program does not permit the number of animals of the species to be reduced below their optimum sustainable population. 16 U.S.C. § 1379(b)(1)(C) and (D).

III. Analysis

The only issue for consideration is whether the Service properly determined that Plaintiffs' permit applications should be denied. As noted in part I above, the dispute in this case involves the meaning of the Act's provisions. Plaintiffs believe the environmental protections of the Act do not apply to recreational activities on Florida's inland waters, and, therefore, argue that the Service lacked the administrative authority to deny their permit applications. Defendants contend, conversely, that they are entitled to summary judgment because the Act applies to the circumstances of this case. . .

As mentioned above, *Section 1371* prohibits the issuance of permits that allow for the taking of marine mammals during the time of the moratorium, unless the permit may be issued pursuant to one of the exceptions in the section. The exception in *Section 1371(a)(5)(A)* grants the Service the authority to allow "citizens of the United States who engage in a specified activity (other than commercial fishing) within a specified geographical region" to engage in that activity if the "incidental" taking of marine mammals caused thereby only has a "negligible impact" on the marine mammal species. 16 U.S.C. § 1371(a)(5)(A).

Plaintiffs do not contend that the exception for takings in *Section 1371(a)(5)(A)* applies to them. Plaintiffs simply argue that the Act does not apply to takings that occur in a state's inland waters when such takings are caused by recreational activities. The "precise question at issue," therefore, is whether *Section 1371* applies to a state's inland waters without limitations for hazards attributable to recreational activities. Based on the terms of *Section 1371*, and the language and design of the Act as a whole, this Court finds that Congress did address this precise question and answered it in the affirmative.

C. Congressional Intent

Congress did not explicitly state that the terms of *Section 1371* apply to a state's inland waters. The findings and policy provisions in *Section 1361*, however, demonstrate a clear congressional intent to protect marine mammals from all man-made threats in all the areas that make up their habitat. Equally clear is the intent of Congress to use *Section 1371* to carry out the objectives in *Section 1361* without any limitation based on geography or the nature of the man-made threat.

In *Section 1361*, Congress recognized that "man's activities" are endangering the existence of marine mammals and declared the "major objective" of the Act to be the prevention of marine mammal species and population stocks from "diminishing beyond the point in which they cease to be a significant functioning element *in the ecosystem of which they are apart.*" 16 U.S.C. § 1361(2) (*emphasis added*). In accordance with this major objective, Congress stated that the "optimum sustainable population" of each species and population stock should be maintained, meaning that the Act was designed to promote the "number of animals which will result in the maximum productivity of the population stock or the species, keeping in mind the carrying capacity of the habitat and the health of the ecosystem of which they form a constituent element." *See* 16 U.S.C. § 1361(2); 16 U.S.C. § 1362(9)(defining "optimum sustainable population"). Additionally, Congress noted that marine mammals are "resources of great international significance" and "should be protected and encouraged to develop to the greatest extent feasible commensurate with sound policies of resource management and that the primary objective of their management should be to maintain the health and stability of the marine ecosystem."

These provisions demonstrate in unambiguous terms that the purpose of the *Act* is to stop the artificial depletion of marine mammals by man's activities so that the optimum number of animals for each marine mammal population stock and species can be achieved. Not only is there is no indication from Congress that it sought to distinguish between the different areas that make up a marine mammal's habitat or the nature of the man-made threat as part of this principal objective, such distinctions would be inapposite to the achievement of the objective. Considering marine mammal habitats in their entirety and eliminating all artificial dangers contained therein was clearly a part of Congress' objective, because natural habitats free from all unnatural hazards are what determine the marine mammals' "optimum sustainable population."

This conclusion that the Act was designed to protect marine mammals from all man-made threats in all the areas inhabited by them, including a state's internal waters, is not only consistent with the terms of *Section 1361* and logically sound, it is supported by the provisions in *Section 1379* granting the federal government exclusive jurisdiction over the conservation and management of marine mammals. Because Congress prohibited the States from enforcing or attempting to enforce any State laws or regulations relating to the taking of any marine mammal "within the State," Congress clearly expected the protections of the Act to apply to all areas within the states, including internal waters. *See* 16 U.S.C. § 1379(a). Plaintiffs' suggestion that the Act does not apply to these areas actually weakens the legal protections offered to marine mammals by nullifying applicable state laws and not replacing them with any federal law. This interpretation produces a rather absurd result for a federal law clearly designed to optimize the number of marine mammals that exist in each population stock or species.

The Act's legislative history also conflicts with Plaintiff's interpretation of the statute. Congress declared that "the purpose of this legislation is to prohibit the harassing, catching and killing of marine mammals by U.S. citizens *or within the jurisdiction of the United States . . ." (emphasis added)*. With respect to Florida manatees in particular, the legislative history demonstrates that Congress understood the operation of recreational motorboats to be one of the principal causes of the artificially low numbers of manatees, and it designed the Act to protect manatees from this hazard in the areas that make up their habitats. *See* 1972 H.R. Rep. No. 92-707 (1972), *reprinted in* 1972 U.S.C.C.A.N. 4144, 4147-4150 (noting that "manatees . . . have been . . . run down by boats . . . and exposed to a multitude of other indignities, all in the interests of profit and recreation;" acknowledging "the operation of powerboats in areas where the manatees are found" as one of the principal hazards to which manatees are exposed; and announcing that "at present the Federal government is essentially powerless to force these boats to slow down or curtail their operations").

Faced with these statements in the legislative history, Plaintiffs contend that the failure to include the word "all" in the phrase "in areas where manatees are found" indicates Congress sought to protect manatees only in some areas that make up the manatee habitat. This omission is insufficient to cast doubt on Congress' intent to protect marine mammals throughout their habitats. First, there is no evidence in the legislative history to support Plaintiffs' interpretation that the phrase "in areas where manatees are found" means "only some areas where manatees are found." Second, the legislative history demonstrates that Congress was aware that many marine mammals lived part of their lives outside of the sea. *Id.* at 4148 ("the bill covers all mammals who spend part or all of their lives in the sea"). With this understanding, it would seem likely that Congress would announce an intention not to protect a marine mammal in a particular area if this was its intention. Third, Plaintiffs' interpretation is inconsistent with the design of the statute as a whole, including the stated objective of the Act to achieve the optimum sustainable population for each marine mammal population stock or species and the federal preemption of state law "within" each state. Finally, there is simply no evidence in the legislative history to support Plaintiffs' theory that the application of the Act to a state's inland waters is conditioned on maritime commercial center activity.

Having determined that the clear objective of the Act is to protect marine mammals from man-made dangers in all areas that make up their natural habitat, the Court now turns to the provisions of *Section 1371*. The terms of this Section clearly demonstrate that it was designed to fulfill the principal objective Congress enumerated in *Section 1361*, without the limitations suggested by Plaintiffs.

The moratorium on takings and permits in *Section 1371* undoubtedly was designed to further the objectives set forth in *Section 1361*, for both of these measures address the ultimate cause Congress identified in that section as the threat to achieving an optimum sustainable population for marine mammals: "man's activities." Additionally, Congress used rather absolute terms to articulate this chosen method of protecting marine mammals, to wit: a "complete cessation" on the taking of marine mammals, during which time "no" permit can be issued that authorizes such activity. By modifying the term "cessation," which by itself is normally understood to mean "the act or fact of putting an end to something," *see* Websters II: New College Dictionary 975 (Houghton Mifflin Co. 1999) (defining "cessation" and "cease"), with the term "complete," Congress clearly designed *Section 1371* to end the taking of marine mammals without regard to the nature of the activity that caused the taking or the precise location within the habitat where the taking occurred.

The exceptions to the moratorium in *Section 1371* also demonstrate that the section is intended to operate to further the Act's objectives. These exceptions are either directly conditioned upon conformity with the Act's objectives, or, as with the exception at issue in this case, are limited by their very terms to avoid any conflict with these objectives. For example, the exception in *Section 1371(a)(1)* allows for the issuance of permits for takings caused by scientific research, public display, photography for education or commercial purposes, or enhancing the survival or recovery of a species or stock . . . [so long as the proposed taking] is *consistent with the purposes and policies of section 1361 of this title" (emphasis added). See also* 16 U.S.C. 1371(a)(2) (providing similar terms); 16 U.S.C. 1371(a)(3)(A) (authorizing the Secretary to waive the moratorium, provided the taking "is in accord with sound principles of resource protection and conservation *as provided in the purposes and policies of this chapter") (emphasis added). Section 1371(a)(5)(A)*, the exception applicable to this case, allows for the "incidental" takings of marine mammals "by citizens of the United States who engage in a specified activity other than commercial fishing" only if such takings have a "negligible impact on a species or stock" and if regulations are promulgated to allow for "the least practicable adverse impact on such species or stock and its habitat." *See* 16 U.S.C. § 1371(a)(5)(A); *see also* 1371(a)(5)(D)(i) (conditioning certain takings on identical terms).

The conditions and limitations incorporated into the exceptions to the moratorium ensure that the Act's overall objective of reaching an optimum sustainable population for each marine mammal population stock or species will not be compromised by activities that the government authorizes through the permit process. Additionally, the fact that the exception at issue in this case is directed at citizens engaging in activities "other than commercial fishing" undermines Plaintiffs' argument that *Section 1371* only applies to takings on inland waters if the takings are caused my maritime commercial center activities.

The legislative history also indicates that *Section 1371* in particular operates to further the Act's objectives without limitations, and accordingly applies to all man-made threats and all the areas that make up the marine mammals' habitats. Congress explained that the purpose of the Act was to prevent takings of marine mammals, "unless taken under the authority of a permit issued by an agency of the Executive Branch." 1972 H.R. REP. NO. 92-707 (1972), *reprinted in* 1972 U.S.C.C.A.N. 4144. It also declared with respect to manatees in particular that passage of the Act "would provide the Secretary of the Interior with adequate authority to regulate or even forbid the use of powerboats *in waters where manatees are found . . ." (emphasis added). Id.* at 4150. Because *Section 1371* governs the Service's authority to issue or deny taking permits, these declarations along with Congress' recognition of the hazards posed by the recreational use of motorboats demonstrate that Congress expected *Section 1371* to apply to activities of any nature and in the areas that constitute a marine mammal's habitat.

Plaintiffs' argument that the provision in *Section 1372* should be engrafted onto *Section 1371* is belied by the unambiguous design of the statute as a whole and *Section 1371* in particular. As an initial matter, this Court is not convinced that the terms of *Section 1372* are as limited as Plaintiffs contend because these provisions also must be construed in the context of the statute as a whole. The legislative history appears to contradict Plaintiff's interpretation of *Section 1372* because it indicates that Congress expected the prohibitions to create a moratorium for at least two years that would prohibit any taking of a marine mammal without a permit. *Id.* at 4153; *see* United States v. Mitchell, 553 F.2d 996, 1000 (1977) ("the Committed reasoned that a de facto moratorium would develop from the prohibitions because any taking without a permit would be deemed unlawful). Even assuming Plaintiffs' reading of *Section 1371* is correct, nothing in *Section 1371*, *Section 1372* or the legislative history supports Plaintiffs' argument. . .

IV. Conclusion

The terms and design of the Act, along with the legislative history, demonstrate clearly that Congress identified man's activities as the undesirable cause of marine mammals' artificially low numbers, and recognized these activities as being both commercial and recreational in nature. Congress' objective was unmistakable: to protect marine mammals from these artificial hazards so that their numbers can reach and maintain equilibrium with their natural habitats. The "complete cessation" on takings and the provisions governing the issuance of permits established in *Section 1371* was clearly designed to further this objective. To hold that *Section 1371* does not extend to certain areas inhabited by marine mammals would divorce this section from the Act's objective by permitting "man's activities" of a recreational nature to continue unabated in areas making up marine mammal habitats. Because the Service's construction and application of the Act is in accord with the unambiguously expressed intent of Congress, the decision to deny Plaintiffs' permits must be upheld.

NOTES & QUESTIONS

1. The MMPA affords federal protection to manatees whether they are endangered or not. What's so special about marine mammals?

2. Besides MMPA regulations, manatees are also protected by a network of seven federal manatee sanctuaries and five state manatee protection zones. "This network was designed to prevent the take of manatees by waterborne activities, including but not limited to, boating and manatee viewing activities, and was established to allow manatees to continue to gain access to critical warm-water areas and important resting and foraging areas." Establishing a Manatee Refuge in Kings Bay, Citrus County, FL, 77 Fed. Reg. 15617, 15617 (2012). But the establishment of such refuges is controversial. In its latest rulemaking on the subject, the FWS received a comment complaining that "a manatee refuge will stop all boating activity and recreation." *Id.* at 15622. The agency responded that "will not stop all boating and recreational activity. It provides for specific prohibitions, including speed and anchoring restrictions, time and area prohibitions, and prohibited activities such as chasing manatees, to avoid and minimize the harassment of manatees. However, boating, fishing, kayaking, and other forms of recreation are still allowed within all or portions of the manatee refuge, except in manatee sanctuaries and temporary no entry areas while they are in effect, as defined in the rule portion of this regulation." Id. Another comment asserted that "[t]he proposed designation of Kings Bay as a manatee refuge infringes on property rights of homeowners that own property on the banks of Kings Bay." *Id.* Or, as the leader of the Citrus County Tea Party put it, "We cannot elevate nature above people. That's against the Bible and the Bill of Rights." Craig Pittman, *Tea Party Members Tackle a New Issue: Manatees*, TAMPA BAY TIMES, July 13, 2011 (quoting Edna Mattos). The agency explained that the rule requiring boating permits contained "exceptions to all riparian property homeowners (their guests, employees, and designees including contractors and lessees) whose property adjoins a manatee sanctuary or no-entry area so they can retain their watercraft access and conduct property maintenance." *Id.* Would you be satisfied with these answers if you wanted to engage in recreational boating in the area? Would you be satisfied if you wanted to visit the area to see the manatees?

3. In its draft environmental assessment for the Kings Bay Manatee Refuge, the FWS asked "[h]ow much are Florida residents willing to pay to cover the costs associated with protecting the manatee?" The agency found that "[i]n 1993 dollars, efforts to protect the manatee population were valued at an estimated $2.6 billion or $14.78 per household (or $4.03 billion or $22.91 per household, when adjusted to reflect 2011 monetary values). Based on surveys of north Florida residents, Fishkind and Associates estimated that adult Florida residents would be willing to pay $30 per year in 1992 dollars (or $47.70 per year when adjusted to reflect 2011 monetary values) to help compensate for the adverse economic effects, if any, of protecting the manatee population." U.S. Dep't of the Interior, FWS Region 4, Draft Environmental Assessment for the

Proposed Kings Bay Manatee Refuge, Crystal River, Florida, at 33 (2011). Should everyone who is willing to pay to protect manatees pay everyone who is unable to engage in recreational boating? For a colorful recounting of the debate, see CRAIG PITTMAN, MANATEE INSANITY: INSIDE THE WAR OVER FLORIDA'S MOST ENDANGERED SPECIES (2010).

Sierra Club v. Commissioner of the Department of Environmental Management

Supreme Judicial Court of Massachusetts, 2003.
791 N.E.2d 325.

■ SPINA, J. The Sierra Club and others (plaintiffs) brought an action . . . seeking declaratory relief against the Secretary (Secretary) of the Executive Office of Environmental Affairs (EOEA), relating to his certificate approving the Supplemental Final Environmental Impact Report (SFEIR) submitted by Wachusett Mountain Associates, Inc. (WMA), for the expansion of facilities at the Wachusett Mountain Ski Area within the Wachusett Mountain State Reservation (reservation). . . The reservation consists of approximately 2,000 acres of land, mostly forested, located in the towns of Princeton and Westminster. Established in 1899 and owned by the Commonwealth, the reservation is managed by the division of forests and parks within the department. In 1958, the Legislature authorized the development of publicly operated ski areas at State reservations and other lands. Various entities operated the ski area at the reservation from 1962 until 1969, when WMA successfully bid for a five-year contract to operate the ski area. Statute 1977, c. 287, authorized the commissioner to enter into a thirty-year renewable lease of "a portion of land on Wachusett Mountain State reservation, for the support of skiing facilities . . . [on] four hundred and fifty acres, more or less." After environmental review under the terms of G.L. c. 30, §§ 61-62H (Massachusetts Environmental Policy Act or MEPA), a commissioner entered into a thirty-year lease for the ski area with WMA.

In 1993, WMA, hoping to expand the ski area by adding new ski trails and widening existing ski trails within the 450 acres under lease, began a new MEPA review process by filing an environmental notification form (ENF) with the Secretary, which, as modified by later documents and changes, is the subject of this controversy. The MEPA review for this project lasted about six years. The plans underwent a significant change when a large area of "old growth forest"[4] was discovered on the slopes of Mt. Wachusett. As a result, WMA modified the proposed location of new ski trails to place all new clearing and widening of ski trails outside of the area where the old growth forest is located, and it filed a corresponding notice of project change.

---

[4] "Old growth forests" are defined in the department's old growth policy (OGP) as stands of trees greater than five to ten acres in area, with no significant sign of human post-European settlement disturbances, with a component of trees that are greater than 50% of the maximum longevity for the particular species, and with a component of younger trees that are filling in the gaps created by natural aging and loss of the older trees. The old growth forest on Mt. Wachusett is specifically mentioned in the OGP as the "only one east of the Connecticut River ... and is the only documented old-growth stand in Massachusetts that has a significant oak component."

During the MEPA review process, in part because of the order of the Secretary to do so, and in part because the existing plans were outdated, the department began review of its resource management plan for the reservation. That review resulted in a new plan, the RMPP, that created several zoning overlays for the mountain, each of which allows, and prohibits, certain activities. The proposed improvements to the ski area are located within the biodiversity significance overlay zone, an area designated in the RMPP as an additional buffer to protect the old growth forest.

On April 1, 1999, the Secretary issued his certificate of compliance under MEPA for the SFEIR. On August 6, 1999, the commissioner issued his § 61 findings, thus completing the MEPA process and clearing the way for WMA to seek permits or approvals. On the same day, the commissioner sent a letter to the president of WMA stating that the department "has reviewed the ski lift upgrade and replacement information submitted by WMA and approves commencement of construction activities related to this aspect of the project." The plaintiffs filed their complaint on August 27, 1999, within thirty days of the issuance of a permit, as required by 301 Code Mass. Regs. § 11.14 (2) (a) (1998).

4. The SFEIR. The commissioner and the WMA argue that the judge erred by concluding that the SFEIR submitted by WMA violated G.L. c. 30, § 62B, and 301 Code Mass. Regs. § 11.07 (1998) because it failed to address the need for the proposed project, it failed to address reasonable alternatives to the new trails and widening of existing trails, and it failed sufficiently to identify and analyze the impacts of the project on the old growth forest. They contend that they were not required to address need, and that the Secretary's certification of the SFEIR was not arbitrary or capricious.

(a) Need. The judge's decision criticized the SFEIR as containing inadequate analysis or information about the need for the expansion of the ski area. Neither the MEPA statute nor the regulations contain any requirement that an EIR should include an analysis of the "need" for the project itself, or that such an analysis be incorporated in the § 61 findings. See G.L. c. 30, §§ 61-62H, and 301 Code Mass. Regs. §§ 11.00 (1998). The statute addresses "need" only as to the question of the need for an environmental impact report. G.L. c. 30, §§ 62A, 62H. Nonetheless, as is often the case, the MEPA submissions here included a variety of statements by the proponent as to its perceived need for the project. These statements included analyses of the changing demographics of skiers in the New England area, showing that the new trails would be used for snowboarders, for free-style skiing, and for ski-race training, and that the type of terrain created in the "alpine park" (including a 250- to 300-foot long "half pipe") is increasingly in demand by a growing percentage of those who use the ski area. The added benefit of increasing skier safety was also included in WMA's statements pertaining to the need for ski trails. The need for additional space in the skier services building and base lodge, increased parking, and improvements to ski lifts and ski lift capacity, as well as to water supplies and snowmaking equipment, were all detailed throughout the MEPA submissions. These submissions adequately described WMA's perceived need for the project, and provided more than was required.

(b) Alternatives. The judge ruled that "an adequate and appropriate EIR must contain . . . a description of reasonable alternatives to the project including a review of the no build option." This language is derived from 301 Code Mass. Regs. § 11.07(6)(f) (2), which requires an EIR to contain a description and analysis of alternatives to the project including: "the alternative of not undertaking the Project (i.e., the no-build alternative) for the purpose of establishing a future baseline in relation to which the Project and its alternatives can be described and analyzed and its potential environmental impacts and mitigation measures can be assessed" (emphasis added). The various MEPA submissions, together with the RMPP, the OGP, and the various studies of the flora and fauna of Mt. Wachusett, together established a thoroughly studied baseline that adequately complied with the requirements of this section.

Other alternatives to the location of the proposed alpine park were raised during the MEPA process. The plaintiffs contend that those alternatives were never adequately studied. The plaintiffs would have both the Secretary and the commissioner conduct an exhaustive search for alternatives that the MEPA statutes do not require. WMA points out that its MEPA submissions made after the filing of its notice of project change constitute an alternative to its original plan, and were made in response to the discovery of old growth forest within which its original plan had contemplated creating new ski trails. WMA argues that there were no further reasonable alternatives "outside the [old growth forest] and inside the existing trail foot-print [within the ski area] that was large enough to contain [the new trails]." We agree.

In the commissioner's memorandum to the board, dated July 11, 2000, he retrospectively summarized the alternative site analysis conducted by WMA during the MEPA process. He stated that the criteria that WMA had sought to meet for a new trail location were: (1) that the trails be outside and not immediately adjacent to the old growth forest administrative boundaries; (2) that the new trails be within the footprint of existing trails, so as not to fragment a currently intact forest ecosystem; (3) that the trail location have a slope of about 15%; and (4) that the trails not be located where they would cross streams. Alternative sites within the ski area that might meet these criteria were assessed. One was rejected because it was "bisected with drainage swales, is too narrow for two full trails, and is close to the old growth forest administrative area." Other areas that were outside of the existing footprint of ski trails were also examined, but rejected either because they would have fragmented large forest areas, crossed streams, or been "partially within or immediately adjacent to the old growth forest." In sum, alternatives were both discussed and considered, and the Secretary's and commissioner's acceptance of the eventually approved plan was not arbitrary or capricious by reason of a failure to consider alternatives.

(c) Environmental impacts. The judge's analysis of the SFEIR led him to conclude that the MEPA submissions failed properly to assess environmental impacts arising from the proposed expansion. The MEPA submissions, and the Secretaries' certifications of each, all discussed and assessed the potential impacts of the project on various aspects of the ecology of the reservation and the surrounding areas. For example, the FEIR discussed the impact of the proposed new trails on the old growth forest, on wildlife habitats and on vegetation, and discussed mitigation measures that would be put in place to minimize the environmental impact. As discussed below, the judge's analysis misapprehended the RMPP, which expressly contemplated expansion of the ski area, including clearing of forest for new trails, as a permitted use within the leased ski area. Environmental impacts were adequately considered. We conclude that the Secretary's certification was not arbitrary or capricious.

5. *Section 61.* Section 61 findings and the RMPP. The commissioner and the WMA argue that the judge erred by concluding that the record did not support the § 61 findings confirming the need for new trails and that all feasible measures had been taken to avoid or minimize environmental damage. They further contend that the judge erred by concluding that construction of new trails and widening of existing trails would violate the RMPP and the OGP.

(a) Need. As stated above, the statutes and regulations governing the MEPA process do not include any requirement for a "need" analysis in the EIR process, nor do they require any discussion of "need" in the agency's § 61 findings. Nonetheless, the commissioner's § 61 findings describe the need for the project as allowing the ski area to increase its capacity as well as its ability to cater to the evolving tastes of its customers for varied skiing terrain.

(b) Feasible measures to avoid or minimize environmental damage. The judge concluded that the commissioner's § 61 findings failed to adequately demonstrate that all feasible measures had been taken to avoid or minimize environmental damage. General Laws c. 30, § 61, requires that departments of the Commonwealth "review, evaluate, and determine the impact on the natural environment of all works, projects or activities conducted by them" and requires them to "use all practicable means and measures to minimize damage to the environment." A finding is required by the statute "describing the environmental impact, if any, of the project and a finding that all feasible measures have been taken to avoid or minimize said impact."

The commissioner's § 61 findings extensively described both the potential sources and nature of environmental impacts arising from the proposed expansion of the ski area, as well as the measures that would be required of WMA to mitigate and minimize the impacts on the environment. The findings addressed the issues of impact on the old growth forest, including so called "edge effects." "Edge effects" are discussed within the RMPP and described as events that "often occur within the transition zone between one type of habitat and a distinctly different type of habitat (e.g., forest and meadow). Edge effects may have either beneficial or negative ecological repercussions." Because there are locations where edge effects come close to the old growth forest, a monitoring program has been incorporated into the RMPP "adjacent to ski trails and at the [reservation] visitor's center, where abrupt edges occur between Old Growth and cleared land. Specific parameters to be monitored include breeding birds and presence of invasive species."

According to the OGP, edge effects may be reduced by maintaining a buffer of other "protection forest" that will consist "in so far as possible [of] forested areas where disturbance is either precluded or minimized." "The location and extent of these buffers will be dealt with in the site-specific management plans that will be prepared for each stand [of old growth forest]."

The commissioner's § 61 findings also discussed the biological integrity of the ski area leasehold, wetlands and water resources, cultural resources, traffic impacts, and offseason events. His findings laid out mitigation measures appropriate to each area of concern. They also responded to comments received from the public. As such, the findings adequately fulfilled the commissioner's obligations under G.L. c. 30, § 61, and were not arbitrary or capricious.

The only basis that the judge stated in support of his conclusion that the commissioner's § 61 findings were inadequate was his determination that an irreconcilable inconsistency existed between the prohibition of commercial silviculture within the biodiversity significance overlay zone and the commissioner's approval of the clearcutting of about twelve and one-half acres of forest within that zone for new and widened ski trails. As discussed below, the two are not inconsistent, and we hold that the commissioner's § 61 findings adequately addressed the requirements of § 61.

(c) The RMPP. The judge determined that the RMPP for Mt. Wachusett and the approval of the proposed expansion were inconsistent. In his opinion, the "RMPP provides no analysis, explanation, or justification for constructing new trails and widening existing trails in the biodiversity significance overlay. . . Thus the absence of [the department's] analysis of how permitting clear cutting of trees over a swath of twelve acres of mature forest in the biodiversity significance overlay can be reconciled with banning partial cutting incident to commercial silviculture compels the conclusion of arbitrary treatment."

WMA argues that, by its own terms, the RMPP contemplates and permits the proposed expansion of the ski area and simultaneously applies the zoning overlays to the reservation. WMA points out that the EIR and the RMPP were "developed in concert" and are part of a "coordinated process . . . for improvement of the ski area which received environmental reviews that were extensive, proper and more than adequate." The proposed expansion is, in its view, "entirely consistent with the management plan for the Reservation as a whole." The commissioner also argues that his § 61 findings and the RMPP are consistent with one another. We agree.

The RMPP, which was adopted by the board on July 11, 2000, under authority of G.L. c. 21, § 2F, sets forth the management objectives for the department's stewardship of the reservation. These management objectives were developed "in specific consideration of the natural, cultural, and recreational resources provided by [the reservation]" and their purpose was to "assist [the department] personnel in making management decisions in the day-to-day operation of the reservation."[5] The department's role, as set forth in the RMPP, is to manage the reservation so that a variety of activities can coexist without interfering with one another or "with the natural and cultural resources present on the reservation."

One of the tools the department adopted to meet this goal was the implementation of land stewardship zoning. The basic principle is to define the appropriate land use for a particular resource area by zoning the land according to a scheme that designates areas (in decreasing order of resource sensitivity) as either environmental protection zones, conservation zones or intensive use zones. In addition, where conditions warrant, the department can establish significance overlay zones that may overlap the underlying zone, completely or in part, to "allow[] management activities to be tailored more specifically to the particular resource, and [those significance overlay zones] may be more restrictive than the environmental protection zone."

The RMPP establishes four significance overlay zones for the reservation. The first, the old growth significance overlay, corresponds to the "administrative limits" of the old growth forest as mapped out on the mountain. Within the old growth significance overlay, "any potentially disruptive activities that might negatively affect the integrity of this ecosystem will be either prohibited or constrained to protect and maintain the integrity of this ecosystem." Although the old growth significance overlay encircles the summit of Mt. Wachusett, it does not overlap the area at the summit where intensive uses were long established (an area that falls under the summit natural and cultural resources significance overlay zone). The RMPP states that "the directives established under the department's Statewide [OGP] apply throughout that portion of [the reservation] designated under the old growth significance overlay."

The second significance overlay created at Mt. Wachusett was the "biodiversity significance overlay" zone, which covers nearly the entire mountain, from the perimeter of the old growth significance overlay to the boundaries of the reservation to the west and north, and to the base of the slopes to the south. The proposed alpine park is entirely within the biodiversity significance overlay, as are the areas where WMA planned to widen existing ski trails.

---

[5] Among the objectives of the RMPP were to: (1) "Manage and protect the natural resources of the reservation to ensure a diverse and sustainable ecosystem ..."; (2) "Maintain the high quality of water delivered by the watersheds of the reservation;" (3) "Manage and protect the cultural resources of the reservation ...;" (4) "Provide and maintain safe, enjoyable, diverse outdoor recreation opportunities, within the limits of the natural and cultural resources of the reservation...."

The RMPP states: "The biodiversity significance overlay provides an additional buffer to the northern and southern flanks of the old growth significance overlay. The biodiversity significance overlay will allow continued use and maintenance of the numerous hiking and skiing trails within the limits of the overlay, including any necessary infrastructure improvements (e.g., dam reconstruction at Echo Lake and Everett Pool, annual ski area work plans). No commercial silvicultural activities will be allowed within the biodiversity significance overlay, however management of early successional vegetation will be undertaken to maintain scenic vistas, restore High Meadow to grassland, and to allow the continuation of the existing utility corridor, until such time that technological advances and financial feasibility enable its discontinuation." (Emphases added.)

Appendix I to the RMPP includes a document entitled "Approval Process for All Construction, Maintenance and/or Alterations at Wachusett Mountain Ski Area." Paragraph A of that document states that "on or before March 15th of each year, [WMA] shall submit to [the department] working plans and specifications and proposed project schedules for all work projects proposed to commence within the following 12 months. Work projects shall include, but not be limited to the erection, modification, addition, removal or alteration of any building(s), lift(s), natural features or resources, or structure of any nature and/or projects involving removing, filling, dredging, drilling, excavating, grading or landscaping within the leased premises." (emphasis added). Thus, although the RMPP's biodiversity significance overlay zone prohibits commercial silviculture, it expressly envisions the type of work that WMA proposes for the leased ski area. The arguments and counterarguments pertaining to the meaning of the RMPP's prohibition on commercial silviculture, and whether that ban applies or does not apply to the clearing of land for new ski trails are rendered extraneous by the scope of the annual ski area work plans permitted within the biodiversity significance overlay zone, and thus on the leased ski area. Because the RMPP permits the type of trail work proposed by WMA, the § 61 findings and the RMPP are not in conflict. . .

NOTES & QUESTIONS

1. The Wachusett Mountain State Reservation is home to wetlands, ponds, and an old growth forest with 350-year-old trees that somehow survived four centuries of settlement in Massachusetts. The first hotel was built on the summit in 1882, making it an early New England ecotourism destination. The Civilian Conservation Corps cut the first skiing trails there in the 1930s. Today the ski area has 22 trails, 110 skiable acres, and eight lifts. The ski area promotes itself as "one of the 'Greenest' mountains in the USA!." Wachusett IS Green," http://www.wachusett.com/TheMountain/GreenInitiatives/tabid/61/Default.aspx.

2. MEPA, like its federal counterpart NEPA, requires state agencies to study the environmental impacts of their actions. Is such an approach more or less likely to properly balance the demands of biodiversity and other agency responsibilities when employed by a state government instead of the federal government?

3. In March 2012, the Massachusetts Department of Conservation & Recreation published draft updated land stewardship zoning guidelines. Those guidelines distinguish between three types of zones: Zone 1, where the management objective is "[p]rotection of sensitive resources from management or other human activities that may adversely impact the resources;" Zone 2, which seeks to "[p]rovide for a balance between the stewardship of natural and cultural resources and recreational opportunities which can be appropriately sustained;" and Zone 3, which "[p]rovide[s] public access to safe and accessible recreational opportunities, as well as administrative and maintenance facilities that meet the needs of DCR visitors and staff." There are different management guidelines for recreation and public access in each zone:

- "In general, recreation activities will be limited to dispersed, low impact, non-motorized recreation and dependent on assessment of specific resource sensitivity and stewardship considerations by resource specialists . . . in conjunction with field staff. Existing trails will be evaluated for compatibility with resource protection goals. Trails will be discontinued if discontinuance furthers sensitive resource protection and does not compromise public safety. Proposals for new activities will be strictly evaluated, and management guidelines will be applied by resource specialists for the protection of resources and to address specific issues." – Zone 1

- "Resources will be managed to support a variety of safe, sustainable recreation opportunities that are compatible with the long-term stewardship and character of natural and cultural resources. New public access may be allowed depending upon existing area trail densities, purpose and need, physical suitability of the site, and specific guidelines for protection of rare species habitat and archaeological resources . . ." – Zone 2

- "Intensive recreation areas will be managed to maintain public health and safety. Agency policies, resource protection and recreational goals will determine activities that are supported in individual properties." – Zone 3

Land Stewardship Zoning Guidelines: Draft Update – March 2012, http://www.mass.gov/dcr/stewardship/rmp/downloads/lsz_guidelines.pdf. How would apply these guidelines to the respective zones? Is land stewardship zoning a promising approach to reconciling recreational uses and biodiversity?

Case study: Cape Hatteras National Seashore

Cape Hatteras is the point on the North Carolina coast where the southerly-flowing cold water Labrador Current and the northerly-flowing warm water Gulf Stream collide. The cape is actually a bend in Hatteras Island, one of the long thin barrier islands that make up the Outer Banks. Cape Hatteras is perhaps most famous for its lighthouse, which was built in 1870, moved one mile inland in 2000 to escape the eroding beach, and remains a popular tourist attraction.

Congress authorized the Cape Hatteras National Seashore in 1937. Another dozen years passed before the federal government acquired enough land to actually establish the national seashore in 1953. Today the Cape Hatteras National Seashore consists of more than 30,000 acres distributed along approximately 671 miles of shoreline. It was the first national seashore, followed later by nine other national seashores and two national lakeshores, all of which are managed by the Park Service pursuant to its Organic Act, 16 U.S.C. 1, "to conserve the scenery and the natural and historic objects and the wild life therein and to provide for the enjoyment of the same in such manner and by such means as will leave them unimpaired for the enjoyment of future generations."

The enabling legislation for Cape Hatteras National Seashore provides that "[e]xcept for certain portions of the area, deemed to be especially adaptable for recreational uses, particularly swimming, boating, sailing, fishing, and other recreational activities of similar nature, which shall be developed for such uses as needed, the said area shall be permanently reserved as a primitive wilderness and no development of the project of plan for the convenience of visitors shall be undertaken which would be incompatible with the preservation of the unique flora and fauna or the physiographic conditions now prevailing in this area." 16 U.S.C. § 459a-2. The enabling legislation further provides that the national seashore shall be "administered, protected, and developed by the National Park Service for national seashore recreational purposes for the benefit and enjoyment of the people." Congress amended the enabling legislation in 1942 even before the national seashore was actually established to allow hunting there. In doing so, Congress renamed the unit the Cape Hatteras National Seashore *Recreational* Area. The NPS made an administrative decision to refer to the Cape Hatteras National Seashore once Congress established national seashores elsewhere throughout the U.S..

The Park Service urged local residents to promote tourism to Cape Hatteras, and they responded by developing businesses and infrastructure need to support increased tourism. They succeeded.

The national seashore is now a popular recreation destination. More than two million people visited it in 2008, an eight-fold increase in visitation since 1955. Seashore visitors participate in a variety of recreational activities, including beach recreation (sunbathing, swimming, shell collecting, etc.), fishing (surf and boat), hiking, hunting, motorized boating, nonmotorized boating (sailing, kayaking, canoeing), nature study, photography, ORV use (beach driving), shellfishing, sightseeing, watersports (surfing, windsurfing, kiteboarding, etc.), and wildlife viewing.

The national seashore also provides a variety of important marshes, tidal flats, and riparian habitats created by its dynamic environmental processes. It is home to both summering and wintering populations of piping plovers, which are listed as threatened under the ESA. The American oystercatcher, Wilson's plover, and colonial waterbirds (least terns, common terns, and black skimmers) are all listed by the North Carolina Wildlife Resources Commission as species of special concern. Besides rare birds, the national seashore hosts five species of sea turtles and one plant (the seabeach amaranth) that are listed under the federal ESA.

In 2011, 15 pairs of piping plovers, 23 pairs of American oystercatchers, and 147 sea turtle nests (of which 137 were for loggerhead turtles) were seen in the national seashore. Those numbers have changed relatively little during the past decade. The threats to each species include hurricanes, predation from small mammals and other birds, and human disturbance from beach goers on foot or in off-road vehicles (ORVs). To protect the rare birds and turtles, the Park Service restricts access to the beach during nesting season. ORVs are excluded from nesting areas, and pedestrian access is restricted from the most sensitive places at the most sensitive times. For example, the Park Service imposes a minimum buffer of 200 meters around American oystercatcher chicks once they hatch. Conflict arises because the section of the beach preferred by the birds and the turtles are often the most desirable for beachgoers and fishing.

The tension between recreation and biodiversity arose early during the history of the national seashore. There were no paved roads on or bridges to Cape Hatteras until the 1950s. Historically, beach driving at the Seashore was for the purpose of transportation, and not recreation. Because the area was sparsely populated, the number of ORVs on the beach was much smaller than it is today. Residents adopted the use of ORVs for commercial netting of fish, while sport fishermen used ORVs to pursue migrating schools of game fish and reach more productive areas, such as Cape Point or the inlets, often a mile or more from the nearest paved surface. The paving of NC-12, the completion of the Bonner Bridge connecting Bodie and Hatteras islands in 1963, and the introduction of the State of North Carolina ferry system to Ocracoke Island facilitated visitor access to the sound and ocean beaches. Improved access, increased population, and the popularity of the sport utility vehicle have resulted in a dramatic increase in vehicle use on Seashore beaches. Seashore visitors use ORVs for commercial and recreational fishing, sightseeing, travel to and from swimming and surfing areas, and pleasure driving. These vehicles supported lots of recreation, but they also provoked objections that the area was becoming "Hatteras Parking Lot."

The proponents of ORV use in the national seashore see is at a historical and cultural tradition that has a minimal impact on the native wildlife. They assert that the continuation of these traditional practices is central to the preservation of the historic social and cultural fabric of Outer Banks villages. Here is how one local official described recreation at Cape Hatteras:

> A common trait of each recreational activity is the challenge offered to the visitor to find just the perfect spot on the beach. One day, the best shells may be in one location, the next day in another. One day the wind may blow from the northeast and chase the visitors to the South Beaches; the next day the wind may blow from the southwest and chase the visitors to the North Beaches. One day the bait in the water will lead the bluefish and Spanish mackerel (and likewise, the fisher-

men) in one direction, and the next day in a different one. Each of these activities . . . is made possible through the mobility afforded by personal, four-wheel-drive vehicles coupled with beaches open to access.

Or, as one local resident explained, "ORV use is the only practical way to gain access to some of the key recreational sites within this uniquely designed seashore. . . Without ORV access, the physically disabled, the elderly and many who suffer from chronic medical conditions are unable to reach the seashore and enjoy the place that is supported by their tax dollars." Moreover, local residents believe that ORV use allows birders to approach much closer to observe birdlife while inside their vehicles than they could as pedestrians

In response to a general increase of ORV use on public lands, President Nixon issued an executive order in 1972 for the purpose of "establish[ing] policies and provid[ing] procedures that will ensure that the use of off-road vehicles on public lands will be controlled and directed so as to protect the resources of those lands, to promote the safety of all users of those lands, and to minimize conflicts among the various uses of those lands." Exec. Order No. 11,644, 37 Fed. Reg. 2877 (Feb. 8, 1972), as amended by Exec. 34617, Sec. 21 Order No. 12,608, 52 Fed. Reg. (September 9, 1987). This executive order required federal agencies to "develop and issue regulations and administrative instructions . . . to provide for administrative designation of the specific areas and trails on public lands on which the use of off-road vehicles may be permitted, and areas in which the use of off-road vehicles may not be permitted, . . ." *Id.* at §3. The Executive Order required that the regulations direct that the designation of such areas and trails: (1) "be based upon the protection of the resources of the public lands, promotion of the safety of all users of those lands, and minimization of conflicts among the various uses of those lands"; and (2) be located in such a way as to (a) "minimize damage to soil, watershed, vegetation, or other resources of the public lands"; (b) "minimize harassment of wildlife or significant disruption of wildlife habitats"; (c) "minimize conflicts between off-road vehicle use and other existing or proposed recreational uses of the same or neighboring public lands"; and (d) "ensure the compatibility of such uses with existing conditions in populated areas, taking into account noise and other factors." *Id.* at § 3(a). Further, such trails and areas were not to be located in designated Wilderness or Primitive Areas, and "shall be located in areas of the National Park system . . . only if the respective agency head determines that off-road vehicle use in such locations will not adversely affect their natural, aesthetic, or scenic values." Id. Public participation in the promulgation of the regulations and designations of the areas and trails was required. *Id.* at § 3(b). The executive order also required the agencies to "monitor the effects" of ORV use on the public lands and "[o]n the basis of the information gathered, they shall from time to time amend or rescind designations of areas or other actions taken pursuant to this order as necessary to further the policy of this order." *Id.* § 8.

The executive order did not have an immediate impact at Cape Hatteras. Beach driving restrictions and wildlife protections on the national seashore were somewhat ad hoc, more responsive than pro-active, and implemented primarily by Superintendent's Orders and on-the-ground decisions. It was not until 2006 that the Park Service developed an Interim Strategy to manage ORVs in the national seashore. The Park Service characterized the Interim Strategy as a temporary measure to employ "while a long-term ORV management plan is developed." The Fish & Wildlife Service issued biological opinion pursuant to the ESA which indicated that the Interim Strategy would cause adverse effects to federally listed species, but which found no jeopardy to those species for purposes of ESA section 7 mainly because of the limited duration of implementation (expected to be no later than the end of 2009).

In October 2007, Defenders of Wildlife and the National Audubon Society, represented by the Southern Environmental Law Center, filed a lawsuit claiming the Interim Strategy violated the ESA and other laws, failed to protect species at Cape Hatteras National Seashore, and failed to comply with the requirements of the ORV executive orders and NPS regulations on ORV use. In December 2007, Dare County, Hyde County, and the Cape Hatteras Access Preservation Alliance, a coalition of ORV/access and fishing groups, were granted Intervenor-Defendant status in the lawsuit. In April 2008, the Plaintiffs, Federal Defendants, and Intervenor-Defendants jointly submitted to the court a consent decree that would be signed by U.S. District Judge Terrence Boyle on April 30, 2008, to settle the lawsuit. The consent decree, which is enforceable by the court, provides for specific species protection measures and required the NPS to complete the ORV management plan/EIS and required special regulation by December 31, 2010, and April 1, 2011, respectively. Consent decree modifications of the Interim Strategy included changes in the size of buffers provided for various species at the Seashore, as well as added restrictions related to night driving. For example, the consent decree prohibited nighttime driving on the beach during the summer, and it required a full beach closure between the hours of sunset and 6AM during the period when sea turtles were about to hatch.

The Park Service then prepared an environmental impact statement that analyzed a number of alternative approaches to resolving the dispute between recreational users and biodiversity protection at Cape Hatteras. It identified six alternatives:

- Alternative A would continue to follow the Interim Strategy;

- Alternative B would manage ORV use according to the Interim Strategy as modified by the 2008 consent decree;

- Alternative C would provide visitors with a degree of predictability regarding areas available for ORV use, as well as vehicle-free areas, based largely on the seasonal resource and visitor use characteristics of various areas in the national seashore;

- Alternative D—the environmentally preferable alternative—would give visitors the maximum amount of predictability regarding areas available for ORV use and vehicle-free areas for pedestrian use with most areas having year-round, rather than seasonal, designations;

- Alternative E would provide for additional flexibility in access for both ORV and pedestrian users, including allowing some level of overnight vehicle use at selected points and spits. Where greater access is permitted, often additional controls or restrictions would be in place to limit impacts on sensitive resources;

- Alternative F—the NPS Preferred Alternative—provides a similar mileage of year-round ORV routes as the other action alternatives but provides more ORV and pedestrian access than alternative D by improving interdunal road access and enhancing pedestrian facilities and opportunities.

Additionally, members of the public offered their own suggestions, including

- the implementation of an escort program, whereby vehicles would be escorted around resource closures by Park Service staff;

- providing a corridor though all species resource closures and buffers;

- move hatched chicks to Pea Island National Wildlife Refuge on the north end of the national seashore or to some other area;

- provide captive rearing of piping plovers and turtles;

- relocate bird and turtle nests;

- implement a range of species management measures such as monitoring nesting activity, a beach watch program, and vehicle escorts;

- create new habitat; and

- fence chicks away from the ORV corridor

The EIS elicited cautious praise from environmental organizations and vehement criticism from local officials and recreational groups. The Coalition for Beach Access claimed:

> Tourists are the lifeblood of the local economy. They stay at motels and rental houses. They eat at the restaurants and buy food from the grocery stores. They put gas in their vehicles. They support the local shops by getting bait and tackle, bathing suits, surf boards and books. They buy souvenirs, local art and T-Shirts to remember their time here on the islands. During the summer, it was difficult to find a place to stay if you didn't have a reservation and there were always long waits to get into restaurants. For decades, Cape Hatteras National Seashore Recreational Area was immune from recession including the fallout from Sept. 11, 2001. Economic downturns that would cripple

the national economy tended to give a boost to the Hatteras economy because people were inclined to go to Hatteras for inexpensive, short-distance vacations. The Consent Decree has taken a heavy toll on the local economy. Without sensible beach access, there is no reason for tourists to come here. Since 2008, successful businesses that are older than the park itself have started to fail. All walks of business are reporting that staffs have been reduced by 25 to 50% and the same for their sales figures. Restaurants are half full in summer and finding a place to stay is now easy. The people who are still working are earning less. Charity organizations are reporting a tremendous increase in the number of families needing their assistance, doubling every year since the Consent Decree took effect. Church donations have decreased. Area banks are reporting that businesses have exhausted most of their lines of credit trying to stay afloat. Dare County now has the highest rate of unemployment in the state of North Carolina.

But the Park Service adopted its preferred plan effective February 2012. The plan requires ORV users to obtain a permit to drive on the beach, it closes section of the beach from April 1 to October 1, and it authorizes additional beach closures when necessary to protect wildlife. The Park Service describes the new plans as "the products of an intensive five-year long planning process that included a high level of public participation through both the National Environmental Policy Act (NEPA) process and negotiated rulemaking, including four rounds of public comment opportunities. The NPS received more than 15,000 individual comments on the draft plan/EIS and more than 21,000 individual comments on the proposed special regulation. In completing the final ORV management plan/EIS and special regulation, the NPS considered all comments, weighed competing interests and ensured compliance with all applicable laws."

That is not the end of the story. Soon after the Park Service implemented its plan in February 2012, local members of Congress introduced legislation to overturn the new plan and to reinstate the Interim Strategy. The "Preserving Access to Cape Hatteras National Seashore Recreational Area Act" provides:

Sec. 2. Reinstatement of Interim Management Strategy.

(a) Management- After the date of the enactment of this Act, Cape Hatteras National Seashore Recreational Area shall be managed in accordance with the Interim Protected Species Management Strategy/Environmental Assessment issued by the National Park Service on June 13, 2007, for the Cape Hatteras National Seashore Recreational Area, North Carolina, unless the Secretary of the Interior (hereafter in this Act referred to as the `Secretary') issues a new final rule that meets the requirements set forth in section 3.

(b) Restrictions- The Secretary shall not impose any additional restrictions on pedestrian or motorized vehicular access to any portion of Cape Hatteras National Seashore Recreational Area for species protection beyond those in the Interim Management Strategy, other than as specifically authorized pursuant to section 3 of this Act."

Sec. 3. Additional Restrictions on Access to Cape Hatteras National Seashore Recreational Area for Species Protection.

(a) In General- If, based on peer-reviewed science and after public comment, the Secretary determines that additional restrictions on access to a portion of the Cape Hatteras National Seashore Recreational Area are necessary to protect species listed as endangered under the Endangered Species Act of 1973 (16 U.S.C. 1531 et seq.), the Secretary may only restrict, by limitation, closure, buffer, or otherwise, pedestrian and motorized vehicular access for recreational activities for the shortest possible time and on the smallest possible portions of the Cape Hatteras National Seashore Recreational Area.

(b) Limitation on Restrictions- Restrictions imposed under this section for protection of species listed as endangered under the Endangered Species Act of 1973 (16 U.S.C. 1531 et seq.) shall not be greater than the restrictions in effect for that species at any other National Seashore.

(c) Corridors Around Closures- To the maximum extent possible, the Secretary shall designate pedestrian and vehicular corridors of minimal distance on the beach or interdunal area around closures implemented under this section to allow access to areas not closed."

H.R. 4094, 112th Cong., 2d Sess. (2012). The bill would also provide that the 2008 consent "shall not apply after the date of the enactment of this Act." *Id.* § 4.

The bill, like the plans it would supersede, generated conflicting opinions. According to Walter Jones, the congressional representative from the Outer Banks, "This bill is about jobs and taxpayers' right to access the recreational areas they own. H.R. 4094 will restore balance and common sense Park Service management in Cape Hatteras National Recreational Area. It will reverse the significant job loss and economic decline that Hatteras Island has experienced since access was cut off to many of the most popular areas of the seashore." By contrast, the Department of the Interior testified that it "supports allowing appropriate public use and access at the Seashore to the greatest extent possible, while also ensuring protection for the Seashore's wildlife and providing a variety of visitor use experiences, minimizing conflicts among various users, and promoting the safety of all visitors. We strongly believe that the final ORV management plan and special regulation will accomplish these objectives far better than the defunct Interim Strategy."

* * * * *

How would you resolve this controversy if you were (a) the Superintendent of the Cape Hatteras National Seashore; (b) a member of the United States House of Representatives from Cape Hatteras; (c) an attorney working for an interested conservation organization; (d) a local restaurant owner; (e) a bird watcher, or (f) an ORV enthusiast? What constraints does the law impose on the possible resolutions? What *should* the law saw about this kind of dispute between recreation and biodiversity?

PART 4

GLOBAL BIODIVERSITY

CHAPTER 14

DOMESTIC LAWS

Chapter Outline:
A. Reliance on Each Country's Own Domestic Laws
B. Extraterritorial Application of Domestic Environmental Laws

A. RELIANCE UPON EACH COUNTRY'S OWN DOMESTIC LAWS

Every nation has laws protecting biodiversity. Some laws seek to manage activities occurring in particular ecosystems, such as forests, coastal areas, or wetlands. Other laws regulate the time, place, and manner of hunting, fishing, logging, and the commercial exploitation of biodiversity. A smaller number of nations have laws specifically protecting endangered or threatened species or ecosystems. And a small, but growing, number of laws protect biodiversity as a whole.

The specific content of the domestic laws concerning biodiversity varies greatly from country to country. Poland prohibits the destruction of anthills in forests. The Bangladesh Fish Act provides seasonal protection to fish and their habitats. Germany requires ten percent of its land to be designated as interconnecting habitat conservation areas to protect biodiversity. Vietnam protects its forests by requiring the use of wood substitutes. Iceland allows only one unwieldy twelve-foot long tool, called a hafur, to be used to capture puffins. South Africa prohibits development that disturbs ecosystems or leads to a loss of biodiversity. Many nations have established nature preserves to protect their notable ecosystems and species from outside threats. Alas, the existence of such laws does not necessarily guarantee the actual preservation of a nation's biodiversity. Enforcement is a serious problem for many national and local governments. Financial resources and technical expertise limit the effective management of ecosystems.

So can individual countries enact and enforce adequate laws to protect the biodiversity that exists within their borders? Are some countries more capable of protecting their biodiversity than other countries? When should the international community, or other nations, take steps to protect the species, ecosystems, and genetic diversity within another country that is unable to accomplish such protection itself? Consider the answers to those questions in light of the following case study of China.

1. CHINA

China is a vast, varied nation that hosts an incredible range of ecosystems and species. Most famously, it is the only home of the giant panda, the symbol of many efforts to protect biodiversity throughout the world today. But China is also the home for more than 1,250,000,000 people. China's

1104

rapid economic growth further challenges efforts to preserve ecosystems, species, and genetic resources. China's efforts to address the needs of its biodiversity are documented in Ministry of Environmental Protection, China's Fourth National Report on Implementation of the Convention on Biological Diversity (Nov. 2008), http://www.cbd.int/doc/world/cn/cn-nr-04-en.pdf; CHINA'S BIODIVERSITY: A COUNTRY STUDY (1997), *available at* http://english.zhb.gov.cn/biodiv/state_dimp_en/country study.html; and CHINA: BIODIVERSITY CONSERVATION ACTION PLAN (1994), and CHINA'S BIODIVERSITY: A COUNTRY STUDY (1997), http://english.zhb.gov.cn/biodiv/state_dimp_en/country study.html. These documents provide the best overview of the status of and efforts to protect biodiversity within China, and they are complemented by countless additional materials, only some of which are cited in the following account.

China's biodiversity

"China's biodiversity ranks eighth in the world and first in the northern hemisphere." China's Agenda 21: White Paper on China's Population, Environment, and Development in the 21st Century 171 (1994). Over 100,000 species of animals and nearly 33,000 plant species exist in 460 different types of ecosystems. Those ecosystems include forests, grasslands, deserts, wetlands, seas and coastal areas, and agricultural ecosystems. China hosts 212 different types of bamboo forests alone. China also has an unusual number of ancient and relic species because of its protection from historic geologic events such as the movement of glaciers. Such species and ecosystem diversity is complemented by an unsurpassed collection of genetic diversity. "The richness of China's cultivated plants and domestic animals are incomparable in the world. Not only did many plants and animals on which human survival depend originate in China, but it also retains large numbers of their wild prototypes and relatives." China's National Report on Implementation of the Convention on Biological Diversity: The Richness and Uniqueness of China's Biodiversity, http://english.zhb.gov.cn/biodiv/state_con_en/china_biodiv_den.htm. A 2005 report estimated that China's biodiversity is valued at nearly five hundred billion dollars.

The biodiversity of China has encountered countless threats for thousands of years, including the cultivation of more and more land for agriculture and the consequences of numerous wars. During the Great Leap Forward of 1958 to 1960, Mao Zedong targeted the "Four Pests": rats, sparrows, flies, and mosquitoes. The attack on sparrows enlisted schoolchildren to knock down nests and to beat gongs so that the sparrows could not find a place to rest. Only after sparrows were virtually eliminated throughout China did the country's leaders recognize the value of the birds in controlling insects. China faces many of the same threats as biodiversity in other countries, with the notable addition of the country's notorious air pollution. Habitat loss is the biggest threat to biodiversity in China. As in many other countries, rapid economic development and continued population growth exert relentless pressure on previously undeveloped areas that offered habitat to a diversity of wildlife and plants. Overgrazing of rangelands, erosion, and the adverse effects of tourism and mining further compromise the condition of ecosystems and species throughout China.

Forests have suffered an especially devastating toll throughout China. Mark Elvin describes "[t]he destruction of the old-growth forests that once covered the greater part of China" as "the oldest story in China's environmental history." The story unfolded because "the original core of classical Chinese culture was hostile to forests, and saw their removal as the precondition for the creation of a civilized world." Trees were cut for fuel, to provide building materials, and as obstacles to farms and other human projects. But the disappearance of the forests caused other, albeit predictable, problems. Deforestation increased erosion, which resulted in huge amounts of sediment collecting along the coasts and the sides of lakes and rivers. Wood became scarce as early as 600 B.C. in some parts of the country. By the nineteenth century, a writer lamented that "[t]hese days, people have used their axes to deforest the mountains." During the twentieth century, China encouraged the wholesale destruction of forests for their timber—which was the country's primary fuel until coal recently replaced it—or simply the removal of trees to facilitate agricultural crops. Trees were cut indiscriminately in a planned effort to generate revenue for local education, health and infrastructure needs. As one villager remembered:

> When I was a child, there were jackals and foxes in the woods, but after the big trees were cut to fuel furnaces during the [Great Leap Forward], there wasn't even a rabbit. New trees grew, but then it was time to "learn from Dazhai." In fact, we didn't need terraces in our area, because the population was sparse. But our per-*mu* production was considered low. So we had to cut the trees. Whoever cut the most got the most political points, and the most gain.

JUDITH SHAPIRO, MAO'S WAR AGAINST NATURE: POLITICS AND THE ENVIRONMENT IN REVOLUTIONARY CHINA (2001). Another writer recalled when he was sent to Fuyuan County in northeastern China "charged with 'opening the wilderness' to convert the land to farmland and with making preparations for war with the Soviet Union:"

> During my five years in the county, beginning in 1969, when I arrived, the old forest was almost completely cut down and some animals were wiped out. One was an amphibious muskrat. During my second year, two hunters and a dog stayed with us. Every day they came back with a huge bag of animals that they were going to sell for two or three *yuan* each. The Army Corps only gave us 36 *yuan* a month, so that was a lot of money to us. So we all went out to hunt the muskrats, and after a few years, they were pretty much all gone. They were easy to hunt because they would stand up and cry out. I caught three. The disappearance of the muskrats affected the whole ecosystem. They eat fish; foxes eat them. It was a change in the whole food chain. Serious harm was done. But their fur was good.

Id. at 167. Fires and pests further degraded forest ecosystems. The result was that forest cover in the lush provinces of southwest China declined from 30% of the land in 1950 to 13% by 1999. The loss of forests, in turn, caused deadly flooding along the Yangtze River and devastated the natural ecosystems and the species within them. Tigers, for example, "stalk their prey from the cover and the shadow provided by forests. The relationship is pretty simple: no forests, no tigers." ROBERT B. MARKS, TIGERS, RICE, SILK, AND SILT: ENVIRONMENT AND ECONOMY IN LATE IMPERIAL SOUTH CHINA 323 (1998). Forests continue to disappear at an alarming rate, with the remaining forests often broken into smaller, fragmented areas. *See, e.g.*, THE ROOT CAUSES OF BIODIVERSITY LOSS 153–182 (Alexander Wood, Pamela Stedman-Edwards & Johanna Mang eds.) (2000) (chapter describing the loss of biodiversity in the forested areas of Deqin County in northern Yunnan Province and Pingwu County in northern Sichuan Province).

Other types of ecosystems confront similar threats. Overgrazing, farming, and plagues of rodents have caused the grassland steppes that account for one-third of China's total area to lose up to half of their grass yields in the past twenty years. Over seven million hectares of wetlands were reclaimed during the past thirty years. Once known as "the province with a thousand lakes," Hubei Province now has only 326 lakes and rivers left. Lime mining and handicraft production by local residents have damaged eighty percent of the coral reefs along the coast of Hainan Island. The overall result is that "continued destruction and deterioration of ecosystems has now become one of the most serious environmental problems in China." CHINA: BIODIVERSITY CONSERVATION ACTION PLAN, *supra*, at 10.

China's notorious pollution affects many of the country's ecosystems. China routinely places multiple cities in the lists of the world's most polluted cities, and air pollution damages croplands, fisheries, and other ecosystems. China's fisheries suffered $130 million in losses from 941 water pollution incidents in 2004 that affected 211,000 hectacres of freshwater ecosystems. A November 2005 factory explosion that polluted the Songhua River required the temporary termination of water supplies in the northwestern city of Harbin and had untold consequences for the freshwater ecosystem. The quantity of water is often a problem for biodiversity as well. Efforts to move freshwater to places where it is scarce, such as Beijing, include such controversial projects as the Three Gorges Dam in central China, which many environmentalists believe will destroy many of the nearby ecosystems. Further south, the planned damming of the Mekong River could destroy a lot. *See* Milton Osborne, River at Risk: The Mekong and the Water Politics of China and Southeast Asia (2005), *available at* www.lowyinstitute.org.

Biodiversity is also threatened by the direct exploitation of many species. "Plants are cut for fuel, building materials, food and medicine. Birds, mammals, reptiles, fish and many invertebrates are hunted and fished virtually everywhere they are available." *Id.* at 13. Commercial trade in wildlife is another serious threat. China is the world's largest exporter and a leading user of endangered species. Enforcement becomes even more difficult because of the huge demand for products derived from endangered species. Traditional Chinese medicine uses tiger bones (for arthritis and rheumatism), rhino horns (for fevers), and bear gall bladders. Nearly every tiger part is used as a tonic, an aphrodisiac, gourmet delicacies or some other purpose. Chinese pharmaceutical factories use 1,400 pounds of rhino horns annually, the product of about 650 rhinos. Panda pelts sell for as much as $10,000 and tiger bones are priced at $500 per pound, and a rhino horn can earn as much as $45,000. Villagers can earn ten years income from one tiger.

These pressures are evidenced in the placement of three native Chinese species among the World Wildlife Fund's list of the top ten most endangered species in the world. The giant panda is the most famous of those three species. Only one thousand pandas are left in the wild, and their numbers are still declining, albeit at a reduced rate. The threats to their survival include the loss of bamboo and habitat, a relatively small number of young pandas, genetic inbreeding, inability to survive in captivity, and poaching. The second species—the black rhinoceros—has suffered a 95% drop in population since 1970 so that only 2,000 are alive today. The third species—the Indo-Chinese tiger—is the most endangered. Estimates of the number of Indo-Chinese tigers alive in the wild range from 50 to 500, and with two of the four native Chinese tiger species already extinct, many fear that this tiger could disappear by the end of the century. The disappearance of native species is obvious in other ways as well. The town of "Wild Yak Gully now has no wild yaks; Wild Horse Sands, no wild horses," and the Town of Moose and the Town of Gazelle have no moose or gazelles. *Id.* at 15. Other notable Chinese species that are endangered include the Yangtze alligator, the white flag dolphin, the crested ibis, and certain Mongolian horses.

China's genetic diversity has suffered as well. "As habitats become fragmented and the total numbers of individuals within a species reduced, the genetic base becomes increasingly narrow. There is less and less opportunity to avoid inbreeding and to maintain genetic diversity. . . In the case of domestic species, the problem is aggravated by intentional selective breeding for a narrow set of desired characteristics." *Id.* at 12. Genetic diversity among plants has dropped as rapid economic development along the coast and agricultural innovations have led to the disappearance of many traditional strains of native plants and crops.

China's efforts to protect its biodiversity

(1) China understands the threats to its biodiversity. In its 2008 Fourth National Report on Implementation of the Convention on Biological Diversity, *supra*, the Ministry of Environment cited China's "remarkable progress" on biodiversity preservation but acknowledged that "China still faces the following obstacles:

(2) Forest ecosystems are not performing due functions. There is a sharp drop in the area and serious degradation of grasslands and wetlands;

(3) There is still serious over-consumption of wildlife resources;

(4) There is severe loss of genetic resources;

(5) Total pollutant emissions are high and the pollution is still serious;

(6) Alien species invasions occur frequently with an increasing tendency;

(7) Nature reserves are distributed unevenly. There are not enough marine and grassland nature reserves. The institutions of nature reserves are not well established and management and conservation infrastructures are insufficient;

(8) Technical support is inadequate;

(9) Funding is inadequate.

Id. at v. China's primary response to the threat to its biodiversity has been the creation of nature reserves. The Dinghushan National Natural Reserve was the first such reserve, established in 1956 in Guangdong Province to protect the subtropical evergreen forests and accompanying rare plants and animals. By 2011, 2,538 reserves covered 15% of China's land. *See* Ruidong Wu et al., *Effectiveness of China's Nature Reserves In Representing Ecological Diver*sity, 9 Front Ecol Environ 383 (2011). More than a dozen of those reserves were for pandas, and the population of pandas in the wild increased from 1,114 in 2000 to 1,596 in 2005. Another reserve covers 45,000 square kilometers and protects 60 endangered animals and 300 rare plants. The newest reserves include 16,800 acres in China's largest freshwater lake that is home to the Yangtze River dolphin, and 100 square kilometers in northwestern China that contains an untouched euphrates poplar forest. By contrast, efforts to establish a tiger reserve failed because of the huge amount of land required by wild tigers, the lack of acceptable sites, and the ignorance about the precise needs of tigers. Forest ecosystems are well represented in the nature reserves. Wetland and coastal ecosystems have been included in reserves since the 1970's, while the creation of reserves for grassland and desert ecosystems are a new priority for the government. More generally, a recent analysis of China's nature reserves concluded:

> In western China, the NR system provides coverage for most ecoregions, biodiversity priority areas, and natural vegetation types, at levels that meet international standards. However, such coverage is much lower in eastern and southern China, even though there are relatively more NRs in these regions of the country. This discrepancy is clearly due to the greater human population density and, consequently, the much higher proportion of land appropriated for human use in the east and south.

Ruiding, supra, at 388.

The nature reserves, however, do not solve all of the problems faced by China's biodiversity. Consider the Zhalong Nature Reserve in northeastern China's Heilonjiang Province is home to nine of the fifteen species of cranes in the world, but in recent years it has suffered from a severe drought, extensive fires, and housing developments built within its borders. The droughts have reduced the wetlands from 36,000 hectares to less than 6,000 hectares, and the government worries that the area could become a "sea of sand" if conditions are not reversed. *China's Major Wetland Shrinking Rapidly*, XINHUA GENERAL NEWS SERVICE, Aug. 10, 2005. Another wetland reserve in northern China was seriously polluted by oil that leaked from a passenger airplane crash in 2004. Most reserves are simply no hunting zones, not affirmative wildlife management areas. For example, over 15,000 people live in ninety villages within Xishuangbanna Nature Reserve in southwestern Yunnan Province, where "they engage in agriculture, forestry, animal production, fisheries, and small-scale retailing and commercial activities." CLEM TISDELL, BIODIVERSITY, CONSERVATION AND SUSTAINABLE DEVELOPMENT: PRINCIPLES AND PRACTICES WITH ASIAN EXAMPLES 147–48 (1999). More generally, "[s]ome engineering projects go on even in the core areas of nature reserves. In other reserves or scenic spots, tourism is promoted to develop the local economy, and while tourism can assist conservation when it is carried out properly, the prospects for quick profits may lead to abuses of the natural systems and species which the reserves protect." CHINA: BIODIVERSITY CONSERVATION ACTION PLAN, *supra*, at 21. Additionally, "illegal hunting and poaching of endangered animal and plant species occurs frequently" in reserves. *Id.* There is no general law regulating the operation of nature reserves. Management difficulties and inadequate funding also threaten many reserves. Reserve administrators and employees are often untrained to protect the species in their care. Most reserves do not even possess a list of species that live there.

The Chinese government is aware of these shortcomings, though, and it has charted an ambitious program to improve the effectiveness of nature reserves in protecting the country's biodiversity. Proposed actions include restrictions on free access to sensitive reserves, better pay and living conditions for reserve personnel (including allowances for families to live in nearby cities), efforts to "improve relations with local people and find ways for them to make a living without depleting the natural resources," and the establishment of new nature reserves "in regions with urgent need of biodiversity conservation," such as the coral reefs of Dongshan Island and seven proposed reserves to conserve wild rice, soybeans, and other agricultural crops. *Id.* at 36–40. Likewise, in 2005, Sichuan Province "closed 78 mines and polluting companies in the giant panda's habitat to provide a better home for the endangered species." *Giant Panda's Home Cleaned Up from Pollution*, XINHUA GENERAL NEWS SERVICE, May. 11, 2005.

The nature reserves are joined by zoos, botanical gardens, and scientific study institutes. China's 28 zoological gardens and 143 zoological exhibition sites contain more than 600 species of animals. Over 13,000 species of plants are contained in more than 100 botanical gardens. Over one thousand scientists work together through the Chinese Research Network of Ecosystems to study and monitor ecosystem diversity. Genetic diversity is protected by "the world's largest resource bank of different varieties of crops, a number of gene and cell banks and 25 germ-plasm nurseries, which hold a total of 350 thousand specimens of germ-plasm for various species of trees and crops." CHINA'S AGENDA 21, *supra*, at 173.

Educational campaigns serve as another primary feature of China's efforts to protect its biodiversity. China has traditionally relied on exhortational campaigns to change people's conduct. China's biodiversity conservation action plan begins with an emphasis on the need "[t]o enhance the nation's awareness of the critical importance of our biodiversity and its conservation is our urgent task of the highest priority." China: Biodiversity Conservation Action Plan, *supra*, at ii. Such an educational focus appears in China's Agenda 21 plan, which calls for media teaching about biodiversity, the promotion of public events such as Earth Day and Bird Loving Week, and the use of a traveling Panda Exhibition. China also held a "National Program for Environmental Education and Publicity" that drew upon the resources of such organizations as the government's environmental departments, the Ministry of Broadcasting and Television, and the Chinese Communist Youth League. One recent program to protect the five thousand remaining *grus nigricollis*—a rare type of crane—is designed to "make the youth conscious of animal protection before they become poachers." Such efforts have helped convince 99% of the Chinese people that environmental pollution and ecological destruction are at least "fairly serious" issues. In particular, anyone who harms a panda must face "the censure of an angry public."

Yet all agree that more environmental education needs to be done. The greatest problem exists in rural areas where people ask why wild animals can no longer survive on their own, and where menus proclaiming "Rare Wild Animals Are Served" still appear in restaurants and hotels. The demand for the products of endangered species remains high. Years of teaching traditional Chinese medicine and delicacies is hard to reverse. How do you convince a billion people to take aspirin instead of rhino horn pills? "Many Chinese still believe that wildlife species are endowed with magical powers capable of curing a myriad of ills, and are angered by pressure from countries such as the United States to ban the sale of endangered species." Daniel C.K. Chow, *Recognizing the Environmental Costs of the Recognition Problem: The Advantages of Taiwan's Direct Participation in International Environmental Law Treaties*, 14 STAN. ENVTL. L.J. 256, 299 (1995). Likewise, many still see tigers as pests, just as many ranchers fear the introduction of wolves and bears into the western United States. More generally, "[b]iodiversity conservation is a new technical term for many officials in the governments at all levels and for citizens who are lacking basic knowledge on biodiversity conservation." CHINA: BIODIVERSITY CONSERVATION ACTION PLAN, *supra*, at 33.

The biodiversity conservation action plan reveals a keen understanding of the importance of gaining public support for the task at hand:

> In general, people want government policies that do not require them to change their lifestyles, provide material benefits and development, and provide benefits today that will be paid for later. Politics to conserve biodiversity would be the opposite, requiring fundamental

changes in people's relationship with the environment, restricting access to resources, foregoing material benefits, and paying today for abstract future benefits. Unless the public is convinced of the value of conserving biodiversity, and the government changes its policies accordingly, the chance of saving biodiversity is small.

Id. at 60. Thus the Chinese government seeks to help the media better publicize the importance of biodiversity conservation, "[w]ork with local theater groups to write and perform plays with a biodiversity message," and teach students of all ages about biodiversity in the nation's schools. *Id.* at 60–62.

Neither China's emphasis on nature reserves nor its use of educational campaigns actually regulates any conduct that threatens biodiversity. The development of Chinese wildlife law mirrors the development of Chinese environmental law (and indeed Chinese law) generally. Interest in the environment and interest in law both lagged until the 1970's, so not surprisingly, there was little Chinese environmental law. The People's Congress approved the Law on Environmental Protection—the first general Chinese environmental statute—in 1978. Article 15 of that law prohibits hunting and exploitation of rare wildlife. Then, in 1982, several provisions regarding environmental protection were added to China's constitution. Article 9 provides for state ownership of natural resources, ensures state protection of natural resources, and prohibits appropriation or damage of natural resources. Article 26 provides that "the State protects and improves the living environment and the ecological environment, prevents and remedies pollution and other public hazards." By 1994, China had enacted twelve national statutes, twenty national administrative regulations, over six hundred local laws and regulations, and three hundred other norms regulating the environment.

Chinese biodiversity law has developed in much the same fashion. To be sure, China's long history contains numerous examples of the law being used to protect the country's biodiversity. An edict issued in 336 A.D. stated that "[t]o take possession of the mountains, or to put the marshes under one's personal protection is tantamount to robbery with violence." The *Respectfully Determined Laws and Precedents of the Great Qing* prescribed that anyone who "thievishly cuts down the trunks of trees, removes soil or stones, opens kilns for charcoal . . . or starts fires to burn the mountains for short-term farming, *he shall be beheaded* as if he had stolen imperial vessels used for sacrifices to the gods." Today, the Forestry Law prohibits the hunting of animals in protected areas. The Water Law provides that the government "shall protect water resources and adopt effective measures to preserve natural flora, plant trees and grow grass, conserve water sources, prevent and control soil erosion and improve the ecological environment." The Grassland Law directs the government to protect grassland ecosystems, vegetation, and rare plants, and it prohibits harmful reclamation and construction activities. Genetic diversity is protected by Plant Variety Regulations, though China may need to strengthen those regulations to comply with the International Convention for the Protection of New Varieties of Plants (UPOV). *See* Lester Ross & Libin Zhang, *Agricultural Development and Intellectual Property Protection for Plant Varieties: China Joins the UPOV*, 17 Pᴀᴄ. Rɪᴍ. L. J. 226 (1999).

One Chinese law seeks to abate the transformation of once fertile grassland ecosystems into lifeless deserts. Nomadic herders have lived in the grasslands of what is now Inner Mongolia for countless generations, but the 1950's brought a wave of Chinese immigrants adding more livestock and seeking to cultivate the naturally arid land bordering the Gobi Desert. Today, expanding desertification claims 2,500 square kilometers at a cost of $6.5 billion to China's economy each year. The effects of the dust have been seen as far away as Colorado, where particulate concentrations rose above permissible levels in April 2001 after the jet stream carried the dust all the way from China. In March 2002, another dust storm dumped 30,000 tons of dirt on Beijing, even as billboards around the city trumpeted the "Green Olympics" to be held there in 2008. The resulting international publicity prompted local television newscasters to affirm the government's resolve to "outwit" the dust storms. The first law to try to match wits with the dust was enacted by the National People's Congress (NPC) in August 2001. The law against desertification:

- States that land occupants have a duty not only to prevent desertification but also to restore areas that have already become desert;

- Promises unspecified preferential policies, tax breaks, subsidies and technical support to offset the cost of this unfunded mandate;

- Creates a new class of protected areas off-limits to development and calls for farmers and herders to be removed from those areas; and

- Authorizes local governments to grant land-use rights of up to 70 years to desertified areas if the landholder promises to undertake restoration efforts.

China Adopts Law to Control Desertification: A November 2001 Report from U.S. Embassy Beijing, *available at* http://www.usembassy-china. org.cn/english/sandt/desertification_law.htm. As Qu Geping, the chair of the NPC Environment and Resources Committee, explained, the antidesertification law was designed to prevent the frequent dust storms that have sounded "a warning bell from nature."

Endangered wildlife is also protected by Chinese law. The Ministry of Forestry established the first list of Rare and Precious Species of China in 1969. A 1983 State Council circular orders that "[a]ll economic activities that affect the breeding and survival of endangered wildlife in their main nesting area should be banned." A general wildlife protection law was enacted in 1989. As of 1990, the List of State's Mainly Protected Wild Animals contained 96 animals; killing any species on that list is prohibited. Over a hundred other species appear on the list of animals to be protected by provincial and local governments; those governments are beginning to enact their own wildlife laws. China tightened its wildlife laws in 1993, bowing to pressure from the United States and international environmental groups.

The existence of such laws is one thing; their actual implementation is another. To be sure, there are examples of very stringent enforcement of wildlife laws in China. The government recently executed numerous poachers for killing endangered pandas. Five poachers were sentenced to death in 1994 after they killed sixteen elephants in a nature reserve in Yunnan province and then engaged in a fierce gun battle with police. In 1995, nineteen hotels and restaurants on Hainan Island were closed and fined $34,000 for serving bear's paw, monkey brains and other wildlife. China has promised to step up such efforts to punish those who kill endangered species for financial gain. *See generally* Charu Sharma, *Chinese Endangered Species at the Brink of Extinction: A Critical Look at the Current Law and Policy in China*, 11 ANIMAL L. 215, 239–43 (2005) (describing additional cases). China has also acted to prohibit patented medicines from containing ingredients taken from endangered species. *See* John Copeland Nagle; *Why Chinese Wildlife Disappears as CITES Spreads*, 9 GEORGETOWN INT'L ENVTL. L. REV. 435 (1997). A fishing ban on the Xiaolangdi Reservoir in central China soon resulted in the rediscovery of the copper cyprinid, a species that had been thought to be extinct. Most recently, China's state forestry agency charged a multinational paper corporation with illegally logging tens of thousands of acres of timber in Yunnan Province, apparently aided by local officials. But the Chinese government admits its failure to adequately enforce the existing laws protecting biodiversity:

> While many laws and regulations intended to protect biodiversity exist, in practice they are often not enforced or enforced strictly, or when the violators are apprehended, the court system treats them very leniently. As a result, illegal hunting and collection of endangered animal and plant species is very widespread, and disputes arise continuously between management of nature reserves and local residents, hindering biodiversity conservation efforts.

CHINA: BIODIVERSITY CONSERVATION ACTION PLAN, *supra*, at 32.

Non-governmental organizations (NGOs) have played a growing role in China's efforts to preserve it biodiversity. The Nature Conservancy is active in Yunnan Province, which hosts abundant biodiversity along the border with Vietnam, Myanmar, and Tibet. One of the organization's projects supports ecotourism, operates a community conservation development fund, and established a comprehensive fisheries management plan in the Lashi Lake watershed that serves as habitat for the endangered blacknecked crane. Other projects target ecosystems that are home to snow leopards, the Yunnan golden monkey, Asiatic black bears, red pandas, and thousands of acres of forests and alpine ecosystems. "In collaboration with the State Environmental Protection Agency (SEPA), the State Forestry Administration (SFA), and the Chinese Academy of Sciences," The Nature Conservancy is "advising and assisting in the development of a national biodiversity conservation action plan," "helping with the revision of China's Nature Reserve Law," "working to improve enforcement and monitoring mechanisms that ensure importation of certified timber and prohibit timber from illegal sources abroad," and "developing global climate change adaptation and carbon sequestration strategies." The Nature Conservancy, Places We Work: China, *available at* http://www.nature.org/ourinitiatives/regions/asia andthepacific/china/index.htm. Even so, "China's leaders . . . have been careful to circumscribe both the number of NGOs and the scope of their activities," so the role that such groups will be able to play in preserving the country's biodiversity remains uncertain. ELIZABETH C. ECONOMY, THE RIVER RUNS BLACK: THE ENVIRONMENTAL CHALLENGE TO CHINA'S FUTURE 130 (2004).

A final part of China's biodiversity strategy is its active participation in international efforts to protect biodiversity. In 1980, China joined the Convention on International Trade in Endangered Species (CITES, which is discussed below at page 1044). In 1992, it signed the Ramsar Convention for the protection of wetlands. That year also saw China become one of the first nations to ratify the Convention on Biological Diversity that was negotiated in Rio de Janeiro (discussed below at page 1054). China then launched a "China Biodiversity Conservation Plan" in 1994, and it discussed the measures needed to protect biodiversity in its white paper documenting China's efforts to further its Agenda 21 environmental commitments. The Agenda 21 strategy states that "[t]he policy for biodiversity conservation in China is 'laying equal stress on both the development and utilization and the conservation and protection of natural resources' and 'he who develops, conserves; he who utilizes, compensates; he who destroys, restores.' "CHINA'S AGENDA 21, *supra*, at 171–72.

But critics question China's resolve to end its trade in endangered species. China resisted international calls for the destruction of existing rhino horn stocks. It declined to become a member of the Global Tiger Forum established by twelve Asian countries in 1994 to protect endangered tigers throughout Asia. It advanced a proposal that would create a farm to raise tigers in order to satisfy the demand for tiger parts, though that idea was withdrawn after environmentalists objected. Its limited efforts to stop that trade have subjected China to international criticism. For example, in 1993 the United States and other countries threatened to sanction China for failing to control the trade in tiger and rhino parts. That the United States decided not to penalize China was viewed as an exercise in diplomacy unrelated to China's actual progress in enforcing the treaty. China's efforts to protect its ecosystems suffer from similar limitations on resources and political will. As one observer writes, China's solid national biodiversity policy "has made very little difference to the peoples of southwest China, where many of the reserves lack staff, funds, infrastructure, or a management plan. The international conservation community has focused on the panda at the expense of other species." John Studley, *Environmental Degradation in China*, CHINA REVIEW (Spring 1999), *available at* http://www.gbcc.org.uk/studley12.htm.

NOTES & QUESTIONS

1. The Chinese government's biodiversity conservation action plan states that "the overall objective of biodiversity in China is to set in place as soon as possible measures for avoiding further damage, and, over the long term, for mitigating or reversing the damage already done." CHINA: BIODIVERSITY CONSERVATION ACTION PLAN, *supra*, at 35. It then identifies several specific objectives designed to achieve that goal: improve the basic research on biodiversity in China, improve the national network of nature reserves and other protected areas, conserve wild species that are significant for biodiversity, conserve genetic resources related to crops and domestic livestock, promote in-site conservation outside nature reserves, establish a nationwide information and monitoring network for biodiversity conservation, and coordinate biodiversity and sustainable development. *Id.* at 35–47. Are these objectives attainable? Are there other goals that China should pursue in its effort to preserve its biodiversity?

2. Can China protect its biodiversity by itself? Could it do so if it received adequate funding and technical assistance from developed nations? How should other nations or the international community encourage or pressure China to protect its biodiversity?

B. EXTRATERRITORIAL APPLICATION OF DOMESTIC ENVIRONMENTAL LAWS

If a country is unable or unwilling to protect the biodiversity that lives within its borders, can another country adopt such protections itself? A country's laws usually only apply to activities that occur in the country's territory or to the country's own citizens, but there are many exceptions to that general rule. A country may also decide to subsidize or otherwise encourage the steps needed to protect biodiversity around the world. The choice of carrots—*e.g.*, providing financial assistance—or sticks—*e.g.*, regulating or sanctioning harmful conduct—often determines the popularity of a country's unilateral efforts to protect biodiversity outside its own borders. The more fundamental question is whether, or in what circumstances, it is appropriate for a country to use its laws to influence the management of ecosystems and species in other parts of the world.

Asian Elephant Conservation Act of 1997
House Report 105–266 Part 1.
United States House of Representatives Committee on Resources, 1997.
105th Congress, 1st Session.

The Committee on Resources, to whom was referred the bill (H.R. 1787) to assist in the conservation of Asian elephants by supporting and providing financial resources for the conservation programs of nations within the range of Asian elephants and projects of persons with demonstrated expertise in the conservation of Asian elephants, having considered the same, report favorably thereon with an amendment and recommend that the bill as amended do pass. . .

PURPOSE OF THE BILL

The purpose of H.R. 1787 is to create an Asian Elephant Conservation Fund and to authorize the Congress to appropriate up to $5 million per year to this Fund for each of the next five fiscal years to finance various conservation projects.

BACKGROUND AND NEED FOR LEGISLATION

In Asia, the relationship between man and elephant dates back almost 5,000 years when elephants were first captured and trained for use in religious ceremonies, war, and as draft animals. In fact, ancient Hindu scriptures frequently refer to elephants, the elephant-headed god Ganesh is revered throughout India, and the white elephant has special religious significance for Buddhists throughout Asia. In Chinese culture, elephants have played a special role in folklore, games, medicine and pageantry.

Asian elephants have also been used in forestry operations for many years. Today, wild elephants are still captured and trained for use in logging operations in Burma. Elsewhere throughout their range, domestic elephants are used for ceremonial, tourism and transportation purposes. These activities provide an important source of income to numerous local communities.

Sadly, the Asian elephant is now in grave danger and unless steps are immediately taken by the international community, the Asian elephant will largely disappear from most of its historical range. To date, the Asian elephant has been declared endangered and placed on the U.S. Endangered Species Act list, on the Red List of Mammals by the International Union for Conservation of Nature and Natural Resources (IUCN)-World Conservation Union, and on Appendix I of the Convention on International Trade in Endangered Species of Wild Fauna and Flora. Placement on Appendix I prohibits all commercial trade in Asian elephant products on a worldwide basis.

Despite these efforts, the population of Asian elephants living in the wild has dramatically fallen to about 40,000 animals, which is less than 10 percent of its elephant cousin (Loxodonta Africana) living in Africa. These wild populations are located in 13 countries in South and Southeast Asia. The largest population of 20,000 Asian elephants, or 50 percent of the total, resides in India; the smallest population of 50 animals is located in Nepal. What is equally distressing is the fact that there are only about 14 populations of 1,000 or more individuals in a contiguous area. Seven of these populations are found in Burma and India. In simple terms, this means that such drastic population fragmentation increases the likelihood of geographic extinctions and greatly reduces the long-term viability of the species. In addition, it has been estimated that there are about 16,000 domesticated elephants.

There are a number of important reasons why there has been a severe decline in the number of Asian elephants. The primary reason is the loss of habitat. All Asian elephants need a shady or forest environment, and this habitat is disappearing rapidly throughout Asia. Due to their sheer size and social structure, elephants need large areas to survive. Since Asian elephants inhabit some of the most densely populated areas of the world, forest clearance for homes and large-scale agricultural crops have resulted in a dramatic loss of thousands of acres of their habitat. In essence, elephants and man are in direct competition for the same resources.

Second, while poaching for ivory has not been an overriding reason for its decline, Asian elephants of both sexes are increasingly being poached for bones, hide, meat and teeth. Hide is used for bags and shoes in China and Thailand, and bones, teeth and other body parts are used in traditional Chinese medicine to cure various ailments. In fact, this type of poaching even threatens domestic elephants that are allowed to free-range in various forests.

Third, Asian elephants are still captured in the wild for domestication. In Burma, the country with the highest demand for work elephants, adult elephants are captured and trained for use in the timber industry. Regrettably, capture operations inevitably result in some mortalities and it does adversely affect the genetic pool of elephants living in the wild.

Finally, conflicts between elephants and people are increasing at an escalating rate. This is a direct result of the dramatic loss of forest habitat and the ensuing competition for the remaining resources. Every year, thousands of acres of agricultural crops are destroyed by elephants looking for food. In many cases, elephants encounter people where they were not found previously, thereby leading to the destruction of human lives and homes.

In countries where governments are concerned with this ever-increasing problem, measures taken are drastic and very expensive. For instance, in Malaysia, there was large-scale shooting of crop-raiding elephants in the late 1960s and, more recently, the construction of electric fences and translocation of problem elephants to protected areas. Other countries like Indonesia are taking short-term measures by capturing large numbers for domestication. However, they have found no long-term use for these domesticated elephants because there has been no traditional relationship between people and working elephants. In countries like Cambodia and Vietnam where no immediate solutions are provided by governmental authorities because of lack of financial resources, people are increasingly taking the law into their own hands and shooting the elephant offenders.

It is also important to understand that effective Asian elephant conservation and management efforts will have a positive effect on other species that reside in the same habitat. In the case of the Asian elephant, these include: the Asiatic wild dog, Clouded leopard, gaur, Great Pied hornbill, Hoolock gibbon, kouprey, Lion-tailed macaque, Malayan sun bear, peacock pheasant, rhinoceros and tiger. It is essential to the survival of these species that the Asian elephant not be allowed to disappear from this planet.

Finally, unlike the African elephant, there is no sport-hunting of Asian elephants and no large stockpiles of Asian elephant ivory in government warehouses in Asia or Southeast Asian countries.

COMMITTEE ACTION

... On Thursday, July 31, 1997, the Subcommittee on Fisheries Conservation, Wildlife and Oceans held a legislative hearing on H.R. 1787, the

Asian Elephant Conservation Act of 1997. The Subcommittee heard testimony from Mr. Marshall P. Jones, Assistant Director for International Affairs, United States Fish and Wildlife Service, Department of the Interior; Dr. Terry Maple, President and Chief Executive Officer, Zoo Atlanta; Dr. Eric Dinerstein, Chief Scientist and Director, World Wildlife Fund; the Honorable Andy Ireland, Senior Vice President, Feld Entertainment, Inc.; Dr. Raman Sukumar, Center for Ecological Sciences, Indian Institute of Science; Dr. Mary C. Pearl, Executive Director, Wildlife Preservation Trust International; and Dr. Michael Stowe, Research Associate, Smithsonian Institution. All witnesses testified in strong support of the bill.

Mr. Marshall Jones of the Interior Department testified that:

On behalf of the Administration, the Service fully supports the enactment of this legislation and congratulates the Congress on its foresight in recognizing and addressing the plight of the Asian elephant. Asian elephants need active protection and management of their habitat, resolution of the deleterious conflicts with humans over land uses, better law enforcement activities to protect against poaching, reduction of captures from the wild, and better care and humane treatment of the remaining captive populations. They also need the restoration of the harmonious relationship that previously existed with humans through community education and awareness activities. It is indeed timely that this Subcommittee is now considering H.R. 1787 (which) acknowledges the problems of forest habitat reduction and fragmentation, conflicts with humans, poaching and other serious issues affecting the Asian elephant. The Act addresses the need to encourage and assist initiatives of regional and national agencies and organizations whose activities directly or indirectly promote the conservation of Asian elephants and their habitat, and it provides for the establishment of an Asian Elephant Conservation Fund, authorized to receive donations and appropriated funds. While many range governments have demonstrated a commitment towards conservation, the lack of international support for their efforts has been a serious impediment. . .

CONGRESSIONAL BUDGET OFFICE COST ESTIMATE

. . . Summary: H.R. 1787 would establish a new fund to support the conservation of Asian elephants. The bill would direct the Secretary of the Interior to use amounts in the new fund to finance eligible conservation efforts, which may include specific projects such as research and education as well as ongoing activities such as law enforcement. For this purpose, the bill would authorize appropriations to the fund of $5 million for each of fiscal years 1998 through 2002. Also, the Secretary would be authorized to accept and use donated funds without further appropriation.

Assuming appropriation of the authorized amounts, CBO estimates that implementing H.R. 1787 would result in additional discretionary spending of about $10 million over the 1998–2002 period (with the remainder of the authorized $25 million estimated to be spent after 2002). The legislation would affect direct spending and receipts by allowing the Secretary to accept and spend donations; therefore, pay-as-you-go procedures would apply. Any such transactions, however, would involve minor, offsetting amounts. H.R. 1787 does not contain any intergovernmental or private-sector mandates as defined in the Unfunded Mandates Reform Act of 1995 (UMRA), and would have no impact on the budgets of state, local, or tribal governments.

NOTES & QUESTIONS

1. Why is the plight of the African elephant a problem for the United States Congress? How does the committee report's description of the need for the legislation explain why it is the United States that should enact such legislation?

2. The U.S. Fish & Wildlife Service proclaims that [t]he 2010 Congressional appropriation of $2 Million to the Asian Elephant Conservation Fund allowed the Service to support 41 crucial elephant conservation projects within Asia, including:

- Build local capacity for Asian elephant research through a hands-on training workshop in Bhutan and develop capacity for Bhutanese and other Asian participants in non-invasive sampling techniques such as fecal DNA sampling and camera trapping, developing study design, protocols for conservation research, project implementation and data analysis, making reliable inferences of results and educational outreach.

- Estimate the Asian elephant population size and distribution, improve local capacity to protect Asian elephants and implement management activities across the Northern Plains of Cambodia.

- Conduct environmental education in local communities, expand community elephant monitoring networks to inform population studies, carry out habitat conservation and human-elephant conflict mitigation strategies and implement a community development fund for economic alternatives to reduce human elephant conflict in China.

- Identify emerging diseases and their prevalence in Asian elephants and determine their impact for future long-term conservation, assess stress levels in populations using new molecular techniques and assess morbidity and mortality in the largest Asian elephant population in Southern India.

- Strengthen protection measures by involving fringe villagers in Manas National Park in the conservation of Asian elephants. Financially support 45 volunteers to enhance protection of Asian elephants and other wildlife and their habitats at Manas National Park in Assam in India.

- Target conservation outreach on Asian elephants in the Western Ghats in India, extend conservation outreach to decision makers by holding workshops and conducting field visits aimed at providing the required exposure to target groups to effect pro-elephant conservation policies, development plans and minimize negative impacts on wild elephants and their habitats.

- Improve Asian elephant monitoring through patrolling and enforcement in Nam Pouy National Protected Area Lao PDR. Develop a system for patrolling and response to illegal activities in Nam Pouy NPA, improve the capacity of law enforcement personnel, NPA staff and local villagers, assess and adapt the patrolling system and provide training in Monitoring Information Systems (MIST)."

FWS, Asian Elephant Conservation Fund (Feb. 2011), http://www.fws.gov/international/semipostal/asefs11.pdf. The FWS awarded 161 grants totaling over $8 million between 2006 and 2010. *Id.* The FWS thus told Congress that the Act "has greatly enhanced the conservation status of the Asian elephant." *Wildlife Conservation Bills: Hearing Before the Subcomm. on Fisheries, Wildlife & Insular Affairs of the House Natural Resources Comm.*, 112th Cong., 1st Sess. (2011) (testimony of Teiko Saito, Assistant Director, International Affairs, FWS).

Reflecting on the first ten years of the Act, a FWS official and an elephant sanctuary director advised:

> The concept of "sustainable development" may require serious re-evaluation; it may be well past the time when any development can be considered, sustainable or otherwise. A better approach would be to think in terms of "sustainable management" of natural resources. With accelerating global climate change and worldwide recognition of the need for restoration and conservation of natural forests for the purposes of carbon sequestration, protection of ecosystem services, and natural disaster mitigation, there is now further possibility of expanding ideas on habitat protection. It is important for conservationists to look at ways to make communities benefit from forest protection and restoration, such as by providing carbon credits directly to the communities involved in habitat protection and restoration efforts.

Meenakshi Nagendran & Heidi S. Riddle, *The U.S. Fish and Wildlife Service Asian Elephant Conservation Fund - The First Ten Years of Support*, 29 GAJAH 45, 48 (2008). Can development and the Asian elephant coexist? How can the Act – or any action by the United States – promote such coexistence?

3. The African Elephant Conservation Act is just one of a number of U.S. statutes designed to assist the protection of biodiversity overseas. The Neotropical Migratory Bird Conservation Act, Pub. L. No. 106–247, 114 Stat. 593 (2000), is the one such statute. The three purposes of the act are "(1) to perpetuate healthy populations of neotropical migratory birds; (2) to assist in the conservation of neotropical migratory birds by supporting conservation initiatives in the United States, Latin America, and the Caribbean; and (3) to provide financial resources and to foster international cooperation for those initiatives." *Id.* § 3. The act seeks to achieve these goals by funding conservation projects, authorizing federal appropriations and private donations to the Neotropical Migratory Bird Conservation Account, sharing information and encouraging meetings among people and organizations involved in protecting the birds, and developing appropriate international agreements. *Id.* §§ 5–7, 9. Which activities should receive the Secretary of the Interior's highest priority in implementing the act?

Listing Six Foreign Birds as Endangered Throughout Their Range

United States Fish and Wildlife Service, 2011.
76 Federal Register 50052.

We, the U.S. Fish and Wildlife Service, determine endangered status for the following six foreign species found on islands in French Polynesia and in Europe, Southeast Asia, and Africa: Cantabrian capercaillie (*Tetrao urogallus cantabricus*); Marquesan imperial pigeon (*Ducula galeata*); the Eiao Marquesas reed-warbler (*Acrocephalus percernis aquilonis*), previously referred to as (*Acrocephalus mendanae aquilonis*); greater adjutant (*Leptoptilos dubius*); Jerdon's courser (*Rhinoptilus bitorquatus*); and slender-billed curlew (*Numenius tenuirostris*), under the Endangered Species Act of 1973 (Act), as amended. [The FWS listed each species as endangered pursuant to the five factors specified in the ESA and described above in chapter 4. Here we excerpt only the agency's discussion of "the inadequacy of existing regulatory mechanisms" for each species.]

I. Cantabrian capercaillie (Tetrao urogallus cantabricus)

Species Description

The Cantabrian capercaillie (*Tetrao urogallus cantabricus*) is a subspecies of the western capercaillie (*T. urogallus*) in the family Tetraonidae. The species in general is a large, very dark grouse of 80 to 115 centimeters (cm) in length (31 to 45 inches (in)), with the female being much smaller than the male. . . The Cantabrian capercaillie once existed along the whole of the Cantabrian Mountain range from northern Portugal through Galicia, Asturias, and Leon, to Santander in northern Spain (IUCN Redbook 1979, p. 1). Currently its range is restricted to both the northern slope (Asturias and Cantabria provinces) and the southern slope (Leon and Palencia provinces) of the Cantabrian Mountains in northwest Spain. The subspecies inhabits an area of 1,700 square kilometers (656 square miles), and its range is separated from its nearest neighboring subspecies of capercaillie (*T. u. aquitanus*) in the Pyrenees mountains by a distance of more than 300 km (186 mi) (Quevedo *et al.* 2006b, p. 268). . . The current population is likely less than 1,000 birds; however, reliable estimates are lacking. . .

This subspecies is currently classified as "in danger of extinction" in Spain under the National Catalog of Endangered Species, which affords it special protection (*e.g.*, additional regulation of activities in the forests of its range, regulation of trails and roads in the area, elimination of poaching, and protection of areas important to young). Although it is classified as "in danger of extinction" . . . illegal hunting still occurs.

In conjunction with this subspecies being listed as "in danger of extinction" under the National Catalog of Endangered Species, a recovery plan for the Cantabrian capercaillie was approved by the Autonomous Community of Castilla and Leon. This official document approves the recovery plan and adopts measures for the protection of the species in the Community of Castilla and Leon. The purpose of the Recovery Plan is to foster necessary actions to allow the species to achieve a more favorable conservation status and to ensure its long-term viability and stop population decline. The Recovery Plan includes requirements that the effects to the Cantabrian capercaillie or its habitat be considered before a plan or activity can be implemented; restricting access to critical areas; suspension of resource exploitation activities following wildlife catastrophic events (*e.g.*, animal epidemics, poisoning, widespread wildfires) to allow for recovery; prohibiting certain activities within critical areas; and specific measures to meet the goals of the Recovery Plan.

The European Union (EU) Habitat Directive 92/43/EEC addresses the protection of habitat and species listed as endangered at the European scale. Several habitat types valuable to capercaillie have been included in this Directive, such as in Appendix I, Section 9, Forests. The EU Bird Directive (79/407/EEC) lists the capercaillie in Annex I as a "species that shall be subject to special habitat conservation measures in order to ensure their survival." Under this Directive, a network of Special Protected Areas (SPAs) comprising suitable habitat for Annex I species is to be designated. This network of SPAs and other protected sites are collectively referred to as Natura 2000. Several countries in Europe, including Spain, are in the process of establishing the network of SPAs. The remaining Cantabrian capercaillie populations occur primarily in recently established Natural Reserves in Spain that are part of the Natura 2000 network (Muniellos Biosphere Reserve). Management of natural resources by local communities is still allowed in areas designated as an SPA; however, the development of management plans to meet the various objectives of the Reserve network is required.

This subspecies is also afforded special protection under the Bern Convention. The Cantabrian capercaillie is listed as "strictly protected" under Appendix II, which requires member states to ensure the conservation of the listed taxa and their habitats. Under this Convention, protections of Appendix-II species include the prohibition of: The deliberate capture, keeping, and killing of the species; deliberate damage or destruction of breeding sites; deliberate disturbance during the breeding season; deliberate taking or destruction of eggs; and the possession or trade of any individual of the species. We were unable to find information on the effectiveness of this designation in preventing further loss of Cantabrian capercaillie or its habitat; however, poaching of protected grouse is known to be common, suggesting that this designation has not been effectively implemented.

In November 2003, Spain enacted the "Forest Law," which addresses the preservation and improvement of the forest and rangelands in Spain. This law requires development of plans for the management of forest resources, which are to include plans for fighting forest fires, establishment of danger zones based on fire risk, formulation of a defense plan in each established danger zone, the mandatory restoration of burned area, and the prohibition of changing forest use of a burned area into other uses for a period of 30 years. In addition, this law provides economic incentives for sustainable forest management by private landowners and local entities. We do not have information on the effectiveness of this law with regard to its ability to prevent negative impacts to Cantabrian capercaillie habitat.

Despite recent advances in protection of this subspecies and its habitat through EU Directives and protection under Spanish law and regulation, populations continue to decline, habitat continues to be degraded, lost, and fragmented, and illegal poaching still occurs. We were unable to find information on the effectiveness of any of these measures at reducing threats to the species. Therefore, we find that existing regulatory mechanisms are inadequate to ameliorate the current threats to the Cantabrian capercaillie throughout its range. . .

II. Eiao Marquesas Reed-Warbler (Acrocephalus percernis aquilonis), Previously Referred to as Eiao Polynesian Warbler (Acrocephalus mendanae aquilonis and Acrocephalus caffer aquilonis)

Species Description

. . . The Eiao Marquesas reed-warbler (Eiao reed-warbler) is a large, insectivorous reed-warbler of the family Acrocephalidae. It is characterized by brown plumage with bright yellow underparts. The Eiao reed-warbler is endemic to the island of Eiao in the French Polynesian Marquesas Archipelago in the Pacific Ocean. The Marquesas Archipelago is a territory of France located approximately 1,600 km (994 mi) northeast of Tahiti. Eiao Island is one of the northernmost islands in the Archipelago and encompasses 40 km^2 (15 mi^2).

Population densities of the Eiao reed-warbler are thought to be high within the remaining suitable habitat; one singing bird was found nearly every 40-50 m (131-164 ft). The total population is estimated at more than 2,000 birds. This population estimate is much larger than the 100-200 individuals last reported in 1987 . . . It is unknown if the population actually increased from 1987 to 2007, or if the differences in the population estimates are a result of using different survey methodologies. We have no reliable information on the population trend of this subspecies. . .

The Eiao reed-warbler is a protected species in French Polynesia. Northern Marquesas reed-warblers (*A. percernis*) are classified as a Category A species under Law Number 95-257. Article 16 of this law prohibits the collection and exportation of species listed under Category A. In addition, under Part 23 of Law 95-257, the introduced myna bird species, which is commonly known to outcompete other bird species, is considered a danger to the local avifauna and is listed as "threatening biodiversity." Part 23 also prohibits importation of all new specimens of species listed as "threatening biodiversity," and translocation from one island to another is prohibited. As described above, Eiao Island is not currently inhabited by humans and we found that overutilization for commercial, recreational, scientific, or educational purposes is not a threat to this subspecies. Furthermore, mynas do not occur on Eiao Island and is not a threat to the Eiao reed-warbler. Although this law may provide adequate protection to this subspecies from these threats, it does not protect the Eiao reed-warbler from current threats such as habitat destruction.

The French Environmental Code, Article L411-1, prohibits the destruction or poaching of eggs or nests; mutilation, destruction, capture or poaching, intentional disturbance, the practice of taxidermy, transport, peddling, use, possession, offer for sale, and the sale or the purchase of non-domesticated species in need of conservation, including northern Marquesas reed-warblers (*A. percernis*). It also prohibits the destruction, alteration, or degradation of habitat for these species. As overutilization for commercial, recreational, scientific, or educational purposes is not a threat to this subspecies, this regulation may provide adequate protection against this threat; however, habitat destruction by overgrazing livestock remains a problem on Eiao Island. Therefore this regulation does not provide adequate protection against threats currently faced by this subspecies.

Hunting and destruction of all species of birds in French Polynesia were prohibited by a 1967 decree; however, destruction of birds which have been listed as "threatening biodiversity" is legal. Furthermore, restrictions on possession of firearms in Marquesas are in place. Hunting is not known to be a threat to the survival of this subspecies.

In addition, the entire Eiao Island was declared an officially protected area in 1971. It is classified as Category IV, an area managed for habitat or species. However, of the nine protected areas in French Polynesia, only one (Vaikivi on Ua Huka) is actively managed. We found no information on the direct effects of this protective status on the Eiao reed-warbler or its habitat. However, Eiao Island is not actively managed and, as discussed under Factor A, the entire island has been heavily impacted by introduced domestic livestock, suggesting this regulatory mechanism is not effective at reducing or ameliorating threats to the species.

In summary, regulations exist that protect the subspecies and its habitat. However, as described under Factor A, habitat destruction continues to threaten this subspecies. Although legal protections are in place, there are none effectively protecting the suitable habitat on the island from damage from overgrazing sheep and other livestock as described in Factor A. Therefore, we find that the existing regulatory mechanisms are inadequate to ameliorate the current threats to the Eiao reed-warbler throughout its range.

III. Greater Adjutant (Leptoptilos dubius)

Species Description

The greater adjutant (*Leptoptilos dubius*) is a very large (145 to 150 cm long (4.7 to 4.9 ft)) species of stork in the family Ciconiidae. This species is characterized by a naked pink head and a low-hanging neck pouch. Its bill is very thick and yellow in color. The plumage ruff of the neck is white,

and other than a pale grey leading edge on each wing, the rest of the greater adjutant's body is dark grey.

This species of bird once was common across much of Southeast Asia,
occurring in India, Bangladesh, Burma, Thailand, Cambodia, Malaysia,
Myanmar, Vietnam, Sumatra, Java, and Borneo. Large breeding colonies
occurred in Myanmar, with the highest concentration found in Pegu; however, this colony collapsed in the mid-1900s.

The current distribution of this species consists of two breeding populations, one in India and the other in Cambodia. Recent sighting records of
this species from the neighboring countries of Nepal, Bangladesh, Vietnam,
and Thailand are presumed to be wandering birds from one of the two populations in India and Cambodia. . .

Although there is evidence of commercial trade across the Cambodia
border into Laos and Thailand, this species is currently not listed under
CITES.

India: The greater adjutant is listed under Schedule I of the Indian
Wildlife Protection Act of 1972 (IWPA). Schedule I provides absolute protection, with the greatest penalties for offenses. This law prohibits hunting,
possession, sale, and transport of listed species. The IWPA also provides for
the designation and management of sanctuaries and national parks for the
purposes of protecting, propagating, or developing wildlife or its environment. As stated above in Factor A, the ongoing loss of habitat through habitat conversion for development and agriculture is a primary threat to this
species. Furthermore, greater adjutant eggs and chicks are known to be
taken for local consumption and trade, and adult birds are known to be poisoned, netted, and trapped for various reasons. Therefore, this regulatory
mechanism is not adequate to ameliorate these threats to this species.

Protected areas in India allow for regulated levels of human use and
disturbance and are managed to prevent widespread clearing and complete
loss of suitable habitat. Although the greater adjutant uses habitat in three
national parks in India, almost all nesting colonies of this species in India
are found outside of protected areas. Some of the species' foraging areas are
also located outside of protected areas. Ongoing loss of habitat through habitat conversion for development and agriculture is a primary threat to this
species; therefore, it appears that regulatory mechanisms outside of protected areas, such as national parks, do not provide adequate protection of
habitat for the greater adjutant.

Cambodia: Areas designated as natural areas by the Ministry of Environment, such as the Tonle Sap Biosphere Reserve, are to be managed for
the protection of the natural resources contained within. Portions of the
Biosphere Reserve have also been designated as areas of importance under
the Convention of Wetlands of International Importance of 1971.

The Mekong River Commission (MRC) was formed between the governments of Cambodia, Lao PDR, Thailand, and Vietnam in 1995 as part of

the Agreement on the Cooperation for the Sustainable Development of the Mekong River Basin. The signatories agreed to jointly manage their shared water resources and the economic development of the river. According to the Asian Development Bank, 13 dams have been built, are being built, or are proposed to be built along the Mekong River. The continued modification of greater adjutant habitat has been identified as a primary threat to this species (Factor A), and this regional regulatory mechanism is not effective at reducing that threat.

Several laws exist in Cambodia to protect the greater adjutant from two of the primary threats to the species: Habitat destruction and hunting. However, they are ineffective at reducing those threats. In Cambodia, Declaration No. 359, issued by the Ministry of Agriculture, Forestry and Fisheries in 1994, prohibits the hunting of greater adjutant. However, reports of severe hunting pressure within the greater adjutant's habitat exist and illegal poaching of wildlife in Cambodia continues.

The Creation and Designation of Protected Areas regulation (November 1993) established a national system of protected areas. In 1994, through Declaration No. 1033 on the Protection of Natural Areas, the following activities were banned in all protected areas:

(1) Construction of saw mills, charcoal ovens, brick kilns, tile kilns, limestone ovens, tobacco ovens;

(2) Hunting or placement of traps for tusks, bones, feathers, horns, leather, or blood;

(3) Deforestation;

(4) Mining minerals or use of explosives;

(5) The use of domestic animals such as dogs;

(6) Dumping of pollutants;

(7) The use of machines or heavy cars which may cause smoke pollution;

(8) Noise pollution; and

(9) Unpermitted research and experiments.

In addition, the Law on Environmental Protection and Natural Resource Management of 1996 sets forth general provisions for environmental protection. Under Article 8 of this law, Cambodia declares that its natural resources (including wildlife) shall be conserved, developed, and managed and used in a rational and sustainable manner.

Protected Areas have been established within the range of the greater adjutant, such as the Tonle Sap Lake Biosphere Reserve. The Tonle Sap Great Lake protected area was designated a multipurpose protected area in

1993. Under this decree, Multiple Use Management Areas are those areas which provide for the sustainable use of water resources, timber, wildlife, fish, pasture, and recreation; the conservation of nature is primarily oriented to support these economic activities. In 1997, the Tonle Sap region was nominated as a Biosphere Reserve under UNESCO's (United Nations Educational, Scientific and Cultural Organization) "Man and the Biosphere Program." The Cambodian Government developed a National Environmental Action Plan (NEAP) in 1997, supporting the UNESCO site goals. Among the priority areas of intervention are fisheries and floodplain agriculture at Tonle Sap Lake, biodiversity and protected areas, and environmental education. NEAP was followed by the adoption of the Strategy and Action Plan for the Protection of Tonle Sap (SAPPTS) in February 1998, and the issuance of a Royal Decree officially creating Tonle Sap Lake Biosphere Reserve (TSBR) on April 10, 2001. The royal decree was followed by a subdecree by the Prime Minister to establish a Secretariat, along with its roles and functions, for the TSBR with the understanding that its objectives could not be achieved without cooperation and coordination among relevant stakeholders.

Joint Declaration No. 1563, on the Suppression of Wildlife Destruction in the Kingdom of Cambodia, was issued by the Ministry of Agriculture, Forestry, and Fisheries in 1996. Although the Japan International Cooperation Agency reported that this regulatory measure was ineffectively enforced, some strides have been made recently through the combined efforts of WCS, the Cambodian Government, and local communities at Tonle Sap Lake. WCS Cambodia reports that the illegal wildlife trade in Cambodia is "enormous" and driven by demand for meat and traditional medicines in Thailand, Vietnam, and China. Substantial progress has been made in protecting seven species of waterbirds at Prek Toal Core Area in the TSBR, increasing populations of some species tenfold by working with the primary management agencies and working at the field level to improve community engagement, law enforcement, and long-term research and monitoring.

The Forestry Law of 2002 strictly prohibits hunting, harming, or harassing wildlife (Article 49). This law further prohibits the possession, trapping, transport, or trade in rare and endangered wildlife (Article 49). However, to our knowledge, Cambodia has not yet published a list of endangered or rare species. Thus, this law is not currently effective at protecting the greater adjutant from threats by hunting.

In 2006, the Cambodian Government created Integrated Farming and Biodiversity Areas (IFBA), including over 161 km (100 mi) of grassland (over 30,000 ha (74,132 ac)) near Tonle Sap Lake to protect the Bengal florican, an endangered bird in that region. The above measures have focused attention on the conservation situation at TSBR and have begun to improve the conservation of the area and its wildlife there, but several management challenges remain. These challenges include overexploitation of flooded forests and fisheries; negative impacts from invasive species; lack of monitoring and enforcement; low level of public awareness of biodiversity values; and uncoordinated research, monitoring, and evaluation of species' populations.

Even though the wildlife laws discussed above exist, greater adjutant habitat within Cambodian protected areas faces several challenges. The legal framework governing wetlands management is institutionally complex. It rests upon legislation vested in government agencies responsible for land use planning (Land Law 2001), resource use (Fishery Law 1987), and environmental conservation (Environmental Law 1996, Royal Decree on the Designation and Creation of National Protected Areas System 1993); however, there is no interministerial coordinating mechanism nationally for wetland planning and management. As a result of this institutional complexity and lack of defined jurisdiction, natural resource use goes largely unregulated. Thus, the protected areas system in Cambodia is ineffective in removing or reducing the threats of habitat modification and hunting faced by the greater adjutant.

Existing regulatory mechanisms in both India and Cambodia are ineffective at reducing or removing threats to the species such as habitat modification and collection of eggs and chicks for consumption. Although progress has been made recently in the protection of nests and birds at specific locations, this has largely been driven by measures from the private sector. We believe that the inadequacy of regulatory mechanisms, especially with regard to lack of law enforcement and habitat protection, is a significant risk factor for the greater adjutant. Therefore, we find that existing regulatory mechanisms are inadequate to ameliorate the current threats to the greater adjutant throughout its range. . .

IV. Jerdon's Courser (Rhinoptilus bitorquatus)

. . . The Jerdon's courser is a rare species of bird that is endemic to the Eastern Ghats of the states of Andhra Pradesh and extreme southern Madhya Pradesh in India (BLI 2009b, unpaginated). The size of the population is not known. Historically, this species was reported in the Khamman, Nellore, and Anantapur districts of Andhra Pradesh and the Gadchiroli District of Maharashtra. Until 1900, its presence was periodically recorded, including some records in the Pennar and Godavari river valleys and near Anantapur. Efforts by various ornithologists in the early 1930s and mid to late 1970s to record the presence of this species failed, leading to the belief that the species was extinct. In 1986, the Jerdon's courser was rediscovered near Reddipalli village.

The area where the species was rediscovered was designated as the Sri Lankamaleswara Wildlife Sanctuary (SLWS). After its rediscovery, it was only observed regularly at a few sites in and around the SLWS, including reports of its presence in Sri Penusula Narasimha Wildlife Sanctuary (SPNWS) in the Cuddapah and Nellore districts, Andhra Pradesh. It has since been found at three additional localities in and around SLWL. . .

The Jerdon's courser is listed under Schedule I of the Indian Wildlife Protection Act of 1972. Schedule I provides absolute protection with the greatest penalties for offenses. This law prohibits hunting, possession, sale, and transport of listed species and allows the State Government to designate an area as a sanctuary or national park for the purpose of protecting, propagating, or developing wildlife or its environment. The Jerdon's courser is also listed as a priority species under the National Wildlife Action Plan (2002-2016) of India. This National Plan includes guidance to expand and strengthen the existing network of protected areas, develop management plans for protected areas in the country, restore and manage degraded habitats outside of protected areas, and control activities such as poaching and illegal trade, among others. We are unaware of any management plans for the protected areas in Andhra Pradesh where the Jerdon's courser occurs. This species is also proposed as a threatened species under section 38 of the Biological Diversity Act, 2002.

The SLWS and SPNWS were established for the purpose of protecting the habitat of the Jerdon's courser. The sanctuaries allow for regulated levels of human use and disturbance while preventing complete loss of scrub habitat. The SLWS and SPNWS are protected by the Forest Conservation Act of 1980. Section 2 of this law restricts the use of forest land for nonforest purposes, such as the fragmentation or clearing of any forest. In addition, the SLWS and SNPWS are designated as Important Bird Areas (IBA) in India. IBAs are sites of international importance for the conservation of birds, as well as other animals and plants, and are meant to be used to focus conservation efforts and reinforce the existing protected areas network. However, designation as an IBA provides no legal protection of these areas.

In 2010, a recovery plan was published for the Jerdon's courser. The plan uses a multi-pronged approach to secure the long-term survival of this species. Elements of the plan include research, monitoring, advocacy, conservation education, habitat management, training, and funding. The actions outlined in the plan involve several national and international groups and the APFD, which has the primary responsibility for the management of Jerdon's courser habitat. Implementation of the recovery plan is dependent on funding (approximately 1.8 million U.S. dollars) and the cooperation of several agencies. Although this plan was published by the APFD and submitted to The Ministry of Environment and Forests, Government of India, we could not determine that implementation of this plan is mandatory or binding; rather the plan is meant to serve as a reference for conservation managers, policy-makers, researchers, decision-makers, and serve as a basis for future conservation actions. Furthermore, as this recovery plan was just published in November 2010, it is too early to determine if this plan will be effective in providing protection to the species. . . In summary, although protections for the species exist, the primary threat to this species is ongoing loss of habitat . . .

V. Marquesan Imperial Pigeon (Ducula galeata)

The Marquesan Imperial Pigeon (*Ducula galeata*), known locally as Upe, is a very large arboreal pigeon belonging to the family Columbidae. . . The pigeon is endemic to the French Polynesian Marquesas Archipelago in

the Pacific Ocean. The Marquesas Archipelago is a territory of France located approximately 1,600 km (994 mi) northeast of Tahiti. Based on
subfossil records, the pigeon was historically present on four islands in the
Marquesas Archipelago, Hiva Oa, Ua Huka, Tahuata, and Nuku Hiva, as
well as the Cook, the Pitcairn, and Society Island chains. At the time of its
discovery, the pigeon was already restricted to Nuku Hiva, a 337 km<2>
(130 sq mi<2>) island. Researchers believe that hunting, degradation of
local forest, invasive weeds and trees, and predation were the probable
causes of its decline. On Nuku Hiva, the pigeon is restricted to 7 sites
which are difficult to access by hunters and livestock. In an effort to protect
the remaining population from extinction due to catastrophic events, the
pigeon was reintroduced to Ua Huka, an island 50 km (31 mi) east of Nuku
Hiva in 2000. Ua Huka was chosen as a reintroduction site primarily because the pigeon was historically found on the island, and due to availability of suitable habitat located in a protected area, a lack of black rats
(*Rattus rattus*), and a smaller human population compared to other
Marquesan islands.

Population estimates on Nuku Hiva have ranged from 75 to 300 birds
since 1975; however, the most recent survey, conducted in 2000, estimated
the population to be approximately 80-150 birds. In 2000, five birds were
translocated to Ua Huka and an additional five translocated in 2003. In
2006, approximately 32 birds were present. In 2008, another survey was
conducted. Two groups of nine and six birds were observed within the initial translocation. . .

The Marquesan imperial pigeon is a protected species in French Polynesia; it is classified as a Category A species under Law Number 95-257.
Article 16 of this law prohibits the collection and exportation of species
listed under Category A. Under Article L411-1 of the French Environmental Code, the destruction or poaching of eggs or nests, mutilation, destruction, capture or poaching, intentional disturbance, the practice of taxidermy, transport, peddling, use, possession, offer for sale, or the sale or the
purchase of nondomestic species in need of conservation is prohibited. The
French Environmental Code also prohibits the destruction, alteration, or
degradation of habitat for these species.

Hunting of this species is believed to be one of the main reasons for the
species' decline. Hunting and destruction of all species of birds in French
Polynesia was prohibited by a decree enacted in 1967. Furthermore, although restrictions on possession of firearms in Marquesas are in place,
firearms are made available through visiting. On Ua Huka, there is an
agreement in force not to hunt pigeons. Although this species is fully protected, and hunting has been banned, illegal hunting of the Marquesan Imperial pigeon still occurs and remains a threat on Nuku Hiva.

The Marquesas Archipelago is designated as an Endemic Bird Area
(EBA) (Manu 2009, unpaginated, BLI 2009c). EBAs are territories less
than 50,000 km<2> (19,300 mi<2>) where at least two bird species with
restricted ranges are found together, and represent priority areas for biodiversity. Nord-Ouest de Nuku Hiva is 9,000 ha area designated as an Im-

portant Bird Area (IBA). Designation as an IBA constitutes recognition of the area as a critical site for conservation of birds. In addition, Nuku Hiva is designated as an Alliance for Zero Extinction (AZE) (Manu 2009, unpaginated). AZEs are considered areas that are in the most urgent need of conservation. Although Nuku Hiva and Ua Huka are designated as areas of importance to the conservation of birds, these designations only serve to identify areas of biodiversity and focus conservation efforts; there is no legal protection of these areas. There is one officially protected area on Ua Huka (Vaikivi), established in 1997, which is actively managed.

In summary, regulations exist to protect the species and its habitat. The threats that affect the species on each island are different. On the island of Ua Huka, also described under Factors A and B, destruction and modification of habitat are not known to threaten this species and illegal hunting is not occurring. This is likely because the protected area on Ua Huka is actively managed, the human population is less substantial, and there is a local agreement preventing hunting on this island. Furthermore, pigeons were reintroduced to Ua Huka due to the absence of threats to the species. Therefore, we find that the inadequacy of existing regulatory mechanisms is not applicable to Ua Huka. However, as described in Factors A and B, habitat destruction continues to threaten this species and illegal hunting continues to occur on the island of Nuku Hiva. Therefore, we find that the existing regulatory mechanisms are inadequate to ameliorate the current threats to the Marquesan imperial pigeon on the island of Nuku Hiva. . .

VI. Slender-Billed Curlew (Numenius tenuirostris)

The slender-billed curlew (*Numenius tenuirostris*) is a species of wading bird, one of the six curlews of the same genus within the family Scolopacidae. . . The species is believed to breed in Northwest Siberia (though the only two confirmed cases of breeding were in 1914 and 1924). The species migrates 5,000-6,000 km (3,100-3,700 mi) towards the west-southwest across Kazakhstan, passing north of the Caspian and Black Seas through southeastern and southern Europe to its wintering grounds in the Mediterranean and Middle East.

The species has been sighted in Eastern Europe, including Russia, Kazakhstan, Ukraine, Bulgaria, Hungary, Romania, and Yugoslavia; in Southern Europe, including Albania, Greece, Italy, and Turkey; in Western Europe, including France and Spain; in North Africa, including Algeria, Morocco, and Tunisia; and in the Middle East, including Iran and. It has also been reported in Slovenia, Uzbekistan, Turkmenistan, Oman, Saudi Arabia, and Yemen.

During the 19th Century, the slender-billed curlew was described as the most common curlew in countries such as Spain, Sicily, Malta, Tunisia, Morocco, and Algeria; described as abundant in Romania, southeast Hungary, and Italy; and regularly recorded in France. Flocks were reported as hundreds, sometimes thousands, strong. Its population density frequently exceeded that of two relative species: The Eurasian curlew (*Nemenius arquata*) and the whimbrel (*Numenius phaeopus*). From 1900 to the 1930s, the species was still regularly recorded, although not as abundant as in the 1800s. By 1940, a decline in slender-billed curlew populations was apparent and the species continued to decline, although flocks of more 100 birds were recorded in Morocco as late as the 1960s and 1970s. In 1978, a flock of 150 birds was observed in Turkey. In the 1970s and 1980s, about 10-15 sightings were reported annually. In the 1990s, annual records consist of sightings of 1 to 3 birds, with the exception of 19 birds sighted in Italy in 1995 and a group of up to 50 wintering along the southern coast of Iran.

No nesting birds have been found since 1924, although in 1996 an adult slender-billed curlew in flight was reported west-north-west of Tara. Juveniles were reported in 1998 and 1999, indicating that the slender-billed curlew is still breeding somewhere. Between 1987 and 1995, 1 to 3 slender-billed curlews were regularly recorded in Merja Zergas (Morocco), the last known regular wintering site; however, it has not been recorded at this location since 1995. Most of the recent records have come from south-eastern Europe in countries along the migration route. However, the last confirmed sighting of a slender-billed curlew was in 2001 in Hungary.

The most recent population estimate is fewer than 50 birds. Surveys were conducted from 1987 through 2000 in various parts of the species' historic breeding range, which covered several thousand kilometers of habitat. No slender-billed curlews were found during these survey efforts. In 2009-10 a search to find this species within the non-breeding range began; this survey involved teams of observers covering 35 countries around the Mediterranean, Middle East, and Indian subcontinent. As of March 2010, no slender-billed curlews have been found, which may mean the population is below an absolute minimum to be able to recover.

As stated above, the slender-billed curlew is listed on Annex I of the European Union (EU) Wild Bird Directive, which includes protection for habitat, bans on activities that directly threaten wild birds, and a network of protected areas for wild birds found within the EU.

The slender-billed curlew is listed in Appendix I of CITES. CITES is an international treaty among 175 nations, including Albania, Algeria, Bulgaria, France, Greece, Hungary, Iran, Italy, Kazakhstan, Morocco, Oman, Romania, Russia, Saudi Arabia, Slovenia, Spain, Tunisia, Turkey, Ukraine, Yemen, and the United States, entered into force in 1975. In the United States, CITES is implemented through the U.S. Endangered Species Act of 1973, as amended. The Secretary of the Interior has delegated the Department's responsibility for CITES to the Director of the Service and established the CITES Scientific and Management Authorities to implement the treaty. Under this treaty, member countries work together to ensure that international trade in animal and plant species is not detrimental to the survival of wild populations by regulating the import, export, and reexport of CITES-listed animal and plant species. As discussed under Factor B, we do not consider international trade to be a threat impacting this species. Therefore, protection under this Treaty is an adequate regulatory mechanism.

The Wild Bird Conservation Act (WBCA) provides restrictions on the importation of slender-billed curlew into the United States. The purpose of the WBCA is to promote the conservation of exotic birds by ensuring that all imports to the United States of exotic birds is biologically sustainable and is not detrimental to the species. The WBCA generally restricts the importation of most CITES-listed live or dead exotic birds except for certain limited purposes such as zoological display or cooperative breeding programs. Import of dead specimens is allowed for scientific specimens and museum specimens. To date, no request for importation of slender-billed curlew into the United States has been received.

This species is also listed in Appendix I of the CMS or Bonn Convention, which includes species threatened with extinction. This convention encourages international cooperation for the conservation of species. Inclusion in Appendix I of CMS means that member states work toward strict protection, conserving and restoring the habitat of the species, controlling other reasons for endangerment, and mitigating obstacles to migration, whereas Appendix II encourages multistate and regional cooperation for conservation.

A Memorandum of Understanding (MOU) was developed under CMS auspices and became effective on September 10, 1994. The MOU area covers 30 Range States in Southern and Eastern Europe, Northern Africa, and the Middle East. The MOU has been signed by 18 Range States and 3 cooperating organizations. In early 1996, a status report was produced and distributed by the CMS Secretariat. An International Action Plan for the Conservation of the Slender-billed Curlew was prepared by BLI in 1996, which was later approved by the European Commission and endorsed by the Fifth Meeting of the CMS. The Action Plan is the main tool for conservation activities for the species under the MOU. Conservation priorities include: effective legal protection for the slender-billed curlew and its look-alikes; locating its breeding grounds and key wintering and passage sites; appropriate protection and management of its habitat; and increasing the awareness of politicians in the affected countries.

The CMS Web site includes an update on the progress being made under the Slender-billed curlew MOU. It states that conservation activities have already been undertaken or are under way in Albania, Bulgaria, Greece, Italy, Morocco, the Russian Federation, Ukraine, and Iran. However, no details of these activities are provided.

In Algeria, Tunisia, and Turkey, the slender-billed curlew is protected; however, we have been unable to determine under what laws it is protected or the provisions of the protection. All *Numenius* species are protected, along with most other waders, in Bulgaria under Ordinance 342, 21/4/86. The penalty for shooting a slender-billed curlew is approximately 450 U.S. dollars (USD). The slender-billed curlew is also protected in Greece and Hungary with penalties of 300-3,000 USD and 1,185 USD with potentially one year in jail, respectively. In the Islamic Republic of Iran, hunting of waders is not allowed and all species of waders are protected. Curlews are not listed as legal quarry species in Italy, and are thus considered protected by Gretton. All curlew species are protected in Morocco; however, other species of waders are not.

Based on the lack of information available on this species (location of breeding and wintering areas), it is difficult to assess the adequacy of existing regulatory mechanisms in preventing the extinction of this species. Although progress is under way in various countries to better protect the habitat, prevent loss of individuals from hunting and misidentification, and educate the public about the precarious status of this species, not all 30 Range States of this species have signed the MOU. Furthermore, many of the range countries have provisions in place to protect the slender-billed curlew; however, legal and illegal hunting continues to be a threat to the species. In countries where the slender-billed curlew is protected from hunting, but other curlews can be legally shot, the slender-billed curlew is still at risk given the similarity of appearance and the inability of hunters to distinguish between species. In addition, enforcement of existing laws is also a problem in many countries. Therefore, we find that the inadequacy of existing regulatory mechanisms is a threat to the continued existence of the slender-billed curlew throughout its range. . .

NOTES & QUESTIONS

1. Why is the plight of these six birds the concern of the United States? Is the United States more or less justified in legislating to protect these birds than it is to protect African elephants? Should the United States defer to the wishes of the governments of the countries in which the birds actually live?

2. Does your answer to the questions in note 1 differ depending on whether the bird lives in a developed country such as Spain or in a developing country such as Cambodia that enjoys less wealth and a less established legal system than the United States?

Defenders of Wildlife v. Lujan

United States Court of Appeals for the Eighth Circuit, 1990.
911 F.2d 117.

■ GIBSON, CIRCUIT JUDGE.

[In 1978, the Fish and Wildlife Service and the National Marine Fisheries Service promulgated a joint regulation providing that the consultation duties imposed by section 7 of the Endangered Species Act apply to the actions of federal agencies in foreign countries. The agencies changed their position in 1986 and issued a new regulation limiting the scope of the consultation duties to federal agency actions within the United States or on the high seas. Environmentalists sued to overturn the 1986 regulation and to require, for example, the Agency for International Development to engage in a section 7 consultation before funding development projects that could jeopardize the habitat of endangered crocodiles, elephants and leopards in Africa.]

. . . It cannot be denied that Congress has chosen expansive language which admits to no exceptions. Reduced to its simplest form, the statute clearly states that each federal agency must consult with the Secretary regarding any action to insure that such action is not likely to jeopardize the existence of any endangered species. We recognize, however, that the use of all-inclusive language in this particular section of the Act is not determinative of the issue. We must search the Act further for clear expression of congressional intent.

The Supreme Court extensively discussed the Act's ambitious purpose in *Tennessee Valley Authority v. Hill*. "The plain intent of Congress in enacting this statute was to halt and reverse the trend toward species extinction, whatever the cost. This is reflected not only in the stated policies of the Act, but in literally every section of the statute." The Court described the Act as "the most comprehensive legislation for the preservation of endangered species ever enacted by any nation."

In the Act, Congress declared that "the United States has pledged itself as a sovereign state in the international community to conserve to the extent practicable the various species of fish or wildlife and plants facing extinction." The Act lists various international agreements which guide this pledge. Congress also committed itself to meeting the international commitments of the United States to existing conservation programs. The Act further declares one of its purposes is to take the appropriate steps to achieve the purposes of the international treaties and conventions just mentioned.

The Act defines "endangered species" broadly and without geographic limitations. Furthermore, the Act sets out a detailed procedure for determining whether a species is endangered. This section states that the Secretary shall determine whether a species is endangered or threatened after taking into account "those efforts, if any, being made by any State or foreign nation . . . to protect such species." The Secretary is instructed to give consideration to species which have been designated as requiring protection from unrestricted commerce by any foreign nation, or pursuant to any international agreement, and species identified as in danger of extinction by any State agency or by any agency of a foreign nation. Moreover, the Secretary is required to give actual notice to and invite comment from each foreign nation in which species proposed for listing as endangered are found.

The Secretary is instructed to publish a list of all species found to be threatened. Defenders asserts, and the Secretary does not contest, that "[a]s of May 1989, of 1,046 species listed as endangered or threatened, 507 were species whose range is outside the United States. In addition, there are 71 listed species whose range includes both United States and foreign territory." The listing process does not distinguish between domestic and foreign species.

The Act contains a section entitled "International Cooperation" which declares that the United States' commitment to worldwide protection of endangered species will be backed by financial assistance, personnel assignments, investigations, and by encouraging foreign nations to develop their own conservation programs. While the Secretary argues that this section and section 1538, dealing with imports and exports of wildlife, embody Congress' complete response to the international problem of endangered species, we are persuaded that this provision cannot be so neatly excised from the larger statutory scheme. Rather, we believe that the Act, viewed as a whole, clearly demonstrates congressional commitment to worldwide conservation efforts. To limit the consultation duty in a manner which protects only domestic endangered species runs contrary to such a commitment.

Based upon the foregoing examination of the Act as a whole, we are convinced that congressional intent can be gleaned from the plain language of the Act. Accordingly, we owe no deference to the Secretary's construction of the Act. *See Chevron*, 467 U.S. at 842–43. Furthermore, "[t]he judiciary is the final authority on issues of statutory construction and must reject administrative constructions which are contrary to clear congressional intent."

We believe that the answer to the extraterritorial issue can be found in the plain words of the statute. Our examination of the statute's legislative history, however, also reinforces our conclusion.

The original Environmental Species Act was enacted in 1973. Soon thereafter, the Secretary initiated a rulemaking process in order to implement the Act. In regard to the consultation requirement at issue here, the Secretary solicited comment from various agencies. Several agencies, including the Army Corps of Engineers, the State Department, and the Defense Department, expressed opposition to extraterritorial application. The Council on Environmental Quality, the Interior Department Solicitor's Office, and the General Counsel's Office of the National Oceanic and Atmospheric Administration, however, took the position that the consultation duty extended to foreign countries. After considering the extensive commentary, the Secretary concluded that Congress intended the duty to extend beyond the United States, and published a final rule on January 4, 1978, providing that: Section 7 . . . requires every Federal agency to insure that its activities or programs in the United States, upon the high seas, and in foreign countries, will not jeopardize the continued existence of a listed species. At that time, the Secretary justified the extraterritorial application by stressing the Act's broad, inclusive language; its legislative history; and its policy implications.

After these regulations were issued, Congress amended the consultation section of the Act to reflect its present version. The amendment was essentially a reorganization to allow additions to the rest of the section. The conference report to these 1978 amendments indicates that no substantive changes were intended. . . In light of the fact that the "existing law" at the time of the 1978 amendments included the prior regulation requiring consultation on foreign projects, we believe that the above language provides strong evidence of the conference committee's tacit approval of the prior regulation. . .

Despite this evidence of congressional intent, in 1983, the Secretary issued a notice of proposed rulemaking to revise the regulation. The proposed regulation eliminated the need for consultation on foreign projects and defined "action" to exclude foreign activities. The Secretary attributed its radical shift on extraterritorial application to "the apparent domestic orientation of the consultation and exemption processes resulting from the [1978] Amendments, and because of the potential for interference with the sovereignty of foreign nations."

We are compelled to reject this justification. We recognize that "[a]n administrative agency is not disqualified from changing its mind," and that "substantial deference is nonetheless appropriate if there appears to be have been good reason for the change." In this situation, however, the reasons offered for the change fall far short when examined in the context of the Act's language and legislative history previously discussed.

The Secretary places great emphasis upon the Act's treatment of the critical habitat clause, as support for its position. According to the Secretary, Congress could not have intended that the critical habitat provisions apply only to domestic projects while the consultation requirement extends to foreign projects. We are not persuaded. The Act reveals an intent to separately address the concerns raised by critical habitats and endangered species. The designation of critical habitat is governed by different procedures and standards than the listing of endangered species. Furthermore, we observe that the Secretary was not troubled by this alleged inconsistency when it promulgated its earlier regulation permitting differing geographic scopes of the two concerns. The evidence reveals that the consultation requirement and the critical habitat designation have been viewed as severable as to their geographical scope.

The Secretary claims that the domestic orientation of the consultation requirement is shown by the exemption provision added by the 1978 amendments. Specifically, the Secretary points out that exemptions are granted only if "the action is of regional or national significance," and require the weighing of public interests, which would be a gross intrusion upon the sovereignty of foreign nations. Again, we are unpersuaded. The exemption clauses provide that "the Governor of the State in which an agency action will occur, if any, . . . may apply to the Secretary for an exemption." This language, when considered with the substantive and persuasive evidence previously discussed, leads us to conclude that the exemption provisions do not limit the consultation requirement geographically. The Secretary also identifies other provisions of the Act which purportedly limit the consultation duty. We have carefully considered these arguments and believe that they do not compel a different result here. They merit no further discussion.

To support its construction of the Act, the Secretary relies heavily upon the canon of statutory construction that statutes are presumed to have domestic scope only. To overcome the presumption that the statute was not intended to have extraterritorial application, there must be clear expression of such congressional intent. We are convinced that evidence of such intent is found both in the words of the Act and in its legislative history as previously set forth. This evidence leaves us with the belief that Congress intended for the consultation obligation to extend to all agency actions affecting endangered species, whether within the United States or abroad.

The Secretary also expresses concerns about the impact on foreign relations stemming from extraterritorial application of the consultation duty. It urges that such a construction would be viewed as an intrusion upon the sovereign right of foreign nations to strike their own balance between development of natural resources and protection of endangered species. We note initially that the Act is directed at the actions of federal agencies, and not at the actions of sovereign nations. Congress may decide that its concern for foreign relations outweighs its concern for foreign wildlife; we, however, will not make such a decision on its behalf.

NOTES & QUESTIONS

1. The Supreme Court reversed the Eighth Circuit because the environmental plaintiffs lacked standing to raise the extraterritoriality issue. *See* Lujan v. Defenders of Wildlife, 504 U.S. 555 (1992). Justice Stevens would have held that the plaintiffs did have standing, but he disagreed with the Eighth Circuit on the merits and would have held that the ESA does not apply extraterritorially. *Id.* at 585–89 (Stevens, J., concurring in the judgment). The issue remains unresolved by the Supreme Court.

2. Judge Gibson acknowledged the rule that statutes are presumed *not* to apply extraterritorially unless Congress clearly says so. Does the evidence cited by the court overcome that presumption? Justice Stevens emphasized the presumption against extraterritoriality in concluding that the ESA's consultation duty does not apply to projects conducted in foreign countries. *See Lujan*, 504 U.S. at 585–89. Is that presumption justified? What is its purpose? Jonathan Turley advocates the contrary presumption "that, unless expressly limited, Congress intends statutes to apply extraterritorially." Jonathan Turley, *"When in Rome": Multinational Misconduct and the Presumption Against Extraterritoriality*, 84 NW. U.L. REV. 598, 655–60 (1990). What is the justification for *that* presumption? Why have any presumption?

3. Similar questions surround the extraterritorial effect of other federal statutes affecting biodiversity. In United States v. Mitchell, 553 F.2d 996 (5th Cir.1977), the defendant U.S. citizen was charged with violating the Marine Mammal Protection Act (MMPA) by capturing dolphins in the Bahamas and taking them to an aquarium in England. The Fifth Circuit reversed Mitchell's conviction because the MMPA did not apply to his actions. The court explained:

> When Congress considers environmental legislation, it presumably recognizes the authority of other sovereigns to protect and exploit their own resources. Other states may strike balances of interests that differ substantially from those struck by Congress. The traditional method of resolving such differences in the international community is through negotiation and agreement rather than the imposition of one particular choice by a state imposing its law extraterritorially.

Id. at 1002.

Numerous federal courts have grappled with the extraterritorial application of the National Environmental Policy Act (NEPA), which requires an environmental impact statement (EIS) of any federal government project that will have a significant effect on the environment. In Environmental Defense Fund, Inc. v. Massey, 986 F.2d 528 (D.C.Cir.1993), the court held that NEPA obligated the National Science Foundation to prepare an EIS before incinerating food wastes in Antarctica. Other NEPA cases have reached differing results. *See* NRDC v. Nuclear Regulatory Comm'n, 647 F.2d 1345 (D.C.Cir.1981) (holding NEPA does not apply extraterritorially to NRC export licensing decisions); Sierra Club v. Adams, 578 F.2d 389 (D.C.Cir.1978) (assuming that NEPA applied to the construction of a highway in South America where the United States had 2/3 of the financial responsibility and controlled construction); NEPA Coalition of Japan v. Aspin, 837 F.Supp. 466 (D.D.C.1993) (rejecting the application of NEPA to the actions at American military installations in Japan); Greenpeace USA v. Stone, 748 F.Supp. 749 (D.Haw.1990) (holding that NEPA does not apply extraterritorially to the transport of U.S. chemical weapons from West Germany to Johnston Atoll for destruction there), *appeal dismissed*, 924 F.2d 175 (9th Cir.1991) (case moot because transport completed); People of Enewetak v. Laird, 353 F.Supp. 811 (D.Haw.1973) (holding that NEPA applies to U.S. trust territories in Pacific).

4. *Should* the ESA apply extraterritorially? What are the costs of using U.S. environmental laws to regulate environmental activities in other countries? Are they outweighed by the environmental benefits? Principle 12 of the Rio Declaration on Environment and Development states that "[u]nilateral actions to deal with environmental challenges outside the jurisdiction of the importing country should be avoided. Environmental measures addressing transboundary or global environmental problems should, as far as possible, be based on international consensus." In a leading discussion of the issue, the editors of the Harvard Law Review proposed a test stating that U.S. environmental statutes should not be applied extraterritorially unless the country in which the activity occurs does not have adequate environmental laws itself. *See Developments in the Law: International Environmental Law*, 104 HARV. L. REV. 1484, 1609–38 (1991). How do those tests differ? Do any of the countries discussed earlier in this chapter—Australia, China, or the Latin American and Caribbean nations—have "inadequate" environmental laws so that the extraterritorial application of the laws of other countries is justified?

United States-Import Prohibition of Certain Shrimp and Shrimp Products

World Trade Organization Appellate Body, 1998.
WT/DS58/AB/R; (98–3899); ABB1998-4.

[In 1987, the United States issued regulations pursuant to the ESA that required shrimp fishers to use Turtle Excluder Devices (TEDs) in areas where many endangered sea turtles are killed when caught in shrimp trawls. Without such devices, sea turtles are captured as shrimp nets drag through the water, and the turtles drown if they cannot escape the nets. TEDs are designed to guide the turtles out of the net while keeping the shrimp within the net. Section 609 of a general congressional appropriations statute enacted in 1989 banned the importation of shrimp from any nation that did not require its shrimp fishers to use the TEDs mandated by the ESA. At first, the State Department interpreted the amendment to apply only to those nations with shrimping fleets in the Gulf of Mexico, the Caribbean Sea, and the western Atlantic Ocean. The Earth Island Institute, an environmental group based in San Francisco, successfully challenged the limited application of the amendment in federal court, and in May 1996 the United States imposed a shrimp embargo on 40 nations that failed to comply with the TED requirements. In response, India, Malaysia, and Pakistan filed a complaint with the World Trade Organization (WTO) contending that the American shrimp importation ban violated international trade agreements.]

113. Article XX of the [General Agreement on Tariffs and Trade] GATT 1994 reads, in its relevant parts:

Article XX *General Exceptions*

Subject to the requirement that such measures are not applied in a manner which would constitute a means of arbitrary or unjustifiable discrimination between countries where the same conditions prevail, or a disguised restriction on international trade, nothing in this Agreement shall be construed to prevent the adoption or enforcement by any Member of measures:

. . . (*b*) necessary to protect human, animal or plant life or health;

. . . (*g*) relating to the conservation of exhaustible natural resources if

such measures are made effective in conjunction with restrictions on domestic production or consumption;

B. *Article XX(g): Provisional Justification of Section 609*

125. In claiming justification for its measure, the United States primarily invokes Article XX(g). Justification under Article XX(b) is claimed only in the alternative; that is, the United States suggests that we should look at Article XX(b) only if we find that Section 609 does not fall within the ambit of Article XX(g). We proceed, therefore, to the first tier of the analysis of Section 609 and to our consideration of whether it may be characterized as provisionally justified under the terms of Article XX(g). . .

1. "Exhaustible Natural Resources". . .

128. . . Textually, Article XX(g) is *not* limited to the conservation of "mineral" or "non-living" natural resources. The complainants' principal argument is rooted in the notion that "living" natural resources are "renewable" and therefore cannot be "exhaustible" natural resources. We do not believe that "exhaustible" natural resources and "renewable" natural resources are mutually exclusive. One lesson that modern biological sciences teach us is that living species, though in principle, capable of reproduction and, in that sense, "renewable", are in certain circumstances indeed

susceptible of depletion, exhaustion and extinction, frequently because of human activities. Living resources are just as "finite" as petroleum, iron ore and other non-living resources. . .

132. We turn next to the issue of whether the living natural resources sought to be conserved by the measure are "exhaustible" under Article XX(g). That this element is present in respect of the five species of sea turtles here involved appears to be conceded by all the participants and third participants in this case. The exhaustibility of sea turtles would in fact have been very difficult to controvert since all of the seven recognized species of sea turtles are today listed in Appendix 1 of the Convention on International Trade in Endangered Species of Wild Fauna and Flora ("CITES"). The list in Appendix 1 includes "all species *threatened with extinction* which are or may be affected by trade."

133. Finally, we observe that sea turtles are highly migratory animals, passing in and out of waters subject to the rights of jurisdiction of various coastal states and the high seas. . . The sea turtle species here at stake, i.e., covered by Section 609, are all known to occur in waters over which the United States exercises jurisdiction. Of course, it is not claimed that *all* populations of these species migrate to, or traverse, at one time or another, waters subject to United States jurisdiction. Neither the appellant nor any of the appellees claims any rights of exclusive ownership over the sea turtles, at least not while they are swimming freely in their natural habitat—the oceans. We do not pass upon the question of whether there is an implied jurisdictional limitation in Article XX(g), and if so, the nature or extent of that limitation. We note only that in the specific circumstances of the case before us, there is a sufficient nexus between the migratory and endangered marine populations involved and the United States for purposes of Article XX(g).

134. For all the foregoing reasons, we find that the sea turtles here involved constitute "exhaustible natural resources" for purposes of Article XX(g) of the GATT 1994.

2. "Relating to the Conservation of [Exhaustible Natural Resources]"

135. Article XX(g) requires that the measure sought to be justified be one which "relates to" the conservation of exhaustible natural resources. [The appellate body concluded that section 609(b)(1) related to the conservation of exhaustible natural resources because that section "is not a simple, blanket prohibition of the importation of shrimp imposed without regard to the consequences (or lack thereof) of the mode of harvesting employed upon the incidental capture and mortality of sea turtles."]

3. *"If Such Measures are Made Effective in conjunction with Restrictions on Domestic Production or Consumption". . .*

144. We earlier noted that Section 609, enacted in 1989, addresses the mode of harvesting of imported shrimp only. However, two years earlier, in 1987, the United States issued regulations pursuant to the Endangered

Species Act requiring all United States shrimp trawl vessels to use approved TEDs, or to restrict the duration of tow-times, in specified areas where there was significant incidental mortality of sea turtles in shrimp trawls. These regulations became fully effective in 1990 and were later modified. They now require United States shrimp trawlers to use approved TEDs "in areas and at times when there is a likelihood of intercepting sea turtles," with certain limited exceptions. Penalties for violation of the Endangered Species Act, or the regulations issued thereunder, include civil and criminal sanctions. The United States government currently relies on monetary sanctions and civil penalties for enforcement. The government has the ability to seize shrimp catch from trawl vessels fishing in United States waters and has done so in cases of egregious violations. We believe that, in principle, Section 609 is an even-handed measure.

145. Accordingly, we hold that Section 609 is a measure made effective in conjunction with the restrictions on domestic harvesting of shrimp, as required by Article XX(g).

C. *The Introductory Clauses of Article XX: Characterizing Section 609 under the Chapeau's Standards*

146. As noted earlier, the United States invokes Article XX(b) only if and to the extent that we hold that Section 609 falls outside the scope of Article XX(g). Having found that Section 609 does come within the terms of Article XX(g), it is not, therefore, necessary to analyze the measure in terms of Article XX(b).

147. Although provisionally justified under Article XX(g), Section 609, if it is ultimately to be justified as an exception under Article XX, must also satisfy the requirements of the introductory clauses—the "chapeau"—of Article XX, that is,

Article XX *General Exceptions*

Subject to the requirement that such measures are *not applied in a manner which would constitute a means of arbitrary or unjustifiable discrimination between countries where the same conditions prevail*, or *a disguised restriction on international trade*, nothing in this Agreement shall be construed to prevent the adoption or enforcement by any Member of measures: (emphasis added)

We turn, hence, to the task of appraising Section 609, and specifically the manner in which it is applied under the chapeau of Article XX; that is, to the second part of the two-tier analysis required under Article XX. . .

2. *"Unjustifiable Discrimination"*

161. We scrutinize first whether Section 609 has been applied in a manner constituting "unjustifiable discrimination between countries where the same conditions prevail." Perhaps the most conspicuous flaw in this measure's application relates to its intended and actual coercive effect on

the specific policy decisions made by foreign governments, Members of the WTO. Section 609, in its application, is, in effect, an economic embargo which requires *all other exporting Members*, if they wish to exercise their GATT rights, to adopt *essentially the same* policy (together with an approved enforcement program) as that applied to, and enforced on, United States domestic shrimp trawlers. As enacted by the Congress of the United States, the *statutory* provisions of Section 609(b)(2)(A) and (B) do not, in themselves, *require* that other WTO Members adopt *essentially the same* policies and enforcement practices as the United States. Viewed alone, the statute appears to permit a degree of discretion or flexibility in how the standards for determining comparability might be applied, in practice, to other countries.[1] However, any flexibility that may have been intended by Congress when it enacted the statutory provision has been effectively eliminated in the implementation of that policy through the 1996 Guidelines promulgated by the Department of State and through the practice of the administrators in making certification determinations. . .

166. Another aspect of the application of Section 609 that bears heavily in any appraisal of justifiable or unjustifiable discrimination is the failure of the United States to engage the appellees, as well as other Members exporting shrimp to the United States, in serious, across-the-board negotiations with the objective of concluding bilateral or multilateral agreements for the protection and conservation of sea turtles, before enforcing the import prohibition against the shrimp exports of those other Members. . .

168. Second, the protection and conservation of highly migratory species of sea turtles, that is, the very policy objective of the measure, demands concerted and cooperative efforts on the part of the many countries whose waters are traversed in the course of recurrent sea turtle migrations. The need for, and the appropriateness of, such efforts have been recognized in the WTO itself as well as in a significant number of other international instruments and declarations. As stated earlier, the Decision on Trade and Environment, which provided for the establishment of the CTE and set out its terms of reference, refers to both the Rio Declaration on Environment and Development and Agenda 21. Of particular relevance is Principle 12 of the Rio Declaration on Environment and Development, which states, in part:

> Unilateral actions to deal with environmental challenges outside the jurisdiction of the importing country should be avoided. *Environmental measures addressing transboundary or global environmental problems should, as far as possible, be based on international consensus.* (emphasis added). . .

---

[1] Pursuant to Section 609(b)(2), a harvesting nation may be certified, and thus exempted from the import ban, if:

(A) the government of the harvesting nation has provided documentary evidence of the adoption of a program governing the incidental taking of such sea turtles in the course of such harvesting that is comparable to that of the United States; and

(B) the average rate of that incidental taking by vessels of the harvesting nation is comparable to the average rate of incidental taking of sea turtles by United States vessels in the course of such harvesting ...

Moreover, we note that Article 5 of the Convention on Biological Diversity states:

> . . . each contracting party shall, as far as possible and as appropriate, cooperate with other contracting parties directly or, where appropriate, through competent international organizations, in respect of areas beyond national jurisdiction and on other matters of mutual interest, for the conservation and sustainable use of biological diversity. . .

169. Third, the United States did negotiate and conclude one regional international agreement for the protection and conservation of sea turtles: The Inter-American Convention. This Convention was opened for signature on 1 December 1996 and has been signed by five countries, in addition to the United States, and four of these countries are currently certified under Section 609. This Convention has not yet been ratified by any of its signatories. The Inter-American Convention provides that each party shall take "appropriate and necessary measures" for the protection, conservation and recovery of sea turtle populations and their habitats within such party's land territory and in maritime areas with respect to which it exercises sovereign rights or jurisdiction. Such measures include, notably,

> the reduction, to the greatest extent practicable, of the incidental capture, retention, harm or mortality of sea turtles in the course of fishing activities, through the appropriate regulation of such activities, as well as the development, improvement and use of appropriate gear, devices or techniques, including the use of turtle excluder devices (TEDs) pursuant to the provisions of Annex III [of the Convention]. . .

172. Clearly, the United States negotiated seriously with some, but not with other Members (including the appellees), that export shrimp to the United States. The effect is plainly discriminatory and, in our view, unjustifiable. The unjustifiable nature of this discrimination emerges clearly when we consider the cumulative effects of the failure of the United States to pursue negotiations for establishing consensual means of protection and conservation of the living marine resources here involved, notwithstanding the explicit statutory direction in Section 609 itself to initiate negotiations as soon as possible for the development of bilateral and multilateral agreements. The principal consequence of this failure may be seen in the resulting unilateralism evident in the application of Section 609. As we have emphasized earlier, the policies relating to the necessity for use of particular kinds of TEDs in various maritime areas, and the operating details of these policies, are all shaped by the Department of State, without the participation of the exporting Members. The system and processes of certification are established and administered by the United States agencies alone. The decision-making involved in the grant, denial or withdrawal of certification to the exporting Members, is, accordingly, also unilateral. The unilateral character of the application of Section 609 heightens the disruptive and discriminatory influence of the import prohibition and underscores its unjustifiability. . .

175. Differing treatment of different countries desiring certification is also observable in the differences in the levels of effort made by the United States in transferring the required TED technology to specific countries. Far greater efforts to transfer that technology successfully were made to certain exporting countries—basically the fourteen wider Caribbean/western Atlantic countries cited earlier—than to other exporting countries, including the appellees. The level of these efforts is probably related to the length of the "phase-in" periods granted—the longer the "phase-in" period, the higher the possible level of efforts at technology transfer. Because compliance with the requirements of certification realistically assumes successful TED technology transfer, low or merely nominal efforts at achieving that transfer will, in all probability, result in fewer countries being able to satisfy the certification requirements under Section 609, within the very limited "phase-in" periods allowed them.

176. When the foregoing differences in the means of application of Section 609 to various shrimp exporting countries are considered in their cumulative effect, we find, and so hold, that those differences in treatment constitute "unjustifiable discrimination" between exporting countries desiring certification in order to gain access to the United States shrimp market within the meaning of the chapeau of Article XX.

3. "Arbitrary Discrimination"

177. We next consider whether Section 609 has been applied in a manner constituting "arbitrary discrimination between countries where the same conditions prevail." We have already observed that Section 609, in its application, imposes a single, rigid and unbending requirement that countries applying for certification under Section 609(b)(2)(A) and (B) adopt a comprehensive regulatory program that is essentially the same as the United States' program, without inquiring into the appropriateness of that program for the conditions prevailing in the exporting countries. Furthermore, there is little or no flexibility in how officials make the determination for certification pursuant to these provisions. In our view, this rigidity and inflexibility also constitute "arbitrary discrimination" within the meaning of the chapeau. . .

185. In reaching these conclusions, we wish to underscore what we have *not* decided in this appeal. We have *not* decided that the protection and preservation of the environment is of no significance to the Members of the WTO. Clearly, it is. We have *not* decided that the sovereign nations that are Members of the WTO cannot adopt effective measures to protect endangered species, such as sea turtles. Clearly, they can and should. And we have *not* decided that sovereign states should not act together bilaterally, plurilaterally or multilaterally, either within the WTO or in other international fora, to protect endangered species or to otherwise protect the environment. Clearly, they should and do.

186. What we *have* decided in this appeal is simply this: although the measure of the United States in dispute in this appeal serves an environmental objective that is recognized as legitimate under paragraph (g) of

Article XX of the GATT 1994, this measure has been applied by the United States in a manner which constitutes arbitrary and unjustifiable discrimination between Members of the WTO, contrary to the requirements of the chapeau of Article XX. For all of the specific reasons outlined in this Report, this measure does not qualify for the exemption that Article XX of the GATT 1994 affords to measures which serve certain recognized, legitimate environmental purposes but which, at the same time, are not applied in a manner that constitutes a means of arbitrary or unjustifiable discrimination between countries where the same conditions prevail or a disguised restriction on international trade. As we emphasized in *United States— Gasoline*, WTO Members are free to adopt their own policies aimed at protecting the environment as long as, in so doing, they fulfill their obligations and respect the rights of other Members under the *WTO Agreement.* . .

NOTES & QUESTIONS

1. Should the United States ban the importation of shrimp from nations that do not require TEDs? The general issue of the proper relationship between free trade and environmental protection has generated enormous controversy and an enormous literature. The arguments on both sides are nicely summarized in DAVID HUNTER, JAMES SALZMAN & DURWOOD ZAELKE, INTERNATIONAL ENVIRONMENTAL LAW AND POLICY 1127–39 (2d ed. 2002); and Michael M. Weinstein & Steve Charnovitz, *The Greening of the WTO*, FOREIGN AFFAIRS, Nov./Dec. 2001, at 147.

2. Why did the WTO conclude that the American ban was illegal? Prior to the establishment of the WTO in 1995, a GATT dispute panel had been less accepting of the effects of American environmental regulation on international trade. The leading dispute involved trade sanctions imposed by the United States pursuant to the Marine Mammal Protection Act banning the importation of tuna from nations that failed to protect dolphins from the effects of tuna fishing. In 1991, a GATT panel held that the import ban violated GATT. *See* General Agreement on Tariffs and Trade: Dispute Panel Settlement Panel Report on United States Restrictions on Imports of Tuna, 30 I.L.M. 1594 (1991). Two years later, another GATT panel reached a similar conclusion concerning the secondary embargo imposed upon intermediary nations who could not prove that any of their shipments to the United States contained tuna that had been caught by nations that failed to take dolphin-safe fishing. *See* General Agreement on Tariffs and Trade: Dispute Settlement Panel Report on United States Restrictions on Import of Tuna, 33 I.L.M. 839 (1994). While the dispute panel reports never took effect, they provoked a hostile response from environmentalists around the world.

3. After the WTO appellate panel issued its decision in the shrimp and sea turtle dispute, the United States agreed to import shrimp from nations that do not require TEDs when it is proved that the shrimp came from boats that used TEDs. In October 2001, a WTO appellate body upheld a renewed United States ban on the importation of shrimp from any nations who could not show that the shrimp were caught by boats using TEDs. The appellate body found that the United States remedied its previous unfair discrimination. The appellate body noted that the United States had made good faith efforts to negotiate a sea turtle conservation agreement with the Indian Ocean and southeast Asian nations affected by the law, and that it had helped those nations with technical advice to adopt fishing methods that were safe for the endangered sea turtles. *See* United States-Import Prohibition of Certain Shrimp and Shrimp Products, Recourse to Article 21.5 by Malaysia (WT/DS58/RW) (Oct. 23, 2001). To the Malaysian press, that decision "signals yet another victory for powerful developed nations to practise double standards and selective protectionism, in the name of conservation and the environment. . . Like all developing countries, [Malaysia] has first to have the resources to care for the forests, oceans, and atmosphere. Denying the country a legitimate source of income [from its small wild shrimp industry] is only going to make it that much tougher, regardless of its willingness, to protect the environment; which of course is not quite the rich countries' real objective." *Turning Turtle on the Environment*, BUSINESS TIMES (Malaysia), Oct. 25, 2001, at 6. How would you respond to Malaysia's complaints?

4. Would the WTO allow the United States to apply section 7 of its Endangered Species Act to conduct occurring in other countries? Could the United States enforce ESA section 9 to a take of endangered species that occurs overseas?

CHAPTER 15

INTERNATIONAL LAW

Chapter Outline:
A. Treaties
B. The Convention on International Trade in Endangered Species
C. The Convention on Biological Diversity
D. Customary Law

The international character of biodiversity leads many to champion the role of international law in protecting it. Species that live in more than one country, and ecosystems that transcend national borders, are obvious candidates for legal actions that apply to every concerned nation. Public international law governs the actions of the governments of countries around the world; only rarely does it govern the activities of private organizations or individuals. Public international law includes treaties and other agreements between two or more nations, and the customary international law norms that govern every nation regardless of its consent. Treaties are the dominant mode of protecting biodiversity, though the types of treaties are almost as diverse as the plants and wildlife they seek to protect. The examples range from three countries that have agreed to protect one lake— *e.g.*, the Agreement on the Protection of Lake Constance Against Pollution, signed by Austria, Germany, and Switzerland in 1992—to the 182 parties to the Convention on Biological Diversity who have agreed to protect the full range of biodiversity throughout the world. But treaties, like contracts, only bind those who agree to them. The conspicuous unwillingness of some countries to approve prominent agreements respecting biodiversity—such as the failure of the United States to ratify the Convention on Biological Diversity—demonstrates the limits of treaties as a means of protecting biodiversity. Customary international law, consisting of those legal principles that have become so prevalent to be deemed law, purports to regulate the actions of the governments whether or not the country has agreed to such legal principles. It thus avoids the consent problem posed by treaties, but it presents its own challenges of defining what constitutes such customary international law and determining what consequences attach to a violation of it. Efforts to craft a customary international law solution to the problems of biodiversity have yet to succeed.

International environmental law generally, and the international law protecting biodiversity, have received vastly increased attention in recent years. While some wildlife treaties date back a century or more, the agreements of the past thirty years have attracted more parties and applied to more species than ever before. The international community came together in Stockholm in 1972, and in Rio de Janeiro in 1992, to grapple with the role of international law in protecting the environment and biodiversity. The accompanying treatises, journals, web sites, and other resources are far too numerous to fully engage in this chapter. Some of the best sources of information about the role of international law in protecting biodiversity include the Convention on Biological Diversity's website's at http://www.biodiv.org/; LAKSHAM D. GURUSWAMY ET AL., INTERNATIONAL ENVIRONMENTAL LAW AND WORLD ORDER: A PROBLEM-ORIENTED COURSEBOOK 792–953 (2d ed. 1999); and DAVID HUNTER, JAMES SALZMAN & DURWOOD ZAELKE, INTERNATIONAL ENVIRONMENTAL LAW AND POLICY 909–1124 (2d ed. 2002).

A. TREATIES

Statement of Dr. William T. Hornaday, Investigation of the Fur-Seal Fisheries: Hearing Before the Senate Committee on Conservation of National Resources on Bill (S. 7242) Entitled "An Act to Protect the Seal Fisheries of Alaska, and for Other Purposes"

61st Congress, 2d Session (1910).

Doctor HORNADAY. I fancy that you have time, gentlemen, to consider only the facts that impinge directly upon the subject of the present hearing. It is my sincere belief that the fate of the fur seal today lies in the hands of this committee, the Secretary of Commerce and Labor, the Secretary of State, the Commissioner of Fisheries, and the President of the United States, and if that small group of men is not instrumental in securing immediately the measures that are absolutely necessary to the preservation of that industry, then I believe that it will be wiped out entirely in the very near future.

First, one word in regard to my own status. By profession I am a zoologist, but when I am at home I draw as much salary for being a practical business man as for my zoological work. My interest in this question is not alone that of a zoologist, nor is it a sentimental interest. As a business man and patriotic citizen I desire to see a very valuable industry saved to the Government and to the people of the United States.

I represent the Camp-Fire Club of America, which is a New on York organization of lawyers, doctors, businessmen, and others, all of whom are sportsmen and lovers of nature. One of the chief objects of the club is the preservation of wild life and forests. Our New York organization is allied with six other clubs, scattered all the way from Jamestown, N.Y., to Los Angeles, Cal. Our own club in New York contains about 350 members. A committee consisting of thirteen members, all of whom, with the exception of myself, are lawyers, has been formed to promote the better protection of wild life. It is called the committee on game protective legislation and preserves, and of it I have the honor to be chairman. One of the first acts of that committee was to consider the case of the fur seal. My expenses here are paid by a special subscription in the club for the work of this committee. I do not come here to represent New York Zoological Society. That organization has not elected to take an active part in the fur-seal matter, for the reason that it has so many interests in other directions.

THE CURSE OF "PELAGIC SEALING"

The present trouble lies first in the fact that the number of fur seals have diminished to a very low point, and secondly, that the situation is entangled with the affairs of other nations, particularly Canada and Japan. The evil at this moment arises from what is call "pelagic sealing," but I shall be careful not to dwell on the details of that, because I know that you are already familiar with it. "Pelagic sealing" means killing seals at sea; and in killing seals at sea all ages and sexes are killed, indiscriminately, and of all that are killed, fully one-half are lost. . .

Owing to the lack of a treaty with Japan, the Japanese seal-hunters have the right to kill seals to within 3 miles of the shores of [the Pribilof Islands of Alaska]. They always have had that right, and during the past fifteen years have exercised it with merciless vigor and persistence. You will remember that about two years ago a party of Japanese landed on one of the Pribilof Islands and actually began to kill the seals on our own soil.

. . . The Canadians may kill fur seals anywhere outside of [the Canadian dead line], which is 60 miles from the shore of the islands, but Americans may not kill seals at sea anywhere.

Now, it is a well attested fact that every year, in the fall, the seals leave these islands and make the most wonderful migration that is made by any aquatic species in the world. It covers nine months in the year, and reaches about 2,000 miles. The months indicated here represent the seasonal progress of the herd. This region forms part of the hunting grounds of the pelagic sealers of Canada, who make their headquarters in Vancouver and Victoria. Until very recently, at least, the pelagic fleet contained about thirty vessels, manned by about twelve hundred men, using about three hundred boats. The sealers know in general the locality of the fur seals at different periods of the year. The migration route has been determined by the logs of the various pelagic sealing vessels that have taken fur seals at various times of the year throughout that great course. The greatest killing in done around the islands and close along the Pacific coast from San Francisco up to Prince William Sound. Between 1883 and 1897 a total of 304,713 skins of seals killed at sea were marketed, and undoubtedly an equal number were lost. In 1895 there were 56,291 seals killed at sea that were secured.

During the breeding season, or from July to October, the mother seals are obliged to leave the islands to go off shore from sixty to a hundred miles for food. The moment the mother seals leave the Japanese 3-mile dead line, the Japanese sealers are after them; and a mother seal, in order to get her food with which to suckle her young, is obliged to run the gauntlet of these Japanese vessels. The destruction of a mother seal means the starvation of the offspring on shore; and uncounted thousands of young seals have perished on our islands from that cause.

In 1895 a member of Congress, Mr. J. B. Crowley, assisted in counting about 30,000 young fur seals that starved to death on the breeding ground because their mothers had been killed while in quest of food.

Now, let us come down to the necessities of the case. It has been my pleasure to study both the life history and the political history of the fur seal during the past thirty years. I have accumulated during that time a great many documents and publications on the subject, and facts derived from men who are familiar with the fur seals and the islands from personal observation. Up to this date several of my personal friends have been advising the Government as experts, and although I have witnessed this awful and wasteful slaughter of the fur seal herd, I have resolutely held my peace until a few weeks ago. Now, however, as the total destruction of this industry is imminent and the fur seal is fast following the American bison, I feel that it is my duty as an American citizen to speak out.

To come directly to the point, from a careful study of the present situation and the past history that has led up to it, especially the Russian history of the fur-seal industry, I am convinced that we must do three things to save our fur-seal herd, as follows:

(1) We must immediately forbid the execution of a new lease for the killing of fur seals on these islands, for reasons that I will presently set forth;

(2) We must secure treaties with Canada, Russia, Japan, and Mexico which will put a stop to pelagic sealing; and

(3) We must declare a closed season for ten years.

TREATIES REGARDING PELAGIC SEALING.

I have been convinced all along that if a new lease is now made, to take the place of that which expires next April, it will greatly complicate the negotiations of our State Department, not only with Canada, but Japan and Russia as well. We believe that the Japanese and Russians are willing to enter into an agreement with us for the suppression of pelagic sealing as soon as we come to satisfactory terms with Canada. Last year our State Department endeavored to negotiate a seal treaty with Japan, but with no result.

Now, what is the state of affairs with Canada? During the past three years the State Department has submitted several propositions to Canada. I do not wish to say much regarding the work of the State Department, but there are some things that really must be said. I understand that certain propositions were submitted by Senator Root, then Secretary of State, and that they have all been rejected. The matter remains as much open and unsettled—and irritating—today as it was four years ago. Now, here is an important fact bearing on this subject:

In 1905 Mr. John Hay, who was then Secretary of State, prepared, with the assistance of Senator Dillingham, the basis of an agreement with the Canadian government that if ratified, would have settled this whole matter and put it on a good foundation for many years to come. That agreement, a copy of which I hold in my hand, proposed that Canada should have a compensation for the suppression of pelagic sealing by her people. The Canadians are not willing to give up their pelagic sealing privileges for nothing, for the simple reason that the Canadians have made much money out of it. Now, Mr. Hay and Sir Mortimer Durand agreed that it was right for Canada to have compensation—in the form of a small percentage of the net annual income from the killing lease—20 percent of whatever the amount might be, and also the privilege of being represented by a commissioner on our islands. Well, just as this was on the point of being ratified into a treaty Secretary Hay died and the whole thing fell to the ground. Mr. Elliott exercised every form of persuasion and insistence that he knew of to induce this Government, through Congress, through cabinet officers and the President, to renew it along those lines, but I am told by Mr. Elliott that it never was done.

At the Paris tribunal, in 1893, we made a treaty with England and Canada, by which the Canadians were estopped from pelagic sealing at the 60-mile limit. We have no absolute treaty with Japan and Russia, and therefore the terms of international law hold good; that is to say beyond the 3-mile limit. We can not protect our fur seals from either Japanese or Russians. Canada is still bound by the Paris award to the 60-mile limit.

A CLEAR FIELD FOR TREATY MAKING

That opinion is extremely important at this time. It will take a year to make these treaties; and it may take even longer. I insist upon it, as representing three hundred and fifty good citizens who are interested in this subject, that the making of any new killing lease at this time would complicate our negotiations with foreign governments, and it might easily be the means of entirely defeating the purpose of our Secretary of State. We believe that the imperative need at the present hour is that this committee shall secure from Congress such action which will enable the Secretary of Commerce and Labor to abandon all thought of now executing a new lease, and at the same time, if possible, provide for a ten-year close season.

There is one other matter that I desire to mention, because it is certain to be brought forward by those who desire the execution of a new slaughtering lease. The law provides that the Secretary of Commerce and Labor shall have the power to restrict, or in other words, to place a limit upon the number of seals that may be killed under the lease, according to his discretion. It is claimed by some of the gentlemen who do not agree with us in the matter, that it is not necessary to have a new act passed, or any new regulation of any kind adopted on the theory that the Secretary of Commerce and Labor has the power to regulate killing operations upon our islands and suspend all killing if he chooses. I do not think that, as professional and business men, this committee is likely to lose sight of this fact: With a new lease in existence, and with thousands of dollars invested in the sealing industry, it will require a Secretary of Commerce and Labor with a tremendous amount of courage to go to the length of stopping the killing privilege entirely, even though he should think it ever so necessary. I do not think that it would be right for this Government to expect any Secretary to assume the entire responsibility of virtually abrogating an existing lease where the holders of the lease have large vested rights, and assuredly would put in large-sized claims for damages. . .

NOTES & QUESTIONS

1. William Hornaday was more than the representative of the Camp-Fire Club of America. He was also "the influential director of the New York Zoological Park. Hunter, taxidermist, polemicist, student of animal morals, advocate of the white man's burden, enthusiast for phrenology and temperance, Hornaday was a passionate man who got under a lot of people's skins. Of all his enthusiasms, biodiversity was the foremost: he spent more than forty years railing against the loss of species." CHARLES C. MANN & MARK L. PLUMMER, NOAH'S CHOICE: THE FUTURE OF ENDANGERED SPECIES 119 (1994); *see also* STEFAN BECHTEL: MR. HORNADAY'S WAR: HOW A PECULIAR VICTORIAN ZOOKEEPER WAGED A LONELY CRUSADE FOR WILDLIFE THAT CHANGED THE WORLD (2012). Hornaday's 1913 book *Our Vanishing Wild Life* "was probably the first book devoted to the biodiversity crisis." MANN & PLUMMER, *supra*, at 120. That book proclaimed that "Labor, Money, and Publicity" are the "three very slender threads" upon which "[t]he fate of wild life in North America hangs." WILLIAM T. HORNADAY, OUR VANISHING WILDLIFE: ITS EXTERMINATION AND PRESERVATION 393 (1913). Hornaday focused on biodiversity in the United States, but he also described the present and future of game in Asia and Africa, the game preserves and game laws of Canada, and British game preserves in Africa and Australia.

Hornaday recounted the battle to save the fur seals in a later book describing efforts to protect biodiversity. *See* WILLIAM T. HORNADAY, THIRTY YEARS WAR FOR WILDLIFE: GAINS AND LOSSES IN THE THANKLESS TASKS (1931). (As an aside, the book is probably the only one ever "dedicated to the Congress of the United States as a small token of appreciation of its generous services to wild life during the decade from 1920 to 1930, in new legislation to provide game sanctuaries, and to reduce excessive killing privileges." *Id.* at vii). Russian fur traders had nearly hunted fur seals to extinction in the decades after 1786, when the explorer * * * Pribylov discovered the islands that were later named after him. The czar then instituted measures to make the seal harvest, and the United States tried to mimic those measures after it purchased Alaska from Russia in 1867. In 1870, the United States entered into a 20 year lease that allowed the Alaskan Commercial Company to kill 100,000 fur seals on the Pribolof Islands. President Grant had sought to protect the seals in 1869 by designating the Pribolof Islands as the nation's first wildlife sanctuary. But pelagic sealing began to replace the killing of the seals on land. The resulting slaughter of the seals involved American, Canadian, Russian, and Japanese ships. In 1886, the federal government seized two Canadian sealing vessels, asserting exclusive American jurisdiction over the waters of the area, but the Paris tribunal mentioned by Hornaday rejected that claim in 1893.

So the fight turned to the establishment of an international treaty. Hornaday credited Henry Wood Elliott as doing 'by far the most to save the Fur Seal industry' had manifested the slightest interest in the fate of the unhappy fur seals. *Id.* at 175, 179. Elliott was a Treasury Department official who undertook an official government mission to Pribolofs soon after the purchase of Alaska, and he sketched dozens of drawings of the seal hunting that occurred there. He later became convinced that the seals were being killed to the brink of extinction. Indeed, he wrote that the slaughter "is due entirely to the greed, cruelty, and avarice of certain men—unspeakable men, who, shielded and panoplied by imperfect law and regulations, have wrought this loot and ruin of our fur-seal herd of Alaska." Henry W. Elliott, *The Loot and the Ruin of the Fur-Seal Herd of Alaska*, 185 NORTH AMERICAN REV. 426, 427–28 (1907). Elliott, like Hornaday, testified before numerous congressional hearings investigating the issue. Hornaday offered the testimony excerpted above before the Senate Committee on Natural Resources on February 26, 1910. As Hornaday described it, it was "a very odd and spectacular Hearing" in which eleven Senators listened to just one witness—Hornaday. "The Committee did not seem to think it worth while to notify or invite any other persons, possibly because no one outside of Congress, save [Elliot], had manifested the slightest interest in the fate of the unhappy fur seals." *Id.* at 175, 179. The result of Hornaday's testimony was an unanimous resolution opposing the renewal of the lease permitting the killing of fur seals and advocating a treaty to prevent pelagic sealing. "And that action," reported Hornaday, "instantly killed the leasing system of seal killing, forever and a day." *Id.* at 176.

Next, "[i]n due course of time and diplomatic procedure, the Department of State completed an excellent treaty with England and Canada, Japan and Russia, which was fully ratified, and which at once put a stop to the wicked and wasteful killing of seals at sea." *Id.* at 181. The 1911 Treaty for the Preservation and Protection of Fur Seals banned pelagic sealing, empowered each country to seize vessels violating that ban, prohibited the importation of unapproved seal skins, and directed each country to supervise seal harvests on the islands' rookeries within their jurisdiction. The treaty also authorized the continuing harvest of the seals (albeit not by killing at sea) and mandated the payment of various sums for existing skins and in lieu of future hunting. Japan withdrew from the treaty on the eve of World War II: in fact, it "may have telegraphed its intention to go to war with the United States when on October 23, 1941, it broadcast a message to the Pribolofs in English rejecting the treaty and announcing plans to 'wage war' on American fur seals wherever they were found." George Reiger, *Song of the Seal*, Audubon, Sept. 1975, at 19. Informal restrictions continued until the original parties entered into the Interim Fur Seal Convention of 1957, which essentially retained the same provisions while adding an explicit policy of "achieving the maximum sustainable productivity of the fur seal resources . . . so that the fur seal population can be brought to and maintained at the levels which will provide the greatest harvest year after year." That interim agreement was continually renewed until 1985. At that time, the dramatic increase in the Pribolof Islands fur seal population from 30,000 in 1910 to as many as 2,500,000 in the 1950's began to be reversed. The 1985 population of about 800,000, combined with listing of the fur seal as threatened under the Endangered Species Act, ended the commercial harvest of the fur seals. Since then, the fur seal population has grown slightly to about 1,000,000. *See generally* MICHAEL J. BEAN & MELANIE J. ROWLAND, THE EVOLUTION OF NATIONAL WILDLIFE LAW 471–78 (3d ed. 1997); SIMON LYSTER, INTERNATIONAL WILDLIFE LAW: AN ANALYSIS OF INTERNATIONAL TREATIES CONCERNED WITH THE CONSERVATION OF WILDLIFE 39–48 (1985).

2. Could the United States have saved the seals without a treaty? Was Hornaday right to insist that the fur seal could only be saved through the efforts of the "small group of men" that he named? What would have happened if the nations involved in pelagic sealing had been unable to reach an agreement? Consider the example of the fisheries of the high seas beyond the jurisdiction of any individual country, which were long treated as "common resources subject to the law of capture. Resources belonged to whoever took the property into possession first." HUNTER, SALZMAN & ZAELKE, *supra*, at 680. The many efforts to establish treaties to govern the use of such fisheries are described *id.* at 703–731.

3. The fur seal treaty was one of the first international agreements to protect biodiversity. The few agreements before then were even more limited in their focus, such as a 1781 convention that protected forests and game birds along the border between France and Basel. *See* P. van Heijnsbergen, International Legal Protection of Wild Fauna and Flora 9 (1997). The fur seal treaty was soon followed by the Migratory Bird Treaty of 1916, which established a number of protections for birds that migrated between the United States and Canada. The ensuing federal statute to enforce the treaty was sustained against a federalism challenge in Missouri v. Holland, 252 U.S. 416 (1920), in which Justice Holmes observed that "[b]ut for the treaty and the statute there soon might be no birds for any powers to deal with." *Id.* at 434–35.

Today there are hundreds of bilateral treaties, regional treaties, and other treaties involving a small number of countries that address certain species or ecosystems. They attempt to protect such biodiversity as:

- *Whales*—The hunting of whales has captured the public's attention at least since the publication of *Moby Dick*. International efforts to regulate the killing of whales began in the 1920's, culminating in the International Convention for the Regulation of Whaling in 1946. The preamble to the convention explained that the parties sought "to provide for the proper conservation of whale stocks and thus make possible the orderly development of the whaling industry." That convention created the International Whaling Commission (IWC), which can designate protected species of whales and govern the hunting of whales. But "[w]ith no clear mandate for whale conservation, a directive to consider the needs of the whaling industry, and a regulatory structure that enables individual nations to frustrate conservation actions by registering objections to them, the IWC has for most of its life served as overseer of successive depletions of individual whale stocks." BEAN & ROWLAND, *supra*, at 480. Then, in 1982, the IWC imposed a moratorium on commercial whaling. Japan, Norway, and the Soviet Union filed objections to the moratorium and continued whaling until the threat of American trade sanctions convinced each nation to accept the moratorium. Those nations, and others, still kill some whales pursuant to a controversial "research" provision contained in the convention, and Alaskan Eskimos and other aboriginal groups engage in subsistence whaling. Moreover, Iceland withdrew from the convention in 1992, and Norway resumed its commercial whaling in 1993 based on the objection it had lodged against the moratorium. The competing perspectives on the proper role of international law in governing whaling are presented in the web sites of the IWC, http://ourworld.compuserve.com/homepages/iwcoffice/;

the Japan Whaling Association, http://wwww.jp-whaling-assn.com/ english/index.htm; and Greenpeace, www.greenpeace.org.chio.html.

- *Polar bears*—The decline in the number of polar bears living in the Arctic ecosystem prompted the Soviet Union to ban polar bear hunting in 1955 and the state of Alaska to prohibit sport hunting in 1972. An international agreement followed in 1973, when Canada, Denmark (acting on behalf of Greenland), Norway, the Soviet Union, and the United States entered into the Agreement on the Conservation of Polar Bears. The agreement is designed to limit the killing and capture of polar bears, to protect their habitat, and to facilitate research efforts. The agreement prohibits the "taking" of polar bears—defined as "hunting, killing and capturing"—but it contains a series of exceptions for scientific purposes, conservation purposes, "local people using traditional methods in the exercise of their traditional rights," and takings "wherever polar bears have or might have been subject to taking by traditional means by its nationals." The agreement also requires each party to "take appropriate action to protect the ecosystems of which polar bears are a part, with special attention to habitat components such as denning and feeding sites and migration patterns." That ecosystem provision poses a particular challenge for the United States because "[t]he most important polar bear on-land denning area in Alaska is in the coastal plain of the Arctic National Wildlife Refuge," which has been eyed for increased oil production. BEAN & ROWLAND, *supra*, at 492.

- *Wetlands*—The Convention on Wetlands of International Importance Especially as Waterfowl Habitat—better known as the Ramsar Convention after the Iranian city in which it was signed in 1971—seeks to better protect the most important of the wetlands that constitute four percent of the world's surface. It was "the first international treaty focused on conservation of a single type of ecosystem." Hunter, Salzman & Zaelke, *supra*, at 1029. Each of the 130 countries that are parties to the convention are required to designate at least one wetland for the List of Wetlands of International Importance. The list contains 1,111 wetlands, such as Karaginsky Island in the Bering Sea along a major bird migration route, a wetland formed during mining construction in the Transvaal region of South Africa in 1930, Kakadu National Park in northern Australia, and the Everglades National Park. (For the entire list, visit the convention's web site at http://www.ramsar.org/ profileindex.htm. The convention's general guidance regarding the ecological, botanical, hydrological, and other international importance of a wetland has been supplemented by more specific quantitative criteria to determine whether a wetland enjoys the requisite importance. Listed sites that are threatened are included in the Montreux Record, which identifies "wetlands requiring urgent national and international conservation attention." Hunter, Salzman & Zaelke, *supra*, at 1031. Once listed, a party must encourage the "wise use" of a wetland. Parties are also required to establish nature reserves containing wetlands. Even though "[t]he inclusion of a wetland in the List does not prejudice the exclusive sovereign rights of the Contracting Party in whose territory the wetland is situated," Ramsar Convention, Art. 2, para. 3, the effect of listing has often been to block harmful development from occurring on or near a listed wetland. *See* HUNTER, SALZMAN & ZAELKE, *supra*, at 1035–36 (citing examples from Canada, Chile, Great Britain, Norway, Pakistan, and South Africa).

- *Antarctica*—The fragile and unique ecosystem of Antarctica lies outside the jurisdiction of any individual nation. Instead, 26 countries now play a role in governing the region pursuant to a treaty established in 1959. That treaty paid scant attention to biodiversity, though, simply authorizing recommendations for the "preservation and conservation of living resources." Antarctica's biodiversity gained international protection in 1980 when many of the same interested nations agreed to the Convention on the Conservation of Antarctic Marine Living Resources (CCAMLR). The convention's preemptive effort to protect the abundant, shrimp-like krill makes it "one of the few international treaties concerned with wildlife conservation to be concluded prior to heavy commercial protection of the species it was designed to protect." SIMON LYSTER, INTERNATIONAL WILDLIFE LAW: AN ANALYSIS OF INTERNATIONAL TREATIES CONCERNED WITH THE CONSERVATION OF WILDLIFE 157 (1985). The convention applies to all "marine living resources" in Antarctica, not just krill, by focusing upon the size of harvested populations, maintaining ecological relationships, and preventing irreversible changes in the marine ecosystem. The Commission for the Conservation of Antarctic Marine Living Resources is charged with establishing a marine reserves and reaching a consensus on any necessary regulations. It relies upon the "two central concepts" of a precautionary approach and an ecosystem approach designed "to preserve the 'health' of the ecosystem by setting conservative (i.e., precautionary) krill catch limits to take account of the needs of the associated species and to preserve the ecological sustainability of all of the species concerned." Ecosystem Approach, *available at* httpwww.ccamlr.org/pu/E/sc/eco-app-intro.htm. The countries responsible for Antarctica agreed to a Protocol on Environmental Protection to the Antarctic Treaty, better known as the Madrid Protocol, in 1992. Two features of the Madrid Protocol are of particular note for Antarctica's biodiversity. It states that "protection of the Antarctic environment and dependent and associated ecosystems, including its wilderness and aesthetic values . . . shall be fundamental considerations in the planning and conduct of all activities" there. The protocol also prohibits the introduction of any exotic animal or plant species to the Antarctic without a permit.

- *Food crops*—In 2000, 56 countries entered into the first international agreement specifically designed to protect genetic diversity. The International Undertaking on Plant Genetic Resources emerged from a Rome meeting of the members of the United Nations Food and Agriculture Organization (FAO). That agreement seeks "to ensure the conservation and sustainable use of plant genetic resources used for food and agriculture and the fair and equitable sharing of the benefits arising from their use." Food and Agriculture Organization of the United Nations, *Agreement Reached on Protecting Plant Genetic Resources*, http://www.fao.org/news/2001/010703Be.html. Two complementary provisions are designed to achieve these goals: a system that facilitates access to gene banks, actual farms, and other sources of agricultural information; and a cost-sharing plan that requires mandatory payments when commercial benefits are gained from the use of the plant genetic resources covered by the system, with most of the collected funds invested in developing countries. The agreement also directs countries to "take measures to protect and promote Farmers' Rights" by protecting traditional knowledge about plant genetic resources, encouraging public participation by farmers in decisions about genetic resources, and promoting the ability of farmers to share equitably in the benefits produced by such resources. In November 2001, the FAO submitted the agreement for adoption by its member states, and by the end of 2001 the agreement had gained the approval of eight of the forty nations needed for it to become effective.

Are such agreements more or less desirable than multinational agreements that seek to protect all kinds of biodiversity? Can you identify the factors that should determine whether an issue is best addressed by a focused treaty with few parties, a broad treaty with many parties, or some other kind of agreement?

4. Not every treaty addressing biodiversity is successful. Scott Barrett argues that "the constraints imposed by sovereignty mean that a treaty has to restructure incentives in order to succeed in altering behavior." Specifically, a successful international treaty that relies upon self-enforcement to address environmental concerns must satisfy three conditions: (1) a treaty must be individually rational, so that each party has an incentive to comply with its terms; (2) a treaty must be collectively rational, which "requires that it not be possible for parties to gain collectively by changing their treaty;" and (3) a treaty must be "fair," and thus "perceived by the parties to be legitimate . . . SCOTT BARRETT, ENVIRONMENT AND STATECRAFT: THE STRATEGY OF ENVIRONMENTAL TREATY-MAKING. xiii-xiv (2003). Barrett describes the Fur Seal Treaty as "ingenious" and "an unqualified success" because it achieved five tasks, "each necessary for success, but each almost useless should any of the others fail. *Id.* at 19, 32. The five tasks that a treaty must accomplish are to: (1) create an aggregate gain, a reason for all countries to come to the bargaining table; (2) distribute that gain such that all countries would prefer that the agreement succeed; (3) ensure that each country would lose by not participating, given that all the others agreed to participate; (4) provide incentives for all the parties to comply with the treaty; and (5) deter entry by third parties" who seek to exploit the natural resource. *Id.* at 33. The Fur Seal Treaty also shows that "resources that lie within a nation's territorial borders can be effectively managed; shared resources are prone to overuse when countries pursue unilateral policies; an effective treaty can improve on unilateralism and make every party better off." *Id.* Are these the appropriate criteria by which to judge a treaty or a prospective treaty? How do the treaties in this chapter fare under these criteria?

B. THE CONVENTION ON INTERNATIONAL TRADE IN ENDANGERED SPECIES

Testimony of John E. Scanlon, Secretary-General of the Convention on International Trade in Endangered Species of Wild Fauna and Flora

(CITES): "Ivory and Insecurity: The Global Implications of Poaching in Africa"

United States Senate Committee on Foreign Relations, 2012.
http://www.foreign.senate.gov/imo/media/doc/Scanlon_Testimony.pdf.

CITES stands at the intersection between trade, environment and development and the Convention is needed more today than it was back in March, 1973 when it was adopted right here in Washington, D.C.

CITES regulates trade in close to 35,000 species of plants and animals, including listed timber and aquatic species, to ensure that such trade is legal, sustainable and traceable. CITES holds records of over 12 million trades, with about 850,000 legal trades being reported by CITES Parties to the Secretariat annually. . .

Illegal trade in wildlife is happening at a scale that poses an immediate risk to both wildlife and to people and their livelihoods. An even greater effort is required, and new approaches need to be taken, if we are to adequately address this risk, including through: employing more formidable and coordinated enforcement responses at Global, regional, sub-regional and national levels; making better use of modern enforcement techniques and technologies; attracting additional financial and human resources at national and international level, and through more effectively suppressing the demand that is driving illegal trade.

Strong and clear political messages from the highest possible levels are also required to combat the illegal trade in wildlife.

The 40th Anniversary of CITES on 3 March, 2013, which coincides with the 16th meeting of the Conference of the Parties in Bangkok, offers an ideal opportunity for Parties to take stock of their law enforcement efforts to date, to agree on enhanced enforcement measures, and to send strong and clear political messages on combating the illegal trade in wildlife. . .

The massive scale of wildlife crime

The effectiveness of CITES implementation at a national level is severely challenged by the extent of illegal trade. The CITES Secretariat does not place a value on illegal wildlife trade but it notes that others have valued it at anything between USD 5-20 billion and USD 8-10 billion a year (excluding timber and marine wildlife).

The estimates of the extent of wildlife crime is further reinforced by the published results of short-term intensive wildlife enforcement actions that are taken by organizations such as INTERPOL and the World Customs Organization, as well as domestic operations such as 'Operation Crash' in the United States of America. Further, according to data submitted by CITES Parties to the Elephant Trade Information System (ETIS), large-scale ivory seizures, defined as seizures of more than 800 kg of ivory, are at an all time high. Such seizures serve as a useful proxy measure for assessing the involvement of organized crime in the trade.

The species affected by illegal trade are not only those in which international commercial trade is prohibited (Appendix I), such as the tiger, but also those in which such trade is regulated to ensure sustainability, such as the Queen conch (Appendix II). The Congressional Research Service Report for Congress of February, 2, 2009 identified some of the most lucrative illicit wildlife commodities as including tiger parts, caviar, elephant ivory, rhino horn, and exotic birds and reptiles – excluding marine and timber species.

The depth of analysis of wildlife crime is poor in comparison to that of other areas of illicit trade - such as the analysis of the illicit trade in drugs through the UNODC World Drugs Reports. UNODC is now working on a series of environmental crime reports, with a focus on wildlife crime. There is a need for a more systematic and thorough global analysis of the illicit trade in wildlife.

However, a more detailed and thorough analysis is available on the illegal killing of, and trade in, African elephants. This is achieved through the four global monitoring and reporting systems for elephants and trade in elephant specimens recognized under CITES, namely:

- the programme for Monitoring the Illegal Killing of Elephants (MIKE), managed by the CITES Secretariat;

- the Elephant Trade Information System (ETIS), managed for CITES by TRAFFIC to track illegal trade in ivory and other elephant specimens;

- annual reports of CITES Parties on the authorized trade in specimens of CITES-listed species, including legal trade in all elephant specimens, compiled by UNEP-WCMC and available on-line through the CITES Trade Data Base; and

- the African and Asian Elephant Database, housing information on elephant population numbers and range, maintained by IUCN through the SSC African Elephant and Asian Elephant Specialist Groups.

These four monitoring and reporting systems are working closely together to deliver timely, integrated, evidence-based reports to the CITES Parties to inform their decision-making.

The CITES Parties and the Secretariat also derive valuable information from multiple other sources, including from intergovernmental bodies involved in tackling illegal wildlife trade, and from non-government organizations taking an active interest in these issues.

CITES' serious and increasing concern with illegal trade in elephants and rhinos

Last year, we witnessed seriously escalating levels of illegal trade in elephant ivory and in rhino horn, which is pushing these species towards extinction. Such trade is putting money in the handsof criminals - including those involved in armed conflicts. It is also depriving local people of livelihoods in many instances, and robbing countries of their natural resources and cultural heritage, as well as of potential revenue—not to mention the costs associated with taking enforcement measures. It must be stopped and elephant and rhino range States need further support to achieve this objective. . .

The need for collaboration in fighting illegal wildlife trade

Fighting poaching and illegal trade in wildlife is about fighting serious crime, especially when dealing with species that attract high returns such as elephant and rhinos. There is a need for collaboration and joint work at multiple levels, including: among range, transit and consumer States; among international entities involved in the fight against wildlife crime; among States at the regional and sub-regional level; and among multiple enforcement authorities at the national level.

Taking enforcement action is a national responsibility. And the men and women who work to protect elephants and rhinos in their habitats every day do extraordinary work under extremely difficult conditions. We applaud the tireless efforts of these officials, who are serving in the front-line. Yet, despite all of these courageous efforts, poaching, and illegal trade continue to increase.

The fight to save these species extends well beyond their habitat. The actual site where an animal is poached can be the start of a long chain of criminality – a chain that may stretch from forests, through rural villages, to large cities, across provincial and national borders, via land, air and sea ports or crossing points, until the animals tusks or horns are finally delivered to clandestine markets, dealers and consumers, often many thousands of kilometers from where the animal was killed.

Anti-poaching personnel acting alone can do little to break these links further up that chain. But Customs and Police can – and that is why the coordinated approach across agencies is critical, both nationally and internationally.

Given the nature and scale of the risk associated with the illegal trade in wildlife, it is now acknowledged that a more organized and sophisticated response needs to be taken by the law enforcement community to tackling the problem.

Responses to the current situation

Coordinated and formidable enforcement support through ICCWC

In recognition of this pressing need, five international organizations joined forces in late 2010 to create the International Consortium on Combating Wildlife Crime (ICCWC). ICCWC exists to support those officers serving in the front line in carrying out their essential duties – and in doing so to work with regional wildlife enforcement networks such as the ASEAN Wildlife Enforcement Network (WEN) and South Asian WEN – networks that have benefitted greatly from support from the United States of America through the State Department and other agencies such as the Department of Justice. To date there are no such networks in Africa, and Central Africa in particular may benefit from such a network.

ICCWC seeks to ensure that perpetrators of serious wildlife crimes will face a more formidable and coordinated response, as distinguished from the present situation where the risk of detection and punishment is all too low. It also seeks to deploy modern techniques and technologies that are applied in different areas to tackling wildlife crime, such as controlled deliveries and the use of wildlife forensics. It also seeks to 'follow the money' and address asset forfeiture and corruption.

ICCWC comprises the CITES Secretariat, INTERPOL, the United Nations Office on Drugs and Crime (UNODC), the World Bank and the World Customs Organization (WCO). The CITES Secretariat chairs the Consortium.

CITES is encouraged by the level of commitment to tackling wildlife crime that has been demonstrated by each participating organization, including the strong personal commitment shown by each executive head – Secretary-General Noble of INTERPOL, Executive Director Fedotov of UNODC, President Zoellick of the World Bank and Secretary-General Mikuriya of WCO. . .

At international level, bold steps are being taken to practice what is being preached regarding better coordination, which is to the benefit of national authorities and regional and sub-regional networks. Further technical, financial and political support is required to continue this effort.

The same level of cooperation is required at the national level if we are going to seriously tackle wildlife crime. And while it takes considerable effort, it is being done, as is evident from the efforts being made in South Africa and the United States of America. Recent significant moves towards national collaboration are also evident in China through the establishment of the National Inter-Agency CITES Enforcement Collaboration Group (NICECG) of China, which has just completed a major nation-wide enforcement operation.

CITES implementation has also recently been brought to the fore at the highest political level. In the joint statement issued after the fourth round of the U.S.-China Strategic and Economic Dialogue held from 3 to 4 May in Beijing, article 47 states that: "We decide to jointly support the wildlife law enforcement efforts and to combat the smuggling of endangered and protected species. China and the United States will attend the Special Investigation Group Meeting held from 20 to 21 June 2012 in Nanning, China, led by ASEAN-WEN. At the meeting, wildlife investigators and forensic experts will identify and recommend improved enforcement and inspection efforts."

ICCWC is also working to raise the profile and awareness of wildlife crime among politicians, diplomats, policy-makers and decision-makers, as well as the judiciary, so that they may better understand why this area deserves to be a high priority for law enforcers and why they should devote further human and financial resources to it. . .

Moving beyond seizures - linking the entire 'enforcement chain'

As reported through ETIS, and noted above, very few large-scale ivory seizures actually result in successful follow-up law enforcement actions, including investigations, arrests, convictions and the imposition of penalties that serve as deterrents. This comment applies to wildlife crime more generally.

While they are essential, enforcement efforts to stop wildlife crime must not just result in seizures – they must result in prosecutions, convictions and strong penalties to stop the flow of contraband. The whole 'enforcement chain' must work together. And this is why the work of ICCWC is so essential in supporting States and regional and sub-regional networks, as the ICCWC partners collectively deal with the entire enforcement system. The recent training by ICCWC (led by WCO) in controlled deliveries is an excellent example of the sorts of measures that are required to track down the criminal syndicates.

Increasing financial resources

In light of the scale of wildlife crime, and the risks to wildlife and people associated with this crime, the financial resources to tackle wildlife crime are clearly inadequate. ICCWC is working with the donor community, as well as with governments, agencies and institutions that may have the money and know-how to assist range, transit and consumer States, and to supply the logistics that many of them need so badly.

All Parties to CITES have also invested their own resources in establishing Management Authorities and putting into place necessary legislation and enforcement measures, some of which require additional support from the international community.

African Elephant Conservation Fund

The United States of America has been active in its support for the African Elephant Conservation Fund, which has benefited from appropriations from the United States Congress, and its support is greatly appreciated and continues to be desperately needed. It can help support the sorts of specific measures that are referred to below.

African Elephant Fund

The African Elephant Fund has also been established in support of the implementation of the African Elephant Action Plan, a plan supported by all 38 range States of the African elephant, and further support is sought for the Fund. The Action Plan includes as its first priority objective: "reduce illegal killing of elephants and illegal trade in elephant products."

Global Environment Facility

The Global Environment Facility (GEF) does not serve as a financial mechanism for CITES, making it extremely difficult to secure GEF funding in support of CITES and enforcement actions in particular. This situation does not reflect the importance of tackling wildlife crime and is being considered by the CITES Standing Committee, which is addressing whether GEF should serve as a financial mechanism for CITES. Any change to existing arrangements would require decisions by the CITES Conference of the Parties and the GEF Assembly.

The CITES Secretariat raised the issue of providing additional funding to tackle wildlife crime in a presentation to the Council of the GEF, in November, 2011. Making GEF a financial mechanism for CITES would open up additional financing opportunities for Parties to enforce the Convention.

In the meantime, the CITES Secretariat has worked with South Africa to develop a CITES-related GEF project that will support the use of modern forensics in tackling poaching of rhinos and the illegal trade in rhino specimens. The project has been signed off by the Chief Executive Officer of GEF and will be considered by the GEF Council in June, 2012.

The World Bank

The World Bank has been very active in mobilizing resources for wildlife crime issues, including illegal timber trade and tiger conservation, and in perusing major initiatives to 'follow the money', which is vital to ensure that criminals do not benefit from the proceeds of their criminal activities.

Foundations, the private sector and non-government organizations

The CITES Secretariat is also seeking to mobilize support from foundations and the private sector to support enforcement actions, and in particular to support the use of modern forensic techniques.

The non-government sector has been very active in raising financial resources in support of elephants and rhinos. . .

NOTES & QUESTIONS

1. The first two CITES appendices contain the lists of species that are "threatened with extinction" and that "may become" threatened with extinction, respectively. Species listed on the third appendix do not require a vote of the parties because they are simply placed there by their host nation. As of 2001, about 5,000 species of animals and 25,000 species of plants were listed on the three appendices. The contested votes concerning the listing of elephants, whales, sturgeon, the Hawksbill sea turtle, and bigleaf mahogany reveal the difficulty in deciding the appropriate treatment of a species. CITES itself does not define the operative terms "threatened with extinction" and "may become" threatened with extinction. The Berne Criteria, adopted at the first CITES conference in 1976, sought to provide guidance regarding the biological and trade information needed to judge the status of a species. Widespread objections to those guidelines resulted in the adoption of the Fort Lauderdale Criteria at the ninth convention of the parties in 1994. The new criteria provide that a species should be included in Appendix I if the species "is or may be affected by trade" and if (1) its wild population is small, (2) its population is limited to a small area, (3) the population is dropping, or (4) either of the first three biological factors will be satisfied within five years. The criteria further specify the quantitative measurements that judge whether a population is small, restricted, or declining. The criteria thus represent an effort to employ objective scientific standards in listing decisions, rather than relying upon ad hoc political reasons. One recent study described the Fort Lauderdale Criteria as "a small but useful attempt to increase the influence of science in the decisionmaking process," but it contended that the criteria "will improve the deliberations of the parties to CITES not so much by increasing the influence of scientific data as by cooling expressive disputes among the parties, encouraging compromise, and promoting further scientific research." Note, *The CITES Fort Lauderdale Criteria: The Uses and Limits of Science in International Conservation Decisionmaking*, 114 HARV. L. REV. 1769, 1792 (2001).

2. The substantive provisions of CITES regulate trade in a species once it is listed. Species listed on Appendix I may be traded only if the exporting and importing countries permit the trade after they determine that the individual animal or bird was obtained properly, the individual will not be used "primarily for commercial purposes," and the survival of the species would not be threatened. Appendix II and III species require an export permit to be traded, but not an import permit. CITES also contains a number of exceptions for animals that were bred in captivity for commercial purposes and plants that were artificially propagated for commercial purposes, specimens that are personal or household effects, specimens collected by scientists and scientific institutions, and specimens that were acquired before the species was listed.

Enforcement of these regulations depends upon the efforts of each country that is a party to the treaty. CITES Article VIII provides that parties "shall take appropriate measures to enforce the provisions of the present Convention and to prohibit trade in specimens in violation thereof." Each party must designate a Management Authority that is responsible for issuing permits and a Scientific Authority that monitors those permits. Note, too, that CITES Article XIV ensures that countries that are party to the treaty are allowed to adopt stricter domestic regulations regarding the trade of species protected by CITES.

The success of CITES depends upon domestic statutes prohibiting trade in the species protected by CITES. The United States Congress, for example, enacted the Endangered Species Act in 1973 in part to enforce the obligations imposed by CITES. How much CITES adds to the efforts of the United States to protect endangered species is questionable. One observer suggests that CITES "is best treated as an extra facility under which any Party can invoke the assistance of law enforcement agencies of other Parties in improving the implementation of its own policies." R.B. Martin, *When CITES Works and When It Does Not*, in Endangered Species, Threatened Convention, *supra*, at 31. By contrast, "CITES is unlikely to work . . . where control of wildlife is not centralized or popularly accepted or where the state bureaucracy is weak and inefficient." *Id.* at 32.

The ability of CITES to control the international trade in endangered species also depends upon the treatment of those countries that are not parties to the treaty. CITES Article X states, "Where export or re-export is to, or import is from, a State not a Party to the Convention, comparable documentation issued by the component authorities in that State which substantially conforms with the requirements of the present Convention for permits and certificates may be accepted in lieu thereof by any Party." This provision anticipates a problem created by the very popularity of CITES, which now has 154 parties: "There are so few countries that are not members of CITES that considerable money can be made from the channeling of illegal trade through these few countries. There is now an economic incentive to not be a member, if you are willing to deal in illegal goods." Favre, *supra*, at 256. Article X responds to that concern by requiring all parties to CITES to trade with non-parties only when there has been substantial compliance with the CITES provisions. What else can be done about countries that are not parties to CITES that countenance trade in endangered species?

3. The ESA implements CITES in the United States. Specifically, it is illegal to "engage in any trade in any specimen contrary to the provisions of the Convention," 16 U.S.C. § 1538(c)(1), and any seized materials "shall be subject to the forfeiture to the United States." *Id.* § 1540(e)(4)(A). The federal courts routinely adjudicate cases involving violations of those provisions, including a decision upholding the federal government's detention of several shipments of bigleaf mahogany from Brazil, which listed the tree on Appendix III of CITES. *See* Castlewood Products, L.L.C. v. Norton, 365 F.3d 1076 (D.C. Cir. 2004).

4. The internet has complicated the effort to control the international trade in rare wildlife. A 2005 report produced by the International Fund for Animal Welfare found 146 live primates, 5,527 elephant products, 526 turtle and tortoiseshells, 2,630 reptile products, and 239 cats for sale—in just one week. "Trade on the Internet is easy, cheap and anonymous," explained the organization's director. How can CITES be employed to address this new problem? What legal tools might be more successful than CITES than regulating internet shopping?

5. How important is CITES given that habitat destruction is a greater threat to biodiversity than trade? David Favre defends CITES as follows:

> Controlling land use decisions within a particular country would be very difficult to do in an international convention, but controlling the move-

ment of animals is possible because the flow of international commerce already goes through identifiable locations which can be monitored. Controlling trade may not provide all of the protection necessary for a species' survival, but it would be impossible to protect most species without controlling trade. Also, the process of listing an animal or plant under this international document will hopefully bring public attention and government action in protecting the habitat of the species listed.

Favre, *supra*, at 30. Conversely, can the international wildlife trade be "a positive tool for conservation," as the sustainable use proponents described by Dickson contend? Is the contrary premise of CITES outdated? Or is it more necessary than ever?

6. One treatise describes "CITES has proved to be the most controversial of the international environmental conventions." Jon Hutton & Barnabas Dickson, *Introduction*, in ENDANGERED SPECIES, THREATENED CONVENTION xv (Jon Hutton & Barnabas Dickson eds. 2000). Another treatise describes CITES as "perhaps the most successful of all international treaties concerned with the conservation of wildlife." SIMON LYSTER, INTERNATIONAL WILDLIFE LAW: AN ANALYSIS OF INTERNATIONAL TREATIES CONCERNED WITH THE CONSERVATION OF WILDLIFE 240 (1985). Who is right? Or could CITES be both successful and controversial? What would you need to know to judge both claims? Additional, thorough overviews of CITES include WILLEM WIJNSTEKERS, THE EVOLUTION OF CITES (6th ed. 2001); DAVID S. FAVRE, INTERNATIONAL TRADE IN ENDANGERED SPECIES: A GUIDE TO CITES (1989); and the CITES web site at http://www.cites.org.

C. THE CONVENTION ON BIOLOGICAL DIVERSITY

United Nations Conference on Environment and Development: Convention on Biological Diversity
31 International Legal Materials 818 (1992).

Preamble

The Contracting Parties,

Conscious of the intrinsic value of biological diversity and of the ecological, genetic, social, economic, scientific, educational, cultural, recreational and aesthetic values of biological diversity and its components,

Conscious also of the importance of biological diversity for evolution and for maintaining life sustaining systems of the biosphere,

Affirming that the conservation of biological diversity is a common concern of humankind,

Reaffirming that States have sovereign rights over their own biological resources,

Reaffirming also that States are responsible for conserving their biological diversity and for using their biological resources in a sustainable manner,

Concerned that biological diversity is being significantly reduced by certain human activities,

Aware of the general lack of information and knowledge regarding biological diversity and of the urgent need to develop scientific, technical and institutional capacities to provide the basic understanding upon which to plan and implement appropriate measures.

Noting that it is vital to anticipate, prevent and attack the causes of significant reduction or loss of biological diversity at source.

Noting also that where there is a threat of significant reduction or loss of biological diversity, lack of full scientific certainty should not be used as a reason for postponing measures to avoid or minimize such a threat,

Noting further that the fundamental requirement for the conservation of biological diversity is the in-situ conservation of ecosystems and natural habitats and the maintenance and recovery of viable populations of species in their natural surroundings,

Noting further that ex-situ measures, preferably in the country of origin, also have an important role to play,

Recognizing the close and traditional dependence of many indigenous and local communities embodying traditional lifestyles on biological resources, and the desirability of sharing equitably benefits arising from the use of traditional knowledge, innovations and practices relevant to the conservation of biological diversity and the sustainable use of its components,

Recognizing also the vital role that women play in the conservation and sustainable use of biological diversity and affirming the need for the full participation of women at all levels of policy-making and implementation for biological diversity conservation,

Stressing the importance of, and the need to promote, international, regional and global cooperation among States and intergovernmental organizations and the non-governmental sector for the conservation of biological diversity and the sustainable use of its components,

Acknowledging that the provision of new and additional financial resources and appropriate access to relevant technologies can be expected to make a substantial difference in the world's ability to address the loss of biological diversity,

Acknowledging further that special provision is required to meet the needs of developing countries, including the provision of new and additional financial resources and appropriate access to relevant technologies,

Noting in this regard the special conditions of the least developed countries and small island States,

Acknowledging that substantial investments are required to conserve biological diversity and that there is the expectation of a broad range of environmental, economic and social benefits from those investments,

Recognizing that economic and social development and poverty eradication are the first and overriding priorities of developing countries,

Aware that conservation and sustainable use of biological diversity is of critical importance for meeting the food, health and other needs of the growing world population, for which purpose access to and sharing of both genetic resources and technologies are essential,

Noting that, ultimately, the conservation and sustainable use of biological diversity will strengthen friendly relations among States and contribute to peace for humankind,

Desiring to enhance and complement existing international arrangements for the conservation of biological diversity and sustainable use of its components, and

Determined to conserve and sustainably use biological diversity for the benefit of present and future generations,

Have agreed as follows:

Article 1. Objectives

The objectives of this Convention, to be pursued in accordance with its relevant provisions, are the conservation of biological diversity, the sustainable use of its components and the air and equitable sharing of the benefits arising out of the utilization of genetic resources, including by appropriate access to genetic resources and by appropriate transfer of relevant technologies, taking into account all rights over those resources and to technologies, and by appropriate funding.

Article 2. Use of Terms

For the purposes of this Convention:

"Biological diversity" means the variability among living organisms from all sources including, inter alia, terrestrial, marine and other aquatic ecosystems and the ecological complexes of which they are part; this includes diversity within species, between species and of ecosystems.

"Biological resources" includes genetic resources, organisms or parts thereof, populations, or any other biotic component of ecosystems with actual or potential use or value for humanity.

"Biotechnology" means any technological application that uses biological systems, living organisms, or derivatives thereof, to make or modify products or processes for specific use.

"Country of origin of genetic resources" means the country which possesses those genetic resources in in-situ conditions.

"Country providing genetic resources" means the country supplying genetic resources collected from in-situ sources, including populations of both wild and domesticated species, or taken from ex-situ sources, which may or may not have originated in that country.

"Domesticated or cultivated species" means species in which the evolutionary process has been influenced by humans to meet their needs.

"Ecosystem" means a dynamic complex of plant, animal and microorganism communities and their non-living environment interacting as a functional unit.

"Ex-situ conservation" means the conservation of components of biological diversity outside their natural habitats.

"Genetic material" means any material of plant, animal, microbial or other origin containing functional units of heredity.

"Genetic resources" means genetic material of actual or potential value.

"Habitat" means the place or type of site where an organism or population naturally occurs.

"In-situ conditions" means conditions where genetic resources exist within ecosystems and natural habitats, and, in the case of domesticated or cultivated species, in the surroundings where they have developed their distinctive properties.

"In-situ conservation" means the conservation of ecosystems and natural habitats and the maintenance and recovery of viable populations of species in their natural surroundings and, in the case of domesticated or cultivated species, in the surroundings where they have developed their distinctive properties.

"Protected area" means a geographically defined area which is designated or regulated and managed to achieve specific conservation objectives.

"Regional economic integration organization" means an organization constituted by sovereign States of a given region, to which its member States have transferred competence in respect of matters governed by this Convention and which has been duly authorized, in accordance with its internal procedures, to sign, ratify, accept, approve or accede to it.

"Sustainable use" means the use of components of biological diversity in a way and at a rate that does not lead to the long-term decline of biological diversity, thereby maintaining its potential to meet the needs and aspirations of present and future generations.

"Technology" includes biotechnology.

Article 3. Principle

States have, in accordance with the Charter of the United Nations and the principles of international law, the sovereign right to exploit their own resources pursuant to their own environmental policies, and the responsibility to ensure that activities within their jurisdiction or control do not cause damage to the environment of other States or of areas beyond the limits of national jurisdiction.

Article 4. Jurisdictional Scope

Subject to the rights of other States, and except as otherwise expressly provided in this Convention, the provisions of this Convention apply, in relation to each Contracting Party:

(a) In the case of components of biological diversity, in areas within the limits of its national jurisdiction; and

(b) In the case of processes and activities, regardless of where their effects occur, carried out under its jurisdiction or control, within the area of its national jurisdiction or beyond the limits of national jurisdiction.

Article 5. Cooperation

Each Contracting Party shall, as far as possible and as appropriate, cooperate with other Contracting Parties, directly or, where appropriate, through competent international organizations, in respect of areas beyond national jurisdiction and on other matters of mutual interest, for the conservation and sustainable use of biological diversity.

Article 6. General Measures for Conservation and Sustainable Use
Each Contracting Party shall, in accordance with its particular conditions and capabilities:

(a) Develop national strategies, plans or programmes for the conservation and sustainable use of biological diversity or adapt for this purpose existing strategies, plans or programmes which shall reflect, inter alia, the measures set out in this Convention relevant to the Contracting Party concerned; and

(b) Integrate, as far as possible and as appropriate, the conservation and sustainable use of biological diversity into relevant sectoral or cross-sectoral plans, programmes and policies.

Article 7. Identification and Monitoring

Each Contracting Party shall, as far as possible and as appropriate, in particular for the purposes of Articles 8 to 10:

(a) Identify components of biological diversity important for its conservation and sustainable use having regard to the indicative list of categories set down in Annex I;

(b) Monitor, through sampling and other techniques, the components of biological diversity identified pursuant to subparagraph (a) above, paying particular attention to those requiring urgent conservation measures and those which offer the greatest potential for sustainable use;

(c) Identify processes and categories of activities which have or are likely to have significant adverse impacts on the conservation and sustainable use of biological diversity, and monitor their effects through sampling and other techniques; and

(d) Maintain and organize, by any mechanism data, derived from identification and monitoring activities pursuant to subparagraphs (a), (b) and (c) above.

Article 8. In-situ Conservation

Each Contracting Party shall, as far as possible and as appropriate:

(a) Establish a system of protected areas or areas where special measures need to be taken to conserve biological diversity;

(b) Develop, where necessary, guidelines for the selection, establishment and management of protected areas or areas where special measures need to be taken to conserve biological diversity;

(c) Regulate or manage biological resources important for the conservation of biological diversity whether within or outside protected areas, with a view to ensuring their conservation and sustainable use;

(d) Promote the protection of ecosystems, natural habitats and the maintenance of viable populations of species in natural surroundings;

(e) Promote environmentally sound and sustainable development in areas adjacent to protected areas with a view to furthering protection of these areas;

(f) Rehabilitate and restore degraded ecosystems and promote the recovery of threatened species, inter alia, through the development and implementation of plans or other management strategies;

(g) Establish or maintain means to regulate, manage or control the risks associated with the use and release of living modified organisms resulting from biotechnology which are likely to have adverse environmental impacts that could affect the conservation and sustainable use of biological diversity, taking also into account the risks to human health;

(h) Prevent the introduction of, control or eradicate those alien species which threaten ecosystems, habitats or species;

(i) Endeavour to provide the conditions needed for compatibility between present uses and the conservation of biological diversity and the sustainable use of its components;

(j) Subject to its national legislation, respect, preserve and maintain knowledge, innovations and practices of indigenous and local communities embodying traditional lifestyles relevant for the conservation and sustainable use of biological diversity and promote their wider application with the approval and involvement of the holders of such knowledge, innovations and practices and encourage the equitable sharing of the benefits arising from the utilization of such knowledge, innovations and practices;

(k) Develop or maintain necessary legislation and/or other regulatory provisions for the protection of threatened species and populations;

(*l*) Where a significant adverse effect on biological diversity has been determined pursuant to Article 7, regulate or manage the relevant processes and categories of activities; and

(m) Cooperate in providing financial and other support for in-situ conservation outlined in subparagraphs (a) to (*l*) above, particularly to developing countries.

Article 9. Ex-situ Conservation

Each Contracting Party shall, as far as possible and as appropriate, and predominantly for the purpose of complementing in-situ measures:

(a) Adopt measures for the ex-situ conservation of components of biological diversity, preferably in the country of origin of such components;

(b) Establish and maintain facilities for ex-situ conservation of and research on plants, animals and micro-organisms, preferably in the country of origin of genetic resources;

(c) Adopt measures for the recovery and rehabilitation of threatened species and for their reintroduction into their natural habitats under appropriate conditions;

(d) Regulate and manage collection of biological resources from natural habitats for ex-situ conservation purposes so as not to threaten ecosystems and in-situ populations of species, except where special temporary ex-situ measures are required under subparagraph (c) above; and

(e) Cooperate in providing financial and other support for ex-situ conservation outlined in subparagraphs (a) to (d) above and in the establishment and maintenance of ex-situ conservation facilities in developing countries.

Article 10. Sustainable Use of Components of Biological Diversity

Each Contracting Party shall, as far as possible and as appropriate:

(a) Integrate consideration of the conservation and sustainable use of biological resources into national decision-making;

(b) Adopt measures relating to the use of biological resources to avoid or minimize adverse impacts on biological diversity;

(c) Protect and encourage customary use of biological resources in accordance with traditional cultural practices that are compatible with conservation or sustainable use requirements;

(d) Support local populations to develop and implement remedial action in degraded areas where biological diversity has been reduced; and

(e) Encourage cooperation between its governmental authorities and its private sector in developing methods for sustainable use of biological resources.

Article 11. Incentive Measures

Each Contracting Party shall, as far as possible and as appropriate, adopt economically and socially sound measures that act as incentives for the conservation and sustainable use of components of biological diversity.

Article 12. Research and Training

The Contracting Parties, taking into account the special needs of developing countries, shall:

(a) Establish and maintain programmes for scientific and technical education and training in measures for the identification, conservation and sustainable use of biological diversity and its components and provide support for such education and training for the specific needs of developing countries;

(b) Promote and encourage research which contributes to the conservation and sustainable use of biological diversity, particularly in developing countries, inter alia, in accordance with decisions of the Conference of the Parties taken in consequence of recommendations of the Subsidiary Body on Scientific, Technical and Technological Advice; and

(c) In keeping with the provisions of Articles 16, 18 and 20, promote and cooperate in the use of scientific advances in biological diversity research in developing methods for conservation and sustainable use of biological resources.

Article 13. Public Education and Awareness

The Contracting Parties shall:

(a) Promote and encourage understanding of the importance of, and the measures required for, the conservation of biological diversity, as well as its propagation through media, and the inclusion of these topics in educational programmes; and

(b) Cooperate, as appropriate, with other States and international organizations in developing educational and public awareness programmes, with respect to conservation and sustainable use of biological diversity.

Article 14. Impact Assessment and Minimizing Adverse Impacts

1. Each Contracting Party, as far as possible and as appropriate, shall:

(a) Introduce appropriate procedures requiring environmental impact assessment of its proposed projects that are likely to have significant adverse effects on biological diversity with a view to avoiding or minimizing such effects and, where appropriate, allow for public participation in such procedures;

(b) Introduce appropriate arrangements to ensure that the environmental consequences of its programmes and policies that are likely to have significant adverse impacts on biological diversity are duly taken into account;

(c) Promote, on the basis of reciprocity, notification, exchange of information and consultation on activities under their jurisdiction or control which are likely to significantly affect adversely the biological diversity of other States or areas beyond the limits of national jurisdiction, by encouraging the conclusion of bilateral, regional or multilateral arrangements, as appropriate;

(d) In the case of imminent or grave danger or damage, originating under its jurisdiction or control, to biological diversity within the area under jurisdiction of other States or in areas beyond the limits of national jurisdiction, notify immediately the potentially affected States of such danger or damage, as well as initiate action to prevent or minimize such danger or damage; and

(e) Promote national arrangements for emergency responses to activities or events, whether caused naturally or otherwise, which present a grave and imminent danger to biological diversity and encourage international cooperation to supplement such national efforts and, where appropriate and agreed by the States or regional economic integration organizations concerned, to establish joint contingency plans.

2. The Conference of the Parties shall examine, on the basis of studies to be carried out, the issue of liability and redress, including restoration

and compensation, for damage to biological diversity, except where such liability is a purely internal matter.

Article 15. Access to Genetic Resources

1. Recognizing the sovereign rights of States over their natural resources, the authority to determine access to genetic resources rests with the national governments and is subject to national legislation.

2. Each Contracting Party shall endeavour to create conditions to facilitate access to genetic resources for environmentally sound uses by other Contracting Parties and not to impose restrictions that run counter to the objectives of this Convention.

3. For the purpose of this Convention, the genetic resources being provided by a Contracting Party, as referred to in this Article and Articles 16 and 19, are only those that are provided by Contracting Parties that are countries of origin of such resources or by the Parties that have acquired the genetic resources in accordance with this Convention.

4. Access, where granted, shall be on mutually agreed terms and subject to the provisions of this Article.

5. Access to genetic resources shall be subject to prior informed consent of the Contracting Party providing such resources, unless otherwise determined by that Party.

6. Each Contracting Party shall endeavour to develop and carry out scientific research based on genetic resources provided by other Contracting Parties with the full participation of, and where possible in, such Contracting Parties.

7. Each Contracting Party shall take legislative, administrative or policy measures, as appropriate, and in accordance with Articles 16 and 19 and, where necessary, through the financial mechanism established by Articles 20 and 21 with the aim of sharing in a fair and equitable way the results of research and development and the benefits arising from the commercial and other utilization of genetic resources with the Contracting Party providing such resources. Such sharing shall be upon mutually agreed terms.

Article 16. Access to and Transfer of Technology

1. Each Contracting Party, recognizing that technology includes biotechnology, and that both access to and transfer of technology among Contracting Parties are essential elements for the attainment of the objectives of this Convention, undertakes subject to the provisions of this Article to provide and/or facilitate access for and transfer to other Contracting Parties of technologies that are relevant to the conservation and sustainable use of biological diversity or make use of genetic resources and do not cause significant damage to the environment.

2. Access to and transfer of technology referred to in paragraph 1 above to developing countries shall be provided and/or facilitated under fair and most favourable terms, including on concessional and preferential terms where mutually agreed, and, where necessary, in accordance with the financial mechanism established by Articles 20 and 21. In the case of technology subject to patents and other intellectual property rights, such access and transfer shall be provided on terms which recognize and are consistent with the adequate and effective protection of intellectual property rights. The application of this paragraph shall be consistent with paragraphs 3, 4 and 5 below.

3. Each Contracting Party shall take legislative, administrative or policy measures, as appropriate, with the aim that Contracting Parties, in particular those that are developing countries, which provide genetic resources are provided access to and transfer of technology which makes use of those resources, on mutually agreed terms, including technology protected by patents and other intellectual property rights, where necessary, through the provisions of Articles 20 and 21 and in accordance with international law and consistent with paragraphs 4 and 5 below.

4. Each Contracting Party shall take legislative, administrative or policy measures, as appropriate, with the aim that the private sector facilitates access to, joint development and transfer of technology referred to in paragraph 1 above for the benefit of both governmental institutions and the private sector of developing countries and in this regard shall abide by the obligations included in paragraphs 1, 2 and 3 above.

5. The Contracting Parties, recognizing that patents and other intellectual property rights may have an influence on the implementation of this Convention, shall cooperate in this regard subject to national legislation and international law in order to ensure that such rights are supportive of and do not run counter to its objectives.

Article 17. Exchange of Information

1. The Contracting Parties shall facilitate the exchange of information, from all publicly available sources, relevant to the conservation and sustainable use of biological diversity, taking into account the special needs of developing countries.

2. Such exchange of information shall include exchange of results of technical, scientific and socio-economic research, as well as information on training and surveying programmes, specialized knowledge, indigenous and traditional knowledge as such and in combination with the technologies referred to in Article 16, paragraph 1. It shall also, where feasible, include repatriation of information.

Article 18. Technical and Scientific Cooperation

1. The Contracting Parties shall promote international technical and scientific cooperation in the field of conservation and sustainable use of bio-

logical diversity, where necessary, through the appropriate international and national institutions.

2. Each Contracting Party shall promote technical and scientific cooperation with other Contracting Parties, in particular developing countries, in implementing this Convention, inter alia, through the development and implementation of national policies. In promoting such cooperation, special attention should be given to the development and strengthening of national capabilities, by means of human resources development and institution building.

3. The Conference of the Parties, at its first meeting, shall determine how to establish a clearing-house mechanism to promote and facilitate technical and scientific cooperation.

4. The Contracting Parties shall, in accordance with national legislation and policies, encourage and develop methods of cooperation for the development and use of technologies, including indigenous and traditional technologies, in pursuance of the objectives of this Convention. For this purpose, the Contracting Parties shall also promote cooperation in the training of personnel and exchange of experts.

5. The Contracting Parties shall, subject to mutual agreement, promote the establishment of joint research programmes and joint ventures for the development of technologies relevant to the objectives of this Convention.

Article 19. Handling of Biotechnology and Distribution of its Benefits

1. Each Contracting Party shall take legislative, administrative or policy measures, as appropriate, to provide for the effective participation in biotechnological research activities by those Contracting Parties, especially developing countries, which provide the genetic resources for such research, and where feasible in such Contracting Parties.

2. Each Contracting Party shall take all practicable measures to promote and advance priority access on a fair and equitable basis by Contracting Parties, especially developing countries, to the results and benefits arising from biotechnologies based upon genetic resources provided by those Contracting Parties. Such access shall be on mutually agreed terms.

3. The Parties shall consider the need for and modalities of a protocol setting out appropriate procedures, including, in particular, advance informed agreement, in the field of the safe transfer, handling and use of any living modified organism resulting from biotechnology that may have adverse effect on the conservation and sustainable use of biological diversity.

4. Each Contracting Party shall, directly or by requiring any natural or legal person under its jurisdiction providing the organisms referred to in paragraph 3 above, provide any available information about the use and safety regulations required by that Contracting Party in handling such or-

ganisms, as well as any available information on the potential adverse impact of the specific organisms concerned to the Contracting Party into which those organisms are to be introduced.

Article 20. Financial Resources

1. Each Contracting Party undertakes to provide, in accordance with its capabilities, financial support and incentives in respect of those national activities which are intended to achieve the objectives of this Convention, in accordance with its national plans, priorities and programmes.

2. The developed country Parties shall provide new and additional financial resources to enable developing country Parties to meet the agreed full incremental costs to them of implementing measures which fulfil the obligations of this Convention and to benefit from its provisions and which costs are agreed between a developing country Party and the institutional structure referred to in Article 21, in accordance with policy, strategy, programme priorities and eligibility criteria and an indicative list of incremental costs established by the Conference of the Parties. Other Parties, including countries undergoing the process of transition to a market economy, may voluntarily assume the obligations of the developed country Parties. For the purpose of this Article, the Conference of the Parties, shall at its first meeting establish a list of developed country Parties and other Parties which voluntarily assume the obligations of the developed country Parties. The Conference of the Parties shall periodically review and if necessary amend the list. Contributions from other countries and sources on a voluntary basis would also be encouraged. The implementation of these commitments shall take into account the need for adequacy, predictability and timely flow of funds and the importance of burden-sharing among the contributing Parties included in the list.

3. The developed country Parties may also provide, and developing country Parties avail themselves of, financial resources related to the implementation of this Convention through bilateral, regional and other multilateral channels.

4. The extent to which developing country Parties will effectively implement their commitments under this Convention will depend on the effective implementation by developed country Parties of their commitments under this Convention related to financial resources and transfer of technology and will take fully into account the fact that economic and social development and eradication of poverty are the first and overriding priorities of the developing country Parties.

5. The Parties shall take full account of the specific needs and special situation of least developed countries in their actions with regard to funding and transfer of technology.

6. The Contracting Parties shall also take into consideration the special conditions resulting from the dependence on, distribution and location

of, biological diversity within developing country Parties, in particular small island States.

7. Consideration shall also be given to the special situation of developing countries, including those that are most environmentally vulnerable, such as those with arid and semi-arid zones, coastal and mountainous areas.

Article 21. Financial Mechanism

1. There shall be a mechanism for the provision of financial resources to developing country Parties for purposes of this Convention on a grant or concessional basis the essential elements of which are described in this Article. The mechanism shall function under the authority and guidance of, and be accountable to, the Conference of the Parties for purposes of this Convention. The operations of the mechanism shall be carried out by such institutional structure as may be decided upon by the Conference of the Parties at its first meeting. For purposes of this Convention, the Conference of the Parties shall determine the policy, strategy, programme priorities and eligibility criteria relating to the access to and utilization of such resources. The contributions shall be such as to take into account the need for predictability, adequacy and timely flow of funds referred to in Article 20 in accordance with the amount of resources needed to be decided periodically by the Conference of the Parties and the importance of burden-sharing among the contributing Parties included in the list referred to in Article 20, paragraph 2. Voluntary contributions may also be made by the developed country Parties and by other countries and sources. The mechanism shall operate within a democratic and transparent system of governance.

2. Pursuant to the objectives of this Convention, the Conference of the Parties shall at its first meeting determine the policy, strategy and programme priorities, as well as detailed criteria and guidelines for eligibility for access to and utilization of the financial resources including monitoring and evaluation on a regular basis of such utilization. The Conference of the Parties shall decide on the arrangements to give effect to paragraph 1 above after consultation with the institutional structure entrusted with the operation of the financial mechanism.

3. The Conference of the Parties shall review the effectiveness of the mechanism established under this Article, including the criteria and guidelines referred to in paragraph 2 above, not less than two years after the entry into force of this Convention and thereafter on a regular basis. Based on such review, it shall take appropriate action to improve the effectiveness of the mechanism if necessary.

4. The Contracting Parties shall consider strengthening existing financial institutions to provide financial resources for the conservation and sustainable use of biological diversity.

Article 22. Relationship with Other International Conventions

1. The provisions of this Convention shall not affect the rights and obligations of any Contracting Party deriving from any existing international agreement, except where the exercise of those rights and obligations would cause a serious damage or threat to biological diversity.

2. Contracting Parties shall implement this Convention with respect to the marine environment consistently with the rights and obligations of States under the law of the sea. . .

NOTES & QUESTIONS

1. The Convention on Biological Diversity resulted from years of international negotiations. In 1972, the Stockholm Convention became the first effort to state binding principles of international environmental law. Discussions about biodiversity continued through the 1980's and culminated at the United Nations Conference on the Environment and Development held in Rio de Janeiro in June 1992. The Convention emerged from Rio with the signatures of nearly every country that attended the conference, and it became effective at the end of 1993. It has become the primary framework for the protection of global biodiversity. As of 2001, 182 countries have ratified the Convention.

But not the United States. The Bush Administration declined to send representatives to Rio in 1992 because of concerns about the nature of the evolving agreement. It emphasized both that it "strongly supports the conservation of biodiversity" and that "international cooperation in this area [is] extremely desirable," but it found "particularly unsatisfactory the text's treatment of intellectual property rights; finances, including, importantly, the role of the Global Environmental Facility (GEF); technology transfer and biotechnology." United States: Declaration Made at the United Nations Environment Programme Conference for the Adoption of the Agreed Text of the Convention on Biological Diversity, 31 I.L.M. 848 (1992). One year later, President Clinton signed the Convention. He then dispatched State Department official (and former Colorado Senator) Timothy Wirth to defend the Convention before a House of Representatives committee. Wirth testified:

> The Administration strongly supports the Convention on Biological Diversity as an important vehicle for the conservation and sustainable use of biodiversity worldwide. It sets in place a global commitment to promote biodiversity conservation and sustainable use for the benefit of this and future generations. U.S. adherence to the Convention is critical for global efforts to conserve and utilize biodiversity and for maintaining our position as the world leader in environmental protection.

> As noted above, no implementing legislation will be required. The existing assemblage of Federal, State and private sector biodiversity programs— comprising numerous State and Federal laws and programs, an extensive system of Federal and State wildlife management areas, marine sanctuaries, parks and forests, and research and education programs—is considered sufficient in meeting our responsibilities under the convention. The Administration does not intend to disrupt the existing balance of State

and Federal authorities through this Convention and, indeed, is committed to expanding and strengthening these productive partnerships. . .

As you know, Mr. Chairman, industry has expressed concerns about the way some of the language in the Convention is drafted, particularly on the issues of intellectual property rights protection, terms of transfer of technology, and participation in U.S. research projects. We share those concerns, but feel we can best protect U.S. interests by:

1. Sending clear messages to the rest of the world as to how the U.S. expects these provisions to be implemented by all Parties;

2. Participating actively in the Convention to protect U.S. intellectual property rights interests; and

3. Depositing with our instrument of ratification statements of understanding on specific issues raised in articles of the convention.

Specifically, we propose to deposit with our instrument of ratification statements of U.S. understanding that make clear our positions on the issues of technology transfer and intellectual property rights, research, funding, sovereign immunity, and the Article 3 Principle. . .

Finally, many have asked what mechanisms are available to the United States to ensure that any decisions of the Conference of the Parties (COP) accord with U.S. interests. First, we will ensure that the COP's rules of procedure, which will be adopted by consensus, are fully acceptable to the United States. Second, we have supported a proposal to require that all decisions concerning the financial mechanism are also made by consensus. Most importantly, however, the Conference of the Parties could not legally bind the United States to a legal interpretation of the Convention that the U.S. did not accept. The United States will have an opportunity to formally accept or reject any amendment or protocol to the Convention.

Timothy E. Wirth, *Ratification Sought for the Convention on Biological Diversity*, 5 DEPT. OF STATE DISPATCH 213, 214–15 (Apr. 18, 1994). But Congress has not been persuaded. The Senate has not ratified the Convention, and there is little prospect that it will in the foreseeable future.

Meanwhile, some environmentalists object to the Convention as well. Professor Lakshman Guruswamy contends that the Convention "may halt the advance of international environmental law on three fronts. . ." First, it rejects the concept of sustainable development by prioritizing economic growth over environmental protection, allowing international resources earmarked for the protection of biodiversity to be expended on economic growth that could destroy biodiversity. Second, it denies state responsibility for damage to the global commons. Finally, it repudiates the idea that the plant, animal, insect, and genetic resources of the world (our biodiversity) are the common heritage of humankind, and that it is the responsibility of the community of nations to protect this heritage. Lakshnan D. Guruswamy, *The Convention on Biological Diversity: A Polemic*, in PROTECTION OF GLOBAL BIODIVERSITY: CONVERGING STRATEGIES 351 (Lakshman D. Guruswamy & Jeffrey A. McNeely eds. 1998).

Notwithstanding these objections, nearly every nation has ratified the Convention. The discussion of the key issues raised by the Convention that follows draws from numerous sources, though it is especially indebted to DAVID HUNTER, JAMES SALZMAN & DURWOOD ZAELKE, INTERNATIONAL ENVIRONMENTAL LAW AND POLICY 932–76 (2d ed. 2002); and to the Convention's web site at http://www.biodiv.org.

2. The Preamble to the Convention states that the conservation of biological diversity is a "common concern of humankind." Can that be disputed? The most frequent complaint with that assertion is that it does not go far enough. As Professor Guruswamy notes, the alternative formulation would have proclaimed biodiversity to be "the common heritage of humankind." How are the two descriptions different? Which is more accurate? The rejected "common heritage of humankind" description was opposed by developing countries who "did not want common heritage applied to all biodiversity, because the concept implies a requirement to allow all States free access to the resource." It was also opposed by industrial countries who worried that "the common heritage principle if applied too far might require benefit sharing or open transfers of technology derived from biodiversity." HUNTER, SALZMAN & ZAELKE, *supra*, at 934.

The Preamble also seeks to balance state sovereignty with state responsibility for the protection of biodiversity. Does it do so successfully? Opponents of the Convention answer no, though for much different reasons. Professor Guruswamy sees the Convention as tilted in favor of national economic development instead of global biodiversity. American complaints, by contrast, insist that the Convention will deprive the United States (and other concerned countries) of the freedom to balance biodiversity and economic development themselves, even if that balance is more favorable toward biodiversity. Still, "the primary rights and responsibilities regarding biodiversity conservation remain at the national level." *Id.* at 936. Is that an accurate assessment of the Convention? If so, why did the signatories adopt an approach that emphasizes domestic laws rather than international law? What does the Convention add that interested countries could not accomplish themselves?

Is there anything surprising in the steps that each country is asked to take to protect its biodiversity? Articles 6 through 11, 14, and 26 each set forth specific duties. Do you agree with Assistant Secretary of State Wirth that the United States already satisfies those requirements? Does the experience of the United States in protecting species and ecosystems suggest any appropriate duties besides those listed in the Convention? The strategies adopted by different countries can be discerned from plans, required by Article 6, that each signatory is required to prepare. *See* CONVENTION ON BIOLOGICAL DIVERSITY, ALL NATIONAL REPORTS, *available at* http://www.biodiv.org/world/reports.asp?t=all.

3. The Convention regulates the biotechnology trade. The nexus between that trade and the preservation of biodiversity is provided by the concern that genetic diversity could suffer if foreigners are allowed to exploit a nation's native plant and animals resources. This became a North-South conflict centered on the appropriate scope of intellectual property rights. The South "wanted to retain the right to control the access of northern industries to 'prospect' for biodiversity in their countries," and "they saw intellectual property rights (IPR) regimes, which protected the patents of biotechnology firms, as a major obstacle to benefit-sharing and ultimately to biodiversity conservation." The South also objected to "biopiracy": the exploitation of traditional knowledge about local biodiversity by multinational bioprospecting companies who seek to patent their "discoveries." For its part, "the North wanted to ensure free and open access to biodiversity so that pharmaceutical and agricultural research firms could expand their efforts to identify potentially valuable plants and animals," and to protect the intellectual property rights of those firms in order to reward and encourage their investments in research and product development. HUNTER, SALZMAN & ZAELKE, *supra*, at 943–44.

Is the Convention's treatment of these concerns—embodied in Articles 15 through 19—satisfactory? Some developing nations object that "the Convention does not explicitly address the global and national roots of biodiversity destruction, and pays mostly lip-service to the genuine needs of disprivileged people everywhere." Anshish Kothari, *Beyond the Biodiversity Convention: A View from India* 67–72, in BIODIPLOMACY: GENETIC RESOURCES AND INTERNATIONAL RELATIONS (V. Sanchez & C. Juma eds. 1994). The United States reads the Convention quite differently. Assistant Secretary Wirth insisted that "the Convention cannot serve as a basis for any Party unilaterally to change the terms of existing agreements involving public or private U.S. entities." He continued:

> On the critical issue of technology transfer, our understandings make clear that any access to and transfer of technology that occurs under the convention must recognize and be consistent with the adequate and effective protection of intellectual property rights (IPR). The U.S. understandings also make clear that the term "fair and most favorable terms" for technology transfer contained in Article 16(2) of the Convention means terms that are voluntarily agreed to by all Parties to the transaction. This lays down the clear marker to all other countries that the Convention cannot be used by any Party to unilaterally impose terms or obligations on any other Party regarding technology transfer.

Wirth, *supra*, at 215. Is Wirth's fear of unilateral actions legitimate? Should the Convention permit such actions? And for another critique, consider Professor Jim Chen, who insists that "[m]ost allegations of biopiracy are so thoroughly riddled with inconsistencies and outright lies that the entire genre, pending further clarification, must be consigned to the realm of 'rural' legend." Jim Chen, *There's No Such Thing as Biopiracy . . . And It's a Good Thing Too*, 36 MCGEORGE L. REV. 1, 5 (2005).

4. Biodiversity can be harmful. The traditional illustrations of that maxim involve the smallpox virus, predators who eliminate their prey, and alien species that wreak havoc when found outside their native ecosystems. Now biotechnology presents far more ominous concerns about the potential effects of genetically modified organisms (GMOs) that are released into the environment. Developing countries have been particularly worried about GMOs because of their concerns that foreign corporations will be insufficiently sensitive to the risks of creating such organisms within their borders. Again, the United States sees the issue differently. Testifying in 1995, Assistant Secretary Wirth explained:

> Industry representatives have also inquired as to U.S. intentions regarding the negotiation of a biosafety protocol under the Convention. We stated at the time we signed the Convention that the need for a protocol must be demonstrated before further steps are considered. At the first intergov-

ernmental meeting relating to the Convention we restated this position, adding that based on our experience, we did not feel that a biosafety protocol to this Convention is warranted. However, should negotiations on a protocol eventually proceed, we will be in a better position to protect U.S. interests if we have a seat at the table. And the United States, in cooperation with U.S. industry and other interested groups, would work to ensure that any protocol is scientifically based and analytically sound.

Wirth, *supra*, at 215.

In 2000, the parties to the Convention adopted the Cartagena Protocol on Biosafety. That protocol allows countries to decide whether or not they are willing to accept agricultural imports that contain GMOs. Commodities that might contain GMOs must be clearly labeled when exported, with heightened notice requirements imposed upon seeds, live fish, and other GMOs that are intentionally released into the environment. The protocol thus embodies the precautionary principle, a common yet contested feature in environmental law that allows regulators to err on the side of caution when faced with uncertain scientific risks. *See* Michael Pollan, *The Year in Ideas: A to Z.; Precautionary Principle*, N.Y. TIMES, Dec. 9, 2001, § 6, at 92 (discussing the role of the precautionary principle in the Biosafety Protocol). The protocol also establishes a Biosafety Clearing House that collects and shares information about GMOs. The protocol became effective in 2003, and it has now been ratified by 129 countries. Most participants at the second meeting of the parties in 2005 praised the progress that had occurred to date, but India complained about the slow pace of implementation, and a coalition of grain shippers were concerned about the costs that could be imposed to comply with the Protocol.

5. So who should pay for all of these efforts? The South agreed to emphasize biodiversity conservation as an international goal in exchange for the North's promise to help pay for that conservation. Was that tradeoff necessary? Should developing countries treat biodiversity as important even if that means that they have pay for its protection themselves? Should developed countries pay for the protection of biodiversity even if the host country does not regard it as especially important? Consider, moreover, the financial obligations contained in Articles 20 and 21. What does Article 20 require of developed nations? Developing nations? What examples are there of "countries undergoing the process of transition to a market economy" who may voluntarily assume the financial responsibilities imposed upon developed countries?

Management of the requisite funds has generated questions of its own. Not surprisingly, the dispute has centered on control of the distribution of the money collected pursuant to the Convention. The American position, as explained by Assistant Secretary Wirth, notes that "U.S. funding for convention-related activities will be handled through periodic contributions to the Global Environment Facility (GEF). The United States has committed to provide $430 million over the next four fiscal years toward the replenishment of the recently restructured GEF; total pledges by all countries will come to slightly more than $2 billion over the replenishment period. In order to make clear how the United States interprets key funding provisions of the convention, the Administration has recommended several understandings to be deposited with our instrument of ratification. . ." Wirth, *supra*, at 214–15. By contrast, many developing countries have objected to the role of the GEF because of its relationship to the

World Bank, which those countries criticize as insufficiently democratic and responsive to the needs of developing nations. The Convention itself does not specify the entity that will oversee the funding efforts, and Article 21 mandates that the chosen entity possess a "democratic and transparent system of governance." The parties to the Convention selected GEF to perform the role described in Article 21, and as modified, GEF continues to be responsible for the funds promised by the Convention. *Cf.* HUNTER, SALZMAN & ZAELKE, *supra*, at 1501–05 (providing an overview of the GEF).

6. Numerous other issues are addressed in the provisions of the Convention not reprinted above. Articles 23 establishes a Conference of the Parties that meets periodically and oversees the implementation of the Convention, while Article 24 creates the Secretariat that performs the daily work of the Convention. Article 27 addresses the resolution of any disputes between parties to the Convention, as complemented by the arbitration procedures detailed in Annex II of the Convention. Article 37 states simply, "No reservations may be made to this Convention," thereby preventing a common strategy by which countries have signed treaties even as they refuse to be bound by key provisions of them. Article 38 permits a country to withdraw from the Convention after giving one year's notice.

D. CUSTOMARY LAW

Beanal v. Freeport–McMoran, Inc.

United States Court of Appeals for the Fifth Circuit, 1999.
197 F.3d 161.

■ STEWART, CIRCUIT JUDGE:

. . . This case involves alleged violations of international law committed by domestic corporations conducting mining activities abroad in the Pacific Rim. Freeport-McMoran, Inc., and Freeport-McMoran Copper & Gold, Inc., ("Freeport"), are Delaware corporations with headquarters in New Orleans, Louisiana. Freeport operates the "Grasberg Mine," an open pit copper, gold, and silver mine situated in the Jayawijaya Mountain in Irian Jaya, Indonesia. The mine encompasses approximately 26,400 square kilometers. Beanal is a resident of Tamika, Irian Jaya within the Republic of Indonesia (the "Republic"). He is also the leader of the Amungme Tribal Council of Lambaga Adat Suki Amungme (the "Amungme"). In August 1996, Beanal filed a complaint against Freeport in federal district court in the Eastern District of Louisiana for alleged violations of international law. Beanal invoked jurisdiction under (1) 28 U.S.C. § 1332, (2) the Alien Tort Statute, 28 U.S.C. § 1350, and (3) the Torture Victim Protection Act of 1991, sec. 1, et seq., 28 U.S.C. § 1350 note. In his First Amended Complaint, he alleged that Freeport engaged in environmental abuses, human rights violations, and cultural genocide. Specifically, he alleged that Freeport mining operations had caused harm and injury to the Amungme's environment and habitat. He further alleged that Freeport engaged in cultural genocide by destroying the Amungme's habitat and religious symbols, thus forcing the Amungme to relocate. Finally, he asserted that Freeport's private security force acted in concert with the Republic to violate international human rights. [The district court dismissed Beanal's claims for failure to state a claim. *See* Beanal v. Freeport-McMoRan, 969 F.Supp. 362 (E.D.La.1997)].

. . . We observed in 1985, "the question of defining 'the law of nations' is a confusing one which is hotly debated, chiefly among academics." Carmichael v. United Technologies Corp., 835 F.2d 109, 113 (5th Cir.1985). However, in Cohen v. Hartman, 634 F.2d 318, 319 (5th Cir.1981) (per curiam), we "held that the standards by which nations regulate their dealings with one another inter se constitutes the 'law of nations.' " These standards include the rules of conduct which govern the affairs of this nation, acting in its national capacity, in relationships with any other nation. The law of nations is defined by customary usage and clearly articulated principles of the international community. One of the means of ascertaining the law of nations is "by consulting the work of jurists writing professedly on public law or by the general usage and practice of nations; or by judicial decisions recognizing and enforcing that law." Courts "must interpret international law not as it was in 1789. but as it has evolved and exists among the nations of the world today." Although Beanal's claims raise complex issues of international law; nonetheless, the task before us does not require that we resolve them. We are only required to determine whether the pleadings on their face state a claim upon which relief can be granted. Although the day may come when we will have to join other jurisdictions who have tackled head-on complex issues involving international law, "this case, however, does not require that we stand up and be counted.". . .

Environmental Torts and Abuses

Next, Beanal argues that Freeport through its mining activities engaged in environmental abuses which violated international law. In his Third Amended Complaint, Beanal alleges the following:

FREEPORT, in connection with its Grasberg operations, deposits approximately 100,000 tons of tailings per day in the Aghwagaon, Otomona and Akjwa Rivers. Said tailings have diverted the natural flow of the rivers and have rendered the natural waterways of the plaintiff unusable for traditional uses including bathing and drinking. Furthermore, upon information and belief, the heavy metal content of the tailings have and/or will affect the body tissue of the aquatic life in said rivers. Additionally, tailings have blocked the main flow of the Ajkwa River causing overflow of the tailings into lowland rain forest vegetation destroying the same.

FREEPORT in connection with its Grasberg operations has diverted the aforesaid rivers greatly increasing the likelihood of future flooding in Timika, the home of the plaintiff, TOM BEANAL.

FREEPORT, in connection with its Grasberg mining operations has caused or will cause through the course of its operations 3 billion tons of "overburden" to be dumped into the upper Wanagon and Carstensz creating the likely risk of massive landslides directly injurious to the plaintiff. Furthermore, said "overburden" creates acid rock damage which has created acid streams and rendering the Lake Wanagon an "acid lake" extremely high in copper concentrations, . . .

However, Freeport argues that Beanal's allegations of environmental torts are not cognizable under the "law of nations" because Beanal fails to show that Freeport's mining activities violate any universally accepted environmental standards or norms. Furthermore, Freeport argues that it would be improper for a United States tribunal to evaluate another county's environmental practices and policies. The district court conducted a thorough survey of various international law principles, treaties, and declarations and concluded that Beanal failed to articulate environmental torts that were cognizable under international law.

Beanal and the amici refer the court to several sources of international environmental law to show that the alleged environmental abuses caused by Freeport's mining activities are cognizable under international law. Chiefly among these are the Principles of International Environmental Law I: Frameworks, Standards and Implementation 183–18 (Phillip Sands ed,. 1995) ("Sands"),[1] and the Rio Declaration on Environment and Development, June 13, 1992, U.N. Doc. A/CONF. 151/5 rev.1 (1992) (the "Rio Declaration").

Nevertheless, "it is only where the nations of the world have demonstrated that the wrong is of mutual and not merely several, concern, by means of express international accords, that a wrong generally recognized becomes an international law violation in the meaning of the [ATS]." Thus, the ATS "applies only to shockingly egregious violations of universally recognized principles of international law." Beanal fails to show that these treaties and agreements enjoy universal acceptance in the international community. The sources of international law cited by Beanal and the amici merely refer to a general sense of environmental responsibility and state abstract rights and liberties devoid of articulable or discernable standards and regulations to identify practices that constitute international environmental abuses or torts. Although the United States has articulable standards embodied in federal statutory law to address environmental violations domestically, *see* The National Environmental Policy Act (42 U.S.C. § 4321 et seq.) and The Endangered Species Act (16 U.S.C. § 1532), nonetheless, federal courts should exercise extreme caution when adjudicating environmental claims under international law to insure that environmental policies of the United States do not displace environmental policies of other governments. Furthermore, the argument to abstain from interfering in a sovereign's environmental practices carries persuasive force especially when the alleged environmental torts and abuses occur within the sovereign's borders and do not affect neighboring countries.[2] Therefore, the dis-

---

[1] Sands features three environmental law principles: (1) the Polluter Pays Principle; (2) the Precautionary Principle; and (3) the Proximity Principle.

[2] Although Beanal cites the Rio Declaration to support his claims of environmental torts and abuses under international law, nonetheless, the express language of the declaration appears to cut against Beanal's claims. Principle 2 on the first page of the Rio Declaration asserts that states have the "sovereign right to exploit their own resources pursuant to their own environmental and developmental policies," but also have "the responsibility to ensure that

trict court did not err when it concluded that Beanal failed to show in his pleadings that Freeport's mining activities constitute environmental torts or abuses under international law.

NOTES & QUESTIONS

1. Is there a customary international law norm requiring the protection of biodiversity? The court explains that "the law of nations"—*i.e.*, customary international law—"is defined by customary usage and clearly articulated principles of the international community." More specifically, the statute governing the International Court of Justice identifies five sources of customary international law: (1) treaties, (2) international custom that provides "evidence of a general practice accepted as law," (3) "the general principles of law recognized by civilized nations," (4) certain judicial decisions and the writings of "the most highly qualified publicists of the various nations," and (5) equity. Statute of the International Court of Justice, June 26, 1945, 1945 U.S.T. Lexis 199, Art. 38. United Nations resolutions, the resolutions of other international organizations, intergovernmental communiqués, and international consensus, are among the other acts and documents that can become relevant to the determination of customary international law. *See generally* LAKSHAM D. GURUSWAMY ET AL., INTERNATIONAL ENVIRONMENTAL LAW AND WORLD ORDER: A PROBLEM-ORIENTED COURSEBOOK 67–170 (2d ed. 1999) (discussing the sources of international law).

Extending these principles to the protection of biodiversity has proved to be difficult. In 1990, Michael Glennon described the state of customary international law related to biodiversity as follows:

It is now possible to conclude that customary international law requires states to take appropriate steps to protect endangered species. Customary norms are created by state practice "followed by them from a sense of legal obligation." Like highly codified humanitarian law norms that have come to bind even states that are not parties to the instruments promulgating them, wildlife protection norms also have become binding on nonparties as customary law. Closely related to this process of norm creation by practice is that of norm creation by convention: customary norms are created by international agreements "when such agreements are intended for adherence by states generally and are in fact widely accepted." Several such agreements are directed at wildlife protection, and CITES is one of them. It is intended for adherence by states generally and is accepted by the 103 states that have become parties. In addition, some nonparties comply with certain CITES documentary requirements so as to trade with parties. CITES is not "rejected by a significant number of states"; only the United Arab Emirates has withdrawn from the agreement. In such circumstances, the International Court of Justice has observed, international agreements constitute state practice and represent law for nonparties.

---

activities within their jurisdiction or control do not cause damage to the environment or other States or areas beyond the limits of national jurisdiction." Beanal does not allege in his pleadings that Freeport's mining activities in Indonesia have affected environmental conditions in other countries.

Moreover, customary norms are created by "the general principles of law recognized by civilized nations." Because CITES requires domestic implementation by parties to it, and because the overall level of compliance seems quite high, the general principles embodied in states' domestic endangered species laws may be relied upon as another source of customary law. Even apart from the CITES requirements, states that lack laws protecting endangered species seem now to be the clear exception rather than the rule. That there exists opinio juris as to the binding character of this obligation is suggested by the firm support given endangered species protection by the UN General Assembly and various international conferences.

While the existence of a norm requiring the protection of endangered species thus seems likely, its scope remains uncertain. To the extent that the norm derives from CITES and laws implementing CITES, that scope would be fairly narrow, for the norm would cover only species in international trade, not those taken for domestic consumption or those endangered by threats to their habitat. Even if it could be shown that major legal systems generally comprise endangered species legislation, more work needs to be done to determine exactly what elements those laws have in common. What constitutes an "endangered species," for example, is debatable. Is it one that is endangered in every state, or only in the state making the assessment? And to what lengths must a state go in protecting a species it finds "endangered"? Must it do everything necessary to protect that species, notwithstanding the cost or the ecological significance of the species? . . .

It thus appears doubtful that a customary norm concerning the elephant or any other endangered species can yet play any significant role in its protection. But the trend cannot be doubted; and once its contours are more clear, the customary norm requiring states to protect endangered species ought to take on the character of an obligation erga omnes. Ordinarily, claims for the violation of an international obligation may be made only by the state to which the obligation is owed. Obligations erga omnes, however, run to the international community as a whole; thus, their breach is actionable by any state since such matters are "[b]y their very nature . . . the concern of all States. . ." [T]hey are obligations erga omnes.

Michael J. Glennon, *Has International Law Failed the Elephant?*, 84 Am. J. of Int'l L. 1, 30–33 (1990). Do any events since 1990 provide sufficient evidence that customary international law now requires nations to prevent the destruction of biodiversity? Why did the Fifth Circuit conclude that the operation of the Grasberg mine does not violate customary international law?

Most legal scholars support the recognition of customary international law norms favoring environmental preservation, and the writings of "the most highly qualified publicists of the various nations" can serve as a source of customary international law. Why has international legal scholarship failed to give rise to customary international law regarding biodiversity? Judge Cabranes offered one answer in Flores v. Southern Peru Copper Corp., 343 F.3d 140 (2d Cir. 2003), a case involving pollution from a copper mine in Peru. Judge Cabranes contrasted earlier legal scholarship "constituting in substantial measure of compilations, explications, and digests" with contemporary scholarship that is "largely theoretical and normative." *Id.* at 157 n.26. He then noted "that compilations and digests are of greater value in providing 'trustworthy evidence of what the law *really* is,' whereas expressly theoretical or normative works make their contribution by setting for th the 'speculations of . . . authors concerning what the law *ought to be*.' " *Id.* (quoting The Paquete Habana, 175 U.S. 677, 700 (1900)).

2. Suppose that the court had determined that the mine did violate customary international law. What remedies would have been available to the plaintiffs? What obligations would the Fifth Circuit's decision have imposed on the government of Indonesia? What other forum has jurisdiction to render a decision that Indonesia has acted in violation of international law? If there is no such forum, or if Indonesia could ignore without sanction any holding that it had violated international law, what would it mean to say that international law protects biodiversity? *Cf.* GURUSWAMY, *supra*, at 49–66 (reviewing the debate concerning the character of customary international law as "law").

3. Tom Beanal has many responsibilities besides lead plaintiff in this case. He is the head of the tribal council of the Amunge community which used to live on the land now occupied by the mine. He has served as deputy chairman of the Papuan People's Congress and is a leading supporter of West Papua's (formerly Irian Jaya) bid for independence from Indonesia. And during a speech in New Orleans—the corporate home of Freeport in 1996—Beanal described the environmental consequences of the Grasberg mine: "Our environment has been ruined and our forests and rivers polluted by waste. The sago forests which serve as our primary food source have become dry, making it hard for us to find food. . . The animals we have hunted in the past have disappeared so we no longer know what to hunt. . . Our water is contaminated by chemicals so we can no longer drink it." *Tom Beanal's Speech at Loyola University in New Orleans* (May 23, 1996), *available at* http://www.corpwatch.org.issues/PID.jsp?/articleid=987.

Two recent reports portray the mine and its effects in starkly different terms. According to a group of Indonesian community organizations, the mine has dumped one billion tons of tailings into the river system and has destroyed extensive habitat of the area's remarkable biodiversity. *See* WALHI-INDONESIAN FORUM FOR ENVIRONMENT, THE ENVIRONMENTAL IMPACTS OF FREEPORT-RIO TINTO'S COPPER AND GOLD MINING OPERATION IN PAPUA (2006), *available at* http://www.eng.walhi.or.id/kampanye/tambang/frpt-reportmay-06/. The owner of the mine, by contrast, emphasizes its compliance with applicable environmental regulations and its funding of numerous biodiversity projects. *See* FREEPORT-MCMORAN COPPER & GOLD INC., THE ELEMENTS OF SUSTAINABLE DEVELOPMENT: 2005 WORKING TOWARD SUSTAINABLE DEVELOPMENT REPORT (2006), *available at* http://www.fcs.com/envir/wtsd/pdf-wtsd/2005/WTSD-ver4.pdf. A travel agency serving Timika—Beanal's hometown—boasts of *both* "the unparalleled bio-diversity" of the area and of the Grasberg mine. "A major attraction of Irian Jaya is the wide variety of flora and fauna with steamy mangrove swamps in the lowland coastal areas rising to tropical rainforests in the island's heart. . . Wildlife diversity is incredible with 640 species of birds including the cassowary and 36 types of Birds of Paradise," along with 800 species of spiders and 2,700 species of orchids, pitcher plants, and giant anthouse plants. At the same time, the agency proclaims that the Grasberg mine "has been called one of the world's great engineering marvels," adding that "[a] virtual tour of the mining operations is available on interactive touchscreen videos in the Irian Jaya Room of the Sheraton Timika." *Welcome to Timika-Irian Jaya-Indonesia.* The mine contains the largest reserves of gold, and the third largest reserves of copper, in the world. Does that explain why, in the words of the Rio Declaration, Indonesia has exercised its "sovereign right to exploit [its] own resources pursuant to [its] own environmental and development policies?"

4. How *should* Indonesia balance its environmental and economic needs? Consider the September 2001 announcement by Freeport that it had agreed to pay $2.5 million and then $500,000 annually to a trust benefitting the Amungme and Kamoro tribal communities who were native to the land now containing the Grasberg mine. Tribal leaders plan to use some of the trust's money to purchase shares of Freeport stock, thus obtaining an ownership interest in the mine. Beanal applauded the agreement, saying, "We used to be on the outside, but now we stand together. We have a stake in this mining operation and we will work hard so that we can share in its success." *Freeport to Establish Trust for Indigenous Communities,* JAKARTA POST, Sept. 26, 2001.

5. Is the court correct that "the argument to abstain from interfering in a sovereign's environmental practices carries persuasive force especially when the alleged environmental torts and abuses occur within the sovereign's borders and do not affect neighboring countries?" One student commentator disagrees because (1) the ATCA's restriction to "shockingly egregious" violations of international law provides sufficient caution in all cases, (2) the ATCA does not require concern for the domestic policies for foreign nations, and (3) there is nothing unique about environmental claims that justifies greater judicial caution than any other violation of international law. *See* Russell Unger, Note, *Brandishing the Precautionary Principle Through the Alien Tort Claims Act,* 9 N.Y.U. ENVTL. L. REV. 638, 646–47 (2001). Should a foreign nation's unwillingness to regulate the destruction of biodiversity within its borders affect the success of an ATCA claim? Does it matter that the Indonesian government has been labeled one of the most corrupt in the world? Or could a foreign nation authorize a lawsuit against an activity that harms biodiversity within the United States?

6. A lawsuit brought by the Indonesian Forum for the Environment claiming violations of Indonesia's own law proved to be more successful than Beanal's customary international law litigation in the United States. In 2001, the South Jakarta District Court held that Freeport had spread misleading information about its environmental activities and violated an Indonesian law concerning environmental management. *Experts Allay Fears Over Freeport Ruling,* Jakarta Post, Aug. 31, 2001. Since then, the Indonesian government has prosecuted the chief executive of another multinational mining corporation for allegedly polluting a bay in North Sulawesi province. *See* Jonathan Hopfer, *Indonesian Prosecutors to Pursue Charges Against Newmont Subsidiary, Top Executive,* 131 BNA DAILY ENV'T REP. A-1 (July 11, 2005). And a senior Indonesian government official proclaimed in 2004 that "illegal loggers are environmental terrorists. They steal millions of dollars worth of revenue and destroy the environment. . . We are seriously considering the death penalty. We want to get the big players." Lely T. Djuhari, *Indonesia Mulls Death Penalty for Illegal Loggers,* Associated Press, Mar. 15, 2004 (quoting Fachir Fahoni). Do these actions suggest that domestic law will remain a more fruitful means of protecting biodiversity than customary international law? Would there be any legal cause of action against such habitat destruction if the mine were located in the United States? What is the ideal legal regime to prevent the loss of biodiversity attributed to an activity like the Grasberg mine?

PART 5

MAJOR THREATS TO BIODIVERSITY AND ECOSYSTEMS

CHAPTER **16** Invasive Species

CHAPTER **17** Climate Change and its Impact on Biodiversity

CHAPTER **18** Biodiversity and Climate Mitigation

CHAPTER **19** Biodiversity and Climate Adaptation

We have already covered a wide range of threats to biodiversity throughout the first four parts of this text. Indeed, if it were not for the many threats to biodiversity and ecosystems, the entire book would never have existed. As human beings have proliferated and set up house and shop, our bit-by-bit impact on the natural functioning of ecosystems has only gotten worse with the passing of time. By the time you reach this point in the book you should have a sense of most traditional threats and how we are addressing them. While the concept of threats is spread throughout the text, a concentrated review of traditional threats to biodiversity can be found in Chapter 2.C.

The purpose of this Part is to focus on two very modern and rapidly growing threats, climate change and invasive species, as these are grand-scale issues that have very quickly reached emergency status. After decades of picking at land development and localized industrial behavior, we are now faced with threats so great that they could (and to some extent will) spell the end of biodiversity as we know it. The magnitude of these threats is such that they are worthy of in-depth treatment in their own Part. This is especially important given that we do not yet have, at the time of this writing, comprehensive legislation to deal with either of these massive problems. As such, we must consider the array of related laws, regulations, and policies, and how they work together to at least partially address these threats. The first chapter focuses on invasive species and the remaining three chapters address issues relating to climate change: 1) its *impact* on biodiversity generally, 2) the relationship between biodiversity and efforts to reduce the *causes* of climate change (aka mitigation), and 3) the role of biodiversity in our process of *adapting* to climate change that is already occurring.

CHAPTER 16

INVASIVE SPECIES

Chapter Outline:
A. An Introduction to the Invasive Species Problem and its Regulation
B. The Ballast-Water Cases: A Survey of the Application of Existing Laws to Invasive Species
C. Invasive Species and Climate Change

A. AN INTRODUCTION TO THE INVASIVE SPECIES PROBLEM AND ITS REGULATION

If you are from the South, or for that matter have ever been there, you are likely familiar with kudzu, the ubiquitous vine that covers nearly everything in some areas. Perhaps you have driven down highways lined with trees you cannot see, only knowing that they are there because the vines form the shape of a tree – a tree that is choking and dying beneath those vines. Kudzu is one of the more widely familiar examples of an invasive species. As with most invasive species, the humans responsible for its introduction meant well.

> One of the most notorious intentional plant introductions in the United States is kudzu, also known as "The vine that ate the south." Kudzu is a perennial vine that is native to Japan and China. In the late 1800s, it was introduced to the United States to be used as a forage crop. In the 1930s, the federal government launched an aggressive campaign to plant kudzu as a solution for soil erosion. The campaign worked, unfortunately too well. Kudzu grew rapidly and spread to other areas, wreaking havoc by choking out beneficial native vegetation. In fact, kudzu has been known to cover almost anything in its path, including power poles, railroad tracks, and even buildings. Ultimately, kudzu was no longer a solution to soil erosion; instead it became an ecological problem itself, causing extensive economic and ecological harm to the United States. Kudzu is as an example of how the government has aggressively promoted and introduced an invasive plant species for a solution to an ecological problem without the adequate knowledge, regulations, and safeguards to prevent the unforeseen and catastrophic consequences that stem from its introduction.

Karen Ray, *Are Biofuel Crops the Next Kudzu?*, 17 SAN JOAQUIN AGRIC. L. REV. 247, 247 (2008).

Human beings have introduced an estimated 25,000 non-native species to the United States, both intentionally and unintentionally. *See* David Pimentel, Lori Lach, Rodolfo Zuniga & Doug Morrison, *Environmental and Economic Costs Associated with Non-Indigenous Species in the United States*, 50 BIOSCIENCE 53 (2000). Some of these non-native species thrive in their new environments and cause significant damage to the native species and ecosystems in which they have relocated. These are the ones we call "invasive." Alongside global climate change in terms of dimension and magnitude, or perhaps even ahead of it, the problem of invasive species is one with profound potential effects on global biodiversity. *See* Peter M. Vitousek et al., *Biological Invasions as Global Environmental Change*, American Scientist, Sept.-Oct. 1996, at 468.

Jane Cynthia Graham, *Snakes on a Plain, or in a Wetland: Fighting Back Invasive Nonnative Animals--Proposing a Federal Comprehensive Invasive Nonnative Animal Species Statute*
25 Tul. Envtl. L.J. 19 (2011).

Forget the war on drugs. What the United States needs is a war on invasive animal species. Burmese pythons swallowing American alligators in the Everglades, Asian carp invading the Great Lakes, and Zebra Mussels in California and the Great Lakes: this is just a sampling of nonnative invasive animal species horrors in the United States. Nonnative invasive animal species create a host of problems, such as environmental degradation, economic waste, public health risks, and personal injuries to humans. Unlike New Zealand, the United States does not have a federal comprehensive invasive species statute that regulates the invasive species problem in a centralized framework. A variety of federal, state, and local laws regulate nonnative invasive species, but they are not well coordinated and do not fully address all the problems associated with invasive species.

* * *

The scope of discussion will be limited to invasive animal species. Executive Order 13,112 defines invasive species as "an alien species whose introduction does or is likely to cause economic or environmental harm or harm to human health." An alien species with respect to a particular ecosystem includes "any species, including its seeds, eggs, spores, or other biological material capable of propagating that species, that is not native to that ecosystem." ...

I. The Scourge of Invasive Species

The spread of nonnative invasive animal species in the United States is correlated with a plethora of problems. The environmental impacts are well known but there are also numerous less obvious impacts related to economic loss, crime and national security, and public health and safety. For example, the removal of marine nonnative species such as zebra mussels costs hundreds of millions of dollars. Recent data shows that "[w]ildlife trafficking is thought to be the third most valuable illicit commerce in the world, after drugs and weapons." This Part examines the link between nonnative species with these harmful impacts.

A. Environmental Degradation

Some nonnative species cause wide-ranging ecological harms to ecosystems. In extreme cases, the proliferation of a nonnative species in an area contributes to the decline and ultimate extinction of native fauna. However, under different circumstances, a nonnative species could have barely any harmful impacts on an ecosystem. This Part looks at the range of different environmental impacts on ecosystems, both direct and indirect.

1. Changes in the Ecosystem Balance

A new species can wreak havoc on an ecosystem's balance. The introduction of a predator can be devastating, especially on islands, lakes, and other isolated areas where native species have evolved in the absence of other predators. In Guam, for example, the nonnative brown treesnake "has eliminated most native vertebrates (birds, bats, and lizards) that pollinate trees and flowers." The discovery of a thirteen-foot Burmese python, which died trying to swallow a whole, live, six-foot alligator, caused biologists in Florida to fear "that the nonnative snakes could threaten a host of other animal species in the Everglades." Giant constrictors (snakes) are capable of eating almost every type of land-dwelling vertebrate, so if a bird or mammal is already rare, a novel predator could tip the balance against the native prey species. Ultimately, this could mean that entire food webs could change through the elimination or depletion of vulnerable native prey species.

Nonnative species may compete with native species for food and breeding habitat. Moreover, they enjoy an advantage over native species in their new habitat because their natural enemies may not be in the area. They can multiply unchecked, competing for valuable resources such as sunlight, water, and nutrients. For example, a single Cuban Tree Frog can lay four thousand eggs at a time, three times more than native tree frogs in Florida. Native species suffer from this intense competi-tion from nonnative invaders. Invasive nonnative species "are the primary cause of species endangerment and have contributed to 68 percent of extinctions in the U.S."

2. Physical Destruction of Habitat

Nonnative species can also alter the physical environment and modify or destroy natural habitats. A prime example is the nutria, a South American semiaquatic rodent that has invaded parts of the U.S. Gulf Coast. Like wild hogs, they burrow underground for food, which destabilizes the soil, uproots or weakens native vegetation, damages crops and lawns, and causes erosion on the banks of rivers and canals in the bayous of coastal Louisiana and other fragile ecosystems.

B. Economic Waste

Economic losses resulting from invasive species are extensive. A 1999 study estimated that the fifty thousand invasive species contribute to approximately $137 billion per year in damages. More recent commentaries suggest this was a conservative estimate, considering the study did not account for the invasive species damages reported to the U.S. Department of Agriculture Wildlife Services and underestimated populations of invasive swine. Although there is extensive research and scholarship on the economic impacts of invasive species, calculating precise values of economic loss can be prohibitively expensive. Investigators assessing past and projected economic damages associated with uncontrolled nutria populations in Maryland, for example, admitted that a precise tally would require additional resources in the thousands—if not millions—of dollars. It is important to keep this in mind for the discussion later in this Article on economic valuation for public nuisance liability and the proposal for a cost recovery statute.

C. Criminal Activity

The illicit wildlife trafficking trade, second only to the drugs and weapons trade, has an estimated worth of $10 to $20 billion a year. Many of the organized crime rings trafficking in drugs and arms are also linked to the illegal wildlife trade. Demand fuels illegal wildlife trafficking. The worldwide markets for exotic pets, rare foods, trophies, and traditional medicines are expansive. Traffickers can make a huge profit with little cost. Animals have been sold for as much as $10,000 each. As long as markets exist in developed nations like the United States, exotic animals will be trafficked from the lesser-developed nations, legally or illegally. The United States is the largest importer of wildlife. The U.S.-Mexico border is notoriously permeable for wildlife smuggling. The demand for exotic species and large payoff for the traffickers creates opportunities for nonnative species introductions into the wild.

D. Public Health and Personal Injury

Nonnative species in the United States detrimentally impact human health by spreading various infectious diseases and causing individual personal injuries. Most live animals imported into the United States, eighty-two percent of which are nonnative to the United States, are never tested for infectious agents. Therefore, a significant proportion of the diseases that those animals harbor are also likely to be foreign. Exotic pets have been linked to outbreaks of rare diseases in humans throughout the United States. For example, the 2003 outbreak of monkeypox in Wisconsin, Illinois, and Indiana was linked to a pet-trade shipment of a Gambian giant rat (Cricetomys gambianus). Wild hogs in Florida are known to carry forty-five different parasitic and infectious diseases, and the Great Green Tree frog, a large Australian frog, is known to carry the deadly pathogen Batrachochytrium dendrobatidis. "Invasive Brown Tree Snakes and Black Spiny-tailed iguana deliver venomous bites." Nonnative species kept as pets, or those that have escaped into the wild, have also been known to attack people in suburbs and cities.

E. Impacts Compounded by Climate Change

The impacts described above may be compounded by the effects of climate change. Research indicates that tropical and subtropical species and diseases will move northward, as habitats in higher latitudes and at higher elevations become warmer and moister. Scientists predict that the number of harmful species invasions will likely increase in a warming North America because tropical species will be able to acclimate more easily to the warmer winter. Furthermore, as the normal ranges of species shift with changing climatic conditions, and some native species go extinct in their formerly hospitable ecosystems, it will become more difficult to determine whether a new species is "nonnative." Assisted migration, a management tool to aid certain endangered and threatened species from becoming extinct, could challenge the notion of what is harmful to an ecosystem. Although assisted migration could lead to the relocated species becoming invasive, not all relocated species threaten the ecosystems into which they are introduced.

These impacts of nonnative species in the United States, including ecological, financial, health, and criminal effects, compounded by the prospect of climate change, will form the "purposes" section of the proposed comprehensive statute. It is within this backdrop that our legal analysis begins.

*   *   *

III. Assessment of Current Federal Invasive Nonnative Species Law

The main federal invasive species laws are the Lacey Act and Executive Order 13,112. While these mechanisms have tools for prevention and enforcement, they lack cost recovery and incentive tools. The Lacey Act is reactive instead of proactive, and Executive Order 13,112 does not have the force of law. Other laws deal with a narrow scope of invasive species regulation. This Part will examine these statutory frameworks and evaluate their effectiveness. The analysis will underscore the need for a federal comprehensive invasive nonnative species statute that has provisions for prevention, liability, enforcement, and incentives.

A. Lacey Act

The Lacey Act is the United States' oldest federal conservation law and is the first line of defense against the trade of nonnative species. However, critics have bemoaned the 110-year-old statute as ineffective. ...

1. Purpose of the Lacey Act

John Lacey, an Iowa Congressman and trusted friend of Theodore Roosevelt, first introduced the Lacey Act to the United States House of Representatives in 1900 citing threats of excessive hunting and harmful nonnative species displacing native populations of birds. The original intent of the Lacey Act was "(1) to authorize the introduction and preservation of

game, song, and insectivorous wild birds, (2) to prevent the 'unwise' introduction of foreign birds and animals, and (3) to supplement state laws for
the protection of game and birds." The Lacey Act "authorized the Department of Agriculture to assist with the reintroduction of game birds and
other wild birds where they had become locally scarce or extinct."

2. Statutory Framework

There are two separate statutory sections under the umbrella of the
Lacey Act, 16 U.S.C. §§ 3371-3377 and 18 U.S.C. § 42.

a. 16 U.S.C. § 3372

This provision makes it unlawful for any person to import, export, or
transport "any fish or wildlife" or "any plant" that is made illegal by "any
law, treaty or regulation of the United States," any Indian tribal law, or
any state or foreign law. It also enforces international treaties to which the
United States is a party. For example, it enforces the Convention on International Trade in Endangered Species of Wild Fauna and Flora (CITES),
which "established a permit system to place trade restrictions on three categories of threatened and endangered plant and animal species."

Because state, foreign, and international laws, treaties, and regulations fall under § 3372, the statute's scope is broad. For example, in *United
States v. Condict*, a defendant was found guilty under § 3372(a) for purchasing and receiving domestic white tailed deer, in violation of Oklahoma
law. In other cases, Lacey Act violations have been found where shellfish
harvesting violated South African, Honduran, or Russian law. Courts have
found that foreign regulations are also applicable as foreign laws under the
Lacey Act. On the other hand, at least one court has found no Lacey Act
violation where a regulation was unpublished. In *United States v. Cannon*,
the defendant killed a coyote on Edwards Air Force Base in violation of the
unpublished Air Force Flight Test Center Instruction 32-8. Since the regulation was unpublished and the record was insufficient to show that the
defendant had actual notice of the base hunting regulations, the Lacey Act
did not apply.

b. 18 U.S.C. § 42

The other section of the Lacey Act, 18 U.S.C. § 42, lists a limited number of forbidden species. These species can only be imported into the United
States if the importer has a permit from the United States Fish and Wildlife Service (Service). The Service implements the injurious wildlife provisions (18 U.S.C. § 42) through regulations contained in 50 C.F.R. part 16 to
prevent the listed species' introduction or establishment through human
movement in the United States. The list aims to protect the health and welfare of humans, the interests of agriculture, horticulture and forestry, and
the welfare and survival of wildlife resources from potential and actual
negative impacts of the species.

The Service considers a variety of factors when evaluating [whether a species should be listed] as injurious[, including: (1)] species' survival capabilities and ability to spread geographically[, (2)] its impacts on habitats and ecosystems, threatened and endangered species, and human beings and resource-based industries[, and (3)] resource managers' ability to control and eradicate the species.

[citing *Injurious Wildlife: A Summary of the Injurious Provisions of the Lacey Act* (18 U.S.C. 42; 50 CFR 16), U.S. Fish & Wildlife Serv. (June 2010), at 2.]

The Service reviews scientific data for factors contributing to injuriousness and factors that reduce or remove injuriousness. A variety of economic analyses are also conducted to determine the economic impacts of potential rulemakings. Currently, there is a petition in the notice and comment period to add nine species of snakes to the list of injurious species to "prohibit the importation of any live animal, gamete, viable egg, or hybrid of these nine constrictor snakes into the United States, except as specifically authorized."

A species can only be added to the injurious species list through the bulky rulemaking process. A 2007 study showed that the average time for a species to be listed has increased to over four years, and only one species has been added by petition in the past decade. Considering the variety of new nonnative species arriving in the United States on a constant basis, this is a startlingly low number. For example, two genera of snakehead fish were listed as injurious wildlife in October 2002. By the time they were listed, the snakeheads already invaded the Potomac River in Maryland and Virginia, and had "spread beyond the possibility of eradication." Furthermore, the idea of listing forbidden animals on a "dirty list" assumes that there is adequate information to know when a species will cause harm. But, it does not authorize the exclusion of animals whose threat is unknown.

c. Authority for Enforcement

The Lacey Act gives enforcement authority to the Secretary of Interior, the Secretary of Transportation, or the Secretary of the Treasury, who may with or without reimbursement, use the personnel, services, and facilities of any other federal agency or any state agency or Indian tribe. The Service has broad authority to detain and inspect any international shipment, mail parcel, vehicle, or passenger baggage and all accompanying documents, whether or not wildlife has been formally declared. According to the Service, "[W]ildlife inspectors are stationed at 38 major U.S. airports, ocean ports, and border crossings, where they monitor imports and exports to ensure compliance with U.S. laws and regulations." In 1999, for example, Service special agents worked on more than fifteen hundred Lacey Act investigations.

d. Penalties Under the Lacey Act

Penalties under the Lacey Act are fixed. The Act provides for both civil and criminal penalties of a modest nature, e.g., knowingly or negligently violating the Act may result in a civil penalty of "not more than $10,000 for each such violation" and criminal penalties, up to five years in prison and a $20,000 fine for each violation of 16 U.S.C. § 3372(a) or (c). In contrast to 16 U.S.C. § 3373, the penalties for 18 U.S.C. § 42(b) are lighter, including fines, imprisonment for not more than six months, or both. Additionally, "all fish or wildlife [or] plants imported, exported, transported, sold, received, acquired, or purchased contrary to the provisions of section 3372," other than subsection (b), or contrary to corresponding regulations, must be subject to forfeiture.

3. Assessment of the Lacey Act's Effectiveness

The effectiveness of the Lacey Act is limited, and does not fulfill the rubric for a comprehensive invasive species statute.

a. Prevention

The Lacey Act is not a strong tool for prevention. The listing process of injurious wildlife is long, and is reactive to a problem rather than proactive. By the time a species is petitioned for listing, the species is already a serious problem. For example, Burmese pythons were documented in the Everglades by the 1980s. Only after the public was energized by a news story of a python attacking a toddler in 2009 was the idea of listing pythons as injurious species under the Lacey Act discussed. As of March 2011, the Service's proposed listing of nine of these large snakes as injurious species under the Lacey Act is still undergoing administrative review, and the introduced legislation in the House of Representatives and Senate is still pending. Meanwhile, the South Florida Water Management District recently reported that the python problem in the Everglades is worsening. The District removed six pythons in February and March 2011 from territories previously thought to be uninvaded, including areas deep in the Everglades. This illustrates how the Lacey Act's drawn out listing process is defective.

Furthermore, the listing process can be duplicative in some cases. While a species remains in limbo waiting to be listed as an injurious species under 18 U.S.C. § 42, a state could pass a law, thus triggering the provisions of 16 U.S.C. § 3372. For example, a 2010 Florida state law banned any person, party, firm, association, or corporation from keeping, possessing, importing, selling, bartering, trading, or breeding several varieties of pythons for personal use. The snakes listed in the Florida statute are almost the same as the ones listed in the introduced federal legislation. The penalties under 16 U.S.C. § 3373 are more severe than 18 U.S.C. § 42. However, the national listing is still important where a species poses a risk between state boundaries and a single state's law does not apply. For example, if Burmese pythons potentially invaded Georgia, the Florida law that applies under 16 U.S.C. § 3373 would not be triggered.

Additionally, once a species is listed as injurious under the Lacey Act, that species' population in the United States does not necessarily decrease. A study showed that out of seven species established by the time of listing, at least five have spread to additional states since the listing. On the other hand, none of the seven species absent from the country at the time of listing subsequently established populations. Two of the species that were present only in captivity (raccoon dog and brushtail possum) did not establish wild populations.

b. Enforcement

Because the Lacey Act enforces laws and regulations from such a large variety of sources, there is no clear guidance as to what specific species are forbidden. As a result, defendants have challenged prosecutions under the Lacey Act when the law was not readily accessible and or unconstitutionally vague. For example, a defendant challenged a Nevada law because the term "wildlife" did not distinguish whether it applied to indigenous or non-indigenous wildlife. *United States v. Tierney*, 38 F. App'x 424, 425-26 (9th Cir. 2002). However, the court held that the statute was not unconstitutionally vague. The issue of notice has been challenged in several cases, as well. Courts have held that the government must prove that the defendant knew "that the fish or wildlife or plants were taken, possessed, transported, or sold in violation of, or in a manner unlawful under, any underlying law, treaty or regulation." 16 U.S.C. §3373(d)(1) (2006); *United States v. Santillan*, 243 F.3d 1125, 1129 (9th Cir. 2001). This second requirement of knowledge is satisfied if the person knows that the possession, etc., violated any law, without regard to whether the person knows which law it violated. This is an example of enforcement that is susceptible to vagueness and ambiguity.

The monetary fines and penalties of the Lacey Act are comparable to New Zealand's penalties. However, New Zealand distinguishes between fines for individuals and corporations; higher fines for corporations (up to $200,000) exceed anything available in the Lacey Act.

c. Cost Recovery and Incentives

While the Lacey Act does have a forfeiture provision, it lacks a cost recovery mechanism. Additionally, it does not promote voluntary actions to curb the spread of invasive species, or other incentives to restore an ecosystem from the damage caused by the release of an invasive species.

In sum, there are a number of ways in which the Lacey Act falls short. The Lacey Act's dirty list is reactive instead of proactive, only listing a species once it is too late. Furthermore, the Lacey Act does not place people on notice of laws in other countries and states that trigger the Lacey Act. It neither includes robust preventative measures, such as a full risk assessment process to keep invasive species from spreading, nor a response and cleanup mechanism to restore ecosystems once they have been harmed. Thus, the Lacey Act is not currently adequate to fully alleviate the problems caused by invasive species.

* * *

C. National Invasive Species Act

On October 26, 1996, Congress enacted the National Invasive Species Act (NISA). A misnomer, NISA amended the Nonindigenous Aquatic Nuisance Prevention Control Act of 1990 and only applies to aquatic nuisance species (ANS). NISA defines ANS as "nonindigenous species that threaten[] the diversity or abundance of native species or the ecological stability of infested waters, or commercial, agricultural, aquacultural or recreational activities dependent on such waters."

1. NISA Mechanisms for Prevention and Regional Coordination

NISA includes mechanisms for voluntary guidelines, monitoring, and risk assessment. First, NISA directs the Coast Guard to implement voluntary national guidelines for ballast-water management in the waters of the United States. These guidelines apply to all vessels with ballast water tanks. NISA also establishes a task force charged with developing and implementing "a program for waters of the United States to prevent introduction and dispersal of aquatic nuisance species; to monitor, control and study such species; and to disseminate related information." The Task Force will

> establish and implement measures . . . to minimize the risk of introduction of aquatic nuisance species to waters of the United States, including (A) [identifying] pathways by which aquatic organisms are introduced . . .; (B) [assessing] the risk that an aquatic organism carried by an identified pathway may become an aquatic nuisance species; and (C) [evaluating] whether measures to prevent introductions of aquatic nuisance species are effective and environmentally sound.

NISA originally had a series of appropriations for invasive species management programs, but these expired in 2002.

2. Effectiveness of NISA

In theory, NISA authorizes the Coast Guard to enforce regulations against vessel operators who have not complied with ballast water disposal regulations and contributed to the spread of aquatic invasive species. However, in practice the effectiveness of NISA is limited. While NISA's statutory language is descriptive and proscriptive, case law suggests that NISA's use is limited. NISA is voluntary, and allows discretion to the appropriate agencies. The United States District Court for the District of Minnesota explained: "The plain language of these NISA sections imposes no limitation on the Coast Guard's discretion to enforce its ballast water regulations. Nor does this language provide meaningful substantive standards." If the Coast Guard decides not to enforce its own ballast regulations, there is no remedy. Moreover, the Coast Guard's mandatory regulations, promulgated through NISA, contain loopholes. Finally, while NISA aims to reduce the spread of aquatic nuisance species through ballast discharges, the law has no impact on terrestrial or avian invasive species.

D. Federal Acts Specific to a Single Invasive Species

Some federal laws authorize plans for the prevention, eradication, and control of a specific species, such as the Brown Tree Snake Control and Eradication Act of 2004. Other laws are tools for federal funding or for Lacey Act injurious species listing. This Part will show that these laws vary in content and would not stand in the way of a comprehensive invasive species statute.

1. Brown Tree Snake Control and Eradication Act of 2004

The Brown Tree Snake Control and Eradication Act of 2004 authorizes funding "to support brown tree snake control, interdiction, research, and eradication efforts carried out by the Department of the Interior and the Department of Agriculture, other Federal agencies, States, territorial governments, local governments, and private sector entities." The Secretary of Interior and Secretary of Agriculture must include "at a minimum the . . . [e]xpansion of science-based eradication and control programs in Guam[,] . . . interagency and intergovernmental rapid response teams[,] . . . efforts to protect and restore native wildlife in Guam or elsewhere in the United States damaged by the brown tree snake," and a variety of sustained research and funding programs. Unlike other statutes that authorize appropriations in cost-share schemes, this statute authorizes specific monetary caps on programs for specific time periods. The statute also establishes quarantine protocols to control the spread of the brown tree snake.

It is unknown how effective this statute has been. The Animal and Plant Health Inspection Service (APHIS) reports that Wildlife Services uses snake trapping and nighttime spotlight searches to reduce the number of snakes in areas where cargo is packed or stored, as well as specially trained Jack Russell terriers to detect any brown tree snakes hidden in outgoing cargo. Regardless, there are still reports of brown tree snakes inflicting harm on Guam's environment.

2. Other Specific Species Statutes with Limited Tools

Other specific species laws provide incentives. Some laws provide assistance to specific states and geographic regions implementing programs. For example, the Nutria Eradication and Control Act authorizes the Secretary of the Interior to provide financial assistance to Maryland and Louisiana for programs to eradicate or control nutria and restore marshland damaged by nutria. The statute places the Federal cost share limit at seventy-five percent. Other statutes are merely tools to include a certain species in the list of injurious species on the Lacey Act.

3. Assessment of Single Species Act Effectiveness

Species specific statutes have benefits for prevention and restoration. Since these laws address a particular species and geographic region, they are individually tailored and aim to fix a concrete problem. Furthermore, the Nutria Eradication and Control Act and Brown Tree Snake Control and

Eradication Act have specific funding sources written into the statute, making the monetary support for these programs more likely.

However, specific species statutes share many of the same challenges as the Lacey Act. First, they are reactive instead of preventative. By the time the statute is passed, the problem might have grown to such a proportion that the solution in the statute is insufficient, or alternatively, the problem has already solved itself. Both houses of Congress have to review and pass the statutes, and then the President has to have an opportunity to review and sign or veto them. The House of Representatives voted on the Captive Primate Safety Act in 2009, but the bill died at the end of the legislative session due to inaction.

Furthermore, if there are hundreds of potentially invasive nonnative species that could cause destruction throughout the United States, why expend resources trying to solve the problem one by one? It does not make sense to pass separate laws for different subspecies at different times, as evidenced by the Asian Carp Act. The slow and protracted nature of the legislative process is ineffective to deal with the rapid spread of invasive species. It is impractical to hope that legislators will draft and submit bills for each and every species that poses a threat to the environment.

E. Nonnative Wildlife Invasion Prevention Act

The proposed Nonnative Wildlife Invasion Prevention Act (NWIPA) died at the end of the 2009-2010 legislative session. However, a review will benefit our analysis. NWIPA would have established a broad prevention framework for nonnative species, prohibiting the possession, barter, or release into the wild of any nonnative wildlife species prohibited under the new risk assessment system. It also would have created a clean list to be published in the Federal Register excluding any animal listed currently in the Lacey Act as an injurious species, or "any species, the importation of which is prohibited by any other Federal law or regulation of the United States due to the likelihood of causing harm to the economy, the environment, or other animal species or human health." A detailed risk assessment process would have evaluated the risk of a species becoming invasive based on a number of factors, including the native range of the species, if the species has caused harm to the economy, the environment, or human health in ecosystems that are similar to those in the United States, the likelihood of establishment and spread of the species in the United States, and the likelihood that the species would harm wildlife, habitats, or ecosystems. A provision would have grandfathered in the possession of individual animals if they were owned before the statute was passed.

F. Summary of Current Legal and Regulatory Invasive Species Landscape

In sum, current federal invasive species laws have limited use, and do not satisfy the framework for a comprehensive invasive species plan. While there are tools for prevention, such as the injurious species listing and prohibitions of all other state and foreign laws regulating the importation of species, they are not comprehensive. There are no detailed statutory provisions for surveillance, quarantines, or special permits for invasive species. Additionally, since the listing process is a dirty list instead of a clean list, the Lacey Act is a reactive tool instead of a preventative tool. While the Executive Order fosters collaboration between different agencies, there is no force behind the law to compel results. NISA is limited to aquatic nuisance species and does not have enforcement power or adequate funding. Species specific statutes are also reactive instead of preventative. Some species specific laws have funding and grant programs, an idea that could be utilized on a national scale. H.R. 669 would have been an improvement for invasive species prevention but was never passed.

NOTES & QUESTIONS

1. Invasive species cause problems both terrestrially and aquatically, and yet we see legislation targeted only at the latter. Why might that be? Can you think of potential difficulties for legislating in the land context that may not be as troublesome in the aquatic context? Or perhaps it is simply a reactive solution to the more rapidly developing problem.

2. While the invasive species phenomenon is present in all ecosystem types world-wide, it is particularly acute in freshwater ecosystem settings, and even more particularly in lakes and rivers. Invasive species became a household name and darling of the media in the summer of 2002 when a fisherman snagged a 26-inch northern snakehead from a pond in Crofton, Maryland. Maryland state biologists reacted with horror when they learned of the catch, and finally tracked the fish down to a man who admitted to having released it in the pond because he grew tired of feeding it as a "pet" in a home fish tank. The snakehead, found throughout Southeast Asia where it is considered a dinnertime delicacy, is considered a "bottomless pit" in terms of appetite for fish native to its newfound country. It also has the ability to wriggle across dry land to find new aquatic haunts. It joins the ranks of 185 aquatic invasive fish species, including such other notables as the Asian swamp eel working its way south in Florida towards the Everglades, the Asian carp, a 100-pound plankton eater working its way up the Mississippi River toward the Great Lakes, and "harmless" Oscars released from fish tanks around the country only to reveal their true colors as voracious carnivores.

Not every introduced species succeeds in its new setting, but it takes only one to throw the existing dynamic equilibrium between species into disarray. In the Great Lakes, for example, ballast water introduced the zebra mussel, which has an amazing capacity to filter water (about 1 liter per day) and to reproduce. It has become the dominant mussel species in the Great Lakes ecosystem and, while it has contributed measurably to increased clarity of the water, that in itself has disrupted the food web in the entire system because light is reaching deeper into the water column. The zebra mussel has quickly moved beyond the Great Lakes and threatens many river systems. Indeed, freshwater mussels already were among the most rapidly vanishing species domestically, and the zebra mussel may push a good number to extinction. The list of similar human-induced ecosystem disruptions is long and growing. For an extensive source of information on the zebra mussel and other invasive plant and animal aquatic species, see National Aquatic Nuisance Species Clearinghouse, http://www.

aquaticinvaders.org.; and the University of Florida's Aquatic, Wetland, and Invasive Plant Information Retrieval System, http://aquat1.ifas.ufl.edu/database.html. We will be looking more closely at the ballast water problem in part B of this chapter.

3. Invasive species can also wreak havoc in forest ecosystems through complex impacts on species dynamics. In the Florida Everglades, for example, cypress forests have been inundated with the Old World climbing fern. Native to tropical Africa, India, and southeast Asia, its competitors and herbivorous feeders are absent here. First appearing in the United States only 30 years ago, possibly by spores blown on prevailing winds, the fast growing fern now drapes trees in an elegant cloak of emerald sequins, a cloak of death. When left unchecked in its new environs, the fern cuts off light supply to its victims, thereby triggering a cascade of effects through the ecosystem. The increase in dead vegetation raises the risk and intensity of fires. The decline in native vegetation displaces insects that depended on it for food and shelter, thus depriving other species that depend on the insects for their food supply, and so on up the food chain. Researchers have found some areas, where the fern has choked the life out of the trees, to be virtually devoid of birds. Spreading too fast to be controlled by mechanical means, and making prescribed fire burns too dangerous, the fern has posed a complicated ecosystem management problem for resource managers throughout Florida. Researchers are currently searching the fern's native ecosystems for specific herbivores that will devour the fern, but only the fern, if they are introduced into the picture here in the United States. *See* Steve Mirsky, *Floral Fiend*, SCIENTIFIC AMERICAN, Nov. 1999, at 24.

Forests also are being attacked from below, by none other than *worms*. Earthworms, ubiquitous in many parts of the country, are not native to the northern United States and Canada—the glaciers scoured them away ages ago. An integral part of these northern forest ecosystems is the layer of "duff" on the forest floor, upon which many species depend for shelter and food. Anglers and other human travelers have introduced earthworms throughout the region, and, not surprisingly, earthworms are voracious consumers of duff. Within five years after worms arrive on the scene, the duff is gone and the worms move on. The worm populations spread outward at a rate of about 20 feet per year, leaving behind a denuded forest floor of little value to native species and, because of higher nutrient levels worms leave behind, highly vulnerable to invasive plant species. The problem is so serious that the University of Minnesota has devoted a website to it, *see Minnesota Worm Watch*, http://www.nrri.umn.edu/worms/, as has the Minnesota Department of Natural Resources, *see Contain Those Crawlers*, http://www.dnr.state.mn.us/exotics/terrestrialanimals/earthworms/index.html.

Would introducing "natural" predators of the fern and worms be a good idea? What do the principles of ecosystem management and adaptive management suggest as an approach to answering that question?

4. The legal response to invasive species has been hampered by the pervasive and invidious nature of the problem. International trade has opened countless pathways to species introductions, making it virtually impossible to cut off all possible avenues. Thus, we seldom know of the invasion before it has happened, and by then it is usually too late. It has proven extremely difficult to eradicate an invasive species from its conquered ecosystem without doing yet more harm to the ecosystem. This has resulted in the unfocused and ineffective efforts discussed in the above excerpt and later in this chapter.

Can you think of a more effective legal framework for preventing invasive species introductions? How about for managing ecosystems after an introduction has occurred and the new species has become dominant? Is this something law can really have any appreciable effect over? Alas, in the end we may, over generations, come to think of the zebra mussel as native to the Great Lakes. We most likely will not have a choice. For a series of scientific studies covering the invasive species issue comprehensively, see *Special Section: Population Biology of Invasive Species*, 17 CONSERVATION BIOLOGY 24 (2003).

5. We edited out Graham's brief description of President Clinton's executive order targeting invasive species, which is fully reproduced below. While being the most broadly applicable legal tool addressing invasive species, it is not legislation and thus carries less force. That said, in a time without comprehensive invasive species legislation to work with, it has served a valuable purpose. Following the executive order, we have included portions of 1) a white paper by the advisory committee to be established per the executive order, broadly defining invasive species for the purposes of federal action planning; and 2) the most current National Invasive Species Management Plan prepared by the Invasive Species Council, which was created by the executive order and directed therein to draft such a plan.

Executive Order 13112, Invasive Species
President of the United States, 1999.
64 Federal Register 6183.

By the authority vested in me as President by the Constitution and the laws of the United States of America, including the National Environmental Policy Act of 1969, Nonindigenous Aquatic Nuisance Prevention and Control Act of 1990, Lacey Act, Federal Plant Pest Act, Federal Noxious Weed Act of 1974, Endangered Species Act of 1973, and other pertinent statutes, to prevent the introduction of invasive species and provide for their control and to minimize the economic, ecological, and human health impacts that invasive species cause, it is ordered as follows:

Section 1. *Definitions.*

(a) "Alien species" means, with respect to a particular ecosystem, any species, including its seeds, eggs, spores, or other biological material capable of propagating that species, that is not native to that ecosystem.

(b) "Control" means, as appropriate, eradicating, suppressing, reducing, or managing invasive species populations, preventing spread of invasive species from areas where they are present, and taking steps such as restoration of native species and habitats to reduce the effects of invasive species and to prevent further invasions.

(c) "Ecosystem" means the complex of a community of organisms and its environment.

(d) "Federal agency" means an executive department or agency, but does not include independent establishments as defined by 5 U.S.C. 104.

(e) "Introduction" means the intentional or unintentional escape, release, dissemination, or placement of a species into an ecosystem as a result of human activity.

(f) "Invasive species" means an alien species whose introduction does or is likely to cause economic or environmental harm or harm to human health.

(g) "Native species" means, with respect to a particular ecosystem, a species that, other than as a result of an introduction, historically occurred or currently occurs in that ecosystem.

(h) "Species" means a group of organisms all of which have a high degree of physical and genetic similarity, generally interbreed only among themselves, and show persistent differences from members of allied groups of organisms.

(i) "Stakeholders" means, but is not limited to, State, tribal, and local government agencies, academic institutions, the scientific community, nongovernmental entities including environmental, agricultural, and conservation organizations, trade groups, commercial interests, and private landowners.

(j) "United States" means the 50 States, the District of Columbia, Puerto Rico, Guam, and all possessions, territories, and the territorial sea of the United States.

Sec. 2. *Federal Agency Duties.*

(a) Each Federal agency whose actions may affect the status of invasive species shall, to the extent practicable and permitted by law,

(1) identify such actions;

(2) subject to the availability of appropriations, and within Administration budgetary limits, use relevant programs and authorities to: (i) prevent the introduction of invasive species; (ii) detect and respond rapidly to and control populations of such species in a cost-effective and environmentally sound manner; (iii) monitor invasive species populations accurately and reliably; (iv) provide for restoration of native species and habitat conditions in ecosystems that have been invaded; (v) conduct research on invasive species and develop technologies to prevent introduction and provide for environmentally sound control of invasive species; and (vi) promote public education on invasive species and the means to address them; and

(3) not authorize, fund, or carry out actions that it believes are likely to cause or promote the introduction or spread of invasive species in the United States or elsewhere unless, pursuant to guidelines that it has prescribed, the agency has determined and made public its determination that

the benefits of such actions clearly outweigh the potential harm caused by invasive species; and that all feasible and prudent measures to minimize risk of harm will be taken in conjunction with the actions.

(b) Federal agencies shall pursue the duties set forth in this section in consultation with the Invasive Species Council, consistent with the Invasive Species Management Plan and in cooperation with stakeholders, as appropriate, and, as approved by the Department of State, when Federal agencies are working with international organizations and foreign nations.

Sec. 3. *Invasive Species Council.*

(a) An Invasive Species Council (Council) is hereby established whose members shall include the Secretary of State, the Secretary of the Treasury, the Secretary of Defense, the Secretary of the Interior, the Secretary of Agriculture, the Secretary of Commerce, the Secretary of Transportation, and the Administrator of the Environmental Protection Agency. The Council shall be Co-Chaired by the Secretary of the Interior, the Secretary of Agriculture, and the Secretary of Commerce. The Council may invite additional Federal agency representatives to be members, including representatives from subcabinet bureaus or offices with significant responsibilities concerning invasive species, and may prescribe special procedures for their participation. The Secretary of the Interior shall, with concurrence of the Co-Chairs, appoint an Executive Director of the Council and shall provide the staff and administrative support for the Council.

(b) The Secretary of the Interior shall establish an advisory committee under the Federal Advisory Committee Act, 5 U.S.C. App., to provide information and advice for consideration by the Council, and shall, after consultation with other members of the Council, appoint members of the advisory committee representing stakeholders. Among other things, the advisory committee shall recommend plans and actions at local, tribal, State, regional, and ecosystem-based levels to achieve the goals and objectives of the Management Plan in section 5 of this order. The advisory committee shall act in cooperation with stakeholders and existing organizations addressing invasive species. The Department of the Interior shall provide the administrative and financial support for the advisory committee.

Sec. 4. *Duties of the Invasive Species Council.*

The Invasive Species Council shall provide national leadership regarding invasive species, and shall:

(a) oversee the implementation of this order and see that the federal agency activities concerning invasive species are coordinated, complementary, cost-efficient, and effective, relying to the extent feasible and appropriate on existing organizations addressing invasive species, such as the Aquatic Nuisance Species Task Force, the Federal Interagency Committee for the Management of Noxious and Exotic Weeds, and the Committee on Environment and Natural Resources;

(b) encourage planning and action at local, tribal, State, regional, and ecosystem-based levels to achieve the goals and objectives of the Management Plan in section 5 of this order, in cooperation with stakeholders and existing organizations addressing invasive species;

(c) develop recommendations for international cooperation in addressing invasive species;

(d) develop, in consultation with the Council on Environmental Quality, guidance to Federal agencies pursuant to the National Environmental Policy Act on prevention and control of invasive species, including the procurement, use, and maintenance of native species as they affect invasive species;

(e) facilitate development of a coordinated network among Federal agencies to document, evaluate, and monitor impacts from invasive species on the economy, the environment, and human health;

(f) facilitate establishment of a coordinated, up-to-date information-sharing system that utilizes, to the greatest extent practicable, the Internet; this system shall facilitate access to and exchange of information concerning invasive species, including, but not limited to, information on distribution and abundance of invasive species; life histories of such species and invasive characteristics; economic, environmental, and human health impacts; management techniques, and laws and programs for management, research, and public education; and

(g) prepare and issue a national Invasive Species Management Plan as set forth in section 5 of this order.

Sec. 5. *Invasive Species Management Plan.*

(a) Within 18 months after issuance of this order, the Council shall prepare and issue the first edition of a National Invasive Species Management Plan (Management Plan), which shall detail and recommend performance-oriented goals and objectives and specific measures of success for Federal agency efforts concerning invasive species. The Management Plan shall recommend specific objectives and measures for carrying out each of the Federal agency duties established in section 2(a) of this order and shall set forth steps to be taken by the Council to carry out the duties assigned to it under section 4 of this order. The Management Plan shall be developed through a public process and in consultation with Federal agencies and stakeholders.

(b) The first edition of the Management Plan shall include a review of existing and prospective approaches and authorities for preventing the introduction and spread of invasive species, including those for identifying pathways by which invasive species are introduced and for minimizing the risk of introductions via those pathways, and shall identify research needs and recommend measures to minimize the risk that introductions will occur. Such recommended measures shall provide for a science-based process to evaluate risks associated with introduction and spread of invasive species and a coordinated and systematic risk-based process to identify, monitor, and interdict pathways that may be involved in the introduction of invasive species. If recommended measures are not authorized by current law, the Council shall develop and recommend to the President through its Co-Chairs legislative proposals for necessary changes in authority.

(c) The Council shall update the Management Plan biennially and shall concurrently evaluate and report on success in achieving the goals and objectives set forth in the Management Plan. The Management Plan shall identify the personnel, other resources, and additional levels of coordination needed to achieve the Management Plan's identified goals and objectives, and the Council shall provide each edition of the Management Plan and each report on it to the Office of Management and Budget. Within 18 months after measures have been recommended by the Council in any edition of the Management Plan, each Federal agency whose action is required to implement such measures shall either take the action recommended or shall provide the Council with an explanation of why the action is not feasible. The Council shall assess the effectiveness of this order no less than once each 5 years after the order is issued and shall report to the Office of Management and Budget on whether the order should be revised.

Sec. 6. *Judicial Review and Administration.*

(a) This order is intended only to improve the internal management of the executive branch and is not intended to create any right, benefit, or trust responsibility, substantive or procedural, enforceable at law or equity by a party against the United States, its agencies, its officers, or any other person.

(b) Executive Order 11987 of May 24, 1977, is hereby revoked.

(c) The requirements of this order do not affect the obligations of Federal agencies under 16 U.S.C. 4713 with respect to ballast water programs.

(d) The requirements of section 2(a)(3) of this order shall not apply to any action of the Department of State or Department of Defense if the Secretary of State or the Secretary of Defense finds that exemption from such requirements is necessary for foreign policy or national security reasons.

WILLIAM J. CLINTON

THE WHITE HOUSE, February 3, 1999.

Invasive Species Definition Clarification and Guidance White Paper

Submitted by the Definitions Subcommittee of the Invasive Species Advisory
Committee (ISAC).
Approved by ISAC April 27, 2006.

Preamble: **Executive Order 13112** – defines an *invasive species* as
"an alien species whose introduction does or is likely to cause economic or environmental harm or harm to human health." In the Executive Summary of the National Invasive Species Management Plan (NISMP) the term *invasive species* is further clarified and defined as **"a species that is non-native to the ecosystem under consideration and whose introduction causes or is likely to cause economic or environmental harm or harm to human health."** To provide guidance for the development and implementation of the NISMP, the National Invasive Species Council (NISC) and the Invasive Species Advisory Committee (ISAC) adopted a set of principles outlined in Appendix 6 of the NISMP. Guiding Principle #1 provides additional context for defining the term *invasive species* and states **"many alien species are non-invasive and support human livelihoods or a preferred quality of life."** However, some alien species (non-native will be used in this white paper because it is more descriptive than alien), for example West Nile virus, are considered invasive and undesirable by virtually everyone. Other non-native species are not as easily characterized. For example, some non-native species are considered harmful, and therefore, invasive by some sectors of our society while others consider them beneficial. This discontinuity is reflective of the different value systems operating in our free society, and contributes to the complexity of defining the term *invasive species*.

NISC is engaged in evaluating and updating the 2001 NISMP and is developing comments for a revised action plan as required by the EO 13112. While there have been numerous attempts to clarify the term *invasive species,* there continues to be uncertainty concerning the use and perceived meaning of the term, and consequently over the prospective scope of actions proposed in the NISMP. Options related to private property use, pet ownership, agriculture, horticulture, and aquaculture enterprises may be affected depending upon the definition, use, and policy implications of the term.

In particular, the desire to consider a non-native species as 'invasive' may trigger a risk/benefit assessment process to determine whether regulatory action is warranted. All these uncertainties have stood and could continue to stand in the way of progress in actions and policy development to prevent new invasions and manage existing invasive species. While it is not the purpose of this white paper to define a risk/benefit assessment process, development of such a process must be open and efficient to minimize the uncertainties.

This white paper is intended to provide a non-regulatory policy interpretation of the term *invasive species* by identifying what is meant, and just as important, what is not meant by the term. ISAC recognizes that biologi-

cal and ecological definitions will not precisely apply to regulatory definitions. We believe, however, that our clarification will apply to *all taxa of
invasive species in all habitats* and furthermore, our explanation will be
functional and acceptable to most stakeholders. ISAC simply wants to clarify what is meant and what is not meant by the term invasive species in the
technical sense and to provide insight into those areas where societal
judgments will be necessary to implement effective public policy.

The utility of our clarification should be in education, conflict resolution, and efficiency in the planning, prevention, control/eradication, and
management of *invasive species.*

***ISAC recommends that NISC adopt the clarifications presented in
this white paper to foster progress for invasive species management
in the United States.***

Introduction

An invasive species is a non-native species whose introduction does or
is likely to cause economic or environmental harm or harm to human, animal, or plant health. The National Invasive Species Management Plan indicates that NISC will focus on non-native organisms known to cause or
likely to cause negative impacts and that do not provide an equivalent or
greater benefit to society. In the technical sense, the term 'invasion' simply
denotes the uncontrolled or unintended spread of an organism outside its
native range with no specific reference about the environmental or economic consequences of such spread or their relationships to possible societal
benefits. However, the policy context and subsequent management decisions necessitate narrowing what is meant and what is not meant by the
term *invasive species.* Essentially, we are clarifying what is meant and not
meant by "causing harm" by comparing negative effects caused by a non-
native organism to its potential societal benefits.

Perception to Cause Harm

Complications concerning the concept of *invasive species* arise from differing human values and perspectives. Differing perceptions of the relative
harm caused or benefit gained by a particular organism are influenced by
different values and management goals. If *invasive species* did not cause
harm, we would not be nearly as concerned. Perceptions of relative benefit
and harm also may change as new knowledge is acquired, or as human values or management goals change.

For a non-native organism to be considered an *invasive species* in the
policy context, the negative effects that the organism causes or is likely to
cause are deemed to outweigh any beneficial effects. Many non-native introductions provide benefits to society and even among species that technically meet the definition of invasive, societal benefits may greatly exceed
any negative effects (for example crops and livestock raised for food). However, in some cases any positive effects are clearly overshadowed by negative effects, and this is the concept of causing harm. For example, water

hyacinth has been popular in outdoor aquatic gardens but its escape to natural areas where its populations have expanded to completely cover lakes and rivers has devastated water bodies and the life they support, especially in the southeastern U.S. And, there are some organisms, such as West Nile virus, that provide almost no benefits to society at all. Such organisms constitute a small fraction of non-native species, but as a consequence of their ability to spread and establish populations outside their native ranges, they can be disastrous for the natural environment, the economies it supports, and/or public health. Because *invasive species* management is difficult and often very expensive, these worst offenders are the most obvious and best targets for policy attention and management.

The negative impact to a native species caused by an *invasive species* might trigger additional negative interactions for other associated native species; i.e., there could be direct and indirect effects. For example, an invasive weed that is undesirable as a food source may outcompete and displace native grasses and broadleaf plants. These displaced native grasses and broadleaf plants may have been primary forage for animals, which subsequently would be displaced to a new location or have their populations reduced because the weed invasion decreased the availability of food in their native plant and animal community. However, negative effects are not always characterized by a cascade of impacts realized throughout the environment. For example, simple displacement of an endangered species by a non-native species might alone provide sufficient justification to consider the non-native organism an *invasive species*.

What We Do Not Mean, What We Do Mean, and the "Gray" Area

Native and Non-native Species

Invasive species are species not native to the ecosystem being considered. Canada geese are native to North America and most of their populations migrate annually. However, in some locations in the U.S. (e.g. suburban Maryland; the Front Range of Colorado) introduced, non-migratory populations of Canada Geese are causing problems – such as fouling lawns, sidewalks, grass parks, and similar areas. While non-migratory populations can cause problems, they are not considered an *invasive species* because they are native. Additionally, Canada geese are of significant financial value to many local economies through waterfowl hunting and simple enjoyment. Mute swans, however, are invasive. Mute swans are native to Europe and Asia but were introduced into North America where their populations have increased dramatically. They compete directly with native waterfowl for habitat, displacing them, and that is why they are considered an *invasive species*. Whitetail deer populations have increased dramatically in the northeastern U.S. and are problems in farms, yards, and natural areas because they consume plants valued by humans; but are not invasive because they are native. Nutria, on the other hand, are another classic example of an *invasive species*. Nutria are native to South America but were introduced into North America where their populations have soared. Nutria compete directly with native muskrats, beavers, and other similar native species for habitat; often causing the displacement of these native species.

Feral Populations

It is also essential to recognize that *invasive species* are not those under human control or domestication; that is, *invasive species* are not those that humans depend upon for economic security, maintaining a desirable quality of life, or survival. However, the essential test is that populations of these species must be under control. Escaped or feral populations of formerly domesticated plants and animals would be considered *invasive species* if all the concepts and conditions are met as outlined in "Weeds Are Examples." Cereal rye being produced on a farm in Kansas is considered very desirable, but feral rye on the breaks of the Poudre River in Colorado would be considered an *invasive species* because it is displacing native plants and the native animal communities they support. Domesticated goats on a farm in Texas are considered highly desirable, but feral goats in Haleakala National Park on Maui are considered an *invasive species*. Feral goats have severely overgrazed areas and eliminated native Hawaiian plants, which were never adapted to grazing. Areas denuded by feral goats have led to increased soil erosion.

A Biogeographical Context

An *invasive species* may be invasive in one part of the country, but not in another. A biogeographical context must be included when assessing whether a non-native species should be considered an *invasive species*. Lake trout are highly desirable in the Great Lakes where they are native, but are considered an *invasive species* in Yellowstone Lake. They compete with native cutthroat trout for habitat, which decreases their populations. Atlantic saltmarsh cordgrass is an essential component of east coast salt marshes, but is highly invasive on the west coast where it covers mudflats and displaces native estuarine plants and the community of animals they support, including huge flocks of migrating waterfowl. Kentucky bluegrass would be considered an *invasive species* in Rocky Mountain National Park in Colorado, but considered non-invasive a mere 60 miles away at a golf course in Denver. English ivy is considered a good ground cover species in the Great Plains and Midwest, but is a highly invasive weed in the forests of the Pacific Northwest and Eastern U.S. where it outcompetes native plants and displaces the associated animal communities.

The "Gray" Area

There are obvious examples of *invasive species* such as snakehead fish, yellow starthistle, or *Phytophthora ramorum* (the organism that causes sudden oak death); and there are obvious examples of species that are not invasive, namely native plants and animals. There are, however, non-native organisms for which it will be difficult to make a determination and these should be subject to assessment. Whether these non-native organisms will be considered *invasive species* will depend upon human values. For example, European honeybees are cultured to produce honey and pollination services, and even though they form wild populations in many parts of the country and occasionally create problems by building hives in the walls of homes or can be a human health problem for individuals that are highly allergic to their sting, most would not consider them an *invasive species* because they produce a desired food product.

Another gray area example would be native termites v. Formosan termites. No one wants termites in their homes but only Formosan termites would be considered an *invasive species* because they are non-native. Smooth brome also serves as another gray area example. It was imported from Russia in the 1890s for forage and was widely planted. It clearly has escaped cultivation and can be found in many natural areas particularly in the western U.S. but in most situations, smooth brome would not be considered an *invasive species* because of its forage value for wildlife and livestock.

Chinese or Oriental clematis serves as another gray area example. Chinese clematis (virgin's bower, orange peel) is a popular ornamental that has been planted worldwide. However, it has escaped cultivation in several western states where its populations can spread, particularly in shrubland, on riverbanks, sand depressions, along roadsides, in gullies, and along riparian forests in hot dry valleys, deserts, and semi-desert areas. Escaped populations of Chinese clematis occur in Idaho, Nevada, Utah, New Mexico, and Colorado but so far, it is considered an *invasive species* only in Colorado where it has spread dramatically from its site of introduction and displaced native plant species.

Environmental Harm

We use environmental harm to mean biologically significant decreases in native species populations, alterations to plant and animal communities or to ecological processes that native species and other desirable plants and animals and humans depend on for survival. Environmental harm may be a result of direct effects of *invasive species*, leading to biologically significant decreases in native species populations.

Examples of direct effects on native species include preying and feeding on them, causing or vectoring diseases, preventing them from reproducing or killing their young, out-competing them for food, nutrients, light, nest sites or other vital resources, or hybridizing with them so frequently that within a few generations, few if any truly native individuals remain. Environmental harm includes decreases in populations of Federally Listed Threatened and Endangered Species, other rare or uncommon species and even in populations of otherwise common native species. For example, over three billion individual American chestnut trees were found in U.S. forests before the invasive chestnut blight arrived and virtually eliminated them. Environmental harm also can be the result of an indirect effect of invasive species, such as the decreases in native waterfowl populations that may result when an invasive wetland plant decreases the abundance of native plants and thus, decreases seeds and other food that they provide and that the waterfowl depend upon.

Environmental harm also includes significant changes in ecological processes, sometimes across entire regions, which result in conditions that native species and even entire plant and animal communities cannot tolerate. For example, some non-native plants can change the frequency and intensity of wildfires, or alter the hydrology of rivers, streams, lakes and wetlands and that is why they are considered *invasive species*. Others can significantly alter erosion rates. For example, trapping far more wind-blown sand than native dune species, or holding far less soil than native grassland species following rainstorms. Some invasive plants and micro-organisms can alter soil chemistry across large areas, significantly altering soil pH or soil nutrient availability. Environmental harm also includes significant changes in the composition and even the structure of native plant and animal communities. For example, the invasive tree *Melaleuca quinquinervia*, can spread into and take over marshes in Florida's Everglades, changing them from open grassy marshes to closed canopy swamp-forests.

Environmental harm may also cause or be associated with economic losses and damage to human, plant and animal health. For example invasions by fire promoting grasses that alter entire plant and animal communities eliminating or sharply reducing populations of many native plant and animal species, can also lead to large increases in fire-fighting costs and sharp decreases in forage for livestock. West Nile virus is a well known human health problem caused by a non-native virus which is commonly carried by mosquitoes. West Nile Virus also kills many native bird species, causing drastic reduction in populations for some species including crows and jays.

Additional Examples of Impacts Caused by Invasive Species

Specific examples of the harm caused by *invasive species* are useful to further clarify the definition. The following list of examples is not meant to be comprehensive, but offers further explanation:

Impacts to Human Health

Respiratory infections: The outbreak of *West Nile virus* in the U.S. began in the Northeast in 1999 and has since spread throughout the country. Infections in humans may result in a flu-like illness and in some cases death. This outbreak has caused illness in thousands of citizens, increased medical costs for affected persons, and decreased productivity due to absence from work. *West Nile virus* also has affected horses and has caused widespread mortality in native birds.

Poisonous plants: Exposure to the sap of *Tree-of-heaven/Chinese sumac tree* has caused inflammation of the heart muscle (myocarditis) in workers charged to clear infested areas. Afflicted personnel experienced fever/chills, chest pain that radiated down both arms, and shortness of breath. Exposure occurred when sap from tree-of-heaven contacted broken skin. Such exposure has caused hospitalization, medical expense, and lost productivity due to absence from work.

Impacts to Natural Resources

Declines in wildlife habitat and timber availability: *Chestnut blight* is a disease of American chestnut caused by a non-native fungal pathogen that was introduced into eastern North America around 1910. The disease eliminated the American chestnut from eastern deciduous forests thereby decreasing timber harvests and wildlife that depended upon the American chestnut for habitat.

European gypsy moth defoliates trees on millions of acres of northeastern and mid-western forests. It currently is found in 19 states causing an estimated $3.9 billion in tree losses and also decreased wildlife habitat.

Decreased soil stabilization and interrupted forest succession: *White pine blister rust* is a disease of white pine species caused by the non-native fungal pathogen *Cronartium ribicola*. It was introduced into eastern North America around 1900 and western North America in 1920. It spread rapidly, killing off native white, whitebark, and limber pines, whose seeds are an important food source for birds, rodents and bears. Elimination of these trees caused by this pathogen alters forest ecosystems, eliminates wildlife forage, and decreases the soil stabilization effects of these trees, snowmelt regulation, and forest succession.

Changes in wildfire frequency and intensity: *Cheatgrass* decreases the interval between the occurrences of wildfires in the Great Basin region from once every 70 to 100 years to every 3 to 5 years because it forms dense stands of fine fuel annually. The decrease in interval between wildlfires causes increased risk to human life and property and also places at risk established communities of plants and animals that we consider desirable.

Excessive use of resources: *Tamarisk* in the desert southwest use more than twice as much water annually as all the cities in southern California, which places this invasive weed in direct competition with humans for the most limiting resource in the southwestern U.S.

Suppressors: *Russian knapweed* exudes toxins from its tissues that inhibit the growth of surrounding plants or eliminates them. Desirable plant communities are placed at risk from *Russian knapweed* invasion, which may result in decreased numbers of wildlife species or livestock that the invaded land otherwise could support. *Russian knapweed* also is very toxic to horses.

Decreased carrying capacity for wildlife and livestock: Expansion of *leafy spurge, yellow starthistle*, or other unpalatable invasive weeds displace desirable forage plants and may allow fewer grazing animals to survive in infested areas.

Impacts to Recreational Opportunities and Other Human Values

Decreased property values: *Asian longhorned beetles* first appeared in New York in 1996 and in Chicago in 1998. Larvae burrow into trees causing girdling of stems and branches, dieback of the crown, and can kill an entire tree. It infests many different tree species in the U.S. and is a threat to urban and rural forests.

Emerald ash borers were first detected in the U.S. in 2002. They currently are found in Michigan, Ohio, and Indiana. Emerald ash borer larvae tunnel under bark of ash trees and could eliminate ash as a street, shade, and forest tree throughout the U.S. Estimated replacement cost in six Michigan counties is $11 billion and an additional $2 million in lost nursery sales.

Dutch elm disease was first introduced into the U.S. in 1927 and occurs in most states. Dutch elm disease has killed more than 60% of elms in urban settings and decreased the value of urban and suburban properties.

Spotted knapweed and *leafy spurge* expansion in the western U.S. have displaced desirable forage plants thereby decreasing the value and sales price of grazingland in the western U.S.

Eurasian watermilfoil was introduced into the U.S in the 1940s and has since spread throughout much of the country. This submersed aquatic plant can form dense mats at the water surface limiting access, recreation, and aesthetics and thus, has decreased the values of shoreline properties in New Hampshire, the Midwest and elsewhere.

Decreased sport fishing opportunities: *Whirling disease* is caused by a parasite (*Myxobolus cerebralis*) that most likely originated in Europe. It was first observed in the U.S. in 1958. The parasite attacks the soft cartilage of young trout causing spinal deformities and causes the fish to exhibit erratic tail-chasing behavior. Heavily infected young trout can die from *Whirling disease* and even if they recover, they remain carriers of the parasite. All species of trout and salmon may be susceptible and angling and the businesses supported by trout and salmon fishing may be at risk if this disease continues to spread.

Smallmouth bass fishing in Lake Erie was closed during bass mating because of *round goby* predation of nests. Fishing was closed because male smallmouth bass aggressively guard nests from predators and are easier to catch by anglers during this time of year. Removal of males by anglers decreased the number of bass offspring because of increased *round goby* predation of unguarded nests. Businesses that smallmouth bass anglers patronize could be adversely affected by such closures.

Altered business opportunities: The concern over *Sudden Oak Death Syndrome* caused by the pathogen *Phytophthora ramorum* is causing drastic changes in available nursery stock by nurseries and landscape businesses. This clearly impacts the profitability of these businesses and choice by consumers and could devastate oak forests nationwide.

Annual harvests of oysters in Long Island Sound averaged over 680,000 bushels during 1991 through 1996. After *Haplosporidium nelsonii* (MSX) invaded in 1997 and 1998, oyster harvests decreased from 1997 through 2002 to an average annual harvest of 119,000 bushels with a low of 32,000 bushels in 2002. The overall ex-vessel value of oyster farming dropped 96% in 10 years from $45 million in 1992 to $2 million in 2002.

Non-native algae introduced into the Hawaiian Islands costs Maui alone about $20,000,000 annually due to algae fouling the beaches and subsequent lost tourism.

Sea lampreys were introduced into Lakes Ontario and Erie during the construction of the Welland Canal and quickly spread to the other Great Lakes. The *sea lamprey* is a parasite that attaches itself to fish, eventually killing them, and has devastated commercial and recreational Lake Trout fishing in the Great Lakes.

Australian spotted jellyfish were introduced into the Gulf of Mexico in 2000 and occurred in such massive numbers that shrimping operations were shut down because jellyfish clogged shrimp nets.

Altered ecosystems and recreational opportunities: The submersed aquatic plant *hydrilla,* forms dense canopies at the water surface that raise surface water temperatures, change pH, exclude light, and consume oxygen, resulting in native plant displacement and stunted sport fish populations. This example of an altered aquatic ecosystem caused by an invasive aquatic weed also negatively affects recreation and businesses that depend upon that human activity.

Summary

Invasive species are those that are not native to the ecosystem under consideration and that cause or are likely to cause economic or environmental harm or harm to human, animal, or plant health. Plant and animal species under domestication or cultivation and under human control are not *invasive species*. Furthermore for policy purposes, to be considered invasive, the negative impacts caused by a non-native species will be deemed to outweigh the beneficial effects it provides. Finally, a non-native species might be considered invasive in one region but not in another. Whether or not a species is considered an *invasive species* depends largely on human values. By attempting to manage *invasive species*, we are affirming our economic and environmental values. Those non-native species judged to cause overall economic or environmental harm or harm to human health may be considered invasive, even if they yield some beneficial effects. Society struggles to determine the appropriate course of action in such cases, but in a democratic society that struggle is essential.

Many *invasive species* are examples of "the tragedy of the commons," or how actions that benefit one individual's use of resources may negatively impact others and result in a significant overall increase in damage to the economy, the environment, or public health. In ISAC's review of Executive Order 113112, the public domain is specifically represented; however, the implementation of the NISMP has prompted concerns over the rights of personal and private property owners. Property rights are of great importance in the U.S. and one outcome of the NISMP should be to recognize the right to self determination by property owners and promote collaboration on *invasive species* management. The right to self determination is an important concept in a democratic society, however, with that right comes personal responsibility and stewardship, which includes being environmentally responsible. The natural environment that our society enjoys, recreates in, and depends upon to support commerce must be conserved and maintained. Effective *invasive species* management is just one aspect of conserving and maintaining our nation's natural environment, the economies it supports, and the high quality of life our society enjoys.

2008-2012 National Invasive Species Management Plan

The National Invasive Species Council, 2008.

Executive Summary

Invasive Species introduced into the United States from around the globe are affecting plant and animal communities on our farms, ranches and coasts; and in our parks, waters, forests, and backyards. As global climate patterns shift, the distribution of species will change, and so will the susceptibility of particular habitats to the impacts of new species introductions. Human activity such as trade, travel and tourism have all increased substantially, increasing the speed and volume of species movement to unprecedented levels. Invasive species are often unintended hitchhikers on cargo and other trade conveyances. Still more species are deliberately introduced as pets, ornamental plants, crops, food, or for recreation, pest control or other purposes. Most nonnative species, including most of our sources of food and fiber, are not harmful; and many are highly beneficial. A small percentage of nonnative species cause great harm to the environment, the economy or human health. Nonnative species that cause harm are collectively known as invasive species.

It is difficult to estimate the total economic harm caused by invasive species, however invasive plants alone result in two to three billion dollars in crop loss each year. Aquatic invasive species clog irrigation canals and pipes that supply water to power plants and factories. Invasive plants, pathogens and parasites cut crop yields and sicken livestock. Humans can be affected directly. Invasive ants cause painful stings. Invasive plant pollen increases the severity of respiratory allergies and the sap of the invasive plant, Giant Hogweed, causes blisters on the skin that can lead to permanent scarring. West Nile Virus (WNV) is an invasive pathogen of humans and animals. As of July 2008, the Centers for Disease Control and

Prevention report that 1,086 deaths in the United States were caused by WNV.

Invasive species (such as kudzu, snakehead fish, zebra mussels, emerald ash borers, sea lamprey, tree of heaven, hydrilla, nutria, West Nile virus, and Sudden Oak Death pathogen) may prey upon, displace or otherwise harm native species. Some invasive species also alter ecosystem processes, transport disease, interfere with crop production, or cause illnesses in animals and humans; affecting both aquatic and terrestrial habitats. For these reasons, invasive species are of national and global concern.

Invasive species populations span geographic and jurisdictional boundaries; thus efforts to manage invasive species must be coordinated across boundaries. In 1999, Executive Order (EO) 13112 established the National Invasive Species Council (NISC), co-chaired by the Secretaries of the Interior, Agriculture, and Commerce. NISC members include the Secretaries of Transportation, State, Defense, Homeland Security, Treasury, and Health and Human Services; the Administrators of the Environmental Protection Agency and the National Aeronautics and Space Administration; as well as the Director of the U.S. Agency for International Development and the U.S. Trade Representative. NISC was charged with providing coordination, planning and overall leadership for federal invasive species programs and reaching out to state, tribal, local and private partners.

EO 13112 also required the Secretary of the Interior to establish the Invasive Species Advisory Committee (ISAC), a group of 30 nonfederal stakeholders from diverse constituencies (representing state, tribal, local and private concerns) around the Nation, to advise NISC on invasive species issues. In addition, EO 13112 called on NISC to prepare and issue the first national plan to deal with invasive species. Completed in 2001, the National Invasive Species Management Plan, *Meeting the Invasive Species Challenge* (2001 Plan), served as a comprehensive "blueprint" for federal action on invasive species, as well as NISC's primary coordination tool. This coordination tool provided the first comprehensive national plan for invasive species action. It called for about 170 specific actions within nine categories of activity, about 100 of which have been established or completed. Actions identified in the 2001 Plan continue to be implemented.

The 2008–2012 *National Invasive Species Management Plan* (2008 Plan) is the first revision of the 2001 Plan, as mandated by EO 13112. This document will direct Federal efforts (including overall strategy and objectives) to prevent, control and minimize invasive species and their impacts within the next five fiscal years (2008 through 2012). If necessary, it may be updated more frequently to reflect changes in circumstances, agency plans and priorities. NISC member agencies, ISAC members, NISC staff, stakeholders and other experts have provided input in drafting this revision, which replaces the 2001 Plan.

The 2008 Plan is focused upon five "Strategic Goals": Prevention; Early Detection and Rapid Response; Control and Management; Restoration; and Organizational Collaboration. To accomplish these strategic goals, crit-

ical support for efforts such as research, data and information management, education and outreach, and international cooperation elements are
included in pertinent sections of the 2008 Plan.

Each of the five strategic goals specifies on-going objectives and the
long-term vision for success in that area. Under each strategic goal, "Objectives" describe what is to be accomplished over the next five years, and
"Implementation Tasks" describe what agencies expect to do in order to accomplish that objective. Within the "Implementation Tasks", there are
"Performance Elements" which allow for measurement of progress towards
accomplishing identified tasks.

The 2008 Plan is not a comprehensive list of all federal invasive species actions. It is a targeted set of priority strategic action plans with objectives and implementation tasks that are intended to be completed in the
next five years. The over-arching strategic goals and strategic action plan
objectives remain consistent with the 2001 Plan. The accomplishment of
specific implementation tasks and performance elements will be dependent
upon agency budgets, and in some cases, legal or regulatory changes.

The 2008 Plan currently requires the work of 35 different "entities"
(typically agencies or bureaus within NISC members' departments and
agencies) to achieve a total of 87 Performance Elements. Participating
agencies are identified either as a "Lead" or a "Participant" to describe
their role in accomplishing a specific Performance Element.

Prevention is the first-line of defense. The Strategic Goal for Prevention calls for preventing the introduction and establishment of invasive
species to reduce their impact on the environment, the economy and health
of the United States.

Even the best prevention efforts cannot stop all invasive species. **Early Detection**, rapid assessment and **Rapid Response** (EDRR) may act as
a critical second defense. The EDRR Strategic Goal calls for developing and
enhancing the capacity in the United States to identify, report and effectively respond to newly discovered and localized invasive species.

The spread of widely established invasive species can be slowed and
their impacts reduced. The **Control and Management** Strategic Goal
calls for containing and reducing the spread of invasive populations to minimize their harmful impacts.

Invasive species can severely undermine the ability of plants and animal communities to recover. The **Restoration** Strategic Goal calls for the
restoration of high-value ecosystems to meet natural resource conservation
goals by conducting restoration efforts on multiple scales.

Invasive species cross jurisdictional boundaries, making coordination
and collaboration critical to success. The **Organizational Collaboration**
Strategic Goal calls for maximizing organizational effectiveness and collab-

oration on invasive species issues among international, federal, state, local and tribal governments, private organizations and individuals.

The problem of invasive species may at times seem overwhelming. However, considerable success is being achieved in the prevention, detection, eradication and control of some invasive species along with increasing emphasis in the restoration of ecosystems that have previously been dramatically affected by invasive species. Additional research and information exchange; new detection and eradication techniques; and innovative control methodologies and collaborative models are increasing our capacity to address invasive species problems. The 2008–2012 National Invasive Species Management Plan takes a strategic approach and builds on existing programs to maximize federal efforts over the next five years to prevent and control invasive species in order to enhance our environment, economy and human health.

NOTES & QUESTIONS

1. Clinton was not the first president to attempt to address the invasive species problem in the absence of legislative authority to regulate more broadly. In 1977, President Carter signed Executive Order 11,987, which directed federal agencies to restrict the importation and introduction of exotic species into ecosystems on federal land. Unfortunately, federal agencies failed to enforce this order, in part because it lacked political support. Clinton's order has led to far greater effort to minimize the problem.

2. Can the executive order and resulting planning actually make a difference? Consider the following viewpoints:

> Executive Order 13,112 explicitly states: "This order is intended only to improve the internal management of the executive branch and is not intended to create any right, benefit, or trust responsibility, substantive or procedural, enforceable at law or equity by a party against the United States, its agencies, its officers, or any other person." As a result, the order does not empower any party to mandate that certain actions are done. For example, the Executive Order states that the Council must "develop, in consultation with the Council on Environmental Quality [CEQ], guidance to Federal agencies pursuant to the National Environmental Policy Act [NEPA] on prevention and control of invasive species, including the procurement, use, and maintenance of native species as they affect invasive species." A thorough review reveals that as of April 15, 2011, this guidance has not been completed. In fact, in 2009, the National Environmental Coalition on Invasive Species wrote a letter to Nancy Sutley of the CEQ, requesting that action be taken to draft this guidance. As of yet, it has not been drafted.

> While Executive Order 13,112 is helpful for coordination and management purposes, it is only a procedural and not a substantive tool. The lack of legal redress available, as detailed in the Executive Order, underlines its inability to be a catalyst for change. The fact that the CEQ NEPA guidance has not been written in over ten years is a symptom of the Executive Order's lack of utility. Furthermore, the Executive Order does not articu-

late funding mechanisms for programs, and states broadly that the programs are "subject to the availability of appropriations."

Jane Cynthia Graham, *Snakes on a Plain, or in a Wetland: Fighting Back Invasive Nonnative Animals—Proposing a Federal Comprehensive Invasive Nonnative Animal Species Statute*, 25 TUL. ENVTL. L.J. 19, 44 (2011).

Why point to this executive order as the leading example of U.S. invasive species policy if it cannot create new legal authority? President Clinton's executive order on invasive species draws on the full range of available legal authority. In other words, Clinton's order asserts the maximum available authority in support of federal NIS [non-indigenous species] efforts. To the extent that the absence of federal NIS policy has been a lack of action, responsibility, or coordination (whether of budgets, people, or institutions), an executive order can help solve these problems since there is (at least in theory) a unitary executive branch, and an executive order is the policy command of the President.

***

The policy directive to all federal agencies whose actions may affect NIS is sweeping. Unfortunately, saying "everyone" has responsibility is a little like saying no one has responsibility.

However, Executive Order 13,112 also creates an Invasive Species Council (the "Council"), made up of cabinet officers with significant responsibility for NIS. The Council was directed to issue an Invasive Species Management Plan (the "Management Plan"). The Council is advised by an advisory committee whose responsibility is to "recommend plans and actions at local, tribal, State, regional, and ecosystem-based levels to achieve the goals and objectives" of the Management Plan.

Executive Order 13,112 uses many of the hottest federal management tricks in the book. The interagency council made up of cabinet officers places responsibility as high as it can go. Involving a wide range of cabinet level officers increases the likelihood of a full airing of views, revelation of conflicts, and perhaps consistency, efficiency and success of enforcement. Requiring a plan provides a device for action and commentary. Creating an advisory committee increases the chance of expert input and invests a number of people and organizations outside the government in the details of the Council's work.

After an extended process of drafting and review, the Council promulgated the first National Invasive Species Management Plan (NISMP or "the Plan") in January 2001. Reflecting a dominant view among U.S. biologists, the NISMP emphasizes the complex biological, economic, and social dynamics that make it hard to even recognize NIS as a problem and make regulating harm from NIS even more difficult.

***

The NISMP proposes some major changes in U.S. law and policy. For example, the Plan proposes that the federal government develop a "risk-based comprehensive screening system for evaluating first-time intention-ally introduced non-native species." Another recommendation is that the federal government should "[i]dentify the pathways by which invasive spe-cies move, rank them according to their potential for ecological and eco-nomic impacts, and develop mechanisms to reduce movement of invasive species." A third recommendation is to "interdict pathways that are recog-nized as significant sources for the unintentional introduction of invasive species."

These may not seem like dramatic policy recommendations. However, if implemented, these recommendations might require much more intensive examination of goods and people as they crossed borders. If a new organ-ism is proposed for import (and perhaps for export), the NISMP system might lead to expensive analysis before trade can proceed. If a new item were shipped in trade, rules might require a close evaluation, perhaps of each shipment, for possible "hitchhikers" – unintentional transport of non-indigenous plants, animals, or other organisms that could become harmful if established.

Marc L. Miller, *Does the WTO Substantially Limit the Ability of Countries to Regulate Harmful Nonindigenous Species?*, 17 EMORY INT'L L. REV. 1059, 1064-70 (2003).

3. So far we have been looking at national-level policy of broad applicability. The following excerpt from Yosemite National Park's invasive management plan provides a glimpse into the on-the-ground work in the fight against inva-sive species.

Invasive Plant Management Program 2012 Work Plan

Yosemite National Park, 2012.
http://www.nps.gov/yose/naturescience/upload/2012IPPWorkPlan.pdf.

INTRODUCTION

The purpose of the Invasive Plant Program (IPP) is to protect Yosemi-te National Park's natural and cultural resources from displacement by non-native invasive plants. Yosemite's large size, just over three quarters of a million acres, can make surveying for and treating invasive plants logisti-cally difficult. This is especially true in remote wilderness. The threat from invasive species is growing and new invasive plant species and populations are found and treated each year. Limited operational resources for invasive plant control make it critical that treatments are efficient and effective and guided by a strategically sound plan.

Invasive plant management in Yosemite National Park is directed by the 2010 Invasive Plant Management Plan Update and the 2008 Invasive Plant Management Plan (2008 IPMP), which both can be found at: http://www.nps.gov/yose/parkmgmt/invasive_docs.htm. Management ac-tions are based upon integrated pest management (IPM), elements of which include prevention, inventory, prioritization, treatment, monitoring, research, education, and outreach. The IPM process includes manual, mechanical, biological, herbicide and cultural (altering management to discourage invasives) methods to ensure that the most effective treatment tools are used to protect resources, while posing the least possible impact to people and the environment.

This work plan addresses Yosemite's most serious invasive plant species. These species are prioritized for control based on the risk that they pose relative to the program's ability to obtain the monetary and personnel resources necessary to mitigate their threat. "High priority" species pose the greatest risk to Yosemite's natural and cultural resources and are treated before medium or low priority invasive species. *Early detection and rapid response* allows populations to be efficiently controlled while they are still small, and minimizes the risk of further spread. Newly discovered invasive plant species and populations may receive elevated priority for control.

Resource managers conduct ongoing internal review with other branches in the Division of Resources Management and Science as well as other park divisions. External consultation with American Indian tribes and groups and other stakeholders during the invasive plant management process also occurs. Managers then derive an appropriate treatment strategy by location for invasive plant infestations. The treatment method for a particular locality depends on the invasive species, plant phenology (timing of plant growth, flowering, and senescence [aging]), and the availability of methods known to be effective and permitted under the IPMP. A range of site-specific considerations is taken into account when selecting the appropriate treatment methods. These may include:

Location	Treatment
Within the bed and banks of a designated Wild and Scenic Rivers	Aquatic herbicides
Wetland and riparian ecosystems	In consultation with Branch of Wildlife Management where necessary. Most areas will be treated using aquatic herbicides.
Terrestrial ecosystems	Herbicide for Himalayan blackberry and other species determined a high priority for treatment.
Archeological sites	Control near archaeological resources would be conducted in consultation with Branch of Anthropology and Archeology.
Traditional-use areas	In consultation with American Indian tribes and groups
Designated Wilderness	The minimum appropriate tool will be used to control invasive species. Herbicide use is allowed if it is determined to be the best tool after a minimum re-

	quirements analysis. Otherwise, manual methods used.
Private in-holdings	Outreach, assistance and treatment with landowner's permission
DNC land assignments	DNC is responsible for treatment of invasive plants. NPS staff will coordinate with DNC to treat high priority weeds
Special status plant habitat	Consultation with botanists in the Branch of Vegetation and Ecological Restoration during planning stage for work that would occur near special status plant populations.
Wildlife species of concern and critical habitat	Consultation with wildlife ecologists during planning stage for work that would occur in critical habitat for species of concern.

Yosemite National Park is consulting with culturally associated American Indian tribes and groups to ensure no adverse effect on traditional cultural properties or traditional cultural use areas. Information sharing and project planning will continue in consultation with the American Indian tribes and groups throughout the planning and implementation of 2012 field season to ensure that concerns are properly addressed and that management recommendations are fully considered. Information sharing includes notifications, meeting and field visits, and this annual work plan, which outlines locations, approximate dates, and methods for invasive plant management activities proposed for the 2012 season.

PREVENTION

Integrated weed management is essential to the Invasive Plant Management Plan. Yosemite focuses on four major programs: 1) Public outreach 2) Equipment inspection 3) Weed-free aggregate 4) Early detection, rapid response

Public outreach Invasive plant managers work to communicate with visitors and local communities. For example, the invasive plant website was overhauled in 2010 and provides abundant information appropriate for both visitors and other land managers. To engage local community members, letters were distributed to all park inholders informing them of management actions and encouraging them to treat invasive plants on their property. Additionally, the invasive plant crew offers consultation and assistance with treatment.

In 2012, the invasive plant managers will be performing the first systematic survey of the park. The survey will be completed with the assistance of volunteers and will provide an opportunity to educate citizen scientists about invasive plants. Mapping will be completed using smartphone technology and will provide a fun, interactive way to engage our partners in citizen science.

Equipment Inspection The Vegetation and Ecological Restoration Branch collaborates with the Division Facilities and Maintainence to inspect all incoming heavy equipment. Heavy equipment is a major source of invasive plant propagules in the park, and the commencement of this program has been very successful in preventing infestations. Most contractors fully comply with this program and few pieces of equipment have to be turned around each year.

Weed-free aggregate Non-native plants are often transported with imported sand and gravel. To prevent invasive plants from being imported, resource managers inspect quarries for invasive plants and work with quarry operators to treat their quarry and therefore reduce the risk of invasive plants coming into the park. This program is rapidly expanding and is now a collaborative effort across agencies. In 2012, four prevention workshops highlighting this program will be held across the state.

Early detection, rapid response Resource managers work hard to ensure that new populations of invasive plants due not expand by treating infestations while they are still small. Resource managers currently perform detailed surveys of recently burned areas as they are highly vulnerable to invasive plants. In 2012, the systematic survey will great increase our early detection rapid response capacity.

SUMMARY OF 2011 WORK

TREATMENT SUMMARIES

Yellow Star-thistle (*Centaurea solstitialis*). Each field season begins with the program's most ambitious and challenging project—the treatment of yellow star-thistle in El Portal. Some slopes in this area are steep enough to require the use of fall protection. In 2011, crews treated 16 canopy acres of yellow star-thistle. They covered all old yellow star-thistle infestations while expanding treatment into new infestations. Because the seedbank only lasts for two to three years, a major reduction in the El Portal star-thistle density began in 2011 and is expected to continue in 2012.

Himalayan and Cut-leaf Blackberry (*Rubus armeniacus* and *R. laciniatus*, collectively referred to as "blackberry"). In 2011, crews treated 36 acres of blackberry along the Merced and Tuolumne rivers. Due to the success of the 2010 treatments, the total amount of herbicide applied to blackberry in 2011 declined slightly, despite expanding treatments into the Merced River corridor and the Tuolumne river watershed.

Wall Hawkweed (*Hieracium murorum*). Crews controlled an infestation of wall hawkweed at the Tacoma housing area in Yosemite Valley. This invasive plant was new to California in 2010 and has the potential to spread rapidly in the park. The infestation site will be monitored and retreated if needed in 2012.

Bull Thistle (*Cirsium vulgare*). Staff and volunteers manually treated bull thistle, the most widespread high-priority species in Yosemite.

Bull thistle is found in Yosemite Valley, Wawona, designated Wilderness, and in some recently burned areas.

Spotted Knapweed (*Centaurea maculosa*). Crews conducted follow up surveys in an ongoing effort to remove an invasive spotted knapweed population in Foresta. Thirty-three plants were found and removed in 2010 and twelve in 2011, thus keeping Yosemite's most noxious and insidious non-native plant under control. Efforts to remove this noxious plant will continue in 2012.

Oxeye Daisy (*Leucanthemum vulgare*). The IPP began intensive management of Oxeye daisy, an aggressive meadow invader in 2010. Crews surveyed 40 gross-infested acres in the Big Meadow burn area and treated 7 acres of daisy. In 2011, the crews treated more than 12 acres of oxeye daisy, almost double the amount treated in 2010.

Velvet Grass and Cheatgrass (*Holcus lanatus and Bromus tectorum*). Velvet grass infests hundreds of acres of Yosemite meadows and cheatgrass heavily infests the foothill woodlands and is spreading into new areas within the park. Effective control methods are not yet available for these two high-priority species. The Yosemite Conservancy is funding much of this work. Park staff are also collaborating with the U.S. Geologic Survey (USGS) on effectiveness studies for velvet grass and cheatgrass control. The goal is to aid in the development of a management strategy through learning more about the biology and potential treatment tactics for these species.

MONITORING

Checking assumptions that water resources are not negatively affected

Water quality is important! Yosemite occasionally resorts to the use of glyphosate near water in order to treat Himalayan blackberry and other high priority invasive plant species that cannot be effectively controlled using manual techniques. Glyphosate is a very safe herbicide and does not readily move in water. However, we wanted to verify that herbicide concentrations did not exceed accepted hazard quotients:

In 2011, we selected two of our largest net infestations (each totaling at least one gross infestation acre within 10 feet from water). We used an aquatic formulation of glyphosate and monitored water quality after the first heavy rain, because that is the most likely time when herbicide would appear in water samples.

Water samples were taken from three locations at two treatment sites for a total of six samples. Two samples were downstream of the patch, and one sample was above the patch to act as the control.

Water samples were submitted to a third party lab for testing. The lowest detectable limit for the lab is 1.8 ug herbicide/liter of water or

(0.0000018g/l). The samples show no trace of herbicide in any water sample. The results will be posted on the YOSE invasive plant team website: http://www.nps.gov/yose/naturescience/invasive-plants.htm.

Monitoring treatment effectiveness

Yosemite invasive plant managers are tracking how much and where herbicides are used in the park. . . Our primary targets are blackberry, yellow star-thistle and oxeye daisy. ... [F]or both blackberry and yellow star thistle the number of gallons of herbicide increased from 2009 to 2010, but a significant decrease occurred between 2010 to 2011. This decrease is attributable to treatment success in 2009 and 2010, and we anticipate further decline in 2012. This trend is also observed when examining the number of canopy acres treated over three years. Canopy acres are the combined area of the individual plants. ... While the number of acres treated decreased from 2010 to 2011, the amount of area covered increased consistently from 2009 to 2011. The gross infested acres, which includes the area between plants in an infestation, shows the amount of area covered by the crews.

Effectiveness monitoring: Our effectiveness monitoring for Himalayan blackberry showed that glyphosate was more effective that aminopyralid. Therefore, we used only glyphosate to control Himalayan blackberry in 2012.

For yellow star thistle, both herbicides work very well, but for restoration reasons, we prefer to use the selective herbicide aminopyralid during the early season, and the non selective glyphosate in late season, hence the weather and the timing of our treatments influence how much of what tool we use. Overall, we used less herbicide on yellow star-thistle in 2011 compared to 2010, attributable to the success of our treatments. A further decline is anticipated in 2012.

The total number of gross infested acres documented in the park is around 430 acres. Bull thistle, blackberry, and a mix of other species (which includes cheat grass), each have over 100 acres documented in the park. Around 65-75% of the known populations of bull thistle, blackberry and oxeye daisy are currently undergoing treatment. Almost the entire yellow star thistle population is currently undergoing treatment.

Himalayan blackberry has been manually and mechanically treated in many easily accessible sites in Yosemite Valley. Even in such easily gentle terrain, the treatments involve heavy soil disturbance and major impacts to desirable native vegetation. Years of diligent re-treatment to secure treatment success, and due to the soil disturbance, the site is often invaded by secondary invasives such as bull thistle and velvet grass. In rocky and remote terrain it isn't possible to remove blackberry roots effectively. Trial plots comparing herbicide use, and handpulling have repeatedly shown that herbicide treatments foster better and more rapid native species recovery.

OVERVIEW OF 2012 WORK PLAN

This plan describes the methods and locations of control actions for high priority invasive species and medium-high priority species. New invasive plant species or new populations of high priority species are found each year. Because the most effective way to protect the park from new invasions is through rapid response to these early detections, it is very likely that, on a limited basis, crews would apply treatments that are not explicitly described in this document and on the maps. Because some plants survive treatment, crews will monitor previously treated sites and retreat as needed. Also this year, USGS and park scientists will initiate an herbicide effectiveness study focused on cheatgrass.

Detailed Planning Maps

This plan includes a set of 37 maps that provide site-specific treatment details to park staff and the public. The maps also act as guide for field crews' decision-making. The maps, which include a total of 8,849 mapped features (individual points, lines or polygons), display invasive plant infestations collected in the field since 1995. Large infestations are shown to scale as polygons. Small patches and individual plants are shown as points.

The maps have some limitations. Infestation locations are only as accurate as the equipment used to map them; a patch mapped using GPS could actually be located up to 20-40 feet from where it appears. Therefore, an infestation may appear to be located in a river or middle of the road. Invasive plant infestations may have expanded or may no longer exist as shown due to effective control. Invasive species often co-occur, showing up on a map as a feature within a feature. The treated area of an infestation can overlay the larger, full infestation.

Treatment techniques

Spot spray targeted application of herbicide is applied to foliage of priority plant species using a backpacker sprayer or a truck-mounted sprayer. Targeted applications result in minimal impact to non-target plants.

Frill cut used on trees or large shrubs, a diagonal cut into the bark is made prior to herbicide application to aid delivery into the target plant

Stump cut used on trees, a tree is cut near ground level before herbicide is applied directly to the stump of the target plant

Hand-pull removal of target plant biomass, including the roots, by hand

Lop and grub above ground plant is cut with loppers and then the (often deeper) root system is dug out; very time intensive

Shovel-shear plant is severed a couple inches under the ground surface using a shovel; some root material remains

Inflorescence removal reproductive parts are removed to prevent spread by seed

Cut and dab plant is lopped a few inches from ground and a paint brush is used to apply herbicide to the stump

Monitoring activities

Survey a systematic search for target plants

Grid survey a line of people collectively search for target plants resulting in a very thorough survey

Map to document infestations; most often using GPS units

GPS Global Positioning System; use of satellite technology to pinpoint location; used to map infestations

Monitor a general term to describe all activities that examine results of management actions; for example, observation of a site after treatment to document outcome of that treatment

Pilot study a quantitative study to assess effectiveness of a treatment new to Yosemite

TREATMENT PLAN FOR HIGH-PRIORITY SPECIES

Cheat grass (*Bromus tectorum*). This plant is widespread in Yosemite and difficult to control. The IPP has not focused control efforts toward cheatgrass in the past but park scientists are continuing an herbicide effectiveness study in collaboration with USGS. Field staff and volunteers will also continue to document its distribution in the park and target some treatments to slow its spread in Wilderness.

Italian thistle (*Carduus pycnocephalus*)(photo to right). This California-listed noxious weed has been found a few times in Yosemite and effectively treated with manual methods. In 2010, populations were discovered within ¼ mile of the park borders in El Portal and Foresta. These areas will be resurveyed and treated if necessary in May. This plant is set to become one of Yosemite's most troublesome plants in the future.

Spotted knapweed (*Centaurea maculosa*). Since its accidental introduction to Foresta in 1990, crews have repeatedly hand-pulled spotted knapweed with the goal of eradicating it from Yosemite. Previously infested areas will be resurveyed in 2012 and individual plants will be hand-pulled. Large patches, while not known or expected, will be sprayed with aminopyralid.

Yellow star-thistle (*Centaurea solstitialis*). Extensive grid surveys have been conducted in El Portal. Manual and mechanical methods have and will continue to be used to treat small populations. Aminopyralid will be used in early season to treat most populations. Plants may be spot sprayed with glyphosate later in the season. Historic populations of yellow star-thistle in Foresta will continue to be monitored. If plants are discovered, they will be hand pulled or sprayed with aminopyralid.

Bull thistle (*Cirsium vulgare*). Bull thistle is presently our most widespread, high-priority invasive plant. It is wind dispersed and quickly invades wet sites after disturbance. New infestations are often observed after prescribed and wildland fires. NPS crews will remove bull thistle where encountered with aminopyralid treatment, hand-pulling or shovel-shearing.

French broom (*Genista monspessulana*). This plant was introduced to El Portal as an ornamental and is spreading quickly. Crews will treat French broom on NPS land with aminopyralid. However, it and other ornamental broom species (*Genista* and *Cytisus*) are present on in-holdings within Yosemite and some of them may be invasive. Public outreach materials and activities are being developed to encourage cooperative resource protection between these landowners and Yosemite National Park.

Velvet grass (*Holcus lanatus*). Although velvet grass is widespread and abundant in Yosemite's meadows; the IPP does not yet have a highly effective treatment prescription. Hand-pulling can enhance the infestation by activating the robust seed bank, and initial herbicide trials did not yield promising results. New treatment prescriptions are being tested through a collaborative research effort with USGS. If study results indicate a viable treatment prescription, crews will begin treatment. Herbicide treatment will focus on small populations within intact native plant communities to halt further displacement of native vegetation. Additionally, small populations found along roads and trails with a high likelihood of dispersal into natural habitats will be a main target.

St. John's Wort (*Hypericum perforatum*). USFS and Mariposa County officials report it is spreading quickly. St.-John's wort is very similar to the native *H. formosum*, but the native species lacks the characteristic translucent glandular dots when held up to the light (see photo). Infestations of St. John's wort will be treated with aminopyralid or glyphosate.

Oxeye daisy (*Leucanthemum vulgare*). Yosemite Invasive Plant managers have noted a dramatic spread in the Big Meadow area in Foresta. Yosemite is continuing systematic mapping and removal operations park-wide. It is treated with aminopyralid.

Perennial pepperweed (*Lepidium latifolium*). A population found in Foresta was removed. Although no plants have been found for several years, monitoring is ongoing to ensure eradication.

Himalayan and cut-leaf blackberry (*Rubus armeniacus* and *R. laciniatus*). Himalayan blackberry constitutes the majority of invasive blackberry; cut-leaf blackberry will be treated the same as Himalayan blackberry. NPS crews will continue to treat largely with glyphosate. However, imazapyr may be used from July-November, particularly on populations that have not been responsive to glyphosate. They will also treat with triclopyr from October-November, particularly where treatment success has been low (particularly *R. laciniatus*). Treatment will be spot-sprays applied with backpack sprayers or with a hand wand from a truck mounted sprayer. Cut-and-dab application trials, conducted in 2009 and 2010, yielded promising results. Crews may choose this method for remote populations or populations located near special status plants or other special resources.

*   *   *

B. THE BALLAST-WATER CASES: A SURVEY OF THE APPLICATION OF EXISTING LAWS TO INVASIVE SPECIES

The most litigated invasive species problem involves the introduction of aquatic invasive species via the discharge of ballast water from cargo ships. As such, the ballast water context provides a useful study of the application of a range of existing laws to invasive species. Ballast water is the water (and whatever is mixed with it) that is drawn into or discharged out of subsurface tanks on cargo ships in order to maintain balance when cargo is added or removed. Because cargo is picked up in one location and delivered to another, the water is drawn into the tanks in one location and released in another, along with any organisms that may have survived the trip.

Via the following three cases we see litigation under the Clean Water Act, the National Environmental Policy Act, the Endangered Species Act, and the interplay between state regulation and the federal legislation directly targeted to this issue. We begin with the Clean Water Act case, as it provides the most detailed explanation of the ballast water situation generally, which will aid in your appreciation of the remaining cases.

Northwest Environmental Advocates v. United States Environmental Protection Agency

United States Court of Appeals for the Ninth Circuit, 2008.
537 F.3d 1006.

■ FLETCHER, CIRCUIT JUDGE.

Plaintiffs in this case are Northwest Environmental Advocates, San Francisco Baykeeper, and The Ocean Conservancy. Plaintiffs-intervenors are the States of Illinois, Michigan, Minnesota, New York, Pennsylvania, and Wisconsin. Plaintiffs and plaintiffs-intervenors challenge a regulation originally promulgated by the Environmental Protection Agency ("EPA") in 1973 exempting certain marine discharges from the permitting scheme of sections 301(a) and 402 of the Clean Water Act ("CWA"). That regulation, 40 C.F.R. § 122.3(a), provides that the following vessel discharges into the navigable waters of the United States do not require permits: discharge of effluent from properly functioning marine engines; discharge of laundry, shower, and galley sink wastes from vessels; and any other discharge incidental to the normal operation of a vessel, including the discharge of ballast water.

The district court concluded that the EPA had exceeded its authority under the CWA in exempting these discharges from permitting requirements. The district court vacated § 122.3(a), effective September 30, 2008. We affirm the decision of the district court.

I. Background

A. The CWA and 40 C.F.R. § 122.3(a)

In 1972, Congress enacted sweeping amendments to the Federal Water Pollution Control Act of 1948. After another round of substantial amendments in 1977, the statute became known as the Clean Water Act. The CWA declares a "national goal that the discharge of pollutants into the navigable waters be eliminated by 1985."

Section 301(a) of the CWA provides that, subject to certain exceptions, "the discharge of any pollutant by any person shall be unlawful." One of these exceptions is for discharges authorized by a permit granted pursuant to the National Pollutant Discharge Elimination System ("NPDES"), a system set forth in section 402 of the Act. The combined effect of sections 301(a) and 402 is that "[t]he CWA prohibits the discharge of any pollutant from a point source into navigable waters of the United States without an NPDES permit." *N. Plains Res. Council v. Fid. Exploration & Dev. Co.,* 325 F.3d 1155, 1160 (9th Cir.2003). The EPA administers the NPDES.

Obtaining a permit under the CWA need not be an onerous process. For example, in appropriate circumstances a discharge may be allowed under a "general permit" requiring only that the discharger submit a "notice of intent" to make the discharge. As we explained in *Natural Resources Defense Council v. U.S. EPA,* 279 F.3d 1180, 1183 (9th Cir.2002):

> NPDES permits come in two varieties: individual and general. An individual permit authorizes a specific entity to discharge a pollutant in a specific place and is issued after an informal agency adjudication process. General permits, on the other hand, are issued for an entire class of hypothetical dischargers in a given geographical region and are issued pursuant to administrative rulemaking procedures. General permits may appropriately be issued when the dischargers in the geographical area to be covered by the permit are relatively homogenous. After a general permit has been issued, an entity that believes it is covered by the general permit submits a "notice of intent" to discharge pursuant to the general permit. A general permit can allow discharging to commence upon receipt of the notice of intent, after a waiting period, or after the permit issuer sends out a response agreeing that the discharger is covered by the general permit.

In 1973, the EPA exempted by regulation several categories of vessel discharges from NPDES permitting requirements under the CWA. The regulation provides that "[t]he following discharges do not require NPDES permits":

> Any discharge of sewage from vessels, effluent from properly functioning marine engines, laundry, shower, and galley sink wastes, or any other discharge incidental to the normal operation of a vessel. This exclusion does not apply to rubbish, trash, garbage, or other such materials discharged overboard; nor to other discharges when the vessel is operating in a capacity other than as a means of transportation[.]

40 C.F.R. § 122.3(a). The CWA expressly exempts sewage discharges from vessels from the permitting process and regulates these discharges by other means. Because § 122.3(a) does not itself exempt sewage discharges but instead merely recognizes the statute's exemption of sewage discharges, the sewage clause in § 122.3(a) is not subject to the *ultra vires* claim made here. *See also Chevron U.S.A., Inc. v. Hammond,* 726 F.2d 483, 493 n. 13 (9th Cir.1984) (contrasting the express statutory exemption of sewage with regulation relating to "deballasting" by ships). Therefore, three categories of discharges exempted by 40 C.F.R. § 122.3(a) are at issue in this case: (1) marine engine discharges; (2) graywater discharges ("laundry, shower, and galley sink wastes"); and (3) "any other discharge incidental to the normal operation of a vessel."

The first proposed draft of the regulation would have excluded only marine engine discharges. The EPA subsequently added the exclusions for graywater and other discharges incidental to normal vessel operations. When promulgating the final regulation in May 1973, the EPA explained its anticipated effect: "Most discharges from vessels to inland waters are now clearly excluded from the permit requirements." The EPA stated that "[t]his type of discharge generally causes little pollution." The EPA stated, further, that the "exclusion of vessel wastes from the permit requirements will reduce administrative costs drastically." Decades later, an EPA administrator declared that in 1973:

> [W]e were faced with many, many other much higher priority situations such as raw sewage being discharged, municipal plants having to be built, very large paper mills or steel mills and the like discharging. At the time we thought that was not an important area to deal with. . . Vessels were not important to the overall scheme of things at that time.

The EPA amended the regulation in 1979 in minor respects that do not affect our analysis.

The text of the CWA does not exempt from NPDES requirements marine engine discharges, graywater discharges, or other discharges incidental to the normal operation of vessels. However, the EPA contended in 1973, and continues to contend, that it has the power to provide these exemptions by regulation. The Administrator of the EPA prefaced the draft January 1973 regulation with a statement that a discharger could discharge lawfully only if the discharger "possesses a valid permit or is excluded from coverage by law *or regulation*." The final rules similarly stated that "[a]ll discharges of pollutants . . . are unlawful . . ., unless the discharger has a permit or is specifically relieved by law *or regulation* from the obligation of obtaining a permit."

The first category exempted by § 122.3(a), marine engine discharges, includes unburned fuel and various kinds of oil. The second category, graywater discharges, can include pathogens such as fecal coliform, *enterococci*, and *E. coli* and pollutants such as ammonia, arsenic, copper, lead, nickel, and zinc. The third category, "any other discharge," includes, among other discharges, ballast water from ships.

Plaintiffs have made clear, both here and in the district court, that their primary environmental concern stems from the discharge of ballast water. We quote a passage from the district court's order granting plaintiffs' motion for permanent injunctive relief that describes the purpose of ballast water and the effects of its discharge:

> Ballast water is water that is taken on by cargo ships to compensate for changes in the ship's weight as cargo is loaded or unloaded, and as fuel and supplies are consumed. Ballast water may be used for a number of different purposes, such as maintaining stability, maintaining proper propeller and bow immersion, and to compensate for off-center weights. Thus, ballast water is essential to the proper functioning of cargo ships, as well as to the safety of its crew.

> Because ballast water is primarily used to compensate for changes in cargo, it is generally taken in or pumped out at the ports along a ship's route. When a ship takes on ballast water, whether freshwater or saltwater, organisms found in that water are typically taken in as well. These organisms are carried in the ballast tanks of the ship until the ship arrives at its next port, where, due to changes in the distribution of the ship's cargo, they may be released into a new ecosystem. Due to the size of ballast tanks on modern cargo ships, and the speed with which these ships can reach their destinations, organisms are increasingly able to survive the journey to a new ecosystem. All told, "more than 10,000 marine species each day hitch rides around the globe in the ballast water of cargo ships." A number of these species are released into U.S. waters in the more than 21 billion gallons of ballast water released in the United States each year.

> If these foreign organisms manage to survive and reproduce in the new ecosystem, they can cause severe problems in the natural and human environment. For example, zebra mussels, native to the Caspian Sea region of Asia, were brought into the Great Lakes in the ballast water of cargo ships. "Zebra mussels have clogged the water pipes of electric companies and other industries; infestations in the Midwest and Northeast have cost power plants and industrial facilities almost $70 million between 1989 and 1995." As another example, according to a 2001 EPA report,

[a]n introduced strain of cholera bacteria, possibly released in the bilge water of a Chinese freighter, caused the deaths of 10,000 people in Latin America in 1991. This cholera strain was then imported into the United States from Latin America in the ballast tanks of ships that anchored in the port of Mobile, Alabama. Fortunately, cholera bacteria were detected in oyster and finfish samples in Mobile Bay . . . and no additional deaths occurred from exposure to this pathogen.

With a lack of natural predators, invasive species can multiply rapidly and quickly take over an ecosystem, threatening native species. Indeed, invasive species "are a major or contributing cause of declines for almost half the endangered species in the United States." Once established, invasive species become almost impossible to remove, leading "[s]cientists, industry officials, and land managers [to] recogniz[e] that invasive species are one of the most serious, yet least appreciated, environmental threats of the 21st century."

In economic terms, invasive species can also have a devastating effect. The Department of Agriculture spends millions of dollars per year to detect and prevent invasive species. One study cited by the [General Accounting Office] concluded that "total annual economic losses and associated control costs [are] about $137 billion a year-more than double the annual economic damage caused by all natural disasters in the United States."

Nw. Envtl. Advocates v. U.S. EPA ("Northwest Environmental Advocates II "), No. 03-05760, 2006 WL 2669042, at *3-4, (N.D.Cal. Sept. 18, 2006).

*   *   *

III. Discussion

*   *   *

2. Text of the CWA

Our first substantive inquiry is whether § 122.3(a) is invalid under the plain meaning of the CWA. Our inquiry is guided by *Chevron*. The Court wrote:

When a court reviews an agency's construction of the statute which it administers, it is confronted with two questions. First, always, is the question whether Congress has directly spoken to the precise question at issue. If the intent of Congress is clear, that is the end of the matter; for the court, as well as the agency, must give effect to the unambiguously expressed intent of Congress.

467 U.S. at 842-43, 104 S.Ct. 2778.

Section 301(a) of the CWA mandates that "the discharge of any pollutant by any person shall be unlawful." This prohibition is "[t]he 'cornerstone' and 'fundamental premise' of the Clean Water Act." *SE Alaska Conservation Council v. U.S. Army Corps of Eng'rs*, 486 F.3d 638, 644 (9th Cir.2007). Section 402 of the CWA provides that a "point source" can obtain a "permit for the discharge of any pollutant or combination of pollutants." "[T]he Act categorically prohibits any discharge of a pollutant from a point source without a permit." *Comm. to Save Mokelumne River v. E. Bay Mun. Util. Dist.*, 13 F.3d 305, 309 (9th Cir.1993).

The text of the statute clearly covers the discharges at issue here. A "discharge of any pollutant" is "any addition of any pollutant to navigable waters from any point source." A "point source" is "any discernable, confined and discrete conveyance, including . . . [a] vessel or other floating craft, from which pollutants are or may be discharged." "[N]avigable waters" are "the waters of the United States, including the territorial seas," which begin near the coast and "extend[ ] seaward a distance of three miles." "Pollutant" is defined as "dredged spoil, solid waste, incinerator residue, sewage, garbage, sewage sludge, munitions, chemical wastes, biological materials, radioactive materials, heat, wrecked or discarded equipment, rock, sand, cellar dirt and industrial, municipal, and agricultural waste discharged into water." The term "biological materials" includes invasive species.

The question before us of whether the CWA authorizes the EPA's regulatory exemptions was answered by the D.C. Circuit more than thirty years ago. *See Natural Res. Def. Council v. Costle* ("*Costle* "), 568 F.2d 1369 (D.C.Cir.1977). The same year that the EPA issued the regulation in our case, the agency promulgated a different but conceptually identical regulation. *Costle* addressed an *ultra vires* challenge to that regulation.

The regulation entirely exempted several categories of point sources from NPDES requirements:

> all silviculture point sources; all confined animal feeding operations below a certain size; all irrigation return flows from areas less than 3,000 contiguous acres or 3,000 noncontiguous acres that use the same drainage system; all nonfeedlot, nonirrigation agricultural point sources; and separate storm sewers containing only storm runoff uncontaminated by any industrial or commercial activity.

Id. at 1372. In a unanimous opinion by Judge Leventhal, the D.C. Circuit held that the EPA acted *ultra vires* in promulgating this regulation.

The analysis of the D.C. Circuit in *Costle,* with which we agree, is dispositive of our case. The only possible textual source of authority for the exemptions at issue in *Costle* (and in our case) is section 402 of the CWA. In relevant part, that section provides that the EPA Administrator

> may, after opportunity for public hearing, issue a permit for the discharge of any pollutant, . . . notwithstanding section 301(a), upon con-

dition that such discharge will meet either (A) all applicable requirements under sections 301, 302, 306, 307, 308, and 403 of this Act, or (B) prior to the taking of necessary implementing actions relating to all such requirements, such conditions as the Administrator determines are necessary to carry out the provisions of this Act.

33 U.S.C. § 1342(a)(1).

Section 402 uses the word "may," but only in the context of "issu[ing] a permit for the discharge of any pollutant." The Administrator "may" issue a permit under two circumstances: either on the condition that the discharge meets all of the requirements specified in the section; or, prior to implementation of those statutory requirements, on such conditions "as the Administrator determines are necessary to carry out the provisions of [the] Act." That is, section 402 allows the Administrator to issue a permit, but it does not provide that the Administrator may entirely exempt certain categories of discharges from the permitting requirement. As the D.C. Circuit concluded, "The use of the word 'may' in § 402 means only that the Administrator has discretion either to issue a permit or to leave the discharger subject to the total proscription of § 301. This is the natural reading, and the one that retains the fundamental logic of the statute." *Costle,* 568 F.2d at 1375.

The D.C. Circuit confirmed the correctness of its reading of the CWA by consulting the legislative history of the Act. It wrote, "[T]he legislative history makes clear that Congress intended the NPDES permit to be the only means by which a discharger from a point source may escape the total prohibition of § 301(a)." *Id.* at 1374. Because the statutory language is unambiguous, we do not need to revisit the legislative history. Congress's intent was clear: "[T]he EPA Administrator does not have authority to exempt categories of point sources from the permit requirements of § 402." *Id.* at 1377.

*   *   *

V. Conclusion

We hold that the district court had subject matter jurisdiction over plaintiffs' suit alleging that the EPA acted *ultra vires* in promulgating § 122.3(a). We affirm the district court, holding that the EPA acted *ultra vires* in promulgating § 122.3(a) and that EPA's denial of plaintiffs' 1999 petition requesting the repeal of § 122.3(a) was not in accordance with law. We affirm the district court's remedial order as a proper exercise of its discretion. Finally, we dismiss for lack of subject matter jurisdiction plaintiffs' petition for review filed directly with this court.

Fednav, Ltd. v. Chester

United States Court of Appeals for the Sixth Circuit, 2008.
547 F.3d 607.

■ KETHLEDGE, CIRCUIT JUDGE.

Plaintiffs-a coalition of shipping companies, non-profit shipping associations, a port terminal and dock operator, and a port association-appeal the district court's dismissal of their constitutional challenges to the so-called Michigan Ballast Water Statute, Mich. Comp. Laws § 324.3112(6), and the regulations promulgated pursuant thereto. We hold that Plaintiffs lack standing to challenge one portion of the statute, and reject their arguments as to its remainder. We therefore affirm.

I.

A.

Congress passed the Nonindigenous Aquatic Nuisance Prevention and Control Act of 1990, 16 U.S.C. § 4701 et seq. ("NANPCA"), to combat the problem of aquatic nuisance species ("ANS") in United States waters. ANS are "nonindigenous species that threaten[ ] the diversity or abundance of native species or the ecological stability of infested waters, or commercial, agricultural, aquacultural or recreational waters dependent on such waters."

In NANPCA, Congress found that "the discharge of untreated water [from] the ballast tanks of vessels . . . results in unintentional introductions of" ANS. Id. § 4701(a)(1). Some oceangoing vessels take on ballast water in foreign harbors to maintain trim, draft, and stability of the vessel when not carrying a full load of cargo. This ballast water "may inadvertently contain aquatic organisms, which are then released when the ballast is discharged in another port." [quoting appellants] In most cases, these organisms die, but in some they thrive in their new environment in the absence of natural predators. In those cases the organisms "may compete with or prey upon native species of plants, fish, and wildlife, may carry diseases or parasites that affect native species, and may disrupt the aquatic environment and economy of affected near-shore areas." 16 U.S.C. § 4701(a)(2).

One such organism is the zebra mussel, which was introduced into the Great Lakes via discharged ballast water in the 1980s. "In June 1988, this small bivalve mollusk, native to the Black, Azov, and Caspian Seas in [E]astern Europe, was discovered on the Canadian side of Lake Saint Clair in the Great Lakes." 58 Fed.Reg. 18330, 18330 (Apr. 8, 1993). It has since spread throughout the Great Lakes. Congress estimated in 1990 that "the potential economic disruption to communities affected by the zebra mussel due to its colonization of water pipes, boat hulls and other hard surfaces" could reach $5 billion by the year 2000. 16 U.S.C. § 4701(4). Moreover, "[a]s a filter-feeding organism, [the zebra mussel] removes vast quantities of microscopic organisms from the water, the same organisms that fish larvae and young fish rely upon for their food supply." 58 Fed.Reg. at 18330.

NANPCA's purpose, therefore, was "to prevent unintentional introduction and dispersal of nonindigenous species into waters of the United States through ballast water management and other requirements." Id. § 4701(b)(1). To that end, NANPCA required the Coast Guard to "issue regulations to prevent the introduction and spread of aquatic nuisance species into the Great Lakes through the ballast water of vessels." *Id.* § 4711(b)(1).

The Coast Guard issued such regulations on May 10, 1993. The regulations require vessels traveling to the Great Lakes and carrying ballast water from beyond the exclusive economic zone ("EEZ") to employ one of three "ballast water management practices": (1) carry out an exchange of ballast water on the waters beyond the EEZ to achieve a minimum ballast water salinity level of thirty parts per thousand; (2) retain the ballast water onboard the vessel; or (3) use an alternative environmentally sound method of ballast-water management that has been approved by the Coast Guard. 33 C.F.R. § 151.1510(a) (2008).

With respect to the saltwater ballast-exchange method, the Coast Guard explained that

> [c]urrently, the most practical method of helping to protect the Great Lakes from foreign organisms that may exist in discharged ballast water is the exchange of ballast water in the open ocean, beyond the continental shelf. Water in the open ocean contains organisms that are adapted to the physical, chemical, and biological conditions (such as high salinity) of the ocean. These organisms will not, or are unlikely to, survive if introduced into a freshwater system.

58 Fed.Reg. at 18330.

The Coast Guard acknowledged the existence of other possible methods, including "discharging ballast water to reception facilities ashore, heating or chemically treating ballast water, disinfecting ballast water with ultraviolet light, depriving ballast water of oxygen, installing filters, and modifying vessel design." *Id.* But the Coast Guard said there was, at that time, "a lack of research and practical experience on the cost, safety, effectiveness, and environmental impact of these methods." *Id.* The Coast Guard has not approved any alternative ballast-water-treatment methods since 1993.

On October 26, 1996, Congress reauthorized and amended NANPCA by enacting the National Invasive Species Act of 1996 ("NISA"), 16 U.S.C. § 4701 et seq. In NISA, Congress noted the continuing problem of ANS and found that "if preventative management measures are not taken nationwide to prevent and control unintentionally introduced nonindigenous aquatic species in a timely manner, further introductions and infestations of species that are as destructive as, or more destructive than, the zebra mussel . . . may occur." 16 U.S.C. § 4701(a)(13). Congress also found that "resolving the problems associated with aquatic nuisance species will require the participation and cooperation of the Federal Government and State governments, and investment in the development of prevention technologies." *Id.* § 4701(15).

NISA directed the Coast Guard to implement voluntary national guidelines for ballast-water management in the waters of the United

States. If the Coast Guard deemed compliance with the voluntary guidelines inadequate, NISA authorized the Coast Guard to convert the voluntary guidelines into mandatory regulations. The Coast Guard did precisely that between 1999 and 2004, promulgating mandatory national regulations for ballast-water management. Those national regulations did not change the 1993 Great Lakes-specific regulations, however, except that vessels equipped with ballast tanks entering the Great Lakes are now required to comply with certain recordkeeping and reporting requirements.

This case ultimately arises from the fact that the Coast Guard's ballast-water regulations contain, for lack of a better term, a loophole. To wit, none of the Coast Guard's ballast-water requirements – neither the 1993 Great-Lakes regulations nor the 2004 national regulations (except for the recordkeeping and reporting requirements) – apply to vessels that declare they have "no ballast on board," so-called "NOBOBs." See 33 C.F.R. § 151.1502 (Great Lakes regulations apply to "each vessel that carries ballast water"); 69 Fed.Reg. 44952, 44955 (July 28, 2004) ("our final rule for mandatory [ballast-water management for U.S. waters] does not address NOBOBs"). The Coast Guard explains that NOBOBs are often fully loaded with cargo, and consequently cannot safely conduct a full ballast-water exchange at sea. Importantly, however, the Coast Guard acknowledges:

> *NOBOBs have the potential to carry [ANS] in their empty tanks via residual ballast water and/or accumulated sediment.* Once NOBOBs enter the Great Lakes, discharge some or all of their cargo and take on ballast water, this water mixes with the residual water and sediment and if this mixed ballast water is subsequently discharged into the Great Lakes, may provide a mechanism for [ANS] to enter the Great Lakes.

70 Fed.Reg. 51831, 51832 (August 31, 2005) (emphasis added).

Recognizing this threat, the Coast Guard announced in 2004 that it "is in the process of establishing ballast-water-discharge standards and evaluating shipboard treatment technologies." 69 Fed.Reg. 44952, 44955. The Coast Guard also stated that "[b]allast water discharge standards will be the subject of future rulemaking." *Id.* In the four years since, however, the Coast Guard has not done any further rulemaking regarding ballast-water discharge standards.

What the Coast Guard has done in the meantime – on August 31, 2005 – is to issue "best management practices" for NOBOBs. These practices encourage NOBOBs to conduct either a mid-ocean ballast-water exchange or a "saltwater flushing of their empty ballast water tanks" prior to entering the Great Lakes. Whether NOBOBs adopt these practices, however, is entirely up to them.

Thus, to summarize, the Coast Guard's ballast-water regulations applicable to the Great Lakes have remained essentially unchanged since 1993. Vessels entering the Great Lakes carrying ballast water from outside the EEZ must either conduct a mid-ocean ballast-water exchange before discharging ballast water into the Great Lakes, or retain their ballast water. NOBOB vessels are essentially unregulated with respect to their ballast-water practices. They are thus free to take on ballast water in the Great Lakes, mix it with any sediment or residual water in their tanks, and then discharge the mixture into the Great Lakes.

B.

Michigan took action to address the problem of ANS in 2005. Specifically, Michigan amended its Natural Resources and Environmental Protection Act to require all vessels "engaging in port operations in" Michigan to obtain a permit from the state. Mich. Comp. Laws § 324.3112(6) (the "Ballast Water Statute"). The Ballast Water Statute provides:

> Beginning January 1, 2007, all oceangoing vessels engaging in port operations in this state shall obtain a permit from the department. The department shall issue a permit for an oceangoing vessel only if the applicant can demonstrate that the oceangoing vessel will not discharge aquatic nuisance species or if the oceangoing vessel discharges ballast water or other waste or waste effluent, that the operator of the vessel will utilize environmentally sound technology and methods, as determined by the [Michigan Department of Environmental Quality], that can be used to prevent the discharge of aquatic nuisance species.

Id.

Pursuant to this provision, the Michigan Department of Environmental Quality ("MDEQ") issued a "Ballast Water Control General Permit" ("General Permit") in 2006. All oceangoing vessels are required to purchase a General Permit before engaging in port operations in Michigan. To obtain a General Permit, a vessel operator is required to fill out a three-page application and pay a $75 application fee and a $150 annual fee. The General Permit authorizes the vessel to engage in port operations in Michigan through January 1, 2012, so long as the vessel complies with the requirements of the General Permit.

To comply with the General Permit, all vessels must submit notification reports to the MDEQ at least twenty-four hours prior to engaging in port operations in Michigan. Each report must include, among other things, the vessel's name, port destination, the date and type of its last ballast-water-management practice (e.g., ballast-water exchange or saltwater flushing), and the total volume or weight of ballast water on board the vessel.

Other reporting requirements depend on whether the vessel will discharge ballast water in Michigan. Vessels that will not discharge ballast water are required to include in the notification report a "certification that ballast water will not be discharged into the waters of the state." Vessels that *will* discharge are authorized to do so only if they first treat their ballast water with one of four methods specified in the General Permit. Those are: (1) hypochlorite treatment, (2) chlorine dioxide treatment, (3) ultraviolet light radiation treatment preceded by suspended solids removal, or (4) deoxygenation treatment. The requirements for each treatment method are detailed in the General Permit.

* * *

II.

* * *

C.

1.

Plaintiffs claim the permit requirement is preempted by federal law. Preemption can be express or implied. Express preemption occurs when Congress "explicitly state[s]" that it intends a statute to have that effect. *Jones v. Rath Packing Co.*, 430 U.S. 519, 525, 97 S.Ct. 1305, 51 L.Ed.2d 604 (1977). Implied preemption comes in two forms, field and conflict preemption. Field preemption occurs when "the scheme of federal regulation is sufficiently comprehensive to make reasonable the inference that Congress 'left no room' for supplementary state regulation." *Ohio Mfrs. Assoc. v. City of Akron*, 801 F.2d 824, 828 (6th Cir.1986). Field preemption also occurs when an "Act of Congress . . . touch[es] a field in which the federal interest is so dominant that the federal system will be assumed to preclude enforcement of state laws on the same subject." *Ray v. Atlantic Richfield Co.*, 435 U.S. 151, 157, 98 S.Ct. 988, 55 L.Ed.2d 179 (1978). Conflict preemption occurs when a provision of state law "actually conflicts with federal law." *City of Akron*, 801 F.2d at 828.

It is undisputed that there is no express preemption here. Congress did not expressly state in NANPCA or NISA that it intended to preempt state law. Federal law will only preempt the permit requirement, therefore, if Congress has occupied the field in which the permit requirement falls, or if the requirement actually conflicts with federal law. We examine each type of implied preemption in turn.

a.

Plaintiffs argue that the permit requirement is subject to field preemption. Specifically, they contend that "two pertinent [federal] statutes" – NISA and NANPCA – leave no room for enforcement of the Ballast Water Statute. Before addressing that contention directly, however, we must do two things: first, define the relevant field; and second, determine whether, as the district court held, that field is one in which state regulation is affirmatively preserved by means of NISA's "savings clause."

NISA neatly defines the relevant field in this case. NISA's purpose is "to prevent unintentional introduction and dispersal of nonindigenous species into waters of the United States through ballast water management and other requirements." 16 U.S.C. § 4701(b)(1). Under the structure of the statute, this purpose encompasses two distinct fields: first, the *"prevention "* of ANS introduction into the Great Lakes, which includes measures "to minimize the risk of introduction of aquatic nuisance species," *id.* § 4722(c)(1) (emphasis added); and second, the *"control "* of ANS dispersal after introduction, which includes measures such as "eradication of infestations, reductions of populations, development of means of adapting human activities and public facilities to accommodate infestations, and prevention of the spread of aquatic nuisance species from infested areas." *Id.* § 4722(e)(1) (emphasis added).

The Ballast Water Statute falls in the field of ANS prevention. The Statute seeks to prevent introduction of ANS into Michigan waters; it says nothing about controlling them *after* introduction. Hence, this field – the prevention of ANS introduction – is the relevant one for our preemption analysis.

We next consider whether NISA's savings clause preserves state regulation in this field. The clause states: "Nothing in this chapter shall affect the authority of any State or political subdivision thereof to adopt or enforce control measures for aquatic species, or diminish or affect the jurisdiction of any State over species of fish and wildlife." 16 U.S.C. § 4725. The district court held that the clause saved the Ballast Water Statute from preemption, reasoning that "[t]he saving clause alone makes it difficult to comprehend that Congress intended to occupy this entire field[.]"

We respectfully disagree. The savings clause concerns a different field than the one at issue here. As Plaintiffs persuasively point out, the clause preserves only state authority to "adopt or enforce *control* measures[.]" 16 U.S.C. § 4725 (emphasis added). The clause is silent as to *prevention* measures. These, as discussed above, are terms of art in NISA. And because the savings clause preserves only state authority to adopt ANS control measures, it is inapposite to the question whether Congress intended to preempt the field of ANS prevention measures.

So we now turn to that question. In doing so, we are guided by the "oft-repeated" principle that Congress' intent is the "ultimate touchstone in every preemption case." *Medtronic, Inc. v. Lohr*, 518 U.S. 470, 485, 116 S.Ct. 2240, 135 L.Ed.2d 700 (1996). "In deciding whether a federal law pre-empts a state statute, our task is to ascertain Congress' intent in enacting the federal statute at issue." *Shaw v. Delta Air Lines, Inc.*, 463 U.S. 85, 95, 103 S.Ct. 2890, 77 L.Ed.2d 490 (1983).

Implied preemption being precisely that – implied – Congress's intent to preempt is often divined inferentially, by measuring the comprehensiveness of federal legislation in the field, or by assessing the dominance of the federal interests reflected in that legislation. *See supra* at Section II.C.1. But those are not the only means of divining Congressional intent. There may be cases where – even absent the direct means of express preemption, on the one hand, or an applicable savings clause, on the other – a statute's text indirectly reveals whether Congress intended its rules to be exclusive in a particular field.

This is such a case. The trail starts with NISA's statement that "resolving the problems associated with aquatic nuisance species will require the participation and cooperation of the Federal Government and State governments." 16 U.S.C. § 4701(15). Thus we know that states can – and indeed must – have a role with respect to ANS "problems"; the question, then, is whether that role is limited to ANS "control," or extends also to "prevention."

Other sections of NISA provide an answer to that question. In § 4723 – entitled, sensibly enough, "Regional coordination" – Congress ordered the creation of a "Great Lakes panel" to "coordinate, where possible, aquatic nuisance species program activities in the Great Lakes region that are not conducted pursuant to this chapter." *Id.* § 4723(a)(1)(D). The term "[a]quatic nuisance species program activities" is defined by § 4722 to include not only ANS "control" measures, *see* § 4722(e), but also ANS "*[p]revention* " measures "to minimize the risk of introduction of aquatic nuisance species to waters of the United States. *Id.* § 4722(c)." Thus we know that Congress contemplated ANS prevention measures "in the Great Lakes region that *are not conducted pursuant to this chapter.*" *Id.* § 4723(a)(1)(D) (emphasis added).

That leaves only the question whether the reference to ANS prevention measures "not conducted pursuant to this chapter" includes measures conducted by the states. For several reasons, we believe that it does. First, the federal statutes addressing the problem of ANS – namely, NISA and NANPCA – of course fall within NISA's "chapter." That suggests that the entities conducting the activities referenced in § 4723(a)(1)(D) are acting pursuant to state, rather than federal, authority. Second, the activities are to be "coordinate[d]" by a "Great Lakes panel" that includes representatives of "State and local agencies[.]" *Id.* § 4723(a)(1). Given that state agencies typically do not "coordinate" the activities of federal agencies, this language too suggests that the referenced activities are conducted by the states.

NISA's next section makes this conclusion inescapable. That section invites (but does not require) state governors to submit "state aquatic nuisance species management plans," *id.* § 4724, to a "Task Force" comprised of senior federal officials, including the Commandant of the Coast Guard, the Secretary of Agriculture, and the Director of the United States Fish and Wildlife Service. *Id.* § 4721. These plans should, among other things, "identify and describe *State and local programs for* environmentally sound *prevention* and control *of the target aquatic nuisance species.*" *Id.* § 4724(a)(2)(A) (emphasis added). That reference standing alone makes clear that Congress intended for state ANS prevention measures to continue after the enactment of NISA.

Moreover, if the Task Force approves a state's plan, the state is eligible to receive grants from the United States Fish and Wildlife Service. Thus, not only does NISA make clear that state ANS prevention measures are permissible; it actually expresses a conditional willingness to *pay* for them.

NISA's text thus reveals that Congress expressly contemplated ANS prevention measures – in the "Great Lakes region" no less, *id.* § 4723(a)(1)(D) – that are conducted by the states. Indeed, it encourages them. Federal law therefore does not preempt the field of ANS prevention measures.

It bears mention that the Coast Guard – which is the agency administering NISA – agrees with our conclusion. The Coast Guard stated in 2004 that

> *the congressional mandate is clearly for a Federal-State cooperative regime in combating the introduction of [ANS] into U.S. waters from ship's [sic] ballast tanks. This makes it unlikely that preemption, which would necessitate consultation with the States under Executive Order 13132, will occur.*

69 Fed.Reg. 32864, 32868 (emphasis added). Moreover, in response to comments requesting that the Coast Guard coordinate its ballast-water-management program with state programs to "eliminate duplicative reporting requirements," the Coast Guard expressly stated that "*each State is authorized under NISA to develop their own regulations if they feel that Federal regulations are not stringent enough.*" *Id.* at 32865 (emphasis added). That is precisely what Michigan has done here.

In 2005, the Coast Guard reiterated its position that NISA does not preempt state ANS prevention measures. Specifically, in response to a comment-similar to Plaintiffs' complaints here-that "a federal approach to preventing invasions in the Great Lakes is needed whereas a State-by-State piece-meal approach is not," the Coast Guard responded:

> The Coast Guard agrees that a federal approach is more amenable than a patch-work of state NOBOB management programs. . . However, *NISA does allow for states to develop their own [ANS] prevention measures.*

70 Fed.Reg. 51831, 51832 (emphasis added). That is an unequivocal recognition that NISA does not preempt the field of ANS prevention. And the Coast Guard made that recognition notwithstanding the same policy objections that Plaintiffs make here.

Plaintiffs assert that the Coast Guard had earlier taken a contrary view. Specifically, in promulgating its 1993 Great Lakes regulations – which required oceangoing vessels carrying ballast water from beyond the EEZ either to conduct a saltwater ballast-water exchange or to retain their ballast water – the Coast Guard made the following statement, under the heading, "Federalism":

> Standardizing the minimum requirements for vessels entering the Great Lakes after operating in waters beyond the EEZ is necessary to effectively help prevent additional introductions of nonindigenous species. Therefore, the Coast Guard intends this rule to preempt State

and local regulations that are *inconsistent* with the requirements of this rule.

58 Fed.Reg. 18330, 18333 (emphasis added).

Contrary to Plaintiffs' contention, however, this statement envisions a conflict-preemption regime, not a field-preemption one. The statement actually implies that the Coast Guard interprets NISA to allow state ANS prevention regulation. Indeed, the whole predicate of this statement is that states *can* impose additional prevention requirements on vessels entering the Great Lakes, so long as those requirements are not "inconsistent with" the Coast Guard's own "minimum" requirements. Thus, contrary to Plaintiffs' assertion, this statement is entirely consistent with the Coast Guard's later statements that NISA does not preempt the field of ANS prevention.

Plaintiffs also argue that the federal interest in "international maritime regulation" supports a finding of field preemption here. It is true, as Plaintiffs point out, that the Supreme Court emphasized the federal interest in "national and international maritime commerce" in *United States v. Locke*, 529 U.S. 89, 108 (2000). But the Locke Court discussed that interest primarily in holding that "in this area there is no beginning assumption that concurrent regulation by the State is a valid exercise of its police powers." *Id.* Accordingly, we have not applied any such "beginning assumption" in favor of preserving state regulatory power here.

What *Locke* does not do is convert a statutory inquiry into a metaphysical one. Plaintiffs essentially argue that certain aspects of maritime commerce are inherently federal and thus not subject to state regulation of any kind. And they cite various passages from *Locke* in support of that argument. Plaintiffs fail to recognize, however, that the passages they cite from *Locke* – concerning, for example, "tanker" operation and staffing, and "tanker" design and construction – are themselves based on a *federal statute*, namely, the Ports and Waterways Safety Act of 1972 ("PWSA"). Thus, contrary to Plaintiffs' implication, the issue in Locke was not whether, in the nature of things, maritime regulation is somehow inherently federal. The issue instead was "the scope of appropriate local regulation *under the PWSA*[.]" *Locke*, 529 U.S. at 108, 120 S.Ct. 1135 (emphasis added). Accordingly, *Locke* held that *"Title II of the PWSA "* – and not some abstract federal interest in maritime regulation – establishes a field preemption regime with respect to "the 'design, construction, alteration, repair, maintenance, operation, equipping, personnel qualification, and manning' of tanker vessels." *Id.* at 112, 120 S.Ct. 1135 (emphasis added).

The problem with Plaintiffs' argument, then, is that it is unmoored to any federal statute. No one contends that the PWSA applies here. The PWSA "applies to a tank vessel[,]" 46 U.S.C. § 3702(a), which is in turn defined to "mean[ ] a vessel that is constructed or adapted to carry, or that carries, *oil or hazardous material in bulk* as cargo or cargo residue[.]" 46 U.S.C. § 2101(39) (emphasis added). None of the Plaintiffs allege that its ships include oil tankers, or that the PWSA otherwise applies in this case. Consequently, *Locke*'s specific holdings regarding the PWSA's preemptive effect upon various aspects of tanker regulation are simply inapposite in this case. Plaintiffs have identified no federal interest that supports a finding that Congress intended to preempt the field of ANS prevention.

b.

"Even where Congress has not completely displaced state regulation in a specific area, state law is nullified to the extent that it actually conflicts with federal law." *Hillsborough County*, 471 U.S. at 713. Conflict preemption occurs when either (1) "compliance with both federal and state regulation is a physical impossibility," *Florida Lime & Avocado Growers, Inc. v. Paul*, 373 U.S. 132, 142-43 (1963); or (2) the state law "stands as an obstacle to the accomplishment and execution of the full purposes and objectives of Congress." *Hines v. Davidowitz*, 312 U.S. 52, 67 (1941).

Here, it is not physically impossible to comply with both Michigan's permit requirement and NISA. Pursuant to the permit requirement, owners of "oceangoing vessels engaged in port operations" in Michigan must pay $225 in fees and fill out several forms. None of those things is impossible.

Nor does the Ballast Water Statute "stand[ ] as an obstacle to the accomplishment and execution of the full purposes and objectives of Congress." *Hines*, 312 U.S. at 67. NISA's purpose is "to prevent unintentional introduction and dispersal of nonindigenous species into waters of the United States through ballast water management and other requirements." 16 U.S.C. § 4701(b)(1). That purpose is shared, not obstructed, by the Ballast Water Statute. The Statute furthers that purpose by requiring vessel owners to provide information to the MDEQ regarding their ballast-water practices. Vessels that do not discharge ballast water in Michigan must provide a certification to that effect. Vessels that will discharge ballast water must submit information such as the date of their last ballast discharge, the origin of their ballast water, and the volume of their proposed discharge. None of this obstructs NISA's purposes in the least.

The permit requirement does not conflict with NISA or the Coast Guard's regulations promulgated pursuant to it. The requirement therefore is not preempted by federal law.

D.

Plaintiffs claim the Ballast Water Statute violates the so-called "dormant" Commerce Clause because, they say, the Statute burdens interstate commerce. It is undisputed – before this Court at least – that the Ballast Water Statute does not "favor in-state economic interests over out-of-state interests." *Brown-Forman Distillers Corp. v. New York State Liquor Auth.*, 476 U.S. 573, 579 (1986). It instead imposes its burdens evenhandedly. Statutes that so impose their burdens "will be upheld unless the burden imposed on such commerce is clearly excessive in relation to the putative local benefits." *Pike v. Bruce Church, Inc.*, 397 U.S. 137, 142 (1970).

The Ballast Water Statute need not provide a perfect solution to the problem of ANS in order to pass this test. Plaintiffs conceded in the district court that "[i]nvasive species pose a serious threat to the ecosystem," and are "an acute problem which must be solved." *See also* Appellants' Br. at 9 ("non-indigenous species may disrupt the local aquatic ecosystem, killing or displacing native fish and plant life"). Moreover, as noted above, Congress predicted in 1990 that-wholly apart from ecological harm-economic harm from the zebra mussel alone could total $5 billion by the year 2000. Thus, to the extent the permit requirement even marginally reduces the problem of ANS introduction, its local benefits would be very large.

In contrast, the burdens imposed by the permit requirement – an application fee of $75, a yearly fee of $150, and the completion of a few forms – are *de minimis. See Ferndale Labs., Inc. v. Cavendish*, 79 F.3d 488, 495 (6th Cir.1996) (rejecting a Commerce Clause challenge to an Ohio statute requiring all wholesalers of prescription drugs to fill out a two-page registration application and pay a $100 annual fee, because, *inter alia*, "[w]e do not consider the $100 fee a burden").

The district court therefore held that Plaintiffs could not, under any circumstances, show that the permit requirement's burdens clearly exceeded its benefits. Plaintiffs argue, however, that the issues of benefit and burden are factual in nature, and that they should be permitted to develop a record on those issues before their claim is adjudicated.

We need not await that factual development to affirm the dismissal of Plaintiffs' claim. Indeed, there is no need to conduct the *Pike* balancing at all. The reason, as explained below, is that the Commerce Clause has not been dormant here.

The Commerce-Clause power belongs to Congress, not the courts. The purpose of the dormant Commerce-Clause doctrine is to "safeguard[ ] Congress' latent power from encroachment by the several States." *Merrion v. Jicarilla Apache Tribe*, 455 U.S. 130, 154 (1982). Accordingly, "we only engage in [dormant Commerce-Clause] review when Congress has not acted or purported to act." *Id.* "Once Congress acts, courts are not free to review state taxes or other regulation under the dormant Commerce Clause." *Id.*

NISA was an exercise of Congress's power under the Commerce Clause. And in enacting NISA, as shown above, Congress expressly contemplated, and indeed encouraged, state participation in ANS prevention measures. We would lose our constitutional bearings if we were to hold that the Commerce Clause, in its dormancy, strikes down state regulation that Congress, in *actively exercising* its power under the Clause, expressly contemplated. We therefore affirm the dismissal of this claim.

E.

Only Plaintiffs' substantive due process claim remains. Plaintiffs argue that, "[b]y purporting to require owners and operators of oceangoing vessels to procure permits to operate even if they do not discharge ballast water containing aquatic nuisance species . . . [,] the Ballast Water Statute deprives plaintiffs of their property without due process of law in contra-vention of the Fourteenth Amendment of the United States Constitution."

It is undisputed that the permit requirement is subject only to ration-al-basis review. Accordingly, the permit requirement "need only be ration-ally related to a legitimate government purpose" to be upheld. *Thompson v. Ashe*, 250 F.3d 399, 407 (6th Cir.2001). This test is "highly deferential; courts hold statutes unconstitutional under this standard of review only in rare or exceptional circumstances." *Doe v. Michigan Dept. of State Police*, 490 F.3d 491, 501 (6th Cir.2007). "[A]ny *conceivable* legitimate governmen-tal interest" will do, *37712, Inc. v. Ohio Dept. of Liquor Control*, 113 F.3d 614, 620 (6th Cir.1997) (emphasis added); and even then it is constitution-ally irrelevant whether the conceivable interest actually underlay the en-actment of the challenged provision.

Here, Michigan has a legitimate state interest in protecting its waters from further introductions of ANS from ballast-water discharges by ocean-going vessels. The permit requirement is rationally related to advancing that interest: it requires vessels to provide the MDEQ with information regarding their ballast water and ballast-water-management practices, thereby allowing the MDEQ to monitor compliance with its requirements. And it requires vessels that say they will not discharge ballast water in Michigan to certify that fact, which may make them more inclined to do as they say, since a false certification is a felony. All of this conceivably could reduce the introduction of new ANS into Michigan waters. The permit re-quirement therefore does not violate Plaintiffs' substantive due process rights.

III.

Michigan, for undisputedly legitimate reasons, has enacted legislation of a type expressly contemplated by Congress. We have no basis to disrupt the result of those democratic processes. The August 15, 2007 order of the district court is affirmed.

San Francisco Baykeeper v. United States Army Corps of Engineers

United States District Court for the Northern District of California, 2002.
219 F.Supp.2d 1001.

■ WILKEN, DISTRICT JUDGE.

The case involves the environmental impact of two construction pro-jects initiated by the Port of Oakland (Port). The first project, the Oakland Harbor Navigation Improvement Project (dredging project), is jointly fund-ed by the Port and Defendant United States Army Corps of Engineers (Corps). It will deepen the channels and berths at the Port from forty-two feet to fifty feet. The second project, the berths project, will create four new container berths and two new cargo terminals at the Port. The berths project is dependent on receipt of a Corps permit to dredge and fill as necessary to create the new berths.

Because of the Corps' involvement in the projects, the consultation provisions of both the National Environmental Policy Act (NEPA), and the Endangered Species Act (ESA), are implicated. Plaintiffs move for summary judgment that Defendant federal agencies violated both NEPA and the ESA by failing adequately to analyze and disclose the potential environmental consequences of the projects. Defendants oppose the motion and cross-move for summary judgment that their consultation and analysis satisfied their statutory obligations.

BACKGROUND

* * *

B. Statutory and Regulatory Requirements

In its capacity as the action agency with respect to the dredging project and the regulating agency with respect to the berths project, the Corps was required to satisfy statutory and regulatory obligations under NEPA and to engage in consultation with Defendant Fish and Wildlife Service (FWS) and Defendant National Marine Fisheries Service (NMFS) pursuant to section 7 of the ESA.

1. NEPA

NEPA is the basic "national charter for protecting the environment." 40 C.F.R. § 1500.1(a). It requires all federal agencies to prepare an environmental impact statement (EIS) for "major federal actions significantly affecting the quality of the human environment." The responsible federal agency may first choose to prepare an environmental assessment (EA), a preliminary document which "briefly provides sufficient evidence and analysis for determining whether to prepare an environmental impact statement or a finding of no significant impact." After considering the EA, the agency may then decide to issue either a finding of no significant impact (FONSI) or a more detailed EIS.

NEPA is procedural in nature. It does not require "that agencies achieve particular substantive environmental results." *Marsh v. Or. Natural Res. Council,* 490 U.S. 360, 371 (1989). Rather, it requires agencies to collect, analyze and disseminate information so that "the agency will not act on incomplete information, only to regret its decision after it is too late to correct." *Id.* Federal agencies comply with NEPA by carrying out this procedural mandate.

2. ESA

Section 7 of the ESA, requires every federal agency to ensure that any action that it funds, authorizes, or carries out is not likely to jeopardize the continued existence of any listed species or adversely modify the critical habitat of any such species. FWS and NMFS (collectively, "consulting agencies") share responsibility for administering the ESA, with FWS responsible for listing terrestrial and freshwater species, and NMFS charged with protecting marine and anadromous species.

If a federal agency determines that a proposed action may affect listed species or their critical habitat, the agency must initiate consultation with the appropriate consulting agency, either FWS or NMFS. An action agency may satisfy the requirements of section 7(a)(2) by initiating either "informal" or "formal" consultation with the appropriate consulting agency. Informal consultation is "an optional process that includes all discussions, correspondence, etc., between the Service and the federal agency . . . designed to assist the [action agency] in determining whether formal consultation is . . . required." "If during informal consultation it is determined by the [action agency], with the written concurrence of the [consulting agency], that the action is not likely to adversely affect listed species or critical habitat, the consultation process is terminated and no further action is necessary."

However, if informal consultation fails to resolve the question of harm to a listed species, the action agency must engage in formal consultation. Formal consultation procedures require the consulting agency to evaluate the effects of the proposed action on the listed species, and issue a "biological opinion" (BO), which states whether the action is likely to jeopardize the continued existence of the species (hereinafter, "jeopardy finding" or "no jeopardy finding"). The issuance of the biological opinion terminates the formal consultation process.

C. Agency Consultation and Analysis

1. NEPA

a) Dredging Project

In February, 1998, the Corps, jointly with the Port, issued a Draft Environmental Impact Statement/Environmental Impact Report (Draft EIS) for the dredging project. In response to the Draft EIS, Plaintiffs submitted a series of comments asserting that the Corps had failed to evaluate the impact of non-native species entering the San Francisco Bay through ballast water discharges. The final EIS for the dredging project was published in May, 1998.

The May, 1998 Final EIS recognized that "discharge of ballast water is the primary mechanism by which exotic marine and freshwater organisms are spread around the world today" and that "the establishment of unwanted species . . . can seriously upset the existing ecological balance at the discharge location." The Final EIS listed several variables that could affect the likelihood that "any particular discharge of ballast water will lead to the introduction of an invasive species." Although the Corps identified several relevant variables, it found that there were too many "uncertainties along the potential path of introduction" to quantify the risk of establishment of an invasive species through ballast water discharge.

Instead, the Corps focused on volume of ballast water discharged, on the theory that a reduction in quantity of ballast water would correlate to a reduced risk of invasive species transported in ballast water. The Corps concluded that, upon completion of the dredging project in 2010, total ballast water discharged would be less than if no project were undertaken. The Corps based this conclusion on the projected increase in the number of post-Panamax vessels using the Port if the project were completed. Because these vessels are wider and more stable, they typically use less ballast water. Consequently, by accommodating these ships in the Port, ballast water discharges would decrease.

Based on the reduction in total ballast water discharged, and the inability to quantify the other factors relevant to the invasive species problem, the Corps concluded that "no increased risk of invasive species introduction can be determined to qualify as a significant cumulative impact of the proposed project." Although it had concluded that there would be no significant impact, the Corps nevertheless identified specific mitigation measures relevant to reducing the risk of invasive species. It recommended that the Port adopt certain of these mitigation measures.

The Corps supplemented the Final EIS with an "Information Report, Corrections, and Updates on the Final EIS/EIR" (Information Report) in March, 1999, and the Port released "Revisions to the Final EIR" (EIR Revisions) in September, 1999. The Information Report and EIR Revisions contained changes in the analysis of the invasive species issue. Specifically, the Final EIS had assumed that the dredging project would result in increased vessel traffic to the Port. A subsequent analysis undertaken in conjunction with the berths project revealed that increased vessel calls were attributable only to the berths project. With only the dredging project, cargo throughput would remain virtually static while ship calls would decrease over time because of the increased use of post-Panamax ships. Consequently, the Corps concluded that the dredging project "would not cause a significant impact from ballast water discharges."

b) Berths Project

As lead agency under the California Environmental Quality Act (CEQA), the Port issued a detailed EIR for the berths project in April, 1999. This document concluded that the berths and dredging projects, in combination, would likely reduce the risk of introducing invasive species into the Bay.

In support of this conclusion, the EIR reasoned as follows. First, the EIR determined that the berths project alone would increase the volume of ballast water discharged by five percent and, therefore, would have a significant adverse impact on the environment. However, the EIR also noted that the combination of all future Port projects would decrease ballast water discharge below the discharge levels if no future projects were implemented and below the levels likely to occur if only the berths project was implemented. Although the EIR presumed a cumulative reduction in ballast water discharge, in recognition of the project specific impact, it nevertheless imposed mitigation measures. In particular, the Port relied on Port Ordinance 3516, which required ships visiting the Port to release ballast water in the ocean, thereby reducing the risk that any invasive species may be introduced into the Bay. The combination of the cumulative reduction in ballast water and the likely consequence of Port Ordinance 3516 led the Port to conclude that "the risk of invasive species introduction via ballast water discharges at the Port [will be reduced] to a level far lower than under either existing conditions or the no-project alternative."

In May, 1999, the Corps completed an Environmental Assessment (EA), rather than a full EIS for the berths project. The Corps incorporated the Port's EIR analysis into its final EA. The Corps issued a Permit Evaluation and Decision Document on December 3, 1999, determining that issuance of the requested permit would result in no significant impact.

2. ESA Consultation

a) FWS Consultation

On January 26, 1998, the Corps initiated formal consultation with FWS pursuant to section 7(a)(2) of the ESA. On June 23, 1998, FWS submitted a draft BO on the effects of the proposed projects on the endangered California least tern and the endangered California brown pelican. After receiving comments on the draft BO, and providing responses, FWS issued a final BO covering both the berths and dredging projects.

The FWS BO noted that ballast water discharges are a major vector for introducing non-native species into the Bay–Delta ecosystem. The biological opinion acknowledged that there "is a probability but not a certainty" that the future introduction of invasive species could affect listed species. However, the BO concluded that because ballast water discharges to the San Francisco Bay would decrease as a consequence of anticipated changes in shipping practices and the Port's open-ocean exchange ordinance, the projects were not likely to jeopardize listed species or their habitat.

b) NMFS Consultation

In March, 1999, the Corps initiated consultation with NMFS to determine the impact of the dredging project on steelhead and winter-run chinook salmon. On August 9, 1999, after reviewing the Corps' Final EIS, NMFS issued a letter of concurrence concluding that the dredging project would not adversely effect listed species or critical habitat.

On September 27, 1999, the Corps initiated formal consultation with NMFS for the berths project. Like FWS, NMFS described the adverse effects of exotic species on the Bay–Delta ecosystem, focusing on the impact to salmonid species. Relying on the anticipated reduction in ballast water discharge, NMFS concluded that the project was not likely to jeopardize listed species or critical habitat.

* * *

DISCUSSION

Plaintiffs' first and second claims for relief relate to the Corps' alleged failure to comply with the analysis and public disclosure requirements of NEPA. The third claim for relief alleges that the Corps failed to comply with section 7(a)(1) of the ESA requiring federal agencies to "carry[ ] out programs for the conservation of endangered species and threatened species." The fourth, fifth and sixth claims for relief address the adequacy of the biological opinions and the letter of concurrence issued by FWS and NMFS.

A. NEPA (First and Second Claims for Relief)

* * *

2. Insufficient Discussion of Invasive Species Problem

Plaintiffs also contend that the dredging project EIS and the berths project EA produced by the Corps were inadequate under NEPA. As noted above, the fundamental purpose of NEPA is to provide disclosure of significant environmental risks before a project is undertaken. Consequently, "an EIS is in compliance with NEPA when its form, content and preparation substantially 1) provide decision-makers with an environmental disclosure sufficiently detailed to aid in the substantive decision whether to proceed with the project in light of its environmental consequences, and 2) make available to the public, information of the proposed project's environmental impact and encourage public participation in the development of that information." *Trout Unlimited v. Morton*, 509 F.2d 1276, 1283 (9th Cir.1974).

Plaintiffs contend that both the dredging project EIS and the berths project EA failed to satisfy this notice function because these documents do not contain sufficient discussions of potential invasive species impacts and causes. Plaintiffs raise three specific areas where they allege that the EIS and EA skirted the vital environmental issues raised by the projects.

First, Plaintiffs contend that the documents contain an insufficient discussion of the potential impacts of invasive species on the San Francisco Bay. Plaintiffs point out that invasive species can lead to multiple, diverse ecological and economic problems. In particular, the transplanting of non-native species creates a significant danger to native species by disrupting the local food chain and altering the physical environment in which local species thrive. Invasive species, therefore, may lead to endangerment or extinction of indigenous species. Plaintiffs argue that the Corps failed to discuss these potential impacts in its EIS or EA and, therefore, failed to satisfy its obligation to provide adequate information on which to base policy.

Defendants contend that the discussion of potential invasive species impacts was reasonable and sufficient under the circumstances. This is so because the Corps was only required to provide a "full and fair discussion of the significant environmental impacts" of the action. Both the EIS and the EA concluded that the projects in question would have no significant adverse environmental impact with respect to invasive species. The Corps, therefore, had no obligation to discuss the potential consequences of the introduction of invasive species into the Bay. In other words, Defendants argue that they had no legal obligation to provide a detailed description of impacts that the projects will not have.

If the Corps' determination that the projects are more likely to have a mitigating effect on the risk of introduction of invasive species was correct, it was not obliged to provide a detailed discussion of the environmental consequences of potential invasive species introduction. Consequently, whether the discussion of invasive species impacts was sufficient is dependent on whether the Corps' determination of risk was adequate. Plaintiffs raise two challenges to the Corps' assessment of the invasive species risk. First, Plaintiffs argue that the Corps failed to consider all of the relevant factors that contribute to the introduction of invasive species. Second, Plaintiffs contend that the Corps' analysis of the one risk factor it did consider—ballast water discharge volume—was flawed.

Plaintiffs argue that in order properly to assess the invasive species risk, the Corps was required to consider the numerous factors that contribute to that risk, including the source of the ballast water, the time in transit, and the location of the discharge of ballast water. In fact, in both the EIS and the EA, the Corps considered all of the risk factors identified by Plaintiffs. However, the Corps concluded that it was unable to base its determination on these factors because no methodology existed to quantify these various risks.

> No established methodology has been developed to quantify the risk that ballast water discharges will result in introduction of invasive species. Nor is there a generally accepted methodology to predict the potential environmental impact of the introduction of invasive species.

> The likelihood that any particular discharge or volume of discharge of ballast water will lead to the introduction of an invasive species and result in environmental impact depends upon a large number of uncertainties along the path of introduction. Information to satisfy these variables as they relate to the myriad of potential invasive species is either unavailable or incomplete, and the cost and complexity of collecting and analyzing such information would be prohibitive.

[citing the administrative record]

> Because of the complexity of the issue, there are currently no models in use to predict which exotic species will become established in a new location.

[citing a different part of the administrative record]

The Corps reasonably concluded that it was unable accurately to quantify the myriad variables that Plaintiffs have identified. Moreover, even assuming that the Corps could accurately quantify these variables, Plaintiffs do not explain how the Corps could translate these variables to meaningful predictions of the projects' environmental impact. Instead of speculating as to what these uncertain impacts might be, the Corps chose a relatively simple model: if the volume of ballast water decreases, the number of invasive species living in that ballast water is likely to decrease, thereby decreasing the possible environmental impact of invasive species. Plaintiffs' suggestions would add complexity to this model without increasing its predictive accuracy. Accordingly, the Corps did not act arbitrarily by relying on the volume of ballast water discharged as the determinative variable in its invasive species analysis.

In order to survive review, however, the ballast water discharge calculations must be founded "in reasoned evaluation of the relevant factors." *Marsh,* 490 U.S. at 378. In its EA for the berths project, the Corps concluded that the combination of the dredging and berths project would both expand capacity at the Port of Oakland and decrease the total ballast water into the Bay. Because the dredging project would increase the percentage of cargo transported by larger, more efficient post-"Panamax" vessels, the number of vessel calls per existing berth is expected to decrease substantially. In addition, the newer vessels are wider and more stable and therefore typically carry only one-fourth of the ballast water required by the older Panamax vessels. On the balance, the total ballast water discharged by vessels calling on the Port of Oakland is expected to drop from 6.0 million metric tons in 1996 to 3.5 million metric tons in 2010.

Plaintiffs take issue with several assumptions underlying this analysis. Plaintiffs contend that the Corps improperly relied on "personal communications" to estimate the ballast water discharge of post-Panamax vessels. Plaintiffs cite no authority that only written information may be relied on in an EIS and the Court declines to impose such a requirement. The individuals who provided the oral information, and their respective capacities, were disclosed in the EIS, thereby enabling verification by interested parties.

In addition, Plaintiffs contend that the Corps used uncertain ballast water volume estimates and arbitrarily based its no significant impact finding on discharge estimates from 2010. Plaintiffs note that, based on the estimates provided by the Port, the project will increase ballast water discharged at the Port in 2003. The discharges under the "with project" scenario are then expected to decrease over time as changes in the fleet mix result in a higher proportion of post-Panamax vessels. Plaintiffs also point out that "equally reasonable" assumptions of discharge volume could lead to an estimated increase in ballast water discharged in 2010.

Plaintiffs concede that the Corps' selection of the year 2010 as a basis for analysis and its ballast water discharge estimates were reasonable assumptions entitled to deference by this Court. Plaintiffs' argument is that given the numerous non-quantifiable risk factors relevant to the invasive species question and the uncertain nature of the Corps' assumptions, the Corps was obliged to recognize this uncertainty and provide a thorough discussion of potential impacts in the event that unanalyzed risks proved relevant or uncertain assumptions proved incorrect. In support of this argument, Plaintiffs rely on 40 C.F.R. § 1502.22. That regulation provides guidelines to agencies faced with "incomplete or unavailable information" when "evaluating reasonably foreseeable significant adverse effects on the human environment." The regulation defines "reasonably foreseeable impacts" as

> impacts which have catastrophic consequences, even if their probability of occurrence is low, provided that the analysis of the impacts is supported by credible scientific evidence, is not based on pure conjecture and is within the rule of reason.

40 C.F.R. § 1502.22(b)(1).

In this case, the Corps was not required to describe the potentially severe consequences of invasive species introduction into the Bay because there was no "credible scientific evidence" that such impacts would occur. The information in the record, much of it submitted by Plaintiffs during the comment period, indicated that there was no established methodology for foreseeing the arrival, survival and impacts of an invasive species. "Predictions of what species will invade, and where and when invasions will occur, remain one of the more elusive aspects of biological invasion science." The National Sea Grant College Program, *The Role of Shipping in the Introduction of Nonindigenous Aquatic Organisms to the Coastal Waters of the United States (other than the Great Lakes) and an Analysis of Control Options* (the Shipping Study), at xxiii. "A more basic problem is that there are generally far too few data to demonstrate how introduced species affect native species. Furthermore, we have no idea under what circumstances such effects ripple or cascade through the food web of the receiving community." Townsend, *Invasion Biology and Ecological Impacts of Brown Trout, Salmo trutta in New Zealand,* Biological Conservation, vol. 78 at 13. In this context, Plaintiffs' proposed discussion of risk factors and potential impacts would have been "based on pure conjecture." 40 C.F.R. § 1502.22(b)(1). The disclosure purpose of NEPA does not require such an exercise.

In sum, the Corps' reliance on ballast water discharge estimates to assess the impact of invasive species was not arbitrary; it was the only quantifiable measurement that correlated with the likelihood of introduction of non-native species. Although other risk factors were considered by the Corps, it reasonably determined that—in the absence of a sound scientific methodology for translating these factors into impact predictions—detailed analysis of these factors would not aid in its assessment of reasonably foreseeable impacts. Because this methodology was not arbitrary, and the Corps used reasonable assumptions to implement this methodology, its conclusion that the projects would decrease the risk of invasive species impacts was likewise not arbitrary. Furthermore, because this conclusion was well-supported, the Corps did not err in failing to provide a detailed description of possible impacts if invasive species were to be established in the Bay.

* * *

B. ESA § 7(a)(2) (Fourth, Fifth and Sixth Claims for Relief)

Plaintiffs contend that neither FWS nor NMFS satisfied the substantive requirements of § 7(a)(2) of the ESA. Specifically, Plaintiffs challenge the agencies' assessment of the projects' effects on the distribution of invasive species in the Bay–Delta ecosystem, arguing that the agencies failed adequately to evaluate the impact that the projects would have on the spread of introduced species through ballast water discharges and hull fouling.

1. Scope of Action Area

First, Plaintiffs argue that the agencies improperly limited the scope of their biological opinions to the immediate vicinity of the proposed projects. Section 7(a)(2) of the ESA requires the consulting agency to assess the biological impact of the proposed action on "all areas to be affected directly or indirectly by the Federal action and not merely the immediate area involved in the action." 50 C.F.R. § 402.02(d) (defining "action area"). Because invasive species can reproduce and spread to the limit of their ecological tolerances, Plaintiffs argue that the proposed actions could indirectly affect listed species found throughout the Bay–Delta ecosystem. Thus, Plaintiffs contend that FWS and NMFS should have evaluated the indirect effects of the projects on each listed species found in the San Francisco Bay estuary. Plaintiffs specifically object to FWS's focus on two endangered species that were identified in biological surveys conducted in the project area from January, 1997 through July, 1997: the California lease tern and the California brown pelican.

FWS's focus on the least tern and brown pelican was not arbitrary and capricious. Because these species were found in close proximity to the project area, they are more likely to be affected by the construction and long-term operation of the projects than other listed species in the Bay–Delta ecosystem. This approach is consistent with the ESA's focus on harm to individual listed species and their habitat rather than on the health of ecosystems as a whole. *See* 16 U.S.C. § 1536(b)(4)(C); *see also* 50 C.F.R. § 402.14(g)(1) (listing "on-site inspection" as a method for gathering "relevant information" during the formal consultation process).

It is true that neither FWS nor NMFS separately assessed the impact that invasive organisms might have on each listed species found in the Bay–Delta ecosystem. The agencies' approach reflects the difficulty inherent in predicting the introduction, dispersal, establishment, and ecological impact of invasive species. Plaintiffs' proposed methodology would require the agencies to assess the indirect effects that changed shipping patterns at the Port of Oakland would have on all listed species in the Bay–Delta ecosystem, or potentially, the West Coast of the United States. Such an analysis would necessarily require a degree of speculation not contemplated by § 7 of the ESA, which focuses on actions that are "likely to jeopardize" the continued existence of listed species. Neither FWS nor NMFS acted arbitrarily by declining to issue a jeopardy biological opinion based on these speculative effects.

2. Relevant Information

Next, Plaintiffs reprise their contention that the agencies ignored factors relevant to the introduction of invasive species. The ESA requires the consulting agencies to "review all relevant information provided by the federal agency or otherwise available." 50 C.F.R. § 402.14(g)(1). Plaintiffs argue that FWS and NMFS arbitrarily based their invasive species analyses on the volume of ballast water discharged without considering other factors that may effect the projects' impact on listed species, including the ballast water's time in transit, the location of its discharge, and the risks associated with hull fouling and other non-ballast-tank-related effects.

The record shows that the consulting agencies investigated a range of factors that affect the transport, introduction, and establishment of invasive species. Nonetheless, because the "no jeopardy" findings of both agencies relied primarily on the Corps' predicted reduction in ballast water volume, Plaintiffs are correct to suggest that other factors were minimized in the agencies' analyses.

However, Plaintiffs must also show that the agencies' decision to focus on the ballast water volume was arbitrary and capricious. Like the Corps, FWS and NMFS reasonably relied on ballast water volume to quantify the highly uncertain effects that changes in shipping patterns would have on the Bay–Delta ecosystem. Accordingly, neither FWS nor NMFS acted arbitrarily by relying on the volume of ballast water discharge as the determinative variable in their invasive species analyses.

3. Ballast Water Projections

The consulting agencies reasonably relied on projected ballast water discharges to support their "no jeopardy" findings. However, in order for that "no jeopardy" finding to survive review, the ballast water discharge calculations must be founded in "reasoned evaluation of the relevant factors." *Marsh,* 490 U.S. at 378. In its berths project EA, the Corps, considering the combined effects of the berths and dredging projects, concluded that although the projects would expand capacity at the Port of Oakland, total ballast water discharge would decrease from 6.0 million tons in 1996 to 3.5 million metric tons in 2010.

Plaintiffs contend that comparing the 2010 "with project" projections with the 1996 data does not provide a rational basis for determining the "effects of the action" under the ESA. Plaintiffs argue that rather than comparing current discharges with post-project ballast water volumes, the consulting agencies should have compared future discharges under "with project" and "without project" scenarios. In other words, Plaintiffs contend that the proper comparison is between expected ballast water discharges after project completion and expected ballast water discharges if the projects were not undertaken at all.

In evaluating the effects of the federal action, the consulting agency must consider the "past and present impacts of all Federal, State, or private actions and other human activities in the action area, the anticipated impacts of all proposed Federal projects in the action area that have already undergone . . . Section 7 consultation, and the impact of State or private actions which are contemporaneous with the consultation in process." 50 C.F.R. § 402.02(d) (defining "effects of the action"). The consulting agency then determines the effects of the action with reference to this "environmental baseline." In the present case, the "without project" scenario estimates the anticipated impacts of human activities not associated with the projects and therefore establishes the environmental baseline against which the projects must be evaluated. Thus, a comparison of the estimated "with project" and "without project" discharges is relevant to assessing the effects of the action.

As previously discussed, the Final Berths Project EIR does in fact compare projected "with project" and "without project" discharges in 2003 and 2010. However, Plaintiffs observe that this comparison reflects less favorably on the "with project" scenario than the comparison with the 1996 data. The Corps' projections show that "with project" ballast water discharges would temporarily increase relative to the "without project" alternative. After this temporary increase, the total ballast water discharge is predicted to be approximately ten percent lower under the "with project" alternative.

These figures reflect the total volume discharged and therefore do not account for the mitigating effects of the open-ocean exchange ordinance, which is intended to reduce significantly discharges to the Bay–Delta ecosystem. The parties dispute the relevance of this mitigation measure to the consulting agencies' no jeopardy conclusion. Defendants contend that their assessment of the effects of the action on listed species must include the projected benefits of the Port's mitigation measure. The mitigation measure to which Defendants refer, Port Ordinance 3516, has been partially and temporarily superceded by the passage of AB 703. However, as noted above, AB 703 will expire on January 1, 2004. Thus, while the agencies are required to consider the effects of AB 703 in assessing impacts through 2003, the ESA does not require them to speculate as to what actions the California legislature will take when the statute expires. See 50 C.F.R. § 402.02(d) (directing consulting agencies to include the impact of "contemporaneous" State actions in the environmental baseline). At a minimum, FWS and NMFS could reasonably rely on Port Ordinance 3516 as insurance against the possibility that the State ballast water management program will not be renewed in 2004.

Even if the effects of AB 703 are considered as part of the environmental baseline, the ultimate inquiry under the ESA is whether the proposed action is "likely to jeopardize the continued existence of a listed species or result in the destruction or adverse modification of critical habitat." Unlike NEPA, the ESA does not explicitly require a consulting agency to consider a "no action" alternative when issuing a biological opinion. Based on their comparison of 1996 and 2010 ballast water discharges, the agencies reasonably concluded that ballast water discharges would decline over time. Because it was reasonable to emphasize ballast water volume over other less quantifiable factors, it was also reasonable to conclude that decreases in the volume of ballast water discharged would decrease the likelihood of jeopardy to a listed species. Regardless of whether this decrease occurs because of the Port's mitigation measures, a State statute, or changes in fleet composition, the effects on listed species remain the same. Furthermore, even when compared with the "without project" alternative, the projects are predicted to result in a long-term decrease in ballast water discharge. Therefore, FWS and NMFS reasonably concluded that the projects are not likely to jeopardize listed species.

4. NMFS's Berths Project Biological Opinion

Plaintiffs also separately contest the adequacy of NMFS's finding that the berth projects would not jeopardize listed species.

a) Independent Evaluation of Berths Project

First, Plaintiffs appear to claim that because the berth project, evaluated independently, would increase ballast water discharges, NMFS acted arbitrary in issuing a "no jeopardy" finding. Plaintiffs' contention lacks merit. In fulfilling its interagency consultation obligations under § 7 of the ESA, the consulting agency must consider the "entire agency action." This includes the effects of the federal action together with the ecological impact of "interrelated and interdependent" actions. In the present case, the berth and dredging projects are closely related elements of the Port of Oakland's modernization program. Accordingly, NMFS's berths project biological opinion did not violate the ESA by considering the ecological effects of the dredging project along with those of the berths project itself.

b) Adequacy of Mitigation Measures

Next, Plaintiffs contend that the consulting agencies failed adequately to analyze the efficacy of open-ocean exchange measures in preventing impacts to listed species. Plaintiffs note that open-ocean exchange is not completely effective in removing non-native species from ballast water tanks. In addition, they observe that compliance with the ordinance is likely to be imperfect. Plaintiffs also observe that neither the port ordinance nor the State statute requires compliance if doing so would jeopardize the safety of the vessel, its crew, or its passengers.

Plaintiffs contend that NMFS acted arbitrarily by adopting the Port of Oakland's view that open-ocean exchange effectively mitigates the adverse effects of invasive species. They note several instances where NMFS considered a "zero discharge standard" for ballast water, before rejecting such options in its final biological opinion. In addition, the record shows that NMFS received comments from Plaintiffs and other members of the public encouraging it to consider alternative mitigation measures, including on-shore ballast water treatment.

In its biological opinion, NMFS explicitly recognized the concerns that Plaintiffs have raised in this action and concluded that the open-ocean exchange is not "100% effective." However, NMFS concluded that "ballast water exchange is the only [currently available] management tool to reduce the risk of ballast-mediated invasion." The record contains ample evidence to support its conclusion. *See, e.g.,* Gregory M. Ruiz & Jeffery Crooks, *Scope of Work for the Proposed Study on Efficacy of Ballast Water Exchange* 3 (Jan. 3, 2001 draft) (noting that "[m]id-ocean exchange is currently the only management strategy available for commercial ships to reduce quantities of non-indigenous coastal plankton in ballast water"); Herbert Engineering Corp., *Ballast Water Management for Containerships* 3 (Sept. 7, 1999) (observing that open-ocean exchange "greatly mitigates the threat of invasions"); Jan. 28, 1999 Letter from Dames & Moore to Jody Zaitlin, Port of Oakland at 3 (concluding that "there is little evidence to support a statement that . . . shore-based treatment is a cost effective option").

In summary, the record supports NMFS's conclusion that open-ocean exchange is an appropriate and effective means for reducing the adverse ecological impact of invasive species. In such cases, the Court is not permitted to substitute its judgment for that of the agency. Therefore, Plaintiffs' contention that NMFS acted arbitrarily in failing to recommend additional mitigation measures to the Corps lacks merit.

Furthermore, Plaintiffs misconstrue NMFS's role in implementing the ESA. First and foremost, the ESA requires the consulting agency to determine whether a federal action is likely to jeopardize the continued existence of an endangered species. If, as in the present case, the agency issues a no jeopardy finding, the consulting agency's role in crafting mitigation measures is limited to making an advisory recommendation to the action agency. Because these recommendations "are not intended to carry any binding legal force," the Court must limit its inquiry to determining whether the mitigation measures effectively prevent the project from jeopardizing listed species. For the reasons stated above, the open-ocean discharge ordinance meets this standard. Accordingly, NMFS did not act arbitrarily by relying on the ordinance to support its no jeopardy finding.

NOTES & QUESTIONS

1. A variety of issues have arisen relating to invasive species under the ESA. As one example, environmental groups have argued that addition of invasive species, or even protection of existing ones, is a "take" in violation of section 9 of the ESA. In *Coalition for a Sustainable Delta v. Koch*, 2009 WL 2151842 (E.D. Cal. 2009), the plaintiffs had argued that game restrictions on the nonindigenous striped bass were allowing it to continue to exist in the Delta ecosystem and consume endangered Chinook salmon, thereby taking them in violation of the ESA. The plaintiffs lost their motion for summary judgment, but the loss

was without prejudice as to this ESA claim, but rather a matter of insufficient evidence for summary judgment (there were conflicting expert opinions regarding the pros and cons of the striped bass for the ecosystem, with some noting that they also eat other predators that would otherwise eat Chinook, and calling them a keystone species). In addition to being an interesting example of take by invasive species, this story also raises the specter of invasive species as keystone species. The striped bass were introduced back in 1879, so a significant amount of time had passed and a new food-web design had taken hold. As the counter-argument went, disrupting this food web by allowing the top predator to be over-fished could have devastating consequences. How should we make such choices after the passage of time? Is there a statute of limitations on vilifying invasive species? If an altered ecosystem is able to reach functionality again, do we go with that, or try to get back what was lost?

2. Beyond merely raising the invasive species issue as something that should be taken into account in a jeopardy analysis, research suggests that for ESA-listed salmon this problem might be greater than the primary factors usually considered in the salmon context (habitat alteration, harvest, hatcheries, and the hydrosystem). *See* Katie A. Barnas, A. Michelle Wargo Rub & Beth L. Sanderson, *Nonindigenous Species of the Pacific Northwest: An Overlooked Risk to Endangered Salmon?*, 59 BIOSCIENCE 243 (2009) (reporting on a study that quantified the impact of nonindigenous species on threatened and endangered salmonids in the Pacific Northwest).

3. The use of herbicides, a common method of responding to invasive plant species, has also been challenged under both NEPA and the ESA, as harmful to fish and wildlife. *See, e.g., League of Wilderness Defenders/Blue Mountains Biodiversity Project v. United States Forest Service*, 2012 WL 2522878 (D. Or. 2012). What other solutions might we have for going after invasive plant species without the use of harmful chemicals? The people of the Chattanooga Tennessee Public Works Department managed to make very productive use of goats—goats who like eating the ubiquitous kudzu vines. While the approach raised some eyebrows (and made some headlines, and even inspired a humorous song), it was actually quite effective, albeit just in the small area of the project. You can read the whole story at: Theo Emery, *In Tennessee, Goats Eat the 'Vine That Ate the South'*, N.Y. TIMES, June 5, 2007, available at http://www.nytimes.com/2007/06/05/us/05goats.html?_r=1. Interestingly, "Chattanooga is not the only city to seek a four-legged alternative to herbicides. For several years, Tallahassee, Fla., fought kudzu with sheep. Spartanburg, S.C., tried using goats, but stopped after they were stolen." *Id.* Might this idea spread? If not, what might be some of the obstacles to such an approach becoming more widely used?

4. In March 2012 the Coast Guard issued a new rule tightening restrictions on ballast water. The summary of the rule states:

> The Coast Guard is amending its regulations on ballast water management by establishing a standard for the allowable concentration of living organisms in ships' ballast water discharged in waters of the United States. The Coast Guard is also amending its regulations for engineering equipment by establishing an approval process for ballast water management systems. These new regulations will aid in controlling the introduc-

tion and spread of nonindigenous species from ships' ballast water in waters of the United States.

33 C.F.R. § 151.1510. Of course, the ballast water saga will likely continue for quite a while longer.

C. INVASIVE SPECIES AND CLIMATE CHANGE

David A. Strifling, *An Ecosystem-Based Approach to Slowing the Synergistic Effects of Invasive Species and Climate Change*
22 DUKE ENVIRONMENTAL LAW & POLICY FORUM 145 (2011).

Introduction

Spring is springing earlier these days, an average of ten days earlier than it did just twenty years ago. This scientific phenomenon, called "spring creep," is often ascribed to climate change. Perhaps unsurprisingly, spring creep affects individual species differently. It is a boon to some and a mortal danger to others. However, scientists researching these effects have identified one common theme: spring creep typically favors "invasive species," defined as non-native species that cause environmental or economic harm, or both, and which generally appear to be adaptable to a broader range of climatic conditions. At one site, for example, invasive species now flower eleven days earlier than native species, almost perfectly matching the spring creep. The earlier flowering time confers an advantage on the invasive species, which compete with native species. Warmer temperatures also facilitate the physical movements of invasive species along previously inaccessible pathways and to previously inhospitable environments. Interestingly, it appears that the invasive species return these favors. By upsetting the delicate balance in native ecosystems, invasive species simultaneously increase that ecosystem's susceptibility to climate change-related stressors, and reduce its potential for carbon sequestration.

Even considered separately, invasive species and climate change are each likely to cause significant damage to human health and the environment, as well as enormous economic losses. For example, invasive species place a heavy strain on agricultural systems, they are responsible for a significant percentage of species extinctions, and they are vectors for the spread of disease. Recent studies estimate that invasive species cause worldwide economic damage of about $1.4 trillion yearly, or about 5% of the global economy. For its part, climate change "may well alter the lives of every person on the planet." The economic damages flowing from climate change are less certain, but recent estimates range from 5 to 20% of worldwide gross domestic product.

To consider these phenomena separately, however, ignores the powerful multiplier effect each one exerts on the other. Although a sizable body of research has addressed policy responses to climate change, very little scholarship has addressed the policy response to the invasive species conundrum. And no scholars appear to have addressed the confluence of the two. This article fills that gap, positing that new scientific evidence showing the synergies between climate change and invasive species compels policymakers to consider climate change and invasive species jointly. The synergy between the two will compound the environmental and economic damages each phenomenon causes, and the policy response to each concern should ideally consider the synergistic effects of the other.

*   *   *

... [F]ederal policymakers should adopt an ecosystem-based approach to controlling invasive species that has the potential to address both threats. Specifically, federal agencies should identify key ecosystems and ecosystem services they wish to preserve against the impacts of climate change and concentrate invasive species prevention and control on those same ecosystems, as well as on the pathways by which invasive species may reach them. Reducing the overall threat of invasive species by supporting ecosystem health is a low-risk strategy to combat the effects of climate change, no matter what level of severity those impacts eventually have.

I. The Synergistic Effect of Climate Change and Invasive Species

The connections between the environmental phenomena of climate change and invasive species are not immediately apparent. Indeed, at first glance they appear entirely disparate. One is believed to be global in nature, largely caused by the releases of certain gases into the atmosphere. The other proceeds at the ecosystem level, as invasive plants and animals slowly rise to replace their native counterparts. The first has been the subject of exhaustive policy debates and negotiations in the United States and abroad, while the second has largely escaped such scrutiny. But these two phenomena have much more in common than the readily apparent production of negative effects on human health, the environment, and the economy. In fact, this part will show that the two are deeply connected in ways that scientists are only beginning to understand. In turn, this means that any adaptation or mitigation measures directed at combating one of the two will have effects on the other, and that policymakers should consider those effects when designing such measures.

A. Climate Change

Nearly twenty years ago, the United Nations Framework Convention on Climate Change defined "climate change" as "a change of climate which is attributed directly or indirectly to human activity that alters the composition of the global atmosphere and which is in addition to natural climate variability observed over comparable time periods." The United States is among 194 parties to the Convention. The "ultimate objective" of the Convention is to "achieve . . . stabilization of greenhouse gas concentrations in the atmosphere at a level that would prevent dangerous anthropogenic interference with the climate system." Unfortunately, even the most optimistic assessment would likely conclude that little progress has been made toward that goal.

A detailed examination of the causes and effects of climate change is beyond the scope of this paper; those issues have been exhaustively studied by scientists, economists, policymakers, and legal scholars. Suffice it to say that although the climate change phenomenon continues to be hotly debated in political circles, there exists a "current scientific consensus that significant global climate change is happening, human activities are a significant contributing cause of that change, and the associated public health and welfare impacts are sufficiently serious to warrant climate change legislation." The most recent report from the Intergovernmental Panel on Climate Change (IPCC) predicted that the continued gradual warming of the globe will, to varying degrees of certainty, cause a host of negative effects including sea-level rise, ocean acidification, and increased frequency of extreme weather events such as cyclones and droughts. The report further predicts that these physical effects will directly affect human health and the environment through decreased agricultural yields, migration of climate refugees from coastal areas, and adverse effects on available water quality and quantity, among many others.

B. Invasive Species

By the late 1990s scientists and policymakers had begun to study climate change intensively, and in 1997, the Kyoto Protocol was adopted. Awareness of the invasive species problem had also increased, but to a lesser extent. In February of 1999, President Bill Clinton issued Executive Order 13,112 (the "Order") to "prevent the introduction of invasive species and provide for their control and to minimize the economic, ecological, and human health impacts that invasive species cause." The Order defined "invasive species" as a non-native species "whose introduction does or is likely to cause economic or environmental harm or harm to human health."

That definition makes plain that not all non-native species are invasive. Most non-native species cause no economic or environmental harm; indeed, many are beneficial, including cattle, wheat, soybeans, and tulips. Nevertheless, "invasive" species in the true sense of the Order's definition "inhabit all regions of the United States and every nation," and they cause significant economic harm in the United States every year. Recent estimates put the worldwide economic damages in excess of $1.4 trillion annually, with the harm in the United States alone at over $120 billion per year.

Moreover, economic damage estimates do not fully value the nonmonetary damages involved in the displacement of native organisms or the destruction of ecosystems. Costs typically not considered include the impact on natural ecosystems, the extinction of native species, lost water-purification capability, aesthetic and recreational impacts, and weakened resistance to impacts of invasions by other species in the future. Instead, the estimates are more likely to focus on the effects on commercial activities such as timber or fishery production.

Invasive species have a long history of wreaking havoc on commerce and the environment. For example, the boll weevil devastated the United States cotton crop for a number of decades in the early twentieth century.

And it is undeniable that recent years have seen growth in both the environmental havoc wreaked by invasive species as well as the legal discord over them. Two examples illustrate these issues: the invasion of Walden Pond in Massachusetts, and the potential invasion of the Great Lakes by several species of Asian carp.

1. Case Study: Walden Pond

Henry David Thoreau spent two years living in semi-isolation at Walden Pond. Walden; or Life in the Woods, published in 1854, documented Thoreau's observations of the surrounding plant and animal life, among other things, and eventually turned the site into a cultural and environmental icon. Today, Thoreau might find much of the flora and fauna unrecognizable. Harvard biologists studying the pond and its surroundings have found that 30% of the plants once found there are already extinct, and another 30% are so rare that they are likely to become extinct soon. Walden "natives" such as lilies, orchids, roses, and dogwoods are less capable of flowering earlier to match the earlier spring. "The winners, by and large, are the non-native plant species." Slowly but surely, the native vegetation is being replaced by invasive species.

In 1851, Thoreau initiated a data-collection effort that is possibly unequaled in the annals of American biology. Beginning that year, and in the 160 years since, biologists have collected local data related to temperature, species abundance, and first flowering date. More recently, Harvard biologists divided the data set into native, invasive, and non-native non-invasive species based on data from the U.S. Department of Agriculture (USDA). The biologists then examined the historical data to determine whether the three types of species differed significantly in their ability to respond to changing seasonal temperatures.

The biologists found that the invasive species tracked seasonal variations in temperature much better than did the native and non-native non-invasive species. Over the past century, the invasive plants' flowering time has shifted to an average of eleven days earlier than that of native species. One species hastened its flowering time by an astonishing twenty-three days. Other studies have shown that this innate ability to quickly adjust to changes in the seasons is not limited to invasive plants. For example, a researcher studying the Sawtooth National Recreational Area in central Idaho found that invasive insects adjust their behaviors to account for season creep on a yearly basis, much more quickly than their native host forests, which can take decades to do so.

During the same period at Walden, the invasive species "significantly increased in abundance . . . relative to native . . . species." According to the researchers, the study provided the strongest proof to date of the synergy between climate change and invasive species. The biologists concluded that "[a]s climate change accelerates, non-native species' ability to respond favorably will likely exacerbate the ecological and economic problems that result from their success."

2. Case Study: Great Lakes

While Walden Pond demonstrates the competitive success of invasive species in certain ecosystems, the saga of the threatened invasion of the Great Lakes by several species of Asian carp illustrates how the lack of a cohesive federal program to control invasive species can lead to staggering litigation and administrative costs. As with Walden Pond, it is a story that begins over a century ago.

During much of the nineteenth century, the cities of Chicago and St. Louis engaged in a struggle to determine which of them would become the economic and population hub of the Midwest; as late as 1870, St. Louis remained the "larger and richer" city. Chicago was handicapped in this pursuit by the flow of its sewage and industrial waste from the Chicago River into the city's primary harbor in Lake Michigan, thus polluting water intakes for its municipal water supply and causing several outbreaks of typhoid fever.

The city, backed by the state of Illinois, solved its problem with an amazing feat of civil engineering, consisting of two massive projects. First, it constructed a series of locks and related facilities to reverse the flow of the Chicago River. Second, to provide an outlet for the reversed flow, it created an artificial connection between the Lake Michigan watershed and the Mississippi River watershed via an entirely manmade body of water, the Chicago Sanitary and Ship Canal.

The practical consequences of the project were remarkable. With a single stroke, Chicago had not only solved the problem of its waste polluting its own harbor, it had in fact diverted that waste to the Mississippi River, where it flowed downstream to its rival St. Louis. Outraged, the state of Missouri promptly sued Illinois in an original action in the U.S. Supreme Court. *Missouri v. Illinois*, 200 U.S. 496 (1906). The Court ultimately ruled in Illinois' favor because it found that sufficient facts did not then exist to justify Missouri's economic and health-related fears. "There is nothing which can be detected by the unassisted senses—no visible increase of filth, no new smell." But the Court also struck a note of caution:

> It is a question of the first magnitude whether the destiny of the great rivers is to be the sewers of the cities along their banks or to be protected against everything which threatens their purity. To decide the whole matter at one blow by an irrevocable fiat would be at least premature.

In the long run, as the Court seemingly recognized, the greatest consequence of Chicago's project may be ecological, not economic. Today, the artificial connection between the Mississippi River and the Great Lakes is no longer primarily a path for untreated sewage; instead, it has become a pathway for an invasion of the Great Lakes.

The story of the invasion dates back almost half a century, to 1963, when the state of Arkansas imported grass carp, a species of Asian carp, for use in aquaculture and research. A decade later, Arkansas introduced two more species of Asian carp, bighead and silver carp, for fish pond vegetation control. The practice eventually spread to fish farms in numerous other states. These species of Asian carp are enormous fish. For example, silver carp can grow to three feet long and weigh up to sixty pounds; bighead carp can grow four and a half feet long and weigh up to eighty pounds. Occasionally, the carp species were accidentally released into the wild, and numerous carp escaped during the flooding of the Mississippi River in the 1990s. Intentionally or accidentally, the Asian carp escaped into the lower Mississippi basin and rapidly migrated through nearly the entire basin, with their populations increasing exponentially.

The spread of the voracious predators did not go unnoticed. In 2006, the U.S. Fish and Wildlife Service (FWS) opined that "Asian carp pose the greatest immediate threat to the Great Lakes ecosystem." By 2009, silver carp had been observed in the Chicago Sanitary and Ship Canal, very near to Lake Michigan. If the carp enter the Great Lakes, they could very well overwhelm native species and thereby devastate a fishery the value of which has been estimated at billions of dollars annually.

Attempting to forestall that outcome, in 2009 the state of Michigan, joined by several other Midwestern states, attempted to launch an original action in the U.S. Supreme Court against Illinois. The petitioning states sought the severance of the connection between the Great Lakes and the Mississippi; in other words, for Chicago to close the canal system.

The petitioning states faced a serious problem. ... [F]ederal law provides scant authority to prevent such an invasion, or to control it after the fact. As such, the petitioning states were forced to root their petition in nuisance-based common law causes of action. Moreover, the petitioning states lacked a statutory vehicle under which to bring the action, and so sought to engage the Supreme Court's jurisdiction via two attempts perhaps best described as long shots. The first attempt was a petition to reopen a set of cases related to Illinois' diversion of water from Lake Michigan that the Court had initially settled in 1929 and had reopened several times since. Second, the petitioning states concurrently requested that the Court exercise its original jurisdiction to enter a preliminary injunction to effectively close the locks and prevent the passage of the carp.

The Supreme Court denied the petitioning states' motion for an injunction on March 22, 2010, *Wisconsin v. Illinois*, 130 S. Ct. 1934 (2010), and a month later the Court denied the petitioners' request to re-open the diversion cases. Since then, President Obama named a "carp czar," John Goss, to coordinate federal efforts to keep the carp out of the Great Lakes, convened a "carp summit" at the White House, and proposed a $78 million plan to keep Asian carp out of the Great Lakes. Meanwhile, in July 2010 Michigan and four other states filed a new lawsuit in federal district court naming as defendants the Army Corps of Engineers and the Metropolitan Water Reclamation District of Greater Chicago. Although the suit adds an Administrative Procedure Act based claim, it primarily relies on the same legal theory as the earlier suits: that the defendants have created an ongoing public nuisance by operating locks, gates, and other infrastructure through which the carp can enter the Great Lakes. *Michigan v. U.S. Army Corps of Eng'rs*, 2010 WL 5018559, at *21 (N.D. Ill. Dec. 2, 2010).

The enormous expenditure of public resources in such high stakes, "long-shot" cases are necessitated by the traditional failure of federal law to address the invasive species problem in any uniform or effective manner ....

C. Synergies

Despite exhaustive study, the effects of climate change are still not fully understood. Every day, however, scientists uncover more about how the climate affects the environment, and vice versa. As the Walden Pond case study demonstrates, scientists have recently begun to examine the direct and indirect synergies between climate change and invasive species. A 2010 study funded by the World Bank revealed evidence of at least three direct synergies between the two.

First, climate change will provide invasive species with new opportunities to compete with native species. For reasons yet unknown, invasive species are typically more adaptable than native species. They can survive in a broader range of conditions and are better able to withstand the rising temperatures and shifting seasons that scientists predict will result from climate change. Moreover, warmer temperatures may facilitate the physical movements of invasive species. This could occur because invasive species will be able to move along new pathways to previously inaccessible environments and higher elevations, or because invasive species will be transported via extreme wind and wave events, which are expected to become more commonplace as climate change takes hold.

Second, some scholars and conservationists have advocated the concept of "assisted migrations," under which humans would facilitate the physical movement of species whose continued existence is jeopardized by changing environmental conditions to a less threatening location. This strategy could end up doing more harm than good if the relocated species becomes invasive in its new location. Professor Jonathan Wiener has advocated a "risk-risk" analysis to fully consider the countervailing risks associated with policymakers' decisions to protect human health and the environment, and a similar analysis would likely be appropriate before any major facilitated movements are undertaken.

Third, the presence of invasive species is likely to increase an ecosystem's susceptibility to climate change-related stressors and to reduce its carbon sequestration potential. For example, certain invasive insects can increase tree mortality rates, and invasive grasses may induce fires in some tropical ecosystems, thus devastating native forests. This will weaken the ecosystem's resistance to climate change.

In addition to these three direct synergies, climate change and invasive species will indirectly influence each other in several respects. First, "disturbance events" such as hurricanes and other natural disasters are expected to become more common due to climate change. By increasing the stress on local ecosystems, such events will make it easier for invasive species to establish themselves. Moreover, well-meaning relief efforts to natural disaster locations may unintentionally result in the direct introduction of new invasive species to nearby ecosystems.

Finally, climate change is likely to change ecosystem functions and interactions in ways that are currently difficult to predict. Given the innate ability of invasive species to survive under a broader range of conditions than native species typically can, this too is likely to favor the proliferation of invasive species over natives. In fact, scientists studying the spring creep phenomenon, like those at Walden Pond, could conceivably point to the rising dominance of invasive species in a particular ecosystem as corroborative evidence of climate change, when coupled with rising temperatures in that same ecosystem.

Considered separately, invasive species and climate change are each likely to cause significant economic losses and damage to the environment and human health. Scientists predict that climate change will cause a panoply of serious, irreversible calamities, threatening "the basic elements of life for people around the world." These impacts will include reduction in drinkable water supplies, eventually threatening up to one-sixth of the world's population; declining crop yields, especially in developing nations; increases in vector-borne diseases, such as malaria; rising sea levels causing increasing floods and even permanent population displacement in coastal areas; mass extinction of species, especially in vulnerable ecosystems; and the potential for abrupt, sudden events such as the collapse of polar ice sheets or the drying of the Amazon rain forest.

Like climate change, invasive species also have the potential to inflict significant damages on human health and the environment. First, invasive species may place a heavy strain on agricultural systems through the introduction of new weeds, pests, and diseases. This will have a domino effect as the weakened agricultural production will cause rising prices at best, and food shortages and security issues at worst, especially in developing nations.

Moreover, invasive species will wreak irreversible havoc on biodiversity. Invasive species are already suspected to be responsible for one-half to two-thirds of species extinctions.

Finally, invasive species are often vectors for the spread of diseases. For example, an increased range for mosquitoes from hot and wet climates may result in a similar geographic increase in the scope of many infectious diseases such as malaria. As of July 2008, the U.S. Centers for Disease Control and Prevention reported that the West Nile Virus, an invasive pathogen common to humans and animals, had caused 1,086 deaths in the United States.

The potential economic impacts are also considerable, albeit "difficult to estimate." Recent studies have estimated that invasive species cause economic damages of about $1.4 trillion annually, or about 5% of the global economy. In the United States, these estimates likely do not include the increasing costs of interstate litigation over invasive species like the Asian carp dispute discussed above.

The economic losses from climate change are more uncertain. As noted above, recent predictions put the estimated economic damages due to that phenomenon at 5 to 20% of global GDP. This means that even without considering synergies, the combined economic damages from invasive species and climate change are in the range of 10 to 25% of global GDP. The synergistic effects discussed above will only increase those damages.

* * *

III. Improving Federal Policy Via an Ecosystem-Based Approach

Existing scholarship exhaustively discusses potential policies and legislation to address the threat of climate change. Re-plowing that ground is beyond the scope of this article. Beginning to address the intractable problem of invasive species is daunting enough for policymakers. Accordingly, this part of the article is limited to broadly sketching out the potential scope of and vehicles for improving the federal response to invasive species, while taking into account and responding to those species' synergistic effects with climate change.

A. The Scope and Substance of an Ecosystem-Based Approach

Several threshold questions confront policymakers beginning to discuss the scope of a new effort to address the invasive species problem. The first, and perhaps the most important of these questions goes to the appropriate target for new resources tasked to the problem. Existing law and policy has typically focused on one of two avenues: attempting either to eradicate or control invasive species that are already present or to prevent the entry of new invasive species. Efforts focused on eradication run headlong into the truth of Dr. Lodge's pronouncement that "invasion is forever," quoted at the beginning of this article. It is exceedingly difficult to institute immediate emergency measures that save food supplies already devastated by invasive pests, or that rescue native species from the brink of extinction.

On the other hand, efforts that focus on prevention, such as NANCPA and the Lacey Act, have weaknesses of their own. Invasive species manifest in new environments by at least three methods: accidental introduction; intentional introduction due to anticipated benefits, where the introduction has unanticipated side effects or spreads beyond its initial confines; and intentional, malicious introduction. It is nearly impossible for a single policy instrument to address all three pathways. Moreover, the Lacey Act depends on a "dirty list" approach, meaning that it only applies to invasive species that have been administratively added to a list of prohibited species. Non-listed species may easily slip through the cracks. A corollary to the "dirty list" approach could be to issue permits for the beneficial introduction of non-native species, but such an approach would carry heavy social costs in the form of an increased administrative load.

An alternative approach is to focus on ecosystem-based protection and adaptation. An ecosystem is "the sum total of the organisms living in a particular place, the interactions between these organisms, and the physical environment in which they interact." In the past few years, methodologies that focus on ecosystem-based environmental protection efforts and policies have gained increasing popularity in a variety of contexts, including climate change. Moreover, such an approach allows a simultaneous focus on fostering resistance and adaptation to both climate change and invasive species. Both threaten the fundamental ecosystem services upon which humans have come to rely over thousands of years.

To date, agencies and policymakers charged with wildlife management have typically analyzed threats to native plants and animals on a species-specific basis. However, that view is changing based on trends in conservation biology that urge a broader focus in light of the interconnectedness of life within particular ecosystems. This approach, while rooted in scientific theory, is not without support in the law. For example, the Congressionally-stated purpose of the ESA is to "provide a means whereby the ecosystems upon which endangered species and threatened species depend may be conserved."

The ecosystem-level approach has similar appeal in the context of invasive species management. Specifically, I suggest that where invasive species threaten ecosystems, agencies should focus on preserving biodiversity within ecosystems and maintaining the functionality of ecosystem services. This would allow agencies to consider the "domino effects" – both positive and negative – that the entry of an invasive species might have for an entire ecosystem, as opposed to effects of the invasion on individual species or particular types of harm, all with the ultimate goal of preserving biodiversity and the ecosystem services described above. Agencies could, perhaps, employ some version of the precautionary principle to determine whether a departure from equilibrium that invasive species cause in a particular ecosystem is likely to have positive or negative consequences. While this is a more complex level of analysis, it will likely yield more helpful results.

An ecosystem-level approach has several potential advantages over traditional, national-level responses to the synergistic problems that invasive species and climate change pose. First, ecosystem-based adaptation has already been recognized as "part of an overall . . . strategy" for responding to climate change. It "uses the range of opportunities for the sustainable management, conservation, and restoration of ecosystems to provide services that enable people to adapt to the impacts of climate change." It also aims to strengthen the defenses of ecosystems and people to climate change by maintaining and increasing the natural resilience of ecosystems. One "key element" of ecosystem-based adaption is "the reduction of other major threats, which when compounded with the effects of climate change would push a system beyond its ability to function properly." Stanley W. Burgiel & Adrianna A. Muir, INVASIVE SPECIES, CLIMATE CHANGE AND

ECOSYSTEM-BASED ADAPTATION: ADDRESSING MULTIPLE DRIVERS OF GLOB-
AL CHANGE 13 (2010). Without doubt, invasive species are one of those
"other major threats," the reduction of which increases the ability of ecosystems to resist the impacts of climate change. The ecosystem-based approach should be able to accommodate this additional consideration.

Second, the identification and prioritization of key ecosystems and ecosystem services to protect against climate change can also provide order to
the federal response to invasive species. Specifically, once those key ecosystems and ecosystem services have been identified, the involved federal
agencies can concentrate prevention and response efforts on the invasive
species that inhabit these prioritized ecosystems as well as on blocking
pathways by which additional invasive species may enter them. This prioritization of critical ecosystems should make the policy response more manageable on both administrative and economic levels, because policymakers
will not need to address every single problem nationwide.

Finally, the flexibility inherent in an ecosystem-based approach will
allow iterative adjustment of federal practices as agencies gain more information about the impending effects of climate change. Within a particular
ecosystem, policymakers might choose to focus on prevention of invasive
species entry through particular pathways, or on control of invasive species
already present. The success or failure of such efforts can inform similar
undertakings at other ecosystems, or could perhaps eventually be generalized to regular procedures to be followed to protect general types of ecosystems. Such an "adaptive management" approach to environmental policy
helps policymakers "respond to uncertainty by undertaking reversible actions and studying outcomes to reduce uncertainty at the next decision
point."

In the specific context of the potential invasion of the Great Lakes, for
example, an ecosystem-based approach has two distinct advantages. First,
had such an approach been in place in the late nineteenth century, the city
of Chicago might have been required, or at least encouraged, to find a different solution to its sewage problems given the obvious issues involved
with connecting two ecosystems that had previously been entirely distinct.
Second, at present, policymakers could choose to address the specific pathways by which the carp may enter the Great Lakes, instead of being forced
to make those decisions on a much larger scale (that is, policymakers would
not have to set policy that would govern all ecosystems everywhere).

Ultimately, the selected strategy must address a broad range of concerns, potentially including federalism issues and ensuring broad-based
participation by state and local policymakers; the extent to which cost-
benefit calculations should play a role in selecting particular ecosystem-
based projects; an information-gathering dimension to allow the best possible decision making; and the selection of a liability scheme for noncompliance.

The liability scheme deserves further emphasis and study because in
the context of invasive species, very small actions can result in enormous

consequences, and this makes the selection of a liability scheme extremely complex. Take, once again, the example of the Asian carp. A negligence-based scheme would likely be unhelpful because those responsible for introducing the carp are unavailable, unable to make good individually on the tremendous economic consequences, or even non-negligent in their actions. Likewise, a strict liability scheme would likely be unworkable because the potential economic harms are so vast that those responsible may be unable to shoulder them.

B. The Policy Vehicle for an Ecosystem-Based Approach

Even if policymakers agreed on the ecosystem-based approach that this article recommends, they would still need to select an appropriate vehicle to implement that approach. There are at least three potential options: a new or amended federal statute, modification of Executive Order 13,112, and unilateral administrative action by one agency or a group of agencies.

A new or amended federal law would give policymakers the most flexibility to fashion a remedy. However, the difficulties of passing a major environmental statute in the modern era have frequently been expounded upon, and these concerns seem especially valid in the current weak economic climate. Most commentators agree that Congress has not enacted a major environmental statute since the Clean Air Act Amendments of 1990, and this difficulty manifested again in Congress's failure to pass a climate change statute in 2010 despite Democratic majorities in both houses of Congress and a Democratic president. Yet, the passage of a less ambitious statute with less economic impact might not be impossible. Congress has passed numerous such statutes recently. For example, in the context of invasive species, Congress has authorized funding in the National Defense Authorization Act for Fiscal Year 2008 and the Water Resources Development Act of 2007. It has also passed several substantive measures, including the Great Lakes Fish and Wildlife Restoration Act of 2006 and the Public Lands Corps Healthy Forests Restoration Act of 2005. A statute of appropriate scope would likely find broad support in Congress.

Executive Order 13,112, which drives much of existing federal policy related to invasive species control, provides another option to implement the ecosystem-based approach. The very text of the Order directs NISC to "encourage planning and action at . . . ecosystem-based levels." This could be accomplished by executive amendment or reissuance of the Order (perhaps the path of least political resistance), or by congressional action to adopt some of the Order's precepts into law. Both approaches are not without flaws, however. Mere amendment or reissuance of the Order would leave it subject to the same difficulties it now faces: the absence of agency prioritization due to the lack of underlying legislative authority, the potential for turf wars among the many agencies that administer the Order, and most worrisome of all, the potential that a future executive could simply discontinue the Order. Congressional adoption of some or all of the Order would eliminate the last concern, but is subject to the same impediments just discussed relating to the difficulty of passing federal environmental legislation. Moreover, any solution based on the Order will have to resolve the "alphabet soup" approach of numerous federal agencies, each with an ill-defined stake in solving invasive species issues.

The third option for an ecosystem-based approach would be for individual agencies to implement it through regulations or in day-to-day practice. For example, the FWS could issue regulations or interpretive guidance pursuant to the ESA that required consideration of potential invasive species impacts when preparing future recovery plans for threatened or endangered species. This approach is the most flexible in terms of allowing expert agency decision makers to select particular ecosystems for prioritization, perhaps based on the presence of endangered native species or other considerations.

This option is limited by the impact that any one agency can impose on the overall invasive species problem, as well as the danger, as with the Order, that a future administration could simply change agency policy. Moreover, some individual agencies may lack the necessary authority to promulgate regulations that address invasive species control or permitting.

Conclusion

It is possible, of course, that federal agencies can continue to muddle through, separately addressing the problems of invasive species and climate change as if operating in a vacuum. Yet federal policy can have the greatest impact on these synergistic threats if it responds with a synergistic response of its own, namely ecosystem-based management. Consideration of the "domino effects" that invasive species can have in an ecosystem will provide agencies and policymakers with a more complete and biologically accurate picture of the potential impacts on the ecosystem. Such an approach could fill many of the gaps in the patchwork of federal laws and policies now governing the invasive species problem, and would be a low-risk method to combat both invasive species and climate change induced impacts, even though we are uncertain as to the precise level of severity of those impacts.

CHAPTER 17

CLIMATE CHANGE AND ITS IMPACT ON BIODIVERSITY

Chapter Outline:
A. Introduction to Anthropogenic Climate Change
B. Impacts on Biodiversity and Ecosystems
C. Problem Areas in Focus
    1. Arctic and Antarctic regions
    2. Fisheries
    3. Forests
    4. Endangered Species Act Listing Process
D. Biodiversity and Geoengineering in Response to Climate Change

A. INTRODUCTION TO ANTHROPOGENIC CLIMATE CHANGE

The terminology of climate change is always evolving: initially we used "global warming," which was a potentially misleading oversimplification, so we shifted to the broader and presently most common "climate change," and the movement is now afoot toward the arguably even more accurate "climate disruption." Whatever you call it (we'll use "climate change" in this edition), "climate change means a change of climate which is attributed directly or indirectly to human activity that alters the composition of the global atmosphere and which is in addition to natural climate variability observed over comparable time periods." United Nations Framework Convention on Climate Change (UNFCCC), Article I.

How does human activity impact something so significant? We have dramatically increased, to an unnatural level, an otherwise natural occurrence known as greenhouse gasses. This name actually goes a long way toward explaining the phenomenon. Under normal atmospheric conditions, energy from the sun enters the atmosphere, after which some of it is absorbed and some (a lot, actually) is sent back into space. How the energy is divided between these two potential outcomes determines the atmospheric temperature. The more it is sent into space, of course, the cooler the atmosphere, and vice versa. Greenhouse gasses absorb and re-emit infra-red radiation, standing in the way of some of the energy-reflection from the earth. When the energy is re-emitted, it goes both into space and back toward the earth. Because this creates a net increase in retained solar radiation, more greenhouse gasses in the atmosphere result in warmer average temperatures within the earth's atmosphere. There are natural greenhouse gasses for which we cannot take the blame (and which are not blameworthy anyway, as without them the earth's atmosphere would be inhospitably cold), but when we emit certain chemicals into the air, particularly carbon dioxide, methane, nitrous oxide, and sulphur hexafluoride, they collect in the atmosphere in unnatural quantities and contribute to the excessive greenhouse effect.

Climate change is rapidly becoming the most infamous global emergency of our time, at least when it comes to the environment. While scientists had already been concerned about it for decades, Al Gore popularized this concern and made the data more accessible in his 2006 documentary, An Inconvenient Truth. Since then, increased public awareness of the issue has placed even greater pressure on governments to work more quickly toward our globally shared goal of delaying the catastrophic consequences that are beginning to appear inevitable at some point in time.

The climate problem is not, however, a novel concern for the U.S. Congress. Indeed, it has passed climate change legislation on several occasions, all well before there was a tipping point of public attention. First was the National Climate Program Act of 1978, which had the "purpose of ... establish[ing] a national climate program that will assist the Nation and the world to understand and respond to natural and man-induced climate processes and their implications." 15 U.S.C. § 2902. In 1990 Congress passed the Global Climate Change Prevention Act, which directs the Secretary of Agriculture to research climate change in relation to agricultural and Forest Service activity. 1990 also saw a couple of other climate-related acts: the Global Change Research Act of 1990, and a 1990 amendment to the Clean Air Act entitled Stratospheric Ozone Protection). That said, the world continues to await more comprehensive U.S. climate change legislation. For an analysis of how we should go about drafting such legislation, see Richard J. Lazarus, *Super Wicked Problems and Climate Change: Restraining the Present to Liberate the Future*, 94 CORNELL L. REV. 1153 (2009). In the meantime, states have been stepping up to fill the void with their own climate laws. A useful discussion of such state programs can be found in Robert B. McKinstry, Jr. & Thomas D. Peterson, *The Implications of the New "Old" Federalism In Climate-Change Legislation: How To Function In a Global Marketplace When States Take the Lead*, 20 PAC. MCGEORGE GLOBAL BUS. & DEV. L.J. 61 (2007).

About a decade before Gore mainstreamed climate awareness, world leaders were working together to reduce greenhouse gasses in the atmosphere and thereby slow the progression of anthropogenic (human-caused) climate change. The Kyoto Protocol, in which certain ratifying countries agreed to reduce their GHG emissions, was adopted in 1997. The stated purpose of the Protocol was "stabilization of greenhouse gas concentrations in the atmosphere at a level that would prevent dangerous anthropogenic interference with the climate system. Such a level should be achieved within a time-frame sufficient to allow ecosystems to adapt naturally to climate change, to ensure that food production is not threatened and to enable economic development to proceed in a sustainable manner."

In 1988 the United Nations Environment Programme (UNEP) and the World Meteorological Association (WMO) established an international working group of leading climate scientists called the Intergovernmental Panel on Climate Change (IPCC), which is now the preeminent authority for assessing climate change. There are, at present, 195 countries with IPCC membership, which means that they have representatives in the group and approval authority for its reports. The work of the IPCC is intended to be purely scientific, with experts assessing the current state of scientific knowledge and reporting it for use in setting policy, but without prescribing policy actions themselves. That said, as you read the following IPCC report, think about how the political influence of such a large international membership might play a role in its content.

Climate Change 2007, Synthesis Report
Intergovernmental Panel on Climate Change, 2008.
http://www.ipcc.ch/pdf/assessment-report/ar4/syr/ar4_syr.pdf.

Definitions of climate change: Climate change in IPCC usage refers to a change in the state of the climate that can be identified (e.g. using statistical tests) by changes in the mean and/or the variability of its properties, and that persists for an extended period, typically decades or longer. It refers to any change in climate over time, whether due to natural variability or as a result of human activity. This usage differs from that in the United Nations Framework Convention on Climate Change (UNFCCC), where climate change refers to a change of climate that is attributed directly or indirectly to human activity that alters the composition of the global atmosphere and that is in addition to natural climate variability observed over comparable time periods.

Warming of the climate system is unequivocal, as is now evident from observations of increases in global average air and ocean temperatures, widespread melting of snow and ice and rising global average sea level

Eleven of the last twelve years (1995-2006) rank among the twelve warmest years in the instrumental record of global surface temperature (since 1850). ... The linear warming trend over the 50 years from 1956 to 2005 (0.13 [0.10 to 0.16]°C per decade) is nearly twice that for the 100 years from 1906 to 2005.

The temperature increase is widespread over the globe and is greater at higher northern latitudes. Average Arctic temperatures have increased at almost twice the global average rate in the past 100 years. Land regions have warmed faster than the oceans. Observations since 1961 show that the average temperature of the global ocean has increased to depths of at least 3000m and that the ocean has been taking up over 80% of the heat being added to the climate system. New analyses of balloon-borne and satellite measurements of lower- and mid-tropospheric temperature show warming rates similar to those observed in surface temperature.

Increases in sea level are consistent with warming. Global average sea level rose at an average rate of 1.8 [1.3 to 2.3]mm per year over 1961 to 2003 and at an average rate of about 3.1 [2.4 to 3.8]mm per year from 1993 to 2003. Whether this faster rate for 1993 to 2003 reflects decadal variation or an increase in the longer-term trend is unclear. Since 1993 thermal expansion of the oceans has contributed about 57% of the sum of the estimated individual contributions to the sea level rise, with decreases in glaciers and ice caps contributing about 28% and losses from the polar ice sheets contributing the remainder.

* * *

Observational evidence from all continents and most oceans shows that many natural systems are being affected by regional climate changes, particularly temperature increases.

There is *high confidence* that natural systems related to snow, ice and frozen ground (including permafrost) are affected. Examples are:

- enlargement and increased numbers of glacial lakes

- increasing ground instability in permafrost regions and rock avalanches in mountain regions

- changes in some Arctic and Antarctic ecosystems, including those in sea-ice biomes, and predators at high levels of the food web.

Based on growing evidence, there is *high confidence* that the following effects on hydrological systems are occurring: increased runoff and earlier spring peak discharge in many glacier- and snowfed rivers, and warming of lakes and rivers in many regions, with effects on thermal structure and water quality.

Locations of significant changes in data series of physical systems (snow, ice and frozen ground; hydrology; and coastal processes) and biological systems (terrestrial, marine, and freshwater biological systems), are shown together with surface air temperature changes over the period 1970-2004.

* * *

There is *very high confidence*, based on more evidence from a wider range of species, that recent warming is strongly affecting terrestrial biological systems, including such changes as earlier timing of spring events, such as leaf-unfolding, bird migration and egg-laying; and poleward and upward shifts in ranges in plant and animal species. Based on satellite observations since the early 1980s, there is *high confidence* that there has been a trend in many regions towards earlier 'greening' of vegetation in the spring linked to longer thermal growing seasons due to recent warming.

There is *high confidence*, based on substantial new evidence, that observed changes in marine and freshwater biological systems are associated with rising water temperatures, as well as related changes in ice cover, salinity, oxygen levels and circulation. These include: shifts in ranges and changes in algal, plankton and fish abundance in high-latitude oceans; increases in algal and zooplankton abundance in high-latitude and high-altitude lakes; and range changes and earlier fish migrations in rivers. While there is increasing evidence of climate change impacts on coral reefs, separating the impacts of climate-related stresses from other stresses (e.g. overfishing and pollution) is difficult.

*   *   *

Changes in the atmospheric concentrations of GHGs and aerosols, land cover and solar radiation alter the energy balance of the climate system and are drivers of climate change. They affect the absorption, scattering and emission of radiation within the atmosphere and at the Earth's surface. The resulting positive or negative changes in energy balance due to these factors are expressed as radiative forcing4, which is used to compare warming or cooling influences on global climate.

Human activities result in emissions of four long-lived GHGs: CO_2, methane (CH_4), nitrous oxide (N_2O) and halocarbons (a group of gases containing fluorine, chlorine or bromine). Atmospheric concentrations of GHGs increase when emissions are larger than removal processes.

Global atmospheric concentrations of CO_2, CH4 and N_2O have increased markedly as a result of human activities since 1750 and now far exceed pre-industrial values determined from ice cores spanning many thousands of years. The atmospheric concentrations of CO_2 and CH4 in 2005 exceed by far the natural range over the last 650,000 years. Global increases in CO_2 concentrations are due primarily to fossil fuel use, with land-use change providing another significant but smaller contribution. It is *very likely* that the observed increase in CH4 concentration is predominantly due to agriculture and fossil fuel use. The increase in N_2O concentration is primarily due to agriculture.

The global atmospheric concentration of CO_2 increased from a pre-industrial value of about 280ppm to 379ppm in 2005. The annual CO_2 concentration growth rate was larger during the last 10 years (1995-2005 average: 1.9ppm per year) than it has been since the beginning of continuous direct atmospheric measurements (1960-2005 average: 1.4ppm per year), although there is year-to-year variability in growth rates. The global atmospheric concentration of CH4 has increased from a pre-industrial value of about 715ppb to 1732ppb in the early 1990s, and was 1774ppb in 2005. Growth rates have declined since the early 1990s, consistent with total emissions (sum of anthropogenic and natural sources) being nearly constant during this period. The global atmospheric N_2O concentration increased from a pre-industrial value of about 270ppb to 319ppb in 2005. Many halocarbons (including hydrofluorocarbons) have increased from a near-zero pre-industrial background concentration, primarily due to human activities.

There is *very high confidence* that the global average net effect of human activities since 1750 has been one of warming ...

The equilibrium climate sensitivity is a measure of the climate system response to sustained radiative forcing. It is defined as the equilibrium global average surface warming following a doubling of CO_2 concentration. Progress since the TAR enables an assessment that climate sensitivity is *likely* to be in the range of 2 to 4.5°C with a best estimate of about 3°C, and is *very unlikely* to be less than 1.5°C. Values substantially higher than 4.5°C cannot be excluded, but agreement of models with observations is not as good for those values.

Feedbacks can amplify or dampen the response to a given forcing. Direct emission of water vapour (a greenhouse gas) by human activities makes a negligible contribution to radiative forcing. However, as global average temperature increases, tropospheric water vapour concentrations increase and this represents a key positive feedback but not a forcing of climate change. Water vapour changes represent the largest feedback affecting equilibrium climate sensitivity and are now better understood than in the TAR. Cloud feedbacks remain the largest source of uncertainty. Spatial patterns of climate response are largely controlled by climate processes and feedbacks. For example, sea-ice albedo feedbacks tend to enhance the high latitude response.

Warming reduces terrestrial and ocean uptake of atmospheric CO_2, increasing the fraction of anthropogenic emissions remaining in the atmosphere. This positive carbon cycle feedback leads to larger atmospheric CO_2 increases and greater climate change for a given emissions scenario, but the strength of this feedback effect varies markedly among models.

*   *   *

Advances since the TAR show that discernible human influences extend beyond average temperature to other aspects of climate, including temperature extremes and wind patterns.

Temperatures of the most extreme hot nights, cold nights and cold days are *likely* to have increased due to anthropogenic forcing. It is *more likely than not* that anthropogenic forcing has increased the risk of heat waves. Anthropogenic forcing is *likely* to have contributed to changes in wind patterns, affecting extra-tropical storm tracks and temperature patterns in both hemispheres. However, the observed changes in the Northern Hemisphere circulation are larger than simulated by models in response to 20th century forcing change.

It is *very likely* that the response to anthropogenic forcing contributed to sea level rise during the latter half of the 20th century. There is some evidence of the impact of human climatic influence on the hydrological cycle, including the observed large-scale patterns of changes in land precipitation over the 20th century. It is *more likely than not* that human influence has contributed to a global trend towards increases in area affected by drought since the 1970s and the frequency of heavy precipitation events.

*   *   *

Continued GHG emissions at or above current rates would cause further warming and induce many changes in the global climate system during the 21st century that would *very likely* be larger than those observed during the 20th century.

* * *

There is now *higher confidence* than in the TAR in projected patterns of warming and other regional-scale features, including changes in wind patterns, precipitation and some aspects of extremes and sea ice.

Projected warming in the 21st century shows scenario-independent geographical patterns similar to those observed over the past several decades. Warming is expected to be greatest over land and at most high northern latitudes, and least over the Southern Ocean (near Antarctica) and northern North Atlantic, continuing recent observed trends.

Snow cover area is projected to contract. Widespread increases in thaw depth are projected over most permafrost regions. Sea ice is projected to shrink in both the Arctic and Antarctic under all SRES scenarios. In some projections, Arctic late-summer sea ice disappears almost entirely by the latter part of the 21st century.

It is *very likely* that hot extremes, heat waves and heavy precipitation events will become more frequent.

Based on a range of models, it is *likely* that future tropical cyclones (typhoons and hurricanes) will become more intense, with larger peak wind speeds and more heavy precipitation associated with ongoing increases of tropical sea-surface temperatures. There is less confidence in projections of a global decrease in numbers of tropical cyclones. The apparent increase in the proportion of very intense storms since 1970 in some regions is much larger than simulated by current models for that period.

Extra-tropical storm tracks are projected to move poleward, with consequent changes in wind, precipitation and temperature patterns, continuing the broad pattern of observed trends over the last half-century.

* * *

Some systems, sectors and regions are *likely* to be especially affected by climate change.

Systems and sectors:

- particular ecosystems:

    o terrestrial: tundra, boreal forest and mountain regions because of sensitivity to warming; mediterranean-type ecosystems because of reduction in rainfall; and tropical rainforests where precipitation declines o   coastal: mangroves and salt marshes, due to multiple stresses

      o   marine: coral reefs due to multiple stresses; the sea-ice biome because of sensitivity to warming

- water resources in some dry regions at mid-latitudes and in the dry tropics, due to changes in rainfall and evapotranspiration, and in areas dependent on snow and ice melt

- agriculture in low latitudes, due to reduced water availability

- low-lying coastal systems, due to threat of sea level rise and increased risk from extreme weather events

- human health in populations with low adaptive capacity.

*   *   *

6.1 Observed changes in climate and their effects, and their causes

Robust Findings

Warming of the climate system is unequivocal, as is now evident from observations of increases in global average air and ocean temperatures, widespread melting of snow and ice and rising global average sea level.

Many natural systems, on all continents and in some oceans, are being affected by regional climate changes. Observed changes in many physical and biological systems are consistent with warming. As a result of the uptake of anthropogenic CO_2 since 1750, the acidity of the surface ocean has increased.

Global total annual anthropogenic GHG emissions, weighted by their 100-year GWPs, have grown by 70% between 1970 and 2004. As a result of anthropogenic emissions, atmospheric concentrations of N_2O now far exceed pre-industrial values spanning many thousands of years, and those of CH4 and CO_2 now far exceed the natural range over the last 650,000 years.

Most of the global average warming over the past 50 years is *very likely* due to anthropogenic GHG increases and it is *likely* that there is a discernible human-induced warming averaged over each continent (except Antarctica).

Anthropogenic warming over the last three decades has *likely* had a discernible influence at the global scale on observed changes in many physical and biological systems.

Key Uncertainties

Climate data coverage remains limited in some regions and there is a notable lack of geographic balance in data and literature on observed changes in natural and managed systems, with marked scarcity in developing countries.

Analysing and monitoring changes in extreme events, including drought, tropical cyclones, extreme temperatures and the frequency and intensity of precipitation, is more difficult than for climatic averages as longer data time-series of higher spatial and temporal resolutions are required.

Effects of climate changes on human and some natural systems are difficult to detect due to adaptation and non-climatic drivers.

Difficulties remain in reliably simulating and attributing observed temperature changes to natural or human causes at smaller than continental scales. At these smaller scales, factors such as landuse change and pollution also complicate the detection of anthropogenic warming influence on physical and biological systems.

The magnitude of CO_2 emissions from land-use change and CH4 emissions from individual sources remain as key uncertainties.

6.2 Drivers and projections of future climate changes and their impacts

Robust findings

With current climate change mitigation policies and related sustainable development practices, global GHG emissions will continue to grow over the next few decades.

For the next two decades a warming of about 0.2°C per decade is projected for a range of SRES emissions scenarios.

Continued GHG emissions at or above current rates would cause further warming and induce many changes in the global climate system during the 21st century that would *very likely* be larger than those observed during the 20th century.

The pattern of future warming where land warms more than the adjacent oceans and more in northern high latitudes is seen in all scenarios.

Warming tends to reduce terrestrial ecosystem and ocean uptake of atmospheric CO_2, increasing the fraction of anthropogenic emissions that remains in the atmosphere.

Anthropogenic warming and sea level rise would continue for centuries even if GHG emissions were to be reduced sufficiently for GHG concentrations to stabilise, due to the time scales associated with climate processes and feedbacks.

Equilibrium climate sensitivity is *very unlikely* to be less than 1.5°C.

Some systems, sectors and regions are *likely* to be especially affected by climate change. The systems and sectors are some ecosystems (tundra, boreal forest, mountain, mediterranean-type, mangroves, salt marshes, coral reefs and the sea-ice biome), low-lying coasts, water resources in some dry regions at mid-latitudes and in the dry topics and in areas dependent on snow and ice melt, agriculture in low-latitude regions, and human health in areas with low adaptive capacity. The regions are the Arctic, Africa, small islands and Asian and African megadeltas. Within other regions, even those with high incomes, some people, areas and activities can be particularly at risk.

Impacts are *very likely* to increase due to increased frequencies and intensities of some extreme weather events. Recent events have demonstrated the vulnerability of some sectors and regions, including in developed countries, to heat waves, tropical cyclones, floods and drought, providing stronger reasons for concern as compared to the findings of the TAR.

Key uncertainties

Uncertainty in the equilibrium climate sensitivity creates uncertainty in the expected warming for a given CO_2-eq stabilisation scenario. Uncertainty in the carbon cycle feedback creates uncertainty in the emissions trajectory required to achieve a particular stabilisation level.

Models differ considerably in their estimates of the strength of different feedbacks in the climate system, particularly cloud feedbacks, oceanic heat uptake and carbon cycle feedbacks, although progress has been made in these areas. Also, the confidence in projections is higher for some variables (e.g. temperature) than for others (e.g. precipitation), and it is higher for larger spatial scales and longer time averaging periods.

Aerosol impacts on the magnitude of the temperature response, on clouds and on precipitation remain uncertain.

Future changes in the Greenland and Antarctic ice sheet mass, particularly due to changes in ice flow, are a major source of uncertainty that could increase sea level rise projections. The uncertainty in the penetration of the heat into the oceans also contributes to the future sea level rise uncertainty.

Large-scale ocean circulation changes beyond the 21st century cannot be reliably assessed because of uncertainties in the meltwater supply from the Greenland ice sheet and model response to the warming.

Projections of climate change and its impacts beyond about 2050 are strongly scenario- and model-dependent, and improved projections would require improved understanding of sources of uncertainty and enhancements in systematic observation networks.

Impacts research is hampered by uncertainties surrounding regional projections of climate change, particularly precipitation.

Understanding of low-probability/high-impact events and the cumulative impacts of sequences of smaller events, which is required for risk-based approaches to decision-making, is generally limited.

6.3 Responses to climate change

Robust findings

Some planned adaptation (of human activities) is occurring now; more extensive adaptation is required to reduce vulnerability to climate change.

Unmitigated climate change would, in the long term, be *likely* to exceed the capacity of natural, managed and human systems to adapt.

A wide range of mitigation options is currently available or projected to be available by 2030 in all sectors. The economic mitigation potential, at costs that range from net negative up to US$100/ tCO_2-equivalent, is sufficient to offset the projected growth of global emissions or to reduce emissions to below current levels in 2030.

Many impacts can be reduced, delayed or avoided by mitigation. Mitigation efforts and investments over the next two to three decades will have a large impact on opportunities to achieve lower stabilisation levels. Delayed emissions reductions significantly constrain the opportunities to achieve lower stabilisation levels and increase the risk of more severe climate change impacts.

The range of stabilisation levels for GHG concentrations that have been assessed can be achieved by deployment of a portfolio of technologies that are currently available and those that are expected to be commercialised in coming decades, provided that appropriate and effective incentives are in place and barriers are removed. In addition, further RD&D would be required to improve the technical performance, reduce the costs and achieve social acceptability of new technologies. The lower the stabilisation levels, the greater the need for investment in new technologies during the next few decades.

Making development more sustainable by changing development paths can make a major contribution to climate change mitigation and adaptation and to reducing vulnerability.

Decisions about macro-economic and other policies that seem unrelated to climate change can significantly affect emissions.

NOTES & QUESTIONS

1. While the assessment in this report may strike you as frightening, it should be noted that it is quite tame. Even at the time it was drafted it was necessarily conservative, due to the rigorous process required for its drafting. Not only are there several draft stages for expert and governmental review, but each member state has to provide *line-by-line approval* for the Executive Summary and Summary for Policy Makers. That said, although consensus is required for

each line, there is a back-up plan for tough situations, allowing for a dissenting view to be noted. Because of the IPCC's highly politicized process, the resulting product is generally going to be relatively conservative.

2. Not only was the report conservative in representing the predictions at the time, but in the few years since we have already learned that the situation is worse than we thought then. *See, e.g.*, Richard A. Betts et al., *When Could Global Warming Reach 4°C?*, 369 PHIL. TRANSACTIONS ROYAL SOC'Y A 67 (2011); Julie Steenhuysen, *Global Warming Worse than Predicted-US Scientist*, REUTERS NEWS, Feb. 14, 2009 (discussing the IPCC report's underestimation of climate change).

3. Were you wondering what the italicized uncertainty terms (*very likely, unlikely, high confidence*, etc.) meant as you read the report? Do you think that you and your classmates may interpret these differently? Well, if this bothered you at all, perhaps this was for good reason. A recent study on how people interpret these terms demonstrated that there was wide variation, which not surprisingly related to the reader's individual political beliefs. The study found that coupling such terms with numerical assessments had significantly greater success in achieving a consensus of understanding. The researchers concluded "that using a dual (verbal—numerical) scale would be superior to the current mode of communication as it (a) increases the level of differentiation between the various terms, (b) increases the consistency of interpretation of these terms, and (c) increases the level of consistency with the IPCC guidelines. Most importantly, these positive effects are independent of the respondents' ideological and environmental views." David V. Budescu et al., *Effective communication of uncertainty in the IPCC reports*, 113 CLIMATIC CHANGE 181–200 (2012).

4. A similar international scientific panel has just been created to focus on biodiversity. The Intergovernmental Platform on Biodiversity and Ecosystem Services (IPBES), sometimes referred to as "the biodiversity IPCC," will work to design reports to aid policy-makers in responding to the crises of biodiversity loss and ecosystem degradation. *See World governments establish biodiversity panel akin to IPCC*, 171 ECOS 2 (2012); *'IPCC for Biodiversity' Gets Final Approval*, 336 SCIENCE 397 (2012).

5. At the time of this writing, the United Nations Conference on Sustainable Development, also known as Rio+20, has just taken place in Rio de Janeiro, 20 years after the historic 1992 United Nations Conference on Environment and Development (UNCED) was held in the same location (hence the name Rio+20). This meeting resulted in a 49-page vision document entitled "The Future We Want." By most accounts, little was actually accomplished at this meeting, apart from committing to future efforts at progress, though a good deal of that was achieved.

> The agreement adopted in Rio calls for the UN General Assembly (UNGA), at its next session, to take decisions on, *inter alia*: designating a body to operationalize the 10-year framework of programmes on sustainable consumption and production; determining the modalities for the third international conference on small island developing states, which is to convene in 2014; identifying the format and organizational aspects of the high-level forum, which is to replace the Commission on Sustainable Development; strengthening the UN Environment Programme (UNEP); constituting a

working group to develop global sustainable development goals (SDGs) to be agreed by UNGA; establishing an intergovernmental process under UNGA to prepare a report proposing options on an effective sustainable development financing strategy; and considering a set of recommendations from the Secretary- General for a facilitation mechanism that promotes the development, transfer and dissemination of clean and environmentally sound technologies.

In addition, the UNGA is called on to take a decision in two years on the development of an international instrument under the UN Convention on the Law of the Sea (UNCLOS) regarding marine biodiversity in areas beyond national jurisdiction. Furthermore, the UN Statistical Commission is called on to launch a programme of work on broader measures to complement gross domestic product, and the UN system is encouraged, as appropriate, to support industry, interested governments and relevant stakeholders in developing models for best practice and facilitate action for the integration of sustainability reporting. The text also includes text on trade-distorting subsidies, fisheries and fossil fuel subsidies.

While many had held out hope that Rio+20 would launch new processes and significantly alter the international framework —from establishing a new High Commissioner for Future Generations, to upgrading the UN Environment Programme to the status of a specialized agency, to identifying significant means of implementation, to establishing concrete targets and a "roadmap" for the green economy—the UNCSD outcome document was much more modest. But while some criticized the document for "kicking the can" down the road and missing an opportunity to boldly redirect sustainable development actions, others focused on the upcoming opportunities within the UNGA and other fora to shape the true Rio+20 legacy.

Earth Negotiations Bulletin, Vol. 27, No. 51, 25 June 2012, pp. 1-2, available at http://www.iisd.ca/download/pdf/enb2751e.pdf (last visited July 1, 2012).

For a brief description of the original Rio meeting and resulting United Nations Framework Convention on Climate Change (UNFCCC), see Ruth Gordon, *Climate Change and the Poorest Nations: Further Reflections on Global Inequality*, 78 U. COLO. L. REV. 1559, 1582-5 (2007).

6. Environmental policy choices always require trade-offs between the cost of restraining economic activity and the benefit to the environment. Although such benefits tend to be difficult to quantify for use in a cost-benefit analysis, there are usually at least somewhat immediate consequences at stake. Climate change creates a bit of a policy analysis time warp, however, in that the economic sacrifices made in one year will have benefits many years later. The next excerpt provides a vivid picture of the stretched-out time frame we are working with when we regulate in this area.

R.T. Pierrehumbert, Climate Change: A Catastrophe in Slow Motion

6 Chicago Journal of International Law 573 (2006).

The word catastrophe usually brings to mind phenomena like tsunamis, earthquakes, mudslides, or asteroid impacts—disasters that are over in an instant and have immediately evident dire consequences. The changes in Earth's climate wrought by industrial carbon dioxide emissions do not at first glance seem to fit this mold since they take a century or more for their consequences to fully manifest. However, viewed from the perspective of geological time, human-induced climate change, known more familiarly as "global warming," is a catastrophe equal to nearly any other in our planet's history. Seen by a geologist a million years from now, the era of global warming will probably not seem as consequential as the asteroid impact that killed the dinosaurs. It will, however, appear in the geological record as an event comparable to such major events as the onset or termination of an ice age or the transition to the hot, relatively ice-free climates that prevailed seventy million years ago when dinosaurs roamed the Earth. It will be all the more cataclysmic for having taken place in the span of one or a few centuries, rather than millennia or millions of years.

Humans have become a major geological force with the power to commit future millennia to practically irreversible changes in global conditions. This is what Bill McKibben refers to as "The End of Nature." As an example of the impact life has on global climate, the imminent global warming caused by humans does not stand out as unique or even unusually impressive. When oxygen-generating photosynthetic algae evolved between one and two-and-one-half billion years ago, they changed the composition of one-fifth of the atmosphere, poisoned much of the previous ecosystem, and more or less terminated the dominant role of methane as a greenhouse gas (oxygenation also, to be fair, set the stage for evolution of multi-celled organisms—the animals and plants we know and love). And when plants colonized land half a billion years ago, they vastly increased the rate at which atmospheric carbon dioxide is converted to limestone in the soil, leading to severe global cooling. One hardly wants to contemplate the kind of environmental impact statement that would have to be filed for either of these innovations.

What makes global warming unique in the four billion year history of the planet is that the causative agents—humans—are sentient. We can foresee the consequences of our actions, albeit imperfectly, and we have the power, if not necessarily the will, to change our behavior so as to effectuate a different future. The conjuncture of foresight and unprecedented willful power over the global future thrusts the matter onto the stage where notions of responsibility, culpability, and ethics come into play. The philosopher Hans Jonas finds in this "imperative of responsibility" a need for a fundamentally new formulation of ethics—one that takes greater cognizance of future generations and of the biosphere at large. It is against this backdrop that the foundation of international institutions capable of dealing with the catastrophe of global warming must be seen.

II. Unique Physical Aspects of the Climate Change Problem: Imposing Our Will on the Next 5000 Generations

In this section I will review the basic physical features that make global warming fundamentally different from all other pollution problems faced by humans. The problem of ozone destruction by chlorofluorocarbons (the "ozone hole" problem) was a small warm-up act sharing some characteristics with the global warming problem. But because the ozone hole problem was somewhat more limited in scope, and abatement of chlorofluorocarbons did not force society to confront any really difficult economic decisions, it is in a qualitatively different class. Human-induced emissions of several gases other than carbon dioxide also contribute to global warming, but in the long run, carbon dioxide is by far the biggest player and the most embedded in economic activity. I will thus restrict my discussion to this gas alone.

Carbon dioxide is present only in very low concentrations in the atmosphere. Immediately before the beginning of the industrial era, you would have needed to sift through a million molecules of air to find 280 molecules of carbon dioxide. If all of the carbon dioxide in the atmosphere were gathered together into a layer near the ground, the layer would be about two meters deep. Most of us would have to stand on a chair to breathe. It is because there is relatively little carbon dioxide in the atmosphere that human economic activity has the prospect of doubling its concentration within the twenty-first century, with greater increases in sight thereafter. It would be much harder for anything we do to significantly change the atmosphere's oxygen content, which makes up about a fifth of the atmosphere. Despite its low concentration, carbon dioxide plays a key role in determining the Earth's climate because this gas greatly retards the efficiency with which the planet loses energy to space by infrared (heat) radiation. The major constituents of the atmosphere are essentially transparent to infrared radiation. Carbon dioxide warms the Earth in the same way a sleeping bag or down comforter warms a person—by reducing the rate of heat loss. For the Earth, this additional blanketing allows the planet to maintain a higher temperature than would otherwise be possible, given the rate of solar energy input from the Sun.

Water vapor is the other major player in the Earth's energy budget, but its concentration in the atmosphere is buffered on a time scale of weeks by the huge oceanic reservoir of water, which can rapidly evaporate into the atmosphere and equally rapidly rain out. Water vapor thus adjusts in response to other changes in climate (principally temperature); rather than being a prime mover, it is a feedback amplifying other causes of climate change, including carbon dioxide increase. This is why water vapor, though an important greenhouse gas, is not regulated under the Kyoto Protocol or under proposed California state-level climate control regulations.

Carbon dioxide, in contrast, has a very long lifetime in the atmosphere and very weak natural sources; therefore, changes in the rate at which carbon dioxide is put into the atmosphere have great leverage over the atmosphere's carbon dioxide content. Carbon dioxide is implicated in virtually all of the great climate shifts in Earth's history, including the coming and going of the Ice Ages; the eons of warm ice-free states that the dinosaurs lived in some seventy million years ago; the collapse of the Earth into a globally frozen state in the Neoproterozoic era some six hundred million years ago; and the maintenance of conditions favorable to life on the very young

Earth, when the Sun was much fainter than it is today. We know from Earth's history that carbon dioxide has an enormous impact on the habitability of our planet, but history also humbles us by revealing major gaps in our understanding of the nature and severity of the impact. For a geologist, the idea of doubling the atmosphere's carbon dioxide concentration is outright terrifying, akin to closing one's eyes and spinning a thermostat dial that has not been touched in a long time, and without even the benefit of knowing quite whether it is a gas furnace or a hydrogen bomb at the nether end of the thermostat's wires.

The unique character of the challenge posed by carbon dioxide pollution derives from a triad of properties. First, human-induced emissions of carbon dioxide constitute a huge disturbance of the natural carbon cycle, causing changes in the atmosphere's carbon dioxide concentration that are large and of unprecedented speed in the annals of geological history. In the absence of fossil fuel burning, the natural carbon dioxide level is maintained by volcanic activity, specifically an escape of about five hundred million metric tons of carbon per year into the atmosphere from the Earth's interior. Fossil fuel burning currently puts about fifteen times this amount into the atmosphere annually, and the rate is increasing exponentially. As a result, the atmospheric carbon dioxide level has already increased from its pre-industrial value of 280 molecules per million to a present value of 370 molecules per million, and this level is expected to reach twice the pre-industrial value before the end of the current century. By way of comparison, carbon dioxide concentration during the two million years prior to the industrial era, encompassing the entire history of the human species, had fluctuated between a low of 180 molecules per million during the Ice Ages and a high of about 300 molecules per million during the inter-glacial periods. One has to go back perhaps ten million years to find another time when the carbon dioxide concentration was as high as we will make it during the next century. Looking a little further into the future, fossil fuel burning could quadruple the pre-industrial concentration within four hundred years under a business-as-usual scenario. This is comparable to the values that climate modelers use to reproduce the steamy, ice-free climate of the Cretaceous that existed some seventy million years ago. To turn back the climate clock seventy million years in the course of a few centuries is not a thing to be undertaken lightly.

Second, the expected changes in temperature caused by the increase of carbon dioxide are of a direction and magnitude unprecedented in the past two million years. During that time, the climate has fluctuated from a maximum global mean warmth approximating values prevailing around 1950 to temperatures about six degrees colder during the major Ice Ages. Simulations of global mean warming associated with a doubling of carbon dioxide lie in the range of two to four degrees Centigrade, with no guarantee that the higher figure truly represents the worst possible case. At the high end of this range, we are talking about a climate change two-thirds as big as the transition to an ice age but with this important difference: the expected warming would be added on top of the maximum temperatures experienced in the past two million years. Therefore, we have no natural analogues to tell us how the complex web of physical and biological interactions would respond to such a drastic climate change. We are driving into unknown territory, and, given the present imperfect state of physical and especially ecological simulations, with a windshield heavily encrusted with mud.

Third, and most significant, the excess carbon dioxide we put in the atmosphere today is removed exceedingly slowly, meaning that the carbon dioxide we emit in the next half-century will alter the climate for millennia to come; even if we wholly ceased using fossil fuels after fifty years, the harm could not be undone. The lifetime of carbon dioxide in the atmosphere is often mistakenly quoted as being on the order of a hundred years; this figure is actually the result of a fallacious and largely meaningless method of aggregating the many physical processes that operate on widely differing time scales into a single number which is supposed to represent the amount of time some extra added carbon dioxide will stay in the atmosphere. The fact is that for each kilogram of carbon dioxide put into the atmosphere today, only a small portion will be rapidly absorbed into the ocean. After five hundred to one thousand years of slow uptake by the ocean, fully one-quarter of that kilogram will remain in the atmosphere. A portion of that will be taken up by the ocean over the next ten thousand years by slow processes related to ocean sediments, but fully 7 percent of our initial kilogram will stick around for hundreds of thousands of years. It has been estimated that fossil fuel exploitation could eliminate the natural ice age cycle for the next half-million years, with presently unforeseeable consequences for the storing and catastrophic release of exotic methane-bearing ices in the ocean. The long reach of our actions over the eons gives us unprecedented power over the future, and with that power comes unprecedented responsibility.

An innocuous-sounding two to four degree Centigrade increase in average global temperature carries along with it much larger regional changes in temperature and precipitation, which can in turn have profound consequences. Polar regions warm more than the average, and already, at the present early stage of warming, one-fifth of Arctic summer sea ice has disappeared. Arctic summer ice may be gone in fifty years, which will have dire consequences for polar bears and other marine mammals. The opening of arctic ports and shipping routes may well prove to be a boon for the market economy (as well as a source of political conflict and territorial disputes), but the increasingly intensive exploitation of the area is hardly likely to be good for natural ecosystems. We are learning, too, that land ice can respond more rapidly to climate than previously thought. The Greenland summer melt zone has expanded dramatically and many of the Greenland glaciers are surging into the ocean. At the opposite pole, the Larsen B ice shelf in the Antarctic has collapsed for the first time in ten millennia. The success of the documentary film March of the Penguins, a straightforward account of a year in the life of the Antarctic's emperor penguins, is a testament to the deep affinity people feel for these brave creatures. Emperor penguins adapted over millions of years to life on the ice. Their life cycle is intimately tied up with the long inland march along sea ice and shelf ice, undertaken to protect their newborns from oceanic predators. The penguins would struggle mightily to undo ten million years of evolution in a century.

In the tropics, temperature changes little in the normal course of the year. How will the Amazon ecosystem respond to the extensive warming and drying predicted by some models? Warm water holds less oxygen than cold water. Throughout the world, then, global warming will stress sensitive freshwater fish living in shallow streams; coastal saltwater shellfish will likely also be affected by the heat. Agricultural diseases, human diseases, and parasite infestations (including potato blight, bark beetles, West Nile, and malaria) can expand their range with warming. Summer heat waves will become more severe, placing particular stress on places that are already barely tolerable during the summer. Some regions will experience extensive droughts, and if the monsoons should cease, the results will be catastrophic for countries such as India. Also, hurricanes draw their energy from warm water, so the intensity (and perhaps also the number) of hurricanes is likely to increase in the future. There are indications that the expected increase in the destructive power of hurricanes is already underway. The impact in low-lying coastal regions may be exacerbated by a sea level rise even greater than currently forecast, if glaciers should prove more responsive to temperature increases than conventionally thought.

Major ocean circulations are also likely to change, with uncertain consequences for the Earth's climate and its oceanic ecosystems. Carbon dioxide becomes an acid when it dissolves in water; the resulting acidification of the ocean will make it harder for coral to form their skeletons. While carbon dioxide in the air acts as a fertilizer for many kinds of plants, meaning that an increase in its concentration could have limited beneficial effects on agricultural plants, this increase could also have adverse and unexpected consequences for land ecosystems (just as dumping phosphate and nitrate fertilizer into the Gulf of Mexico has not proved beneficial for the environment).

In addition, historical evidence shows that the climate system has abrupt switches built into it, and that climate changes in fits and starts rather than along a smooth, gentle curve. Notwithstanding the movie The Day After Tomorrow, this does not mean that global warming risks bringing on an ice age. Rather, what we risk is a switch to a climate that has much more dramatic swings in it from one decade to the next, making adaptation much more difficult. The last ten thousand years, which embrace the entire history of civilization, have had an unusually steady climate, and we are uncertain about what it would take to disrupt this happy state of affairs.

Many of the above impacts are in the realm of the possible rather than the probable, and it is presently difficult to say how large such impacts would be, or even how probable they are. However, a cogent case has been made that one should pay more attention to low-risk but potentially catastrophic events, as opposed to the current focus on the "most probable" case. Those who would sneer that such an application of the "precautionary principle" would lead to paralysis are relying on an extreme caricature of the principle that has little resemblance to the way it is used in practice. For example, if one is thinking about driving down a mountain road at night and has faulty headlights, knows that the ravine ahead has a rickety bridge over it, and has heard that there has been a storm that may have washed the bridge away, one would be quite justified in driving slowly or perhaps even postponing the trip, even if it was not known for certain that the bridge had been swept away. No doubt, those who disdain the "precautionary principle" would be quite happy to load their whole family in the car and put the pedal to the floor.

The global nature of the climate change problem has some novel policy implications and also creates some opportunities. The atmosphere is well-mixed with regard to carbon dioxide. From the standpoint of climate change, carbon dioxide released in Sydney, Australia is in every regard interchangeable with carbon dioxide released in Beijing, China or Edmonton, Canada. The atmosphere truly is a global commons with respect to carbon dioxide, making emissions trading schemes far more benign than would be the case for pollutants, such as mercury, which have locally lethal impacts. The harm caused by the emission of carbon dioxide in Edmonton is not felt primarily, if at all, in Edmonton. This scenario means that one is confronted with an especially severe form of the free rider problem. A particularly unstable situation is created when a major emitter like the United States perceives (foolishly) that it will suffer minimal harm from the impacts of climate change and perceives (also foolishly) that actions taken to reduce emissions will derail its economy.

Because of the extremely long-term impact of each additional year's carbon dioxide emissions, the calculus of delay is completely changed as compared to other pollution problems. Ordinarily, in the face of uncertainty, a certain amount of delay could be justified; technology improves so as to make abatement cheaper, and one could wait to get a peek at the growing impacts to see just how deleterious they actually are. For many kinds of pollution, bad decisions are, to some extent, reversible. For example, suppose that at some point society has decided that it can no longer afford stringent restrictions on particulate emissions by power plants. It holds to this decision despite the possibility that a rather modest rollback in tax cuts for the wealthy could easily cover the costs. Such a society, in essence, places a higher value on the ability of wealthy individuals to afford new Hummers than it does on the health of children and other vulnerable populations. A future generation with different values may ultimately have to live with the guilt of a large number of preventable deaths of children from asthma and other respiratory ailments. However, a feeling of guilt is all that future generations are burdened with since the adverse impacts will disappear within a few years of action taken by more enlightened leaders. We do not have even this dubious luxury with respect to global warming. If we wait forty or fifty years before taking serious action, the die will have been cast and a thousand generations of our descendants will have to live with the consequences of the climate we bequeathed them.

The problem of long-term consequences is compounded by the long lead time for developing new energy infrastructure and technology and by the long capital life—well over a half-century—of newly built electric power plants. Investments being made today, investments that the coming generation will be reluctant to write down, are committing the world economy to another half-century of runaway carbon dioxide emissions. We are, in fact, rapidly running out of time to act.

NOTES & QUESTIONS

1. Although we are already beginning to experience some of the consequences of climate change, and can expect to see it get worse within most of our lifetimes, the worst of it will likely fall on future generations. Today's economic restraint is an investment in a future that policy-makers will not themselves see. How might this temporal distance impact our choices? We are also paying a price today for the actions of our ancestors over the last two centuries (much of the American industrial revolution took place in the nineteenth century). Are we now to be the sandwich generation, paying for both the mistakes of the past and the survival of the future? What duty does our generation owe to future generations?

There is an intriguing new litigation trend, directly targeting this duty issue, as described in the following blog-post:

> In a CPRBlog post in May 2011, I discussed the lawsuits filed on behalf of children against all 50 states and several federal agencies alleging that these governmental entities have violated the common law public trust doctrine by failing to limit greenhouse gas emissions that contribute to climate change. The suits were filed by Our Children's Trust, an Oregon-based nonprofit. The claims sought judicial declaration that states have a fiduciary duty to future generations with regard to an "atmospheric trust" and that states and the federal government must take immediate action to protect and preserve that trust. At the time, I opined that although these claims were novel and would likely have little, if any, immediate effect on state climate policy, they relied on what has proved to be a flexible and powerful common law doctrine in at least some states. As a result, I concluded there was likely to be significant variation in results between the states on creating opportunities for a new forum for consideration of climate change harms and potential legal responses. Now, just over a year later, some lower courts have issued decisions in the cases and, as expected, the results vary widely from state to state.

> The public trust doctrine is a concept dating back to Roman law which holds that there are certain natural resources that are forever subject to government ownership and must be held in trust for the use and benefit of the public. In the United States, plaintiffs have used the public trust doctrine successfully to prevent states and other governmental entities from conveying public trust resources such as submerged lands or municipal harbors into private ownership, to create public beach access, and to otherwise ensure public access to water-based resources. Until the 1970s, however, the doctrine had little to do with environmental protection and instead was used almost exclusively to prevent the privatization of water-

based resources or to preserve public access to fishing, boating, or commerce. Since that time, however, with the help of an influential law review article by Professor Joseph Sax, some states, like California, Louisiana, and Hawaii, have applied the common law doctrine to protect rivers, lakes, and other water-based resources as well as land-based resources such as birds and other wildlife. As I have discussed in my scholarly work on the public trust doctrine, other states have bolstered their common law public trust doctrine by relying on state constitutional provisions and state statutes mandating governmental protection of environmental resources. In this way, these states use the common law, state constitutions, and state statutes together to protect what I call generally "public trust principles." Despite these developments, however, there are still states that have a much more limited version of the common law public trust doctrine, with courts in those states limiting the doctrine's reach to ensuring continuing public ownership of water-based resources rather than using it for environmental protection purposes.

This brings us to the current lawsuits, which argue that the common law public trust doctrine is broad enough to encompass an "atmospheric trust" and that states have a duty to protect and preserve this trust resource for the benefit of present and future generations. As relief in the state court lawsuits, the plaintiffs sought a declaration that an atmospheric trust exists and that defendants have a duty to protect and preserve it. So how have courts responded? Not surprisingly, courts in several states, including Colorado, Oregon, Arizona, Washington, Arkansas, and Minnesota dismissed the cases early on, finding no basis for an "atmospheric trust" under state common law. Most of these states do not have a history of broad common law public trust doctrine protection for environmental resources, instead limiting the common law doctrine to its historic protection of submerged lands and access to navigable waters. In California, the plaintiffs voluntarily dismissed the case to pursue settlement talks. This too is not surprising because California has already been a leader in enacting statutes and regulations to reduce greenhouse gas emissions and is also one of the states most likely to recognize an atmospheric trust under common law doctrine. Thus, the ultimate goals of the plaintiffs and the State of California are much more aligned than in other states around the country.

Two victories for the petitioners, though, come from recent decisions in the New Mexico and Texas courts. In New Mexico, in January, on a motion to dismiss, the district court stated that the atmosphere could be recognized as within the public trust doctrine's protection and allowed the plaintiffs leave to amend their complaint to refine the relief they sought and to specify the government actions causing harm. Then, on Monday, a district court in Austin, Texas issued a ruling rejecting the Texas Commission on Environmental Quality's conclusion that the public trust doctrine is exclusively limited to the conservation of water in the state. Instead, the court held that the public trust doctrine is much broader, and includes all of the natural resources of the state, including air quality. In reaching this decision, the court expressly stated that the public trust doctrine "is not simply a common law doctrine" but is incorporated into the Texas Constitution, which (1) protects "the conservation and development of all the resources of the State," (2) declares conservation of those resources "public rights and duties," and (3) directs the Legislature to pass appropriate laws to protect these resources. The court also relied upon the Texas Clean Air Act as an additional ground of Commission authority to act in this case "to protect against adverse effects, including global warming."

The decisions in the public trust cases to date highlight both the diversity of approaches to the public trust doctrine from state to state and the continuing ability of the doctrine to create new grounds for natural resource protection in the courts. As I noted in my post last year, it is unlikely these lawsuits will result in any quick decisions by courts to order their state agencies to set limits on greenhouse gas emissions. It is also unlikely that a majority of states will expressly recognize an atmospheric trust under state common law—the doctrine is simply not well-developed enough in most states to make such a jump. Nevertheless, the variety of approaches to this doctrine among the states in our federalist system means that some state courts may be able to shape the public trust doctrine based on their own state common law, statutes, and constitution to recognize the modern threat to natural resources caused by climate change. The decisions so far are a classic example of federalism at work as well as evidence of the continuing power and potential of the public trust doctrine to protect the natural resources when regulation fails to meet present-day environmental protection needs.

Alexandra Klass, *Federalism at Work: Recent Developments in Public Trust Lawsuits to Limit Greenhouse Gas Emissions*, at http://www.progressivereform. org/CPRBlog.cfm?idBlog=8092FA68-ADF9-7258-98BF80BAC5FA4AA7.

2. The use of cost-benefit analysis is common in making policy decisions, as well as implementation choices. When the benefit is to accrue in the future, it is common to "discount" that benefit, using mathematical formulae similar to compounding interest, only in the reverse direction. The result of such processes is that, just as a dollar today may be worth two dollars in ten years, we also determine that two dollars in ten years is worth only a dollar today. When we evaluate environmental benefits in the future, and apply such discounting methods to them, they can be worth very little to our cost-benefit analysis today. For an excellent discussion (and criticism) of the justifications underlying intergenerational discounting in the climate change context, see Richard L. Revesz & Matthew R. Shahabiand, *Climate Change and Future Generations*, 84 S. CAL. L. REV. 1097 (2011). For an enlightening analysis of the impact of discounting on policy, see Daniel A. Farber, *From Here to Eternity: Environmental Law and Future Generations*, 2003 U. ILL. L. REV. 289 (2003).

Of course, we can always count on Cass Sunstein to provide a different perspective. He and Arden Rowell propose that we are looking at the problem in the wrong way:

> There is an elaborate debate over the practice of "discounting" regulatory benefits, such as environmental improvements and decreased risks to health and life, when those benefits will not be enjoyed until some future date. Economists tend to think that, as a general rule, such benefits should be discounted in the same way as money; many philosophers and lawyers doubt that conclusion on empirical and nor-

mative grounds. Both sides frequently neglect a simple point: if regulators are interested in how people currently value risks that will not come to fruition for a significant time, they can use people's current willingness to pay to reduce those risks. And if the question involves people's willingness to pay in the future, what is being discounted is merely money, not regulatory benefits as such. No one seeks to discount health and life as such—only the money that might be used to reduce threats to these goods. If willingness to pay to reduce risk is the appropriate metric for allocating regulatory resources, discounting merely adjusts that metric to make expenditures comparable through time. To be sure, cost-benefit analysis with discounting can produce serious problems of intergenerational equity; but those problems, involving the obligations of the present to the future, require an independent analysis. Failing to discount will often hurt, rather than help, future generations, and solutions to the problem of intergenerational equity should not be conflated with the question of whether to discount.

Cass R. Sunstein & Arden Rowell, *On Discounting Regulatory Benefits: Risk, Money, and Intergenerational Equity*, 74 U. CHI. L. REV. 171 (2007).

3. Might our obligation to mitigate climate change go beyond such economic analyses entirely? Might it go beyond our duty to future generations of human beings? What would Aldo Leopold say? He argued for an ethical duty to the natural world itself, called a land ethic, which resulted in a very simple (yet tough to follow) command: "A thing is right when it tends to preserve the integrity, stability, and beauty of the biotic community. It is wrong when it tends otherwise." ALDO LEOPOLD, A SAND COUNTY ALMANAC AND SKETCHES HERE AND THERE 262 (1949).

4. Is it possible that some people and businesses will actually benefit from climate change? Considering the changes taking place and how they vary from one region to the next, which areas might see the greatest short-term benefits from advancing climate change? How might these temporary advantages be harnessed? Could doing so jeopardize the movement to mitigate climate change? For a discussion of these issues see J.B. Ruhl, *What Should We Do About the Climate Change Winners?*, http://papers.ssrn.com/sol3/papers.cfm?abstract_id=1953928.

5. Of course, we are not all on the same page when it comes to the existence of climate change, at least not in the lay-person community. Even today there remains a significant percentage of Americans who seriously doubt that these changes are taking place, or at least that we have caused them. This phenomenon betrays different views of science, economics, ethics, media, and ultimate values, as explored in great depth in MIKE HULME, WHY WE DISAGREE ABOUT CLIMATE CHANGE: UNDERSTANDING CONTROVERSY, INACTION AND OPPORTUNITY (2009).

Researchers from Yale and George Mason University have conducted surveys of nearly a thousand Americans in order to determine where people stand on climate change. The following is a summary of the results.

Anthony Leiserowitz, Edward Maibach, Connie Roser-Renouf & Nicholas Smith, *Global Warming's Six Americas in May* 2011

Yale Project on Climate Change Communication, 2011.
http://environment.yale.edu/climate/files/SixAmericasMay2011.pdf.

Introduction

This report extends and updates an ongoing program of research analyzing Americans' interpretations of and responses to climate change. The research segments the American public into six audiences that range along a spectrum of concern and issue engagement from the Alarmed, who are convinced of the reality and danger of climate change, and who are highly supportive of personal and political actions to mitigate the threat, to the Dismissive, who are equally convinced that climate change is *not* occurring and that no response should be made. The Six Americas are not very different demographically, but are dramatically different in their beliefs and actions, as well as their basic values and political orientations. The groups were first identified in a nationally representative survey conducted in the fall of 2008, and were re-assessed in January and June of 2010. The current report is the fourth in the series; in it we provide new insights into the informational needs of the six groups, their understanding of the health impacts of global warming, beliefs about current environmental impacts of global warming in the U.S., and support for local adaptation and mitigation policies. ...

[Editor's note: The survey resulted in six groups, from the most concerned to disbelievers, which broke down as follows: Alarmed (12%), Concerned (27%), Cautious (25%), Disengaged (10%), Doubtful (15%), and Dismissive (10%).]

Segment Size

The proportion of the population in each of the Six Americas has remained relatively stable over the past year, with 39 percent of Americans in the two groups most concerned about climate change - the Alarmed and the Concerned - and a quarter of the population in the two groups least concerned about the issue - the Dismissive and Doubtful. The high level of concern found in the fall of 2008, on the eve of the recession and prior to the release of stolen emails (known as climategate), remains an unmatched benchmark for engagement with the issue of climate change.

Uncertainty

Uncertainty on the issue remains high: More than a third of Americans agreed that they could easily change their minds about global warming – especially those in the Disengaged (73%) and Cautious (58%) segments. While 70 percent of the Dismissive said they do not need any more information to form a firm opinion on the issue, majorities of all other groups said they need at least a little more information before making up their minds, including 91 percent of the Concerned, 89 percent of the Cautious, and 86 percent of the Disengaged. Close to half of the Disengaged (47%) said they need a lot more information to form a firm opinion.

Questions about Global Warming

Most Americans have many questions about global warming: If given the chance to talk to an expert on the issue, four of the Six Americas would ask nine or more questions, out of a possible 13. The question that the largest number of Americans would ask is how experts know that global warming is caused by human activities, rather than natural changes in the environment. The Alarmed and Concerned would most like to know what the nations of the world can do to reduce global warming, and if there's still time to do so. The Disengaged would most like to ask whether global warming is actually occurring, and what harm it will cause. And the Cautious, Doubtful and Dismissive would most like to have an expert explain how experts know that global warming is happening and is caused by human activities.

Self-Perceived Knowledge

Of the Six Americas, the Dismissive were the most likely to say they are well-informed about global warming, with 91% saying they were very or fairly well-informed. Among the Alarmed, 85% said they were very or fairly well-informed, followed by two-thirds of the Concerned the Doubtful. The Disengaged were most likely to say they were *not* well-informed, with only 2% saying they were very well-informed.

Cause of Global Warming

Three-quarters or more of the Alarmed and Concerned groups said global warming is caused primarily by human activities, while 85 percent or more of the Doubtful and Dismissive said either it is caused by natural changes in the environment or it is not happening. The Cautious and Disengaged were more divided, with the Cautious almost evenly split between human and natural causes, and the Disengaged more likely to believe that natural changes are responsible (47%) than human activities (36%).

Perceptions of Scientific Agreement

Only in the Alarmed and Concerned groups were a majority aware that most scientists think global warming is occurring. Majorities in the other four groups said that either there was a lot of disagreement among scientists or that they didn't know. Even among the Alarmed and Concerned, however, awareness of the *strength* of scientific agreement is low: While approximately 97% of publishing climate scientists agree that climate change is occurring and that it is caused primarily by human activities, this high level of scientific agreement is recognized by only 44 percent of the Alarmed, 18 percent of the Concerned, 12 percent of the Cautious, and 5 percent or fewer of the Disengaged, Doubtful and Dismissive.

Inferences about Global Warming from Recent Weather

Because Americans do not clearly distinguish between weather and climate, they may be inclined to infer whether climate change is occurring from recent weather. The results presented here suggest that the groups that are most undecided about global warming - the Cautious and Disengaged - are the most likely to use weather events in this way: Majorities of both groups agreed that last winter's record snowstorms made them question the reality of global warming, *and* that last summer's heat waves strengthened their belief in global warming. Conversely, the groups with stronger opinions - the Alarmed, Concerned, Doubtful and Dismissive - were more likely to say that recent weather strengthened what they already believed: The record heat waves last summer strengthened belief in global warming for 83 percent of the Alarmed and 75 percent of the Concerned, but the record snowstorms last winter made only 32 percent of the Alarmed and 39 percent of the Concerned question the reality of global warming. Conversely, 93 percent of the Dismissive and 82 percent of the Doubtful said that the heat waves did not strengthen their belief in global warming. The snowstorms, however, led 53 percent of the Dismissive and 45 percent of the Doubtful to question the reality of global warming.

Risk Perceptions

Consistent with prior studies, we found that global warming was perceived as having greater impacts on distant people and places, with the greatest harm expected for people in developing nations, future generations, and other species. Within this general pattern, risk perceptions were much higher among the Alarmed and Concerned, with 100 percent of the Alarmed believing future generations and other species will be harmed a great deal or a moderate amount, as compared to 0 percent of the Dismissives.

Local Risk Perceptions

When asked about types of *local* harm expected from global warming, respondents said they expected the greatest impacts to be on agriculture, followed by native plants and wild birds and animals. More than half of the Cautious, Concerned and Alarmed expected that these four will experience moderate to great harm, and among the Alarmed, the proportions rose to more than 95 percent.

Human Health Impacts

The majority of Americans expected that global warming will increase deaths and injuries in the U.S. due to floods, hurricanes, winter storms and wildfires; 53 percent also expected increases in heat stroke, and half anticipated increased malnutrition due to spikes in food prices. Fewer than half said there will be increases in lung diseases, such as asthma, and in infectious diseases carried by insects and infected water. Within the segments, the anticipation of these health impacts was very high among the Alarmed and Concerned, and relatively high among the Cautious. Very few of the

Disengaged, Doubtful and Dismissive expected health impacts from global warming, however. Roughly two-thirds of the Disengaged said that they don't know whether global warming will have each of these impacts, while the Doubtful and Dismissive said there will be no impacts.

Current Impacts in the U.S.

Close to half of Americans believe that global warming is already causing or worsening a variety of environmental problems in the U.S. The current impacts most likely to be perceived were coastline erosion and flooding (52%), droughts (50%), hurricanes (49%), rivers flooding (48%) and wildfires (45%). As with health impacts, attribution of these impacts to global warming was higher among the Alarmed and Concerned. Two-thirds or more of the Disengaged said they didn't know; half of the Doubtful said the impacts are not happening and another third said they didn't know; and about 90 percent of the Dismissive said the impacts are not happening.

Trust in Sources

Three-quarters of Americans said they trust the National Oceanic and Atmospheric Administration (NOAA) and scientists as sources of information on global warming. While three-quarters or more of the Disengaged, Cautious, Concerned and Alarmed said they trust these two sources, only half of the Doubtful said they trust them. Among the Dismissive, only a quarter trusted NOAA and 30 percent trusted scientists, and yet these were their two most trusted sources of the 10 assessed. Overall, majorities trusted a number of other government agencies: The U.S. Centers for Disease Control and Prevention (CDC), the Environmental Protection Agency (EPA), the National Park Service, and the Department of Energy (DOE). Trust in President Obama was highly polarized, with 77 percent of the Alarmed saying they trusted him, as compared to 21 percent of the Doubtful and 3 percent of the Dismissive. The mainstream news media and congressional representatives were the least trusted sources, with fewer than 10 percent of any audience segment saying they strongly trusted them.

Issue Priorities

Two-thirds of Americans said that developing sources of clean energy should be a high or very high priority for the president and Congress, and half said that global warming should be. Both issues were marked by polarization among the six audiences, although the differences were smaller for clean energy: 98 percent of the Alarmed said that clean energy should be a high or very high priority, as compared to 24 percent of the Dismissive. By comparison, 96% of the Alarmed said global warming should be a priority, but none of the Dismissive thought it should be.

Support for Local Climate and Energy Policies

Three-quarters of Americans said they would like their communities to build more bike paths and bike lanes, and to increase the availability of public transportation. This support extended across the six audience groups, with 60 percent of the Dismissive saying they supported these policies, as compared to more than 90 percent of the Alarmed. A number of other policies received support from majorities of four of the six segments: Majorities of the Alarmed, Concerned, Cautious and Disengaged supported requiring new homes to be more energy efficient; changing zoning rules to reduce the need for a car and commuting times; and promoting the construction of energyefficient apartment buildings. The one policy receiving stronger support from the Dismissive than other groups was building a local nuclear power plant. A majority of the Dismissive (57%) supported this, while majorities of all other groups opposed it.

Protecting Local Resources

Because they do not perceive climate change to be a danger, few of the Dismissive or Doubtful favored local community action to protect their resources; fewer than a third of the Doubtful and 11 percent or less of the Dismissive expressed support for protecting any local resource. Among the other four groups, however, protecting local resources was perceived as important: Half or more of each group expressed support for protecting *all* of the resources that applied to their communities, including the water supply, public health, agriculture, natural resources, the sewer system and public property.

Political Activism

Political activism around the issue of global warming appears to be more prevalent among the groups that favor national action on the issue than among the groups that oppose it: 28 percent of the Alarmed and 10 percent of the Concerned said that they have contacted a political official about global warming, and almost all of these contacts were in support of action to reduce warming. By comparison, 7 percent of the Dismissive and 5 percent of the Doubtful had contacted officials to express opposition to mitigation policies. The Alarmed and Concerned were also more likely to have posted comments online about global warming than the Doubtful and Dismissive. A majority of the Alarmed (54%) and 22 percent of the Concerned have supported organizations working to reduce global warming; few members of the other four groups have supported global warming organizations.

B. IMPACTS ON BIODIVERSITY AND ECOSYSTEMS

While climate change is causing problems in many different ways, in this text we are primarily concerned about the impact it is having on biodiversity. This is no small inquiry, as biodiversity may well be the catastrophe's greatest victim. We have already seen relatively dramatic changes in habitat and species behavior, and it is very clear that what has taken place so far is only the tip of the iceberg.

Thomas R. Karl, Jerry M. Melillo, & Thomas C. Peters eds., *Global Climate Change Impacts in the United States*

Cambridge University Press, 2009.
http://downloads.globalchange.gov/usimpacts/pdfs/climate-impacts-report.pdf.

Ecosystems

The natural functioning of the environment provides both goods – such as food and other products that are bought and sold – and services, which our society depends upon. For example, ecosystems store large amounts of carbon in plants and soils; they regulate water flow and water quality; and they stabilize local climates. These services are not assigned a financial value, but society nonetheless depends on them. Ecosystem processes are the underpinning of these services: photosynthesis, the process by which plants capture carbon dioxide from the atmosphere and create new growth; the plant and soil processes that recycle nutrients from decomposing matter and maintain soil fertility; and the processes by which plants draw water from soils and return water to the atmosphere. These ecosystem processes are affected by climate and by the concentration of carbon dioxide in the atmosphere.

The diversity of living things (biodiversity) in ecosystems is itself an important resource that maintains the ability of these systems to provide the services upon which society depends. Many factors affect biodiversity including: climatic conditions; the influences of competitors, predators, parasites, and diseases; disturbances such as fire; and other physical factors. Human-induced climate change, in conjunction with other stresses, is exerting major influences on natural environments and biodiversity, and these influences are generally expected to grow with increased warming.

Ecosystem processes, such as those that control growth and decomposition, have been affected by climate change.

Climate has a strong influence on the processes that control growth and development in ecosystems. Temperature increases generally speed up plant growth, rates of decomposition, and how rapidly the cycling of nutrients occurs, though other factors, such as whether sufficient water is available, also influence these rates. The growing season is lengthening as higher temperatures occur earlier in the spring. Forest growth has risen over the past several decades as a consequence of a number of factors – young forests reaching maturity, an increased concentration of carbon dioxide in the atmosphere, a longer growing season, and increased deposition of nitrogen from the atmosphere. Based on the current understanding of these processes, the individual effects are difficult to disentangle.

A higher atmospheric carbon dioxide concentration causes trees and other plants to capture more carbon from the atmosphere, but experiments show that trees put much of this extra carbon into producing fine roots and twigs, rather than new wood. The effect of carbon dioxide in increasing growth thus seems to be relatively modest, and generally is seen most strongly in young forests on fertile soils where there is also sufficient water to sustain this growth. In the future, as atmospheric carbon dioxide continues to rise, and as climate continues to change, forest growth in some regions is projected to increase, especially in relatively young forests on fertile soils.

Forest productivity is thus projected to increase in much of the East, while it is projected to decrease in much of the West where water is scarce and projected to become more so. Wherever droughts increase, forest productivity will decrease and tree death will increase. In addition to occurring in much of the West, these conditions are projected to occur in parts of Alaska and in the eastern part of the Southeast.

Large-scale shifts have occurred in the ranges of species and the timing of the seasons and animal migration, and are very likely to continue.

Climate change is already having impacts on animal and plant species throughout the United States. Some of the most obvious changes are related to the timing of the seasons: when plants bud in spring, when birds and other animals migrate, and so on. In the United States, spring now arrives an average of 10 days to two weeks earlier than it did 20 years ago. The growing season is lengthening over much of the continental United States. Many migratory bird species are arriving earlier. For example, a study of northeastern birds that migrate long distances found that birds wintering in the southern United States now arrive back in the Northeast an average of 13 days earlier than they did during the first half of the last century. Birds wintering in South America arrive back in the Northeast an average of four days earlier.

Another major change is in the geographic distribution of species. The ranges of many species in the United States have shifted northward and upward in elevation. For example, the ranges of many butterfly species have expanded northward, contracted at the southern edge, and shifted to higher elevations as warming has continued. A study of Edith's checkerspot butterfly showed that 40 percent of the populations below 2,400 feet have gone extinct, despite the availability of otherwise suitable habitat and food supply. The checkerspot's most southern populations also have gone extinct, while new populations have been established north of the previous northern boundary for the species.

For butterflies, birds, and other species, one of the concerns with such changes in geographic range and timing of migration is the potential for mismatches between species and the resources they need to survive. The rapidly changing landscape, such as new highways and expanding urban areas, can create barriers that limit habitat and increase species loss. Failure of synchronicity between butterflies and the resources they depend upon has led to local population extinctions of the checkerspot butterfly during extreme drought and low-snowpack years in California.

Tree species shifts

Forest tree species also are expected to shift their ranges northward and upslope in response to climate change, although specific quantitative predictions are very difficult to make because of the complexity of human land use and many other factors. This would result in major changes in the character of U.S. forests and the types of forests that will be most prevalent in different regions. In the United States, some common forests types are projected to expand, such as oak-hickory; others are projected to contract, such as maple-beech-birch. Still others, such as spruce-fir, are likely to disappear from the United States altogether.

In Alaska, vegetation changes are already underway due to warming. Tree line is shifting north-ward into tundra, encroaching on the habitat for many migratory birds and land animals such as caribou that depend on the open tundra landscape.

Marine species shifts and effects on fisheries

The distribution of marine fish and plankton are predominantly determined by climate, so it is not surprising that marine species in U.S. waters are moving northward and that the timing of plankton blooms is shifting. Extensive shifts in the ranges and distributions of both warmwater and coldwater species of fish have been documented. For example, in the waters around Alaska, climate change already is causing significant alterations in marine ecosystems with important implications for fisheries and the people who depend on them.

In the Pacific, climate change is expected to cause an eastward shift in the location of tuna stocks. It is clear that such shifts are related to climate, including natural modes of climate variability such as the cycles of El Niño and La Niña. However, it is unclear how these modes of ocean variability will change as global climate continues to change, and therefore it is very difficult to predict quantitatively how marine fish and plankton species' distributions might shift as a function of climate change.

Breaking up of existing ecosystems

As warming drives changes in timing and geographic ranges for various species, it is important to note that entire communities of species do not shift intact. Rather, the range and timing of each species shifts in response to its sensitivity to climate change, its mobility, its lifespan, and the availability of the resources it needs (such as soil, moisture, food, and shelter). The speed with which species can shift their ranges is influenced by factors including their size, lifespan, and seed dispersal techniques in plants. In addition, migratory pathways must be available, such as northward flowing rivers which serve as conduits for fish. Some migratory pathways may be blocked by development and habitat fragmentation. All of these variations result in the breakup of existing ecosystems and formation of new ones, with unknown consequences.

Extinctions and climate change

Interactions among impacts of climate change and other stressors can increase the risk of species extinction. Extinction rates of plants and animals have already risen considerably, with the vast majority of these extinctions attributed to loss of habitat or over-exploitation. Climate change has been identified as a serious risk factor for the future, however, since it is one of the environmental stresses on species and ecosystems that is continuing to increase. The Intergovernmental Panel on Climate Change has estimated that if a warming of 3.5 to 5.5°F occurs, 20 to 30 percent of species that have been studied would be in climate zones that are far outside of their current ranges, and would therefore likely be at risk of extinction. One reason this percentage is so high is that climate change would be superimposed on other stresses including habitat loss and continued overharvesting of some species, resulting in considerable stress on populations and species.

Fires, insect pests, disease pathogens, and invasive weed species have increased, and these trends are likely to continue.

Forest fires

In the western United States, both the frequency of large wildfires and the length of the fire season have increased substantially in recent decades, due primarily to earlier spring snowmelt and higher spring and summer temperatures. These changes in climate have reduced the availability of moisture, drying out the vegetation that provides the fuel for fires. Alaska also has experienced large increases in fire, with the area burned more than doubling in recent decades. As in the western United States, higher air temperature is a key factor. In Alaska, for example, June air temperatures alone explained approximately 38 percent of the increase in the area burned annually from 1950 to 2003.

Insect pests

Insect pests are economically important stresses on forest ecosystems in the United States. Coupled with pathogens, they cost $1.5 billion in damage per year. Forest insect pests are sensitive to climatic variations in many stages of their lives. Changes in climate have contributed significantly to several major insect pest outbreaks in the United States and Canada over the past several decades. The mountain pine beetle has infested lodgepole pine in British Columbia. Over 33 million acres of forest have been affected, by far the largest such outbreak in recorded history. Another 1.5 million acres have been infested by pine beetle in Colorado. Spruce beetle has affected more than 2.5 million acres in Alaska and western Canada. The combination of drought and high temperatures also has led to serious insect infestations and death of piñon pine in the Southwest, and to various insect pest attacks throughout the forests of the eastern United States.

Rising temperatures increase insect outbreaks in a number of ways. First, winter temperatures above a certain threshold allow more insects to survive the cold season that normally limits their numbers. Second, the longer warm season allows them to develop faster, sometimes completing two life cycles instead of one in a single growing season. Third, warmer conditions help expand their ranges northward. And fourth, drought stress reduces trees' ability to resist insect attack (for example, by pushing back against boring insects with the pressure of their sap). Spruce beetle, pine beetle, spruce budworm, and woolly adelgid (which attacks eastern hemlocks) are just some of the insects that are proliferating in the United States, devastating many forests. These outbreaks are projected to increase with ongoing warming. Trees killed by insects also provide more dry fuel for wildfires.

Disease pathogens and their carriers

One consequence of a longer, warmer growing season and less extreme cold in winter is that opportunities are created for many insect pests and disease pathogens to flourish. Accumulating evidence links the spread of disease pathogens to a warming climate. For example, a recent study showed that widespread amphibian extinctions in the mountains of Costa Rica are linked to changes in climatic conditions which are thought to have enabled the proliferation of an amphibian disease.

Diseases that affect wildlife and the living things that carry these diseases have been expanding their geographic ranges as climate heats up. Depending on their specific adaptations to current climate, many parasites, and the insects, spiders, and scorpions that carry and transmit diseases, die or fail to develop below threshold temperatures. Therefore, as temperatures rise, more of these disease-carrying creatures survive. For some species, rates of reproduction, population growth, and biting, tend to increase with increasing temperatures, up to a limit. Some parasites' development rates and infectivity periods also increase with temperature. An analysis of diseases among marine species found that diseases were increasing for mammals, corals, turtles, and mollusks, while no trends were detected for sharks, rays, crabs, and shrimp.

Invasive plants

Problems involving invasive plant species arise from a mix of human-induced changes, including disturbance of the land surface (such as through over grazing or clearing natural vegetation for development), deliberate or accidental transport of non-native species, the increase in available nitrogen through over-fertilization of crops, and the rising carbon dioxide concentration and the resulting climate change. Human-induced climate change is not generally the initiating factor, nor the most important one, but it is becoming a more important part of the mix.

The increasing carbon dioxide concentration stimulates the growth of most plant species, and some invasive plants respond with greater growth rates than native plants. Beyond this, invasive plants appear to better tolerate a wider range of environmental conditions and may be more successful in a warming world because they can migrate and establish themselves in new sites more rapidly than native plants. They are also not usually dependent on external pollinators or seed dispersers to reproduce. For all of these reasons, invasive plant species present a growing problem that is extremely difficult to control once unleashed.

Deserts and drylands are likely to become hotter and drier, feeding a self-reinforcing cycle of invasive plants, fire, and erosion.

The arid Southwest is projected to become even drier in this century. There is emerging evidence that this is already underway. Deserts in the United States are also projected to expand to the north, east, and upward in elevation in response to projected warming and associated changes in climate.

Increased drying in the region contributes to a variety of changes that exacerbate a cycle of desertification. Increased drought conditions cause perennial plants to die due to water stress and increased susceptibility to plant diseases. At the same time, non-native grasses have invaded the region. As these grasses increase in abundance, they provide more fuel for fires, causing fire frequency to increase in a self-reinforcing cycle that leads to further losses of vegetation. When it does rain, the rain tends to come in heavy downpours, and since there is less vegetation to protect the soil, water erosion increases. Higher air temperatures and decreased soil moisture reduce soil stability, further exacerbating erosion. And with a growing population needing water for urban uses, hydroelectric generation, and agriculture, there is increasing pressure on mountain water sources that would otherwise flow to desert river areas.

The response of arid lands to climate change also depends on how other factors interact with climate at local scales. Large-scale, unregulated livestock grazing in the Southwest during the late 1800s and early 1900s is widely regarded as having contributed to widespread desertification. Grazing peaked around 1920 on public lands in the West. By the 1970s, grazing had been reduced by about 70 percent, but the arid lands have been very slow to recover from its impacts. Warmer and drier climate conditions are expected to slow recovery even more. In addition, the land resource in the Southwest is currently managed more for providing water for people than for protecting the productivity of the landscape. As a result, the land resource is likely to be further degraded and its recovery hampered.

Coastal and near-shore ecosystems are already under multiple stresses. Climate change and ocean acidification will exacerbate these stresses.

Coastal and near-shore marine ecosystems are vulnerable to a host of climate change-related effects including increasing air and water temperatures, ocean acidification, changes in runoff from the land, sea-level rise, and altered currents. Some of these changes have already led to coral bleaching, shifts in species ranges, increased storm intensity in some regions, dramatic reductions in sea ice extent and thickness along the Alaskan coast, and other significant changes to the nation's coastlines and marine ecosystems.

The interface between land and sea is important, as many species, including many endangered species, depend on it at some point in their life cycle. In addition, coastal areas buffer inland areas from the effects of wave action and storms. Coastal wetlands, intertidal areas, and other near-shore ecosystems are subject to a variety of environmental stresses. Sea-level rise, increased coastal storm intensity, and rising temperatures contribute to increased vulnerability of coastal wetland ecosystems. It has been estimated that 3 feet of sea-level rise (within the range of projections for this century) would inundate about 65 percent of the coastal marshlands and swamps in the contiguous United States. The combination of sea-level rise, local land sinking, and related factors already have resulted in substantially higher relative sea-level rise along the Gulf of Mexico and the mid-Atlantic coast, more so than on the Pacific Coast. In Louisiana alone, over one-third of the coastal plain that existed a century ago has since been lost, which is mostly due to local land sinking. Barrier islands are also losing land at an increasing rate (see Southeast region), and they are particularly important in protecting the coastline in some regions vulnerable to sea-level rise and storm surge.

Coral reefs

Coral reefs are very diverse ecosystems that support many other species by providing food and habitat. In addition to their ecological value, coral reefs provide billions of dollars in services including tourism, fish breeding habitat, and protection of coastlines. Corals face a host of challenges associated with human activities such as poorly regulated tourism, destructive fishing, and pollution, in addition to climate change-related stresses.

Corals are marine animals that host symbiotic algae which help nourish the animals and give the corals their color. When corals are stressed by increases in water temperatures or ultraviolet light, they lose their algae and turn white, a process called coral bleaching. If the stress persists, the corals die. Intensities and frequencies of bleaching events, clearly driven by warming in surface water, have increased substantially over the past 30 years, leading to the death or severe damage of about one-third of the world's corals.

The United States has extensive coral reef ecosystems in the Caribbean, Atlantic, and Pacific oceans. In 2005, the Caribbean basin experienced unprecedented water temperatures that resulted in dramatic coral bleaching with some sites in the U.S. Virgin Islands seeing 90 percent of the coral bleached. Some corals began to recover when water temperatures decreased, but later that year disease appeared, striking the previously bleached and weakened coral. To date, 50 percent of the corals in Virgin Islands National Park have died from the bleaching and disease events. In the Florida Keys, summer bleaching in 2005 was also followed by disease in September.

But rising temperature is not the only stress coral reefs face. As the carbon dioxide concentration in the air increases, more carbon dioxide is absorbed into the world's oceans, leading to their acidification. This makes less calcium carbonate available for corals and other sea life to build their skeletons and shells. If carbon dioxide concentrations continue to rise and the resulting acidification proceeds, eventually, corals and other ocean life that rely on calcium carbonate will not be able to build these skeletons and shells at all. The implications of such extreme changes in ocean ecosystems are not clear, but there is now evidence that in some ocean areas, such as along the Northwest coast, acidification is already occurring.

Arctic sea ice ecosystems are already being adversely affected by the loss of summer sea ice and further changes are expected.

Perhaps most vulnerable of all to the impacts of warming are Arctic ecosystems that rely on sea ice, which is vanishing rapidly and is projected to disappear entirely in summertime within this century. Algae that bloom on the underside of the sea ice form the base of a food web linking microscopic animals and fish to seals, whales, polar bears, and people. As the sea ice disappears, so too do these algae. The ice also provides a vital platform for ice-dependent seals (such as the ringed seal) to give birth, nurse their pups, and rest. Polar bears use the ice as a platform from which to hunt their prey. The walrus rests on the ice near the continental shelf between its dives to eat clams and other shellfish. As the ice edge retreats away from the shelves to deeper areas, there will be no clams nearby.

The Bering Sea, off the west coast of Alaska, produces our nation's largest commercial fish harvests as well as providing food for many Native Alaskan peoples. Ultimately, the fish populations (and animals including seabirds, seals, walruses, and whales) depend on plankton blooms regulated by the extent and location of the ice edge in spring. As the sea ice continues to decline, the location, timing, and species composition of the blooms is changing. The spring melt of sea ice in the Bering Sea has long provided material that feeds the clams, shrimp, and other life forms on the ocean floor that, in turn, provide food for the walruses, gray whales, bearded seals, eider ducks, and many fish. The earlier ice melt resulting from warming, however, leads to later phytoplankton blooms that are largely consumed by microscopic animals near the sea surface, vastly decreasing the amount of food reaching the living things on the ocean floor. This will radically change the species composition of the fish and other creatures, with significant repercussions for both subsistence and commercial fishing.

Ringed seals give birth in snow caves on the sea ice, which protect their pups from extreme cold and predators. Warming leads to earlier snow melt, which causes the snow caves to collapse before the pups are weaned. The small, exposed pups may die of hypothermia or be vulnerable to predation by arctic foxes, polar bears, gulls, and ravens. Gulls and ravens are arriving in the Arctic earlier as springs become warmer, increasing the birds' opportunity to prey on the seal pups.

Polar bears are the top predators of the sea ice ecosystem. Because they prey primarily on ice-associated seals, they are especially vulnerable to the disappearance of sea ice. The bears' ability to catch seals depends on the presence of sea ice. In that habitat, polar bears take advantage of the fact that seals must surface to breathe in limited openings in the ice cover. In the open ocean, bears lack a hunting platform, seals are not restricted in where they can surface, and successful hunting is very rare. On shore, polar bears feed little, if at all.

In addition, the rapid rate of warming in Alaska and the rest of the Arctic in recent decades is sharply reducing the snow cover in which polar bears build dens and the sea ice they use as foraging habitat. Female polar bears build snow dens in which they hibernate for four to five months each year and in which they give birth to their cubs. Born weighing only about 1 pound, the tiny cubs depend on the snow den for warmth.

About two-thirds of the world's polar bears are projected to be gone by the middle of this century. It is projected that there will be no wild polar bears left in Alaska in 75 years.

Continued warming will inevitably entail major changes in the sea ice ecosystem, to the point that its viability is in jeopardy. Some species will become extinct, while others might adapt to new habitats. The chances of species surviving the current changes may depend critically on the rate of change. The current rates of change in the sea ice ecosystem are very rapid relative to the life spans of animals including seals, walruses, and polar bears, and as such, are a major threat to their survival.

The habitats of some mountain species and coldwater fish, such as salmon and trout, are very likely to contract in response to warming.

Animal and plant species that live in the mountains are among those particularly sensitive to rapid climate change. They include animal species such as the grizzly bear, bighorn sheep, pika, mountain goat, and wolverine. Major changes have already been observed in the pika as previously reported populations have disappeared entirely as climate has warmed over recent decades.70 One reason mountain species are so vulnerable is that their suitable habitats are being compressed as climatic zones shift upward in elevation. Some species try to shift uphill with the changing climate, but may face constraints related to food, other species present, and so on. In addition, as species move up the mountains, those near the top simply run out of habitat.

Fewer wildflowers are projected to grace the slopes of the Rocky Mountains as global warming causes earlier spring snowmelt. Larkspur, aspen fleabane, and aspen sunflower grow at an altitude of about 9,500 feet where the winter snows are deep. Once the snow melts, the flowers form buds and prepare to bloom. But warmer springs mean that the snow melts earlier, leaving the buds exposed to frost. (The percentage of buds that were frosted has doubled over the past decade.) Frost does not kill the plants, but it does make them unable to seed and reproduce, meaning there will be no next generation. Insects and other animal species depend on the flowers for food, and other species depend on those species, so the loss is likely to propagate through the food chain.

Shifts in tree species on mountains in New England, where temperatures have risen 2 to 4°F in the last 40 years, offer another example. Some mountain tree species have shifted uphill by 350 feet in the last 40 years. Tree communities were relatively unchanged at low and high elevations, but in the transition zone in between (at about 2,600 feet elevation) the changes have been dramatic. Cold-loving tree species declined from 43 to 18 percent, while warmer-loving trees increased from 57 to 82 percent. Overall, the transition zone has shifted about 350 feet uphill in just a few decades, a surprisingly rapid rate since these are trees that live for hundreds of years. One possibility is that as trees were damaged or killed by air pollution, it left an opportunity for the warming-induced transition to occur more quickly. These results indicate that the composition of high elevation forests is changing rapidly.

Coldwater fish

Salmon and other coldwater fish species in the United States are at particular risk from warming. Salmon are under threat from a variety of human activities, but global warming is a growing source of stress. Rising temperatures affect salmon in several important ways. As precipitation increasingly falls as rain rather than snow, it feeds floods that wash away salmon eggs incubating in the streambed. Warmer water leads eggs to hatch earlier in the year, so the young are smaller and more vulnerable to predators. Warmer conditions increase the fish's metabolism, taking energy away from growth and forcing the fish to find more food, but earlier hatching of eggs could put them out of sync with the insects they eat. Earlier melting of snow leaves rivers and streams warmer and shallower in summer and fall. Diseases and parasites tend to flourish in warmer water. Studies suggest that up to 40 percent of Northwest salmon populations may be lost by 2050.

Large declines in trout populations are also projected to occur around the United States. Over half of the wild trout populations are likely to disappear from the southern Appalachian Mountains because of the effects of rising stream temperatures. Losses of western trout populations may exceed 60 percent in certain regions. About 90 percent of bull trout, which live in western rivers in some of the country's most wild places, are projected to be lost due to warming. Pennsylvania is predicted to lose 50 percent of its trout habitat in the coming decades. Projected losses of trout habitat for some warmer states, such as North Carolina and Virginia, are up to 90 percent.

Some of the benefits ecosystems provide to society will be threatened by climate change, while others will be enhanced.

Human well-being depends on the Earth's ecosystems and the services that they provide to sustain and fulfill human life. These services are important to human well-being because they contribute to basic material needs, physical and psychological health, security, and economic activity. A recent assessment reported that of 24 vital ecosystem services, 15 were being degraded by human activity. Climate change is one of several human-induced stresses that threaten to intensify and extend these adverse impacts to biodiversity, ecosystems, and the services they provide. Two of many possible examples follow.

Forests and carbon storage

Forests provide many services important to the well-being of Americans: air and water quality maintenance, water flow regulation, and watershed protection; wildlife habitat and biodiversity conservation; recreational opportunities and aesthetic and spiritual fulfillment; raw materials for wood and paper products; and climate regulation and carbon storage. A changing climate will alter forests and the services they provide. Most of these changes are likely to be detrimental.

In the United States, forest growth and long-lived forest products currently offset about 20 percent of U.S. fossil fuel carbon emissions. This carbon "sink" is an enormous service provided by forests and its persistence or growth will be important to limiting the atmospheric carbon dioxide concentration. The scale of the challenge of increasing this sink is very large. To offset an additional 10 percent of U.S. emissions through tree planting would require converting one-third of current croplands to forests.

Recreational opportunities

Tourism is one of the largest economic sectors in the world, and it is also one of the fastest growing; the jobs created by recreational tourism provide economic benefits not only to individuals but also to communities. Slightly more than 90 percent of the U.S. population participates in some form of outdoor recreation, representing nearly 270 million participants, and several billion days spent each year in a wide variety of outdoor recreation activities.

Since much recreation and tourism occurs outside, increased temperature and precipitation have a direct effect on the enjoyment of these activities, and on the desired number of visitor days and associated level of visitor spending as well as tourism employment. Weather conditions are an important factor influencing tourism visits. In addition, outdoor recreation and tourism often depends on the availability and quality of natural resources, such as beaches, forests, wetlands, snow, and wildlife, all of which will be affected by climate change.

Thus, climate change can have direct effects on the natural resources that people enjoy. The length of the season for, and desirability of, several of the most popular activities – walking; visiting a beach, lakeshore, or river; sightseeing; swimming; and picnicking – are likely to be enhanced by small near-term increases in temperature. Other activities are likely to be harmed by even small increases in warming, such as snow- and ice-dependent activities including skiing, snowmobiling, and ice fishing.

The net economic effect of near-term climate change on recreational activities is likely to be positive. In the longer term, however, as climate change effects on ecosystems and seasonality become more pronounced, the net economic effect on tourism and recreation is not known with certainty.

NOTES & QUESTIONS

1. The ocean is the world's largest habitat, covering over 70% of the planet and containing over half of all living species on earth. In spite of this, ocean acidification tends to get short shrift in the conversations about climate change, but it is a very serious problem.

> Changes in ocean chemistry will probably affect marine life in three different ways: (1) decreased carbonate ion concentration could affect the calcification process for calcifying organisms (e.g., corals); (2) lowered pH could affect acid-base regulation, as well as a variety of other physiological processes; and (3) increased dissolved CO_2 could alter the ability of primary producers to photo-synthesize.

Cheryl A. Logan, *A Review of Ocean Acidification and America's Response*, 60 BIOSCIENCE 819 (2010) (recommended reading for a more in-depth analysis of these issues).

2. The National Oceanic and Atmospheric Administration has a program to monitor ocean acidification, but as yet we have engaged in little response to the problem. Other countries have begun to take action, however. A useful review of the harms caused by ocean acidification, as well as the governmental responses to the issue, can be found in Heidi R. Lamirande, *From Sea to Carbon Cesspool: Preventing the World's Marine Ecosystems from Falling Victim to Ocean Acidification*, 34 SUFFOLK TRANSNAT'L L. REV. 183 (2011).

3. While NOAA begins to look at ocean acidification, the broader issue of climate change impacts on biodiversity generally also requires attention. The U.S. agency tasked with such concerns is, as you may have gathered by now, the Fish & Wildlife Service. The Service has released a report on the problems created by climate change as well as the agency's plan to address them. When you read the following excerpt, consider how the information presented compares with what you read in the previous one.

Rising to the Urgent Challenge: Strategic Plan for Responding to Accelerating Climate Change

U.S. Fish & Wildlife Service, 2010.
http://www.fws.gov/home/climatechange/pdf/CCStrategicPlan.pdf.

Over the 21st century, the U.S. Fish and Wildlife Service and the Department of the Interior envision a North American continent continuing to be altered by accelerating climate change, but managed to sustain diverse, distributed, and abundant populations of fish and wildlife through conservation of healthy habitats in a network of interconnected, ecologically functioning landscapes.

While many species will continue to thrive, we also envision that some populations and species may decline or be lost, and some will only survive in the wild through our direct and continuous intervention. We will be especially challenged to conserve species and habitats that are particularly vulnerable to climate-driven changes, but we will dedicate our absolute best efforts and expertise to the task, understanding fully that we must continue to meet our obligations for conserving trust species. We will need to make choices and set priorities and, working with our partners, apply ourselves where we can make the greatest difference.

We see climate change as an issue that will unite the conservation community like no other issue has since the early 1960s, when Rachel Carson sounded an alarm about pesticides. We envision a new era of collaborative conservation in which members of the conservation community work interdependently, building knowledge, sharing expertise, and pooling resources as we craft explicit landscape-scale goals and pursue these goals together. We foresee unparalleled opportunities to engage with, and enlist the involvement of, private citizens, businesses and industry, nongovernmental organizations, and national and international governments at all levels to conserve fish and wildlife in the face of climate change.

Climate change is an immense, serious, and sobering challenge — one that will affect fish and wildlife profoundly. At the same time, climate change is galvanizing the conservation community in ways we have not seen since a half-century ago, when Silent Spring alerted the world to the hazards of overuse of pesticides and launched a worldwide environmental movement.

As concern for climate change and its impacts grows, so do the opportunities for the Service and members of the conservation community to pool our talents, imagination, creativity, and spirit of public service to reduce and manage those impacts in ways that sustain fish and wildlife. Working interdependently and collaboratively, the Service will mount a bold response to climate change, on the ground, where our actions have the most impact; and in other settings where policies, priorities, and budgets are shaped and tough choices and decisions are made.

Across the Service, our employees have initiated action to address climate change. Some employees are monitoring sea level rise and exploring ways of safeguarding our coastal National Wildlife Refuges and the trust resources they support. Others are working tirelessly with water managers to ensure fish and wildlife resources are considered meaningfully in water allocation decisions, particularly in the Southwest, where climate change is likely to exacerbate drought. Some are busy calculating the Service's carbon footprint and devising innovative ways to help the Service become carbon neutral. Still other employees are reaching out to our workforce and our external partners to help them better understand the direction and magnitude of climate change and its effects on fish and wildlife.

It remains for the Service to do two things: First, we must focus the talents, creativity and energy of our employees on a common set of strategies, goals, objectives and actions for addressing climate change impacts. Second, we must provide employees with additional support in terms of knowledge, technology, and resources to enable them to realize their full potential in conserving fish and wildlife in the face of climate change.

* * *

"Warming of the climate system is unequivocal, as is now evident from observations of increases in global average air and ocean temperatures, widespread melting of snow and ice, and rising global average sea level. . . Most of the observed increase in global average temperatures since the mid-20th century is very likely due to the observed increase in anthropogenic greenhouse gas concentrations." So concludes the Intergovernmental Panel on Climate Change (IPCC) in its Fourth Assessment Report published in 2007. There is no longer any doubt that the Earth's climate is changing at an accelerating rate and that the changes are largely the result of human-generated greenhouse gas concentrations in the atmosphere caused by increasing human development and population growth. Climate change has manifested itself in rising sea levels, melting sea ice and glaciers, changing precipitation patterns, growing frequency and severity of storms, and increasing ocean acidification.

A growing body of evidence has linked accelerating climate change with observed changes in fish and wildlife, their populations, and their habitats in the United States. Polar bear population declines have already been noted in Canada, and extirpations of Bay checkerspot butterfly populations in the San Francisco Bay area are also documented. Across the continental United States, climate change is affecting the migration cycles and body condition of migratory songbirds, causing decoupling of the arrival dates of birds on their breeding grounds and the availability of the food they need for successful reproduction.

Climate change has very likely increased the size and number of wildfires, insect outbreaks, pathogens, disease outbreaks, and tree mortality in the interior West, the Southwest, and Alaska and will continue to do so. In the aquatic environment, evidence is growing that higher water temperatures resulting from climate change are negatively impacting cold- and cool-water fish populations across the country. Along our coasts, rising sea levels have begun to affect fish and wildlife habitats, including those used by shorebirds and sea turtles that nest on our coastal National Wildlife Refuges. In the oceans, subtropical and tropical corals in shallow waters have already suffered major bleaching events driven by increases in sea surface temperatures.

The immensity and urgency of the climate change challenge are indeed sobering. The IPCC's Fourth Assessment Report estimates that approximately 20 – 30 percent of the world's plant and animal species assessed as of 2006 are likely to be at increasingly high risk of extinction as global mean temperatures exceed a warming of 2 – 3°C above preindustrial levels.

CLIMATE CHANGE AND ITS IMPACT ON BIODIVERSITY

Global average temperature increases of 0.74°C are already documented, and temperature increases in some areas are projected to exceed 3.0°C over the next decade. The IPCC further concludes that substantial changes in structure and functioning of terrestrial ecosystems are very likely to occur with a global warming of more than 2 – 3°C above preindustrial levels. These changes will have predominantly negative consequences for biodiversity and ecosystem goods and services (e.g., water and food).

The IPCC also reports that the resilience of many ecosystems around the world is likely to be exceeded this century by an unprecedented combination of climate change; disturbances associated with climate change, such as flooding, drought, wildfire, and insects; and other global change-drivers, including land-use changes, pollution, habitat fragmentation, urbanization, and growing human populations and economies. These projected changes have enormous implications for management of fish and wildlife and their habitats around the world.

Climate change has the potential to cause abrupt ecosystem changes and increased species extinctions. These changes will reduce the ability of natural systems to provide many societal goods and services — including the availability of clean water, our planet's lifeblood — which in turn will impact local, regional, and national economies and cultures. Clearly, we cannot delay in addressing climate change effects on fish and wildlife. They demand urgent attention and aggressive action.

*   *   *

Climate change is the transformational conservation challenge of our time, not only because of its direct effects, but also because of its influence on the other stressors that have been and will continue to be major conservation priorities.

Many other issues, such as the spread and control of invasive species; the mounting pressures on limited water supplies; the need for robust fire management to help conserve natural systems; the harm to species from exposure to environmental contaminants; continued changes in land use, specifically habitat loss; and the impacts of all of these factors on biodiversity, have been and will continue to pose tremendous challenges to sustaining healthy, vibrant ecosystems.

Climate change does not replace these other threats or render them less important; they must remain priorities in the years ahead. It is, however, essential that we understand how climate change will exacerbate these threats and pose new ones. For example, climate change will allow the range of some invasive species to expand, perhaps markedly. Climate change will also make some regions drier, further complicating what are already very challenging efforts to capture water and deliver it to natural systems. These changes in precipitation patterns will also affect fire regimes. Our employees and partners will need to take this into account in their management activities so as to protect both the natural world and the places where people live.

In addition, climate change will have many unforeseen impacts on land use and development. For example, rising seas will result in immense pressure to build sea walls and other structures to protect coastal development. These actions will impact the fish and wildlife that rely upon nearby beaches, salt marshes and other natural habitats. Furthermore, climate change may divert development pressure from coastal areas to relatively higher ground as people seek to escape places threatened by rising seas. Together, all of these stressors will have impacts on species that are imperiled today, and they could cause others to become imperiled for the first time.

One of the major challenges of addressing climate change effects on fish and wildlife is identifying and addressing uncertainty in our understanding of future climate change and how that change will affect ecological systems. Our understanding of future climate change is based largely on projections from global climate models (also known as General Circulation Models) that are run using different greenhouse gas emissions scenarios developed by the IPCC. These projections contain a degree of uncertainty resulting from the inability of climate models to perfectly simulate the climate system, particularly at regional geographic scales and less than decadal time intervals; and uncertainty over which greenhouse gas emissions scenario will be realized in the future. As the IPCC has stated, the emissions scenarios are "based on assumptions concerning... future socio-economic and technological developments that may or may not be realized, and are therefore subject to substantial uncertainty." There also remains much uncertainty over how climate change will affect ecological systems at different scales, especially in its interactions with such non-climate stressors as land-use changes.

Finally, unanticipated impacts of climate change have already occurred and are likely to occur in the future. These impacts are difficult to predict based on our current understanding of climate and ecological systems, adding further uncertainty to our ability to predict the future. We must account for this uncertainty as we design, implement and evaluate our plans in response to climate change and as we carry out our management, regulatory and monitoring programs. We must learn as we go, using new knowledge and results of focused research to reduce uncertainty. As we learn more about climate change, we will be better able to refine our planning, decisions, and management actions to reflect that greater understanding.

NOTES & QUESTIONS

1. After the above assessment portion, the FWS climate change strategy document goes on to list "Seven Bold Commitments," and "Three Progressive Strategies: Adaptation, Mitigation, and Engagement," which will be discussed further in the following chapters on mitigation and adaptation to climate change.

2. The current administration describes climate change as "the single biggest threat to wildlife," but how realistic is the hope that it can make a difference without further legislation? Given all that you have learned from the earlier

chapters in this casebook, what powers might the FWS have to address these problems? Which aspects of ESA implementation might create an opening to consider the impacts of climate change?

C. PROBLEM AREAS IN FOCUS

1. ARCTIC AND ANTARCTIC REGIONS

The polar regions of the planet have evolved as ecosystems heavily dependent upon their colder temperatures and icy world, so a warming climate can make irreversible changes to the habitat. Because ice melts at a set temperature (0 degrees Celsius or 32 degrees Fahrenheit), ice-dependent habitats are especially prone to an early tipping point for complete devastation. With numerous species in need of such habitat, their rapid decline is ringing the alarms of the scientific and governmental communities. The following excerpts discuss these regions, the first focusing largely on the Arctic, followed by a case excerpt discussing the ribbon seal's loss of habitat, and the final segment focuses on Antarctica.

Dr. Ahmed Djoghlafa, *Climate Change and Biodiversity in Polar Regions*

8 Sustainable Development Law & Policy 14 (2008).

INTRODUCTION

Polar ecosystems are home to an array of plants and animals that survive in some of the most extreme conditions in the world. For example, the seas surrounding the Antarctic are rich in plankton, which support a rich marine food chain, while the Arctic itself supports many mammals and plays an important role in the annual cycle of migratory birds. The scientific studies carried out at the occasion of the celebration of the International Polar Year have provided additional evidence of the rich, unique nature of the marine Arctic environment. Indeed the biodiversity of the Arctic is fundamental to the livelihoods of Arctic peoples. However, the Millennium Ecosystem Assessment, along with recent reports from the Intergovernmental Panel on Climate Change, have made us aware that climate change negatively impacts existing ecosystems and is one of the main drivers of biodiversity loss. Particular attention is now being paid to Polar Regions, where evidence of the impacts of climate change have been observed and widely reported. Indeed, Polar Regions are currently experiencing some of the most rapid and severe climate change on Earth, which will contribute to environmental and socio-economic changes, many of which have already begun. During the twentieth century, Arctic air temperatures increased by approximately five degrees Celsius, which is an increase that is ten times faster than the observed global-mean surface temperature. An additional warming of about four to seven degrees Celsius in the Arctic is predicted over the next hundred years. Moreover, Polar Regions are particularly threatened by climate change since Polar species and societies have developed very specialized adaptations to the harsh conditions found at the poles, thus making them extremely vulnerable to dramatic changes in these conditions.

OBSERVED AND PROJECTED IMPACTS

Walruses, polar bears, seals, and other marine mammals that rely on sea ice for resting, feeding, hunting, and breeding are particularly threatened by climate change. For example, studies reveal that in 1980, the average weight of female polar bears in western Hudson Bay, Canada, was 650 pounds. While in 2004, their average weight was only 507 pounds. It is believed that the progressively earlier breakup of the Arctic sea ice is responsible for the decrease in the polar bears' average weight, as this ice loss reduces their hunting season and food intake. Although for a different reason, reduced sea-ice extent is also believed to have caused a fifty percent decline in emperor penguin populations in Terre Adélie. Populations of krill and other small organisms may also decline as ice recedes. Due to the high importance of krill in various food chains, the entire marine food web could be adversely affected.

Climate change is already affecting the livelihood of indigenous peoples in the Arctic. Losses in biodiversity affect the traditional practices of indigenous people, particularly fishing and hunting. For example, the Saami people have observed changes in reindeer grazing pastures, while the Inuit people of Canada have observed reductions in the ringed seal population, their single most important source of food.

CLIMATE CHANGE AND INDIGENOUS AND LOCAL COMMUNITIES IN THE ARCTIC

Due to its unique nature, climate, and sensitivity to climate changes, the Arctic is an important early warning system as far as climate change is concerned. The findings of the Intergovernmental Panel on Climate Change show that eleven of the last twelve years (1995-2006) rank among the twelve warmest years in the instrumental record of global surface temperatures since 1850. In the past one hundred years, average temperatures in the Arctic increased by almost twice the global average rate. Consequently, the annual average Arctic sea ice extent has shrunk by 2.1 to 3.1 percent per decade. Further, temperatures at the top of the permafrost layer have generally increased up to three degrees Celsius since the 1980s. It is projected that higher temperatures will contribute to continuing snow contraction and widespread increases in thaw depth over permafrost regions. Also, the gradual melting of the Greenland ice sheet is projected to contribute to sea level rise, even beyond the year 2100.

The consequences of climate change are becoming more visible in the Arctic, and are greatly influencing the environment, animals, and living conditions of humans, especially the indigenous peoples who strongly depend on the Arctic ecosystem and natural resources. The Arctic indigenous peoples, their life, culture, and traditional knowledge, are adapted to and largely dependent on the cold and extreme physical conditions of the region. Over the years, they have adapted to the challenges brought about by the Arctic geography and climate. Although the Arctic climate has always undergone change, the ongoing changes in the climate are taking place at such an alarming speed that indigenous communities are having severe difficulties coping.

The Arctic Climate Impact Assessment ("ACIA"), commissioned by the Arctic Council, provides important insight into the impacts of climate change in the Arctic region. Over a period of five years, an international team of over three hundred scientists, others experts, and members of indigenous communities prepared this assessment. The ACIA Report identifies a range of climate change impacts including: rising temperatures in the Arctic with worldwide implications; shifts in Arctic vegetation zones; changes in animal species' diversity, ranges, and distribution; and increased exposure to storms by coastal communities.

The ACIA Report devotes a separate chapter to address matters concerning the changing Arctic from an indigenous perspective. Indigenous peoples have provided case studies addressing the situation in Kotzebue, the Aleutian and Pribilof Islands Region, the Yukon Territory, Denendeh, Nunavut, Greenland, Sápmi, and Kola. An important common theme or observation in the case studies is that the weather in the Arctic region has become more variable and less predictable by traditional means.

The Arctic Climate Impact Assessment recognizes that further research is required to understand environmental changes occurring in the Arctic, as well as the ways in which people view these changes. It states that in both cases, there is a growing, but still insufficient, body of research to draw on, in particular in those Arctic areas where few or no current records of indigenous observations are available. The assessment concludes that further research needs to detect and interpret climate change, and to determine appropriate response strategies.

Center for Biological Diversity v. Lubchenco

United States District Court for the Northern District of California, 2010.
758 F.Supp.2d 945.

■ LAPORTE, UNITED STATES MAGISTRATE JUDGE.

In this civil action for declaratory and injunctive relief, Plaintiffs Center for Biological Diversity and Greenpeace (collectively, "Plaintiffs") allege that Defendants Jane Lubchenco, Administrator of the National Oceanic and Atmospheric Administration ("NOAA"), Gary Locke, the United States Secretary of Commerce, and the National Marine Fisheries Service ("NMFS") violated the Endangered Species Act ("ESA"), 16 U.S.C. §§ 1531, et seq., in failing to list the ribbon seal as threatened or endangered. ... For the reasons stated at the hearing and in this Order, the Court denies Plaintiffs' Motion for Summary Judgment and grants Defendants' Cross–Motion for Summary Judgment.

RIBBON SEAL

The ribbon seal primarily inhabits Russia's Sea of Okhotsk and the Bering and Chukchi Seas off of western Alaska. The species is strongly associated with the sea ice during its whelping, mating and molting periods from mid-March through June. Most of the rest of the year is spent at sea, and the ribbon seal is rarely seen on land. Ribbon seals can live twenty to thirty years, and females give birth to one pup every year after four to five years of age. The pup is nursed for three to four weeks and then abandoned to fend for itself. Once the sea ice melts with the onset of sub-Arctic summer in June, ribbon seals spread throughout their range.

Sea ice is essential to ribbon seal survival. However, the sea ice habitat has been shrinking. For example, there is evidence that for the period from 1979 through 2006, the sea ice extent in the Okhotsk Sea declined by 9.3% per decade. One estimate states that the summer sea ice habitat in the Bering and Okhotsk Seas is projected to decline by 40% by mid-century. Loss of Arctic sea ice (distinct from the sea ice in the Bering Sea and Okhotsk Sea) could increase shipping through the area, and therefore through some parts of the ribbon seals' habitat. Expansion of commercial fishing could impact ribbon seals through bycatch and through competition for prey.

Because ribbon seals rely on the sea ice for breeding, whelping, nursing and molting, declines in sea ice could impact ribbon seals. Declining sea ice areas could also lead to declining birth rates if females cannot find quality ice on which to give birth. Survival of weaned pups can be affected if they do not have sufficient ice to haul out while they are learning to swim. Dr. Rey, a ribbon seal expert, has explained how losses of sea ice have already probably resulted in high pup mortality ("The case of the ribbon seal is most urgent . . . Pups remain on or near the ice during a 4–week molting period, when they begin to feed. However, during 2006 and 2007, little sea ice remained beyond mid-May, depriving the pups of their habitat and requiring a high-energy demand for aquatic life. It is highly unlikely that the pups could meet this demand, probably resulting in high mortality during the following summer."). Sea ice loss can also affect adults that need the ice to molt.

Andrew Clarke, Climate Change and the Antarctic marine ecosystem

www.vliz.be/imisdocs/publications/120077.pdf.

The Antarctic climate has changed throughout time and on a wide range of temporal scales. Southern Ocean bottom temperatures have changed dramatically over the past 60 Ma, as has been demonstrated by palaeotemperature studies of benthic foraminifera isolated from deep-sea sediment cores. Glaciation of the Antarctic continent probably began 36–40 Ma BP, and throughout its existence the continental ice-cap has varied in volume and the extent to which it has covered the continental shelves. A key driver of this variability has been Milankovitch cyclicity, long-term variations in the Earth's orbit which affect received solar radiation on time-scales ranging from <20,000 to >100,000 years. These variations affect the timing and duration of seasons, and the extent of the tropical and polar regions. For the last 15 Ma there has been consistent cooling of the Southern Ocean, and this is the period that has driven the evolution of the Antarctic climate and biota we observe today.

Climatic and tectonic changes on geological and Milankovitch scales have produced a generally rich and diverse Antarctic marine fauna adapted to cope with this variability, by slow growth, longevity and intermittent recruitment. The marine fauna of Antarctica is generally rich and diverse, though some taxa are more speciose than others (notably species-rich groups include amphipod and isopod crustaceans, echinoderms and pycnogonids). In contrast, the Southern Ocean has very few decapod crustaceans, and is dominated by only one group of teleost fish. Climate change is likely to influence this biodiversity through three processes, namely direct temperature effects on organisms, oceanographic shifts and changes in the dynamics of sea-ice. In some cases, any effects may be exacerbated by changes in UV flux as a result of changes in the seasonal development of the ozone hole. At present, there is evidence for small temperature changes in both shallow and deep waters around Antarctica, and for some associated oceanographic changes. There is also some evidence for changes in sea-ice distribution and dynamics, though here it is difficult to distinguish a climate-change signal from natural long-period variability in the system. The clearest evidence for long-term changes in sea-ice dynamics comes from the Amundsen and Bellingshausen Seas, where there has been a decrease in winter sea-ice cover of about 10% since satellite records began. The atmospheric climate of the Antarctic Peninsula is warming faster than almost anywhere else on the planet, with warming being most evident in winter, and this may be related to the changes in sea-ice dynamics observed in the Amundsen and Bellingshausen Seas. In contrast, the climate of the Antarctic continent shows no consistent pattern, and some places have even displayed a slight cooling.

Data for biological responses to climate change in Antarctica are few, although there are strong indications of changes in population dynamics of some seabirds in relation to sea-ice. Climate change has already affected the breeding distribution of pygoscelid penguins, but no change has yet been observed for plankton or benthos. Some marine invertebrates have been shown to live near their maximum temperature limits (a situation analogous to that of some tropical corals) and would therefore seem liable to extinction should seawater temperatures rise significantly in the near future. How the fate of individual sensitive species relates to the response of whole ecological assemblages is, however, far from clear.

The dynamics of sea-ice are complex, and can influence the population dynamics of many zooplankton which depend on sea-ice at stages in their life-cycle. An excellent example of this is the Antarctic krill, Euphausia superba, which is widely regarded as a keystone species in the food web at lower latitudes in the Southern Ocean. Young krill hatch along the western Antarctic Peninsula and are carried in the strong Antarctic Circumpolar

Current to South Georgia, where they form a major part of the diet of many higher predators (fish, squid, seabirds and marine mammals). This means that variations in krill supply driven by changes in sea-ice dynamics thus influence the breeding success of dependent predators at South Georgia.

Demonstrating long-term changes in the biodiversity of marine systems is hindered by the paucity of data and the overwhelming effects of man's activities, even in Antarctica. Important insights into the potential effects of future climate change come from examining historical changes in the fauna, and from comparison of the two polar regions. To understand the impact of climate change on the Antarctic ecosystem as a whole, one needs to understand the structure of the food web. Although often portrayed as a simple, two-step linear food chain (diatoms to krill to whales, the classic Antarctic food chain of many textbooks), the Southern Ocean food web is similar to other marine food webs in that it is nonlinear, incorporates a microbial loop and has a significant flux to benthos. The major difference from nonpolar food webs is the role of sea-ice. The food web structure and its non-linear dynamics make prediction of future responses very difficult. The removal of great whales might have resulted in a regime shift to a system dominated by fur seals and squid. Currently, we cannot predict the biological consequences of climate change on the Antarctic. Rather than focusing on individual taxa, the impact of climate change on assemblages needs to be investigated.

2. FISHERIES

If you have ever tried to care for a home aquarium, you know that fish are extremely sensitive to even the slightest alterations in water temperature or chemistry. Given that climate change has a substantial impact on both of these characteristics of water bodies, it places a heavy burden on fisheries. Climate change also impacts the timing and quantity of water, by altering the amount of precipitation that falls as snow. Think of snow as a time-release capsule for water delivery – it stores the water in the winter and then gradually releases it in the warmer months. Ecosystems developed based on a certain rate of delivery, and can suffer when that timing is altered.

Natural Resources Defense Council v. Kempthorne

United States District Court for the Eastern District of California, 2007.
506 F.Supp.2d 322.

■ WANGER, DISTRICT JUDGE.

I. INTRODUCTION

This case concerns the effect on a threatened species of fish, the Delta smelt (Hypomesus transpacificus), of the coordinated operation of the federally-managed Central Valley Project ("CVP") and the State of California's State Water Project ("SWP"), among the world's largest water diversion projects. Both projects divert large volumes of water from the California

Bay (Sacramento–San Joaquin) Delta ("Delta") and use the Delta to store water.

For over thirty years, the projects have been operated pursuant to a series of cooperation agreements. In addition, the projects are subject to ever-evolving statutory, regulatory, contractual, and judicially-imposed requirements. The Long–Term Central Valley Project and State Water Project Operations Criteria and Plan ("2004 OCAP" or "OCAP") surveys how the projects are currently managed in light of these evolving circumstances. At issue in this case is a 2005 biological opinion ("BiOp"), issued by the United States Fish and Wildlife Service ("FWS" or "Service") pursuant to the Endangered Species Act ("ESA"), which concludes that current project operations described in the OCAP and certain planned future actions will not jeopardize the continued existence of the Delta smelt or adversely modify its critical habitat.

The Delta smelt is a small, slender-bodied fish endemic to the Delta. Historically, Delta smelt could be found throughout the Delta. Although abundance data on the smelt indicates that the population has fluctuated wildly in the past, it is undisputed that, overall, the population has declined significantly in recent years, to its lowest reported volume in fall 2004.

In this case, Plaintiffs, a coalition of environmental and sportfishing organizations, challenge the 2005 BiOp's no jeopardy and no adverse modification findings as arbitrary, capricious, and contrary to law under the Administrative Procedure Act, 5 U.S.C. §§ 702 et seq. Before the court for decision is Plaintiffs' motion for summary judgment. Among other things, Plaintiffs allege that the BiOp fails to consider the best available science, relies upon uncertain (and allegedly inadequate) adaptive management processes to monitor and mitigate the potential impacts of the OCAP, fails to meaningfully analyze whether the 2004 OCAP will jeopardize the continued existence of the Delta smelt, fails to consider the OCAP's impact upon previously designated critical habitat, and fails to address the impacts of the entire project.

*   *   *

F. Relationship Between Smelt and "X2."

Smelt are euryhaline (tolerant of a wide range of salinities), but generally occur in water with less than 10–12 parts per thousand (ppt) salinity. For a large part of its life span, Delta smelt are thought to be associated with the "freshwater edge of the mixing zone," where the salinity is approximately 2 parts per thousand (often referred to as "X2"). The summer TNS index increases dramatically whenever X2 is located between Chipps and Roe islands. Whenever the location of X2 shifts upstream of the confluence of the Sacramento and San Joaquin, either as a result of water diversions or natural conditions, smelt abundance decreases.

*   *   *

3. Global Climate Change Evidence.

Plaintiffs next argue that the BiOp ignored data about Global Climate Change that will adversely affect the Delta smelt and its habitat. This is potentially significant because the BiOp's conclusions are based in part on the assumption that the hydrology of the water bodies affected by the OCAP will follow historical patterns for the next 20 years (explaining that CALSIM II modeling involved making "adjustments to historic water supplies . . . by imposing future level land use on historical meteorological and hydrologic conditions").

In a July 28, 2004 comment letter, Plaintiff NRDC directed FWS's attention to several studies on the potential effects of climate change on water supply reliability, urging that the issue be considered in the BiOp. The comment letter stated:

> The best scientific data available today establishes that global climate change is occurring and will affect western hydrology. At least half a dozen models predict warming in the western United States of several degrees Celsius over the next 100 years. Such sophisticated regional climate models must be considered as part of the FWS' consideration of the best available scientific data.

> Unfortunately, the Biological Assessment provided by the Bureau to FWS entirely ignores global climate change and existing climate change models. Instead, the BA projects future project impacts in explicit reliance on seventy-two years of historical records. In effect, the Biological Assessment assumes that neither climate nor hydrology will change. This assumption is not supportable.

> In California, a significant percentage of annual precipitation falls as snow in the high Sierra Nevada mountains. Snowpack acts as a form of water storage by melting to release water later in the spring and early summer months. The effects of global climate change are expected to have a profound effect on this dynamic. *Among other things, more precipitation will occur as rain rather than snow, less water will be released slowly from snowpack "storage" during spring and summer months, and flooding is expected to increase. These developments will make it more difficult to fill the large reservoirs in most years, reducing reservoir yields and will magnify the effect of CVP operations on downstream fishes.* These developments will also dramatically increase the cost of surface storage relative to other water supply options, such as conservation.

> While the precise magnitude of these changes remains uncertain, judgments about the likely range of impacts can and have been made. See e.g., U.S. Global Climate Action Report—2002; Third National Communication of the United States Under the United Nations Framework Convention on Climate Change at 82, 101 (2002). The Service can and must evaluate how that range of likely impacts would affect CVP operations and impacts, including the Bureau's ability to

provide water to contractors while complying with environmental standards. We therefore request that the Service review and consider the work cited above, as well as the background and Dettinger presentation at a recent climate change conference held in Sacramento, June 9–11, 2004 and climate change reports.

A second presentation by Michael Dettinger at a December 8–9, 2004 CALFED meeting, attended by FWS staff, concluded that "warming is already underway . . ."; that this would result in earlier flows, more floods, and drier summers; and that "California water supplies/ecosystems are likely to experience [ ] changes earliest and most intensely." Following Dettinger's presentation, members of CALFED noted "the need to reevaluate water storage policies and ERP [Ecosystem Recovery Program] recovery strategies, all of which would be affected by projected climate changes." The record reflects that extreme water temperatures can have dramatic impacts upon smelt abundance.

In addition to the specific studies and data cited by NRDC, FWS scientists recognized the issue of climate change warranted further consideration. At a June 2003 symposium entitled "Framing the issues for Environmental and Ecological Effects of Proposed Changes in Water Operations: Science Symposium on the State of Knowledge," a number of questions regarding climate change were raised, including: "How does the proposed operations plan account for the potential effects of climate change (e.g., El Nino or La Nina, long term changes in precipitation and runoff patters, or increases in water temperature)?"

Plaintiffs argue that, despite this evidence that climate change could seriously impact the smelt by changing Delta hydrology and temperature, the BiOp "did not so much as mention the probable effects of climate change on the delta smelt, its habitat, or the magnitude of impacts that could be expected from the 2004 OCAP operations, much less analyze those effects." Defendants and Defendant–Intervenors respond by arguing (1) that the evidence before FWS at the time the BiOp was issued was inconclusive about the impacts of climate change; and (2) that, far from ignoring climate change, the issue is built into the BiOp's analysis through the use of X2 as a proxy for the location and distribution of Delta smelt.

a. Inconclusive Nature of Available Information Regarding the Impacts of Global Climate Change on Precipitation.

Federal Defendants and the State Water Contractors characterize Mr. Dettinger's presentation, as reflecting "a great deal of uncertainty that climate change will impact future precipitation." The presentation is entitled "Climate Change Uncertainties and CALFED Planning." Dettinger acknowledges that, although current climate models "yield consistent warming scenarios for California", there is no similar consensus regarding the impact of warming on future precipitation. Federal Defendants suggest that FWS "responsibly refused to engage in sheer guesswork, and properly declined to speculate as to how global warming might affect delta smelt." But, the NRDC letter cited a number of studies in addition to Mr.

Dettinger's presentations, all of which predict that anticipated climate change will adversely impact future water availability in the Western United States.

At the very least, these studies suggest that climate change will be an "important aspect of the problem" meriting analysis in the BiOp. *Pacific Coast Fed'n*, 265 F.3d at 1034. However, as with the 2004 FMWT data, the climate change issue was not meaningfully discussed in the biological opinion, making it impossible to determine whether the information was rationally discounted because of its inconclusive nature, or arbitrarily ignored.

Plaintiffs argue that "[r]egardless of the uncertainty involved in predicting the consequences of climate change, FWS had an obligation under the ESA to address the probable effects on Delta smelt." In response, the State Water Contractors quote the following passage from *Bennett v. Spear*, 520 U.S. 154, 176–177 (1997), in support of the proposition that the ESA intended to preclude exactly this kind of argument:

> The obvious purpose of the requirement that each agency "use the best scientific and commercial data available" is to ensure that the ESA not be implemented haphazardly, on the basis of speculation or surmise. While this no doubt serves to advance the ESA's overall goal of species preservation, we think it readily apparent that another objective (if not indeed the primary one) is to avoid needless economic dislocation produced by agency officials zealously but unintelligently pursuing their environmental objectives.

But, this passage from *Bennett* was part of a broader discussion holding that persons who are economically burdened by a decision made under the ESA fall within the zone of interests the statute protects for the purposes of standing. *Bennett* sheds little light on the current inquiry—whether and to what extent the data that was before the FWS regarding climate change should have been considered and addressed in the BiOp.

b. X2 as a Proxy for Climate Change.

The State Water Contractors argue that the approaches taken in the DSRAM [Delta Smelt Risk Assessment Matrix] are "more than adequate to deal with the projected impacts of climate change—assuming they occur." For example, Plaintiffs' suggestion that climate change will produce earlier flows, more floods, and drier summers is addressed by the DSRAM's X2 trigger. Flow level changes will be reflected in the position of X2. If climate change alters water temperatures, DSRAM also includes a temperature trigger, that monitors the temperature range within which successful Delta smelt spawning occurs.

The DSRAM offers no assurance that any mitigating fish protection actions will be implemented if the X2 criteria is triggered. That X2 indirectly monitors climate change does not assuage Plaintiffs' concerns that the

BiOp has not adequately analyzed the potential impact of climate change on the smelt.

The BiOp does not gauge the potential effect of various climate change scenarios on Delta hydrology. Assuming, arguendo, a lawful adaptive management approach, there is no discussion when and how climate change impacts will be addressed, whether existing take limits will remain, and the probable impacts on CVP–SWP operations.

FWS acted arbitrarily and capriciously by failing to address the issue of climate change in the BiOp. This absence of any discussion in the BiOp of how to deal with any climate change is a failure to analyze a potentially "important aspect of the problem."

There is no basis to determine what weight FWS should ultimately give the climate change issue in its analysis.

Plaintiffs' motion for summary adjudication is GRANTED as to this claim.

3. FORESTS

Herman Shugart et al., *Forests & Global Climate Change: Potential Impacts on U.S. Forest Resources*

Pew Center on Global Climate Change, 2003.
http://www.c2es.org/docUploads/forestry.pdf.

Executive Summary

Climate change is expected to have far-reaching consequences for forests and, subsequently, timber production in the United States. Although studies have shown that forests have adapted to temperature increases of 2-3°C (3.6-5.4°F) in the past, these changes occurred over thousands of years. Current climate predictions suggest that average global mean temperatures could rise 1.5-5.8°C (2.7-10.4°F) over this century alone. Such rapid changes in a relatively short period of time could affect forests significantly. Understanding how climate change will affect future forests and markets, however, is a complex task. Ecological and economic processes are exceptionally complicated, and understanding how integrated ecological and economic systems will respond to changing climate conditions remains a challenge. In spite of a number of remaining uncertainties, this report describes the many important insights into this process discovered over the last 10-20 years of research.

This report explores the potential effects of climate change on both natural and managed forest ecosystems, which differ significantly in their potential responses to climate change. Managed forests, such as forest plantations, receive significant amounts of human intervention in the form of planting, thinning and other management activities. These interventions have the potential to ameliorate the adverse effects of climate change. However, large areas of forest are considered natural and receive minimal direct human management, and thus may be more vulnerable to the effects of climate change. This duality within the forest sector makes it more difficult to state with precision what the overall economic impacts of climate change on forests will be. Further, the ecological changes caused by climate change could have large implications both for non-market attributes (e.g., biodiversity) and for other economic sectors associated with forests (e.g., recreation and water supply). The economic analysis in this report, however, focuses strictly on timber market impacts.

One of the most important ways that researchers discover clues about how forest ecosystems will respond to climate change is to explore the historical record for data regarding the impacts of past climate changes. This record indicates that individual tree species respond to warming either by changing their ranges or by increasing or decreasing their abundance. More recently, researchers have developed sophisticated models to explore how species distributions may change as climate changes. These changes could include increases or decreases in forest area, changes from one forest type to another, or movements of specific species from place to place.

In addition to species migration, it is important to consider how climate change could affect the productivity of forests (i.e., annual growth in forests). Existing studies show both positive and negative impacts on overall productivity, depending on the climate scenario. Further, some locations could experience higher productivity while others experience lower productivity. For example, forests in the southern United States are generally sensitive to the effects of drying, and productivity is more likely to decline there, while productivity is generally predicted to rise in the northern United States in response to low to moderate warming.

Understanding how productivity will change is complicated by an incomplete understanding of the effects of higher atmospheric carbon dioxide (CO_2) concentrations on plant growth and ecosystem processes (so-called "carbon fertilization"). Experimental evidence suggests that carbon fertilization is likely to increase individual tree growth. Some evidence also suggests that the CO_2 effect makes trees use water more efficiently, thereby making them less vulnerable to drought. Other evidence, however, suggests that the effects of carbon fertilization decline as trees age and at wider spatial scales where forest losses from other processes become important. Unfortunately, most measurements have been made on individual trees in experimental conditions, and not on entire forest ecosystems. In natural forests, and even in managed industrial forests, enhanced growth in trees could be offset by increased natural mortality elsewhere in the system. This is certainly the case for plantation forests where foresters usually predict increased thinning with higher growth in well-stocked stands.

While more precise regional estimates will be made as climate models provide a fuller understanding of regional climate change, and as ecological impacts become clearer, the existing results suggest that timber production could shift northward. Although some shifting will occur throughout most U.S. forests, the shifts would be strongest if the area suitable for southern softwoods expands northward. Hence, southern forests and markets appear most susceptible to climate change, in part because southern species are sensitive to drying effects, and in part because northward migration would erode the comparative advantage for timber production currently enjoyed by southern producers. Southern forests are also the most important economically since they account for well over one-half of U.S. production.

Changes in the frequency and intensity of disturbances like forest fires, pest infestations, and windthrow (i.e., from large storm events) are likely to have large consequences for the structure of both natural and managed forests. Natural forests, in particular, will be heavily influenced by changes in disturbances. Because disturbance has long been an important issue in forest management, managers have a number of tools available for adapting industrial and other managed forests as conditions change. Large-scale disturbances, however, can have substantial effects on markets. For example, although disturbances can cause substantial forest dieback, such ecological damages have the potential to cause short-term increases in timber supply, depressing timber prices for consumers.

As with agriculture, forest landowners have many options for adapting to the types of changes likely to occur with climate change, such as by salvaging dead and dying timber and by shifting to species that are more productive under the new climatic conditions. The long time lags between planting and harvesting trees, however, complicate the decisions for landowners. Adaptation can also occur at the market level, such as changing the types of species used in producing end products. End products are made from a wider variety of species today than 30 years ago; such adaptations help protect the market from large-scale changes in supply.

The following summarizes the current understanding of the potential impacts of climate change on U.S. forests and timber markets over the next century:

1. Tree species generally are expected to migrate northward or to higher altitudes in response to increased temperatures. While species will adapt over time by moving from one region to another, differential rates of change may cause significant differences in the types of natural stands in the future. Rates will depend critically on (a) how fast seeds migrate into new regions that are climatically suitable for a species after a climate change, (b) changes in the spread of insects and disease, (c) the spread of wildfire in different climates, and (d) human interventions to promote species migration.

2. Forest productivity is expected to change, but the changes could be positive or negative. Forests could become more or less productive, depending on how much climate changes (including both temperature and precipitation), how forests respond to higher carbon concentrations in the atmosphere, whether mortality changes, and whether disturbance-induced dieback increases or decreases. Many of these factors are expected to vary from region to region, suggesting that economic impacts are likely to differ among regions in the United States.

3. The effect of additional carbon dioxide in the atmosphere on forested ecosystems ("carbon fertilization") is complex and uncertain, but it has large implications for understanding how forest productivity will change. Most studies suggest that forest area and productivity will increase if carbon fertilization enhances forest growth, but will decline if carbon fertilization does not occur. Plant-level experiments suggest that carbon fertilization will enhance tree growth, at least for some period of time. Scaling these results up to the ecosystem level is complex, but available studies suggest that carbon fertilization will be limited by competition, disturbance, and nutrient limitations. It is important to continue developing a better understanding of carbon fertilization effects, particularly at the ecosystem scale.

4. Changes in the frequency and severity of forest disturbance, such as storm damage, fires, and pests are likely to affect forest structure and function. The impact on markets, while generally negative, can be ameliorated by salvage. At the market level, salvage associated with disturbances can increase timber supply and reduce prices in the short-term, which benefits consumers. However, increased disturbance and lower prices generally have negative effects on landowners.

5. United States timber markets have low susceptibility to climate change because of the large stock of existing forests, technological change in the timber industry, and the ability to adapt. The United States currently consumes less timber than grows within the country each year, providing a cushion if climate change has short-term impacts on supply. Further, companies already substitute a wide array of species in end products, so that if particular species are negatively affected by climate change, markets can adapt by changing the types of species used in the production of end products. In addition, landowners can assist natural migration of timber by planting southern species in the North.

6. Economic studies have tended to find small negative to positive overall effects on timber production in the United States. While the studies have looked at a wide range of potential climate change effects across species within the United States, the net productivity effects used by the studies have tended to be positive over the long-term. Higher forest productivity translates into increased timber yield, increased timber inventory, increased supply, and lower prices. Lower prices generate overall net benefits, although they primarily benefit consumers at the expense of landowners. Lower forest productivity has the opposite effect.

7. Northern states may gain from climate change if productivity increases and if southern species move north, while southern states may lose production. Producers in southern regions are the most vulnerable to climate change because they have a large share of the nation's current timber production capital, and the highly productive species in that region are sensitive to potential drying effects. Northern states are generally predicted to gain productivity and market share during climate change.

8. Understanding the economic effects of climate change on timber production is limited by scientific understanding of several key factors that control the response of natural and managed forests to climate change. Additional research is needed to enable ecologists and foresters to develop a more robust understanding of future changes in U.S. climate, ecosystem responses to climate change, the relationship between forest productivity and timber yield, and adaptation options available to foresters. Future clarification of these uncertainties will permit more informed assessments of the economic impacts of climate change to the forestry sector.

4. ENDANGERED SPECIES ACT LISTING PROCESS

Endangered and Threatened Wildlife and Plants; Emergency Listing of the Miami Blue Butterfly as Endangered, and Emergency Listing of the Cassius Blue, Ceraunus Blue, and Nickerbean Blue Butterflies as Threatened Due to Similarity of Appearance to the Miami Blue Butterfly, Part II

United States Fish & Wildlife Service, 2011.
76 Federal Register 49542.

Background

The Miami blue is a small, brightly colored butterfly approximately 0.8 to 1.1 inches (1.9 to 2.9 centimeters [cm]) in length (Pyle 1981, p. 488) with a forewing length of 0.3 to 0.5 inches (8.0 to 12.5 millimeters) (Minno and Emmel 1993, p. 134). Wings of males are blue above (dorsally), with a narrow black outer border and white fringes; females are bright blue dorsally, with black borders and an orange/red and black eyespot near the anal angle of the hindwing (Comstock and Huntington 1943, p. 98; Minno and Emmel 1993, p. 134). The underside is grayish with darker markings outlined with white and bands of white wedges near the outer margin. The ventral hindwing has two pairs of eyespots, one of which is capped with red; basal and costal spots on the hindwing are black and conspicuous (Minno and Emmel 1993, p. 134). The winter (dry season) form is much lighter blue than the summer (wet season) form and has narrow black borders (Opler and Krizek 1984, p. 112). Seasonal wing pattern variation may be caused by changes in humidity, temperature, or length of day (Pyle 1981, p. 489). Miami blue larvae are bright green with a black head capsule, and pupae vary in color from black to brown (Minno and Emmel 1993, pp. 134-135). . .

Summary of Factors Affecting the Species

Section 4 of the Act (*16 U.S.C. 1533*), and its implementing regulations at 50 CFR part 424, set forth the procedures for adding species to the Federal Lists of Endangered and Threatened Wildlife and Plants. Under section 4(a)(1) of the Act, we may determine a species to be endangered or threatened due to one or more of the following five factors: (A) The present or threatened destruction, modification, or curtailment of its habitat or range; (B) overutilization for commercial, recreational, scientific, or educational purposes; (C) disease or predation; (D) the inadequacy of existing regulatory mechanisms; or (E) other natural or manmade factors affecting its continued existence. Listing actions may be warranted based on any of the above threat factors, singly or in combination. Each of these factors is discussed below.

A. The Present or Threatened Destruction, Modification, or Curtailment of Its Habitat or Range

The Miami blue has experienced substantial destruction, modification, and curtailment of its habitat and range (see Background, above), with an estimated > 99 percent decline in area occupied (FWC 2010, p. 11). Although many factors likely contributed to its decline, some of which may have operated synergistically, habitat loss, degradation, and fragmentation are undoubtedly major forces that contribute to its imperilment (Calhoun *et al.* 2002, pp. 13-19; Saarinen 2009, p. 36). . .

Climate Change and Sea Level Rise

Climatic changes, including sea level rise, are major threats to south Florida, including the Miami blue and its habitat. Known occurrences and suitable habitat are in low-lying areas and will be affected by rising sea level. In general, the Intergovernmental Panel on Climate Change (IPCC) reported that the warming of the world's climate system is unequivocal based on documented increases in global average air and ocean temperatures, unprecedented melting of snow and ice, and rising average sea level (IPCC 2007, p. 2; 2008, p. 15). Sea level rise is the largest climate-driven challenge to low-lying coastal areas and refuges in the subtropical ecoregion of southern Florida (U.S. Climate Change Science Program [CCSP] 2008, pp. 5-31, 5-32). The long-term record at Key West shows that sea level rose on average 0.088 inches (0.224 cm) annually between 1913 and 2006 (National Oceanographic and Atmospheric Administration [NOAA] 2008, p. 1). This equates to approximately 8.76 inches (22.3 cm) in 100 years (NOAA 2008, p. 1).

In a technical paper following its 2007 report, the IPCC (2008, p. 28) emphasized it is very likely that the average rate of sea level rise during the 21st century will exceed that from 1961 to 2003, although it was projected to have substantial geographical variability. Partial loss of the Greenland and Antarctic ice sheets could result in many feet (several meters) of sea level rise, major changes in coastlines, and inundation of low-lying areas (IPCC 2008, pp. 28-29). Low-lying islands and river deltas will incur the largest impacts (IPCC 2008, pp. 28-29). According to CCSP (2008, p. 5-31), much of low-lying, coastal south Florida "will be underwater or inundated with salt water in the coming century." This means that most occupied, suitable, and potential habitat for Miami blue will likely be either submerged or affected by increased flooding.

The 2007 IPCC report found a 90 percent probability of an additional 7 to 23 inches and possibly as high as many feet (several meters) of sea level rise by 2100 in the Keys. This would cause major changes to coastlines and inundation of low-lying areas like the Keys (IPCC 2008, pp. 28-29). The IPCC (2008, pp. 3, 103) concluded that climate change is likely to increase the occurrence of saltwater intrusion as sea level rises. Since the 1930s, increased salinity of coastal waters contributed to the decline of cabbage palm forests in southwest Florida (Williams *et al.* 1999, pp. 2056-2059), expansion of mangroves into adjacent marshes in the Everglades (Ross *et al.* 2000, pp. 9, 12-13), and loss of pine rockland in the Keys (Ross *et al.* 1994, pp. 144, 151-155).

Hydrology has a strong influence on plant distribution in these and other coastal areas (IPCC 2008, p. 57). Such communities typically grade from salt to brackish to freshwater species. In the Keys, elevation differences between such communities are very slight (Ross *et al.* 1994, p. 146), and horizontal distances are also small. Human developments will also likely be significant factors influencing whether natural communities can move and persist (IPCC 2008, p. 57; CCSP 2008, p. 7-6). For the Miami blue, this means that much of the butterfly's habitat in the Keys, as well as habitat in other parts of its historical range, will likely change as vegetation changes. Any deleterious changes to important host plants and nectar sources could further diminish the likelihood of the subspecies' survival and recovery.

The Nature Conservancy (TNC) (2010, p. 1) used Light Detection and Ranging (LIDAR) remote sensing technology to derive digital elevation models and predict future shorelines and distribution of habitat types for Big Pine Key based on sea level rise predictions ranging from the best case to worst case scenarios described by current scientific literature. In the Keys, models predicted that sea level rise will first result in the conversion of habitat and eventually the complete inundation of habitat. In the best case scenario, a rise of 7 inches (18 cm) would result in the inundation of 1,840 acres (745 ha) (34 percent) of Big Pine Key and the loss of 11 percent of the island's upland habitat (TNC 2010, p. 1). In the worst case scenario, a rise of 4.6 feet (140 cm) would result in the inundation of about 5,950 acres (2,409 ha) (96 percent) and the loss of all upland habitat (TNC 2010, p. 1). Although the Miami blue no longer occurs on Big Pine Key, it was historically found on this island. If modeling is accurate, under the worst case scenario, even upland habitat on Big Pine Key will become submerged, thereby making the butterfly's potential recolonization or survival at this and other low-lying locations in the Keys very unlikely.

Similarly, using a spatially explicit model for the Keys, Ross *et al.* (2009, p. 473) found that mangrove habitats will expand steadily at the expense of upland and traditional habitats as sea level rises. Most of the upland and transitional habitat in the central portion of Sugarloaf Key is projected to be lost with a 0.2-meter rise (0.7-foot rise) in sea level; a 0.5-meter rise (1.6-foot rise) in sea level can result in a 95 percent loss of upland habitat by 2100 (Ross *et al.* 2009, p. 473). Furthermore, Ross *et al.* (2009, pp. 471-478) suggested that interactions between sea level rise and pulse disturbances (*e.g.,* storm surges or fire [see Factor E]) can cause vegetation to change sooner than projected based on sea level alone.

Scientific evidence that has emerged since the publication of the IPCC Report (2007) indicates an acceleration in global climate change. Important aspects of climate change seem to have been underestimated previously, and the resulting impacts are being felt sooner. For example, early signs of change suggest that the 1 [degrees] C of global warming the world has experienced to date may have already triggered the first tipping point of the Earth's climate system—the disappearance of summer Arctic sea ice. This process could lead to rapid and abrupt climate change, rather than the gradual changes that were forecasted. Other processes to be affected by projected warming include temperatures, rainfall (amount, seasonal timing, and distribution), and storms (frequency and intensity) (see Factor E).

The MIT scenarios combine various levels of sea level rise, temperature change, and precipitation differences with population, policy assumptions, and conservation funding changes. All of the scenarios, from small climate change shifts to major changes, will have significant effects on the Keys.

We have identified a number of threats to the habitat of the Miami blue which have operated in the past, are impacting the subspecies now, and will continue to impact the subspecies in the foreseeable future. Based on our analysis of the best available information, we find that the present and threatened destruction, modification, or curtailment of the subspecies' habitat is a threat to the subspecies throughout all of its range. We have no reason to believe that this threat will change in the foreseeable future. The decline of butterflies in south Florida is primarily the result of the long-lasting effects of habitat loss, degradation, and modification from human population growth and associated development and agriculture. Environmental effects resulting from climatic change, including sea level rise, are expected to become severe in the future and result in additional losses. Although efforts have been made to restore habitat in some areas, the long-term effects of large-scale and wide-ranging habitat modification, destruction, and curtailment will last into the foreseeable future. . .

Determination of Status

We have carefully assessed the best scientific and commercial information available regarding the past, present, and future threats to the Miami blue butterfly. The habitat and range of the subspecies are threatened with destruction, modification, and curtailment from human population growth, associated development and agriculture, and environmental effects resulting from climatic change. Due to the few metapopulations, small population size, restricted range, and remoteness of occupied habitat, collection is a significant threat to the subspecies and could potentially occur at any time. Additionally, the subspecies is currently threatened by a wide array of natural and manmade factors. Existing regulatory mechanisms do not provide adequate protection for the subspecies. As a result, impacts from increasing threats, singly or in combination, are likely to result in the extinction of the subspecies because the magnitude of threats is high.

Section 3 of the Endangered Species Act defines an endangered species as "* * * any species which is in danger of extinction throughout all or a significant portion of its range" and a threatened species as "* * * any species which is likely to become an endangered species within the foreseeable future throughout all or a significant portion of its range." Based on the immediate and ongoing significant threats to the Miami blue butterfly throughout its entire occupied range and the fact that the subspecies is restricted to only one or possibly two populations, we have determined that the subspecies is in danger of extinction throughout all of its range. Since threats extend throughout the entire range, it is unnecessary to determine if the Miami blue butterfly is in danger of extinction throughout a significant portion of its range. Therefore, on the basis of the best available scientific and commercial information, we have determined that the Miami blue butterfly meets the definition of an endangered species under the Act. Consequently, we are listing the Miami blue butterfly as an endangered species throughout its entire range.

Endangered and Threatened Wildlife and Plants; 12-Month Finding on a Petition To List the Nueces River and Plateau Shiners as Threatened or Endangered

United States Fish & Wildlife Service, 2011.
76 Federal Register 48777.

. . . On June 25, 2007, we received a petition dated June 18, 2007, from Forest Guardians (now WildEarth Guardians), requesting that 475 species in the southwestern United States, including the Nueces River and plateau shiners, be listed under the Act and critical habitat be designated. We acknowledged the receipt of the petition in a letter to the petitioner, dated July 11, 2007. In that letter we also stated that the petition was under review by staff in our Southwest Regional Office.

On March 19, 2008, WildEarth Guardians filed a complaint alleging that the Service failed to comply with its mandatory duty to make a preliminary 90-day finding on the June 18, 2007, petition to list 475 southwest species. We subsequently published an initial 90-day finding for 270 of the 475 petitioned species on January 6, 2009, concluding that the petition did not present substantial information that listing of those 270 species may be warranted. This initial 90-day finding did not include the Nueces River and plateau shiners. Subsequently, on March 13, 2009, the Service and WildEarth Guardians filed a stipulated settlement agreement, agreeing that the Service would submit to the Federal Register a finding as to whether their petition presented substantial information indicating that the petitioned action may be warranted for the remaining 192 southwestern species by December 9, 2009. On December 16, 2009 *(74 FR 66866),* we published a second 90-day finding for the remaining 192 southwestern species, which included a determination that listing the Nueces River and plateau shiners may be warranted, and initiated a status review. This notice constitutes the 12-month finding on the June 18, 2007, petition to list the Nueces River and plateau Shiners as threatened or endangered with critical habitat.

Population Abundance

There has been much speculation and very little research actually surveying and documenting the abundance of the Nueces River and plateau shiners. . . Even though there have been claims in the scientific literature that the Nueces River and plateau shiners were declining, these claims appear to be unsubstantiated by actual survey data. On the other hand, a recent study conducted by Edwards *et al.* (2008, pp. 1-30) that surveyed abundance of the Nueces River and plateau shiners found large numbers of these species. In conclusion, there is insufficient evidence to determine population trends for either species.

Summary of Information Pertaining to the Five Factors

Section 4 of the Act *(16 U.S.C. 1533)* and implementing regulations (50 CFR part 424) set forth procedures for adding species to, removing species from, or reclassifying species on the Federal Lists of Endangered and Threatened Wildlife and Plants. Under section 4(a)(1) of the Act, a species may be determined to be endangered or threatened based on any of the following five factors:

(A) The present or threatened destruction, modification, or curtailment of its habitat or range;

(B) Overutilization for commercial, recreational, scientific, or educational purposes;

(C) Disease or predation;

(D) The inadequacy of existing regulatory mechanisms; or

(E) Other natural or manmade factors affecting its continued existence.

In making this finding, information pertaining to the Nueces River and plateau shiners in relation to the five factors provided in section 4(a)(1) of the Act is discussed below. In making our 12-month finding on the petition, we considered and evaluated the best available scientific and commercial information. We reviewed the petition, information available in our files, and other available published and unpublished information. We also consulted with recognized fish experts and biologists with TPWD and The Nature Conservancy. . .

Factor E. Other Natural or Manmade Factors Affecting Its Continued Existence

Global climate change, and associated effects on regional climatic regimes, is not well understood, but model predictions are that temperatures in the southwestern United States will continue to increase, with extreme weather events (such as heat waves, drought, and flooding) occurring with more frequency (Archer and Predick 2008, p. 24). Also, there is some scientific information suggesting that fish in streams in southwestern North America may be vulnerable to extirpation or extinction due to global climate change because many fish species are already living near their lethal thermal limits (Mathews and Zimmerman 1990, p. 26). Endemic species, like the Nueces River shiner, which only inhabits the spring-fed headwaters of the Nueces River, could be more vulnerable to rising stream temperatures because they may not be able to move to more suitable areas. On the other hand, spring-fed streams have nearly constant environmental conditions, such as temperature, due to the constancy of groundwater chemistry and discharge (Hoagstrom *et al.* 2011, p. 22). Thus, areas with substantial connections to aquifers may sustain endemic fishes because groundwater responds slowly to climate change, buffering against fluctuations in climate conditions (Hoagstrom *et al.* 2011, p. 22). Additionally, we are not aware of any research that has been conducted on water temperature tolerance of the Nueces River shiner. Because the Nueces River shiner's water temperature tolerance is unknown, the point at which rising stream temperatures may impact the species is also unknown.

Likewise, recent models on climate change have indicated that annual mean precipitation in the southwestern United States is likely to decrease (Intergovernmental Panel on Climate Change (IPCC) 2007, p. 887). Decreased precipitation could result in diminished water flows, which may cause losses in habitat diversity, reduce stream productivity, and degrade water quality (Norris *et al.* 2005, p. 1). While it appears reasonable to assume that climate change could affect the Nueces River shiner by reduced water flows, we lack sufficient certainty to know specifically how climate change will affect the species. We have not identified, nor are we aware of, any data on an appropriate scale to evaluate habitat or population trends for the Nueces River shiner within its range, or to make predictions on future trends and whether the species will actually be impacted.

There are multiple hypothetical outcomes associated with climate change that could potentially affect the Nueces River shiner, but we lack predictive local or regional models on how climate change will specifically affect the Nueces River shiner or its habitat. Currently, we have no certainty regarding the timing, magnitude, or effects of impacts. Therefore, we find at this time that it is not possible to make reliable predictions of climate change effects on the status of the Nueces River shiner due to current limitations in available data and climate models. Based on the best available information and our current knowledge and understanding, we find that the Nueces River shiner is not in danger of extinction now or in the foreseeable future as a result of natural or other manmade threats affecting its continued existence.

D. BIODIVERSITY AND GEOENGINEERING IN RESPONSE TO CLIMATE CHANGE

While the primary responses to climate change are falling into the categories of mitigation and adaptation (each of which have their own chapters following this one), there remains significant concern that even our best possible efforts in these areas will not be adequate to the massive task at hand. For this reason, some are getting creative, devising plans to alter the earth's functioning on just as grand a scale as we have done to get into this mess in the first place. With creativity comes both potential for the otherwise unachievable and also great risk, however. Some look at the geoengineering proposals as sheer genius, while others see it as completely crazy to play with the planet on such a massive scale. For our purposes, however, the matter of greatest interest is the implications of geoengineering for biodiversity.

Impacts of Climate-Related Geoengineering on Biological Diversity

United Nations Environment Programme & Convention on Biological Diversity, Subsidiary Body on Scientific, Technical and Technological Advice, 2012

Biodiversity, ecosystems and their services are critical to human well-being. Protection of biodiversity and ecosystems requires that drivers of biodiversity loss are reduced. The current main direct drivers of biodiversity loss are habitat conversion, over-exploitation, introduction of invasive species, pollution and climate change. These in turn are being driven by demographic, economic, technological, socio-political and cultural changes. Human-driven climate change due to greenhouse-gas emissions is becoming increasingly important as a driver of biodiversity loss and the degradation of ecosystem services. A rapid transition to a low-carbon economy is the best strategy to reduce such adverse impacts on biodiversity. However, on the basis of current greenhouse-gas emissions, their long atmospheric residence times and the relatively limited action to date to reduce future emissions, the use of geoengineering techniques has also been suggested as an additional means to limit the magnitude of human-induced climate change and its impacts.

Proposed climate-related geoengineering techniques

In this report, climate-related geoengineering is defined as a deliberate intervention in the planetary environment of a nature and scale intended to counteract anthropogenic climate change and its impacts. Geoengineering techniques include increasing the reflectivity of the Earth's surface or atmosphere, and removing greenhouse gases from the atmosphere; other approaches have also been proposed. This definition of geoengineering encompasses a wide spectrum of possible actions to counteract (or remedy) global warming and its associated consequences. The commonality of those actions is that they could produce global cooling, if applied at sufficient scale. Geoengineering can therefore be differentiated from actions that mitigate (reduce or prevent) anthropogenic greenhouse-gas emissions. Carbon capture and storage (CCS) linked to fossil fuel combustion is not here considered as geoengineering, although some geoengineering techniques may involve the same or similar processes of managed carbon storage. Afforestation/reforestation and large scale land-management changes are, however, included, notwithstanding that such measures are already deployed for climate-change mitigation and other purposes, and that they involve minimal use of new technologies.

Sunlight reflection methods (SRM), also known as solar radiation management, aim to counteract warming and associated climatic changes by reducing the incidence and subsequent absorption of short-wave solar radiation, reflecting a small proportion of it back into space. They are expected to rapidly have an effect once deployed at the appropriate scale, and thus have the potential to reduce surface global temperatures within a few months or years if that were considered desirable. SRM would not address the root cause of human-driven climate change arising from increased greenhouse-gas concentrations in the atmosphere: instead they would mask the warming effect of accumulating greenhouse gases. They would introduce a new dynamic between the warming effects of greenhouse gases and the cooling effects of SRM with uncertain climatic implications, especially at the regional scale. SRM would not directly address ocean acidification. SRM proposals include:

1. *Space-based approaches:* reducing the amount of solar energy reaching the Earth by positioning sun-shields in space with the aim of reflecting or deflecting solar radiation;

2. *Changes in stratospheric aerosols*: injecting sulphates or other types of particles into the upper atmosphere, with the aim of increasing the scattering of sunlight back to space;

3. *Increases in cloud reflectivity:* increasing the concentration of cloud-condensation nuclei in the lower atmosphere, particularly over ocean areas, thereby whitening clouds with the aim of increasing the reflection of solar radiation;

4. *Increases in surface albedo:* modifying land or ocean surfaces with the aim of reflecting more solar radiation out to space.

SRM could be implemented separately or in combination, at a range of scales.

Carbon dioxide removal (CDR) techniques aim to remove CO_2, a major greenhouse gas, from the atmosphere, allowing outgoing long-wave (thermal infra-red) radiation to escape more easily. In principle, other greenhouse gases, such as nitrous oxide (N_2O), and methane (CH_4), could also be removed from the atmosphere or reduced at source, but such approaches are currently highly speculative. Proposed CDR techniques include:

Ocean fertilization: the enrichment of nutrients in marine environments with the intention of stimulating plant production, hence CO_2 uptake from the atmosphere and the deposition of carbon in the deep ocean;

Enhanced weathering: artificially increasing the rate by which CO_2 is naturally removed from the atmosphere by the weathering (dissolution) of carbonate and silicate rocks;

Increasing carbon sequestration through ecosystem management: through, for example: afforestation, reforestation, or measures that enhance natural carbon storage in soils and wetlands

Biological carbon capture, using harvested biomass and subsequent carbon storage: for example, through biochar, the long term storage of crop residues or timber, or bio-energy with carbon capture and storage; and

Direct, chemical capture of carbon from the atmosphere and its subsequent storage, for example, with storage as liquid CO_2 in geological formations or in the deep ocean.

CDR approaches involve two steps: (1) CO_2 capture from the atmosphere; and (2) long-term storage (sequestration) of the captured carbon. In the first three techniques, these two steps are very closely linked, although the permanence of the storage may be variable and technique-specific; in the fourth and fifth, capture and storage may be separated in time and space. Ecosystem-based approaches such as afforestation, reforestation or the enhancement of soil carbon are already employed as climate-change mitigation activities, and are not universally regarded as geoengineering technologies. CDR techniques act relatively slowly: to have a significant impact on the climate, such interventions, individually or collectively, would need to involve the removal from the atmosphere of several Gt C/yr (gigatonnes of carbon per year), maintained over decades. This seems unlikely to be achievable for several proposed CDR approaches.

There is no single geoengineering approach that currently meets all three basic criteria for effectiveness, safety and affordability. Different techniques are at different stages of development, mostly theoretical, and many are of doubtful effectiveness. Few, if any, of the approaches proposed above can be considered well-researched; for most, the practicalities of their implementation have yet to be investigated, and mechanisms for their governance are potentially problematic. Early indications are that several of the techniques, both SRM and CDR, are unlikely to be effective at the global scale.

* * *

Potential impacts on biodiversity of SRM geoengineering

SRM, if effective in abating the magnitude of warming, would reduce several of the climate-change related impacts on biodiversity. Such techniques are also likely to have other, unintended impacts on biodiversity. Assessment of the totality of those impacts is not straightforward: not only are the effects of specific SRM measures uncertain, but the outcome of the risk assessment will depend on the alternative, non-SRM strategy used as the 'control' for comparisons. Because climate change is projected to occur, climate-change scenarios provide relevant controls for assessing the risks and benefits of geoengineering, including the implications for biodiversity.

Model-based analyses and evidence from volcanic eruptions indicate that uniform dimming of sunlight by 1-2% through an unspecified atmospheric SRM measure could, for most areas of the planet, reduce future temperature changes projected under unmitigated greenhouse gas emissions. Overall, this would reduce several of the adverse impacts of projected climate change on biodiversity. These benefits would vary regionally, and might be negligible or absent for some areas. However, only limited research has been done; uniform dimming is a theoretical concept and may not be achievable; and many uncertainties remain concerning the effects of different atmospheric SRM measures and their geo-spatial consequences, for the hydrological cycle as well as for heat distribution. It is therefore not yet possible to predict effects with any confidence.

SRM would introduce a new dynamic between the heating effects of greenhouse gases and the cooling due to sunlight reduction. There are no known palaeo-precedents for the radiative impacts of high greenhouse-gas concentrations to be balanced by reduced light quantity; thus the stability of that combination is uncertain, and it is not clear what specific environmental challenges an "SRM world" might present to individual species and ecosystems, either on a short-term or a long-term basis.

The amount of anthropogenic CO_2 in the atmosphere is unaffected by SRM. Thus SRM would have little effect on ocean acidification and its associated impacts on marine biodiversity, nor the impacts (positive or negative) of elevated atmospheric CO_2 on terrestrial ecosystems. Some indirect effects of SRM on atmospheric CO_2 are possible; e.g., if such techniques prevent the temperature-driven release of additional CO_2 from natural systems. Nevertheless, SRM cannot be considered as an alternative to emission mitigation or CDR in terms of avoiding detrimental effects on the (marine) biosphere.

Rapid termination of SRM, that had been deployed for some time and masking a high degree of warming due to continued greenhouse-gas emissions, would almost certainly have large negative impacts on biodiversity and ecosystem services. Those adverse consequences would be more severe than those resulting from gradual climate change, since the opportunity for adaptation, including through population migration, would be much reduced.

Stratospheric aerosol injection, using sulphate particles, would affect the overall quantity and quality of light reaching the biosphere; have relatively minor effects on atmospheric acidity; and could also contribute to stratospheric ozone depletion. All these unintended impacts have implications for biodiversity and ecosystem services. Stratospheric aerosols would decrease the amount of photosynthetically active radiation (PAR) reaching the Earth by 1-2%, but would increase the proportion of diffuse (as opposed to direct) radiation. This would be expected to affect community composition and structure. It may lead to an increase of gross primary productivity (GPP) in forest ecosystems whilst decreasing ocean productivity. However, the magnitude and nature of effects on biodiversity are likely to be mixed, and are currently not well understood. Increased ozone depletion, primarily in the polar regions, would cause an increase in the amount of ultra violet (UV) radiation reaching the Earth, although potentially offset by the UV scattering of the aerosol particles themselves.

Cloud brightening is a more localised SRM proposal, with its application likely to be limited to specific ocean areas. The predictability of its climatic impacts is currently uncertain; nevertheless regional cooling with associated atmospheric and oceanic perturbations are likely, with potentially significant effects on terrestrial and marine biodiversity and ecosystems. Unintended impacts could be positive as well as negative.

Surface albedo changes would need to be deployed over very large land areas (sub-continental scale) or over much of the global ocean to have substantive effects on the global climate, with consequent impacts on ecosystems. Strong localized cooling could have a disruptive effect on regional weather patterns. For instance, covering deserts with reflective material on a scale large enough to be effective in addressing the impacts of climate change would greatly reduce habitat availability for desert fauna and flora, as well as affecting its customary use.

Potential impacts on biodiversity of CDR geoengineering techniques

Carbon dioxide removal techniques, if effective and feasible, would be expected to reduce the negative impacts on biodiversity of climate change and, in most cases, of ocean acidification. By removing CO_2 from the atmosphere, CDR techniques reduce the concentration of the main causal agent of anthropogenic climate change, Acidification of the surface ocean would also be reduced, but the effect of CDR on the ocean as a whole will depend on the location of long-term carbon storage. CDR methods are generally slow in affecting the atmospheric CO_2 concentration, with further substantial time-lags in the climatic benefits. Several of the techniques are of doubtful effectiveness, because of limited scalability.

Individual CDR techniques may have significant unintended impacts on terrestrial, and/or ocean ecosystems, depending on the nature, scale and location of carbon capture and storage. In some biologically-driven processes (ocean fertilization; afforestation, reforestation and soil carbon enhancement), carbon removal from the atmosphere and its subsequent storage are very closely linked. In these cases, impacts on biodiversity are likely to be limited to marine and terrestrial systems respectively. In other cases, the steps are discrete, and various combinations of capture and storage options are possible. Thus the carbon that is fixed within land biomass, for example, could be either: dumped in the ocean as crop residues; incorporated into the soil as charcoal; or used as fuel with the resultant CO_2 chemically removed at source and stored either in sub-surface reservoirs or the deep ocean. In these cases, each step will have different and additive potential impacts on biodiversity, and potentially separate impacts on marine and terrestrial environments.

Ocean fertilization involves increased biological primary production with associated changes in phytoplankton community structure and species diversity, and implications for the wider food web. Ocean fertilization may be achieved through the external addition of nutrients (Fe, N or P) or, possibly, by modifying ocean upwelling. If carried out on a climatically significant scale, changes may include an increased risk of harmful algal blooms, and increased benthic biomass. Potential effects on fisheries are uncertain. If Fe is used to stimulate primary production, increases in one region may be offset, to some degree, by decreases elsewhere. Ocean fertilization is expected to increase the midwater production of methane and nitrous oxide; if released to the atmosphere, these greenhouse gases would significantly reduce the effectiveness of the technique. Large-scale ocean fertilization would slow near-surface ocean acidification but increase acidification (and potential anoxia) in mid- and deep-water. The small-scale experiments conducted to date indicate that this is a technique of doubtful effectiveness for geoengineering purposes.

Enhanced weathering would involve large-scale mining and transport of carbonate and silicate rocks, and the spreading of solid or liquid materials on land or sea. The scale of impacts (that may be positive as well as negative) on terrestrial and coastal ecosystems will depend on the method and scale of implementation. CO_2 is naturally removed from the atmosphere by the weathering (dissolution) of carbonate and silicate rocks. This process could be artificially accelerated by techniques that include releasing calcium carbonate or other dissolution products of alkaline minerals into the ocean or spreading abundant silicate minerals such as olivine over agricultural soils. In the ocean, this technique could, in theory, be used to counter ocean acidification; the practicalities have yet to be tested.

The impacts on biodiversity of ecosystem carbon storage through afforestation, reforestation, or the enhancement of soil and wetland carbon depend on the method and scale of implementation. If managed well, such approaches have the potential to increase or maintain biodiversity. Afforestation, reforestation and land-use change are already being promoted as climate change mitigation options, and are not considered by many to be geoengineering. Much guidance has already been developed, by the Convention on Biological Diversity and others, to maximize the biodiversity benefits of these approaches and minimize the disadvantages (e.g., planting assemblages of native species rather than exotic monocultures).

Production of biomass for carbon sequestration on a scale large enough to be climatically significant is likely to either compete for

land with food and other crops or involve large-scale land-use change, with impacts on biodiversity as well as greenhouse-gas emissions that may partially offset (or even exceed) the carbon sequestered as biomass. The coupling of biomass production with its use as bioenergy in power stations equipped with effective carbon capture at source has the potential to be carbon negative. The net effects on biodiversity and greenhouse-gas emissions would depend on the approaches used. The storage or disposal of biomass may have impacts on biodiversity separate from those involved in its production. Removal of organic matter from agricultural ecosystems is likely to have negative impacts on agricultural productivity and biodiversity, and may increase the need for fertilizer application to maintain soil fertility.

The impacts of long-term storage of biochar (charcoal) in different soil types and under different environmental conditions are not well understood. Important issues that need to be resolved include the stability of carbon in the biochar, and effects on soil water retention, N_2O release, crop yields, mycorrhizal fungi, soil microbial communities and detritivores.

Ocean storage of terrestrial biomass (e.g., crop residues) is expected to have a negative impact on biodiversity. The deposition of ballasted bales would likely have significant local physical impacts on the seabed due to the sheer mass of the material. Wider, long-term indirect effects of oxygen depletion and deep-water acidification could be regionally significant if there were cumulative deposition, and subsequent decomposition, of many gigatonnes of organic carbon.

Chemical capture of CO_2 from ambient air would require a large amount of energy. Some proposed processes may also have high demand for freshwater, and potential risk of chemical pollution from sorbent manufacture; otherwise they would have relatively small direct impacts on biodiversity. Removal of CO_2 from the ambient air (where its concentration is 0.04%) is much more difficult and energy intensive than its capture from flue gases of power stations (where levels are about 300 times higher, at ~12%); it is therefore unlikely to be viable without additional carbon-free energy sources. CO_2 extracted from the atmosphere would need to be stored either in the ocean or in sub-surface geological reservoirs with additional potential impacts; alternatively, it could be converted to carbonates and bicarbonates.

Ocean CO_2 storage will necessarily alter the local chemical environment, with a high likelihood of biological effects. Effects on midwater and seafloor ecosystems are likely through the exposure of marine invertebrates, fish and microbes to pH reductions of 0.1 - 0.3 units. Near-total destruction of deep seafloor organisms can be expected if lakes of liquid CO_2 are created. Chronic effects on ecosystems of direct CO_2 injection into the ocean over large ocean areas and long time scales have not yet been studied, and the capacity of ecosystems to compensate or adjust to such CO_2 induced shifts is unknown.

Leakage from CO_2 stored in sub-seafloor geological reservoirs, though considered unlikely if sites are well selected, would have biodiversity implications for benthic fauna on a local scale. CO_2 storage in sub-seafloor geological reservoirs is already being implemented at pilot-scale levels. Its effects on lithospheric microbial communities seem likely to be severe, but have not been studied.

CHAPTER 18

BIODIVERSITY AND CLIMATE MITIGATION

Chapter Outline:
A. What is Climate Mitigation?
B. Is the Endangered Species Act a Viable Tool for Mitigation of GHG Emissions?
C. The Current Federal Approach to Endangered Species and Climate Mitigation
D. Climate Mitigation through Renewable Energy: Conflicts with Endangered Species

One of the essential responses to the problem of climate change is an effort to mitigate our contribution to the rapidly developing phenomenon. Climate mitigation – and the vast array of policy avenues for achieving it – is a big enough topic for its own casebook, so our main concern is the relationship between biodiversity and climate mitigation efforts. Before going there, however, we must first understand the basic concept of climate mitigation as well as the typical methodologies applied to reduce our impact on global climate. We can then consider the wisdom and practicality of using our legal tools designed for the protection of biodiversity (given that many species are especially climate-sensitive and all are climate-dependent at some point) as leverage to force reductions in greenhouse gasses. Once we have considered the policy implications of this avenue, we will take a look at the present federal approach to the issue. Finally, given the importance of renewable energy in the struggle to reduce our dependence on fossil fuels (and thereby cut greenhouse gas emissions), it is important that we consider the significant tension between biodiversity and renewable energy development.

A. WHAT IS CLIMATE MITIGATION?

It is fairly simple logic to observe that those who are causing an ongoing problem are in the best position to fix it, if only by ceasing to engage in their harmful activity. By this reasoning we can see that what is needed, in order to mitigate climate change, is for those who are emitting greenhouse gasses (GHGs) to stop doing so. Of course, in reality it is far more complicated than that. We have become highly dependent on the use of fossil fuels and corresponding release of GHGs, in a wide range of contexts (e.g., manufacturing, transportation, and consumer energy). We cannot stop emitting GHGs overnight, but we can certainly begin to prioritize and minimize, at least gradually.

Emission of GHGs is perhaps the most perfect example of an externality possible, given the vast number of people impacted (everyone!). Externalities are costs that are shared with many people who are neither the decision-maker nor the beneficiary of the action in question. The classic example is traditional (localized) pollution from a factory. Suppose the factory pollutes the air in an area populated by several million people, who are forced to breathe in the harmful chemicals, resulting in diminished health and well-being. Assuming the absence of regulation or litigation, the harm to outsiders will not play a role in the cost-benefit analysis used in designing the factory. The shared harm is worth only as much as its impact on the decision-maker, which is far less than its total value, so it carries less weight against the benefits of operating the factory or costs of technological tools to reduce pollution. This results in less efficient decision-making, so externalities are best regulated.

In addition to operating as an externality, GHG emissions pose both commons and free rider problems as well. For goods that are capable of either sustainable use or total and final consumption, a private owner will likely use the good sustainably in order to maximize the total yield (which might be a pasture for grazing, trees in a forest, or fish in a fishery, for example). If the good is freely available to all, however (a common good), the rational user will take as much as he can as fast as possible, knowing that the good will be depleted no matter what he does and wanting to get the largest possible share. This concept is most famously detailed in ecologist Garrett Hardin's *The Tragedy of the Commons*. The commons problem works best with consumable resources, but is typically applied to the traditional pollution context via treating clean air or clean water as the common good, and polluting it as the taking or using up of that good. It is easy to see how this applies in the context of GHGs. A stable climate is the good that is being destroyed, and seeing that it will be destroyed no matter what one actor does, the actor will go ahead and profit by engaging in an industry that emits GHGs.

While the tragedy of the commons demonstrates why there is no incentive to cut GHGs in the pessimistic context of global devastation, the free rider problem applies in the opposite context, in which there are substantial global efforts to reduce GHGs. For the individual emitter whose contribution of GHGs is not sufficient alone to have a significant impact on climate change, and absent regulatory force, there is no incentive to join in this effort. The rest of the world can solve the problem of climate change at no expense to this entity, so the rational choice is to keep business as usual. For a discussion of these and other collective action problems, as well as individual psychological factors in the context of climate mitigation choices, see Andrew Green, *Self Control, Individual Choice, and Climate Change*, 26 VA. ENVTL. L.J. 77 (2008).

What the application of these theories demonstrates is that GHGs are not going to decline unless there is significant regulatory pressure to reduce emissions. The term "climate mitigation" encompasses the wide variety of approaches that might be taken to force a reduction in GHG emissions. It also contemplates the reduction of GHGs via reforestation, in light of the carbon-absorbing nature of forests (indeed, by some measures, deforestation has had a greater impact on climate than the entire transportation industry). This chapter will consider whether the protection of biodiversity, while certainly related to climate change, is a feasible *legal tool* for climate mitigation.

First, we will take a more detailed look at the need for climate mitigation, as well as the scope of the GHG problem, via the following excerpt of a report from the Organisation for Economic Co-Operation and Development (OECD). The OECD is a forum comprised of 30 member countries, which work together to analyze the economic, social, and environmental issues that arise as a result of the modern globalization trend. The OECD consults with governments on a range of policy issues. The representatives of member countries meet to engage in comparison of policy experiences, consideration of common problems, identification of best practices, and coordination of domestic and international policies. The OECD member countries consist of the world's major economies, including the United States.

Climate Change Mitigation: What Do We Do?
Organisation for Economic Co-Operation and Development (OECD), 2008.

World GHG emissions have roughly doubled since the early 1970s, and on current policies could rise by over 70% during 2008-2050. Historically, energy-related GHG emissions were predominantly from the richer developed countries of the OECD, so that the rise in GHG concentration from the industrial revolution to today is largely accounted for by economic activity in these countries. Today, however, two-thirds of the flow of new emissions into the atmosphere is accounted for by developing countries outside the OECD, and without new policies this share is set to rise further to 2050.

Greenhouse gases are emitted by many economic activities. Quantitatively, the largest share is accounted for by power generation (electricity production and transformation were responsible for 26% of global emissions in 2004), followed by industry generally (about 19%) and transportation (13%). It is important to note that deforestation and forest degradation (about 17%) are estimated to account for more emissions globally than the entire transport sector.

Figure 2 illustrates the likely build-up of GHG concentrations to 2100 based on a "business as usual" scenario and without any climate policies beyond those currently in place. It also shows the ultimate extent of global warming associated with these GHG concentrations. The OECD baseline scenario assumes world economic growth averaging just over 3.5% in purchasing-power-parity terms up to 2050, with a gradual catch-up in living standards of developing countries to those of the developed ones. In terms of emissions and resulting concentrations, the baseline is quite close to the average of other recent studies; some are more optimistic, but others less so.

Figure 2. Greenhouse gas concentration and world temperature would rise sharply
without new policy action

(Projected trends in greenhouse gas concentration and associated temperature increases
in the absence of new climate change policies)

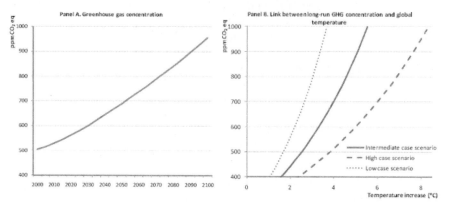

Note: The scenarios embed different values for the climate sensitivity parameter. This parameter measures the impact on temperature of a doubling of concentration and determines the link between long-run GHG concentration and global temperature at the steady state. Because of the inertia of the system, steady-state temperatures may be reached several decades after concentration stabilisation. The climate sensitivity parameter equals 4.5 in the "high case" scenario, 3 in the "intermediate case" scenario, and 2 in the "low case" scenario.

Source: Magicc 5.3, OECD ENV-Linkages model and IPCC (2007), AR4.

There are clearly grounds for concern. The mid-range estimate for global warming to the end of the century, close to 4° Celsius compared with preindustrial levels, brings temperature to a level where destructive climate events are not improbable; and the temperature would keep rising into the next century even if concentration were to stabilise at that point. It has to be noted that in many respects the OECD baseline scenario is not a particularly pessimistic one. Energy intensity – the amount of energy used to produce a given level of gross domestic product (GDP) – is assumed to fall continuously, partly because as living standards across the world converge, GDP shifts steadily towards less energy-intensive products. At the same time, ongoing efficiency gains are expected in the use of energy, partly as a result of high energy prices.

Some might argue that the problem just cannot be this bad, and at least two lines of argument deserve brief comment here. One is that the rise in oil and other energy prices in recent years should, if sustained, trigger major changes in behaviour that would in turn curb emissions. The second is that the baseline scenario underestimates the capacity for technological innovation to find solutions to problems.

There is of course an important element of truth in the energy price argument, although volatile oil prices do not provide clear signals to motivate long-term changes in behaviour. ... The price of oil is projected to keep rising as conventional oil becomes increasingly scarce relative to demand because of the depletion of oil reserves. But while oil is scarce, other hydrocarbons – notably non-conventional oils such as the Canadian tar sands and coal – are much less so. So the OECD baseline shows the price of coal, in particular, as leveling off even as more coal is being used. The problem is that non-conventional oil and coal are actually more carbon-intensive than petroleum, so that the estimated CO2 intensity per unit of energy consumed rises by some 35% between now and 2050. In other words, any possible reduction in emissions due to less use of motor transport due to high oil prices is mostly offset by a shift to more CO2-intensive coal in power generation.

When it comes to the argument that innovation will save the day, it is certainly true that innovation policies will play a central role in making a mitigation strategy affordable. But Research and Development (R&D) efforts, however intensive, cannot by themselves accomplish enough if the incentives to deploy new technologies are weak. Figure 4 seeks to illustrate this point by presenting an alternative scenario that includes an aggressive world-wide policy of investing in abatement-related R&D, raising such spending four-fold from current levels as a share of global GDP back to the peak levels observed in the early 1980s, but without applying any other policies to reduce emissions.

While such an R&D-led approach clearly yields some results, OECD estimates suggest that these are not nearly enough to stabilise GHG concentration levels by the end of the century. In fact, even a 30-fold increase in worldwide public R&D spending on low-carbon technologies, raising it to about 1% of global GDP annually, would not be enough to achieve this target. The essential problem is that, even if innovative and effective technologies emerge, they will not be intensively used until their costs come down close to those of existing competing technologies, unless incentives are put in place for people to use them. Such cost falls typically take a very long time. Carbon capture and storage (CCS) technology provides a telling and extreme example of this challenge. This technology is still new and expensive. Intensive R&D efforts would in all likelihood bring costs down steadily. But this technology would not be widely used in power generation unless there were significant incentives to cut carbon emissions, since otherwise it reduces generating efficiency and hence raises costs without providing any return.

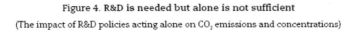

Figure 4. R&D is needed but alone is not sufficient

(The impact of R&D policies acting alone on CO_2 emissions and concentrations)

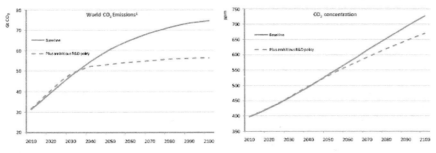

1. CO_2 emissions excluding emissions from land use, land-use change and forestry. Emissions of non-CO_2 gases are not covered by the model used in this analysis and are therefore excluded from these simulations.

Source: WITCH model simulations.

What Can Be Done?

Faced with the consequences and costs of inaction, governments have reached a consensus internationally that global emissions need to be cut significantly. ... The OECD has simulated a number of possible scenarios for ambitious reductions in GHG emissions along with their economic and environmental impacts compared with those of the baseline scenario with no new policy action. Figure 5 presents the time path of GHG emissions associated with these scenarios.

For illustrative purposes the economic issues involved in designing a comprehensive approach to reducing emissions are explored here primarily by examining one mitigation reference scenario. This scenario eventually stabilises GHG concentrations at a level equal to 550 parts per million (ppm) of CO2 (or about 450 ppm CO2 only), while allowing a moderate overshooting of this level over an interim period. It has to be emphasised that this scenario has no specific normative significance. Indeed, many countries have taken the view that a more ambitious objective would be appropriate as would be required, for instance, to cap the extent of global warming at 2°Celsius. But for illustrative purposes, this [document] focuses on one scenario and uses this to examine quantitatively how different policy assumptions might affect overall results.

Major changes in behaviour and production methods will be needed to achieve GHG mitigation at the lowest possible cost. Mitigation is achieved by reducing both the energy intensity of GDP and the carbon intensity of energy used. As a side effect of these changes, GDP growth will also be affected... . Under the mitigation reference scenario examined here, it is estimated that the average growth of the world economy over the period 2008-2050 would be some 0.13 percentage points lower than in the absence of climate change policies. The impact on GDP growth is small in the early years, but increases significantly after 2025. By 2050, the level of world GDP is estimated to be some 4.8% below what it would be in the absence of climate change policies. The reason for this GDP loss is that substantial human and capital resources will have to be shifted to working on GHG mitigation, thus reducing the resources available for producing other goods and services. While abatement obviously generates other benefits in terms of avoided climate change damage, such benefits are not always directly captured in conventional GDP, and are not reflected here.

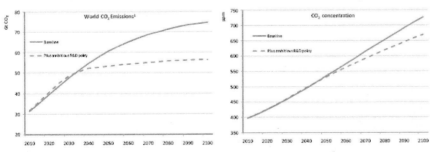

Figure 5. **Stabilising the climate will ultimately require large emission cuts**

(Greenhouse gas emissions in an illustrative 550 ppm stabilisation concentration scenario, 2005-2100)

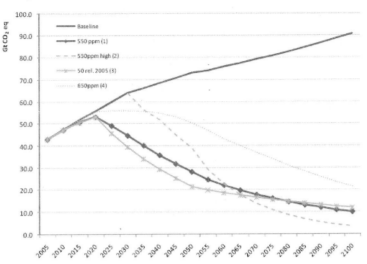

1. Stabilisation at 550ppm CO_2 eq all gases included (corresponding to about 450ppm CO_2 only) with modest overshooting.

2. Stabilisation at 550ppm CO_2 eq all gases included (corresponding to about 450ppm CO_2 only) with high overshooting.

3. 50% GHG emission cut in 2050 with respect to 2005 levels.

4. Stabilisation at 650ppm CO_2 eq all gases included (corresponding to about 550ppm CO_2 only) without overshooting.

Source: OECD ENV-Linkages model.

Ambitious GHG abatement is economically rational, but it will not be cheap. The costs would be lower if a less stringent emissions pathway were chosen, or if greater overshooting of the target were allowed. For instance, allowing more interim overshooting (to over 600 ppm instead of about 560 ppm) could lower the GDP loss in 2050 to around 2%. But such overshooting would come at the price of greater risks of irreversible damage from climate change and would merely postpone some of the costs farther in the future. It is also the case that the cost estimate presented could be lower if certain mitigation options not built into the reference scenario were taken into account. Three of these [are] related to energy subsidies, reforestation and the emergence of major new low-carbon technologies[]. On the other hand, the cost estimates may be optimistic in that they assume that all world emission sources are covered and that the large required shifts in resources all take place smoothly, without transitional costs.

NOTES & QUESTIONS

1. The OECD report describes GHG abatement as economically rational in spite of its heavy cost. Do you agree? Does this question depend upon how we define economically rational? Suppose we define it selfishly, focusing only on those alive today – would that change the equation?

2. Does the advice seem realistic? What did you think of the assumption, admitted to in the last sentence of this excerpt, that all sources would be covered?

Given how severe the cutting is even with that assumption, is it even possible for the actually covered sources to go further to compensate for the rogues?

3. We all, as individuals living in the world, contribute to GHG emissions. Collectively this is significant. Are you willing to change your behavior? What options do you have? Do any of the theories discussed in the text before the OECD excerpt apply to you?

4. A few years ago a significant climate mitigation hurdle was jumped in *Massachusetts v. EPA*, 549 U.S. 497 (2007). The Court held that the Environmental Protection Agency (EPA) had the authority to regulate greenhouse gas emissions under the Clean Air Act, and indeed was required to make a finding as to whether GHGs endanger public health or welfare. *Id.* at 534. In an exceptional moment for environmentalists, the Court placed its stamp of legitimacy on climate mitigation via GHG reduction, stating that "[a] well-documented rise in global temperatures has coincided with a significant increase in the concentration of carbon dioxide in the atmosphere. Respected scientists believe the two trends are related." *Id.* at 504-05.

The EPA has begun to take climate mitigation steps since *Massachusetts v. EPA*. On December 7, 2009, the EPA published a finding that six greenhouse gases constitute a threat to public health and welfare, and that motor vehicle emissions cause and contribute to the climate change problem. On May 13, 2010, EPA set greenhouse gas emissions thresholds determining the point at which permits are required for new and existing industrial facilities (stationary sources). This final rule "tailors" these requirements to apply to only the largest greenhouse gas emitters: power plants, refineries, and cement production facilities. On March 27, 2012, EPA proposed a "Carbon Pollution Standard for New Power Plants" that would set national limits on the amount of carbon pollution that power plants are allowed to emit. The proposed rule applies only to new fossil-fuel-fired electric utility generating units.

B. IS THE ENDANGERED SPECIES ACT A VIABLE TOOL FOR MITIGATION OF GHG EMISSIONS?

Can the EPA manage climate mitigation on its own, or does it make sense for the Fish & Wildlife Service to come after GHG emitters for the harm they are doing to ecosystems, including the habitat of threatened and endangered species? We know that the ESA prohibits such behavior (jeopardizing or taking listed species or destroying their habitat), so what, if anything, should we do about it? And, for that matter, can we make all the necessary causal links come together for proper ESA enforcement against GHG emitters? Consider the arguments in the next two article excerpts. First, Gerhart makes a case that the ESA cannot be successfully used to stop actions that emit GHGs, in spite of the devastating impact that climate change has on some listed species. Next, Ruhl explains why we would not want to litigate this issue in any event, but rather leave it to the agencies to sort out how to use the ESA to the benefit of climate-impacted species, which should be primarily in the adaptation context.

Matthew Gerhart, *Climate Change and the Endangered Species Act: The Difficulty of Proving Causation*

36 Ecology Law Quarterly 167 (2009).

In recent years, the Fish and Wildlife Service (FWS) and the National Marine Fisheries Service (NMFS) have received several petitions to list species under the Endangered Species Act (the ESA) based on the impacts of climate change. In 2006, NMFS listed two species of coral as threatened, due in large part to the effects of climate change on the oceans where the corals exist. In 2007, FWS announced that it would receive public comments on a petition to list several penguin species under the ESA. In a more highly publicized decision, FWS proposed to list the polar bear as a threatened species. That proposal followed in the wake of several studies that found that increased temperatures have reduced the extent of seasonal pack ice, which has reduced the availability of seals, polar bears' main food source.

Once FWS lists a species, it is only a matter of time, before an environmental group files suit under the ESA to stop a project on the basis that greenhouse gas emissions harm a listed species. Frustrated at the federal government's refusal to regulate greenhouse gas emissions, states and environmental groups have increasingly resorted to litigation to force legislative action; states and environmentalists have already tried to use the Clean Air Act, the National Environmental Policy Act, and common law to address the impacts of climate change. Undoubtedly, environmental groups will also view the ESA as a legal tool for forcing action on climate change. This was confirmed when the policy director at the Center for Biological Diversity, which filed petitions to list the staghorn and elkhorn coral (and the polar bear), stated, "We think this victory on coral critical habitat actually moves the entire Endangered Species Act onto a firm legal foundation for challenging global-warming pollution."

How will climate change affect the workings of the Endangered Species Act? In some respects, the ESA will continue to function as it has for over thirty years. For example, suppose that FWS lists the polar bear as threatened and a private individual were to hunt a polar bear. Section 9 of the ESA would apply, and the individual would be guilty of a prohibited "take." If the federal government proposed oil drilling in polar bear habitat, and FWS concluded that the oil drilling would likely jeopardize the survival of polar bears as a species, section 7 would prohibit the federal government from going forward with the project.

The analysis becomes more complex, however, when the threat to the polar bear comes not from these traditional activities but from climate change and the greenhouse gas emissions that cause it. Suppose that a federal agency is involved in a project to build a coal-fired power plant in Ohio. Would section 7 of the ESA require the federal government to analyze the impacts of the coal plant on the survival and recovery of the polar bear species? Could a plaintiff argue that a coal plant in Ohio has violated section 9 by releasing carbon dioxide, which contributes to global warming, which causes disappearance of the sea ice, which caused a particular polar bear to drown in open water?

*   *   *

A. Climate Change, Section 7, and Causation

Section 7 prohibits agencies from taking actions that would jeopardize the survival of a listed species or result in the adverse modification of habitat of a listed species. What matters for section 7 purposes is the impact of the agency action on the species as a whole—not the harm to individual organisms. To take the example of polar bears, a valid section 7 claim would need to show that an agency action harmed not just one or two polar bears, but jeopardized polar bears as a species.

Thus, in order to apply section 7 to a climate change case, a plaintiff would need to prove two causation elements. First, the plaintiff would need to demonstrate that climate change causes harm to the survival or recovery of a species, rather than harm to merely a few organisms. Second, the plaintiff would need to show that the specific agency action at issue causes jeopardy or adverse modification. For climate change, this means showing that a particular agency action causes climate change.

Plaintiffs will likely have little difficulty establishing that climate change threatens the survival or recovery of a listed species. NMFS, by listing the elkhorn and staghorn corals as threatened, has already recognized that species may warrant listing on the basis of changes caused by climate change. FWS, in proposing to list the polar bear as threatened, has indicated a similar willingness to accept that climate change may imperil the survival of a species. Given these developments, I proceed under the assumption that there is no logical or doctrinal barrier to a plaintiff's proving that climate change threatens the survival or recovery of a species. I do not suggest that this will be easy to prove, but the problem is an evidentiary one, not a doctrinal one.

Even if a plaintiff can prove that climate change jeopardizes a listed species, can a plaintiff prove that a specific agency action causes climate change? Answering this question requires an understanding of the case law concerning causation under section 7. Two causation issues that arise in the case law are particularly relevant to climate change. First, when a federal agency proposes an action, how far must it look to determine the impacts of the proposed action? Under the ESA, this inquiry is resolved through the "action area." Second, what is the baseline against which the incremental impact of a proposed action is measured? Under the ESA, this issue is addressed through the "environmental baseline." The legal definitions of the "action area" and the "environmental baseline" illustrate the challenges plaintiffs will face in proving that an agency action impacted a species via climate change.

B. Action Area

A significant causation obstacle in a climate change case is that the effects of greenhouse gas emissions may appear in places far removed from the source of the emissions. To return to the polar bear example, emissions in the lower forty-eight states affect polar bears in Alaska. Assuming polar bears were listed as threatened, would a federal action that would lead to greenhouse gas emissions in California require an assessment of the potential impacts on polar bears in Alaska under section 7?

Courts have addressed this issue, in part, through the concept of "action area," which is the area in which a federal agency must assess the impacts of its proposed action. Courts have upheld the joint NMFS and FWS regulations that define "action area" as "all areas to be affected directly or indirectly by the Federal action and not merely the immediate area involved in the action." The federal agency must analyze the effects of its proposed action on the listed species even if those impacts occur on lands not owned and managed by the agency. However, courts have held that the "action area" does not necessarily include the species' entire habitat; it includes only those areas in which the proposed federal action will have an effect on the species.

Two cases illustrate the legal requirements for defining an "action area." In *Defenders of Wildlife v. Babbitt*, plaintiffs challenged the biological opinions of several federal agencies' actions that could affect the endangered Sonoran pronghorn. The National Park Service (NPS) and Bureau of Land Management argued that they needed to analyze the impacts of their proposed actions only in the immediate area of the action, and did not need to consider impacts on lands they did not manage. NPS argued that for its proposed activities in Organ Pipe Cactus National Monument, the Service needed to analyze only the impacts on the pronghorn within the monument.

Evidence in NPS's Biological Opinion, however, indicated that a road running through the monument could prevent pronghorn from traveling through it, and thereby sever the pronghorn into two populations, one east of the monument, and one west. Thus, the evidence suggested that NPS's proposed federal actions within the monument would have effects on pronghorn outside of it. As a result, the court held that the regulations prohibit the agency from limiting the action area to the park.

In *Native Ecosystems Council v. Dombeck*, two environmental groups sued to stop a timber sale because the U.S. Forest Service (USFS) had failed to analyze adequately the impacts of the action on threatened grizzly bears. The agency action in question was a 226-acre timber sale. In the Biological Assessment for the timber sale, USFS selected an action area extending 16.5 miles to the west of the timber sale and 1.5 miles to the east of the boundary of the timber sale. Plaintiffs claimed that the selection of this action area was arbitrary and capricious.

The Ninth Circuit asserted that ordinarily an agency is entitled to deference in selecting the action area, since the decision involves application of scientific expertise. USFS failed in this instance, however, to provide any evidence that justified its choosing the particular boundaries in question. Accordingly, the court held that USFS had failed to comply with the regulations, which required it to construe the action area based on the areas that would "actually be affected by the timber sale (by determining, for instance, where displaced bears might wander)."

Furthermore, the environmental group plaintiffs presented evidence that the action area chosen by USFS excluded certain areas in which the proposed action would affect grizzly bears. The Biological Assessment stated that the timber sale would cause grizzly bears to move outside the timber sale, and a sheep grazing allotment was just beyond the eastern boundary of the Biological Assessment's action area. If the bears moved onto the grazing allotments, they faced the risk of being "removed or killed due to conflicts with livestock." The court determined that USFS had acted arbitrarily by failing to justify its exclusion of the grazing allotment from the action area.

C. Action Area and Climate Change

The concept of the "action area" addresses one causation issue—when an entity acts, what is the geographic scope of the effects for which it is responsible? The action area answers this question by limiting the effects for which the agency is responsible to the geographic area where the agency action has direct and indirect effects on the listed species, as evidenced by the record, even if the impacts occur on lands not owned or managed by the action agency. To date, the chains of causation in section 7 cases have been tightly linked, as far is geography is concerned: a timber sale caused grizzly prey to avoid the action area, so the grizzlies moved outside of the area as well; a road into a national monument restricted the movement of pronghorn outside of the monument.

Climate change strains the concept of "action area" because the effects of greenhouse gas emissions occur around the globe. To return to the polar bear example, a potential plaintiff might argue that a federal action related to a proposed coal plant in Ohio requires an assessment of the impact that the plant's greenhouse gas emissions will have on polar bears in Alaska. There is nothing in existing regulations or case law that would prevent the Ohio coal plant's action area from extending to impacts in Alaska. Based on traditional action area requirements, the plaintiff could submit evidence in the record that greenhouse gas emissions from other coal plants in Ohio have an indirect effect on polar bears in Alaska, and thus the action area should include polar bear habitat in Alaska.

The policy problem with making such an argument is that the action area expands exponentially if an agency is required to consider the possible impacts of the emissions from the project on all listed species. It may be important that courts normally remedy section 7 violations with injunctive relief, and monetary damages are simply not available in the ESA context, although civil penalties are. This may alleviate some of the concerns voiced in a recent public nuisance suit, in which a district court declined to impose liability on entities for harm from climate change, in part because of the court's reluctance to impose expansive liability. However, a prior lawsuit based on the theory that harm from climate change is a public nuisance was dismissed as well, even though the plaintiffs sought only injunctive relief. As a result, it is unclear whether the absence of a request for money damages in a section 7 suit will alleviate the concerns expressed by courts in recent cases seeking relief from entities alleged to have contributed to global warming. Even with the limited scope of remedies available for section 7 violations, it seems reasonable to assume that many courts would hesitate to interpret section 7 as requiring federal agencies to consider the impacts of their actions' emissions on all listed species.

D. The Environmental Baseline

Once the proper action area is established, the section 7 jeopardy analysis attempts to quantify the incremental impact of an agency action upon a listed species. The joint regulations require FWS and NMFS, when conducting section 7 consultations, to evaluate "the current status of the listed species or critical habitat" and "the effects of the action and cumulative effects on the listed species or critical habitat." The current status of the species is determined through the "environmental baseline," which is defined in the joint regulations as the past and present impacts of all Federal, State, or private actions and other human activities in the action area, the anticipated impacts of all proposed Federal projects in the action area that have already undergone formal or early section 7 consultation, and the impact of State or private actions which are contemporaneous with the consultation in process.

What information is included in the environmental baseline often determines whether the agency will find that the action jeopardizes a listed species. Likewise, the manner in which the agency measures the project's effects against the environmental baseline can determine the outcome of the jeopardy analysis.

To clarify the use of the environmental baseline in the section 7 jeopardy analysis, I will use a hypothetical. Imagine that FWS determines that to survive as a species, the northern spotted owl needs a minimum of one hundred mature individuals, each of which needs a minimum of one thousand acres of suitable habitat. Assume that at present, there are only eighty owls, some of which have access to one thousand acres of habitat, and some of which have access to less than one thousand acres of habitat. The species does not have the minimum population size and the minimum habitat necessary to survive as a species. Consequently, the species is in jeopardy status.

Given this set of facts, I will work through three scenarios. First, suppose that the National Forest Service proposes a timber sale. The timber sale will occur in habitat that is not suitable for spotted owls, and will thus have no impact on the spotted owl. As a result, the agency action will not jeopardize the spotted owl. Note that the spotted owl will still be in jeopardy status, since, after the agency action, there will still be only eighty owls, some of which have inadequate habitat. Nonetheless, the proposed timber sale will not violate section 7, because the agency action has not caused any deterioration in the status of the species.

In the second scenario, the Forest Service proposes a timber sale and as part of the project, the agency proposes to create two thousand acres of habitat for spotted owls. After the agency action, the number of spotted owls with one thousand acres of suitable habitat will increase, but fewer than one hundred owls will have suitable habitat. There will still be too few owls and too little habitat to survive as a species. Thus, after the proposed timber sale, the survival of the spotted owl will remain jeopardized. Nevertheless, the agency action will not violate section 7, because the agency action has not worsened the plight of the spotted owl—in fact, it is has improved it.

In the third scenario, USFS proposes a timber sale that will destroy five thousand acres currently used by spotted owls. In this scenario, it is possible that the agency action will violate section 7. Before the proposed action, the spotted owl was in jeopardy—the environmental baseline was so poor that the spotted owl was already likely to face extinction. Nonetheless, the proposed timber sale will violate section 7 if it harms the spotted owl by hastening its extinction. Very few cases have addressed whether a species must experience a threshold quantity of harm to its chance of survival in order to trigger a section 7 violation. FWS has taken the position that an agency action violates section 7 only if it produces a significant adverse effect on a species' chance of survival.

These three scenarios illustrate two critical aspects of the jeopardy analysis. First, the jeopardy analysis requires the agency to assess the effects of the action once those effects are added to the environmental baseline. A biological opinion cannot simply mention the environmental baseline and then analyze the impacts of the action independently from the species' actual baseline status. Second, the jeopardy analysis looks only at the incremental impact of the agency action, when that impact is added to the environmental baseline. The jeopardy analysis does not require an agency to combine all impacts to make an aggregate jeopardy determination. Nonetheless, a degraded environmental baseline makes a jeopardy finding more likely.

National Wildlife Federation v. National Marine Fisheries Service provides a useful summary of the role of the environmental baseline in the section 7 jeopardy analysis. The National Wildlife Federation sued NMFS based on its 2004 Biological Opinion, which concluded that operation of dams and related facilities of the Federal Columbia River Power System would not jeopardize thirteen species of salmon.

To determine whether the proposed action would jeopardize the salmon, NMFS measured the baseline conditions and then estimated the effects of the proposed agency action. NMFS then compared the effects of the agency action to the baseline conditions; since the effects of the action were no worse than the baseline conditions, NMFS concluded that the proposed action would not jeopardize the salmon. NMFS contended that to conclude otherwise would expand the meaning of "agency action" to include preexisting harms to the species. NMFS argued that under such an approach, once baseline conditions put a species in jeopardy, any agency action would violate section 7—a scheme which the agency found to be untenable.

The Ninth Circuit rejected NMFS's approach, ruling that a biological opinion must assess whether the proposed agency action, when added to the environmental baseline and cumulative effects of other agency actions, will jeopardize the species. This does not mean that when baseline conditions already place a species in jeopardy, an agency action automatically violates section 7:

> Agency action can only "jeopardize" a species' existence if that agency action causes some deterioration in the species' pre-action condition. . . [A]n agency may not take action that will tip a species from a state of precarious survival into a state of likely extinction. Likewise, even where baseline conditions already jeopardize a species, an agency may not take action that deepens the jeopardy by causing additional harm.

Since NMFS failed to incorporate a degraded baseline into the jeopardy analysis, and NMFS did not add the action's effects to the environmental baseline, the court held that the biological opinion was legally insufficient.

E. Environmental Baseline and Climate Change

As previously discussed, agency regulations require that a section 7 consultation result in a biological opinion that calculates an environmental baseline, the impacts of the proposed action, and the cumulative effects of other actions. The agency then adds all of these effects together to determine whether the proposed action will cause jeopardy or adverse modification of critical habitat.

This process has interesting implications when the impacts of a proposed action are greenhouse gas emissions. An agency, or an industry intervenor, could claim that the environmental baseline is a level of greenhouse gas emissions that already commits us to warming for at least several decades, if not centuries, and thus that any proposed agency action is irrelevant—harmful warming will occur anyway.

Support for this position comes from the Intergovernmental Panel on Climate Change (the IPCC), which released its Fourth Assessment Report in 2007. The report cites models indicating that even if global greenhouse gas emissions were immediately cut to zero, the climate would continue to warm over the next several decades. Even if the more modest goal of cutting emissions to 2000 levels was achieved, the climate would be expected to warm by 0.1 degree Celsius each decade for the next two decades.

These long-term effects of emissions stem from the rate at which greenhouse gases are removed from the atmosphere. Different greenhouse gases persist in the atmosphere for different lengths of time. The IPCC report expresses the lifetime of a greenhouse gas as the length of time that it takes for a gas to reduce to 37 percent of its initial volume. The lifetime of methane is twelve years, hydrochlorofluorocarbon-22 (a refrigerant) is twelve years, and nitrous oxide is 110 years. Carbon dioxide has no specific lifetime, but the report states that it takes roughly one hundred years to reduce an amount of carbon dioxide by half. Roughly 20 percent of the amount of carbon dioxide emitted remains in the atmosphere for millennia.

What is the significance of greenhouse gas lifecycles for calculating the environmental baseline in a section 7 suit? It means that an agency could claim that the environmental baseline is an amount of greenhouse gases that commits us to warming for at least several decades. An agency could then claim that if jeopardy will result to the listed species, that jeopardy results from the emissions that are already in the atmosphere, rather than from the proposed agency action.

To illustrate, I return to the polar bear example. Imagine that it can be determined that an increase in atmospheric and sea temperatures of a certain magnitude will reduce the extent of the sea ice which will in turn jeopardize the survival of polar bears. While it does not matter what this magnitude is for my purposes, assume that it is three degrees Celsius above current temperatures. Further, imagine that a defendant can show that the present atmospheric concentration of greenhouse gases commits us to a warming of three degrees Celsius over the next century, even if emissions are immediately cut to zero. Such a defendant could plausibly claim that the proposed action does not jeopardize the survival of the polar bear, because the polar bear is already in jeopardy due to past emissions.

Ultimately, then, plaintiffs face two hurdles under section 7. Given the current models of climate change, defendants have ample evidence to argue that the present concentration of greenhouse gases is such that climate change will occur for many years. As a result, defendants can argue that past actions, instead of present actions, caused the climate change and consequently caused the harm of which the plaintiffs complain.

Furthermore, a defendant can argue that the emissions from a proposed action do not contribute significantly to climate change, and thus do not result in jeopardy. In support of this argument, a defendant could point to FWS position that only significant adverse impacts to a species' chance of survival violate section 7. This jeopardy analysis hinges on the quantity of harm to a species' chance of survival needed to constitute a section 7 violation. If an agency action that causes any deterioration in a species' baseline condition results in jeopardy, then proposed actions that emit virtually any amount of greenhouse gases will likely jeopardize a species sensitive to climate change. By contrast, if courts uphold the FWS position that only significant adverse impacts on a species' chance of survival violate section 7, very few actions that emit greenhouse gases will result in jeopardy—

since few actions emit enough greenhouse gases to have a significant impact on climate change.

NOTES & QUESTIONS

1. As you might expect, there are similar issues standing in the way of using the section 9 take prohibition to go after GHG emitters. Gerhart discusses them in the second half of his article excerpted above. To summarize:

> Three aspects of climate change translate into three distinct problems for proving causation under section 9. First, a huge number of sources emit greenhouse gases at any given time, and each source emits only a small fraction of global emissions. The sheer volume of emitters poses a problem because of the traditional requirement that an entity be liable for harm only if its conduct is a substantial factor in bringing about the harm.

> The persistence of greenhouse gas emissions in the atmosphere is also problematic, because any current harm is attributable not only to current emitters, but to past emitters as well. Consequently, it is it even more difficult to establish that any given emitter's emissions are a substantial factor in causing climate change harm.

> Third, it is nearly impossible to trace the lifecycle of greenhouse gas emissions from a particular source, which renders it virtually impossible to trace particular emissions to particular climate change harms. This aspect of greenhouse gas emissions poses a legal problem because of the traditional rule that an entity is liable only to the particular person whose injuries the entity actually caused.

Matthew Gerhart, *Climate Change and the Endangered Species Act: The Difficulty of Proving Causation*, 36 ECOLOGY L.Q. 167, 183–4 (2009).

2. Aside from the doctrinal issues with the ESA's applicability to GHG emissions, can you imagine the practical implications? How might the scope of enforcement be limited? Indeed, it is not necessary for one to be completely persuaded by the doctrinal arguments Gerhart makes. Even if we can see some potential for getting past the causation issue and applying the ESA to GHG emissions, the idea of actually going forward with such an approach is quite daunting, as described by one of the editors of this casebook:

> To be sure, as with the listing decision, the FWS consultation decision depends on a three-part causal chain: greenhouse gas emissions cause tropospheric warming, which in turn causes secondary climate change effects, which in turn cause ecological changes that adversely affect the species. Although determining whether these downscale effects actually occur may be difficult to say in particular scenarios, the point is that they could occur. Unless the FWS intends on ruling out that possibility entirely - a difficult proposition after Massachusetts v. EPA - it stands to reason that consultations under Section 7(a)(2) should consider the possible direct, indirect, and cumulative effects of greenhouse gas emissions and climate change.

***

As with the Section 9 take prohibition, however, the problem with fitting climate change into the consultation framework is that it exhibits more certainty at macro levels than at micro levels. Consider, for example, the proposed coal-fired power plant in Florida and its effects on the pika in the Sierra Nevada Mountains. It would seem quite a stretch to conclude that the power plant emissions will jeopardize the pika. Yet, at a macro level the analysis is rather straight forward: the power plant emits greenhouse gases (a direct effect of the action), greenhouse gases are reasonably certain to warm the troposphere (an indirect effect of the action), a warming troposphere is reasonably certain to adversely alter ecological conditions for the pika, and it is reasonably expected that such ecological changes will bring an end to the pika. At the micro level, however, it becomes difficult to link the individual plant's emissions as the jeopardizing agent for the pika, given that all greenhouse gas emissions worldwide are subject to the same macro analysis. Other than quantity of emissions, the FWS would have no reasoned basis for distinguishing between the power plant in Florida, a farm in Kansas, or an elementary school in Oregon. All have an adverse effect on the pika - and some arguably have more of an effect - but given the small proportion of total greenhouse gas emissions that each represents, the FWS can likely justify finding that none of the emitting land uses jeopardizes the species.

Given these attributes of greenhouse gas emission effects on climate, it is difficult to conceive of how the agency would go about aggressively regulating greenhouse gas emissions through the jeopardy consultation program. The FWS does not have the pollution control expertise of the EPA, nor does any provision of the ESA explicitly provide authority to engage in emissions regulation. Given that all emission sources contribute to warming effects, the threat of jeopardy findings would have to be applied universally to all sources. This, in turn, might induce emission sources to engage in emission offsets (e.g., by purchasing forestation credits) or technological and operational emission reductions. But is the FWS equipped to assume the role of nation-wide regulator of farms, industrial facilities, auto emissions, and everything else? In short, the idea that all emission sources present jeopardy conditions to each and every climate-threatened species would prove too much, and likely render the ESA and the FWS political targets in the first degree.

J.B. Ruhl, *Climate Change and the Endangered Species Act: Building Bridges to the No-Analog Future*, 88 B.U. L. REV. 1, 44-47 (2008).

3. Even in the face of seemingly insurmountable doctrinal and practical obstacles, there remain those who believe that the ESA can and should be used to go after GHG emissions, especially in light of the conspicuous absence of any targeted federal legislation on the matter.

The notion that there is no causal connection between greenhouse gas emissions and the decline of the polar bear (or other species) is demonstrably incorrect. The connection between greenhouse gas emissions and sea ice reductions—and the effect that sea ice decline has on polar bears—is supported by voluminous scientific literature and, indeed, is the central reason for the decision to place the polar bear on the list of threatened and endangered species. Just as there is no requirement to link the thinning of any particular bald eagle egg to any particular molecule of DDT to demonstrate that authorization of the use of DDT may result in a taking of bald eagles, there is no requirement to link any particular molecule of carbon dioxide or other greenhouse pollutant to the death of an individual bear. As the Supreme Court stated in Tennessee Valley Authority, section 7 "admits of no exception," and affords endangered species "the highest of priorities." The administration's attempt to create an exception for the most important threat to biodiversity the Earth has ever seen is almost certainly doomed to failure.

Anna T. Moritz et al., *Biodiversity Baking and Boiling: Endangered Species Act Turning Down the Heat*, 44 TULSA L. REV. 205, 226 (2008); see also Ari N. Sommer, *Taking the Pit Bull off the Leash: Siccing the Endangered Species Act on Climate Change*, 36 B.C. ENVTL. AFF. L. REV. 273 (2009).

4. To the extent that the ESA is capable of serving as a tool to protect listed species from the perils of climate change, what might be the best way to apply it? Which of its provisions work best in this context, and at what stage? And who should do the work to figure this out? In the next excerpt, J.B. Ruhl points out the downsides to allowing litigation to lead the way, especially in the mitigation context.

J.B. Ruhl, *Climbing Mount Mitigation: A Proposal for Legislative Suspension of Climate Change "Mitigation Litigation"*

1 Washington & Lee Journal of Energy, Climate, & the Environment 71 (2010).

[The portion of this article excerpted here] focuses on the dysfunctional effects litigation designed to force agencies into regulating greenhouse gas emissions under existing laws, what I call "mitigation litigation," is likely to have on agency policy development. As strong proponents of mitigation litigation have described their agenda, it is simply that "we must launch a thousand arrows immediately." And they have been launched. For example, with over $6 million of funding already committed, the Center for Biological Diversity recently formed the Climate Law Institute to, among other things, "establish legal precedents requiring existing environmental laws such as the Clean Air Act, Endangered Species Act, National Environmental Policy Act, Clean Water Act, and the California Environmental Quality Act to be fully implemented to regulate greenhouse gas emissions." Even disregarding the inherently poor attributes of litigation for making national policy in general—i.e., that it is not transparent, it limits public participation, it is piecemeal, it can lead to inconsistent results, it takes a long time to reach conclusion, etc.—mitigation litigation is an especially awful platform for developing national climate change policy. Using the Endangered Species Act as a case study, I argue that, while it has pushed a few agencies into examining the role of existing authorities, mitigation litigation in the long run will lead to an uncoordinated and ineffective climate change policy. Existing legislation, if creatively applied within the bounds of permissible agency statutory interpretation, offers many opportunities for agencies to pursue mitigation and adaptation policies, but not all such opportunities necessarily should be employed to the maximum an agency's policy discretion might allow. The pursuit of mitigation litigation against federal agencies has been designed to push them into emissions mitigation regulation "because it's there," with no clear vision of how to do so at the agency level and no plan for how to coordinate a government-wide climate change policy initiative that includes both mitigation and adaptation.

Targeting agencies with this kind of mitigation litigation forces the federal government to build a mitigation policy through ad hoc, agency-by-agency litigation. To be sure, in the George W. Bush Administration, mitigation litigation under existing laws moved some agencies off center and in the direction of formulating climate change policies. Indeed, *Massachusetts v. EPA* may in retrospect be seen as the jolt needed to put existing laws in play in the climate change policy dialogue. But continuing down the mitigation litigation path will not bring about a coherent, integrated, multi-scalar national climate change policy.

* * *

I define mitigation litigation as any litigation effort designed to force an agency to employ, or to not employ, existing regulatory authority to regulate greenhouse gas emissions or limit a regulated action on the basis of its greenhouse gas emissions. As the Climate Law Institute's mission statement suggests, the primary fronts for the initiative have been the Clean Air Act, Endangered Species Act, and National Environmental Policy Act. Thus far, however, the first wave of mitigation litigation has produced very little mitigation regulation policy. To be sure, courts have interpreted existing statutes to require agencies to integrate climate change into decision making, but they have imposed no particular outcome. For example, the Supreme Court in *Massachusetts v. EPA* pushed the agency toward regulating greenhouse gas automobile emissions under the Clean Air Act, but observed that "EPA no doubt has significant latitude as to the manner, timing, content and coordination of its regulations with those of other agencies." Clearly, the Climate Law Institute effort is designed to focus the next litigation thrust on shaping the policies the EPA and other agencies develop now that they know they cannot so easily avoid making decisions about how to address climate change under their authorizing statutes. As valuable as the first wave of mitigation litigation was for putting existing laws on the climate change policy playing board, however, the launching of the second wave portends only folly.

Nowhere is the potential fallout from this single-minded litigation-led quest for the mitigation peak more evident than in the debate over how to integrate the Endangered Species Act (ESA) into climate change policy. I previously have outlined the scope of discretion agencies have under the existing ESA to engage in climate change mitigation and adaptation measures. Like the Clean Air Act and most other existing environmental laws, the ESA does not mention climate change but is riddled with provisions that offer varying ranges of discretion to agencies to formulate climate change mitigation and adaptation policies, making it a sitting duck for mitigation litigation. In particular, Section 7(a)(2) of the ESA provides:

Each Federal agency shall, in consultation with and with the assistance of the Secretary, insure that any action authorized, funded, or carried out by such agency (..."action agency") is not likely to jeopardize the continued existence of any endangered species or threatened species or result in the destruction or adverse modification of habitat of such species which is determined . . . to be critical . . .

The statute and implementing regulations build an elaborate procedure for carrying out these consultations under which the agency proposing the action (known as the "action agency") must consult with, depending on the species, either the Fish and Wildlife Service (FWS) or the National Marine Fisheries Service (NMFS) through a series of steps designed to predict the impact of the action on listed species, with the ultimate product being a "biological opinion" from the FWS or NMFS "setting forth the [agency's] opinion, and a summary of the information on which the opinion is based, detailing how the agency action affects the species or its critical habitat."

The substantive content for conducting the consultation analysis is defined primarily in joint FWS/NMFS regulations. "Jeopardize" is defined there as "to engage in an action that reasonably would be expected, directly or indirectly, to reduce appreciably the likelihood of both the survival and recovery of a listed species in the wild by reducing the reproduction, numbers, or distribution of that species." "Action" is defined as "all activities or programs of any kind authorized, funded, or carried out, in whole or in part, by Federal agencies in the United States or upon the high seas." "Effects of the action" include "the direct and indirect effects of an action on the species or critical habitat, together with the effects of other activities that are interrelated or interdependent with that action, that will be added to the environmental baseline." The "indirect effects" are "those that are caused by the proposed action and are later in time, but still are reasonably certain to occur."

On the one hand, greenhouse gas emissions and their climate change consequences arguably can be plausibly fit into this framework. Greenhouse gas emissions from actions carried out, funded, or authorized by federal agencies contribute to tropospheric warming, the indirect effects of which could at some later time adversely affect a protected species. Although determining whether these effects actually occur may be difficult to do reliably in particular scenarios, the point is that they could occur.

On the other hand, there are considerable legal, scientific, and practical difficulties with fitting climate change into the consultation framework at the level of detail necessary to evaluate particular federal agency actions, even relatively large or programmatic actions. Consider, for example, a proposed coal-fired power plant in Florida and its effects on the polar bear in the Arctic. The argument for applying the ESA goes as follows: the power plant emits greenhouse gases (a direct effect of the action), greenhouse gases are reasonably certain to warm the troposphere (an indirect effect of the action), a warming troposphere is reasonably certain to adversely alter ecological conditions for the polar bear, and it is reasonably expected that such ecological changes will bring an end to the polar bear as a species.

While that chain of events makes for an easy connect-the-dots story, in fact any effort to link the individual plant's emissions as the jeopardizing agent for the polar bear species would meet obvious objections stemming from the fact that *all* greenhouse gas emissions worldwide are subject to the same causal analysis. Acting through an incredibly complex temporal and spatial causal chain beginning over a century ago, all greenhouse gas molecules are equally to blame for whatever impact climate change has on a species. It is not possible, therefore, to "upscale" current emissions from a particular source and "downscale" them in real time to a particular impact on the ground, which is precisely what the Section 7 consultation process would require the FWS and NMFS to do for every action funded, carried out, or authorized by federal agencies. As a federal court recently explained in deciding the causation requirement of Article III standing had not been met in a claim that current greenhouse gas emissions are causing a public nuisance:

> The undifferentiated nature of greenhouse gas emissions from all global sources and their worldwide accumulation over long periods of time . . . makes clear that there is no realistic probability of tracing any particular alleged effect of global warming to any particular emissions by any specific person, entity, [or] group at any particular point in time . . . [T]he genesis of global warming is attributable to numerous entities which individually and cumulatively over the span of centuries created the effects . . . [I]t Is not plausible to state which emissions—emitted by whom and at what time in the last several centuries and at what place in the world—"caused . . . alleged global warming related injuries.

Every source of greenhouse gas emissions funded, carried out, or authorized by a federal agency, therefore, is on the same footing with respect to causation of jeopardy for a climate-threatened species. In other words, going down the mitigation road with Section 7 would subject a vast segment of our nation's economy to greenhouse gas regulation under the ESA, with no principled way of distinguishing between emission sources for purposes of assigning "jeopardizing" causal status. Either all federal actions would trigger jeopardy status and be subject to regulation by the FWS and NMFS, or the FWS and NMFS would have to adopt arbitrary thresholds for assigning jeopardy status (e.g., quantity or efficiency of emissions) that would face difficult legal challenges.

Indeed, the suggestion that Section 7 could, in Clean Air Act like fashion, arbitrarily apply only to "major" greenhouse gas emission sources but lay off the small ones fundamentally misses the basic theme of the jeopardy prohibition. Moritz et al. argue, for example, that the FWS and NMFS "could set a threshold level for consultation, as long as it was reasonable and sufficiently protective of listed species." But they do not point to authority in Section 7 or elsewhere in the ESA for differentiating between sources in terms of *legal* status if there is no scientific basis for differentiating the sources' *causal* status. The regulatory definition of jeopardy, they point out, is "to reduce *appreciably* the likelihood of both the survival and recovery of a listed species in the wild," which they suggest opens the door to an emissions level threshold. But consider how "appreciably" would be measured once a species is in jeopardy of not surviving and recovering. Jeopardy itself can be thought of as a threshold the ESA prohibits federal agencies from crossing based on the status of the species in question. After a species is listed, it is not the case that no further degradation of the species' condition or its habitat is permitted. Rather, the "incidental take authorization" procedures of Sections 7 and 10 allow public and private actions to cause harm and even death to individuals of the species with FWS and NMFS approval, with the jeopardy prohibition of Section 7 acting as a threshold of maximum tolerance. Hence, in reality there is an increment of "likelihood of survival and recovery" that additional federal and nonfederal actions erode through these incidental take authorizations. At some point, that increment is sufficiently eroded that the next action requiring incidental take authorization would trigger a jeopardy finding regardless of its "size." In the polar bear's case, in other words, conditions could reach the point that the species can tolerate no additional net increase in emissions of greenhouse gases without moving the likelihood of survival and recovery dangerously close to zero. At that point, if we want to entertain this causal story at the micro scale of discrete land uses, *zero* additional emissions of greenhouse gases from *any* source could escape a jeopardy finding.

Moreover, the idea that the ESA can differentiate between "major" and "minor" sources, regulating the former and leaving the latter outside the scope of consultation, turns the "cumulative effects" problem on its head in violation of Section 7. If Moritz et al. believe establishing causation is not a problem for applying Section 7 to emissions from "major" sources, then it follows that it also is not a problem for applying Section 7 to the cumulative effects of "minor" sources. Rarely does one hear environmental protection interest groups lobby in favor of an exemption from Section 7 for projects destroying under 20 acres of forest habitat of an endangered bird, or for projects diverting under 10 acre feet of water for an endangered fish, or for projects releasing under 10 pounds of pesticides for an endangered reptile. I wouldn't either. Why, then, would anyone be comfortable regulating only "major" sources of greenhouse gas emissions under the ESA, other than as an expedient to regulate major sources of greenhouse gas emissions and avoid the political and legal complications of regulating all causal sources? Why would greenhouse gas emissions from, say, hundreds of thousands of farms receiving federal subsidies not cross the jeopardy threshold but emissions from a single large power plant would?

Moritz et al. overlook that Section 7 regulations specifically prohibit this distortion by requiring that cumulative impacts be considered. The precise question under review in a Section 7 consultation is whether "the action, *taken together with cumulative effects*, is likely to jeopardize the continued existence of listed species." Cumulative effects are "those effects of future State or private activities, not involving Federal activities, that are reasonably certain to occur within the action area of the Federal action subject to consultation," and the action area includes "all areas to be affected directly or indirectly by the Federal action and not just the immediate area involved in the action." This means that for greenhouse gas emission sources, if Section 7 is applied to them, the action area is the entire planet and thus *all* greenhouse emissions from *all* sources subject to United States jurisdiction anywhere in the world would have to be included in the cumulative effects component of the consultation. Rather obviously, no source, no matter how small, could escape a jeopardy finding under this causal reasoning once the cumulative effects sources are factored into the consultation. In short, there is no way under Section 7 to have your cake and eat it too; if one believes greenhouse gas emissions can be regulated under Section 7 notwithstanding the tenuous causal theory supporting that view, every source of greenhouse gas emissions the federal government carries out, funds, or authorizes will, because of how cumulative effects and the action area are defined, be found to reduce appreciably the likelihood of both the survival and recovery of all climate-threatened listed species in the world.

My suggestion that this application of Section 7 is not a practical use of the ESA and should be avoided to the extent permitted under the agencies' discretion has been met with accusations that I am "rationaliz[ing] for a preferred policy approach rather than a meritorious legal argument." This critique seems out of place with the recognition, endorsed by a long list of environmental law professors, that "there is a legitimate debate to be had over how well the current structure of the ESA serves to address climate change in general, or climate change impacts on listed species in particular," and that "it is unclear whether consultation would halt...power plants, require significant changes to the projects, or have no impact at all." Other legal commentary recognizes the difficulties of establishing the necessary causation under the ESA and suggests that either my or the Moritz et al. perspective finds plausible support in ESA law. Proponents of using the ESA as the lynchpin of our nation's greenhouse gas regulation regime thus seem no less susceptible to the charge of preferring a policy outcome than am I. Moritz et al. suggest, for example, that "[o]nly by fully implementing the ESA to help avoid rapid and catastrophic climate change can we keep it the strongest and most relevant biodiversity protection statute that the world has ever seen," and that "[t]here is absolutely no reason why we should not require these agencies to adopt all feasible measures to reduce emissions immediately through the Section 7 process," but that is just their "preferred policy approach."

I make no bones about my "preferred policy approach;" it is to promote the ESA as one of the nation's focused climate change *adaptation* statutes, for which I argue the ESA is especially well designed, and leave greenhouse gas emission regulation to agencies that are better equipped at pollution control science and technology, such as the EPA. The question boils down to whether my "preferred policy approach" fits within the range of discretion the FWS and the NMFS enjoy under Section 7; that is, whether courts would find the agencies' position that causation cannot be established within the meaning of Section 7 is a reasonable interpretation of the statute entitled to judicial deference. I believe a "meritorious legal argument" can be made that they would.

To be sure, under my approach the FWS and NMFS would have no room to dodge the ESA's mandate at least to consider the *effects* of climate change on actions and species as part of the environmental baseline required to be accounted for in all consultations under Section 7. That is, after all, a necessary ingredient of using the ESA to assist species adaptation. The mitigation litigation cause wants much more, however...

*   *   *

[T]here has to be a better way of going about integrating existing laws into a national climate change policy than having interest groups and federal agencies flail about in piecemeal litigation and defensive rulemakings. Federal agencies must act, but they ought to be able to act at least initially without the specter of mitigation litigation looming. A coordinated, multi-scalar national climate change policy is too important to have in place, and soon, to allow it to be forged by courts interpreting existing laws through ad hoc litigation around the nation.

NOTES & QUESTIONS

1. Ruhl proposes that, instead of the "mitigation litigation" approach, we need:

> federal legislation that would suspend for two years all causes of action against agencies designed to force them to develop climate change policies under existing legislation. During this period agencies would conduct coordinated statutory and policy studies, develop and finalize regulatory proposals, and suggest legislative amendments, after which any litigation about the final regulations would be channeled through a prescribed judicial review forum.

J.B. Ruhl, *Climbing Mount Mitigation: A Proposal for Legislative Suspension of Climate Change "Mitigation Litigation"*, 1 WASH. & LEE J. ENERGY, CLIMATE, & ENV'T 71, 76 (2010).

2. What do you think the wildlife agencies would do with this freedom? Should they make an effort to address GHGs at all, or set a policy from the start that this will not be their approach? What would you do?

C. THE CURRENT FEDERAL APPROACH TO ENDANGERED SPECIES AND CLIMATE MITIGATION

It appears that the FWS would agree with the arguments in the previous section, as it has taken a largely hands-off approach to the regulation of greenhouse gasses. This has resulted in a good deal of struggle with environmentalists wishing to use every possible weapon against GHG emitters. Because of the extent to which climate change is destroying essential habitat, the agency issued a guidance memo for regional directors to apply when consulting on actions that would emit GHGs.

United States Department of the Interior, Fish and Wildlife Service, Memorandum of May 14, 2008.

To: Regional Directors, Regions 1-8

From: Director

Subject: Expectations for Consultations on Actions that Would Emit Greenhouse Gases

Recently, questions have been raised regarding compliance with section 7 of the Endangered Species Act concerning emissions of greenhouse gases (GHG), how these emissions contribute to global climate change, and any effects they may cause to listed species and designated critical habitats. These questions became evident as we analyzed the climate change information relevant to the polar bear listing determination. Based on our review of the information and issues considered during the analysis of the polar bear's status, I am writing to establish an analytical framework within which the Service will be able to assist Federal action agencies (including the Service itself when intra-Service consultation is appropriate) in achieving procedural and substantive compliance with the Act.

We recognize the primacy of a Federal action agency's role in determining how to conform its proposed actions to the requirements of section 7 and its responsibility to make the initial determination as to whether consultation is required on its action. As part of its ESA responsibilities, an action agency must examine the effects of its action in order to determine if consultation is necessary. Based on the attached memorandum to me from the Director of the U.S. Geological Survey, however, the Service does not anticipate that the mere fact that a Federal agency authorizes a project that is likely to emit GHG will require the initiation of section 7 consultation. Consultation is required for proposed Federal actions that may affect a listed species. The determination of whether consultation is triggered requires an examination of whether the direct and indirect effects of a particular action reach the regulatory threshold of "may affect". GHG that are projected to be emitted from a facility would not, in and of themselves trigger section 7 consultation for a particular action unless it is established that the emissions from the proposed action cause an indirect effect to listed species or critical habitat. To constitute an indirect effect, the impact to the species must be later in time, must be caused by the proposed action, and must be reasonably certain to occur. The best scientific data available today do not allow us to draw a causal connection between GHG emissions from a given facility and effects posed to listed species or their habitats, nor are there sufficient data to establish that such impacts are reasonably certain to occur. Without sufficient data to establish the required causal connection – to the level of reasonable certainty – between a new facility's GHG emissions and impacts to listed species or critical habitat, section 7 consultation would not be required to address impacts of a facility's GHG emissions.

A question has also been raised regarding the possible application of section 7 to effects that may arise from oil and gas development activities conducted within the habitat of listed species. It is clear that any direct effects of oil and gas development operations, such as drilling activities, vehicular traffic to and from drill sites, and other on-site operational support activities that pose adverse effects to listed species and their critical habitat would need to be evaluated through the section 7 consultation process. It is also clear that any indirect effects from oil and gas development activities, such as impacts from the spread of contaminants (accidental oil spills, or the unintentional release of other contaminants) that are caused by the oil and gas development activities under consultation and that are reasonably certain to occur, (e.g., that are outside of the footprint of the action and spread into habitat areas used by listed species) would also need to be evaluated through the section 7 consultation process.

However, the future effects of any emissions that may result from the consumption of petroleum products refined from crude oil pumped from a particular drilling site would not constitute indirect effects and therefore would not be considered during section 7 consultations. The best scientific data available to the Service today do not provide the degree of precision needed to draw a causal connection between the oil produced at a particular drilling site, the GHG emissions that may eventually result from the consumption of the refined petroleum product, and a particular impact to listed species or their habitats. At present there is a lack of scientific or technical knowledge to determine a relationship between oil and gas leasing, development, or production activity and the effects of the ultimate consumption of petroleum products (GHG emissions). There are discernible limits to the establishment of a causal connection, such as uncertainties regarding the amount of production from a field; whether any or all of that production will be refined for plastics or other products that will not be burned; what mix of vehicles or factories might use the product; and what mitigation measures might offset consumption. Furthermore, there is no traceable nexus between the ultimate consumption of the petroleum product and any particular effect to listed species or their habitats. In short, the emissions effects resulting from the consumption of petroleum derived from an oil field would not constitute an indirect effect of any Federal agency action to approve the development of that field.

As we move into and adapt to this new field of consultations, we must recognize the needs of our fellow agencies for assistance and consultation in the broadest sense. While the foregoing discussion describes our expectations with regard to certain types of Federal actions, you need to be prepared to respond to any Federal agency that believes it may have a compliance duty under section 7 for its programs or actions affecting the production of GHGs. As new information and knowledge about emissions and specific impacts to species and their habitats is developed, we will adapt our framework for consultations accordingly. This is particularly important as more regionally-based models are developed and refined to the level of specificity and reliability needed for the Service to execute its implementation of the Act's provisions ensuring consistency with the statute's best available information standard. Regional Directors are expected to brief the Director as these new models and sources of information ripen at the appropriate scale prior to incorporation into implementing the Act.

NOTES & QUESTIONS

1. Do you agree with this approach? Would you do more?

2. On the same day as the FWS consultation memo was released, the Department of the Interior announced that it was listing the polar bear as threatened, as well as creating a special 4(d) rule applicable to the polar bear. This was the end result of a three-year process initiated by the Center for Biological Diversity, which had filed a petition in 2005 to list the polar bear as threatened due to climate-change-induced melting of its sea-ice habitat. Delays in responding to the petition led to litigation, which resulted in the final listing. However, because the Secretary felt pressured into this listing by "the legal standards under the ESA," he simultaneously issued a special rule "tailored to the conservation needs of the polar bear." Kempthorne explained both actions – the listing and the special 4(d) rule – in a press conference announcement.

Remarks by Secretary Kempthorne
Press Conference on Polar Bear Listing, May 14, 2008.

Today I am listing the polar bear as a "threatened" species under the Endangered Species Act.

I believe this decision is most consistent with the record and legal standards of the Endangered Species Act – perhaps the least flexible law Congress has ever enacted.

I am also announcing that this listing decision will be accompanied by administrative guidance and a rule that defines the scope of impact my decision will have, in order to protect the polar bear while preventing unintended harm to the society and economy of the United States.

* * *

The fact is that sea ice is receding in the arctic. Last year, arctic sea ice fell to the lowest level ever recorded by satellite, 39% lower than the long-term average from 1979 to 2000.

I asked the U.S. Geological Survey to project future sea ice and its relationship to polar bears. They produced a peer-reviewed analysis of computer models. All ten computer models projected declines in September sea ice, averaging 30% by the middle of this century.

My hope is that the projections from these models are wrong, and that sea ice does not further recede. But the best science available to me currently says that is not likely to happen in the next 45 years.

Although the population of bears has grown from a low of about 12,000 in the late 1960's to approximately 25,000 today, our scientists advise me that computer modeling projects a significant population decline by the year 2050. This, in my judgment, makes the polar bear a threatened species – one likely to become in danger of extinction in the foreseeable future.

I have accepted the science presented to me by the Fish and Wildlife Service and the U.S. Geological Survey. I have also accepted these professionals' best scientific and legal judgments that the loss of sea ice, not oil and gas development or subsistence activities, are the reason the polar bear is threatened.

Polar bears are already protected under the Marine Mammal Protection Act, which has more stringent protections for polar bears than the Endangered Species Act does. The oil and gas industry has been operating in the Arctic for decades in compliance with these stricter protections. The Fish and Wildlife Service says that no polar bears have been killed due to encounters associated with oil and gas operations.

The most significant part of today's decision is what President Bush observed about climate change policy last month. President Bush noted that "The Clean Air Act, the Endangered Species Act and the National Environmental Policy Act were never meant to regulate global climate change."

The President is right. Listing the polar bear as threatened can reduce avoidable losses of polar bears. But it should not open the door to use the ESA to regulate greenhouse gas emissions from automobiles, power plants, and other sources. That would be a wholly inappropriate use of the Endangered Species Act. ESA is not the right tool to set U.S. climate policy.

The Endangered Species Act neither allows nor requires the Fish and Wildlife Service to make such interventions. The Service must articulate a causal connection between the effects of any action and loss of a polar bear. As the U.S. Geological Survey has advised me, the best scientific data available do not demonstrate significant impacts on individual polar bears from specific power plants, resource projects, government permits, or other indirect effects of activities in the lower 48 states that are potentially reviewable under the "consultation" requirements of the ESA.

The President is right when he says: "There is a right way and wrong way to approach reducing greenhouse gas emissions. The American people deserve an honest assessment of the costs, benefits and feasibility of any proposed solution. Discussions with such far-reaching impact should not be left to unelected regulators and judges but should be debated openly and made by the elected representatives of the people they affect."

This Administration has taken real action to deal with the challenges of climate change. The Administration and the private sector plan to dedicate nearly a billion dollars to clean coal research and development. Our incentives for power production from wind and solar energy have helped to more than quadruple its use. We have worked with Congress to make available more than $40 billion in loan guarantees to support investments that will avoid, reduce, or sequester greenhouse gas emissions or air pollutants.

To make sure that the Endangered Species Act is not misused to regulate global climate change, I will take the following specific actions:

First, to provide clarity and certainty to those regulated under the Endangered Species Act, the Fish and Wildlife Service will propose what is known as a 4(d) rule that states that if an activity is permissible under the stricter standards imposed by the Marine Mammal Protection Act, it is also permissible under the Endangered Species Act with respect to the polar bear. This rule, effective immediately, will ensure the protection of the bear while allowing us to continue to develop our natural resources in the arctic region in an environmentally sound way.

Second, Director Hall will issue guidance to Fish and Wildlife Service staff that the best scientific data available today cannot make a causal connection between harm to listed species or their habitats and greenhouse gas emissions from a specific facility, or resource development project, or government action.

Third, the Department will issue a Solicitor's Opinion further clarifying these points.

Fourth, the ESA regulatory language needs to be clarified. We will propose common sense modifications to the existing regulation to provide greater certainty that this listing will not set backdoor climate policy outside our normal system of political accountability.

I sought to reform the Endangered Species Act with Senators Harry Reid and Max Baucus and the late John Chaffee when I served in the United States Senate. I had lived with the consequences of ESA decisions as Governor of Idaho. As Secretary I have now experienced the reality that the current ESA is among the most inflexible laws Congress has passed. It prevents me, as Secretary, from taking into account economic conditions and adverse consequences in making listing decisions.

In many ways, the polar bear poses a unique conservation challenge. With most threatened and endangered species, we can identify a localized threat that we can seek to address. The threat to the polar bear, however, comes from global influences and their effect on sea ice.

While the legal standards under the ESA compel me to list the polar bear as threatened, I want to make clear that this listing will not stop global climate change or prevent any sea ice from melting. Any real solution requires action by all major economies for it to be effective. That's why I'm taking administrative and regulatory action to make certain the ESA isn't abused to make global warming policies.

* * *

This has been a difficult decision. But in light of the scientific record and the restraints of the inflexible law that guides me, I believe it was the only decision I could make.

NOTES & QUESTIONS

1. Secretary Kempthorne expressly noted that climate change is the reason for the polar bear listing, but he went on to say that the ESA will not protect the polar bear from this threat. Ultimately, does this listing decision have any impact at all? Note the effort to tie it to the MMPA, only prohibiting what was already prohibited there, and excluding what is exempt under that regime. If there is a traditional take of a polar bear, now both statutes can apply. Apart from having direct enforcement value (which is arguably lacking here), what are some of the other possible benefits to having the polar bear listed?

2. In the Omnibus Appropriations Act of 2009, Congress gave the Obama administration an opportunity to withdraw the special 4(d) rule, but after a period of consideration the new administration declined to do so. Secretary Salazar stated that polar bear recovery was a high priority for the administration, but that "the Endangered Species Act is not the proper mechanism for controlling our nation's carbon emissions." The new administration did, however, toss out another one of the Bush administration's lame duck regulations, which would have more broadly altered the section 7 consultation requirement, cutting back on the range of contexts which might be considered the proximate cause of jeopardy. Do you think this was a fair compromise? Would you have decided differently about whether to keep the polar bear rule? What might the consequences be of eliminating that rule?

3. What would have happened if the polar bear were listed as endangered? Recall from Chapter 6 that species listed as endangered receive their take protection from the ESA directly, whereas threatened species must be protected from take via regulation. If the polar bear had been listed as endangered, there would have been no potential for this special rule. Can you imagine how that might have played out? It will have to happen at some point (a species is listed as endangered because of climate change), so then what sort of litigation might we expect to see? Do you think that the choice to list the polar bear as threatened rather than endangered may have been outcome driven?

4. It should come as no surprise that the choice to list the polar bear as threatened, as well as the issuance of a special 4(d) rule limiting its protections, would spark litigation. The following two opinions are the result of this litigation (at least so far, at the time of this writing). The first, from June 2011, addresses the threatened listing. The second, from October 2011, focuses in on the 4(d) rule, which naturally requires some discussion regarding the applicability of the ESA to climate mitigation.

In Re Polar Bear Endangered Species Act Listing and § 4(d) Rule Litigation

United States District Court for the District of Columbia, 2011.
794 F.Supp.2d 65.

■ SULLIVAN, UNITED STATES DISTRICT JUDGE.

In May 2008, the U.S. Fish and Wildlife Service ("FWS" or "the Service") issued its final rule listing the polar bear as a "threatened species" under the Endangered Species Act of 1973. *See* Determination of Threatened Status for the Polar Bear (*Ursus maritimus*) *Throughout Its Range, 73 Fed. Reg. 28,212 (May 15, 2008)* (the "Listing Rule"). The Service concluded that the polar bear is likely to become endangered within the foreseeable future because of anticipated impacts to its sea ice habitat from increasing Arctic temperatures, which have been attributed to global greenhouse gas emissions and related atmospheric changes. Numerous plaintiffs have challenged the Listing Rule under the Endangered Species Act ("ESA" or "the Act"), *16 U.S.C. §§ 1531-1544*, and the Administrative Procedure Act ("APA"), *5 U.S.C. §§ 551-559, 701-706*, claiming that the Service's decision to list the polar bear as a threatened species was arbitrary and capricious and an abuse of agency discretion. Pending before the Court are the parties' cross-motions for summary judgment.

As the briefing in this case makes clear, the question of whether, when, and how to list the polar bear under the ESA is a uniquely challenging one. The three-year effort by FWS to resolve this question required agency decision-makers and experts not only to evaluate a body of science that is both exceedingly complex and rapidly developing, but also to apply that science in a way that enabled them to make reasonable predictions about potential impacts over the next century to a species that spans international boundaries. In this process, the Service considered over 160,000 pages of documents and approximately 670,000 comment submissions from state and federal agencies, foreign governments, Alaska Native Tribes and tribal organizations, federal commissions, local governments, commercial and trade organizations, conservation organizations, nongovernmental organizations, and private citizens. In addition to relying on its own experts, the agency also consulted a number of impartial experts in a variety of fields, including climate scientists and polar bear biologists.

In view of these exhaustive administrative proceedings, the Court is keenly aware that this is exactly the kind of decision-making process in which its role is strictly circumscribed. Indeed, it is not this Court's role to determine, based on its independent assessment of the scientific evidence, whether the agency could have reached a different conclusion with regard to the listing of the polar bear. Rather, as mandated by the Supreme Court and by this Circuit, the full extent of the Court's authority in this case is to determine whether the agency's decision-making process and its ultimate decision to list the polar bear as a threatened species satisfy certain minimal standards of rationality based upon the evidence before the agency at that time.

For the reasons set forth below, the Court is persuaded that the Listing Rule survives this highly deferential standard. After careful consideration of the numerous objections to the Listing Rule, the Court finds that plaintiffs have failed to demonstrate that the agency's listing determination rises to the level of irrationality. In the Court's opinion, plaintiffs' challenges amount to nothing more than competing views about policy and science. Some plaintiffs in this case believe that the Service went too far in protecting the polar bear; others contend that the Service did not go far enough. According to some plaintiffs, mainstream climate science shows that the polar bear is already irretrievably headed toward extinction throughout its range. According to others, climate science is too uncertain to support any reliable predictions about the future of polar bears. However, this Court is not empowered to choose among these competing views. Although plaintiffs have proposed many alternative conclusions that the agency could have drawn with respect to the status of the polar bear, the Court cannot substitute either the plaintiffs' or its own judgment for that of the agency. Instead, this Court is bound to uphold the agency's determination that the polar bear is a threatened species as long as it is reasonable, regardless of whether there may be other reasonable, or even more reasonable, views. That is particularly true where, as here, the agency is operating at the frontiers of science.

. . . [T]he Court finds that the Service's decision to list the polar bear as a threatened species under the ESA represents a reasoned exercise of the agency's discretion based upon the facts and the best available science as of 2008 when the agency made its listing determination. . .

I. BACKGROUND

A. Statutory Background

Congress enacted the ESA "to provide a means whereby the ecosystems upon which endangered species and threatened species depend may be conserved, [and] to provide a program for the conservation of such endangered species and threatened species."[2] *16 U.S.C. § 1531(b).* An "endangered species" is "any species which is in danger of extinction throughout all or a significant portion of its range." *Id. § 1532(6).* A "threatened species" is "any species which is likely to become an endangered species within the foreseeable future throughout all or a significant portion of its range." *Id. § 1532(20).* The term "species" is defined in the Act to include species, subspecies, and "any distinct population segment of any species of vertebrate fish or wildlife which interbreeds when mature." *Id. § 1532(16).*

---

[2] Under the conservation program established by the ESA, a designation of "endangered" triggers a broad range of protections, including a prohibition on "taking" individual members of the species. *See 16 U.S.C. § 1538(a)(1)(B); see also id. § 1532(19)* (defining the term "take" to mean "harass, harm, pursue, hunt, shoot, wound, kill, trap, capture, or collect, or to attempt to engage in any such conduct"). The Act authorizes the Secretary to extend these prohibitions, in whole or in part, to threatened species as well. *Id. § 1533(d).* In addition, the Secretary shall "issue such regulations as he deems necessary and advisable to provide for the conservation of [threatened] species." *Id.*

The ESA requires the Secretary of the Interior to publish and maintain a list of all species that have been designated as threatened or endangered. *Id. § 1533(c).* Species are added to and removed from this list after notice and an opportunity for public comment, either on the initiative of the Secretary or as a result of a petition submitted by an "interested person." *Id. §§ 1533(b)(1), (3), (5).* The Secretary of the Interior and the Secretary of Commerce are responsible for making listing decisions. *Id. §§ 1532(15), 1533(a)(2).* The Secretary of the Interior has jurisdiction over the polar bear. *See 50 C.F.R. § 402.01(b).*

A listing determination is made on the basis of one or more of five statutorily prescribed factors:

> (a) the present or threatened destruction, modification, or curtailment of the species' habitat or range;

> (b) overutilization for commercial, recreational, scientific, or educational purposes;

> (c) disease or predation;

> (d) the inadequacy of existing regulatory mechanisms; or

> (e) other natural or manmade factors affecting the species' continued existence.

16 U.S.C §§ 1533(a)(1)(A)-(E); see also 50 C.F.R. § 424.11(c). The agency must list a species if "any one or a combination" of these factors demonstrates that the species is threatened or endangered. *50 C.F.R. § 424.11(c).*

The ESA further provides that the decision to list a species must be made

> solely on the basis of the best scientific and commercial data available . . . after conducting a review of the status of the species and after taking into account those efforts, if any, being made by any State or foreign nation, or any political subdivision of a State or foreign nation, to protect such species . . .

> 16 U.S.C. § 1533(b)(1)(A).

B. Factual and Procedural Background

Polar bears are marine mammals that are described as "ice-obligate," meaning that they are evolutionarily adapted to, and indeed completely reliant upon, sea ice for their survival and primary habitat. They depend upon sea ice for critical functions such as hunting ice-dependent seals (their primary source of food), migrating between feeding areas and land-based maternity dens, and traveling long distances in search of mates or food. Over most of their range, polar bears remain on the ice year-round. The international Polar Bear Specialist Group - the authoritative source for information on the world's polar bears - has identified nineteen polar bear populations located within five countries in the ice-covered regions of the

Northern Hemisphere: the United States (in Alaska), Canada, Denmark (in Greenland), Norway, and Russia.

On February 16, 2005, the Center for Biological Diversity submitted a petition to the Secretary of the Interior to list the polar bear as a threatened species under the ESA due to observed and anticipated declines in the Arctic sea ice upon which the polar bear relies for survival. FWS ultimately issued a final rule listing the polar bear as a threatened species on May 15, 2008. At the time of listing, there were estimated to be approximately 20,000 to 25,000 polar bears worldwide, distributed throughout the species' range. These estimates further indicated that two of the nineteen polar bear populations were increasing in numbers (Viscount Melville Sound and M'Clintock Channel); six populations were stable (Northern Beaufort Sea, Southern Hudson Bay, Davis Strait, Lancaster Sound, Gulf of Boothia, Foxe Basin); and five populations were declining (Southern Beaufort Sea, Norwegian Bay, Western Hudson Bay, Kane Basin, Baffin Bay). Insufficient data were available to identify trends for the remaining six populations (Barents Sea, Kara Sea, Laptev Sea, Chukchi Sea, Arctic Basin, East Greenland).

In its Listing Rule, FWS acknowledged that sea ice conditions across the Arctic had changed over the past several decades. Specifically, the agency cited data indicating that the summer/fall ice melt season in the Arctic lengthened by approximately two weeks per decade between 1979 and 2005. The agency also cited data indicating that September (i.e., minimum) sea ice extent was at an all-time low during the period between 2002 and 2007. FWS further noted that scientists had observed significant recent declines in winter (i.e., maximum) sea ice extent, cumulative annual sea ice extent, and overall sea ice age and thickness.

Relying on complex climate models and related data from the International Panel on Climate Change ("IPCC") - which FWS acknowledged to be the leading international body in climate change science - FWS attributed these changes in sea ice to increased Arctic temperatures caused by greenhouse gas emissions and related changes in atmospheric and oceanic circulation. As FWS described, due to a reported lag time in response between when greenhouse gases are emitted into the atmosphere and when the impacts of those emissions are felt on the ground, the IPCC concluded that the global climate system is committed to a continued warming trend through the end of the 21st century. Indeed, FWS noted that average projected warming levels through mid-century were generally consistent across all IPCC climate models, regardless of differences in possible emission levels over that period. FWS looked also to IPCC models of Arctic sea ice, which similarly projected declines in ice extent through the end of the 21st century. As FWS noted, the ten models that most accurately reflected historical sea ice changes prior to 2007 all projected a decline in September sea ice extent of over thirty percent (30%) by mid-century. On the basis of these IPCC models and associated analysis, FWS concluded that it could confidently predict a significant decline in the polar bear's sea ice habitat over the next 40 to 50 years.

FWS further concluded that the extent of anticipated declines in sea ice will significantly impact polar bear population health. As FWS described, sea ice losses have been tied to nutritional stress in polar bears because of lower overall numbers of ice-dependent prey, decreased access to the prey that remain, shorter hunting seasons and longer seasonal fasting periods, and higher energetic demands from traveling farther and swimming longer distances across open water to reach sea ice. FWS determined that this nutritional stress and other related factors will likely result in a decline in the physical condition of polar bears, leading to lower overall body weights and reduced cub survival rates. FWS further found that consistent declines in physical condition and reproductive success will ultimately lead to population-level declines. . .

Based on a voluminous administrative record, including the studies described above, and input from fourteen peer reviewers and numerous polar bear specialists, climate scientists, experts in Traditional Ecological Knowledge ("TEK"), state and federal agencies, foreign governments, Alaska Native tribes and tribal organizations, federal commissions, local governments, commercial and trade organizations, conservation organizations, nongovernmental organizations, and private citizens, FWS concluded that the polar bear was threatened throughout its range at the time of listing, within the meaning of the ESA. Specifically, FWS determined that all polar bear populations will be affected by substantial losses of sea ice within the foreseeable future (which it defined as 45 years), although different populations will be affected at different rates and to different degrees. FWS further found that polar bears are unlikely to adapt to these anticipated habitat changes.

However, notwithstanding these findings, FWS concluded that the polar bear was not endangered in any portion of its range at the time of listing. The agency determined that at the time of listing the species was generally abundant throughout its range, the species continued to occupy the full extent of its historical range, and it had yet to experience precipitous population declines in any portion of its range. Even in the Western Hudson Bay population, where a statistically-significant decline had been observed, the species continued to reproduce normally. According to FWS, these countervailing facts demonstrated that the polar bear was not "in danger of extinction" at the time it made its listing decision, although the agency reiterated that the species would likely become an endangered species by mid-century.

The publication of the Listing Rule triggered lawsuits by a number of organizations and individuals . . .

II. STANDARD OF REVIEW

The Service's listing decisions are subject to review under the APA. Under APA review, federal agency actions are to be held unlawful and set aside where they are "arbitrary, capricious, an abuse of discretion, or otherwise not in accordance with law." *5 U.S.C. § 706(2)(A)*. . .

III. DISCUSSION

A. The Service Articulated a Rational Basis for Its Conclusion that the Polar Bear Met the Definition of a Threatened Species at the Time of Listing

1. Plaintiff CBD's Claim that the Polar Bear Should Have Been Considered Endangered at the Time of Listing

. . . [Plaintiff Center for Biological Diversity (CBD)] contends that the agency's conclusion is flawed because FWS improperly ignored or discounted relevant factors. This Court disagrees. The Court is not persuaded that the agency ignored or otherwise failed to consider any of the information cited by plaintiff CBD. All of that information—including the population modeling data and polar bear monitoring reports—is included in the voluminous administrative record that was before the agency and, indeed, much of that data was cited by the agency as a basis for designating the polar bear as a threatened species. Notably, CBD cites to the agency's findings in the Listing Rule itself for much of the evidence that it claims the agency ignored.

To the extent that CBD is asking this Court to find that FWS drew improper conclusions from the scientific information it considered, the Court declines to do so. Although the evidence emphasized by CBD is very troubling, the Court finds that the agency acted well within its discretion to weigh the available facts and scientific information before it in reaching its conclusion that the polar bear was not endangered at the time of listing. Where an agency has exercised its Congressionally-authorized discretion to weigh the relevant factors, and it has made a listing determination based on a reasoned choice, the Court will not disturb its conclusion. . .

2. Joint Plaintiffs' Claim that the Polar Bear Should Not Have Been Considered Threatened at the Time of Listing

The Court turns now to Joint Plaintiffs' claim that FWS similarly misinterpreted and misapplied the ESA when it concluded that the polar bear is likely to become endangered within the foreseeable future and thus qualified for threatened status at the time the agency made its listing determination. . . A threatened species under the ESA is a species that is "likely to become an endangered species within the foreseeable future throughout all or a significant portion of its range." *16 U.S.C. § 1532(20)*. Joint Plaintiffs claim that FWS failed to prove that the polar bear is sufficiently "likely" to become endangered within the meaning of this definition. Specifically, Joint Plaintiffs contend that FWS failed to demonstrate a 67-90% likelihood that the polar bear will become endangered within the foreseeable future.

. . . Having carefully reviewed the administrative record, the Court is not persuaded that FWS adopted a numerical standard of 67-90% probability in determining whether the polar bear is "likely" to become endangered. Although the only arguable definition of the term "likely" in the Listing

Rule appears in the response to comments that Joint Plaintiffs have highlighted, the Court agrees with the federal defendants that this lone statement does not demonstrate the agency's intent to adopt the IPCC's numerical standards for all purposes, including statutory construction.

Indeed, a close review of the record belies any such intention. The record reveals that FWS used the terms "likely" and "very likely" interchangeably throughout its Listing Rule. The Court concludes that if FWS had intended to imbue these terms with the mathematical precision urged by Joint Plaintiffs for the purposes of statutory construction, it would have used these terms more deliberately. . .

The Court turns now to Joint Plaintiffs' argument that the Service's choice of a "foreseeable future" timeframe over which the polar bear is likely to become endangered was arbitrary and capricious. In its Listing Rule, FWS defined the "foreseeable future" as "the timeframe over which the best available scientific data allow us to reliably assess the effects of threats on the polar bear," and it concluded based on record evidence that it could confidently predict potential impacts to the polar bear from sea ice losses over a 45-year period. . .

The federal defendants respond that FWS reasonably defined the foreseeable future as 45 years because it found that it could make confident forecasts about polar bear population trends up to that point, based on climate modeling and other reliable data. Specifically, the federal defendants assert, climate change projections from the IPCC AR4 supported a 45-year foreseeable future timeframe at the time of listing. As the federal defendants describe, model outcomes reported in the IPCC AR4, which FWS accepted as the best available science on climate change, consistently predict a certain base level of overall warming through mid-century, regardless of whether actual emissions increase or decrease over that period. According to FWS, therefore, at the time the agency made its listing decision minimum impacts to Arctic sea ice could be predicted with confidence for up to fifty years but projections became more speculative beyond that point.

As the federal defendants point out, FWS also acknowledged that a 45-year period roughly corresponds to three polar bear generations. However, according to the federal defendants, the agency found this correlation to be relevant because population status projections will generally be even more reliable if they correspond in some way to the life history characteristics of the species. Specifically, the federal defendants assert, FWS determined that population projections that can be made over multiple polar bear generations are more reliable than projections that only span one generation. The federal defendants contend that it was not irrational for FWS to rely on biological factors in this way to support its choice of a foreseeable future timeframe for its listing decision. . .

As with the term "likely," Congress has not defined the term "foreseeable future" under the ESA, and FWS has not promulgated any regulations or other policy guidance defining the term. At least one court has recognized that what is "foreseeable" is likely to vary from species to species depending on a number of factors and, therefore, a bright-line rule of foreseeability is inappropriate. *See W. Watersheds Project v. Foss, No. 06-1574, 2005 U.S. Dist. LEXIS 45753, at *44-45 (E.D. Pa. Aug. 19, 2005)* (noting that "the definition of 'foreseeable future' may vary depending on the particular species - for example, 'foreseeable future' may be defined differently for a sequoia tree . . . than for the slickspot peppergrass, which is an annual or biennial plant"). In the absence of a quantitative standard, a "foreseeable future" determination is made on the basis of the agency's reasoned judgment in light of the best available science for the species under consideration. *See id.* (declining to establish a bright-line rule but noting that the agency must articulate a satisfactory explanation for its definition).

Having carefully considered the parties' arguments and the administrative record, the Court rejects Joint Plaintiffs' argument that the choice of a 45-year foreseeable future timeframe for the polar bear was arbitrary and based on improper considerations. Contrary to Joint Plaintiffs' assertions, FWS does not appear to have based its choice solely on biological factors, even at the proposed rule stage. To the extent this Court considers the agency's proposed rule, which is not the action before it on review, the Court finds that the agency sufficiently explained that its decision was based on "IUCN criteria,[36] the life-history and population dynamics of polar bears, documented changes to date in both multi-year and annual sea ice, and the direction of projected rates of change of sea ice in future decades," which all supported a 45-year or three-generation timeframe for the foreseeable future. Moreover, the final Listing Rule indicates that the climate change projections found in the IPCC AR4—and not biological factors— were the primary basis for the Service's determination of the foreseeable future timeframe. In light of the IPCC AR4 findings, the Court is satisfied that the agency articulated a rational basis for its choice. . .

In Re Polar Bear Endangered Species Act Listing and § 4(D) Rule Litigation

United States District Court for the District of Columbia, 2011.
818 F.Supp.2d 214.

■ SULLIVAN, DISTRICT JUDGE.

On May 15, 2008, the U.S. Fish and Wildlife Service ("the Service" or "the agency") published its final rule listing the polar bear as a threatened species under the Endangered Species Act ("ESA"). This Court recently upheld the Listing Rule as a reasonable exercise of agency discretion. The two cases currently before the Court arise from a related agency rule, Special Rule for the Polar Bear, 73 Fed. Reg. 76,249 (December 16, 2008) ("Special Rule"), which specifies the protective mechanisms that apply to the polar bear as a result of its threatened status.

---

[36] A 45-year time period for the foreseeable future is consistent with the work of the international Polar Bear Specialist Group, which reassessed the status of the polar bear in June 2005 for the purposes of the International Union for the Conservation of Nature's ("IUCN") Red List classification, a list of species considered to be threatened. Although the standards for Red Listing classification differ from ESA listing standards, FWS nonetheless found the IUCN assessment to be instructive.

Section 4(d) of the ESA requires the Service to promulgate such rules as it deems "necessary and advisable to provide for the conservation of [threatened] species." Although the polar bear is already regulated in the United States under the Marine Mammal Protection Act ("MMPA"), as well as treaties and other international agreements, the Service determined that it is nonetheless necessary and advisable for the conservation of the species to extend additional ESA protections to the polar bear, pursuant to Section 4(d). Among other things, the Service's Special Rule aims to address the threat of direct impacts to individual bears and their habitat from oil and gas exploration and development activities within the species' current range.

The plaintiffs in this case have challenged the agency's Special Rule for the polar bear under the ESA, the National Environmental Policy Act ("NEPA"), and the Administrative Procedure Act ("APA"). Pending before the Court are the parties' cross-motions for summary judgment. Plaintiffs claim, first, that the Service's Special Rule violates the ESA because it fails to provide for the conservation of the polar bear. Specifically, plaintiffs contend that the Service cannot effectively provide for the conservation of the polar bear without addressing global greenhouse gas emissions, which the agency itself identified as the cause of increasing Arctic temperatures that are expected to lead to a significant decline of the polar bear's sea ice habitat. Plaintiffs argue that the Service purposely and unlawfully crafted its Special Rule in such a way as to avoid addressing this threat, in contravention of the ESA's conservation mandate.

The Court understands plaintiffs' frustration. However, as this Court has previously observed, climate change poses unprecedented challenges of science and policy on a global scale, and this Court must be at its most deferential where the agency is operating at the frontiers of science. Here, the Service concluded based on the evidence before it that Section 4(d) of the ESA is not a useful or appropriate tool to alleviate the particular threat to the polar bear from climate change caused by global greenhouse gas emissions, and plaintiffs have offered no compelling evidence to the contrary. Although the Court is sensitive to plaintiffs' arguments for a strong mechanism to combat the effects of global climate change, the Court finds that the agency's conclusion was not arbitrary, capricious, or contrary to law. The Court is therefore prohibited from substituting either the plaintiffs' or its own judgment for that of the agency. The question before the Court, then, is whether the Service reasonably concluded that its Special Rule provides for the conservation of the polar bear even if it does not reverse the trend of Arctic sea ice loss. As will be discussed below, the Court is persuaded that the agency has done so. Accordingly, with respect to plaintiffs' ESA claim, the Court **DENIES** plaintiffs' motion for summary judgment and **GRANTS** the federal defendants' and defendant-intervenors' motions for summary judgment.

In addition to their claims under the ESA, plaintiffs claim that the Service violated NEPA by failing to analyze the potential environmental impacts of its Special Rule, which is generally required for all "major Federal actions significantly affecting the quality of the human environment." With respect to this claim, the Court agrees with plaintiffs. The Court declines to recognize the broad NEPA exemption that the federal defendants urge.

Accordingly, and for the reasons discussed below, the Court finds that the Service was required to conduct at least an initial assessment to determine whether its Special Rule for the polar bear warranted a full "environmental impact statement" ("EIS"). Here, the Service conducted no analysis whatsoever; as a result, its Special Rule for the polar bear violates NEPA. Accordingly, with respect to plaintiffs' NEPA claim, the Court **GRANTS** plaintiffs' motion for summary judgment and **DENIES** the federal defendants' and defendant-intervenors' motions for summary judgment. The Court finds that vacatur of the final Special Rule is the appropriate remedy for the Service's NEPA violation. Upon vacatur of the final Special Rule, the prior May 15, 2008, interim final Special Rule for the polar bear shall remain in effect until further Order of the Court.

I. BACKGROUND

A. Statutory and Regulatory Background

*   *   *

2. MMPA

The MMPA has governed the management of polar bear populations in the United States since 1972. Congress enacted the MMPA to preserve and replenish marine mammal populations. The MMPA imposes a general moratorium on the taking and import of marine mammals and marine mammal products. Under the MMPA, the term "take" is defined as "to harass, hunt, capture, or kill, or attempt to harass, hunt, capture, or kill any marine mammal."

Like the ESA, the MMPA provides some limited exceptions to its moratorium on taking marine mammals. The Secretary may issue permits authorizing the incidental, but not intentional, taking of a marine mammal while engaging in an otherwise lawful activity, provided such take "will have a negligible impact" on the species.

*   *   *

B. Factual and Procedural Background

On May 15, 2008, the Service published its final rule listing the polar bear as a threatened species under the ESA throughout its range. Concurrent with the Listing Rule, the agency also published a special rule for the polar bear pursuant to Section 4(d) of the ESA. The Secretary made this Interim Final Special Rule effective immediately. Following a 60–day comment period, on December 16, 2008, the Secretary replaced the Interim Final Special Rule with a substantially similar final rule for the polar bear.

The Service's final Special Rule for the polar bear was subsequently codified at 50 C.F.R. § 17.40(q).

The agency's final Special Rule extends all of the take prohibitions available under Section 9 of the ESA to the polar bear, with two exceptions. First, the rule provides that none of these prohibitions will apply to any activity that is already authorized or exempted under the MMPA, the Convention on International Trade in Endangered Species of Wild Fauna and Flora, [hereinafter "CITES"], or both, provided that the person carrying out the activity has complied with all applicable terms and conditions. In other words, under the Service's Special Rule for the polar bear, any activity that is already permitted or exempted under the MMPA or CITES will not require additional authorization under the ESA.

The Service determined that this exception is appropriate because polar bear populations in the United States were effectively managed and protected under the MMPA and CITES for thirty years prior to the publication of the Listing Rule. Indeed, the agency noted, "none of the activities currently regulated under the MMPA and CITES are factors that threaten the polar bear throughout all or a significant portion of its range." Further, after comparing their relevant provisions, the agency found that "[m]any provisions . . . under the MMPA and CITES are comparable to or stricter than similar provisions under the ESA, including the definitions of take, penalties for violations, and use of marine mammals." Accordingly, the Service concluded that an additional overlay of ESA authorization procedures for activities currently permitted under the existing regulatory regime is not necessary or advisable to provide for the conservation of the polar bear:

> The comparable or stricter provisions of the MMPA and CITES, along with the application of the ESA regulations for any activity that has not been authorized or exempted under the MMPA and CITES . . ., address those negative effects on polar bears that can foreseeably be addressed under sections 9 and 10 of the ESA. It would not contribute to the conservation of the polar bear to require an unnecessary overlay of redundant authorization processes that would otherwise be required under the general ESA threatened species regulations.

Second, the Service's Special Rule provides that none of the ESA's Section 9 prohibitions will apply to any taking of polar bears that is incidental to, but not the purpose of, carrying out an otherwise lawful activity, unless that taking is caused by an activity occurring within the current range of the polar bear in the United States. In other words, under the Service's Special Rule, an "incidental take" of a polar bear that is not otherwise authorized under the MMPA and is caused by an activity occurring *within* the range of the polar bear will be considered a prohibited taking under the ESA and will be subject to penalties under both statutes. By contrast, an unauthorized incidental take of a polar bear caused by an activity occurring *outside* the current range of the polar bear will not be considered a prohibited taking under the ESA and will only be subject to penalties under the MMPA.

In support of this provision, the Service explained that for activities occurring within the polar bear's range, "overlay of the incidental take prohibitions under [the ESA] is an important component of polar bear management because of the timing and proximity of potential takes of polar bears." As the agency described, future oil and gas development activities in Alaska may result in unauthorized incidental takes of polar bears that could be reduced or avoided by imposing additional penalties under the ESA. By contrast, the Service determined that an overlay of additional penalties and permitting procedures outside the range of the polar bear is "not necessary for polar bear management and conservation." "If it is shown that a particular activity conducted outside the current range of the species is reasonably likely to cause the incidental taking of a polar bear, whether lethal or nonlethal," the agency explained, "any incidental take that occurs is a violation of the MMPA" and, accordingly, will be subject to "the full array of the statute's civil and criminal penalties."

In sum, the Service generally characterized its Special Rule as follows:

> Under this final special rule, if an activity is authorized or exempted under the MMPA or CITES, we will not require any additional authorization under the ESA regulations associated with that activity. However, if the activity is not authorized or exempted under the MMPA or CITES and the activity would result in an act that would be otherwise prohibited under the ESA regulations, the [take] prohibitions apply, and permits would be required under our ESA regulations. The special rule further provides that any incidental take of polar bears that results from activities that occur outside of the current range of the species is not a prohibited act under the ESA.

Accordingly, pursuant to Section 4(d) of the ESA, the Service concluded that this complementary management regime is "necessary and advisable to provide for the conservation of the polar bear."

With respect to the primary threat identified in the Listing Rule—i.e., loss of sea ice habitat and related effects—the agency concluded that no additional ESA protections are necessary or advisable because that threat "would not be alleviated by the additional overlay of provisions in the general threatened species regulations . . . or even the full application of the provisions in section 9 and 10 of the ESA." Indeed, the Service concluded, "[n]othing within our authority under section 4(d) of the ESA, above and beyond what we have already required in this final special rule, would provide the means to resolve this threat." In response to comments, the Service further explained, citing a policy memorandum issued by its Director on May 14, 2008, that "the future indirect impacts of individual [greenhouse gas] emitters cannot be shown to result in 'take' based on the best available science at this time."

*   *   *

III. DISCUSSION

Plaintiffs argue that the final Special Rule for the polar bear is arbitrary, capricious, and contrary to both the ESA and NEPA. Before reaching the merits of plaintiffs' claims, the Court [held, in response to an intervenor's challenge, that the rule was final agency action subject to review in the courts.]

* * *

The Court turns now to the merits of plaintiffs' ESA claim.

B. Plaintiffs' ESA Claim

In its Special Rule for the polar bear, the Service found that it is necessary and advisable to extend Section 9 take prohibitions to the polar bear, but that it is not necessary for the conservation of the species to apply those prohibitions to (1) activities that are currently authorized or exempted under the MMPA or CITES; or (2) activities that are occurring outside the range of the species but may incidentally impact polar bears. The Service determined that extending limited additional ESA protections to the polar bear is particularly appropriate in light of the comparable protections available under the MMPA, which apply to activities that impact polar bears regardless of where those activities occur.

Plaintiffs claim that the Service's Special Rule fundamentally violates the ESA because it fails to provide sufficiently for the conservation of the polar bear. Plaintiffs' claim relies in large part on two threshold assumptions: first, that the plain language of the ESA requires the agency to "provide for the conservation" of threatened species; and second, that the Service cannot "reduce" the protections that would automatically apply to the polar bear under 50 C.F.R. § 17.31, which extends all Section 9 take prohibitions to all threatened species, without demonstrating a valid conservation basis for diverging from that default rule. The Court will address each of these threshold issues in turn.

1. Whether the Service's Special Rule Must Be Necessary and Advisable to Provide for the Conservation of the Polar Bear

Section 4(d) of the ESA reads, in relevant part:

[W]henever any species is listed as a threatened species . . . the Secretary shall issue such regulations as he deems necessary and advisable to provide for the conservation of such species. The Secretary may by regulation prohibit with respect to any threatened species any act prohibited under section 9(a)(1), in the case of fish or wildlife.

Plaintiffs assert that the plain language of this section establishes a strict standard that all special rules promulgated under Section 4(d) must be "necessary and advisable to provide for the conservation of [the] species."

In accordance with controlling D.C. Circuit precedent, the Court must reject plaintiffs' plain-language reading of Section 4(d), and it finds that the statute is ambiguous on this point. *See Sweet Home Chapter of Cmties. for a Great Oregon v. Babbitt,* 1 F.3d 1, 8 (D.C.Cir.1993). However, in its Special Rule, the Service in fact adopted the standard urged by plaintiffs: "[T]he regulations promulgated under section 4(d) of the ESA provide the Secretary the discretion to determine what prohibitions, exemptions, or authorizations are *necessary and advisable* for a species, *so long as the regulation provides for the conservation of that species.*" (emphasis added). Indeed, the Service premised its Special Rule on a finding that the rule is necessary and advisable to provide for the conservation of the polar bear.[14]

The Court finds that the Service's assessment of its obligations under Section 4(d), as set forth in its Special Rule for the polar bear, constitutes a reasonable and permissible interpretation of the ESA. Accordingly, the Court upholds the Service's interpretation under step two of the *Chevron* framework, and it will review the Special Rule for the polar bear pursuant to the "necessary and advisable" standard adopted by the agency.

2. Whether the Service Must Demonstrate a Valid Conservation Basis for Departing from 50 C.F.R. § 17.31(a)

A second fundamental premise of plaintiffs' ESA claim is that the Service cannot "reduce" the protections that would otherwise apply to the bear under the Service's general regulations for threatened species, set forth at 50 C.F.R. § 17.31(a), without demonstrating a valid conservation basis for not applying the default rule. Plaintiffs note that "for more than 30 years, it has been the Service policy and administrative practice to extend the ESA's full protections against take to threatened species as the most effective approach for ensuring their conservation." Therefore, plaintiffs argue, any departure from this longstanding practice must have a valid conservation purpose ("Fundamentally, in order to provide a conservation 'benefit' to the polar bear, the benefits to the polar bear from the Special Rule must outweigh the benefits of any protections polar bears would enjoy in the absence of a Special Rule.").

The Court finds this argument unpersuasive. Plaintiffs are correct that, in the absence of a special rule, management of the polar bear under the ESA would be governed by the general rule set out at 50 C.F.R. § 17.31(a), which extends all of the Section 9 take prohibitions to all threatened species. However, section 17.31 also authorizes the Service to issue special rules for particular species pursuant to Section 4(d). This regulation provides that where the agency chooses to issue a special rule, that rule "will contain all the applicable prohibitions and exceptions" and "none of

---

[14] In their briefs, the federal defendants contend that the Service's Special Rule falls within the agency's broad discretionary authority under the second sentence of Section 4(d) and, therefore, the Service was not required to find that its Special Rule is necessary and advisable for the conservation of the polar bear. However, this Court can only uphold an agency decision based on the grounds relied upon by the agency itself and not the *post hoc* rationalizations of agency counsel. *See Burlington Truck Lines v. United States,* 371 U.S. 156, 168–69, 83 S.Ct. 239, 9 L.Ed.2d 207 (1962) ("[A] reviewing court ... must judge the propriety of [agency] action solely by the grounds invoked by the agency.").

the provisions of [paragraph (a)] . . . will apply." *Id.* § 17.31(c). Nothing in the regulation, or in the ESA itself, requires the agency to demonstrate a conservation basis for *not* applying the general regulation at 50 C.F.R. § 17.31(a).

Indeed, courts have recognized that the ESA does not require regulations protecting threatened species from taking at all. Section 4(d) itself merely provides that the Secretary "*may* . . . prohibit with respect to threatened species *any* act prohibited under section 9(a)(1)" (emphasis added). *See, e.g., Louisiana, ex rel. Guste v. Verity,* 853 F.2d 322, 333 (5th Cir.1988) ("In addition to this mandatory duty [to issue regulations that are necessary and advisable to provide for the conservation of the species] . . ., the ESA also provides the Secretary authority to prohibit by regulation the taking of any threatened species of fish and wildlife." (emphasis omitted)); *Trout Unlimited v. Lohn,* 559 F.3d 946, 962 n. 12 (9th Cir.2009) (noting that Section 4(d) does not require regulations protecting threatened species from taking and that "[t]he combination of the discretionary 'may' and the phrase 'necessary and advisable' grant [the Service] much leeway in crafting regulations"); *Defenders of Wildlife v. Kempthorne,* No. 04–1230, 2006 WL 2844232, at *2, 2006 U.S. Dist. LEXIS 71137, at *7–8 (D.D.C. Sept. 29, 2006) (noting that the Secretary may, but is not required to, extend prohibitions of Section 9 to threatened species). *See also* S.Rep. No. 93–307, at 8 (1973), 1973 U.S.C.C.A.N. 2989, 2997 ("Once an animal is on the threatened list, the Secretary has an almost infinite number of options available to him with regard to the permitted activities for those species. He may, for example, permit taking, but not importation of such activities, or he may choose to forbid both taking and importation but allow the transportation of such species.").

Accordingly, the Court finds that the Service was not required to demonstrate that diverging from the general regulation at 50 C.F.R. § 17.31(a) is necessary and advisable to provide for the conservation of the polar bear. Rather, the relevant question before the Court is whether the Service reasonably concluded that the specific prohibitions and exceptions set forth in its Special Rule are necessary and advisable to provide for the conservation of the polar bear. The Court turns now to that question.

3. Whether the Service Reasonably Concluded that its Special Rule Is Necessary and Advisable to Provide for the Conservation of the Polar Bear

The ESA defines "conservation" as "the use of all methods and procedures which are *necessary* to bring any endangered species or threatened species to the point at which the measures provided . . . are no longer necessary." Whereas the ESA itself prescribes certain measures that Congress deemed necessary to provide for the conservation of endangered species, Congress has generally delegated to the Secretary of the Interior the responsibility of determining what measures are necessary for the conservation of threatened species. *See WildEarth Guardians v. Salazar,* 741 F.Supp.2d 89, 105 (D.D.C.2010) ("Congress delegated to the Secretary the authority to determine the extent to which the ESA protects threatened species."). In this case, the Service determined that it is necessary and advisable to extend Section 9 take prohibitions to the polar bear but that it is *not* necessary for the conservation of the species to apply those prohibitions to activities that are currently authorized or exempted under the MMPA or CITES, or to activities that are occurring outside the range of the species that may incidentally impact polar bears.

Plaintiffs contend that the Service's Special Rule cannot be necessary and advisable to provide for the conservation of the polar bear because it does not address the primary threat to the species from greenhouse gas emissions and the loss of its sea ice habitat. Specifically, plaintiffs argue that the Service purposefully chose not to extend the full Section 9 take prohibitions to the polar bear "in order to . . . exempt greenhouse gas emissions from the reach of the ESA." Although it is undisputed that the Special Rule does not address greenhouse gas emissions, the Court is persuaded that the rule nonetheless survives rational basis review.

As a threshold matter, and contrary to plaintiffs' assertions, nothing in the Special Rule expressly exempts greenhouse gas emissions from regulation under the ESA or any other statute. To the extent the Service discussed greenhouse gases in the preamble to its Special Rule, the Service noted that anticipated sea ice losses as a result of greenhouse gas emissions "would not be alleviated" by an additional overlay of incidental take provisions under the ESA. The Service further explained in response to comments that "[t]here is currently no way to determine how the emissions from a specific action both influence climate change and then subsequently affect specific listed species, including polar bears." In other words, because climate modeling does not currently allow the agency to draw a causal connection between the greenhouse gas emissions from a specific source and the impact on a particular polar bear, the Service determined that it cannot identify when a "take" has occurred for the purposes of enforcing the incidental take provisions of the ESA against an individual greenhouse gas emitter (explaining that "the future indirect impacts of individual [greenhouse gas] emitters cannot be shown to result in 'take' based on the best available science at this time."). Accordingly, the Service concluded that even extending the full take prohibitions of the ESA to the polar bear would not effectively address the threat to the species from sea ice losses caused by global greenhouse gas emissions.

The administrative record amply supports the Service's conclusion. In a memorandum summarizing the most recent findings on this issue by the leading international climate science research organizations, the United States Geological Survey determined that "[i]t is currently beyond the scope of existing science to identify a specific source of CO2 emissions and designate it as the cause of specific climate impacts at an exact location." Similarly, in a memorandum to the Service, the Environmental Protection Agency Office of Air and Radiation observed that "[t]he climate change research community has not yet developed tools specifically intended for evaluating or quantifying end-point impacts attributable to the emissions of [greenhouse gases] from a single source, and we are not aware of any scientific literature to draw from regarding the climate effects of individual, facility-level [greenhouse gas] emissions." Based on these findings, the Service Director issued a subsequent policy memorandum in which he concluded that "[t]he best scientific data available today do not allow us to draw a causal connection between [greenhouse gas] emissions from a given facility and effects posed to listed species or their habitats." The Department of the Interior has echoed these conclusions in a similar policy memorandum:

> Given the nature of the complex and independent processes active in the atmosphere and the ocean acting on [greenhouse gases], the causal link simply cannot currently be made between emissions from a proposed action and specific effects on a listed species or its critical habitat. Specifically, science cannot say that a tiny incremental global temperature rise that might be produced by an action under consideration would manifest itself in the location of a listed species or its habitat. Similarly, any observed climate change effect on a member of a particular listed species or its critical habitat cannot be attributed to the emissions from any particular source. Rather it would be the consequence of the collective greenhouse gas accumulation from natural sources and the world-wide anthropogenically produced [greenhouse gas] emissions since at least the beginning of the industrial revolution.

Notably, plaintiffs do not contradict this record evidence. Rather, at bottom, plaintiffs' complaint appears to be that the Special Rule pre-emptively forecloses the option of citizen enforcement actions against greenhouse gas emitters in the contiguous United States. The citizen suit provision of the ESA authorizes "any person" to commence a civil suit on her own behalf to enforce certain provisions of the statute, including penalties for prohibited takings of listed species. Plaintiffs have expressed a concern that, because no incidental take of a polar bear that occurs outside the range of the species will be considered a prohibited taking within the meaning of the ESA as a result of the Service's Special Rule, no grounds exist for citizen enforcement actions against greenhouse gas emitters operating outside the range of the species in Alaska. By precluding citizen enforcement in these circumstances, plaintiffs contend, the Service has unlawfully eliminated a potentially useful tool for addressing greenhouse gas emissions and, ultimately, Arctic sea ice loss. However, although plaintiffs would undoubtedly prefer a broad citizen enforcement option, the Court is not persuaded that the Special Rule is arbitrary and capricious on these grounds.[16]

---

[16] The Court notes that nothing in the Special Rule would preclude a citizen suit against a greenhouse gas emitter operating without incidental take authorization *within* the range of the polar bear. Moreover, although the MMPA does not contain a citizen suit provision, nothing in the Special Rule precludes the agency itself from pursuing an enforcement action against a greenhouse gas emitter for an unauthorized incidental take of a polar bear under the MMPA, assuming a violation of that statute can be identified. Further, nothing in the Service's Special Rule prohibits the agency from taking steps to address the primary threat to the polar bear to the extent feasible within its authority under other provisions of the ESA ("[N]othing in this special rule, the MMPA, or CITES precludes us from developing and implementing a recovery plan or entering into a treaty or conservation agreement that addresses the specific threats to the polar bear as outlined in the listing rule.").

The Court is satisfied that the Service articulated a rational basis for the prohibitions and exceptions set forth in its Special Rule. The Service determined that an additional overlay of ESA permitting procedures and penalties within the range of the polar bear is necessary and advisable to provide for the conservation of the species due to the timing and proximity of potential takings of polar bears from oil and gas exploration and development activities in Alaska. Specifically, the Service concluded that ESA penalties, including citizen enforcement actions, may be necessary to avoid or otherwise reduce these direct impacts. The Service found no evidence to suggest that extending the ESA incidental take provisions outside the range of the polar bear would produce similar conservation benefits, however. With respect to these indirect impacts, in the event that an incidental take can be identified and attributed to a specific cause originating outside the species' range, the Service found that the incidental take provisions of the MMPA are sufficient to address that violation ("[T]he Service will pursue any violation under the MMPA for incidental take that has not been authorized, and all MMPA penalties would apply."). Accordingly, the Service concluded that an additional overlay of ESA incidental take permitting procedures and penalties outside the range of the polar bear is not necessary for the conservation of the species. The Court finds that the agency's conclusions follow from the evidence before it, and the Service has articulated a rational basis for limiting the extent of the Section 9 take prohibitions to the current range of the polar bear.

Moreover, the Court finds that the Service reasonably concluded that a complementary management regime encompassing the MMPA, CITES, and the ESA is necessary and advisable to provide for the conservation of the polar bear. The Service conducted an exhaustive analysis in which it determined that the MMPA is comparable to, or even stricter than, the take provisions of the ESA in most respects. Accordingly, the Court finds that the Service reasonably chose to minimize administrative redundancy after it determined that doing so would not sacrifice significant conservation benefits.

In sum, having carefully considered the parties' arguments and the full administrative record, the Court finds that the Service reasonably determined that the prohibitions and exceptions set forth in its Special Rule for the polar bear are "necessary and advisable to provide for the conservation of [the] species," in accordance with Section 4(d) of the ESA. Particularly in view of Congress's broad delegation of authority to the Secretary to determine what measures are necessary and advisable to provide for the conservation of threatened species, plaintiffs have failed to carry their burden to demonstrate that the agency's conclusions were arbitrary and capricious.

The question at the heart of this litigation—whether the ESA is an effective or appropriate tool to address the threat of climate change—is not a question that this Court can decide based upon its own independent assessment, particularly in the abstract. The answer to that question will ultimately be grounded in science and policy determinations that are beyond the purview of this Court. … The question this Court must decide is whether the agency has articulated a rational basis for the protections set forth in its Special Rule for the polar bear. For the reasons set forth above, the Court finds that the Service has done so. Accordingly, with respect to plaintiffs' ESA claim, the Court **DENIES** plaintiffs' motion for summary judgment and **GRANTS** the federal defendants' and defendant-intervenors' motions for summary judgment.

NOTES & QUESTIONS

1. The Court held in favor of the plaintiffs on their NEPA claim, which led to vacatur of the final rule pending an Environmental Assessment under NEPA. A draft replacement of the controversial 4(d) Rule, along with a draft environmental assessment as required by the court, was filed on April 19, 2012. The new 4(d) Rule is substantially the same as the previous one, but had to be reissued due to the NEPA violation. For now, the polar bear continues to be protected at the level described in the opinions above. Can this present status of ESA non-coverage be anything more than a temporary arrangement? What might happen next? Can you think of legislative or regulatory actions that could more permanently resolve the problems that the polar bear brought to light?

2. A NEPA Environmental Assessment requires the consideration of action alternatives, as well as the no-action alternative. The FWS draft Environmental Assessment proposes the following four alternatives:

> *Alternative 1*: Under the no action alternative, no 4(d) special rule would be promulgated for polar bear conservation under the ESA.
>
> *Alternative 2 – Proposed Alternative*: Rule is the final 4(d) special rule published in the *Federal Register* on December 16, 2008. This 4(d) rule, in most instances, adopts the existing conservation regulatory requirements under the MMPA and CITES as the appropriate regulatory provisions for the polar bear. In addition, this special rule provides that any incidental take of polar bears resulting from an activity that occurs outside the current range of the polar bear is not a prohibited act under the ESA. This special rule does not affect any existing requirements under the MMPA, including incidental take restrictions, or CITES, regardless of whether the activity occurs inside or outside the range of the polar bear.
>
> *Alternative 3*: Rule is the interim 4(d) special rule published in the *Federal Register* on May 15, 2008. There is only one substantive difference between Alternative 2 and Alternative 3 Alternative 3 provides that any incidental take of polar bears resulting from activities that occur outside Alaska is not a prohibited act under the ESA. Thus, the geographic range of incidental take exemption under the ESA differs between "outside Alaska" (Alternative 3) and "outside the current range of the polar bear" (Alternative 2).
>
> *Alternative 4*: Rule is the same as the final 4(d) special rule, but without the provisions of Paragraph 4. Alternative 4 does not contain a provision to expressly exempt any geographic areas from the prohibitions in §17.31 of the ESA regarding incidental taking of polar bears. All three versions of

the special rule (i.e., alternatives 2, 3 and 4) adopt the existing conservation regulatory requirements under the MMPA and CITES as the appropriate regulatory provisions for the polar bear.

U.S. Fish & Wildlife Service, Proposed Special Rule for the Polar Bear and Draft Environmental Assessment Under Section 4(d) of the Endangered Species Act, Questions & Answers, http://alaska.fws.gov/fisheries/mmm/polarbear/pdf/Q&APolarBear4(d)041312.pdf.   Can you think of any other alternatives that might have been worth consideration?

3. The polar bear was provided with a critical habitat designation, though not without litigation to push it forward. The following is an excerpt from the FWS press release regarding that designation:

> WASHINGTON, D.C. – The Department of the Interior's U.S. Fish and Wildlife Service today designated more than 187,000 square miles of onshore barrier islands, denning areas and offshore sea-ice as critical habitat for the threatened polar bear under the Endangered Species Act.
>
> The designation identifies geographic areas containing features considered essential for the conservation of the bear that require special management or protection.
>
> "This critical habitat designation enables us to work with federal partners to ensure their actions within its boundaries do not harm polar bear populations," said Tom Strickland, Assistant Secretary for Fish and Wildlife and Parks. "Nevertheless, the greatest threat to the polar bear is the melting of its sea ice habitat caused by human-induced climate change. We will continue to work toward comprehensive strategies for the long-term survival of this iconic species."
>
> The designation of critical habitat under the ESA does not affect land ownership or establish a refuge, wilderness, reserve, preserve, or other conservation area. It does not allow government or the public access to private lands. A critical habitat designation does not affect private lands unless federal funds, permits, or activities are involved.
>
> The final designation, contained in a final rule that was submitted on November 23, 2010 to the Federal Register, encompasses three areas or units: barrier island habitat, sea ice habitat and terrestrial denning habitat. Barrier island habitat includes coastal barrier islands and spits along Alaska's coast, and is used for denning, refuge from human disturbances, access to maternal dens and feeding habitat and travel along the coast. Sea ice habitat is located over the continental shelf, and includes ice over water up to 300 m (984 ft) in depth extending to the outer limits of the U.S. Exclusive Economic Zone, 321 km (200 miles) from shore.
>
> Terrestrial denning habitat includes lands within 32 km (20 miles) of the northern coast of Alaska between the Canadian border and the Kavik River and within 8 km (5 miles) between the Kavik River and Barrow, Alaska. Approximately 96 percent of the area designated as critical habitat is sea ice habitat.

***

The ESA requires that, to the maximum extent prudent and determinable, the Secretary of the Interior designate critical habitat at the time the species is added to the federal list of threatened and endangered species. However, the Service determined that additional time was needed to conduct a thorough evaluation and peer–review of a potential critical habitat designation, and thus did not publish a proposed designation when the listing's final rule was announced. As part of the settlement of a subsequent lawsuit brought by a group of conservation organizations, the Department of the Interior agreed to publish a Final Rule designating critical habitat for the polar bear. Today's announcement fulfills the terms of that agreement.

Polar bears evolved for life in the harsh arctic environment, and are distributed throughout most ice-covered seas of the Northern Hemisphere. They are generally limited to areas where the sea is ice-covered for much of the year; however, they are not evenly distributed throughout their range. They are most abundant near the shore in shallow-water areas, and in other places where currents and ocean upwelling increases marine productivity and maintains some open water during the ice-covered season.

Polar bears are completely dependent upon Arctic sea-ice habitat for survival. They use sea ice as a platform to hunt and feed upon seals, as a habitat on which to seek mates and breed, as a platform to move to onshore maternity denning areas, and make long-distance movements, and occasionally for maternity denning. Most populations use onshore habitat partially or exclusively for maternity denning.

Throughout most of their range, polar bears remain on the sea ice year-round or spend only short periods on land. ...

U.S. Department of the Interior News Release: U.S. Fish and Wildlife Service Announces Final Designation of Polar Bear Critical Habitat, http://alaska.fws.gov/fisheries/mmm/polarbear/pdf/news_release_11_24_10_critical_habitat_final.pdf.

D. Climate Mitigation through Renewable Energy: Conflicts with Endangered Species

The largest share of GHG emissions comes from power generation (electricity production and transformation were responsible for 26% of global emissions in 2004). Because of this, one of the most promising routes to climate mitigation is the development of renewable energy sources such as wind, solar energy, and hydropower. Indeed, scientists have proposed plans to move completely, as in 100 percent, to these energy sources within a couple of decades. *See* Mark Z. Jacobson & M.A. Delucchi, *A Path to Sustainable Energy by 2030*, 301 Scientific American 58–65 (November 2009) (scientists from Stanford and U.C. Davis outline their plan to achieve this goal, thereby "eliminating all fossil fuels"). Nearly everything you can find to read about renewable energy is positive and often exuberantly optimistic about the panacea it may be for all the world's problems, allowing us to have our energy cake and eat it too (and worry less about reducing consumption).

That said, before we leave our worries behind and celebrate, we must resolve one potentially difficult issue for renewable energy, especially these three favored brands, which is that they conflict with another important goal, protecting biodiversity. Wind, solar, and hydro energy all have one thing in common: they destroy habitat as well as directly kill wildlife, including listed species and their habitat. Can these problems be reconciled with the movement toward renewable energy, allowing us to partake of its many benefits? At least for now, we regularly see renewable energy progress impeded by the need for ESA compliance. As you read the following three excerpts, one from each of these renewable energy contexts, think about how we might maximize our access to renewable energy while minimizing its impacts on vulnerable species.

Animal Welfare Institute v. Beech Ridge Energy

United States District Court for the District of Maryland, 2009.
675 F.Supp.2d 540.

■ TITUS, DISTRICT JUDGE.

This is a case about bats, wind turbines, and two federal polices, one favoring protection of endangered species and the other encouraging development of renewable energy resources. It began on June 10, 2009, when Plaintiffs Animal Welfare Institute ("AWI"), Mountain Communities for Responsible Energy ("MCRE"), and David G. Cowan (collectively, "Plaintiffs") brought an action seeking declaratory and injunctive relief against Defendants Beech Ridge Energy LLC ("Beech Ridge Energy") and Invenergy Wind LLC ("Invenergy") (collectively, "Defendants"). Plaintiffs allege that Defendants' construction and future operation of the Beech Ridge wind energy project ("Beech Ridge Project"), located in Greenbrier County, West Virginia, will "take" endangered Indiana bats, in violation of § 9 of the Endangered Species Act ("ESA").

*   *   *

I. The Endangered Species Act

*   *   *

The ESA's plain language, citizen-suit provision, legislative history, and implementing regulations, as well as case law interpreting the Act, require that this Court carefully scrutinize any activity that allegedly may take endangered species where no ITP has been obtained.

II. The Indiana Bat

The FWS originally designated the Indiana bat (*Myotis sodalis*) as in danger of extinction in 1967 under the Endangered Species Preservation

Act of 1966, the predecessor to the ESA. The species has been listed as endangered since that time. The Indiana bat is in the genus *Myotis* and shares some morphological similarities with other *Myotis* species. It closely resembles the little brown bat (*Myotis lucifugus*) and the northern long-eared bat (*Myotis septenrionalis*). An Indiana bat weighs approximately one quarter of an ounce (approximately seven grams), its forearm length is 1 3/8 inches to 1 5/8 inches (35-41 millimeters), and its head and body length is 1 5/8 inches to 1 7/8 inches (41-49 millimeters).

The current range of the Indiana bat includes approximately twenty states in the mid-western and eastern United States, including West Virginia. ...

The Indiana bat population has declined since it was listed as an endangered species in 1967, and was estimated by the FWS in 2007 at approximately 468,184. However, research suggests that the West Virginia population of hibernating Indiana bats has increased since 1990, with an estimated current population of about 17,000. Approximately three percent of Indiana bats are located in West Virginia.

The Indiana bat is an insectivorous, migratory bat whose behavior varies depending on the season. In the fall, Indiana bats migrate to caves, called hibernacula. The bats engage in a "swarming" behavior in the vicinity of the hibernacula, which culminates in mating. Indiana bats ordinarily engage in swarming within five miles of hibernacula, but may also engage in swarming beyond the five mile radius. During swarming, the bats forage for insects in order to replenish their fat supplies. In mid-November, Indiana bats typically enter hibernation and remain in hibernacula for the duration of winter.

In April and May, Indiana bats emerge from hibernation. After engaging in "staging," typically within five miles of the hibernacula, they fly to summer roosting and foraging habitat. In the summer, female Indiana bats form maternity colonies in roost trees, where they give birth to "pups," and raise their young. Studies suggest that reproductive female Indiana bats give birth to one pup each year. Male Indiana bats spend their summers alone or in small temporary groups in roost trees, changing roost trees and locations throughout the summer. Roost trees generally consist of snags, which are dead or dying trees with exfoliating bark, or living trees with peeling bark.

Like other bats, Indiana bats navigate by using echolocation. Specifically, bats emit ultrasonic calls and determine from the echo the objects that are within their environment. Call sequences are typically composed of multiple pulses.

The FWS published the original recovery plan for the Indiana bat in 1983 and a draft revised plan in 1999. In April 2007, the FWS published the current Draft Recovery Plan. The current plan provides substantial background information regarding the behavior of the Indiana bat and the many threats that endanger the species. The plan also sets forth a recovery program designed to protect the Indiana bat and ultimately remove it from the Federal List of Endangered and Threatened Wildlife.

III. Wind Turbines and Bat Mortality

Research shows, and the parties agree, that wind energy facilities cause bat mortality and injuries through both turbine collisions and barotrauma. Barotrauma is damage caused to enclosed air-containing cavities (e.g., the lungs, eardrums, etc.) as a result of a rapid change in external pressure, usually from high to low. The majority of bat mortalities from wind energy facilities has occurred during fall dispersal and migration, but bat mortalities have also occurred in the spring and summer. At the Mountaineer wind energy facility in West Virginia, which is located approximately 75 miles from the Beech Ridge Project, a post-construction mortality study resulted in an estimated annual mortality rate of 47.53 bats per turbine.

The construction of wind energy projects may also kill, injure, or disrupt bat behavior. For example, the cutting of trees may kill or injure roosting bats and destroy potential roosting sites.

IV. The Beech Ridge Project

Defendant Invenergy is the fifth largest wind developer in the United States, with an aggregate wind-energy generating capacity of nearly 2,000 megawatts. Beech Ridge Energy, a wholly-owned subsidiary of Defendant Invenergy, intends to construct and operate 1226 wind turbines along 23 miles of Appalachian mountain ridgelines, in Greenbrier County, West Virginia. The first phase of the project currently consists of 67 turbines and the second phase consists of 55 turbines.

The footprint for the transmission line will be approximately 100 acres and the footprint for the wind turbines will be approximately 300 acres. The lowest turbines are located at an elevation of approximately 3,650 feet above sea level and the highest are at approximately 4,350 feet. The towers are 263 feet tall and the rotors have a diameter of 253 feet. When the blade is pointing straight up at twelve o'clock, the turbine is 389 feet tall, and when the blade is pointing straight down at six o'clock, the bottom point of the blade is 137 feet off the ground.

The Beech Ridge Project will cost over $300 million to build and will produce 186 megawatts of electricity, equivalent to the amount of electricity consumed by approximately 50,000 West Virginia households in a typical year. The project is projected to operate for a minimum of twenty years. Invenergy has signed a twenty-year contract with Appalachian Power Company to sell all output from the first 105 megawatts of power. Sixty-seven turbines, the number of turbines in the first phase of the project, are required to produce this amount of electricity.

* * *

XI. Presence of Indiana Bats at the Beech Ridge Project Site

When confronting the issue of whether Indiana bats are present at the Beech Ridge Project site, the parties analyzed a variety of factors, including: (i) the existence of hibernacula in the vicinity of the turbines; (ii) the physical characteristics of the Beech Ridge Project site; (iii) the mist-net data collected during the pre-construction surveys; and (iv) the acoustic data recorded by Libby.

*   *   *

E. Indiana Bats are Present at the Beech Ridge Project Site

Considering all of the evidence in the record, the Court concludes by a preponderance of the evidence that there is a virtual certainty that Indiana bats are present at the Beech Ridge Project site during the spring, summer, and fall. (Indiana bats are not likely to be present during winter, when the bats are hibernating.)

First, the Court finds that the close proximity of Indiana bat hibernacula to the project site, one cave located at 6.7 miles and another at 9.6 miles from the nearest turbines, supports a conclusion that Indiana bats are likely present at the Beech Ridge Project site. Indiana bats have been observed to travel far in excess of these distances in the spring, summer, and fall.

Second, the Court finds that the physical characteristics of the site also make the presence of Indiana bats more likely. The project site contains suitable roosting snags, and construction has further augmented the environment by creating habitat "sinks" that attract Indiana bats. Although the high elevation of the site makes it less likely, but not impossible, that maternity colonies are present during the summer, Indiana bats may still use the site during migration, fall swarming, and spring staging.

Third, the Court concludes that the acoustic data, collected by an entrepreneurial BHE subcontractor, confirms to a virtual certainty the presence of Indiana bats. Both Robbins and Gannon presented compelling testimony that their analysis of the AnaBat data identified Indiana bat calls. Because only four hours of acoustic data was collected over a mere two night period-during one summer survey session when Indiana bats are least likely to be present-more extensive acoustic surveys during different seasons and at different locations at the project site would almost certainly yield a greater number of Indiana bat calls.

Based on the evidence of nearby hibernacula, the physical characteristics of the project site, the acoustic data, and the behavioral traits of Indiana bats, the Court concludes by a preponderance of the evidence that Indiana bats are present at the Beech Ridge Project site during the spring, summer, and fall.

XII. Likelihood of a Take of Indiana Bats at the Beech Ridge Project Site

It is uncontroverted that wind turbines kill bats, and do so in large numbers. Defendants contend, however, that Indiana bats somehow will escape the fate of thousands of their less endangered peers at the Beech Ridge Project site.

Defendants argue that Indiana bats do not fly at the height of the turbine blades. Lacki and Tyrell stated that Indiana bats are "edge foragers," meaning they tend to forage for food directly below or at the tree canopy. Lacki opined that Indiana bats are not going to be in locations, such as the area above the tree canopy, where "their foraging approach is likely to render them vulnerable." Tyrell speculated that the tree canopy at the Beech Ridge Project site is 60 to 80 feet above the ground, which is below the lowest part of the rotor swept area.

However, Plaintiffs' expert Kunz, one of the leading bat biologists in the country, stated that with the development of acoustic technology and thermal cameras, there is growing research that bats can fly as high as a kilometer or more above the ground, and that Indiana bats may also fly at these altitudes. Kunz explained that bats fly above the tree canopy as warm air carries insects high above the surface of the earth. Kunz opined that "the fact that Indiana bats were detected at ground level . . . suggests that they would also would also equally likel[y] be detected higher up in the rotor swept region." Moreover, the height at which Indiana bats forage has no relation to how high they fly during migration.

Defendants also point out that no Indiana bat has been confirmed dead at any wind power project in the country, which they contend supports a conclusion that Indiana bats, unlike other bat species, are somehow able to avoid harm caused by wind turbines.

However, other *Myotis* species have been reported killed at wind power projects. *See, e.g.,* Edward B. Arnett et al., *Patterns of Bat Fatalities at Wind Energy Facilities in North America,* 72 J. of Wildlife Mgmt. 61, 64 (2008). Plaintiffs' experts opined that biologically, Indiana bats are no less vulnerable than other *Myotis* species to turbine collisions and barotrauma.

In addition, post-construction mortality studies are generally inefficient (for example, due to scavenging), thus making the chances of finding the carcass of a rare species even smaller. At trial, Gannon criticized those mortality studies – like those proposed at the Beech Ridge Project site – that survey only a subset of the turbines: "[i]f you've got a haystack, and you're only looking at a very small portion of that haystack, what's the odds that you're going to find something rare in the haystack?"

Plaintiffs' experts opined as follows regarding the likelihood that Indiana bats will be harmed by the Beech Ridge Project:

- *Robbins:* "Because the only logical scientific conclusion based on the foregoing is that Indiana bats are very likely-if not certainly-present on the Beech Ridge project site during spring, summer, and fall, it is still my opinion that there is a high likelihood that Indiana bats will be killed and injured by this project."

- *Gannon:* "Since, in my opinion, there exists an extremely high likelihood of Indiana bat presence on the project site during spring, summer, and fall based on the current evidence, my position remains that Indiana bats are very likely to be killed and injured by the [Beech Ridge Project]."

- *Kunz:* "Because Indiana bats are very likely to be present on the Beech Ridge project site during three seasons of each year when turbines operate, it continues to be my opinion that there is a high likelihood that Indiana bats will be killed and/or injured by this project during its twenty-year lifespan."

The Court agrees with these very credible expert opinions. The Court finds that there is no reason why Indiana bats would not fly at a height of 137 to 389 feet above the ground, within the rotor swept area of the turbines at the Beech Ridge Project site. Plaintiffs have presented compelling evidence that Indiana bats behave no differently than other *Myotis* species that have been killed by wind turbines and Defendants have failed to rebut this fact. Furthermore, the Court is not surprised that no dead Indiana bat has yet been found at any wind project because few post-mortality studies have been conducted, mortality searches are generally inefficient, and Indiana bats are rare.

Based on the evidence in the record, the Court therefore concludes, by a preponderance of the evidence, that, like death and taxes, there is a virtual certainty that Indiana bats will be harmed, wounded, or killed imminently by the Beech Ridge Project, in violation of § 9 of the ESA, during the spring, summer, and fall.

XIII. Effectiveness of Discretionary Post-Construction Adaptive Management Techniques

Defendants point to adaptive management after completion of construction as the appropriate way to address any perceived threat to Indiana bats. Even if adaptive management is ultimately the best way to reduce the risk of death and injury to Indiana bats posed by the Beech Ridge Project, Defendants are not currently *required* to implement *any* minimization or mitigation techniques. The West Virginia Public Service Commission's August 28, 2006 Order contains only precatory language.

Specifically, the Order states only that Defendants must *"consult"* with the TAC regarding the *"potential* for adaptive management" and agree to *"test* adaptive management strategies." Only if (i) the project causes "significant levels of bat or bird mortality"-*numbers which are not defined;* and (ii) adaptive management techniques are "proven effective"-a level of effectiveness which is not established; and (iii) adaptive management techniques are "economically feasible"-*the feasibility of which will be determined by the project developers*-must Beech Ridge Energy make a "good faith effort to work with the Commission" to implement adaptive management strategies. The Order states that adaptive management is discretionary and it imposes no consequences on Defendants if they fail to adopt necessary minimization and mitigation strategies.

Moreover, because Defendants repeatedly ignored letters from the FWS recommending additional preconstruction surveys and surveying techniques, the Court has little confidence that Defendants will actually implement any adaptive management strategies recommended by the TAC. At trial, Groberg, Vice President of Business Development for Invenergy and the lead developer of the Beech Ridge Project, testified that "I didn't want to commit to implementing anything that I couldn't put some bounds on." Defendants will likely continue to exhibit similar restraint.

In addition, the Court is highly skeptical of Defendants' ability and desire, without proper oversight, to identify Indiana bats during the course of ordinary business while the turbines are operating. Mortality studies are typically inefficient and are not comprehensive. Furthermore, the limited scope of the pre-construction surveys suggests that any post-construction monitoring will be ineffective. Rommé ignored repeated formal letters from the Service recommending that BHE perform three years of pre-construction surveys, conduct surveys during fall swarming and spring staging, and use other survey methods, including acoustic detection. In addition, BHE neither provided the acoustic data to any of the regulators nor analyzed it using either technology available at the time, if any, or improved technology as it has become available. It was not until this litigation began that BHE attempted to analyze the acoustic data. BHE's actions in this case and on behalf of other clients give the Court little reason to have any confidence in the effectiveness of any proposed post-construction monitoring advocated by Defendants.

Because entirely discretionary adaptive management will not eliminate the risk to Indiana bats, the Court has no choice but to award injunctive relief.

XIV. Injunctive Relief

Because the Court has found that the Beech Ridge Project will take Indiana bats, injunctive relief is appropriate under § 11 of the ESA. The question, then, is what form that injunctive relief should take. The ITP process is available to Defendants to insulate themselves from liability under the ESA and, while this Court cannot require them to apply for or obtain such a permit, it is the only way in which the Court will allow the Beech Ridge Project to continue.

The Court sees little need to preclude the completion of construction of those forty turbines already under construction, but does believe that any construction of additional turbines should not be commenced unless and until an ITP has been obtained. The simple reason for this is that the ITP process may find that some locations for wind turbines are entirely inappropriate, while others may be appropriate.

There is, by the same token, no reason to completely prohibit Defendants from operating wind turbines now under construction once they are completed. However, in light of the record developed before this Court, that operation can only occur during the periods of time when Indiana bats are in hibernation, i.e., from November 16 to March 31. Outside this period, determining the timing and circumstances under which wind turbine operation can occur without danger of the take of an Indiana bat is beyond the competence of this Court, but is well within the competence of the FWS under the ITP process.

Accordingly, the Court will enjoin all operation of wind turbines presently under construction except during the winter period enumerated above. However, the Court invites the parties to confer with each other and return to the Court, if agreement can be reached, on the conditions under which the wind turbines now under construction would be allowed to operate, if at all, during any period of time outside of the hibernation period of Indiana bats.

XV. Conclusion

As noted at the outset, this is a case about bats, wind turbines, and two federal policies, one favoring the protection of endangered species, and the other encouraging development of renewable energy resources. Congress, in enacting the ESA, has unequivocally stated that endangered species must be afforded the highest priority, and the FWS long ago designated the Indiana bat as an endangered species. By the same token, Congress has strongly encouraged the development of clean, renewable energy, including wind energy. It is uncontroverted that wind turbines kill or injure bats in large numbers, and the Court has concluded, in this case, that there is a virtual certainty that construction and operation of the Beech Ridge Project will take endangered Indiana bats in violation of Section 9 of the ESA.

The two vital federal policies at issue in this case are not necessarily in conflict. Indeed, the tragedy of this case is that Defendants disregarded not only repeated advice from the FWS but also failed to take advantage of a specific mechanism, the ITP process, established by federal law to allow their project to proceed in harmony with the goal of avoidance of harm to endangered species

*   *   *

This Court has concluded that the only avenue available to Defendants to resolve the self-imposed plight in which they now find themselves is to do belatedly that which they should have done long ago: apply for an ITP. The Court does express the concern that any extraordinary delays by the FWS in the processing of a permit application would frustrate Congress' intent to encourage responsible wind turbine development. Assuming that Defendants now proceed to file an application for an ITP, the Court urges the FWS to act with reasonable promptness, but with necessary thoroughness, in acting upon that application.

The development of wind energy can and should be encouraged, but wind turbines must be good neighbors. Accordingly, the Court will, albeit reluctantly, grant injunctive relief as discussed above.

NOTES & QUESTIONS

1. In March 2012 the FWS released an 82-page document outlining its Land-Based Wind Energy Guidelines. While not mandatory for wind developers, these guidelines were designed to provide those in the industry with the information they need to minimize conflicts with wildlife. From the executive summary:

> As the Nation shifts to renewable energy production to supplant the need for carbon-based fuel, wind energy will be an important source of power. As wind energy production increases, both developers and wildlife agencies have recognized the need for a system to evaluate and address the potential negative impacts of wind energy projects on species of concern. These voluntary Guidelines provide a structured, scientific process for addressing wildlife conservation concerns at all stages of land-based wind energy development. They also promote effective communication among wind energy developers and federal, state, and local conservation agencies and tribes. When used in concert with appropriate regulatory tools, the Guidelines form the best practical approach for conserving species of concern. The Guidelines have been developed by the Interior Department's U.S. Fish and Wildlife Service (Service) working with the Wind Turbine Guidelines Advisory Committee. They replace interim voluntary guidance published by the Service in 2003.

> The Guidelines discuss various risks to "species of concern" from wind energy projects, including collisions with wind turbines and associated infrastructure; loss and degradation of habitat from turbines and infrastructure; fragmentation of large habitat blocks into smaller segments that may not support sensitive species; displacement and behavioral changes; and indirect effects such as increased predator populations or introduction of invasive plants. The Guidelines assist developers in identifying species of concern that may potentially be affected by their proposed project, including migratory birds; bats; bald and golden eagles and other birds of prey; prairie and sage grouse; and listed, proposed, or candidate endangered and threatened species. Wind energy development in some areas may be precluded by federal law; other areas may be inappropriate for development because they have been recognized as having high wildlife value based on their ecological rarity and intactness.

***

The most important thing a developer can do is to consult with the Service as early as possible in the development of a wind energy project. Early consultation offers the greatest opportunity for avoiding areas where development is precluded or where wildlife impacts are likely to be high and difficult or costly to remedy or mitigate at a later stage. By consulting early, project developers can also incorporate appropriate wildlife conservation measures and monitoring into their decisions about project siting, design, and operation.

Adherence to the Guidelines is voluntary and does not relieve any individual, company, or agency of the responsibility to comply with laws and regulations. However, if a violation occurs the Service will consider a developer's documented efforts to communicate with the Service and adhere to the Guidelines. The Guidelines include a Communications Protocol which provides guidance to both developers and Service personnel regarding appropriate communication and documentation.

The Guidelines also provide Best Management Practices for site development, construction, retrofitting, repowering, and decommissioning. ...

U.S. Fish and Wildlife Service Land-Based Wind Energy Guidelines, March 23, 2012, http://www.fws.gov/windenergy/docs/WEG_final.pdf.

2. Given how valuable wind power is to mitigating climate change, along with how valuable such mitigation is to endangered species, what is the appropriate attitude for wildlife folks to have toward wind development? Should it receive special treatment under the ESA? Should it get a pass from ESA enforcement? Or should we expect the industry to work within the limitations of the ESA just like all others before them? *See* J.B. Ruhl, *Harmonizing Commercial Wind Power and the Endangered Species Act through Administrative Reform*, http://papers.ssrn.com/sol3/papers.cfm?abstract_id=2070891.

Julie Cart, *Saving Desert Tortoises is a Costly Hurdle for Solar Projects: Brightsource Energy Has Spent $56 Million So Far To Protect the Threatened Creatures, But Calamities Have Befallen the Effort*

Los Angeles Times, March 4, 2012.

Reporting from Ivanpah Valley, Calif. — Stubborn does not come close to describing the desert tortoise, a species that did its evolving more than 220 million years ago and has since remained resolutely prehistoric.

Its slowpoke take on biological adaptation has exposed modern vulnerabilities. The persnickety reptile is today beset by respiratory infections and prone to disease. Its only defenses are the shell on its back and the scent of its unspeakably foul urine.

How this creature the size of a shoe box became the single biggest obstacle to industrial-scale solar development in the Mojave Desert is turning into a true story of the survival of the fittest.

At the $2.2-billion BrightSource Energy solar farm in the Ivanpah Valley, the tortoise brought construction to a standstill for three months when excavation work found far more animals than biologists expected.

BrightSource has spent $56 million so far to protect and relocate the tortoises, but even at that price, the work has met with unforeseen calamity: Animals crushed under vehicle tires, army ants attacking hatchlings in a makeshift nursery and one small tortoise carried off to an eagle nest, its embedded microchip pinging faintly as it receded.

History has shown the tortoise to be a stubborn survivor, withstanding upheavals that caused the grand dinosaur extinction and ice ages that wiped out most living creatures. But unless current recovery efforts begin to gain traction, this threatened species could become collateral damage in the war against fossil fuels.

Costly conservation efforts by state and federal agencies and solar companies have created a mishmash of strategies that one scientist says amounts to a "grand science experiment," said Jeff Lovich, who studies the impact of renewable energy projects on desert tortoises for the U.S. Geological Survey.

"One could argue that they are nature's greatest success story," Lovich said. "Yet over half the world's turtles are in dire need of help. The common denominator is humans. They may not survive us."

An ideal site

BrightSource's project at Ivanpah is the first large-scale solar plant to enter the desert tortoise regulatory maze. Its experience is a case study for how the booming solar industry must deal with the reptile.

Long before construction began, BrightSource was warned that the site was thick with tortoises, more so than any of the other dozen solar farms planned for that part of the Mojave.

But BrightSource wanted the site because it is ideal for generating solar power. So the company negotiated with state and federal agencies to hash out meticulously detailed protocols for collecting and relocating tortoises, also agreeing to monitor them for five years after they were moved.

The company made its first concession to the tortoise during planning, giving up about 10% of its expected power output in a redesign that reduced the project footprint by 12% and the number of 460-foot-tall "power towers" from seven to three.

BrightSource also agreed to install 50 miles of intricate fencing, at a cost of up to $50,000 per mile, designed to prevent relocated tortoises from climbing or burrowing back into harm's way.

The first survey of tortoises at the site found just 16. Based on biological calculations, the U.S. Fish and Wildlife Service issued BrightSource a permit to move a maximum of 38 adults, and allowed a total of three accidental deaths per year during three years of construction. Any more in either category and the entire project would be shut down.

The limit put the company under enormous pressure, as more and more tortoises began cropping up and BrightSource's project came closer to the federal thresholds.

The pressure boiled over after company biologists discovered an adult female tortoise with its carapace crushed in October 2010, during a media tour of the site. Biologists concluded that a vehicle struck the animal and ordered it euthanized.

A flurry of emails ensued. Steve DeYoung, then a BrightSource vice president, wrote to a federal biologist: "How in God's name could anyone blame us? It is completely unconscionable that we would be blamed for this. I simply cannot sit back and watch this happen."

Ultimately, the death was not attributed to the project. But other mishaps occurred, many of them documented in 36 boxes of project files stored at the Bureau of Land Management office in Needles.

The reports read like medical charts: a juvenile had his right forelimb gnawed by rodent, a tortoise died of heat distress after being caught in the black plastic erosion fencing, hatchlings were set upon by army ants, which killed four babies still in their eggs and injured four others.

The project's bottom line took on an inevitable arc: as tortoise numbers rose, costs went up.

BrightSource, which was paying to have as many as 100 biologists to be on the site at one time, began seeing red. The company warned that tortoise mitigation was jeopardizing Ivanpah's viability. In an email to a BLM official, DeYoung complained that tortoises were at that point costing the company as much as $40 million. "This truly could kill the project," he wrote.

BrightSource lawyer Jeffrey D. Harris wrote to the California Energy Commission to suggest that if the Ivanpah crashed because of tortoises, the state's renewable energy goals would meet the same fate.

By February 2011, all parties realized that the site contained more tortoises than allowed under the permit. Two months later, state and federal agencies ordered construction suspended until a new biological assessment could be completed.

When BLM officials inquired about the slow pace of the work, Amy Fesnock, BLM's lead biologist for endangered species, sent an email up the BLM food chain stating that many requests for data were apparently being ignored by BrightSource.

Referring to BrightSource Energy by the shorthand BSE, Fesnock wrote, "The 'crisis' that this project is in is purely of BSE's making. If we continue to reward their bad behavior — contorting ourselves to solve the problems that they keep creating, we have no hope of them not creating a new problem for us to solve."

Fesnock told The Times recently that her issues with former BrightSource project managers had been resolved and called the work of the company's biologists "phenomenal."

At Ivanpah today, 166 adult and juvenile tortoises have been collected and moved to a nine-acre holding facility. The objective is to release them into the "wild," on the other side of the fence from the solar facility.

Tools of survival

Desert tortoises were not always so scarce. They thrived in a harsh environment with the few tools nature provided.

To ward off predators, they spritz pungent bladder contents around their burrows, where they spend as much as 95% of their lives. When tortoises hear thunder — signaling a desert storm — they come topside and lower the side of their shells like bulldozer blades to gouge out water catchments. They can increase their body mass by 30% to 40% by guzzling water in this way, a quenching that can sustain them for more than two years without another drop.

The animals were once so abundant that Southern Californians used to bring the small ones home from desert trips as souvenirs, and the animals lived quiet lives in suburban backyards.

Once the tortoise was added to the endangered species list in 1990, however, a reverse diaspora occurred. Panicked moms and dads streaked back to the Mojave to release the now-protected tortoise. The story does not end there, nor does it end well. The former captives brought with them disease that spread and killed tortoises across the Mojave.

About the same time, desert recreation increasingly began to include off-road vehicles, which crushed either the animals or their burrows. The dust kicked up by the machines exacerbated the animal's propensity for upper respiratory infections.

As Southern California's exurbs marched east, trash dumps came with them, bringing ravens — one of the tortoise's most effective predators. Finally, roadways crossing the desert to connect population centers and provide for recreation along the Colorado River laid down an asphalt moat that, as much as anything, defined the new de facto tortoise habitat.

BrightSource's difficulties with the tortoise raise hackles among people who believe government protections afforded to animals are too extreme. Even before solar power entered the picture, state and federal agencies had spent nearly $200 million since 1990 toward the care and feeding of the desert tortoise.

California requires developers to provide two acres of suitable tortoise habitat for every acre of habitat taken. But the scale of the solar development coming to Western deserts is so vast that it renders the formula unworkable. Not enough alternative land exists.

Instead, solar developers may now pay to close off-road vehicle routes, rehabilitate degraded habitat on federal land, fund public education programs and erect miles of special fencing to keep the tortoises off highways and out of solar energy sites.

Homing instinct

Tortoise relocation is a formidable issue. Moved animals nearly always attempt to plod home, piloted by an uncanny sense of direction.

"If I pick you up and drop you off in Kansas, wouldn't you try to come back to California?" Fesnock asked. Tortoises live long and have good memories, she said. "They know when they are not at home. They know where the water is. They know where the food is."

For now, wildlife officials are still unsure if they will release animals this spring because a drought is expected this summer.

To date, just one desert tortoise has been relocated at Ivanpah.

Last October, a tagged female, BS-71, had been in a holding pen for four months and wasn't adapting. She endlessly paced her enclosure. Over and over the animal attempted to climb the wire mesh, gaining some height, then usually ending up flipping on her back.

Unable to bear the sight of the tortoise's apparent distress any longer, BrightSource lead biologist Mercy Vaughn sought permission to release the female to the wild. The request has since been dubbed the "Mercy Rule."

After gaining approval from the U.S. Fish and Wildlife Service, filling out paperwork, providing medical testing — a tortoise under stress is more susceptible to disease — Vaughn was finally cleared to free the homesick tortoise.

The animal was placed in a purple plastic bin and carried deep into the desert. While a dozen people looked on, some filming the event, the tortoise was gently placed at the entrance of a burrow. She hesitated for a moment, then shuffled down into the gloom.

Moments later BS-71 reemerged, blinked and began munching grass.

NOTES & QUESTIONS

1. On July 24, 2012, the U.S. Department of the Interior issued the following press release regarding its environmental impact statement for solar energy development:

WASHINGTON, D.C. - As part of President Obama's all-of-the-above energy strategy, the Department of the Interior, in partnership with the Department of Energy, will publish the Final Programmatic Environmental Impact Statement (PEIS) for solar energy development in six southwestern states—Arizona, California, Colorado, Nevada, New Mexico, and Utah.

The final Solar PEIS represents a major step forward in the permitting of utility-scale solar energy on public lands throughout the west.

Today's announcement builds on the historic progress made in fostering renewable energy development on public lands. When President Obama took office, there were no solar projects permitted on public lands; since 2009, Interior has approved 17 utility-scale solar energy projects that, when built, will produce nearly 5,900 megawatts of energy—enough to power approximately 1.8 million American homes. Thanks to steps already taken by this administration, renewable energy from sources like wind and solar have doubled since the President took office.

The Solar PEIS will serve as a roadmap for solar energy development by establishing solar energy zones with access to existing or planned transmission, the fewest resource conflicts and incentives for development within those zones. The blueprint's comprehensive analysis will make for faster, better permitting of large-scale solar projects on public lands.

"This blueprint for landscape-level planning is about facilitating faster, smarter utility-scale solar development on America's public lands," said Secretary of the Interior Ken Salazar. "This is a key milestone in building a sustainable foundation for utility-scale solar energy development and conservation on public lands over the next two decades."

"Developing America's solar energy resources is an important part of President Obama's commitment to expanding American-made energy, increasing energy security, and creating jobs," said Energy Secretary Steven Chu. "This new roadmap builds on that commitment by identifying public lands that are best suited for solar energy projects, improving the permitting process, and creating incentives to deliver more renewable energy to American homes and businesses."

The Solar PEIS planning effort has focused on identifying locations on Bureau of Land Management (BLM) lands that are most suitable for solar energy development. These areas are characterized by excellent solar resources, good energy transmission potential, and relatively low conflict with biological, cultural and historic resources. The Final PEIS identifies 17 Solar Energy Zones (SEZs), totaling about 285,000 acres of public lands, as priority areas for utility-scale solar development, with the potential for additional zones through ongoing and future regional planning processes. The blueprint also allows for utility-scale solar development on approximately 19 million acres in "variance" areas lying outside of identified SEZs. In total, the Final PEIS estimates a total development of 23,700 megawatts from the 17 zones and the variance areas, enough renewable energy to power 7 million American homes.

"Input from stakeholders has been extremely valuable throughout this process," said Acting BLM Director Mike Pool. "Their comments have helped to refine the zones to make sure they're 'smart from the start', to improve the transmission analyses and to build effective incentives into this blueprint for solar development."

Key elements of the Final Solar PEIS:

- Establishes an initial set of 17 Solar Energy Zones on 285,000 acres across 6 Western States;

- Outlines a process for industry, the public and other interested stakeholders to propose new or expanded zones; efforts already underway include California's Desert Renewable Energy Conservation Plan and the West Chocolate Mountains Renewable Energy Evaluation, Arizona's Restoration Energy Design Project, and other local planning efforts in Nevada and Colorado;

- Includes strong incentives for development within zones, including faster and easier permitting, improved mitigation strategies, and economic incentives;

- Sets a clear process that allows for development of well-sited projects on approximately 19 million acres outside the zones;

- Protects natural and cultural resources by excluding 78 million acres from solar energy development;

- Identifies design features (best practices) for solar energy development to ensure the most environmentally responsible development and delivery of solar energy; and

- Establishes a framework for regional mitigation plans and a strategy for monitoring and adaptive management; the first mitigation pilot for the Dry Lake Solar Energy Zone is already underway.

In support of more detailed system-level analyses of transmission needs, the BLM is engaged in ongoing transmission planning efforts, including through the Transmission Expansion Planning Policy Committee and the Western Electricity Coordination Council's transmission study.

The July 27 *Federal Register* Notice of Availability for the Final PEIS will begin a 30-day protest period, after which Secretary Salazar may consider adopting the document through a Record of Decision. ...

Obama Administration Releases Roadmap for Solar Energy Development on Public Lands, July 24, 2012, http://solareis.anl.gov/documents/docs/PressRelease_Final_Solar_PEIS.pdf.

Notably absent from the press release is any mention of conflicts with wildlife or habitat. Of course, these issues are addressed in the PEIS itself, as they are the primary environmental concern with solar energy development (perhaps you have seen the viral billboard image by the Vote Solar Initiative saying "When there's a huge solar energy spill, it's just called a 'nice day'"). Why make no mention of the issue to the press? Might conflicts with endangered species make for bad PR in the push to expand solar energy development? The PEIS suggests mitigation measures for when conflicts with species cannot be avoided. Shouldn't such trade-offs be part of the general public's consideration of the issue?

2. How might we get more of the benefits of solar energy with less of the environmental cost? Consider the significant portion of U.S. land that has already

been developed, already wiping out the habitats that once were there. Every building in the country has a roof. Every street light has a post to which a panel can be affixed to power that street light. Can you think of some possible reasons behind our primary focus on undeveloped lands for solar energy? Which approach works best within our existing framework of property rights and corporate innovation? Have you ever considered placing solar panels on your home? If not, what are the primary hurdles that stand in your way, and what (administratively) might be done to relieve them?

Alabama Power Company v. Federal Energy Regulatory Commission

United States Court of Appeals for the District of Columbia Circuit, 1992.
979 F.2d 1561.

■ RANDOLPH, CIRCUIT JUDGE:

This case is here on petitions for review of orders of the Federal Energy Regulatory Commission directing Alabama Power Company to increase the minimum amounts of water regularly released from its Jordan Dam on the Coosa River and refusing to stay those orders. The principal question is whether the Commission, in these rulings, complied with sections 7(a)(2) and 7(a)(4) of the Endangered Species Act.

From its source near Rome, Georgia, the Coosa River flows southwestwardly 286 miles through Alabama to its confluence with the Alabama River. Dams of the Alabama Power Company along the river have created an uninterrupted series of impoundments, with the exception of a 7.5 mile reach of the river directly below the Jordan Dam, where a riverine environment still exists. The dam, located several miles north of Montgomery and built in 1928 pursuant to a 50-year license to provide hydroelectric power, impounds the Jordan Reservoir. During relicensing proceedings in 1980, the Commission ordered Alabama Power to conduct a "study to determine what minimum flow release is necessary to insure protection of downstream fisheries and recreation within the operational constraints of the generating units."

Alabama Power's study, completed in 1984, disclosed a considerable variance in the flow of the Coosa River at the Jordan Dam, ranging from a low of several dozen cubic feet per second (cfs) in October to a high of several hundred thousand cfs in April in any given year. The company recommended that the minimum flow of the river be set at 188 cfs, a figure corresponding to the estimated seepage from the dam. The United States Fish and Wildlife Service and the Alabama Department of Conservation and Natural Resources opposed this plan, stating that the "leakage flow release would further degrade an already depressed fishery," "reduce an already limited recreational resource," and "potentially degrade water quality." In the interests of fishing and recreational boating, both agencies recommended a minimum continuous discharge rate of 4,475 cfs between June and February, and a doubling of that rate during March, April, and May.

During the rest of the 1980's, the proceeding moved along at the customary pace until the snails were detected. In 1988, Dr. Robert Hershler reported the existence of *Tulotoma magnifica* in the Jordan Dam tailwater, a discovery of some note because mollusk experts-malacologists-considered the species extinct. The only previously known populations, located in other sections of the Coosa River, met their doom in the 1960's when additional hydroelectric dams were constructed and the snail's habitat was flooded. This is not to suggest that in the stretch of river below the Jordan Dam, the snail itself, although not its significance, could have gone undetected, especially by Coosa River fishermen. Tulotoma grows to the size of a golf ball. Long ago, when the Coosa River was in its natural state, Indians ate these gill-breathing snails and used their shells as ornaments. Because tulotoma prefers "cool, oxygenated, clean, free-flowing waters," the snail is generally found in riffles and shoals, spending the daylight hours clinging to the undersides of large rocks.

With the discovery of the tulotoma snail, and the consequent prospect that the Interior Department would eventually list the creature as endangered, Alabama Power argued for the first time in 1990 that the Commission's judgment about minimum continuous flows ought to give more attention to protecting the snails. There is no need to recount at this stage the details of the proceedings leading to the Commission's final order on rehearing on July 31, 1991. It is enough to point out that the Commission rejected Alabama Power's request for a stay of an interim order requiring a minimum continuous release of 2,000 cfs from June through February, and 4,475 cfs from March through May; for a stay of the Commission's decision affirming this order; and for a stay pending the company's petition for rehearing. On December 20, 1990, while the petition for rehearing was pending, Alabama Power implemented the new flow regime ordered on November 20, 1990.

One event of note occurred thereafter, on June 1, 1991, when Alabama Power abruptly reduced the continuous flow of water from 4,475 cfs to 2,000 cfs. This had the utterly predictable result of leaving a good many tulotoma high and dry. Many of the stranded snails perished. Alabama Power puts the number at "high hundreds to low thousands" and places the blame on the Commission's order, with which it was "simply complying." The Commission, in its July 31, 1991, decision on rehearing, responded to the catastrophe by modifying the original order to require the company to ramp down the flows from May 29 to May 31 each year.

After Dr. Hershler's discovery in 1988, the Interior Department's Fish and Wildlife Service started the process for listing *Tulotoma magnifica* as an endangered species under the Endangered Species Act. The Service published its proposed listing of tulotoma on July 11, 1990. The proposal generated two comments, both from Alabama agencies supporting the listing. The final rule, published on January 9, 1991, became effective February 8, 1991. Since that time, federal law has protected tulotoma from capture, harm or relocation.

The legal effect of the Service's proposing tulotoma for listing was to trigger the requirement, in section 7(a)(4) of the Endangered Species Act, that the Commission "confer" with the Secretary of the Interior about any agency action "likely to jeopardize the continued existence" of the species. After tulotoma made the list, section 7(a)(2) of the Act, required the Commission, "in consultation with and with the assistance of the Secretary," to "insure" that any agency action would not be likely to have this effect; and to "use the best scientific and commercial data available" in fulfilling the Act's directive. As Alabama Power sees it, the Commission's continuous flow orders and denials of stays after July 11, 1990, when the Service proposed tulotoma for listing, violated section 7(a)(4), and its order on rehearing issued after tulotoma's listing violated section 7(a)(2).

As to section 7(a)(4), there is no doubt that the Commission satisfied its duty to "confer" with the Secretary's designee, the Fish and Wildlife Service. The Service was deeply involved in these proceedings from their onset in 1980, when it recommended continuous flows in order to improve the fishery in the Jordan Dam tailwater. By the time the Commission issued its order in late 1990 directing Alabama Power to implement the continuous flow regime, it had already heard from the Service about the effect on the snail. On May 1, 1990, the Service informed the Commission in writing that continuous minimum flows at the Jordan Dam, far from having an adverse impact on the tulotoma snail, "would improve the quality and quantity of the aquatic habitat for this species." Thereafter, in a meeting with Commission staff on December 13, 1990, and through a letter dated December 24, 1990, the Service provided further technical advice. Section 7(a)(4) demanded nothing more. The duty to confer arises only when the agency action is "likely to jeopardize the continued existence" of the species. As both the Service and the Commission evaluated the situation, the continuous flow order would have no such consequence.

When Alabama Power complains that the Service was more intent on improving the fishery than in protecting the snail it makes the mistake of supposing that these objectives are somehow inconsistent. Numerous species of fish thrive in the same aquatic environment needed by tulotoma snails. Well-oxygenated, clean, continuous flowing water with riffles and pools and a substrate consisting of rocks and gravel could describe many of the finest trout streams in the nation. While the Coosa River below Jordan Dam is not a coldwater stream and is not favored with trout, the fish it holds-spotted bass, blue catfish, channel catfish, crappie, hybrid striped bass, white bass, and freshwater drum-benefit from the same conditions. Like trout, some of these species feed on the caddisflies, mayflies, and stoneflies found predominantly in riffles. Alabama Power's own study also disclosed that more larval fish were found in these sections of the Jordan Dam tailwater, thus indicating that the fish were using the riffle/runs as a nursery and spawning ground. The continuous flow regime therefore held the promise of simultaneously improving the fishery and the habitat of the tulotoma snail.

As far as section 7(a)(4) is concerned, the Commission fulfilled its duty, "in consultation" with the Service, of insuring that continuous flows would not be "likely to jeopardize the continued existence" of the snail. After the Service listed tulotoma, the Commission, at Alabama Power's urging, requested "formal consultation" with the Service on the effect of the new minimum flows on the snail. In making this request, the Commission may have done even more than the Act required of it. The regulations of the Fish and Wildlife Service provide that formal consultation is unnecessary when, "as a result of informal consultation with the Service," the agency determines, "with the written concurrence of the Director, that the proposed action is not likely to adversely affect any listed species or critical habitat." At any rate, the Service acceded to the Commission's request on March 4, 1991, and began developing its "Biological Opinion" regarding the likely effect of the agency action. For its part, the Commission deferred final action on Alabama Power's rehearing petition. The Service issued its Biological Opinion on July 10, 1991, after receiving comments from the Commission and Alabama Power. The Opinion concluded that the "mainstream Coosa River population of tulotoma may benefit from the Commission's Orders"; and that "the minimum continuous flows ordered by the Commission increase the amount of habitat available to the snail and significantly alleviate the impacts of low flows and extreme flow fluctuations which occurred almost daily prior to December 20, 1990." The Commission then denied Alabama Power's rehearing petition, but-as mentioned earlier-modified its previous order by requiring a gradual decrease of the flow during the transition from the May rate to the lower rate of release in effect from June to February.

The Commission's violation of section 7(a)(2), according to Alabama Power, stemmed from its failure to conduct a "study of the snail's habitat needs and life cycle in those conditions which existed prior to the implementation of the minimum flow order." One might wonder how this argument can be squared with the findings by the Service and the Commission that the pre-existing flow regime had been harmful to the snail. No one could seriously urge jeopardizing the snail in order to study how to avoid jeopardizing it. Alabama Power saw things differently. The company enlisted the services of a malacologist, Dr. Fred G. Thompson, submitting his affidavit to the Commission on December 13, 1990. In Dr. Thompson's opinion, there was insufficient evidence about the snail to enable anyone to conclude that increased flows would not have adverse effects. He advocated maintaining the status quo for 1½ to 2 years to permit a "baseline study" of the snail. Relying on this affidavit, Alabama Power submits that the Commission did not "use the best available scientific and commercial data available," as section 7(a)(2) requires.

We reject this argument for the following reasons. In the first place, the affidavit could have related only to section 7(a)(4), not section 7(a)(2): when the company filed the affidavit, the Service had only proposed tulotoma for listing. The Commission's obligation at that stage was not to consult, but to "confer," and to confer only if its action would be "likely to jeopardize" the snail's existence. Significantly, Dr. Thompson's affidavit expressed no opinion that the snails would likely be jeopardized. Rather, he "question[ed]" the Service's conclusion that the snails would benefit from the increased flows. Furthermore, section 7(a)(4) does not have a "best-scientific-evidence-available" requirement such as the one contained in section 7(a)(2). Yet not until February 8, 1991, when the snail was listed, did section 7(a)(2) become applicable. By that time, Dr. Thompson's proposal had become moot. Alabama Power had already begun complying with the Commission's continuous flow order, which went into effect on December 20, 1990. "All baseline data, requisite to a full and complete study," Dr. Thompson stated, "will be virtually eliminated" once the flows are released, making it "virtually impossible to conduct a significant and meaningful 'comparative' study. . ." In other words, a worthwhile baseline study could not have been performed from that point forward according to the company's own expert. *Roosevelt Campobello International Park v. EPA,* 684 F.2d 1041 (1st Cir.1982), which Alabama Power invokes for the proposition that section 7(a)(2) required the Commission to conduct a baseline study, is beside the point. Section 7(a)(2) does not demand the impossible.

Alabama Power's remaining arguments do not warrant discussion. These have been considered and rejected.

The petition for review is denied.

NOTES & QUESTIONS

1. Considering what a hydropower dam does, blocking a river and requiring the water to pass through its turbines in order to generate power, it is easy to imagine what the greatest issue would be: the fish species that must travel up and down the river (or, to be more accurate, down and up). How do you think this is resolved? For a survey of the fish/dam saga, as well as a general discussion of the environmental impact of dams, see Kyle J. Mathews, *Who Controls the Fate of the Fish? Interagency Fighting Over Section 10(J) of the Federal Power Act,* 74 S. Cal. L. Rev. 1165 (2001).

2. The National Geographic website provides a concise and interesting background on hydropower, including some useful facts about how it works and how heavily we have come to rely on it:

> Hydropower is electricity generated using the energy of moving water. Rain or melted snow, usually originating in hills and mountains, create streams and rivers that eventually run to the ocean. The energy of that moving water can be substantial, as anyone who has been whitewater rafting knows.

> This energy has been exploited for centuries. Farmers since the ancient Greeks have used water wheels to grind wheat into flour. Placed in a river, a water wheel picks up flowing water in buckets located around the wheel. The kinetic energy of the flowing river turns the wheel and is converted into mechanical energy that runs the mill.

> In the late 19th century, hydropower became a source for generating electricity. The first hydroelectric power plant was built at Niagara Falls in 1879. In 1881, street lamps in the city of Niagara Falls were powered by

hydropower. In 1882 the world's first hydroelectric power plant began operating in the United States in Appleton, Wisconsin.

A typical hydro plant is a system with three parts: an electric plant where the electricity is produced; a dam that can be opened or closed to control water flow; and a reservoir where water can be stored. The water behind the dam flows through an intake and pushes against blades in a turbine, causing them to turn. The turbine spins a generator to produce electricity. The amount of electricity that can be generated depends on how far the water drops and how much water moves through the system. The electricity can be transported over long-distance electric lines to homes, factories, and businesses.

Hydroelectric power provides almost one-fifth of the world's electricity. China, Canada, Brazil, the United States, and Russia were the five largest producers of hydropower in 2004. One of the world's largest hydro plants is at Three Gorges on China's Yangtze River. The reservoir for this facility started filling in 2003, but the plant is not expected to be fully operational until 2009. The dam is 1.4 miles (2.3 kilometers) wide and 607 feet (185 meters) high.

The biggest hydro plant in the United States is located at the Grand Coulee Dam on the Columbia River in northern Washington. More than 70 percent of the electricity made in Washington State is produced by hydroelectric facilities.

Hydropower is the cheapest way to generate electricity today. That's because once a dam has been built and the equipment installed, the energy source—flowing water—is free. It's a clean fuel source that is renewable yearly by snow and rainfall.

Hydropower is also readily available; engineers can control the flow of water through the turbines to produce electricity on demand. In addition, reservoirs may offer recreational opportunities, such as swimming and boating.

But damming rivers may destroy or disrupt wildlife and other natural resources. Some fish, like salmon, may be prevented from swimming upstream to spawn. Technologies like fish ladders help salmon go up over dams and enter upstream spawning areas, but the presence of hydroelectric dams changes their migration patterns and hurts fish populations. Hydropower plants can also cause low dissolved oxygen levels in the water, which is harmful to river habitats.

Hydropower: Going with the Flow, http://environment.nationalgeographic .com/environment/global-warming/hydropower-profile/.

CHAPTER 19

BIODIVERSITY AND CLIMATE ADAPTATION

Chapter Outline:
A. What is Climate Adaptation?
B. The Tools of the Adaptation Trade: Ecosystem Resilience, Adaptive Management, and Assisted Migration
    1. Ecosystem Resilience
    2. Adaptive Management
    3. Assisted Migration
    4. Bringing it all Together in the Florida Everglades, A Case Study
    5. Letting Go of the Past
C. The Federal Approach to Adapting Wildlife and Ecosystems to Climate Impacts
    1. The Endangered Species Act and Climate Adaptation
    2. Inter-Agency Planning for Ecosystems and Climate Adaptation

A. WHAT IS CLIMATE ADAPTATION?

The last two chapters have made it quite clear that we need to find a way to reduce our GHG emissions with the goal of slowing down (and eventually halting) our impact on global climate. However, we have also learned that climate change is already underway, that it operates with a multi-decade lag time, and that we are neither economically nor politically capable of immediate and/or complete cessation of GHG emissions. In other words, we will be stuck with climate change for at least a few decades, likely longer, and it is likely to get worse before it gets better. *See* T.M.L. Wigley, *The Climate Change Commitment*, 307 SCIENCE 1766 (2005). What will this mean for our ecosystems and the species that depend on them?

In this chapter we will consider the need to adapt to climate change, primarily in terms of adapting species and ecosystems to direct climate-induced alterations to the environment, but also with regard to addressing the negative impacts that human adaptations may have on species and ecosystems. We will review some of the key scientifically-supported methods of reducing the impact climate change will likely have on wildlife, as well as the relationship between the federal government (including the ESA) and those methods. But first we must answer the question heading this section. This analysis begins with a look at a Pew Center summary of adaptation basics, including its societal role and strategies for success, which is followed by several interpretations of the concept by legal scholars.

William E. Eastering III, Brian H. Hurd & Joel B. Smith, *Coping with Global Climate Change: The Role of Adaptation in the United States*

Pew Center on Global Climate Change, 2004.
http://www.c2es.org/docUploads/Adaptation.pdf.

Executive Summary

Climate change resulting from increased greenhouse gas concentrations has the potential to harm societies and ecosystems. In particular, agriculture, forestry, water resources, human health, coastal settlements, and natural ecosystems will need to adapt to a changing climate or face diminished functions. Reductions in emissions of greenhouse gases and their concentration in the atmosphere will tend to reduce the degree and likelihood that significantly adverse conditions will result. Consideration of actions—e.g., mitigation policy—that can reduce this likelihood is reasonable and prudent, and has generally been the primary focus of public attention and policy efforts on climate change. However, recognition is increasing that the combination of continued increases in emissions and the inertia of the climate system means that some degree of climate change is inevitable. Even if extreme measures could be instantly taken to curtail global emissions, the momentum of the earth's climate is such that warming cannot be completely avoided. Although essential for limiting the extent, and indeed the probability, of rapid and severe climate change, mitigation is not, and this paper argues, should not be, the only protective action in society's arsenal of responses.

Adaptation actions and strategies present a complementary approach to mitigation. While mitigation can be viewed as reducing the likelihood of adverse conditions, adaptation can be viewed as reducing the severity of many impacts if adverse conditions prevail. That is, adaptation reduces the level of damages that might have otherwise occurred. However, adaptation is a risk-management strategy that is not free of cost nor foolproof, and the worthiness of any specific actions must therefore carefully weigh the expected value of the avoided damages against the real costs of implementing the adaptation strategy.

Adaptation to environmental change is a fundamental human trait and is not a new concept. Throughout the ages, human societies have shown a strong capacity for adapting to different climates and environmental changes, although not always successfully. As evidenced by the widespread and climatically diverse location of human settlements throughout the world, humans have learned how to thrive in a wide variety of climate regimes, ranging from cold to hot and from humid to dry. The resilience and flexibility exhibited in the patterns of human settlements evidence an inherent desire and some measure of capacity to adapt.

For human systems, the success of adaptation depends critically on the availability of necessary resources, not only financial and natural resources, but also knowledge, technical capability, and institutional resources. The types and levels of required resources, in turn, depend fundamentally on the nature and abruptness of the actual or anticipated environmental change and the range of considered responses.

The processes of adaptation to climate change in both human and natural systems are highly complex and dynamic, often entailing many feedbacks and dependencies on existing local and temporal conditions. The uncertainties introduced by the complexity, scale, and limited experience with respect to anthropogenic climate change explain the limited level of applied research conducted thus far on adaptation, the reliance on mechanistic assumptions, and the widespread use of scenarios and historical analogues. In addition, many social, economic, technological and environmental trends will critically shape the future ability of societal systems to adapt to climate change. While such factors as increased population and wealth will likely increase the potential level of material assets that are exposed to the risks of climate change, greater wealth and improved technology also extend the resources and perhaps the capabilities to adapt to climate change. These trends must be taken into account when evaluating the nature and scale of future adaptive responses and the likelihood that they will succeed.

The implications of climate change are more dire for natural systems, because it will be difficult for many species to change behavior or migrate in response to climate change. While biological systems might accommodate minor (or slowly occurring) perturbations in a smooth continuous fashion, even minor changes in climate may be disruptive for many ecosystems and individual species. In addition, many of the world's species are currently stressed by a variety of factors including urban development, pollution, invasive species, and fractured (or isolated) habitats. Such conditions, coupled with the relatively rapid rate of anticipated climate change, are likely to challenge many species' resiliency and chances for successful adaptation.

Key insights and findings on adaptation and its potential for success are summarized below:

1) Adaptation and mitigation are necessary and complementary for a comprehensive and coordinated strategy that addresses the problem of global climate change. By lessening the severity of possible damages, adaptation is a key defensive measure. Adaptation is particularly important given the mounting evidence that some degree of climate change is inevitable. Recognizing a role for adaptation does not, however, diminish or detract from the importance of mitigation in reducing the rate and likelihood of significant climate change.

2) The literature indicates that U.S. society can on the whole adapt with either net gains or some costs if warming occurs at the lower end of the projected range of magnitude, assuming no change in climate variability and generally making optimistic assumptions about adaptation. However, with a much larger magnitude of warming, even making relatively optimistic assumptions about adaptation, many sectors would experience net losses and higher costs. The thresholds in terms of magnitudes or rates of change (including possible non-linear responses) in climate that will pose difficulty for adaptation are uncertain. In addition, it is uncertain how much of an increase in frequency, intensity, or persistence of extreme weather events the United States can tolerate.

3) To say that society as a whole "can adapt" does not mean that regions and peoples will not suffer losses. For example, while the agricultural sector as a whole may successfully adapt, some regions may gain and others may lose. Agriculture in many northern regions is expected to adapt to climate change by taking advantage of changing climatic conditions to expand production, but agriculture in many southern regions is expected to contract with warmer, drier temperatures. Individual farmers not benefiting from adaptation may lose their livelihoods. In addition, other individuals or populations in these and other regions can be at risk, because they could be adversely affected by climate change and lack the capacity to adapt. This is particularly true of relatively low-income individuals and groups whose livelihoods are dependent on resources at risk from climate change.

4) Adaptation is not likely to be a smooth process or free of costs. While studies and history show that society can on the whole adapt to a moderate amount of warming, it is reasonable to expect that mistakes will be made and costs will be incurred along the way. People are neither so foolish as to continue doing what they have always done in the face of climate change, nor so omniscient as to perfectly understand what will need to be done and to carry it out most efficiently. In reality, we are more likely to muddle through, taking adaptive actions as necessary, but often not doing what may be needed for optimal or ideal adaptation. Additionally, adaptation is an on-going process rather than a one-shot instantaneous occurrence. Compounding society's shortcomings, a more rapid, variable, or generally unpredictable climate change would add further challenges to adaptation.

5) Effects on ecosystems, and on species diversity in particular, are expected to be negative at all but perhaps the lowest magnitudes of climate change because of the limited ability of natural systems to adapt. Although biological systems have an inherent capacity to adapt to changes in environmental conditions, given the rapid rate of projected climate change, adaptive capacity is likely to be exceeded for many species. Furthermore, the ability of ecosystems to adapt to climate change is severely limited by the effects of urbanization, barriers to migration paths, and fragmentation of ecosystems, all of which have already critically stressed ecosystems independent of climate change itself.

6) Institutional design and structure can heighten or diminish society's exposure to climate risks. Long-standing institutions, such as disaster relief payments and insurance programs, affect adaptive capacity. Coastal zoning, land-use planning, and building codes are all examples of institutions that can contribute to (or detract from) the capacity to withstand climate changes in efficient and effective ways.

7) Proactive adaptation can reduce U.S. vulnerability to climate change. Proactive adaptation can improve capacities to cope with climate change by taking climate change into account in long-term decision-making, removing disincentives for changing behavior in response to climate change (such as removing subsidies for maladaptive activities), and introducing incentives to modify behavior in response to climate change (such as the use of market-based mechanisms to promote adaptive responses). Furthermore, improving and strengthening human capital through education, outreach, and extension services improves decision-making capacity at every level and increases the collective capacity to adapt.

NOTES & QUESTIONS

1. The organization that developed this report has since shifted its focus to energy development in the context of climate change. In a November 2011 press release, the Center issued the following press release:

> The Center for Climate and Energy Solutions (C2ES), a new nonprofit organization promoting strong policy and action to address the twin challenges of energy and climate change, was launched today at an event in Washington, D.C.
>
> The independent, nonpartisan Center is the successor to the Pew Center on Global Climate Change, which was widely recognized in the United States and abroad as an influential voice on climate issues. Pew Center founder and president Eileen Claussen assumes the new role of C2ES president.
>
> "There is greater need than ever for common sense and common ground in the search for climate and energy solutions," Claussen said. "These challenges are real, and we can't afford to deny or ignore them. We need stronger action here and around the world to keep these challenges from becoming crises. As C2ES, we bring the same team and the same commitment to fact-based analysis and pragmatic solutions."
>
> C2ES's launch marks the Center's transition from the long-time support of The Pew Charitable Trusts to a broader base of charitable, corporate and public support. Three Strategic Partners – Entergy, HP and Shell – have made substantial multi-year funding commitments to the new organization. Other major contributors include the Alcoa Foundation, Bank of America, GE, The Energy Foundation, Duke Energy, and the Rockefeller Brothers Fund.
>
> "We are deeply indebted to The Pew Charitable Trusts for its many years of extraordinary support. Without Pew, we could not possibly be the organization we are today," Claussen said. "But it's time we stand on our own two feet, and thanks to our many supporters, we can. We're especially thankful that, even amid such economic and political uncertainty, so many in the business and philanthropic communities are so deeply committed to our mission."
>
> Rebecca Rimel, president and CEO of The Pew Charitable Trusts, congratulated C2ES on its launch. "As a highly respected, nonpartisan voice for climate change solutions, the Center has played a pivotal role in this debate since 1998," Rimel said. "All of us at Pew could not be prouder of

their work to bring together leaders from the business, governmental and scientific communities to address this complex issue. While we applaud their important accomplishments to date, we are excited to see the Center transition to this new chapter and wish them continued success."

Claussen said that the principal activities of the Arlington, Va.-based organization will include:

- Providing timely, impartial information and analysis on the scientific, economic, technological and policy dimensions of climate and energy challenges;

- Working with policymakers and stakeholders to promote practical, effective climate and energy policies at the state, national and international levels;

- Convening multi-stakeholder initiatives, such as ongoing efforts to accelerate the deployment of plug-in electric vehicles and expand the use of captured CO_2 for enhanced oil recovery;

- Continuing to convene the Business Environmental Leadership Council (BELC) – with more than 40 leading corporations, the largest U.S.-based group of companies supporting policy and action to address climate and energy; and

- Partnering with companies and others through the Make an Impact program to educate consumers and employees on ways to reduce their energy use and carbon footprints.

C2ES's establishment was announced by board chair Theodore Roosevelt IV at an event at the Newseum. The program featured a discussion of the climate and energy policy outlook with Claussen, Entergy Chairman and CEO Wayne Leonard, former Senator John Warner, and Resources for the Future president Phil Sharp, moderated by NBC News correspondent Anne Thompson.

"These issues are critical to our environment, our security, our competitiveness, and the well-being of countless people around the globe," Roosevelt said. "Only a sensible centrist approach can bring us lasting solutions. I'm very proud to help lead C2ES's efforts to bring people together around pragmatic strategies that meet our energy needs while protecting the global climate."

Leonard noted the strong intersection of climate and energy issues for Entergy. "As the electric utility company that serves customers along the disappearing Louisiana coastline, Entergy knows firsthand the risks and ultimate consequences of climate change for coastal communities and the Gulf Coast's energy infrastructure," Leonard said. "We also know that it is not too late to reduce the risks of climate change. We congratulate the Pew Center for offering an essential, highly credible voice on these issues over many years, and we look forward to working closely with the Center for Climate and Energy Solutions to build support for practical, effective solutions."

GE Chairman and CEO Jeff Immelt commended Claussen on C2ES's launch. "I welcome the formation of the Center for Climate and Energy Solutions, and look forward to working with Eileen Claussen and the other companies participating in this important effort. America needs a strong national energy policy that promotes diverse and reliable energy supplies, ensures affordable energy for American businesses and families, reduces greenhouse gases, and protects our national security. Eileen is a critical thought leader on energy and climate issues; under her leadership, the Center for Climate and Energy Solutions will bring credible information and analysis to one of the most important policy issues of our time."

Center For Climate And Energy Solutions Launched In Washington, D.C.: Eileen Claussen to Lead New Organization, Successor to Pew Center on Global Climate Change, Press Release November 9, 2011, http://www.c2es.org/newsroom/releases/C2ES-launch-announcement.

2. The press release notes that the change in Center focus is a result of significant funding from a group of mega-corporations, including energy-related companies. What was your reaction to this development? Does it suggest the end of an honestly independent body of researchers capable of reporting accurate information even if it conflicts with corporate economic interests? What is a "sensible centrist approach"? Will the future reports be geared toward industry lobbying? On the other hand, might this be a positive development, demonstrating genuine corporate interest in reconciling their activities with the needs of the environment?

3. In the next excerpt, Professor Craig provides us with a more in-depth introduction to climate adaptation, followed by an argument that it is essential that we turn more legal attention to the matter. Immediately following that is an excerpt from Professor Camacho, who sets forth the "typology of government adaptation strategies."

Robin Kundis Craig, *"Stationarity Is Dead"–Long Live Transformation: Five Principles for Climate Change Adaptation Law*

34 Harvard Environmental Law Review 9 (2010).

I. Climate Change Adaptation Versus Climate Change Mitigation

A. An Introduction to Climate Change Adaptation and Its Differences from Mitigation

In the United States, much of the legal attention to climate change, whether expressed through litigation, legislation, or scholarship, has focused on mitigation—that is, on the mechanisms for reducing global emissions of greenhouse gases, especially carbon dioxide, and lowering the concentrations of those gases in the atmosphere. For example, the Massachusetts v. EPA litigation at the Supreme Court was about mitigation because it addressed EPA's authority and duty to regulate carbon dioxide emissions from motor vehicles. Almost all of the climate change legislation and programs that the states, regional organizations, and Congress have been considering or implementing are mitigation measures designed to reduce total emissions of carbon dioxide and other greenhouse gases. Legal scholars, in turn, have debated the merits of the litigation, legislative, and programmatic efforts to reduce greenhouse gas emissions.

Climate change mitigation efforts remain crucial, and this Article does not intend to suggest otherwise. In 2007, the Intergovernmental Panel on Climate Change ("IPCC") reported that "[u]nmitigated climate change would, in the long term, be likely to exceed the capacity of natural, managed and human systems to adapt." Thus, without mitigation efforts, mass destruction of both natural systems and human societies becomes an increasingly likely eventuality.

At the same time, however, the IPCC noted that "[a]daptation is necessary in the short and longer term to address impacts resulting from the warming that would occur even for the lowest stabilisation scenarios assessed." In other words, adaptation must become a co-strategy with mitigation efforts for dealing with climate change, because "[r]isks associated with climate change could greatly increase vulnerability unless adaptation is stepped up." Moreover, adaptation efforts may have immediate benefits for socio-ecological systems by decreasing vulnerability to future changes, "reducing sensitivity to climatic risks," and increasing the adaptive capacity of both humans and the ecological systems upon which they depend.

According to the IPCC, climate change adaptation refers to "the adjustment in natural or human systems in response to actual or expected climatic stimuli or their effects, which moderates harm or exploits beneficial opportunities." Ideally, these adjustments should "enhance resilience or reduce vulnerability to observed or expected changes in climate," such as "investment in coastal protection infrastructure to reduce vulnerability to storm surges and anticipated sea-level rise." In practice, adaptation measures can be as broad-ranging as the scope of climate change impacts themselves; they can "include anticipatory and reactive actions, private and public initiatives, and can relate to projected changes in temperature and current climate variations and extremes that may be altered with climate change."

Thus, whereas mitigation efforts focus on shaping human behavior to reduce the ultimate cause of climate change—increased greenhouse gas concentrations in the atmosphere—adaptation strategies must rely upon the (sometimes limited) abilities of species, ecosystems, and socio-ecological systems to respond to continuous alterations in baseline conditions. Ecological literature describes these abilities through the closely related concepts of resilience and adaptive capacity. Resilience refers to the ability of a species, ecosystem, or socio-ecological system to cope with change. More precisely, resilience is:

> the capacity of linked socio-ecological systems to absorb recurrent disturbances such as hurricanes or floods so as to retain essential structures, processes, and feedbacks. Resilience reflects the degree to which a complex adaptive system is capable of self-organization (versus lack of organization or organization forced by external factors) and the de-

gree to which the system can build capacity for learning and adaptation.

Similarly, adaptive capacity refers to "the regenerative ability of ecosystems and their capability in the face of change to continue to deliver resources and ecosystem services that are essential for human livelihoods and societal development." Resilience reflects a system's ability to absorb impacts and continue to function, while adaptive capacity refers to a system's ability to change to adjust to new conditions.

As a matter of international law, climate change adaptation is a component of the United Nations Framework Convention on Climate Change, to which the United States is a party. In particular, Article IV of the Convention requires parties to "cooperate in preparing for adaptation to the impacts of climate change." While the parties to the Convention have pursued this duty less intensively than their duty to mitigate (as evidenced by the Kyoto Protocol and post-Kyoto negotiations), they are beginning to pursue adaptation measures.

Nevertheless, climate change impacts also create particular problems for specific places and peoples. As such, a global legal response is insufficient to deal with the localized details of climate change impacts, which will require legal reforms at the national, state, and local levels as well. The next section reviews the kinds of climate change impacts that are occurring and likely to occur with this local/state/national nexus in mind.

B. The Need to Turn Legal Attention to Climate Change Adaptation

Climate change adaptation will be necessary for at least the next several decades, and probably centuries. ... [C]limate change effects are already being felt, and such impacts will continue to increase through at least the twenty-first century even if atmospheric greenhouse gas concentrations are stabilized quickly, which is unlikely. Continued climate change impacts are inevitable because carbon dioxide persists in the atmosphere for "'a few centuries, plus 25 percent . . . lasts essentially forever,'" and "[t]he warming from our . . . emissions would last effectively forever, too." Thus, even if the world immediately implements comprehensive efforts to significantly reduce emissions of carbon dioxide and other greenhouse gases, there will be a substantial time lag between implementation of those efforts and either actual stabilization of greenhouse gas concentrations in the atmosphere or cessation of climate change impacts. As a result, the world is probably already committed to a 2°C increase in average global temperature.

One example of delayed climate change impacts will be sea level rise. Increased greenhouse gas concentrations in the atmosphere cause increased average global air temperatures. Much of this heat is transferred to the oceans, causing a slow expansion of their volume. At the same time, warming temperatures cause land-based ice and glaciers to melt, increasing the total amount of water in the seas. As a result, according to the IPCC:

> Sea level rise under warming is inevitable. Thermal expansion would
> continue for many centuries after GHG concentrations have stabilised,
> for any of the stabilisation levels assessed, causing an eventual sea
> level rise much larger than projected for the 21st century... The long
> time scales of thermal expansion and ice sheet response to warming
> imply that stabilisation of GHG concentrations at or above present
> levels would not stabilise sea level for many centuries.

Other climate change-driven alterations in ecological, meteorological, and
climatic conditions will also be facts of life, at least until the end of this
century and almost certainly much longer.

Climate change adaptation is not only a long-term problem; it is a
complex problem. First, climate change is affecting atmospheric, land,
freshwater, and ocean temperatures—but not uniformly. Temperatures
toward the poles are increasing faster than temperatures near the equator,
and land temperatures are rising faster than temperatures in the ocean.
These temperature changes are already altering weather patterns, leading
to fewer cold nights and frosts and more frequent hot days and hot nights,
heat waves, heavy precipitation events, and "intense tropical cyclone activity in the North Atlantic." As a result, climate change impacts will vary
from location to location, necessitating different specific adaptation strategies in different places.

Second, many of these climate change-driven ecological changes are
likely to become both worse and more complex in the coming decades, because even the IPCC's fairly conservative analysis projects changes of 0.1°C
to 0.2°C per decade for the rest of this century. Contraction of snow- and
ice-covered areas, increasing extreme heat events, increased intensity of
tropical cyclones, and a poleward shift of such storms, are all likely results.
Water supplies are especially vulnerable:

> There is high confidence that by mid-century, annual river runoff and
> water availability are projected to increase at high latitudes (and in
> some tropical wet areas) and decrease in some dry regions in the mid-
> latitudes and tropics. There is also high confidence that many semi-
> arid areas (e.g. Mediterranean Basin, western United States, southern
> Africa and north-eastern Brazil) will suffer a decrease in water re-
> sources due to climate change.

Moreover, as noted, changes in glacial, Arctic, and Antarctic ecosystems
have already been observed as a result of changes in snow, ice, and frozen
ground, while other areas are experiencing alterations in hydrological patterns and shifts of species poleward and upward, to higher elevations. The
IPCC concluded in 2007 that many other ecosystems are also likely to experience significant stresses and alterations as a result of climate change.

Third, climate change impacts all sectors of socio-ecological systems.
The changes in water resource availability alone will directly affect agriculture in low-latitude regions and human health throughout the world. Temperature impacts create a multiplicity of problems for humans and are al-

ready affecting several important economic and social activities, including: (1) agriculture, particularly with respect to the timing of spring planting and the availability of a summer irrigation supply; (2) forest management, especially with respect to fires and pests; and (3) public health efforts, especially with regard to heat-related mortality, changes in infectious disease vectors such as mosquitoes, and changes in allergenic pollens.

Climate change impacts operate on complex ecosystems and set in motion feedback loops and nonlinear changes, neither of which are entirely (or even mostly) predictable through existing knowledge and modeling. For example, one of the consequences of the mountain pine beetle's spread through Canada, with the resulting death of millions of acres of trees, is an increase in carbon dioxide emissions from the decaying trees and a decreased ability of the remaining forest to act as a carbon sink. Researchers predict that the beetle's expansion and ravages—which are themselves almost certainly the result of early climate change impacts—may release 270 megatonnes of carbon dioxide by 2020, an amount that equals Canada's emission reduction commitment under the Kyoto Protocol. This is an example of a positive feedback loop: increasing greenhouse gas concentrations in the atmosphere result in warming temperatures that allow the mountain pine beetle to expand its range, killing trees and resulting in increasing concentrations of carbon dioxide in the atmosphere, which will warm temperatures further and, at least for a while, allow the beetle to expand even farther northward.

Differential sensitivities of ecosystems add another layer of complexity to climate change impacts, and hence to adaptation strategies. Tundra, boreal forests, mountain regions, and the sea ice biome are primarily sensitive to warming, but Mediterranean-type ecosystems and tropical rainforests are most likely to be impacted by reductions in precipitation, while coastal ecosystems are most vulnerable to sea level rise and more severe storm events. The most complex problems may occur in coral reefs, mangroves, and salt marshes, which will be impacted by several climate change-induced stresses—increased temperatures, sea level rise, and changes in water quality—simultaneously.

Moreover, the crossing of ecosystem thresholds, like those in the Arctic tundra, and the conversion of ecosystems to new and probably irreversible states of being (e.g. the Arctic shrubland) is not only possible, but a source of real concern for the future. As the IPCC rather cautiously acknowledged, "[a]nthropogenic warming could lead to some impacts that are abrupt or irreversible, depending upon the rate and magnitude of the climate change." More dramatically, but with a necessary sense of urgency, Ted Nordhaus and Michael Shellenberger have opined that:

> To describe these challenges as problems of pollution is to stretch the meaning of the word beyond recognition. Global warming is as different from smog in Los Angeles as nuclear war is from gang violence. The ecological crises we face are more global, complex, and tied to the basic functioning of the economy than were the problems environmentalism was created to address forty years ago. Global warming threat-

ens human civilization so fundamentally that it cannot be understood as a straightforward pollution problem, but instead as an existential one. Its impacts will be so enormous that it is better understood as a problem of evolution, not pollution.

Given what we already know about climate change impacts, adaptation requires a constructive legal and social response to continuous, interacting, often unpredictable, and perhaps irreversible changes in multiple sectors. These changes affect the most basic elements of human support systems: water supply, agriculture, public health, ecosystem stability, and in some areas like the Arctic and coastal regions, the very existence of land to live on. Nevertheless, comparatively little attention has been paid in the United States to the legal principles that should inform and govern climate change adaptation. Legal institutions need to begin to address adaptation challenges, and the sooner they do so, on a reasoned basis, the more proactive, rational, and cost-effective climate change adaptation measures can be. Moreover, while climate change adaptation efforts will need to pervade all aspects of law and society, a logical and manageable place to begin the discussion of climate change adaptation law is to set out principles for environmental regulation and natural resource management.

C. Mitigation Versus Adaptation as a Legal Problem

Recognizing that environmental regulation and natural resource management should address the need for climate change adaptation is just the first step in adapting the relevant laws to the realities of climate change. As the previous discussion suggests, adaptation is inherently a far more complex legal problem than mitigation. Despite some proposals (many sounding as though they came straight from science fiction) for short-term technological "fixes" to the problem of increasing greenhouse gas concentrations, climate change mitigation efforts have one clear and essential regulatory goal: substantially reduce overall emissions of greenhouse gases worldwide, preferably sooner rather than later. Even the basic regulatory mechanisms available to accomplish this goal are fairly limited in number: mandated reductions for each regulated emitter ("command-and-control" regulation), cap-and-trade programs, mandated changes in manufacturing processes, taxes and other economic incentives such as subsidies, or some combination thereof.

Of course, the conceptual simplicity of mitigation law does not mean that creating and implementing such law will be easy. Indeed, the almost two decades of international negotiations on the subject and the failures of many nations to adopt mitigation laws attest to the numerous political, economic, technological, and practical difficulties in establishing a functional mitigation legal regime. Participating nations have been less than successful in achieving their Kyoto Protocol commitments, demonstrating that inertia remains an important practical limitation to mitigation progress and that new technologies and social norms are probably necessary before mitigation efforts can be successful.

Even so, climate change adaptation law will be dealing with complexity at another order of magnitude because, as noted, the effects of climate change will themselves be complex—ever-changing, often unpredictable, and subject to feedback mechanisms that may not be completely understood and that may change over time, often leading to nonlinear alterations of ecosystems and their services. Moreover, adaptation law will have to cope with multiple layers of governmental interest, since many adaptation strategies will have to be intensely local in implementation, while adaptation principles and goals may need to operate on a larger state, watershed, regional, or national scale.

The complexity of climate change adaptation makes it both a more interesting and a more vexing legal problem than climate change mitigation. In the broadest perspective, adaptation measures must embrace all aspects of human society simultaneously, from national security to changes in economic productivity; from energy production and distribution to national and regional infrastructure redevelopment; from food production, distribution, and agricultural practices to water supply; from local government planning and land use regulation to environmental regulation and natural resource management. Equally important, governments must implement whatever adaptation measures they choose while the ground is figuratively and literally shifting under society's feet—that is, while the focus of the adaptation measures itself may no longer have a stable identity.

Therefore, it is worth emphasizing that climate change adaptation law and policy, by definition, cannot be preservationist. The point should not be—and in many areas and sectors, cannot be—to preserve as much of the current status quo as possible, or even to make a shift to a new and stable status quo.

Instead, even if we restrict our focus to environmental and natural resources law, as this Article does, climate change adaptation law will often require both a new way of thinking about what regulation is supposed to accomplish and different kinds of legal frameworks for accomplishing those new goals.

Alejandro E. Camacho, *Adapting Governance to Climate Change: Managing Uncertainty through a Learning Infrastructure*

59 Emory Law Journal 1 (2009).

II. Adapting to Climate Change

Exceptional uncertainty is the core challenge that natural resource governance faces from climate change. Ecologists and other scientists are being forced to reconsider long-held assumptions and methodologies for studying natural systems, and agencies are being pressed to prepare for problems they have never faced before. In short, adapting to climate change necessitates the coordination and mobilization of scientific and management information to a degree never attempted. To be sure, government institutions must develop a suite of strategies to both prevent further climatic change and foster suitable adaptations to its effects on natural and human systems. More importantly, natural resource governance must develop an infrastructure that enhances the capacity of public and private actors to assess and manage an uncertain regulatory environment.

A. The Need for Adaptation

Despite the sizeable uncertainty that accompanies any comprehensive effort to manage the effects of climate change, climate change adaptation is a vital complement to mitigation activities that seek to curb further climatic change. On the one hand, focusing more attention on adaptation should certainly not supplant vital efforts to abate greenhouse gas emissions. Extensive evidence compiled by thousands of independent scientists indicates that without swift, comprehensive efforts to substantially reduce emissions, the effects of climate change on natural systems will undoubtedly be more severe. ... Emissions reduction through efforts, such as the currently pending Waxman-Markey American Clean Energy and Security Act of 2009, that seek a cap-and-trade or emission tax system to mitigate greenhouse gas emissions should not be merely an afterthought, but rather a vital part of any sensible response to climate change.

On the other hand, no amount of abatement, even if enacted tomorrow, is likely to diminish the effects of climate change for several decades. Evidence suggests that the effects of global warming are already being experienced in the United States, and climate change is likely to continue for decades, even in the event of significant reduction of emissions. Countless people and ecosystems are and will continue to be threatened by the effects of climate change, at least until abatement measures show results.

Climate change thus will increasingly place considerable stress on the perpetually limited resources allocated to manage natural resources. Government institutions must be tactical in trying to expand the capacity to address existing regulatory vulnerabilities while anticipating and averting severe climate change effects. Unfortunately, legislators and regulators in the United States and elsewhere have only begun to consider the role of adaptation in combating climate change.

B. A Typology of Government Adaptation Strategies

Greater attention must be given to reducing the existing and future adverse effects of climate change on natural resources. To advance this endeavor, this section proposes a framework for classifying government adaptation measures according to three particularly relevant parameters: (1) whether the adaptation primarily anticipates or reacts to effects from climate change; (2) whether the strategy focuses exclusively, partially, or only indirectly on projected climate change effects; and (3) whether the strategy is a "substantive" response to the direct effects of climate change, or an indirect "procedural" adaptation of a process for deciding among substantive adaptations. All of these government strategies likely have a role to play in any comprehensive approach to climate change adaptation. However, as detailed here, the uncertainty attributable to climate change, and the inevitable scarcity of resources allocated for natural resource governance, counsel for an emphasis on proactive, procedural strategies directed at addressing existing key regulatory vulnerabilities likely to be exacerbated by climate change. Such strategies can provide a basis for government regulators to manage uncertainty and reduce the risk of regulatory waste.

1. Proactive and Reactive Strategies

The timing of an adaptation's implementation is likely to have significant repercussions on the cost and success of the strategy. A proactive adaptation "takes place before impacts of climate change are observed." Such strategies seek to formulate long-term strategies for infrastructure, education, outreach, and improving collective capacities to adapt, as well as create incentives to change behaviors suited to the shifting climate. However, such strategies are susceptible to the considerable uncertainty inherent in predictive modeling. Therefore, to be successful, proactive strategies must be designed to adapt to a range of possible effects and must be nimble enough to respond to new information obtained during implementation.

In contrast, a reactive adaptation is "a deliberate response to a climatic shock or impact, in order to recover and prevent similar impacts in the future." Such strategies have the key inherent advantage of being subject to less uncertainty, as they are only implemented in response to actualized risks. However, various intrinsic problems exist with reactive approaches. Because they are only implemented after-the-fact, "a high degree of ecosystem and infrastructure damage is likely to occur before reactive measures are taken." Due to "inefficiencies in the response when it is needed, wasted investments made in ignorance of future conditions, or potentially even greater damages because precautionary actions were not taken," reactive adaptations may be more vulnerable to higher long-term administrative costs and damages. The limitations of reactive strategies are particularly problematic when addressing high-cost or irreversible impacts of long-term and expensive investments, or when otherwise important to prevent (and not merely respond to) climate effects. Unfortunately, such circumstances are quite common in the context of climate change, particularly in the context of threats to certain biological resources.

Thus, in adapting to the effects of climate change on ecological resources it is better to prevent negative consequences by employing proactive adaptations based on the precautionary principle. Reactive adaptations should be left to circumstances in which proactive strategies were unsuccessful in identifying and preventing a hazard from occurring. Establishing a systematic approach for cultivating successful proactive adaptations is thus crucial to developing effective adaptation strategies.

2. Exclusive, Co-benefit, or No-Regret Strategies

Another variable for distinguishing among adaptation strategies emphasizes the orientation of the adaptation in terms of the benefit provided. Exclusive adaptations are directed exclusively at reducing the effects of climate change. A co-benefit strategy is in part directed at reducing vulnerabilities related to climate change but is also expected to produce other public benefits. No-regrets adaptations are directed at providing net benefits irrespective of the effects of climate change.

Due to existing uncertainties about such effects, prudent regulators should seek to maximize the use of no-regrets adaptations. No-regrets strategies reduce the risks of regulatory waste from uncertainty because they are a net benefit to their particular natural and/or regulatory system regardless of whether (or to what extent) the projected effects of climate change occur. However, given the magnitude and speed of impacts anticipated by climate change, it is doubtful that reliance on no-regrets strategies alone could forestall all the heretofore unknown effects of climate change. Because the exact effects of climate change remain uncertain, regulators also should seek to adopt partial or co-benefit adaptations that maximize supplementary public benefits in order to minimize the risks from costly adaptations. Only as a precaution against particularly large or catastrophic risks should regulators consider employing exclusive adaptations that lack other public benefits.

3. Substantive and Procedural Strategies

In classifying potential adaptation strategies, perhaps the most important distinction is one that has not been identified in the scientific or legal literature: whether the adaptation is primarily a substantive or procedural strategy. This distinction considers whether the strategy principally seeks to address the direct effects of climate change (substantive), or to change a process for deciding among substantive adaptations (procedural).

a. Substantive Governmental Strategies

Most of the strategies mentioned by natural resource managers and discussed in the growing scholarly literature on climate change adaptation are substantive. For example, many proposed adaptations focus on altering the environment to minimize the direct effects of sea level rise and severe weather events such as storm intensity, floods, and droughts. These sorts of direct, discrete adaptations, such as physical removal of invasive species or construction of breakwaters, rock sills, levees, or dams, tend to be reactive.

Other substantive adaptations seek to alter the way private actors interact with the immediate environment to reduce the effect of climate change, often through the disclosure of information or changes to regulations that encourage or mandate particular private conduct. For example, regulatory adaptations that address increased risks to coastal resources could include (1) public information disclosure or education initiatives regarding flood risk; (2) early warning systems; (3) changes to government flood insurance; (4) subsidies or changes to zoning or building codes to increase the capacity of private property to withstand climate events; (5) modifications to permit programs to reduce coastal erosion, such as prohibitions on private seawalls; or (6) relocations of private structures from flood-prone areas through government acquisition.

On a larger scale, substantive adaptations also include agency management planning, varying from site-specific to program-wide plans. An example of a program-wide plan is EPA's new National Water Strategy, which seeks to modify EPA's water programs to address climate change effects. As adaptation strategies necessarily are specific to their application, the list of potential discrete or concrete strategies for any particular plan may be extensive. Management planning strategies being considered include the creation of additional protected areas, wildlife corridors, and replicate ecosystems; increased protection of vulnerable genotypes, species, and communities; ecosystem restoration; and "assisted migration" of species.

b. Procedural Governmental Strategies

Though most commenters have focused on substantive strategies that seek to minimize or reverse the adverse effects of climate change on natural systems, the most crucial adaptations may take the more indirect form of procedural governmental strategies. Rather than focusing on directly managing the effects of climate change—or the natural systems or human conduct that may exacerbate such effects—this category is intended to encompass strategies that manage the regulatory programs and processes that develop more direct strategies. Such approaches might seek to change the decision-making process officials use to select direct adaptation strategies. At their broadest level, such approaches might also seek a more fundamental transformation of the government institutions society relies on to manage natural resources. For example, procedural adaptation strategies should be created to flexibly manage the considerable uncertainty surrounding climate change to avert and minimize the harm from mistakes throughout the regulatory process.

The concept of "adaptive management" was originally proposed by scientists in the 1970s who sought a more effective approach to natural resource management in response to the significant uncertainty that regularly exists in ecosystems. This increasingly influential model seeks to address information gaps in management plans that surface during plan formation by including systematic monitoring procedures for obtaining more data to adjust the management strategies during implementation.

At the broadest level, procedural adaptation strategies may also include large-scale modifications to governance—that is, how regulators manage the programs that govern natural systems and how societies manage these regulators. Such approaches might include wholesale changes to existing statutory regimes or programs, the creation of new programs or agencies, or other fundamental changes to decision-making processes for regulating or managing natural resources. A few observers have discussed the need to make systemic or large-scale governance changes to respond to climate change. Yet, ... few recognize the need to increase the adaptive capacity of natural resource programs and governance to manage the uncertainty that climate change brings.

C. The Value of Procedural Strategies

Though the value of direct substantive adaptations may be more apparent in comprehensive attempts to address the effects of climate change, a central assertion of this Article is that procedural strategies that transform existing approaches to natural resource governance are even more vital given the uncertainties that exist for addressing the impacts of a warming climate. For all the reasons that apply regarding the effects from climate change, substantive government adaptations—and in particular those seeking to regulate or manage ecosystems—are subject to the uncertainties of climate change as impact models are downscaled to specific locations. This uncertainty is compounded by the limited information that exists regarding the suitability and efficacy of possible adaptation strategies. For example, captive breeding and assisted migration strategies are less likely to work if climate change effects are rapid or substantial, yet the speed and magnitude of change are largely unknown for particular ecosystems. This uncertainty is again amplified because analyses of such strategies are rare, particularly in response to climate change, and protocols identifying when such strategies may be appropriate often do not exist. Additionally, some strategies are likely to conflict with other conservation methods or resource uses, and the optimal reconciliation of such conflicts is debatable.

However, uncertainty over the exact future consequences and optimal substantive strategies should not lead to the conclusion that regulators and the public can afford to neglect adaptation. As is often the case when inexorable uncertainty exists in assessing long-term environmental harms, the key question is not whether something should be done. Indeed, the United States is already investing enormously in climate change adaptation, though most of these costs are not counted as such because they are treated as facets of more conventional management activities, such as drought relief or storm damage recovery, and are aimed at problems such as water resource planning for which climate change is only one stressor. The key question is, based on the best available data, what strategies are likely to be most effective and cost efficient at averting or minimizing potential damage from climate change.

Procedural strategies can serve as the crucial bridge between uncertainty and the need for adaptation. Designed properly, such strategies are crucial for helping managers and regulators manage the substantial uncertainty about both the effects of climate change and the efficacy and side effects of substantive adaptation responses. Furthermore, larger-scale governance strategies can be cultivated that seek to create and disseminate information to regulatory actors, stakeholders, and the public to minimize uncertainty about climate change effects, substantive adaptations, and smaller-scale procedural adaptations. Procedural strategies can thus serve to strengthen the adaptability of existing processes and help avoid and adjust over- and under-regulation in response to climate change.

NOTES & QUESTIONS

1. Professor Camacho suggests that we need to accept uncertainty with regard to our climate future, which means not wedding ourselves to specific substantive adaptation strategies. Of course, accepting uncertainty and deferring decision-making does not come easily to most people. As a result, there has developed a field of climate prediction for the purpose of guiding adaptation planning. The term "climate prediction" suggests a means of escape from the dreaded state of uncertainty, yet of course the results of such work are always expressed in probabilities, as we simply do not know what is going to happen. Do you think that having probabilities for the potential climate future is helpful to planning for adaptation? A pair of scientists from the UK argue that the generation of such probabilities may do more harm than good, given the difficulties in accurately estimating climate probabilities coupled with human nature to act on them anyway. *See* Suraje Dessai & Mike Hulme, *Does climate adaptation policy need probabilities?*, 4 Climate Policy 107 (2004).

2. Both Professors Craig and Camacho argue that we need to work harder on developing our adaptation framework, but not everyone agrees. In the next piece we see an argument against focusing too much effort on adaptation.

Matthew D. Zinn, *Adapting to Climate Change: Environmental Law in a Warmer World*
34 Ecology Law Quarterly 61 (2007).

The public debate about climate change is shifting. For years, the disputants have disagreed mainly about (1) whether the climate is changing, and (2) assuming it is, whether or to what extent humanity bears responsibility for it. How one answers those questions has largely determined whether one supports or opposes policies to mitigate climate change, that is, to reduce atmospheric concentrations of carbon dioxide and the other greenhouse gases that cause climatic warming. Recently, however, some opponents of mitigation have staked out a new position. They argue that mitigation is far too socially costly or simply infeasible and therefore suggest that we should instead direct our limited resources to adapting to the change. One journalist has summarized the climate change skeptics' position as follows:

> It is a planet where global warming isn't happening or, if it is happening, isn't happening because of human beings. Or, if it is happening because of human beings, it isn't going to be a big problem. And, even if it is a big problem, we can't realistically do anything about it other than adapt. The dichotomy of mitigation and adaptation is a false one. We have passed the point of such a binary choice, if ever there were such a point. Given inertia in the climate system, even immediate and radical steps to reduce greenhouse gas emissions cannot prevent the climate from warming; they can only moderate it. Some adaptation is therefore inescapable, and the real debate must be about how much we should seek to mitigate and how much we should leave to adaptation.

This Article seeks to inform that debate by describing how an adaptation-preferring climate policy – one that wholly or mostly rejects mitigation—is potentially fraught with two related problems. First, adaptation has its own potentially severe adverse environmental impacts that would compound the direct or primary effects of climate change and that thus comprise indirect or secondary environmental impacts of climate change. For example, climate change will reduce mountain snowpack on which western states rely to provide natural water storage. Building more dams to make up for that loss would destroy riparian and upland habitat above the dams and fundamentally alter aquatic ecosystems below them. Worse still, the stresses of climate change will undermine the capacity of natural systems to assimilate the environmental impacts caused by climate adaptation. Many species will alter their distributions to adapt to new climatic conditions, a process that may cause stress for the species and interfere with reproduction or survival. Anthropogenic habitat destruction or fragmentation, such as that caused when we relocate our communities away from rising tides or increasingly flooding rivers, may compound the stress on these species. An adaptation-preferring climate policy thus risks creating a perverse synergy by failing to moderate the severity of climate change and its stresses on natural systems and simultaneously requiring adaptations that produce their own severe, and in some cases synergistic, impacts on those systems.

Adaptation's effects are not foreordained, but the task of avoiding them poses the second complication of an adaptation-preferring climate policy: adaptation may undermine the effectiveness of environmental law. Though the welter of complex regulatory regimes developed over the last forty years is in many ways flawed, it nonetheless has had some notable successes in moderating our environmental impacts. We have markedly reduced air pollution in some regions; pulled a few species, such as the gray wolf and bald eagle, back from the brink of extinction; curtailed emissions of stratospheric ozone-depleting chemicals; and sharply reduced the industrial effluent discharged to our streams and rivers. Those successes might suggest that we can also apply existing regimes, or design new ones, to moderate the harm that climate adaptations might otherwise cause. This view, however, may be unduly optimistic; the prospects for effective environmental law appear to be bleaker in a warmer world. This Article suggests that climate change stands to undermine the ability of environmental law to moderate both the new impacts of adaptation and the ongoing impacts of run-of-the-mill economic activity.

Two concerns counsel this pessimism. The first is that climate change and adaptation would exacerbate some of the challenges of institutional capacity that have historically troubled environmental law. Complexity and coordination problems are likely to be even more troublesome where climate change requires large-scale and widely distributed adaptations. Experience suggests that we lack the capacity to plan for and choose among the numerous necessary adaptations in order to minimize their massively cumulative and synergistic environmental effects. While we have had some success in reducing emissions of individual air or water pollutants, for example, nothing in the history of environmental law suggests that we can carry out the kind of large-scale, panoptic planning needed to manage the host of impacts that would be caused by adaptation to unchecked climate change.

The second concern is less one of capacity than of will. There are reasons to think that public ardor for environmental protection might cool as the climate warms. This Article hypothesizes that in the face of environmental changes that upset settled ways of living, such as rising sea levels or more frequent and severe storm activity, attitudes toward the environment and its preservation will not remain static. The environmental changes caused by a warming climate could undermine public commitment to environmental stewardship in a variety of ways. Climate change will disrupt some human relationships with the natural environment that have been important to public support for environmental protection. Disasters exacerbated by climate change, such as hurricanes, floods, or disruption of water supplies, may transform public conceptualization of the environment from an amenity or luxury good worth protecting to a hostile force requiring control. Finally, the simple fact of an environment constantly in flux may undermine the notion of "the environment" as an entitlement that must be preserved. In this context, faced with the challenges posed by climate change, we may be unable to muster the "republican moment" that some have argued gave birth to the late twentieth-century effusion of environmental law.

Most analysis of the intersection of climate change and environmental law understandably focuses on mitigation, viz., how environmental law might alter the course of climate change. This Article, by contrast, imagines the converse: how unchecked climate change, in a world of adaptation rather than mitigation, might alter environmental law. ...

This vision of climate adaptation is stark. It suggests that a choice today to reject climate change mitigation may produce a kind of path dependence, requiring massive future environmental interventions with massive new environmental harms. These harms would occur in a natural environment increasingly less able to accommodate them and in a legal environment less able to prevent them. At the least, this means that climate policy must take into account the environmental costs of adaptation, as best they can be estimated, on the assumption that they will not be avoided. The literature and public debate about climate adaptation have yet to grapple with this problem. Moreover, if we value our own concern for the environment and wish that concern to continue into the future, we should consider binding ourselves to the mast by adopting a mitigation-preferring policy. In doing so, we may better preserve our ability, and our commitment, to protect our environment.

Despite its dystopian vision of a future dominated by climate adaptation rather than mitigation, this Article concludes with some guarded optimism. Growing public support for mitigation and proliferating state experimentation with mitigation policies may avoid the need for the most aggressive and damaging adaptations. The longer we wait to implement those policies, however, the more adaptation we will require and the greater the environmental costs we may have to accept.

NOTES & QUESTIONS

1. What do *you* think? Is there a serious danger that adaptation efforts would direct us away from mitigation efforts? Might we become so convinced of our ability to adapt that we lose all concern for the continued warming trend? This seems unlikely; indeed most scholarly work recommending adaptation expressly notes that mitigation remains important as well. *See, e.g.*, J.B. Ruhl, *Climate Change Adaptation and the Structural Transformation of Environmental Law*, 40 ENVTL. L. 363, 370-71 (2010) ("It is not, in other words, an either-or choice between mitigation and adaptation. The time when such a choice could have been made—when starting to install a meaningful mitigation regime could have obviated the need to ever have to think about adaptation—is long since past by many decades."); Peter Hayes, *Resilience as Emergent Behavior*, 15 Hastings W.-Nw. J. Envtl. L. & Pol'y 175, 175 (2009) ("[T]he main game is now adaptation which renders mitigation no less urgent, but shifts the political equation in dramatic ways that cannot be ignored any longer."); Ileana M. Porras, *The City and International Law: In Pursuit of Sustainable Development*, 36 Fordham Urb. L.J. 537, 593 (2009) ("Most climate change experts and policy-makers recognize that adaptation and mitigation are not mutually exclusive strategies but must, on the contrary be employed in tandem.").

2. Of course, adaptation efforts will certainly expensive, so we should hope to need them as little as possible and for as short a time as possible, but by most accounts some need is already spilt milk. The high cost of adaptation raises the question of who should pay for it. Professor Dan Farber analyzes the options, including sending the bill to the beneficiaries, the emitters, the public, or the winners. Daniel A. Farber, *Adapting to Climate Change: Who Should Pay*, 23 J. LAND USE & ENVTL. L. 1 (2007).

B. THE TOOLS OF THE ADAPTATION TRADE: ECOSYSTEM RESILIENCE, ADAPTIVE MANAGEMENT, AND ASSISTED MIGRATION

Moving from the what (and whether) to the how, we next look at some of the key methods that are, or will be, employed in the effort to bring as many species as possible into the next climate era. After providing introductions to several approaches for adapting wildlife to climate change, we see a blend of them in action in the Florida Everglades. Finally, we will consider the need to change our entire way of thinking about conservation in order to facilitate our move forward into our new climate future.

1. ECOSYSTEM RESILIENCE

First, we need resilient ecosystems, ready to withstand the changes that come. This will sometimes entail restoration, in cases where we have weakened ecosystems without actually destroying them, recognizing that just because they have remained intact thus far does not mean they are prepared to adapt to climate change. Restoration can bring back the strength and vitality needed to survive change. In other circumstances the primary concern may be connectivity, allowing species greater room for movement, given the likelihood of increased movement in response to climate change. Further, connectivity is important even in a pre-climate-change world, as fragmentation weakens ecosystems and reduces the size and variability of populations. For this reason, connectivity will be an important factor in ecosystem resilience to climate change.

The original concept of ecosystem resilience, as well as several later evolutions of the concept, came to us from C.S. Holling:

> Humanity strongly influences biogeochemical, hydrological, and ecological processes, from local to global scales. We currently face more variable environments with greater uncertainty about how ecosystems will respond to inevitable increases in levels of human use. At the same time, we seem to challenge the capacity of desired ecosystem states to cope with events and disturbances. The combination of these two trends calls for a change from the existing paradigm of command-and-control for stabilized "optimal" production to one based on managing resilience in uncertain environments to secure essential ecosystem services. The old way of thinking implicitly assumes a stable and infinitely resilient environment, a global steady state. The new perspective recognizes that resilience can be and has been eroded and that the self-repairing capacity of ecosystems should no longer be taken for granted. The challenge in this new situation is to actively strengthen the capacity of ecosystems to support social and economic development. It implies trying to sustain desirable pathways and ecosystem states in the face of continuous change.

> Holling, in his seminal [1973] paper, defined ecosystem resilience as the magnitude of disturbance that a system can experience before it shifts into a different state (stability domain) with different controls on structure and function and distinguished ecosystem resilience from engineering resilience. Engineering resilience is a measure of the rate at which a system approaches steady state after a perturbation, that is, the speed of return to equilibrium, which is also measured as the inverse of return time. Holling [later, in 1996,] pointed out that engineering resilience is a less appropriate measure in ecosystems that have multiple stable states or are driven toward multiple stable states by human activities.

> Here, we define resilience as the capacity of a system to absorb disturbance and reorganize while undergoing change so as to retain essentially the same function, structure, identity, and feedbacks. The ability for reorganization and renewal of a desired ecosystem state after disturbance and change will strongly depend on the influences from states and dynamics at scales above and below. Such cross-scale aspects of resilience are captured in the notion of a panarchy, a set of dynamic systems nested across scales. Hence, resilience reflects the degree to which a complex adaptive system is capable of self-organization (versus lack of organization or organization forced by ex-

ternal factors) and the degree to which the system can build and increase the capacity for learning and adaptation.

Carl Folke, Steve Carpenter, BrianWalker, Marten Scheffer, Thomas Elmqvist, Lance Gunderson & C.S. Holling, *Regime Shifts, Resilience, and Biodiversity in Ecosystem Management*, 35 ANNUAL REVIEW OF ECOLOGY, EVOLUTION, AND SYSTEMATICS 557, 558 (2004).

We know we want ecosystem resilience, but how will achieving it fit into our existing structure for federal land management?

Robert L. Glicksman, *Ecosystem Resilience to Disruptions Linked to Global Climate Change: An Adaptive Approach to Federal Land Management*
87 Nebraska Law Review 833 (2009).

IV. ACCOMMODATING CLIMATE CHANGE THROUGH RESILIENCE

It is perhaps unfair to place undue blame for the failure of the existing federal land management and cross-cutting statutes to specifically require agencies to address climate change, or even to prescribe decisionmaking techniques for land and resource management that are up to the task of dealing with the phenomenon of climate change. The statutes by and large were adopted before climate change became a prominent concern. Further, the magnitude and complexity of the issues raised by climate change far exceed any resource management issue experienced by either Congress or the land management agencies. Similar excuses are not available to land managers who have buried their heads in the ground or failed to take advantage of the discretion they do enjoy to craft strong programs for anticipating climate change, enhancing the resilience of the resources they manage, and laying the groundwork for dealing with the potential for climate change which puts valuable federal lands and resources at risk.

* * *

A. Recommendations for Resource Management in the Face of Climate Change

The changes recommended here encompass changes to the enabling legislation of the federal land management agencies, the manner in which the agencies prepare for and make decisions that implement that legislation, and some of the cross-cutting (or overlay) statutes that both govern all of the land management agencies and determine the degree to which their decisions are subject to accountability checks such as judicial review. One commenter on a draft of this Article at the meeting at which the symposium papers were first presented described the net impact of these recommendations as fostering an "institutional resilience" that would facilitate the ability of the land management agencies to set the stage for the physical and biological resilience that will be needed to protect the integrity of federal lands and resources in the face of climate change.

1. The federal land management agencies need to adapt their planning processes (with legislative directives, if necessary) to afford priority to climate change issues and to emphasize the long-term consequences of climate change. As Congress recognized when it adopted FLPMA, "the national interest will be best realized if the public lands and their resources are periodically and systematically inventoried and their present and future use is projected through a land use planning process coordinated with other Federal and State planning efforts." Similarly, Congress directed the NFS under the NFMA to "use a systematic interdisciplinary approach [to planning] to achieve integrated consideration of physical, biological, economic, and other sciences." The organic statute for the National Wildlife Refuges requires the FWS to prepare conservation plans for all units within the System to help achieve the agency's statutory mission of conserving wildlife and its habitat for the benefit of present and future generations. Even the NPS, whose narrowly defined mission makes planning somewhat less vital to the implementation of its mission than is true of the other land management agencies, is required by its organic act to develop general management plans for each unit of the National Park System.

The existence of statutorily-imposed planning requirements, however, assures neither intelligent nor effective land and resource management. As the U.S. Climate Change Science Program's 2008 report recognizes, the usefulness of management plans may be limited by factors that include a failure to adequately address evolving issues, a failure to identify actions worthy of priority attention, reliance on outdated management goals, and the use of a planning horizon that is too short. Some of these flaws have hampered the efforts of the federal land management agencies to prepare for climate change. Climate change represents the greatest and most sustained challenge that has ever faced federal land managers. Yet, climate change considerations are apparently not addressed at all, and certainly not in any depth, in many current planning efforts. In interviews with the GAO, planners from the NPS, NFS, and FWS confessed to confusion about the nature of their agencies' mandates to deal with climate change and to uncertainty about how to build climate change considerations into the planning and management process. As one observer put it, land use plans are "an accountability tool . . . What is not in a plan tends to be considered unimportant."

The U.S. Climate Change Science Program's conclusions are consistent with the GAO's findings. Its 2008 report found that some management systems have failed to recognize climate change as a "significant problem or stressor" and that, more generally, agency policies and plans are not flexible enough to deal effectively with uncertainty and change. The report singles out effective management of shifts in species distributions and prevention of possible species extirpations as the likely consequences of these policy and planning failures. These failures represent the antithesis of planning to enhance resilience.

To overcome these problems, it is essential that top agency officials make climate change a priority in the planning process and clearly convey that message throughout their organizations. The Climate Change Science Program's 2008 report recommends the use of flexible and long-term planning horizons, an emphasis that runs counter to the proclivity of decisionmakers to focus on immediate crises and short-term objectives. In addition, planners should seek out opportunities to coordinate with those planning for nearby but separate management units, whether those are within the same or different federal lands systems. According to the report, "[m]anagement plans that are allowed to incorporate climate change adaptation strategies but that have not yet done so provide a blank canvas of opportunity."

2. The land management agencies, in the planning process as well as in other contexts, must rely heavily on the management technique known as adaptive management. The Interior Department's most recent NEPA regulations define adaptive management as "a system of management practices based on clearly identified outcomes and monitoring to determine whether management actions are meeting desired outcomes; and, if not, facilitating management changes that will best ensure that outcomes are met or re-evaluated. Adaptive management recognizes that knowledge about natural resource systems is sometimes uncertain." Biologists have distinguished among different types of adaptive management. The one endorsed here is active adaptive management, which involves "learning about environmental impacts by creating specific scientific experiments designed to test hypotheses."

Adaptive management is a planning and management device tailor-made for dealing with uncertainty. The vast majority of scientists no longer disagree that climate change has begun or that human activities that generate GHG emissions are largely responsible for causing it. Yet major uncertainties remain over the timing, extent, and distribution of climate change and its associated impacts. The planning process must provide resource managers with sufficient flexibility to deal with unanticipated effects of climate change. Adaptive management can provide that flexibility.

According to some observers, some federal land management systems have long relied on static policies that fail to reflect the "dynamic management actions," such as adaptive management, needed to tackle climate change. But all of the federal land management agencies already appear to rely on adaptive management to some extent. As indicated above, the Interior Department's NEPA regulations incorporate adaptive management into the NEPA evaluation process. In addition, the FWS has listed "providing a basis for adaptive management by monitoring progress, evaluating plan implementation, and updating refuge plans accordingly" as one of the eight goals of planning for the National Wildlife Refuge System. The agency has recognized, however, that it needs to provide additional guidance dealing with the principles of adaptive management and monitoring. Similarly, the Forest Service has characterized land management planning as "an adaptive management process that includes social, economic, and ecological evaluation; plan development, plan amendment, and plan revision; and monitoring." To carry out that process, the agency in the latest iteration of its planning regulations has included a prohibition on the implementation of a project or activity (such as a timber sale) approved under a plan until the responsible official either establishes an environmental management system for the Forest System unit concerned or conforms the project or activity to a multi-unit, regional, or national level system.

According to the U.S. Climate Change Science Program, "[c]limate change creates new situations of added complexity for which an adaptive management approach may be the only way to take management action today while allowing for increased understanding and refinement tomorrow." Yet, the land management agencies must be careful how they implement an adaptive management approach. The courts are not always impressed with the process and may regard it as a mechanism for achieving an end-run around statutory planning requirements. In one case, for example, the Ninth Circuit held that the BLM violated the requirement that management decisions conform to preexisting plans by changing resource management plan provisions without a formal amendment. The court rejected the agency's claim that its actions constituted mere efforts to "maintain" the plan, and that formal amendment was therefore unnecessary under BLM regulations. The court refused to allow the BLM to conduct timber sales in a manner inconsistent with the plan by characterizing the actions it took as adaptive management modifications that were contemplated by the plan and made necessary by newly available information. In another case, a federal district court found that the Forest Service violated the NFMA, and a land and resource management plan adopted under it that required monitoring of the effects of grazing on forest resources, when it stated in an environmental impact statement that it would develop and implement a monitoring plan through an "iterative process" that was part of an adaptive management strategy. The court found that these references provided an inadequate explanation of how the agency would comply with the plan's requirements.

The courts have reached similar results in cases in which the Fish and Wildlife Service relied on its commitment to engage in adaptive management to justify its failure to discuss mitigation measures in a biological opinion issued under the ESA[, as in *Natural Res. Def. Council, Inc. v. Kempthorne*, 506 F. Supp. 2d 322 (E.D. Cal. 2007)]. Although the court acknowledged that adaptive management can be beneficial and that flexibility is an essential incident of adaptive management, it concluded that the agency failed to strike an appropriate balance between the dual needs of flexibility and certainty in that it did not provide reasonable assurance that the admitted adverse effects of the project would actually be mitigated. These cases caution that the land management agencies should not use reliance on adaptive management as an excuse for deferring real planning in favor of a "don't-worry-about-it-now-because-we'll-figure-out-what-we-need-to-do-when-it-happens" approach.

3. Planning and project level decisions are only as good as the information on which they are based. Resource managers have stressed the need for better information, both about baseline resource conditions on the

federal lands and about the potential effects of climate change on particular ecosystems or federal land units. Agency officials have bemoaned the paucity of computational models capable of projecting small-scale climate-related changes. Absent that information, it is difficult to anticipate problems or plan for their resolution. In addition, if agencies employ adaptive management techniques, they will need the resources to monitor conditions on an ongoing basis to allow them to adjust management approaches in light of prior successes or failures.

As the U.S. Climate Change Science Program has recognized, "[a]daptation is predicated upon research and scientific information." Gaps in scientific information due to budgetary restrictions that limit the degree to which agencies can implement adequate monitoring programs, coupled with the scientific uncertainties surrounding the effects of climate change on particular ecosystems, are likely to hamstring efforts to address climate change in a fashion that protects federal lands and resources. To make matters worse, the agencies may lack personnel with adequate training, expertise, or experience to interpret the data and put it to good use even if it exists. Particularly at a time when economic difficulties make expansions of agency budgets unlikely, these constraints are potentially significant ones.

The Climate Change Science Program suggests collaboration and information-sharing among agencies as one palliative. It also recommends the adoption of uniform training, information-gathering, and assessment techniques to facilitate information-sharing among the agencies. In addition, Professor Wendy Wagner has provided an important set of recommendations for supplying missing information about the health and environmental effects of industrial and developmental activity. These reforms may be useful in reducing data gaps that plague effective planning and action to combat the effects of climate change. She suggests, for example, the creation of incentives to produce missing information by basing regulatory standards on worst-case predictions. The severity of regulation could then be reduced if regulated entities produce credible information that risks or harms have been exaggerated. This approach need not be confined to federal land users. If it were applied to large producers of GHGs, such as auto manufacturers, industrial companies would have incentives to plug the data gaps with information that might be useful to federal land managers. One problem is that many of those responsible for the products or activities that generate the most GHGs, like the auto companies and the operators of coal-fired power plants, are typically not federal land users subject to management by the federal land management agencies. This method of reducing data gaps concerning climate change would therefore likely require changes in laws beyond those that govern federal land management.

Another way to provide new resources to federal land managers, in a time of shrinking resources, would be to sell instead of give away emissions allowances under any cap-and-trade scheme that Congress includes in climate change legislation. The government may then allocate part of the revenues it accumulates to efforts by federal land managers to prepare for and react to climate change. The indelible images of Hurricane Katrina in 2005 graphically illustrate the dangers of shoddy preparation.

4. The effects of climate change are not bounded by human jurisdictional designations. If climate change exacerbates wildfire risks in a national park, it will also do so for adjacent National Forest System lands. The U.S. Climate Change Program's 2008 report on Adaptation Options finds that experience gained from natural resource management programs teaches us "that it may be necessary to define the management scale beyond the boundaries of a single habitat type, conservation area, or political or administrative unit to encompass an entire ecosystem or region." It adds, "Although a single national park or national forest may have limited capacity for adaptation, the entire system of parks and forests and refuges in a region may have the capacity for adaptation." Ultimately, "[t]he scale of the challenge posed by climate disruption and the uncertainty surrounding future changes demand coordinated, collaborative responses that go far beyond traditional 'agency-by-agency' responses to stressors or threats."

Accordingly, land managers must make greater efforts to coordinate management of the nation's public lands and resources, both among themselves and with state and local resource managers. Greater information sharing among the land management agencies would represent one step toward this goal. Coordinated planning is another. The land management agencies typically plan for the management and use of discrete units, making it difficult "to fully consider the matrix in which [these units] are embedded and the extent to which those attributes may vary over time in response to drivers external to the management system. Climate change adaptation opportunities may be missed if land and water resources are thought of as distinct, static, or out of context of a regional and even continental area."

Inter-agency cooperation to plan for an entire ecosystem is not unprecedented. In response to the controversy created by the application of NEPA and the ESA to logging and related activities within the habitat of the northern spotted owl, President Clinton in 1993 created an inter-agency, interdisciplinary team called the Forest Ecosystem Management Assessment Team. The Team recommended that the NFS and the BLM manage the lands in question by using an ecosystem management approach. In response, the two agencies in 1994 adopted the Northwest Forest Plan. The Plan covered 24.5 million acres of land managed by the NFS and the BLM in Washington, Oregon, and northern California that is within the range of the northern spotted owl. When the validity of the Plan was challenged, the courts upheld it. The Plan had two principal goals: protection of the long-term health of the forest ecosystem, and provision of a sustainable supply of timber and other forest products. One analyst deemed the Plan "a grand experiment in ecosystem planning . . . [that] could determine the fate of hundreds of species." The point is not that the Northwest Forest Plan was a complete success. Rather, the point is that there may be more flexibility to arrange inter-agency planning efforts than is normally assumed.

There are limits to that flexibility, however. Only Congress, for example, has the authority to create or change the boundaries of wilderness areas. As a result, if the land management agencies themselves are not capable of planning beyond the confines of the individual units they manage, either because the existing organic statutes prevent them from doing so or because of the fear of ceding jurisdiction and power to others, Congress should require that they do so and establish appropriate processes.

5. As indicated above, one of the most significant effects of climate change will be species migrations. As a result, what is desert today may be grassland tomorrow, and what is tundra this year may be temperate forests the next. Joshua Tree National Park may soon be devoid of Joshua trees. These kinds of shifts in the nature of the resources found in particular federal land units may require dramatic changes in the management directives that govern these units. To address these kinds of ecosystem disruptions, the President, the land management agencies, and Congress should use available authority to change the status of particular land units, alter the mix of permissible uses, and alter the boundaries of adjacent units (e.g., a national wildlife refuge next to a national forest) to accommodate species migrations and other climate-related changes in the condition and location of resources such as wildlife.

To a certain extent, the land management agencies have authority to shift the nature of permissible uses within the lands they manage. For example, within limits, the Secretary of the Interior has the authority under FLPMA to make, modify, or revoke withdrawals. FLPMA also delegates to the Secretary the power to modify or terminate classifications as part of the land use planning process. The Forest Service and the BLM also have broad discretion under their organic acts to determine the extent to which each of the multiple uses authorized on their lands should be permitted. In addition, the President has the power to reserve lands for particular uses and to exclude others. The Antiquities Act, for example, allows the President to reserve as national monuments federal lands of historic or scientific interest. The agencies and the President should use these powers when appropriate to enhance the capacity of federal lands and resources to adjust to the ecosystem disturbances resulting from climate change. If a major restructuring of the federal land system map becomes necessary, however, Congress will need to take the lead in altering that map to enhance the resilience of federal lands and resources in the face of climate change.

2. ADAPTIVE MANAGEMENT

Holly Doremus et al., *Making Good Use of Adaptive Management*

Center for Progressive Reform Paper # 1104, 2011.
http://ssrn.com/abstract=1808106.

What Is Adaptive Management?

The concept of adaptive natural resource management was developed in the 1970s by ecologist C.S. "Buzz" Holling and fisheries biologist Carl Walters. They argued that limited knowledge about natural systems called for a structured, iterative approach to environmental management. The goal of this approach was to reduce uncertainty over time by systematically incorporating learning into management. They called for managers to design their actions as scientific experiments, monitoring the outcomes, and adjust management direction in light of what the experiments revealed.

The Elements of Adaptive Management

The essence of adaptive management is a commitment to learning and a systematic approach to doing so. Detailed definitions of adaptive management abound, but there is general agreement that it embraces these elements:

- **Explicitly stated goals** and **measurable indicators** of progress toward those goals;

- An **iterative approach** to decision-making, providing the opportunity to adjust decisions in light of subsequent learning;

- **Systematic monitoring** of outcomes and impacts;

- **Feedback loops** so that monitoring and assessment produce **continuous and systematic learning** that in turn is incorporated into subsequent rounds of decision-making;

- Explicit **acknowledgement and characterization of risks and uncertainties**, identification of key uncertainties for management purposes; and

- An overarching goal to **reduce uncertainty over time.**

A distinction is often made between "active" and "passive" adaptive management. In active adaptive management, management actions are designed as experiments to test hypotheses about the system. For example, forest managers uncertain of the effect of post-fire logging on sensitive species might decide to log some areas while leaving others untouched. Passive adaptive management does not rely on deliberate experiments, instead choosing the strategy thought most likely to work but using monitoring to inform refinement of the models and updating of the management hypotheses. In a passive adaptive management strategy, forest managers would implement post-fire logging in the locations and to the extent they believe it will promote desired forest conditions. They would intensively monitor the outcome and be prepared to learn that at least some elements of their initial decisions were mistaken. Both active and passive adaptive management should be distinguished from ordinary trial-and-error, a less structured decision-making approach in which management interventions are tried *seriatim*, evaluated on an *ad hoc* basis, and either retained or discarded based upon a general assessment of how well they achieve their goals.

Adaptive management is frequently coupled with collaborative or consensus-based decision-making. The two are, however, conceptually distinct. Adaptive management is a process for learning and adjusting management. In theory, it can be used with any sort of decision-making process that the particular management context permits. Consensus-based or collaborative management processes apply specific procedures to making management decisions, engaging a variety of stakeholders and attempting to reach consensus rather than imposing actions in a top-down way.

Managers should exercise special caution in using adaptive management in conjunction with consensus-based decision making because the need for consensus adds a potentially insurmountable barrier to changing management direction in response to new information. Adaptive management provisions, for example, are increasingly popular in hydropower relicensing settlement agreements, which often have a very large number of parties. Some settlement agreements require that all parties agree on changes to management in response to monitoring data. That sort of provision inhibits management adjustment simply because it is difficult to get all the parties together to consider changes. Though there may be other benefits from requiring stakeholder consensus, divergent stakeholder interests also tend to make management changes difficult because the parties may not agree on what has been learned or what changes are desirable.

Adaptive Management in Practice

Since the mid-1990s, the concept of adaptive management has held a prominent place in natural resource management policy in the United States, embraced by agency heads and line managers alike and increasingly finding its way into agency guidance, regulations, and statutory mandates. The concept is not without controversy, however. Resource users and the regulated community sometimes argue that adaptive management does not provide sufficient regulatory certainty, exposing them to the risk of costly unanticipated changes and making long-term planning difficult or impossible. For their part, many environmentalists argue that adaptive management places too much open-ended discretion in the hands of agency managers, reducing accountability and exposing environmental values to the risks of agency capture and bureaucratic inertia.

As practiced by resource management agencies, adaptive management often falls well short of the scientific ideal. Statutory and agency definitions of adaptive management vary widely, as do the objectives and implementa-

tion protocols of the agencies and programs. Most of the definitions employed are decidedly imprecise. Key questions – including how learning will be accomplished, exactly how it will improve management decisions, and how managers will be held accountable to statutory goals – typically are not addressed. As a result, in many cases the term "adaptive management" has become at best uninformative and at worst a smokescreen for unbounded agency discretion and a wobbly commitment to program objectives.

When Is Adaptive Management Appropriate?

Because uncertainty is typical of environmental and natural resource problems, adaptive management is an important tool. When misused, however, it can provide an excuse to delay politically uncomfortable decisions and to inhibit effective public oversight. The first step for policymakers considering prescribing adaptive management or managers considering implementing it should be to evaluate its fit in the particular context.

Adaptive Management Can Help Address Incomplete Understanding and Changing Systems

Adaptive management can help address two challenges common to environmental problems: incomplete understanding and changing systems. Environmental systems are frequently highly complex and poorly understood. Gaps in baseline data are common. Furthermore, many natural processes and systems are inherently dynamic and non-linear, producing unforeseen and even unforeseeable changes in the natural system on a human time scale. Superimposing rapid global climate change on systems that were already dynamic has made the situation even more complicated.

In light of uncertainties and environmental change, it may be difficult to identify management strategies that will achieve applicable management goals. Those circumstances call for provisional management decisions and the structured learning adaptive management can provide. Adaptive management is especially appropriate when uncertainties make management choices difficult, but the prospects for reducing uncertainty appear good.

Adaptive Management Is Not Always the Answer

Adaptive management should only be used in contexts where it is likely to improve management. It seeks to insure progress over time toward meeting the objectives of a management experiment in the face of scientific uncertainty, while collecting, synthesizing, and applying new scientific information. It is an iterative process that collects information and applies it to determine whether ongoing management is on track or needs to be adjusted to changed conditions or newly learned information.

But adaptive management is not a panacea. It requires more resources than conventional management, because doing it right requires taking the time to carefully analyze the system at the outset, monitor the results, and periodically reassess and revise. It imposes unfamiliar demands on management institutions for long-term commitment of human and financial resources. It imposes greater demands on stakeholders, because they must monitor decisions and the decision-making process over the life of the project. Because it implies that decisions are always tentative, adaptive management may also increase or extend controversy and conflict, Finally, it may require trading the anticipated best outcome in the short-term for long-term learning and improvement.

Because of these costs, adaptive management should not be undertaken lightly. Managers should not assume that it is the right strategy for every management context. It should be used only if the management improvements it promises over time justify the trade-offs it imposes.

When to Use Adaptive Management

In order to ensure that adaptive management is employed only where it is appropriate, before deciding to implement it, resource managers should undertake, and policymakers should require, an explicit, formalized analysis of the prospects for learning and its expected value for management. That analysis, which should be reviewed by leading technical experts outside the management agency and periodically re-examined, can serve valuable internal and external ends. Internally, it can force managers to confront their assumptions about the system and their information needs, providing the kind of intellectual discipline that prepares the groundwork for learning. A thorough pre-adoption review of the prospects for adaptive management can lead to a better adaptive management program if one is ultimately adopted. Externally, it can provide a different kind of discipline, enhancing accountability to management goals by forcing managers to explain how they expect adaptive management to help them achieve those goals.

The Three Prerequisites for Adaptive Management

Adaptive management is premised on the assumption that learning is both plausible and valuable. It makes logical sense only if three conditions are satisfied. First, there must be an information gap that is important to management choices. Second, it must seem possible to fill that gap on a management-relevant timescale. Third, it must seem possible to adjust the initial decision over time in response to new information.

- **Information gaps**. Adaptive management is useful only if learning is needed in order to achieve management goals. Unless information gaps limit resource managers' ability to evaluate their choices, they do not need adaptive management to facilitate later adjustment. Because there is so much we do not know about natural systems, this requirement will rarely turn policymakers away from adaptive management. Nonetheless, directly confronting it is important. Defining important information gaps requires the definition of clear management goals, an essential but often overlooked element of successful adaptive management. Explicitly identifying information gaps focuses attention on areas where learning would be most helpful. It is also the first step in identifying why information is missing, and how it might be obtained.

- **Good prospects for learning**. The second requirement for successful adaptive management is the ability to learn. Adaptive management will not improve management outcomes unless important information gaps are narrowed over time. Although it can be difficult to evaluate the likelihood or cost (in resources and time) of learning, making a rough stab at that analysis is crucial to understanding whether adaptive management will be useful. It should take into account the sources of uncertainty, potentially confounding environmental variables, the ability to experiment and the resolving power of available experiments.

- **Opportunities for adjustment**. Finally, adaptive management requires the ability to change management direction in response to learning. Initial management steps must not become immediately locked in, either formally by law or informally by reason of their practical effect. Adaptive management cannot help when there is no way to correct an initial mistake, as when the decision in question is to allow irreversible alteration of the environment. For example, EPA should not rely on adaptive management to ensure that mountaintop removal mining does not violate water quality standards unless it knows that the water quality effects of filling streams with mine debris are reversible.

NOTES & QUESTIONS

1. While we may be able to largely agree at this point that adaptive management is desirable, whether we are capable of doing it is an entirely different question. While courts generally favor the idea of adaptive management, the actual agency efforts to design such programs are generally unsatisfying. In any case, the early case-law in this area demonstrates that "adaptive management procedures, no matter how finely crafted, cannot substitute for showing that a plan will meet substantive management criteria required by law." J.B. Ruhl & Robert L. Fischman, *Adaptive Management in the Courts*, 95 MINN. L. REV. 424, 427 (2010). Could this rigid loyalty to pre-set legal standards stand in the way of our ability to evolve toward more adaptive management?

2. While the above adaptive management material serves us well in this chapter as an introduction to the field for the purpose of considering the range of climate adaptation tools, students wishing to learn about adaptive management in greater depth and detail will find a good deal more on it in Chapter 7 of this text.

3. ASSISTED MIGRATION

Alejandro E. Camacho, *Assisted Migration: Redefining Nature and Natural Resource Law under Climate Change*
27 Yale Journal on Regulation 171 (2010).

A growing number of conservationists, resource managers, and scientific and legal scholars are suggesting the use of an experimental and controversial strategy to help the world's biota adapt to the considerable projected adverse effects of anthropogenic climate change. "Managed relocation," alternatively dubbed "assisted migration" and "assisted colonization," is the intentional transfer of flora or fauna to a new region in response to climatic change. In other words, assisted migration involves the deliberate movement of non-human refugees to a new area for which they are believed to be better suited due to projected changes in climate. Decisions on whether, when, and how to use this novel form of species translocation will undoubtedly have substantial consequences for biota and ecological systems. Yet such questions also make plain how climate change necessitates fundamental changes in American natural resource management.

* * *

III. The Ethics of Assisted Migration

Though the scholarly literature on assisted migration has primarily focused on questions of scientific viability and legal feasibility, at their core the arguments animating debates about assisted migration are normative—not whether it can be safely and effectively used, but whether it should ever be used as a climate change adaptation strategy. As detailed in this Part, assisted migration ignites long-smoldering tensions in American natural resources policy. Assisted migration commits natural resource management to active and long-term human manipulation and control, running counter to imbedded conservation ideals that aim to allow natural systems to function apart from human interference. Likewise, it pits claims that preserving species diversity is vital for the functioning of human and natural systems against emerging models of resource management that seek to focus on protecting native ecosystems. Finally, assisted migration's focus on managing resources for future climatic conditions contravenes longstanding public land preservation and restoration goals that view nature as context-specific and historical.

This Part concludes that though scientific uncertainty or predicted harms to biological or man-made systems may sometimes counsel against employing assisted migration in a particular case, categorical ethical claims against the use of assisted migration are unfounded. First, any attempts to safeguard notions of wild and uncontrolled natural systems are belated and artificial in a world in which climate change was caused by human alterations of the environment. Second, though a singular focus on protecting endangered species would be myopic, so would a fixation on maintaining preexisting biota, particularly as such a focus provides little guidance on the appropriate means and ends of resource management in a climate change world. Third, there is scant ethical foundation for categorically arresting the evolution of preexisting ecosystems or dedicating increasing levels of limited resources to actively trying to return ecosystems to what is essentially an arbitrary historic state. Accordingly, legislators and regulators should not reject the use of assisted migration. Rather, they should support and integrate into natural resource decisionmaking robust scientific research that helps reduce uncertainties regarding translocations, identify circumstances where the likely ecological benefits of assisted migration are high compared to the probable costs, and minimize risks of harm from experimental use of this strategy.

A. Challenges to Conventional Natural Resource Management

Assisted migration is unsettling to many because it raises challenges to a number of central features of natural resource law and management. First, assisted migration is premised on a very active human management of and interference with biological systems, eroding a historically influential conservation aim of keeping natural processes uncontrolled and wild. Second, assisted migration would allow resource managers to engage in management activities focused on protecting endangered species but potentially at the expense of preexisting native species and ecological communities. Lastly, assisted migration's orientation toward anticipating future conditions and transforming resources to maximize future value, however defined, is incongruous with the prevalent conservation objective that seeks to preserve or restore preexisting resources.

1. Attempting To Shield a Wild and Organic Nature

In addressing the effects of climate change on biological systems, natural resource managers ultimately will have the choice of four basic options. The first is doing nothing, allowing existing biological communities and landscapes to change and often decline in ecological function and biodiversity without human management. Another is to rely on passive resource management strategies, such as linking existing preserves with corridors. These strategies would focus on increasing the capacity of native species and biological communities to better accommodate and adapt to climate changes, but would involve little active human management of such interactions. Third, managers could actively manage biological communities and landscapes to preserve them as they were before the onset of anthropogenic climate change. Such strategies would include activities like preventing invasions, engaging in irrigation activities, and regulating biotic interactions over time. Finally, managers could actively manage biological communities and landscapes to convert them into something deemed more compatible with new climatic conditions. One way to understand the argument in favor of assisted migration is that the last of these options is the best available alternative. Proponents of assisted migration must trust in the capacities of active human management.

However, such a strategy necessarily conflicts with another recognized goal of natural resource management and law that focuses on preventing or minimizing human interference with, or manipulation of, untarnished natural processes and areas. In this view, what first and foremost should be preserved or restored through conservation management is not a preexisting landscape or ecosystem, but rather the concept of uninhibited nature, that humans are not actively in control. Many, beginning perhaps with John Muir, have emphasized the instrumental and intrinsic value of a wild nature. Numerous commentators have stressed its spiritual value, asserting that wilderness allows individuals opportunities for spiritual restoration through the observance of divine creation or God. Others have focused on nature's ability to remove the daily stress of life. Some note the economic benefits a wild nature provides to both users and non-users, while others focus on the value that untouched nature provides ecologists as an invaluable template to learn from when trying to restore damaged ecosystems. Finally, others have emphasized the value of the mere existence of nature unsullied by humans. At least some of these commentators claim that maintaining or restoring ecological systems to this "natural" state is normatively desirable, morally required, or both.

In natural resources law, this ethical perspective is best embodied by the Wilderness Act of 1964, which protects wilderness lands from active human manipulation. Wilderness areas may "contain ecological, geological, or other features of scientific, educational, scenic, or historical value." However, the defining characteristic of wilderness is that it is "untrammeled . . . undeveloped Federal land retaining its primeval character and influence, without permanent improvements or human habitation, which is protected and managed so as to preserve its natural conditions." These areas are protected not primarily for their ecological, geological, scenic, or historical value; they are preserved principally because they are wild, essentially uncontrolled by humankind. The NPS asserts that it prefers to allow wilderness lands to recover naturally from natural disturbances, without human manipulation, though they allow for active management to reverse prior human disturbance of natural conditions. Several public agencies emphasize the value of minimal human interference in non-wilderness areas as well.

This view leans heavily on a dualism between humans and nature. Wild, relatively undisturbed, natural systems are accepted as normatively good. In contrast, active human management is presumed to be interference or even artifice. Active management in some sense leads to a resource that is really an artifact shaped by human craft, a product of external human agency rather than purely "natural" forces. Active human intervention may be morally appropriate only in exceptional circumstances, such as restoration to reverse prior human disturbance, though some strongly criticize even such efforts.

Assisted migration potentially erodes if not destroys this conception of nature as wild and natural. Assisted migration is expressly active human intervention and management; humans take it upon themselves to control and change biota and biotic interactions. Because assisted migration promotes the removal, introduction, and sustained management of biological units, it ensures an exceptionally active level of natural resource management. Assisted migration challenges the distinction between what is a given of the natural world and what is acceptable for human manipulation.

Some might claim that by engaging in assisted migration, natural resource managers would be treating nature as a "zoological theme park" – a human artifact. It would be impossible to engage in assisted migration and not view the landscape or ecosystem in which the assisted species is introduced as at least in part artifactual, a human creation. Allowing assisted migration would require the tacit approval of active and enduring human manipulation of ecosystems as a principled (or at least acceptable) form of natural resource conservation. Similar to innovations in biotechnology for manipulating genes or embryos, assisted migration raises concerns regarding the hubris of playing God. To the extent that assisted migration could be portrayed as a mechanism for reversing or overcoming a prior human disturbance of a natural system—climate change—it might be possible to navigate around concerns about the propriety of active management of ecosystems. However, the employment of assisted migration would be at least a partial rejection of the intrinsic value of a wild and unmanaged nature. It would be an implicit and likely anthropocentric determination that other considerations are more essential or valuable.

Finally, for some the argument against assisted migration might focus on the increased level of moral culpability that should accompany more active human management of ecosystems in contexts of substantial uncertainty. To some extent, this differentiation is akin to the legal and moral distinctions between responsibility for the commission and omission of an act. In this view, all else being equal, a natural resource management agency is less culpable if it allows a species to go extinct by not engaging in assisted migration than if it engages in assisted migration and the introduced population causes harm. This is not a question of whether the risk of harm of species extinction is greater than the risk of harm of introduction; setting that aside, such a critique asserts that by acting the agency is more culpable than if it does not act.

2. Allowing the Elevation of Endangered over "Native"

In addition, because assisted migration involves the translocation of vulnerable species to new areas, it seems to set arguments for endangered species protection against concerns embedded in natural resource law and management for safeguarding preexisting biological communities. The underlying argument for the use of assisted migration is the longstanding and widely held value of protecting biodiversity. As stated earlier, global climate change threatens the existence of many vital and productive ecosystems and their biological constituencies. Proponents of assisted migration suggest that new active management techniques such as assisted migration will be essential for combating the loss of species and ecosystem health. This line of reasoning draws not only from the extensive literature championing the instrumental and intrinsic value of species diversity, but particularly from the federal ESA's focus on protecting species from extinction.

Many have emphasized and documented the instrumental benefits to humans of biodiversity and avoiding species extinctions. These include the potential medical or pharmacological benefits derived directly or indirectly from biota. Many also argue that species and genetic diversity maintain ecosystem functions and foster long-term stability in natural systems that provide value to humans. This claim relies in part on the precautionary principle: because the detrimental effects of species extinction on ecosystem function and scientific knowledge are potentially considerable and likely irreversible, we should work toward sustaining and preserving all species and prioritize efforts to avert extinctions.

Others focus on the aesthetic or recreational benefits to humans of promoting a diverse natural resource base through the protection of endangered species. Though certainly more subjective, such interests have nonetheless been an important motivation for proponents of assisted migration claiming a special connection to a particular vulnerable species. For example, the founder of Torreya Guardians, Connie Barlow, has asserted: "'I kept visiting these spindly trees and thinking, nobody understands you but I do,' . . . 'I made a personal commitment to do whatever it took to save them.'" Such arguments undoubtedly have a powerful resonance for many, having historically played a significant role in helping motivate species protection laws such as the federal ESA. Finally, some argue that the ESA is motivated by the conviction that species have intrinsic value regardless of their potential utility to humans. In this view, there is a societal responsibility to take special steps to protect those species most threatened with extinction.

Though few scholars have attempted to explore it in the context of climate change, any species-focused justification for assisted migration directly challenges a prevalent theme of natural resource policy that seeks to protect and restore native ecosystems. As explained earlier and further detailed in the next subsection, much of modern conservation law (and public land management in particular) is motivated by the objective of protecting native ecosystems. In particular, much of contemporary American natural resource law is designed to protect species that preexisted European settlement and inhibit those that did not. Though in the past conservation of both endangered species and native ecosystems could be accomplished if endangered species conservation were limited to the species' existing or historic range, assisted migration would promote endangered species conservation to the potential detriment of other preexisting biota.

Moreover, a growing number of interjurisdictional governance regimes have been emerging in response to concerns over regulatory fragmentation and the recognition that effective natural resource management "requires consideration of connected ecosystem components." These regulatory processes seek to focus on "ecosystem-based" management that emphasizes the importance of protecting ecosystem diversity and health, rather than just focusing on preventing species extinctions. Accordingly, any species-specific focus of assisted migration would run counter to recent trends toward more holistic ecosystem conservation.

In fact, various regulators, conservation groups, and legal scholars have contended that a crucial motivating factor of the keystone conservation law dedicated to species protection—the federal ESA—is the protection of native ecosystems. The ESA does treat species as the focal target for protection. However, it also explicitly mentions ecosystem protection as a purpose for the law. Legislative history indicates that Congress intended ecosystem protection to be a "basic" and "essential" goal of the Act, and courts have agreed. Congress's 1982 amendments to the ESA authorizing habitat conservation plans (HCPs) responded to substantial criticisms of the ESA's species focus, and the subsequent dominance of HCPs in ESA implementation further developed existing ecosystems as a focal unit under the ESA. In this view, endangered species serve as an indicator of native ecosystem health, enabling resource managers to protect ecosystems by gauging the fitness of particularly vulnerable constituents. The primary intent of such laws, from this perspective, is not preventing the extinction of particular species but some other measure of ecosystem health, such as genetic or population diversity or a more holistic ecological "sustainability" or "integrity."

Therefore, by focusing only on particular species vulnerable to climate change, assisted migration potentially elevates the importance of an individual endangered species over that of native ecosystems. A judgment is being made regarding the relative value of a vulnerable species to be introduced vis-à-vis the biotic communities that already exist and may be harmed by the introduction. In this light, a persistent focus on protecting endangered species through assisted migration arguably contravenes the growing trend in existing natural resource management—including the ESA—that emphasizes native ecosystem protection.

3. Current Dominance of Historical, Contextual Preservation

Finally, assisted migration also departs from widespread natural resource goals that regard nature as contextual and seek to preserve and restore native biological systems to a historical benchmark. As detailed earlier, the preservation and restoration of native resources to a historic baseline is a core feature of modern American natural resources law. There certainly are historical and current differences in the management of the various federal resource lands. This is particularly so between those lands initially established to be managed for use (for example, general national forest and BLM lands) and those established with an explicit preservation focus (for example, national parks, Federal Wildlife Refuges, and wilderness areas). However, today even national forests and BLM lands are subject to a host of regulations that seek to preserve or restore existing ecological resources to historical conditions through measures that include avoiding, limiting, and removing non-native species.

Much of natural resources management is grounded in an early version of preservation and restoration ecology that is premised on stationarity, "the idea that natural systems fluctuate within an unchanging envelope of variability." Reserves – the fundamental strategy of conventional natural resources management – embody this model of ecology that emphasizes stasis and natural stability. The few management techniques that seek to revise resource management to integrate the now-dominant "dynamic equilibrium" model of ecology still assume that any variability in ecosystems is bounded and manageable.

A primary goal of the reserve strategy has been to protect and preserve preexisting resources (such as native biota) within reserved areas while working to remove or keep non-native species out. Natural resource managers are trained in a professional ethic that focuses on preventing or undoing the human alteration of nature. For many, the influential "Leopold Report," commonly considered a foundational (even "scriptural") authority for modern national park management, represents this preservation ethic. One of its most quoted passages recommends as the primary goal of park management that "the biotic associations within each park [should] be maintained, or where necessary recreated, as nearly as possible in the condition that prevailed when the area was first visited by the white man." Active management may be acceptable and even necessary, but generally only to the extent that it is needed to restore the landscape or maintain it in a historic condition.

Similarly, native species have been accepted in natural resource management as a normative, intrinsic good, while only non-native species can be regarded as harmful or invasive. Virtually every definition of "invasive" in the scientific literature requires for the species to be non-indigenous, with some actually treating non-indigenous as synonymous with invasive. Likewise, federal law creates a dichotomy between indigenous species and exotics. Federal definitions of invasive include as a necessary prerequisite that the species is non-native. In contrast, even if a native species causes serious harm to human health or economic or environmental harm, it is commonly not considered invasive.

This preservationist management focus draws on the premise that nature is supposed to be contextual and historical. For many, conservation ethics is rooted in a sense of place and is context-specific. Even the Torreya Guardians, who ardently argue for the employment of assisted migration for protecting Torreya taxifolia, formulate their reasoning for moving the endangered plant north at least partially in restorative terms.

Assisted migration directly contradicts this focal management goal of preserving or restoring natural resources to a static historic baseline. Under a policy of assisted migration, management would not rely principally on preserving preexisting biota or excluding non-native species. Rather, managers would deliberately seek to introduce and integrate non-native species in direct contradiction with conventional natural resource preservation principles as exemplified by the Leopold Report. The goal of such efforts could no longer be to restore or maintain the landscape as it was prior to human disturbance, or to embed natural resources in a context-specific history.

Assisted migration would strain the natural/man-made and native/non-native poles that exist in natural resource management. Without a native ecological baseline, what does "natural" mean anymore? Native species or ecosystems, long accepted as valuable, would be expected to yield to non-native species in the name of conservation. For those who consider non-native to be synonymous with invasive (and thus harmful by definition), assisted migration would be completely unacceptable. Even those who consider non-native status to be just one prerequisite of invasiveness—in other words, those who would require a species to also be widespread or harmful to be considered invasive—would still have to accept that the value of the introduced non-native species could outweigh that of the native ecosystem.

Assisted migration also could help refute the idea that a place has a unique and organic biota and history. In this critique, assisted migration would not just save a few organisms. At a minimum, assisted migration creates entirely new assemblages of species; at its extreme, assisted migration has the potential to redesign the biota of Earth. Assisted migration makes it virtually impossible to maintain a context-specific intuition of nature. For example, the prevalent association of Yellowstone National Park with its iconic elk, bison, and bears reflected in the park's conservation strategies has little place in a conservation approach that contemplates removal of such fauna to a new landscape. Without a historical ecological baseline, it is unclear what natural resource managers would use to decide what would be an ethical or appropriate management strategy.

B. In Defense of Assisted Migration

Assisted migration is undoubtedly controversial because it challenges the human-nature dualism, native ecosystem focus, and preservationist goal of contemporary natural resource management. As detailed in this Section, however, these various features of natural resource management make little sense in a world of climate change. It is increasingly evident that human activity is affecting natural systems throughout the globe. Moreover, in a world in which the climate is rapidly changing, committing ever-increasing resources to the preservation or restoration of existing resources and landscapes will be increasingly costly and potentially detrimental to the health of ecological systems.

The goal of maintaining or restoring native ecological systems with respect to a particular historic baseline may previously have been tenable and even advantageous as a rough heuristic for limiting resource exploitation. However, climate change suggests that it might be wasteful and even counterproductive. Rather than unconditionally rejecting assisted migration as a potential climate change adaptation strategy, scientists should focus on developing scientific data to assist analyses of the risks and benefits of assisted migration in particular circumstances. More broadly, agencies and policymakers should seek to develop regulatory institutions and goals that better reflect the realities of a dynamic world in which human effects and ecological change are inescapable.

1. Active Management for Species Protection

Arguments based on a normative commitment to keeping natural systems wild and uncontrolled—nd thus the binary distinction between humans and nature—lack persuasive power, particularly in an era of anthropogenic climate change. Humanity is inseparable from nature. Humans have helped shape natural systems for tens of thousands of years, and there are few if any examples of nature today that are pristine and independent from humanity. The signatures of humanity exist even in deep and remote locations. Indeed, anthropogenic climate change itself has already ensured human interaction with virtually every natural system on the planet.

As such, human involvement in natural systems is inevitable. Though there are extensive ecological and other benefits from natural resource conservation, one of those benefits cannot be that wilderness and other undeveloped landscapes remain unaffected by humanity. The critical query cannot be whether human activities, and in particular natural resource management strategies such as assisted migration, interact with and affect nature—they unquestionably do. Rather, the important analysis is whether the effects of a particular human activity are, on the whole, beneficial. Natural resource management must seek to minimize the negative (and maximize the positive) consequences of human activities on natural systems. In view of this, assisted migration could be a defensible adaptation strategy in certain circumstances.

The dualist critique of assisted migration as interference with nature becomes even weaker when one considers that the alternative strategies to assisted migration could be just as intrusive and dangerous. Management of ecosystems to preserve them as they were before the onset of anthropogenic climate change is as active a form of management as the intentional movement of species, as would be any attempt to restore ecosystems to a preexisting state. Furthermore, though less active than assisted migration, there is scant evidence that creating corridors is categorically less likely to lead to ecological harm to the receiving ecosystem than active movement by humans via assisted migration. Similarly, though less intrusive than active strategies like assisted migration, passive resource management strategies such as setting aside land preserves are still a form of human interaction with and influence on natural systems. Some in fact argue that wilderness areas are "the most astonishingly unnatural places on earth" because society takes "human beings out of nature altogether and mak[es] wilderness of it." In short, any adaptation strategy—and even the absence of an express adaptation strategy for species conservation—will have substantial effects on ecological systems. A human-nature dichotomy simply is not a useful standard for evaluating resource management strategies.

In fact, though some may consider the feature of active human involvement to militate against the use of assisted migration, there actually is a credible argument for an ethical duty to at least consider more active approaches like assisted migration as a way to reverse the effects of climate change. This is borne out by a closer review of the legal and ethical distinction between responsibility for omission and commission. Though the law may acknowledge a general distinction between responsibility for acting and failing to act, this is certainly not the case when there is a special relationship or other obligation to act. At least government agencies, established with the duty of conserving shared natural resources for the public, could not rely on a decreased culpability for failing to act. In addition, because current global climate change is at least in part anthropogenic, there may in fact be an affirmative moral and legal duty for public entities to act. In contexts involving preceding acts that led to harm, some have reasoned that there is an affirmative duty to take reasonable steps to reverse or mitigate the negative effects of the initial act. As such, doing nothing or taking less aggressive steps to reverse the harms of climate change might be more morally problematic than the intentional movement of species out of their native range.

2. Balancing Endangered and Preexisting Species

As detailed earlier, the experience of the federal ESA has demonstrated that a solitary focus on protecting endangered species is misguided. However, categorical ethical claims against the use of assisted migration based on a fidelity to keeping native ecosystems intact are similarly problematic. An absolutist approach that focuses on maintaining currently existing (or restoring previously occurring) biota is of suspect value for managing perpetually changing ecological communities, particularly in light of the rapid and convulsive effects of global climate change.

The lack of a broader management focus has been an insightful critique of endangered species management laws, but establishing a consensus on what ecosystem management is and should be has been very elusive. The definition of ecosystem management in the academic literature is contested, and professed applications of it by regulatory authorities vary considerably. Many interpretations rely on procedural themes that may be quite valuable but do not provide substantive limitations or guidance on what to focus on in managing an ecosystem. Moreover, those interpretations of ecosystem management that do discuss substantive themes emphasize concepts which are vague, pliable, and particularly confounding in light of climatic change. These include the protection of ecological or biological integrity or health, sustainability, and broadening the management focus to include not only species but also genetic, population, and ecosystem diversity.

A core problem with such a focus is that because ecosystems are always in flux, any attempt to manage such dynamic systems is fraught with ambiguity. As difficult as managing a resource area for a particular species may be, developing broadly accepted standards and limitations for managing for the integrity or sustainability of a multitude of genotypes, populations, species, and ecosystems is an exponentially greater challenge. Some are thus understandably concerned that a rejection of managing for particular species in favor of ecosystem management can be a recipe for standardless resource regulation.

Some understandings of ecosystem-centered natural resource management provide sufficient flexibility to allow the use of assisted migration when beneficial to humans. These interpretations explicitly include the integration of human-centered values as an important part of ecosystem-based management. For such approaches, there is an express recognition that humans are and should be significant influences on natural systems. In such a view, the categorical rejection of assisted migration becomes impossible except in the unlikely event that one could establish that under no circumstances could the benefits to humans of introducing a non-native endangered species outweigh the risks. Otherwise, the only way to determine if the use of assisted migration is warranted is through a case-specific analysis that considers the social and ecological benefits and costs of translocating a particular species to a particular site.

Other attempts to elaborate on these substantive themes of ecosystem management emphasize preservation and even reintroduction to protect naturalness, natural disturbance regimes, the representation of ecosystems across natural ranges of variations, or viable populations of native diversity. These interpretations thus emphasize promoting the preservation or restoration of nativity, using some predetermined historic baseline to guide resource management strategies. However, given that ecosystems have been and "naturally" are continually in flux – often as a result of human activity – it is difficult to identify an unassailable ethical basis for categorically dismissing the use of assisted migration as unnatural. Any such rejection would more soundly be based on a judgment that, in the particular circumstances, maintaining the assemblage of present species is of more value (historic or otherwise) than the assemblage that would exist with the introduction of a new endangered species. Yet, as is detailed in the next subsection, such a determination will be increasingly difficult as climate changes cause ecological systems to transform.

3. Anticipatory Management for Impending Change

Though the preservation or restoration of landscapes may promote scientific, aesthetic, or other human interests, categorically freezing biota at a particular period in the past or future has no objective ethical foundation. In fact, climate change will make accomplishing preservation or restoration objectives increasingly difficult. Any sensible analysis of assisted migration should consider the diminishing gains and escalating costs of preserving and restoring to a historic baseline before rejecting the use of assisted migration.

One might reasonably question the prudence of relying on a natural resource management approach that seeks to restore past (or preserve existing) ecosystems or landscapes as inert and unchanging phenomena. Many commentators have discussed how much of conventional natural resource law and management historically has focused on maintaining the "balance of nature," fallaciously treating ecosystems as static assemblages. Ecosystems are now universally understood as naturally dynamic, not in equilibrium but rather ever-changing. Instability may even be necessary for many species to exist. As such, any attempt to identify and preserve ecosystems rooted in the notion of an original steady state is problematic. Thus, ethical claims against assisted migration based on it being antithetical to the preservation or restoration of native ecosystems appear to be incongruous with prevailing knowledge of ecological systems.

Indeed, climate change is likely to alter ecosystems in fundamental ways, causing many new, no-analog biotic assemblages and communities to form. Why would these newly formed communities be natural and moral, while introducing species into such communities would be artificial and unethical – particularly if members of an introduced species might have migrated to such a location had they not been trapped by human-caused dispersal barriers (such as agriculture and urban areas)? Accordingly, the possibility of intervening in ecological systems through assisted migration to improve their function or to advance other public values should not be unconditionally rejected on ethical grounds.

A corollary of this contention is linked with previously stated concerns about relying on a simplistic dualism of nature and humanity: the pervasive native/non-native distinction is a short-sighted human construct that only accounts for a tiny fragment of evolutionary time. Viewed under a longer timeline, humans are simply a part of nature, and species movements in and out of particular landscapes are unexceptional and widespread. Consequently, the critical inquiry is not whether human activities such as assisted migration tamper with nature or depart from a historical norm; rather, the important objective is to minimize the negative and maximize the positive consequences from resource management strategies and other human activities.

Accordingly, scientists and regulators should not categorically reject assisted migration. ... [S]cientists should work to substantiate the ecological benefits and risks of assisted migration, and legislators must develop a regulatory framework that integrates such scientific information into management decisions. More importantly, natural resource law must evolve to recognize that natural systems – as well as information about them – necessarily change over time, and that assessments of their value unavoidably involve judgments that are not exclusively a scientific inquiry.

NOTES & QUESTIONS

1. As you likely gathered from Professor Camacho's defense, assisted migration is a controversial policy. For a discussion of some of the issues of contention, see Jason S. McLachlan et al., *A Framework for Debate of Assisted Migration in an Era of Climate Change*, 21 CONSERVATION BIOLOGY 297 (2008).

2. Given that we do not have specific legislation directly targeting assisted migration, how might the prospect fit into our existing structure of federal laws, regulations, and policies? For an analysis of possible avenues as well as roadblocks, see Julie Lurman Joly & Nell Fuller, *Advising Noah: A Legal Analysis of Assisted Migration*, 39 ENVTL. L. REP. NEWS & ANALYSIS 10413 (2009).

4. BRINGING IT ALL TOGETHER IN THE FLORIDA EVERGLADES, A CASE STUDY

While it is important to understand such climate adaptation tools as maintaining ecosystem resilience and connectivity, restoration, adaptive management, assisted migration, and the imposition of protective laws, it is also essential to remember that they are all part of a single holistic process. The value of studying the manner in which these methods interact with one another, both positively and negatively, cannot be overstated.

The following excerpt from *Center for Biological Diversity v. Salazar*, while substantially edited, is nonetheless longer than the usual case excerpt. This is because it so beautifully weaves together the considerations of nearly all these approaches to climate adaption, perfectly demonstrating their tensions with and complements to one another, which cannot be fully appreciated in just a few pages. While not itself a case about climate adaptation, the story it tells us reveals the key strengths, weaknesses, and relationships among the various tools of the climate adaptation trade (or trade-offs it faces), including:

- Restoration;

- adaptive management;

- static habitat needs versus the need for change;

- fragmentation versus connectivity;

- conflicts between the ESA and efforts at restoration and/or adaptive management;

- managed systems versus natural systems;

- differing treatment for species whose habits have been altered to the point that original habitat conditions may no longer serve them;

- conflicts among multiple listed species;

- conflicts with Native American tribes;

- the choice to trust in adaptive management, even where more certain protections are available, where that certainty comes at a high price;

- accepting that risk of uncertainty in the hope of achieving more;

- comparing long-term versus short-term species needs;

- the potential danger inherent in what the court calls "ESA myopia"; and

- consideration of public comment, peer review, and stakeholder interests.

These are many of the issues that will arise as we both proactively and reactively adapt species and ecosystems to climate change. Thus, the story of the sparrow and the Everglades makes for a valuable case study, perhaps giving us a glimpse of what to expect as we head down the climate adaptation road. As you read it, consider how the analysis might apply to other contexts you have read about in the last three chapters on climate change.

Center for Biological Diversity v. Salazar

United States District Court, District of Columbia, 2011.
770 F.Supp.2d 68.

■ COLLYER, DISTRICT JUDGE.

Did the Secretary of the U.S. Department of the Interior appropriately exercise executive discretion when he failed to designate the area containing sub-population A of the Cape Sable seaside sparrow as critical habitat because the designation would most likely interfere with the Comprehensive Everglades Restoration Plan which will return more natural water flows to the Everglades? Balancing these competing interests is complex and difficult but the result is left to the Secretary, defendant Kenneth Salazar, and his designees. As long as his decision will not result in the extinction of the species, the Secretary has broad discretion. The Secretary insists that sub-population A will persist, albeit in far less area, and that the exclusion will not result in the extinction of the bird. Plaintiffs attack his reasoning and conclusions. In the end, it is a judgment call that the Secretary is empowered to make. As the Secretary has provided a rational basis for his determinations, summary judgment will be granted to the defendants.

I. FACTUAL BACKGROUND

A. The Endangered Species Act

*   *   *

Section 4 of the ESA guides the Secretary in the decision-making process of designating critical habitat for a species. In full, the provision reads:

The Secretary shall designate critical habitat, and make revisions thereto, under subsection (a)(3) of this section on the basis of the best scientific data available and after taking into consideration the economic impact, the impact on national security, and any other relevant impact, of specifying any particular area as critical habitat. The Secretary may exclude any area from critical habitat if he determines that the benefits of such exclusion outweigh the benefits of specifying such area as part of the critical habitat, unless he determines, based on the best scientific and commercial data available, that the failure to designate such critical habitat will result in the extinction of the species concerned.

16 U.S.C. § 1533(b)(2). In other words, the ESA empowers the Secretary to exclude an area that would otherwise qualify as critical habitat if he finds the benefits of excluding the area are greater than the benefits of designating the area. However, the Secretary's discretion to exclude critical habitat comes to an end when the failure to designate the area would result in the extinction of the species.

The ESA provides an array of vital protections to listed species and their designated critical habitat. Relevant here, federally backed actions that "may affect" a listed species or its critical habitat invoke the consultation requirements of Section 7 of the ESA. When triggered, Section 7(a)(2) of the ESA requires that "[e]ach Federal agency shall, in consultation with and with the assistance of the Secretary, insure that any action authorized, funded, or carried out by such agency . . . is not likely to jeopardize the continued existence of any endangered species or threatened species or result in the destruction or adverse modification of habitat of such species." Formal consultation culminates in a biological opinion from the Service, which determines whether the agency action would jeopardize the species or adversely modify its habitat. "If jeopardy or adverse modification is found, the Secretary shall suggest those reasonable and prudent alternatives" that the Secretary believes would avoid the jeopardy or adverse modification.

B. The Cape Sable Seaside Sparrow

This matter represents the continued involvement of the Court in the Service's efforts to protect the Cape Sable seaside sparrow (*Ammodramus maritimus mirabilis*) ("Sparrow"), which began in December of 2000 when essentially the same parties brought suit to, inter alia, force the Service to revise the Sparrow's critical habitat designation. *See generally Biodiversity Legal Found. v. Norton,* 285 F.Supp.2d 1 (D.D.C.2003). The Sparrow is endangered and first received federal protection when it was determined to be "threatened with extinction" on March 11, 1967. The Sparrow is restricted to areas in and around the southern tip of the Everglades in Florida.

The Sparrow exists in six distinct sub-populations which live in six spatially distinct regions. The sub-populations are separated by areas of unsuitable habitat, and although the distances between them range from only two to twenty miles, the birds rarely move between these regions. The flocks are referred to as Sparrow sub-populations A through F. Sub-population A ("Sub A") is located west of the Shark River Slough—a free-flowing channel of water serving as the southern Everglades' primary drainage point into the Florida Bay—while the other sub-populations are all farther east, on the other side of the Shark River Slough. The habitat of Sub A falls within and adjacent to the western portion of Everglades National Park and the southeastern corner of Big Cypress National Preserve.

Sub A is considered critically important to the species as a whole due to its location and separation from the other sub-populations. The detachment of Sub A "might provide the species with a measure of protection against extinction if some calamity were to wipe out the other five sub-populations." *Miccosukee Tribe of Indians v. United States*, 566 F.3d 1257, 1262 (11th Cir. 2009). Although Sub A was one of the largest flocks in 1992, its numbers then declined and have remained relatively low ever since. *See* Biological Opinion on Proposed Continuation of the Interim Operational Plan, U.S. Fish and Wildlife Service (Nov. 17, 2006) ("2006 BiOp") at 28–29 (estimating Sub A at 2,608 birds in 1992, to a low of 16 birds in 2004, 96 birds in 2005, and 112 birds in 2006). The cumulative Sparrow population in 2006 was estimated at 3,088 birds.

The generally sedentary and non-migratory Sparrow has particular habitat requirements which limit its distribution, further complicated by the fact its preferred habitat has been diminished by natural and man-made occurrences. *See, e.g., Biodiversity Legal Found.*, 285 F.Supp.2d at 4–5 (noting how hurricanes in 1935 and 1960 and man-made changes to the hydrology of the Everglades have altered the Sparrow's habitat and occurrence). The Sparrow's "distribution is limited to the short-hydroperiod wet-lands at the downstream end of the greater Everglades system on the southern tip of mainland Florida." The birds predominately occur in fresh-water wet prairies known as "marl prairies." The prairies indulge the Spar-rows with areas of clumped grasses with open space allowing the birds to move on the ground and build nests in the grasses, at approximately four-teen to eighteen centimeters off the ground.

Under prior natural hydrologic conditions in the Everglades, before the implementation of manmade water controls, water from Lake Okeechobee flowed southward through the Everglades and spilled into Florida Bay, the flow volume depending on the seasonal rains. As the seasonal rains flowed southward, the Shark River Slough would overflow into the surrounding marl prairies leaving them flooded for three to seven months of the year. The timing and extent of marl prairie flooding is now heavily regulated.

The Sparrow's breeding season correlates with the dry season when most areas of the marl prairie are either dry or only covered by shallow wa-ter. As water levels begin to rise, commonly in the summer months, nesting becomes significantly more likely to fail as the nests become more detecta-ble to predators or are flooded by the rising waters. The end of breeding season overlaps the summer rains, as the birds are not prone to initiate nesting if water levels reach a depth greater than ten centimeters. Due to its habitat requirements, the Sparrow avoids areas with permanent water cover or long-hydroperiod wetlands. Due to this, the hydrology of an area is a crucial component to the Sparrow's survival.

C. Critical Habitat Designation & Prior Litigation

The Service initially designated critical habitat for the Sparrow on Au-gust 11, 1977, which was corrected on September 22, 1977. The Service re-leased a first recovery plan for the Sparrow in April 1983. In February 1999, the Service found that certain water projects implemented by the Army Corps of Engineers would jeopardize the Sparrow if continued and thus required the implementation of reasonable and prudent alternatives. A revised Recovery Plan for the Sparrow was then issued in May 1999. The Service's goal is to reclassify the Sparrow from endangered to threatened:

> This objective will be achieved: if the loss of functional Cape Sable seaside sparrow habitat, as a result of current and past water management practices, and the invasion of woody and exotic plant species, is eliminated; if Cape Sable seaside sparrow habitat west of Shark River Slough and in Taylor Slough, which has been degraded by current and past water management practices, is restored . . .

To accomplish this goal, the 1999 Recovery Plan concluded that, among other actions, the Service needed to "[r]eview and revise the current critical habitat designation based on distribution surveys." The Service stated that "[c]ritical habitat should, at minimum, include habitat west of Shark River Slough that supports one of the two core subpopulations." The Service recognized that protection of the area where Sub A occurs was necessary to the Sparrow's survival but also advocated for the restoration of natural water flows. "Existing short-hydroperiod marl prairie must be protected and enhanced for Cape Sable seaside sparrows if the population is to survive." "Current water management practices must be changed to restore more natural timing, volume, and placement of water flows."

*   *   *

... The Proposed Rule encompassed seven critical habitat units, comprising approximately 156,350 acres of land. Units 1 and 2, amounting to approximately 71,290 acres, were the only proposed habitat west of the Shark River Slough and the only units to support Sub A. In the Final Rule, the Secretary excluded Units 1 and 2 from the designation, thus no area west of the Shark River Slough where Sub A occurs is designated critical habitat.

D. Comprehensive Everglades Restoration Plan

Within the last century the Everglades has endured an unrelenting encroachment as man pushed back its reach and subjugated its natural flow. The Eleventh Circuit described this transformation:

> For centuries, a broad, shallow sheet of fresh water that covered most of South Florida flowed south from Lake Okeechobee to the Florida Bay. This phenomenon was the 'river of grass' or Everglades, which supported unique and fragile flora and fauna. As so often happens with natural treasures, people sought to control and manipulate the Everglades for their own ends. After the State of Florida's efforts to tame the Everglades failed, in 1948 the Army Corps of Engineers got involved.

> The Corps undertook the Central & Southern Florida Flood Project, which it hoped would control flooding, divert water away from developing areas, provide a source for irrigating crops, facilitate recreation,

and "enhance" wildlife. In order to bend the water to its will, the Corps created thousands of miles of canals and levees supported by scores of pumps, gates, and dams. This massive plumbing project drained the northern portion of the original Everglades for agricultural use and diverted water into distinct, deeper Water Conservation Areas for controlled release into the southern part of the original area, which became Everglades National Park.

Miccosukee Tribe of Indians, 566 F.3d at 1261. In the 1940's, the U.S. Army Corps of Engineers constructed the Central & South Florida Project ("C & SF Project") as a water supply and flood control system for South Florida. The C & SF Project consists of approximately 1,600 kilometers of canals and levees, 150 water control structures, and 16 major pump stations.

Under the C & SF Project "water flow into Everglades National Park is controlled by floodgates and levees in Water Conservation Areas 3A and 3B to the north. A series of floodgates (S–12s) . . . at the north end of Shark River Slough allows managers to release water" from the water conservation areas southward, spilling into the western region of the Everglades National Park where Sub A is found. Jeffrey R. Walters, *et al., The AOU [American Ornithologists' Union] Conservation Committee Review of the Biology, Status, and Management of Cape Sable Seaside Sparrows: Final Report,* 117(4) The Auk 1093 (2000) ("AOU Conservation Report") at 1096.

Critically, the "system has disrupted the natural volume, timing, quality and flow of surface and ground water throughout the Everglades" resulting in severe degradation to South Florida's ecosystem. The Sparrow has particularly suffered from the significant alteration of its habitat's hydrologic conditions caused by the C & SF Project. Specifically, it appears that the C & SF Project increased the frequency and duration of flooding in the Sparrow's western habitat, adversely affecting Sub A's nesting opportunities, while it over-drained the remaining Sparrow sub-populations' eastern habitat, rendering that area especially susceptible to naturally occurring fires.

The Service and other stakeholders implemented several corrective plans to mitigate the disastrous effects that water management practices of the 1990's had on Sub A. Following the Service's February 1999 biological opinion finding certain water projects would likely jeopardize the Sparrow and adversely modify its critical habitat, an Interim Structural and Operational Plan ("ISOP") was implemented in December 1999 to ensure more favorable hydrologic conditions within the Everglades National Park for the Sparrow. The ISOP called for greater restrictions on the amount of water released from Water Conservation Area 3A ("WCA 3A") via the S–12 structures, resulting in decreased water flow into Sub A's habitat, and increased flows into the eastern portions of the Everglades National Park. "The net effect of these ISOP structural and operation modifications was to move water away from western Shark Slough, which was too wet for the sparrow nesting, to regions . . . on the east side of [Everglades National Park], which were too dry for maintenance of sparrow habitat." A 2002 Interim Operational Plan ("IOP") was also concerned with reducing water flows into the western Shark River Slough area, and increasing water delivery to the eastern portion of the Everglades National Park. Yet other plans and projects have been implemented which address the needs of the Sparrow.

Under the grip of the law of unintended consequences, however, these corrective plans produced untoward results. Some argue that the greater retention of water for longer periods of time in WCA 3A, intended for Sparrow conservation, precipitated abnormally high water levels in WCA 3A. The higher water levels in WCA 3A are thought to have imposed adverse effects on other endangered species and on members of the Miccosukee Tribe of Indians of Florida ("Tribe")—who reside on more than 100,000 acres of WCA 3A land—by flooding culturally significant sites. Thus, as the flow of water is restrained from certain regions, the diverted excess flow and any accompanying consequences create tensions among the goals and priorities of the various Everglades' stakeholders.

On the immediate horizon, the Comprehensive Everglades Restoration Project ("CERP") promises the most far reaching and transformative alteration to the complicated system of water management that pervades Florida and the Everglades in particular. CERP is composed of a multitude of smaller projects intended to restore the Everglades to its most natural self possible. The Service explains the goals of CERP:

> CERP has been described as the world's largest ecosystem restoration effort and includes more than 60 major components. The overarching objective of CERP is the restoration, preservation and protection of the south Florida ecosystem while providing for other water-related needs of the region. It covers 16 counties over an 18,000–square–mile area, and centers on an update of the Central & Southern Florida (C & SF) Project.

> The remaining Everglades no longer exhibit the functions and richness that defined the pre-drainage ecosystem. There has been a substantial reduction in the size of the Everglades. Water volumes, flow patterns, and water quality within the Everglades ecosystem have been substantially altered. The changes that have taken place in the natural system have led to decreases in native animal and plant populations. Compartmentalization caused by construction of physical barriers such as canals, levees, and roads, or even hydrologic barriers (such as the Water Conservation Areas) has fragmented the system by creating a series of poorly connected natural areas. CERP is intended to reverse the course of the declining health of the ecosystem.

> Increasing spatial extent and improving habitat quality can provide a base for improving species abundance and diversity. Improving the connectivity of habitats may also improve the range of many animals and their prey-base and provide for a more natural balance of species within the system. The goal of Everglades restoration is to return the pattern, timing, and volume of water flows to the Everglades landscape to conditions similar to those which occurred prior to the first ef-

forts to control the water in the Everglades, which occurred around 1900.

The Combined Structural Operation Plan is considered one of the first major steps in restoration. Ultimately, CERP is intended to improve and supercede the IOP and other water management plans that have been implemented thus far.

*   *   *

III. ANALYSIS

The question before the Court is whether the Secretary properly exercised his discretion to exclude Units 1 and 2 from the Sparrow's critical habitat designation. The Secretary concedes that Units 1 and 2 contain the physical constituent elements essential to the Sparrow's conservation and thus would qualify as critical habitat. The Secretary contends he nonetheless appropriately excluded the Units after determining that the benefits of exclusion were greater than the benefits of inclusion and that exclusion would not result in the extinction of the Sparrow.

The Service excluded the Units primarily on the grounds that designation would essentially require that the habitat in, and the current hydrologic regime for, Units 1 and 2 be statically maintained which almost certainly would conflict with the fluid and transformative revitalization that CERP pledges to materialize in the Everglades. Looming in this determination, of course, is the strong possibility that a significant portion of Units 1 and 2 would cease to be suitable habitat for the Sparrow as hydrologic conditions adjust under CERP. The Service explains:

> The Service is in a difficult position in this case: the agency is charged with implementing the ESA with respect to *all* species. Here, there is tension between conservation of sparrow habitat in the short-term, and restoration of the natural hydrologic conditions that will benefit all species in the Everglades in the long-term. The Secretary weighed these competing interests, as envisioned under the ESA, and reasonably exercised his discretion to exclude proposed Units 1 and 2.

The Secretary also asserts that exclusion will not result in the extinction of the Sparrow. Plaintiffs counter that the Secretary's basis for omitting Units 1 and 2 from the Sparrow's critical habitat is inconsistent and fails this Court's standard of review and that exclusion would, indeed, lead to the extinction of the Sparrow.

The Service has long recognized that Sparrow sub-population A is critical to survival of the species. Sub A may provide a bulwark against extinction if some calamity were to befall the eastern sub-populations, whose habitat is often overly-dried as a result of current water controls, and which experience more frequent naturally-occurring fires and human intrusion into their areas. Separated from these populations by the Shark River Slough, Sub A lives in the marl prairie where it can nest in the grasses high enough to protect against water and snakes and low enough to protect against other predators. Yet, the population of Sub A fell from more than 2,600 birds in 1992 to 16 birds in 2004 and approximately 112 birds in 2006, most likely due in large part to the Army Corps of Engineers' system of releasing water into the Everglades directly north of Sub A nesting sites in the 1990's. Final Rule at 62,738 ("concentrated releases of water from the S–12 structures from 1992 to 1995, above and beyond existing water depth and seasonal rainfall, directly led to the deep-water conditions west of Shark River Slough. These in turn probably caused habitat in the range of Population A to be unsuitable for breeding, and we conclude that this likely played a major role in the apparent decline of Population A"). Following the Service's finding of imminent peril to the Sparrow in 1999, various plans have come into effect, beginning in 2000, which have afforded more favorable hydrologic conditions for the birds of Sub A.

In originally proffering the designation of Unit 1 as critical habitat in the Proposed Rule, the Service noted that because of the historic damage caused to Sub A's habitat by water management practices, "special management of hydrologic conditions [would be] necessary" for the Sparrow to continue in that area. Unit 2 was proposed as critical habitat designation because it "is the only remaining large area of suitable habitat within the cordgrass marsh—marl prairie transitional zone that sparrows historically occupied." The area covered by Unit 2 is considered part of Sub A's habitat, but it is "relatively isolated from the rest of the area supporting this subpopulation" and because its vegetation differed from that of the other proposed units, the Service concluded "its condition and suitability is influenced by a different set of factors than in other units."

Public comment on the Proposed Rule illustrates the mixed viewpoints and potential complications associated with the area encompassed by the Sparrow habitat west of the Shark River Slough. To be sure, some commentators applauded the inclusion of Units 1 and 2 and some argued that yet "more innovative and aggressive elements" would be necessary to save the Sparrow. One commentator added:

> Adding Unit 1 to critical habitat designation is a crucial and well justified step to protect what historically was a major subpopulation (A), the restoration of which recent analyses . . . suggest is essential to recovery. It would be difficult to argue that critical habitat designation is not necessary for this area because current management is sufficient, given that prior water management is implicated in the dramatic decline of the subpopulation, and that it has not recovered under current water management. However, it will be essential to integrate management of the area as critical habitat for sparrows with the overall Everglades restoration effort known as CERP, in which hopes for spatially expansive, long-term habitat preservation and restoration reside.

> Jeffrey Walters, Virginia Polytechnic Institute and State University: Peer Review (Jan. 2, 2007).

Public comment included contentions that designating Units 1 and 2 would prove incompatible with the goals of CERP. The U.S. Army Corps of Engineers cautioned:

> Of particular concern is the statement in the rule that special management of hydrologic conditions is necessary for Unit 1. The weight of the best available, peer-reviewed, scientific information indicates that the area in and around the proposed critical habitat Unit 1 was much wetter historically than the conditions which exist today in the managed system. The hydrologic premise upon which the CERP was designed is to restore a less managed, more free-flowing system through the removal of structures which impound and compartmentalize the ecosystem. The CERP plan recommends removal of the L–28 Levee and the S–12 gate spillway structures upstream of Unit 1 and replacement of the S–12 facilities with a series of bridges to allow for a more natural, free-flowing, rain-driven water regime between the Water Conservation Areas, Big Cypress National Preserve and the Everglades National Park. The requirement for special management considerations and protections to meet the Primary Constituent Element (PCE) for hydrologic regime in Unit 1 is incompatible with the CERP Plan and the restoration targets upon which it is based. The economic analysis did not address the potential costs of wholesale revisions to the CERP plan which may be needed to meet any such PCE hydrologic regime requirements nor did it consider other relevant impacts such as reduction in restoration benefits to the Everglades ecosystem, impacts to other endangered and threatened species, impacts to level of service of flood protection and costs for additional mitigation features that may be required.

Thus, the designation of habitat west of the Slough would necessitate artificial water management which the Corps and other commentators believed irreconcilable with CERP's pursuit of unshackling, to the greatest extent possible, the water flow in the Everglades from human intervention and structures. Another commentator noted, in the introduction to his peer review, the problems with the water management regime that he believed would be inherent in designating Units 1 and 2:

> The Capes [sic] Sable Seaside Sparrow (the sparrow) has existed for centuries in the area of Everglades National Park. Sparrows have weathered extreme flooding and drought, numerous hurricanes, frequent fire, etc. well before people arrived and modified the natural hydrology of the ecosystem. While most look with disdain at the canals, levees, pumps, gates, and other water control structures that lace south Florida, and have embarked upon a multi-billion dollar program, i.e. the Comprehensive Everglades Restoration Plan (CERP) to eliminate as many structures as possible, the Fish and Wildlife Service (FWS) is now proposing a Critical Habitat designation that will require 'special management considerations' (code for institutionalizing in perpetuity the current use of water control structures to artificially manage water flows into western Shark River Slough at lower levels

than before human intervention). It would seem to even the most casual of observers that if we move toward restoring the natural flows and levels, under which the sparrows lived for 100s of years, the artificial management of flows that is being proposed . . . would be unnecessary. Especially since for 9 years, this artificial management has shown no indications of helping the sparrow, and has caused much damage to other areas of the Everglades. But no, the Fish and Wildlife Service is attempting, via the Endangered Species Act (ESA) provisions for Critical Habitat, to create a perpetual requirement for a very specific hydrologic goal, which is diametrically counter to restoration of the Everglades and, has not proven helpful, but detrimental to the sparrow.

Dr. Terry L. Rice: PEER REVIEW (Sept. 16, 2007).

Some comments stated that maintaining an artificial water regime for Units 1 and 2 would conflict with the conservation and protection of other species within the Everglades. The Florida Fish and Wildlife Conservation Commission acknowledged that it was statutorily obligated to protect the Sparrow but that it also stood strongly in support of CERP and expressed concern about the possible effects of designating Units 1 and 2 on the conservation efforts for other species. The Commission expressed its belief that water management practices under the ISOP and IOP plans—which were designed to protect the Sparrow on the west side of the Shark River Slough—had adversely affected species in other areas, such as the snail kite, apple snail, and roseate spoonbills. The Commission predicted the same harmful water management practices would continue if Units 1 and 2 were designated. The Commission agreed that Units 1 and 2 would likely become wetter under Everglades restoration and would no longer support Sparrow nesting, but the Commission nonetheless asserted that designation would conflict with the "broad overall ecosystem restoration goals as envisioned under the CERP." The Commission recommended that the Service "continue to give strong and careful consideration to the potential unintended effects that designation of critical habitat in Units 1 and 2 may pose for the restoration of the greater Everglades ecosystem."

The Miccosukee Tribe memorialized its belief that water management practices implemented to secure favorable breeding conditions for Sub A, and which they believed would continue if Units 1 and 2 were designated, were causing negative impacts on Tribal lands. As one example, the Tribe plants corn on tree islands for religious and subsistence purposes. The Tribe commented that as of 2007, about half of the tree islands, approximately 60% of their acreage, had disappeared in WCA 3A due to flooding they believed was caused by water management meant to save Sub A. Once destroyed, tree islands "cannot be replaced except in geologic time frames or with prohibitively expensive restoration." The Tribe also argued that the flooding of WCA 3A had precipitated a drop in the population of the endangered Everglade Snail Kite.

The Tribe further rejected the assumption that decreased water flows from the S–12 structures into Sub A's habitat would allow the bird to flourish. The Tribe asserted that this "invalid assumption" had caused severe damage to WCA 3A and its inhabitants yet has "not helped Subpopulation A, which declined in numbers under actions allegedly being taken to protect it." The Tribe lamented that designation of Units 1 and 2 would necessitate the continuation of water management efforts to unnaturally dry out Sub A's habitat by closing the S–12 structures which would "perpetuate nearly a decade of artificial conditions." The inclusion of Units 1 and 2 arguably breached the "promise of the Federal government to the Miccosukee Tribe that these lands would be preserved in their natural state *in perpetuity,* and will prevent the restoration of the Tribe's traditional Everglades homeland." Ultimately, designation would "create *unnatural and artificial* conditions for the [Sparrow] that will in all likelihood prevent *natural* conditions in the Everglades from ever being restored."

When the Secretary responded in the Final Rule to all the comments, he informed commentators who favored the designation of proposed Units 1 and 2: "Upon further evaluation of the proposed critical habitat designation, we have found that the benefits of excluding proposed Unit 1 [and Unit 2] outweigh the benefits of inclusion and that such exclusion will not result in the extinction of the species. Therefore, we have excluded Unit 1 [and Unit 2] from critical habitat." The Secretary acknowledged that "some habitats currently occupied by sparrows, particularly in the vicinity of sparrow subpopulation A, may have been wetter historically than they are presently, and conditions may become wetter in some portions of this area under restoration. This was a consideration in our decision to exclude these areas from the designation."

The Secretary explicitly relied upon Section 4(b)(2) of the ESA to exclude Units 1 and 2 from designation, having found the benefits of exclusion to outweigh the benefits of inclusion, and having also determined from the best available scientific information, that exclusion would not result in the extinction of the Sparrow. Because the issue here is whether the Secretary has exercised his discretion in a reasonable manner, the Court quotes him extensively. The Secretary first explained the benefits of designating Units 1 and 2. He found the principal regulatory benefit of inclusion would be that federally backed activity affecting the habitat would require consultation pursuant to Section 7 of the ESA, to ensure the activity would not destroy or adversely affect the critical habitat. The Secretary acknowledged the potential that rising water levels in Units 1 and 2 under CERP would trigger the ESA's adverse modification consultation requirements. "A benefit of inclusion would be that in certain CERP alternative scenarios, . . . the adverse-modification standard may result in a determination of destruction or adverse modification of designated critical habitat . . . and result in implementation of Reasonable and Prudent Alternatives that would protect the sparrow habitat *as it presently exists.*"

The Secretary determined, however, that the benefits of adverse modification consultation under Section 7 were lessened because current management plans already consider the needs of the Sparrow. The Secretary forecast that the Service and other Department of the Interior representatives would be intimately involved in the planning, implementation, and oversight of CERP, and would ensure that the projects considered endangered species. The Sparrow also "occurs almost exclusively on public land managed for conservation purposes, which include the protection of listed species." The majority of both Units 1 and 2 are subsumed by the Everglades National Park and Big Cypress National Preserve, each of which operates under a general management plan that calls for the maintenance of habitats and protection of threatened and endangered species. The management plan for Big Cypress National Preserve specifically addresses the needs of the Sparrow, including efforts to understand the Sparrow's decline in the area and efforts to strengthen the Sparrow's numbers in the Preserve.

The Secretary explained the limitations in this instance of protection afforded by critical habitat designation as compared with broader management plans:

> We believe that conservation achieved through implementing management plans is typically greater than would be achieved through multiple site-by-site, project-by-project, section 7 consultations that consider critical habitat and are conducted at varying points in time. Management plans commit resources consistently to habitat protection, but also to long-term proactive management of habitats for listed species and conservation benefit to other species, and generally ensure consistent consideration of listed species. Section 7 consultations involving critical habitat only commit Federal agencies to prevent destruction and adverse modification to critical habitat caused by a particular project. They do not commit agencies to conservation, long-term management, or providing benefits to critical habitat or sparrow areas not affected by the proposed project. Thus, any management plan that considers enhancement, recovery, or restoration as the management standard, or which explicitly addresses the listed species, may provide more benefits for the conservation of this listed species than result from the prohibition of destruction or adverse modification of critical habitat alone.

The Secretary acknowledged that the management plans have no control over hydrologic conditions in the habitat.

The Secretary also noted that representatives of the various agencies that manage the properties that contain proposed critical habitat units convene annually for the sole purpose of discussing efforts to bolster the Sparrow population. "These protections and management assurances will remain in place regardless of critical habitat designation." The Secretary emphasized that the purpose of CERP is to restore "conditions that closely resemble those to which the sparrow adapted before water management changes in the 20th century" and that the "hydrologic management plans for the region are developed in conjunction with the Service and are subject to consultation under section 7 of the Act under the jeopardy standard." Thus, the Secretary concluded that "the benefits of inclusion in the form of ensuring consideration of sparrow habitat through section 7 consultation and improving awareness of opportunities for sparrow conservation during Everglades restoration are small."

The Secretary then enumerated the benefits of exclusion. The Secretary was unequivocal that "[p]ossibly the greatest benefit of exclusion would be the removal of a potential constraint to the CERP and other Everglades restoration projects." CERP is intended to restore hydrologic conditions and vegetation that mimic those existing before human hydrologic manipulation. "Consequently, changes in the extent and location of unfavorable and favorable habitat conditions for sparrows are also likely to occur." The Secretary explained that "[t]this expectation is at odds with evaluation of critical habitat under section 7 of the Act." "Critical habitat designation establishes static boundaries on the landscape and requires evaluation of proposed alterations of the habitat within the critical habitat boundaries." "In essence, the requirement to prevent changes from occurring within designated critical habitat boundaries may prevent the change that is intended under CERP." Despite the availability of best available scientific evidence suggesting that CERP would benefit the Sparrow, critical habitat designation of proposed Units 1 and 2 would likely "have the result of limiting the overall environmental benefits of Everglades restoration."

The Secretary also stated that a further potential benefit of exclusion, as CERP comes to fruition, would be less intensive hydrologic management to maintain the Sparrow. As manmade intervention is deconstructed through CERP, another benefit of exclusion would be avoiding the compartmentalization required of designation that which runs counter to ecosystem-wide restoration, in that restoration instead seeks to increase the connectivity of habitats and water flow. The Secretary also referred to the numerous comments he had received from the public, the Tribe, and "other resource management agencies expressing opposition and concern about the proposed designation because of potential conflicts with restoration." The Secretary explained that since "the process of planning and implementing CERP projects is a multi-agency, multi-stakeholder collaborative process, exclusion of proposed Units 1 and 2 would provide great benefit in terms of completing the collaborative process of Everglades restoration planning with a goal of achieving a broad variety of environmental benefits, including enhancement of listed species habitats and populations."

The Secretary acknowledged that the area where Sub A occurs will likely experience greater water incursion under CERP thereby raising questions about the sustainability of that area to host the Sparrow. The Secretary explained there was less concern that changing conditions under CERP would adversely affect the eastern sub-populations. "These issues are less of a concern in the eastern sparrow subpopulations, which currently support most of the sparrow population and the best available information suggests will support a large amount of sparrow habitat after CERP is complete." The Secretary determined that "[b]ased on the best available scientific information, we believe that restoration, when complete, will provide habitat that will be sufficient to support a secure sparrow population."

"In light of this information, exclusion of proposed Units 1 and 2, the areas within sparrow subpopulation A, would be beneficial to achieving full restoration benefits under CERP and other Everglades restoration projects." Exclusion would allow "conservation efforts to focus on activities intended to advance restoration of the broader Everglades ecosystem, which includes sparrow habitat, instead of focusing resources on regulatory compliance with critical habitat."

Based on these considerations, the Secretary determined that the benefits of excluding proposed Units 1 and 2 would outweigh the benefits of including the Units. The Secretary explained he chose Units 1 and 2 for exclusion as opposed to other units because "there are differences in the degree of benefit among the different areas." "The benefits of exclusion are greatest in those areas where there is the greatest degree of uncertainty in the ultimate outcome of restoration and its effects on current sparrow habitat, and the greatest potential impacts in terms of the potential incompatibility with or limitation of the planned restoration of the ecosystem." The Secretary found exclusion benefits to be greatest with Units 1 and 2.

Lastly, in amalgamating all the factors previously cited, the Secretary determined that excluding Units 1 and 2 would not result in the extinction of the Sparrow. In its motion for summary judgment, the Secretary adds that "excluding proposed Units 1 and 2 from the critical habitat designation will not result in elimination of the subpopulation [A], let alone extinction of the species." "The protections in place through consultation under Section 7 of the ESA, combined with existing management plans and the involvement of the Service in the Everglades restoration process, provide a rational basis for the Service's conclusion that exclusion of proposed Units 1 and 2 will not result in extinction of the sparrow."

* * *

The balance between designating a crucial swath of critical habitat for the Sparrow, a single species, and greater flexibility for restoration of the Everglades to benefit the entire ecosystem and its many inhabiting species, is left to the Secretary's discretion as long as it does not result in extinction of the species. The Secretary has provided a rational basis for his decision to exclude the Units and the Court defers to his conclusion. ...

The Secretary concluded the most significant benefit of exclusion was that designation of Units 1 and 2 could erect a significant roadblock to the implementation of Everglades restoration, a position well-supported by the record. CERP originates from the well-documented belief that the restoration process will provide a substantial benefit to the entire Everglades ecosystem, including the Sparrow and other endangered species. The Secretary also considered the opposition of the Tribe and state entities to the designation and found exclusion would benefit the collaborative process required of the multi-stakeholder restoration process. The Secretary considered the very real benefits of inclusion that would accrue to the Sparrow by securing its habitat as it currently exists on the western side of the Slough. However, the Secretary determined that even absent critical habitat designation, Sub A would still be afforded some protection under management plans that take into consideration its status as an endangered species, the involvement and intervention of the Service in CERP implementation, and the jeopardy consultation requirement of Section 7 of the ESA. That the Secretary decided to avoid potentially severe impediments to a process that promises so much long-term benefit to all the species of the Everglades cannot be called arbitrary or capricious.

* * *

[T]he Secretary readily admits that "there is a large degree of uncertainty that is inherent in planning Everglades restoration." The anticipated hydrologic consequences of restoration on Units 1 and 2 are varied and necessarily involve a degree of scientific uncertainty inherent in a predictive and novel comprehensive restoration effort. Yet, the record supports the view that water levels might rise in most of the area comprising Units 1 and 2, and the Court defers to the Secretary's evaluation of the inherent uncertainty.

* * *

The Secretary also considered that any federally-backed actions, including CERP, that are found to jeopardize the continued existence of the Sparrow would trigger consultation requirements under Section 7 of the ESA and the possible implementation of reasonable and prudent alternatives to avoid the jeopardy. The Secretary points to the fact that a jeopardy finding by the Service in 1999 culminated in cooperation with the Corps to implement measures to mitigate adverse water flows into Sub A's habitat even though the area was not designated as critical habitat. To be sure, given the underlying purpose of exclusion, a future jeopardy determination may be met with alternatives that do not require the imposition of water management controls. However, the manipulation of water levels, while perhaps the most effective short-term guarantee for Sub A, is not the only measure of protection in the Secretary's arsenal.

* * *

The Service prepared its Proposed Rule in a hurry, forced by court deadlines and possibly with ESA myopia. When evaluating the best available scientific information limited to the Sparrow, it proposed that Units 1 and 2 be designated critical habitat. Push-back from other stakeholders forced a re-evaluation—the exact purpose of public comment and peer review. With a broader view of conservation of the Sparrow, other species in the Everglades, and the Everglades' ecosystem itself, the Service determined that Sub A would persist without designation; that the Sparrow would not become extinct and would, in fact, prosper in a restored Everglades; that designation of Units 1 and 2 would hamper Everglades restoration; and that these considerations rendered exclusion of Units 1 and 2 more beneficial overall than inclusion. In other words, designation of the Units as critical habitat would impose a static restriction on an area that is beginning a dynamic and somewhat unpredictable revitalization. The Service has been remarkably candid and straightforward about the difficult choices it faced and its reasoning for the Final Rule.

The Court acknowledges the continuing precarious position of the Sparrow. Plaintiffs raise legitimate and pressing concerns inherent in the Secretary's final designation of critical habitat. These are extremely difficult and complex decisions. The brake on the Secretary's discretion in making such a decision is that it cannot result in a species becoming extinct. The record supports the Secretary's finding that exclusion of Units 1 and 2 from critical habitat will not result in the Sparrow's extinction; Sub A may or may not be adversely affected by CERP while sub-populations B–F should enjoy some amelioration of habitat and possibly thrive. The very complexity of these issues shows that more than one reasonable conclusion could be drawn; under such circumstances, the Secretary is entitled to exercise his discretion.

5. LETTING GO OF THE PAST

There is one more climate adaptation tool to consider – one that is sufficiently conceptually different from the others to keep a bit separate. It is arguably more psychological than anything else, though the suggested attitudinal shift has a practical motive. Some refer to this proposal as the "end of conservation," which language might make the pill a little tougher to swallow. To put it into slightly more comforting terminology, given that it is about a psychological shift and perhaps in need of some softening of the blow, let's call it "acceptance," or "letting go of the past." This seedling movement is not about giving up on the principles behind conservation, but instead looks at the new reality of climate change and asks some tough questions: which goals are still realistic, and can we better achieve them by letting go of the unrealistic ones? As you read the next article, ask yourself what you are ready to let go of. Could desperately clinging to our historical landscape accelerate our move toward having no landscape at all?

Alejandro E. Camacho, Holly Doremus, Jason S. McLachlan & Ben A. Minteer, *Reassessing Conservation Goals in a Changing Climate*
Issues in Sci. & Tech., Summer 2010, at 21.

Climate change poses a hierarchy of significant challenges for conservation policy. First, the sheer scale of climate change calls for conservation efforts to be vastly stepped up. Second, the pace and extent of expected climate change will probably undermine the effectiveness of traditional conservation tools focused on protecting designated areas from human intrusion. The search for novel conservation strategies that will stand up to global shifts in climate highlights a third challenge: New conditions and new tools require a reassessment of our conservation goals. This third challenge has so far not been the subject of much debate, but merits closer and more systematic attention. The debate may be uncomfortable, but avoiding it complicates the tasks of prioritizing conservation efforts and choosing

conservation tools. More important, the failure to explicitly identify conservation goals that acknowledge climate change is likely to lead to failure to achieve those goals.

The threat of climate change to conservation policy is daunting. Climate change is altering habitats on a grand scale. Species around the world are shifting their ranges to accommodate warming trends. Under any reasonable projection of greenhouse gas emissions, the rate of change will accelerate in coming decades. For species with small populations or specialized habitat requirements, climate change poses special challenges. Although the U.S. Fish and Wildlife Service recently declined to list it as endangered or threatened, the American pika remains an excellent example. The pika, a heat-sensitive mammal that is native to the mountaintops of the American West, can only move so far uphill and cannot migrate to higher or more northerly mountains because it cannot survive the intervening low-elevation habitat.

Unfortunately, the magnitude of impending climate change also worsens the prospects for species whose conservation status is not currently directly tied to climatic limitations. For example, the Florida torreya is an endangered conifer found only in a handful of stands along a 35-mile stretch of the Apalachicola River in Florida and Georgia. These populations are currently threatened by an outbreak of a thus-far unidentified disease. Species such as torreya, currently threatened by multiple stresses such as disease, invasive species, and human development, are common throughout the world. Climate change will make their conservation more difficult.

Overall, climatic shifts will place at risk many more species, communities, and systems than are currently protected. The magnitude and details of the extinction threat are uncertain, but that uncertainty is itself a challenge to conservation efforts, because conservation planning and implementation are long-term efforts. There is little doubt that future demands will strain the resources available for conservation, which have long been stretched thin.

Inadequate conventional tools

Our dominant conservation strategy, the designation of reserves, is mismatched to a world that is increasingly dynamic. The reserve strategy rests on the assumption that nature can be protected in sanctuaries walled off from human effects. But no reserve is immune to changes in atmospheric composition, temperature, and rainfall. Furthermore, no reserve manager has or is likely to be given authority to control the entire spectrum of activities that produce greenhouse gas emissions. In a changing climate, reserves may become inhospitable to the resources they are intended to protect. For example, preserves designed to conserve Florida torreya may, even now, not be adequate to protect and promote the growth of existing populations, which are declining. Large climate shifts could further undermine their effectiveness. Similarly, mountain reserves will do little to save pika populations, because no reserve can hold back the changing climate.

What proportion of the world's species will find themselves limited by existing conservation strategies? Estimates of climate-driven extinction range as high as one-third of all species, including plants, vertebrates, invertebrates, fungi, and microbes. In addition to species extinctions, climate change threatens genetic diversity within species, as well as the ecosystem functions performed by species and ecological communities, such as providing fresh water and controlling pest populations. Currently, we do not have the ecological knowledge to forecast the magnitude of these effects accurately. However, static reserve systems will probably not be able to accommodate the biotic shifts projected to occur in coming decades.

The expectation that current reserves will prove ineffective has spurred the development of more exotic and novel conservation tools. Ex-situ conservation efforts aimed at preserving rare species and genotypes that have been lost in the wild are enjoying new popularity. New strategies have also been proposed, notably including managed relocation, defined as the deliberate relocation of species, genotypes, or ecological communities to new locations where they have a greater chance of persisting under emerging climate conditions. The Torreya Guardians, a grassroots conservation group, has introduced torreya to forests in North Carolina, far north of the species' historical range. They argue that northern climates are superior for the growth of torreya and for its resistance to disease. Opponents of managed relocation respond that the deliberate introduction of non-native species, even for conservation purposes, courts the disastrous consequences associated with invasive species. It is still in the early stages, but a robust dialogue has been sparked about the appropriate use of these new tools.

Reevaluating existing goals

The third challenge of climate change—the challenge to established conservation goals—has not yet received enough sustained attention. Confronting this challenge is essential to effectively dealing with the first two, because the priorities necessary in a resource-constrained world cannot be sensibly set, nor can conservation strategies be selected and evaluated without reference to the underlying goals. Many observers have noticed that climate change will make it difficult to achieve established conservation goals. None, however, has grappled in a concrete way with how those goals might need to be reconsidered. In fact, existing conservation goals are insufficiently examined under current conditions. Climate change simply makes the consequences of continuing to avoid that examination more apparent.

There are, of course, many different conservation goals and many different conservation contexts. Here we focus on public conservation efforts, for which both the goals and the strategies are necessarily open to public debate. Public conservation goals are complex and often surprisingly opaque. It is useful to distinguish between the "why" and the "what" aspects of those goals; that is, between the guiding principles that motivate public conservation efforts and the conservation targets selected.

The principles can be quite abstract. They include maintaining useful resources for present and future generations, providing durable opportunities for nonconsumptive environmental experiences, and protecting elements of nature for their own sake. Frequently, multiple principles motivate political action. The potential for tension between those principles is often ignored.

Conservation policy targets give tangible form to the general motivating principles. They must be concrete and identifiable to make policy implementation and enforcement practicable. Conservation targets are commonly tied to the preservation of existing conditions or elements of nature, or the restoration of conditions thought to have existed at some historical reference point. Examples include the preservation or recovery of viable populations of native species; the preservation of iconic landscapes in what is believed to have been their historical condition; and the maintenance of existing ecosystem services. Targets may serve one or more motivating principles. Species protection, for example, simultaneously preserves useful or potentially useful resources, protects the opportunity for specific experiences, and fulfills ethical obligations to protect species for their own sake.

Climate change complicates the achievement of conventional conservation targets in ways that make it necessary to unpack their relationship to the underlying motivating principles, and to sort out priorities among those principles. Changing climate conditions may, for example, make it impossible to maintain the combination of goals we have come to expect of landscapes designated as reserves: historical continuity, protection of current features, and "naturalness," in the sense that ecological processes occur with only limited human direction or assistance.

Managed relocation

Proposals for managed relocation bring those tensions sharply into focus. The world is becoming a very different climatic place. It will not be possible to preserve some current species in the wild if the climate envelope they require disappears. Other species may survive only if they are moved to locations to which they have no known historic tie. That in turn may affect the native biota of the receiving location in ways that are difficult to predict.

Conservation targets, therefore, may need to change, or new mechanisms for making tradeoffs between conflicting targets may need to be developed. The prospects are daunting, because if targets such as historical continuity or protecting existing constituents of natural systems are relaxed, new end points are not obvious. In other words, it may appear that there is no viable substitute for current conservation targets. Especially because of the political pressures that can be brought to bear against conservation, reopening discussion on those targets presents real risks for conservation advocates. It is not surprising that the conservation community has not been anxious to debate goals.

But there are also costs to avoiding the goals debate. The issue of managed relocation illustrates the kinds of questions that must be confronted when setting priorities or choosing strategies, and why those questions can't be answered without a clearer understanding of the principles behind conservation policy.

First, if it is sometimes desirable to move species beyond their historic range, what differentiates "good" translocations from "bad" ones? A 1999 presidential executive order allows the deliberate introduction of exotic species if the benefits are thought to outweigh the harms. Is that the right test for managed relocation? If so, how should harm be evaluated? Should relocation be acceptable if, for example, it affects the abundance of native species at the target site but does not rapidly eliminate any of those species?

Second, if historic conditions are no longer the touchstone, how can we identify desirable end points? Is the goal to help species disperse as they would do on their own without anthropogenic habitat fragmentation or anthropogenic acceleration of the rate of climate change? Is that an appropriate and measurable objective? Are more–culturally defined end points needed in light of the challenges that climate change presents to traditional understandings of naturalness, nativeness, and wilderness? Can such end points be made operational?

Third, how should the effects of managed relocation on receiving communities be distributed? Given resource limitations, it is highly unlikely that a candidate species will be transferred to all potential receiving habitats. Governments will almost certainly have to choose. That raises the possibility that decisions will be made solely on the basis of the political power, or lack thereof, of target communities. Should an environmental justice analysis be an element of conservation decisions? Should such an analysis be applied only to strategies that alter historic conditions, or to conventional preservation strategies as well?

Fourth, who should make these choices, and through what processes? Decisions about who decides are particularly complex and uncertain, given the prevailing piecemeal nature of natural resource governance. For the many migrations and translocations that are likely to cross political borders, a host of local, state, federal, multinational, and international authorities with different and often incompatible objectives may be implicated. This is true regardless of whether the primary threat to species survival is climate change, overhunting, habitat loss, the spread of disease, or a synergistic combination of anthropogenic threats and rapid environmental change. For example, some conservationists recently proposed relocating the Iberian lynx, an endangered species that scientists fear will become the first large cat to go extinct within the past 2,000 years. Translocations are proposed from its rapidly shrinking and fragmenting habitat in Spain to what is viewed as a more suitable range in Scotland. Yet the current international system of fragmented and generally uncoordinated authority was not designed to manage broad shifts in climatic and environmental conditions—or to facilitate such long-term, active management of landscape-scale movements of vegetation and wildlife across different jurisdictions.

In addition, what roles should scientists, regulators, direct stakeholders, and the public play in untangling and resolving these difficult tradeoffs? Making a historic baseline the target limits management discretion to some extent, at least if the baseline is reasonably clear. By limiting discretion, a historic baseline keeps the decisions about tradeoffs in the hands of the public. Removing the constraint of historical continuity gives unelected regulators more discretion, so that decisions become more technocratic. At the same time, those decisions may become less scientific, if unconstrained regulators decide to use cost/benefit analysis or tools other than science to make those choices.

We do not pretend to have the answers to these difficult questions. We believe they should be the subject of broad discussion involving, at least, conservation scientists (who can help society understand the biological consequences of different choices), lawyers and resource managers (who can help ensure that policy targets can be put into effect), ethicists (who can help clarify the motivations for conservation and their relationship to choices of targets and tools), and the public (who will inevitably be affected by both conservation outcomes and the costs of implementing conservation programs). Such a discussion is needed now, before resource managers implement potentially irreversible strategies with poorly understood consequences.

One way to begin the discussion might be through the creation of an interdisciplinary advisory group that could provide a forum for a "deliberative community" of the sort recommended by Ben Minteer and Jim Collins of Arizona State University in a December 6, 2005, article in *Conservation Biology*. Such a committee could develop a set of principles and a broad domestic policy framework under the auspices of the National Academy of Sciences, or perhaps in a parallel effort at the international level, under the International Union for the Conservation of Nature. In any case, the composition of the group is more important than the conveyor, because the group would be asked to deal with the inherently interdisciplinary tasks of exploring the challenges that climate change poses to conservation principles and targets, identifying potential conflicts, and suggesting frameworks for evaluating tradeoffs and choosing among options. Although decisions on these questions ultimately require value choices that are the province of democratically accountable authorities, such an interdisciplinary advisory group could provide valuable guidance and help put the issues on the political agenda.

Although humans have long claimed a stewardship role in the management of the world's natural resources, the precise contours of that role are called into question by climate change. Managed relocation and similar interventionist strategies to conserve species signal a shift to a far more activist and hands-on approach to conservation. That shift may make many environmental scientists and conservation professionals uncomfortable. Indeed, the heavy human hand required for such efforts, creating the possibility of destructive meddling in ecological systems, opens it up to charges of managerial arrogance, especially by those who place a premium on ecological integrity as a policy goal. Such criticisms of aggressive anthropocentrism and technological dominance have become a mainstay of contemporary preservationist thought. Yet the emerging effects of climate change on natural systems make clear that substantial human intervention has already occurred, and the ecological and human costs of failing to intervene to sustain and promote ecological health and function may be immense.

Ultimately, then, climate change forces us to decide whether we want to be curators seeking to restore and maintain resources for their historical significance; gardeners trying to maximize aesthetic or recreational values; farmers attempting to maximize economic yield; or trustees at- tempting to actively manage and protect wild species from harm even if that sometimes requires moving them to a more hospitable place.

NOTES & QUESTIONS

1. Are you a curator, gardener, farmer, or trustee? Which of the values of "nature" would you most prefer to maintain into the future?

2. If you are intrigued by these issues, you might enjoy the earliest (and perhaps most devastating) book on our no-turning-back circumstances and the corresponding need to reassess our relationship with nature, BILL MCKIBBEN, THE END OF NATURE (1989).

C. THE FEDERAL APPROACH TO ADAPTING WILDLIFE AND ECOSYSTEMS TO CLIMATE IMPACTS

1. THE ENDANGERED SPECIES ACT AND CLIMATE ADAPTATION

J.B. Ruhl, *Climate Change and the Endangered Species Act: Building Bridges to the No-Analog Future*
88 Boston University Law Review 1 (2008).

IV. Using the ESA To Carry Species to the No-Analog Future

The task ahead of the FWS is daunting, and it must use [its] discretion ... to develop a plan soon, lest climate change sweep away its mission along with its charges. ... [M]anifestations of climate change already are well underway and already have had adverse impacts on some species. More can be expected. Indeed, the FWS must assume that more climate change impacts will unfold even if the global community takes measures to mitigate greenhouse gas emissions. ... [T]his assumption poses complex policy questions for the FWS, though ... the agency has considerable flexibility in how it answers them. It has the discretion, within bounds, to adopt passive or aggressive policies for how to integrate climate change in ESA programs.

With that foundation established, what should define the agency's set of operating assumptions about how the global community responds generally to climate change – pessimism or optimism? A worst case scenario would have the global community utterly fail to contain greenhouse gas emissions and, as a result, climate change spiraling into chaos for centuries. In that scenario, the FWS might as well pack up its bags and close shop, as climate change will become an unassailable force in ecological reshuffling, overwhelming any management of ecosystems or species. Exercising the ESA, in other words, is pointless in this scenario.

On the other hand, the agency also cannot afford to assume a Pollyanna future in which the global community comes together tomorrow, drastically reduces emissions, somehow sucks carbon dioxide out of the troposphere, and reaches 1990 overall levels by the end of this decade. The message of Massachusetts v. EPA is that a regulatory agency can't assume someone else will address the climate change problem. Each agency must "whittle away" with whatever knife Congress has provided it.

The ESA will be best served if the FWS adopts a cautious optimism that recognizes the limits of the ESA but keeps the statute relevant. Conceding that some human-induced climate change is inevitable even in the best of circumstances does not concede that it will be perpetual and chaotic. Rather, the FWS can reasonably assume that the global community will eventually arrest greenhouse gas emissions to a benchmark level and that, as a consequence, climate regimes will eventually settle into a new "natural" pattern of variation. We have no analog for what that pattern will be, and the transition from the present to that future will be, by all appearances, a rocky ride, but in all probability we will get there. The job of the ESA is to help as many species as is reasonably possible get there with us – to serve as their bridge across the climate change transition into the no-analog future.

Ironically, to do this will take some humility and restraint. Going for the jugular by regulating greenhouse gas emissions is not where the ESA can be of most help to imperiled species. There is little to be gained for the FWS or for climate-threatened species by having the agency go down this road. The agency has no explicit authority to do so, does not have the expertise to do so, and would risk undermining the political viability of the ESA by doing so. Rather, the FWS can provide expert assistance to the agencies more appropriately charged with regulating greenhouse gas emissions, such as the EPA, by advising them about the effects of climate change on species.

As for its direct role in addressing climate change, the FWS can employ the ESA most effectively by identifying species threatened by climate change, identifying which of those can be helped through the ESA's habitat-based programs, and devising a management plan - one that uses regulatory action as well as recovery planning – to build each such species its bridge. Indeed, this strategy allows the FWS to dispense with the distinction between human-induced and natural climate variation. Climate change is climate change – it does not matter to the species what is causing it. What does matter to them is whether and in what shape they survive it.

This brings us to the six policy choice pressure points raised [earlier in the article]. To implement the proposed bridge policy, I suggest the FWS approach the policy choices as follows:

Identifying Climate-Threatened Species. The agency's objective should be to use the ESA to define and monitor the ecological reshuffling effects of climate change. The agency should aggressively identify species threatened by climate change. Early identification of species threatened by climate change and of the critical habitat they require for survival through climate change transition will help in defining the extent of ecological reshuffling and guide human adaptation programs. Early identification also will provide the basis for listing species as threatened, which provides more flexibility in terms of regulatory effects and recovery efforts.

Regulating Greenhouse Gas Emissions. The agency's objective should be to not squander agency resources in a futile effort for which the ESA is simply not equipped. The FWS should not attempt to use its Section 7 and Section 9 regulatory programs in an effort to regulate greenhouse gas emissions. As for the take prohibition, listing species as threatened early will allow the agency to remove greenhouse gas emissions from consideration under Section 9 while keeping the take prohibition active with respect to other contributing threats. If an animal species is in endangered status, meaning Section 9 necessarily applies in full force, difficulties in establishing the burden of proof would support the exercise of prosecutorial discretion not to attempt to regulate greenhouse gas emissions. Under the Section 7 consultation program, project-specific jeopardy analyses should promote other federal agencies to consider ways of reducing greenhouse gas emissions, but should not lead to jeopardy findings.

Regulating Non-Climate Effects To Protect Climate-Threatened Species. The agency's objective should be to support the bridge function of the ESA and to reduce the adverse impacts on species from human adaptation to climate change. Where a species weakened by climate change is also threatened by other anthropogenic sources, such as loss of habitat, and where the agency reasonably believes addressing the non-climate threats will help carry the species through the climate change transition, the agency should use Section 7 and Section 9 regulatory powers to the extent necessary. In particular, where human adaptation to climate change exacerbates threats to a species, the agency should aggressively employ its regulatory presence through Section 7 consultations and enforcement of the Section 9 take prohibition. The agency also must monitor the impacts of human adaptation on species that face no direct or secondary ecological threat from climate change and employ Section 7 and Section 9 powers accordingly. Clearly, however, innovative approaches will be needed, such as market-based incentives and regional planning efforts, to facilitate human adaptation measures as much as species can tolerate.

Designing Conservation and Recovery Initiatives. The agency's objective should be to get as many species with a long-term chance at survival and recovery through the transition to the other side of climate change as is realistically possible. The agency must initially differentiate between species that are unlikely to survive climate change under any circumstances and those that are likely to benefit from assistance in their home ecosystems. Agency resources should not be wasted in developing recovery plans or other conservation measures for non-recoverable species. For species that appear likely to withstand climate change under the ESA's protection, recovery plans should identify the expected intensity of assistance required to manage or respond to primary and secondary ecological effects. Conservation measures for species that require intensive assistance, particularly in Section 10 HCPs, should be designed around adaptive management techniques that involve ample monitoring and considerable room for adjustment of management actions in order to account for the possibility that continuing climate change will alter the effectiveness of those actions.

Species Trade-Offs. The agency's objective should be to not contribute to ecological reshuffling through its species management efforts. Where the measures described above are complicated by species trade-offs – when helping one may harm another – the agency should adopt an ecosystem-based management approach modeled on promoting long-term species diversity and ecosystem multi-functionality. When ecological models do not point to a particular management action to serve those goals, general default priorities, such as assisting top-level predators and resisting induced invasions, may help mediate between species in conflict.

Dealing with the Doomed. The agency's objective should be to avoid accelerating the decline of species who stand no chance of surviving climate change, but not to take measures on their behalf which could pose threats to other species. Under this standard, assisted migration should be employed for such a species only if the FWS has assembled conclusive evidence of the extinction threat, a quantitative model showing the likely success of assisted migration for the species with de minimis anticipated effects on other species, and an assisted migration management plan including long term monitoring and active adaptive management. Human adaptation measures that could accelerate the extinction of the species, which could cascade to affect other species, should be regulated under Section 7 and Section 9 as for any other listed species.

NOTES & QUESTIONS

1. Can you detect elements of the "acceptance" arguments from the end of the previous section in the proposals here? Imagine how difficult it would be to make trade-off choices without first accepting that we cannot preserve our historic ecosystems as they are or were.

2. How has ESA implementation taken climate adaptation into account thus far? The following case discusses the requirement that FWS or NMFS consider climate impacts in the context of jeopardy consultations. It also provides us

with an interesting example of designing an adaptive management plan within an incidental take statement.

Pacific Coast Federation of Fishermen's Associations v. Gutierrez

United States District Court, Eastern District of California, 2008.
606 F. Supp.2d 1122.

■ WANGER, UNITED STATES DISTRICT JUDGE.

I. Introduction.

Before the Court are the parties' cross-motions for summary judgment arising from an October 22, 2004, Biological Opinion ("BiOp") issued by the United States National Marine Fisheries Service ("NMFS" also referred to as "NOAA Fisheries," used interchangeably), in response to the United States Bureau of Reclamation's ("Bureau") initiation of formal and early consultation with NMFS. This is one of a series of cases that address through this and other Biological Opinions, the potential adverse impacts of ongoing Central Valley Project ("CVP") and California State Water Project ("SWP") operations on fish, here, salmonid species, caused by the Long-Term Central Valley Project and State Water Project Operations Criteria and Plan ("2004 OCAP") completed June 30, 2004.

A. The Water Projects.

The CVP is an "extensive system of dams, tunnels, canals and reservoirs that stores and regulates water for California's Central Valley and southward." *Westlands Water District v. Department of Interior*, 376 F.3d 853, 861 (9th Cir.2004). The CVP supplies 200 water districts, "providing water for about 30 million people, irrigating California's most productive agricultural region and generating electricity at nine power plants." The Projects move water through their Delta pumping facilities to provide flood protection, power generation, and water service to otherwise barren areas of Central California for agricultural, municipal, and environmental uses. The CVP was taken over by the United States in 1935, has since been a Federal enterprise, and is the largest Federal water management project in the United States. The Federal government has administered the CVP since 1935. The Bureau administers the CVP.

The SWP is the "largest State-built water project in the country, (and) is managed by the California Department of Water Resources ('DWR')". *Natural Res. Def. Council v. Norton*, No. 05-01207-OWW 2006 WL 39094, *1 (E.D.Cal. Jan. 5, 2006). "The CVP and SWP share certain facilities and coordinate operations with one another pursuant to a Coordinated Operating Agreement ('COA'). The COA which originated in 1986, has evolved over time to reflect, among other things, changing facilities, delivery requirements and regulatory restrictions."

For over thirty years, the projects have been operated pursuant to a series of cooperation agreements. In addition, the projects are subject to ever-evolving statutory, regulatory, contractual, and judicially-imposed requirements. The 2004 OCAP is a baseline description of the Projects' operating facilities and operating environment.

The Bureau and DWR requested the initiation of formal ESA § 7 consultation for Project operations and proposed operations on March 15, 2004 and March 12, 2004, respectively. Among proposed changes in operations are the expansion of the Projects' capacity and increased pumping out of the Delta. The BiOp was intended to address the potential adverse impacts of ongoing (for the next twenty-five years) CVP and SWP operations on the salmonid species.

The original BiOp concludes that the effects of proposed Project operations under the 2004 OCAP are not likely to jeopardize the continued existence of the Sacramento River winter-run Chinook ("winter-run Chinook"), and are not likely to adversely modify the critical habitat for the winter-run Chinook listed as endangered January 4, 1994. The BiOp further concludes that proposed operations under the 2004 OCAP are not likely to jeopardize the continued existence of the Central Valley spring-run Chinook ("spring-run Chinook"), listed as threatened on September 16, 1999, or Central Valley steelhead ("CV steelhead") listed as threatened on March 19, 1998.

Following the issuance of the BiOp, NOAA Fisheries listed as threatened, a population segment of the North American Green Sturgeon located in the Delta Region. NOAA designated critical habitat in the Delta region affected by the CVP for two Evolutionarily Significant Units ("ESUs") of Chinook salmon and five ESUs of steelhead. As a result, the Bureau, on April 26, 2006, requested reinitiation of ESA § 7 consultation on the 2004 NMFS BiOp.

Project operations affect a variety of salmonid species including the endangered Sacramento River winter-run Chinook salmon ("winter-run Chinook"), the threatened Central Valley spring-run Chinook salmon ("spring-run Chinook"), threatened Central Valley steelhead ("CV steelhead"), threatened Southern Oregon/Northern California Coast Coho salmon; and threatened Central California Coast steelhead.

After reinitiation of consultation, Federal Defendants sought to dismiss, remand or stay this case. That motion was denied on all grounds. A motion to dismiss Plaintiffs' Seventh Claim under the National Environmental Protection Act ("NEPA") for lack of jurisdiction was granted June 15, 2007. Plaintiffs' challenge the Bureau's "early consultation" with NMFS and the adoption of the 2004 BiOp.

* * *

III. Factual Background.

* * *

B. Description of Proposed Action in the BiOp.

The purpose of the proposed action is to continue to operate the CVP and SWP in a coordinated manner to divert, store, and convey Project water. In addition to current day operations, several future facilities and actions are included in the consultation. These include (1) increased flows in the Trinity River, (2) an intertie between the California Aqueduct and the Delta-Mendota Canal, (3) the Freeport Regional Water Project, (4) water transfers, and (5) renewal of long term CVP water service contracts and future deliveries. The proposed actions will come online at various times in the future, except for increased flows in the Trinity River, which are presently being implemented in accordance with the Trinity River Record of Decision. The proposed action is: (a) continued operation of the CVP and SWP without these actions, and (b) implementing these operations as they come online.

C. Mitigation Measures.

The BiOp includes mitigation measures principally related to: (1) movement of the 56°F Sacramento River Temperature Compliance Point from Bend Bridge upstream to Balls Ferry; (2) maintaining the carryover storage for Shasta Reservoir at 1.9 million acre-feet ("MAF") as a target; (3) the operation of Red Bluff Diversion Dam ("RBDD") to provide unimpeded fish passage upstream and downstream at RBDD.

Plaintiffs complain about mitigation measures that are to be implemented in the future including, but not limited to, (1) Environmental Water Account assets; (2) increased exports resulting from the South Delta Improvement Program; (3) utilization of the Environmental Water Account to augment water flows.

D. Species Life History and Population Dynamics.

1. Chinook Salmon.

a. General Life History of Chinook Salmon.

Chinook salmon exhibit two generalized fresh water life histories known as "stream-type" and "ocean-type." Stream-type Chinook salmon enter fresh water months before spawning and reside in fresh water for a year or more following emergence. Ocean-type Chinook salmon spawn soon after entering fresh water and migrate to the ocean as fry or parr within their first year. Spring-run Chinook exhibit a stream-type life form where adults enter fresh water in the spring and spawn in the fall. Spring-run Chinook juveniles typically spend a year or more in fresh water before emigrating towards the sea. Winter-run Chinook exhibit characteristics of both stream-type and ocean-type life histories. Adult winter-run Chinook enter freshwater in winter or early spring and delay spawning until spring or early summer (stream-type). Juvenile winter-run Chinook migrate to the sea after only four to seven months of river life (ocean-type). Adequate instream flows and cool water temperatures are more critical for the survival of Chinook salmon exhibiting a stream-type life history due to over-summering by adults and/or juveniles.

Chinook salmon mature between two and six plus years of age. Freshwater entry and spawning timing generally are thought to be related to local water temperature and flow regimes. Chinook salmon runs are designated on the basis of adult migration timing. Both spring-run and winter-run Chinook tend to enter freshwater as immature fish, migrate far upriver, and delay spawning for weeks or months.

During their upstream migration, adult Chinook salmon require stream flows sufficient to provide olfactory and other orientation cues to locate their natal streams. Adequate stream flows are necessary to allow adult passage to upstream holding habitat. The preferred temperature is 38°F to 56°F. Adult winter-run Chinook enter San Francisco Bay from November through June and migrate past RBDD from mid-December through early August. The majority of the winter-run Chinook pass RBDD from January through May, and passage peaks in mid-March. The timing of migration may vary due to river flows, dam operations, and water year type. Adult spring-run Chinook enter the Delta from the Pacific Ocean beginning in January and enter natal streams from March to July. Spring-run Chinook utilize mid to high elevation streams that provide appropriate temperatures and sufficient flow, cover, and pool depth to allow over-summering while conserving energy and allowing their gonadal tissue to mature.

Spawning Chinook salmon require clean, loose gravel in swift, relatively shallow riffles or along the margins of deeper runs, and suitable water temperatures, depths, and velocities. Spawning typically occurs in gravel beds that are located at the tails of holding pools. The upper preferred water temperature for spawning Chinook salmon is 55°F to 57°F. Winter-run Chinook spawning occurs primarily from mid-April to mid-August, with peak activity occurring in May and June in the Sacramento River between Keswick dam and RBDD. The majority of spawning winter-run Chinook are three years old (between 56% and 87%). Spring-run Chinook spawning occurs between September and October depending on water temperatures.

The optimal water temperature for egg incubation is 44°F to 54°F. Incubating eggs are vulnerable to adverse effects from floods, siltation, desiccation, disease, predation, poor gravel percolation, and poor water quality. The length of time required for eggs to develop and hatch is variable and depends on water temperature. The lower and upper temperatures resulting in 50% pre-hatch mortality were 37°F and 61°F, respectively, when the incubation temperature was constant. Winter-run Chinook fry begin to emerge from the gravel in late June to early July and continue through October, generally at night. Spring-run Chinook fry emerge from the gravel from November to March and spend about three to fifteen months in freshwater habitats before emigrating to the ocean.

When juvenile Chinook salmon reach a length of 50 to 75 millimeters, they move into deeper water with higher current velocities. Emigration of juvenile winter-run Chinook past RBDD may begin as early as mid-July, typically peaks in September, and can continue through March in dry years. From 1995 to 1999, all winter-run Chinook outmigrating as fry passed RBDD by October, and all outmigrating pre-smolts and smolts passed RBDD by March. Spring-run Chinook emigration is highly variable. Some may begin outmigrating soon after emergence, while others over-summer and emigrate as yearlings with the onset of intense fall storms. The emigration period for spring-run Chinook extends from November to early May, with up to sixty-nine percent young-of-the-year outmigrants passing through the lower Sacramento River and Sacramento-San Joaquin Delta during this period.

*   *   *

VI. Law and Analysis.

*   *   *

D. NMFS Claims.

*   *   *

2. Global Climate Change and the Effects on the Hydrology of Northern California Rivers.

Plaintiffs contend that, at the time the BiOp was being formulated, the best available science demonstrated that global climate change would significantly change the hydrology of Northern California's river systems. According to Plaintiffs, the BiOp's analysis relies on temperature and hydrology models that assume the same monthly temperature, hydrologic, and climatic conditions experienced in the Project area from 1922 through 1994 will continue for the future twenty-five year duration of the 2004 OCAP operations.

NMFS admits that an explanation of its conclusions on the effects of global climate change should have been included in the BiOp. NMFS states it will address global climate change in its ongoing, reinitiated ESA § 7 consultation consistent with *NRDC v. Kempthorne*. The DI also concede further explanation of the effects of global climate change is needed.

The § 7 formal consultation process is designed to "insure" that any agency action "is not likely to jeopardize the continued existence of any endangered species or threatened species or result in the destruction or adverse modification of habitat of such species which is determined . . . to be critical . . ." "In fulfilling the requirements of [this section] each agency shall use the best scientific and commercial data available."

An agency has wide discretion to determine what is "the best scientific and commercial data available." *San Luis & Delta-Mendota Water Auth. v.*

Badgley, 136 F.Supp.2d 1136, 1151 (E.D.Cal.2000) (citing *Southwest Ctr. for Biological Diversity v. United States Bureau of Reclamation,* 143 F.3d 515, 523 n. 5 (9th Cir.1998)). "The ESA does not explicitly limit the Secretary's analysis to apolitical considerations." *Southwest,* 143 F.3d at 523 n. 5.An agency must make its decision about jeopardy based on the best science available at the time of the decision, and may not defer that jeopardy analysis by promising future studies to assess whether jeopardy is occurring. While uncertainty is not necessarily fatal to an agency decision, an agency may not entirely fail to develop appropriate projections where data "was available but [was] simply not analyzed." *Greenpeace v. National Marine Fisheries Service,* 80 F.Supp.2d 1137, 1149-50 (W.D.Wash.2000).

NRDC v. Kempthorne addressed 2004 OCAP and Project impacts on the Delta smelt and determined that the FWS acted arbitrarily and capriciously by failing to address the issue of global climate change in that Biological Opinion, finding, "the absence of any discussion in the BiOp of how to deal with any climate change is a failure to analyze a potentially important aspect of the problem." *Kempthorne,* 506 F. Supp 2d. at 370.

During the time period when NMFS was formulating this BiOp, readily available scientific data existed regarding the potential effects of global climate change on the hydrology of the Project area river systems including:

(1) Studies showing that radiative forcing (warming) had begun to increase steeply around 1970 and is expected to continue into the foreseeable future. Scientists predicted this warming would produce less snowfall, more rainfall, and earlier snowmelt, leading to major reductions in the Sierra snowpack and decreases in summer stream flow.

(2) Plaintiffs NRDC and The Bay Institute expressed their concern to the Bureau in July 2003 that the Draft OCAP and Draft OCAP Biological Assessment failed to consider climate change effects and provided references for several studies and reports on climate change effects on water availability in the Western United States. These concerns were ignored.

The BiOp does not discuss this global climate change data or mention that NMFS, at a minimum, considered this data. Instead, the BiOp relies on past hydrology and temperature models that assume the historical monthly temperature, hydrologic, and climatic conditions experienced from 1922 through 1994 will continue for 25 years through the duration of the 2004 OCAP operations. These assumptions were challenged as without basis in then-available science.

Plaintiff's motion for summary adjudication is GRANTED as to the climate change claim issue based on NMFS's total failure to address, adequately explain, and analyze the effects of global climate change on the species. Federal Defendants' cross-motion is DENIED.

3. Sufficiency of Adaptive Management Plan and Mitigation Measures.

Plaintiffs dispute that the adaptive management plan and all formulated action and mitigation measures are sufficient, certain, or enforceable.

The principal action measures are: (1) movement of the Sacramento River temperature compliance point (TCP) upstream from Bend Bridge to Balls Ferry; (2) changing the 1.9 MAF COS requirement for Shasta Reservoir to a target; and (3) the operation of the RBDD. Plaintiffs further complain about future use of Environmental Water Account assets to reduce Project effects and the potential for increased exports resulting from the South Delta Improvement Project.

As Federal Defendants and DI correctly observe, the action-mitigation measures described in the Population Impacts section of the BiOp are made part of the "Terms and Conditions" of the BiOp, each of which is a specific part of the Incidental Take Statement ("ITS"), enforceable under civil and criminal law, the ITS provides take coverage for Project operations. The ITS characterizes the "Terms and Conditions" as "non-discretionary" and that Reclamation and DWR must comply or ensure compliance by their contractor(s) "with the following terms and conditions, which implement the reasonable and prudent measures described above."

Each of the operational concerns Plaintiffs advance, Sacramento River temperature controls, Shasta Reservoir COS and RBDD passage and operations are specifically prescribed by the BiOp's Terms and Conditions and are subject to enforceable definite and certain requirements as specifically analyzed below. It is well established that any biological opinion's ITS constitutes a permit authorizing the agency action to "take" the endangered or threatened species so long as the agency respects those terms and conditions.

By contrast, the Delta Smelt BiOp in the *NRDC v. Kempthorne* case, prescribed mitigation measures in a Delta Smelt Risk Assessment Matrix that had no finite standards which were enforceable through the ITS. Adaptive management of mitigation measures delineated by the ITS Terms and Conditions has been employed for a number of years and DI argue, these measures are working to increase winter-run population and returning adults from a low of 186 in 1994 to nearly 10,000 in 2003. DI refer to returning adult spring-run from 1,403 fish in 1993 to more than 8,500 in 2000 and 2003. The efficacy of this analysis has been discussed above.

a. Temperature Control.

Project operations affect salmon which travel from their spawning grounds to and from the ocean. The BiOp contains the following reasonable and prudent measure:

Reclamation shall manage the cold water supply within Shasta Reservoir and make cold water releases from Shasta Reservoir to provide suitable habitat for Sacramento River winter-run Chinook salmon, Central Valley spring-run Chinook salmon, and Central Valley Steelhead in the Sacramento River between Keswick Dam and Bend Bridge.

The Supreme Court has defined the word "shall" used in a BiOp to generally indicate a command that admits of no discretion on the part of the person instructed to carry out the directive.

The following temperature control obligation is non-discretionary in the BiOp:

Reclamation shall target daily average water temperatures in the Sacramento River between Keswick Dam and Bend Bridge as follows:

I. Not in excess of 56°F at compliance locations between Balls Ferry and Bend Bridge from April 15 through September 30 and not in excess of 60°F at the same compliance locations between Balls Ferry and Bend Bridge from October 1 through October 31, provided operations and temperature forecast demonstrate the capability to achieve and sustain compliance.

This 56°F requirement was established by State Water Resources Control Board Order 90-5, issued May 2, 1990. Consultation is required with the SWRCB if the Bureau seeks to designate a temperature compliance point upstream of RBDD. Because hydrologic conditions can limit controllability of upstream operations to an inopportune period of time or upstream of Bend Bridge, the Bureau must maintain daily average water temperature at 56°F at Bend Bridge or other locations upstream, depending upon actual hydrology. This is necessary because mortality of eggs and pre-emergent fry commences at 57°F and reaches 100% at 62°F.

In dry and critical years the Bureau must initiate consultation with concerned agencies regarding temperature control. In fact, in all but two "wet" years since 1993, the Bureau and NMFS have re-consulted to adjust the temperature compliance point upstream of Bend Bridge toward Balls Ferry in accordance with the fact that most salmon redds and incubating eggs are located above Balls Ferry. Unlike the Delta Smelt Remedial Action Matrix, here, a finite 56°F enforceable temperature requirement is set between Balls Ferry and Bend Bridge, with adaptive management only used where compliance cannot be achieved, and actual reinitiation of consultation with NMFS is required before the Bureau announces annual CVP water delivery allocations.

Recognizing that in lower storage years at Shasta, the temperature compliance point has been adjusted using finite criteria:

May 1 Shasta Cold

Water Volume Below 52°F	Compliance Target
<3.3 MAF	Balls Ferry
>3.3 MAF but < 3.6 MAF	Jellys Ferry
>3.6 MAF	Bend Bridge

This temperature control protocol requires maintenance of the 56°F ceiling. In the event of noncompliance, consultation and alternative compliance is required and has actually occurred and water allocation measures have been implemented in 8 of 10 years prior to the 2004 BiOp. No more is required.

b. Shasta Carryover Storage.

For Shasta COS, the ITS non-discretionary Terms and Conditions specify:

> Reclamation shall target a minimum end-of-year (September 30) carryover storage in Shasta Reservoir of 1.9 MAF for improvement of cold water resources in the following water year.

Plaintiffs maintain that the use of the term "target" eliminates a definite and enforceable requirement for Shasta Reservoir COS that was mandated by the 1993 BiOp. DI rejoin that the record shows there was never a mandatory requirement for carryover at Shasta that applied in all years. Although the 1.9 MAF is a target, the Bureau must consult with NMFS before it announces water delivery allocations for any year that annual water conditions do not support temperature control compliance at Balls Ferry. NMFS may object to delivery allocations that reduce the ability to meet temperature control at the location which exists to protect spawning adults and incubating eggs. The Bureau must still reinitiate consultation with NMFS before the first water allocation announcement in February if the Bureau's forecast projects carryover storage levels drop below 1.9 MAF at the end-of-water-year.

* * *

d. Red Bluff Diversion Dam.

To provide upstream and downstream passage at RBDD the BiOp includes the following requirements:

> Reclamation shall implement all measures practicable to provide unimpeded passage upstream and downstream at the Red Bluff Diversion Dam during the period of September 1 through June 30 each year.

A. As a minimum, Reclamation shall provide unimpeded upstream and downstream passage at the Red Bluff Diversion Dam from September 15 through May 14 each year.

B. NOAA Fisheries will review proposals for early gate closures (prior to May 15) of up to ten days, one time per year, only in emergency situations where the alternative water supplies (i.e., new 4th Pump at Red Bluff Pumping Plant and Stony Creek) are unable to meet TCCA demands. Reclamation will reopen the gates for a minimum of five consecutive days, prior to June 15 of the same year in a manner that will be least likely to adversely affect water deliveries.

C. Reclamation shall further investigate and implement all practicable opportunities, including improvement to fish ladders, to improve or provide unimpeded upstream and downstream passage at Red Bluff Diversion Dam from May 15 through June 30 and September 1 through September 15 each year.

D. Reclamation in coordination with FWS and DFG, shall further investigate the results of blockage or delays in the migration of adult Sacramento winter-run Chinook salmon and Central Valley spring-run Chinook salmon at the RBDD as a result of gate closures between May 15 and June 30 and from September 1 through September 15. Written reports shall be provided by to NOAA Fisheries as investigations are completed.

These enforceable Terms and Conditions are imposed with the mandatory "shall" and impose a non-discretionary obligation during specified time periods. If early closure of the RBDD gates is necessary, adaptive management may be implemented by NMFS.

e. The Environmental Water Account.

Plaintiffs raise again the argument that mitigation measures cannot rely upon "environmental water" because there is no finite certainty the environmental water account will be adequately funded in the future. The Court has previously ruled that:

> The EWA is simply a means by which the SWP and the CVP can obtain water by purchasing it from willing sellers. EWA water may be used either to protect fish or to compensate Project water users for reduced exports at the Project pumps. If money is unavailable to fund the EWA, Defendants are nonetheless required to prevent smelt take from exceeding permissible take limits.

> There is a difference between the DSRAM's failure to require mitigation actions in response to trigger events, designed to assure the commitment of necessary resources to smelt protection, and the duty to have available or acquire those necessary resources. A court must leave to the agency the application of its expertise and authority to

manage the complex hydrological, legal, financial, physical and logistical aspects of protecting the Delta smelt.

NRDC v. Kempthorne, 506 F.Supp.2d at 358-59. There is no reason to disturb this ruling.

f. South Delta Improvement Program.

This issue has also been decided in the Smelt BiOp Order:

The SDIP is a separate addition that may or may not be constructed. Project operations under the 2004 OCAP in no way depend upon the SDIP. There is no prohibition to addressing future operations, if and when the construction of the SDIP will occur, in a separate consultation.

In this case the SDIP was treated in the BiOp as a matter for early consultation. Early consultation regarding salmonids does not result in incidental take protection. The reasoning of the *Kempthorne* decision has equal applicability. There is no legal impediment to address future operations of the SDIP, if and when it will be constructed, a separate ESA § 7 consultation must then be performed.

In this case, the BiOp's mitigation measures are included in the Terms and Conditions of the Incidental Take Statement, are declared to be "nondiscretionary" by the BiOp, and are enforceable. For all the reasons described above, the mitigation measures are definite, and sufficiently certain to be enforceable. Their prescription and implementation are within the agency's reasonable discretion to which deference is owed. These measures strike the appropriate balance between the needs of certainty and flexibility prescribed by law.

Plaintiffs' motion for summary adjudication regarding mitigation measures and adaptive management is DENIED. Federal Defendants' cross-motion for summary judgment is GRANTED.

*   *   *

VII. Conclusion.

It is not the Court's prerogative nor within its competence to usurp the executive function to perform the Agency's work to determine whether Project operations will or will not jeopardize the winter-run Chinook, fall-run Chinook, or CV steelhead species or adversely modify their critical habitat. These responsibilities are by law committed to the discretion and expertise of the expert agency, NMFS, and action agency, the Bureau. The Court's authority is limited to determining the lawfulness of the Agencies' actions or inactions.

The 2004 BiOp did not analyze the recovery of the three species and any effect global climate change will have over the next 25 years, the relevant duration of Project operations. The BiOp is incomplete and in the respects specifically identified, inexplicably inconsistent as to the species' survival and recovery. The BiOp is unlawfully silent on critical habitat effects.

An entire failure to consider an important aspect of the problem and a failure to explain contradictory record evidence make the BiOp arbitrary and capricious. Under the APA, a reviewing court must then remand the BiOp to the consulting agency. The court is without authority to proceed to decide the merits of the dispute until the Agencies have had the opportunity to discharge their statutory duties under the ESA. NMFS must provide rational and fact-based grounds for its new biological opinion based on the best science available.

SO ORDERED.

2. INTER-AGENCY PLANNING FOR ECOSYSTEMS AND CLIMATE ADAPTATION

The following two reports provide insight into the current U.S. policy goals for climate adaptation. The first broadly applies to a range of federal programs operating throughout federal lands. The second comes directly from the wildlife agencies (FWS and NOAA chairing a committee with members from other federal, state, and tribal agencies), as the result of a congressional request tied to the Department of the Interior's Fiscal Year 2010 appropriations, and thus provides a more direct glimpse at the plans within the ESA-implementing agencies. Congress specifically urged DoI "to develop a national, government-wide climate adaptation strategy to assist fish, wildlife, plants, and related ecological processes in becoming more resilient, adapting to, and surviving the impacts of climate change." The reports are very long, so these are the executive summaries included for each.

U.S. Global Change Research Program (USGCRP), *Preliminary Review of Adaptation Options for Climate-Sensitive Ecosystems and Resources*

U.S. Environmental Protection Agency, 2008.

Executive Summary

Climate variables are key determinants of geographic distributions and biophysical characteristics of ecosystems, communities, and species. Climate change[1] is therefore affecting many species attributes, ecological interactions, and ecosystem processes. Because changes in the climate system will continue into the future regardless of emissions mitigation, strategies for protecting climate-sensitive ecosystems through management will be increasingly important. While there will always be uncertainties associ-

---

[1] Climate change refers to any change in climate over time, whether due to natural variability or as a result of human activity. This usage differs from that in the United Nations Framework Convention on Climate Change, which defines "climate change" as: "a change of climate which is attributed directly or indirectly to human activity that alters the composition of the global atmosphere and which is in addition to natural climate variability observed over comparable time periods."

ated with the future path of climate change, the response of ecosystems to climate impacts, and the effects of management, it is both possible and essential for adaptation to proceed using the best available science.

This report provides a preliminary review of adaptation options for climate-sensitive ecosystems and resources in the United States. The term "adaptation" in this document refers to adjustments in human social systems (*e.g.*, management) in response to climate stimuli and their effects. Since management always occurs in the context of desired ecosystem conditions or natural resource management goals, it is instructive to examine particular goals and processes used by different organizations to fulfill their objectives. Such an examination allows for discussion of specific adaptation options as well as potential barriers and opportunities for implementation. Using this approach, this report presents a series of chapters on the following selected management systems: National Forests, National Parks, National Wildlife Refuges, Wild and Scenic Rivers, National Estuaries, and Marine Protected Areas. For these chapters, the authors draw on the literature, their own expert opinion, and expert workshops composed of resource management scientists and representatives of managing agencies. The information drawn from across these chapters is then analyzed to develop the key synthetic messages presented below.

Many existing best management practices for "traditional" stressors of concern have the added benefit of reducing climate change exacerbations of those stressors. Changes in temperature, precipitation, sea level, and other climate-related factors can often exacerbate problems that are already of concern to managers. For example, increased intensity of precipitation events can further increase delivery of non-point source pollution and sediments to rivers, estuaries, and coasts. Fortunately, many management practices that exist to address such "traditional" stressors can also address climate change impacts. One such practice with multiple benefits is the construction of riparian buffer strips that (1) manage pollution loadings from agricultural lands into rivers today and (2) establish protective barriers against increases in both pollution and sediment loadings due to climate changes in the future. While multiple benefits may result from continuing with today's best practices, key adjustments in their application across space and time may be needed to ensure their continued effectiveness in light of climate change.

Seven "adaptation approaches" can be used for strategic adjustment of best management practices to maximize ecosystem resilience to climate change. As defined in this report, the goal of adaptation is to reduce the risk of adverse environmental outcomes through activities that increase the resilience of ecological systems to climate change. Here, resilience refers to the amount of change or disturbance that a system can absorb without undergoing a fundamental shift to a different set of processes and structures. Managers' past experiences with unpredictable and extreme events have already led to some existing approaches that can be adjusted for use in adapting to longer-term climate change. The specific "adaptation approaches" described below are derived from discussions of existing (and new) management practices to maintain or increase ecosystem resilience, drawn from across the chapters of this report.

Protecting key ecosystem features involves focusing management protections on structural characteristics, organisms, or areas that represent important "underpinnings" or "keystones" of the overall system. **Reducing anthropogenic stresses** is the approach of minimizing localized human stressors (*e.g.*, pollution, fragmentation) that hinder the ability of species or ecosystems to withstand climatic events. **Representation** refers to protecting a portfolio of variant forms of a species or ecosystem so that, regardless of the climatic changes that occur, there will be areas that survive and provide a source for recovery. **Replication** centers on maintaining more than one example of each ecosystem or population such that if one area is affected by a disturbance, replicates in another area provide insurance against extinction and a source for recolonization of affected areas. **Restoration** is the practice of rehabilitating ecosystems that have been lost or compromised. **Refugia** are areas that are less affected by climate change than other areas and can be used as sources of "seed" for recovery or as destinations for climate-sensitive migrants. **Relocation** refers to human-facilitated transplantation of organisms from one location to another in order to bypass a barrier (*e.g.*, urban area).

Each of these adaptation approaches ultimately contributes to resilience, whether at the scale of individual protected area units, or at the scale of regional/national systems. The approaches above are not mutually exclusive and may be implemented jointly. The specific management activities that are selected under one or more approaches above should then be based on considerations such as: the ecosystem management goals, type and degree of climate effects, type and magnitude of ecosystem responses, spatial and temporal scales of ecological and management responses, and social and economic factors.

Levels of confidence in these adaptation approaches vary and are difficult to assess, yet are essential to consider in adaptation planning. Due to uncertainties associated with climate change projections as well as uncertainties in species and ecosystem responses, there is also uncertainty as to how effective the different adaptation approaches listed above will be at supporting resilience. It is therefore important to assess the confidence within the expert community that these approaches will support a degree of resilience that may allow ecosystems to persist without major losses of ecosystem processes or functions. Using one of the methodologies presented in the Intergovernmental Panel on Climate Change's guidelines for estimating uncertainties, the authors of this report developed their confidence estimates by considering two separate but related elements of confidence. The first element is the amount of available evidence (high or low) to support the determination that the effectiveness of a given adaptation approach is well-studied and understood. Evidence might consist of any of the following sources: peer-reviewed and gray literature, data and observations, model results, and the authors' own experience with each adaptation approach. The second element is the level of agreement or consensus throughout the scientific community about the different lines of evidence on the effectiveness of the adaptation approach.

The resulting confidence estimates vary, both across approaches and across management systems. Reducing anthropogenic stresses is one approach for which there is considerable scientific confidence in its ability to promote resilience for virtually any situation. Confidence in the other approaches—including protecting key ecosystem features, representation, replication, restoration, identifying refuges, and especially relocation—is much more variable. Despite this variability, many of the individual adaptation options under these approaches may still be effective. In these cases, a more detailed assessment of confidence for individual adaptation options is needed, based on a clearer understanding of how the ecosystem in question functions, the extent and type of climate change that will occur there, the resulting ecosystem impacts, and the projected ecosystem response to the adaptation option.

One method for integrating confidence estimates into resource management given uncertainty is adaptive management. Adaptive management is a process that promotes flexible decision-making so that adjustments are made in decisions as outcomes from management actions and other events are better understood. This method supports managers in taking action today using the best available information while also providing the possibility of ongoing future refinements through an iterative learning process.

The success of adaptation strategies may depend on recognition of potential barriers to implementation and creation of opportunities for partnerships and leveraging. In many cases, perceived barriers associated with legal or social constraints, restrictive management procedures, limitations on human and financial capital, and gaps in information may be converted into opportunities. For example, there may be a possibility to address difficulties associated with information or capacity shortages through leveraging of human capital. Existing staff could receive training on addressing climate change issues within the context of their current job descriptions and management frameworks, but a critical requirement for success of this activity would be to ensure that employees feel both valued as "climate adaptation specialists" and empowered by their institutions to develop and implement innovative adaptive management approaches that might be perceived as "risky." As a second example, partnerships among managers, scientists, and educators can go a long way toward efficiently closing information gaps. With good communication and coordination, scientists can target their research to better inform management challenges, resource managers can share data and better design monitoring to test scientific hypotheses, and outreach specialists can better engage the public in understanding and supporting adaptation activities. Two additional categories of opportunities that are especially promising are highlighted below.

The Nation's adaptive capacity can be increased through expanded collaborations among ecosystem managers. When managers seize opportunities to link with other managers to coordinate adaptation planning, they are able to broaden the spatial and ecological scope of potential adaptation options with a shared vision for increasing adaptive capacity. For example, many management units are nested within or adjacent to other systems. Collaboration across systems allows individual units to be, in effect, extended beyond their official boundaries to encompass entire ecosystems or regions; the result is a larger array of options for responding to future climate change impacts. Collaboration may also enhance research capacity and offer opportunities to share data, models, and experiences. In addition to overcoming limiting factors such as inadequate resources and mismatches of management unit size with ecosystem extent, collaborations may also be used to create flexible boundaries that follow unanticipated changes in ecosystems or species in response to climate change. Exercising opportunities for collaboration has the advantage of reducing uncertainties associated with attaining management goals under climate change because (1) the increase in the geographic range over which resources can be managed and the associated increase in available adaptation options makes success more likely, and (2) the increase in the resource base, in research capabilities, and in the size of data sets through data sharing and coordinated monitoring reduces statistical uncertainties and increases the probability of success.

The Nation's adaptive capacity can be increased through creative re-examination of program goals and authorities. Anticipated climate-induced changes in ecosystems and species and the uncertain nature of some of those changes will necessitate dynamic management systems that can accommodate and address such changes. Existing management authorities may be malleable enough to allow for changing conditions and dynamic responses, and with creative re-examination of those authorities their full capabilities could be applied. For example, federal land and water managers may be able to strategically apply traditional legislative authorities in non-traditional ways to coordinate management outside of jurisdictional boundaries. Similarly, while management policies can sometimes be limiting, the iterative nature of management planning may allow priorities and plans to be revisited on a cyclical basis to allow for periodic adjustments. Greater agility in program planning can increase the probability of meeting management goals by overcoming implementation barriers associated with narrowly defined and interpreted authorities.

Establishing current baselines, identifying thresholds, and monitoring for changes will be essential elements of any adaptation approach. Climate changes may cause ecological thresholds to be exceeded, leading to abrupt shifts in the structure of ecosystems. Threshold changes in ecosystems have profound implications for management because such changes may be unexpected, large, and difficult to reverse. If these ecosystems cannot then be restored, actions to increase their resilience will no longer be viable. Understanding where thresholds have been exceeded in the past and where (and how likely) they may be exceeded in the future allows managers to plan accordingly and avoid tipping points where possible. Activities taken to prevent threshold changes include establishing current baseline conditions, modeling a range of possible climate changes and system responses, monitoring to identify relevant ecological changes, and responding by implementing adaptation actions at appropriate scales and times. Current baselines capture a benchmark set of conditions for the ecological attributes or processes that are critical for maintaining that system and the current set of ecosystem services that the public has come to expect from that system. Developing a range of quantitative or qualitative visions of the future (scenarios) and planning adaptation responses for that range provide an approach for addressing the large uncertainties associated with any single projection of the future. Sensitivity analyses for any given scenario explore key attributes of the system and their response to systematic changes in the climate drivers. Such analyses may allow managers to identify thresholds beyond which key management goals may become unattainable. Directed monitoring then supports managers' ability to detect changes in baseline conditions, informs their decisions about the timing of adaptation actions, and helps them evaluate the effectiveness of their actions. With such information, a program that has the authority to, for example, acquire land interests and water rights to restore a river to its historic flows would better be able to determine how, when, and where to use this authority.

Beyond "managing for resilience," the Nation's capability to adapt will ultimately depend on our ability to be flexible in setting priorities and "managing for change." Prioritizing actions and balancing competing management objectives at all scales of decision making is essential, especially in the midst of shifting budgets and rapidly changing ecosystems. Using a systematic framework for priority setting would help managers catalog information, design strategies, allocate resources, evaluate progress, and inform the public. This priority-setting could happen in an ongoing way to address changing ecological conditions and make use of new information. Over time, our ability to "manage for resilience" of current systems in the face of climate change will be limited as temperature thresholds are exceeded, climate impacts become severe and irreversible, and socioeconomic costs of maintaining existing ecosystem structures, functions, and services become excessive. At this point, it will be necessary to "manage for change," with a re-examination of priorities and a shift to adaptation options that incorporate information on projected ecosystem changes. Both "managing for resilience" and "managing for change" require more observation and experimentation to fill knowledge gaps on how to adapt to climate change. This report presents a preliminary review of existing adaptation knowledge to support managers in taking immediate actions to meet their management goals in the context of climate change. However, this is only a first step in better understanding this burgeoning area of research in adaptation science and management. It will be necessary to continuously refine and add to this body of knowledge in order to meet the challenge of preserving the Nation's lands and waters in a rapidly changing world.

The National Fish, Wildlife and Plants Climate Adaptation Strategy: Public Review Draft

U.S. Fish & Wildlife Service et al., 2012.
http://www.wildlifeadaptationstrategy.gov/public-review-draft.php.

Executive Summary

The climate is changing, and the effects are being seen in the nation's valuable natural resources and in the economies and communities that depend on plants, animals, and ecosystems. Measurements unequivocally show that average temperatures in the United States have risen two degrees Fahrenheit (°F) over the last 50 years. The science strongly supports the finding that the underlying cause of these changes is the accumulation of heat-trapping carbon dioxide (CO_2) and other greenhouse gases (GHG) in the atmosphere. If GHG emissions continue, the planet's temperature is predicted to rise by an additional 2.0 to 11.5 °F by the end of the century, with accompanying increases in extreme weather events and sea levels.

Faced with a future climate that will be unlike that of the recent past, the nation has no choice but to adapt to the changes. In 2009, Congress recognized the need for a national government-wide climate adaptation strategy for fish, wildlife, plants, and ecosystems, asking the Council on Environmental Quality (CEQ) and the Department of the Interior (DOI) to develop such a strategy. CEQ and DOI responded by assembling an unprecedented partnership of federal, state, and tribal fish and wildlife conservation agencies to draft the *Strategy*. More than 100 diverse technical and scientific experts from across the country participated in drafting the Strategy for the partnership.

The result is The National Fish, Wildlife and Plants Climate Adaptation Strategy (hereafter *Strategy*). The *Strategy* is the first joint effort of three levels of government (federal, state, and tribal) that have primary authority and responsibility for the living resources of the United States to identify what must be done to help these resources become more resilient, adapt to, and survive a warming climate. It is designed to inspire and enable natural resource managers, legislators, and other decision makers to take effective steps towards climate change adaptation over the next five to ten years.

The *Strategy* is guided by nine principles. Those principles include collaborating across all levels of government, working with non-government entities such as private landowners and other sectors like agriculture and energy, and engaging the public. It's also important to use the best-available science—and to identify where science and management capabilities must be improved or enhanced. When adaptation steps are taken, it's crucial to carefully monitor actual outcomes in order to adjust future actions to make them more effective, an iterative process called adaptive management. And given the size and urgency of the challenge, we must begin acting now.

The *Strategy* details how climate change is expected to affect the eight major ecosystem types in the United States. [These are later listed as "forests, grasslands, shrublands, deserts, tundra, inland waters, coastal, and marine systems."] Warmer temperatures and changing precipitation patterns are expected to cause more fires and more pest outbreaks like the mountain pine beetle epidemic in forests, for instance, while boreal forest will move north into what is now tundra. Grasslands and shrublands are likely to be invaded by non-native species and suffer wetland losses from drier conditions, which would decrease nesting habitat for waterfowl. Deserts are expected to get hotter and drier, accelerating existing declines in species like the Saguaro cactus.

Climate change is expected to be especially dramatic in the Arctic, with temperatures in northern Alaska projected to climb 13 to 26 °F. That would change tundra into shrublands, and bring more fires. In addition, the thawing of frozen organic material in soils would release huge amounts of greenhouse gases, contributing to climate change. Rivers, streams, and lakes face higher temperatures that harm coldwater species like salmon and trout populations, while sea level rise threatens coastal marshes and beaches, which are crucial habitats for many species. Among those at risk: the diamondback terrapin and the piping plover.

Since water absorbs CO2 from the air, the rising levels of the gas in the atmosphere have caused the oceans to become 30 percent more acidic since 1750. That's already affecting the reproduction of species like oysters. As the pH of seawater continues to drop, major impacts on aquatic ecosystems and species are expected.

The *Strategy* describes steps that can be taken to combat these impacts and conserve ecosystems and make them more resilient. Proposed strategies and actions along with checklists to monitor progress are organized under seven major goals in the *Strategy*: (1) conserving and connecting habitat; (2) managing species and habitats; (3) enhancing management capacity; (4) supporting adaptive management; (5) increasing knowledge; (6) increasing awareness and motivating action; and (7) reducing stresses not caused by climate change. Many proposed actions describe types of conservation activities that management agencies have traditionally undertaken, but that will continue to be useful in a period of climate change but that will continue to be useful in a period of climate change. Others are designed to respond to the new challenges posed by climate change.

The most robust approach for helping fish, wildlife, and plants adapt to climate change is conserving enough suitable habitat to sustain diverse and healthy populations. Many wildlife refuges and habitats could lose some of their original values, as the plants and animals they safeguard are forced to more hospitable climes. As a result, there's a growing need to identify the best candidates for new conservation areas, and to provide corridors of habitat that allow species to migrate.

This *Strategy* envisions innovative opportunities for creating additional habitat. Paying farmers in the Great Plains to take some of their land

out of production and then restoring prairie grass and sagebrush on the land could offset the projected population declines from climate change of the threatened lesser prairie chicken, according to one analysis. Similarly, adjusting rice farming practices in Louisiana could provide valuable new resources for a variety of waterfowl and shorebirds whose habitat is now disappearing because of wetland loss and sea level rise.

It's also possible to use applied management to make habitats and species more resistant to climate change so they continue to provide sustainable cultural, subsistence, recreational, and commercial use. Stream and habitat restorations that narrow and deepen streams or that ensure a steady supply of cold groundwater can keep water temperatures low enough to maintain healthy trout populations even when air temperatures rise.

Climate change adaptation requires new ways of assessing information, new management tools and professional skills, increased collaboration across jurisdictions, and review of laws, regulations, and policies. Climate change impacts are occurring at scales much larger than the operational scope of individual organizations and agencies, and successful adaptation to climate change demands a strong collaboration among all jurisdictions. Landscape Conservation Cooperatives, Migratory Bird Joint Ventures, National Fish Habitat Partnerships, and other existing and emerging partnerships are useful vehicles to promote collaboration.

Predicting how individual species and ecosystems will react to climate change will frequently be difficult. Adapting to uncertain impacts requires coordinated observation and monitoring, information management and decision support systems, and a commitment to adaptive management approaches. The National Ecological Observatory Network is one example of a coordinated observation system. Coordinated information management systems that link and make available data currently developed by separate agencies or groups will increase access to and use of this information by resource managers, planners, and decision makers. Vulnerability assessments can help managers develop and prioritize adaptation efforts and inform management approaches.

New research is needed to increase knowledge about the specific impacts of climate change on fish, wildlife, plants, and habitats and their adaptive capacity to respond. The use of models has already produced useful information for planning for climate change impacts. More refined models at temporal and spatial scales appropriate to adaptation are required. Methods to objectively quantify the value of ecosystem services provided by well-functioning ecosystems are needed.

Adaptation efforts will be most successful if they have broad public and political support and if key groups and people are motivated to take action themselves. Efforts to increase awareness and motivate action should be targeted toward elected officials, public and private policy makers, groups that are interested in learning more about climate change, private landowners, and natural resource user groups. Engaging these stakeholders early and repeatedly to increase awareness of climate change, to develop integrated adaptation responses, and to motivate their participation and action is key to making this *Strategy* work.

Reducing existing stresses on fish, wildlife, and plants can be some of the most effective, and doable, ways to increase resilience to climate change. Reducing and mitigating the ongoing habitat degradation associated with human development such as pollution and loss of open space is critical and requires collaboration with land use planners. Taking steps to reduce stresses not related to climate, such as fighting invasive species like water hyacinth, can help natural systems cope with the additional pressures imposed by a changing climate.

In addition, the *Strategy* emphasizes that actions to help plants, wildlife, fish, and natural systems adapt to climate change can be coordinated with measures taken in other sectors, such as agriculture and industry, to increase the benefits for all sectors. Reducing stormwater runoff not only reduces risks of flooding in cities, for example, it also reduces the threat that toxic algal blooms will affect aquatic ecosystems.

The *Strategy* is also designed to build upon and complement many existing adaptation and conservation efforts. Notable among those are the U.S. Global Change Research Program and the National Climate Assessment it produces every four years; the Interagency Climate Change Adaptation Task Force that coordinates U.S. federal agency adaptation efforts; State Wildlife Action Plans; and Landscape Conservation Cooperatives. Implementing the *Strategy* will require coordination and collaboration among these and many other entities. The *Strategy* proposes creation of a coordination body to oversee its implementation and engage with conservation partners.

Admittedly, the task ahead is a daunting one. However, we can begin to take effective action to reduce risks and increase resiliency of valuable natural resources. This *Strategy* is a call to action. Unless the nation begins a serious effort to undertake this task now, we risk losing priceless living systems—and the benefits and services they provide—as the climate changes.

INDEX